WORLD LIST OF
SCIENTIFIC PERIODICALS

PUBLISHED IN THE YEARS

1900—1960

ENGLAND:	BUTTERWORTH & CO. (PUBLISHERS) LTD. LONDON: 88 Kingsway, W.C.2
AFRICA:	BUTTERWORTH & CO. (AFRICA) LTD. DURBAN: 33–35 Beach Grove
AUSTRALIA:	BUTTERWORTH & CO. (AUSTRALIA) LTD. SYDNEY: 6–8 O'Connell Street MELBOURNE: 473 Bourke Street BRISBANE: 240 Queen Street
CANADA:	BUTTERWORTH & CO. (CANADA) LTD. TORONTO: 1367 Danforth Avenue, 6
NEW ZEALAND:	BUTTERWORTH & CO. (NEW ZEALAND) LTD. WELLINGTON: 49–51 Ballance Street AUCKLAND: 35 High Street
U.S.A.:	BUTTERWORTH INC. WASHINGTON, D.C.: 7235 Wisconsin Avenue, 14

WORLD LIST OF

SCIENTIFIC PERIODICALS

PUBLISHED IN THE YEARS

1900—1960

FOURTH EDITION

Edited by

PETER BROWN, B.A.

of the British Museum

and

GEORGE BURDER STRATTON, M.B.E.

Librarian, Zoological Society of London

VOLUME 1, A–E

(1–18907)

LONDON

BUTTERWORTHS

1963

Made and printed in Great Britain by
William Clowes and Sons, Limited, London and Beccles

PREFACE TO THE FOURTH EDITION

THE third edition of the *World List of Scientific Periodicals* was published in 1952 and reprinted in 1958. In 1957 work started on the preparation of the fourth edition and has continued steadily to the end of 1963. This task has been very great, for the number of periodicals to be included has now reached the figure of over sixty thousand.

During these years the World List Association suffered a severe blow in losing its Chairman, the late Dr. E. J. Holmyard, who retired owing to ill health shortly before his death. His great qualities, wide experience and sympathetic understanding were of inestimable value to the Association.

The printing and publishing of this edition has been undertaken for the Association by Butterworths in continuation of the agreement under which the third edition was published, whereby they have been responsible for the cost of production. The cost of preparation of the work, which is borne by the Association, has inevitably increased to a sum much greater than that for previous editions. The Association records with gratitude the receipt of two grants towards this cost amounting to £7,200 from the Royal Society of London out of their Parliamentary grant-in-aid of scientific publications. The compilation of this edition would have been impossible without this financial help.

It is with regret that the Association must announce that this fourth edition of the *World List of Scientific Periodicals* published in the years 1900–1960 is the last that can appear in this format. Apart from increasing costs the great labour of compilation is now beyond the resources of an Association without permanent staff and which has to rely upon the part-time services of public-spirited experts who have carried out their task with admirable devotion. As the Association saw no prospect of the publication of a fifth edition, which should ideally appear in about ten years' time, it sought alternative means of keeping the list up to date. The Association has been fortunate in concluding an agreement with The National Central Library, by which the list will be in effect continued through the publication of annual supplements of the *British Union Catalogue of Periodicals*. A list of new publications and corrections will appear as a supplement to BUCOP and it is possible, if demand justifies it, that the annual lists will be gathered into quinquennial issues. This arrangement has further the bibliographical value of avoiding the duplication of publications that would otherwise occur. The Council of Management of the *World List of Scientific Periodicals* is confident that this arrangement will meet the needs of the users of the List.

The first three editions of the *World List* were edited by the late Mr. W. A. Smith, whose preface to the third edition concludes on a sadly prophetic note; he died when work was about to start on the fourth edition. The editorial task then devolved on Mr. P. Brown and Mr. G. B. Stratton to whom all users of the *World List* are greatly indebted for their unremitting and devoted labours. Mr. Stratton has been associated with the preparation of all the editions of the *World List*, from the first covering the period 1900–1921.

Finally I wish to record the thanks of the Association to its secretary, Miss Grace Gay, who has for so long dealt so efficiently with the voluminous correspondence involved.

L. HARRISON MATTHEWS
Chairman
World List of Scientific Periodicals

16 October, 1963

EDITORS' NOTE

THIS, the fourth edition of the *World List of Scientific Periodicals*, is the first to be prepared without the editorship of Mr. W. A. Smith. Although he had previously considered that the third edition would be his last he was in fact preparing himself at the close of 1956 to face once more the arduous task of editing another *World List* when he was suddenly taken ill and died in January 1957. The present editors can do no more than express the hope that this edition, which is to be the last *World List* to appear in this form, has come near to equalling its predecessors.

This present edition is of exactly the same pattern as the previous editions, but now covering the period 1900 to 1960. It includes periodicals concerned with the natural sciences and technology of which issues were published during this period of sixty-one years. Periodicals first published at any time before 1900 are listed so long as they continued publication into the twentieth century; changes of title taking place before 1900 are not shown. At the other end of the period a change of title taking place after 1960 is noted, but no separate entries have been made for the post-1960 titles.

Our largest source of information for periodicals for the years 1900 to 1950 has naturally been the third edition of the *World List*. Many of these entries have been revised in the light of further information and some titles of periodicals published during that period but not included in earlier editions of the *World List* have been added. On the other hand, some ten thousand titles which appeared in the third edition have been excluded from the present edition as being of social or commercial interest rather than scientific. The period 1951 to 1960 was one of greatly increased publication of scientific and technological periodicals, with the result that entries for periodicals published during these ten years account for about a quarter of this present edition of the *World List*.

The *World List* is not a catalogue of periodicals but a finding list of titles arranged in alphabetical order of the important words of the titles. We have not followed exactly the arrangement of titles in the previous editions but have regarded *all* nouns and adjectives as being important words in this respect. For this reason we would advise users of previous editions as well as new users of the *World List* to consult the revised 'Explanation of the Arrangement' on page xi.

We have attempted to include in this edition every means we could to assist users in finding entries. Words used in the arrangement of the titles are in bold type. The majority of entries can be found in the alphabetical arrangement without any difficulty, but in a large number of cases we have included cross references where entries may be sought under alternative forms. Titles in the Cyrillic and Greek alphabets are arranged according to their transliterated form, but the transliteration and original alphabet are both given in the entries; titles in other non-Roman alphabets are given only in transliteration. The transliteration of Cyrillic and Greek characters is in accordance with the method recommended by the Royal Society, modified and published as British Standard 2979:1958. It was with regret that we had to decide that time would not permit us to supplement this *World List* with a Societies index.

The abbreviations in this edition have been prepared in general accordance with the forthcoming *British Standard for the Abbreviation of Titles of Periodicals* but do not show very great differences from the abbreviations given in previous editions of the *World List*. Where new abbreviations have been introduced it has in general been with the aim of assisting users of the abbreviations to reconstruct the full title sufficiently to be able to find this title in an alphabetically arranged list such as the *World List*. We have given many abbreviations fuller forms (even leaving some words unabbreviated) at the beginning of titles so that there should not be any uncertainty about the exact word in question. The work of revising the abbreviations has had to be secondary to our main task of recording the full titles and holdings and although we have attempted to ensure that there are no inconsistencies we fear that shortage of time may have led to our leaving some; we can only hope that they are few in number. Details of the abbreviations, together with a select list of abbreviations and their full forms are given in the 'Note on the Abbreviation of Titles' on page xvii.

Dates of publication (or coverage) of a title are shown in brackets after the abbreviation. Where we have been unable to establish the date of the first issue the final date, if known, has been shown by an asterisk following the holding of the first library listed as having the last issue, e.g. **L**.BM. 39–48*.

We are greatly indebted to the librarians who have contributed information about the periodical holdings of their libraries for this edition. We are, however, sorry that a few libraries who have provided information for the previous editions have not done so for this edition, with the result that their holdings of periodicals are not shown as fully as they might have been. Without the valuable assistance provided by the contributing libraries, not only would we have been unable to record holdings but we would probably have remained unaware of the existence of many new titles. We have attempted, as far as time would allow, to record in accordance with the information received the holdings of every contributing library for every title unless a holding was for only a very short period of a periodical's life and the title was well represented in a good coverage of other libraries. We welcome the inclusion in this edition of new libraries. We are particularly glad to have received some information of the periodicals held at the National Lending Library for Science and Technology. This important library was not officially opened until 1962, so that it has not been possible to record fully its extensive holdings; nevertheless, through the courtesy of the Director, Dr. D. J. Urquhart, and Miss R. M. Bunn, reference is made to a considerable number of titles held in the library. Contained in the stock of the National Lending Library for Science and Technology are many periodicals transferred from the Science Museum and we are much indebted to Miss H. J. Parker and Miss G. M. Turner for the details of the titles transferred. It may be that some titles credited as being held by **L**.SC. are now located in **Y**. Details of the libraries and the symbols used to designate them are given below in the 'Note on Libraries and Holdings' on page xiii.

The *World List* attempts to list not only those periodicals which are held by the contributing British libraries, but also those of which, so far as is known, there is no copy in this country. We are well aware that for this fourth edition the short time left to us after we had recorded the information provided by the libraries prevented us from searching out all the titles not so reported and that for the period 1951 to 1960 the present edition falls short of the standard set by previous editions in this respect. There are however, a number of published lists of periodicals for this period and we would refer users to these where they are unable to find information about a title in this *World List*.

We cannot pretend that we, as new editors, have found the task of compiling this fourth edition of the *World List of Scientific Periodicals* an easy one, and, therefore, we are all the more indebted to the people who have helped us in its preparation. In this respect it gives us much pleasure to record our special thanks to Mr. G. W. F. Claxton of the British Museum (Natural History) and Messrs. R. A. Fish, L. G. Ellis and R. Langstaff of the Zoological Society of London for the generous assistance given throughout the preparation of this edition. To Butterworths, our publishers, we are much indebted for their helpful and understanding consideration of the problems involved in producing the *World List*, and for giving us the benefit of their advice on many points.

For both of us it has been a task which has had to be fitted into what would otherwise have been our leisure hours. It is with some relief that we view the completion of our task, as well as a certain amount of satisfaction with many of the things we have been able to do, though this must inevitably be tinged with some dissatisfaction that there was not time to do all that we might have wished.

P.B.
G.B.S.

EXPLANATION OF THE ARRANGEMENT

An attempt has been made, subject to a few conventions described below, to record the exact titles of periodicals and to arrange these titles in strict alphabetical order of the important words, i.e. *all* nouns and adjectives (in only very few particular instances have verbs, adverbs and prepositions had to be considered also).

1. The words considered in the arrangement of titles are in bold type. The place of publication, where this has been used to determine the arrangement of entries with the same titles, has not, however, been printed in bold type.

2. The following words in titles are disregarded for the purposes of arrangement:

(*a*) All articles, except when as suffixes forming part of a noun;

(*b*) All prepositions, verbs, adverbs, pronouns and conjunctions, except when forming the first word of a title or to distinguish otherwise identical titles.

All nouns and adjectives disregarded in the arrangement of the titles in previous editions of the *World List* now count, e.g.

Fortschritte auf dem **Gebiet** der **Chemie,**
Bericht über die **Tätigkeit** der **Gesellschaft,**
Journal of the **Royal Statistical Society,**
Mitteilungen der **K. Akademie** der **Wissenschaften,**
Journal of the **State Department** of **Agriculture,**
Annales de l'**Académie r.** de **physique.**

(*Note.* The foreign titular adjectives Königlich, Kaiserlich, Kaiserlich-Königlich, royale are shortened to **K., KK.,** and **r.** and included as such in the arrangement.)

3. In many headings variant forms, singulars and plurals, older and more recent forms, have been brought together and recorded in one form, e.g.

Anais for Anais and Annaes,
Årbog for Årbog and Aarbog,
Archivos for Archivos and Arquivos,
Bulletin for Bulletin and Bulletins,
Compte rendu for Compte rendu and Comptes rendus,
Zentralblatt for Zentralblatt and Centralblatt.

General cross references have been included for the alternative forms. At the beginning of a title **Report** is used for both 'Report' and 'Annual Report', but the forms **Biennial Report, Annual Meteorological Report,** etc. are not changed.

4. Titles with initial letters are arranged in a separate sequence at the beginning of the letter, e.g.

A.A. Journal. Architectural Association,
A.A.A.S. Bulletin. American Association for the Advancement of Science,
A.C.E.C. Ateliers de construction électriques de Charleroi,
AEC Gazette. Associated Equipment Co.

5. Hyphenated forms are to be read as if forming a single complete word.

6. German ä, ö, ü are arranged as if they were ae, oe, ue but in any other language these letters are arranged as a, o, u. No other diacritical marks affect the arrangement.

7. In those periodicals in which the arrangement of words in the title cannot be established, a cross reference is frequently provided from an alternative form, but users should be prepared for an inversion of words such as shown in the following examples:

(*a*) Transposition of a geographical name.
    Journal of the Department of Agriculture of New Jersey.
    Journal of the New Jersey Department of Agriculture.

(*b*) Transposition of the name of an Institution with a sub-section.

> Bulletin de l'Institut colonial de Marseille, Section des matières grasses.
> Bulletin de la Section des matières grasses de l'Institut colonial de Marseille.

(*c*) Transposition of the name of the publishing Institution from beginning to end of a title.

> Bulletin. Northwestern University.
> Northwestern University Bulletin.

8. An article forming the first word of a title is not shown, with the result that a title beginning 'Der deutsche' is entered as 'Deutsche', e.g.

> **Deutsche Arzt.**
> **Deutsche Techniker.**

9. Where a title has been reported in various forms or languages every attempt has been made to bring these together under one form of title and in one language, leaving cross references at the other forms of title, but identification of these variants has not always been possible. Translations of periodicals issued under a different title have been entered separately.

10. Where a title has undergone an actual change a separate entry has been made under the new title where the change is considerable or significant, and the date of the change is shown. (N.B. Where no dates are given for the whole life of a title the date of change may be indicated in one of the holdings by an asterisk.) Continuations are shown in brackets at the foot of the entry. Minor changes may be included within one title. At times where insufficient information about a change has been available a cross reference (occasionally with an abbreviation) has been included for one of the forms.

11. Supplements to periodicals have been entered separately where these supplements are known to have a separate and definite title; otherwise the existence of supplements is merely noted in brackets at the foot of the entry.

12. As the Cyrillic and Greek titles are transliterated in accordance with the 'British' system published in British Standard 2979:1958 there are a number of differences in the arrangement of these titles as compared with earlier editions. The most important of these are as follows:

Greek Χ is arranged as **h** instead of **ch**, e.g.

> **Hēmika** Χημικα

and ' is arranged as ' instead of **h**, e.g.

> **'Ellēnikē** Ἑλληνικη

Russian ѣ is arranged as **ê** instead of **ye**, e.g.

> **Vêstnik** Вѣстникъ

and ы is arranged as **ȳ** instead of **ui**, e.g.

> **Promȳshlennost'** Промышленность

Ukrainian and White Russian г is arranged as **h** instead of **g** and и is arranged as **ȳ** instead of **i**, e.g.

> **Heofȳzȳchna** Геофизична

NOTES ON LIBRARIES AND HOLDINGS

LIBRARY SYMBOLS

L. = London.

A.   Royal Agricultural Society of England.
AM.   Ministry of Agriculture, Fisheries and Food.
AN.   Royal Anthropological Institute of Great Britain and Ireland.
AS.   Royal Astronomical Society.
AV.   Ministry of Aviation Central Library.
B.   Bedford College (University of London).
BA.   Royal Institute of British Architects.
BM.   British Museum, Bloomsbury.
BM^N. British Museum (Natural History), South Kensington.
C.   Chemical Society.
CB.   Chester Beatty Research Institute.
D.   British Dental Association.
DI.   Industrial Diamond Information Bureau.
E.   Royal Entomological Society of London.
EB.   Commonwealth Institute of Entomology.
EE.   Institution of Electrical Engineers.
FA.   National Farmers' Union.
FO.   British Food Manufacturing Industries Research Association. *See* **Lh.**FO. (removed to Leatherhead).
G.   Royal Geographical Society.
GH.   Guy's Hospital, Wills Library.
GL.   Geological Society of London.
GM.   Geological Survey and Museum.
H.   Ministry of Health Library.
HO.   Horniman Museum and Library.
HQ.   Department of Scientific and Industrial Research Headquarters.
HS.   Royal Horticultural Society.
I.   Iron and Steel Institute and the Institute of Metals.
IC.   Imperial Chemical Industries Ltd. Headquarters.
IN.   John Innes Horticultural Institution. *See* **Ba.**I. (removed to Bayfordbury).
K.   Royal Botanic Gardens, Kew.
KC.   King's College (University of London).
L.   Linnean Society of London.
LE.   British Leather Manufacturers' Research Association.
LI.   Lister Institute of Preventive Medicine.
M.   London Mathematical Society.
MA.   British Medical Association.
MC.   Medical Research Council.
MD.   Royal Society of Medicine.
MI.   Institution of Mining and Metallurgy.
MIE. Institution of Mining Engineers.
MIR. Motor Industry Research Association. *See* **Li.**M. (removed to Lindley, near Nuneaton).
MO.   Meteorological Office (removed to Bracknell, Berks).
MT.   Institute of Metals. *See* **L.**I. (now joint Library).
MY.   Commonwealth Mycological Institute, Kew.
NC.   Nature Conservancy.
NF.   British Non-Ferrous Metals Research Association.

NP.   Northern Polytechnic and National College of Rubber Technology.
OP.   Institute of Ophthalmology.
OS.   School of Oriental and African Studies.
P.   Patent Office.
PG.   Royal Photographic Society of Great Britain.
PH.   Pharmaceutical Society of Great Britain.
PL.   British Plastics Federation.
PR.   Research Association of British Paint, Colour and Varnish Manufacturers, Teddington.
PS.   British Psychological Society.
PT.   Institute of Petroleum.
QM.   Queen Mary College (University of London).
R.   Royal Society.
RA.   British Institute of Radiology.
RI.   Royal Institution of Great Britain.
S.   Royal College of Surgeons of England.
SB.   St. Bride Printing Library.
SC.   Science Museum.
SH.   Royal Society of Health.
SI.   British Scientific Instrument Research Association.
SL.   School of Slavonic and East European Studies (University of London).
SU.   Ministry of Supply. *See* **L.**AV.
TD.   London School of Hygiene and Tropical Medicine.
TP.   Tropical Products Institute.
U.   University of London, Senate House.
UC.   University College London, Gower Street.
UCH. University College Hospital Medical School.
V.   Royal College of Veterinary Surgeons.
VC.   Royal Veterinary College (University of London).
Z.   Zoological Society of London.

Abd. = Aberdeen: M. Scottish Home Department, Marine Laboratory; P. Public Library; R. Rowett Research Institute, The Reid Library; S. Macaulay Institute for Soil Research; T. Torry Research Station, D.S.I.R.; U. University.

Abs. = Aberystwyth: A. Welsh Plant Breeding Station, Plas Gogerddan; N. National Library of Wales; U. University College of Wales.

Ba. = Bayfordbury, Herts: I. John Innes Institute.

Bil. = Billingham, Durham: OC. Heavy Organic Chemicals Division, I.C.I.

Bl. = Belfast: U. Queen's University of Belfast.

Bm. = Birmingham: C. British Cast Iron Research Association; N. Birmingham Natural History and Philosophical Society; P. Birmingham Public Libraries; T. College of Technology; U. University.

Bn. = Bangor: U. University College of North Wales.

NOTES ON LIBRARIES AND HOLDINGS

Br. = Bristol: A. Agricultural and Horticultural Research Station, University of Bristol; P. Bristol Public Libraries; U. University.

Bra. = Bradford: D. Society of Dyers and Colourists; P. Central Public Library.

C. = Cambridge: A. School of Agriculture; AB. National Institute of Agricultural Botany; AN. School of Anatomy; AP. Institute of Animal Pathology, *See* **C.**V.; APH. Institute of Animal Physiology; B. Balfour Library, Department of Zoology; BI. Colman Library, Department of Biochemistry; BO. Botany School; C. Cavendish Laboratory (Raleigh Library); CH. Chemical Laboratory; E. Haddon Library, Faculty of Archaeology and Anthropology; ENG. Department of Engineering; GD. Department of Geodesy and Geophysics; GE. Department of Genetics; GG. Department of Geography; L. Low Temperature Research Station, D.S.I.R.; MC. MacCurdy Library, Medical Psychology Laboratory; MD. Department of Medicine; MI. Department of Mineralogy and Petrology; MO. Molteno Institute of Biology and Parasitology; MS. Post-Graduate Medical School, Addenbrooke's Hospital; MT. Department of Metallurgy; N. Newton Library, *See* **C.**B.; O. The Observatories; P. Cambridge Philosophical Library; PA. Department of Pathology; PH. Physiological Laboratory; PO. Scott Polar Research Institute; PS. Psychological Laboratory; R. Department of Radiotherapeutics; S. Department of Geology, Sedgwick Museum; SI. Sidney College; SJ. St. John's College; SL. Statistical Laboratory; SP. Solar Physics Observatory, *See* **C.**O.; T. Trinity College; UL. University Library; V. Departments of Veterinary Clinical Studies and Animal Pathology; Z. Department of Zoology, *See* **C.**B.

Cn. = Croydon: R. Research Association of British Rubber Manufacturers, *See* **Sy.**R. (removed to Shawbury, near Shrewsbury).

Co. = Coventry: T. Lanchester College of Technology.

Cr. = Cardiff: I. South Wales Institute of Engineers; M. National Museum of Wales; MD. Welsh National School of Medicine; MS. Cardiff Medical Society; N. Cardiff Naturalists' Society, c/o National Museum of Wales; P. Central Library; U. University College of South Wales and Monmouthshire.

Db. = Dublin Libraries (Dublin Institute for Advanced Studies, Institute for Industrial Research and Standards, Medical Research Council of Ireland; National Library of Ireland, Royal College of Physicians of Ireland, Royal College of Surgeons of Ireland, Royal Dublin Society, Royal Irish Academy, Trinity College, University College, Veterinary College of Ireland).

Dm. = Dove Marine Laboratory, Cullercoats.

Dn. = Dundee: U. Queen's College (University of St. Andrews).

Do. = Dorking: F. Fire Service College, Abinger Common.

E. = Edinburgh: A. National Library of Scotland; AB. Commonwealth Bureau of Animal Breeding and Genetics; AG. Institute of Animal Genetics; AR. Animal Breeding Research Organisation; B. Royal Botanic Garden; C. Royal Physical Society (Housed with **E.**T. and **E.**U.); CE. Cerebos Group Library, A. & R. Scott Ltd.; D. Geological Survey of Great Britain; E. Faculty of Actuaries; F. Royal Scottish Museum; G. Royal Scottish Geographical Society; HW. Heriot-Watt College; I. Royal Medical Society; J. Edinburgh Geographical Society; L. Royal Scottish Society of Arts; M. Meteorological Office (Air Ministry); N. Royal (Dick) Veterinary College; O. Royal Observatory; P. Royal College of Physicians; PO. Poultry Research Centre; Q. Edinburgh Mathematical Society; R. Royal Society of Edinburgh; S. Royal College of Surgeons; SW. Institute of Seaweed Research and Arthur D. Little Research Institute, Inveresk; T. Central Public Library; U. University of Edinburgh; V. National Museum of Antiquaries of Scotland; W. Edinburgh and East of Scotland College of Agriculture.

El. = Elstree: FE. Fire Research Station, D.S.I.R.

Ep. = Epsom: D. Distillers Company Ltd., Great Burgh.

Ex. = Exeter: U. Roborough Library, University of Exeter.

Fa. = Royal Aircraft Establishment, Farnborough.

Fr. = Freshwater Biological Association, Windermere Laboratory, Ambleside.

G. = Glasgow: E. Institution of Engineers and Shipbuilders in Scotland; F. Royal Faculty of Physicians and Surgeons; G. Glasgow Geological Society; I. West of Scotland Iron and Steel Institute; M. Mitchell Library; ME. Mechanical Engineering Research Laboratory, D.S.I.R.; MG. Mining Institute of Scotland (Incorporated in **G.**T.); N. Andersonian Naturalists of Glasgow; PH. Corporation of Glasgow, Health and Welfare Department; T. Royal College of Science and Technology, The Andersonian Library; U. Glasgow University.

H. = Hull: U. University of Hull.

Ha. = Harmondsworth: RD. Road Research Laboratory, D.S.I.R.

Hu. = Hurley, near Maidenhead: G. Grassland Research Institute.

Je. = Imperial Chemical Industries, Jealott's Hill Research Station.

Lc. = Leicester: A. Leicester Colleges of Art and Technology.

Ld. = Leeds: P. Library of Commerce, Science and Technology, Central Library; PL. Philosophical and Literary Society (Incorporated in **Ld.**U.); U. Brotherton Library, University of Leeds; W. Wool Industries Research Association.

Lh. = Leatherhead: FO. British Food Manufacturing Industries Research Association; P. Printing, Packaging and Allied Trades Research Association.

Li. = Lindley, near Nuneaton: M. Motor Industry Research Association.

Lo. = Fisheries Laboratory, Ministry of Agriculture, Fisheries and Food, Lowestoft.

Lv. = Liverpool: M. Liverpool Medical Institution; P. Liverpool Public Libraries; U. University.

M. = Manchester: C. Cotton, Silk and Man-made Fibres Research Association, Shirley Institute; D. Imperial Chemical Industries, Dyestuffs Division; M. Manchester Museum (Housed with **M.**U.); MS. Medical Library, The University; P. Manchester Public Libraries, Technical Library; T. Manchester College of Science and Technology; U. University.

xiv

Ma. = Great Malvern: T. Royal Radar Establishment.

Md. = Maidstone: H. Joint Library of East Malling Research Station and Commonwealth Bureau of Horticulture and Plantation Crops.

Mi. = Scottish Marine Biological Association, Marine Station, Millport, Isle of Cumbrae.

N. = Nottingham: P. Public Libraries; T. Nottingham and District Technical College; U. University.

Nu. = Nutfield: B. Brewing Industry Research Foundation.

Nw. = Newcastle: A. King's College; P. Central Library.

O. = Oxford: A. Ashmolean Museum; AEC. Agricultural Economics Research Institute; AP. Bureau of Animal Population; B. Bodleian Library; BI. Department of Biochemistry; BO. Botany Department; BS. Science Library, Balliol College; CC. Corpus Christi College; CH. Christ Church; E. Exeter College; EP. Institute of Experimental Psychology; F. Department of Forestry, Commonwealth Forestry Institute; G. School of Geography; H. Hope Department of Entomology; O. University Observatory; OR. Edward Grey Institute of Field Ornithology; PC. Physical Chemistry Laboratory; PH. University Laboratory of Physiology; R. Radcliffe Science Library; RE. Department of Agriculture; RH. Rhodes House; SJ. St. John's College; T. Taylor Institution; UC. University College; Z. Department of Zoology and Comparative Anatomy.

Pit. = Pitlochry, Perthshire: F. Freshwater Fisheries Laboratory, D.S.I.R.

Pl. = Plymouth: M. Marine Biological Association of the United Kingdom.

Pr. = Princes Risborough: FT. Forest Products Research Laboratory, D.S.I.R.

R. = Reading: D. National Institute for Research in Dairying; U. University.

Rn. = Renfrew: B. Research Department, Babcock and Wilcox, Ltd.

Rt. = Rothamsted Experimental Station, Harpenden.

Sa. = St. Andrew's University.

Sal. = Commonwealth Bureau of Helminthology, St. Albans; F. Research Association of British Flour-Millers, Cereals Research Station.

Sh. = Sheffield: G. Society of Glass Technology; IO. Sheffield Interchange Organisation, Science and Commerce Library, Central Library; M. Midland Institute of Mining Engineers, The University, St. George's Square; P. Central Library; S. Safety in Mines Research Establishment; SC. University Library of Applied Science; U. University.

Sil. = National Institute of Agricultural Engineering, Silsoe.

Sl. = Slough: I. Imperial Chemical Industries Ltd., Paints Division; P. Pest Infestation Laboratory, D.S.I.R.; RI. Radio Research Station, D.S.I.R.

St. = Stoke on Trent: R. British Ceramic Research Association.

Ste. = Imperial Chemical Industries Ltd., Nobel Division, Stevenston Ayrshire.

Sw. = Swansea: I. Royal Institution of South Wales; U. University College of Swansea.

Sy. = Shrewsbury: R. Research Association of British Rubber Manufacturers, Shawsbury, Nr. Shrewsbury.

Te. = Teddington, Middlesex: C. National Chemical Laboratory, D.S.I.R.; N. National Physical Laboratory, D.S.I.R.

W. = Commonwealth Bureau of Animal Health and Central Veterinary Laboratory of the Ministry of Agriculture, Weybridge.

Wa. = Watford, Hertfordshire: B. Building Research Station, Garston, D.S.I.R.; W. Water Pollution Research Laboratory, Stevenage, D.S.I.R.

We. = Wealdstone, Middlesex: K. Kodak Ltd.

Wd. = Imperial Chemical Industries Ltd., General Chemicals Division, Widnes, Lancashire.

Wl. = Wallingford, Buckinghamshire: H. Hydraulics Research Station, D.S.I.R.

Wo. = National Institute of Oceanography, Wormley.

Y. = National Lending Library for Science and Technology, Boston Spa, Yorkshire.

HOLDINGS

Method of showing library holdings explained by examples:

[1952–] **L.**BM^N.; K.; P.; R.; **Abs.**A.; U. 59–; **Dn.**U. 62–; **E.**B.; **G.**U.; **Y.**

means this periodical commenced publication in 1952, that **L.**BM^N.; K.; P.; R.; **Abs.**A.; **E.**B.; **G.**U.; **Y.** have complete sets; **Abs.**U. has from 1959 and **Dn.**U. from 1962.

[1920–45] **L.**BM.; P.; S.; TD. 36–37; **Br.**U.; **C.**P. 24–45; **O.**B. [C. of: 2134; > 7356, 1925–33; C. as: 8472]

means this periodical ran under the title shown from 1920 to 1945 with the exception of a break between 1925 and 1933 when it has the title listed at 7356; that it was preceded by the title at 2134 and followed by the title at 8472; that **L.**BM.; P.; S.; **Br.**U.; and **O.**B. have complete sets; **L.**TD. has 1936 to 1937 and **C.**P. 1924 to 1945.

[1933–41: 51–] **L.**BA.; BM.; **C.**UL. imp.; **Db.** v. imp.; **Ld.**U. (curr.); **M.**T. (5 yr.); **Y.** 52–. [Suspended 1942–46; > 4776, 1946–50]

means this periodical ran under this title from 1933 to 1941 and recommenced publication in 1951, was not issued between 1942 and 1946 and from 1946 to 1950 has the title listed at 4776; that **L.**BA.; BM. have complete sets **C.**UL. has an imperfect set, **Db.**, a very imperfect set, **Ld.**U. retains current issues only, **M.**T. retains the last 5 years, and **Y.** has from 1952.

The date at which four figures are given has been moved forward to 1860. Until 1860 all four figures are given, beyond that only the last two. Where a library holding is given as commencing in 61 or 62 it implies 1861 or 1862 where the journal was in publication prior to 1860, otherwise the holding began in 1961 or 1962.

[1846–60] **L.**BM.; BM^N.; R. 1859–97; **G.**U. 61–60

means **L.**BM. and BM^N. have complete sets, **L.**R. has from 1859 to 1897 and **G.**U. from 1861 to 1960.

[1898–] **L.**BM.; R.; **G.**U. 61–; **Ld.**U. 62–

means **L.**BM. and R. have complete sets, **G.**U. has from 1961 and **Ld.**U. from 1962.

NOTE ON THE ABBREVIATION OF TITLES

As in previous editions of the *World List*, each title is followed by an abbreviated form of the title. This abbreviated form is printed in italics. For this fourth edition the abbreviations have, as far as possible, been prepared in accordance with the forthcoming British Standard for the Abbreviation of Titles of Periodicals. In general, the abbreviations are the same as those for previous editions, except that a deliberate attempt has been made in the abbreviations to differentiate cognate forms of certain words. This has been done particularly for cognate forms and cognate words when occurring at the beginning of titles where ability to reconstruct exactly the full word is likely to be of the greatest importance for tracing a title in an alphabetically arranged list. At the beginnings of titles, therefore, some words have been abbreviated to a lesser degree and some words have been left unabbreviated. Contracted, rather than abbreviated forms have frequently proved suitable for differentiating these cognate forms.

Abbreviations (where letters from the end of a word have been omitted) end with a full stop. Contractions (where letters from the middle of a word have been omitted) are not followed by a full stop. Abbreviated titles ending with a contraction or with an unabbreviated word are not followed by a full stop.

Abbreviated nouns begin with a capital letter; abbreviated adjectives and other words (with the few exceptions shown below) begin with a small letter; except that the first word of an abbreviated title always begins with a capital letter.

A few adjectives of honour occurring before the names of institutions and abbreviated to a single letter are represented by a capital letter, e.g.

> *R. Soc.* for Royal Society,

but *imp. Acad.* for Imperial Academy,

> *Acad. r.* for Académie royale.

Adjectives in the English language formed from proper names begin in their abbreviated form with a capital letter (the decision in the forthcoming British Standard to discontinue this practice was reached too late for the large number of alterations to be made in this World List), e.g.

> *Am.* for American, but *am.* for americano.

Articles are not shown in the abbreviated titles except in some instances when forming the suffix to a noun.

Prepositions, verbs, adverbs, pronouns and conjunctions are not shown in the abbreviated titles except when forming the first word of a title or very occasionally either to distinguish otherwise identical abbreviated titles or to clarify an abbreviated title. Conjunctions are shown abbreviated or in full when connecting broken compound words, e.g.

> *Mitt. dt. Ges. Nat.- u. Völkerk.*
>
> *Meddr Danm. Fisk.- og Havunders.*

Singular and plural forms of words are distinguished in the abbreviated titles only where it is of importance for identification to do so or occasionally for the sake of clarity.

All single-word titles are left unabbreviated, even if consisting of a long compound word.

In compound words the abbreviation frequently consists of the abbreviation of each of the elements of the compound word, but without a full stop after the first abbreviation unless this word is followed by a hyphen in the full form, e.g.

> *EntwMech.*
>
> *MaterPrüf.*
>
> *Auto.-Rdsch.*
>
> *eisenbtech.*

In such compounds, for the sake of clarity, some words forming the first element are left unabbreviated, but frequently with a more drastic abbreviation of the second element. In the case of compound adjectives, a hyphen is occasionally introduced into the abbreviation to avoid confusion, e.g.

> *Naturw.* (as opposed to *Nat.* and *Wiss.*)
>
> *auto.-tech.* (as opposed to *eisenbtech.*)

SELECT LIST OF ABBREVIATIONS USED

This list of abbreviations and their corresponding full forms is intended as a guide to reconstructing the full title of a periodical from an abbreviation in *World List* form.

The mark * before an abbreviation indicates that, although this is the abbreviation used generally, a longer form is used to differentiate variants or cognates when the word occurs at the beginning of a title. This longer form, if it is still an abbreviation, will be found in the list in brackets; the use of unabbreviated forms will be found by referring to entries in the *World List* beginning with these words.

When the full word is followed by *etc.* it indicates that the same abbreviation is used for cognate forms in the same or in another language. As a result, in this list no distinction is made in these instances between abbreviations for nouns and adjectives (elsewhere indicated by the use of an initial capital letter for nouns and an initial small letter for adjectives), e.g.

Acad.—Academy etc. indicates that *Acad.* is the abbreviation used for Academy, Académie, Academia, and *acad.* for academic, académique, academica.

* Activ.—Activity *etc.* indicates that *Activ.* is the abbreviation generally used for Actividad, Actividades, Activité, Activités, Activity, Activities, but that these words are differentiated in abbreviated titles by longer forms when they occur at the beginning of a title.

In this list abbreviations are shown for nouns except where the abbreviation shown is always used for the adjectival form, the cognate noun form being less drastically abbreviated at the beginning of titles, or where an adjectival form is met with more frequently, e.g. Anat.—Anatomy *etc.* indicates not only that other cognate nouns are represented by *Anat.* but also that cognate adjectives are indicated by *anat.*; *aeronaut.—aeronautical *etc.* indicates that cognate adjectives are represented by *aeronaut.* while cognate nouns are represented by *Aeronaut.* only when they do not come at the beginning of titles, where a longer or unabbreviated form is used; curr.—current *etc.* indicates not only that other cognate adjectives are represented by *curr.* but also that cognate nouns are indicated by *Curr.*

Normally the place of imprint is omitted except when needed to distinguish periodicals with the same title, e.g.

Annali idrologici.	Bologna.	*Annali idrol., Bologna*
Annali idrologici.	Roma.	*Annali idrol., Roma*
Ethnos.	Lisboa.	*Ethnos, Lisb.*
Ethnos.	Mexico.	*Ethnos, Méx.*
Ethnos.	Stockholm.	*Ethnos, Stockh.*

or to distinguish titles with the same abbreviated title, e.g.

Botanische Studien	*Bot. Stud., Jena*
Botaniska studier	*Bot. Stud., Lund*

Details of variant forms of abbreviation for words when occurring at the beginning of a title are shown here only for abbreviations with the initial letters A to E. The variant forms for abbreviations with initial letters later in the alphabet will be shown in the subsequent volumes.

a.	annual *etc.*	*Activ.	Activities *etc.*	Aeropl.	Aeroplane		
Abh.	Abhandlungen	(Activid.)	Actividades	ärztl.	ärztlich		
*Abridg.	Abridgement *etc.*	*Actual.	Actualités *etc.*	Afd.	Afdeling		
Abschr.	Abschrift	(Actualid.)	Actualidades	Afh.	Afhandling		
Abstr.	Abstracts	addit.	additional *etc.*	*Afr.	African *etc.*		
Abt.	Abteilung	Additam.	Additamenta	Ag.	Agency *etc.*		
Acad.	Academy *etc.*	Adhes.	Adhesives *etc.*	Aggiorn.	Aggiornamenti		
Acc.	Accession	*Adm.	Administration *etc.*	*agr.	agrarian *etc.*		
Accad.	Accademia	Admty	Admiralty	*agric.	agricultural *etc.*		
Access.	Accessory *etc.*	(admve)	administrative	Agron.	Agronomy *etc.*		
Accid.	Accident *etc.*	Adv.	Advances	Aircr.	Aircraft		
Acct	Account	advd	advanced	Airpl.	Airplane		
Acet.	Acetylene *etc.*	advg	advancing	Akad.	Akademie *etc.*		
Achiev.	Achievements	advis.	advisory *etc.*	Aktinom.	Aktinometrie *etc.*		
Acoust.	Acoustics *etc.*	Advmt	Advancement	Aktiv.	Aktivität *etc.*		
acrid.	acridological *etc.*	Aerodyn.	Aerodynamics *etc.*	Akush.	Akusherstvo		
Act.	Actes	Aerol.	Aerology *etc.*	Akust.	Akustik *etc.*		
actinom.	actinometric *etc.*	*aeronaut.	aeronautical *etc.*	Akvar.	Akvarium *etc.*		

LIST OF ABBREVIATIONS

Ala.	Alabama	
alg.	algemeen	
Aliment.	Alimentation *etc.*	
allg.	allgemein	
allm.	allmän *etc.*	
*Alm.	Almanach *etc.*	
(Alman.)	Almanaque	
alp.	alpine *etc.*	
alphab.	alphabetical *etc.*	
Als.	Alsace	
Alumin.	Aluminium	
Am.	American *etc.*	
Amat.	Amateur	
Amst.	Amsterdam	
amtl.	amtlich	
An.	Anales	
Anaesth.	Anaesthesia *etc.*	
Anal.	Analele	
Analg.	Analgesia *etc.*	
analyt.	analytical *etc.*	
Anat.	Anatomy *etc.*	
Anesth.	Anesthesia *etc.*	
angew.	angewandt	
Anh.	Anhang	
Anim.	Animal	
Ann.	Annals	
Annln	Annalen	
Annlr	Annaler	
Annls	Annales	
*annot.	annotated *etc.*	
(Annotnes)	Annotationes	
Annu.	Annuaire	
Annuar.	Annuario	
anorg.	anorganisch *etc.*	
anorm.	anormal	
Anot.	Anotaciones	
Anst.	Anstalt	
*anthrop.	anthropological *etc.*	
Antrop.	Antropologia *etc.*	
Anu.	Anuario	
Anvisn.	Anvisning	
Anwend.	Anwendung	
Anz.	Anzeiger	
Apar.	Aparato	
apl.	aplicado *etc.*	
Appar.	Apparatus	
appl.	applied *etc.*	
Applic.	Application *etc.*	
*Arb.	Arbeiten *etc.*	
*Årb.	Årbog, Årbok	
Arch.	Archiv	
Archf	Archief	
*archit.	architectural *etc.*	
Archo	Archivio	
Archos	Archivos	
Archs	Archives	
Archvm	Archivum	
Archwm	Archiwum	
Arct.	Arctic	
Argent.	Argentina	
Arh.	Arhiv	
Ark.	Arkiv	
Arkh.	Arkhiv	
Arkhit.	Arkhitektura *etc.*	
Arkit.	Arkitektur *etc.*	
årl.	årlig	
Arquit.	Arquitectura *etc.*	
Årsb.	Årsbok	
Årsberätt.	Årsberättelse	
Årsberetn.	Årsberetning	
Årsskr.	Årsskrift	
Artic.	Articles	
artif.	artificial	
Ask.	Askeri	
Asoc.	Asociación *etc.*	
Ass.	Association *etc.*	
astr.	astronomical *etc.*	
Astronaut.	Astronautics *etc.*	
Astrophys.	Astrophysics *etc.*	
Atmos.	Atmosphere *etc.*	
*atom.	atomic *etc.*	
Attiv.	Attività	
Attual.	Attualità	
ausl.	ausländisch	
Aust.	Australian *etc.*	
australas.	Australasian	
Ausz.	Auszüge	
Auth.	Authority	
Auto.	Automobile *etc.*	
autom.	automatic *etc.*	
Automn	Automation	
automot.	automotive	
aux.	auxiliary *etc.*	
Avd.	Avdelning	
Avh.	Avhandlingar	
Aviat.	Aviation *etc.*	
Avto.	Avtomobil' *etc.*	
avtom.	avtomaticheskiĭ *etc.*	
Azerb.	Azerbaĭdzhan *etc.*	
Azet.	Azetylen	
B. Aires	Buenos Aires	
Bact.	Bacteriology *etc.*	
Bd	Board	
Beibl.	Beiblätter	
Beih.	Beihefte	
Beil.	Beilage	
Beitr.	Beiträge	
Belg.	Belgique *etc.*	
Beob.	Beobachtungen	
Ber.	Bericht	
Berätt.	Berättelse	
Beretn.	Beretning	
Bergb.	Bergbau	
Berl.	Berlin	
Betr.	Betrieb	
bett.	better	
Bez.	Bezirk	
Bgham	Birmingham	
biann.	biannual	
Biblfía	Bibliografía	
biblfich.	bibliograficheskiĭ	
Biblfija	Bibliografija	
Biblfiya	Bibliografiya	
Biblphia	Bibliographia	
biblphic	bibliographic	
biblphical	bibliographical	
Biblphie	Bibliographie	
Biblphien	Bibliographien	
Biblphies	Bibliographies	
Biblphy	Bibliography	
Bibltca	Biblioteca	
Biblthca	Bibliotheca	
Biblthk	Bibliothek	
Bibltque	Bibliothèque	
Bidr.	Bidrag	
bienn.	biennial	
Bih.	Bihang	
Bijdr.	Bijdrag	
Bilj.	Bilješke	
Bilt.	Bilten	
bi.-m.	bi-monthly	
bimens.	bimensile *etc.*	
Biochem.	Biochemistry *etc.*	
Biochim.	Biochimica	
Biodyn.	Biodynamics *etc.*	
Biofiz.	Biofizika *etc.*	
biokhem.	biokhemicheskiĭ	
Biokhim.	Biokhimiya	
*Biol.	Biology *etc.*	
Biophys.	Biophysics *etc.*	
Biul.	Biuletyn	
Bk	Book	
*Bl.	Blätter *etc.*	
Bldg	Building	
Bldr	Builder	
Boll.	Bollettino	
Bolm	Boletim	
Boln	Boletin	
*bot.	botanical *etc.*	
Bpest	Budapest	
Br.	British *etc.*	
Bras.	Brasil *etc.*	
Brch	Branch	
Brux.	Bruxelles	
Buc.	Bucureşti	
Bul.	Buletinul	
Bulg.	Bulgaria *etc.*	
Bull.	Bulletin	
Bült.	Bülteni	
Bum.	Bumaga *etc.*	
Bur.	Bureau	
Butll.	Butlleti	
Byul.	Byuletin'	
Byull.	Byulleten'	
C. r.	Compte rendu	
Cah.	Cahiers	
*Cal.	Calendario *etc.*	
Calc.	Calcium	
Calif.	California	
Camb.	Cambridge	
*Can.	Canadian *etc.*	
Cann.	Canning	
Čas.	Časopis	
*Cat.	Catalogue *etc.*	
Cem.	Cement	
*cent.	central *etc.*	
Chal.	Chaleur	
*chem.	chemical *etc.*	
chf	chief	
chil.	chilena	
child.	children	
*Chim.	Chimica *etc.*	
Chin.	Chinese	
Chir.	Chirurgia *etc.*	
*Chron.	Chronicle *etc.*	
*Ciênc.	Ciência	
cient.	científica	
Cim.	Ciment	
*Circ.	Circular *etc.*	
Circol.	Circolare	
(Circul.)	Circulaire	
Cirug.	Cirugía	

Cirurg. Cirurgia
civ. civil etc.
*clim. climatological etc.
*clin. clinical etc.
Col. Colegio
*coll. collected etc.
*Coll. College etc.
Colln Collection
colon. colonial etc.
Com. Comité etc.
comb. combined
Combust. Combustion
Comm. Committee etc.
comml commercial
Commn Commission
Commnr Commissioner
Commonw. Commonwealth
*Commun. Communication etc.
(Communs) Communications
(Communtnes) Communicationes
comp. comparative
*Comun. Comunicaciones etc.
(Comunicaz.) Comunicazione
Concr. Concrete
*Conf. Conference etc.
Congr. Congress etc.
Cons. Conseil
Conserv. Conservation etc.
*Constr. Construction etc.
*Contr. Contributions etc.
*Conv. Convention etc.
Corr. Correo etc.
Corros. Corrosion etc.
Cott. Cotton
Coun. Council
*Cron. Cronaca etc.
Crón. Crónica etc.
*čsl. československsk
(čslka) československsk
(čslký) československský
Cst Coast
cstl coastal
Ctry Country
Cty County
Cuad. Cuadernos
*Cult. Culture etc.
curr. current etc.
Cy City
Cytol. Cytology etc.
Czas. Czasopismo
Czech. Czechoslovak etc.

Danm. Danmark
Darb. Darbai
Darst. Darstellung
Def. Defence etc.
Delt. Deltion
*dent. dental etc.
Dep. Department etc.
(depl) departmental
Derg. Dergisi
Derm. Dermatology etc.
derzh. derzhavnÿĭ
*Des. Design
*Descr. Description etc.
(descrve) descriptive

Dev. Development etc.
Dif. Difesa
Dig. Digest
Dir. Direction etc.
Dis. Disease
*Diss. Dissertation etc.
Distr. District
*Div. Division etc.
(divl) divisional
dly daily
Dnev. Dnevnik
doct. doctoral
*Docum. Document etc.
(Documn) Documentation
(Docums) Documents
Dokl. Dokladÿ
Dolg. Dolgozatok
Dom. Dominion
Dopov. Dopovidi
Doświad. Doświadczalnictwo
dřev. dřevarski
Društ. Društvo
dt. deutsch
Dtl. Deutschland

E. East
east. eastern
Éc. École
econ. economic etc.
Edn Edition
Effic. Efficiency etc.
Egy. Egyétem etc.
eidg. eidgenössisch
ekon. ekonomisch etc.
eksp. eksperimental'nÿĭ etc.
*Elect. Electricity etc.
(electl) electrical
elekt. elektrisch etc.
Elem. Element etc.
Elett. Elettricità etc.
Emp. Empire
Émul. Émulation
Endocr. Endocrinology etc.
Enf. Enfance
Engl. England etc.
Engng Engineering
Engr Engineer
Ens. Ensaio etc.
Enst. Enstitüsü
Ent. Entomology etc.
Erdb. Erdbeben
Erdk. Erdkunde
Ergänz. Ergänzungen
Ergebn. Ergebnisse
Ert. Értesitö
Esc. Escola
Esp. Espana etc.
Establ. Establishment
Estaç. Estaçao
Estac. Estacion
*Estud. Estudios etc.
Ethnogr. Ethnography etc.
Ethnol. Ethnology etc.
Étud. Études etc.
Eur. Europe etc.
Évk. Évkonyve
*Exp. Experiment etc.
(expl) experimental

Explor. Exploration etc.
Explos. Explosives etc.
Ext. Extension
ezhedn. ezhednevnÿĭ
Ezheg. Ezhegodnik
ezhem. ezhemesyachnÿĭ etc.

Fabr. Fabrik
Fac. Faculty etc.
Fact. Factory
Fak. Fakultat etc.
Farm. Farmacia etc.
faun. faunistica etc.
Fd Food
Fdn Foundation
Fed. Federation etc.
Fert. Fertility
Fertil. Fertiliser
Finl. Finland
fís. física etc.
Fisch. Fischerei
Fish. Fisheries
Fishg Fishing
Fisk. Fiskeri
Fiz. Fizika etc.
Fiziol. Fiziologiya etc.
Fla Florida
Fld Field
Fm Farm
Fmg Farming
Fmr Farmer
Fndry Foundry
Förd. Förderung
Földt. Földtani
Foll. Folletos
Foly. Folyoirat
Fond. Fondation
for. foreign
For. Forestry
För. Förening
Forb. Forbund
Förb. Förbund
Foren. Forening
Forh. Forhandlinger
Förh. Förhandlingar
Formul. Formulaire
Fors. Forsøk
Förs. Försög etc.
Forsch. Forschung
Forsk. Forskning
forst. forstlich
Förteckn. Förteckning
Fortschr. Fortschritte
fr. français etc.
Fys. Fysik etc.

G. Giornale
Ga Georgia
Gac. Gaceta
Gaz. Gazette etc.
Gazz. Gazzetta
Gdn Garden
Gdng Gardening
Gdnr Gardener
Geb. Gebiet
gen. general etc.
Geneesk. Geneeskunde
Genet. Genetics etc.

LIST OF ABBREVIATIONS

Geod.	Geodesy *etc.*	Irrig.	Irrigation *etc.*	Madr.	Madrid
Geofis.	Geofisica *etc.*	Isl.	Island *etc.*	Mag.	Magazine
Geofiz.	Geofizika *etc.*	Issled.	Issledovanie	Magn.	Magnetism *etc.*
Geofys.	Geofysik *etc.*	Ist.	Istituto	Magy.	Magyar
Geogr.	Geography *etc.*	It.	Italy *etc.*	Mal.	Maladie *etc.*
Geol.	Geology *etc.*	Izd.	Izdanie	Man.	Manual *etc.*
Geophys.	Geophysics *etc.*	Izslêd.	Izslêdovanie	Manchr	Manchester
ger.	geral	Izv.	Izvestiya	mar.	marine *etc.*
Germ.	German			marit.	maritime
Ges.	Gesellschaft	J.	Journal	Masch.	Maschin
ges.	gesammt	Jaarb.	Jaarboek	Mash.	Mashina *etc.*
Gesch.	Geschichte *etc.*	jaarl.	jaarlijks	Mat.	Matematik *etc.*
Gesundh.	Gesundheit	jährl.	jährlich	Mater.	Material *etc.*
Gig.	Gigiena	Jap.	Japanese	Math.	Mathematics *etc.*
Ginec.	Ginecologia *etc.*	Jb.	Jahrbuch	Méc.	Mécanique
Glasn.	Glasnik	Jber.	Jahresbericht	Mech.	Mechanics *etc.*
Godiš.	Godišnjak *etc.*	Jel.	Jelentései	Mechaniz.	Mechanization
Godish.	Godishnik *etc.*	Jh.	Jahresheft	Med.	Medicine *etc.*
gos.	gosudarstvennŷĭ	Jorn.	Jornal	Meddn	Meddelanden
Gosp.	Gospodarstvo *etc.*	Jschr.	Jahresschrift	Meddr	Meddelelser
Govt	Government	jt	joint	Meded.	Mededelingen
Gt Br.	Great Britain	Jta	Junta	Meet.	Meeting
Gynaec.	Gynaecology *etc.*	Jübers.	Jahresübersicht	Mem.	Memoirs
Gynäk.	Gynäkologie *etc.*	Julk.	Julkaisja	Mém.	Mémoires
Gynéc.	Gynécologie *etc.*	Jversl.	Jaarverslag	meml	memorial
		Jverz.	Jahresverzeichnis	Mems	Memorias
half-y.	half-yearly			mens.	mensual *etc.*
Harv.	Harvard	k.	Königlich, kaiserlich,	ment.	mental *etc.*
Hand.	Handelingen		*etc.*	Met.	Meteorology *etc.*
Handb.	Handbook *etc.*	Kab.	Kabinet	Metall.	Metallurgy *etc.*
Handl.	Handlingar	Kal.	Kalender	Meth.	Method
Heat.	Heating	kem.	kemisk *etc.*	Méx.	México *etc.*
hebd.	hebdomadaire	Khim.	Khimiya *etc.*	mezhdunar.	mezhdunarodnŷĭ
Heiz.	Heizung	Khir.	Khirurgiya *etc.*	Mf.	Manufacture
Her.	Herald *etc.*	Khoz.	Khozyaĭstvo *etc.*	mfg	manufacturing
Helv.	Helvetia *etc.*	Kiad.	Kiadványei	Mfr	Manufacturer
Herb.	Herbage *etc.*	Kisérl.	Kisérleti	Mgmt	Management
Hig.	Higiene *etc.*	Klin.	Klinik *etc.*	Min.	Mining *etc.*
Highw.	Highway	Kom.	Komitet *etc.*	Miner.	Mineral *etc.*
Hist.	History *etc.*	Komm.	Komission *etc.*	Minist.	Ministry *etc.*
Hlth	Health	Közl.	Közlemények	Mins	Minutes
Hort.	Horticulture *etc.*	Kwart.	Kwartalnik *etc.*	misc.	miscellaneous *etc.*
Hosp.	Hospital	Ky	Kentucky	Miss.	Mississippi
hosp.	hospodářski *etc.*			Mitt.	Mitteilungen
Hung.	Hungary *etc.*	Lab.	Laboratory *etc.*	Mkt	Market
Hydrogr.	Hydrography *etc.*	Landb.	Landbouw *etc.*	Mktg	Marketing
Hydrol.	Hydrology *etc.*	Landw.	Landwirtschaft *etc.*	Mo.	Missouri
Hyg.	Hygiene *etc.*	Lap.	Lapok	mod.	modern
		Lar.	Laryngology *etc.*	mon.	monthly
Idrogr.	Idrografia *etc.*	Lav.	Lavori	monat.	monatliche
Idrol.	Idrologia *etc.*	Leafl.	Leaflet	Monit.	Moniteur *etc.*
Ig.	Igiene *etc.*	Leath.	Leather	Monogr.	Monograph *etc.*
Ill.	Illinois	Lect.	Lecture	Mosk.	Moskva
ill.	illustrated	Leist.	Leistung	Mt	Mount
Immun.	Immunology *etc.*	lek.	lékařsk *etc.*	Mübers.	Monatsübersicht
imp.	imperial	Lepid.	Lepidoptera *etc.*	munic.	municipal
Improv.	Improvements	Lepr.	Leprosy	Mus.	Museum *etc.*
ind.	industrial *etc.*	les.	lesnoĭ	Muz.	Muzeum *etc.*
Inf.	Information *etc.*	lesn.	lesnick *etc.*	Mverz.	Monatsverzeichnis
Ing.	Ingenieur *etc.*	Let.	Letopis		
Insp.	Inspection *etc.*	List.	Listok	N.	North
Inst.	Institute *etc.*	Lit.	Literature *etc.*	N.S.W.	New South Wales
Instn	Institution	Loco.	Locomotive	N.Y.	New York
Instrum.	Instrument *etc.*	Lond.	London	N.Z.	New Zealand
int.	international *etc.*	Lpz.	Leipzig	nac.	nacional
Intell.	Intelligence			Nachr.	Nachrichten
Invest.	Investigation *etc.*	maand.	maandelijks	NachrBl.	Nachrichtenblatt
Ir.	Irish	Mach.	Machine *etc.*	nar.	narodnŷĭ

nat.	natural *etc.*	Penn.	Pennsylvania	Rd	Road
natn.	national	period.	periodical *etc.*	Rdsch.	Rundschau
Naturg.	Naturgeschichte *etc.*	Petrol.	Petroleum *etc.*	Rec.	Record *etc.*
naturh.	naturhistorisch	Pfl.	Pflanze	rec.	recent
Naturw.	Naturwissenschaft *etc.*	Pharm.	Pharmacy *etc.*	Rech.	Recherche
nauch.	nauchnyĭ	Pharmac.	Pharmacology *etc.*	Recl	Recueil
naut.	nautical	Pharmn	Pharmacien *etc.*	Ref.	Reference *etc.*
nav.	naval	Pharmst	Pharmacist	Refrig.	Refrigeration
Ned.	Nederland *etc.*	Photogr.	Photography *etc.*	Reg.	Region *etc.*
neft.	neftyanoĭ *etc.*	Phys.	Physics *etc.*	Relac.	Relaciones
Newsl.	Newsletter	Physiol.	Physiology *etc.*	Relat.	Relatorio
nord.	nordisk *etc.*	Pl.	Plant	Relaz.	Relazione
norm.	normal *etc.*	Plann.	Planning	Rens.	Renseignement
Not.	Notices	Plast.	Plastics *etc.*	Rep.	Report
Notat.	Notationes	Plr	Planter	Rép.	Répertoire
Notic.	Noticias	Pol.	Polska *etc.*	Repr.	Reprints
Notiz.	Notiziario	Polytech.	Polytechnic *etc.*	Reprio	Repertorio
Notul.	Notulae *etc.*	pop.	popular *etc.*	Reprium	Repertorium
nouv.	nouveau *etc.*	Port.	Portugal *etc.*	Reptr	Reporter
Nov.	Novosti	Pr.	Prace, Práce	Res.	Research
nth.	northern	pract.	practical *etc.*	Result.	Resultados *etc.*
nucl.	nuclear *etc.*	prakt.	praktisch *etc.*	Résult.	Résultats
Nurs.	Nursing	prat.	pratica *etc.*	Rev.	Review
Nutr.	Nutrition *etc.*	Přehl.	Přehled	Revta	Revista
		prelim.	preliminary *etc.*	Rheum.	Rheumatism *etc.*
Obozr.	Obozrenie	Print.	Printing	Rhod.	Rhodesia
Obs.	Observatory *etc.*	Probl.	Problems *etc.*	Ric.	Ricerche
Obsções	Observações	Proc.	Proceedings	Riv.	Rivista
Obsnes	Observaciones	Prod.	Produce *etc.*	Rly	Railway
Obsns	Observations	prof.	professional *etc.*	Roč.	Ročenka
Obshch.	Obshchestvo	Prog.	Progress *etc.*	Roczn.	Rocznik
Obstet.	Obstetrics *etc.*	Progm.	Programme *etc.*	Rom.	România *etc.*
Obz.	Obzor	Prom.	Promyshlennost' *etc.*	Ross.	Rossiya *etc.*
occ.	occasional	Propr.	Propriétaires	Rozhl.	Rozhledy
Oceanogr.	Oceanography *etc.*	Prot.	Protection *etc.*	Rozpr.	Rozpravy *etc.*
öff.	öffentlich	Prov.	Province *etc.*	Rubb.	Rubber
Öst.	Österreich *etc.*	Przegl.	Przegląd	rur.	rural
Of.	Oficio *etc.*	Przem.	Przemysł	Russ.	Russia *etc.*
Off.	Office *etc.*	Przyr.	Przyroda *etc.*	russk.	russkiĭ *etc.*
Offr	Officer	Psikhiat.	Psikhiatriya *etc.*	rÿb.	rÿbnÿĭ
Ont.	Ontario	Psiquiat.	Psiquiatría *etc.*		
Opt.	Optics *etc.*	Psychol.	Psychology *etc.*	S	San *etc.*
Optn	Optician	Pubbl.	Pubblicazioni	S.	South
Org.	Organisation *etc.*	publ.	public *etc.*	sächs.	sächsisch
Orn.	Ornithology *etc.*	Publ.	Publikace *etc.*	Saermeld.	Saermelding
Orsz.	Országos	Publnes	Publicaciones	Saertr.	Saertrykk
Orv.	Orvosok	Publs	Publications	Saf.	Safety
Osp.	Ospedale	Publtiës	Publicatiës	Sällsk.	Sällskap
Oss.	Osservatorio	Publtnes	Publicationes	Saml.	Samling
Ossni	Osservazioni			Samml.	Sammlung
Otch.	Otchet	Q./q.	Quarterly	Sanid.	Sanidad
Otd.	Otdel *etc.*	Quad.	Quaderni	sanit.	sanitary *etc.*
Otol.	Otology *etc.*	quadr.	quadrennial	Sb.	Sbornik
Overs.	Oversigt	Qd	Queensland	Sber.	Sitzungsbericht
Overz.	Overzicht	Queb.	Quebec	Sch.	School
Oxf.	Oxford	quinq.	quinquennial	Schr.	Schriften
				Schritt.	Schrifttum
P.-v.	Procès-verbaux	R./r.	Royal *etc.*	schweiz.	schweizerisch
Pacif.	Pacific	Rab.	Rabot *etc.*	Sci.	Science *etc.*
Palaeont.	Palaeontology *etc.*	Rad.	Radovi	scient.	scientific
Palest.	Palestine	Radiogr.	Radiography *etc.*	Scotl.	Scotland
Pam.	Pamiętnik	Radiol.	Radiology *etc.*	Scott.	Scottish
Pamph.	Pamphlet	Rak.	Raksti	Scr.	Scripta
państ.	państwowy *etc.*	Rap.	Raport *etc.*	Séanc.	Séances
Pap.	Paper(s)	Rapp.	Rapport *etc.*	Secr.	Secretary *etc.*
Pat.	Patent	Rass.	Rassegna	Sect.	Section *etc.*
Path.	Pathology *etc.*	Rast.	Rastenie *etc.*	seism.	seismic *etc.*
Patol.	Patologia	Rc.	Rendiconti	sel.	selected *etc.*

sel'.   sel'skiĭ
Selecc.   Selecciones
Selsk.   Selskap
Sem.   Semaine *etc.*
Semin.   Seminar *etc.*
Ser.   Series *etc.*
Sér.   Série
Serv.   Service *etc.*
settim.   settimana
Sh.   Sheet
Shipbldg   Shipbuilding
Shipp.   Shipping
Shk.   Shkola
Shum.   Shumarstvo *etc.*
Silvic.   Silviculture *etc.*
sint.   sinteticheskiĭ *etc.*
sism.   sismic *etc.*
sist.   sistematicheskiĭ *etc.*
Sitz.   Sitzungen
Sk.   Skole
skand.   skandinavisk *etc.*
Skr.   Skrifter
Skyr.   Skyrsla
Slov.   Slovenia *etc.*
Soc.   Society *etc.*
somm.   sommaire
Sonderdr.   Sonderdruck
Soobshch.   Soobshcheniya *etc.*
sots.   sotsialisticheskiĭ *etc.*
Sov.   Sovet *etc.*
sovrem.   sovremennȳĭ
spec.   special
Spec.   Species
Specif.   Specification
Spectrogr.   Spectrography *etc.*
Spectrosc.   Spectroscopy *etc.*
sper.   sperimentale *etc.*
Spis.   Spisanie
sprav.   spravochnȳĭ
Spraw.   Sprawozdania
St   Saint
St.   State *etc.*
Sta.   Stantsiya *etc.*
Stand.   Standard
Standard.   Standardisation
Statist.   Statistics *etc.*
Staz.   Stazione
sth.   southern
Stn   Station
Stomat.   Stomatology *etc.*
Str.   Strasse
Strassb.   Strassburg
Stroit.   Stroitel'stvo *etc.*
Struct.   Structure *etc.*
Stud.   Studies *etc.*
Styr.   Styrelse
submar.   submarine
süddt.   süddeutsch
Sug.   Sugar
šum.   šumarsk *etc.*
Summ.   Summary *etc.*
Suom.   Suomen *etc.*
Supl.   Suplemento
Suppl.   Supplement *etc.*
Surf.   Surface
Surg.   Surgery *etc.*
Surv.   Survey *etc.*
Sved.   Svedeniya

Sver.   Sverige
Swed.   Swedish
Symp.   Symposia *etc.*
Synd.   Syndicate *etc.*
Synth.   Synthesis *etc.*
Szk.   Szkoła

Tabl.   Tables
Tät.   Tätigkeit
Tag.   Tagung
Tasm.   Tasmania
tead.   teaduste
Tec.   Tecnica
téc.   técnica
tech.   technical *etc.*
Techn   Technician
Technol.   Technology *etc.*
Teh.   Tehnica *etc.*
Tek.   Teknik *etc.*
Tekh.   Tekhnika *etc.*
Tekst.   Tekstil *etc.*
Telegr.   Telegraphy *etc.*
Teleph.   Telephony *etc.*
Telev.   Television *etc.*
Terap.   Terapia *etc.*
Text.   Textile *etc.*
Ther.   Therapeutics *etc.*
Tidskr.   Tidskrift
Tidsskr.   Tidsskrift
Tiedon.   Tiedonantoja
Tijdschr.   Tijdschrift
Timb.   Timber
Tn   Town
Tob.   Tobacco
Toim.   Toimetised
Tört.   Története
Tow.   Towarzystwo
Trab.   Trabajos *etc.*
Tract.   Tractor *etc.*
Traff.   Traffic
Trans.   Transactions
Transl.   Translation
Transp.   Transport *etc.*
Transpn   Transportation
Trav.   Travaux
trienn.   triennial
trimest.   trimestriel *etc.*
trop.   tropical *etc.*
Trud.   Trudove
Tsem.   Tsement
Tsirk.   Tsirkulyar
Tuberc.   Tuberculosis *etc.*
Tuberk.   Tuberkulose *etc.*
Tuinb.   Tuinbouw
Turk.   Turkey *etc.*

U.K.   United Kingdom
U.N.   United Nations
U.S.   United States
Uchen.   Ucheniya *etc.*
Übers.   Übersicht
Uff.   Ufficio *etc.*
Ugeskr.   Ugeskrift
Uitg.   Uitgave
Uitk.   Uitkomst
Ukr.   Ukraina *etc.*
Umieję̨t.   Umiejętności
Umjetn.   Umjetnosti

Un.   Union *etc.*
Unders.   Undersøgelse *etc.*
Univ.   University *etc.*
univl   universal
Unters.   Untersuchung
Urol.   Urology *etc.*
Urug.   Uruguay *etc.*
Usp.   Uspekhi
Util.   Utilisation *etc.*
Uurim.   Uurimused

Va   Virginia
Valt.   Valtion
Vap.   Vapeur
var.   various *etc.*
věd.   vědecké
Veg.   Vegetable
Venez.   Venezuela
Ver.   Verein
Verb.   Verband
Verein.   Vereinigung
Veren.   Vereniging
Vergl.   Vergleich *etc.*
Verh.   Verhandlung *etc.*
Vermess.   Vermessung
Veröff.   Veröffentlichung
Vers.   Verslagen
Versamml.   Versammlung
Verwalt.   Verwaltung
Verz.   Verzeichnis
Vesn.   Vesnik
Vest.   Vestnik
vet.   veterinary *etc.*
Vetensk.   Vetenskapen *etc.*
Vibr.   Vibration
Vidensk.   Videnskaber *etc.*
Vinic.   Viniculture *etc.*
Visn.   Visnȳk
Vissch.   Visscherij
Vitam.   Vitamins *etc.*
Vitic.   Viticulture *etc.*
Vjber.   Vierteljahrsbericht
Vjest.   Vjestnik
Vjhft   Vierteljahrsheft
Vjschr.   Vierteljahrsschrift
Vlugbl.   Vlugblad
Vlugschr.   Vlugschrift
Vopr.   Voprosȳ
Vortr.   Vorträge
vrach.   vrachebnȳĭ
vses.   vsesoyuznȳĭ
vȳchisl.   vȳchislitel'nȳĭ
Vȳr.   Vȳročni

W.   West
Wash.   Washington
Wass.   Wasser
Wat.   Water
Wbl.   Wochenblatt
Weath.   Weather
Weld.   Welding
west.   western
Wett.   Wetter
Wiad.   Wiadomości
Wildl.   Wildlife
Wirt.   Wirtschaft *etc.*
Wiss.   Wissenschaft *etc.*
Witt.   Witterung

Wk	Work	Zap.	Zapiski	Zesz.	Zeszyty
wkly	weekly	Zashch.	Zashchita *etc.*	Zh.	Zhurnal
Wld	World	Zašt.	Zaštita *etc.*	Zheleznod.	Zheleznodorozhnik
Wschr.	Wochenschrift	Zav.	Zavod *etc.*		*etc.*
Wydaw.	Wydawnictwa	Zbirn.	Zbirnik	Zhivot.	Zhivotnovodstvo *etc.*
Wydz.	Wydział	Zborn.	Zbornik	Zir.	Ziraat
		Železn.	Železnice *etc.*	Znan.	Znanosti
Yayin.	Yayinlari	Zem.	Zement	Zool.	Zoology *etc.*
Yb.	Yearbook/Year book	Zeměd.	Zemědelstvi *etc.*	Zpr.	Zprávy
yill.	yillik	Zeml.	Zemledelie *etc.*	Ztg	Zeitung
		Zent.	Zentrum *etc.*	Zuck.	Zucker
Z.	Zeitschrift	Zentbl.	Zentralblatt		

WORLD LIST OF SCIENTIFIC PERIODICALS
(1900-60)

A

1 **A.A. Journal.** Architectural Association. London. *A.A. Jl* [1948–] **L.**BA.; BM.; P. (5 yr.); SH. (1 yr); U. 51–; **Abs.**N.; **C.**UL.; **E.**A.; **Lv.**P. 54–; **O.**B.; **Y.** [*C. of:* 3981]

2 **A.A.A.S. Bulletin.** American Association for the Advancement of Science. Lancaster, Pa. *A.A.A.S. Bull.* [1942–46] **L.**P.; **Dn.**U. imp.; **Hu.**G. imp.; **Nw.**A.

3 **AAF Review.** American Air Force. Washington. *AAF Rev.* [1946–] **L.**AV. 49–; BM.; **F.**A. 54–. [*C. of:* 1537]

4 **AB Metal Digest.** Evanston. *AB Metal Dig.* **L.**P. (curr.)

    A.B.C.M. Quarterly Safety Summary. *See* 41644.
    A.B.C.M. Safety Summary. *See* 48455.

5 **ABM-Noticiário.** Associação brasileira de metais. São Paulo. *ABM-Noticiário* **L.**P. (curr.)

6 **A.B.M.A.C. Bulletin.** American Bureau for Medical Aid to China. New York. *A.B.M.A.C. Bull.* [1939–]
    ABT. *See* 303.

7 **AC.** International Asbestos-Cement Review. Zürich. *AC* [1956–] **L.**BA.; P. 57–; **Y.**

8 **ACA Monograph.** American Crystallographic Association. Milwaukee. *ACA Monogr.* **L.**P. 53–. [*C. of:* 127]

9 **A.C.E.C.** Ateliers de constructions électriques de Charleroi. *A.C.E.C.* [1948–] **L.**EE; P. 48–50; **Bm.**T. 51–; **E.**HW. 50–; **Lc.**A. 53–; **Ld.**P.; U. 54–; **Lv.**P. 52–; **M.**P.; T. (10 yr.); **Nw.**A.; **R.**U. 53–; **Sh.**IO. 50–53; **Y.** [*English language edition at:* 10 and 11; *C. from:* 13681]

10 **ACEC Charleroi.** Ateliers de constructions électriques de Charleroi. Charleroi. *ACEC Charleroi* [1950–54] **L.**P.; QM. 54; **Lc.**A. 53–54; **R.**U. 53–54; **Sa.** [*English language edition of:* 9; *C. as:* 11]

11 **ACEC Review.** Ateliers de constructions électriques de Charleroi. Charleroi. *ACEC Rev.* [1955–] **L.**AV. 57–; P.; QM.; **Bl.**U. 59–; **Co.**T. 60–; **Lc.**A.; **R.**U.; **Sa.**; **Y.** [*English language edition of:* 9; *C. of:* 10]

12 **A.C.E.C. Revue.** Ateliers de constructions électriques de Charleroi. Charleroi. *A.C.E.C. Revue* [1922–38] **L.**EE; P. 25–38; UC. 27–30; **Bm.**U. 26–38 imp.; **Br.**U. 23–38; **G.**M. 27–37; **M.**P.; **N.**T. (5 yr.); **Nw.**A.; **Y.** [*C. in:* 13681]
    ACEMI. Association canadienne des étudiants en médecine et des internes. Montréal. *See* 12861.

13 **ACI Bibliography.** American Concrete Institute. Detroit. *ACI Biblphy* [1955–] **L.**P.
    A.C.S.I.L. Bulletin. Admiralty Centre for Scientific Information and Liaison. *See* 9213.
    A.C.S.I.L. Library Bulletin. Admiralty Centre for Scientific Information and Liaison. [*Contained in:* 9213]

14 **A.C.V. Gazette.** Associated Commercial Vehicles Group. London. *A.C.V. Gaz.* [1951–59] **L.**BM.; **F.**A.; **M.**P. 54–59. [*C. of:* and *Rec. as:* 20]
    A.D.A. Information Bulletin. Aluminium Development Association. *See* 23411.

15 **A.D.A. Newsletter.** American Dental Association. Chicago. *A.D.A. Newsl.* **L.**D.

16 **ADB Magazine.** Bruxelles. *ADB Mag.* **L.**P. 57–.
    ADC Gazette. Associated Equipment Co. *See* 20.

17 **ADEF.** Asociación de empleados de farmacía. Buenos Aires. *ADEF* [1931–] [>46846, 1938–39]

18 **ADM.** Revista de la Asociación dental mexicana. México. *ADM* **L.**D. 44–; MD. 55– imp.

19 **ADM Nutrition Reviews.** Minneapolis. *ADM Nutr. Rev.*
    AE. Aktiebolaget Atomenergi. *See* 1633ª.

19ª **AE** and **CI Reporter.** African Explosives and Chemical Industries. Johannesburg. *AE & CI Reptr* [1957–] **L.**BM.

20 **AEC Gazette.** Associated Equipment Co. London. *AEC Gaz.* [1926–50: 59–] **L.**BM.; P. (1 yr); **F.**A.; **M.**P.; **Y.** [*Issues for 1927 and 1928 entitled 'ADC Gazette'.* [>14, 1951–59]

21 **AEC Technical Information Bulletin.** Atomic Energy Commission. Washington. *AEC tech. Inf. Bull.* [1960–] **L.**P; SC.

21° **AEc. Technical Publications.** Mississippi Agricultural Experiment Station. State College. *AEc tech. Publs* [1959–] **L.**P.

22 **AECL.** Atomic Energy of Canada Ltd. Chalk River, Ont. *AECL* [1953–] **L.**P.; SC.

23 **A.E.E.W. Memoranda.** Atomic Energy Establishment, Winfrith. *A.E.E.W. Memor.* [1959–] **L.**BM.; P.; SC. 59–.

24 **A.E.E.W. Report.** Atomic Energy Establishment, Winfrith. *A.E.E.W. Rep.* [1959–] **L.**BM.; P.; SC.

24ª **A.E.E.W. Translations.** Atomic Energy Establishment, Winfrith. *A.E.E.W. Transl.* [1960–] **L.**BM.; P.; SC.

    A.E.G.-Journal Berlin. *See* 27.

25 **A.E.G. Mitteilungen.** Allgemeine Elektrizitäts-Gesellschaft. Berlin. *A.E.G. Mitt.* [1917–] **L.**EE. 28–40 imp.; P. 23– imp.; **Br.**U. 21–25; **G.**M. 27–31; **Y.** [*C. of:* 32305; *Suspended* 1944–51]

26 **A.E.G. Progress.** Allgemeine Elektrizitäts-Gesellschaft. Berlin. *A.E.G. Prog.* [1925–] **L.**AV. 57–; EE. 26–38 imp.; I. (4 yr.); P. 25–38: 55–; UC. 29–30; **Br.**U. 29–38: 56–; **G.**M 27–38 imp.; **M.**P. 27–30; **Sil.** 31–; **Sy.**R. 28–31.

27 **A.E.G.-Zeitung.** Allgemeine Elektrizitäts-Gesellschaft. Berlin. *A.E.G.-Ztg* [1889–14] **L.**P. 09–14.

27ᵃ **A.E.I.** John Thompson Nuclear Energy Company. *A.E.I.* [1957–] **L.**BM.

28 **AEI Automation Review.** Associated Electrical Industries. London. *AEI Automn Rev.* [1960–] **Bl.**U.

29 **AEI Electrical Distribution.** Associated Electrical Industries. *AEI elect. Distrib.* [1960] **L.**AV. [*C. in:* 30]

30 **AEI Engineering Review.** Associated Electrical Industries. London. *AEI Engng Rev.* [1960–] **L.**AV.; BM.; C.; EE.; IC.; NF.; P.; SI.; U.; UC.; **Abs.**U.; **Bl.**U.; **Bm.**C.; T.; U.; **Bn.**U.; **Br.**U.; **C.**ENG.; **Co.**T.; **Dn.**U.; **E.**R.; U.; **G.**T.; **H.**U.; **Ld.**P.; U.; **Lv.**P.; **M.**C.; P.; T.; **Ma.**T.; **Nw.**A.; **O.**R.; **Sh.**SC.; **Sil.**; **Sy.**R.; **Y.** [*C. of:* 5687, 31701 and 49717]

31 **AEI News.** Associated Electrical Industries. London. *AEI News* **L.**EE. 46– imp.; **M.**T. (1 yr)

32 **AEI Radio** and **Electronic Components Review.** Associated Electrical Industries. London. *AEI Radio electron. Compon. Rev.* [1960–] **L.**AV.

33 **AEI Research Laboratory Reprints.** Associated Electrical Industries. Rugby. *AEI Res. Lab. Repr.* [1960–] **L.**P. imp.; **Ld.**P.; **Sa.** [*C. of:* 45862]

34 **AEI Review** of **Work** and **Progress.** Associated Electrical Industries. *AEI Rev. Wk Prog.* [1960–] **L.**BM.; P.; **Y.**

34ᵃ **AEI Technical Monograph.** Associated Electrical Industries. *AEI tech. Monogr.* [1960–] **L.**P.; **Y.**

A.E.R.E. AM. Atomic Energy Research Establishment. *See* 2567.

35 **A.E.R.E. Inf./Bib.** Atomic Energy Research Establishment. Harwell. *A.E.R.E. Inf./Bib.* **L.**BM. 55–; P. 56–.

35ᵃ **A.E.R.E. Lectures.** Harwell. *A.E.R.E. Lect.* **L.**BM.; SC. 59–. [*Issued in various series*]

36 **A.E.R.E. Lib./Trans.** Atomic Energy Research Establishment. Harwell. *A.E.R.E. Lib./Trans.* **L.**BM. 55–; P. 54–.

37 **A.E.R.E. List** of **Publications** available to the **Public.** Atomic Energy Research Establishment. Harwell. *A.E.R.E. List Publs Publ.* [1955–] **L.**BM.; CB.; MO. 57–; P.; **Y.** [*C. of:* 38]

38 **A.E.R.E. List** of **Unclassified Reports.** Atomic Energy Research Establishment. Harwell. *A.E.R.E. List unclass. Rep.* [1953–55] **L.**CB. [*C. as:* 37]

39 **A.E.R.E. Memoranda.** Atomic Energy Research Establishment. Harwell. *A.E.R.E. Memor.* [1958–] **L.**BM.; SC. [*Issued in several series*]

39ᵃ **A.E.R.E. Note.** Atomic Energy Research Establishment. Harwell. *A.E.R.E. Note* [1956–] **L.**BM.; P. [*Issued in various series*]

40 **A.E.R.E. Reading List.** Atomic Energy Research Establishment. Harwell. *A.E.R.E. Read. List.* [1958–] **L.**BM.; P. 58–61; SC.

41 **A.E.R.E. Reports.** Atomic Energy Research Establishment. Harwell. *A.E.R.E. Rep.* [1948–] **L.**BM.; P.; SC. [*These reports have various series with prefix letters and the series start at various times from 1948 onwards*]

42 **A.E.R.E. Technical Note.** Atomic Energy Research Establishment. Harwell. *A.E.R.E. tech. Note* [1956–] **L.**P. 56–58.

42° **A.E.R.E. Translation.** Atomic Energy Research Establishment. Harwell. *A.E.R.E. Transl.* [1954–] **L.**BM.; P.

43 **A.E.R.E. Unclassified Reports** and their Availability in the Published Literature. Atomic Energy Research Establishment. Harwell. *A.E.R.E. unclass. Rep.* [1954–] **L.**BM. 55–; P.; SC.

A.E.S. Bulletin. Amateur Entomologists' Society. *See* 9285.

A.E.S. Leaflet. Amateur Entomologists' Society. *See* 28234.

A.E.S. Pamphlet. Amateur Entomologists' Society. *See* 36864.

43° **A.E.S.D. Data Sheet.** Association of Engineering and Shipbuilding Draughtsmen. *A.E.S.D. Data Sh.* **L.**BM. 42–.

44 **A.E.T.F.A.T. Index.** Association pour l'étude taxonomique de la flore d'Afrique tropicale. Bruxelles. *A.E.T.F.A.T. Index* **L.**BMᴺ. 53–; **O.**F. 53–.

AEÜ. Archiv der elektrischen Übertragung. *See* 4064.

45 **AGA-Journal.** Svenska Aktiebolaget Gasaccumulator. Stockholm. *AGA-Jl* **L.**P. 33–.

A.G.A. Monthly. American Gas Association. *See* 1970.

46 **A.G.A.E.M. Bulletin.** Association of Gas Appliances and Equipment Manufacturers. New York. *A.G.A.E.M. Bull.* [1936–41]

47 **AGARD Bibliography.** Advisory Group for Aeronautical Research and Development. Paris. *AGARD Biblphy* [1959–] **L.**BM.; P.; SC.

48 **AGARD Memorandum.** Advisory Group for Aeronautical Research and Development. Paris. *AGARD Memor.* [1952–] **L.**P. 53–54; QM.; **M.**U. 52–53.

49 **AGARD Papers** and **Proceedings.** Advisory Group for Aeronautical Research and Development. Paris. *AGARD Pap. Proc.* [1952–] **L.**P. 52–56; QM.

50 **AGARD Report.** Advisory Group for Aeronautical Research and Development. Paris. *AGARD Rep.* [1955–] **L.**P.; QM.; SC. 56–; **Br.**U.; **M.**U. imp.

51 **AGARDograph.** Advisory Group for Aeronautical Research and Development. Paris. *AGARDograph* [1954–] **L.**BM. 55–; P. imp.; SC.; **Bl.**U. 55– imp.; **Br.**U. 55– imp.

52 **AGFA Cinetechnical News.** Wolfen. *AGFA cinetech. News* [1957–] **L.**P.

53 **AGFA-Reprod-Mitteilungen.** Leverkusen. *AGFA-Reprod-Mitt.* [1953–] **L.**P.

54 **A.G.M.A. News Bulletin.** *AGMA News Bull.* [1947–] **Y.**

54° **A.G.S. Handbooks.** American Geographical and Statistical Society. London, New York. *A.G.S. Handb.* [1957–] **L.**BM.

54ᵉ **A.H.S.B. Report.** Authority Health and Safety Branch, United Kingdom Atomic Energy Authority. Risley. *A.H.S.B. Rep.* [1959–] **L.**BM.; P.; SC. [*Issued in various series*]

55 **A.I. Digest.** Columbia. *A.I. Dig.* [1957–] **E.**AB.; AR.

56 **A I A.** Asociación de ingenieros agronomos. Montevideo [1956–] **L.**MY.; **C.**A.; **E.**AB.; **Hu.**G.; **Sil.** [*C. of:* 46316]

57 **A I A Aerospace.** Aerospace Industries Association. *A I A Aerospace* [1960–] **L.**AV. [*C. of:* 56]

58 **A I A Planes.** Aerospace Industries Association. *A I A Planes* [1945–59] **L.**AV. 51–59. [*C. as:* 57]

59 **A.I.B.S. Bulletin.** American Institute of Biological Sciences. Washington. *A.I.B.S. Bull.* [1951–] **L.**P. 55–; **Y.**

60 **A.I.Ch.E. Journal.** American Institute of Chemical Engineers. New York; Richmond, Va. *A.I.Ch.E. Jl* [1955–] **L.**C.; P.; SC.; **Bm.**T. 59–; **Db.** 56–; **E.**U.; **Ep.**D.; **G.**T.; **Ld.**U. 58–; **M.**D.; T.; U.; **N.**U. 57–; **Rn.**B. 57–; **Sh.**SC.; **Ste.** 57–; **Wd.**; **Y.**

61 **A.I.E.E. Standards.** American Institute of Electrical Engineers. New York. *A.I.E.E. Stand.* **M.**P. 25–30 imp.

62 **A.I.F. News.** Agricultural, Insecticide and Fungicide Association. New York. *A.I.F. News* [1942–] **L.**MY. 47–.

62° **A.I.H.P. Notes.** American Institute of the History of Pharmacy. Madison. *A.I.H.P. Notes* [1955–57]

63 **A.I.M.E. Series.** American Institute of Mining Engineers. New York. *A.I.M.E. Ser.* **L.**BM. 32–.
　　A.I.M.M.E. Transactions. American Institute of Mining and Metallurgical Engineers. *See* 53550.

64 **A.I.R.** Archives of Interamerican Rheumatology. Rio de Janeiro. *A.I.R.* [1958–] **L.**MA.; MD.

65 **ALA rotante.** Roma. *ALA rotante* **L.**P. 60–.

66 **A.L.B. Mitteilungen.** Arbeitsgemeinschaft für landwirtschaftliches Bauwesen. Frankfurt-a-M. *A.L.B. Mitt.* [1950–55] **L.**AM.; Sil. 53–55. [*C. as:* 58500]

67 **A.L.S. Quarterly Notes.** Agricultural Land Service. London. *A.L.S. q. Notes* [1949–52] **L.**AM.; **C.**A. [*C. as:* 27988]

68 **A.M.A. American Journal** of **Diseases** of **Children.** Chicago. *A.M.A. Am. J. Dis. Child.* [1951–55] **L.**GH.; MA.; MC. 51–53; MD.; S.; TD.; U.; UCH.; **Abd.**R.; U.; **Bl.**U.; **Bm.**U.; **Br.**U.; **C.**V.; **Cr.**MD.; **Db.**; **Dn.**U.; **E.**P.; U.; **G.**F.; U.; **Ld.**U.; **Lv.**M.; **M.**MS.; **Nw.**A.; **O.**R.; **R.**D.; **Sh.**U. [*C. of:* 2010; *C. as:* 81]

69 **A.M.A. Archives** of **Dermatology.** New York, etc. *A.M.A. Archs Derm.* [1956–60] **L.**CB.; MA.; MD.; RA.; TD.; U.; UCH.; **Abd.**U.; **Bl.**U.; **Bm.**U.; **Br.**U.; **C.**UL.; **Cr.**MD.; **Db.**; **Dn.**U.; **E.**P.; U.; **G.**F.; T.; U. imp.; **Ld.**U.; **Lv.**M.; U.; **M.**MS.; **Nw.**A.; **O.**R.; **Sh.**U. [*C. of:* 70; *C. as:* 4211]

70 **A.M.A. Archives** of **Dermatology** and **Syphilology.** New York, etc. *A.M.A. Archs Derm. Syph.* [1951–54] **L.**CB.; MA.; MD.; RA.; TD.; U.; UCH.; **Abd.**U.; **Bl.**U.; **Bm.**U.; **Br.**U.; **C.**UL.; **Cr.**MD.; **Db.**; **Dn.**U.; **E.**P.; U.; **G.**F.; T.; U. imp.; **Ld.**U.; **Lv.**M.; U.; **M.**MS.; **Nw.**A.; **O.**R.; **Sh.**U. [*C. of:* 4212; *C. as:* 69]

71 **A.M.A. Archives** of **General Psychiatry.** Chicago. *A.M.A. Archs gen. Psychiatry* [1959–60] **L.**GH.; MA.; MC.; MD.; OP.; PS.; S.; U.; UC.; **Abd.**U.; **Bl.**U.; **Bm.**U.; **Br.**U.; **C.**APH.; PH.; PS.; **Cr.**MD.; **Db.**; **Dn.**U.; **E.**U.; **G.**F.; U.; **Ld.**U.; **M.**MS.; **Nw.**A.; **O.**PH.; R.; **Sh.**U. [*C. from:* 76; *C. as:* 4224]

72 **A.M.A. Archives** of **Industrial Health.** Chicago. *A.M.A. Archs ind. Hlth* [1955–50] **L.**AM.; AV.; C.; CB.; H.; MA.; MC.; MD.; P.; PR.; SH.; TD.; **Abd.**U.; **Bl.**U.; **Bm.**C.; **Cr.**MD.; **Dn.**U.; **E.**U.; **Ep.**D.; **G.**U.; **Ld.**P.; U.; **Lv.**P. 59–60; **M.**C.; D.; MS.; **Nw.**A.; **Sh.**S.; **Ste.**; **Wd.** [*C. of:* 73; *C. as:* 4219]

73 **A.M.A. Archives** of **Industrial Hygiene** and **Occupational Medicine.** Chicago. *A.M.A. Archs ind. Hyg.* [1951–54] **L.**AM.; AV.; C.; CB.; H.; MA.; MC.; MD.; P.; PR.; SH.; TD.; **Abd.**U.; **Bl.**U.; **Bm.**C. 52–54; **Dn.**U. 53–54; **E.**U.; **Ep.**D.; **G.**U.; **Ld.**U.; **M.**C.; D.; MS.; **Nw.**A.; **Sh.**S.; **Ste.**; **Wd.** [*C. of:* 4238; *C. as:* 72]

74 **A.M.A. Archives** of **Internal Medicine.** Chicago. *A.M.A. Archs internal Med.* [1951–60] **L.**C.; GH.; H. 56–57; MA.; MC.; MD.; PH.; S.; TD.; U.; UC.; UCH. 51–56 imp.; **Abd.**R.; U.; **Bl.**U.; **Br.**U.; **C.**PA.; V. 53–60; **Cr.**MD.; **Db.**; **Dn.**U.; **E.**P.; U.; **G.**F.; U.; **Ld.**U.; **Lv.**M.; U.; **M.**MS.; **Nw.**A.; **O.**R.; **Sh.**U. [*C. of:* and *Rec. as:* 4259]

75 **A.M.A. Archives** of **Neurology.** Chicago. *A.M.A. Archs Neurol.* [1959–60] **L.**GH.; MA.; MC.; MD.; OP.; PS.; S.; U.; UC.; **Abd.**U.; **Bl.**U.; **Bm.**U.; **Br.**U.; **C.**APH.; PH.; PS.; **Cr.**MD.; **Db.**; **Dn.**U.; **E.**U.; **G.**F.; U.; **Ld.**U.; **M.**MS.; **Nw.**A.; **O.**PH.; R.; **Sh.**U. [*C. from:* 76; *C. as:* 4312]

76 **A.M.A. Archives** of **Neurology** and **Psychiatry.** Chicago. *A.M.A. Archs Neurol. Psychiatry* [1951–59] **L.**GH. 56–59; MA.; MC.; MD.; OP.; PS.; S.; U.; UC.; **Abd.**U.; **Bl.**U.; **Bm.**U.; **Br.**U.; **C.**APH.; PH.; PS.; **Cr.**MD.; **Db.**; **Dn.**U. 55–59; **E.**U.; **G.**F.; U. imp.; **Ld.**U.; **M.**MS.; **Nw.**A.; **O.**PH.; R.; **Sh.**U. [*C. of:* 4314; *C. as:* 71 and 75]

77 **A.M.A. Archives** of **Ophthalmology.** New York. *A.M.A. Archs Ophthal.* [1951–60] **L.**MA.; MD.; OP.; S.; U.; **Abd.**U.; **Bl.**U.; **Bm.**U.; **Br.**U.; **C.**MS.; **Dn.**U.; **E.**P.; S.; U.; **G.**F.; **Ld.**U.; **Lv.**M.; **M.**MS.; **Nw.**A.; **O.**R.; **Sh.**U.; **Y.** [*C. of:* and *Rec. as:* 4321]

78 **A.M.A. Archives** of **Otolaryngology.** Chicago. *A.M.A. Archs Otolar.* [1951–60] **L.**C.; CB.; MA.; MD.; U.; UCH.; **Abd.**U.; **Bl.**U.; **Br.**U.; **Cr.**MD.; **Dn.**U.; **E.**S.; **G.**F.; **Ld.**U.; **Lv.**M.; **M.**MS.; **Nw.**A.; **Sh.**U. [*C. of:* and *Rec. as:* 4326]

79 **A.M.A. Archives** of **Pathology.** Chicago. *A.M.A. Archs Path.* [1951–60] **L.**CB. imp.; LI.; MA.; MD.; OP.; S.; TD.; U.; UCH.; **Abd.**U.; **Bm.**U.; **Br.**U.; **C.**PA.; V. 53–60; **Cr.**MD.; **Db.**; **Dn.**U.; **E.**N.; PO.; U.; **G.**F.; U.; **Ld.**U.; **M.**MS.; **Nw.**A.; **O.**P.; R.; **Sh.**U.; **W.**; **Y.** [*C. of:* and *Rec. as:* 4330]

80 **A.M.A. Archives** of **Surgery.** Chicago. *A.M.A. Archs Surg.* [1951–60] **L.**CB.; MA.; MD.; S.; U.; **Bl.**U.; **Bm.**U.; **Br.**U.; **C.**APH.; **Cr.**MD.; **Db.**; **Dn.**U.; **E.**S.; U.; **G.**F.; **Lv.**M.; **M.**MS.; **O.**R.; **Sh.**U. [*C. of:* and *Rec. as:* 4372]

81 **A.M.A. Journal** of **Diseases** of **Children.** Chicago. *A.M.A. J. Dis. Child.* [1956–60] **L.**GH.; H.; MA.; MD.; S.; TD.; U.; UCH.; **Abd.**R.; U.; **Bl.**U.; **Bm.**U.; **Br.**U.; **C.**V.; **Cr.**MD.; **Db.**; **Dn.**U.; **E.**P.; U.; **G.**F.; U.; **Ld.**U.; **Lv.**M.; **M.**MS.; **Nw.**A.; **O.**R.; **R.**D.; **Sh.**U. [*C. of:* 68; *C. as:* 2010]

82 **AMCA Bulletin.** American Mosquito Control Association. Albany. *AMCA Bull.* [1948–] **Y.**

84 **AMHS Journal.** American Material Handling Society. Boston, Mass. *AMHS Jl* **L.**P. [*C. of:* 29568; *Issued in:* 32968]

85 **A.M.M.** Organo de la Asociación médica mexicana. México. *A.M.M.* [1923–25] [*C. as:* 46319]

86 **A.M.T.D.A. Journal.** Agricultural Machinery and Tractor Dealers' Association. London. *A.M.T.D.A. Jl* [1949–52] **L.**AM.; BM.
　　A.N.A.R.E. Interim Reports. *See* 23773.

87 **A.N.A.R.E. Reports.** Australian National Antarctic Research Expeditions. Melbourne. *A.N.A.R.E. Rep.*
Series A. Narrative, Geography, Geology, Glaciology **L.**BM.
Series B. Zoology **L.**BM.; BM^N. 50–; Z.; **Wo.**
Series C. Terrestrial Magnetism [1952–] **L.**BM.; MO.
Series D. Meteorology [1948–] **L.**BM.

88 **ANSCO Abstracts.** Binghampton, N.Y. *ANSCO Abstr.* **L.**P. 54–61*.

88ᶜ **AO.** Atualidades odontológicas. São Paulo. *AO*

88ᵉ **A.O.P. News.** Association of Optical Practitioners. London. *A.O.P. News* [1957–] **L.**BM.; **Bm.**T.; **C.**UL.; **Db.**; **O.**R. [*C. of:* 89]

89 **A.O.P. Newsletter.** Association of Optical Practitioners. London. *A.O.P. Newsl.* [1948–57] **L.**BM.; **Bm.**T. 56–57; **C.**UL.; **Db.** imp.; **O.**R. [*C. as:* 88ᵉ]

90 **AOPA Pilot.** Aircraft Owners and Pilots Association. Chicago. *AOPA Pilot* [1958–] **L.**AV.

91 **A.O.P.I.** Associazione orticola professionale italiana. Firenze. *A.O.P.I.*

92 **A.O.S. Journal.** London. *A.O.S. Jl* [1907–10] **L.**AM.; BM. [*C. as:* 15888]

94 **A.P.C.A. Abstracts.** Air Pollution Control Association. Pittsburgh. *A.P.C.A. Abstr.* [1955–] **L.**MO. 58–; P. 58–; TD. 58–; **Y.**

95 **A.P.C.A. News.** Air Pollution Control Association. Pittsburg, Wilmerding. *A.P.C.A. News* **L.**MO. 57–59; P. (curr.).

96 **A.Ph.A. Monographs.** American Pharmaceutical Association. Washington. *A.Ph.A. Monogr.* [1935–] **L.**SC.

97 **A.P.I. Standards.** American Petroleum Institute. Dallas. *A.P.I. Stand.* [1930–] **L.**P.

APPITA. Australian Pulp and Paper Industry Technical Association. *See* 3733.

98 **A.P.R.** Australasian Photo Review. Sydney. *A.P.R.* [1938–] **L.**PG.; **We.**K. [*C. of:* 5346]

98ᵒ **APV Bulletin.** Aluminium Plant and Vessel Company. *APV Bull.* **L.**BM. 49–.

99 **A.R.C. Report Series.** Agricultural Research Council. London. *A.R.C. Rep. Ser.* [1935–] **L.**BM.; P. **Bm.**P.; **Bn.**U.; **Bra.**P. 56–; **C.**A.; APH. 49–; **Ld.**P. 39–; **O.**R.; RE.; **Rt.**; **Y.**

99ᵒ **A.R.D.E. Translation.** Armament Research and Development Establishment. Fort Halstead. *A.R.D.E. Transl.* **L.**P. 57–.

ARMA Engineering. American Bosch Arma Corporation. *See* 4814.

100 **ARS Journal.** American Rocket Society. Easton. *ARS Jl* [1959–] **L.**AV.; P.; **Bl.**U.; **Bm.**P.; T.; **F.**A.; **G.**U.; **Lv.**P.; **M.**U.; **N.**U.; **Y.** [*C. of:* 25331]

101 **ARU.** Internationale Automobil-Rundschau. Zürich. *ARU* [1952–] **L.**P. 54–.

102 **A.S.A. Bulletin.** American Standards Association. New York. *A.S.A. Bull.* **L.**P. 30–32*; [*C. as:* 23288]

103 **A Sc W Journal.** Association of Scientific Workers. London. *A Sc W Jl* [1955–] **L.**BM.; P. (curr.); **Abs.**N.; **Bm.**C.; P.; **C.**UL.; **E.**A.; T.; **Ex.**U.; **O.**B.; R.; **Y.** [*C. of:* 49272]

104 **A.Sc.W.S.A. Research Memoranda.** Cape Town. *A.Sc.W.S.A. Res. Memor.* [1943–]

105 **A.S.E. Journal.** Ahsanullah School of Engineering. Dacca. *A.S.E. Jl* **L.**BM. 34–38.

106 **ASEA-Journal.** Allmänna svenska elektriska Aktiebolaget. Västerås. *ASEA-Jl* [1924–] **L.**BM. 51–; EE.; P.; SI. 46–; U. 49–; UC. 29–30; **Bl.**U. 26–; **Bm.**U. 26–39: 47–; **Bn.**U. 46–; **Br.**U. 53–; **C.**ENG. 47–; **F.**A. 46–; **G.**M. 27–39 imp.; T. (5 yr.); **Ld.**P. 49–; **Lv.**P. 46–; **M.**P. 27– v. imp.; T. 46–; U. 46–; **Nw.**A. 27–37; **Sh.**IO. 32–; **Y.**

107 **ASEA Research.** Allmänna svenska elektriska aktiebolaget. Västerås. *ASEA Res.* [1958–] **L.**AV.; P.; **Br.**U.; **Co.**T. 58; **Bl.**U.; **G.**E.; **Ld.**P.; U.; **Ma.**T.; **Y.**

108 **ASEA-Revue.** Allmänna svenska elektriska aktiebolaget. Västerås. *ASEA-Revue* [1928–] **Sy.**R. 52–; **Y.**

109 **ASEA Tidning.** Allmänna Svenska Elektriska aktiebolaget. Västerås. *ASEA Tidn.* [1909–] **L.**P. 43–; **Y.**

110 **ASEA Zeitschrift.** Allmänna svenska elektriska aktiebolaget. Västerås. *ASEA Z.* [1956–] **Y.**

ASGROW Monographs. Associated Seed Growers. New Haven. *See* 4974.

111 **ASHRAE Journal.** American Society of Heating, Refrigerating and Air-Conditioning Engineers. New York. *ASHRAE Jl* [1959–] **L.**AM.; IC.; P.; SC.; **Lv.**P.; U.; **M.**P.; **Ma.**T.; **Sh.**SC.; **Wd.**; **Y.** [*C. of:* 42429 and *part of:* 22009]

112 **ASL Research Report.** American Scientific Laboratories. Madison. *ASL Res. Rep.*

113 **ASLE Transactions.** American Society of Lubrication Engineers. New York, London. *ASLE Trans.* [1959–] **L.**BM.; P.; SC.; **Abs.**N.; **Bl.**U.; **Co.**T.; **G.**T.; U. 61–; **Ld.**U. 59; **Lv.**P.; **M.**P.; U.; **O.**R.; **Sh.**SC.; **Sil.**; **Y.** [*C. of:* 28833]

114 **A.S.M. Review** of **Metal Literature.** American Society of Metals. Cleveland. *A.S.M. Rev. metal Lit.* [1944–] **L.**I.; NF.; P. 54–; SC.; **Bm.**C. 44–47; P. 45–; T.; **Lv.**P. 50– imp.; **M.**P. imp.; T.; **Rn.**B.; **Sh.**IO.; SC. 50–; **Y.**

115 **A.S.M.E. Mechanical Catalogue** and **Directory.** *A.S.M.E. mech. Cat.* [1939–55] **L.**P. 39: 41; **G.**M. 39–47: 55. [*C. of:* and *Rec. as:* 29750]

A.S.M.E. Transactions. *See* 53570.

116 **A.S.N.H.S. Journal.** Association of School Natural History Societies. Carshalton. *A.S.N.H.S. Jl* [1950–52] **C.**UL. [*C. as:* 50764]

116ᵒ **ASPAS.** Madrid. *ASPAS* [1950–] **C.**A. 51–.

117 **A.S.R.E. Circular.** New York. *A.S.R.E. Circ.* [1924–31]

118 **A.S.R.E. Journal.** New York. *A.S.R.E. Jl* [1914–22] **L.**P. 20–22; **Lv.**U. [*C. of:* 53572; *C. as:* 42429]

119 **A.S.S.T. Handbook.** Cleveland. *A.S.S.T. Handb.* [1927–29] [*C. as:* 34142]

120 **ASTA Publications.** Association of Short-Circuit Testing Authorities. London. *ASTA Publs* [1939–] **L.**BM.; P.; **Y.**

121 **A.S.T.E. Journal.** American Society of Tool Engineers. Detroit. *A.S.T.E. Jl* [1932–35] [*C. as:* 53358]

122 **A.S.T.E. Research Report.** American Society of Tool Engineers. Detroit. *A.S.T.E. Res. Rep.* [1954–] **L.**P.

    A.S.T.M. Bulletin. *See* 9356.
    A.S.T.M. Proceedings. *See* 38910.
    A.S.T.M. References on **Fatigue.** *See* 42414.

123 **A.S.T.M. Standards.** Philadelphia. *A.S.T.M. Stand.* [1916–] **L.**BM.; C. 21–; I. 18–; MT. 21–; NF. 18–; P.; PR. 21–; PT. 21–30; **Bl.**U. 16–27; **Bm.**C. (curr.); P. 25–; U. 21–; **C.**ENG. (curr.); **G.**I. 18–; M. 24–; U. 49–; **Ld.**P.; U.; W. 27–; **Lv.**U. 21–; **M.**C.; P.; U. imp.; **Sh.**P. 21: 27–; **St.**R. 39–; **Sw.**U. 33–36 imp.; **Y.** [*From 1910–15 issued in* 58003]

124 **A.S.T.M. Standards** on **Electrical Insulating Materials.** Philadelphia. *A.S.T.M. Stand. electl insul. Mater.* **Y.**

125 **A.S.T.M. Standards** on **Textile Materials.** Philadelphia. *A.S.T.M. Stand. Text. Mater.* **Ld.**W. 35–; **M.**C.; P. 48–51; **Y.**

126 **A.S.T.M. Tentative Standards.** Philadelphia. *A.S.T.M. tentat. Stand.* [1917–38] **L.**P.; PT.; **G.**U. 24–38; **Ld.**W. 28–38 imp.; **M.**U. 21: 27: 28; **Sw.**U. 33–36 imp. [*Issued in* 58003 *for 1914–15; in* 38910 *for 1916–38; and subsequently in* 123]

127 **ASXRED Monographs.** American Society for X-Ray and Electron Diffraction. Washington. *ASXRED Monogr.* [1944–46] **L.**BM.ᴺ. imp.; P.; SC. [*C. as:* 8]

128 **ATA.** Associazione tecnica dell' automobile. Torino. *ATA* **L.**P. 58–; **Li.**M. 54–; **Y.**

129 **ATA ricerche.** Associazione tecnica dell' automobile. Torino. *ATA Ric.* **L.**P. 52–59. [*Supplement to:* 128]

    ATB Metallurgie. Mons. *See* 31482.

130 **A.T.C. Gazette.** *A.T.C. Gaz.* [1941–46] **Bm.**P. [*C. as:* 1550]

131 **A.T.E. Journal.** Automatic Telephone and Electric Company. Liverpool. *A.T.E. Jl* [1953–] **L.**AV.; BM.; EE.; P.; **Bl.**U. 56–; **Bm.**T. 58–; **Bn.**U.; **Br.**U.; **C.**UL.; **Co.**T. 62–; **Db.** 58–; **F.**A.; **Lv.**P.; **M.**P.; **Ma.**T.; **Sa.**; **Y.** [*C. of:* 51029]

    A.T.M. Archiv für technisches Messen. *See* 4166.

131° **ATPAS Bulletin.** Technical Publications Committee, Association of Teachers of Printing and Allied Subjects. Chatham. *ATPAS Bull.* [1952–] **L.**BM.

    A.T.S. Transactions of the Danish Academy of Technical Sciences. *See* 53685.

132 **ATS Review.** Associated Technical Societies of Detroit. Detroit. *ATS Rev.* [1929–33] [*C. of:* 9419]

    ATZ. Automobiltechnische Zeitschrift. *See* 5502.

133 **ATZ.-Beihefte.** Automobiltechnische Zeitschrift. Stuttgart. *ATZ.-Beih.* [1935–] **L.**P. 35. [*Supplement to:* 5502]

    AVC. Agricultural and veterinary chemicals. *See* 1426.

134 **A.W.A. Technical Review.** Sydney, etc. *A.W.A. tech. Rev.* [1935–] **L.**AV. 41– imp.; BM.; EE. imp.; MO.; P. 36–; SI. 38–; UC.; **Bm.**U; **Br.**U. 56–; **C.**UL.; **E.**U.; **F.**A. 53–; **G.**U. imp.; **Ld.**U. 37–; **M.**U. 37–; **Ma.**T. 48–; **O.**R. 37–; **R.**U. 48–; **Y.**

135 **AWF-Mitteilungen.** Ausschuss für wirtschaftliche Fertigung. Berlin, Frankfurt am Main. *AWF.-Mitt.*

[1918–] **L.**P. 18–27: 59–. [*From 1918–22 forms part of:* 6516; *from 1922–27 part of:* 29497; *and from 1959 part of:* 58892]

136 **AWF-Qualitätskontrolle.** Ausschuss für wirtschaftliche Fertigung. Frankfurt am Main. *AWF-QualKontr.* **L.**P. 59–. [*Supplement to* and *forms part of:* 58892]

137 **AWF-Sperrgetriebe.** Ausschuss für wirtschaftliche Fertigung. Berlin. *AWF-Sperrgetriebe* [1955–56] **L.**P. [*C. as:* 55812]

137° **A.W.R.E. Report.** Atomic Weapons Research Establishment. Aldermaston. *A.W.R.E. Rep.* [1956–] **L.**BM.

138 **A.W.R.E. Translation.** Atomic Weapons Research Establishment. Aldermaston. *A.W.R.E. Transl.* [1956–] **L.**BM.; P.; SC.; **Y.** [*Issued in various series*]

139 **A.W.S. Bibliographies.** American Welding Society. New York. *AWS Biblphies* **L.**P.

140 **Aanteekeningen** van het **verhandelde** in de **sectievergaderingen** van het **Prov. Utrechtsch genootschap** van **kunsten** en **wetenschappen.** Utrecht. *Aanteek. Verhand. Sectievergad. prov. utrecht. Genoot.* [1845–21] **L.**R.; **Db.** 00–21; **E.**A. 85–21; C. 12–20; R. [*C. in:* 56275]

    Aarbog. *See* Årbog.
    Aarbok. *See* Årbok.

141 **Aarde** en haar **volken.** Haarlem. *Aarde* [1865–]
    Aarsberetning. *See* Årsberetning.
    Aarskrift. *See* Årskrift.
    Aarsoversigt, Aarsoversikt. *See* **Årsoversigt, Årsoversikt.**

142 **Abbott Memorial Lecture.** University of Nottingham. *Abbott memor. Lect.* [1927–] **Bl.**U.; **O.**R.; **Y.**

143 **Abeille.** Alger. *Abeille, Alger*

144 **Abeille.** Paris. *Abeille, Paris* [1864–45] **L.**BM. 64–00; BMᴺ.; E.; **C.**B. 64–72; UL. 64–68: 22–45; **O.**H. 64–73 imp.

145 **Abeille.** Québec. *Abeille, Québ.* [1919–28] **Rt.** 26–28. [*C. as:* 147]

146 **Abeille** et sa **culture.** Huy. *Abeille Cult.* [1893–]

147 **Abeille** et l'**érable.** Québec. *Abeille Érable* [1928–] **Rt.** 34–40: 46–53 imp. [*C. of:* 145]

148 **Abeille** de **France.** *Abeille Fr.* **Y.**

149 **Abeille méridionale.** Toulouse. *Abeille mérid.*

150 **Abeille rhodanienne.** Marseille. *Abeille rhodan.* [1934–]

151 **Abeilles** et **ruchers.** Limoges. *Abeilles Ruch.*

152 **Abel's Photographic Weekly.** New York. *Abel's photogr. Wkly* [1907–34] **L.**PG. 11–34 imp. [*C. as:* 39951]

153 **Aberdeen University Studies.** Aberdeen. *Aberd. Univ. Stud.* [1900–] **L.**BM.; BMᴺ. 07–15 imp.; U. imp.; **Abd.**U.; **Abs.**N. imp.; **Bm.**U. 00–28 imp.; **Br.**U. imp.; **Db.** imp.; **E.**A. imp.; C. 09–; H. 02–; R. 04–; U.; **G.**U. imp.; **Ld.**U. imp.; **Lv.**U.; **M.**U. imp; **Nw.**A. 00–07 imp.; **O.**B.; **Sa.**

154 **Aberdeen-Angus.** Buenos Aires. *Aberd.-Angus, B. Aires* **O.**R. 39– imp.; **Y.**

155 **Aberdeen-Angus Review.** Aberdeen. *Aberd.-Angus Rev.* [1919–] **Abd.**U. 19–40: 46–48; **Bn.**U. 56–; **C.**A. 21–; **Db.** 57–; **Ld.**U. 25–; **N.**U. (curr.); **O.**RE. 26–40; **Y.**

156 Aberystwyth Studies. University of Wales. Aberystwyth. *Aberyst. Stud.* [1912–36] **L**.BM. imp.; BM^N.; U.; **Abd**.U.; **Abs**.N.; U.; **Bl**.U.; **Bm**.U.; **Br**.U. 24–36; **C**.UL.; **Cr**.M.; P.; U.; **Db**.; **E**.U.; **G**.U.; **Ld**.U.; **Lv**.U.; **M**.U. 12–34; **N**.U.; **O**.B.; **Sw**.U.

157 Abhandlungen aus dem Aerodynamischen Institut an der **Technischen Hochschule, Aachen.** *Abh. aerodyn. Inst. Aachen* [1921–34] **L**.AV. 21–32; P. 26–34; SC.

158 Abhandlungen der Agrikulturwissenschaftlichen Gesellschaft in Finnland. Helsingfors. *Abh. agrikwiss. Ges. Finnl.* [1911–26] **Rt**. imp. [*C. in:* 51435]

159 Abhandlungen der Akademie der Wissenschaften zu Göttingen. Göttingen. *Abh. Akad. Wiss. Göttingen* Mathematisch-physikaliche Klasse. [1923–] **L**.BM.; BM^N.; MO. 58–; P.; R.; SC.; U. 57–; **Abs**.N.; **C**.P.; UL.; **Db**.; **E**.R.; **O**.R.; **Sa**. 56–. [*C. of:* 232; *also supplement*]

 Abhandlungen der Akademie der Wissenschaften zu **Mainz.** *See* 246.

160 Abhandlungen des Archivs für Molluskenkunde. Frankfurt. *Abh. Arch. Molluskenk.* [1922–29] **L**.BM^N.; **C**.UL.

161 Abhandlungen aus der Augenheilkunde und ihren Grenzgebieten. Berlin. *Abh. Augenheilk.* [1926–38] **L**.MD. [*C. as:* 6812]

162 Abhandlungen der Badischen Landeswetterwarte. Karlsruhe. *Abh. bad. Landeswetterw.* **L**.MO. 22–32.

163 Abhandlungen der Bayerischen Akademie der Wissenschaften. München. *Abh. bayer. Akad. Wiss.* Math.-phys. Kl. [1829–] **L**.BM. 1832–; BM^N. 1829–39; C. 1829–30; G. 1829–16; GL. 00–; GM. 24–; L.; MD. 1852–92: 03–06; MO. 13–33; P. 1829–25; RI. 1829–36; S. 1829–14; SC. 36–44: 49–; UC. 29–36; Z.; **Abd**.U. 1860–; **C**.P. 1832–; UL.; **Db**.; **E**.C. 1832–1841: 09–14 imp.; O. 1844–14; R.; U. 1829–39; **G**.U. imp.; **Lv**.U. 83–06; **M**.U. 09–14: 24–30 imp.; **Nw**.A. 1832–39; **O**.B. 1832–; R. 1832–; **Pl**.M. 09– imp.; **Sa**. 1832–; **Y**.

164 Abhandlungen und **Berichte des Deutschen Museums.** Berlin, etc. *Abh. Ber. dt. Mus.* [1929–] **L**.P. 29–39 imp.; SC.; **Y**.

165 Abhandlungen und **Berichte des K. Zoologischen** u. **anthropologisch-ethnographischen Museums** zu **Dresden.** *Abh. Ber. K. zool. anthrop.-ethn. Mus. Dresden* [1886–22] **L**.BM.; BM^N.; Z.; **Bl**.U. 86–07; **C**.UL. [*C. as:* 166]

166 Abhandlungen und **Berichte der Museen für Tierkunde und Völkerkunde** zu **Dresden.** *Abh. Ber. Mus. Tierk. Völkerk. Dresden* [1923–39] **L**.BM.; BM^N. 23–34; Z.; **C**.UL. [*C. of:* 165; *C. as:* 173]

167 Abhandlungen und **Berichte** aus dem **Museum für Natur-** und **Heimatkunde** (*afterwards* **Naturkunde** und **Vorgeschichte**) in **Magdeburg.** *Abh. Ber. Mus. Nat-. u. Heimatk.* (*Naturk. Vorgesch.*) *Magdeburg* [1905–48] **L**.BM. 05–09; BM^N.; GL. 05–12; L. 05–12; UC. 05–12; Z. 05–25 imp.; **Db**.; **E**.R. 05–12; **G**.N. 05–12 imp.; **Lv**.U. 05–12. [*C. as:* 169]

168 Abhandlungen und **Berichte des Naturhistorichen Museums** zu **Görlitz.** *Abh. Ber. naturh. Mus. Görlitz.* [1953] **L**.SC.; **Bl**.U.; **Db**. [*C. of:* 251; *C. as:* 170]

169 Abhandlungen und **Berichte** für **Naturkunde** und **Vorgeschichte.** Magdeburg. *Abh. Ber. Naturk. Vorgesch.* [1948–] **L**.BM^N.; **Db**.; **Y**. [*C. of:* 167]

170 Abhandlungen und **Berichte des Naturkundes-museums-Forschungsstelle.** Görlitz. *Abh. Ber.* *NaturkMus.-ForschStelle, Görlitz* [1954–] **L**.BM.; BM^N.; **Bl**.U.; **Db**. [*C. of:* 168]

171 Abhandlungen und **Berichte des Naturkundlichen Museums 'Mauritianum'.** Altenburg. *Abh. Ber. naturk. Mus. 'Mauritianum'* [1958–] **L**.BM^N [*C. of:* 32673]

172 Abhandlungen und **Berichte der Pommerschen naturforschenden Gesellschaft.** Stettin. *Abh. Ber. pommersch. naturf. Ges.* **L**.BM^N. 20–29★. [*C. as:* 17108]

173 Abhandlungen und **Berichte** aus dem **Staatlichen Museum** für **Tierkunde. Forschungsinstitut.** Dresden, Leipzig. *Abh. Ber. st. Mus. Tierk., Dresden* [1953–] **L**.BM.; BM^N.; Z. (zool.); **C**.UL.; **Y**. [*C. of:* 166]

 Abhandlungen und **Berichte der technischen Gewerbeakademie in Chemnitz.** *See* 174.

174 Abhandlungen und **Berichte der technischen Staatslehranstalten in Chemnitz.** *Abh. Ber. tech. StLehranst. Chemnitz* [1912–28]

175 Abhandlungen und **Berichte des Vereins der Naturfreunde** zu **Greiz.** *Abh. Ber. Ver. NatFreunde Greiz*

176 Abhandlungen und **Berichte des Vereins für Naturkunde** zu **Cassel.** *Abh. Ber. Ver. Naturk. Cassel.* **L**.BM^N. 87–13; **Bl**.U. 95–19; **E**.R. 94–; **G**.N. 94–12 imp.

177 Abhandlungen aus der **Braunkohlen-** und **Kali-industrie.** Halle (Saale). *Abh. Braunkohl.- u. Kali-Ind.* **L**.P. 21–36.

178 Abhandlungen der Braunschweigischen wissen-schaftlichen Gesellschaft. Braunschweig. *Abh. braun-schw. wiss. Ges.* [1949–] **L**.BM.; BM^N.; I. 51–; U.; **Br**.U.; **C**.P.; UL.; **Db**.; **E**.U.; **M**.U.; **Y**.

 Abhandlungen der Deutschen Akademie der Wis-senschaften zu **Berlin. Geomagnetisches Institut Potsdam.** *See* 207.

179 Abhandlungen der Deutschen Akademie der Wissenschaften zu **Berlin.** *Abh. dt. Akad. Wiss. Berl.*
 Mathematisch-naturwissenschaftliche Klasse [1945–49] **L**.BM.; BM^N.; GL.; LI.; P.; R.; SC.; SI.; UC.; Z.; **Abd**.U.; **C**.P.; **Db**.; **E**.R.; U.; **G**.U.; **O**.B.; R.; **Sa**.; **Y**.
 Klasse für Mathematik und allgemeine Natur-wissenschaften [1950–54] **L**.BM.; BM^N.; GL.; LI.; P.; R.; RI. 54; UC.; Z.; **Abd**.U.; **C**.P.; **Db**.; **E**.R.; U.; **G**.U.; **O**.B.; R.; **Sa**.; **Y**.
 Klasse für medizinische Wissenschaften [1950–54] **L**.SC.; **C**.P. 53–54; **O**.R. 54; **Y**.
 Klasse für technische Wissenschaften [1950–54] **L**.SC. 53–54; **C**.P.; **Y**.
 Klasse für Chemie, Geologie und Biologie [1955–] **L**.BM.; BM^N.; GL.; P.; R.; RI.; SC.; U.; UC.; Z.; **Abd**.U.; **C**.P.; **Db**.; **E**.R.; U.
 Klasse für Mathematik, Physik und Technik [1955–] **L**.BM.; P.; R.; SC.; U.; **G**.U.; **O**.R.; **Y**.
 Klasse für Medizin [1954–] **L**.SC.; **C**.P.; **O**.R.; **Y**.
 Klasse für Bergbau, Hüttenwesen und Montangeo-logie [1958–] **L**.SC.
[*C. of:* 264]

180 Abhandlungen der Deutschen Bunsen-Gesellschaft für **angewandte physikalische Chemie.** Halle. *Abh. dt. Bunsen-Ges.* [1909–29] **L**.P.; **Bl**.U. 14; **E**.U. 09–20; **Lv**.U. 09–20.

181 Abhandlungen der Deutschen kältetechnischen Verein. Karnlsruhe. *Abh. dt. kältetech. Ver.* [1950–] **L**.P. [*C. of:* 32554]

182 **Abhandlungen** des **Deutschen meteorologischen Diensts** in der **sowjetisch besetzten Zone Deutschlands.** Berlin. *Abh. dt. met. Diensts sowj. besetz. Zone* **L.**MO. 50–.

183 **Abhandlungen** des **Deutschen naturwissenschaftlich-medizinischen Vereins** für **Böhmen, 'Lotos'.** Prag. *Abh. dt. naturw.-med. Ver. Böhm.* [1896–] **L.**BM^N. 96–15; **C.**P.; **E.**R. 10–42; **G.**N. 07– imp.

184 **Abhandlungen** des **Deutschen Seefischereivereins.** Berlin. *Abh. dt. SeefischVer.* [1897–22] **L.**AM.; BM^N.; P.; **Abd.**M. 97–99; **C.**UL.; **Db.** 00–16; **E.**U.; **Lo.**; **Lv.**U. imp.; **Pl.**M.

185 **Abhandlungen** zur **exakten Biologie.** Berlin. *Abh. exakt. Biol.* [1939–] **C.**UL.; **Pl.**M.

186 **Abhandlungen** aus der **Fischerei** und deren **Hilfswissenschaften.** Berlin, Radebeul. *Abh. Fisch. Hilfswiss.* [1949–51] **Abd.**M.; **Fr.**; **Lo.**; **Pit.**F.; **Pl.**M. [*C. of* and *Rec. as:* 58592]

187 **Abhandlungen** aus dem **Fritz-Haber-Institut** der **Max-Planck-Gesellschaft.** Berlin. *Abh. Fritz-Haber-Inst.* **L.**R. 52–.

188 **Abhandlungen** aus dem **Gebiet** der **Auslandskunde.** Hamburg. *Abh. Geb. Auslandsk.* [1920–] **L.**BM.; BM^N. (natur.) 20–41; **G.**U. 20–35; **O.**B. [*C. of:* 219]

189 **Abhandlungen** aus dem **Gebiet** der **Bäder-** und **Klimaheilkunde.** Berlin. *Abh. Geb. Bäder- u. Klimaheilk.* [1938–]

190 **Abhandlungen** aus dem **Gebiet** der **Feuerversicherungswissenschaft.** Hannover. *Abh. Geb. FeuerversichWiss.* [1910–16] [*C. as:* 209]

191 **Abhandlungen** aus dem **Gebiet** der **Geburtshilfe** u. **Gynaekologie.** Mitteilungen aus der 2. Frauenklinik der Universität Budapest. *Abh. Geb. Geburtshilfe Gynäk., Bpest* [1909–13] **E.**P.

192 **Abhandlungen** aus dem **Gebiet** der **klinischen Zahnheilkunde.** Berlin. *Abh. Geb. klin. Zahnheilk.* [1914–]

193 **Abhandlungen** aus dem **Gebiet** der **Krebsforschung** u. **verwandten Gebieten.** Berlin. *Abh. Geb. Krebsforsch.*

194 **Abhandlungen** aus dem **Gebiet** der **Naturwissenschaften** hrsg. vom Naturwissenschaftlichen Verein in Hamburg. *Abh. Geb. Naturw., Hamburg* [1846–31] **L.**BM.; BM^N.; L.; R.; Z.; **C.**B. 84–01; UL.; **Db.** 83–31; **E.**R. 76–31 imp.; **G.**N. 1846–12 imp.; **Ld.**U. 19–31. [*C. in:* 279]

195 **Abhandlungen** aus dem **Gebiet** der **Psychotherapie** und **medizinischen Psychologie.** Stuttgart. *Abh. Geb. Psychother. med. Psychol.* [1925–31] [*C. of:* 58793]

196 **Abhandlungen** aus dem **Gebiet** der **Sexualforschung.** Bonn. *Abh. Geb. Sexualforsch.* **L.**BM. 18–31.

197 **Abhandlungen** aus dem **Gebiet** der **Vogelzugsforschung.** Biologische Anstalt auf Helgoland. Berlin. *Abh. Vogelzugsforsch. Helgoland.* **L.**BM^N. 30–31; **O.**OR. 30–31.

198 **Abhandlungen** aus der **Geburtshilfe** und **Gynäkologie.** Berlin. *Abh. Geburtshilfe Gynäk.* **L.**MD. 27–.

199 **Abhandlungen** des **Geographischen Instituts** der **Freien Universität.** Berlin. *Abh. geogr. Inst. frei. Univ.* [1953–] **L.**G.

200 **Abhandlungen** der **Geologischen Bundesanstalt.** Wien. *Abh. geol. Bundesanst., Wien* [1852–] **L.**BM. 1852–27; BM^N.; G. 1852–85 imp.; GL.; GM.; L. 1852–90; R. 1852–29; **C.**P. 1852–70; UL.; **Db.**; **E.**D. 1852–27; R.

201 **Abhandlungen** des **Geologischen Dienstes.** Berlin. *Abh. geol. Dienst.* [1951–] **L.**BM.; BM^N.; GL.; GM.; **Br.**U.; **C.**UL.; **G.**U.; **O.**R. [*C. of:* 203]

202 **Abhandlungen** des **Geologischen Landesamtes** in **Baden-Württemberg.** Freiburg i. Br. *Abh. geol. Landesamt. Baden-Württ.* [1953–] **L.**BM^N.; **Y.**

203 **Abhandlungen** der **Geologischen Landesanstalt.** Berlin. *Abh. geol. Landesanst.* [1948–51] **L.**BM.; BM^N.; GL.; GM.; SC.; **Br.**U. 48–51; **C.**UL.; **G.**U.; **O.**R. [*C. of:* 267; *C. as:* 201]

204 **Abhandlungen** der **Geologischen Landesuntersuchung** des **Bayerischen Oberbergamtes.** München. *Abh. geol. Landesunters. bayer. Oberbergamt.* [1929–38] **L.**BM^N.; GL. 30–38; GM.; SC. [*C. of:* 20933; *C. as:* 32708]

Abhandlungen der **Geologischen Reichsanstalt.** Wien. *See* 200.

205 **Abhandlungen** zur **geologischen Spezialkarte** von **Elsass-Lothringen.** Strassburg. *Abh. geol. SpezKarte Els.-Loth.* [1875–05] **L.**BM^N.; GL.; GM.

206 **Abhandlungen** aus dem **Geologisch-palaeontologischen Institut** der **Universität Greifswald.** *Abh. geol.-palaeont. Inst. Greifswald* **L.**BM^N. 20–39; SC. 20–37.

207 **Abhandlungen** des **Geomagnetischen Instituts** und **Observatoriums Potsdam-Neimagh.** Potsdam. *Abh. geomagn. Inst. Obs. Potsdam-Neimagh* [1954–] **L.**MO.; SC. 57–; **Db.**; **Y.** [*C. of:* 208]

208 **Abhandlungen** des **Geophysikalischen Instituts.** Potsdam. *Abh. geophys. Inst., Potsdam* **L.**MO. 39–54*. [*C. as:* 207]

209 **Abhandlungen** aus dem **gesamten Gebiete** der **Versicherungswissenschaften.** Hannover. *Abh. ges. Geb. VersichWiss.* [1917–19] [*C. of:* 190]

210 **Abhandlungen** aus dem **Gesamtgebiet** der **Hygiene.** Leipzig. *Abh. Gesamtgeb. Hyg.* [1928–36] **L.**TD.

211 **Abhandlungen** aus dem **Gesamtgebiet** der **Kriminalpsychologien:** Heidelberger Abhandlungen. Berlin. *Abh. Gesamtgeb. KrimPsychol.* [1912–29] **L.**BM. 12–21.

212 **Abhandlungen** aus dem **Gesamtgebiet** der **Medizin.** Wien. *Abh. Gesamtgeb. Med.* [1923–]

213 **Abhandlungen** zur **Geschichte** der **Mathematik.** Leipzig. *Abh. Gesch. Math.* [1877–12] **L.**BM.; R. 99–12; UC. 77 02; **E.**U. 02–12; **G.**U.; **M.**U.; **O.**R.; Sa.

Abhandlungen zur **Geschichte** der **mathematischen Wissenschaften.** *See* 213.

214 **Abhandlungen** zur **Geschichte** der **Medizin.** Breslau. *Abh. Gesch. Med.* [1902–06] **L.**UC.; **G.**F. 03–06; **O.**R.

215 **Abhandlungen** zur **Geschichte** der **Medizin** und der **Naturwissenschaften.** Berlin. *Abh. Gesch. Med. Naturw.* [1934–]

216 **Abhandlungen** zur **Geschichte** der **Naturwissenschaften** und der **Medizin.** Erlangen. *Abh. Gesch. Naturw. Med.* [1922–25] **L.**BM.; P.; **Bm.**U.; **C.**UL.

217 **Abhandlungen** aus der **Geschichte** der **Veterinärmedizin.** Leipzig. *Abh. Gesch. VetMed.* [1925–]

218 **Abhandlungen** auf den **Grenzgebieten** der **inneren Sekretion.** Budapest. *Abh. Grenzgeb. inn. Sekret.* [1923–36]

Abhandlungen der **Grossherzoglichen Hessischen geologischen Landesanstalt.** *See* 222.

219 **Abhandlungen** des **Hamburgischen Kolonialinstituts.** Hamburg. *Abh. hamburg. KolonInst.* [1910–20] L.BM.; BM[N]. 13–20 imp.; G.U.; O.B. [*C. as:* 188]

220 **Abhandlungen** der **Heidelberger Akademie** der **Wissenschaft.** Heidelberg. *Abh. heidelb. Akad. Wiss.* Math.-Nat. Kl. [1910–] L.BM.; BM[N]. 10–37: 44; P.(A.) 24–32; SC. 26–44; UC. 24–31; C.P.; Db.; E.R.

221 **Abhandlungen. Herder-Gesellschaft** und **Herder-Institut.** Riga. *Abh. Herder-Ges. u. Herder-Inst.* [1925–35] L.BM[N]. 25–27: 35.

222 **Abhandlungen** der **Hessischen geologischen Landesanstalt.** Darmstadt. *Abh. hess. geol. Landesanst.* [1884–] L.BM[N]. 84–28; GL. 84–36 imp.; GM.; SC. 89–28; C.UL. 84–99.

223 **Abhandlungen** des **Hessischen Landesamtes** für **Bodenforschung.** Wiesbaden. *Abh. hess. Landesamt. Bodenforsch.* [1950–] L.BM[N].; GL.; C.A.; Lv.U.; Y.

Abhandlungen aus dem **Institut** für **Bodenkunde** in **Puławy.** *See* 38397.

224 **Abhandlungen. Institut** für **elektrische Anlagen** und **Hochspannungstechnik.** Karlsruhe. *Abh. Inst. elekt. Anl. HochspannTech., Karlsruhe* [1955–] L.P.

225 **Abhandlungen** aus dem **Institut** von **Ernst Beckmann, Laboratorium** für **angewandte Chemie** der **Universität Leipzig.** *Abh. Inst. Ernst Beckmann* [1906–09]

226 **Abhandlungen** aus dem **Institut** für **Metallhüttenwesen** und **Elektrometallurgie** der **Technischen Hochschule** zu **Aachen.** Halle, Aachen. *Abh. Inst. Metallhüttenw. Elektrometall. Aachen* L.NF. 32–38; P. 15–19: 58–.

227 **Abhandlungen. Institut** für **Tierzucht** und **Molkereiwesen** an der **Universität Leipzig.** *Abh. Inst. Tierz. Molkereiw, Lpz.* L.P. 27–.

228 **Abhandlungen** des **Instituts** für **Seefischerei.** Wesermunde. *Abh. Inst. Seefisch., Wesermunde* [1929–] **Abd.**M. 29–30.

229 **Abhandlungen** des **Instituts** für **wissenschaftliche Heimatforschung.** Riga. *Abh. Inst. wiss. Heimatforsch., Riga* L.BM. 36–.

Abhandlungen der **Internationalen Vereinigung** für **Brückenbau** und **Hochbau.** *See* 30707.

230 **Abhandlungen** aus dem **juristisch-medizinischen Grenzgebiete.** Wien. *Abh. jurist.-med. Grenzgeb.* [1926–27]

Abhandlungen der **K. Bayerischen Akademie** der **Wissenschaften.** *See* 163.

231 **Abhandlungen** des **K. Bayerischen hydrotechnischen Bureaus.** München. *Abh. K. bayer. hydrotech. Bur.*

Abhandlungen der **K. Böhmischen Gesellschaft** der **Wissenschaften.** *See* 48194.

232 **Abhandlungen** der **K. Gesellschaft** der **Wissenschaften** zu **Göttingen.** Göttingen. *Abh. K. Ges. Wiss. Göttingen* Math.-physik. Kl. [1894–23] L.BM.; MO. 08–23 imp.; R.; SC.; Abs.N.; C.P.; UL.; Db.; E.R. imp.; O.R. [*C. as:* 159]

Abhandlungen der **K. Preussischen Akademie** der **Wissenschaften.** *See* 264.

Abhandlungen der **K. Preussischen geologischen Landesanstalt.** *See* 265.

Abhandlungen des **K. Preussischen meteorologischen Instituts.** *See* 266.

Abhandlungen der **K. Sächsischen Gesellschaft** der **Wissenschaften.** *See* 269.

233 **Abhandlungen** des **K. Sächsischen meteorologischen Instituts.** Dresden. *Abh. K. sächs. met. Inst.* L.MO. 96–01; Db. 00–01.

Abhandlungen des **K. Ungarischen astrophysikalischen Observatoriums** von **Konkoly's Stiftung** in **Budapest-Svabhegy.** *See* 32742.

234 **Abhandlungen** der **K. K. Geographischen Gesellschaft** in **Wien.** *Abh. K. K. geogr. Ges. Wien* [1899–22] L.BM.; G.; MO. 99; R.; E.G. 99–14; O.G. 02–07 imp.; R.U. 99–09 imp.

Abhandlungen der **K. K. Geologischen Reichsanstalt.** Wien. *See* 200.

Abhandlungen der **K. K. Zoologisch-botanischen Gesellschaft** in **Wien.** *See* 283.

Abhandlungen der **Kaiser Leopoldinisch-Carolinischen Deutschen Akademie** der **Naturforscher.** *See* 35356.

235 **Abhandlungen** aus dem **Kaiser-Wilhelm-Institut** für **Chemie.** Berlin-Dahlem. *Abh. Kaiser-Wilhelm-Inst. Chem.* L.P. 13–20*; Br.U. 13–15.

236 **Abhandlungen** aus dem **Kaiser-Wilhelm-Institut** für **Eisenforschung** zu **Düsseldorf.** *Abh. Kaiser-Wilhelm-Inst. Eisenforsch.* [1920–44] L.P. imp. [*Contained in* 32555; *C. as:* 247]

237 **Abhandlungen** aus dem **Kaiser-Wilhelm-Institut** für **physikalische Chemie** und **Elektrochemie.** Berlin-Dahlem. *Abh. Kaiser-Wilhelm-Inst. phys. Chem.* [1911–] L.UC. 11–33; C.P. 29–35; UL. 29–.

238 **Abhandlungen** aus der **Kinderheilkunde** und ihren **Grenzgebieten.** Berlin. *Abh. Kinderheilk.* [1924–37] L.BM.; MD.; S.; Bm.U. 31–37; C.UL. [*C. as:* 6813]

239 **Abhandlungen** für die **Kunde** des **Morgenlandes.** Leipzig. *Abh. Kunde Morgenlandes* [1859–] L.BM.; G. 1859–06; C.UL.; Db. 1859–10; E.U. 1860–89; O.B.

240 **Abhandlungen** zur **Landeskunde** der **Provinz Westpreussen.** Danzig. *Abh. Landesk. Prov. Westpreuss.* [1890–] L.BM. 90–20; O.B. 97–19.

241 **Abhandlungen** aus dem **Landesmuseum** für **Naturkunde** zu **Münster** in **Westfalen.** *Abh. Landesmus. Naturk. Münster* [1940–] L.BM[N].; Z.; Y. [*C. of:* 242]

242 **Abhandlungen** aus dem **Landesmuseum** der **Provinz Westfalen.** Münster. *Abh. Landesmus. Prov. Westf.* [1936–39] L.BM[N].; E.B.; G.N. [*C. of:* 282; *C. as:* 241]

243 **Abhandlungen** zur **Larvalsystematik** der **Insekten.** Berlin. *Abh. Larvalsyst. Insekten* [1957–] L.BM[N].; Y.

Abhandlungen aus dem **Mathematischen Seminar** der **Hamburgischen Universität.** *See* 244.

244 **Abhandlungen** aus dem **Mathematischen Seminar, Universität Hamburg.** Hamburg. *Abh. math. Semin. Univ. Hamburg* [1921–] L.M.; R. 29–; SC. 37–; U. 49–; UC. 22–38; Bl.U.; Br.U.; C.P.; UL.; Dn.U.; E.Q.; R. 22–29; G.U. 21–57; M.U. imp.; Sh.U. 49–; Sw.U. 21–22.

245 **Abhandlungen** über den **mathematischen Unterricht** in **Deutschland.** Leipzig. *Abh. math. Unterr. Dtl.* [1909–16] **L.**BM. 09–12 imp.; **G.**U. 09–13; **O.**B. 09–12 imp.

246 **Abhandlungen. Mathematisch-naturwissenschaftliche Klasse. Akademie** der **Wissenschaften** und der **Literatur, Mainz.** *Abh. math.-naturw. Kl. Akad. Wiss. Mainz* [1950–] **L.**BM.; BM^N. 57–; P. 54–; R.; SC.; U.; **Db.**; **Y.**

247 **Abhandlungen** aus dem **Max-Planck-Institut** für **Eisenforschung.** Dusseldorf. *Abh. Max-Planck-Inst. Eisenforsch.* [1946–] **L.**P. [*C. of:* 236; *contained in:* 4063 and 50716]

248 **Abhandlungen** aus dem **Mineralogisch-geologischen Institut** der **K. Ungarischen Stephan Tisza Universität** in **Debrecen.** *Abh. miner.-geol. Inst. Debrecen* **L.**BM^N. 31–37.

249 **Abhandlungen** und **Monographien** aus dem **Gebiet** der **Biologie** und **Medizin.** Bern. *Abh. Monogr. Geb. Biol. Med.* [1920–23]

250 **Abhandlungen** der **Naturforschenden Gesellschaft** zu **Danzig.** *Abh. naturforsch. Ges. Danzig* [1924–] **L.**BM.; BM^N.; L.; **Bl.**U.; **C.**P.; **E.**R. [*C. in:* 48817]

251 **Abhandlungen** der **Naturforschenden Gesellschaft** zu **Görlitz.** *Abh. naturforsch. Ges. Görlitz* [1827–52] **L.**BM.; BM^N. 1827–42; R. 1827–33; **Bl.**U. 75–52 imp.; **Db.** 00–52; **G.**N. 1860–11 imp. [*C. as:* 168]

252 **Abhandlungen** der **Naturforschenden Gesellschaft** zu **Halle.** *Abh. naturforsch. Ges. Halle* [1853–19] **L.**BM.; BM^N.; GL. 00–14; L. 1853–06; R. 1853–14; S. 1860–06; SC. 1853–06; Z. 1853–14; **C.**UL.; **Db.** 1855–19; **E.**R. 80–19; **O.**R. 1853–14.

253 **Abhandlungen** der **Naturhistorischen Gesellschaft** zu **Nürnberg.** *Abh. naturhist. Ges. Nürnberg* [1852–] **L.**AN. 98–36; BM^N.; GL. 00–13; Z. 1852–98; **C.**UL.; **Db.** 81–39; **E.**B. 06–12; **G.**N. 81–13 imp.

254 **Abhandlungen** hrsg. vom **Naturwissenschaftlichen Verein** zu **Bremen.** *Abh. naturw. Ver. Bremen* [1868–] **L.**BM.; BM^N; K. 68–39; R. 68–32; SC. 68–38: 49–; Z.; **Abd.**U. 75–14; **Bl.**U. 68–26; **C.**UL.; **Db.**; **E.**B. 84–14; C. 80–14 imp.; J. 88–; R. 68: 94–; **G.**N.

Abhandlungen des **Naturwissenschaftlichen Vereins** mit **Fränkischen Museum** für **Naturkunde.** Würzburg. *See* 258.

256 **Abhandlungen** des **Naturwissenschaftlichen Vereins** in **Regensburg.** *Abh. naturw. Ver. Regensb.* [1849–18] **L.**BM^N.

257 **Abhandlungen** des **Naturwissenschaftlichen Vereins** für **Schwaben** e V. in **Augsburg.** Augsburg. *Abh. naturw. Ver. Schwaben* [1936–] **L.**BM. 49–; BM^N. 36: 49–; **Y.** [*Also supplement*]

258 **Abhandlungen** des **Naturwissenschaftlichen Vereins** e. V. **Würzburg** mit Fränkischen Museum fur Naturkunde. Würzburg. *Abh. naturw. Ver. Würzburg* [1956–] **L.**BM^N.; **Y.**

Abhandlungen der **Naturwissenschaftlichen** (früher **Zoologisch-mineralogischen**) **Vereins** in **Regensburg.** *See* 256.

259 **Abhandlungen** aus der **Neurologie, Psychiatrie, Psychologie** und ihren Grenzgebieten. Berlin. *Abh. Neurol. Psychiat. Psychol.* [1917–38] **L.**MD.; **C.**UL. 27–38; **E.**P. [*C. as:* 6814]

260 **Abhandlungen** des **Österreichischen Dokumentationszentrum** für **Technik** und **Wirtschaft.** Wien. *Abh. öst. DokumZent. Tech. Wirtsch.* [1951–] **Y.**

Abhandlungen der **Pamir Expedition.** *See* 54518.

261 **Abhandlungen** zur **Physiologie** der **Gesichtsempfindungen** aus dem **Physiologischen Institut** zu **Freiburg** i. B. *Abh. Physiol. Gesichtsempf.* [*C. as:* 262]

262 **Abhandlungen** zur **Physiologie** der **Sinne.** Leipzig. *Abh. Physiol. Sinne* [1925] [*C. of:* 261]

263 **Abhandlungen** zur **praktischen Geologie** und **Bergwirtschaftslehre.** Halle. *Abh. prakt. Geol. BergwLehre* [1925–32] **L.**GM.; SC.

264 **Abhandlungen** der **Preussischen Akademie** der **Wissenschaften.** Berlin. *Abh. preuss. Akad. Wiss.* Phys.-math. Kl. [1804–44] **L.**BM.; BM^N.; G. 08–12; L. 1830–44; MD. 1814–1815; P. imp.; R.; RI. 1840–43; S. 1804–14; U. 39–44; UC. 73–44 imp.; Z. 1822–21: 39–44 imp.; **Abd.**U.; **C.**P.; UL.; **Db.**; **E.**R.; U.; **G.**U. 1801–39; **Lv.**U. 25–44; **Nw.**A. 1839–63; **O.**B.; R.; **Sa.** [*C. as:* 179]

265 **Abhandlungen** der **Preussischen geologischen Landesanstalt.** Berlin. *Abh. preuss. geol. Landesanst.* [1872–38] **L.**BM.; BM^N. imp.; GL. 00–38; GM.; SC. 28–38; **Br.**U. 89–38 imp.; **C.**UL.; **G.**U. 89–38. [*C. as:* 268]

266 **Abhandlungen** des **Preussischen meteorologischen Instituts.** Berlin. *Abh. preuss. met. Inst.* [1888–34] **L.**MO.; **E.**M. [*C. as:* 57694]

267 **Abhandlungen** des **Reichsamts** für **Bodenforschung.** Berlin. *Abh. Reichsamts Bodenforsch.* [1942–44] **L.**BM.; BM^N.; GL.; GM.; SC.; **Br.**U.; **C.**UL.; **G.**U.; **O.**R. [*C. of:* 268; *C. as:* 203]

Abhandlungen des **Reichsamts** für **Wetterdienst.** Berlin. *See* 57694.

268 **Abhandlungen** der **Reichsstelle** für **Bodenforschung.** Berlin. *Abh. Reichsstelle Bodenforsch.* [1940–41] **L.**BM.; BM^N.; GL.; GM.; SC.; **Br.**U.; **C.**UL.; **G.**U.; **O.**R. [*C. of:* 265; *C. as:* 267]

269 **Abhandlungen** der **Sächsischen Akademie** der **Wissenschaften.** Leipzig. *Abh. sächs. Akad. Wiss.* Math.-Phys. Kl. [1852–] **L.**AS. 1852–14; BM.; BM^N.; P.; R.; SC.; U. 45–; UC. 1832–36; **Abd.**U. imp.; **C.**P. 1852–44; UL.; **Db.**; **E.**C. 78–; R.; **G.**U.; **Ld.**U. 20–; **Lv.**U. 21–; **M.**U. 91–14 imp.; **O.**R.; **Sa.**; **Y.**

270 **Abhandlungen** des **Sächsischen geologischen Landesamts.** Leipzig. *Abh. sächs. geol. Landesamts* [1927–39] **L.**BM^N.; GM. [*C. as:* 32698]

271 **Abhandlungen** über **Salvarsan.** München. *Abh. Salvarsan*

272 **Abhandlungen** zur **Sammlung mathematischer Modelle.** Leipzig. *Abh. Samml. math. Modelle* [1907–11]

273 **Abhandlungen** der **Schweizerischen paläontologischen Gesellschaft.** Zürich. *Abh. schweiz. paläont. Ges.* [1874–39] **L.**BM.; BM^N.; GL.; GM.; R. 74–17; UC.; Z.; **Br.**U. 74–88: 96–97; **C.**S.; UL. 74–81; **Db.** 74–05; **G.**U. 81–39; **O.**R. [*C. as:* 48952]

274 **Abhandlungen** hrsg. von der **Senckenbergischen naturforschenden Gesellschaft.** Frankfurt a. M. *Abh. senckenb. naturforsch. Ges.* [1854–] **L.**BM. 1854–18; BM^N.; E. 76–; EB. (ent.) 86–; GL. 00–; GM. 84–; L.; R.; S. 1854–00; Z.; **C.**P. 83–32; UL.; **Db.**; **E.**C. 14–; G.; R. imp.; **G.**N. 76–05 imp.; **Lv.**U. 97–57; **O.**R.; **Sa.**; **Y.**

275 **Abhandlungen** aus der **sowjetischen Physik.** Berlin. *Abh. sowj. Phys.* [1951–55] **L.**P. 54; **Br.**U. 1951–53. [*Supplement to:* 50371; *C. as:* 37701]

Abhandlungen der **Sowjet-Sektion** der **Internationalen Assoziation** für das **Studium** des **Quartärs.** Leningrad, Moskau. *See* 55056.

276 **Abhandlungen** zur **theoretischen Biologie.** Berlin. *Abh. theor. Biol.* [1919–31] **L.**SC. 26–31; **C.**UL.; **Pl.**M. [*Superseded by:* 185]

277 **Abhandlungen** zur **Theorie** der **organischen Entwicklung.** Berlin. *Abh. Theor. org. Entw.* [1926–31] **L.**L.; Z.; **C.**B.; **E.**P.; **O.**R.; **Pl.**M. [*C. of:* 56953]

Abhandlungen der **Tschernyschewsky-Staats-Universität.** Saratov. *See* 55433.
Abhandlungen des **Ukrainischen wissenschaftlichen Instituts** in **Berlin.** *See* 55094.
Abhandlungen des **Ukrainischen wissenschaftlich-forschenden geologischen Instituts.** *See* 58348.

278 **Abhandlungen** des **Vereins** für **naturwissenschaftliche Erforschung** des **Niederrheins.** Krefeld. *Abh. Ver. naturw. Erforsch. Niederrheins* [1913–16] **L.**BM^N.

279 **Abhandlungen** und **Verhandlungen** des **Naturwissenschaftlichen Vereins** in **Hamburg.** *Abh. Verh. naturw. Ver. Hamburg.* [1937–] **L.**BM^N.; Z. 57–; **Db.**; **Ld.**U. [*C. of:* 194 and 56057] [*Suspended* 1938–56]

280 **Abhandlungen** und **Vorträge** aus dem **Gebiet** der **Mathematik, Naturwissenschaften** und **Technik.** Leipzig. *Abh. Vortr. Geb. Math. Naturw. Tech.* [1916–24] **L.**SC. 20–24.

281 **Abhandlungen** und **Vorträge** zur **Geschichte** der **Naturwissenschaften.** Leipzig. *Abh. Vortr. Gesch. Naturw.* **L.**BM. 06–13.

282 **Abhandlungen** aus dem **Westfälischen Provinzial-Museum** für **Naturkunde.** Münster i. W. *Abh. westf. ProvMus. Naturk.* [1930–35] **L.**BM^N.; Z.; **E.**B. [*C. as:* 242]

283 **Abhandlungen** der **Zoologisch-botanischen Gesellschaft** in **Wien.** *Abh. zool.-bot. Ges. Wien* [1901–] **L.**BM^N.; E. (ent.) 01–24; EB. 01–29; K. (bot.) 01–36; L. 01–39; R.; Z.; **C.**P. 20–29; UL. 01–11; **E.**R. imp.; **O.**R.

284 **Abiks loodusevaatlejale.** Tartu. *Abiks Loodusevaat.* [1951–] **L.**BM^N.; **Fr.**

284ᶜ **Ability.** Hubbard Association of Scientologists. Phoenix. *Ability* [1955–] **L.**BM.

285 **Ablesungen** der **Meteorologischen Station Greifswald.** *Ables. met. Stn Greifswald*

286 **Abolitionist.** London. *Abolitionist* [1899–48] **E.**A.; **O.**B. [*C. as:* 3601]

287 **Abrasive** and **Cleaning Methods.** New York. *Abras. clean. Meth.* **L.**P. 36–37.

288 **Abrasive Industry.** Cleveland. *Abras. Ind.* [1921–36] **L.**NF. 23–36; P.; **Bm.**P. 32–36; **Sh.**IO. 24–36. [*C. as:* 289]

289 **Abrasives.** Cleveland. *Abrasives* [1937–38] **L.**P.; **Bm.**P.; **Sh.**IO. [*C. of:* 288]

Abrégé du **Bulletin** de la **Société hongroise** de **géographie.** *See* 19766.

290 **Abridged** and **Full Translations** and **Extended Summaries** filed at the **Commonwealth Bureau** of **Plant Breeding** and **Genetics.** Cambridge. *Abridged full Transl. Commonw. Bur. Pl. Breed. Genet.* [1931–] **L.**BM; **C.**A.; **Y.**

291 **Abridged Reports** of **Tests. National Institute** of **Agricultural Engineering.** Silsoe. *Abridged Rep. Tests natn. Inst. agric. Engng* [1956–] **L.**BM; **Rt.**

292 **Abridged Scientific Publications. Research Laboratory. Eastman Kodak Co.** Rochester, N.Y. *Abridged scient. Publs Eastman Kodak Co.* [1913–] **L.**BM. 35–; C.; CB. 49–; P.; PG. 15–; U.; UC. 15–; **Abs.**N. imp.; **Bl.**U. 15– imp.; **Bm.**P. 31–; U. 35–47; **Bn.**U. 35–38; **Br.**U. 26–; **C.**P. 15–; UL. 54–; **Cr.**U. 35–38; **Db.** 38–; **Dn.**U. 26–; **E.**U. 25–; **F.**A. 29– imp.; **G.**U. 27–49; **H.**U. 13–32; **Ld.**U. 17–; W. 15–49; **Lh.**P. 42–; **Lv.**P. 35–50; **M.**C.; D. 19– imp.; P. 19–25; **N.**U. 35–38; **O.**R. 35–38; **Sa.** 35–38; **We.**K.; **Y.**

293 **Abridged Weekly Weather Report** for **Canberra.** Canberra. *Abridged wkly Weath. Rep. Canberra* **L.**MO. 47– imp.

294 **Abridgments** of **Specifications** [of Patents]. London. *Abridg. Specif.* [1855–] **L.**BM.; MO. 75–10 imp.; NF.; P.; QM.; 31–39; U. 31–; **Abs.**N. 12–; **Bm.**P.; U. 1855–19; **Br.**P.; **Bra.**P.; **C.**UL.; **Cr.**I. 1855–49; P.; **Db.** 00–; **E.**F.; J. 04–; **G.**E. 1855–40; **Ld.**P.; U.; **Lv.**P.; U. 1855–08; **M.**C.; P.; T. 01–; **N.**P.; **Nw.**P.; **O.**R.; **Rt.** 1855–25; **Sh.**P. 00–; **Sw.**I. 77–.

Abstract. *See* **Abstracts.**
Abstract Bulletin. *See* **Abstracts Bulletin.**

296 **Abstracts** on **Agricultural** and **Horticultural Engineering.** Silsoe. *Abstr. agric. hort. Engng* [1950–51] **L.**AM.; BM.; P.; **Bm.**P.; **C.**A.; **Db.**; **Je.**; **Md.**H.; **N.**U.; **O.**B.; R.; RE.; **R.**U.; **Sil.** [*C. as:* 1338]

297 **Abstracts: Agricultural, Industrial** and **Economic Research.** Territory of Hawaii. Honolulu. *Abstr. agric. ind. econ. Res. Hawaii* [1952–] **Rt.**

Abstracts. Air Ministry. London. *See* 360.
Abstracts. Air Pollution Control Association, Pittsburgh. *See* 94.
Abstracts. American Gas Association. *See* 298.

298 **Abstracts. American Gas Institute.** New York. *Abstr. Am. Gas Inst.* **L.**P. 11–18*. [*C. of:* and *Rec. as:* 9162]

299 **Abstracts. American Potash Institute.** Washington. *Abstr. Am. Potash Inst.* [1960–] **L.**P. [*Replaces:* 28668]

300 **Abstracts** of **Articles** on **Fatigue** of **Metals** under **Repeated Stress.** American Society for Testing Materials. Philadelphia. *Abstr. Art. Fatigue Metals* **L.**P. 28–30*. [*C. in:* 31497]

301 **Abstracts. Automobile Research Association.** Brentford. *Abstr. Auto. Res. Ass.* [1942–45] **L.**SC.; **Bm.**C.; **Sil.**; **Sy.**R. [*C. as:* 359]

Abstracts. Automobile Research Committee. *See* 301.
Abstracts. B.S.F.A. British Steel Foundry Association. *See* 5684.

302 **Abstracts** of **Bacteriology.** Baltimore. *Abstr. Bact.* [1917–25] **L.**AM.; LI.; MC.; MD.; P.; S.; SH. 17–19; TD.; U.; UCH.; V. 24–25; **Abd.**U. 24–25; **Abs.**N.; **Br.**U.; **C.**PA.; UL.; **Cr.**MD.; **Db.** 21–25 imp.; **E.**B.; N. 18–25 imp.; W.; **G.**U.; **Ld.**U. 25; **Lv.**U.; **N.**U. 17–20; **Nw.**A.; **R.**D.; U.; **Rt.**; **Sh.**U.; W. 20–25. [*C. in:* 7057]

303 **Abstracts** of **Bioanalytic Technology.** Chicago. *Abstr. bioanalyt. Technol.* [1953–] **L.**P.; **Ld.**U.; **M.**MS. 54–; **Y.** [*Also supplements*]

304 **Abstracts. British Baking Industries Research Association.** Chorleywood, Herts. *Abstr. Br. Baking Ind. Res. Ass.* [1953–] **L.**AM.; BM.; P.; **G.**T.; **Lh.**FO; **R.**D. 53–59; **Y.** [*C. of:* 5724]

305 **Abstracts. British Ceramic Society.** Stoke-on-Trent. *Abstr. Br. Ceram. Soc.* [1939–41] **L.**P. [*Supplement to:* 53620; *C. of:* 321; *C. as:* 8767]

    Abstracts. British Electrical and Allied Industries Research Association. *See* 17319.

    Abstracts. British Food Manufacturing Industries Research Association. *See* 326.

306 **Abstracts. British Gelatine and Glue Research Association.** London. *Abstr. Br. Gel. Glue Res. Ass.* [1949–] **L.**AM.; BM.; P. 54–; PR. 50–; SC. 56–; **We.**K.

    Abstracts. British Internal Combustion Engine Research Association. *See* 5664.

    Abstracts. British Leather Manufacturers' Research Association. *See* 5671.

307 **Abstracts. British Plastics Federation.** London. *Abstr. Br. Plast. Fed.* [1945–] **L.**BM.; C.; P.; PR. 57–; SC.; SI. 54–; **E.**A.; **F.**A. (ser. 7) 52–; **G.**U. (ser. 14) 59–; **Lh.**P. 47–; **Lv.**P. 59–; **M.**D. 56– imp.; **O.**R.; **Sy.**R. 45–50: 55–.

308 **Abstracts. British Rubber Producers Research Association.** London. *Abstr. Br. Rubb. Prod. Res. Ass.* **L.**BM.; **Sy.**R, 39–41 imp.

    Abstracts. British Steel Castings Research Association. *See* 5684.

    Abstracts. British Steel Founders' Association. *See* 5684.

309 **Abstracts of Bulgarian Scientific Literature.** Sofia. *Abstr. Bulg. scient. Lit.*
    Biology and Medicine [1958–] **L.**BM.; MA.; MC.; MD.; TP.; **Y.**
    Chemistry and Chemical Technology [1958–] **L.**BM.; C. (5 yr.); P.; **Y.**
    Geology and Geography [1957–] **L.**BM.; **G.**U.; **Y.**
    Agriculture and Forestry [1962–] **L.**BM.
    [*English edition of:* 42403ᵃ]

310 **Abstracts Bulletin. Aluminium Laboratories Ltd., London.** *Abstr. Bull. Alumin. Labs, Lond.* [1930–] **L.**P. 49–59; **F.**A. 41–46.

311 **Abstracts Bulletin. Aluminium Laboratories Ltd., Montreal.** Kingston, Can. *Abstr. Bull. Alumin. Labs, Montreal* [1946–] **L.**AV. imp.; P. 54–59; **Bm.**T. 56–; U.; **Br.**U. 48–; **C.**UL.; **G.**E. 51–; U. 48–59; **Li.**M. (1 yr.); **Lv.**P. 58–; **M.**U. 46–59 imp.; **Nw.**A. 48–; **O.**R.; **Sw.**U.

312 **Abstracts Bulletin. Building Research Laboratory.** Victoria, Australia. *Abstr. Bull. Bldg Res. Lab., Vict.* **L.**BA. 48–.

313 **Abstracts Bulletin. Geological Survey of South Australia.** Adelaide. *Abstr. Bull. geol. Surv. S. Aust.* [1950–] **L.**GM.; MI.

314 **Abstracts-Bulletin of the Incandescent Lamp Dept. of the Nela Research Laboratory.** *Abstr.-Bull. incand. Lamp Dep. Nela Res. Lab.* [1917–30] **L.**C.; NF.; P.; UC.; **Bm.**U. 17–25 imp.; **Br.**U. 17–25; **E.**R.; **G.**U.; **Lv.**U.; **M.**U.; **Nw.**A.; **R.**U. 17–25. [*C. of:* 318; *C. as:* 317]

315 **Abstracts Bulletin. Insect Control Committee.** National Research Council. Washington. *Abstr. Bull. Insect Control Comm., Wash.* **G.**PH. 46–47.

316 **Abstracts Bulletin. Institute of Paper Chemistry.** Appleton. *Abstr. Bull. Inst. Pap. Chem.* [1958–] **L.**P.; PR.; **Lh.**P.; **M.**C.; **Y.** [*C. of:* 10639]

Abstracts from the **Bulletin** of the **Institute** of **Physical** and **Chemical Research.** Tokyo. *See* 401.

317 **Abstracts Bulletin of the Lamp Development Laboratory.** Cleveland, Ohio. *Abstr. Bull. Lamp Dev. Lab.* [1939–] **L.**C.; NF.; P.; UC.; **G.**U.; **Lv.**U.; **M.**U.; **Nw.**A. [*C. of:* 314]

318 **Abstracts Bulletin of the Physical Laboratory of the National Electric Lamp Association,** Cleveland, Ohio. Chicago. *Abstr. Bull. phys. Lab. natn. elect. Lamp Ass.* [1913] **L.**C.; NF.; P.; UC.; **E.**R.; **G.**U.; **Lv.**U.; **M.**U.; **Nw.**A.; **R.**U. [*C. as:* 314]

319 **Abstracts of Canning Technology.** Washington. *Abstr. Cann. Technol.* [1923–30]

320 **Abstracts. Central Board of Irrigation. India.** Simla. *Abstr. cent. Bd Irrig. India* [1943–] **L.**P. 53–; **Hu.**G. 48–; **Rt.** 48–; **Y.** [*C. from:* 9722]

321 **Abstracts. Ceramic Society.** Tunstall. *Abstr. Ceram. Soc.* [1917–38] **L.**P. [*Supplement to:* 53653; *C. of:* 336; *C. as:* 305]

322 **Abstracts of Chemical Papers,** issued by the Bureau of Chemical Abstracts. London. *Abstr. chem. Pap.* [1924–25] **L.**BM.; BMᴺ.; LE.; P.; PR.; TD.; UC.; **Bm.**U.; **Bn.**U.; **Br.**U.; **C.**BI.; SJ.; UL.; **Db.** 25; **E.**R.; **G.**M.; T.(a); **Ld.**P.; W.; **Lv.**P.; **M.**C.; T.; U.; **N.**T.; **O.**R.; **Rt.**; **Sh.**S.; **Sw.**U. [*C. as:* 8768; *Issued from* 1871–1923 *in:* 25779]

323 **Abstracts of the Chlordane, Endrin and Heptachlor Literature.** Velsicol Chemical Corporation. *Abstr. Chlordane Endrin Heptachlor Lit.* **L.**TP. 58–.

    Abstracts of Current Articles on Water Treatment, National Aluminate Corporation. Chicago. *See:* 33916.

324 **Abstracts of Current Literature. Institute for Research in Agricultural Engineering, University of Oxford.** *Abstr. curr. Lit. Inst. Res. agric. Engng* [1931–37] **L.**AM.; BM.; P.; **Abs.**A.; N. 35–37; **Br.**U.; **C.**A.; **O.**AEC.; R.; **R.**U.; **Rt.**; **Sil.**

324° **Abstracts** from **Current Literature. Research Council** of the **British Whiting Federation.** Welwyn. *Abstr. curr. Lit. Res. Coun. Br. Whiting Fed.* [1956–] **L.**BM. [*Formerly issued in:* 9637]

325 **Abstracts of Current Publications. Safety** in **Mines Research Establishment.** Sheffield. *Abstr. curr. Publs Saf. Mines Res. Establ.* [1952–] **L.**AV. 56– imp.; BM.; MI. imp.; P.; SC.; TD. 54–; **Ld.**P. 53–; **O.**R.; **Sh.**S.; **Sy.**R. 57–. [*Replaces:* 33398]

326 **Abstracts** from **Current Scientific** and **Technical Literature. British Food Manufacturing Industries Research Association.** Leatherhead. *Abstr. curr. scient. tech. Lit. Br. Fd Mfg Ind. Res. Ass.* [1947–] **L.**AM.; BM.; P. 53–; **Br.**A. 49–; **Lh.**P. 49–; **M.**C.; **Md.**H. 48–55 imp.; **Y.**

327 **Abstracts of the Current Technical Literature** of **Engineering.** London. *Abstr. curr. tech. Lit. Engng* [1939–41] [*Contained in:* 26218]

328 **Abstracts of Declassified Documents. U.S. Atomic Energy Commission.** Washington. *Abstr. declass. Docum. U.S. atom. Energy Commn* [1947–48] **L.**P.; **C.**UL. [*C. as:* 35437]

329 **Abstracts of Dissertations** approved for the Ph.D., M.Sc., and M.Litt. degrees in the **University** of **Cambridge.** *Abstr. Diss. Univ. Camb.* [1925–57] **L.**BM. 40–57; BMᴺ.; C. 28–29: 43–47 imp.; GL. 28–57; MD. 51–57;

P. 51–57; SC.; U. 31–57; UC.; **Abs.**A. 32–57; U.; **Bl.**U. 26–57; **Bm.**U.; **C.**A.; B. 49–57; ENG. 53–57; S.; UL.; **Cr.**U. imp.; **E.**U.; **G.**U. 26–57; **Ld.**U.; **N.**U.; **O.**B. [*C. as:* 53305]

330 **Abstracts** of **Dissertations** for the degree of Doctor of Philosophy, **Oxford University.** *Abstr. Diss. Oxf. Univ.* **L.**BM. 28–47; BM[N]. 28–47; SC. 28–47; U. 31–; **C.**UL.; **O.**B. 29–; R. 29–.

331 **Abstracts** of **Dissertations** for the Degree of Doctor of Philosophy, **Stanford University.** Palo Alto. *Abstr. Diss. Stanford Univ.* [1924–52] **C.**A. 39–52; **Rt.** 51–52. [*C. in:* 17024]

332 **Abstracts** of **Dissertations** for the Degree of Doctor of Philosophy, **University** of **Virginia.** Charlottesville. *Abstr. Diss. Univ. Va* **L.**U. 31–; **G.**U. 31–; **O.**B. 32–; **Y.**

333 **Abstracts** of **Doctoral Dissertations. Ohio State University.** Columbus. *Abstr. doct. Diss. Ohio St. Univ.* [1929–] **L.**BM[N]. 29: 41–45; **C.**A. 46–; **Y.**

334 **Abstracts** of **Doctoral Dissertations. Pennsylvania State College.** *Abstr. doct. Diss. Pa St. Coll.* [1938–55] **C.**A.; **R.**D.; **Y.** [*C. in:* 17024]

335 **Abstracts** of **Doctoral Dissertations. University** of **Nebraska.** Lincoln. *Abstr. doct. Diss. Univ. Neb.* **L.**BM[N]. 47–53*; **C.**A. 42: 44: 47–53; **O.**B. 47–53. [*C. in:* 17024]

Abstracts of **Doctors' Dissertations. Ohio State University.** *See* 333.

336 **Abstracts. English Ceramic Society.** Tunstall. *Abstr. Engl. Ceram. Soc.* [1905–16] **L.**P. [*Supplement to:* 53706; *C. as:* 321]

337 **Abstracts** of **German Patent Applications** open to Public Inspection. Frankfurt. *Abstr. Germ. Pat. Applic.* [1950–52] **L.**P.

338 **Abstracts. Institute** of **Petroleum.** London. *Abstr. Inst. Petrol.* **L.**BM.; RI. 39–.

Abstracts. Institution of **Mining** and **Metallurgy,** London. *See* 22634.

Abstracts. International Institute for the **Conservation** of **Museum Objects.** London. *See* 22629.

339 **Abstracts** of **Japanese Medicine.** Amsterdam, etc. *Abstr. Jap. Med.* [1960–] **L.**BM.; MD.; **Bl.**U.; **Ld.**U.; **Y.**

Abstracts from **Journal** of the **Iron** and **Steel Institute** of **Japan.** *See* 52914.

340 **Abstracts Journal: Metallurgy.** New York, London. *Abstr. J. Metall.* [1957–] **L.**AV.; BM.; P.; **Bm.**C.; **G.**T.; **O.**R.; **Sh.**SC.; **Y.** [*From* 1958 *issued in two sections: A. Scientific and B. Technology; Selections in English translation from:* 42405; *See also* 25407ᵃ]

Abstracts Journal for **Metallurgy** of the **USSR.** *See* 340.

341 **Abstracts** from **Kagaku-kenkyu-jo-hōkōku.** Tokyo. *Abstr. Kagaku-Kenkyu-jo-Hōkōku* [1950–57] **L.**C.; P.; **Abs.**U.; **Bm.**U.; **Bn.**U.; **Ld.**U.; **M.**C.; **O.**R.; **Y.** [*C. of:* 401; *C. as:* 402]

342 **Abstracts** of **Literature** relating to **Combustion Apparatus.** Combustion Appliance Makers' Association. London. *Abstr. Lit. Combust. Appar.* [1937–38] **L.**SC. [*C. of:* 45841; *C. as:* 11593]

343 **Abstracts** of the **Literature** of **Industrial Hygiene.** Cambridge, Mass. *Abstr. Lit. ind. Hyg.* [1919–49] **L.**BM.; C. 28–49; MD.; P.; TD.; **Abs.**N.; **Br.**U.; **C.**UL.; **E.**A.; U.; **G.**U.; **Ld.**U. 29–49; **M.**MS.; U.; **O.**R. 20–49. [*Supplement to:* 26159]

344 **Abstracts** of **Literature** on the **Manufacture** and **Distribution** of **Ice Cream.** Harrisburg, Pa. *Abstr. Lit. Mf. Distrib. Ice Cream* [1927–35] **L.**P. 34–35. [*C. in:* 25873]

Abstracts of **Literature** on **Milk** and **Milk Products,** Journal of Dairy Science. *See* 25873.

345 **Abstracts** of **Literature** on the **Production, Processing** and **Distribution** of **Fresh Milk.** Washington. *Abstr. Lit. Prod. Process. Distrib. fresh Milk* [1931–34] **R.**D. [*C. in:* 25873]

346 **Abstracts** of the **Literature** on **Semiconducting** and **Luminescent Materials** and their **Applications.** New York, London. *Abstr. Lit. semicond. lumin. Mater.* [1953–56] **L.**AV.; BM.; P.; SC.; UC.; **E.**A.; **G.**U.; **Sh.**SC. [*C. as:* 49507]

347 **Abstracts** of **Mean Meteorological Readings** of **Kuala Lumpur Observatory.** Kuala Lumpur. *Abstr. mean met. Read. Kuala Lumpur Obs.* **L.**MO. 00–16.

348 **Abstracts** of **Mean Meteorological Readings, Pahang Observatory.** *Abstr. mean. met. Read. Pahang Obs.* **L.**MO. 01–24. [*C. in:* 351]

349 **Abstracts** of **Mean Meteorological Readings** of the **Seremban Observatory.** Negri Sembilan. *Abstr. mean met. Read. Seremban Obs.* **L.**MO. 03–12.

350 **Abstracts** of **Medicine** for the **General Practitioner.** *Abstr. Med. gen. Practnr* [1960] **E.**P. [*C. as:* 16183]

350° **Abstracts** of the **Meeting** of the **Japan Gibberellin Research Association.** Tokyo. *Abstr. Meet. Japan Gibberellin Res. Ass.* **Md.**H. 60–.

351 **Abstracts** of **Meteorological Observations, Federated Malay States.** Kuala Lumpur. *Abstr. met. Obsns F.M.S.* [1925–38] **L.**MO. [*C. of:* 348, 353, 354, 355, 356; *C. as:* 33383]

352 **Abstracts** of the **Meteorological Observations.** Georgetown, Demerara. *Abstr. met. Obsns, Georgetown*

353 **Abstracts** of **Meteorological Readings, Perak.** *Abstr. met. Read. Perak* **L.**MO. 99–24. [*C. in:* 351]

354 **Abstracts** of **Meteorological Readings, Selangor.** *Abstr. met. Read. Selangor* **L.**MO. 09–24. [*C. in:* 351]

355 **Abstracts** of **Meteorological Readings, State of Negri Sembilan.** *Abstr. met. Read. St. Negri Sembilan* **L.**MO. 10–24. [*C. in:* 351]

356 **Abstracts** of **Meteorological Readings, State of Pahang.** *Abstr. met. Read. St. Pahang* **L.**MO. 10–24. [*C. in:* 351]

357 **Abstracts** on **Military** and **Aviation Ophthalmology** and **Visual Sciences.** Washington. *Abstr. milit. Aviat. Ophthal.* [1953–] **L.**MD.

358 **Abstracts** of **Minutes. Royal Irish Academy** Dublin. *Abstr. Minutes R. Ir. Acad.* [1869–30] **L.**BM. 02–30; SC. 13–30; **Abs.**N. 15–30; **Db.**; **E.**R. 04–30; **O.**B. 10–30; R. [*C. as:* 39637]

359 **Abstracts. Motor Industry Research Association.** Brentford. *Abstr. Mot. Ind. Res. Ass.* [1946–54] **L.**BM.; P. 52–54; **Bm.**C; **Br.**U. 48–54; **Sil.**; **Sy.**R. [*C. of:* 301; *C. as:* 33622]

360 **Abstracts** and **Notices. Air Ministry.** London. *Abstr. Not. Air Minist.*

361 **Abstracts** of **Observations** and **Results, Southport Meteorological Observatory.** Southport. *Abstr. Obsns Results Southport met. Obs.* **L.**MO. 05–46 imp. [*C. as:* 30666°]

362 **Abstracts** of **Orthopedic Surgery.** Washington. *Abstr. orthop. Surg.* [1949−] **L.**MD.; S. 49–50.

363 **Abstracts** of **Papers. Agricultural Education Association.** London. *Abstr. Pap. agric. Educ. Ass.* **Bn.**U. 08–33 imp.; **Rt.** 08–.

364 **Abstracts** of **Papers** on **Agricultural Research** in **Great Britain** and **Northern Ireland.** London. *Abstr. Pap. agric. Res. Gt Br.* [1926–30] **Abs.**A.; **C.**A.; **G.**U. imp.; **O.**AEC.; **R.**U. 26–29; **Rt.**; **Sa.** 28–30.

365 **Abstracts** of **Papers. American Chemical Society.** Washington. *Abstr. Pap. Am. chem. Soc.* **L.**C. 41–; P. 54– imp.; SC. 42–; **Bl.**U. 57–; **C.**CH. 47–; **G.**M. 56–; U. 59–; **H.**U. 58–; **Ld.**U. 58–; **Lv.**P. 51–53: 56–; **M.**C. 57–; D. 43–; **N.**U. 56–; **O.**BI; **Y.**

366 **Abstracts** of **Papers. American Society** for **Horticultural Science.** Ithaca, N.Y. *Abstr. Pap. Am. Soc. hort. Sci.* **Md.**H. 54–.

367 **Abstracts** of **Papers. Belfast Association** of **Engineers.** Belfast. *Abstr. Pap. Belfast Ass. Engrs* **L.**P. 14–19*; **Abs.**N. 14–19. [*C. as:* 36999]

368 **Abstracts** of **Papers. Brighton** and **Sussex Natural History** and **Philosophical Society.** Hove. *Abstr. Pap. Brighton nat. Hist. Soc.* [1855–38] **L.**BM. 87–38; BM^N.; HO. 04–38; R. 99–24; UC. 87–38 imp.; **Bl.**U.; **Cr.**N. 80–38; **G.**N. 02–38 imp. [*C. as:* 42871]

369 **Abstracts** of **Papers. Grassland Division, D.S.I.R., New Zealand.** Palmerston. *Abstr. Pap. Grassld Div. D.S.I.R., N.Z.* [1955–] **Rt.** 55.

370 **Abstracts** of **Papers. Houghton Poultry Research Station.** Houghton. *Abstr. Pap. Houghton Poult. Res. Stn* [1956–] **C.**A.

370° **Abstracts** of **Papers. Japan Society** of **Civil Engineers.** Tokyo. *Abstr. Pap. Japan Soc. civ. Engrs*

370ᵉ **Abstracts** of **Papers** of the **Journal** of the **Japanese Society** of **Internal Medicine.** *Abstr. Pap. J. jap. Soc. internal Med.* **Abd.**R. 60–.

371 **Abstracts** of **Papers. Minnesota Academy** of **Sciences.** Minneapolis. *Abst. Pap. Minn. Acad. Sci.* [1932–36] [*C. as:* 39406]

372 **Abstracts** of **Papers. National Physical Laboratory.** Teddington. *Abstr. Pap. natn. phys. Lab.* [1936–38] **L.**BM.; MO. 36; NF.; P.; U.; **C.**P.; **E.**R.; **G.**I.; M.; U.; **Ld.**P.; U.; **M.**P. 37–38; **O.**R. 37–38. [*C. of:* 14861]

373 **Abstracts** of **Papers. Royal Society** of **London.** *Abstr. Pap. R. Soc. Lond.* **L.**P. 38–41; R.; **C.**P. 37–; **M.**P. 39–40; **Pl.**M. 37–40.

374 **Abstracts** of **Papers** on **Scientific Hydrology.** Tokyo. *Abstr. Pap. scient. Hydrol., Tokyo* **L.**MO. 36.

375 **Abstracts** of **Papers** in **Scientific Transactions** and **Periodicals.** London. *Abstr. Pap. scient. Trans. Period.* [1919–20] **L.**BM.; P.; UC.; **Br.**U.; **C.**UL.; **E.**A.; R.; **G.**E.; **Ld.**U.; **Lv.**P.; **M.**U.; **Nw.**A.; **O.**R. [*C. as:* 18082]

376 **Abstracts** of **Papers. Society** of **American Bacteriologists.** Baltimore. *Abstr. Pap. Soc. Am. Bact.* [1949] **L.**TD.; **R.**D. [*C. of:* 39385; *C. as:* 5701]

377 **Abstracts** of **Physics Papers.** Chinese Physical Society. Peking. *Abstr. Phys. Pap., Peking*

378 **Abstracts** of **Physiological Researches.** Baltimore. *Abstr. physiol. Res.* [1916–]

379 **Abstracts** of **Proceedings** of the **Association** of **Life Insurance Medical Directors.** New York. *Abstr. Proc. Ass. Life Insur. med. Dir.* [1889–40] **L.**MD. 19–40. [*C. as:* 53603]

380 **Abstracts** of the **Proceedings. Boston Society** of **Natural History.** Boston. *Abstr. Proc. Boston Soc. nat. Hist.* **Ld.**U. 37–38.

381 **Abstracts** of the **Proceedings** of the **Geological Society.** London. *Abstr. Proc. geol. Soc., Lond.* [1856–52] **L.**BM. 76–52 imp.; BM^N.; G. 80–52; GL.; L. 87–52; UC. 36–52 imp.; **Abs.**U. 00–17 imp.; **Bn.**U. 48–52; **C.**S. 52; UL. 00–52; **Db.** 48–52; **E.**R. 81–52 imp.; **Ld.**U. 18–44 imp.; **Lv.**U. 68–17 imp.; **O.**R. 80–52; **Sw.**U. 82–99. [*C. as:* 39218]

381ᵃ **Abstracts** of **Proceedings. Indian Central Cotton Committee.** Bombay. *Abstr. Proc. Indian cent. Cott. Comm.* [1921–32] **L.**BM. 31–32; **M.**C. imp. [*C. as:* 51375]

382 **Abstracts** of **Proceedings** of the **Linnaean Society** of **New York.** New York. *Abstr. Proc. Linn. Soc. N.Y.* [1888–32] **L.**BM^N.; G. 89–94 imp.; R. 88–07; Z. 91–14; **Db.** 90–32. [*C. as:* 39349]

383 **Abstracts** of the **Proceedings** of the **Linnean Society** of **London.** *Abstr. Proc. Linn. Soc. Lond.* **L.**BM^N. 95–; E.; L.; **Db.** 00–.

384 **Abstracts** of **Proceedings. Linnean Society** of **New South Wales.** Sydney. *Abstr. Proc. Linn. Soc. N.S.W.* **L.**BM. 82– imp.; BM^N. 82– imp.; E. 23–; L. 77–; Z. 82–99: 47– imp.; **Dm.** 36–; **E.**B. 28–; R. 94 imp.; **Y.**

385 **Abstracts. Proceedings** of the **New York Pathological Society.** New York. *Abstr. Proc. N.Y. path. Soc.* [1927–] **L.**LI. 27–38: 42–45; MA. 27–38; S. 27–49; **C.**P. 27–33: 46–; PA. 27–33: 42– imp.; **E.**U. [*Reprinted from* 4330; *a continuation of:* 39516]

386 **Abstracts** of the **Proceedings** of the **Royal Entomological Society** of **London.** *Abstr. Proc. R. ent. Soc.* [1935–36] **L.**BM.; BM^N.; E.; EB.; HO.; L.; UC.; Z.; **Abs.**N.; **Bn.**U.; **C.**B.; P.; UL.; **Cr.**M.; P.; **Db.**; **E.**A.; **G.**U.; **Ld.**U.; **O.**B.; R. [*C. as:* 39634, *Section C*]

387 **Abstracts** of **Proceedings. Royal Society** of **New South Wales.** Sydney. *Abstr. Proc. R. Soc. N.S.W.* **L.**BM^N. 97–03; Z. 97–99; **Ld.**U. 97–03.

388 [**Abstracts** of the **Proceedings**] **Société linnéenne** de **Normandie.** Caen. *Abstr. Proc. Soc. linn. Normandie* **L.**BM^N. 12–19; **Cr.**N. 14–23.

389 **Abstracts** of **Proceedings. Society** of **Agricultural Bacteriologists.** Reading. *Abstr. Proc. Soc. agric. Bact.* [1938–44] **L.**BM.; TD.; **C.**UL.; **R.**D. [*C. of:* 37101; *C. as:* 390]

390 **Abstracts** of **Proceedings. Society** for **Applied Bacteriology.** Reading. *Abstr. Proc. Soc. appl. Bact.* [1945–] **L.**BM.; KC. 54–; **R.**D. [*C. of:* 389]

391 **Abstract** of the **Proceedings** of the **Zoological Society** of **London.** *Abstr. Proc. zool. Soc. Lond.* [1904–36] **L.**BM^N.; SC.; Z. [*C. as:* 39835]

392 **Abstracts** of **Psychiatry** for the **General Practitioner.** Belle Mead, N.J. *Abstr. Psychiatry gen. Practnr* [1958–] **Ld.**U.

393 **Abstracts** of **Published Papers** and **List** of **Translations. C.S.I.R.O., Australia.** Melbourne. *Abstr. publd Pap. List. Transl. C.S.I.R.O. Aust.* [1952–56] **L.**P.; **Abd.**R.; **C.**A.; **F.**A.; **Hu.**G.; **R.**D. 53–56; **Y.** [*C. as:* 12910]

394 **Abstracts** of **Published Research Papers** from **National Laboratories** and **Sponsored Research Projects** of **C.S.I.R., India.** New Delhi. *Abstr. publ. Res. Pap. natn. Labs C.S.I.R. India* **L.**P. 58–. [*Supplement to:* 26864]

395 **Abstracts** of **Recent Published Material** on **Soil** and **Water Conservation.** Soil Conservation Service. Washington. *Abstr. rec. publ. Mater. Soil Wat. Conserv.* [1949–] **L.**BM.; P. 51–; **O.**F.; **Y.**

396 **Abstracts** and **References. Radio Research Board.** London. *Abstr. Refs Radio Res. Bd* **L.**BM.; MO. 26–; SC. 22–; **C.**ENG. 27–; **O.**ED. 30–.

397 **Abstracts Reports** of the **Geological Survey** of **Western Australia.** Perth. *Abstr. Rep. geol. Surv. West. Aust.* **E.**D. 11–.

    Abstracts from **Reports. Institute** of **Physical** and **Chemical Research, Tokyo.** *See* 402.

    Abstracts from **Reports. Scientific Research Institute, Tokyo.** *See* 341.

    Abstracts. Research and **Development Division, British Steel Founders Association.** *See* 5685.

398 **Abstracts** of the **Results** of **Meteorological Observations** taken at **Alipore Observatory.** Calcutta. *Abstr. Results met. Obsns Alipore Obs.* **L.**MO. 77–10.

399 **Abstracts Review. American Paint** and **Varnish Manufacturers Association.** Washington. *Abstr. Rev. Am. Paint Varn. Mfrs Ass.* **L.**P. 28–30*; PR. 29–30; **Y.** [*C. as:* 400]

400 **Abstracts Review. National Paint, Varnish** and **Lacquer Association.** Washington. *Abstr. Rev. natn. Paint Varn. Lacq. Ass.* [1933–] **L.**P.; PR.; **Y.** [*C. of:* 399]

401 **Abstracts** from **Rikwagaku-kenkyu-jo-iho.** *Abstr. Rikwagaku-Kenkyu-jo-Iho* [1928–43] **L.**C. 28–35; M. imp.; P.; UC.; **Abs.**U.; **Bm.**U.; **Bn.**U.; **E.**R.; **G.**U.; **Ld.**U.; **M.**C.; **O.**R.; **R.**U.; **Sa.**; **Sw.**U.; **Y.** [*C. as:* 341]

402 **Abstracts** from **Rikagaku-Kenkyū-sho-hōkōku.** Tokyo. *Abstr. Rikagaku-Kenkyū-sho-Hōkōku* [1958–] **L.**P.; **Abs.**U.; **Bm.**U.; **Bn.**U.; **G.**U.; **Ld.**U.; **M.**C.; **O.**R.; **Y.** [*C. of:* 341]

403 **Abstracts. Scientific Department, National Coal Board.** London. *Abstr. scient. Dep. natn. Coal Bd*
    Abstracts A. Technical Coal Press. **L.**P.56–.
    Abstracts B. Industrial Health. **L.**P. 57–.
    Abstracts C. Coal Measures. **L.**P. 56–.
    Abstracts D. Fluid Mechanics. **L.**P. 56–.
    Abstracts E. Gasification and Hydrogenation of Coal. **L.**P. 57–.
    Abstracts F. Underground Gasification of Coal. **L.**P. 57–.

404 **Abstracts** of **Scientific** and **Technical Papers** published in **Egypt** and Papers received from [other Middle East countries]. Cairo. *Abstr. scient. tech. Pap. Egypt* [1955–59] **L.**MO. 55–; MY.; P.; TP. imp.; SC. [*Incorporates:* 14474; *Forms* Pt. 2 *of:* 11680; *C. as:* 405]

405 **Abstracts** of **Scientific** and **Technical Papers** published in **U.A.R.** and Papers received from [other Middle East countries]. Cairo. *Abstr. scient. tech. Pap. U.A.R.* [1959–] **L.**MY.; P.; SC.; TP. imp. [*C. of:* 404; *Forms* Pt. 2 *of:* 11680 and 17079]

406 **Abstracts** from the **Scientific** and **Technical Press** issued by the **Directorates** of **Scientific Research** and **Technical Development, Air Ministry.** London. *Abstr. scient. tech. Press Air Minist.* **L.**MO. 26–39. [*C. as:* 407]

407 **Abstracts** from the **Scientific** and **Technical Press. Ministry** of **Aircraft Production.** London. *Abstr. scient. tech. Press Minist. Aircr. Prod.* **L.**MO. 40–44. [*C. of:* 406 and 18860]

408 **Abstracts** from the **Scientific** and **Technical Press. Royal Aeronautical Society.** London. *Abstr. scient. tech. Press R. aeronaut. Soc.* [1940–44] **L.**BM.; P.; **N.**U.; **Sy.**R. 43–44 imp. [*Formerly* and *subsequently issued in:* 1074]

409 **Abstracts** of **Scientific** and **Technical Progress.** Bulletin. Cairo. *Abstr. scient. tech. Prog., Cairo* [1955–] **O.**B. 55.

410 **Abstracts** of **Scientific** and **Technical Publications. Massachusetts Institute** of **Technology.** Cambridge, Mass. *Abstr. scient. tech. Publs Mass. Inst. Technol.* [1928–32] **L.**BM^N.; C.; GM.; P.; **Ld.**U.

411 **Abstracts** bearing on **Shellac Research Literature.** London. *Abstr. Shellac Res. Lit.* [1928–46] **L.**BM.; P. imp.; SC.; **G.**U. 43–44; **Rt.** 44–45; **Sy.**R. [*Reprinted from* 46195]

    Abstracts. Society of **Chemical Industry.** London. *See* 26920.

412 **Abstracts** of **Soviet Medicine.** Amsterdam. *Abstr. Sov. Med.* [1957–]
    A. Basic medical sciences. **L.**LI. 58–; MA.; MC.; MD.; TD.; UC.; **Bl.**U.; **Br.**U.; **Cr.**U.; **E.**U.; **G.**F.; U.; **Ld.**U.; **M.**MS.; **O.**R.; **Sh.**U.; **Y.**
    B. Clinical medicine. **L.**MA.; MD.; TD.; **Bl.**U.; **Br.**U.; **E.**U.; **G.**F.; U.; **Ld.**U.; **M.**MS.; **O.**R.; **Sh.**U.; **Y.** [*From* 1961 *the parts combine: Forms a section of:* 18709]

412° **Abstracts. Symposium** on **Molecular Structure** and **Spectroscopy.** Columbus. *Abstr. Symp. mol. Struct. Spectrosc.* **L.**P. 52–.

    Abstracts of the **Technical Literature** on **Archaeology** and the **Fine Arts.** London. *See* 22629.

    Abstracts from **Technical Periodicals. British Internal Combustion Engine Research Association.** *See* 5664.

413 **Abstracts** of **Thermometrical** and **Rainfall Observations, Negri Sembilan.** *Abstr. thermometr. Rainf. Obsns Negri Sembilan* **L.**MO. 09–24. [*C. in:* 351]

414 **Abstracts** of **Thermometical** and **Rainfall Observations, Pahang.** *Abstr. thermometr. Rainf. Obsns Pahang* **L.**MO. 08–30 imp.

415 **Abstracts** of **Thermometrical** and **Rainfall Observations, Selangor.** *Abstr. thermometr. Rainf. Obsns Selangor* **L.**MO. 89–24 imp. [*C. in:* 351]

416 **Abstracts** of **Theses. Cornell University.** Ithaca. *Abstr. Thes. Cornell Univ.* **C.**A. 37–47.

417 **Abstracts** of **Theses** for **Doctorates. University** of **Durham.** *Abstr. Thes. Doct. Univ. Durham* **L.**BM. 32–; BM^N. 31–39; **N.**U. 31–39; **Nw.**A. 31–38.

418 **Abstracts** of **Theses,** etc., **Graduate School. University** of **Pittsburgh.** *Abstr. Thes. Univ. Pittsburgh* **L.**U. 31–.

419 **Abstracts** of **Theses. Louisiana State University.** Baton Rouge. *Abstr. Thes. La St. Univ.* [1935–] **L.**BM.; U. imp.; **O.**B.

420 **Abstracts** of **Theses. Massachusetts Institute** of **Technology.** Cambridge, Mass. *Abstr. Thes. Mass. Inst. Technol.* **G.**U. 51–; **Y.**

421 **Abstracts** of **Theses. University** of **Chicago.** Chicago. *Abstr. Thes. Univ. Chicago.* Science series. **L.**BM^N. 22–32; P. 22–29; **O.**B. 23–32.

422 **Abstracts** of **Theses** accepted by the **University** for **Higher Degrees.** Aberdeen. *Abstr. Thes. Univ. Aberd.* [1931–37] **L.**BM^N.; **Abd.**U.; **C.**UL.; **G.**M. 34–37; **N.**U.imp.; **O.**B.

423 **Abstracts** of **Theses. University** of **Washington.** Seattle. *Abstr. Thes. Univ. Wash.* [1914–] **L.**BM. 31–46; **C.**A.

424 **Abstracts** of **Theses. Vanderbilt University.** Nashville. *Abstr. Thes. Vanderbilt Univ.* **O.**B. 31–.

425 **Abstracts** of **Tuberculosis.** Baltimore. *Abstr. Tuberc.* [*Supplement to:* 2143]

426 **Abstracts** from **Wildlife Disease.** Washington. *Abstr. Wildl. Dis.* [1959–] **L.**MD.

Abstracts of the **Works** of the **Zoological Institute** of the **Moscow State University.** *See* 48637 and 54904.

427 **Abstracts** of **World Medicine.** British Medical Association. London. *Abstr. Wld Med.* [1947–] **L.**BM.; CB.; D.; GH.; H.; MA.; MC.; MD.; OP.; P. 57–; QM. 47–55 imp.; S.; SH. (1 yr.); TD.; U.; UC.; UCH. 47–54; VC.; **Abd.**R.; **Abs.**N.; **Bl.**U.; **Bm.**T. 54–; U.; **Br.**U.; **C.**MD.; **Cr.**MD.; MS.; **Db.**; **Dn.**U.; **E.**A.; I.; N.; U.; **Ep.**D.; **G.**F.; U.; **Ld.**U.; **Lv.**M.; P. 57–; **M.**MS.; P. 56–; **O.**R.; **Sa.** 51–; **Y.**

428 **Abstracts** of **World Surgery, Obstetrics** and **Gynaecology.** London. *Abstr. Wld Surg. Obstet. Gynaec.* [1947–52] **L.**CB.; D.; GH.; H.; MA.; MC.; MD.; OP.; S.; TD.; U.; UC.; **Abd.**R.; U.; **Abs.**N.; **Bl.**U. imp.; **Bm.**U.; **Br.**U.; **C.**UL.; **Cr.**MD.; MS. 48–52; **Db.**; **Dn.**U.; **E.**A.; N.; P.; S.; U.; **Ep.**D. 47–51; **G.**F.; U.; **Ld.**U.; **Lv.**M. **M.**MS.; **O.**R.; **Sa.** [*C. in:* 427]

Abstracts. Zinc Development Association. *See* 58216.

429 **Academia odontológica.** Medellin. *Acad. odont. Medellin*

430 **Academy Architecture** and **Architectural Review.** London. *Acad. Archit. archit. Rev.* [1889–31] **L.**BA.; BM.; P. 89–25; **Abs.**N. 20–31; **Bm.**P. 28–31; **Cr.**P. 90–05 imp.; **Db.**; **E.**A. 89–22 imp.; T.; **G.**M. 93–31; **Ld.**P. 16–21; **Lv.**P. imp.; **M.**P. 89–10; **O.**B. imp.

431 **Academy Review** of the **California Academy** of **Periodontology.** San Francisco. *Acad. Rev. Calif. Acad. Periodont.* **L.**D.

432 **Acadian Naturalist.** Fredericton, N.B. *Acadian Nat.* [1943–47] **L.**BM^N. [*C. of:* 11251]

433 **Acarologia.** Abbeville, Paris. *Acarologia* [1959–] **L.**AM.; BM^N.; TD.; Z.; **Bn.**U.; **Y.**

434 **Accademia medica.** Genova, Torino. *Accad. med.* [1929–] **L.**MA. 30–38 imp.; MD. 37–38. [*C. of:* 8385]

435 **Accession Lists. Industrial Diamond Information Bureau.** London. *Acc. Lists ind. Diam. Inf. Bur.* [1946–48] **L.**SI. [*C. in:* 6729]

Accessions to the **Engineering Libraries** of **Praha, Brno** and **Bratislava.** *See* 38722.

436 **Accessoire** de **pharmacie,** etc. Paris. *Access. Pharm.*

437 **Accessory** and **Garage Equipment.** London. *Access. Gar. Equip.* [1956–] **L.**BM.; P.; **Y.**

438 **Acciaio** e **costruzioni metalliche.** Milano. *Acciaio Costruz. metall.* [1955–59] [*C. of* and *Rec. as:* 15978]

439 **Acciaio inossidabile.** Milano. *Acciaio inoss.* **L.**P. 60–; **Y.**

439° **Accident Prevention** in **Nonferrous-Metal Processing Plants.** U.S. Bureau of Mines. Washington. *Accid. Prev. nonferr.-Metal Process. Pl.* [1954–] **L.**BM.

440 **Accidents.** London. *Accidents* [1949–] **L.**AV. 49–59; BM.; P.; TD. imp.; **Cr.**U.; **M.**P.; **Ma.**T. 59–; **Sy.**R. [*C. of* 22460]

441 **Accidents** and their **Prevention. Institute** of **Welding.** London. *Accid. Prev. Inst. Weld.* [1957–] **L.**BM.; P.

442 **Acción científica internacional.** Madrid. *Acción cient. int.* [1936–]

443 **Acción médica.** Buenos Aires. *Acción méd., B. Aires* **L.**MA. 32–40 imp.

444 **Acción médica.** La Paz, Bolivia. *Acción méd., La Paz* [1942–]

445 **Acción médica.** México. *Acción méd., Méx.*

446 **Account** of the **Operations** of the **Great Trigonometrical Survey** of **India.** Calcutta. *Acct Ops gt trig. Surv. India* [1870–10] **L.**AS.; BM. 76–10; SC.; U.; **Abd.**U.; **Bm.**U. 70–80: 10; **C.**O.; **E.**A. 70–06; R.; U.; **G.**U.; **Lv.**U.; **O.**B.

447 **Acero** y **energía.** Barcelona. *Acero Energ.* **L.**I. (3 yr.); P. 55–; **Y.** [*Also Número especial*]

448 **Acetilén** és **karbid.** Budapest. *Acet. Karb., Bpest*

449 **Acetylen** in **Wissenchaft** u. **Industrie.** Halle a. S. *Acet. Wiss. Ind.* **L.**P. 10–30*. [*C. as:* 5625]

Acetylene. London. *See* 451.

Acetylene-Gas Journal. *See* 450.

450 **Acetylene Journal.** Chicago. *Acet. J.* [1899–30] [> 25414 and 25415, 1917–19; *C. in:* 57299]

Acetylene Lighting and **Welding Journal.** *See* 451.

Acetylene Welding. Moscow. *See* 5602.

451 **Acetylene** and **Welding Journal.** London. *Acet. Weld. J.* [1903–24] **L.**BM.; MT. 23–24; NF. 22–24; P. 12–24; **Bm.**C. 22–24; **G.**M. 11–24. [*C. as:* 57304]

452 **Achema-Jahrbuch.** Deutsche Gesellschaft für Chemisches Apparatewesen. Leipzig. *Achema-Jb.* [1925–] **L.**BM.; P. imp.; **Ld.**U.; **Y.**

Achievements of **Science** and of **Advanced Research** in **Agriculture.** Moscow. *See* 17170.

453 **Acht** en **opbouw.** Amsterdam. *Acht Opb.* [1930–43] **L.**BA. 34–40.

454 **Acier.** Paris. *Acier, Paris* [1932–] **L.**P. 36– imp.; **Y.**

455 **Acier—Stahl—Steel.** Bruxelles. *Acier, Brux.* [1955–] **L.**KC. 57–; P.; **C.**ENG. (4 yr.); **G.**U. 62–; **Ld.**U. 59–; **Sh.**SC. 57–; **Y.** [*C. of:* 36475]

456 **Aciers fins** et **spéciaux français.** Paris. *Aciers fins spéc. fr.* **L.**P. 54–; **G.**E. (3 yr.); **Y.**

457 **Aciers** au **nickel.** Paris. *Aciers Nickel* Série B. **Y.**

Aciers spéciaux et leur **emplois, métaux** et **alliages.** *See* 458.

458 **Aciers spéciaux, métaux** et **alliages.** Paris. *Aciers spéc.* **L.**I. 27–34*; NF. 28–34; P. 27–34; **Bm.**U. 25–28; **Sh.**IO. 27–29: 31–32. [*C. as:* 31510]

459 **Acme International Bulletin.** Chicago. *Acme int. Bull.* **L.**P. 28–29.

460 **Acologist.** Farmington, Minn. *Acologist*

460° **Acosa News.** Aluminium Company of South Africa. Pietermaritzburg. *Acosa News* [1957–] **L.**BM.

461 **Acqua** nell' **agricoltura,** nell' **igiene** e nell' **industria.** Roma. *Acqua Agric. Ig. Ind.*

462 **Acqua** nei **campi** e nell' **abitato.** Milano. *Acqua Campi Abit.*

463 **Acqua** e **gas.** Roma. *Acqua Gas* [1929–] [*C. of:* 23136]

464 **Acquario.** Associazione italiana acquariofili. Roma. *Acquario* [1949–] **L.**Z. 49–52 imp.
     Acque e **bonifiche.** *See* 465.

465 **Acque, bonifiche, costruzione.** Roma. *Acque Bonif. Costruz.* [1933–] **Y.** [*C. of:* 467]

466 **Acque gassate.** Roma. *Acque gass.*

467 **Acque** e **trasporti.** Roma. *Acque Trasp.* [1917–32] [*C. as:* 465]
     Acquets techniques. *See* 33877.

468 **Acridological Abstracts.** London. *Acrid. Abstr.* [1950–] **L.**NC. 60–; P. 58–.

469 **Acropole.** São Paulo. *Acropole* **L.**BA. 51–

470 **Acrylo-News.** New York. *Acrylo-News* [1956–] **Sy.**R.

471 **Acta Academiae åboensis.** Abo. *Acta Acad. åbo.* Mathematica et physica [1922–] **L.**C.; G.; M.; P. 54–; R. 27–52; U.; UC.; **Abd.**U.; **Abs.**U.; **Bl.**U.; **Bm.**U.; **Br.**U. 22–27; **C.**P.; UL.; **Db.**; E.R. 25–; U.; **G.**T.; U.; **M.**U. 22–37; **N.**U. 22–27; **O.**R.; **R.**U.; **Y.**
     Acta Academiae R. scientiarum Upsaliensis. *See* 27819ª.
     Acta Academiae scientiarum čechoslovenicae basis brunensis. *See* 38287.

472 **Acta Academiae scientiarum naturalium moravo-silesiacae.** Brno. *Acta Acad. Sci. nat. moravo-siles.* [1948–53] **L.**BM.; BM^N.; L. 50–53; UC.; **C.**P.; UL.; **Db.**; E.R.; **O.**B.; R. [*C. of:* 772; *C. as:* 38287]

473 **Acta adriatica.** Institut za oceanografija i ribarstvo u Splitu FNR Jugoslavija. *Acta adriat.* [1932–] **L.**AM.; BM. 48–; BM^N.; SC.; Z.; **Abd.**M.; **Bn.**U. 54– imp.; **C.**P.; UL. 48–; **Dm.** 41: 48–; **Fr.** 55–; **Lv.**U. imp.; **Mi.** 38–; **Pl.**M.; **Wo.**; **Y.** [*Not published* 1942–47]

474 **Acta aerophysiologica.** Hamburg. *Acta aerophysiol.* [1933–34]
     Acta agralia fennica. *See* 51436.

475 **Acta agralia vadensia.** Wageningen. *Acta agral. vadens.* [1934–] **L.**BM^N. 34; **Abs.**A. 34; **C.**A.; **Rt.** 34–36; **Y.**

476 **Acta agricultura suecana.** Stockholm. *Acta agric. suec.* [1945–49] **L.**AM.; K.; **Abd.**R.; S.; **Abs.**A.; U.; **Bn.**U. imp.; **C.**A.; AB.; GE.; **E.**AB.; **Hu.**G.; **Md.**H.; **O.**R.; **R.**D.; **Rt.**; **Sal.**; **Y.** [*C. as:* 477]

477 **Acta agriculturae scandinavica.** Stockholm. *Acta Agric. scand.* [1950–] **L.**AM.; BM. 53–; HS.; K.; **Abd.**R.; S.; **Abs.**A.; U.; **C.**A.; AB.; **Db.**; **E.**AB.; **Hu.**G.; **Md.**H.; **N.**U.; **O.**R.; RE.; **R.**D.; U. 52–; **Rt.**; **Sal.** 50–56; **Sil.** 54–; **Y.** [*C. of:* 476; *also supplements*]

478 **Acta agriculturae sinica.** Peking. *Acta Agric. sin.* [1952–] **L.**AM. 58–60; P.; R. 56–; **C.**A. 56–; **Rt.** 55–; **Sil.** 59–; **Y.** [*C. of:* 13928; *Suspended:* 1960]

479 **Acta agrobotanica.** Warszawa. *Acta agrobot.* [1953–] **L.**AM.; BM^N.; MY 54–; SC.; **C.**A. 54–; **Pl.**M.; **Rt.**

480 **Acta agromechanica sinica.** Peking. *Acta agromech. sin.* [1957–] **L.**BM.; **Sil.**

481 **Acta agronomica.** Facultad de agronomía, Universidad nacional de Colombia. Palmira. *Acta agron., Palmira* [1950–] **L.**AM.; K.; L.; MY. 51–; TP. 58–; **Abd.**R.; **Br.**A.; **C.**A.; **E.**AB.; **Hu.**G.; **Ld.**U.; **Md.**H.; **N.**U.; **Y.**

482 **Acta agronomica Academiae scientiarum hungaricae.** Budapest. *Acta agron. hung.* [1950–] **L.**AM.; BM.; P.; **C.**A.; UL.; **E.**AB. 52–56; **Hu.**G.; **Md.**H. 52–; **Pl.**M. 50–53; **Rt.**; **Sal.** 52–54; **Y.**
     Acta agronomica hungarica. *See* 482.
     Acta albertina. Regensburg. *See* 483.

483 **Acta albertina ratisbonensia.** Regensburg. *Acta albert. ratisb.* [1951–] **L.**BM^N.; **Db.**; **Y.** [*C. of:* 6308]

484 **Acta allergologica.** København. *Acta allerg.* [1948–] **L.**MA.; MC.; MD.; **Bm.**U. 49–; **C.**PA. 53–; **G.**U. 48–51; **Ld.**U.; **Lv.**M. 48: 50– imp.; **M.**MS.; **Nw.**A.; **O.**R.; **W.**; **Y.** [*Also supplements*]

485 **Acta americana.** Inter-American Society of Anthropology and Geography. Washington. *Acta am.* [1943–]

486 **Acta anaesthesiologica.** Padova. *Acta anaesth., Padova* [1950–] **Bl.**U. 50–60.

487 **Acta anaesthesiologica belgica.** Bruxelles. *Acta anaesth. belg.* [1950–] **L.**MA. 52–; MD.; S. [*From* 1952 *forms supplement to:* 538]

488 **Acta anaesthesiologica scandinavica.** Aarhus. *Acta anaesth. scand.* [1957–] **L.**MA.; MD.; S.; **Cr.**MD.; **E.**U.; **Ld.**U.; **Lv.**M.; **M.**MS.; **Sh.**U. 59–; **Y.**

489 **Acta anatomica.** Basel, New York. *Acta anat.* [1945–] **L.**BM^N.; MA.; MD.; S.; SC.; U. 50–; **Bl.**U.; **Bm.**U.; **C.**AN.; APH.; **Cr.**U.; **Dn.**U. 50–; **E.**U.; **G.**U. 56–; **Ld.**U.; **M.**MS.; **Nw.**A. 57–; **O.**R.; **Sa.**; **Sh.**U. 57–; **Y.** [*Also supplements*]

490 **Acta anatomica nipponica.** Tokyo. *Acta anat. nippon.* [1928–]

491 **Acta anatomica sinica.** Peking. *Acta anat. sin.* [1953–]

492 **Acta anthropobiologica.** Budapest. *Acta anthropobiol.* [1947–] **L.**AN.; BM.; SC. 47.

493 **Acta anthropologica.** México. *Acta anthrop., Méx.* **L.**AN. 46–; BM. 45–.

494 **Acta anthropologica Universitatis Lodziensis.** Lodz. *Acta anthrop. Univ. lodz.* [1949–]

495 **Acta arachnologica.** Tokyo. *Acta arachn., Tokyo* [1936–] **L.**BM^N. 44–; Z. 49–51 imp.; **C.**B. 55–; **Y.**

496 **Acta arctica.** København. *Acta arct.* [1943–] **L.**BM.; Z. (zool.) 52–; **C.**PO.; **Y.**

497 **Acta argentina** de **fisiología** y **fisiopatología.** Córdoba. *Acta argent. Fisiol. Fisiopat.* [1950–] **L.**MD. 50–54.

498 **Acta arithmetica.** Warszawa, Kraków. *Acta arith.* [1935–39: 58–] **L.**M.; SC.; UC.; **Br.**U. 35–39; **C.**UL. 35–39; E.R. 58–; **G.**U.; **M.**U. imp.; **O.**R.; **Sh.**U. [*Suspended* 1940–57]

499 **Acta astronomica.** Warszawa, Kraków. *Acta astr.* [1925–] **L.**AS.; SC.; **C.**O.; **G.**U. imp.; **Ld.**U. 25–39: 56; **M.**U. 47– imp.; **O.**O.; **Y.** [*From* 1925–55 *in series*]

500 **Acta astronomica sinica.** Peking. *Acta astr. sin.* **L.**P. 58–; **M.**U. 55– imp.

501 **Acta balneologica polonica.** Cracoviae. *Acta baln. pol.* [1937–]

502 **Acta belgica** de **arte medicinali** et **pharmaceutica militari.** Bruxelles. *Acta belg. Arte med. Pharm. milit.* [1955–] **L.**MA.; MD. [*C. of:* 2678]

503 **Acta biochimica polonica.** Warszawa. *Acta biochim. pol.* [1954–] **L.**C. 58–; LI.; MC.; P.; SC.; **Abd.**R. 60–; **Db.**; **Dn.**U.; **R.**D.; **Rt.** 56; **Y.**

504 **Acta biochimica sinica.** Peking, Shanghai. *Acta biochim. sin* [1958–] **L.**C.; MC. imp.; P. 59–; **C.**CH. imp.

505 **Acta biologiae experimentalis.** Varsovie, etc. *Acta Biol. exp., Vars.* [1928–] **L.** B M N. imp.; LI. 28–35; R.; UC. 36–; Z. 50–; **C.**A.; BI. 28–38; MO. 47–; P.; **Db.**; **E.**AG. 47–50: 56–; **G.**U. 38– imp.; **Ld.**U. 28–39; **Lv.**U.; **Pl.**M. imp.; **Rt.**; **Y.**

506 **Acta biologiae experimentalis sinica.** Peking. *Acta Biol. exp. sin.* [1953–] **L.**BM.; BM N. 60–; MC. 58–; **Bn.**U. 60–; **C.**A. 57–; **Y.** [*C. of:* 13930]

Acta biologica. Fukuoka. *See* 49714.

507 **Acta biologica.** Acta Universitatis szegediensis. Szeged. *Acta biol., Szeged* [1955–] **L.**BM N.; U.; Z. 55–56; **C.**P.; **Y.** [*See also:* 2682]

508 **Acta biologica Academiae scientiarum hungaricae.** Budapest. *Acta. biol. hung.* [1950–] **L.**AM. 51–52; BM.; BM N.; C. 54–; P. 54–; R.; SC.; Z.; **Abd.**R.; **Bl.**U.; **Br.**A.; **C.**A. 50–53; P.; UL.; **Db.**; **E.**AB. 50–51; R.; **Hu.**G.; **O.**R.; **Pl.**M.; **Y.** [*Also supplements* 1957–] [*C. of:* 22496]

509 **Acta biologica belgica.** Bruxelles. *Acta biol. belg.* [1941–43] **L.**LI.; TD.; V.; Z.; **C.**MO.; UL.; **Ex.**U.; **Lv.**M.; **R.**D.

510 **Acta biologica cracoviensia.** Kraków. *Acta biol. cracov.* [1958–]

    Série botanique. **L.**BM N.; **Bl.**U.; **C.**P.; **Pl.**M.

    Série zoologique. **L.**BM N.; Z.; **Bl.**U.; **C.**P.; **Pl.**M.

Acta biologica hungarica. *See* 507.

Acta biologica latvica. *See* 28164.

511 **Acta biologica** et **medica.** Gdańsk. *Acta biol. med., Gdańsk* [1957–] **L.**MD.; **Pl.**M. 61–.

512 **Acta biologica** et **medica germanica.** Berlin. *Acta biol. med. germ.* [1958–] **L.**MD. 58 imp.: 61–; **Y.**

513 **Acta biologica venezuelica.** Caracas. *Acta biol. venez.* [1951–] **L.**BM N.; Z.; **Fr.**; **Mi.**; **Ld.**U. 52–59; **Pl.**M.

514 **Acta biotheoretica.** Leiden. *Acta biotheor.* [1935–] **L.**BM.; BM N.; SC.; UC.; **Bl.**U. (Ser. a) **C.**P. 58–; **E.**R.; **H.**U. 35–53; **M.**U.; **O.**R.; **Y.**

515 **Acta borealia.** Tromsø. *Acta boreal.* [1951–]

    A. Scientia. **L.**BM.; BM N.; L. 52–; R.; UC.; **Abd.**M.; **C.**P. 53–; PO.; **Dm.**; **E.**B.; R.; **Lo.**; **Lv.**U.; **M.**U.; **Pl.**M.; **Y.** [*C. of:* 54389]

516 **Acta botanica.** Acta Universitatis Szegediensis. Szeged. *Acta bot., Szeged* [1942–49] **L.**DM N.; U. imp. [*See also:* 2682]

517 **Acta botanica Academiae scientiarum hungaricae.** Budapest. *Acta bot. hung.* [1954–] **L.**BM.; BM N.; K.; SC.; **C.**P.; **Y.**

518 **Acta botanica bohemica.** Prag. *Acta bot. bohem.* [1922–] **L.** B M N. 22–36; K. 22–43; L. 22–38; **Bl.**U. 22–38; **C.**A.; BO.; **E.**B.; **Md.**H. 32–38; **O.**BO. 22–38.; **Rt.** 22–38.

Acta botanica colombiana. Bogota. *See* 33883.

518° **Acta botanica croatica.** Zagreb. *Acta bot. croat.* [1957–] **L.**BM.; BM N.; K.; MY. [*C. of:* 520]

519 **Acta botanica fennica.** Helsingforsiae. *Acta bot. fenn.* [1925–] **L.** B M N.; R.; L.; NC.; R. 25–53; SC.; **Bl.**U.

27–; **Bn.**U. 54–; **C.**P.; PO.; **Cr.**U 27–; **Db.** 27–; **E.**B.; R.; **G.**U.; **Lv.**U.; **Nw.**A. 27–; **O.**BO. 54–; R. 28–; **Y.**

Acta botanica horti bucurestiensis. *See* 28846.

Acta botanica hungarica. *See* 516.

520 **Acta botanica Instituti botanici Universitatis zagrebiensis.** Zagreb. *Acta bot. Inst. bot., Zagreb* [1925–56] **L.**BM.; BM N.; K.; MY. [*C. as:* 518°]

521 **Acta botanica neerlandica.** Amsterdam. *Acta bot. neerl.* [1952–] **L.**BM N.; K.; L.; R.; SC.; **Abs.**A.; U. 59–; **Bl.**U.; **Bn.**U. 59–; **C.**BO.; **Dn.**U. 62–; **E.**B.; R.; **G.**U.; **Ld.**U.; **M.**U.; **N.**U.; **O.**BO.; F. 55– imp.; **R.**U.; **Rt.**; **Sa.**; **Sh.**U.; **Y.** [*C. of:* 34459 and 42368]

522 **Acta botanica sinica.** Peking. *Acta bot. sin.* [1951–] **L.**BM N.; K.; P. 53–; R. 55–; **Bn.**U. 58–; **C.**A. 56–; P. 55–; **O.**F. 58–; **Rt.** 52–; **Y.** [*Suspended* 1960]

523 **Acta botanica taiwanica.** Taipei. *Acta bot. taiwan.* [1947–] **L.**BM N.; K.; **C.**A.; **E.**B.; R.

524 **Acta brevia neerlandica** de **physiologia, pharmacologia, microbiologia,** e.a. Amsterdam. *Acta brev. neerl. Physiol.* [1931–49] **L.**LI. 34–35; MC. imp.; MD. 32–49; UC. 34–35; **Bm.**U. 43–49; **C.**P.; **E.**U.; **R.**D. 47–49. [*C. in:* 727]

525 **Acta brevia sinensia.** British Council. London. *Acta brev. sinensia* [1943–45] **L.**EB.; P.; TD.; **Bm.**U. 44–45; **Pl.**M. imp.; **Rt.** 45. [*C. in:* 49007]

526 **Acta cancrologica.** Budapest. *Acta cancr., Bpest* [1934–37] **L.**BM.; MD.

527 **Acta cancrologica jugoslavica.** Belgrade. *Acta cancr. jugosl.* [1939–40]

528 **Acta cardiologica.** Bruxelles. *Acta cardiol.* [1946–] **L.**MA.; MD.; U. 52–; UCH. 51–53.

529 **Acta carsologica.** Ljubljana. *Acta carsol.* [1955–] **L.**BM N.; E.R.; **Y.** [*C. of:* 38119]

530 **Acta chemica fennica.** Helsingforsiae. *Acta chem. fenn.* [1928–] **L.**C. 31–; **C.**CH. 59–; **Y.**

Acta chemica, mineralogica et **physica.** Szeged. *See* 625.

532 **Acta chemica scandinavica.** København. *Acta chem. scand.* [1947–] **L.**B.; BM.; C.; CB. 54–; KC.; LI.; MA. 50–; MC.; P.; QM.; RI.; SC.; TP. imp.; U. 50–; UC.; **Abd.**U.; **Abs.**U. 53–; **Bl.**U.; **Bm.**T.; U.; **Bn.**U.; **Br.**A. 57–; U.; **C.**APH.; BI.; CH.; P.; UL.; **Cr.**U. 57–; **Db.**; **E.**R. 57–; SW. 54– imp.; U.; **Ep.**D.; **Ex.**U.; **G.**T.; U.; **Lv.**P. 54–; U.; **Ld.**U.; W. 54–; **M.**C.; D.; T.; U. 48–; **N.**U.; **Nw.**A.; **O.**R.; **R.**D. 48–; U.; **Rt.**; **Sw.**U. 47–48; **Y.**

533 **Acta chimica Academiae scientiarum hungaricae.** Budapest. *Acta chim. hung.* [1951–] **L.**BM.; C.; MA. 53–; MD.; P.; R.; **Abd.**R. 51–56; **Bl.**U.; **Br.**A.; **C.**P.; UL.; **Db.**; **Y.** [*C. of:* 22497]

Acta chimica hungarica. *See* 533.

534 **Acta chimica sinica.** Peking. *Acta chim. sin.* **L.**C. 56–; MC. 58– imp.; P. 52–; PR. 59–; R. 55–; **Bn.**U. 58–; **C.**CH. 58–; P. 58; **Db.** 56–; **E.**R. 58; **Y.** [*C. of:* 25796]

535 **Acta chimica Societatis scientiarum lodziensis.** Łódź. *Acta chim. Soc. Sci. lodz.* [1955–] **L.**BM.; C. 58–; **O.**R.; **Y.** [*Previously issued in:* 38355]

536 **Acta chirurgiae orthopaedicae** et **traumatologiae čechoslovaca.** Praha. *Acta Chir. orthop. Traum. čech.* [1950–] **L.**MA.; MD. 50–51. [*C. of:* 48609]

537 **Acta chirurgiae plasticae.** Praha. *Acta Chir. plast.* [1959–] **L.**MD.; **Y.**

537° **Acta chirurgica.** Zagreb. *Acta chir., Zagr.* [1950–52] [*C. as:* 540]

538 **Acta chirurgica belgica.** Bruxelles. *Acta chir. belg.* [1946–] **L.**MA.; MD.; S.; **M.**MS. 46–54 imp. [*C. of:* 25806]

539 **Acta chirurgica italica.** Padova. *Acta chir. ital.* [*C. of:* 541]

540 **Acta chirurgica iugoslavica.** Beograd. *Acta chir. iugosl.* [1954–] **L.**BM.; MA. [*C. of:* 537°]

541 **Acta chirurgica patavina.** Padova. *Acta chir. patav.* [*C. as:* 539]

542 **Acta chirurgica scandinavica.** Stockholm. *Acta chir. scand.* [1919–] **L.**BM.; MA. 32–; MC. 19–26: 43–48; MD. 20–; S.; U. 50–; **Abd.**U. 40–; **Bl.**U. imp.; **Bm.**U. 19–23: 47–; **Br.**U. 20–; **C.**MD.; **Db.** 23–; **Dn.**U. 47–; **E.**P.; S. 29–; U.; **G.**F. 47–; **Ld.**U. 52–; **Lv.**M. 36– imp.; U. 20–22; **M.**MS.; **Nw.**A. 19–26: 30–; **O.**R. 19–23; **Sa.** 19–23; **Sh.**U. 22–23: 57–; **Y.** [*C. of:* 34983 Afd. 1.; *Also supplements*]

543 **Acta cientifica potosina.** San Luis Potosi. *Acta cient. potosina* [1957–] **L.**BM[N].; K.

544 **Acta cientifica venezolana.** Caracas. *Acta cient. venez.* [1950–] **L.**BM. 51–; P. 58–; **Abd.**R.; **C.**UL.; **R.**D. 53–; **Sa.**; **Y.**

545 **Acta clínica.** Rio de Janeiro. *Acta clín., R. de Jan.*

546 **Acta clínica.** Sevilla. *Acta clín., Sevilla* **L.**MA. 48–.

547 **Acta clinica belgica.** Bruxelles. *Acta clin. belg.* [1946–] **L.**MA.; MD.; **Bm.**U.; **Y.**

548 **Acta** et **commentationes Imperialis universitatis jurjevensis.** *Acta Comment. imp. Univ. jurjev.* [1893–17] **L.**BM. 98–17 imp.; **C.**UL. 98–13; **Db.** 95–17; **E.**R. imp.; **O.**B. 93–13. [*C. as:* 549]

 Acta et **commentationes Universitatis dorpatensis.** *See* 549.

549 **Acta** et **commentationes Universitatis tartuensis.** Dorpat. *Acta Comment. Univ. tartu.* [1921–]
 (*a*) Mathematica, physica, medica. **L.**BM.; BM[N]. 31–39; L. 21–40 imp.; R. 21–37 imp.; **Abd.** U.; **Bm.**U.; **C.**P. 31–; UL.; **Db.**; **E.**R. 21–40; U.; **G.**U.; **Lv.**U.; **M.**U. 21–40; **Nw.**A.; **O.**B.
 (*c*) Annales. **L.**BM.; BM[N]. 29–37; U.; **Bm.**U.; **C.**UL.; **E.**R. 29–39; **G.**U.; **Ld.**U.; **Lv.**U. 29–. [*C. of:* 548]

550 **Acta crystallographica.** Cambridge, Copenhagen. *Acta crystallogr.* [1948–] **L.**B.; BM.; BM[N].; C.; GM.; I.; IC.; P.; PR.; QM.; R.; RI.; SC.; U.; UC.; **Abd.**U.; **Abs.**N.; U. 59–; **Bl.**U.; **Bm.**T. 48–52: 59–; U.; **Bn.**U.; **C.**C.; CH.; MI.; UL.; **Cr.**U.; **Db.**; **Dn.**U.; **E.**A.; U.; **Ep.**D. 48–54; **Ex.**U. 58–; **F.**A.; **G.**T. 49–; U.; **H.**U.; **Ld.**U.; W. 48–54; **Lv.**P. 56–; U.; **M.**C.; D.; P.; T.; U.; **Ma.**T. 52–; **N.**U.; **Nw.**A.; **O.**R.; **R.**U.; **Rn.**B. 51–; **Rt.**; **Sh.**IO.; U.; **St.**R.; **Ste.**; **Sw.**U. imp.; **Wd.**; **Y.**

 Acta culturae et **praeparationis plantarum.** *See* 29567.

551 **Acta cytologica.** Chicago. *Acta cytol.* [1957–] **L.**MA.; MD.; **Abd.**U.; **Dn.**U. 62–; **G.**U.

552 **Acta davosiana.** Davos, Berne. *Acta davos.* [1933–] **L.**MA.; MD. 35–59 imp.; **O.**R. 36–.

553 **Acta dermatologica.** Kyoto. *Acta derm., Kyoto* [1923–] **L.**LI. 23–28 imp.; MD.; TD. 28–31 imp.; **Lv.**U. 25–.

554 **Acta dermato-venereologica.** Stockholm. *Acta derm.-vener., Stockh.* [1920–] **L.**MA. 45–; MD. imp.; TD. 36–49; U. 50–; **Bl.**U. 61–; **Cr.**MD. 55–; **Dn.**U. 62–; **G.**F. 50–; U. 52–; **Ld.**U.; **Lv.**M. 34–36. [*Also supplements*]

555 **Acta electronica.** Paris. *Acta electron.* [1956–] **L.**AV. 57–; EE.; P.; **Y.**

556 **Acta embryologiae** et **morphologiae experimentalis.** Palermo. *Acta Embryol. Morph. exp.* [1957–] **L.**SC. 61–; **E.**AG.; U.; **Y.**

557 **Acta endocrinologica.** Bucarest. *Acta endocr., Buc.* **L.**MA. 46–?*; MD. 47– [*C. of:* 12156; *C. as:* 18016]

558 **Acta endocrinologica.** Copenhagen. *Acta endocr., Copenh.* [1948–] **L.**CB.; MA.; MC.; MD.; SC.; U. 50–; UC.; **Abd.**U. 57–; **Bl.**U. imp.; **Bm.**U.; **C.**BI. 52–; **Cr.**MD. 57–; **Dn.**U. 60–; **E.**U.; **G.**U. 57–; **Ld.**U. imp.; **M.**MS.; **N.**U. 57–; **Nw.**A. 55–; **O.**R.; **R.**D.; **Sa.**; **Sh.**U. 55–; **Y.** [*Also supplements*]

559 **Acta endocrinologica cubana.** Habana. *Acta endocr. cub.* [1953–] **L.**MA.

560 **Acta endocrinologica** et **gynaecologica hispano-lusitana.** Porto. *Acta endocr. gynaec. hisp.-lusit.* [1947–50] [*C. in:* 561 and 592]

561 **Acta endocrinologica iberica.** Porto. *Acta endocr. iber.* [1951–53] **L.**MA. [*C. of:* 560; *C. as:* 46598]

562 **Acta endocrinologica ucrainica.** Kharkov. *Acta endocr. ucrain.* **L.**MA. 46–; **Br.**U. 36–39.
 Acta entomologica. Prag. *See* 48611.
 Acta entomologica. Takeuchi Entomological Laboratory. Kyoto. *See* 52845.

563 **Acta entomologica fennica.** Helsinki. *Acta ent. fenn.* [1947–] **L.**BM[N].; E.; EB.; SC.; Z.; **C.**B.; MO. 48–; **Md.**H.; **O.**H.; **Rt.**

564 **Acta entomologica sinica.** Peking. *Acta ent. sin.* [1953] **L.**BM[N].; Z. [*C. of:* 2731]

565 **Acta española neurológica** y **psiquiátrica.** Madrid. *Acta esp. neurol. psiquiát.* [1940] **L.**MD. [*C. as:* 824]

566 **Acta ethnographica Academiae scientiarum hungaricae.** Budapest. *Acta ethnogr. hung.* [1950–] **L.**AN.; BM.; **O.**B.
 Acta ethnographica hungarica. *See* 566.

567 **Acta ethnologica.** København. *Acta ethnol., Kbh.* [1936–38] **L.**BM.; **Cr.**M.; **E.**U. imp. [*C. in:* 19831]

568 **Acta Facultatis medicae Universitatis brunensis.** Brno. *Acta Fac. med. Univ. brun.* **L.**MD. 60–.
 Acta Facultatis medicae zagrebiensis. *See* 41888.
 Acta Facultatis medicinae skopiensis. *See* 21421.
 Acta Facultatis medicinae Universitatis lithuaniensis. *See* 28561.
 Acta Facultatis rerum naturalium Universitatis Carolinae. *See* 50629.

569 **Acta Facultatis rerum naturalium Universitatis comenianae.** Bratislava. *Acta Fac. Rerum nat. Univ. comen., Bratisl.* [1956–]
 Series Chimia. **L.**C. 59–.
 Series Zoologia. **L.**BM[N].; **O.**H.
 Acta Facultatis rerum naturalium Universitatis slovacae Bratislavae. *See* 48655.

570 **Acta** pro **fauna** et **flora universali.** Bucureşti. *Acta Fauna Flora univers.* [1932–]
 Botanica. **L.**BM[N]. 32–38; K.
 Zoologica. **L.**BM[N]. 32.
 Acta faunistica entomologica Musei nationalis Pragae. *See* 48612.

571 **Acta fisioterapica iberica.** Barcelona. *Acta fisioter. iber.*

Acta florae rossicae. Tartu. *See* 56507.

572 **Acta florae Sueciae.** Stockholm. *Acta Flor. Suec.* [1921] L.BM^N.; K.; Bl.U.

573 **Acta forestalia fennica.** Helsingforsiae. *Acta for. fenn.* [1912–] L.BM^N. 26–; K.; L.; NC. 46– imp.; Abd.U.; Bm.U. 23–; Bn.U. 19–37 imp.; C.P.; PO. 50–; Db.; E.B.; R. 12–20: 56–; Lv.U. 12–30; O.F.; Y.

574 **Acta gastro-enterologica belgica.** Bruxelles. *Acta gastro-enter. belg.* [1946–] L.MA.; MD.; Abd.R. [*C. of:* 25653]

575 **Acta genetica** et **statistica medica.** Basle, New York. *Acta genet. Statist. med.* [1948–] L.MA.; MD.; SC.; TD.; Abs.A. 48–54; Ba.I. 48–57; Bl.U. 48–58; Bm.U.; C.GE.; E.AG.; G.U.; O.R.; Y. [*Also supplements*]

576 **Acta geneticae medicae** et **gemellologiae.** Roma. *Acta Genet. med. Gemell.* [1952–] L.MA.; MD.; SC.; C.GE.; E.AR.; Y.

Acta geobotanica. Amsterdam. *See* 55930.

576^c **Acta geodetica** et **cartographica sinica.** Peking. *Acta geod. cartogr. sin.* [1957–] Y.

Acta geografica. Ljubljana. *See* 20954.

577 **Acta geographica.** Acta Universitatis szegediensis. Szeged. *Acta geogr., Szeged* [1955–] L.BM.; U.; Y.

578 **Acta geographica.** Societas geographica Fenniae. Helsingforsiae. *Acta geogr., Helsingf.* [1927–] L.AN.; BM.; G.; GL.; SC. 27–58; C.GG.; P.; UL.; Db.; E.G.; R.; O.B.; F. 49– imp.; Pl.M.; R.U.

Acta geographica. Łódź. *See* 581.

579 **Acta geographica.** Société de géographie de Paris. *Acta geogr., Paris* [1947–] L.BM.; U.; C.GG. 48–; PO.; Db.; E.G.; R.; G.U. imp.; Ld.U. 50– imp.; Y.
also Bibliographie mensuelle [1950–59] L.BM. 56–59; U. 54–59; C.GG.; Db. 51–59; G.U. 51–59; Ld.U.
then Supplément bibliographique [1959–] L.B.; BM.; U.; C.GG.; G.U.; Ld.U.

580 **Acta geographica sinica.** Peking. *Acta. geogr. sin.* L.G. 56–; E.G. (curr.); Y.

581 **Acta geographica Universitatis lodziensis.** Łódź. *Acta geogr. Univ. lodz.* [1948–] L.G.; Y.

582 **Acta geologica Academiae scientiarum hungaricae.** Budapest. *Acta geol. hung.* [1952–] L.BM.; BM^N.; GL.; GM.; R. 53–; SC.; C.P. 56–; G.U.; Y.

Acta geologica hungarica. *See* 582.

583 **Acta geologica lilloana.** Tucuman Republic, Argentina. *Acta geol. lilloana* [1956–] C.S.; Y.

584 **Acta geologica polonica.** Warszawa. *Acta geol. pol.* [1950–] L.BM. imp.; BM^N.; GL.; GM.; P. 57–; SC.; C.S.; Db.; E.R. 54–; G.U. imp.; Lv.U.; Sa.; Y.

585 **Acta geologica sinica.** Peking. *Acta geol. sin.* L.BM.; BM^N. 61–; GL. 56–; GM. 56–; Db. 56–; Y. [*See also* 10342]

586 **Acta geologica taiwanica.** Taipei. *Acta geol. taiwan.* L.BM^N.; GL.; GM.; Br.U.; C.P.; S.; Db. 54–; E.R.; Y.

587 **Acta geophysica polonica.** Warszawa. *Acta geophys. pol.* [1953–] L.BM.; MO.; P. imp.; SC.; C.UL.; Y.

588 **Acta geophysica sinica.** Peking. *Acta geophys. sin.* L.GM. 56–; MO. 56–. [*C. of:* 25799]

589 **Acta gerontologica.** Milano. *Acta geront.* [1951–] L.MA.; MD. 54–; Abd.R.

590 **Acta ginecologica.** Madrid. *Acta ginec.* [1950–] L.MA.

591 **Acta gnathologica.** København. *Acta gnath.* L.D. 36–39 imp.

592 **Acta gynaecologica** et **obstetrica hispanolusitana.** Porto. *Acta gynaec. obstet. hisp.-lusit.* [1951–] L.MA. [*C. of:* 560]

593 **Acta gynecologica scandinavica.** Uppsala. *Acta gynec. scand.* [1921–25] L.BM. 21–23; MD.; Abs.N.; C.UL.; Db. 24–25; M.MS. 22–25; O.R. [*C. as:* 681]

594 **Acta haematologica.** Basel, New York. *Acta haemat.* [1948–] L.MA.; MC. 60–; MD.; Bl.U. 54–; C.MD.; Cr.MD. 57–; Dn.U.; G.U.; Ld.U. 53–; Sh.U. 57–; Y.

595 **Acta haematologica japonica.** Kyoto. *Acta haemat. jap.* [1937–] L.MD. 61–; Y.

596 **Acta hepatologica.** Hamburg. *Acta hepat.*

596^c **Acta hepato-splenologica.** Stuttgart. *Acta hepatosplenol.* [1954–] L.MA. 59–.

597 **Acta histochemica.** Jena. *Acta histochem.* [1954–] L.MD.; SC.; UC.; G.U.; M.MS.; R.U.; Y. [*Also supplements*]

598 **Acta historica scientiarum naturalium** et **medicinalium.** København. *Acta hist. Sci. nat. med.* [1942–] L.BM.; O.R. 43–.

599 **Acta Horti Bergiani.** Meddelanden från Kongl. Svenska Vetenskaps-Akademiens trädgård, Bergielund. Stockholm. *Acta Horti Bergiani* [1890–] L.BM.; BM^N.; HS. 90–07: 14–; K.; L.; SC.; C.BO. 97–07: 58; E.R.; O.BO. 07–; Y.

Acta Horti botanici Tadshikistanici. *See* 24513.

Acta Horti botanici Universitatis Asiae mediae. *See* 783 (8b).

601 **Acta Horti botanici Universitatis imperialis jurjevensis.** Jurjev. *Acta Horti bot. Univ. imp. jurjev.* [1900–14] L.BM^N.; K.; E.B.

602 **Acta Horti botanici Universitatis latviensis.** Riga. *Acta Horti bot. Univ. latv.* [1926–39] L.BM.; BM^N.; HS.; K.; L.; Abs.U.; C.A.; BO. 26–33; Cr.U.; E.B.; R. 26–35 imp.; G.U. imp.; Lv.U.; M.U. 26: 36–38; O.BO. 26–33; R.

603 **Acta Horti gothoburgensis.** Meddelanden från Göteborgs botaniska trädgard. Göteborg. *Acta Horti gothoburg.* [1924–] L.BM^N.; HS.; K.; L.; SC.; Db.; E.B. 24; Md.H. 52–; O.BO. 56; Y.

Acta Horti petropolitani. St. Petersburg. *See* 54587 and 54551.

604 **Acta humboldtiana.** Seria geographica et ethnographica. Wiesbaden. *Acta humboldt.* L.BM. 59–.

605 **Acta hydrobiologica.** Kraków. *Acta hydrobiol., Kraków* [1959–] L.AM.; BM^N.; Z.; Bn.U.; Y. [*C. of:* 7203]

606 **Acta hydrobiologica sinica.** Peking. *Acta hydrobiol. sin.* Fr. 55–.

607 **Acta hydrologica, limnologica** et **protistologica.** Den Haag. *Acta hydrol. limnol. protistol.* Br.U. 48–; O.R. 48–.

608 **Acta hydrophysica.** Berlin. *Acta hydrophys.* [1953–] L.MO. imp.; P.; Abd.M.; Wo.; Y.

609 **Acta hymenopterologica.** Tokyo. *Acta hymenopt., Tokyo* [1958–] L.BM^N.; O.H.; Y.

610 **Acta ibérica radiológica-cancerológica.** Madrid. *Acta ibér. radiol.-cancer.* [1952–] L.CB. 52–54; MD. imp.; E.P. [*C. of:* 41851]

611 **Acta ichthyologica Bosniae** et **Hercegovinae.** Sarajevo. *Acta ichthyol. Bosn. Herceg.* [1954–] L.BM[N]; SC. 54–56; **Fr.**; **Lo.**; **Mi.**

Acta Instituti agronomici stauropolitani. *See* 55064.

612 **Acta Instituti anatomici Universitatis Helsingforsiae.** *Acta Inst. anat. Univ. Helsingf.* [1928–] L.S. 46–53; UC. 35–; **Bm.**U. 28–37; **Br.**U. 39–; **Y.**

613 **Acta Instituti baltici.** Hamburg. *Acta Inst. balt.* [1950–] L.BM.

Acta Instituti botanici. Erivan. *See* 54491.

Acta Instituti botanici Academiae scientiarum SSR Armeniae. *See* 54490.

Acta Instituti botanici Academiae scientiarum URSS. *See* 54489.

614 **Acta Instituti defensionis plantarum latviensis.** Riga. *Acta Inst. Defens. Pl. latv.* L.EB. 30–32; UC. 22–40. [*C. in:* 625]

615 **Acta Instituti entomologici Choui.** Shensi. *Acta Inst. ent. Choui* L.BM[N]. 47.

Acta Instituti et **horti botanici dorpatensis.** *See* 616.

616 **Acta Instituti** et **horti botanici tartuensis.** Tartu. *Acta Inst. Hort. bot. tartu.* [1926–] L.BM[N]. 26–37; K. 26–38; L. 26–38; **Db.**; **E.**B.; **Lv.**U.; **M.**U. 26–38 imp.

617 **Acta Instituti** et **horti botanici Universitatis Carolinae Pragensis.** Prague. *Acta Inst. Horti bot. Univ. Carol. Prag.* [1946–] **Rt.**

618 **Acta Instituti** et **Musei zoologici Universitatis atheniensis.** *Acta Inst. Mus. zool. Univ. athen.* [1935–] L.BM[N]. 35–39; E. 35–39; EB. 35–39; L. 35–39; Z. 35–37; **Bl.**U. 35–39; **Br.**U. 35–38; **C.**UL. 35–39; **E.**R. 35–39; **Pl.**M. 35.

619 **Acta Instituti** et **Musei zoologici Universitatis tartuensis.** Tartu. *Acta Inst. Mus. zool. Univ. tartu.* [1929–] L.Z. 29; **Abs.**U. 29–38.

620 **Acta Instituti psychologiae Universitatis zagrebiensis.** Zagreb. *Acta Inst. Psychol. Univ. zagreb.* [1936–37]

621 **Acta japonica medicinae tropicalis.** Taihoku. *Acta jap. Med. trop.* [1939–41] L.BM[N]. 39; EB.; LI. 39; TD. imp. [*C. as:* 680]

622 **Acta lapponica.** Stockholm. *Acta lapp.* [1938–] L.AM.; BM.; **C.**PO.

623 **Acta leidensia** edita cura et sumptibus Scholae medicinae tropicae. Lugduni Batavorum. *Acta leidensia* [1926–] L.BM. 46–; EB.; LI.; MD. 26: 46; TD.; **Bm.**U. 26–34; **Y.**

624 **Acta limnologica.** Lund. *Acta limnol.* [1948–] L.BM. 51–; BM[N]. 48–50; SC.; **Dm.** 50–.

625 **Acta litterarum** ac **scientiarum R. Universitatis hungarica Francisco-Josephina.** Szeged. *Acta Litt. Scient. R. Univ. hung. Francisco-Josephina.*
    Sectio scientiarum naturalium [1922–27] L.BM.; BM[N].
    Divided into
      Acta biologica [1928–37] L.BM.; BM[N].; MD. 32–36.
    and
      Acta chemica, mineralogica et physica [1928–38] L.BM.; BM[N].; GM.; UC.

    Sectio scientiarum mathematicarum [1922–38] L.BM.; M.; SC.; UC.
    Sectio medicorum [1927–37] L.BM.; MD. 36–37; UC. 32.
[*Replaced by:* 788]

626 **Acta mathematica.** Stockholm, Uppsala. *Acta math., Stockh.* [1882–] L.BM.; M. 00–; R.; SC. 82–91: 29–; U. 50–; UC.; **Abd.**U.; **Abs.**N. 16–; U.; **Bl.**U.; **Bm.**U.; **Br.**U.; **C.**P.; SJ.; T.; UL.; **Cr.**U. 49: 55–; **Db.**; **E.**R.; U.; **Ex.**U. 01–; **G.**U.; **H.**U.; **Ld.**U.; **Lv.**M.; **M.**U.; **N.**U. 82–41: 52–; **Nw.**A.; P. 82–36; **O.**R.; **R.**U.; **Sa.**; **Sh.**U.; **Sw.**U. 21–; **Y.**

627 **Acta mathematica Academiae scientiarum hungaricae.** Budapest. *Acta math. hung.* [1950–] L.BM.; R.; SC.; **C.**P.; UL.; **Db.**; **E.**R.; **G.**U. 51–; **Ld.**U. 50–51; **M.**U. 55–; **O.**R.; **Y.** [*C. of:* 22498]

Acta mathematica hungarica. *See* 627.

628 **Acta mathematica sinica.** Peking. *Acta math. sin.* [1951–] L.P. 53–; R. 55–; **Db.** 56–; **E.**R. 57–; **G.**U. 57–; **Y.** [*C. of:* 25801]

629 **Acta mechanica sinica.** Peking. *Acta mech. sin.* [1957–] L.P. 59–.

630 **Acta medica.** Fukuoka. *Acta med., Fukuoka* [1927–] L.TD. 56–; **Y.**

631 **Acta medica.** Rio de Janeiro. *Acta med., Rio de J.* [1938–43] L.MD. 43; TD. imp.

632 **Acta medica Academiae scientiarum hungaricae.** Budapest. *Acta med. hung.* [1950–] L.BM.; CB. 57; MA.; MD.; R.; S. 51–55; TD.; UCH. 50–54; **Abd.**R. 51–54; **Br.**U.; **C.**P.; UL.; **Db.**; **E.**R.; **M.**MS.; **Nw.**A.; **O.**R.; **Y.** [*C. of:* 22499]

633 **Acta medica** et **biologica.** Niigata. *Acta med. biol., Niigata* [1953–] L.LI.; MA.; MC.; MD.; PH. 56–; S.; **Br.**U.; **Lv.**M.; **Y.**

634 **Acta medica chirurgica brasiliense.** Rio de Janeiro. *Acta med. chir. bras.* [1953–] L.MA.; MD.; TD. [*C. of:* 46766]

635 **Acta medica costarricense.** San José. *Acta med. costarric.* [1957–] L.MD.

636 **Acta medica hidalguense.** Hidalgo. *Acta med. hidalguense.*

Acta medica hokkaidonensia. *See* 22247.

Acta medica hungarica. *See* 632.

637 **Acta medica iranica.** Tehran. *Acta med. iran.* [1956–] L.MD.; S. 56–59.

638 **Acta medica italica.** Milano. *Acta med. ital.* [1935–]

639 **Acta medica italica** di **malattie infettive** e **parassitarie.** Roma, Napoli. *Acta med. ital. Mal. infett.* [1946–] L.MA.; TD. 47–.

640 **Acta medica iugoslavica.** Beograd. *Acta med. iugosl.* [1947–] L.BM. 51–; MA.; MC.; MD.; S.; TD.; **G.**F. imp.; **Y.**

Acta medica, Kyushu University. *See* 630

641 **Acta medica latina.** Paris. *Acta med. lat.* [1928–]

642 **Acta medica nagasakiensia.** Nagasaki. *Acta med. nagasak.* L.MD. 60– imp.; **Y.**

643 **Acta medica orientalia.** Jerusalem, Tel Aviv. *Acta med. orient.* [1941–58] L.MA. 45–58; MD.; TD. 42–58; **Bl.**U. 45–48; **M.**MS. 53. [*C. as:* 24233]

644 **Acta medica patavina.** Padova. *Acta med. patav.* L.MA. 54– imp.

645 **Acta medica philippina.** Manila. *Acta med. philipp.* [1939–] **L.**MA.; MD. 39–41; TD. 39–41.

646 **Acta medica polonica.** Cracovie. *Acta med. pol., Cracovie* [1949] **L.**MD.

647 **Acta medica polonica.** Varsoviae. *Acta med. pol., Vars.* [1960–] **L.**MD.

648 **Acta medica scandinavica.** Stockholm. *Acta med. scand.* [1919–] **L.**BM.: GH. 20–; H. 23–; MA. 24–; MC.; MD.; S. 21–; TD. 21–; U. 50–; **Abd.** U. 25–; **Bl.**U. 21– imp.; **Bm.**U.; **Br.**U.; **C.**APH. 61–; PA. 20–; R. 52–; **Cr.**MD. 41– imp.; **Db.** 35–52 imp.; **Dn.**U. 49–; **E.**P.; U.; **G.**F. 23– imp.; U. 21–; **Ld.**U. imp.; **Lv.**M. 28– imp.; U. imp.; **M.**MS.; **Nw.**A. 28–; **O.**R.; **Sh.**U. 48–; **Y.** [*C. of:* 34983 Afd. 2; *Also supplements*]
Acta medica szegediensis. *See* 625.

650 **Acta médica** de **Tenerife.** Santa Cruz. *Acta méd. Tenerife* [1952–] **L.**MA.

651 **Acta medica turcica.** Ankara. *Acta med. turc.* [1948–] **L.**LI. 48; MA. imp.; MD. 55–59 imp.; TD. imp.; U. 49–.

652 **Acta medica U.R.S.S.** Moscow. *Acta med. U.R.S.S.* [1938–40] **L.**BM.; MD. 38–39; S. 38–39; **Br.**U. imp.; **E.**S. 38–39; **O.**R.

653 **Acta médica venezolana.** Caracas. *Acta méd. venez.* [1953–] **L.**MA. 55– imp.; MD. 59–.

654 **Acta médica veterinaria.** Madrid. *Acta méd. vet., Madr.* [1955–] **L.**V.; **Y.**

655 **Acta medica veterinaria.** Napoli. *Acta med. vet., Napoli* [1955–] **W.**
Acta Medicinae facultatis Vytauti magni universitatis Caunae. *See* 28561.

655° **Acta medicae historiae patavina.** Padova. *Acta med. Hist. patav.* [1955–] **L.**BM.

656 **Acta medicinae legalis** et **socialis.** Liège. *Acta Med. leg. soc.* [1948–] **L.**MA. 52–; **Dn.**U. 50–.

657 **Acta medicinae Okoyama.** Okoyama. *Acta Med. Okoyama* [1952–] **L.**LI.; MA.; MC.; MD.; TD. 56–; **Br.**U. 57–; **E.**U.; **G.**U. 54–; **Lv.**U.; **O.**R.; **Sal.**; **Y.** [*C. of:* 3859]

658 **Acta medicinalia** in **Keijo.** Keijo. *Acta medicin. Keijo* [1928–29] **L.**C.; EB.; MC.; MD.; S.; TD.; **Bl.**U.; **Bm.**U.; **Br.**U.; **C.**UL.; **E.**P.; U.; **Ld.**U.; **Lv.**U.; **M.**U.; **Nw.**A.; **O.**R.; **Sa.** [*C. of:* 32607; *C. as:* 27295]

659 **Acta metallurgica.** Toronto, New York. *Acta metall.* [1953–] **L.**AV. imp.; BM. 56–; C.; P.; RI.; SC.; **Abd.**U.; **Bl.**U. 53–57; **Bm.**C. 56–; T.; **Bn.**U.; **Cr.**U.; **E.**A. 57–; U. 55–; **F.**A.; **G.**I.; T.; U. 58–; **Ld.**U.; **Lv.**P.; **M.**P. 56–; T.; U.; **Ma.**T.; **N.**U. 55–; **Nw.**A.; **O.**B.; R.; **R.**U.; **Rn.**B.; **Sh.**S. 58–; SC.; U. 59–; **Sw.**U.; **Y.**

660 **Acta metallurgica sinica.** Peking. *Acta metall. sin.* [1956–] **L.**P. 59–; **Y.**

661 **Acta meteorologica sinica.** Peking. *Acta met. sin.* **L.**MO. 55–; **Y.**

662 **Acta microbiologica Academiae scientiarum hungaricae.** Budapest. *Acta microbiol. hung.* [1954–] **L.**BM.; MA.; MC.; MD.; P.; R.; SC.; TD.; **Rt.**; **W.**; **Y.**
Acta microbiologica hellenica. *See* 16481.
Acta microbiologica hungarica. *See* 662.

663 **Acta microbiologica polonica.** Warszawa. *Acta microbiol. pol.* [1951–] **L.**A.; AM.; BM. 54–; BM^N. imp.; MY. imp.; SC.; TD.; **Abd.**S.; **Br.**A.; **C.**A.; **Db.**; **Hu.**G.; **Lv.**U. imp.; **Y.**

664 **Acta microbiologica sinica.** Peking. *Acta microbiol. sin.* [1953–] **L.**EB. 57–; MC. 58–; P. 59–; **Y.**

665 **Acta mineralogica** et **petrographica.** Acta Universitis Szegediensis. Szeged. *Acta miner. petrogr., Szeged* [1943–] **L.**BM^N.; GL.; U.; UC.; **Y.**

666 **Acta monographica Instytut zoologiczny.** Kraków. *Acta monogr. Inst. zool., Kraków* [1947–] **L.**BM.; R.; Z.; **Rt.** (sel. issues)
Acta monographiae. Warszawa. *See* 33261.

667 **Acta morphologica.** Gorki. *Acta morph., Gorki* [1935–]

668 **Acta morphologica Academiae scientiarum hungaricae.** Budapest. *Acta morph. hung.* [1951–] **L.**BM.; CB. 57; MA.; MD.; R.; TD.; UC.; UCH. 51–54; **Br.**U.; **C.**UL.; **Db.**; **E.**R.; **Y.**
Acta morphologica hungarica. *See* 668.

669 **Acta morphologica neerlando-scandinavica.** Utrecht. *Acta morph. neerl.-scand.* [1956–] **L.**MD.; SC.; UC.; **Bl.**U.; **Br.**U.; **C.**AN.; **E.**AG.; **Ld.**U.; **M.**MS.; **O.**R.; **R.**U.; **Sh.**U. [*C. of:* 672]
Acta Musei historiae naturalis. Kraków. *See* 38367.
Acta Musei et horti botanici Bohemiae borealis. *See* 48672.

670 **Acta Musei macedonici scientiarum naturalium.** Skopje. *Acta Mus. maced. Sci. nat.* [1953–] **L.**BM^N.; Z.; **Fr.**; **Pl.**M.; **Y.** [*C. of:* 2850]
Acta Musei moraviensis. Brno. *See* 13415.
Acta Musei nationalis Pragae. *See* 48633.
Acta Musei reginaehradecensis. Hradec Kralové. *See* 38353.
Acta Musei Silesiae. Opava. *See* 13422.
Acta mycologica hungarica. *See* 29187.

671 **Acta naturalia islandica.** Reykjavik. *Acta nat. islandica* [1946–] **L.**BM^N.; C.PO.; **Lo.** 55–; **O.**R.; **Y.**

672 **Acta neerlandica morphologiae normalis** et **pathologicae.** Utrecht. *Acta neerl. Morph.* [1937–49] **L.**MD.; UC.; **Bl.**U.; **Br.**U.; **C.**AN.; **E.**AG.; **Ld.**U.; **M.**MS.; **O.**R.; **R.**U.; **Sh.**U. 48–49. [*C. as:* 669]

673 **Acta neurochirurgica.** Wien. *Acta neurochir.* [1950–] **L.**MA. 52–; MD.; S.; **M.**MS.

674 **Acta neurologica.** Napoli. *Acta neurol.* [1946–] **L.**MA.; MD. 49–.

675 **Acta neurologica latinoamericana.** Buenos Aires. *Acta neurol. latinoam.* [1955–] **L.**MA.; **O.**R.

676 **Acta neurologica** et **psychiatrica belgica.** Bruxelles. *Acta neurol. psychiat. belg.* [1948–] **L.**MA.; MD. [*C. of:* 25657]

677 **Acta neuropsiquiátrica argentina.** Buenos Aires. *Acta neuropsiq. argent.* [1954–] **L.**MA.; U.; **Dn.**U. 56–; **M.**MS.; **O.**R.

678 **Acta neuro-psychiatrica.** Istanbul. *Acta neuropsych., Istanbul*

679 **Acta neurovegetativa.** Wien. *Acta neuroveg.* [1950–] **L.**MA. 53–; MD.; SC.; **M.**MS.; **Y.** [*Also supplements*]

680 **Acta nipponica medicinae tropicalis.** Taihoku. *Acta nippon. Med. trop.* [1942] **L.**EB.; TD. [*C. of:* 621]

680° **Acta nutrimenta sinica.** Peking. *Acta nutr. sin.* [1956–] **Y.**

681 **Acta obstetrica** et **gynecologica scandinavica.** Helsingfors, etc. *Acta obstet. gynec. scand.* [1926–] **L.**MA. 46–; MD.; **Abs.**N.; **Bm.**U. 30–; **Db.** 26–39 imp.; **Dn.**U. 57–; **E.**S. 54–; U. 44–; **G.**F. 40–56 imp.: 59–; **Ld.**U. 28– imp.; **Lv.**M. 26–40; **M.**MS.; **O.**B.; R.; **Sh.**U. 55–; **Y.** [*C. of:* 593; *Also supplements*]

Acta odontologica. Tokyo. *See* 53344.

682 **Acta odontologica scandinavica.** Stockholm. *Acta odont. scand.* [1939–] L.D.; MA. 47–; MD. 41:55– imp.; S. 55–; Bl.U. 57–; Br.U. 55–; Db. 53–; Dn.U. 43–; E.U. 55–; Ld.U.; M.MS. 55–; Sh.U. 55–. [*Also supplements*]

682° **Acta oeconomico-entomologica sinica.** Peking. *Acta oecon.-ent. sin.* [1958–] L.EB.

Acta operum Facultatis rerum naturalium Universitatis slovacae Bratislavae. *See* 48655.

683 **Acta ophthalmologica.** Kjøbenhavn. *Acta ophthal.* [1923–] L.MA. 38–; MD.; OP.; S. 46–; U. 51–; E.S.; M.MS. 23–28: 56–; Sa. 22–26 imp.; Y. [*Also supplements*]

684 **Acta ophthalmologica orientalia.** Jerusalem. *Acta ophthal. orient.* [1938–] L.MD. 38–40. [*Replaces:* 19812]

Acta ophthalmologica polonica. *See* 27525.

685 **Acta ornithologica.** Warszawa. *Acta orn., Warsz.* [1933–] L.AM. 49– imp.; BM^N.; L.; U. 49–; Z.; Bl.U.; C.P.; Cr.M.; Db.; E.R.; G.N. 33–38; Ld.U. 33–57; Lv.U.; Nw.A.; O.OR. imp.; Pl.M. imp.; Y.

Acta ornithologica Musei zoologici polonici. *See* 685.

686 **Acta orthopaedica belgica.** Bruxelles. *Acta orthop. belg.* L.MA. 46–; MD. 48–; S. 46–; M.MS. 55–. [*C. of:* 11864]

687 **Acta orthopaedica italica.** Reggio Calabria, Roma. *Acta orthop. ital.* [1955–] L.MD.

688 **Acta orthopaedica scandinavica.** København. *Acta orthop. scand.* [1930–] L.MA.; MD.; S. 39–; U. 50–; Br.U. 57–; E.S.; G.F. 49–; Ld.U. 45–; Lv.M. 35–39: 45–; M.MS. 48–; Sa. 53–; Y. [*Also supplements*]

689 **Acta ortopédica-traumatólogica ibérica.** Madrid. *Acta ortopéd.-traum. ibér.* [1953–56] L.MA.; MD.; TD. [*C. of:* 14429; *C. as:* 46855]

690 **Acta oto-laryngologica.** Stockholm. *Acta oto-lar.* [1918–] L.MA. 46–; MD.; S. 18–35; U. 50–; Abd.U. 24–28: 51; Bl.U. 59–; Br.U. imp. 54–; E.S.; G.F. 20– imp.; Ld.U. 49–; Lv.M. 14–48 imp.; M.MS. 54–; Nw.A. 32–; Y. [*C. of:* 34969; *Also supplements*]

691 **Acta oto-laryngologica orientalia.** Jerusalem. *Acta oto-lar. orient.* [1945–] L.MA. 45 imp.: 47–; MD.

692 **Acta oto-rhino-laryngologica belgica.** Bruxelles. *Acta oto-rhino-lar. belg.* [1947–] L.MA.; MD. [*C. of:* 11865]

693 **Acta otorinolaringológica española.** Madrid. *Acta otorinolar. esp.*

694 **Acta oto-rino-laringológica ibéro-americana.** Barcelona. *Acta oto-rino-lar. ibéro-am.* Lv.M. 50–.

Acta paediatrica. Madrid. *See* 708.

695 **Acta paediatrica.** Stockholm, Uppsala. *Acta paediat., Stockh.* [1921–] L.LI. 21–55; MA. 25–; MC. 21–29: 46–; MD.; U. 50–; UCH. 57–; Abd.U.; Bl.U. 49–; Bm.U.; Br.U.; C.MD. 48–; Cr.MD. 57–; MS. 21–34 imp.; Db. 21–41: 49–53 imp.; Dn.U.; E.P.; U. 45–; G.F. 21–47: 59–; U. 21–32: 37; Ld.U. 58–; Nw.A. [*Also supplements*]

696 **Acta paediatrica Academiae scientiarum hungaricae.** Budapest. *Acta paediat. hung.* [1960–] L.MD.

697 **Acta paediatrica belgica.** Bruxelles. *Acta paediat. belg.* [1946–] L.MA.; MD. 48–; Y.

Acta paediatrica hungarica. *See* 696.

698 **Acta paediatrica japonica.** Tokyo. *Acta paediat. jap.* Y.

699 **Acta paediatrica latina.** Parma, Reggio Emilia. *Acta paediat. lat.* [1948–] L.MA. 50–; MD. 56–60.

699° **Acta palaeobotanica.** Instytut botaniki. Polska akademia nauk. Cracovia. *Acta palaeobot, Cracov.* [1960–] L.BM^N.

700 **Acta palaeontologica polonica.** Warszawa. *Acta palaeont. pol.* [1956–] L.BM^N.; GL.; GM.; QM.; Z.; Br.U.; C.S.; E.R.; Y.

701 **Acta palaeontologica sinica.** Peking. *Acta palaeont. sin.* [1953–] L.BM.; BM^N.; GL. 56–; R. 56–; C.S. 55–; Db. 56–; E.R. 57–; Y.

702 **Acta paracelsica.** München. *Acta paracels.* [1930–32] G.U.

703 **Acta parasitologica lithuanica.** Vilnius. *Acta parasit. lith.* [1958–] L.BM^N.; Y.

704 **Acta parasitologica polonica.** Warszawa. *Acta parasit. pol.* [1953–] L.BM^N.; L.; MA.; SC.; TD. 59–; Z.; G.U. 60–; Sal.

705 **Acta pathologica.** Belgradiae. *Acta path., Belgr.* [1937–]

706 **Acta pathologica japonica.** Tokyo. *Acta path. jap.* [1951–] L.CB. 51–53; MA.; MC. 51–53: 56–57; MD.; S. 51–53:56–; TD. 51–53; UC.; Y.

707 **Acta pathologica** et **microbiologica scandinavica.** Kjøbenhavn. *Acta path. microbiol. scand.* [1924–] L.CB. 54–; LI. 52–; MA. 38–; MC. 24–35: 41–; MD.; S. 39–; TD.; U. 50–; UCH. 52–; Abd.U. 52–; Bl.U. 47–; Bm.U. 39–; Br.U.; C.PA. 53–; UL. 50–; V. 54–; Dn.U. 51–; E.U. 55–; G.F. 54–; U.; Ld.U.; M.MS. 47–; Nw.A. 31–; O.P. 28–; Sh.U. 48–; W. 32–; Y. [*Also supplements*]

708 **Acta pediatrica española.** Madrid. *Acta pediat. esp.* [1943–] L.MA.; MD. 44–.

709 **Acta pedologica sinica.** Nanking. *Acta pedol. sin.* Rt. 53–. [*C. of:* 12247]

710 **Acta phaenologica.** Nederlandsche phaenologische vereeniging. 's-Gravenhage. *Acta phaenol.* [1932–35] L.AM.; BM^N.; Abs.A.; E.W.; O.F.

711 **Acta pharmaceutica hungarica.** Budapest. *Acta pharm. hung.* [1953–] L.PH. imp.; Y. [*C. of:* 21692]

712 **Acta pharmaceutica internationalis.** København. *Acta pharm. int.* [1950–53] L.C.; P. 50–51; PH.; G.T.; N.U.

713 **Acta pharmaceutica jugoslavica.** Zagreb. *Acta pharm. jugosl.* [1951–] L.P. 58–; PA. imp.; Y.

714 **Acta pharmaceutica sinica.** Peking. *Acta pharm. sin.* [1953–] L.MC. 58–; MD. 58–; P. 59–; PH. 56–. [*C. of:* 25803]

715 **Acta pharmaciae historica.** Den Haag. *Acta Pharm. hist.* [1959–]

716 **Acta pharmacologica sinica.** Peking. *Acta pharmac. sin.* L.R. 56–.

717 **Acta pharmacologica** et **toxicologica.** København. *Acta pharmac. tox.* [1945–] L.MA. 47–; MC. imp.; MD.; SC.; U.; UC.; Bm.U.; Br.U.; C.APH.; R. 46–; UL.; Cr.MD.; E.R.; U.; G.U.; M.MS.; N.U.; Nw.A.; Sh.U. 47–; Y. [*Also supplements*]

718 **Acta phtisiologica.** Paris. *Acta phtisiol.* [1952–] L.MA.

719 **Acta physica Academiae scientiarum hungaricae.** Budapest. *Acta phys. hung.* [1951–] L.BM.; C.; GM.; P.; R.; **C.**P.; UL.; **Db.**; E.R.; **F.**A.; **M.**U.; O.R.; **Pl.**M. 51–55; **Y.** [*C. of:* 22500]

720 **Acta physica austriaca.** Wien. *Acta phys. austriaca* [1947–] L.BM.; P.; SC.; UC.; **Bm.**U.; **Br.**U. 47–50; **C.**P.; **Db.**; **E.**U.; **G.**U.; **M.**U. imp.; O.R.; **Sa.**; **Y.**

721 **Acta physica** et **chemica.** Acta Universitatis Szegediensis. Szeged. *Acta phys. chem., Szeged* [1955–] L.U.; **C.**CH. 57–; P. 57–; **Sh.**U. 58–; **Y.**
   Acta physica hungarica. *See* 719.

722 **Acta physica polonica.** Warszawa. *Acta phys. pol.* [1932–] L.BM. 50–; I. (curr.); P.; R. 32–39; SC. 32–39: 47–; U.; UC.; **Bn.**U. 56–61; **Br.**U. 37–; **C.**P.; UL.; **Db.** 56–; E.R.; G.U. 52– imp.; **Nw.**A. 51–; **Sa.** 39– imp. [*C. of:* 15256]

723 **Acta physica sinica.** Peking. *Acta phys. sin.* [1951–] L.P. imp.; **Db.** 57–; E.R. 57–. [*C. of:* 13932]

724 **Acta physico-chimica URSS.** Moscow. *Acta phys.-chim. URSS* [1934–47] L.AV. 40–46 imp.; C. imp.; I. imp.; IC.; P. 34–37 imp.; UC. 34–39; **Br.**U.; **C.**P.; UL. 40–47; **Dn.**U. 39–47: V. imp.; E.R.; G.U. 40–47 imp.; **Ld.**U.; W. 40–47 imp.; **M.**C. 39–41; T. 34–40: 45–47; U. imp.; **Nw.**A. 43–47; O.BS. 34–39; R.; **Sh.**S. 46–47; **St.**R. 46–47; **Y.** 42–46.

725 **Acta physiologica Academiae scientiarum hungaricae.** Budapest. *Acta physiol. hung.* [1950–] L.B. 58–; BM.; C. 52–; CB. 57–; MA.; MC. 55–; MD.; R.; UC.; **Abd.**R.; **Bl.**U.; **C.**P.; UL.; **Cr.**MD. 58–; **Db.**; G.U.; O.R.; **Rt.**; **Sh.**U.; **Y.** [*C. of:* 22501; *Also supplements*]
   Acta physiologica hungarica. *See* 725.

726 **Acta physiologica latinoamericana.** Buenos Aires. *Acta physiol. latinoam.* [1950–] L.MD.; SC.; UC.; **Abd.**U.; **E.**U. 50–52; G.U.; **R.**D.; **Y.**

727 **Acta physiologica** et **pharmacologica néerlandica.** Amsterdam, etc. *Acta physiol. pharmac. néerl.* [1950–] L.BM.; BM^N. 50–52; MC.; MD.; SC.; U.; Z. 50–52; **Abs.**U. 58–; **Br.**U.; **C.**APH.; P.; PH.; UL.; **Cr.**MD.; **Db.**; **Dm.** 50–52; E.R. 50–52; R.; **Nw.**A.; **Pl.**M.; **R.**D.; **Sh.**U.; **Y.** [*C. of:* 524 and 4307]

728 **Acta physiologica polonica.** Warszawa. *Acta physiol. pol.* [1950–] L.BM.; MA.; MD.; SC.; UC. 54–; **Y.**

729 **Acta physiologica scandinavica.** Stockholm, etc. *Acta physiol. scand.* [1940–] L.B. 52–; LI.; MA. 46–; MC.; MD.; NC. 59–; OP. 46–; P. 57–; S. 46–; SC.; U. imp.; UC.; VC. 41– imp.; **Abd.**R. 62–; U.; **Abs.**U. 58–; **Bl.**U.; **Bm.**U.; **Br.**U.; **C.**APH.; PH.; **Cr.**MD. 58–; U. 55–; **Db.**; **Dn.**U. 46– imp.; **E.**P.; U.; G.U.; **Ld.**U.; **M.**MS.; **N.**U. 54–; O.BI.; PH.; R.; **Pl.**M.; **R.**D. 47–; U.; **Sa.** 53–; **Sh.**U.; **Y.** [*Replaces:* 49873; *Also supplements*]

730 **Acta physiologica sinica.** Peking. *Acta physiol. sin.* [1955–] L.MC. 58–; **Y.** [*C. of:* 13933]

731 **Acta physiotherapica** et **rheumatologica belgica.** *Acta physiother. rheum. belg.* [1946–55] L.MA.; MD. 47–55. [*C. as:* 25656]

732 **Acta phytochimica.** Tokyo. *Acta phytochim., Tokyo* [1922–49] L.BM^N. 28–39 imp.; C.; K. 22–39; P. 22–39; R. 22–39; SC. 22–39; UC.; **Abd.**U. 22–39 imp.; **Bm.**U. 28–40; **Br.**U. 23–49 imp.; **C.**BI. 22–38; BO. 22–37; P.; G.U. 30–39; **Ld.**U. 23–29; **Lv.**U. 22–39; **M.**U. 22–40.

733 **Acta phytogeographica suecica.** Uppsala. *Acta phytogeogr. suec.* [1929–] L.BM.; BM^N.; K.; L.; NC. 31–;

SC.; **Bl.**U.; **C.**BO.; P. 53–; E.R. 35–; **Fr.** 40–; G.U. 55–; **Lv.**U. 31– imp.; **M.**U. 40–48: 52; O.BO. 31–; **Rt.** 33; **Sa.** 58–; **Y.**

734 **Acta phytopathologica sinica.** Peking. *Acta phytopath. sin.* [1955–] L.MY.; **C.**A. 57–.
   Acta phytotaxonomica. Peking. *See* 737.

736 **Acta phytotaxonomica** et **geobotanica.** Kyoto. *Acta phytotax. geobot., Kyoto* [1932–] L.BM^N. imp.; K. 32–45; SC. 32–43: 54–; **E.**B.; **Y.**

737 **Acta phytotaxonomica sinica.** Peking. *Acta phytotax. sin.* [1951–] L.BM^N.; K.; O.F. 58–.

738 **Acta phytotherapeutica.** Amsterdam. *Acta phytother.* [1954–] **Y.**
   Acta Poloniae maritima. *See* 1633^a.

739 **Acta Poloniae pharmaceutica.** Warszawa. *Acta Pol. pharm.* [1937–] L.BM. 47–; MD. 51–; PH. 47– imp.; **Y.**

740 **Acta polonici mathematici.** Warszawa. *Acta pol. math.* [1954–] L.SC.

741 **Acta polytechnica.** Stockholm. *Acta polytech.*
   Series (*a*). Chemistry, including Metallurgy [1947–56] L.I.; P 50–56; **Bm.**U.; **G.**E.; T.; **Sh.**IO.; SC.; **Y.**
   Series (*b*). Civil Engineering and Building Construction [1947–57] L.I.; P. 50–57; SI.; **Bm.**U.; **G.**E.; T.; **M.**U. 50–57; **Sh.**IO.; **Y.**
   Series (*c*). Electrical Engineering [1947–57] L.EE.; I.; P. 50–57; SI.; **Bm.**U.; T.; **G.**E.; **Nw.**A.; **Sh.**IO.; SC.; **Y.**
   Series (*d*). Mechanical Engineering [1947–57] L.AV. 47–55; I.; P. 50–57; **Bm.**U.; **G.**E.; T.; **M.**U. 51–52; **Sh.**IO.; SC.; **Y.**
   Series (*e*). Physics and Applied Mathematics [1947–54] L.AV.; I.; P. 50–53; SI.; **Bm.**U.; **G.**E.; T.; **Sh.**IO.; SC.; **Y.**
   then
   Physics including Nucleonics [1955–57] L.I.; SI.; **Bm.**U.; **G.**E.; T.; **Sh.**IO.; SC.; **Y.**
[*C. as:* 742]

742 **Acta polytechnica scandinavica.** Stockholm. *Acta polytech. scand.* [1958–]
   Series (*a*). Chemistry, including Metallurgy. L.I.; P.; **Bm.**U.; **G.**E.; T.; **Sh.**IO.; SC.; **Y.**
   Series (*b*). Civil Engineering and Building Construction. L.I.; P.; **Bm.**U.; **G.**E.; T.; **M.**U.; **Sh.**IO.; SC.; **Y.**
   Series (*c*). Electrical Engineering. L.EE.; I.; P.; SI.; **Bm.**U.; T.; **G.**E.; **Nw.**A.; **Sh.**IO.; SC.; **Y.**
   Series (*d*). Applied Mathematics and Computing Machinery. L.I.; P.; **Bm.**U.; **G.**E.; T.; **Sh.**IO.; SC.; **Y.**
   Series (*e*). Mechanical Engineering. L.AV.; I.; P.; **Bm.**U.; **G.**E.; T.; **Sh.**IO.; SC.; **Y.**
   Series (*f*). Physics including Nucleonics. L.AV.; I.; P.; SI.; **Bm.**U.; **G.**E.; T.; **Sh.**IO.; SC.; **Y.**
[*C. of:* 741]

743 **Acta Pontificiae Academiae scientiarum.** Citta del Vaticano. *Acta pontif. Acad. Sci.* [1937–] L.BM.; BM^N.; EE. 39–40 imp.; MO. 37; **Br.**U. 44–48; **Db.**; **E.**C. 38–40 imp.; R. [*C. of:* 5758]
   Acta psychiatrica. *See* 744.

743^c **Acta průhoniciana.** Průhonice. *Acta průhon.* **Md.**H. 60–.

744 **Acta psychiatrica** et **neurologica** (*afterwards* **scandinavica**). Kjøbenhavn. *Acta psychiat. neurol. scand.* [1926–61] **L.**BM.; MA. 37–39; MD.; PS. 38–; U. 50–; UC.; **Bl.**U. 26–29 imp.: 59–61; **Db.** 49–; **Dn.**U. 61; **Ld.**U. 56–61; **Nw.**A. 56–61; **Sh.**U. 59–61. [*Also supplements; C. as:* Acta psychiatrica scandinavica *and* Acta neurologica scandinavica]

745 **Acta psychologica.** Hague. *Acta psychol.* [1935–] **L.**BM.; PS.; **Bl.**U. 60–; **Br.**U. 49–; **C.**PS. 46–; UL.; **Db.** 49–; **E.**U.; **H.**U. 60–; **O.**B.; EP. 49–; **R.**U.

745ᶜ **Acta psychologica fennica.** Helsingissä. *Acta psychol. fenn.* [1951–] **L.**BM

745ᵉ **Acta psychologica gothoburgensia.** Stockholm. *Acta psychol. gothoburg.* [1956–] **L.**BM.

746 **Acta psychologica taiwanica.** Taipei. *Acta psychol. taiwan.* [1958–] **Y.**

747 **Acta psychotherapeutica, psychosomatica** et **orthopaedagogica.** Basel, New York. *Acta psychother. psychosom. orthopaedag.* [1953–] **L.**MD.

748 **Acta radiologica.** Stockholm. *Acta radiol.* [1921–] **L.**MA. 29–; MD.; P. 21–29; RA.; S. 39–; U. 27–; UCH. 49–; **Abd.**R. 31–; U. 31–; **Bl.**U.; **Br.**U. 31–; **C.**AN. 26–41 imp.; R.; **Dn.**U. 52–; **E.**S. 47–; U. imp.; **G.**F. 32– imp.; **Ld.**U. imp.; **M.**MS. 51–; **O.**R. 47–; **Sh.**IO. 31–; **Y.** [*Also supplements*]

Acta radiologica et **cancerologica Bohemiae** et **Moraviae.** *See* 749.

749 **Acta radiologica** et **cancerologica bohemoslovenica.** Praga. *Acta radiol. cancer. bohemoslov.* [1938–54] **L.**BM.; CB. [*Not published* 1941–48; *C. as:* 13611]

750 **Acta radiológica interamericana.** Buenos Aires. *Acta radiol. interam.*

751 **Acta Regiae Scientiarum universitatis hungaricae budapestinensis.** Budapestini. *Acta R. Sci. Univ. hung. Bpest* **L.**SC. 16–19; **E.**U. 16–19; **O.**B. 89– imp.

752 **Acta Regiae Scientiarum universitatis hungaricae debreceniensis a Stephano Tisza nominatae.** Debrecen. *Acta R. Sci. Univ. hung. Debrecen* [1914–] **E.**U. 36–42.

Acta Regiae Societatis physiograpnicae lundensis. *See* 786 avd. 2.

Acta rerum naturalium Districtus ostraviensis. *See* 48658.

753 **Acta rheumatica.** Amsterdam. *Acta rheum., Amst.* [1929–39] **L.**BM. 30–39; H.; MA.; MD.; S. 32–39; **Bm.**U. 32–38; **Br.**U.; **C.**UL. 30–39; **O.**R. 30–39.

Acta rheumatologica. Amsterdam. *See* 753.

754 **Acta rheumatológica latinoamericana.** Buenos Aires. *Acta rheum. latinoam.* [1958–] **L.**MA.

755 **Acta rheumatologica scandinavica.** Stockholm. *Acta rheum. scand.* [1955–] **L.**MA.; MD.; **E.**P.; **G.**F.; **M.**MS.

756 **Acta salmanticensia.** Salamanca. *Acta salmant.*
  1. Ciencias [1945–] **L.**BM.; SC.; **C.**P. 54–; **G.**U.; **O.**R. 54–.
  2. Medicina [1954–] **C.**P.; **G.**U.; **O.**R.

757 **Acta Scholae medicinalis** in **Gifu.** Gifu. *Acta Sch. med. Gifu* [1953–]

758 **Acta Scholae medicinalis Universitatis** in **Kioto.** Kioto. *Acta Sch. med. Univ. Kioto* [1916–] **L.**GH. 16–39

imp.; L. 16–27; MA. 32–; MC. 53–; MD.; R.; S. 16–39; TD.; Z. 16–39; **Abd.**R. 49–; U.; **Bl.**U.; **Bm.**U.; **Br.**U.; **C.**B. imp.; UL.; **Cr.**MD. 16–25 imp.; **Db.** 16–34 imp.; **Dn.**U.; **E.**P.; R.; U. imp.; **G.**U.; **Ld.**U. 23–29; **Lv.**U.; **M.**U. 16–39; **Nw.**A. 25–30; **O.**R.; **Rt.** 16–18 imp.; **Sa.**; **Y.**

759 **Acta scientia sinica.** Peking. *Acta scient. sin.* [1952–54] **L.**BM. imp.; P.; SC.; **C.**P.; **Ld.**U. 53–54. [*C. as:* 49135]

760 **Acta scientiarum mathematicarum.** Acta Universitatis szegediensis. Szeged. *Acta Sci. math., Szeged* [1941–] **L.**BM. imp.; KC. 49–; M.; U.; **E.**R. 49–; **G.**U. 51–; **Y.**

761 **Acta scientiarum naturalium Universitatis pekinensis.** Peking. *Acta Sci. nat. Univ. pekin.* [1955–] **C.**P.

762 **Acta scientifica.** Observatorio de **física cósmica.** San Miguel. *Acta scient. Obs. Fís. cósm, S Miguel* **L.**MO. 50–.

Acta Societatis biologiae Latviae. Riga. *See* 28164.

763 **Acta Societatis botanicorum Poloniae.** Warszawa. *Acta Soc. Bot. Pol.* [1923–] **L.**BMᴺ.; HS. imp.; K. 23–47; L.; MY. 29–38: 46–; QM. 27–52 imp.; SC.; U. 46; **Bl.**U. 27– imp.; **Bm.**U. 27–28; **Br.**U. 27–; **C.**A. 30–57; BO.; UL. 49–; **Db.**; **E.**B.; U. 46–; **Fr.** 56–; **Ld.**U. 25–28; **Lv.**U.; **M.**U. imp.; **O.**BO.; **Pl.**M.; **Rt.** 27– imp.; **Sa.** 56–; **Y.**

Acta Societatis entomologicae Bohemiae. *See* 13398, 13401 and 48308.

Acta Societatis entomologicae Čechoslovenicae. *See* 13398, 13401 and 48038.

764 **Acta Societatis entomologicae jugoslavensis.** Beograd. *Acta Soc. ent. jugosl.* [1926–31] **L.**BMᴺ.; EB.

Acta Societatis entomologicae Serbo-Croato-Slovenae. Beograd. *See* 764.

765 **Acta Societatis entomologicae stauropolitanae.** Stavropol. *Acta Soc. ent. stauropol.* [1925–38] **L.**BMᴺ.; EB.

766 **Acta Societatis** pro **fauna** et **flora fennica.** Helsingforsiae. *Acta Soc. Fauna Flora fenn.* [1875–] **L.**BMᴺ.; E. 75–05 imp.; K.; L.; NC. 44–; R. 75–53; SC. 35–; Z. imp.; **Bl.**U. 29–; **Bm.**N. 26–; **C.**P. 06–; PO. 37–; UL.; **Cr.**U 37–; **Db.** 81– imp.; **E.**B.; F. 92–21 imp.; R.; **Fr.** 37–; **G.**N.; **Lv.**U. 21–29; **M.**U. 06–09; **O.**OR. 98–38; R.; **Pl.**M. 88–; **Y.**

Acta Societatis internationalis veterinariorum et **zootechnicorum.** Madrid. *See* 59300.

767 **Acta Societatis medicorum fennicae 'Duodecim'.** Helsinki. *Acta Soc. Med. fenn. 'Duodecim'* [1919–45] **L.**GH. 34–40; MC. 19–25; MD. 19–30; S.; **Br.**U. 21–45; **Db.** 31–41 imp.; **E.**U. [*From* 1930–1945 issued in *two series:* Ser. A, *C. as:* 2830, Ser. B, *C. as:* 2831 and 2699]

Acta Societatis medicorum suecanae. *See* 51582.

768 **Acta Societatis medicorum upsaliensis.** Uppsala. *Acta Soc. Med. upsal.* [1950–] **L.**BM.; MA.; MC.; MD.; S.; TD.; **Abd.**R.; **Bm.**U.; **C.**UL.; **E.**S. 56–; **Nw.**A. [*C. of:* 55723]

769 **Acta Societatis ophthalmologicae japonicae.** Tokyo. *Acta Soc. ophthal. jap.*

770 **Acta Societatis pathologicae japonicae.** Tokyo. *Acta Soc. path. jap.* [1933–] **L.**CB. 33–39; LI. 35–39; MC.; MD. 33–34; S. 33–38; TD. 33–39. [*C. of:* 53792]

Acta Societatis pediatricae hellenicae. *See* 16482.

771 **Acta Societatis scientiarum fennicae.** Helsing-forsiae. *Acta Soc. Sci. fenn.* [1842–26: Ser. A. 27–; Ser. B. 31–] **L.**AS. 1842–26: (*a*); BM.; BM^N.; G. 88–; MO. 37–38; P. 88–06; R.; UC. 83– imp.; Z. imp.; **Abd.**U. 07–; **Abs.**U. 08–; **Bm.**U. 1847– imp.; **C.**P.; UL. 1842–88; **Db.**; **E.**R. imp.; **G.**U. 97– imp.; **Ld.**U. 95–96: 08–; **Lv.**U. 83– imp.; **M.**R.; **Mi.** (*b*); **O.**R.; **Sh.**U. 08–.

772 **Acta Societatis scientiarum naturalium mora-vo-silesiacae.** Brno. *Acta Soc. Sci. nat. moravo-siles.* [1924–47] **L.**BM.; BM^N.; UC.; **C.**P.; UL.; **Db.**; **E.**R.; **Ld.**U. 24; **O.**B. (*b*): (*c*) 29–37; R. (*a*). [*C. as:* 472]
  Acta Societatis zoologicae bohemoslovenicae. *See* 56429.
  Acta Societatis zoologicae čechoslovenicae. *See* 56429.

773 **Acta stomatologica hellenica.** Athenae. *Acta stomat. hell.* **L.**D.

774 **Acta Svenska tekniska vetenskapsakademien i Finland.** Helsingfors. *Acta svenska tek. VetAkad. Finl.* [1926–] **L.**P.; **Y.**

775 **Acta technica.** Praha. *Acta tech., Praha* [1956–61] **L.**P.; SC.; **Y.** [*C. as:* Acta technica ČSAV]

776 **Acta technica Academiae scientiarum hungaricae.** Budapest. *Acta tech. hung.* [1950–] **L.**AV.; BM.; I. 51–; MI.; P. 51–; **Bm.**C. 51–; **C.**UL.; **Db.**; **Ld.**U.; **Lv.**P. 57–; **Y.**
  Acta technica ČSAV. *See* 775.
  Acta technica hungarica. *See* 776

777 **Acta theriologica.** Warszawa. *Acta theriol.* [1955–] **L.**AM.; BM^N.; MC. 58–; NC. 59–; SC.; Z.; **Bl.**U.; **C.**P.; **Dm.** 59–; **E.**R.; **G.**N. 57–59; **Ld.**U. 55–57; **Lo.** 56–; **M.**P.; **O.**R.; **Pl.**M.; **Y.**

778 **Acta tropica.** Basel. *Acta trop.* [1944–] **L.**BM.; E. 44–47; EB.; MC.; MD.; SC.; TD.; TP. 45–49 imp.; **C.**A. 51–; E.; UL.; **E.**U. 58–; **Nw.**A.; **O.**R.; **Y.** [*Also supplements*]

779 **Acta tuberculosea belgica.** Bruxelles. *Acta tuberc. belg.* [1948–] **L.**MA. [*C. of:* 47081]
  Acta tuberculosea graeca. *See* 50088^c.

780 **Acta tuberculosea japonica.** Kyoto. *Acta tuberc. jap.* [1951–] **L.**LI.; MC.; MD.; TD.; **Y.**

781 **Acta tuberculosea scandinavica.** Copenhagen. *Acta tuberc. scand.* [1925–] **L.**MA.; MC.; MD.; TD. 48–; U. 52–; **Bl.**U. 28–58 imp.; **Br.**U. 25–57; **Cr.**MD.; **O.**P. 29–; **Y.** [*Also supplements*]

782 **Acta Unionis internationalis** contra **cancrum.** Bruxelles, Paris. *Acta Un. int. Cancr.* [1936–] **L.**CB.; H. 50–; MD. 36–39; S. 59–; U. 48–; **C.**R.; **O.**R. 39–; **Y.**
  Acta Universitatis agriculturae. Praha. *See* 48709.
  Acta Universitatis agriculturae et **silviculturae.** Brno. *See* 48707.

783 **Acta Universitatis Asiae mediae.** Tashkent. *Acta Univ. Asiae mediae*
  1*c.* Psychology [1929–30] **L.**L.
  5*a.* Mathematics [1929–41] **L.**AS.; UC.; **E.**U. 33–41.
  5*b.* Astronomy [1927–32] **L.**AS; U.C; **C.**P. 27; **E.**U. 32.
  6. Chemistry [1928–41] **L.**BM^N.; C. 28–38; **C.**P.; **E.**U. 33–37.
  7*a.* Geology [1928–29] **L.**BM.^{N}.; GL.
  7*d.* Pedology [1930–36] **L.**BM^N.; **E.**U. 30.

  8*a.* Zoology [1927–38] **L.**BM^N.; L. 29–38; **E.**U. 34–38; **Lv.**U. 28–38.
  8*b.* Botany [1927–39] **L.**BM^N.; K. 29–31; L. 29–37; **E.**U. 31–39; **Lv.**U.
  8*c.* Ecology [1933–39] **L.**BM^N.; **E.**U.
  9. Medicine [1928–30] **L.**BM^N.; **C.**P.
  10. Agriculture [1929–36] **L.**BM^N.; **C.**P.; **Lv.**U.;
  11. Technics [1929] **L.**UC.; SC.; **E.**U.
  12*a.* Geography [1928–38] **L.**BM^N.; **C.**P.; **E.**U. 31–38; **Lv.**U.
  12*b.* Ethnography [1928–29] **L.**BM^N.; **C.**P.; **Lv.**U.
  13. Varia [1934] **L.**BM^N.; **C.**P.
  Nova Ser. [1945–] **L.**BM^N. 45–46 imp.
  Acta Universitatis bergensis. *See* 3921.

784 **Acta Universitatis Carolinae.** Pragae. *Acta Univ. Carol.* [1954–]
  Biologica. **L.**BM^N.; K.; SC.; **Bl.**U.; **C.**A.; **E.**U.; **Y.**
  Geologica. **L.**BM^N.; GL.; K.; **E.**U.; **Y.**
  Medica. **Bl.**U. 59–; **E.**U.; **Y.** [*Also supplements*]
  [*New series formed in* 1958 *when joined with:* 55568]

785 **Acta Universitatis debreceniensis** de **Ludovico Kossuth** nominatae. Budapest. *Acta Univ. debrecen.* [1954–] **L.**BM. 54–56; BM^N.; **G.**U.; **O.**B.; **Y.**
  Acta Universitatis gotoburgensis. *See* 21494.
  Acta Universitatis latviensis. *See* 28163.
  Acta Universitatis litterarum r. hungaricae de-breceniensis. *See* 752.

786 **Acta Universitatis lundensis.** Lund. *Acta Univ. lund.* [1864–] **L.**BM.; BM^N.; GL. 06– imp.; L.; R.; U. 18–; UC. (ser. 2) 05–28 imp.; Z. 64–71: (ser. 2) 05–; **Abd.**U.; **Abs.**U. 51–; **Bm.**U. 13–31; **C.**A. 32–48 imp.; P.; UL.; **Db.**; **Dm.** 05–55 imp.; **E.**B.; J. 73–; R.; **G.**U. 65: 18: 28–; **Lv.**U. 89–11 imp.; **M.**U.; **O.**R. 65–; **Pl.**M. 06–49 imp.; **Sa.** 01–; **Y.**
  Acta Universitatis palackianae olomucensis. *See* 48656.
  Acta Universitatis stockholmiensis. Contributions in **Geology.** *See* 50940.

788 **Acta Universitatis szegediensis.** Szeged. *Acta Univ. szeged.* [*Replaces:* 625]
  Sectio scientiarum naturalium.
    Acta biologica. Pars botanica [1939] **L.**BM^N.; Pars zoologica [1939] **L.**BM^N.
    Acta chemica, mineralogica et physica [1939–40] **L.**BM.; BM^N.; GM.; UC.
  then in series issued separately:
    Acta biologica [1955–] *See* 508.
    Acta botanica [1942–49] *See* 517.
    Acta geographica [1955–] *See* 577.
    Acta mineralogica, petrographica [1943–] *See* 665.
    Acta physica et chemica [1955–] *See* 721.
    Acta scientiarum mathematicarum [1941–] *See* 760.
    Acta zoologica [1942–51] *See* 806.

789 **Acta Universitatis tanaitici.** Rostov. *Acta Univ. tainait.* **E.**U. 19–25.

790 **Acta Universitatis tsinghuanensis.** Peking. *Acta Univ. tsinghuan.* [1955–] **L.**P.

791 **Acta Universitatis voronegiensis.** Voronezh. *Acta Univ. voroneg.* [1925–] **L.**BM^N. 25–38; C. 25–31; UC.; Z. 25–27; **Bl.**U. 37–39; **E.**R. 35–39. [*Published in sections*]

792 **Acta urologica.** Budapest. *Acta urol., Bpest* [1947–] **L.**MA.; MD.; **G.**U. 47–49; **Ld.**U.

793 **Acta urologica.** Kyoto. *Acta urol., Kyoto* [1955–]

794 **Acta urologica belgica.** Bruxelles. *Acta urol. belg.* [1955–] [*C. of:* 25659]

795 **Acta vertebratica.** Stockholm. *Acta vertebr.* [1957–] **L.**BM.; BM^N.; NC.; SC.; Z.; **O.**AP.; R.

796 **Acta veterinaria.** Beograd. *Acta vet., Beogr.* [1951–] **L.**V. 51–57 imp.; **E.**AB. 51–52; **W.**; **Y.**

797 **Acta veterinaria Academiae scientiarum hungaricae.** Budapest. *Acta vet. hung.* [1948–] **L.**AM.; BM. 51–; V. 48–49; **Abd.**R. 60–; **C.**UL.; V. 51–54; **E.**AB. 51–54; **W.** 51–; **Y.**

    Acta veterinaria Facultatis medicinae veterinariae Universitatis Belgradensis. See 796.

    Acta veterinaria hungarica. See 797.

798 **Acta veterinaria japonica.** Tokyo. *Acta vet. jap.* [1956–] **L.**V.; **W.**; **Y.**

799 **Acta veterinaria neerlandica.** Utrecht. *Acta vet. neerl.* [1933–34] **W.**

800 **Acta veterinaria scandinavica.** Copenhagen. *Acta vet. scand.* [1959–] **L.**MA.; MD.; VC.; **Abd.**R.; **C.**A.; **W.**; **Y.** [*Also supplements*]

800° **Acta veterinaria et zootechnica sinica.** Peking. *Acta vet. zootech. sin.* [1956–] **Y.**

801 **Acta virologica.** Prague. *Acta virol., Prague* [1957–] **L.**MA.; MC.; TD.; **G.**U.; **Ld.**U. 60–; **W.**; **Y.** [*International journal in English Edition*]

802 **Acta vitaminologiae.** Wilno. *Acta Vitam., Wilno* [1938–39] **L.**LI.; **Abd.**R. imp.

803 **Acta vitaminologica.** Milano. *Acta vitam., Milano* [1947–] **L.**C.; MA.; MD. 48–; SC. 48–; **Abd.**R. 49–.

804 **Acta zooecologica.** Tokyo. *Acta zooecol., Tokyo* **L.**BM^N. 36.

805 **Acta zoologica.** Stockholm. *Acta zool., Stockh.* [1920–] **L.**BM^N.; SC. 57–; UC.; Z.; **Abd.**U. 20–32; **Bm.**U. 23–; **Bn.**U. 50–; **Br.**U.; **C.**B.; P. 25–52; UL.; **E.**R.; **Ld.**U.; **M.**U.; **Nw.**A.; **O.**R.; **Pl.**M.; **R.**U.; **Sw.**U. 57–; **Y.**

806 **Acta zoologica.** Acta Universitatis szegediensis. Szeged. *Acta zool., Szeged* [1942–51]

807 **Acta zoologica Academiae scientiarum hungaricae.** Budapest. *Acta zool. hung.* [1954–] **L.**BM.; BM^N.; SC.; Z.; **Pl.**M. 58–59; **Y.**

    Acta zoologica colombiana. See 28827.

808 **Acta zoologica cracoviensia.** Kraków. *Acta zool. cracov.* [1956–] **L.**BM^N.; Z.; **C.**B.; **E.**R.; **Fr.**; **O.**H.; **Y.**

809 **Acta zoologica fennica.** Helsinforsiae. *Acta zool. fenn.* [1926–] **L.**BM^N.; EB.; L.; NC.; R. 26–54; SC.; Z.; **Abd.**M.; **Abs.**U. 26–27; **Bl.**U.; **Bn.**U. 55–; **Br.**U.; **C.**B. 36–; P.; PO.; **Cr.**U.; **Db.**; **E.**R.; **Fr.**; **G.**N.; U. 36– imp.; **Lo.** 50– imp.; **Lv.**U.; **O.**R.; OR. 27–41: 45–51; **Pl.**M.; **Wo.** 55: 58; **Y.**

    Acta zoologica hungarica. See 807.

810 **Acta zoologica lilloana.** Tucumán. *Acta zool. lilloana* [1943–] **L.**BM^N.; E. 44–; Z.; **C.**B.; **Ld.**U. 50–52; **O.**H.; **R.**U. 43–44; **Y.**

811 **Acta zoologica mexicana.** México. *Acta zool. mex.* [1955–] **L.**BM^N.; Z.; **G.**N.; **Sal.**

812 **Acta zoologica et oecologica Universitatis lodziensis.** Łódź. *Acta zool. oecol. Univ. lodz.* [1951–] **L.**BM^N.

813 **Acta zoologica sinica.** Peking. *Acta zool. sin.* [1949–] **L.**BM^N. 56–; R. 55–; Z. 56–; **Bn.**U. 58–; **E.**R. 57–; **Fr.** 55–; **Pl.**M. 56; **Y.**

814 **Acta zoologica taiwanica.** Taipei. *Acta zool. taiwan.* [1948–] **Pl.**M. 48.

815 **Actas. Academia de ciencias exactas, físicas y naturales.** Lima. *Actas Acad. Cienc. Lima* [1938–39] **L.**R.; **Db.** [*C. as:* 817]

816 **Actas de la Academia nacional de ciencias en Cordoba.** *Actas Acad. nac. Cienc. Cordoba* [1875–89: 21–] **L.**BM. 75; BM^N. 75–38; E. 75–86 imp.; GL. 21–38; L. 21–28; MO. 24; R. 75–89: 21–38; Z. 75–84; **E.**R. 75–89: 21–28 imp.

817 **Actas. Academia nacional de ciencias exactas, físicas y naturales de Lima.** *Actas Acad. nac. Cienc. Lima* [1939–] **L.**R.; **Db.**; **E.**R. 47–. [*C. of:* 815]

818 **Actas das assembléas geraes. Academia das sciencias de Lisboa.** *Actas Assembl. ger. Acad. Sci. Lisb.* [1899–] **L.**BM.; G.; GL. 99–15; L. 99–12; UC.; **C.**UL.; **E.**B.; R. 99–19; U. 99–16; **M.**R.; **O.**R. 99–15.

818° **Actas Ciba.** Productos químicos Ciba. Buenos Aires. *Actas Ciba*

819 **Actas de la Clínica Yodice.** Buenos Aires. *Actas Clín. Yodice* [1953–]

820 **Actas de la Conferencia latino-americana de neurología, psiquiatría y medicina legal.** Buenos Aires, etc. *Actas Conf. lat.-am. Neurol.* [1928–] **C.**UL.; **O.**R. 29.

820° **Actas. Congreso argentino de psicología.** Tucumán. *Actas Congr. argent. Psicol.* [1955–]

821 **Actas. Congreso internacional de biología.** Montevideo. *Actas Congr. int. Biol.* [1930–32] **Bl.**U.; **E.**R. [*Supplement to:* 4653]

822 **Actas. Congreso nacional de ciencias naturales.** Lisboa. *Actas Congr. nac. Cienc. nat. Lisb.* **Dm.** 42–.

823 **Actas dermo-sifilográficas.** Madrid. *Actas dermosifilogr.* [1909–] **L.**MA. 47–; MD. 24–39: 48–.

824 **Actas españolas de neurología y psiquiatría.** Madrid. *Actas esp. Neurol. Psiquiat.* [1941–] **L.**MD. 41–43. [*C. of:* 565]

825 **Actas do Instituto de micología.** Recife. *Actas Inst. Micol., Recife* [1960–] **L.**BM^N.

826 **Actas luso-españolas de neurología y psiquiatría.** Madrid. *Actas luso-esp. Neurol. Psiquiat.* **L.**MA. 47–.

827 **Actas y memorias. Congreso de historia y geografía hispano-americano.** Madrid. *Actas Mems Congr. Hist. Geogr. hisp.-am.* **L.**BM. 14: 21.

828 **Actas y memorias del Congreso de naturalistas españoles.** Zaragoza. *Actas Mems Congr. Nat. esp.* **L.**BM^N. 08.

829 **Actas y memorias. Sociedad española de antropología, etnografía y prehistoria.** Madrid. *Actas Mems Soc. esp. Antrop.* [1921–] **L.**AN.; BM^N. 21–35; UC.; **C.**AN. 21–26; E.

830 **Actas, resoluciones y memorias del Congreso meteorológico nacional** convocado por la Sociedad científica 'Antonio Alzate'. México. *Actas Resol. Mems Congr. met. nac., Méx.*

831 **Actas de la semana de geográficos. Sociedad argentina de estudios geográficos.** San Juan. *Actas Semana Geogr. Soc. argent. Estud. geogr.* **O.**B. 51–.

832 **Actas das sessões da primeira classe. Academia das sciencias de Lisboa.** *Actas Sess. prim. Cl. Acad. Sci. Lisb.* [1899–] **L.**BM.; G. 99–10; L. 99–13; UC.; **E.**B.; R. 99–10; **M.**R. 01–; **O.**B.

833 **Actas** das **sessões** da **Sociedade** de **geographia** de **Lisboa.** *Actas Sess. Soc. Geogr. Lisb.* [1876–] **L.**G. 76–94; **C.**UL. 83–95; **E.**O. 86–03; **G.**U. 83.

Actas de la **Sociedad científica** de **Chile.** *See* 850.

834 **Actas. Sociedad española** para el **estudio** de la **esterilidad.** Madrid. *Actas Soc. esp. Estud. Esteril.* [1953–] **L.**MD. 53–55.

835 **Actas** de la **Sociedad española** de **historia natural.** Madrid. *Actas Soc. esp. Hist. nat.* [1897–00] **L.**BM.; BM^N.; Z.; **E.**C.; **G.**N.

836 **Actas** de la **Sociedad oftalmológica hispanoamericana.** Barcelona. *Actas Soc. oftal. hisp.-am.* **L.**MD. 04–10 imp.

Actas da **Sociedade** de **biologia** do **Rio de Janeiro.** *See* 5080°.

838 **Actas** y **trabajos. Asociación argentina** para el **estudio** de las **enfermedades transmisibles.** Perón. *Actas Trab. Asoc. argent. Estud. Enferm. transmis.*

839 **Actas** y **trabajos. Conferencia nacional** de **profilaxis antituberculosa.** Rosario de Santa Fé. *Actas Trab. Conf. nac. Profil. antituberc., Rosario* **L.**BM. 19.

840 **Actas** y **trabajos. Congreso médico latinoamericano.** Barcelona, etc. *Actas Trab. Congr. méd. lat.-am.* **L.**BM. 01–03; **O.**R. 01.

841 **Actas** y **trabajos** del **Congreso médico nacional.** Habana. *Actas Trab. Congr. méd. nac., Habana*

842 **Actas** y **trabajos. Congreso nacional** de **cirugía** de la **República Argentina.** Buenos Aires. *Actas Trab. Congr. nac. Cirug. Repúb. Argent.* [1928–] **Br.**U. 28–30.

843 **Actas** y **trabajos. Congreso nacional** de **medicina.** Buenos Aires. *Actas Trab. Congr. nac. Med., B. Aires* **L.**BM. 34; **Br.**U. 22 imp.: 31; **G.**F. 31; **O.**B. 27: 31–35.

844 **Actes** de l'**assemblée générale. Institut international** d'**agriculture.** Rome. *Act. Assem. gén. Inst. int. Agric.* **L.**AM. 08–46; **Bl.**U. 13–46. [*C. of:* 39856]

845 **Actes. Camargue réserve zoologique** et **botanique.** Chateauroux. *Act. Camargue Rés. zool. bot.* [1930–] **M.**P. 30–32.

846 **Actes** et **comptes rendus. Association coloniessciences.** Paris. *Act. C.r. Ass. Colon.-Sci.* [1925–40] **L.**SC. 31–40; **O.**F. 39.

Actes du **Congrès. Association française** pour l'**avancement** des **sciences.** *See* 15161.

847 **Actes** de l'**Institut botanique** de l'**Université** d'**Athènes.** *Act. Inst. bot. Univ. Athèn.* [1940–] **L.**BM^N.

848 **Actes** du **Muséum** d'**histoire naturelle.** Rouen. *Act. Mus. Hist. nat. Rouen* [1860–] **L.**BM^N. 1860–31; SC. 25–; **C.**UL. 11–31; **Rt.** 11–31.

Actes de la **Société helvétique** des **sciences naturelles.** *See* 56067.

849 **Actes** de la **Société linnéenne** de **Bordeaux.** *Act. Soc. linn. Bordeaux* [1830–] **L.**BM.; BM^N.; GL. 00–; K. 73–36; L. 75–; UC. 87–; Z. 1858–40 imp.; **C.**UL. 26–; **Cr.**N. 15–36; **Db.** 1832–; **G.**N. 76–01; **Ld.**U. 98–28.

850 **Actes** de la **Société scientifique** du **Chili.** Santiago. *Act. Soc. scient. Chili* [1892–] **L.**BM. 92–93; BM^N. 92–35 imp.; GL. 92–36 imp.; MD. 33–35; R. 92–95; Z. 92–09; **Db.** 92–07; **E.**R. 92–09: 26–35 imp.; **G.**N. 92–09 imp.; **Lv.**U. 92–09 imp.

851 **Actinic Practitioner** and **Electrotherapist.** London. *Actinic Practnr Electrother.* [1928–29] **L.**BM.; S.; **Abs.**N.; **O.**R. [*C. as:* 8850]

852 **Actinometric Bulletin.** Tokyo. *Actinom. Bull., Tokyo* [1930–?] **L.**MO. 30–40. [*C. in:* 45028]

853 **Actinoterapia.** Napoli. *Actinoterapia* [1915–31] **L.**RA. 23–24.

854 **Action agricole.** Paris. *Action agric.* [1919–]

855 **Action cinématographique.** Paris. *Action cinématogr.* [1936–]

856 **Action forestière** et **piscicole.** Paris. *Action for. pisc.* **O.**F. 47–51.

857 **Action médicale.** Montréal. *Action méd.* [1925–]

858 **Action pharmaceutique.** Cahors. *Action pharm.*

859 **Action scientifique internationale.** Paris. *Action scient. int.* [1934–]

860 **Action vétérinaire.** Paris. *Action vét.*

861 **Actions chimiques** et **biologiques** des **radiations.** Paris. *Actions chim. biol. Radiat.* [1955–] **L.**P.

862 **Activator.** New Jersey Zinc Co. New York. *Activator* [1935–] **L.**P.; **Y.**

863 **Actividad antarctica argentina.** Buenos Aires. *Actividad antarct. argent.* [1959–] **L.**BM^N.

863° **Actividades petroleras.** Caracas. *Activid. petrol.* **O.**R. 51–.

864 **Activitas nervosa superior.** Praha. *Activitas nerv. sup.* [1959–]

865 **Activité** de la **Commission géodésique baltique.** Helsinki. *Activité Commn géod. balt.* [1938–] **L.**AS.; BM.; P. 38–47; **C.**PO.; **O.**R. [*C. of:* 15171]

866 **Activité géomagnetique.** Istanbul, Kandilli. *Activité géomagn., Istanbul* **E.**M. 55– imp.

867 **Activité** de l'**Institut** d'**hygiène** des **mines.** Bruxelles. *Activité Inst. Hyg. Mines, Brux.* **L.**MI. 54–.

868 **Activities** of **F.A.O.** under the **Expanded Technical Assistance Program.** Rome. *Activ. F.A.O. expand. tech. Assist. Progm* [1950–] **L.**BM. 50–55; **G.**M.; **Ld.**P.

869 **Activity.** London. *Activity* **Lh.**P. 41–56★.

870 **Activity. Agricultural Research Centre.** Helsinki. *Activity agric. Res. Cent., Helsinki* **Md.**H. 58–.

871 **Actos universitarios.** Universidad nacional de La Plata. La Plata. *Actos univ. La Plata* **Bm.**U. 17–; **O.**B. 11–17 imp.

872 **Actual Announcements.** Woods Hole Oceanographic Institution. *Actual Announc. Woods Hole oceanogr. Instn* **Lo.** 31–41.

873 **Actualidad médica.** Granada. *Actualidad méd., Granada* **L.**MA. 46–; TD. imp.

874 **Actualidad médica peruana.** Lima. *Actualidad méd. peru.* [1935–] **L.**MA.; MD. 36–37; TD. 40–.

875 **Actualidad pediátrica.** Granada. *Actualidad pediát.* [1952–] **L.**MA.

876 **Actualidades biológicas.** Instituto Rocha Cabal. Coimbra. *Actualid. biol.* **L.**S. 29–34; UC. 29–34; **Y.**

877 **Actualidades científicas.** Observatorio de San Miguel, Argentina. *Actualid. cient. Obs. S Miguel* [1938–] **L.**MO. 38–39.

878 **Actualidades médicas.** Rutherford. N.J. *Actualid. méd., Rutherford, N.J.* [1929–32]

879 **Actualidades médicas (mundial).** Buenos Aires. *Actualid. méd. (mund.), B. Aires.*

880 **Actualidades médico-sanitárias.** Rio de Janeiro. *Actualid. méd.-sanit.* [1945–] **L.**TD. 48–.

881 **Actualité automobile.** Paris. *Actualité auto.* **L.**AV. 48–.

882 **Actualité chimique** et **industrielle.** Paris. *Actualité chim. ind.* [1937–]

883 **Actualité médicale.** Paris. *Actualité méd.* [1889–14]

884 **Actualité scientifique.** Paris. *Actualité scient.* **L.**P. 14–19*. [*C. in:* 47528]

885 **Actualité thérapeutique.** Paris. *Actualité thér.*

886 **Actualités agronomiques.** Paris. *Actual. agron.* Sér. B. [1951–] **L.**BM^N.; **C.**A.
Sér. C. Epiphyties [1954–] **L.**BM.; BM^N.; **C.**A.; **Rt.**

887 **Actualités biochimiques.** Paris. *Actual. biochim.* [1946–] **L.**CB. 46–47 imp.

888 **Actualités biologiques.** Association française de biologie médicale. *Actual. biol.* [1954–]

888^c **Actualités cardiologiques internationales.** Paris. *Actual. cardiol. int.* [1950–]

889 **Actualités** de **chimie contemporaine.** Paris. *Actual. Chim. contemp.* **L.**SC. 22–.

890 **Actualités** de **clinique thérapeutique.** Paris. *Actual. Clin. thér.* [1950–]

891 **Actualités gynécologiques.** Paris. *Actual. gynéc.* [1954–]

892 **Actualités hématologiques.** Paris. *Actual. hémat.* [1951–]

893 **Actualités marines.** Québec. *Actual. mar., Québ.* [1957–] **L.**BM^N. 58–; **Lo.** 58–; **Wo.** 58–.

894 **Actualités médicales.** Paris. *Actual. méd.*

895 **Actualités médico-chirurgicales.** Marseille. *Actual. méd.-chir., Marseille* [1933–]

896 **Actualités médico-chirurgicales.** New York. *Actual. méd.-chir., N.Y.* [1944–]

897 **Actualités neurophysiologiques.** Paris. *Actual. neurophysiol.* **L.**MD. 59–.

898 **Actualités odontostomatologiques.** Paris. *Actual. odontostomat.* [1947–] **L.**D.; **Dn.**U.

899 **Actualités pharmacologiques.** Paris. *Actual. pharmac.* [1950–] **Y.**

900 **Actualités scientifiques.** Paris. *Actual. scient.* **L.**P. 04–12; **Db.** 24–.

901 **Actualités scientifiques** et **industrielles.** Paris. *Actual. scient. ind.* [1931–] **L.**SC. 32–49; **C.**UL.; **E.**C.; R.; **O.**R. [*C. of:* 15403]

902 **Acuario.** La Habana. *Acuario* [1953–] **L.**BM^N.; Z.

903 **Acustica.** Zürich, Stuttgart. *Acustica* [1951–] **L.**EE; P.; RI.; SC.; **Abs.**U.; **E.**U. 54–; **G.**U.; **Ld.**U.; **Li.**M.; **M.**C.; **Nw.**A.; **Rn.**B. 52–; **Wd.** 52– imp.; **Y.** [*Akustische Beihefte at:* 1641]

904 **Aczél** és **vas.** Budapest. *Aczél Vas* [*Supplement to:* 1842]

905 **Addisonia.** New York. *Addisonia* [1916–] **L.**BM^N. 16–41; HS.; K. 16–55; **C.**BO. 16–31; **E.**B.

906 **Additamenta faunistica coleopterorum.** Reit in Dinkl. Hamburg. *Additam. faun. Coleopt.* **L.**BM^N. 46.

907 **Additional Series. Royal Botanic Gardens, Kew.** *Addit. Ser. Kew* [1898–] **L.**AM. 98–20 imp.; BM.; BM^N. 98–36; K. 98–36; L.; P.; **Abs.**N. 00–; **Bm.**P.; **Db.** 00–; **E.**A. 98–22; B.; F. 98–20 imp.; **Lv.**P. 98–36; **M.**U. 98–15; **O.**R. 98–36; **Rt.** 98–36 imp. [*Supplement to:* 11133; *For Kew Bulletin Additional Series See* 27381]

908 **Adhäsion.** Berlin. *Adhäsion* [1957–] **L.**P.; PR. 58–; **Lh.**P.; **Sy.**R.; **Y.** [*C. of:* 20818]

909 **Adhesives Age.** New York. *Adhes. Age.* [1958–] **L.**P.; **Sy.**R.; **Y.**

910 **Adhesives** and **Resins.** London. *Adhes. Resins* [1953–60] **L.**BM.; LE. 53–57; NP.; P.; TP. imp.; **Bm.**P.; **C.**UL.; **E.**A.; **Ep.**D. 54–60; **F.**A.; **G.**M.; **Lc.**A.; **Lv.**P.; **M.**P.; **O.**B.; R.; **Sy.**R.; **Y.**

Administration Report. Acting Director of Fisheries, Ceylon. *See* 13643.

911 **Administration Report. Agricultural Department, Madras.** *Adm. Rep. agric. Dep. Madras* **Md.**H. 54–.

Administration Report. Department of Agriculture, British Guiana. *See* 913^c.

912 **Administration Report. Department of Agriculture, Mysore.** *Adm. Rep. Dep. Agric. Mysore* **Y.**

913 **Administration Report** of the **Department** of **Fisheries, Madras.** *Adm. Rep. Dep. Fish. Madras* **L.**Z. 52–; **Y.** [*Previous reports published in:* 29088]

913^c **Administration Report** of the **Director** of **Agriculture, British Guiana.** Georgetown. *Adm. Rep. Dir. Agric. Br. Guiana* [1928–49] **L.**BM. 41–49; BM^N. 36–45 imp.; K. 28–44 imp.; MY. 37–49; P. 28–41; **C.**A.; **Hu.**G.; **Md.**H. 30–44; **O.**G.; RE.; **Rt.** imp.; **Sal.** 30–44. [*C. of:* 43442; *C. as:* 43471]

Administration Report. Director of **Agriculture, Ceylon.** *See* 13642.

914 **Administration Report** of the **Director** of **Agriculture, Trinidad** and **Tobago.** *Adm. Rep. Dir. Agric. Trin.* [1926–] **L.**BM^N.; EB.; K.; MY.; **C.**A.; **Hu.**G. 31–; **Md.**H. 33–; **O.**RE. (10 yr.); **Rt.** imp.; **Sal.** 31– imp.; **Y.** [*C. of:* 43309]

Administration Report. Director of **Fisheries, Ceylon.** *See* 13643.

Administration Report. Marine Biology. Ceylon. *See* 13646.

915 **Administration Report** of the **Meteorological Reporter** to the **Government** of **Bengal.** Calcutta. *Adm. Rep. met. Reptr Govt Bengal* [1869–1906] **L.**MO. [*C. as:* 918]

Administration Report of the **Meteorological Reporter** to the **Government, North-West Provinces** and **Oudh.** Allahabad. *See* 917.

917 **Administration Report** of the **Meteorological Reporter** to the **Government, United Provinces** of **Agra** and **Oudh.** Allahabad. *Adm. Rep. met. Reptr Govt Unit. Prov. Agra Oudh* **L.**MO. [*C. of:* 916; *C. as:* 917^c]

917^c **Administration Report** of the **Meteorologist** at **Allahabad.** Allahabad. *Adm. Rep. Met. Allahabad* **L.**MO. 07–15. [*C. of:* 917]

918 **Administration Report** of the **Meteorologist, Calcutta.** *Adm. Rep. Met. Calcutta* [1907–] **L.**MO. 07–10. [*C. of:* 915]

918° **Administration Report. Petroleum Department, Trinidad** and **Tobago.** Port-of-Spain. *Adm. Rep. Petrol. Dep. Trin.* **L.**BM. 48–.

919 **Administration Report. Scientific Department. United Planters' Association of Southern India.** Coonoor. *Adm. Rep. scient. Dep. un. Plrs' Ass. south. India* **Br.**A. 48–49.

919° **Administration Report. Works** and **Hydraulics Department, Trinidad** and **Tobago.** Port-of-Spain. *Adm. Rep. Wks Hydraul. Dep. Trin.* [1949–] **L.**BM.

920 **Administrative Medicine. Transactions** of the **Conferences. Josiah Macy Jr. Foundation.** New York. *Admve Med. Trans. Conf. Josiah Macy Jr Fdn* [1953–] **L.**MD.; **Dn.**U.; **E.**U.; **O.**R. 54–; **Y.**

921 **Administrative Report, Agricultural Department, Kerala.** Ernabulam. *Admve Rep. agric. Dep. Kerala* **C.**A. 57–.

922 **Administrative Report. East Malling Research Station.** East Malling. *Admve Rep. E. Malling Res. Stn* **Br.**A. 52–; **Y.**

923 **Administrative Report. Inland Fisheries Branch, California Department of Fish** and **Game.** *Admve Rep. inland Fish. Brch Calif.*

924 **Administrative Report. Trinidad** and **Tobago Cocoa Board.** *Admve Rep. Trin. Tobago Cocoa Bd* **C.**A. 56–; **Y.**

925 **Adrenal Cortex. Transactions** of the **Conferences. Josiah Macy Jr. Foundation.** New York. *Adren. Cortex Trans. Conf. Josiah Macy Jr Fdn* [1949–53] **L.**MD.; **Dn.**U.; **E.**U.; **O.**R. 53.

926 **Advance Reports. British Nylon Spinners Technical Information.** Pontypool. *Advance Rep. Br. Nylon Spinn. tech. Inf.* [1957–] **L.**P.; **Ld.**P.; **M.**C.; **Y.**

927 **Advance Reports. Bureau** of **Mines, Quebec Province.** Quebec. *Advance Rep. Bur. Mines Queb.*

928 **Advanced Management.** New York. *Advd Mgmt* [1939–] **L.**AV. 55–; P.; **Bm.**U.; **Cr.**U. 53–. [*C. of:* 26912]

929 **Advanced Materials Technology.** Niagara Falls. *Advd Mater. Technol.* **L.**P. (curr.)

930 **Advanced Therapeutics.** New York. *Advd Ther.*

931 **Advancement** of **Science.** London. *Advmt Sci., Lond.* [1939–] **L.**AM.; AN.; AV.; B.; BM.; BM^N.; C.; D.; DI. 45–57; E.; EE. imp.; GL.; I.; IC. 41–; MA.; MD.; MO.; NC. imp.; P.; PR.; R.; RI.; SC.; U.; UC.; V. 49– imp.; VC.; Z.; **Abd.**M.; U.; **Abs.**N.; U.; **Bl.**U.; **Bm.**T.; **Br.**P.; **Bra.**P. 39–45; **C.**APH. 60–; B.; BO.; P.; SJ.; **Cr.**M.; P.; U.; **Db.**; **Dn.**U.; **E.**AG. 29–53 imp.; AR.; D.; R.; T.; U.; **Ex.**U.; **F.**A. 42–; **Fr.**; **G.**E.; M.; T.; **H.**U.; **Hu.**G. 50–; **Lc.**A. 39–53; **Ld.**P.; W. 48–; **Lo.** 39–59; **Lv.**P.; U.; **M.**C.; P.; T.; U.; **Md.**H. 39–50; **Mi.**; **N.**P.; U. imp.; **Nw.**A.; **O.**BO. 39–53; G.; R.; **Pl.**M.; **R.**D. 42–; **Rt.**; **Sa.**; **Sh.**U.; **Ste.**; **Sw.**U.; **W.** 43–; **Wo.** 48– imp.; **Y.** [*Replaces:* 42873]

932 **Advancement** of **Science. Addresses** delivered at the **Annual Meetings** of the **British Association** London. *Advmt Sci., Br. Ass.* [1920–38] **L.**BM.; **Abs.**A. 30–33; **Bn.**U. 26–33; **Bra.**P. 28–38; **E.**A.; U.; **Lv.**P.; **M.**U. 21–38; **O.**AEC.; **Sa.**

933 **Advances** in **Aeronautical Sciences.** *Adv. aeronaut. Sci.* [1959–] **L.**BM.; SC.; **Co.**T.

934 **Advances** in **Agronomy.** New York. *Adv. Agron.* [1949–] **L.**AM.; C.; P.; VC. 49–58; **Abd.**R. 49–52; S.; U.; **Abs.**A.; **Bl.**U.; **G.**U.; **Hu.**G.; **Je.**; **Ld.**P.; **Lv.**P. 49: 53: 55–; **M.**U. 51: 57–; **Md.**H.; **N.**U.; **Nw.**A.; **O.**RE.; **Pl.**M. 49; **R.**U.; **Rt.**; **Y.**

935 **Advances** in **Analytical Chemistry** and **Instrumentation.** New York, London. *Adv. analyt. Chem. Instrum.* [1960–] **L.**BM.; BM^N.; P.; SC.; **Ld.**U.; **Y.**

936 **Advances** in **Applied Mechanics.** New York. *Adv. appl. Mech.* [1948–] **L.**IC.; P.; SC.; **Bl.**U.; **Bm.**U.; **Bn.**U; **Br.**U.; **C.**UL.; **Co.**T.; **Cr.**U.; **Db.**; **Dn.**U. 48–56; **E.**U.; **Ex.**U.; **Ld.**P.; **M.**T.; U.; **N.**U.; **Nw.**A.; **O.**R.; **Sh.**SC.; U.; **Sw.**U.; **Y.**

937 **Advances** in **Applied Microbiology.** New York, London. *Adv. appl. Microbiol.* [1959–] **L.**BM.; C.; MD.; SC.; TD.; **Abd.**R.; **Bl.**U.; **Br.**U.; **Cr.**U.; **H.**U.; **Ld.**U.; **Y.**

938 **Advances** in **Astronautical Sciences.** New York *Adv. astronaut. Sci.* [1957–] **L.**P. 59–; SC.; **Y.**

939 **Advances** in **Biological** and **Medical Physics.** New York. *Adv. biol. med. Phys.* [1948–] **L.**C.; CB.; MC.; MD.; SC.; TD.; UC.; UCH.; VC. 51–; **Abd.**R. 48–60; U.; **Bl.**U.; **Bm.**U.; **Br.**U.; **E.**U.; **Ex.**U.; **G.**U.; **Lv.**P. 53–; **M.**MS.; **Nw.**A.; **O.**R.; **R.**D.; U.; **Sh.**U. 51–; **Y.**

940 **Advances** in **Biology** of the **Skin.** Oxford. *Adv. Biol. Skin* [1960–] **L.**MD.; **Y.**

941 **Advances** in **Cancer Research.** New York. *Adv. Cancer Res.* [1953–] **L.**CB.; KC.; MD.; QM.; S. 53–58; SC.; UC.; UCH. 55–; **C.**PA.; **Cr.**MD.; **Dn.**U.; **E.**U.; **G.**U.; **Ld.**U.; **Lv.**P.; **O.**R.; **Y.**

942 **Advances** in **Carbohydrate Chemistry.** New York. *Adv. Carbohyd. Chem.* [1945–] **L.**AM. 50–; B.; C.; CB.; IC.; LI.; MC.; MD.; P.; SC.; TD.; TP. imp.; **Abd.**R.; U.; **Abs.**U.; **Bn.**U.; **Br.**U.; **C.**APH.; BI.; CH.; **Cr.**U.; **Db.**; **Dn.**U.; **E.**U.; **Ex.**U.; **G.**U.; **Ld.**P. 55–; U.; **Lv.**P. imp.; **M.**D.; P.; T.; U.; **N.**U.; **O.**R.; **R.**D. 54–; U.; **Rt.**; **Sa.**; **Sw.**U.; **Y.**

Advances in **Cardiology.** Basle. *See* 20221.

943 **Advances** in **Catalysis** and Related Subjects. New York. *Adv. Catalysis* [1948–] **L.**C.; P.; QM.; RI.; SC.; UC.; **Abd.**U.; **Bl.**U.; **Bm.**U.; **Bn.**U. 57–; **Br.**U.; **C.**UL.; **Cr.**U.; **Db.**; **Dn.**U. 52–55 imp.; **Ex.**U.; **G.**U.; **H.**U.; **Ld.**P.; U.; **Lv.**U.; **M.**D.; U.; **N.**U.; **Nw.**A. 48–53: 55–; **O.**R.; **R.**U.; **Sa.**; **Sh.**SC.; **Sw.**U.; **Y.**

944 **Advances** in **Chemical Engineering.** New York. *Adv. chem. Engng* [1956–] **L.**C.; P.; SC.; **Bm.**P.; **Ld.**P.; U. 56–58; **M.**P.; **N.**U.; **Nw.**A.; **Rn.**B.; **Sh.**SC.; **Sw.**U.; **Y.**

945 **Advances** in **Chemical Physics.** New York. London. *Adv. chem. Phys.* [1958–] **L.**BM. 61–; C.; P.; QM.; SC.; **Abs.**U.; **Bn.**U.; **Br.**U.; **C.**CH.; **Dn.**U.; **Ex.**U.; **G.**U.; **H.**U.; **Ld.**U.; **M.**P.; U.; **Sh.**U.; **Y.**

Advances in **Chemistry.** Moscow. *See* 55771.

946 **Advances** in **Chemistry Series.** Washington. *Adv. Chem. Ser.* [1950–] **L.**P.; SC.; **Ld.**P. 51–; **Rt.** imp.; **Wd.**

947 **Advances** in **Clinical Chemistry.** New York, London. *Adv. clin. Chem.* [1958–] **L.**C.; MD.; QM.; SC. 58–59; **Dn.**U.; **E.**U.; **G.**U.; **Y.**

948 **Advances** in **Colloid Science.** New York. *Adv. Colloid Sci.* [1942–50] **L.**C.; CB.; IC.; P.; RI.; SC.; **Abd.**U. 42–46; **Bl.**U.; **Bn.**U.; **Br.**U. imp.; **C.**BI. 42–46; UL. 50; **E.**U.; **Ex.**U.; **G.**U. 44–50; **Ld.**P.; U.; **Lv.**U.; **M.**P.; T.; U.; **N.**U.; **Nw.**A.; **O.**R.; **R.**D. 42–46; U.; **Rt.**

949 **Advances** in **Computers.** New York, London. *Adv. Comput.* [1960–] **L.**P.; SC.; **Bn.**U.; **Cr.**U.; **G.**U.; **Ld.**U.; **Y.**

950 **Advances** in **Cryogenic Engineering.** New York. *Adv. cryogen. Engng* [1957–] **L.**P.; SC.; **Ld.**U.; **Y.**

951 **Advances** in **Electronics.** New York. *Adv. Electronics* [1948–52] **L.**P.; QM.; SC.; SI.; U.; **Abd.**U.; **Bl.**U.; **Bn.**U.; **Co.**T.; **Db.**; E.U.; **Ex.**U.; **G.**U.; **H.**U.; **Ld.**P.; U.; **Lv.**P.; **M.**P.; U.; **N.**U.; **Nw.**A.; **O.**R.; **R.**U.; **Sa.**; **Y.** [*C. as:* 952]

952 **Advances** in **Electronics** and **Electron Physics.** New York. *Adv. Electronics Electron Phys.* [1953–] **L.**BM.; P.; QM.; SC.; SI.; U.; **Abd.**U.; **Bl.**U.; **Bn.**U.; **Br.**U. 54–; **Co.**T.; **Db.**; E.U.; **Ex.**U.; **Fr.** 55–; **G.**U.; **H.**U.; **Ld.**P.; U.; **Lv.**P.; **M.**P.; U.; **N.**U.; **Nw.**A.; **O.**R.; **R.**U.; **Sa.**; **Sh.**SC. 60–; **Y.** [*C. of:* 951]

953 **Advances** in **Enzymology** and Related Subjects of Biochemistry. New York. *Adv. Enzymol.* [1941–] **L.**AM.; BM. 56–; C.; CB.; IC.; KC.; LE.; LI.; MC.; MD.; P. 50–; PH.; QM.; RI.; S.; SC.; TD.; U.; UC.; UCH.; **Abd.**R. imp.; U.; **Abs.**U.; **Ba.**I. 41–45: 55–; **Bl.**U.; **Bm.**U.; **Bn.**U.; **Br.**A.; U.; **C.**APH.; B. 41–52; BI.; BO.; CH.; T.; **Cr.**U.; **Db.**; **Dn.**U.; **E.**HW. 48– imp.; U. 55–; **Ex.**U.; **G.**U. imp.; **Hu.**G. 41–43; **Ld.**P. 56–; U.; **Lv.**P. imp.; U.; **M.**MS.; T.; U.; **N.**U.; **Nw.**A.; **O.**BI.; BO.; PH.; R.; **Pl.**M. 45–48; **R.**D.; U.; **Rt.**; **Sa.**; **W.**; **Y.**

    Advances in **Experimental Biology.** Moscow. *See* 55769.

954 **Advances** in **Fluorine Chemistry.** London. *Adv. Fluor. Chem.* [1960–] **L.**BM.; C.; P.; SC.; **Bl.**U.

955 **Advances** in **Food Research.** New York. *Adv. Fd Res* [1948–] **L.**AM.; C.; P.; SC.; TD.; TP. 58–; **Abd.**R.; **Bl.**U.; **Bm.**P.; U.; **Bn.**U.; **Br.**A. 53–; **C.**UL.; **Db.**; E.U.; **G.**U.; **Ld.**U.; **Lv.**P.; **M.**T.; **N.**U.; **Nw.**A. 48–57; **R.**D.; U.; **Y.**

956 **Advances** in **Genetics.** New York. *Adv. Genet.* [1947–] **L.**AM.; B.; BM.; BM^N.; CB.; IC.; KC.; MD.; QM.; SC.; UC.; VC.; Z.; **Abd.**U.; **Abs.**A.; U.; **Ba.**I.; **Bl.**U.; **Bm.**U.; **Bn.**U.; **C.**B.; BO.; GE.; **Cr.**U. 48–; **Db.**; **Dn.**U. 61–; **E.**AR.; U.; **Ex.**U.; **G.**U.; **Ld.**U.; **Lv.**P. imp.; U.; **M.**U.; **Md.**H.; **N.**U.; **Nw.**A.; **O.**BO.; R.; RE. 47–58 imp.; **R.**D.; U.; **Sh.**U.; **Sw.**U.; **Y.**

957 **Advances** in **Geophysics.** New York. *Adv. Geophys.* [1952–] **L.**MO.; P.; SC.; **Abd.**M.; U.; **Bl.**U.; **Bn.**U. 59–; **Cr.**U.; **Dn.**U.; E.U.; **G.**U.; **Ld.**P. 56–; U. 56–58; **Lv.**P.; **M.**U.; **R.**U.; **Sa.**; **Sh.**U.; **Y.**

958 **Advances** in **Inorganic Chemistry** and **Radiochemistry.** New York. *Adv. inorg. Chem. Radiochem.* [1959–] **L.**BM.; C.; P.; SC.; **Bl.**U.; **Bn.**U.; **Br.**U.; **Co.**T.; **Cr.**U.; **Dn.**U.; **G.**U.; **Ld.**P.; **M.**U.; **Y.**

959 **Advances** in **Insecticide Research.** Jerusalem. *Adv. Insect. Res.* [1951–] **Rt.** 51.

960 **Advances** in **Internal Medicine.** London, New York. *Adv. internal Med.* [1942–] **L.**BM. 42–49; MD.; SC. 49–; UCH. 49–; VC. 55–; **Abd.**U. 50–52; **Bm.**U.; **Br.**U.; **C.**UL.; **Cr.**MD. 58–; **Dn.**U. 52–; E.U.; **Lv.**M.; **M.**MS.; **O.**R.; **Sh.**U.

    Advances in **Mathematical Sciences.** Moscow. *See* 55672.

    Advances in **Modern Biology.** Moscow. *See* 55675.

961 **Advances** in **Nuclear Engineering.** London. *Adv. nucl. Engng* [1957–] **L.**BM.; **C.**UL.; **Y.**

962 **Advances** in **Organic Chemistry.** New York. *Adv. org. Chem.* [1960–] **L.**C.; MC.; P.; SC.; **Bn.**U.; **Dn.**U.; **G.**U.; **Ld.**U.

963 **Advances** in **Pediatrics.** New York, London. *Adv. Pediat.* [1942–] **L.**BM. 42–49; MD.; UCH.; **Bl.**U.; **Bm.**U.; **Br.**U.; **C.**UL.; **Cr.**MD. 47–; **Dn.**U.; E.U.; **Lv.**M.; **M.**MS.; **Nw.**A.; **O.**R.; **Sh.**U.

964 **Advances** in **Pest Control Research.** New York, London. *Adv. Pest Control Res.* [1957–] **L.**AM.; C.; P.; TD.; UC.; **Abd.**U.; **Bl.**U. 57–60; **Bm.**P.; **Bn.**U.; **Br.**A.; **C.**UL.; **G.**U.; **Je.**; **Ld.**U.; **M.**P.; **Md.**H.; **N.**U.; **O.**R.; **R.**U.; **W.**; **Y.**

965 **Advances** in **Petroleum Chemistry** and **Refining.** New York, London. *Adv. Petrol. Chem. Refin.* [1958–] **L.**BM.; C.; P.; SC.; **Bm.**P.; **Cr.**U.; **Ld.**P.; U.; **M.**P.; **O.**R.; **Y.**

966 **Advances** in **Physical Sciences.** Washington. *Adv. phys. Sci.* [1957] **L.**P. [*English translation of:* 55770; *C. as:* 50353]

967 **Advances** in **Physics.** London. *Adv. Phys.* [1952–] **L.**AV. imp.; B.; BM.; C.; CB.; EE.; MO.; NP.; P.; QM.; R.; RI.; SC.; SI.; U.; **Abd.**U.; **Abs.**N. 55–; **Bl.**U.; **Bm.**P.; T.; **Bn.**U.; **Br.**P.; U. 52–58 imp.; **C.**CH.; P.; UL.; **Cr.**U.; **Db.**; **Dn.**U.; **E.**A.; R.; U.; **Ex.**U.; **F.**A.; **G.**M.; T.; U.; **Ld.**P. 58–; **Lv.**P. 53–; **M.**C.; D.; P.; T.; U.; **Ma.**T.; **N.**T. 60–; U.; **Nw.**A.; **O.**BS. 54–; **R.**U.; **Sa.**; **Sh.**S. 56–; SC.; U.; **Sw.**U.; **Y.** [*Supplement to:* 37579]

    Advances in **Polymer Science.** Berlin. *See* 20217.

968 **Advances** in **Protein Chemistry.** New York. *Adv. Protein Chem.* [1944–] **L.**AM.; C.; CB.; IC.; LE.; LI.; MC.; MD.; P.; PH.; RI.; SC.; TD.; TP. imp.; U.; UC.; **Abd.**R.; S.; U.; **Abs.**U.; **Ba.**I.; **Bl.**U.; **Bm.**U.; **Bn.**U.; **Br.**U.; **C.**A. 49–; APH.; B.; BI.; CH.; MO. 48–; **Cr.**U.; **Db.**; **Dn.**U.; E.U.; **Ex.**U.; **G.**U.; **H.**U.; **Ld.**P. 52–; U.; **Lv.**P.; **M.**D.; MS.; T.; U.; **N.**U.; **Nw.**A.; **O.**PH.; R.; **R.**D.; U.; **Rt.**; **Sa.**; **Sh.**U.; **Sw.**U.; **Y.**

969 **Advances** in **Research** and **Application.** New York. *Adv. Res. Appl.* [1943–]

    Advances in **Research** and **Applications, Solid State Physics.** *See* 50050.

970 **Advances** in **Space Science** and **Technology.** New York. *Adv. Space Sci. Technol.* [1959–] **L.**P.; SC.; **Bl.**U.; **G.**U; **Ld.**U.; **Y.**

971 **Advances** in **Spectroscopy.** New York. *Aav. Spectrosc.* [1959–] **L.**BM.; BM^N.; C.; P.; SC.; **Bl.**U.; **Br.**U. 59; **Cr.**U.; **Dn.**U. 61–; **G.**U.; **Ld.**U.; **M.**U.; **Sh.**SC.; **Y.**

972 **Advances** in **Steel Technology.** Geneva. *Adv. Steel Technol.* [1952–] **L.**P.

973 **Advances** in **Surgery.** New York. *Adv. Surg.* [1949] **L.**MD.; S.; UC.; UCH.; **Abd.**U.; **Br.**U.; E.A.; U.; **Ld.**U.; **Lv.**M.; **Nw.**A.; **O.**R.

    Advances in **Tuberculosis Research.** Basle. *See* 20250.

974 **Advances** in **Veterinary Science.** New York. *Adv. vet. Sci.* [1953–] **L.**AM.; MD.; TD.; V.; VC.; **Abd.**R.; **Bn.**U.; **Br.**U.; **C.**APH.; **E.**AB.; AR.; **Lv.**P.; **N.**U.; **Nw.**A.; **R.**U.; **W.**; **Y.**

975 **Advances** in **Virus Research.** New York. *Adv. Virus Res.* [1953–] **L.**AM.; BM.; CB.; LI. 57–; MC.; MD.; QM. 57–; SC.; TD.; U.; UC.; **Ba.**I.; **Bl.**U.; **Br.**U.; **C.**V.; **Db.**; **Dn.**U.; E.U.; **Ex.**U.; **G.**U.; **Ld.**U.; **Lv.**P. 54–; **Md.**H.; **N.**U.; **O.**BO.; **R.**U.; **Sh.**U.; **Y.**

976 **Advances** in **X-ray Analysis.** New York. *Adv. X-ray Analysis* [1960–] **L.**P.; **Y.**

    Advances in **Zootechnical Sciences.** Moscow. *See* 55676.

977 **Advancing Fronts** in **Chemistry.** New York. *Advg Fronts Chem.* [1945–] **L.**SC. 45–46.

978 **Advisory Bulletin. Agricultural Department University College, Wales.** Aberystwyth. *Advis. Bull. agric. Dep. Univ. Coll. Aberyst.* [1925–27] **L.**P. 25; **Abs.**A.; N.; U.; **C.**A.; **O.**R.; **Rt.**; **Sw.**U.

979 **Advisory Bulletin. War Food Production.** Welsh Plant Breeding Station. Aberystwyth. *Advis. Bull. War Fd Prod.* [1940–45] **L.**BM.; P.; **Abs.**A.; **Bl.**U. 40–41 imp.; **O.**R.; RE.; **Rt.**

980 **Advisory Circular. Rubber Research Institute of Ceylon.** Dartonfield. *Advis. Circ. Rubb. Res. Inst. Ceylon* [1951–] **L.**MY.; P.; **C.**A.; **O.**RE.; **Rt.**; Y. [*C. of:* 981]

981 **Advisory Circular. Rubber Research Scheme, Ceylon.** Peradeniya, etc. *Advis. Circ. Rubb. Res. Scheme Ceylon* [1930–50] **L.**MY. 43–50; P. imp.; **C.**A.; **O.**RE. 50 imp.; **Rt.**; Y. [*C. as:* 980]
    Advisory Group for **Aeronautical Research** and **Development.** *See:* **AGARD.**

982 **Advisory Leaflet. Board** of **Agriculture, Isle of Man.** Peel. *Advis. Leafl. Bd Agric. I.o.Man* **L.**P. 32; **C.**A. 32–.

982° **Advisory Leaflet. Department** of **Agriculture, Mauritius.** Port Louis. *Advis. Leafl. Dep. Agric. Maurit.* [1951–] **L.**BM.

983 **Advisory Leaflet. Department** of **Agriculture, Scotland.** Edinburgh. *Advis. Leafl. Dep. Agric. Scotl.* [1949–] **L.**AM.; BM.; P.; **Abd.**U.; **Bn.**U. 51–; **C.**A.; **Ld.**U.; **M.**P.; **O.**RE.; **Rt.**; Y. [*C. of:* 28270]

984 **Advisory Leaflet. Division** of **Plant Industry, Department** of **Agriculture** and **Stock, Queensland.** Brisbane. *Advis. Leafl. Div. Pl. Ind. Qd* [1937–] **L.**EB. (ent.); Y.

985 **Advisory Leaflet. Forest Service, Queensland.** Brisbane. *Advis. Leafl. Forest Serv. Qd* [1938–] **O.**F. 38–39.

986 **Advisory Leaflet. Ministry** of **Agriculture** and **Fisheries.** London. *Advis. Leafl. Minist. Agric. Fish.* [1930–] **L.**AM.; BM^N.; EB. (ent.) 31–; H. 35–; MA.; **Abs.**N.; **Bm.**P. 44–; U. 43–45 imp.; **Bn.**U.; **C.**A.; **E.**A. 31–; **M.**P.; **N.**U. 31– imp.; **O.**AEC. imp.; AP. (pest.); R.; RE.; **Rt.**; Y.

987 **Advisory Leaflet. Ministry** of **Works.** London. *Advis. Leafl. Minist. Wks* [1948–] **L.**P.; **Ld.**P.

988 **Advisory Leaflet. Royal Agricultural Society** of **England.** London. *Advis. Leafl. R. agric. Soc. Engl.* [1946–] Y.

989 **Advisory Leaflet. UPASI Scientific Department.** United Planters' Association of Southern India. *Adv. Leafl. UPASI scient. Dep.* [1951–] Y.

990 **Advisory Leaflet. West** of **Scotland Agricultural College.** Glasgow. *Advis. Leafl. W. Scotl. agric. Coll.* [1949–] **L.**BM.; **Br.**A. 57– imp.; **O.**R.; **Rt.** 50– imp.; Y.

991 **Advisory Note. Cement** and **Concrete Association.** London. *Advis. Note Cem. Concr. Ass.* [1957–] **L.**BM.; P.; **Ld.**P.; Y.

992 **Advisory Note. Food Investigation Board.** London. *Advis. Note. Fd Invest. Bd* [1950–] **L.**BM.; **Bm.**P.; **C.**A.; **Pl.**M.

993 **Advisory Pamphlet. Biological Branch, Department** of **Agriculture, Victoria.** Melbourne. *Advis. Pamphl. biol. Brch Dep. Agric. Vict.* [1942–]

994 **Advisory Report. Harper Adams Agricultural College.** Newport, Salop. *Advis. Rep. Harper Adams agric. Coll.* [1923–] **L.**AM. 26–39; BM. 26–; P. 26–39; **Abs.**A. 26–; **Bm.**P.; **C.**A. 26–; **Rt.**

995 **Aednik.** Revel. *Aednik*

996 **Ægir.** Mánaðarrit Fiskifélags Islands um fiskiveiðar og farmennsku. Reykjavik. *Ægir* **L.**AM.; **Abd.**M. 49; **Ld.**U. 05–38; **Lo.** 37–45: 58– imp.

997 **Aequatoria.** Coquilhatville. *Aequatoria* **L.**AN. 47–.

998 **Aera.** American Electric Railway Association. New York. *Aera* [1912–32] [*C. of:* 25508]

999 **Aereo.** Roma. *Aereo* [1922–23]

1000 **Aerial.** Chelmsford. *Aerial* [1953–] **L.**AV.; BM.; P. (curr.); **F.**A.; Y.

1001 **Aerial Age.** New York. [22–23] *Aerial Age* **L.**P. [*C. of:* 1002]

1002 **Aerial Age Weekly.** New York. *Aerial Age Wkly* [1915–22] **L.**AV. 20–22; P. 19–22. [*C. as:* 1001]

1003 **Aerial Forest Survey Research Note.** Ottawa. *Aerial Forest Surv. Res. Note, Ottawa* [1942] **O.**F.

1004 **Aerial League Bulletin.** London. *Aerial Leag. Bull.* **L.**BM. 19*. [*C. as:* 1541]

1005 **Aerial Survey Review.** London. *Aerial Surv. Rev.* [1952–] **L.**K. 57–; P. (curr.); **Rt.**

1006 **Aerial Year Book.** London. *Aerial Yb.* **M.**P. 20–; **O.**B. 20.

1007 **Aëro.** Budapest. *Aëro, Bpest*

1008 **Aero.** Helsingfors. *Aero, Helsingf.* [1921–]

1009 **Aero.** London. *Aero, Lond.* [1909–13] **L.**BM.; P.; SC.; **Db.** 09–12; **G.**M. 12–13; **M.**P. 10–11 imp.; **O.**B.

1010 **Aéro.** Marseille. *Aéro, Marseille*

1011 **Aero.** München. *Aero, Münch.* [1950–] **L.**P. 57–; Y.

1012 **Aéro.** Paris. *Aéro, Paris* [1908–35]

1013 **Aero** and **Airways.** London. *Aero Airways* [1935] **L.**BM.; P. [*C. of:* 1625]

1014 **Aéro-** i **avtomobil'naya zhizn'.** S. Peterburg. Аэро и автомобильная жизнь. *Aero- i avto. Zhizn'*

1014° **Aero bilten.** Beograd. *Aero Bilt.* [1953–] **L.**BM.

1015 **Aero Club** of **America Bulletin.** New York. *Aero. Club Am. Bull.* [1909–11] [*C. as:* 19730]

1016 **Aero Digest** (including Aviation Engineering). New York. *Aero Dig.* [1924–56] **L.**AV.; BM. 36–56; P. 33–56; **F.**A. 35–39: 45–56; **Lv.**P. 50: 53–56. [*C. of:* 1067]

1017 **Aero Equipment Review.** Minneapolis. *Aero Equip. Rev.* [1936–39]

1018 **Aero Field.** Birmingham. *Aero Fld* [1926–] **L.**BM. 26–30; **Abs.**N.; **Bm.**P.; U. 26–29; **E.**A. 26–30; **O.**B.

1019 **Aéro France.** Paris. *Aéro Fr.* [1951–] **L.**AV. 60–; Y.

1020 **Aero Mechanic.** Seattle. *Aero Mechanic* [1939–]

1021 **A****ro Mechanics.** New York. *Aero Mech.* [1929–30] [*C. as:* 1022]

1021° **Aero mundial.** *Aero mund.* English edition. **L.**AV. 54–57.

1022 **Aero News** and **Mechanics.** New York. *Aero News Mech.* [1930] [*C. of:* 1021; *C. in:* 49041]

1023 **Aero Research Aircraft Bulletin.** Duxford. *Aero Res. Aircr. Bull.* [1957–] **Br.**U.

1024 **Aero Research Technical Notes.** Duxford. *Aero Res. tech. Notes* [1943–58] **L**.BM.; LE.; NP.; P.; SC.; **Bm**.P.; **Fr.** 56–58; **Lc**.A. 57–58; **Lv**.P. 53–58; **M**.C.; P.; **N**.U.; **Sy**.R. [*C. as:* 14015]

Aero Space Engineering. Easton. *See* 1105.

1025 **Aero World.** New York. *Aero Wld* [1916–17]

1026 **Aerocraft.** London. *Aerocraft* [1909–10] **L**.BM. imp.; P.

1027 **Aerodrome Abstracts.** Road Research Board. West Drayton. *Aerodrome Abstr.* [1942–48] **L**.BA. 43–48; P.; **Bm**.P.; **G**.U.; **M**.P.; **O**.R. 43–45.

1028 **Aerodynamics Note.** Melbourne. *Aerodyn. Note* **L**.P. 42–; **Br**.U. 53–; **Y.**

Aerodynamics Reports. Aeronautical Research Laboratories, Melbourne. *See* 42634.

1029 **Aerodynamics Technical Memorandum.** Melbourne. *Aerodyn. tech. Memor.* **L**.P. 55–.

1030 **Aerologiai havi jelentés.** Budapest. *Aerol. Havi Jel.* **L**.MO. 38–49*.

1031 **Aerological Bulletin.** Meteorological and Geophysics Institute. Djakarta. *Aerol. Bull., Djakarta* [1957–] **L**.MO.; **G**.U.

1032 **Aerological Data** of **Darien.** Tokyo. *Aerol. Data Darien* **L**.MO. 44–45.

1033 **Aerological Data** of **Japan.** Tokyo. *Aerol. Data Japan* **L**.MO. 47–; **Y.**

1034 **Aerological Data** of **Korea.** Tokyo. *Aerol. Data Korea* **L**.MO. 42–44.

1035 **Aerological Data** of **Manchuria.** Tokyo. *Aerol. Data Manchuria* **L**.MO. 42–44.

Aerological Monthly Weather Report of **Hungary.** *See* 1030.

1036 **Aerological Summary, Southern Rhodesia.** Salisbury. *Aerol. Summ. South. Rhod.* **L**.MO. 36–39.

Aerologische Beobachtungen. Berlin. *See* 16902.

1037 **Aerologische Beobachtungen** des **Österreichischen Flugwetterdienstes.** Wien. *Aerol. Beob. öst. FlugwettDienst.* **L**.MO. 30–38; **E**.M. 30–38.

1038 **Aerologische Berichte. Aeronautisches Observatorium, Lindenberg.** Berlin. *Aerol. Ber., Berl.* **L**.MO. 26–35; **E**.M. 26–35. [*C. in:* 16902]

1039 **Aerologische Berichte. Zentralanstalt** für **Meteorologie** und **Geodynamik.** Wien. *Aerol. Ber., Wien* **L**.MO. 52–; **Y.**

1040 **Aerologische Monatsübersicht.** Preussisches Aeronautisches Observatorium, Lindenberg. Berlin. *Aerol. Mübers.* **L**.MO. 33–35. [*C. of:* 27856]

1041 **Aërologische waarnemingen.** Station Ukkel. *Aërol. Waarn.*

Aerologischer Monatsbericht von **Ungarn.** *See* 1030.

1042 **Aerologiska iakttagelser** i **Göteborg-Torslands.** Stockholm. *Aerol. Iakttag. Göteborg* **L**.MO. 45–.

1043 **Aerologiska iakttagelser** i **Östersund-Frösön.** Stockholm. *Aerol. Iakttag. Östersund* **L**.MO. 49–.

Aerologiska iakttagelser, Stockholm. *See* 4902.

1044 **Aerologiska iakktagelser** i **Stockholm-Bromma.** Stockholm. *Aerol Iakttag. Stockh.-Bromma* **L**.MO. 46–.

1045 **Aerologiska observationer** i **Finland.** Helsingfors. *Aerol. Obsnr Finl.* **L**.MO. 52–.

1046 **Aerølogiske observationer** i **Danmark.** København. *Aerøl. Obsnr Danm.* **L**.MO. 52–.

1047 **Aerølogiske observationer** i **Grønland.** København. *Aerøl. Obsnr Grønl.* **L**.MO. 53–.

1048 **Aerologist.** Chicago. *Aerologist* **L**.P. 25–34; TD. 32–35. [*C. in:* 22009]

1049 **Aerology Bulletin.** Navy Department. Washington. *Aerology Bull., Wash.* **L**.MO. 47–54 imp.

1050 **Aerology Series.** Navy Department. Washington. *Aerology Ser., Wash.* **L**.MO. 43–46.

1051 **Aéro-manuel.** Répertoire sportif, technique et commercial de l'aéronautique. Paris. *Aéro-Manuel* [1911–14]

1052 **Aéro-mécanique.** Bruxelles. *Aéro-Méc.* **L**.P. 08–14*.

1053 **Aeromedica acta.** Soesterberg. *Aeromed. Acta*

1054 **Aeromodeller.** London. *Aeromodeller* [1935–] **L**.AV. 58–; BM.; P. 46–; SC.; **C**.UL.; **E**.A.; **G**.M. 45–; **O**.R.; **Sh**.P. (5 yr.); **Y.**

1055 **Aëronauta.** Budapest. *Aëronauta*

1056 **Aéronaute.** Paris. *Aéronaute* **L**.BM. 85–07; P. 68–11*; SC. 68–06. [*C. in:* 52480]

1057 **Aeronautic Review.** Washington. *Aeronautic Rev.* [1928–30] [*C. of:* and *Rec. as:* 34087]

1058 **Aeronautica.** Arnhem. *Aeronautica, Arnhem* [1927–] **L**.AV. 27–29.

1059 **Aeronautica.** Buenos Aires. *Aeronautica, B. Aires* **L**.AV. 46.

1060 **Aeronautica.** Milano. *Aeronautica, Milano* [1927–32]

1061 **Aeronautica.** Santiago de Chile. *Aeronautica, Santiago* **L**.AV. 44–46.

1062 **Aeronautica.** Valencia. *Aeronautica, Valencia* [1937–]

1063 **Aeronautica.** Washington. *Aeronautica, Wash.* [1949–] **L**.AV. 52–55; **Br**.U. 49–56; **F**.A.

1064 **Aeronautica argentina.** Cordoba. *Aeronautica argent.* [1934–]

1065 **Aeronautical Abstract Cards.** Amsterdam. *Aeronaut. Abstr. Cards* [1958–] **L**.AV.

1066 **Aeronautical Classics.** London. *Aeronaut. Class.* [1910–11] **L**.BM.; P.; **E**.R.

1067 **Aeronautical Digest.** New York. *Aeronaut. Dig.* [1922–24] **L**.AV. [*C. as:* 1016]

1068 **Aeronautical Engineering.** London. *Aeronaut. Engng, Lond.* **L**.P. 29–31. [*Supplement to* 1092]

1069 **Aeronautical Engineering.** New York. *Aeronaut. Engng, N.Y.* [1929–33] **L**.AV.; P.; UC. 31–33.

1070 **Aeronautical Engineering Catalog.** New York. *Aeronaut. Engng Cat.* [1944–58] **L**.P. 45–58 imp. [*C. as:* 1107]

1071 **Aeronautical Engineering Index.** New York. *Aeronaut. Engng Index* [1947–59] **L**.AV.; P. 48–59; **Br**.U.; **F**.A.; **M**.U. 56. [*C. as:* 1108]

1072 **Aeronautical Engineering Review.** New York, Easton Pa. *Aeronaut. Engng Rev.* [1942–58] **L**.AV. 46–58; BM.; P.; QM. 52–58; SC.; **Bm**.T. 51–58; **Br**.U.; **C**.ENG. 56–58; **F**.A. 42: 47–58; **G**.T. 54–58; **Ld**.U.; **M**.T. [*C. of:* 25423; *C. as:* 1105]

1073 **Aeronautical Industry.** East Stroudsburg, Pa. *Aeronaut. Ind.* [1930–31]   [*C. of:* 1564; *C. in:* 1622]

1074 **Aeronautical Journal.** London. *Aeronaut. J.* [1897–22] **L.**AV.; BM.; MO. 04–10: 12–13: 18–22; P.; UC. 20–22; **Abs.**N. 12–22; **Bl.**U. 19–22; **Bm.**P. 22; U. 18–22; **Bn.**U. 19-22 imp.; **Br.**P. 12–21; U. 16: 18–22; **C.**UL. 01–22; **Db.** 09–22; **E.**A. 01–22; R. 13–22; U. 19–22; **F.**A. 10–22; **G.**E. 97–16; U. imp.; **Ld.**U. 18–22; **Lv.**U. 19–22 imp.; **M.**P. 97–11; U. 19–22; **O.**R.; **Sa.** 19–22; **Sh.**IO. 16–22.   [*C. as:* 26793]

1075 **Aeronautical News Bulletin.** Amsterdam. *Aeronaut. News Bull.* [1958–] **L.**AV.

1076 **Aeronautical Quarterly.** London. *Aeronaut. Q.* [1949–] **L.**AV.; BM.; P.; QM.; SC.; **Abd.**U.; **Bl.**U. 57–; **Bm.**P.; U.; **Bn.**U.; **Br.**U.; **Co.**T.; **Cr.**U.; **Db.**; **E.**U. 57–; **Ex.**U.; **F.**A.; **G.**M.; U.; **Lv.**P. 52–; **M.**P.; U.; **N.**U. 57–; **Nw.**A.; **Sa.** imp.; **Sh.**U.; **Sw.**U. 57–; **Y.**

1077 **Aeronautical Reader's Guide.** Institute of the Aeronautical Sciences. New York. *Aeronaut. Read. Guide* [1940–41]   [*C. in:* 25422]

1078 **Aeronautical Report.** National Research Council. Ottawa. *Aeronaut. Rep., Ottawa* [1959–] **L.**P.; **Y.**   [*C. of:* 27937]

1079 **Aeronautical Research Report.** Council for Scientific and Industrial Research, Australia. Melbourne. *Aeronaut. Res. Rep., Melb.* [1948–49] **L.**BM.; P.; **Abs.**U.; **Bl.**U.; **Bn.**U.; **Lv.**P.; **M.**P.; U. imp.; **O.**R.   [*C. of: and Rec. as:* 42597]

Aeronautical Review. Easton. *See* 25423.

1080 **Aeronautical World.** Glanville, Ohio. *Aeronaut. Wld, Glanville* **L.**P. 02–03*.

1081 **Aeronautical World.** Whittier, Calif. *Aeronaut. Wld, Whittier* [1928–31] **L.**P. 29–30.

1082 **Aeronautics.** London. *Aeronautics, Lond.* [1907–21] **L.**AV.; BM. 08–21 imp.; P.; RI. 09–14; SC. imp.; **Abs.**N. 12–21; **Bm.**P.; **Br.**P. 12–21; **Co.**T. 18–21; **Db.**; **E.**A. 08–15 imp.; **Lv.**P. 09–21; U. 13–21; **O.**B. 08–21.

1083 **Aeronautics.** London. *Aeronautics, Lond.* [1939–] **L.**AV.; BM.; MO. (I yr); P.; SC.; **Abs.**N.; **Bl.**U. 58–; **Br.**U. 46–; **Cr.**P. (5 yr.); **Db.** 46–; **E.**A.; T. imp.; **F.**A. 46–; **G.**M. 43–; **M.**P. 41–; **O.**B.; **Sh.**IO. (5 yr.); **Y.** [–62*]

1084 **Aeronautics.** New York. *Aeronautics, N.Y.* [1908–15] **L.**P.   [*C. of:* 2076; *C. in:* 1082]

1085 **Aeronautics Bulletin.** Washington. *Aeronautics Bull., Wash.* **L.**BM. 31–.

1086 **Aeronautics Bulletin.** Department of Commerce, etc., Philippine Is. Manila. *Aeronautics Bull., Manila* [1932–] **L.**P. 32–37 imp.

1087 **Aéronautique.** Paris. *Aéronautique* [1919–40] **L.**AV.; BM.; P.; **Bm.**U. 24–40 imp.

1088 **Aeronave.** Buenos Aires. *Aeronave* **L.**AV. 47–49.

1089 **Aérophile.** Paris. *Aérophile* [1893–] **L.**AV. 93–38; BM.; P. 10–47 imp.; SC.

1090 **Aerophone** and **Auto Age.** Montreal. *Aerophone Auto Age*

1091 **Aeropilot.** London. *Aeropilot* [1934–37] **O.**B.

1092 **Aeroplane.** London. *Aeroplane* [1911–58] **L.**AV. 34–58; BM.; P. 14–58; SC. 19–58; **Abs.**N. 40–58; **Bl.**U. 37–58 imp.; **Bm.**U. 28–33: 47–58; **Bra.**P. 55–58; **Db.** 13–14; **Dn.**U. 19–58; **E.**A.; T. 40–58; **F.**A.; **G.**M. 23–58; **Lv.**P. 41–58; **M.**P. 38–58; U. 21–22; **Nw.**A. 48–58; **O.**B. 12–58; **Sh.**IO. 41–58; **Y.**   [*C. as:* 1093]

1093 **Aeroplane** and **Astronautics.** London. *Aeropl. Astronaut.* [1959–] **L.**AV.; BM.; P.; SC.; **Abs.**N.; **Bl.**U.; **Bm.**U.; **Br.**P (2 yr.); U. 60–; **Bra.**P.; **Dn.**U.; **E.**A.; T.; **F.**A.; **G.**M.; **Li.**M. (I yr.); **Lv.**P.; **M.**P.; **Ma.**T.; **Nw.**A.; **O.**B.; **Sh.**P.; **Sil.**; **Y.**   [*C. of:* 1092]

1094 **Aeroplane Production Year Book.** London. *Aeropl. Prod. Yb.* [1943–47] **L.**BM.; **Lv.**P. 43–45; **O.**R.   [*C. as:* 1581]

1095 **Aeroplane Spotter.** London. *Aeropl. Spotter* [1941–48] **L.**BM.; P.; **Bl.**U. 42–48 imp.; **Bm.**P.; **G.**M. imp.; **M.**P. 41–43 imp.; **O.**B.

1096 **Aeroplane Supplement.** Gloster Aircraft Co. London. *Aeropl. Suppl.* **L.**SC. 28.

1097 **Aéroplanes.** Paris. *Aéroplanes* **L.**P. 10–12*.

1098 **Aeroporika nea** (kai **astronautike**). Athenais. Αεροπορικα νέα (και αστροναυτικη). *Aeropor. nea* [1953–] **L.**AV. 53–60 imp.; **Y.**

1099 **Aéro-revue.** Lyon. *Aéro-Revue, Lyon* [1907–08]
Aéro-revue. Zürich. *See* 48905.
Aéro-revue suisse. *See* 48905.

1100 **Aerosettimana.** Milan. *Aerosettimana* **L.**BM. 53–; P. (curr.); **Y.** [*Supplement to:* 1663]

1101 **Aerosol Age.** New York, Paterson N.J. *Aerosol Age* [1956–] **L.**P. 59–; **Lh.**P. 57–; **Y.**

1102 **Aerosol Bulletin.** Zürich. *Aerosol Bull.* [1959–] **L.**P.

1103 **Aerosol News.** Wilmington. *Aerosol News* [1956–] **L.**P. 58–.

1104 **Aerospace Accident** and **Maintenance Review.** Washington. *Aerospace Accid. Maint. Rev.* [1960–] **L.**AV.; P.; **Y.**   [*C. of:* 1575]

1105 **Aero/Space Engineering.** Easton, New York. *Aero/Space Engng* [1958–60] **L.**AV.; BM.; P.; QM.; **Br.**U.; **G.**T.; **Ld.**U.; **Lv.**P.; **M.**T.; **Y.**   [*C. of:* 1072; *C. as:* 1106]

1106 **Aerospace Engineering.** Easton. *Aerospace Engng* [1960–] **L.**AV.; BM.; P.; QM.; **Br.**U.; **G.**T.; **Ld.**U.; **Lv.**P.; **M.**T.; **Y.**   [*C. of:* 1105]

1107 **Aero/Space Engineering Catalog.** New York. *Aero/Space Engng Cat.* [1959–] **L.**P.   [*C. of:* 1070]

1108 **Aerospace Engineering Index.** New York. *Aerospace Engng Index* [1960–] **L.**P.   [*C. of:* 1071]

1108° **Aerospace Management.** Philadelphia. *Aerospace Mgmt* [1960–] **L.**AV.; **Y.**   [*C. of:* 1590]

1109 **Aerospace Medicine.** Washington. *Aerospace Med.* [1959–] **L.**AV.; MA.; MD.; S.; SC.; **Abd.**U.; **Bm.**U.; **C.**UL.; **E.**U.; **M.**MS.; **Y.**   [*C. of:* 25644]

1110 **Aerospace Medicine** and **Biology.** An annotated bibliography. Washington. *Aerospace Med. Biol.* [1954–] **L.**BM.; P.; SC.   [*C. of:* 5566]

1110° **Aerospace Safety.** *Aerospace Saf.* **L.**AV. 61–.

1111 **Aerosphere.** New York. *Aerosphere* **Bm.**P. 39: 41–43.

1112 **Aérostation.** Paris. *Aérostation* [1904–14]

1113 **Aerosul.** Lisboa. *Aerosul* **L.**AV. 44.

1114 **Aérotechnique.** Paris. *Aérotechnique* [1923–38] **L.**P.   [*C. in:* 48995]

1115 **Aerotecnica.** Milano. *Aerotecnica, Milano* [1925–31] **L.**P. imp.

1116 **Aerotecnica.** Roma. *Aerotecnica, Roma* [1925–] **L.**AV. imp.; BM. 34–; P.; SC. 31–39: 51–; **F.**A. 46–; **Y.** [*C. of:* 5169]

1117 **Aerovox Research Worker.** Brooklyn, N.Y. *Aerovox Res. Wkr* [1928–] **L.**P. 40–.

1118 **Ärzteblatt für das Sudetenland.** Aussig. *Ärztebl. Sudetenl.* [1938–39] [*C. of:* 1131]

1119 **Ärzteblatt für Südwestdeutschland.** Stuttgart. *Ärztebl. Südwestdtl.* [1938–] [*C. of:* 1120]

1120 **Ärzteblatt** für **Württemberg.** Stuttgart. *Ärztebl. Württ.* [1934–38] [*C. of:* 30580; *C. as:* 1119]

1121 **Ärztliche Forschung.** Bad Wörishafen. *Ärztl. Forsch.* [1947–] **L.**MA.; MD. 52–; S. 52–56 imp.; **G.**U. 52–; **Y.**

1122 **Ärztliche Korrespondenz.** Berlin, Wien. *Ärztl. Korr.* **L.**MA. 36–37 imp.; MD. 37–38.

1123 **Ärztliche Laboratorium.** Wurzburg. *Ärztl. Lab.*

1124 **Ärztliche Mission.** Gütersloh. *Ärztl. Mission* [1906–]

1125 **Ärztliche Mitteilungen.** Leipzig. *Ärztl. Mitt., Lpz.* [1899–28]

1126 **Ärztliche Mitteilungen.** Strassburg. *Ärztl. Mitt., Strassb.*

1127 **Ärztliche Monatshefte.** Schwarzenburg. *Ärztl. Mh.* **L.**MD. 50 imp.

1128 **Ärztliche Monatshefte** für **berufliche Fortbildung.** Bern. *Ärztl. Mh. berufl. Fortbild.* **L.**MA. 47–; MD. 59–; **Br.**U. 47–.

1129 **Ärztliche Monatsschrift.** Berlin. *Ärztl. Mschr., Berl.* [1924–29]

1130 **Ärztliche Monatsschrift.** Leipzig. *Ärztl. Mschr., Lpz.* [1898–02]

1131 **Ärztliche Nachrichten.** Prag. *Ärztl. Nachr.* [1915–38] **L.**MA. 37 imp. [*C. as:* 1118]

1132 **Ärztliche Praxis.** Leipzig. *Ärztl. Prax., Lpz.* [1898–07] [*C. as:* 58463]

1133 **Ärztliche Praxis.** Wien. *Ärztl. Prax., Wien* [1927–] **L.**MD. 33–44; **Y.**

1134 **Ärztliche Psychologie.** Leipzig. *Ärztl. Psychol.* **C.**PS. 14–.

1135 **Ärztliche Rundschau.** München. *Ärztl. Rdsch.* [1891–36]

1136 **Ärztliche Sachverständigenzeitung.** Berlin. *Ärztl. SachverstZtg* [1895–] **L.**S. 95–04; **E.**U. 08–13.
Ärztliche Sammelblätter. *See* 1137.

1137 **Ärztliche Sammelmappe.** Berlin. *Ärztl. Sammelmappe* [1923–25] [*C. of:* 30567; *C. as:* 42474]

1138 **Ärztliche Standeszeitung.** Wien. *Ärztl. Standesztg* [1910–24] [*C. of:* 22038]

1139 **Ärztliche Vierteljahrsrundschau.** Bonn. *Ärztl. VjrRdsch.*

1140 **Ärztliche Wochenschrift.** Berlin. *Ärztl. Wschr.* [1946–] **L.**MA.; MC.; MD.; P.; **C.**UL.; **E.**A.; **O.**R.

1141 **Ärztliche Zeitung.** Berlin. *Ärztl. Ztg* [1937–] [*C. of:* 16653]

1142 **Ärztliche Zentral-Zeitung.** Wien. *Ärztl. Zent-Ztg*

1143 **Ärztlicher Bericht** des **K. K. Allgemeinen Krankenhauses** zu **Prag.** *Ärztl. Ber. K. K. allg. Krankenh. Prag* [*C. as:* 25002]

1144 **Ärztlicher Praktiker.** Frankfurt. *Ärztl. Praktr* [1930–]

1145 **Ärztlicher Zentralanzeiger.** Hamburg. *Ärztl. ZentAnz.* [1885–22]

1146 **Ärztliches Jahrbuch.** Frankfurt a. M. *Ärztl. Jb.*

1147 **Ärztliches Jahrbuch** für **Österreich.** Wien. *Ärztl. Jb. Öst.* **L.**MD. 22–.

1148 **Ärztliches Jahrbuch** von **Ungarn.** Budapest. *Ärztl. Jb. Ung.*

1149 **Ärztliches Korrespondenzblatt** für **Niedersachsen.** Hannover. *Ärztl. KorrBl. Niedersachsen*

1150 **Ärztliches Taschenbuch** der **Wiener medizinischen Wochenschrift.** Wien. *Ärztl. Taschenb. Wien. med. Wschr.* **L.**MD. 36–. [*C. of:* 30557]

1151 **Ärztliches Vereinsblatt** für **Deutschland.** Leipzig. *Ärztl. Vereinsbl. Dtl.*
Ärztlich-pharmazeutische Korrespondenz. *See* 30561.

1152 **Æsculap.** Berlin. *Æsculap., Berl.* [1902–05]

1153 **Aesculap.** Budapest. *Aesculap, Bpest*

1154 **Æsculape.** Paris. *Æsculape* [1911–] **L.**BM. 11–40: 50–; MA. 50–; MD. 23–40; S. 23–40; **Br.**U. 23–26 imp.; **C.**PA. 54–; **Cr.**MD. 26–28 imp.; **Db.** 23–27; **Dn.**U. 11–28 imp.

1155 **Aesculapian.** Brooklyn, N.Y. *Aesculapian, Brooklyn* [1908–09] **L.**S.; **M.**MS.; **O.**B. [*C. of:* 30266; *C. as:* 10916]

1156 **Aesculapian.** New Orleans. *Aesculapian, New Orl.*

1157 **Ätherische Öle, Riechstoffe, Parfümerien, Essenzen** und **Aromen.** Hannover. *Äther. Öle* [1951–54] **L.**C. 52–54. [*C. as:* 47774]

1158 **Afinidad.** Organo de la Asociación de químicos. Barcelona. *Afinidad* **L.**C. 45– imp.; P. 56–; **Y.**

1159 **Afra.** Cahiers d'entomologie. Paris. *Afra* [1930–36] **L.**BMᴺ.; E.

1160 **Africa médica.** Lisboa. *Africa méd.* [1934–] **L.**TD. 34–47.

1161 **African Abstracts:** a quarterly review of ethnographic, etc., studies. London. *Afr. Abstr.* [1950–] **L.**AN.; BM.; HO.; **E.**U.; **G.**U.; **Nw.**A.; **O.**B.

1162 **African Air Review.** Johannesburg. *Afr. Air Rev.* [1946–] **L.**BM.

1162ᶜ **African Architect.** Johannesburg. *Afr. Archit.* [1911–14] **L.**BM.

1162ᵉ **African Beekeeping.** Cape Town. *Afr. Beekeep.* [1958–]

1162ᵍ **African Bottling Industries.** Johannesburg. *Afr. Bottl. Inds* [1950–] **L.**BM.

1163 **African Chemist** and **Druggist.** Johannesburg. *Afr. Chem. Drugg.* [1921–35] **L.**MA. 29–34. [*C. in:* 50174]

1164 **African Engineering.** London. *Afr. Engng* [1905–14] **L.**BM.; **O.**R. 06–14.

1165 **African Industries.** London. *Afr. Inds* [1921–30] **L.**BM.; **O.**F. 24–30.

1166 **African Manual** on **Mining,** etc. London. *Afr. Manual Min.* **L.**BM. 27–49; MI. 49; **Bm.**P. 34–35; **C.**UL. 28–39; **G.**M. 27–29: 34–39: 48–49; **Lv.**P. 38–39: 48–; **O.**RH. 28–39.

1166ᵃ **African Oxygen.** Johannesburg. *Afr. Oxyg.* [1955–] **L.**BM. [*C. of:* 57295ᵃ]

1167 **African Oxygen** and **Acetylene Journal.** Germiston. *Afr. Oxyg. Acet. J.* [1934–38] **L.**BM. [*C. as:* 36655ᵃ]

1167ᶜ **African Roads** and **Transport.** Johannesburg. *Afr. Rds Transp.* [1942–] **L.**BM. 47–.
African Soils. *See* 50054.

1168 **African Studies.** Johannesburg. *Afr. Stud.* [1942–] **L.**AN.; BM.; **Bl.**U. 58–; **Bm.**U.; **E.**U. 49–; **Nw.**A. 50–; **Sh.**U. 58–; **Y.** [*C. of:* 5755]

1169 **African Sugar** and **Cotton Journal.** Durban. *Afr. Sug. Cott. J.* [1927] **L.**TP. [*C. of:* 1170 and 50131]

1170 **African Sugar** and **Cotton Planter.** *Afr. Sug. Cott. Plr* [1924–27] [*C. of:* 34085; *C. as:* 1169]

1171 **African Violet.** African Violet Society of Great Britain. *Afr. Violet* [1954–] **L.**BM.; HS. 54–55.

1172 **African Violet Magazine.** Knoxville. *Afr. Violet Mag.* [1947–] **L.**HS. 52–; K. 53.

1173 **African Wild Life.** Johannesburg. *Afr. wild Life* [1946–] **L.**BM.; BMᴺ.; Z.; **Y.**

1173ᶜ **African Wool, Cotton** and **Textile Industries.** *Afr. Wool Cott. Text. Inds* [1952–] **L.**BM.
Africander Cattle Journal. *See* 1173ᶜ.
Africa-Tervuren. *See* 15427ᶜ.

1173ᵉ **Afrikanerbees joernaal.** Bloemfontein. *AfrikBees J.* [1953–] **L.**BM.

1174 **Afrique française chirurgicale.** Alger. *Afr. fr. chir.* [1943–] **L.**MA.; MD. 44– imp.; S.; **Br.**U. 46– imp.; **Dn.**U. 57–; **M.**MS. 46– imp.

1175 **Afrique médicale.** Alger. *Afr. méd.* [1905–14] [*C. of:* 47395]

1176 **Afrique minière.** Paris. *Afr. min.*

1177 **Aga nyheter.** Lidingö. *Aga Nyhet.* **L.**P. 45–58.
Aga-Baltic nyheter. *See* 1177.

1178 **Âge de l'aluminium.** Paris. *Âge Alumin.*

1179 **Âge de fer.** Paris. *Âge Fer*

1180 **Âge nucléaire.** Paris. *Âge nucl.* [1956–58] **L.**P.; **M.**U. 57–58. [*C. in:* 18048]
Âge préhistorique. Brunn. *See* 38543.

1181 **Age of Steel.** St. Louis, Mo. *Age Steel* [1857–02] [*C. as:* 24172]

1182 **Agenda** and **Abstracts** of the **Scientific Meetings** of the **Zoological Society** of **London.** *Agenda Abstr. scient. Mtgs zool. Soc. Lond.* [1939–] **L.**SC.; Z. [*Suspended* 1940–44; *C. of:* 39835 Sect. C]

1183 **Agenda chimistului.** Bucureşti. *Agenda chim.* [1936–]

1184 **Ager.** Revista agropecuaria. Madrid. *Ager* **Hu.**G. 47–49 imp.

1185 **Agfa Diamond.** New York. *Agfa Diam.* [1936–42] **L.**PG. 37–42 imp. [*C. as:* 3534]

1186 **Agfa Photoblätter.** Berlin. *Agfa Photobl.* [1924–33] **L.**P. 30–33; PG. 30–33 imp. [*C. as:* 37599]

1187 **Agfa Röntgenblätter.** Berlin. *Agfa RöntgBl.* [1931–40] **L.**P. 31–39; PG. 39.

1188 **Agfa X-ray Journal.** Berlin. *Agfa X-ray J.* **L.**P. 35–39.

1189 **Aggiornamenti** di **fisiologia.** Firenze. *Aggiorn. Fisiol.* [1950–] **E.**U. [*Supplement to:* 4400]

1190 **Aggiornamenti** sulle **malattie** da **infezione.** Roma. *Aggiorn. Mal. Infez.* [1955–] **L.**MA.; MD.; TD.; **Nw.**A.

1191 **Aggiornamenti** di **terapia oftalmologica.** Pisa. *Aggiorn. Ter. oftal.* [1949–] **L.**MD.; OP.

1192 **Aggiornamento pediatrico.** Roma. *Aggiorn. pediat.* [1950–] **L.**MA

1193 **Aging.** Washington. *Aging* [1951–] **L.**MD. imp.; SH. (1 yr.); TD. 53– imp.; **G.**F. 53– imp.; **Y.**

1194 **Agra Medical College Journal.** Agra. *Agra med. Coll. J.* [1948–]

1195 **Agra University Journal** of **Research: Science.** Agra. *Agra Univ. J. Res.* [1952–] **L.**BM.; BMᴺ.; C. 53–; L. 53–; P.; SC.; U.; **Abs.**N. 54–; **Bl.**U. 53–; **Bm.**U. 54–; **C.**A. 54–; P.; UL.; **Db.** 53–; **E.**R. 53–; U. 54–; **G.**U.; **Ld.**U. 55–; **Y.**

1196 **Agrarfrage** und die **gegenwärtige Bauernbewegung.** Moskau. *Agrarfrage* [1935–] **L.**AM.; BM.; **Abs.**N.; **C.**A. [*C. of:* 1209]
Agrarian and **Agricultural Index.** Moscow. *See* 22866.

1197 **Agrarien.** Clemson. *Agrarien* [1938–]

1198 **Agrarmeteorologische Bibliographie.** Deutscher Wetterdienst. Bad Kissingen. *Agrarmet. Biblphie* [1949–53] **L.**MO.; P. 50–53; **E.**R. 50–53. [*C. as:* 1201]

1199 **Agrarmeteorologische Monatsübersicht.** Meteorologisches Amt für N.W. Deutschland. Hamburg. *Agrarmet. Mübers, Hamburg* [1947–48] **L.**MO. [*C. in:* 57749]

1200 **Agrarmeteorologischer Literaturbericht.** Deutscher Wetterdienst. Bad Kissingen. *Agrarmet. Lit.Ber.* [1954–] **L.**MO. 54–56; **Rt.** (1 yr)

1201 **Agrarmeteorologischer Monatsbericht.** Agrarmeteorologische Versuchs- und Beratungsstelle, Deutscher Wetterdienst. Giessen. *Agrarmet. Mber., Giessen* [1953–] **L.**MO. 53–55; P.; **E.**R. [*C. of:* 1198]

1202 **Agrarmeteorologischer Monatsbericht** für die **französische Südzone.** Seelbach bei Lahr. *Agrarmet. Mber. fr. Südzone* **L.**MO. 48.

1203 **Agrarmeteorologischer Monatsbericht** für den **Rheingau.** Geisenheim. *Agrarmet. Mber. Rheingau* [1953–] **L.**MO. 53–55. [*C. of:* 33088]

1204 **Agrarmeteorologischer Monatsbericht, Trier.** *Agrarmet. Mber. Trier* [1954–58] **L.**MO. [*C. of:* 57468ᶜ; *C. in:* 33123]

1205 **Agrarmeteorologischer** und **phänologischer Jahresbericht.** Badischer Landeswetterdienst. Freiburg. *Agrarmet. phänol. Jb., Freiburg* **L.**MO. 48–49.

1206 **Agrarmeteorologischer Witterungsbericht. Französischer Besatzungsgebiet.** Seelbach. *Agrarmet. WittBer. fr. BesatzGeb.* **L.**MO. 47–48.

1207 **Agrarnaya literatura SSSR.** Moskva. Аграрная литература СССР. *Agrar. Lit. SSSR* [1929–31] [*C. of:* 18874 and 49468]

1208 **Agrárni archiv.** Praha. *Agrárni Arch.* [*C. as:* 13409]

1209 **Agrar-Probleme.** Institut agraire international. Moskau. *Agrar-Probl.* [1928–34] **L.**AM. imp.; BM. 32–34; **Abs.**A. 28–31; N. 30–34; **C.**A. [*C. as:* 1196]

1210 **Agrartörténeti szemle.** Budapest. *Agrartört. Szle* [1957–] **L.**AM.

1210ᵃ **Agrártudomány.** Budapest. *Agrártudományi* [1949–] **L.**BM. 51–.

1211 **Agrártudományi egyetem Agrárközgazdasági kar kiadványai.** Budapest. *Agrártud. Egyet. agrárközg. Kar Kiad.* [1955–] **Rt.** 55; **Y.**

1212 **Agrártudományi egyetem Agronómiai kar kiadványai.** Budapest. *Agrartud. Egyet. agron. Kar Kiad.* [1954–57] **C.**A.; **Hu.**G.; **Rt.**; **Y.**

1213 **Agrártudományi egyetem Állattenyészetési karának közleményei.** Gödöllö-Budapest. *Agrartud. Egyet. állattenyész. Kar. Közl.* [1955–57] **L.**AM. 56–57; **C.**A.; **E.**AB.; AG.; W; **Hu.**G. 55–56; **N.**U. 56–57; **Y.**

1214 **Agrártudományi egyetem Erdömérnöki karának évkönyve.** Sopron. *Agrartud. Egyet. erdömern. Kar. Évk.* [1950] **Db.**; **O.**F.; **Rt.** [*C. of:* 18337; *C. as:* 18360]

1215 **Agrártudományi egyetem Kert- és szölögazdaságtudományi karának évkönyve.** Budapest. *Agrártud. Egyet. kert- és szölögtud. Kar. Évk.* [1950–53] **L.**HS. 50–52; MY. 51–53; **N.**U. 50–52; **Rt.** [*Issued as part of series at:* 1216]

1216 **Agrártudományi egyetem Kert- és szölögazdasagtudományi karának közlemenyei.** Budapest. *Agrártud. Egyet. kert- és szölögtud. Kar. Közl.* [1948–52] **L.**AM.; **Br.**A. 48–49; **Rt.** [*C. as:* 27358]

1217 **Agrártudományi egyetem Központi könyvtárának kiadványaí.** Budapest. *Agrártud. Egyet. Közp. Könyvtár. Kiad.* [1957–] **Y.**

1217ᵃ **Agrártudományi egyetem Mezögazdaságtudományi karának évkönyve.** Budapest. *Agrártud. Egyet. mezögtud. Kar. Évk.* [1950–] **C.**A.

1218 **Agrártudományi egyetem Mezőgazdaságtudományi karának közleményei.** Gödöllö. *Agrartud. Egyet. mezögtud. Kar. Közl., Gödöllö* **Abd.**R. 58–; **C.**A. 58–; **Y.**

1219 **Agrártudományi egyetem tudományos tájekoztatója.** Gödöllö. *Agrartud. Egyet. Tudom. Tájekozt.* [1960–] **Y.**

1220 **Agrártudományi szemle.** Budapest. *Agrartud. Szle* [1947–] **C.**A.; **Hu.**G. 47.

1221 **Agrarwirtschaft.** Hannover. *Agrarwirtschaft* [1952–] **L.**AM.; **Abs.**U.; **C.**A.; **O.**AEC.; **Y.**

1222 **Agrarwissenschaft.** Braunschweig. *Agrarwissenschaft* [1952–] **C.**A.

1223 **Agraurul.** Bucureşti. *Agraurul*

1224 **Agressologie.** Paris. *Agressologie* [1960–] **L.**MD.; **Y.**

1225 **Agri hortique genetica.** Landskrona. *Agri Hort. Genet.* [1943–] **L.**AM. 53–; K.; QM. 50; **Abs.**A.; **C.**A.; AB.; GE. 50–; **Hu.**G. 49–; **Y.**

1225ᶜ **Agricola.** México. *Agricola* [1939–] [*C. of:* 8030]

1226 **Agricola floreale.** San Remo. *Agricola flor.* **L.**HS. 30–40.

1227 **Agricoltore agrigentino.** Girgenti. *Agricoltore agrigent.* **L.**EB. 14.

1228 **Agricoltore ferrarese.** Ferrara. *Agricoltore ferrar.* [1876–] **Y.**

1229 **Agricoltore d'Italia.** Roma. *Agricoltore Ital.*

1230 **Agricoltore dell'Italia centrale.** Roma. *Agricoltore Ital. cent.*

1231 **Agricoltura.** Anoia. *Agricoltura, Anoia* [1910–14]

1232 **Agricoltura:** attualitá italiana e straniere. Roma. *Agricoltura, Roma* [1952–] **L.**AM. imp.; **C.**A. 60–; **Y.**

1233 **Agricoltura bolognese.** Bologna. *Agricoltura bologn.* [1915–39]

1234 **Agricoltura coloniale.** Firenze, Roma. *Agricoltura colon.* [1907–44] **L.**EB. 19–44; K.; TP.; **Hu.**G. 35–42 imp.; **Md.**H. 30–44; **Rt.** 38–40. [*C. as:* 47820]

1235 **Agricoltura italiana.** Pisa. *Agricoltura ital., Pisa* **L.**BM. 07–17; **C.**UL. 74–80.

1236 **Agricoltura italiana.** Roma. *Agricoltura ital., Roma* [1950–] **L.**AM. 50–51; **Y.**

1237 **Agricoltura libica.** Tripoli. *Agricoltura lib.* [1937–] **L.**TP; **C.**A.; **Rt.** 39–40. [*C. of:* 8501]

1239 **Agricoltura razionale.** Roma. *Agricoltura raz.* [*C. as:* 35470]

1240 **Agricoltura di Terra di Lavoro.** Caserta. *Agricoltura Terra di Lavoro* **L.**EB. 14–16.

1242 **Agricoltura toscana.** Firenze. *Agricoltura tosc.* [1946–52] **C.**A. 49–52.

1243 **Agricoltura delle Venezie.** Venezia. *Agricoltura Venezie* [1947–] **L.**AM.; **C.**A.; **Y.**

1244 **Agricoltura veterinaria.** Roma. *Agricoltura vet.* **L.**AM. 49–50.

1245 **Agricom.** E. Lansing, Mich. *Agricom* [1953–] **L.**AM.

1246 **Agriculteur de Bretagne.** Rennes. *Agriculteur Bret.* [1923–]

1247 **Agricultor.** Santiago de Chile. *Agricultor, Santiago* [1916–21] [*C. of:* and *Rec. as:* 8126]

1248 **Agricultor costarricense.** San José. *Agricultor costarric.* [1943–] **Y.**

1249 **Agricultor mexicano y hogar.** Juarez. *Agricultor mex.* [1896–] **L.**MY. 23–24.

1250 **Agricultor venezolano.** Caracas. *Agricultor venez.* [1936–] **L.**AM. (10 yr.); BM. 38–; **C.**A. (3 yr.); **Hu.**G. 43–; **Md.**H. 53– imp.; **Y.**

1251 **Agricultura.** Bogota. *Agricultura, Bogota* [1936–] **L.**BM. 36–40; **Abs.**A. 40–; **C.**A. [*C. of:* 7547]

1252 **Agricultura.** Ciudad Trujillo. *Agricultura, Ciud. Truj.* [1946–] **L.**BM. 55–. [*C. of:* 46272]

1253 **Agricultura.** Guatemala. *Agricultura, Guatem.* [1923–24]

1253ᵃ **Agricultura.** Jogjakarta. *Agricultura, Jogjakarta* [1960–]

1254 **Agricultura.** Lima. *Agricultura, Lima*

1255 **Agricultura.** Lisboa. *Agricultura, Lisb.* [1959–] **L.**AM.; BM.; **C.**A.; **Md.**H. 60–; **Y.**

1256 **Agricultura.** Louvain. *Agricultura, Louvain* **L.**AM. 53–; P. 55–; TP. 49–51; **C.**A. 33–; **Rt.** 46–; **Y.** [*C. of:* 47218]

1257 **Agricultura.** Madrid. *Agricultura, Madr.* [1929–] **L.**AM. (5 yr.); **C.**UL.; **Hu.**G. 32– imp.; **Rt.** 31–33 imp.; **Sil.** 52–54; **Y.**

1258 **Agricultura.** México. *Agricultura, Méx.* [1937–39]

1259 **Agricultura.** San Cristobal, R.D. *Agricultura, S Cristobal* **L.**AM. (10 yr.)

1260 **Agricultura.** Santiago de las Vegas, Cuba. *Agricultura, Santiago, Cuba* **C.**A. 31–.

1261 **Agricultura.** Tegucigalpa. *Agricultura, Tegucigalpa* [1948–] **L.**AM. 54–.

1262 **Agricultura.** Washington. *Agricultura, Wash.* [1925–33] [*C. as:* 49533]

1263 **Agricultura** de las **Américas.** *Agricultura Am.* [1956–] **Sil.** [*C. of:* 22839]

1264 **Agricultura: Bau-Buildings-Bâtiments.** Lund. *Agricultura Bau-Bldgs-Bâtim.* [1960–] **C.**A.; **Sil.**

1265 **Agricultura, comércio** e **industrias.** Asunción. *Agricultura, Comérc. Inds, Asunción* [1941–] **O.**F. 41–42 imp.

1266 **Agricultura** al **dia.** Santurce. *Agricultura Dia* [1955–] **L.**AM. 56– imp.

1267 **Agricultura española.** Valencia. *Agricultura esp.*

1268 **Agricultura especial.** Buenos Aires. *Agricultura espec.* [1935–] **Abs.**A. 35–37.

1269 **Agricultura experimental.** Rio Piedras. *Agricultura exp., R. Piedras* [1941–43] **C.**A.

1270 **Agricultura experimentală.** Cluj. *Agricultura exp., Cluj* [1927–28] **Rt.**

1271 **Agricultura** y **ganadería.** Bogota. *Agricultura Ganad., Bogota* [1940–] **L.**BM.

1272 **Agricultura** y **ganadería.** Santiago de Chile. *Agricultura Ganad., Santiago* [1955–] **Y.**

1273 **Agricultura** y **ganadería tropical.** México. *Agricultura Ganad. trop.* [1943–]

1274 **Agricultura guipuzcoana.** San Sebastian. *Agricultura guipuzc.* **O.**R. 03–06.

1276 **Agricultura moderna.** Habana. *Agricultura mod., Habana* [1943–]

1277 **Agricultura moderna.** Lisboa. *Agricultura mod. Lisb.*

1278 **Agricultura nacional.** Lisboa. *Agricultura nac., Lisb.*

1279 **Agricultura** e **pecuaria.** Rio de Janeiro. *Agricultura Pec.* [1938–]

1280 **Agricultura sinica.** Nanking. *Agricultura sin.* [1934–36] **L.**AM.; BM^N.; EB.; MY.; P.; **C.**A.; **Hu.**G. imp.; **Md.**H.; **Rt.**

1281 **Agricultura técnica.** Santiago de Chile. *Agricultura téc.* [1944–] **L.**AM. v. imp.; MY. 44–46; TP. 49–57 imp.; **C.**A.; **Hu.**G.; **Md.**H. 49–; **Rt.** imp.; **Y.** [*C. of:* 7665]

1282 **Agricultura técnica** en **México.** México. *Agricultura téc. Méx.* [1955–] **L.**AM.; BM.; **C.**A.; **Rt.**; **V.**

1283 **Agricultura tropical.** Bogota. *Agricultura trop.* [1945–] **L.**AM. imp.; MY. 52– imp.; **C.**A. 52–; **Hu.**G. imp.; **Rt.** 46– imp.; **Y.**

1284 **Agricultura venezolana.** Caracas. *Agricultura venez.* [1936–]

1285 **Agricultura** y **zootécnia.** Habana. *Agricultura Zootéc.* [1921–]

1286 **Agricultural Aviation.** The Hague. *Agric. Aviat.* [1959–] **L.**AM.; AV.; P.; **O.**RE. (3 yr.); **Sil.**; **Y.**
　　Agricultural Bulletin. Albany, N.Y. *See* 1298^a.

1288 **Agricultural Bulletin.** Chelmsford. *Agric. Bull., Chelmsford* [1943–45] **C.**A.

1289 **Agricultural Bulletin.** Christchurch, N.Z. *Agric. Bull., Christchurch, N.Z.* **O.**RE. 51–.

1290 **Agricultural Bulletin.** Cork. *Agric. Bull., Cork* [1925–] **L.**BM.; **C.**A.; **Db.**; **O.**R.; **Y.**

1292 **Agricultural Bulletin.** Wellington, N.Z. *Agric. Bull., Wellington, N.Z.* **L.**BM. 34–.

1293 **Agricultural Bulletin. Bermuda Department** of **Agriculture.** Hamilton. *Agric. Bull. Bermuda* [1922–] **L.**EB. imp.; K. 23–45 imp.; MY. 22–43; TP. 24–39; **C.**A. 34–39: 58–; **Md.**H. 37–39 imp.; **Rt.** 24–39; **Y.** [*Suspended* 1946–54]

1294 **Agricultural Bulletin. Canterbury Chamber** of **Commerce.** Canterbury, N.Z. *Agric. Bull. Canterbury, N.Z.* **Hu.**G. 53–; **O.**RE. 51–; **Sil.** 46–.

1295 **Agricultural Bulletin. Department** of **Agriculture, Northern Rhodesia.** Lusaka. *Agric. Bull. Dep. Agric. North. Rhod.* **Rt.** 55.

1295^a **Agricultural Bulletin. Economic Reform Club** and **Institute.** London. *Agric. Bull. econ. Reform Club* [1943–46] **L.**BM. [*C. as:* 48276]
　　Agricultural Bulletin. Essex W.A.E.C. *See* 1288.

1296 **Agricultural Bulletin. Federated Malay States.** Kuala Lumpur. *Agric. Bull. F.M.S.* [1912–21] **L.**AM.; BM.; BM^N.; EB.; K.; MY. imp.; P.; TP. imp.; **Abs.**A.; U; **C.**A.; P.; **Db.**; **Md.**H. 12–21 imp.; **Rt.**; **Sy.**R. [*C. from:* 1301; *C. as:* 29307]

1297 **Agricultural Bulletin** of **Iraq.** Baghdad. *Agric. Bull. Iraq.* **L.**TP. 22–27.

1298 **Agricultural Bulletin** of the **Malay Peninsula.** Singapore. *Agric. Bull. Malay Penins.* [1891–00] **L.**BM.; BM^N.; K.; L.; MY.; **Rt.**; **Sy.**R. [*C. as:* 1301]

1298^a **Agricultural Bulletin. New York State.** Albany. *Agric. Bull., N.Y. St.* **L.**AM. 39– imp.; **Y.** [*C. of:* 11302]

1299 **Agricultural Bulletin, Palestine.** Jerusalem. *Agric. Bull. Palest.* [1940–] **L.**BM^N. 40–41; **Abs.**A.; **E.**AB. 40–41. [*C. of:* 33386]

1300 **Agricultural Bulletin** of the **Saga University.** Saga. *Agric. Bull. Saga Univ.* [1953–] **C.**A. 55–; **Md.**H. 57–.

1301 **Agricultural Bulletin** of the **Straits** and **Federated Malay States.** Singapore. *Agric. Bull. Straits F.M.S.* [1901–12] **L.**AM.; BM.; BM^N.; HS. 07–12; K.; L.; MY. imp.; PH. 01–09; TP.; **C.**A.; **E.**B.; **Lv.**U.; **Rt.**; **Sy.**R. [*C. of:* 1298; *C. as:* 1296 *and* 20616]

1302 **Agricultural Census. Kenya Colony.** Nairobi. *Agric. Census Kenya* **L.**BM^N. 24–33.

1303 **Agricultural Chemicals.** Baltimore, etc. *Agric. Chem* [1946–] **L.**AM. imp.; C.; EB. imp.; MY. 47–; P.; TP.; **Abs.**U. 56–; **Br.**A. 47–; **C.**A. 48–52; **E.**P. 50–; **Hu.**G. 49–; **Je.**; **Ld.**U. 48–; **M.**P. 53– imp.; **Md.**H. 49–; **O.**RE. 47–; **Rt.** 47–; **Y.**

1304 **Agricultural Chronicle.** London. *Agric. Chron.* [1901–07] **L.**BM.; P. 02–06; **O.**R. 02–07. [*C. as:* 29059]

1305 **Agricultural Circular. Department** of **Agriculture, Fiji.** *Agric. Circ. Fiji* [1920–25] **L.**BM^N.; EB.; TP.; **C.**A. [*C. of:* 33501]
　　Agricultural Circular. Ministry of **Agriculture, Egypt.** *See* 14296.

1306 **Agricultural College Extension Bulletin. Ohio State University.** Columbus. *Agric. Coll. Ext. Bull. Ohio*

1307 Agricultural College Journal, Osmania University. Hyderabad-Deccan. *Agric. Coll. J. Osmania Univ.* [1954–58] **C.**A. [*C. as:* 27763]

1308 Agricultural Conservation. U.S. Department of Agriculture. Washington. *Agric. Conserv.* **L.**BM^N. 36–.

1309 Agricultural Co-operation. Horace Plunkett Foundation. London. *Agric. Co-op.* [1925] **M.**P. [*C. as:* 57983]

1309° Agricultural Department Bulletin. Department of **Agriculture, Ceylon.** Colombo. *Agric. Dep. Bull. Ceylon* **L.**BM. 51–. [*C. of:* 9968]

1310 Agricultural Development Bulletin. Imperial Chemical Industries. London. *Agric. Dev. Bull.* [1950–] **L.**BM.; **O.**RE.

1311 Agricultural Development Paper. Agricultural Division, F.A.O. Washington. *Agric. Dev. Pap. F.A.O.* [1949–] **L.**BM.; **C.**A.; **Db.**; **Ld.**P.; **O.**RE. 50– imp.

1312 Agricultural Economic Bibliographies. Washington. *Agric. econ. Biblphies* [1925–42] **L.**AM.; BM^N. 25–28; **Abs.**U. 27–38; **Rt.** [*C. in:* 6700]
   Agricultural Economics. London. *See* 17433.

1313 Agricultural Economics. Reading. *Agric. Econ., Reading* [1927–] **L.**BM.; **O.**R. 27; **Rt.** imp.

1314 Agricultural Economics Bulletin. Agricultural Experiment Station, University of Hawaii. Honolulu. *Agric. Econ. Bull., Honolulu* [1950–] **C.**A.; **Y.**

1315 Agricultural Economics Literature. Washington. *Agric. Econ. Lit.* [1927–42] **L.**AM.; **O.**AEC.; **R.**U. 31–40; **Rt.** [*C. in:* 6700]

1316 Agricultural Economics Research. Washington. *Agric. Econ. Res.* [1949–] **L.**AM.; BM.; **Abs.**U.; **Br.**U.; **C.**A.; P. 50–; **Db.**; **E.**R.; **Ld.**U. 54–; **M.**C. (2 yr.); U. 51– imp.; **O.**AEC.; **R.**D.; U.; **Sa.** 50–; **Y.**

1317 Agricultural Economist and **Horticultural Review.** London. *Agric. Econst hort. Rev.* [1870–16] **L.**AM. 93–95: 02–04; BM.; P.; U. 08–14; UC. 08–15; **Abs.**N. 12–16; U. 00–15 imp.; **Bm.**U. 05–16; **Db.** 07–14; **E.**A. 85–05; **G.**M. 08–15; U. 09–14; **Ld.**P. 10–14; **M.**U. 08–14; **O.**B. 95–16; **Sa.** 08–14.

1318 Agricultural Engineering. London. *Agric. Engng, Lond.* **L.**BM. 22–23*.

1319 Agricultural Engineering. St. Joseph, Mich., Ames, Ia. *Agric. Engng, St Joseph, Mich.* [1920–] **L.**AM. 30–; P. 21– imp.; SC. 32–; TP. 48–; **Abd.**R. 48–60; U. 47–; **Abs.**A. 52–; N. 45–; R. 48–; **Br.**A. 51–54; **C.**A. 33–; **Db.** 56–; **Ld.**U. 40–; **N.**U. 40–; **O.**AG.; RE. 49–59; **R.**D. 47–; U. 46–; **Rt.** 32–; **Sil.** imp.; **Y.**

1320 Agricultural Engineering Publications. Tennessee Valley Authority. Knoxville. *Agric. Engng Publs T.V.A.*

1321 Agricultural Engineering Record. Askham Bryan. *Agric. Engng Rec., Askham* [1945–49] **L.**A.; AM.; BM.; HS.; P.; TP. imp.; U.; **Abd.**S.; U. 47–49; **Abs.**A.; **Ba.**I.; **Bm.**P.; **Br.**A.; **C.**A.; UL.; **Cr.**P.; **Db.**; **E.**A.; B.; **Ld.**U.; **Lv.**P.; **M.**P.; **Md.**H.; **N.**U.; **O.**AEC.; R.; RE.; **R.**D.; U.; **Rt.**; **Sil.**

1322 Agricultural Engineering Record. Oxford. *Agric. Engng Rec., Oxf.* [1940] **L.**BM.; P.; TP.; **Abs.**A.; **Bm.**P.; **C.**A.; UL.; **M.**P.; **Md.**H.; **O.**AEC.

1323 Agricultural Engineers' Yearbook. St. Joseph, Mich. *Agric. Engrs' Yb.* [1955–] **Abd.**U.

1324 Agricultural Experiments. Minneapolis. *Agric. Exp.* [1901–06]

1326 Agricultural Extension Bulletin. Department of **Agriculture, University** of **Saskatchewan.** *Agric. Ext. Bull. Univ. Saskatch.* **C.**A. 22– imp.

1327 Agricultural Extension Bulletin. North Dakota Agricultural College. *Agric. Ext. Bull. N. Dak.*

1328 Agricultural Gazette. London. *Agric. Gaz., Lond.* [1874–25] **L.**AM. 74–04 imp: 19; BM.; P. 74–12; **Abd.**U. 20–25; **Abs.**N. 12–25; U. 09–25; **Db.**; **E.**A. 85–25; **O.**B. 85–25; RE. 74–84; **R.**D. 23–25; U. 75–76: 84–86; **Rt.** 75–01: 21–25. [*C. in:* 19129]

1329 Agricultural Gazette. British Solomon Islands Protectorate. Sydney. *Agric. Gaz. Br. Solomon Isl.* [1933–36] **L.**AM.; EB.; TP.; **C.**A.; **O.**RH.

1330 Agricultural Gazette of **Canada.** Ottawa. *Agric. Gaz. Can.* [1914–24] **L.**A.; AM.; BM.; BM^N.; EB.; K.; P. 24; S.; TP.; **Db.**; **E.**N. 19–24 imp.; **Rt.**

1331 Agricultural Gazette of **New South Wales.** Sydney. *Agric. Gaz. N.S.W.* [1890–] **L.**AM.; BM. 90–13; BM^N.; E. 90–01; EB.; IC. 47–; K.; L. 90–23; MY. 23–; P. 10–53; TP.; **Abd.**R. 57–; **Abs.**A.; N. imp.; U. 04–33 imp.; **C.**A. 09– imp.; AB. 28–; P. 24–; **Db.** 93–; **E.**AB. 33–; W. 03–12 imp.; N. 17– imp.; **Hu.**G. 52–; **Je.** 47–; **Ld.**U. 29–; W. 39–; **Md.**H. 30–; **N.**U. 48–; **O.**RH. 92– imp.; **R.**D. 36–; U. 13–; **Rt.**; **Sa.** 91–05; **Sal.** 34–; **Sil.** 45–; **Y.**

1332 Agricultural Gazette of **Tasmania.** Hobart. *Agric. Gaz. Tasm.* [1892–15] **L.**AM. 97–04: 11–15; EB. 15; P. 05–15; TP. 93–15; **Abs.**N. 11–15; **Cr.**P. 11–15 imp.; **Rt.** 15.

1333 Agricultural Grange News. Seattle. *Agric. Grange News* [1912–27] [*C. as:* 21531]

1334 Agricultural History. Washington. *Agric. Hist.* [1927–] **L.**AM.; BM. 58–; U. 59–; UC. 55–; **Bm.**U.; **Br.**U. 49–; **C.**A.; **E.**W. 48–; **N.**U. 51–; **O.**AEC. 30–; **R.**U.; **Rt.** [*C. of:* 36990]

1335 Agricultural History Review. London, etc. *Agric. Hist. Rev.* [1953–] **L.**A.; AM.; BM.; KC. 55–; QM.; SC.; U.; **Abd.**U.; **Abs.**N.; U.; **Bl.**U.; **Bm.**P.; **Bn.**U.; **Br.**U.; **C.**A.; UL.; **Cr.**U.; **Db.**; **Dn.**U. 61–; **E.**A.; U.; V.; **G.**U.; **H.**U.; **Hu.**G.; **Ld.**U.; **N.**U.; **O.**B.; R.; RE.; **R.**D.; T.; U.; **Sa.**; **Sh.**U.; **Sil.** imp.; **Sw.**U.

1336 Agricultural History Series. U.S. Department of Agriculture. Washington. *Agric. Hist. Ser.* [1941–] **Bm.**U.; **C.**A.

1337 Agricultural and **Home Economics Research Progress.** Pullman. *Agric. Home Econ. Res. Prog.* **L.**P. 56–.

1338 Agricultural and **Horticultural Engineering Abstracts.** Silsoe. *Agric. hort. Engng Abstr.* [1951–] **L.**AM.; BM. 58–; EB. 56–; MY. 56–; P.; TP.; **Abd.**R. 57–; **Abs.**U. imp.; **Bm.**P.; **Bn.**U. 57–; **Br.**U. 56–; **C.**A.; **Db.**; **E.**AB. 60–; **Je.**; **Ld.**P. 60–; **Li.**M. (3 yr.); **Md.**H.; **N.**U.; **O.**B.; R.; RE.; **R.**D. 56–; U. **Sil.**; **Y.** [*C. of:* 296]

1339 Agricultural Index. New York. *Agric. Index* [1916–] **L.**AM. 17– imp.; BM. 55–; FA. 49–; P. 16–30; **Abd.**U. 16–24; **Abs.**N.; **Db.** 45–; **E.**AG. 49–53; U.; W. 47– imp.; **G.**M. 16–25; **Ld.**U. 45–; **Lv.**P. 45–; **M.**P.; **Md.**H. 28–46; **R.**D. 16–48; U.; **Rt.** 16–50.

1340 Agricultural and **Industrial Bulletin.** Kansas City. *Agric. ind. Bull.*

1341 **Agricultural** and **Industrial Progress** in **Canada.** Montreal. *Agric. ind. Prog. Can.* [1919–] **Br.**P. (2 yr.); **O.**AEC. 46–47.

Agricultural Information Bulletin. Washington. *See* 1447.

1342 **Agricultural Information Series.** U.S. Department of Agriculture. Washington. *Agric. Inf. Ser.* [1944–] **C.**A.

1343 **Agricultural, Insecticide** and **Fungicide Association News.** New York. *Agric. Insect. Fung. Ass. News* **L.**MY. 47–49 imp.

1344 **Agricultural Institute Review.** Ottawa. *Agric. Inst. Rev.* [1945–] **L.**AM.; FA. 47–; P.; **C.**A.; **E.**AB. 46–48 imp.; **Hu.**G.; **Md.**H. 53–; **O.**RE. (2 yr.); **R.**D. 52–; **Rt.** 47–; **Sal.** 47–; **Y.** [*C. of:* 12912]

1345 **Agricultural Ireland.** Dublin. *Agric. Ire.* [1941–] **Abs.**U.; **Hu.**G. 45– imp.; **O.**RE. (1 yr).

1346 **Agricultural Journal.** Victoria, B.C. *Agric. J., Vict. B.C.* [1916–25] **L.**AM.; EB. imp.; P.; TP. imp.; **Rt.**

1347 **Agricultural Journal** of the **Bihar** and **Orissa Department** of **Agriculture.** Patna. *Agric. J. Bihar Orissa* [1913–17] **L.**AM.; BM.; EB.; TP.; **C.**A.; **Rt.**

Agricultural Journal of **British Columbia.** *See* 1346.

1348 **Agricultural Journal** of **British East Africa.** *Agric. J. Br. E. Afr.* [1908–14] **L.**AM.; EB.; P.; TP.; **C.**A.; **Rt.**

1349 **Agricultural Journal** of **British Guiana.** Georgetown. *Agric. J. Br. Guiana* [1928–39] **L.**AM.; E.; EB.; K.; MY.; P.; TP.; Z.; **C.**A.; P.; **Hu.**G. 30–39; **Md.**H. 30–39 imp.; **Rt.**; **Sal.** 34–39. [*C. of:* 25672; *Suspended* 1932 –33]

1350 **Agricultural Journal** of the **Cape** of **Good Hope.** Cape Town. *Agric. J. Cape G. H.* [1888–10] **L.**AM. 98–10; BM. 89–09; BM^N. 96–10 imp.; K. 97–10; P.; TP. 97–10 imp.; **Abs.**N. 00–09 imp.; **E.**B. 05–10; **Lv.**U. 07–10; **Rt.** 08–10 imp. [*Superseded by:* 1358]

1351 **Agricultural Journal.** **Department** of **Agriculture, Fiji.** Suva. *Agric. J. Dep. Agric. Fiji* [1928–] **L.**AM. 41– imp.; BM.; BM^N.; EB.; K.; MY. 29– imp.; TP. imp.; V. 29–46 imp.: 47–; **Abd.**R. (curr.); **Abs.**A. 48–; **Br.**A. 49– imp.; **C.**A.; **E.**AB.; W. 37– imp.; **Hu.**G.; **Md.**H. imp.; **O.**RE. 31– imp.; **R.**D. 38–; **Rt.**; **Sal.** 31– imp.; **Y.**

1352 **Agricultural Journal, Department** of **Science** and **Agriculture, Barbados.** Bridgetown. *Agric. J. Dep. Sci. Agric. Barbados* [1932–40] **L.**AM.; BM^N.; EB.; K. 32–39; MY.; TP.; **C.**A.; **Hu.**G. 37–40; **Md.**H. 32–39; **O.**RH.; **Rt.**; **Sal.** 37–40. [*C. of:* and *Rec. as:* 43440]

1353 **Agricultural Journal** of **Egypt.** *Agric. J. Egypt* [1911–28] **L.**AM. 11–20: 23–25; BM. 11–20; EB. 11–20: 25–28; K.; TP. 11–20; **C.**A. 11–25; **E.**R. 11–20; **Rt.**

1354 **Agricultural Journal** of **India.** Pusa. *Agric. J. India* [1906–30] **L.**AM.; BM.; BM^N.; C. 06–19 imp.; E. 06: 12–13: 18–28; EB. 18–30; HO. 18–27; K.; L.; MY. 15–30 imp.; P.; TP. 06–30; **Abs.**N. imp.; **Bl.**U. 06–10; **Bm.**U. 06–24; **C.**A.; P.; **Cr.**P. 11–13 imp.; **Db.** 17–30; **E.**N. 17–30 imp.; R. 06–21; W. 06–25 imp.; **Hu.**G. 07–30 imp.; **Lv.**U. 06–10; **M.**C. 14–30; U. 06–25 imp.; **Md.**H. 30; **Nw.**A.; **O.**R. 09–25 imp.; **Rt.**; **Sal.** 30. [*C. as:* 1448, 22985 and 23031]

1355 **Agricultural Journal** and **Mining Record.** Pietermaritzburg. *Agric. J. Min. Rec.* [1898–03] **L.**K.; P. imp.; TP.; **Rt.** [*C. as:* 34083]

1356 **Agricultural Journal** of the **Mozambique Company.** Beira. *Agric. J. Mozamb. Co.* [1911–12] **L.**AM.; K. 11; TP.

1357 **Agricultural Journal** of **South Africa.** Johannesburg. *Agric. J. S. Afr.* [1915–19] **L.**AM.; BM. 17–19; TP. 15–18; **Rt.** 15–19. [*C. of:* and *Rec. as:* 51399]

Agricultural Journal of the **Transvaal.** *See* 54147.

1358 **Agricultural Journal** of the **Union** of **South Africa.** Pretoria. *Agric. J. Un. S. Afr.* [1911–14] **L.**AM.; BM^N.; EB.; K.; P.; TP.; UC.; **Abd.**U. 11–13; **Abs.**N.; U. 12–13 imp.; **C.**A.; **Cr.**P. imp.; **E.**B.; U.; W. 11–14 imp.; **Ld.**U.; **Lv.**U.; **Nw.**A.; **O.**R.; **R.**U.; **Rt.** [*C. of:* 54147; *C. as:* 25891]

1359 **Agricultural Leaflets. Agricultural Department, Burma.** Rangoon. *Agric. Leafl. Agric. Dep. Burma*

1360 **Agricultural Leaflets. Department** of **Agriculture, F.M.S.** Kuala Lumpur. *Agric. Leafl. Dep. Agric. F.M.S.* [1934–36] **L.**P.; **C.**A.

1361 **Agricultural Leaflets. Department** of **Agriculture, Palestine.** Jerusalem. *Agric. Leafl. Dep. Agric. Palest.* **Rt.** 28–34 imp.

1362 **Agricultural Leaflets, Horticulture. Department** of **Agriculture, Palestine.** *Agric. Leafl. Hort. Dep. Agric. Palest.* **L.**BM^N. 28–33 imp.

1363 **Agricultural Ledger.** Calcutta. *Agric. Ledger* [1892–12] **L.**AM.; BM.; BM^N. imp.; C.; K.; P.; PH.; TP.; **Bm.**U. 08–12 imp.; **Db.**; **E.**B.; F. 00–12; U. 92–99; **G.**U. 92–00 imp.; **Nw.**A.; **O.**R.; **Rt.**

1364 **Agricultural Ledger. Special Veterinary series.** Calcutta. *Agric. Ledger, spec. vet. Ser.* [1896–05] **L.**AM. 96–99; P.; **C.**UL.; **Rt.** 97–05.

1365 **Agricultural Lime Information.** London. *Agric. Lime Inf.* [1957–] **Abs.**A.; **Bn.**U.; **R.**U.; **Rt.** 58.

1366 **Agricultural Lime News Bulletin.** Washington. *Agric. Lime News Bull.* [1920–27]

1367 **Agricultural Literature** of **Czechoslovakia.** Prague. *Agric. Lit. Czech.* [1960–] **L.**AM.; P.; **Bn.**U.; **C.**A.

1368 **Agricultural Literature References** to **Boron** and **Minor Elements.** London. *Agric. Lit. Refs Boron* [1948–57] **L.**K. 52–57; MY. 49–57; **Md.**H.; **Rt.** 49–57. [*C. as:* 8540]

Agricultural Literature of the **U.S.S.R.** *See* 49468.

Agricultural Machinery. Moscow. *See* 49469.

1369 **Agricultural Machinery Journal.** London. *Agric. Mach. J.* [1947–] **L.**AM. 49–; BM.; FA.; P. 49–; **Abd.**U. 53–; **C.**A. (2 yr.); **Nw.**A.; **Sil.**; **Y.**

Agricultural Machinery and **Tractor Dealers' Association Journal.** *See* 86.

1370 **Agricultural Mechanization Series.** Geneva. *Agric. Mechaniz. Ser.* [1956–] **L.**BM.; **O.**RE.

1371 **Agricultural Merchant.** London. *Agric. Merch.* **L.**AM. 40– imp.; BM. 20– imp.; **Abs.**A. 52–; U. 42– imp.; **C.**A. (2 yr.); **E.**CE. 56–; **Hu.**G. 53–; **Ld.**U. 59–; **O.**AEC. 47–; **Sil.** 54–.

Agricultural Meteorology. Tokyo. *See* 25441.

1372 **Agricultural News.** Bridgetown, W. Indies. *Agric. News, Bridgetown* [1902–22] **L.**AM. 02–06; BM.; BMᴺ.; EB.; HS.; K.; MY. 05: 12–22; P.; TP. 02–21; **Abd.**U. 14–22; **Abs.**N. 14–22; U. 14–19 imp.; **Bm.**U. 15–22 imp.; **C.**A. 17–22; **E.**B. imp.; **G.**U. 14–22; **Ld.**U. 14–19; **Lv.**U. imp.; **M.**U. 14–22; **Nw.**A. 15–22 imp.; **O.**RE. 08–22 imp.; **Rt.**; **Sa.** 14–22; **Sw.**U. 22.

1373 **Agricultural News.** Durban. *Agric. News, Durban* **L.**BM. 17–20 imp.

1374 **Agricultural News. Shell Petroleum Co.** London. *Agric. News Shell Petrol. Co.* [1956–] **Abs.**U. 57–.

1375 **Agricultural News Bulletin.** Nanking. *Agric. News Bull., Nanking* [1947] [*C. as:* 33387]

1376 **Agricultural News Letter.** Du Pont de Nemours and Co. Wilmington, Del. *Agric. News Lett.* [1935–] **L.**MY. 35–40; P. (curr.); TP. 38–40; **C.**A. (5 yr.); **M.**U. 35–40 imp.; **Md.**H. 47–.

1377 **Agricultural Newsletter** from the **Netherlands.** The Hague. *Agric. Newsl. Neth.* [1951–] **L.**AM.; BM. 54–; P.; **O.**AEC. 52–; **Rt.** 56; **Sil.** imp.

1378 **Agricultural Notes. Porto Rico Agricultural Experiment Station.** Mayaguez. *Agric. Notes Porto Rico agric. Exp. Stn* [1924–] **C.**A.; **Rt.** 25–37 imp.

1379 **Agricultural Notes. Yorkshire N. Riding Agricultural Education Committee.** Leeds. *Agric. Notes Yorks. N. Riding* [1943–] **L.**AM.

1380 **Agricultural Outlook** for **Canada.** Ottawa. *Agric. Outl. Can.* [1954–] **L.**BM.; **O.**AEC. 57–.

1381 **Agricultural Outlook Digest.** Washington. *Agric. Outl. Dig.* [1952–] **O.**AEC.

1381ᵃ **Agricultural Production Series. Bureau** of **Fisheries, Philippine Islands.** Manila. *Agric. Prod. Ser. Bur. Fish. Philipp. Isl.* **L.**BM. 54–.

1382 **Agricultural Progress.** London, etc. *Agric. Prog.* [1924–] **L.**AM.; BM.; IC. 37–; VC. 53–; **Abd.**R. 24–60; U.; **Abs.**A.; N.; U. 25–35: 49–; **Bl.**U. 29– imp.; **Bn.**U. 24–40; **Br.**U.; **C.**A.; **Cr.**P. 24–35 imp.; UL.; **Db.**; **E.**A.; AB. 48–; AG. 49–52; AR. 24–56; U.; W. 24–40 imp.; **Hu.**G. 25– imp.; **Je.** 30–; **Ld.**U. 29–39: 48–; **Lv.**P 24–40; **N.**U.; **O.**AEC.; R.; RE.; **R.**D.; U.; **Rt.**; **Sil.** 33–50 imp.; **Y.**

1383 **Agricultural Progress** in **South Carolina.** Charleston. *Agric. Prog. S. Carol.* **Y.**

1384 **Agricultural Record.** Dublin. *Agric. Rec., Dubl.* [1948–] **Bl.**U. imp.; **Db.**; **Rt.** 55.

1385 **Agricultural Record.** London. *Agric. Rec., Lond.* [1908–11] **L.**A.; AM.; BM.; P.; **Bm.**P.; U.; **C.**UL.; **O.**R. [*C. of:* 16019; *C. as:* 25754]

1386 **Agricultural Records.** Agricultural Experiment Station, Institute of Agriculture and Natural History. Tel-Aviv. *Agric. Recs, Tel-Aviv* **L.**P. 27.

1387 **Agricultural Register.** Oxford. *Agric. Regist.* [1933–39: 56–] **L.**AM.; BM.; **Bm.**U. 33–39; **Bn.**U. 33–39; **Br.**P. 34–38; **C.**A.; **G.**M. 33–39; U. 34–38; **Ld.**U. 33–39; **M.**P. 33–39; **N.**U. 33–39; **O.**AEC.; B.; RE.; **R.**D. 33–38; U. 33–39.

1388 **Agricultural Report. Colonial Sugar Refining Company,** Ltd. Sydney. *Agric. Rep. colon. Sug. Refg Co.* **L.**EB. 16–23; **C.**A. 17–35 imp.

1389 **Agricultural Report. Cornwall County Council.** *Agric. Rep. Cornwall* **L.**AM.; **Ld.**U.; **Rt.** 97–11.

1390 **Agricultural Report. Foreign Office. Miscellaneous Series.** London. *Agric. Rep. F.O. misc. Ser.* **L.**BM. 86–; **E.**A. 86–; **Lv.**P. 00–; **Rt.** 99–08.

1391 **Agricultural Research.** London. *Agric. Res., Lond.* [1925–30] **L.**A.; AM.; BM.; C.; HS.; P.; V.; **Abd.**R. 27–30; U.; **Abs.**N.; **Bl.**U. imp.; **Bm.**U. 25–26; **Bn.**U.; **Br.**U.; **C.**A.; UL.; **Cr.**P.; **Hu.**G.; **Ld.**U.; **M.**U.; **Nw.**A.; **O.**R.; RE.; **R.**D.; U.; **Rt.** [*C. as:* 19154]

1392 **Agricultural Research.** Nanking. *Agric. Res., Nanking* [1935–] **C.**A. 35–36; **Ld.**U. 36 imp.

1393 **Agricultural Research.** New Delhi. *Agric. Res., New Delhi* **Y.**

1393ᶜ **Agricultural Research.** Department of Agricultural Technical Services, Republic of South Africa. Pretoria. *Agric. Res., Pretoria* [1960–] **C.**A.

1394 **Agricultural Research.** Taipei. *Agric. Res., Taipei* [1950–] **L.**EB.; **C.**A.; **Rt.**; **Y.** [*Issue for* 1951 *entitled* Agricultural Research Quarterly]

1395 **Agricultural Research.** Washington. *Agric. Res., Wash.* [1953–] **L.**AM.; P. 59–; TP. imp.; **Abd.**R. 61–; **C.**A.; **E.**AB.; **Md.**H. imp.; **Sil.** 60–; **Y.**

1396 **Agricultural Research Bulletin.** Calcutta. *Agric. Res. Bull., Calcutta* [1940–]

1396ᵃ **Agricultural Research Bulletin.** Jealotts' Hill Research Station. Bracknell. *Agric. Res. Bull., Bracknell* [1932–36]

Agricultural Research Council Reports. London. *See* 99.

1398 **Agricultural Research Institute** and **Agricultural Board Reporter.** Washington. *Agric. Res. Inst. agric. Bd Reptr* **L.**P. (curr.)

1399 **Agricultural Research Memoirs. Indian Central Jute Committee.** Calcutta. [1943–] *Agric. Res. Mem. Indian cent. Jute Comm.* **L.**BMᴺ. 43; **C.**A.; **E.**R. 43; **Rt.** 53– imp.

1400 **Agricultural Research News Notes.** Ministry of Agriculture, Lima. *Agric. Res. News Notes, Lima*

Agricultural Research Quarterly. Taipei. *See* 1394.

1401 **Agricultural Research** in **Review.** Baltimore. *Agric. Res. Rev., Baltimore* **Hu.**G. 30–41: 54–.

1402 **Agricultural Research Review.** Cairo. *Agric. Res. Rev., Cairo* [1958–] **L.**AM.; **C.**A.; **Md.**H.; **Y.** [*English edition of the Arabic journal*]

1404 **Agricultural Research** and **Teaching** at **Cambridge.** Cambridge. *Agric. Res. Teach. Camb.* [1957–] **O.**R.; **Rt.**; **Y.**

1405 **Agricultural Research Work** in the **Sudan.** London. *Agric. Res. Wk Sudan* **Md.**H. 27–29.

1406 **Agricultural Returns.** Board of Agriculture. London. *Agric. Returns, Lond.* [1866–01] **L.**BM.; MO. 86–01; **Abd.**U. 83–01; **Abs.**N.; **Bm.**P.; U. 01; **C.**A.; **Cr.**P. 69–01; **Db.** 00–01; **E.**A.; **Ld.** P. 78–93; U. 91–01; **Lv.**P. 00–01; **M.**P.; U. 93–01; **Nw.**A. 96–00; P. 93–01; **O.**AEC.; RE. 93–01; **Rt.** [*C. as:* 1418]

1407 **Agricultural Review.** Kansas City. *Agric. Rev., Kans. Cy* [1916–31] [*C. of:* 10134; *Superseded by:* 34626]

1408 **Agricultural Review.** London. *Agric. Rev., Lond.* [1955–58] **L.**A.; AM.; BM.; FA.; P.; SC.; TP.; VC.; **Abd.**R.; S.; U.; **Abs.**A.; U.; **Bl.**U.; **Bn.**U.; **Br.**A.; U.; **C.**A.; APH.; UL.; V.; **E.**A.; AB.; CE. 57–58; PO.; U.; W.;

Ep.D.; **G.**M.; **Hu.**G.; **Ld.**U.; **Md.**H.; **N.**U.; **Nw.**A. **O.**AEC.; R.; RE.; **R.**D.; T.; U.; **Sil.**; **Y.** [*C. of:* 8752]
  Agricultural Science. Budapest. *See* 1210ᵃ.
  Agricultural Science. Cairo. *See* 1846.

1409 Agricultural Science. Nanking. *Agric. Sci., Nanking* [1923–27]

1410 Agricultural Science and **Genetics Newsletter.** Washington, D.C. *Agric. Sci. Genet. Newsl.* **Abs.**A. 43–45 imp.; **R.**D. 44–45.
  Agricultural Sciences. Sofia. *See* 58936.
  Agricultural Series, F.A.O. *See* 18909.
  Agricultural Settlement Series Circular. British Columbia Department of Agriculture. Vancouver. *See* 14112.

1410ᵃ Agricultural Show Bulletin. London. *Agric. Show Bull.* [1958–] **L.**BM.

1411 Agricultural Situation I.I.A. Rome. *Agric. Situ., Rome* [1929–33] **L.**AM.; BM.; **Bl.**U.; **O.**RE.; **R.**U.; **Rt.** 29–31. [*C. as:* 57851]

1412 Agricultural Situation. Washington. *Agric. Situ., Wash.* **L.**AM. (2 yr.); BM. 27–; BMᴺ. 33–; TP. 33– imp.; **Abs.**U. 47– imp.; **C.**A. (5 yr.); **E.**W. 48– imp.; **O.**AEC. 38–; **R.**D. 47–; U. 53–.

1413 Agricultural Situation in **India.** Delhi. *Agric. Situ. India* [1948–] **L.**AM.; TP. 49–50; **O.**AEC. 50–; **Y.**

1414 Agricultural Situation and **Outlook.** Ottawa. *Agric. Situ. Outl., Ottawa* **O.**AEC. 34–39; **Rt.** 37–38.

1415 Agricultural Statistics of **British India.** Calcutta. *Agric. Statist. Br. India* **L.**AM. 84–39; BM. 90–; **Abs.**N. 06–26; **Bm.**U. 02– imp.; **E.**A. 84–13; U. 12–39 imp.; **O.**I. 84–39; G. 31–.

1416 Agricultural Statistics. Department of Agriculture for **Ireland.** Dublin. *Agric. Statist. Dep. Agric. Ire.* [1900–] **L.**AM.; BM.; U. 10–17 imp.; **Bm.**P. 00–16; **Cr.**P. 05– imp.; **Db.**; **E.**A.; W. 12– imp.; **G.**M. 00–20; **Ld.**U. 01–20; **Lv.**P. 25–30; **M.**P. 01–; **Nw.**P. 12–; **O.**AEC. 00–33; B.; G. 02–16 imp.; RE. 05–17; **Rt.**; **Y.**

1417 Agricultural Statistics. Department of Agriculture for **Scotland.** Edinburgh. *Agric. Statist. Dep. Agric. Scotl.* [1912–] **L.**AM.; BM.; MO. 12–15; U. 12–21; **Abd.**U.; BL. 39– imp.; **Bm.**P.; U. 39–; **Bn.**U. 29–38; **C.**A. 31–; UL. 21–; **Cr.**P. imp.; **E.**A.; AG. (1, 2) 39–49; **G.**M. 21–; **Ld.**P. 39–; U.; **Lv.**P. 21–44; **M.**P.; **Md.**H. 45–; **O.**AEC.; G. 24– imp.; R. 21–; RE. 12–19: 26–.

1418 Agricultural Statistics. Ministry of Agriculture, Fisheries, and Food. London. *Agric. Statist. Minist. Agric., Lond.* [1902–] **L.**BM.; BMᴺ. 26–36 imp.; H. 21–39; MO. 02–27; U. imp.; **Abd.**U.; **Abs.**A.; N.; **Bl.**U. 39–; **Bm.**P.; U. imp.; **Bn.**U. 04–; **Bra.**P. 54–; **C.**A.; **Cr.**P.; **Db.**; **E.**A.; **G.**M.; **H.**U. 29–; **Ld.**P. 07 imp.; U.; **Lv.**P. 21–45; **M.**P.; U. 02–38 imp.; **Md.**H. 32–39; **Nw.**P.; **O.**AEC.; B. 02–05: 22–; G. imp.; RE.; **R.**D. 30–; U. 20–; **Rt.**; **Sh.**P. [*C. of:* 1406]

1419 Agricultural Statistics. U.S. Department of Agriculture. Washington. *Agric. Statist. U.S.* [1936–] **L.**AM.; BM.; BMᴺ. 37–; P.; UC.; **Bl.**U. 43–44: 47; **C.**A.; **Lv.**P.; **M.**P.; **Md.**H. 37–; **O.**AEC.; RE. 36–53; RH.; **R.**D. 41–; U. 36–42.; **Y.**

1420 Agricultural Statistics Report. Province of **British Columbia.** Victoria. *Agric. Statist. Rep. Prov. Br. Columb.* **M.**P. 13–; **Md.**H. 24– imp.; **Y.**

1421 Agricultural Students' Association, Armstrong College. Newcastle-upon-Tyne. *Agric. Stud. Ass. Armstrong Coll.* **L.**AM. 00–36; **Nw.**A. 00–15; **Rt.** 00–.

1422 Agricultural Students' Gazette. Royal Agricultural College. Cirencester. *Agric. Stud. Gaz., Cirenc.* [1875–15] **L.**AM. 82–15; BM. 89–15; **Abs.**A. 95–15 imp.; N. 12–15; **Br.**U. 75–14; **E.**C. 83–15; F. 82–15; **Nw.**A. 94–15; **Rt.** [*C. as:* 48160]

1423 Agricultural Studies. University of Hawaii. *Agric. Stud. Univ. Hawaii* [1927–30] **L.**P. 27; **C.**A imp.
  Agricultural Studies, F.A.O. *See* 18910.

1424 Agricultural Surveys. Department of Agriculture, Burma. Rangoon. *Agric. Survs Dep. Agric. Burma* **L.**BM. 10–; **C.**A. 30–36; **Rt.** 10–36.

1425 Agricultural Topics. Aberystwyth. *Agric. Topics* [1944–] **Abs.**A.; N.; U. 44–46 imp.; **Rt.**

1426 Agricultural and **Veterinary Chemicals.** London. *Agric. vet. Chem.* [1960–] **L.**AM.; BM.; EB.; **C.**A.; **Ld.**U. 60–61; **Sil.**; **W.**; **Y.**

1427 Agricultural Work Simplification Review. Lafayette. *Agric. Wk Simplif. Rev.* [1956–] **C.**A.; **Sil.** [*C. of:* 57845]

1428 Agricultural Yearbook. Washington. *Agric. Yb.* [1923–25] **L.**AM.; BM.; BMᴺ.; EB.; K.; MY. 25; P.; UC.; Z.; **Abd.**U.; **Bl.**U.; **Bm.**P.; U.; **Bn.**U.; **C.**A.; GG. 23–24; P.; UL.; **Db.**; **E.**U.; **G.**M.; N.; **Ld.**U.; **Lv.**P.; **M.**P.; **N.**U.; **Nw.**A. 25; **O.**AEC. 24–25; RE.; **Rt.** [*C. of:* 58172; *C. as:* 57984]

1429 Agriculture. Allahabad. *Agriculture, Allahabad* [1951–] **Rt.** 54.

1430 Agriculture. Ceylon University Agricultural Association. Colombo. *Agriculture, Colombo* **L.**BM. 58–.

1431 Agriculture. London. *Agriculture, Lond.* [1939–] **L.**A.; AM.; B. 39–53; BM.; BMᴺ.; EB.; FA.; H.; HS.; IC.; MO.; MY.; NC.; P.; RI. 39–57; SC.; TP.; V.; VC.; U.; **Abd.**R.; S.; U.; **Abs.**A.; U.; **Ba.**I.; **Bl.**U.; **Bm.**U.; **Bn.**U. **Br.**A.; P.; U.; **Bra.**P.; **C.**AB.; APH. 49–; BO.; UL.; V. 49–; **Cr.**M.; P.; U. imp.; **Db.**; **Dn.**U. 44–; **E.**A.; AB.; AG.; N.; PO. 51–; U.; **G.**M.; **H.**U. 57–; **Hu.**G.; **Je.**; **Ld.**P.; U.; W.; **Lv.**P.; **M.**P.; U. imp.; **Md.**H.; **N.**U. 43–; **Nw.**A.; P.; **O.**RE.; **R.**D. 55–; U.; **Rt.**; **Sal.**F.; **Sh.**P. **Sil.**; **W.** 49–; **Y.** [*C. of:* 26486]

1432 Agriculture. Montréal. *Agriculture, Montréal* [1944–] **L.**AM. 46–; **Hu.**G. 48– imp.; **Md.**H. 48–; **Y.**
  Agriculture. Sofia. *See* 58967.

1433 Agriculture. Téhéran. *Agriculture, Téhéran*
  Agriculture. Varsovie. *See* 48112 and 48113.

1434 Agriculture Abroad. Ottawa. *Agriculture abroad* [1945–] **L.**AM.; BM. 57–; **Abs.**U. 52–; **C.**A.; **O.**AEC.; **R.**U. 53–.

1435 Agriculture in the **Americas.** Washington. *Agriculture Am.* [1941–47] **L.**AM. 47; BMᴺ.; FA. 46–47; TP.; **C.**A.; **Hu.**G.; **Lv.**P. imp.; **Md.**H.; **O.**AEC. 47; **Rt.** [*C. in:* 19917]

1436 Agriculture and **Animal Husbandry** in **India.** Calcutta. *Agriculture Anim. Husb. India* [1933–39] **L.**AM. 33–37; BMᴺ. 33–35 imp.; EB. imp.; V.; **C.**A.; **M.**C. 36; **Md.**H.; **Nw.**A.; **O.**I.; **Rt.**; **Sal.** [*C. of:* 46181]

1437 Agriculture and **Animal Husbandry, Uttar Pradesh.** Lucknow. *Agriculture Anim. Husb. Uttar Pradesh* [1950–57] **L.**EB. 50–56 imp.; K.; **Abs.**A. imp.; **C.**A. imp.; **E.**AB. 50–55 imp.; **Md.**H. 50–54 imp.; **R.**D. 54; **Rt.** imp.

1438 Agriculture in **British Guiana.** Georgetown. *Agriculture Br. Guiana* [1952–] **C.**A.; **Y.**

1439 **Agriculture Correspondence.** Ministry of Agriculture and Forestry. Nanking. *Agriculture Corresp., Nanking* O.F. 45– (for.).

1440 **Agriculture** et **élévage** au **Congo belge.** Bruxelles. *Agriculture Élév. Congo belge* L.K. 27–31.

1441 **Agriculture** and **Forestry Notes.** College of Agriculture and Forestry, University of Nanking. *Agriculture For. Notes Univ. Nanking* Md.H. 39–41.

1442 **Agriculture** and **Forestry Series.** College of Agriculture and Forestry, University of Nanking. *Agriculture For. Ser. Univ. Nanking*

1443 **Agriculture** and **Forestry Series.** Pan-American Union. Washington, D.C. *Agriculture For. Ser. Pan-Am. Un.*

1444 **Agriculture Handbook.** Forest Service, U.S. Department of Agriculture. Washington. *Agric. Handb. Forest Serv. U.S.* [1949–] O.F.; **Y.**

1445 **Agriculture** and **Horticulture.** Tokyo. *Agriculture Hort., Tokyo* Md.H. 53–; **Rt.** 51; **Y.**

1446 **Agriculture** et l'**horticulture** à l'**école.** Bordeaux. *Agriculture Hort. Éc.*

1447 **Agriculture Information Bulletin.** Washington. *Agriculture Inf. Bull.* [1949–] L.BM.; **Br.**A. 58– imp.; **C.**A.; O.F. imp.; RE. 50– imp.; **Rt.**; **Y.**
Agriculture in Israel. *See* 21739.

1448 **Agriculture** and **Live-Stock** in **India.** Delhi. *Agriculture Live-Stk India* [1931–39] L.AM.; BM.; BM^N.; EB.; MY.; TD.; TP.; V.; **Abd.**R.; **Abs.**A.; **C.**A.; P.; UL.; E.AB.; U.; W. imp.; **M.**C.; **Md.**H.; **Nw.**A.; O.RE.; **Rt.**; **Sal.** [*C. from:* 1354; *C. as:* 22968]
Agriculture of **Maine.** *See* 44370.

1449 **Agriculture Monographs.** U.S. Department of Agriculture. Washington. *Agriculture Monogr.* [1950–55] L.BM.; BM^N.; K.; Z. 51; **C.**A.; O.F. imp.; RE. imp.; **Rt.**; **Y.**

1450 **Agriculture** in **Northern Ireland.** Belfast. *Agriculture North. Ire.* [1960–] L.AM.; BM.; **Abd.**R. 60–; **Bn.**U.; **C.**A.; **G.**U.; **Ld.**U.; **Md.**H.; O.RE. (3 yr.); **Y.** [*C. of:* 33390 and 33601]

1451 **Agriculture nouvelle.** Paris. *Agriculture nouv.* [1891–]

1452 **Agriculture Overseas.** Ministry of Agriculture and Fisheries. London. *Agriculture overseas* [1946–49] L.AM.; BM.; **Ld.**P.; O.G.; RE.; **Rt.**; **Y.**

1453 **Agriculture Pakistan.** Karachi. *Agriculture Pakist.* [1949–] L.AM.; BM^N.; EB. 60–; TP. 53–; **C.**A.; E.AB. 58–; **Md.**H.; O.RE. (2 yr.); **R.**D.; **Rt.**; **Y.**

1454 **Agriculture polonaise** et des pays de l'Est européen. Varsovie. *Agriculture pol.* [1931–32] L.AM.; **C.**A.; **Rt.** [*C. of:* 56697; *C. as:* 18534]

1455 **Agriculture pratique.** Paris. *Agriculture prat.* [1937–38: 49–] L.A. 49– imp.; AM.; P.; **Abs.**N.; **C.**A.; **Db.**; **Hu.**G. 49–53 imp.; **Rt.**; **Y.** [*C. of:* 25462: 1938–40 *merged in:* 47057]

1456 **Agriculture pratique** des **pays chauds.** Paris. *Agriculture prat. Pays chauds* [1901–14: 30–32] L.BM. 01–14; EB. 30–32; K. 01–13; P. 01–14; TP. imp.; **C.**A. 30–31; **Rt.** 30–31; **Sy.**R. 01–13. [1914–30 *published in* 1490]

1456ª **Agriculture Research Digest.** Bracknell. *Agriculture Res. Dig.* [1943–] E.W. 43–50.
Agriculture in **Scotland.** *See* 43297.

1457 **Agriculturist.** Grand Island, Neb. *Agriculturist*
Agri-hortique genetica. Landskrona. *See* 1225.

1458 **Agrikultur-Zeitung.** Wien. *Agrikultur-Ztg*

1459 **Agrimotor Magazine.** Chicago. *Agrimotor Mag.* L.P. 17–22*.

1460 **Agro.** Buenos Aires. *Agro* [1959–] L.AM. 60–.

1461 **Agrobiologiya.** Moskva. Агробиология. *Agrobiologiya* [1942–] L.AM. 42–49: 60–; BM.; MY. 55–; P. 59–; **C.**A. 46– imp.; **Hu.**G. 46–50 imp.; **Md.**H. 54–; **N.**U. 56–; **Rt.** 46–; **Y.** 47. [*C. of:* 57976]

1462 **Agrobotanika. Orszagos agrobotanikai intezet közlemenyei.** Budapest. *Agrobotanika* **C.**A. 59–.
Agrochemistry and **Soil Science.** Budapest. *See* 1467.

1464 **Agrochimica.** Pisa. *Agrochimica* [1956–] L.AM. 61–; P. 58; **Br.**A. 57–; **C.**A.; **Ld.**U.; N.U.; R.U.; **Rt.**; **Y.**
Agrogeological Publications. Helsinki. *See* 1466.
Agrogeologisia julkaisuja. *See* 1466.
Agrogeologisia karttoja. Helsinki. *See* 1465.

1465 **Agrogeologiska kartor.** Geologiska kommission. Helsingfors. *Agrogeol. Kart.* [1916–56] L.AM. 37–56; BM.; BM^N. 16–23; GL. 00–; GM.; **Bn.**U. 24–56; **C.**A.; N.U. 56; **Rt.**; **Y.**

1466 **Agrogeologiska meddelanden.** Helsingfors. *Agrogeol. Meddn* L.AM. 38–58; BM^N. 24; **Abs.**A. 35–58; **Bn.**U. 27–58; **Br.**A. 41–58 imp.; **C.**A. 13–58; N.U. 55–58. **Rt.** 13–46; **Y.**

1467 **Agrokémia** és **talajtan.** Budapest. *Agrokém. Talajt.* [1951–] L.A.; AM. 59–; C.; **Abs.**A.; **Br.**A.; **C.**A. 51; **Db.**; **Hu.**G.; **Y.**

1468 **Agrokémiai kutató intézet évkönyve.** Budapest. *Agrokém. Kutató Intéz. Évk.* [1950–] L.BM.; **Y.**

1469 **Agrolesomelioratsiya.** Moskva. Агролесомелиорация. *Agrolesomelioratsiya* [1956–] **Rt.** 57.

1470 **Agro-meteorological Bulletin.** Meteorological Service, Israel. Hakirya. *Agro-met. Bull. Israel* [1959–] **Y.**

1471 **Agrometeorological Bulletin.** Station Wad Medani. Khartoum. *Agromet. Bull., Khartoum* L.MO. 58–.
Agronom. Kiev. *See* 1512.

1472 **Agronom.** Moskva. Агроном. *Agronom, Mosk.* [1924–29] [*C. in:* 50597]

1473 **Agronome.** Namur. *Agronome, Namur*

1474 **Agronome praticien.** Compiègne. *Agronome Pratn* [1930–]

1475 **Agronomía.** Buenos Aires. *Agronomía, B. Aires* [1930–] [*C. of:* 46375]

1476 **Agronomía.** Habana. *Agronomía, Habana* [1924–]

1477 **Agronomía.** La Molina, Peru. *Agronomía, La Molina* [1936–]

1478 **Agronomía.** Lima. *Agronomía, Lima* L.AM. 48–; **C.**A. 49–; **Hu.**G. 57–; **Y.**

1479 **Agronomia.** Escola nacional de agronomia. Rio de Janeiro. *Agronomia, Esc. nac. Agron. Rio de J.* [1945–] L.EB. [*C. of:* 7358]

1480 **Agronomia.** Sociedade brasiliera de agronomia. Rio de Janeiro. *Agronomia, Soc. bras. Agron. Rio de J.* [1930–] **Y.**

1481 **Agronomía.** Sociedad agronómica de Chile. Santiago. *Agronomía, Santiago* [1915–] **Hu.**G. 50–. [*C. of:* 46270]

1482 **Agronomia angolana.** Luanda. *Agronomia angol.* [1948–] **L.**BM. 54–; BM^N.; TP. 48–56; **C.**A.; **Hu.**G.; **Md.**H. 48–50; **O.**F.; **Rt.**; **Y.**

1483 **Agronomia lusitana.** Sacavém, etc. *Agronomia lusit.* [1939–] **L.**AM. imp.; BM.; BM^N.; EB.; K. 39–46; L. imp.; MY.; QM. 42–imp.; TP. 44–; **Abd.**R. 44–; S.; **Abs.**A.; **Ba.**I. 41–; **Br.**A. 43–; **C.**BO.; **E.**B.; W.; **Hu.**G. 45–; **Lv.**U. 52–; **Md.**H.; N.U.; **O.**F.; R.U. 42–53; **Rt.**; **Sil.** 52–; **Y.**

1484 **Agronomía sulriograndense.** Buenos Aires. *Agronomía sulriogr.* [1954–] **L.**TP. imp.

1485 **Agronomía tropical.** Revista del Instituto nacional de agricultura. Maracay. *Agronomía trop.* [1951–] **L.**BM^N. 57–; MY.; **C.**A.; **Hu.**G.; **Y.**

1486 **Agronomía y veterinaría técnica y practica rural.** Buenos Aires. *Agronomía Vet. téc. pract. rur.* [1951–] **L.**AM. 52–; V. 52–; **C.**V. 57–; **E.**AB. 55–; **Y.**

    Agronómiai kar kiadványai, Agrartudományi egyetem, Budapest. *See* 1212.

1487 **Agronomic Series Bulletin.** Department of Agriculture, Nyasaland. Zomba. *Agronomic Ser. Bull. Nyasald* [1926–] **O.**F. 30: 39; **Rt.** 26–30.

1488 **Agronomica.** Roma. *Agronomica* [1956–] **Abs.**U.; **Y.**

1489 **Agronomicheskīya izvêstīya Saratovskoĭ gubernii.** Saratov. Агрономическія извѣстія Саратовской губерніи. *Agron. Izv. Saratov. Gub.*

1490 **Agronomie coloniale.** Paris. *Agron. colon.* [1913–39] **L.**EB. 18–39; K.; MY. 21–39; TP.; **C.**A. 36–39; **Md.**H. imp. [*C. of:* 1492; *C. as:* 1491]

1491 **Agronomie tropicale.** Nogent-sur-Marne, etc. *Agron. trop., Nogent* [1946–] **L.**AM. 50–; EB.; K.; P. 50– imp.; **C.**A.; **Hu.**G.; **Md.**H.; **O.**F.; R.U. 55–; **Rt.**; **Sil.** imp.; **Sy.**R.; **Y.** [*C. of:* 1490]

1492 **Agronomie tropicale.** Société d'études d'agriculture tropicale. Uccle. *Agron. trop., Uccle* [1909–13] **L.**EB.; K.; TP. [*C. as:* 1490]

1493 **Agronomo argentino.** Rosario. *Agronomo argent.* [1928–30]

1494 **Agronomski glasnik.** Zagreb. *Agron. Glasn.* [1951–] **L.**BM. 57–; **Hu.**G. 56–; **Y.**

1495 **Agronomy.** Current Literature. U.S. Department of Agriculture. Washington. *Agronomy, U.S. Dep. Agric.* **C.**A. [*C. in:* 37870]

1496 **Agronomy Abstracts.** American Society of Agronomy. Davis, Cal., etc. *Agron. Abstr.* [1953–] **L.**P. 55–; **C.**A.; **Y.**

1497 **Agronomy Bulletin.** College of Agriculture, Sun Yat-Sen University. Canton. *Agron. Bull., Canton* **C.**A. 33–49 imp.

1498 **Agronomy Bulletin.** School of Agriculture, University of Sydney. Sydney. *Agron. Bull. Univ. Sydney* **C.**A. 58–.

1499 **Agronomy Circular.** Nebraska College of Agriculture. Lincoln, Neb. *Agron. Circ. Neb.*

1500 **Agronomy Information Circulars.** North Carolina Agricultural Experiment Station. Raleigh. *Agron. Inf. Circ., N. Carol.* **C.**A.

1501 **Agronomy Journal.** Washington, etc. *Agron. J.* [1949–] **L.**AM.; P.; TP.; **Abd.**U. **Abs.**A.; S.; U. 50–; **Ba.**I.; **Bl.**U. 53–; **Bm.**U.; **Bn.**U.; **Br.**A. 49–55; **C.**A.; AB.; **Cr.**N.; **Db.**; **E.**W.; **G.**GE. 50–; U. 53–; **Hu.**G.; Je.; **Ld.**U.; **Md.**H.; N.U.; **Nw.**A.; **O.**RE. imp.; **R.**D. 51–; U.; **Sil.**; **Y.** [*C. of:* 25532]

1501° **Agronomy [News.** Madison. *Agron. News* **C.**A. 56–.

1502 **Agronomy Review.** Lincoln, N.Z. *Agron. Rev.* [1948–49] **Abs.**A.; **Ba.**I.; **C.**A.; **Db.**; **E.**W. imp.; **Rt.**

1503 **Agronoomia.** Tartu. *Agronoomia* [1921–] **C.**A. 28–40; **Hu.**G. 37–38; **Rt.** 37–40.

1504 **Agros.** Lisboa. *Agros, Lisb.* [1917–] **Hu.**G. 45– imp.; **O.**AEC. 45–; F. 43– imp.; **Y.**

1505 **Agros.** Pelotas. *Agros, Pelotas* [1948–] **C.**A. 50–; **Hu.**G. 51–.

1506 **Agrostologist.** London. *Agrostologist* [1936–] **Bn.**U. 38–39.

1507 **Agrotécnia.** Havana. *Agrotécnia*

1508 **Agrotekhnika.** Khar'kov. Агротехника. *Agrotekhnika* [1932–]

1509 **Agrotikē zōē.** en Athēnais. Ἀγροτικὴ ζωή. *Agrot. Zoe* [1927–29] [*C. of:* 34438; *C. as:* 34437]

1510 **Agrotikos tahudromos.** en Athēnais. Ἀγροτικὸς Ταχυδρόμος. *Agrot. Tahudr.* **Y.**

1511 **Agyagipari ujság.** Budapest. *Agyagip. Ujs.*

    Ahrens Sammlung chemischer und chemisch-technischer Vorträge. *See* 48508.

1512 **Ahronom.** Kȳyiv. Агроном. *Ahronom* [1923–28] **Rt.**

1513 **Aichi Journal** of **Experimental Medicine.** Nagoya. *Aichi J. exp. Med.* [1923–24] **L.**LI.; MD.; S.; TD.; UC.; Z.; **Bl.**U.; **Bm.**U.; **Br.**U.; **C.**UL.; **E.**R.; U.; **G.**U.; **Ld.**U.; **Lv.**U.; **Nw.**A.; **O.**R.; **Sa.** [*C. as:* 34045]

1514 **Ailes.** Journal hebdomadaire de la locomotion aérienne. Paris. *Ailes* [1921–] **L.**AV. 37–; **Y.**

1515 **A'in Shams Science Bulletin.** Cairo. *A'in Shams Sci. Bull.* [1956–] **L.**K.; QM.

1516 **Ainslie's Nautical Almanac.** South Shields. *Ainslie's naut. Alm.* [1868–41] **L.**BM. 87–41; **Abs.**N. 13–41; **E.**A. 98–41 imp.; **O.**B. 98–41.

1517 **Air.** London. *Air, Lond.* [1909–20] **L.**BM.

1518 **Air.** Aeronautical Institute. London. *Air, aeronaut. Inst.* [1916–18] **L.**BM. imp.; P.; **Abs.**N.; **Bm.**P.; **G.**M.; **O.**R.

1519 **Air.** Air League of the British Empire. London. *Air, Air Leag.* [1927–31] **L.**BM.; SC.; **Bm.**U. 28–31; **C.**UL.; **O.**B. [*C. in:* 1522]

1520 **Air.** Paris. *Air, Paris* [1919–60] **L.**AV. 21–30: 38–39: 48–60 imp.; **Y.** [*C. as:* 1535°]

1521 **Air Affairs.** Washington. *Air Affairs* [1946–] **L.**AV. 46–50.

1522 **Air and Airways.** London. *Air Airways* [1931–33] **L.**BM.; SC.; **Bm.**U.; **C.**UL.; **O.**B. [*C. of:* 1519 and 1624; *C. as:* 1625]

1523 **Air Almanac.** London, Washington. *Air Alm.* [1937–] **L.**AS. 43–; BM.; **Bm.**P. 45–; **G.**M.; **Lv.**P.; **M.**P.; **N.**P. 40–; **O.**R.; **Y.**

1524 **Air Annual** of the **British Empire.** London. *Air A. Br. Emp.* [1929–39] **L.**BM.; P.; **Abs.**N.; **Bm.**P.; U.; **C.**UL.; **Cr.**P.; **Db.**; **E.**A.; **G.**M.; U.; **Ld.**P. 29–37; **Lv.**P.; **M.**P.; **Nw.**P. imp.; **O.**B.

1525 **Air BP.** London. *Air BP* [1956–] **L.**AV.; BM.; P. (curr.); **Y.**

1526 **Air Commerce Bulletin.** Washington. *Air Commerce Bull.* [1929–39] **L.**AV.; MO. 37–39; P. 38–39 imp. [*C. as:* 14445]

1527 **Air comprimé.** Paris. *Air compr.* [1955–] **L.**P.; **Y.**

1528 **Air Conditioning** and **Controls.** London. *Air Condit. Controls* [1960–] **L.**BM.; P.; **Y.**

1529 **Air Conditioning** with **Fluid Fuels.** New York. *Air Condit. fluid Fuels* [1932–33]

1530 **Air Conditioning, Heating** and **Ventilation.** New York. *Air Condit. Heat. Vent.* [1955–] **L.**P.; SC.; TD.; **Lv.**P. 59–; **Y.** [*C. of:* 22012]

1531 **Air Conditioning** and **Oil Heat.** New York. *Air Condit. Oil Heat* [1936–42] [*C. of:* 36120; *C. in:* 20428]

1532 **Air Conditioning** and **Refrigeration News.** Detroit. *Air Condit. Refrig. News* [1936–] [*C. of:* 17619]

1533 **Air Conditioning Trends.** Chicago. *Air Condit. Trends* [1932–33]

1534 **Air Craft.** New York. *Air Craft*

1535 **Air Engineering.** Detroit. *Air Engng* [1959–] **L.**P. 60–; **Y.**

1535ᵉ **Air** et l'**espace.** Paris. *Air Espace* [1960–] **L.**AV.; **Y.** [*C. of:* 1520]

1536 **Air Facts.** New York. *Air Facts* **L.**AV. 50–55; **Y.**

1537 **Air Force.** Washington. *Air Force* **L.**BM. 43–46*. [*C. as:* 3]

1538 **Air Force Review.** Toronto. *Air Force Rev.* [1940–44] [*C. as:* 5571]

1539 **Air Force Survey** in **Geophysics.** Bedford Mass. *Air Force Surv. Geophys.* **L.**MO. 52– imp.; P. 59–.

1540 **Air Freight.** London. *Air Freight* [1954–59] **L.**BM.; P.; AV.; **Lv.**P. [*C. as:* 20337]

1541 **Air League Bulletin.** London. *Air Leag. Bull.* **L.**BM. 20–; SC. 26–27. [*C. of:* 1004]

1542 **Air News.** Mount Morris, Ill. *Air News* [1945–46] **L.**AV. [*C. of:* 1559]

1542ᵃ **Air Observations. Royal Observatory, Hong Kong.** *Air Obsns R. Obs. Hong Kong* [*C. from:* 31630]

1543 **Air Pilot.** London. *Air Pilot* **L.**MO. (1 yr.); **Bm.**P. 34–; **G.**M. 29–; **O.**B. 24–.

1544 **Air Pollution Bibliography.** Washington. *Air Pollut. Biblphy* [1957–59] **L.**BM.; H.; MO.; P.; SC.

Air Pollution Control Association News. *See* 95.

1544ᵃ **Air Pollution News.** National Smoke Abatement Society. London. *Air Pollut. News* [1957–] **L.**BM.

1545 **Air Power.** London. *Air Pwr, Lond.* [1953–60] **L.**AV.; BM.; **Abs.**N.; **C.**UL.; **E.**A.; **F.**A.; **G.**M.; **Lv.**P.; **O.**B. [*C. of:* and *Rec. as:* 48162]

1546 **Air Power.** New York. *Air Pwr, N.Y.* [1918–20] [*C. of:* 34435]

1547 **Air Power News.** London. *Air Pwr News* **L.**P. (curr.)

1548 **Air Progress.** New York. *Air Prog.* [1938–]

1549 **Air Repair.** Pittsburgh, Louisville. *Air Repair* [1951–55]

1550 **Air Reserve Gazette.** *Air Reserve Gaz.* [1946–] **Bm.**P.; **C.**UL. [*C. of:* 130]

1551 **Air Revue.** Bruxelles. *Air Revue* [1955–59] **L.**P.; **Y.** [*C. as:* 1599]

1552 **Air** et la **route.** Journal mensuel de l'aviation et de l'automobile. Paris. *Air Route*

1553 **Air Scout.** New York. *Air Scout* [1918–19]

1554 **Air Service Information Circular.** Washington. *Air Serv. Inf. Circ.* **L.**BM. 22–23 imp.

1555 **Air Service Journal.** New York. *Air Serv. J.* **L.**AV. 18–19*; BM. 17–19. [*C. as:* 1589]

1556 **Air** et **soleil.** Paris. *Air Sol.* [1917–39]

1557 **Air Surgeon's Bulletin.** Dayton, Ohio. *Air Surg. Bull.* **L.**MD. 44–45.

1558 **Air Survey Research Papers.** War Office, London. *Air Surv. Res. Pap.* **L.**P. 44–46; **M.**P. 45–; **O.**R. 45–.

1559 **Air Tech:** the magazine of aircraft maintenance and operation. New York. *Air Tech* [1942–45] **L.**AV. 43–45. [*C. as:* 1542]

1560 **Air Techniques.** Paris. *Air Techniq.* [1957–] **L.**AV. 58– imp.; P.; **Y.**

1561 **Air Trails.** New York. *Air Trails* **L.**BM. 28–31; **O.**B. 28–31.

1562 **Air Transport** and **Airport Engineering.** London. *Air Transp. Airport Engng* [1945–] **L.**BM.; **Abs.**N.; **O.**B.

1563 **Air Transport** and **Civil Aviation.** London, New York. *Air Transp. civ. Aviat.* [1943–48] **L.**BM.; **F.**A. 45–47; **M.**P.; **O.**B.

1564 **Air Transportation.** East Stroudsburg, Pa. *Air Transpn, E. Stroudsburg* [1927–30] [*C. as:* 1073]

1565 **Air Transportation.** Flushing, N.Y. *Air Transpn, Flushing, N.Y.* [1932–34] [*C. of:* 1614; *C. as:* 1569]

1566 **Air Transportation.** New York. *Air Transpn, N.Y.* [1942–] **L.**AV. 57– imp.; **Bm.**P. 43–; **Y.**

1567 **Air Treatment Engineer.** London. *Air Treat. Engr* [1938–50] **L.**BA.; BM.; EE. 47–50 imp.; P.; **C.**UL. 45–50; **E.**A. 45–50; **G.**M. 47–50; **M.**P. 39–50; **O.**B.; R.; **Sil.** 49–50. [*C. as:* 22006]

1568 **Air University Quarterly Review.** Montgomery, Washington. *Air Univ. q. Rev.* [1947–] **L.**BM. 52–; **O.**B. 55–.

1569 **Air World.** Flushing, N.Y. *Air Wld, Flushing, N.Y.* [1934] [*C. of:* 1565]

1570 **Air World.** New York. *Air Wld, N.Y.* [1943–]

1571 **Aircraft.** London. *Aircraft, Lond.* [1916–19] **L.**AV.; BM.; P. 17–19. [*C. as:* 1583]

1572 **Aircraft.** Melbourne. *Aircraft, Melb.* [1921–] **L.**AV. 45– imp.; **Y.**

1573 **Aircraft.** Sydney. *Aircraft, Sydney*

1574 **Aircraft.** Toronto. *Aircraft, Toronto* [1951–] **L.**AV.; **Y.** [*C. of:* 1577]

1574ᵃ **Aircraft Accident Digest.** International Civil Aviation Organization. Montreal. *Aircr. Accid. Dig.* [1951–] **L.**BM.

1575 **Aircraft Accident** and **Maintenance Review.** Washington. *Aircr. Accid. Maint. Rev.* [1946–60] **L.**AV.; 54–60; P. 59–60. [*C. as:* 1104]

1576 **Aircraft Age.** Kansas City. *Aircr. Age* [1929–33]

1577 **Aircraft** and **Airport.** Ottawa, etc. *Aircr. Airport* L.AV. 47–50*; **Y.** [*C. as:* 1574]

1578 **Aircraft Annual.** London. *Aircr. A., Lond.* [1949: 57–] L.BM.; C.UL.; E.A.; O.R. [>1595, 1954–55]

1579 **Aircraft Annual.** New York. *Aircr. A., N.Y.* [1944–]

1580 **Aircraft Bulletin.** Ciba (A.R.L.) Ltd. Duxford. *Aircr. Bull.* [1957–] L.P.

1581 **Aircraft Development** and **Production.** London. *Aircr. Dev. Prod.* [1948–] L.BM.; G.M.; Lv.P.; M.P.; O.R. [*C. of:* 1094]

1582 **Aircraft Engineer.** London. *Aircr. Engr* L.BM.; P. 26–; Lv.P. 26–28. [*Supplement to:* 19608]

1583 **Aircraft Engineering.** London. *Aircr. Engng* [1919–21] L.BM.; P.; C.ENG. [*C. of:* 1571]

1584 **Aircraft Engineering.** London. *Aircr. Engng* [1929–] L.AV.; BM.; I. (3 yr.); KC. 55–; P.; QM. 35–; SC.; Abs.N.; Bl.U. 55–; Bm.P. 34–; U. 46–; Bn.U. 40–45; Br.P. 38–; U. 38–; C.ENG.; UL.; Co.T. 43–; Db.; Dn.U. 52–; E.A.; T. 36–; Ex.U. 48–; F.A.; G.M. 51–; T. 30–; U. 46–; Ld.U. 37–; Lv.P. 32–; U. 57–; M.P. 30–; T. 39–; U. 41– imp.; Ma.T. 58–; N.U. 55–; O.ED.; R.; Sh.P. 38–; SC. 57–; **Y.**

1585 **Aircraft Engines** of the **World.** New York. London. *Aircr. Eng. Wld* L.P. 46–; SC. 45–.

1586 **Aircraft** of the **Fighting Powers.** Leicester. *Aircr. fight. Pwrs* [1940–46] L.BM.; Bm.P.; G.U.; Lv.P.; M.P.; O.B.

1587 **Aircraft Heating Digest.** Columbus, Ohio. *Aircr. Heat. Dig.* [1949–] L.P. 49–57.

1588 **Aircraft Journal.** East Hartford, Conn. *Aircr. J., E. Hartford* [1941–43]

1589 **Aircraft Journal.** New York. *Aircr. J., N.Y.* [1919–20] L.AV.; BM. [*C. of:* 1555]

1590 **Aircraft** and **Missiles.** Philadelphia. *Aircr. Missiles* [1959–60] L.AV. [*C. of:* 1591; *C. as:* 1108ᶜ]

1591 **Aircraft** and **Missiles Manufacturing.** Philadelphia. *Aircr. Missiles Mfg* [1958–59] L.AV. [*C. as:* 1590]

1591ᵃ **Aircraft News.** Pretoria. *Aircr. News* [1956–] L.BM.

1592 **Aircraft Operator's Bulletin.** London. *Aircr. Oper. Bull.*

1593 **Aircraft Production.** London. *Aircr. Prod., Lond.* [1938–] L.AV.; BM.; I. (2 yr.); P.; PL. 45–; SC.; Bm.P.; T. 53– imp.; U.; Br.P. (1 yr); C.UL.; E.A.; T.; F.A. 44–; Ld.U. 60–; Lv.P. 53–; M.P.; T.; Ma.T. 58–; O.R.; Sh.P.; **Y.**

1594 **Aircraft Production.** Los Angeles. *Aircr. Prod., Los Ang.* [1943–]

1595 **Aircraft Today.** London. *Aircr. today* [1954–55] L.BM.; C.UL.; E.A.; O.R. [*C. of:* and *Rec. as:* 1578]

1596 **Aircraft Year Book.** London. *Aircr. Yb., Lond.* L.BM. 23.

1597 **Aircraft Year Book.** New York. *Aircr. Yb., N.Y.* L.P. 19–22; Bm.P. 32–.

1598 **Aireview.** Tokyo. *Aireview, Tokyo* L.AV. 53– imp.; **Y.**

1599 **Airevue.** Bruxelles. *Airevue* [1959–] L.P.; **Y.** [*C. of:* 1551]

1600 **Airfields Circular.** Shell International Petroleum. London. *Airflds Circ.* L.P. 59–.

1601 **Airflow.** Newark, N.J. *Airflow* [1941–]

1602 **Airframe** and **Equipment Engineering Report.** Washington. *Airframe Equip. Engng Rep.* **Y.**

1603 **Airlift.** Washington. *Airlift* [1959–] L.AV. F.A.; Lv.P. [*C. of:* 1905]

1604 **Airman.** Manston, Kent. *Airman* L.BM. 21*.

1605 **Airman's Year Book.** London. *Airman's Yb.* [1934–35] L.BM.; Bm.P.; M.P. 35; O.B.

1606 **Airplane Patent Digest.** New York. *Airpl. Pat. Dig.* [1932–] L.P.; F.A 44–. [*C. of* 37193]

1607 **Airplanes.** Chicago. *Airplanes* [1936–]

1608 **Airport** and **Airline Management.** London. *Airport Airline Mgmt* [1960–] L.AV.; BM.; P.; **Y.** [*C. of:* 1615]

1609 **Airport Bulletin.** Washington. *Airport Bull.* [1935–] L.BM.

1610 **Airport Construction** and **Management.** Los Angeles. *Airport Constr. Mgmt* [1929–30]

1611 **Airports.** Charlotte, N.C. *Airports, Charlotte* [1944–] L.AV. 45–48. [*C. of:* 2123]
Airports. Flushing, N.Y. *See* 1614.

1612 **Airports.** Washington. *Airports, Wash.* [1954–58] L.AV. 58. [*C. as:* 1617]

1613 **Airports** and **Air Transportation.** London. *Airports Air Transpn* [1946–57] L.AV. 48–57; BM. P.; F.A.; **Y.** [*C. of:* 1616; *C. as:* 1615]

1614 **Airports** and **Airlines.** Flushing, N.Y. *Airports Airlines* [1928–32] [*C. as:* 1565]

1615 **Airports** and **Airport Engineering.** London. *Airports & Airport Engng* [1957–60] L.AV. 58–60; BM.; P.; **Y.** [[*C. of:* 1613; *C. as:* 608]

1616 **Airports** and **Ground Engineering.** London. *Airports Grnd Engng* [1943–46] L.P.; **Y.** [*C. as:* 1613]

1617 **Airports** and **Heliports.** Washington. *Airports Heliports* [1958] L.AV. [*C. of:* 1612]

1618 **Airship.** London. *Airship* [1934–39] L.BM.; P.; SC. 35–39. [*C. as:* 1619]

1619 **Airship** and **Aero History.** London. *Airship Aero Hist.* [1947–49] L.BM.; SC. [*C. of:* 1618]

1620 **Airship** and **Aeronautical Engineer.** London. *Airship aeronaut. Engr* [1908–09] L.BM.; P.

1621 **Airspeed Bulletin.** Portsmouth. *Airspeed Bull.* [1936–39] L.P.

1622 **Airway Age.** New York. *Airway Age* [1928–31] L.AV. 30; P. 30–31. [*C. of:* 49941; *C. in:* 5560]

1623 **Airway Bulletin.** U.S. Department of Commerce. Washington. *Airway Bull.* L.BM. 27–.

1624 **Airways.** London. *Airways* [1924–31] L.BM.; Bm.U. 28–31 imp.; C.UL.; O.B. [*C. in:* 1522]

1625 **Airways** and **Airports.** London. *Airways Airports* [1933–35] L.BM.; SC.; Bm.U.; C.UL.; Dn.U.; Lv.P.; O.B. [*C. of:* 1522; *C. as:* 1013]

1626 **Aisa.** México. *Aisa* [1946–] L.MA. imp.; MD.; TD. 47– imp.; Br.U. 47– imp.; G.U. 46–52.

1627 **Akadēmaikē iatrikē.** en Athēnais. Ἀκαδημαϊκή ἰατρική. *Akad. Iatr.* L.MA. 49–.

1628 **Akadémiai értesitő.** Magyar tudományos akadémia. Budapest. *Akad. Ért.* [1840–51] **L.**BM. 90–51; RI. 50–51; **Bl.**U. 50–51; **Db.** 50; E.R.1860–89 imp.: 50–51.

1629 **Akademisk afhandling.** Dissertatio Academica.— Inaugural Dissertation at the University of Upsala. Upsala. *Akad. Afh. Upsala* **L.**BM^N. 13–; **Lv.**P. 84–18.

1630 **Akademiya arkhitekturў.** Moskva. Академия архитектуры. *Akad. Arkhit.* [1934–38] **L.**BA. 34–35. [*C. of:* 50284]

1631 **Åkerbruket** och **husdjursskötseln.** Stockholm. *Åkerbr. Husdjurssköt.*

1632 **Akita Medical Journal.** Akita. *Akita med. J.* **Akitaken ishikai zasshi.** *See* 1632.

1633 **Akitu.** Takeuchi Entomological Laboratory. Shinomiya Yamashina. Kyoto. *Akitu* [1937–] **L.**BM^N. 37 imp. [*Suspended* 1944–54]

1633^a **Akta** do **dziejów Polski** na **morzu.** Gdańsk. *Akta Dziej. Pol. Morzu* **L.**BM. 51–.

1634 **Aktinometrické merania** v **ČSR.** Praha. *Aktinom. Merania ČSR* **L.**MO. 55–.

1635 **Aktinometrische Monatsbericht.** Tiflis. *Aktinom. Mber.* **L.**MO. 28–29.

1635^a **Aktivisti sanitar.** Tiranë. *Aktivisti sanit.* **L.**BM. 57–.

1636 **Aktiviteits-overzicht. Rijksstation** voor **plantenveredeling.** Lemberge (Melle). *Aktiv.-Overz. Rijksstn PlVered. Abs.*A. 47–.

1637 **Aktuarské vědy:** pojistná matematika. Praha. *Aktu. Vědy* [1929–] **E.**E. **Aktuelle Probleme** der **Dermatologie.** *See* 16195.

1638 **Akusherka.** Odessa. Акушерка. *Akusherka*

1639 **Akusherstvo i ginekologiya.** Leningrad, Moskva. Акушерство и гинекология. *Akush. Ginek.* [1936–] **L.**BM. 55–; MA. 47–; MD. 45–; **Y.** 55– imp. [*C. of:* 21215 and 59129]

1640 **Akusticheskiĭ zhurnal.** Moskva. Акустический журнал. *Akust. Zh.* [1955–] **L.**AV. 59–; BM.; P.; SC.; **C.**P. 56–; **Y.** 56–. [*English translation at:* 50347; *English abstracts at:* 25417^c]

1641 **Akustische Beihefte.** Zürich, Stuttgart. *Akust. Beih.* [1951–] **L.**EE.; P.; RI.; **Abs.**U.; **M.**C. 51–56: 61; **G.**U.; **Ld.**U.; **Nw.**A.; **O.**R. [*Supplement to:* 903]

1642 **Akustische Zeitschrift.** Berlin, etc. *Akust. Z.* 1936–43] **L.**AV. 37–44; P.; SC. 36–42; **Nw.**A. 36–39: 43. [*Replaced by:* 1641]

1643 **Akvariet.** Medlemsblad for Akvarieforeningen. Kjøbenhavn. *Akvariet*

1644 **Akvaristické listy.** Praha. *Akvar. Listy* **L.**Z. 58–.

1645 **Akvarĭum i komnatnȳya rastenĭya.** Moskva. Акваріумъ и комнатныя растенія. *Akvar. komnat. Rast.*

1645^c **Akvárium** a **terárium.** Praha. *Akvár. Terár.,Praha* [1958–] **L.**Z.

1646 **Akvárium** és **terrárium.** Budapest. *Akvár. Terrár., Bpest.* [1956–] **L.**Z. 58–.

1647 **Ala.** Firenze. *Ala* [1945–]

1648 **Ala d'Italia.** Milano. *Ala Ital.* [1922–] **L.**AV. 36–42; BM. 34–43 imp.; **Y.**

1649 **Alabama Conservation.** Montgomery. *Ala. Conserv.* [1940–]

1650 **Alabama Farmer.** Auburn. *Ala. Fmr* [1919–]

1651 **Alabama Forest News.** Montgomery. *Ala. Forest News*

1652 **Alabama Game** and **Fish News.** Montgomery. *Ala. Game Fish News*

1653 **Alabama Medical Journal.** Birmingham, Ala. *Ala. med. J.* [1888–11]

1654 **Alabama Mental Health.** Montgomery. *Ala. ment. Hlth*

1655 **Alam attib.** Damascus. *Alam Attib* [1953–] **L.**MA. imp.

1656 **Alambic.** Bruxelles. *Alambic* **L.**P. (curr.)

1657 **Ålands försöksfält.** Helsinki. *Ålands FörsFält* **C.**A. 48–52.

1658 **Ålands sjöfartstidning.** Organ för sjöfart, jordbruk, fiske. Mariehamn. *Ålands SjöfTidn.*

1659 **Alas.** Revista quincenal de aeronáutica. Madrid. *Alas* [1922–28]

1660 **Alaska Medicine.** Anchorage. *Alaska Med.* [1959–] **L.**MD.

1661 **Alaska** and **North-West Mining Journal.** Seattle, Wash. *Alaska N.-W. Min. J.* [1913–21] [*C. of:* 36705; *C. as:* 36683^c]

1662 **Alaska's Health.** Juneau. *Alaska's Hlth* [1943–] **L.**TD. 51– imp.; **C.**PO. imp.

1663 **Alata.** Milano. *Alata* [1945–] **L.**BM. 48–; P. 55–; **Y.**

1664 **Alauda.** Études et notes ornithologiques. Dijon. *Alauda* [1929–] **L.**BM^N.; NC. 29–39: 49–50: 55–; Z.; **Br.**U.; **C.**B.; **O.**OR. 29–39; **Y.**

1665 **Alba agricola.** Pavia. *Alba agric.* [1903–25]

1666 **Alba-Kundendienst.** Hanau. *Alba-Kundendienst* [1936–39] **L.**P.

1667 **Albany Medical Annals.** Albany. *Albany med. Ann.* [1880–] **L.**MD. 05–07: 14–; **Br.**U. 03–08; **G.**F. 97–17 imp.; **M.**MS. 07–21 imp.

1668 **Alberta Medical Bulletin.** Edmonton. *Alberta med. Bull.*

1669 **Alberta Oil Review.** Edmonton. *Alberta Oil Rev.* [1915–] **O.**G. 44–.

1670 **Albiswerk-Berichte.** Zürich. *Albiswerk-Ber.* [1949–] **L.**P. 52–.

1671 **Albrecht** v. **Graefes Archiv** für **Ophthalmologie.** Leipzig. *Albrecht v. Graefes Arch. Ophthal.* [1854–] **L.**BM.; MA. 27–; MD.; OP.; S. 1854–49; U. 50–; **Abd.**U.; **Bl.**U. 97–15; **Bm.**U.; **Db.** 83–99 imp.; **C.**UL.; **E.**S.; U. 1854–20; **G.**F. 1854–1860: 69–85; U.; **Lv.**M. 01–07; **M.**MS. 1854–20; **O.**R.; **Sa.** 94–16; **Y.**

1672 **Albrecht-Thaer-Archiv.** Berlin. *Albrecht-Thaer-Arch.* [1956–] **L.**AM. 59–; P.; SC. 59–; **C.**A.; **Rt.** 56; **Y.**

1673 **Alchemist.** Glasgow University Alchemist Club. Glasgow. *Alchemist, Glasg.* **G.**M. 25–40; U. 25–; **O.**B. 27–30.

1674 **Alchemist.** Leeds. *Alchemist, Leeds* [1920–58] **L.**BM. 49–58 imp.; PH. 49–58; **E.**HW. 53–58; **G.**T. 53–58; **Lc.**A.; **Sa.** 48–50. [*C. as:* 37499]

1675 **Alchemistische Blätter.** Berlin. *Alchem. Bl.* [1927–29] **L.**C. [*C. as:* 4043]

1676 **Alcmeone**: rivista trimestrale di storia della medicina. New York. *Alcmeone* [1939–] **L**.MA. 47–.

1676ᶜ **Alcoa Aluminium News Letter.** Pittsburgh. *Alcoa Alumin. News Lett.* [*C. of:* 1854]

1677 **Alcool** et **dérivés.** Paris. *Alcool Dérivés* [1952–59] **L**.P. 54–59 imp.

1678 **Alcool industriel.** Paris. *Alcool ind.*

1679 **Alcool industriel** et ses **applications.** Paris. *Alcool ind. Appl.*

1680 **Aldea.** Revista de agricultura. San Sebastián. *Aldea*

1681 **Aleia.** Athenai. Αλεια. *Aleia*

1682 **Alemara.** Cairo. *Alemara* **L**.BA. 40–48.

1683 **Alembic Club Reprints.** Edinburgh. *Alembic Club Repr.* [1893–] **L**.BM.; PH.; SC.; U.; **Abd**.U.; **Br**.U. 93–58; **E**.R.; U.; **H**.U. 29– imp. **Nw**.A. [*Suspended* 1912–28]

1684 **Alemite Industrial Lubrication.** Chicago. *Alemite ind. Lubric.* **L**.P. 29–32. [*C. of:* 28832]

1685 **Alergía.** Buenos Aires. *Alergía, B. Aires* [1947–] **L**.MA.

1686 **Alergía.** México. *Alergía, Méx.* [1953–] **L**.MA.; **Y.**

1687 **Alergología.** Madrid. *Alergología* [1951–] **L**.MA.; MD. [*Supplement to:* 35291.]

1688 **Alessandria medica.** Alessandria. *Alessandria med.*

1689 **Alexander Blair Hospital Bulletin.** Detroit. *Alexander Blair Hosp. Bull.*

1690 **Alexandria Journal** of **Agricultural Research.** Alexandria. *Alex. J. agric. Res.* [1953–] **C**.A.; **E**.AB. imp.

1691 **Alexandria Medical Journal.** Alexandria. *Alex. med. J.* [1955–] **L**.MA. 56–; MD. 58–; S. 58–; **Abd**.R.

1692 **Alexanor.** Revue des lépidoptéristes français. Paris. *Alexanor* [1959–] **L**.BMᴺ.; **Y.**

1693 **Alfalfa Abstracts.** Kansas City. *Alfalfa Abstr.* [1950–] **L**.P. 58–; **C**.A.

    Alfred Hospital Clinical Reports. Melbourne. *See* 14613.

1694 **Alföldi tudományos gyüjtemény.** Szeged. *Alföldi Tud. Gyűjt.* [1948–] **L**.BM. [*C. of:* 1694ᶜ]

1694ᶜ **Alföldi tudományos intézet évkönyve.** Szeged. *Alföldi Tud. Intéz. Évk.* [1946] **L**.BM. [*C. as:* 1694]

1695 **Algemeen hollandsch landbouwblad.** Arnhem. *Alg. holl. LandbBl.* [1932–34] [*Replaces* 1697; *Replaced by* 22249]

1696 **Algemeen landbouwweekblad** voor **Nederlandsch-Indië.** Bandoeng. *Alg. LandbWbl. Ned.-Indië* **Sy**.R. 30–46 imp.

1697 **Algemeen nederlandsch landbouwblad.** Arnhem. *Alg. ned. LandbBl.* [1915–31] [*Replaced by:* 1695]

1698 **Algemeen zuivel- en melkhygienisch weekblad.** Rotterdam. *Alg. zuivel- en melkhyg. Wbl.* [1922–] **Y.** [*C. of:* 1699]

1699 **Algemeen zuivelblad.** Rotterdam. *Alg. Zuivelbl.* [1921–22] [*C. as:* 1698]

    Alger-mathématiques. *See* 41219.
    Alger-sciences physiques. *See* 41219.

1700 **Algérie agricole.** Alger. *Algér. agric.*

1701 **Algérie médicale.** Alger. *Algér. méd.* **L**.MA. 46–; MD. 46– imp.; S. 46–; SH. (1 yr); TD. 35–; **Br**.U. 46–; **Dn**.U. 55– imp.; **Ld**.U. 46–; **M**.MS. 46–. [*C. of:* 26409]

1702 **Algérie viticole.** Alger. *Algér. vitic.*

1703 **Algodão.** Rio de Janeiro. *Algodão* [1934–]
    Algodón. Buenos Aires. *See* 7898.

1704 **Algodón.** Lima. *Algodón, Lima* [1940–] **M**.C.

1705 **Alienist** and **Neurologist.** St. Louis, Mo. *Alien. Neurol.* [1880–20] **L**.BM.; MD. 86–15 imp.; **Br**.U. 91–04 imp.

1706 **Aligarh Muslim University Publications.** Aligarh Musl. Univ. Publs
    Zoological Series [1948–] **L**.Z.; **Bl**.U. 56–.

1707 **Alimentary Review.** Jersey City. *Aliment. Rev.* [1901–09]

1708 **Alimentation** et **agriculture.** F.A.O. Rome. *Aliment. Agric.* **O**.R. 47–.

1709 **Alimentation animale.** Noyon. *Aliment. anim., Noyon*

1710 **Alimentation** des **animaux.** Paris. *Aliment. Anim.*

1711 **Alimentation moderne** et les **industries annexes.** Paris. *Aliment. mod.* [1897–25]
    Alimentation et la **vie.** *See* 12197.

1712 **Alimentazione animale.** Roma. *Alimentaz. anim.* **Abd**.R. 61–; **Hu**.G. 59–.

1713 **Alind Chronicle.** Kundara. *Alind Chron.* [1951–] **L**.P. imp.

1714 **Aliso.** Anaheim, Claremont. *Aliso* [1948–] **L**.BMᴺ.; K.; **Bl**.U.; **Y.**

1715 **Alkaloidal Clinic.** Chicago. *Alkal. Clin.* [1894–05] **L**.MD. 95–02. [*C. as:* 2002]

1716 **Alkaloidchemie.** Stuttgart. *Alkaloidchemie*

1717 **Alkohol-Industrie.** Düsseldorff. *Alkohol-Ind.* [1954–] **L**.P.; **Y.** [*C. of:* 16644]

1718 **Alkoholkérdés.** Budapest. *Alkoholkérdés* [1910–]

1719 **All** the **World's Aircraft.** London. *All Wld's Aircr.* [1909–] **L**.BM.; P.; QM. 34–37: 45–46; SC.; **Abs**.N. 13–; **Bm**.P. 17–32 imp.; **Br**.P. 32–; **Bra**.P. imp.; **C**.UL.; **Cr**.P. 19–; **Db**.; **G**.M. imp.; U. 43–47: 52–; **Ld**.P. 38–; **Lv**.P. 24– imp.; **M**.P. 12–; **Nw**.P. 14–22 imp.; **O**.B.; **Sh**.P. 27– imp.; **Y.**
    All the **World's Airships.** *See* 1719.

1720 **All** the **World's Fighting Ships.** London. *All Wld's fight. Ships* [1898–] **L**.BM.; P. 50– imp.; SC. 06– imp.; **Br**.P. 29–; **Bra**.P. imp.; **C**.UL. 03; **Db**.; **G**.M.; **Ld**.P. 37– imp.; **Lv**.P. 09– imp.; **M**.P. 04–; **O**.B.; **Sh**.P. imp.; **Y.**

1721 **Allahabad Farmer.** Allahabad. *Allahabad Fmr* [1925–] **E**.AB. 30–48: 52–; **Hu**.G. 51– imp.; **O**.AEC. 45–; **R**.D. 44–; **Rt**. 33–; **Y.**

1722 **Allahabad University Studies.** Allahabad. *Allahabad Univ. Stud.* **L**.BM. 49–; BMᴺ. 25–40; TD. 25–26; UC. 32–38; **C**.P.; UL.; **E**.U. 30–38 imp.; **Lv**.U.; **O**.B. 11: 37–38.

1722ᵃ **Állam** és **jog.** Budapest. *ÁllamJog* [1952–] **L**.BM.

1722ᵇ **Állam-** és **jogtudományi intézet tudomanyos könyvtára.** Budapest. *Állam- és jogtud. Intéz. Tud. Könyv.* **L**.BM. 53–.

1722° **Állam** és **kőzigazgatás.** Budapest. *Állam Kőzigazg.* [1949–] **L.**BM.

Allamorvos. *Supplement to:* 21687.

Allan Hancock Foundation Publications. *See* 1723, 15601 and 42718.

1723 **Allan Hancock Pacific Expedition.** Los Angeles. *Allan Hancock Pacif. Exped.* [1935–] **L.**BM[N].; L.; Z.; **Abd.**M.; **C.**P.; **Db.**; **Dm.** 38– imp.; **E.**R. 43–; **Lo.**; **Lv.**U.; **Pl.**M.

Állandó havi értesitő. *Supplement to:* 21696.

1724 **Állategészség.** Budapest. *Állategészség*

1725 **Állategészségi szemle.** Budapest. *Állateg. Szle*

1726 **Állategészségügy állatorvostudományi szaklap.** Budapest. *Állateg. állatorvostud. Szakl.* **W.** 32–.

1727 **Állategészségügyi értesitő.** Budapest. *Állateg. Ért.*

1728 **Állategészségügyi évkönyv.** Budapest. *Állateg. Évk.* **L.**BM. 80–10; **W.** 26–.

1729 **Állatok védelme.** Kolozsvár. *Állatok Véd.*

1730 **Állatorvosi közlöny.** Budapest. *Állatorv. Közl.* **W.** 33–.

1731 **Állatorvosi lapok.** Veterinarius. Budapest. *Állatorv. Lapok* [1878–] **Sal.** 33–34; **W.** 32–.

1732 **Állattani közlemények.** Budapest. *Állatt. Közl.* [1902–] **L.**BM[N].; L. 25–43; MD. 31–; **E.**R. 04–39; **Y.**
Állattani tanulmányok. *See* 51080.

1733 **Állattenyésztés.** Budapest. *Állattenyésztés* [1952–] **Abd.**R. 58–; **C.**A. 53–; **E.**AB. 57–; **R.**D. 53–; **Y.**

1734 **Állattenyésztési** és **tejgazdasági-lapok.** Budapest. *Állatteny. Tejgazd.-Lapok.*

1735 **Állatvédelem.** Budapest. *Állavédelem*

1736 **All-Bengal Kala-Azar Conference.** Calcutta. *All-Bengal Kala-Azar Conf.* **L.**TD. (no. 2) 25.

1737 **Allen Engineering Review.** Bedford. *Allen Engng Rev.* (1939–] **L.**BM.; P.; **G.**E. (2 yr.); **Sh.**IO. 55–; **Y.**

1738 **Allergia.** Athenai. 'Αλλεργία. *Allergia*

1739 **Allergie.** Deutsche Gesellschaft für Allergieforschung. Stuttgart. *Allergie, Stuttg.* [1952–]. [*Supplement to:* 16765]

1740 **Allergie** und **Asthma.** Leipzig. *Allergie Asthma* [1955–] **L.**MD. 59–.

1740° **Allergie-** und **Asthmaforschung.** Leipzig. *Allerg.- u. Asthmaforsch.* [1961–] **L.**MD. [*Supplement to:* 1740]

1741 **Allergy.** Japanese Society of Allergy. Tokyo. *Allergy, Tokyo* [1952–]

1742 **Allergy Abstracts.** St. Louis, Mo. *Allergy Abstr.* [1937–] **L.**MD. 45–; U. 50–; **Dn.**U. 49–; **Y.** [*From 1944 issued with* 25481]

1743 **Allevamenti.** Palermo. *Allevamenti* **L.**EB. 21–24.

1744 **Allgäuer Molkereizeitung.** Kempten. *Allgäu. MolkZtg*

1745 **Allgäuer Monatsschrift** für **Milchwirtschaft** u. **Viehzucht.** Biberach. *Allgäu. Mschr. Milchw.* [1913–]

1746 **Allgemeine Automobilzeitung.** Berlin-München. *Allg. AutoZtg, Berl.* [1900–] **L.**P. 14–23.

1747 **Allgemeine Automobilzeitung.** Wien. *Allg. AutoZtg, Wien* [1900–23] **L.**P.

1748 **Allgemeine Bauzeitung.** Wien. *Allg. Bauztg* [1836–19] **L.**BA. 1836–10; BM. 1836–18; P. 1836–13; **E.**F. 80–01.

1749 **Allgemeine Bauzeitung.** Wien, etc. *Allg. Bauztg* [1946–] **L.**BM.; P. (1 yr); **Y.**

1750 **Allgemeine botanische Zeitschrift** f. **Systematik, Floristik, Pflanzengeographie,** etc. Karlsruhe. *Allg. bot. Z.* [1895–27] **L.**BM[N].; K.; L.; **M.**U. 95–12 imp.

1751 **Allgemeine Brauer-** u. **Mälzerzeitung.** Stuttgart. *Allg. Brau.- u. MälzZtg* [*C. of:* 16673]

1752 **Allgemeine deutsche Bäderzeitung.** Breslau. *Allg. dt. Bäderztg* [1904–27]

1753 **Allgemeine deutsche Mühlenzeitung.** Berlin. *Allg. dt. MühlZtg* **Sal.**F. 38–39.
Allgemeine Elektrizitäts Gesellschaft Zeitung. *See* 27.

1754 **Allgemeine Fischereizeitung.** München. *Allg. FischZtg* [1886–] **L.**AM. 49–55 imp.; BM[N]. 94–18; **Db.** 02–; **G.**U. 57–; **Lv.**U. 93–33 imp.; **Pl.**M. 94–04; **Y.**

1755 **Allgemeine Fischwirtschaftszeitung.** Bremerhaven. *Allg. FischwZtg* [1950–] **L.**AM. 57–; **Lo.** 57–; **Y.**

1757 **Allgemeine forst-** und **holzwirtschaftliche Zeitung.** Wien. *Allg. forst- u. holzw. Ztg* [1946–50] **O.**F. [*C. of:* 57544; *C. as:* 1759]

1758 **Allgemeine Forstzeitschrift.** München. *Allg. Forstz.* **O.**F. 49–; **Y.**

1759 **Allgemeine Forstzeitung.** Wien. *Allg. Forstztg* [1950–] **O.**F.; **Y.** [*C. of:* 1757]

1760 **Allgemeine Forst-** u. **Jagdzeitung.** Frankfurt a. M. *Allg. Forst- u. Jagdztg* **C.**BO. 08–13; UL. 07–; **E.**B. 91–05; **O.**F. 1841–; RE. 90–00; **Y.**

1761 **Allgemeine Gärtnerzeitung.** Berlin. *Allg. Gärtnerztg* **L.**MY. 41–45.

1762 **Allgemeine Glas-** und **Keram-Industrie.** Haida i. B. *Allg. Glas- u. Keramind.* [1910–] **Sh.**G. 24–.

1763 **Allgemeine medizinische Zentralzeitung.** Berlin. *Allg. med. ZentZtg* [1832–33] **L.**BM. 1842–14; **Br.**U. 89–91; **C.**PH. 1855–1856.

1764 **Allgemeine milchwirtschaftliche Zeitschrift.** Berlin. *Allg. milchw. Z.*

1765 **Allgemeine Milchzeitung.** Hamburg. *Allg. Milchztg*
Allgemeine militärärztliche Zeitung. *Supplement to:* 30564.

1766 **Allgemeine Molkereizeitung.** Stuttgart. *Allg. MolkZtg*

1767 **Allgemeine Oel-** und **Fettzeitung.** Berlin. *Allg. Oel- u. Fettztg* [1904–] **L.**C. 32–40 imp.; PR. 31–39; TP. 31–43 imp.

1768 **Allgemeine österreichische Chemiker-** u. **Techniker-Zeitung.** Wien. *Allg. öst. Chem.- u. TechZtg* [1883–34] **L.**BM. 18–19; P. 08–34. [*C. in:* 7273]

1769 **Allgemeine Papierrundschau.** Baden-Baden, etc. *Allg. PapRdsch.* [1949–] **L.**P. 56–; **Y.** [*C. of:* 34547]

1770 **Allgemeine Schlosser-** und **Maschinenbauerzeitung.** Dresden, etc. *Allg. Schlosser- u. MaschBauZtg* **L.**P. 57–; **Y.**

1771 **Allgemeine Textil-Zeitschrift** und **Textil-Ring.** Pössneck. *Allg. TextZ.* [1943–45] **L.**P. 44; **M.**C. 44–45 imp.

1772 **Allgemeine Textilzeitung.** Wien. *Allg. Text-Ztg*

1773 **Allgemeine Vermessungsnachrichten.** Liebenwerda. *Allg. VermessNachr.* [1889–54] **L.**P. 39–40; **Y.** [*C. in:* 6988]

1774 **Allgemeine Wärmetechnik.** Dissen. *Allg. Wärmetech.* [1951–] **L.**KC. 56–; P. 52–; **Y.** [*C. of:* 4085]

1775 **Allgemeine Wiener medizinische Zeitung.** Wien. *Allg. wien. med. Ztg* [1856–15] **L.**MD. 73–80: 12: 14; S. 1856–14; **Abd.**U. 86–14; **E.**U. 85–15; **Ld.**U. 85–09.
     Allgemeine zahntechnische Revue. Budapest. *See* 1841.

1776 **Allgemeine Zeitschrift** für **Bierbrauerei** und **Malzfabrikation.** Wien. *Allg. Z. Bierbrau.* **L.**P. 10–28*.

1777 **Allgemeine Zeitschrift** für **Entomologie.** Schöneberg-Berlin. *Allg. Z. Ent.* [1901–04] **L.**BM[N].; E.; UC.; Z.; **C.**B. [*C. of:* 22800; *C. as:* 58896]

1778 **Allgemeine Zeitschrift** für **Psychiatrie.** Berlin. *Allg. Z. Psychiat.* [1844–49] **L.**BM., MD.; S. 1847–39; UC. 82–90; **E.**P.; **M.**MS. 74–79; **Sa.** 98–04.

1779 **Allgemeine Zeitschrift** für **Psychotherapie** und **psychische Hygiene.** Leipzig. *Allg. Z. Psychother.* [1928–]

1780 **Allgemeine Zellforschung** und **mikroskopische Anatomie.** Berlin. *Allg. Zellforsch. mikrosk. Anat.* [1939–45] **L.**Z.; **C.**B.; **E.**U. [*C. from:* and *Rec. as:* 58906]

1781 **Allgemeiner Anzeiger** für **Berg-, Hütten-** und **Maschinenindustrie** u. **Zentralanzeiger** für **Metallindustrie.** Strassburg. *Allg. Anz. Berg- Hütten- u. MaschInd.*

1782 **Allgemeiner Anzeiger** für die **chemische Industrie.** Zürich. *Allg. Anz. chem. Ind., Zürich*

1783 **Allgemeiner Anzeiger** d. **chemischen Industrie.** Pfullingen. *Allg. Anz. chem. Ind., Pfullingen*

1784 **Allgemeiner Anzeiger** für die **gesamte Milchwirtschaft.** Hildesheim. *Allg. Anz. ges. Milchw.*

1785 **Allgemeiner Anzeiger** für die **Mineralwasserindustrie.** Landshut. *Allg. Anz. MinerWassInd.*

1786 **Allgemeiner Bericht** u. **Chronik** der in **Österreich** beobachteten Erdbeben. Wien. *Allg. Ber. Chron. Öst. beob. Erdb.* **L.**UC. 04–21; **E.**R. 04–21; **M.**U. 06–15 imp.; **O.**O. 04–15.

1787 **Allgemeiner deutscher Anzeiger** für **chemische Industrien.** Berlin. *Allg. dt. Anz. chem. Ind.*

1788 **Allgemeiner landwirtschaftlicher Anzeiger.** *Allg. landw. Anz.*
     Allgemeiner technischer Anzeiger für **Ungarn.** *See* 1842.

1789 **Allgemeinverständliche naturwissenschaftliche Abhandlungen.** Berlin. *Allgverst. naturw. Abh.* [*C. as:* 34303]

1790 **Alliages cuivreux.** *Alliages cuivr.* **Bm.**P. 47–48.

1791 **Alliages légers.** *Alliages légers* **Bm.**P. 47–48.

1792 **Alliance Coater.** Toronto. *Alliance Coater* **L.**P. 53–.

1793 **Allied Radio** and **Electronic News.** Chicago. *Allied Radio electronic News* [1944–]

1794 **Allied Veterinarian.** Indianapolis. *Allied Vet.* [1930–] **W.** 42–.

1795 **Allier vinicole.** Moulins. *Allier vinic.*
     All-India Conference of **Medical Research Workers.** *See* 38814.

1796 **All-India Hospital Assistants' Journal.** Bombay. *All-India Hosp. Assist. J.* [1907–09] **C.**MD. [*C. as:* 23037]

1797 **Allionia.** Bollettino dell'Istituto ed orto botanico dell'Università di Torino. Torino. *Allionia* [1952–] **L.**BM[N].; HS.; **C.**A.; **O.**BO. [*C. of:* 28193]

1798 **Allis-Chalmers Electrical Review.** Milwaukee. *Allis-Chalmers elect. Rev.* [1936–] **L.**AV. 53– imp.; P. 37–; **Y.**

1799 **Allis-Chalmers Operation** and **Maintenance Review.** Milwaukee. *Allis-Chalmers Op. Maint. Rev.* [1943–]

1800 **Allmän hälso-** och **sjukvård.** Stockholm. *Allm. Hälso- o. Sjukv.* **L.**H. 36–.

1801 **Allmän svensk trädgårdstidning.** *Allm. svensk TrädgTidn.* **L.**HS. 34–45 imp.
     Allmänna svenska elektriska aktiebolagets journal. *See* 106.

1802 **Allmänna svenska läkartidningen.** Stockholm. *Allm. svenska LäkTidn* [1903–18] [*C. of:* 17539; *C. as:* 51583]

1803 **Alloy Casting Bulletin.** New York. *Alloy Cast. Bull.* **L.**I. 44–; **Y.**

1804 **Alloy Digest.** *Alloy Dig.* **F.**A. 53–.

1805 **Alloy Metals Review.** Widnes. *Alloy Metals Rev.* [1936–] **L.**BM., EE. 46– imp.; I.; P.; **Bm.**T. 36–52; **F.**A. 54–; **G.**E. 43–; I. imp.; **Lv.**P. 36–47; V. imp.: 53–; **M.**P.; **Sh.**IO.; **Y.**

1806 **Alloy Pot.** New York. *Alloy Pot* [1948–] **L.**P. [*C. of:* 59219]

1807 **Alloys** of **Iron Research.** Engineering Foundation. New York. *Alloys Iron Res.* [1927–30] **L.**P. 28–30.

1808 **Alloys** and **Metals Review.** London. *Alloys Metals Rev.* [1959–] **L.**P.; **Y.**

1809 **Alluminio.** Milano. *Alluminio* [1932–] **L.**I. (1 yr); IC. 48–; NF. 47–; P.V. imp.; **Y.**

1810 **All-Wave Radio.** New York. *All-Wave Radio* [1935–38] [*C. in:* 41800]

1811 **Almanacco astronomico.** Bologna. *Almcco astr.* **L.**SC. 56–; **Y.** [*Supplement to:* 14699]

1812 **Almanach** der **Akademie** der **Wissenschaften** in **Wien.** *Alm. Akad. Wiss. Wien* [1851–46] **L.**BM.; BM[N]. 03–46; P. 66–39; SC. 75–95: 33–37; UC. 04–07; **Bm.**U. 36–46; **C.**UL.; **Db.** 03–06; **E.**R. 97–46; **G.**U. 1855–06 imp.; **O.**B. 1856–46; **Y.** [*C. as:* 1818]

1813 **Almanach České akademie (Čísaře Františka Josefa)** pro **védy, slovesnost** a **uméní.** Praha. *Alm. čes. Akad.* [1891–] **L.**BM.; BM[N]. 05–40; **E.**R. imp.; **M.**U. 26–37 imp.
     Almanach České akademie véd a **uméní.** *See* 1813.

1814 **Almanach** für die **deutschen See-** und **Küstenfischerei.** Hamburg. *Alm. dt. See- u. Küstenfisch.* [1899–] **L.**AM. 99–51 imp.
     Almanach der **K. Akademie** der **Wissenschaften** in **Wien.** *See* 1812.

1815 **Almanach** der **K. Bayerischen Akademie** der **Wissenschaften** zu **München.** *Alm. K. bayer. Akad. Wiss.* [1843–09] **E.**R. imp. [*Superseded by:* 24697]

1816 **Almanach Lázeńský Republiky Československé.** Praha. *Alm. Láz. Repub. čsl.* [1920–] **L.**BM. [*C. of:* 1817]

1817 **Almanach léčebných míst, lázní a letních sidel českých.** v Praze. *Alm. léč. Míst Lázní letn. Sidel čes.* **L.**BM. 01–14*. [*C. as:* 1816]

1818 **Almanach. Österreichische Akademie** der **Wissenschaften.** Wien. *Alm. öst. Akad. Wiss.* [1947–] **L.**BM.; BM^N.; SC.; **Bm.**U.; **C.**UL.; **E.**R.; **O.**B.; **Y.** [*C. of:* 1812]

1819 **Almanach** des **sciences.** Paris. *Alm. Sci.* [1948–52] **L.**BM. 51–52; P. 51–52; U.; **Sw.** U.

1820 **Almanak handa íslenskum fiskimönnum.** *Alm. ísl. Fisk.*

1821 **Almanaque aeronáutico. Instituto** y **observatorio** de **marina.** San Fernando. *Alm. aeronáut. S Fernando*

1822 **Almanaque agrícola** de **Guatemala.** Guatemala. *Alm. agríc. Guat.* **Md.**H. 49.

1823 **Almanaque agrícola** de **Puerto Rico.** San Juan. *Alm. agríc. P. Rico.*

1824 **Almanaque astronómico** de **Chile.** Santiago. *Alm. astr. Chile*

1825 **Almanaque** del **Ministerio** de **agricultura** y **ganadería** de la **nación.** Buenos Aires. *Alm. Minist. Agric. Ganad., B. Aires* [1926–] **L.**AM. 29–52 imp.; BM. 33–; EB. 39–45; MY. 27: 39–52 imp.; **Abs.**U. 51–52; **E.**AB. 39–49; **Md.**H. 39–44; **O.**R. 35– imp.; **Sal.** 39–44; **Y.**

1826 **Almanaque náutico. Instituto** y **observatorio** de **marina San Fernando.** Cadiz. *Alm. náut. S Fernando* [1791–] **L.**AS. 1830–; BM. 1791– imp.; **C.**O. 1831–; **E.**O. 1855– imp.; R. 1853–68; **O.**O. 01–; **Y.**

1827 **Almanaque salvadorêñõ.** Servicio meteorologico nacional. San Salvador. *Alm. salvador.* **L.**MO. 57–.

1829 **Almoner.** A journal of medical social work. London. *Almoner* [1948–] **L.**BM.; H.; MA.; **Sh.** (1 yr); U.; **Cr.**MD.; **Db.**; **G.**PH. 55–; **H.**U.; **Ld.**U.; V. imp.; **M.**MS.; **Nw.**A. 51–.

1830 **Alox Technical Bulletin.** Niagara Falls. *Alox tech. Bull.* [1947–] **L.**P.

1831 **Alpe.** Rivista forestale italiana. Milano. *Alpe* **C.**A. 29–38*; **O.**F. 28–38. [*C. as:* 47855]

1832 **Alpes industrielles.** Grenoble. *Alpes ind.* [1928] **L.**P. [*C. from:* 2729; *C. as:* 51267°]

1833 **Alpes industrielles** et **annales** de l'**énergie.** Grenoble. *Alpes ind. Annls Énerg.* **L.**BM. 25*; P. 25. [*C. as:* 2729]

1834 **Alpha Omegan.** Philadelphia. *Alpha Omegan* **L.**D. 48–; **Bl.**U. 48–.

1835 **Alphabet** and **Image.** London. *Alphabet Image* [1946–48] **L.**BM.; SB.; U.; **Bm.**P.; **Br.**P.; **Cr.**P.; **E.**HW.; **Lv.**P.; **O.**B. [*Replaced:* 55389; *C. as:* 22812]

1836 **Alphabetical Lists of Patentees** and **Inventions.** Washington. *Alphab. Lists Pat. Invent., Wash.* **L.**P. 72–; **E.**F. 93–12; **G.**M. 10–; **Ld.**P. 87–.

1837 **Alpine Journal.** London. *Alp. J.* [1863–] **L.**BM.; G.; RI. 63–45; U.; **Abs.**N. 00–; **Bl.**U. 99–16; **Bm.**P.; U.; **Br.**P. 08–48 imp.; U. 63–94 imp.; **C.**PO. 31–; UL.; **Cr.**P. 92–32; **Db.**; **E.**A.; T. 00–16 imp.; **G.**M. 94–; **Lv.**P.; **M.**P.; R.; **N.**U. 86–; **O.**B. imp.; F. 28–; G. 84–12 imp.

1838 **Alpský věstník.** Praha. *Alp. Věst.* **Abs.**N. imp.

1839 **Alpwirtschaftliche Monatsblätter.** Solothurn. *Alpw. Mbl.* **L.**BM. 67–; **Hu.**G. 44–; **Y.**

1840 **Alta frequenza.** Milano. *Alta Freq.* [1932–] **L.**AV. 48–50: 55–; EE. imp.; P.; SC. 37–; **Bn.**U. 49–; **Br.**U. 55–57; **F.**A. 39–; **Ma.**T. 37–39: 45–47; **Y.**

1841 **Általános fogtechnikai szemle.** Budapest. *Ált. fogtech. Szle*

1842 **Általános műszaki értesitő.** Budapest. *Ált. műsz. Ért.*

1843 **Általános szeszipari közlöny.** Budapest. *Ált. szeszip. Közl.*

1844 **Altersforschung.** Wünschelburg-Heuscheuer. *Altersforschung* [1935–37] [*Replaced by:* 58471]

1845 **Altersprobleme.** Chisinau. *Altersprobleme* [1937–] **L.**MD. 37. [*C. of:* 33094]

1846 **Aluloum azziraiya.** Cairo. *Aluloum Azzir.* [1948–] **C.**A.

1847 **Alumínium.** Budapest. *Alumínium, Bpest* [1949–53] **L.**P. [*Supplement to:* 5759 *and* 5760]

1848 **Aluminium.** Paris. *Aluminium, Paris* **L.**P. 95–01*. [*C. as:* 25939]

1849 **Aluminium. Aluminium Zentrale.** Berlin. *Aluminium, Alumin. Zent.* [1919–44: 51–] **L.**AV. 33– imp.; DI. 51–57 imp.; I. 22–43: 51–; P. 33– imp.; **Bm.**P. 38; **Y.** [*C. of:* 1850 *and* 21921]

1850 **Aluminium. Carl Schmalfeldt** G.m.b.H. Berlin. *Aluminium, Carl Schmalfeldt* **L.**AV. 26–32*; I. 22–32; NF. 23–32 imp.; P. 24–32. [*C. in:* 1849]

Aluminium Abstract Bulletin. London. *See* 310.

1851 **Aluminium Broadcast.** London. *Alumin. Broadc.* [1930–34] **L.**P. [*C. in:* 28578]

1852 **Aluminium Courier.** London. *Alumin. Cour.* [1947–] **L.**AM. (2 yr.); AV. 52–; BA.; BM.; I.; P.; **E.**A. 50–; **G.**E. (3 yr.); **Ld.**P. (5 yr.); **Lv.**P. 53–; **M.**T. (5 yr.); **N.**T. (5 yr.); **O.**B. 50–; **Sil.** (1 yr); **Y.**

Aluminium Development Association Research Report. *See* 45945.

Aluminium Laboratories Ltd. Abstract Bulletin. *See* 310.

Aluminium Laboratories Ltd. Development Bulletin. *See* 16925.

Aluminium Laboratories Ltd. Research Bulletin. *See* 45783.

1852° **Aluminium** and **Magnesium.** New York. [1944–47] *Alumin. Magnes.* **L.**AV.; NF.; P. 45–47.

1853 **Aluminium News.** Montreal. *Alumin. News* [1948–] **L.**BA.; I. (curr.); P. (curr.)

1854 **Aluminium News Letter.** Pittsburgh. *Alumin. News Lett.* **Sh.**10. 37–45. [*C. as:* 1676°]

1855 **Aluminium** and the **Non Ferrous Review.** London. *Alumin. non-ferr. Rev.* [1935–] **L.**NF. 35–43 imp.; P. 35–48; **Bm.**P. 36–; **C.**UL.; **E.**A.; **O.**R.

1856 **Aluminium Service Bulletin.** Pittsburgh. *Alumin. Serv. Bull.*

1857 **Aluminium suisse.** Zurich. *Alumin. suisse* [1951–] **L.**BA.; P. 58–; **Y.**

1858 **Aluminium Technique.** London. *Alumin. Tech.* [1939–] **L.**NF. 39–41; P.

1859 **Aluminium Wire Review.** Port Tennant, Swansea. *Alumin. Wire Rev.* [1958–] **L.**AV.

1860 **Aluminium World.** New York. *Alumin. Wld* **L.**P. 94–02*. [*C. as:* 31416]

1861 **Aluminium-Archiv.** Berlin. *Alumin.-Arch.* **L.**NF. 36–41.

1862 **Aluminium-Merkblatt.** Düsseldorf. *Alumin-Merkbl.* [1950–] **L.**P.

1863 **Aluminium-nyt.** København. *Alumin.-Nyt* [1952–] **L.**P.; SC.

1864 **Aluminiumnytt.** Oslo. *Aluminiumnytt* **L.**P. 60– [*C. of:* 34037]

1865 **Aluminium-Zeitschrift.** Berlin. *Alumin-Z.* [1929] **L.**P. [*C. as:* 21921]
Aluminum. *See as* **Aluminium.**

1867 **Alveare.** Trento. *Alveare* [1928–33] [*C. in:* 3697]

1868 **Älvsborg läns norra hushällningsällskaps tidskrift.** *Älvsborg Läns norra HushällnSällsk. Tidskr.* **Y.**

1869 **Älvsborg läns södra hushällningssällskaps kvartalskrift.** Boras. *Älvsborg Läns södra HushällnSällsk. KvartSkr.* **Y.**

1870 **Amaçonas medico.** Manaos. *Amaçonas med.* **L.**TD. 18–22*; **Lv.**U. 18–20.
Amalgamated Wireless Technical Review. Sydney. *See* 134.

1871 **Amani Memoirs.** London. *Amani Mem.* **O.**F. 28–; **Rt.** 30–41.

1872 **Amateur Aquarist** and **Reptilian Review.** London. *Amat. Aquar.* [1924–27] **L.**Z.; **Abs.**N.; **C.**UL.; **Cr.**M.; **M.**P.; **O.**R.; **Pl.**M. [*C. as:* 3773]

1873 **Amateur Astronomer.** New York. *Amat. Astr.* [1929–36]

1874 **Amateur de champignons.** Paris. *Amat. Champign.* **L.**K. 07–24.

1875 **Amateur Cine World.** London. *Amat. Cine Wld* [1934–] **L.**BM.; PG.; **Abs.**N. 47–; **Bm.**P. 44–; **Br.**P. (2 yr.); **E.**A.; T. 53–; **M.**P. 54–; **Nw.**A. 47–; **O.**B. 34–43; **Sh.**IO. 56–; **Sil.** 49–53 imp.; **We.**K.

1876 **Amateur Entomologist.** London. *Amat. Ent.* [1939–] **L.**BM.; BMᴺ.; E.; Z. 41–; **C.**UL.; **O.**AP.; H.; R.; **Rt.** imp.; **Y.** [*C. from:* 18266]

1877 **Amateur Mechanic** and **Work.** London. *Amat. Mech. Wk* [1924–26] **L.**BM.; P.; **G.**M.; **Lv.**P.; **M.**P.; **O.**B.; **Sh.**IO. [*C. of:* 57841; *C. in:* 18195]

1878 **Amateur de papillons.** Paris. *Amat. Papillons* [1922–48] **L.**BMᴺ.; E.; **O.**H. [*C. as:* 47197]

1879 **Amateur Photographer.** London. *Amat. Photogr.* [1884–] **L.**AV. (1 yr); BM.; P. 10–; PG.; SC. 08–; **Abs.**N. 13–; **Bm.**P.; **Br.**P. (2 yr.); **Bra.**P. 05–; **C.**UL.; **Db.** 21–; **E.**A. 92–; T. 36–; **G.**M. 00– imp.; **Ld.**P. 86–; **Lv.**P. imp.; **M.**P.; **Nw.**A. 47–; **O.**B.; **Sa.** 88–89: 07–17 imp.; **Sh.**IO. 57–; **We.**K.; **Y.**

1880 **Amateur Scientist.** New York. *Amat. Scient.* [1937–38]
Amateur Wireless and **Electronics.** *See* 1881.

1881 **Amateur Wireless** and **Radiovision.** London. *Amat. Wireless* [1922–31] **L.**BM.; **Abs.**N.; **E.**A.; **O.**B. [*C. in:* 38416]

1882 **Amatores herbarii.** Kobe. *Amatores Herb.* [1932–] **L.**K. 58–.

1883 **Amatus lusitanus:** revista de medicina e cirurgia. Lisboa. *Amatus lusit.* [1941–] **L.**MA. 42; MD. 42; S. 42–48.
Amazonas medico. *See* 1870.

1884 **Ambassador,** incorporating International Textiles. London. *Ambassador* [1946–] **L.**P. (1 yr); **Bra.**P. 47–; **Ld.**P. 52–; U.; **M.**C. 49–55; **O.**B.; **Y.** [*C. of:* 23951]

1885 **Amber-Hi-Lites.** Philadelphia. *Amber-Hi-Lites* [1949–] **L.**P.; **Br.**A. 58–; **Y.**

1886 **Ambix.** Society for the Study of Alchemy and Early Chemistry. London. *Ambix* [1937–] **L.**BM.; C.; E.; NP. 53–; P.; PA.; R.; RI.; SC.; U.; UC.; **Abs.**N.; U.; **Br.**P. imp.; U.; **C.**UL.; **E.**A.; R.; **G.**U.; **Ld.**U.; **O.**R.; **Sh.**U.; **Y.**

1887 **Ambulance** de "l'Océan." La Panne. *Ambul. Océan* [1917–19] **L.**BM.; MD.; S.; **O.**R.

1888 **Amech.** Revista mensual de la Asociación médica chilena. Santiago. *Amech*

1889 **Ameghiniana.** Revista de la Asociación paleontológica argentina. Buenos Aires. *Ameghiniana* [1957–] **L.**BMᴺ.

1890 **América científica.** New York. *Am. cient.*

1891 **América clínica.** New York. *Am. clín.* [1940–]

1892 **América indigena.** México. *Am. indig.* [1941–] **L.**AN. 45–; **Y.**

1893 **American Agricultural Magazine.** Grand Rapids. *Am. agric. Mag.*

1894 **American Alpine Journal.** New York. *Am. alp. J.* [1929–] **L.**G. 29–31; **C.**PO. imp.

1895 **American Amateur Photographer.** New York. *Am. amat. Photogr.* [1889–07] **L.**BM. 93–98 imp.; PG. 90–07. [*C. as:* 2118]

1896 **American Anatomical Memoirs.** Philadephia. *Am. anat. Mem.* [1918–] **L.**SC.; UC.; **C.**AN. 18–41; UL.; **E.**U.; **G.**U. 18–41; **O.**R.; **Sa.** 18–42. [*C. of:* 31095]

1897 **American Annual** of **Photography.** New York. *Am. A. Photogr.* [1887–53] **L.**BM. 86: 94: 13–16; P. 10–31; PG. imp.; **Abs.**N. 13–15; **Bm.**P. 36–53; **Bra.**P. 37–51; **C.**UL. 27–; **Cr.**P. 27–49 imp.; **G.**M. 37–53; **Ld.**P. 89–53 imp.; **M.**P. 88–53; **O.**B. 00–53 imp.; **We.**K. 05–53 imp.
American Anthropological Association Bulletin. *See* 9292.

1898 **American Anthropologist.** Lancaster, Pa. *Am. Anthrop.* [1888–] **L.**AN.; BM.; BMᴺ. 55–; HO. 23–; U. 47–; UC. 99–; **Abd.**U. 58–; **Abs.**N. 99–24; U. 38–; **Bl.**U. 99–15: 46–49: 58–; **Bm.**U. 39–; **Br.**U. 99 ; **C.**E. 16–; UL.; **E.**F.; T. 88–29 imp.; U. 47–; **Ex.**U. 54–; **G.**U. 48–; **H.**U. 46–; **Ld.**U. 48–; **Lv.**P. 57–; **Nw.**A. 49–; **O.**R.; **R.**U. 20–51 imp.; **Sa.** 48–53; **Sh.**U. 59–.

1899 **American Antiquity.** Menasha. *Am. Antiq.* [1935–] **L.**AN. 40–; BM.; **C.**E.; PO. 50–; UL. 49–.

1900 **American Architect** and **Architecture.** New York. *Am. Archit.* [1876–38] **L.**P. 76–28; **G.**M. 23–38; **Lv.**U. 08–38; **M.**P. 91–38.

1901 **American Association** of **Public Health Bulletin.** Oak Park, Ill. *Am. Ass. publ. Hlth Bull.*

1902 **American Astronomical Society Publications.** Ann Arbor, Mich. *Am. astr. Soc. Publs* [1918–46] **L.**AS.; BM.; **C.**O.; **E.**O.; **M.**U.; **O.**O.; R. 18. [*C. of:* 40876]

1903 **American Automobile.** New York. *Am. Auto.* Overseas edition [1924–61] **L.**BM. 55–61; P. 34–61 imp.; **Li.**M. 59–61; **Y.** [*C. as:* Automobile International]

1904 **American Automobile Digest.** Cincinnati, O. *Am. Auto. Dig.* [1918–25] [*C. as:* 5486 and 5487]

1905 **American Aviation.** Washington. *Am. Aviat.* [1937–59] **L.**AV. 43–59; **F.**A. 47: 55–59; **Lv.**P. 57–59. [*C. of:* 1603]

1906 **American Bee Journal.** Chicago, etc. *Am. Bee J.* [1861–] **L.**AM. 61–33 imp.; BM. 69–70; **Abs.**A. 52–55; **C.**B. 20–27; **Rt.** 19– imp.; **Sa.** 28: 34–37; **Y.**

1907 **American Biology Teacher.** Lancaster, Pa. *Am. Biol. Teach.* **Sw.**U. 60–.

1908 **American Bloodstock Review.** Lexington, Ky. *Am. Bloodstk Rev.* [1941–]

1909 **American Botanist.** Joliet, Ill. *Am. Bot.* **L.**BM^N. 01–31; K. 01–.

1910 **American Bottler.** New York. *Am. Bottl.* **L.**BM. 19–23 imp.; P. 82–. [> 1921, 1888–1905]

1911 **American Boxmaker.** Chicago. *Am. Boxmkr* [1910–] **Lh.**P. 46–.

1912 **American Breeders' Magazine.** Washington. *Am. Breed. Mag.* [1910–13] **L.**AM.; AN.; HS. 13; UC.; Z. v. imp.; **Ba.**I.; **C.**GE.; **Db.**; **E.**AB.; **Ld.**W.; **O.**R. [*C. as:* 26087]

1913 **American Brewer.** New York. *Am. Brew.* [1868–] **Bm.**U. 46–; **Nu.**B. 51–; **Y.**

1914 **American Brewers' Review.** Chicago. *Am. Brew. Rev.* [1887–] **Nu.**B. 09–18: 35–39 imp.

1915 **American Builder** and **Building Age.** Chicago. *Am. Bldr* [1917–] [*C. of:* 1922]

1916 **American Building Association News.** Chicago, Ill. *Am. Bldg Ass. News*

1917 **American Butter** and **Cheese Review.** New York. *Am. Butter Cheese Rev.* [1939–48] **R.**D. 47–48. [*C. from:* 2136; *C. as:* 1935]
American Butter Review. *See* 1917.

1918 **American Cage Bird Magazine.** Chicago. *Am. Cage Bird Mag.* **L.**Z. 59–62.

1919 **American Camellia Quarterly.** *Am. Camellia Q.* **L.**HS. 52–.

1920 **American Camellia Society Yearbook.** *Am. Camellia Soc. Yb.* **L.**HS. 46–.

1921 **American Carbonator** and **American Bottler.** New York. *Am. Carbonator* **L.**P. 88–05*. [*C. of:* and *Rec. as:* 1910]

1922 **American Carpenter** and **Builder.** Chicago. *Am. Carp. Bldr* [1905–17] [*C. as:* 1915]

1923 **American Cattle Producer.** Denver. *Am. Cattl Prod.* [1919–]
American Caver. *See* 11244.
American Ceramic Society Bulletin. *See* 9305.

1924 **American Chemical Journal.** Baltimore. *Am. chem. J.* [1879–13] **L.**BM^N. 02–13; C.; P.; PH. 02–06; RI.; SC.; UC.; **Abd.**U.; **Abs.**U.; **Bm.**T. 06–13; **Br.**P. 09–13; **C.**P.; UL. 80–13; **Db.**; **Dn.**U. 05–13; **E.**C. 79–84 imp.; R.; U.; **Ld.**U. 90–13; **Lv.**U. 06–13; **M.**D.; U. 80–13; **O.**R.; **Sa.** [*C. in:* 25500]

1925 **American Chemical Society Directory** of **Graduate Research.** Washington. *Am. chem. Soc. Dir. Grad. Res.* **L.**SC. 58–.

1926 **American Chemical Society. News Edition.** *Am. chem. Soc. News Edn* [1939–41] **L.**AM.; AV.; C.; G.; IC.; LE. 40–41; MC.; NF.; P.; PH.; PR.; PT.; SC.; TP.; UC.; **Abd.**U.; **Abs.**U.; **Bm.**P.; T.; U.; **Br.**P.; U.; **C.**P.; UL.; **Cr.**U.; **Db.**; **E.**HW.; U.; **Ep.**D. 41; **Ex.**U.; **F.**A.; **G.**M.; **Ld.**U.; W.; **Li.**M.; **Lv.**U.; **M.**D.; P.; U. 40–41; **N.**U.; **Nw.**A.; **O.**B.; **R.**D.; **Rt.**; **Sa.**; **Sh.**G.; P.; S.; **Sy.**R.; **Sw.**U.; **Wd.** [*C. of:* 23198; *C. as:* 13736]

1927 **American Child Health Association. Publications.** *Am. Child Hlth Ass. Publs* **L.**MD. 23–.

1928 **American Cinematographer.** Los Angeles. *Am Cinematogr.* [1920–] **L.**P. 59–; PG. 22–; **F.**A. 48–; **Nw.**A. 47–; **We.**K. 29–.

1929 **American City Magazine.** New York. *Am. Cy Mag.* [1909–] **L.**BA. 30–; **G.**M.; **Ha.**RD. 47–; **Lv.**P. 60–; **Nw.**A. 48–.

1930 **American Coal Journal.** Chicago, Ill. *Am. Coal J.* [1908–] [*C. of:* 48051]

1931 **American College** of **Radiology Bulletin.** Chicago. *Am. Coll. Radiol. Bull.*

1932 **American Cotton Ginner.** Little Rock, Ark. *Am. Cott. Ginn.* [1925–27] [*C. of:* 4770; *C. as:* 1974]

1933 **American Cotton Grower.** Atlanta. *Am. Cott. Grow.* [1935–40]

1934 **American Creamery** and **Poultry Produce Review.** New York. *Am. Cream. Poult. Prod. Rev.* [1930–37] [*C. of:* 34709; *C. as:* 2136]

1935 **American Dairy Products Manufacturing Review.** New York. *Am. Dairy Prod. Mfg Rev.* [1951–53] **R.**D. [*C. of:* 1917; *C. in:* 2090]

1936 **American Dairyman.** Chicago. *Am. Dairym.* [1941–44] **R.**D. 43–44. [*C. as:* 22109]

1937 **American Dental Journal.** Chicago. *Am. dent. J.* [1902–18]

1938 **American Dental Surgeon.** Chicago. *Am. dent. Surg.* [1925–32] **L.**D. 26–31; GH. 26–31; MD. [*Incorporating* 16568]

1939 **American Dentist.** Chicago. *Am. Dent.* [1915–20]

1940 **American Documentation.** Cambridge, Mass. *Am. Docum.* [1950–] **L.**AV. 54–; BM.; P.; SC.; U.; **Bm.**P.; **Br.**U.; **C.**UL.; **Db.**; **Ep.**D. 57–; **F.**A. 52–; **Lv.**P.; **M.**C. 56–59; D. 56–; P.; T.; **O.**B.; **Y.** [*C. of:* 25904]

1941 **American Drop Forger.** Pittsburgh. *Am. Drop Forg.* [1915–20] **L.**I. 16–20; P. 20. [*C. as:* 20075]

1942 **American Drug Index.** Philadelphia, Montreal. *Am. Drug Index* [1956–] **L.**BM.; MD.; P.; **O.**R.

1943 **American Druggist.** New York. *Am. Drugg.* [1871–] **L.**PH. 32–41.

1944 **American Dyestuff Reporter.** New York. *Am. Dyestuff Reptr* [1917–] **L.**C. 45–; IC. 46–; LE. 45–60; P. 26–; **Bra.**D. 47– imp.; P. 26–; **Lc.**A. 54–55; **Ld.**P. 53–; U. 38–; W. 27–; **Lv.**P. 59–; **M.**C. 22–; P. 38–; T. 29–; **Y.**

1945 **American Egg** and **Poultry Review.** New York. *Am. Egg Poult. Rev.* [1940–] [*C. from:* 2136]

1946 **American Electro-therapeutic** and **X-Ray Era.** Chicago. *Am. electro-ther. X-Ray Era* [1901] [*C. as:* 4218]

1947 **American Engineer.** Jersey City. *Am. Engr, Jersey Cy* [1935–] **Y.** [*Replaces:* 1948]

1948 **American Engineer.** New York. *Am. Engr, N.Y.* [1931–34] [*Replaced by:* 1947]

1949 **American Engineer** and **Railroad Journal.** New York. *Am. Engr Railrd J.* [1893–13] **L.**BM.; **P.** 12–13; [*C. as:* 41904]

1950 **American Engineering** and **Industry.** New York. *Am. Engng Ind.* [1924–]

1951 **American Ephemeris** and **Nautical Almanac.** Washington. *Am. Ephem.* [1855–] **L.**AS.; BM.; G.; **M.** 17–; **MO.** 24–; **R.** 65–34; **U.** 10–15; **UC.** 16–; **C.**O. 65–; **UL.**; **Db.** 73–; **E.**O. imp.; **R.** 17–; **G.**M. 14–; **U.** 1855–61; 95–; **Ld.**U. 97–42 imp.; **M.**U. 51–; **O.**O. 80–; **Wo.** 30–; **Y.** [*From* 1960 *same text as:* 5037: *Also* Aeronautical supplement]

1952 **American Fabrics.** New York. *Am. Fabrics* [1946–] **Lc.**A. 53–54; **Ld.**P. 58–.

1953 **American Fern Journal.** Port Richmond. *Am. Fern J.* [1910–] **L.**BM^N.; K.; **L.** 29–; **E.**U. 56–; **M.**U. 52–; **O.**BO. 48–57 imp.; **Y.**

1954 **American Fertilizer** (*afterwards* and Allied Chemicals). Philadelphia, Pa. *Am. Fertil.* [1894–51] **L.**P. 01–31; **TP.** 08–51; **Rt.** 13–51. [*C. as:* 19022]

1955 **American Fish Culturist.** St. Johnsburg, Vt. *Am. Fish Cult.* [1904–05] [*C. in:* 19386]

1956 **American Florist.** Chicago. *Am. Flor.* [1885–31] **L.**HS. 13–18.

1957 **American Food Journal.** Chicago. *Am. Fd J.* [1906–28]

1958 **American Food Manufacturer.** New York. *Am. Fd Mfr* [1916] [*C. in:* 1957]

1959 **American Forester.** Seattle, Wash. *Am. Forester*

1960 **American Forester Review.** San Francisco. *Am. Forester Rev.*

1961 **American Forestry.** Washington. *Am. For.* [1911–24] **L.**EB. 14–19; **C.**F. 15–24; **Db.** 15–24; **G.**M. 14–24; **O.**F. 14–24; RE. 14–20. [*C. as:* 1962]

1962 **American Forests** and **Forest Life.** Washington. *Am. Forests & Forest Life* [1924–] **C.**F.; **Db.**; **G.**M.; **O.**AP. 41–54; F. [*C. of:* 1961]

1963 **American Foundryman.** Chicago. *Am. Foundryman* [1938–55] **L.**I.; **P.** 38–54 imp.; **Bm.**C. imp.; **Sh.**IO. 39–55. [*Replaces:* 9317; *C. in:* 32942]

1964 **American Fruit Grower Magazine.** Cleveland. *Am. Fruit Grow. Mag.* [1918–] **L.**AM.; **Ba.**I. 53–; **C.**A. 40–; **Md.**H. 41– imp.; **Sil.** 47–49 imp: 50–.

1965 **American Fruits.** Rochester, N.Y. *Am. Fruits* [1904–16] [*C. as:* 2102]

1966 **American Fur Breeder.** St. Peter, Minn., etc. *Am. Fur. Breed.* [1928–] **W.** 60–.

1967 **American Fur Growers' Magazine.** Bremen, O. *Am. Fur Grow. Mag.* [1926–34]

1968 **American Game.** American Game Protective Association. New York. *Am. Game* [1925–35] **O.**AP. [*C. of:* 9318; *C. as:* 2176]

1969 **American Gardening.** New York. *Am. Gdng* [1872–04] [*C. in:* 57412]

1970 **American Gas Association Monthly.** New York. *Am. Gas Ass. Mon.* [1919–] **L.**P. imp.; **Lv.**P. 59–; **M.**P. 52–; T.; **Sh.**P. (5 yr.); **Y.** [*Replaces:* 20647]

1971 **American Gas Engineering Journal.** New York. *Am. Gas Engng J.* [1917–] **L.**BM. 18–19; **C.** 46–; **P.**; **Sh.**P. (5 yr.) [*C. of:* 1972]

American Gas Journal. *See* 1971.

1972 **American Gas Light Journal.** New York. *Am. Gas Lt J.* **L.**P. 10–16*. [*C. as:* 1971]

1973 **American Geologist.** Minneapolis. *Am. Geol.* [1888–05] **L.**BM.; BM^N.; GL.; GM.; SC. imp.; **C.**S. imp.; **E.**R.; **O.**R. [*C. as:* 17418]

1974 **American Ginner** and **Cotton Oil Miller.** *Am. Ginn. Cott. Oil Miller* [1927–38] [*C. of:* 1932; *C. in:* 15986]

1975 **American Glass Review.** *Am. Glass Rev.* [1927–] [*C. of:* 21376]

1976 **American Gynæcological** and **Obstetrical Journal.** New York. *Am. gynæc. obstet. J.* [1891–01] **L.**MD. 94–01; **Br.**U.; **M.**MS.

1977 **American Gynecology.** New York. *Am. Gynec.* [1902–03] **L.**MD.; **Br.** U.

1978 **American Health.** New Haven. *Am. Hlth* [1908–09]

1979 **American Heart Journal.** St. Louis. *Am. Heart J.* [1925–] **L.**GH. imp.; MA.; MD.; S.; U. 50: 52–; UCH.; **Abd.**U. 38–; **Bl.**U. 29– imp.; **Bm.**U. 44–; **Br.**U. 27–; **Cr.**MD. 36–; **Db.** 37–; **Dn.**U. 47– imp.; **E.**U.; **G.**F.; U.; **Ld.**U. 29– imp.; **Lv.**M. 33–; **M.**MS. 46–; **Nw.**A. 28–35 imp.: 38–; **O.**R.; **Sh.**U. 39–; **Y.**

1980 **American Helicopter.** New York. *Am. Helicopter* [1945–60] **L.**AV.; **P.** 58–60; **TP.** 54–58 imp.; **F.**A.; **Y.**

1981 **American Helicopter Quarterly.** Bridgeport. *Am. Helicopter Q.* [1946–] **L.**P. [*C. of:* 49518]

1982 **American Highways.** Washington. *Am. Highw.* **L.**P. 29–; **Y.**

1983 **American Homœopathist.** New York. *Am. Homœop.* [1877–01] [*C. as:* 2121]

1984 **American Horologist** and **Jeweler.** Denver, Calif., etc. *Am. Horol. Jeweler* [1936–] **L.**AV. 49–51; **P.**; SC. 41–; **Y.**

1985 **American Horse Breeder.** Boston. *Am. Horse Breed.* [1882–35]

1986 **American Horticultural Council News.** Washington. *Am. hort. Coun. News* **L.**HS. 53–.

1987 **American Horticultural Magazine.** Washington. *Am. hort. Mag.* [1960–] **C.**A.; **Md.**H.; **Y.** [*C. of:* 34131]

1987^c **American Horticultural Society Gardeners Forum.** Washington. *Am. hort. Soc. Gdnrs Forum* **Md.**H. 57–.

1988 **American Hortigraphs** and **Agronomic Review.** New York. *Am. Hortigr. agron. Rev.* [1930–37] **Rt.** 32: 34 imp.

1989 **American Indian Magazine.** Washington. *Am. Indian Mag.* [1916–20] **L.**AN. 16–19. [*C. of:* 41554]

1990 **American Industrial Hygiene Association Journal.** Chicago. *Am. ind. Hyg. Ass. J.* [1958–] **L.**H.; MA.; MD.; **P.** 59–; TD.; **Bl.**U.; **Bm.**C.; **E.**U.; **Ep.**D.; **G.**U.; **M.**MS.; **Sh.**S.; U.; **Y.** [*C. of:* 1991]

1991 **American Industrial Hygiene Association Quarterly.** *Am. ind. Hyg. Ass. Q.* [1946–57] **L.**H. 56–57; MA. 55–57; TD. 47–57; **Bl.**U. imp.; **E.**U.; **Ep.**D. 56–57; **G.**U.; **M.**MS.; **Sh.**S. 55–57; U. [Nos. 1–6 *issued as supplement in:* 23244; *C. as:* 1990]

1992 **American Ink Maker.** New York. *Am. Ink Mkr* [1923–] **L**.P. 35–42 imp.: 57–; PR. 31–; **Lh**.P. 38– imp.; **Lv**.P. 55–; **M**.D. 35–; **Y**.

American Institute of **Chemical Engineers Journal.** *See* 60.

1994 **American Institute** of **Crop Ecology.** Washington. *Am. Inst. Crop Ecol.* [1950–] **M**.U. 50–58; **O**.RE.; **Rt**.; **Y**. [*C. of:* 23808]

1995 **American Journal** of **Anatomy.** Baltimore. *Am. J. Anat.* [1901–] **L**.MA. 48–; MC. 20–; MD. 08–; S.; SC. 21–; U. 49–; UC.; VC. 46–; **Abd**.U.; **Bl**.U. 16–23; **Bm**.U.; **Br**.U.; **C**.AN.; APH. 48–; B. 01–14: 20–; **Cr**.U.; **Db**.; **Dn**.U. 26–; **E**.P.; S.; U.; **G**.U.; **Ld**.U. 02–; **Lv**.U. imp.; **M**.MS.; **Nw**.A. 01–14: 16– imp.; **O**.R.; **R**.D. 47–; **Sa**.; **Sh**.U.; **W**. 39–58; **Y**.

1996 **American Journal** of **Anesthesia** and **Analgesia.** Kansas City [1914–26] *Am. J. Anesth. Analg.* [*Supplement to:* 2061]

1997 **American Journal** of **Botany.** Lancaster, Pa. *Am. J. Bot.* [1914–] **L**.AM. 40–; B.; BM[N].; HS. 14–35 imp.; K.; L.; NC. 48– imp.; QM. 49–; SC. 24–; U. 48–; UC. 28– imp.; **Abd**.U.; **Abs**.A. 30–; U. 27–; **Ba**.I.; **Bl**.U. 25–; **Bm**.P. 21–; U.; **Bn**.U.; **Br**.A. 55–; U.; **C**.BO.; P. 14–35; **Cr**.U. 30–; **Db**.; **Dn**.U. 52–; **E**.B. 20–; SW. 46–; **Ep**.D. 47–; **Ex**.U. 28–; **Fr**. 50–; **G**.U.; **H**.U.; **Hu**.G.; **Je**. 47–; **Ld**.U.; **Lv**.U.; **M**.U.; **Md**.H. 28–; **N**.U. imp.; **Nw**.A. 16–; **O**.BO.; **Pl**.M.; 14–30; **R**.U.; **Rt**. 19–; **Sh**.U. 36–; **Sw**.U. 22–; **Y**.

1998 **American Journal** of **Cancer.** New York. *Am. J. Cancer* [1931–40] **L**.BM.; CB.; H. 33–40; MC.; MD.; RA.; S.; UCH.; **Abd**.R.; **Bl**.U. 31–38 imp.; **Bm**.U.; **Br**.U.; **C**.R.; UL.; **Dn**.U. 35–40; **E**.PO. 33–40; S.; U.; **G**.F.; U.; **Lv**.M.; **M**.MS.; **O**.R.; **Sh**.IO. [*C. of:* 25746; *C. as:* 13287]

1999 **American Journal** of **Cardiology.** New York. *Am. J. Cardiol.* [1958–] **L**.MA.; MD.; **Cr**.MD.; **Dn**.U.; **Ld**.U.; **M**.MS.; **Y**.

2000 **American Journal** of **Care** for **Cripples.** New York. *Am. J. Care Crippl.* [1914–19] **L**.BM. 16–19 imp.; S. 18–19; **Abs**.N. 19; **Br**.P. 19; **C**.UL. 15: 19; **Lv**.P. 19; **Nw**.P. 19; **O**.B. 15–19 imp.

2001 **American Journal** of **Chiropractic Research.** Los Angeles. *Am. J. chiropr. Res.* [1941–]

2002 **American Journal** of **Clinical Medicine.** Chicago. *Am. J. clin. Med.* [1906–24] **L**.MD. 06–08: 10: 17–24 imp. [*C. of:* 1715; *C. as:* 14599]

2003 **American Journal** of **Clinical Nutrition.** New York, etc. *Am. J. clin. Nutr.* [1954–] **L**.AM.; H.; MA. 55–; MD.; TD.; U.; **Abd**.R.; **Dn**.U. 58–; **E**.U.; **G**.F.; U.; **Lv**.P. 59–; **R**.D.; **Y**. [*C. of:* 25826]

2004 **American Journal** of **Clinical Pathology.** Baltimore. *Am. J. clin. Path.* [1931–] **L**.CB. 51–; H. 47–; MA. 38–; MD.; S.; TD. 48–; U. 52–; UCH. 51–; **Bl**.U. 36– imp.; **Bm**.U. 32–; **Br**.U.; **C**.APH. 55–; PA. 53–; **Cr**.MD.; **Db**. 51–; **Dn**.U. 43–; **E**.U. 45–; **G**.F. 47–; U.; **Ld**.U. 38–; **M**.MS. 46–; **Nw**.A. 57–; **O**.R. 38–; **W**. 43–56; **Y**.

2005 **American Journal** of **Clinical Pathology. Technical Supplement.** Baltimore. *Am. J. clin. Path. tech. Suppl.* [1937–] **L**.MA.; MD.; S.; **Bm**.U.; **C**.MD. 51–; **G**.U.; O R.; **Y**.

2006 **American Journal** of **Cosmetology.** New York. *Am. J. Cosmet.* [1941–]

2007 **American Journal** of **Dental Science.** Madison. *Am. J. dent. Sci.* [1838–09] **L**.D. 1839–1860: 94–95; S. 1859–1860; **Br**.U. 1838–1857.

2008 **American Journal** of **Dermatology** and **Genito-urinary Diseases.** St Louis. *Am. J. Derm. genito-urin. Dis.* **L**.MD. 97–12* imp. [*C. as:* 55748]

2009 **American Journal** of **Digestive Diseases.** Fort Wayne, New York. *Am. J. dig. Dis.* [1934–] **L**.MA. 37–; MD.; S.; UC. 55–; **Abd**.R.; U. 40–; **Bl**.U. 37– imp.; **Br**.U. 37–55 imp.; **C**.PA. 37–; **Cr**.MD. 52–53; **E**.U.; **G**.F. 37– imp.; U.; **Ld**.U. 46–; **M**.MS.; **Nw**.A. imp.; **O**.R. 49–; **Y**.

American Journal of **Digestive Diseases** and **Nutrition.** *See* 2009.

2010 **American Journal** of **Dieases** of **Children.** Chicago. *Am. J. Dis. Child.* [1911–50: 60–] **L**.GH. 38–50: 60–; H.; MA. 20–50: 60–; MC. 24–50; MD.; S. imp.; TD. 26–50: 60–; U. 50: 60–; UCH. 22–50: 60–; **Abd**.R.; U. 27–50: 60–; **Bl**.U. 25–50: 60–; **Bm**.U. 14–50: 60–; **Br**.U. 20–50 imp.: 60–; **C**.V.; **Cr**.MD. 33–50: 60–; **Db**.; **Dn**.U. 28–50: 60–; **E**.P.; U. 23–50: 60–; **G**.F. 40–50 imp.: 60–; U. imp.; **Ld**.U. 21–50; **Lv**.M. 14–50 imp.: 60–; **M**.MS. 14–50 imp.: 60–; **Nw**.A.; **O**.R. 32–50: 60–; **R**.D. 35–50; **Sh**.U. 23–50: 60–; **Y**. [> 68, 1951–55 and 81, 1956–60]

2011 **American Journal** of **Electrotherapeutics** and **Radiology.** New York. *Am. J. Electrother. Radiol.* [1916–25] **L**.MD.; RA. 24–25; **Abd**.U. [*C. of:* 25418; *C. as:* 37680]

2012 **American Journal** of **Enology** and **Viticulture.** Delano, Davis. *Am. J. Enol. Vitic.* [1954–] **Md**.H. 60–; **Y**. [*C. of:* 38897]

2013 **American Journal** of **Eugenics.** Chicago. *Am. J. Eugen.* [1907–10]

2014 **American Journal** of **Gastroenterology.** New York. *Am. J. Gastroent., N.Y.* [1954–] **L**.MA.; MD.; S. 54–58; **G**.F.; **O**.R. [*C. of:* 46206]

2015 **American Journal** of **Gastro-Enterology.** Philadelphia. *Am. J. Gastro-Ent., Philad.* [1911–14] [*C. in:* 39889]

2016 **American Journal** of **Hospital Pharmacy.** Ann Arbor. *Am. J. Hosp. Pharm.* [1958–] **L**.H.; PH.; **Y**. [*C. of:* 9353]

2017 **American Journal** of **Human Genetics.** Baltimore. *Am. J. hum. Genet.* [1949–] **L**.CB.; MA. 50–; MD.; SC.; TD.; U.; **Ba**.I.; **Bl**.U.; **C**.GE.; **Dn**.U. 56–; **E**.AG.; AR.; U. 51–; **G**.U.; **Ld**.U.; **Y**.

2018 **American Journal** of **Hygiene.** Baltimore, etc. *Am. J. Hyg.* [1921–] **L**.BM[N]. 39–; EB.; H. 33– imp.; LI.; MA. 30–; MC.; MD.; SC. 38–; SH.; TD.; UCH.; **Abd**.R. 21–52; **Br**.U. 38–; **C**.APH. imp.; MO.; V. 49–56 imp.: 57–; **Cr**.MD. 40–; **Db**. 30–43: 54–; **E**.U. 53–; **G**.M.; U. **Ld**.U.; **Lv**.P. 60–; U.; **M**.MS.; **Nw**.A. 53–; **O**.R. 34–; **Sal**. imp.; **W**. 36–; **Y**. [*Also Monograph series*]

2019 **American Journal** of **Individual Psychology.** Chicago. *Am. J. indiv. Psychol.* [1945–56] **L**.BM. 52–56; MA. 52–56. [*C. as:* 26155]

2020 **American Journal** of **Insanity.** Utica. *Am. J. Insan.* [1844–21] **L**.BM.; MD.; PS. 03–15; **C**.UL.; **Db**. 98– 21 imp.; **Dn**.U. 03–21; **E**.P. imp.; S. 14–21 imp.; **M**.MS. 1845–75; **Sa**. 03–21. [*C. as:* 2050]

2021 **American Journal** of **Mathematics.** Baltimore. *Am. J. Math.* [1878–] **L**.BM.; M. 00–; QM. 57–; R.; SC.; U. 47– imp.; UC. 86–; **Abd**.U.; **Abs**.U. 78–20: 58–; **Bl**.U.; **Bm**.U.; **Br**.U.; **C**.P.; T. 78–22; UL.; **Cr**.U. 78–05: 59–; **Db**.; **E**.C. 80–84; Q. 92–; R.; U.; **G**.U. 93–; **H**.U.; **Ld**.U.; **Lv**.U.; **M**.U. 79–; **N**.U.; **Nw**.A.; P. 78–37; **O**.R.; **R**.U. 55–; **Sa**.; **Sh**.U. 78–31 imp.: 48–; **Sw**.U. 24–40 imp.: 60–; **Y**.

2022 American Journal of **Medical Jurisprudence.** Boston. *Am. J. med. Jurispr.* [1938–39] Nw.A.

2023 American Journal of the **Medical Sciences.** Philadelphia. *Am. J. med. Sci.* [1827–] L.CB. 58–; GH. 1828–; H. 06– imp.; MA.; MC. 19–; MD.; S.; TD. 1857– imp.; U. 52–; UCH. 93–00: 37–; **Abd.**U. 1837– imp.; **Bl.**U. 1849– imp.; **Bm.**U. 70–; **Br.**U.; **C.**APH. 20– imp.; P. 81–85; PA. 1847– imp.; **Cr.**MD. 00–; **Db.** 1841– imp.; **Dn.**U. 82– imp.; **E.**I. 1848–22; P.; S. 84–53; U. 73–; **G.**F. 1827–92 imp.: 98–; U. 1841–; **Ld.**U. 77– imp.; **Lv.**M. imp.; U. 85–06; **M.**MS.; Nw.A. imp.; **O.**R. 65–; **Sa.** 82–; **Sh.**U. 85–; Y.

2024 American Journal of **Medical Technology.** Detroit, etc. *Am. J. med. Technol.* [1935–] L.MA. 46–; Y. [*C. of:* 9351]

2025 American Journal of **Medicine.** New York. *Am. J. Med.* [1946–] L.CB. 58–; MA. 47–; MD.; S. 47–; U. 52–; UCH. 49–; **Abd.**U. 49–; **Bl.**U. imp.; **Bm.**U.; **Br.**U.; **C.**APH. 61–; MD. 53–; **Cr.**MD.; **Dn.**U. 52–; **E.**U.; **G.**F. 47– imp.; U. 47–; **M.**MS. 48–; Nw.A. 49: 53–; **O.**R. 49–; Y.

2026 American Journal of **Mental Deficiency.** Albany. *Am. J. ment. Defic.* [1940–] L.H. 49–; MA. 46–; MD.; TD. 47–; U. 49–; **Br.**U. imp.; **Dn.**U. 61–; **Sh.**U. 56–; Y. [*C. of:* 26748]

2027 American Journal of **Neuropathy.** Philadelphia. *Am. J. Neuropathy* [1911]

2028 American Journal of **Nursing.** Philadelphia. *Am. J. Nurs.* [1900–] E.U. 57–.

2029 American Journal of **Obstetrics** and **Diseases** of **Women** and **Children.** New York. *Am. J. Obstet. Dis. Wom.* [1868–19] L.BM.; MD.; S.; U. 88–09 imp.; UCH. 99–19 imp.; **Abd.**U. 78–19; **Bl.**U. 94–19; **Br.**U.; **Db.** 81–19; **Dn.**U. 76–07 imp.; **E.**P.; S. 78–19; **G.**F. 71–19; U. 85–86; **Ld.**U. 82–19 imp.; **Lv.**M. imp.; **M.**MS.; Nw.A. 00–19; **Sa.** 76–07; **Sh.**U. 93–14. [*C. as:* 2030]

2030 American Journal of **Obstetrics** and **Gynecology.** St. Louis. *Am. J. Obstet. Gynec.* [1920–] L.CB. 54–; MA. 22–; MC. 42–; MD.; S.; U. 52–; UCH. 22–23: 27–; **Abd.**U. 25–; **Bl.**U. 28–; **Bm.**U.; **Br.**U. 21–; **C.**MS. 59–; UL.; V. 46– imp.; **Cr.**MD.; **Db.** 23–; **Dn.**U. 29– imp.; **E.**S.; U.; **G.**F. imp.; U. 21– imp.; **Ld.**U.; **Lv.**M. 22–; **M.**MS.; Nw.A. 28–36 imp.: 37–; **O.**R. 37–; **R.**D. 47–52; **Sh.**U. 46–; W. 46–54; Y. [*C. of:* 2029]

2031 American Journal of **Occupational Therapy.** New York. *Am. J. occup. Ther.* L.MA. 55–.

2032 American Journal of **Ophthalmology.** St. Louis. *Am. J. Ophthal.* [1884–] L.CB. 46–; LI. 56–; MA. 93–; MD.; OP. 91–; S.; U. 52–; **Bl.**U. 18– V. imp.; **Bm.**T. 58–; U. 46–; **Br.**U. 84–17: 21–; **C.**MS. 59–; **Cr.**MD. 33–; **Db.** 21–25; **Dn.**U. 18–; **E.**S. 14–; **Ld.**U. 46–; **Lv.**M. 20–; **M.**MS. 48–; **O.**R. 18–; **Sa.** 04–24 imp.; Y.

2033 American Journal of **Optometry** and Archives of the American Academy of Optometry. Minneapolis. *Am. J. Optom.* [1924–] L.MA. 53–; MD. 53–; OP. 53–; SC. 35–; UC. 53–; **Bm.**T. 52–; **E.**HW. 53–; Y.

2034 American Journal of **Orthodontics.** St. Louis, etc. *Am. J. Orthod.* [1938–] L.D.; MA. 47–; MD.; RA.; S. 42–53; UCH. 57–; **Bl.**U. 44–; **Bm.**U. 45–; **Br.**U. 49–; **Dn.**U. 48–; **E.**U. 49–; **Ld.**U. 38–47; **M.**MS.; Nw.A. 38–42 imp.: 43–; Y. [*C. of:* 23880; *See also* 36305]

American Journal of **Orthodontics** and **Oral Surgery.** *See* 2034 and 36305.

2035 American Journal of **Orthopedic Surgery.** Boston. *Am. J. orthop. Surg.* [1903–18] L.MD.; S.; **G.**F. 03–16 imp. [*C. of:* 53558; *C. as:* 26624]

2036 American Journal of **Orthopsychiatry.** Menasha, Wis., etc. *Am. J. Orthopsychiat.* [1930–] L.B. 51–; MA. 46–; MD.; PS.; U. 50–; **Abd.**U. 43–; **Bm.**U. 48–; **Br.**U. 37– imp.; **C.**MC. 53–; **Cr.**MS. 60–; **Dn.**U. 55–; **E.**U. 48–; **G.**PH. 58–; U. 48–; **Ld.**U. 48–; **Sa.** 48–; Y.

2037 American Journal of **Pathology.** Boston, etc. *Am. J. Path.* [1925–] L.CB. 25–37: 44–; LI.; MA.; MC.; MD.; OP. 51–; S.; TD.; U. 50–; UC.; UCH.; **Abd.**R.; U.; **Bl.**U.; **Bm.**U.; **Br.**U. 28–; **C.**APH.; MO. 25–37; PA.; V. 53–; **Cr.**MD.; **Db.**; **Dn.**U.; **E.**N. 43–; U.; **G.**F.; U.; **Ld.**U.; **M.**MS.; Nw.A.; **O.**P.; R.; **R.**D. 25–38; **Sh.**U.; W.; Y. [*C. of:* 26438]

2038 American Journal of **Pharmaceutical Education.** Lincoln, Nebraska., etc. *Am. J. pharm. Educ.* [1937–] **Lv.**P.; N.U. 45–; Y.

2039 American Journal of **Pharmacy.** Philadelphia. *Am. J. Pharm.* [1829–] L.C. 84– imp.; K. 84–30 imp.; MA. 46–; P. 10–; PH. 1835–; **Bm.**T. 03–04: 29–34; **Db.** 74–82; **Dn.**U. 03–; **E.**U. 32–; **Lc.**A. 33–53; **M.**MS. 85–98; N.U. 29–32: 47–; Y.

2040 American Journal of **Photography.** Philadelphia. *Am. J. Photogr.* [1879–00] L.P. 86–00; PG. 86–00 imp.; **Abs.**N. 90–91. [*Merged into:* 37594]

2041 American Journal of **Physical Anthropology.** Washington. *Am. J. phys. Anthrop.* [1918–] L.AN.; BM.; BM^N.; MA. 49–; MD. 42–; S. 18–50; SC. 18–27: 33–; U. 50–; UC.; **Abd.**R. 37–50; U.; **Bm.**U.; **C.**AN.; E.; UL.; **Cr.**U.; **Db.** 21–; **Dn.**U. 52–; **E.**U.; **G.**U. 24–; **Ld.**U.; **O.**R.; **R.**U.; **Sa.**; **Sh.**U. 43–; Y.

2042 American Journal of **Physical Medicine.** Baltimore. *Am. J. phys. Med.* [1952–] L.BM.; H.; MA.; MD.; P.; SC.; **Bm.**P.; U.; **Br.**U.; **C.**PS.; UL.; **Db.** 54–; **E.**A.; U.; **G.**M.; U.; **Ld.**P.; U.; **M.**P.; T.; **O.**B.; **R.**U.; **Sh.**P.; U.; Y. [*C. of:* 35810]

2043 American Journal of **Physical Therapy.** Chicago. *Am. J. phys. Ther.* L.MD. 24–36 imp. [*C. in:* 14599]

2044 American Journal of **Physics.** Lancaster, Pa. *Am. J. Phys.* [1940–] L.AV. 44– imp.; B. 54–; I. 47–; KC. 55–; P. 42–; QM. 50–; RI.; SC.; U.; UC. 43–; **Abd.**U. 52–; **Abs.**U. 46–; **Bm.**T. 50–; **Br.**U. 40– imp.; **C.**P. 40–; **Cr.**U.; **Db.**; **Dn.**U. 44–; **E.**HW. 44– R. 44–; U.; **Ex.**U. 50–; **F.**A. 46–; **G.**T. 40–; U.; **H.**U.; **Ld.**P. 58–; U.; **Lv.**P. 46–; **M.**P. 50–; U. 51–; N.U. 45–; Nw.A.; **O.**R. 42–; **R.**U.; **Sa.** 51–; **Sh.**U. 54–; **Sw.**U. 57–58; Y. [*C. of:* 2122]

2045 American Journal of **Physiologic Therapeutics.** Chicago. *Am. J. physiol. Ther.* **Br.**U. 10–11.

2046 American Journal of **Physiological Optics.** Southbridge, Mass. *Am. J. physiol. Opt.* [1920–26] L.P. 22–26; OP.; S.; UC.; **Bm.**U.; **C.**C.; **Dn.**U.; **M.**MS. 20–24; U.; **O.**R.; **Sa.** 24–26 imp.

2047 American Journal of **Physiology.** Boston, etc. *Am. J. Physiol.* [1898–] L.B. 08–; BM^N. 98–08; CB. 54–; H. 34–55; LI.; MA. 42–; MC.; MD.; OP. 50–; PH. 28–; RI. 98–33; S.; SC.; TD. 11–45 imp.: 46–; U.; UC.; VC. 46– imp.; **Abd.**R. 23–; U.; **Bl.**U.; **Bm.**U. 07–; **Bn.**U. 49–; **Br.**U. 07–; **C.**APH.; BI. 54–; PA. 29–; PH.; V. 54–; **Cr.**MD. 56–; U.; **Db.**; **Dn.**U.; **E.**N. 43–; P.; PO. 51–; U.; **G.**F. 47–51: 59–; U.; **Lc.**A. 55–; **Ld.**U. 02–; **Lv.**U.; **M.**MS.; N.U. 53–; Nw.A. 98–01: 07–; **O.**PH.; R.; UC. 20–; **Pl.**M. 09– imp.; **R.**D. 31–; **Sa.** 56–; **Sh.**U.; W. 49–56: 61–; Y.

2048 **American Journal** of **Proctology.** New York. *Am. J. Proctol.* [1950–] **L.**MA.; MD.

2049 **American Journal** of **Progressive Therapeutics.** Chicago. *Am. J. prog. Ther.* [1904–06] [*C. of:* 2179]

2050 **American Journal** of **Psychiatry.** Baltimore. *Am. J. Psychiat.* [1921–] **L.**BM.; H. 50–; MA. 30–33: 37–; MD.; PS. 21–54 imp.; U. 51–; **Abd.**U. 42– imp.; **Bl.**U. 32– V. imp.; **Bm.**U. 44–; **Br.**U. 33– imp.; **C.**MC.; UL.; **Db.** 22–33: 46–; **Dn.**U. 56–; **E.**P.; S.; U. 44– imp.; **M.**MS. 47–; **Nw.**A. 21–32 imp.: 36–; **O.**R. 37–; **Sa.**; **Sh.**U. 54–; **Y.** [*C. of:* 2020]

2051 **American Journal** of **Psychoanalysis.** New York. *Am. J. Psychoanal.* [1941–]

2052 **American Journal** of **Psychology.** Worcester, etc. *Am. J. Psychol.* [1887–] **L.**AN.; B. 51–; BM.; MA. 46–; MD. 05–; PS.; U.; UC. 08–; **Abd.**U. 92–32: 46–; **Bl.**U. 35– imp.; **Bm.**P.; U. 98–; **Br.**U. 24–; **C.**PH. 87–04 imp.; PS.; UL. 17–; **Cr.**P. 03–51; **Dn.**U. 48–54: 61–; **E.**P.; U.; **Ex.**U. 24–25: 29–31: 56–; **G.**U.; **H.**U. 33– imp.; **Ld.**U. 20–; **Lv.**U. 09–; **M.**P. 53–; R. 07–; **N.**U. 50– imp.; **O.**EP.; N.; R.; **R.**U.; **Sh.**U. 95– imp.; **Y.**

2053 **American Journal** of **Psychotherapy.** Lancaster, Pa., etc. *Am. J. Psychother.* [1947–] **L.**B. 30–43 imp.: 46–; MA. 52–; MD.; **Dn.**U. 55–.

2054 **American Journal** of **Public Health** (*afterwards* and the **Nation's Health**). New York. *Am. J. publ. Hlth* [1912–] **L.**AM. 54–; H. 22–; LI. 38–; MA. 30–; MD.; SC. 32–; SH. 25–; TD.; **Abd.**R. 43– imp.; U. 19–; **Bl.**U. 30– imp.; **Bm.**U. 37–; **Br.**U. 42– imp.; **Cr.**MD. 37–; **Dn.**U. 16– imp. **E.**U. 26–; **G.**PH. 35–45: 50–; **M.**MS. 48–; **Nw.**A. 40–; **O.**R. 32–; **R.**D. 17–; **Sh.**S. 55–; **W.** 36–54. [*C. of:* 25530]

2055 **American Journal** of **Public Hygiene** and Journal of the Massachusetts Association of Boards of Health. Boston, etc. *Am. J. publ. Hyg.* **L.**MD. 08–10*; TD. 05–10. [*C. of:* 26387; *C. as:* 25530]

2056 **American Journal** of **Roentgenology** (*afterwards* **Radium Therapy** and **Nuclear Medicine**). New York. *Am. J. Roentg.* [1913–] **L.**BM. 18–; CB.; H. 42–53 imp.; MA. 30–; MC. 27–44; MD.; MT. 24–; P. 20–29; RA.; S.; SC. 30–; U. 52–; UCH. 42– imp.; **Abd.**U. 35– imp.; **Abs.**N. 49–; **Bl.**U. 45– v. imp.; **Bm.**U. 43–; **Bn.**U. 27–33: 48–57; **Br.**U. 19– imp.; **Cr.**MD. 23– imp.; **Db.** 19–28: 34–; **Dn.**U. 52–; **E.**A. 49–; S. 20–; U. 29–; **Ex.**U. 22–30; **G.**F. 47– imp.; **Ld.**U. 45–; **Lv.**M. 27– imp.; **M.**MS. 28–; **Nw.**A. 35–; **O.**R. 49–; **Sh.**IO. 31–; **Y.** [*C. of:* 2139]

2057 **American Journal** of **School Hygiene.** Worcester. *Am. J. Sch. Hyg.* [1917–21] [*C. as:* 48784]

2058 **American Journal** of **Science.** New Haven. *Am. J. Sci.* [1818–] **L.**B. 1839– imp.; BM.; BMᴺ.; C. 1843–; EE. 06–28; G.; GL. 00–; GM.; H. 45–; I. 72– imp.; K.; P.; QM. 58–; RI. 1830–; S. 78–12; SC. 14–; Z. 1846–; **Abd.**U. 1846–; **Abs.**U. 35–; **Bl.**U. imp.; **Bm.**P.; U. 67– imp.; **Br.**P. imp.; U.; **C.**MI. 96–; P.; PO. 51–; S. 24–; UL.; **Cr.**U. 19–; **Db.** 1852–; **E.**D. 1836–1856: 74–; R.; T. 1818–32; U. imp.; **Ex.**U. 56–; **G.**F. 1818–1844; M. 77–; U. 1846– imp.; **Ld.**PL. 00–; U. 64–73: 85–; T. 29–; **H.**U. 31–; **Lv.**P. 53–; U.; **M.**P.; U. 1818–69: 40– imp.; **N.**U. 00–; **Nw.**A.; **O.**R.; **R.**U. 22–; **Rt.** 47–; **Sa.**; **Sh.**SC. 1859–; **Sw.**U. 54–; **Y.**

2059 **American Journal** of **Science. Radiocarbon Supplement.** New Haven. *Am. J. Sci. Radiocarbon Suppl.* [1959–60] **L.**BM.; BMᴺ.; P.; SC.; **C.**BO.; **E.**R.; **H.**U. [*Supplement to:* 2058; *C. as:* Radiocarbon]

2060 **American Journal** of **Stomatology.** New York. *Am. J. Stomat.* [1929–31] **L.**D. 30 imp. [*C. of:* 2160]

2061 **American Journal** of **Surgery** (*formerly* and Gynecology). New York. *Am. J. Surg.* [1890–] **L.**BM. 29–; GH. 05–28; MA. 26–; MD. 04–; RA. 29–35; S. 07–; U. 51–; **Abd.**U. 26–; **Bl.**U. 27– imp.; **Bm.**U. 46–; **Br.**U. 10–56; **C.**UL. 29–; **Cr.**MD. 26–; **Db.** 29–; **Dn.** U. 26–; **E.**S. 35–; U. 25–26: 46–; **G.**F. 28– imp.; U. 26–; **Ld.**U. 41–; **Lv.**M. 09–; **M.**MS. 25–; **Nw.**A. 18–35 imp.: 37–; **O.**R. 29–; **Sh.**U. 55–; **Y.**

2061ᶜ **American Journal** of **Syphilis, Gonorrhea** and **Venereal Diseases.** St. Louis, etc. *Am. J. Syph. Gonorrhea vener. Dis.* [1955–] **L.**MA.; MD.; S.; TD.; **Bl.**U.; **G.**F.; **Ld.**U.; **Lv.**M.; **Nw.**A. [*C. of:* 2062]

2062 **American Journal** of **Syphilis** and **Neurology.** St Louis, Mo. *Am. J. Syph. Neurol.* [1917–54] **L.**MA. 38–54; MD.; S. 17–54; TD.; **M.**MS. 17–21; **Nw.**A. 46–54; UCH. 21–25; **Bl.**U. 46–54 imp.; **Db.** 21–23; **G.**F.; **Ld.**U.; **Lv.**M. 37–51; U. [*C. as:* 2061ᶜ]

2063 **American Journal** of **Tropical Diseases** and **Preventive Medicine.** New Orleans. *Am. J. trop. Dis. prev. Med.* **L.**TD. 13–16*; **Lv.**U. 13–16. [*C. in:* 30358]

2064 **American Journal** of **Tropical Medicine.** Baltimore. *Am. J. trop. Med.* [1921–51] **L.**BMᴺ.; EB.; H. 33–40; MA.; MC.; MD.; TD.; TP. 49–51; **Bl.**U. 37–41 imp.; **Bm.**U. 44–51; **E.**U. 38–51; **Lv.**U.; **Nw.**A.; **O.**R. 37–51; **Sal.** 48–51; **Sh.**U. 48–51; **W.** 36–51. [*C. as:* 2065]

2065 **American Journal** of **Tropical Medicine** and **Hygiene.** Baltimore. *Am. J. trop. Med. Hyg.* [1952–] **L.**BMᴺ.; EB.; MA.; MC.; MD.; TD.; TP. imp.; **Bl.**U.; **Bm.**U.; **C.**MO.; **E.**U.; **Lv.**U.; **Nw.**A.; **O.**R.; **Sal.**; **Sh.**U.; **W.** 52–55; **Y.** [*C. of:* 2064 and 26524]

2066 **American Journal** of **Urology** and **Sexology.** New York. *Am. J. Urol. Sex.* [1904–20] **L.**MD. 04–06; S. 12–16; **M.**MS. 05–15. [*C. in:* 30267 *and later replaced by* 26885]

2067 **American Journal** of **Veterinary Medicine.** Chicago. *Am. J. vet. Med.* [1910–20] **L.**V.; **E.**N. 17–18. [*C. of:* 32241; *C. as:* 56641]

2068 **American Journal** of **Veterinary Research.** Chicago. *Am. J. vet. Res.* [1940–] **L.**AM. 51–; EB. 41–; LI.; MA. 46–; MC.; MD. 42–; V.; VC. 46– imp.; Z. 58–; **Abd.**R. 41–; **Bl.**U. 58–; **Bn.**U. 62–; **Br.**U.; **C.**A. 41–; APH. 48–; V.; **Db.** 43–; **E.**N.; PO. 49–; **Ld.**U. 54–; **Nw.**A. 41–; **O.**R. 58–; **R.**D. 41–; **Sal.** 44–49: 57–; **W.**; **Y.**

2069 **American Journal** of **Veterinary Science.** Chicago. *Am. J. vet. Sci.* [1958–] **L.**V.; UC.; **Abd.**R.; **Abs.**U.; **W.** [*C. of:* 35072 Sect. I]

2070 **American Lumberman.** Chicago. *Am. Lumberman* [1899–]

2071 **American Machine** and **Tool Record.** Chicago. *Am. Mach. Tool Rec.* [1911–30] [*C. in:* 38260]

2072 **American Machinist.** New York. *Am. Mach., N.Y.* [1877–60] **L.**BM. 35–60; DI. 50–60 imp.; P. 56–60; **C.**ENG. 04–31; **Cr.**U. 16–60; **Db.** 11–60; **G.**M. 82–01; T. 85–08 imp.; **Ld.**P. 91–02; **Lv.**P. 53–56 v. imp.: 58–60; U. 00–15 imp.; **Sh.**IO. 56–60; **Y.** [*From* 1900–32 *also formed part of* 2073; *C. as:* 2075]

2073 **American Machinist. European Edition.** London. *Am. Mach., Lond.* [1900–32] **L.**BM.; NF. 22–32; P. 10–32; **Bm.**P. 18–32; U. 04–32; **Bra.**P. 27–32; **Db.**; **G.**M. 02–32; U. 03–32; **M.**P. 25–32; T.; **Sh.**P. 19–32; SC. [*C. as:* 29077. *Contains the complete text of* 2072 *and a European section*]

2074 **American Machinist. German edition.** Zeitschrift für praktischen Maschinenbau. Berlin. *Am. Mach., Berl.*

2075 **American Machinist/Metalworking Manufacturing.** New York. *Am. Mach./Metalwkg Mfg* [1960–] **L.**BM.; DI.; P.; **Cr.**U.; **Db.**; **Li.**M. (1 yr); **Lv.**P.; **Sh.**IO.; **Y.** [*C. of:* 2072]

2076 **American Magazine** of **Aeronautics.** New York. *Am. Mag. Aeronaut.* **L.**P. 07–08. [*C. as:* 1084]

2077 **American Manufacturer** and **Iron World.** Pittsburg. *Am. Mfr Iron Wld* [1902–06] **L.**P.; **Bm.**U. imp.; **G.**M. 06; **Nw.**A.

2078 **American Marine Engineer.** New York. *Am. mar. Engr* [1906–]

2079 **American Marine Standard.** Washington. *Am. mar. Stand.* [1925–] **L.**P.

2080 **American Mathematical Monthly.** Springfield. *Am. math. Mon.* [1894–] **L.**BM. 16–; SC.; U. 57–; UC.; **Abd.**U. 51–; **Bm.**T. 53–; **C.**P. 21–; **Co.**T. 62–; **Db.** 42–; **E.**Q. 32–; R. 20–; U. 52–; **G.**U. 13–; **Lv.**P. 59–; **M.**U. 17–; **N.**U. 30–; **O.**UC. 58–; **Sa.** 47–; **Y.**

American Mathematical Society Notices. Ann Arbor. *See* 35276.

2082 **American Mathematical Society Translations.** Providence. *Am. math. Soc. Transl.* [1950–] **L.**SC.; **C.**P. 55; **Db.**; **Dn.**U. 55–59; **G.**U.; **H.**U. 55–; **M.**P. 55–; U. 51–52: 55–; **N.**U. 55–; **Nw.**A. 55–; **Sa.** 55–; **Sh.**U. 55–; **Y.**

2083 **American Medical Compend.** Toledo. *Am. med. Compend* [1884–]

2084 **American Medical Journal.** St. Louis, Mo. *Am. med. J.* (1873–16)

2085 **American Medical Monthly.** Baltimore. *Am. med. Mon.* [1883–04]

2086 **American Medical Practitioner.** New York. *Am. med. Practnr* [1944–]

2087 **American Medicine.** Philadelphia. *Am. Med.* [1901–36] **L.**MA. 31–36 imp.; MD. 06–36; S. 01–05: 07; **Br.**U. 01–14; **C.**PA. 01–14; **G.**F. 01–11 imp.; **Lv.**M. 01–36.

2088 **American Midland Naturalist.** Notre Dame, Ind. *Am. Midl. Nat.* [1909–] **L.**BM*N*.; K.; NC. 51–; SC. 26–; Z.; **C.**B. 33–; **Cr.**N. 27–47 imp.; **Db.**; **E.**B. 43–; **G.**N. 09–51; **Ld.**U.; **Lv.**U. 35–; **M.**U. 13–15 imp.; **Mi.** imp.; **Nw.**A. imp.; **O.**AP. 37–; F. 41–52; OR. 33–42 imp.; **Sal.** 57–; **Y.** [*C. of:* 31787]

2089 **American Midland Naturalist. Monographs.** Notre Dame. *Am. Midl. Nat. Monogr.* [1944–] **L.**BM.; BM*N*.; SC. 44–51; Z. (zool.)

2090 **American Milk Review.** New York. *Am. Milk Rev.* [1939–] **L.**AM. 58–60; **Abs.**U. 59–; **R.**D.; **Y.** [*C. from:* 31847]

2091 **American Miller** and **Processer.** Chicago, etc. *Am. Miller Processer* [1873–] **L.**BM. 21–30; P.; **E.**CE. 55–; **Sal.**F. 28–; **Y.** [>34143, 1930–31 and 34090, 1931–34]

2092 **American Mineralogist.** Lancaster, etc. *Am. Miner.* [1916–] **L.**B.; BM*N*.; DI. 44–; GL.; GM.; P. 54–; QM. 49–; SC.; **Abd.**S. 50–; U.; **Abs.**U. 55–; **Bl.**U. 55–; **Bm.**U.; **Br.**U.; **C.**MI.; UL.; **Cr.**U. 49–; **Db.** 53–; **E.**F. 16–39; R.; U.; **Ex.**U. 38–; **F.**A. 47–; **G.**T. 48–; U. 18– imp.; **H.**U. 20– imp.; **Ld.**U.; **M.**U. 23–; **N.**U. 53–; **Nw.**A. 39–; **O.**R.; **R.**U. 21–; **Rt.** 46–; **Sa.** 30–; **Sh.**SC.; **St.**R. 51–; **Sw.**U. 21–; **Y.**

2093 **American Mining Congress Monthly Bulletin.** Washington. *Am. Min. Congr. mon. Bull.* [1910–13] [*C. as:* 32002]

2094 **American Mining Digest.** Denver. *Am. Min. Dig.* [1937–38]

2095 **American Mining Review.** Los Angeles. *Am. Min. Rev.* [1907–09] [*C. of:* and *Rec. as:* 28803]

2096 **American Monthly Microscopical Journal.** Washington. *Am. mon. microsc. J.* [1880–02] **L.**BM. 89–02; BM*N*.; P.; **Bl.**U. 90–02 imp.; **C.**UL. 80–86; **Db.** 81–02; **M.**U. 80–01 imp.; **O.**R.; **Pl.**M.

2097 **American Museum Journal.** New York. *Am. Mus. J.* [1900–18] **L.**BM*N*.; GM. 15–18; HO. 02–18 imp.; Z.; **C.**P. 12–18; **Cr.**M. 13–18; **Db.**; **E.**F. 11–18 imp.; R.; **Lv.**P. [*C. as:* 34215]

2098 **American Museum Novitates.** New York. *Am. Mus. Novit.* [1921–] **L.**BM*N*.; GL. imp.; GM.; UC.; Z. 24–; **Abd.**M. (fish.); **C.**P.; **Dm.**; **E.**R.; **Lv.**P. 21–39 imp.; U. 40– imp.; **Nw.**A. 26–31 imp.: 53–; **O.**R.; **Pl.**M. 50–.

2099 **American Naturalist.** Lancaster, Pa. *Am. Nat.* 1867–] **L.**AM. 20–31; BM.; BM*N*.; CB. 48–; E. 67–82: 90–91; EB. 92–11 imp.; GM. 79–81 imp.: 87–15; K.; L.; NC. 50–; SC.; U. 50–; UC. 07–37; Z. imp.; **Abd.**U. 43–; **Abs.**A. 20–; **Ba.**I. 16–; **Bm.**P.; U. 04–08: 34–; **Bn.**U.– 13– imp.; **Br.**U. 67–97: 13–21: 36–; **C.**B.; GE. 18–; UL.; **Cr.**U. 86–09; **Db.**; **Dn.**U. 85– imp.; **E.**A. 02–07; AG. 47–; AR. 48–; R. 67–75: 89–16; U. 73–99; imp.: 00–; **Ex.**U. 37–; **G.**M. 78–; U. 24– imp.; **Ld.**P. 73–17; U.; **Lv.**P. 00–21; U. 08–; W. 28–31; **M.**U. imp.; **N.**U. 53–; **Nw.**A. 20–; **O.**R.; **Pl.**M. 21– imp.; **Rt.** 19–; **Sh.**U. 46–; **Y.**

2100 **American Nautical Almanac.** Washington. *Am. naut. Alm.* [1866–59] **L.**BM.; **Db.** 00–59; **E.**O. imp.; R. 70–81; **G.**M. 15–38. [*C. as:* 9001]

2101 **American Neptune.** Salem, Mass. *Am. Neptune* [1941–] **L.**BM.; SC.; **E.**A.; U. imp.; **Lv.**P.; **Y.**

2102 **American Nurseryman.** Rochester. *Am. Nurserym.* [1916–] **Md.**H. 61–; **O.**F. 41–; **Sil.** 60–. [*C. of:* 1965]

2103 **American Nut Journal.** Rochester, N.Y. *Am. Nut J.* [1914–31]

2104 **American OSE Review.** New York. *Am. OSE Rev.* [1942–] **L.**MA. 47–.

2105 **American Oil Journal.** Kansas City. *Am. Oil J.* [1917–19]

2106 **American Optical Messenger.** San Francisco. *Am. opt. Mess.* [1937–]

2107 **American Orchid Society Yearbook.** *Am. Orchid Soc. Yb.* **L.**HS. 49–.

2108 **American Ornithology.** Worcester. *Am. Orn.* [1901–05] **L.**BM*N*.; Z.

2109 **American Orthodontist.** Kansas City. *Am. Orthod.* [1907–12] **L.**D. 10–12.

2110 **American Orthoptic Journal.** Rochester. *Am. orthopt. J.* [1951–] **L.**MA.; MD.; OP.

2111 **American Paint Journal.** St. Louis. *Am. Paint J.* [1916–] **L.**PR. 28–; S.; **Sl.**I. 49–; **Y.**

2112 **American Paper Converter.** Chicago. *Am. Pap. Converter* [1946–53] **Lh.**P. [*C. of:* 36957ᵃ; *C. as:* 36960]

2113 **American Pecan Journal.** Waco, Tex. *Am. Pecan J.* [1940–]

2114 **American Perfumer.** New York. *Am. Perfumer* [1960–] **L.**C.; P.; TP.; **Ld.**U. 63–; **Lv.**P.; **Y.** [*C. of:* 2115]

2115 **American Perfumer** and **Aromatics.** New York.
Am. Perfumer Arom. [1955–60] **L.**C.; **P.**; **TP.**; **Lv.**P. 59–60;
Y.
    Documentary edition. [1960] **L.**P.; **Y.**
[*C. of:* 2116; *C. as:* 2114]

2116 **American Perfumer** and **Essential Oil Review.**
New York. *Am. Perfumer ess. Oil Rev.* [1906–55] **L.**C.
46–55 imp.; **P.** 10–32: 55; **TP.** 50–55; **Bm.**U. 14–18 imp.;
Y. [*C. as:* 2115]
    American Petroleum Institute Quarterly. New
York. *See* 41436.

2117 **American Photo-Engraver.** St. Louis, Mo.
Am. Photo-Engraver [1908–] **L.**SB. 11–14; **Lh.**P. 39– imp.

2118 **American Photography.** New York. *Am. Photogr.*
[1907–53] **L.**P. 07–23: 42–47; **PG.**; **Bm.**P. 45–53; **Nw.**A.
47–53; **We.**K. 39–53. [*C. of:* 1895; *C. in:* 37646°]

2119 **American Physical Education Review.** Springfield, Mass. *Am. phys. Educ. Rev.* [1896–29] **L.**MD. 00:
04–29; **TD.** 27–29; **Bm.**U. 12–27; **Ex.**U. 24–29. [*C. as:*
26082]

2120 **American Physician.** Philadelphia. *Am. Physn,
Philad.* [1920–26] [*C. of:* 30215]

2121 **American Physician.** Rahway, N.J. *Am. Physn,
Rahway* [1903–08] [*C. of:* 1983]

2122 **American Physics Teacher.** Lancaster, Pa.
Am. Phys. Teach. [1933–39] **L.**RI.; **SC.**; **U.**; **C.**P.; **Cr.**U.;
E.U.; **G.**T.; **U.**; **H.**U. 37–39; **Nw.**A. 37–39; **R.**U. [*C. as:*
2044]

2123 **American Pilot** and **Aircraftsman.** Charlotte,
N.C. *Am. Pilot AircrMan* [1939–44] [*C. as:* 1611]

2124 **American Plants.** San Diego, Cal. *Am. Pls*
[1907–10] **L.**K.

2125 **American Pomology.** Ames, Ia. *Am. Pomol.*
[1931–34]

2126 **American Potato Journal.** Washington. *Am.
Potato J.* [1926–] **L.**AM. 48– imp.; **IC.** 45–; **MY.** 43–; **P.**;
Abd.R. 42–52; **Ba.**I. 55–; **C.**A. 33–; **AB.** 47–; **Db.** 57–;
Dn.U. 61–; **E.**U. 51–54; **Hu.**G. 53–; **Je.** 45–; **Md.**H.
41–52 imp.; **N.**U. 58–; **Rt.** 47–; **Sil.** 59–; **Y.** [*C. of:*
38190]

2127 **American Potato Yearbook.** New York. *Am.
Potato Yb.* **L.**AM. 48–; **C.**A. 48–; **Hu.**G. 57–; **Md.**H.
49–52; **Y.**

2128 **American Poultry Journal.** Chicago. *Am.
Poult. J.* [1874–]

2129 **American Practitioner.** Louisville, Ky. *Am.
Practnr, Louisville* [1870–15] **L.**MD. 86–13; **S.** 86–14; **Br.**U.
86–05; **E.**S. 86–10. [*C. in:* 2066]

2130 **American Practitioner.** Philadelphia. *Am.
Practnr, Philad.* [1946–49] **L.**BM.; **MA.**; **MD.**; **Bl.**U.; **C.**UL.;
Db.; **E.**A.; **U.**; **O.**B. [*C. as:* 2131]

2131 **American Practitioner** and **Digest of Treatment.**
Philadelphia. *Am. Practnr Dig. Treat.* [1950–] **L.**BM.;
D.; **MA.**; **MD.**; **Bl.**U. 50–56; **C.**UL.; **Db.**; **E.**A.; **U.**; **O.**R.; **Y.**
[*C. of:* 2130 and 16987]

2132 **American Pressman.** St. Louis. *Am. Pressman*
[1890–] **L.**SB. 93–00: 09–12: 32–42: 46–; **Lh.**P. 37– imp.
    American Primrose Society Quarterly. *See*
41437.

2133 **American Printer.** New York. *Am. Printer*
[1900–54] **L.**P. 12–31; **SB.**; **E.**HW. 29–54 imp.; **T.** 91–30
imp.; **Lh.**P. 37–54 imp. [*C. as:* 2134]

2134 **American Printer** and **Lithographer.** New York.
Am. Printer Lithogr. [1954–58] **L.**SB.; **E.**HW.; **Lh.**P.
[*C. of:* 2133; *C. in:* 23643]

2135 **American Produce Grower.** Chicago. *Am.
Prod. Grow.* [1926–30] [*C. in:* 1964]

2136 **American Produce Review.** New York. *Am.
Prod. Rev.* [1937–39] [*C. of:* 1934; *C. as:* 1917, 1945
and 2090]

2137 **American Professional Pharmacist.** New York.
Am. prof. Pharm. [1935–] **L.**PH. 38–; **G.**T. 55–56; **N.**U.
49–. [*Replaces:* 38422]

2137° **American Project Series.** Center for International
Studies, Massachusetts Institute of Technology. New
York. *Am. Proj. Ser.* [1958–] **L.**BM.

2138 **American Psychologist.** Lancaster, Pa. *Am.
Psychol.* [1946–] **L.**PS.; **Bl.**U. 60–; **Dn.**U. 48– imp.;
H.U. 59–; **Ld.**U.; **O.**EP.; **Sw.**U. 60–.

2139 **American Quarterly** of **Roentgenology.** Pittsburg. *Am. Q. Roentg.* [1906–13] **L.**RA. [*C. as:* 2056]

2140 **American Review** of **Respiratory Diseases.**
Baltimore. *Am. Rev. resp. Dis.* [1959–] **L.**H.; **MA.**; **MC.**;
MD.; **TD.**; **Bl.**U.; **Bm.**U.; **Br.**U.; **C.**UL.; **Cr.**MS.; **E.**P.; **U.**;
G.PH.; **U.**; **Ld.**U.; **Lv.**M.; **O.**P.; **PH.**; **R.**; **Sh.**U.; **W.**; **Y.**
[*C. of:* 2143]

2141 **American Review** of **Soviet Medicine.** New
York. *Am. Rev. sov. Med.* [1943–48] **L.**MA.; **MC.** 46–48;
MD.; **S.**; **TD.**; **Bm.**U.; **Br.**U.; **E.**U. 45–48; **O.**R.

2142 **American Review** of **Tropical Agriculture.**
Mexico. *Am. Rev. trop. Agric.* [1909–10] **L.**HS.; **K.**
[*C. as:* 46275]
    American Review of **Tuberculosis.** *See* 2143.

2143 **American Review** of **Tuberculosis** and **Pul-
monary Diseases.** New York. *Am. Rev. Tuberc.
pulm. Dis.* [1917–59] **L.**H. 33–59; **MA.** 30–59; **MC.**; **MD.**;
TD.; **U.** 50–59; **UCH.** 36–40; **Bl.**U. 46–59; **Bm.**U. 48–59;
Br.U.; **C.**UL. 18–59; **Cr.**MD. 51–59; **Db.** imp.; **E.**P.;
U. 37–59; **G.**F. 51–59 imp.; **PH.** 24–27: 37–59; **U.** 46–49:
53–59 imp.; **Ld.**U. 47–59; **Lv.**M. 21–59; **M.**MS. 35–59
imp.; **Nw.**A. 18–59 imp.; **O.**P. 49–59; **PH.** 28–59; **R.**;
R.D. 17–36; **Sh.**U. 44–59; **W.** 39–59. [*C. as:* 2140]

2144 **American Rhododendron Society Yearbook.**
Am. Rhodod. Soc. Yb. **L.**HS. 49. [*C. of:* 47717; *C. as:*
47719]

2145 **American Rifleman.** Washington. *Am. Rifleman* [1924–] **L.**SC. 41–; **Ste.**

2146 **American Road Builder.** Washington. *Am. Rd
Bldr* **L.**P. (curr.)
    American Roofer and **Modern Roofing.** *See*
2147.

2147 **American Roofer** and **Siding Contractor.** New
York. *Am. Roofer Siding Contractor* [1911–] **Y.**

2148 **American Rose Annual.** Harrisburg, Pa. *Am.
Rose A.* [1916–] **L.**HS.; **Abs.**N.; **Ba.**I.; **Y.**

2149 **American Rose Magazine.** Harrisburg, Pa., etc.
Am. Rose Mag. [1933–] **L.**HS.; **Abs.**N.; **Ba.**I. 51–;
Bn.U. 63–. [*Replaces:* 2150]

2150 **American Rose Quarterly.** West Grove, Pa.
Am. Rose Q. [1930–32] **L.**HS.; **SC.**; **Abs.**N. [*Replaced
by:* 2149]

2151 **American Scientist.** New Haven, Conn., etc.
Am. Scient. [1942–] **L.**BM^N. 48–; **CB.** (2 yr.); **L.** 46–53;
MA. 47–; **P.** 44–; **SC.**; **U.** 50–; **Bm.**U. 49–; **C.**P. 46–; **UL.**
46–; **Fr.** 43–50 imp.; **Pl.**M. 43– imp.; **Rt.** 52–; **Y.** [*C. of:*
49732]

2152 **American Shipbuilder.** New York. *Am. Ship-bldr* **L.**P. 94–07*.

2153 **American Shoemaking.** Boston. *Am. Shoemkg* [1901–] **L.**P. 19–31. [*C. of:* 28329]
  American Silk Journal. *See* 2154.

2154 **American Silk** and **Rayon Journal.** New York. *Am. Silk Rayon J.* [1882–38] **L.**P. 10–23; **M.**C. 36–38 imp. [*C. in:* 42226]

2155 **American Society** of **Anesthesiologists News-letter.** *Am. Soc. Anesth. Newsl.* **L.**D.

2156 **American Society** of **Heating** and **Ventilating Engineers Guide.** New York. *Am. Soc. Heat. Vent. Engrs Guide* [1922–37] **L.**P. 25–37. [*C. of:* 22013]
  American Society for Testing Materials Standards *and* **Tentative Standards.** *See* 123 and 126.

2157 **American Standards.** New York. *Am. Stand.* **L.**P. 23–.

2158 **American Standards Year Book.** New York. *Am. Stand. Yb.* [1929–] **L.**P.; **Bm.**P. 45–. [*C. of:* 58004: 1934–37 *not published*]

2159 **American Statistician.** *Am. Statistn* [1947–] **L.**AM. imp.; BM.; **C.**GE.; SL.; **F.**A. 49–50; **Ld.**U. 62–; **Sh.**IO. 50–; **Y.** [*C. of:* 9358]

2160 **American Stomatologist.** New York. *Am. Stomat.* [1927–29] **L.**MD. [*C. as:* 2060]

2161 **American Stone Trade.** Chicago. *Am. Stone Trade* [1910–36] **L.**GM. 11–15; P. 10–21. [*C. of:* 48044]

2162 **American Sugar Bulletin.** New York. *Am. Sug. Bull.* [1916–24]

2163 **American Sugar Industry.** Chicago. *Am. Sug. Ind.* [1904–13] [*C. of:* 5893; *C. as:* 51276]

2164 **American Surgeon.** Baltimore. *Am. Surg.* [1951–] **L.**MA.; MD.; S. [*C. of:* 50255]

2165 **American Swedish Engineer.** East Orange, N.J. *Am. Swed. Engr* [*C. of:* 9355]

2166 **American Telephone Journal.** New York. *Am. Teleph. J.* [1900–08] **L.**EE. 02–08; P. 08. [*C. in:* 52807]

2167 **American Therapist.** New York. *Am. Ther.* [1892–05]

2168 **American Thresherman** and **Farm Power.** Madison, Wis. *Am. Thresherman* [1898–32]

2169 **American Tomato Yearbook.** Westfield, N.J. *Am. Tomato Yb.* **C.**A. 51–; **Md.**H. 52–.

2170 **American Tung News.** Picayune. *Am. Tung News* [1949–] **L.**TP. 54– imp.; **Y.**

2171 **American Tung Oil News.** Pensacola, Fla. *Am. Tung Oil News* [1934–37]

2172 **American Tung Oil Topics.** New Orleans. *Am. Tung Oil Top.* [1954–] **L.**P.; PR.; TP. imp.; **Y.**

2173 **American Vegetable Grower.** Willoughby. *Am. Veg. Grow.* [1955–] **Md.**H.

2174 **American Veterinary Review.** New York. *Am. vet. Rev.* [1879–15] **L.**V. imp.; **Br.**U. 94–15 imp.; **W.** 04–15. [*C. as:* 25545]

2175 **American Vinegar Industry.** New York. *Am. Vinegar Ind.* [1921–23] [*C. as:* 20387]

2176 **American Wildlife.** Washington. *Am. Wildl.* [1935–41] **O.**AP. [*C. of:* 1968]

2177 **American Woods.** U.S. Forest Service. Washington. *Am. Woods* [1932–54] **O.**F.

2178 **American Wool** and **Cotton Reporter.** Boston. *Am. Wool Cott. Reptr* [1908–51] **Bra.**P. 27–42; **Ld.**W. 47–51. [*C. of:* 57820; *C. as:* 2184]

2179 **American X-ray Journal.** St. Louis, Mo. *Am. X-Ray J.* [1897–04] [*C. as:* 2049]

2180 **American Yearbook** of **Anesthesia** and **Analgesia.** New York. *Am. Yb. Anesth. Analg.* [1915–18] **L.**MC.; MD.; S.; **G.**F. 15.

2181 **American Year-book** of **Medicine** and **Surgery.** Philadelphia. *Am. Yb. Med. Surg.* [1896–00] **L.**BM. 99–00; MA.; MD.; S.; **Br.**U.; **M.**MS. 98–00; **O.**R. [*C. as:* 48598]

2182 **American Zinc, Lead** and **Copper Journal.** Joplin, Mo. *Am. Zinc Lead Copp. J.* [1915–38] **L.**NF. 23–38 imp.

2183 **America's First Zoo.** Philadelphia. *Am.'s first Zoo* [1949–] **L.**BM^N.; z. [*Replaces:* 19198]

2184 **America's Textile Reporter.** Boston, Mass. *Am.'s Text. Reptr* [1951–] **Ld.**W. [*C. of:* 2178]

2185 **Ames Forester.** Ames, Iowa. *Ames Forester* [1913–53] **L.**K.; **O.**F. 23–53 imp.

2186 **Aminco Laboratory News.** American Instrument Co. Silver Spring, Md. *Aminco Lab. News* **Y.**

2187 **Amino acides, peptides, protéines.** Paris. *Amino Acides* [1957–] **L.**MD.; S. 57–59; **Bl.**U.; **G.**U.

2188 **Aminoacidosi.** Torino. *Aminoacidosi*

2189 **Aminsteel News.** New York. *Aminsteel News* [1930–32] [*C. as:* 50889]

2190 **Amis** de l'**hygiène.** Nantes. *Amis Hyg.* [1948–] **L.**TD. 48–59.
  Amis du **Musée océanographique** du **Monaco.** *See* 12434.

2191 **Amis** des **roses.** Lyon. *Amis Roses* [1908–] **L.**HS.; **Y.**

2192 **Ammohouse Bulletin.** Wellington, N.Z. *Ammohouse Bull.* [1957–] **L.**AM.; **Lo.**

2193 **Amoeba:** Amateur Biological Club of Japan. Tokyo. *Amoeba, Tokyo* [1928–33] **L.**BM^N. 28–30.

2194 **Amoy Fisheries Bulletin.** Amoy, Chosen. *Amoy Fish. Bull.* [1950–] **Abd.**R. 50–51; **Dm.**; **Pl.**M. 50.

2195 **Amoy Marine Biological Bulletin.** *Amoy mar. biol. Bull.* [1936–] **L.**AM. 36–37; **Abd.**M. 36–37.

2196 **Ampco Welding News.** Milwaukee. *Ampco Weld. News* **L.**P. 52–.

2196° **Ampelografiya SSSR.** Moskva. Ампелография CCCP. *Ampelogr. SSSR* [1946–] **L.**BM.

2197 **Amphenol Engineering News.** Chicago. *Amphenol Engng News* [1948–] **L.**P.

2198 **Amplion Magazin.** Frankfurt a. M. *Amplion Mag., Frankf. a. M.*

2199 **Amplion Magazine.** London. *Amplion Mag., Lond.* [1925–27] **L.**BM.; **Bm.**U. imp.; **O.**R.; **Sa.**

2200 **Ampurias.** Barcelona. *Ampurias* [1939–] **L.**AN. 41–; BM. 50–; **Bl.**U. 49–; **Cr.**U. 49–; **Db.**; **E.**U. 47–; v. 45–.

2201 **Amsterdam Naturalist.** Amsterdam. *Amst. Nat.* [1950] **L.**BM^N.; z.; **Bl.**U.; **Bn.**U.; **Pl.**M. [*C. as:* 5865]

2202 **Amtliche Pflanzenschutzbestimmungen.** Berlin. *Amtl. PflSchutzbestimm.* [1924–43: 51–] **L.**AM. 51–; BM. 51–; EB.; MY. 24–39: 52–; **Br.**A. 51–; **Md.**H. 38–39 imp.; **O.**AP. 32–39; F. 24–39. [>37458, 1949–51; *Supplement to:* 34019]

2203 **Amtsarzt.** Jena. *Amtsarzt, Jena* **L.**BM. 36–.

2204 **Amtsarzt.** Wien. *Amtsarzt, Wien* [1909–19]

2205 **Amurskii zemledêlets.** Blagovêshchensk. Амурскій земледѣлецъ. *Amursk. Zemled.*

2206 **Anaconda Publications.** Waterbury, Conn. *Anaconda Publs* **L.**P. (Publ. B, C, E) 38– imp.

2207 **Anadolu kliniği.** Istanbul. *Anad. Klin.* [1933–] **L.**MA. 47–.

2208 **Anaesthesia.** London. *Anaesthesia* [1946–] **L.**BM. CB. 48–; D. 48–; MA.; MD.; S.; U. 50–; UCH. 49–; **Abs.**N. 58–; **Bl.**U. imp.; **Br.**U.; **C.**MS. 58–; UL.; V. 53–; **Cr.**MD.; **Db.**; **Dn.**U. 49–; **E.**A.; S.; U.; **Ld.**U.; **Lv.**M.; **M.**MS.; **O.**R.; **Wd.** 58–; **Y.**

2209 **Anaesthesist.** Berlin, etc. *Anaesthesist* [1952–] **L.**MA.; MD.; S. 58–; **Cr.**MD. 54–; **E.**U.; **Ld.**U.; **Y.**

2210 **Anahuac.** Organo de la aviación nacional. México *Anahuac* [1942–]

2211 **Anais da Academia brasileira de ciencias.** Rio de Janeiro. *Anais Acad. bras. Cienc.* [1929–] **L.**BMN.; C. 44–; GM.; I. (2 yr.); MC. 49–; P. 57–; R. 31–; SC.; TD. 40–; **C.**P. 47–; **E.**D. imp.; R.; **Pl.**M. 36; **Y.** [*C. of:* 46927]

    Anais da Academia brasileira de sciencias. Rio de Janeiro. *See* 2211.

2212 **Anais da Academia de medicina do Rio de Janeiro.** Rio de Janeiro. *Anais Acad. Med. Rio de J.*

2213 **Anais actinométricos.** Instituto geofísico. Oporto. *Anais actinomét.* **L.**BM.; MO. 54–.

2214 **Anais da assistencia a psicopatas.** Rio de Janeiro. *Anais Assist. Psicopatas* [1931–40] **L.**TD. [*C. as:* 4647]

2215 **Anais da Associação brasileira de química.** São Paulo. *Anais Ass. bras. Quím.* [1951–] **L.**BMN.; I. 51–54; **Y.** [*C. of:* 2217]

2216 **Anais da Associacão dos geógrafos brasileiros.** Rio de Janeiro, São Paulo. *Anais Ass. Geógr. bras.* [1945–] **L.**G. 53–; **E.**U. 45.

2217 **Anais da Associaçao química do Brasil.** São Paulo. *Anais Ass. quím. Bras.* [1942–50] **L.**C.; I. 47–50. [*C. as:* 2215]

2218 **Anais Azevedos.** Laboratorios Azevedos. Sociedade industrial farmacêutica. Lisboa. *Anais Azevedos* [1949–] **Y.**

2219 **Anais botânicos do Herbário 'Barbosa Rodrigues.'** Santa Catarina. *Anais bot. Herb. 'Barbosa Rodrigues'* [1949–53] **L.**BMN.; K.; L. 52–53; MY. 52–53; **Hu.**G. [*C. as:* 49452]

2220 **Anais brasileiros de dermatologia e sifilografia.** Rio de Janeiro. *Anais bras. Derm. Sif.* [1925–] **L.**MA. 46–; MD. 25: 29–30 imp.; TD. 27: 42–43: 47– imp.

2221 **Anais brasileiros de gynecologia.** Buenos Aires. *Anais bras. Gynec.* [1936–] **L.**MA. 37–.

2222 **Anais da Catedra de higiene.** Rio de Janeiro. *Anais Cat. Hig., Rio de J.*

2223 **Anais da Clinica ginecológica da Faculdade de medicina da Universidade de São Paulo.** São Paulo. *Anais Clin. ginec. Univ. S Paulo*

2224 **Anais do Colegio anatómico brasileiro.** Rio de Janeiro. *Anais Col. anat. bras.*

2225 **Anais da Colonia de psychopathas.** Rio de Janeiro. *Anais Colon. Psychopathas, Rio de J.* **L.**MD. 29.

2226 **Anais da Conferencia algodoeira.** Rio de Janeiro, etc. *Anais Conf. algod., Rio de J.* **L.**EB. 16–18.

2227 **Anais. Congresso açúcareiro nacional.** Rio de Janeiro. *Anais Congr. açúc. nac., Rio d. J.* [1950–] **L.**P. 50.

2228 **Anais. Congresso brasileiro de hygiene.** Bello Horizonte. *Anais Congr. bras. Hyg.* [1923–]

2229 **Anais. Congresso brasileiro de ortopedia e traumatologia.** Rio de Janeiro. *Anais Congr. bras. Ortop. Traum.* **Br.**U. 40.

2230 **Anais do Congresso brasileiro de urologia.** Rio de Janeiro. *Anais Congr. bras. Urol.* [1935–] **L.**BM.

2230° **Anais. Departamento estadual de saúde.** Espírito Santo, Brasil. *Anais Dep. est. Saúde, Espírito Santo* **L.**TD. 48–50.

2231 **Anais de enfermagem.** Rio de Janeiro. *Anais Enferm.* [1932–37]

2232 **Anais da Escola de minas.** Ouro Preto. *Anais Esc. Min., Ouro Preto* **L.**GL. 00–07; **Lv.**U. 84–08 imp.

2233 **Anais da Escola superior de agricultura 'Luiz de Queiroz.'** Piracicaba. *Anais Esc. sup. Agric. 'Luiz Queiroz'* [1944–] **L.**AM.; MY. 53–; **C.**A.; **Md.**H. 48–; **Rt.**

2234 **Anais da Escola superior de medicina veterinaria.** Lisboa. *Anais Esc. sup. Med. vet., Lisb.* **W.** 50–.

2235 **Anais da Estação agrária nacional.** Lisboa. *Anais Estaç. agr. nac., Lisb.* **Rt.** (ser. A) 24–25.

2236 **Anais da Faculdade de ciências do Porto.** *Anais Fac. Ciênc. Porto* [1921–] **L.**BM.; BMN. 27–55; R.; UC. 27–; **C.**P. 21–55; **Db.** 27–; **E.**Q. (curr.); **O.**R. 27–. [*C. of:* 2274]

2237 **Anais da Faculdade de farmácia e odontologia do Estado de Rio de Janeiro.** Niterói. *Anais Fac. Farm. Odont. Est. Rio de J.*

2238 **Anais da Faculdade de farmácia e odontologia, Universidade de São Paulo.** *Anais Fac. Farm. Odont. Univ. S Paulo* [1943–] **L.**MD. 56–; PH. 54– imp.; **Y.**

2239 **Anais da Faculdade de farmácia do Porto.** *Anais Fac. Farm. Porto* [1939–] **Y.**

    Anais da Faculdade de farmácia, Universidade de Porto. *See* 2239.

2240 **Anais da Faculdade fluminense de medicina, da Universidade de Rio de Janeiro.** *Anais Fac. flumin. Med. Univ. Rio de J.*

2241 **Anais da Faculdade de medicina do Porto.** Porto. *Anais Fac. Med. Porto* **L.**S. 21.

2242 **Anais da Faculdade de medicina de Pôrto Alegre.** Pôrto Alegre. *Anais Fac. Med. Pôrto Alegre* [1938–] **L.**TD. 38–49.

2243 **Anais da Faculdade de medicina, Universidade da Bahia.** Salvador. *Anais Fac. Med. Univ. Bahia* **L.**TD. 44–55*; **E.**R. 44–45; **Lv.**M. 44–45. [*C. as:* 4536°]

2244 **Anais da Faculdade de medicina da Universidade de Minas Gerais.** Bello Horizonte. *Anais Fac. Med. Univ. Minas Gerais* [1929–] **L.**LI; TD. 29–45; **M.**U. 30.

2245 **Anais da Faculdade de medicina da Universidade do Recife.** Recife. *Anais Fac. Med. Univ. Recife* [1934–] **L.**MD. 54: 56–; TD. v. imp.

2246 **Anais** da **Faculdade** de **medicina** da **Universidade** de **São Paulo.** *Anais Fac. Med. Univ. S Paulo* [1926–57] **L.**BM^N.; EB.; LI. 32–38: 46–57; MA. 28: 33–35; MD. 28–57; TD. 26–39; UC. 26–33; **Br.**U.; **E.**U. 26–35; **G.**U. 52–57; **Lv.**U. 30–57; **O.**R. 26: 28–57. [*C. as:* 46644]

2247 **Anais** da **Faculdade nacional** de **farmácia.** Rio de Janeiro. *Anais Fac. nac. Farm. Rio de J.*

2248 **Anais** da **Faculdade nacional** de **odontologia** da **Universidade** do **Brasil.** Rio de Janeiro. *Anais Fac. nac. Odont. Univ. Bras.* [1948–] **L.**D.; MA. 54–.

2249 **Anais** da **Faculdade** de **odontologia** e **farmácia** da **Universidade** de **Minas Geraes.** *Anais Fac. Odont. Farm. Univ. Minas Geraes* [1936–] **Bl.**U. 39; **Bm.**U. 36–38; **Br.**U. 36–39; **O.**R. 55–.

Anais da **Faculdade** de **sciências** do **Porto.** *See* 2236.

2250 **Anais** de **farmácia** e **química** de **São Paulo.** São Paulo. *Anais Farm. Quím. S Paulo* **L.**MA. 53–; PH. 57–.

2251 **Anais** do **Instituto geobiológico La Salle** de **Canoas.** *Anais Inst. geobiol. La Salle Canoas* **L.**BM^N. 50.

2252 **Anais** do **Instituto geofísico** do **Infante D. Luis.** Lisboa. *Anais Inst. geofís. Infante D. Luis* [1947–] **L.**BM. 54–; MO. [*C. of:* 2267, Part I.]

2253 **Anais** do **Instituto** de **medicina tropica.** Lisboa. *Anais Inst. Med. trop., Lisb.* [1943–] **L.**BM^N.; EB.; H.; LI. 45–; MA.; MC. 45– imp.; MD.; TD.; **Abd.**R. 50–61; **Br.**U.; **C.**MO. 43: 53–; UL.; **Db.** 43–50 imp.; **O.**R.; **Sal.**; **Y.** [*Also supplements; Replaces* 4559]

2254 **Anais** do **Instituto Pinheiros.** São Paulo. *Anais Inst. Pinheiros* [1938–] **L.**MD. 38.

2255 **Anais** do **Instituto** de **psiquiatria** da **Universidade** do **Brasil.** Rio de Janeiro. *Anais Inst. Psiquiat. Univ. Bras.* **L.**MD. 44–47. [*C. as:* 25386]

2256 **Anais** do **Instituto superior** de **agronomia** da **Universidade técnica** de **Lisboa.** Lisboa. *Anais Inst. sup. Agron. Univ. téc. Lisb.* [1920–] **L.**AM. 50–; BM. 51–; K. 25–; MY.; **C.**A. 25–; **Md.**H. 30–; **N.**U. 54–; **R.**U. 25–37; **Rt.** imp.; **Sil.** 42–; **Y.**

2257 **Anais** do **Instituto** do **vinho** do **Porto.** *Anais Inst. Vinho Porto* [1940–] **Y.**

2258 **Anais. Junta** de **investigações coloniais.** Lisboa. *Anais Jta Invest. colon.* [1947–51] **L.**BM^N.; G. 51; **O.**F. 48–51; **Y.** [*C. of:* 2260; *C. as:* 2259]

2259 **Anais. Junta** de **investigações** do **ultramar.** Lisboa. *Anais Jta Invest. Ultramar* [1952–] **L.**BM^N.; G.; **O.**F.; **Y.** [*C. of:* 2258]

2260 **Anais** da **Junta** das **missões geográficas** e de **investigações coloniais.** Lisboa. *Anais Jta Miss. geogr.* [1946–47] **L.**BM^N.; **Y.** [*C. as:* 2258]

2261 **Anais** de **maternidade** de **São Paulo.** São Paulo. *Anais Matern. S Paulo* [1955–] **L.**MA.

2262 **Anais** de **medicina homoeopatica.** Rio de Janeiro. *Anais Med. homoeop.* [1882–22] **L.**BM. 01.

2263 **Anais meteorológicos** das **colónias.** Lisboa. *Anais met. Colón.* **L.**G. 22–31; MO. 27–46*. [*C. as:* 3633]

2264 **Anais** de **microbiologia.** Universidade do Brasil. Rio de Janeiro. *Anais Microbiol.* [1951–] **L.**LI.; MC.; MD.; TD.; **Br.**U.

2265 **Anais** do **Museu paulista.** São Paulo. *Anais Mus. paul.* [1922–] **C.**UL.; **Db.** 25–; **O.**B.

2266 **Anais. Observatorio astronómico** da **Universidade, Coimbra.** *Anais Obs. astr. Univ. Coimbra* [1929–] **L.**AS. (sect. 1): (sect. 3) 40–; SC. (sect. 1) 34–; **Y.** (sect. 1).

2267 **Anais** do **Observatorio** do **Infante D. Luiz.** Lisboa. *Anais Obs. Infante D. Luiz*
Part I. Observações de Lisbõa. **L.**MO.; UC. 32–46; **Db.** 04–11: 13–46; **E.**M. imp.; R. 01–11; **G.**U. 63–88; **O.**G. imp. [*C. as:* 2252]
Part II. Observações das estações meteorológicas. **E.**M. [*C. as:* 3633]
Part III. Observações sismológicas. **E.**M. 40–45. [*C. as.* 3633]

2268 **Anais** de **oto-rino-laringologia.** Recife. *Anais Oto-rino-lar.* **L.**MD. 35–38.

2269 **Anais paranaenses** de **tuberculose** e **doenças torácicas.** Parána. *Anais parana. Tuberc.* [1956–] **L.**MA.; S. 56–58.

2270 **Anais paulistas** de **medicina** e **cirurgia.** São Paulo. *Anais paul. Med. Cirurg.* [1913–] **L.**MA. 28–31: 33–37: 46–; MD. imp.; S. 33– imp.; TD. imp.; **Bl.**U. 45– imp.; **Lv.**M. 31–43 imp.; U. 18–30 imp.; **O.**R. 33–. [*Also supplements*]

2271 **Anais portugueses** de **psiquiatria.** Lisboa. *Anais port. Psiquiat.* [1949–] **L.**BM. 56–; MD. imp.

2272 **Anais** da **Reunião sud-americana** de **botânica.** Rio de Janeiro. *Anais Reun. sud-am. Bot.* [1938–] **O.**F. 38; **Rt.** 38.

2273 **Anais** de **sciencias naturaes.** Porto. *Anais Sci. nat.* [1894–06] **L.**BM. 94–05; BM^N.; E. 94–03; Z.; **Bl.**U. 94–03 imp.; **Cr.**N. 94–03; **Db.** 94–03; **Lv.**U.; **Pl.**M.

2274 **Anais scientificos** da **Academia polytecnica** do **Porto.** Coimbra. *Anais scient. Acad. polytec. Porto* [1905–21] **L.**BM^N.; GL.; R.; UC.; **Bl.**U. 05–19; **Bm.**N.; **C.**P.; UL. 05–17; **Db.**; **E.**C.; Q.; R. 06–19 imp.; **G.**U. 05–18; **Lv.**U. 05–15 imp.; **O.**R. [*C. of:* 25399; *C. as:* 2236]

2275 **Anais** do **Seminario brasileiro** de **herbicidas** e **ervas daninhas.** Rio de Janeiro. *Anais Semin. bras. Herbicidas* [1956–]

2275c **Anais** dos **Serviços** de **veterinária** e **indústria animal, Moçambique.** Lourenço Marques. *Anais Servs Vet. Ind. anim. Moçamb.* **L.**BM. 50–.

2276 **Anais** da **Sociedade** de **biologia** de **Pernambuco.** Recife. *Anais Soc. Biol. Pernamb.* [1938–] **L.**BM^N. 38–39 imp.; EB. 38–53; K. 57–; MY. 53–; SC.; TD. 55– imp.

2277 **Anais** da **Sociedade** de **medicina** de **Pernambuco.** Pernambuco. *Anais Soc. Med. Pernamb.* [1949–] **L.**MD. 50–.

2278 **Anais** da **Sociedade** de **pharmacia** e **chimica.** São Paulo. *Anais Soc. Pharm. Chim., S Paulo*

2279 **Anais** da **Sociedade rural brasileira.** São Paulo. *Anais Soc. rur. bras.* **L.**EB. 20–21*. [*C. as:* 46981]

2280 **Analecta médica.** México. *Analecta méd.* [1940–50] **L.**MA. 40: 47–50; MD. imp.; S. 41–50 imp.; TD. 42–50 v. imp. [*C. as:* 46701]

2281 **Analecta terapeutica.** Barcelona. *Analecta terap.* [1932–]

2282 **Analele Academiei române.** Bucureşti. *Anal. Acad. rom.* [1867–] **L.**BM.; BM^N. 81–08 (nat. hist.): 09–44 imp.; MO. 67–90; **C.**UL. 91–; **Db.** 86–; **E.**R. 79– imp. [Memoriile Sectiunii stiintifice, *published in* Analele *until* 1922, *were issued separately from* 1923]

2283 **Analele Facultăţii** de **agronomie** din **Cluj.** Cluj. *Anal. Fac. Agron. Cluj* [1944–47] **L.**AM.; **Abs.**A.; **C.**A.; **Rt.** 46–47. [*C. of:* 9111; *C. as:* 3621]

2284 **Analele genito-urinare.** Bucureşti. *Anal. genito-urin.*

2286 **Analele Institutului** de **cercetări agronomice** al **Academia Republicii populare Romine.** Bucureşti. *Anal. Inst. Cerc. agron.* [1930–] **L.**AM.; EB.; MY. 30–46; P.; **Abs.**A. imp.; **C.**A.; **Hu.**G. 56–; **Ld.**U. 30–38; **M.**U. 30–46; **Y.** [*From* 1958 *issued in* Ser. A. Agroclimatológie, Pedologie, Agrochimie şi amelioraţii: Ser. B. Agrotehnica, Pǎşani şi Finèţe: Ser. C. Fiziologie, Genetică, Ameliorare, Protecţia Plantelor şi Tehnologie]

2287 **Analele Institutului** de **cercetări si experimentaţie forestieră.** Bucureşti. *Anal. Inst. Cerc. Exp. for.* [1934–] **O.**F. 34–39.

2288 **Analele Institutului** de **cercetări piscicole** al **României.** Bucureşti. *Anal. Inst. Cerc. pisc. Rom.* **L.**BMᴺ. 42–56; **Abd.**M. 56–60; **Fr.** 56–60; **Pl.**M. 56.

2289 **Analele Institutului** de **cercetări zootehnice.** Bucureşti. *Anal. Inst. Cerc. zooteh.* **E.**AB. 47–56. [*C. of:* 2291; *C. as:* 28856]

2290 **Analele Institutului meteorologic** al **României.** Bucureşti. *Anal. Inst. met. Rom.* [1885–07] **L.**BM. 86–88; MO. 85–02; **Db.** 85–02; **E.**M. 85–02 imp.; R.; imp.; **O.**G. 85–92. [*C. in:* 2294]

2291 **Analele Institutului national zootehnic.** Bucureşti. *Anal. Inst. natn. zooteh.* [1932–?] **Br.**U. 32–39 imp.; **C.**A. 42–43; **E.**AB. 32–38. [*C. as:* 2289]

2292 **Analele Institutului** de **patologie** şi de **bacteriologie.** Bucureşti. *Anal. Inst. Patol. Bact.* **Br.**U. 94–95.

2292ᵃ **Analele Institutului Victor Babes** din **Bucureşti.** Bucureşti. *Anal. Inst. Victor Babes* **L.**MD. Ser. AIIa 38–45.

Analele minelor dîn **România.** *See* 2841.

2293 **Analele Ministeriului lucrărilor publice.** Bucureşti. *Anal. Minist. Lucrăr. publ.* **L.**BM. 20–.

2294 **Analele Observatorului astronomic** si **meteorologic.** Bucureşti. *Anal. Obs. astr. met.* [1885–] **E.**R. 07–09. [*From* 1908 *incorporates* 2290]

2295 **Analele** de **psihologie.** Bucureşti. *Anal. Psihol.* [1934–]

2296 **Analele romîno-sovietice.** Bucureşti. *Anal. rom.-sov.* [1955–]
　　Seria: Agricultura. **L.**AM.; **C.**A.
　　Seria: Biologie. **L.**AM.; BMᴺ. 57–; **C.**A.; BO. 57.
　　Seria: Silvicultura. **L.**AM.; **O.**F.

2297 **Analele Spitalului Bârlad** şi **Elena Beldiman.** Bârlad. *Anal. Spital. Bârlad Elena Beldiman*

2298 **Analele ştiinţifice** de **Universităţii 'Al. I. Cuza'** din **Iaşi.** Iaşi. *Anal. ştiinţ. Univ. Al. I. Cuza* [1955–]
　　Sect. I. Mathematică, fizică, chimie. **L.**BM.; C.; G.; P. 58–; **G.**U.; **Y.**
　　Sect. II. Stiinţe naturale. **L.**BM.; BMᴺ.; K.; P.; Z. 58–; **Abd.**M.; **Y.** [*C. of:* 2915]

2299 **Analele Universităţii C. I. Parhon.** Bucureşti. *Anal. Univ. C. I. Parhon*
　　Seria ştiintelor naturii [1956–] **L.**BMᴺ.; **Y.**

2300 **Anales** de la **Academia argentina** de **geografia.** Buenos Aires. *An. Acad. argent. Geogr.* [1957–] **L.**G.; **O.**B.; **Y.**

2301 **Anales** de la **Academia** de **biología.** Santiago. *An. Acad. Biol., Santiago* [1935–36] **L.**BMᴺ.; MD.; TD.; Z.

2302 **Anales** de la **Academia chilena** de **ciencias naturales.** Santiago de Chile. *An. Acad. chil. Cienc. nat.* **L.**BM. 48–; BMᴺ. 38– imp.; U. 53–; **R.**U. 53– imp. [*Published in* 47018]

2303 **Anales** de la **Academia** de **ciencias exactas, físicas** y **naturales.** Universidad de Buenos Aires. *An. Acad. Cienc. exact. fís. nat. B. Aires* **E.**R. 17.

2304 **Anales** de la **Academia** de **ciencias médicas, físicas** y **naturales** de la **Habana.** *An. Acad. Cienc. méd. fís. nat. Habana* [1864–] **L.**BM. 11–; BMᴺ. 64–11; S. 11–26: 37–40; TD. 12 imp.: 45–; Z. 13–20; **Lv.**U. 11–19; **O.**R. 37–.

Anales. Academia de **farmacía.** Madrid. *See* 2504.

Anales de l'**Academia** y **laboratorio** de **ciencias médicas** de **Catalunya.** Barcelona. *See* 2554.

Anales. Academia de **medicina.** Madrid. *See* 2505.

2306 **Anales** de la **Academia** de **medicina** de **Barcelona.** Barcelona. *An. Acad. Med. Barcelona* [1930–]

2307 **Anales** de la **Academia** de **medicina** de **Medellin.** *An. Acad. Med. Medellin* [1887–04: 20–49] [*C. in:* 3594]

2308 **Anales. Academia mexicana** de **ciencias exactas físicas** y **naturales.** México. *An. Acad. mex. Cienc. exact. fís. nat.* [1903–09] **E.**R. 03.

2309 **Anales** de la **Academia nacional** de **agronomía** y **veterinaria** de **Buenos Aires.** *An. Acad. nac. Agron. Vet. B. Aires* [1932–] **Abs.**A.; **C.**A. 32–34.

2310 **Anales** de la **Academia nacional** de **ciencias exactas, físicas** y **naturales** de **Buenos Aires.** *An. Acad. nac. Cienc. exact. fís. nat. B. Aires* [1927–] **L.**BM. 44–; BMᴺ. 59–; SC. 45– imp.; **E.**R. 58–. [*Suspended* 1933–38]

2311 **Anales. Academia nacional** de **medicina** de **Lima.** *An. Acad. nac. Med. Lima* [1919]

2312 **Anales** de la **Academia** de **obstetricia, ginecología** y **pediatría.** Madrid. *An. Acad. Obstet. Ginec. Pediat., Madr.* [1909–12]

2313 **Anales. Administración nacional** de **bosques.** Buenos Aires. *An. Adm. nac. Bosques, B. Aires* [1956–] **O.**F.; **Y.**

2314 **Anales agronómicos.** Santiago de Chile. *An. agron., Santiago* [1906–14] **L.**AM. 06–11 imp.; BM. 06; **Ld.**U. 06–10; **O.**B. 06.

2315 **Anales** de **anatomía.** Granada. *An. Anat., Granada*

2316 **Anales argentinos** de **oftalmología.** Rosario. *An. argent. Oftal.*

2317 **Anales** de **arqueología** y **etnología.** Mendoza. *An. Arqueol. Etnol., Mendoza* [1947–] **L.**AN. [*C. of:* 2410]

Anales de la **Asociación española** para el **progreso** de las **ciencias.** *See* 14045.

2318 **Anales** de la **Asociación mexicana** de **orthodoncia.** México. *An. Asoc. mex. Orthod.* **L.**D. 42.

2319 **Anales** de la **Asociación química argentina.** Buenos Aires. *An. Asoc. quím. argent.* [1955–] **L.**C.; P.; **Y.** [*C. of:* 2531: *Also supplements*]

2320 **Anales** de la **Asociación** de **química** y **farmacía** del **Uruguay.** Montevideo. *An. Asoc. Quím. Farm. Urug.* **L.**S. 33–; **Y.**

2321 **Anales** de la **Asociación veterinaria** de **higiena bromatológica.** Madrid. *An. Asoc. vet. Hig. bromat., Madr.* [1953–] **L.**V.

2322 **Anales** del **Ateneo** de **clínica médica.** Buenos Aires. *An. Aten. Clín. méd.* [1931–33]

2324 **Anales** del **Ateneo** de **clínica quirúrgica.** Montevideo. *An. Aten. Clín. quir.* [1935–]

2325 **Anales** del **Ateneo. Instituto** de **maternidad. Hospital Rawson.** Buenos Aires. *An. Aten. Inst. Matern. Hosp. Rawson* [1942–]

2326 **Anales** del **Ateneo médico Leonés.** Leon. *An. Aten. méd. Leonés*

2327 **Anales** del **Ateneo** de **patología** y **clínica médica.** Hospital Torcuato de Alvear. Buenos Aires. *An. Aten. Patol. Clín. méd. Hosp. Torcuato Alvear* [1935–] **Bl.**U.

2328 **Anales** de **bromatologia.** Madrid. *An. Bromat.* [1949–] **L.**C. 53–; P.; **Abd.**R. 54–; **Y.**

2329 **Anales** de la **Casa** de **salúd Valdecilla.** Santander. *An. Casa Salúd Valdecilla* **L.**MD. 32–36 imp.

2330 **Anales** de la **Catedra** de **clínica médica** del **Dr. E. S. Mazzei.** Buenos Aires. *An. Cat. Clín. méd. Mazzei* **L.**MA. 46–.

2331 **Anales** de la **Catedra** de **patología** y **clínica** de la **tuberculosis.** Universidad de Buenos Aires. *An. Cat. Patol. Clín. Tuberc. B. Aires* [1939–] **L.**MA. 39–42: 45–; TD. 42– imp.; U.; **E.**U.

2332 **Anales** de la **Catedra** de **radiología** y **fisioterapía** de la **Universidad** de **Buenos Aires.** *An. Cat. Radiol. Fisioter. Univ. B. Aires* [1940–]

2333 **Anales** del **Centro** de **investigaciones tisiológicas.** Buenos Aires. *An. Cent. Invest. tisiol., B. Aires* [1934–36] **L.**MD. [*C. as:* 40639]

2334 **Anales cervantinos.** Madrid. *An. cervant.* [1951–] **L.**BM.; **Ld.**U.

2335 **Anales** de **ciencias naturales.** Instituto José de Acosta. Madrid. *An. Cienc. nat. Inst. José Acosta* **L.**BM[N]. 40–41.

2336 **Anales científicos** de la **Asociación médica** del **Centro Gallego** de **Buenos Aires.** Buenos Aires. *An. cient. Asoc. méd. Cent. Gallego* [1952–] **L.**MA.

2337 **Anales científicos paraguayos.** Asunción. *An. cient. parag.* **L.**BM[N]. 01–24; EB. 01–20; K. 05–18 imp.

2338 **Anales** del **Círculo médico argentino.** Buenos Aires. *An. Círc. méd. argent.* **Db.** 87–.

2339 **Anales** de **cirugía.** Buenos Aires. *An. Cirug., B. Aires* [1942–] [*Spanish edition of* 3191]

2340 **Anales** de **cirugía.** Habana. *An. Cirug., Habana*

2341 **Anales** de **cirugía.** Rosario. *An. Cirug., Rosario* [1935–] **L.**MA.; MD. imp.; S. 51–53.

2342 **Anales climatalógicos.** Servicio meteorológico nacional. Buenos Aires. *An. clim., B. Aires* **L.**MO. 28–44.

2343 **Anales** de **Clínica** del **Hospital Juarez.** México. *An. Clín. Hosp. Juarez* [1931–] **Br.**U. 31.

2344 **Anales** de la **Clínica** de **Nuestra Señora** del **Carmen.** Burgos. *An. Clín. Nuestra Señora del Carmen*

2345 **Anales** de la **Clínica** del **Prof. C. Jiménez Díaz.** Madrid. *An. Clín. Prof. Jiménez Díaz* [1928–] **L.**MD. [*C. as:* 2426]

2346 **Anales** del **Colegio oficial** de **veterinarios** de **Barcelona.** Barcelona. *An. Col. of. Vet. Barcelona* [1956–] **L.**U.

2347 **Anales** de la **Comisión geodésica mexicana,** Tacubaya. México. *An. Comn geod. mex.* **C.**O. 04–.

2347a **Anales** de la **Comisión** de **investigación científica. Provincia** de **Buenos Aires gobernación.** La Plata. *An. Comn Invest. cient. Prov. B. Aires* [1960–] **L.**BM[N].

2348 **Anales** del **Comité nacional** de **plantas medicinales.** Madrid. *An. Com. nac. Pl. med. Madr.*

2349 **Anales** del **Congreso nacional** de la **industría minera.** Lima. *An. Congr. nac. Ind. min., Lima* [1919–21] **L.**BM[N]. 21; I.; MI.; P.; **Bl.**U.; **Bm.**U.; **E.**C. 21; R.; **Sh.**M.

2350 **Anales** del **Congreso panamericano** de **ingenieria,** de **minas** y **geología.** Santiago. *An. Congr. panamer. Ing. Minas Geol.* [1942–] **L.**MI. 42.

2351 **Anales** del **Congreso sul-riograndense** de **historia** e **geografía.** Rio Grande do Sul. *An. Congr. sul.-riogr. Hist. Geogr.* [1936–]

2352 **Anales Dalmacio García Izcara** del **Colegio oficial** de **veterinarios.** Valencia. *An. Dalmacio García Izcara* [1949–] **L.**V. 49–52.

2353 **Anales** del **Departmento científico** del **Consejo** de **salúd pública.** Montevideo. *An. Dep. cient. Cons. Salúd públ., Montevideo* **L.**S. 33–34.

2354 **Anales** del **Departmento** de **ganadería** y **agricultura** del **Uruguay.** Montevideo. *An. Dep. Ganad. Agric. Urug.*

2355 **Anales. Departmento** de **investigaciones científicas, Universidad nacional** de **Cuyo.** Mendoza. *An. Dep. Invest. cient. Univ. nac. Cuyo* **L.**MO. 52–53.

2356 **Anales** del **Departmento nacional** de **higiene.** Buenos Aires. *An. Dep. nac. Hig., B. Aires* **L.**EB. 19–30; LI. 19–21; TD. 19–36; **Lv.**U. 13–25.

2357 **Anales** del **Desarrollo.** Granada. *An. Dessarrollo* **L.**MC. 60–.

2358 **Anales** de la **Dirección** de **fomento.** Lima. *An. Dir. Fom., Lima* **L.**EB. 13.

Anales de la **Dirección general** de **industría minera.** Buenos Aires. *See* 2360.

2359 **Anales** de la **Dirección** de **meteorología.** Buenos Aires. *An. Dir. Met., B. Aires* **L.**MO. 30–31; **M.**P. 24–28.

Anales. Dirección de **minas** y **geología.** Buenos Aires. *See* 2360.

2360 **Anales. Dirección nacional** de **minería.** Buenos Aires. *An. Dir. nac. Min., B. Aires* [1947–] **L.**BM.; BM[N]. 47; MI.; **Y.**

2360o **Anales. Dirección nacional** de **química.** Buenos Aires. *An. Dir. nac. Quím., B. Aires*

2361 **Anales** de la **Dirección** de **sanidad nacional.** Caracas. *An. Dir. Sanid. nac., Caracas* [1919–23] **L.**BM.; S.; TD. 19–22 imp.; **Ld.**U.; **Lv.**U.

2362 **Anales** del **Dispensario público nacional** para **enfermedades** del **aparato digestivo.** Buenos Aires. *An. Dispens. públ. nac. Enferm. Apar. digest.*

2363 **Anales** de **edafología** y **agrobiología.** Madrid. *An. Edafol. Agrobiol.* [1960–] **L.**A.; AM.; BM.; BM^N.; SC.; **Abd.**S.; **Abs.**A.; **Bn.**U.; **Br.**A.; **C.**A.; **Db.**; **Hu.**G.; **Ld.**U.; **Md.**H.; **Rt.**; **Y.** [*C. of:* 2364]

2364 **Anales** de **edafología** y **fisiología vegetal.** Madrid. *An. Edafol. Fisiol. veg.* [1949–59] **L.**A. 55–59 imp.; AM. 55–59; BM^N.; SC.; **Abd.**S.; **Abs.**A. 50–59; **Bn.**U.; **Br.**A.; **C.**A.; **Db.**; **Hu.**G. 52–59; **Ld.**U. 53–59; **Md.**H.; **Rt.** [*C. of:* 2407; *C. as:* 2363]

2365 **Anales. Escuela** de **farmacía. Universidad nacional mayor** de **San Marcos.** Lima. *An. Esc. Farm. Univ. S Marcos* [1939–45] [*C. as:* 46529]

2366 **Anales** de la **Escula nacional** de **ciencias biológicas.** México. *An. Esc. nac. Cienc. biol., Méx.* [1938–] **L.**AM. 45–48; BM.; BM^N.; EB. 38–55; LI. 47–; MD. 38–39; MY. 38–45: 48: 53–; TD. 38–48 imp.; **C.**A. 39–55; **Db.**; **G.**U. 45–48; **Ld.**U. 38–55 imp.; **M.**U. imp.; **R.**U. 53–58; **Rt.** 38: 45–47; **Y.**

2367 **Anales** de la **Escuela** de **peritos agrícolas** y **superior** de **agricultura.** Barcelona. *An. Esc. Perit. agríc., Barcelona* [1941–] **L.**AM. 50–; BM^N.; **Hu.**G. 50–; **Md.**H.; **Y.**

2368 **Anales** de la **Escuela superior** de **veterinaria** de **Madrid.** *An. Esc. sup. Vet. Madr.* **L.**V. 35.

2369 **Anales** de la **Escuela** de **veterinaria** del **Uruguay.** Montevideo. *An. Esc. Vet. Urug.* **W.** 31–.

2370 **Anales españoles** de **odontoestomatología.** Madrid. *An. esp. Odontoestomat.* **L.**D. 42–.

2371 **Anales** de la **Estación experimental** de **Aula Dei.** Zaragoza. *An. Estac. exp. Aula Dei* [1948–] **L.**AM. 50–; BM.; BM^N.; **Abs.**A.; **Ba.**I.; **Br.**A.; **C.**A.; **Hu.**G. 51–; **Md.**H.; **Rt.** imp.; **Y.**

2372 **Anales** de **Faculdade** de **medicina** de **Porto Alegre.** *An. Fac. Med. Porto Alegre*

2373 **Anales** de la **Facultad** de **biología** y **ciencias médicas.** Santiago de Chile. *An. Fac. Biol. Cienc. méd., Santiago* [1934–] **L.**U. 34–36.

2374 **Anales** de la **Facultad** de **ciencias físicas** y **matemáticas, Universidad** de **Concepción.** *An. Fac. Cienc. fís. mat. Univ. Concepción* [1952–] **L.**SC.

Anales de la **Facultad** de **ciencias médicas, Universidad** de **Lima.** *See* 2382.

2375 **Anales** de la **Facultad** de **ciencias médicas. Universidad nacional** de **La Plata.** Buenos Aires. *An. Fac. Cienc. méd. Univ. nac. La Plata* [1937–] **L.**MD. 37; **Bl.**U.; **Dn.**U. 45–; **G.**U. 37–39; **Ld.**U. 44–49.

2376 **Anales** de la **Facultad** de **ciencias médicas. Universidad nacional** del **Paraguay.** Asunción. *An. Fac. Cienc. méd. Univ. nac. Parag.* [1928–] **L.**TD. 28–31: 45–48 imp.

2377 **Anales** de la **Facultad** de **ciencias. Universidad mayor** de **San Marcos.** Lima. *An. Fac. Cienc. Univ. S Marcos*

2378 **Anales** de la **Facultad** de **ciencias** de **Zaragoza.** *An. Fac. Cienc. Zaragoza*

2379 **Anales** de la **Facultad** de **farmacía** y **bioquímica. Universidad nacional** de **San Marcos.** Lima. *An. Fac. Farm. Bioquím. Univ. S Marcos* [1950–] **L.**C. 51–; MA.; PH. 50–54 imp.; **Abd.**R.; **Y.**

2379° **Anales** de la **Facultad** de **ingeniería, Universidad** de **Concepción.** *An. Fac. Ing. Univ. Concepción* [1952–] **L.**SC.

2380 **Anales** de la **Facultad** de **medicina** y **farmacía.** La Habana. *An. Fac. Med. Farm., Habana* [1930–]

2381 **Anales** de la **Facultad** de **medicina. Universidad** de **Montevideo.** *An. Fac. Med. Univ. Montevideo* [1916–] **L.**MA. 46–; MD. 16–27: 34; S. 19–33: 46–; TD. 16–18 imp.: 21–; **Bl.**U. 46– imp.

2382 **Anales** de la **Facultad** de **medicina. Universidad nacional mayor** de **San Marcos** de **Lima.** *An. Fac. Med. Univ. S Marcos* [1862–04: 18–] **L.**MA. 40–; MD. 18; TD. 18–47 v. imp.; **Br.**U. 18– imp.; **Lv.**U. 18: 26.

2383 **Anales** de la **Facultad** de **medicina. Universidad** de **Zaragoza.** *An. Fac. Med. Univ. Zaragoza* **Bm.**U. 19–22; **Br.**U. 19–22.

2384 **Anales** de la **Facultad** de **odontología. Universidad** de la **República oriental** del **Uruguay.** Montevideo. *An. Fac. Odont. Univ. Urug.* [1955–] **L.**MD. imp.; **Wd.**

2385 **Anales** de la **Facultad** de **química** y **farmacía, Universidad** de **Uruguay.** Montevideo. *An. Fac. Quím. Farm. Univ. Urug.* [1952–56] **L.**P. 54–56; **Y.** [*C. as:* 2386]

2386 **Anales** de la **Facultad** de **química, Universidad** de la **República** del **Uruguay.** Montevideo. *An. Fac. Quím. Univ. Repúb. Urug.* [1960–] **L.**P.; **Y.** [*C. of:* 2385]

2387 **Anales** de la **Facultad** de **veterinaria** de **Léon, Universidad** de **Oviedo.** *An. Fac. Vet. Léon* [1955–] **L.**AM. 59–; **C.**V. 55–56.

2388 **Anales** de la **Facultad** de **veterinaria** de la **Universidad** de **Madrid.** Madrid. *An. Fac. Vet. Univ. Madr.* [1949–52] **L.**V. 50–52; **Abd.**R.; **Abs.**U. 50–52. [*C. as:* 2427]

Anales de la **Facultad** de **veterinaria. Universidad** de **Montevideo.** *See* 2389.

2389 **Anales** de la **Facultad** de **veterinaria** del **Uruguay.** Montevideo. *An. Fac. Vet. Urug.* [1937–] **L.**V. 37–39 imp.: 54; **Hu.**G. 54–; **W.** 44–.

2390 **Anales** de **farmacía** y **bioquímica.** Bogotá. *An. Farm. Bioquím., Bogotá*

2391 **Anales** de **farmacía** y **bioquímica.** Buenos Aires. *An. Farm. Bioquím., B. Aires* [1930–] **L.**PH. 42–46 imp.

2392 **Anales** de **farmacía hospitalaria.** Madrid. *An. Farm. hosp.* [1957–]

2393 **Anales** de **física** y **química.** Madrid. *An. Fís. Quím.* [1941–47] **L.**C.; P.; SC.; **C.**P. [*C. of:* and *Rec. as:* 2506]

2394 **Anales gráficos.** Buenos Aires. *An. gráf.* [1910–] **L.**SB. 13–24.

2395 **Anales hidrográficos.** Buenos Aires. *An. hidrogr., B. Aires*

2396 **Anales hidrológicos.** Servicio meteorológico nacional. Buenos Aires. *An. hidrol., B. Aires* **L.**MO. 47–49.

2397 **Anales hispano-americanos** de **hidrología médica** y **climatología.** Madrid. *An. hisp.-am. Hidrol. méd.*

2398 **Anales** del **Hospital** de **niños.** Buenos Aires. *An. Hosp. Niños, B. Aires* **L.**MD. 38.

2399 **Anales** del **Hospital** de **niños** e **Instituto** de **puericultura** de **Rosario.** *An. Hosp. Niños Rosario* **L.**MD. 36–38.

2400 **Anales** del **Hospital** de **San José** y **Santa Adela.** Madrid. *An. Hosp. S José, Madr.* [1929–]

2401 **Anales** del **Hospital** de la **Santa Cruz** y **San Pablo.** Barcelona. *An. Hosp. S Cruz, Barcelona* **Lv.**U. 27– imp.

2402 **Anales hospitalários.** Lima. *An. hosp., Lima* [1922–]

2403 **Anales** de **ingeniería.** Bogotá. *An. Ing., Bogotá* [1887–] **L.**P. 25–; **Y.**

2403ᶜ **Anales** del **Instituto Barraquer.** Barcelona. *An. Inst. Barraquer* [1959–] **L.**MD.

2404 **Anales** del **Instituto** de **biología. Universidad** de **México.** *An. Inst. Biol. Univ. Méx.* [1930–] **L.**BMᴺ.; E. 30–31; EB.; K.; L. 37– imp.; MD. 46–; TD.; Z. 56–; **Bl.**U. 32– imp.; **Bm.**N.; **C.**A. 37–; UL.; **Db.** 38–; **E.**R.; **Lv.**U. 51–53; **Pl.**M.; **Rt.**; **Sal.**

2405 **Anales** del **Instituto botánico A. J. Cavanillo.** Madrid. *An. Inst. bot. A. J. Cavanillo* [1950–] **L.**BM.; BMᴺ.; K.; L.; MY. 51–; **C.**BO.; **Db.**; **Hu.**G.; **O.**BO.; **Y.** [*C. of:* 2453]

2406 **Anales** del **Instituto Corachán.** Barcelona. *An. Inst. Corachán* [1949–] **L.**MD. imp.; S. 50–; **Ld.**U. 51–; **M.**MS. 50–; **O.**R. 49–.

2407 **Anales** del **Instituto español** de **edafología, ecología** y **fisiología vegetal.** Madrid. *An. Inst. esp. Edafol.* [1942–48] **L.**BMᴺ.; SC.; **Abd.**U.; **Bn.**U.; **Br.**A.; **C.**A.; **Db.**; **Md.**H. 47–48; **Rt.** [*C. as:* 2364]

2408 **Anales** del **Instituto español** de **hematología** y **hemoterapía.** Madrid. *An. Inst. esp. Hemat.*

2409 **Anales** del **Instituto étnico nacional.** Buenos Aires. *An. Inst. étnico nac., B. Aires* [1948–] **L.**BM. 51–.

2410 **Anales. Instituto** de **etnografiá americana.** Mendoza. *An. Inst. Etnogr. am.* [1940–46] **L.**AN.; C.; U. 41–46. [*C. as:* 2317]

2411 **Anales** del **Instituto** de **farmacología española.** Madrid. *An. Inst. Farmac. esp.* [1952–] **L.**MA.; SC. 55–.

2413 **Anales. Instituto** de **física, Universidad nacional autónoma** de **México.** México. *An. Inst. Fís. Univ. Méx.* [1955–] **L.**P.

2414 **Anales** del **Instituto físico-geográfico** y del **Museo nacional** de **Costa Rica.** San José. *An. Inst. fís.-geogr. C. Rica* **L.**BMᴺ. 89–96; G. 89–91; MO. 89–46; **E.**M. 89–93.

2415 **Anales** del **Instituto fitotécnico** de **Santa Catalina.** Buenos Aires. *An. Inst. fitotéc. S Catalina* [1939–] **L.**AM. 39–42; **C.**A. 39–42; **Rt.** imp.

2416 **Anales** del **Instituto forestal** de **investigaciones** y **experiencias.** Madrid. *An. Inst. for. Invest. Exp.* [1956–] **O.**F.; **Y.**

2417 **Anales** del **Instituto general** y **técnico** de **Valencia** *An. Inst. gen. téc. Valencia* **L.**BMᴺ. 16–23.

2418 **Anales** del **Instituto** de **geofísica, Universidad nacional autónoma** de **México.** Mexico City. *An. Inst. Geofís. Univ. Méx.* [1955–] **L.**MO.; **Wo.**; **Y.**

2419 **Anales** del **Instituto** de **geología** de **México.** *An. Inst. Geol. Méx.* [1930–] **L.**BMᴺ.; GM.; MI. 30–36: 46–; **Bm.**U.; U.; **C.**S.; **E.**R.; **G.**N.; **M.**U. imp.; **Nw.**A. 30–46 imp.; **Y.** [*C. of:* 2420]

2420 **Anales** del **Instituto geológico** de **México.** *An. Inst. geol. Méx.* [1917–29] **L.**BMᴺ.; GL. 17–20; GM.; MI.; **Bl.**U.; **Bm.**N.; U. 17–27; **C.**P.; S.; **E.**F. 17–20; R.; **G.**MG.

19–20 imp.; N. 25–29; T. 17–20; **Lv.**U. 17–20; **M.**U. imp.; **Nw.**A.; **O.**R. 17–20.; **Y.** [*C. of:* 37157; *C. as:* 2419]

2421 **Anales** del **Instituto** de **higiene** de **Montevideo.** *An. Inst. Hig. Montevideo* [1947–] **L.**EB. 47–51; TD. 47–50.

2422 **Anales** del **Instituto** de **ingenieros** de **Chile.** Santiago. *An. Inst. Ing. Chile* **L.**EE. 36–40 imp.: 45–.

2423 **Anales** del **Instituto** de **investigaciones científicas** y **tecnológicas. Universidad nacional** del **Litoral.** Santa Fé. *An. Inst. Invest. cient., S Fé* **L.**C. 32–33.

2424 **Anales** del **Instituto** de **investigaciones científicas. Universidad** de **Nuevo Leon.** Monterrey. *An. Inst. Invest. cient., Monterrey* [1944–]

2425 **Anales. Instituto** de **investigaciones físicas** aplicadas a la **patología humana.** Buenos Aires. *An. Inst. Invest. fís. Patol. hum.* [1940–]

2426 **Anales** del **Instituto** de **investigaciones médicas** y de la **Clínica médica** del **Prof. C. Jiménez Díaz.** Barcelona. *An. Inst. Invest. méd. Clín. méd. Prof. Díaz* [1941–] **L.**LI. 46–48; MD. 48. [*C. of:* 2345]

2427 **Anales** del **Instituto** de **investigaciones veterinarias.** Madrid. *An. Inst. Invest. vet.* [1953–] **L.**V.; **Abd.**R.; **Abs.**U.; **E.**AB. [*C. of:* 2388]

2428 **Anales. Instituto José Celestino Mutis.** *An. Inst. José Celestino Mutis* **Y.**

2429 **Anales** del **Instituto Madinaveitia.** Madrid. *An. Inst. Madinaveitia* **L.**BM. 25–29.

2430 **Anales** del **Instituto** de **maternidad** y **asistencia social.** Buenos Aires. *An. Inst. Matern., B. Aires* [1940–] **L.**MA. 42: 44–; TD. 44–45: 47.

2431 **Anales** del **Instituto** de **medicina experimental.** Caracas. *An. Inst. Med. exp., Caracas* [1942–] **L.**BM. 45–.

2432 **Anales** del **Instituto** de **medicina experimental 'Angel H. Roffo.'** Buenos Aires. *An. Inst. Med. exp. 'Angel H. Roffo'* [1952–54] **L.**CB.; LI.; MD.; TD.; **Br.**U.; **G.**U.; **M.**MS.; **O.**P. [*C. of:* 2433; *C. as:* 2446]

2433 **Anales** del **Instituto** de **medicina experimental** para el **estudio** y **tratamiento** del **cáncer.** Buenos Aires. *An. Inst. Med. exp. Estud. Trat. Cáncer, B. Aires* [1949–51] **L.**CB.; LI.; MD.; TD.; **Br.**U.; **G.**U.; **M.**MS.; **O.**P. [*C. of:* 7833; *C. as:* 2432]

2434 **Anales** del **Instituto** de **medicina experimental** de **Valencia.** *An. Inst. Med. exp. Valencia* [1943–] **L.**MD. 44–; TD. 43–45; **O.**R. 43–.

2435 **Anales** del **Instituto** de **medicina legal. Universidad** de **Buenos Aires.** *An. Inst. Med. leg. Univ. B. Aires* [1928–]

2436 **Anales** del **Instituto** de **medicina regional.** Perón. *An. Inst. Med. reg., Perón*

2437 **Anales** del **Instituto** de **medicina regional.** Tucumán. *An. Inst. Med. reg., Tucumán* [1944–] **L.**EB. 44–57; MD. 48–; TD.

2438 **Anales** del **Instituto médico nacional.** México. *An. Inst. méd. nac., Méx.* [1894–15] **L.**K. 94–97; TD. 04–14; **Bm.**U. 94–14 imp.; **Lv.**U. 10–15. [*C. as:* 7670]

2439 **Anales** del **Instituto modelo** de **clínica médica.** Buenos Aires. *An. Inst. modelo Clín. méd., B. Aires* [1915–] **L.**MD. 32–34 imp.; TD. 17–25.

2440 **Anales** del **Instituto municipal** de **higiene** de **Zaragoza.** Zaragoza. *An. Inst. munic. Hig. Zaragoza* [1952–] **R.**D.; **Y.**

2441 **Anales. Instituto nacional** de **antropología** e **historia.** México. *An. Inst. nac. Antrop. Hist., Méx.* [1939–] **L.**AN.; U.

2442 **Anales. Instituto nacional** de **investigaciones agronómicas.** Madrid. *An. Inst. nac. Invest. agron.* [1952–] **L.**AM.; BM.; BM^N. 55–; K. 54–; TP. imp.; **Abd.**R.; **Br.**A.; **C.**A.; **Db.**; **E.**AG.; R.; **Hu.**G.; **Md.**H.; **N.**U. 53–; **Sil.**; **Y.**
　　Anales del **Instituto nacional** de **microbiologia.** Buenos Aires. *See* 46643.

2443 **Anales** del **Instituto nacional** de **parasitología.** Asunción. *An. Inst. nac. Parasit., Asunción* [1928–32] **L.**BM.; BM^N.; UC.; **Lv.**U.

2444 **Anales** del **Instituto** de **neurología.** Montevideo. *An. Inst. Neurol., Montevideo* [1927–] **L.**MD. 27; S. 27–; **E.**R. 27–39.

2445 **Anales** del **Instituto** y **Observatorio** de **marina** de **San Fernando.** *An. Inst. Obs. Mar. S Fernando* **L.**R. 70–85; **C.**O. 92–; P. 96–; **Db.** 70–; **E.**M. 73– imp.; O. 70–; **O.**G. 70–38.

2446 **Anales** del **Instituto** de **oncología 'Angel H. Roffo'.** Buenos Aires. *An. Inst. Oncol. 'Angel H. Roffo'* [1955–] **L.**CB.; LI.; MD.; TD.; **Br.**U.; **G.**U.; **M.**MS.; **O.**P. [*C. of:* 2432]

2447 **Anales** del **Instituto** de **psicología.** Buenos Aires. *An. Inst. Psicol., B. Aires* [1935–]

2448 **Anales** del **Instituto radio-quirúrgico** de **Guipuzcoa.** San Sebastian. *An. Inst. radio-quir. Guipuzcoa* **L.**CB. 56–; S. 40–41: 43–44.

2449 **Anales. Instituto técnico** e **industrial** del **Perú.** Lima. *An. Inst. téc. ind. Perú*

2450 **Anales** del **Instituto traumatológico.** Santiago. *An. Inst. traum., Santiago*

2451 **Anales** de **investigación textil.** Barcelona. *An. Invest. text.* [1949–] **M.**C. 49–50.

2452 **Anales** de **investigaciones agronómicas.** Madrid *An. Invest. agron.* [1952–] **Abs.**A. 54–.

2453 **Anales** del **Jardin botánico** de **Madrid.** *An. Jard. bot. Madr.* [1940–50] **L.**K.; L.; MY. 45–50; **Db.** 46–50; **Hu.**G. 47–50; **O.**BO.; **Rt.**; **Y.** [*C. as:* 2405]

2454 **Anales** de la **Junta** para **ampliación** de **estudios** y **investigaciones científicas.** Madrid. *An. Jta Ampl. Estud. Invest. cient., Madr.* **L.**BM. 09–; M. 18.

2455 **Anales** del **Laboratorio central S.C.I.S.P.** Cochabamba, Bolivia. *An. Lab. cent. S.C.I.S.P.*

2456 **Anales** de **lactología** y **química agrícola** de **Zaragoza.** Zaragoza. *An. Lactol. Quím. agríc. Zaragoza* [1960–] **Y.**

2457 **Anales** de **mecánica** y **electricidad.** Madrid. *An. Mec. Elect.* **L.**EE. 40– imp.; I. 48–; P.; **Y.**

2458 **Anales** de **medicina** y **cirugía.** Barcelona. *An. Med. Cirug., Barcelona* **L.**MA. 45–; MD. 45– imp.; PS. 48–; **Ld.**U. 48–.

2459 **Anales** de **medicina** y **cirugía.** Málaga. *An. Med. Cirug., Málaga*

2460 **Anales** de **medicina** y **cirugía.** Trujillo. *An. Med. Cirug., Trujillo* [1940–]

2461 **Anales** de **medicina interna.** Madrid. *An. Med. interna* [1932–36] **L.**MA.; MD. 36; **O.**R.

2462 **Anales** de **medicina legal, psiquiatría** y **anatomía patológica.** Barcelona. *An. Med. leg. Psiquiat. Anat. patol.* [1933–]

2463 **Anales** de **medicina pública.** Santa Fé. *An. Med. públ.* [1949–] **L.**TD.

2464 **Anales médico-quirúrgicos.** Madrid. *An. méd.-quir.* [1954–] **L.**MA.

2465 **Anales médicos.** Cádiz. *An. méd., Cádiz*

2466 **Anales médicos** de **Concepción.** Concepción. *An. méd. Concepción* [1944–] **L.**TD. 45– imp.

2467 **Anales médicos** de **Puerto Rico.** *An. méd. P. Rico* [1912] **Lv.**U.

2468 **Anales médicos** de la **Sociedad médica** del **A.B.C.** (Americano británico Cowdray) **hospital** de **México.** México. *An. méd. Soc. méd. A.B.C. Hosp. Méx.* [1956–] **L.**MA.; MD. 57–62 imp.

2469 **Anales** del **Ministerio** de **agricultura. Sección** de **geología, mineralogía** y **minería.** Buenos Aires. *An. Minist. Agric. Secc. Geol. Min. Miner., B. Aires* **L.**BM^N. 12–23 imp.; GM. 05– imp.; MI. 13–22 imp.; **G.**G. 05– imp.; **Lv.**U. 10.

2470 **Anales** del **Museo argentino** de **ciencias naturales 'Bernardino Rivadavia' Buenos Aires.** Buenos Aires. *An. Mus. argent. Cienc. nat.* [1931–47] **L.**BM.; BM^N.; G.; GM.; K.; L.; R.; UC. imp.; Z.; **Abs.**U.; **Bl.**U. 31–45 imp.; **C.**P.; **Db.**; **E.**B.; G.; R. 31–45; **Lv.**P.; **Pl.**M.; **Wo.** 31–32. [*C. of:* 2478]
　　Anales del **Museo** de la **Ciudad Eva Perón.** *See* 2473.

2472 **Anales** del **Museo** de **historia natural** de **Montevideo.** *An. Mus. Hist. nat. Montevideo* [1924–] **L.**BM^N.; L.; Z. 24–53 imp.; **Abs.**U.; **C.**P.; **E.**R.; **Pl.**M. 53– imp. [*Replaces:* 2479]

2473 **Anales** del **Museo** de **La Plata.** Buenos Aires. *An. Mus. La Plata* [1890–] **L.**AN. (anthrop.) 50–; BM.; BM^N. 91–30: 36– imp.; GL. 00–; L. 95–; R. 91–30; SC. (anthrop.) 50–; Z. imp.; **C.**E. 07–08; P. 25–; UL. 25–; **Db.** 00–; **E.**G. 07–; R. 25–; **Lv.**U. 95–30 imp.; **O.**R. 90–94; **Pl.**M. 53; **Y.** (anthrop.). [*Published in sections*]

2474 **Anales** del **Museo nacional** de **arqueología, historia** y **etnología** de **México.** *An. Mus. nac. Arqueol. Méx.* [1877–] **L.**AN. 03–35 imp.; BM. 77–09; BM^N. 77–05: 25–37; U. 27–; **O.**B. 77–05: 13–35 imp.

2475 **Anales** del **Museo nacional** de **Bolivia.** La Paz. *An. Mus. nac. Bolivia* **L.**BM. 20–.

2476 **Anales** del **Museo nacional** de **Chile.** Santiago. *An. Mus. nac. Chile* [1891–10] **L.**BM.; BM^N.; L.

2477 **Anales** del **Museo nacional David J. Guzman.** *An. Mus. nac. David J. Guzman*

2478 **Anales** del **Museo nacional** de **historia natural** de **Buenos Aires.** *An. Mus. nac. Hist. nat. B. Aires* [1864–31] **L.**BM.; BM^N.; E. 95–02; G. 95–31; GL. 00–13; GM. 13–31; K. 26–31; L.; R.; UC. 96–31 imp.; Z.; **Abs.**U. 26–31; **Bl.**U. 95–31; **C.**P. 13–31; **Cr.**N. 95–06; **Db.** 95–31; **E.**B. 08–31; G. 95–31; R. 85–31; **G.**N. 95–09 imp.; **Lv.**P. imp.; U. 95–25 imp.; **M.**U. 95–25; **Pl.**M. 95–31; **Wo.** 20–31 imp. [*C. as:* 2470]
　　Anales del **Museo nacional** de **México.** *See* 2474.

2479 **Anales** del **Museo nacional** de **Montevideo** *An. Mus. nac. Montevideo* [1894–11] **L.**BM.; BM^N.; L.; MO. 95; UC. 96–08; Z. 96–05 imp.; **Bl.**U. 99–11 imp.; **Bm.**N. 09–11; **C.**BO. 96–11; **E.**R.; **G.**M. 94–09; **Lv.**U. 96–06; **Pl.**M. 98–08. [*Replaced by:* 2472]

2480 **Anales** del **Museo nacional. República** de **El Salvador.** San Salvador. *An. Mus. nac. Repúb. Salvador* [1903–11] **L.**BM. 03; BM^N.; G. 03–09; GM. 03–10; **Lv.**U. 05–11; **M.**U. 06.

2481 **Anales. Museo** de **Nahuel Huapí.** Buenos Aires. *An. Mus. Nahuel Huapí* [1945–] **L.**BM.; **Y.**

2482 **Anales** de **neurocirugía.** Buenos Aires. *An. Neurocirug.* **L.**MD. 56–. [*C. of:* 4621]

2483 **Anales neuropsiquiátricos.** Bogotá. *An. neuropsiquiát.*

2484 **Anales** del **Observatorio astronómico y meteorológico** de **San Salvador.** *An. Obs. astr. met. S Salvador* **L.**MO. 17–; **E.**R. 95: 17–37 imp. [*C. as:* 2489]

2485 **Anales** del **Observatorio. Colegio 'Nuestra Señora** de **Montserrat'.** Habana. *An. Obs. Col. 'Nuestra Señora de Montserrat', Habana* **L.**MO. 11–22; **O.**G. 11–.

2486 **Anales** del **Observatorio meteorológico nacional Ciudad Universitaria.** Bogotá. *An. Obs. met. nac. Ciud. Univ.* **L.**MO. 41–. [*C. of:* 2490]

Anales del **Observatorio meteorológico** de **San Salvador.** *See* 2484 *and* 2489.

2488 **Anales** del **Observatorio nacional meteorológico** de **'La Aurora'.** Guatemala. *An. Obs. nac. met. 'La Aurora'* [1928–] **L.**MO. 28–39 imp. [*Not published* 1932–38]

2489 **Anales. Observatorio nacional meteorológico** de **San Salvador.** *An. Obs. nac. met. S Salv.* **L.**MO.; SC.; **Db.** 51–. [*C. of:* 2484]

2490 **Anales. Observatorio nacional** de **San Bartolomé.** Bogotá. *An. Obs. nac. S Bartolomé* [1923–36] **L.**BM. 30–36; MO.; **E.**M.; **M.**P. 23–25. [*C. as:* 2486]

2491 **Anales** de la **Oficina meteorológica argentina.** Buenos Aires. *An. Of. met. argent.* [1878–] **L.**G. 89–90; MO. 81–28; **E.**G. 12–; M.; R.; **Ex.**U. 82–13; **G.**U.

2492 **Anales. Oficina meteorológica** de la **provincia** de **Buenos Aires.** *An. Of. met. Prov. B. Aires*

2493 **Anales** de la **Oficina química** de la **provincia** de **Buenos Aires.** La Plata. *An. Of. quím. Prov. B. Aires* **Rt.** 27–28.

2494 **Anales** de **oftalmología.** México. *An. Oftal.* [1898–17] **L.**MD. 04–15; OP. 06–15. [*C. as:* 2529]

2495 **Anales** de **oftalmología y oto-rino-laringología** del **Paraguay.** *An. Oftal. Oto-rino-lar. Parag.*

2496 **Anales** de **ortopedia y traumatología.** México, D.F. *An. Ortop. Traum., Méx.*

2497 **Anales** de **oto-rino-laringología** del **Uruguay.** Montevideo. *An. Oto-rino-lar. Urug.* [1931–] **L.**MA. 40– imp.; MD. 32–.

2498 **Anales** de **parques nacionales.** Buenos Aires. *An. Parq. nac., B. Aires* [1952–] **L.**BM^N. 58–; **Y.**

2499 **Anales** de **pediatría.** Barcelona. *An. Pediat.* [1934–35] **L.**MA. imp.; MD. imp.

2500 **Anales. Policlínica** de **enfermedades infecciosas** del **Profesor adjunto Dr. Carlos Alberto Videla.** Buenos Aires. *An. Policlín. Enferm. infecc. Prof. Videla* **L.**TD. 42–44.

2501 **Anales** de **psicología.** Buenos Aires. *An. Psicol.* [1909–10] **L.**BM.

2502 **Anales** de **psicotécnia.** Rosario, R.A. *An. Psicotéc.* [1941–]

2503 **Anales** de **química** y **farmacía.** Santiago de Chile. *An. Quím. Farm.* [1931–]

2504 **Anales. R. Academia** de **farmacía.** Madrid. *An. R. Acad. Farm., Madr.* **L.**MA. 46–; PH. 42– imp.; **Y.**

2505 **Anales** de la **R. Academia** de **medicina.** Madrid. *An. R. Acad. Med., Madr.* [1879–] **L.**BM. 79–13; MD. 33–35: 47–; **O.**R.

Anales de la **R. Academia nacional** de **medicina.** Madrid. *See* 2505.

2506 **Anales** de la **R. Sociedad española** de **física y química.** Madrid. *An. R. Soc. esp. Fís. Quím.* [1903–40: 48–] **L.**AV.(*a*) 58–; C.; I (3 yr.); P. 24–; QM. 50–; SC. 27–; **C.**P.; **G.**U. (*b*) 56–; **Y.** [>2393, 1941–47; *from* 1948 *issued in Sér. A. Física; Sér. B. Química*]

2507 **Anales** de **radiología.** Habana. *An. Radiol.*

2508 **Anales** de **rehabilitación.** México. *An. Rehabil.* [1955–] **L.**MD.

2509 **Anales** y **revista mensual** de **medicina, cirugía** y **especialidades.** Valencia. *An. Rev. mens. Med. Cirug.*

2510 **Anales** de la **Sala VIII. Hospital F. J. Muniz.** Buenos Aires. *An. Sala VIII Hosp. F.J. Muniz* [1939–]

2511 **Anales** del **Sanatorio Pedralbes.** Barcelona. *An. Sanat. Pedralbes* **L.**MD. 44.

2512 **Anales** del **Sanatorio Valdés.** México. *An. Sanat. Valdés*

2513 **Anales** de **sanidad militar.** Buenos Aires. *An. Sanid. milit.* [1899–00] [*C. as:* 46922]

2514 **Anales** de la **Sección** de **orientación profesional, Escuéla** del **trabajo.** Barcelona. *An. Secc. Orient. prof. Esc. Trab., Barcelona* [1928–30] **L.**P. 29–30. [*C. of:* 2555; *C. as:* 2556]

2515 **Anales** de la **Secretaria** de **comunicaciones** y **obras públicas.** México. *An. Secr. Comun. Obr. públ., Méx.* **G.**U. 19–21.

2516 **Anales** del **Servicio** de **traumatología, cirugía ortopédica** y **accidentes** del **trabajo** del **Hospital provincial** de **Valencia.** Valencia. *An. Serv. Traum. Cirug. ortopéd. Hosp. prov. Valencia.*

2517 **Anales. Servicio** de **traumatología** del **Dr. Lopez-Trigo.** *An. Serv. Traum. Lopez-Trigo* **L.**MA. 45–.

2518 **Anales sismológicos. Servicio meteorológico nacional.** Buenos Aires. *An. sism., B. Aires* **L.**MO. 48–53.

2519 **Anales** de la **Sociedad agronómica** de **Santiago.** *An. Soc. agron. Santiago* [1911–13] [*C. as:* 46270]

2520 **Anales** de la **Sociedad** de **biología** de **Bogotá.** *An. Soc. Biol. Bogotá* [1943–] **L.**MA. 45–55; TD. 45–.

2521 **Anales** de la **Sociedad científica argentina.** Buenos Aires. *An. Soc. cient. argent.* [1876–] **L.**BM. 76–18; BM^N.; EB. 10– imp.; G. 99–10 imp.; GL. 00–; M.; MY. 21–; S. 32–39; UC. 28–; **C.**P. 25–; UL. 26–; **Db.** 28–; **E.**G. 10–; R. 25–; U. 10–20 imp.; **Y.**

2522 **Anales** de la **Sociedad científica argentina. Sección Santa Fé.** *An. Soc. cient. arg. Secc. S Fé* [1934–] **L.**BM^N. 34–43; **E.**R. [*C. of:* 2523]

2523 **Anales** de la **Sociedad científica** de **Santa Fé.** *An. Soc. cient. S Fé* [1929–33] **L.**BM^N.; **E.**R. 29–30. [*C. as:* 2522]

Anales de la **Sociedad española** de **física** y **química.** *See* 2506.

2524 **Anales** de la **Sociedad española** de **hidrología médica.** Madrid. *An. Soc. esp. Hidrol. méd.* **L.**MD. 24–31 imp.

2525 **Anales** de la **Sociedad española** de **historia natural.** Madrid. *An. Soc. esp. Hist. nat.* [1872–02] **L.**BM.; BM^N.; R. 72–01; Z.; **C.**UL.; E.C. 94–02; **G.**N. 73–00.

2526 **Anales** de la **Sociedad española** de **meteorología.** Madrid. *An. Soc. esp. Met.* **L.**MO. 27–29.

2527 **Anales** de la **Sociedad** de **geografía** e **historia** de **Guatemala.** *An. Soc. Geogr. Hist. Guatem.* [1924–] **L.**BM^N.; G. 27–32; E.G. 27–.

2528 **Anales. Sociedad médico-quirúrgica** del **Guayaquil.** *An. Soc. méd.-quir. Guayaquil* [1920–] **Lv.**U. 21–24: 29–.

2529 **Anales** de la **Sociedad mexicana** de **oftalmología** y **oto-rino-laringología.** México. *An. Soc. mex. Oftal. Oto-rino-lar.* [1916–] **L.**MA. 47–; MD. 23–; OP. 47–. [*C. of:* 2494]

2530 **Anales** de la **Sociedad otorinolaringológica andaluzza.** Córdoba. *An. Soc. otorinolar. andal.*

2530° **Anales** de la **Sociedad peruana** de **historia** de la **medicina.** Lima. *An. Soc. peru. Hist. Med.* [1939–]

2531 **Anales** de la **Sociedad química argentina.** Buenos Aires. *An. Soc. quím. argent.* [1913–54] **L.**C.; P. 26–54.; **Y.** [*C. as:* 2319]

2532 **Anales** de la **Sociedad rural argentina.** Buenos Aires. *An. Soc. rur. argent.* [1866–] **L.**A. 42: 44; AM. 08– imp.; EB. 17–26; **Abs.**N. 94– imp.; **C.**UL. 17–23; **Db.** 17–; O.R. 39–; **Y.**

2533 **Anales** de la **Sociedad veterinaria** de **zootecnia.** Madrid. *An. Soc. vet. Zootec., Madr.* [1947–51] **L.**AM. 51; V.; E.AB. 48–51. [*C. as:* 59300]

2534 **Anales** de **tisiología.** Buenos Aires. *An. Tisiol., B. Aires* [1924–27] [*C. as:* 4664]

2535 **Anales** de **tisiología** y **climatología.** Cosquin. *An. Tisiol. Clim.* [1942–]

2536 **Anales** de la **Universidad** de **Buenos Aires.** *An. Univ. B. Aires* [1888–02] **L.**UC. 99–00; **Abd.**U. 01–02; **C.**UL.; **Db.**; E.U. imp.; O.B. [*C. as:* 47010]

2537 **Anales** de la **Universidad central** del **Ecuador.** Quito. *An. Univ. cent. Ecuad.* **L.**BM^N. 26– imp.; L. 91– imp.; **Y.**

2538 **Anales** de la **Universidad central** de **Venezuela.** Caracas. *An. Univ. cent. Venez.* **L.**TD. 25–39 v. imp.; **C.**UL. 00–; **Ld.**U. 53; O.B. 25–; **Sa.** 04–08; **Y.**

2539 **Anales** de la **Universidad** de **Chile.** Santiago. *An. Univ. Chile* [1843–] **L.**BM.; BM^N. 61– imp.; Z. 1843–72 imp.; **Abd.**U. 92–09; **C.**UL. 02–; **Db.** 99– imp.; **G.**U. 92–40 imp.; **M.**U. 92–40 imp.; O.B. 91– imp.; **Sa.** 92– imp.

2540 **Anales** de la **Universidad** de **Costa Rica.** San José. *An. Univ. Costa Rica* **Bn.**U. 56–59 imp.

2541 **Anales** de la **Universidad** de **Madrid.** *An. Univ. Madr.* [1932–36] **L.**U.; **Bm.**U.; **Ld.**U. (cienc.) 32–35 imp.; **M.**U. 32–34.

2542 **Anales** de la **Universidad nacional mayor** de **San Marcos.** Lima. *An. Univ. nac. mayor S Marcos* [1949–] [*C. of:* 8182]

2543 **Anales** de la **Universidad nacional** del **Paraguay.** Asunción. *An. Univ. nac. Parag.* [1899–07: 36–] **L.**BM. 03–07; **Db.** 00–07.

2544 **Anales** de la **Universidad** de **Oviedo.** *An. Univ. Oviedo* [1901–10] **L.**BM. 01–07; UC.; **C.**UL.; **Db.** 03–10; **O.**B.

2545 **Anales** de la **Universidad** de **Santo Domingo.** Trujillo. *An. Univ. S Domingo* [1937–] **L.**BM^N. imp.; MA. 40–45; MD. 44–46; **Br.**U. 39–; **G.**U. 39–.

2546 **Anales** de la **Universidad** del **Uruguay.** Montevideo. *An. Univ. Urug.* [1891–] **Abd.**U. 93–20 imp.; **Bm.**U. 91–10.

2547 **Anales** de la **Universidad** de **Zaragoza.** *An. Univ. Zaragoza* [1917–] **L.**BM.; O.B. 17–27 imp.

2548 **Anales universitários** del **Perú.** Lima. *An. univ. Perú* **Abd.**U. 96–04.

2549 **Anales** de **vias digestivas, sangre** y **nutrición.** Habana. *An. Vias dig.* [1930–32] **L.**TD.; **Lv.**U

2550 **Anales** de **zoología aplicada.** Santiago de Chile. *An. Zool. apl.* [1914–22] **L.**BM^N. imp.; EB. imp.

2551 **Anali Instituta** za **eksperimentalno šumarstvo.** Jugoslovenska akademija znanosti i umjetnosti. Zagreb. *Anali Inst. eksp. Šum., Zagr.* [1955–] **O.**F.

2552 **Anali medicine** i **chirurgije.** Beograd. *Anali Med. Chir., Beogr.* [1927–]

2553 **Analisi** e **preparazione** dei **minerali.** *Analisi Prep. Miner.* [1959–] **L.**SC.

2553° **Analiticheskiĭ kontrol' proizvodstva** v **azotnoĭ promÿshlennosti.** Аналитический контроль произ-водства в азотной промышленности. *Analit. Kontrol' Proizv. azot. Prom.* [1956–] **L.**BM.; **Y.** 58–.

2554 **Anals** de l'**Academia** y **laboratori** de **cienciès médiques** de **Catalunya.** Barcelona. *Anals Acad. Lab. Cienc. méd. Catalunya*

2555 **Anals. Institut** d'**orientació professional.** Barcelona. *Anals Inst. Orient. prof. Barcelona* [1920–27] **L.**P. 20–23. [*C. as:* 2514]
　　Anals de **medecina.** Barcelona. *See* 2305.

2556 **Anals** d'**orientació profesional.** Barcelona. *Anals Orient. prof.* [1930] [*C. of:* 2514]

2557 **Analyse** des **contraintes.** Paris. *Analyse Contraintes* [1952–] **L.**P. 53–; **Y.**

2558 **Analyses. Météorologie nationale.** Paris. *Analyses Mét. natn., Paris* **L.**MO. 58–.

2559 **Analysis.** Rivista di critica della scienza. Milano. *Analysis, Milano* [1946–] **L.**K. 50–; U. 47–.

2560 **Analyst.** London. *Analyst, Lond.* [1876–] **L.**AM. 99–23: 48– imp.; AV. 41– imp.; BM.; BM^N. 54–; C.; CB. 47–; H. 46– imp.; I. 10–; IC. 77–79: 10–; LE. 19–; MA. 00–; MC. 48–60; MD. 37–; NF. 25–; NP. 54–; P. imp.; PH.; PR. 30–; QM. 53–; RI. (curr.); SC. 82–; SI. 16–; TP. 93– imp.; U. 47–; UC.; **Abd.**M. 50–; R. 35–; S. 98–; U. 92–; **Abs.**N. 12–; U. 00– imp.; **Bl.**U. 25– imp.; **Bm.**C. 30–; P. 79–; T.; U. 80–; **Bn.**U. 84– imp.; **Br.**A. 44–; P. 07– imp.; U. 94–01: 29–; **Bra.**D. 48– imp.; P. 21–; **C.**APH. 37–; UL.; **Cr.**MD. 31–48; U. 30–; **Db.** 88–; E.A. 85–; CE. 25–; HW. 35–; PO. 48–; SW. 46–57; U. 86–; W. 92– imp.; **Ep.**D. 30–; **Ex.**U. 52–; **F.**A. 42–; **Fr.** 55–; **G.**T. 98–; U. 76–15: 24–; **Hu.**G. 47–; **Je.** 29–; **Ld.**P. 25–; U.; W. 30–; **Lh.**P. 39–; **Lv.**P. 38–; U. 93– imp.; **M.**C.; D. 15– imp; MS. 81–; P. 81–; T. 27–; U. 52–; **Md.**H. 44–; **Mi.** 44–; **N.**T. 45–47; U. 21–; **Nw.**A. 76–84: 06–; O.R. 79–; **R.**D. 02–; U. 92–; **Rn.**B. 52–; **Rt.** 35–; **Sa.** 33–46; **Sal.**F. 43–; **Sh.**P. 29–; S. 40–; **Sil.** 53–; **St.**R. 94–; **Ste.** 76–78: 10–; **Sw.**U. 58–; **Sy.**R. 25–; W. 37–; **Wd.** 15–; **We.**K. 21–; **Wo.** 53–; **Y.**

2561 **Analyst.** 's-Gravenhage. *Analyst, 's-Grav.* [1946–58] **Y.** [*C. as:* 13789]

2562 **Analytica chimica acta.** New York, Amsterdam, etc. *Analytica chim. Acta* [1947–] **L.**AM. 54–; BM.; BM^N. 57–; C.; I.; IC.; NC. 56–57; NF.; P. PR. 51–; RI.; SC.; U.; UC.; **Abd.**S.; U. **Bm.**C. 48–; U.; **Bn.**U.; **Br.**A.; U.; **C.**CH.; **Co.**T. 54–58; **E.**A.; SW. 47–52; U.; **Ep.**D.; **Ex.**U. 58–; F.A.; **G.**T.; U.; **Ld.**U.; **Lv.**P. 56–; U.; **M.**C.; D.; P. 56–; T.; U.; **Md.**H.; **N.**U.; **Nw.**A.; O.R.; **Pit.**F.; R.U. 58–; **Rt.**; **Sh.**S.; **St.**R.; **Ste.**; **Wd.**; **We.**K. 58–; **Y.**

2563 **Analytical Abstracts.** Cambridge. *Analyt. Abstr.* [1954–] **L.**AM.; AV.; BM.; BM^N.; C.; CB.; GH.; LE.; MA.; MC.; MD.; NC.; NF.; NP.; P.; PH.; PR.; QM.; R.; RI. (curr.); SC.; SI.; TD.; TP. imp.; U.; UC.; VC. imp.; **Abd.**R.; S.; U.; **Abs.**N.; U.; **Bl.**U.; **Bm.**C.; P.; T.; U.; **Bn.**U.; **Br.**A.; P.; U.; **Bra.**P.; **C.**A.; APH.; BI.; UL.; **Co.**T.; **Cr.**U.; **Db.**; E.A.; HW.; PD.; U.; W.; **Ex.**U.; F.A.; **Fr.**; G.M.; T.; U.; **H.**U.; **Je.**; **Lc.**A.; **Ld.**P.; U.; W.; **Lh.**P.; **Lo.**; **Lv.**P.; U.; **M.**C.; MS.; P.; T.; U.; **Md.**H.; **N.**P.; T. 55–57; U.; **Nw.**A.; O.BI.; R.; **Pit.**F.; R.D.; U.; **Rn.**B.; **Rt.**; **Sh.**IO.; S.; U.; **Sil.**; **St.**R.; **Ste.** 57–; **Sw.**U.; **Sy.**R.; W.; **We.**K.; **Wo.**; **Y.** [*Replaces:* 8749, Sect. C]

2564 **Analytical Biochemistry.** New York, London. *Analyt. Biochem.* [1960–] **L.**C.; MC.; MD.; P.; SC.; **Abd.**R.; **Bl.**U.; **Bn.**U.; **C.**APH.; **H.**U.; **Ld.**U.; **M.**C.; **Y.**

2565 **Analytical Chemistry.** Easton, Pa., etc. *Analyt. Chem.* [1947–] **L.**AM. 47–; AN.; AV.; B. 47–52: 60–; BM. 48–; BM^N. 54–; C.; CB. 48–; H.; I.; IC.; LE.; LI.; MC.; MI. 48–51 imp.; NC. 55–; NF.; NP.; P.; PH.; PL. 48–; PR.; PT.; RI.; SC.; SI.; TD. 48–; TP.; U.; UC.; **Abd.**R.; S. 48–; U.; **Abs.**U.; **Bl.**U.; **Bm.**C.; P.; T.; **Bn.**U.; **Br.**A.; P.; **Bra.**D.; **C.**APH.; BI.; CH.; MI.; P.; UL.; **Cr.**P. 47–51; U.; **Db.**; **Dn.**U.; **E.**CE.; HW.; SW. 49–; U.; F.A.; **Fr.**; G.M.; T.; U.; **H.**U. 57–; **Hu.**G. 48–; **Je.** 48–; **Lc.**A.; **Ld.**P.; U.; W.; **Lh.**P.; **Li.**M. (3 yr.); **Lo.** 60–; **Lv.**P.; U.; **M.**C.; D.; T.; U.; **Ma.**T. 55–; **Md.**H.; **Mi.**; **N.**T. 42–; U.; **Nw.**A.; O.BI.; **Pit.**F. 48–; **Pl.**M.; R.D.; **Rn.**B.; **Rt.**; **Sa.**; **Sal.**F.; **Sh.**P.; S.; SC.; U.; **St.**R.; **Ste.**; **Sy.**R.; W. 57–; **Wd.**; **We.**K.; **Wo.** 54–; **Y.** [*C. of:* 23196]

2566 **Analytical Digest.** Chicago. *Analyt. Dig.* **Li.**M. 48–.

2567 **Analytical Method.** Atomic Energy Research Establishment. London. *Analyt. Meth. A.E.R.E.* [1959–] Unclassified issues **L.**P.; SC.; **Bm.**P.

2568 **Anatomia e chirurgia.** Roma. *Anat. Chir., Roma* [1956–] **L.**MA.

2569 **Anatomical Record.** Philadelphia, etc. *Anat. Rec.* [1906–] **L.**BM^N.; CB. 49–; MA. 48–; MC. 20–; MD.; S.; SC.; U. 49–; UC.; VC. 46–; Z. 18–23; **Abd.**U.; **Bl.**U. 20–23; **Bm.**U.; **Bn.**U. 49–; **Br.**U.; **C.**AN.; APH. 25– imp.; UL.; **Cr.**U.; **Db.**; **Dn.**U. 28–; **E.**AG. 51–; P.; PO. 48–; U.; **G.**U. 06: 61–; **Ld.**U.; **Lv.**U. imp.; **M.**MS.; **N.**U. 53–; **Nw.**A. 17–; O.R.; **Pl.**M. 44–; R.D. 46–; U. 51–; **Sa.**; **Sh.**U.; **Sw.**U. 57–; W. 45–58.; **Y.**

2570 **Anatomie der Japaner.** Kyoto. *Anat. Jap.* **O.**R. 28–.

2571 **Anatomische** und **entwicklungsgeschichtliche Monographien.** Leipzig. *Anat. entwgesch. Monogr.* [1909–14] **L.**SC.
Anatomische Hefte. Abt. I. *See* 3798. Abt. 2. *See* 18380.

2572 **Anatomische Nachrichten.** Jena. *Anat. Nachr.*

2573 **Anatomischer Anzeiger.** Jena. *Anat. Anz.* [1886–] **L.**BM.; BM^N.; L. 86–43; MA. 49–; MD.; S. 86–50;

SC.; UC.; Z.; **Abd.**U. 03–; **Bl.**U. imp.; **Bm.**U.; **Bn.**U. 96–98; **Br.**U.; **C.**AN. 86–40: 48; APH. 41–; B.; PH. 96–20; **Cr.**U.; **Db.** 13–14: 29–; **Dn.**U.; E.P.; R. 90–; S. 97–23 imp.; U.; **G.**U. imp.; **Ld.**U. imp.; **Lv.**U.; **M.**MS.; **Nw.**A. 03–14; O.R.; **Pl.**M. 92–; R.U.; **Sa.**; **Sh.**U. 04–; **Y.** [*Also supplements*]

2574 **Anatomischer Bericht.** Jena. *Anat. Ber.* [1922–44] **L.**BM.; S. 22–42; UC.; **Bl.**U.; **Bm.**U. 36–44; **Br.**U. 40–44; **C.**AN.; E.U.; **G.**U.; O.R. 22–29; **Sa.**

2575 **Anatomiske skrifter.** Aarhus. *Anat. Skr.* [1954–] **L.**S.; UC.

2576 **Anbudstidende.** Oslo. *Anbudstidende* [1932–] [*Supplement to:* 34994]

2577 **Ancient India.** Delhi. *Ancient India* [1946–] **L.**AN.; BM.; U. 47–; **Bl.**U.; **Br.**U.; **C.**UL.; **Db.**; E.R.; U.; **G.**U. 46–49.

2578 **Ancre médicale.** Lyon. *Ancre méd.*

2579 **Andhra Agricultural Journal.** Bapatla. *Andhra agric. J.* [1954–] **C.**A.; **Rt.** 55–56; **Y.**

2580 **Andhra University Memoirs** in **Oceanography.** Waltair. *Andhra Univ. Mem. Oceanogr.* [1954–] **L.**BM^N.; **Dm.**; **Lv.**U.; **Mi.**; **Pl.**M.; **Wo.**; **Y.**

2581 **Andina.** Santiago. *Andina* **L.**G. 30–32 imp.

2582 **Anestesia.** Bogotá. *Anestesia, Bogotá.*

2583 **Anestesia.** Rio de Janeiro. *Anestesia, Rio de J.*

2584 **Anesthesia Abstracts.** Minneapolis. *Anesth. Abstr.* [1937–] **L.**MD.; S. 37–39: 47–; **Cr.**MD. 43–; **Nw.**A.

2585 **Anesthesia** and **Analgesia Current Researches.** Elmira, N.Y. *Anesth. Analg. curr. Res.* [1957–] **L.**D.; GH.; MA.; MC.; MD.; S.; UC.; UCH.; **Abd.**U.; **Bl.**U.; **Br.**U.; **Cr.**MD.; **Db.**; **Dn.**U.; E.U.; **G.**U.; **Ld.**U.; **Lv.**M.; **M.**MS.; **Nw.**A.; O.R.; **Sh.**U.; **Y.** [*C. of:* 16200]

2586 **Anesthesia Digest.** Cleveland. *Anesth. Dig.*

2587 **Anesthésie et analgésie.** Paris. *Anesth. Analg.* [1935–56] **L.**MA.; MD. 35–39; S. 37–56; **Cr.**MD.; **Db.**; E.U.; **M.**MS. 35–39. [*C. as:* 2588]

2588 **Anesthésie, analgésie, réanimation.** *Anesth. Analg. Réanim.* [1957–] **L.**MA.; S.; **Cr.**MD.; **Db.**; E.U. [*C. of:* 2587]

2589 **Anesthesiology.** Lancaster, Pa., etc. *Anesthesiology* [1940–] **L.**D. 41– imp.; MA.; MD.; S.; U. 48–; UCH. 51–; **Abd.**U. 45–; **Bl.**U. imp; **Cr.**MD. 45–; **Db.** 49–; **Dn.**U. 51–; E.S. 47–; U.; **Ld.**U.; **Lv.**M. 46–; **M.**MS.; **Nw.**A. 47–; O.R.; **Wd.** 51–; **Y.**

2590 **Ancxos das Memorias** do **Instituto de Butantan, Seccão de botanica.** São Paulo. *Anex. Mems Inst. Butantan Secc. Bot.* [1921–22] **L.**BM^N.; K.; TD.; E.B.; R. (Ofiol.) 21–22; O.F. [*Supplement to:* 31190; *C. as:* 4485]

2591 **Angéiologie et annales** de la **Société française d'angéiologie** et **d'histopathologie.** Paris. *Angéiologie*

2592 **Angestellte Arzt.** Köln. *Angest. Arzt*

2593 **Angewandte Botanik.** Berlin. *Angew. Bot.* [1919–] **L.**AM. 19–30; K. 19–43; MY. 26–43 imp.; P.; SC.; **Abs.**A. 30–43 imp.; **C.**UL. 27–; **Db.**; **M.**C. 32–39; U. 19–25; **Md.**H. 31–38: 42–; O.BO. 43–; **Y.** [*C. of:* 25120]

2594 **Angewandte Chemie.** Berlin, etc. *Angew. Chem.*
[1932–] L.AV. 35–49 imp.; BM. 47–; C. 32–41; CB. 54–;
IC.; KC. 53–; LE. 57–; LI. 54–55; MC. 59–; P.; PR.; QM. 50–
53; SC. 32–42: 47–; U. 38–39; UC.; **Abd.**U. (*a*) 58–;
Abs.U. 50–; **Bl.**U. 52–; **Bm.**U.; **Br.**U. 60–; **C.**CH.;
Cr.U. 59–; **E.**U. 32–40: 47–; **Ep.**D. 32–39: 48–; **F.**A. 47–;
G.T. 58–; U.; **Ld.**U.; W. 32–39; **Lv.**P. 47–52 imp.: 54–;
U.; **M.**C. 32–38; D. 32–41: 47–; P. 56–; T.; U. imp.;
N.U. 56–; **Nw.**A. 39–44: 47–; **Sa.** 55–; **Sh.**U. 58–; **St.**R.
32–38; **Ste.** imp.; **Sw.**U. 57–; **Te.**C.; **Wd.** 32–44: 47–; **Y.**
[*C. of:* 58475; 1947–48 *forms Ausgabe A.* (*Wissenschaft-
licher Teil*); *See* 2595 *and* 13783 *for Ausgabe B: an
International Edition in English published from* 1962]

2595 **Angewandte Chemie. Ausgabe B., Technisch-
wirtschaftlicher Teil.** Berlin. *Angew. Chem. Ausg.*
B [1947–48] **L.**BM.; C.; I.; IC.; P.; PR.; QM.; SC.; UC.;
Bm.U.; **C.**CH.; **E.**U.; **Ep.**D.; **F.**A.; **G.**U.; **Ld.**U.; W.;
Lv.P.; **M.**D.; T.; U. imp.; **Nw.**A.; **Wd.** [*C. of:* 13816; *C.
as:* 13793]

2596 **Angewandte Geographie.** Halle a. S. *Angew.*
Geogr. [1902–21] **L.**BM.; G. 02–14.

2597 **Angewandte Meteorologie.** Berlin. *Angew. Met.*
[1951–] **L.**MO.; P.; SC. 57–; **Y.** [*Supplement to:* 58725]

2598 **Angewandte Parasitologie.** Jena. *Angew. Parasit.* [1960–] **L.**BM.; EB.; W.; **Y.**

2599 **Angewandte Pflanzensoziologie.** Stolzenau.
Angew. PflSoziol. [1951–] **Hu.**G.; **O.**F.; **R.**U.; **Y.**

2600 **Angiología.** Barcelona. *Angiología* [1949–] **L.**MA.;
MD.; **M.**MS.

2601 **Angiology.** Baltimore. *Angiology* [1950–] **L.**MA.;
Bl.U. 61–; **Cr.**MD.; **E.**U.; **G.**F.; **Lv.**M.; **M.**MS.; **Y.**

2601ᵃ **Angkasa.** Djakarta. *Angkasa* [1949–]

2602 **Angle Orthodontist.** Chicago, etc. *Angle Orthod.*
[1931–] **L.**D.; MA. 47–; **Bl.**U. 49–; **Bm.**U. 45–; **Br.**U. 48–;
Dn.U. 50–; **E.**U. 53–; **Ld.**U. 59–; **M.**MS. 51–; **Nw.**A. 57–.

2603 **Angling.** London. *Angling* [1936–] **L.**AM. 47–;
BM.; **C.**UL.; **Fr.** 51–56; **O.**R.

2604 **Angling** in **Malaya.** Malacca. *Angl. Malaya*
[1953–] **L.**BM. 57–; BM.

2605 **Anglo-German Medical Review.** Stuttgart.
Anglo-Germ. med. Rev. [1960–] **L.**MD.; **Bl.**U.

2606 **Anilinokrasochnaya promÿshlennost'.** Moskva.
Анилинокрасочная промышленность. *Anilin. Prom.*
[1931–35]

2607 **Animadversiones systematicae ex Herbario
Universitatis Tomskensis.** Tomsk. *Animadv. syst.
Herb. Univ. Tomsk.* [1927–] **L.**BM. imp.; K. 31–.

2608 **Animadversiones systematicae ex Museo zoologico Instituti biologici Universitatis Tomskensis.**
Tomsk. *Animadv. syst. Mus. zool. Univ. Tomsk.* **L.**BM.
35–36.

2609 **Animal Ailments.** London. *Anim. Ailm.* [1923]
L.BM.; **E.**A.; **O.**B. [*C. as:* 2626]

2610 **Animal Behaviour.** London. *Anim. Behav.*
[1958–] **L.**AM.; B.; BM.; BM.; L.; KC.; MD.; NC.; QM.;
S.; SC.; U.; UC.; V.; VC.; Z.; **Abd.**M.; R.; **Bl.**U.; **Bm.**P.; U.;
Bn.U.; **Br.**U.; **C.**A.; APH.; B.; PS.; UL.; V.; Z.; **Cr.**U.; **Db.**;
E.A.; AR.; PO.; U.; **G.**U.; **Hu.**G.; **Ld.**U.; **Lo.**; **Lv.**U.;
M.U.; **N.**U.; **Nw.**A.; **O.**AP.; EP.; F.; OR. imp.; R.; **Pl.**M.;
R.D.; U.; **Sw.**U. 54–; **W.**; **Y.** [*C. of:* 8848]

2611 **Animal Breeding Abstracts.** Edinburgh, Farnham Royal. *Anim. Breed. Abstr.* [1933–] **L.**AM.; BM.;
BM. 33–34 imp.; CB. 56–; K. 27–43 imp.; MC. 47–; NC.
48– imp.; P.; SC.; TP. 47–; V.; VC.; UC.; Z.; **Abd.**R.; U.
47–; **Abs.**A. 33–34; N.; **Bn.**U. 46–; **Br.**U.; **C.**A.; APH.
53–; GE.; V. 40: 47–; **E.**A.; AB.; AG. 40–42: 46–52; AR.;
N. 39–; PO.; U. 40–42: 46–; W. imp.; **H.**U.; **G.**U. 38–;
Ld.U. imp.; W.; **N.**U. imp.; **O.**AP. 47–; R.; RE. 51–; **R.**D.;
Rt.; **Sal.**; W.; **Y.** [*C. of:* 41470 *and* 42414°]

2612 **Animal Health.** London. *Anim. Hlth* [1955–]
L.AM.; BM.; NC. 56–; Z. 57–; **C.**A.; UL.; **E.**A.; **O.**R.

2612° **Animal Health** and **Forestry Publications.**
Colonial Advisory Council of Agriculture. *Anim. Hlth
For. Publs* [1950–] **O.**RE.

2613 **Animal Health Leaflet.** Ministry of Agriculture,
Fisheries and Food. London. *Anim. Hlth Leafl.* [1948–]
L.AM.; BM. imp.; EB. (ent.); **Bn.**U.; **Bra.**P.; **C.**A.;
Lv.P.; **N.**U.; **M.**P.; **O.**RE.; **Y.**

2614 **Animal Health Review Series.** Imperial Agricultural Bureaux. *Anim. Hlth Rev. Ser.* [1938–] **Abs.**U.

2615 **Animal Health Yearbook.** F.A.O. Rome. *Anim.
Hlth Yb.* **G.**M. 57–; **Y.**
　　Animal Husbandry. Moscow. *See* 56518, ser. *h.*

2616 **Animal Husbandry.** Tokyo. *Anim. Husb., Tokyo*
[1947–] **Y.**

2617 **Animal Husbandry Circular.** Department of
Agriculture. Saskatschewan. *Anim. Husb. Circ., Sask.*

2618 **Animal Industry.** Tokyo. *Anim. Ind., Tokyo*
Y.

2619 **Animal Industry Series.** Taipei. *Anim. Ind.
Ser., Taipei* [1951–] **C.**A. imp.

2620 **Animal Kingdom.** New York. *Anim. Kingd.*
[1942–] **L.**BM.; Z.; **O.**AP.; OR.; 48–; **Y.** [*C. of:* 11312]

2621 **Animal Production.** Edinburgh. *Anim. Prod.*
[1959–] **L.**AM.; BM.; V.; VC.; **Abd.**R.; U.; **Abs.**N.; U.; **Bl.**U.;
Bn.U.; **Br.**U.; **C.**A.; APH.; **Db.**; **E.**AB.; AG.; AR.; U.; **G.**U.
61–; **Hu.**G.; **Ld.**U.; **N.**U.; **O.**R.; RE.; **R.**D.; **Y.** [*C. of:*
39033]

2622 **Animal World.** London. *Anim. Wld* [1869–]
L.AM. 54–; BM.; **E.**A.; **G.**M. 86–19; **O.**B. 70– imp.

2623 **Animal Year Book.** London. *Anim. Yb.* [1931–
38] **L.**BM.; BM.; Z.; **M.**P.; **O.**AP.; B.

2624 **Animal** and **Zoo Magazine.** London. *Anim.
Zoo Mag.* [1938–41] **L.**BM.; Z. [*C. of:* 59248]
　　Animalia fennica. *See* 51418.

2625 **Animals' Advocate.** London. *Anims' Advoc.*
[1922–34] **L.**BM.; V. 27–34 imp. [*C. as:* 2630]

2626 **Animals** and their **Ailments.** London. *Anims
Ailm.* [1924–27] **L.**BM.; **E.**A.; **O.**R. [*C. of:* 2609]

2627 **Animals Defender** and **Anti-Vivisectionist.**
London. *Anims Def. Anti-Vivisect.* [1957–] **L.**BM.; MD.;
V.; **Bm.**U.; **C.**UL.; **Db.**; **E.**A.; **G.**M.; U. imp.; **Lv.**P.;
O.B. [*C. of:* 2628]

2628 **Animals Defender** (*afterwards* and **Zoophilist**).
London. *Anims Def. Zoophil.* [1915–56] **L.**BM.; MD.; V.
32–56; **Bm.**U. 23–56; **C.**UL.; **Db.**; **Dn.**U. 16–21 imp.;
E.A.; **G.**M. 15–27; U. imp.; **Lv.**P. 49–56; **O.**B. [*C. of:*
59297; *C. as:* 2627]

2628° **Animals' Friend.** London. *Anims' Friend* [1894–]
L.BM. 96–; **Abs.**N. 11– imp.; **E.**A. 94–23 imp.; **O.**B. 94–
30.

2629 **Animals' Guardian.** London. *Anims' Guard.*
[1890–20] **L.**BM. 91–20; **Abs.**N. 13–20; **O.**B. 03–16. [*C.
as:* 3599]

2630 **Animals' Magazine.** London. *Anims' Mag.* **L.**V. 34–37 imp. [*C. of:* 2625]

2630° **Animals and Zoo.** Tokyo Zoological Park Society. Tokyo. *Anim. Zoo, Tokyo* **L.**Z. 58–59.

2631 **Animaux.** Association française pour la défense des animaux. Paris. *Animaux* **L.**V. 50– imp.

2632 **Anjou médical.** Angers. *Anjou méd.*

2633 **Ankara üniversitesi Fen fakültesi mecmuasi.** Ankara. *Ankara Üniv. Fen Fak. Mecm.* [1948–] [*Foreign language edition at:* 15079]

2633ᵃ **Ankara üniversitesi Fen fakültesi yayinlari.** *Ankara Üniv. Fen Fak. Yayinl.* Botanik. **L.**BMᴺ. 52–.
Ankara üniversitesi Tip fakültesi mecmuasi. *See* 651.

2634 **Ankara üniversitesi Veteriner fakültesi dergisi.** Ankara. *Ankara Üniv. vet. Fak. Derg.* **E.**AB. 57.

2634° **Ankara üniversitesi Ziraat fakültesi yilliği.** *Ankara Üniv. Zir. Fak. Yill.* **L.**BMᴺ. 53–.
Ankara yüksek Ziraat enstitüsü. *See* 58208.

2635 **Anleitungen für die chemische Laboratoriumspraxis.** Berlin. *Anleit. chem. LabPrax.* [1938–]

2636 **Anleitungen** der **Deutschen Gesellschaft** für **Züchtungskunde.** *Anleit. dt. Ges. Züchtungsk.*
Annaes. *See* **Anais**

2637 **Annale** van die **Universiteit** van **Stellenbosch.** Kaapstad. *Annale Univ. Stellenbosch* [1923–] **L.**BMᴺ.; **K.** (sect. a) 23–46 imp.; **SC.** (sect. a); **UC.** 26–; **Bm.**U.; **C.**UL.; **E.**U.; **Lv.**U.; **M.**U. (sect. a); **O.**B.; **Y.**
Annalele. *See* **Analele.**

2638 **Annalen.** Abteilung für **Wasserwirtschaft, Schweizerische Landeshydrographie.** Berne. *Annln Abt. Wasserw. schweiz. Landeshydrogr.* **L.**MO. 15–18.
Annalen der Belgische vereniging voor **tropische geneeskunde.** *See* 2933.

2639 **Annalen** von der **Bosscha-Sterrenwacht.** Lembang. *Annln Bosscha-Sterrenw.* [1925–] **L.**AS.; **C.**O. 28–; **SP.** 28–; **E.**R. 31–33 imp.; **M.**U. 27–51 imp.; **O.**O.
Annalen der Chemie. *See* 27138.

2640 **Annalen** der **Elektrohomöopathie** und **Gesundheitspflege.** Genf. *Annln Elektrohomöop. GesundhPflege* **L.**S. 89–04*. [*C. as:* 48599]

2641 **Annalen** der **Elektrotechnik.** Darmstadt. *Annln Elektrotech.* [1906–10] **L.**EE.; **P.** [*C. in:* 52524]

2642 **Annalen** für das **gesamte Hebammenwesen** des **In-** und **Auslandes.** Berlin. *Annln ges. HebammWes.* [1910–14] **Lv.**M. 10–12. [*C. of:* 58607]

2643 **Annalen** für **Gewerbe** u. **Bauwesen,** hrsg. v. Glaser. Berlin. *Annln Gew. Bauwes.* [1877–21] **L.**BM.; **I.** 79–97; **P.** 10–21 imp.; **Y.** [*C. as:* 21327]

2644 **Annalen** der **Grossherzoglichen Sozietät** für die **gesammte Mineralogie** in **Jena.** Neustadt-in-Jena. *Annln grossh. Soz. ges. Miner. Jena*

2645 **Annalen** für **Hydrographie.** Seehydrographischer Dienst, Deutsche demokratische Republik. Stralsund. *Annln Hydrogr., Stralsund* [1954–] **Abd.**M.; **Wo.** [*C. from:* 2646]

2646 **Annalen** der **Hydrographie** u. **maritime Meteorologie.** Deutsche Seewarte. Berlin. *Annln Hydrogr. Berl.* [1875–44] **L.**BM.; BMᴺ. 38–44; **G.** 87–44; **MO.**; **P.** 10–33; **SC.** 30–40; **UC.** 07–12 imp.; **Abd.**M. 20–44; **Lo.** 20–44; **Lv.**U. 00–44; **Nw.**A. 28–32; **O.**G. 11–16; **Pl.**M. 03–44; **Wo.** 25–39 imp. [*C. as:* 2645 *and* 16733]

Annalen der **K. Ingenieur-Hochschule** in **Moskau.** *See* 24366.
Annalen der **K. landwirtschaftlichen Hochschule Schwedens.** *See* 27808.
Annalen K. Museum voor **Midden-Africa.** Reeks 4to. *See* 2847; Reeks 8vo. *See* 2846.
Annalen der **K. Nicolaus Universität.** *See* 24368.

2647 **Annalen** der **K. Universitätssternwarte** in **Strassburg.** Karlsruhe. *Annln K. UnivSternw. Strassb.* [1896–25] **L.**AS.; BM.; R.; **C.**O.; P.; **Db.**; **E.**O.; **O.**O. 96–12. [*C. as:* 2873]
Annalen des **K. K. Naturhistorischen Museums.** Wien. *See* 2650.
Annalen der **K.K. Universitätssternwarte** in **Wien.** *See* 2656.

2648 **Annalen** der **landwirtschaftlichen Meteorologie.** Peterburg. *Annln landw. Met.*

2649 **Annalen** der **Meteorologie.** Meteorologischer Amt für Nordwestdeutschland. Hamburg. *Annln Met., Hamburg* [1948–] **L.**MO. 48–59; **SC.**; **C.**PO.; **Db.**; **E.**R.; **Lo.** 57– imp.; **O.**R.
Annalen der **mijnen** van **België.** *See* 2838.
Annalen van het **Museum** van **Belgisch Congo.** *See* 2846, 2847, 2848 and 2849.

2650 **Annalen** des **Naturhistorischen Museums** in **Wien.** Wien. *Annln naturh. Mus. Wien* [1886–] **L.**BM.; BMᴺ.; E.; EB.; GL. 00–; GM.; K.; L.; R.; UC.; Z.; **Bl.**U. 90– imp.; **C.**P.; S.; **Db.** 02–; **Dm.** 37: 58; **E.**B. 14–; C. 86–39 imp.; D. 13–21; R.; **G.**U. 25–33; **Lv.**U. imp.; **M.**U. 95– imp.; **Nw.**A. 12–; **O.**R.; **Pl.**M. 14–; **Y.**

2651 **Annalen** der **Physik,** etc. Leipzig, etc. *Annln Phys.* [1799–] **L.**AV. 21–43 imp.; BM.; C.; EE. 77–39; IC. 75–40; M. 00–; MD. 77–93; MO. 18–39 imp.: 42–; P.; PH. 91–07; QM. 50– imp.; R.; RI. 1824–; SC. imp.; U. 50–; UC. 62– imp.; **Abd.**U. 1846–; **Abs.**U. 93– imp.; **Bl.**U. imp.; **Bm.**P.; U.; **Bn.**U. 1845–42: 47–; **Br.**U. 1845–; **C.**C. 77–; P. 1824–; T. 75–11; UL.; **Cr.**U. imp.; **Db.**; **Dn.**U. 77–; **E.**O. imp.; R. 1824–; U.; **Ex.**U. 1824–00: 15–; **G.**F. 1834–1853; M. 78–15 imp.; U. imp.; **H.**U. 1824–40: 48–; **Ld.**U. 71–; **Lv.**P. 93–08 imp.: 54–: U. 77–; **M.**C. 20–39: 48–; D. 47–; P. 55–; U.; **Ma.**T. 41–44: 48–; **N.**P. 99–04; U. 98–; **Nw.**A. 1835–1837: 70–43; **O.**BS. 74–40 imp.; R.; **R.**U. 77–; **Sa.**; **Sh.**SC. 78–31; U. 77–; **Ste.** 13–40; **Sw.**U. 89–98: 21–34; **Te.**N. 1860–67: 77–42: 48–; **Y.** [*See also:* 5901]
Annalen der **Physik: Beiblätter.** *See* 5901.
Annalen des **Physikalischen Zentral-Observatoriums.** St. Petersburg. *See* 28485.

2652 **Annalen** der **Schweizerischen balneologischen Gesellschaft.** Aarau. *Annln schweiz. baln. Ges.*

2653 **Annalen** der **Schweizerischen meteorologischen Zentralanstalt.** Zürich. *Annln schweiz. met. ZentAnst.* [1864–] **L.**MO.; **E.**M. imp.; R. 20–; **O.**G. imp.; R. 00: 11; **Y.**

2654 **Annalen** der **städtischen allgemeinen Krankenhäuser** zu **München,** *Annln städt. allg. Krankenh. Münch.* [1874–] **L.**BM. 78–12; MD. 78–10; S. 78–10; -M.MS. 78–95.

2655 **Annalen** der **Sternwarte** in **Leiden.** s' Gravenhage. *Annln Sternw. Leiden* [1868–] **L.**AS.; BM.; R.; UC. 06–; **Bl.**U. 90–97; **C.**O.; SP. 02–; **Db.** 68–75; **E.**O. imp.; R.; **M.**U. 70– imp.; **O.**O.; **Y.**
Annalen van de **Sterrenwacht** in **Leiden.** *See* 2655.
Annalen. Universität des **Saarlandes.** *See* 2989.

2656 **Annalen** der **Universitätssternwarte** in **Wien.**
Wien. *Annln UnivSternw. Wien* [1821–] **L.**AS. 1821–
27; BM.; R. 1821–01; **C.**O.; **E.**O. 1835–; **O.**O. 84–12.

    Annalen der **Veterinärfakultät** der **Landwirt-
schaftlichen Hochschule** in **Wologda.** *See* 55134.

    Annalen der **Weissruthenischen staatlichen
Akademie** der **Landwirtschaft** in **Gorki.** *See* 58276.

    Annaler. K. Landbrukshögskolans. Stockholm.
See 27808.

    Annaler. Stockholms observatorium. *See* 50941.

2657 **Annaler. Uppsala astronomiska observatorium.** Uppsala. *Annlr Uppsala astr. Obs.* **L.**AS. 39–;
M.U. 39– imp.

2658 **Annales** de l'**ACFAS.** Association canadienne-
française pour l'avancement des sciences. Montréal.
Annls ACFAS [1935–] **L.**BM.; BM^N.; **Db.**; **Y.**

2659 **Annales** de l'**abeille.** Paris. *Annls Abeille* [1958–]
L.BM; BM^N.; P. 60–; Z.; **Y.** [*Forms* Sér. C bis *of:* 2785^c]

    Annales Academiae disciplinae silvaticae, Sop-
ron. *See* 18360.

    Annales Academiae horti- et **viticulturae,**
Budapest. *See* 27358.

2659ᵃ **Annales. Academiae medicae cracoviensis.**
Annls Acad. med. cracov. **Y.**

    **Annales Academiae regiae scientiarum up-
saliensis.** *See* 27819.

    Annales Academiae scientiarum fennicae. *See*
51415.

2659ᶜ **Annales Academiae sinicae.** Taipei. *Annls
Acad. sin.* [1954–]

2660 **Annales** de l'**Académie ethnographique** de la
Gironde. Bordeaux. *Annls Acad. ethnogr. Gironde*

2661 **Annales** de l'**Académie** de **Mâcon.** Mâcon.
Annls Acad. Mâcon [1853–] **L.**BM.

2662 **Annales** de l'**Académie national** des **sciences,
belleslettres** et **arts** de **Bordeaux.** Bordeaux. *Annls
Acad. natn. Sci. Bordeaux*

2663 **Annales** de l'**Académie** des **sciences, belles-lettres**
et **arts** de **Clermont-Ferrand.** Clermont-Ferrand.
Annls Acad. Sci. Clermont-Ferrand

2664 **Annales. Académie** des **sciences coloniales.**
Paris. *Annls Acad. Sci. colon.* [1925–] **L.**LI.; SC. 25–38.

    Annales de l'**Académie** des **sciences techniques** à
Varsovie. *See* 48056.

    Annales de l'**Académie tchécoslovaque** de l'**agri-
culture.** *See* 48606.

2665 **Annales agricoles.** Paris. *Annls agric.*

2666 **Annales agricoles** de l'**Afrique occidentale
française** et **étrangère.** Paris. *Annls agric. Afr.
occid. fr.* [1937–38] **L.**EB.; **C.**A.

2667 **Annales agricoles vaudoises.** Lausanne. *Annls
agric. vaud.* [1923–] **C.**A.; **Y.**

2668 **Annales agronomiques.** Paris. *Annls agron.*
[1875–02: 31–] **L.**A. 40–; AM.; BM.; C. 75–02; HS.
31–40: 50–; IC. 32–39: 48–; K. 31–; P. 95–02: 31–;
TP. 49–; U. 96–02; **Abd.**R. 31– imp.; S. 37–; U. 96–02:
31–; **Abs.**A. 31–; **Ba.**I. 40–; **Bn.**U. 34–; **Br.**A. 37–51;
U. 37–; **C.**A.; **E.**B. 86–02; **Hu.**G. 50–; **Ld.**U. 75–02; **Md.**H.
31– imp.; **O.**RE.; **R.**U. 31–; **Rt.**; **Sil.** 56–; **Y.** [>2906,
03–30; *The new series,* 1950–, *forms* Sér. A *of:* 2785^c]

2669 **Annales** de l'**amélioration** des **plantes.** Paris.
Annls Amél. Pl. [1951–] **L.**AM.; BM.; HS. 53–; TP.; **Abs.**A.;
Br.A. 53– imp.; **C.**A.; **Hu.**G.; **Md.**H.; **O.**RE. 51–59; **R.**U.
55–; **Rt.**; **Y.** [*Forms* Sér. B. *of:* 2785^c]

2670 **Annales** d'**anatomie pathologique.** Paris. *Annls
Anat. path.* [1956–] **L.**MA.; MD.; S.; **Bm.**U. **E.**S.; **Ld.**U.;
M.MS.; **O.**R.; **Y.** [*C. of:* 2671]

2671 **Annales** d'**anatomie pathologique** et d'**anatomie
normale médico-chirurgicale.** Paris. *Annls Anat.
path. Anat. norm. méd.-chir.* [1926–47] **L.**MA. 37–39;
MD.; S.; UCH. 28–29; **Bl.**U. 32–47; **Bm.**U.; **E.**S.; **G.**F.
38–39; **Ld.**U. imp.; **Y.** [*C. of:* 2672 and 10932; *not
published* 1941–46; *C. as:* 2670]

2672 **Annales** d'**anatomie pathologique médico-
chirurgicale.** Paris. *Annls Anat. path. méd.-chir.*
[1924–25] **L.**MD.; **E.**S. [*C. in:* 2671]

    Annales Association canadienne-française pour
l'**avancement** des **sciences.** *See* 2658.

2673 **Annales** de l'**Association** des **ingénieurs** sortis des
écoles de **Gand.** Gand. *Annls Ass. Ingrs Éc. Gand*
[1876–56] **L.**P. 26–56; **E.**L.; T. 83–01: 24–30. [*Suspended*
1941–45; *C. as:* 47096]

2674 **Annales. Association** des **ingénieurs** et des
techniciens de l'**industrie minière** de **Roumanie.**
Annls Ass. Ingrs Techns Ind. min. Roum.

2675 **Annales. Association internationale** pour le
calcul analogique. Bruxelles. *Annls Ass. int. Calcul
analog.* [1958–] **L.**P.; **G.**U.

2676 **Annales** de l'**Association** des **naturalistes** de
Levallois-Perret. *Annls Ass. Nat. Levallois-Perret*
[1894–36] **L.**BM^N.; E. 99–31; GL. 13–31; Z. 06–36.

    Annales astronomiques. Observatoire de **Zi-
ka-wei.** *See* 2859.

2677 **Annales** d'**astrophysique.** Paris. *Annls Astrophys.* [1938–] **L.**AS.; BM.; P. 51–; SC.; UC. 47–; **Bl.**U. 47–;
Br.U. 43–46; **C.**UL. 43–47; **E.**O.; **Ex.**U. 48–; **Ld.**U. 38:
47–; **M.**U. imp.; **O.**O.; R. 43–; **R.**U.; **Sa.**; **Sh.**U. 57–; **Y.**
[*Also supplements*]

2678 **Annales belges** de **médecine militaire.** Bruxelles. *Annls belg. Méd. milit.* [1948–54] **L.**MA.; MD.
[*C. of:* 4361; *C. as:* 502]

2679 **Annales belges** de **stomatologie.** Bruxelles.
Annls belg. Stomat. [1912–39] **L.**D. 30–39. [*C. in:*
4368]

2680 **Annales biologicae Universitatis budapestiensis.**
Budapest. *Annles biol. Univ. bpest.* [1950] **L.**BM.; BM^N.
[*C. in:* 2683]

2681 **Annales biologicae Universitatis debreceniensis.** Debrecen. *Annls biol. Univ. debrecen.* [1950]
L.BM.; BM^N. [*C. in:* 2683]

2682 **Annales biologicae Universitatis szegediensis.**
Szeged. *Annls biol. Univ. szeged.* [1950] **L.**BM.; BM^N.;
Y. [*C. in:* 2683]

2683 **Annales biologicae Universitatum hungariae.**
Budapest. *Annls biol. Univ. Hung.* [1952–54] **L.**BM.;
BM^N.; (K. pars Debrecin.); **C.**A.; **Rt.**; **Y.** [*C. of:* 2680,
2681 and 2682]

2684 **Annales** de **biologie.** Paris. *Annls Biol.* [1911]
C.UL.; **Lv.**U.

2685 **Annales** de **biologie animale, biochimie** et
biophysique. Paris. *Annls Biol. anim. Biochim. Biophys.* [1960–] **L.**BM.; **Abd.**R. 61–; **C.**A.; APH.; **W.**; **Y.**
[*Forms* Ser. E. bis *of:* 2785^c]

2686 **Annales** de **biologie appliquée.** Paris. *Annls
Biol. appl.* [1921–]

2687 **Annales** de **biologie clinique.** Paris. *Annls Biol. clin.* [1943–] **L.**MA. 45–; MD. 45–; TD. 46–.

2688 **Annales** de **biologie lacustre.** Bruxelles. *Annls Biol. lacustre* [1906–26] **L.**AM.; BMᴺ.; Z.; **C.**B. 13–26; **Db.**; **E.**R. 06–16; **Fr.**; **Ld.**U.; **Lo.**; **O.**R. [*C. as:* 42360]

2689 **Annales biologiques.** Conseil permanent international pour l'exploration de la mer. Copenhague. *Annls biol., Copenh.* [1939–] **L.**AM.; BM.; BMᴺ.; L. 48–; MO.; R.; UC.; Z.; **Abd.**M.; U. 46–; **Bm.**U.; **Bn.**U.; **C.**B.; **Dm.**; **E.**M.; R.; U.; **H.**U. 52–; **Lo.**; **Lv.**U.; **M.**U. imp.; **Mi.**; **O.**R.; **Pl.**M.; **Wo.** 43–; **Y.**

2690 **Annales bogoriensis.** Bogor. *Ann. bogor.* [1950–] **L.**BM.; BMᴺ.; K.; L.; SC.; UC.; **Bn.**U.; **C.**BO.; P.; UL.; **Db.**; **E.**B.; U.; **G.**U.; **Ld.**U.; **M.**U.; **Md.**H.; **O.**BO.; **Pl.**M.; **Y.** [*C. of:* 3135]

    Annales botanici Societatis zoologicae-botanicae fennicae Vanamo. *See* 51409.

2691 **Annales** de la **brasserie** et de la **distillerie.** Paris. *Annls Brass. Distill.* [1898–34] **L.**P.; **Bm.**U. 14–34; **Nu.**B. 32–33. [*C. as:* 2741]

2692 **Annales bryologici.** The Hague. *Annls bryol.* [1928–39] **L.**BM.; BMᴺ.; K.; L.; **Bm.**U. 28; **C.**BO.; UL.; **Cr.**M. 28–31; **E.**B.; **G.**U.; **Ld.**U.; **M.**U.; **O.**BO. [*C. in:* 2710]

    Annales et **bulletin. Société r.** des **sciences médicales** et **naturelles** de **Bruxelles.** *See* 2963.

2693 **Annales** du **Bureau central météorologique** de **France.** Paris. *Annls Bur. cent. mét. Fr.* [1877–20] **L.**BM. 86–15; MO.; R.; SC.; E.M.
    Annales du **Bureau** des **longitudes.** *See* 2694.

2694 **Annales** du **Bureau** des **longitudes** et de l'Observatoire astronomique de Montsouris. Paris. *Annls Bur. Longit.* [1877–] **L.**AS. 77–49; BM. imp.; MO. 49–; R. 77–03; SC. 83– imp.; **Br.**U. 77–82; **C.**O.; **E.**O.; R. 38–.

2695 **Annales** du **Centre** d'**études** et de **documentation paléontologiques.** Paris. *Annls Cent. Étud. Docum. paléont.* [1950–57] **L.**BMᴺ. 53–57; GM. 53–57. [*C. as:* 2919ᶜ]

2696 **Annales** de **chimie.** Paris. *Annls Chim.* [1914–] **L.**BM.; C.; MA. 54–; P.; PH. 47–; R.; RI.; SC.; U.; UC.; **Abd.**U.; **Bm.**U.; **Bn.**U. 39–; **Br.**P. 14–19; U.; **C.**CH. 14–38; P.; UL.; **Cr.**U.; **Db.**; **Dn.**U. 21– imp.; **E.**R.; U.; **Ex.**U. 47–; **F.**A. 46–; **G.**U.; **Ld.**U.; **Lv.**P. 56–; **M.**C. 20–27; D. 24–; U.; **Nw.**A.; **O.**BS. 14–34; R.; **Sa.**; **Y.** [*C. from:* 2698]

2697 **Annales** de **chimie analytique.** Paris. *Annls Chim. analyt.* [1896–46] **L.**C. 01–46; MT. 20–46 imp.; P. 10–46; PR. 34–40; SC. 31–46; **Db.** 44–46; **Nw.**A. 36–46. [*C. as:* 13909]

2698 **Annales** de **chimie** (*afterwards* et de **physique**). Paris. *Annls Chim. Phys.* [1789–13] **L.**BM.; BMᴺ. 1789–03; C.; GH. 1789–1817; IC. 11–13; MD.; P.; PH.; QM. 1816–89 imp.; R.; RI.; SC.; U.; UC. 1820–13 imp.; **Abd.**U.; **Bl.**U.; **Bm.**P. imp.; U.; **Bn.**U. 1789–93; **Br.**P. 09–13; U. 1789–1793; 1816; 1826–1837; 1840–13; **C.**CH.; P.; UL.; **Cr.**U.; **Db.**; **E.**A. 1789–06; R.; U.; **G.**F. 1789–1854; M. 1816–1827 imp.; U.; **Ld.**U.; **Lv.**M. 1789–62 imp.; U.; **M.**C. 20–27; U.; **Nw.**A.; **O.**BS.; R.; **Rt.** 1853–1858; **Sa.**; **Ste.** 11–13. [*C. as:* 2696 and 2892]

2699 **Annales chirurgiae** et **gynaecologiae Fenniae.** Helsinki. *Annls Chir. Gynaec. Fenn.* [1946–] **L.**BM 51–; MA.; MD.; S.; **Br.**U.; **E.**S. 55– imp.; U. 51–; **G.**F. 53–; [*C. from:* 767 Ser. B.; *Also supplements*]

2700 **Annales** de **chirurgie infantile.** Paris. *Annls Chir. infant.* [1960–] **L.**MD.

2701 **Annales** de **chirurgie plastique.** Paris. *Annls Chir. plast.* **L.**S. [*Issued in* 49484]

2702 **Annales climatologiques** de l'**Observatoire** de **Ksara.** Liban. *Annls climat. Obs. Ksara* [1957–] **L.**MO.; **Y.** [*C. of:* 2866 Ser. C]

2703 **Annales climatologiques. Service** météorologique du **Cameroun** sous tutelle française. Danala. *Annls climat. Serv. mét. Cameroun* **L.**MO. 52–.

2704 **Annales** de la **Clinique chirurgicale** du **Prof. Pierre Delbet.** Paris. *Annls Clin. chir. Delbet* **L.**BM. 13–.

2705 **Annales** de **clinique** et **radiodiagnostique.** Paris. *Annls Clin. Radiodiagn.* [*Published in:* 49484]

2706 **Annales. Collège internationale** pour l'**étude scientifique** des **techniques** de **production mécanique.** *Annls Coll. int. Étude scient. Tech. Prod. méc.* [1953–] **L.**P.; SC. 54–.

2707 **Annales** de la **Commission** pour l'**étude** des **raz** de **marée.** Union géodesique et géophysique internationale. Paris. *Annls Commn Étud. Raz Marée* **Lv.**U. 31–35.

2708 **Annales** de la **Commission internationale** d'**agriculture.** Paris. *Annls Commn int. Agric.* [1927–37] [*C. as:* 2709]

2709 **Annales** de la **Confédération internationale** de l'**agriculture.** Paris. *Annls Conféd. int. Agric.* [1937–] [*C. of:* 2708]

2710 **Annales cryptogamici** et **phytopathologici.** Waltham, Mass. *Annls cryptog. phytopath.* [1944–] **L.**BM.; BMᴺ.; K.; **Bn.**U.; **C.**UL.; **E.**B.; **G.**U. 44–54; **Ld.**U.; **O.**BO.; **Rt.**; **Y.**

2711 **Annales** de **cryptogamie exotique.** Paris. *Annls Cryptog. exot.* [1928–35] **L.**BMᴺ.; K.; MY. [*C. as:* 47459]

2712 **Annales** de **dermatologie** et de **syphiligraphie.** Paris. *Annls Derm. Syph.* [1868–] **L.**MA. 80– imp.; MD.; S. 68–49: 53; UCH. 89– imp.; **Br.**U. 94–15 imp.; **Db.** 48–49; **Dn.**U. 20– v. imp.; **E.**P.; S. 90–22; **G.**U. 52–; **Ld.**U. 85–; **Lv.**M. 90–21 imp.: 53–56; **M.**MS. 19–33; **Nw.**A. 29–36.

2713 **Annales** de la **Direction générale** des **eaux** et **forêts.** Paris. *Annls Dir. gén. Eaux Forêts* [1912–] **L.**AM. 34–37; P. 20–37. [*C. of:* 2714]

2713ᶜ **Annales. Direction générale** du **génie rural** et de l'**hydraulique agricole.** Paris. *Annls Dir. gén. Génie rur.* **L.**BM. 50–.

2714 **Annales. Direction** de l'**hydraulique** et des **améliorations agricoles.** Paris. *Annls Dir. Hydraul. Amélior. agric.* [1903–11] **L.**P. [*C. of:* 10086; *C. as:* 2713]

2715 **Annales** de l'**École nationale** d'**agriculture** d'**Alger.** Alger. *Annls Éc. natn. Agric. Alger* [1958–] **L.**AM.; EB.; **Br.**A.; **Hu.**G.; **Md.**H.; **Y.** [*C. of:* 2770]

2716 **Annales** de l'**École nationale** d'**agriculture** de **Grignon.** Paris. *Annls Éc. natn. Agric. Grignon* [1910–] **L.**AM. 10–39 imp.; P. 10–16; **Br.**A. 20–39; **C.**A. 37–48; UL. 20–; **Rt.**

2717 **Annales** de l'**École nationale** d'**agriculture** de **Montpellier.** Montpellier. *Annls Éc. natn. Agric. Montpellier* [1884–] **L.**AM. 84–06; BM.; EB. 13–; MY.; **C.**A. 30–; **Dn.**U. 85–89; **Md.**H. 39–; **Rt.** 33–39.

2718 **Annales** de l'**École nationale** d'**agriculture** de **Rennes.** Rennes. *Annls Éc. natn. Agric. Rennes* [1907–] L.AM. 53–; EB. 13; MY. 07–09; **Br.**A. 50–; **C.**A. 51–.

2719 **Annales** de l'**École nationale** des **eaux** et **forêts** et de la **station** de **recherches** et **expériences forestières.** Nancy. *Annls Éc. natn. Eaux Forêts, Nancy* [1923–] L.K.; P.; **Abd.**S.; **Bn.**U.; **C.**UL.; **E.**U.; **Fr.** 35–; **O.**F.; **Y.**

2720 **Annales** de l'**École nationale supérieure agronomique.** Toulouse. *Annls Éc. natn. sup. agron., Toulouse* [1953–] L.AM.; BM[N]. 57–; K. 57–; **C.**A.; **N.**U. 54–.

2721 **Annales** de l'**École** de **plein exercise** de **médecine** et de **pharmacie** de **Marseille.** *Annls Éc. plein Exerc. Méd. Pharm. Marseille* **M.**MS. 93–12.

Annales de l'**École polytechnique** de **Budapest.** *See* 33779.

Annales de l'**École royale supérieure** d'**agriculture** de la **Suède.** *See* 27806.

2723 **Annales** de l'**École supérieure** de **médecine** et de **pharmacie** de l'**Indochine.** Hanoi. *Annls Éc. sup. Méd. Pharm. Indochine* [1935–] L.TD. 35–39.

Annales de l'**École supérieure** des **mines** de l'**Oural.** *See* 24538.

2724 **Annales** de l'**École supérieure** des **sciences.** Dakar. *Annls Éc. sup. Sci., Dakar* [1954–57] L.BM[N].; **C.**P.; **Dm.**; **Pl.**M. 57–; **Rt.**; **Y.** [*C. as:* 2737]

Annales d'**électrobiologie** et de **radiologie.** *See* 2725.

Annales d'**électro-homéopathie** et d'**hygiène.** *See* 2640.

2725 **Annales** d'**électrothérapie** et d'**électrodiagnostique.** Paris. *Annls Électrothér. Électrodiagn.* [1898–14] L.MD. 02–14; UC. 01–03 imp.

2726 **Annales** d'**endocrinologie.** Paris. *Annls Endocr.* [1939–] L.C. 46–; MA.; MC. 39: 44–54: 58–; MD.; SC. 47–; **Bm.**U.; **C.**A.; **E.**U.; **O.**R. 49–; **R.**D. 47–; **Y.**

2727 **Annales** de l'**énergie.** Grenoble. *Annls Énerg., Grenoble* [1928–] L.P. 28–31. [*C. from:* 2729]

2728 **Annales** de l'**énergie.** Lyon. *Annls Énerg., Lyon* [1921–24] L.BM.; P. [*C. in:* 1833]

2729 **Annales** de l'**énergie** et les **Alpes industrielles.** Grenoble. *Annls Énerg. Alpes ind.* L.P. 25–27★. [*C. of:* 8333; *C. as:* 1832 and 2727]

2730 **Annales** de l'**enfance.** Paris. *Annls Enfance* [1926–34]

Annales entomologici fennici. *See* 51423.

2731 **Annales entomologici sinici.** Peking. *Annls ent. sin.* [1950–52] L.BM[N]. 51–52; E. 50–51. [*C. as:* 564]

2732 **Annales** des **épiphyties.** Paris. *Annls Épiphyt.* [1920–] L.AM.; BM.; BM[N].; EB.; HS. 52–; IC. 47–; K.; L. 34–; MY. 34–38: 50–; P. 58–; Z. 50–; **Abs.**U. 50–; **Br.**A. 34– imp.; **C.**A. 34–; BO. 34–38; MO. 34–38; **E.**W. 45– imp.; **Hu.**G. 35–46: 50–; **Md.**H. 21– imp.; **O.**AP. 34–47; R. 34–37; **R.**U. 20–36; **Y.** [*C. of:* 2918: *The new series, 1950– forms series C of:* 2785[c]]

Annales des **épiphyties** et de **phytogénétique.** Paris. *See* 2732.

Annales d'**essais** de **semences.** Leningrad. *See* 58337.

Annales pro **experimentis foresticis.** Zagreb. *See* 21358.

Annales Facultatis agronomicae Universitatis agriculturae. Budapest. *See* 1217[a].

Annales Facultatis disciplinae silvaticae Universitatis agriculturae. Sopron. *See* 1214.

Annales de la **Faculté agronomique** de **Cluj.** *See* 2283.

Annales de la **Faculté forestière.** Beograd. *See* 21357.

2735 **Annales** de la **Faculté française** de **médecine** et de **pharmacie** de **Beyrouth.** Beyrouth. *Annls Fac. fr. Méd. Pharm. Beyrouth* [1932–]

2736 **Annales** de la **Faculté** des **sciences** de **Marseille.** Marseille. *Annls Fac. Sci. Marseille* [1891–] L.BM.; BM[N].; K. (bot.); L.; M.; P. 56–; R.; SC. 91: 35–; UC.; **Bl.**U. 91–09; **Bm.**N. 07–09; U. 91–05; **C.**P.; **Db.**; **E.**B.; Q.; R.; **Ld.**U. 47–; **Lv.**U. imp.; **M.**U. 01–36 imp.; **Y.**

2737 **Annales** de la **Faculté** des **sciences, Université** de **Dakar.** Dakar. *Annls Fac. Sci. Univ. Dakar* [1959–] L.BM[N].; TD.; **C.**P.; **Dm.** 59; **Pl.**M.; **Rt.**; **Y.** [*C. of:* 2724]

2738 **Annales** de la **Faculté** des **sciences** de l'**Université** de **Toulouse** pour les **sciences mathématiques** et **physiques.** Paris. *Annls Fac. Sci. Univ. Toulouse* [1887–] L.M.; R.; UC.; **Abs.**N. 19–; U. 87–35; **C.**P.; UL.; **Db.** 05–; **E.**Q. 09–; R.; **Ex.**U. 01–39; **G.**U. 56–; **O.**R.; **Sw.**U. 24–25; **Y.**

Annales des **falsifications.** *See* 2740.

2739 **Annales** des **falsifications** et de l'**expertise chimique.** Paris. *Annls Falsif. Expert. chim.* [1960–] L.AM.; BM.; C.; P.; **Lh.**FO.; **R.**D.; **Y.** [*C. of:* 2740]

2740 **Annales** des **falsifications** et des **fraudes.** Paris. *Annls Falsif. Fraudes* [1908–59] L.AM. 52–59; BM. 52–59; C. imp.; H. 08–19: 33–40; P.; **Lh.**FO. 52–59; **R.**D. 17–25: 51–59; **Y.** [*C. of:* 47331; *C. as:* 2739]

2741 **Annales** des **fermentations.** Paris. *Annls Ferment.* [1935–] L.P. 35–43; **Bm.**U. 35–43; **C.**BI. 35–42; **Ep.**D. 35–42; **Nu.**B. 35–38. [*C. of:* 2691]

2742 **Annales françaises** de **chronométrie.** Besançon. *Annls fr. Chronom.* [1931–] L.AS.; BM.; DI. 47–; P. 33–; SC.; **Db.** 49–; **E.**O.; R. 31; **O.**R. 40–; **Y.** [*C. of:* 9793]

Annales françaises de **chronométrie: documentation.** *See* 12458.

2743 **Annales** de **Gembloux.** Bruxelles. *Annls Gembloux* [1905–] L.A. 48– imp.; AM.; EB. 19–33; MY. 52–56 imp.; **Ba.**I. 46–; **C.**A. 36–; UL. 36–; **Db.** 10–; **Hu.**G. 48–; **Md.**H. 46–; **Rt.** 46–; **Y.** [*C. of:* 23605]

2744 **Annales** de **génétique.** Paris. *Annls Génét.* [1958–] **C.**A.; GE.; **E.**AG.; U.; **Y.**

2745 **Annales** du **génie chimique.** Toulouse. *Annls Génie chim.* [1957–] L.P.; SC.; **G.**T.; **Wd.**

2746 **Annales** de **géographie.** Paris. *Annls Géogr.* [1891–] L.B. 22– imp.; BM.; G.; NC. 56–; QM. 27– imp.; SC. 91–40: 46–; U. 99–; UC. 28–41: 46–; Z. 91–03; **Abd.**U. 32–; **Abs.**U. 15– imp.; **Bl.**U. 21–22: 57–; **Bm.**U.; **Br.**U.; **C.**GG. 27–; PO. 41–; **Ex.**U. imp.; **G.**M. 00–; U.; **Db.**; **Dn.**U. 35–; **E.**G.; U. 08– imp.; **Ex.**U. imp.; **G.**M. 00–40: 47–; U.; **H.**U. 28–; **Ld.**U.; **Lv.**P. 48–; U. 12–; **N.**U. 00–; **Nw.**A. 29–; **O.**B.; G.; **R.**U.; **Rt.** 47–; **Sa.** 35–; **Sh.**U. 10–39: 46–; **Sw.**U 32–; **Y.**

2747 **Annales** de **géologie** et de **paléontologie.** Palerme, Turin. *Annls Géol. Paléont.* [1886–30] L.BM. 86–18; BM[N].; GL. 00–30; GM.; SC.; **C.**S.; **E.**U.

2748 **Annales géologiques** de **Madagascar.** Tananarive. *Annls géol. Madagascar* [1958–] L.BM.; BM[N].; GL.; MI.; **Y.** [*C. of:* 2750]

2749 **Annales géologiques** des **pays helléniques.**
Athènes. *Annls géol. Pays hell.* **L.**BM. 57–; BM^N. 47–;
Ld.U. 57–; **Y.**
　Annales géologiques de la **Péninsule balkanique.**
See 21061.

2750 **Annales géologiques** du **Service** des **mines,
Madagascar.** Tananarive. *Annls géol. Serv. Mines
Madagascar* [1931–57] **L.**BM. 49–57; BM^N.; GL.; MI. 48–
57; **Y.** [*C. as:* 2748]
　Annales de **géomorphologie.** *See* 58602.

2751 **Annales** de **géophysique.** Paris. *Annls Géophys.*
[1944–] **L.**AS.; BM. 54–; GM. 56–; MO.; P.; SC.; SI. 47–;
UC. 47–; **Bl.**U.; **C.**GD.; **Db.**; **Lv.**U.; **Nw.**A.; **O.**R.; **R.**U.;
Sh.U. 57–; **Y.**
　Annales de **glaciologie.** *See* 58643.

2752 **Annales** de **Grignon.** Châteauroux. *Annls Grignon* **L.**AM. 01–05.
　Annales Guébhard. *See* 2753.

2753 **Annales Guébhard-Séverine.** Neuchâtel. *Annls
Guébhard-Séverine* [1930–] **L.**BM^N.; GL.; GM.; P.; **Bn.**U.
34–; **Db.**; **Ex.**U. 30–54; **Lv.**U.; **M.**C. 51–53; U. 30–37:
44–; **Y.** [*C. of:* 2780]

2754 **Annales** de **gynécologie** et d'**obstétrique.** Paris.
Annls Gynéc. Obstét. [1874–19] **L.**MD.; S. 88–19; UCH. 99–
13; E.P. 79–19; U. 79–19; **G.**F. 04–08: 12–15; **Ld.**U.
92–15; **Lv.**U. 09–12; **M.**MS. 85–18. [*C. in:* 21683]

2755 **Annales Hébert.** Paris. *Annls Hébert* [1892–12]
L.BM^N.; **C.**S. 92–06. [*Replaced by* 2756]

2756 **Annales Hébert** et **Haug.** Paris. *Annls Hébert
Haug* [1949–] **L.**BM^N.; **C.**S. 49–52. [*Replaces* 2755]

2757 **Annales** d'**histochimie.** Nancy. *Annls Histochim.* [1956–] **L.**MA.; MD.; SC.; **Ld.**U.; **O.**R.; **Y.**

2758 **Annales** d'**histoire naturelle** de l'**Aisne.** Saint-
Quentin. *Annls Hist. nat. Aisne* **L.**BM^N. 47–48.

2759 **Annales** d'**histoire naturelle. Délégation** en
Perse. Paris. *Annls Hist. nat. Délég. Perse* [1908–13]
L.BM.; BM^N.; **C.**UL.; **G.**U. 08–11.

2760 **Annales historico-naturales Musei nationalis
hungarici.** Budapest. *Annls hist.-nat. Mus. natn. hung.*
[1903–] **L.**BM.; BM^N.; E.; EB.; GL. 35–; L.; SC.; Z.; **Abs.**U.
49–57; **C.**P.; UL.; **Dm.** 13–; **E.**B. 35–; D. 14–19; J. 03–12;
Ld.U. 29–; **Lv.**U. 06–; **Y.** [*C. of:* 52870]

2761 **Annales homéopathiques** de l'**Hôpital Saint-
Jacques.** Paris. *Annls homéop. Hôp. St-Jacques*
　Annales d'**hydrographie.** St. Pétersbourg. *See*
58286.

2762 **Annales hydrographiques.** Paris. *Annls hydrogr.* [1848–] **L.**BM.; G.; GL. 00–; MO. 62–; R. 1849–91; SC.
17–; **C.**P. 34–; UL. 15–; E.R. 40–; **Lv.**U. 18–21 imp.;
O.B. 92– imp.; **Wl.**H. 18–54; **Wo.** 52–; **Y.**

2763 **Annales** d'**hydrologie** et de **climatologie médicales.** Paris. *Annls Hydrol. Clim. méd.* [1854–95: 05–22]
L.MD. 10–22; S. 74–77. [*C. as:* 2948]

2764 **Annales** d'**hygiène** et de **médecine coloniales.**
Paris. *Annls Hyg. Méd. colon.* [1898–14] **L.**EB. 13–14;
H. 98–13; MD. 06; TD.; E.U. 02–14; **Lv.**U. 11–14. [*C. as:*
2819]

2765 **Annales** d'**hygiène pratique.** Etampes. *Annls
Hyg. prat.*

2766 **Annales** d'**hygiène publique.** Tokyo. *Annls Hyg.
publ., Tokyo*

2767 **Annales** d'**hygiène publique, industrielle** et
sociale. Paris. *Annls Hyg. publ. ind. soc.* [1923–51]
L.BM.; H.; MA. 24–51; MD.; S. 23–39; SH. 29–51; TD.;
Abd.U.; **C.**UL.; E.P.; R. imp.; U.; **G.**F. 23–26; **Lv.**M.
23–27: **O.**R. [*C. of:* 2768]

2768 **Annales** d'**hygiène publique** et de **médecine
légale.** *Annls Hyg. publ. Méd. lég.* [1829–22] **L.**BM.; H.;
MD.; P. 10–22; S.; **Abd.**U.; **Br.**U. 1829–1854; **C.**UL.;
Db. 1829–90 imp.; E.P.; R. 1837–22 imp.; S. 93–19 imp.;
U.; **G.**F.; U. 1829–64; **Lv.**M. imp.; **M.**MS. 1852–19; **O.**R.
[*C. as:* 2767]

2769 **Annales** de l'**Institut** d'**actinologie.** Paris. *Annls
Inst. Actinol., Paris* [1926–]

2770 **Annales** de l'**Institut agricole** et des **services** de
recherches d'**experimentation agricole** de l'**Algérie.**
Alger. *Annls Inst. agric. Algér.* [1939–57] **L.**AN. imp.;
EB.; **Br.**A. 46–57; **C.**A.; **Hu.**G. 49–57; **Md.**H.; **Rt.**; **Sil.**
39–53; **Y.** [*C. as:* 2715]
　Annales de l'**Institut agronomique** de **Moscou.**
See 24428.
　Annales de l'**Institut** d'**analyse physico-chimique.**
Petrograd. *See* 24387.

2772 **Annales** de l'**Institut central ampélologique
r. hongrois.** Budapest. *Annls. Inst. cent. ampélol. r.
hong.* [1900–14] **L.**AM. 01–05; BM.; K. 05–13; MY. 02: 03:
13; **C.**UL.
　Annales de l'**Institut central** de **météorologie.**
Budapest. *See:* 36415^a.

2774 **Annales** de l'**Institut chirurgical** de **Bruxelles.**
Bruxelles. *Annls Inst. chir. Brux.*

2775 **Annales** de l'**Institut colonial** de **Marseille.**
Paris. *Annls Inst. colon. Marseille* [1893–06] **L.**BM.;
BM^N.; K. [*C. as:* 2843]
　Annales de l'**Institut** d'**essais** de **semences** au
Jardin impérial botanique de **Pierre le Grand.**
See 58340.

2776 **Annales** de l'**Institut** d'**études maritimes** de **Belgique.** Bruxelles, etc. *Annls Inst. Étud. marit. Belg.*
[1931–47] **L.**AM.; **Dm.** 31–35; **Lo.** [*C. as:* 30733]

2777 **Annales** de l'**Institut expérimental** du **tabac** de
Bergerac. Paris. *Annls Inst. exp. Tab. Bergerac*
[1950–] **L.**P.; **C.**A.; **Md.**H. 52–; **Rt.**; **Y.** [*C. of:* 31130]
　Annales de l'**Institut fédéral** de **recherches
forestières.** Zürich. *See* 32724.

2778 **Annales** de l'**Institut Fourier.** Université de
Grenoble, etc. *Annls Inst. Fourier Univ. Grenoble*
[1949–] **L.**M.; SC.; U.; **Bl.**U.; **C.**P.; UL.; **Db.**; E.R.; **Ld.**U.;
M.U. 52–; **Nw.**A. 52–; **Y.** [*C. from:* 2993]

2779 **Annales. Institut** des **fruits** et **agrumes coloniaux.** Paris. *Annls Inst. Fruits Agrumes colon.*
[1951–] **Rt.** 53– imp.

2780 **Annales** de l'**Institut** de **géophysique** et **sciences
diverses.** Fondation Guébhard-Séverine. Neuchâtel.
Annls Inst. Géophys. Fond. Guébhard-Séverine [1924–29]
L.BM^N.; GL. 25–29; GM.; **Db.**; **Lv.**U. 27–29; **M.**U.; **Sa.**
imp.; **Y.** [*C. as:* 2753]

2781 **Annales** de l'**Institut Henri Poincaré.** Paris.
Annls Inst. Henri Poincaré [1930–] **L.**BM.; M. 31–; P. 51–;
SC. 31–37: 46–; U. 56–; UC. imp.; **Br.**U.; **C.**P.; **Db.**; E.R.;
G.U. imp.; **M.**U. 46–; **O.**R.; **Y.**

2782 **Annales** de l'**Institut** d'**hydrologie** et de **climatologie.** Paris. *Annls Inst. Hydrol. Clim., Paris* [1923–] **L.**BM.; MD. 25–34; MO. 50–56; **C.**UL.; **O.**R.; **Y.**

Annales de l'**Institut industriel** du **Caucase** du **nord** à Novotcherkassk. *See* 24496.

Annales de l'**Institut industriel** de **Novotcherkassk** du nom **Serge Ordzhonikidze.** *See* 24442.

Annales de l'**Institut** de **laiterie** de **Vologda.** *See* 55140.

2783 **Annales** de l'**Institut** de **médecine légale** de l'**Université** de **Lyon.** Lyon. *Annls Inst. Méd. lég. Univ. Lyon* [1913–]

Annales de l'**Institut météorologique hongrois.** *See* 36415ᵃ.

Annales de l'**Institut** des **mines** de l'**Impératrice Cathérine II** à **St. Pétersbourg.** *See* 58287.

Annales de l'**Institut** des **mines** à **Léningrad.** *See* 58287.

Annales de l'**Institut** des **mines** à **Petrograd.** *See* 58331.

2785 **Annales** de l'**Institut national agronomique.** Paris. *Annls Inst. natn. agron., Paris* [1876–] **L.**AM. 77– imp.; BM.; **Br.**A. 49–; **C.**A. 37–; **Db.** 09–; **Hu.**G.; **Ld.**U. 76–13; **Md.**H. 47–; **Rt.**; **Y.**

2785ᶜ **Annales** de l'**Institut national** de la **recherche agronomique.** Paris. *Annls Inst. natn. Rech. agron., Paris*

Sér. A. Annales agronomiques [1950–] *See* 2668.

Sér. A bis. Annales de physiologie végétale [1959–] *See* 2891.

Sér. B. Annales de l'amélioration des plantes [1951–] *See* 2669.

Sér. C. Annales des épiphyties [1950–] *See* 2732.

Sér. C bis. Annales de l'abeille [1958–] *See* 2659.

Sér. D. Annales de zootechnie [1952–] *See* 2998.

Sér. E. Annales de technologie agricole [1952–] *See* 2981.

Sér. E bis. Annales de biologie animale, biochemie et biophysique. *See* 2685.

Annales de l'**Institut national zootechnique** de **Roumanie.** *See* 2291.

2786 **Annales** de l'**Institut océanographique.** Monaco, Paris. *Annls Inst. océanogr., Monaco* [1909–] **L.**BMᴺ.; G. 10–; SC. 24–; Z. 48–; **Abd.**M. 24–40 imp.; **Bn.**U. 31– imp.; **C.**B. 09–14; **Db.**; **E.**R.; **Lo.** 24– imp.; **Lv.**U.; **M.**U. 09–17: 24–; **Mi.**; **Pl.**M.; **Wo.** 58–.

2787 **Annales** de l'**Institut Pasteur.** Paris. *Annls Inst. Pasteur, Paris* [1887–] **L.**BM.; BMᴺ. 87–94: 31–; C.; CB.; EB. 13–39; H. 87–40: 50–; IC. 87–30: 47–; LI.; MA.; MC. imp.; MD.; P.; PH. 87–08; R.; RI.; S.; SC. 92–; TD.; U. 50–; UC. 94–96; UCH. 03–; V. imp.; **Abd.**U.; **Abs.**N. 14–; **Bl.**U.; **Bm.**U. 94–; **Br.**U. 93–; **C.**MO. 87–14; P. 07–; PA.; PH. 02–12; UL.; V. 24–; **Cr.**MD. 97– imp.; **Db.** imp.; **Dn.**U. 87–57; **E.**B. 87–05; N. 17– imp.; P.; U.; **G.**F. 92–35 imp.; T. 53–; U.; **Ld.**U. 97–; **Lv.**U.; **M.**MS.; U. 51–57; **Nw.**A. 07–; **O.**P. 28–; PH. 28–; R.; **Pl.**M. 21–; **R.**D. 06–; U. 47–; **Rt.**; **Sh.**U. 92–; **Ste.** 87–30 imp.; **W.** 14–; **Y.**

2788 **Annales** de l'**Institut Pasteur** de **Lille.** *Annls Inst. Pasteur Lille* [1948–] **L.**MC.; MD.; P.; TD.; **Y.**

Annales de l'**Institut** de **pathologie** et de **bactériologie** de **Bucarest.** *See* 2292.

2789 **Annales** de l'**Institut** de **physique** du **globe** de l'**Université** de **Paris.** *Annls Inst. Phys. Globe Univ. Paris* [1922–] **L.**BM.; MO. 23–; P. 29–; R.; U.; **C.**UL.; **Db.**; **E.**M.; U.; **G.**U.; **M.**U. 22–49; **O.**R. [*C. from:* 2693]

2790 **Annales** de l'**Institut** de **physique** du **globe** de l'**Université** de **Strasbourg.** *Annls Inst. Phys. Globe Univ. Strasb.*

(1) Météorologie [1936–] **L.**MO.; SC. 36–40: 46–; **O.**G. 36–37. [*Replaces:* 3270]

(2) Séismologie [1936–] **L.**AS. 36–; SC. 39–. [*Replaces:* 3270]

(3) Géophysique [1936–] **L.**AS.; P. 37–; SC.; **C.**GD. 40–.

2791 **Annales** de l'**Institut phytopathologique Benaki.** Athènes. *Annls Inst. phytopath. Benaki* [1935–] **L.**AM. 39– imp.; BM. 51; BMᴺ. 35–51 imp.; EB.; K. 35–52 imp.; **Br.**A.; **C.**A.; BO. 54–; **Md.**H.; **Rt.** imp.; **Y.**

Annales de l'**Institut** de **platine.** Léningrad. *See* 24383.

Annales de l'**Institut polytechnique** du **Don** du **Césarévitch Alexis** à **Novotcherkassk.** *See* 24300.

Annales de l'**Institut polytechnique** de l'**Empereur Alexandre II** à **Kiev.** *See* 24408.

2792 **Annales** de l'**Institut polytechnique** de **Grenoble.** Grenoble. *Annls Inst. polytech. Grenoble* [1952–54] **L.**P. imp.

Annales de l'**Institut polytechnique** au **nom** de **M. J. Kalinin.** Léningrad. *See* 24419.

Annales de l'**Institut polytechnique** à **Novotcherkassk.** *See* 24328.

Annales de l'**Institut polytechnique** de l'**Oural.** *See* 24537.

Annales de l'**Institut polytechnique Pierre** le **Grand** à **St. Pétersbourg.** *See* 24486.

Annales de l'**Institut polytechnique Pierre** le **Grand** à **St. Pétersbourg. Section technique.** *See* 24485.

2793 **Annales** de l'**Institut r. météorologique** de **Belgique.** Bruxelles. *Annls Inst. r. mét. Belg.* **L.**BM. 19.

Annales de l'**Institut** de **recherches agronomique** de **Roumanie.** *See* 2286.

Annales. Institut de **recherches forestières** de **Serbie.** *See* 41886.

2794 **Annales** de l'**Institut scientifique chérifien.** Casablanca. *Annls Inst. scient. chérif.* **L.**MO. 34–. [*C. from:* 30856]

2795 **Annales** de l'**Institut technique** du **bâtiment** et des **travaux publics.** Paris. *Annls Inst. tech. Bâtim.* [1936–] **L.**BA.; P. 36–40: 48–; PR. 36–40; **C.**ENG. 56–; **Y.**

2796 **Annales Instituti agrorum culturae experiendae, Debrecen.** Budapest. *Annls Inst. Agrorum Cult. exp. Debrecen* [1950–] **C.**A.

2797 **Annales Instituti biologiae pervestigandae hungarici.** Tihany. *Annls Inst. Biol. pervest. hung.* [1949] **L.**BMᴺ.; LI.; Z.; **C.**A.; **E.**R.; **O.**AP.; **Y.** [*C. of:* 4184; *C. as:* 2798]

2798 **Annales Instituti biologici, Tihany, Hungaricae academiae scientiarum.** Tihany. *Annls Inst. biol. Tihany* [1950–] **L.**BMᴺ.; L.; LI.; MC.; Z.; **C.**A.; **E.**R.; **Fr.**; **O.**AP.; **Pl.**M.; **Y.** [*C. of:* 2797]

2799 **Annales Instituti geologici publici hungarici.** *Annls Inst. geol. publ. hung.* **L.**P.; **Y.**

Annales Instituti ad **investigandum agrochemicam.** *See* 1468.

2800 **Annales Instituti** ad **investigandum irrigationis** et **emendationis soli.** Budapest. *Annls Inst. Invest. Irrig. Emend. Soli, Bpest* [1950–] **C.**A.

2801 **Annales Instituti** ad **investigandum pecuariae.** Budapest. *Annls Inst. Invest. Pecuar., Bpest* [1950–] **C.**A.

2802 **Annales Instituti obstetrici** et **gynecologici Universitatis helsingiensis.** Helsinki. *Annls Inst. obstet. gynec. Univ. helsing.* [1925–] **L.**MA. 42–; MD. 30.

2803 **Annales Instituti pathologico-anatomici Universitatis helsingiensis.** Helsinki. *Annls Inst. path.-anat. Univ. helsing.* **L.**MA. 42–; UCH. 46–52; **C.**PA. 46–52.
    Annales Instituti protectionis plantarum hungarici. *See* 35384ª.
    Annales Instituti r. hungarici geologici. *See* 24857 and 32534.

2804 **Annales Instituti terrae frugibus procreandis Martonvásár.** Budapest. *Annls Inst. Terrae Frug. procr. Martonvásár* [1950–] **C.**A.

2805 **Annales internationales** de **chirurgie gastro-intestinale.** Le Mans. *Annls int. Chir. gastro-intest.* **Br.**U. 13–14.

2806 **Annales internationales** de **médecine physique** et de **physio-biologie.** Anvers. *Annls int. Méd. phys. Physio-Biol.* [1937–38] **L.**MD.; S. [*C. of: and Rec. as:* 2821]

2807 **Annales** du **Jardin botanique** de **Buitenzorg.** *Annls Jard. bot. Buitenz.* [1876–40] **L.**BM. 76–20; BMᴺ.; K.; L.; R. 82–24; SC.; UC.; **Abd.**U. 76–32; **Bn.**U.; **Br.**U. 76–10; **C.**BO.; UL. 76–02: 25–40; **Db.**; **E.**B.; **G.**U.; **Ld.**U.; **Lv.**U. imp.; **M.**U.; **O.**BO. 85–40. [*C. as:* 3135]

2808 **Annales** du **Laboratoire** d'**études** de la **soie.** Lyon. *Annls Lab. Étud. Soie, Lyon*
    Annales du **Laboratoire** de **physiologie végétale** de l'**Université libre** de **Bruxelles.** *See* 2890.

2809 **Annales des laboratoires. Société** des **brevets lumière,** Laboratoires A. Lumière de physiologie expérimentale et de pharmacodynamie. Lyon. *Annls Labs Soc. Brev. Lum. Labs Lum. Physiol. exp.* **L.**MA. 37–38; MD. 24–.

2810 **Annales des maladies** de l'**oreille** et du **larynx.** Paris. *Annls Mal. Oreille Larynx* [1875–30] **L.**BM. 75–15; MD. 75–30; S. 75–30; **Abd.**U. 06–30 imp.; **Bm.**U. 01–08; **Cr.**MD. 03–13; **G.**F. 86–14 imp.; **M.**MS. 87–08. [*C. in:* 2879]

2811 **Annales** des **maladies** des **organes génito-urinaires.** Paris. *Annls Mal. Org. génito-urin.* [1883–11] **L.**MD.; S.; **Bm.**U. 97–00; **E.**S.; **G.**F. 03–05; **M.**MS. 88–11. [*C. as:* 27077]

2812 **Annales des maladies vénériennes.** Paris. *Annls Mal. vénér.* [1906–] **L.**MD.; S. 06–12. [*C. of:* 51692]

2813 **Annales** de **médecine.** Paris. *Annls Méd.* [1914–56] **L.**GH. 20–30; MA. 16–22: 29–31: 35–56; MC. 14–54 imp.; MD.; S. 14–51 imp.; **Abs.**U. 28–40; **Bl.**U. 20–35; **Bm.**U.; **Br.**U. 17–38 imp.; **C.**UL. 20–56; **Cr.**MD. 22–34; **Db.** 14–34 imp.; **Dn.**U.; **E.**P.; U. 20–56; **G.**U.; **Ld.**U.; **Lv.**M. 28–31; **M.**MS. 20–40 imp.; **Nw.**A. 21–40 imp.; **O.**R.

2814 **Annales** de **médecine** et de **chirurgie.** Paris. *Annls Méd. Chir.* [1927–] **L.**MD. 27–29.

2815 **Annales** de **médecine** et de **chirurgie infantiles.** Paris. *Annls Méd. Chir. infant.* [1897–14]

2816 **Annales** de **médecine** de **France,** des **colonies** et des **pays** de **protectorat.** Paris. *Annls Méd. Fr.*

2817 **Annales** de **médecine haïtienne.** Port-au-Prince. *Annls Méd. haïti.* [1923–]

2818 **Annales** de **médecine légale,** de **criminologie** et de **police scientifique.** Paris. *Annls Méd. lég. Crimin. Police scient.* [1921–] **L.**MA. 34–; MD.; **E.**U.

2819 **Annales** de **médicine** et de **pharmacie coloniales.** Paris. *Annls Méd. Pharm. colon.* [1920–39] **L.**EB.; MD. 37–38; TD.; **Lv.**U.; **Sal.** 28–39 imp. [*C. of:* 2764; *C. as:* 30013]

2820 **Annales** de **médecine physique.** Lille. *Annls Méd. phys.* [1958–] **L.**MD.

2821 **Annales** de **médecine physique** et de **physio-biologie.** Anvers. *Annls Méd. phys. Physiobiol.* [1907–] **L.**S. 33–39. [*C. of:* 2952; >2806, 1937–38]

2822 **Annales** de **médecine praticienne** et **sociale.** Paris. *Annls Méd. prat. soc.* [1947–56] **L.**MA.; MC. [*C. of:* 2824]

2823 **Annales** de **médecine pratique.** Marseille. *Annls Méd. prat.* [1914]

2824 **Annales** de **médecine sociale.** Lyon. *Annls Méd. soc.* [1941–] **L.**MA. 47–; MD.; TD. [*C. as:* 2822]

2825 **Annales** de **médecine thermale.** Vichy. *Annls Méd. therm.* [1888–]

2826 **Annales** de **médecine vétérinaire.** Bruxelles. *Annls Méd. vét.* [1852–] **L.**EB. 13–30; MD. 97–05; V. 65–14 imp: 19–; **W.** 05– imp.; **Y.**

2827 **Annales** des **médecins praticiens** de **Lyon** et du **Sud-Est.** Lyon. *Annls Méds Pratns Lyon*
    Annales médicales. Sofia. *See* 30537.

2828 **Annales médicales** et **bulletin** de **statistique** de l'**Hôpital** d'**enfants Hamidié.** Constantinople. *Annls méd. Bull. Statist. Hôp. Enfants Hamidié* [1903–]

2829 **Annales médicales** de **Vittel.** Vittel. *Annls méd. Vittel* [1930–]

2830 **Annales medicinae experimentalis** et **biologiae Fenniae.** Helsinki. *Annls Med. exp. Biol. Fenn.* [1947–] **L.**BM. 51–; GH.; LI. 48; MA.; MC.; MD.; S.; SC.; TD.; **Br.**U.; **E.**U.; **M.**MS. 56–; **Y.** [*C. of:* 767, Ser. A; *Also supplements*]

2831 **Annales medicinae internae Fenniae.** Helsinki. *Annls Med. intern. Fenn.* [1946–] **L.**H. 51–; MA.; S.; TD.; **Bl.**U. 59–; **Br.**U.; **E.**U. 50–; **G.**F. 51–; **Nw.**A.; **Y.** [*C. from:* 767, Ser. B; *Also supplements*]

2832 **Annales médico-chirurgicales.** Dour. *Annls méd.-chir., Dour*

2833 **Annales médico-chirurgicales.** Paris. *Annls méd.-chir., Paris* [1936–]

2834 **Annales médico-chirurgicales** du **centre.** Tours *Annls méd.-chir. Cent., Tours* [*C. of:* 53397]

2835 **Annales médico-chirurgicales** de l'**Hôpital Saint Justine** de **Montréal.** Montréal. *Annls méd.-chir. Hôp. St Justine Montréal* [1930–]

2836 **Annales médico-psychologiques.** Paris. *Annls méd.-psychol.* [1843–] **L.**BM.; MA. 46–; MD. 00–; PS. 21–; S. 1843–46; U. 50–; UC. 81–92; **Br.**U. 1844–48; **C.**UL. 1843–78; **E.**P.; U. 45–; **G.**F. 1843–11 imp.; U.; **Ld.**U. 61–; **M.**MS. 1843–19; **Y.**

2837 **Annales mensuelles. Société nantaise** des **amis** de l'**horticulture.** Nantes. *Annls mens. Soc. nant. Amis Hort.* [1914–24] **L.**HS. [*C. of:* 2902ᶜ; *C. as:* 11035]
    Annales de **Merck.** *See* 31358.

2837ª **Annales météorologiques** de l'Observatoire **r.** de **Belgique.** Uccle. *Annls mét. Obs. r. Belg.* [1867–09] **L.**MO. 76–09.
    Annales des **mines.** Paris. *See* 2839.

2838 **Annales** des **mines** de **Belgique.** Bruxelles. *Annls Mines Belg.* [1896–] **L.**I. imp.; MI.; 07–12 imp.: 52–54 imp.: 56–; MIE. 96–39: 48– imp.; P. 10–; SC.; **Cr.**U. 10– imp.; **G.**MG. 09– imp.; **M.**U. 06–25 imp.; **N.**P. 00–05 imp.; **Nw.**A. 53–; **Sh.**M. 06–38; S. 49–; SC. 07–36; **Ste.** 96: 12–; **Y.**

2839 **Annales** des **mines** et des **carburants.** Paris. *Annls Mines Carbur., Paris* [1794–] **L.**BM. 1816–; BMᴺ. 1794–12; GL. 00–; I. 63– imp.; MI. 09– imp.; MIE. 50–55 imp.: 56–; P. 1817–; PT. 43–46; SC. 1817–39: 47–; **Bl.**U. 1855–20; **Bm.**P. 1816–11; U. 1851– imp.; **C.**P. 1817–39: 47, UL. 1816–; **Cr.**P. 1794–1822 imp.; U. 64– imp.; **Db.**; E.R. imp.; U. 1794–66; **G.**U. 1816– imp.; **Ld.**U. 77–; **Lv.**U. 1794–1858; **M.**U. 1816– imp.; **N.**U. 56–; **Nw.**A. 1846–76; **O.**R. 1794–34; **Sh.**M. 81–97; S. 1859–67: 24–39: 47–; **Ste.** 32–39: 47–; **Y.**

2840 **Annales** des **mines** et de la **géologie.** Tunis. *Annls Mines Géol., Tunis* [1947–] **L.**MI. imp.; **Y.**

2841 **Annales** des **mines** de **Roumanie.** Bucarest. *Annls Mines Roum.* [1918–] **L.**BM. 20–; BMᴺ. 20–; PT. 24–31; **G.**MG. 20–21 imp.

2842 **Annales** du **Ministère** de l'**agriculture.** Paris. *Annls Minist. Agric., Paris* **L.**AM. 02– v. imp.; P. 02. [*C. of:* 11107]

2843 **Annales** du **Musée colonial** de Marseille. *Annls Mus. colon. Marseille* [1907–] **L.**BMᴺ. 07–54; K. 07–46; TP. 07: 09–52: 54; **Lv.**U. 07–10 imp.; **Md.**H. 30–38. [*C. of:* 2775]

2844 **Annales** du **Musée géologique** du **Boulonnais.** Boulogne-sur-mer. *Annls Mus. géol. Boulonnais* **L.**BMᴺ. 24–29.
    Annales du **Musée géologique Pierre le Grand.** *See* 54540.

2845 **Annales** du **Musée d'histoire naturelle** de **Marseille.** Marseille. *Annls Mus. Hist. nat. Marseille* [1882–] **L.**BM.; BMᴺ. 82–37; L. 82–40; R. 82–85; S. 84–99 imp.; SC. 82–12: UC. 82–99: 08; Z.; **Abd.**M. 82–99 imp.: 34; **Bm.**U. 00–37 v. imp.; **C.**B. 83–05; UL.; **Db.**; **G.**U. 98–40; **Lv.**U. imp.; **M.**U. 86–37; **O.**R.; **Pl.**M. 83–19; **Sa.** 82–24 imp.

2846 **Annales** du **Musée r.** de l'**Afrique central.** Série in 8vo. Tervuren. *Annls Mus. r. Afr. cent. Sér. 8vo.* [*C. of:* 2848 *which see for details of series issued*]

2847 **Annales** du **Musée r.** de l'**Afrique central.** Série in 4to. Tervuren. *Annls Mus. r. Afr. cent. Sér. 4to* [1960–] Zoologie. **L.**BMᴺ.; EB. (ent.); G.; L.; Z.; **Abd.**U.; **E.**F. imp.; G.; R.; **Lv.**U.; **O.**R.; **Y.** [*C. of:* 2849 *which see for other series issued*]

2848 **Annales** du **Musée r.** du **Congo belge.** Série in 8vo. Tervuren. *Annls Mus. r. Congo belge Sér. 8vo*
    Sciences géologiques [1948–] **L.**BM.; BMᴺ.; GL. imp.; **C.**S.; **Db.**; **E.**R.; **Y.**
    Sciences zoologiques [1948–] **L.**BM.; BMᴺ.; EB. (ent.); SC.; Z.; **Db.**; **E.**R.; **O.**H. 51–;.
    Sciences historiques et économiques [1947–] **L.**BM. 47–50; BMᴺ.; SC.; **Db.**
    Sciences de l'homme [1951–] **L.**BM.; BMᴺ.; SC.; **Db.**
    [*In* 1960 *the name of the Museum changed, see* 2846]

2849 **Annales** du **Musée r.** du **Congo belge.** Bruxelles, Série in 4to. Tervuren. *Annls Mus. r. Congo belge Sér. 4to*
    Minéralogie, géologie, paléontologie [1908–] **L.**BM.; BMᴺ.; G. 08–60; GL. 08–13; L.; **Abd.**U.; **C.**UL.; **E.**F. imp.; G.; R.; **M.**P. 08–39; **O.**R.; **Sa.** 08–32; **Y.**
    Botanique [1898–] **L.**BMᴺ 98–10; G. 03–; K. 98–13; L.; SC. 07–13; **Abd.**U.; **E.**F.; G.; R.; **O.**R.; **Sa.** 98–13 imp.
    Zoologie [1898–58] **L.**BMᴺ.; EB. 54–58; G. 03–58; L.; Z.; **Abd.**U.; **E.**F. imp.; G.; R.; **Lv.**U.; **M.**P. 98–39; **O.**H. 03–50 imp.; R. 03–58; **Pl.**M. 98–12; **Sa.** 98–55; **Y.**
    Anthropologie et ethnographie [1899–] **L.**AN.; BM. 99–08; BMᴺ. 99–47; G. 03–; **Abd.**U.; **E.**F. imp.; **G.**R.; **M.**P. 98–39; **Sa.** 99–39; **Y.**
    Le pays et ses habitants; documents historiques [1903–] **L.**BMᴺ. 03–04; G.; **Abd.**U.; **E.**F. imp.; Q.; R.
    Miscellanées [1924–] **L.**BM.; G.; L.; **Abd.**U.; **E.**F.; G.; R.
    Nouvelle série. Sciences de l'homme [1951–] **L.**BMᴺ.; **Abd.**U.; **E.**F.; G.; R.
    [*In* 1960 *the name of the Museum changed, see* 2847]
    Annales du **Musée zoologique.** Académie impériale des sciences. St. Pétersbourg. *See* 18893.
    Annales des **musées tchéco-slovaques.** *See* 13617.

2850 **Annales Musei Serbiae meridionalis.** Skopje. *Annls Musei Serb. merid.* [1939–] **L.**BMᴺ.; **Ld.**U. 39; **Pl.**M. 39. [*C. as:* 670]

2851 **Annales Musei zoologici polonici.** Warszawa. *Annls Mus. zool. pol.* [1930–53] **L.**AM. 47–53; BM.; BMᴺ.; E.; EB.; L.; SC.; U. 39–53; UC. 34–37; Z.; **C.**P.; **Cr.**M.; **Db.**; **Dm.**; E.F.; R.; **Fr.** 33–53; **G.**N. 34–53; **Ld.**U. imp.; **Lv.**U.; **O.**H.; **Pl.**M.; **Rt.** 47–53 imp. [*C. of:* 38374; *C. as:* 2997]

2852 **Annales mycologici.** Berlin. *Annls mycol.* [1903–44] **L.**AM.; BM.; BMᴺ. imp.; K.; L.; MY.; **Abs.**N. 24–40; **Br.**A. 03–18; U. 03–20; **C.**BO.; **Cr.**U. 03–14; **Db.**; **E.**B.; **Lv.**U. 24–40; **M.**U.; **Nw.**A. 03–31: 39–40: 42–43; **R.**U. 32–40; **Rt.** 23–39. [*C. as:* 51636]

2853 **Annales** de la **nutrition** et de l'**alimentation.** Paris. *Annls Nutr. Aliment.* [1947–] **L.**A. 59–; AM. 50–; BM. 50–; MA.; MD.; SC.; TP. 60–; **Abd.**R.; **C.**A. 50–; **E.**U. 50–; **G.**U.; **M.**MS. 48–; **R.**D.; U. 51–; **Y.**

2854 **Annales** de l'**Observatoire d'astronomie physique** de **Paris.** Paris. *Annls Obs. Astr. phys. Paris* [1896–26] **L.**AS.; BM.; R.; **C.**O.; **Db.**; **E.**O.; R.; **O.**O. 06–26. [*C. as:* 2872ª]
    Annales de l'**Observatoire astronomique, magnétique et météorologique** de **Toulouse.** *See* 2855.
    Annales de l'**Observatoire astronomique** de l'**Academia sinica.** *See* 2859.

2855 **Annales** de l'**Observatoire astronomique** et **météorologique** de **Toulouse.** Toulouse. *Annls Obs. astr. mét. Toulouse* [1873–] **L.**AS.; BM.; MO. 73–16 imp.; R. 73–05; SC. 99–16: 33–; **C.**O.; **E.**O.; R. 73–12; **Lv.**U. 73–10 imp.; **M.**U. 48–; **O.**O.

2856 **Annales** de l'**Observatoire astronomique** de **Moscou.** Moscou. *Annls Obs. astr. Mosc.* [1874–29] **L.**AS.; **C.**O.; **E.**O.; R.; **O.**O. 75–27.

2857 **Annales** de l'**Observatoire astronomique** de **Tokyo.** Tokyo. *Annls Obs. astr. Tokyo* [1889–50] **L.**AS. 94–50; BM. 21–50; **C.**O.; **E.**O.; **O.**O. [*C. as:* 3192]

2858 **Annales** de l'**Observatoire astronomique** de l'**Université impériale, Kharkow.** *Annls Obs. astr. Univ. imp. Kharkow* **C.**O. 04–; **E.**R. 04.

2859 **Annales** de l'**Observatoire astronomique** de **Zô-sé.** Chang Hai, Nanking. *Annls Obs. astr. Zô-sé* [1907–] **L.**AS.; **M**O. 27; SC.; **C.**SP. 17–; **E.**O. imp.; **M.**U. 07–57 imp.; **O.**O.

Annales de l'**Observatoire** de **Besançon.** *See* 2869ª.

2861 **Annales** de l'**Observatoire** de **Bordeaux.** *Annls Obs. Bordeaux* [1885–] **L.**AS.; BM.; R. 85–07; **C.**O.; **Db.**; **E.**O.; **O.**O. 85–17.

Annales de l'**Observatoire géophysique central.** Vladivostok. *See* 28479.

2862 **Annales** de l'**Observatoire** de **Houga.** Toulouse. *Annls Obs. Houga* [1942–] **L.**AS.

2863 **Annales** de l'**Observatoire impérial** de **Rio de Janeiro.** Rio de Janeiro. *Annls Obs. imp. Rio de J.* [1882–] **L.**BM.; **C.**O.; **E.**M. 94–12; O.; R. 82–89 imp.

Annales de l'**Observatoire** de l'**Institut météorologique hongrois.** Budapest. *See* 36413ª.

2865 **Annales** de l'**Observatoire** de **Kiev.** Kiev. *Annls Obs. Kiev* [1879–] **C.**O. 84–; **O.**O. 93–14.

2866 **Annales** de l'**Observatoire** de **Ksara.** Liban. *Annls Obs. Ksara* [1921–] **L.**MO. imp.; **Y.** [*C. as:* 2702 and 2916]

Annales de l'**Observatoire magnétique** et **météorologique** de l'**Université** à **Odessa.** *See* 18881.

2867 **Annales** de l'**Observatoire météorologique, physique** et **glaciaire** du **Mont Blanc.** Paris. *Annls Obs. mét. phys. glac. Mt Blanc* [1893–17] **L.**BM.; MO. imp.; R.; SC. 93–05; **Bl.**U.; **C.**UL.; **Db.** 96–17; **E.**M.; R. 96–05; **O.**G.; R. 93–05.

Annales de l'**Observatoire** de **Montsouris.** *See* 2868.

2868 **Annales** de l'**Observatoire municipal** de **Paris.** *Annls Obs. mun. Paris* [1900–12] **L.**MO. 00–10; **E.**M. 06–07; **O.**R. [*Replaces:* 3295]

2869 **Annales** de l'**Observatoire national** d'**Athènes.** *Annls Obs. natn. Athènes* [1894–] **L.**AS. 98–; BM. 98–12; GL. 98–12; MO.; SC. 98–; **C.**O. 12–; **Db.** 98–; **E.**M.; O. 98–; R. 98–; **O.**G. 98–. [*Suspended:* 1917–25; *See also:* 2922]

2869ª **Annales** de l'**Observatoire national** de **Besançon.** Astronomie et géophysique. Besançon. *Annls Obs. natn. Besançon* [1934–] **L.**AS.; **M.**U. 55–; **O.**R. 39–.

2870 **Annales** de l'**Observatoire** de **Nice.** Paris. *Annls Obs. Nice* [1887–] **L.**AS. 87–11; BM. 87–11; R. 87–05; **C.**O. 99–; **Db.** 04–; **E.**O.; R. 87–11; **G.**U. 87–90; **O.**O. 99–11.

2871 **Annales** de l'**Observatoire** de **Paris.** Paris. *Annls Obs. Paris*
(a) Mémoires [1855–25] **L.**AS.; BM. 82–13; R. 1855–24; UC. 92–08; **Abd.**U. 1858–12; **Br.**U. 1855–77; **C.**O.; UL.; **Db.** 00–25; **E.**M.; R.; **G.**U. 61–25; **M.**U. 1855–77 imp.; **O.**O. 1861–25; R. 1855–89; **Sa.** 1855–95.
(b) Observations [1858–17] **L.**AS.; BM. 68–06; R.; UC. 92–08; **Abd.**U. 1858–12; **Br.**U. 1858–77; **C.**O.; UL.; **Db.** 00–25; **E.**M.; R. 1858–07; **G.**U. 1858–06 imp.; **M.**U. 1858–67 imp.; **O.**O.; R. 1858–14; **Sa.** 1858–95.

2871ª **Annales** de l'**Observatoire** de **Paris.** **Section** d'**astrophysique** á **Meudon.** Paris. *Annls Obs. Paris Sect. Astrophys. Meudon* [1930–48] **L.**AS. [*C. of:* 2872ª]

Annales de l'**Observatoire physique central** de **Nicolas.** *See* 28485.

2872 **Annales** de l'**Observatoire r.** de **Belgique.** Bruxelles. *Annls Obs. r. Belg.* [1834–] **L.**AS.; BM. 78–; MO. 1834–09; SC.; UC.; 78–; **Abd.**U. 04–; **Bm.**U. 87–; **C.**O.; UL.; **Db.**; **E.**M. 76–03; O.; R. imp.; U. 78–23 imp.; **Lv.**U. 87–07; **M.**U. 87–; **O.**G. 67–12 imp.; R. 1834–18 imp.; **Sa.** 1834–68: 04–07.

2872ª **Annales** de l'**Observatoire, Section** de **Meudon.** Paris. *Annls Obs. Sect. Meudon, Paris* [1928–29] **L.**AS. [*C. of:* 2854; *C. as:* 2871ª]

2873 **Annales** de l'**Observatoire** de **Strasbourg.** *Annls Obs. Strasb.* [1926–] **L.**AS.; BM.; R.; **C.**O.; P.; **Db.**; **E.**O.; **M.**U. 26–56 imp.; **O.**O. [*C. of:* 2647]

2874 **Annales** d'**oculistique.** Paris. *Annls Oculist.* [1838–] **L.**BM.; MA. 94–; MD.; OP.; U. 50–; **Abd.**U. 69–; **Br.**U. 85: 95; **C.**UL. 1838–69; **Db.** 64– imp.; **E.**S. 1843– imp.; **G.**F. 61–35; **Lv.**M. 77–19; **M.**MS. 1850–79; **Nw.**A. 92–05: 07–14: 16–27; **O.**R. 67–; **Sa.** 92–24; **Y.**

2875 **Annales odonto-stomatologiques.** Lyon. *Annls odonto-stomat.* **L.**D. 44–.

2876 **Annales. Office météorologique** de la **ville Nice.** *Annls Off. mét. Nice* **L.**MO. 32–55.

2877 **Annales** de l'**Office nationale** de **combustibles liquides.** Paris. *Annls Off. natn. Combust. liq.* [1926–39] **L.**P. 30–39; PT. 26–38. [*C. as:* 47317]

2878 **Annales** d'**optique oculaire.** Paris. *Annls Opt. ocul.* [1952–] **Y.**

2879 **Annales** d'**oto-laryngologie.** Paris. *Annls Otolar.* [1931–] **L.**MA.; MD.; S. 31–60; U.; **E.**S.; **G.**F. 31–32; U. 52–; **Nw.**A. 47–48; **Y.** [*C. of:* 2810 and 4263]

2880 **Annales paediatriae Fenniae.** Helsinki. *Annls Paediat. Fenn.* [1954–] **L.**MA.; MD.; **Abd.**U.; **Br.**U. [*Also supplements*]

2881 **Annales paediatrici.** Basel. *Annls paediat.* [1938–] **L.**KC. 53–; MA. 38–42; MD.; **Abd.**R.; **Bl.**U. 58–; **Bm.**U.; **C.**UL.; **E.**P.; **G.**F. 38–41; **Nw.**A.; **Sh.**U. 52–55; **Y.** [*C. of:* 24770]

2882 **Annales paediatrici japonici.** Kyoto. *Annls paediat. jap.* [1955–] **L.**MA.; MD.; TD.; **C.**UL.; **O.**R.; **Y.** [*C. of:* 36376]

2883 **Annales** de **paléontologie.** Paris. *Annls Paléont.* [1906–] **L.**BMᴺ.; GL.; GM.; RI. 06–38; SC.; UC. 25–; Z.; **Bl.**U. 55–; **Bm.**U.; **Br.**U.; **C.**B.; S.; **Db.**; **E.**F.; **G.**U. 16–; **Ld.**U.; **M.**U. imp.; **N.**U. 06–32: 56–; **Nw.**A. 50–; **O.**R.; **Y.**

Annales de **palethnologie.** *See* 47522.

2884 **Annales** de **parasitologie humaine** et **comparée.** Paris. *Annls Parasit. hum. comp.* [1923–] **L.**BMᴺ.; EB.; KC. 53–; LI. 23–32; MA. 46–; MC. 23–54 imp.; MD.; MY.; TD.; V. 23–30; Z. 49–; **Abd.**R. 23: 25–56; **Abs.**U. 58–; **Br.**U. 49–; **C.**MO.; V. 23–34: 38– imp.; **E.**U.; **G.**U.; **Lv.**U.; **Sal.**; **W.**; **Y.**

2885 **Annales pharmaceutiques belges.** Bruxelles. *Annls pharm. belg.* [1950–] **L.**PH. imp.; **Y.** [*C. of:* 37469]

2886 **Annales pharmaceutiques françaises.** Paris. *Annls pharm. fr.* [1943–] **L.**BM.; C.; MA. 45–; P.; PH.; SC.; U.; **Bm.**T.; **C.**UL.; **Db.**; **Dn.**U.; **E.**P.; R.; U.; **G.**T. 54–; U.; **N.**U.; **O.**B.; R.; **Y.** [*C. of:* 26661 and 11671]

2887 **Annales** de **pharmacie.** Louvain. *Annls Pharm.* [1895–14]

2888 **Annales** de **physicothérapie.** Paris. *Annls Physicothér.* [1901–]

2889 **Annales** de **physiologie** et de **physicochimie biologique.** Paris. *Annls Physiol. Physicochim. biol.* [1925–] **L.**BM.; C. 37–39; MD.; UC. 25–29; **Abd.**R. 35–40; **C.**P.; **E.**U. 25–39; Ld.U.; O.PH. 25–39.

2890 **Annales** de **physiologie végétale.** Bruxelles. *Annls Physiol. vég., Brux.* [1956–] **Br.**A. 57–; **C.**A.; O.BO.; **Rt.**

2891 **Annales** de **physiologie végétale.** Paris. *Annls Physiol. vég., Paris* [1959–] **L.**AM.; BM.; **Md.**H.; **Rt.**; **Sil.** 57–; **Y.** [*Forms Ser. A bis of:* 2785ᶜ]

2892 **Annales** de **physique.** Paris. *Annls Phys.* [1914–] **L.**BM.; C.; IC.; MO. 24–31; P.; RI.; SC.; U.; UC.; **Abd.**U.; **Abs.**U.; **Bl.**U.; **Bm.**U.; **Bn.**U. 21– imp.; **Br.**P. 14–39; U.; **C.**P.; UL.; **Cr.**U.; **Db.**; **Dn.**U. 21–23 imp.; **E.**R.; U.; **Ex.**U. 45–; **F.**A. 46–; **G.**U.; **H.**U.; Ld.U.; **Lv.**P. 56–; U.; **M.**C. 20–27; U.; **N.**U. 57–; **Nw.**A.; O.BS. 14–34; R.; **R.**U. 51–; **Sa.**; **Sh.**U. 48–; **Ste.**; **Y.** [*C. from:* 2698]

2893 **Annales** de **physique** du **globe** de la **France** d'**outre mer.** Paris. *Annls Phys. Globe Fr. outre mer* [1934–39] **L.**BM.; MO.

2894 **Annales** des **planteurs** de **caoutchouc** de l'**Indo-Chine.** Saïgon. *Annls Plrs Caoutch. Indo-Chine* **Sy.**R. 11–18⋆. [*C. as:* 12332]

2895 **Annales polonici mathematici.** Warszawa, Kraków. *Annls pol. math.* [1954–] **L.**M.; R.; SC.; U.; **C.**P.; **E.**G. 58–; **G.**U. imp.; **Y.** [*C. of:* 2961]

2896 **Annales** des **ponts** et **chaussées.** Paris. *Annls Ponts Chauss.* [1831–] **L.**BM.; P. 01–; SC. 1869–14: 26–; **Bm.**P.; U. 1831–80: 18–; **C.**UL.; **Db.** 1831–00 imp.; **E.**R. 40–54; U. 1831–1845; **G.**U. imp.; **Ha.**RD. 34–; **Sh.**SC. 24–; **Wl.**H. 47–57; **Y.**

2897 **Annales** des **postes, télégraphes** et **téléphones.** Paris. *Annls Post. Télégr. Téléph.* [1910–] **L.**BM. 19–; EE. 10–39; P. 10–39.

2898 **Annales** de **protistologie.** Paris. *Annls Protist.* [1928–36] **L.**BMᴺ.; Z.; **Cr.**U.; **Fr.**; **Pl.**M.

2899 **Annales** de la **psychologie zoologique.** Paris. *Annls Psychol. zool.* [1901–02]

2900 **Annales** de **radioélectricité.** Paris. *Annls Radioélect.* [1945–] **L.**AV. imp.; EE.; P.; **Bm.**P.; **C.**ENG. 52–; P. 55–; **Ma.**T. 47–52; **Sh.**SC. 57–; **Sw.**U. 47– imp.; **Y.**

2901 **Annales** de la **recherche forestière** au **Maroc.** Rabat. *Annls Rech. for. Maroc* [1951–] **O.**F.
Annales de la **recherche médicale.** Paris. *See* 37227ᶜ.

2902 **Annales Regiae scientiarum universitatis hungaricae debreceniensis a Stephano Tisza nominatae.** Debrecen. *Annls R. Sci. Univ. hung. Debrecen* [1916–]

2902ᶜ **Annales** et **résumés** des **travaux** de la **Société nantaise** d'**horticulture.** Nantes. *Annls Résum. Trav. Soc. nantaise Hort.* [*C. as:* 2837]

2903 **Annales** de **roentgénologie** et **radiologie.** Paris. *Annls Roentg. Radiol.* [1922–28] **L.**P. 26–28. [*International edition of* 56503]

2904 **Annales roumaines** de **mathematique.** Bucarest. *Annls roum. Math.* [1935–] **E.**R. 35–37.
Annales Sabariensis. Szombathely. *See* 18695.

2905 **Annales** de la **santé.** Paris. *Annls Santé*

2906 **Annales** de la **science agronomique française** et **étrangère.** Paris. *Annls Sci. agron. fr.* [1884–30] **L.**AM.; BM.; BMᴺ. 84–91; MY. 89–06; P. 10–30; **Abd.**U. 96–30; **Abs.**N. 24–30; **Br.**U. 14–30; **C.**A.; **Db.**; O.BO. 84–98; **Rt.** [*C. as:* 2668 N.S. 1931–]

2907 **Annales** des **sciences** et **arts appliqués** aux **industries textiles.** Verviers. *Annls Sci. Arts appl. Ind. text.* [1937–39] **L.**P.; U.; **E.**U.; **M.**C.

2908 **Annales** des **sciences chimiques** et **physiques.** Paris. *Annls Sci. chim. phys.* **L.**C. 14–.
Annales des **sciences horticoles.** Varsovie. *See* 48068.

2909 **Annales** des **sciences naturelles.** Paris. *Annls Sci. nat.* [1824–]
(a) Botanique, etc. **L.**BM.; BMᴺ.; GM. 1824–02; HS.; K.; L.; MD. 1824–88; NC. 54–; P. 1834–09; PH. 1858–38 imp.; R.; SC.; U. 1844–63; UC. 1834–; **Abd.**U. imp.; **Abs.**U. 11– imp.; **Bl.**U. 1834–; **Bm.**U.; **Bn.**U. 23–; **Br.**P. 1824–39 imp.; U. 64–74: 05–; **C.**BO. 1834–20: 39–; UL.; **Db.**; **E.**B.; R. 1827–; U. 1824–30; **G.**F. 1824–02; U.; Ld.U. 78–; **Lv.**P. 1824–32; U. 94–; **M.**U. 1851– imp.; **Mi.** 47–; **N.**U. 95– imp.; **Nw.**A. 1841–17 imp.; O.BO. 1834–; R.; **R.**U. 47–; **Sa.** 1834–; **Sh.**U. 64– imp.; **Y.**
(b) Zoologie, etc. **L.**AM. 91– imp.; B. 64–87; BM.; BMᴺ.; GL. 00–14; GM. 1824–02; L.; MD. 1824–88; NC. 54–; PH. 1858–85; R.; S. 1824–32; SC.; U. 1844–63; Z.; **Abd.**U. 1844–32; U. 13–27; **Bl.**U. 1834–; **Bm.**U.; **Br.**P. 1824–39 imp.; U. 64–74: 05–; **C.**B. 1834–00; UL.; **Db.**; **E.**B.; R. 1827–; U.; **G.**F. 1824–02; U.; Ld.U. 1844–; **Lo.** 91– imp.; **Lv.**P. 1824–32; U. 1854–; **M.**U. 1851– imp.; **Mi.** 47–; **N.**U. 38–; **Nw.**A. 1841– imp.; R.; **Pl.**M. 54–; **R.**U. 50–; **Sa.** 1834–; **Y.**

2910 **Annales** des **sciences psychiques.** Paris. *Annls Sci. psych.* [1891–19] **L.**BM.; **Bm.**U.; O.R. 91–93.
Annales scientifiques de la **Chaire de botanique** à **Charkov.** *See* 34392.

2911 **Annales scientifiques** de l'**École normale supérieure.** Paris. *Annls scient. Éc. norm. sup., Paris* [1864–] **L.**BM.; M. 31–; P. 10–39; R. 30–; RI. 64–28; SC. 64–28: 31–33: 52–; U. 21–23: 57–; UC. 31–35; **Abd.**U. 64–36; **Abs.**N. 21–; U.; **Br.**U. 64–23; **C.**P. 84–; UL.; **Db.**; **E.**R. 66– imp.; U. 72–; **G.**U.; **H.**U. 29–40: 46–; **Lv.**U. 26–; **M.**U. 21– imp.; **N.**U. 64–83: 94–; **Nw.**A. 57–; O.R.; **Sa.** 64–83: 21–22; **Sw.**U. 11–; **Y.**

2912 **Annales scientifiques** de **Franche-Comté.** Besançon. *Annls scient. Franche-Comté* [1947–49] **L.**BMᴺ.; L.; U. imp.; **Br.**U. 49; **C.**UL.; **Db.**; **G.**U.; **M.**U. [*C. as:* 2914]

2913 **Annales scientifiques textiles belges.** Bruxelles. *Annls scient. text. belg.* [1953–] **L.**P.; Ld.W.; **M.**C.; P. 58–; T.; **Y.**

2914 **Annales scientifiques** de l'**Université** de **Besançon.** *Annls scient. Univ. Besançon* [1950–] **L.**BM.; BMᴺ. imp.; GL.; L.; P. (chim.; math.; mécan; phys.); SC.; U.; Z. (zool.) 50–; **Bn.**U. (bot.) 58–; (zool.) 59–; **Br.**U. (geol.); **C.**BO. 54–; P. (zool.); S. (geol.); UL.; **Db.**; **Dm.**; **G.**U.; **M.**U.; **Nw.**A. 54–; O.BO (bot.) 54–; Z. (zool.) 54–; **Sa.**; **Y.** [*Issued in series:* Botanique, Chimie, Climatologie, *afterwards* Climatologie comtoise et jurassienne, Géologie, Hydrographie, Mathématiques, Mécanique et physique théorique, Médecine, *afterwards* et pharmacie, Météorologie, Physique, Zoologie et physiologie. *C. of* 2912]

2915 **Annales scientifiques** de l'**Université** de **Jassy.** Jassy. *Annls scient. Univ. Jassy* [1900–48] **L.**BM^N. 00–38: (nat. hist.) 39–48; GL. 00–34; P. 24–34; R. 00–08; UC. imp.; UL.; Z. 00–36; **C.**P. 00–36; UL. 00–36; **E.**Q. 24–36; U. 15–36; **G.**U. imp.; **M.**U. 31–36; **O.**R. [*Replaced by:* 2298]

Annales du **Secteur** d'**analyse physico-chimique,** Institut de chemie générale. Leningrad. *See* 24491.

Annales du **Secteur** du **platine** et des **autres métaux précieux,** Institut de chimie générale. Léningrad. *See* 24492.

Annales de la **section dendrologique** de la **Société botanique** de Pologne. *See* 48081.

Annales Sectionis horti- et **viticulturae Universitatis agriculturae,** Budapest. *See* 1215.

2916 **Annales séismologiques** de l'**Observatoire** de **Ksara.** Ksara. *Annls séism. Obs. Ksara* [1956–] **Y.** [*C. of:* 2866]

2917 **Annales** du **Service botanique** et **agronomique** de la **Direction générale** de l'**agriculture.** Tunisie. *Annls Serv. bot. agron. Tunis.* [1920–] **L.**BM^N. 49–; MY. 21–; **Ba.**I. 39–; **C.**A. 30–; **Ld.**U. 29–; **Md.**H. 29–; **Rt.**

Annales du **Service botanique** de la **Direction générale** de l'**agriculture, Tunisie.** *See* 2917.

2918 **Annales** du **Service** des **épiphyties.** Paris. *Annls Serv. Épiphyt.* [1912–19] **L.**AM.; BM^N.; EB.; K.; MY. 12–13; **C.**MO.; **R.**U. 19; **Rt.** [*C. as:* 2732]

2919 **Annales** du **Service** d'**études** des **grandes forces hydrauliques.** Paris. *Annls Serv. Étud. gr. Forces hydraul.*

2919ᶜ **Annales** des **Services** d'**information géologique** du **Bureau recherches géologiques, géophysique** et **minières.** Paris. *Annls Servs Inf. géol. Bur. Rech. géol. géophys. min.* [1958–] **L.**BM^N.; GM. [*C. of:* 2695]

2920 **Annales. Service météorologique** de la **France** d'**outre mer.** Paris. *Annls Serv. mét. Fr. outre mer* **L.**MO. 51–.

2921 **Annales** du **Service météorologique** de l'**Indochine.** Hanoi. *Annls Serv. mét. Indochine* [1928–37] **L.**MO.; **E.**M.

2922 **Annales. Service météorologique nationale** de **Grèce. Observations météorologiques.** Athènes. *Annls Serv. mét. natn. Grèce Obsns mét.* [1930–] **L.**AS.; MO.; **C.**O.; **E.**M. [*See also* 2869]

2923 **Annales** du **Service** des **mines.** Comité spécial du Katanga. Bruxelles. *Annls Serv. Mines Katanga* [1930–] **L.**BM.; BM^N.; GL.; MI. 30–31: 33–38: 45–; **Bm.**U.; **Br.**U.; **C.**P. 30; S.; **Y.**

2924 **Annales** du **Service** de **physique** du **globe** et de **météorologie, Casablanca.** Rabat. *Annls Serv. Phys Globe Mét., Casabl.* **L.**MO. 34–; **Wo.** 56–; **Y.**

2925 **Annales** des **services techniques** d'**hygiène** de **Paris.** *Annls Servs tech. Hyg. Paris* [1913–38] **L.**MO.; **O.**G. (met. sect.) 21–37. [*C. in:* 3313]

2926 **Annales silesiae.** Wrocław. *Annls Silesiae* [1960–] **L.**BM^N; **Y.**

Annales Societatis culturalis comit. **castriferrei** et civit. **Sabariae** et **Musei** comit. **castriferrei.** Szombathely. *See* 18695.

Annales Societatis historico-naturalis fukuokensis. *See* 20442.

2927 **Annales Societatis rebus naturae investigandis** in **Universitate tartuensi constitutae.** Tartu. *Annls*

Soc. Reb. Nat. invest. Univ. tartu. [1934–43] **L.**BM^N.; GL. 34–40; **Cr.**N. 34–37. [*C. of:* 40277; *C. as:* 28797]

Annales Societatis scientiarum faeroensis. *See* 20362.

Annales Societatis zoologicae-botanicae fennicae Vanamo. *See* 51408.

2928 **Annales. Société académique** de **Nantes.** *Annls Soc. acad. Nantes* **O.**B. 1830–18.

2929 **Annales** de la **Société** d'**agriculture** de **Lyon.** Lyon. *Annls Soc. Agric. Lyon* [1838–21] **L.**BM.; BM^N.; L.; P. 1838–17; R. 93–04; Z. 69–11; **C.**UL.; **Db.** 1838–10 imp.; **E.**R. imp.; **O.**B. 1838–17.

2930 **Annales. Société** des **amis** des **sciences** et du **Muséum** de **Rouen.** *Annls Soc. Amis Sci. Mus. Rouen* **L.**BM^N. 42–46.

2931 **Annales** de la **Société belge** de **chirurgie.** Bruxelles. *Annls Soc. belge Chir.* [1893–01] **Br.**U. 98–01; **C.**P. 94–01; **M.**MS. 98–00. [*C. as:* 25806]

2932 **Annales** de la **Société belge** pour l'**étude** du **pétrole,** de ses dérivés et succedanés Gand. *Annls Soc. belge Étud. Pétrole* [1937–]

2933 **Annales** de la **Société belge** de **médecine tropicale.** Bruxelles. *Annls Soc. belge Méd. trop.* [1920–] **L.**EB.; MA. 45–; MC. 45–; MD. 38–; TD.; **C.**MO.; **Lv.**U.; **Sal.** 57–; **W.** 32–38: 51–; **Y.**

2934 **Annales** de la **Société belge** de **microscopie.** Bruxelles. *Annls Soc. belge Microsc.* [1874–07] **L.**BM^N. 80–07; P. 84–07; **C.**P. 94–07; **Db.** 00–07; **E.**C. 84–07 imp.

2935 **Annales** de la **Société belge** de **neurologie.** Bruxelles. *Annls Soc. belge Neurol.* **L.**BM. 98–02.

2936 **Annales** de la **Société belge** d'**urologie.** Bruxelles. *Annls Soc. belge Urol.*

2937 **Annales** de la **Société botanique** de **Lyon.** Lyon. *Annls Soc. bot. Lyon* [1873–22] **L.**BM.; BM^N.; K.; L. 73–01; **E.**R. 79–82: 09–22.

2938 **Annales. Société économique** d'**agriculture** du **département** des **Landes.** Mont-de-Marsan. *Annls Soc. écon. Agric. Dép. Landes*

2939 **Annales** de la **Société** d'**émulation** de **Bruges.** *Annls Soc. Émul. Bruges* [1839–] **L.**BM.; **C.**UL.; **M.**R.; **O.**B.

2940 **Annales** de la **Société** d'**émulation** du **département** des **Vosges.** Épinal. *Annls Soc. Émul. Dép. Vosges* **L.**BM. 1831–.

2941 **Annales** de la **Société entomologique.** Levallois-Perret. *Annls Soc. ent., Levallois-Perret*

2942 **Annales** de la **Société entomologique** de **Belgique.** Bruxelles. *Annls Soc. ent. Belg.* [1857–24] **L.**BM. 1859–12; BM^N.; E.; EB. 09–24; L.; Z.; **Bl.**U. 93–13; **Bm.**N. 81–13; **C.**UL.; **Db.** 00–24; **G.**N. 93–14; **M.**U. 13–14; **Nw.**A. 1857–61; **O.**H.; R. [*C. in:* 9373]

2943 **Annales** de la **Société entomologique** de **France.** Paris. *Annls Soc. ent. Fr.* [1832–] **L.**BM. 1834–92; BM^N.; E.; EB. 76– imp.; L. 1832–13; NC. 55–; R. 1832–95; SC. 71–; Z. 1833–; **Bn.**U. 50–; **Br.**U. 86–15: 22–32; **C.**UL.; **Db.** 78–; **Fr.** 20–54; **G.**N. 86–38; **Ld.**U. 93–imp.; **N.**U. 45–; **O.**H.; R. 20–21; **Rt.** 18–32; **Y.**

Annales de la **Société entomologique** de **Québec.** *See* 3146.

Annales. Société de **géographie.** Paris. *See* 2746.

2944 **Annales** de la **Société géologique** de **Belgique.** Liège. *Annls Soc. géol. Belg.* [1874–] **L.**BM.; BM^N.; GL.; GM.; R. 74–32; SC. 74–94: 26–; **Abs.**U. 30–48: 57–; **Bm.**U. 37–; **C.**MI. 30–46; P.; S.; **E.**J.; U. 46–; **G.**U.; **Ld.**U. 46–; **Lv.**U. imp.; **M.**U. 92–31 imp.; **Nw.**A. 74–27; **Sh.**M. 74–06; **Y.**

2945 **Annales** de la **Société géologique** du **Nord.** Lille. *Annls Soc. géol. N.* [1870–] **L.**BM^N.; GL.; GM.; UC. imp.; **C.**S.; **Db.** 77–; **E.**G. 97–; R. 75–; **Lv.**U. 76– imp.; **M.**U. 74–26; **Nw.**A. 54–; **Y.**

Annales de la **Société géologique** de **Pologne.** *See* 48073.

2946 **Annales** de la **Société d'histoire naturelle** de **Toulon.** Toulon. *Annls Soc. Hist. nat. Toulon* [1910–45] **L.**BM^N. [*C. as:* 2969]

2947 **Annales** de la **Société d'horticulture** et d'**histoire naturelle** de l'**Hérault.** Montpellier. *Annls Soc. Hort. Hist. nat. Hérault* **L.**HS. 99–39 imp.; K. imp.

2948 **Annales** de la **Société d'hydrologie médicale** de **Paris.** Paris. *Annls Soc. Hydrol. méd. Paris* [1923–] **L.**MD. 23–35; S. 34–39. [*C. of:* 2763]

2949 **Annales** de la **Société des lettres, sciences** et **arts** des **Alpes-Maritimes.** Nice. *Annls Soc. Lett. Sci. Arts Alpes-Marit.* **L.**BM. 65–; UC. 65–75.

2950 **Annales** de la **Société linnéene** de **Lyon.** *Annls Soc. linn. Lyon* [1826–37] **L.**AN. 24–36; BM. 1845–37; BM^N.; E. 1845–87 imp.; K. 23–37 imp.; L. 1836–36; NC. 24–35; R. 1853–04; Z. 1853–37; **Br.**P. 85–06; **C.**UL. 1845–37; **Db.** 1845–1853; **E.**B. 24–27; R. 05–37; **G.**N. 76–37; **O.**R. 1845–37; **Pl.**M. 21–37.

2951 **Annales** de la **Société** de **médecine légale** de **Belgique.** Charleroi. *Annls Soc. Méd. lég. Belg.* [1889–]

2952 **Annales** de la **Société** de **médecine physique** d'**Anvers.** *Annls Soc. Méd. phys. Anvers* [1903–06] [*C. as:* 2821]

2953 **Annales** de la **Société** de **médecine** de **St. Étienne.** St. Étienne. *Annls Soc. Méd. St Étienne*

2954 **Annales. Société médicale** de **Neufchâteau.** *Annls Soc. méd. Neufchâteau*

2955 **Annales** de la **Société médico-chirurgicale** d'**Anvers.** Anvers. *Annls Soc. méd-chir. Anvers*

2956 **Annales** de la **Société médico-chirurgicale** du **Brabant.** Bruxelles. *Annls Soc. méd.-chir. Brabant*

2957 **Annales** de la **Société médico-chirurgicale** de **Liége.** Liège. *Annls Soc. méd.-chir. Liége*

2958 **Annales** de la **Société nationale** de l'**horticulture** de **France.** Paris. *Annls Soc. natn. Hort. Fr.* [1955–] **L.**BM^N.; HS.; K.; **Md.**H.; **Y.**

2959 **Annales** de la **Société nationale** de **médecine** de **Lyon.** Lyon. *Annls Soc. natn. Méd. Lyon*

2960 **Annales** de la **Société obstétricale** de **France.** Toulouse. *Annls Soc. obstét. Fr.*

2961 **Annales** de la **Société polonaise** de **mathématique.** Krakow. *Annls Soc. pol. Math.* [1922–52] **L.**R. 23–48: 50–52; UC.; **C.**P.; **E.**Q.; R.; **O.**R. 48–52; **Y.** [*C. as:* 2895]

2962 **Annales** de la **Société r. malacologique** de **Belgique.** Bruxelles. *Annls Soc. r. malacol. Belg.* [1863–02] **L.**BM. 65–02; BM^N.; L.; R.; Z.; **Bl.**U. 78–02 imp.; **Db.** 00–12; **E.**C.; **G.**N. 75–02; **Lv.**U. 80–02; **M.**U. imp. [*C. as:* 2965]

2963 **Annales. Société r.** des **sciences médicales** et **naturelles** de **Bruxelles.** *Annls Soc. r. Sci. méd. nat. Brux.* [1892–] **L.**MC.; S.; SC. 20–39: 48– imp.; U. 05–24; **C.**P. 99–; **E.**U. 22–33; **Lv.**U. 99–; **Y.**

2964 **Annales** de la **Société r. zoologique** de **Belgique.** Bruxelles. *Annls Soc. r. zool. Belg.* [1923–] **L.**BM.; BM^N.; GL.; L.; R. 23–39; SC. 38–39: 46–; Z.; **Bl.**U.; **Bm.**U. 23–25; **C.**B 53–; P.; **Db.**; **Dm.** 30–; **E.**C.; **G.**N.; **Ld.**U.; **Lv.**U.; **M.**U. 23–50; **Pl.**M. 50–; **Sa.** 25–26; **Y.** [*C. of:* 2965]

2965 **Annales** de la **Société r. zoologique** et **malacologique** de **Belgique.** Bruxelles. *Annls Soc. r. zool. malacol. Belg.* [1903–22] **L.**BM.; BM^N.; GL.; L.; R.; Z.; **Bl.**U.; **Bm.**U. 13–22; **C.**P.; **Db.**; **Dm.** 13–22; **E.**C.; **G.**N.; **Ld.**U. 21–22; **Lv.**U.; **M.**U. [*C. of:* 2962; *C. as:* 2964]

2966 **Annales** de la **Société** des **sciences industrielles** de **Lyon.** Lyon. *Annls Soc. Sci. ind. Lyon*

2967 **Annales** de la **Société** des **sciences naturelles** de la **Charente-Inférieure.** La Rochelle. *Annls Soc. Sci. nat. Charente-Infér.* [1854–41] **L.**BM^N. 79–41. [*C. as:* 2968]

2968 **Annales** de la **Société** des **sciences naturelles** de la **Charente-Maritime.** *Annls Soc. Sci. nat. Charente-Marit.* [1946–] **L.**BM^N. [*C. of:* 2967]

2969 **Annales** de la **Société** des **sciences naturelles** de **Toulon.** Toulon. *Annls Soc. Sci. nat. Toulon* [1946–] **L.**BM^N. 46–47. [*C. of:* 2946]

2970 **Annales** de la **Société scientifique** de **Bruxelles.** Louvain. *Annls Soc. scient. Brux.* [1875–] **L.**BM.; BM^N. 75–34: (*b*) 35–46; C. (*b*) 27–; SC. 75–98: 30–40; SI. 47–; **Abs.**U. 00–21 imp.; **Br.**U. 27–29; **C.**P. 24–; **Db.** 23–; **E.**R.; **Y.** [*From* 1927 *divided into series*]

Annales de la **Société suisse** de **balnéologie.** *See* 2652.

Annales de la **Société zoologique suisse** et du **Muséum** d'**histoire naturelle** de **Genève.** *See* 47595.

2971 **Annales** de la **Société** de **zymologie pure** et **appliquée.** Gand. *Annls Soc. Zymol.* [1929–30] [*C. as:* 2999]

2972 **Annales** de la **soudure autogène** et de l'**acétylène.** Paris. *Annls Soud. autog. Acét.*

2973 **Annales** de **spéléologie.** Paris. *Annls Spéléol.* [1959–] **L.**BM^N.; **Y.** [*C. of:* 35194]

2974 **Annales** de la **Station aquicole** de **Boulogne.** *Annls Stn aquic. Boulogne* [1892–14] LBM. 92–11; BM^N. 92–12; Z. 06–11; **Abd.**M. 92–93: 05; **Db.** 92–11; **Dm.** 92–12; **Lo.**; **Pl.**M. 92–11.

2975 **Annales** de la **Station centrale** de **hydrobiologie appliquée.** Paris. *Annls Stn cent. Hydrobiol. appl.* [1945–] **L.**AM. 45–50; SC.; **Db.**; **Fr.**; **Lo.**; **Pit.**F.

2976 **Annales** de la **Station limnologique** de **Besse.** Clermont-Ferrand. *Annls Stn limnol. Besse* **L.**BM^N. 09–10.

2977 **Annales. Station océanographique** de **Salammbô.** Tunis. *Annls Stn océanogr. Salammbô* [1925–] **L.**BM^N.; SC. 54–; **Abd.**M. 54–; **Dm.**; **Lv.**U. 54–; **Mi.**; **Pl.**M.; **Wo.** 55–.

Annales de **stratigraphie** et de **paléontologie** du **Laboratoire** de **géologie** de la **Faculté** des **sciences** de l'**Université** de **Paris.** *See* 2755.

Annales suisses des **sciences appliquées** et de la **technique.** *See* 48906.

2978 **Annales techniques.** Paris. *Annls tech.* [1906] [*Replaces:* 47599]

2979 **Annales techniques** de l'**aviation civile.** Paris. *Annls tech. Aviat. civ.* [1947–48]

2980 **Annales** de **technologie agricole.** Paris. *Annls Technol. agric.* **Md.**H. 38.

2981 **Annales** de **technologie agricole.** Paris. *Annls Technol. agric.* [1952–] **L.**BM.; P. 58–; TD.; **Bl.**U. 55–; **O.**R. 55–; **R.**D. 53–; U. imp.; **Rt.**; **Y.** [*Forms* Sér. E *of:* 2785ᶜ]

2982 **Annales** des **télécommunications.** Paris. *Annls Télécommun.* [1946–] **L.**AV. 59–; BM. 52–; EE.; P.; SC. 47–; **Y.**

2983 **Annales** de **thérapeutique dermatologique** et **syphiligraphique.** Paris. *Annls Thér. derm. syph.* [1901–09]

2984 **Annales** des **travaux agricoles scientifiques.** Béograd. *Annls Trav. agric. scient.* **L.**MY. 38–40.

2985 **Annales** des **travaux publics** de **Belgique.** Bruxelles. *Annls Trav. publ. Belg.* [1843–] **L.**BM.; P. 10–; **Bm.**U. 21–; **C.**UL. 1843–87; E.U. 1843–1847; **Ha.**RD. 45–; **Y.**

2986 **Annales Universitatis fennicae aboensis.** Åbo. *Annls Univ. fenn. åbo.* [1922–33] **L.**BM.; BMᴺ.; **C.**P. (ser. A). [*C. as:* 2991]

2987 **Annales Universitatis litterarum regiae hungaricae Francisco-Josephinae kolozsvariensis.** Kolozsvár. *Annls Univ. Litt. r. hungaricae kolozsvár.* **G.**U. 85–13 imp.; **O.**B. 83–15 imp.; **Sa.** 03–13.

2988 **Annales Universitatis Mariae Curie-Skłodowska.** Lublin. *Annls Univ. Mariae Curie-Skłodowska* [1946–]
   Sect. A. Mathematica **C.**P.; **Db.**; **Ld.**U. 53–; **Y.**
   AA. Physica, chemia **L.**C.; **Db.**; **Ld.**U. 53–; **Rt.**; **Y.**
   B. Geographia, geologia, mineralogia et petrographia **L.**BMᴺ.; GL.; MO. 53–; **C.**A.; GG. 50–55; **Db.**; E.G.; **Rt.**; **Y.**
   C. Biologia. **L.**AM. 47–; AN.; BMᴺ.; EB.; L.; S.; Z.; **Bl.**U.; **C.**A.; P.; **Db.**; **Dm.**; **Fr.** 54–; **Ld.**U. 52–; **Lv.**U.; **Pl.**M.; **Rt.**; **Y.**
   D. Medicina. **L.**EB.; MD. 46–47; S.; TD.; **Y.**
   DD. Medicina veterinaria **L.**EB.; TD. 49–; **W.**; **Y.**
   E. Agricultura **L.**AM.; BMᴺ.; EB.; **Br.**A.; **C.**A.; **Hu.**G. 47–; **Sil.**; **W.**; **Y.**
   F. Ethnologia **L.**AN.; SC.; **Db.**; G.
   [*Also supplements*]

2989 **Annales Universitatis saraviensis.** Saarbrücken *Annls Univ. sarav.*
   1. Wissenschaften/Sciences [1952–] **L.**BM.; DMᴺ.; P.; SC.; U.; **Bl.**U.; **G.**U.; **Pl.**M. 52; **Y.**
   2. Medizin/Médecine [1953–] **L.**BM.; U.; **Db.**; **G.**U.; **Y.**

2990 **Annales Universitatis scientiarum budapestinensis** de **Rolando Eötvös** nominatae. Budapest. *Annls Univ. Scient. bpest. Rolando Eötvös*
   1. Sectio biologica [1957–] **L.**BM.; BMᴺ.; **Rt.** 57; **Y.**
   2. Sectio mathematica [1958–] **L.**BM.; E.R.; **G.**U.; **Y.**
   3. Sectio geologica [1957–] **L.**BM.; **Y.**
   4. Sectio chemica [1959–] **L.**BM.; P.; **Y.**

2991 **Annales Universitatis turkuensis.** Turku. *Annls Univ. turku.* [1935–]

Ser. A. Physico-mathematica-biologica **L.**BMᴺ.; **C.**P. [*C. of:* 2986]

2992 **Annales** de l'**Université d'Ankara.** *Annls Univ. Ankara* **G.**U. 48–.

2993 **Annales** de l'**Université** de **Grenoble.** Paris. *Annls Univ. Grenoble* [1889–48] **L.**R. 45–48; UC. 95–05; **Abd.**U. (sci.-méd.) 24–48; **C.**UL. 90–48; **Db.** 95–48; E.U. 11–48; **M.**U. 01–23: (sci.-méd.) 24–35 imp.; **O.**B. imp.; **Sa.** (sci.-méd.) 24–38. [*C. as:* 2778]
   Annales de l'**Université impériale** de **Kharkow.** See 58291.

2994 **Annales** de l'**Université** de **Lyon.** Lyon. *Annls Univ. Lyon* [1891–] **L.**BM. (*a–c*) 40–; BMᴺ.; GL. 91–27 imp.; GM. (geol.) 99–; M. (*a*); P. (*b*) 57–; R. 92–34; SC. 07–33 imp.: 36–; **C.**P.; **Db.** 99–; **Dm.** 92–48 imp.; E.R.; **M.**U. imp.; **Nw.**A. 36: 42–46; **O.**B. 37–. [*Issued in series*]
   Annales de l'**Université** de **Minsk.** See 58474.
   Annales de l'**Université** de **Moscou.** See 55429.

2995 **Annales** de l'**Université** de **Paris.** Paris. *Annls Univ. Paris* [1926–] **L.**B. imp.; BM.; MD. 36–; SC. 26–41: 47–; **C.**UL.; **Cr.**P. 26–55 imp.; **Db.**; E.U.; **Ex.**U.; **G.**T. 52–; U.; **Ld.**U.; **Lv.**P. 32–38: 47–50 imp.: 51–; U.; **M.**U.; **Nw.**A. 26–40: 47–; **O.**B.; **Sa.**; **Y.**

   Annales. Vasvarmegyi muzeum. Szombathely. See 18695.

2997 **Annales zoologici.** Warszawa. *Annls zool., Warsz.* [1954–] **L.**AM.; BM.; BMᴺ.; E.; EB.; L.; SC.; U.; Z.; **Bl.**U.; **C.**P.; V.; **Cr.**M.; **Db.**; E.F.; R.; **Fr.**; **G.**N. 54–58; **Ld.**U. 54–60; **Lo.** 57–; **Lv.**U.; **M.**P.; **O.**H.; **Pl.**M.; **Rt.**; **Y.** [*C. of:* 2851]
   Annales zoologici Musei polonici historiae naturalis. See 2851, 2997, 38374 and 38411.
   Annales zoologici Societatis zoologico-botanicae fennicae. Vanamo. See 51409.

2998 **Annales** de **zootechnie.** Paris. *Annls Zootech.* [1952–] **L.**AM.; BM.; UC.; VC.; Z. 58–; **Abd.**R. 60–; **Bl.**U. 55–; **C.**APH. 55–; **E.**AB. 52–; AG. 55–; AR. 56–; **Hu.**G. 55–; **Ld.**W. 55–; **O.**R. 55–; **R.**D. 53–; **W.** 61–; **Y.** [*Forms* Sér. D *of:* 2785ᶜ]

2999 **Annales** de **zymologie.** Gand. *Annls Zymol.* [1931–40] [*C. of:* 2971; *C. as:* 47175]

3000 **Annales-Bulletins** de l'**Academia asiatica.** Téhéran. *Annls-Bull. Acad. asiat., Téhéran* **L.**BMᴺ. 31–33. [*C. of:* 10607]

3001 **Annali** della **Accademia d'agricoltura** di **Torino.** Torino. *Annali Accad. Agric. Torino* [1840–] **L.**AM. 05–29 imp.; BM.; **Abs.**N. 94–24 imp.; **C.**A. 48–; **Y.**

3002 **Annali. Accademia italiana** di **scienze forestali.** Firenze. *Annali Accad. ital. Sci. for.* [1953–] **O.**F.; R.; **Y.**

3002ᶜ **Annali. Accademia** del **Mediterraneo.** *Annali Accad. Medit.* [1952–]

3003 **Annali** di **agricoltura.** Roma. *Annali Agric.* [1878–21] **L.**AM. 78–12; BM.; BMᴺ. 79–86: 12; P. 82–99 imp.; **Abs.**N. 00–12 imp.; **Db.** 87–11. [*C. as:* 35476]

3004 **Annali** di **botanica.** Roma. *Annali Bot.* [1903–] **L.**BMᴺ. 03–38; K. 03–43; **Abs.**A. 28–32; **C.**UL.; E.B.; **Y.** [*C. of:* 3502]

3005 **Annali** del **Centro sperimentale agrario** e **zootecnico** della **Libia.** Tripoli. *Annali Cent. sper. agr. zootec. Libia* [1938–41] **L.**SC.; **C.**A.

3006 **Annali** di **chimica**. Roma. *Annali Chim.* [1950–] **L.**C.; P.; PH.; SC.; **Abd.**R. 50–52; **C.**P. 60–; **O.**R. 57–; **Y.** [*C. of:* 3007]

3007 **Annali** di **chimica applicata**. Roma. *Annali Chim. appl.* [1914–49] **L.**C.; P. imp.; PH. 41–49; SC. 23–40: 48–49; **C.**P. 14–19; **M.**T. 14–19. [*C. as:* 3006]

3008 **Annali** di **chimica farmaceutica**. Roma. *Annali Chim. farm.* [1938–] **L.**BM. 38–39 imp. [*Issued as Supplement to:* 19105]

3009 **Annali** della **Clinica** delle **malattie mentali** e **nervose** della **R. Università** di **Palermo**. *Annali Clin. Mal. ment. nerv. Univ. Palermo* [1898–35] **L.**MA. 33–35; MD. 34–35.

3010 **Annali** di **clinica medica**. Palermo. *Annali Clin. med.* [1910–31]

3011 **Annali** di **clinica odontoiatrica** e dell'Istituto superiore 'George Eastman'. Roma. *Annali Clin. odont.* [1931–38] **L.**D. 35–38. [*C. of:* 16144]

3012 **Annali** di **elettricità medica** e **terapia fisica**. Napoli. *Annali Elett. med. Terap. fis.* [1902–]

3013 **Annali** della **Facoltà agraria** e **forestale**. Firenze. *Annali Fac. agr. for., Firenze* [1937–38] **L.**MY.; **C.**A.; **E.**U.; **O.**F. [*C. of:* 3091]

3014 **Annali** della **Facoltà** di **agraria** di **Portici** della **R. Università** di **Napoli**. *Annali Fac. Agr. Portici* [1936–51] **L.**AM.; BM.; BM^N.; EB.; GL.; HS. 36–39; MY. 36–48; **C.**UL.; **Db.**; **G.**U.; **Md.**H.; **Rt.** [*C. of:* 3092; *C. as:* 3024]

    Annali della **Facoltà** di **agraria** della **R. Università** di **Pisa**. *See* 3017.

    Annali della **Facoltà** di **agraria** della **R. Università** degli **studi** di **Perugia**. *See* 3018.

3015 **Annali** della **Facoltà** di **agraria**, **Università** di **Bari**. *Annali Fac. Agr. Univ. Bari* [1939–] **L.**AM.; **C.**A.; **Hu.**G. 47; **Rt.** 42–.

3016 **Annali** della **Facoltà** di **agraria**, **Università** di **Milano**. Milano. *Annali Fac. Agr. Univ. Milano* [1952–] **C.**A.; UL. 55–; **Hu.**G. 54–; **Md.**H. 55–; **O.**R. 55–.

3017 **Annali** della **Facoltà** di **agraria** della **Università** di **Pisa**. *Annali Fac. Agr. Univ. Pisa* [1938–] **L.**EB.; **C.**A.; **Md.**H. 51–; **Rt.** 43–; **Y.** [*C. of:* 8390]

3018 **Annali** della **Facoltà** di **agraria** della **Università** degli **studi** di **Perugia**. *Annali Fac. Agr. Univ. Perugia* [1942–] **Abd.**S. 48– imp.; **Br.**A. 49–; **C.**A.; **Rt.** 55.

3019 **Annali** della **Facoltà** di **medicina** e **chirurgia**, **Università** di **Bari**. *Annali Fac. Med. Chir. Univ. Bari* **L.**MA. 45–.

3020 **Annali** della **Facoltà** di **medicina** della **Università** di **Perugia**. *Annali Fac. Med. Univ. Perugia* **Db.** 98–00; **M.**U. 11–12.

3021 **Annali** della **Facoltà** di **medicina veterinaria** di **Torino**. Torino. *Annali Fac. Med. vet. Torino* [1950–] **L.**V. 50–51; **W.**

3022 **Annali** della **Facoltà** di **medicina veterinaria**. **Università** di **Pisa**. *Annali Fac. Med. vet. Univ. Pisa* [1948–] **L.**V.; **C.**V. 53–56; **E.**AB.; **W.**

3023 **Annali** della **Facoltà** di **scienze agrarie** della **Università** di **Palermo**. *Annali Fac. Sci. agr. Univ. Palermo* [1950–] **C.**A.; **Y.**

3024 **Annali** della **Facoltà** di **scienze agrarie** della **Università** degli **studi** di **Napoli**. Portici. *Annali Fac. Sci. agr. Univ. Napoli* [1951–] **L.**AM.; BM.; BM^N.; EB.; GL.; **C.**A.; UL.; **Db.**; **G.**U.; **Md.**H.; **Rt.**; **Y.** [*C. of:* 3014]

3025 **Annali** di **farmacoterapia** e **chimica biologica**. Milano. *Annali Farmacoter. Chim. biol.* [1824–00] **L.**BM.; C. 98–00; P. 98–00; **C.**UL. 99–00.

3026 **Annali** di **freniatria** e **scienze affini**. Torino. *Annali Freniat.* [1888–13]

3027 **Annali** di **geofisica**. Roma. *Annali Geofis.* [1948]– **L.**BM. 61–; GL.; MO.; SC.; U.; **C.**GD.; P.; **Db.** 49–; **E.**R.; **Lv.**U. 48–49; **M.**U. 48–52 imp.; **Y.**

    Annali di **geomorfologia**. *See* 58602.
    Annali di **glaciologia**. *See* 58643.

3028 **Annali** **idrografici**. Genova. *Annali idrogr., Genova* **L.**BM^N. 00–28; MO. 32*; **Lv.**U. 00–24. [*C. as:* 3035]

3029 **Annali** **idrografici**. Venezia. *Annali idrogr., Venezia* [1925] **L.**MO. [*C. of:* 8198; *C. as:* 3043]

3030 **Annali** **idrologici**. Bari. *Annali idrol., Bari* **L.**MO. 32–.

3031 **Annali** **idrologici**. Bologna. *Annali idrol., Bologna* [1930–] **L.**MO. imp.; **Y.** [*C. of:* 8271]

3032 **Annali** **idrologici**. Cagliari. *Annali idrol., Cagliari* **L.**MO. 54–; **Y.**

3033 **Annali** **idrologici**. Catanzaro. *Annali idrol., Catanzaro* [1927–] **L.**MO. 27–28: 51–. [*C. of:* 8273]

3034 **Annali** **idrologici**. Chieti. *Annali idrol., Chieti* **L.**MO. 26–29.

3035 **Annali** **idrologici**. Genova. *Annali idrol., Genova* [1932–] **L.**MO. [*C. of:* 3028]

3036 **Annali** **idrologici**. Milano. *Annali idrol., Milano* **L.**MO. 28–35.

3037 **Annali** **idrologici**. Napoli. *Annali idrol., Napoli* [1938–] **L.**MO. [*C. of:* 8275]

3038 **Annali** **idrologici**. Palermo. *Annali idrol., Palermo* **L.**MO. 43–. [*C. of:* 8276]

3039 **Annali** **idrologici**. Parma. *Annali idrol., Parma* [1924–] **L.**MO.; **Lv.**U. 50–; **Y.** [*C. of:* 8197]

3040 **Annali** **idrologici**. Pescara. *Annali idrol., Pescara* **L.**MO. 55–.

3041 **Annali** **idrologici**. Pisa. *Annali idrol., Pisa* **L.**MO. 50–.

3041^a **Annali** **idrologici**. Roma. *Annali idrol., Roma* **L.**MO. 51–. [*C. of:* 8278]

3042 **Annali** **idrologici**. Torino. *Annali idrol., Torino* **L.**MO. 26–35.

3043 **Annali** **idrologici**. Venezia. *Annali idrol., Venezia* [1926–] **L.**MO. 26–34: 46–. [*C. of:* 3029]

3044 **Annali** **d'igiene sperimentale**. Torino, Roma. *Annali Ig. sper.* [1889–48] **L.**BM. 91–48; EB. 13–48; LI. 98–08: 19–40 imp.; MA. 32–40 imp.; MC. 17–40 imp.; MD. 35–48 imp.; SH. 27–40; TD. 00–48; **C.**MO. 96–37; PA. 92–99; **Lv.**U. 91–48 imp. [*C. as:* 35474]

3045 **Annali** **d'ingegneria**. Napoli. *Annali Ing.*

3046 **Annali** di **Ippocrate**. Milano. *Annali Ippocrate* [1906–12]

3047 **Annali** **Isnardi** di **auxologia normale** e **patologica**. Napoli. *Annali Isnardi Auxol.* [1954–] **L.**MA. 57–; MD. 57–.

3048 **Annali** dell'**Istituto Carlo Forlanini**. Roma. *Annali Ist. Carlo Forlanini* [1937–] **L.**MA.; TD. 55–; **Y.**

3049 **Annali** dell'**Istituto Maragliano** per lo **studio** e la **cura** della **tubercolosi.** Genova. *Annali Ist. Maragliano* [1904–39] **L.**GH. 31–39; LI. 31–39; MA. 31–39 imp.; MD. 31–39; **Bm.**U. 08–12 imp. [>4384, 1924–30; *C. as:* 4394]

3050 **Annali** dell'**Istituto navale** di **Napoli.** *Annali Ist. nav. Napoli*

3051 **Annali** dell'**Istituto psichiatrico** della **R. Università** di **Roma.** *Annali Ist. psichiat. R. Univ. Roma*

3052 **Annali** dell'**Istituto sperimentale** per lo **studio** e la **difesa** del **suolo.** Firenze. *Annali Ist. sper. Stud. Dif. Suolo* [1954–] **Rt.**

3053 **Annali** dell'**Istituto sperimentale zootecnico** di **Roma.** *Annali Ist. sper. zootec. Roma* [1933–] **Abd.**R. 33: 45–; **E.**AB.; **R.**D.

3054 **Annali** dell'**Istituto superiore** di **scienze** e **lettere** di **Santa Chiara.** Napoli. *Annali Ist. sup. Sci. Lett. S Chiara* [1948–59] **L.**BM^N. [*C. as:* 3089]

3055 **Annali italiani** di **chirurgia.** Napoli. *Annali ital. Chir.* [1922–] **L.**MA. 46–; **Br.**U. 22–37 imp.; **M.**MS. 25–38 imp.

3056 **Annali italiani** di **dermatologia** e **sifilografia.** Napoli. *Annali ital. Derm. Sif.* **L.**MA. 48–; MD. 47–.

3057 **Annali italiani** di **pediatria.** Cagliari. *Annali ital. Pediat.*

3058 **Annali** del **Laboratorio autonomo** di **chimica agraria** in **Forlì.** *Annali Lab. auton. Chim. agr. Forlì* [1910–] [*C. of:* 3095]

3059 **Annali** del **Laboratorio** di **chimica agraria** della **R. Università** di **Milano.** *Annali Lab. Chim. agr. R. Univ. Milano* [1935–] **C.**A. 35–45.

3060 **Annali** del **Laboratorio chimico centrale** delle **Gabelle.** Roma. *Annali Lab. chim. cent. Gabelle* **L.**C. 97–12.

3061 **Annali** del **Laboratorio** di **medicina legale** dell' **Università** di **Bologna.** Imola. *Annali Lab. Med. leg. Univ. Bologna*

3062 **Annali. Laboratorio** di **ricerche** sulle **fermentazioni, Lazzaro Spallanzani.** Milano. *Annali Lab. Ric. Ferment. Spallanzani* [1930–] **L.**BM.; P. 30–37; **Rt.** 39.

3063 **Annali** di **laringologia** ed **otologia, rinologia** e **faringologia.** Empoli. *Annali Lar. Otol. Rinol. Faring.*

3064 **Annali lateranensi.** Roma. *Annali lateran.* [1937–] **L.**AN.; BM.; HO.; **Nw.**A. 52–.

3065 **Annali** dei **lavori pubblici.** Roma. *Annali Lavori pubbl.* [1924–42] **L.**BM. 34–42; MO. 24–25; P. [*C. of:* and *Rec. as:* 21241]

3066 **Annali** del **Manicomio provinciale** di **Catanzaro.** *Annali Manic. prov. Catanzaro*

3067 **Annali** del **Manicomio provinciale** di **Perugia.** Perugia. *Annali Manic. prov. Perugia* [*C. as:* 3081]

3068 **Annali** di **matematica pura** ed **applicata.** Milano. *Annali Mat. pura appl.* [1858–] **L.**BM.; M. 67–04; R.; SC. 34–; U. 56–; UC.; **Abd.**U. 1858–18; **Abs.**N. 23–; **Bl.**U. 07–; **Br.**U.; **C.**P. 1858–65 imp.: 36–; UL.; **Db.**; **Dn.**U. 34–; **E.**Q. 45–; U.; **Lv.**U. 00–06; **N.**U. 47–; **Nw.**P. 09–25; **O.**R.; **Y.**

3069 **Annali** di **medicina navale** e **coloniale.** Roma. *Annali Med. nav. colon.* [1895–50] **L.**MA. 47–50; MD. 14–19; TD. 04–50; **Lv.**U. 11–50. [*C. as:* 3070]

3070 **Annali** di **medicina navale** e **tropicale.** Roma. *Annali Med. nav. trop.* [1951–] **L.**MA.; TD.; **Lv.**U. [*C. of:* 3069]

3071 **Annali** di **merceologia siciliana.** Istituto di merceologia. Catania. *Annali Merceol. sicil.* [1932–] **Rt.** 32–33.

3072 **Annali Merck.** Milano. *Annali Merck*

3073 **Annali** di **microbiologia** (*afterwards* ed **enzimologia**). Milano. *Annali Microbiol.* [1949–] **L.**SC. 54–; **R.**D.; **Rt.**; **Y.**

Annali del **Museo civico** di **storia naturale** di **Genova.** *See* 3074.

3074 **Annali** del **Museo civico** di **storia naturale Giacomo Doria.** Genova. *Annali Mus. civ. Stor. nat. Giacomo Doria* [1870–] **L.**BM.; BM^N.; E.; EB. 93–; L.; Z.; **C.**P. 84–19; UL. 78–; **Cr.**N. 34–; **E.**R. 72–; **Ld.**U. 35–; **O.**H. 35–45; R.; **Pl.**M. 52–.

3075 **Annali** del **Museo libico** di **storia naturale.** Tripoli. *Annali Mus. libico Stor. nat.* **L.**BM^N. 39–53.

3076 **Annali** del **Museo Pitrè.** Palermo. *Annali Mus. Pitrè* [1950–] **L.**AN. 51–.

3077 **Annali** di **neuropsichiatria** e **psicoanalisi.** Napoli. *Annali Neuropsich. Psicoanal.* [1954–] **L.**MA. [*Replaces:* 3078]

3078 **Annali** di **nevrologia.** Napoli. *Annali Nevrol.* [1883–31] **L.**MD. 04–31 imp. [*Formed part of:* 34602 *for* 1924–26; *Replaces:* 3077]

3079 **Annali** di **odontologia.** Roma. *Annali Odont.* [1916–] **L.**D. 22–31; MD. imp. [>4386, 1934–37]

3080 **Annali** di **oncologia sperimentale.** Torino. *Annali Oncol. sper.*

3081 **Annali** dell'**Ospedale psichiatrico provinciale** in **Perugia.** *Annali Osp. psichiat. prov. Perugia* **L.**MD. 29–. [*C. of:* 3067]

3082 **Annali** dell'**Osservatorio** di **economia agraria** di **Bologna.** *Annali Oss. Econ. agr. Bologna*

3083 **Annali** dell'**Osservatorio** di **economia agraria** per la **Lombardia.** Milano. *Annali Oss. Econ. agr. Lombardia*

3084 **Annali** dell'**Osservatorio** di **economia agraria** di **Portici.** Roma. *Annali Oss. Econ. agr. Portici* **Md.**H. 40; **O.**AEC. 40.

3085 **Annali** dell'**Osservatorio** di **economia agraria** per la **Toscana.** Firenze. *Annali Oss. Econ. agr. Toscana*

3086 **Annali** del **Osservatorio vesuviano.** Napoli. *Annali Oss. vesuv.* **L.**BM. 24–25; GL. 25–35 imp.

3087 **Annali** di **ostetricia** e **ginecologia.** Napoli. *Annali Ostet. Ginec.* [1879–] **L.**MA. 29– imp.; MD.; S. 79–40; **Br.**U. 94–02; **Dn.**U. 04–07; **E.**P. imp.

Annali di **ottalmologia.** Pavia. *See* 3088.

3088 **Annali** di **ottalmologia** e **clinica oculista.** Pavia. *Annali Ottal. Clin. ocul.* [1871–] **L.**MA. 51–; MD. 07– imp.; OP. 71–15: 22; U. 50–; **G.**F. 04–06; **M.**MS. 71–79.

3089 **Annali** del **Pontificio Istituto superiore** di **scienze** e **lettere** di **Santa Chiara.** Napoli. *Annali pont. Ist. sup. Sci. Lett. S Chiara* [1960–] **L.**BM^N. [*C. of:* 3054]

Annali della **R. Accademia** d'**agricoltura** di **Torino.** *See* 3001.

3089^c **Annali** del **R. Istituto** di **clinica chirurgica** di **Roma.** Roma. *Annali R. Ist. Clin. chir. Roma*

3090 **Annali** del **R. Istituto** di **patologia chirurgica** e **della Clinica chirurgica propedeutica.** Padova. *Annali R. Ist. Patol. chir.* **L.**S. 09–13 imp.; **Lv.**U. 09–12.

3091 **Annali** del **R. Istituto superiore agrario** e **forestale nazionale.** Firenze. *Annali R. Ist. sup. agr. for. naz.* [1914–36] **L.**MY. 24–36; **C.**A. 28–36; **E.**U. 19–36 imp.; **O.**F. [*C. as:* 3013]

3092 **Annali** del **R. Istituto superiore agrario** di **Portici.** *Annali R. Ist. sup. agr. Portici* [1926–35] **L.**AM.; BM.; BM^N.; EB.; GL.; MY.; **C.**P.; UL.; **Db.**; **Md.**H.; **Rt.** [*C. of:* 3105; *C. as:* 3014]
   Annali del **R. Istituto superiore forestale nazionale.** Firenze. *See* 3091.

3093 **Annali** del **R. Istituto tecnico Antonio Zanon** in **Udine.** Udine. *Annali R. Ist. tec. Antonio Zanon*
   Annali del **R. Laboratorio autonomo** di **chimica agraria** in **Forlì.** *See* 3058.
   Annali del **R. Osservatorio vesuviano.** *See* 3086.

3094 **Annali** della **R. Scuola** d'**ingegneria** di **Padova.** *Annali R. Scu. Ing. Padova* **L.**P. 26.
   Annali della **R. Scuola normale superior, Pisa.** *See* 3104.

3095 **Annali** della **R. Stazione agraria** di **Forlì.** Forlì. *Annali R. Staz. agr. Forlì* [1872–09] [*C. as:* 3058]
   Annali della **R. Stazione chimico-agraria sperimentale** di **Roma.** *See* 3109.
   Annali della **R. Stazione sperimentale agraria** di **Modena.** *See* 3111.

3096 **Annali** della **R. Stazione sperimentale** di **agrumicoltura** e **frutticoltura** in **Acireale.** Acireale. *Annali R. Staz. sper. Agrumic. Fruttic. Acireale* [1912–48] **L.**AM.; EB.; K. 12–37; MY. 19–48; **C.**A. 32–48; **Md.**H.; **Rt.** 12–37. [*C. of:* 8199]

3097 **Annali** dei **RR. Istituti tecnico** e **nautico** di **Livorno.** Livorno. *Annali RR. Ist. tec. naut. Livorno*

3098 **Annali** di **radiologia diagnostica.** Bologna. *Annali Radiol. diagn.* [1939–] **L.**MA. 43–. [*C. of:* 3099]

3099 **Annali** di **radiologia** e **fisica medica.** Bologna. *Annali Radiol. Fis. med.* [1934–38] [*C. of:* 47963; *C. as:* 3098]

3100 **Annali, ricerche** e **studi** di **geografia.** Genova. *Annali Ric. Stud. Geogr.* **E.**G. (curr.)

3101 **Annali** della **sanità pubblica.** Roma. *Annali Sanità pubbl.* [1948–] **L.**H.; MA.; MD.; TD.; **Y.** [*C. of:* 35034]

3102 **Annali Schiapparelli.** Rassegna trimestra di terapia, farmacologia e chimica farmacologica. Torino. *Annali Schiapparelli* [1927–]

3103 **Annali Sclavo.** Rivista di microbiologia e di immunologia. Milan. *Annali Sclavo* [1959–] **L.**MA.

3104 **Annali** della **Scuola normale superiore.** Pisa. *Annali Scu. norm. sup., Pisa* [1871–] Scienze fisiche e matematiche. **L.**BM.; M. 71–12 (curr.); U. 56–; UC.; **C.**P. 32–; **E.**Q. 32–; R. 32–; **G.**U. 52–; **N.**U. 57–; **O.**R.; **Y.**

3105 **Annali** della **Scuola superiore** di **agricoltura** in **Portici.** Napoli. *Annali Scu. sup. Agric. Portici* [1878–25] **L.**AM. 99–25; BM. 07–29; BM^N.; EB. 24–25; GL. 00–25; MY. 20–25; **Bl.**U. 99–08; **Bm.**U. 78–03; **C.**P. 07–25; UL. 99–25; **Db.** 08–25; **G.**U. 99–25; **Lv.**U. 07–08; **O.**R. 99–04 imp.; **Rt.** 99–25. [*C. as:* 3092]

3106 **Annali** della **Società agraria provinciale.** Bologna. *Annali Soc. agr. prov., Bologna*

3107 **Annali. Società** degli **ingegneri** e degli **architetti italiani.** Roma. *Annali Soc. Ing. Archit. ital.* [1886–20] [*Replaced by:* 21225]

3108 **Annali** della **sperimentazione agraria.** Roma. *Annali Sper. agr.* [1930–41: 47–] **L.**A. 47– imp.; AM.; BM. 51–; C. 48–; EB. 47–; MY. 47–; P. 53–; UC. 32–; **Abd.**R. 50–; **Bn.**U. 33–; **Br.**A. imp.; U.; **C.**A.; **E.**AB. 48–; W. imp.; **Hu.**G. 47–; **Ld.**U. 60–; **Md.**H. 47–; **R.**D. imp.; U. 32–; **Rt.**; **Y.** [*Also supplements*]

3109 **Annali** della **Stazione chimico-agraria sperimentale** di **Roma.** Roma. *Annali Staz. chim.-agr. sper. Roma* [1906–41: 48–] **L.**A. 49: 51–52; AM. 31–55 imp.; C. 55–; K. 06–09; **C.**A. 30–; **Hu.**G. 49–; **Rt.**

3110 **Annali** della **Stazione chimico-agrario sperimentale** di **Udine.** *Annali Staz. chim.-agr. sper. Udine* [1871–] **Rt.** 25.

3111 **Annali** della **Stazione sperimentale agraria** di **Modena.** *Annali Staz. sper. agr. Modena* [1927–] **L.**AM. 27–31 imp.; MY. 27–37; **C.**A. 27–37; **Rt.** [*C. of:* 50875]

3112 **Annali** della **Stazione sperimentale** per le **malattie infettive** del **bestiame.** Napoli. *Annali Staz. sper. Mal. infett. Best.* [1911–22] **L.**EB. 13–22; V.; **Bm.**U. 11–19; **C.**UL.; **E.**U. 11–18; **G.**U. 13–20; **Lv.**U.; **O.**R. 11–13.

3113 **Annali. Stazione sperimentale** di **risicoltura** e delle **colture irrigue.** Vercelli. *Annali Staz. sper. Risicolt.* [1953–] **L.**P.; TP.; **C.**A.

3114 **Annali** di **stomatologia.** Roma. *Annali Stomat.* [1952–] **L.**D.; MA.

3115 **Annali** di **tecnica agraria.** Roma. *Annali Tec. agr.* [1928–] **L.**AM. 28–37; **C.**A. 34–39.
   Annali. Ufficio centrale di **meteorologia** e **geofisica.** *See* 3116.

3116 **Annali** dell'**Ufficio centrale meteorologico** e **geodinamico italiano.** Roma. *Annali Uff. cent. met. geodin. ital.* [1879–15: 21–25] **L.**MO. imp.; SC. 88–15: 21–25; **Db.** 82–15: 21–25; **E.**M. 79–15: 21–23. [*C. as:* 31309]

3117 **Annali** dell'**Ufficio presagi.** Ministero dell'aeronautica. Roma. *Annali Uff. presagi Minist. Aeronaut.* **L.**G. 27–31; MO. 27–35; **E.**M.

3118 **Annali** dell'**Università** di **Ferrara.** Ferrara. *Annali Univ. Ferrara*
   Nuove serie
     Sezione 3. Biologia animale [1951–] **L.**BM^N.; **Y.**
     Sezione 4. Botanica [1951–] **L.**BM^N.; **Y.**
     Sezione 5. Chimica pura ed applicata [1954–] **L.**P.; **Y.**
     Sezione 6. Fisiologia e chimica biologica [1952–] **Y.**
     Sezione 7. Scienze matematiche [1952–] **L.**SC.
     Sezione 9. Scienze geologiche e paleontologiche (*afterwards* Scienze geologiche e mineralogiche) [1951–] **L.**BM^N.; **Y.**
     Sezione 13. Anatomia e fisiologia comparate [1956–] **L.**BM^N.
     Sezione 15. Paleontologia umana e paletnologia [1959–] **L.**BM^N.; **Y.**

3119 **Annali** delle **Università toscana.** Pisa. *Annali Univ. tosc.* [1846–31] **L.**BM. 1846–15; BM^N.; GL. 00–25; MD. 01–26 imp.; **C.**UL. 1846–72; **Db.** 19–; **O.**B. 1846–17. [*C. in:* 3104]

3120 **Annali** delle **utilizzazione** delle **acque.** Roma. *Annali Util. Acque* [1924–27] **L.**P.

3121 **Annali** della **Vasca nazionale** per le **esperienze** di **architettura navale** in **Roma.** *Annali Vasca naz. Esper. Archit. nav.* [1931–] **L.**P. 31–42; **G.**E. 31–39; **Lv.**U.

3122 **Annali** del **Villagio sanatoriale** di **Sondalo.** Sondrio. *Annali Vill. sanat. Sondalo* [*Supplement to:* 3101]
    Annals of the **Agricultural College** of **Sweden.** *See* 27808 and 28133.

3123 **Annals** of the **Agricultural Experiment Station.** Government-General of Chosen. Suigen. Chosen. *Ann. agric. Exp. Stn Chosen* [1928–] **L.**AM. 37–38; **E**B. 37–38 imp.; **K.** imp.; **M**Y. 37–39.

3124 **Annals** of **Agricultural Science.** University of A'in Shams. Cairo. *Ann. agric. Sci. Univ. A'in Shams* [1956–] **L.**AM.; **E**B.; **K.**; **Abd.**R.; **Abs.**U.; **Br.**A.; **C.**A.; **Ld.**U.; **Md.**H.; **N.**U.; **Rt.**

3125 **Annals** of the **Allegheny Observatory.** Allegheny, Pa. *Ann. Allegheny Obs.*

3126 **Annals** of **Allergy.** Minneapolis, etc. *Ann. Allergy* [1943–] **L.**MA. 46–; **M**D.; **U.** 50–; **Lv.**M. 48–; **M.**MS. 54–; **O.**R. 58–.; **Y.**

3127 **Annals** of the **Andersonian Naturalists' Society.** Glasgow. *Ann. Anderson. Nat. Soc.* [1893–36] **L.**BM. 93–14; **B**M[N]. 93–14; **Abd.**U. 93–14; **Abs.**N. 36; **C.**UL. 00–14; **E.**C. 93–00; **D.** 93–14; **G.** 93–14; **R.** 93–25; **G.**F. 93; **M.**; **N.**; **T.** 93–00; **U.** 93–08.

3128 **Annals** of **Animal Psychology.** Tokyo. *Ann. Anim. Psychol., Tokyo* **O.**Z. 53–.

3129 **Annals** of **Applied Biology.** Cambridge. *Ann. appl. Biol.* [1914–] **L.**AM.; **B**M.; **B**M[N].; **E**B.; **H**S.; **I**C. 29–; **K.**; **M**D. 49–; **M**Y.; **N**C. imp.; **P.**; **Q**M. 55–; **S**C.; **T**D.; **T**P. 26–; **U.** 14–18: 30– imp.; **U**C.; **Z.**; **Abd.**U.; **Abs.**A.; **N.**; **U.** 14–38: 43–; **Ba.**I. 42–; **Bl.**U. 37–; **Bm.**U.; **Bn.**U.; **Br.**A.; **U.**; **C.**A.; **AB.** 30–; **B.** BO.; UL.; **Cr.**M. 20–; **U.** 16– imp.; **Db.**; **Dn.**U. 61–; **E.**A.; **U.**; **W.** 14–24 imp.; **Ep.**D. 58–; **Ex.**U. 14–32; **Fr.** 14–16: 26–; **G.**M.; **T.** 25–31; **U.**; **H.**U.; **Hu.**G. imp.; **Je.** 29–; **Ld.**U.; **Lo.** 23–26: 57–; **Lv.**U.; **M.**P.; **U.**; **Md.**H.; **Mi.** 47–; **N.**U.; **Nw.**A. imp.; **O.**H. 14–55 imp.; **R.**; **R**E.; **Pl.**M.; **R.**D. 22–31; **U.**; **Rt.**; **Sa.** 36–; **Sh.**U. 32–; **Sil.** 47–; **Y.**

3130 **Annals** of **Archaeology** and **Anthropology.** Liverpool. *Ann. Archaeol. Anthrop.* [1908–48] **L.**AN.; **B**M.; **U.**; **U**C. 08–27; **Abs.**N.; **U.** 21–48; **Bm.**P.; **U.**; **Br.**P. 29–39; **U.**; **C.**E.; **UL.**; **Db.**; **E.**A.; **U.**; **V.**; **Ex.**U. 23–48; **G.**M.; **U.**; **Ld.**U. 08–27; **Lv.**P. 08–40; **U.**; **M.**P.; **Nw.**A. 10–36 imp.; **O.**B.; **Sa.** 08–16; **Sh.**U.

3131 **Annals** of the **Association** of **American Geographers.** Minneapolis, etc. *Ann. Ass. Am. Geogr.* [1911–] **L.**B. imp.; **B**M. imp.; **G.** 12–; **S**C. 33–; **U.** 40–; **U**C.; **Abd.**U.; **Abs.**U. imp.; **Bl.**U. imp.; **Bm.**U.; **C.**GG. 38–40: 48–; **UL.**; **Db.** 40–; **E.**G.; **U.** 21–; **Ex.**U.; **G.**U. 33– imp.; **H.**U.; **Ld.**U.; **Lv.**P. 58–; **N.**U.; **Nw.**A. 11–22: 40: 46–; **O.**G.; **R.**U.; **Rt.** 47–; **Sa.** 49–; **Sh.**U.; **Sw.**U.; **Y.**
    Annals of the **Astronomical Observatory** of **Harvard College.** *See* 3150.

3132 **Annals** of the **Astrophysical Observatory** of the **Smithsonian Institution.** Washington. *Ann. astrophys. Obs. Smithson. Instn* [1900–] **L.**AS.; **B**M.; **M**O.; **P.**; **R.**; **S**C.; **U.** 00–42; **U**C. 00–13; **Abd.**U. 00–42; **Bl.**U. 00–22; **Bm.**U.; **Br.**U. 00–22; **C.**O.; **P.** 00–32; **UL.**; **Db.**; **E.**F.; 00–08; **O.**; **R.** 00–42; **U.**; **G.**U. 08–42; **Ld.**U. 02–; **Lv.**P. 42–; **U.**; **M.**P. 00–22; **U.** 00–42; **O.**R.; **Sa.** 00–42.

3133 **Annals** of **Biochemistry** and **Experimental Medicine.** Calcutta. *Ann. Biochem. exp. Med.* [1941–] **L.**C. 41–50 imp.; **C**B. 58–; **M**C. 57–; **M**D. 51–; **S.** 55–58; **S**C.; **T**D.; **Abd.**R. imp.; **Br.**U. 55–; **C.**P. 57–; **R.**D. 50–52: 55–; **Sal.** 55–; **Y.**
    Annals of the **Biological Research Institute,** Perm. *See* 54483.
    Annals of **Biology.** Moscow. *See* 3199.
    Annals of **Blue Hill Meteorological Observatory.** *See* 3150.

3134 **Annals** of the **Bolus Herbarium** of the **South African College.** Cape Town. *Ann. Bolus Herb.* [1914–28] **L.**BM[N].; **H**S.; **K.**; **L.**; **Abs.**N.; **C.**BO.; **UL.**; **Db.**; **E.**B.; **M.**U.; **O.**BO. 14–18; **R.**
    Annals of the **Bosscha Observatory.** *See* 2639.

3135 **Annals** of the **Botanic Garden, Buitenzorg.** *Ann. bot. Gdn Buitenz.* [1941–49] **L.**BM[N].; **K.**; **L.**; **R.**; **S**C.; **U**C.; **Bn.**U.; **C.**BO.; **UL.**; **Db.**; **E.**B.; **U.**; **G.**U.; **Ld.**U.; **Lv.**U.; **M.**U.; **Md.**H.; **O.**BO.; **Pl.**M. [*C. of:* 2807; > 51691, 1943; *C. as:* 2690]

3136 **Annals** of **Botany.** London. *Ann. Bot.* [1887–] **L.**AM. 13–; **B.**; **B**M.; **B**M[N].; **H**O. 12–; **H**S.; **K.**; **L.**; **N**C. 55–; **P.** 87–94: 09–; **P**H.; **Q**M.; **R**I.; **S**C.; **U.**; **U**C.; **Abd.**U.; **Abs.**A. 33–; **N.** 12–; **U.**; **Ba.**I.; **Bl.**U.; **Bm.**P.; **T.** 45–; **U.**; **Bn.**U.; **Br.**A. 27–49: 59–; **U.**; **C.**AB. 26–; **BO.**; **Cr.**M. 26–; **U.**; **Db.**; **Dn.**U. 26–; **E.**A.; **B.**; **H**W. 53–; **R.**; **S**W. 46–54: 57–; **T.**; **U.**; **Ex.**U. 00–; **Fr.** 53–; **G.**M.; **N.** 87–51; **T.** 10–22; **U.**; **H.**U.; **Hu.**G. 37–; **Ld.**P. 87–27; **U.**; **Lv.**P. imp.; **U.**; **M.**P.; **U.**; **Md.**H. 23–; **N.**U.; **Nw.**A.; **P.** 87–16; **O.**BO.; **R.**; **R**E. 37–; **Pit.**F. 49–; **R.**U.; **Rt.**; **Sa.**; **Sh.**U.; **Sil.** 58–; **Sw.**U. 22–; **Y.** [*Memoirs at:* 3137]

3137 **Annals of Botany Memoirs.** London. *Ann. Bot. Mem.* [1950–] **L.**BM.; **B**M[N].; **O.**R.; **Y.**
    Annals of the **CAAS.** Czechoslovak Academy of Agricultural Sciences. *See* 48606 and 48607.
    Annals of the **Cape Observatory.** *See* 3185.

3138 **Annals** of the **Carnegie Museum.** Pittsburg. *Ann. Carneg. Mus.* [1901–] **L.**BM[N].; **Z.**; **Bm.**U. 03–; **C.**P.; **Dn.**U. imp.; **O.**R. 01–09 imp.; **Sa.** 01–04; **Y.**

3139 **Annals** of **Clinical Medicine.** Baltimore. *Ann. clin. Med.* [1922–27] **L.**MD.; **Bl.**U. imp. [*C. of:* 3164; *C. as:* 3154]

3140 **Annals** of the **Computation Laboratory** of **Harvard College.** Cambridge. Mass. *Ann. Computn Lab. Harv.* [1946–] **L.**SC.; **O.**R.; **Y.**

3141 **Annals** of the **Cyprus Natural History Society.** Nicosia. *Ann. Cyprus nat. Hist. Soc.* [1908–13] **L.**BM. 10–13; **B**M[N].; **Z.** 11–13; **Db.** 08–09; **O.**R. 10–13.
    Annals of the **Czechoslovak Academy** of **Agriculture.** *See* 48606 and 48607.

3142 **Annals** of **Dearborn Observatory, Northwestern University.** Evanston, Ill. *Ann. Dearborn Obs.* [1915–] **L.**AS.; **S**C.; **C.**O.; **E.**O.; **M.**U. 15–58 imp.; **O.**O.

3143 **Annals** of **Dentistry.** Albany. *Ann. Dent.* [1936–] **L.**D. imp. [*C. of:* 26557]

3144 **Annals** of **Durban Museum.** Durban. *Ann. Durban Mus.* [1914–47] **L.**BM. 14–21; **B**M[N].; **E.** 19–21; **E**B.; **L.** 14–32; **R.**; **Z.**; **Abs.**N.; **C.**UL.; **Cr.**M.; **Dm.** 17–47; **E.**F.; **Lv.**U. 14–21; **M.**U.; **Pl.**M. [*C. as:* 17284]

3145 **Annals** of the **Entomological Society** of **America.** Columbus, O., etc. *Ann. ent. Soc. Am.* [1908–] **L.**AM. 54–; BM^N.; E.; EB.; QM. 50–; SC.; 33–; Z.; **Bm.**U.; **Bn.**U. 15– imp.; **C.**B.; UL.; **Cr.**U. 60–; **E.**U.; **G.**U.; **H.**U. 51–; **Ld.**U. 30–; **N.**U.; **O.**H. 15–55 imp.; R.; **Rt.**; **Sw.**U. 60–; **Y.**

3146 **Annals** of the **Entomological Society** of **Quebec.** *Ann. ent. Soc. Queb.* [1956–] **L.**AM.; BM^N.; EB.; **C.**A.; B.; **Ld.**U. 60–; **O.**H.; **Rt.**; **Y.**

3147 **Annals** of **Eugenics.** London. *Ann. Eugen.* [1925–54] **L.**AN. 25–39; BM.; H. 25–39; MA. imp.; MC. 25–28; MD.; RI.; SC.; TD.; U.; UC.; **Abd.**U. 25–31: 47–54; **Abs.**N.; U. 26–31: 41–54; **Ba.**I. 34–54; **Bl.**U.; **Bm.**P.; U.; **Br.**U. 47–54; **C.**A. 34–54; GE. 35–54; SL. 34–54; UL.; **Cr.**MD. 46–54; **Db.**; **E.**A.; AG.; S. 27–30; U. 34–54; **G.**F. 25–52; M.; PH. 25–33; U.; **Ld.**U. 47–54; W. 37–51; **M.**C. 36–52; MS. 46–54; P. 25–40; **Nw.**A. 46–54; **O.**R.; **R.**D. 34–45; **Rt.** 34–54; **Sa.**; **Sh.**U. 53–54. [*C. as:* 3151]
Annals of **Food Technology** and **Chemistry.** Warszawa. *See* 48082.

3148 **Annals** of **General Practice.** Sydney. *Ann. gen. Pract.* [1956–] **L.**MA.
Annals of **Geomorphology.** *See* 58602.
Annals of **Glaciology.** Berlin. *See* 58643.

3149 **Annals** of **Gynecology** and **Paediatry.** Boston. *Ann. Gynec. Paediat.* [1887–09] **L.**MD. 89–01; **G.**F. 92–98. [*C. as:* 3163]

3150 **Annals** of **Harvard College Observatory.** Cambridge, Mass. *Ann. Harv. Coll. Obs.* [1855–] **L.**AS.; BM.; MO. 89–27 imp.; R. 1855–51; SC.; UC. 1857–13 imp.; **Bm.**U. 03–08; **C.**O.; UL.; **Cr.**P. 90–00 imp.; **Db.** 00–08; **E.**O.; R.; U. 90–97; **G.**U. 86–91; **M.**U. 1855–54 imp.; **Nw.**A. 25–; **O.**O.; R.; **Sa.** 1855–67. [*Meteorology* 1928 *appears in* 35611]

3151 **Annals** of **Human Genetics.** London. *Ann. hum. Genet.* [1954–] **L.**BM.; MA.; MD.; RI.; SC.; TD.; U.; UC.; **Abd.**U.; **Abs.**N.; U.; **Ba.**I.; **Bl.**U.; **Bm.**P.; U.; **Br.**U.; **C.**A.; GE.; SL.; UL.; **Cr.**MD.; **Db.**; **Dn.**U. 55–; **E.**A.; AG.; AR.; U.; **G.**M.; U.; **Ld.**U.; **M.**MS.; **Nw.**A.; **O.**R.; **Rt.**; **Sa.**; **Sh.**U.; **Y.** [*C. of:* 3147]
Annals of the **Institute** of **Forest Research, Prague.** *See* 48677.

3152 **Annals** of the **Institute** of **Laryngology** and **Otology.** London. *Ann. Inst. Lar. Otol.* [1949–] **L.**MA.; MD.
Annals of the **Institute** of **Physico-Chemical Analysis.** Leningrad. *See* 24388.

3153 **Annals** of the **Institute** of **Statistical Mathematics.** Tokyo. *Ann. Inst. statist. Math., Tokyo* [1949–] **L.**SC.; **Abd.**U.; **C.**P.; SL.; **Y.**

3154 **Annals** of **Internal Medicine.** Ann Arbor, etc. *Ann. intern. Med.* [1927–] **L.**CB. 58–; GH. 46–; MA. 34–; MD.; S.; TD. 46–; U. 50–; UCH. 49–; **Abd.**R. 41–; U. 47–; **Bl.**U. imp.; **Bm.**U. 44–; **Br.**U. 28– imp.; **C.**MS. 59–; **Db.** 53–; **Dn.**U. 53–; **E.**U. 30–; **G.**F. 44–; U. 31–; **Lv.**M.; **M.**MS. 33–; **O.**R. 31–; **Y.** [*C. of:* 3139]

3155 **Annals** of the **International Geophysical Year.** London. *Ann. int. geophys. Yr* [1957–] **L.**MO.; P.; **Bl.**U. imp.; **Bm.**P.; U.; **C.**UL.; **E.**A.; **Ld.**P.; **M.**P.; U. 57–59; **O.**R. 60–; **Sa.**; **Y.**
Annals. Leningrad State University of the name of A. S. Boubnoff. *See* 55428.

3156 **Annals** of **Lowell Observatory.** Flagstaff, Ariz. *Ann. Lowell Obs.* [1898–05] **L.**AS.; BM.; SC.; **C.**O. 90–05; **Cr.**P.; **E.**O.; **O.**O.; R.

3157 **Annals** of the **Lund Observatory.** Lund. *Ann. Lund Obs.* [1926–] **L.**AS.; SC. 31–42; **M.**U. 31–57 imp.; **O.**O. 31–.

3158 **Annals** and **Magazine** of **Natural History.** London. *Ann. Mag. nat. Hist.* [1838–] **L.**AM. 20–; BM. 1841–; BM^N.; E.; EB. 28–46; GL. 00–; GM.; HO. 05–; L.; NC. 55–; PH. 90–06; QM. 48–; R.; SC.; U.; UC. 1842–; Z.; **Abd.**M. 48– imp.; U.; **Abs.**N.; U. 37–; **Bl.**U.; **Bm.**P.; U. 28–; **Bn.**U. 48–; **Br.**P. 05–18; U. 1838–1849: 24–; **Bra.**P. 72–52; **C.**B.; BO. 1838–77; P.; UL. 1841–; **Cr.**M. imp.; U. 38–; **Db.**; **Dn.**U. 1852–01 imp.; **E.**A.; D. 1847–15; F. 1858–; R.; T. 88–; U.; **Ex.**U. 56–; **G.**F. 1838–1844: 1858–76; M. 78–; U.; **Ld.**P. imp.; U. 1838–36: 48–; **Lo.** 20–; **Lv.**P.; U. imp.; **M.**P. 74–; U. imp.; **Md.**H. 26–58; **Mi.** 46–; **N.**U. 53–; **Nw.**A.; **O.**H. 1838–27 imp.; R.; **Pl.**M.; **R.**U. 2c–; **Sa.**; **Sal.** 22–42; **Sh.**U. 25–; **Y.**
Annals. Manchuria Research Society. *See* 54927.

3159 **Annals** of **Mathematical Statistics.** Ann Arbor, etc. *Ann. math. Statist.* [1930–] **L.**BM. 51–; M.; NC.55–; SC.; UC. 47–; **Abd.**U. 47–; **Bl.**U.; **Bm.**U. 40–; **Br.**A. 54–; U. 60–; **C.**GE.; P.; SL.; UL.; **Db.** 39–; **Dn.**U. 49–; **E.**Q.; R. 38–; **Ep.**D. 37–; **Ex.**U. 56–; **F.**A. 45–; **G.**T. 54–; U.; **Hu.**G. 58–; **Ld.**U.; W. 48–52; **M.**C. 38–; D. 43–; U.; **N.**U. 51–; **Nw.**A. 30–34: 45–; **O.**R.; **R.**D. 49–; **Rt.**; **Sa.** 52–; **Sh.**IO. 51–; U. 48–; **Sw.**U. 45–; **Wd.** 57–; **Y.**

3160 **Annals** of **Mathematics.** Princeton, etc. *Ann. Math.* [1884–] **L.**BM. 52–; M. 85– imp.; QM. 50–; R. 30–; SC. 99–; U. 48–; UC. 88–; **Abd.**U. 38–; **Abs.**U. 31–; **Bl.**U. 29–; **Bm.**T. 47–49; U. 28–; **Br.**U. 28–; **C.**P.; UL.; **Cr.**U. 48–; **Db.** 99–; **Dn.**U. 19–; **E.**A. 00–11; Q. imp.; R.; **Ex.**U. 36–; **G.**T. 58–; U. 99–; **H.**U. 46–; **Ld.**U. imp.; **Lv.**P. 53–; U. 24–31; **M.**U. 08–; **N.**U. imp.; **Nw.**A. 30–; **O.**R. 84–11: 20–; **R.**U. 46–; **Sa.** 35–; **Sh.**U. 24–; **Sw.**U. 45–; **Y.**

3161 **Annals** of **Mathematics Studies.** Princeton. *Ann. Math. Stud.* [1940–] **L.**U. 42–; **Bl.**U. 40–56 imp.; **M.**U. 42– imp.; **Sw.**U.

3162 **Annals** of **Medical History.** New York. *Ann. med. Hist.* [1917–42] **L.**BM. 23–42; MC.; MD.; S.; TD. 24–42 imp.; **Bm.**U.; **Br.**U.; **C.**PA. 29–42; UL. 23–42; **Cr.**MD.; **Dn.**U. 17–31; **E.**P.; **G.**U.; **Ld.**U. 23–42; **Lv.**M.; **M.**MS. 33–42; **Nw.**A.; **O.**R.; **Sa.**

3163 **Annals** of **Medical Practice.** Boston. *Ann. med. Pract.* [1910] [*C. of:* 3149]

3164 **Annals** of **Medicine.** Hagerstown, Md. *Ann. Med., Hagerstown* [1920–21] [*C. as:* 3139]

3165 **Annals** of **Missouri Botanical Garden.** St. Louis, Mo. *Ann. Mo. bot. Gdn* [1914–] **L.**BM^N.; HS.; K.; L.; MY. 14–55; SC.; TP. 14–56; UC. 14–23; **Abd.**U.; **Abs.**A. 52–; **Bn.**U. imp.; **C.**P.; **Cr.**N.; **Db.**; **E.**B.; F.; R.; **Ep.**D. 47–; **Hu.**G. 44–; **Ld.**U.; **Lv.**U.; **M.**U. imp.; **O.**BO. 43–; **Pl.**M. 14–55; **Rt.**; **Y.** [*C. of:* 44582]

3166 **Annals** of the **Natal Museum.** Pietermaritzburg, etc. *Ann. Natal Mus.* [1906–] **L.**AM. imp.; BM.; BM^N.; GM.; HO. 19–; K.; L.; R. 06–49; UC.; Z.; **Abs.**N. 09–; **C.**B.; P.; UL.; **Db.**; **E.**A.; F.; R.; **G.**N. 09–37; **Lo.** imp.; **Lv.**U.; **M.**U.; **Mi.** 47–; **O.**R.; **Pl.**M. imp.; **Y.**

3167 **Annals** of the **New York Academy** of **Sciences.** New York. *Ann. N.Y. Acad. Sci.* [1823–] **L.**BM. 1823–06; BM^N.; C. 42–54 imp.; CB. 47– imp.; GL. (geol.); L. 77–; MC. 41–; MD. 42– imp.; P. 77–; R.; RI. 87–; SC.; U. 51–; UC. 40–; VC. 56–; Z.; **Abd.**M. 98–04; U. 55–; **Bl.**U. imp.; **Bm.**U. 79–; **Bn.**U. 16– imp.; **Br.**P. 98–05;

U. 07– imp.; **C.**APH. 51–; P. 79–; R. 56– imp.; UL. 79–85;
Db. 1853–; **Dn.**U. 55–; **E.**B. 79–; C. 77– imp.; G. 06–;
G.U. 87– imp.; **Ld.**U. 43– imp.; **Lv.**P. 53–; U. 79– imp.;
M.U. 82–89: 11–19 imp.; **Nw.**A. 38–43: 52–; **O.**B. 02–;
BI.; **Pl.**M. 98–; **Sh.**U. 59–; **Y.**

Annals of the **Observatory** of **Lund.** *See* 3157.

3168 **Annals** of **Occupational Hygiene.** London, etc.
Ann. occup. Hyg. [1958–] **L.**BM.; MD.; P.; TD.; **Bl.**U.;
Cr.MD.; **Dn.**U. 59–; **O.**R.; **Y.**

3169 **Annals** of **Ophthalmology.** St. Louis. *Ann.*
Ophthal. [1892–17] **L.**MA. 02–17; MD.; OP. imp.; **Br.**U.
94–95; **Dn.**U. 97–17 imp.; **Sa.** 97–15 imp.

3170 **Annals** of the **Orgone Institute.** New York.
Ann. Orgone Inst. [1947–] **L.**MA.; **C.**UL. [*C. of:* 23888]

3171 **Annals** of **Oriental Research.** Madras University. Madras. *Ann. orient. Res.* [1937–] **L.**BM. [*C. of:*
26619]

3172 **Annals** of **Otology, Rhinology,** and **Laryngology.**
St. Louis. *Ann. Otol. Rhinol. Lar.* [1897–] **L.**MA. 09–17;
37–; MD. 04–06: 12–; S. 11–; U. 50–; UCH. 51–; **Abd.**U.
37–; **Bl.**U. 40– imp.; **Br.**U. 09– imp.: 38: 43–; **Cr.**MD.
33–; **Db.** 24–29 imp.; **Dn.**U. 97–98: 24–35 v. imp.:
47–; **E.**S. 20–; U. 39–; **G.**U. 20– imp.; **Ld.**U. 37–; **Lv.**M.
36–; **M.**MS. 23–; **Nw.**A. 26–; **Y.**

3173 **Annals** of **Physical Medicine.** London. *Ann.*
phys. Med. [1952–] **L.**BM.; GH. 54–; MA.; MD.; S.; **C.**UL.;
E.A.; **Ld.**U. 56–; **Lv.**M.; **O.**B.; R.; **Y.**

3174 **Annals** of **Physics.** Baltimore etc. *Ann. Phys.*
[1957–] **L.**KC.; P.; QM.; RI. 59–; SC.; U.; **Bl.**U.; **Bm.**U.;
Bn.U.; **Br.**U.; **C.**P.; R.; **Db.**; **E.**U.; **F.**A.; **G.**T.; U.; **Ld.**U.;
M.P.; T.; U.; **Ma.**T. 57–59; **N.**U.; **O.**R.; **R.**U.; **Sa.**; **Sh.**U.;
Sw.U.; **Y.**

3175 **Annals** of the **Phytopathological Society** of
Japan. Tokyo. *Ann. phytopath. Soc. Japan* [1918–]
L.AM. 27–40 imp.; BM^N. 18–34 imp.; K. 18–23; MY.;
E.B. 18–21; **Rt.** 50–; **Y.**

3176 **Annals** of the **Pickett-Thomson Research
Laboratory.** London. *Ann. Pickett-Thomson Res. Lab.*
[1924–34] **L.**BM.; MA.; MD.; SH.; TD.; V. 27–34; **Abs.**N.;
Bm.U. 27–29; **Br.**U. 25: 30: 32–34; **C.**UL.; **Cr.**MD.;
Db.; **E.**U.; **G.**PH. 30; **Lv.**U.; **O.**R.

3177 **Annals** of **Psychical Science.** London. *Ann.*
psych. Sci. [1905–10] **L.**BM.; U.; **Bm.**U. 05–09; **C.**UL.;
Db. imp.; **G.**M.; **M.**P. **O.**R. 05–09.

3178 **Annals** of the **Queensland Museum.** Brisbane.
Ann. Qd Mus. [1891–11] **L.**BM. 00–08; BM^N.; E. 01–11
imp.; EB. imp.; GL. 91–00; L.; R. 91–97; SC. 91–00 imp.;
UC. imp.; Z. imp.; **Bl.**U. 91: 97–11; **Bm.**N.; U.; **C.**P. 92–
11; UL. 91–10; **Db.**; **E.**C. 95–11; F. imp.; R.; **Ld.**U. imp.;
Lv.U. 92–11; **M.**U.; **O.**R. 00–11; **Pl.**M. imp. [*C. as:*
31061]

3179 **Annals** of the **Research Institute** for **Microbial
Diseases.** Osaka. *Ann. Res. Inst. microb. Dis.* [1950–]
L.LI. 54–; MC. 54–57.

3180 **Annals** of the **Rheumatic Diseases.** London.
Ann. rheum. Dis. [1939–] **L.**BM.; GH. 49–; H.; MA.;
MC. 46–58; MD.; S.; U. 50–; UCH. 52–; **Abd.**U.; **Abs.**N.
44–; **Bl.**U.; **Bm.**U.; **Br.**U.; **C.**MS. 59–; UL.; **Cr.**MD. imp.;
U. 58–; **Db.**; **Dn.**U. 46–; **E.**A.; U.; **G.**F. 47–; **Ld.**U.;
Lv.M. 46–; **M.**MS.; **O.**R.; **Sh.**U. 54–; **Y.** [*C. of:* 47695]

3181 **Annals** of **Roentgenology.** New York. *Ann.*
Roentg. [1920–] **L.**MD.; RA. 20–31.

Annals of the **Royal Agricultural College** of
Sweden. *See* 27808.

3182 **Annals** of the **Royal Botanic Garden, Calcutta.**
Calcutta. *Ann. R. bot. Gdn Calcutta* [1887–39] **L.**BM.;
BM^N.; K.; L.; P. 87–31; R.; **Abd.**U.; **Bl.**U. 93–39; **C.**UL.;
Db.; **Dn.**U. 89–13 imp.; **E.**A. 87–18; B.; R. 87–36; U.;
G.U.; **M.**U. 87–05; **O.**B.; BO. 87–38; **Sa.** 87–08.

3183 **Annals** of the **Royal Botanic Gardens** of **Peradeniya.** Colombo. *Ann. R. bot. Gdns Peradeniya*
[1901–56] **L.**BM.; BM^N.; HS. 01–52; K. 01–32; L.; MY.
15–56 imp.; P. 24–45; SC.; TP. 34–56; UC. 05–56; **Abs.**N.
imp.; **Bl.**U. 24–56; **Bm.**U. 24–56; **Bn.**U. 24–56; **Br.**U.
25–56; **C.**A.; BO. 01–29; P. 24–56; UL. 04–56; **Cr.**U.
24–56; **Db.** 24–56; **E.**B. imp.; R. 01–32 imp.; U. 24–56;
G.U. 24–56; **Ld.**U. 24–56; **Lv.**U. 24–56; **M.**U.; **Md.**H.
32–56; **Nw.**A. 01–32; **O.**R. 24–56; **Rt.** 19–56 imp.;
Sa. 24–56. [*From 1924 to 1956 published as Section A of*
13655; 1957 onwards incorporated in 13656, Biological
Sciences]

3184 **Annals** of the **Royal College** of **Surgeons** of
England. London. *Ann. R. Coll. Surg.* [1947–] **L.**BM.;
CB.; D.; GH.; MA.; MC.; MD.; OP.; S.; U.; UCH.; **Abd.**U.;
Abs.N. 56–; **Bl.**U.; **Bm.**U.; **Br.**U.; **C.**MD.; PA.; UL.;
Cr.MD.; **Db.**; **E.**A.; I. 47–56; S.; U.; **G.**F.; U.; **Ld.**U.;
Lv.M.; **M.**MS.; **Nw.**A.; **O.**R.; **Y.**

3185 **Annals** of the **Royal Observatory, Cape Town.**
London. *Ann. R. Obs. Cape Town* [1886–] **L.**AS. 98–;
BM.; R.; SC. 98–; UC.; **Abd.**U.; **Abs.**N. 12– imp.; **C.**O.; UL.;
Db.; **E.**O.; R. 86–55; U. 86–31; **G.**M. imp.; U. 98–38 imp.;
Ld.U. 86–39 imp.; **M.**P. imp.; U.; **Nw.**A. 27–; **O.**O.; R.;
Sa.

3186 **Annals** of the **Royal Observatory** of **Edinburgh.**
Ann. R. Obs. Edinb. [1902–10] **L.**AS.; BM.; SC.; **Abd.**U.;
Bm.P.; **Db.**; **E.**O.; R.; U.; **Ld.**U.; **Lv.**U. 06–10; **M.**P.;
U.; **O.**O.; R.; **Sa.**

3187 **Annals** of **Science.** London. *Ann. Sci.* [1936–]
L.BM.; BM^N.; C.; MD.; NP. 54–; P.; QM.; R.; RI.; S.; SC.;
U.; UC.; **Abd.**U.; **Abs.**N.; U. 48–; **Bl.**U.; **Bm.**P.; U.; **Bn.**U.;
Br.U.; **C.**UL.; **Cr.**M.; U.; **Db.**; **E.**A.; R.; U.; **G.**T. 55–; U.;
Ld.U.; **Lv.**P. 52–; **M.**P.; U. 51–52; **N.**P.; U.; **O.**R.; **R.**U.;
Rt.; **Sa.**; **Sh.**U.; **Sw.**U. 36–39; **Y.** [*Suspended* Jan.
1943–June 1945]

3188 **Annals** of **Scottish Natural History.** Edinburgh.
Ann. Scot. nat. Hist. [1892–11] **L.**BM.; BM^N.; E. 92–00;
K.; L.; Z.; **Abd.**P.; U.; **Abs.**U.; **Bn.**U.; **Br.**U.; **C.**B.; BO.
93–95; P.; UL.; **Cr.**M. 96–97; **Db.**; **Dn.**U. imp.; **E.**A.;
B.; F.; G.; R.; U.; **G.**M.; N.; U.; **Ld.**U.; **M.**U.; **Mi.**; **O.**AP.;
BO.; OR.; R.; **Pit.**F.; **Pl.**M.; **Sa.** [*C. of:* and *Rec. as:*
49316]

3189 **Annals** of the **Solar Physics Observatory.** Cambridge. *Ann. sol. Phys. Obs.* [1915–] **L.**AS.; BM.; MO.
20– imp.; R.; SC. 30–49; U.; **Abd.**U.; **Abs.**N. 15–20;
Bm.U. 49–; **Db.** 30–; **E.**O.; R. 15–38; **M.**U. 15–49 imp.;
O.O. 30–; R. 30–; **Y.**

3190 **Annals** of the **South African Museum.** Cape
Town. *Ann. S. Afr. Mus.* [1898–] **L.**AN. 07–36; BM.;
BM^N.; E. 98–32 v. imp.; GL.; K. 11–32 imp.; L.; R.; UC.
03–24 imp.; Z.; **Abd.**U. 08–13 imp.; **Abs.**N. 08– imp.;
Bm.U. imp.; **Br.**U. 03– imp.; **C.**P.; S. (paleont.) 03–;
UL.; **Db.**; **Dm.** 03– imp.; **E.**A.; D. 13– imp.; F. 23–;
R.; U. 98–23 imp.; **Lo.** 54– imp.; **Lv.**U. 06–; **M.**U.; **O.**R.;
Pl.M.; **Wo.** 08– v. imp.; **Y.**

Annals of the **State Institute** of **Experimental
Agronomy, Petrograd.** *See* 24358.

3191 **Annals** of **Surgery.** London, Philadelphia. *Ann. Surg.* [1885-] L.BM. 92-; CB. 43-; GH. 97-; MA. imp.; MD.; S.; U. 94-16: 50-; UC. 41-; UCH. 89-; **Abd.**R. 03-17; U. 03-; **Abs.**N. 12-; **Bl.**U. 01-; **Bm.**U. 96-; **Br.**U.; **C.**PA. 85-96: 05-10 imp.; UL. 92-; **Cr.**MD. 19-; MS. 93-; **Db.**; **Dn.**U.; E.A. 92-; P.; S.; U. 89- imp.; **G.**F.; M. 90-19; U.; **Ld.**U.; **Lv.**M. 96-; U. 04-14; **M.**MS.; **Nw.**A. 92-; **O.**R. 92-; **Sa.** 97-28; **Sh.**U. 87-33: 46; **Y.**

Annals of the **Tadjïk Astronomical Observatory.** *See* 55070.

Annals of the **Tchernyshev Museum.** *See* 18883.
Annals of the **Thermotechnical Institute, Moscow.** *See* 24522.

3192 **Annals** of the **Tokyo Astronomical Observatory.** *Ann. Tokyo astr. Obs.* [1951-] L.AS.; BM.; SC.; **C.**O.; E.O.; **M.**U.; **O.**O.; **Y.** [*C. of:* 2857]

3193 **Annals** of the **Transvaal Museum.** Pretoria. *Ann. Transv. Mus.* [1908-] L.BM.; BM^N.; K. imp.; L. 08-41; R.; TP. 58-; UC.; Z.; **Abs.**U. 26-; **C.**P.; UL.; **Dm.** 09- imp.; E.R.; U. 17-; **Ld.**U.; **Lv.**U.; **M.**U. 08-52 imp.; **O.**R.; **Pl.**M. 08-58; **Y.**

3194 **Annals** of **Tropical Medicine** and **Parasitology.** Liverpool. *Ann. trop. Med. Parasit.* [1907-] L.BM.; BM^N.; E. 18-27 imp.; EB.; H. 48-; KC. 53-; LI. 07-50; MA.; MC.; MD.; P. 07-31; S. 07-48; SC.; TD.; TP. 57-; UCH. 12-; V.; Z. 07-48: 58-; **Abd.**R.; U.; **Abs.**N. 15-; **Bm.**U. 46-; **Bn.**U. 22-; **Br.**U. 07-12; **C.**MO.; P.; UL.; **Cr.**MD. 30-54; **Db.**; E.A.; P.; U.; **Ex.**U. 28-33; **G.**F. imp.; U.; **Ld.**U. 38-; **Lv.**P. 08-56 v. imp.; U.; **Nw.**A. 56-; **O.**R.; **R.**D. 13-20; **Sal.** imp.; **Sh.**U. 46-; **W.**23-; **Y.** [*C. of:* 31018, *which recommenced publication in* 1924. *Both journals now current*]

3195 **Annals** of **Tuberculosis.** Tenri, Nara. *Ann. Tuberc., Tenri* [1950-] L.MA.; MC.; MD.; TD.

3196 **Annals** of the **Ukrainian Academy** of **Arts** and **Sciences** in the **United States.** New York. *Ann. Ukrain. Acad. U.S.* [1951-] L.BM.; **Db.**; E.A. 51-; U. 51-55 imp.; **G.**U.

Annals of the **University of Stellenbosch.** *See* 2637.

3197 **Annals** of **Western Medicine** and **Surgery.** Los Angeles. *Ann. west. Med. Surg.* [1947-52] L.BM. imp.; MA. 48-52 imp.; MD.; S.; TD.; **Bl.**U. imp.

Annals of the **White Russian Agricultural Institute.** *See* 54473.

3198 **Annals** of **Zoology.** Agra. *Ann. Zool., Agra* [1955-] L.BM^N.; SC.; Z. 56-; **Bl.**U.; E.R.

3199 **Annalÿ biologii.** Moskva. Анналы биологии. *Annalÿ Biol.* [1959-] L.BM^N.; Z.; **Bl.**U.; **C.**A.; P.; **Y.** 59.

3200 **Annalÿ. Mechnikovskiĭ institut.** Kharkiv. Анналы. Мечниковский институт. *Annalÿ mechnik. Inst., Kharkiv* [1935-] L.TD. 36-37; V. 36-37 imp.

3201 **Année aéronautique.** Paris. *Année aéronaut.* [1919-] L.BM. 25-; P. 25-30; SC. 25-34.

Année automobile. *See* 5495.

3202 **Année biologique.** Paris. *Année biol.* [1895-] **L.**B. 46-; BM.; BM^N.; EB. 49-; K. 95-17: L.; SC.; U. 17-; UC. 95-29; Z. 95-37 imp.; **Abd.**U. 95-13; **Br.**U. 95-96: 20-; **C.**B. 95-03; UL. 95-05: 25-; **Db.** 95-23; **G.**U. imp.; **H.**U. 47-; **Ld.**U. 46-; **Lv.**U. 46-47; **M.**U. 95-98; **O.**R.; **Pl.**M. 20-; **Rt.** 45-47; **Sa.** 95-18; **Sal.** 45-47; **Y.**

3203 **Année cartographique.** Paris. *Année cartogr.* [1891-14] L.BM.; **O.**B.; G. imp.

3204 **Année clinique.** Paris. *Année clin.* [1945-]

3205 **Année électrique, électrothérapique** et **radiographique.** Paris. *Année élect. électrothér. radiogr.* [1900-13] L.MD. 02-13 imp.; P.; UC. 08: 12.

3206 **Année électro-radiologique.** Paris. *Année électroradiol.* [1934-35] L.MA.

3207 **Année endocrinologique.** Paris. *Année endocr.* [1949-] L.SC.; **Y.**

3208 **Année ferroviaire.** Paris. *Année ferrov.* [1947- L.SC. 49-53.

3209 **Année forestière.** Paris. *Année for.*

3210 **Année médicale pratique.** Paris. *Année méd. prat.* [1922-] L.MA. 27: 29-40; **Br.**U. 25: 32.

3211 **Année médico-chirurgicale.** Paris. *Année méd.-chir.*

3212 **Année obstétricale.** Paris. *Année obstét.* L.MA. 25.

3213 **Année odonto-stomatologique** et **maxillo-faciale** Paris. *Année odonto-stomat. maxillo-fac.*

3214 **Année pédiatrique.** Paris. *Année pédiat.* L.MA. 34: 36; MD. 36.

3215 **Année pharmaceutique.** Paris. *Année pharm.*

3216 **Année psychologique.** Paris. *Année psychol.* [1894-] **L.**B. 12-; BM.; MD. 07-; PS. 09-; U. 07-14: 30-34; UC.; **Abd.**U.; **Bm.**P. 23-; U. 10-; **C.**PS.; UL.; E.P.; U.; **G.**U.; **H.**U. 94-38: 51-53; **Ld.**U.; **M.**R. 20-; **Nw.**A. 22-23; **O.**EP. 94-98: 11-23 imp.: 29-; R.; **R.**U. 48-; **Sa.** 95-; **Sh.**U. 04-19.

3217 **Année scientifique** et **industrielle.** Paris. *Année scient. ind.* [1856-13] L.BM.; P.; RI.; S. 63-01; SC.; **Bm.**P. 78-13; **C.**UL. 1857-13; E.U. 66-13 imp.; **G.**N. 1857-1859: 79-13; U. 1858-13; **Nw.**A. 00-13 imp.; **O.**R.; **Sa.** 1857-13.

3218 **Année technique.** Paris. *Année tech.* L.BM. 02-06★; P. 00-06; SC. 03-04.

3219 **Année thérapeutique.** Paris. *Année thér.* [1920-] L.MA. 31-39; MD. 20-24 imp.: 42-43: 60; **M.**MS. 22.

3220 **Annotated Account** of **Fungi** received at the **Imperial Bureau** of **Mycology.** Kew. *Annot. Acct Fungi imp. Bur. Mycol.* [1925-41] L.BM.; BM^N.; K.; MY.; **Bm.**U.; **C.**A.; BO.; UL.; **O.**R.; **Rt.** [*C. as:* 33896]

3221 **Annotated Bibliography** of **Cortisone, A.C.T.H.** and **Related Hormonal Substances.** London. *Annot. Biblphy Cortisone* [1950-51] L.MD.; **Bl.**U.

3222 **Annotated Bibliography** of **Economic Geology.** [Urbana, Ill.] *Annot. Biblphy econ. Geol.* [1928-] L.BM^N.; GL.; GM.; MI. 46-; P. 28-51; SC.; **C.**MI.; E.F. 28-38; U.; **G.**U. imp.; **Nw.**A.; **O.**G. 29-31; R.; **Y.**

3223 **Annotated Bibliography** on **Hydrology** and **Sedimentation, United States** and **Canada.** Washington. *Annot. Biblphy Hydrol. Sediment. U.S. & Can.* [1950-] L.MO.; P. [*C. of:* 3224]

3224 **Annotated Bibliography** on **Hydrology, United States** and **Canada.** Washington. *Annot. Biblphy Hydrol. U.S. & Can.* [1941-50] L.MO.; P. [*C. as:* 3223]

3225 **Annotated Bibliography** of **Influenza.** Washington. *Annot. Biblphy Influenza* [1960-] L.MD.

3226 **Annotated Bibliography** of **Medical Mycology.** Kew. *Annot. Biblphy med. Mycol.* [1943-50] L.BM.; H.; MC.; MD.; S.; SH.; TD.; U.; **Bl.**U.; **C.**UL.; V.; E.A.; U.; **G.**U.; **Ld.**U.; **Nw.**A.; **O.**R.; **R.**U.; **Sh.**U. [*C. as:* 46216]

3227 **Annotated Bibliography** on **Snow, Ice** and **Permafrost.** Wilmington. *Annot. Biblphy Snow Ice* **L.**MO. 53–.

3228 **Annotated Bibliography** on the **Use** of **Organolithium Compounds** in **Organic Synthesis.** Minneapolis. *Annot. Biblphy Use Organolithium Compounds* [1949–] **L.**P.

3229 **Annotated Bibliography** of **Vitamin E.** New York. *Annot. Biblphy Vitam. E* [1950–] **G.**U.; **Y.**

3230 **Annotated Equilibrium Diagram Series.** Institute of Metals. London. *Annot. Equilib. Diag. Ser.* [1943–] **L.**BM.; I.; P.; SC.; **O.**R.

3231 **Annotation** of the **Oceanographical Research.** Imperial Fisheries Institute, Tokyo. *Annotn oceanogr. Res., Tokyo* [1926–29] **L.**AM.; Abd.M.; E.R. 28–29; Lo.; Lv.U.; Pl.M. imp.

3232 **Annotationes ornithologiae orientalis.** Tokyo. *Annotnes Orn. orient.* [1927–33] **L.**BM^N. 27–29; **O.**OR.
　　Annotationes phoneticae. Berlin. *Supplement to:* 56972.

3233 **Annotationes zoologicae japonenses.** Tokyo. *Annotnes zool. jap.* [1897–] **L.**BM. 97–14; BM^N.; EB. 97–40; L. 97–40; R. 97–40; SC. 97–40: 45: 50–; UC. 06–10; Z.; **Bl.**U. 97–40 imp.; **Bm.**N. imp.; **Bn.**U. 97–40 imp.; **Br.**U. imp.; **C.**UL.; **Cr.**U. 01–39 imp.; **Db.**; **Dm.** 04: 07: 25–27; **Dn.**U. imp.; **E.**F. 99–39 imp.; R.; U. 97–12; **Ld.**U. 03–33 imp.; **Lv.**U.; **N.**U. 35–40; **O.**H. 30–40 imp.; R. 98– imp.; **Pl.**M.; **Sa.** 97–32; **Y.**

3233^c **Annotirovannȳi ukazatel' literaturȳ** po **radio-élektronike.** Аннотированный указатель литературы по радиоэлектронике. *Annotir. Ukaz. Lit. Radioélektron.* **L.**BM.; Sil. 62–; **Y.** 57–.

3234 **Announcement Cards, Harvard College Observatory.** *Announc. Cards Harvard Coll. Obs.* [1936–] **L.**AS.
　　Annuaire de l'**Académie** de **médecine I. P. Pavlov.** Plovdiv. *See* 21423^a.
　　Annuaire de l'**Académie** de **médecine 'Valko Chervenkov'.** Sofia. *See* 21423^b.

3235 **Annuaire** de l'**Académie r.** de **Belgique.** Bruxelles. *Annu. Acad. r. Belg.* [1933–] **L.**BA.; BM.; BM^N.; G.; GL.; M.; P. 32–35; SC.; U. 32–39: 52–; UC.; Z. 40–; **Abd.**U.; **Bm.**N. imp.; **C.**P.; **Db.**; **E.**B. imp.; C.; R. imp.; **G.**U. imp.; **Ld.**U. imp.; **Lv.**U.; **Nw.**A.; **O.**B. 34–. [*C. of:* 3236]
　　Annuaire de l'**Académie rurale 'G. Dimitrov'.** Sofia. *See* 21425^a.

3236 **Annuaire** de l'**Académie** des **sciences, des lettres, et des beaux-arts** de **Belgique.** Bruxelles. *Annu. Acad. Sci. Belg.* [1835–32] **L.**BA. 1846–32; BM.; BM^N.; E. 75–24 imp.; G. 90–32; GL. 00–32; M. 90–32; P. 68–32; SC. 1846–32; U. 82–32; UC. 90–32; Z. 71–05; **Abd.**U. 00–32; **Bm.**N. 86–32 imp.; **C.**P. 08–32; T. 1849–11; UL. 1835–08; **Db.**; **E.**B. 77–32 imp.; C. 70–32 imp.; R. imp.; **G.**U. 68–32 imp.; **Ld.**U. 27–32; **Lv.**U. 74–32; **Nw.**A. 82–32. [*C. as:* 3235]

3237 **Annuaire** de l'**Académie** des **sciences** de **Paris.** *Annu. Acad. Sci. Paris* **L.**BM. 33–; BM^N. 97: 17– imp.; SC. 33–; **Bm.**P. 17–; **C.**UL. 18–; **Db.** 27–; **E.**U. 18–; **M.**U. 18– imp.; **O.**R. 17–; **Y.**

3238 **Annuaire aérologique.** Service météorologique de l'aviation. Sofia. *Annu. aérol. Serv. mét. Aviat., Sof.* **L.**MO. 32–35.

3239 **Annuaire agricole** de la **Suisse.** Berne. *Annu. agric. Suisse* [1900–32] **L.**AM.; EB. 14–32; MY. 23–32; C.A. 28–32; **Db.**; **Rt.**; **Y.** [*C. in:* 28117]

3240 **Annuaire. Association française** des **techniciens** du **pétrole.** Paris. *Annu. Ass. fr. Techns Pétrole* **Y.**

3241 **Annuaire** de l'**Association minière d'Alsace** et de **Lorraine.** *Annu. Ass. min. Als. Lorr.* **L.**SC. 23–.
　　Annuaire de l'**Association suisse** pour l'**aménagement** des **cours** d'eau. *See* 24842.

3242 **Annuaire** de l'**Association suisse** des **électriciens.** Zurich. *Annu. Ass. suisse Électns* **L.**P. (1 yr).

3243 **Annuaire. Association technique** de **fonderie.** Paris. *Annu. Ass. tech. Fond.* **L.**P. 35–38.

3243^c **Annuaire. Association technique** de l'**industrie papetière.** Paris. *Annu. Ass. tech. Ind. pap.* **L.**P. (curr.); **Y.**

3244 **Annuaire. Association technique maritime** et **aéronautique.** Paris. *Annu. Ass. tech. marit. aéronaut.*
　　Annuaire astronomique. Léningrad. *See* 5051.

3245 **Annuaire astronomique** et **météorologique.** Paris. *Annu. astr. mét., Paris* **L.**BM. 95:50–; SC. 93– imp.

3246 **Annuaire astronomique** de l'**Observatoire r.** de **Belgique.** Bruxelles. *Annu. astr. Obs. r. Belg.* [1901–13] **L.**BM.; MO. 01; SC.; U. 06–13 imp.; UC. 08–13; **Abd.**U.; **Bm.**U.; **Db.**; **E.**O.; R.; U.; **G.**U. 01–07; **Lv.**U. 05–07; **M.**U.; **O.**R. 01–08; **Sa.** 01–07. [*Replaces:* 3296 *from* 1901–1913]

3247 **Annuaire belge** de l'**électricité.** Bruxelles. *Annu. belge Élect.*

3248 **Annuaire** du **Bureau** d'**études géologiques** et **minières coloniales.** Paris. *Annu. Bur. Étud. géol. min. colon.* [1937–] **L.**SC. [*C. of:* 3257]
　　Annuaire du **Bureau hydrographique international.** *See* 58087.

3249 **Annuaire** publié par le **Bureau** de **longitudes.** Paris. *Annu. Bur. Longit.* [1796–] **L.**AS. 1828–; BM. 72–; G. 20–; MO. 95: 18: 25– imp.; SC. 1833–10 imp.; **Abd.**U. 1828–22; **Br.**U. 64–65: 73–99; **C.**O. 1836–; UL. 07–10; **Db.** 00–; **E.**O. 02–; R. 1830–1847: 81– imp.; U. 1818–16 imp.; **G.**U. 1828– imp.; **Lv.**U. 1804–1844; **M.**U. 1820: 1824–1847: 1858–79 imp.; **N.**U. 06–14 imp.; **Sa.** 1823–; **Y.**

3250 **Annuaire. Chambre syndicale** des **constructeurs** de **navires** et de **machines marines.** Paris. *Annu. Chamb. synd. Constr. Nav.* **Y.**

3251 **Annuaire** de la **Chambre syndicale française** des **mines métalliques.** Paris. *Annu. Chamb. synd. fr. Mines métall.*

3252 **Annuaire** de **chimie.** Paris. *Annu. Chim.* [1945–51] **L.**U.

3253 **Annuaire** de la **chimie industrielle.** Paris. *Annu. Chim. ind.*

3254 **Annuaire climatologique.** Bruxelles. *Annu. clim., Brux.* [1956–] **L.**MO.

3255 **Annuaire** du **Comité central** des **forges** de **France.** Paris. *Annu. Com. cent. Forges Fr.* **L.**I.

3256 **Annuaire** du **Comité central** des **houillères** de **France.** Paris. *Annu. Com. cent. Houill. Fr.* **Sh.**S. 25–.

3257 **Annuaire. Comité** d'**études minières** pour la **France** d'**outre-mer.** Paris. *Annu. Com. Étud. min. Fr. d'outre-mer* **L.**SC. 31–36★. [*C. as:* 3248]

3257ᶜ **Annuaire** du **Comité géologique. Institut géologique** de **Roumanie.** Bucureşti. *Annu. Com. géol. Roum.* [*Abridged French translation of:* 3618]

3258 **Annuaire** de la **Confédération** des **sociétés scientifiques françaises.** Paris. *Annu. Conféd. Socs scient. fr.*

3259 **Annuaire** du **Conservatoire** et du **Jardin botaniques** de **Genève.** Genève. *Annu. Conserv. Jard. bot. Genève* [1897–22] **L.**BMᴺ.; ᴋ.; **C.**ʙᴏ.; ᴘ.; **E.**ʙ. [*C. as:* 13293]

3259ᶜ **Annuaire** de la **construction navale.** *Annu. Constr. nav.* **Y.** 28– imp.

3260 **Annuaire** des **corrections** de **cartes.** Service central-hydrographique de la marine. Paris. *Annu. Correct. Cartes* **L.**sᴄ. 34–.

Annuaire du **Département** des **forêts, Lithuanie.** *See* 32215.

3261 **Annuaire** de **documentation coloniale comparée.** Institut colonial international. Bruxelles. *Annu. Docum. colon. comp.* **L.**ʙᴍ. 27–; sᴇ. 27–; **C.**ᴜʟ. 27–.

Annuaire de la **Faculté d'agronomie** et de **sylviculture, Université** de **Skopje.** *See* 21421ª.

Annuaire de la **Faculté d'agronomie** et **sylviculture, Université** de **Plovdiv.** *See* 21421ᵇ.

Annuaire de la **Faculté agronomique** et **forestière, Université** de **Belgrade.** *See* 21430.

Annuaire de la **Faculté agronomique, Université** de **Plovdiv.** *See* 21421ᵇ.

Annuaire de la **Faculté** de **médecine, Université** de **Plovdiv.** *See* 21423ᶜ.

Annuaire de la **Faculté** de **philosophie** de l'**Université** de **Skopje.** Section des sciences naturelles et mathématique. *See* 21420.

Annuaire de la **Fédération** des **industries chimiques** de **Belgique.** *See* 39916.

3262 **Annuaire** de la **Fédération internationale** des **ingénieurs-conseils.** Bruxelles. *Annu. Féd. int. Ing.-Cons.* **L.**sᴄ. 28–.

Annuaire géologique et **minéralogique** de la **Russie.** *See* 18877.

Annuaire hydrographique de **Pologne.** *See* 48063.

3262ª **Annuaire hydrographique** de la **Suisse.** *Annu. hydrogr. Suisse* **Y.** 24–.

Annuaire hydrologique. Prague. *See* 41320.

3263 **Annuaire hydrologique** de la **France.** Paris. *Annu. hydrol. Fr.* **L.**ʙᴍ. 49–; **O.**ɢ. 39–; **Y.**

3263ª **Annuaire hydrologique** de la **France** d'**outre-mer.** Paris. *Annu. hydrol. Fr. d'outre-mer* [1951–] **L.**ʙᴍ.

3263ᵇ **Annuaire** de l'**industrie électronique.** *Annu. Ind. électron.* **Y.** 52–.

Annuaire de l'**Institut biologique** à **Sarajevo.** *See* 21428.

Annuaire de l'**Institut chimico-technologique.** Sofia. *See* 21423.

3264 **Annuaire** de l'**Institut** de **France.** Paris. *Annu. Inst. Fr.* [1796–] **L.**ʙᴍ. 1811–; ɢʟ. 24–; ᴍᴏ. 99–33: 39; **Abs.**ɴ. 11–; **Bm.**ᴜ. 21–; **E.**ʀ. 21–; **G.**ᴜ. 93– imp.; **O.**ʙ. 1861–.

Annuaire de l'**Institut géologique** de **Roumanie.** *See* 3618.

Annuaire de l'**Institut géologique r. hongrois.** *See* 24857 and 32534.

3265 **Annuaire** de l'**Institut géophysique** de la **République tchécoslovaque.** Prague. *Annu. Inst. géophys. Répub. tchéc.* **L.**ᴍᴏ. 27–38.

3266 **Annuaire. Institut** de **météorologie** et de **physique** du **globe** de l'**Algérie.** Alger. *Annu. Inst. Mét. Phys. Globe Algér.* [1938–] **L.**ᴍᴏ.

3267 **Annuaire** de l'**Institut météorologique** de **Bulgarie.** Sofia. *Annu. Inst. mét. Bulg.* [1899–] **L.**ᴍᴏ. 99–20: 23–23: 39; **E.**ᴍ. 09–17; ʀ. 99–32 imp.; **O.**ɢ. 09–27. [*See also* 31640ª]

Annuaire de l'**Institut météorologique** de **Pologne.** *See* 48071.

3268 **Annuaire** de l'**Institut météorologique** de la **République tchécoslovaque.** Prague. *Annu. Inst. mét. Répub. tchéc.* [1916–47] **L.**ᴍᴏ. [*C. as:* 48040ª]

Annuaire de l'**Institut miniére** et **géologique.** Sofia. *See* 21423ᶜ.

Annuaire de l'**Institut océanographique** du **Royaume** de **Yougoslavie.** *See* 21429.

3269 **Annuaire** de l'**Institut** de **physique** du **globe.** Paris. *Annu. Inst. Phys. Globe, Paris* [1919–] **E.**ᴍ.; **O.**ʙ. 19–20.

3270 **Annuaire** de l'**Institut** de **physique** du **globe.** Strasbourg. *Annu. Inst. Phys. Globe, Strasb.*
     Météorologie [1915–35] **L.**ᴍᴏ.; **O.**ɢ. 15: 19–35. [*C. of:* 16908]
     Séismologie [1919] **L.**ᴍᴏ. [*Superseded by:* 2790]
     Archives de l'**Institut r.** de **bactériologique Câmara Pestana.** Lisbonne. *See* 4637.

3271 **Annuaire. Institut r. colonial belge.** Bruxelles. *Annu. Inst. r. colon. belge* **L.**ʙᴍᴺ. 46; **C.**ᴜʟ. 18–.

Annuaire. Institut des **recherches agronomiques.** Skopje. *See* 21421ᶜ.

3273 **Annuaire** de l'**Institut séismologique** de **Béograd, microséismique** et **macroséismique.** Béograd. *Annu. Inst. séism. Béogr. microséism. macroséism.* [1948–] **L.**ʙᴍ. imp.; ᴍᴏ.; **Y.** [*C. of:* 3291]

3274 **Annuaire** des **Instituts** de **recherches agronomiques** de la **République tchécoslovaque.** Prague. *Annu. Insts Rech. agron. Répub. tchéc.* [1924–] **C.**ᴀ.

3275 **Annuaire international** de l'**acétylène.** Paris. *Annu. int. Acét.* **L.**ᴘ. 07–12.

3276 **Annuaire international** de **législation agricole.** Rome. *Annu. int. Lég. agric.* [1911–43] **L.**ᴀᴍ.; ʙᴍ;. ᴇʙ. 11–24; **Abd.**ᴜ. 16–43; **Abs.**ɴ. 19–43; **N.**ᴜ. 18–43 imp.; **O.**ʙ. 11; **R.**ᴜ. 11–21; **Rt.** [*C. as:* 58085]

3277 **Annuaire international** des **mines** et de la **métallurgie.** Paris. *Annu. int. Min. Métall.* **L.**sᴄ. 27–28.

Annuaire international de **statistique agricole.** *See* 23958.

Annuaire de la **littérature agraire, U.R.S.S.** *See* 49468.

Annuaire magnétique. Dansk meteorologiske Institut. *See* 29139 and 29140.

3278 **Annuaire** de la **marine marchande.** Paris. *Ann. Mar. march.* **L.**ᴀᴍ. 10–39 imp.

3279 **Annuaire** des **mathématiciens.** Paris. *Annu. Mathns* **L.**sᴄ. 01–02*.

3280 **Annuaire médical belge.** Bruxelles. *Annu. méd. belge* **L.**ᴍᴅ. 28– imp.

3281 **Annuaire médical égyptien.** Le Caire. *Annu. méd. égypt.* **L.**MD. 28.

3282 **Annuaire médical** et **pharmaceutique** de la **France.** Paris. *Annu. méd. pharm. Fr.* **L.**S. 88–13.

3283 **Annuaire médical suisse.** Berne. *Annu. méd. suisse* **L.**MD. 20.

3284 **Annuaire** et **mémoires** du **Comité** d'**études historiques** et **scientifiques** de l'**Afrique occidentale.** Gorée. *Annu. Mém. Com. Étud. hist. scient. Afr. occ.* [1916–17] **L.**AN.; BM^N.; G. [*C. as:* 9852]

3285 **Annuaire** de **métallurgie.** Paris. *Annu. Métall.*

Annuaire météorologique d'**Alsace** et de **Lorraine.** *See* 3270.

Annuaire météorologique de **Copenhague.** *See* 31675.

3286 **Annuaire météorologique** et **géophysique, Sahara.** *Annu. mét. géophys. Sahara* **Y.**

3286° **Annuaire météorologique** et **géophysique, Algérie** du **nord.** *Annu. mét. géophys. Algér. N.* **Y.** 39–.

3287 **Annuaire météorologique** et **hydrographique.** Luxembourg. *Annu. mét. hydrogr., Luxemb.* [1949–] **L.**MO.

Annuaire météorologique de l'**Institut météorologique central** de **Bulgarie.** *See* 31640ª.

Annuaire météorologique. Institut météorologique r. des **Pays-Bas.** *See* 31656.

3288 **Annuaire météorologique** d'**Islande.** Reykjavik. *Annu. mét. Isl.* [1920–] **L.**MO. 20–23; **E.**M.; **Ld.**U. 23. [*C. from:* 31675]

3289 **Annuaire météorologique. Observatoire r.** de **Belgique.** Bruxelles. *Annu. mét. Obs. r. Belg.* [1901–] **L.**BM. 01–20; MO. 01–10; **Db.** 14–; **O.**G. 01–20. [*C. from:* 3296]

Annuaire météorologique. Service hydrométéorologique de la **R.P.F.** de **Yougoslavie.** *See* 31683.

3290 **Annuaire météorologique** de la **Station** de **géographie mathématique.** Gand. *Annu. mét. Stn Geogr. math., Gand* **L.**MO. 11–13.

3291 **Annuaire microséismique** et **macroséismique.** Béograd. *Annu. microséism. macroséism., Béogr.* [1921–40] [*C. as:* 3273]

Annuaire du **Musée zoologique** de l'**Académie impériale** des **sciences** de **St. Pétersbourg.** *See* 18893.

3292 **Annuaire** du **Muséum national** d'**histoire naturelle.** Paris. *Annu. Mus. natn. Hist. nat.* [1939–] **L.**BM. 53–; BM^N.; **Db.**; **Dm.** 53: 59; **O.**BO. imp.; **Pl.**M. 53; **Y.**

3293 **Annuaire** des **observations météorologiques** de l'**Observatoire** au **Lomnicky Stit.** Prague. *Annu. Obsns mét. Obs. Lomnicky Stit* **L.**MO. 40–53. [*C. as:* 48040°]

3294 **Annuaire** des **observations météorologiques** de l'**Observatoire météorologique** et **géophysique** d'**état** de **Stara Dala.** Bratislava. *Annu. Obsns mét. Obs. mét. géophys. Stara Dala* **L.**MO. 45–48. [*C. as:* 48040^b]

Annuaire de l'**Observatoire aérologique** à **Belgrade.** *See* 21427.

Annuaire. Observatoire astronomique de **Belgrade.** *See* 21428ª.

Annuaire de l'**Observatoire météorologique** et **magnétique** de l'**Université impériale** à **Odessa.** *See* 18881.

Annuaire de l'**Observatoire** de **Montsouris.** *See* 3295.

3295 **Annuaire** de l'**Observatoire municipal** de **Paris,** dit Observatoire de Montsouris. Paris. *Annu. Obs. mun. Paris* [1872–00] **L.**SH. 84–90; **O.**G. 72–97; **R.** 84–00. [*Replaced by:* 2868]

3296 **Annuaire** de l'**Observatoire r.** de **Belgique.** Bruxelles. *Annu. Obs. r. Belg.* [1834–] **L.**BM.; MO. 1835–00 imp.; SC. 22–; **U.** 24–28; UC. 14–; **Abd.**U. 14–; **Bm.**U. 14–30; **C.**O.; **P.** 92–; UL.; **Db.** 1835–; **E.**M. 73–16; O.; **R.**; **U.** 14–26; **M.**U. 1834–78: 14–; **O.**R. [*Replaced by:* 3246 and 3289 from 1901 to 1913]

Annuaire phénologique. Service hydrométéorologique de la **R.P.F.** de **Yougoslavie.** *See* 19285.

3296° **Annuaire** des **produits chimiques** et de la **droguerie.** Paris. *Annu. Prod. chim. Drog.* **Lv.**P. 50– imp.

3297 **Annuaire sanitaire international.** Genève. *Annu. sanit. int.* **Abd.**U. 24–25.

3297° **Annuaire** de la **santé animale.** *Annu. Santé anim.* **Y.** 59–.

3298 **Annuaire séismique.** Béograd. *Annu. séism., Béogr.* [1920–]

3299 **Annuaire** du **Service météorologique** de l'**Afrique occidentale française.** Dakar. *Annu. Serv. mét. Afr. occid. Fr.*
   1. Fréquences. **L.**MO. 36–37.
   2. Bulletin séismique. **L.**MO. 36–37.

3300 **Annuaire** de la **Société belge** d'**astronomie.** Bruxelles. *Annu. Soc. belge Astr.* **L.**BM. 96–14.

3301 **Annuaire. Société** de **chimie physique.** Paris. *Annu. Soc. Chim. phys.*

3302 **Annuaire** de la **Société chimique** de **France.** Paris. *Annu. Soc. chim. Fr.* **L.**SC. (curr.); **Y.**

Annuaire de la **Société dendrologique** de **Pologne.** *See* 48074.

3303 **Annuaire** de la **Société française** d'**économie alpestre.** Paris. *Annu. Soc. fr. Écon. alp.* [1921–27] **O.**F. [*C. as:* 17439]

3304 **Annuaire** de la **Société française** des **ingénieurs techniciens** du **vide.** Paris. *Annu. Soc. fr. Ingrs Techns Vide* **Y.**

3305 **Annuaire** de la **Société française** de **physique.** Paris. *Annu. Soc. fr. Phys.* **E.**R. 12–51; **M.**U. 12– imp.

Annuaire de la **Société géologique** de **Pologne.** *See* 48073.

3306 **Annuaire. Société** de l'**industrie minérale.** Saint-Étienne. *Annu. Soc. Ind. minér.*

3307 **Annuaire** de la **Société** des **ingénieurs civils** de **France.** Paris. *Annu. Soc. Ingrs civ. Fr.* [1848–] **L.**BM. 11–; SC. 30–38: 52–; **G.**E. 1858–; **Nw.**A. 10–13: 15–30; **Y.**

3308 **Annuaire** de la **Société internationale** des **électriciens.** Paris. *Annu. Soc. int. Électns* **L.**BM. 00–.

3309 **Annuaire** de la **Société** de **médecine** de **Paris.** Paris. *Annu. Soc. Méd. Paris* **L.**MD. 51–.

3310 **Annuaire** de la **Société météorologique** de **France.** Paris. *Annu. Soc. mét. Fr.* [1853–24] **L.**BM. MO.; **C.**UL.; **Db.** 1853–1856; **E.**R. 1853–76 imp. [*C. as* 31654]

Annuaire de la **Société paléontologique Russie.** *See* 18887.

Annuaire de la **Société** des **sciences** et des **lettres** de **Varsovie.** *See* 50669.

3311 **Annuaire** de la **Station agronomique** de l'**État** à **Gembloux.** Gembloux. *Annu. Stn agron. Gembloux* [1912–28] **L.**AM. EB. 12–13; SC. 13; **Rt.** 12–13. [*Replaced by:* 10577]

3312 **Annuaire statistique** de la **santé publique.** Bruxelles. *Annu. statist. Santé publ., Brux.* **L.**H. 51–.

3313 **Annuaire statistique** de la **ville** de **Paris.** Paris. *Annu. statist. Ville Paris* [1938–] **L.**MO (mét.)

3314 **Annuaire. Syndicat général** de l'**industrie** des **cuirs** et **peaux** de la **France.** Paris. *Annu. Synd. gén. Ind. Cuirs Peaux Fr.*

3315 **Annuaire. Syndicat** des **mécaniciens chaudronniers** et **fondeurs** de **France.** Paris. *Annu. Synd. Mécns Chaudr. Fond. Fr.*

3315° **Annuaire** de l'**Union belge** des **ingénieurs navals.** *Annu. Un. belge Ingrs nav.* **Y.** 41–.
    Annuaire de l'**Université** de **Sofia.** *See* 21424.

3316 **Annuaire** des **vétérinaires militaires.** Alfort. *Annu. Vét. milit.*

3317 **Annual Administration Report** of the **Petroleum Department** of **Trinidad** and **Tobago.** Trinidad. *A. Adm. Rep. Petrol. Dep. Trin.* **L.**MI. 42–.

3318 **Annual Administration Report. Tea Scientific Section, United Planters' Association** of **Southern India.** Madras. *A. Adm. Rep. Tea scient. Sect. un. Plrs Ass. south. India* **Md.**H. 48–; **Y.**

3319 **Annual Announcement. Peking Union Medical College.** Peking. *A. Announc. Peking Un. med. Coll.*

3320 **Annual Announcement. Woods Hole Oceanographic Institution.** Woods Hole, Mass. *A. Announc. Woods Hole oceanogr. Instn* [1931–41] **L.**BM^N. 34–41; **Abd.**M.; **E.**R.; **Lv.**U.; **Pl.**M.

3320ª **Annual Automobile Review.** Lausanne. *A. Auto. Rev.* [1954–55] **L.**BM.; **Ld.**P.; **Lv.**P. [*C. as:* 5495]

3321 **Annual Biology Colloquium. Oregon Agricultural** (*afterwards* **State**) **College.** Corvallis. *A. Biol. Colloq. Ore. St. Coll.* [1940–] **L.**BM. 49–; BM^N. 44– **C.**UL. 49–; **H.**U. 49–; **Y.**

3322 **Annual Blueberry Open House.** New Jersey Blueberry Research Laboratory. Pemberton. *A. Blueberry Open House* **Md.**H. 41–.

3323 **Annual Booklet. Association** of **Growers** of the **New Varieties** of **Hops.** Faversham. *A. Bookl. Ass. Grow. new Var. Hops* **Md.**H. 52–.

3324 **Annual Booklet. Nova Scotia Fruit Growers Association.** Kentville. *A. Bookl. Nova Scotia Fruit Grow. Ass.* **Md.**H. 34–35.

3325 **Annual Bulletin. Academy** of **Medicine** of **Jerusalem.** *A. Bull. Acad. Med. Jerusalem* [1926–27]

3325° **Annual Bulletin. Beach Erosion Board, U.S. Army.** Washington. *A. Bull. Beach Eros. Bd* [1947–] **Y.**

3326 **Annual Bulletin. Colorado College.** Colorado. Springs. *A. Bull. Colo. Coll.* **L.**BM. 05–.

3327 **Annual Bulletin. Connecticut Forestry Association.** Hartford, Conn. *A. Bull. Conn. For. Ass.* [1902–05] [*C. as:* 40959]

3328 **Annual Bulletin. Department** of **Agriculture, Nigeria.** Lagos. *A. Bull. Dep. Agric. Nigeria* [1922–36] **L.**AM.; BM^N.; EB.; K.; P.; **Abs.**A. 30–36; **C.**A.; **Ld.**U. 22–30; **Md.**H. 25–32; **O.**RE.; **Rt.**

3329 **Annual Bulletin** of the **Department** of **Agriculture, Northern Rhodesia.** Livingstone. *A. Bull. Dep. Agric. North. Rhod.* [1931–33] **L.**BM^N.; EB. 32; K.; **Abs.**A.; **C.**A.; **Md.**H. 32–33; **O.**F.

3330 **Annual Bulletin. Department** of **Animal Health, Northern Rhodesia.** Livingstone. *A. Bull. Dep. Anim. Hlth North. Rhod.* **L.**EB. 32–; **C.**A. 32–; **W.** 31–.

3331 **Annual Bulletin** of **Divisional Reports** of the **Department** of **Agriculture, Fiji.** Suva. *A. Bull. div. Rep. Dep. Agric. Fiji* [1931–38] **L.**BM^N. imp.; EB.; V. 32–37 imp.; **C.**A.; **Md.**H.; **O.**RH.; **Sal.**

3332 **Annual Bulletin** of **Electric Energy Statistics** for **Europe.** Geneva. *A. Bull. elect. Energy Statist. Eur.* [1956–] **L.**BM.; **Bm.**U.; **M.**P.

3333 **Annual Bulletin. International Commission** on **Irrigation** and **Drainage.** New Delhi. *A. Bull. int. Commn Irrig. Drain.* [1952–] **L.**P.; **C.**A.; **Sh.**SC. 54–; **Sil.** 55–; **Y.**

3334 **Annual Bulletin. Société jersiaise.** Jersey. *A. Bull. Soc. jersiaise* [1957–] **L.**BM.; BM^N.; SC.; **C.**UL.; **O.**B.; **Pl.**M.; **Y.** [*C. of:* 9393]

3335 **Annual Cancer Report. United Birmingham Hospitals.** *A. Cancer Rep. un. Bgham Hosps* [1953–] **L.**CB.; MD.; UCH.; **Dn.**; U. 54–; **E.**P.; **G.**U.

3336 **Annual Climatological Bulletin** of the **Meteorological Institute.** Athens. *A. clim. Bull. met. Inst., Athens* **L.**MO. 52–.

3337 **Annual Climatological Review. Philippine Islands.** Manila. *A. clim. Rev. Philipp. Isl.* [1952–] **L.**MO.; **Y.**

3337° **Annual Clinical Record. Cardiff Royal Infirmary.** Cardiff. *A. clin. Rec. Cardiff R. Infirm.* [1948–] **L.**BM.

3338 **Annual** of the **Club** of **Natural Science** and **Geography** of the **Y.M.C.A.** Harbin. *A. Club nat. Sci. Geogr. Y.M.C.A., Harbin* **L.**BM^N. 33.

3339 **Annual Collected Papers. American Society** of **Tool Engineers.** Detroit. *A. coll. Pap. Am. Soc. Tool Engrs* [1956–] **L.**P.

3339° **Annual Concrete Conference. College** of **Engineering, University** of **North Dakota.** *A. Concr. Conf. Univ. N. Dak.* [1953–] **Y.**
    Annual Conference . . . *See also* **Proceedings** of **Annual Conference . . .**

3339ᵉ **Annual Conference** on **Applications** of **X-Ray Analysis.** *A. Conf. Appl. X-ray Analysis* **Y.** 59–.
    Annual Conference on **High Energy Nuclear Physics.** *See* 38928.

3340 **Annual Conference. Lankenau Hospital.** Philadelphia. New York. *A. Conf. Lankenau Hosp.* **Dn.**U. 60.
    Annual Conference. National Association for the **Prevention** of **Consumption.** *See* 34095.

3341 **Annual Conference** on **Protein Metabolism.** Bureau of Biological Research, Rutgers University. New Brunswick. *A. Conf. Protein Metab. Rutgers Univ.* **L.**MD. 52–.

3341° **Annual Conference Report** on **Cotton Insect Research** and **Control.** Beltsville Md. *A. Conf. Rep. Cott. Insect Res. Control* **L.**P. 60–.

3342 **Annual Conference** on the **Weights** and **Measures** of the **United States.** Bureau of Standards. Washington. *A. Conf. Wghts Meas. U.S.* **L.**BM. 05–17; P. 07–; U. 05–12; **G.**M. 12–25; **Lv.**U. 15–22 imp.; **M.**U. 05–07.

Annual Congress. *See also* **Proceedings of Annual Congress** ...

3343 **Annual Congress. British Small-Animal Veterinary Association.** London. *A. Congr. Br. small-Anim. vet. Ass.* [1958–] **L.**BM.; MD.; **Br.**U.; **O.**R.

3344 **Annual Congress. British Veterinary Association.** *A. Congr. Br. vet. Ass.* **L.**BM.; **Br.**U. 49–; **Y.**

3345 **Annual Congress. National Veterinary Medical Association** of **Great Britain** and **Ireland.** London. *A. Congr. natn. vet. med. Ass.* [1926–] **L.**BM.; MD.; **C.**UL.; **O.**R.

Annual Convention. *See also* **Proceedings** of **Annual Convention.**

Annual Convention. Atlantic Deeper Water-Ways Association. *See* 44928.

3345° **Annual Convention. Ceylon Veterinary Association.** Kandy. *A. Conv. Ceylon vet. Ass.* [1955–] **L.**BM.

Annual Convention. National Electric Light Association. New York. *See* 39453.

3346 **Annual Convention New York State Waterways Association.** Albany. *A. Conv. N.Y. St. WatWays Ass.*

3347 **Annual** of **Czechoslovak Medical Literature.** Praha. *A. Czech. med. Lit.* [1956–] **L.**MD.; **Abd.**R.; **E.**P. [*Supersedes 6584*]

3348 **Annual Departmental Report. Director** of **Agriculture, Fisheries** and **Forestry.** Hong Kong. *A. dep. Rep. Dir. Agric. Fish. For., Hong Kong* [1951–] **L.**BM.; BM^N.; **Lo.**53–; **Md.**H.; **O.**F.; **Y.**

3349 **Annual Departmental Report. Fisheries.** Hong Kong. *A. dep. Rep. Fish., Hong Kong* [1945–47] **L.**BM.; **Y.**

3350 **Annual Dew Summary. Meteorological Service, Israel.** Hakirya. *A. Dew Summ. Isr.* [1945–] **L.**MO. 45–52.

Annual Divisional Report. Department of **Agriculture, British Guiana.** *See* 43533.

3351 **Annual Epidemiological Report.** Health Organisation, League of Nations, Geneva. *A. epidem. Rep. Hlth Org.* [1932–38] **L.**BM.; H.; MC.; MD.; SH.; TD.; **Abd.**R. 34–37; **Bl.**U.; **Dn.**U.; **G.**PH.; **M.**P. imp.; **Sh.**U. [*C. of:* 50848; *Superseded by:* 3352]

3352 **Annual Epidemiological** and **Vital Statistics.** World Health Organisation, Geneva. *A. epidem. vital Statist.* [1939–] **L.**BM.; CB. 52–; H.; MC.; MD.; SH.; U.; TD.; **Bl.**U. 55–; **Dn.**U.; **G.**PH.; **M.**P.; **Sh.**U.; **Y.** [*Supersedes:* 3351]

3353 **Annual General Report. Department** of **Agriculture,** etc., for **Ireland.** Dublin. *A. gen. Rep. Dep. Agric. Ire.* [1900–23] **L.**AM.; BM.; BM^N. 02–18 imp.; P.; **Abs.**N. 01–23 imp.; **Abd.**U. 00–18; **Bn.**U.; **C.**A. 00–08; **Cr.**U. 10–23 imp.; **Db.**; **E.**F. 00–05; **G.**M. 19–23; **Ld.**U. 06–13; **Nw.**P. 11–23; **O.**AEC. 12–23; B. 19–23; G. 10–21; RE. 05–23. [*C. as:* 20861]

3354 **Annual General Report. Ministry** of **Agriculture, Northern Ireland.** Belfast. *A. gen. Rep. Minist. Agric. North. Ire.* [1921–] **L.**AM.; MO. 28–34; MY. 23–31; **Abs.**A. 22–37 imp.; N.; U. 23–51; **Bl.**U. 21–34; **Bm.**P.; **Bn.**U.; **Br.**A. 57–; U. 21–34; **C.**A.; **E.**A.; **G.**U. 26–; **Ld.**U.; **O.**AEC. 30–34; F. 51–; R. 21–25 imp.; RE 21–40; **Rt.**

3355 **Annual Geological Report. Somaliland Agricultural** and **Geological Department.** London. *A. geol. Rep. Somalild* **L.**GL. 27–; UC. 29.

3356 **Annual Handbook. British Medical Association.** London. *A. Handb. Br. med. Ass.* [1921–] **L.**BM.; BM^N.; MD.; **Abd.**U. 24–; **Abs.**N. 22–; U. 22–; **Bm.**U. 22–; **Br.**U. 22–; **C.**UL.; **G.**U.; **O.**R. [*C. of:* 21783]

3357 **Annual Index** of **Literature** on **Coal Utilisation.** London. *A. Index Lit. Coal Util.* **L.**BM.; SC. 39–.

3358 **Annual Journal. Association** of **Municipal** and **Sanitary Engineers** and **Surveyors—South African District.** Cape Town. *A. J. Ass. mun. sanit. Engrs S. Afr. Distr.* [1948–53] **Y.** [*C. as:* 3359]

3359 **Annual Journal. Institution** of **Municipal Engineers, South African District.** Cape Town. *A. J. Inst. mun. Engrs S. Afr. Distr.* [1954–] **L.**P.; **Y.** [*C. of:* 3358]

3360 **Annual Journal** of the **National Federation** of **Textile Works Managers' Associations.** Manchester. *A. J. natn. Fed. Text. Wks Mgrs Ass.* [1931–] **L.**P. imp.; **M.**C.; P. 31–37. [*C. of:* 26520]

3361 **Annual Journal. Royal Lancashire Agricultural Society.** Preston. *A. J. R. Lancs. agric. Soc.* [1917–58] **L.**A. imp.; AM. imp.; BM.; P. 17–32; **Abs.**N.; **C.**A. 31–58; **Ld.**U. 46: 52–58; **Lv.**P. 24–58; **M.**P.; **R.**D. 20–23; **Rt.** 48; **W.** 43–50; 53–58; **Y.** [*C. of:* 26820; *C. as:* 48170]

Annual Journal. South African District Institution of **Municipal Engineers.** *See* 3358.

3361° **Annual Lectures. National Institutes** of **Health.** Washington. *A. Lect. natn. Insts Hlth* [1954–] **L.**BM.

3363 **Annual Magazine. Notts. Mining Students' Association.** Nottingham. *A. Mag. Notts. Min. Stud. Ass.* **L.**P. 21–57*; **N.**T. 21–41. [*C. as:* 50598]

3363ª **Annual Medical** and **Health Report, Antigua.** St. Johns. *A. med. Hlth Rep. Antigua* [1955–] **L.**BM. [*C. of:* 3370ª]

3363ᵇ **Annual Medical** and **Health Report, Fiji.** Suva. *A. med. Hlth Rep. Fiji* **L.**BM. 36–38. [*C. of:* 3366]

Annual Medical and **Health Report, Nigeria.** *See* 3376.

3364 **Annual Medical Report. East Africa Protectorate.** Nairobi. *A. med. Rep. E. Afr. Prot.* [1911–19] **L.**TD.; **Lv.**U. [*C. as:* 3367]

3365 **Annual Medical Report, Falkland Islands.** Stanley. *A. med. Rep. Falkl. Isl.* **L.**TD. 17–21; **O.**RH. 33–.

3366 **Annual Medical Report, Fiji.** Suva. *A. med. Rep. Fiji* **L.**EB.; TD. [*C. as:* 3363ᵇ]

3367 **Annual Medical Report, Kenya.** Nairobi. *A. med. Rep. Kenya* [1920–28] **L.**EB. 27–28; MD. 22–28; TD.; **Lv.**U. [*C. of:* 3364; *C. as:* 44436]

3368 **Annual Medical Report. King Edward VII Sanatorium,** Midhurst. *A. med. Rep. King Edw. VII Sanat. Midhurst.*

Annual Medical Report, Nyasaland. *See* 3377.

Annual Medical Report, Somaliland Protectorate. *See* 3378.

3369 **Annual Medical Report, Tanganyika Territory.** London. *A. med. Rep. Tanganyika* [1918–25] **L.**BM. 21–25; EB.; MD. 21–25; TD. [*C. as:* 3379]

3370 **Annual Medical Report. Trudeau Sanatorium.** *A. med. Rep. Trudeau Sanat.* L.MD. 21– imp.

Annual Medical Report, Uganda Protectorate. *See* 3380.

3370ᵃ **Annual Medical** and **Sanitary Report, Antigua.** St. Johns. *A med. sanit. Rep. Antigua* [1935–54] L.BM. [*C. as:* 3363ᵃ]

3370ᵇ **Annual Medical** and **Sanitary Report, British Solomon Islands.** *A. med. sanit. Rep. Br. Solomon Isl.* L.BM. 37–.

3371 **Annual Medical** and **Sanitary Report, Colony** of **Gibraltar.** *A. med. sanit. Rep. Colony Gibraltar* L.BM. 45–.

3372 **Annual Medical** and **Sanitary Report, Cyprus.** Nicosia. *A. med. sanit. Rep. Cyprus* L.EB. 11–44*; TD. 13–44 imp.; O.RH. 30–37: 40–44. [*C. as:* 44470]

3373 **Annual Medical** and **Sanitary Report, Gambia.** London, etc. *A. med. sanit. Rep. Gambia* L.EB. 14–43*; MD. 22–38; TD. 07–43; Lv.U. 09–43; O.G. 43. [*C. as:* 44447]

3374 **Annual Medical** and **Sanitary Report, Grenada.** London. *A. med. sanit. Rep. Grenada* [1927–] L.TD.; Lv.U.; O.RH. 35–42. [*C. of:* 30309]

3375 **Annual Medical** and **Sanitary Report, Leeward Islands.** *A. med. sanit. Rep. Leeward Isl.* L.BM. 46–.

3376 **Annual Medical** and **Sanitary Report, Nigeria.** Lagos. *A. med. sanit. Rep. Nigeria* L.EB. 17–30*; MO. (north.) 13; TD. 05–30; Lv.U. 16–30; O.RH. 29–30. [*C. as:* 44437. From 1905–13 issued in two parts, *Northern* and *Southern*]

3377 *Annual Medical* and **Sanitary Report, Nyasaland Protectorate.** Zomba. *A. med. sanit. Rep. Nyasaland* L.EB. 26–42*; L.TD. 08–42.

Annual Medical and **Sanitary Report, Sierra Leone.** *See* 44438.

3378 **Annual Medical** and **Sanitary Report, Somaliland Protectorate.** London. *A. med. sanit. Rep. Somaliland* L.EB. 25–29; TD. 10– imp.

3379 **Annual Medical** and **Sanitary Report, Tanganyika.** Tanga. *A. med. sanit. Rep. Tanganyika* [1926–36] L.BM.; EB.; MD.; TD.; E.U. 30–36; G.M. 28. [*C. of:* 3369; *C. as:* 44440]

3380 **Annual Medical** and **Sanitary Report, Uganda Protectorate.** Entebbe. *A. med. sanit. Rep. Uganda* L.EB. 20–35*; TD. 12–25; O.RH. 20–35. [*C. as:* 44441]

3381 **Annual Meeting. American Association** of **Orthodontists.** St. Louis. *A. Mtg Am. Ass. Orthod.* [1938–] [*C. of:* 3382]

3382 **Annual Meeting. American Society** of **Orthodontists.** St. Louis. *A. Mtg Am. Soc. Orthod.* [1907–37] L.D. 30–31. [*C. as:* 3381]

Annual Meeting. Canadian Diamond Drilling Association. *See* 52218ᶜ.

3383 **Annual Meeting. Central Council for District Nursing.** London. *A. Mtg cent. Coun. Distr. Nurs.* O.R. 44–.

Annual Meeting. International Acetylene Association. *See* 39296.

3383ᶜ **Annual Meeting. Inter-Society Cytology Council.** *A. Mtg inter-Soc. Cytol. Coun.* [1954–] Y.

3384 **Annual Meeting. National Anti-vaccination League.** *A. Mtg natn. Anti-vacc. Leag.* O.R. 25–.

3385 **Annual Meteorological Bulletin, Bangkok.** *A. met. Bull. Bangkok* L.MO. 37–41. [*C. as:* 3386]

3386 **Annual Meteorological Data, Bangkok.** *A. met. Data Bangkok* L.MO. 46–. [*C. of:* 3385]

3387 **Annual Meteorological Report Falkland Islands Dependencies Bases.** Port Stanley. *A. met. Rep. Falkl. Isl.* L.MO. 51–.

3388 **Annual Meteorological Report, Fiji.** Suva. *A. met. Rep. Fiji* [1928–39] L.MO.; C.A. 29–39; E.M. [*C. of* and *Rec. as:* 31601]

3388ᵃ **Annual Meteorological Report, Gambia.** Bathurst. *A. met. Rep. Gambia* L.BM. 47–.

3389 **Annual Meteorological Report, Isthmian Canal Commission.** Culebra. *A. met. Rep. Isthmian Canal Commn* L.MO. 1910. [*C. in:* 33555]

3390 **Annual Meteorological Report.** Nanking. *A. met. Rep., Nanking* L.G. 28–29; MO. 28–34; E.R. 28–29; O.G. 28–29.

3391 **Annual Meteorological Report, Straits Settlements.** Singapore. *A. met. Rep. Straits Settl.* L.MO. 85–16.

3392 **Annual Meteorological Return, Bermuda.** *A. met. Ret. Bermuda* L.MO. 21–49.

3393 **Annual Meteorological Summary** with **Comparative Data. U.S. Weather Bureau.** Washington. *A. met. Summ. U.S.* L.BM. 30–48*; MO. 39–48 imp.; O.G. 35–39 imp. [*C. as:* 28746ᵃ].

3394 **Annual Meteorological Summary, Edmonton, Calgary, Halifax N.S., Winnipeg, Regina, Vancouver Airport** and **City.** Toronto. *A. met. Summ. Edmonton etc.* [1951–] L.MO.

3395 **Annual Meteorological Summary, Fiji.** Suva. *A. met. Summ. Fiji* L.MO. 50–; Y.

3396 **Annual Meteorological Summary** of **Toronto.** *A. met. Summ. Toronto* Y.

3397 **Annual Meteorological Tables. Falkland Islands** and **Dependencies Meteorological Service.** Port Stanley. *A. met. Tables Falkl. Isl.* [1951–] L.BM. 52–; MO.; C.PO.; G.U.; Ld.U.; Y.

Annual Minutes. Hawaii Territorial Medical Association. *See* 53734.

Annual of the **Office** of **Naval Intelligence.** *See* 57980.

3397ᶜ **Annual Petroleum** and **Natural Gas Statistical Yearbook.** Division of Mineral Resources, Saskatchewan. *A. Petrol. nat. Gas statist. Yb. Sask.* [1955–] L.BM.

Annual Proceedings. American Electroplaters Society. *See* 38849.

Annual Proceedings. American Pharmaceutical Manufacturers Association. *See* 38875.

Annual Proceedings. American Society of **Brewing Chemists.** *See* 38894.

3398 **Annual Proceedings. Associated** and **Technical Societies** of **South Africa.** Johannesburg. *A. Proc. ass. tech. Socs S. Afr.* Y.

3399 **Annual Proceedings. Gifu College** of **Pharmacy.** *A. Proc. Gifu Coll. Pharm.* Y.

3400 **Annual Proceedings. Institute** of **Australian Foundrymen.** Melbourne. *A. Proc. Inst. Aust. Foundrymen* [1939–] L.NF.; P. 41–.

3401 **Annual Proceedings. Institute** of **Vitreous Enamellers.** London. *A. Proc. Inst. vitr. Enam.* [1935–50] **L.**BM.; C. 41–42; I. imp.; NF. 36–38; P.; **Bm.**C.; P.; **C.**UL.; **E.**A.; **O.**R. [*C. as:* 39277]

3402 **Annual Proceedings. International Commission** for the **Northwest Atlantic Fisheries.** Halifax, N.S. *A. Proc. int. Commn NW. Atlant. Fish.* [1954–] **L.**BMᴺ. **Abd.**M.; **Bn.**U. 55–; **C.**PO.; **E.**A. 55–; **Fr.** 55–; **Lo.**; **Pl.**M.; **Wo.**; **Y.** [*C. of:* 44188]

3403 **Annual Proceedings. Maryland Pharmaceutical Association.** Baltimore. *A. Proc. Md pharm. Ass.*
Annual Proceedings. Pacific Northwest Industrial Waste Conference. *See* 39573.

3404 **Annual Proceedings. Railway Fuel** and **Traveling Engineers' Association.** Chicago. *A. Proc. Rly Fuel travel. Engrs' Ass.* [1937–] **L.**P. 37–46.

3405 **Annual Proceedings** and **Report. Medical Officers** of **Schools Association.** London. *A. Proc. Rep. med. Offrs Sch. Ass.* [1926–] **L.**MD.; TD. 36–47 imp. **Abs.**N.; **C.**UL.; **O.**R.

3406 **Annual Proceedings. Sheet** and **Strip Metal Users' Association.** London. *A. Proc. Sheet Strip Metal Users' Ass.* [1946–] **L.**NF.; **Sh.**IO. 47–.

3407 **Annual Progress Report. Bay Marine Piling Survey.** San Francisco. *A. Prog. Rep. Bay mar. Piling Surv.* **Lv.**U. 21–23.

3408 **Annual Progress Report. Beaudette Foundation** for **Biological Research.** Solvang, Cal. *A. Prog. Rep. Beaudette Fdn* [1958–] **L.**BMᴺ.

3409 **Annual Progress Report. Co-operative Punchcard Climatological Program.** Institute of Atmospheric Physics, University of Arizona. Tucson. *A. Prog. Rep. co-op. Punchcard clim. Prog.* **L.**MO. 55–; **Y.**

3409° **Annual Progress Report. Department** of **Lands, Mines** and **Surveys, Fiji.** Suva. *A. Prog. Rep. Dep. Lds Mines Surv. Fiji* [1952–] **L.**BM.

3410 **Annual Progress Report. Division** of **Forest Research, Department** of **Lands** and **Forests.** Ontario. *A. Prog. Rep. Div. Forest Res., Ontario* **O.**F. 49–50. [*C. as:* 3425]

3411 **Annual Progress Report** on **Forest Administration** in the **Presidency** of **Bengal.** *A. Prog. Rep. Forest Adm. Pres. Bengal* **Abs.**N. 10–.

3411ª **Annual Progress Report** on **Forest Administration** in the **Province** of **Bihar.** *A. Prog. Rep. Forest Adm. Prov. Bihar* [1938–] **L.**BM. [*C. from:* 3412]

3412 **Annual Progress Report** on **Forest Administration** in the **Province** of **Bihar** and **Orissa.** *A. Prog. Rep. Forest Adm. Prov. Bihar Orissa* [1913–36] **L.**BM.; **Y.** [*C. as:* 3411ª and 3412ª]

3412ª **Annual Progress Report** on **Forest Administration** in the **Province** of **Orissa.** Cuttack. *A. Prog. Rep. Forest Adm. Prov. Orissa* [1938–] **L.**BM. [*C. from* 3412]

3413 **Annual Progress Report** of the **Geological Survey** of **Queensland.** Brisbane. *A. Prog. Rep. geol. Surv. Qd* **L.**BMᴺ. 99–01.

3414 **Annual Progress Report** of the **Geological Survey. Western Australia.** Perth. *A. Prog. Rep. geol. Surv. West. Aust.* [1897–39] **L.**BM.; BMᴺ.; G. 97–01; GL. 00–39; P. 97–00; UC. 08–39 imp.; **Bm.**U. 98–39; **Db.** 13–39; **E.**D. 99–39; J. 99–11; R. 02–39 imp.; **G.**G. 98–23 imp.; **Ld.**U. 98–39; **Lv.**U. 08–39 imp.; **Sa.** [*C. as:* 43902]

3415 **Annual Progress Report. Institute** of **Astrophysics, University** of **Toronto.** Toronto. *A. Prog. Rep. Inst. Astrophys. Toronto* **L.**MO. 57–; **Y.**

3416 **Annual Progress Report** on **Marine Borer Activity. Forest Department, Mombasa.** *A. Prog. Rep. mar. Borer Activ.* [1956–] **O.**F. 57–.

3416° **Annual Progress Report** of the **Pakistan Forest Institute.** Peshawar. *A. Prog. Rep. Pakistan Forest Inst.* **L.**BMᴺ. 60–.

3417 **Annual Progress Report** of the **Scheme** for **Research** on the **Manufacture** of **Sugar Candy.** Kanpur. *A. Prog. Rep. Scheme Res. Mf. Sug. Candy* [1951–] **L.**P. 51–54.

3418 **Annual Progress Report** of the **Sugar Research** and **Testing Station,** Bilari, District Moradabad. Kanpur. *A. Prog. Rep. Sug. Res. Test. Stn Bilari* [1951–] **L.**P. 51–52.

3419 **Annual Public Health Report. Bihar** and **Orissa.** *A. publ. Hlth Rep. Bihar Orissa* [1936–] **O.**I. [*C. of:* 3450]

3419° **Annual Public Health Report. Bombay.** *A. publ. Hlth Rep. Bombay* **Y.** 24–.

3420 **Annual Publication** of the **Colorado College Scientific Society.** Colorado Springs. *A. Publ. Colo. Coll. scient. Soc.*

3420ª **Annual Rainfall, Australia.** *A. Rainf. Aust.* **Y.** 55–.

3421 **Annual Rainfall Statistics, Sudan Meteorological Service,** Khartoum. *A. Rainf. Statist. Sudan* **L.**MO. 40–.

3422 **Annual Rainfall Summary. Meteorological Service, Israel.** Hakirya. *A. Rainf. Summ. Israel* **L.**MO. 41–; **Y.**
Annual Report. *See* **Report.**

3423 **Annual Report Series. Mellon Institute** of **Industrial Research,** University of Pittsburgh. *A. Rep. Ser. Mellon Inst. ind. Res.* [1951–] **L.**P. [*C. of:* 44488]

3424 **Annual Reprint** of the **Reports** of the **Council** on **Pharmacy** and **Chemistry, American Medical Association.** Chicago. *A. Repr. Rep. Coun. Pharm. Chem.* [1910–54] **L.**P. [*Reprints from* 25520]

3424° **Annual Research Memoirs Summary. Central Water** and **Power Research Station, Poona.** *A. Res. Mem. Summ. cent. Wat. Pwr Res. Stn Poona* **Y.** 58–.

3425 **Annual Research Progress Report. Division** of **Forest Research, Department** of **Lands** and **Forests.** Ontario. *A. Res. Prog. Rep. Div. Forest Res., Ontario* [1951–] **O.**F. [*C. of:* 3410]

3426 **Annual Research Publication. Central Irrigation** and **Hydrodynamics Research Station, Poona.** *A. Res. Publ. cent. Irrig. Hydrodyn. Res. Stn Poona*

3427 **Annual Research Report. Laboratory** of **Chemical** and **Solid State Physics, Massachusetts Institute** of **Technology.** Cambridge, Mass. *A. Res. Rep. Lab. chem. solid St. Phys. M.I.T.* **Y.**

3428 **Annual Return** of **Statistics** relating to **Forest Administration** in **British India.** Delhi. *A. Return Statist. Forest Adm. Br. India* **Bn.**U. 37–40.

3429 **Annual Review. Academy** of **Natural Sciences** of **Philadelphia.** Philadelphia. *A. Rev. Acad. nat. Sci. Philad.* [1935–] **L.**BM.; BMᴺ. 35; E.; GL.; UC.; **Abs.**U.; **Bl.**U.; **C.**UL.; **Dm.**; **Ld.**U.; **Lv.**U.; **Nw.**A.; **O.**R.; **Pl.**M. [*C. of:* 46178]

3430 **Annual Review** of **Analytical Chemistry.** American Chemical Society. New York. *A. Rev. analyt. Chem.* [1949–] **L.**SC. [*Contained in:* 23197]

3430ᵃ **Annual Review. Asphalt Roads Association.** Westminster. *A. Rev. Asph. Rds Ass.* [1956–] **L.**BM.

3430ᶜ **Annual Review. Australian Mineral Industry.** *A. Rev. Aust. Miner. Ind.* **Y.**

3431 **Annual Review** in **Automatic Programming.** Oxford. *A. Rev. autom. Progrmg* [1960–] **L.**BM.; P.; SC.; **Cr.**U.; **G.**U.; **Ld.**U.; **Y.**

3432 **Annual Review** of the **Biochemical** and **Allied Research** in **India.** Bangolore. *A. Rev. biochem. all. Res. India* [1936–] **L.**C. 36–37; P.; SC.; **C.**A.; **Hu.**G. 40–46; **R.**D. 52–; **Rt.** 36–41. [*C. of:* 7006]

3433 **Annual Review** of **Biochemistry.** Stanford University. Palo Alto. *A. Rev. Biochem.* [1932–] **L.**AM.; B.; BM.; C.; CB.; IC. 35–; KC. 57–; LE.; LI.; MA. 37– imp.; MC.; MD.; OP. 32: 37–39: 42–; P.; PH.; QM. imp.; RI. 37–; S.; SC.; TD.; U. 32–36: 39–; UC.; UCH.; VC.; **Abd.**R.; S. 49–; U.; **Abs.**A. 51–54; U. 45–; **Ba.**I. 37–; **Bl.**U.; **Bm.**P.; U. 37–39: 41–; **Bn.**U.; **Br.**A. 34–; U.; **C.**A.; APH.; B.; BI.; BO.; CH.; MO. 46–; P.; T. 46–; UL. 46–50; V. 55–; **Cr.**MD. 34– imp.; U. 38–; **Db.**; **Dn.**U. 46–; **E.**HW.; U.; **Ex.**U. 37–; G.T.; U.; **H.**U.; **Hu.**G. 48–; **Je.**; **Lc.**A. imp.; **Ld.**P. 45–; U.; **Lv.**P.; U.; **M.**C.; MS.; P. 35–53; T.; U.; **Md.**H. 37–61; MI.; **N.**P. 45–; U.; **Nw.**A.; **O.**BO. 35–; BS.; P. 33–; PH.; R.; S. 36–; UC.; **Pl.**M.; **R.**D.; U.; **Rt.**; **Sa.**; **Sal.**F.; **Sh.**U.; **Sw.**U.; **W.** 46–; **Wd.** 44: 50–; **Y.**

3434 **Annual Review. Canterbury Agricultural College.** Lincoln, N.Z. *A. Rev. Canterbury agric. Coll. N.Z.* [1950–] **L.**AM.; V.; **Abs.**A.; **Br.**A.; **C.**A.; **Md.**H.; **N.**U.; **Sal.**; **Y.** [*C. of:* 42967]

3435 **Annual Review. Department** of **Agriculture, Kenya.** Nairobi. *A. Rev. Dep. Agric. Kenya* **C.**A. 50–.

3436 **Annual Review** of **Entomology.** Stanford, Palo Alto. *A. Rev. Ent.* [1956–] **L.**AM.; BM.; BMᴺ.; E.; P.; QM.; SC.; **Abd.**U.; **Bl.**U.; **Bm.**U.; **Bn.**U.; **Br.**A.; U.; **C.**B.; V.; **Dn.**U.; **E.**U.; **Fr.**; **H.**U.; **Je.**; **Ld.**P.; U.; **Md.**H.; **N.**U.; **O.**F.; H.; R.; **R.**U.; **Rt.**; **Sw.**U.; **Y.**

3436ᶜ **Annual Review. Fisheries Council** of **Canada.** *A. Rev. Fish. Coun. Can.* **Y.**

3437 **Annual Review** of **Medicine.** Stanford University. Palo Alto. *A. Rev. Med.* [1950–] **L.**BM.; CB.; MA.; MC.; MD.; S. 56–; SC.; VC.; **Abd.**R.; **Br.**U.; **C.**V. 52–; **Cr.**U. 55–; **Dn.**U. 61–; **E.**U.; **G.**U. 58–; **M.**MS.; **N.**U. 56–; **Sh.**U. 55–.

3438 **Annual Review** of **Microbiology.** Stanford University. Palo Alto. *A. Rev. Microbiol.* [1947–] **L.**AM.; B.; BM. 50–; BMᴺ.; C.; CB.; IC.; LE.; LI.; MC.; MD.; MY.; PH.; QM.; SC.; TD.; UC.; **Abd.**R.; S.; U.; **Abs.**A. 51–; U.; **Bl.**U.; **Bm.**U.; **Bn.**U.; **Br.**A.; U.; **C.**APH.; BI.; BO.; GE.; MO.; PA.; V.; **Cr.**U.; **Db.**; **Dn.**U.; **E.**U.; HW.; **Ex.**U. 50–51: 56–; **Fr.** 52–; **G.**T.; U.; **H.**U.; **Hu.**G. 51–; **Je.**; **Lc.**A. 48–; **Ld.**P. 54–; U.; **Lv.**P.; **M.**C. 57–60; P. 55–; T.; U.; **Md.**H.; **Mi.**; **N.**U.; **Nw.**A.; **O.**BO.; F. 47–48; R.; RE.; **R.**D.; U.; **Rt.**; **Sw.**U. 59–; **W.** 48–; **Y.**

3439 **Annual Review** of **Nuclear Science.** Stanford, Palo Alto. *A. Rev. nucl. Sci.* [1952–] **L.**B. 56–; BM.; CB. 53–; C.; P.; QM. 56–; RI. 53–; SC.; **Abd.**U.; **Bl.**U.; **Bm.**P.; **Bn.**U.; **Br.**U. 52–53; **Db.**; **Dn.**U. 52–59; **E.**U.; **Ex.**U.; **F.**A.; **G.**U.; **Ld.**P. 56–; U.; **Lo.** 58–; **Lv.**P.; **M.**U.; **N.**U.; **R.**U.; **Sa.**; **Y.**

3440 **Annual Review** of **Oilseeds, Oils, Oilcakes** and **other Commodities.** London. *A. Rev. Oilseeds* [1923–] **L.**AM. 32–; BM. 49–; PR. 26–; **Ld.**P. 46– imp.; **M.**P. 25–.

3441 **Annual Review** of the **Paint Industry.** New York. *A. Rev. Paint Ind.* [1953–] **L.**P.

3442 **Annual Review** of **Pharmacology.** *A. Rev. Pharmac.* **L.**P.; **Y.**

3443 **Annual Review** of **Physical Chemistry.** Stanford University. Palo Alto. *A. Rev. phys. Chem.* [1950–] **L.**B.; BM.; C.; CB.; I. 57–; KC.; LE. 50–58; P.; QM.; RI.; SC.; U.; **Abd.**S.; U.; **Abs.**U. 56–; **Bl.**U.; **Bm.**T.; **Bn.**U.; **Br.**U.; **C.**APH.; **Cr.**U.; **Db.**; **Dn.**U.; **E.**U.; **Ex.**U. 56–; **G.**U.; **H.**U.; **Ld.**P. 52–; U.; **Lv.**P.; U.; **M.**C.; D.; P.; T.; U.; **N.**U.; **Nw.**A.; **O.**E. 50–57; PC.; **R.**U.; **Rt.**; **Sh.**U.; **Sw.**U.; **Wd.**; **Y.**

3444 **Annual Review** of **Physiology.** Stanford University. Palo Alto. *A. Rev. Physiol.* [1939–] **L.**B.; BM.; CB.; LI.; MA. 40–43: 47–; MC.; MD.; OP.; PH.; RI. 50–; S.; SC.; TD.; U.; UC.; UCH.; VC.; **Abd.**R.; U. 47–; **Abs.**U. 44–; **Bl.**U.; **Bm.**P.; U.; **Bn.**U.; **Br.**U.; **C.**APH.; B.; BI.; MO.; PH.; V. 54–; **Cr.**MD. 48–; U.; **Db.**; **Dn.**U.; **E.**AB.; E. 40: 42: 50–57; U.; **G.**U.; **H.**U. 55–; **Ld.**U.; **Lo.** 51–; **M.**MS.; U.; **Mi.** 47–; **N.**U.; **Nw.**A.; **O.**BS.; EP. 47–; N.; P.; PH. 53–; R.; **Pl.**M.; **R.**D.; U.; **Sa.**; **Sh.**U.; **W.**; **Y.**

3445 **Annual Review** of **Plant Physiology.** Stanford University. Palo Alto. *A. Rev. Pl. Physiol.* [1950–] **L.**AM.; B.; BM.; C.; QM.; SC.; UC. 58–; VC. 50–58; **Abd.**S.; U.; **Abs.**A. 55–; U.; **Ba.**I.; **Bm.**P. 54–; **Bn.**U.; **Br.**A.; U.; **C.**BI.; BO.; **Cr.**U.; **Db.**; **Dn.**U. 60–; **E.**HW.; U.; **Ex.**U.; **Fr.**; **G.**U.; **H.**U.; **Hu.**G.; **Je.**; **Lv.**P. 52–; U.; **Md.**H.; **N.**U.; **Nw.**A.; **O.**BO.; F.; RE.; UC.; **Pl.**M.; **R.**U.; **Rt.**; **Sa.**; **Sh.**U.; **Wd.**; **Y.**

3446 **Annual Review** of **Psychology.** Stanford University. Palo Alto. *A. Rev. Psychol.* [1950–] **L.**B.; BM.; MD.; U.; VC. 56–; **Abd.**U. 52–; **Bl.**U.; **Br.**U.; **C.**PS.; **Dn.**U.; **E.**U.; **Ex.**U. 33–; **G.**U.; **H.**U.; **N.**U.; **Nw.**A.; **O.**EP.; **R.**U.; **Sh.**U.; **Y.**

3446ᶜ **Annual Review. Rubber Research Institute** of **Ceylon.** Dartonfield. *A. Rev. Rubb. Res. Inst. Ceylon* [1960–] **L.**BM.; MY.; P.; **Je.**; **Md.**H.; **Y.** [*C. of:* 45181]
Annual Review of **Shipping, Shipbuilding, Marine Engineering,** etc. *See* 25850.

3446ᵉ **Annual Review. Solartron Electronic Group.** Thames Ditton. *A. Rev. Solartron electronic Grp* [1958–] **L.**BM.

3447 **Annual Review** of **World Production** and **Consumption** of **Fertilizers.** F.A.O. Rome. *A. Rev. Wld Prod. Consum. Fertil.* [1953–] **L.**BM.; **G.**M.; **Ld.**U.; **Md.**H.; **O.**AEC.; **O.**R.; **R.**T. [*C. of:* 19323]

3448 **Annual Reviews** of **Petroleum Technology.** London. *A Revs Petrol. Technol.* [1937–40] **L.**C.; I.; IC.; P.; SC.; **Abs.**N.; **C.**UL.; **G.**T. 38; **Ld.**P.; **M.**P. 40; **O.**R.; **Wd.** [*C. of:* 37431; *C. as:* 46227]

3449 **Annual Ring.** University of Toronto. Toronto. *A. Ring* **Bn.**U. 49– imp.; **O.**F. 49–.

3450 **Annual Sanitary Reports. Bihar** and **Orissa.** Patna. *A. sanit. Rep. Bihar Orissa* **L.**MD. 12–26; S. 12–35*; **O.**I. 12–35. [*C. as:* 3419]

3451 **Annual Scientific Bulletin** of the **Royal Agricultural College.** Cirencester. *A. scient. Bull. R. agric. Coll.* [1909–13] **L.**AM.; BM.; MO. 12–13; **Abs.**A.; N. 11–13; **Ld.**U. 10–13; **Nw.**A. 10–13; **O.**R. 09–11; **Rt.**
Annual Scientific Supplement to **Urania.** Kraków. *See* 55736.

3451ᵃ **Annual Soils Conference.** University of Minnesota. *A. Soils Conf. Univ. Minn.* **Y.** 54–.

3451ᵇ **Annual Soot** and **Dustfall Report.** Smoke Abatement League. *A. Soot Dustf. Rep.* **Y.** 31–.

3451ᶜ **Annual Statement** of **Rainfall** in the **United Provinces** of **Agra** and **Oudh** (*formerly* in the North-Western Provinces and Oudh). Allahabad. *A. Statem. Rainf. Unit. Prov. Agra Oudh* **L.**MO. 77: 99–13*. [*C. as:* 33394]

3452 **Annual Statistical Report. American Iron** and **Steel Association** (Institute). *A. statist. Rep. Am. Iron Steel Ass.* **L.**I. 73–; SC. 23–; **G.**I. 16–40 imp.; **Y.**

3453 **Annual Statistical Summary** of the **Ministry** of **Fuel** and **Power.** Coal Mining Industry. London. *A. statist. Summ. Minist. Fuel Pwr Coal Min. Ind.* **L.**BMᴺ. 45–.

Annual Statistics for the **United Kingdom, British Iron** and **Steel Federation.** *See* 24176.

3454 **Annual Summary** of **Chemical Laboratory Reports** from **Natal Sugar Factories.** Durban. *A. Summ. chem. Lab. Rep. Natal Sug. Fact.*

3455 **Annual Summary** of the **Indian Weather Review.** Calcutta. *A. Summ. Indian Weath. Rev.* [1891–] **L.**MO.; **Abs.**N. 11– imp.; **E.**M.; R.; 97– imp.; **Ld.**U. 01–08: 15; **O.**R. [Part D. *C. as:* 49394]

3456 **Annual Summary. Meteorological Department.** Weymouth. *A. Summ. met. Dep., Weymouth*

3457 **Annual Summary** of **Observations. British West African Meteorological Service, Nigeria.** *A. Summ. Obsns Br. W. Afr. met. Serv.* **L.**MO. 49–; **Y.** [*C. of:* 31583]

Annual Summary of **Observations, Gambia.** *See* 31570.

3458 **Annual Summary** of **Observations** in **Ghana.** Meteorological Service. Accra. *A. Summ. Obsns Ghana* [1952–] **L.**MO. 52–. [*C. of:* 3459]

3459 **Annual Summary** of **Observations** in the **Gold Coast.** Lagos. *A. Summ. Obsns Gold Coast* [1951] **L.**MO. [*C. as:* 3458]

3460 **Annual Summary** of **Observations. Meteorological Department, Sierra Leone.** Freetown. *A. Summ. Obsns met. Dep. Sierra Leone* **L.**BM. 52–; MO. 49–; **Bl.**U. 54–; **E.**M. 49– imp.; **Y.** [*C. of:* 44510]

3461 **Annual Survey** of **American Chemistry.** New York. *A. Surv. Am. Chem.* [1927–35] **L.**C.; IC.; P. 27–29; SC.; U.; **Abd.**U.; **Bm.**P. 34–35; **Ld.**W. [*C. of:* 51497]

3462 **Annual Survey** of the **British Textile Industry.** London. *A. Surv. Br. Text. Ind.*

3463 **Annual Survey** of **Psychoanalysis.** New York. *A. Surv. Psychoanal.* [1952–] **L.**BM.; MD.; U.

3464 **Annual Survey** of **Research** in **Pharmacy.** Baltimore. *A. Surv. Res. Pharm.* [1933–]

Annual Survey. Synthetic Methods of **Organic Chemistry.** *See* 51684.

Annual Symposium on **Antibiotics.** *See* 3585.

3465 **Annual Symposium** on **Fundamental Cancer Research.** London. *A. Symp. fund. Cancer Res.* **Dn.**U. 58; **Y.**

3465ᶜ **Annual Symposium** on **Problems** in **Air Pollution.** Franklin Institute. *A. Symp. Probl. Air Pollut.* [1957–] **Y.**

3466 **Annual Symposium. School** of **Forestry, Louisiana State University** and **Agricultural** and **Mechanical College.** Baton Rouge. *A. Symp. Sch. For. La St. Univ.* [1952–] **O.**F.

3467 **Annual Tables** of **Physical Constants** and **Numerical Data.** Princeton, N.J. *A. Tables phys. Const.* [1941–] **L.**C.; P.; SC.; **C.**UL.; **E.**R. 41–45; **O.**R. [*Replaces:* 23832ᶠ and 51774]

3468 **Annual Technical Report. Council** of **Scientific** and **Industrial Research, India.** *A. tech. Rep. C.S.I.R India* **Y.**

3468ᶜ **Annual Transactions** and **Year Book. Kansas Engineering Society.** *A. Trans. Yb. Kans. Engng Soc.* **Y.** 28–.

3469 **Annual Veterinary Report, British Somaliland.** Berbera. *A. vet. Rep. Br. Somalild* **W.** 24–.

Annual Volume. Institute of **Marine Engineers.** *See* 53759.

3470 **Annual Weather Report. Meteorological Service, Israel.** Hakirya. *A. Weath. Rep. Israel* [1949–] **Y.**

Annual Wool Digest. Sydney. *See* 16338.

3471 **Annual Wool Review.** Boston, Mass. *A. Wool Rev.* **Ld.**U. 01–.

Annuario [Portuguese]. *See* **Anuário.**

Annuario [Spanish]. *See* **Anuario.**

3473 **Annuario** della **Accademia** d'Italia. Roma. *Annuar. Accad. Ital.* **L.**BM.; C. 29–37; EE. 30–37; U. 30–; UC. 29–; **Abd.**U. 29–37; **E.**C. 24–38 imp.; R. 29–37; **O.**B. 29–.

3474 **Annuario** della **Accademia** dei **Lincei.** Roma. *Annuar. Accad. Lincei* **L.**BM. 86–; U. 29–37: 50–; **Db.** 86– imp.; **E.**R. 88: 01: 05: 25– imp.; **O.**B. 25–39.

3475 **Annuario** dell'**Accademia pontaniana.** Napoli. *Annuar. Accad. pontan.*

3476 **Annuario** della **Accademia** delle **scienze** di **Torino.** *Annuar. Accad. Sci. Torino* **E.**R. 77–78: 32–34.

3477 **Annuario** dell'**aeronautica italiana.** Milano. *Annuar. Aeronaut. ital.* [1929–]

3478 **Annuario** dell'**agricoltura italiana.** Roma. *Annuar. Agric. ital.* [1948–] **L.**AM. 48–50; BM. 49–; **O.**AEC.; B.

Annuario astronomico. Trieste. *See* 3497.

3479 **Annuario astronomico** del **Osservatorio** di **Pino-Torinese.** Torino. *Annuar. astr. Oss. Pino-Torin.* **C.**O. 05–; **E.**O. 09–26 imp.

Annuario astronomico del **R. Osservatorio** di **Pino-Torinese.** *See* 3479.

3480 **Annuario biografico** del **Circolo matematico** di **Palermo.** *Annuar. biogr. Circ. mat. Palermo* **Abs.**U. 12: 28; **E.**C. 12–14; **O.**R. 12.

3481 **Annuario** di **chimica scientifica** ed **industriale.** Torino. *Annuar. Chim. scient. ind.* **L.**C. 19–21.

3482 **Annuario** del **Circolo matematico** di **Catania.** *Annuar. Circ. mat. Catania* **L.**UC. 21: 23.

3484 **Annuario** dell'**economia agraria italiana.** Roma. *Annuar. Econ. agr. ital.* **L.**AM. 47–.

Annuario idrografico della **Svizzera.** *See* 3262ᵃ.

3486 **Annuario** dell'**industria metallurgica italiana.** *Annuar. Ind. metall. ital.* **L.**P. 32.

3487 **Annuario** dell'**industria mineraria, metallurgica** e **chimica italiana.** Torino. *Annuar. Ind. miner. metall. chim. ital.*

3488 **Annuario** per le **industrie chimiche** e **farmaceutiche.** Roma. *Annuar. Ind. chim. farm.*

3489 **Annuario** degli **Istituti scientifici italiana.** Roma. *Annuar. Ist. scient. ital.* O.B. 18.

3490 **Annuario** dell'**Istituto** e **museo** de **zoologia** dell'**Università** di **Napoli.** *Annuar. Ist. Mus. Zool. Univ. Napoli* [1949–] L.BM.; BM^N.; EB.; R. 49–54; Z.; C.P.; E.R.; Lv.U. Pl.M. [*C. of:* 3505]
   Annuario dell'**Istituto** di **sperimentazione** per la **chimica agraria** in **Torino.** *See* 3519.

3491 **Annuario** della **Istituzione** d'**agraria. R. Scuola superiore** di **agricoltura.** Milano. *Annuar. Ist. Agr. Milano* Rt. 92–16.

3492 **Annuario** del **Laboratorio** di **chimica generale** e **tecnologia** della **R. Accademia navale** in **Livorno.** Milano. *Annuar. Lab. Chim. gen. Tecnol. Livorno*

3493 **Annuario marittimo.** Triesti. *Annuar. maritt.* L.BM. 1854–13; MO. 75.

3494 **Annuario meteorologico. Istituto geofisico** e **geodetico.** Messina. *Annuar. met., Messina* L.MO. 37–38.

3495 **Annuario. Ministerio** dell'**aeronautico, aviazione civile** e **traffico aero.** Roma. *Annuar. Minist. Aeronaut.* L.MO. 26–32.
   Annuario del **Museo zoologico** della **Università** di **Napoli.** *See* 3505.
   Annuario. Osservatorio astrofisico di **Catania.** *See* 3506.

3496 **Annuario. Osservatorio astrofisico** di **Arcetri, Istituto** di **studi superiori.** Firenze. *Annuar. Oss. astr. Arcetri, Firenze* L.SC. 57–.

3497 **Annuario** del **Osservatiorio astronomico** di **Trieste.** *Annuar. Oss. astr. Trieste* E.R. 34–.

3498 **Annuario. Osservatorio** di **fisica terrestre** del **Seminario Arcivescoville.** Como. *Annuar. Oss. Fis. terr., Como* L.MO. 43– imp.

3499 **Annuario. Osservatorio geofisico** del **Seminario Patriarcale.** Venezia. *Annuar. Oss. geofis., Venezia* L.MO. 28–38 imp.

3500 **Annuario. Osservatorio** di **Messina.** *Annuar. Oss. Messina* L.MO. 04–09.

3501 **Annuario** della **Pontificia Accademia** delle **scienze.** Città del Vaticano. *Annuar. pontif. Accad. Sci.* [1929–] L.BM. 36–37; EE. 36–37; SC. 33–37; Bl.U. 33–34; E.C. 36–37; R.
   Annuario della **R. Accademia** d'**Italia.** *See* 3473.
   Annuario. R. Accademia dei **Lincei.** Roma. *See* 3474.
   Annuario. R. Accademia delle **scienze** di **Torino.** *See* 3476.

3502 **Annuario** del **R. Istituto botanico** di **Roma.** Roma. *Annuar. R. Ist. bot. Roma* [1884–02] L.BM. 84–00; BM^N.; K. 84–01; C.UL.; E.B. [*C. as:* 3004]

3503 **Annuario** del **R. Istituto sperimentale agrario** in **Sidi Mesri.** *Annuar. R. Ist. sper. agr. Sidi Mesri* [1923–] C.A. 28–.

3504 **Annuario** del **R. Istituto veneto** di **scienze, lettere** ed **arti.** Venezia. *Annuar. R. Ist. veneto Sci.* [1938–] L.BM. 38–.

3505 **Annuario R. Museo zoologico** della **R. Università** di **Napoli.** Napoli. *Annuar. R. Mus. zool. R. Univ. Napoli* [1862–48] L.AM. 01–35; BM. 01–48; BM^N.; EB.

09–48; R. 01–48; Z.; C.P. 01–48; UL.; Db. 01–15; E.R. 01–48 imp.; Lv.U. 05–48; Pl.M. [*C. as:* 3490]

3506 **Annuario R. Osservatorio astrofisico** di **Catania.** *Annuar. R. Oss. astrofis. Catania* E.R. 27–35 imp.
   Annuario del **R. Osservatorio astronomico** di **Trieste.** *See* 3497.

3507 **Annuario** della **R. Società italiana** d'**igiene.** Milano. *Annuar. R. Soc. ital. Ig.*

3508 **Annuario** della **R. Stazione bacologica sperimentale** di **Padova.** *Annuar. R. Staz. bacol. sper. Padova* L.EB. 24–37*; C.BI. 34–37; P. 23–37.
   Annuario della **R. Stazione chimico-agraria sperimentale** di **Torino.** *See* 3519.

3509 **Annuario** della **R. Stazione** di **patologia vegetale.** Roma. *Annuar. R. Staz. Patol. veg. Roma*

3510 **Annuario sanitario italiano.** Milano. *Annuar. sanit. ital.*

3511 **Annuario scientifico** ed **industriale.** Milano. *Annuar. scient. ind.* [1863–27] L.P. 89–25.

3512 **Annuario. Scuola** d'**applicazione** per gl'**ingegneri.** R. Università romana. Roma. *Annuar. Scu. Appl. Ing. R. Univ. romana* Db. 93–.

3513 **Annuario** della **Società chimica.** Milano. *Annuar. Soc. chim., Milano*

3514 **Annuario** della **Società italiana** delle **scienze.** Roma. *Annuar. Soc. ital. Sci.* Db. 27–; E.R. 24–38.

3515 **Annuario** della **Società R.** di **Napoli.** *Annuar. Soc. R. Napoli* L.BM^N. 39.

3516 **Annuario** di **statistica agraria.** Roma. *Annuar. Statist. agr.* L.AM. 39–; BM. 56–.

3517 **Annuario** di **statistica forestale.** Roma. *Annuar. statist. for.* L.BM. 51–.

3518 **Annuario** di **statistica industriale.** Roma. *Annuar. Statist. ind.* L.BM. 56–.
   Annuario della **Stazione bacologica sperimentale** di **Padova.** *See* 3508.

3519 **Annuario** della **Stazione chimico-agraria sperimentale** di **Torino.** Torino. *Annuar. Staz. chim.-agr. sper. Torino* [1871–] L.P. 52–; Br.A. 41–; Rt. 14–; Y.

3520 **Annuario. Stazione sperimentale** di **viticoltura** (*afterwards* e di **enologia**) di **Conegliano.** Treviso. *Annuar. Staz. sper. Vitic. Enol. Conegliano* L.EB. 24–; Md.H. 23–36.

3521 **Annuario storico-meteorologico italiano** dell' **Osservatorio** del **R. Collegio Carlo Alberto, Moncalieri.** Torino. *Annuar. stor.-met. ital.*

3521° **Annuario termotecnico italiano.** *Annuar. termotec. ital.* [1958–] Y.

3522 **Annuario tessile italiano.** Milano. *Annuar. tess. ital.*

3523 **Annuario** dell'**Ufficio presagi.** Ministerio dell' aeronautica. Roma. *Annuar. Uff. presagi Minist. Aeronaut.* L.G. 32–.

3525 **Annuario** della **Università** di **Pisa.** *Annuar. Univ. Pisa* L.MD. 00–16 imp.

3526 **Annuary** of the **American Institute** of **Architects.** Washington, D.C. *Annuary Am. Inst. Archit.* [1909–31: 36–] L.SC. 27–.

3527 **Año academico** de la **R. Academia** de **ciencias naturales** y **artes.** Barcelona. *Año Acad. R. Acad. Cienc. nat., Barcelona* L.BM. 99– imp.; BM^N. 96–26 imp.; MO. 15–20; M.U. 19–28: 52.

3528 **Anode.** Butte, Montana. *Anode* [1915–]

3529 **Anomalo.** Rivista di antropologia criminale e psichiatria. Napoli. *Anomalo* [1889–22]

3530 **Años pluvimetricos, Venezuela.** Caracas. *Años pluvimetr. Venez.* **L.**MO. 21–28 imp. [*C. in:* 46138ᵃ]

3531 **Anotaciones pediátricas.** Medellin. *Anot. pediát.* [1954–] **L.**MA.

3532 **Ansaldo.** Genova. *Ansaldo* [1926–33] **L.**P.

3533 **Ansco Abstracts.** Binghampton, N.Y. *Ansco Abstr.* **L.**P. 54–; **Y.**

3534 **Ansconian.** Binghampton, N.Y. *Ansconian* [1943–] **L.**PG. imp. [*C. of:* 1185]

3535 **Anstalts-Umschau.** Kulmbach. *Anst.-Umsch.* [1927–57] **L.**H. 56–57. [*Not published* 1944–48; *C. as:* 27744]

3536 **Ansul News Notes.** Ansul Chemical Company. *Ansul News Notes* **L.**P. imp. [*C. as:* 34804]

3537 **Antarctic News Bulletin.** Washington. *Antarctic News Bull.* [1950–] **C.**PO.

3538 **Antarctic Record.** Reports of the Japanese Antarctic Research Expedition. Tokyo. *Antarctic Rec.* [1957–] **L.**BMᴺ.; MO.

3539 **Antenna.** Milano. *Antenna, Milano.* **L.**AV. 57–; P. 60–; **Y.**

3540 **Antenna.** Rio de Janeiro. *Antenna, Rio de J.* **L.**AV. 58–.

3541 **Antenne.** Zeitschrift für drahtlose Nachrichten-übermittlung. Berlin. *Antenne* [1913–25] **L.**P. 13–14.

3542 **Anthologica medica dermatologica.** Milano. *Anthol. med. derm.*

3543 **Anthracite Forest Protector.** Hazleton, Pa. *Anthrac. Forest Prot.* [1926–]

3544 **Anthracite Survey Papers.** Philadelphia. *Anthrac. Surv. Pap.* [1940–] **O.**F.

3545 **Anthrax Investigation Board Reports.** *Anthrax Invest. Bd Rep.* **Bra.**P. 06–18.
   Anthropologia hungarica. *See* 3607.

3546 **Anthropologica.** Ottawa. *Anthropologica* [1955–] **L.**AN.; BM.; BMᴺ. 59–.

3547 **Anthropologica sinica.** Peiping. *Anthrop. sin.* [1939–]

3548 **Anthropological Briefs.** New York. *Anthrop. Briefs* [1942–]

3549 **Anthropological Bulletins. University** of **Chicago.** Chicago. *Anthrop. Bull. Univ. Chicago*

3550 **Anthropological Bulletins** from the **Zoological Survey** of **India.** Calcutta. *Anthrop. Bull. zool. Surv. India* [1931–] **L.**AN. 31–34; BMᴺ. 31–34; **Db.**; **E.**R. 31.

3551 **Anthropological Handbooks.** American Museum of Natural History. New York. *Anthrop. Handb. Am. Mus. nat. Hist.* [1954–] **L.**AN.

3552 **Anthropological Papers** of the **American Museum** of **Natural History.** New York. *Anthrop. Pap. Am. Mus. nat. Hist.* [1907–] **L.**AN.; BM. 44–; BMᴺ.; **Abs.**U. 28–; **C.**E. 08–; P. 27–; **Db.**; **E.**R.; **Lv.**P. 07–36 imp.; **O.**R.; **Y.**

3553 **Anthropological Papers. Bureau** of **American Ethnology.** Washington. *Anthrop. Pap. Bur. Am. Ethnol.* [1938–] **L.**AN.; **E.**R.; **G.**U. 49–; **M.**P.

3554 **Anthropological Papers. Museum** of **Anthropology, University** of **Michigan,** Ann Arbor, Mich. *Anthrop. Pap. Mus. Anthrop. Univ. Mich.* [1949–] **L.**AN.; BM.; BMᴺ.; SC.; **Abd.**U.; **Bl.**U.; **Sa.**; **Y.**

3555 **Anthropological Papers. University** of **Alaska.** College. *Anthrop. Pap. Univ. Alaska* [1952–] **L.**AN.; BM.; **C.**PO.

3556 **Anthropological Papers** of the **University** of **Arizona.** Tucson. *Anthrop. Pap. Univ. Arizona* [1959–] **L.**BM.; BMᴺ.

3557 **Anthropological Papers. University** of **Calcutta.** *Anthrop. Pap. Univ. Calcutta* [1920–] **L.**AN. 27–; **E.**F.; **O.**B. 35–; **Y.**

3558 **Anthropological Papers** of the **University** of **Texas.** Austin. *Anthrop. Pap. Univ. Tex.* [1933–] **L.**AN.; **Br.**U.; **O.**R.

3559 **Anthropological Publications** of the **Pennsylvania University Museum.** Philadelphia, Pa. *Anthrop. Publs Pa Univ. Mus.* [1909–24] **L.**AN.; BM.; UC. 09–16; **Abs.**N. 19–24; **Lv.**U.

3560 **Anthropological Quarterly.** Washington. *Anthrop. Q.* [1953–] **L.**AN.; **Nw.**A. [*C. of:* 38661]

3561 **Anthropological Records. University** of **California.** Berkeley. *Anthrop. Rec. Univ. Calif.* [1937–] **L.**AN.; BM.; BMᴺ.; UC.; **Abd.**U.; **Br.**U.; **C.**E.; P. imp.; **Db.**; **E.**C.; G.; R.; **O.**B.; **Y.**

3562 **Anthropological Report, New Guinea.** Melbourne. *Anthrop. Rep. New Guinea* [1925–] **L.**AN. 25–31.

3563 **Anthropological Series. Boston College Graduate School.** Chestnut Hill, Mass. *Anthrop. Ser. Boston Coll.* [1936–] **L.**AN. 36–39.

3564 **Anthropological Series. Catholic University** of **America.** Washington. *Anthrop. Ser. Cath. Univ. Am.* [1930–] **L.**AN.

3564ᶜ **Anthropological Series. Department** of **Natural Resources, Saskatchewan.** *Anthrop. Ser. Sask.* [1955–] **L.**BM.

3565 **Anthropological Series. National Museum** of **Victoria.** Melbourne. *Anthrop. Ser. natn. Mus. Vict.* [1956–] **L.**AN.

3566 **Anthropological Studies. Louisiana Department** of **Conservation.** New Orleans. *Anthrop. Stud. La Dep. Conserv.* **L.**BM. 35–; U. 35–36.
   Anthropological Studies from **Yale University.** *See* 57959.
   Anthropologie. Kiev. *See* 3611.

3567 **Anthropologie.** Paris, *Anthropologie, Paris* [1890–] **L.**AN.; BM.; BMᴺ. 01–; HO. 13–; MD. 08–16; R.; S. 90–34; UC. 90–37; **Abd.**U.; **Abs.**N. 22–; U. 22–; **Bl.**U.; **Bm.**U. 12–; **Br.**U. 90–09: 28–; **C.**AN. 90–39; E.; UL.; **Cr.**U. 53–; **Db.**; **E.**R.; U.; V.; **G.**U.; **M.**P.; **O.**R.; **Sa.**; **Y.**

3568 **Anthropologie.** Institut d'anthropologie de l'Université Charles à Prague. *Anthropologie, Prague* [1923–43] **L.**AN.; BMᴺ. 28–41 imp.; S. 23–31 imp.; **Bl.**U. 23–38; **Br.**U. 28–43; **C.**UL.

3569 **Anthropologische Forschungen.** Wien. *Anthrop. Forsch.* [1950–] **L.**AN.; **O.**R.

3570 **Anthropologischer Anzeiger.** Stuttgart. *Anthrop. Anz.* [1924–] **L.**AN. 24–42; BM. 56–; BMᴺ. 56–; S. 24–39; **Bm.**U.; **C.**AN. 24–39; UL.; **O.**B. 56–; **Y.** [*Also supplement*]

3571 **Anthropologist.** Delhi. *Anthropologist* [1954–] L.AN.

3572 **Anthropology** in **British Colombia.** Victoria, B.C. *Anthropology Br. Columb.* [1950–] L.AN.

3573 **Anthropology** in **British Columbia. Memoir.** Victoria, B.C. *Anthropology Br. Columb. Mem.* [1952–] L.AN.

3574 **Anthropology Design Series.** Chicago. *Anthropology Design Ser.* [1924–] L.AN.

3575 **Anthropology Reports, Papua.** Sydney. *Anthropology Rep. Papua* [1921–36] L.AN. imp.; BM.; BM^N. imp.

3576 **Anthropomorphology.** Freeport, N.Y. *Anthropomorphology* [1936–37]

3577 **Anthropophyteia.** Leipzig. *Anthropophyteia* L.BM.

3578 **Anthropos.** Internationale Zeitschrift für Völker- u. Sprachenkunde. Wien, etc. *Anthropos* [1906–] L.AN.; BM.; HO. 42–; UC. 06–37; Abs.N. 06–22; Bm.U. 42–; C.E.; Db. 42–; E.U. 27–; G.U. 06: 11–; Lv.P. 58–; M.R.; Nw.A. 53–; O.B.; Sa. 40–.
Anthropos-Bibliothek. *See* 3579.

3579 **Anthropos-ethnologische Bibliothek.** Münster i. W. *Anthropos-ethnol. Biblthk* [1909–] L.AN.; BM.

3580 **Anthropozoikum.** Praha. *Anthropozoikum* [1951–] L.AN.; BM.; BM^N.

3581 **Antibiotic Medicine** (*afterwards* and **Clinical Therapy**). New York, Washington. *Antibiotic Med. clin. Ther.* [1955–] L.BM.; MA.; MD.; PH.; S.; TD.; V. Bl.U.; C.UL.; E.A.; Ep.D.; G.U.; Ld.U.; Lv.M.; O.B.; R. [*Ceased publication in* 1961]

3582 **Antibiotic Medicine** and **Clinical Therapy. British edition.** London. *Antibiotic Med. clin. Ther. Br. Edit.* [1956–57] L.BM.; H.; LI.; MA.; MD.; V.; Bl.U.; C.UL.; G.U.

3583 **Antibiotica** et **chemotherapia.** Fortschritte, advances, progrès. Basel, New York. *Antibiotica Chemother.* [1954–] L.BM.; MD.; P.; UC.; Y.
Antibióticos y quimioterápicos. *See* 3583.

3584 **Antibiotics.** New York. *Antibiotics* [1959–] L.MD; Y. [*English translation of:* 3587]

3585 **Antibiotics Annual.** New York. *Antibiotics A.* [1953–60] L.AM. 53–60; CB. 57–58; MD. 53–60; P.; SC.; TD.; Abd.U. 55–60; Br.U. 54–60; Ld.U.; N.U.; O.R. 56–60; W. 53–60. [*C as:* 3592]

3586 **Antibiotics** and **Chemotherapy.** New York. *Antibiotics Chemother.* [1951–] L.AM. 53–; C.; H. 56–; MA.; MC.; MD.; P. 56–; PH.; SC. 53–; TD.; Bl.U.; Br.U.; Cr.MD.; E.U.; Ep.D.; G.T. 53–; U. imp.; Ld.U. imp.; Lv.M. 56–; M.MS. 53–; N.U. 53–; R.D. imp.; W. 53–; Y.

3587 **Antibiotiki.** Moskva. Антибиотики. *Antibiotiki* [1948–] L.BM.; MA. 59–; Y. [*English translation at:* 3584]

3588 **Anti-Cancer Journal.** London. *Anti-Cancer J.* L.BM. 22–.

3589 **Anti-Corrosion Manual.** London. *Anti-Corros. Man.* [1958–] L.BM.; P.; SC.; Bm.P.

3590 **Anti-Locust Bulletin.** Anti-Locust Research Centre. London. *Anti-Locust Bull.* [1948–] L.BM.; BM^N.; E.; EB.; L.; MO imp.; Z.; Bm.U.; Br.U.; C.B.; E.U.; Lv.U. 55–; M.P. 55–; O.AP. imp.; B.; H.; R.; Rt.; Y.

3591 **Anti-Locust Memoir.** Anti-Locust Research Centre. London. *Anti-Locust Mem.* [1946–] L.BM.; BM^N.; E.; EB.; L.; MO.; Z.; Bm.U.; Br.U.; C.B.; E.U.; O.AP.; B.; H.; R.; Z. imp.; Y.

3592 **Antimicrobial Agents Annual.** New York. *Antimicrob. Ag. A.* [1960–] L.AM.; MD.; P.; SC.; TD.; Abd.U.; Br.U.; Ld.U.; N.U.; O.R.; W.

3593 **Antincendio** (*afterwards* e **protezione civile**). Roma. *Antincendio Prot. civ.* [1949–] L.P.; Y.

3594 **Antioquía médica.** Medellin. *Antioquía méd.* [1950–] L.H. 55–; MA.; TD. [*C. of:* 2307 and 7621]

3595 **Antiquity** and **Survival.** The Hague. *Antiq. Survival* [1953–] L.BM.; BM^N.; HO.

3596 **Antiseptic.** Edinburgh and Madras. *Antiseptic* [1904–] L.MD. 27–; S. 24–58; Abd.R. 43– imp.; Bl.U. 45–53 v. imp.; Br.U. 05: 23–49; Y.

3597 **Anti-Tuberculosis Bulletin.** Manila. *Anti-Tuberc. Bull.*

3598 **Antivaccinator.** Leipzig. *Antivaccinator*

3599 **Antivivisection Journal.** London. *Antivivis. J.* [1921–40] L.BM.; V. 33–40; Abs.N. [*C. of:* 2629; *C. as:* 34810]

3600 **Anti-Vivisection News.** London. *Anti-Vivis. News* [1953–56] L.BM.; V. [*C. of:* 34810; *C. in:* 2627]
Antivivisection News Sheet. *See* 34810.

3601 **Anti-Vivisectionist.** London. *Anti-Vivisectionist* [1949–] L.BM.; C.UL.; E.A. [*C. of:* 286]

3602 **Antologia agraria.** Alba. *Antol. agr.*

3603 **Antonie van Leeuwenhoek.** Nederlandsch tijdschrift voor hygiene, microbiologie en serologie. (Journal of microbiology and serology.) Amsterdam. *Antonie van Leeuwenhoek* [1934–] L.AM. 58–; IC. 46–; LI. 52–; MD. 51–; SC. 37–; TD. imp.; Br.A. 59–; E.U. 54–; G.T. 39– imp.; U. 51–; Rt. 47–; Sh.U. 48–; Y. [*Replaces:* 34469]

3603° **Antropología.** Manaus. *Antropología, Manaus* [1957–]

3604 **Antropologia.** São Paulo. *Antropologia, S Paulo* [1946–] L.AN.

3605 **Antropología** y **etnología.** Madrid. *Antrop. Etnol.* [1949–] L.AN.; Db.

3606 **Antropología, etnología** y **arqueología.** Museo nacional de historia natural. Buenos Aires. *Antrop. Etnol. Arqueol.* L.BM. 03–19.

3607 **Antropologiai füzetek.** Budapest. *Antrop. Füz.* [1923–28] L.AN.

3608 **Antropológica.** Caracas. *Antropológica* [1956–] L.AN.

3609 **Antropologicheskiĭ zhurnal.** Moskva. Антропологический журнал. *Antrop. Zh.* [1932–] L.AM. 32–37 imp.; BM. 34: 36–37. [*C. of:* 48335]

3610 **Antropologja i etnologja.** Lwów. *Antropologja Etnol.* [1926–33]

3611 **Antropolohiya.** Kabinet antropolohiÿ im. F. Vovka. Kÿyiv. Антропологія. Кабінет Антропологии ім. Ф. Вовка. *Antropolohiya* [1927–30] L.AN.

3612 **Anuar aerologic.** Bucureşti. *Anuar aerol.* L.MO. 53–.

3613 **Anuar Facultăţii** de **ştiinţe agricole Chişinău.** Iaşi. *Anuar Fac. Sti. agric. Chişinău*

3614 **Anuar general** al **agriculturei, comercului** şi **industriei României.** Bucureşti. *Anuar gen. Agric. Comerc. Ind. Rom.* **L.**BM. 05: 08.

3615 **Anuar** de **geografie** şi **antropogeografie.** Bucureşti. *Anuar Geogr. Antropogeogr.*

3616 **Anuar hidrografico.** Bucureşti. *Anuar hidrogr.* **L.**MO. 38–50. [*C. as:* 3617]

3617 **Anuar hidrologic.** Bucureşti. *Anuar hidrol.* [1951–] **L.**MO. [*C. of:* 3616]

3618 **Anuar Institutului geologic** al **României.** Bucureşti. *Anuar Inst. geol. Rom.* [1907–] **L.**BM[N]. 07–43; GL.; GM.; UC. 07–30; **Db.**; E.D. imp.; J. 07–11; G.N.; Lv.U. 07–22; **Y.** [*Abridged French translation at:* 3257°]

3619 **Anuar Institulului** de **patologie** şi **igiena animala.** Bucureşti. *Anuar Inst. Patol. Ig. anim.* [1950–58] **L.**V. 55–58; **W.** 53–58. [*C. as:* 28857]

3620 **Anuar Institutului** de **seruri** si **vaccinuri Pasteur.** Bucureşti. *Anuar Inst. Seruri Vacc. Pasteur* [1956–57] **W.** [*C. as:* 28858]

3621 **Anuar lucrărilor ştiinţifice. Institutul agronomic 'Dr. Petru Coroza'.** Cluj. *Anuar Lucr. ştiinţ. Inst. agron. Cluj* [1957–] **L.**AM.; **C.**A. [*C. of:* 2283]

3622 **Anuar lucrărilor ştiinţifice. Institutul agronomic 'N. Bălcescu'.** Bucureşti. *Anuar Lucr. ştiinţ. Inst. agron., Buc.* **C.**A. 57–.

Anuar lucrărilor ştiinţifice. Institutul agronomic 'Professor Ion Ionescu de la **Brad'.** Iaşi. *See* 28853.

3623 **Anuar Museului** de **geologiă** şi de **paleontologia.** Bucureşti. *Anuar Mus. Geol. Paleont., Buc.* [1894–10] **L.**BM[N]. 94–96; GL. 10; UC.

3623° **Anuar Observatorul** din **Bucureşti.** *Anuari Obs. Buc.* **L.**BM. 58–.

Anuar ştiinţifice. Institutul agronomic 'Professor Ion Ionescu de la **Brad'.** Iaşi. *See* 28853.

3624 **Anuari. Junta** de **ciències naturals.** Barcelona. *Anuari Jta Ciènc. nat.* [1916–18] **L.**BM[N].; GL. 18; Z.; Bl.U. 17. [*C. as:* 31141]

3625 **Anuario. Academia** de **ciencias.** Veracruz. *Anu. Acad. Cienc., Veracruz* **L.**MO. 50.

Anuario de la **Academia** de **ciencias exactas, físicas y naturales.** Madrid. *See* 3669.

3625ª **Anuário** da **Academia polytechnica** do **Porto.** *Anu. Acad. polytech. Porto* **L.**BM[N]. 79–09.

3626 **Anuário académico. Academia** das **ciências** de **Lisboa.** *Anu. acad. Lisb.* [1932–] **L.**BM.; BM[N]. 36– imp.; **Db.** 37–; E.C. 37–43; **Y.**

3627 **Anuário açucareiro.** Rio de Janeiro. *Anu. açuc.* **L.**P. 50–.

3628 **Anuario** de **aeronáutica.** Madrid. *Anu. Aeronaut.*

3629 **Anuario agrícolo** de los **territorios españoles** del **Golfo** de **Guinea.** Madrid. *Anu. agríc. Terr. esp. Golfo Guinea* **C.**A. 44–.

3630 **Anuario agropecuario.** Buenos Aires. *Anu. agropec.* [1935–] **L.**BM.; **M.**P.

3631 **Anuario** de **arquitectura y técnica.** Buenos Aires. *Anu. Arquit. Téc.* [1932–38]
Anuario automovitístico. *See* 4595.

3632 **Anuário brasileiro** de **economia florestal.** Rio de Janeiro. *Anu. bras. Econ. flor.* [1948–] **O.**F.

3633 **Anuário climatológico** de **Portugal.** Lisbõa. *Anu. clim. Port.* [1947–]
Pt. 1 and 3: Continente e ilhas do Atlântico-norte. **L.**BM. 54–; MO.; UC.; E.M.; G.U.; **Y.** [*C. of:* 2267]
Pt. 2 and 4: Territorios ultramarinos. **L.**BM. 54–; MO.; E.M.; **Y.** [*C. of:* 2263]

3633ª **Anuário** del **Collegio Pedro II.** Rio de Janeiro. *Anu. Coll. Pedro II* [1914–] **L.**BM.; UC. 14–27; **O.**B.

3634 **Anuario. Dirección** de **hidrografía.** Madrid. *Anu. Dir. Hidrogr., Madr.*

3635 **Anuário. Escola** de **engenharia** de **São Carlos.** São Paulo. *Anu. Esc. Engen. S Carlos* **G.**U. 53–.

3636 **Anuário** da **Escola médico-cirúrgica** de **Lisboa.** Lisboa. *Anu. Esc. méd.-cirúg. Lisb.*

3637 **Anuário** da **Escola médico-cirúrgica** do **Pôrto.** Pôrto. *Anu. Esc. méd. cirúrg. Pôrto* [1906–07] [*C. as:* 3642]

3638 **Anuario. Escuela nacional** de **ciencias biológicas.** México. *Anu. Esc. nac. Cienc. biol., Méx.* **L.**BM[N]. 38:43; **Db.** 43–.

3639 **Anuario** de **estadística agrícola.** Montevideo. *Anu. Estad. agric., Montevideo* **L.**AM. 13–29 imp.

3640 **Anuario estadístico** de **agricultura.** Santiago. *Anu. estad. Agric., Santiago* **L.**AM. 07–42 imp.

3641 **Anuário. Faculdade** de **filosofia, ciencias y letras.** Universidade de São Paulo. *Anu. Fac. Filos. Cienc. Letr. Univ. S Paulo* **G.**U. 51.

3642 **Anuário** da **Faculdade** de **medicina** do **Pôrto.** Pôrto. *Anu. Fac. Med. Pôrto* [1907–] **L.**S. 07–10. [*C. of:* 3637]

3643 **Anuario. Facultad** de **ciencias físicas matemáticas y astronómicas.** La Plata. *Anu. Fac. Cienc. fís. mat. astr., La Plata* [1910–] **L.**M. 14–16; **Bm.**U. 14–; **Db.** 14–; E.C. 14–15; R. 14–15: 26–37; Ld.U. 11; **M.**U. 11–19; **O.**B. 11–21.
Anuario. Facultad de **ciencias fisicomatemáticas, La Plata.** *See* 3643.

3643° **Anuário fluviométrico.** Serviço de águas, Brasil. Belo Horizonte. *Anu. fluviométr. Bras.* [1940–] **Y.** 45–.

3644 **Anuario hidrográfico.** Buenos Aires. *Anu. hidrogr., B. Aires* **L.**MO. 42–44. [*C. as:* 3646]

3645 **Anuario hidrográfico** de la **marina** de **Chile.** Valparaiso. *Anu. hidrogr. Mar. Chile* [1874–28] **L.**BM.; G. 75–15 imp.; **C.**UL. 81–28; E.G. 01–28; Ld.U. 17; **O.**B. 00–03.

3646 **Anuario hidrológico.** Buenos Aires. *Anu. hidrol., B. Aires* [1945–] [*C. of:* 3644]

3647 **Anuario** de la **Inspección general** de **sanidad.** Madrid. *Anu. Insp. gen. Sanid., Madr.* **L.**TD. 20–24.

3648 **Anuario** del **Instituto geográfico militar** de la **República Argentina.** Buenos Aires. *Anu. Inst. geogr. milit. Repúb. Argent.* **L.**G. 12–26; **Y.**

3649 **Anuario** del **Instituto** de **geología.** México. *Anu. Inst. Geol., Méx.* [1932–] **L.**BM[N].; MI. 32–34; E.R. 32–36.

3650 **Anuario. Instituto tropical** de **investigaciones científicas.** San Salvador. *Anu. Inst. trop. Invest. cient. S Salv.* [1950–] **L.**BM[N].; **Db.**

3651 **Anuario médico** de **España.** Madrid. *Anu. méd. Esp.* **L.**MD. 27.

3652 **Anuario médico y farmaceutico.** Buenos Aires. *Anu. méd. farm., B. Aires* **L.**MD. 12–13.

3653 **Anuario meteorológico, Bogotá.** *Anu. met.,
Bogotá* **L.**MO. 48–.

3653ᶜ **Anuario meteorológico, Bolivia.** La Paz. *Anu.
met. Bolivia* **Y.**46–.

3654 **Anuario meteorológico** de **Chile.** Santiago.
Anu. met. Chile **L.**G. 04–14; MO. 11–; **C.**O. 20–; **E.**M.
11–22; R. 11–25 imp.; **M.**P. 20–24.

3655 **Anuario meteorológico, Colombia.** Chinchina.
Anu. met. Colombia **L.**MO. 50–.

3656 **Anuario meteorológico, Montevideo.** *Anu.
met., Montevideo* **L.**MO. 01–04: 07.

3657 **Anuário meteorologico** do **Observatorio** de
João Capelo. Loanda. *Anu. met. Obs. João Capelo*
L.BM. 56–; MO. 53–. [*C. of:* 17915]

3658 **Anuario meteorológico** de **Venezuela.** Maracay.
Anu. met. Venez. [1950–] **L.**BM. 51–; MO.

3659 **Anuario** de **minería, metalurgía** e **industrias
químicas** de **España.** Madrid. *Anu. Min. Metal.
Ind. quím. Esp.*

3660 **Anuário** do **Ministério** de **agricultura, industria**
e **commercio** do **Brazil.** Rio de Janeiro. *Anu.
Minist. Agric. Ind. Braz.*

3661 **Anuario** de **observaciones** de la **Oficina central**
del **Colegio** de **ingenieros** de **Venezuela.** Caracas.
Anu. Obsnes Of. cent. Col. Ing. Venez.

3662 **Anuário** de **observações. Observatorio Campos
Rodriques.** Lourenço Marques. *Anu. Obsçes Obs.
Campos Rodriques* [1951–]
    1. Astronómicas.   2. Meteorológicas.   **L.**AS.;
MO.; **E.**M. 51–; **O.**G.; **Y.**   [*C. of:* 42495]

3663 **Anuario. Observatorio astronómico nacional**
de **La Plata.** *Anu. Obs. astr. nac. La Plata* **C.**O. 87–;
E.O. 87–92.

3664 **Anuario** del **Observatorio astronómico nacional**
de **Tacubaya.** México. *Anu. Obs. astr. nac. Tacubaya*
L.BM. 81–88; MO. 84–35 imp.; SC. 81–; **Bl.**U. 87–49
imp.; **C.**O. 84–; **Db.** 86–; **E.**G. 99–; O.; R. 84–35; **Ld.**U.
88–34 imp.; **Nw.**A. 29–; **Y.**

3665 **Anuario** del **Observatorio astronómico nacional**
de la **Universidad** de **Chile.** Santiago de Chile. *Anu.
Obs. astr. nac. Univ. Chile* [1897–] **L.**BM. 03– imp.; G.
04–07; MO. 97–00: 03–07; SC. 36–; **C.**O. 06–; **E.**O.;
O.R. 03–06; **Y.**
    Anuario del **Observatorio nacional** de **Santiago.**
See 3665.

3666 **Anuário** publ. pelo **Observatorio** do **Rio de
Janeiro.** Rio de Janeiro. *Anu. Obs. Rio de J.* [1885–]
L.MO. 85–32; UC. 28–; **Abd.**U. 88–; **C.**O.; UL. 88–; **Db.**
00–; **E.**G. 99–; M.; O.; R. 88– imp.

3668 **Anuário** do **pesca maritima** no **Estado** do **São
Paulo.** *Anu. Pesca mar. S Paulo* **Dm.** 44; **Pl.**M. 44.

3669 **Anuario** de la **R. Academia** de **ciencias exactas,
físicas** y **naturales.** Madrid. *Anu. R. Acad. Cienc.,
Madr.* [1857–] **L.**GL. 00–29; **Db.** 88– imp.; **E.**R. 88–89:
95–36 imp.

3670 **Anuario** del **R. Observatório** de **Madrid.** Madrid.
Anu. R. Obs. Madr. [1859–] **L.**BM. 1859–79; MO. 1860–21
imp.; R. 1860–; SC. 1859–80: 25–; **Bm.**U. 71–72; **C.**O.
62– imp.; **E.**M. 77–21; O. 63– imp.; **M.**U. 52–60; **Y.**

3671 **Anuario** de la **R. Sociedad geográfica** de **Madrid.**
Anu. R. Soc. geogr. Madr. **L.**BM. 10–21 imp.

3672 **Anuario** del **Servicio meteorológico** de la
Dirección del **territorio marítimo.** Valparaiso.
Anu. Serv. met., Valparaiso [1899–09] **L.**BM.; MO.; **E.**M.
05; R. 04–09; **O.**R.

3673 **Anuário** dos **Serviços hidráulicos, Portugal.**
Lisboa. *Anu. Servs hidrául. Port.* **L.**BM. 53–; **Y.**

3674 **Anuario** de la **Sociedad** de **estudios vascos.**
Vittoria. *Anu. Soc. Estud. vascos* **L.**AN. 21–34.

3675 **Anuário** da **Sociedade broteriana.** Coimbra.
Anu. Soc. broteriana [1935–] **L.**HS.; **Bl.**U.; **O.**F.

3675ᵃ **Anuário** da **Universidade** de **Coimbra.** *Anu.
Univ. Coimbra* **L.**BMᴺ. 96–12; **E.**C. 94–12 imp.
    Anuarul, Anuarulŭ. *See* **Anuar.**

3676 **Anvil.** Davy and United Engineering Company.
Sheffield. *Anvil* **L.**BM. 56–; P. (curr.); **Y.**

3676ᶜ **Anvisning.** Norges byggforskningsinstitutt.
Oslo. *Anvisn. Norg. ByggforskInst.* [1953–59] **L.**P. 54–
59; **Y.** 54–59.   [*C. as:* 21777ᵃ]

3677 **Anvisning. Statens Byggeforsknings Institut.**
København. *Anvisn. St. Byggeforsk. Inst.* **L.**BM. 51– imp.;
Y.

3678 **Anwendungsbeispiele** für **Araldit.** Basel. *An-
wendBeisp. Araldit* [1951–] **L.**P.

3679 **Anza- és csecsemóvédelem.** Budapest. *Anza-
és Csecsemóv.* [1928–] **L.**TD.   [*Supplement to:* 34517]
    Anzeiger der **Akademie** der **Wissenschaften** in
Krakau. *See* 10659.

3680 **Anzeiger** der **Akademie** der **Wissenschaften,
Wien.** *Anz. Akad. Wiss. Wien* Mathematische-natur-
wissenschaftliche Klasse [1864–46] **L.**BM.; BMᴺ.; C. 01–10
imp.; GL. 00–46; HS. 20–26; L.; P. 38–46; PH. 64–95; R.; Z.
73–46 imp.; **Abs.**N. 33–46; **Bm.**U. 31–46; **C.**P. 08–46;
PH. 77–87; UL.; **E.**U. 01–39; **Lv.**U. 81–46.   [*C. as:* 3689]

3681 **Anzeiger** für **Berg-, Hütten-** u. **Maschinenwesen.**
Essen. *Anz. Berg- Hütt.- MaschWes.*

3682 **Anzeiger** für **Berg-, Hütten-, Metall-** u. **Maschinenindustrie.** Leipzig-Gohlis. *Anz. Berg-
Hütt.- Metall- u. MaschInd.*

3683 **Anzeiger** für die **Draht-Industrie.** Berlin. *Anz.
Drahtind.* [1892–] **L.**P. 10–14.

3684 **Anzeiger** der **Ethnographischen Abteilung** des
Ungarischen National-Museums. Budapest. *Anz.
ethnogr. Abt. ung. NatnMus.* [1902–35] [*For Hungarian
edition, see* 29230]

3685 **Anzeiger** des **Germanischen Nationalmuseums.**
Nürnberg. *Anz. germ. NatnMus.* [1884–] **L.**BM. 96–
UC. 84–07.

3686 **Anzeiger** für **Hütten-, Metall-** u. **Maschinenwesen.** Halle a. S. *Anz. Hütt.- Metall- u. MaschWes.*

3687 **Anzeiger** für **Industrie** u. **Technik.** Frankfurt a.
M. *Anz. Ind. Tech.*
    Anzeiger der **K. Akademie** der **Wissenschaften,
Wien.** *See* 3680.

3688 **Anzeiger** für den **Maschinen-** u. **Werkzeug-
Handel** von **Uhland.** Leipzig. *Anz. Masch.- Werkz.-
Hand. Uhland*

3689 **Anzeiger. Österreichische Akademie der Wissenschaften.** Wien. *Anz. öst. Akad. Wiss.* Matema-
tische-naturwissenschaftliche Klasse [1947–] **L.**BM.;
BMᴺ.; GL.; L.; P.; R.; SC.; Z.; **Abs.**N.; **Bm.**U.; **C.**P.;
UL.; **Lv.**U. [*C. of:* 3680]

3690 **Anzeiger** der **Ornithologischen Gesellschaft** in **Bayern.** München. *Anz. orn. Ges. Bayern* [1919–] L.BM^N. 19–39; Lv.U. 25–; O.OR.

3691 **Anzeiger** für **Schädlingskunde.** Berlin, Hamburg. *Anz. Schädlingsk.* [1925–] L.AM. 54–; BM^N.; EB. imp.; TD. 54–; M.U. imp.; O.F. [*Not published 1945–47*]

3692 **Aparato respiratório y tuberculosis.** La Paz, Bolivia. *Apar. resp. Tuberc., La Paz* [1940–]

3693 **Aparato respiratório y tuberculosis.** Santiago de Chile. *Apar. resp. Tuberc., Santiago* [1935–] L.MA. 43–; MD. imp.

Aperçu de la **presse technique.** Prague. *See* 38572.
Aperçu des **travaux** des **commissions agraires.** St. Pétersbourg. *See* 54184.

3694 **Aperture.** San Francisco. *Aperture* [1952–] L.PG.

3695 **Apiary Circular.** Apiary Branch, Department of Agriculture. Victoria. *Apiary Circ., Victoria* L.BM. 54–; **Y.**

3696 **Apicoltore.** Milano. *Apicoltore* [1868–20] L.AM. 84–95. [*C. in:* 3699]

3697 **Apicoltore** d'**Italia.** Ancona. *Apicolt. Ital.* [1934–] [*C. of:* 1867 and 3699]

3698 **Apicoltore moderno.** Torino. *Apicolt. mod.* [1910–] **Y.**

3699 **Apicoltura italiana.** Milano. *Apic. ital.* [1905–33] [*C. in:* 3697]

3700 **Apicoltura razionale.** Firenze. *Apic. razion.*

3701 **Apiculteur.** Paris. *Apiculteur* L.AM. 1856–23 imp.; BM. 90–; EB. 13–25; Rt. 20–22 imp.; **Y.**

3702 **Apiculteur** d'**Alsace** et de **Lorraine.** Strasbourg. *Apicult. Als.-Lorr.* [1873–]

3703 **Apiculteur belge.** Renaix. *Apicult. belge*

3704 **Apiculteur praticien.** Paris. *Apicult. Pratn* [1856–] L.AM. 1856–95; E.B. 13–25.

3705 **Apicultor.** Barcelona. *Apicultor*

3706 **Apicultor chileno.** Santiago. *Apicult. chil.* [1931–]

3707 **Apicultorul lunar.** Chişinău. *Apicult. lunar*

3708 **Apicultural Abstracts.** London. *Apic. Abstr.* [1950–] L.BM. 53–; W. [*Reprinted from:* 5876]

3709 **Apiculture.** Paris. *Apiculture*

3710 **Apiculture belge.** Eghezée. *Apic. belge* [1928–36] [*Replaces:* 3713]

3711 **Apiculture française.** Paris. *Apic. fr.* [1919–] [*C. of:* 47149]

3712 **Apiculture nouvelle.** Paris. *Apic. nouv.* [1906–20]

3713 **Apiculture rationelle.** Eghezée. *Apic. ration.* [1913–27] [*Replaced by:* 3710]

3714 **Aplikace matematiky.** Praha. *Aplik. mat.* [1956–] L.P. 60–; SC.; C.P.; G.U. imp.; Ld.U.; O.R.; **Y.**

3715 **Apollo.** Organ für Photographie. Dresden. *Apollo* L.PG. 95–14; E.U. 38–; Lv.P. 30–.

3716 **Apollonia.** Sydney. *Apollonia* L.D. 46–.

3717 **Apollonian.** Boston. *Apollonian* [1926–] L.D. 42 imp.

3718 **Apotekarski vjesnik.** Zagreb. *Apot. Vjesn.*

3719 **Apothecary.** Boston. *Apothecary* [1903–] [*C. of:* 34636]

3720 **Apotheek.** Amsterdam. *Apotheek* [1933–] L.C. 33–35. [*Supplement to:* 37482]

3721 **Apothekar-Zeitung.** Marienbad. *Apothekar-ztg*

3722 **Apotheke.** Ründeroth. *Apotheke*

3723 **Apothekenhelferin.** Stuttgard. *Apothekenhelferin* L.P. (curr.); **Y.** [*Supplement to:* 16658]

3724 **Apotheker** im **Drogenfach.** Berlin. *Apoth. Drogenfach*

3725 **Apotheker** im **Osten.** Berlin. *Apotheker Osten* [1942–]

3726 **Apothekerzeitung.** Berlin. *Apothekerzeitung, Berl.* [1886–53] L.P. 12–14 imp.; PH. 99–34; SC. 97–13: 26–53. [> 16658, 1934–48; *C. in:* 37517]

3727 **Apothekerzeitung.** New York. *Apothekerzeitung, N.Y.* [1918–32] [*C. of:* 16649]

3728 **Appalachia.** Appalachian Mountain Club. Boston. *Appalachia* L.BM. 79–; BM^N. 76–08; G. 79–; SC. 86–; C.GG. 45–50 v. imp.; PO. 51–; E.R. 76–78; **Y.**

3729 **Apparatebau.** Hannover. *Apparatebau* L.P. 28–44 imp.; SC. 32–.

3730 **Appareillage.** Paris. *Appareillage* [1951–] L.P. [*C. of:* 5781]

3731 **Apparent Places** of **Fundamental Stars.** London, Heidelberg, etc. *Appar. Places fund. Stars* [1941–] L.AS.; BM.; SC.; Bl.U. 58–; G.M.; Ld.P. 45– imp.; Lv.P. 42–; O.R.; **Y.**

3732 **Appel médical.** Paris. *Appel méd.* [*C. as:* 52837]

3733 **Appita.** Australian Pulp and Paper Industry Technical Association. Sydney. *Appita* [1957–] L.P. 57–; TP. 59–; O.F. 57– imp.; **Y.** [*C. of:* 38996]

3734 **Apple Research Digest.** Yakima, Wash. *Apple Res. Dig.* [1946–] Md.H. 55–59 imp.; Sil. 53–57.

Application Note. **Radio Corporation** of **America.** *See* 41704.

3735 **Application Report.** Radio Division, Siemens **Edison Swan** Ltd. London. *Applic. Rep. Radio Div. Siemens Edison Swan* [1958–] L.P.; **Y.**

3736 **Application Sheets.** Heenan and **Froude** Ltd. Worcester. *Applic. Sh. Heenan & Froude* [1953–] L.P. imp.

3737 **Applications** of **Electricity** to **Railways.** Bibliography of Periodical Articles. Association of American Railroads. Washington. *Applics Elect. Rlys* L.P. 42–55; **Y.**

Applications and **Industry.** Transactions of the American Institute of Electrical Engineers. *Applics Ind. See* 53544, Part 2.

3738 **Applications** du **nickel.** Centre d'information du nickel. Paris. *Applics Nickel, Paris* **Y.**

3739 **Applications thermiques** de l'**électricité.** Lille. *Applics therm. Élect.* [1957–] L.P. 58–.

3740 **Applied Anthropology.** Cambridge, Mass., Philadelphia. *Appl. Anthrop.* [1941–48] L.AN. 47–48; BM.; MD.; U.; Bm.U. 42–48; Ld.U. imp.; O.R. [*C. as:* 22484]

3740° **Applied Anthropology Newsletter.** *Appl. Anthrop. Newsl.* G.U. 51–55.

3741 **Applied Chemistry** in **Manufacturer Arts,** etc. Paris. *Appl. Chem. Mfr Arts*

3742 **Applied Electronics Annual.** London. *Appl. Electron. A.* [1951–56] L.BM.; P.; E.A.; M.P. 51; O.B.; R.; **Y.**

3743 Applied Forestry Notes. Northern Rocky Mountain Forest Experiment Station. Missoula, Montana. *Appl. For. Notes North. Rocky Mtn Forest Exp. Stn* O.F. 39.

3744 Applied Forestry Notes. U.S. Forest Service. Washington. *Appl. For. Notes U.S.* O.F. 21–22.

3745 Applied Hydraulics (*afterwards* and **Pneumatics**). Cleveland. *Appl. Hydraul. Pneumat.* [1948–60] L.AV. 55–60; MO. imp.; P. 52–60; F.A.; G.ME. 52–60; T. 54–60; Sh.IO. 57–60; Sil. 52–60; Y. [*C. as:* 22527]

3746 Applied Magnetics. Valparaiso. *Appl. Magn.* [1953–] L.P.

3747 Applied Mass Spectrometry. London. *Appl. Mass Spectrom.* C.UL. 53.

Applied Mathematics and **Mechanics.** Moscow. *See* 38658.

Applied Mathematics and **Mechanics.** Pergamon Press. New York, London. *See* 36677.

3748 Applied Mathematics and **Mechanics.** Office of Technical Services. New York. *Appl. Math. Mech., N.Y.* Y. 57–. [*English abstracts of:* 38658]

3749 Applied Mathematics Series. U.S. Bureau of Standards. Washington. *Appl. Math. Ser.* [1948–] L.P. imp.; SC.; C.P.; Db.; E.R.; M.U. imp.; Rt. 52– imp.; Y.

Applied Mathematic Series. University of Toronto. *See* 55679.

Applied Mechanics. Transactions of the American Society of Mechanical Engineers. *See* 25573.

3750 Applied Mechanics Reviews. Easton, Pa., etc. *Appl. Mech. Rev.* [1948–] L.AV.; B. 54–; DI. 48–56; I.; IC.; KC.; P.; QM.; R.; SC.; SI.; Abd.U.; Bl.U. 60–; Bm.T. 49–55; U.; Bn.U.; Br.U.; C.ENG.; P.; Co.T. 63–; Cr.U. 51–; Db.; Dn.U. 51–; E.R.; SW. U. 56–; F.A.; G.E.; T.; U.; Ld.U.; Li.M.; Lv.P. 49–51 imp.: 53–; M.C.; T.; U.; N.T.; U.; Nw.A.; O.R. 56–; R.U.; Rn.B. 55–; Sa. 51–; Sh.IO. 49–; S. 55–; SC.; Sil. 52–; St.R. 48–55; Sw.U.; Wo. 58–; Y.

3751 Applied Microbiology. Baltimore. *Appl. Microbiol.* [1953–] L.AM.; MA.; MD.; P. 54–; SC.; TD.; TP. 59–; U. 54–; Abd.S. 55–; C.APH. 62–; Cr.U. 59–; E.W. 53–; Ep.D.; G.T.; U.; Je.; Ld.U. 54–; Lh.FO.; P. 56–; Lv.P. 54–; M.D. 57–; U. 54–; N.U.; O.R. 56–; R.D.; T.; U.; Sh.U. 54–; W. 60–; Y.

3752 Applied Photography. Rochester, N.Y. *Appl. Photogr.* [1931–36]

3753 Applied Photography. Rochester, N.Y. *Appl. Photogr.* C.APH. 57–.

3753° Applied Physics Quarterly. *Appl. Phys. Q.* L.SC. 60–.

3754 Applied Plastics. London. *Appl. Plast.* [1958–] L.BM.; NP.; P.; PL.; Lv.P. 60–; Sy.R.; Y.

Applied Pneumatics. Richmond. *See* 25579.

3755 Applied Psychology Monographs. Stanford University. Palo Alto. *Appl. Psychol. Monogr.* [1943–48] L.BM. 44:46–48; Br.U. 45–46; O.B. 44–48. [*C. in:* 40456]

3756 Applied Science. Toronto. *Appl. Sci.* [1907–16] L.P. 10–16; M.U. [*C. of:* 53705; *C. as:* 54092]

3756° Applied Science and **Technology in Germany.** D.S.I.R. London. *Appl. Sci. Technol. Germ.* L.AV. 61–; Y.

3757 Applied Science and **Technology Index.** New York. *Appl. Sci. Technol. Index* [1958–] L.AV.; BM.; P.; U.; Abs.N.; Bm.P.; T.; Br.P.; Cn.R.; Db. 58–; F.A.; G.M.; T.; U.; Ld.P.; Li.M.; Lv.P.; M.D.; P.; Nw.P.; Sh.P. [*C. from:* 23175]

3758 Applied Scientific Research. The Hague. *Appl. scient. Res.* [1947–]
(A) Mechanics, Heat, Chemical Engineering, Mathematical Methods. L.AV.; BM.; I.; P.; RI.; SC.; SI.; Bl.U.; Bm.U.; Br.U.; C.ENG. 49–; P.; E.R.; F.A. 51–; G.T.; U. 49–; Ld.U.; Lh.P.; Li.M.; M.C.; D.; P.; T.; U. imp.; N.U. 49–; Nw.A.; O.R.; R.D.; U.; Sa.; Sh.S.; SC.; Ste.; Sw.U. 57–; Wd. 47–56; Y.
(B) Electrophysics, Acoustics, Optics. L.BM.; P.; RI.; SC.; SI.; Bl.U.; Bm.U.; Br.U.; C.ENG. 50–; P.; E.R.; F.A. 51–; G.T.; U. 50–; Ld.U.; Lh.P.; M.C.; D.; P.; T.; U. imp.; N.U. 55–; Nw.A.; O.R.; R.D. 54–; U.; Sa.; Sh.S.; SC.; Ste.; Sw.U. 57–; Wd. 47–56; Y.

3759 Applied Spectroscopy. New York, etc. *Appl. Spectrosc.* [1952–] L.AV. 56– imp.; C. 55–; SC. 52–; C.B. 54–; NC. 58–; P. 54–; SI.; TP. 58–; Bm.C.; G.U. 55–; M.D. 54–; O.R. 55–; W. 59–; Wd. 54–; Y. [*C. of:* 12230]

3760 Applied Statistics. London, Edinburgh. *Appl. Statist.* [1952–] L.AM.; AV.; B.; BM.; EE.; MA.; P.; SC.; U.; Abd.R.; U. 54–; Abs.A.; Bl.U.; Bm.P.; Br.A. 54–; C.GE.; SL.; Co.T. 62–; Dn.U. 52–56; E.A.; HW. 54–; R.; U.; UC.; Ep.D.; G.M.; PH. 52–57; T. 54–; H.U.; Lc.A.; Ld.P.; U.; W.; Lh.FO.; P.; Lv.P.; M.C.; D.; P.; N.P. 57–; U.; Nw.A.; O.B.; Sa.; Sh.S.; U.; Sil.; St.R.; Ste.; Sy.R.; Wd.; Y.

3761 Applied Statistics in Meteorology. *Appl. Statist. Met.* Y.

3762 Applied Therapeutics. Toronto. *Appl. Ther.* L.MD. 61–.

3763 Approach. Naval Aviation Safety Review. Norfolk Va. *Approach* [1955–] L.AV. 58–59; BM.; P.; Y.

3764 Aptechnoe delo. Moskva. Аптечное дело. *Aptech. Delo* [1952–] L.BM. 54–; MA. 56–; P. 59–; PH. 55–; Y. 53–55: 56–.

3765 Aptekarska poshta. Lovech'. Аптекарска поща. *Aptek. Poshta*

3766 Apteryx. Providence, R.I. *Apteryx* [1905]

3767 Apuntes de **historia natural.** Buenos Aires. *Apunt. Hist. nat.* [1909–10] L.BMᴺ.; K.

3768 Aqua. Water Supply Association. London. *Aqua, Lond.* [1952–] L.P.; SH. (1 yr) Y.

3769 Aqua. Melbourne. *Aqua, Melb.* Hu.G. 55–.

3770 Aquaria-Nachrichten. St. Gallen. *Aquaria-Nachr.* [1954–]

3771 Aquarienfische in **Wort** und **Bild.** Stuttgart. *AquarFische* L.BMᴺ. 34–39; Z. 34–.

3772 Aquarien- und **Terrarien-Zeitschrift.** Stuttgart. *Aquar.- u. Terrar.-Z.* [1951–] L.BMᴺ.; Z.; Y. [*C. of:* 16659]

3773 Aquarist and **Pondkeeper.** London. *Aquarist Pondkpr* [1928–] L.AM. 47– imp.; BM.; BMᴺ. 33–; HO.; Z.; Abs.N.; C.GE. 57–; UL.; Cr.M.; E.A.; Fr. 56–; Lo. 53–; M.P.; N.P. 38–40; O.R.; Pit.F. 51–; Pl.M. 28–41 imp.; Y. [*C. of:* 1872]

3774 Aquarist's Journal. Leicester. *Aquarist's J.* L.BM 46–47; Z. 46 imp.

3775 **Aquarium.** Berlin. *Aquarium, Berl.* L.BM^N. 27–40 imp.; Z. 27–40.

3776 **Aquarium.** Den Haag. *Aquarium, Den Haag* L.BM^N. 52– imp.

3777 **Aquarium.** Paris. *Aquarium, Paris* [1934–36]

3778 **Aquarium.** Philadelphia. *Aquarium, Philad.* [1912–14] L.Z. imp.

3779 **Aquarium.** Philadelphia. *Aquarium, Philad.* [1932–] L.BM^N.; Z.

3780 **Aquarium Bulletin.** Brooklyn, N.Y. *Aquar. Bull.* [1917–19] [*C. of:* 9638]

3781 **Aquarium Journal.** San Francisco. *Aquar. J.* [1928–] L.BM^N. 52–; Z. 47–; Pl.M. 46–47 imp.

3782 **Aquarium News.** Brooklyn, N.Y. *Aquar. News, N.Y.* [1921–]

3783 **Aquarium News.** Rochester, N.Y. *Aquar. News, Rochester* [1934–38]

3784 **Aquarium Review.** London. *Aquar. Rev.* [1928–34] L.BM. 32–34 imp.

3785 **Aquatic Life.** Philadelphia. *Aquat. Life* [1915–]

3786 **Aquila.** Magyar ornithologiai központ folyóirata. Budapest. *Aquila* [1894–] L.BM^N. imp.; EB. 12–39; L. 52–; Z.; C.B. 94–13: 31–38; Db. 07–; E.R. imp.; Lv.U. 04–06; M.U. 02–11; O.OR. 98– imp.; Y.

3786° **Arachnological News.** Arachnological Society of Eastern Asia. Kansai Branch. Osaka. *Arachn. News* [1952–] L.BM^N.

3787 **Aradhegyalja.** Szölöszeti és borászati hetilap. Borosjenó. *Aradhegyalja*

3788 **Aradi mernök és épitészegylet közlönye.** Arad. *Aradi Mern. Épitész. Közl.*

3789 **Aradvidéki iparegyesület heti értesitöje.** Arad. *Aradvid. Iparegy. Ért.*

3790 **Aranata Journal** of **Agriculture.** Malabou. *Aranata J. Agric.* [1953–] L.AM.; BM. 57–; MY. 53–55; TP.; **Br.**A. 57–; C.A.; Md.H.; Rt.; Y.

3791 **Arbeider** fra den **Botaniske Have i Kjöbenhavn.** Kjöbenhavn. *Arb. bot. Have Kbh.* L.K. 20–.

3792 **Arbeider** fra den **Danske arktiske Station paa Disko.** Kjöbenhavn. *Arb. danske arkt. Stn Disko* L.BM^N. 10–; Y.

3793 **Arbeider** fra **Rigshospitalets Födeafdeling A** og **Gynækologisk Afdeling.** København. *Arb. Rigshosp. Födeafd. A, Kbh.* L.MD. 23–32; Db. 26–32.

3794 **Arbeider** fra **Rigshospitalets Födeafdeling B** øg **Gynækologisk Afdeling M.** København. *Arb. Rigshosp. Födeafd. B, Kbh.* L.MD. 26–32.

3795 **Arbeiten** der **Agrikultur-chemischen Versuchsstation Halle** a. S. der Landwirtschaftskammer für Sachsen. Berlin. *Arb. agrik.-chem. VersStn Halle*

3796 **Arbeiten** aus dem **Ambulatorium** und der **Privatklinik** für **Ohren-, Nasen- u. Halsleiden von Stetter.** Königsberg. *Arb. Ambul. v. Stetter*

3797 **Arbeiten** aus dem **Anatomischen Institut** der **K. Japanischen Universität** zu **Sendai.** Tokyo. *Arb. anat. Inst. Sendai* [1918–42] L.BM.; L. 18–39; MD.; R. 18–39; S.; UC. 18–39; Z. 19–39; **Abs.**N. 18–25; **Bl.**U. 18–39; **Bm.**U.; **Br.**U.; **C.**PA. 19–39 imp.; UL.; **Cr.**U. imp.; Db.; **Dn.**U.; E.P.; R.; S. 36–39; T. 20–37 imp.; U.; **G.**U.; **Ld.**U. 20–42; Lv.U. 18–25; **M.**P.; U. 18–

39; N.U. 34–38 imp.; Nw.A. 20–39; O.R.; Sa. 18–39. [*C. in:* 53331]

Arbeiten aus dem **Anatomischen Institut** der **Universität** zu **Kyoto.** *See* 3825.

3798 **Arbeiten** aus **anatomischen Instituten.** Wiesbaden. *Arb. anat. Inst., Wiesbaden* [1891–21] L.BM.; S.; SC.; UC.; **Abd.**U.; **Bl.**U.; **C.**AN.; B. 91–14; UL.; E.P.; S. 00–21; U.; **G.**F. 91–14; U.; **Ld.**U. 91–16; **M.**MS. 05–21; O.R. [*C. as:* 58473]

3799 **Arbeiten** aus dem **Anatomischen** und **zootomischen Institut** der **K. Universität Münster.** Leipzig. *Arb. anat. zootom. Inst. Münster*

3800 **Arbeiten** aus der **Anstalt** für **Hessische Landesforschung** an der **Universität Giessen.** *Arb. Anst. hess. Landesforsch.* L.G. 30–32.

3801 **Arbeiten** der **Arbeitsgemeinschaft deutscher Rinderzüchter.** Hannover. *Arb. ArbGemeinsch. dt. Rinderzüchter* [1951–] C.A. [*C. of:* 3890]

3802 **Arbeiten** aus dem **Bakteriologischen Institut** der **Technischen Hochschule** zu **Karlsruhe.** Karlsruhe, Wiesbaden. *Arb. bakt. Inst. Karlsruhe* [1894–03] L.BM.; BM^N.; S.; E.P. imp.

3803 **Arbeiten** aus dem **Bakteriologischen Laboratorium** des **städtischen Schlachthofes in Berlin.** Leipzig. *Arb. bakt. Lab. städt. Schlachth. Berl.*

3804 **Arbeiten** aus der **Bayerischen Landesanstalt** für **Pflanzenbau** und **Pflanzenschutz.** München. *Arb. bayer. Landesanst. PflBau* [1926–32] L.BM^N.

3805 **Arbeiten** und **Berichte** aus der **Süddeutschen Versuchs-** und **Forschungsanstalt** für **Milchwirtschaft.** Weihenstephan. *Arb. Ber. süddt. Vers.-u. ForschAnst. Milchw.* [1950–] R.D.

Arbeiten aus der **biologischen Abteilung** für **Land- u. Forstwirtschaft.** Berlin. *See* 3806.

Arbeiten aus der **biologischen Anstalt** für **Land-u. Forstwirtschaft.** Berlin. *See* 3806.

3806 **Arbeiten** aus der **biologischen Bundesanstalt** für **Land- u. Forstwirtschaft.** Berlin. *Arb. biol. BundAnst. Land- u. Forstw.* [1900–43] L.AM. 30–39; BM.; BM^N.; EB.; HS. 29–39; K. 00–25; MY. 22–43; P. 00–39; C.A. 30–43; UL.; Db.; Md.H. 31–39; O.RE. 00–39; Rt.

3807 **Arbeiten** aus dem **biologischen Institut** in **München.** München. *Arb. biol. Inst. Münch.* L.BM^N. 21.

Arbeiten der **biologischen Meeresstation** am **Schwarzen Meer in Varna.** *See* 54423.

Arbeiten aus der **biologischen Meeresstation** in **Stalin.** *See* 54429.

3808 **Arbeiten** der **biologischen Noworossijsk Station.** *Arb. biol. Noworossijsk Stn* Pl.M. 30–36 imp.

Arbeiten der **biologischen Oka-Station.** Murom, Nizhnij-Novgorod. *See* 41752.

Arbeiten aus der **biologischen Reichsanstalt** für **Land- u. Forstwirtschaft.** Berlin. *See* 3806.

Arbeiten der **biologischen Station** zu **Kossino.** *See* 54792.

3809 **Arbeiten** der **biologischen Station Lunz.** *Arb. biol. Stn Lunz* [1954–] Fr.; Pl.M.

Arbeiten der **biologischen Wolga-Station.** Saratov. *See* 41759.

Arbeiten aus der **biologischen Zentralanstalt** für **Land- u. Forstwirtschaft.** Berlin. *See* 3806.

3810 **Arbeiten** aus dem **botanischen Institut** des **K. Lyzeum Hosianum in Braunsberg.** Braunsberg. *Arb. bot. Inst. Braunsberg* L.BM^N. 01–26* imp.; K. 03–26 imp.

3811 **Arbeiten. Bundesforschungsanstalt** für **Forst-**
und **Holzwirtschaft.** Reinbek. *Arb. BundForsch-
Anst. Forst- u. Holzw.* **O.**F. 57– imp.; **Y.**

3812 **Arbeiten** aus der **chirurgischen Abteilung** des
städtischen Krankenhauses Moabit zu **Berlin.**
Leipzig. *Arb. chir. Abt. Krankenh. Moabit Berl.*

3813 **Arbeiten** aus der **chirurgischen Klinik** der **K.
Universität Berlin.** Berlin. *Arb. chir. Klin. K. Univ.
Berl.* **L.**s. 86–06; **E.**s. 86–02.

3814 **Arbeiten** aus dem **chirurgischen Sanatorium Dr.
Jaklin** in **Pilsen.** Pilsen. *Arb. chir. Sanat. Jaklin
Pilsen*

3815 **Arbeiten** der **chirurgischen Universitätsklinik
Dorpat.** Leipzig. *Arb. chir. UnivKlin. Dorpat* [1903–]

3816 **Arbeiten** aus der **Deutschen Forschungsanstalt**
für **Psychiatrie** in **München.** Berlin. München.
Arb. dt. ForschAnst. Psychiat. Münch. [1916–]

3817 **Arbeiten** der **Deutschen Gesellschaft** für **Züchtungskunde.** Hannover. *Arb. dt. Ges. Züchtungsk.*
[1909–] **E.**AB. 33–42 imp.

3818 **Arbeiten** der **Deutschen Landwirtschaftsgesellschaft.** Berlin, etc. *Arb. dt. LandwGes.* [1894–] **L.**AM.
94–33 imp.: 47–; P. 10–33; **Abs.**N. 26–; **C.**A. 18–27: 49–;
O.RE. 04–14 imp.; **Rt.** 94–33.

3819 **Arbeiten** der **Deutschen Landwirtschaftsgesellschaft** für **Österreich.** Wien. *Arb. dt. LandwGes.
Öst.*

3820 **Arbeiten** des **Deutschen milchwirtschaftlichen
Reichsverbands.** *Arb. dt. milchw. Reichsverb.* [1915–]
L.P. 20–21. [*C. of:* 48799: *Suspended* 1922–1930]

3821 **Arbeiten** aus der **Deutschen psychiatrischen Universitätsklinik** in **Prag.** Berlin. *Arb. dt. psychiat.
UnivKlin. Prag.*

3822 **Arbeiten** der **Deutschen Sektion** des **Landes-
Kulturrates** für das **Königreich Böhmen.** Prag. *Arb.
dt. Sekt. LandeskultRat. Böhm.*

3823 **Arbeiten** der **Deutschen wissenschaftlichen
Kommission** für **internazionale Meeresforschung.**
Arb. dt. wiss. Komm. int. Meeresforsch. **E.**R. 09–10.

3823° **Arbeiten** der **Deutsch-nordischen Gesellschaft**
für **Geschichte** der **Medizin,** der **Zahnheilkunde** und
der **Naturwissenschaften.** Greifswald. *Arb. dt.-nord.
Ges. Gesch. Med.* [1923–]

3824 **Arbeiten** aus **Dr. Unnas Klinik** für **Hautkrank-
heiten** in **Hamburg.** Berlin. *Arb. Dr. Unnas Klin.
Hamburg*

3825 **Arbeiten** aus der **dritten Abteilung** des **Anatomischen Institutes** der **Kaiserlichen Universität
Kyoto.** *Arb. 3ten. Abt. anat. Inst. Kyoto.*
> Ser. A. [1930–35] **L.**LI.; MA.; MD.; S.; SC.; UC.;
> **Bl.**U. 34–35; **Bm.**U.; **E.**U. 30–33.
> Ser. B. [*not issued*]
> Ser. C. [1930–45] **L.**LI. 30–37; MA. 30–37; MD.;
> s. 30–35; SC.; UC.; **Bl.**U. 34–38; **Bm.**U. 30–35;
> **E.**U. 30–33; **G.**F. 38.
> Ser. D. [1930–44] **L.**LI. 30–37; MA. 30–37; MD.;
> s. 30–38; UC.; **Bl.**U. 34–38; **Bm.**U. 30–35; **E.**U.
> 30–33; **G.**F. [Serie D. *C. in:* 28921]

3826 **Arbeiten** aus dem **Elektrotechnischen Institut** der
**Grossherzoglichen Badischen technischen Hoch-
schule Fridericiana** zu **Karlsruhe.** Berlin. *Arb.
elektrotech. Inst. Karlsruhe* **L.**P. 20–24; **M.**U. 08–29.

3827 **Arbeiten** aus dem **Elektrotechnischen Institut.
K. technische Hochschule, Aachen.** Berlin. *Arb.
elektrotech. Inst. Aachen* [1924–33] **L.**P.; **Nw.**A. 28–33.

3828 **Arbeiten** zur **Entwicklungspsychologie.** Leipzig.
Arb. EntwPsychol. **L.**BM.14–.

3829 **Arbeiten** des **Fischereiinstituts** der **Universität
Königsberg.** *Arb. FischInst. Univ. Königsberg* **Abd.**M.
28–34 imp.; **Dm.** 29–30.
> **Arbeiten** der **Fischereiwirtschaftlichen Station**
in **Jakutsk.** *See* 55230.

3830 **Arbeiten** aus dem **Forschungsinstitut** für **Hygiene**
und **Immunitätslehre.** Berlin-Dahlem. *Arb. Forsch-
Inst. Hyg. ImmunLehre* **L.**MD. 26–30.

3831 **Arbeiten** des **Forschungsinstitutes** für **Kartoffel-
bau.** Berlin. *Arb. ForschInst. KartoffBau* [1919–27]
L.AM.; BM.; MY.; P.; **Db.**; **M.**U. imp.; **Rt.** [*C. in:* 32309]

3832 **Arbeiten** auf dem **Gebiet** der **chemischen Physiologie.** Bonn. *Arb. Geb. chem. Physiol.* [1903–36]
Lv.U. 06–12; **M.**MS. 20.

3833 **Arbeiten** auf dem **Gebiet** der **experimentellen
Physiologie.** Jena. *Arb. Geb. exp. Physiol.* [1908–10]

3834 **Arbeiten** auf dem **Gebiet** der **Grossgasindustrie.**
Leipzig. *Arb. Geb. Grossgasind.* [1909–18] **L.**P.

3835 **Arbeiten** auf dem **Gebiet** der **pathologischen
Anatomie** und **Bakteriologie** an dem **Pathologisch-
anatomischen Institut** zu **Tübingen.** Leipzig. *Arb.
Geb. path. Anat. Bakt.* [1891–22] **L.**BM.; MD. 91–14; S.;
C.UL. 91–14; **Dn.**U. 91–14; **E.**P. imp.; **G.**F. 91–08;
Lv.U. 02; **O.**R.
> **Arbeiten** der **Geburtshilflich-gynäkologischen
Klinik.** Helsingfors. *See* 2802.

3836 **Arbeiten** aus dem **Geographischen Institut.**
Leipzig. *Arb. geogr. Inst., Lpz.* [1951–] **L.**G. 52–.

3837 **Arbeiten** aus dem **Geographischen Institut,
Universität** des **Saarlandes.** Saarbrücken. *Arb. geogr. Inst., Saarbr.* [1956–] **L.**G.

3838 **Arbeiten** des **Geographischen Instituts** der
Deutschen Universität in **Prag.** *Arb. geogr. Inst. dt.
Univ. Prag* [1921–] **L.**BM^N. 21–31 imp.

3838° **Arbeiten** des **Geologischen Instituts, Universität** des **Saarlandes.** Saarbrücken. *Arb. geol. Inst.,
Saarbr.* **L.**SC. 52–.

3839 **Arbeiten** zur **Geschichte** der **Kenntnis** der
Medizin im **Rheinland** und in **Westfalen.** Jena.
Arb. Gesch. Kennt. Med. Rheinl. Westf. [1929–33]
> **Arbeiten** der **Gorkischen landwirtschaftlichen
Versuchs-Station.** *See* 54557.
> **Arbeiten** aus dem **Heiz-** und **Lüftungsfach.** *See*
21165.

3840 **Arbeiten** aus dem **Hirnanatomischen Institut** in
Zürich. Wiesbaden. *Arb. hirnanat. Inst. Zürich* [1905–
16] **L.**MD.; UC.; **Abd.**U. 05–06; **E.**U.

3841 **Arbeiten** aus dem **Hydrobiologischen Laborato-
rium, Kastanienbaum.** Luzern. *Arb. hydrobiol. Lab.
Kastanienbaum* **L.**SC. 26–.
> **Arbeiten** der **Hydrobiologischen Station** zu
Kossino. *See* 54792.
> **Arbeiten** der **Hydrobiologischen Station** am See.
Glubokoje. *See* 54549.

3842 **Arbeiten** der **Hydrometeorologischen Abteilung, Tashkent.** *Arb. hydromet. Abt. Tashk.* **L.**MO. 27–33.

3843　**Arbeiten** aus dem **Hygieneinstitut** der **Universität Greifswald.** *Arb. HygInst. Univ. Greifswald* **L.**MD. 22–23.

3844　**Arbeiten** aus dem **Hygienischen Institut** der **K. Tierärztlichen Hochschule** zu **Berlin.** Berlin. *Arb. hyg. Inst. K. tierärztl. Hochsch. Berl.*

Arbeiten des **Ichtyologischen Laboratoriums** der **Kapsi-Wolgaschen Fischerei-Verwaltung** in **Astrachan.** *See* 54583.

Arbeiten aus dem **Institut** für **Anatomie** und **Physiologie** des **Zentralnervensystems** an der **Wiener Universität.** *See* 3864.

3845　**Arbeiten** aus dem **Institut** zur **Erforschung** der **Infektionskrankheiten** in **Bern** und den **wissenschaftlichen Laboratorien** des **Schweizer Serum-** und **Impf-Instituts.** Jena. *Arb. Inst. Erforsch. Infekt-Krankh. Bern*

3846　**Arbeiten** aus dem **Institut** für **Geschichte** der **Naturwissenschaft.** Heidelberg. *Arb. Inst. Gesch. Naturw.* [1924–] **L.**SC. 24–25.

3847　**Arbeiten** aus dem **Institut** für **Paläobotanik** und **Petrographie** der **Brennsteine.** Berlin. *Arb. Inst. Paläobot.* [1929–] **L.**BM^N. 29–34; GM.; L. 29–34.

3848　**Arbeiten** aus dem **Institut** für **Seefischerei.** Hamburg. *Arb. Inst. Seefisch.* [1951–] **Abd.**M. 54– imp.; **Pl.**M. 53– imp.

3849　**Arbeiten** aus dem **Institut** für **Tierzucht, Vererbungs-** und **Konstitutionsforschung.** München. *Arb. Inst. Tierzucht* [1959–] **C.**A.

Arbeiten des **Instituts** für **Geophysik** und **Meteorologie** an der **Universität Lettlands.** *See* 28178.

3850　**Arbeiten** aus der **K. Frauenklinik** in **Dresden.** Leipzig. *Arb. K. Frauenklin. Dresd.*

3851　**Arbeiten** aus dem **K. Gesundheitsamte.** Berlin. *Arb. K. GesundhAmt.* [1886–17] **L.**BM.; H. imp.; LI.; MC. 00–17; MD.; P. 10–17; R. 86–14; TD.; **Abd.**U.; **C.**UL.; **Db.** 86–88; **E.**P.; U.; **G.**F. 86–14 imp.; U. 06–17; **Lv.**U.; **M.**MS. 86–92: 06–17; **O.**R.; **R.**D. 13–15. [*C. as:* 3878; *Supplement to:* 56187]

3852　**Arbeiten** aus den **K. Hygienischen Instituten** zu **Dresden.** Dresden. *Arb. K. hyg. Inst. Dresd.* **L.**BM. 03–08.

3853　**Arbeiten** aus dem **K. Institut** für **experimentelle Therapie** zu **Frankfurt a. M.** Jena. *Arb. K. Inst. exp. Ther. Frankf. a. M.* [1906–20] **L.**LI.; MC.; MD.; S.; TD. 07–20 imp.; **E.**P.; U.; **Lv.**U. [*C. as:* 3883]

3854　**Arbeiten** des **K. Preussischen Aeronautischen Observatoriums** bei **Lindenberg.** Braunschweig. *Arb. K. preuss. aeronaut. Obs.* [1917–] **L.**MO. 19–33; **Ld.**U. [*C. of:* 18385]

3855　**Arbeiten** aus der **K. Psychiatrischen Klinik** zu **Würzburg.** Jena. *Arb. K. psychiat. Klin. Würzburg* [1906–18]

Arbeiten des **Kaiser-Wilhelm Instituts** für **Kohlenforschung** in **Mülheim Ruhr.** *See* 21143.

Arbeiten der **Klinik** für **Ohren-, Hals-** und **Nasenleiden,** Universität Moskau. *See* 54772.

Arbeiten der **Landwirtschaftlichen Akademie Bonn-Poppelsdorf.** *See* 28071.

Arbeiten aus dem **Landwirtschaftlichen Institut** der **Universität, Halle.** *See* 27790.

3856　**Arbeiten** des **Landwirtschaftlichen Vereins** in **Breslau.** *Arb. landw. Ver. Bresl.*

3857　**Arbeiten** der **Landwirtschaftlichen Versuchsstation.** Limburgerhof. *Arb. landw. VersStn Limburgerhof* **C.**A. 14–.

Arbeiten der **Limnologischen Station** zu **Kossino.** *See* 54834.

3858　**Arbeiten. Max-Planck-Institut** für **Arbeitsphysiologie.** Dortmund. *Arb. Max-Planck-Inst. ArbPhysiol.*

Arbeiten des **Medizinisch-chemischen Laboratoriums** der **K. Universität** zu **Tomsk.** *See* 54842.

3859　**Arbeiten** aus der **Medizinischen Fakultät** zu **Okayama.** Okayama. *Arb. med. Fak. Okayama* [1933–51] **L.**LI. 33–38; MC. 33–38; MD.; TD. 33–40; UC. 33–40; **E.**U.; **Lv.**U. [*C. of:* 3861; *C. as:* 657]

3860　**Arbeiten** aus der **Medizinischen Klinik** zu **Leipzig.** Jena. *Arb. med. Klin. Lpz.* [1912–23] **E.**P. imp.

3861　**Arbeiten** aus der **Medizinischen Universität** zu **Okayama.** *Arb. med. Univ. Okayama* [1928–32] **L.**LI.; MC.; MD.; TD.; UC.; **E.**U.; **Lv.**U. [*C. as:* 3859]

Arbeiten der **Medizinisch-naturwissenschaftlichen Abteilung** der **Wissenschaftlichen Stefan-Tisza-Gesellschaft.** *See* 33836.

Arbeiten des **Meteorologischen Instituts** der **Lettländischen Universität.** *See* 28178.

Arbeiten aus dem **Mikrobiologischen Institut** der **Volksunterrichtskommissariats.** Moskau. *See* 54846.

3862　**Arbeiten** über **morphologische** und **taxonomische Entomologie** aus **Berlin-Dahlem.** *Arb. morph. taxon. Ent. Berl.* [1934–44] **L.**BM^N.; E.; EB.; Z.; **C.**B. 34–39; **Db.**; **E.**R.; **Ld.**U.; **O.**H.

3863　**Arbeiten** des **Naturforschervereins** zu **Riga.** Riga. *Arb. NatForschVer. Riga* [1847–] **L.**BM^N. 1847–37; SC.; **Db.** 08–.

3864　**Arbeiten** aus dem **Neurologischen Institut** an der **Wiener Universität.** Wien. *Arb. neurol. Inst. wien. Univ.* [1892–35] **L.**MD. 02: 04: 14–35; S. 92–20; UCH. 03–15 imp.; **Bl.**U. 92–19; **Bm.**U. 24–26; **C.**PH. 92–09; UL. 20–35; **O.**R. 92–33.

Arbeiten der **Nord-Kaukasischen Assoziation wissenschaftlicher Institute.** *See* 55030.

Arbeiten der **Ost-sibirischen Staatsuniversität.** *See* 55149.

3865　**Arbeiten** zur **Pädagogik** und **psychologischen Anthropologie.** Langensalza. *Arb. Pädag. psychol. Anthrop.* [1939–]

3866　**Arbeiten** aus der **parasitologischen Abteilung, Institut** für **Hygiene** und **Schule** für **Volksgesundheit** in **Zagreb.** Zagreb. *Arb. parasit. Abt. Inst. Hyg. Zagreb* [1929–]

3867　**Arbeiten** aus dem **Pathologischen Institut** zu **Leipzig.** *Arb. path. Inst. Lpz.* **E.**U. 08.

3868　**Arbeiten** aus dem **Pathologischen Institut** der **Universität Helsingfors.** Berlin. *Arb. path. Inst. Univ. Helsingf.*

3869　**Arbeiten** aus dem **Paul Ehrlich-Institut** und dem **Georg Speyer-Haus** und dem **Ferdinand-Blum-Institut** zu **Frankfurt a. M.** *Arb. Paul Ehrlich-Inst.* [1947–] **L.**LI.; MC.; MD.; S. 47–52; TD.; **E.**P.; **Lv.**U.; Y. [*C. of:* 3882]

3870　**Arbeiten** aus dem **Pharmakologischen Institut** der **Universität Wien.** *Arb. pharmak. Inst. Wien* [1925–] **L.**UC. 25–26; **E.**U. 26–36.

3871 **Arbeiten** aus dem **Pharmazeutischen Institut** der **Universität Berlin.** Berlin. *Arb. pharm. Inst. Berl.* [1903–] L.P. 03–13; C.UL. 12.

3872 **Arbeiten** aus dem **Pharmazeutischen Institut** der **Universität Hamburg.** *Arb. pharm. Inst. Hamburg* L.MC. 28–; MD. 72–78.

3873 **Arbeiten** über **physiologische** und **angewandte Entomologie** aus **Berlin-Dahlem.** *Arb. physiol. angew. Ent. Berl.* [1934–44] L.AM.; BM^N.; E.; EB.; Z.; E.R.; Lv.U.; O.R.; Rt.

3874 **Arbeiten** aus dem **Physiologischen Laboratorium** der **Würzburger Hochschule.** Würzburg. *Arb. physiol. Lab. würzb. Hochsch.* [1872–30] L.S. 99–29 imp.; UC. 99–02; Lv.U. 08–12.

3875 **Arbeiten** des **Phytopalaeontologischen Laboratoriums** der **Universität Graz.** *Arb. phytopalaeont. Lab. Univ. Graz* L.BM^N. 24–26; SC. 26–.

3876 **Arbeiten** aus der **Privat-Frauen-Klinik** von **A. Mackenrodt.** Berlin. *Arb. Privat-Frauenklin. A. Mackenrodt*

3877 **Arbeiten** aus dem **Psychologischen Institut.** München. *Arb. psychol. Inst., München* L.PS. 33–38.

3878 **Arbeiten** aus dem **Reichsgesundheitsamte.** Berlin. *Arb. ReichsgesundhAmt.* [1918–42] L.AM. 26–31; BM.; H. 18–39 imp.; LI. 18–39; MC. 18–39; MD. 18–35 imp.; P. 18–39; TD.; **Abd.**U. 18–32; C.UL.; E.P.; U. 18–40; G.U. 18–39; Lv.U.; **M.**MS. 18–24; O.R. 18–34. [*C. of:* 3851]

3879 **Arbeiten** des **Reichsnährstandes.** Berlin. *Arb. Reichsnährstand.* [1935–44] Abs.H.

3880 **Arbeiten** zur **rheinischen Landeskunde.** Bonn. *Arb. rhein. Landesk.* [1952–] L.G.; MO. 54–55.

3881 **Arbeiten** aus dem **Sero-bakteriologischen Institute** der **Universität Helsinki.** *Arb. sero-bakt. Inst. Univ. Helsinki* [1928–] L.LI. 35–38: 43– imp.; TD. 39–.

3882 **Arbeiten** aus dem **Staatlichen Institut** für **experimentelle Therapie** und **Forschungsinstitut** für **Chemotherapie** zu **Frankfurt a. M.** *Arb. st. Inst. exp. Ther. Frankf. a. M.* [1938–46] L.LI.; MC.; MD.; S.; TD. 38–44; E.P.; Lv.U.; Y. [*C. of:* 3883; *C. as:* 3869]

3883 **Arbeiten** aus dem **Staatsinstitut** für **experimentelle Therapie** und dem **Georg Speyer-Haus** zu **Frankfurt a. M.** Jena. *Arb. StInst. exp. Ther. Frankf. a. M.* [1920–37] L.LI.; MC.; MD.; S.; TD. 21–37; E.P.; U.; Lv.U. [*C. of:* 3853; *C. as:* 3882]

Arbeiten der **Station** zur **Bekämpfung** der **Pflanzenschädlinge.** Kiev. *See* 54768.

3884 **Arbeiten** aus dem **Systematisch-zoologischen Institut** der **Lettländischen Universität.** Riga. *Arb. syst.-zool. Inst., Riga* L.EB. 29; Abs.U. 39–43.

Arbeiten Tomsker Staatsuniversität. *See* 55084.

3885 **Arbeiten** aus dem **Treub-Laboratorium.** Weltevreden. *Arb. Treub-Lab.* L.BM^N. 27.

Arbeiten der **Turkmenischen landwirtschaftlichen Hochschule, Aschkabad.** *See* 55109.

Arbeiten des **Ukrainischen Instituts** für **angewandte Botanik.** *See* 55119.

3886 **Arbeiten** des **Ungarischen biologischen Forschungs-Institutes.** Tihany. *Arb. ung. biol. ForschInst.* [1928–46] L.BM^N.; L.; LI. 30–46 imp.; MC.; MD. 30–46; UC. 29–38; Z. 44–46; C.A. 30–46; E.R.; **Fr.** imp.; O.AP.; Pl.M.; Rt. [*C. of:* 4681; *C. as:* 4184]

Arbeiten des **Unteren-Wolgagau-Museums.** Saratov. *See* 54918.

3888 **Arbeiten** der **Versuchsstation** für **Molkereiwesen** in **Kiel.** Leipzig. *Arb. VersStn Molkereiw. Kiel* L.P. 01–09.

Arbeiten des **Wissenschaftlichen Forschungs-Instituts** beim **Kubanischen landwirtschaftlichen Institut.** *See* 54880.

Arbeiten aus dem **Wissenschaftlichen Institut** für **Fischereiwirtschaft.** Moskau. *See* 44881.

3889 **Arbeiten** der **wissenschaftlichen Kongresse** der **Agronomen Lettlands.** Riga. *Arb. wiss. Kongr. Agron. Lettl.* C.A. 25–26.

Arbeiten der **Wissenschaftlichen Zentralversuchsstation** für **Weinbau** in **Odessa.** *See* 38540.

Arbeiten der **Woronesher Filiale** des **Wissenschaftlichen Forschungsinstituts** für **Teichwirtschaft, U.d.S.S.R.** *See* 55144.

Arbeiten aus dem **Yüksek ziraat enstitüsü,** Ankara. *See* 58207.

Arbeiten der **Zentralen Forschungsstation** für **Seide** und **Seidenraupenzucht.** Moskau. *See* 55103.

3890 **Arbeiten** des **Zentralverbandes deutscher Rinderzüchter.** Hannover. *Arb. ZentVerb. dt. Rinderz.* [1947–50] C.A. [*C. as:* 3801]

3891 **Arbeiten** des **Zentralverbandes deutscher Schafzüchter.** Hannover. *Arb. ZentVerb. dt. Schafz.* [1947–51] C.A. 47; E.AB. 47–48.

3892 **Arbeiten** aus dem **Zoologischen Institut** zu **Graz.** Leipzig. *Arb. zool. Inst. Graz.* L.Z. 86–89 imp.; **Dm.** 16–30 v. imp.

3893 **Arbeiten** aus dem **Zoologischen Institut** der **Universität Innsbruck.** *Arb. zool. Inst. Univ. Innsbruck* [1924–28] L.BM^N.

3894 **Arbeiten** aus den **Zoologischen Instituten** der **Universität Wien** u. der **Zoologischen Station** in **Triest.** Wien. *Arb. zool. Inst. Univ. Wien* [1878–15] L.BM.; BM^N.; L.; S.; SC.; 78–14; UC.; Z. 81–15; **Bm.**U. 78–88; C.B.; UL.; **Dn.**U. 81–15; E.R. 78–14; U.; G.U.; Lv.U. 08–15; **M.**U. 78–93; O.R.; Pl.M.

3895 **Arbeiten** aus dem **Zootomischen Institut** der **Universität** zu **Stockholm.** Stockholm. *Arb. zootom. Inst. Univ. Stockh.* C.B. 19–; Y.

Arbeiten der **Zweiten Abteilung** der **Wissenschaftlichen Stefan Tisza Gesellschaft.** *See* 33836.

3896 **Arbeitsbericht.** **Akademie** für **Raumforschung** und **Landesplanung.** Hannover. *Arbeitsber. Akad. Raumforsch.* [1953–] Db.; Y.

3897 **Arbeitsbericht.** **Bundesforschungsanstalt** für **Forst-** und **Holzwirtschaft.** Hamburg. *Arbeitsber. BundForschAnst. Forst- u. Holzw.* O.F. 53–; Y.

3898 **Arbeitsblätter.** **Institut** für **Ausbautechnik** im **Hochbau.** Dresden. *Arbeitsbl. Inst. Ausbautech. Hochbau* [1957–] L.P.

3899 **Arbeitsmedizin.** Leipzig. *Arbeitsmedizin* L.TD. 44– imp.; Y.

3900 **Arbeitsphysiologie.** Berlin. *Arbeitsphysiologie* [1928–44: 49–54] L.MA. 49–54; MC. 28–31; MD. 28–32; P. 53–54; SC.; TD.; U. 49–54; UC.; **Abd.**R. 49–54; **Bm.**U. 38–54; C.UL.; E.U. 49–54; G.U.; Ld.U. 59–54; O.R.; **Sh.**U. 28–39. [*C. as:* 23988]

3901 **Arbeitspsychologie** und **praktische Psychologie.** München. *Arbeitspsychol. prakt. Psychol.* [1939–] [*C. of:* 58493]

3902 **Arbeitstagung Festkörperphysik.** Berlin. *Arbeitstag. FestkörpPhys.* [1952–] **L.**P.

3903 **Arbeitswissenschaftlicher Auslandsdienst.** Darmstadt. *Arbeitswiss. AuslDienst* [1952–58] **L.**P. imp.
Arbejder. *See* **Arbeider.**

3904 **Arbeten** från **Karolinska institutets Patologiska avdelning.** *Arb. Karol. Inst. patol. Avd.* [1925–] **L.**UCH. 34–.

3905 **Arbeten** och **småtryck** från **Första medicinska kliniken i Stockholm.** *Arb. Småtryck första med. Klin. Stockh.* **L.**MD. 29: 31–.

3906 **Arbeten. Symbolae botanicae upsaliensis.** *Arb. Symb. bot. upsal.* **O.**F. 42– imp.
Arbeten från **Zootomiska institutet** vid **Stockholms högskola.** *See* 3895.

3907 **Arbezol-Revue.** Zürich. *Arbezol-Revue* **L.**P. (curr.); **Y.**

3909 **Årbog. Danmarks tekniske Museum.** København. *Årbog Danm. tek. Mus.* [1958–] **L.**SC. 60–.

3910 **Årbog** for den **dansk Fiskerflaade.** København. *Årbog dansk Fiskerfl.* **L.**AM. 25–27 imp. [*C. as:* 19568]

3911 **Årbog** for **Dansk Ingeniørforening.** Kjøbenhavn. *Årbog dansk Ingrfor.* [1924–] **Y.**

3911ᵃ **Årbog. Dansk Kedelforening.** København. *Årbog dansk Kedelfor.* [1954–] [*C. of:* 6084]

3912 **Årbog. Dansk Post-** og **Telegrafvæsen.** København. *Årbog dansk Post- og Telegrafv.*

3913 **Årbog** for **gartneri.** Almindelig Dansk Gartnerforening. København. *Årbog Gart.* [1919–] **L.**AM. 39: 46–; **Md.**H. 45: 48–; **Rt.** 21–36; **Y.**

3914 **Årbog. Norges geologiske undersøgelse.** Kristiania. *Årbog Norg. geol. Unders.* [1890–] **L.**BM.; BMᴺ.; GL. 00–; GM.; **G.**U. 16. [*See also:* 34994]
Årbog for **Universitets zoologiske Museum.** København. *See* 17304.

3914ᵃ **Årbok** for **beitebruk** i **Norge.** *Årbok Beitebr. Norge* **Abd.**R. 26–31: 34–37: 40–47; **Abs.**A. 17–47; **C.**A. 44–.

3915 **Årbok. Forsvarets forskningsinstitutt.** Oslo. *Årbok Forsvar. ForskInst.* [1949–52] **L.**P. 50–52; **Y.**

3916 **Árbók** hins **íslenzka fornleifafélags.** Reykjavík. *Árbók ísl. Fornleifaf.* **L.**UC. 80–; **E.**R. 30–; U. 80–.

3917 **Årbok. Kongelige Norske videnskabers selskab. Museet.** Trondhjem. *Årbok K. norske Vidensk. Selsk. Mus.* [1951–] **L.**BM.; BMᴺ.; L.; **Dm.**; **Pl.**M.; **Y.**

3917ᵒ **Årbok. Norsk farmaceutisk selskap.** Oslo. *Årbok norsk farm. Selsk.*

3918 **Årbok. Norsk polarinstitutt.** Oslo. *Årbok norsk Polarinst.* [1960–] **L.**BMᴺ.; SC.

3920 **Årbok. Norske videnskapsakademi** i **Oslo.** *Årbok norske VidenskAkad.* [1925–] **L.**BM.; BMᴺ.; UC.; Z. imp.; **Bl.**U.; **C.**P.; SJ. 25–39; **Db.**; **E.**C.; R.; **G.**U. 39–45; **Lv.**U.; **O.**B.; **Pl.**M.; **Sa.** 37: 39; **Y.**

3921 **Årbok** for **Universitetet** i **Bergen.** Bergen. *Årbok Univ. Bergen*
    Matematisk-naturvitenskapelig serie [1960–] **L.**AM.; AN.; BM.; BMᴺ.; G.; GL.; L.; MA.; MO.; R.; Z.; **Abd.**M.; **Bl.**U.; **Bn.**U.; **C.**B.; E.; P.; **Cr.**M.; **Db.**; **Dm.**; **E.**C.; G.; J.; R.; V.; **G.**N.; U.; **Lv.**U.; **M.**U.; **O.**R.; **Pl.**M.; **Rt.**; **Sw.**U.; **Y.** [*C. of:* 55569]
    Medisinsk serie [1960–] **L.**BM.; **Bl.**U.; **Cr.**M.; **E.**R.; **O.**R.; **Y.**

3923 **Arbor.** Aberdeen University Forestry Society. Aberdeen. *Arbor, Aberd.* [1944–] **L.**BM. 53–; BMᴺ. 55–; **Abd.**U.; **Bn.**U.; **Db.** 47–; **E.**U. 44–48 imp.: 56; **O.**F.

3924 **Arbor.** Revista generale del Consejo superiore de investigaciones científicas. Madrid. *Arbor, Madr.* [1944–] **L.**BM. imp.; **E.**U.

3925 **Arboretum Bulletin.** Seattle, Wash. *Arboretum Bull., Seattle* [1936–] **L.**HS. 45–55.

3926 **Arboretum Bulletin** of the **Associates.** Morris Arboretum. Philadelphia. *Arboretum Bull. Ass. Morris Arbor.* [1935–41] **L.**BM.; BMᴺ.; HS. 41; K.; **E.**R.; **Lv.**U. 37–41 imp.; **M.**U.; **O.**R.; **Pl.**M.; **Rt.** [*C. as:* 33683]

3927 **Arboretum kórnickie.** Poznań. *Arboretum kórn.* [1955–] **L.**BMᴺ. 57–; K.; **Md.**H.; **Rt.**; **Y.** [*C. of:* 38402]

3927ᵒ **Arboretum Leaves.** Ohio. *Arboretum Leaves* **O.**F. 60–.

3928 **Arboretum News.** University of Wisconsin, Madison. *Arboretum News Univ. Wisc.* [1952–] **Pl.**M.

3929 **Arboriculture.** Chicago. *Arboriculture* [1902–09]

3930 **Arboriculture fruitière.** Paris. *Arboric. fruit.* [1954–59] **Md.**H.; **Y.** [*C. of:* and *Rec. as:* 38082]

3931 **Arboriculturist.** Kent, Ohio. *Arboriculturist* [1935–]

3932 **Arborist's News.** Columbus. *Arborist's News* [1935–] **Y.**

3933 **Arbre.** Paris. *Arbre* [1915–40] [*C. of:* 12462]

3934 **Arbres** et **fruits.** Lille. *Arbres Fruits* **Md.**H. 46–50 imp.

3935 **Arc Quarterly Bulletin.** London. *Arc. q. Bull.* **L.**P. 41–.

3936 **Arc Welding Foundation News.** Cleveland. *Arc Weld. Fdn News* [1937–38]

3937 **Arcachon-Médical.** Paris. *Arcachon-méd.*

3938 **Arch Dam Investigations Bulletin.** Engineering Foundation. New York. *Arch Dam Invest. Bull.* **L.**P. 25–27*.

3939 **Archæological** and **Ethnological Papers** of the **Peabody Museum, Harvard University.** Cambridge, Mass. *Archæol. ethnol. Pap. Peabody Mus.* [1888–01] **L.**AN.; BM.; G.; **Abs.**N.; **C.**E.; **G.**M. 96–01; **Lv.**U.; **O.**B. [*C. as:* 37086]

3940 **Archaeometry.** Oxford. *Archaeometry* [1958–] **L.**BM.; BMᴺ.; **Abs.**N.; **Cr.**M.; **G.**U.
    Archeia. Ἀρχεια. *See* **Arheia.**
    Archeion. Ἀρχειον. *See* **Arheion.**

3941 **Archeion.** Archivio di storia della scienza. Roma, *Archeion* [1927–43] **L.**BM.; MD. 40–43; P.; SC.; UC.; **C.**UL.; **G.**U.; **O.**R. [*C. of:* 4449; *C. as:* 4262]

3942 **Archeologické rozhledy.** Praha. *Archeol. Rozhl.* [1949–] **L.**BMᴺ.; **Y.**

3943 **Archief** voor de **cacao** en **anderere kleine cultuures** in **Nederlandsch-Indië.** Semarang. *Archf Cacao Ned.-Indië* [1927–28] **L.**EB.; MY.; P.; TP. [*C. in:* 3944]

3944 **Archief** voor de **koffiecultuur** in **Indonesië.** Soerabaia. *Archf Koffiecult. Indonesië* [1925–] **L.**EB. 25–33; MY. 25–33: 47–; P. 25–55; TP. 25–30; **C.**A. 31–55; **Md.**H. 30– imp.; **Y.** [*Suspended* 1942–47]
    Archief voor de **koffiecultuur** in **Nederlandsch-Indië.** *See* 3944.

3945 **Archief** voor de **rubbercultuur.** Soerabaia, Buitenzorg. *Archf Rubbercult.* [1948–53] **L.**MY.; P.; TP.; **C.**A.; **Md.**H.; **Rt.**; **Sy.**R.; **Y.** [*C. of:* 3946; *C. as:* 4355]

3946 **Archief** voor de **rubbercultuur** in **Nederlandsch-Indië.** Soerabaia, etc. *Archf Rubbercult. Ned.-Indië* [1917–41] **L.**MY. 27–41; P. 26–41; TP.; **C.**A.; **Md.**H. 30–41; **Rt.** 33–41; **Sy.**R.; **Y.** [*C. as:* 3945]

Archief van **sociale geneeskunde** en **hygiëne.** Brussel. *See* 4287.

3947 **Archief** voor de **suikerindustrie** in **Nederland** en **Nederlandsch-Indië.** *Archf SuikInd. Ned. en Ned.-Indië* [1940–] **L.**C. 40–41; MY. 40–41; P. 40–42; **C.**A.; **Rt.** [*C. of:* 3948; *Suspended* 1942–47]

3948 **Archief** voor de **suikerindustrie** in **Nederlandsch-Indië.** Soerabaia. *Archf Suik. Ind. Ned.-Indië* [1910–34] **L.**BM^N. 27–31 imp.; K. 22–34; MY. 24–29; P. 14–34 imp.; **C.**A. 16–34 imp.; **Rt.** imp. [*C. as:* 3947]

3949 **Archief** voor de **theecultuur.** Batavia. *Archf Theecult.* [1948–55] **L.**MY.; P.; **C.**A.; **Md.**H.; **Rt.** [*C. of:* 3950; *Replaces:* 4374]

3950 **Archief** voor de **theecultuur** in **Nederlandsch-Indië.** Buitenzorg, etc. *Archf Theecult. Ned.-Indië* [1927–41] **L.**EB. 27–33; K. 27–33; MY. imp.; P.; TP.; **C.**A. 27–33; **Md.**H. 30–41; **Rt.** 33–41 imp.; [*C. of:* 30128 and 53037; *Replaced by:* 3949]

3951 **Archief. Zeeuwsch genootschap** der **wetenschappen.** Vlissingen. *Archf zeeuw. Genoot. Wet.* **L.**BM 78–18; BM^N. 1856–06.

3952 **Archimede.** Rivista per gli insegnanti e i cultori di matematiche pure e applicati. Firenze. *Archimede* [1949–] **L.**SC. 57–.

3953 **Archimedes.** Deutsches Patentblatt. Berlin. *Archimedes, Berl.*

3954 **Archimedes.** South African Science Survey. Pretoria. *Archimedes, Pretoria* [1957–] **L.**BM.; **Y.**

3955 **Architect.** London. *Architect, Lond.* [1869–93: 19–26] **L.**BA.; BM.; UC. 80–85; **Abs.**N. 19–26; **Bm.**P.; **Bra.**P. 72–93: 19–26; **Cr.**P. 81–93: 19–26; **Db.**; **E.**A.; F. 80–93: 19–20; T. 89–93: 19–26; **G.**M. 77–93: 19–26; **Ld.**P. 73–93: 19–26; **M.**P. 74–93: 19–26; **Nw.**P.; **O.**B. 19–26; **Sh.**P. [> 3963, 1893–18; *C. as:* 3962]

3956 **Architect.** Perth, W. Australia. *Architect, Perth* [1939–] **L.**BA.

Architect. Prague. *See* 50871.

3957 **Architect.** San Francisco. *Architect, S Francisco* [1915–19] [*C. of:* 36686; *C. as:* 9078]

3958 **Architect** and **Builder.** Cape Town. *Architect Bldr, Cape Tn* [1917–29] **L.**BM. [*C. as:* 3960]

3958° **Architect** and **Builder.** Cape Town. *Archit. Bldr, Cape Tn* [1950–] **L.**BM.

3959 **Architect** and **Builder.** Kansas City. *Architect Bldr, Kans Cy* [1904–07] [*C. of:* 27231; *C. in:* 57399]

3960 **Architect, Builder** and **Engineer.** Cape Town. *Architect Bldr Engr, Cape Tn* [1930–] **L.**BA. 30–41; BM. [*C. of:* 3958]

3961 **Architect, Builder** and **Engineer.** Vancouver, B.C. *Architect Bldr Engr, Vancouver*

3962 **Architect** and **Building News.** London. *Architect Bldg News* [1926–] **L.**BA.; BM.; H. (curr.); P. (5 yr.); U. 46–; **Abs.**N.; **Bm.**P.; T. 48–; **Br.**P. (2 yr.); **Bra.**P.; **C.**UL.; **Cr.**P.; **Db.**; **E.**A.; T.; **G.**M.; **Lc.**A. 36–47: 53–; **Ld.**P.; **Lv.**P. 56–; **M.**P.; T.; **N.**T. 54– imp.; **Nw.**A. 34–; P.; **O.**B.; **Sh.**P.; **Y.** [*C. of:* 3955]

3963 **Architect** and **Contract Reporter.** London. *Architect Contract Reptr* [1893–18] **L.**BA.; BM.; **Abs.**N. 12–18; **Bm.**P.; **Bra.**P.; **Cr.**P.; **Db.**; **E.**A.; **E.**F.; T.; **G.**M.; **Ld.**P.; **M.**P.; **N.**P. 00–18; **Nw.**A. 97–19 imp.; P.; **O.**B. 17–18; **Sh.**P. [*C. of:* and *Rec. as:* 3955]

3964 **Architect** and **Engineer** of **California.** San Francisco. *Architect Engr Calif.* [1905–] **L.**BA. 45–.

3965 **Architect** and **Surveyor.** London. *Architect Surv.* [1956–] **L.**BA.; BM.; P.; SC.; **Bm.**P.; T.; **Br.**P.; **Cr.**P.; **E.**A.; **Lv.**P.; **M.**P.; **O.**B.; **Y.** [*C. of:* 37184]

3966 **Architecte.** Paris. *Architecte, Paris* [1906–35] **L.**BA. 24–35; **Lv.**U. 27–35. [*Suspended* 1914–23]

Architecte. Prague. *See* 50871.

3967 **Architects'** and **Builders' Journal.** London, Baltimore. *Architects' Bldrs' J.* [1910–19] **L.**BA.; BM.; P.; SC.; **Abs.**N. 12–19; **Bm.**P. 18–19; **Db.** 10–14; **E.**A.; **G.**M.; **Lv.**P.; **M.**P.; T. 11–19; **O.**B. [*C. of:* 9037; *C. as:* 3970]

3968 **Architects'** and **Builders' Magazine.** New York. *Architects' Bldrs' Mag.* [1882–11] **L.**BA. 99–11. [*C. as:* 4014]

3969 **Architects' Detail Sheets.** London. *Architects' Det. Sh.* [1952–] **L.**BM.; **Ld.**P.

3970 **Architects' Journal.** London. *Architects' J.* [1920–] **L.**BA.; BM.; P. (5 yr.); PG. 31–; SC.; SH. (1 yr); U. 47–; **Abs.**N.; **Bm.**P.; T. 47–; **Bra.**P. 39–; **C.**UL.; **Cr.**P. (5 yr.); **Db.** 38–; **E.**A.; T. 30–; U. 56–; **G.**M.; PH. 38–48; **Lc.**A. 39–; **Ld.**P.; **Lv.**P.; U. 21–; **M.**P.; T.; **N.**T. (5 yr.); **Nw.**A. 34–; P. 30–; **O.**B.; **Sh.**IO. 45–; U. 39–;

Information sheets. **L.**P.

[*C. of:* 3967]

3971 **Architects' Magazine.** London. *Architects' Mag* [1900–07] **L.**BM.; P.; **C.**UL.; **E.**A.; **O.**B. [*C. of:* and *Rec. as:* 26914]

3972 **Architects' Working Details.** London. *Architects' wkg Det.* [1953–] **L.**BM.; **Ld.**P.

3973 **Architect's World:** a monthly digest. New York. *Architect's Wld* **L.**BM. 38–; SC. 13– imp.

3974 **Architects' Yearbook.** London. *Architects' Yb.* [1945–] **L.**BA.; BM.; **Bra.**P.; **G.**M.; **Ld.**P.; **Lv.**P.; **R.**U. 53–; **Sh.**U. 47: 57–.

3975 **Architectura.** Amsterdam. *Architectura, Amst.* **L.**BA. 27–39*. [*C. of:* 36249; *C. in:* 8622]

3976 **Architectura.** Berlin. *Architectura, Berl.* [1933] **L.**BA.

3977 **Architectura.** Maassluis. *Architectura, Maassluis*

Architectura. 's-Gravenhage. *See* 8622.

3978 **Architectura** y **construcción.** Santiago. *Architectura Constr.* **L.**BA. 45–56.

3979 **Architectural Annual.** Washington. *Archit. A.*

3980 **Architectural Association Brown Book.** London. *Archit. Ass. brown Bk* **Abs.**N. 16–20*; **C.**UL. 06–20; **O.**B. 06–20. [*C. as:* 3984]

3981 **Architectural Association Journal.** London. *Archit. Ass. J.* [1905–47] **L.**BA.; BM.; P.; SC. 26–; **Abs.**N. 15–47; **C.**UL.; **E.**A.; **O.**B. [*C. of:* 3982; *C. as:* 1]

3982 **Architectural Association Notes.** London. *Archit. Ass. Notes* [1887–05] **L.**BA.; BM. 96–05; P. [*C. as:* 3981]

3983 Architectural Association Sketch Book. London. *Archit. Ass. Sketch Bk* [1867–17: 23] **L.**BM. 73–23; **Abs.**N. 14–17; **Bm.**P. 14–; **Br.**P. 06–13; **C.**UL.; **Db.** 06–23; **E.**A. 71–23; F. 95–17; **G.**M. 95–23 imp.; **Lv.**U. 67–70: 23; **O.**B. 97–23.

3984 Architectural Association Year Book. London. *Archit. Ass. Yb.* [1921–] **L.**BM.; **Abs.**N.; **O.**B. [C. of: 3980]

3985 Architectural and **Building Journal** of **Queensland.** Brisbane. *Archit. Bldg J. Qd* **L.**BA. 23–25: 29–30.

3986 Architectural Concrete. Portland Cement Association. Chicago. *Archit. Concr.* [1930–] **L.**BA. 36–44; **Y.**

Architectural Culture. Tokyo. *See* 27313.

3987 Architectural Design. London. *Archit. Design* [1947–] **L.**BM.; P. (5 yr.); SC.; TD. 53–; U.; **Abs.**N.; **E.**A.; **G.**T. (1 yr); **Lc.**A.; **M.**P.; T.; **Nw.**A.; **O.**B.; **Sh.**IO.; U.; **Y.** [C. of: 3988]

3988 Architectural Design and **Construction.** London. *Archit. Design Constr.* [1930–46] **L.**BM.; SC. 32–46; **Abs.**N.; **E.**A.; **Lc.**A. 44–46; **M.**P. 45–46; T. 46; **Nw.**A. 37–46; **O.**B.; **Sh.**IO. 44–46; U. 35–46. [C. as: 3987]

3989 Architectural Digest. Los Angeles. *Archit. Dig.* [1914–]

3990 Architectural Forum. Boston, New York. *Archit. Forum* [1917–] **L.**BA.; BM. 52–; U. 40–; UC. 20–; **Bl.**U. 47–; **Bm.**P. 44–; T. 45–; **Br.**P. 31–; **C.**UL. 27–; **G.**T. 27–52: (1 yr); **Lc.**A. 53–; **Ld.**P. 30–; **Lv.**P. 22–; U. 21–; **M.**P. 22–39: 56–; **Nw.**A. 47–; **Sh.**U. 29–. [C. of: 8736]

3991 Architectural History. York. *Archit. Hist.* [1958–] **L.**BA.; BM.; **Bl.**U.; **Ld.**P.; **Sh.**U.

3992 Architectural Information from the **Cement** and **Concrete Association.** London. *Archit. Inf. Cem. Concr. Ass.* [1939–]

3993 Architectural Metals. Chicago. *Archit. Metals* [1955–] **Y.**

3994 Architectural Progress. Cincinnati. *Archit. Prog.*

3995 Architectural Prospect. London. *Archit. Prosp.* [1948–] **L.**BA.; BM.; **E.**A.; **G.**M. 56–; **O.**B. 48–49.

Architectural Prospect. Incorporation of Architects in Scotland. *See* 40241.

3996 Architectural Quarterly of **Harvard University.** Cambridge, Mass. *Archit. Q. Harv. Univ.*

3997 Architectural Record. New York. *Archit. Rec.* [1891–] **L.**BM. 11–; P. 11–25; **Bm.**P. 44–; **Br.** P. 32–; **Db.** 13–; **G.**M. 38–; **Lv.**P. 59–; **M.**P. 38–; T. 53–57; **O.**R.; **Sh.**U. 28–.

3998 Architectural Record of **Design** and **Construction.** London. *Archit. Rec. Design Constr.* **L.**P. 37*. [C. in: 3988]

3999 Architectural Review. Boston. *Archit. Rev., Boston* [1890–21] **Lv.**U. 04–21; **Nw.**P. 97–21. [C. in: 1900]

4000 Architectural Review. London. *Archit. Rev., Lond.* [1896–] **L.**BA.; BM.; H. 55–; NP. 26– imp.; P. 96–28; U.; UC. 96–37 imp.; **Abs.**N. 12–; **Bl.**U. imp.; **Bm.**P.; U. imp.; **Br.**P. 29–; **Bra.**P.; **C.**UL.; **Cr.**P. imp.; U. 50–; **Db.**; **E.**A.; H. 96–24; T.; U. 32–; **G.**M.; U. 48– imp.; **Lc.**A. 97–16: 40–; **Lv.**P.; U. 00–; **M.**P.; T. 11–; **N.**P.; **Nw.**A. 46–; P.; **O.**B.; **R.**U. 47–; **Sh.**P. 97–; **Y.**

4001 Architectural Science Review. Sydney. *Archit. Sci. Rev.* [1958–] **L.**P. 59–; SC.; **Sh.**SC.61–.

4002 Architectural Survey. Dublin. *Archit. Surv.* [1953–] **L.**BM.; **O.**B. 54–.

4003 Architectural and **Topographical Record.** London. *Archit. topogr. Rec.* [1908] **L.**BM.; **Bm.**P.; **Db.**; **E.**A.; **G.**M.; **M.**P.; **O.**B.

4004 Architectural Yearbook. University of Illinois. Urbana. *Archit. Yb., Urbana* **L.**BM. 12–17; **O.**B. 15–17.

4005 Architecture. London. *Architecture, Lond.* [1922–31] **L.**BA.; BM.; P. 22–25; **Abs.**N.; **Bm.**P.; **Br.**P. 22–25; **Cr.**P.; **E.**A.; **G.**M.; **Lv.**P.; U.; **M.**P.; **O.**B. [C. of: 26914; C. in: 9034]

4006 Architecture. New Orleans. *Architecture, New Orl.*

4007 Architecture. New York. *Architecture, N.Y.* [1900–36] **L.**BA. 23–36; BM. 23–36; **G.**M. 22–36; **Lv.**U. 07–36. [C. in: 1900]

4008 Architecture. Paris. *Architecture, Paris* [1888–] **L.**BA. 07–39; **Bm.**P. 07–09.

4009 Architecture. Sydney. *Architecture, Sydney* [1916–55] **L.**BA. 22. [C. as: 4011]

4010 Architecture d'aujour d'hui. Boulogne. *Architecture aujour d'hui* [1930–] **L.**BA. 31–; BM. 50–; **Bl.**U. 47– imp.; **Db.** 45–; **G.**T. 57–; **Lc.**A. 57–; **M.**P. 56–; **Nw.**A. 47–; **Sh.**U. 36–40: 45–46; **Y.**

4011 Architecture in Australia. Sydney. *Architecture Aust.* [1955–] **Y.** [C. of: 4009]

4012 Architecture—bâtiment—construction. Montréal. *Architecture—Bâtim.—Constr.* **L.**BA. 48–.

4013 Architecture and **Building.** London. *Architecture Bldg, Lond.* [1954–] **L.**BA.; BM.; H. 58–; NP. **Bm.**T.; **Br.**P. (2 yr.); **C.**UL.; **Cr.**P. 57–; **E.**A.; U. 58–; **F.**A. 54–55; **G.**M.; **Lc.**A. 58–; **Lv.**P.; **M.**T. 54–57; **Nw.**P. 54–; **O.**R.; **Sh.**U.; [C. of: 9040]

4014 Architecture and **Building.** New York. *Architecture Bldg, N.Y.* [1911–32] **L.**BA. 11–13; P. 15–17. [C. of: 3968]

4014° Architecture and **Building, Tasmania.** Hobart. *Architecture Bldg Tasm.* **Y.**

4015 Architecture Chronicle. Moscow. *Architecture Chron., Mosc.* [1944–] **L.**BA. 44–45.

Architecture and **Construction.** Moscow. *See* 4776ᵃ.

4016 Architecture et la **construction** dans l'ouest. Rouen. *Architecture Constr. Ouest* [1897–14]

Architecture contemporaine. Moscou. *See* 50364.

4017 Architecture and **Design.** Salisbury, Rhodesia. *Architecture Design* [1956–] **L.**BA.

4018 Architecture française. *Architecture fr.* [1940–] **L.**BA.; BM.; **Db.** 54–; **Dm.** 51–; **Y.**

4019 Architecture Illustrated. London. *Architecture ill.* [1930–57] **L.**BA.; BM.; **Abs.**N.; **C.**UL.; **Db.**; **E.**A.; **M.**P. 35–57; **Nw.**A. 34–57; **O.**B. [C. in: 23174]

4020 Architecture moderne. Paris. *Architecture mod.*

4021 Architecture du **sud-ouest.** Bordeaux. *Architecture Sud-Ouest*

4022 Architecture suisse. Lausanne, Berne. *Architecture suisse*

4023 **Architecture, urbanisme, habitation.** Louvain. *Architecture Urban. Habit.* L.BA. [*C. of:* 17991]

4024 **Architecture usuelle.** Revue technique. Dourdan. *Architecture usuelle*

4025 **Architekt.** Essen. *Architekt, Essen* L.BA. 53–.

4026 **Architekt.** Kraków. *Architekt, Kraków*

4027 **Architekt.** Wien. *Architekt, Wien*

4028 **Architekt S I A.** Spolek československých inženýrů. v Praze. *Architekt S I A* [1902–] L.BA. 36–39: 46–.

4029 **Architekten.** Kjøbenhavn. *Architekten* [*C. as:* 4797]

4030 **Architektenzeitung.** Berlin. *Architektenzeitung*

4031 **Architekten- u. Baumeister-Zeitung.** Wien. *Architekten- u. Baumeisterztg*

4032 **Architektonický obzor.** *Architekton. Obzor*

4033 **Architektonische Rundschau.** Esslingen. *Architekton. Rdsch.* [1885–15] Lv.P. 85–14.

4034 **Architektur** und **Wohnform.** Stuttgart. *Architektur Wohnform* [1946–] L.BA. 52–; BM. 54–. [*C. of:* 23651]

4035 **Architektura.** Warszawa. *Architektura* [1947–] L.BA.; BM. 52–; Y.

4036 **Architektura i budownictwo.** Warszawa. *Architektura Budown.* L.BA. 35–39.

4037 **Architektura Č S R.** Praha. *Architektura Č S R* [1939–] L.BA. 39: 45–47; BM. imp.; Y. [*C. of:* 50866, 50871 and 51216]

4038 **Architetti.** Firenze. *Architetti* L.BA. 50–53.

4039 **Architettura.** Milano. *Architettura* [1921–] L.BA. 21–40; BM. 33–.

4040 **Architettura cantiere.** Milano. *Architettura cantiere* [1957–] L.BA.; Db.; M.T.

4041 **Architettura, cronache e storia.** Roma, Milano. *Architettura Cron. Stor.* [1955–] L.BA.; BM.

4042 **Architettura italiana.** Torino. *Architettura ital.* [1905–] L.BA. 05–40.

4043 **Archiv für alchemistische Forschung.** Berlin. *Arch. alchem. Forsch.* [1930] L.C. [*C. of:* 1675]
   Archiv für Anatomie und Entwicklungsgeschichte
   See 4044: *Forms* Anatomische Abteilung.

4044 **Archiv für Anatomie** und **Physiologie.** Leipzig. *Arch. Anat. Physiol.* [1796–19] L.BM. 1834–14; BM^N. 1796–88; MC. (physiol.) 90–19; MD. 00–19; R.; S. 77–19; SC. 1834–19; Z.; Abd.U. 1834–19; Bl.U. 1834–19; Bm.U.; Bn.U. 00–19 imp.; Br.U. 1854–1857: 06; C.AN. 1834–19; B. 69–05; PA. (physiol.) 77–89; PH. 1834–19; UL. 1826–19; Cr.U. 98–18; Db. 1858–19; Dn.U. 89–18 imp.; E.P.; U.; G.F. 1826–1830: 1834–01; U.; Lv.U. 95–19 imp.; M.MS.; U. 86–04; N.U. 1852–78; O.R.; Sa.; Sh.U. 99–19.

4045 **Archiv für Anthropologie.** Braunschweig. *Arch. Anthrop.* [1866–42] L.AN.; BM.; BM^N. 66–88; MD. 66–88; S. 66–35; SC. 66–39 imp.; Abd.U. 88–38; Bm.U.; C.UL.; Db. 90–42; Dn.U. 03–28; E.P.; U. 04–39; V. 04–10; G.U. 66–39; O.R.

4046 **Archiv für Anthropologie** und **Geologie Schleswig-Holsteins** und der benachbarten Gebiete. Kiel. *Arch. Anthrop. Geol. Schlesw.-Holst.* L.BM^N. 95–13; GM. 96–13.

4047 **Archiv** und **Atlas** der **normalen** und **pathologischen Anatomie** in **typischen Röntgenbildern.** Hamburg. *Arch. Atlas norm. path. Anat.* [1900–] L.BM.; Abd.U.; E.P.; G.U. imp. [*Supplement to:* 20210]

4048 **Archiv für Augenheilkunde.** Wiesbaden. *Arch. Augenheilk.* [1869–37] L.BM. 79–37; MD. 00–37; OP.; C.UL. 79–37. [*C. in:* 1671]

4049 **Archiv für Balneologie** und **medizinische Klimatologie.** Berlin. *Arch. Balneol. med. Klim.* [1925–] L.MD. 25–26.

4050 **Archiv der Balneotherapie** und **Hydrotherapie.** Halle. *Arch. Balneother. Hydrother.* [1897–01]

4051 **Archiv für Bevölkerungswissenschaft** und **Bevölkerungspolitik.** Leipzig. *Arch. BevölkWiss. BevölkPol.* L.AN. 43.

4052 **Archiv für Bienenkunde.** Leipzig, Berlin, etc. *Arch. Bienenk.* [1919–] L.AM. 20–23: 30 imp.; BM.; Rt. imp; Y.
   Archiv der Biologischen Wolga-Station. See 33244.

4053 **Archiv für Biontologie.** Berlin. *Arch. Biontol.* [1906–31] L.BM^N.; Z. 06–24; C.P. 06–20; UL. 06–20; E.C. 06–09; R. 06–20; G.U. 06–20.

4054 **Archiv für Buchbinderei.** Halle a. S. *Arch. Buchbind.* [1901–] L.BM. 31–; P. 01–31; SB. 01–13 v. imp.

4055 **Archiv der Bulgarischen landwirtschaftlichen Gesellschaft.** Sofia. *Arch. bulg. landw. Ges.* [1946–?] [*C. as:* 58936]

4056 **Archiv für Chemie** und **Mikroskopie in ihrer Anwendung** auf den öffentlichen Verwaltungsdienst. Wien. *Arch. Chem. Mikrosk.* [1908–18]

4057 **Archiv für Dermatologie** und **Syphilis.** Wien u. Leipzig. *Arch. Derm. Syph.* [1869–55] L.MA. 89–14: 38–55; MD.; S. 69–48; TD. 26–41; U. 50–55; UCH. 69–31; E.P.; S. 92–22; M.MS. 69–31. [*C. as:* 4105]

4058 **Archiv der Deutschen Landwirtschaftsgesellschaft.** Hannover, Berlin. *Arch. dt. LandwGes.* L.AM. 50–; C.A. 49–; Y.

4059 **Archiv des Deutschen Landwirtschaftsrats.** Berlin. *Arch. dt. LandwRats* [1876–33] L.AM. 99–01; Db. 13–33; O.RE. 07–25.

4060 **Archiv für Druck** und **Papier.** Berlin. *Arch. Druck Pap.* [1955–] L.BM.; P.; SB.; Lh.P.; M.P.; Y.

4061 **Archiv für Eisenbahntechnik.** Darmstadt. *Arch. EisenbTech.* L.P. 54–. [*Supplement to:* 17555]

4062 **Archiv für Eisenbahnwesen.** Berlin. *Arch. EisenbWes.* [1881–43] L.BM. 78–43.

4063 **Archiv für das Eisenhüttenwesen.** Düsseldorf. *Arch. EisenhüttWes.* [1927–43: 48–] L.C. 40; I.; NF. 27–33; P.; SC. 28–44: 49–; Bm.C.; U. 48–; C.ENG. 53–; MT.; G.T. imp.; U. 55–; M.U. imp.; Sh.IO. 29–; SC. imp.; St.R. 28–43: 48–; Y. [*Supplement to:* 50716]

4064 **Archiv für** die **elektrischen Übertragung.** Wiesbaden. *Arch. elekt. Übertr.* [1947–] L.EE. imp.; P. imp.; SC.; SI. 56–; C.P.; Y.

4065 **Archiv für Elektrotechnik.** Berlin. *Arch. Elektrotech.* [1912–] L.AV. 41–44 imp.; BM. 17–19: 55–; EE. 12–43 imp.; P. imp.; SC. 21–; Bm.P. 27–; U. 12–14; Bn.U. 24– imp.; C.P. 30–; UL. 13–; Db. 48–; Dn.U. 48–; G.T.; U.; Ld.U. 24–; Lv.P. 53–; U.; M.P. 12–13: 56–; T. 24– imp.; U.; N.U. 55–; Nw.A. 21– imp.; Sh.S. 32–; SC. 32– imp.; Sw.U. 50–; Y.

4065° **Archiv für Energiewirtschaft.** *Arch. EnergWirt.* Y.

4066 **Archiv** für **Entwicklungsgeschichte** der **Bakterien.** Berlin. *Arch. EntwGesch. Bakt.* [1931–]

4067 **Archiv** für **Entwicklungsmechanik** der **Organismen.** Leipzig. *Arch. EntwMech. Org.* [1894–23] **L.**AM. imp.; BM.; BM^N.; L.; SC. 95–23; UC. 95–23; Z.; **Ba.**I.; **Bm.**U. 94–22; **C.**AN.; B.; **E.**AG.; P.; U.; **Fr.** 12–14; **G.**U.; **Lo.** imp.; **M.**U. 05–23; **O.**R.; **Pl.**M.; **Sa.** 97–23 imp. [*C. in:* 4128]

4068 **Archiv** des **Erdmagnetismus.** Potsdam. *Arch. Erdmagn.* [1903–]

4069 **Archiv** für **Erzbergbau, Erzaufbereitung, Metallhüttenwesen.** Berlin. *Arch. Erzbergb.* **L.**P. 31–36*. [*Supplement to:* 31444]

4070 **Archiv** für **experimentelle u. klinische Phonetik.** Berlin. *Arch. exp. klin. Phon.* **L.**P. 13–14. [*Supplement to:* 5925]

4071 **Archiv** für **experimentelle Pathologie** und **Pharmakologie.** Leipzig. *Arch. exp. Path. Pharmak.* [1873–25] **L.**MC. 97–25; MD.; PH. 85–14; S.; TD. 00–25; U. 03–20; UC.; UCH. 12–14; **Abd.**U.; **Bl.**U.; **Bm.**U. 73–00: 20–25; **C.**PH.; UL.; **Db.** imp.; **Dn.**U.; **E.**P.; U.; **G.**M. 81–14; U. 85–25; **Ld.**U. 85–25; **Lv.**U.; **M.**MS.; **N.**U. 73–87; **O.**R.; **Sa.** 99–03 imp.; **Y.** [*C. as:* 34398]

4072 **Archiv** für **experimentelle Veterinärmedizin.** Leipzig, Berlin. *Arch. exp. VetMed.* [1952–] **L.**V.; VC. 60–; **W.**; **Y.** [*C. of:* 18742]

4073 **Archiv** für **experimentelle Zellforschung.** Jena. *Arch. exp. Zellforsch.* [1925–44] **L.**CB.; MD. 25–33; SC.; UC.; **Bm.**U. 28–31; **C.**AN. 25–39; **G.**U.; **Ld.**U. 25–33; **M.**U.; **O.**R.

4074 **Archiv** für **Feuerschutz, Rettungs- u. Feuerlöschwesen.** Leipzig. *Arch. Feuerschutz*

4075 **Archiv** für **Fischereigeschichte.** Berlin. *Arch. FischGesch.* [1913–17] **L.**P.; **C.**B.

4076 **Archiv** für **Fischereiwissenschaft.** Braunschweig, Hamburg. *Arch. FischWiss.* [1948–] **L.**BM^N.; P.; **Abd.**M.; **Lo.** 50–; **Pit.**F.; **Pl.**M.; **Y.** [*Also supplements*]

4077 **Archiv** für **Forstwesen.** Berlin. *Arch. Forstw.* [1952–] **L.**AM.; P. 55– imp.; **Bm.**U. 53–; **O.**F.; **Y.**
    Archiv für **Frauenkunde** und **Eugenetik.** *Arch. Frauenk. Eugen.* See 4078.

4078 **Archiv** für **Frauenkunde** und **Konstitutionsforschung.** Wurzburg, etc. *Arch. Frauenk. KonstForsch.* [1914–33] **L.**BM.

4079 **Archiv** der **Freunde** der **Naturgeschichte** in **Mecklenburg.** Rostock. *Arch. Freunde NatGesch. Mecklenb.* [1954–] **L.**BM^N.; L.; SC.; **Abs.**U.; **C.**P.; UL.; **Db.**; **G.**U.; **Lv.**U.; **O.**R.; **Y.** [*C. of:* 4173]

4080 **Archiv** für **Gartenbau.** Berlin. *Arch. Gartenb.* [1953–] **L.**AM.; SC. 54–; **C.**A.; **Md.**H.; **Sil.** 60–; **Y.**

4081 **Archiv** für **Geflügelkunde.** Berlin. *Arch. Geflügelk.* [1926–39: 53–] **L.**AM. 53–; **Abd.**R. 36–39: 53–; **C.**A.; **E.**AB. 27–39; PO. 26–39 imp.: 55–; **R.**U. 53–; **W.** 33–38: 58–; **Y.** [>4102, 1940–42]

4082 **Archiv** für **Geflügelzucht** und **Kleintierkunde.** Berlin. *Arch. Geflügelz. Kleintierk.* [1952–] **L.**AM.; **C.**A.; **R.**U.; **Y.**
    Archiv für die **gesamte Physiologie** des **Menschen** und der **Tiere.** See 37461.

4083 **Archiv** für die **gesamte Psychologie.** Leipzig. *Arch. ges. Psychol.* [1903–44] **L.**B.; BM.; MD. 05–32; PS. 03–24: 27–44; U. 03–22; UC. 03–41 imp.; **Bm.**U. 08–22;

C.PS.; UL.; **Cr.**U. 11–14; **Db.**; **E.**P.; U.; **G.**U.; **Ld.**U. 03–30; **M.**P.; **O.**B.; **Sa.** 13–30; **Sh.**U. 06–24 imp.

4084 **Archiv** für die **gesamte Virusforschung.** Wien. *Arch. ges. Virusforsch.* [1939–] **L.**AM. 51–; LI. 39; MA. 44–; MC.; MD.; SC.; TD.; U. 48–; **Bl.**U. 55–; **Br.**U. 59–; **C.**PA. 55–; **Dn.**U. 39–57; **E.**U. 40–; **G.**U.; **Md.**H. 39–44 imp.; **Sh.**U. 54–; **W.** 51–; **Y.**

4085 **Archiv** für die **gesamte Wärmetechnik.** Dissen. *Arch. ges. Wärmetech.* [1950] [*C. as:* 1774]

4086 **Archiv** für **Geschichte** und **Landeskunde Vorarlbergs.** Bregenz. *Arch. Gesch. Landesk. Vorarlb.* [1904–16]

4087 **Archiv** für **Geschichte** der **Mathematik,** der **Naturwissenschaften** und der **Technik.** Leipzig. *Arch. Gesch. Math. Naturw. Tech.* [1927–31] **L.**BM.; P.; SC.; UC.; **G.**U. 29–31. [*C. of:* 4089; *C. as:* 41674]

4088 **Archiv** für **Geschichte** der **Medizin.** Leipzig. *Arch. Gesch. Med.* [1907–28] **L.**BM.; MD.; UC.; **C.**UL.; **E.**P.; **G.**F. 07–14; **O.**R. [*C. as:* 51243]

4089 **Archiv** für die **Geschichte** der **Naturwissenschaften** und der **Technik.** Leipzig. *Arch. Gesch. Naturw. Tech.* [1909–22] **L.**BM.; P. 09–22; SC. 09–22; UC.; **G.**U. 09–14; **O.**R. [*C. as:* 4087]

4090 **Archiv** für **Geschwulstforschung.** Dresden, Leipzig. *Arch. Geschwulstforsch.* [1949–] **L.**CB.; MA.; MD.; U.; **Abd.**R.; **C.**R. 52–; **Y.**

4091 **Archiv** für **Gewerbepathologie** und **Gewerbehygiene.** Berlin. *Arch. Gewerbepath. Gewerbehyg.* [1930–61] **L.**MC. 30–49; MA. 54–61; MD.; PS. 30–32; TD.; **Y.** [*Not issued* 1945–53; *C. as:* Internationales Archiv für Gewerbepathologie und Gewerbehygiene]

4092 **Archiv** für **Gynaekologie.** Berlin. *Arch. Gynaek.* [1870–] **L.**BM.; MD.; S. 70–14: 19; **Abd.**U.; **Bm.**U. 70–85: 98–18: 48–; **Br.**U. 09; **C.**UL.; **Cr.**MD. 81–91; **Db.** 70–39; **Dn.**U. 00–31; **E.**P.; S. 70–40 imp.; U.; **G.**F. 70–14; M. 70–14; U.; **Lv.**M. 28–33; **M.**MS. 70–23; **Y.**

4093 **Archiv** für **Homöopathie.** Dresden. *Arch. Homöop.*

4094 **Archiv** für **Hydrobiologie.** Stuttgart. *Arch. Hydrobiol.* [1905–] **L.**BM.; BM^N.; L. 05–49; P. 55–; SC.; Z.; **Bl.**U. 62–; **Bn.**U. 59–; **C.**B.; UL.; **Fr.** 05–11: 14–16: 24–; **G.**U. 48–; **Lo.** 26–42: 49–; **Lv.**U. 09–; **O.**R.; Z. 05–24; **Pit.**F. 52–; **Pl.**M.; **Y.** [*C. of:* 20139; *Also supplements*]
    Archiv für **Hydrobiologie** und **Planktonkunde.** *Arch. Hydrobiol. Planktonk.* See 4094.

4095 **Archiv** für **Hygiene** und **Bakteriologie.** München u. Berlin. *Arch. Hyg. Bakt.* [1883–] **L.**H. 89–19: 56–; LI. 83–40: 43; MC. 02–51 imp.; P. 09–31; S. 83–40; SC. 35–40: 50–; TD.; **Abd.**U. 94–52; **Bl.**U.; **C.**PA. 90; UL.; **E.**P.; U.; **G.**U.; **Lv.**U. 83–07; **O.**P. 28–; R. 83–33; **R.**D. 14–44 imp.: 50–; **Y.**

4096 **Archiv** für **Insektenkunde** des **Oberrheingebietes** und der angrenzenden Länder. Freiburg i. B. *Arch. Insektenk. Oberrheingeb.* [1926–30] **L.**BM^N.; EB. [*C. of:* 32288]

4097 **Archiv** für **japanische Chirurgie.** Tokyo. *Arch. jap. Chir.* [1924–] **L.**MA. 52– imp.; MC. 53– imp.; MD. 33–; S. 52–; **Y.**

4098 **Archiv** der **Julius Klaus-Stiftung** für **Vererbungsforschung, Sozialanthropologie** und **Rassenhygiene.** Zürich. *Arch. Julius Klaus-Stift. VererbForsch.* [1925–] **L.**SC.; **Ba.**I.; **C.**A. 46–; GE.; **E.**AG. 48–; U. 48–; **Y.**

4099 Archiv für **Kinderheilkunde.** Stuttgart. *Arch. Kinderheilk.* [1880–] L.MA. 02–14: 28–; MD.; S. 80–40; U. 80–07; **Abd.**R. 46–50; **Bm.**U. 97–05; **Dn.**U. 00–02; E.P.; S. 98–03 imp.; G.U. 25– imp.; **M.**MS. imp.

4100 Archiv zur **Klärung** der **Wünschelrutenfrage.** München. *Arch. Klär. Wünschelrutenfrage* L.P. 31★.

4101 Archiv für **klassifikatorische** und **phylogenetische Entomologie.** Wien. *Arch. klassif. phylogen. Ent.* [1928–30] L.BM^N. imp.; E.

4102 Archiv für **Kleintierzucht.** Berlin. *Arch. Kleintierz.* [1940–42] **Abd.**R. 40; **C.**A.; E.AB. [*C. of:* and *Rec. as:* 4081]

4103 Archiv für **klinische Chirurgie.** Berlin. *Arch. klin. Chir.* [1861–44] L.MD.; S.; UCH. 90–14: 20–28; **Abd.**U.; **Bm.**U. 94–14; **Br.**U. 65–38 imp.; **C.**UL.; **Db.** 66–19 imp.; **Dn.**U. 02–20; E.P.; S.; **G.**F. 61–14; **Ld.**U. 76–07; **Lv.**M. 61–14; **M.**MS. 61–24. [*C. in:* 4104]

4104 Archiv für **klinische Chirurgie** vereinigt mit **Deutsche Zeitschrift** für **Chirurgie.** Berlin. *Arch. klin. Chir.* [1947–] L.MA.; MD.; S. 47–53: 58–; G.U.; **Ld.**U. [*C. of:* 4103 and 16855]

4105 Archiv für **klinische** und **experimentelle Dermatologie.** Wien. *Arch. klin. exp. Derm.* [1956–] L.MA.; MD.; TD.; U.; E.P.; **Ld.**U. 58–; Y. [*C. of:* 4057]

4106 Archiv für **Kreislaufforschung.** Dresden. *Arch. Kreislaufforsch.* [1937–] L.MD. [*Supplement to:* 58694]

4107 Archiv für **Kriminalanthropologie** und **Kriminalistik.** Leipzig. *Arch. KrimAnthrop.* [1898–16] E.S. 05–14 imp. [*C. as:* 4108]

4108 Archiv für **Kriminologie.** Leipzig. *Arch. Kriminol.* [1917–] L.PS. 22–30; E.S. 20–22. [*C. of:* 4107]

4109 Archiv für **Kurzwellen-Technik.** Hamburg. *Arch. Kurzwell.-Tech.* L.P. 55–.

4110 Archiv für **Lagerstättenforschung.** Berlin. *Arch. LagerstättForsch.* [1910–] L.BM.; BM^N.; GL. 41–51; GM.; P.; SC. 36–51; **Br.**U. 44–51; G.U. imp.

4111 Archiv für **Landes-** u. **Volkskunde** der **Provinz Sachsen** nebst angrenzenden Landesteilen. Halle a. S. *Arch. Landes- u. Volksk. Prov. Sachsen* [1891–19] L.BM.; **O.**B. 93–19; G. 93–19.

4112 Archiv des **Landmaschinenwesens.** Technische Schriftenschau. Berlin. *Arch. LandmaschWes.* L.P. 27–44 imp. [*Supplement to:* 52454]

4113 Archiv für **Landtechnik.** Berlin. *Arch. Landtech.* [1959–] L.AM.; P.; **C.**A.; **Sil.**; Y.

4114 Archiv für **Land-** und **Forstwirtschaft.** Wien. *Arch. Land- u. Forstw.* [1883–]

4115 Archiv für **Laryngologie** u. **Rhinologie.** Berlin. *Arch. Lar. Rhinol.* [1894–21] L.MD.; S.; **Cr.**MD. 94–14; **Db.** 01–13; E.P.; S. 20–21; **G.**F.; **Lv.**M. 94–13; **M.**MS. 07–21. [*C. in:* 58649]

4116 Archiv für **Lebensmittelhygiene.** Hannover. *Archiv. Lebensmittelhyg.* [1955–] L.MD.; V.; **R.**D. 55; Y. [*C. of:* 28343]

4117 Archiv für **Lichttherapie** u. verwandte Gebiete. Berlin. *Arch. Lichtther.* [1899–04]

4118 Archiv der **Mathematik.** Karlsruhe, etc. *Arch. Math.* [1948–] L.B. 59–; SC.; U.; UC.; **Bl.**U.; **C.**P.; E.R.; G.U. 60–; **M.**U.; **O.**R.; **Sh.**U.; **Sw.**U. 54–; Y.

4119 Archiv for **Mathematik** og **Naturvidenskab.** Kristiania (Oslo). *Arch. Math. Naturv.* [1876–] L.BM.;

BM^N.; M.; R.; SC. 18–; UC.; Z.; **C.**UL. 76–23; **Db.** 96–; **Dm.** 82–; E.C. 89– imp.; R.; G.U. 99–; **M.**U. 06–23 imp.; **O.**R. 76–01; **Pl.**M. 89–; Y.

4120 Archiv der **Mathematik** u. **Physik.** Leipzig, Berlin. *Arch. Math. Phys.* [1841–20] L.BM. 1843–20; M. 1852–1860; R.; UC. 1841–70; **Bl.**U. 1841–1862; **Br.**U. 1841–98; **C.**UL.; **Db.**; E.U.; G.U.; O.R.

4121 Archiv für **mathematische Logik** und **Grundlagenforschung.** Stuttgart. *Arch. math. Logik GrundlForsch.* [1950–] L.SC. 59–; U.; **Ld.**U. 57–; **O.**B.; Y.

4122 Archiv für **mathematische Wirtschafts-** und **Sozialforschung.** Leipzig. *Arch. math. Wirtsch.- u. Sozialforsch.* [1935–] **C.**UL.; **O.**B.

4123 Archiv Mecklenburgischer Naturforscher. Rostock. *Arch. mecklenb. Naturf.* [1923–] L.BM. 23–24; BM^N.; L.; **C.**P.; E.R. 23: 25–27: 36: 54–.

Archiv für **medizinische Wissenschaften.** Leningrad, Moskau. *See* 4784.

4124 Archiv für **Metall-Finisching.** Saulgau/Württemberg. *Arch. Metall-Finisch.* [1954–58] L.P. [*Published with:* 31494; *C. as:* 20589]

4125 Archiv für **Metallkunde.** Heidelberg. *Arch. Metallk.* [1946–49] L.I.; IC.; NF.; P.; **Bm.**U.; **F.**A.; G.U. [*C. of:* 27686; *C. as:* 57345]

4126 Archiv für **Meteorologie, Geophysik** und **Bioklimatologie.** Wien. *Arch. Met. Geophys. Bioklim.* [1948–]

Ser. A. Meteorologie und Geophysik. L.MO.; SC.; **Db.**; E.U.; Y.

Ser. B. Allgemeine und biologische Klimatologie. L.MO.; SC.; **Db.**; E.U.; Y.

4127 Archiv für **Mikrobiologie.** Berlin, Heidelberg. *Arch. Mikrobiol.* [1930–] L.BM^N.; MY. 48–; SC. 30–43: 49–; **C.**UL.; E.W. 55–; **Fr.** 50–; **G.**T. 53–; U. 61–; **Ld.**U. 62–; **Mi.** 56–; **O.**R.; **R.**D.; U. 52–; **Rt.** 48–; Y. [*Not published* 1944–47]

4128 Archiv für **mikroskopische Anatomie** und **Entwicklungsmechanik.** Bonn. *Arch. mikrosk. Anat. EntwMech.* [1865–25] L.B. 10–21 imp.; BM.; BM^N.; H. 89–92; L.; MD.; S.; SC.; UC.; Z. imp.; **Abd.**U.; **Bl.**U. 97–19 imp.; **Bm.**U. 98–25; **Br.**U. 07–08; **C.**B.; PH. 65–06; UL. 65–22; **Cr.**U. 74–24; **Db.**; **Dn.**U. imp.; E.P.; S. 92–22 imp.; U. 95–25; G.U.; **Ld.**U. 89–25; **Lv.**U. 97–99: 24–25; **M.**MS. 76–92; U.; **N.**U. 65–79; **O.**R.; **Pl.**M. 94–23; **Sa.** [*C. as:* 57615]

4129 Archiv für **Molluskenkunde.** Frankfurt a. M. *Arch. Molluskenk.* [1920–] L.BM^N.; SC. 43–; Z.; **C.**UL.; **Db.**; G.U. 30–; Y. [*C. of:* 34032]

4130 Archiv für **Naturgeschichte.** Berlin. *Arch. Naturgesch.* [1835–44] L.BM.; BM^N.; L. 1835–09; S. 1835–14; SC.; Z. imp.; **Abd.**U. 74–04; **C.**B. 77–05; P. 1835–20 imp.; UL.; **Db.** 1835–1855; E.R. 1860–09; U. 1835–39; G.U. 1835–39 imp.; **O.**H. 1835–1842; R.; **Pl.**M. 32–39; **Sa.** 1835–26. [*From* 1932–44 *forms Abt. B. of:* 58900]

Archiv für die **Naturkunde Estlands.** Tartu. *See* 17478^c.

4132 Archiv für die **Naturkunde Liv-, Est-** u. **Kurlands.** Dorpat. *Arch. Naturk. Liv- Est- u. Kurlands* [1854–05] L.BM. 17–03; BM^N.; GL. 00–05; Z. (biol.): (mineral.) 70–89; E.C.; R. imp. [*C. as:* 4133]

4133 Archiv für die **Naturkunde** des **Ostbaltikums.** Dorpat. *Arch. Naturk. Ostbalt.* [1920–23] L.BM^N.; GL.; Z. 20–22; E.R. [*C. of:* 4132; *C. as:* 17478^c]

4133° **Archiv** für **Naturschutz.** *Arch. NatSchutz* **Y.**

4133° **Archiv** für **Naturschutz** und **Landschaftsforschung.** *Arch. NatSchutz LandschForsch.* **Y.**

4134 **Archiv** für die **Naturwissenschaftliche Landesdurchforschung** von **Böhmen.** Prag. *Arch. naturw. LandDurchforsch. Böhm.* [1869–15] L.BM.; BM^N.; GL. 69–12; GM. 72–12; L.; Z. 69–15 imp.; C.UL.; E.R. 69–15; G.M. 69–13. [*C. as:* 4152]

4135 **Archiv** für **öffentliche Gesundheitspflege** in **Elsass-Lothringen.** Strassburg. *Arch. öff. Gesundh-Pflege Els.-Lothr.* [*C. as:* 50981]

4136 **Archiv** für **Ohrenheilkunde.** Wurzburg, Leipzig. *Arch. Ohrenheilk.* [1864–15] L.MA. 79–07; MD.; S.; UC. 00–09; **Abd.**U. 69–15; **Bm.**U. 90–03; **Db.** 99–12; **E.**P.; S. 07–15 imp.; **G.**F. 99–13 imp.; **M.**U. [*C. as:* 4137]

4137 **Archiv** für **Ohren-, Nasen-** u. **Kehlkopfheilkunde.** Leipzig. *Arch. Ohr.-, Nas.- u. KehlkHeilk.* [1916–] L.MA. 47–; MD.; S. 64–69; **Abd.**U. 16–36; C.UL. 47–; E.P.; S. imp.; G.U. 47–; M.U. [*C. of:* 4136]
  Archiv des **Omsker medizinischen Instituts.** *See* 4786.
  Archiv für **Ophthalmologie.** *See* 1671.

4138 **Archiv** für **Optik.** Leipzig. *Arch. Optik* [1907–08] L.AS.; P.; SC. 08.

4139 **Archiv** für **Orientforschung.** Berlin. *Arch. Orientforsch.* [1926–] C.UL.; Cr.U. 45–; E.U. 52–.

4140 **Archiv** für **Orthopädie, Mechanotherapie** u. **Unfallchirurgie.** Wiesbaden. *Arch. Orthop. Mechanother. Unfallchir.* [1903–17] L.MD. [*C. as:* 4141]

4141 **Archiv** für **orthopädische** und **Unfallchirurgie.** Wiesbaden. *Arch. orthop. Unfallchir.* [1918–] L.MD.; UCH. 27–35; **Y.** [*C. of:* 4140]
  Archiv für **pathologische Anatomie** und **Physiologie.** *See* 56730.

4142 **Archiv** für **Pelzkunde.** Frankfurt a. Main *Arch. Pelzk.* [1951–] L.BM^N.; **Y.**

4143 **Archiv** für **Pflanzenbau.** Berlin. *Arch. PflBau* [1930–34] L.MY. 31–34; **Abs.**A. 30–31; C.UL. 30–32; R.U. 30–32; **Rt.** [*C. of:* 37449]

4144 **Archiv** for **Pharmaci** og **Chemi.** Kjøbenhavn. *Arch. Pharm. Chemi* L.BM. 1844–; PH. 1859–05: 38–; **Y.**

4145 **Archiv** der **Pharmazie** (und **Berichte der Deutschen pharmazeutischen Gesellschaft**). Berlin, Mannheim. *Arch. Pharm., Berl.* [1822–] L.C. 72– imp.; P. 10–23; PH.; SC. 34–44: 50–; TP. 06– imp.; **Bl.**U. 1855–62; **Bm.**T. 35–38; C.CH. 1845–; **Dn.**U. 03–; E.U. 74–; **G.**T. 34–; U. 38–; **Ld.**U. 59 ; **M.**T. 1859–67: 73–91: 93–38: 50–; **N.**U. 50–; **Nw.**A.; O.R. 1835–; **Y.**

4146 **Archiv** für **physikalisch-diätetische Therapie** in der **ärztlichen Praxis.** Berlin. *Arch. phys.-diätet. Ther.* [1899–20] L.MD. 99–11.

4147 **Archiv** für **physikalische Medizin** und **medizinische Technik.** Leipzig. *Arch. phys. Med. med. Tech.* [1905–14] L.MD.; P. 06–14.

4148 **Archiv** für **physikalische Therapie, Balneologie** und **Klimatologie.** Leipzig. *Arch. phys. Ther. Baln. Klim.* [1949–]
  Archiv für **Physiologie.** *See* 4044: *Forms* Physiologische Abteilung.

4149 **Archiv** für **Post** und **Telegraphie.** Berlin. *Arch. Post Telegr.* [1873–40] L.BM. 89–40; P. 89–31. [*C. as:* 38157]

4150 **Archiv** für das **Post-** und **Fernmeldewesen.** Frankfurt. *Arch. Post- u. Fernmeldew.* [1949–] L.P.; **Y.**

4151 **Archiv** na **přírodovědecké prozkoumání Moravy.** Oddêl botanický. v Brně. *Arch. přírodov. Prozk. Moravy Odd. bot.*

4152 **Archiv** pro **přírodovědecký výzkum Čech.** Praha. *Arch. přírodov. Výzk. Čech* [1915–] L.BM.; BM^N. 15–43; L.; C.UL.; E.R. 15–48. [*C. of:* 4134]

4153 **Archiv** für **Protistenkunde.** Jena. *Arch. Protistenk.* [1902–44: 52–] L.BM.; BM^N.; H. 07–24 imp.; L. 02–43; LI. 02–39: 54–; MC. 02–44; MD.; R.; SC.; TD.; UC. 02–39; Z.; **Abd.**U. 21–36; **Bl.**U. 02–11: 61–; **Bm.**U. 02–14; **Bn.**U. 44–; **Br.**U.; C.B.; MO. 02–22; **Db.** 07–14; **Dn.**U. 02–31; E.P.; U.; **Ex.**U.; **Fr.** 02–14: 34–; G.U.; **Ld.**U.; **Lv.**U. imp.; M.U. imp.; O.R.; Pl.M.; **Rt.**; **Y.**

4154 **Archiv** für **Psychiatrie** und **Nervenkrankheiten.** Berlin, etc. *Arch. Psychiat. NervKrankh.* [1868–] L.MA. 38–; MD.; U. 49–; UC. 05–24; **Abd.**U. 68–32; **Bm.**U. 68–85: 01–04: 22–25 imp.; C.PH. 68–05; UL.; **Db.** 96–28; E.P.; U. 68–33; **Ld.**U. 55–; **Lv.**U. 68–04; M.MS. 68–24: 48–; **Nw.**A. 68–81; O.R. 68–33; **Y.**

4155 **Archiv** für **Rassen-** u. **Gesellschaftsbiologie** einschliessend **Rassen-** u. **Gesellschaftshygiene.** Leipzig-Berlin. *Arch. Rass.- u. GesBiol.* [1904–43] L.AN. 04–14: 29; BM. 12–; UC.; **Br.**U. 10–18; C.B.; **Dn.**U. 04–13; **Sa.** 35–37.

4156 **Archiv** für **rationelle Therapie.** Lorch. *Arch. ration. Ther.* [1906–14]

4157 **Archiv** für **Rettungswesen** u. **erste ärztliche Hilfe.** Berlin. *Arch. Rettungsw.* [1912–22]

4158 **Archiv** für **Schiffbau** und **Schiffahrt.** Hamburg. *Arch. Schiffb. Schiff.* [*C. of:* 32274]

4159 **Archiv** für **Schiffs-** u. **Tropenhygiene.** Leipzig. *Arch. Schiffs- u. Tropenhyg.* [1897–40] L.EB. 09–40; H. 33–39; LI. 10–40; MC.; MD. 00–40; S. 09–40; TD.; C.MO.; E.P.; U.; **Lv.**U.; **Sal.** 31–40. [*C. as:* 16830]

4160 **Archiv** für **Schreib-** und **Buchwesen.** Wolfenbüttel. *Arch. Schreib- u. Buchw.* [1927–35] L.P. 27–29.

4161 **Archiv** für **Sexualforschung.** Heidelberg. *Arch. SexForsch.* [1915–16] L.BM.

4162 **Archiv** für **soziale Hygiene** und **Demographie.** Leipzig. *Arch. soz. Hyg. Demogr.* [1911–34] L.MD. 25–34; TD.; E.P. [*C. of:* 33145 *and* 58824]

4163 **Archiv** für **soziale Medizin** und **Hygiene.** Leipzig. *Arch. soz. Med. Hyg.* [1904–05] [*C. of:* 33145; *C. as:* 50375]

4164 **Archiv** für **Sprach-** und **Stimmheilkunde** und **angewandte Phonetik.** Berlin. *Arch. Sprach- u. Stimmheilk.* L.MD. 37–39.

4165 **Archiv** für **Stadthygiene.** Berlin. *Arch. Stadthyg.* L.P. 14*. [*C. of:* 58826; *C. as:* 58688]

4166 **Archiv** für **technisches Messen.** München. *Arch. tech. Messen* [1931–] L.AV. 37– imp.; DI. 47–; EE. imp.; HQ. 49–; P. 32–; SC. imp.; UC. 36–; **F.**A. 49–; **M.**C. 31–39: 52–; **Y.**

4167 **Archiv** für **Tierernährung.** Berlin. *Arch. Tierernähr.* [1950–] **Abd.**R.; C.A.; APH. 50–58; R.D.; U.; **Y.**

4168 **Archiv** für **Tierernährung** und **Tierzucht.** Berlin. *Arch. Tierernähr. Tierz.* [1931–33] L.P. 31; **Abd.**R. 32–33. [*C. of:* 53188]

4169 **Archiv** für **Tierzucht.** Berlin. *Arch. Tierz.* [1958–] E.AB.; R.D.; **Y.**

4170 **Archiv** für **Toxikologie.** Berlin. *Arch. Tox.* [1954–] L.MA.; MD.; C.UL.; E.U.; G.U.; Lv.U.; **Y.** [*C. of:* 48515]

4171 **Archiv** für **Unfallheilkunde, Gewerbehygiene** u. **Gewerbekrankheiten.** Stuttgart. *Arch. Unfallheilk. Gewerbehyg.* L.S. 96–01.

4172 **Archiv** für **Verdauungskrankheiten.** Berlin. *Arch. VerdauKrankh.* [1895–38] L.MD. imp.; UC. 95–05; **Br.**U. 98–00; **Db.** 07–38; E.P.; G.U. 04–38; M.MS. 04–24; O.R. 95–03. [*C. as:* 20683]

4173 **Archiv** des **Vereins** der **Freunde** der **Naturgeschichte** in **Mecklenburg.** Güstrow. *Arch. Ver. Freunde Naturg. Mecklenb.* [1847–40] L.BM. 1847–22; BMᴺ.; L. 86–27 imp.; Abs.U. 27; C.P. 25–40; UL. 1847–65; Lv.U. 82–40 imp. [*Replaced by:* 4079]

4174 **Archiv** des **Vereins** für **Siebenbürgische Landeskunde.** Hermannstadt. *Arch. Ver. siebenb. Landesk.* L.BM. 64–; BMᴺ. 1843–1851.

4175 **Archiv** für **vergleichende Ophthalmologie.** Leipzig. *Arch. vergl. Ophthal.* [1909–14] L.MD.; C.PH.

4176 **Archiv** für **Virusforschung.** *Arch. Virusforsch.* [1939–] L.MC.

4177 **Archiv** für **Völkerkunde.** Wien. *Arch. Völkerk.* [1946–] L.AN.; BM.; HO.; **Bm.**U.

4178 **Archiv** für **Wärmewirtschaft** und **Dampfkesselwesen.** Verein Deutscher Ingenieure. Berlin. *Arch. Wärmew. DampfkWes.* [1920–44] L.P. 21–44; G.U. 33–44 imp. [*C. in:* 8705]

4178ᵃ **Archiv** und **Wissenschaft.** München. *Arch. Wiss.* [1957–] O.B.

4179 **Archiv** für **wissenchaftliche Botanik.** Berlin. *Arch. wiss. Bot.* [1925] L.BMᴺ.; K.; C.BO.; G.U.; R.U. [*C. as:* 37873]

4180 **Archiv** für **wissenschaftliche** u. **praktische Tierheilkunde.** Berlin. *Arch. wiss. prakt. Tierheilk.* [1875–44] L.BM.; LI. 26–35; MD.; S. 75–32; TD. 99–31; V.; Abd.U. 86–40; C.MO. 75–94; UL. 04–44; V. 36–40: 44; Lv.U. 75–09; M.MS. 06–24; O.R.; W. 04–44.

4181 **Archiv** der **Wissenschaftlichen Gesellschaft** für **Land-** und **Forstwirtschaft.** Freiburg i. B. *Arch. wiss. Ges. Land- u. Forstw.* [1949–] C.A. 49–50; O.F.

4182 **Archiv** für **Zahnheilkunde.** Dresden. *Arch. Zahnheilk.* [1920–21]

Archiv und **Zeitschrift** für **Chirurgie.** *See* 4104.

4183 **Archiv** für **Zellforschung.** Leipzig. *Arch. Zellforsch.* [1908–23] L.L.; SC.; Z.; Ba.I.; C.B.; BO. 08–17; E.U.; G.U.; Lv.U. 14–15; O.R.; Pl.M. 08–20. [*C. as:* 58905]

4184 **Archiva biologica hungarica.** Tihany. *Archiva biol. hung.* [1947–48] L.BMᴺ.; L.; LI.; MC.; Z.; C.A.; E.R.; Fr. 48; O.AP.; Pl.M.; Rt. [*C. of:* 3886; *C. as:* 2797]

4185 **Archiva cardio-rheumatológica hispanica.** Barcelona. *Archiva cardio-rheum. hisp.*

4186 **Archiva medica belgica.** Bruxelles. *Archiva med. belg.* [1946–59] L.; MA.; MD.; SH. (1 yr); TD.; Abd.R.; Bl.U.; Br.U. 50–59; Db.; Ld.U.; Nw.A.

Archiva veterinară. Bucureşti. *See* 4755.
Archive. *See* **Archives.**

4187 **Archives** de l'agriculture du **Nord** de la **France.** Lille. *Archs Agric. N. Fr.*

4188 **Archives** d'anatomie, d'histologie et d'embryologie. Strasbourg. *Archs Anat. Histol. Embryol.* [1922–] L.S. 22–58; UC.; Z. imp.; Bm.U.; C.AN.; E.U. 33–; O.R.; **Y.**

4189 **Archives** d'anatomie microscopique. Paris. *Archs Anat. microsc.* [1897–40] L.BM.; BMᴺ.; SC. 33–40; UC.; Z. 23–39; Br.U. 20–23; C.B.; UL. 20–40; Db. 20–28; E.P.; U. 12–23; G.U. 03–40; M.MS.; O.R.; Pl.M. 09–10. [*C. as:* 4190]

4190 **Archives** d'anatomie microscopique et de morphologie expérimentale. Paris. *Archs Anat. microsc. Morph. exp.* [1946–] L.BM.; BMᴺ.; MA. 48–; SC.; UC.; Z.; Bl.U. 56–; Bn.U. 48–; C.B.; UL.; E.P.; G.U.; M.MS.; N.U. 58–; O.R.; **Y.** [*C. of:* 4189]

Archives d'anatomie pathologique. *See* 37227°.

4191 **Archives. Andrew Todd McClintock Memorial Foundation** for the **Study** of **Diseases** of the **Alimentary Canal.** Wilkes-Barre. *Archs Andrew Todd McClintock Fdn* [1925] L.MA.; S.; Abd.U.; M.MS.

4192 **Archives** d'anthropologie criminelle de **médecine légale** et de **psychologie normale** et **pathologique.** Lyon. *Archs Anthrop. crim.* [1886–14] L.BM.; E.P.

4193 **Archives** of **Antibiotics.** Kyoto. *Archs Antibiot., Kyoto* [1947–53]

4194 **Archives balkaniques** de **médecine, chirurgie** et leurs **specialités.** Paris. *Archs balkan. Méd. Chir.* [1939–] L.S. 39–40.

4195 **Archives belges** de **dermatologie** et de **syphiligraphie.** Bruxelles. *Archs belg. Derm. Syph.* [1938–] L.MA. 47–; MD.; G.U. 52–.

4196 **Archives belges** de **médecine militaire.** Bruxelles. *Archs belg. Méd. milit.* [1848–14] [*C. as:* 4290]

4197 **Archives belges** de **médecine sociale, hygiène, médecine** du **travail** et **médecine légale.** Bruxelles. *Archs belg. Méd. soc.* [1941–] L.H. 46–; MA. 46–; SH. (1 yr); TD.; Bl.U. 61–; **Y.** [*C. of:* 4287]

4198 **Archives belges** du **Service** de **santé** de l'armée. Liége. *Archs belg. Serv. Santé Armée* [1938–40] L.MA.; MD.; Br.U. [*C. of:* 4290; *C. as:* 4361]

4199 **Archives** of **Biochemistry.** New York. *Archs Biochem.* [1942–51] L.C.; CB.; IC.; LI.; MD.; P. 48–51; SC.; TD. 50–51; U. 45: 47–51; UC.; UCH.; Abd.R.; U.; Bl.U.; Bm.U.; Bn.U. 46–51; Br.A. 49; C.A.; APH.; BI.; CH.; R. 48–51; Db.; Dn.U.; E.U.; Ep.D.; G.U. 43–51; Je. 48–51; Ld.U.; W. 43–51; M.MS.; Md.H. 42: 49–51; N.U.; Nw.A. 43–51; O.BI.; PH.; R.; R.D.; U.; W. 48–51; Rt.; Sa.; Sal.F. 48–51; Sh.U.; W. [*C. as:* 4200]

4200 **Archives** of **Biochemistry** and **Biophysics.** New York. *Archs Biochem. Biophys.* [1952–] L.B. 60–; BM.; C.; CB.; IC.; LI.; MC.; MD.; P.; QM. 58–; SC.; TD.; U.; UC.; UCH.; Abd.R.; U.; Ba.I.; Bl.U.; Bm.U.; Bn.U.; C.A.; APH.; BI.; CH.; R.; Db.; Dn.U.; E.U.; Ep.D.; G.U.; H.U. 52–; Je.; Ld.U.; W.; M.MS.; U. 58–; Md.H.; N.U.; Nw.A.; O.BI.; PH.; R.; R.D.; U.; W.; Rt.; Sa.; Sal.F.; Sh.U.; Sw.U.; W.; **Y.** [*C. of:* 4199]

Archives of **Biological Sciences.** Belgrade. *See* 4745.

4200° **Archives** de **biochimie** et **cosmétologie.** *Archs Biochim. Cosm.* **Y.**

4201 **Archives** de **biologie.** Paris, etc. *Archs Biol., Paris* [1880–] **L.**B. 36–40 imp.; BM.; BM^N.; L.; MC. 34–40: 46–; MD. 08–; R. 80–39; RI. 80–29; S. 80–50; SC.; UC.; Z.; **Bm.**U. 40–; **Bn.**U. 23–; **C.**B. 80–33; P. 26–; UL.; **Cr.**U. 28–39: 55–; **Db.**; **Dn.**U. 84–09 imp.; **E.**P.; R.; U.; **Ex.**U. 36–; **Ld.**U.; **Lv.**U.; **M.**U.; **Nw.**A. 39–; **O.**R.; **Pl.**M.; **Sa.** 80–35; **Y.**

Archives de **biologie médicale.** *See* 37227°.

Archives de **biologie** de la **Société** des **sciences** et des **lettres** de **Varsovie.** *See* 4707.

4202 **Archives** de **biothérapie.** Paris. *Archs Biothér.*

Archives bohèmes de **médecine.** *See* 48623.

Archives bohèmes de **médecine clinique.** *See* 48620.

4203 **Archives** de **botanique. Bulletin mensuel.** Caen. *Archs Bot. Bull. mens.* [1927–30] **L.**BM^N.; K.; L. 28–30; **C.**UL.; **E.**B.; **M.**U. 27–29 imp.

4204 **Archives** de **botanique. Mémoires.** Caen. *Archs Bot. Mém.* [1927–36] **L.**BM^N.; K.; L. 28–36; **C.**UL.; **M.**U. 27–30 imp.; **E.**B.

4205 **Archives** of **British Columbia.** Victoria, B.C. *Archs Br. Columb.* **L.**BM^N. 14–31.

4206 **Archives** of the **Cambridge Forestry Association.** Cambridge. *Archs Camb. For. Ass.* [1919–20] **L.**BM.; **Bm.**U. 20; **C.**P.; UL.; **O.**R. [*C. as:* 25733]

4207 **Archives** of **Clinical Cancer Research.** New York. *Archs clin. Cancer Res.* [1925–30]

4208 **Archives** of **Clinical Oral Pathology.** New York. *Archs clin. oral Path.* [1937–40] **L.**D.; **Br.**U.

4209 **Archives cliniques, radiologiques** et **thérapeutiques** de **rhumatologie.** Lyon. *Archs clin. radiol. thér. Rhum.* [1936–38] **L.**MA.; MD. [*Replaced by:* 4352]

Archives of **Coffee Cultivation.** Djakarta. *See* 3944.

4210 **Archives** of **Criminal Psychodynamics.** Washington, D.C. *Archs. crim. Psychodyn.* [1955–] **L.**MA.; **Dn.**U.

Archives of **Criminology** and **Forensic Medicine.** Kharkov. *See* 4783.

Archives de **dermatologie** et **syphiligraphie.** Istanbul. *See* 16607.

4211 **Archives** of **Dermatology.** New York, etc. *Archs Derm.* [1960–] **L.**CB.; MA.; MD.; RA.; TD.; U.; UCH.; **Abd.**U.; **Bl.**U.; **Bm.**U.; **Br.**U.; **C.**UL.; **Cr.**MD.; **Db.**; **Dn.**U.; **E.**P.; U.; **G.**F.; T.; U. imp.; **Ld.**U.; **Lv.**M.; U.; **M.**MS.; **Nw.**A.; **O.**R.; **Sh.**U.; **Y.** [*C. of:* 69]

4212 **Archives** of **Dermatology** and **Syphilology.** New York, etc. *Archs Derm. Syph.* [1920–50] **L.**CB. 46–50; MA.; MD.; RA. 42–50; TD.; U. 50; UCH.; **Abd.**U. 46–50; **Bl.**U. 29–50; **Bm.**U. 44–50; **Br.**U. imp.; **C.**UL.; **Cr.**MD. 31–50; **Db.**; **Dn.**U. 48–50; **E.**P.; S. 20: 22; U. 27–50; **G.**F. 21–50 imp.; T. 46–50 imp.; **Ld.**U.; **Lv.**M. 26–50 imp.; U.; **M.**MS. 23–50; **Nw.**A. 45–50; **O.**R. 32–50; **Sh.**U. 44–50. [*C. of:* 25869; *C. as:* 70]

4213 **Archives dermato-syphiligraphiques** de la **Clinique** de l'**Hôpital Saint-Louis.** Paris. *Archs dermatosyph. Clin. Hôp. S-Louis* [1929–] **L.**MD.

4214 **Archives** of **Diagnosis.** New York. *Archs Diagn.* [1908–22] **L.**MD. 12–15; **Br.**U. 13–15; **M.**MS. 20.

4215 **Archives** of **Disease** in **Childhood.** London. *Archs Dis. Childh.* [1926–] **L.**BM.; GH.; H. 38–; LI. 36–; MA.; MD.; S.; TD.; U. 49–; UCH.; **Abd.**R. 31–32: 37–; U. 27–; **Abs.**N.; **Bl.**U.; **Bm.**U.; **Br.**U.; **C.**UL.; **Cr.**MD.;

MS. 31–; **Db.** 33–; **Dn.**U.; **E.**A.; S.; U.; **G.**F. 26– imp.; PH.; **Ld.**U.; **Lv.**M.; P. 56–; **M.**MS.; **Nw.**A.; **O.**R.; **Sh.**U. 45–; **Y.**

4216 **Archives** de **Doyen;** revue médico-chirurgicale illustrée. Paris. *Archs Doyen* [1910–12] **L.**S. 10–11; SC. 10–11.

4217 **Archives** d'**électricité médicale,** etc. Paris. *Archs Élect. méd.* [1893–47] **L.**MD.; P. 10–38; RA. 23–29; S. 08–14; **E.**P. 97–15. [*Suspended* 1914–25; *C. in:* 26760]

4218 **Archives** of **Electrology** and **Radiology.** Chicago. *Archs Electrol. Radiol.* [1904] [*C. of:* 1946]

4219 **Archives** of **Environmental Health.** *Archs envir. Hlth* [1950–] **L.**AM.; AV.; C.; CB.; H.; MA.; MC.; MD.; P.; PR.; SH.; TD.; **Bl.**U.; **Bm.**C. 52–54; **Dn.**U. 53–54; **E.**P.; U.; **Ep.**D.; **G.**U.; **Ld.**U.; **M.**C.; MS.; **Nw.**A.; **Ste.**; **Wd.**; **Y.** [*C. of:* 72]

4220 **Archives** de la **flore jurassienne.** Besançon. *Archs Flore jurass.* [1900–06] **L.**BM^N.; K.

4221 **Archives françaises** de **pathologie générale** et **expérimentale** et d'**anatomie pathologique.** Paris. *Archs fr. Path. gén. exp.* [1922–24]

4222 **Archives françaises** de **pédiatrie.** Paris. *Archs fr. Pédiat.* [1942–] **L.**MA. 44–; MD.; S.; **Bl.**U. 58–; **Bm.**U.; **Cr.**MD. 53– imp. [*Replaces:* 47203]

4223 **Archives franco-belges** de **chirurgie.** Bruxelles. *Archs fr.-belg. Chir.* [1916–36] **L.**MD. 21–34; S. 21–36 imp.; **Br.**U. 23–36 imp. [*C. of:* 4342]

4224 **Archives** of **General Psychiatry.** Chicago. *Archs gen. Psychiat.* [1960–] **L.**GH.; MA.; MC.; MD.; OP.; PS.; S.; U.; UC.; **Abd.**U.; **Bl.**U.; **Bm.**U.; **Br.**U.; **C.**APH.; PH.; PS.; **Cr.**MD.; **Db.**; **Dn.**U.; **E.**U.; **G.**F.; **Ld.**U.; **M.**MS.; **Nw.**A.; **O.**PH.; R.; **Sh.**U.; **Y.** [*C. of:* 71]

4225 **Archives générales** de **chirurgie.** Paris. *Archs gén. Chir.* [1907–14] **L.**MD.; S. 08–14; **Bm.**U. 07–13 imp.

4226 **Archives générales françaises** de **thérapeutique physique.** Paris. *Archs gén. fr. Thér. phys.* [1904–12] **L.**MD. [*C. in:* 47522]

4227 **Archives générales** d'**hydrologie.** Paris. *Archs gén. Hydrol.* [1890–08]

4228 **Archives générales** de **kinésithérapie.** Paris. *Archs gén. Kinésithér.* [*C. of:* 47119]

4229 **Archives générales** de **médecine.** Paris. *Archs gén. Méd.* [1823–14] **L.**GH. 1845–11; MA.; MD.; S.; U. 80–05; **Abd.**U. 1828–11 imp.; **C.**UL.; **Db.** imp.; **Dn.**U. 03–13; **E.**P.; S. 1858–13; **G.**F. 90–14; **Ld.**U. imp.; **Lv.**M. 1823–10; **M.**MS.; **Nw.**A. 1849–81; **O.**R. 1854–14; **Sa.** 1823–82.

4230 **Archives géologiques** du **Cambodge,** du **Laos** et du **Viet Nam.** Saigon. *Archs géol. Cambodge, Laos Viet Nam* [1952] **L.**GM. [*C. as:* 4231]

4231 **Archives géologiques** du **Viêt-Nam.** Saigon. *Archs géol. Viêt-Nam* [1953–] **L.**BM^N. 61–; GL.; GM.; **Y.** [*C. of:* 4230]

Archives d'**histoire** de la **médecine turque.** *See* 55341.

4232 **Archives** d'**histoire naturelle.** Paris. *Archs Hist. nat., Paris* [1925–35] **L.**Z.

4233 **Archives** d'**histoire naturelle.** Bulletin mensuel de la Société 'la Ségusia'. Lyon. *Archs Hist. nat., Lyon*

4234 **Archives** for **History** of **Exact Sciences.** *Archs Hist. exact Sci.* [1960–] **L.**sc.; **Bl.**U.; **G.**U.; **Ld.**U.; **Y.**

4235 **Archives** de l'**horlogerie.** Bienne. *Archs Horlog.* [1925–] **L.**P. 25–40; 52–.

4236 **Archives hospitalières.** Paris. *Archs hosp.* [1933] **L.**MA. [*C. of:* 10460]

4237 **Archives hospitalières.** Paris. *Archs hosp.* **L.**H. 47–48; **Nw.**A. 35–46 imp.
Archives d'**hydrobiologie** et d'**ichthyologie.** Suwalki. *See* 4699.
Archives d'**hygiène.** Athènes. *See* 4737.

4238 **Archives** of **Industrial Hygiene** and **Occupational Medicine.** Baltimore. *Archs ind. Hyg.* [1950] **L.**AV.; C.; MA.; MC.; MD.; P.; PR.; TD.; **Bl.**U.; **Br.**U.; **Cr.**MD.; **E.**U.; **G.**U.; **Ld.**P.; U.; **M.**C.; D.; MS.; **Nw.**A.; **Sh.**S.; **Ste.**; **Wd.** [*Replaces:* 26159 and 35806; *C. as:* 73]

4239 **Archives** de l'**Ingénieur-Conseil.** Paris. *Archs Ingr-Cons.* **L.**P. 02–.

4240 **Archives** de l'**Institut botanique** de l'**Université** de **Liége.** Bruxelles, etc. *Archs Inst. bot. Univ. Liége* [1897–] **L.**BMᴺ.; K. 97–45; L. 07–; UC. 34–; **Bm.**U. 29–39; **Bn.**U. 28–51; **Br.**U. 27: 38; **C.**BO. 97–27: 32–34; P.; **Db.**; **E.**B.; **Ld.**U. 28–; **M.**U. 97–27; **N.**U.; **O.**BO. 97–27: 38; **Rt.** 28–; **Sa.** 00–06: 27; **Y.**

4241 **Archives. Institut grand-ducal** de **Luxembourg.** Luxembourg. *Archs Inst. gr.-duc. Luxemb.* [1906–]
Section des sciences naturelles, physiques et mathématiques. **L.**BM. 51–; BMᴺ. 31– imp.; R.; **E.**R.; **Lv.**U. 17; **Y.** [*C. of:* 41058]

4242 **Archives** de l'**Institut** d'**Hessarek.** Téhéran. *Archs Inst. Hessarek* [1939–] **L.**BMᴺ. 40–; EB. 46–; MA. 53– imp.; MC. 46–; TD. 46–; V. 46–; **Rt.** 46–; **W.**; **Y.**

4243 **Archives** de l'**Institut** de **médecine légale** et de **médecine sociale** de **Lille.** Lille. *Archs Inst. Méd. lég. Lille* **L.**TD. 47.
Archives de l'**Institut** de **microbiologie** et **hygiène** d'**Azerbaidjan.** *See* 4781.

4244 **Archives** de l'**Institut** de **paléontologie humaine. Mémoires.** Paris. *Archs Inst. Paléont. hum.* [1927–] **L.**AN.; BM.; BMᴺ.; **Abd.**U. imp.; **Bm.**U.; **C.**UL.

4245 **Archives** de l'**Institut Pasteur** d'**Algérie.** Alger. *Archs Inst. Pasteur Algér.* [1923–] **L.**BMᴺ.; EB.; LI.; MA. 28–30 imp.; MC. imp.; MD.; SC. 47–; TD.; **Bm.**U. 23–30; **C.**MO.; PA. 23–51 imp.; V. 52–; **Lv.**U.; **O.**P. 27–; **W.** 33– imp.; **Y.**

4246 **Archives** de l'**Institut Pasteur** de la **Guyane française.** Cayenne. *Archs Inst. Pasteur Guyane fr.* [1954–] **L.**BMᴺ.; EB.; P.; TD.; **Abd.**R. 56–58. [*C. of:* 4247]

4247 **Archives** de l'**Institut Pasteur** de la **Guyane** et du **territoire** de l'**Inini.** Cayenne. *Archs Inst. Pasteur Guyane Terr. Inini* [1951–53] **L.**BMᴺ.; EB.; TD. [*C. of:* 41070; *C. as:* 4246]

4248 **Archives** de l'**Institut Pasteur hellénique.** Athènes. *Archs Inst. Pasteur hellén.* [1923–31: 55–] **L.**MC. 23–31; TD. 23–30; **Ld.**U. 55–; **Y.**

4249 **Archives** de l'**Institut Pasteur** de l'**Iran.** Téhéran *Archs Inst. Pasteur Iran* [1948–] **L.**BMᴺ. 48; TD.

4250 **Archives** de l'**Institut Pasteur** du **Maroc.** Casablanca. *Archs Inst. Pasteur Maroc* [1932–] **L.**EB.; TD. 44– imp.; **C.**MO.; **W.** 38–.

4251 **Archives** de l'**Institut Pasteur** de la **Martinique.** Fort-de-France. *Archs Inst. Pasteur Martinique* [1948–] **L.**H.; TD.

4252 **Archives** de l'**Institut Pasteur** de **Tananarive.** Tananarive. *Archs Inst. Pasteur Tananarive*

4253 **Archives** de l'**Institut Pasteur** de **Tunis.** Tunis. *Archs Inst. Pasteur Tunis* [1906–] **L.**AM. 55– imp.; BMᴺ.; EB. imp.; LI. 06: 12: 17–39: 40–41; MA. 29–; MC. 07– imp.; MD.; R. 06–42; S. 26–42; SC. 24–; TD.; UC. 24–42 v. imp.; **Bm.**U. 25–42; **C.**MO. 07–; PA. imp.; V. 55–; **Lv.**U.; **O.**P. 25–; **Sal.** 40–42; **W.** 32–42; **Y.** [> 4257, 1921–22; *Suspended* 1944–54]

4254 **Archives** de l'**Institut prophylactique.** Paris. *Archs Inst. prophyl.* [1929–] **L.**MD.; TD. 29–39 v. imp.; **Dn.**U. 38–39 imp.
Archives de l'**Institut r.** de **bactériologie Camara Pestana.** *See* 4637.

4255 **Archives** de l'**Institut** du **radium** de l'**Université** de **Paris** et de la **Fondation Curie.** Paris. *Archs Inst. Radium Univ. Paris* **L.**MA. 27–39.
Archives de l'**Institut Razi.** *Archs Inst. Razi See* 4242.

4256 **Archives** de l'**Institut** de **recherches agronomiques** de l'**Indochine.** Saïgon. *Archs Inst. Rech. agron. Indochine* [1950] **C.**A.; **Md.**H. [*C. as:* 4350]

4257 **Archives** des **Instituts Pasteur** de l'**Afrique** du **Nord.** Tunis. *Archs Insts Pasteur Afr. N.* [1921–23] **L.**BMᴺ.; EB.; MC.; MD.; R.; TD.; **Bm.**U.; **C.**MD.; MO.; **Lv.**U. [*C. of:* and *Rec. as:* 4253]

4258 **Archives** des **Instituts Pasteur** d'**Indo-Chine.** Saïgon. *Archs Insts Pasteur Indo-Chine* [1925–44] **L.**BMᴺ. 25–41; EB.; LI. 25–38; MC. 25–41; MD.; TD.; **Bm.**U.; **Cr.**MD. 25–32 imp.; **Lv.**U.
Archives of **Interamerican Rheumatology.** *See* 64.

4259 **Archives** of **Internal Medicine.** Chicago. *Archs intern. Med.* [1908–50: 60–] **L.**C. 26–50: 60–; GH. 19–50: 60–; MA.; MC. 17–50: 60–; PH. 38–50: 60–; S. 14–50: 60–; TD.; UC. 10–50: 60–; UCH. 19–50: 60–; **Abd.**R.; U. 23–50: 60–; **Bl.**U. imp.; **Br.**U. imp.; **C.**PA. imp.; **Cr.**MD. 12–50: 60–; **Db.** 12–50: 60–; **Dn.**U. 31–50: 60–; **E.**P.; U. 26–50: 60–; **G.**F.; U.; **Ld.**U. 09–50: 60; **Lv.**M. 23–50: 60–; U. 13–50: 60–; **M.**MS.; **Nw.**A. 17–50: imp: 60–; **O.**R.; **Sh.**U. 17–50: 60–; **Y.** [>74, 1951–60]

4260 **Archives internationales** des **brucelloses.** Ardèche. *Archs int. Brucell.* [1938–] **L.**MA. 38; TD.

4261 **Archives internationales** de **chirurgie.** Gand. *Archs int. Chir.* [1903–14] **G.**F. 03–08.
Archives internationales d'**ethnographie.** *See* 24004.

4262 **Archives internationales** d'**histoire** des **sciences.** Paris. *Archs int. Hist. Sci.* [1947–] **L.**BM.; BMᴺ. 56–; MA.; MD.; P.; R.; SC.; U. 58–; UC.; **Bl.**U. imp.; **Bm.**U.; **C.**UL.; **E.**R. 47–55; **Ex.**U. 56–; **G.**U.; **Ld.**U.; **M.**U.; **N.**U. 56–; **O.**R.; **Sw.**U. 48–55 imp.; **Y.** [*C. of:* 3941]
Archives internationales d'**hygiène scolaire.** *See* 23830.

4263 **Archives internationales** de **laryngologie,** d'**otologie** et de **rhinologie.** Paris. *Archs int. Lar. Otol. Rhinol.* [1887–30] **L.**D. 28–30; MD. 98–30 imp.; S.; **Br.**U. 22–23; **E.**S. 22–30; **G.**F. 87–14: 22–30; **O.**R. 92–93. [*C. in:* 2879]

4264 **Archives internationales** de **médecine expérimentale.** Liége. *Archs int. Méd. exp.* [1924–46] **L.**MD.; TD. 30–39; **C.**PA. 24–39. [*C. in:* 47075]

4265 **Archives internationales** de **médecine légale.** Liége, Bruxelles. *Archs int. Méd. lég.* [1924–46] [*C. in:* 4197]

4266 **Archives internationales** de **neurologie.** Paris. *Archs int. Neurol.* [1910–] **L.**BM.; MA. 45–; MD. 11–25 imp.; S.; **Abd.**U. 10–32; **E.**P.; **M.**MS. 10–14. [*C. of:* 4311]

4267 **Archives internationales** de **pharmacodynamie** et de **thérapie.** Bruxelles–Paris., Gand. *Archs int. Pharmacodyn. Thér.* [1895–] **L.**C. 38–40 imp.; KC. 56–; MA. 45–; MC. 95–40: 55–; MD.; P. 56–; S. 95–18: 55–; SC. 35–; UC.; **Abd.**U.; **Br.**U. 49–; **C.**APH. 50–; PA. 95–02: 08–13; PH. 03–07 imp.: 25–; UL.; **Cr.**MD imp.; **Dn.**U. 99–; **E.**P. 25–; U.; **G.**U.; **Ld.**U. 36–; **M.**MS. 95–18; **O.**R.; **Sh.**U. 59–; **Y.**

Archives internationales de **photogrammétrie.** See 24006.

4268 **Archives internationales** de **physiologie.** Liége. et Paris. *Archs int. Physiol.* [1904–54] **L.**MA. 49–54; MC.; MD.; SC. 30–54; U. 40–54; UC. 04–40; **Abd.**U.; **Bm.**U. 46–54; **C.**APH. 30–54; P. 22–54; PH.; **Db.**; **Dn.**U. 04–29; **E.**P.; U.; **G.**U. 49–54; **Ld.**U. 27–54; **Lv.**U.; **M.**MS.; **O.**R.; **Pl.**M. 27–54. [*C. as:* 4269]

4269 **Archives internationales** de **physiologie** et de **biochimie.** Liège, Paris. *Archs int. Physiol. Biochim.* [1955–] **L.**MA.; MC.; MD.; S.; U.; **Abd.**U.; **Bm.**U.; **C.**APH.; P.; PH.; **Db.**; **E.**P.; U.; **G.**U.; **Ld.**U.; **Lv.**U.; **M.**MS.; **O.**R.; **Pl.**M.; **Y.** [*C. of:* 4268]

4270 **Archives italiennes** de **biologie.** Pisa, Turin. *Archs ital. Biol.* [1882–36: 57–] **L.**BM[N]. 82–11; LI.; MC. 03–24 imp.: 57–; MD.; S. 82–18; SC. 10–13: 57–; UC.; **Abd.**U. 08–12: 27–; **Bm.**U. 57–; **C.**APH. 59–; PH. 82–19; UL.; **Db.**; **Dn.**U. 90–16 imp.; **E.**P.; R.; U. 82–25: 57–; **G.**U.; **Ld.**U. 57–; **Lv.**U. 82–31; **M.**MS. 05–15: 57–; **O.**R.; **Y.** [>35350, 1938; 47068, 1938–39; and 47826, 1940]

4271 **Archives des laboratoires** des **hôpitaux d'Alger.** *Archs Labs Hôp. Alger* [*C. as:* 47396]

4272 **Archives des maladies** de l'**appareil digestif** et de la **nutrition.** Paris. *Archs Mal. Appar. dig.* [1907–] **L.**MA. 38–; MD. 21–; TD. 44–49; **Bl.**U. 28–40 imp.; **Lv.**U. 08–12 imp.; **M.**MS.; **O.**R. 49–.

4273 **Archives des maladies** du **cœur,** des **vaisseaux** et du **sang.** Paris. *Archs Mal. Cœur* [1908–] **L.**GH.; MA. 29–40: 45–; MD.; S. 11–; U. 50–; UCH. 48–; **Br.**U. 29–; **C.**PA. 08–17 imp.; **Cr.**MD. 22–50 imp.; **Db.** 46–47; **E.**P. 08–13: 28– imp.; **G.**F. 08–39: 59–; **Lv.**M. 08–26; **M.**MS. 46–49: 56–; **Nw.**A. 51–; **O.**R.; **Y.**

4274 **Archives des maladies professionelles** de **médecine** du **travail** et de **sécurité sociale.** Paris. *Archs Mal. prof. Méd. trav.* [1938–] **L.**MA.; MD. 38–39; TD.; **Ld.**U. 39–53; **Y.**

4275 **Archives des maladies** des **reins** et des **organes génito-urinaires.** Paris. *Archs Mal. Reins* [1922–36] **L.**MD.; **Cr.**MD. 22–24.

4276 **Archives marocaines.** Paris. *Archs maroc.* [1904–34] **L.**BM.; G. 04–06 imp.; **G.**U.; **O.**B.

Archives of Mechanical Engineering. Warsaw. See 4691.

4277 **Archives** de **médecine.** Athènes. *Archs Méd., Athènes* **L.**TD. 11–19 imp.

4278 **Archives** de **médecine** et de **chirurgie spéciales.** Paris. *Archs Méd. Chir. spéc.* [1900–10]

4279 **Archives** de **médecine** des **enfants.** Paris. *Archs Méd. Enf.* [1898–] **L.**MD.; S. 08–; **E.**P.; **G.**F. 98–40; U. 06–28; **Lv.**M. 21–38 imp.

4280 **Archives** de **médecine expérimentale** et d'**anatomie pathologique.** Paris. *Archs Méd. exp. Anat. path.* [1889–19] **L.**LI. 01–04; MC.; MD.; S.; **Abd.**U. 15–19; **C.**PA. 95–17; **Db.**; **Dn.**U.; **E.**P. 89–16; U.; **G.**U.; **Ld.**U.; **Lv.**U. imp.; **M.**MS. 89–16; **Nw.**A.; **O.**R.

4281 **Archives** de **médecine génerale** et **coloniale.** Marseille. *Archs Méd. gén. colon.* [1932–39] **L.**MD. 35–39; TD. [*C. of:* 47406; *C. as:* 4282]

4282 **Archives** de **médecine générale** et **tropicale.** Marseille. *Archs Méd. gén. trop.* [1950–] **L.**MA.; MD.; TD. [*C. of:* 4281]

4283 **Archives** de **médecine navale.** Paris. *Archs Méd. nav.* [1864–10] **L.**BM. 71–10; S.; TD. 77: 89–10; **E.**P.; U. 98–02; **Lv.**U. [*C. as:* 4285]

4284 **Archives** de **médecine** et de **pharmacie militaires.** Paris. *Archs Méd. Pharm. milit.* [1883–35] **L.**BM. 83–19; MD. 08–35; S. 89–35; TD. 13–35; **Br.**U. 19–35 imp. [*C. as:* 47567]

4285 **Archives** de **médecine** et de **pharmacie navales.** Paris. *Archs Méd. Pharm. nav.* [1911–40] **L.**BM.; MD. 11–19: 25–40; S. 11–39; TD. 11–36; **E.**P.; **Lv.**U. [*C. of:* 4283; *C. as:* 47388]

4286 **Archives** de **médecine sociale.** Paris. *Archs Méd. soc.* [1945–51] **L.**H. 47–49; MA.; MD.; SH.; TD.; U. 48–51; **Abd.**R. 47; **C.**MD. 47–51; **Nw.**A. 48–50; **O.**R. 49–51.

4287 **Archives** de **médecine sociale** et d'**hygiène** et **Revue** de **pathologie** et de **physiologie** du **travail.** Bruxelles. *Archs Méd. soc. Hyg.* [1938–40] **L.**H.; MA.; TD.; **Bm.**U; **Y.** [*C. as:* 4197]

4288 **Archives of Medical Hydrology.** London. *Archs med. Hydrol.* [1922–] **L.**BM.; GH. 25–37; GL. 25–28; MD.; S. 22–39; TD. 22–39; **Abs.**N.; **Bm.**U. 23–; **Br.**U.; **Db** 29–; **Dn.**U. 25–39 imp.; **Ld.**U. 25–39; **Lv.**U. 30–; **M.**MS. 22–38 imp.; **Nw.**A. 26–39 imp.; **O.**R. 25– imp.; **Sa.** 25–; **Y.** [*Not published* 1940–47]

4289 **Archives médicales** d'**Angers.** Angers. *Archs méd. Angers* [1897–]

4290 **Archives médicales belges.** Bruxelles. *Archs méd. belg.* [1917–36] **L.**MA. 29–36; MD.; **C.**MD.; **O.**R. 17–22. [*C. of:* 4196; *C. as:* 4198]

4291 **Archives médicales** de **Clermont-Ferrand.** *Archs méd. Clermont-Ferrand*

4292 **Archives médicales françaises.** Paris. *Archs méd. fr.* [1917–]

4293 **Archives médicales** de **Toulouse.** Toulouse. *Archs méd. Toulouse* [1895–14]

4294 **Archives médico-chirurgicales** de l'**appareil respiratoire.** Paris. *Archs méd.-chir. Appar. resp.* [1926–46] **L.**MA.; MD. [*C. as:* 26028]

4295 **Archives médico-chirurgicales** de **Normandie.** Le Havre. *Archs méd.-chir. Normandie* [1910–] **L.**MD. 59– imp.

4296 **Archives médico-chirurgicales** du **Poitou.** Poitiers. *Archs méd.-chir. Poitou* [1906–08] [*C. as:* 4297]

4297 **Archives médico-chirurgicales** de **Provence.** Poitiers. *Archs méd.-chir. Provence* [1909–] [*C. of:* 4296]

4298 Archives mensuelles d'obstétrique et de **gynécologie.** Paris. *Archs mens. Obstét. Gynéc.* [1912–19] L.MD.; E.P.; G.F. 13–14. [*C. of:* 35681; *C. in:* 21683]

4299 Archives of the **Middlesex Hospital. Clinical series.** London, etc. *Archs Middx Hosp. clin. Ser.* [1909–20] L.BM.; MD.; S.; U.; **Abs.**N. 12–15; **Bm.**U. 09–15 imp.; **Br.**U. 09–13 imp.; **C.**PA. imp.; UL.; **Cr.**MD. 09–15; E.P.; G.F. 09–15; U. 09–15; O.R. 09–15.

4300 Archives of the **Middlesex Hospital. New series.** London. *Archs Middx Hosp. new Ser.* [1951–55] L.BM.; GH.; U.; **Abd.**U.; **Bl.**U.; **Br.**U.; **Dn.**U.; E.A.; U. 51–53; G.F.; U.; **Lv.**M.; **Nw.**A.; O.R.

4301 Archives of the **Middlesex Hospital. Report** from the **Cancer Research Laboratories.** *Archs Middx Hosp. Rep. Cancer Res. Labs* [1902–14] L.BM.; CB.; D.; MD.; S.; TD. 04; U.; UCH. 04–14 imp.; **Abd.**U.; **Abs.**N. 12–14; **Bl.**U. 04–14 imp.; **Bm.**U. imp.; **Br.**U. 04–13; **C.**PA. 11–14; UL.; **Cr.**MD. 04–14; **Db.** 04–14; **Dn.**U.; E.U. 04–06 imp.; G.F.; U.; **Ld.**U.; **Lv.**U. 03–13 imp.; O.R. [*C. of:* 42966]

Archives de **minéralogie** de la **Société** des **sciences** de **Varsovie.** *See* 4705.

4302 Archives de **morphologie générale** et **expérimentale.** Paris. *Archs Morph. gén. exp.* [1921–37] L.BM.; BM^N.; UC.; **C.**AN.; O.R.; **Pl.**M. 21–30.

4303 Archives du **Musée Teyler.** Haarlem. *Archs Mus. Teyler* [1866–] L.BM.; BM^N. 66–53; R.; RI.; SC. 68–53; Z. 66–04: 29; **Abs.**U. 22–; **Bl.**U. 66–87; **C.**P. 68–; UL.; **Db.**; **Dm.** 12–53; E.B.; O.; R. 66–53; **Lv.**U. 83–; O.R.

Archives du **Musée zoologique** de l'**Université** de **Moscou.** *See* 48683.

Archives du **Muséum** d'histoire **naturelle.** Paris. *See* 4305.

4304 Archives du **Muséum** d'histoire **naturelle** de **Lyon.** Lyon. *Archs Mus. Hist. nat. Lyon* [1872–39] L.BM.; BM^N.; GL.; GM. 72–12; R. 72–12; RI. 77–12; SC. 09–39; Z. 72–99; **C.**P. 26–39; UL.; **Db.** 72–07; E.D. 76–39 imp.; **M.**U. 72–12 imp.; O.R. [*C. as:* 35353]

4305 Archives du **Muséum national** d'histoire **naturelle.** Paris. *Archs Mus. natn. Hist. nat., Paris* [1926–] L.BM^N.; GL.; K.; L.; R. 26–33; Z.; **C.**P. 26–42: 52–; UL.; **Db.**; E.R.; O.R.; Y. [*C. of:* 35352; *Suspended* 1943–51]

4306 Archives néerlandaises de **phonétique expérimentale.** La Haye. *Arch. néerl. Phon. exp.* [1927–] L.BM.; UC.; **C.**UL. 27–47; **Db.** 29–; **Dm.**; E.R.; G.U.; **Nw.**A. 29–47.

4307 Archives néerlandaises de **physiologie** de l'**homme** et des **animaux.** Amsterdam. *Archs néerl. Physiol.* [1916–47] L.BM^N.; L.; MC.; MD.; R.; S. 20–29; SC. 32–47; UC.; Z.; **Bl.**U. 16–36; **Bm.**U. 25–28: 44–47; **Br.**U. 16–19; **C.**B.; P.; PH. 16–43; UL.; **Dm.** 18–47; E.R.; U.; G.U.; **Lv.**U.; **Nw.**A. 17–47 imp.; O.PH.; R.; **Sh.**U. [*Forms Ser.* 3° *of* 4308; *C. in:* 727]

4308 Archives néerlandaises des **sciences exactes** et **naturelles.** Haarlem. *Archs néerl. Sci.* [Ser. 1 & 2: 1866–11; Ser. 3ᵃ. 1911–33; Ser. 3ᵇ. 1911–30; Ser. 3°=4307; Ser. 4=37670] L.AV. 98–31; BM.; BM^N.; C.; GL. 66–31; K. 66–15; M.; P.; R.; RI.; SC.; U. 66–93 imp.; UC.; Z. 66–18; **Abd.**U.; **Abs.**U. 12–33; **Bm.**U. 03–33; **C.**P.; UL.; **Db.**; **Dm.** 12–30; E.R.; G.U. 86–15; **Ld.**U.; **Lv.**U.; **M.**C. 86–10; **Mi.**; O.R. [Ser. 3ᵃ Sciences exactes, *C. in:* 37671; Ser. 3ᵇ Sciences naturelles; *C. in:* 4309]

4309 Archives néerlandaises de **zoologie.** Leiden. *Archs néerl. Zool.* [1934–] L.AM.; BM^N.; L.; R.; RI. 51–; SC.; UC.; Z.; **Abd.**M.; **Abs.**U.; **Bl.**U. 62–; **Bn.**U.; **C.**B.; P.; **Db.**; **Dm.**; E.R.; G.U. 56–; Lo.; **Lv.**U.; O.R.; **Pl.**M.; **Sal.** 34–40; **Sw.**U. 58–; **Wo.** 51–; Y. [*Supersedes* 53223 and 4308, Ser. 3ᵇ]

4310 Archives de **neurologie.** Bucarest. *Archs Neurol., Buc.* L.MD. 37–39; S. 37–39.

4311 Archives de **neurologie.** Paris. *Archs Neurol., Paris* [1880–09] L.BM.; MA.; MD.; **Abd.**U.; **Bm.**U. 80–85; **Br.**U. 80–07 imp.; **Dn.**U. 92–94 imp.; E.P. imp.; **M.**MS. 81–09. [*C. as:* 4266]

4312 Archives of **Neurology.** Chicago. *Archs Neurol., Chicago* [1960–] L.GH.; MA.; MC.; MD.; OP.; PS.; S.; U.; UC.; **Abd.**U.; **Bl.**U.; **Bm.**U.; **Br.**U.; **C.**APH.; PH.; PS.; **Cr.**MD.; **Db.**; **Dn.**U.; E.U.; G.F.; **Ld.**U.; **M.**MS.; **Nw.**A.; O.PH.; S.; **Sh.**U.; Y. [*C. of:* 75]

4313 Archives of **Neurology** from the **Pathological Laboratory** of the **London County Asylums.** Claybury, Sussex. *Archs Neurol. path. Lab., Claybury* [1899–07] L.BM.; GH.; H.; LI. 03–07; MC.; MD.; S.; TD.; U. 02–07; UC. 07; **Bl.**U.; **Bm.**U.; **Br.**U.; **C.**UL. 03–07; **Db.**; **Dn.**U.; E.P.; U. 02–07; G.F. 03; **Ld.**U.; **Lv.**U.; **M.**MS.; **Nw.**A. 02–07; O.R. [*C. as:* 4315]

4314 Archives of **Neurology** and **Psychiatry.** Chicago. *Archs Neurol. Psychiat., Chicago* [1919–50] L.GH. 50; MA. 34–50; MC.; MD.; OP. 49–50; PS.; S. 20–50; U. 50; UC.; **Abd.**U. 22–50; **Bl.**U. 32–50 imp.; **Bm.**U. 31–50; **Br.**U. 35–50; **C.**APH. 40–50; PH.; PS.; **Db.**; E.S. 47–50; U.; G.F. 25–50 imp.; **Ld.**U. 31–50; **Lv.**M. 42–46 imp.; **M.**MS. 20–50; **Nw.**A. 26: 33–50 imp.; O.PH. 27–50; R.; **Sh.**U. 44–50. [*C. as:* 76]

4315 Archives of **Neurology** and **Psychiatry.** London. *Archs Neurol. Psychiat., Lond.* [1909–50] L.BM.; H.; LI. 09–22; MC.; MD.; S.; TD. 09–11; U.; UC. 09–22; UCH. 09–11; **Abd.**U. 31–50; **Bl.**U. 09–14; **Bm.**U.; **Br.**U.; **C.**PA. 09–22; **Db.** 09–18; **Dn.**U. 09–14; E.P.; U. 09–22; G.F. 09–11; **Ld.**U. 09–39; **Lv.**U. 09–18; **Nw.**A. 09–11; O.R. 09–31. [*C. of:* 4313]

4316 Archives of **Neurology** and **Psychopathology.** Utica, N.Y. *Archs Neurol. Psychopath.* [1898–01] L.BM.; S. 98; UC. 98–99; **Lv.**U. 98–00.

4317 Archives of **Occupational Therapy.** Baltimore. *Archs occup. Ther.* [1922–24] **C.**UL. [*C. as:* 35810]

4318 Archives de l'**Office indochinois** du **riz.** Saïgon. *Archs Off. indochin. Riz*

Archives of the **Ophthalmological Society** of **N. Greece.** *See* 4366.

4319 Archives d'**ophthalmogie.** Paris. *Archs Ophthal., Paris.* [1880–36] L.MD.; OP.; S.; **Bl.**U. 06–12; **Bm.**U. 82–99; **Br.**U. 89–02; **Db.** 89–24; E.S.; **Ld.**U. 92–00; O.R. 12–36; **Sa.** 88–16. [*C. as:* 4320]

4320 Archives d'**Ophthalmologie** et **revue générale** d'**ophthalmogie.** Paris. *Archs Ophthal. Rev. gén. Ophthal.* [1937–] L.MA.; MD.; OP.; S.; TD. 38–40; U. 50–; E.S.; O.R. [*C. of:* 4319]

4321 Archives of **Ophthalmology.** New York. *Archs Ophthal., N.Y.* [1869–50: 60–] L.BM. 69–36; MA. 79–50: 60–; MD.; OP.; S.; U. 97–05: 08: 60–; **Abd.**U. 38–50 imp.: 60–; **Bl.**U. 36–50 imp.: 60–; **Bm.**U. imp.; **Br.**U. 76–50 imp.: 60–; **C.**MS.; **Db.** 83–04; **Dn.**U. 91–50 imp.: 60–; E.P.; S. 89–50 imp.: 60–; U. 45–50: 60–; G.F.; **Ld.**U. 92–50: 60–; **Lv.**M. 69–93: 24–50: 60–; **M.**MS. 69–01: 31–50: 60–; **Nw.**A. 01–08: 13: 29–50: 60–; O.R.; **Sa.** 90–23; **Sh.**U. 29–39: 44–50: 60–; Y. [*C. as:* and *Rec. of:* 77]

4322 Archives of **Optometry.** Philadelphia. *Archs Optom.* [1922–23] [*C. in:* 36255]

4323 **Archives** of **Oral Biology.** London, New York. *Archs oral Biol.* [1959–] L.BM.; D.; MD.; S.; SC.; **Abs.**N.; **Bl.**U.; **Br.**U.; **Cr.**U.; **Dn.**U.; Ld.U.; **Sh.**U.; Y.

4324 **Archives orientales** de **médecine** et de **chirurgie.** Paris. *Archs orient. Méd. Chir.* [1899–01] [*C. in:* 22869]

4325 **Archives** of **Orthodontics.** Bruxelles. *Archs Orthod.* [1948–] L.D.; Bl.U. 52.

4326 **Archives** of **Otolaryngology.** Chicago. *Archs Otolar.* [1925–50: 60–] L.CB. 46–; MA.; MD.; S. 61–; U. 50–; UCH. 47–; **Abd.**U.; **Bl.**U. 34–; **Br.**U. 48–; **Dn.**U.; E.S. 45–; G.F.; Ld.U. 46–; Lv.M.; M.MS. 47–; Nw.A.; **Sh.**U. 44–; Y. [*C. as:* and *Rec. of:* 78]

4327 **Archives** of **Otology.** New York. *Archs Otol.* [1879–08] L.MD.; S.; **Abd.**U. 04–08; **Bm.**U. 79–07 imp.; **Br.**U. 70–08 imp.; **Cr.**MD. 06–08; **Db.** 83–03; **Dn.**U. 81–96; E.S. 89–08; G.F.; U. 03–08; Ld.U. 96–00; Lv.M. 79–92; M.MS. 80–93; O.R.

4328 **Archives** de **parasitologie.** Paris. *Archs Parasit.* [1898–19] L.BM.N.; LI. 98–05; MD. 03–14; TD.; V. 98–04; Z. 98–12; **Abd.**U. 06–14; **C.**B. 98–07; MO.; **Db.** 98–00; E.P.; G.F.; U. 11–12; Lv.U. 98–14; O.R.

Archives of **Pathological Anatomy** and **Pathological Physiology.** Moscow. *See* 4787.

4329 **Archives** of the **Pathological Institute, London Hospital.** London. *Archs path. Inst., Lond.* [1906–08] L.BM.; MD.; S.; TD.; **C.**UL.; **Db.**; G.F.; Lv.U.; M.MS.; O.R.

4330 **Archives** of **Pathology.** Chicago. *Archs Path.* [1926–50: 60–] L.CB. imp.; MA.; MC.; MD.; S.; TD.; UC. 26–27; UCH.; **Abd.**U.; **Bl.**U. 29–31 imp.; **Bm.**U. imp.; **Br.**U.; **C.**APH. 61–; PA.; **Cr.**MD.; **Db.**; **Dn.**U.; E.N. 43–50: 60–; PO. 48–50: 60–; U.; G.F. 48–50: 60–; U.; Ld.U.; Lv.M. 28–31; M.MS.; Nw.A.; O.P. 49–50: 60–; R.; **Sh.**U. 42–50: 60–; Y. [*C. as:* and *Rec. of:* 79]

Archives of **Pathology** and **Laboratory Medicine.** *See* 4330.

4331 **Archives** of **Pediatrics.** New York. *Archs Pediat.* [1884–] L.MA.; MD.; **Abd.**R. 33–; **Bl.**U. 23– v. imp.; **Br.**U. 94–53 imp.; **Db.** 15–17 imp.; E.P.; S. 84–31; G.F.; Lv.M. 84–91: 21–29; M.MS. 84–57; Nw.A. 24–35; Y.

4332 **Archives** of **Philosophy, Psychology** and **Scientific Methods.** New York. *Archs Phil. Psychol. scient. Meth.* [1905–06] L.BM.; E.U.; G.U.

4333 **Archives** of **Physical Medicine.** Omaha. *Archs phys. Med.* [1945–52] L.MA.; MD.; RA.; S.; U. 50–52; **Bl.**U. 47–52; **Cr.**MD.; E.U. [*C. of:* 4335; *C. as:* 4334]

4334 **Archives** of **Physical Medicine** and **Rehabilitation.** Omaha. *Archs phys. Med. Rehabil.* [1953–] L.MA.; MD.; RA.; U.; **Bl.**U.; **Cr.**MD.; E.U.; M.MS. 57–; Y. [*C. of:* 4333]

4335 **Archives** of **Physical Therapy** (**X-ray, Radium**). Omaha. *Archs phys. Ther.* [1926–44] L.MA. 36–44; MD.; RA.; S.; **Cr.**MD. 33–44; E.U. 43–44. [*C. of:* 26763; *C. as:* 4333]

4336 **Archives** of **Physiological Therapy.** Boston. *Archs physiol. Ther.* [1905–06]

4337 **Archives** de **physique biologique.** Paris. *Archs Phys. biol.* [1921–44] L.SC. 27–44; **C.**B.; **Pl.**M. 21–38 imp.

4338 **Archives** de **plasmologie générale.** Bruxelles, Paris. *Archs Plasmol. gén.* [1912]

Archives polonaises de **médecine interne.** *See* 38052.

Archives polonaises des **sciences biologiques** et **médicales.** *See* 38035°.

4339 **Archives** of the **Population Association** of **Japan.** Tokyo. *Archs Pop. Ass. Japan* [1952–] L.TD. 52–53.

4340 **Archives portugaises** des **sciences biologiques.** Lisbonne. *Archs port. Sci. biol.* [1921–] L.BM.N. 21–53; EB. 21–36; LI. 36–50; R. 36–53; S. 36–; TD. 34–38 imp.; Z. 36–52; Y.

4341 **Archives** du **praticien.** Paris. *Archs Pratn* [1910–]

Archives for **Printing, Paper** and **Kindred Trades.** *See* 4060.

4342 **Archives provinciales** de **chirurgie.** Paris. *Archs prov. Chir.* [1892–15] L.MD.; **Br.**U. 96–04. [*C. as:* 4223]

4343 **Archives** of **Psychoanalysis.** Stamford, Conn. *Archs Psychoanal.* [1926–27]

4344 **Archives** de **psychologie.** Genève, Paris. *Archs Psychol., Genève* [1902–] L.BM.; MD. 27–29; PS.; UC.; **Br.**U. 47–; **C.**PS.; E.P.; U.; G.U.; Ld.U.; O.B.; EP. 47–. [*C. of:* 4345]

4345 **Archives** de **psychologie** de la **Suisse romande.** Genève. *Archs Psychol. Suisse romande* [1901] L.BM.; UC.; E.P.; G.U.; Ld.U.; O.B. [*C. as:* 4344]

4346 **Archives** of **Psychology.** New York. *Archs Psychol., N.Y.* [1906–45] L.BM.; MD. 37–45; PS.; **C.**UL. 08–45; G.U. [*C. from:* 4332; *C. in:* 40456]

4347 **Archives** of the **Public Health Laboratory** of the **University** of **Manchester.** *Archs publ. Hlth Lab. Univ. Manchr* [1906] L.MD.; P.; S.; **Abd.**U.; **C.**UL.; Lv.U.; M.MS.; U.

4348 **Archives** of **Radiology** and **Electrotherapy.** London. *Archs Radiol. Electrother.* [1915–23] L.BM.; CB.; GH. 15–21; MD.; P.; RA.; RI. 16–23; S.; **Br.**U. 20–23; **C.**P. 19–23; UL.; **Cr.**MD. 22–23; **Db.**; **Dn.**U. imp.; E.A.; P.; S.; G.F.; U.; Lv.M.; M.MS.; O.R. [*C. of:* 4353; *C. as:* 8888]

4349 **Archives** for **Rational Mechanics** and **Analysis.** Berlin. *Archs ration. Mech. Analysis* [1957–] L.AV.; P.; SC.; UC.; **Bl.**U.; **Bn.**U.; **Br.**U.; **C.**P.; **Db.**; **Ex.**U.; G.T.; U. 60–; **H.**U.; **M.**C.; T.; U.; **N.**U.; **Sh.**U.; **Sw.**U.; Y.

4350 **Archives** des **recherches agronomiques** au **Cambodge,** au **Laos** et au **Vietnam.** Saigon. *Archs Rech. agron. Cambodge Laos Vietnam* [1951–52] **C.**A.; Md.H. [*C. of:* 4256; *C. as:* 4351]

4351 **Archives** des **recherches agronomiques** et **pastorales** au **Viêt Nam.** Saigon. *Archs Rech. agron. past. Viêt Nam* [1953–] **C.**A. 53–55; Md.H. 53–55. [*C. of:* 4350]

4352 **Archives** de **rhumatologie.** Lyon. *Archs Rhum.* [1946–] L.MA.; MD. [*C. of:* 4209]

4353 **Archives** of the **Roentgen Ray.** London. *Archs Roentg. Ray* [1896–15] L.BM.; CB.; GH. 98–15; MD. 99–15; P. 10–15; RA.; RI.; S.; SI. 99–04 imp.; **Abs.**N. 12; **Bm.**U. 99–04; **Br.**U. imp.; **C.**UL.; **Db.**; **Dn.**U. 06–15 imp.; E.A.; P.; S.; **Ex.**U. 11–15; G.F. 96–13; M. 96–00; U. 02–15; Lv.M. 02–15; M.MS. imp.; O.R.; Sa. 06–08. [*C. as:* 4348]

4354 **Archives roumaines** de **pathologie expérimentale** et de **microbiologie.** Paris, Bucureşti. *Archs roum. Path. exp. Microbiol.* [1928–38: 42–] L.EB.; LI.; MA. 57–; MC. imp.; MD.; TD.; **Bl.**U. 59–; **C.**MO.; **O.**P.; **W.** 45–.

4355 **Archives** of **Rubber Cultivation.** Bogor, Djakarta-Kota. *Archs Rubb. Cult.* [1954–] L.MY.; P.; TP.; **C.**A.; **Cn.**R.; **M.**D.; **Md.**H.; **Rt.**; **Sy.**R.; **Y.** [*C. of:* 3945]

Archives russes d'**anatomie,** d'**histologie** et d'**embryologie.** *See* 48308.

Archives russes de **pathologie,** de **médecine clinique** et de **bactériologie.** *See* 48309.

Archives russes de **protistologie.** *See* 48310.

4356 **Archives** des **sciences.** Genève. *Archs Sci., Genève* [1948–] L.AS.; BMᴺ.; C.; E. 48–53; EE.; GL.; MO.; P.; QM. 56–; RI.; SC.; Z.; **Bl.**U.; **Bn.**U. imp.; **C.**P.; UL. 49–; **Cr.**N. imp.; **Db.**; **Dm.**; **E.**M.; R.; U.; **G.**U.; **H.**U.; **Lv.**U.; **Pl.**M.; **Y.** [*C. of:* 4360]

Archives des **sciences biologiques.** Belgrade. *See* 4745.

4357 **Archives** des **sciences biologiques** (*afterwards* **Arkhiv biologicheskikh nauk.** Архив биологических наук). St. Pétersbourg, Moscou. *Archs Sci. biol., St Pétersb.* (*Arkh. biol. Nauk*) [1892–41] L.BM. 92–13; MA. 29–41; MC. 25–41; MD. 39–41; R. 92–14; S. 92–08; TD. 23–41; UC. 92–35; **C.**P. 35–41 imp.; **Db.** 92–12; **E.**R. 92–40; U. 96–14; **Lv.**M. 33–37 imp.; U. 01–13; **O.**R. 92–14: 35–39.

4358 **Archives** des **sciences médicales.** Paris. *Archs Sci. méd.* [1896–00] L.S.; **C.**PA.

4359 **Archives** des **sciences physiologiques.** Paris. *Archs Sci. physiol.* [1947–] L.MA.; MC. 47: 49: 52–; MD.; SC.; **Abd.**R. 49–; U.; **Br.**U.; **C.**PH.; **E.**U.; **G.**U. **M.**MS.; **Y.**

4360 **Archives** des **sciences physiques** et **naturelles.** Genève, Lausanne, Paris. *Archs Sci. phys. nat.* [1846–47] L.BM. 1846–24; BMᴺ.; C. 67–68: 01–47; EE. 06–47; P.; R. 78–32; RI. 78–47; S. 1846–32; SC.; UC. 26–30; **Bl.**U. 1855: 69–39; **Br.**U. 79–26; **C.**P. 80–94; PH. 78–81; UL.; **Db.**; **E.**C. 82–07 imp.; M. 22–47; R. imp.; U.; **G.**U.; **Lv.**U. 26–47; **R.**D. 17–25. [*C. as:* 4356]

Archives. Section des **sciences naturelles, physiques** et **mathématiques, Institut grand-ducal** de **Luxembourg.** *See* 4241.

Archives séismologiques. Beograd. *See* 49416.

4361 **Archives** du **Service** de **santé** de l'**armée belge.** Bruxelles. *Archs Serv. Santé Armée belge* [1945–47] L.MA.; **Br.**U. [*C. of:* 4198; *C. as:* 2678]

4362 **Archives sismiques** de **Roumanie.** Bucarest. *Archs sism. Roum.*

4363 **Archives** de la **Société française** de **biologie médicale.** Paris. *Archs Soc. fr. Biol. méd.* [*Published in:* 49484]

4364 **Archives** de la **Société internationale** de **gastroentérologie.** Bruxelles. *Archs Soc. int. Gastro-entérol.* L.MD. 36–37.

4365 **Archives** de la **Société internationale** d'**histoire** de la **médecine.** Paris. *Archs Soc. int. Hist. Méd.* [1936–]

4366 **Archives** de la **Société** d'**ophthalmologie** de la **Grèce** du **nord.** Salonika. *Archs Soc. Ophthal. Grèce N.* [1952–] L.MA. 53–; OP.

4367 **Archives** de la **Société** des **sciences médicales** et **biologiques** de **Montpellier** (et du **Languedoc méditerranéen**). *Archs Soc. Sci. méd. biol. Montpellier* [1927–]

L.LI.; MA.; MC. 29–39; MD.; S. 27–39 imp.; U. 32–39; UC. 27–39; **Bl.**U. imp.; **Bm.**U.; **Br.**U. imp.; **Db.**; **E.**U. 27–39; **G.**U. imp.; **Ld.**U.; **Lv.**U.; **M.**MS. 27–37; **Nw.**A. 27–39 imp.; **O.**R. imp.; **Sa.** [*C. of:* 12169]

4368 **Archives** de **stomatologie.** Liège. *Archs Stomat., Liège* [1947–] L.D. [*C. of:* 2679 and 4378]

4369 **Archives** de **stomatologie** et **Journal** de l'**anesthésie.** Paris. *Archs Stomat., Paris* [1900–13]

4370 **Archives suisses** d'**anthropologie générale.** Génève. *Archs suisses Anthrop. gén.* [1914–] L.AN.; BM.; U.; UC. 14–22; **Bl.**U. 14–20; **Bm.**P.; **E.**U.; **M.**U. 14–29 imp.; **Y.** [*Suspended* 1923–27]

Archives suisses de **neurologie** et de **psychiatrie.** *See* 48908.

4371 **Archives suisses** d'**ornithologie.** Berne. *Archs suisses Orn.* [1932–49] L.BMᴺ.; Z.; **Br.**U. 42–49; **O.**OR.

4372 **Archives** of **Surgery.** Chicago. *Archs Surg., Chicago* [1920–50: 60–] L.CB. 48–50: 60–; MA. 24–50: 60–; MD.; S.; U. 50: 60–; **Abd.**U. 23–; **Bl.**U. 27–31: 47–50: 60–; **Bm.**U. 47–50: 60–; **Br.**U.; **C.**APH. 49–50: 60–; **Cr.**MD. 27–50: 60–; MS. 91–10: 60–; **Db.** 25–50: 60–; **E.**S. imp.; U. 22–24: 35–50: 60–; **G.**F. 38–50: 60–; **Lv.**M. 25–50: 60–; **M.**MS.; **Nw.**A. 20–34; **O.**R. 32–50: 60–; **Sh.**U. 20–32: 44–50: 60–; **Y.** [*C. as:* and *Rec. of:* 80]

4373 **Archives** of **Surgery.** London. *Archs Surg., Lond.* [1889–00] L.BM.; MD.; S.; UCH. 89–94; **Bm.**U.; **Br.**U.; **C.**AP. 90–00; UL.; **Cr.**MS. 91–00; **Db.**; **Dn.**U.; **E.**P. imp.; S.; **G.**F.; M.; U.; **Ld.**U.; **Lv.**M.; U.; **M.**MS.; **Nw.**A. 89–99; **O.**R. 93–00; **Sh.**U.

4374 **Archives** of **Tea Cultivation.** Bogor. *Archs Tea Cultiv.* [1959–] L.P.; **C.**A.; **Md.**H. 59–; **Rt.**; **Y.** [*C. of:* 3949]

4375 **Archives** of **Therapeutics.** New York. *Archs Ther., N.Y.* [1925–27] [*C. of:* 53041]

4376 **Archives** de **thérapeutique.** Paris. *Archs Thér., Paris* [1898–17] Lv.U. 08–14 imp.

Archives trimestrielles. Institut grand-ducal de **Luxembourg.** *See* 4241.

4377 **Archives urologiques** de la **clinique** de **Necker.** Paris. *Archs urol. Clin. Necker* [1913–32] L.MD.; **Cr.**MD. 21–29.

4378 **Archives wallones** de **stomatologie.** Liège. *Archs wallon. Stomat.* [1946] L.D. [*C. in:* 4368]

4379 **Archives** de **zoologie expérimentale** et **générale.** Paris. *Archs Zool. exp. gén.* [1872–] L.AM. 92–; BM.; BMᴺ.; L.; QM. 50–; R.; S. 72–50; SC.; UC. 78–42; Z.; **Abd.**U.; **Bm.**U.; **Bn.**U. 48–; **C.**B.; UL.; **Db.** 78–; **Dm.** 17: 27–31; **E.**R.; U.; **Ex.**U. 54–; **G.**U.; **Ld.**U.; **Lo.** 92–; **Lv.**P. 72 31; U. 08–; **M.**R.; U. imp.; **Mi.** 44–; **N.**U. 56–; **Nw.**A. 38–; **Pl.**M.; **Rt.** 18–28; **Sa.**; **Sh.**U. 89–33 imp.; **Sw.**U. 56–; **Y.**

Archivi. *See* **Archivio.**

4380 **Archivio** di **anatomia patologica** e **scienze affini.** Palermo. *Archo Anat. patol.*

4381 **Archivio** di **antropologia criminale, psichiatria** e **medicina legale.** Torino. *Archo Antrop. crim. Psichiat. Med. leg.* [1909–49] L.AN. 09–37; BM.; MD. 28–39. [*C. of:* 4438; *C. as:* 31966]

4382 **Archivio** per l'**antropologia** e la **etnologia.** Firenze. *Archo Antrop. Etnol.* [1871–] L.AN.; BM.; S. 71–35: 39–45; UC. 13–20 imp.; **Abs.**U. 71–81; **Y.**

4383 **Archivio** ed **atti** della **Società italiana** di **chirurgia.** Roma. *Archo Atti Soc. ital. Chir.* L.S. 87–38 imp.

4384 **Archivio** di **biologie applicata** alla **patologia,** alla **clinica** e all'**igiene.** Genova. *Archo Biol. appl. Patol.* [1924–30] L.GH.; LL.; MD.; **Br.**U. 24–28. [*C. of:* and *Rec. as:* 3049]

4385 **Archivio botanico** per la **sistematica, fitogeografia** e **genetica.** Forli. *Archo bot. Sist. Fito-geogr. Genet.* [1925–] L.BM^N.; K.

4386 **Archivio Chiavaro.** Roma. *Archo Chiavaro* [1934–37] L.MD. [*C. of:* and *Rec. as:* 3079]

4387 **Archivio** di **chimica, farmacognosia** e **scienze affini.** Roma. *Archo Chim. Farmacogn.* [*C. of:* 4396]

4388 **Archivio** di **chimica scientifica** ed **industriale.** Torino. *Archo Chim. scient. ind.*

4389 **Archivio** di **chirurgia infantile.** Roma. *Archo Chir. infant.* [1934–35] L.MD.

4390 **Archivio** di **chirurgia ortopedica** e di **medicina.** Milano. *Archo Chir. ortoped. Med.*

4391 **Archivio** di **chirurgia** del **torace.** Firenze. *Archo Chir. Torace* [1947–] L.MD.; E.U.

4392 **Archivio 'De Vecchi'** per l'**anatomia patologica** e la **medicina clinica.** *Archo De Vecchi* L.MA. 44–; MD. 45–.

4393 **Archivio** di **dermatologia sperimentale** e **funzionale.** Milano. *Archo Derm. sper. funz.*

4394 **Archivio E. Maragliano** di **patologia** e **clinica.** Genova. *Archo E. Maragliano* [1946–] L.LI.; MA.; MD.; **Y.** [*C. of:* 3049]

4395 **Archivio** per la **etnografia** e la **psicologia** della **Lunigiana.** Spezia. *Archo Etnogr. Psicol. Lunigiana*

4396 **Archivio** di **farmacognosia** e **scienze affini.** Roma. *Archo Farmacog.* [1912–17] [*C. as:* 4387]

4397 **Archivio** di **farmacologia sperimentale** e **scienze affini.** Roma. *Archo Farmac. sper.* [1902–] L.C. 19–40 imp.; GH. 06–29 imp.; MD. 36–40; S. 33: 35–40; TD. 18–28; **C.**PH. 02–04; **Dn.**U. 02–31 imp.; E.U. 10–14; Lv.U. 06–12 imp.

4398 **Archivio** di **farmacologia** e **terapeutica.** Palermo. *Archo Farmac. Terap.* [1893–12] L.MD. 95–01; **C.**UL. 93–; **Dn.**U. 02–10.

4399 **Archivio fascista** di **medicina politica.** Parma. *Archo fasc. Med. polit.*

4400 **Archivio** di **fisiologia.** Firenze. *Archo Fisiol.* [1903–] L.MA. 46–; MC. 30–44 imp.; SC. 32–; U. 03–21; UC.; **Bm.**U. 03–27; **C.**APH. 49–; PH. 03–26; PS. 13–; **Cr.**U. 03–15; E.P.; U.; Ld.U.; Lv.U. 03–31; O.R.; **Y.**

4401 **Archivio generale** di **neurologia** e **psichiatria** (e **psicoanalisi**). Napoli. *Archo gen. Neurol. Psichiat.* [1920–38] L.MA. 26–37; MD.; PS.; **C.**PS. [*Replaced by:* 4440]

4401° **Archivio internazionale** di **etnografia** e **preistoria.** Torino. *Archo int. Etnogr. Preist.* [1958–] L.BM.
Archivio internazionale di **fotogrammetria.** See 24006.

4402 **Archivio internazionale** di **medicina** e **chirurgia.** Napoli. *Archo int. Med. Chir.* [1885–09]

4403 **Archivio internazionale** di **radiobiologia.** Bologna. *Archo int. Radiobiol.* [1934–35] [*C. of:* 41821; *C. as:* 41821°]

4404 **Archivio internazionale** di **studi neurologici.** Firenze. *Archo int. Studi neurol.* [1950–] L.MD.

4405 **Archivio** dell'**Istituto biochimico italiano.** Milano. *Archo Ist. biochim. ital.* [1929–] L.C. 29–39; MA. 29–36; MD. 40– imp. [*Suspended* 1944–53]

4406 **Archivio italiano** di **anatomia** e di **embriologia.** Firenze. *Archo ital. Anat. Embriol.* [1902–] L.MC. 40–45; MD. 19–; UC.; Z. 04–; **Bm.**U.; **C.**AN.; E.U.; G.U. 24–; **M.**MS. 48–; O.R. 25–.

4407 **Archivio italiano** di **anatomia** e **istologia patologica.** Milano, etc. *Archo ital. Anat. Istol. patol.* [1930–] L.MA. 32–40.

4408 **Archivio italiano** di **chirurgia.** Bologna. *Archo ital. Chir.* [1919–] L.MA. 28–; MC. 19–27 imp.; MD. 26–40: 49–; **Br.**U. 22– imp.

4409 **Archivio italiano** di **dermatologia, sifilografia** e **venereologia.** Bologna. *Archo ital. Derm. Sif. Vener.* [1925–58] L.MA. 48–58; MD. 42–58. [*C. as:* 4410]

4410 **Archivio italiano** di **dermatologia, venereologia** e **sessiologia.** Bologna. *Archo ital. Derm. Vener.* [1959–] L.MA.; MD. [*C. of:* 4409]

4411 **Archivio italiano** di **ginecologia.** Napoli. *Archo ital. Ginec.* [1898–14] L.MD. imp.

4412 **Archivio italiano** di **laringologia.** Napoli. *Archo ital. Lar.* [1881–] L.MA. 49–; MD. 94–; G.F. 96–37.

4413 **Archivio italiano** dei **malattie** dell'**apparato digerente.** Bologna. *Archo ital. Mal. Appar. dig.* [1931–] L.MA. 48–; MD. 61–; **Abd.**R. 48–58.

4414 **Archivio italiano** per le **malattie** della **trachea, bronchi, esofago.** Parma. *Archo ital. Mal. Trachea* [1933–] L.MD. 37–40.

4415 **Archivio italiano** di **medicina interna.** Roma. *Archo ital. Med. intern.* [1898–01]

4416 **Archivio italiano** di **medicina sperimentale.** Torino. *Archo ital. Med. sper.* [1937–39] L.MD. 38–39. [*C. as:* 30468]

4417 **Archivio italiano** di **oftalmoiatria.** Pavia. *Archo ital. Oftal.* [1922–26] [*C. of:* 4431]

4418 **Archivio italiano** di **otologia, rinologia** e **laringologia.** Torino-Palermo. *Archo ital. Otol. Rinol. Lar.* [1893–] L.MA. 02–; MD. 98–; S. 01–06; **Abd.**U. 23–32 imp.; **M.**U.

4419 **Archivio italiano** di **patologia** e **clinica** dei **tumori.** Modena. *Archo ital. Patol. Clin. Tum.* [1957–] L.MD.

4420 **Archivio italiano** di **pediatria** e **puericoltura.** Bologna. *Archo ital. Pediat. Pueric.* [1932–] L.MA. 46–; MD.; **Abd.**R. 48–.

4421 **Archivio italiano** di **psicologia.** Torino. *Archo ital. Psicol.* [1920] **C.**PS., Ld.U. 20–25.

4422 **Archivio italiano** di **scienze farmacologiche.** Milano, etc. *Archo ital. Sci. farmac.* [1932–42: 48–] L.MC.; MD. imp.; **C.**APH. 60–; **Cr.** MD. 32–39 imp.; E.U. 32–39: 48–; **Y.**

4423 **Archivio italiano** di **scienze mediche coloniali.** Tripoli. *Archo ital. Sci. med. colon.* [1920–49] L.EB. 20–28; MA. 48–49; MD. 37–39; TD.; E.B. 20–28; Ld.U. 20–22; Lv.U. [*C. as:* 4424]

4424 **Archivio italiano** di **scienze mediche tropicali** e di **parassitologia.** Tripoli. *Archo ital. Sci. med. trop. Parassit.* [1950–] L.MA.; TD.; Lv.U.; **Y.** [*C. of:* 4423]

4425 **Archivio italiano** di **urologia.** Bologna. *Archo ital. Urol.* [1924–] L.MA. 28–32 imp.; MD. 43–.

4426 **Archivio** di **medicina** e **chirurgia.** Milano. *Archo Med. Chir.* [1932–] L.MD. 37–40.

4427 **Archivio** di **medicina interna.** Parma. *Archo Med. interna*

4428 **Archivio** di **neurochirurgia.** Firenze. *Archo Neurochir.*

4429 **Archivio** di **neurologia.** Napoli. *Archo Neurol.*

4430 **Archivio** di **oceanografia** e **limnologia.** Roma. *Archo Oceanogr. Limnol.* [1941–] L.BM^N.; G.; Z.; Abd.M.; Dm.; E.G.; Fr. 41–; Lo.; Lv.U.; Mi.; Pl.M. 49–; Wo. 54–; Y. [*C. of:* 31304]

4431 **Archivio** di **oftalmoiatria.** Pavia. *Archo Oftal.* [1913–17] [*C. as:* 4417]

4432 **Archivio** di **ortopedia.** Milano. *Archo Ortop.* [1884–] L.MA. 31–; MD. 28–; Br.U. 95–46 imp.

4433 **Archivio** dell'**Ospedale** al **mare.** Venezia. *Archo Osp. Mare* [1949–] L.MA.

4434 **Archivio** di **ostetricia** e **ginecologia.** Napoli. *Archo Ostet. Ginec.* [1894–] L.MA. 37–; MD. 94; E.P. 04–.

4435 **Archivio** di **ottalmologia.** Palermo, Napoli. *Archo Ottal.* [1893–] L.MA. 47–; MD. 93: 16–42: 46–58 imp.; OP. 97–; U. 50.

4436 **Archivio di patologia** e **clinica infantile.** Napoli. *Archo Patol. Clin. infant.* [1902–03]

4437 **Archivio di patologia** e **clinica medica.** Bologna. *Archo Patol. Clin. med.* [1921–] L.MA. 28–; MD. 28–; S. 46–58; Br.U. 25–; Db. 21–22.

4438 **Archivio di psichiatria, antropologia criminale,** etc. Torino e Roma. *Archo Psichiat. Antrop. crim.* [1880–08] L.AN.; BM. [*C. as:* 4381]

4439 **Archivio** di **psicologia collettiva** e **scienze affini.** Cosenza. *Archo Psicol. collett.*

4440 **Archivio** di **psicologia, neurologia** e **psichiatria.** Milano. *Archo Psicol. Neurol. Psichiat.* [1939–] L.BM. 53–; MA. 46–; MD. 39: 45; PS. imp. [*Replaces:* 4401]

4441 **Archivio 'Putti'** di **chirurgia** degli **organi** di **movimento.** Firenze. *Archo 'Putti'* [1949–] L.MD. 57–.

4442 **Archivio** di **radiologia.** Napoli. *Archo Radiol.* [1925–] L.BM. 33–; MA. 40–42; MD. 37–40.

4443 **Archivio scientifico** di **medicina veterinaria.** Torino. *Archo scient. Med. vet.* [*C. of:* 4444]

4444 **Archivio scientifico** della **R. Società** ed **Accademia veterinaria italiana.** Torino. *Archo scient. R. Soc. Accad. vet. ital.* [1903–12] [*C. as:* 4443]

4445 **Archivio** di **scienza ospedaliera.** Bergamo. *Archo Sci. osped.*

4446 **Archivio** di **scienze biologiche.** Napoli, etc. *Archo Sci. biol.* [1919–] L.C. 37–56 imp.; PH.; SC. 27–; UC.; Abd.R. 46–; C.PH. 19–26; E.U. 21–29; O.PH.; Y.

4447 **Archivio** di **scienze** della **cerebrazione** e dei **psichismi.** Napoli. *Archo Sci. Cerebraz.* [1944–]

4448 **Archivio** per le **scienze mediche.** Torino. *Archo Sci. med.* [1876–] L.BM.; MD. 31–40: 46:΅60– imp.; S. 90–42: 47–; C.PA. 96–23; PH. 76–91; Lv.U. 76–03.

4449 **Archivio** di **storia** della **scienza.** Roma. *Archo Stor. Sci.* [1919–26] L.BM.; P.; SC.; UC.; C.UL.; G.U.; O.R. [*C. as:* 3941]

4450 **Archivio** per lo **studio** della **fisiopatologia** e **clinica** del **ricambio.** Milano. *Archo Stud. Fisiopatol. Clin. Ricam.* [1933–]

Archivio svizzero di **neurologia** e **psichiatria.** *See* 48908.

4451 **Archivio** di **tisiologia** e delle **malattie** dell'**aparato respiratorio.** Napoli. *Archo Tisiol.* [1946–] L.MA.; MC. 50–; MD. 47–.

4452 **Archivio veterinario italiano.** Milano. *Archo vet. ital.* [1950–] L.V.; Br.U. 57–; E.AB. 50–54 imp.; R.D.; W. 53–; Y.

4454 **Archivio zoologico italiano.** Napoli. *Archo zool. ital.* [1902–] L.BM.; BM^N.; L. 12–50; SC. 33–; Z.; Bn.U. 55–; G.U.; O.R.; Pl.M.

Archivo. *See also* **Archivos.**

4455 **Archivo de anatomia** e **anthropologia.** Lisboa. *Archivo Anat. Anthrop.* [1912–] L.AN.; BM^N.; MD. 12–22; S.; SC. 13–; UC. 12–38; Bl.U.; Bm.U.; Br.U.; C.AN. 12–21: 29; UL.; Db. 14–28 imp.; E.U.; G.U. 12–41; Ld.U.; Lv.U.; M.U. 12–40 imp.; N.U. 12–21 imp.; Nw.A. 12–21; O.R. 12–21; R.U. 14–41 imp.; Sa. 12.

4456 **Archivo de biología vegetal teorica y aplicada.** Buenos Aires. *Archivo Biol. veg. teor. apl.* [1943–]

4457 **Archivo de ciencias biológicas** y **naturales teoricas** y **aplicades.** Buenos Aires. *Archivo Cienc. biol. nat. teor. apl.* L.BM^N. 61–.

4458 **Archivo das colónias.** Lisboa. *Archivo Colón., Lisb.* [1917–] L.BM.; E.G. 18–.

4459 **Archivo fitotécnico** del **Uruguay.** Montevideo. *Archivo fitotéc. Urug.* [1935–] L.AM. 37–53 imp.; C.A. 35–53; Hu.G. 35–40; Sil. 49–54; Y.

4460 **Archivo geográfico** de la **península ibérica.** Barcelona. *Archivo geogr. Peníns. ibér.* [1916] L.BM.

4461 **Archivo** de **medicina.** Porto. *Archivo Med., Porto*

4462 **Archivo** de **medicina legal.** Lisboa. *Archivo Med. leg.* [1922–] L.BM.; C. 30–35; MD. 31–; S. 22–35; UC. 30–; Bl.U. 30–42; Bm.U. imp.; Br.U. 22–23; C.UL. 30–; Db. 30–35; E.R. 22–35 imp.; G.F. 30–35; U. 30–35; Ld.U. 33–35; M.MS. 22–23; O.R. 30–35.

4464 **Archivo** de **patologia.** Lisboa. *Archivo Patol.* [1925–] L.BM. 54–; CB. 38–; H. 51–; MA. 46–; Cr.MD. 47–; O.R. 30–.

4465 **Archivo da repartição de antropologia criminal, psicologia experimental** e **identificação civil** do **Porto.** *Archivo Repart. Antrop. crim. Porto* [1931–] L.AN.

4466 **Archivo** y **revista** de **hospitales.** Habana. *Archivo Revta Hosp., Habana* [1935–]

4467 **Archivo** de **trabalhos** da **Faculdade** de **medicina** do **Porto.** *Archivo Trab. Fac. Med. Porto* L.MD. 41–43.

4468 **Archivos americanos** de **medicina.** Buenos Aires. *Archos am. Med.* [1925–] L.MA. 46–.

4469 **Archivos de anatomía.** Santiago de Compostela. *Archos Anat., Santiago* **Archivos de anatomia** e **anthropologia.** Lisboa. *See* 4455.

4470 **Archivos** de **anatomia patológica, patologia correlativa** e **neuro-ergenologia.** Coimbra. *Archos Anat. patol., Coimbra* [1946–] L.CB. 46–48. [*C. of:* 4628]

4471 **Archivos argentinos** de **dermatología.** Buenos Aires. *Archos argent. Derm.* [1951–] L.MA.; MD.

4472 **Archivos argentinos** de **enfermedades** del **aparato digestivo** y de la **nutrición.** Buenos Aires. *Archos argent. Enferm. Apar. dig.* [1925–] L.MA. 28–40; MD. 36–; TD. 28– imp.

4473 **Archivos argentinos** de **enfermedades** del **aparato respiratório** y **tuberculosis.** Buenos Aires. *Archos argent. Enferm. Apar. resp.* [1933–] L.MA. 33–40; MD. 36–; Lv.M. 35–39 imp.

4474 **Archivos argentinos** de **kinesiología.** Buenos Aires. *Archos argent. Kinesiol.* [1948–50] L.MD. 49–50.

4475 **Archivos argentinos** de **neurología.** Buenos Aires. *Archos argent. Neurol.* [1927–41] L.MD.; S.; UC. 33–41; UCH. 27–30; Br.U. 32–41 imp.; O.R. [*Replaced by:* 4621]

4476 **Archivos argentinos** de **pediatría.** Buenos Aires. *Archos argent. Pediat.* [1930–] L.MA. 37–39; MD. 37– imp. [*C. of:* 4589]

4477 **Archivos argentinos** de **reumatología.** Buenos Aires. *Archos argent. Reum.*

4478 **Archivos argentinos** de **tisiología.** Buenos Aires. *Archos argent. Tisiol.* [1938–] L.MD. 41–44. [*C. of:* 4664]

4479 **Archivos** de la **Asociación** para **evitar** la **ceguera** en **México.** México. *Archos Asoc. evit. Ceguera Méx.* [1942–] L.MA. 56–; MD. 46–; O.P. imp.

4480 **Archivos** de la **Asociación peruana** para el **progreso** de la **ciencia.** Lima. *Archos Asoc. peru. Prog. Cienc.* [1921–22] L.GL.; P.; U.; UC.; Bl.U.; Bm.U.; C.UL.; E.C. 22; M.U.
Archivos de **assistencia** a **psicopatas** do **Estado** de **São Paulo.** See 4645.

4481 **Archivos** de **biologia.** Lisboa. *Archos Biol., Lisb.*

4482 **Archivos** de **biologia.** São Paulo. *Archos Biol., S Paulo* [1915–] L.MA. 46–; TD. 36–54 v. imp.; Y.

4483 **Archivos** de **biología** de **Montevideo.** *Archos Biol. Montev.* Lv.U. 29–.

4484 **Archivos** de **biologia** e **tecnologia.** Curitiba. *Archos Biol. Tecnol., Curitiba* [1946–] L.BM^N.; EB.; v. 47–; Z.; Rt.; Y.
Archivos de **biologia vegetal teorica** y **aplicada.** Buenos Aires. See 4456.

4485 **Archivos** de **botânica** do **Estado** de **São Paulo.** *Archos Bot. Est. S Paulo* [1925–27: 38–] L.BM^N.; K.; L. 38–; TD. 25–27; E.B. 25–27; O.F. 27: 38–. [*C. of:* 2590]

4486 **Archivos brasileiros** de **cardiologia.** São Paulo. *Archos bras. Cardiol.* [1948–] L.MA.

4487 **Archivos brasileiros** de **cirurgia** e **ortopedia.** Recife. *Archos bras. Cirug. Ortop.* [1935–] Lv.M. 35–39. [*C. of:* 4505]

4488 **Archivos brasileiros** de **endocrinologia** (e **metabologia**). Rio de Janeiro. *Archos bras. Endocr. Metab.* [1951–] L.MA. 57–; MC. imp.; MD.; Abd.R. 58–; Br.U. 57–; G.U. 57–; Y.

4489 **Archivos brasileiros** de **hygiene mental.** Rio de Janeiro. *Archos bras. Hyg. ment.* [1925–]

4490 **Archivos brasileiros** de **medicina.** Rio de Janeiro. *Archos bras. Med.* [1911–] L.MA. 29– imp.; MD. imp.; TD. imp.

4491 **Archivos brasileiros** de **medicina naval.** Rio de Janeiro. *Archos bras. Med. nav.* [1940–]

4492 **Archivos brasileiros** de **neuriatria** y **psychiatria.** Rio de Janeiro. *Archos bras. Neuriat. Psychiat.* [1919–] L.S. 29–36.

4493 **Archivos brasileiros** de **nutrição.** Rio de Janeiro. *Archos bras. Nutr.* [1944–] L.AM. 47– imp.; BM. 60–; H. 51– imp.; MD. 46–; TD. 44–50 v. imp.; Abd.R. 44– imp.; R.D. 47–; Y.

4494 **Archivos brasileiros** de **oftalmologia.** São Paulo. *Archos bras. Oftal.* [1938–] L.MA. 51–; MD.; OP. 47–.

4495 **Archivos brasileiros** de **profilaxia** da **cegueira.** Bahia. *Archos bras. Profil. Cegueira* [1939–42]

4496 **Archivos brasileiros** de **psicotécnica.** Rio de Janeiro. *Archos bras. Psicotéc.* [1949–]

4497 **Archivos brasileiros** de **psychiatria, neurologia** e **sciencias affins.** Rio de Janeiro. *Archos bras. Psychiat. Neurol.*

4498 **Archivos brasileiros** de **urologia.** São Paulo. *Archos bras. Urol.*

4499 **Archivos** de **bromatologia.** Rio de Janeiro. *Archos Bromat.* [1953–] Y.

4500 **Archivos** de **cardiología** y **hematología.** Madrid. *Archos Cardiol. Hemat.* [1920–36]

4501 **Archivos chilenos** de **morfología.** Santiago. *Archos chil. Morf.* [1933–] L.BM^N. 33–35; S. 49–54.

4502 **Archivos chilenos** de **oftalmología.** Santiago. *Archos chil. Oftal.* [1944–] L.MA.; OP.

4503 **Archivos** de **cirugía experimental.** Buenos Aires. *Archos Cirug. exp.* [1938–] L.S. 38.

4504 **Archivos** de **cirurgia clinica** e **experimental.** São Paulo. *Archos Cirurg. clin. exp.* [1937–] L.MA. 49–; MD. 54–; O.R. 39–.

4505 **Archivos** de **cirurgia** e **ortopedia.** Recife. *Archos Cirurg. Ortop.* [1933–35] [*C. as:* 4487]

4506 **Archivos** de **clinica.** Rio de Janeiro. *Archos Clin.* [1945–51] L.MA.; MD. 48–51; TD. 48–51. [*C. in:* 4490]

4507 **Archivos** de **clinica ginecológica.** Rio de Janeiro. *Archos Clin. ginec.*

4508 **Archivos** de la **Clínica** e **Instituto** de **endocrinología.** Montevideo. *Archos Clín. Inst. Endocr., Montev.* [1937–40] L.MD.

4509 **Archivos** de **clinica médica.** Porto. *Archos Clin. méd.* [1925–] L.BM.; S. 25–56 imp.; O.R. 25–30 imp.

4510 **Archivos. Clínica obstétrica** y **ginecológica 'Eliseo Canton'.** Buenos Aires. *Archos Clín. obstét. ginec. Eliseo Canton* [1942–]

4511 **Archivos** de **clinica oftalmológica** e **oto-rino-laringológica.** Porto Alegre. *Archos Clin. oftal. oto-rinolar.* [1934–39] L.MD. 35: 37–39.

4512 **Archivos** das **clinicas cirúrgicas.** Coimbra. *Archos Clins cirúrg., Coimbra* [1928–] L.S. 35.

4513 **Archivos** del **Colegio médico** de **El Salvador.** San Salvador. *Archos Col. méd. El Salv.* [1947–] L.MA.; MD. 60–; TD. 48–.
Archivos das **colónias.** Lisboa. See 4458.

4514 **Archivos** de la **Conferencia** de **médicos** del **Hospital Ramos-Mejia.** Buenos Aires. *Archos Conf. Méd. Hosp. Ramos-Mejia* [1917–32] [*C. as:* 4607]

4515 **Archivos. Consejo** de **higiene** de **Valparaíso.** *Archos Cons. Hig. Valparaíso*

4516 **Archivos** de **criminología, neuropsiquiatría** y **disciplinas conexas.** Quito. *Archos Crim. Neuropsiq.* [1937–]

4517 **Archivos cubanos** de **cancerología.** Habana. *Archos cub. Cancer.* [1942–59] **L**.CB. 47–59; MA. 44–59; MD. 43–59; S. 43–59; **G**.U. 57–59.

4518 **Archivos** de **dermatologia** y **sifiligraphia** de **São Paulo.** *Archos Derm. Sif. S Paulo* [1937–] **L**.MA. 37–45 imp.; MD. 43–; TD. imp.

4519 **Archivos** de las **enfermedades** del **corazón** y de los **vasos.** Barcelona. *Archos Enferm. Corazón* **L**.MA. 47–.

4520 **Archivos** de **entomologia.** Pelotas. *Archos Ent., Pelotas* [1959–] Série A. **L**.BM^N.

4521 **Archivos** da **Escola médico-cirúrgica** de (**Nova**) **Goa.** Bastora. *Archos Esc. méd.-cir. (Nova) Goa* [1927–] **L**.AN. 27–37 imp.; EB. 27–38 imp.; LI. (*a*) 28–37 imp.: (*b*) 27–37; MY. 28–38; TD. (*a*): (*b*) 27–37; **Bm**.U. 27–38; **Br**.U. (*a*) 28–35: (*b*) 27–34; **C**.MO 32–38: 50–; **G**.U. (*a*) 27–38 imp.: 55–: (*b*) 28–37; **Lv**.U.; **O**.R. imp. [*C. of:* 4562]

4522 **Archivos** da **Escola superior** de **agricultura** e **medicina veterinaria,** Nictheroy. Rio de Janeiro. *Archos Esc. sup. Agric. Med. vet. Nictheroy* [1917–33] **L**.BM^N.; EB.; GL. imp.; MY.; V.; Z. 20–27; **Bl**.U. 17–28; **C**.A.; PH.; **E**.B.; C. 22–33 imp.; R.; **Lv**.U.; **M**.U. 17–23 imp.

4523 **Archivos** da **Escola superior** de **veterinaria** da **Universidade rural, Estado** de **Minas Gerais.** Belo Horizonte. *Archos Esc. sup. Vet. Est. Minas Gerais* [1943–] **L**.V.; Z. 55– imp.; **C**.V. 51–56; **E**.AB.; **Hu**.G. 50– imp.; **R**.D. 52–; **Sal**.; W.; Y.

4524 **Archivos** de la **Escuela** de **farmacía** de la **Facultad** de **ciencias médicas** de **Córdoba.** *Archos Esc. Farm. Córdoba* **L**.BM^N. 36–39.

4525 **Archivos españoles** de **morfología.** Valencia. *Archos esp. Morf.* [1941–] **L**.MD. 41–51 (imp.); **E**.U. imp.; **Nw**.A. imp.; Y.

4526 **Archivos españoles** de **enfermedades** de l'**aparato digestivo,** etc. Madrid. *Archos esp. Enferm. Apar. dig.* [1918–34] [*Replaced by:* 46494]

4527 **Archivos españoles** de **medicina interna.** Barcelona. *Archos esp. Med. interna* [1955–] **L**.MA.; MD. imp. [*C. of:* 4576]

4528 **Archivos españoles** de **neurología, psiquiatría** y **fisioterapía.** Madrid. *Archos esp. Neurol. Psiquiat. Fisioter.*

4529 **Archivos españoles** de **oncología.** Madrid. *Archos esp. Oncol.* [1930–33]

4530 **Archivos españoles** de **pediatría.** Madrid. *Archos esp. Pediat.* [1917–36] **L**.MA. 30–36 imp.

4531 **Archivos españoles** de **tisiología.** Barcelona. *Archos esp. Tisiol.* [1919–22] **L**.MC.

4532 **Archivos españoles** de **urología.** Madrid. *Archos esp. Urol.* [1944–] **L**.MA. 47–; MD. 45–.

4533 **Archivos** de **estudios médicos aragoneses.** Zaragoza. *Archos Estud. méd. aragon.* [1952–] **L**.MA.

4534 **Archivos** da **Faculdade** de **higiene** e **saúde pública** da **Universidade** de **São Paulo.** São Paulo. *Archos Fac. Hig. Saúde públ. Univ. S Paulo* [1947–] **L**.LI; MA.; MD. 59–; TD.

4536ᶜ **Archivos** da **Faculdade** da **medicina, Universidade** da **Bahía.** *Archos Fac. Med. Univ. Bahía* [1946–] **L**.MA.; TD. 46–53; **E**.R. 46–51; **Lv**.M. 46–51; **O**.R. [*C. of:* 2243]

4536ᵈ **Archivos** da **Faculdade nacional** de **medicina.** Rio de Janeiro. *Archos Fac. nac. Med., Rio de J.* [1946–] **L**.TD.

4536ᵉ **Archivos** de la **Facultad** de **ciencias médicas.** Quito. *Archos Fac. Cienc. méd., Quito*

4537 **Archivos** de la **Facultad** de **medicina** de **Zaragoza.** Zaragoza. *Archos Fac. Med. Zaragoza* [1953–] **L**.MA.

4538 **Archivos** de **farmacía** y **bioquímica** de **Tucuman.** *Archos Farm. Bioquím. Tucuman* [1943–] **L**.MA. 46–; MD.; PH.; SH.; Y.

Archivos fitotécnicos del **Uruguay.** *See* 4459.

4539 **Archivos** da **Fundação hospitalar Octavio Mangabeira.** Bahia. *Archos Fund. hosp. Mangabeira* [1954–] **L**.MA.

4540 **Archivos** de **gastro-enterología** y **nutrición.** Habana. *Archos Gastroent. Nutr.* **Lv**.U. 25–26.

Archivos geográficos de la **peninsula ibérica.** *See* 4460.

4541 **Archivos** de **ginecopatía, obstetricia** y **pediatría.** Barcelona. *Archos Ginecop. Obstet. Pediat.* [1889–23]

4542 **Archivos** de **higiene.** Buenos Aires. *Archos Hig., B. Aires* **L**.MA. 08–09.

4543 **Archivos** de **higiene.** Rio de Janeiro. *Archos Hig., Rio de J.* [1927–] **L**.TD. 17–30; 36–54 imp.; **Lv**.U. 27–30. [*Suspended* 1931–34]

4544 **Archivos** de **higiene** e **saúde pública.** São Paulo. *Archos Hig. Saúde públ.* [1936–] **L**.BM.; EB. 41–; LI. 41–42: 46–47; MA. 44–; SH. (1 yr); TD.; **Rd**. 53–; Y.

4545 **Archivos** de **histología normal** y **patológica.** Buenos Aires. *Archos Histol. norm. patol.* [1942–] **C**.PA. 42–46: 55–58; **O**.R.

4546 **Archivos** de **historia médica** de **Venezuela.** Caracas. *Archos Hist. méd. Venez.* [1934–35]

4547 **Archivos** de **historia** da **medicina portugueza.** Porto. *Archos Hist. Med. port.* **O**.R. 10–15.

4548 **Archivos** del **Hospital clinico** de **niños Roberto del Rio.** *Archos Hosp. clin. Niños Roberto Rio* [1930–] **L**.MA. 31–37 imp: 45–.

4549 **Archivos** del **Hospital** de la **Cruz roja** de **Barcelona.** Barcelona. *Archos Hosp. Cruz roja Barcelona* [1956–] **L**.MA.; MD. (imp.) [*C. as:* 4603]

4550 **Archivos. Hospital Israelita.** Buenos Aires. *Archos Hosp. israel., B. Aires.*

4551 **Archivos** del **Hospital municipal** de la **Habana.** *Archos Hosp. munic. Habana*

4552 **Archivos** del **Hospital Pereira Rossell.** Montevideo. *Archos Hosp. Pereira Rossell, Montev.* [1938–] **L**.MD. 38–39.

4553 **Archivos** del **Hospital Rosales.** San Salvador. *Archos Hosp. Rosales, S Salv.*

4554 **Archivos** del **Hospital Santo Tomás.** Panamá. *Archos Hosp. S Tomás, Panamá* [1946–] **L**.MA. 46–49; TD. 46–49.

4555 **Archivos** del **Hospital universitario.** Habana. *Archos Hosp. univ., Habana* [1949–] **L**.MA.; MD.; TD.; **Br**.U.

4556 **Archivos** del **Hospital Vargas.** Caracas. *Archos Hosp. Vargas* [1959–] **L**.BM.; MD.; **G**.U.

4557 **Archivos** de los **hospitales.** Buenos Aires. *Archos Hosps, B. Aires*

4558 **Archivos** dos **hospitals** da **Santa Casa** de **São Paulo.** São Paulo. *Archos Hosps S Casa S Paulo* [1954–] **L.**MA.

Archivos de **hygiene.** Rio de Janeiro. *See 4543.*

4559 **Archivos** de **hygiene** e **patologia exóticas.** Lisboa. *Archos Hyg. Patol. exót., Lisb.* [1905–26] **L.**BM^N. 05–15; EB. 09–26; MD. 05–18; TD.; UC. 05–16; **Abd.**U. 05–18; **Lv.**U. imp.; **O.**R. 05–18 imp. [*Replaced by:* 2253]

Archivos de **hygiene** e **saúde pública.** São Paulo. *See 4544.*

4560 **Archivos iberoamericanos** de **historia** de la **medicina** y de **antropología médica.** Madrid. *Archos iberoam. Hist. Med.*

4561 **Archivos** do **Ibit.** Bahia. *Archos Ibit* **L.**MA. 53–.

4562 **Archivos indo-portugueses** de **medicina** e **historia natural.** Nova Goa. *Archos indo-port. Med. Hist. nat.* [1921–27] **L.**MY.; TD.; **Bm.**U. imp.; **O.**R. imp. [*C. as:* 4521]

4563 **Archivos. Instituto aclimatación.** Almeria. *Archos Inst. Aclim., Almeria* [1953–] **L.**BM.^N; L.; Z.; **Hu.**G.; **Y.**

Archivos do **Instituto bacteriológico Câmara Pestana.** *See 4637.*

4564 **Archivos** del **Instituto** de **biología** do **exército.** Madrid. *Archos Inst. Biol. Exérc., Madr.* **L.**MA. 44–; TD. 44–53.

4565 **Archivos** do **Instituto** de **biologia** do **exército.** Rio de Janeiro. *Archos Inst. Biol. Exérc., Rio de J.*

4566 **Archivos** do **Instituto** de **biologia vegetal.** Rio de Janeiro. *Archos Inst. Biol. veg., Rio de J.* [1934–38] **L.**BM.; BM^N.; EB.; MY. imp.; **C.**A.; Z.; P.; **E.**R.; **G.**U. 34–37; **Lv.**U.; **Nw.**A.; **O.**R.; **Rt.** [*C. as:* 4646]

4567 **Archivos** do **Instituto biológico.** São Paulo. *Archos Inst. biol., S Paulo* [1934–] **L.**AM. imp.; BM^N.; E. imp.; EB.; L.; LI. imp.; MA. 46–; MC. 49–; MY.; TD.; V. 34–54; Z.; **C.**A.; MO. 34–40: 45–52; **E.**B.; **Lv.**U.; **Md.**H.; **Pl.**M. 38–39; **Rt.**; **Sal.** 45–; **W.**; **Y.** [*C. of:* 4568]

4568 **Archivos** do **Instituto biológico** de **defesa agricola** e **animal.** São Paulo. *Archos Inst. biol. Def. agric. anim., S Paulo* [1928–33] **L.**AM. imp.; BM^N.; E. imp.; EB.; L.; LI. imp.; MY.; TD. 29–33; V.; Z.; **C.**A.; **E.**B. 29–33; **Lv.**U.; **Md.**H.; **Rt.**; **W.** [*C. as:* 4567]

4569 **Archivos** do **Instituto brasileiro** para **investigação** da **tuberculose.** Bahia. *Archos Inst. bras. Invest. Tuberc.* [1937–] **L.**MA. 48–; TD. 43–45: 49–54.

4570 **Archivos** del **Instituto** de **cardiología de México.** *Archos Inst. Cardiol. Méx.* [1944–] **L.**MA. imp.; MD.; **C.**UL.; **O.**R. [*C. of:* 4587]

4571 **Archivos** del **Instituto** de **cirugía** de la **Provincia** de **Buenos Aires Prof. Dr. Luis Güemes.** *Archos Inst. Cirug. Prov. B. Aires* **L.**MD. 46; S. 46.

4572 **Archivos Instituto** de **estudios africanos.** Madrid. *Archos Inst. Estud. afr.* [1948–] **Y.**

4573 **Archivos** del **Instituto** de **farmacología experimental.** Madrid. *Archos Inst. Farmac. exp., Madr.* [1949–] **L.**MD. 59–; **Y.**

4574 **Archivos** do **Instituto** de **farmacologia** e **terapeútica experimental,** Universidade de Coimbra. *Archos Inst. Farmac. Univ. Coimbra* [1931–] **Y.**

4575 **Archivos** do **Instituto** de **medicina Le Gal** de **Lisboa.** Lisboa. *Archos Inst. Med. Le Gal Lisb.*

4576 **Archivos** del **Instituto** de **medicina práctica.** Barcelona. *Archos Inst. Med. práct.* [1949–54] **L.**MA. [*C. as:* 4527]

4577 **Archivos** do **Instituto médico-legal.** Rio de Janeiro. *Archos Inst. méd.-leg., Rio de J.* [1931–32] [*C. as:* 4600]

4578 **Archivos** del **Instituto nacional** de **hidrología** y **climatología médicas.** Habana. *Archos Inst. nac. Hidrol. Clim. méd., Habana* [1946–47] **L.**MD.

4579 **Archivos** del **Instituto nacional** de **higiene** de **Alfonso XIII.** Madrid. *Archos Inst. nac. Hig. Alfonso XIII* [1922–26] **L.**LI.; MD. 22–24; TD.; **Lv.**U. imp. [*C. of:* 7836]

4580 **Archivos** do **Instituto** de **patologia geral** da **Universidade** de **Coimbra.** *Archos Inst. Patol. ger. Univ. Coimbra* [1931–]

4581 **Archivos** do **Instituto** de **pesquisas agronómicas.** Pernambuco. *Archos Inst. Pesq. agron., Pernambuco* [1938–] **L.**AM.; **C.**A. 38–.

4582 **Archivos** do **Instituto** de **pesquisas veterinarias Desiderio Finamor.** Porto Alegre. *Archos Inst. Pesq. vet. Desiderio Finamor*

4583 **Archivos** do **Instituto químico-biológico** do **Estado** de **Minas Gerais.** Belo Horizonte. *Archos Inst. quím.-biol. Minas Gerais* [1945–] **L.**MD.; TD.

4584 **Archivos** do **Instituto vital Brazil.** Niteroi. *Archos Inst. vital Brazil* [1923–27] **L.**BM^N.; EB. [*C. as:* 7417]

4585 **Archivos internacionales** de la **hidatidosis.** Montevideo. *Archos int. Hidatid.* [1934–] **L.**MA. 46–; MD. 34–51: 56– imp.; S. 34–56; TD. 34–46.

4586 **Archivos** do **Jardim botânico.** Rio de Janeiro. *Archos Jard. bot., Rio de J.* [1915–] **L.**BM.; BM^N.; K.; L. imp.; MY. 17– imp.; UC. imp.; **Abd.**U.; **Bl.**U. 18–; **Bm.**U. 25; **Br.**U. 15–30 imp.; **C.**BO.; P.; **Db.**; **E.**B.; R. 15–18; **G.**U. 25– imp.; **Hu.**G. 49–; **Ld.**U. 25–; **Lv.**U. 15–33; **M.**U.; **Nw.**A. 17–; **O.**R. imp.; **Rt.**; **Sa.**; **Y.** [*Suspended* 1934–46]

4587 **Archivos latino-americanos** de **cardiología** y **hematología.** México. *Archos lat.-am. Cardiol. Hemat.* [1930–43] **L.**MA. 32–43; MD. 40–43; **C.**UL.; **O.**R. [*C. as:* 4570]

4588 **Archivos latino-americanos** de **neurología, psiquiatría, medicina legal.** Neuronio. *Archos lat.-am. Neurol. Psiquiat. Med. leg.* [1939–]

4589 **Archivos latino-americanos** de **pediatría.** Buenos Aires. *Archos lat.-am. Pediat.* **L.**MD. 19–26 imp. [*C. as:* 4476]

4590 **Archivos latinos** de **medicina** y de **biología.** Madrid. *Archos lat. Med. Biol.* [1903]

4591 **Archivos latinos** de **rinología, laringología, otología.** Barcelona. *Archos lat. Rinol. Lar. Otol.* [1890–05] [*C. as:* 4638]

4592 **Archivos** de **lepra.** Bogotá. *Archos Lepra, Bogotá* [1929–35] **L.**BM. 32–35; MA. 29–33; MD. 32–35 imp.; S. 29–33; TD.; **Lv.**M. imp.; U. imp.

4593 **Archivos** do **manicômio judiciario Heitor Carrilho.** Rio de Janeiro. *Archos Manicôm. judic. Heitor Carrilho* **L.**MA. 51–54.

4594 **Archivos** de **medicina, cirugía** y **especialidades.** Madrid. *Archos Med. Cirug. Espec.* [1920–36] **L.**MA. 29–36; MD. 28–36; **E.**U. imp.; **Lv.**U.

4595 Archivos de **medicina e cirugía** de **Pernambuco.** Pernambuco. *Archos Med. Cirug. Pernambuco*

4596 Archivos de **medicina experimental.** Madrid. *Archos Med. exp.* [1948–] **L.**BM.; MA.; MD.; **Bl.**U.; **Br.**U.; E.U.; **Lv.**M. 48–51. [*C. of:* 53424]

4597 Archivos de **medicina infantil.** Habana. *Archos Med. infant., Habana* [1932–] **L.**MA. 33–; MD. 37–; RA. 42–; TD.

4598 Archivos de **medicina interna.** Habana. *Archos Med. interna, Habana* **L.**MA. 52– imp.; MD. 35–42; **C.**UL.

4599 Archivos de **medicina legal.** Buenos Aires. *Archos Med. leg., B. Aires.* [1931–]

4600 Archivos de **medicina legal e identificação.** Rio de Janeiro. *Archos Med. leg. Ident., Rio de J.* [1931–] **L.**MD. 33–39; S. 34–40. [*C. of:* 4577]

4601 Archivos de **medicina práctica.** La Coruña. *Archos Med. práct., La Coruña*

4602 Archivos médico-quirúrgicos y del **trabajo.** Barcelona. *Archos méd.-quir. Trab., Barcelona* [1945–] **L.**MA. 45–48 imp.; TD. 45–48.

4602ª Archivos médicos. Porto Alegre. *Archos méd., Porto Alegre* [1930] [*C. of:* and *Rec. as:* 4639]

4603 Archivos médicos de **Barcelona.** Barcelona. *Archos méd. Barcelona* [1957–] **L.**MA.; MD. [*C. of:* 4549]

4604 Archivos médicos de **Cuba.** La Habana. *Archos méd. Cuba* [1952–] **L.**MA.; MD.; TD. imp.; **Br.**U. 54–57. [*C. of:* 4611]

4605 Archivos médicos ferrocarrileros. México. *Archos méd. ferrocarr., Méx.* [1939–]

4606 Archivos médicos da Fôrça pública de **São Paulo.** São Paulo. *Archos méd. Fôrça públ. S Paulo*

4607 Archivos médicos del **Hospital Ramos-Mejia.** Buenos Aires. *Archos méd. Hosp. Ramos-Mejia* [1933–] [*C. of:* 4514]

4608 Archivos médicos mexicanos. Monterrey. *Archos méd. mex.* [1943–] **L.**MA. 46–.

4609 Archivos médicos municipais. São Paulo. *Archos méd. munic., S Paulo.* [1949–] **L.**MA.; TD. 49–54 imp.

4610 Archivos médicos panameños. Panamá. *Archos méd. panam.* [1952–] **L.**MA.; TD. [*C. of:* 7576]

4611 Archivos médicos de **San Lorenzo.** La Habana. *Archos méd. S Lorenzo* [1950–51] **L.**MA.; MD. [*C. as:* 4604]

4612 Archivos médicos del **Servicio sanitario** del **ejército** (y **Boletin** de **sanidad dental**). Santiago. *Archos méd. Serv. sanit. Ejérc. Boln Sanid. dent.* [1938–] [*C. of:* 46921]

4613 Archivos mexicanos de **neurología y psiquiatría.** México. *Archos mex. Neurol. Psiquiat.* [1951–] **L.**MA. [*C. of:* 4623]

4614 Archivos mexicanos de **venereosifilía y dermatología.** México. *Archos mex. Venereosif. Derm.* [1942–]

4615 Archivos mineiros de **leprologia.** Belo Horizonte. *Archos mineir. Leprol.* [1941–] **L.**MA. 46; TD. 52– v. imp.

4616 Archivos. Museu etnográfico, Universidad de **Buenos Aires.** *Archos Mus. etnogr. Univ. B. Aires* [1930] **L.**AN.

4617 Archivos do **Museu Bocage.** Lisboa. *Archos Mus. Bocage* [1930–56] **L.**BMN. imp.; Z. [*C. as:* 46879]

4618 Archivos do **Museu nacional.** Rio de Janeiro. *Archos Mus. nac., Rio. de J.* [1876–] **L.**AM.40–; BM.76–17; BMN.; E. 76–92: 45: 51; EB. 23–; GL. 00–34; L. imp.; R. 76–92; U. 76– 01: 45–; UC. 87–92: 95; Z. imp.; **Abd.**U. 77–81; **Bl.**U. 79– imp.; **Bm.**U. 78–92: 45; **C.**B. 45–; P.; V. 45–; **Cr.**M. 45–; **Db.**; E.B. 05–; C. 77–34 imp.; J. 80–; R. 87–; **Fr.** 45–; **G.**F. 92–21; M. 92– imp.; U. 43–; **Lv.**P. 76–29; U. 78–26; **M.**U. imp.; **Nw.**A. 45–; **O.**R. 76–05: 40; **Pl.**M. 45–; **Rt.** 45–; **Wo.** 29–; Y.

4619 Archivos do **Museu paranaense.** Curitiba. *Archos Mus. parana.* [1941–] **L.**BMN. 41–54; EB. 41–51; Y. [*From* 1954 *in series:* Antropología; Geología]

4620 Archivos de **neurobiología.** Madrid. *Archos Neurobiol.* [1920–] **L.**MD. 20–32; S. 54–; **O.**PH. 20–28.
   Archivos de **neurobiología, psicología, fisiología, histología, neurología** y **psiquitría.** Madrid. *See* 4620.

4621 Archivos de **neurocirugía.** Buenos Aires. *Archos Neurocirug.* [1944–54] **L.**MD.; S. 44–47; UC.; **Br.**U.; **O.**R. [*Replaces:* 4475] [*C. as:* 2482]

4622 Archivos de **neurología** y **psiquiatría.** La Habana. *Archos Neurol. Psiquiat., Habana* [1947–] **L.**MA. 54–.

4623 Archivos de **neurología y psiquiatría** de **México.** *Archos Neurol. Psiquiat. Méx.* [*C. as:* 4613]

4624 Archivos de **neuropsiquiatria.** São Paulo. *Archos Neuropsiquiat., S Paulo* [1943–] **L.**MA.; MD.; S.

4625 Archivos de **oftalmología.** La Paz. *Archos Oftal., La Paz* [1936–]

4626 Archivos de **oftalmología** de **Buenos Aires.** *Archos Oftal. B. Aires* [1925–] **L.**MA. 45–; MD. 26–; OP.; E.S. 36–51 imp.

4627 Archivos de **oftalmología hispano-americanos.** Madrid. *Archos Oftal. hisp.-am.* [1901–36] **L.**MD. 04–24. [*Replaced by:* 4659]
   Archivos de **patologia.** Lisboa. *See* 4464.

4628 Archivos de **patologia geral** e de **anatomia patológica.** Coimbra. *Archos Patol. geral Anat. patol.* **L.**MD. 35–40*. [*C. as:* 4470]

4629 Archivos de **pediatría.** Barcelona. *Archos Pediat., Barcelona* [1950–] **L.**MA.

4630 Archivos de **pediatría.** Rio de Janeiro. *Archos Pediat., Rio de J.* [1928–] **L.**MD. 31–32 imp.

4631 Archivos de **pediatría** del **Uruguay.** Montevideo. *Archos Pediat. Urug.* [1930–] **L.**MA. 34–; MD. 37–; TD. 41–53 imp. [*Replaces:* 8134]

4632 Archivos peruanos de **higiene mental.** Lima. *Archos peru. Hig. ment.* [1937–] [*Replaces:* 7751]

4633 Archivos peruanos de **patología y clínica.** Lima. *Archos peru. Patol. Clín.* [1947–] **L.**MA.

4634 Archivos de la **Policlínica.** Habana. *Archos Policlín., Habana*

4635 Archivos portugueses de **oftalmologia.** Lisboa. *Archos port. Oftal.* [1949–] **L.**MD. 53–; OP.

4636 Archivos de **psiquiatría** y **criminología.** Buenos Aires. *Archos Psiquiat. Crim.* [1903–13] **L.**BM. 11–13. [*Replaced by:* 46451]

4637 **Archivos** do **R. Instituto bacteriológico Câmara Pestana.** Lisboa. *Archos R. Inst. bact. Câmara Pestana* [1906–] **L.**BM^N.; EB. 09–52; H. 42–; LI. 49–; MC.; MD. 06–42 imp.; R. 08–52; TD.; UC.; **Abd.**U. 06–24; **Bm.**U. 06–32; **Br.**U.; **C.**UL.; **G.**U. 34–37; Lv.U.; O.R.

Archivos da **repartição** de **antropologia criminal, psicologia experimental e identificação civil** do **Porto.** *See* 4465.

Archivos y **revista** de **hospitales.** Habana. *See* 4466.

4638 **Archivos** de **rinología, laringología, otología.** Barcelona. *Archos Rinol. Lar. Otol.* [1906–18] [*C. of:* 4591]

4639 **Archivos rio-grandenses** de **medicina.** Porto Alegre. *Archos rio-grand. Med.* [1919–30: 31–] **L.**TD. **Lv.**U. 19–22 imp. [> 4602ª, *June–August* 1930]

4640 **Archivos** de **salud pública.** Buenos Aires. *Archos Salud públ., B. Aires* **Lv.**M. 47–49.

4641 **Archivos** del **Sanatório quirúrgico** del **Doctor Figueroa.** México. *Archos Sanat. quir. Figueroa*

4642 **Archivos** de **saúde pública.** Belo Horizonte. *Archos Saúde públ., Belo Horiz.* **L.**TD. 38.

4643 **Archivos** da **Seccão** de **biologia e parasitologia.** Museo zoológico da Universidade de Coimbra. *Archos Secç. Biol. Parasit. Mus. zool. Univ. Coimbra* [1929–39] **L.**BM^N.; E. 29–33; EB.; Z.; **Bl.**U.; **C.**P.; **E.**F.; R.; U. 29–35; **Lv.**U.

4644 **Archivos** da la **Secretaría** de **salud pública** de la **nación.** Buenos Aires. *Archos Secr. Salud públ., B. Aires* [1946–] **L.**D. 47– imp.; H. 46–50 imp.; MA.; MD. 46–49; TD. 46–49; **Bl.**U. 47–49; **Ld.**U. 46–48.

4644° **Archivos. Servicio** de **vías urinarias** del **Hospital Rawson.** Buenos Aires. *Archos Serv. Vías urin. Hosp. Rawson*

4645 **Archivos** do **Serviço** de **assistencia à psicopatas** do **Estado** de **São Paulo.** *Archos Serv. Assist. Psicopatas S Paulo* [1936–47] **L.**MD. 38–39.

4646 **Archivos** do **Serviço florestal** do **Brasil.** Rio de Janeiro. *Archos Serv. flor. Bras.* [1939–] **L.**BM.; BM^N.; MY. 51–; **Bl.**U. 47–; **C.**A.; P.; E.R.; **G.**U.; **Ld.**U. 52–; **Lv.**U.; **Nw.**A. 47–; **O.**F.; R.; **Rt.**; Y. [*C. of:* 4566]

4647 **Archivos** do **Serviço nacional** de **doenças mentais.** Rio de Janeiro. *Archos Serv. nac. Doênç. ment., Rio de J.* [1940–] [*C. of:* 2214]

4648 **Archivos** do **Serviço nacional** de **lepra.** Rio de Janeiro. *Archos Serv. nac. Lepra, Rio de J.* [1943–] **L.**TD. 43–47 imp.

4650 **Archivos** do **Serviço** de **vias urinarias** da **Policlínica geral** do **Rio de Janeiro.** *Archos Serv. Vias urin. Policlín. geral Rio de J.* [1930–]

4651 **Archivos** de la **Sociedad americana** de **oftalmología** y **optometría.** Bogotá. *Archos Soc. am. Oftal. Optom.* [1958–] **L.**MD. 59–.

4652 **Archivos** de la **Sociedad argentina** de **anatomía normal** y **patológica.** Buenos Aires. *Archos Soc. argent. Anat.* [1939–] **L.**MA.

4653 **Archivos** de la **Sociedad** de **biología** de **Montevideo.** *Archos Soc. Biol. Montev.* [1929–] **L.**BM^N.; MA. 31: 45–; R.; **Bl.**U.; **C.**B. 43–; P.; **Db.**; **E.**R.; **Hu.**G. 49–55; **Lv.**U.; **N.**U. 29–33.

4654 **Archivos** de la **Sociedad** de **cirujanos** de **Chile.** Santiago. *Archos Soc. Ciruj. Chile* [1949–] **L.**MA. 51–.

4655 **Archivos** de la **Sociedad** de **cirujanos** de **hospital.** Santiago de Chile. *Archos Soc. Ciruj. Hosp., Santiago* [1931–] **L.**MA. 46–47; MD. 45–.

4656 **Archivos** de la **Sociedad cubana** de **oftalmología.** La Habana. *Archos Soc. cub. Oftal.* [1951–] **L.**MA. 52–; MD. 51–52 imp.

4657 **Archivos** de la **Sociedad** de **estudios clínicos** de la **Habana.** Habana. *Archos Soc. Estud. clín. Habana* [1881–] **L.**MA. 37–; MD. 37–40; TD. 27–41: 47–51 imp.

4658 **Archivos** de la **Sociedad médica** de **Valparaíso.** *Archos Soc. méd. Valparaíso* [1926–] **Br.**U. 26–29.

4659 **Archivos** de la **Sociedad oftalmológica hispano-americana.** Barcelona. *Archos Soc. oftal. hisp.-am.* [1942–] **L.**MA. 45–; MD. 42: 47–; U. 50–; Y. [*Replaces:* 4627]

4660 **Archivos** da **Sociedade** de **medicina e cirurgia** de **São Paulo.** *Archos Soc. Med. Cirurg. S Paulo*

4661 **Archivos** da **Sociedade** de **medicina legal e criminologia** de **São Paulo.** São Paulo. *Archos Soc. Med. leg. Crim. S Paulo* [1930–]

4662 **Archivos sudamericanos** de **oftalmología.** Santiago de Chile. *Archos sudam. Oftal.* [1936–]

4663 **Archivos** de **terapéutica** de las **enfermedades nerviosas** y **mentales.** Barcelona. *Archos Terap. Enferm. nerv. ment.*

4664 **Archivos** de **tisiología.** Buenos Aires. *Archos Tisiol.* [1928–37] [*C. of:* 2534; *C. as:* 4478]

4665 **Archivos** de **tisiología** y **pneumología.** Montevideo. *Archos Tisiol. Pneumol.* [1940–] **L.**MD. 41–43.

Archivos de **trabalhos** da **Faculdade** de **medicina** do **Porto.** *See* 4467.

4666 **Archivos universal** de **medicina.** Fichas médicas. Extratos de revistas médicas estrangeiras. Rio de Janeiro. *Archos universal Méd. Fichas méd.*

4667 **Archivos** de la **Universidad** de **Buenos Aires.** *Archos Univ. B. Aires* [1926–] **L.**BM^N. 26–48 imp.; **C.**UL.; O.B.

Archivos da **Universidade** da **Bahia. Faculdade** de **medicina.** *See* 4536°.

4669 **Archivos** da **Universidade** de **Lisboa.** *Archos Univ. Lisb.* [1914–] **L.**U. 14–20; UC. 25–; **Abd.**U. 14–20; **Abs.**U. 14–16; **Bm.**U. 14–20; **C.**UL.; **Db.**; **E.**U. 14–20; **Lv.**U.; **M.**U. 14–45; O.R. 14–20; Sa. 14–20.

4670 **Archivos uruguayos** de **ginecología** y **obstetricia.** Montevideo. *Archos urug. Ginec. Obstet.* **L.**MD. 28.

4671 **Archivos uruguayos** de **medicina, cirugía** y **especialidades.** Montevideo. *Archos urug. Med. Cirug.* [1932–] **L.**LI. 32–37: 57–; MA. 33– imp.; MD.; S. 32–58; TD.; E.U.; **Nw.**A.

4672 **Archivos venezolanos** de **cardiología** y **hematología.** Caracas. *Archos venez. Cardiol. Hemat.* [1935–1936]

4673 **Archivos venezolanos** de **nutrición.** Caracas. *Archos venez. Nutr.* [1950–] **L.**AM. 53–; BM.; TD. imp.; R.D.; Sa.; Y.

4674 **Archivos venezolanos** de **patología tropical** y **parasitología médica.** Caracas. *Archos venez. Patol. trop. Parasit. méd.* [1948–] **L.**EB. 48–54; MA.; TD. 48–54 imp.; Y.

4675 **Archivos venezolanos** de **psiquiatría** y **neurología.** Caracas. *Archos venez. Psiquiat. Neurol.*

4676 **Archivos venezolanos** de **puericultura** y **pedia-tría.** Caracas. *Archos venez. Puericult. Pediat.* [1939-] **L.**BM.; MA. 46-; MD. 43- imp.; TD. 39-42 imp.: 51-.

4677 **Archivos venezolanos** de la **Sociedad** de **oto-rino-laringología, oftalmología, neurología.** Caracas. *Archos venez. Soc. Oto-rino-lar.* [1940-] **L.**MA. 45-; MD. 43-46: 51 imp.; TD. 40-43 imp.

4678 **Archivos** de **veterinaria práctica.** La Coruña. *Archos Vet. práct., La Coruña* [1951]

4679 **Archivos** de **zoologia** do **Estado** de **São Paulo.** *Archos Zool. Est. S Paulo* [1940-] **L.**AN. 47-; EB.; BM^N.; Z.; **C.**UL.; **Db.**; **E.**R.; **Nw.**A. 40-43: 47-; **Y.**

4680 **Archivos** de **zootecnia.** Córdoba. *Archos Zootecnia* [1952-] **L.**AM.; BM^N. 53- imp.; V. 54-; **E.**AB.; **R.**D.; **W.**; **Y.**

4681 **Archivum balatonicum.** Budapest. *Archvm balaton., Bpest* [1926-27] **L.**BM^N.; L.; LI.; MC.; SC.; **E.**R.; **Fr.**; **O.**AP. 27; **Pl.**M.; **Rt.** [*C. as:* 3886]

4683 **Archivum chirurgiae oris.** Bologna. *Archvm Chir. Oris, Bologna* [1931-35] **L.**S.

4684 **Archivum chirurgicum.** Budapest. *Archvm chir., Bpest* [1948-49] [*C. as:* 29246]

4685 **Archivum chirurgicum neerlandicum.** Arnhem. *Archvm chir. neerl.* [1949-] **L.**MA.; MD.; S.; **Br.**U.; **Cr.**MD. 55-; **Db.** 50-; **E.**S. 50-; U.; **G.**F.; U.; **Ld.**U. 50-; **Lv.**M. 55-; **M.**MS. 54-; **Nw.**A. 50: 55-; **O.**R. 56-.

4686 **Archivum histologicum japonicum.** Okoyama. *Archvm histol. jap.* [1950-] **C.**P.

4687 **Archivum melitense.** Malta Historical and Scientific Society. Valetta. *Archvm melit.* [1910-39] **L.**BM. 10-37; BM^N. 10-39.

Archivum Societatis zoologicae-botanicae fennicae 'Vanamo'. *See* 51413.

4688 **Archivum stomatologiae.** Budapestini. *Archvm Stomat., Bpest*

4689 **Archivum zoologicum.** Budapestini. *Archvm zool., Bpest* [1909-10] **L.**BM^N.; E.; Z.

4690 **Archiwum automatyki i telemechaniki.** Warszawa. *Archwm Automat. Telemech.* [1956-] **L.**P. 60-; **Y.**

4691 **Archiwum budowy maszyn.** Warszawa. *Archwm Budowy Masz.* [1954-] **L.**AV.; BM.; P.; **E.**R.; **Y.**

4691^a **Archiwum chemji i farmacji.** Warszawa. *Archwm Chem. Farm.* [1934-37] **L.**P.

4692 **Archiwum elektrotechniki.** Warszawa. *Archwm Elektrotech.* [1952-] **L.**BM. 53-; EE. imp; P.; SC.; **Y.**

4693 **Archiwum etnograficzne.** Poznań. *Archwm etnogr.* [1936-37]

4693^c **Archiwum etnologiczne.** Łódź. *Archwm etnol.* [1951-] **L.**BM.

4694 **Archiwum górnictwa.** Warszawa. *Archwm Górn.* [1956-] **L.**BM. imp.; MI.; MIE.; P.; **G.**U.; **Ld.**U. 58-; **Sh.**M.; **Y.** [*C. from:* 4695]

4695 **Archiwum górnictwa i hutnictwa.** Kraków, Warszawa. *Archwm Górn. Hutn.* [1953-55] **L.**BM.; MI.; MIE; P.; **G.**U.; **Sh.**M.; **Y.** [*C. as* 4694 and 4698]

4695^c **Archiwum higeny.** Wilno. *Archwm Hig.* [1926-36]

4696 **Archiwum historji i filozofji medycyny.** Poznań. *Archwm Hist. Filoz. Med.* [1924-47] [*C. as:* 4697]

4697 **Archiwum historji medycyny.** Warszawa. *Archwm Hist. Med.* [1948-] **L.**MD. 57-; Y [*C. of:* 4696]

4698 **Archiwum hutnictwa.** Kraków, Warszawa. *Archwm Hutn.* [1956-] **L.**BM.; MI.; P.; **Sh.**M.; **Y.** [*C. from:* 4695]

4699 **Archiwum hydrobiologji i rybactwa.** Suwałki. *Archwm Hydrobiol. Ryb.* [1926-47] **L.**AM.; BM^N. 26-38: 47; SC.; Z. 28-47 imp.; **Dm.** 30-34: 38; **E.**R. 33-47; **Fr.** 28-38: 47; **Lo.** 26-32: 47; **Lv.**U. 31-47; **Pl.**M. 26-39. [*C. of:* 4709; *C. as:* 38051]

4700 **Archiwum hydrotechniki.** Warszawa, Kraków. *Archwm Hydrotech.* [1954-] **L.**BM.; **E.**R.; **Y.**

4701 **Archiwum hygieny.** Wilno. *Archwm Hyg.* [1926-] **L.**TD. 26-36 imp.

4702 **Archiwum immunologii i terapii doświadczalnej.** Warszawa, Wrocław. *Archwm Immun. Terap. doświad.* [1953-] **L.**MA.; **G.**U.; **Y.**

4703 **Archiwum inżynierii lądowej.** Warszawa. *Archwm Inżyn. lądow.* [1955-] **L.**P. 69-; **Y.**

4704 **Archiwum mechaniki stosowanej.** Warszawa, Kraków. *Archwm Mech. stosow.* [1949-] **L.**AV. 52- imp.; BM. 54-; **E.**R. 52; **Ld.**U. 60- **O.**R. 54-; **Y.**

4705 **Archiwum mineralogiczne.** Warszawa. *Archwm miner.* [1925-] **L.**BM^N.; GL. imp.; **Db.** 30-; **Lv.**U. [*Not issued* 1939-1953]

4706 **Archiwum nauk antropologicznych.** Warszawa. *Archwm Nauk antrop.* [1921-30] **L.**AN.

4707 **Archiwum nauk biologicznych.** Lwów. *Archwm Nauk biol.* [1921-] **L.**BM^N. 21-39; R. 29-39; DB. 46-.

4708 **Archiwum naukowe.** Lwów. *Archwm nauk.* [1902-19] **L.**BM. [*C. as:* 4710]

4709 **Archiwum rybactwa polskiego.** Bydgoszcz. *Archwm Ryb. pol.* [1925] **L.**BM.; Z. imp. [*C. as:* 4699]

4710 **Archiwum Towarzystwa naukowego we Lwowie.** Lwów. *Archwm Tow. nauk. Lwow.* [1921-39] **L.**BM.; BM^N. (Wydz. III.) 21-39. [*C. of:* 4708]

4711 **Arclight Review.** Colchester. *Arclight Rev.* **L.**AV. 57-; P. 56-; **C.**ENG. 45-; **Lv.**P. 56-; **M.**T. (1 yr).

4712 **Arcos.** Revue des applications de la soudure à l'arc. Bruxelles. *Arcos* **L.**NF. 46-; P. 13- imp.; **Y.**

4713 **Arcos Technical Bulletin.** Philadelphia. *Arcos tech. Bull.* **L.**P. 38-.

4714 **Arcs** and **Sparks.** United Carbon Products Co. Bay City, Mich. *Arcs Sparks* **L.**P. curr.

4715 **Arctic:** Journal of the Arctic Institute of North America. Montreal, New York, etc. *Arctic* [1948-] **L.**BM. 60-; G.; GM. 54-; MO. 48-53; SC. 49-; **Abd.**U. 51-; **C.**GG. 48-54 imp.; PO.; **E.**G.; **H.**U. 49-; **Ld.**U.; **Lo.** 50-; **O.**AP; **Pl.**M.; **Wo.** 54-; **Y.**

4716 **Arctic Bibliography.** Washington. *Arct. Biblphy* [1953-] **L.**BM.; P. 54- imp; SC.

4717 **Arctic Circular.** Ottawa. *Arct. Circ.* [1948-] **L.**G.; **C.**PO.; **O.**AP.

4718 **Arctic News.** Toronto. *Arct. News* **C.**PO. 44-.

4719 **Arctic News Letter.** Montreal, New York. *Arct. News Lett.* [1948-] **L.**MO. 49-53; **C.**PO.; **Ld.**U. 48-49; **Pl.**M 49-57 imp.

4720 **Arctic Service News.** R. and H. Chemicals Dept., E.I. Du Pont de Nemours and Co. Wilmington. *Arct. Serv. News Du Pont de Nemours* [1935-] **L.**P. 38-41 imp.

4721 **Arctica.** Leningrad. *Arctica, Leningr.* [1933-37] **L.**BM^N.; SC.; **C.**PO.; **O.**AP. 33-36. [*C. in:* 38764]

4722 **Ardea.** Nederlandsche ornithologische vereeniging. Wageningen. *Ardea* [1912–] **L.**BM[N].; NC. 12–43: 46–50; Z. 40–; **Br.**U.; **C.**B.; **E.**F. 24–; **O.**OR. imp.; **Y.**

4723 **Ardealul medical.** Cluj. *Ardeal. med.* **L.**MA. 48–.

4724 **Ardeola.** Revista iberica de ornithología. Madrid. *Ardeola* [1954–] **L.**BM[N].; Z.; **C.**B.; **O.**OR.; **Y.**

4725 **Arecanut Journal.** Kozhikode, Calcutta. *Arecanut J.* **C.**A. 59–; **Md.**H. 56–.
Arerugi. *See* 1741.

4726 **Argentina austral.** Buenos Aires. *Argent. austral* **C.**PO 49–.

4727 **Argentina odontológica.** Buenos Aires. *Argent. odont.*

4728 **Argentor.** Journal of the National Jewellers' Association, London. *Argentor* [1946–53] **L.**BM.; DI.; U.; **Bm.**P.; **O.**B. 48–53.

4729 **Argeologiese navorsing** van die **Nasionale Museum, Bloemfontein.** *Argeol. Navors. nas. Mus. Bloemfontein* [1928–39] **L.**BM[N]. 32–39; GL.; GM.; SC.; Z.; **Bl.**U.; **C.**P. imp.; **E.**R. 28–35; **Lv.**U. [*C. in:* 34434]

4730 **Argile.** Paris. *Argile* [1938–] **L.**P. 38; **St.**R. 46–.

4731 **Argomenti** di **farmacoterapia.** Corregio, Emilia. *Argom. Farmacoter.*

4732 **Argus.** Journal of modern production practice. Birmingham. *Argus, Bham* [1957–] **L.**AV.; P.; **Y.**

4733 **Argus.** Rivista di tutte le reviste mediche. Roma. *Argus, Roma*

4734 **Argus** des **collectivités.** Paris. *Argus Collect.* [1951–] **L.**H. 58–.

4735 **Argus médical.** Paris. *Argus méd.* [1907–13]

4736 **Argus vétérinaire.** Paris. *Argus vét.*
'**Arheia iatrikēs.** Ἀρχεία ἰατρικῆς. *See* 4277.

4737 '**Arheia ugieinēs.** en Athenais. Ἀρχεία ὑγιεινῆς. *Arheia Ug.* [1937–] **L.**MA. 47–; MD. 37–40; H. 47–; TD. imp.

4738 '**Arheion 'ellēnikēs paidiatrikēs etairias.** Athēnai. Ἀρχειον ἑλληνικής παιδιατρικής ἑταιρίας. *Arheion ell. paidiat. etair.*

4739 '**Arheion neurologias.** Athēnai. Ἀρχειον νευρολογίας. *Arheion neurol.*

4740 **Arhimēdēs.** Ἀθηνēσιν. Ἀρχιμήδης. *Arhimēdēs*

4741 **Arhitectura.** Bucureşti. *Arhitectura* **L.**BA 35–37. [*C. as:* 4741[a]]

4741[a] **Arhitectura R.P.R.** Bucureşti. *Arhit. R.P.R.* [1953–] **L.**BA. 56–; BM. 57–; **Y.** [*C. of:* 4741]

4741[c] **Arhitekt.** Ljubljana. *Arhitekt* [1951–] **L.**BM.

4742 **Arhitektōriki.** Ἀθηνēσιν. Ἀρχιτεκτωρικι. *Arhitektōriki* **L.**BA. 57–; **Y.**

4743 **Arhitektura.** Zagreb. *Arhitektura* **L.**BA. 52–.

4744 **Arhiv** za **arbanasku starinu, jezik** i **etnologiju.** Beograd. Архив за арбанаску старину, језик и етнологију. *Arh. arban. Star. Jezik Etnol.*

4745 **Arhiv bioloških nauka.** Beograd. *Arh. biol. Nauka* [1949–]. **L.**BM[N]. 49–50: 55–; EB.; MC. 23–40; MY.; **C.**B. 49–51; **Db.** 49–; **Fr.** 50 imp.: 53–; **Pl.**M. 49–50; **Y.**

4746 **Arhiv** zu **farmaciju.** Beograd. *Arh. Farm.* [1951–] **L.**PH. 56–.

4747 **Arhiv** za **hemiju** i **farmaciju.** Zagreb. *Arh. Hem. Farm.* [1927–37] **L.**C.; P. 28–37; SC. 29–37. [*C. as:* 4748]

4748 **Arhiv** za **hemiju** i **tehnologiju.** Zagreb. *Arh. Hem. Tehnol.* [1938–39] **L.**C.; P.; SC. [*C. of:* 4747; *C. as:* 4751]

4749 **Arhiv** za **higijenu rada.** Zagreb. *Arh. Hig. Rada* [1950–] **L.**BM. 51–; MA.; TD.; **Cr.**MD.; **O.**R.; **Y.**

4750 **Arhiv** za **kemiju.** Zagreb. *Arh. Kem.* [1946–55] **L.**BM.; C.; P.; SC.; **Ld.**U. 49–55; **Lv.**P. 54–55; **O.**R. 54–55; **Y.** [*C. of:* 27307; *C. as:* 16067]

4751 **Arhiv** za **kemiju** i **tehnologiju.** Zagreb. *Arh. Kem. Tehnol.* [1939–40] **L.**C.; P.; SC.; [*C. of:* 4748; *C. as:* 27307]

4752 **Arhiv** za **medicinu rada.** Zagreb, Beograd. *Arh. Med. Rada* [1946–] **L.**TD. 47–48.

4753 **Arhiv Ministarstva poljoprivrede** i **šumarstva.** Beograd. *Arh. Minist. Poljopr. Šum.* [1934–40] **L.**AM. 34–39; EB. 38–40; SC.; **C.**A. [*C. as:* 4754]

4754 **Arhiv** za **poljoprivredne nauke** (i **tehniku.**) Beograd. *Arh. poljopr. Nauke Teh.* [1946–] **L.**AM. 46–52 imp.; EB.; MY. 52–; **Abs.**A. 51–; **C.**A.; **Hu.**G. 51–; **Md.**H.; **Rt.** imp.; **Sil.** 51–52; **Y.** [*C. of:* 4753]

4754[c] **Arhiv** za **zastitu majke** i **djeteta.** Zagreb. *Arh. Zast. Majke Djet.* [1957–] **L.**MA 58– imp.

4755 **Arhiva veterinara.** Bucureşti. *Arhiva vet.* [1904–] **L.**TD. 20–30; V. 09–39 imp.; **Lv.**U. imp.

4756 **Arid Zone.** UNESCO. Paris. *Arid Zone* [1958–] **L.**BM.; MO.; **Bm.**P.; **Bn.**U.; **Dn.**U.; **Ld.**P.; **O.**F.; R.; RE.; **Rt.**; **Y.** [*C. of:* 4758]

4757 **Arid Zone Programme.** UNESCO. Paris. *Arid Zone Progm.* [1952–53] **Bn.**U.; **Dn.**U. 53; **O.**F.; RE. [*C. as:* 4758]

4758 **Arid Zone Research.** UNESCO. Paris. *Arid Zone Res.* [1955–57] **L.**MO.; **Bn.**U. imp.; **Dn.**U.; **O.**F.; R.; RE. imp.; **Rt.** [*C. of:* 4757; *C. as:* 4756]

4759 **Aristote.** Science et médecine. Paris. *Aristote* [1926–]
Arizona Bureau of **Mines Bulletin.** *See* 9670.

4760 **Arizona Highways.** Phoenix. *Ariz. Highw.* **L.**BM[N]. 61–.

4761 **Arizona Medical Journal.** Phoenix. *Ariz. med. J.* [1912–16]

4762 **Arizona Medicine.** Phoenix. *Ariz. Med.* [1944–] **L.**MA. 47–; TD. 44–55. [*Replaces:* 50272]

4763 **Arizona Mining Journal.** Phoenix. *Ariz. Min. J.* [1917–27] **L.**SC. 26–27. [*C. as:* 32025]

4764 **Arizona Mining Review.** Prescot. *Ariz. Min. Rev.*

4765 **Arizona Public Health News.** Phoenix. *Ariz. publ. Hlth News* **L.**TD. 31–39. [*C. of:* 33406]
Arizona University Bulletin.
Anthropological Papers. *See* 3556.
Biological Science Bulletin. *See* 7077.
Bureau of Mines. *See* 9670.
Physical Science Bulletin. *See* 37678.

4766 **Arizona Wild Life Magazine.** Bisbee. *Ariz. wild Life Mag.* [1928–38] [*Replaced by:* 4767]

4767 **Arizona Wildlife** and **Sportsman.** Phoenix. *Ariz. Wildl. Sportsm.* [1939–] [*Replaces:* 4766]

4768 **Arkansas Dental Journal.** Conway. *Arkans. dent. J.*

4769 **Arkansas Farm Research.** Fayetteville. *Arkans. Fm Res.* [1952–] **L.**AM.; MY.; P. curr.; **C.**A.; **Hu.**G.; **Md.**H.; **N.**U.; **Y.**

4770 **Arkansas Ginner.** Little Rock, Ark. *Arkans. Ginner* [1924–25] [*C. as:* 1932]

4771 **Arkansas Malaria Bulletin.** Little Rock. *Arkans. Malaria Bull.* [1945–50] **L.**TD. 49–50. [*C. as:* 4772]

4772 **Arkansas Vector Control Bulletin.** Little Rock. *Arkans. Vector Control Bull.* [1950–] **L.**TD. 50–52. [*C. of:* 4771]

4773 **Arkhimedes.** Helsinki. *Arkhimedes* [1949–] **L.**P.; SC.; **Y.**

Arkhitekt. Sofiya. Архитект. *See* 50618.

4774 **Arkhitektura.** Sofiya. Архитектура. *Arkhitektura, Sof.* [1954–] **L.**BM.

4774[a] **Arkhitektura Moskvȳ.** Moskva. Архитектура Москвы. *Arkhit. Mosk.* [1953–] **L.**BM.

4774[b] **Arkhitektura narodov SSSR.** Moskva. Архитектура народов СССР. *Arkhit. Narod. SSSR* [1951–] **L.**BM.

4775 **Arkhitektura za rubêzhom.** Moskva. Архитектура за рубѣжом. *Arkhit. Rubêzh.* [1934–] **L.**BA. 34–36.

4776 **Arkhitektura SSSR.** Moskva. Архитектура СССР. *Arkhit. SSSR* [1933–41: 51–] **L.**BA. 55–; BM. 35–41; **Y.** 52–. [*Published as the organ of various institutions at different periods. From 1946–50 > 4776[d]*]

4776[a] **Arkhitektura sovetskikh obshchestvennȳkh sooruzheniï.** Moskva. Архитектура советских общественных сооружений. *Arkhit. sov. obshch. Sooruzh.* [1954–] **L.**BM.

4776[b] **Arkhitektura sovetskikh promȳshlennȳkh sooruzheniï.** Moskva. Архитектура советских промышленных сооружений. *Arkhit. sov. prom. Sooruzh.* [1954–] **L.**BM.

4776° **Arkhitektura i stroitel'stvo.** Kiev. Архитектура и строительство. *Arkhit. Stroit., Kiev* [1953–56] [*C. as:* 51017]

4776[d] **Arkhitektura i stroitel'stvo.** Moskva. Архитектура и строительство. *Arkhit. Stroit., Mosk.* [1946–50] **L.**BA.; BM. 47–50; **Y.** 48–50. [*C. of and Rec. as:* 4776]

4776[e] **Arkhitektura i stroitelstvo.** Sofiya. Архитектура и строителство. *Arkhit. Stroit., Sof.* [1951–] **L.**BM. 52–.

4777 **Arkhitektura i stroitel'stvo Leningrada.** Leningrad. Архитектура и строительство Ленинграда. *Arkhit. Stroit. Leningr.* [1936–60] **L.**BA. 55–60; BM. 55–60 imp.; **Y.** 55–60. [*C. as:* 51017[a]]

4778 **Arkhitektura i stroitel'stvo Moskvȳ.** Архитектура и строительство Москвы. *Arkhit. Stroit. Moskvȳ* [1952–] **L.**BM. 53–; **Y.** 56–.

4779 **Arkhitektura Ukrainskoï SSR.** Moskva. Архитектура Украинской ССР. *Arkhit. ukr. SSR* [1954–] **L.**BM.

4780 **Arkhiv anatomii, gistologii i émbriologii.** Leningrad, Moskva. Архив анатомии, гистологии и эмбриологии. *Arkh. Anat. Gistol. Embriol.* [1931–] **L.**MA 57–; S. 57–; SC. 37–39: 57–; **Db.**; **Sh.**U. 59; **Y.** 54: 57–. [*C. of:* 48308]

4781 **Arkhiv Azerbaïdzhanskogo instituta mikrobiologii i gigienȳ.** Baku. Архив Азербайджанского института микробиологии и гигиены. *Arkh. azerb. Inst. Mikrobiol. Gig.* **L.**TD. 29.

Arkhiv biologicheskikh nauk. Moskva. Архив биологических наук. *See* 4357.

Arkhiv istorii nauki i tekhniki. Leningrad. Архив истории науки и техники. *See* 54653, ser. 1.

4782 **Arkhiv klinicheskoï i éksperimental'noï meditsinȳ.** Moskva. Архив клинической и экспериментальной медицины. *Arkh. klin. éksp. Med.* [1922–24]

4783 **Arkhiv kriminologiï i sudebnoï meditsinȳ.** Khar'kov. Архив криминологіи и судебной медицины. *Arkh. Krim. sudeb. Med.*

4784 **Arkhiv meditsinskikh nauk.** Moskva. Архив медицинских наук. *Arkh. med. Nauk* [1929] **L.**MA imp.; MD.; TD. [*C. as:* 56842]

4785 **Arkhiv na Ministerstvo na narodnoto prosvêshtenie.** Sofiya. Архивъ на Министерство на народното просвѣщение. *Arkh. Minist. nar. Prosvêsh., Sof.*

4786 **Arkhiv Omskogo meditsinskogo instituta.** Omsk. Архив Омского медицинского института. *Arkh. omsk. med. Inst.* [1930–] **L.**BM; TD. 30–31; **E.**U.; **Nw.**A. [*C. of:* 36179]

4787 **Arkhiv patologii.** Moskva. Архив патологии. *Arkh. Patol.* [1946–] **L.**BM. 49–; CB. 55–; MA. 47; MD.; **O.**R. 47–; **Y.** 51–55: 58–. [*C. of:* 4788]

4788 **Arkhiv patologii, anatomii i patologicheskoï fiziologii.** Moskva. Архив патологии, анатомии и патологической физиологии. *Arkh. Patol. Anat. patol. Fiziol.* [1935–41] [*C. as:* 4787]

4789 **Arkhiv Russkago protistologicheskago obshchestva.** Petrograd. Архив Русскаго протистологическаго общества. *Arkh. russk. protist. Obshch.* [1922–23] **L.**BM[N].; TD.; **Lv.**U. 22. [*C. as:* 48310]

4790 **Arkhiv Sovetskogo klinicheskogo instituta dlya usovershenstvovaniya vracheï.** Petrograd. Архив Советского клинического института для усовершенствования врачей. *Arkh. sov. klin. Inst.*

4791 **Arkhiv teoreticheskoï i prakticheskoï meditsinȳ.** Baku. Архив теоретической и практической медицины. *Arkh. teor. prakt. Med.* [1923] [*C. as:* 59196]

4792 **Arkhiv veterinarnȳkh nauk.** Архивъ ветеринарныхъ наук. *Arkh. vet. Nauk* [1876–17] **L.**EB. 14.

4793 **Arkhȳtektura radyans'koyi Ukrayini.** Kȳyiv. Архітектура радянської України. *Arkhȳt. radyan. Ukr.* [1938–]

4794 **Arkitekt.** Istanbul. *Arkitekt* **L.**BA.; **Y.** [*C. of:* 31865]

4795 **Arkitekten.** Helsingfors. *Arkitekten, Helsingf.* [1903–] **L.**BA 29–. [*Suspended* 1918–19]

4797 **Arkitekten.** København. *Arkitekten, Kbh.* [1929–] **L.**BA.; NP.; **Y.** [*C. of:* 4029]

4798 **Arkitekten, Maanedshæfte.** Kjøbenhavn. *Arkitekten, Maanedsh.* **L.**BA. 27–; NP. 53–. [*C. in:* 4797]

4799 **Arkitekten, Ugehæfte.** Kjøbenhavn. *Arkitekten, Ugeh.* **L.**BA 45–. [*C. in:* 4797]

4801 **Arkitektur.** Stockholm. *Arkitektur, Stockh.* [1901–22]

4801° **Arkitektur.** Stockholm. *Arkitektur, Stockh.* [1959–] **L.**BA.; **Nw.**A.; **Y.** [*C. of:* 12728, Upplaga A]

4802 **Arkiv** för **astronomi.** Stockholm. *Ark. Astr.* [1950–] **L.**AS.; BM.; MO.; R.; RI.; SC.; **Br.**U.; **C.**P.; UL.; **Db.**; **E.**R.; **G.**U.; **M.**U.; **Nw.**A.; **Y.** [*C. from:* 4809]

4803 **Arkiv** för **botanik.** Uppsala, Stockholm. *Ark. Bot.* [1903–] **L.**BM.; BM^N.; G.; GL. 03–48; K.; L.; MC. 55–; R.; SC.; UC. 12–; **Abd.**U. 03–52; **Bl.**U. 03–17; **Bn.**U. 48–; **C.**BO. 31– imp; P.; UL.; **Db.**; **E.**B. 05–; C.; J.; P.; R.; **G.**U. 49–; **H.**U. 36–; **Ld.**U. 03–16: 24–; **Lv.**M.; U.; **M.**U. imp.; **O.**BO. 31–; R. 03–33; **Pl.**M.; **Sa.** 49–; **Y.** [*C. of:* 36053]

4804 **Arkiv** för **fysik.** Stockholm. *Ark. Fys.* [1949–] **L.**AS.; BM.; C. 51–; MO.; P.; R.; RI. SC.; U.; **Abd.**U. 49–54; **Br.**U.; **C.**P.; UL.; **Db.**; **E.**R.; **Ex.**U. 56–; **G.**T. 55–; U.; **M.**U. imp.; **Nw.**A.; **R.**U. 58–; **Sa.**; **Y.** [*C. from:* 4809]

4805 **Arkiv** för **geofysik.** Stockholm. *Ark. Geofys.* [1950–] **L.**AS.; BM.; GL.; I.; MO.; P.; R.; RI.; SC.; **C.**P.; UL.; **Db.**; **E.**R.; **G.**U.; **Wo.** 51: 59 imp.; **Y.**

4806 **Arkiv** för **kemi.** Stockholm. *Ark. Kemi* [1949–] **L.**BM.; C.; LI. 58–; MA.; P.; QM. 57–; R.; RI.; SC.; UC.; **Abd.**U. 49–53; **Cr.**U. 58–; **Db.**; **E.**R. U.; **G.**U.; **M.**C.; **Nw.**A.; **Pl.**M.; **Sh.**U. 56–; **Y.** [*C. from:* 4807]

4807 **Arkiv** för **kemi, mineralogi** och **geologi.** Uppsala. *Ark. Kemi Miner. Geol.* [1903–49] **L.**BM; BM^N.; C.; GL.; GM.; I. 47–49; MA. 46–49; P. 08–49; R.; SC.; **Abd.**U.; **Bl.**U. 03–17; **C.**P.; UL.; **Db.**; **E.**C.; J.; P.; R.; U.; **G.**U.; **Ld.**U. imp.; **M.**U. 13–24 imp.; **N.**U. 45–49; **O.**R.; **Pl.**M. [*C. from:* 36053; *C. as:* 4806 and 4810]

4808 **Arkiv** för **matematik.** Stockholm. *Ark. Mat.* [1949–] **L.**BM. 60–; M.; MO.; R.; RI.; SC.; U.; UC. 53–; **Br.**U.; **C.**P.; UL.; **Db.**; **E.**Q.; R.; **G.**U.; **Ld.**U.; **M.**U.; **N.**U. 54–; **Nw.**A.; **Y.** [*C. from:* 4809]

4809 **Arkiv** för **matematik, astronomi** och **fysik.** Uppsala. *Ark. Mat. Astr. Fys.* [1903–49] **L.**BM.; BM^N.; EE. 30–49 imp.; GL.; MO.; P.; R.; RI.; SC.; UC.; **Abd.**U.; **Abs.**U. 03–21; **Bl.**U. 03–17; **Bm.**U. 48–49; **Br.**U. imp.; **C.**O.; P.; UL.; **Db.**; **E.**C.; O.; Q. 27–49; R.; **Ld.**U.; **Lv.**U. 24–49; **M.**U. 47–49; **Nw.**A.; **O.**R. [*C. from:* 36053; *C. as:* 4802, 4804 and 4808]

4810 **Arkiv** för **mineralogi** och **geologi.** Stockholm. *Ark. Miner. Geol.* [1949–] **L.**BM.; BM^N.; GL.; I.; RI.; SC.; **Abd.**U. 49–52; **Br.**U.; **C.**P.; UL.; **Db.**; **E.**R.; U.; **G.**U.; **M.**U.; **Pl.**M.; **Y.** [*C. from:* 4807]

4811 **Arkiv** för **zoologi.** Uppsala. *Ark. Zool.* [1903–] **L.**B. 59–; BM.; BM^N.; E.; FR. 13–; G.; GL. 03 57; L.; MC. 50–; NC. 59–; R.; SC.; UC.; Z.; **Abd.**U. 03–53; **Bl.**U. 03–17: 42–; **Bm.**U.; **Br.**U. 32–; **C.**B. 03–25; P.; UL.; **Db.**; **Dm.**; **E.**C.; J.; R.; **G.**U. 49–; **Ld.**U. 03–16: 25–; **Lv.**U.; **Mu.** 36–40 imp.; **Mi.**; **Nw.**A. 51–; **O.**H. 16–39; R.; **Pl.**M.; **Y.** [*C. from:* 36053]

4812 **Arkkitehti.** Helsinki. *Arkkitehti* [1921–] [*For the Swedish edition, see* 4795]

Arktis. Copenhagen. *See* 56136.

4813 **Arktis.** Internationale Studiengesellschaft zur Erforschung der Arktis mit dem Luftschiff Gotha. *Arktis, Gotha* [1928–31] **L.**G.; MO.; **C.**PO.; **O.**AP. imp.

4814 **Arma Engineering.** American Bosch Arma Corporation. Garden City, N.Y. *Arma Engng* [1959–] **L.**AV.; **Y.**

4815 **Armagh Observatory Contributions.** Armagh. *Armagh Obs. Contr.* [1941–] **L.**AS.; BM. 50–; **Bl.**U.; **C.**UL.; **Db.**; **M.**U. 49–58; **O.**R.

4816 **Armagh Observatory Leaflet.** Armagh. *Armagh Obs. Leafl.* [1950–] **L.**AS.; SC.; **Bl.**U. 52–; **Db.**; **M.**U. 50–59.

4817 **Armed Forces Chemical Journal.** Washington. *Armed Forces chem. J.* [1946–] **L.**P. 48–; **Y.**

4818 **Armed Forces Medical Library Catalogue.** Washington. *Armed Forces med. Libr. Cat.* [1952–] **L.**BM.; BM^N.; D.; GH.; MA.; MC.; MD.; P.; S. 52–54; **Abd.**U.; **Bm.**P.; **Br.**U.; **C.**UL.; **Db.**; **Dn.**U.; **E.**A.; P.; R.; S.; U.; **G.**F.; M.; U.; **Lv.**M.; U.; **M.**MS.; R.; **O.**B.; R.; **Sa.**; **Sh.**U. [*C. of:* 4834]

4819 **Armed Forces Medical Library News.** Washington. *Armed Forces med. Libr. News* [1952–] **L.**MD.; TD. [*C. of:* 4835]

4820 **Armierter Beton.** Berlin. *Armierter Beton* [1908–19] **L.**P. 16–19*.

4821 **Armour Engineer.** Chicago. *Armour Engr* [1909–35] **L.**P. 28–35. [*C. as:* 4822]

4822 **Armour Engineer** and **Alumnus.** Chicago. *Armour Engr Alumnus* [1935–41] **L.**P. [*C. of:* 4321; *C. as:* 22774]

4823 **Armour's Analysis.** Chicago. *Armour's Analysis* [1952–] **L.**AM. (1 yr)

Armourers and **Braziers Journal.** Sheffield. *See* 26887.

4824 **Arms** and **Explosives.** London. *Arms Explos.* [1892–20] **L.**BM.; IC.; P.; **Db.**; **E.**A. 92–05; **O.**B.; **Ste.**

4825 **Armstrong Tire News.** West Haven, Conn. *Armstrong Tire News* [1943–] **L.**PR. imp.; **Sy.**R. 58–.

4826 **Armstrong-Saurer Bulletin.** London. *Armstrong-Saurer Bull.* [1932–35] **L.**P.; **Sy.**R.

4827 **Armstrong-Siddeley Air Mail.** *Armstrong-Siddeley Air Mail* [1928–] **L.**P. 28–33; SC.; **Bm.**U.

4828 **Armstrong-Whitworth Record.** London. *Armstrong-Whitworth Rec.* **L.**P. 31–33.

4829 **Armurerie liégoise.** Liège. *Armur. liége.* [1911–] **L.**P. 11–48; **Ste.** 23–30.

4830 **Army Air Force Technical Data Digest.** Ohio. *Army Air Force Data Dig.* **L.**PG.

4831 **Army Dental Bulletin.** Washington. *Army dent. Bull.* **L.**D. 42–43 imp. [*C. of:* 16519]

4832 **Army Medical Bulletin.** Carlisle, Pa. *Army med. Bull.* [1922–43] **L.**MD. 42–43; **Br.**U. 27–43 imp. [*Replaces:* 30506; *C. as:* 12504]

4833 **Army Medical Department Bulletin.** London. *Army med. Dep. Bull.* [1941–45] **L.**MD.; S.; TD.

Army Medical Journal. Prague. *See* 56854.

4834 **Army Medical Library Author Catalogue.** Washington. *Army med. Libr. Author Cat.* [1949–51] **L.**BM.; BM^N.; D.; GH.; MA.; MC.; MD.; P.; S.; **Abd.** U.; **Bm.**P.; **Br.**U.; **C.**UL.; **Db.**; **Dn.**U.; **E.**A.; P.; R.; S.; U.; **G.**F.; M.; U.; **Lv.**M.; U.; **M.**MS.; R.; **O.**R.; R.; **Sa.**; **Sh.**U. [*C. of:* 22926; *C. as:* 4818]

4835 **Army Medical Library Newsletter.** Washington. *Army med. Libr. Newsl.* [1945–52] **L.**MD.; TD. [*C. as:* 4819]

4836 **Army Medical Services Magazine.** Aldershot. *Army med. Servs Mag.* [1948–] **L.**D.; S. 48–50; **Db.**; **E.**A. 48–53.

4837 **Army Motors.** Baltimore. *Army Mot.* [1940–]

4838 **Army Ordnance.** Washington. *Army Ordn.* [1920–] **Ste.** 20–47 imp.

4839 **Army Veterinary Bulletin.** Carlisle Barracks, Pa. *Army vet. Bull.* [1942–43] **L.**V. [*C. of:* 56633; *C. in:* 12504]

4840 **Arnoldia.** Arnold Arboretum. Cambridge, Mass. *Arnoldia* [1941–] **L.**BM^N. 43–; HS. 41; K.; SC.; **E.**B.; **Y.** [*C. of:* 11534]

4841 **Aromatics.** New York. *Aromatics* [1927–32] [*C. of:* 34679; *C. in:* 1943]

4842 **Arquitecto peruano.** Lima. *Arquitecto peru.* [1937–] **L.**BA. 48–.

4843 **Arquitectos.** Lisboa. *Arquitectos* [1938–42] **L.**BA.

4844 **Arquitectura.** Habana. *Arquitectura, Habana* [1917–] **L.**BA. 37–.

4844° **Arquitectura.** Lisboa. *Arquitectura, Lisb.* **L.**BM. 44–52 imp.

4845 **Arquitectura.** Madrid. *Arquitectura, Madr.* [1918–36: 59–] **L.**BA. 32–; BM. 33–. [>46826, 1941–58]

4846 **Arquitectura.** México. *Arquitectura, Méx.* [1939–] **L.**BA. 46–.

4847 **Arquitectura.** Montevideo. *Arquitectura, Montev.* [1914–] **L.**BA. 30–.

4848 **Arquitectura** y **arte decorativo.** Santiago de Chile. *Arquit. Arte decor.* [1929–]

4849 **Arquitectura** y **construcción.** Barcelona. *Arquit. Constr.* [1897–22]

4850 **Arquitectura** y **decoración.** México. *Arquit. Decor.* [1937–] **L.**BA.

4851 **Arquitectura** y lo **demás.** México. *Arquit. Demás* [1945–] **L.**BA.

4852 **Arquitectura** de **hoy.** Buenos Aires. *Arquit. hoy* [1947–48] **L.**BA. [*South American edition of* 4010]

4853 **Arquitectura portuguesa** (e **cerâmica** e **edificâçáo, reunidas**). *Arquit. port.* [1908]

4853° **Arquitetura** e **engenharia.** *Arquit. Engen.* **Y. Arquivo.** *Arq. See* **Archivo** and **Archivos. Arquivos.** *Arqs See* **Archivos.**

4854 **Arrow Press Student Publications.** Leighton Buzzard. *Arrow Press Stud. Publs* [1948–] **L.**P. 48–56; **Y.**

4855 **Arrow Press Technical Publications.** Leighton Buzzard. *Arrow Press tech. Publs* [1946–53] **L.**BM.; P.; **Y.** [*C. as:* 20666]

4856 **Ars medica.** Revista de medicina, cirugía y especialidades. Barcelona. *Ars med.* [1925–26] **Br.**U. 27–29 imp.

4857 **Ars medici.** Bruxelles, Gand. *Ars Med., Brux.* [1946–] **L.**MA. 47–; MD. 48–; **Bl.**U. 46–47.

4858 **Ars medici.** Liesthal. *Ars Med., Liesthal* [1911–] **L.**MA. 46–; MD. imp.

4859 **Ars medici.** Wien. *Ars Med., Wien* [1923–39] **L.**BM. 24–39; H. 33–39; MA. 31–39; MD.; **Abs.**N. 29–39; **Bm.**U. 23–27; **Br.**U. 23; **C.**UL.; **Lv.**U. 23–26 imp.; **Nw.**A. 28–39; **O.**R. 24–36. [*American edition of:* 4858]

4860 **Ars typographica.** New York. *Ars typogr.* [1918–26] **L.**BM.; SB. 25–26; **Abs.**N. 26; **M.**P. 25–26; **O.**R. 25–26. [*Suspended* 1920–25]

4861 **Årsberättelse. Föreningen för växtförädling** av **strogstrad.** Stockholm, etc. *Årsberätt. För. Växtförädl Strogstr.* **L.**P. 43–; **C.**A. 49; **O.**F. 42–.

4862 **Årsberättelse. Hydrografiska byrån.** Stockholm. *Årsberätt. hydrogr. Byr.* **L.**MO. 08–18; **E.**M. 13–18 imp.

4862° **Årsberättelse. Jordbrukstekniska förening.** *Årsberätt. jordbrtek. För.* **Y.** 28–.

4863 **Årsberättelse** från **K. Veterinär-institutet.** Stockholm. *Årsberätt. K. VetInst., Stockh.* **L.**AM.

4864 **Årsberättelse. Kemiska station** och **frökontrollanstalt, Kalmar.** *Årsberätt. kem. Stn FrökontrAnst., Kalmar*

4865 **Årsberättelse. Kemiska station** och **frökontrollanstalt, Örebro.** *Årsberätt. kem. Stn FrökontrAnst.* **Örebro Rt.** 93–31.

4866 **Årsberättelse. Kemiska station, Halmstad.** *Årsberätt. kem. Stn Halmstad*

4867 **Årsberättelse** från **Malmö museum.** Malmö. *Årsberätt. Malmö Mus.* **L.**BM. 26–; **C.**FT. 34–47 imp.

4868 **Årsberättelse. Stadskemistens laboratorium.** Göteborg. *Årsberätt. Stadskem. Lab., Göteborg*

4869 **Årsberättelse. Statens meteorologisk-hydrografiska anstalt.** Stockholm. *Årsberätt. St. met.-hydrogr. Anst.* **L.**MO. 35– imp. [*C. from:* 4902]

4870 **Årsberättelse. Sveriges geologiska undersökning.** Stockholm. *Årsberätt. Sver. geol. Unders.* **Br.**U. 40–; **Db.** (*Aa.*) 29–: (*Ba.*) 33–: (*C.*) 31–: (*Ca.*) 11–.

4870° **Årsberättelse. Sveriges meteorologiska** och **hydrologiska institut.** Stockholm. *Årsberätt. Sver. met. hydrol. Inst.* **Y.** 35–.

4871 **Årsberetning. Chr. Michelsens institutt** for **videnskap** og **åndsfrihet.** Bergen. *Årsberetn. Chr. Michelsens Inst.* **Y.**

4872 **Årsberetning** fra **Danmarks fiskeri-** og **havundersøgelser.** København. *Årsberetn. Danm. Fisk.-Havunders.* [1951–] **L.**BM^N.; **Abd.**M.; **Dm.** 51–52; **E.**R.; **Lo.** 51–55; **Lv.**U; **Pl.**M. 51–52; **Y.**

4873 **Årsberetning. Dansk fiskeriforening.** Kjøbenhavn. *Årsberetn. dansk FiskForen.* **Db.** 04–09.

Årsberetning. Danske landhusholdningsselskab. *See* 4876.

4874 **Årsberetning** fra **Fiskeriministeriets Forsøgslaboratorium.** København. *Årsberetn. FiskMinist. ForsLab.* **L.**BM. 52–.

4874° **Årsberetning** vedrørende **Frøpatologisk Kontrol. Statens Plantetilsyn.** København. *Årsberetn. frøpatol. Kontrol* [1952–] **Y.**

4875 **Årsberetning** fra **J. E. Ohlsens enkes plantepatologiske laboratorium.** København. *Årsberetn. J. E. Ohlsens Enkes plpatol. Lab.* **Md.**H. 40–45.

4876 **Årsberetning** om det **K. Danske landhusholdningsselskabs virksomhed.** Kjøbenhavn. *Årsberetn. K. danske LandhushSelsk. Virks.* **L.**AM. 90–39; MO. 61–72; **C.**A. 30–39.

Årsberetning fra **Kommissionen for Danmarks fiskeri-** og **havundersøgelser.** *See* 4872.

ARS

4877 Årsberetning. Landbrukets priscental. Ski. *Årsberetn. Landbr. Priscent.* C.A. 22–; O.AEC. 45–.

4878 Årsberetning for de meteorologiske institutjoner i Norge. Oslo. *Årsberetn. met. Inst. Norge* [1938–] C.PO. 38–39; Db.; E.M.; Y. [*C. of:* 35061]

4879 Årsberetning. Norges branntekniske Laboratorium. Trondheim. *Årsberetn. Norg. branntek. Lab.* L.P. 54–.

4880 Årsberetning. Norges byggforskningsinstitutt. Oslo. *Årsberetn. Norg. ByggforskInst.* [1954–] L.P. 57–; Y.

4881 Årsberetning vedkommende Norges fiskerier. Bergen. *Årsberetn. Norg. Fisk.* L.AM. 94– imp.; Abd.M. 32–44 imp.: 45–; C.PO. 27–; Db. 00–; Dm. 23; Lv.U. 00– imp.; Mi. 03–26 imp.; Pl.M. 00–.

4882 Årsberetning fra Norges landbrukshøiskole. Oslo. *Årsberetn. Norg. LandbrHøisk.* [1927–] L.MO. 40–42; Abs.A.; N.; Dm. 27–38; Ld.U.; Md.H. 44–45; Nw.A. 27–45 imp.; Rt. [*C. of:* 4913]

4882° Årsberetning. Norges standardiserings-forbund. *Årsberetn. Norg. Stand.-Forb.* Y. 34–.

4883 Årsberetning från Norges tekniske Høiskole (Høgskole). Trondhjem. *Årsberetn. Norg. tek. Høisk. (Høgsk.)* L.P. 38–; Y.

4884 Årsberetning. Norges teknisk-naturvitenskapelige forskningsråd. Oslo. *Årsberetn. Norg. tek.-naturv. ForskRåd* [1946–] L.BM. 48–; P. 52–; Y.

4885 Årsberetning. Norsk meteorologisk institut. Oslo. *Årsberetn. norsk met. Inst.* L.MO. 67–76: 19–; E.M. 10–45; R. 24–; O.G. 13– imp.

4886 Årsberetning. Norsk treteknisk institutt. Blindern. *Årsberetn. norsk tretek. Inst.* Y.

4887 Årsberetning angaaende de offentlige foranstaltninger til landbrukets fremme. Kristiania. *Årsberetn. off. Foranst. Landbr. Frem.* L.AM. 91–; C.A. 31–.

4888 Årsberetning og regnskap. Fiskerimuseet i Bergen og Selskabet for de norske fiskeriers fremme. *Årsberetn. Regnsk. FiskMus. Bergen* [1958–] L.BM^N. [*C. of:* 6113]

4889 Årsberetning for Selskabet for de norske fiskeriers Fremme. Bergen. *Årsberetn. Selsk. norske Fisk. Frem.* [1879–51] L.BM. 82–00; BM^N. 10–51; Abd.M. 89–00 imp.; Db. 90–51; Lv.U. 94–01; Pl.M. 84–51 imp. [*C. as:* 6113]

4890 Årsberetning. Skogsinsektlaboratorium. Springforbi. *Årsberetn. Skogsinsektlab.* L.BM^N. 48–.

4890^a Årsberetning. Statens skadedyrlaboratorium. Springforbi. *Årsberetn. St. Skadedyrlab.* L.BM. 49–; FB. 48–; Br.A. 48–; N.U. 56–; O.AP. 48-imp.

4891 Årsberetning. Sundhedsstyrelse, Danmark. *Årsberetn. SundhStyr. Danm.* L.H. 18– imp.

4892 Årsberetning angaaende sundhedstilstanden. København. *Årsberetn. Sundhedstilst.* L.H. 07–38 v. imp.: 50–; G.PH. 30–38.

4892° Årsberetning fra Syndssygehospitalerne i Danmark. København. *Årsberetn. Syndssygehosp. Danm.* L.BM. 50–.

Årsberetning. Tromsø Museum. *See* 54388.

4893 Årsberetning. Veterinærdirektoratet. København. *Årsberetn. VetDir.* L.AM. 24– imp.; BM. 48–; V. 26–; W. 26–; Y.

Årsberetning fra veterinærfysikater. *See* 4893.

4894 Årsberetning. Veterinærsundhedsråd. København. *Årsberetn. VetSundhRåd* L.BM. 47–; Y.

4895 Årsberetning. Zoologisk museum. Oslo. *Årsberetn. zool. Mus., Oslo.* L.BM^N. 51–; Pl.M. 51–.

4896 Årsbok från Alnarps trädgårdars försöksverksamhet. Alnarp. *Årsb. Alnarps Trädg. FörsVerks.* C.A. 27–36*. [*C. in:* 29789°]

4897 Årsbok. Centralskogssällskap skogskultur. Årsberättelse för verksamheten. Helsingfors. *Årsb. CentSkogssällsk. Skogskult.* O.F. 51–.

4897° Årsbok. Finlands flottareförening. Helsinki. *Årsb. Finl. FlottFör.* O.F. 51–.

Årsbok. Finska vetenskaps-societet. *See* 4911.

4898 Årsbok. Göteborgs och Böhus läns havsfiskeförening. Göteborg. *Årsb. Göteborgs Böhus Läns Havsfiskeför.* L.AM. 26– imp.; Abd.M. 31–32: 45–50.; Dm. 22–24: 26–38; Lo. 26–50 imp.; Pl.M. 26– imp.; Y.

4899 Årsbok. Hydrografiska byrån. Helsinki. *Årsb. hydrogr. Byr., Helsinki* [1910–] L.MO.

4900 Årsbok. Hydrografiska byrån. Stockholm. *Årsb. hydrogr. Byr., Stockh.* [1908–18] L.GM.; MO.; E.M. 12: 16.

Årsbok. K. Svenska vetenskapsakademien. *See* 27812.

Årsbok. K. vetenskapssamhället i Uppsala. *See* 27819.

Årsbok. K. vetenskaps-societeten, Uppsala. *See* 27820.

Årsbok. Societas scientiarum fennica. *See* 4911.

4902 Årsbok. Statens meteorologisk-hydrografiska anstalt. Stockholm. *Årsb. St. met.-hydrogr. Anst.* [1919–45] L.MO.; Db.; E.C. 20–45; M. [*C. of:* 29342; *C. as:* 408]

Årsbok. Statens naturvetenskapliga forskningsråd, Brömma. *See* 50781.

4903 Årsbok. Statens provnings-anstalt. Stockholm. *Årsb. St. ProvnAnst.* L.P. 21. [*C. as:* 29861]

4904 Årsbok. Svenska flottledsförbundet. Stockholm. *Årsb. svenska Flottledsförb.* [1925–] O.F. 52–.

4905 Årsbok. Svenska gasverks-föreningen. Stockholm. *Årsb. svenska Gasverksför.* L.P. 46–49.

4906 Årsbok. Sveriges geologiska undersökning. Stockholm. *Årsb. Sver. geol. Unders.* [1907–] L.BM^N.; Gl.I. 45–; Br.U.; C.MI. 23–; PO. 23– imp.; E.D.; R. 23–; Y.

4907 Årsbok. Sveriges lantbruksförbund. Stockholm. *Årsb. Sver. LantbrFörb.* C.A. 44–47.

4908 Årsbok. Sveriges meteorologisk och hydrologiska institut. Stockholm. *Årsb. Sver. met. hydrol. Inst.* [1946–] L.MO.; P.; C.PO.; Db.; E.C.; M.; R. 20: 27: 40; Rt. 45–; Y. [*C. of:* 4902. *Also supplements*]

4909 Årsbok. Sydsvenska geografiska sällskapet. Lund. *Årsb. sydsvenska geogr. Sällsk.* L.G. 25–26*. [*C. as:* 51552]

4910 Årsbok. Vetenskaps-societeten i Lund. *Årsb. VetenskSoc. Lund* L.BM^N. 24–31; UC. 22–; Lv.U. 37–; O.B. 24–35.

4911 Årsbok-Vuosikirja. Societas scientiarum fennica. Helsingfors. *Årsb/Vuosik. Soc. Scient. fenn.* [1922–] L.BM^N. 52–; MO. 50–; R. 31–; Z. 24–; Abd.M. 50–52; Bm.U.; C.P.; Db.; E.R.; Lv.U.; O.R.; Y.

4912 Arsenal médico-chirurgical contemporain. Paris. *Arsenal méd.-chir. contemp.*

Årshefter. Tromsø Museums. *See* 54389.

4912° Årsmeddelelser. Dansk astronautisk Forening. København. *Årsmeddr dansk astronaut. Foren.* [1950–] **Y.**

4913 Årsmelding fra **Norges landbrukshøgskole.** Oslo. *Årsmeld. Norg. LandbrHøgsk.* [1923–27] **Abs.**A.; N. 25–27; **Ld.**U.; **Nw.**A.; **Rt.**; **Y.** [*C. of:* 35000; *C. as:* 4882]

4914 Årsmelding. Norges landbrukssvitenskapelige forskningsråd. Oslo. *Årsmeld. Norg. landbrvit. ForskRåd* **C.**A. 58–.
    Årsmelding om det **norske skogsvæsen.** *See* 22865.
    Årsoversigt samlet ved **Statens plantepatologiske forsøg.** *See* 37892.

4915 Årsoversikt over **forsøksvirksomheten** i **jord-** og **plantekultur.** Kontoret for Landbruksforskning. Oslo. *Årsovers. ForsVirks. Jord- og PlKult.* **C.**A. 55–.

4915° Årsredogörelse. Sveriges standardiserings kommission. *Årsredog. Sver. Stand. Kommn.* **Y.** 31–.

4916 Årsrit Fiskifélags Íslands. Reykjavik. *Årsr. Fiskif.Ísl.* [1932–]
    I. Fiskirannsoknir. **L.**AM. 32–36; BM^N. 33–37; Z. 32–37 imp.; **Abd.**M. 32–37; **C.**B. 32–37; **Fr.** 32–37; **Wo.** 32–37.
    II. Fiskirtrannsóknir. **L.**AM. 32–36; BM^N. 33–37; P. 42–; **Abd.**M. 37–46; **C.**B. 32–37; **Fr.** 32–37; **Wo.** 32–37.

4917 Årsrit ræktunarfélags Nordurlands. Akureyri. *Årsr. Ræktunarf. Nordurlands*

4918 Årsrit. Skógraektarfélags Íslands. Reykjavik. *Årsr. Skógraektarf. Ísl.* **C.**PO. 46–; **O.**F. 46–; **Rt.** 39–.

4918° Årsskrift utgiven av **Åbo akademi.** Åbo. *Årsskr. Åbo Akad.* [1917–] **L.**BM. 47–.

4919 Årsskrift från **Alnarps lantbruks-, mejeri-** och **trädgårds-institut.** Alnarp. *Årsskr. Alnarps Lantbr.- Mejeri- och Trädg.-Inst.* **Abs.**A. 48–49. [*See also:* 6072]
    Årsskrift. Göteborgs högskola. *See* 21493.

4920 Årsskrift. K. Veterinær- og **Landbohøjskole.** København. *Åsskr. K. Vet.- Landbohøjsk.* [1917–] **L.**AM.; BM. 49–; MY. 56–; **Br.**A. 51–; **Ld.**U. 56–; **Y.**

4921 Årsskrift. Norsk planteskolelag. Oslo. *Årsskr. norsk. PlSkLag* **Md.**H. 56–.

4922 Årsskrift. Norske skogplanteskoler. Oslo. *Årsskr. norske SkogplSk.* **O.**F. 50–.

4922ᵃ Årsskrift. Sveriges pomologiska förening. *Årsskr. Sver. pomol. För.* **Y.** 28–.

4922ᵇ Årstryck. Göteborgs naturhistoriska museum. *Årstr. Göteborgs naturhist. Mus.* **Y.** 56–.

4923 Ārsts. Latvijas Ārstu biedrības žurnals. Riga. *Ārsts* [1939–] [*C. of:* 28162]

4924 Art dentaire. Paris. *Art dent.* **L.**D. 47–48.

4925 Art and **Industry.** London. *Art Ind.* [1936–58] **L.**BA. 40–58; BM.; P. 54–58; U. 46–58; **Bm.**C. 46–58; **Cr.**P.; **E.**A.; **G.**M.; **Lv.**P.; **M.**P.; **N.**P.; **Sh.**IO.; **Sil.** 47–58. [*C. of:* 15010; *C. as:* 16634]

4926 Art médical. Nice. *Art méd., Nice* [1924–]

4927 Art médical. Paris. *Art méd., Paris* [1855–12]

4928 Art médical d'**Anvers.** *Art méd. Anvers* **L.**MA. 32–40 imp.; S. 34–40.

4929 Art del **Pagés.** Revista agrícola. Barcelona. *Art Pagés*

4930 Art photographique. Bruxelles. *Art photogr., Brux.* [1920–] **L.**PG. 28–30 imp.

4931 Art photographique. Paris. *Art photogr., Paris* **L.**PG. 03–06 imp.

4932 Art et **technique.** Bruxelles. *Art Tech., Brux.* **L.**P. 13–14*.

4933 Art et **technique.** Paris. *Art Tech., Paris* [1927–32]

4934 Arte medica. Napoli. *Arte med.* [1899–02]

4935 Arte ostetrica. Milano. *Arte ostet.* [1887–]

4936 Arteries of **Industry.** Compoflex Co. London, Oldham. *Arteries Ind.* [1956–] **L.**BM.; **M.**C. (1 yr)

4937 Artes textiles. Ghent. *Artes text.* [1953–] **L.**BM.

4938 Arthritis and **Rheumatism.** New York. *Arthritis Rheum.* [1958–] **L.**MA.; MD.; **G.**F.; **Ld.**U.; **M.**MS.; **Y.**

4939 Arthropoda. Organo oficial de la Asociación argentina de artropodología. Buenos Aires. *Arthropoda* [1947–] **L.**BM^N. 47–50; EB.; Z. 47.

4940 Arthur Dehon Little Memorial Lectures. Cambridge, Mass. *Arthur Dehon Little mem. Lect.* [1946–] **L.**P. imp.; **Y.**

4941 Articles on **Fatigue.** Philadelphia. *Artic. Fatigue* [1950] **Br.**U. [*C. as:* 42414]
    Articles pour l'**investigation** de la **syphilis.** *See* 6072.

4942 Articulator. Sydney. *Articulator* **L.**D. 48 imp.

4943 Artículos científicos publicados en **América latina.** Montevideo. *Artic. cient. Am. lat.* [1949–51] **L.**MO; P.; **C.**A.; **Y.**

4944 Artificial Earth Satellites. New York, London. *Artif. Earth Satell.* [1960–] **L.**P. [*English translation of:* 24222°]

4945 Artificial Insemination Report. Milk Marketing Board. Thames Ditton. *Artif. Insem. Rep. Milk Mktg Bd* **O.**AEC. 47–.

4946 Artificial Limbs. Washington. *Artif. Limbs* [1954–] **L.**P.

4947 Artificial Silk World. London. *Artif. Silk Wld* [1928–29] **L.**BM.; P.; **Abs.**N.; **C.**UL.; **E.**A.; **M.**C.; P.; T.; **O.**B. [*C. as:* 42217]

4948 Artificial Silk Year Book. Manchester. *Artif. Silk Yb.* **O.**B. 27–30.

4948° Artigos de **divulgação. Instituto** de **botânica.** Lisboa. *Artig. Divulg. Inst. Bot., Lisb.* **Y.** 57–.

4949 Artis. Amsterdam. *Artis, Amst.* [1955–] **L.**Z.

4950 Artois médical. Paris. *Artois méd.*

4951 Arts and **Crafts.** London. *Arts Crafts* [1904–06: 27–29] **L.**BM.; SB. 04–06; **G.**M. 04–06.

4952 Arts de **feu.** Paris. *Arts Feu* [1938–] **L.**BM.

4953 Arts et **manufactures.** Paris. *Arts Mfres* [1951–] **L.**P.; **G.**E. 55–; **Y.**

4954 Arts et **métiers.** Revue technique. Paris. *Arts Métiers* [1920–38] **L.**MT.; P.; SC. [*C. as:* 23620]

4955 **Arts** and **Science Studies.** Oklahoma Agricultural and Mechanical College. *Arts Sci. Stud. Okla. agric. mech. Coll.* Biological Science Series [1950–] **Y.**

4956 **Arts** et **techniques sonores.** Paris. *Arts Tech. sonores* [1953–] **L.**P. [*Published in:* 47579]

4957 **Arvernia biologica.** Clermont-Ferrand. *Arvernia biol.* [1930–] **L.**BM^N. 30–34; **C.**P.

4958 **Arxius** de **cirugía.** Barcelona. *Arx. Cirug.*

4959 **Arxius** de l'**Escola superior** d'**agricultura.** Barcelona. *Arx. Esc. sup. Agric., Barcelona* [1921–] **Md.**H. 34–38.

4960 **Arxius** de l'**Institut de ciencias.** Barcelona. *Arx. Inst. Cienc.* [1911–24] **L.**BM. 11; BM^N.; SC. 16–24; **C.**P.; **Db.** 22–24; **Sa.** imp.; **Y.** [*C. as:* 4963]

4961 **Arxius** d'**odontologia.** Barcelona. *Arx. Odont.* [1933–36]

4962 **Arxius** de **psicologia** i **psiquiatria infantil.** Barcelona. *Arx. Psicol. Psiquiat. infant.*

4963 **Arxius** de la **Secció de ciències. Institut** d'**estudis catalans.** Barcelona. *Arx. Secc. Ciènc. Inst. Estud. catalans* **L.**BM^N. 47–; SC.; **Db.** 47–; **Y.** [*C. of:* 4960]

4964 **Arzneimittel-Forschung.** Aulendorf. *Arzneimittel-Forsch.* [1951–] **L.**C. 61–; CB. 54–; MA.; MD.; P.; PH.; SC.; U.; **G.**U.; **Ld.**U. 55–; **Y.**

4965 **Arzneipflanzenumschau.** Berlin. *Arzneipflanzenumschau* [1946–] **L.**C. 47–; MA.; P.47–; PH.; **E.**U. 49–. [*Supplement to:* 37522]

4966 **Asa Gray Bulletin.** Ann Arbor. *Asa Gray Bull.* [1952–] **L.**BM^N.

4966° **Asahi Camera.** The Japanese Journal of Photography. Tokyo. *Asahi Camera* **L.**PG. 27–41 imp: 53–.

4967 **Asbestology.** New York. *Asbestology* [1923–33] **L.**P. imp.

4968 **Asbestos.** Philadelphia. *Asbestos, Philad.* [1919–] **L.**BM. 21–; MI. 54–55; P. 33–48; **Ld.**P. 47–; **Sy.**R.; **Y.**

4969 **Asbestos.** Rochdale. *Asbestos, Rochdale* [1918–21] **L.**BM.; P.; **Abs.**N.; **E.**F. 18–20; **O.**R. 18–20.

4970 **Asbestos Bulletin.** Guildford. *Asbestos Bull.* [1960–] **L.**P.

4971 **Asclepios.** Paris. *Asclepios* [1926–]
Asea Journal. Västerås. *See* 106.
Asea Research. Västerås. *See* 107.
Asea revue. Västerås. *See* 108.
Asea tidning. Västerås. *See* 109.

4972 **Asepsie.** Paris. *Asepsie* [1908–14]

4973 **Asfalti, bitumi, catrami.** Milano. *Asfalti Bitumi Catrami* [1929–] **L.**P. 50–; **Ha.**RD. 42–; **Y.**

4974 **Asgrow Monographs.** Associated Seed Growers. New Haven. *Asgrow Monogr.* [1949–] **Y.**

4975 **Ashen sihhiye dergisi.** Istanbul. *Ashen sihh. Derg.* [1949–] **L.**TD. 49–52. [*C. of:* 4988]
Ashrae Journal. *See* 111.

4976 **Ash's Journal.** London. *Ash's J.* [1917–18] **L.**BM. 17; D.; MD. [*C. of:* 4977; *C. as:* 16538]

4977 **Ash's Monthly.** London. *Ash's Mon.* [1911–16] **L.**D.; MD. 14–16 imp. [*C. of:* 4978; *C. as:* 4976]

4978 **Ash's Quarterly Circular.** London. *Ash's q. Circ.* [1908–10] **L.**D. [*C. of:* 41506; *C. as:* 4977]

4979 **Asia.** New York. *Asia* [1917–] **L.**BM.; UC. 30–38; **C.**UL. 19–; **E.**A. 19–; **O.**B. 19–. [*C. of:* 25490]

4980 **Asia Major.** *Asia maj.* [1949–] **L.**BM.; HO.; **E.**A.

4981 **Asian** and **Indian Skyways.** Bombay. *Asian Indian Skyways* [1959–] **L.**AV.; P.; **Y.** [*C. of:* 23076]

4982 **Asian Medical Journal.** Tokyo. *Asian med. J.* [1958–] **L.**MA.; MD. 60–; **Y.**

4983 **Asian Printer.** Tokyo. *Asian Print.* [1958–] **L.**P.

4984 **Asiatic Society Monographs.** London. *Asiat. Soc. Monogr.* [1902–] **L.**BM.; **Abs.**N. 15–; **Bm.**P.; **C.**UL.; **E.**U. 02–16; **G.**M.; U.; **Lv.**P. 07–29 imp.; **M.**R. imp.; **O.**B.

4985 **Asie française.** Bulletin mensuel du Comité de l'Asie française. Paris. *Asie fr.* **C.**UL. 21–24; **O.**B. 21–24; **Sa.** 21–24. [*C. of:* 9850]

4986 **Asistencia pública.** México. *Asist. públ.* [1941–43] **L.**MA. imp. [*C. as:* 48493]

4987 **Askania-Warte.** Berlin. *Askania-Warte* [1936–] **L.**P. imp.; **Y.**

4988 **Askeri sihhiye mecmuasi.** İstanbul. *Ask. sihh. Mecm.* **L.**TD. 43–49*. [*C. as:* 4975]

4989 **Askeri tibbi baytarı mecmuası.** İstanbul. *Ask. Tibbi Bayt. Mecm.* [1933–37] **L.**V. 34–37. [*C. of:* and *Rec. as:* 4991]

4990 **Askeri veteriner dergisi.** Ankara. *Ask. vet. Derg.* [1949–] **L.**V.; **W.**; **Y.** [*C. of:* 4991]

4991 **Askeri veteriner mecmuasi.** İstanbul. *Ask. vet. Mecm.* [1923–48] **L.**V. 38–48 imp. [> 4989; 1933–37; *C. as:* 4990]

4992 **Asklēpios.** en Athēnais. 'Ασκλήπιος. *Asklepios* [1930–]
Asociación médica mexicana. *See* 85.

4993 **Aspen Report.** Lake States Forest Experiment Station, University Farm, St. Paul, Minn. *Aspen Rep.* [1947–] **O.**F. imp.

4994 **Asphalt.** Asphalt Roads Association. London. *Asphalt* [1948–] **L.**P.; **Y.**

4995 **Asphalt Institute Quarterly.** New York. *Asph. Inst. Q.* [1949–53] **L.**BM.; **L.**P. (curr.)

4996 **Asphalt Paving Publications.** Asphalt Association. New York, etc. *Asph. Pav. Publs*

4997 **Asphalt** und **Strassenbau.** Berlin. *Asph. Strassenb.* [1930–32] **L.**C.; P. [*Supplement to:* 37405]

4998 **Asphalt** und **Teer, Strassenbautechnik.** Berlin. *Asph. Teer* [1929] **L.**P. 29–44 [*C. of:* 5000]

4999 **Asphalte.** Paris. *Asphalte* [1953–] **L.**P.; **Y.**

5000 **Asphalt-** u. **Teerindustriezeitung** u. Zeitschrift für Bodenbelegung, Dachdeckung u. Imprägnierung. Berlin. *Asph.- u. TeerindZtg* [1901–29] **L.**P. 10–29. [*C. as:* 4998]

5001 **Assam Forest Bulletin.** Shillong. *Assam Forest Bull.* [1930] **O.**F. [*C. as:* 5003]

5002 **Assam Forest Records. Botany.** Shillong. *Assam Forest Rec. Bot.* [1934: 37] **L.**BM^N. (bot.) 37; **E.**R.; **O.**F.

5003 **Assam Forest Records. Silviculture.** Shillong. *Assam Forest Rec. Silvic.* [1934–] **E.**R.; **O.**F. [*C. as:* 5001]

5004 **Assemblée générale** de l'**Union géodésique** et **géophysique internationale.** *Assembl. gén. Un. géod. géophys. int.* [1922–] **L.**MO. imp.; SC. 26–54; **O.**R. 39–.

5005 **Assises** de **médecine.** Paris. *Assises Méd.*

5006 **Assistenza sanitaria.** Roma. *Assist. sanit.* **L.**MA. 33-39 imp.

Associated Commercial Vehicles Ltd Gazette. *See* 14.

Associated Electrical Industries. [*For publications whose titles begin with this name*] *See* **AEI.**

5007 **Association** of **Agriculture Review.** London. *Ass. Agric. Rev.* [1948-] **L.**AM. 48-56; BM.; U.; **Abs.**A. 49-; **Bl.**U. 48-52; **Br.**A.; **C.**A.; UL. 50-56; **O.**AEC.; B.; R.; **Sil.** 53-.

5008 **Association** of **British Chemical Manufacturers' Information.** *Ass. Br. chem. Mfrs' Inf.* [1929-] **L.**PR. 29-39.

Association for **Computing Machinery Journal.** New York. *See* 25607.

5009 **Association** of **Engineering** and **Shipbuilding Draughtsmen. Technical Section.** [**Papers.**] Gateshead-on-Tyne. *Ass. Engng Shipbldg Draughtsmen* [1919-] **L.**BM.; P.; **Bm.**P. 21-; T. 20- imp.; **Br.**P. 23- imp.; U. 21-28: 32- imp.; **Bra.**P. (Lect.) 22-28: (Pamph.) 49-; **C.**UL. 30-; **G.**M. 25-32: 38-; T. 27-; U. 37-; **Ld.**P.; **Lv.**P. 32- imp.; U.; **M.**P. 35-; T. 20-; **O.**R. 31-; **Sh.**P.; **Sw.**U. 26-28.

5010 **Association générale aéronautique.** Paris. *Ass. gén. aéronaut.*

Association of **Green Crop Driers Yearbook.** *See* 58012.

5011 **Association médicale.** Paris. *Ass. méd.* [*C. of:* 25618]

5012 **Association météorologique** d'**Orthez.** Orthez. *Ass. mét. Orthez*

5013 **Association** of **Public Lighting Engineers.** [**Papers.**] London. *Ass. publ. Ltg Engrs* **L.**P. 28-30. [*C. of:* 23710]

5014 **Association** of **Supervising Electricians.** London. *Ass. superv. Electns* **L.**P. 15-17. [*C. as:* 34096]

5015 **Astarte.** Short Papers published by the Zoological Department, Tromsø Museum. Tromsø. *Astarte* [1951-] **L.**BMᴺ.; L.; SC.; **Abd.**M.; **C.**P.; PO.; **Dm.**; **Lo.**; **Lv.**U.; **Pl.**M.; **Y.** [*C. of:* 54389]

5016 **Astrakhanskiĭ sbornik.** Astrakhan. Астраханскій сборникъ, издаваемый Петровскимъ обществомъ изслѣдователей Астраханскаго края. *Astrakh. Sb.*

5017 **Astrofilo.** Rivista illustrata del cielo. Milano. *Astrofilo*

5017° **Astrofizikas laboratorijas atsevisks iespiedums.** Riga. *Astrofiz. Lab. Atsev. Iesp.* [1958-]

Astrofizikas laboratorijas raksti. Latvijas PSR Zinatnu Akademija. *See* 54458.

5018 **Astrographic Catalogue. Royal Observatory.** Edinburgh. *Astrogr. Cat. R. Obs., Edinb.* [1950-] **L.**BM.; **Db.**

5019 **Astronaut.** Manchester Interplanetary Society. Manchester. *Astronaut, Manchr* [1937-] **L.**BM.

Astronaut. Thiokol Chemical Corporation, Bristol, Pa. *See* 53086ᵃ.

5020 **Astronautica.** Barcelona. *Astronautica, Barcelona* [1955-]

5021 **Astronautica.** Torino. *Astronautica, Torino* **L.**P. 60-.

5022 **Astronautica acta.** International Astronautical Federation. Wien, London. *Astronautica Acta* [1955-] **L.**AV.; BM.; P.; SC.; UC.; **F.**A. 57-; **G.**U.; **Y.**

5023 **Astronautical Abstracts.** London. *Astronaut. Abstr.* [1959-] **L.**AV.; BM. [*Issued in:* 25714]

5024 **Astronautical Sciences Review.** Palo Alto. *Astronaut. Sci. Rev.* [1959-] **L.**AV. 60-; P.

5025 **Astronautics.** New York. *Astronautics, N.Y.* [1932-44] **L.**P.; **Bm.**P.; **G.**U. [*C. of:* 9328; *C. as:* 25531]

5026 **Astronautics.** American Rocket Society. Easton. *Astronautics, ARS* [1956-] **L.**AV. 58-; P. 57-; SC. 57-; **F.**A.; **Y.**

5027 **Astronautics.** Journal of the American Astronautical Society. New York. *Astronautics, Am. astronaut. Soc.* [1954-] **L.**P. [*C. as:* 25632]

5028 **Astronautik.** Frankfurt am Main. *Astronautik, Frankf.* [1952-] **Y.**

5029 **Astronautik.** Stockholm. *Astronautik, Stockh.* [1958-] **L.**AV.; P.; **Y.**

5030 **Astronautische Forschungsberichte.** Bremen. *Astronaut. ForschBer.* [1957-] **L.**P.

5031 **Astronom-amatér.** Praha. *Astronom-Amatér* [1934]

Astronomical Bulletin. Leningrad. *See* 5050.

5032 **Astronomical Bulletin. Carter Observatory.** Wellington, N.Z. *Astr. Bull. Carter Obs.* [1940-] **L.**AS.; BM.; MO.; SC. 46-; **E.**O.; R.; **M.**U. 40-57 imp.

Astronomical Circular. Bureau of **astronomical Information,** Academy of Sciences, U.S.S.R. *See* 5054.

Astronomical Circular. Observatory of the **Kiev State University.** *See* 5053.

5033 **Astronomical Circular. Tashkent Astronomical Observatory.** Tashkent. *Astr. Circ. Tashkent* [1932-] **L.**AS.; **E.**O.; R.; **O.**O.

5034 **Astronomical Contributions** of **Boston University.** Boston. *Astr. Contr. Boston Univ.* [1958-] **Y.**

5035 **Astronomical Contributions** from the **University** of **Manchester.** Manchester. *Astr. Contr. Univ. Manchr*
Series I. Jodrell Bank Annals. *See* 25343.
Series II. Jodrell Bank Reprints. *See* 25344.
Series III. [1952-] **L.**BM.; **M.**U.; **Sa.**

5036 **Astronomical Digest.** Plainfield, N.J. *Astr. Dig.* [1932-33]

5037 **Astronomical Ephemeris.** London. *Astr. Ephem.* [1960-] **L.**AS.; B.; BM.; G.; MO.; QM.; R.; SC.; U.; UC.; **Abs.**N.; **Bl.**U.; **Bm.**N.; P.; **Br.**P.; **Bra.**P.; **C.**PO.; **Cr.**P.; **Db.**; **E.**A.; O.; R.; U.; **G.**M.; U.; **H.**U.; **Ld.**P.; U.; **Lo.**; **Lv.**P.; **M.**P.; U.; **N.**U. (10 yr.); **Nw.**A.; P.; **O.**B.; G.; O.; **Sa.**; **Sh.**P.; SC.; **Sw.**U.; **Y.** [*C. of:* 34399: *same text as:* 1951]

5038 **Astronomical Handbook.** Wellington, N.Z. *Astr. Handb.* [1949] [*C. of:* 35659; *C. as:* 34723]

5038° **Astronomical Handbook. Weather Bureau, Philippine Islands.** Manila. *Astr. Handb., Manila* **L.**BM. 55-.

5039 **Astronomical Herald.** Tokyo. *Astr. Her., Tokyo* **L.**SC. 50; **Y.**

5040 **Astronomical Journal.** Dudley Observatory, Cambridge, Mass. Albany, etc. *Astr. J. Dudley Obs.* [1849-] **L.**AS.; BM.; SC.; **C.**O.; UL.; **E.**O.; **G.**U. 95-; **Ld.**U.; **M.**U.; **O.**O.; R. 91-26; **Sa.** 42-; **Y.**

5040ᵃ **Astronomical Journal.** Office of Technical Services. New York. *Astr. J., N.Y.* **Y.** 57–. [*English abstracts of:* 5055]

5041 **Astronomical** and **Magnetical** and **Meteorological Observations** made at the **R. Observatory, Greenwich.** London. *Astr. magn. met. Obsns R. Obs. Greenw.* [1848–24] **L.**AS.; BM.; P.; SC.; UC.; **Abd.**U.; **Abs.**N. 08–24; U. 01–30; **Bl.**U.; **Bm.**P.; U.; **C.**P.; UL.; **Db.**; **E.**M.; O.; R.; S.; U. imp; **G.**M. 82–24; U.; **Ld.**P. 85–24; U.; **Lv.**P. 1860–24; U. 78–24; **M.**P. 06–24; U. 1848–73 imp.; R.; **Sa.**; **Sh.**U. 01–24. [*C. as:* 35640]

5042 **Astronomical Newsletter.** Harvard College Observatory, *later* Laboratoire d'astronomie de Lille. Cambridge, Mass., Lille. *Astr. Newsl.* [1948–] **L.**AS.; SC.; **M.**U.; **Sa.** 53–. [*C. of:* 33395]

Astronomical Observations. Prague. *See* 22516.

5043 **Astronomical Observations** made at the **Observatory** of **Cambridge.** Cambridge. *Astr. Obsns Camb.* [1828–] **L.**AS.; BM.; SC. 1828–26; **Abs.**N. 19–; **C.**O.; **Db.**; **E.**O.; R. 1828–28; U.; **G.**U. 1828–43; **M.**U. 1828–1860; **O.**O.; R. 66–.

5044 **Astronomical Observations** and **Researches** made at **Dunsink.** Dublin. *Astr. Obsns Res. Dunsink* [1870–00] **L.**AS.; BM. 79–00; SC.; **Bm.**P.; **Db.**; **E.**O.; R.; U.; **G.**U.; **O.**O.; R.

5045 **Astronomical Observations. Rousdon Observatory.** Rousdon. *Astr. Obsns Rousdon Obs.* [1882–00] **L.**AS. 82–90; BM.

5046 **Astronomical Papers** prepared for the use of the **American Ephemeris** and **nautical almanac.** Washington. *Astr. Pap., Wash.* [1879–] **L.**AS. 82–; BM.; 79–12; **C.**O.; **Db.**; **E.**O.; R.; **G.**U. 79–91; **M.**U. 90–55 imp.; **O.**O. 79–05; R. 79–91; **Y.**

5047 **Astronomical Papers** published by the **Lehigh University.** Sayre Astronomical Observatory, South Bethlehem. *Astr. Pap. Lehigh Univ.* [1907–] **C.**O.; **E.**O.; **O.**R. 07.

5048 **Astronomical Papers** of the **University of California.** Los Angeles. *Astr. Pap. Univ. Calif.* [1939–] **L.**AS.; SC.; **Db.**; **E.**R.; **M.**U. 43–; **Y.**

5048ᶜ **Astronomical Phenomena** for the **Year.** U.S. Naval Observatory. Washington. *Astr. Phenom. Yr* **L.**BM. 51–.

5049 **Astronomical Results** from **Observations** made at the **Royal Observatory, Greenwich.** London. *Astr. Results Obsns Greenw.* [1920–] **L.**AS.; BM.; R.; SC.; UC.; **Abd.**U.; **Abs.**N.; **Bm.**P.; **Db.**; **E.**O.; R.; U.; **G.**M.; **O.**R. [*C. of:* 46074]

5049ᵃ **Astronomical Review. Carter Observatory,** Wellington, N.Z. *Astr. Rev. Carter Obs.* **Y.**

5049ᶜ **Astronomical Tables** for **Hong Kong.** Royal Observatory, Hong Kong. *Astr. Tabl. Hong Kong* [1960–] **Y.**

5050 **Astronomicheskiĭ byulleten'.** Leningrad. Астрономическій бюллетень. *Astr. Byull.* **E.**R. 27–30*.

5051 **Astronomicheskiĭ ezhegodnik.** Gosudarstvennȳĭ vȳchislitel'nȳĭ institut. Petrograd, Moskva. Астрономическій ежегодник. Государственный вычислительный институт. *Astr. Ezheg.* [1922–] **L.**BM. 42–; SC. 26–; **M.**U. 52–53: 55–57; **O.**R. 50–.

5052 **Astronomicheskiĭ sbornik.** L'vovskiĭ gosudarstvennȳĭ universitet im. I. Franko. L'vov. Астрономическій сборник. Львовский государственный университет им. И. Франко. *Astr. Sb.* **M.**U. 54.

5053 **Astronomicheskiĭ tsirkulyar. Astronomicheskaya observatoriya, Kievskiĭ gosudarstvennyiĭ universitet.** Астрономический циркуляр. Астрономическая обсерватория, Киевский государственный университет. *Astr. Tsirk. astr. Obs. kiev. gos. Univ.* [1946–] **L.**AS. 46–47.

5054 **Astronomicheskiĭ tsirkulyar. Byuro astronomicheskikh soobshcheniĭ, Akademiya nauk SSSR.** Kazan'. Астрономический циркуляр. Бюро астрономических сообщений, Академия наук СССР. *Astr. Tsirk. Byuro astr. Soobshch.* [1943–] **L.**AS; SC. 51–; UC. 50; **M.**U. 52–.

5055 **Astronomicheskiĭ zhurnal.** Moskva. Астрономический журнал. *Astr. Zh.* [1928–] **L.**AS.; BM.; P. 58–; SC. 24–32: 42–50 imp.: 53–; **C.**P. 28–32: 58–; **E.**R. 38– imp.; **M.**U. 51– imp.; **O.**O. 33–39: 44–. [*C. of:* 48311; *English translation at:* 50339; *English abstracts at:* 5040ᵃ]

5056 **Astronomicheskoe obozrênie.** Nikolaev. Астрономическое обозрѣніе. *Astr. Obozr.*

5057 **Astronomie.** Bulletin de la Société astronomique de France. Paris. *Astronomie* [1911–] **L.**AS.; BM. 39–; QM. 16–25 imp; SC.; **E.**R.; **Ld.**U. 12–19; **Sh.**P. 11–21; **Y.** [*C. of:* 11853]

5057ᶜ **Astronomijos observatorijos biuletenis.** Vilnius. *Astr. Obs. Biul., Viln.* [1910–] **Y.**

5058 **Astronomische Abhandlungen.** Kiel, etc. *Astr. Abh., Kiel* [1901–44] **L.**AS.; BM. 01–13; SC.; UC. 22–44; **Abd.**U. 06–35; **Cr.**P. 11–24 imp.; UL.; **G.**U. 01–37; **O.**O. [*Supplement to:* 5067]

5059 **Astronomische Abhandlungen** der **Hamburger Sternwarte** in **Bergedorf.** Hamburg. *Astr. Abh., Hamburg* **L.**AS. 09–; BM. 04–; **Bl.**U. 09–13; **C.**O. 09–; **E.**O. 09–; R. 08–13; **M.**U. 09–40 imp.; **O.**O. 09–13.

Astronomische Abhandlungen. K. Ungarisches astrophysikalisches Observatorium von **Konkolys' Stiftung** in **Budapest-Svábhegy.** *See* 32742.

Astronomische Arbeiten des **K. K. Gradmessungsbureau.** *See* 41331.

5060 **Astronomische Beobachtungen** auf der **K. Sternwarte** zu **Berlin.** Berlin. *Astr. Beob. K. Sternw. Berl.* [1840–04] **L.**AS.; BM.; SC.; **C.**O.; **E.**O.

5061 **Astronomische Beobachtungen** auf der **K. Universitätssternwarte** zu **Königsberg.** *Astr. Beob. K. Univ Sternw. Königsberg* [1815–] **L.**AS. 1815–38; BM. 1815–99; R. 1815–1848; **C.**O.; UL. 13–22; **E.**O.; R. 1821–03 imp.; **G.**U. 1815–1858; **O.**O. 03–.

5062 **Astronomische Beobachtungen** an der **K.K. Sternwarte** zu **Prag.** *Astr. Beob. K.K. Sternw. Prag* [1884–09] **L.**AS.; BM. 05–09; **C.**O.; **Db** 00–09; **E.**O. 84–91; R. 84–91: 00–09. [*C. as:* 41338]

5063 **Astronomische Beobachtungen** auf der **Sternwarte** der **K. Christian-Albrechts-Universität** zu **Kiel.** Liepzig. *Astr. Beob. Sternw. K. Univ. Kiel* [1905–] **L.**AS. 05–12; **Bl.**U. 05–12; **C.**O.; **E.**O.

5064 **Astronomische Korrespondenz.** Hamburg. *Astr. Korresp.*

5065 **Astronomische Mitteilungen.** Zürich. *Astr. Mitt., Zürich* [1867–] **L.**AS.; MO. 76–; SC. 27–; **C.**O. 95–; **E.**O. 76–; **M.**U. 40– imp.

5066 **Astronomische Mitteilungen** der **K. Sternwarte** zu **Göttingen.** *Astr. Mitt. K. Sternw. Göttingen* [1869–20] L.AS.; C.O.; E.O.; O.O. 69–13. [*C. as:* 56246]

5067 **Astronomische Nachrichten.** Kiel, etc. *Astr. Nachr.* [1823–] L.AS. imp.; BM.; SC. 74–40: 48–; UC. 00–39; **Abd.**U. 1828–32; **Bl.**U. 1823–02; **Br.**U. 1823–89 imp.; C.O.; UL.; **Db.** 1836– imp.; E.O.; R.; U. 1823–21 imp.; **Ex.**U. 90–05 imp.; G.U. imp.; **Ld.**U. 24–; **M.**U. imp.; O.O. 1824–; R.; Sa. 83–84: 01–06: 35–; Y.

5068 **Astronomische Rundschau.** Herausgegeben von der Manora-Sternwarte in Lussinpiccolo. Lussinpiccolo. *Astr. Rdsch.* L.AS. 99–09*; O.O. 99–01.

5069 **Astronomischer Jahresbericht.** Berlin, etc. *Astr. Jber.* [1899–] L.AS.; BM. 99–37: 44–; SC. 30–37: 44–; C.O.; UL.; E.O. imp.; M.U.; O.O.; Y.

5070 **Astronomisch-geodätische Arbeiten. Geodätisches Institut.** Berlin. *Astr.-geod. Arb., Berl.* L.AS 70–; E.O. 70; Y.

5071 **Astronomisch-geodätische Arbeiten. K. Bayerische Kommission** für die **internationale Erdmessung.** München. *Astr.-geod. Arb., Münch.* L.BM. 96–18; SC. 1961–.
  Astronomisch-geodätische Arbeiten des **K. u. K. Militär-geographischen Instituts** in **Wien.** *See* 41332.

5072 **Astronomisch-geodätische Arbeiten** in der **Schweiz.** Zürich. *Astr.-geod. Arb. Schweiz.* [1907–] L.AS.; SC. 21–; **C.**GD. 10–; O. 10–; UL. 07–11; E.R. 07–51; O.R. 44–; Y. [*C. of:* 48935]

5073 **Astronomisch-geodätisches Jahrbuch.** Astronomisches Rechen-Institut in Heidelberg. *Astr.-geod. Jb.* [1949–57] L.AS; SC. 53–56.

5074 **Astronomisch-nautische Ephemeriden.** Triest. *Astr.-naut. Ephem.*

5075 **Astronomiska iakttagelser** och **undersökningar** på **Stockholms observatorium.** Uppsala and Stockholm. *Astr. Iakttag. Unders. Stockh. Obs.* [1880–34] L.AS.; G. 88–08; R. 03–34; SC.; **Bl.**U. 85–09; C.O.; UL. 80–88; E.O.; R.; M.U. 32; O.O. 98–34. [*C. as:* 50941]

5076 **Astrophysica norvegica.** Oslo. *Astrophys. norv.* [1934–] L.AS.; BM.; MO.; P.; R. 49–; SC.; U. 39–; UC.; **Bl.**U.; **C.**P.; **Db.**; **Dn.**U.; E.C. 34–46; M.; O.; R.; M.U.; O.O.; R.; Sa.; Y. [*C. of:* 41342]

5077 **Astrophysical Journal.** University of Chicago. Chicago and New York. *Astrophys. J.* [1895–] L.AS.; BM.; MO. 11–31; NP. 53–; P.; QM. 50–; RI.; SC.; U. 50–; UC. **Abd.**U. 04–; **Abs.**U. 07–; **Bl.**U. 12–; **Bm.**U.; **Bn.**U. 33– imp.; **Br.**U. 06–; **C.**P.; SJ. 98–; UL.; **Cr.**P. 99–15 imp.; U. 07–50; **Db.**; **Dn.**U. 55–; E.A. 50–; O.; R.; U.; **Ex.**U. 22–33: 37–40: 42–; G.T. 31–; U.; H.U. 95–18: 29–38; **Ld.**U.; **Lv.**P. 99–05; U. 24–; M.U. imp.; **Ma.**T. 55–; **Nw.**A. 06–; O.O.; R.; Sa.; **Sh.**U.; **Sw.**U. 21–34: 54–; Y.

5078 **Astrophysical Journal. Supplement Series.** Chicago. *Astrophys. J. Suppl. Ser.* [1954–] L.AS.; SC.; **Bn.**U.; E.A.; **Ld.**U.; O.O.; **Sw.**U.; Y. [*Supplement to:* 5077]

5079 **Astrophysical Monographs.** Yerkes Observatory. Chicago. *Astrophys. Monogr. Yerkes Obs.* L.BM. 37–.
  Asxred Monograph. *See* 127.

5080 **Atas. Instituto** de **micologia.** Universidade do Recife. *Atas Inst. Micol.* [1960–] L.BM^N.

5080° **Atas** da **Sociedade** de **biologia** do **Rio** de **Janeiro.** *Atas Soc. Biol. Rio de J.* [1957–] L.BM.; BM^N.; Z.

5081 **Atelier.** Sydney Technical College Architectural Club. Sydney. *Atelier, Sydney*

5082 **Atelier moderne.** Paris. *Atelier mod.*

5083 **Atelier des Photographen** u. **allgemeine Photographenzeitung.** Halle a. S. *Atelier Photogr.* [1894–33] L.P. 06–28; PG. imp. [*C. as:* 20809]
  Ateliers des **constructions électriques** de **Charleroi.** *See* ACEC.

5084 **Ateliers** des **constructions électriques** de **Delle.** Lyon-Villeurbaune. *Ateliers Constr. élect. Delle* [1929–35] L.P. [*C. as:* 16474]

5085 **Ateliers** des **constructions électriques** du **Nord** et de l'**Est.** *Ateliers Constr. élect. N. et E.*

5086 **Ateneo medico.** Roma. *Ateneo med.*

5087 **Ateneo parmense.** Organo della Facoltà (Società) di medicina dell'Università di Parma. *Ateneo parmense* [1929–] L.MA. 33–; MD. 36–; UC. 35–40; **Bm.**U. 29–30; **C.**UL.; O.R. 29–30; Y. [*C. of:* 8462]

5088 **Ateneo veneto.** Venezia. *Ateneo veneto* L.R. 81–05; **Db.** 00–.

5089 **Ateneum wileńskie.** Wilno. *Ateneum wileń.* [1923–]

5090 **Athēna.** Athēnēsin. Ἀθηνᾶ. *Athēna, Athēn.* [1889–] L.BM. 89–13; BM^N. 20; M.R. 01–; O.B.

5091 **Athena:** rassegna mensile di biologia, clinica e terapia. Roma. *Athena, Roma* [1932–] L.MA. 36–37: 47–; S. (1 yr); **Lv.**U.
  Athmosphaera. Budapest. *See* 22729.

5092 **Atividades** do **Serviço** de **caça** e **pesca.** Rio de Janeiro. *Ativ. Serv. Caça Pesca* L.BM. 34–.

5093 **Atlanta Journal-record** of **Medicine.** Atlanta, Ga. *Atlanta J.-Rec. Med.* [1899–18] M.MS. 06–09.
  Atlanta University Publications. *See* 9532.

5094 **Atlanten.** Medlemsblad for Foreningen De Danske Atlanterkavs'oer. Kjøbenhavn. *Atlanten*

5095 **Atlantic Fisherman.** Boston. *Atlant. Fisherman* [1920–53] [*C. as:* 34115]

5096 **Atlantic Medical Journal.** Harrisburg. *Atlant. med. J.* [1923–28] [*C. of:* and *Rec. as:* 37325]

5097 **Atlantic Naturalist.** Washington, D.C. *Atlant. Nat.* [1950–] Y. [*C. of:* 57797]

5098 **Atlantic Salmon Journal.** *Atlant. Salmon J.* [1952–] Pit.F.

5099 **Atlantic Waterways.** Philadelphia. *Atlant. WatWays* [1921] [*C. of:* 9533]

5100 **Atlantide Report.** Scientific Results of the Danish Expedition to the Coasts of Tropical West Africa, 1945–1946. Copenhagen. *Atlantide Rep.* [1950–] L.BM.; Z.; **Abd.**M.; **Lv.**U.; Mi.; **Pl.**M.; Wo. 50–51.

5101 **Atlas.** Buenos Aires. *Atlas, B. Aires* [1954–] Y.

5102 **Atlas Compressed Air Review.** Stockholm. *Atlas compr. Air Rev.* [1949–52] L.P.; Y. [*Replaced by:* 15145]

5102° **Atlas Copco Comments.** Stockholm. *Atlas Copco Comm.* [1958–] Y.

5103 **Atlas Diesel Bulletin.** Stockholm. *Atlas Diesel Bull.* [1934–] L.P. 34–37. [*C. of:* 9534]

5103° **Atlas flory polskiej.** Kraków. *Atlas Flory pol.* [1930–] L.BM.

5104 **Atlas geologiczny Galicyi.** Kraków. *Atlas geol. Galicyi* [1887-] **L.**BM.; BM^N. 87-11; GM. 87-08; **E.**R. 87-11 imp.

5105 **Atmosphère.** Paris. *Atmosphère*

5106 **Atmosphere Control.** Cambridge. *Atmosphere Control* [1937-] **L.**BM.

5107 **Atmosphere Pollution Bulletin.** Monthly Summary of Observations and Abstracts of Literature. London. *Atmosphere Pollut. Bull.* **L.**AM. 52-; BM.; SA. 46-; TD. 46-; **G.**PH. 46-; **St.**R. 46-.

5108 **Atmospheric Pollution Abstracts.** London. *Atmosph. Pollut. Abstr.* **L.**BM.; **Cr.**MD. 33-; **G.**PH. 46-.

5109 **Atoll Research Bulletin.** Washington. *Atoll Res. Bull.* [1951-] **L.**BM^N.; K.; SC.; TP.; **E.**U. 52-; **Mi.** 52-; **O.**R.; **Y.**

5110 **Atom.** Brooklyn, N.Y. *Atom, Brooklyn*

5111 **Atom.** London. *Atom, Lond.* [1956-] **L.**AM. 59-; AV.; BM.; P.; QM. 57-; SC. 57-; **Abs.**N. 57-; **Bl.**U. 59-; **Bm.**T.; **Bn.**U. 57-; **C.**CH. 57; **Ld.**P. 57-; **Lo.**; **Lv.**P.; **M.**U.; **Sa.**; **Wo.** 57-; **Y.** [*Summaries of:* 45500°]

5112 **Atom Industry.** London, New York. *Atom Ind.* [1955-] **L.**BM.; P. (curr.); **Bn.**U.; **C.**UL.; **E.**A.; **O.**R.

5113 **Atom** und **Strom.** Frankfurt a. Main. *Atom Strom* [1955-] **L.**P.; SC.; **Y.** [*Supplement to:* 17829]

5114 **Atom Wirtschaft.** Düsseldorf. *Atom Wirtsch.* [1955-] **L.**P. 57-; **Y.**

5115 **Atombrief.** Regensburg. *Atombrief* **Br.**P. 58-.

5115° **Atomenergie** pro **pace.** München. *Atomenergie Pace* [1955] [*C. as:* 5133]

5116 **Atomes.** Tous les aspects scientifiques d'un nouvel âge. Paris. *Atomes* [1946-] **L.**P.; **Bm.**U. 46-47; **Y.**

5117 **Atomes** et **radiations.** Physique, biologie, médecine. Paris. *Atomes Radiat.* [1946-47] **L.**SC.; **E.**U.

5118 **Atomic Digest.** London. *Atom. Dig.* [1952-] **L.**BM.

5118° **Atomic Energy.** Office of Technical Services. Washington. *Atom. Energy, Off. tech. Servs* [1957-] **L.**P.; **Y.** [*English abstracts of:* 5136]

5118ᵉ **Atomic Energy.** Significant references. Library of Congress. Washington. *Atom. Energy, Libr. Congr.* [1946-51] **L.**BM. 48-51.

5119 **Atomic Energy.** Australian Atomic Energy Authority. Sydney. *Atom. Energy, Sydney* [1957-] **L.**BM.

5119° **Atomic Energy** in **Biophysics, Biology** and **Medicine.** Oak Ridge. *Atom. Energy Biophys. Biol. Med.* [1948] [*C. in:* 35437]

Atomic Energy Establishment, Winfrith. [*For periodicals whose titles begin with this name*] *See* **A.E.E.W.**

5120 **Atomic Energy** in **Industry.** Minutes of Conferences. New York. *Atom. Energy Ind.* [1952-] **L.**P.

5121 **Atomic Energy Newsletter.** New York. *Atom. Energy Newsl.* [1949-] **L.**CB. 54-.

Atomic Energy Research Establishment. [*For publications whose titles begin with this name*] *See* **A.E.R.E.**

Atomic Energy Review. General Electric Company. London. *See* 20501.

5123 **Atomic Energy Year Book.** London. *Atom. Energy Yb.* [1949] **L.**P.; SC.; U.; **C.**UL.; **E.**A.; T.; **G.**M.

5123° **Atomic Power Review.** Johannesburg. *Atom. Pwr Rev.* [1956-] **L.**BM.

5124 **Atomic Scientists Journal.** London. *Atom. Scient. J.* [1953-56] **L.**AM. 55-56; BM.; CB. 54-56; QM.; SC.; **Bl.**U. 55-56; **Bm.**P.; U.; **Bn.**U.; **Br.**P.; **C.**UL.; **G.**M.; U. 54-56; **Ld.**U.; **Lo.** 54-56; **O.**R.; **Sa.** [*C. of:* 5125; *C. in:* 34692]

5125 **Atomic Scientists News.** London. *Atom. Scient. News* [1947-53] **L.**BM.; QM.; SC.; **Bm.**P. 51-53; U.; **Br.**P.; **C.**UL.; **G.**M. 51-53; **Ld.**U.; **O.**R. [*C. as:* 5124]

Atomic Weapons Research Establishment. [*For periodicals whose titles begin with this name*] *See* **A.W.R.E.**

5126 **Atomic World.** London. *Atom. Wld* [1958-59] **L.**AM.; AV.; BM.; C.; I.; IC.; P.; RI.; SC.; SI.; TP.; **Abs.**U.; **Bm.**P.; T.; **Bn.**U.; **Br.**A.; **E.**A.; AC.; T.; **Ep.**D.; **Ex.**U.; **F.**A.; **G.**M.; **Lh.**FO; **Lo.**; **Lv.**P.; **M.**D.; P.; **Rn.**B.; **Sh.**IO. [*C. of:* 5132; *C. in:* 13760]

5127 **Atomics.** London. *Atomics* [1949-53] **L.**AM.; AV. 52-53; BM.; C.; I.; IC.; P.; SC.; SI.; TP.; **Abs.**U. 50-53; **Bm.**P. 51-53; T.; **Bn.**U.; **Br.**A. 51-53; **E.**A.; AC. 52-53; T.; **Ep.**D. 51-53; **Ex.**U.; **F.**A. 52-53; **G.**M.; **Lo.**; **Lv.**P.; **Pl.**M. 49-52; **Sh.**IO. [*From 1945-49 issued in* 38253; *C. as:* 5129]

5128 **Atomics** and **Atomic Engineering.** London. *Atomics atom. Engng* [1953] **L.**AM.; AV.; BM.; C.; I.; IC.; P.; SC.; SI.; TP.; **Abs.**U.; **Bm.**P.; T.; **Bn.**U.; **Br.**A.; **E.**A.; AC.; T.; **Ep.**D.; **Ex.**U.; **F.**A.; **G.**M.; **Lo.**; **Lv.**P.; **Sh.**IO. [*C. of* 5127; *C. as:* 5129]

5129 **Atomics** and **Atomic Technology.** London. *Atomics atom. Technol.* [1953-55] **L.**AM.; AV.; BM.; C.; I.; IC.; P.; SC.; SI.; TP.; **Abd.**S. 54-55; **Abs.**U.; **Bm.**P.; T.; **Bn.**U.; **Br.**A.; **E.**A.; AC.; T.; **Ep.**D.; **Ex.**U.; **F.**A.; **G.**M.; **Lo.**; **Lv.**P.; **M.**P. 55; **Rn.**B. 55; **Sh.**IO. [*C. of:* 5128; *C. as:* 5131]

5130 **Atomics** and **Energy.** Johannesburg. *Atomics Energy* [1956-] [*Supplement to:* 23278°]

5131 **Atomics: Engineering** and **Technology.** London. *Atomics Engng Technol.* [1956] **L.**AM.; AV.; BM.; C.; I.; IC.; P.; SC.; SI.; TP.; **Abs.**U.; **Bm.**P.; T.; **Bn.**U.; **Br.**A.; **E.**A.; AC.; T.; **Ep.**D.; **Ex.**U.; **F.**A.; **G.**M.; **Lo.**; **Lv.**P.; **M.**P. 55; **Rn.**B. 55; **Sh.**IO. [*C. of:* 5129; *C. as:* 5132]

5132 **Atomics** and **Nuclear Energy.** London. *Atomics nucl. Energy* [1957-58] **L.**AM.; AV.; BM.; C.; I.; IC.; P.; SC.; SI.; TP.; **Abs.**U.; **Bm.**P.; T.; **Bn.**U.; **Br.**A.; **E.**A.; AC.; T.; **Ep.**D.; **Ex.**U.; **F.**A.; **G.**M.; **Lo.**; **Lv.**P.; **M.**P.; **Rn.**B.; **Sh.**IO. [*C. of:* 5131; *C. as:* 5126]

5133 **Atomkernenergie.** München. *Atomkernenergie* [1956-] **L.**P.; SC.; **Y.** [*C. of:* 5115°]

5134 **Atomkraftwerk.** Wien. *Atomkraftwerk* [1958-] **L.**P.; **Y.** [*Supplement to* and *published in:* 35553]

5135 **Atomlight.** Boston, Mass. *Atomlight* [1957-] **L.**P. 59-; **Y.**

5136 **Atomnaya énergiya.** Moskva. Атомная энергия. *Atomn. Energ.* [1956-] **L.**AV. 58-; BM.; P.; SC. 57-; U.; **Y.** [*English translation at:* 50341 *and* 50342; *abstracts at:* 5118°]

5137 **Atomnaya énergiya. Prilozhenie.** Moskva. Атомная энергия. Приложение. *Atomn. Energ. Prilozh.* [1958-] **L.**P.

5137° **Atomnaya tekhnika** za **rubezhom.** Атомная техника за рубежом. *Atomn. Tekh. Rubezh.*

5138 **Atomo** e **industria.** Roma. *Atomo Ind.* [1957-]

5139 **Atompraxis.** Karlsruhe. *Atompraxis* [1955–] **L.**BM.; P. 57; **Y.**

5140 **Atoms** for **Peace Digest.** Washington. *Atoms Peace Dig.* [1955–60] **L.**AV. 58–60; BM.; P. imp.; QM.; **Bn.**U. imp.; **Br.**P. (1 yr); **Cr.**P.; **Ex.**U.; **G.**E. (3 yr.); M.; **Lv.**P.; **M.**P.; **N.**P. 56–60; **O.**R.; **R.**U.; **Sa.** [*C. as:* 49029] **Atomwirtschaft.** *See* 5114.

5141 **Atoom.** Amsterdam. *Atoom* [1946–48] **L.**SC. [*C. in:* 57457]

5142 **Atoomenergie** en haar **toepassingen.** Den Haag. *Atoomenergie Toepass.* [1959–] **L.**P.; **Br.**P. (1 yr.); **Lv.**P.; **M.**P.; **Y.** [*C. of:* 41710]

5143 **Atskats** uf **Bio-entomologiskas stazijas darbibu.** Latvijas lauksaimneezibas centralbeedriba. Riga. *Atsk. bio-ent. Sta. Darb.* **L.**EB. 13–22*. [*C. as:* 5304]

5144 **Atti** dell'**Accademia** dei **fisiocritici** di **Siena.** Siena. *Atti Accad. Fisiocr. Siena* [1761–] **L.**BM.; BM[N]. 1761–32; MA. (sez. med.-fis.) 47–; R. 1761–1774: 1841: 89–55 imp.; **Db.** 74– imp.; **O.**R. 35–; **Y.** (Sez. med.-fis.).

5145 **Atti** dell'**Accademia** dei **georgofili** di **Firenze.** Firenze. *Atti Accad. Georgof. Firenze* **L.**BM. 71–13. [*C. as:* 21113]

5146 **Atti** dell'**Accademia gioenia** di **scienze naturali.** Catania. *Atti Accad. gioenia Sci. nat.* [1825–] **L.**BM.; BM[N].; M. 04–29 imp.; R. 1825–28: 35–54; SC. 1825–1833; UC. 04–29; **C.**UL. 1825–18; **Db.** 1825–1845: 88– imp.; **E.**R. 65–.

5147 **Atti. Accademia italiana** della **vite** e del **vino siena.** Firenze. *Atti Accad. ital. Vite Vino siena* **Md.**H. 49–.

5148 **Atti** dell'**Accademia ligure** di **scienze** e **lettere.** Genova. *Atti Accad. ligure* [1941–] **L.**BM[N].; R.; SC. 43–; **Abd.**M. 43–; **Bl.**U.; **C.**P. 43–; **Db.** 47–; **E.**R. 43–53; **H.**U. 43–; **Lo.** 47–; **Pl.**M. 43–. [*C. of:* 5267]

5149 **Atti** dell'**Accademia lucchese** di **scienze, lettere** ed **arti.** Lucca. *Atti Accad. lucchese* [1821–] **L.**BM. 1840–; **C.**UL.; **Db.** 1821–1845; **O.**B.

5150 **Atti** dell'**Accademia medica lombarda.** Milano. *Atti Accad. med. lomb.* [1931–40] **L.**S. 39–40; **Y.** [*C. of and Rec. as:* 5254]

5151 **Atti** dell'**Accademia medico-chirurgica** di **Perugia.** Perugia. *Atti Accad. med.-chir. Perugia* [1949–] **L.**MA. 50–.

5152 **Atti** dell'**Accademia medico-fisica fiorentina.** Firenze. *Atti Accad. med.-fis. fiorent.*

5153 **Atti** dell'**Accademia nazionale** dei **Lincei. Memorie.** Roma. *Atti Accad. naz. Lincei Memorie* Classe di scienze fisiche e matematiche. [1876–] **L.**BM. 95–; BM[N].; C.; EE. 06–31; G.; GL. 00–; K. 76–89 imp.: 46–57; L. 76–38 imp.; M. 76–89; P. 94–; R.; SC.; U.; UC.; Z.; **Abd.**U. 94–; **Abs.**N. 51–; U. 46– imp.; **Bl.**U. 15–19; **Bm.**U. 10–35: 46–; **C.**P.; T. 76–31; UL.; **Db.**; **E.**C. 01–; R. imp.; U. 99–12; **F.**A. 55–; **G.**U. 76–19 imp.; **Ld.**U. 04–; **M.**U. 76–13: 46–50 imp.; **Nw.**A. 55–; **O.**R.; **Sa.** 48–52; **Y.** [1940–44 *represented in* 5220].

5154 **Atti** dell'**Accademia nazionale** dei **Lincei. Rendiconti.** Roma. *Atti Accad. naz. Lincei Rc.* Classe di scienze fisiche, matematiche e naturali [1884–] **L.**BM.; BM[N].; C.; EB. 23–39; EE. 06–; G.; GL. 00–; HQ. 51–; I. 84–20 imp.; K. (bot.) 84–39 imp.; L.; M. imp.; MC. 25–39; MO. 13–33; P. 02–; R.; S. 20–52; SC. 85–; U. imp.; Z.; **Abd.**U.; **Abs.**N. 90–; **Bl.**U. 84–24 imp.; **Bm.**N. 22–; U. 10–14: 25–32: 46–; **Bn.**U. 96–55 imp.; **Br.**U. 21–33; **C.**P.; T. 92–39;

UL. 92–; **Db.**; **E.**C.; J.; O. imp.; R.; U. 98–14; V. 96–; **G.**U. 84–23; **Lv.**U. 05–; **M.**U. 84–39 imp.; 46–50; **Nw.**A. 28–32: 55–; **O.**R.; **Sa.**; **Y.** [1939–43 *represented in* 5221]

5155 **Atti** dell'**Accademia nazionale** dei **Lincei. Rendiconti** delle **sedute solenni.** Roma. *Atti Accad. naz. Lincei Rc. Sed. solen.* [1892–] **L.**BM.; C. 92–98: 50–; EE. 06–39; G.; GL. 00–; L.; M. 92–13; R.; SC. 01–38; UC. Z. 50–; **Abd.**U.; **Bl.**U.; 01–28; **Bm.**U. 11–13; **C.**P. 29–; UL.; **Db.**; **E.**C. 92–39; **G.**U. 92–26 imp.; **Lv.**U. 05–; **O.**B.; **Sa.**

5156 **Atti** dell'**Accademia olimpica.** Vicenza. *Atti Accad. olimp.* **Dm.** 08–25.

5157 **Atti** dell'**Accademia peloritana.** Messina. *Atti Accad. pelorit.* [1878–] **L.**BM[N]. 15–53; UC. 00: 02; **C.**P. 05–13; **Db.** 05–; **E.**R. 05–13.

5158 **Atti** dell'**Accademia pontificia** dei **Nuovi Lincei.** Roma. *Atti Accad. pontif. Nuovi Lincei* [1847–35] **L.**BM. 1847–13; BM[N]. 71–35; EB. 12–33; R.; SC. 1851–35; **Db.** 79–35; **E.**R. imp.; **G.**U. 1847–06 imp.; **M.**R. 1851–35; **Nw.**P. 08–17; **O.**B. 1847–69. [*C. as:* 743]

5159 **Atti** dell'**Accademia properziana** del **Subasio** in **Assisi.** Assisi. *Atti Accad. properz. Subas. Assisi*

5160 **Atti** dell'**Accademia scientifica veneto-trentino-istriana.** Padova. *Atti Accad. scient. veneto-trent.-istriana* [1872–35] **L.**BM. 04–35; BM[N].; Z. 72–02; **Bl.**U. 87–35 imp.; **E.**C. 79–35; **G.**N. 79–34. [*C. in:* 5210]

5161 **Atti** dell'**Accademia** delle **scienze.** Torino. *Atti Accad. Sci., Torino* [1865–] **L.**BM.; BM[N].; GL. 00–; L.; M. 03– imp.; P.; R. 65–55; RI. 49–; SC. 65–27; UC. 90–45; Z.; **Abd.**U. 01–; **Abs.**N. 81–; **Bl.**U. 12–32 imp.; **C.**P. 74–; UL.; **Db.**; **E.**C. L. 00–; R. 65–32; U. 94–19 imp.; **G.**U. 81– imp.; **Lv.**U. 26–; **O.**R.; **Sa.** 53–; **Y.**

5162 **Atti** dell'**Accademia** delle **scienze fisiche** e **matematiche.** Napoli. *Atti Accad. Sci. fis. mat., Napoli* [1863–] **L.**BM. 63–16; BM[N].; GL. 00–33 imp.; L. imp.; M. 88–14; R. 63–35; UC. 88–; **Bm.**N. 01–14; **C.**P. 88–; UL.; **Db.**; **E.**J. 87–14; R. imp.; **G.**U. 88–14; **Lv.**U. 88–89; **M.**U. 02–14; **O.**R. 63–35.

5163 **Atti** dell'**Accademia** delle **scienze** dell'**Istituto** di **Bologna. Memorie.** Bologna. *Atti Accad. Sci. Ist. Bologna Memorie.* Classe di scienze fisiche. [1954–] **L.**BM.; BM[N].; M.; P.; SC.; UC.; **Bm.**N.; **C.**UL.; **Db.**; **E.**C.; R.; **Lv.**U.; O.R. [*C. of:* 31300]

5164 **Atti** dell'**Accademia** delle **scienze** dell'**Istituto** di **Bologna. Rendiconti.** Bologna. *Atti Accad. Sci. Ist. Bologna Rc.* Classe di scienze fisiche. [1953–] **L.**BM.; BM[N].; M.; P.; R. 54–56; **Abs.**N.; **Bm.**N.; **Lv.**U. [*C. of:* 42554]

5165 **Atti** dell'**Accademia** di **scienze, lettere** ed **arti.** Palermo. *Atti Accad. Sci. Lett., Palermo* [1845–] **L.**BM.; BM[N].; R. 1845–1859: 84–02; SC. 1845–1859: 38–; UC. 1853–1859; **Db.** 92–.

5166 **Atti** dell'**Accademia** di **scienze, lettere** ed **arti.** Udine. *Atti Accad. Sci. Lett., Udine* **L.**BM. 53; **Y.** **Atti** della **Accademia** di **scienze, lettere** ed **arti** degli **Agiati** in **Rovereto.** *See* 5199.

5167 **Atti** dell'**Accademia** delle **scienze mediche** e **naturali** in **Ferrara.** Ferrara. *Atti Accad. Sci. med. nat. Ferrara* [1824–]

5168 **Atti** dell'**Associazione elettrotecnica italiana** Milano. *Atti Ass. elettrotec. ital.* [1896–13] **L.**EE. [*C. as:* 17926]

5168° **Atti. Associazione genetica italiana.** Roma. *Atti Ass. genet. ital.* **L.**SC. 53–; **C.**A. 54–.

Atti. Associazione geofisica italiana. *See* 5186.

5169 **Atti** dell'**Associazione italiana** di **aerotecnica.** Roma. *Atti Ass. ital. Aerotec.* [1920–24] **L.**AV.; P.; SC. [*C. as:* 1116]

5170 **Atti** dell'**Associazione italiana** di **ingegneria chimica.** Milano. *Atti Ass. ital. Ing. chim.* **L.**P. 60–.

5171 **Atti** dell'**Ateneo** di **scienze, lettere** ed **arti.** Bergamo. *Atti Ateneo Sci. Lett., Bergamo*

5172 **Atti** del **Centro italiano** de **ricerche subacquei.** *Atti Cent. ital. Ric. subacq.* **Pl.**M. 56–.

5173 **Atti** del **Centro nazionale meccanico agricolo.** Torino. [1952–] *Atti Cent. naz. mecc. agric.* **L.**AM.; P. 56–; **Rt.** 56.

5174 **Atti** della **Clinica oto-rino-laringoiatrica** della **R. Università** di **Roma.** Roma. *Atti Clin. oto-rinolar. R. Univ. Roma* **L.**MD. 26–30.

5175 **Atti** della **Clinica otorinolaringologica** della **R. Università** di **Napoli.** *Atti Clin. otorinolar. R. Univ. Napoli* **L.**MD. 38–39.

5176 **Atti** del **Collegio** degli **ingegneri** ed **architetti.** Bologna. *Atti Coll. Ing. Archit., Bologna.*

5177 **Atti** del **Collegio** degli **ingegneri** ed **architetti.** Milano. *Atti Coll. Ing. Archit., Milano* [1868–19] **L.**P. 16–19.

5178 **Atti** del **Collegio** degli **ingegneri** ed **architetti.** Novara. *Atti Coll. Ing. Archit., Novara*

5179 **Atti** del **Collegio** degli **ingegneri** ed **architetti.** Palermo. *Atti Coll. Ing. Archit., Palermo* [1878–15]

5180 **Atti** del **Collegio** degli **ingegneri** ed **architetti.** Parma. *Atti Coll. Ing. Archit., Parma*

5181 **Atti** del **Collegio** degli **ingegneri navali** e **meccanici.** Genova. *Atti Coll. Ing. nav. mecc., Genova*

5182 **Atti** del **Collegio toscano architetti** ed **ingegneri.** Firenze. *Atti Coll. tosc. Archit. Ing.* [1900–]

5183 **Atti** del **Collegio veneto** degli **ingegneri.** Venezia. *Atti Coll. veneto Ing.*

5183° **Atti** del **Congresso geografico italiano.** Genova. *Atti Congr. geogr. ital.* [1893–]

5184 **Atti** del **congresso nazionale** dell'**Associazione meccanica italiana.** Milano. *Atti Congr. naz. Ass. mecc. ital.* **L.**P. 56–; SC. 42–; **Y.** 56–.

5185 **Atti** del **congresso. Unione matematica italiana.** *Atti Congr. Un. mat. ital.* [1941–] **L.**SC. 42–.

5186 **Atti** dei **convegni. Associazione geofisica italiana.** Roma. *Atti Conv. Ass. geofis. ital.* **L.**MO. 57; **Y.** 52–.

5187 **Atti** dei **convegni. Fondazione Alessandro Volta.** Roma. *Atti Conv. Fond. Aless. Volta* [1931–] **L.**C. 31; P.; SC. 53–; UC. 32–; **Br.**U. 32; **E.**R. 32.

5188 **Atti. Convegno** per il **commercio estero** della **ceramica.** Vizenza. *Atti Conv. Comm. estero Ceram.* [1950] **L.**P. [*C. as:* 5190]

5189 **Atti. Convegno** di **geologia nucleare.** Roma. *Atti Conv. Geol. nucl.* [1955–] **L.**P.

5189° **Atti. Convegno** sugli **idrocarburi gassosi.** Piacenza. *Atti Conv. Idrocarb. gass.* [1957] **L.**P. [*C. of:* 5193; *See* International Congresses Section for continuation.*]

5190 **Atti. Convegno nazionale** della **ceramica.** Vicenza. *Atti Conv. naz. Ceram.* [1952–] **L.**P. [*C. of:* 5138]

5191 **Atti** del **Convegno nazionale. Lega italiana** per la **lotta** contro il **cancro.** *Atti Conv. naz. Lega ital. Lotta Cancro*

5192 **Atti** del **Convegno nazionale** di **tecnica navale.** Genova. *Atti Conv. naz. Tec. nav.* [1948–] **G.**E. 48–49.

5193 **Atti. Convegno nazionale** sulle **utilizzazioni** del **metano.** Piacenza. *Atti Conv. naz. Util. Metano* [1952–54] **L.**P. [*C. as:* 5189°]

5194 **Atti** del **convegno. Società italiana** di **scienze farmaceutiche.** Milano. *Atti Conv. Soc. ital. Sci. farm.* [1954–] **L.**P.

5195 **Atti** della **Fondazione** e **contributi** dell' **Istituto nazionale** di **ottica.** Firenze. *Atti Fond. Contrti Ist. naz. Ottica* [1953–] **L.**P.; SI.; **Y.** [*C. of:* 5196]

5196 **Atti** della **Fondazione 'Giorgio Ronchi'** e **contributi** dell'**Istituto nazionale** di **ottica.** Firenze. *Atti Fond. Giorgio Ronchi* [1946–52] **L.**P.; SI.; **Y.** [*C. as:* 5195]

5197 **Atti** della **Fondazione scientifica Cagnola.** Milano. *Atti Fond. scient. Cagnola* [1856–42] **L.**BM.; BM^N. 1856–88: 15–42; R. 1860–42; UC. 93–42; **Db.** 63–42; **M.**U. 06–37.

5198 **Atti** di **guidonia.** *Atti Guidonia* **L.**AV. 39–42.

5199 **Atti** dell' **I. R. Accademia roveretana** di **scienze, lettere** ed **arti** degli **Agiati.** Rovereto. *Atti I.R. Accad. roveret. Sci.* [1913–] **L.**BM.

5200 **Atti** dell'**Istituto botanico** della **Università** e **Laboratorio crittogamico** di **Pavia.** Milano. *Atti Ist. bot. Univ. Lab. crittogam. Pavia* [1888–] **L.**BM.; BM^N.; K.; L. 02–; MY. imp.; SC. 21; **Ba.** I. 44–; **Br.**A. 43–; **C.**A. 43–; UL.; **Db.**; **E.**R. 02–04; **Hu.**G. 29–50; **Md.**H. 27– imp.; **Rt.**; **Sil.** 50–; **Y.** [*Also supplement*]

5201 **Atti** dell'**Istituto geologico, Università** di **Pavia.** *Atti Ist. geol. Pavia* [1943–] **L.**BN^N.; GL. 47; **Ld.**U. 60–.

5202 **Atti** dell'**Istituto d'incoraggiamento** alle **scienze naturali.** Napoli. *Atti Ist. Incoragg. Sci. nat.* [1811–] **L.**BM.; BM^N. 1811–04: 08; P. 1811–13; R. 1811–1855: 98–01: 09–12; S. 1811–28; **C.**UL.; **Db.** imp.; **E.**R. 93–12 imp.; **Lv.**U. 08–13; **O.**R. 1811–72.

Atti. Istituto lombardo di **scienze** e **lettere.** *See* 42539.

5203 **Atti. Istituto** di **scienza** delle **costruzioni.** Bari. *Atti Ist. Sci. Costr.* **L.**B. 58–.

5204 **Atti. Istituto sperimentale** di **meccanica agraria.** Milano. *Atti Ist. sper. Mecc. agr.*

5205 **Atti** del **Istituto veneto** di **scienze, lettere** ed **arti.** Venezia. *Atti Ist. veneto Sci.* Scienze mat. e nat. [1841–] **L.**BM.; BM^N.; L. 1860–; M. 83–13; MD. 44–; P. 55–; R. 1855–39: 44–; SC. 80–93: 37–; UC. 83–36 imp.; **C.**UL. 25–; **E.**J. 74–09; R. 1858– imp.; **Nw.**A. 09–; **Y.**

5206 **Atti** dei **Laboratori scientifici A. Mosso** sul **Monte Rosa** della **R. Università** di **Torino.** *Atti Lab. scient. A. Mosso* **E.**U. 23–39; **M.**MS. 23.

Atti del **Laboratorio crittogamico, Pavia.** *See* 5200.

5207 **Atti** e **memorie** dell'**Accademia d'agricoltura, scienze** e **lettere** di **Verona.** Verona. *Atti Memorie Accad. Agric. Sci. Lett. Verona* [1900–] **L.**BM. 49–; **C.**A. 32–; **O.**B. 57–. [*C. of:* 31269]

5208 Atti e **memorie** dell'**Accademia patavina** di **scienze, lettere** ed **arti.** Padova. *Atti Memorie Accad. patavina* [1948–] L.BM.; BM^N.; P. (parte 2) 58–; SC.; **Y.** [*C. of:* 5210]

5209 Atti e **memorie. Accademia** di **scienze, lettere** ed **arti.** Modena. *Atti Memorie Accad. Sci. Lett., Modena* [1926–] L.BM.; BM^N.; E.R.; O.B. [*C. of:* 31302]

5210 Atti e **memorie** dell'**Accademia** di **scienze, lettere** ed **arti.** Padova. *Atti Memorie Accad. Sci. Lett., Padova* [1885–43] L.BM.; BM^N.; GL. 00–20; SC. 36–43; E.R. 85–12 imp.; T. 93–06: 19–20. [*C. as:* 5208]

5211 Atti e **memorie** dell'**Accademia** di **storia** dell'**arte sanitaria.** Roma. *Atti Memorie Accad. Stor. Arte sanit.* L.MD. 35–40. [*C. of* 8297; *Supplement to:* 42149]

5211° Atti e **memorie. Accademia toscana** di **scienze** e **lettere 'La Columbaria'.** Firenze. *Atti Memorie Accad. tosc. Sci. Lett.* L.BM. 51–52.

5212 Atti e **memorie** dell'**Associazione medico-chirurgica** di **Alessandria.** *Atti Memorie Ass. med.-chir. Alessandria*

5213 Atti e **memorie** dell'**I. R. Società agraria** di **Gorizia.** Gorizia. *Atti Memorie I. R. Soc. agr. Gorizia*

5214 Atti e **memorie** de **Lo Scoltenna, circolo scientifico,** etc. Modena. *Atti Memorie Lo Scoltenna*

    Atti e **memorie. R. Accademia** di **scienze lettere** et **arti, Modena.** *See* 5209.

5215 Atti e **memorie** della **R. Accademia virgiliana.** Mantova. *Atti Memorie R. Accad. virgil.* [1863–] L.BM. 68–17; G.U. 68: 09–23 imp.

5216 Atti e **memorie. Società lombarda** di **medicina.** *Atti Memorie Soc. lomb. Med.* [1933–] L.MA. 34–35 imp.; S. 35–39.

5217 Atti del **Museo civico** di **storia naturale** di **Trieste.** Trieste. *Atti Mus. civ. Stor. nat. Trieste* [1884–] L.BM^N.; R. 84–03: 26–54; E.R.; G.N. 03; Pl.M. 08.

5218 Atti e **notizie. Associazione italiana** di **metallurgia.** Milano. *Atti Notiz. Ass. ital. Metall.* [1946–] L.P. 52–; **Y.**

    Atti della **Pontificia Accademia** delle **scienze, Nuovi Lincei.** *See* 5158.

5219 Atti della **Prima associazione italiana** fra gli **utenti** di **caldaie** a **vapore.** *Atti prima Ass. ital. Utenti Cald. Vap.*

    Atti della **R. Accademia** dei **fisiocritica** di **Siena.** *See* 5144.

    Atti della **R. Accademia** dei **georgofili** di **Firenze.** *See* 5145.

    Atti della **R. Accademia Gioenia** di **scienze naturali.** *See* 5146.

5220 Atti della **R. Accademia d'Italia. Memorie.** Roma. *Atti R. Accad. Ital. Memorie.* Classe di scienze fisiche, matematiche e naturali. [1940–44] L.BM^N. 41–44; EB. (ent.); R.; U. imp.; Z.; C.; P.; SC.; Z. (zool.); M.U.; Sa. [*Replaced* 5153 *and* 31298 *during the war years*]

5221 Atti della **R. Accademia d'Italia. Rendiconti.** Roma. *Atti R. Accad. Ital. Rc.* Classe di scienze fisiche, matematiche e naturali. [1939–43] L.BM.; BM^N.; C.; EB.; EE.; G.; GL.; L.; MC.; MD.; P.; R.; SC.; U. imp.; Z.; **Abd.**U.; **Abs.**N.; **Bm.**N.; **Br.**U.; **C.**P.; UL.; **Db.**; E.C.; J.; O.;

R.; V.; **Lv.**U.; **M.**U.; **O.**R.; **Sa.** [*C. of:* and *Rec. as:* 5154]

    Atti della **R. Accademia ligure** di **scienze** e **lettere.** *See* 5148.

    Atti della **R. Accademia lucchese** di **scienze lettere** ed **arti.** *See* 5149.

5222 Atti della **R. Accademia medico-chirurgica.** Napoli. *Atti R. Accad. med.-chir., Napoli.*

    Atti della **R. Accademia nazionale** dei **Lincei. Memorie.** *See* 5153.

    Atti della **R. Accademia nazionale** dei **Lincei. Rendiconti.** *See* 5154.

    Atti della **R. Accademia nazionale** dei **Lincei. Rendiconti** delle **sedute solenni.** *See* 5155.

5223 Atti della **R. Accademia Pontaniana.** Napoli. *Atti R. Accad. pontan.* [1810–33]. L.BM. 1832–33; BM^N.; R. 1810–1819: 90–13: 24–28; UC. 03–28 imp.; **Db.** 90–33; G.U. 90–99: 04–13.

    Atti della **R. Accademia** delle **scienze.** Torino. *See* 5161.

5224 Atti della **R. Accademia** delle **scienze mediche.** Palermo. *Atti R. Accad. Sci. med., Palermo* E.J. 61–12.

    Atti della **R. Istituto veneto** di **scienze, lettere** ed **arte.** *See* 5205.

5225 Atti della **R. Stazione agraria sperimentale.** Palermo. *Atti R. Staz. agr. sper., Palermo.*

    Atti della **R. Università** di **Genova.** *See* 5271.

5226 Atti e **rassegna tecnica** della **Società** degli **ingegneri** e degli **architetti** di **Torino.** *Atti Rass. tec. Soc. Ing. Archit. Torino* L.P.

5227 Atti e **relazioni. Accademia pugliese** delle **scienze.** Bari, Verona. *Atti Relaz. Accad. pugl. Sci.* [1942–]

    Parte 2—Classe di scienze fisiche, mediche e naturali. L.MD. 53–; O.R. 52–.

5228 Atti e **rendiconti. Accademia dafnica** di **scienze, lettere** ed **arti** in **Acireale.** Acireale. *Atti Rc. Accad. dafnica Acireale* L.BM. 95–02.

5229 Atti e **rendiconti** della **R. Accademia** degli **zelanti.** Acireale. *Atti Rc. R. Accad. Zelanti* [1889–00] L.BM. 91–00*; BM^N.; R. 93–00; C.P. 95–00. [*C. as:* 42545]

5230 Atti, resoconti, memorie. Congresso nazionale di **locomozione aerea.** *Atti Resoc. Memorie Congr. naz. Locom. aerea* L.BM. 10.

5231 Atti della **riunione annuale. Associazione nazionale** di **ingegneria sanitaria.** *Atti Riun. a. Ass. naz. Ing. sanit.* L.P. 55–.

5232 Atti della **riunione scientifica. Sezione piedimontese, Società italiana** di **nipiologia.** Milano, Torino. *Atti Riun. scient. Sez. piedmont. Soc. ital. Nipiol.* L.MD. 49.

5233 Atti del **Seminario matematico** e **fisico** dell'**Università** di **Modena.** *Atti Semin. mat. fis. Univ. Modena* [1947–] C.P. 58–; **Db.**; Rt. 49–51.

5234 Atti del **Sindicato provinciale fascista ingegneri** di **Genova.** *Atti Sind. prov. fascista Ing. Genova*

5235 Atti del **Sindicato provinciale fascista ingegneri** di **Milano.** *Atti Sind. prov. fascista Ing. Milano* Sil. 35–39 imp.

5236 Atti della **Società agronomica italiana.** Roma. *Atti Soc. agron. ital.* Rt. 20–.

5237 Atti della **Società** fra i **cultori** delle **scienze mediche** e **naturali** in **Cagliari.** *Atti Soc. Cult. Sci. med. nat. Cagliari* [1927–35] [*C. of:* 8440; *C. as:* 42171]

5238 **Atti** della **Società** di **cultura medica novarese.** Novara. *Atti Soc. Cult. med. novarese* **L.**MD. 43–.

5239 **Atti** della **Società** di **dermatologia e sifilografia** e delle **sezione interprovinciali.** Bologna. *Atti Soc. Derm. Sif., Bologna* **L.**MD. 38.

Atti della **Società elvetica** di **scienze naturali.** *See* 56067.

5240 **Atti** della **Società freniatrica italiana.** Genova. *Atti Soc. freniat. ital.*

5241 **Atti** della **Società** degli **ingegneri** e degli **architetti** di **Trieste.** *Atti Soc. Ing. Archit. Trieste*

5242 **Atti** della **Società italiana** di **anatomia.** *Atti Soc. ital. Anat.* [1929–] **L.**BM^N.; Z. 31–. [*Supplement to:* 33217]

5243 **Atti** della **Società italiana** di **cancerologia.** Milano. *Atti Soc. ital. Cancer.* [1958–] **L.**MD.

5244 **Atti** della **Società italiana** di **cardiologia.** Roma. *Atti Soc. ital. Cardiol.* **L.**MD. 43. [*Supplement to:* 19781]

5245 **Atti** della **Società italiana** di **genetica** ed **eugenica.** Roma. *Atti Soc. ital. Genet. Eugen.*

5245^a **Atti. Società italiana** di **oftalmologia.** Roma. *Atti Soc. ital. Oftal.* [1924–29] [*C. as:* 5262]

5246 **Atti** della **Società italiana** di **ostetricia e ginecologia.** Roma. *Atti Soc. ital. Ostet. Ginec.* [1894–]

5247 **Atti** della **Società italiana** di **patologia.** Pavia. *Atti Soc. ital. Patol.*

5248 **Atti** della **Società italiana** per il **progresso** delle **scienze.** Roma. *Atti Soc. ital. Prog. Sci.* [1907–] **L.**M.; P. 23–38 imp.; UC. 17–; **Abd.**U.; **C.**P.; **Db.**

5249 **Atti** della **Società italiana** di **scienze naturali,** e del **Museo civile** di **storia naturale.** Milano. *Atti Soc. ital. Sci. nat.* [1859–] **L.**BM. 1859–20; BM^N.; GL. 00–; R.; SC. 1859–70: 55–; UC. 1860–94 imp.; Z. 1860–; **C.**P. 68–79: 38–; UL.; **Cr.**N. 13– imp.; **Db.** 66–; **Dm.** 17–40; **E.**C. 69–; R. 70–89 imp.; **G.**N. 00– imp.; **Lv.**U. 23–imp.; **Pl.**M. 06–; **Y.**

5250 **Atti** della **Società italiana** delle **scienze veterinarie.** Faenza. *Atti Soc. ital. Sci. vet.* [1947–] **L.**V.; VC.; **Abd.**R. 58–; **C.**V. 52–; **R.**D.; **W.**; **Y.**

5251 **Atti** della **Società italiana** di **storia critica** delle **scienze mediche** e **naturali.** Faenza, etc. *Atti Soc. ital. Stor. crit. Sci. med. nat.* **O.**R. 07–09★.

5252 **Atti** della **Società italiana** di **urologia.** Roma. *Atti Soc. ital. Urol.* **L.**MD. 22–.

5253 **Atti** della **Società ligustica** di **scienze naturali** e **geografiche.** Genova. *Atti Soc. ligust. Sci. nat. geogr.* [1890–35] **L.**BM.; BM^N.; R.; SC. 22–35; **Pl.**M. 04–35 imp. [*C. as:* 5267]

5254 **Atti** della **Società lombarda** di **scienze mediche** e **biologiche.** Milano. *Atti Soc. lomb. Sci. med. biol.* [1912–] **L.**CB. 55–; MA. 51–; MD. 51–; **Y.** [*See also:* 5150]

5255 **Atti** della **Società medica** di **Bolzano.** Bolzano. *Atti Soc. med. Bolzano* **L.**MA. 54–.

5256 **Atti** della **Società** di **medicina legale** in **Roma.** *Atti Soc. Med. leg. Roma* [1908–]

5257 **Atti** della **Società medico-biologica** di **Milano.** Milano. *Atti Soc. med.-biol. Milano.*

5258 **Atti** della **Società medico-chirurgica** di **Bolzano.** Bolzano. *Atti Soc. med.-chir. Bolzano* **L.**MD. 48–.

5259 **Atti** della **Società medico-chirurgica** di **Padova.** *Atti Soc. med.-chir. Padova* [1923–30] [*C. as:* 5259^a]

5259^a **Atti** della **Società medico-chirurgica** di **Padova** e **Bolletino** della **Facoltà** di **medicina** e **chirurgia** della **Università** di **Padova.** *Atti Soc. med.-chir. Padova* [1931–] **L.**MA. 45–; **Br.**U. 32–35. [*C. of:* 5259]

Atti della **Società milanese** di **medicina** e **biologia.** *See* 5257.

5260 **Atti. Società napoletana** di **chirurgia.** Napoli. *Atti Soc. napol. Chir.*

5261 **Atti** della **Società** dei **naturalisti** e **matematici.** Modena. *Atti Soc. Nat. Mat.* [1866–] **L.**BM. 83–; BM^N.; SC. 25–; Z. 75– imp.; **C.**UL. 83–; **E.**C. 87–; R. 83– imp.; **Y.**

5262 **Atti** della **Società oftalmologica italiana.** Roma. *Atti Soc. oftal. ital.* [1930–] **L.**OP. 47–. [*C. of:* 5245^a]

5263 **Atti** della **Società oftalmologica lombarda.** Genova. *Atti Soc. oftal. lomb.* [1946–] **L.**MD.; OP.

5264 **Atti. Società peloritana** di **scienze fisiche, matematiche** e **naturali.** Messina. *Atti Soc. pelorit. Sci. fis. mat. nat.* [1955–] **L.**BM^N.; P. 58–; SC.; Z.; **Db.**; **E.**R.; **Pl.**M.

5265 **Atti** della **Società regionali** di **ostetrica** e di **ginecologia.** Torino. *Atti Soc. reg. Ostet. Ginec.* [*Supplement to* and *C. as:* 31962^c]

5266 **Atti** della **Società romana** di **antropologia.** Roma. *Atti Soc. romana Antrop.* [1893–10] **L.**AN.; BM.; **E.**V. 01–09; **O.**R. [*C. as:* 47825]

5267 **Atti** della **Società** di **scienze** e **lettere** di **Genova** Genova. *Atti Soc. Sci. Lett. Genova* [1936–40] **L.**BM.; BM^N.; R.; SC. 36–39; **Pl.**M. [*C. of:* 5253; *C. as:* 5148]

5268 **Atti** della **Società** per gli **studi** della **malaria.** Roma. *Atti Soc. Studi Malar.* [1899–14] **L.**TD.; **Lv.**U.

Atti della **Società toscana** di **scienze naturali** residente in **Pisa.** (a) Memorie. *See* 31319. (b) Processi verbali. *See* 39853.

Atti della **Società veneto-trentina** di **scienze naturali.** *See* 5160.

5269 **Atti ufficiali** del **Congresso nazionale** dei **viticoltori** ed **enologi italiani.** *Atti uff. Congr. naz. Vitic. Enol. ital.*

5270 **Atti ufficiali** del **Convegno internazionale** delle **comunicazioni.** Genova. *Atti uff. Conv. int. Comun.* **L.**SC. 53–.

5271 **Atti** della **Università** di **Genova.** Genova. *Atti Univ. Genova* [1869–] **L.**BM.; BM^N. 69–23; **E.**R. 92: 02.

5272 **Attività medica italiana.** Pisa. *Attiv. med. ital.* [1919–22] [*C. of:* 24261]

5273 **Attività** del **sole.** R. Osservatorio astrofisico di Catania. *Attiv. Sole* **L.**AS. 21–32.

5274 **Attività tecnica** di **officina.** Torino. *Attiv. tec. Off.*

5275 **Attualità** di **chemioterapia.** Milano. *Attual. Chemioter.*

5276 **Attualità** di **laboratorio.** Milano. *Attual. Lab.* **L.**P. 59–.

5277 **Attualità medica.** Milano. *Attual. med., Milano* [1912–] **L.**TD. 14–16.

5278 **Attualità medica.** Roma. *Attual. med., Roma* [1936] **L.**EB. 36–37; I.; LI 36–37; MA. 36–40; MD. 36–39; TD. 36–44. [*C. of:* 22737. *Supplement to:* and *amalgamated with:* 3044]

5279 **Attualità mediche.** Firenze. *Attual. med., Firenze*

5280 **Attualità zoologiche.** Torino. *Attual. zool.* [1933–59] L.z.; **Bn.**U. 57–59; **Y.** [*Supplement to:* 4454]

5281 **Attualità zootecnica.** Milano. *Attual. zootec.* **Atualidades odontologicas.** São Paulo. *See* 88°.

5282 **Auburn Engineer.** Auburn, Ala. *Auburn Engr* [1925–] L.P. 25–32.

5283 **Auburn Veterinarian.** Auburn, Ala. *Auburn Vet.* [1945–] L.v. 46–53 imp.; **W.** 48–.

5284 **Auckland Lily Society Bulletin.** Auckland, N.Z. *Auckland Lily Soc. Bull.* L.HS. 56–.

5285 **Auckland University College Reprints.** Auckland, N.Z. *Auckland Univ. Coll. Repr.* L.BM^N. (bot.) 46–: (chem.) 47; **Pl.**M. (bot.) 49– imp.

5286 **Audio.** Lancaster, Pa., etc. *Audio* [1954–] L.AV. imp.; EE.; P.; SC.; **E.**U.; **F.**A.; **Ld.**U. 62–; **Li.**M. (5 yr.); **M.**P.; **Ma.**T.; **Y.** [*C. of:* 5287]

5287 **Audio Engineering.** New York, Santa Barbara. *Audio Engng* [1947–54] L.AV.; EE.; P. 51–54; SC.; **E.**U.; **F.**A. 52–54; **Ma.**T. imp. [*C. of:* 41779; *C. as:* 5286]

5288 **Audio Record.** New York. *Audio Rec.* L.P. 51–.

5289 **Audiocraft.** *Audiocraft* [1956–58] L.AV. [*C. in:* 22148]

5290 **Audiotecnica.** Torino. *Audiotecnica* [1958–] L.P. 60–; **Li.**M.

5291 **Audiotecnica News.** Torino. *Audiotecnica News* **Li.**M. 55: 58–.

5292 **Audio-Visual Communication Review.** Washington. *Audio-vis. Commun. Rev.* [1953–] **Y.**

5292° **Audio-Visual Instruction.** *Audio-vis. Instruct.* **Y.**

5293 **Audubon Field Notes.** National Audubon Society and United States Fish and Wildlife Service. New York. *Audubon Fld Notes.* L.BM^N. 62–

5294 **Audubon Magazine.** Harrisburg, etc. *Audubon Mag.* [1941–] L.BM^N.; NC. 41–49; Z. 45–; **E.**F.; **O.**AP.; OR.; **Y.** [*C. of:* 7133]

5295 **Audubon Warbler.** Portland, Ore. *Audubon Warbler* [1937–]

5296 **Audubon Yearbook.** Crawfordsville. *Audubon Yb.* [1931–] [*C. of:* 23090]

5297 **Aufbau.** Wien. *Aufbau* [1946–] L.BA.; U. 46–47.

5298 **Aufbereitungs-Technik.** Zeitschrift für die Aufbereitung fester Rohstoffe. Wiesbaden. *Aufbereitungs-Tech.* [1960–] L.P.; **Ld.**U.; **Y.**

5299 **Aufsätze** und **Reden** der **Senckenbergischen naturforschenden Gesellschaft.** Frankfurt am Main. *Aufs. Reden senckenb. naturf. Ges.* [1947–] L.BM.; BM^N.; **Y.**

5300 **Aufzeichnungen** des **Anemometers.** Institut für kosmische Physik der Universität Prag. Prag. *Aufzeichn. Anemomet. Inst. kosm. Phys. Prag* L.MO. 14–23.

5301 **Aufzeichnungen** des **Architekten-** u. **Ingenieur-Vereins** für **Niederrhein** u. **Westfalen.** Köln. *Aufzeichn. Archit.- u. IngVer., Köln*

5302 **Augsburger technische Zeitung.** Augsburg. *Augsburger tech. Ztg*

5303 **Augsne** un **raža.** Riga. *Augsne Raža* [1951–] L.BM.; P. 57–; **C.**A. 51–59; **Db.**; **Rt.**; **Y.** 52–59.

5304 **Augu aizsardzibas Instituta darbibas pārsakts.** Riga. *Augu aizsardz. Inst. darb. Pārs.* [1923–] L.EB. 23–29. [*C. of:* 5143]

5305 **Aujourd'hui.** Art et architecture. Boulogne-sur-Seine. *Aujourd'hui* [1955–] **Y.**

5306 **Auk.** A quarterly journal of ornithology. Cambridge, Mass. *Auk* [1884–] L.BM.; BM^N.; L. 06–13; NC. 97–43: 54–; Z.; **Abd.**U. 52–; **Bm.**P. 20–; **Br.**U.; **C.**B.; **Db.**; **E.**F. 84–39; **G.**N.; **M.**U. 84–16 imp.; **O.**OR.; R. 28–42; **Y.**

5307 **Aural News.** London. *Aural News* [1946–] L.H. 47–.

5308 **Aurore médicale.** Paris. *Aurore méd.*

5309 **Aurum.** School of Mines, Rapid City. *Aurum*

5310 **Aus dem Archiv der Deutschen Seewarte.** Hamburg. *Aus Arch. dt. Seew.* [1878–44] L.MO.; SC. 24–44; **Abd.**M. 20–43; **E.**M. 78–43 imp.; **M.**U. 89–14 imp.; **Pl.**M. 20–43 imp.
Aus dem Draeger-Werk. *See* 17183.

5311 **Aus Natur** und **Museum.** Bericht der Senckenbergischen naturforschenden Gesellschaft. Frankfurt. *Aus Natur Mus.* [1922–26] L.BM.; BM^N.; E.; EB.; GL.; L.; UC.; Z.; **Abs.**U.; **Bl.**U. imp.; **Br.**U.; **C.**P.; UL.; **Cr.**M.; **Db.** 25–26; **E.**C. 25–26; **Ld.**U. 25–26; **Lv.**U.; **M.**U.; **O.**R.; **Pl.**M. [*C. of:* 6347; *C. as:* 34189]

5312 **Aus Natur** und **Technik.** Zürich. *Aus Natur Tech.* [1919–26] [*Supplement to:* 34193]

5313 **Aus Naturwissenschaft** und **Technik.** Göttingen. *Aus Naturw. Tech.*

5314 **Aus den Veröffentlichungen** der **Oberlausitzischen Gesellschaft** der **Wissenschaften** zu **Görlitz.** Görlitz. *Aus Veröff. oberlausitz. Ges. Wiss.*

5315 **Ausgewählte Schweisskonstruktionen.** Fachausschuss für Schweisstechnik, Verein deutscher Ingenieure. Berlin. *Ausgew. Schweisskonstr.* [1930–] L.SC. 30–34.

5316 **Ausländische Zeitschriftenschau** auf dem **Gebiet** des **Bauwesens** und der **Architektur.** Wien. *Ausl. ZSchau Geb. Bauwes. Archit.* [1952] L.P.

5317 **Ausland-Nachrichtendienst** für die **chemische Industrie.** Berlin. *AuslNachrDienst. chem. Ind.*

5318 **Ausland-Nachrichtendienst** für die **Hüttenindustrie.** Berlin. *AuslNachrDienst Hüttenind.*

5319 **Ausland-Nachrichtendienst** für die **Landwirtschaft.** Berlin. *AuslNachrDienst Landw.*

5320 **Ausland-Nachrichtendienst** über **Metalle.** Berlin. *AuslNachrDienst Metalle*

5321 **Ausland-Nachrichtendienst** über **Textilen.** Berlin. *AuslNachrDienst Text.*

5322 **Auslands-Informationen** für **Ernährung** und **Landwirtschaft.** Hamburg. *Auslands-Inf. Ernähr. Landw.* L.AM. (3 yr.)

5323 **Auslands-Nachrichten.** Aus technischen Zeitschriften des Auslandes. Berlin. *Auslands-Nachr.*

5324 **Auslandswegweiser.** Kolonialinstitut, Hamburg. *Auslandswegweiser* L.BM. 19–21*.

5325 **Auslegeschrift.** Deutsches Patentamt. München. *Auslegeschr. dt. PatAmt* [1957–] L.P. [*C. of:* 37205]

5326 **Auslegungen** des **K. Ungarischen Patentamts.** Budapest. *Ausleg. K. ung. PatAmt.*

5327 **Auspicium.** Ringfundberichte der Vogelwarte Helgoland und der Vogelwarte Radolfzell. Wilhelmshaven. *Auspicium* [1959–] L.BM^N.; Z.

5328 **Ausschuss** für **wirtschaftliche Betriebsführung.** Wien. *Aussch. wirtsch. BetrFühr., Wien* **L.**C.24–31.

5329 **Austin Technical News.** Birmingham. *Austin tech. News* [1942–] **L.**DI. 44–; P. 51–; PR. 43–; **Bm.**C. (curr.); P. 43–; **Lv.**P. 56–; **Y.**

5330 **Austral Avian Record.** London. *Austral avian Rec.* [1912–27] **L.**BM.; BM^N.; Z.; **C.**UL.; **Db.**; **O.**B. 12–22; OR.

5331 **Australasian Annals** of **Medicine.** Sydney. *Australas. Ann. Med.* [1952–] **L.**MA.; MD.; TD. (10 yr.); **Bl.**U. 53– imp.; **Cr.**MS. 60–; **Dn.**U. 59–; **G.**F.; U. 56–; **M.**MS. 54–; **Nw.**A. 56–; **O.**R. [C. of: 39630]

5332 **Australasian Beekeeper.** West Maitland. *Australas. Beekpr* [1899–] **L.**AM. 29–31; **Rt.** 25–32 imp.: 50–; **Sa.**; **Y.**

5333 **Australasian Chemist** and **Metallurgist.** Broken Hill. *Australas. Chem. Metall.*

5334 **Australasian Engineer.** Sydney. *Australas. Engr* [1915–] **L.**BM. 25–; I. 46–; P. 55–; **Y.**

5335 **Australasian Engineering** and **Machinery.** London. *Australas. Engng Mach.* **L.**BM. 11–17.

5336 **Australasian Herbarium News.** Sydney. *Australas. Herb. News* [1947–] **L.**BM^N.; L. 47–49; **C.**BO. 47; **E.**B.

5336° **Australasian Irrigator** and **Pasture Improver.** *Australas. Irrig. Past. Improver* **Y.**

5337 **Australasian Journal** of **Medical Technology.** Sydney. *Australas. J. med. Technol.* [1955–] **L.**P.

5338 **Australasian Journal** of **Pharmacy.** Melbourne. *Australas. J. Pharm.* **L.**PH. 85–19: 25–; **N.**U. 49–; **Y.**

5339 **Australasian Leather Trades Review.** Sydney. *Australas. Leath. Trades Rev.* **L.**LE. 47–.

5340 **Australasian Manufacturer Plastics Review.** Sydney. *Australas. Mfr Plast. Rev.* [1935–37] **L.**P.

5341 **Australasian Medical Congress.** [Transactions.] *Australas. med. Congr.* [1905–27] **L.**MA. 05–11; MD.; S.; TD. 08; U. 05–08; **Abd.**U. 08; **Br.**U. 08: 23; **C.**UL. 08–21; **Db.** 05–08; **E.**R. 08–20; S. 08; U. 08–27; **G.**F. 08; U. 08; **Lv.**U. 05–08; **O.**R. 08: 20. [C. of: 23767]

5342 **Australasian Medical Gazette.** Sydney. *Australas. med. Gaz.* [1881–14] **L.**BM. 07–14; GH. 03–14; MD.; S.; TD. 05–14 imp.; **Abd.**U. 00–14; **Abs.**N. 12–14; **Br.**U. 84–07; **C.**UL. 96–14; **Db.** 96–14; **E.**A. 96–13; P. 96–97; **G.**F. 83–97 imp.; U. 99–14 imp.; **Lv.**M. 05–10; U. 12–14; **M.**MS. 83–14; **O.**R. 96–14. [C. in: 30252]

5342° **Australasian Oil** and **Gas Journal.** *Australas. Oil Gas J.* **Y.**

5343 **Australasian Pastoralists' Review.** Melbourne. *Australas. Past. Rev.* [1891–00] **L.**AM.; **E.**U. 98–99. [C. as: 37190]

5344 **Australasian Pharmaceutical Notes** and **News.** Sydney. *Australas. pharm. Notes News* **L.**MA. 38–; MD. 39–.

5345 **Australasian Photographic Review.** Sydney. *Australas. photogr. Rev.* **L.**PG. 01–02*. [C. as: 5346]

5346 **Australasian Photo-Review.** Sydney. *Australas. Photo-Rev.* [1903–37] **L.**PG. [C. of: 5345; C. as: 98]

5347 **Australasian Plating** and **Finishing.** Melbourne. *Australas. Plat. Finish.*

5348 **Australasian Printer.** Sydney. *Australas. Print.* [1950–] **L.**P. 55–; SB. 56–; **Lh.**P.

5349 **Australian Agricultural Newsletter.** London. *Aust. agric. Newsl.* **L.**AM. (1 yr)

5350 **Australian Amateur Mineralogist.** Adelaide. *Aust. amat. Miner.* [1955–] **L.**BM^N.; **Y.**

5351 **Australian Aviation Newsletter.** *Aust. Aviat. Newsl.* **L.**AV. 56–.

5352 **Australian Aviation Yearbook.** Melbourne. *Aust. Aviat. Yb.* [1947–] **L.**BM.

5353 **Australian Aviculture.** Melbourne. *Aust. Avicult.* [1947–] **L.**Z. 47–60. [C. of: 33406°]

5354 **Australian Brewing** and **Wine Journal.** Melbourne. *Aust. Brew. Wine J.* [1930–59] **Nu.**B. imp. [C. as: 5431]

5355 **Australian Chemical Abstracts.** Melbourne. *Aust. chem. Abstr.* [1939–] **L.**P. 39–50. [Supplement to: 26722]

5356 **Australian Chemical Engineering.** *Aust. chem. Engng* **Y.**

5357 **Australian Civil Engineering** and **Construction.** Melbourne. *Aust. civ. Engng Constr.* [1959–] **L.**BM.; P.; **Y.** [C. from: 15045]

5358 **Australian Corrosion Engineering.** *Aust. Corros. Engng* **Y.**

5359 **Australian Cotton Grower.** Sydney. *Aust. Cott. Grow.* [1924] **L.**BM. [C. as: 5360]

5360 **Australian Cotton Grower, Farmer** and **Dairyman.** Sydney. *Aust. Cott. Grow. Fmr Dairym.* [1925–26] **L.**BM. [C. of: 5359]

5361 **Australian Culturist.** Melbourne. *Aust. Culturist* [C. as: 20391]

5362 **Australian Dairy Review.** Melbourne. *Aust. Dairy Rev.* [1922–] **L.**BM. 45–; FA. 46–; **Abs.**U. 59–; **R.**D. 40–.

5363 **Australian Dental Journal.** Sydney. *Aust. dent. J.* [1956–] **L.**D.; MD.; S.; **Bl.**U.; **Bm.**U.; **E.**U.; **Dn.**U.; **Ld.**U.; **Nw.**A. [C. of: 5383, 16536 and 41663]

5364 **Australian Dental Mirror.** Brisbane. *Aust. dent. Mirr.* [1936–47] **L.**D. [C. of: 41664; C. as: 41663]

5365 **Australian Dental Summary.** Sydney. *Aust. dent. Summ.* [1926–29] **L.**D. imp. [C. in: 16536]

5366 **Australian Dried Fruit News.** Mildura, etc. *Aust. dried Fruit News* [1925–] **L.**MY. 50–; P. (curr.); **Y.**

5366° **Australian Electrical World.** *Aust. elect. Wld* **Y.**

5367 **Australian Food Manufacture.** Melbourne. *Aust. Fd Mf.* **L.**AM. 51–; **Y.**

5368 **Australian Forester.** Canberra. *Aust. Forester* **O.**F. 29–33 imp.

5369 **Australian Forestry.** Canberra. *Aust. For.* [1936–] **Abd.**U. imp.; **Bn.**U. 48–; **C.**A. 36–51; **O.**F.; **Y.**

5370 **Australian Forestry Journal.** Sydney. *Aust. For. J.* [1918–31] **L.**BM.; MY. 23–31; **Db.**; **O.**R.; F. 19–31.

5371 **Australian Foundry Trade Journal.** Sydney. *Aust. Found. Trade J.* [1949–53] **Bm.**C. [C. as: 20288]

5372 **Australian Geographer.** Sydney. *Aust. Geogr.* [1928–] **L.**B. 46– imp.; BM. 35–; G.; **Abd.**U. 45–; **Abs.**A. 41–; **Bm.**U. 29–; **C.**GG. v. imp.; PO. 45–; **Dn.**U. 36–; **E.**G.; U.; **G.**U. 52– imp.; **Lv.**P. 59–; **N.**U. 32– imp.; **O.**G. 29–; RH. imp.; **Sh.**U. imp.; **Y.**

5373 **Australian Geographical Society Reports.** Melbourne. *Aust. geogr. Soc. Rep.* [1952–] **L.**BM^N.

5374 **Australian Industrial** and **Mining Standard.** Melbourne. *Aust. ind. Min. Stand.* [1917–18] L.MT. [*C. of:* 5422; *C. as:* 23176]

5375 **Australian Irrigator—Pasture Improver.** Sydney. *Aust. Irrig.—Past. Improver* Hu.G. 58–.

5376 **Australian Journal** of **Agricultural Economics.** Sydney. *Aust. J. agric. Econ.* [1957–] C.A.

5377 **Australian Journal** of **Agricultural Research.** Melbourne. *Aust. J. agric. Res.* [1950–] L.AM.; BM.; BM^N.; C.; EB.; HQ.; L.; MC.; MY.; NC.; P.; SI. 57–; TD. (10 yr.); V.; VC.; **Abd.**R.; S.; U.; **Abs.**A.; U.; **Bn.**U.; **Br.**A.; **C.**A.; APH.; P.; UL.; V.; **Cr.**U.; **Db.**; **E.**AB.; AR.; U.; W.; **Ex.**U.; **G.**U.; **H.**U.; **Hu.**G.; **Ld.**W.; **Lv.**P.; **M.**P.; T. (10 yr.); U.; **Md.**H.; **N.**U.; **Nw.**A.; **O.**BO.; RE.; **Pl.**M.; **R.**D.; U.; **Rt.**; **Sa.**; **Sal.**F.; **Sh.**U.; **Sil.**; **Sw.**U.; **W.**; **Y.**

5378 **Australian Journal** of **Applied Science.** Melbourne. *Aust. J. appl. Sci.* [1950–] L.AM.; AV.; BM.; C.; HQ.; LE.; P.; RI.; SC.; U.; **Abd.**S.; U.; **Bm.**P.; **Bn.**U.; **Br.**U.; **C.**P.; UL.; **Cr.**U.; **Db.**; **E.**AR.; U.; **Ex.**U.; **F.**A.; **G.**U.; **H.**U.; **M.**C.; P.; T.; U.; **Ma.**T.; **N.**U.; **Nw.**A.; **R.**D.; U.; **Rt.**; **Sa.**; **Sil.**; **Sw.**U.; **Wd.** 50–56; **Y.**

5379 **Australian Journal** of **Biological Sciences.** Melbourne. *Aust. J. biol. Sci.* [1953–] L.AM.; AV. 54–; BM.; BM^N.; C.; E.; EB.; K.; L.; LE.; MA. 54–; MC.; MD.; MY.; NC. 48–49: 54–; P.; R.; SC.; TD.; UC.; V.; VC.; Z.; **Abd.**M.; R.; S.; U.; **Abs.**U.; **Bl.**U.; **Bm.**P.; U.; **Bn.**U.; **Br.**A.; U.; **C.**A.; APH.; BI.; P.; UL.; V.; **Cr.**U.; **Db.**; **Dn.**U.; **E.**AB.; AG.; AR.; HW.; R.; U.; **Ex.**U.; **G.**U.; **Hu.**G.; **Je.**; **Ld.**U.; W.; **Lv.**P.; **M.**C.; U.; **Md.**H.; **N.**U.; **Nw.**A.; **O.**AP.; BO.; R.; **R.**D.; V.; **Rt.**; **Sa.**; **Sal.**; **Sh.**U.; **Sw.**U.; **W.**; **Y.** [*C. of:* 5392 Ser. B]

5380 **Australian Journal** of **Botany.** Melbourne. *Aust. J. Bot.* [1953–] L.AM.; BM.; BM^N.; K.; L.; MC.; MY.; NC.; P.; R.; SC.; TD. (10 yr.); UC.; **Abs.**A.; U.; **Bl.**U.; **Bm.**P.; **Br.**A.; U.; **C.**A.; UL.; **Cr.**U.; **E.**AW.; R.; W.; U.; **Ex.**U.; **G.**U.; **H.**U.; **Hu.**G.; **Ld.**U.; **Lv.**P.; U.; **M.**C.; U.; **Md.**H.; **N.**U.; **Nw.**A.; **O.**BO.; RE.; **R.**D.; U.; **Sa.**; **Sal.**; **Sh.**U.; **Sw.**U.; **Y.**

5381 **Australian Journal** of **Chemistry.** Melbourne. *Aust. J. Chem.* [1953–] L.AM.; AV.; BM.; C.; LE.; MO.; NF.; P.; PR.; R.; RI.; SC.; U.; UC.; **Abd.**S.; U.; **Abs.**U.; **Bl.**U.; **Bm.**C.; P.; U.; **Bn.**U.; **Br.**U.; **C.**APH.; BI.; C.; CH.; P.; UL.; **Cr.**U.; **Dn.**U.; **E.**R.; U.; **Ex.**U.; **F.**A.; **G.**T.; U.; **H.**U.; **Hu.**G.; **Ld.**U.; W.; **Li.**M.; **Lv.**P.; U.; **M.**C.; D.; P. 56–; U.; **N.**U.; **Nw.**A.; **O.**AP.; R.; **R.**D.; **Sa.**; **Sh.**U.; **Sw.**U.; **Y.** [*C. from:* 5392, Ser. A]

5382 **Australian Journal** of **Dairy Technology.** Melbourne. *Aust. J. Dairy Technol.* [1946–] L.AM. imp.; P. 60–; **Abd.** R. 58–; **Abs.**U.; **C.**A. 48–; **N.**U.; **R.**D.; **Y.**

5383 **Australian Journal** of **Dentistry.** Melbourne. *Aust. J. Dent.* [1897–55] L.D. 29–55; MD. 01–55 imp.; S. 98–55; **Bl.**U. 54–55; **Bm.**U. 46–55; **Dn.**U. 51–55; **Ld.**U. 46–55; **M.**MS. 33–55. [*C. in:* 5363]

5384 **Australian Journal** of **Dermatology.** Sydney. *Aust. J. Derm.* [1951–] L.MA.; MD.; **Br.**U.; **Dn.**U.

5384° **Australian Journal** of **Experimental Agriculture** and **Animal Husbandry.** Melbourne. *Aust. J. exp. Agric. Anim. Husb.* [1961–] **Abd.**R.; **C.**A.; **O.**RE.; **Y.**

5385 **Australian Journal** of **Experimental Biology** and **Medical Science.** Adelaide. *Aust. J. exp. Biol. med. Sci.* [1924–] L.BM^N.; C. 56–; EB. 58–; GH.; L.; LI.; MA. 29–; MC.; MD.; R.; S. 41–; SC.; SH. 39–54; TD.; UC.; UCH. 53–; V. 43–; VC. 45–; Z.; **Abd.** R. 29–; U. 28–32; 44–56; **Ba.**I. 24–32; **Bl.**U.; **Bm.**U.; **Bn.**U. imp.; **Br.**U.;

C.APH. 49–; BI.; P.; V. imp.; **Cr.**U. 24–32; **Db.**; **E.**R.; U.; W. 27–37; **Ex.**U. 24–33; **G.**F. 50–; T. 54–; U.; **Hu.** G. 38–; **Ld.**U.; **Lv.**U.; **M.**MS.; **N.**U. imp.; **Nw.**A.; **O.**BO. 24–30; PH.; R.; **Pl.**M.; **R.**D. 52–; U.; **Rt.**; **Sa.** 25–45; **Sw.**U. 24–33; **W.** 31–; **Y.**

5386 **Australian Journal** of **Instrument Technology.** Melbourne. *Aust. J. Instrum. Technol.* [1944–] L.MO.; P. 54–; SI.; **Y.**

5387 **Australian Journal** of **Marine** and **Freshwater Research.** Melbourne. *Aust. J. mar. Freshwat. Res.* [1950–] L.AM.; BM.; BM^N.; L.; P.; SC.; VC.; Z.; **Abd.**M.; R. 57–; U.; **Abs.**U. imp.; **Bl.**U.; **Bn.**U.; **Br.**U.; **C.**APH.; B.; P.; **Cr.**U.; **Db.**; **Dm.**; **E.**SW. 51–54; U.; **Fr.**; **G.**U.; **Lo.**; **Lv.**P.; U.; **M.**U.; **Mi.**; **N.**U.; **Nw.**A.; **O.**AP.; Z.; **Pit.**F.; **Pl.**M.; **R.**U.; **Sa.**; **Sal.**; **Sh.**U.; **Sw.**U.; **Wo.**; **Y.**

5387° **Australian Journal** of **Optometry.** *Aust. J. Optom.* **Y.**

5388 **Australian Journal** of **Physics.** Melbourne. *Aust. J. Phys.* [1953–] L.AS.; AV.; BM.; C.; EE.; LE.; MO.; NF.; P.; PR.; R.; RI.; SC.; SI. 57–; UC.; **Abd.**S.; U.; **Abs.**U.; **Bl.**U.; **Bm.**C.; P.; U.; **Bn.**U.; **Br.**U.; **C.**BI.; C.; CH.; P.; UL.; **Cr.**U.; **Db.**; **Dn.**U.; **E.**R.; U.; **Ex.**U.; **F.**A.; **G.**U.; **H.**U.; **Ld.**U.; W.; **Li.**M.; **Lv.**P.; **M.**C.; D.; T.; U.; **Ma.**T.; **N.**U.; **Nw.**A.; **O.**AP.; R.; **R.**D.; **Sa.**; **Sh.**U.; **Sw.**U.; **Y.** [*C. from:* 5392 Ser. A]

5389 **Australian Journal** of **Physiotherapy.** Sydney. *Aust. J. Physiother.* **Br.**U.

5390 **Australian Journal** of **Psychology.** Carlton, Victoria, etc. *Aust. J. Psychol.* [1949–] L.BM. 52–; PS.; UC.; **Bm.**U.; **O.**B.; EP.; **Sw.**U. 59–. [*Also Monograph supplement*]

5391 **Australian Journal** of **Science.** Sydney. *Aust. J. Sci.* [1938–] L.AV. 56–58; BM. 58–; BM^N.; C. 49–54; HQ. 45–; I. 50–; K. 56–; P.; SC.; **Abs.**A. 46–; **C.**A.; BO. 55–57; **Hu.**G.; **Ld.**U.; W.; **N.**U. 57–; **Nw.**A. 53–; **O.**BO. 38–54; R.; **Rt.**; **Sa.** 52–; **W.**R. 48–; **Y.**

5392 **Australian Journal** of **Scientific Research.** Melbourne. *Aust. J. scient. Res.* [1948–52]
Series A. Physical Sciences. L.AS.; BM.; C.; EE.; HQ.; LE.; MO.; NF.; P.; PR.; R.; SC.; TD.; U.; UC.; **Abd.**S.; U.; **Abs.**A. 49–52; **Bl.**U.; **Bm.**C. 48–50; U.; **Bn.**U.; **Br.**U.; **C.**C.; CH.; P.; UL.; **Cr.**U.; **Db.**; **Dn.**U.; **E.**R.; U.; **Ex.**U.; **F.**A.; **G.**U.; **H.**U.; **Hu.**G.; **Ld.**U.; **Li.**M.; **Lv.**P.; **M.**C.; D.; T.; U.; **Ma.**T.; **N.**U.; **Nw.**A.; **O.**AP.; R.; RE.; **R.**D.; **Sa.**; **Sh.**U.; **Sw.**U. [*C. from:* 25865; *C. as:* 5381 and 5388]
Series B. Biological Sciences. L.AM.; BM.; BM^N.; C.; E.; EB.; K.; L. 50–52; LE.; MC.; MD.; MY.; P.; R.; SC.; TD.; UC.; V. 49–52 imp.; Z.; **Abd.**M.; R.; S.; U.; **Abs.**U.; **Bl.**U.; **Bm.**U.; **Bn.**U.; **Br.**A.; U.; **C.**A.; APH.; BI.; P.; UL.; V.; **Cr.**U.; **Db.**; **E.**AR.; R.; U.; **Ex.**U.; **G.**U.; **Hu.**G.; **Je.**; **Ld.**U.; W.; **Lv.**P.; **M.**C.; U.; **Md.**H.; **N.**U.; **Nw.**A.; **O.**AP.; BO.; R.; **R.**D.; **Rt.**; **Sa.**; **Sal.** 50–52; **Sh.**U.; **Sw.**U. [*C. from:* 25865; *C. as:* 5379]

5393 **Australian Journal** of **Zoology.** Melbourne. *Aust. J. Zool.* [1953–] L.AM.; BM.; BM^N.; E.; L.; MC.; QM.; P.; R.; SC.; TD. (10 yr.); UC.; V.; VC.; Z.; **Abd.**M.; U.; **Abs.**U.; **Bl.**U.; **Bm.**P.; **Br.**U.; **C.**A.; APH.; B.; P.; UL.; V.; **Cr.**U.; **E.**AB.; AR.; R.; U.; W.; **Ex.**U.; **Fr.**; **G.**U.; **Hu.**G.; **Ld.**U.; W.; **Lv.**P.; U.; **M.**U.; **N.**U.; **Nw.**A.; **O.**AP.; Z.; **R.**D.; U.; **Rt.**; **Sa.**; **Sal.**; **Sh.**U.; **Sw.**U.; **W.** 55– imp.; **Y.**

5394 **Australian Leather Journal.** Melbourne. *Aust. Leath. J.* **Y.**

5395 Australian Machinery and **Production Engineering.** Sydney. *Aust. Mach. Prod. Engng* [1948–] **L.**P. 56–; **Y.**

5396 Australian Mechanical Engineering. Melbourne. *Aust. mech. Engng* [1960–] **L.**BM.; NF.; P.; **Bm.**C.; **Y.** [*C. from:* 15045]

5397 Australian Medical Journal. Melbourne. *Aust. med. J.* [1856–14] **L.**MD. imp.; S.; TD. 11–14; **Br.**U. 84–95; **Db.** 11–14; **Lv.**U. 12–14; **M.**MS. imp. [> 23768, 1895–09; *C. in:* 30252]

5398 Australian Milk and **Dairy Products Journal.** Sydney. *Aust. Milk Dairy Prod. J.* **R.**D. 45–.

5398° Australian Mineral Industry Review. Canberra. *Aust. Miner. Ind. Rev.* [1955–] **L.**BM.

5399 Australian Mineral Industry. Statistics. Melbourne. *Aust. Miner. Ind. Statist.* [1948–] **L.**BM. 54–; GL.; MI.; NF.; **Y.**

5400 Australian Mining and **Engineering Review.** Melbourne. *Aust. Min. Engng Rev.* [1908–10] **L.**MI. [*C. as:* 32011]

5401 Australian Mining Standard. Melbourne. *Aust. Min. Stand.* [1885–14] **L.**MT.; P. [*C. as:* 5422]

5402 Australian Monthly Weather Report and **Meteorological Abstract.** Melbourne. *Aust. mon. Weath. Rep.* [1910–13] **L.**MO.; TD. 12; **E.**M.

5403 Australian Museum Magazine. Sydney. *Aust. Mus. Mag.* [1921–] **L.**BM.; BM^N.; Z. imp.; **Cr.**M.; **Db.**; **E.**F. imp.; **Pl.**M. 21–31; **Y.** [–61*; *C. as:* Australian Natural History]

    Australian Museum Memoirs. *See* 30882.
    Australian Museum Records. *See* 42292.
    Australian National Antarctic Research Expeditions Interim Reports. *See* 23773.
    Australian National Antarctic Research Expeditions Reports. *See* 87.

5403° Australian National Clay. *Aust. natn. Clay* [1959–] **Y.**

    Australian Natural History. *See* 5403

5404 Australian Naturalist. Sydney. *Aust. Nat.* [1906–] **L.**BM.; BM^N.; K. 06–44 imp.; L.; Z.; **Y.**

5405 Australian and **New Zealand General Practitioner.** Melbourne. *Aust. N.Z. gen. Practnr* [1953–] **L.**MA.; MD.; **Br.**U.; **Ld.**U.; **Lv.**M.; **M.**MS. [*C. of:* 20853]

5406 Australian and **New Zealand Journal** of **Surgery.** Sydney. *Aust. N.Z. J. Surg.* [1931–] **L.**BM.; GH.; MA.; MD.; RA. 42–; S.; U. 45–; UCH. 49–; **Abd.**U. 31–41; **Bl.**U. 37–; **Br.**U.; **Cr.**MD.; **Db.**; **Dn.**U. 36– imp.; **E.**A.; S.; U.; **G.**F.; **Lv.**M.; **M.**MS. 31–44 imp.; **Nw.**A.; **O.**R. [*C. of:* 25843]

5407 Australian and **New Zealand Rose Annual.** Melbourne. *Aust. N.Z. Rose A.* [1943–] **Ba.**I.; **Y.** [*C. of:* 5417]

5408 Australian Official Journal of **Patents,** Trade Marks and Designs. Melbourne. *Aust. off. J. Pat.* [1904–] **L.**BM.; P. 05–; **Bm.**P.; **Ld.**U. 09–14; **Lv.**P. 53–; U. 09–20 imp.; **M.**P.; U. 06–14 imp.; **O.**B. 04–20; **Sy.**R. 51–; **Y.**

5409 Australian Orchid Review. Sydney. *Aust. Orchid Rev.* [1936–] **L.**K.; **Y.**

5409° Australian Paint Journal. Sydney. *Aust. Paint J.* [1960–] **Y.** [*C. of:* 36764]

5410 Australian Pastoralist. Brisbane. *Aust. Past.*

5411 Australian Photographic Journal. Sydney. *Aust. photogr. J.* [1892–10] **L.**PG. [*C. as:* 21884]

5412 Australian Plant Disease Recorder. Sydney. *Aust. Pl. Dis. Rec.* [1949–] **L.**MY.; **C.**A.

5412° Australian Plants. Society for Growing Australian Plants. Picnic Point, N.S.W. *Aust. Pl* [1959–] **L.**BM^N.

5413 Australian Plastics. Sydney. *Aust. Plast.* [1945–56] **L.**IC. 47–56; P. 51–56; PL.; **Sy.**R.; **Y.** [*C. as:* 5415]

5414 Australian Plastics and **Allied Trades Review.** Melbourne. *Aust. Plast. all. Trades Rev.* [1933–35] **L.**P. [*C. as:* 37929]

5415 Australian Plastics and **Rubber Journal.** Sydney. *Aust. Plast. Rubb. J.* [1956–] **L.**IC.; P.; PL. 57–; **Sy.**R.; **Y.** [*C. of:* 5413]

5416 Australian Plastics Yearbook. Sydney. *Aust. Plast. Yb.* **L.**PL. 50–.

5416° Australian Radiation Records. Melbourne. *Aust. Radiat. Rec.* [1953–] **L.**BM.

5417 Australian Rose Annual. Melbourne. *Aust. Rose A.* **Ba.**I. 28–42*. [*C. as:* 5407]

5418 Australian Science Abstracts. Sydney. *Aust. Sci. Abstr.* [1922–57] **L.**BM^N; C. 22–38; MC.; P.; SC.; **C.**A. 31–57; P. 35–57; **Db.** 22–38; **E.**R. 23–38; **Hu.**G.; **O.**B.; BO. 22–38; R.; **Y.** [*From* 1938 *published as Supplement to:* 5391; *Replaced by:* 5419]

5419 Australian Science Index. Melbourne. *Aust. Sci. Index* [1957–] **L.**P.; **Abd.**R.; **C.**P.; **Md.**H. 59–; **R.**D.; **Y.** [*Issue for* 1957 *published in* 12910; *Replaces:* 5418]

5419° Australian Scientist. *Aust. Scient.* **Y.**

5420 Australian Standard Specifications of the **Australian Commonwealth Engineering Standards Association.** Sydney. *Aust. stand. Specif.* [1928–] **L.**P.

5421 Australian Standards Quarterly. Sydney. *Aust. Stand. Q.* [1948–] **Y.** [*C. of:* 48355]

5422 Australian Statesman and **Mining Standard.** Melbourne. *Aust. Statesm. Min. Stand.* [1914–17] **L.**MI. 14–16; MT.; P. 14–16. [*C. of:* 5401; *C. as:* 5374]

5423 Australian Sugar Journal. Brisbane. *Aust. Sug. J.* [1909–] **L.**AM. (4 yr.); P. 26–; **Bm.**U. 39–40; **C.**A. (1 yr); **Ep.**D. 40–; **Rt.** 46–; **Y.**

5423° Australian Sugar Yearbook. Brisbane. *Aust. Sug. Yb.* **Y.** 59–.

5424 Australian Surveyor. Brisbane. *Aust. Surv.* [1928–] **L.**BM. 31–; P.; **Y.** [*C. of:* 41670 and 51522]

5425 Australian Technical Journal. Sydney. *Aust. tech. J.*

5426 Australian Timber Journal. Sydney. *Aust. Timb. J.* **O.**F. 39– imp.; **Y.**

5426° Australian Tobacco Journal. Mareeba. *Aust. Tob. J., Mareeba* **Md.**H. 61–.

5427 Australian Tobacco Journal. Melbourne. *Aust. Tob. J., Melb.*

5428 Australian Veterinary Journal. Sydney. *Aust. vet. J.* [1927–] **L.**EB. 55–; MA. 28–34; MD.; TD. 27–50; V.; VC. 49– imp.; **Abd.**R. 33–; **Bn.**U. 62–; **Br.**U. 34– imp.; **C.**A.; APH. 36–; V.; **Db.**; **E.**AB. 33–; N.; **Ld.**W. 37–; **Lv.**U.; **R.**D. 39–; **Sal.** imp.; **W.** 31–; **Y.** [*C. of:* 25643]

5429 **Australian Welding Engineer.** Melbourne. *Aust. Weld. Engr* [1927–28]   [*C. as:* 29766]

5429° **Australian Welding Journal.** Sydney. *Aust. Weld. J.* [1957–]

5430 **Australian Wild Life.** Journal of the Wild Life Preservation Society of Australia. Sydney. *Aust. Wild Life* [1934–] **L.**BM. 49–; BM[N].; NC.

5431 **Australian Wine, Brewing** and **Spirit Review.** Melbourne. *Aust. Wine Brew. Spirit Rev.* [1959–] **Nu.**B.; **Y.**   [*C. of:* 5354]

5432 **Australian Zoologist.** Sydney. *Aust. Zool.* [1914–] **L.**BM. 54–; BM[N].; E. 14–32; L.; SC.; Z.; **Bm.**U.; **C.**AN. 14–43; P.; UL.; **Db.**; **E.**C. 14–15; F.; **Lv.**P. 14–48; U.; **M.**U. 14–16 imp.; **O.**R. 14–25 imp.; **Pl.**M. imp.

Austrian Documentation covering the fields of **Building** and **Architecture.** *See* 35913.

5433 **Austrian Medical Bulletin.** London. *Austrian med. Bull.* [1945–46] **L.**D.; S.; **O.**R.

5434 **Austria-Patent-Reporter.** Wien. *Austria-Pat.-Reptr* [1954–] **L.**P.

5435 **Austroflug.** Wien. *Austroflug* [1951–] **L.**AV. 56–58; **Y.**

5436 **Auszüge** aus den **Inaugural-Dissertationen. Medizinische Fakultät** in **Bern.** *Ausz. Inaug.-Diss. med. Fak. Bern* **O.**R. 21–33.

5437 **Auszüge** aus der **Literatur** der **Zellstoff-** und **Papierfabrikation.** Berlin. *Ausz. Lit. Zellstoff-PapFabr.* [1924–] **L.**P. 24–40.

5438 **Auszüge** aus den **Patentanmeldungen.** München. *Ausz. PatAnmeld.* [1955–] **L.**P.; **Ld.**P.

5439 **Auszüge** aus den **Patentschriften.** Berlin. *Ausz. PatSchr.* [1877–] **L.**P.; **Sh.**G. 27–39.

5440 **Auszüge** aus den **Protokollen** der **Gesellschaft praktischer Ärzte** zu **Riga.** *Ausz. Protok. Ges. prakt. Ärzte Riga*

5441 **Auszüge** aus den **Protokollen** der **Medizinischen Gesellschaft** zu **Jurjev.** *Ausz. Protok. med. Ges. Jurjev*

5442 **Auto.** London. *Auto, Lond.* [1931–] **L.**BM.; P. 31; **Y.**   [*C. of:* 5514]

5442[a] **Auto.** Venezia. *Auto, Venezia* [1955–] **L.**BM.

5442° **Autó** és **motorujság.** Budapest. *Autó Motorujs.* [1921] **Sy.**R. 31–38 imp.

5443 **Autocar.** London. *Autocar* [1895–] **L.**AV. 42–; BM.; P.; SC.; **Abs.**N. 13–15; **Bm.**P. 02–; U. 20–; **Br.**P. (2 yr.); **Bra.**P. 55–; **C.**UL.; **Db.** 08–14; **E.**A. 97– imp.; **G.**M. 97– imp.; **Li.**M. 46–48 imp.: 49–; **Lv.**P. 02–; **M.**P.; **O.**B.; **Sh.** 10 (5 yr.); **Sy.**R. (1 yr); **Y.**

5444 **Autocar Road Tests.** London. *Autocar Rd Tests* [1951–] **L.**BM.; P.; **Bm.**P.; **E.**A.; **Ld.**P. 53–; **Li.**M.; **M.**P.   [*Issued with:* 5443]

5445 **Autogene Metallbearbeitung.** Halle a. S. *Autogene Metallbearb.* [1908–45] **L.**AV. 33–44; I. 24–39; P. 14–45.   [*C. in:* 17868]

5446 **Autogenschweisser.** Wien. *Autogenschweisser* [1928–]

5447 **Autogiro News.** Philadelphia. *Autogiro News* **L.**P. 31–35.

5448 **Autogummi.** København. *Autogummi* **Sy.**R. 35–38 imp.

Auto-Jahr. Lausanne. *See* 5495.

5449 **Automaten-Markt.** Braunschweig. *Automaten-Markt* [1949–] **L.**P.; **Y.**

5450 **Automatic Age.** Chicago. *Autom. Age*

5451 **Automatic Control.** New York. *Autom. Control, N.Y.* [1954–] **L.**AV. 57–; **F.**A. 57–; **M.**T. 57–58; **Sw.**U. 57–; **Y.**

5452 **Automatic Control.** Tokyo. *Autom. Control, Tokyo* **Y.**

5453 **Automatic Data Processing.** London. *Autom. Data Process.* [1958–] **L.**AV.; BM.; P.; **Bm.**T.; **Cr.**U.; **Ep.**D.; **Ld.**U. 61–; **O.**B.; **Y.**

5454 **Automatic Electric Review.** Chicago. *Autom. elect. Rev.* [1932–] **L.**P. 32–42.   [*C. from:* 5459]

5455 **Automatic Electric Technical Journal.** Chicago. *Autom. elect. tech. J.* [1948–56: 60–] **L.**P.; **Y.** [> 20884, 1957–59]

5456 **Automatic Heat** and **Air Conditioning.** Chicago. *Autom. Heat Air Condit.* [1933–40]   [*C. in:* 37964°]

5457 **Automatic Heating.** Toronto. *Autom. Heatg*

5458 **Automatic Machining.** Rochester, N.Y. *Autom. Machg* [1955–] **L.**P. 59–; **Y.**   [*C. of:* 49322]

5458° **Automatic Programming Information.** *Autom. Progm. Inf.* [1960–] **L.**AV.

5459 **Automatic Telephone.** Chicago. *Autom. Teleph.* [1913–31] **L.**P. imp.; **Dn.**U. 22–31 imp. [*C. as:* 5454 and 51030]

5460 **Automatic Telephone** and **Electric Company Journal.** *See* 131.

5460° **Automatic Vending.** *Autom. Vend.* **Y.**

5461 **Automatic Welding.** London. *Autom. Weld., Lond.* [1959–] **L.**AV.; BM.; P.; **Abs.**N.; **Y.** [*English translation of:* 5603]

5461[a] **Automatic Welding.** Office of Technical Services. New York. *Autom. Weld., N.Y.* **Y.** 57–. [*English abstracts of:* 5603]

5462 **Automatic World.** Oldham. *Autom. Wld* [1959–] **L.**BM.

5463 **Automatica** si **electronica.** Bucureşti. *Automatica Electron.* [1957–] **L.**AV. 61–; **Lv.**P.; **Y.**

5463° **Automatics.** Office of Technical Services. Washington. *Automatics, Wash.* **Y.** 57–. [*English abstracts of:* 5605]

5463[d] **Automatics** and **Telemechanics.** Office of Technical Services. Washington. *Automatics Telemech., Wash.* **Y.** 57–. [*English abstracts of:* 5606]

5463° **Automatie.** *Automatie* **Y.**

5464 **Automatik Teknik.** København. *Automatik Tek.* [1952–] **L.**P.; **Y.**

5465 **Automation.** Cleveland. *Automation, Cleveland* [1954–] **L.**BM. 56–; P. (curr.); **Ld.**P. 56–; **Lv.**P. 59–; **Y.** [*Also supplements*]

5466 **Automation.** London. *Automation, Lond.* [1956] **L.**BM.; P.; QM.; SI.; **E.**A.; **G.**M.; **O.**R.   [*C. of:* 23744; *C. as:* 5471]

5467 **Automation.** Paris. *Automation, Paris* [1954–] **L.**P. 57–; **N.**T. (5 yr.); **Y.**

5468 **Automation Age.** London. *Automn Age* [1955–56] **L.**BM.; P.; **Bn.**U.; **C.**UL.; **G.**M.; **O.**B.   [*C. as:* 5469]

5469 **Automation** and **Automatic Equipment News.**
London. *Automn autom. Equip. News* [1956–] L.AV.
58– imp.; BM.; P.; **Bn.**U.; 56–58; **C.**UL.; **G.**M.; T. 57–;
M.C. 56–57; **O.**B.; **Y.** [*C. of:* 5438]

5470 **Automation Express.** New York. *Automn Express*
[1958–] **L.**P.; **Sh.**SC. 61–.

5471 **Automation** in **Industry.** London. *Automn Ind.*
[1956–57] **L.**BM.; P.; SI.; **E.**A.; **G.**M.; T. 57. [*C. of:*
5466; *C. as:* 23731]

5472 **Automation Progress.** London. *Automn Prog.*
[1956–] **L.**AV. 57–; BM.; EE. 57–; P.; SI.; **C.**UL.; **E.**A.;
Lv.P. 57–; **M.**C.; **N.**T. (5 yr.); **O.**B.; **Sw.**U. 57–; **Y.**

5473 **Automation** and **Remote Control.** Pittsburgh.
Automn remote Control [1956–] **L.**P. 58–; **Dn.**U. 59–;
G.U. 58–; **Ld.**U. 59–; **N.**T. 60–; **N.**U.; **Sh.**SC. 60–; **Y.**
[*English translation of:* 5606]

5474 **Automatisace.** Praha. *Automatisace* [1958] **L.**P.;
Y. [*C. as:* 5478]

5475 **Automatisering.** 's-Gravenhage. *Automatisering*
[1957–] **L.**P. 57–59.

Automatisierung. Berlin. *See* 58723.

5476 **Automatisierung.** Heidelberg. *Automatisierung*
[1956–] **L.**P. 58–; **Y.**

5477 **Automatisme.** Paris. *Automatisme* [1956–] **L.**P.;
Bl.U. 60–; **Bm.**U.; **Sw.**U.; **Y.**

5478 **Automatizace.** Praha. *Automatizace* [1959–] **L.**AV.
61–; P.; **Y.** [*C. of:* 5474]

5479 **Automazione** e **automatismi.** Milano. *Automaz.
Automatismi* [1957–] **L.**AV. 61–; P.; **Y.**

5480 **Automazione** e **strumentazione.** Milano. *Automaz. Strument.* [1960–] **L.**P.; **Y.** [*C. of:* 51044]

5481 **Automobil.** Praha. *Automobil, Praha* [1957–]
L.BM.; P. 58–; **Y.**

5482 **Automobile.** New York. *Automobile* [1902–17]
L.P. 10–17. [*C. as:* 5510]

5483 **Automobile agricole.** Paris. *Auto. agric.* [1907–
09] **L.**P. [*C. as:* 20899]

Automobile and **Automotive Industries.** *See*
5482.

5484 **Automobile belge.** Bruxelles. *Auto. belge*

5485 **Automobile** and **Carriage Builders' Journal.**
London. *Auto. Carr. Bldrs' J.* [1902–49] **L.**BM.; P.;
O.B. 04–49. [*C. of:* 13373; *C. as:* 33719]

5486 **Automobile Digest.** Cincinnati. *Auto. Dig.*
[1925–] [*C. from:* 1904]

5487 **Automobile Digest** and **Register.** New York.
Auto. Dig. Reg. [1925–42] [*C. from:* 1904; *C. as:* 5507].

5487° **Automobile Discussions.** Institution of Mechanical Engineers. London. *Auto. Discuss.* [1954–] **L.**BM.

5488 **Automobile Electricity.** London. *Auto. Elect.*
[1925–39] **L.**BM.; P.; **Bm.**U. 27–30; **C.**UL. 27–39; **O.**R.
26–39. [*Supplement to and C. in:* 33722]

5489 **Automobile Electricity Wiring Diagram.** London. *Auto. Elect. Wir. Diag.* [1925–] **L.**BM.; P. [*From
1941 forms Supplement to and published in:* 33722]

5490 **Automobile Engineer.** London. *Auto. Engr*
[1910–12: 14–] **L.**AV. imp.; BM.; I. (2 yr.); P.; SC. 10–16:
24–; **Abs.**N. 25–; **Bm.**C. (6 mo.); P. 23–; T. 21; U. 27–;
Br.P. 43–; U.; **C.**ENG. 38–; U.; **Co.**T. 44–; **Cr.**U. 18–;
Db. 20–; **Dn.**U. 19–; **E.**A. 29–; T. 36–; **F.**A. 27–; **G.**E.;
M. 14–; T. (1 yr); **Ld.** P. 23–; U. 37–; **Li.**M.; **Lv.**P. 43–47:

53–; U.; **M.**P. 23–; T.; U. 21–; **Nw.**A. 21–; P. 54–; **O.**R.;
Sh.IO. 23–; SC. 34–; **Sil.** 40–; **Y.** [> 23797, 1912–14]

5491 **Automobile Engineering.** London. *Auto. Engng*
L.BM. 10–; P. 11–20; **Lv.**U. 12–; **O.**R. 12–20 imp.

5492 **Automobile Facts** and **Figures.** Detroit. *Auto.
Facts Fig.* [1901–] **Ld.**P. 30– imp.

5493 **Automobile** nell'**industria,** nel **commercio,** nello
sport. Napoli. *Auto. Ind., Napoli*

5494 **Automobile Industries.** *Auto. Inds* **L.**BM.; P.;
Sil.; **Y.** [*English translation of:* 5611]

5494ᵇ **Automobile Industry.** Office of Technical
Services. New York. *Auto. Ind., N.Y.* **Y.** 57–. [*English
abstracts of:* 5611]

Automobile and **Motor Review.** *See* 5482.

5495 **Automobile Year.** Lausanne. *Auto. Yr* [1957–]
L.BM.; P. 58–; **Ld.**P.; **Lv.**P. [*C. of:* 3320ᵃ]

5496 **Automobile-aviation.** Bruxelles. *Auto.-Aviat.*

5497 **Automobil-** und **Motorenfabrikation.** Berlin.
Auto.- u. MotFabr.

5498 **Automobilia.** Paris. *Automobilia* **L.**P. 24–25.

5499 **Automobilismus.** Basel. *Automobilismus*

5500 **Automobil-Revue.** Bern. *Auto.-Revue, Bern*

5501 **Automobilrundschau.** Mitteleuropäischer
Motorwagen-Verein. Berlin. *AutoRdsch.* [1913–] **L.**P.
13–29.

Automobil- u. flugtechnische Zeitschrift. *See*
33746.

5502 **Automobiltechnische Zeitschrift.** Berlin, etc.
Auto.-tech. Z. [1929–] **L.**AV. 31–43; P. imp.; SC.; **F.**A. 37–
42; **Ha.**RD. 45–; **Li.**M.; **Sy.**R. 29–39 imp.; **Y.** [*C. of:*
5523 and 33746]

Automobiltechnische Zeitschrift. Beihefte. *See*
133.

5503 **Automobil-** und **Flugverkehr.** Charlottenburg.
Auto.- u. Flugverk.

5504 **Automotion.** Paris. *Automotion*

5505 **Automotive Abstracts.** Cleveland, O. *Automot.
Abstr.* [1923–34] **L.**P. 25–33 imp.; SC.; **Lv.**U. 25–34.
[*C. in:* 5510]

5506 **Automotive** and **Aviation Industries.** Philadelphia. *Automot. Aviat. Inds* [1942–47] **L.**P.; **Bm.**C.
45–47. [*C. of:* and *Rec. as:* 5510]

5507 **Automotive Digest.** Cincinnati. *Automot. Dig.,
Cincinnati* [1942–] [*C. of:* 5487]

5508 **Automotive Digest.** Toronto. *Automot. Dig.,
Toronto* [1956–] **Sy.**R

5509 **Automotive Electrical Engineer.** Chicago. *Automot. elect. Engr* [1921–26] **L.**SC. 25–26. [*C. as:* 50385]

5510 **Automotive Industries.** New York, Philadelphia.
Automot. Inds [1917–] **L.**AV. 30– imp.; BM. 54–; NF. 23–;
P. imp.; QM. 55– imp.; **Bm.**U. 27–; **F.**A. 34– v. imp.;
Li.M. 33–; **Lv.**P. 59–; U. 22–; **Nw.**A. 54–; **Y.** [*C. of:*
5482; > 5506, 1942–47]

Automotive Industry. Moscow. *See* 5611.

5511 **Automotive Manufacturer.** New York. *Automot.
Mfr* [1919–27] **L.**P. [*C. of:* 22467]

5512 **Auto-Moto-Avion** et **Revue** du **Sport.** Anvers.
Auto-Moto-Avion

5513 **Auto-motociclo.** Milano. *Auto-motociclo*

5514 **Automotor Journal.** London. *Automotor J.* [1896–31] **L.**BM.; P. 10–31. [*C. as:* 5442]

5515 **Automóvil industrial.** Barcelona. *Automóv. ind.*

5516 **Automóviles.** Tokyo. *Automóviles, Tokyo* **L.**BM. 56.

5517 **Autonautique.** Paris. *Autonautique* **L.**P. 05–08★.

5517° **Autopackaging.** Birmingham. *Autopackaging* [1955–] **L.**BM.

5518 **Auto-Presse-Dienst.** Reichsverband der Automobilindustrie. *Auto-Presse-Dienst*

5519 **Autorekord.** München. *Autorekord*

5520 **Auto-Review.** Bourges. *Auto-Rev., Bourges*

5521 **Auto-riassunti e riviste** dei **lavori italiani** di **medicina interna,** etc. Torino. *Auto-riass. Riv. Lav. ital. Med. interna*

5522 **Autoroulotte,** revue mensuelle de l'industrie automobile, etc. Paris. *Autoroulotte*

5522ª **Autostrade.** Roma. *Autostrade* [1959–] **Ld.**U. 62–.

5523 **Auto-Technik.** Berlin. *Auto-Technik* **L.**P. 26–29★. [*C. in:* 5502]

5523° **Autotecnica.** *Autotecnica* **Y.**

5524 **Auto-Vapeur.** Paris. *Auto-Vapeur* **L.**P. 09★.

5525 **Auto-volt.** Paris. *Auto-volt* [1929–] **Li.**M. 59–; **Y.**

5526 **Auvergne médicale.** Clermont-Ferrand. *Auvergne méd.* **L.**MA. 47–50. [*C. as:* 12972]

5527 **Auxiliary Products Literature. I.C.I. Dyestuffs Division.** London. *Aux. Prod. Lit. I.C.I. Dyest. Div.* [1959–] **L.**P.; **Ld.**P.; **Y.** [*C. of:* 5528]

5528 **Auxiliary Products Pamphlets. I.C.I. Dyestuffs Division.** Manchester. *Aux. Prod. Pamph. I.C.I. Dyest. Div.* [1933–58] **L.**P.; **Ld.**P. 50–58 imp.; **Y.** [*C. as:* 5527]

5529 **Avance médical.** La Habana. *Avance méd.* [1940–] **L.**TD. 41–45 imp.

5530 **Avelsföreningens** för **svensk röd** och **vit boskap tidskrift.** Stockholm. *Avelsför. svensk röd vit Bosk. Tidskr.* [1947–57] **E.**AB.; **AG.** [*C. in:* 51553]

5531 **Avenir médical.** Lyon. *Avenir méd., Lyon* **L.**MA. 31–32: 47–.

5532 **Avenir médical.** Paris. *Avenir méd., Paris* [*C. as:* 55560°]

5533 **Avenir** de la **pharmacie.** Nîmes. *Avenir Pharm.*

5534 **Avenir** de la **science.** Paris. *Avenir Sci.* [1936–39]

5535 **Avenir textile.** Paris. *Avenir text.* [1912–32] **M.**C. 20–27: 29–32; **T.** 20–32. [*C. as:* 19432]

5536 **Average Monthly Weather Résumé** and **Outlook.** Washington. *Aver. mon. Weath. Résumé Outl.* **L.**MO. 48–.

5537 **Avertering.** København. *Avertering* [1936–] **L.**PG. 38–40 imp.

Avhandlingar. K. tekniska högskolan. Stockholm. *See* 27817.

Avhandlingar. Sveriges geologiska undersökning. *See* 51607.

Avhandlingar och **uppsatser. Sveriges geologiska undersökning.** *See* 51607.

5538 **Avhandlinger** ugitt av det **Norske videnskapsakademi i Oslo.** *Avh. norske VidenskAkad. Oslo* Matematisk naturvidenskapelig Klasse. [1925–] **L.**BM.; BNᴺ.; R.; UC.; Z. 32–; **Bl.**U.; **C.**P.; SJ. 25–37; **Db.**; **E.**C. imp.; R. 27–; **G.**U. 37: 40; **Ld.**U. 27: 37–; **Lv.**U.; **Nw.**A. 52–; **O.**R.; **Pl.**M. [*C. of:* 20095]

5539 **Avia.** Buenos Aires. *Avia, B. Aires* [1934–49] **L.**AV. 47–49. [*C. as:* 52652]

5540 **Avia.** Den Haag. *Avia, Haag* **L.**AV. 45–51★. [*C. as:* 5542]

5541 **Avia.** Paris. *Avia, Paris* **L.**P. 09–20.

5542 **Avia vliegwereld.** Den Haag. *Avia Vliegwld* [1952–] **L.**AV. [*C. of:* 5540]

5543 **Aviação e astronautica.** Rio de Janeiro. *Aviaç. Astronaut.* [1946–]

5544 **Aviación.** Barcelona. *Aviación, Barcelona*

5545 **Aviación.** Lima. *Aviación, Lima* **L.**AV. 52–54.

5546 **Aviación.** Los Angeles. *Aviación, Los Ang.* [1942–] [*C. from:* 21521]

5547 **Aviación.** México. *Aviación, Méx.* [1928–29]

5548 **Avian Diseases.** Ithaca, N.Y. *Avian Dis.* [1957–] **L.**MD.; VC.; **Br.**U.; **W.**

5549 **Aviapromyšhlennost'.** Moskva. Авиапромышленность. *Aviapromyšhlennost'* [1932–37] **L.**AV. 33: 37. [*C. as:* 5578]

5550 **Aviaticus.** Jahrbuch der deutschen Luftfahrt. Berlin. *Aviaticus* [1931–] **L.**BM.

5551 **Aviatikai ertesítő.** Budapest. *Aviat. Ert.*

5552 **Aviation.** Dublin. *Aviation, Dublin* [1935–37] **L.**BM.

5553 **Aviation.** New York. *Aviation, N.Y.* [1922–47] **L.**AV.; BM.; P.; **Bm.**P.; **C.**UL.; **F.**A. 24–47 imp.; **M.**P. 32–47. [*C. of:* 5557; *C. as:* 5576]

5554 **Aviation** and **Aeronautical Engineering** and **Aircraft Journal.** New York. *Aviat. aeronaut. Engng* [1916–20] **L.**AV.; P.; **Bm.**P.; **C.**UL. [*C. as:* 5557]

5555 **Aviation Age.** New York. *Aviat. Age* [1950–58] **L.**AV.; P. 57–58; SC.; **F.**A. 52–58. [*C. of:* 5569; *C. as:* 50377]

5556 **Aviation Age Research** and **Development Technical Handbook.** New York. *Aviat. Age Res. Dev. tech. Handb.* [1957–58] **L.**P. [*Supplement to:* 5555; *C. as:* 50378]

5557 **Aviation** and **Aircraft Journal.** New York. *Aviat. Aircr. J.* [1920–21] **L.**AV.; BM.; P.; **Bm.**P.; **C.**UL. [*C. of:* 5554; *C. as:* 5553]

5558 **Aviation** and **Automotive Equipment.** East Stroudsberg. *Aviat. automot. Equip.* [1947] [*C. of:* 5561]

5559 **Aviation civile.** Édition générale. Paris. *Aviat. civ.* [1956–] **L.**AV. 57– imp.

5560 **Aviation Engineering.** New York. *Aviat. Engng* [1928–33] **L.**P. 30–33. [*C. in:* 1016]

5561 **Aviation Equipment.** New York. *Aviat. Equip.* [1941–46] [*C. as:* 5558]

5562 **Aviation Maintenance.** New York. *Aviat. Maint.* [1943–46] [*C. as:* 5563]

5563 **Aviation Maintenance** and **Operations.** New York. *Aviat. Maint. Ops* [1946–49] [*C. of:* 5562; *C. as:* 5569]

5564 **Aviation Mechanics.** New York. *Aviat. Mech.*

5565 **Aviation Mechanics Bulletin.** New York. *Aviat. Mech. Bull.* **L.**AV. 55–59 imp.

5566 **Aviation Medicine.** An annotated Bibliography. Washington. *Aviat. Med.* [1952–53] **L.**BM.; P.; SC. [*C. as:* 1110]

5567 **Aviation Meteorological Reports.** Meteorological Office. London. *Aviat. met. Rep.* [1934–46] **L.**MO.; **Bm.**U. 39–46 imp.

5568 **Aviation News.** New York. *Aviat. News* [1944–] **L.**AV. 44–46.

5569 **Aviation Operations.** New York. *Aviat. Ops* [1949–50] **L.**AV.; SC. [*C. of:* 5563; *C. as:* 5555]

5570 **Aviation Report.** London. *Aviat. Rep.* **L.**AV. 52–.

5571 **Aviation Review.** Toronto. *Aviat. Rev.* [1944–] [*C. of:* 1538]

5572 **Aviation Safety Digest.** Melbourne. *Aviat. Saf. Dig.* [1953–] **L.**AV. imp.; **Do.**F.

5573 **Aviation Series. U.S. Weather Bureau.** Washington. *Aviat. Ser. U.S. Weath. Bur.* **L.**BM.; MO. 54–.

5574 **Aviation Service Magazine.** Chicago. *Aviat. Serv. Mag.* [1943–]

5575 **Aviation Times.** Tokyo. *Aviat. Times* [1953–] **L.**AV. 58– imp.

5576 **Aviation Week** (including **Space Technology**). New York. *Aviat. Week* [1947–] **L.**AV.; BM.; P.; SC.; **Bm.**P.; **Br.**U. 60–; **C.**UL.; **Cr.**U. 61–; **F.**A.; **M.**P.; **Ma.**T. 58–; **Sh.**IO. 57–; **Y.** [*C. of:* 5553]

5577 **Aviation Year Book.** London. *Aviat. Yb.* [1930–] **L.**AV. 43–49; BM. 30–31; **Abs.**N.; **C.**UL.; **Cr.**P. 30–31; **E.**A.; **O.**B. 30–31.

5578 **Aviatsionnaya promyshlennost'.** Moskva. Авиационная промышленность. *Aviats. Prom.* **L.**AV. 41. [*C. of:* 5549]

5579 **Aviatsionnyĭ astronomicheskiĭ ezhegodnik.** Leningrad. Авиационный астрономический ежегодник. *Aviats. astr. Ezheg.* [1930–]

5580 **Aviatsionnyĭ zhurnal.** Savastopol'. Авіаціонный журнал. *Aviats. Zh.*

5581 **Aviatsiya i khimiya.** Moskva. Авиация и химия. *Aviats. Khim.* [1926–31] [*C. in:* 27403]

5581° **Aviatsiya i kosmonavtika.** Авиация и космонавтика. *Aviats. Kosmonavt.*

5582 **Aviazione civile** attraverso il **mondo.** *Aviaz. civ. Mondo*

5583 **Avicula.** Giornale ornitologico italiano. Siena. *Avicula* [1897–10] **L.**BM.[N].; Z.

5584 **Aviculteur.** Paris. *Aviculteur* **L.**P. 98–10 imp.

5585 **Aviculteur** du **Berry.** Bourges. *Aviculteur Berry*

5586 **Avicultura española.** Valencia. *Avicult. esp.* [*C. as:* 5595]

5587 **Avicultura práctica.** Arenys de Mar. *Avicult. práct., Arenys*

5588 **Avicultura práctica.** Santiago de Chile. *Avicult. práct., Santiago*

5589 **Avicultura técnica.** Barcelona. *Avicult. téc.* [1948–] **L.**AM. 51–58 imp.

5590 **Avicultural Magazine.** Hertford. *Avicult. Mag.* [1894–] **L.**BM. 00–; BM[N].; Z.; **Abs.**N. 12–; **Bl.**U. 32–35; **Br.**U. 94–19: 29–; **C.**B. 95–; UL. 95–; **Db.** 98–; **E.**A. 96–; **F.** 30–45; **M.**P. 96–40; **N.**U. 95–55; **O.**OR. 25–; R.; **Sh.**IO. 26–; **Y.**

5591 **Aviculture** et l'**apiculture** du **Sud-Est.** Lyon. *Avicult. Apicult. S.-E.*

5592 **Aviculture belge.** Renaix. *Avicult. belge*

5593 **Aviculture commerciale** et **internationale.** Charleville. *Avicult. comm. int.*

5594 **Aviculture pratique.** Paris. *Avicult. prat.* **L.**P. 12–14*.

5595 **Avígan.** Ganadería—avicultura—producciones pecuarias. Valencia. *Avígan* [*C. of:* 5586]

5596 **Avión.** Madrid. *Avión, Madr.* **L.**AV. 46– imp.

5597 **Avion.** Paris. *Avion, Paris* [1926–]

5598 **Avis microsismique** de **Hongrie.** Budapest. *Avis microsism. Hong.*

5599 **Avis sismiques.** Bucureşti. *Avis sism., Buc.*

5600 **Avocetta.** *Avocetta* [1955–] **O.**OR 55–56.

5601 **Avon News Sheet.** Avon India Rubber Co. *Avon News Sh.* **Sy.**R. 54–.

5602 **Avtogennoe delo.** Moskva. Автогенное дело. *Avtog. Delo* [1930–53] **L.**BM. 51; I. 32–37: 48–50: 53; P. 48–53; **Y.** 48–53 imp.

5603 **Avtomaticheskaya svarka.** Kiev. Автоматическая сварка. *Avtom. Svarka* [1950–] **L.**I. 51–; P. 57–; **Db.** 53–; **Y.** 50–55 imp.: 56–. [*English translation at:* 5461; *English abstracts at:* 5461[a]]

5604 **Avtomaticheskiĭ kontrol' i izmeritel'naya tekhnika.** Kiev. Автоматический контроль и измерительная техника. *Avtom. Kontrol'* [1957–] **L.**P.; **Y.**

5604° **Avtomaticheskoe regulirovanie aviadvigateleĭ:** sbornik stateĭ. Автоматическое регулирование авиадвигателей: сборник статей. *Avtom. Regul. Aviadvig.* [1959–] **Y.**

5604[g] **Avtomaticheskoe upravlenie i vychislitel'naya tekhnika.** Автоматическое управление и вычислительная техника. *Avtom. Uprav. vychisl. Tekh.* [1958–] **Y.**

5605 **Avtomatika.** Kiev. Автоматика. *Avtomatika* [1957–] **L.**I. 57; P.; **Y.** [*English abstracts at:* 5463[a]]

5606 **Avtomatika i telemekhanika.** Moskva. Автоматика и телемеханика. *Avomatika Telemekh.* [1934–] **L.**AV. 48– imp.; BM. 46–; I. 59–; P. 55–; SC. 39: 49: 55– imp.; SI. 58–; **C.**P. 56–; **Sw.**U. 58–; **Y.** 46–52: 55– imp. [*English translation at:* 5473; *English abstracts at:* 5463[d]]

5607 **Avtomatika, telemekhanika i svyaz'.** Moskva Автоматика, телемеханика и связь. *Avtomatika Telemekh. Svyaz'* [1957–] **L.**BM. 58–; P.; **Y.**

5607° **Avtomatizatsiya proizvodstvennykh protsessov.** Автоматизация производственных процессов. *Avtomatiz. proizv. Protsess.* **Y.** 58–.

5608 **Avtomobil'.** Moskva. Автомобиль. *Avtomobil'* [1941–53] **Y.** 43–51. [*C. of:* 33713; *C. as:* 5614]

5609 **Avtomobil' i vozdukhoplavanie.** Moskva. Автомобиль и воздухоплаваніе. *Avto. Vozdukh.*

5610 **Avtomobilist.** Moskva. Автомобилистъ. *Avtomobilist*

5611 **Avtomobil'naya promyshlennost'.** Moskva. Автомобильная промышленность. *Avto. Prom.* [1946–50: 58–] **L.**BM. 58–; P. 58–; SC.; **Li.**M. 59–; **Sil** 58–; **Y.** 58–. [*From* 1950–57 > 5612; *English translation at:* 5494; *English abstracts at:* 5494[b]]

5612 **Avtomobil'naya i traktornaya promўshlennost'.** Moskva. Автомобильная и тракторная промышленность. *Avto. traktor. Prom.* [1950–57] **L.**BM. 53–57; P.; **Sil.**; **Y.** 51: 53–57.

5613 **Avtomobil'nўe dorogi.** Moskva. Автомобильные дороги. *Avto. Dorogi* **L.**P. 55–; **Y.** 55–.

5614 **Avtomobil'nўï transport.** Moskva. Автомобильный транспорт. *Avto. Transp.* [1953–] **L.**P. 55–; **Y.** 54–. [*C. of:* 5608]

5615 **Avtomobil'nўya novosti.** Moskva. Автомобильныя новости. *Avto. Nov.*

5616 **Avtotraktornoe.** Moskva. Автотракторное. *Avtotraktornoe*

5617 **Avulso. Centro** de **estudos zoológicos, Universidade** do **Brasil.** Rio de Janeiro. *Avulso Cent. Estud. zool. Univ. Bras.* [1959–] **L.**BM[N].; z.

5618 **Avulso** do **Departamento nacional** da **producção mineral.** Rio de Janeiro. *Avulso Dep. nac. Prod. miner., Rio de J.* **L.**BM[N]. 39– imp.; **E.**D. 34– imp.

5619 **Avulso. Divisão** de **fomento** da **producção mineral.** Rio de Janeiro. *Avulso Div. Fom. Prod. miner., Rio de J.* [1936–] **L.**GL. imp.; MI. imp.; **Y.**

5620 **Avulso. Laboratorio central** da **producção mineral.** Rio de Janeiro. *Avulso Lab. cent. Prod. miner., Rio de J.* **L.**MI. 43–.

Avulso. Serviço de **fomento** da **producção mineral.** Rio de Janeiro. *See* 5619.

5621 **Avulso. Universidade rural** de **Pernambuco.** Pernambuco. *Avulso Univ. rur. Pernambuco*

5622 **Ayrshire Cattle Society's Journal.** Ayr. *Ayrsh. Cattle Soc. J.* [1929–] **L.**BM. 53–; **Abs.**U. 46– imp.; **Bn.**U. 39– imp.; **E.**AR. (curr.); **Ld.**U.; **Nw.**A. 29–30; **O.**B. 50–; R. 50–; **R.**D.; U. 29–40: 47–.

5622° **Azerbaĭdzhanskiĭ khimicheskiĭ zhurnal.** Baku. Азербайджанский химический журнал. *Azerb. khim. Zh.* [1960–] **L.**P.

5623 **Azerbaĭdzhanskiĭ meditsinskiĭ zhurnal.** Baku. Азербайджанский медицинский журнал. *Azerb. med. Zh.*

5624 **Azerbaĭdzhanskoe neftyanoe khozyaĭstvo.** Baku. Азербайджанское нефтяное хозяйство. *Azerb. neft. Khoz.* [1921–] **L.**BM. 35–41 imp.; P. 40; PT. 35–39; **Y.** 47: 56: 58–.

Azērbaycan kimya zhürnali. Baki. *See* 5622°.

5625 **Azetylen in Wissenschaft** und **Industrie.** Halle. *Azet. Wiss. Ind.* [1931–32] **L.**P. [*C. of:* 449]

5626 **Azetylenschweissung.** Neueste Forschungsergebnisse. Halle. *Azetylenschweissung* [1927] [*C. as:* 48901]

5627 **Azienda ospedaliera.** Alessandria. *Azienda osp.* [1951–] **L.**H. 59–.

5628 **Azione sanitaria.** Milano. *Azione sanit.* [1921–]

5629 **Azione veterinaria.** Roma. *Azione vet.* [1932–] **L.**BM. 34–; TD. 32–39; V. 32–40; **W.** [*C. of:* 33032]

B

5630 **BA.** The magazine of Baird-Atomic, Inc. Cambridge, Mass. *BA* [1959–] **L**.P.

B.A.N.Z. Antarctic Research Expedition Report. *See* 42783.

5632 **BASF.** Badische Anilin- und Soda-Fabrik. Ludwigshafen. *BASF* [1951–] **L**.P.

5633 **BBA Journal.** British Belting & Asbestos Ltd. Cleckheaton. *BBA Jl* **Sy**.R. 58–.

5634 **B.B.C. Engineering Monographs.** British Broadcasting Corporation. London. *B.B.C. Engng Monogr.* [1955–] **L**.BM.; SC.; **Bl**.U.; **Co**.T.; **Y**.

5635 **B.B.C. Mitteilungen.** Brown, Boveri et Cie. Baden. *B.B.C. Mitt.* **L**.EE. 19–21 imp.

5636 **B.B.C. Nachrichten.** Brown, Boveri et Cie. Mannheim. *B.B.C. Nachr.* [1914–] **L**.AV. 60–; EE. 39–43 imp.; P. 54–.

BBZ. Bergbau-, Bohrtechniker- und Erdölzeitung. *See* 6136.

5637 **B. C. Farmer** and **Gardener.** Victoria. *B. C. Fmr Gdnr* **Sil.** 50.

5638 **B.C. Forest Service Publications.** Victoria. *B.C. Forest Serv. Publs* **Y**.

5639 **B.C. Professional Engineer.** Vancouver. *B.C. prof. Engr* [1950–] **L**.I. 53–; **Y**. [*C. of:* 7249]

5640 **B.C.'s Health.** Victoria, B.C. *B.C.'s Hlth* [1951–53] **L**.TD. [*C. of:* 21957; *C. in:* 8783ᶜ]

5641 **B.C.A.C.** Bulletin of the British Conference on Automation and Computation. London. *B.C.A.C.* [1958–61] **L**.AV.; BM.; P. (curr.); **O**.R.; **Sil**.

5642 **B.C.F.G.A. Quarterly Report.** British Columbia Fruit Growers' Association. Kelowna. *B.C.F.G.A. q. Rep.* **Md**.H. 60–.

B.C.I.R.A. Bulletin. British Cast Iron Research Association. *See* 9607.

5643 **B.C.I.R.A. Journal.** British Cast Iron Research Association. Birmingham. *B.C.I.R.A. Jl* [1960–] **L**.AV.; BM.; NF.; P.; SC.; **Bm**.C.; U.; **Cr**.U.; **Lv**.P.; **O**.R.; **Sh**.SC. 60–; **Y**.

5644 **B.C.O.R.A. Quarterly Bulletin.** British Colliery Owners' Research Association. *B.C.O.R.A. q. Bull.* [1944–46] **L**.MI.; MIE.; **Bm**.P.; **Ld**.U. 45–46; **O**.R.; **Sh**.M.; P.

5645 **B.C.R.A. Bibliography.** British Coke Research Association. London. *B.C.R.A. Biblphy* [1952–] **L**.P.

5645ᵃ **B.C.S.A. Publications.** British Constructional Steelwork Association. London. *B.C.S.A. Publs* [1950–] **L**.BM.; P.; **Br**.U.; **Y**.

5646 **BCSO Review** of **Science** in **U.S.A.** British Commonwealth Scientific Office, North America.

London. *BCSO Rev. Sci. U.S.A.* [1952–54] **L**.BM.; P. 53–54; QM.; **G**.M.; **Y**. [*C. as:* 35253]

B.C.U.R.A. Annual Report. British Coal Utilization Research Association. *See* 42879.

B.C.U.R.A. Monthly Bulletin. British Coal Utilisation Research Association. *See* 33409.

5647 **B.C.U.R.A. Quarterly Gazette.** British Coal Utilisation Research Association. London. *B.C.U.R.A. q. Gaz.* [1948–] **L**.EE. 55–; I.; LE. 54–; NF.; P.; RI. (curr.); SC.; SI.; **Bm**.C.; **C**.CH.; UL.; **E**.A.; D.; **Lh**.P.; **Li**.M. (1 yr); **Lv**.P. 52–; **M**.C. (1 yr); **N**.T. 54–; **Rn**.B. 56–; **Sh**.IO.; **Sil**. 53–; **Sy**.R.; **Y**.

B.C.U.R.A. Quarterly Progress Reports. British Coal Utilisation Research Association. London. *See* 41576.

B.C.U.R.A. Report. British Coal Utilisation Research Association. *See* 42879.

5648 **BD-orientering.** Boligdirektorat. Oslo. *BD-Orient.* **L**.BM. 56–; P. [*Supplement to* and *issued in:* 12723]

5649 **B.D.I.M. Information.** Bureau of Dairy Industry, U.S. Department of Agriculture. Washington. *B.D.I.M. Inf.* **L**.P. 44–.

B.D.W. Bericht des Deutschen Wetterdienstes. *See* 6203–6205.

5649ᵃ **B.E.A.-Information.** British Engineers' Association. London. *B.E.A.-Inf.* **L**.BM. 46–.

5649ᶜ **B.E.A. Monthly Journal.** British Electricity Authority. London. *B.E.A. mon. J.* **L**.BM. [*C. as:* 8800]

B.E.A.M.A. *See* **Beama.**

5650 **B.E. Bib.** British Electricity Authority. *London.* *B.E. Bib.* [1950–55] **L**.P.; SC. [*C. as:* 12871]

5651 **B. E. Trans.** British Electricity Authority. London. *B. E. Trans* [1949–55] **L**.BM.; P. [*C. as:* 12871ᵃ]

5652 **B.E.L.R.A. Medical Series.** British Empire Leprosy Relief Association. London. *B.E.L.R.A. med. Ser.* **L**.BM.; **O**.B.; R.

5653 **B.E.L.R.A. Quarterly Magazine.** British Empire Leprosy Relief Association. London. *B.E.L.R.A. q. Mag.* [1938–] **L**.BM.; **M**.P. 45 **O**.R.

5654 **B.E.M.A. Bulletin.** Bristol and West of England Engineering Manufacturers' Association. Bristol. *B.E.M.A. Bull.* **L**.BM. 57–.

5655 **B.E.N.A. Bulletin.** British Empire Naturalists' Association. Guildford. *B.E.N.A. Bull.* [1951–] **L**.BM.

5656 **B.E.T.R.O. Review.** British Export Trade Research Organization. *B.E.T.R.O. Rev.* **L**.PT. 48–; **Bm**.U. 48–; **E**.A. 48–.

BEW Mitteilungen. *See* 32305.

5657 **B.F. Goodrich Bulletin.** Goodrich Rubber Co. of Canada. Kitchener, Ont. *B.F. Goodrich Bull.*

5658 **BFG-Referat.** Bundesforschungsanstalt für Getreideverarbeitung. Berlin. *BFG-Ref.* [1960–61] **L**.P. [*C. of:* 55716; *Replaced by:* Documenta cerealia]

5659 **B. and G. Technical Review.** *B. & G. tech. Rev·* **L**.HS. 48–; **Ba**.I. (curr.); **Sil**. 52–57.

5660 **B.H.P. Technical Bulletin.** Broken Hill Proprietary Co. Shortland, N.S.W. *B.H.P. tech. Bull.* [1957–] **Bm**.C.

5661 **B.H.P. Technical News.** Broken Hill Proprietary Co. Newcastle, N.S.W. *B.H.P. tech. News* [1957–] **Bm**.C.

5662 **BHRA—NEL Joint Report.** British Hydromechanics Research Association—National Engineering Laboratory. Glasgow. *BHRA—NEL jt Rep.* [1959–] **L**.P.; **SC**.; **Br**.U. 59–.

5663 **BICC Bulletin.** British Insulated Callender's Cables. London. *BICC Bull.* [1950–] **L**.AV. 58–; **BM**.; P. (curr.); **G**.E. (1 yr); **Ma**.T. 57–.

5664 **BICERA Abstracts.** British Internal Combustion Engine Research Association. Slough. *BICERA Abstr.* **L**.AV. 57–; **BM**.; P.; **SC**. 56–; **F**.A. 53–; **Sil**. (1 yr).

5665 **BICERA Bulletin.** British Internal Combustion Engine Research Association. Slough. *BICERA Bull.* [1956–] **L**.BM.; P.; **G**.E. (1 yr); **Li**.M.; **Y**.

5665ᵃ **B.I.M.C.A.M. Handbook.** British Industrial Measuring and Control Apparatus Manufacturers' Association. London. *B.I.M.C.A.M. Handb.* [1953–] **L**.BM.

5665ᵇ **B.I.O.S. Report.** British Intelligence Objectives Sub-Committee. London. *B.I.O.S. Rep.* [1946–49] **L**.BM.; P. [*C. as:* 5665ᶜ]

5665ᶜ **B.I.O.S. Surveys.** British Intelligence Objectives Sub-Committee. London. *B.I.O.S. Surv.* [1950–] **L**.BM.; P. [*C. of:* 5665ᵇ]

B.I.R. Yearbook. London. *See* 58018.

5666 **B.I.S. News Bulletin.** British Industrial Solvents. Hull. *B.I.S. News Bull.* [1947–48] **L**.BM. [*C. as:* 7157]

5667 **BISOL News Sheet.** British Industrial Solvents. London. *BISOL News Sh.* **L**.P. 55–.

5668 **BISOL Technigram.** British Industrial Solvents. London. *BISOL Technigram* [1953–] **L**.P.

5669 **B.I.S.R.A. Survey.** British Iron and Steel Research Association. London. *B.I.S.R.A. Surv.* [1952–] **L**.BM.; P.; **E**.A. **O**.R.; **Y**.

5670 **B.K.S. Bulletin.** British Kinematograph Society. London. *B.K.S. Bull.* [1940–41] **L**.BM.; P.; PG.; [*C. in:* 25715]

5671 **B.L.M.R.A. Journal.** British Leather Manufacturers' Research Association. London. *B.L.M.R.A. Jl* [1958–] **L**.AM.; AV.; BM.; SI.; **Cn**.R.; **Lh**.P.; **Y**. [*C. of:* 33520]

B.L.M.R.A. Report. British Leather Manufacturers' Research Association. *See* 42900.

5672 **B.L.R.A. Bulletin.** British Launderers' Research Association. London. *B.L.R.A. Bull.* [1936–] **L**.SI. 46–; **Lh**.P. 43–; **Y**.

5673 **B.L.R.A. Communication.** British Launderers' Research Association. London. *B.L.R.A. Commun.* **L**.P. 49–; **Y**.

5673ᶜ **B.L.R.A. Reports.** British Launderers' Research Association. London. *B.L.R.A. Rep.* **Y**.

B.M.B. London. *See* 8906.

BMQ. Boston. *See* 8552.

5674 **B.M.W.-Blätter.** Bayerische Motorenwerke A.G. München. *B.M.W.-Bl.* **L**.P. 30–39.

5675 **B.M.W.-Flugmotoren-Nachrichten.** München. *B.M.W.-Flugmot.-Nachr.* **L**.P. 29–30.

5676 **B.N.F. Review.** British Non-Ferrous Metals Research Association. Birmingham. *B.N.F. Rev.* [1949–] **L**.AV. 51– imp.; DI.; **Rn**.B. (1 yr). [*C. of:* 5677]

5677 **B.N.F.M.R.A. Research Supplement.** British Non-Ferrous Metals Research Association. *B.N.F. M.R.A. Res. Suppl.* [1949–50] [*C. as:* 5676]

5677ᵃ **BNL.** Brookhaven National Laboratory. Publications. Upton, N.Y. *BNL* **Y**.

5678 **BP-Kurier.** Hamburg. *BP-Kurier* **L**.P. (curr.)

5678ᶜ **BP Progress.** Shell Mex & BP. London. *BP Prog.* [1958–] **L**.BM.

Irish edition. Dublin. **L**.BM.

5679 **B.P.S.—**Birmingham Photographic Society Journal. Birmingham. *B.P.S.* [1905–] **L**.BM. 11–15; PG. imp.; **Bm**.P.

B.R.A. Review. British Rheumatic Association. *See* 8939.

BRAB Conference Report. *See* 45838.

5680 **BRI Occasional Report.** Building Research Institute. Tokyo. *BRI occ. Rep.* [1960–] **Y**.

5680ᶜ **B.R.P.R.A. Technical Bulletin.** British Rubber Producers' Research Association. London. *B.R.P.R.A. tech. Bull.* [1954–59] **L**.BM.; P.; **Ld**.P.; **Y**. [*C. as:* 52001ᵃ]

5681 **B.R.U. Bulletin.** Building Research Unit. Roorkee, U.P. *B.R.U. Bull.* [1949–] **L**.SC.

B.S. Journal. Bristol Siddeley. *See* 8745.

5682 **B.S.A. Tools Division Journal.** Birmingham. *B.S.A. Tools Div. J.* [1958–61] **L**.DI.; P.; **Bm**.P.; **Lv**.P. [*C. of:* and *Rec. as:* 5683]

5683 **B.S.A. Tools Group Journal.** Birmingham. *B.S.A. Tools Grp J.* [1950–58: 61–] **L**.AV. 56–57; BM.; DI. 56–58; P. imp.; **Bm**.P. 53–58: 61–; **Co**.T. (curr.); **Lv**.P. 56–58: 61–; **Y**. [> 5682, 1958–61]

5683ᵃ **B.S.B.I. Conference Reports.** Botanical Society of the British Isles. London. *B.S.B.I. Conf. Rep.* [1949–] **L**.BM.

5684 **B.S.C.R.A. Abstracts.** British Steel Castings Research Association. Sheffield. *B.S.C.R.A. Abstr.* [1952–] **L**.AV. 54– imp.; BM.; DI. 53–; P.; SC. 53–; **G**.M.; **Ld**.U.; **Rn**.B. (1 yr); **Y**.

5684ᶜ **B.S.C.R.A. Journal.** British Steel Castings Research Association. Sheffield. *B.S.C.R.A. Jl.* **L**.AV. 56–58.

B.S.C.R.A. Reports. *See* 42913.

5685 **B.S.F.A. Bulletin.** British Steel Founders' Association. Sheffield. *B.S.F.A. Bull.* [1946–] **L**.I.; P.; **Bm**.C.; **Sh**.IO. (5 yr.); **Y**.

5685ᶜ **B.S.I. Information Sheet.** British Standards Institution. London. *B.S.I. Inf. Sh.* [1954–] **L**.AV. 55; BA.; BM.; MI.; PR.; **Bn**.U.; **Br**.U.; **Dn**.U.; **E**.A.; **M**.P.; **Rt**.; **Sw**.U.; **Sy**.R.; **Y**. [*C. of:* 33529; *C. as:* 5686]

5686 **B.S.I. News.** British Standards Institution. London. *B.S.I. News* [1956–] **L.**AM. (curr.); AV.; BA.; BM.; MC. (1 yr); MI.; PR.; TD. (2 yr.); **Bl.**U.; **Br.**U.; **Cn.**R.; **Co.**T. (1 yr); **Dn.**U.; **E.**A.; **G.**U.; **Li.**M. (1 yr); **M.**P.; **R.**D.; **Rt.**; **Sil.**; **Sw.**U.; **Sy.**R.; **Y.** [*C. of:* 5685°]

B.S.I. Report. British Standards Institution. *See* 8950.

5686° **B.S.I.R.A. Research Report.** British Scientific Instrument Research Association. *B.S.I.R.A. Res. Rep.* **Y.** [*Issued in various series.*]

5687 **B. T.-H. Activities** and **Developments.** British Thomson-Houston Co. Rugby. *B. T.-H. Activ. Dev.* **L.**AV. 49–60*; IC. 46–60; NF. 49–60; P. 38–60; SI. 47–50; **Bl.**U. 56–60; **Bm.**U. 32–40; **Bn.**U. 31–60 imp.; **Br.**U. 31–60; **C.**ENG. 43–60; **Cr.**I. 49–60; **Dn.**U. 49–60; **E.**U. 40–60; **G.**E. 59–60; **Lc.**A. 51–60; **Ld.**U. 30–60 imp.; **Lv.**P. 53–60; **M.**P. 46–60; T. 42: 49–60; **Ma.**T. 38–60; **Sh.**IO. 48–60; **Y.** [*C. in:* 30]

5688 **B. T.-H. Infra-red Bulletin.** British Thomson-Houston Co. Watford. *B. T.-H. infra-red Bull.* [1943–] **L.**P. 43–45.

5689 **B. T.-H. Lighting Bulletin.** British Thomson-Houston Co. Watford. *B. T.-H. Ltg Bull.* [1943–48] **L.**P.

B. T.-H. Research Laboratory Papers. British Thomson-Houston Co. *See* 36998.

5690 **B. T.-H. Technical Monographs.** British Thomson-Houston Co. *B. T.-H. tech. Monogr.* **L.**BM.; P. 51–; **O.**B. 50–; R. 50–; **Y.**

B. T. L. Bulletin and **Laboratory Notes.** Baird and Tatlock. London. *See* 10792.

5692 **B. T. P. News.** British Titan Products Co. Billingham. *B.T.P. News* [1953–] **L.**BM. [*C. of:* 5693]

5693 **B. T. P. News Sheet.** British Titan Products Co. Billingham. *B.T.P. News Sh.* [1950–53] **L.**BM. [*C. as:* 5692]

5694 **B. T. P. Publications.** British Titan Products Co. York. *B.T.P. Publs* **L.**P. 54–.

5694° **B. T. R. Technical Society Papers.** Taplow. *B.T.R. tech. Soc. Pap.* **L.**P. 52–.

B. T. Z. *See* 7273.

BUMED Gazette. *See* 12682.

BUMED News Letter. *See* 12683.

B. V. M. Beten, vallar, mossar. *See* 6495.

BWK. Brennstoff–Wärme–Kraft. *See* 8705.

5696 **B. W. P. A. News Sheet.** British Wood Preserving Association. London. *B.W.P.A. News Sh.* **L.**P. (curr.); **Y.**

5697 **Babel.** Revue internationale de la traduction. Bonn. *Babel* [1955–] **L.**AV.; NP. 57–; SC.

5698 **Bacillus.** Chicago. *Bacillus* [*C. as:* 22763]

5699 **Bacterial Therapist.** Detroit, Mich. *Bact. Ther.* [*C. as:* 55828]

5700 **Bacteriological News.** Baltimore. *Bact. News* [1951–] **R.**D. [*C. of:* 34851]

5701 **Bacteriological Proceedings.** Society of American Bacteriologists. Baltimore. *Bact. Proc.* [1950–] **L.**CB. 58–; TD.; UC.; **Bl.**U.; **C.**PA.; **O.**R. 51–; **R.**D.; **Y.** [*C. of:* 376]

5702 **Bacteriological Reviews.** Baltimore. *Bact. Rev.* [1937–] **L.**AM.; C. 46–54 imp.; CB. 54–; H.; IC.; LI.; MA.; MC.; MD.; MY. 47–49; P. 37–47: 50–; PH. 41–; QM. 50–; S. 37–52 imp.; SC.; TD.; TP. 59–; U. 43–; UC. 40– imp.; UCH.; **Abd.**R. 42–; S. 50–; U.; **Abs.**U. 47–; **Bm.**U.; **Bn.**U. 48– imp.; **Br.**A. 48–; U.; **C.**APH. 44–; BI.; GE. 49–; PA.;

UL. 48–; V. 48–; **Cr.**MD. 52–; U. 47–; **Db.**; **Dn.**U.; **E.**AG. 49–52: 59–; U.; **Ep.**D. 39–; **Fr.** 42–43 imp.: 47–; **G.**F. 38–; T.; U.; **Je.**; **Lc.**A. 52–; **Ld.**U.; **Lh.**FO. 45–; P. 44–55; **M.**D. 46–; MS. 42–49; **N.**U.; **Nw.**A.; **O.**P. 38–; PH. 48–; R.; **Pl.**M.; **R.**D.; U.; **Rt.** 38–; **Sh.**U.; W.; **Wd.** 37–56; **Y.**

5703 **Badania** z dziejów społecznych i gospodarczych. Poznań. *Badan. Dziej. społ. gosp.* [1925–]

5704 **Badania fizjograficzne** nad **Polską zachodnią.** Poznań. *Badan. fizjogr. Pol. zachod.* [1948–] **L.**BM.; BM^N.; **Db.**; **Dm.**

5705 **Badania geograficzne** nad **Polską północno-zachodnią.** *Badan. geogr. Pol. północnozachod.* [1926–] **L.**BM.

5706 **Badische Blätter** für **angewandte Entomologie.** Freiburg i. B. *Bad. Bl. angew. Ent.* [1926–29] **L.**BM^N.; EB. [*C. of:* 5707]

5707 **Badische Blätter** für **Schädlingsbekämpfung.** Freiburg i. B. *Bad. Bl. SchädlBekämpf.* [1923–25] **L.**BM^N.; EB. [*C. as:* 5706]

5708 **Badische Feuerwehrzeitung.** Baden-Baden. *Bad. Feuerwehrztg*

5708° **Badische geographische Abhandlungen.** Karlsruhe. *Bad. geogr. Abh.* [1926–38] **L.**G. 31–38. [*C. as:* 35562]

5709 **Badische geologische Abhandlungen.** Karlsruhe. *Bad. geol. Abh.* [1929–39] **L.**BM^N.; GM. 29–37. [*C. as:* 35563]

5710 **Baessler-Archiv.** Beiträge zur Völkerkunde. Leipzig. *Baessler-Arch.* [1910–] **L.**AN. 11–43; BM.; HO. 10–16; **C.**UL. 11–; **O.**B.

5711 **Bahia médica.** Bahia. *Bahia méd.* [1930–] **L.**LI. 33–38; TD. 33–46 v. imp.

5712 **Bahia odontológica.** Bahia. *Bahia odont.*

5713 **Bahia rural.** Bahia. *Bahia rur.* [1933–]

5714 **Bahnarzt.** Wien. *Bahnarzt* [*C. of:* 35914 and 58556]

5715 **Bahningenieur.** *Bahningenieur* [1934–]

5716 **Bailey Bulletin.** Stockport. *Bailey Bull.* [1954–] **L.**P.

5717 **Baileya.** Quarterly journal of horticultural taxonomy. New York. *Baileya* [1953–] **L.**BM^N.; K.; L. 54–; **Ba.**I.; **Br.**U.; **C.**BO.; **E.**W. 55–; **R.**U. 55–; **Y.**

5717^a **Baird** and **Tatlock Bulletin.** Chadwell Heath. *Baird & Tatlock Bull.* [1960–] **Y.** [*See also:* 10792]

5718 **Bakelite Plastics** in **Packaging.** London. *Bakelite Plast. Packg* **L.**P. (curr.).

5719 **Bakelite Plastics Review.** London. *Bakelite Plast. Rev.* [1959–] **L.**P.; **Y.**

5720 **Bakelite Progress.** Bakelite, Ltd. London. *Bakelite Prog.* [1931–] **L.**P. (curr.); **Bm.**C. (curr.); **Sy.**R. 48–56; **Y.**

5721 **Bakelite Review.** New York. *Bakelite Rev.* [1929–] **L.**P. 53–58; **Sy.**R. 30–34 imp.; **Y.**

5722 **Bakers' Digest.** Chicago. *Bakers' Dig.* [1940–] **L.**P.; **Y.** [*C. of:* 5723]

5723 **Bakers' Technical Digest.** Chicago. *Bakers' tech. Dig.* [1936–39] **L.**P. [*C. of:* 49713; *C. as:* 5722]

5723^a **Bakhovskie chteniya.** Institut biokhimii im. A. N. Bakha. Moskva. Баховские чтения. Институт биохимии им. А. Н. Баха. *Bakhov. Chten.* **L.**BM.; **Y.** 57: 59.

5724 **Baking Abstracts.** Chorley Wood. *Baking Abstr.* [1948–52] **L.**AM.; BM.; P.; **G.**T.; **Lh.**FO.; P.; **R.**D. [*C. as:* 304]

5725 **Baking Industry.** Chicago. *Baking Ind.* **L.**AM. 51–60 imp.

5726 **Baking Technology.** Chicago. *Baking Technol.* [1922–27] **L.**C.; P. 24–27. [*C. as:* 25498]

5727 **Baldwin.** Baldwin Locomotive Works. Philadelphia. *Baldwin* [1944–51] **L.**P.; **C.**ENG. 47–51; **Sy.**R. 44–46. [*C. as:* 5728]

5728 **Baldwin Locomotives.** Philadelphia. *Baldwin Loco.* [1922–43] **L.**P. 23–40; SC. 31–40. [*C. as:* 5727]

5729 **Baldwin-Southwark.** Baldwin-Southwark Corporation. Philadelphia. *Baldwin-Southwark* [1936–41] **L.**P.; **Sy.**R. 38–41. [*C. in:* 5728]

5730 **Baldwin Testing Topics.** *Baldwin Test. Top.* [1944–] **L.**AV. 44–52 imp.

5731 **Balearica.** Boletín del Centro de estudios ornitológicos de Baleares. Palma de Mallorca. *Balearica* [1956–] **L.**BM^N.; **O.**OR. 56–57.

Bǎlgarsk. *See* **Bǔlgarsk.** Български

5732 **Balik** ve **balikçilik.** Istanbul. *Balik Balikç.* **Pl.**M. 54–.

5733 **Balkan-kutatásainak tudományos eredményei.** Budapest. *Balkan-Kutat. Tud. Eredm.* [1923–] **L.**BM^N. 23: 26.

5734 **Ball Bearing Journal.** Luton. *Ball Bearing J.* [1926–] **L.**AV. 52– imp.; I. (2 yr.); BM. 52–; P.; **Bm.**T. 49–; **G.**M. 26–40 imp.; **Ld.**P. (5 yr.); **Ma.**T. 59–; **Nw.**A. 26–40; **Sh.**IO. 47–; **Y.** [*Suspended* 1941–46]

5735 **Ballonier.** Amsterdam. *Ballonier* **L.**SC. 37–40.

5736 **Balloon** and **Kite Data.** Meteorological Service, Canada. *Balloon Kite Data Can.* **L.**BM. 15–; MO. 15–17.

5737 **Balneologe.** Berlin. *Balneologe* [1934–] **L.**MD. [*C. of:* 58627]

5738 **Balneologia.** Bucureşti. *Balneologia, Buc.*

5739 **Balneologia** et **balneotherapia.** *Balneol. Balneother.* **G.**U. 58–.

5740 **Balneologia polska.** Warszawa. *Balneol. pol.* [1951–] **Y.**

5741 **Balneologiai lapok.** Bártfafürdői hirlap főlytatása. Budapest. *Balneol. Lap.* [*C. of:* 5771]

5742 **Balneologische Zeitung.** Berlin. *Balneol. Ztg*

5743 **Balneologische Zentralzeitung.** Berlin. *Balneol. ZentZtg*

5743^e **Balneotherapeutische Revue.** Wien. *Balneother. Revue* [*Supplement to:* 22040]

5744 **Baltijas lauksaimneeks.** Rias. *Balt. Lauks.*

5745 **Baltijas tirgotajs.** Rias. *Balt. Tirg.*

5746 **Baltimore Engineer.** Baltimore. *Baltimore Engr* [1926–] **L.**P. 26–48 imp.

5747 **Baltimore Health News.** Baltimore. *Baltimore Hlth News* [1932–] **L.**H. 40–; SH. (1 yr); TD.

5748 **Baltische pharmazeutische Monatshefte.** Libau. *Balt. pharm. Mh.*

5749 **Bambou.** Mons. *Bambou* [1906–08] **L.**BM^N.; K.

5750 **Bamidgeh.** Bulletin of Fish Culture in Israel. Nir-David. *Bamidgeh* [1949–] **L.**AM. 54–; BM. 54–; MI. 56–; **Abd.**M. 56–; **Fr.** 55–; **Pit.**F. 57–; **Y.**

5751 **Banana Bulletin.** Murwillumbah, N.S.W. *Banana Bull.* [1936–] **L.**P. (curr.); **Md.**H. 57–.

5752 **Bandzeitung.** Zeitschrift für die Textilindustrie. Ronsdorf. *Bandzeitung*

5753 **Bankatinwinning.** Banka. *Bankatinwinning* [1922–]

5754 **Bankfield Museum Notes.** Halifax. *Bankfield Mus. Notes* [1901–39] **L.**BM.; BM^N. 01–12; HO.; P. imp.; SC. 12–22; **Abs.**N. 12–18; **C.**UL.; **Cr.**U. 12–18; **E.**F. 08–14 imp.; **Ld.**P.; U. 14–39 imp.; **Lv.**P. 01–23 imp.; **M.**U. 01–18; **O.**B.

5755 **Bantu Studies** and **General South African Anthropology.** Johannesburg. *Bantu Stud.* [1921–41] **L.**AN.; BM.; **Bm.**U.; **E.**U. imp.; **Nw.**A. 29–35. [*C. as:* 1168]

5756 **Bánya-** és **kohómérnöki osztály.** Közleményei. M. kir Jozsef Nador müszaki és gazdaságtudomány egyetem, Bányá-, kohó- és erdömérnöki kar. *Bánya- és kohómérn. Oszt.* [1934–?] **L.**I. 34–38: 40–; P. 33–40 imp.; **Bm.**C. 40–47; **Ld.**U. 34: 39–43. [*C. of:* 50086; *C. as:* 5757]

5757 **Bányamérnöki** és **földmérőmérnöki karok közleményei Soproni müszaki egyetemi karok.** *Bányamérn. földmérőmern. Karok Közl. Soproni* **Ld.**U. 55–. [*C. of:* 5756]

5758 **Bányamérnöki** és **földmérőmérnöki könyvtári közlemények.** Sopron. *Bányamérn. földmérőmern. Könyv. Közl.* [1954–] **Y.**

5759 **Bányászati** és **kohászati lapok.** Búdapest, Selmecz. *Bányász. kohász. Lap.* [1868–50] **L.**BM. 50; **Y.** 33–50. [*C. as:* 5760 *and* 27583]

5759^a **Bányászati kutato intezet kőzleményei.** Budapest. *Bányász. Kut. Intez. Kőzl.* **Y.** 60–.

5760 **Bányászati lapok.** Budapest. *Bányász. Lap.* [1951–] **L.**BM.; **Y.** [*C. from:* 5759]

5761 **Barcelona quirúrgica.** Barcelona. *Barcelona quir.*

5762 **Barlangkutatás.** Höhlenforschung. Budapest. *Barlangkutatás* [1913–27] **L.**BM^N.; GL. 14.

5763 **Barlby Investigation Report.** British Oil and Cake Mills, Ltd. London. *Barlby Invest. Rep.* [1955–] **C.**A.

5764 **Barnard Classification Bulletin.** London. *Barnard Classif. Bull.* [1956–] **L.**BM.; MD.

5764^a **Baroid News Bulletin.** Houston. *Baroid News Bull.* **L.**P. (curr.).

5764^b **Baromfiipar.** Budapest. *Baromfiipar* **Y.** 61–.

5765 **Baromfitenyésztés.** Budapest. *Baromfitenyésztés* **Y.**

5766 **Baromfitenyésztési lapok.** Budapest. *Baromfiteny. Lap.*

5767 **Barrel** and **Box.** Chicago. *Barrel Box* [1895–29] **L.**P. [*C. as:* 5768]

5768 **Barrel** and **Box** and **Packages.** Chicago. *Barrel Box Pack.* [1929–] **L.**P. 29–31; **Lh.**P. 49–. [*C. of:* 5767]

5769 **Barrell's Paper Annual.** Lawrence, Mass. *Barrell's Pap. A.* [1942–] **L.**P. 51.

5770 **Bártfa fürdő.** Bártfa. *Bártfa Fürdő* [*C. as:* 5771]

5771 **Bártfafürdői hirlap.** Bártfa. *Bártfafürdői Hirl.* [*C. of:* 5770; *C. as:* 5741]

5772 **Barthels Mitteilungen** aus der **Löt-** und **Heiz-technik.** Dresden. *Barthels Mitt.* [1919–33] **L.**P. 26–33 imp.

5773 **Bartonia.** Philadelphia Botanical Club. Philadelphia. *Bartonia* [1908–] **L.**K.; **E.**B. 09–39.

5774 **Baserritarra.** Defensor de los intereses agropecuarios de Guipúzcoa. San Sebastián. *Baserritarra*
Basf. Ludwigshafen. *See* 5632.
Basic Documents. **World Meteorological Organization.** *See* 57044°.

5775 **Basic Radio Propagation Predictions.** Washington. *Bas. Radio Propag. Predict.* **L.**MO 46–; P (curr.); **Sil.** (1 yr); **Y.** (Ser. D).

5776 **Baskerville Chemical Journal.** New York. *Baskerville chem. J.* [1950–] **Y.**

5777 **Basler Beiträge** zur **Geographie** und **Ethnologie.** Basel. *Basler Beitr. Geogr. Ethnol.* [1960–] **Y.**

5778 **Basler Veröffentlichungen** zur **Geschichte** der **Medizin** und der **Biologie.** Basel. *Basler Veröff. Gesch. Med. Biol.* [1953–] **L.**SC.

5779 **Bassa corte.** Bellinzona. *Bassa corte, Bellinzona* [1938–]

5780 **Bassa corte.** Genova. *Bassa corte, Genova* [1920–35] [*C. as:* 14964]

5781 **Basse tension.** Villeurbanne. *Basse Tension* **L.**P. 46–50*. [*C. as:* 3730]

5782 **Basse-Cour.** Betoncourt par Vernois. *Basse-cour* [1935–]

5783 **Bassini.** Rivista medico-scientifica. Milano. *Bassini* [1956–] **L.**MA.

5784 **Basteria:** Tijdschrift van de Nederlandsche malacologische vereeniging. Lisse. *Basteria* [1936–] **L.**BM^N.; Z.; **Pl.**M. 36–46; **Y.**

5785 **Bastien typographica.** London. *Bastien typogr.* [1935–47] **L.**BM. [*C. of:* 55382]

5786 **Bateleur.** A quarterly journal of African Ornithology. Nairobi. *Bateleur* [1928–31] **L.**BM^N.; **O.**OR.

5786° **Bateson Lecture.** John Innes Horticultural Institution. Bayfordbury. *Bateson Lect.* [1953–] [*First two lectures issued in:* 22112]

5787 **Baths** and **Bath Engineering.** London. *Baths Bath Engng* [1934–50] **L.**BM.; P. 34–40 imp.; **C.**UL.; **O.**R.; **Wa.**W. 36–41. [*Replaced by:* 5787°; *Suspended* May 1941–June 1949]

5787° **Baths Service.** London. *Baths Serv.* [1950–] **L.**BM.; P.; **O.**R. [*Replaces:* 5787]

5788 **Bâtiment moderne.** Paris. *Bâtim. mod.*

5789 **Bâtiments** et **travaux publics.** Paris. *Bâtims Trav. publ.*

5790 **Bâtir:** revue mensuelle illustrée d'architecture, d'art et de décoration. Bruxelles. *Bâtir, Brux.* [1932–] **L.**BA. 33–39; **Y.** 51–.

5791 **Bâtir.** Revue technique de la Fédération nationale du bâtiment. Paris. *Bâtir, Paris* [1950–] **L.**P. 53–; **N.**U. 55–; **Y.**

5792 **Battelle Technical Review.** Columbus. *Battelle tech. Rev.* [1952–] **L.**AV.; DI. 55–; P.; PR. 53–; SI.; TP imp.; **Bm.**P.; T. 54–; **Br.**U.; **G.**T. (3 yr.); **Lh.**P.; **Li.**M. (5 yr.); **Lv.**P. 56–; **Sh.**S. 55–; **Sy.**R.; **Y.** [*C. of:* 16181]

5793 **Batterien;** Galvanische Elemente, Akkumulatoren. Berlin. *Batterien* [1932–] **L.**P. 33–. [*For English edition see* 20588]

5794 **Batumskĭ sel'skĭ khozyain.** Batum. Батумскiй сельскiй хозяинъ. *Batum. sel'. Khozyain*

5795 **Bau.** Jahrbuch des Bauwesens. Mannheim. *Bau, Mannheim* [1952–] **L.**P.

5796 **Bau.** Bau- und Architekturzeitschrift. Wien. *Bau, Wien* **L.**BA 52–; **Y.**

5797 **Bau** und **Betrieb.** München. *Bau Betr.* [1949–] **L.**P. 49–55. [*Supplement to:* 20674]

5798 **Bau** und **Holz.** Wien. *Bau Holz* [1950–] **L.**P. 54–56.

5799 **Bau** und **Möbelschreiner.** Stuttgart. *Bau Möbelschreiner* [1946–] **L.**P. 55–.

5800 **Bau** und **Werk.** Wien. *Bau Werk* [1938–] **L.**P. [*C. of and Rec. as:* 58746]

5801 **Bauen** auf dem **Lande.** Frankfurt/Main. *Bauen Lande* [1959–] **L.**AM.; P. [*C. of:* 58500]

5802 **Bauen** und **Wirtschaft.** Berlin. *Bauen Wirtsch.* **L.**C. 28–. [*Supplement to:* 53351]

5803 **Bauen** und **Wohnen.** Ravensburg, München. *Bauen Wohn., Ravensb.* [1946–] **L.**BA. 47–; BM. 56–; **Y.**

5804 **Bauen** und **Wohnen.** Zürich. *Bauen Wohn., Zürich* [1947–] **L.**BA. 47–52; **Bm.**P. 54–; **G.**T. 57–; **Lv.**P. 55–; **M.**T. 58–.

5805 **Bauforschung.** Stammheim. *Bauforschung* [1945–] **L.**P.

5806 **Baugewerbe.** Berlin. *Baugewerbe*

5807 **Baugewerkszeitung.** Berlin. *Baugewerkszeitung*

5808 **Baugilde.** Berlin. *Baugilde* [1919–] **L.**BA. 25–26: 29–39.

5809 **Bauhelfer.** Berlin. *Bauhelfer*

5810 **Bauhinia.** Zeitschrift der Basler botanischen Gesellschaft. Basel. *Bauhinia* [1955–] **L.**BM^N.; K.; **Y.** [*C. of:* 32294]

5811 **Bauhütte.** Leipzig. *Bauhütte* [1858–] **L.**BM. 1858–14.

5812 **Bauindustrie.** Generalanzeiger für das gesamte Bauwesen Deutschlands. Ulm. *Bauindustrie.*

5813 **Bauingenieur.** Berlin. *Bauingenieur* [1920–] **L.**BA. 39–42; P. imp.; **Br.**U. 24– imp.; **C.**ENG. 38: 53–; **M.**P. 26–32; **Y.** [*Suspended* 1943–48]

5814 **Bauingenieur-Zeitung.** Berlin. *Bauingr-Ztg*

5815 **Baujournal.** Wien. *Baujournal*

5816 **Baukeramik.** Wien. *Baukeramik*

5817 **Baukunst.** Stuttgart. *Baukunst*

5818 **Baukunst** und **Werkform.** Heidelberg. *Baukunst Werkform* [1947–] **L.**BA. 47–56; BM. 56–.

5819 **Bau-** und **Werkkunst.** Wien. *Bau- u. Werkkunst* [1927–] **C.**UL. [*C. of:* 35986]

5820 **Baulicher Luftschutz.** Berlin. *Baulicher Luftschutz* [1937–44] **L.**AV. 43–44; P. 37–40 [*Supplement to:* 20679]

5821 **Bau-Markt.** Düsseldorf. *Bau-Markt* [1957–] **L.**P. [*C. of:* 16873]

5822 **Baumaschine.** Leipzig. *Baumaschine* **L.**P. 13–14*.

5823 **Baumaschine** und **Bautechnik.** Wiesbaden. *Baumasch. Bautech.* [1954–] **L.**P.; **Y.**

5824 Baumeister. München. *Baumeister* [1902–] **L**.BA. 30–44: 48–; NP. 57–; **G**.T. 57–; **Lv**.P. 55–; **Y.**
Baumgartens Jahresbericht. *See* 24941.

5825 Bauplanung und **Bautechnik.** Berlin. *Bauplan. Bautech.* [1947–] **L**.P.; **Y.** [> 37829, 1950–52]

5826 Baupraxis. Stuttgart. *Baupraxis* [1949–] **L**.P.

5827 Baurú odontológico. São Paulo. *Baurú odont.*

5828 Baurundschau. Wochenschrift für das gesamte Architektur- und Bauwesen Nord- und Westdeutschlands. Hamburg. *Baurundschau* **L**.BA. 47–; **Y.**

5829 Bausch and **Lomb Magazine.** Rochester, N.Y. *Bausch & Lomb Mag.* [1923–] **L**.P. 29–50: 54– imp.

5830 Bausch and **Lomb Review.** Rochester, N.Y. *Bausch & Lomb Rev.* [1951–] **L**.P. 51–54.

5831 Bausch and **Lomb Today.** Rochester, N.Y. *Bausch & Lomb today* **L**.P. (curr.)

5832 Bau- und **Kunstschlosser.** Lübeck. *Bau- u. Kunstschlosser*

5833 Baustoffindustrie. Berlin. *Baustoffindustrie* [1958–] **L**.P.; **Y.**

5834 Bautechnik. Berlin. *Bautechnik* [1923–] **L**.BA 39–40: 44–45; P. 45–; SC. 36–; **C**.ENG. 38: 50–; **Lv**.P. 56–; U. 29–; **Sw**.U. 55–; **Y.**

5835 Bautechnik-Archiv. Berlin. *Bautech.-Arch.* [1947–] **L**.P.; **Y.**

5836 Bautechniker. Wien. *Bautechniker*
Bautechnische Auskunft, etc. *See* 20247.

5837 Bautechnische Gesteinsuntersuchungen. Mitteilungen aus dem Mineral-geologischen Institut der K. Technischen Hochschule, Berlin. *Bautech. Gesteinsunters.* [1910–21] **L**.GM.; P.; SC.

5838 Bautechnische Mitteilungen des Deutschen Beton-Vereins. Bonn. *Bautech. Mitt. dt. Beton-Ver.* **L**.P. 27–39 imp.

5839 Bautechnische Mitteilungen des Stahlwerksverbandes, Düsseldorf. Düsseldorf. *Bautech. Mitt. Stahlwksverb. Düsseldorf*

5840 Bautechnische Zeitschrift. Strausberg. *Bautech. Z.*

5841 Bautenschutz. Berlin. *Bautenschutz* [1930–42] **L**.P. [*Supplement to:* 6499]

5842 Bau-Trichter. Berlin. *Bau-Trichter.* Ausgabe A. **L**.P. 57–.

5842ᵃ Bau-Unternehmer und **Lieferant.** *Bau-Untern. Lief.* [*Supplement to:* 55848]

5843 Bauwelt. Berlin. *Bauwelt* [1910–45: 52–] **L**.BA. 26–44 imp.; P. 40–43; **Y.** [> 34539, 1946–52]

5844 Bauwelt. Bautechnische Luftschutz. Berlin. *Bauwelt bautech. Luftschutz* **L**.P. 36–37.

5845 Bauwerk. Berlin. *Bauwerk* [1947–] **L**.P.; **Y.**

5846 Bauwoche. Düsseldorf. *Bauwoche* [*C. of:* 57373]

5846ᵃ Bauzeitung. Berlin. *Bauzeitung* **Y.** 62–.

5847 Bayer Colorist. Leverkusen. *Bayer Colorist* [1955–] **L**.P.; **M**.D.

5848 Bayerische Baugewerkszeitung. München. *Bayer. Baugewksztg* [*C. of:* 33787]

5849 Bayerische Landesanstalt für **Pflanzenbau** und **Pflanzenschutz.** München. *Bayer. Landesanst. PflBau* **L**.MY. 02–27.

5850 Bayerische Milchzeitung. München. *Bayer. Milchztg*

5851 Bayerische Vorgeschichtsfreund. München. *Bayer. VorgeschFreund* [1921–] **L**.AN. 21–28.

5852 Bayerisches Ärzteblatt. München. *Bayer. Ärztebl.* **L**.MA. 48–.

5853 Bayerisches Industrie- u. **Gewerbeblatt.** München. *Bayer. Ind.- u. GewBl.* [1869–37] **L**.BM. 69–14; P. 10–37.

5854 Bayerisches landwirtschaftliches Jahrbuch. München. *Bayer. landw. Jb.* [1955–] **L**.MY. 56–; Abs.A. 58–; **C**.A.; **Hu**.G.; **Rt.** 56–; **Y.** [*C. of:* 28115 and 58765; *also supplements*]

5855 Bayerisches Tierärzteblatt. München. *Bayer. Tierärztebl.*

5856 Bayınıdırlık dergisi. İstanbul. *Bayinid. Derg.* **L**.SC. 45–.

5857 Baylor Dental Journal. Dallas, Tex. *Baylor dent. J.* [1939–]

5858 Baylor University Bulletin. Waco, Tex. *Baylor Univ. Bull.* [1898–] **L**.BMᴺ. (nat. hist.) 09–39.

5859 Baytari mecmua. Revue vétérinaire de Stamboul. İstanbul. *Bayt. Mecm.* [1923–]

5860 Beama. London. *Beama* [1920–23] **L**.BM.; EE.; P.; **Abs**.N.; **Br**.U.; **C**.UL.; **E**.A.; **G**.M.; **Lv**.U.; **M**.P.; **O**.R.; **Sw**.U. [*C. of:* 5861; *C. as:* 57888]

5860° Beama Handbook. British Electrical and Allied Manufacturers' Association. London. *Beama Handb.* **Lv**.P. 56–.

5861 Beama Journal. London. *Beama J.* [1915–] **L**.BM.; EE. I. (1 yr); P. 16–; **Abs**.N.; P. 37–; T. 47– imp.; U. 37–; **Bn**.U. 37– imp.; **Br**.U. 21–; **C**.UL.; **Cr**.I. 49–; **Db.** 26–; **Dn**.U. 52–; **E**.A.; **F**.A. 56–; **G**.E. (3 yr.); M. 19–; T. 37–; U. 37–; **Ld**.P. 49–; U. 23–; **Lv**.P. 30– imp.; **M**.P.; U. 37–; **N**.U. 54–; **Nw**.A. 37–; **O**.R.; **Sh**.P. (5 yr.); **Sil.** (1 yr); **Y.** [> 5860, 1920–23 and 57888, 1924–37]

5862 Beama News Sheet. London. *Beama News Sh.* **L**.BM. 39–; EE. 43– imp.

5862° Beama Publications. London. *Beama Publs* **L**.P. 44–.

5863 Beama Special Publications. London. *Beama spec. Publs* [1925–26] **L**.BM.; **C**.UL.; **O**.R. 26.

5864 Bearing Engineer. New York. *Bearing Engr* [1941–] **L**.P. imp.; **Ld**.P. (5 yr.).

5865 Beaufortia. Miscellaneous Publications of the Zoological Museum Amsterdam. *Beaufortia* [1951–] **L**.BMᴺ.; Z.; **Bl**.U.; **Bn**.U. 52–; **Db.**; **E**.U.; **Pl**.M.; **Y.** [*C. of* 2201]

5866 Beaumont Foundation Lectures. Wayne County Medical Society. Detroit. *Beaumont Fdn Lect.* **L**.BM. 23–; **C**.UL. 22–.

5867 Beaver. Winnipeg. *Beaver* [1920–] **C**.PO. 38–; **E**.G.; **O**.AP. imp.

5867ᵃ Bechuanaland Protectorate Temperature Returns. Rainfall. *Bechuanaland Prot. Temp. Returns Rainf.* **Y.**

5868 Beckacite Nachrichten. *Beckacite Nachr.* **L**.PR. 59–.

5869 Beckman Bulletin (*afterwards* and **Infrared Notes**). Pasadena. *Beckman Bull.* [1951–] **L**.P. 53–57. [*Overseas edition published from* 1956, *see* 5871]

5870 **Beckman Infrared Notes.** Fullerton. *Beckman infrared Notes* [1955–57] **L**.P. 56–57. [*C. in:* 5869]

5871 **Beckman International Bulletin.** Fullerton. *Beckman int. Bull.* [1956–] **L**.P. [*Overseas edition of:* 5869]

5872 **Bedfordshire Naturalist.** Bedford. *Beds. Nat.* [1947–] **L**.BM.; BM^N.; L.; NC.; **C**.UL.; **Cr**.M.; **O**.AP.; OR. [*C. of:* 25652]

5873 **Bedrijf** en **techniek.** Amsterdam. *Bedr. Tech.* [1946–] **L**.P. 55–; **Y**.

5874 **Bedrijfsfotographi.** Vaklad voor allen die de fotographie in hum bedrijf toepassen. Bloemendal. *Bedrijfsfotographi* **L**.PG. 31–40 imp.

5875 **Beds** and **Hunts Farmer.** Bedford. *Beds Hunts Fmr* [1947–] **Sil.** (1 yr).

5876 **Bee Craft.** Kent and Surrey Bee-Keepers' Association. Rochester. *Bee Craft* [1919–] **L**.AM. imp.; BM. 34–; P. 33–; **Ba**.I. (curr.); **Bm**.P. 31–; **Rt.** 24–; **Sa.** 29: 32; **Y**.

5877 **Bee Kingdom.** Cairo. *Bee Kingdom* [1930–] **L**.AM.; 30–38 v. imp.; **Rt.** 30–33; **Sa.** 39.

5878 **Bee World.** Oxford, etc. *Bee Wld* [1919–] **L**.AM. imp.; BM.; BM^N. 60–; E. 59–; EB. 21–; NC. 54–; Z. 59–; **Abd**.U. 47–; **C**.UL. 47–; **Cr**.U. 61–; **Db.** 56–; **E**.T.; **M**.P.; **Md**.H. 50–; **O**.R. 47–; **Rt.**; **Y**.

5879 **Beech Utilization Series.** Upper Darby, Pa. *Beech Util. Ser.* [1951–] **L**.P. 58–; **O**.F.; **Y**.

5880 **Beef Situation.** Canberra. *Beef Situ.* [1953–] **L**.AM.; **Abs**.U. 53–55; **Bn**.U.

5881 **Bee-Hive.** Pratt and Whitney Aircraft Co. Hartford, Conn. *Bee-Hive* [1926–61] **L**.AV. 46–; P. 29–; **Y**. [*C. as:* United Aircraft Quarterly Bee-Hive]

5882 **Beekeeper.** Peterboro, Ont. *Beekeeper* [1921–33] **L**.EB. (ent.) 21–31; **Sa.** 28–31 imp. [*C. of:* 13161; *C. in:* 13123]

5883 **Beekeeper's Gazette.** London. *Beekeep. Gaz., Lond.* [1911–] **L**.BM.; **O**.R. 11–33.

5884 **Beekeeper's Gazette.** Mohill, Dublin. *Beekeep. Gaz., Mohill* [1901–33] **L**.AM. 22–33; **Abs**.N. 28–33; **Sa.** 15–18: 21–25.

5885 **Bee-keeper's Record.** Liverpool, London. *Beekeep. Rec.* [1882–54] **L**.AM. 82–54 v. imp.; BM.; SC. 36–54; **Abs**.N. 12–54; **G**.M. 09–54; **Lv**.P. 45–54; **O**.R. 82–36. [*C. in:* 8758]

5886 **Beekeeping.** Exeter. *Beekeeping* [1935–] **L**.BM.; **Rt.** 47– imp.
Beekeeping. Moscow. *See* 37256.

5887 **Bee-keeping Annual.** London, etc. *Beekeeping A.* [1928–] **L**.AM. 28–51 v. imp.; BM.; **Abs**.N.; **C**.UL 35–; **E**.A.; **O**.R.; **Sa.** 28–42.

5888 **Beekeeping Division Leaflet.** Forest Department, Tanganyika. Dar-es-Salaam. *Beekeeping Div. Leafl., Tanganyika* [1954–] **Rt.**

5889 **Beekeeping Division Pamphlet.** Forest Department, Tanganyika. Dar-es-Salaam. *Beekeeping Div. Pamph. Tanganyika* [1955–] **Bn**.U.; **O**.F.; **Rt.**

5890 **Beekeeping** in **South Africa.** Johannesburg. *Beekeeping S. Afr.*

5891 **Beerenobstschrifttum.** Referate aus der in- und ausländischen Literatur. Rethmar über Lehrte. *Beerenobstschrifttum* **Md**.H. 56–.

5892 **Beet Grower.** Dublin. *Beet Grow.* [1947–55] **L**.AM.; **C**.A.; **Db.** [*C. as:* 6542]

5893 **Beet Sugar Gazette.** Chicago. *Beet Sug. Gaz.* [1899–04] [*C. as:* 2163]

5894 **Beetle Bulletin.** British Industrial Plastics Ltd. London. *Beetle Bull.* [1951–] **L**.BM. 53–; P. (curr.); **Bm**.T. 56–; **M**.C. (2 yr.); **Sy**.R.

5895 **'Beetle' Magazine.** British Industrial Plastics Ltd. London. *'Beetle' Mag.*

5896 **Begleitwerk** zur **geognostischen Spezialkarte** von **Württemberg.** Stuttgart. *Begleitwk geogn. Spez-Karte Württ.* **L**.GM. 68–.

5897 **Behavior Monographs.** Cambridge, Mass. *Behav. Monogr.* [1911–22] **L**.B.; **Br**.U.; **C**.PS.; **G**.U.; **O**.R. imp.; **Pl**.M. 11–13 imp. [*C. as:* 15129]

5898 **Behavioral Science.** Ann Arbor. *Behavl Sci.* [1956–] **L**.B.; MA.; MD.; PS.; SC.; **Bm**.U.; **C**.P.; **G**.U.; **Ld**.U.; **O**.B.

5899 **Behaviour;** an international journal of comparative ethnology. Leiden. *Behaviour* [1947–] **L**.AM.; B.; BM.; BM^N.; KC.; QM.; SC.; U.; VC. 58–; Z.; **Bm**.U.; **Br**.U.; **C**.B.; PS. 53–; **E**.U.; **Ex**.U. 56–; **Fr.** 47–57; **G**.U.; **H**.U.; **Hu**.G. 47–55; **Ld**.U.; **Lo.** 55–; **Lv**.U.; **Mi.**; **N**.U. 56–; **O**.AP.; EP.; R.; **Pit**.F. 53–; **Pl**.M.; **R**.U.; **Rt.**; **Y**. [*Also supplements*]

5900 **Behaviour Science Bibliographies.** Yale University, New Haven. *Behav. Sci. Biblphies* [1955–] **L**.BM.

5901 **Beiblätter** zu den **Annalen** der **Physik.** Leipzig. *Beibl. Annln Phys.* [1877–19] **L**.BM.; BM^N. 77–02; C.; EE.; 77–14; IC. 87–19 imp.; MD. 77–14; P.; R. 77–14; SC.; UC.; **Abd**.U. 77–14; **Bl**.U.; **Bm**.U.; **Br**.U.; **C**.P.; T. 77–11; UL.; **Cr**.U.; **Db.**; **Dn**.U.; **E**.R.; U.; **G**.M. 78–15; U.; **H**.U.; **Ld**.U.; **Lv**.U.; **M**.U.; **Nw**.A. imp.; **O**.BS.; **R**.U. 05–19; **Sa.**; **Sh**.U. 92–09. [*C. in:* 37702]

5902 **Beiblatt** zu den **Veröffentlichungen** des **Geobotanischen Instituts Rübel.** Zürich. *Beibl. Veröff. geobot. Inst. Rübel* [1922–33] **L**.BM^N. 22–28; **Bl**.U.; **C**.UL.; **O**.R.
Beiheft. *See* **Beihefte.** [Notification of supplements with no separate title will in general be found with the entry for a periodical.]
Beihefte zu **angewandte Chemie** und **Chemie-ingenieur Technik.** *See* 5917.

5903 **Beihefte** zum **Archiv** für **Fischereiwissenschaft.** Bundesforschungsanstalt für Fischerei. Hamburg. *Beih. Arch. FischWiss.* [1960–] **L**.BM^N. [*Supplement to:* 4076]

5904 **Beihefte** zum **Archiv** für **Schiffs-** und **Tropenhygiene.** Leipzig. *Beih. Arch. Schiffs- u. TropHyg.* [1897–] **L**.EB. 07–; S. 09–35; **Sal.** 31–35. [*Supplement to:* 4159]

5905 **Beihefte** zum **Botanischen Zentralblatt.** Cassel. *Beih. bot. Zbl.* [1891–43] **L**.BM^N imp.; HS. 91–42; K.; L. 91–42; SC. 05–04: (*a*) 05–44: (*b*) 05–42; **Bl**.U. 92–00; **Bm**.U.; **Bn**.U. 91–00; **Br**.U.; **C**.BO.; UL.; **Dn**.U.; **E**.B.; R. 91–11; **G**.U.; **H**.U. 29–32; **Ld**.U.; **Lv**.U. 91–04; **M**.C. 91–04; U.; **O**.BO. [*Supplement to:* 8598]

5906 **Beihefte** zum **Geologischen Jahrbuch.** Hannover. *Beih. geol. Jb.* [1951–] **L**.BM^N.; GL.; **Db.**; **Y**. [*Supplement to:* 21051]

5907 **Beihefte** zum **Gesundheits-Ingenieur.** Berlin. *Beih. Gesundh.-Ingr* [1913–] **L**.P. [*Supplement to:* 21165]

5908 **Beihefte** zu den **Jahrbücher** der **Zentralanstalt** für **Meteorologie** und **Geodynamik.** Wien. *Beih. Jb. ZentAnst. Met. Geodyn., Wien* **L.**MO 28–32. [*Supplement to:* 24871]

Beihefte zu **Mikrochemie.** Wien. *See* 31809.

5909 **Beihefte** zu den **Mitteilungen** des **Sächsisch-Thüringischen Vereins** für **Erdkunde** zu **Halle** an der **Saale.** *Beih. Mitt. sächs.-thür. Ver. Erdk.* **O.**B. 34–40 imp. [*Supplement to:* 32715]

5910 **Beihefte** zum **Repertorium specierum novarum regni vegetabilis.** Berlin. *Beih. Repert. Spec. nov. Regni veg.* [1911–] **L.**BM.; BM^N. imp.; K.; L. 14–43 imp.; SC. 53–; **C.**UL.; **E.**B.; **O.**BO. 11–44 imp. [*Supplement to:* 42592]

5911 **Beihefte** zur **Schweizerischen Bienenzeitung.** Aarau. *Beih. schweiz. Bienenztg* [1941–] **Rt.** [*Supplement to:* 48928]

5911ᶜ **Beihefte** zur **Sydowia.** Horn. *Beih. Sydowia* **Y.** [*Supplement to:* 51636]

5912 **Beihefte** zum **Tropenpflanzer.** Berlin. *Beih. Tropenpfl.* [1900–] **L.**BM^N. 00–12; EB. 13–; K.; P. 10–30; **Md.**H. 11–13 imp. [*Supplement to:* 54392]

5913 **Beihefte** zur **Zeitschrift Ernährung.** Leipzig. *Beih. Z. Ernähr.* [1937–] [*Supplement to:* 18474]

5914 **Beihefte** zur **Zeitschrift Geologie.** Berlin. *Beih. Z. Geol.* [1952–] **L.**BM^N.

5915 **Beihefte. Zeitschrift** für die **gesamte Kälte-Industrie.** Berlin. *Beih. Z. ges. Kälte-Ind.* [1927–] **L.**P. [*Supplement to:* 58617]

5916 **Beihefte** zu den **Zeitschriften** des **Schweizerischen Forstvereins.** Bern. *Beih. Zn schweiz. Forstver.* [1925–] **O.**F.

5917 **Beihefte** zu den **Zeitschriften** des **Vereins deutscher Chemiker.** Berlin. *Beih. Zn Ver. dt. Chem.* [1933–50] **L.**P. imp. [*C. as:* 33264ᵃ]

5918 **Beihefte. Zentralblatt** für **Gewerbehygiene** und **Unfallverhütung.** Leipzig. *Beih. Zbl. Gewerbehyg.* [1925–] **L.**P.; **Ste.** 25–39. [*Supplement to:* 59029]

5918ᵃ **Beilage** zur **Wetterkarte.** Wetteramt Schleswig. *Beil. WettKarte Schlesw.* **Y.** 60–. [*Supplement to:* 57471]

Beilsteins Handbuch der **organischen Chemie.** *See* 21826.

5919 **Beiträge** zur **ärztlichen Fortbildung.** Prag. *Beitr. ärztl. Fortbild.*

5920 **Beiträge** zur **ärztlichen Praxis.** Prag. *Beitr. ärztl. Prax.* [1931–34] [*C. as:* 38472]

5921 **Beiträge** zur **Agrargeographie.** Bern. *Beitr. Agrargeogr.*

5922 **Beiträge** zur **Agrarwissenschaft.** Hannover. *Beitr. Agrarwiss.* [1947–] **C.**A. 47–48; **Rt.**

5923 **Beiträge** zur **allgemeinen Botanik.** Berlin. *Beitr. allg. Bot.* [1916–23] **Ld.**U. 18–23.

5924 **Beiträge** zur **Anatomie funktioneller Systeme.** Leipzig. *Beitr. Anat. funkt. Syst.* [1930–] **C.**AN. 30–40.

5925 **Beiträge** zur **Anatomie, Physiologie, Pathologie** und **Therapie** des **Ohres** der **Nase** und des **Halses.** Berlin. *Beitr. Anat. Physiol. Path. Ther. Ohr. Nase Hals.* [1908–26] **E.**P. [*C. as:* 37187]

5926 **Beiträge** zur **angewandten Geophysik.** Leipzig. *Beitr. angew. Geophys.* [1933–] **L.**AM.; BM.; MO.; SC.33–40; **Abd.**U. 33–39; **C.**UL.; **Ld.**U.; **Lo.** 33–35; **M.**U. 33–44. [*C. of:* 18373]

5927 **Beiträge** zur **Anthropologie Elsass-Lothringens.** Strassburg. *Beitr. Anthrop. Els.-Loth.* [1898–02] **L.**AN.; BM.

5928 **Beiträge** zur **Anthropologie** und **Urgeschichte Bayerns.** München. *Beitr. Anthrop. Urgesch. Bayerns* [1876–15] **L.**BM.; BM^N.; **C.**UL.; **O.**B.

5929 **Beiträge** zur **Augenheilkunde.** Hamburg, Leipzig. *Beitr. Augenheilk.* [1890–18] **L.**MD. 90–15; OP. 90–15; **E.**S. 90–93.

5930 **Beiträge** zur **Bauwissenschaft.** Berlin. *Beitr. Bauwiss.*

5931 **Beiträge** zur **Biologie** der **Pflanzen.** Breslau. *Beitr. Biol. Pfl.* [1870–] **L.**BM.; BM^N.; K. 70–39; L. 70–48; MD. 70–17 imp.; SC. 70–39: 57–; **Abd.**U. 70–57; **Br.**U. 75–31; **C.**BO. 75–; UL.; **Db.** 70–04; **E.**B.; P.; **G.**F. 77–11; U.; **Ld.**U. 70–39; **M.**U.; **N.**U. 81–91; **Nw.**A. 75–02; **O.**BO.; R. 87–19; **Y.**

5932 **Beiträge** zur **chemischen Physiologie** u. **Pathologie.** Braunschweig. *Beitr. chem. Physiol. Path.* [1901–08] **L.**BM.; C.; LI. 01–07; MC.; MD.; P. 06–08; S.; TD.; U.; UC.; **Abd.**U.; **Bl.**U.; **Br.**U. 06–07; **C.**BI.; PH.; **Db.**; **Dn.**U.; **E.**P.; U.; **G.**U.; **Lv.**U.; **M.**MS.; **O.**R. [*C. in:* 7017]

5933 **Beiträge** der **Deutschen Akademie** der **Landwirtschaftswissenschaften.** Berlin. *Beitr. dt. Akad. LandwWiss.* **Db.** 52–.

5934 **Beiträge** zur **Entomologie.** Berlin. *Beitr. Ent.* [1951–] **L.**AM.; BM^N.; E.; SC.; Z.; **Bn.**U.; **Db.**; **E.**R.; **Fr.**; **Ld.**U. 51–59; **Md.**H.; **O.**H.; **Y.**

5935 **Beiträge** zur **entwicklungsmechanischen Anatomie** der **Pflanzen.** Jena. *Beitr. entwmech. Anat. Pfl.*

5936 **Beiträge** zur **Erkenntnis** des **Uranismus.** Leipzig-Amsterdam. *Beitr. Erk. Uranism.*

5937 **Beiträge** zur **experimentellen Therapie.** Berlin. *Beitr. exp. Ther.* **L.**MD. 99–05; **C.**UL.; **Lv.**U. 02–06.

5938 **Beiträge** zur **Förderung** der **Landeskultur.** Berlin. *Beitr. Förd. Landeskult.* **Hu.**G. 31–38.

5939 **Beiträge** zur **forensischen Medizin.** Berlin. *Beitr. forens. Med.*

5940 **Beiträge** zur **Fortpflanzungsbiologie** der **Vögel** mit **Berücksichtigung** der **Oologie.** Berlin. *Beitr. FortpflBiol. Vögel* [1924–44] **L.**BM^N.; Z. 42–44 imp.; **C.**B. imp.; **E.**AB. 34–39; **O.**OR imp.

5941 **Beiträge** zur **Freiburger Wissenschafts-** und **Universitätsgeschichte.** Freiburg. *Beitr. freiburg. Wiss.- u. UnivGesch.* [1952–] **L.**BM.

5942 **Beiträge** zur **Geburtshilfe** u. **Gynäkologie.** Leipzig. *Beitr. Geburtsh. Gynäk.* [1898–15] **L.**MD.; **Dn.**U. 98–06; **E.**P.

5943 **Beiträge** zur **geobotanischen Landesaufnahme** der **Schweiz.** Zürich & Leipzig. *Beitr. geobot. Landesaufn. Schweiz* [1916–] **L.**BM.; BM^N.; SC.; **E.**B.; R.; **M.**U.; **Y.**

5944 **Beiträge** zur **Geologie.** Berlin. *Beitr. Geol.* [1959–] **L.**SC.

5945 **Beiträge** zur **Geologie** der **Schweiz.** Bern. *Beitr. Geol. Schweiz*
Geotechnische Serie [1899–] **L.**BM^N.; GL.; GM.; SC. 19–imp.; **C.**UL.; **E.**R.; **Y.**
Hydrologie [1934–] **L.**GL.; GM.; SC.; **C.**UL.; **E.**R.; **Y.**

5946 **Beiträge** zur **Geologie** von **Thüringen.** Jena. *Beitr. Geol. Thür.* [1925–] **L.**BM^N.; GM.

5947 **Beiträge** zur **geologischen Erforschung** der **deutschen Schutzgebiete.** Berlin. *Beitr. geol. Erforsch. dt. Schutzgeb.* [1911–28] **L.**BM. 13–28; BM^N.; GL. 12–28; GM. 12–28.

5948 **Beiträge** zur **geologischen Karte** der **Schweiz.** Bern. *Beitr. geol. Karte Schweiz* [1862–] **L.**BM.; BM^N.; G. 05–; GL. 00–; GM.; **Bm.**U. 05–; **C.**UL.; **E.**R. 63– imp.
Beiträge zur **geologischen Karte** der **Turkei.** *See* 29082.

5949 **Beiträge** zur **Geophysik.** Leipzig. *Beitr. Geophys.* [1887–] **L.**AM. 30–42; BM.; G.; GL. 00–30; GM.; MO.; P. 58–; R. 87–39; SC. 87–45: 49; **Abd.**U. 26– imp.; **C.**UL.; **Db.** 26–; **E.**U. 87–40; **Ld.**U. 26–32; **Lo.**30–42: 45–59; **M.**U. imp.; **Nw.**A. 38–42: 44–; **O.**R.; **Y.**

5949° **Beiträge** zur **gerichtlichen Medizin.** Leipzig. *Beitr. gericht. Med.* [1911–] **L.**BM. [*Not published* 1944–48]

5950 **Beiträge** zur **Geschichte** der **Landwirtschaftswissenschaften.** Berlin. *Beitr. Gesch. LandwWiss.* [1954–] **L.**SC.; **Y.**

5951 **Beiträge** zur **Geschichte** der **Medizin.** Wien. *Beitr. Gesch. Med., Wien* [1911–12]

5952 **Beiträge** zur **Geschichte** der **Medizin.** Wien. *Beitr. Gesch. Med., Wien* [1948]

5953 **Beiträge** zur **Geschichte** der **Medizin.** Zürich, etc. *Beitr. Gesch. Med., Zürich* **O.**R. 25–26.

5954 **Beiträge** zur **Geschichte** der **Meteorologie.** Berlin. *Beitr. Gesch. Met.* **L.**MO. 14–22.

5955 **Beiträge** zur **Geschichte** der **Naturwissenschaft.** Erlangen. *Beitr. Gesch. Naturw.* **O.**R. 11–21 imp.

5956 **Beiträge** zur **Geschichte** der **Pharmazie** und ihrer **Nachbargebiete.** Berlin. *Beitr. Gesch. Pharm.* [1955–] [*Supplement to:* 37522]

5957 **Beiträge** zur **Geschichte** der **Technik** und **Industrie.** Jahrbuch des Vereins Deutscher Ingenieure. Berlin. *Beitr. Gesch. Tech. Ind.* [1909–32] **L.**P.; SC. 29–32. [*C. as:* 52474]

5958 **Beiträge** zur **Geschichte** der **Tierheilkunde.** Magdeburg. *Beitr. Gesch. Tierheilk.*

5959 **Beiträge** zur **Geschichte** der **Veterinärmedizin.** Berlin. *Beitr. Gesch. VetMed.* [1938–] [*Replaces:* 13703]

5960 **Beiträge** zur **Giftkunde.** Berlin. *Beitr. Giftk.*

5961 **Beiträge** zur **Heilkunde.** Berlin. *Beitr. Heilk.*

5962 **Beiträge** zur **Hydrographie** des **Grossherzogtums Baden.** Karlsruhe. *Beitr. Hydrogr. Baden* **L.**MO 84–00 imp.

5963 **Beiträge** zur **Hydrographie Österreichs.** Wien. *Beitr. Hydrogr. Öst.* **L.**BM. 03–18; MO. 96–99: 13–18 imp.: 49–.

5964 **Beiträge** zur **Hygiene** und **Epidemiologie.** Leipzig. *Beitr. Hyg. Epidem.* [1943–] **L.**TD.; **Y.**

5965 **Beiträge** zum **Internationalen geophysikalischen Jahr.** Göttingen. *Beitr. int. geophys. Jahr* [1958–] **L.**BM^N. [*Issued in:* 159]

5965° **Beiträge** zur **Karzinomforschung.** Berlin-Wien. *Beitr. Karzinomforsch.* **E.**P.

5966 **Beiträge** zur **Kenntnis** der **atmosphärischen Elektrizität.** Wien. *Beitr. Kennt. atmos. Elekt.* **L.**MO. 00– imp.

5967 **Beiträge** zur **Kenntnis einheimischer Pilze.** Jena. *Beitr. Kennt. einh. Pilze* **O.**BO. 95–15.

5968 **Beiträge** zur **Kenntnis** der **Land-** und **Süsswasserfauna Deutsch-Südwestafrikas.** Hamburg. *Beitr. Kennt. Land- u. Süsswasserfauna Dt.-SüdwAfr.* **L.**BM^N. 14–28.

5969 **Beiträge** zur **Kenntnis** des **Meeres** und seiner **Bewohner.** Jena. *Beitr. Kennt. Meer. Bewohn.* **L.**BM. 04.

5970 **Beiträge** zur **Kenntnis** der **Meeresfauna Westafrikas.** Hamburg. *Beitr. Kennt. Meeresfauna Westafr.* [1914–32] **L.**BM.; BM^N.; **Pl.**M.

5971 **Beiträge** zur **Kenntis** des **Orients.** Berlin. *Beitr. Kennt. Orient.* [1902–17] **L.**BM. 04–17; **C.**UL. 05–17; **O.**B. 03–17.

5972 **Beiträge** zur **Kenntnis** des **Russischen Reichs** und der **angrenzenden Länder Asiens.** St. Petersburg. *Beitr. Kennt. russ. Reichs* [1839–00] **L.**BM.; BM^N. 1839–90; SC. 1839–96; Z. imp.; **C.**UL.; **O.**B.; **Sa.**
Beiträge zur **Kinderforschung** u. **Heilerziehung.** *See* 58676.

5973 **Beiträge** zur **Klinik** der **Infektionskrankheiten** u. zur **Immunitätsforschung,** mit Ausschluss der Tuberkulose. Würzburg. *Beitr. Klin. InfektKrankh.* [1912–] **L.**MD 13–14.

5974 **Beiträge** zur **Klinik** der **Tuberkulose** und zur **spezifischen Tuberkuloseforschung.** Würzburg. *Beitr. Klin. Tuberk.* [1903–] **L.**H. 39–43; MA. 47–; MC. 19–22; MD.; **C.**PA. 03–08; **Dn.**U. 11–14; **E.**P.; **Y.**

5975 **Beiträge** zur **klinischen Chirurgie.** Tübingen. *Beitr. klin. Chir.* [1883–] **L.**BM.; MA. 34–43; MD. 84–; S. 83–49: 58–; U. 49–; UCH. 09–13: 22–34; **Abd.**U. 84–14; **Br.**U. 08–10; **C.**MD. 98–06 imp.; PA. 98–00: 05–06; **E.**S. 85–; U. 08–15 imp.; **G.**F. 85–14.

5976 **Beiträge** zur **Kryptogamenflora** der **Schweiz.** Bern. *Beitr. KryptogFlora Schweiz* [1898–] **L.**BM.; BM^N. 98–24; K. 98–45 imp.; L.; **O.**BO.; **Y.**

5977 **Beiträge** zur **Krystallographie** und **Mineralogie.** Heidelberg. *Beitr. Krystallogr. Miner.* [1914–] **L.**BM.; BM^N.; GL.; GM.; **M.**U. 14–26.

5978 **Beiträge** zur **Küstenkunde.** Berlin. *Beitr. Küstenk.* [1910–16] **O.**G. 10–13. [*Supplement to:* 2646]

5979 **Beiträge** zur **Landeskunde** der **Rheinlande.** Bonn. *Beitr. Landesk. Rheinl.* [1922–40] [*C. as:* 8522]

5980 **Beiträge** zur **Lokomotivgeschichte.** Darmstadt. *Beitr. LokoGesch.* [1937] **L.**P.; SC.

5981 **Beiträge** zur **Mineralogie** von **Japan.** Tokyo. *Beitr. Miner. Japan* [1905–15: 35–] **L.**BM. 05–12; BM^N. 05–15.

5982 **Beiträge** zur **Mineralogie** und **Petrographie.** Berlin, etc. *Beitr. Miner. Petrogr.* [1957–] **L.**BM^N.; P.; SC.; **C.**MI.; **Ld.**U.; **Y.** [*C. of:* 22034]

5983 **Beiträge** zur **Naturdenkmalpflege.** Berlin. *Beitr. NatDenkmPflege* [1910–37] **L.**BM^N.

5984 **Beiträge** zur **Naturgeschichte** des **Menschen.** Jena. *Beitr. Naturg. Mensch.* [1908–10] **L.**BM.
Beiträge zur **Naturgeschichte Ostasiens.** *Beitr. Naturg. Ostasiens* [*Supplement to:* 163]

5985 **Beiträge** zur **Naturkunde Niedersachsens.** Osnabrück. *Beitr. Naturk. Niedersachs.* [1948–] **L.**BM^N.; **Y.**

5986 **Beiträge** zur **Naturkunde Preussens.** Königsberg. *Beitr. Naturk. Preuss.* [1868–12] **L.**BM.; BM[N].; GL. OO–12; **C.**UL. 68–OO; **O.**R.

5987 **Beiträge** zur **naturkundlichen Forschung** in **Oberrheingebiet.** Karlsruhe i B. *Beitr. naturk. Forsch. Oberrheingeb.* [1941–42] **L.**BM[N]. [*C. of* and *Rec. as:* 5988]

5988 **Beiträge** zur **naturkundlichen Forschung** in **Südwestdeutschland.** Karlsruhe. *Beitr. naturk. Forsch. SüdwDtl.* [1936–] **L.**BM[N].; SC. [> 5987, 1941–42]

5989 **Beiträge** zur **naturwissenschaftlichen Erforschung Badens.** Freiburg i. B. *Beitr. naturw. Erforsch. Badens* **L.**BM[N]. 28–33. [*Issued with* 32292]

5989[a] **Beiträge** zur **neotropischen Fauna.** Jena. *Beitr. neotrop. Fauna* [1956–] **L.**Z.

5990 **Beiträge** zur **pädagogischen Pathologie.** Gütersloh. *Beitr. pädag. Path.*

5991 **Beiträge** zur **Paläontologie** u. **Geologie Österreich-Ungarns** u. des **Orients.** Wien & Leipzig. *Beitr. Paläont. Geol. Öst.-Ung.* [1880–15] **L.**BM.; BM[N].; GL. OO–15; GM.; R. 82–14; **C.**UL. 82–14; **Db.**; **G.**U. 05–15; **O.**R. 96–15.

5992 **Beiträge** zur **paläontologischen Kenntnis** des **Böhmischen Mittelgebirges.** Prag. *Beitr. paläont. Kennt. böhm. Mittelgebirges*

5993 **Beiträge** zur **Pappelforschung.** Berlin. *Beitr. Pappelforsch.* [1956–] **O.**F.

5994 **Beiträge** zur **Pathologie** der **Verdauungsorgane.** Berlin. *Beitr. Path. VerdauOrg.* [1905–] **E.**P.; **Lv.**U. 05.

5995 **Beiträge** zur **pathologischen Anatomie** und zur **allgemeinen Pathologie.** Jena. *Beitr. path. Anat.* [1886–] **L.**BM.; MA. 49–; MC. 86–32; MD.; S. 86–49; UCH. 88–39 imp.; **Abd.**U.; **Bl.**U. imp.; **Bm.**U. 02–; **Br.**U. 93–57; **C.**PA. imp.; UL.; **Cr.**MD. 30–39; **Db.** 93–; **Dn.**U.; **E.**P.; S. 86–22 imp.; U. 92–; **G.**U. 28–; **Ld.**U.; **Lv.**U. 86–32; **M.**MS.; **Nw.**A. 13–14: 37–; **O.**R.; **Sh.**U. 07–16; **Y.**

5996 **Beiträge** zur **Pflanzenzucht.** Berlin. *Beitr. PflZucht* [1911–29] **L.**AM. 11–24; **Abs.**A. 12–29; **Br.**U. 13–14; **C.**A.

5997 **Beiträge** zur **Philosophie** und **Psychologie.** Stuttgart. *Beitr. Phil. Psychol.*

5998 **Beiträge** zur **Physik** der **Atmosphäre.** Frankfurt am Main. *Beitr. Phys. Atmos.* [1956–] **L.**MO.; P. 57–; SC. imp.; **M.**U.; **Y.** imp. [*C. of:* 5999]

5999 **Beiträge** zur **Physik** der **freien Atmosphäre.** Leipzig. *Beitr. Phys. frei. Atmos.* [1904–45] **L.**MO. 04–42; SC. imp; **M.**U. imp.; **Y.** [*C. as:* 5998]

6000 **Beiträge** zur **physikalischen Erforschung** der **Erdrinde.** Berlin. *Beitr. phys. Erforsch. Erdrinde* **L.**GM. 29–.

6001 **Beiträge** zur **Physiologie.** Berlin. *Beitr. Physiol.* [1914–34] **L.**S. 22–24; UC.

6002 **Beiträge** zur **Physiologie** und **Pathologie** der **Verdauung** und **Ernährung.** Leiden. *Beitr. Physiol. Path. Verdau. Ernähr.*

Beitrage zur **physiologischen Optik.** Leningrad. *See* 38770.

6003 **Beiträge** aus der **Plasmaphysik.** Berlin. *Beitr. Plasmaphys.* [1960–] **L.**P.; **Y.**

Beiträge zur **praktischen** und **theoretischen Hals-Nasen-** und **Ohrenheilkunde.** Berlin. *See* 37187.

6004 **Beiträge** zur **Praxis** des **Formens** u. **Giessens.** Berlin. *Beitr. Prax. Form. Giess.*

6005 **Beiträge** zur **psychiatrischen Klinik.** Wien, Berlin. *Beitr. psychiat. Klin.* [1902–03] **L.**BM.; **E.**P.

6006 **Beiträge** zur **Psychologie** der **Aussage.** Leipzig. *Beitr. Psychol. Aussage* [1903–06] **E.**U.; **M.**U. 04–06. [*C. as:* 58486]

6007 **Beiträge** zur **Psychologie** u. **Philosophie.** Leipzig. *Beitr. Psychol. Phil.* [1896–05] **L.**BM.

6008 **Beiträge** zur **Rassenkunde.** Leipzig. *Beitr. Rassenk.* [1906–13] **L.**BM.; **C.**UL.

6009 **Beiträge** zur **Sexualforschung.** Stuttgart. *Beitr. SexForsch.* [1952–] **L.**BM.; MD.

6010 **Beiträge** zur **Silikosforschung.** Bochum. *Beitr. Silikosforsch.* [1949–] **L.**MD. imp.; TD.; **Cr.**MD. 51–; **Y.** [*Also supplements*]

6010° **Beiträge** zur **Substanz-Forschung.** Dornach. *Beitr. Subst.-Forsch.* [1952–] **L.**BM.

6011 **Beiträge** zur **Sukkulentenkunde** und **-pflege.** Berlin. *Beitr. Sukkulentenk.* **L.**BM[N]. 39.

6012 **Beiträge** zur **Syphilisforschung.** Wiesbaden. *Beitr. SyphForsch.*

6013 **Beiträge** zur **Systematik** und **Ökologie mitteleuropäischer Acarina.** Erlangen. Leipzig. *Beitr. Syst. Ökol. mitteleur. Acarina* [1957–] **L.**Z.; **Rt.**

6014 **Beiträge** zur **taxonomischen Zoologie.** Pössneck. *Beitr. tax. Zool.* [1949–] **L.**BM[N]; Z. 49.

6015 **Beiträge** zur **Tierheilkunde.** Berlin. *Beitr. Tierheilk.*

6016 **Beiträge** zur **Tierkunde** und **Tierzucht.** Leipzig. *Beitr. Tierk. Tierz.* **L.**BM[N]. 38–; Z. 51.

Beiträge zur **ukrainischen Ethnologie.** *See* 29656.

Beiträge zur **Völkerkunde.** *See* 5710.

6017 **Beiträge** zur **Vogelkunde.** Leipzig. *Beitr. Vogelk.* [1949–] **L.**BM[N].; SC. 57–; **Y.**

6018 **Beiträge** zur **Wasser-, Abwasser-** und **Fischereichemie** aus dem **Flusswasser-Untersuchungsamt** in **Magdeburg.** *Beitr. Wass.- Abwass.- u. FischChem.* [1946–] **Wa.**W.

6019 **Beiträge** zur **Wirtschaft, Wissenschaft** und **Technik** der **Metalle** und ihrer **Legierungen.** Berlin. *Beitr. Wirtsch. Wiss. Tech. Metalle* [1937–]

6020 **Beiträge** zur **wissenschaftlichen Botanik.** Stuttgart. *Beitr. wiss. Bot.* [1895–06] **L.**BM.; BM[N].; L.; **C.**UL.; **O.**BO. 95–01.

6021 **Beizerei.** Duisberg. *Beizerei* [1936–40] **L.**P. imp. [*Supplement to:* 17964]

6022 **Beiztechnik.** Hamburg. *Beiztechnik* [1952–57] **L.**P. [*C. as:* 31465]

6023 **Bekämpfung** der **Aufzuchtkrankheiten.** Hannover. *Bekämpf. Aufzuchtkrankh.* **W.** 25–.

6024 **Bekämpfung** der **Säuglingssterblichkeit** in **Halle a. S.** *Bekämpf. SäuglSterbl. Halle*

6024° **Bekanntmachungen. Amt** für **Erfindungs-** und **Patentwesen.** Berlin. *Bekanntm. Amt Erfind.- u. PatWes.* [1960–] **L.**P.

6025 **Beknopt verslag. Centrum** voor **onkruidonderzoek.** Ghent. *Beknopt Versl. Cent. Onkruidonderz.* **C.**A. 58–.

Beknopt verslag van de **werkzaamheden** van den **Gezondheidsraad.** *See* 24673.

6026 **Bekroonde verhandelingen. Utrechtsch geno-otschap** voor **kunsten** en **wetenschappen.** 's Graven-hage. *Bekr. Verh. utrecht. Genoot. Kunst. Wet.*

6027 **Belgique apicole.** Erquelinnes. *Belg. apic.* **Rt.** 55–; **Y.**

6028 **Belgique automobile.** Bruxelles. *Belg. auto.* **Y.**

6029 **Belgique laitière.** Brussels. *Belg. lait.* **L.**AM. 48– imp.; BM. 51–; **R.**D. 51–.

6030 **Belgique médicale.** Gand. *Belg. méd.*
Belgisch archief van **sociale geneeskunde** en **hygiëne.** *See* 4197.
Belgisch tijdschrift voor **fysische geneeskunde** en **reumatologie.** *See* 25656.

6031 **Belgisch tijdschrift** voor **geneeskunde.** Gent. *Belg. Tijdschr. Geneesk.* [1945–] **L.**MA.; MC.; MD. 46–48; **Bl.**U. 48–.
Belgisch tijdschrift voor **stomatologie.** *See* 47079.
Belgisch zuivelbedrijf. *See* 6029.

6032 **Belgische diamantfabrikant.** Antwerp. *Belg. DiamFabr.* **L.**DI. 59–.

6033 **Belgische diamantnijverheid.** Antwerp. *Belg. DiamNijv.* **L.**DI. 47–.

6034 **Belgische** en **nederlandsche kleiindustrie.** Nieuwpoort. *Belg. ned.Kleiind.* [1927–]
Belgische optieker. *See* 36268.
Belgische wetenschappelijke textielannalen. *See* 2913.

6035 **Bell Laboratories Record.** New York. *Bell Labs Rec.* [1925–] **L.**AV. 45– imp.; DI. 45–; EE.; I. 38–; NF. 45–; P.; SC. 28–; SI. 37–; UC. (curr.); T.; U. 30– imp.; **Bn.**U. 61–; **Co.**T. 59–; **E.**HW. 50–; **F.**A. 45–; **Ld.**U. 29–41 imp.; **Lv.**P. 59–; **Ma.**T. 37–; **N.**U. 36–; **Sy.**R. 42–; **Y.**

6036 **Bell System Technical Journal.** New York. *Bell Syst. tech. J.* [1922–] **L.**AV. 29– imp.; B. 33–; DI. 43–; EE. imp.; I. (4 yr.); IC. 47–; P.; QM. 26– imp.; RI. 47–; SC. 25–; SI. 31– imp.; U. 50–; UC. 27–; **Abd.**U. 30– imp.; **Bl.**U. 37– imp.; **Bm.**C. 46–; P. 35–; T. 51–; U. 29–; **Bn.**U. imp.; **Br.**U. 23–; **C.**C.; ENG. 47–; P. 51–; UL.; **Co.**T. 40–; **Cr.**U. 32–; **Db.** 23– imp.; **Dn.**U.; **E.**HW. 25–; U. 38–; **F.**A.; **G.**T. 30–37: 54–; U. 26– imp.; **H.**U. 24–; **Ld.**U.; **Lv.**P. 48–; U. 29–; **M.**C. 28– imp.; P. 36–; T.; U. 55–; **Ma.**T. 25–; **N.**T. 53–; U. 35–; **Nw.**A.; **O.**ED. 30–; R. 47–; **R.**U. 32–; **Sa.** 45–; **Sh.**SC. 49–; U. 24– imp.; **Sil.** 34– imp.; **We.**K. 24–50; **Wo.** 58–; **Y.**

6037 **Bell Telephone Magazine.** New York. *Bell Teleph. Mag.* [1941–] **L.**I. 48–; P. imp. [*C. of:* 6038]

6038 **Bell Telephone Quarterly.** New York. *Bell Teleph. Q.* [1922–40] **L.**P.; **Br.**U. 23–24; **Ma.**T. 37–40. [*C. as:* 6037]

6039 **Bell Telephone System Technical Publications.** New York. *Bell Teleph. Syst. tech. Publs* **L.**P. 27– imp.; SC. 30–; UC. 32–; **Bl.**U. 20– imp.; **C.**P. 39–; **M.**C. 29– imp.; **R.**U. 32–; **Y.** [*See also* 52299]

6040 **Belmontia.** Miscellaneous publications in botany. Wageningen. *Belmontia* [1957–]
1. Taxonomy. **L.**BM^N.; K.; **Bl.**U.
2. Ecology. **L.**BM^N.; K.; NC.; **Bl.**U.
3. Horticulture. **L.**BM^N.; K.; **Bl.**U.
4. Incidental. **L.**BM^N; K.; NC.; **Bl.**U.

6041 **Belorusskaya meditsinskaya mȳsl'** (*afterwards* **dumka**). Minsk. Белорусская медицинская мысль (*afterwards* думка). *Belorussk. med. Mȳsl' (Dumka)* [1924–29]

6042 **Belorusskaya veterinariya.** Vitebsk. Белорус-ская ветеринария. *Belorussk. Vet.* [1926–29] **L.**V. 28–29 imp.
Belra Medical Series. *See* 5652.

6043 **Belting Transmission, Tools** and **Supplies.** Chicago. *Belt. Transm. Tools Supplies* **L.**P. 20–27★; **G.**M. 21–27; **Sy.**R. 26–27. [*C. as:* 38260]

6044 **Bendix Radio Engineer.** Baltimore. *Bendix Radio Engr* [1944–]

6045 **Bengal Agricultural Journal.** Dacca. *Beng. agric. J.* [1921–26] **L.**AM.; EB.; **Abs.**U. 21; **Ld.**U. 21–23; **Nw.**A.

6046 **Bengal Forest Bulletin. Silvicultural Series.** Calcutta. *Beng. Forest Bull. silvicult. Ser.* [1936–] **O.**F.

6047 **Bengal Forest Magazine.** Calcutta. *Beng. Forest Mag.* [1936–38] **O.**F.

6047° **Bengal Immunity Research Institute Pamphlets.** Calcutta. *Beng. Immun. Res. Inst. Pamph.* **Y.**

6048 **Bengal Public Health Bulletin.** Calcutta. *Beng. publ. Hlth Bull.* [1940–] **L.**TD. imp.

6049 **Bengal Public Health Journal.** Calcutta. *Beng. publ. Hlth J.* [1939–] **L.**TD. imp.

6050 **Bengal Public Health Report.** Calcutta. *Beng. publ. Hlth Rep.* [1922–] **E.**U.; **Lv.**U.; **O.**I.

6050ᵃ **Bengal Tanning Institute Publications.** *Beng. Tanng Inst. Publs* **L.**LE. 21–41.

6051 **Benjamin Ward Richardson Memorial Lecture.** London Model Abattoir Society. London. *Benjamin Ward Richardson mem. Lect.* [1922–34] **L.**P.

6052 **Bennis Bulletin.** Bennis Combustion Ltd. Manchester. *Bennis Bull.* [1955–] **L.**BM.; P.

6052° **Bentonitovȳe glinȳ Ukrainȳ.** Sovet po izucheniyu proizvoditel'nȳkh sil USSR. Akademiya nauk Ukrain-skoï SSR. Бентонитовые глины Украины. Совет по изучению производительных сил УССР. Академия наук Украинской ССР. *Bentonit. Glinȳ Ukr.* **Y.** 59.

6053 **Beobachtete chromosphärische Eruptionen.** Freiburg. *Beobachtete chromosph. Erupt., Freiburg* **L.**MO. 50–51.
Beobachtungen der K. **Universitäts-Sternwarte** zu **Jurjew** (Dorpat). *See* 41335.

6054 **Beobachtungen** an der K.K. **Zentralanstalt** für **Meteorologie** u. **Erdmagnetismus.** Wien. *Beob. K.K. ZentAnst. Met. Erdmagn.* **L.**MO. 67–04★; **E.**M. 79–00. [*C. as:* 33079]

6055 **Beobachtungen** aus dem **Magnetischen Observatorium** der K. **Marine** in **Wilhelmshaven.** *Beob. magn. Obs. K. Mar. Wilhelmsh.* **L.**UC. 02–11. [*C. as:* 56188]

6055° **Beobachtungen** des **Meteorologischen Observatoriums, Bremen.** *Beob. met. Obs. Bremen* **L.**MO. 21–24.
Beobachtungen angestellt im **Meteorologischen Observatorium** der K. **Universität Moskau.** *See* 33973.
Beobachtungen des **Meteorologischen Observatoriums** der **Lettländischen Universität.** *See* 28179.

6056 **Beobachtungen** des **Meteorologischen Observatoriums** der **Universität Innsbruck.** *Beob. met. Obs. Univ. Innsbruck* **L.**MO. 91–93: 98–49; **E.**M. 13–40; R. 00–07; 10–11; **O.**G. 98–31 imp.

6057 Beobachtungen der **Meteorologischen Station** der **K. Marine** zu **Wilhelmshaven.** Berlin. *Beob. met. Stn K. Mar. Wilhelmsh.* L.UC. 94–12 imp.; E.R. 80–05.
Beobachtungen der **Meteorologischen Stationen** im **Königreich Bayern.** *See* 16903.
Beobachtungen der **Observatorien** und aus dem **Bereich** der **Deutschen Seewarte.** *See* 16907.
Beobachtungen des **Tifliser physikalischen Observatoriums.** *See* 33977.

6058 Beobachtungsergebnisse der von den **forstlichen Versuchsanstalten** des **Königreichs Preussen,** etc., eingerichteten **forstlich-meteorologischen Stationen.** Berlin. *BeobErgebn. forst. VersAnst. Preuss. forstl.-met. Stnen* [1875–01] L.BM.; MO. 72–97.

6059 Beobachtungsergebnisse der **K. Sternwarte** zu **Berlin.** Berlin. *BeobErgebn. K. Sternw. Berl.* [1881–14] L.AS.; SC.; C.O.; E.O.; O.O. 09–14. [*C. in:* 56184]
Beobachtungssystem der **Deutschen Seewarte.** *See* 16907.

6060 Beobachtungszirkular der **Astronomischen Nachrichten.** Kiel. *BeobZirk. astr. Nachr.* [1919–39] L.AS.; UC.; C.O. [*C. as:* 34015]

6061 **Berajah.** Zoographia infinita. Leipzig. *Berajah* [1905–37] L.BM.[N].; Z.; O.OR. imp.

6062 Berättelse om **allmänna hälsotillståndet Stockholm.** Stockholm. *Berätt. allm. Hälsotillst. Stockh.*

6062° Berättelse. **Föreningen skogsträdförädling.** Uppsala. *Berätt. För. SkogstrFörädl.* L.P. 60–.

6063 Berättelse. **Föreningen** för **växtförädling** av **fruktträd, Balsgård.** Fjalkestad. *Berätt. För. Växtförädl. Frukttr. Balsgård* Br.A. 55–.

6064 Berättelse öfver **Göteborgs** och **Bohus Läns hafsfisken.** Göteborg. *Berätt. Göteb. Bohus Läns Hafsfisk.* [1885–12] Abd.M. [*C. as:* 21498[a]]

6065 Berättelse. **Kemiska station** och **frökontrollanstalt, Skara.** Skara. *Berätt. kem. Stn Frökontrollanst. Skara*

6066 Berättelse. **Kemiska station, Hernösand.** Hernösand. *Berätt. kem. Stn Hernösand*

6067 Berättelse över **Skogssällskapets verksamhet.** Göteborg. *Berätt. Skogssällsk. Verks., Göteborg.* O.F. 49–51*. [*C. as:* 51219]

6068 Berättelse över **Statens Provningsanstalt.** Stockholm. *Berätt. St. ProvnAnst.* L.P. 20–29.

6069 Berättelse från **Styrelsen** för **cancerföreningen** i **Stockholm.** *Berätt. Styr. Cancerför. Stockh.* L.MD. 24–; Bn.U. 29–38.

6070 Berättelse över **Svenska smorprovningarnas verksamhet.** Stockholm. *Berätt. svenska Smorprovn. Verks.* L.AM. 21–.

6071 Berättelse över **Svenska väginstitutets verksamhet.** *Berätt. svenska Väginst. Verks.*

6072 Berättelse om **verksamheten** vid **Alnarps landtbrucks-** och **mejeriinstitut.** Malmö. *Berätt. Verks. Alnarps Landtbr.- o. Mejeriinst.* Abs.U. 44–46; C.A. 32–; Rt. 99–.

6073 Berättelse över **verksamheten** vid **K. Veterinärhögskolan.** Stockholm. *Berätt. Verks. K. VetHögsk.* L.AM. 14–33; W. 20–23.

6074 Berättelse över **verksamheten** vid **kemisk-växtbiologiska anstalten** och **frökontrollanstalten** i

Lulea. *Berätt. Verks. kem.-växtbiol. Anst. Lulea* Abs.A. 33–37; C.A. 33–; Rt. 33–37.

6075 Berättelse över **verksamheten** vid **Malmöhus läns hushållningssällskaps marknadsplats** och **Veterinärbakteriologiska laboratorium.** Malmö. *Berätt. Verks. Malmöhus Läns HushållnSällsk. Markn. vet.-bakt. Lab.* W. 24.

6076 Berättelse över **verksamheten** vid **Statens veterinärbakteriologiska anstalt.** Stockholm. *Berätt. Verks. St. vet.-bakt. Anst.* L.V. 11–35; W. 28–.

6077 Berättelse över **verksamheten** vid **Veterinärhögskolan** under **Lasaret.** Trollhatten. *Berätt. Verks. VetHögsk. Lasaret*
Beregnung. *See* 24209.

6078 Beretning. **Akademiet** for de **tekniske Videnskaber.** København. *Beretn. Akad. tek. Vidensk., Kbh.* [1939–] L.P. 39–54; Y.

6079 Beretning om det **Animale vaccine institut.** Kristiania. *Beretn. anim. Vacc. Inst., Krist.*

6080 Beretning om **Bornholms landøkonomiske Forening.** Aakirkeby. *Beretn. Bornholms landøkon. Foren.* Rt. 15–.

6081 Beretning om **Botanisk haves Virksomhed.** København. *Beretn. bot. Hav. Virks.* L.BM[N]. 49–.

6082 Beretning fra **Carlsbergfondet.** København. *Beretn. Carlsbergfond.* [1940–]

6083 Beretning fra **Chr. Michelsens Institut** för **videnskap** og **åndsfrihet.** Bergen. *Beretn. Chr. Michelsens Inst. Vidensk. Åndsfrihet* [1931–] L.BM.; R. 31–39; U. 31–39; E.R.; O.B.; Pl.M. 31–39; Sa.; Y.

6084 Beretning om **Dansk Braendsels-** og **Kontrolsforenings Virksomhed.** København. *Beretn. dansk Braends.- og Kontrolsforen. Virks.* [1922–53] C.UL. 22–53. [*C. as:* 3911[a]]

6085 Beretning fra **Dansk fotografisk Forening.** Kjøbenhavn. *Beretn. dansk fotogr. Foren.* L.PG. 92–02*. [*C. as:* 16367]

6086 Beretning. **Dansk Frøkontrol.** Kjøbenhavn. *Beretn. dansk Frøkontrol*

6086° Beretning. **Dansk Standardiseringsråd.** København. *Beretn. dansk StandRåd* L.BM. 51–; Y.
Beretning fra den **Danske biologiske Station.** *See* 6102.

6087 Beretning fra **Faellesudvalget** for **prøvedyrkning** af **Køkkenurter.** København. *Beretn. Faellesudv. Prøvedyrk. Køkkenurter* Md.H. 44–50.

6087[a] Beretning om **fængselvesenet** i **Danmark.** København. *Beretn. Fængselv. Danm.* L.BM. 51–.

6088 Beretning. **Finsens medicinske Lysinstitut.** Kjøbenhavn. *Beretn. Finsens med. Lysinst.* L.BM. 20.

6089 Beretning om **folkemaengden** og **sundhedstilstanden.** Kristiania (Oslo). *Beretn. Folkemaengd. SunhStilst.* L.H. 82–23 imp.

6090 Beretning fra **Forsøgslaboratoriet.** København. *Beretn. Forsøgslab.* [1915–] L.BM.; Abd.R. 17: 21–; C.A.; E.AB. 21– imp.; Y. [*C. of:* 6095]

6091 Beretning om **Godningsforsögene.** Sjaelland. *Beretn. GodnForsög.* Rt. 14–23.

6092 Beretning vedrørende **Grønland.** København. *Beretn. Grønl.* [1950–] C.PO.; Y. 55–.

6093 **Beretning. K. Selskab** for **Norges vel.** (Kristiania) Oslo. *Beretn. K. Selsk. Norg. Vel* **Abs.**A. 28–.

6094 **Beretning** fra den **K. Veterinær-** og **Landbohøjskole.** Kjøbenhavn. *Beretn. K. Vet.- og Landbohøjsk.* **L.**V. 21–; **Abs.**A. 20–46 imp.

6095 **Beretning** fra den **K. Veterinær-** og **Landbohøjskoles Laboratorium** for **landøkonomiske Forsøg.** Kjøbenhavn. *Beretn. K. Vet.- og Landbohøjsk. Lab. landøkon. Forsøg* **L.**AM. 88–14* imp.; BM. 93–14; **C.**A. 89–14 imp.; **Rt.** 83–14. [*C. as:* 6090]

6096 **Beretning** om **Landboforeningernes Virksomhed** for **Planteavlen** paa **Sjælland.** *Beretn. Landboforen. Virks. PlAvl. Sjælland* **L.**AM. 19– imp.; **C.**A. 32–; **Db.** 06– imp.; **Rt.** 07–.

6097 **Beretning** om **Landbrugsraadets Virksomhed.** Kjøbenhavn. *Beretn. LandbrRaad. Virks.* [1919–] **L.**AM. imp.; **Y.**

6098 **Beretning** fra **Landsforeningen** til **Bekaempelse** af **Børnelammelse** og dens **Folger.** Kjøbenhavn. *Beretn. Landsforen. Bekaemp. Børnelamm.* **L.**H. 48–.

6099 **Beretning. Landsforeningen** mod **Børnelammelse—Polio.** Hellerup. *Beretn. Landsforen. Børnelamm.* [1952–] **L.**MD.; **Y.**

6100 **Beretning** fra **Landsforeningen** til **Kræftens Bekæmpse.** Kjøbenhavn. *Beretn. Landsforen. Kræft. Bekæmp.* **L.**MD. 32–.

6101 **Beretning** om **lokale Markforsøk.** Odense. *Beretn. lok. Markforsøk* **Rt.** 03–17*. [*C. as:* 6110]

6102 **Beretning** til **Ministeriet** for **Landbrug** og **Fiskeri** fra den **Danske biologiske Station.** *Beretn. Minist. Landbr. Fisk. dan. biol. Stn* **L.**BM. 46–.

Beretning om de **Lolland-Falster Landboforeningers virksomhed** for **Planteavlen.** *See* 6108.

6103 **Beretning** om **Nordiske jordbrugsforskeres forenings Kongres.** *Beretn. nord. JordbrForsk. Foren. Kongr.* **C.**A. 35–. [*Contained in:* 34958]

6104 **Beretning** om **Norges geografiske opmålings virksomhet.** Oslo. *Beretn. Norg. geogr. Opmål. Virks.* **Y.**

6104[c] **Beretning** om **Norges landbrukshøgskoles føringsforsøkene.** *Beretn. Norg. LandbrHøgsk. Føringsfors.* **Y.**

6105 **Beretning** om **Norges sjøkartverks virksomhet.** Oslo. *Beretn. Norg. Sjøkartvks Virks.* [1953–] **C.**PO.

6106 **Beretning** om det **Norske myrselskaps forsøksstation.** Oslo. *Beretn. norske Myrselsk. Forsøksstn* [1908–22] **L.**SC. 11–22 imp. [*C. as:* 30644]

Beretning om det **norske skogsvæsen.** *See* 22865.

6107 **Beretning** fra **Oslo helseråd.** Oslo. *Beretn. Oslo Helseråd* **L.**H. 25– imp.; **Y.**

6108 **Beretning** om **Planteavlen** paa **Lolland-Falster.** Nykøbing. *Beretn. PlAvl. Lolland-Falster* **C.**A. 38–46*; **Rt.** 12–46. [*C. as:* 37883]

6109 **Beretning** om **Planteavlen** i de **samvirkende Lolland-Falsterske Landboforeninger.** Nykøbing. *Beretn. PlAvl. samv. Lolland-Falster. Landboforen.* [1954–] **C.**A.; **Rt.** [*C. of:* 37882]

6110 **Beretning** om **Planteavlsarbejdet** i **Landboforeningerne** paa **Fyn.** Odense. *Beretn. PlAvlsarb. Landboforen. Fyn* [1919–] **Rt.** [*C. of:* 6101]

6111 **Beretning** om **Planteavlsarbejdet** i **Landboforeningerne** i **Jylland.** *Beretn. PlAvlsarb. Landboforen. Jyll.* **C.**A. 48–.

6112 **Beretning** om **Planteavlsarbejdet** i de **samvirkende jydske Husmandsforeninger.** Aarhus, Kjøbenhavn. *Beretn. PlAvlsarb. samv. jydske Husm.Foren.* [1918–46] **Rt.** 18–31: 45–46. [*C. of:* 6116; *C. as:* 37884]

6113 **Beretning** og **regnskap. Selskabet** for de **norske fiskeriers fremme.** *Beretn. Regnsk. Selsk. norske Fisk. Frem.* [1951–57] **L.**BM[N].; **Pl.**M. [*C. of:* 4889; *C. as:* 4888]

6114 **Beretning** og **regnskap. Skogbrukets** og **skogindustrienes forskningsforening.** Oslo. *Beretn. Regnsk. Skogbr. Skogind. ForskForen.* **O.**F. 51–.

6115 **Beretning** fra de **samvirkende danske Landboforeningers plantepatologiske Forsøgsvirksomhed.** Kjøbenhavn. *Beretn. samv. danske Landboforen. plpatol. Forsøgsvirks.* **L.**EB. (ent.) 08–13; **Rt.** 09–12 imp.

6116 **Beretning** om die **samvirkende jydske Husmandsforeningers Planteavlsarbejder.** Aarhus. *Beretn. samv. jydske HusmForen. PlAvlsarb.* **Rt.** 16–17*. [*C. as:* 6112]

6117 **Beretning** om **skadeinsekter** og **plantesykdommer** i **land-** og **havebruket.** Kristiania. *Beretn. Skadeinsekt. PlSykd.* **L.**EB. 11–33.

Beretning om den **Skandinaviske Matematikerkongress.** *See* 15193.

6118 **Beretning** om det **Skandinaviske Naturforskermøde.** Kjøbenhavn. *Beretn. skand. NatForskMøde* **M.**U. 29.

6119 **Beretning** fra **Statens Forsøksgård** på **Moistad.** *Beretn. St. Forsøksgård. Moistad* **C.**A. 29–.

6120 **Beretning** fra **Statens Forsøksmejeri.** Kjøbenhavn. *Beretn. St. Forsøksmejeri* [1925–] **L.**AM. 25–39; P. 51–; **C.**A.; **R.**D.; **Y.**

6121 **Beretning** fra **Statens forsøksvirksomhed** i **plantekultur.** Kristiania, Lyngby. *Beretn. St. Forsøksvirks. PlKult.* **L.**EB. (ent. 13–; MY. 18–44; **Rt.** 08–19.

6122 **Beretning** fra **Statens Planteavlsudvalg.** Kjøbenhavn. *Beretn. St. PlAvlsudv.* **L.**AM. 09–39: 45–; SC. 25–; **Br.**A. 54–55 imp.; U. 28–; **C.**A. 08–; **Db.** 04–; **Rt.** 09–; **Y.**

6123 **Beretning. Statens Redskabsprøven.** Kjøbenhavn. *Beretn. St. RedskPrøv.* **L.**P. 14–55*; **C.**A. 30–55; **Rt.** 14–55. [*See also:* 50782; *C. as:* 29949]

6124 **Beretning** om **sundhetstilstanden** og **medicinalforholdene.** Oslo. *Beretn. SundhStilst. MedForh.* **L.**MD. 1853–20.

6124[a] **Beretning** fra **Tjæreforskningsudvalget.** København. *Beretn. TjæreforskUdv.* [1949–] **L.**P. 51–.

6125 **Beretning** om **veterinærvæsenet** i **Norge.** Oslo *Beretn. VetVæs. Norge* **L.**AM. 90–.

6126 **Bergakademie.** Bergakademie Freiburg. Berlin. *Bergakademie* [1948–] **L.**MI. 56–; P.; **Y.**

6127 **Bergbau.** Gelsenkirchen. *Bergbau, Gelsenkirchen* [1888–] **L.**P. 14–; **Sh.**S. 39–42: 50–; **Y.**

6128 **Bergbau.** Hagen. *Bergbau, Hagen* [1950–] **L.**MI. 51–56; MIE. 57–.

6129 **Bergbau** und **Energiewirtschaft.** Berlin. *Bergb. Energiew.* [1948–51] **L.**P. [*C. in:* 6133 and 18049]

6130 **Bergbau** und **Hütte.** Wien. *Bergb. Hütte* **C.**A. 31–33.

6131 **Bergbau-Archiv.** Essen. *Bergb.-Arch.* L.MIE. 47–; P. 47– imp.; SC.; **Ld.**U. 48–; **Sh.**S. 55–; **Y.**

6132 **Bergbau-Rundschau.** Bochum. *Bergb.-Rdsch.* [1949–61] L.MI.; MIE. 55–61; P. 57–61; **Sh.**S. 51–61.

6133 **Bergbautechnik.** Berlin. *Bergbautechnik* [1951–] L.MI. 54–55; MIE. 56–; P.; **Sh.**S. 55–; **Y.** [*C. from:* 6129]

6134 **Bergbauwissenschaften.** Goslar. *Bergbauwissenschaften* [1954–] L.MI.; P.; **Sh.**S. 55–; **Y.**

6135 **Bergbauzeitung.** Wien. *Bergbauzeitung* [1950] L.MI.; P. [*C. of:* 6136; *C. as:* 33375]

6136 **Bergbau-, Bohrtechniker- und Erdölzeitung.** Wien. *Bergb.-, Bohrtech.- u. Erdölztg* [1949–50] L.MI.; P. [*C. of:* 7273; *C. as:* 6135]

6137 **Bergcultures.** Djakarta. *Bergcultures* [1926–57] L.MY. 29–57 imp.; TP. 35–57 imp.; **C.**A. 31–57; **Md.**H.; **Rt.** 26–42: 52; **Sy.**R. 39–40 imp.: 48–57. [*C. as:* 31333]

6138 **Berge** der **Welt.** Schweizerische Stiftung für alpine Forschungen. *Berge Welt* [1946–] L.SC. 46–52.

6139 **Bergens museums årbog.** Afhandlinger og aarsberetning. Bergen. *Bergens Mus. Årb.* [1886–47] L.AM. 10–28; AN. 16–47; BM.; BM^N.; G. 10–47; GL.; L.; MO. 41–47; R.; SC. 00–47; Z. 92–47; **Abd.**M. 92–47; **Bl.**U. 88–47; **Bn.**U. 03–47; **C.**B.; E. 01–47; P.; **Cr.**M. 92–47; **Db.** 00–47; **Dm.** 15–47; **Dn.**U. 93–16 imp.; **E.**C. 89–47; G.; J.; R.; U. 86–25; V.; **G.**N.; U. 31–47; **Lo.** 92–47 imp.; **Lv.**U.; **M.**U.; **Mi.**; **O.**G. 41–42; R.; **Pl.**M. 92–47; **Rt.** 44–47; **Sa.** 86–30; **Wo.** 03–47 imp. [*C. as:* 55569]

6140 **Bergens museums årsberetning.** Bergen. *Bergens Mus. Årsberetn.* [1886–48] L.AN. 17–48; BM.; GL.; L. 15–48; MO. 40–48; SC. 00–48; Z. imp.; **Abd.**M. 05–48; **Bn.**U. 47–48; **C.**B.; PO. 32–48; **Dm.** 15–40; **G.**U. 30–47; **Lo.** 86–91; **Lv.**U. imp.; **M.**U.; **Pl.**M.; **Rt.** 44–48; **Sa.** 10–30 imp. [*C. as:* 55570]

6141 **Bergens museums skrifter.** Bergen. *Bergens Mus. Skr.* [1878–43] L.A. 09–25: 31–43; BM^N.; L.; R. 09–25: 31–43; Z. (zool.); **Abd.**M. 78–36 imp.; **Bl.**U. 09–25; **C.**E. 89–43; **Dm.** 15–43; **E.**C. 12–43 imp.; P. imp.; R. 09–43; U. 09–25; **G.**N. 09–17; **Lv.**U.; **M.**U. 09–43; **Pl.**M. 09–43 imp. [*C. as:* 55572]

6142 **Bergens sjøfartsmuseums årshefte.** Bergen. *Bergens Sjøfartsmus. Årsh.* [1928–] L.SC.

6143 **Bergfreiheit.** Essen. *Bergfreiheit* L.P. 58–; **Sh.**S. 56–; **Y.**

6144 **Bergknappe.** Essen-Ruhr. *Bergknappe*

6145 **Berg- und hüttenmännische Monatshefte.** Wien. *Berg- u. hüttenm. Mh.* [1938–] L.BM.; C. imp.; GL.; I.; MI. 47–; NF. 49–; P. imp.; **Sh.**S. 55–; **Y.** [*C. of:* 6148: *Suspended* 1944–46]

6146 **Berg- und hüttenmännische Rundschau.** Kattowitz. *Berg- u. hüttenm. Rdsch.* [1904–21] L.P.

6147 **Berg- und hüttenmännische Zeitung.** Leipzig. *Berg- u. hüttenm. Ztg* [1842–04] L.BM. 91–04; BM^N. imp.; I. 62–04; MI. 79–83; P.; SC. [*C. in:* 21407]

6148 **Berg- und hüttenmännisches Jahrbuch** der **K.K. Montanistischen Hochschulen** zu **Leoben** und **Příbram.** Wien. *Berg- u. hüttenm. Jb.* [1851–37] L.BM. 95–37; C. 23–37; GL. 00–37; I. 73–37 imp.; P. 10–37; SC. [*C. as:* 6145]

6149 **Berg-** und **Hüttenmann.** Dresden. *Berg- u. Hüttenm.*

6150 **Bergmann-Mitteilungen.** Berlin. *Bergmann-Mitt.* L.P. [1923–30].

6151 **Berg-Technik.** Halle. *Berg-Tech.* [1927–29] [*C. of:* 8684; *C. in:* 23964]

6152 **Bergverksnyt.** Kristiania. *Bergverksnyt*

6153 **Bergwerk** und **Hütte.** Berlin. *Bergwk Hütte* [1931–32] L.P. [*C. of:* and *Rec. as:* 27201]

6154 **Bergwerke** und **Salinen** im **niederrheinisch-westfälischen Bergbaubezirk.** Essen. *Bergwke Salin. niederrhein. BergbBez.*

Bergwerkszeitung. Charkow. *See* 21479.

6155 **Bergwirtschaftliche Mitteilungen.** Berlin. *Bergwirtsch. Mitt.* [1910–15] L.GL. 10–14; GM.; P.; **E.**D. 13–15; **O.**R. [*C. in:* 58785]

6156 **Bericht** und **Abhandlungen** des **Klubs** für **Naturkunde.** Brünn. *Ber. Abh. Klubs Naturk., Brünn* L.BM^N. 96–06*. *C. as:* 6277]

6157 **Bericht** und **Abhandlungen** der **Wissenschaftlichen Gesellschaft** für **Luftfahrt.** München. *Ber. Abh. wiss. Ges. Luftfahrt* [1920–26] L.P.; SC. 23. [*Supplement to:* 58595]

6158 **Bericht. Abwassertechnische Vereinigung.** München. *Ber. abwassertech. Verein.* [1949–] L.P.

6159 **Bericht** der **Aeromechanischen Versuchsanstalt** in **Wien.** *Ber. aeromech. VersAnst., Wien* [1928] L.P.

6160 **Bericht** van de **Afdeeling Handelsmuseum** van de **K. Vereeniging Indisch instituut.** Amsterdam. *Ber. Afd. Handelsmus. K. Vereen. indisch Inst.* [1945–47] L.BM^N.; EB. (ent.); K.; SC.; **M.**C. (selected issues); **Rt.**; **Y.** [*C. of:* 6161; *C. as:* 6162]

6161 **Bericht** van de **Afdeeling Handelsmuseum** van het **Koloniaal instituut** te **Amsterdam.** *Ber. Afd. Handelsmus. kolon. Inst. Amst.* [1920–44] L.BM^N.; EB. (ent.) 22–44; K.; SC.; **M.**C. (selected issues); **Rt.** [*C. as:* 6160]

6162 **Bericht** van de **Afdeling tropische producten** van de **K. Instituut** voor de **tropen.** Amsterdam. *Ber. Afd. trop. Prod. K. Inst. Trop.* [1948–] L.BM^N.; EB.; K.; **M.**C. (selected issues); **Rt.**; **Y.** [*C. of:* 6160]

Bericht der **Akademiker Borodin biologischen Süsswasser-Station.** Leningrad. *See* 54984.

6163 **Bericht** van het **Algemeen proefstation** der **A.V.R.O.S.** Medan. *Ber. alg. Proefstn A.V.R.O.S.* [1956–57] **Md.**H. [*C. as:* 11603]

6164 **Bericht** über die **allgemeine** und **spezielle Pathologie.** Berlin. *Ber. allg. spez. Path.* [1948–] L.MD.; U. 50–; **C.**APH. 51–53; **Y.**

6165 **Bericht** des **Allgemeinen ärztlichen Kongresses** für **Psychotherapie.** Leipzig. *Ber. allg. ärztl. Kongr. Psychother.*

6166 **Bericht** über den **Annaberg-Buchholzer Verein** für **Naturkunde.** Annaberg. *Ber. Annaberg-Buchholzer Ver. Naturk.* L.BM^N. 85–30.

6167 **Bericht** über die **Arbeiten** der **K. Bayerischen Moorkulturanstalt.** München. *Ber. Arb. K. bayer. MoorkultAnst.* [*C. as:* 28115]

6168 **Bericht** über die **Arbeiten** der **Versuchs-** und **Lehranstalt** für **Brauerei** in **Berlin.** *Ber. Arb. Vers.- u Lehranst. Brau. Berl.* L.P. 53–; **Nu.**B. 46–54.

Bericht abgegeben von dem **Arbeitsausschuss** zur **Untersuchung** des **Wassers** und des **Planktons** der **finnischen Binnengewässer.** *See* 42390.

6169 Bericht. Arbeitsgemeinschaft Ferromagnetismus. Stuttgart. *Ber. ArbGemeinsch. Ferromagn.* [1958–] **L.**P.; SC. 59–; **Y.**

6170 Bericht. Arbeitsgruppe Teerstrassen. Forschungsgesellschaft für das **Strassenwesen e. V.** Berlin-Charlottenburg. *Ber. ArbGruppe Teerstr. ForschGes. StrWes.* **L.**P. 35–.

6170° Bericht über die **Arbeitstagung** der **Arbeitsgemeinschaft** der **Saatzuchtleiter.** Gumpenstein. *Ber. ArbTag. ArbGemeinsch. Saatzuchtleiter* **Hu.**G. 53–.

6171 Bericht des **Astrophysikalischen Instituts Königsstuhl-Heidelberg.** *Ber. astrophys. Inst. Königsstuhl Heidelb.* **C.**O. 99–.

6172 Bericht des **Astrophysikalischen Observatoriums Nizbor.** Praha. *Ber. astrophys. Obs. Nizbor* [1909–12]

6172° Bericht zur **Atomkernenergie.** Frankfurt a. M. *Ber. Atomkernenerg.* **L.**P. 59–.

6173 Bericht über den **Aufbau** und die **Tätigkeit** der **Physikalisch-technischen Anstalt.** Braunschweig. *Ber. Aufb. Tät. phys-tech. Anst., Braunschw.*

6174 Bericht des **Ausschusses** für **Versuche** im **Eisenbau.** Berlin. *Ber. Aussch. Vers. Eisenb., Berl.* **L.**P.(A) 15–21.

6175 Bericht des **Ausschusses** für **Versuche** im **Stahlbau.** Berlin. *Ber. Aussch. Vers. Stahlb., Berl.* **L.**P.(B) 30–35*. [*C. as:* 6189]

6176 Bericht der **Bayerischen botanischen Gesellschaft** zur **Erforschung** der **heimischen Flora.** München. *Ber. bayer. bot. Ges.* [1891–] **L.**BMᴺ. imp.; **K.** 91–38 imp.; **L.** 91–14; **Bl.**U. 34– imp.; **E.**B. 91–14; **G.**N. 54–.

6177 Bericht des **Bayerischen Gewerbemuseums** in **Nürnberg.** *Ber. bayer. GewMus.* [*C. of:* 24888]

6178 Bericht der **Beteiligung Deutschlands** an der **internationalen Meeresforschung.** Berlin. *Ber. Beteil. Dtl. int. Meeresforsch.* [1902–08] **L.**AM.; MO.; SC. 05–08; **C.**UL.; **Lo.**; **Lv.**U.; **Pl.**M. 05–08. [*C. as:* 6206]

Bericht der **Biologischen Borodin Station.** Leningrad. *See* 54984.

6179 Bericht über den **Botanischen Garten** und das **Botanische Institut** in **Bern.** *Ber. bot. Garten Bern* **L.**BMᴺ. 44–; **O.**B. 17–; BO. 53–.

6180 Bericht des **Botanischen Vereins** in **Landshut.** Landshut. *Ber. bot. Ver. Landshut* **L.**BMᴺ. 66–00*; **L.** 74–00. [*C. as:* 6306]

6181 Bericht der **Bundesanstalt** für **Pflanzenbau** und **Samenprüfung** in **Wien.** *Ber. Bundesanst. PflBau Wien* [*C. as:* 24898]

6182 Bericht der **Bundesanstalt** für **Pflanzenschutz** in **Wien.** *Ber. Bundesanst. PflSchutz Wien* **L.**EB. 21–26; MY. 23–26.

6183 Bericht der **Čechoslovakischen Normalisierungsgesellschaft.** Prag. *Ber. čsl. NormGes.* **L.**P. 26–37.

6184 Bericht der **Chemischen Gesellschaft** zu **Frankfurt a. M.** *Ber. chem. Ges. Frankfurt*

6185 Bericht des **Chemischen Staatslaboratoriums** in **Hamburg.** Hamburg. *Ber. chem. StLab. Hamburg* **L.**BM. 84–.

6186 Bericht des **Chemischen Untersuchungsamts** für die **Provinz Rheinhessen.** *Ber. chem. UntersAmts Prov. Rheinhessen*

6187 Bericht des **Chemischen Untersuchungsamts** der **Stadt Breslau.** Berlin. *Ber. chem. UntersAmts Stadt Breslau*

6188 Bericht über **Dampfkesselrevisionen** im **Bezirk** der **K. Bergwerksdirektion** zu **Saarbrücken.** *Ber. DampfkRevis. Bez. K. Bergwksdir. Saarbrücken*

6189 Bericht des **Deutschen Ausschusses** für **Stahlbau.** Berlin. *Ber. dt. Aussch. Stahlb.* **L.**P. (*a*) 37–43 imp.; SC (*b*) 35–43. [*C. of:* 6175]

6190 Bericht des **Deutschen Beton-Vereins.** Berlin, etc. *Ber. dt. Betonver.* **L.**P. 10–37 imp. [*C. as:* 56960]

6191 Bericht der **Deutschen botanischen Gesellschaft.** Berlin. *Ber. dt. bot. Ges.* [1883–] **L.**BM. 83–20; BMᴺ. 83–42; HS. 28–40; **K.**; **L.** 83–43; PH. 83–14; **R.** 83–16; SC.; UC. 84–24 imp.; **Abd.**U. 83–10; **Abs.**U. 83–20 imp.; **Bl.**U. 61–; **Bm.**U.; **Bn.**U.; **Br.**U.; **C.**BO.; UL.; **Cr.**U. 83–30 imp.; **Db.**; **E.**B. imp.; **Ex.**U. 29–39: 44–; **G.**U.; **Ld.**U.; **Lv.**U. 09– imp.; **M.**U. 87–; **N.**U.; **Nw.**A.; **O.**BO.; **Pl.**M. 07–; **R.**U. 05–; **Rt.** 90–; **Sa.** 57–; **Sh.**U.; **Y.**

6192 Berichte der **Deutschen chemischen Gesellschaft.** Berlin. *Ber. dt. chem. Ges.* [1868–44] **L.**AV.; B. imp.; BM. 68–41; BMᴺ.; C.; CB. 81–44; IC. 68–41; LE. 19–39; LI. 68–39: 41–44; MC. 79–43; NF.; P. imp.; PH. 73–43 imp.; RI. 68–39; SC. imp.; TD. 94–44; TP. 39–44; U.; UC. 71–39; **Abd.**U.; **Abs.**N. 01–06 imp. U.; **Bl.**U. imp.; **Bm.**P. 98–13: 26–44; U.; **Bn.**U. imp.; **Br.**A. 86–09; U.; **C.**BI. 68–40; CH.; P.; UL.; **Cr.**U. 68–39; **Db.**; **Dn.**U.; **E.**HW. 78–13: 15–17: 32–38; U. 68–39 imp.; **Ep.**D. 84–44; **Ex.**U. 78–03: 25–44; **F.**A. 41–43; **G.**T.; U.; **H.**U. 82–19: 29–39; **Je.** 00–44; **Ld.**U.; **Lv.**P. 83–17; U.; **M.**C.; P. 28–39; T.; U. imp.; **N.**U. 75–44; **Nw.**A. imp.; **O.**BS. 68–15; R.; **R.**U. 84–44; **Rt.**; **Sa.**; **Sh.**U.; **Ste.** 68–28; **Sw.**U.; **Wd.** 84–43. [*Suspended* 1945–46; *C. as:* 13806]

Bericht der **Deutschen Forschungsanstalt** für **Luftfahrt.** *See* 16253.

6193 Bericht der **Deutschen Gesellschaft** für **Zahn-, Mund-** und **Kieferheilkunde.** München. *Ber. dt. Ges. Zahn- Mund- u. Kieferheilk.* **L.**D. 34: 37.

6194 Bericht des **Deutschen Hopfenbau-Vereins.** Nürnberg. *Ber. dt. HopfenbVer.* [*C. as:* 32356]

6195 Bericht der **Deutschen keramischen Gesellschaft** (und des **Vereins deutscher Emailfachleute e.V.**). Berlin. *Ber. dt. keram. Ges.* [1920–] **L.**C. 49–; P. imp.; SC. 20–40: 50–; **Ld.**U. 58–; **M.**U. 27–43 imp.; **Sh.**IO. 49–; **St.**R. 26–44: 50–; **Y.** [> 32901 *for the first five issues of* 1949]

6196 Bericht zur **deutschen Landeskunde.** Remagen, Stuttgart. *Ber. dt. Landesk.* **L.**G. 49–; **Ld.**U. 50–.

Bericht der **Deutschen ophthalmologischen Gesellschaft.** *See* 6414.

6197 Bericht der **Deutschen pharmazeutischen Gesellschaft.** Berlin. *Ber. dt. pharm. Ges.* [1891–23] **L.**C. 07–23; P. 14–23; PH.; **C.**UL. [*C. in:* 4145]

6198 Bericht der **Deutschen physikalischen Gesellschaft.** Braunschweig. *Ber. dt. phys. Ges.* [1903–19] **L.**B.; BM.; C. 07–19; P.; RI.; SC.; UC.; **Abd.**U.; **Bl.**U. 03–15; **Bm.**P. 03–11; U.; **Br.**U.; **C.**UL.; **Db.**; **E.**R.; U.; **G.**U.; **Ld.**U.; **M.**U.; **O.**R.; **Sa.**; **Sh.**U. [*Replaced by:* 58769]

6199 Bericht der **Deutschen Studiengemeinschaft Hubschrauber.** Stuttgart. *Ber. dt. StudGemeinsch. Hubschrauber* **L.**P. 56–.

6200 Bericht des **Deutschen Verbandes** für **Materialforschung.** *Ber. dt. Verb. MaterForsch.* [1955–] [*Published in:* 20122]

6201 **Bericht** des **Deutschen Vereins** für **Volkshygiene.** Berlin. *Ber. dt. Ver. Volkshyg.*

6202 **Bericht** der **Deutschen Versuchsanstalt** für **Luftfahrt.** Köln. *Ber. dt. VersAnst. Luftf.* [1955–] **L.**P.; SC.

6203 **Bericht** des **Deutschen Wetterdienstes.** Bad Kissingen. *Ber. dt. Wetterd., Bad Kissingen* [1953–] **L.**MO.; **E.**R.; **Md.**H.; **Rt.**; **Y.** [*C. of:* 6205]

6204 **Bericht** des **Deutschen Wetterdienstes.** Offenbach. *Ber. dt. Wetterd., Offenbach* **L.**MO. 57–.

6205 **Bericht** des **Deutschen Wetterdienstes** in der **U.S. Zone.** Bad Kissingen. *Ber. dt. Wetterd. U.S. Zone* [1947–52] **L.**MO.; SC.; **E.**R.; **Md.**H. [*C. as:* 6203]

6206 **Bericht** der **Deutschen wissenschaftlichen Kommission** für **Meeresforschung.** Berlin, etc. *Ber. dt. wiss. Kommn Meeresforsch.* [1919–] **L.**AM. 25– imp.; BM^N.; P. 27–; SC. 39–; **Abd.**M. 25–; **Bn.**U. 55–; **Dm.** 25–38; Lo. 25–; **Lv.**U.; **Mi.** 50–; **Pl.**M. imp.; **Wo.** 50–; **Y.** [*C. of:* 6178]

Bericht über **deutsch-koloniale Baumwollunternehmungen.** *See* 56044.

Bericht E.M.P.A. *See* 6208 *and* 6208°.

6207 **Bericht** des **Eidgenössischen Flugzeugwerks Emmen.** *Ber. eidg. Flugzwks Emmen*

6208 **Bericht** der **Eidgenössischen Materialprüfungsanstalt.** Zürich. *Ber. eidg. MaterPrüfAnst.* **L.**SC. 25–27*. [*C. as* 6208°]

6208° **Bericht** der **Eidgenössischen Materialprüfungs- und Versuchsanstalt** für **Industrie Bauwesen** und **Gewerbe.** Zurich. *Ber. eidg. MaterPrüf.- u VersAnst. Ind. Bauw. Gew.* **L.**P. 48–; **M.**C. (selected issues); **Y.** [*C. of:* 6208]

Bericht des **Entomologischen Bureau** zu **Stavropol** am **Kaukasus.** *See* 36534.

6209 **Bericht** des **Entomologischen Kränzchens** zu **Königsberg i. Pr.** *Ber. ent. Kränzch. Königsberg* **L.**BM^N. 08–28.

6210 **Bericht** über die **Ergebnisse** der **Beobachtungen** an den **Regenstationen** der **K. Livländischen gemeinnützigen** und **ökonomischen Sozietät.** Jurjew (Dorpat). *Ber. Ergebn. Beob. Regenstnen, Dorpat* **L.**MO. 85–05: 13; **E.**R. 87–91.

6211 **Bericht** über die **Ergebnisse** der **Deutschen landwirtschaftlichen Pflanzenschutzforschung.** Bonn. *Ber. Ergebn. dt. landw. PflSchutzforsch.* [*C. as:* 20122]

6212 **Bericht** über die **Ergebnisse** der **Forstverwaltung** im **Reglerungs Bezirk Frankfurt a. O.** Frankfurt a. O. *Ber. Ergebn. Forstverw. Frankf. a. O.* [*C. of:* 46061]

6213 **Bericht. Europäischer Kongress** der **Mineral-** und **Tafelwasser-Industrie.** *Ber. eur. Kongr. Mineral- u. Tafelwass.-Ind.* 2. Luzern. 1954. **L.**P.

6214 **Bericht** des **Fachausschusses** für **Anstrichtechnik.** Verein Deutscher Ingenieure. Berlin. *Ber. Fachaussch. Anstrichtech. V.D.I.* [1929–] **L.**P. 29–34.

6215 **Bericht** der **Fachgruppe Staubtechnik.** Verein deutscher Ingenieure. Düsseldorf. *Ber. Fachgr. Staubtech. V.D.I.* **L.**P. 55–.

6216 **Bericht** aus **Forschung** und **Hochschulleben. Technische Hochschule Carolo-Wilhelmina** zu **Braunschweig.** Braunschweig. *Ber. Forsch. HochschLeben tech. Hochsch. Braunschw.* [1952–] **L.**BM^N. 52–54; P.; **Y.**

6217 **Bericht** der **Forschungsanstalt** für **Landwirtschaft.** Braunschweig-Völkenrode. *Ber. ForschAnst. Landw., Braunschw.* **C.**A. 50–.

6218 **Bericht** des **Forschungsinstituts** für **Bastfasern** in **Sorau N.L.** *Ber. ForschInst. Bastfas. Sorau*

6219 **Bericht** des **Forschungsinstituts** der **čechoslovakischen Zuckerindustrie.** Prag. *Ber. ForschInst čsl. ZuckInd.* [1924–42] **L.**MY. 27–39; P. 24–27; **C.**A. 26–42. [*C. of:* 6427]

6220 **Bericht** des **Forschungsinstituts** für **Osten** und **Orient.** Wien. *Ber. ForschInst. Ost. Orient* **L.**BM. 17–.

6221 **Bericht** über die **Fortschritte** der **Eisenbahntechnik.** Leipzig. *Ber. Fortschr. EisenbTech.* [1867–02] **L.**P.

6222 **Bericht** über die **Fortschritte** der **Geologie.** Leipzig. *Ber. Fortschr. Geol.*

6223 **Bericht. Frankfurter Verein** zur **Bekämpfung** der **Schwindsuchtsgefahr.** Frankfurt a. M. *Ber. frankf. Ver. Bekämpf. SchwindsGef.*

6224 **Bericht** der **Freiberger geologischen Gesellschaft.** Freiberg. *Ber. freiberg. geol. Ges.* [1915–] **L.**BM^N. 21–44 imp.; GM. [*C. of:* 24951]

6225 **Bericht** über das **Geobotanische Forschungsinstitut Rübel** in **Zürich.** *Ber. geobot. ForschInst. Rübel* **L.**NC. 56–; SC. 18–; **Db.** 18–; **Hu.**G. 31–; **Rt.** 35–.

6226 **Bericht** der **Geologischen Gesellschaft** in der **Deutschen Demokratischen Republik.** Berlin. *Ber. geol. Ges. D.D.R.* [1955–] **L.**BM^N.; GM.; **Y.**

6227 **Bericht** der **Geologischen Kommission** der **Königreiche Kroatien-Slavonien.** Agram. *Ber. geol. Kommn Königr. Kroat.-Slav.*

6228 **Bericht** der **Geologischen Kommission, Schweizerische naturforschende Gesellschaft.** Bern. *Ber. geol. Kommn schweiz. naturf. Ges.* **L.**G. 29–30; GL. 28–.

Bericht über die **gesamte Biologie.** Abt. A. *See* 6440. Abt. B. *See* 6230.

6229 **Bericht** über die **gesamte Gynäkologie** und **Geburtshilfe.** Berlin. *Ber. ges. Gynäk. Geburtsh.* [1923–] **L.**BM.; MD. 23–44; **Bm.**U.; **M.**MS. 23–24.

6230 **Bericht** über das **gesamte Physiologie** und **experimentelle Pharmakologie.** Berlin. *Ber. ges. Physiol. exp. Pharm.* [1920–43: 48–] **L.**BM^N. 20–40; IC. 20–31; MC. 20–57; MD. 20–44; SC. imp.; TD. 20–39; U. 50–; UC. 20–44: 54–55; **Abd.**R. 20–33: 51–; U. 20–39; **Bm.**U. 20–39; **Br.**U. 27–50 imp.; **C.**APH. 49–54; BI. 20–40; PH. 20–39: 49–; **Dn.**U. 20–22; **E.**U. 20–40; **G.**U.; **M.**MS. 20–24; **Ste.** 20–31; **Y.** [*C. of:* 58991]

6231 **Bericht** der **Gesellschaft** für **Kohlentechnik.** Halle. *Ber. Ges.Kohlentech.* [1921–33] **L.**P.

6232 **Bericht. Gesellschaft** für **praktische Energiekunde.** Karlsruhe. *Ber. Ges. prakt. Energiek.* [1952–53] **L.**P. [*C. as:* 38494]

6233 **Bericht** der **Gesellschaft** für **Seuchenbekämpfung.** Frankfurt a. M. *Ber. Ges. Seuchenbekämpf.*

6234 **Bericht** der **Gesellschaft** für **Völker-** u. **Erdkunde** zu **Stettin.** Greifswald. *Ber. Ges. Völk.- u. Erdk. Stettin* [1897–10] **L.**G. 97–02; **Bl.**U. 99–10; **C.**E. 97–05.

6235 **Bericht** der **Gesellschaft** für **Zeitmesskunde** und **Uhrentechnik.** Berlin. *Ber. Ges. Zeitmess. Uhrentech.* [1926–30] **L.**P. [*C. as:* 48864]

6236 **Bericht** über die **Gesundheitsverhältnisse** u. **Gesundheitsanstalten** in **Nürnberg.** *Ber. Gesundh-Verh. Nürnberg*

6237 **Bericht** der **Grossherzoglichen Wein-** u. **Obstbauschule** in **Oppenheim a. Rh.** *Ber. grossh. Wein- u. ObstbSch. Oppenheim*

6238 **Bericht** über das **Hamburgische Museum** für **Kunst** und **Gewerbe.** Hamburg. *Ber. hamburg. Mus. Kunst Gew.* **L.**BM. 84–.

6239 **Bericht** der **Hamburgischen Station** für **Pflanzenschutz.** Hamburg. *Ber. hamburg. Stn PflSchutz* **L.**AM.; EB. 98–31. [*C. in:* 24989]

6240 **Bericht** über die **Hauptversammlung** des **Deutschen Forstvereins.** Berlin. *Ber. Hauptvers. dt. Forstver.* **O.**F. 19–37 imp.

6241 **Bericht** des **Hygienischen Instituts** über die **Nahrungsmittelkontrolle** in **Hamburg.** Hamburg. *Ber. hyg. Inst. NahrMittelkontrolle Hamburg* **L**v.U. 96–05.

6241ᵃ **Bericht. Indonesisch instituut** voor **rubberonderzoek.** Bogor. *Ber. indon. Inst. RubbOnderz.* **Y.**

6242 **Bericht** des **Instituts** für **Agrarraumforschung** der **Humboldt-Universität** zu **Berlin.** Berlin. *Ber. Inst. Agrarraumforsch. Berl.*

6242ᶜ **Bericht** des **Instituts** für **gewerbliche Wasserwirtschaft** und **Luftreinhaltung.** Köln. *Ber. Inst. gew. Wasserw. Luftreinh.* **L.**P. 59–.

6243 **Bericht** des **Instituts** für **mechanische Technologie** und **Materialkunde.** K. Technische Hochschule, Berlin. *Ber. Inst. mech. Technol. Materialk.* [1928–] **L.**P. 28–35.

6244 **Bericht** des **Instituts** für **Tabakforschung.** Dresden. *Ber. Inst. TabForsch.* [1954–] **L.**P.; **Md.**H.; **Y.**

6245 **Bericht** der **Internationalen Gesellschaft** zur **Erhaltung** des **Wisents.** Berlin. *Ber. int. Ges. Erhalt. Wisents* [1923–37] **L.**Z.

6246 **Bericht** des **Internationalen meteorologischen Komitees.** Berlin. *Ber. int. met. Kom.* **L.**BM. 07–; MO. 85–.

6247 **Bericht** über die **K. Bayerische Akademie** für **Landwirtschaft** und **Brauerei** in **Weihenstephan.** Freising. *Ber. K. bayer. Akad. Landw. Brau.* [*C. of:* 24997]

6248 **Bericht** aus der **K. Bayerischen biologischen Versuchsstation.** München. *Ber. K. bayer. biol. Vers-Stn* [1908–09] **L.**BMᴺ.; SC.; Z.; **Db.**; **Pl.**M.

6249 **Bericht** der **K. Gärtnerlehranstalt** zu **Dahlem.** Berlin. *Ber. K. GärtLehreanst. Dahlem* **L.**AM.; K. 06–07; L. 29–50 imp. [*C. of:* 24995]

6250 **Bericht** der **K. Lehranstalt** für **Obst-** und **Gartenbau** zu **Proskau.** Oppeln. *Ber. K. Lehranst. Obst- u. Gartenb. Proskau* **L.**EB. 11. [*C. of:* 24998; *C. as:* 33995]

6251 **Bericht** der **K. Lehranstalt** für **Wein-, Obst-** und **Gartenbau** zu **Geisenheim.** Berlin. *Ber. K. Lehranst. Wein- Obst- u. Gartenb. Geisenheim* [1897–] **L.**AM. 03–09; P. 26–; **Br.**A. 01–37; U. 97–37 imp.; **O.**RE. 16–12. [*See also:* 6424]

6252 **Bericht** der **K. Saatzuchtanstalt** an der **K. Akademie** für **Landwirtschaft** und **Brauerei** in **Weihenstephan.** München. *Ber. K. SaatzAnst. Weihenstephan*

6253 **Bericht** der **K. Württembergischen Weinbau-Versuchsanstalt.** Weinsberg. *Ber. K. württ. Weinb-VersAnst.*

6254 **Bericht** des **Knopf-Museum Heinrich Waldes.** Prag. *Ber. Knopf-Mus.* [1916–] **L.**P. 16–19.

6255 **Bericht** des **Kohlenstaubausschusses** des **Reichskohlenrat.** Berlin. *Ber. KohlStaubaussch. ReichskohlRat* [1926–30] **L.**P. imp. [*C. as:* 6397, Sect. C.]

6256 **Bericht** des **Komitees** für **Abwasserfragen.** Prag. *Ber. Kom. AbwassFrag., Prag* **L.**P. 15–18.

6257 **Bericht** der **Kommission** für **geophysikalische Forschungen** der **Deutschen Gesellschaft** der **Wissenschaften** und **Künste** für die **Tschechoslowakische Republik.** Prag. *Ber. Kommn geophys. Forsch., Prag* **L.**MO. 33–37.

6258 **Bericht** der **Kommission** für **ozeanographische Forschungen.** Wien. *Ber. Kommn ozeanogr. Forsch.* [1892–] **L.**BMᴺ. 92–12; MO. 95–07; **Db.** 92–09; **E.**U.92–09; **L**v.U. 92–18; **Pl.**M. 92–24.

6259 **Bericht** über den **Kongress** für **experimentelle Psychologie.** Leipzig. *Ber. Kongr. exp. Psychol.* [1904–38] **L.**BM. 06–12; PS. 04–24; **C.**UL.; **E.**U. 06; **G.**U. 06–14; **M.**U.

6260 **Bericht** über die **Korrosionstagung, Verein deutscher Eisenhüttenleute.** Berlin. *Ber. KorrosTag. Ver. dt. Eisenhüttenl.* [1931–] **L.**P. 31–38.

6261 **Bericht** über **Krankheiten** und **Beschädigungen** der **Kulturpflanzen.** Hauptstelle für Pflanzenschutz in Landsberg a. d. Warthe. *Ber. Krankh. Beschäd. Kulturpfl., Landsberg* **O.**AP. 24–31.

6262 **Bericht** über **Krankheiten** und **Beschädigungen** der **Kulturpflanzen.** K. Biologische Anstalt für Land- u. Forstwirtschaft. Berlin. *Ber. Krankh. Beschäd. Kulturpfl., Berl.* **L.**EB. 05–08*.

6263 **Bericht** des **Laboratoriums** für **Kraftfahrzeuge** an der **K. Technischen Hochschule** zu **Berlin.** Berlin & München. *Ber. Lab. Kraftfahrz. Berl.* [1911–12] **L.**SC.; **M.**U.

6264 **Bericht** des **Laboratoriums** für **Verbrennungskraftmaschinen** an der **Technischen Hochschule, Stuttgart.** *Ber. Lab. VerbrennKraftmasch. Stuttg.* [1931–] **L.**P. 31–34.

6264ᶜ **Bericht** zur **Landesforschung** und **Landesplanung.** Wien. *Ber. Landesforsch. Landesplan.* **Y.** 61–.

6265 **Bericht** über **Landtechnik.** München, Frankfurt/Main. *Ber. Landtech.* [1947–] **L.**BM.; **C.**A. [*Also supplements.*]

6266 **Bericht** über **Landwirtschaft.** Berlin. *Ber. Landw.* [1907–] **L.**AM. 23–39; P. 07–31; **Abs.**N. 13; **O.**AP. 07–08 v. imp.: 09–11 imp.; **Y.** [*Also supplements*]

6267 **Bericht** über **Land-** und **Forstwirtschaft** im **Ausland.** Berlin. *Ber. Land- u. Forstw. Ausl.* **L.**AM. 02–16.

6268 **Bericht** über **Land-** und **Forstwirtschaft** in **Deutsch-Ostafrika.** Heidelberg. *Ber. Land- u. Forstw. Dt.-Ostafr.* [1902–11] **L.**BM.; BMᴺ.; EB. 03–11; K.; **Rt.** 04–11.

6269 **Bericht** der **Landwirtschaftlich-chemischen Versuchs-** und **Samen-Kontrol-Station** zu **Riga.** *Ber. landw.-chem. Vers.- u. Samenkontrolstn Riga* **Rt.** 72–81: 90–00 imp.

6270 **Bericht** über das **landwirtschaftliche Versuchsfeld** der **K. Universität Breslau** in **Rosenthal.** Berlin. *Ber. landw. VersFeld K. Univ. Breslau Rosenthal*

6271 **Bericht** aus der **Land-** u. **forstwirtschaftlichen Abteilung** der **Deutsch-chinesischen Hochschule.** Tsingtau. *Berl. land- u. forstw. Abt. dt.-chin. Hochsch.*

6272 **Bericht** des **Landwirtschaftlichen Instituts** der **Universität Halle.** Leipzig. *Ber. landw. Inst. Univ. Halle*

6273 **Bericht** des **Landwirtschaftlichen Instituts** der **Universität Königsberg i. Pr.** Berlin. *Ber. landw. Inst. Univ. Königsb.* [1898–21] **L.**P.
    Bericht der **Landwirtschaftlichen Landes-Versuchsstation** zu **Saratow.** *See* 24490.

6274 **Bericht** der **Landwirtschaftlichen Versuchsstation, Münster i. W.** *Ber. landw. VersStn Münster*

6275 **Bericht. Lehr-** und **Forschungsanstalt** für **Gartenbau** in **Berlin-Dahlem.** Berlin. *Ber. Lehr- u. ForschAnst. Gartenb. Berl.-Dahlem* [*Supplement to* and *published in:* 28071]

6276 **Bericht. Lehr-** und **Forschungsanstalt** für **Wein-, Obst-** und **Gartenbau** zu **Geisenheim** am **Rhein.** *Ber. Lehr- u. ForschAnst. Wein- Obst- u. Gartenb. Geisenheim* **Md.**H. 46–. [*C. of:* 6424; *see also:* 6251]

6277 **Bericht** des **Lehrerklubs** für **Naturkunde.** Brünn. *Ber. Lehrerklubs Naturk., Brünn.* [1906–] **L.**BM^N. 06–15. [*C. of:* 6156]

6278 **Bericht** über die **Leistungen** und **Fortschritte** der **Augenheilkunde.** Karlsruhe. *Ber. Leist. Fortschr. Augenheilk.* [1878–23] **L.**MD. 92–23 imp.; OP. 05–23; **C.**UL. 95–23. [*Supplement to:* 4048]

6279 **Bericht** über die **Leistungen** auf dem **Gebiet** der **Anatomie** des **Zentralnervensystems.** Bonn. *Ber. Leist. Geb. Anat. ZentralnervSyst.* **L.**GH.; MD. 05–10; **Abd.**U.; **Bm.**U.; **C.**MD.; UL.; **E.**P.; **M.**MS. [*Supplement to:* 12868]

6280 **Bericht** der **Limnologischen Flussstation Freudenthal.** Göttingen. *Ber. limnol. Flussstn Freudenthal* [1952–] **L.**BM^N.; **Fr.** 53–; **Pl.**M.; **Y.** [*C. of:* 25032]

6281 **Bericht** über die **Literatur** der **Binnengewässerkunde.** *Ber. Lit. Binnengewässerk.*

6282 **Bericht** des **Mathematischen Vereins** der **Universität Berlin.** Berlin. *Ber. math. Ver. Univ. Berl.*

6283 **Bericht** des **Mathematischen Vereins** an der **Universität Göttingen.** *Ber. math. Ver. Univ. Göttingen*

6284 **Bericht. Max-Planck-Institut** für **Eisenforschung.** Düsseldorf. *Ber. Max-Planck-Inst. Eisenforsch.* **L.**P. 55–; **Y.**

6285 **Bericht** über die **Meteorologische Station, Nürnberg.** Nürnberg. *Ber. met. Stn Nürnberg*

6286 **Bericht** der **Meteorologischen Kommission** des **Naturforschenden Vereins** in **Brünn.** Brünn. *Ber. met. Kommn Brünn.* **L.**MO. 05–07; **E.**J. 83–10.

6287 **Bericht** des **Meteorologisch-geophysikalischen Institutes** und seines **Taunus-Observatoriums.** Braunschweig. *Ber. met.-geophys. Inst., Braunschw.* **L.**MO. 13–19.
    Bericht des **Mikrobiologischen Staats-Instituts** zu **Rostow am Don.** *See* 24359.

6288 **Bericht** des **Milchwirtschaftlichen Instituts** zu **Hameln.** *Ber. milchw. Inst. Hameln* **Rt.** 94–01.

6289 **Bericht** und **Mitteilungen** veranlasst durch die **Internationale mathematische Unterrichtskommission.** Leipzig u. Berlin. *Ber. Mitt. int. math. UnterrKommn* **L.**BM. 10–11; M. 15–; SC. 15–; **G.**U. 10–16 imp.; **Ld.**U. 09–11; **O.**B. 10–11. [*C. of:* 32532]

6290 **Bericht** des **Museums Francisco-Carolinum.** Linz. *Ber. Mus. Francisco-Carol.* [*C. as:* 25042]

6291 **Bericht** des **Museums** für **Völkerkunde** in **Basel.** *Ber. Mus. Völkerk. Basel* **L.**AN. 18–; HO. 34–; **Cr.**M. 13–.

6292 **Bericht** des **Museums** für **Völkerkunde** in **Leipzig.** *Ber. Mus. Völkerk. Lpz.* [*C. as:* 24846]
    Bericht der **Museumskommissionen. Naturhistorisches Museum, Bern.** *See* 6353.
    Bericht des **Museumsvereines** für das **Comitat Trencsén.** *See* 25169.

6293 **Bericht** des **Museumsvereins** oder **Vereins** für **Kunde** der **Natur** und der **Kunst** im **Fürstentum Hildesheim** und in der **Stadt Goslar.** Hildesheim. *Ber. MusVer. Hildesheim* **L.**BM^N. 92–06.

6294 **Bericht** der **Naturforschenden Gesellschaft Augsburg.** Augsburg. *Ber. naturf. Ges. Augsburg* **L.**BM.; BM^N. 48–.

6295 **Bericht** der **Naturforschenden Gesellschaft** in **Bamberg.** *Ber. naturf. Ges. Bamberg* **L.**BM^N. 1860–; SC. 61–; **Db.** 29–.

6296 **Bericht** der **Naturforschenden Gesellschaft** zu **Freiburg i. Br.** *Ber. naturf. Ges. Freiburg. i. B.* [1855–] **L.**BM. 86–; BM^N.; GL.; GM. 06–; L. 85–; R. 86–35; S. 86–03; SC. 1858–; Z. 67: 86– imp.; **C.**A. 71–; P. 10–; UL. 86–; **Db.** 86–; **E.**C. 86–; R. 04–; **Ld.**U. 30–; **Lv.**U. 86–; **Nw.**A. 06–34 imp.; **O.**R. 1858–.

6297 **Bericht** der **Naturforschenden Gesellschaft, Solothurn.** *Ber. naturf. Ges. Solothurn* **L.**BM^N. 48–51.

6298 **Bericht** der **Naturforschenden Gesellschaft Uri.** Altdorf. *Ber. naturf. Ges. Uri* **L.**MO. 35–37 imp.

6299 **Bericht** der **Naturhistorischen Gesellschaft** zu **Hannover.** Hannover. *Ber. naturhist. Ges. Hannover* [1954–] **L.**BM^N.; **E.**R.; **Ld.**U.; **Y.** [*C. of:* 25045]

6300 **Bericht** des **Naturhistorischen Museums** in **Lübeck.** *Ber. naturhist. Mus. Lübeck* **L.**BM^N. 1853–36 imp.; **E.**R. 59–.

6301 **Bericht** der **Naturwissenschaftlichen Gesellschaft, Bayreuth.** Bayreuth. *Ber. naturw. Ges. Bayreuth*

6302 **Bericht** der **Naturwissenschaftlichen Gesellschaft** zu **Chemnitz.** *Ber. naturw. Ges. Chemnitz* **L.**BM^N. 1859–33; **E.**R. 75–31.

6303 **Bericht** der **Naturwissenschaftlichen Sektion** des **Vereins 'Botanischer Garten'** in **Olmütz.** *Ber. naturw. Sekt. Ver. 'bot. Garten' Olmütz*

6304 **Bericht** des **Naturwissenschaftlichen Vereins, Bielefeld** und **Umgegend.** Bielefeld. *Ber. naturw. Ver. Bielefeld* **L.**L. 11–; **Lv.**U. 14–21.

6305 **Bericht** des **Naturwissenschaftlichen Vereins** in **Dessau.** *Ber. naturw. Ver. Dessau* **L.**BM^N. 24–37.

6306 **Bericht** des **Naturwissenschaftlichen Vereins, Landshut.** Landshut. *Ber. naturw. Ver. Landshut* [1900–28] **L.**BM^N. 00–10; L. 00–04. [*C. of:* 6180]

6307 **Bericht** des **Naturwissenschaftlichen Vereins** zu **Passau.** *Ber. naturw. Ver. Passau* [1857–] **L.**BM^N. 1857–25; **C.**P. 82–85; **G.**N. 1858–.

6308 **Bericht** des **Naturwissenschaftlichen Vereins** zu **Regensburg.** *Ber. naturw. Ver. Regensburg* [1886–30] **L.**BM. 88–30; BM^N.; **Db.** 03–30. [*Replaced by:* 483]

6308^c **Bericht** des **Naturwissenschaftlichen Vereins** für **Sachsen** und **Thüringen.** *Ber. naturw. Ver. Sachs.* [*Supplement to:* 58737]

6309 **Bericht** des **Naturwissenschaftlichen Vereins** für **Schwaben** und **Neuburg.** Augsburg. *Ber. naturw. Ver. Schwaben* [1857–33: 60–] **L.**BM^N.; **C.**P. 28: 30; **E.**R. 11: 24–27; **Y.**

6310 **Bericht** des **Naturwissenschaftlichen Vereins** zu **Zerbst.** *Ber naturw. Ver. Zerbst*

6311 **Bericht** des **Naturwissenschaftlich-medizin-ischen Vereins** in **Innsbruck.** *Ber. naturw.-med. Ver. Innsbruck* [1870–] **L.**BM.; BM^N.; R. 70–34; **C.**UL.; **Db.** imp.; **E.**J. 76–13; R. 70–87; **O.**R. 70–00.

6312 **Bericht. Nederlands vlasinstituut.** Wageningen. *Ber. Ned. Vlasinst.* [1950–] **C.**A.

6313 **Bericht** über die **neueren Leistungen** in der **Ohrenheilkunde.** Leipzig. *Ber. neu. Leist. Ohrenheilk.* **L.**MD. 90–91: 97–10.

6314 **Bericht** over **nieuwe bestrijdsmiddelen. Plantenziektenkundige dienst.** Wageningen. *Ber. nieuwe Bestrijdsmidd. plziektenk. Dienst*

6315 **Bericht** des **Nordoberfränkischen Vereins** für **Natur-, Geschichts- u. Landeskunde.** Hof. *Ber. nordoberfränk. Ver. Naturk.* **L.**BM^N. 96–34.

6316 **Bericht** der **Notgemeinschaft** der **deutschen Wissenschaft.** Berlin. *Ber. Notgemeinsch. dt. Wiss.* **L.**BM.; P. 51; **O.**R. 24–33 imp.

6317 **Bericht** der **Oberhessischen Gesellschaft** für **Natur- u. Heilkunde.** Giessen. *Ber. oberhess. Ges. Nat.- u. Heilk.* [1847–] **L.**BM. 1847–19; BM^N. 1847–36; GL. 00–; L. 1849–; P. 65–39; SC. 04–27: 54–; Z. 1854–82; **Abs.**U. 23–; **Bl.**U. 79–22; **Bm.**N. 06– imp.; **C.**P.; **Db.** 1849–; **E.**B. 62–; J. 76–19; R. 83–; **G.**N. 62–22; **Lv.**U. 79–; **Nw.**A. 1847–99.

6318 **Bericht** des **Ōhara Instituts** für **landwirtschaftliche Biologie.** Kuraschiki. *Ber. Ōhara Inst. landw. Biol.* [1954–] **L.**AM.; BM^N.; C.; HS.; L.; MY.; U.; **Abs.**A.; N.; **Ba.**I.; **C.**A.; P.; **Db.** imp.; E.; **Hu.**G.; **Ld.**U.; **Lv.**U.; **M.**U.; **Md.**H.; **Rt.**; **Y.** [*C. of:* 6319]

6319 **Bericht** des **Ōhara Instituts** für **landwirtschaftliche Forschungen, Okayama Universität.** Kuraschiki. *Ber. Ōhara Inst. landw. Forsch.* [1916–53] **L.**AM.; BM^N. imp.; C. 34–43; EB. 16–41; HS.; K. 16–41; L.; MY. 19–41; P. 16–38; U. 18–53 imp.; **Abs.**A.; N. 29–53; **Ba.**I. 30–53 imp. **C.**A.; P. 29–53; **Db.** 17–53; **E.**AB. 32–38; B.; R. 31–53; **Hu.**G. 42–53; **Ld.**U. 31–41: 53; **Lv.**U.; **Md.**H. 31–53; **O.**F. 16–41; **Rt.**; **Y.** [*No issue:* 1944–50; *C. as:* 6318]

Bericht über die **Ophthalmologische Gesellschaft.** Heidelberg. *See* 6419.

6320 **Bericht** über die **ordentliche Hauptversammlung** des **Vereins deutscher Fabriken feuerfester Produkte.** Köln & Berlin. *Ber. ord. Hauptvers. Ver. dt. Fabr. feuerfester Prod.* **L.**P. 83–19 imp.

6321 **Bericht** der **Ornithologischen Station Lotos.** Liboch. *Ber. orn. Stn Lotos*

6322 **Bericht** des **Ornithologisch-oologischen Vereins** zu **Hamburg.** *Ber. orn.-oolog. Ver. Hamburg*

6322^c **Bericht** des **Osteuropa-Institutes** an der **Freien Universität Berlin.** Berlin. *Ber. Osteur. Inst. Berl.* [1952–] Reihe Medizin. **Y.**

6323 **Bericht** über die **Petroleumindustrie.** Berlin. *Ber. PetrolInd.* **L.**P. 39–40. [*Issue for* 1939 *published in* 37405 *as a supplement; issue for* 1940 *published in* 35888 *as a supplement; C. as:* 31930]

6324 **Bericht** über **Pflanzenschutz** der **Abteilung** für **Pflanzenkrankheiten** des **Kaiser-Wilhelm-Instituts** für **Landwirtschaft** in **Bromberg.** Berlin. *Ber. PflSchutz Bromberg* **L.**EB. 08–09.

6325 **Bericht** der **Physikalisch-medizinischen Gesellschaft** zu **Würzburg.** *Ber. phys.-med. Ges. Würzb.* [1936–] **L.**BM^N. 36–39: 51–; L. imp.; z. 36–37; **C.**P.; **Db.** imp.; **E.**R. 27–; **O.**R.; **Y.** [*C. of:* 56064]

6326 **Bericht** aus dem **Physiologischen Laboratorium** des **Landwirtschaftlichen Instituts** der **Universität Halle.** Berlin. *Ber. physiol. Lab. landw. Inst. Univ. Halle* **Rt.** 72–01 imp. [*C. as:* 27790]

6327 **Bericht. Plantenziektenkundige Dienst.** Wageningen. *Ber. plziektenk. Dienst* **L.**EB. (ent.) 48–.

6328 **Bericht** der **Preussischen landwirtschaftlichen Versuchs- und Forschungsanstalten** in **Landsberg.** Berlin. *Ber. preuss. landw. Vers.- u. ForschAnst. Landsberg* [*Supplement to* and *published in:* 28071]

6329 **Bericht** der **Preussischen Versuchs-** und **Forschungsanstalt** für **Getreideverarbeitung** und **Futterveredelung** in **Berlin.** Berlin. *Ber. preuss. Vers.- u. ForschAnst. Getreideverarb. Futtervered. Berl.* [*Supplement to* and *published in:* 28071]

6330 **Bericht** der **Preussischen Versuchs- und Forschungsanstalt** für **Milchwirtschaft** in **Kiel.** Berlin. *Ber. preuss. Vers.- u. ForschAnst. Milchw. Kiel* [*Supplement to* and *published in:* 28071]

6331 **Bericht** der **Preussischen Versuchs- und Forschungsanstalt** für **Tierzucht** in **Tschechnitz.** Berlin. *Ber. preuss. Vers.- u. ForschAnst. Tierzucht Tschechnitz* [*Supplement to* and *published in* 28071]

6332 **Bericht** der **Preussischen Versuchsanstalt** für **Waldwirtschaft.** Eberswalde. *Ber. preuss. VersAnst. Waldw.* **O.**F. 34–37.

6333 **Bericht** über die **psychiatrische Literatur.** Berlin. *Ber. psychiat. Lit.*

6334 **Bericht** aus der **Psychiatrischen Klinik** der **Universität Würzburg.** Würzburg. *Ber. psychiat. Klin. Univ. Würzb.*

6335 **Bericht** over **rassenkeuze.** 's Gravenhage. *Ber. Rassenkeuze* **L.**BM. 50–; P. 48–; **Y.** [*Supplement to:* 28981]
Bericht des **Reichsamts** für **Bodenforschung.** Wien. *See* 6337.

6336 **Bericht. Reichskuratorium** für **Technik** in der **Landwirtschaft.** Berlin. *Ber. Reichskurat. Tech. Landw.* **L.**P. 28.

6337 **Bericht** der **Reichsstelle** für **Bodenforschung.** Wien. *Ber. Reichsstelle Bodenforsch., Wien* [1940–44] **L.**BM^N.; **C.**UL.; **E.**R. [*C. of:* and *Rec. as:* 56022]

6338 **Bericht** der **Rheinischen Gesellschaft** für **wissenschaftliche Forschung.** Bonn. *Ber. rhein. Ges. wiss. Forsch.*

6339 **Bericht** van de **Rijksdienst** voor het **oudheidkundig bodemonderzoek.** Amersfoort. *Ber. Rijksdienst oudheidk. Bodemonderz.* **L.**BM^N. 50–; **Db.** 54–.

6339ᶜ **Bericht. Sächsische Akademie** der **Wissenschaften.** Leipzig. *Ber. sächs. Akad. Wiss. Math.-nat.* Klasse **L.**BM.; P.; **Db.** 44–.

     Bericht der **Saratower Naturforschergesellschaft.** *See* 24488.

6340 **Bericht** von **Schimmel** u. **Co., Leipzig,** über **aetherische Oele, Riechstoffe,** usw. Leipzig. *Ber. Schimmel u. Co., Lpz. aeth. Oele* **L.**C. 09–47★; P. 94–47 imp.; **Bm.**U. 28–29. [*C. as:* 6400]

6341 **Bericht** der **Schweizerischen botanischen Gesellschaft.** Bern. *Ber. schweiz. bot. Ges.* [1891–] **L.**BM.; BMᴺ.; IC. 47–; K.; SC. 35–; U. 50–; **Bn.**U. 47–; **C.**BO. 47–; UL. 91–29; **E.**B. 10–26; R. imp.; **Ld.**U.; **Lv.**U. 41– imp.; **Md.**H. 49; **Y.**

     Bericht der **Schweizerischen Gesellschaft** für das **Studium** der **Ersatzbrennstoffe.** Bern. *See* 6342.

6342 **Bericht** der **Schweizerischen Gesellschaft** für das **Studium** der **Motorbrennstoffe.** Bern. *Ber. schweiz. Ges. Stud. Motorbrennstoffe* [1932–] **L.**P. 32; **Y.**

6343 **Bericht** der **Schweizerischen Versuchsanstalt.** St. Gallen. *Ber. schweiz. VersAnst. St Gallen* **L.**P. 20–25. *Then in:*
         Abt. 1: Textilindustrie. **L.**P. 28–29★. [*C. as:* 25094 Abt. 1]
         Abt. 2: Lederindustrie. **L.**P. 26–29★. [*C. as:* 25094 Abt. 2]

6344 **Bericht** der **Schweizerischen Versuchsanstalt** für **Obst-, Wein-** u. **Gartenbau** in **Wädenswil.** Bern. *Ber. schweiz. VersAnst. Obst- Wein- u. Gartenb.* [1907–43] **L.**EB. 07–16; **Ba.**I. 24–28: 40–43; **Br.**U.; **Md.**H. [*C. as:* 24918]

6345 **Bericht** des **Schwyz. naturforschenden Gesellschaft.** Einsiedeln. *Ber. schwyz. naturf. Ges.* **L.**BMᴺ. 32–.

6346 **Bericht** der **Senckenbergischen Bibliothek** zu **Frankfurt a. M.** *Ber. senckenb. Bibltk* **L.**BMᴺ. 09–37; **E.**R. 31–; **G.**U. 33–35.

6347 **Bericht** der **Senckenbergischen naturforschenden Gesellschaft** in **Frankfurt a. M.** Frankfurt a. M. *Ber. senckenb. naturf. Ges.* [1869–21] **L.**BM.; BMᴺ.; E. 76–12: 14–21; EB. 13–21; GL. 00–21; GM. imp.; K. 69–11; L.; R. 69–18; S. 69–75; UC. 94–21; Z.; **Bl.**U. 92–21 imp.; **Br.**U. 06–21; **C.**P.; UL. 71–20 imp.; **Cr.**M. 05–21; **Db.** 70–21; **E.**B. 70–21 imp.; C. 85–19; J. 89–15; R.; **G.**N. 75–21 imp.; **Ld.**U. 82–13 imp.; **Lv.**U. 87–21; **M.**U. 18–21; **O.**R.; **Pl.**M. imp. [*C. as:* 5311]

6348 **Bericht** über die **Sitzungen** der **Medizinischen Gesellschaft** zu **Leipzig.** *Ber. Sitz. med. Ges. Lpz.*

6348ᶜ **Bericht. Sonderausschuss Radioaktivität.** Stuttgart. *Ber. SondAussch. Radioakt.* [1958–] **L.**P.

6349 **Bericht** der **Staatlichen Höhlenkommission.** Wien. *Ber. st. Höhlenkommn, Wien.* **L.**BMᴺ. 20.

6350 **Bericht** des **Staatlichen Instituts** für **experimentelle Therapie** in **Frankfurt a. M.** *Ber. st. Inst. exp. Ther. Frankfurt*

6351 **Bericht** der **Staatlichen Lehr-** und **Forschungsanstalt** für **Gartenbau** in **Weihenstephan.** *Ber. st. Lehr- u. ForschAnst. Gartenb. Weihenstephan* **Br.**A. 23–30; **Md.**H. 29–30. [*Replaced by:* 25101]

6352 **Bericht** des **Städtischen Marktamtes** über den **Schlachthof,** und die **Lebensmittelkontrolle** in **Karlsbad.** *Ber. städt. Marktamtes Schlachthof, Karlsbad* **W.** 30–.

6353 **Bericht** des **Städtischen naturhistorischen Museums.** Bern. *Ber. städt. naturhist. Mus., Bern* **L.**BMᴺ. 71–.

6354 **Bericht** über die **städtischen Sammlungen** für **Wissenschaft** und **Kunst** zu **Mainz.** Mainz. *Ber. städt. Samml. Wiss.Kunst Mainz*

6355 **Bericht** des **Strahlungs-klimatologischen Stationssetzes** im **Deutschen Nordseegebiet.** Braunschweig. *Ber. Strahl-klim. Stnssetz. dt. Nordseegeb.* **L.**MO. 28–30.

6356 **Bericht** über die **Tätigkeit** des **Bakteriologischen Instituts** der **Landwirtschaftskammer Niederschlesien.** Breslau. *Ber. Tät. bakt. Inst. LandwKamm. Niederschles.* **W.**29–.

6357 **Bericht** über die **Tätigkeit** des **Bakteriologischen Instituts** der **Landwirtschaftskammer** für die **Provinz Sachsen.** Halle a. S. *Ber. Tät. bakt. Inst. LandwKamm. Prov. Sachs.* **W.** 20–.

6358 **Bericht** über die **Tätigkeit** des **Chemischen Laboratoriums** des **Städtenwässerungsamts.** Nürnberg. *Ber. Tät. chem. Lab. StädtenwässAmts, Nürnberg* **L.**P. 24–28.

6359 **Bericht** über die **Tätigkeit** des **Chemischen Untersuchungsamts** für die **Provinz Oberhessen.** Giessen. *Ber. Tät. chem. UntersAmts Prov. Oberhessen*

6360 **Bericht** über die **Tätigkeit** des **Chemischen Untersuchungsamts** der **Stadt Dortmund.** Dortmund. *Ber. Tät. chem. UntersAmts Dortmund*

6360ᵃ **Bericht** über die **Tätigkeit** des **Chemischen Untersuchungsamts** der **Stadt Elberfeld.** *Ber. Tät. chem. UntersAmts Elberfeld.* [*Supplement to:* 25052]

6361 **Bericht** über die **Tätigkeit** des **Deutschen Ausschusses** für den **mathematischen** und **naturwissenschaftlichen Unterricht.** Leipzig u. Berlin. *Ber. Tät. dt. Aussch. math. naturw. Unterr.* **L.**BM. 08–11; **E.**U. 08–12; **O.**B. 09–12.

6362 **Bericht** über die **Tätigkeit** der **Deutschen Forschungsanstalt** für **Lebensmittelchemie.** München. *Ber. Tät. dt. ForschAnst. LebensmittChem.* **L.**P. 53–.

6363 **Bericht** über die **Tätigkeit** der **Deutschen Versuchsanstalt** für **Lederindustrie** zu **Freiberg i. S.** *Ber. Tät. dt. VersAnst. Lederind.* **L.**P. 10–.

6364 **Bericht** über die **Tätigkeit** der **Eidgenössischen agrikulturchemischen Anstalt.** Bern. *Ber. Tät. eidg. agrikchem. Anst.* [*C. of:* 6382]

6365 **Bericht** über die **Tätigkeit** der **eidgenössischen landwirtschaftlichen Versuchsanstalt Zürich-Oerlikon.** Bern. *Ber. Tät. eidg. landw. VersAnst. Zürich-Oerl.* **Abd.**S. 47–; **Br.**A. 38–52 imp.

6366 **Bericht** über die **Tätigkeit** des **Hygienischbakteriologischen Instituts.** Dortmund. *Ber. Tät. hyg.-bakt. Inst.*

6367 **Bericht** über die **Tätigkeit** des **Instituts** für **angewandte Geodäsie.** Frankfurt a. M. *Ber. Tät. Inst. angew. Geod.* **L.**AS. 52–; SC. 56–. [*C. of:* 56169]

     Bericht über die **Tätigkeit** des **Instituts** für **Erdmessung.** Frankfurt a. M. *See* 6367.

6368 **Bericht** über die **Tätigkeit** des **Instituts** für **Grünlandwirtschaft.** Braunschweig-Völkenrode. *Ber. Tät. Inst. Grünlandw.* **Hu.**G. 54–.

6369 **Bericht** über die **Tätigkeit** des **Instituts** für **Hygiene** und **Bakteriologie** zu **Gelsenkirchen** und der **bakteriologischen Laboratorien** in **Bochum,** etc. Wattenscheid. *Ber. Tät. Inst. Hyg. Bakt. Gelsenkirchen*

6370 **Bericht** über die **Tätigkeit** der **K. Agrikulturbotanischen Anstalt** in **München.** *Ber. Tät. K. agrikbot. Anst. Münch.* **L.**AM. 05–07.
Bericht über die **Tätigkeit** des **K. Preussischen meteorologischen Instituts.** *See* 6380.

6371 **Bericht** über die **Tätigkeit** der **K. Ungarischen Reichsanstalt** für **Meteorologie** und **Erdmagnetismus** und des **Observatoriums** in **Ógyalla.** Budapest. *Ber. Tät.K. ung. Reichsanst. Met. Erdmagn.* **L.**MO. 00–08; **E.**O. 00–02. [*For Hungarian edition, see* 29207]
Bericht über die **Tätigkeit** der **K. K. Landwirtschaftlich-chemischen Versuchsstation** in **Wien.** *See* 6383.

6372 **Bericht** über die **Tätigkeit** der **Landwirtschaftlichen Untersuchungs-** und **Forschungsanstalt.** Kiel. *Ber. Tät. landw. Unters.- u. ForschAnst.,Kiel* **Abd.**S. 48– imp.

6373 **Bericht** über die **Tätigkeit** der **Landwirtschaftlichen Versuchsstation, Darmstadt.** Darmstadt. *Ber. Tät. landw. VersStn Darmstadt*

6374 **Bericht** über die **Tätigkeit** des **Milchwirtschaftlichen Instituts** zu **Proskau.** Oppeln. *Ber. Tät. milchw. Inst. Proskau*

6375 **Bericht** über die **Tätigkeit** der **Naturwissenschaftlichen Gesellschaft Isis.** Bautzen. *Ber. Tät. naturw. Ges. Isis* [1906–24] **L.**BM^N.; **G.**N. 06–20. [*C. of:* 49812; *C. as:* 24221]

6375ᶜ **Bericht** über die **Tätigkeit** der **Naturwissenschaftlichen Gesellschaft, St. Gallen.** *See* 6381.

6376 **Bericht** über die **Tätigkeit** des **Naturwissenschaftlichen Vereins** in **Troppau.** *Ber. Tät. naturw. Ver. Troppau* **L.**BM^N. 95–05.

6377 **Bericht** über die **Tätigkeit** des **Offenbacher Vereins** für **Naturkunde.** Offenbach a. M. *Ber. Tät. offenbach. Ver. Naturk.* **L.**BM^N. 1860–32; **E.**R. 87–32.

6378 **Bericht** über die **Tätigkeit** der **Physikalisch-technischen Bundesanstalt.** Braunschweig. *Ber.Tät. phys.-tech. Bundesanst.* [*C. of:* 6379; *Supplement to* and *issued with:* 57693]

6379 **Bericht** über die **Tätigkeit** der **Physikalisch-technischen Reichsanstalt.** Charlottenburg. *Ber. Tät. phys.-tech. Reichsanst.* [1919–?] **L.**P. 33–; **E.**R. 19–32 imp. [*C. of:* 51791; *C. as:* 6378]

6380 **Bericht** über die **Tätigkeit** des **Preussischen meteorologischen Instituts.** Berlin. *Ber. Tät. preuss. met. Inst.* **L.**BM. 07–; MO. 86–33; SC. 25–; **Db.** 91–; **E.**M. 01–33 imp.; **R.** 91–93: 29–.

6381 **Bericht** über die **Tätigkeit** der **St. Gallischen naturwissenschaftlichen Gesellschaft.** St. Gallen. *Ber. Tät. St Gall. naturw. Ges.* [1858–01: 39–] **L.**BM^N.; **R.** 1858–01: **Z.** 1858–01. [>24835, 1901–38]

6382 **Bericht** über die **Tätigkeit** der **Schweizerischen agrikulturchemischen Anstalt, Bern** (Liebefeld). Bern. *Ber. Tät. schweiz. agrikchem. Anst.* **L.**P. 13–38. [*C. as:* 6364]

6383 **Bericht** über die **Tätigkeit** der **Staatlichen landwirtschaftlich-chemischen Versuchsstation.** Wien. *Ber. Tät. st. landw.-chem. VersStn* **L.**AM.; **Rt.** 06–07.

6384 **Bericht** über die **Tätigkeit** der **Städtischen Untersuchungsanstalt** für **Nahrungs-** u. **Genussmittel.** Nürnberg. *Ber. Tät. städt. UntersAnst. Nahr.- u. Genussmitt., Nürnberg*

6385 **Bericht** über die **Tätigkeit** der **technischen Aufsichtsbeamten.** Berlin. *Ber. Tät. tech. Aufsichtsbeamten* **L.**C. 25–39.

6386 **Bericht** über die **Tätigkeit** des **Untersuchungsamtes** der **Landwirtschaftskammer** für die **Provinz Ostpreussen.** Königsberg. *Ber. Tät. UntersAmt. LandwKamm. Ostpreuss.*

6387 **Bericht** über die **Tätigkeit** der **Versuchsanstalt** für **Brauindustrie** in **Böhmen** zu **Prag.** Wien. *Ber. Tät. VersAnst. Brauind. Böhm.* **L.**P. 98–08★.

6388 **Bericht** über die **Tätigkeit** der **Versuchs- u. Kontrollstation** der **Landwirtschaftskammer** für **das Herzogtum Oldenburg.** Oldenburg. *Ber. Tät. Vers.- u. Kontrollstn LandwKamm. Oldenburg*
Bericht über die **Tätigkeit** der **Versuchsstation. Landwirtschaftlich-chemische Versuchs-** u. **Samenkontrollstation** am **Polytechnikum** zu **Riga.** *See* 6269.

6389 **Bericht** über die **Tätigkeit** der **Versuchsstation** und **Lehranstalt** für **Molkereiwesen** zu **Kleinhof-Tapiau.** Königsberg i. Pr. *Ber. Tät. VersStn Molkereiw. Kleinhof-Tapiau*

6390 **Bericht** über die **Tätigkeit** der **Versuchs- u. Samenkontrollstation** der **Landwirtschaftskammer** für die **Provinz Westpreussen** zu **Danzig.** Danzig. *Ber. Tät. Vers.- u. Samenkontrollstn LandwKamm. Westpreuss.*

6391 **Bericht** über die **Tätigkeit** der **Zentralanstalt** für **Meteorologie** und **Geodynamik.** Wien. *Ber. Tät. ZentAnst. Met. Geodyn., Wien* **L.**MO. 34–35.

6392 **Bericht** über die **Tätigkeit** der **Tagung** in **Braunschweig. Nordwestdeutscher Forstverein.** Braunschweig. *Ber. Tag. Braunschw. NWdt. Forstver.* **O.**F. 48–.

6392ᵃ **Bericht** über die **Tagung** der **Freien Vereinigung** für **Mikrobiologie.** *Ber. Tag. frei. Verein. Mikrobiol.* [*Supplement to:* 58989]

6393 **Bericht** über die **Tagung. Internationale Tagung** für **Brückenbau** und **Hochbau.** Wien. *Ber. Tag. int. Tag. Brückenb.* **L.**P. 28★.

6394 **Bericht** über die **Tagung** des **Reichsvereins deutscher Feuerwehringenieure.** Berlin. *Ber. Tag. Reichsver. dt. Feuerwehringre* **L.**P. 25–30.
Bericht. Technische Hochschule Carolo-Wilhelmina zu **Braunschweig.** *See* 6216.

6395 **Bericht** über die **technische Prüfung. Kuratorium** für **Technik** in der **Landwirtschaft.** Frankfurt. *Ber. tech. Prüf. Kurat. Tech. Landw.* **L.**P. 58–.

6396 **Bericht** der **technisch-wirtschaftlichen Sachverständigausschüsse** des **Reichskohlenrats.** Berlin. *Ber. tech.-wirtsch. SachverstAussch. ReichskohlRats* A. Kohlenbergbau. B. Kohlenverwendung. C. Kohlenstaubtechnik [*C. of:* 6449ᶜ]. D. Feuerungstechnik [*C. of:* 19338]. E. Kohlentrocknungstechnik. **L.**P. (C) 32–33: (D) 32–38. [*Sect. C, D C. in:* 52602]

6397 **Bericht** der **technisch-wissenschaftlichen Abteilung** des **Verbands keramischer Gewerke** in **Deutschland.** Bonn. *Ber. tech.-wiss. Abt. Verb. keram. Gewerke Dtl.* **L.**P. 14–19★.

6398 **Bericht** des **Telegraphenversuchsamts.** Berlin. *Ber. TelegrVersAmts, Berl.* **L.**SC. 13–18.
Bericht der **Tomsker Staats-Universität.** *See* 24371.

6399 **Bericht** des **Ukrainischen biochemischen Instituts** zu **Charkow.** *Ber. ukr. biochem. Inst.* **C.**UL. 26–.

Bericht der **Ungarischen pharmazeutischen Gesellschaft.** *See* 29190.

6400 **Bericht** von **Variochem VVB Schimmel** u. **Co.** Leipzig. *Ber. Variochem VVB Schimmel* [1948–55] **L.**C.; P. [*C. of:* 6340; *C. as:* 31862]

6401 **Bericht** des **Verbandes** der **Laboratoriumsvorstände** an **Deutschen Hochschulen.** Leipzig. *Ber. Verb. LabVorst. dt. Hochsch.* **Abd.**U. 98–12.

6402 **Bericht** über die **Verbreitung** der **Reblaus** im **Österreich.** Wien. *Ber. Verbreit. Reblaus Öst.* **L.**AM. 91–12.

Bericht der **Vereinigung** zur **Bekämpfung** der **Säuglingssterblichkeit.** *See* 6024.

Bericht der **Vereinigung Industrielle Kraftwirtschaft.** *See* 55818.

6403 **Bericht** des **Vereins deutscher Emailfachleute.** Bonn. *Ber. Ver. [dt. Emailfachl.* [1949–52] [*Published in:* 6195; *C. as:* 32811]

6404 **Bericht** des **Vereins deutscher Fabriken feuerfester Producte.** Berlin. *Ber. Ver. dt. Fabr. feuerfest. Prod.* [1881–] **L.**P. 83–19.

Bericht des **Vereins deutscher Ingenieure.** *See* 55806.

6405 **Bericht** des **Vereins** für **Feuerungsbetrieb** und **Rauchbekämpfung** in **Hamburg.** Hamburg. *Ber. Ver. FeuerBetr. Hamburg* **L.**P. 08–34.

Bericht des **Vereins** für **Kunde** der **Natur** und **Kunst** im **Fürstentum Hildesheim** und der **Stadt Goslar.** *See* 6293.

6406 **Bericht** des **Vereins schlesischer Ornithologen.** Neisse. *Ber. Ver. schles. Orn.* **L.**BM^N. 26–30; **O.**OR. 26–39 imp.

6407 **Bericht** des **Vereins** zum **Schutze** und zur **Pflege** der **Alpenpflanzen.** Bamberg. *Ber. Ver. Schutze Pflege Alpenpfl.*

6408 **Bericht** über das **Vereinsjahr** erstattet vom **Verein** der **Geographen** an der **Universität Wien.** *Ber. VerJahr Ver. Geogr. Univ. Wien* **L.**G. 84–87 imp. [*C. in:* 20987]

6409 **Bericht** über die **Verhandlungen** der **allgemeinen Versammlung deutscher Pomologen.** Ludwigsburg. *Ber. Verh. allg. Versamml. dt. Pomol.*

6410 **Bericht** über die **Verhandlungen** der **Deutschen Gesellschaft** für **Chirurgie.** Leipzig. *Ber. Verh. dt. Ges. Chir.* **L.**BM. 89–; MD. 00–. [*Supplement to:* 58994]

Bericht über die **Verhandlungen** der **K. Sächsischen Gesellschaft der Wissenschaften.** *See* 6411.

6411 **Bericht** über die **Verhandlungen** der **Sächsischen Akademie** der **Wissenschaften** zu **Leipzig.** *Ber. Verh. sächs. Akad. Wiss.* [1846–] Math.-Phys. Kl. **L.**AS. 1846–13; BM. BM^N. 1846–39: 41: 49– imp.; P. 1849–38: 43–; R.; SC. 1857– imp.; U. 44–; UC. 1846–39 imp.; **Abs.**N. 21–; **C.**P. 1849–54 imp.; UL.; **Db.**; **E.**C. 74–11; R. imp.; **G.**U. 1846–35; **Ld.**U. 20–; **Lv.**U. 86–; **M.**U. 1849–13; **O.**R.; **Sa.** 1846–22; **Y.**

6412 **Bericht** über die **Verhandlungen** des **Verbandstages deutscher Bahnärzte.** Nürnberg. *Ber. Verh. VerbTag. dt. Bahnärzte*

6413 **Bericht** über die **Versammlung** des **Badischen Forstvereins.** Freiburg i. Br. *Ber. Versamm. bad. Forstver.* [*C. of:* 55987]

6414 **Bericht** über die **Versammlung** der **Deutschen ophthalmologischen Gesellschaft** (in **Heidelberg**). München u. Wiesbaden. *Ber. Versamm. dt. ophthal. Ges.* [1920–] **L.**MD.; OP.; **Bm.**U. 20–25; **E.**S. 27–. [*C. of:* 6419: *Suspended between* 1940–48]

6415 **Bericht** über die **Versammlung** des **Elsasslothringischen Forstvereins.** Barr. *Ber. Versamm. els.-loth. Forstver.*

6416 **Bericht** über die **Versammlung** des **Forstvereins** für das **Grossherzogtum Hessen.** Darmstadt. *Ber. Versamm. Forstver. Hessen*

6417 **Bericht** über die **Versammlung** des **Märkischen Forstvereins.** Potsdam. *Ber. Versamm. märk. Forstver.*

6418 **Bericht** über die **Versammlung** des **Oberrheinischen geologischen Vereins.** Stuttgart. *Ber. Versamm. oberrhein. geol. Ver.* [1871–10] **L.**BM^N. 82–10; GL. 00–10; **G.**M. 77–10. [*C. as:* 25038]

6419 **Bericht** über die **Versammlung** der **Ophthalmologischen Gesellschaft.** Heidelberg, etc. *Ber. Versamm. ophthal. Ges.* [1871–18] **L.**MD. 75–18; OP. 77–18; S. 77–01; **Bm.**U. 82–18 imp.; **Br.**U. 86–06; **Db.** 71–11; **E.**S. 13; **G.**F. 11–12. [*C. as:* 6414]

6420 **Bericht** über die **Versammlung** des **Pfälzischen Forstvereins.** Speyer. *Ber. Versamm. pfälz. Forstver.*

Bericht über die **Versammlung** des **Preussischen botanischen Vereins.** Königsberg. *See* 25081.

6421 **Bericht** über die **Versammlung** des **Sächsischen Forstvereins.** Tharandt. *Ber. Versamm. sächs. Forstver.*

6422 **Bericht** über die **Versammlung** der **Tuberkuloseärzte.** Berlin. *Ber. Versamm. TuberkÄrzte* **L.**MD. 03–09.

6423 **Bericht** über die **Versammlung** des **Württembergischen Forstvereins.** Stuttgart. *Ber. Versamm. württ. Forstver.*

6424 **Bericht** der **Versuchs-** und **Forschungsanstalt** für **Wein-, Obst-** und **Gartenbau** zu **Geisenheim** am **Rhein.** Berlin. *Ber. Vers.- u. ForschAnst. Wein- Obst- u. Gartenb. Geisenheim* **L.**P. 27–34; **Md.**H. 27–37. [*C. as:* 6276; *See also:* 6251]

6425 **Bericht** des **Versuchsfeldes** für **Werkzeugmaschinen** an der **Technischen Hochschule, Berlin.** Berlin. *Ber. VersFeld. WerkzMasch. tech. Hochsch. Berl.* **L.**P. 12–32.

6426 **Bericht** der **Versuchsgrubengesellschaft.** Gelsenkirchen. *Ber. VersGrubGes.* [1929–] **L.**P. 29–35; **Sh.**S. 29–48.

6426° **Bericht** der **Versuchs-** und **Lehranstalt** für **Brauerei** in **Berlin.** *Ber. Vers.- u. Lehranst. Brau. Berl.* **Y.**

6427 **Bericht** der **Versuchsstation** für **Zuckerindustrie** in **Prag.** Prag. *Ber. VersStn. ZuckInd. Prag* [1896–23] **L.**P. 12–23; **Rt.** 01–01. [*C. as:* 6219]

6428 **Bericht** der **Versuchsstation** für **Zuckerrohr** in **West-Java.** Leipzig. *Ber. VersStn ZuckRohr W.-Java* **L.**BM^N. 90–96.

6429 **Bericht** über die **Versuchswirtschaft, Lauchstädt.** Berlin. *Ber. VersWirtsch. Lauchstädt*

6430 **Bericht** des **Veterinärinstituts** der **Universität Leipzig.** Leipzig. *Ber. VetInst. Univ. Lpz.*

6431 **Bericht** über das **Veterinärwesen** im **Königreich Sachsen.** Dresden. *Ber. VetWes. Sachs.* **W.** 25-.

6432 **Bericht** über die **Vollversammlung** des **Deutschen Veterinärrates.** Berlin. *Ber. Vollversamm. dt. VetRat.* **W.** 30-.

6433 **Bericht** und **Vorträge** der **Deutschen Akademie** der **Landwirtschaftswissenschaften** zu **Berlin.** Berlin. *Ber. Vortr. dt. Akad. LandwWiss.* [1954-] **Abd.**R. 55-; **C.**A. 55-.

6434 **Bericht** über die **Vorträge** der **Tierärztlichen Abteilung** der **Gesellschaft deutscher Naturforscher** und **Ärzte.** *Ber. Vortr. tierärztl. Abt. Ges. dt. NatForsch. Ärzte* **W.** 33-.

Bericht über die **Wandersammlung** des **Westpreussischen botanisch-zoologischen Vereins.** *See* 6436.

6435 **Bericht** über die **Wanderversammlung** des **Deutschen Photographen-Vereins.** *Ber. Wanderversamm. dt. PhotogrVer.* **L.**P. 03-07.

6436 **Bericht** des **Westpreussischen botanisch-zoologischen Vereins.** Danzig. *Ber. westpreuss. bot.-zool. Ver.* [1878-40] **L.**BM.; BM^N. 78-39; **Bl.**U. 08-37 imp.; **C.**P. 08-37; **Db.** 08: 12; **Dm.** 78-22 imp.; **E.**R. 09-37; **G.**N. 08-37 imp.

6437 **Bericht** der **Wetterauischen Gesellschaft** für die **gesamte Naturkunde** zu **Hanau.** *Ber. wetterau. Ges. ges. Naturk.*

6438 **Bericht** über die **Wetter-** u. **Krankheitsverhältnisse Nürnbergs.** Nürnberg. *Ber. Wett.- u. KrankhVerhält. Nürnbergs*

6439 **Bericht** des **Wiener Stadtphysikates.** Wien. *Ber. wien. Stadtphysik.* **L.**BM. 85-93; TD. 79- imp.; **Lv.**U. 94-96.

6440 **Bericht** über die **wissenschaftliche Biologie.** Berlin. *Ber. wiss. Biol.* [1926-] **L.**BM^N. 26-52; MD.; SC. 26-44: 49-; U. 50-; UC. 26-39; **Abd.**U. 26-32; **Bm.**U. 26-29: 48-; **C.**BI. 26-39; **Db.** 30-; **E.**AB. 30-40; **G.**U.; **Ld.**W. 28-29 imp.; **Nw.**A. 54-; **Y.**

Bericht der **wissenschaftlichen Forschungs-Institute** in **Odessa.** *See* 59168.

6441 **Bericht** der **Wissenschaftlichen Gesellschaft 'Philomathie'** in **Neisse.** Neisse. *Ber. wiss. Ges. 'Philomathie' Neisse*

6442 **Bericht** über die **wissenschaftlichen Leistungen** im **Gebiete** der **Entomologie.** Berlin. *Ber. wiss. Leist. Geb. Ent.* **L.**BM. 1840-13; BM^N. 1854-95; E. 1838-11; EB. 1838-15 imp.; **C.**P. 63-66; UL. 71-; **Db.** 67-; **Nw.**A. 1850-1860; **O.**H. 1838-91; R. 79-13.

6443 **Bericht** über die **wissenschaftlichen Leistungen** in der **Naturgeschichte** der **niederen Tiere.** Berlin. *Ber. wiss. Leist. NatGesch. nied. Tiere* **L.**BM. 80-; R. 80-09; SC. 66-83; **C.**UL. 1857-85; **E.**R. 80-15.

Bericht des **Wissenschaftlichen Meeresinstituts.** Moskau. *See* 54577, 54855 and 54976.

6444 **Bericht** über die **wissenschaftlichen Unternehmungen** des **Deutsch-österreichischen Alpenvereins.** Wien. *Ber. wiss. Untern. dt.-öst. Alpenver.*

6445 **Bericht** des **Zentralverbands Preussischer Dampfkessel-Überwachungsvereine.** Frankfurt a. Oder. *Ber. ZentVerb. preuss. DampfkÜberwVer.* **L.**P. 11-37. [1932-33 *not published*]

6446 **Bericht. Zoologische Gesellschaft** in **Hamburg.** Hamburg. *Ber. zool. Ges. Hamburg* **L.**BM^N. 62-86.

6447 **Bericht** über das **Zoologische Museum** zu **Berlin.** *Ber. zool. Mus. Berl.* **L.**BM^N. 01-26 imp.; EB. 16-26; TD. 11-15; **E.**R. 11-26; **Lv.**U. 11-15; **Pl.**M. 16-26.

6448 **Bericht. Zoologisches Staatsinstitut** und **Zoologisches Museum.** Hamburg. *Ber. zool. StInst. zool. Mus. Hamburg* **L.**BM^N. 25-29.

6449 **Bericht** aus der **Zweiten geburtshülflich gynäkologischen Klinik** in **Wien.** Wien. *Ber. zweit. geburtsh. gynäk. Klin. Wien* **L.**MD. 97-02.

Berichte. *See* **Bericht.**

Berichten. *See* **Bericht.**

6449° **Berichtfolge** des **Kohlenstaubausschusses** des **Reichskohlenrates.** Berlin. *BerFolge Kohlenstaubaussch. ReichskohlRat.* **L.**P. 26-31*. [*C. as:* 6396, A-C]

6449^d **Berita. Balai penjelidikan perusahaan gula.** Djakarta. *Berita Balai Penjel. Perusah. Gula* [1958-] [*C. of:* 30074]

6450 **Berita** dari **Djawatan perikanan laut.** *Berita Djaw. Perik. Laut* [1949-] **Abd.**M. 49-52.

6450° **Berita Departemen kesehatan R. I.** Djakarta. *Berita Dep.Keseh. R.I.* [1951-]

6451 **Berita Gunung berapi.** Vulcanological Survey of Indonesia. Bandung. *Berita Gunung Berapi* [1952-] **L.**GM.

6452 **Berita hygiene.** Djakarta. *Berita Hyg.* [1948-] **L.**TD. 50- imp.

6452^a **Berita I. S. P. K.** Ikatan sardjana pertanian dan kehutanan. Jogjakarta. *Berita I. S. P.K.* [1959-]

6452^b **Berita ilmu penjakit anak.** Djakarta. *Berita Ilmu Penjakit Anak* [1957-]

6452° **Berita industri gula.** Jogjakarta. *Berita Ind. Gula* [1960-]

6452^d **Berita MIPI.** Madjelis ilmu pengetahuan Indonesia. Djakarta. *Berita MIPI* [1957-]

6452^e **Berita pelaut Indonesia.** Djakarta. *Berita Pelaut Indonesia* [1946-]

6453 **Berita perikanan.** Djakarta. *Berita Perik.* [1949-] **L.**AM.; **Lo.** [*C. of:* 56761]

6453^a **Berita. Pusat djawatan kehewanan.** Bogor. *Berita Pusat Djaw.Kehew.* [1952-] **Y.**

6454 **Berita tuberculosea indonesiensis.** Djakarta. *Berita tuberc. indones.* [1954-].

6455 **Berliner Ärzteblatt.** Berlin-Charlottenburg. *Berl. Ärztebl.*

6456 **Berliner Ärztekorrespondenz.** Berlin. *Berl. Ärztekorr.*

6457 **Berliner akademische Nachrichten.** Berlin. *Berl. akad. Nachr.* [*C. of:* 6458]

6458 **Berliner akademische Wochenschrift.** Berlin. *Berl. akad. Wschr.* [*C. as:* 6457]

6459 **Berliner Anzeiger.** Offizielles Organ der Berliner medizinischen Gesellschaft. Berlin. *Berl. Anz.*

6460 **Berliner Architekturwelt.** Berlin. *Berl. ArchitWelt* [1898-19] **L.**BA.; **E.**T. 99-13; **G.**M. 98-16; **Ld.**P. 98-14; **Lv.**P. 00-19; **M.**P. 98-14; **Sh.**P. 99-14.

6461 **Berliner astronomisches Jahrbuch.** Berlin. *Berl. astr. Jb.* [1830-] **L.**AS.; BM.; SC. 29-39: 45-; **C.**O.; UL.; **Db.**; **E.**O.; U. imp.; **G.**U. 1830-59; **M.**U. 1831-1847: 90-97; **O.**O.; **Sa.** 1830-15.

6462 **Berliner Chemical Review.** J.J. Berliner. N.Y. *Berl. chem. Rev.* [1943–]

6463 **Berliner Dentistenzeitung.** Berlin. *Berl. Dent-Ztg*

6464 **Berliner entomologische Zeitschrift.** Berlin. *Berl. ent. Z.* [1857–13] **L**.BM.; BM[N].; E.; L.; Z.; **Bn**.U. 02–03; **C**.UL.; **E**.F. 81–13; **O**.H. 1857–92; R.   [*C. in:* 16693].

6465 **Berliner geographische Arbeiten.** Berlin. *Berl. geogr. Arb.* [1932–] **L**.BM.; G. 33–; GL. 32–37.

6466 **Berliner homöopathische Zeitschrift.** Berlin-Zehlendorf. *Berl. homöop. Z.* [*C. of:* 58512; *C. as:* 16857]

6467 **Berliner Klinik.** Berlin. *Berl. Klin.* [1888–31] **L**.MD. 08–30 imp.; S.; **E**.P.; **M**.MS. 88–20.

6468 **Berliner klinische Wochenschrift.** Berlin. *Berl. klin. Wschr.* [1864–21] **L**.MA. 93–19 imp.; MC. 15–21; MD.; S.; **Abd**.U.; **Bm**.U. 90–95; **Br**.U.; **C**.PA. 98–21; UL. 78–21; **Cr**.MS 89–97; **Db**. 82–21; **Dn**.U. 82–99; **E**.P.; S. imp.; U. 83–21; **G**.F.; **Ld**.U.; **Lv**.M. 64–14; U. 64–14: 20–21; **M**.MS.; **O**.R. 91–21; **Sh**.U. 64–13.   [*C. in:* 27532]

6469 **Berliner klinisch-therapeutische Wochenschrift.** Berlin. *Berl. klin.-ther. Wschr.* [*C. as:* 16736]

6470 **Berliner Kraftfahrzeug-Handwerk.** Berlin. *Berl. Kraftfahrz.-Handwk* [1951–] **L**.P. 55–.

6471 **Berliner Mechaniker.** Berlin. *Berl. Mech.* [1955–] **L**.P.

6472 **Berliner medizinische Zeitschrift.** Berlin. *Berl. med. Z.* [1950–51] **L**.MA.; MD.   [*C. as:* 16901]
Berliner Molkerei-Zeitung. *See* 33061.

6473 **Berliner und Münchener tierärztliche Wochenschrift.** Berlin. *Berl. Münch. tierärztl. Wschr.* [1938–] **L**.LI. 38–40; MD. 48–; V.; **Abd**.R. 38–40: 51–; **C**.V. 53–; **E**.U.; **Sal**.; W.; Y.   [*C. of:* 6476 and 33795:>53181, 1944–45]

6474 **Berliner Nachrichtenblatt** der **Interessengruppe** für **Maschinen-** u. **Elektrotechniker** (Bezirk Gross-Berlin) des **Deutschen Technikerverbandes.** Berlin. *Berl. NachrBl. InteressGruppe Masch.- u. Elektrotech.*

6475 **Berliner Substitutes** and **New Materials Survey.** New York. *Berliner Subst. new Mater. Surv.* [1943–]
Berliner Textil-Zeitung. *See* 53021.

6476 **Berliner tierärztliche Wochenschrift.** Berlin. *Berl. tierärztl. Wschr.* [1885–38] **L**.LI. 24–38; MD. 91–13; TD. 14–30; V. 94–38 imp.; **E**.U. 31–38; **Sal**. 24–38; W. 05–38.   [*C. in:* 6473]

6477 **Berliner Zweigverein** der **Deutschen meteorologischen Gesellschaft.** Berlin. *Berl. Zweigver. dt. met. Ges.* **L**.MO. 85–25 imp.

6477° **Berner Beiträge** zur **Geschichte** der **Medizin** und der **Naturwissenschaften.** Bern. *Berner Beitr. Gesch. Med. Naturw.* [1942–] **O**.R.

6478 **Bernstein-Forschungen.** Berlin. *Bernstein-Forsch.* [1929–] **L**.E. 29–33; P. 29–39.

6479 **Berufsdermatosen.** Aulendorf. *Berufsdermatosen* [1953–] **L**.MA. 54–55; MD. 59–; TD.   [*C. of:* 16612]

6480 **Berufsforum.** Berlin. *Berufsforum* **L**.P. (curr.)   [*Supplement to:* 22266]

6481 **Berufsgenossenschaft.** Berlin. *Berufsgenossenschaft.* **L**.P. 60–.

6482 **Beschrijvende rassenlijst. Instituut** voor **plantenveredeling.** Wageningen. *Beschrijv. RassLijst Inst. PlVered.* **L**.AM. 48–.

6483 **Beschrijvende rassenlijst** voor **landbouwgewassen.** Wageningen. *Beschrijv. RassLijst LandbGewassen* **L**.AM. 43–; Y.

6484 **Beskrifning** till **kartbladet.** Stockholm. *Beskrif. Kartbl.* **L**.GM. 62–.

6485 **Beskrifning** offentliggjord af **K. Patentbyrån** Stockholm. *Beskrif. K. PatByr.*

6486 **Beskrivningar** över **mineralfyndigheter.** Stockholm. *Beskriv. MinerFynd.*

6487 **Besondere Mitteilungen** zum **Deutschen gewässerkundlichen Jahrbuch.** Bielefeld. *Besond. Mitt. dt. gewässerk. Jb.* **L**.MO. 50–; Y.

6488 **Besondere Mitteilungen. Jahrbuch** für die **Gewässerkunde Nord-Deutschlands.** Berlin. *Besond. Mitt. Jb. Gewässerk. NDtl.* **L**.MO. 27–37 imp. [*Supplement to:* 24751]

6489 **Bessarabskoe sel'skoe khozyaĭstvo.** Kishinev. Бессарабское сельское хозяйство. *Bessarab. sel'. Khoz.*

6490 **Bessemer Monthly.** Grove City, Pa. *Bessemer Mon.* **L**.P. 13–30*.   [*C. as:* 15896]

6491 **Bestiame** ed i **campi.** Portomaggiore. *Bestiame Campi*

6492 **Bestimmungs-Tabellen** der **europäischen Coleopteren.** Wien. *Bestimm.-Tab. eur. Coleopt.* **L**.BM[N]. 80–39 imp.; E. 80–.

6493 **Betegsegélyző.** Győr. *Betegsegélyző*
Beteiligung Deutschlands an der **internationalen Meeresforschung. Bericht.** *See* 6178.

6495 **Beten, vallar, mossar.** Uppsala. *Beten Vallar Mossar* [1949–61] **L**.P.; **Abs**.A. 49–52; **C**.A. 49–53; **Rt**. [*C. of:* 51598; *replaced by* Svensk valltidskrift]

6496 **Bethlem Maudsley Hospital Gazette.** London. *Bethlem Maudsley Hosp. Gaz.* [1954–] **L**.BM.; MA.

6497 **Beton.** Herstellung, Verwendung. Düsseldorf. *Beton* [1951–] **L**.P.; **Wa**.B.; Y.

6498 **Beton armé.** Paris. *Beton armé* **L**.P. 59–; Y.

6499 **Beton** und **Eisen.** Berlin. *Beton Eisen* [1902–] **L**.P. 10–40; SC. 27–; **Wa**.B. 05–39: 41–49.   [>6502, 1943–44, *and combined with* 5834, 1944–49]

6500 **Beton** og **jernbeton.** København. *Beton Jernbeton* [1949–56] **L**.P. imp.; **Wa**.B.   [*C. in:* 34951]

6501 **Beton litteratur referater.** København. *Beton Litt. Ref.* [1959–] **L**.P.; Y.   [*Supplement to:* 6514]

6502 **Beton** und **Stahlbetonbau.** Berlin. *Beton Stahlbetonb.* [1943–44: 50–] **L**.P.; SC.; **Ld**.U. 55–; Y.   [*C. of:* 6499, 1944–49 *appeared in* 5834]

6503 **Beton i zhelezobeton.** Moskva. Бетон и железобетон. *Beton Zhelezobeton* [1955–] **L**.BM.; P. 57–; **Wa**.B.; Y. 57–.   [*English abstracts at:* 15373[a]]

6504 **Betonbau.** Wien. *Betonbau* [*C. as:* 58513]

6505 **Betong.** Stockholm. *Betong* **Wa**.B. imp. [*C.in:* 34951]

6506 **Betonkalender.** Berlin. *Betonkalender* **L**.P. 07–30 imp.

6507 **Betonstein Jahrbuch.** Wiesbaden. *Betonstein Jb.* [1958–] **L**.P.

6508 **Betonsteinzeitung.** Wiesbaden. *Betonsteinzeitung* **L**.P. 47– imp.; **Wa**.B. 35–40: 48–; Y.

6509 **Betonstrasse.** Berlin, etc. *Betonstrasse* [1926–] **L**.P. 36–41; **Wa**.B. 37–41.

6510 **Betonstrassen.** Wildegg. *Betonstrassen* **L**.P. 52–; **Ha**.RD.

6511 **Betonstrassenbau** in **Deutschland.** Berlin. *BetonstrBau Dtl.* [1925–]

6512 **Betonszemle.** Budapest. *Betonszemle*

6513 **Beton-Taschenbuch.** Berlin. *Beton-Taschenb.* **L**.P. 07–15.

6514 **Beton-teknik.** København. *Beton-Tek.* [1935–] **L**.P. 58–; **Y.**

6515 **Beton-Zeitung.** Halle. *Beton-Ztg* [1907–12] **L**.BM. 08–12; P. 08–12.

6516 **Betrieb.** Berlin. *Betrieb* [1918–22] **L**.AV.; P.

6517 **Betriebstechnik.** Elektro- u. maschinentechnische Zeitschrift. Frankfurt a. M. *Betriebstechnik Frankf.*

6518 **Betriebstechnik.** München. *Betriebstechnik, Münch.* [1960–] **L**.P.

6519 **Better Analysis.** Cambridge, Mass. *Bett. Analysis* [1949–54] **L**.P. 50–54

6520 **Better Analysis Newsletter.** Cambridge, Mass. *Bett. Analysis Newsl.* [1953–] **L**.P. 53–56.

6521 **Better Blasting.** Washington, Delaware. *Bett. Blast.* **L**.P. curr.

6521° **Better Building Report.** College of Engineering and Architecture, Pennsylvania State University. University Park. *Bett. Bldg Rep.* [1959–] **L**.P.

6522 **Better Crops** with **Plant Food.** New York. *Bett. Crops* [1923–] **L**.AM. 57–; IC. 47–; P. 61–; **Abd**.S. 41–; **Br**.A. 55–; **C**.A. 45–; **Hu**.G. 48–; **Je**. 47–; **Md**.H. 46–; **O**.RE. (1 yr); **Rt.** 38– imp.; **Y.**

6523 **Better Enameling.** Cicero, Ill. *Bett. Enam.* [1930–52] **L**.P. 49–52; **Bm**.C. 35–41: 44–52.

6524 **Better Eyesight.** New York. *Bett. Eyesight* [1919–30] **L**.BM.; **C**.UL. 20–30; **O**.R. 19–22.

6525 **Better Farm Equipment** and **Methods.** St. Louis. *Bett. Fm Equip. Meth.*

6526 **Better Farming.** Chicago. *Bett. Fmg*

6527 **Better Fibers.** *Bett. Fibers* [1959–] **L**.TP.

6528 **Better Fruit.** Portland, Ore. *Bett. Fruit* [1906–] **L**.AM. 47–; EB. 22–42; MY. 23–43; **Md**.H. 30–.

6529 **Better Health.** London. *Bett. Hlth* [1927–] **L**.BM. 33–; H. 39–; MA. 37–57 v. imp.; SH. (1 yr); TD. imp.; **Abs**.N.; **G**.PH. 29–; **O**.R. 27–30.

6530 **Better Highways.** Columbus, Ohio. *Bett. Highw.* [1926–33] **L**.P.

6531 **Better Methods.** Chicago. *Bett. Meth.* **L**.P. (curr.)

6532 **Betterave** et les **industries agricoles.** Valenciennes. *Betterave Ind. agr.* [1891–36]

6533 **Betteravier français.** Paris. *Betteravier fr.* **L**.AM. 52–; **Y.**

6534 **Betteraviste.** Amiens. *Betteraviste*

6534° **Bettis Technical Review.** Pittsburgh. *Bettis tech. Rev.* [1957–]

6534ᵉ **Bevezetés a magyar förténelem forásaiba** és **irodalmába.** Budapest. *Bevez. magy. Förtén. Forás. irodalm.* [1951–] **L**.BM.

6535 **Bevolkingsrubbercultuur** in **Nederlandsch-Indië.** Weltevreden. *BevolkRubbCult. Ned.-Indië* **Rt.** 25–27*.

6536 **Beyer-Peacock Quarterly Review.** Manchester. *Beyer-Peacock q. Rev.* [1927–32] **L**.P.; **M**.P. imp.; U.

6537 **Bezopasnost' truda** v **promÿshlennosti.** Moskva. Безопасность труда в промышленности. *Bezopas. Truda Prom.* [1957–] **L**.BM. 58–; P.; **Y.**

6537° **Bezpečnost a hygiena práce.** Praha. *Bezpeč. Hyg. Práce* [1951–] **Y.**

6538 **Bezpieczeństwo i higiena pracy.** Warszawa. *Bezpiecz. Hig. Pracy* [1947–52] **L**.MA. 51–52; TD. 51–52. [*C. as:* 35836]

6539 **Bhagirath.** Delhi. *Bhagirath* [1954–] **L**.P. 55–.

6539° **Bianco e nero.** Studi cinematografici. Roma. *Bianco nero* [1949–] **L**.BM. 56–.

6540 **Bi-annual Report. East Indies Institute** of **America.** New York. *Biann. Rep. E. Indies Inst. Am.* **L**.SC. 41–43*.

6541 **Bi-annual Report** of the **Southeast Asia Institute.** New York. *Biann. Rep. S.E. Asia Inst..*

6542 **Biatas.** Dublin. *Biatas* [1956–] **L**.AM.; **C**.A. [*C. of:* 5892]

6543 **Bibliografia brasileira** de **botânica.** Rio de Janeiro. *Biblfia bras. Bot.* [1957–] **L**.SC.

6544 **Bibliografia brasileira** de **matemática** e **física.** Rio de Janeiro. *Biblfia bras. Mat. Fís.* [1955–] **L**.P.; SC.

6545 **Bibliografia brasileira** de **química.** Rio de Janeiro. *Biblfia bras. Quím.* [1957–] **L**.P.; SC.; **Y.**

6545° **Bibliografia brasileira** de **química tecnológica.** *Biblfia bras. Quím. tecnol.* [1954–]

6546 **Bibliografia elettrotecnica (straniera).** Milano. *Biblfia elettrotec. (stran.)* [1949–] **L**.AV. 57–; **Y.** [*C. of:* 17927]

6547 **Bibliografia farmaceutica.** Milano. *Biblfia farm.* [1957–] **L**.MA.

6547° **Bibliografia geodetica italiana.** Roma. *Biblfia geod. ital.* **L**.SC. 31–.

6548 **Bibliografia geografica** della **regione Italia.** Firenze. *Biblfia geogr. Reg. Ital.* **O**.G. 01–03.

6549 **Bibliografia geografii polskiej.** Warszawa. *Biblfia Geogr. pol.* [1956–] **L**.MO.; SC.

6550 **Bibliografia geologica italiana.** Roma. *Biblfia geol. ital.* [1886–34] **L**.BMᴺ.

6551 **Bibliografia geologică a Romãniei.** Bucureşti. *Biblfia geol. Rom.* **L**.GM. 26–; **Lv**.U. 26–29.

6552 **Bibliografia geologiczna Polski.** Warszawa. *Biblfia geol. Pol.* [1921–] **L**.BM. 50–; P.; **Y.**
Bibliografía hidrológica, España. *See* 6648.

6553 **Bibliografia hidrológica** do **Império português.** Lisboa. *Biblfia hidrol. Imp. port.* [1949–] **L**.BM.

6554 **Bibliografia hydrologiczna polska.** *Biblfia hydrol. pol.* [1936–] **L**.MO. 37–; P. 45; **Y.**

6555 **Bibliografia** sull'**imballaggio.** Roma. *Biblfia Imball.* **L**.P. 54–. [*Supplement to:* 8255]

6556 **Bibliografia italiana.** Roma. *Biblfia ital.* [1929–]
    A. Scienze matematiche, fisiche e biologiche
    L.BM.; EB. 31–; MC. 29–38; SC.; **C.**UL.; **E.**R.
    B. Medicina
    L.BM.; MC. 29–38; MD. 29–33; SC.; **C.**UL.; **E.**R.
    C. Ingegneria, etc.
    L.BM.; SC.; **C.**UL.; **E.**R.
    D. Agricoltura
    L.BM.; EB. 31–; SC.; **C.**UL.; **E.**R.
    [*C. of* 6570]

6557 **Bibliografia italiana** di **elettrotecnica.** Padova. *Biblfia ital. Elettrotec.* [1950–] **L.**AV. 57–; P.; **Db.**; **Nw.**A.; **Y.** [*C. of:* 8254]

6558 **Bibliografia italiana** di **idraulica.** Padova *Biblfia ital. Idraul.* [1950–] **L.**HQ. 54–; P. 55–.

6559 **Bibliografia** sul **maneggio meccanico** dei **materiali.** Roma. *Biblfia Maneggio mecc. Mater.* **L.**P. 55–. [*Supplement to:* 8255]

6560 **Bibliografia matematica italiana.** Roma. *Biblfia mat. ital.* [1950–] **L.**BM.; SC.; U.; **Y.**

6561 **Bibliografía médica argentina.** Buenos Aires. *Biblfía méd. argent.* **L.**MD. 34.

6562 **Bibliografía médica internacional.** Madrid. *Biblfía méd. int.* [1941–] **L.**MD. 41–44; TD. 42–45 imp.

6563 **Bibliografia médica portuguesa.** Lisboa. *Biblfia méd. port.* [1940–] **L.**BM. 51–; TD.

6564 **Bibliografia medico-biologica.** Roma. *Biblfia med.-biol.* [1939–]

6565 **Bibliografía metalúrgica y mecánica.** Madrid. *Biblfía metal. mec.* [1953] **L.**P. [*C. of:* 31504; *Translation of:* 31472; *Published in:* 46782]

6566 **Bibliografia meteorologica italiana.** Roma. *Biblfia met. ital.* **L.**MO. 26.

6566° **Bibliografía** de **obras** sobre **hidrología. República argentina.** *Biblfía Obras Hidrol. Repúb. Argent.* **Y.**

6567 **Bibliografia ortopedica.** Bologna. *Biblfia ortop.* [1920–] **L.**BM.; MA. 32–39 imp.; MD.; S. 20–40; **Br.**U. 29– imp.; **M.**MS. 31–40 imp.

6568 **Bibliografia polarografica.** Roma. *Biblfia polarogr.* [1949–] **L.**P.; **C.**CH. imp.

6568° **Bibliografia prac** z **dziedziny ewolucjonizmu.** Warszawa. *Biblfia Prac Dziedz. Ewol.* [1953–] **Y.**

6569 **Bibliografía química argentina.** Buenos Aires. *Biblfía quím. argent.* [1934–] **L.**P. [*Supplement to:* 2319]

6570 **Bibliografia scientifico-tecnica italiana.** Bologna. *Biblfia scient.-tec. ital.* [1928] **L.**BM.; MC.; **C.**UL.; **E.**R. [*C. as:* 6556]

6571 **Bibliografia tessile.** Milano. *Biblfia tess.* [1953–56] **L.**P.; **M.**C. [*C. as:* 17091]

6572 **Bibliografia** sul **traffico cittadino.** Roma. *Biblfia Traff. citt.* **L.**P. 55–. [*Supplement to:* 8255]

6573 **Bibliografias. Instituto** de **biología.** Chapultepec, D.F. *Biblfias Inst. Biol., Chapultepec* **L.**BM^N. 31.

6574 **Bibliŏgraficheskiĭ ukazatel' Imperatorskago tekhnicheskago obshchestva** po **zhelêzno-dorozhnomu dêlu.** St. Petersburg. Библіографическій указатель Императорскаго техническаго общества по желѣзно-дорожному дѣлу. *Biblfich. Ukaz. imp. tekh. Obshch. zhel.-dorozh. Dêlu*

Bibliografie lesnického písemnictví Čech a Moravy (a **Sleska).** *See* 6592.

6575 **Bibliografie zemědělská a lesnická, československa literatura.** Praha. *Biblfie zěměd. lesn. čsl. Lit.* [1954–55] **L.**AM.; P. [*C. as:* 38566]

6576 **Bibliografija Jugoslavije.** Beograd. *Biblfija Jugosl.* [1950–] Serija B. Prirodne i primenjene nauke. **L.**BM.; P. 52–; SC. 52–.

Bibliografija. Latvijas PSR zinātņu akademijas. *See* 28176.

6577 **Bibliografiya kartograficheskoĭ literaturŷ i kart.** Moskva. Библиография картографической литературы и карт. *Biblfiya kartogr. Lit. Kart* [1939–40] **L.**BM. [*C. of* and *Rec. as:* 27263]

6577° **Bibliografiya** po **uslovnŷm refleksam.** Moskva. Библиография по условным рефлексам. *Biblfiya uslov. Refleksam* [1955–] **L.**BM.

Bibliografja hydrologiczna. *See* 6554.

6578 **Bibliographia biotheoretica.** Leiden. *Biblphia biotheor.* [1925–] **L.**BM^N.; SC. 25–29: 38–; UC.; **E.**R.; **O.**R. 44–; **Y.** [*Issued in series*]

6579 **Bibliographia chimica.** Leipzig. *Biblphia chim.* [1922–26] **L.**P. imp.; **G.**U. imp.; **Ld.**U. 22–23. [*C. in:* 13823]

6580 **Bibliographia forestalis.** Berlin. *Biblphia for.* [1941–]

6581 **Bibliographia genetica.** 's Gravenhage. *Biblphia genet.* [1925–] **L.**BM^N.; L. 25–52; NC.; QM. 30–33; SC.; UC.; Z.; **Abs.**A.; **Ba.**I.; **Bl.**U. 25–34; **Bm.**U. 41–; **C.**GE.; UL.; **E.**AG.; U.; **G.**U.; **Lv.**U.; **M.**U.; **N.**U.; **O.**R.; **R.**U.; **Rt.**; **Sa.**

6582 **Bibliographia geologica.** Bruxelles. *Biblphia geol.* [1897–06] **L.**BM^N.; P.; **Abd.**U.; **Db.** 00–06.

6583 **Bibliographia medica.** Paris. *Biblphia med.* [1900–02] **L.**MA.; MD.; S.; **E.**P.; **G.**U.; **M.**MS. 00–01.

6584 **Bibliographia medica čechoslovaka.** Praha. *Biblphia med. čsl.* [1947–] **L.**BM. 49–; MD. 47–50; **G.**U.

6585 **Bibliographia medica helvetica.** Basel. *Biblphia med. helv.* [1943–] **L.**BM.; D. 43; MA.; MD. 43: 52–53; U.; **C.**P.; PO.; **E.**U.; **O.**R.

6585° **Bibliographia medica latina.** Roma. *Biblphia med. lat.* [1954–] **L.**BM.

6586 **Bibliographia** şi **notiţe meteorologice.** Bucureşti. *Biblphia Not. met., Buc.* **L.**MO. 01–05.

6587 **Bibliographia oceanographica.** Romae, etc. *Biblphia oceanogr.* [1928–] **L.**AM. 28–47 imp.; BM.; MO.; P. 49–; **Abd.**M.; **Bn.**U. 48–; **C.**P. 36–; PO.; **Dm.** imp.; **Lo.**; **Lv.**U.; **Mi.**; **Nw.**A. 28–44; **Pl.**M. imp.; **Wo.** 34– imp.

6588 **Bibliographia odontologica.** Wien. *Biblphia odont.* **L.**BM^N. 33 imp.

6589 **Bibliographia oto-rhino-laryngologica japonica.** *Biblphia oto-rhino-lar. jap.*

6589^a **Bibliographia phonetica.** *Biblphia phon.* [*Supplement to:* 56972]

6590 **Bibliographia physiologica.** Leipzig, Wien. *Biblphia physiol.* [1905–26] **L.**MD. 05–13; S. 05–14; U. 05–13; **Bl.**U. 05–13; **Br.**U. 05–13: 22; **C.**UL.; **Db.** 05–13; **Dn.**U. 05–12; **E.**U. 06–13; **G.**U. 05–13; **Ld.**U. 05–12; **Lv.**U. 05–09; **M.**MS. 06–08; **O.**R. 05–13; **Sa.** 05–14. [*Suspended* 1915–21: *Supplement to:* 59064]

6591 **Bibliographia scientiae naturalis helvetica.** Bern. *Biblphia Sci. nat. helv.* [1948–] **L.**BM.; SC.; **Ld.**U. 48–52: 56– imp.; **O.**R.; **Y.** [*C. of:* 6675]

6592 **Bibliographia silviculturae Bohemiae** et **Moraviae** (et **Silesiacae**). Prag. *Biblphia Silvic. Bohem. Morav.* [1934–]

6593 **Bibliographia technica.** Berlin. *Biblphia tech.* [1924–25] **L.**P.; SC. 25.

6594 **Bibliographia zoologica.** Lipsiae. *Biblphia zool.* [1896–34] **L.**BM. 96–14; BM^N.; R. 96–16; S. 96–12; SC. 96–12; UC. 99–25; Z.; **Abd.**U.; **Bm.**P.; U. 96–26 imp.; **C.**UL.; **Cr.**M. 96–14; **Db.**; **E.**F. 96–12; R.; U.; **G.**U.; **H.**U.; **Lv.**U.; **M.**U. 96–12; **Mi.** 97–34 imp.; **N.**U. 04–12; **Nw.**A. 96–12; **O.**R.; **Pl.**M.; **R.**U.; **Sa.**; **Sh.**U. 98–14.
    Bibliographic Bulletin. Permanent Inter-African Bureau for **Tsetse Fly** and **Trypanosomiasis.** *See* 9561.

6595 **Bibliographic Contributions. Geological Society** of **America.** Washington. *Biblphic Contr. geol. Soc. Am.* [1933–34] **L.**BM^N.; GL.; SC.; **Bl.**U.; **Bm.**U.; **Br.**U.; **C.**P.; S.; **O.**R. [*C. as:* 6728]

6596 **Bibliographic Contributions. Philippine Bureau** of **Science.** Manila. *Biblphic Contr. Philipp. Bur. Sci.* [1937–] **L.**SC.

6597 **Bibliographic Index.** New York. *Biblphic Index* [1937–] **L.**AM. 37–60; BM.; P.; SC.; SI. 37–48; TD.; **G.**M.; **Lv.**P. 38–; **Y.**

6598 **Bibliographic Index. Permanent International Association** of **Road Congresses.** Paris. *Biblphic Index perm. int. Ass. Rd Congr.* **L.**P. 32–33*. [*C. in:* 9475]
    Bibliographic Series Bulletin. Mellon Institute of **Industrial Research.** Pittsburgh. *See* 6601.

6599 **Bibliographic Series. Division** of **Forest Products. C.S.I.R.O.** Melbourne. *Biblphic Ser. Div. Forest Prod. C.S.I.R.O.* **O.**F. 44– imp.

6600 **Bibliographic Series. Institute** of **Paper Chemistry.** Appleton. *Biblphic Ser. Inst. Pap. Chem.* **L.**P. 42– imp.; **Y.**

6600° **Bibliographic Series. Library Branch, Quartermaster Food** and **Container Institute** for the **Armed Forces.** Chicago. *Biblphic Ser. Libr. Brch Quarterm. Fd Contain. Inst. armed Forc.* [1953–] **Y.**

6601 **Bibliographic Series. Mellon Institute** of **Industrial Research.** *Biblphic Ser. Mellon Inst. ind. Res.* [1922–] **L.**P. 33–; SC.; **M.**P. 27–35 imp.; **Y.**

6602 **Bibliographic Series. Technical Library, Quartermaster Research** and **Development Laboratories.** Philadelphia. *Biblphic Ser. tech. Libr. Quarterm. Res. Dev. Lab.* **Y.**

6603 **Bibliographic Survey** of **Corrosion.** Houston. *Biblphic Surv. Corros.* [1948–] **L.**P. 48–55; SC.; **Y.**
    Bibliographical Annual. Geology of the **U.S.S.R.** *See* 21028.
    Bibliographical Bulletin. Department of **Agriculture.** Washington. *See* 6604.
    Bibliographical Bulletin. International Association of **Medical Press.** Rome. *See* 8228.
    Bibliographical Bulletin. Permanent Inter-African Bureau for **Tsetse** and **Trypanosomiasis.** *See* 9561.

6604 **Bibliographical Bulletin. United States Department** of **Agriculture Library.** Washington. *Biblphical Bull. U.S. Dep. Agric. Libr.* [1943–] **L.**BM.; BM^N. imp.; EB. (ent.); P. 43–54; **C.**A.; **Lv.**P. 44–; **O.**F. 46– imp.; **Y.**

6605 **Bibliographical Bulletin** for **Welding** and **Allied Processes.** Paris. *Biblphical Bull. Weld.* [1949–] **L.**NF.; P.; SC.; **C.**ENG. 51–; **Rn.**B.; **Y.** [*C. of:* 10124]

6606 **Bibliographical Contributions. Library** of **Engineering Societies.** New York. *Biblphical Contr. Libr. Engng Socs* **L.**P. 15.

6607 **Bibliographical Contributions** from the **Lloyd Library.** Cincinnati. *Biblphical Contr. Lloyd Libr.* [1911–18] **L.**BM^N.; G.; HO.; HS.; K.; L.; P.; U.; UC.; **Abd.**U. 11–17; **Bm.**N. 11–16; **Db.**; **E.**B.; D.; J. 11–17; R. 14–18; **Lv.**U. imp.; **Nw.**A.; **O.**BO.; **Rt.**

6608 **Bibliographical Contributions. United States Department** of **Agriculture Library.** Washington. *Biblphical Contr. U.S. Dep. Agric. Libr.* [1919–38] **L.**AM.; BM^N. 19–27; EB. (ent.) 22–30; P.; SC.; **C.**A. 22–38; **Rt.** 22–38. [*C. as:* 28525]

6608° **Bibliographical List** of **Japanese Learned Journals.** Tokyo. *Biblphical List Jap. learn. J.* Natural sciences. [1957–]

6609 **Bibliographical Lists. United States Geological Survey.** Washington. *Biblphical Lists U.S. geol. Surv.* [1934–]

6610 **Bibliographical Monographs. Commonwealth Bureau** of **Plant Breeding** and **Genetics.** Cambridge, etc. *Biblphical Monogr. Commonw. Bur. Pl. Breed.* [1930–] **O.**BO. 32– imp.
    Bibliographical Monographs. Imperial Bureau of **Plant Breeding** and **Genetics.** *See* 6610.

6611 **Bibliographical Notes. Northern Coke Research Committee.** Newcastle-upon-Tyne. *Biblphical Notes nth. Coke Res. Comm.* [1927–30] **L.**P. [*C. as:* 6742]

6612 **Bibliographical Series. Agricultural College** and **Research Institute.** Coimbatore. *Biblphical Ser. agric. Coll. Coimbatore* [1940–]

6613 **Bibliographical Series. Geographical Branch, Department** of **Mines** and **Technical Surveys, Canada.** *Biblphical Ser. geogr. Brch Dep. Mines tech. Surv. Can.* [1950–] **Y.**

6614 **Bibliographical Series. International Atomic Energy Agency.** Vienna. *Biblphical Ser. int. atom. Energy Ag.* [1960–] **L.**P.

6615 **Bibliographical Series. Iron** and **Steel Institute.** London. *Biblphical Ser. Iron Steel Inst.* [1936–] **L.**BM.; I.; P.; SC.; **O.**B.; **Y.**

6615° **Bibliographical Series. Ministry** of **Aviation.** London. *Biblphical Ser. Minist. Aviat.* [1960–] **L.**AV.; BM.; P.; SC.
    Bibliographical Series. Science Library. London. *See* 49043.

6616 **Bibliographical Service. Institut für Schiffahrtsforschung.** Bremen. *Biblphical Serv. Inst. Schiffahrtsforsch.* [1954–57] **L.**P. [*C. as:* 42410]

6617 **Bibliographical Survey** of **Instrument Parts.** London. *Biblphical Surv. Instrum. Parts* [1954–] **L.**BM.

6618 **Bibliographie actinométrique.** Union géodésique et géophysique internationale. *Biblphie actinom.* **L.**MO. 84–35.

6619 **Bibliographie der aerologischen Literatur.** Berlin. *Biblphie aerol. Lit.* **L.**MO. 29–39: 43–44; **E.**M. 29–39.
    Bibliographie agricole tchèque. *See* 13585.

6620 **Bibliographie d'agriculture tropicale.** Rome. *Biblphie Agric. trop.* L.BM 38–.

6621 **Bibliographie anatomique.** Revue des travaux en langue française. Paris et Nancy. *Biblphie anat.* [1893–18] L.BM^N.; L.; UC.; C.AN.; Dn.U. 93–14; E.P.; G.U. 93–14; Ld.U.; Lv.U. 96–18; O.R. 12–18.

6622 **Bibliographie des ausländischen forst- und holzwirtschaftlichen Schrifttums.** Tharant. *Biblphie ausl. forst- u. holzw. Schrifft.* [1955] L.SC.; O.F. [*C. as:* 6632]

6623 **Bibliographie der Biochemie und Biophysik.** Berlin. *Biblphie Biochem. Biophys.* [1910] L.P. [*C. as:* 6624]

6624 **Bibliographie der Biologie.** Berlin. *Biblphie Biol.* [1911] L.P. [*C. of:* 6623]

6625 **Bibliographie cartographique française.** *Biblphie cartogr. fr.* L.SC. 49–; O.G. 38–45.

6626 **Bibliographie cartographique internationale.** *Biblphie cartogr. int.* [1946–] L.BM.; SC.; C.GG. imp.; Ld.U. imp.; R.U. 46–47.
   Bibliographie choisie d'hydrologie, Canada. See 49426.

6627 **Bibliographie der deutschen naturwissenschaftlichen Literatur.** Berlin. *Biblphie dt. naturw. Lit.* [1901–14] L.BM.; BM^N.; C.; P.; SC. 01–05; U.

6628 **Bibliographie der an den deutschen technischen Hochschulen erschienenen Doktor-Ingenieur-Dissertationen.** Berlin. *Biblphie dt. tech. Hochsch. Dr-Ing.-Diss.*

6629 **Bibliographie deutscher Übersetzungen aus den Sprachen der Völker der Sowjetunion und der Länder der Volksdemokratie.** Berlin. *Biblphie dt. Übersetz. Sprachen Völk. SowjUn.* [1952–] Abt. 1. Wissenschaftliche Literatur. L.BM.; HQ. (1 yr.); P. 58–; Y.

6630 **Bibliographie ethnographique du Congo belge et des régions avoisinantes.** Bruxelles. *Biblphie ethnogr. Congo belge* [1925–] L.AN.; E.R.

6631 **Bibliographie des forstlichen Schrifttums Deutschlands.** Freiburg i. Br. *Biblphie forst. Schrifft. Dtl.* L.P. 57–; O.F. 52–.

6632 **Bibliographie des forst- und holzwirtschaftlichen Schrifttums.** Hamburg. *Biblphie forst- u. holzw. Schrifft.* [1956–] L.P.; SC.; TP.; O.F.; Y. [*C. of:* 6622]

6633 **Bibliographie der Freiburger Forschungshefte.** Berlin. *Biblphie freiburg. ForschHft.* [1951–] L.P.

6634 **Bibliographie géodésique internationale.** Bruxelles. *Biblphie géod. int.* [1928–] L.AS.; BM.; P.; SC. 28–30: 35–; U.; Bl.U. 35–39; C.GD.; UL.; Ld.U.; Y.
   Bibliographie géographique. See 6637.

6635 **Bibliographie géographique annuelle.** Paris. *Biblphie géogr. a.* [1891–14] L.B. 93–95: 98–14; BM.; U. 98–14; Abs.U. 99–14; Bl.U. 04–14; Br.U.; E.U. 06–14; Ld.U. 93–14; R.U.; Sh.U. 93–14. [*C. as:* 6637: 1891–92 forms part of text in 2746]

6636 **Bibliographie géographique de l'Égypte.** Le Caire. *Biblphie géogr. Egypte* L.BM. 28–29.

6637 **Bibliographie géographique (internationale).** Paris. *Biblphie géogr. int.* [1915–] L.B.; BM.; SC. 45–; TD. 24–; U.; UC. 22–38; Abd.U. 20–; Abs.U.; Bl.U.; Bm.P. 24–; U.; Br.U.; C.GG. 24–; UL. 23–; E.G. 28–; U.; Ex.U. 15–31: 47–; G.U. 15–44; H.U. 40–; Ld.U.; N.U.; Nw.A.

24–; O.B. 25–; G.; R.U.; Sh.U.; Sw.U. 39–44; Y. [*C. of:* 6635]

6638 **Bibliographie géohydrologique-Portugal.** Lisboa. *Biblphie géohydrol.-Port.* L.MO. 24–; P. 24–; Y.

6638° **Bibliographie géologique du Congo belge et du Ruanda Urundi.** Bruxelles. *Biblphie géol. Congo belge Ruanda Urundi* [1952–] L.BM.; Y.
   Bibliographie géologique et minéralogique de la République tchécoslovaque. See 31936.
   Bibliographie géologique de Pologne. See 6836.

6639 **Bibliographie géologique de la Tunisie.** Tunis. *Biblphie géol. Tunis.* [1954–] Y.

6640 **Bibliographie der gesamten inneren Medizin und ihrer Grenzgebiete.** Berlin. *Biblphie ges. inn. Med.* L.MD. 12: 13: 20*; P. 10. [*C. as:* 24965]

6641 **Bibliographie der gesamten Kinderheilkunde.** Berlin. *Biblphie ges. Kinderheilk.* L.MD. 12:13:20–22*; E.P. 11–22. [*C. as:* 24966]

6642 **Bibliographie der Hals-, Nasen- und Ohrenheilkunde.** Berlin. *Biblphie Hals- Nas.- u. OhrHeilk.* [1922] L.BM.; S.; C.UL.; E.S. [*C. as:* 24979]

6643 **Bibliographie der Haut- und Geschlechtskrankheiten.** Berlin. *Biblphie Haut- u. GeschlKrankh.* [1921] L.MD. [*C. as:* 24982]

6644 **Bibliographie hydrologique-Argentina.** Buenos Aires. *Biblphie hydrol.-Argent.* L.MO. 54–; P. 54–; Y.

6645 **Bibliographie hydrologique du bassin du Nil.** Cairo. *Biblphie hydrol. Bass. Nil* L.P. 84–.

6646 **Bibliographie hydrologique-Belgique.** Bruxelles. *Biblphie hydrol.-Belg.* L.MO. 38–; P. 38–; Y.

6647 **Bibliographie hydrologique-Danemark.** København. *Biblphie hydrol.-Danem.* L.MO. 37–; Y.

6648 **Bibliographie hydrologique-Espagne.** Madrid. *Biblphie hydrol.-Espagne* L.MO. 40–; P.; Y.

6649 **Bibliographie hydrologique-Estonie.** Tallinn. *Biblphie hydrol.-Eston.* L.MO. 38.

6650 **Bibliographie hydrologique-France.** Paris. *Biblphie hydrol.-Fr.* L.MO. 37–; P. 46–; Y.

6651 **Bibliographie hydrologique-Italie.** Rome. *Biblphie hydrol.-Ital.* L.MO. 35–; P. 37–; Y.

6652 **Bibliographie hydrologique-Lithuanie.** Kaunas. *Biblphie hydrol.-Lithuan.* L.MO. 38; Y.

6653 **Bibliographie hydrologique-Norvège.** Oslo. *Biblphie. hydrol-Norv.* L.MO. 40–; Y.

6654 **Bibliographie hydrologique-Pays-Bas.** De Bilt. *Biblphie hydrol.-Pays-Bas* L.MO. 37–; Y.
   Bibliographie hydrologique-Pologne. See 6554.

6655 **Bibliographie hydrologique-Suède.** Stockholm. *Biblphie hydrol.-Suède* L.MO. 37–; Y.

6656 **Bibliographie hydrologique-Suisse.** Zürich. *Biblphie hydrol.-Suisse* L.MO. 39–; Y.

6657 **Bibliographie hydrologique-Tchechoslovaquie.** Praha. *Biblphie hydrol.-Tchech.* L.MO. 34–.

6658 **Bibliographie hydrologique - Yougoslavie.** *Biblphie hydrol.-Yougosl.*

6659 **Bibliographie de l'hygiène du bâtiment et de l'usine.** Paris. *Biblphie Hyg. Bâtim. Usine*
   Bibliographie d'hygiène industrielle. See 6730.

6660 **Bibliographie** der **inneren Medizin.** Berlin. *Biblphie inn. Med.* [1910–] **L.**P. 10.

Bibliographie internationale annotée des **applications industrielles** de la **statistique.** The Hague. *See* 23858.

6661 **Bibliographie internationale** de **météorologie générale.** Paris. *Biblphie int. Mét. gén.* [1933–34] **L.**MO.; SC.; **C.**SP.; **O.**G. [*C. of:* 6667; *C. as:* 6668]

6662 **Bibliographie** der **isländischen Forst-** und **Holzwirtschaften.** Schrifttums. *Biblphie isl. Forst- u. Holzw.* **L.**MY. 56–.

6663 **Bibliographie Klima** und **Mensch.** Deutscher Wetterdienst (*formerly* in der U.S. Zone). Bad Kissingen. *Biblphie Klima Mensch* [1945–] **L.**MO.

Bibliographie de **médecine** du **travail.** *See* 6743.
Bibliographie médicale polonaise. *See* 38039.

6665 **Bibliographie mensuelle** de l'**astronomie.** Société astronomique de France. Paris. *Biblphie mens. Astr.* [1933–43] **L.**AS. 40–43 imp.; **Bl.**U.; **Bm.**P.; **C.**SP.; **E.**R. [*C. as:* 18863]

Bibliographie mensuelle de la **Société** de **géographie.** Paris. *See* 579.

6666 **Bibliographie mensuelle** de l'**Union radio scientifique internationale.** *Biblphie mens. Un. Radio scient. int.*

6667 **Bibliographie météorologique.** Paris. *Biblphie mét.* [1921–32] **L.**MO. [*C. as:* 6661]

6668 **Bibliographie météorologique internationale.** Paris. *Biblphie mét. int.* [1935–] **L.**MO.; SC.; **O.**G. [*C. of:* 6661]

6669 **Bibliographie météorologique suisse.** Zurich. *Biblphie mét. suisse* **Y.**

6670 **Bibliographie méthodique trimestrielle.** **Communauté européenne** du **charbon** et de l'**acier.** Luxembourg. *Biblphie méth. trimest. Commun. eur. Charb. Acier* [1956–] **Bl.**U.; **Dn.**U.; **M.**P. [*C. of:* 10969]

6671 **Bibliographie** der **Neurologie** und **Psychiatrie.** Berlin. *Biblphie Neurol. Psychiat., Berl.* [1910–13] **L.**MD. 11–12; UC. [*C. as:* 24967]

6672 **Bibliographie** der **Pflanzenschutzliteratur.** Berlin. *Biblphie PflSchutzlit.* [1914–] **L.**AM. 14–37: 40– imp.; EB. 14–39; HS. 28–51; K.; P. imp.; SC.; **Abs.**A. 14–36; **C.**A. 31–36; **Db.**; **Ld.**U. 40–52; **M.**U.; **Md.**H. 29–37: 53–; **O.**AP. 32–37; F. 14–36; **Rt.**; **Y.** [*C. of:* 24955]

6673 **Bibliographie** der **Philosophie** und **Psychologie.** Leipzig. *Biblphie Phil. Psychol., Lpz.* [1920–] **C.**UL.

6674 **Bibliographie** der **schweizerischen Landeskunde.** Bern. *Biblphie schweiz. Landesk.* **L.**BM. 94–15; MO. 27.

6675 **Bibliographie** der **schweizerischen naturwissenschaftlichen** und **geographischen Literatur.** Bern. *Biblphie schweiz. naturw. geogr. Lit.* [1925–47] **Ld.**U. 28–47; **O.**R. [*C. as:* 6591]

6676 **Bibliographie** des **sciences géologiques.** Paris. *Biblphie Sci. géol.* [1923–] **L.**BM.; BM^N.; GL.; GM.; SC.; **Bl.**U. 23–24; **E.**C. 24–39 imp.; R.; **Lv.**U. 23–25: 46–; **Nw.**A. 24–29.

6677 **Bibliographie** des **sciences** et de l'**industrie.** Paris. *Biblphie Sci. Ind.* **L.**BA. 48–.

6678 **Bibliographie scientifique.** Bulletin de l'Institut international de bibliographie scientifique. Paris *Biblphie scient.*

6679 **Bibliographie scientifique française.** Paris. *Biblphie scient. fr.* [1902–] **L.**BM^N. (sect. I) 02–33: (sect. II) 02–48 imp.; GL. 09–; **Br.**U. 20–23 imp.; **C.**UL.; **Db.** 03–; **E.**R. 20–23; U.; **M.**U. 20–23; **O.**B.; **Sa.** 20–23.

6680 **Bibliographie scientifique suisse.** Berne. *Biblphie scient. suisse* **L.**SC. 34–.

6681 **Bibliographie signalétique. Météorologie nationale.** Paris. *Biblphie signal. Mét. natn.* **L.**MO. 46–.

6682 **Bibliographie** des **travaux scientifiques.** Paris. *Biblphie Trav. scient.* [1895–22] **L.**BM^N.; SC. 97–17; **O.**B.

6683 **Bibliographie** der **Veröffentlichungen.** **Hygienisches Institut** der **Hansestadt Hamburg** und **Akademie** für **Staatsmedizin.** Hamburg. *Biblphie Veröff. hyg. Inst. Hamb.* **L.**P. 50–.

6684 **Bibliographie** der **Veterinärmedizin.** Berlin. *Biblphie VetMed.* **L.**P. 10.

Bibliographie de la **Yougoslavie.** Série B. Sciences naturelles et appliquées. *See* 6576.

6684ᵃ **Bibliographien** des **deutschen Wetterdienstes.** Bad Kissingen. *Biblphien dt. Wetterd.* [1950–] **L.**MO.; **Md.**H. 55–; **Y.**

6685 **Bibliographies. Armstrong Siddeley Motors, Ltd.** Coventry. *Biblphies Armstrong Siddeley Mot.*

Bibliographies. Commissariat à l'**énergie atomique.** Saclay. *See* 49536ᵃ.

6686 **Bibliographies. Commonwealth Bureau of Animal Genetics.** Edinburgh. *Biblphies Commonw. Bur. Anim. Genet.* **L.**AM.; **C.**A. 30–.

6687 **Bibliographies. Commonwealth Bureau** of **Plant Genetics.** Cambridge. *Biblphies Commonw. Bur. Pl. Genet.* [1930–] **L.**AM.; **C.**A.; **O.**R.

6688 **Bibliographies. Commonwealth Bureau** of **Soil Science.** Harpenden. *Biblphies Commonw. Bur. Soil Sci.* [1932–] **L.**AM.; **C.**A.

6689 **Bibliographies** de la **Haute Autorité, Communauté européenne** du **charbon** et de l'**acier.** Luxembourg. *Biblphies hte Autor. Commun. eur. Charb. Acier* [1955–] **L.**P.; **G.**U. 59–.

Bibliographies. Imperial Bureau of Animal Genetics. Edinburgh. *See* 6686.
Bibliographies. Imperial Bureau of **Plant Genetics.** Cambridge. *See* 6687.
Bibliographies. Imperial Bureau of **Soil Science.** Harpenden. *See* 6688.

6690 **Bibliographies. Leeds** and **Northrup Co.** Philadelphia. *Biblphies Leeds & Northrup Co.*

6691 **Bibliographies** in **Paint Technology.** London. *Biblphies Paint Technol.* [1959–] **L.**P.; SC. 60–.

6692 **Bibliographische Monatsschrift. Internationale Zeitschrift** für die **gesamte Medizin.** Hamburg. *Biblphische Mschr. int. Z. ges. Med.*

Bibliographischer Anzeiger. Internationaler ständiger Verband der **Strassenkongresse.** *See* 6598.

6693 **Bibliographischer Jahresbericht** über **soziale Hygiene, Demographie** und **Medizinalstatistik.** Jena. *Biblphisch. Jber. soz. Hyg.* [1900–]

6694 **Bibliographischer Semesterbericht** der **Erscheinungen** auf dem **Gebiet** der **Neurologie** und **Psychiatrie.** Jena. *Biblphisch. SemBer. Ersch. Geb. Neurol. Psychiat.*

6695 **Bibliography** and **Abstracts** on **Electrical Contacts.** A.S.T.M. *Biblphy Abstr. elect. Contacts* **Bm.**P. 44–.; **Y.**

6696 **Bibliography. Admiralty Centre** for **Scientific Information** and **Liaison.** London. *Biblphy Admty Cent. scient. Inf. Liaison* [1951–] **L.**P. imp.

Bibliography. Advisory Group for **Aeronautical Research** and **Development, NATO.** *See* 47.

6697 **Bibliography. Aeronautical Research Laboratories.** Melbourne. *Biblphy aeronaut. Res. Lab., Melb.* [1954–]

6698 **Bibliography** of **Aeronautics.** Department of Docks. New York. *Biblphy Aeronaut. Dep. Docks* [1938–] **L.**SC. 38–41.

6699 **Bibliography** of **Aeronautics.** National Advisory Committee for Aeronautics. Washington. *Biblphy Aeronaut. N.A.C.A.* [1909–32] **L.**BM.; P.; SC.; **Bm.**P.; **Br.**U. 17–32; **G.**M. 09–31.

6700 **Bibliography** of **Agriculture.** U.S. Department of Agriculture. Washington. *Biblphy Agric., Wash.* [1942–] **L.**AM.; BM^N. 52–; EB. 43–; K. 50–; MY.; P.; SC.; TD. 43–; TP.; **Abd.**R. 44–; **Abs.**A. 52–; U. 48– imp.; **Ba.**I. 44–; **Bm.**P. 46–; U. 43–46; **Br.**A. 54–; **C.**A. 43–; **Db.**E.B. 46–; **Hu.**G.; **Ld.**P. (5 yr.); **M.**C. 50–; U. 54–; **Md.**H.; **N.**U. 43–; **O.**AEC.; F.; RE (2 yr.); **R.**D. 44–52; **Rt.** imp.; **Sal.** 44– imp.; **W.** 44–; **Y.**

6701 **Bibliography** on **Aircraft Noise.** Supplements. London. *Biblphy Aircr. Noise* [1956–] **L.**P.

6702 **Bibliography** of **American Economic Entomology.** *Biblphy Am. econ. Ent.* [1860–05] **L.**BM^N. 89–05; P. imp.

6703 **Bibliography** of **American Literature** relating to **Refrigeration.** Chicago. *Biblphy Am. Lit. Refrig.* **L.**P. 18–21.

6704 **Bibliography** on **Applications** of **Electricity** to **Railways.** American Railroad Association. *Biblphy Applic. Elect. Rlys* **L.**SC. 34–55; **Bm.** P. 33–.

Bibliography of **Applied Geophysics.** London. *See* 49050.

Bibliography. British Coke Research Association. *See* 5645.

6705 **Bibliography. British Scientific Instruments Research Association.** London. *Biblphy Br. scient. Instrum. Res. Ass.* **Y.**

6706 **Bibliography. British Welding Research Association.** London. *Biblphy Br. Weld. Res. Ass.* [1945–] **L.**P.; **Bl.**U. [*C. of:* 6733]

6707 **Bibliography. Building** (and **Road**) **Research Board** (**Laboratory**). Gartson, Herts. *Biblphy Bldg Rd Res. Bd (Lab.)* [1933–] **L.**P. imp.

6708 **Bibliography** of **Canadian Biological Publications.** Toronto. *Biblphy Can. biol. Publs* [1946–] **L.**BM^N. 46–49; NC. 46–49; **Abd.**M.; **Dm.** 46–48; **Fr.**; **O.**AP. 46–49; **Pl.**M. 46–49.

6708^a **Bibliography** of **Canadian Plant Geography.** Toronto, Ottawa. *Biblphy Can. Pl. Geogr.* **O.**BO. 28–51.

6709 **Bibliography** on **Cast Iron.** American Foundrymen's Association. *Biblphy cast Iron*

6709^a **Bibliography. Central Technical Information Service, Central Electricity Generating Board.** London. *Biblphy cent. tech. Inf. Serv. cent. Elect. gener. Bd* **Y.**

6710 **Bibliography** of **Chemical Reviews.** *Biblphy chem. Rev.* [1958–] **Bl.**U.; **Cr.**U.; **Te.**C.; **Y.**

6711 **Bibliography** on **Communication Theory.** Genève. *Biblphy Commun. Theory* **L.**P. 53–.

6712 **Bibliography** of **Diamond Tools** and related subjects. London. *Biblphy Diam. Tools* [1944–47] **L.**BM.; BM^N. 46–47; DI.; P.; SI. 46–47; **Bm.**P. [*C. as:* 6729]

6713 **Bibliography. Division** of **Building Research, National Research Council, Canada.** Ottawa. *Biblphy Div. Bldg Res. Can.* [1951–] **L.**MO. imp.; P.; SC.; **Y.**

Bibliography of **Experimental Tank Work.** *See* 49050.

6714 **Bibliography** of **Forestry.** Statens skogsforskningsinstitut. Stockholm. *Biblphy For., Stockh.* [1951–] **O.**F.

6715 **Bibliography** of **Forestry** and **Forest Products.** F.A.O. *Biblphy For. Forest Prod. F.A.O.* [1948–52] **L.**BM.; MY.; **Bn.**U. imp.; **Pr.**FT.; **Rt.**

6716 **Bibliography. Gas Turbine Power Plant.** National Gas Turbine Establishment. Whetstone, Leics. *Biblphy Gas Turb. Pwr Pl.* [1947–] **L.**P. 47–53.

6717 **Bibliography** of the **Geology** of **Missouri.** Rolla. *Biblphy Geol. Mo.* **L.**BM^N. 56–; **Ld.**U.

6717^a **Bibliography. Geology** of the **North of England.** London. *Biblphy Geol. N. Engl.* **L.**BM^N. 84–32.

6718 **Bibliography** on **Glass Structure.** Columbus. *Biblphy Glass Struct.* [1956–] **L.**P.

6719 **Bibliography** of **Helminthology.** St. Albans. *Biblphy Helminth.* [1930–33] **L.**AM.; BM.; TD.; UC.; **C.**A.; **N.**U.; **O.**R.; **Sal.** [*C. in:* 22058]

6720 **Bibliography. Highway Research Board.** Washington. *Biblphy Highw. Res. Bd* [1947–] **L.**P. 49– imp.; **Y.**

6721 **Bibliography** of **Hydrology, Australia.** *Biblphy Hydrol. Aust.* **L.**MO. 37–.

6722 **Bibliography** of **Hydrology, Great Britain.** London. *Biblphy Hydrol. Gt Br.* **L.**MO.

6723 **Bibliography** of **Hydrology** in **India.** *Biblphy Hydrol. India* **L.**P. 36–.

6724 **Bibliography** of **Hydrology, Ireland.** Dublin. *Biblphy Hydrol. Ire.* **L.**MO. 34–; P. 34–; **Y.**

6725 **Bibliography** of **Hydrology, Israel.** *Biblphy Hydrol. Israel* **L.**P. 21–; **Y.**

6726 **Bibliography** of **Hydrology, United States** of **America.** Washington. *Biblphy Hydrol. U.S.A.* [1935–40] **L.**MO. 38–40; **C.**PO. [*C. in:* 3224]

6727 **Bibliography** of **Illumination.** New York. *Biblphy Illum.* **L.**P. 24–30.

6728 **Bibliography** and **Index** of **Geology,** exclusive of **North America.** Washington. *Biblphy Index Geol.* [1934–] **L.**B.; BM^N.; GL.; KC. 35–42: 49–54; P. 34–44; SC.; **Abd.**U. 34–37: 47–; **Abs.**U.; **Bl.**U.; **Bm.**U.; **Br.**U.; **C.**GG. 35–; P.; S.; **Cr.**U. 38–54; **E.**D. 37–; R.; U. imp.; **Lv.**U.; **M.**U.; **N.**U.; **Nw.**A.; **O.**R.; **R.**U.; **Sh.**SC.; **Sw.**U.; **Y.** [*C. of:* 6595]

6729 **Bibliography** of **Industrial Diamond Applications.** London. *Biblphy ind. Diam. Applic.* [1947–57] **L.**AV. 52–57; BM.; BM^N.; C. 49; DI.; MI. 49–57; NF. 49–57; P.; PR.; SC.; SI.; **Bm.**P.; T. 54–57; **Ld.**U.; **M.**P.; **Sh.**IO. 47–57; **Sy.**R. [*C. of:* 6712; 1952–57 *issued with* 23189; *C. as:* 23187]

6730 **Bibliography** of **Industrial Hygiene.** International Labour Office. Geneva. *Biblphy ind. Hyg.* [1923–41] **L.**P.; SC. 28–41; SH.; TD.; U. 40–41; **Bm.**U. 34–40; **Br.**U.; **C.**UL. 24–41; **E.**U. 23–33; **M.**MS.; P.; **O.**B. 25–41. [*C. as:* 6743]

6731 **Bibliography** of **Information** on **Servomechanisms** and related subjects. Nottingham. *Biblphy Inf. Servomech.* [1950–55] **L.**BM.; P.; **Sil.** [*C. as:* 6763ᶜ]

6732 **Bibliography** of **Insecticide Materials** of **Vegetable Origin.** London. *Biblphy Insect. Mater. Veg. Orig.* [1953–] **L.**BM.; P.; TP.; **Je.** [*C. of:* 41439]

6733 **Bibliography. Institute** of **Welding.** London. *Biblphy Inst. Weld.* [1940–45] **L.**P. 44–45 imp.; **Bl.**U. [*C. as:* 6706]

6734 **Bibliography** on **Irrigation, Drainage, River Training** and **Flood Control.** New Delhi. *Biblphy Irrig.* [1958–] **L.**P.; SC.

6735 **Bibliography** of **Literature** on **Agricultural Meteorology.** London. *Biblphy Lit. agric. Met.* [1926–] **L.**MO.; **C.**A.; **E.**R. 26–29; **Md.**H. 36–; **Rt.**; **Sa.** 36–37.

6736 **Bibliography** of **Literature** on **Potash** as a **Plant Nutrient.** Washington. *Biblphy Lit. Potash Pl. Nutr.* [1939–] **L.**P. 39–54; **O.**BO. imp.; **Rt.**; **Y.**
Bibliography of **Lubrication.** *See* 49050.

6737 **Bibliography** on **Medical Electronics.** New York. *Biblphy med. Electron.* **L.**P. 58–.

6738 **Bibliography** of **Medical Reviews.** Washington. *Biblphy med. Rev.* [1955–] **L.**BM. 57–; CB.; H.; MD.; P. 57–; S. 57–61; TD.; V. 57–; **Bl.**U.; **Br.**U. 57–; **C.**APH. 57–; **Cr.**U.; **Dn.**U. 57–; **E.**U.; **G.**U.; **Ld.**U.; **Lv.**P.; **Y.**

6739 **Bibliography** of **Meteorological Literature.** Royal Meteorological Society. London. *Biblphy met. Lit.* [1920–48] **L.**BM.; GL. 36–48; MO.; QM. 20–29 imp.; P.; SC.; SH. 22–31; U. 42–48; **Bl.**U. 21–48; **Bm.**P. 21–25; U. 22–31; **Br.**U. 32–48; **C.**UL.; **Db.** 22–48; **E.**A.; R.; U.; **M.**U. 31–48 imp.; **Md.**H. 27–48 imp.; **O.**B.; G.

6740 **Bibliography. Mond Nickel Company Ltd.** London. *Biblphy Mond Nickel Co.* **L.**P. 59–.

6741 **Bibliography** of **North American Geology.** Washington. *Biblphy N. Am. Geol.* **L.**KC. 51–55; P. 45–.

6742 **Bibliography. Northern Coke Research Committee.** Newcastle-upon-Tyne. *Biblphy nth. Coke Res. Comm.* [1930–31] **L.**P. [*C. of:* 6611]

6743 **Bibliography** of **Occupational Medicine.** I.L.O. Geneva. *Biblphy occup. Med.* [1948–50] **L.**MD.; P.; SC.; TD.; U.; **Bm.** T.; **Br.**U.; **Cr.**U.; **O.**B. [*C. of:* 6730]

6744 **Bibliography** of **Paper Making** (*afterwards* and **U.S. Patents**). Technical Association of the Pulp and Paper Industry. New York. *Biblphy Pap. Mak.* **L.**P. 00–; SC. 33–; **O.**F. 47–.

Bibliography of **Periodical Articles. Application** of **Electricity** to **Railways.** *See* 6704

6747 **Bibliography** of **Periodical Publications** on **Papermaking** and allied subjects. Papermakers' Association. London. *Biblphy period. Publs PapMak.* **L.**P. 20–32*; SC. 21–32.

6748 **Bibliography** of **Pharmacology** and **Chemotherapy.** *Biblphy Pharmac. Chemother.* **Bm.**P. 40–.

6749 **Bibliography** of **Poultry Diseases.** New Brunswick. *Biblphy Poult. Dis.* [1936–] **C.**A.; **W.** 42–.

6750 **Bibliography** on **Pre-stressed Concrete.** London. *Biblphy pre-stress. Concr.* [1951–] **L.**BM.; P.; SC.

6751 **Bibliography** of the **Publications** from the **Laboratories** and **Clinics** of the **Peiping Union Medical College,** Peiping. *Biblphy Publs Lab. Clin. Peiping Un. med. Coll.* [1915–] **L.**LI. 15–38; MD.; **M.**MS. 25–37 imp.

6752 **Bibliography** of **Published Information** on **Infra-Red Spectroscopy.** London. *Biblphy publd Inf. infra-red Spectrosc.* [1953–54] **L.**AV.; BM.; P.; **Bm.**P.; **M.**D.; P. [*C. as:* 50577]
Bibliography of **Pulp** and **Paper Making.** New York. *See* 6744.

6753 **Bibliography** of **Pulp** and **Paper Manufacture.** *Biblphy Pulp Pap. Mf.* **L.**SC. 34–.

6754 **Bibliography** of **References** to **Literature** on **Agriculture** and allied subjects. London. *Biblphy Refs Lit. Agric.* [1937–38] **L.**P.

6755 **Bibliography. Research Council, British Whiting Federation.** Bedford. *Biblphy Res. Coun. Br. Whiting Fed.* [1950–] **L.**P. 50–51; **Y.**

6755ᶜ **Bibliography. Research Department, Metal Box Company.** London. *Biblphy Res. Dep. Metal Box Co.* **L.**P. 59–.

6756 **Bibliography** of **Research Projects Reports. U.S. Federal Works Agency.** Washington. *Biblphy Res. Proj. Rep., Wash.* **Bm.**P. 40–.

6757 **Bibliography** of **Rubber Literature,** excluding Patents. New York. *Biblphy Rubb. Lit.* [1935–] **L.**P.; **Y.**

6758 **Bibliography** of **Scientific** and **Industrial Reports. U.S. Department of Commerce.** Washington. *Biblphy scient. ind. Rep., Wash.* [1946–49] **L.**AV. imp.; BM. imp.; P.; **Bm.**C.; P. 48–50; **Ld.**W.; **Sy.**R. [*C. as:* 6771]

6759 **Bibliography** of **Scientific Publications** of **South Asia.** Delhi. *Biblphy scient. Publs S. Asia* [1949–54] **L.**BM. 51–54; MY.; P.; SC.; TD. imp.; TP.; **C.**A.; **E.**U.; **Rt.**; **Y.** [*C. as:* 6760]

6760 **Bibliography** of **Scientific Publications** of **South** and **South East Asia.** New Delhi. *Biblphy scient Publs S. & SE.Asia* [1955–] **L.**AV. imp.; BM.; MY.; P.; SC.; TD. imp.; TP.; **C.**A.; **E.**U.; **Rt.**; **Y.** [*C. of:* 6759]

6761 **Bibliography** of **Seismology.** Dominion Observatory. Ottawa. *Biblphy Seism.* [1929–] **L.**MO.; P.; SC.; **Ld.**U. [*Published in:* 40988]

6762 **Bibliography Series, National Housing Center.** Washington. *Biblphy Ser. natn. Hous. Cent., Wash.* **L.**P. 59–.

6763 **Bibliography Series, Philippine Bureau** of **Mines.** Manila. *Biblphy Ser. Philipp. Bur. Mines* [1953–] **L.**BM.; GM.; **Y.**

6763ᶜ **Bibliography** on **Servomechanisms** and related subjects. Nottingham. *Biblphy Servomech.* [1960–] **L.**BM.; P.; **G.**ME. (2 yr.); **Sil.** [*C. of:* 6731]

6764 **Bibliography. Sheep Biology Laboratory.** Commonwealth Scientific and Industrial Research Organization, Australia. Prospect, N.S.W. *Biblphy Sheep Biol. Lab. C.S.I.R.O. Aust.* **C.**A. 59–.

6764ᶜ **Bibliography. Society** of **Vertebrate Palaeontology.** Cambridge, Mass. *Biblphy Soc. vert. Palaeont.* **L.**BMᴺ. 45–.

6765 **Bibliography** on **Soil Mechanics.** Institution of Civil Engineers. London. *Biblphy Soil Mech.* [1950–] **L.**P.; SC.

6766 **Bibliography** of **Soil Science, Fertilizers** and **General Agronomy.** Harpenden. *Biblphy Soil Sci.* [1931–] **L.**P.; SC.; **Abs.**U. 34–; **Bm.**P. 34–; U.; **Bn.**U.; **Br.**U.; **Cr.**U.; **G.**U. 44–; **Hu.**G.; **Je.**; **Ld.**P. 40–; U. 35–; **Lv.**P. 44–; **O.**F.; RE.; **R.**U.; **Rt.**; **Y.**

6767 **Bibliography** of **Spectrophotometric Methods** of **Analysis** for **Inorganic Ions.** Philadelphia. *Biblphy spectrophot. Meth. Analysis inorg. Ions* [1959–] **L.**P.

6768 **Bibliography** and **Subject Index** of **South African Geology.** Pretoria. *Biblphy Subj. Index S. Afr. Geol.* [1959–] **L.**BM[N].; SC.

6769 **Bibliography** of **Systematic Mycology.** Kew. *Biblphy system. Mycol.* [1947–] **L.**MY.; NC.; P.; SC.; **Br.**U. 50–57; **O.**BO. 58–; **Y.** [*Until* 1958 *issued in:* 31875]

6770 **Bibliography. Technical Library, Armstrong Siddeley Motors.** Coventry. *Biblphy tech. Libr. Armstrong Siddeley Mot.* **L.**P. 52–; **Y.**

6771 **Bibliography** of **Technical Reports.** Washington. *Biblphy tech. Rep., Wash.* [1949–54] **L.**AV. 50–54; MO. 54; P.; **Bm.**C.; P.; **Cn.**R.; **Ld.**W.; **M.**T. 54; **Sy.**R. [*C. of:* 6758; *C. as:* 55408]

6772 **Bibliography** on **Tidal Hydraulics.** Vicksburg. *Biblphy tidal Hydraul.* [1954–] **L.**P. [*Volume for* 1954 *forms* Vol. 2 *of:* 43153]

6773 **Bibliography** of **Trace Elements** in **Foods.** Ministry of Health. London. *Biblphy Trace Elem. Fds* [1947–] **L.**P. 47–54; SC. 47–54.

6774 **Bibliography** of **Translations** from **Russian Scientific** and **Technical Literature.** Library of Congress. Washington. *Biblphy Transl. Russ. scient. tech. Lit.* [1953–56] **L.**AV. imp.; BM.; P.; SC.; **Bm.**T.; **M.**U. 53–54 imp.; **Y.** [*C. in:* 54107]

6775 **Bibliography** of **Tropical Agriculture.** International Institute of Agriculture. Rome. *Biblphy trop. Agric.* [1931–42] **L.**AM.; EB.; **C.**A.

6776 **Bibliography. United States Soil Conservation Service.** Washington. *Biblphy U.S. Soil Conserv. Serv.* **O.**F. 40.

6777 **Bibliography. United Steel Companies,** Ltd. Rotherham. *Biblphy un. Steel Co.* **L.**P. 59–.

Bibliography of **Yugoslavia.** Series B. Natural and applied sciences. *See* 6576.

6777° **Biblioteca** de **antropologie.** Bucureşti. *Bibltca Antrop.* [1958–] **L.**BM.

6778 **Biblioteca argentina** de **ciencias naturales.** Buenos Aires. *Bibltca argent. Cienc. nat.* [1948–] **L.**BM.; BM[N]. 48–50; **Bl.**U.; **Pl.**M. 50; **Wo.** 48; **Y.**

6779 **Biblioteca** del **Boletín** de **minas y petroleo.** Bogota. *Bibltca Boln Minas Petrol.* [1929–] **L.**BM. [*Supplement to:* 9757]

6780 **Biblioteca cerculuí tehnic.** Bucureşti. *Bibltca Cerc. teh.*

6781 **Biblioteca científica** del **Observatorio** de **física cósmica.** San Miguel, R. Argentina. *Bibltca cient. Obs. Fís. cósm., S Miguel* [1938–] **L.**AS. 38–39; MO. 38–41 imp. [*C. of:* 6782]

6782 **Biblioteca científica** del **Observatorio** de **San Miguel.** San Miguel. *Bibltca cient. Obs. S Miguel* [1935–38] **L.**AS. 37–38; SC. [*C. as:* 6781]

6783 **Biblioteca geografica** dell'**Istituto geografico De Agostini.** Novara-Roma. *Bibltca geogr. Ist. geogr. De Agostini* **L.**BM. 13.

6784 **Biblioteca** del **Instituto agrícola catalán** de **San Isidro.** Barcelona. *Bibltca Inst. agríc. catalán* **Db.** 09–.

6785 **Biblioteca** del **medico.** Bollettino delle pubblicazioni nuove di medicina e scienze affini. Milano. *Bibltca Med.*

6786 **Biblioteca pro-vulgarización agrícola.** Santiago de Chile. *Bibltca Pro-vulg. agríc.*

6787 **Biblioteca scientifica sovietica.** Roma. *Bibltca scient. sov.* [1949–50] **L.**MD.

6788 **Biblioteca** di **scienze moderne.** Torino. *Bibltca Sci. mod.* **O.**B. 99–19 imp.

6788ª **Biblioteca** de la **Sociedad científica** del **Paraguay.** Asunción. *Bibltca Soc. cient. Parag.* **L.**BM[N]. 28–37 imp.

6788° **Biblioteca Societăţii** de **ştiinţe matematice** şi **fizice** din **R. P. R.** Bucureşti. *Bibltca Soc. Şti. mat. fiz.* [1953–]

6789 **Biblioteca ştiinţa evreiască.** Iaşi. *Bibltca Şti. evr.*

6790 **Biblioteca** di **studi coloniali.** Istituto coloniale italiano. Roma. *Bibltca Stud. colon.* **L.**G. 10–11.

6791 **Biblioteca zootechnica.** Bucarest. *Bibltca zootech.* [1924–] **E.**AB. imp.

6791° **Bibliotechka gal'vanotekhnika.** Библиотечка гальванотехника. *Bibltchka gal'vanotekh.* **Y.** 58–.

6791ᶠ **Bibliotechka zuboreza-novatora.** Библиотечка зубореза-новатора. *Bibltchka zuboreza-nov.* [1957–] **Y.** 58–.

6792 **Bibliotechno-bibliograficheskiĭ byulleten'. Kazakhstanskiĭ filial, Tsentral'naya nauchnaya biblioteka, Akademiya nauk SSSR.** Moskva. Библиотечно-библиографический бюллетень. Казахстанский филиал, Центральная научная библиотека, Академия наук СССР. *Bibltchno-biblfich. Byull. kazakh. Fil. tsent. nauch. Bibltka* [1958–] **L.**SC.

6793 **Biblioteczka rolnicza.** Warszawa. *Bibltczka roln.*

6794 **Bibliotek** for **læger.** Kjøbenhavn. *Bibltk Læger* [1821–] **L.**BM.; MA. 46–; **Db.** 78–87: 06–14: 17–31 imp.

6794° **Biblioteka** po **avtomatike.** Библиотека по автоматике. *Bibltka Avtom.* [1958–] **Y.** imp.

6795 **Biblioteka Centralnog higienskog zavoda.** Beograd. *Bibltka cent. hig. Zav.* [1937–]

6795° **Biblioteka matematicheskogo kruzhka.** Библиотека математического кружка. *Bibltka mat. Kruzhka* **Y.** 59–.

6795ᵈ **Biblioteka morskogo sbornika.** Библіотека морского сборника. *Bibltka morsk. Sb.* [*Supplement to:* 33689]

6795° **Biblioteka 'Nikola Tesla'.** Beograd. *Bibltka Nikola Tesla* **L.**BM. 52–.

6795ᶠ **Biblioteka teplotekhnika.** Библиотека теплотехника. *Bibltka Teplotekhn.* **Y.** 59.

6796 **Biblioteka vozdukhoplavanīya.** S.-Petersburg. Библіотека воздухоплаванія. *Bibltka Vozdukh.* [1909–10] [*C. as:* 56554].

6797 **Biblioteka warszawska.** Warszawa. *Bibltka warsz.* [1841–14] **L.**BM.

6798 **Bibliotheca africana.** Innsbruck. *Biblthca afr.* [1924–34] **L.**AN.

6799 **Bibliotheca biotheoretica.** Leiden. *Biblthca biotheor.* [1941–] **L.**BM[N]. 41–54; UC.; Z.; **E.**R.; **O.**R.; **Y.**

6800 **Bibliotheca botanica.** Stuttgart. *Biblthca bot.* [1886–] **L.**BM^N. imp.; K. 86–38; L. 86–48; SC.; **Bm.**U. 86–30; **C.**UL.; **E.**B.; **G.**U. 86–38; Ld.U.; **M.**U. 86–58; **O.**BO.

6801 **Bibliotheca cardiologica.** Basel. *Biblthca cardiol.* **L.**MD. 39–.

6801° **Bibliotheca cartographica.** Remagen. *Biblthca cartogr.* [1957–] **L.**BM.; G.; SC.

6802 **Bibliotheca gastroenterologica.** Basel & New York. *Biblthca gastroent.* [1960–] **L.**MD.; **Y.** [*Supplement to:* 20683]

6803 **Bibliotheca genetica.** Leipzig. *Biblthca genet.* [1917–29] **L.**K. (bot.) 22–29; SC.; **Ba.**I.; **R.**U.

6804 **Bibliotheca geographica.** Berlin. *Biblthca geogr.* [1891–12] **L.**BM.; BM^N.; G.; SC.; **C.**UL.; **O.**B.; G.; **R.**U. 93–06 imp.

6805 **Bibliotheca haematologica.** Basel & New York. *Biblthca haemat.* [1955–] **L.**MA.; MD. [*Supplement to:* 594]

6806 **Bibliotheca hispana.** Madrid. *Biblthca hisp.* Sección segunda. Matemáticas, astronomía, física, etc. [1943–] **Bm.**U. 48–; SC. 45–; **E.**R. 43; **Y.**

6807 **Bibliotheca javanica.** Weltevreden. *Biblthca javan.* [1930–] **L.**AN.; BM.; **C.**UL.; **O.**B. 30.

6808 **Bibliotheca mathematica.** Leipzig. *Biblthca math.* [1884–14] **L.**BM.; SC. 00–14; UC.; **Bm.**U. 87–14; **C.**UL.; **G.**U. 87–96: 00–14; Ld.U. 00–14; **O.**R.; **R.**U. imp.

6809 **Bibliotheca medica.** Stuttgart. *Biblthca med.* [1893–08] **L.**BM.; S.

6810 **Bibliotheca microbiologica.** Basel & New York. *Biblthca microbiol.* [1960–] **L.**MD. [*Supplement to:* 37224]

6811 **Bibliotheca 'Nutritio et dieta'.** Basel & New York. *Biblthca 'Nutr. Dieta'* [1960–] **L.**MD.; **Abd.**R.; **Y.** [*Supplement to:* 35503]

6812 **Bibliotheca ophthalmologica.** Basel. *Biblthca ophthal.* [1939–] **L.**MD. [*C. of:* 161]

6813 **Bibliotheca paediatrica.** Basel. *Biblthca paediat.* [1945–] **L.**S. 49–; **C.**UL.; **Nw.**A. 46–. [*Supplement to* 2881; *C. of:* 238]

6813ᵃ **Bibliotheca physiographica slovaca.** Bratislava. *Biblthca physiogr. slov.* [1944–] **L.**BM.

6814 **Bibliotheca psychiatrica et neurologica.** Berlin. *Biblthca psychiat. neurol.* [1948–] **L.**MD.; **C.**UL.; **E.**P. [*C. of:* 259]

6815 **Bibliotheca radiologica.** Basel & New York. *Biblthca radiol.* [1959–] **L.**MD. [*Supplement to:* 41847]

6817 **Bibliotheca tuberculosea.** Basel, New York. *Biblthca tuberc.* **L.**MD. 48–.
   Bibliotheca zoologica. Stuttgart. *See* 59255.

6818 **Bibliotheca zoologica II.** Bearbeitet v. O. Taschenberg. Leipzig. *Biblthca zool. II.* [1886–23] **L.**AM. 86–13; BM.; BM^N.; S.; Z.; **Bm.**U. 86–88; **E.**U.; **Mi.** 86–05; **O.**B.; Pl.M.; **Sa.**

6819 **Bibliotheca zoologica rossica.** Academia scientiarum imperialis. St. Petersburg. *Biblthca zool. ross.* [1905–] **L.**BM^N.

6820 **Bibliothek von Coler.** Berlin. *Biblthk v. Coler*

6821 **Bibliothek der gesamten medizinischen Wissenschaften für praktische Ärzte und Spezialärzte.** Wien & Leipzig. *Biblthk ges. med. Wiss.*

6822 **Bibliothek der gesamten Technik.** Hannover. *Biblthk ges. Tech.* **L.**P. imp.

6823 **Bibliothek für Luftschiffahrt und Flugtechnik.** Berlin. *Biblthk Luftschiff. Flugtech.* **L.**BM. 09–20; P. imp.

6824 **Bibliothēkē tou Geōrgou.** en Athēnais. Βιβλιοθήκη τοῦ Γεώργου. *Biblthkē Georg.* [1916–]

6825 **Bibliothèque d'agriculture coloniale.** Paris. *Bibltque Agric. colon.* **L.**SC. 09–11 imp.

6826 **Bibliothèque du cancer.** Paris. *Bibltque Cancer* **L.**BM. 23–.

6827 **Bibliothèque coloniale internationale** Bruxelles. *Bibltque colon. int.* **L.**BM. 95–14; SE. 95–27.
   Bibliothèque de l'École des hautes études. Paris. Bulletin des sciences mathématiques. *See* 11669.

6828 **Bibliothèque de l'École des hautes études.** Paris. Section des sciences naturelles. *Bibltque Éc. ht. Étud., Paris Sect. Sci. nat.* **L.**BM^N. 69–90.

6829 **Bibliothèque de la faune des colonies françaises.** *Bibltque Faune Colon. fr.* **L.**BM^N. 28–31.

6830 **Bibliothèque des géographes arabes.** Paris. *Bibltque Géogr. arab.* [1927–] **O.**B.
   Bibliothèque géologique de la Russie. *Supplement to* 24344.

6831 **Bibliothèque d'histoire scientifique.** Paris. *Bibltque Hist. scient.* **L.**BM. 08.

6832 **Bibliothèque des jeunes naturalistes.** Société canadienne d'histoire naturelle. Montréal. *Bibltque jeunes Nat.* **L.**BM^N. 32–55.
   Bibliothèque de navigation aérienne. Saint-Pétersbourg. *See* 6796.

6833 **Bibliothèque polytechnique internationale.** Paris. *Bibltque polytech. int.*

6834 **Bibliothèque des sciences mathématiques.** Paris. *Bibltque Sci. math.*

6835 **Bibliothèque des sciences pharmacologiques.** *Bibltque Sci. pharmac.*
   Bibliothèque universelle. *See* 4360.

6836 **Bibljografja geologiczna Polski.** Warszawa. *Bibljogr. geol. Pol.* [1914–] **L.**BM^N. 14–35; GL.; GM.; P.; **E.**D. imp.; **Lv.**U.

6837 **Bibljoteka botaniczna.** Warszawa. *Bibljot. bot.* [1925–33]

6838 **Bibljoteka puławska.** Państwowy instytut naukowego gospodarstwa wiejskiego. Puławy. *Bibljot. puław.* [1923–] **C.**A. 23–47 imp.

6839 **Bibljoteka Zakładu architektury polskiej.** Warszawa. *Bibljot. Zakł. Archit. pol.* [1927–38] **L.**BM.
   Bicera Abstracts. *See* 5664.
   Bicera Bulletin. *See* 5665.

6840 **Bidrag till Finlands hydrografi.** Helsingfors. *Bidr. Finl. Hydrogr.* **L.**MO. 08–27 imp.

6841 **Bidrag till kännedom om Finlands natur och folk.** Utgifna af Finska vetenskaps-societeten. Helsingfors. *Bidr. Känn. Finl. Nat. Folk* [1858–] **L.**BM.; BM^N.; MO. 85–32 imp.; P. 86–05; Z.; **Bm.**U. 61– imp.; **Br.**U.; **C.**P. 71–; **Db.**; **E.**R. 71–; **G.**U. 00– imp.; **Lv.**U. 80– imp.; **O.**B. 82–.

6842 **Biedermanns Zentralblatt für Agrikulturchemie und rationellen Landwirtschaftsbetrieb.** Leipzig. *Biedermanns Zbl. AgrikChem.* [1872–31: Abt. A. 31–36] **L.**AM. 11–36; P. 03–36; SC. 27–36; **Abd.**U. 04–32; **Br.**A. 00–18; U. 00–13; **E.**W. 29–32; **Je.** 27–36; **O.**RE. 86–36; **R.**U. 13–31; **Rt.** 90–31. [*For* Abt. B. *see* 53187]
   Bieënvriend. *See* 39966°.

6843 **Biene.** Aschaffenburg. *Biene, Aschaffenb.*

6844 **Biene.** Böhmisch-Leipa. *Biene, Böhm.-Leipa*

6845 **Biene.** Giessen. *Biene, Giessen*

6846 **Biene.** Holyoke, Mass. *Biene, Holyoke*

6847 **Biene** und ihre **Zucht.** Bühl. *Biene Zucht*

6848 **Bienen- u. Obstbau-Zeitung** für **Bayern.** Neustadt a. d. H. *Bienen- u. ObstbZtg Bayern*

6849 **Bienenpflege.** Ludswigsburg. *Bienenpflege, Ludwigsb.* **L.**AM.

6850 **Bienenpflege.** Weinsberg. *Bienenpflege, Weinsberg*

6851 **Bienenvater.** Wien. *Bienenvater, Wien* [1869–38] **L.**AM. 69–95.

6852 **Bienenvater** aus **Böhmen.** Reichenberg. *Bienenvater Böhm.*

6853 **Bienenwirt.** Brussel. *Bienenwirt*

6854 **Bienenwirtschaft** im **Kuntzsch-Betrieb.** Nowawes. *Bienenw. Kuntzsch-Betr.*

6855 **Bienenwirtschaftliches Zentralblatt.** Hannover. *Bienenw. Zbl.* **L.**AM. 90–93.

6856 **Bienenzeitung.** Grevenmacher. *Bienenzeitung, Grevenmacher*

6857 **Bienenzeitung** für **Schleswig-Holstein.** Husum-Neumünster. *Bienenztg Schlesw.-Holst.*

6858 **Biennial Crop Pest** and **Horticultural Report. Oregon Agricultural College Experiment Station.** Corvallis. *Bienn. Crop Pest hort. Rep. Ore.* [1911–20] **L.**EB. 11–14; P. 13–14; Md.H. 11–12. [*C. as:* 16095]

6859 **Biennial Progress Report. Louisiana Forestry Commission.** Baton Rouge. *Bienn. Prog. Rep. La For. Commn* [1944–] **O.**F.

    Biennial Report of the **Agricultural College Survey** of **North Dakota.** *See* 6934.

    Biennial Report. Agricultural Experiment Station, Hawaii University. *See* 6885.

    Biennial Report. Agricultural Experiment Station, Stillwater, Oklahoma. *See* 6935ᵃ.

    Biennial Report. Agricultural Experiment Station, Utah. *See* 6960.

6860 **Biennial Report** of the **Agricultural Research Council.** London. *Bienn. Rep. agric. Res. Coun.* **Ld.**P. 31–37: 56–; **O.**F. 31–.

6861 **Biennial Report** of the **Alaska Development Board.** Juneau. *Bienn. Rep. Alaska Dev. Bd* **C.**PO. 45–.

6862 **Biennial Report** of the **Arizona State Water Commissioners.** Tucson. *Bienn. Rep. Ariz. St. Wat. Commnrs*

6863 **Biennial Report. Biological Experiment Station. University** of **Illinois,** Urbana. *Bienn. Rep. biol. Exp. Stn Univ. Ill.*

6864 **Biennial Report** of the **Board** of **Commissioners** of **Agriculture** and **Forestry** of the **Territory** of **Hawaii.** Honolulu. *Bienn. Rep. Bd Commnrs Agric. For. Hawaii* **L.**EB. 03–58* imp.; **O.**F. 31–32: 43–58. [*C. as:* 43251]

6865 **Biennial Report** of the **British Coal Utilisation Research Association.** London. *Bienn. Rep. Br. Coal Util. Res. Ass.* [1938–] **L.**P. 41–.

6866 **Biennial Report** of the **California Agricultural Experiment Station.** Berkeley. *Bienn. Rep. Calif. agric. Exp. Stn* **O.**F. 38–.

6867 **Biennial Report** of the **California Department** of **Public Health.** *Bienn. Rep. Calif. Dep. publ. Hlth*

    Biennial Report. California Fish and **Game Commission.** *See* 6950.

6868 **Biennial Report** of the **California State Board** of **Forestry.** Sacramento. *Bienn. Rep. Calif. St. Bd For.*

6869 **Biennial Report. California State Commission** of **Horticulture.** Sacramento. *Bienn. Rep. Calif. St. Commn Hort.* **L.**P. 92–11.

6869ᶜ **Biennial Report. Commissioner of Agriculture, Vermont.** Montpelier. *Bienn. Rep. Commnr Agric. Vt* **Y.**

6870 **Biennial Report** of the **Commonwealth Forestry Bureau.** Oxford. *Bienn. Rep. Commonw. For. Bur.* [1941–] **O.**F.

6871 **Biennial Report** of the **Connecticut Agricultural College.** Hartford. *Bienn. Rep. Conn. agric. Coll.* **L.**BM. 02–.

6872 **Biennial Report** of the **Connecticut Commissioners** of **Fisheries** and **Game.** Hartford. *Bienn. Rep. Conn. Commnrs Fish. Game* **L.**BM. 04–.

6873 **Biennial Report** of the **Connecticut Department** of **Agriculture.** *Bienn. Rep. Conn. Dep. Agric.* [1934–] **L.**BM.; P.; **O.**B. [*C. of:* 43175]

6874 **Biennial Report. Connecticut Geological** and **Natural History Survey.** *Bienn. Rep. Conn. geol. nat. Hist. Surv.* **L.**GL. 03–; P. 03–; **O.**R. 03–04.

6875 **Biennial Report** of the **Connecticut Highway Commissioner.** Hartford. *Bienn. Rep. Conn. Highw. Commnr* **O.**R. 05–09: 13–16.

6876 **Biennial Report** of the **Connecticut State Park** and **Forest Commission.** Hartford. *Bienn. Rep. Conn. St. Pk Forest Commn* **O.**F. 40–44*.

6877 **Biennial Report. Delaware Board** of **Game** and **Fish Commissioners.** *Bienn. Rep. Del. Bd Game Fish Commnrs* [*C. as:* 42834]

6877ᶜ **Biennial Report. Department** of **Agriculture** and **Inspection, State of Nebraska.** Lincoln. *Bienn. Rep. Dep. Agric. Insp. St. Neb.* **Y.**

    Biennial Report. Department of Conservation and **Development, North Carolina.** *See* 6931.

    Biennial Report. Department of **Fish** and **Game, State of California.** *See* 6948.

6878 **Biennial Report. Department of Forests** and **Waters.** Harrisburg. *Bienn. Rep. Dep. Forests Wat., Harrisburg* **O.**F. 52–54.

    Biennial Report. Division of **Fish** and **Game, California.** *See* 6949.

    Biennial Report. Division of **Mines** and **Geology, Washington State.** *See* 6966.

6879 **Biennial Report** of the **Florida Department** of **Agriculture.** Tallahassee. *Bienn. Rep. Fla Dep. Agric.*

6880 **Biennial Report** of the **Florida Forest Service.** Tallahassee. *Bienn. Rep. Fla Forest Serv.* [1929–] **Y.**

6880ᵃ **Biennial Report. Florida Geological Survey.** Tallahassee. *Bienn. Rep. Fla geol. Surv.* [1941–] **L.**BMᴺ.; **Dn.**U.; **Y.** [*C. of:* 6881]

6881 **Biennial Report. Florida State Board** of **Conservation.** Tallahassee. *Bienn. Rep Fla St. Bd Conserv.* [1934–40] **L.**BM^N.; **Y.** [*C. as:* 6880ᵃ]

6881° **Biennial Report. Forest Commissioner, Maine.** Augusta. *Bienn. Rep. Forest Commnr Me* **Y.**

6881° **Biennial Report. Forestry Division, Forestry** and **Recreation Commission, New Hampshire.** Concord. *Bienn. Rep. For. Div. New Hamp.* **Y.**

6882 **Biennial Report** of the **Forestry Division** of the **Louisiana Department** of **Conservation.** New Orleans. *Bienn. Rep. For. Div. La*

    Biennial Report. Geological Survey, Missouri Bureau of **Geology** and **Mines.** *See* 6918.

6883 **Biennial Report** of the **Geological Survey, State** of **Illinois.** *Bienn. Rep. geol. Surv. Ill.* **Bm.**U. 11–14.

6884 **Biennial Report. Georgia Department** of **Forestry.** Atlanta. *Bienn. Rep. Ga Dep. For.* **O.**F. 43–.

6885 **Biennial Report. Hawaii University Agricultural Experiment Station.** Honolulu. *Bienn. Rep. Hawaii Univ. agric. Exp. Stn* **O.**F. 44–.

6886 **Biennial Report** of the **Idaho State Board** of **Land Commissioners.** Boise. *Bienn. Rep. Idaho St. Bd Ld Commnrs* **O.**F. 43–.

6887 **Biennial Report. Illinois State Laboratory** of **Natural History.** Urbana. *Bienn. Rep. Ill. St. Lab. nat. Hist.* **L.**BM^N. 87–00.

    Biennial Report of the **Imperial Forestry Bureau.** *See* 6870.

6888 **Biennial Report** of the **Inspector** of **Coal Mines** of the **State** of **Montana.** Helena. *Bienn. Rep. Insp. Coal Mines Mont.* **L.**P. 05–10.

6888° **Biennial Report** of **Iowa Book** of **Agriculture.** Des Moines. *Bienn. Rep. Iowa Bk Agric.* [1954–] **Y.** [*C. of:* 24114]

6889 **Biennial Report. Kansas Agricultural Experiment Station, Manhattan.** Topeka. *Bienn. Rep. Kans. agric. Exp. Stn* [1920–38] **L.**EB.; P.; **Abs.**A. 22–38 imp.; **Bm.**P.; **Br.**U.; **C.**A.; **Rt.**; **Y.** [*C. of:* and *Rec. as:* 44267]

6890 **Biennial Report** of the **Kansas State Board** of **Agriculture.** Topeka. *Bienn. Rep. Kans. St. Bd Agric.* **L.**AM.; P. 77– imp.; **Bm.**P. 81–; **C.**A. 13–.

6891 **Biennial Report. Kansas State Board** of **Health.** Topeka. *Bienn. Rep. Kans. St. Bd Hlth*

6892 **Biennial Report. Kansas State Entomological Commission.** Topeka. *Bienn. Rep. Kans. St. ent. Commn* [1907–] **L.**EB. 07–46 imp.

6893 **Biennial Report. Kansas State Horticultural Society.** Topeka. *Bienn. Rep. Kans. St. hort. Soc.* **L.**EB. 20–51*; **Lv.**P. 23–40 imp.; **Md.**H. 40–41.

6894 **Biennial Report. Kansas State Water Commission.** *Bienn. Rep. Kans. St. Wat. Commn*

6895 **Biennial Report. Kentucky Bureau** of **Agriculture.** Frankfort. *Bienn. Rep. Ky Bur. Agric.* **G.**M. 84–85: 88–89.

6896 **Biennial Report. Kentucky State Board** of **Health.** Louisville. *Bienn. Rep. Ky St. Bd Hlth*

6896° **Biennial Report. Louisiana Department** of **Agriculture** and **Immigration.** Baton Rouge. *Bienn. Rep. La Dep. Agric.* **Y.**

6897 **Biennial Report** of the **Louisiana Department** of **Conservation.** New Orleans. *Bienn. Rep. La Dep. Conserv.*

6898 **Biennial Report** of the **Louisiana Rice Experiment Station.** Crowley. *Bienn. Rep. La Rice Exp. Stn* **L.**P. 30–; **C.**A. 28–.

6899 **Biennial Report. Louisiana State Board** of **Health.** New Orleans. *Bienn. Rep. La St. Bd Hlth* **L.**TD. 12–; **Lv.**U. 12– imp.

6900 **Biennial Report. Louisiana State Crop Pest Commission.** Baton Rouge. *Bienn. Rep. La St. Crop Pest Commn* **L.**EB. 08–09.

6901 **Biennial Report** of the **Louisiana State Department** of **Agriculture.** Baton Rouge. *Bienn. Rep. La St. Dep. Agric.*

6902 **Biennial Report. Louisiana State Live Stock Sanitary Board.** Baton Rouge. *Bienn. Rep. La St. live Stk sanit. Bd* [1908–48] [*C. in:* 6901]

6903 **Biennial Report** of the **Louisiana State Museum.** Baton Rouge. *Bienn. Rep. La St. Mus.* [1908–] **L.**BM^N. 08–39; HO. 10– imp.; K. 18–21 imp.; L. 12–13; **E.**F. imp.; P. 08–23 imp.; **Lv.**U. 12–21; **M.**U. 08–31; **O.**B. 12–23. [*C. of:* 44353]

6904 **Biennial Report. Maine State Forest Service.** Augusta. *Bienn. Rep. Me St. Forest Serv.*

6905 **Biennial Report** of the **Marine Fishing Program.** Florida. *Bienn. Rep. mar. Fishg Progm.* **Pl.**M. 49.

6906 **Biennial Report** of the **Massachusetts Agricultural Experiment Station.** Amherst. *Bienn. Rep. Mass. agric. Exp. Stn* [1924–28] **L.**AM.; EB.; K.; P.; **C.**A.; **Db.** [*C. of:* and *Rec. as:* 44414]

6907 **Biennial Report. Michigan Department** of **Agriculture.** Lansing. *Bienn. Rep. Mich. Dep. Agric.* [1924–] **L.**P.; **Y.**

6908 **Biennial Report. Michigan Department** of **Conservation.** Lansing. *Bienn. Rep. Mich. Dep. Conserv.* **O.**AP. (game) 27–; F. 37–; **Y.**

6909 **Biennial Report** of the **Michigan State Board** of **Fish Commissioners.** Lansing. *Bienn. Rep. Mich. St. Bd Fish Commnrs* **L.**P. 83–04 imp.

6910 **Biennial Report. Minnesota Commissioner** of **Highways.** *Bienn. Rep. Minn. Commnr Highw.* **Y.**

6911 **Biennial Report. Minnesota Department** of **Conservation.** St. Paul. *Bienn. Rep. Minn. Dep. Conserv.* **O.**F. 37 ; **Y.**

6912 **Biennial Report** of the **Minnesota Industrial Commission.** St. Paul. *Bienn. Rep. Minn. ind. Commn*

6913 **Biennial Report. Minnesota State Dairy** and **Food Commissioner.** Mineapolis. *Bienn. Rep. Minn. St. Dairy Fd Commnr*

6914 **Biennial Report** of the **Mississippi State Forest** and **Park Service.** Jackson. *Bienn. Rep. Miss. St. Forest Park Serv.* **O.**F. 38–.

6915 **Biennial Report** of the **Mississippi State Geological Survey.** Jackson. *Bienn. Rep. Miss. St. geol. Surv.* **L.**BM^N. 14– imp.; P. 21–25; **Sh.**M. 05–31; **Y.**

6916 **Biennial Report** of the **Mississippi State Live Stock Sanitary Board.** Jackson. *Bienn. Rep. Miss. St. live Stk sanit. Bd*

6917 **Biennial Report** of the **Mississippi State Plant Board.** Jackson. *Bienn. Rep. Miss. St. Pl. Bd* [1918–31] **L.**EB.

6918 **Biennial Report** of the **Missouri Bureau** of **Geology** and **Mines.** Jefferson City, Mo. *Bienn. Rep. Mo. Bur. Geol. Mines* **L.**BMᴺ. 91–; GL. 91–49; GM. 91–; UC. 03–; **Bm.**U. 07–29; **Lv.**U. 91– imp.

6919 **Biennial Report** of the **Missouri State Fruit Experiment Station.** Mountain Grove. *Bienn. Rep. Mo. St. Fruit Exp. Stn* **L.**EB. 13–14.

6920 **Biennial Report. Montana State Board** of **Entomology.** Helena. *Bienn. Rep. Mont. St. Bd Ent.* **L.**BMᴺ. 27–30; EB. 14–32*.

Biennial Report of the **Nebraska Department** of **Agriculture.** *See* 6877ᶜ.

6922 **Biennial Report. Nebraska State Board** on **Irrigation, Highways** and **Drainage.** *Bienn. Rep. Neb. St. Bd Irrig.*

6923 **Biennial Report** of the **Nebraska State Entomologist.** Lincoln. *Bienn. Rep. Neb. St. Ent.* **L.**EB. 07–08.

6924 **Biennial Report** of the **Nevada State Board** of **Stock Commissioners.** Carson City. *Bienn. Rep. Nev. St. Bd Stk Commnrs* **L.**V. 19–34.

6925 **Biennial Report. Nevada State Department** of **Agriculture.** Carson City. *Bienn. Rep. Nev. St. Dep. Agric.* **L.**V. 34–.

6926 **Biennial Report. Nevada State Inspector** of **Mines.** Carson City. *Bienn. Rep. Nev. St. Insp. Mines* **Y.**

6927 **Biennial Report** of the **Nevada State Rabies Commission.** Carson City. *Bienn. Rep. Nev. St. Rabies Commn*

6928 **Biennial Report** of the **New Hampshire Forestry Commission (Department).** Concord. *Bienn. Rep. New Hamp. For. Commn* **O.**F. 26–.

6929 **Biennial Report. New Hampshire State Board** of **Health.** *Bienn. Rep. New Hamp. St. Bd Hlth*

6930 **Biennial Report. New Mexico Bureau** of **Mines** and **Mineral Resources.** Socorro. *Bienn. Rep. New Mex. Bur. Mines Miner. Resour.* [1951–] **L.**MI.; **Y.** [*C. of:* 44710]

6931 **Biennial Report. North Carolina Department** of **Conservation** and **Development.** Chapel Hill. *Bienn. Rep. N. Carol. Dep. Conserv. Dev.* [1926–] **L.**BMᴺ. 26–32; **O.**F. 35–36: 43–44; **Y.** [*C. of:* 6932]

6932 **Biennial Report** of the **North Carolina Geological Survey.** Chapel Hill. *Bienn. Rep. N. Carol. geol. Surv.* [1891–26] **L.**BMᴺ. [*C. as:* 6931]

6933 **Biennial Report. North Carolina State Department** of **Agriculture.** Raleigh. *Bienn. Rep. N. Carol. St. Dep. Agric.* **L.**P. 99–.

6934 **Biennial Report. North Dakota State Department** of **Health.** Devils Lake. *Bienn. Rep. N. Dak. St. Dep. Hlth* **L.**P. 01–12; **Y.**

6935 **Biennial Report** of the **North-east Louisiana Experiment Station.** St. Joseph. *Bienn. Rep. N.E. La Exp. Stn* [1930–42] **L.**P.; **C.**A. [> 51387, 1932–35; *C. in:* 44351]

6935ᵃ **Biennial Report. Oklahoma Agricultural Experiment Station.** Stillwater. *Bienn. Rep. Okla. agric. Exp. Stn* **Md.**H. 44–; **Y.**

6936 **Biennial Report. Oregon Agricultural Experiment Station.** *Bienn. Rep. Ore. agric. Exp. Stn* **L.**AM.; EB. 18–51*; P. 89–02: 28–51; **Abs.**A. 22–51; **Br.**A. 18–30; U. 18–51; **C.**A.; **Lv.**P. 18–51; **Md.**H. 24–51; **Rt.** 18–30. [*C. as:* 44833]

6937 **Biennial Report** of the **Oregon Soil Investigations.** *Bienn. Rep. Ore. Soil Invest.*

6938 **Biennial Report. Oregon State Fish Commission.** *Bienn. Rep. Ore. St. Fish Commn* **Dm.** 47–49: 59; **Y.**

6940 **Biennial Report. Oregon State Game Commission.** *Bienn. Rep. Ore. St. Game Commn*

6941 **Biennial Report. Oregon State Live Stock Sanitary Board.** *Bienn. Rep. Ore. St. live Stk sanit. Bd*

6942 **Biennial Report. Oregon State Reclamation Commission.** *Bienn. Rep. Ore. St. Reclam. Commn*

6943 **Biennial Report. Pennsylvania Board** of **Fish Commissioners.** Harrisburg. *Bienn. Rep. Pa Bd Fish Commnrs*

6944 **Biennial Report. Pennsylvania Board** of **Game Commissioners.** Harrisburg. *Bienn. Rep. Pa Bd Game Commnrs*

6945 **Biennial Report. Potlach Timber Protective Association.** Potlach, Idaho. *Bienn. Rep. Potlach Timb. prot. Ass.* [1941–] **Y.** [*C. of:* 14983]

6946 **Biennial Report** of the **Shell-Fish Commissioners, Connecticut.** Hartford. *Bienn. Rep. Shell-Fish Commnrs Conn.*

6947 **Biennial Report** of the **South Dakota Department** of **Agriculture.** Pierre, S.D. *Bienn. Rep. S. Dak. Dep. Agric.*

6948 **Biennial Report. State of California, Department** of **Fish** and **Game.** Sacramento. *Bienn. Rep. St. Calif. Dep. Fish Game* [1950–] **L.**BMᴺ. imp.; z. imp.; **Lo.**; **Pl.**M.; **Y.** [*C. of:* 6949]

6949 **Biennial Report. State of California, Division** of **Fish** and **Game.** Sacramento. *Bienn. Rep. St. Calif. Div. Fish Game* [1926–50] **L.**BMᴺ. imp.; z. imp.; **Bl.**U.; **Dm.** 46–50; **Fr.** 32–50; **Lo.** 46–50; **Pl.**M.; **Y.** [*C. of:* 6950; *C. as:* 6948]

6950 **Biennial Report. State of California, Fish** and **Game Commission.** Sacramento. *Bienn. Rep. St. Calif. Fish Game Commn* **L.**BMᴺ. 21–26* imp.; z. 18–26 imp.; **Lv.**U. 09–20; **Pl.**M. 09–26. [*C. as:* 6949]

Biennial Report. State Department of Health, North Dakota. *See* 6934.

6951 **Biennial Report** of the **State Engineer** to the **Governor** of **Colorado.** Denver. *Bienn. Rep. St. Engr Colo.* **L.**P. 85–34 imp.

6952 **Biennial Report** of the **State Engineer, Oregon.** *Bienn. Rep. St. Engr Ore.* **Y.**

6953 **Biennial Report** of **State Entomologist, West Virginia.** Morgantown. *Bienn. Rep. St. Ent. W. Va* **L.**EB. 13–14.

6953ᶜ **Biennial Report. State Forester, Oregon.** Salem. *Bienn. Rep. St. Forester Ore.* **Y.**

6954 **Biennial Report. State Geological Survey** of **North Dakota.** Bismarck. *Bienn. Rep. St. geol. Surv. N. Dak.* **L.**BMᴺ. 02–10; GM. 02–.

6955 **Biennial Report** of the **State Geologist, South Dakota.** Vermilion. *Bienn. Rep. St. Geol. S. Dak.* **L.**BMᴺ. 13–32 imp.

6955ᶜ **Biennial Report. State Highway Commission, Arkansas.** Little Rock. *Bienn. Rep. St. Highw. Commn Arkansas* **Y.**

6956 **Biennial Report** of the **State Inspector** of **Coal Mines, Colorado.** *Bienn. Rep. St. Insp. Coal Mines Colo.* [*C. as:* 45366]

6957 **Biennial Report. State Inspector** of **Coal Mines, State of Washington.** Olympia. *Bienn. Rep. St. Insp. Coal Mines Wash.*
Biennial Report. State Inspector of **Mines, Nevada.** See 6926.

6957ᶜ **Biennial Report. State Plant Board** of **Florida.** Gainesville. *Bienn. Rep. St. Pl. Bd Fla* **Y.**

6958 **Biennial Report** of the **Storrs Agricultural Experiment Station.** Connecticut. *Bienn. Rep. Storrs agric. Exp. Stn* [1906–] **L.**P. 06–23; **Abs.**A. 15–50 imp.; **Br.**A. 20–37: 50–; **Cr.**P. 06–23; **Md.**H. 49–; **Rt.** [*C. of:* 45378; *Suspended* 1938–48]

6959 **Biennial Report** of the **Texas State Board** of **Health.** Austin, Tex. *Bienn. Rep. Tex. St. Bd Hlth*

6960 **Biennial Report. Utah Agricultural Experiment Station.** *Bienn. Rep. Utah agric. Exp. Stn* [1923–] **L.**P.; **Abs.**A. 26–46 imp. [*Issued as part of* 12563]

6961 **Biennial Report. Vermont Department** of **Agriculture.** St. Albans, Vt. *Bienn. Rep. Vt Dep. Agric.* **L.**P. 24–.

6962 **Biennial Report. Vermont Department** of **Natural Resources.** Burlington. *Bienn. Rep. Vt Dep. nat. Resour.* **O.**F. 41–42: 45–.

6963 **Biennial Report. Washington Geological Survey.** Tacoma. *Bienn. Rep. Wash. geol. Surv.* [1903–] **L.**BMᴺ.; **GL.** [*C. of:* 45599]

6964 **Biennial Report. Washington State Department** of **Agriculture.** Olympia. *Bienn. Rep. Wash. St. Dep. Agric.* **L.**EB. 13–30.

6965 **Biennial Report. Washington State Department** of **Health.** Seattle. *Bienn. Rep. Wash. St. Dep. Hlth*

6966 **Biennial Report. Washington State Division** of **Mines** and **Geology.** Olympia. *Bienn. Rep. Wash. St. Div. Mines Geol.* **L.**BMᴺ. 21– imp.; **Y.**

6967 **Biennial Report. West Virginia Department** of **Agriculture.** Morgantown. *Bienn. Rep. W. Va Dep. Agric.* **L.**EB. 17–52; **Y.**

6968 **Biennial Report. Wisconsin Department** of **Agriculture.** Madison. *Bienn. Rep. Wis. Dep. Agric.* **L.**EB. 15–32.

6969 **Biennial Report. Wisconsin Geological** and **Natural History Survey.** Madison. *Bienn. Rep. Wis. geol. nat. Hist. Surv.* **E.**D. 97–01 imp.; **Lv.**P. 97–12.

6970 **Biennial Report. Wisconsin State Conservation Commission.** Madison. *Bienn. Rep. Wis. St. Conserv. Commn* **Y.**

6971 **Biennial Report. Wyoming Board** of **Agriculture.** Laramie. *Bienn. Rep. Wyo. Bd Agric.*

6972 **Biennial Report. Wyoming Game** and **Fish Commissioner.** *Bienn. Rep. Wyo. Game Fish Commnr*

6973 **Biennial Report** of the **Wyoming State Geologist.** Cheyenne. *Bienn. Rep. Wyo. St. Geol.* **L.**BMᴺ. 20–28; **GM.** 22–.

6974 **Bière** et les **boissons fermentées.** Paris. *Bière Boiss. ferm.* [1899–13] **L.**P.

6975 **Bihang** till **Göteborgs K. vetenskaps-** och **vitterhets-samhälles handlingar.** Göteborg. *Bih. Göteb. K. Vetensk.- o. Vitt.-Samh. Handl.* [1928–] **L.**BMᴺ.; R. 31–52; **Bl.**U.; **C.**P. 32–; **Db.**; **E.**R.; **O.**B. 37–; **Pl.**M. 36–. [1883–27 *published in* 21494; *also supplements*]

6976 **Bihang** till **K. Svenska vetenskapsakademiens handlingar.** Stockholm. *Bih. K. svenska VetenskAkad. Handl.* [1872–03] **L.**AS.; BM.; BMᴺ.; E. 88–03; G.; GL.; K.; R.; SC.; UC. 87–03; Z. (zool.); **Bl.**U.; **C.**P.; UL.; **Db.**; **E.**C.; J. 96–02; R.; **Ld.**U.; **Lv.**U. imp.; **Pl.**M. (bot.) 89–03: (zool.) 80–03 imp. [*C. as:* 4803, 4807, 4809 *and* 4811]

6977 **Bihang** till **meteorologiska iakttagelser** i **Sverige.** Stockholm. *Bih. met. Iakttag. Sver.* **L.**MO. 06–18 imp.
Bihar and **Orissa Agricultural Journal.** Patna. See 1347.

6978 **Bihar University Journal.** Bihar. *Bihar Univ. J.* [1956–] **Bm.**U.

6979 **Biharmegyei iparosol közlönye.** Nagyvárad. *Biharm. Iparos. Közl.*

6980 **Bijdragen** tot de **biologie** uit het **Physiologisch laboratorium** der **Universiteit** van **Amsterdam.** *Bijdr. Biol. physiol. Lab. Univ. Amst.* **L.**S. 09–45; **E.**U. 09–.

6981 **Bijdragen** tot de **dierkunde.** Leiden. *Bijdr. Dierk.* [1848–] **L.**BM. 1848–88; BMᴺ.; L. 1848–29; R. 1848–39; Z.; **C.**B. 1848–13; UL.; **E.**R. 1858–; **Lv.**U. 69–; **Pl.**M.; **Y.**

6982 **Bijdragen** tot de **geschiedenis** der **geneeskunde.** Amsterdam, Haarlem. *Bijdr. Gesch. Geneesk.* [1921–] [*Supplement to:* 34468]

6982ᶜ **Bijdragen** tot de **geschiedschrijving** van de **posterijen, telegrafie** en **telefonie** in **Nederland.** 's-Gravenhage. *Bijdr. GeschSchrijv. Post. Telegr. Telef. Ned.* [1947–] **L.**BM.

6983 **Bijzondere publicatiës** van het **Bosbouwproefstation.** Buitenzorg, Bogor. *Bijz. Publ. BosbProefstn, Buitenz.* [1948–] **O.**F. 49– imp.; **Y.**

6984 **Biken's Journal.** Journal of the Research Institute for microbial diseases. Osaka. *Biken's J.* [1958–] **L.**MC.; **C.**APH.

6985 **Bilancia idrologico** del **bacino** del **Po.** *Bilancia idrol. Bacino Po* **L.**MO. 16–22*. [*C. as:* 8197]

6986 **Bild** und **Ton.** Zeiss Ikon A.G. Dresden. *Bild Ton, Zeiss Ikon* **L.**P. 34– imp. [*Not published* 1940–51]

6987 **Bild** und **Ton.** Zeitschrift für Film- und Fototechnik. Berlin. *Bild Ton, Berl.* [1948–] **L.**PG. 49–; **Wd.**K. 48–56; **Y.**

6988 **Bildmessung** und **Luftbildwesen.** Berlin. *Bildmess. Luftbildw.* [1924–] **L.**P. 32– imp.; **Y.** [*Supplement to:* 1773; *not published* 1944–53]
Bilješke. Biološko-okeanografski institut. Split. See 6989.

6989 **Bilješke. Institut** za **oceanografiju** i **ribarstvo.** Split. *Bilj. Inst. Oceanogr. Ribarst.* [1951–] **L.**BMᴺ.; Z.; **Bn.**U. 55–; **C.**P.; **Dm.**; **Lo.** 52–; **Lv.**U.; **Pl.**M.; **Wo.**; **Y.**

6990 **Biljna.** Zagreb. *Biljna* **Hu.**G. 55–57.

6991 **Biljna proizvodnja.** Zagreb. *Biljna Proizv.* [1948–57] **L.**BM. 54–57; **Hu.**G. 54–57; **Md.**H. 56–57.

6991[a] **Biljna zastita.** Zagreb. *Biljna Zast.* [1957–] **Y.**

6991[b] **Bilteknisk fagblad.** Oslo. *Biltek. Fagbl.* **Y.**

6991[c] **Bilten dokumentacija inostrane stručne literature.** Beograd. *Bilt. Dokum. inost. struč. Lit.* [1950–51] **L.**BM. 51; **Y.** [*C. as:* 6991[d] *and* 6991[o]]

6991[d] **Bilten dokumentacija stručne literature.** Beograd. *Bilt. Dokum. struč. Lit.* [1952–54]
    A. Poljoprivreda, šumarstvo. **L.**BM.; **Y.** [*C. as:* 6991[h]]
    B. Mašinska tehnika, elektrotehnika. **L.**BM.; **Y.** [*C. as:* 6991[g]]
    C. Geologija, rudarstvo, metalurgija. **L.**BM.; **Y.** [*C. as:* 6991[i]]
    D. Hemija, hemiska industrija **L.**BM.; **Y.** [*C. as:* 6991[f]]
    E. Građevinska tehnika, arhitektura, saobraćaj. **L.**BM.; **Y.** [*C. as:* 6991[e]]
    Bilten sadržaja stranih časopisa. *See* 6991[o].

6991[e] **Bilten dokumentacije za građevinarstvo, arhitekturu i saobraćaj.** Beograd. *Bilt. Dokum. Građev. Arhit. Saobr.* [1955–] **L.**BM.; HQ. (1 yr); **Y.** [*C. of:* 6991[d] Ser. E.]

6991[f] **Bilten dokumentacije za hemiju i hemisku industriju.** Beograd. *Bilt. Dokum. Hem. hem. Ind.* [1955–] **L.**BM.; HQ. (1 yr); **Y.** [*C. of:* 6991[d] Ser. D.]

6991[g] **Bilten dokumentacije za mašinstvo i elektrotehniku.** Beograd. *Bilt. Dokum. Maš. Elektroteh.* [1955–] **L.**BM.; **Y.** [*C. of:* 6991[d] Ser. B.]

6991[h] **Bilten dokumentacije za poljoprivredu, šumarstvo, duvansku i drvnu industriju.** Beograd. *Bilt. Dokum. Poljopriv. Šum.* [1955–] **L.**BM.; **Y.** [*C. of:* 6991[d] Ser. A.]

6991[i] **Bilten dokumentacije za rudarstvo, metalurgiju i geologiju.** Beograd. *Bilt. Dokum. Rudarstvo Metal. Geol.* [1955–] **L.**BM.; HQ. (1 yr); **Y.** [*C. of:* 6991[d] Ser. C.]

6991[j] **Bilten. Drushtvo na matematicharite i fizicharite od Narodna Republika Makedonija.** Skopje. Билтен. Друштво на математичарите и физичарите од Народна Републжка Македонија. *Bilt. Drusht. Mat. Fiz. nar. Repub. Maked.* [1950–] **L.**BM. 51–.

6991[k] **Bilten. Glavni savez zemljoradničkih zadruga NR Srbije.** Beograd. Билтен. Главни савез земљорадничких задруга НР Србије. *Bilt. glav. Savez zeml. Zadr. NR Srb.* [1953–] **L.**BM.

6991[l] **Bilten naučne dokumentacije za farmaciju.** Beograd. *Bilt. nauč. Dokum. Farm.* [1955–] **Y.**

6991[m] **Bilten naučne dokumentacije za medicinu, farmaciju i veterinu.** Beograd. *Bilt. nauč. Dokum. Med. Farm. Vet.* [1953–] **Y.**

6991[n] **Bilten. Odeljenje materijalno-tehničkog snabdevanja.** Glavna direkcija jugoslovenskih železnica. Beograd. *Bilt. Odel. mater.-teh. Snabd.* [1952–] **L.**BM.

6991[o] **Bilten sadržaja stranih časopisa.** Beograd. *Bilt. Sadrž. stran. Čas.* [1952–]
    A. Poljoprivreda i šumarstvo. **L.**BM.; **Y.**
    B. Mašinska tehnika i elektrotehnika. **L.**BM.; **Y.**
    C. Geologija, rudarstvo, metalurgija. **L.**BM.; **Y.**
    D. Hemija, hemiska industrija. **L.**BM.; **Y.**
    E. Građevinska tehnika, arhitektura, saobraćaj. **L.**BM.; **Y.**
    [*C. from:* 6991[c]]

6991[p] **Bilten Saveza jugoslovenskih laboratorija** za **ispitivanje** i **istrazivanje materijala** i **konstrukcija.** Beograd. *Bilt. Saveza jugosl. Lab. Ispit. Istrav. Mater. Konstr.* [1958–] **Y.**

6991[q] **Bilten. Savezna sanitarna inspekcija.** Beograd. *Bilt. savez. sanit. Insp.* [1951–] **L.**BM.

6992 **Bilten vetseruma.** Beograd. *Bilt. Vetser.* [1948–] **W.** 49–.

6993 **Biltmore Botanical Studies.** Biltmore Herbarium. Biltmore, N.C. *Biltmore bot. Stud.* [1901–02] **L.**BM. 01; BM[N].; K.; **E.**B. 01; **M.**P.

6994 **Bi-monthly Bulletin** of the **American Institute** of **Mining Engineers.** New York. *Bi-m. Bull. Am. Inst. Min. Engrs* [1905–08] **L.**P. imp.; **Db.**; **Nw.**A. imp. [*C. as:* 9326]

6995 **Bi-monthly Bulletin. American Iron** and **Steel Institute.** New York. *Bi-m. Bull. Am. Iron Steel Inst.* [*C. of:* 33404]

Bi-monthly Bulletin. British Coal Utilisation Research Association. *See* 33409.

Bi-monthly Bulletin. Division of Zoology, **Pennsylvania Department** of **Agriculture.** *See* 7002.

6996 **Bi-monthly Bulletin. North Dakota Agricultural Experiment Station.** Fargo. *Bi-m. Bull. N. Dak. agric. Exp. Stn* [1938–58] **L.**AM.; EB. imp.; **Abd.**R.; **Hu.**G. 51–58; **O.**F. imp.; **R.**D. 41–58; **Rt.** imp.; **Sil.** 50–51 imp. [*C. as:* 35081]

6997 **Bi-monthly Bulletin** of the **Ohio Agricultural Experiment Station.** Wooster. *Bi-m. Bull. Ohio agric. Exp. Stn* [1925–46] **L.**AM. 29–40 imp.; EB.; MY.; **Abs.**A. 45–46; **C.**A. 32–46; **O.**F. 37–46 imp.; **R.**D. 29–46; **Rt.** [*C. of:* 33477; *C. as:* 19044]

6998 **Bi-monthly Bulletin** of the **University College** of **Medicine.** Richmond, Va. *Bi-m. Bull. Univ. Coll. Med., Richmond Va* [*C. as:* 14550]

6999 **Bi-monthly Bulletin. Western Washington Agricultural Experiment Substation, Puyallup.** Washington. *Bi-m. Bull. west. Wash. agric. Exp. Substn Puyallup* [1921–] **L.**EB. 21–25. [*C. of:* 33496]

7000 **Bi-monthly Progress Report. Division** of **Forest Biology.** Ottawa. *Bi-mon. Prog. Rep. Div. Forest Biol., Ottawa* [1951–61] **L.**EB.; MY.; **Bn.**U.; **O.**F. [*C. from:* 19952; *C. as:* Bimonthly Progress Report. Forest Entomology and Pathology Branch, Department of Forestry.

Bi-monthly Progress Report. Forest Biology Division, Canada. *See* 7000.

7001 **Bi-monthly Progress Report** on **Forest Insect Investigations.** Ottawa. *Bi-mon. Prog. Rep. Forest Insect Invest.* [1951–] **L.**EB.; **O.**F. [*C. of:* 19952]

7002 **Bi-monthly Zoological Bulletin. Pennsylvania Department** of **Agriculture.** Harrisburg. *Bi-m. zool. Bull. Pa Dep. Agric.* [1911–16] **L.**BM[N]. imp.; EB.; Z. [*C. of:* 59258]

7003 **Binæringerne.** Florø. *Binæringerne*

7004 **Binnengewässer.** Stuttgart. *Binnengewässer* [1925–] **L.**BM[N].; SC.; Z. imp.; **Bn.**U. 32–50 imp.; **Fr.** imp.; **G.**U.; **O.**AP. 26–27: 50–51; Z. 26–29 imp.

7005 **Bioanalysis.** Chicago. *Bioanalysis* [1958–] **L.**SC. [*Supplement to:* 303]

7006 **Biochemical** and **Allied Research** in **India.** Bangalore. *Biochem. all. Res. India* [1930–35] **L.**C. 32–35; **C.**A.; **Rt.** 32–35. [*C. as:* 3432]

7007 **Biochemical** and **Biophysical Research Communications.** New York, London. *Biochem. biophys. Res. Commun.* [1959–] **L.**BM.; MC.; MD.; P.; SC.; TD.; UC.; **Abd.**R.; T.; **Bl.**U.; **Br.**A.; **C.**APH. 62–; BI.; R.; **Cr.**U.; **Dn.**U.; **G.**U. 61–; **Ld.**U.; **M.**C. 59–61; U.; **O.**BI.; **W.** 61–; **Y.**

7008 **Biochemical Bulletin.** Lancaster, N.Y. *Biochem. Bull.* [1911–16] **L.**BM.; LI.; MD. imp.; U. imp.; **Abd.**U. 11–13; **Bl.**U. imp.; **C.**UL.; **Db.** 11–15 imp.; **E.**U.; **O.**R. 11–13 imp.; **Pl.**M. 13–14 imp.; **Rt.**; **Sa.** 11–12.

Biochemical Journal. Kiev. *See* 7030°.

7009 **Biochemical Journal.** Liverpool, Cambridge. *Biochem. J.* [1906–] **L.**AM. 48–; B.; BM.; C.; CB. 26–; IC.; KC. 57–; LE. 19–; LI.; MA. 11–; MC.; MD.; NC. 17–20: 56–; OP. 40–; P. 10–; PH. 06–22; QM. 20–23 imp.: 50–; RI.; S.; SC.; TD.; TP. imp.; U. 26–; UC.; UCH. 06–37; VC.; **Abd.**M. 50–; R.; S. 43–; U.; **Abs.**N.; U. 49–; **Bl.**U.; **Bm.**P.; T. 34–49 imp.: 59–; **Bn.**U. 11– imp.; **Br.**A. 21–; U.: **C.**A.; APH.; BI.; BO. 26–40: 47–; CH. 44–; MO. 38–; P. 06–12; PH. 06–28: 33–; UL.; V. 51–; **Cr.**MD. 32– imp.; U. 06–15; **Db.**; **Dn.**U. 13–; **E.**A.; CE. 55–; P.; SW. 47–56; U.; W. 13–; **Ep.**D.; **Ex.**U.; **Fr.** 27–38: 48–57; **G.**F. 42–; M. 21–; T.; U.; **H.**U. 47–; **Hu.**G. 30–; **Je.** 32–; **Ld.**U.; W. 27–; **Lh.**FO. 13–; **Lo.** 07–12: 21–; **Lv.**P. 46–; U.; **M.**C. 20–; MS.; P. 38–; T. 23–; **Md.**H. 21–; **Mi.** 25–; **N.**T. 49–; U.; **Nw.**A.; **O.**BI.; BO. 40–; BS. 54–; N.; P. 28–; PH. 13–; R.; UC. 39–; **Pl.**M.; **R.**D.; U.; **Rt.**; **Sa.**; **Sal.**F. 43–; **Sh.**IO. 30–48; U. 08–; **Ste.** 35–58; **Sw.**U. 41– imp.; **W.** 28–; **Wd.** 48–; **We.**K. 49–57; **Y.**

7010 **Biochemical Pharmacology.** London, New York. *Biochem. Pharmac.* [1958–] **L.**BM.; C.; CB.; MA.; MC.; MD.; P.; S.; SC.; TP.; UC.; **Bl.**U.; **C.**APH.; **Dn.**U.; **G.**U.; **Ld.**U.; **O.**BI.; R.; **Y.**

7011 **Biochemical Preparations.** New York. *Biochem. Prep.* [1949–] **L.**B.; BM.; C.; CB.; LI.; P.; SC.; TD.; UC.; VC.; **Abd.**R.; **Bl.**U.; **Bm.**U.; **Bn.**U.; **Br.**U.; **C.**BI.; CH.; UL.; **Cr.**U.; **Db.**; **Dn.**U.; **E.**A. 49–55; U.; **Ex.**U.; **H.**U.; **Ld.**P.; **Lv.**P.; **N.**U.; **R.**U.; **Rt.**; **Sa.**; **Y.**

7012 **Biochemical Researches.** Columbia University, New York. *Biochem. Res.*

7013 **Biochemical Society Symposia.** Cambridge. *Biochem. Soc. Symp.* [1947–] **L.**CB.; MD.; P. imp.; QM. imp.; S.; SC.; U.; UCH.; VC.; **Abd.**T.; U.; **Abs.**U. imp.; **Bl.**U.; **C.**APH.; BI.; **Db.**; **E.**U.; **G.**U. 48–; **M.**MS.; U.; **N.**U. 53–; **O.**B. 51– imp.; R.; **Pl.**M. 49–; **R.**U.; **Y.**

7014 **Biochemie.** Magdeburg. *Biochemie*

7015 **Biochemische Monatsblätter.** Leipzig. *Biochem. Mbl.* [1924–32]

7016 **Biochemische Tagesfragen.** Stuttgart. *Biochem. Tagesfragen*

7017 **Biochemische Zeitschrift.** Berlin. *Biochem. Z.* [1906–] **L.**AM. 20–23; BM.; C. imp.; IC. 06–31: 38–40; LI.; MA. 47–; MC. imp.; MD.; P. 09–; S. 08–52; SC. 06–44: 47–; TD.; U.; UC.; **Abd.**R.; U. 36– imp.; **Bl.**U.; **Bm.**U. 21–; **Bn.**U. 57–; **Br.**U.; **C.**APH. 40–; BI.; CH. 47–52; PH. 06–14; **Cr.**U. 06–13: 26–; **Db.**; **Dn.**U. 08–; **E.**P.; SW. 41–; U.; **G.**U.; **Ld.**U. 06–14: 47–; **Lo.** 20–23; **Lv.**P. 53–; U.; **M.**C. 20–39: 51–; MS.; P. 56–; **Nw.**A. 29–; **O.**BI.; PH. 06–28; R.; **Pl.**M. 21–32; **R.**D. 20– imp.; U. 50–; **Sh.**U.; **Ste.** 06–31: 38–40: 48–58; **Y.** [*Incorporating* 5932; *not published* 1945–46]

7018 **Biochemisches Zentralblatt.** Berlin, etc. *Biochem. Zbl.* [1902–10] **L.**C. 02–06; IC.; LI.; MC.; MD.; P.; TD.; U. 05–10; UC. 06–07; **Abd.**U.; **Bl.**U. imp.; **Bm.**U.;

Br.U. 02–08; **C.**BI.; PH.; **Db.**; **Dn.**U.; **E.**P.; U.; **G.**U. 07–10; **Ld.**U.; **Lv.**U.; **M.**MS.; **O.**R.; **R.**U. 04–10; **Ste.** [*C. in:* 58991]

Biochemistry. Leningrad, Moscow. *See* 7031.

7019 **Biochemistry.** New York. *Biochemistry, N.Y.* [1956–] **L.**C.; MC. imp.; MD. 57–; P.; R. 58–; **Abd.**R. 62–; T. 59–; **Bl.**U.; **Bn.**U. 60–; **C.**APH.; BI. 59–; **Cr.**U. 58–; **G.**T.; U.; **Ld.**U. 59–; **M.**U.; **N.**U. 57–; **O.**R. 58–; **Rt.** 57–; **Sw.**U. 59–; **Y.** [*English translation of:* 7031]

7020 **Biochimica.** Bologna. *Biochimica* [1924–]

7021 **Biochimica applicata.** Roma. *Biochim. appl.* [1954–] **L.**C. 58–; SC. 59–; **Y.**

7022 **Biochimica et biophysica acta.** New York and Amsterdam. *Biochim. biophys. Acta* [1947–] **L.**AM. 49–; B.; BM.; C.; CB.; IC.; LI.; MA.; MC.; MD.; P.; QM.; RI.; S. 61–; SC.; TD. 59–; TP. 50–; U.; **Abd.**R.; U.; **Abs.**U. 58–; **Ba.**I. 56–; **Bl.**U.; **Bm.**T.; U.; **Bn.**U.; **Br.**A. 56–; U.; **C.**APH.; BI.; CH.; PH.; R.; **Cr.**MD. 57–; U. 56–; **Db.**; **Dn.**U.; **E.**A.; AG. 47–52; HW. 47–58; SW. 48–; U.; **G.**U.; **Ld.**U.; W.; **M.**C.; P.; U.; **Md.**H. 47–59; **N.**U.; **Nw.**A. 52–; **O.**BI.; PH.; R.; **R.**D.; U. 48–; **Rt.**; **Sa.** imp.; **Sh.**U.; **Sw.**U. 59–; **Y.**

7023 **Biochimica e terapia sperimentale.** Milano. *Biochim. Terap. sper.* [1909–] **L.**C. 39–40; MA. 29–; MD. 26– imp.; SC. 35–; TD. 26–; V. 36–40 imp.; **W.** 22–.

7024 **Biodynamica.** Normandy, Mo. *Biodynamica* [1934–] **L.**SC.; **C.**A. 34–55; BI. 24–38; **Ld.**U. 34–39 imp.; **Y.**

7025 **Biodynamics.** Phoenixville, Pa. *Biodynamics* [1941–] **M.**U. 47–; **Y.**

7026 **Biofizika.** Moskva. Биофизика. *Biofizika* [1956–] **L.**BM.; C.; P. 57–; SC. 58–; **Bm.**T. 59–; **C.**P.; **Y.** 57–. [*English translation at:* 7124]

7027 **Biogeographica.** Biogeographical Society of Japan. Tokyo. *Biogeographica* [1935–42] **L.**BM^N. 35–42 imp.; Z. imp.; **O.**R. 35–41.

7028 **Bio-Graphic Quarterly.** Ottawa. *Bio-graphic Q.* [1955–] **Abs.**A.

7029 **Biographical Memoirs** of **Fellows** of the **Royal Society.** London. *Biogr. Mem. Fellows R. Soc.* [1955–] **L.**B.; BM.; BM^N.; C.; EE.; LI.; MC.; MD.; P.; PH.; QM.; R.; RI.; S.; SC.; [TD. imp.; U.; UC.; UCH.; **Bl.**U.; **Bm.**P.; U.; **Bn.**U. 58–; **C.**B.; GE.; P.; SJ.; UL.; **Cr.**U.; **Db.**; **Dn.**U.; **E.**A.; U.; **G.**M.; U.; **H.**U.; **Ld.**P.; U.; **M.**C.; P.; U.; **N.**U.; **Nw.**A.; **O.**R.; **Pl.**M.; **Rt.**; **Sh.**U.; **Y.** [*C. of:* 35566]

7030 **Biographical Memoirs. National Academy** of **Sciences.** Washington. *Biogr. Mem. natn. Acad. Sci.* [1877–] **L.**AS. 19: 29–39; BM^N. 02– imp.; MO. 19–45 v. imp.; P. 02–; SC. 86–52 imp.; UC. 07– imp.; **Abd.**U. 07–37 imp.; **Bm.**U. 19–; **C.**P. 34–; UL. 19–; **E.**R. 02–44; **G.**U. 86–41 imp.; **H.**U. 13–39 imp.; **Ld.**U. 02–; **Lv.**U. 19: 29–; **M.**U. imp.; **N.**U. 29–39; **Nw.**A. 02–39 imp.; **O.**R. 29–; **Pl.**M. 57–.

7030° **Biokhemichnyĭ zhurnal.** Ky̆yiv. Біохемічний журнал. *Biokhem. Zh.* [1938–41] **L.**C.; MD. 39–40; TD. imp.; UC.; **Abd.**R. 38–40 imp.; **C.**BI. 38–39; **E.**U. 39–40; **Hu.**G. [*C. of:* and *Rec. as:* 55485]

7031 **Biokhimiya.** Leningrad, Moskva. Биохимия. *Biokhimiya* [1936–] **L.**BM. 43–; C.; CB. 57–; MC. 43–45: 54–; MD. 43–; P. 48–; SC. 37–; **Abd.**R. 37– imp.; T. 47–59; **Abs.**A.; **Bn.**U. 45–46 imp.; **C.**APH. 56–; BI.; **E.**AB. 40; R. 43–45; **Hu.**G. 36–54; **Md.**H. 44–; **N.**U. 47–; **R.**D. 54–; **Rt.** 48–; **Y.** 49–54 imp.: 57–. [*English translation at:* 7019]

7032 **Biokhimiya chaĭnogo proizvodstva.** Leningrad. Биохимия чайного производства. *Biokhim. chain. Proizv.* **Y.** 59–.

7033 **Biokhimiya plodov i ovoshchei.** Moskva. Биохимия плодов и овощей. *Biokhim. Plodov Ovoshch.* [1949–] **L.**BM.; P. 58–; **Y.** 58–.

7034 **Biokhimiya vinodeliya.** Moskva. Биохимия виноделия. *Biokhim. Vinodel.* [1947–] **L.**BM. 48–; P.; **Br.**A. 50–; **Y.**

7035 **Biokhimiya zerna.** Moskva. Биохимия зерна. *Biokhim. Zerna* [1951–60] **L.**BM.; P. 58–60; **Y.** [*C. as:* 7036]

7036 **Biokhimiya zerna i khlebopecheniya.** Moskva. Биохимия зерна и хлебопечения. *Biokhim. Zerna Khlebopech.* [1960–] **L.**BM.; P.; **Y.** [*C. of:* 7035]

7037 **Bioklimatische Beiblätter der Meteorologischen Zeitschrift.** Braunschweig. *Bioklim. Beibl.* [1933–] **L.**MO. 34–43; P. 36–43; SC. 33–39; **E.**M. 34–39; **O.**AP. 34–39.

7038 **Biologe.** München. *Biologe* [1931–44] **C.**A. 35–41 imp.

7039 **Biologen-Kalender.** Leipzig. *Biologen-Kal.* **L.**P 14*.

7040 **Biologi.** Türk biologi derneginin yayın organı. İstanbul. *Biologi* [1950–]

7041 **Biológia.** Casopis Slovenskej akademie vied. Bratislava. *Biológia, Bratisl.* [1953–] **L.**BM^N.; L.; Z. imp.; **C.**A. 56–58; **G.**U. 57–; **O.**H. 59–; **Y.** [*C. of:* 7090]

7042 **Biologia.** Biological Society of Pakistan. Lahore. *Biologia, Lahore* [1955–] **L.**BM^N.; MY.; Z.; **C.**P.; **Pl.**M.; **Y.**

7043 **Biologia:** a monthly newsletter supplement to Chronica Botanica. Waltham, Mass. *Biologia, Waltham* [1947–51] **L.**B.; BM.; BM^N.; L.; **Abs.**U.; **Bl.**U.; **Bm.**P.; U.; **C.**BO.; **E.**A.; AG.; U.; **G.**U.; **Ld.**U.; **Md.**H.; **O.**BO.; F.; **R.**U.; **Rt.** [*C. in:* 13983]

7044 **Biologia centrali-americana.** London. *Biologia cent.-am.* [1879–15]
 (a) Botany. **L.**BM.; BM^N.; K. 79–88; SC. 79–90; Z.; **Bm.**P.; **Db.**; **E.**A. 79–12; **O.**R.
 (b) Zoology. **L.**BM.; BM^N.; SC. 79–90; Z.; **Bm.**P.; **Db.**; **E.**A. 79–12; F.; **O.**R.; **Sa.** 89–15.

7045 **Biologia generalis.** Archiv für die allgemeinen Fragen der Lebensforschung. Vienna & New York. *Biologia gen.* [1925–] **L.**BM^N. 25–51; SC. 39–51; UC. 25–30; **C.**UL.; **E.**AG. 25–26: 29: 34–35; **Pl.**M. 25.

7046 **Biologia medica.** Milano. *Biologia med., Milano* [1925–36]

7047 **Biologia médica.** Rio de Janeiro, Niterói. *Biologia méd., Niterói* [1934–] **L.**LI. 34–46; MD. 45–; TD. 35–46 v. imp.; **Sal.** 45–46.

7048 **Biologia neonatorum.** Basel. *Biologia Neonat.* [1959–] **L.**MA.; MD.; UC.; **Br.**U.; **C.**AN.; APH.; **Cr.**MD.; **Dn.**U.; **E.**U.; **Y.** [*C. of:* 18639]

7049 **Biologia plantarum.** Praha. *Biologia Pl.* [1959–] **L.**BM.; **Br.**A.; **C.**A.; **Md.**H.; **O.**RE.; **Pl.**M.; **Y.** [*C. from:* 13589]

7050 **Biológiai közlemények.** Budapest. *Biol. Közl.* [1954–]
 Pars biologica. **Y.**
 Pars anthropologica. **Y.**

7051 **Biologica.** Revue scientifique du médecin. Paris. *Biologica, Paris.* [1911–14] **L.**BM^N.; MD. 11–13; **C.**B. 11–12.

7052 **Biológica.** Trabajos del Instituto de biología de la Universidad de Chile. Santiago. *Biológica, Santiago* [1944–] **L.**BM^N.; EB.; K. 55–; L.; MC.; MD. 44–45; MY. imp.; R.; RI. 55–; S.; TD.; Z.; **Abd.**R. 55–; **Br.**U.; **C.**B.; MO.; P.; UL.; V. 54–55; **Dn.**U. 52–; **E.**AG. 52–; C.; R.; U. 52–; **G.**U. 46– imp.; **Ld.**U. 48–49: 52–; **Lv.**M.; **M.**MS.; **Mi.**; **Nw.**A. 52–; **O.**AP.; Z. 52– imp.; **Pl.**M.; **Rt.** 47–; **Sal.** 47–; **Y.**

7053 **Biologica.** Biological Club of Nippon. Tokyo. *Biologica, Tokyo* [1931] **L.**BM^N.

7054 **Biologica.** Raccolta di scritti di biologia. Torino. *Biologica, Torino* [1906–08] **L.**BM^N.; Z. 06–07; **E.**U.

7055 **Biologica hungarica.** Budapest. *Biologica hung.* [1923–26] **L.**BM^N.; **C.**UL.

7056 **Biologica latina.** Milano. *Biologica lat.* [1948–] **L.**MA.

7057 **Biological Abstracts.** Menasha, Philadelphia. *Biol. Abstr.* [1926–] *From* 1939 *also issued in sections:* A. General biology. B. Basic medical sciences. C. Microbiology, immunology, Public health and parasitology. D. Plant sciences. E. Animal sciences. *During* 1941–53 *the further sections were issued:* F. Animal production and veterinary sciences. G. Food and nutrition research. H. Human biology. J. Cereals and cereal products. **L.**AM.; B. 26–55: (*a–e*) 56–: (*h*) 46–53; BM. 37–; BM^N.; CB.; E. 26–32; HS. (*d*) 49–55; K. 26–54: (*a, c, d*) 55–; L.; LI. (*c*) 39–; MD. 26–34; MY. 26–52 imp.; NC. 27–32: 41–; P.; QM.; R.; SC.; TD.; TP. 48–53; U.; UC.; V. 26–37: (*c*) 54–: (*f*) 42–53; Z.; **Abd.**U.; **Abs.**A. (*d, j*) 51–53; N.; S. (*a, c, e*) 55–; U. **Ba.**I. (*a, d*) 39–; **Bl.**U.; **Bm.**P.; U.; **Bn.**U.; **Br.**A. 26–49: (*a, d, e, g*); U.; **C.**A. (*a, d*): 44–; AN. 26–32; APH. 48–; B.; BO.; GE. 26–31: 36–37: 48–55: (*a*) 56; R. 47–56; V. (*a, b, c, e*) 55–; **Cr.**MD.; U.; **Db.**; **Dn.**U.; **E.**AB. 26–38: (*a, b*) 39–55; AG. 45–53; AR. 47–; B. (*d*): (*j*) 49–53; F. 26–46; N.; PO. 48–; SW. 39–52; U.; W.; **Ep.**D. 45–; **Ex.**U. 27–; **Fr.**; **G.**F. 27–36: 51–; M.; T.; U.; **H.**U.; **Hu.**G. (*d*) 39–; **Je.** 34–41: 48–; **Lc.**A. 46–; **Ld.**U. 26–31; W. (*a, b*): (*f*) 26–38: 48–53; **Lo.** 27–37: 51–; **Lv.**P. 59–; U.; **M.**MS. (*b*) 51–; P.; U.; **Md.**H. 27–56: (*a, c–e*) 57–; **Mi.**; **N.**U.; **Nw.**A.; **O.**BO. 26–39: (*a, d*) 39–: (*c*) 47–; F.; R.; RE.; Z. 26–35; **Pit.**F. imp.; **Pl.**M.; **R.**D. 26–37; U.; **Rt.**; **Sa.**; **Sal.** 26–49; F.; **Sh.**U.; **Sw.**U.; **W.**; **Wo.** 54–; **Y.** [*C. of:* 302 and 8561]

7057° **Biological Antioxidants.** Transactions of Conferences, Josiah Macy Jr. Foundation. New York. *Biol. Antioxyd. Trans. Confs Josiah Macy jr Fdn* [1946–50]

7058 **Biological Bulletin** of Fukien Christian University. Foochow. *Biol. Bull. Fukien Christ. Univ.* [1936–] **L.**BM^N. 36–47; Z. 39–47.

7059 **Biological Bulletin. Marine Biological Laboratory, Woods Hole, Mass.** *Biol. Bull. mar. biol. Lab., Woods Hole* [1899–] **L.**AM. 21–31; B. 42–46: 56–; BM^N.; CB. 49–; EB. 02– imp.; L.; MC. 23–; MD. 26–; NC. 54–; P. 13–; QM. 50–; R. 23–; SC.; U. 50–; UC. 02–; Z.; **Abd.**M. 37–; U. 43–; **Abs.**U. 46–; **Ba.**I. 41–55; **Bl.**U. 39– imp.; **Bm.**U. 31–; **Bn.**U. 09– imp.; **Br.**U. 10–; **C.**B.; P. 06–; **Cr.**U. 37–; **Db.** 02–12: 22–; **Dm.** 18–; **E.**AG. 23–29:31; R. 23–U; **Ex.**U. 10–; **Fr.** 20–24; **G.**U.; **H.**U. 32–; **Ld.**U. 21–; **Lo.** 21–; **Lv.**U. 02–; **M.**U. 14–; **Mi.** 32–; **N.**U. 47–; **O.**R.; Z. 04–11; **Pl.**M.; **R.**U. 54–; **Sa.** 02–imp.; **Sw.**U. 27– imp.; **Y.**

7060 **Biological Bulletin** of the **Normal College, Shiang Chyn University,** Canton. *Biol. Bull. Normal Coll., Canton* **L.**BM^N. 35–36 imp.

7061 **Biological Bulletin** of **St. John's University.** Shanghai. *Biol. Bull. St John's Univ., Shanghai* [1931–35] **L**.BM[N].; **Pl**.M.

7062 **Biological Bulletin. Washington Department** of **Game.** *Biol. Bull. Wash. Dep. Game*

7063 **Biological Flora** of the **British Isles.** British Ecological Society. Cambridge, etc. *Biol. Flora Br. Isl.* [1941–] **L**.NC.; **Bl**.U.; **O**.AP.; BO. [*Reprinted from:* 25919]

7064 **Biological Investigation** of the **Water Purification Plants** of **Calcutta Corporation.** Calcutta. *Biol. Invest. Wat. Purif. Pl. Calcutta* **L**.BM. 29–.

7065 **Biological Journal.** Biological Society of the University of St. Andrews. Edinburgh. *Biol. J. Univ. St. Andrews* [1960–] **L**.BM.; BM[N].; Z.; **Abs**.N.; **Dn**.U.; **Y**.

7066 **Biological Journal** of **Okayama University.** Okayama. *Biol. J. Okayama Univ.* [1952–] **L**.BM[N].; SC.; Z. 57–; **C**.A.; **E**.U.; **Lv**.U. imp.; **Pl**.M.

7067 **Biological Leaflet.** Washington, D.C. *Biol. Leafl.* [1933–] **L**.BM[N].; **Y**.

7068 **Biological Magazine.** University of St. Andrews. *Biol. Mag. Univ. St Andrews* [1954–] **Sa**.

Biological Notes. Montreal. *See* 35193.

Biological Notes. Illinois Natural History Survey Division. *See* 7069.

7069 **Biological Notes. Natural History Survey Division, State of Illinois.** Urbana. *Biol. Notes nat. Hist. Surv. Div. St. Ill.* **L**.BM[N]. 33– imp.; Z. 49– imp.; **E**.R. 38– imp.; **Y**.

7070 **Biological Papers** of the **University of Alaska.** College. *Biol. Pap. Univ. Alaska* [1957–] **L**.BM[N]. 57–; Z. imp.; **O**.AP.

7071 **Biological Papers. University of Minnesota.** Minneapolis. *Biol. Pap. Univ. Minn.* [1958–] **Db**.

7072 **Biological Pharmacology.** London. *Biol. Pharmac.* [1958–] **L**.BM.; **Dn**.U.

7073 **Biological Psychiatry.** *Biol. Psychiat.* [1959–] **G**.U.

7073° **Biological Records. Cave Research Group** of **Great Britain.** *Biol. Rec. Cave Res. Grp Gt Br.* [1954–] **L**.BM[N].; NC.; **Y**. [*C. of:* 7082°]

7074 **Biological Reports. Department** of **Fisheries. State** of **Washington.** Seattle. *Biol. Rep. Dep. Fish. St. Wash.* **Lo**. 49–.

Biological Results of the **Fishing Experiments** carried out by **F.I.S. Endeavour.** *See* 59263.

Biological Results of the **Japanese Antarctic Research Expedition.** *See* 50494.

7074° **Biological Review** of the **City College, New York.** *Biol. Rev. Cy Coll. N.Y.*

7075 **Biological Reviews.** Cambridge. *Biol. Rev.* [1926–] **L**.AM. 48–; B.; BM[N].; C. 47–; GL.; IC. 37–; L.; LI. 33–; MC.; MD.; NC. 50–; NP. 47–; QM.; R.; RI. 54–; SC.; TD.; U.; UC.; VC.; Z.; **Abd**.M.; U.; **Abs**.N.; U.; **Ba**.I.; **Bm**.U.; **Bn**.U. imp.; **Br**.U.; **C**.AN.; APH.; B.; BI.; BO.; GE. 40–; MO.; P.; PH. 48–; S.; V.; U.; **Cr**.N.; U.; **Db**.; **Dn**.U.; **E**.A.; AG. 27–; B. 37–; R.; SW. 47–; U.; **Ex**.U.; **Fr**.; **G**.T. 47–; U.; **H**.U.; **Hu**.G. 48–; **Ld**.U.; **Lo**.; **Lv**.U.; **M**.MS.; P. 46–; U.; **Md**.H. 29–; **Mi**.; **N**.U.; **Nw**.A.; **O**.BI.; BO.; BS. 55–; R.; UC. 39–; Z.; **Pit**.F. 51–; **Pl**.M.; **R**.D. 52–; U.; **Rt**.; **Sa**.; **Sh**.U.; **Sw**.U.; **W**. 50–; **Wo**. 54–; **Y**. [*C. of:* 39046]

Biological Reviews and **Biological Proceedings** of the **Cambridge Philosophical Society.** *See* 7075.

7075° **Biological Science.** Tokyo. *Biol. Sci., Tokyo* [1949–] **Y**.

7076 **Biological Science Bulletin. Florida State Museum.** *Biol. Sci. Bull. Fla St. Mus.*

7077 **Biological Science Bulletin. University** of **Arizona.** Tucson. *Biol. Sci. Bull. Univ. Ariz.* [1933–] **L**.BM.; BM[N].; SC.; U.; **O**.R.

7078 **Biological Science Series. Oklahoma Agricultural** and **Mechanical College.** *Biol. Sci. Ser. Okla. agric. mech. Coll.* [*C. of:* 7081]

7079 **Biological Series. Catholic University** of **America.** Washington. *Biol. Ser. Cath. Univ. Am.* [1937–43] **L**.BM.; SC. [*C. of:* 15617; *C. as:* 7082]

7080 **Biological Series. Michigan State University** of **Agriculture Museum.** East Lansing. *Biol. Ser. Mich. St. Univ. Agric. Mus.* [1957–] **Abs**.U.; **Bl**.U.

Biological Series. Museum, Michigan State University of **Agriculture.** *See* 7080.

7081 **Biological Series. Oklahoma Agricultural** and **Mechanical College.** *Biol. Ser. Okla. agric. mech. Coll.* [*C. as:* 7078]

7082 **Biological Studies. Catholic University** of **America.** Washington. *Biol. Stud. Cath. Univ. Am.* [1943–] **L**.BM. 48–; BM[N].; SC. [*C. of:* 7079]

7082° **Biological Supplement. Cave Research Group** of **Great Britain.** *Biol. Suppl. Cave Res. Grp Gt Br.* [1938–53] **L**.BM[N]. [*C. as:* 7073°]

7083 **Biological Symposia.** Lancaster, Pa. *Biol. Symp.* [1940–] **L**.CB. 42–46 imp.; MD. 41–; S. 41–47; SC. 47–; UC. 41–; Z.; **Bm**.U. 41–; **C**.A.; BI. 41–; **E**.U.; **Ld**.U. 41–47; **N**.U. 41–47 imp.; **O**.R. 41–; **R**.U.; **Sa**. [*Suspended in* 1947]

Biological Transactions. Committee of **Silesian Publications.** *See* 38285.

7084 **Biologicheskie izvestiya,** izdavaemȳe pri **Gosudarstvennom biologicheskom nauchno-issledovatel'skom institute** im. **K. A. Timiryazeva.** Moskva. Биологические известия, издаваемые при Государственном биологическом научно-исследовательском институте имени К. А. Тимирязева. *Biol. Izv. gos. biol. nauchno-issled. Inst. K. A. Timiryazeva* **L**.BM[N]. 23.

Biologicheskiĭ sbornik. L'vovskiĭ gosudarstvennȳĭ universitet. Биологический сборник. Львовский государственный университет. *See* 7087.

7085 **Biologicheskiĭ zhurnal.** Gosudarstvennoe biologicheskoe i meditsinskoe izdatel'stvo. Moskva. Биологический журнал. Государственное биологическое и медицинское издательство. *Biol. Zh.* [1932–38] **L**.BM[N].; UC.; **C**.A.; **E**.AB.; R. [*C. of:* 59134; *C. as:* 59172]

7086 **Biologicheskiĭ zhurnal,** izd. pri zoologicheskom otd. Imp. Obshchestva lyubiteleĭ estestvoznaniya, antropologii i etnografii. Moskva. Біологическій журналъ, изд. при зоологическом отд. Имп. Общества любителей естествознания, антропологіи и этнографіи. *Biol. Zh. zool. Otd. imp. Obshch. Lyub. Estest.* [1910–12] **L**.SC.

7087 **Biologichnii zbirnik.** L'vivs'kiĭ derzhavnii universitet. L'vov. Біологічний збірник. Львівский державний університет. *Biol. Zbirn., L'vov* [1958–] **L**.P. [*C. of:* 34387[a]]

7087° **Biologické listy.** *Biol. Listy* [*Supplement to:* 13411]

7088 **Biologické práce Slovenskej akademie vied.** Bratislava. *Biol. Práce* Sek. biol. a lek. vied [1956–] **L.**BM^N.; z. imp.; **Y.** [*C. of:* 38379]

7089 **Biologické spisy Vysoké školy zvěrolékařské.** Brno. *Biol. Spisy vys. Šk. zvěrolék., Brno* [1922–36] **L.**BM.; BM^N.; MA.; SC.; U.; UC.; V.; **C.**P.; **E.**R.; **Ld.**U. 24–29 imp.; **Lv.**U.; **O.**B.; R.; **W.** [*C. as:* 50631]

7090 **Biologický sborník.** Slovenskej akademie vied a uméni. Bratislava. *Biol. Sb., Bratisl.* [1949–52] **L.**BM^N.; L. 51–52; z. [*C. of:* 38720 *and* 38721; *C. as:* 7041]

7091 **Biológico.** São Paulo. *Biológico* [1935–] **L.**EB. 37–; MY. 37–; SC.; **C.**A. 42–; **Md.**H. 47–; **Y.**

7092 **Biologie** et **médecine.** Paris, etc. *Biologie Méd.* [1947–] **L.**MA. 48–; TD. 48– imp.

7093 **Biologie médicale.** Paris. *Biologie méd.* [1903–] **L.**CB. 56–; MA. 29–40: 46–; MD. 23–; S. 22–40: 46–; SC. 61–; TD. 21–22: 25–26 v. imp.; **Bm.**U. 07–14; **C.**PH. 08–13; **E.**U. 27–40; **Y.** [*Also supplements*]

7094 **Biologie** der **Person.** Berlin. *Biologie Person*

7095 **Biologie** der **Tiere Deutschlands.** Berlin. *Biologie Tiere Dtl.* [1922–] **L.**BM^N.; EB. 22–38; L. 23–38; z. 22–40 imp.; **C.**B.; **Lv.**U. 22–28; **O.**R. 22–38.

7096 **Biologie** van de **Zuiderzee** tijdens haar **drooglegging: mededeelingen.** *Biologie Zuidersee Droogl.* [1928–] **Dm.** 28–44; **Fr.**

7097 **Biologisch jaarboek.** Antwerpen. *Biol. Jaarb.* [1934–] **L.**BM^N.; SC.; **Y.** [*Replaces:* 8588]

7098 **Biologische Abhandlungen.** Würzburg-Versbach. *Biol. Abh.* [1952–] **L.**BM^N.; NC.; **O.**OR.; z.; **Y.** [*C. of:* 36392]

7099 **Biologische Arbeit.** Freiburg i. B. *Biol. Arb.*

7100 **Biologische Heilkunst.** Dresden. *Biol. Heilkunst* **L.**MA. 33–34 imp.; MD. 32–34 imp.

Biologische Mitteilungen herausgegeben von dem **Staatlichen biologischen Timiriazeff Institut.** *See* 7084.

7101 **Biologische Untersuchungen.** Hrsg. von G. Retzius. Stockholm. *Biol. Unters.* [1890–21] **L.**BM. 90–14; BM^N.; MD.; R.; S.; z. imp.; **E.**P.; U. 90–14; **G.**U. 90–14; **Lv.**U. 90–14; **O.**R.

Biologische Zeitschrift. Moskau. *See* 7086.

7102 **Biologisches Zentralblatt.** Leipzig. *Biol. Zbl.* [1881–] **L.**AM. 93–40; B. 50–; BM.; BM^N.; L. 81–49; MA. 47–; MD.; NC. 54–; P. 54–; QM. 50–; SC. 81–39: 43–; UC. 81–39; z.; **Abd.**U. 82–28; **Ba.**I.; **Bl.**U. 46–52 imp.; **Bm.**U.; **Bn.**U. 55–; **Br.**U. imp.; **C.**B.; UL.; **Cr.**U. 27–39: 49–; **Db.**; **Dn.**U. imp.; **E.**AG. 46–; B. 00–05; R. imp.; U. imp.; **G.**U.; **Ld.**U.; Lo. 93–61; **Lv.**U. 96–44; **M.**U. imp.; **Md.**H. 48–; **N.**U. 81–91 imp.; **O.**R.; **Pl.**M. 88–; **Rt.** 23– imp.; **Sa.** 22– imp.; **Y.**

7103 **Biologisk Selskabs Forhandlinger.** Kjøbenhavn. *Biol. Selsk. Forh., Kbh.*

7104 **Biologiske Meddelelser.** K. Danske Videnskabernes Selskab. Kjøbenhavn. *Biol. Meddr* [1917–] **L.**BM. 19–; BM^N.; L.; MA. 46–; MC. 25–; R. 19–; RI. 51–; S. 17–39; SC.; U.; UC. 17–28; z.; **Abd.**U.; **Bm.**U. 32–; **Bn.**U. 54–; **C.**P.; **Db.**; **Dm.**; **E.**R.; U. 33–; **G.**U.; **Ld.**U. 17–38; **Lv.**U.; **O.**F. 30– imp.; R.; **Pl.**M.; **Sa.** 33–; **Y.**

7105 **Biologiske Skrifter.** K. Danske Videnskabernes Selskab. København. *Biol. Skr.* [1939–] **L.**BM.; BM^N.; G.; GL.; L.; MA. 45–; MC.; R.; RI. 50–; SC.; U.; Z.; **Abd.**U.; **Bm.**U.; **Bn.**U.; **C.**P.; **Db.**; **Dm.**; **E.**C.; O.; R.; U.; **G.**U.; **Ld.**U.; **Lv.**U.; **O.**B.; F. 41–; R.; **Pl.**M.; **Sa.**; **Y.** [*C. of:* 27623]

7106 **Biologist.** Denver, Colorado. *Biologist* [1916–] **Biologiya.** Smolensk. Биология. *See* 34349 ser. biol.

7106^a **Biologiya** i **khimiya** v **sredneĭ shkole** (*afterwards* v **shkole.**). Moskva. Биология и химия в средней школе (*afterwards* в школе). *Biologiya Khim. sredn. Shk.* [1934–36] [*C. as:* 7106^b and 27404^a]

7106^b **Biologiya** v **shkole.** Moskva. Биология в школе. *Biologiya Shk.* [1937–] [*C. from:* 7106^a]

7107 **Biology.** London. *Biology, Lond.* [1935–42] **L.**BM.; SC. 38–42; TD. 41–42; **Abs.**N.; U.; **Bm.**U. 42; **Br.**U.; **C.**UL.; **Cr.**U. 39–42; **Db.**; **E.**A.; U. **Ex.**U. 36–42; **G.**PH. 35–37; **O.**R.; **Sw.**U. [*C. as:* 7109]

7108 **Biology.** California Institute of Technology. Pasadena. *Biology, Pasadena* **O.**BO. 57–. **Biology Colloquium.** Oregon. *See* 3321.

7109 **Biology** and **Human Affairs.** London. *Biology hum. Affairs* [1943–] **L.**AM. (9 yr.); BM.; TD. imp.; **Abs.**N.; U.; **Bm.**U.; **Br.**P. 48–; U.; **C.**UL.; **Cr.**U.; **Db.**; **E.**A.; U.; **Ex.**U. 43–55; **G.**M. 48–; **M.**P. 48–; **Nw.**A. 48–; **O.**R.; **Sh.**U. 46–; **Sw.**U.; **Y.** [*C. of:* 7107]

7110 **Biology Reports.** Cheltenham. *Biology Rep.* [1957–] **L.**BM^N.

7111 **Biology Student.** Baltimore. *Biology Stud.* [1930–31]

7112 **Biološki glasnik.** Hrvatsko prirodoslovno društvo. Zagreb. *Biol. Glasn.* [1956–] **L.**AM.; BM^N. 57–; K.; L.; Z.; **Bl.**U.; **C.**P.; **Db.**; **Fr.**; **Hu.**G.; **Rt.**; **Y.** [*C. of:* 21350 Biol. Sek.]

7113 **Biološki věstník.** Ljubljana. *Biol. Věst.* [1952–] **L.**Z. imp.; **Fr.**; **Y.**

7114 **Biomedica internazionale.** Roma. *Biomed. int.*

7115 **Biometric Bulletin.** Worcester, Mass. *Biometric Bull.* [1936–38]

7116 **Biometrics.** American Statistical Association. Washington. *Biometrics* [1947–] **L.**LE. 52–; MC. 56– imp.; NC.; SC.; U.; **Abd.**M.; R. 54–; S. 51–; U.; **Abs.**A. 52–; U. 56–; **Ba.**I.; **Bm.**T. 57–; **Bn.**U. 56–; **Br.**A.; **C.**GE. 48–; SL.; **E.**AG.; AR. 05–; PO. 56–; SW. 47: 52–53; U.; **Ep.**D.; **Ex.**U. 56–; **G.**U.; **Hu.**G. 50–; **Je.**; **Ld.**U.; W. 54–; **Lo.** 51–; **M.**C. 52–; D.; U.; **Md.**H. 49–; **Mi.** 58–; **Nw.**A. 53–; **O.**AP.; R.; **R.**D.; **Rt.**; **Sh.**IO. 51–; U.; **Sil.** 53–; **W.** 53–58; **Wd.** 56–; **Y.** [*C. of:* 7117]

7117 **Biometrics Bulletin.** American Statistical Association. Washington. *Biometr. Bull.* [1945–46] **L.**SC. 46; U.; **Abd.**M.; U.; **Ba.**I.; **Br.**A.; **C.**GE.; SL.; **E.**U.; **Ep.**D.; **G.**U.; **Je.**; **Ld.**U.; **M.**U.; **O.**AP.; R.; **R.**D.; **Rt.**; **Sh.**U. [*C. as:* 7116]

7118 **Biométrie-praximétrie.** Brussels. *Biométr.-Praxim.* [1960–] **L.**SC.

7119 **Biometrika.** Cambridge, London. *Biometrika* [1901–] **L.**AM.; AN.; AV. 56–; B. 35–; BM.; BM^N.; IC.; LE. 51–; MA. 09–; MD.; NC. 15– imp.; QM. 35–; R.; RI.; S. 01–46; SC.; TD.; UC.; UCH. 01–38; Z.; **Abd.**M.; R.; U.; **Abs.**N.; **Ba.**I. 56–; **Bl.**U. imp.; **Bm.**P.; T. 57–; U.; **Bn.**U. 49–; **Br.**U.; **C.**AN. 01–15; B. 01–23; GE. 30–; PS. 43–; SL. 01–17: 32–; **Db.**; **Dn.**U.; **E.**A. 01–03; AG. 48–; AR. 57–; P.; T.; U.; **Ep.**D. 47–; **Ex.**U. 56–; **F.**A. 43–; **Fr.** 54–; **G.**M.; PH. 07–15; T. 52–; U.; **Hu.**G. 38–; **Je.** 49–; **Ld.**U.; W. 36–; **Lo.**; **Lv.**P. 18–32; U.; **M.**C. 20–: D. 32–; P.; U.; **Md.**H. 26: 28–N.U.; **Nw.**A.; **O.**R.; Z. 01–19; **Pl.**M. 01–13; **R.**D. 38–; **Rt.**; **Sa.** 52–; **Sh.**IO. 47–; S. 50–; U.; **Ste.** 52–; **Sw.**U. 47–; **Wd.** 54–; **Y.** [*Also* Biometrika Tables for Statisticians]

7120 **Biometrische Zeitschrift.** Berlin. *Biometr. Z.* [1959–] **L.**SC.; **Y.**

7121 **Bio-morphosis.** Internationale Zeitschrift für Morphologie und Biologie des Menschen und der höheren Wirbeltiere. Basel. *Biomorphosis* [1938–39] **L.**BM^N.; **S.**; SC.; **Bl.**U.; **C.**AN.

7122 **Bionutrition.** Paris. *Bionutrition* [1910–12] **Bm.**U.

7123 **Biophysical Journal.** New York. *Biophys. J.* [1960–] **L.**MD.; SC.; **C.**APH.; P.; **G.**U.; **Ld.**U.; **Pl.**M.; **Y.**

7124 **Biophysics.** London & New York. *Biophysics* [1957–] **L.**BM.; CB.; MD.; P.; RI.; UC.; **C.**P. 58–; R. 59–; UL.; **E.**A.; U.; **O.**R.; **Te.**N. 60–; **Y.** [*English translation of:* 7026]

7125 **Biophysikalisches Zentralblatt.** Berlin. *Biophys. Zbl.* [1905–10] **L.**P.; TD.; U.; **Bl.**U.; **Br.**U. 05–08; **Db.**; **Dn.**U.; **E.**U.; **Lv.**U. 07–09; **M.**MS.; **O.**R. [*C. in:* 58991]

7126 **Bios.** Rivista di biologia sperimentale e generale. Genova. *Bios, Genova* [1913–] **L.**Z. 13–15.

7127 **Bios.** Revue mensuelle des sciences naturelles théoriques et appliquées. Haguenau. *Bios, Haguenau*

7128 **Bios.** Abhandlungen zur theoretischen Biologie und ihrer Geschichte. Leipzig. *Bios, Lpz.* [1934–]

7129 **Bioscope.** London. *Bioscope* [1907–32] **L.**BM.; P. 09–18; **G.**M. 29–32. [*C. in:* 27452]

7129^a **Biospéologica.** Archives de recherches expérimentales. Paris. *Biospéologica* [1907–] [*Contained in:* 4379]

7130 **Biota.** Instituto salesiano 'Pablo Albera'. Magdalena del Mar. *Biota* [1954–] **L.**BM^N.; K.; **C.**A.; **Dm.** 55–; **Mi.**; **Y.**

7131 **Biotypologie.** Paris. *Biotypologie* [1932–] **L.**BM.; SČ.; MD. 46–; **O.**R.; **Y.**

7132 **Bird Calendar.** Cleveland Bird Club. Cleveland. *Bird Cal.* [1905–42] [*C. as:* 7142]

7133 **Bird Lore.** New York. *Bird Lore* [1889–40] **L.**BM^N. 07–40 imp.; Z. 99–37 v. imp.; **E.**F. 99–40 imp.; **Ld.**U. 30–33 imp.; **O.**OR. 24–40 imp. [*C. as:* 5294]

7134 **Bird Migration.** Bulletin of the British Trust for Ornithology. Oxford. *Bird Migrat.* [1958–] **L.**BM.; BM^N.; NC.; Z.; **Ld.**U.; **O.**OR.; **Y.**

7135 **Bird Notes.** Ashbourne. *Bird Notes* [1903–25] **L.**BM.; BM^N. 06–25; Z.; **N.**U. [*C. of:* 19919]

7136 **Bird Notes** and **News.** London. *Bird Notes News* [1903–] **L.**AM. 41–; BM.; BM^N. 03–12 imp.: 30–; HO. 06–; NC. 50–; PG. 51–; SC. 22–; U. 47–; Z. 06–; **Abs.**N.; **Br.**U. 31–59 imp.; **C.**UL.; **Db.** 08 ; **E.**A.; F. 03–14; **G.**M. 08–47; **Ld.**P. 03–25; **M.**P. 47–; U. 09–38 imp.; **O.**B. 03–24; OR. 30–; **Y.**

7137 **Bird Report. Merseyside Naturalists' Association.** Liverpool. *Bird Rep. Merseyside Nat. Ass.* [1953–] **Br.**U. 53–55; **M.**P. [*C. of:* 7138]

7138 **Bird Report** and **Natural History Notes** from the **Liverpool Area.** Liverpool. *Bird Rep. nat. Hist. Notes Lpool* [1952] **Br.**U.; **M.**P. [*C. as:* 7137]

7139 **Bird Study.** Journal of the British Trust for Ornithology. London, Oxford. *Bird Study* [1954–] **L.**AM. 55–; BM.; BM^N.; L.; NC.; SC.; U.; Z.; **Abd.**U.; **Abs.**N.; **Bl.**U.; **Br.**U.; **C.**B.; UL.; **Cr.**M. imp.; P. 55–; **E.**T.; **G.**M.; **Ld.**U.; **Lv.**P.; **M.**P.; **O.**AP.; OR.; R.; **Sa.**; **Y.** [*C. of:* 9635]

7140 **Bird-Banding.** A journal of ornithological investigation. Boston. *Bird-Banding* [1930–] **L.**AM. 57–; BM^N.; NC. 41–50 imp.; Z. 38–; **Br.**U. imp.; **C.**B. 44–; **O.**OR.

7141 **Birdland.** *Birdland* [1946–] **O.**OR.

7142 **Bird-Life.** Cleveland. *Bird-life* [1943] [*C. of:* 7132; *C. as:* 14498]

7143 **Birds.** New Zealand Native Bird Protection Society. *Birds, N.Z.* **L.**Z. 31–33* imp. [*C. as:* 19935]

7144 **Birds** and **Country Magazine.** London. *Birds Ctry Mag.* [1950–] **L.**BM.; NC. 60–; Z.; **C.**UL.; **E.**A.; **O.**R. [*C. of:* 7147]

7145 **Birds Illustrated.** Brentford. *Birds Illust.* [1955–] **L.**BM.; BM^N.

7146 **Birds** in **London.** Committee on Bird Sanctuaries in the Royal Parks. London. *Birds Lond.* [1947–] **Ld.**P.

7147 **Birds Month** by **Month.** London. *Birds Month by Month* [1948–50] **L.**BM.; Z.; **C.**UL.; **E.**A.; **O.**R. [*C. as:* 7144]

7148 **Bird-Watcher.** Association of Bird-Watchers and Wardens. *Bird Watcher* [1939–]

7149 **Birmingham Engineering** and **Mining Journal.** Birmingham. *Bgham Engng Min. J.* [1910–15] **L.**BM.; P.; **Abs.**N. 15; **Bm.**P.; U.; **C.**UL.; **O.**R. [*C. of:* 55573]

7150 **Birmingham Medical Review.** Birmingham. *Bgham med. Rev.* [1872–] **L.**BM.; D. 39–; GH. 79– imp.; MA. 98–; MD.; S.; SH. (1 yr); **Abs.**N. 26–; **Bl.**U. 30–; **Bm.**P.; U.; **Br.**U. 78– imp.; **C.**UL. 91–; **Cr.**MD. 51– imp.; MS. 01–07; **Db.** 86–; **E.**A. 91–; P. 85–18; **G.**F. 72–15: 55–; **Lv.**M. 81–18 imp.: 30–; U. 26–; **M.**MS.; **Nw.**A. 26–; **O.**R. 91–; **Y.** [*Suspended:* 1919–25; –61*: *C. as:* Midland medical Review]

7151 **Birmingham Metallurgical Society Journal.** *Bgham metall. Soc. J.* [1919–] **L.**AV. 58–61; BM.; C. 40–; I. imp.; IC. 44–; MI. 53–; NF.; P.; **Bm.**C. 46–; P.; T.; U.; **C.**UL. 20–; **Ld.**U.; **M.**U. 19 imp.; **Nw.**A. 29–; **O.**B. 19–28; **Sh.**P. 22–; **Y.** [*C. of:* 39010]

Birmingham Photographic Society Journal. See 5679.

7152 **Birmingham University Chemical Engineer.** Birmingham. *Bgham Univ. chem. Engr* [1949–] **L.**HQ. 50–; P.; **Bm.**P.; U.; **M.**D. 56– imp.; **O.**R.; **Wd.**; **Y.**

Birmingham University Mining and **Petroleum Technical Magazine.** See 7154.

7153 **Birmingham University Mining Society Magazine.** Birmingham. *Bgham Univ. Min. Soc. Mag.* **Bm.**U. 14–15*.

7154 **Birmingham University Mining Society Technical Magazine.** Birmingham. *Bgham Univ. Min. Soc. tech. Mag.* [1921–] **L.**BM. 21–29; MI. 44: 51; MIE. 47–48: 52–53: 55–; P.; **Bm.**P.; U. 24– imp.

7155 **Birra** e **malto.** Milano. *Birra Malto* [1954–] **Nu.**B.

7156 **Biscuit Maker** and **Plant Baker.** London. *Bisc. Mkr* [1950–] **L.**AM.; BM.; P. 63–; **G.**T.; **Lv.**P.

Bisol News Sheet. See 5667.

Bisol Technigram. See 5668.

Bisra Survey. See 5669.

7157 **Bistander.** British Industrial Solvents. Hull. *Bistander* [1948–] **L.**BM. [*C. of:* 5666]

Bitamin. Kyôto. See 56785.

7158 **Bitidningen.** Sveriges biodlares riksförbund. *Bitidningen* **Sa.** 24: 26; **Y.**

7159 **Bitki koruma bülteni.** Ankara. *Bitki Koruma Bült.* [1952–] **L.**AM. 59–; BM^N. 59–; EB.; MY. 52–53; TP.

7160 **Bitumastic Bulletin.** Westfield, N.J., etc. *Bitumastic Bull.* [1940–] **L.**P. imp.

7161 **Bitume actualités.** Paris. *Bitume Actual.* [1956–] **L.**P.

7162 **Bitumen.** Berlin, Hamburg. *Bitumen, Berl.* [1931–] **L.**P. 31– imp.; **Ha.**RD. 32–; **Wa.**B. 33–39: 55–; **Y.** [*Not published* May 1942–May 1950]

7163 **Bitumen.** Fachzeitung für die Asphalt-, Teer- u verwandte Industrie. Wiesbaden. *Bitumen, Wiesbaden* [1902–16] [*C. as:* 52671]

7164 **Bitumen, Teere, Asphalte, Peche** und **verwandte Stoffe.** Heidelberg. *Bitumen Teere Asph.* [1950–] **L.**P. imp.; PR. 53–; PT. 51–; **Ha.**RD. 50–; **Wa.**B. 59–; **Y.**

7165 **Bituminous Coal Research.** Pittsburgh. *Bitum. Coal Res.* **L.**P. 52– imp.

7166 **Bituminous Protective Coatings Bulletin.** London. *Bitum. prot. Coat. Bull.* **L.**PR. (v. imp.).

7167 **Biuletenis. Lietuvos misku pramones moksline-technine draugija.** Vilnius. *Biul. liet. misk. Pram. moksl.-tech. Draug.* [1959–] **O.**F.

7168 **Biuletyn. Drogowy instytut badawczy.** Warszawa. *Biul. drog. Inst. badaw.* **L.**P. 31–33.

7169 **Biuletyn farmaceutyczny.** Organ farmacji polskiej poza granicami kraju. London [1946–] *Biul. farm.* **L.**PH.

7170 **Biuletyn geomagnetyczny.** Warszawa. *Biul. geomagn.* [1956–] **L.**MO.

7171 **Biuletyn Głównej biblioteki lekarskiej.** Warszawa. *Biul. głów. Bibltki lek.* [1952–] **L.**BM. 57–; MA. 57–.

7171^c **Biuletyn informacji naukowo-technicznej. Instytut techniki budowlanej.** Warszawa. *Biul. Inf. nauk.-tech. Inst. Tech. budow.* [1959–] **Wa.**B.; **Y.**

7172 **Biuletyn informacyjny delegata Ministra oświaty** do **spraw ochrony przyrody.** *Biul. Inf. Deleg. Minist. Ośw. Spraw Ochr. Przyr.* [1948–] **O.**AP. [*C. of:* 55754]

7173 **Biuletyn informacyjny GIMO.** Główny instytut metalurgii i odlewnictwa. Katowice. *Biul. Inf. GIMO* [1950–] **L.**P. [*Supplement to:* 22507]

7174 **Biuletyn Instytutu budownictwa mieszkaniowego.** Warszawa. *Biul. Inst. Budow. mieszk.* [1953–] **L.**P.; **Wa.**B. [*Supplement to* and *published in:* 40329]

7175 **Biuletyn Instytutu geologicznego.** Warszawa. *Biul. Inst. geol.* [1953–] **L.**BM^N.; GL.; GM.; SC.; UC.; **C.**S. imp.; **G.**U. imp.; **Lv.**U.; **Y.** [*C. of:* 7190]

7176 **Biuletyn Instytutu gospodarki komunalnej.** **L.**P. 60–. *Biul. Inst. Gosp. komun.* [*Supplement to:* 20700]

7177 **Biuletyn Instytutu i laboratorium badawcze przemysłu spożywczego.** Warszawa. *Biul. Inst. Lab. badaw. Przem. spożyw.* [1951–] **L.**P. 59–. [*Supplement to* and *published in:* 40402]

7178 **Biuletyn Instytutu medycyny morskiej** w **Gdańsku.** Warszawa. *Biul. Inst. Med. morsk. Gdańsku* [1950–] **Y.** [*C. of:* 7193]

7179 **Biuletyn Instytutu organizacji i mechanizacji budownictwa.** *Biul. Inst. Org. Mech. Budow.* [1951–] **L.**P. 58–. [*Supplement to* and *published in:* 40329]

7180 **Biuletyn Instytutu roślin leczniczych.** Poznań. *Biul. Inst. Rośl. leczn.* [1957–] **L.**PH. imp.; **C.**A.; **Rt.**; **Y.** [*C. of:* 7194]

7181 **Biuletyn Instytutu techniki budowlanej.** Warszawa. *Biul. Inst. Tech. budow.*
   Ser. A. **L.**P. 56–; **Y.** [*Supplement to* and *published in:* 24084]
   Ser. B. **L.**P. 58–; **Y.** [*Supplement to* and *published in:* 40329]
   Ser. C. **Y.**

7182 **Biuletyn Instytutu weterynarii** w **Puławach.** Puławy. *Biul. Inst. wet. Puław.* [1957–] **W.**

7183 **Biuletyn inżynieryjno-budowlany.** Londyn. *Biul. inżyn.-budow.* [1955–] **L.**BM.; P. [*C. of:* 7201, Sek. inż.]

7184 **Biuletyn. Karpacka stacja geologiczna.** Warszawa. *Biul. karp. Sta. geol.* [1928–] **L.**BM^N. 28–29; GM. [*C. of:* 7198]

7185 **Biuletyn kwarantanny i ochrony roślin.** Warszawa. *Biul. Kwarant. Ochr. Rośl.* [1957–] **L.**AM. imp.

7186 **Biuletyn Morskiego instytutu rybackiego** w **Gdyni.** *Biul. morsk. Inst. ryb. Gdyni* [1948–50] **L.**BM^N.; Z.; **Abd.**M.; **Db.** 50; **E.**R.; **Pl.**M. [*C. of:* 7199; *C. as:* 38366]
   Biuletyn Morskiego laboratorium rybackiego w **Gdyni.** *See* 7186.
   Biuletyn naukowy Instytutu roślin leczniczych. Poznań. *See* 7180.
   Biuletyn naukowy Państwowego instytutu naukowego leczniczych surowców roślinnych w **Poznaniu.** *See* 7194.

7187 **Biuletyn Observatorjum astronomicznego** w **Wilnie.** *Biul. Obs. astr. Wilnie* [1921–] I. Astronomia. II. Meteorologia. **L.**AS.; MO. (II) 21–39; SC. 28–; **E.**O.; **Lv.**U. (II) 28–; **M.**U. (I) 33; **O.**O.

7188 **Biuletyn Obserwatorium astronomicznego** w **Toruniu.** Toruń. *Biul. Obs. astr. Torun.* [1946–] **L.**BM.; **M.**U. 46–58.

7189 **Biuletyn Obserwatorium seismologicznego** w **Warszawie.** Warszawa. *Biul. Obs. seism. Warsz.* [1940–] **L.**AS.; BM^N. 40–47; **Y.**

7190 **Biuletyn Państwowego instytutu geologicznego.** Warszawa. *Biul. pánst. Inst. geol.* [1938–53] **L.**BM^N.; GL.; GM.; UC.; **C.**S. imp.; **E.**D. 35–52 imp.; **G.**U. imp.; **Lv.**U. [*C. of:* 38150 and 50668; *C. as:* 7175]

7191 **Biuletyn Państwowego instytutu hydrologiczno-meteorologicznego.** Warszawa. *Biul. państ. Inst. hydrol.-met.* **L.**MO. 47–.

7192 **Biuletyn Państwowego instytutu książki.** Łódź. *Biul. państ. Inst. Książki* [1947–] **L.**BM.; **Y.**

7193 **Biuletyn Państwowego instytutu medycyny morskiej i tropikalnej** w **Gdańsku.** Warszawa. *Biul. państ. Inst. Med. morsk. trop. Gdańsku* [1948–50] **Y.** [*C. as:* 7178]

7194 **Biuletyn Państwowego instytutu naukowego leczniczych surowców roślinnych** w **Poznaniu.** Poznań. *Biul. państ. Inst. nauk. leczn. Surow. rośl. Poznan.* [1955–56] [*C. as:* 7180]

7195 **Biuletyn peryglacjalny.** Łódź. *Biul. peryglac.* [1954–] **L.**BM.; BM^N.; GL.; SC.; **O.**R.

7195^c **Biuletyn. Polski komitet normalizacyjny.** Warszawa. *Biul. pol. Kom. Norm.* **L.**BM. 58–.

7196 **Biuletyn sekcji weterynarynej.** Warszawa. *Biul. Sekc. wet.*

7197 **Biuletyn Śląskiej stacji geofizycznej** w **Raciborzu.** *Biul. śląsk. Sta. geofiz. Raciborzu* **L.**BM^N. 48; MO. 31–37 imp.; **Y.**

7198 **Biuletyn. Stacja geologiczna** w **Borysławiu.** Borysław. *Biul. Sta. geol. Borysław.* [1923–27] **L.**BM^N.; GM.; SC.; **Bm.**U.; **Lv.**U. 25. [*C. as:* 7184]

7199 **Biuletyn Stacji morskiej** w **Helu.** *Biul. Sta. morsk. Helu* [1937–38] **L.**AM.; **Abd.**M.; **Dm.**; **Lo.**; **Pl.**M. [*C. as:* 7186]

7200 **Biuletyn statystyczny.** Warszawa. *Biul. statyst.* [1957–] **L.**H.; T.P.; **Y.**

7201 **Biuletyn Stowarzyszenia techników polskich** w **W. Brytanji.** London. *Biul. Stow. Tech. pol. W. Br.* [1942–58] **L.**P. 55–58 [*Replaced by:* 52468] Sekcja inżynieryjno-budowlana [1955] **L.**BM. [*C. as:* 7183]

7202 **Biuletyn Towarzystwa geofizyki.** Warszawa. *Biul. Tow. geofiz.* [1931–] **L.**G. 31; **Lv.**U. 32–37; **O.**R. 32–.

7203 **Biuletyn Zakładu biologii stawów.** Kraków. *Biul. Zakł. Biol. Stawów* [1954–58] **L.**BM^N. 57–58; **Fr.** 56–58. [*C. as:* 605]

7204 **Black Bag.** Journal of the Medical Faculty of Bristol University. Bristol. *Black Bag* [1937–] **L.**BM. 46–; MA. 46–; S. 52–; **Br.**U.

7205 **Black Diamond.** New York. *Black Diam.* [1885–] **Cr.**P. 16–21.

7206 **Black Hills Engineer.** Rapid City, S.D. *Black Hills Engr* [1923–] **L.**P. 27–49 imp.

7207 **Black Lechwe.** Northern Rhodesia Game Preservation and Hunting Association. Lusaka. *Black Lechwe* [1959–]

7208 **Black Rock Forest Bulletin.** Cornwall-on-the-Hudson. *Black Rock Forest Bull.* [1930–] **L.**BM^N. 31–; K.; P.; S.; **O.**F.; **Rt.**; **Y.**

7209 **Black Rock Forest Papers.** Cornwall-on-the-Hudson. *Black Rock Forest Pap.* [1935–] **L.**BM^N.; P.; **O.**F.; **Rt.**; **Y.**

7210 **Black** and **White. Metal edition.** E. F. Houghton & Co. Philadelphia. *Black White* [1927–31] **L.**P.

7211 **Blad för Bergshandteringens vänner** inom **Örebro län.** Stockholm. *Blad Bergshandt. Vänn. Örebro* **L.**I. 47–; **Y.**

7212 **Bladen** voor **hygiënische therapie.** Amsterdam. *Bladen hyg. Ther.* [*C. as:* 53228]

7213 **Blätter** tür **Aquarien-** und **Terrarienkunde.** Stuttgart. *Bl. Aquar.- u. Terrarienk.* [1890–38] **L.**BM^N.; Z. 01–14: 27–38 imp. [*C. in:* 57760]

7214 **Blätter. Dechema-Erfahrungsaustausch** auf dem **Gebiet** des **chemischen Apparatenwesens.** Frankfurt-am-Main. *Bl. Dechema-ErfahrAustausch Geb. chem. ApparWes.* **L.**P. 54–.

7215 **Blätter für deutsche Vorgeschichte.** Danzig. *Bl. dt. Vorgesch.* [1924–38] **L.**AN.

7216 **Blätter für Elektro-Homöopathie.** Regensburg. *Bl. Elektro-Homöop.*

7217 **Blätter für Elektrotechnik.** Potsdam. *Bl. Elektrotech.*

7218 **Blätter für Erfindungen** und **Industrie.** Budapest. *Bl. Erfind. Ind.*

Blätter für gerichtliche Medizin. *See* 20355.

7219 **Blätter für Geschichte** der **Technik.** Wien. *Bl. Gesch. Tech.* [1932–38] **L.**P.; SČ. [*C. as:* 7227]

7220 **Blätter für Kakteenforschung.** Volksdorf. *Bl. Kakteenforsch.* [1934–38]

7220^c **Blätter für klinische Hydrotherapie.** Leipzig, etc. *Bl. klin. Hydrother.* [1891–08] **L.**MD. 91–04. [*C. as:* 33142]

7221 **Blätter für landwirtschaftliche Marktforschung.** Berlin. *Bl. landw. Marktforsch.* **L.**AM. 30–33.

7222 **Blätter für Maschinenbau.** Potsdam. *Bl. MaschBau*

7223 **Blätter** für den **Nachwuchs.** Stuttgart. *Bl. Nachwuchs* **L.**P. 50–. [*Supplement to:* 19008 and *afterwards to:* 16699]

7224 **Blätter für Naturkunde** und **Naturschutz Niederösterreichs.** Wien. *Bl. Naturk. Naturschutz Niederöst.* [1913–] **L.**BM^N. 13–29.

7225 **Blätter für Naturschutz.** Berlin & Wien. *Bl. Naturschutz*

7226 **Blätter für Patent-, Muster- u. Zeichenwesen.** Berlin. *Bl. Pat.-, Muster- u. Zeichenw.* [1894–] **L.**AV. 94–45 imp.; P. [*Not published* 1945–47]

7226^a **Blätter für Pflanzenbau** und **Pflanzenzüchtung.** Tetschen a. Elbe. *Bl. PflBau PflZücht.* [1923–38] **C.**A. 32–38; **Cr.**N. 33–38 imp.

7227 **Blätter für Technikgeschichte.** Wien. *Bl. TechGesch.* [1939–] **L.**P.; SC.; **Y.** [*C. of:* 7219]

7228 **Blätter für Untersuchungs-** und **Forschungs-Instrumente.** Emil Busch A.G. Rathenow. *Bl. Unters.- u. Forsch.-Instrum.* **L.**P. 37–39.

7229 **Blätter** aus dem **Walde.** Zeitschrift der Niederösterreichischen Forstvereins. Wien. *Bl. Walde*

7230 **Blätter für Zahnheilkunde.** Zurich. *Bl. Zahnheilk.*

7231 **Blätter für Zuckerrübenbau.** Berlin. *Bl. ZuckRübenb.* [*C. of:* 24872]

Blakeney Point Joint Management and **Scientific Report.** *See* 42823^c.

7232 **Blakeney Point Publications.** London. *Blakeney Pt Publs* **L.**UC. 12–.

7233 **Blanchisserie, teinturerie.** Paris. *Blanchiss. Teintur.* **L.**P. 54–; **Y.**

7234 **Blasberg-Mitteilungen.** Solingen-Merscheid. *Blasberg-Mitt.* [1951–] **L.**P.

7235 **Blast Furnace** and **Steel Plant.** Pittsburgh. *Blast Furn. Steel Pl.* [1915–] **L.**I.; P. 18– imp.; **Bm.**C. 22–; P. 27–; U. 17–30: 46–; **G.**I. 31– imp.; T. 30–; **Ld.**U. 46–; **Lv.**P. 58–; **M.**U. 28–; **Sh.**IO. 24–; **St.**R. 38–; **Sw.**U. 26–58; **Y.** [*Previously published* 1913–15 *as a part of* 24174]

7236 **Blast Pipe.** Birmingham. *Blast Pipe* **Bm.**P. 48–.

Blatt. *See* **Blätter.**

7237 **Blech.** Coburg. *Blech* [1954–] **L.**P. 57–.

7238 **Bleck-** och **plåtslagaren.** Malmö. *Bleck- o. Plåtslag.*

7239 **Blick** in die **sowjetische Landwirtschaft.** Berlin. *Blick sowj. Landw.* [1952–]

7240 **Blood.** The Journal of hematology. New York. *Blood* [1946–] **L**.CB.; H. 47–; LI.; MA.; MC. 51–; MD.; SC. (special issues) 47–48; TD.; U. 52–; UCH. 50– imp.; **Abd.**R. 52–; U.; **Abs.**U.; **Bl.**U.; **Bm.**U.; **Bn.**U.; **Br.**U.; **C.**APH. 48– imp.; MD.; R. 50–58; UL. v. imp.; **Db.**; **Dn.**U.; **E.**AR. 56–; U.; **G.**F. imp.; U.; **Ld.**U.; **M.**MS.; **Nw.**A.; **O.**R.; **W.** 46–58; **Y.**

7241 **Blood Clotting** and **Allied Problems.** Transactions of Conferences. Josiah Macy Jr Foundation. New York. *Blood Clott. all. Probl. Trans. Confs Josiah Macy Jr. Fdn* [1948–52]

7242 **Blood Group News.** Copenhagen. *Blood Grp News* [1948–] **L.**MA.; SC.; **E.**AG. 51– imp.; AR. 59; **Y.**

7243 **Bloodstock Breeders' Review.** London. *Bloodstk Breed. Rev.* [1912–] **L.**BM. v. imp.; VC. 48–; **Abs.**N. 13–; **C.**UL. 21–; **E.**A.; **O.**R.; **Y.**

7244 **Blue Hill Notes.** Blue Hill Meteorological Observatory. Milton, Mass. *Blue Hill Notes* [1938–] **L.**MO. 38–42; SC.

7245 **Blue Hill Observatory Reprints.** Milton, Mass. *Blue Hill Obs. Repr.* [1940–] **L.**MO.; SC.

7246 **Blue Print.** Mt. Vernon. *Blue Print* **L.**BA. 48–.

7247 **Blühende Kakteen.** Deutsche Kakteen-Gesellschaft. Berlin. *Blüh. Kakt.* [1900–21] **L.**BM.; K.; **E.**B.; **M.**P. 01–08.

7248 **Blue-Jay:** Bulletin of the Yorkton Natural History Society. Yorkton, Sask. *Blue-Jay* [1942–] **L.**BM^N. 42–48.

7249 **Blueprint.** Association of Professional Engineers of the Province of British Columbia. Vancouver. *Blueprint* **L.**SC. 45–50*. [*C. as:* 5639]

7250 **Blumea.** Tijdschrift voor de systematiek en de geografie der planten. Leiden. *Blumea* [1934–] **L.**BM^N.; HS.; K.; L.; SC.; UC.; **C.**BO. imp.; UL.; **Cr.**U. 34–52; **E.**B.; **G.**N.; **H.**U. 34–45; **Hu.**G. 34–53; **O.**BO. 54–. [*C. of:* 30133; *also supplements*]

7250° **Blumen-** und **Pflanzenbau.** Berlin. *Blumen- u. PflBau* [1934–] **L.**R. [*C. of:* 20622]

7251 **Blut.** München. *Blut* [1955–] **L.**CB.; MA.; MD.; UC.; **G.**U.

7252 **Bluttransfusion.** *Bluttransfusion* [1952–]

7253 **Blyttia.** Norsk botanisk forenings tidsskrift. Oslo. *Blyttia* [1943–] **L.**BM^N.; K.; SC.; **C.**A. 49–; **Y.** [*C. of:* 29928]

7254 **Board.** London. *Board* [1958–] **L.**P.; TP. 60–.

7255 **Bocagiana.** Museu municipal do Funchal. Funchal. *Bocagiana* [1959–] **L.**BM^N.; **Dm.**; **Lo.**; **Pl.**M.; **Y.**

7256 **Bodemkundige studien.** Stichting voor bodemkartering. Wageningen. *Bodemk. Stud.* [1956–] **Rt.** **Boden** und **Pflanze.** *See* 58978.

7257 **Bodenkultur.** Wien. *Bodenkultur.* [1947–57: 57– in series below] **L.**AM.; TP.; **Abd.**R.; **Br.**A.; U.; **C.**A.; **Hu.**G.; **Md.**H.; **O.**AEC.; **Rt.**; **Y.**
A. Biologisch-technischer Teil. **L.**AM.; TP.; **Abd.**R.; **Br.**A.; U.; **C.**A.; **Hu.**G.; **Md.**H.; **O.**AEC.; **Rt.**; **Y.**
B. Agrarwirtschaftlicher Teil. **L.**AM.; TP.; **Abd.**R.; **Br.**A.; U.; **C.**A.; **Hu.**G.; **Md.**H.; **O.**AEC.; **Rt.**; **Y.**

7258 **Bodenkunde** und **Bodenkultur.** Berlin. *Bodenk. Bodenkult.* [1951–] **Rt.**

7259 **Bodenkunde** und **Pflanzenernährung.** Berlin. *Bodenk. PflErnähr.* [1936–45] **L.**AM.; C.; P. 36–40; **Abd.**S.

36–40; **C.**A.; **E.**W. 36–40; **Ex.**U. 36–39; **Ld.**U.; **Rt.** [*C. of:* and *Rec. as:* 58766]
Bodenkundliche Forschungen. Berlin. *See* 50026.

7260 **Böhmerwald.** Prachatitz. *Böhmerwald*

7261 **Boeing Magazine.** Seattle. *Boeing Mag.* [1944–] **L.**AV. 55–57 [*C. of:* 7262]

7262 **Boeing News.** Seattle. *Boeing News* [1934–44] **L.**AV. 43–44 [*C. as:* 7261]

7263 **Boeing School News.** Boeing School of Aeronautics. Oakland, Cal. *Boeing Sch. News* [1935–42]

7264 **Boer** en **tuinder.** Scheveningen. *Boer Tuinder* **L.**AM. (curr.)

7265 **Bogatstva Rossii.** Petrograd. Богатства России. *Bog. Ross.* [1920–26] **L.**BM.

7266 **Bogatstva sêvera.** Velikiĭ Ustyug. Богатства cêвера. *Bog. Sêv.*

7267 **Bohemià centralis.** Regionálně vědecký sborník. Pražského kraje. *Bohem. cent.*
Řada A.-Přiridní [1959–] **L.**BM^N.

7268 **Bohren-Sprengen-Räumen.** Mannheim. *Bohren-Sprengen-Räumen* [1960–] **L.**P.; **Y.** [*C. of:* 7271]

7269 **Bohrhammer.** Herne, Bochum. *Bohrhammer* **L.**P. 54–.

7270 **Bohrhammer.** English edition. Herne. *Bohrhammer Engl. Edn* [1921–31] **L.**P. 28–31; **Sh.**S. 27–31.

7271 **Bohr-** und **Sprengpraxis.** Mannheim. *Bohr- u. Sprengprax.* [1952–59] **L.**P. [*C. as:* 7268]

7272 **Bohrtechnik-Brunnenbau, (Rohrleitungsbau).** Berlin. *Bohrtech. Brunnenb.* [1950–] **L.**P.; **Y.**

7273 **Bohrtechnikerzeitung.** Wien. *Bohrtechnikerzeitung* [1935–] **L.**P.; SC. [*C. as:* 6136;]*From* 1941–44: 47 *combined with* 35886]

7274 **Boie Dental Review.** Manila. *Boie dent. Rev.* [1936–] [*C. from:* 46341]

7275 **Boiler Maker.** London. *Boiler Mkr, Lond.* [1901–31] **L.**BM. 07–18: 21–31.

7276 **Boiler Maker** and **Plate Fabricator.** New York. *Boiler Mkr Plate Fabr., N.Y.* [1904–37] **L.**P. 07–37. [*C. of:* 33703]
Boiler and **Turbine Manufacture.** Moscow. *See* 27714.

7277 **Bois** et **forêts** des **tropiques.** Paris. *Bois Forêts Trop.* [1947–] **L.**TP. 49–; **Bn.**U.; **E.**U.; **O.**F.; **Pr.**FT. 47–; **Y.**

7278 **Bois** et **résineux.** Bordeaux. *Bois Résin.* **O.**F. 49–52 imp.; R. 49–51.

7278° **Bois** et **scieries menuiserie** et **bâtiment.** Paris. *Bois Scieries* **Y.**

7279 **Boissiera.** Genève. *Boissiera* [1936–] **L.**BM^N.; **C.**P. [*Supplement to:* 13293]

7280 **Boisson.** Bruxelles. *Boisson* **L.**P. 57–58; **Y.**

7281 **Boissons douces, boissons légères;** les fruits et leurs dérivés. Paris. *Boissons douces* [1954–57] **L.**AM.; TP.; **Br.**A. [*C. of:* 20395]

7282 **Boj** proti **tuberkulose.** Praha. *Boj Tuberk.* **L.**MA. 46–. [*C. of:* 56466]

7283 **Bokmakierie.** South African Ornithological Society. Cape Town, Johannesburg. *Bokmakierie* [1948–] **L.**BM.; BM^N. 50–; Z. 50–; **O.**OR. imp.; **Y.**

7284 **Boletim** da **Academia** das **ciências** de **Lisboa.**
Coimbra. *Bolm Acad. Ciênc. Lisb.* [1929–] **L.**BM. 54–;
BM^N. 29–42: 51–; GL.; U. 31–; **Db.**; **E.**B.; C. 29–39; **Y.**
[*C. of:* 25400]

7285 **Boletim** da **Academia nacional** de **farmácia.**
Rio de Janeiro. *Bolm Acad. nac. Farm., Rio de J.*

7286 **Boletim** da **Academia nacional** de **medicina.**
Rio de Janeiro. *Bolm Acad. nac. Med., Rio de J.*
Boletim da **Academia** das **sciências** de **Lisboa.**
See 7284.

7287 **Boletim actinométrico** de **Portugal.** Lisboa.
Bolm actinom. Port. **L.**MO. 55–.

7287° **Boletim** da **Agência geral** das **colónias** do
ultramar. Lisbõa. *Bolm Ag. ger. Colón. Ultramar*
E.G. (curr.)

7288 **Boletim agrícola** e **pecuária.** Colónia de Moçambique. Lourenço Marques. *Bolm agríc. pecuár.*
Moçamb. [1928–] **L.**EB. 28–33; K. imp.

7289 **Boletim** da **agricultura.** Bahia, Brasil. *Bolm*
Agric., Bahia **L.**BM^N. 29–31 imp.

7290 **Boletim** de **agricultura.** Lisboa. *Bolm Agric.,*
Lisb. [1933–] **L.**AM. 33–36.

7291 **Boletim** de **agricultura.** Loanda. *Bolm Agric.,*
Loanda **L.**K. 12*.

7292 **Boletim** de **agricultura.** Nova Goa. *Bolm*
Agric., Nova Goa **L.**EB. 19–20*. [*C. as:* 7373]

7293 **Boletim** de **agricultura.** São Paulo. *Bolm Ag-*
ric., S Paulo [1900–] **L.**AM. 00–37 imp.; BM^N. 21–39; EB.
17–52; K. 06–36; MO. 24–32; TP. 37–50 imp.; **C.**P. 32–
37; **Lv.**U. 08– imp.; **Rt.** 11–41; **Y.**

7294 **Boletim** de **agricultura** do **Departamento** de
produção vegetal. Belo Horizonte. *Bolm Agric.*
Dep. Prod. veg., Belo Horiz. [1952–] **Y.**

7295 **Boletim** de **agricultura, zootechnia** e **veterin-**
aria. Secretaria de agricultura de Minas Geraes.
Bello Horizonte. *Bolm Agric. Zootech. Vet. Minas Geraes*
[1928–] **Abs.**A. 29–.

7296 **Boletim** de **antropologia.** Ceara. *Bolm Antrop.*
[1957–] **L.**BM.

7297 **Boletim anual** da **Estação experimental** de **can-**
na de **assucar.** Rio de Janeiro. *Bolm a. Estaç. exp.*
Canna Assuc., Rio d. J. **C.**A. 32–.

7298 **Boletim anual.** Instituto **astronómico** e **me-**
teorológico. Pôrto-Alegre. *Bolm a. Inst. astr. met.,*
Pôrto-Alegre **L.**MO. 18–33. [*C. of:* 16279]

7299 **Boletim anual** do **Serviço meteorológico** de
Minas Geraes. Bello Horizonte. *Bolm a. Serv.*
met. Minas Geraes [1919–22] **L.**MO. [*C. of:* 16280; *C. us:*
7328]

7300 **Boletim** de **assistência médica** aos **indígenas** e
da **luta contra** a **moléstia** do **sono.** Luanda. *Bolm*
Assist. méd. Indíg., Luanda **L.**TD. 28–29; **Lv.**U. 28.

7301 **Boletim. Associação brasileira** de **metais.**
São Paulo. *Bolm Ass. bras. Metais* **L.**P. 57–.

7302 **Boletim. Associação brasileira** de **normas téc-**
nicas. Rio de Janeiro. *Bolm Ass. bras. Norm. téc.*
[1953–] **Y.**

7303 **Boletim** da **Associação brasileira** de **odontologia.**
Rio de Janeiro. *Bolm Ass. bras. Odont.*

7304 **Boletim** da **Associação brasileira** de **farma-**
ceuticos. Rio de Janeiro. *Bolm Ass. bras. Farm.*
[1930–32] **Y.** [*C. as:* 46324]

7305 **Boletim** da **Associação brasileira** de **química.**
São Paulo. *Bolm Ass. bras. Quím.* [1952–] **L.**C.; **Y.** [*C.*
of: 7310]

7306 **Boletim** da **Associação farmacêutica** de **Pernam-**
buco. Recife. *Bolm Ass. farm. Pernambuco*

7307 **Boletim** da **Associação** da **filosofia natural.**
Porto. *Bolm Ass. Filos. nat.* **L.**BM^N. 38–53.

7308 **Boletim** da **Associação** dos **geógrafos brasileiros.**
São Paulo. *Bolm Ass. Geogr. bras.* **L.**G. 44.

7309 **Boletim** da **Associação portuguesa** de **fotogra-**
metria. Lisboa. *Bolm Ass. port. Fotogram.* [1938–]

7310 **Boletim** da **Associação química** do **Brasil.** Rio
de Janeiro. *Bolm Ass. quím. Bras.* [1942–51] **L.**C.
49–51; SC. 47–51. [*C. as:* 7305]

7311 **Boletim bibliográfico. Academia** das **sciências**
de **Lisboa.** *Bolm biblfco Acad. Sci. Lisb.* [1910–19]
L.BM. 10–17; GL. 14–19 imp.; L. 10–13; U.; UC.; **C.**UL.;
E.B.; C. 14–19; R.; U.; **M.**R.; **O.**B. 11–18.

7312 **Boletim bibliográfico. Centro** de **documenta-**
ção científica, Instituto de **investigação científica** de
Angola. Luanda. *Bolm biblfco Cent. Docum. cient.*
Angola [1959–] **O.**F.

7313 **Boletim bibliográfico. Directoria** de **estatística**
da **producção, Ministério** da **agricultura.** Rio de
Janeiro. *Bolm biblfco Dir. Estat. Prod., Rio de J.* **L.**AM.
48–51 imp.

7314 **Boletim bibliográfico** de **geofísica** y **oceano-**
grafia americanas. Tacubaya. *Bolm biblfco Geo-*
fís. Oceanogr. am. **L.**MO. 58–.

7315 **Boletim** de **bioestatística** e **epidemiologia.** Rio
de Janeiro. *Bolm Bioestat. Epidem.*

7316 **Boletim biológico.** Clube zoológico do Brasil.
São Paulo. *Bolm biol. Clube zool. Bras.* [1933–39] **L.**BM^N.;
EB.; TD.; Z. imp.; **Abs.**U. 33–37. [*C. of:* 7317]

7317 **Boletim biológico.** Laboratorio de parasitologia.
Faculdade de medicina de São Paulo. *Bolm biol. Lab.*
Parasit. Fac. Med. S Paulo [1926–32] **L.**BM^N.; EB. imp.;
TD.; Z. 31; **Abs.**U. imp.; **E.**U. imp.; **Lv.**U. imp. [*C. as:*
7316]

7318 **Boletim carioca** de **geografía.** Rio de Janeiro.
Bolm carioca Geogr. [1948–] **L.**G. 50–; **Bm.**U. 50–.

7319 **Boletim** da **Casa** do **dentista brasileiro.** Rio de
Janeiro. *Bolm Casa Dent. bras.* [1941–]

7320 **Boletim** da **Casa** do **Douro.** Régua. *Bolm Casa*
Douro [1946–] **Y.**

7321 **Boletim. Centro** de **estudos, Hospital** da **aero-**
naútica do **Galeãa.** Rio de Janeiro. *Bolm Cent.*
Estud. Hosp. Aeronaút. Galeãa

7322 **Boletim** do **Centro** de **estudos** do **Hospital** dos
servidores do **estado.** Rio de Janeiro. *Bolm Cent.*
Estud. Hosp. Serv. Estado [1949–] **L.**MD. imp.; SH. (1 yr);
TD. 51– imp.

7322^a **Boletim. Centro** de **estudos** e **pesquisas** de
geodesia, Universidade do **Paraná.** Curitiba. *Bolm*
Cent. Estud. Pesq. Geod. Univ. Paraná **Y.**

7322^b **Boletim. Centro** de **estudos** da **Policlínica** de
pescadores. *Bolm Cent. Estud. Policlín. Pesc.* [1954–]
L.BM. 55–.

7322° **Boletim** do **Centro** de **pesquisas Hermann von**
Ihering. Porto Alegre. *Bolm Cent. Pesq. Hermann von*
Ihering [1957–] **L.**Z. 57–59.

7323 **Boletim climatológico** do **Estação meteoroló-gico** de **Bafata,** Guiné. Bissau. *Bolm clim. Estaç. met. Bafata* **L.**MO. 54.

7324 **Boletim climatológico** do **Estação meteoro-lógico** de **Bissau-Bra,** Guiné. Bissau. *Bolm clim. Estaç. met. Bissau-Bra* **L.**MO. 54.

7325 **Boletim climatológico** do **estação meteorológico** de **Bolama,** Guiné. Bissau. *Bolm clim. Estaç. met. Bolama* **L.**MO. 54–55.

7326 **Boletim climatológico** do **Monte Estoril.** Lisboa. *Bolm clim. Mt. Estoril* **L.**BM. 55–. [*English language edition at:* 14517]

7327 **Boletim climatológico** do **Praia da Rocha.** Lisboa. *Bolm clim. Praia Rocha* **L.**BM. 55–; MO. 40–; **Y.** [*C. of:* 7364]

7328 **Boletim climatológico. Serviço meteoro-lógico, Minas Geraes.** *Bolm clim. Serv. met. Minas Geraes* **L.**MO. 23–29; SC. 25–; **M.**P. 30–; **O.**G. 27–28; **Rt.** 25–29. [*C. of:* 7299]

7329 **Boletim clínico** e de **estatística** dos **hospitais civis** de **Lisboa.** Lisboa. *Bolm clín. Estat. Hosp. civ. Lisb.* [1943–] **L.**MA.; MD. 48–; S. 57–; TD. [*C. of:* 7332]

7330 **Boletim clínico** e de **estatística** do **Hospital colonial** de **Lisboa.** Lisboa. *Bolm clín. Estat. Hosp. colon. Lisb.* [1948–50] **L.**MD.; TD. [*C. as:* 7331]

7331 **Boletim clínico** e **estatístico** do **Hospital** do **Ultramar.** Lisboa. *Bolm clín. estat. Hosp. Ultra-mar* [1951–] **L.**MA. 52–; MD.; TD. [*C. of:* 7330]

7332 **Boletim clínico** dos **Hospitais civis** de **Lisboa.** *Bolm clín. Hosp. civ. Lisb.* [1937–42] **L.**MA. imp.; TD. [*C. as:* 7329]

7333 **Boletim. Colegio brasileiro** de **cirurgiões.** Rio de Janeiro. *Bolm Col. bras. Cirurg.* **L.**MA. 46–; S. 41–52: 56–57.

7334 **Boletim** da **Commissão executiva** do **leite.** Rio de Janeiro. *Bolm Comm. exec. Leite, Rio de J.* [1942–46] **L.**AM. 44–46; SC. [*C. as:* 7425]

7335 **Boletim** da **Commissão geographica** e **geologica** do **Estado** de **Minas Geraes.** Rio de Janeiro. *Bolm Comm. geogr. geol. Minas Geraes* [1889–] **L.**G. imp.

7336 **Boletim. Commissão geographica** e **geologica** do **Estado** de **São Paulo. Serviço meteorologico.** São Paulo. *Bolm Comm. geogr. geol. S Paulo Serv. met.* [1889–06] **L.**BM.; G.; S.; **E.**G. 90–06. [*C. as:* 7464]

7337 **Boletim. Commissão reguladora** das **cereais** do **arquipelaga.** Acores. *Bolm Comm. regul. Cer. Arqui-pelaga* **Hu.**G. 46–.

7337ᶜ **Boletim** do **Conselho nacional** de **geografia** do **Brasil.** Rio de Janeiro. *Bolm Cons. nac. Geogr. Bras.* [1943] **L.**BM.; **E.**G. [*C. as:* 7376]

7338 **Boletim. Conselho nacional** de **pesquisas** do **Brasil.** Rio de Janeiro. *Bolm Cons. nac. Pesq. Bras.* [1955–] **L.**BM.; BMᴺ.; **Bl.**U.; **Y.**

7338ᵃ **Boletim** do **Conselho** de **pesquisas, Universidade** do **Paraná.** Curitiba. *Bolm Cons. Pesq. Univ. Paraná Ser. Botânica.* **L.**BMᴺ. 60–.

7338ᵉ **Boletim cultural** da **Guiné portuguesa.** Lisboa. *Bolm cult. Guiné port.* [1946–] **L.**BM.; BMᴺ.; TP. imp.

7339 **Boletim cultural. Museu** de **Angola.** Luanda. *Bolm cult. Mus. Angola* [1960–] **L.**BMᴺ.

7340 **Boletim** dos **cursos** de **aperfeiçoamento** e **especi-alização. Centro nacional** de **ensino** e **pesquisas agronômicas.** Rio de Janeiro. *Bolm Curs. Aperfeiç. Espec. Cent. nac. Ensino Pesq. agron., Rio de J.* [1943–] **Y.**

7341 **Boletim. Departamento** de **estradas** de **Roda-gem.** São Paulo. *Bolm Dep. Estr. Rodagem* **Y.**

7342 **Boletim** do **Departamento médico** do **Serviço civil** do **Estado São Paulo.** São Paulo. *Bolm Dep. méd. Serv. civ. S Paulo* [1953–] **L.**BM. 54–.

7343 **Boletim. Departamento nacional** da **producção mineral.** Rio de Janeiro *Bolm Dep. nac. Prod. min., Rio de J.* [1934–] **L.**BMᴺ.; GL.; SC.; **E.**D. imp.

7344 **Boletim** do **Departamento** de **química, Univer-sidade** de **São Paulo.** *Bolm Dep.Quím. Univ. S Paulo* [1955–] **L.**C. 55–57.

7345 **Boletim diaro. Instituto** de **meteorologia.** Rio de Janeiro. *Bolm diaro Inst. Met., Rio de J.* **L.**MO. 28–44: 51–.

7346 **Boletim. Directoria** de **agricultura, Bahia.** *Bolm Dir. Agric. Bahia* **L.**AM.

7347 **Boletim. Directoria** de **organização** e **defesa** da **producção.** Rio de Janeiro. *Bolm Dir. Org. Def. Prod., Rio de J.* **L.**BM. 34–.

7348 **Boletim** da **Directoria** da **producção animal, Rio Grande** do **Sul.** Pôrto Alegre. *Bolm Dir. Prod. anim. Rio Grande Sul* **Hu.**G. 50–.

7349 **Boletim** da **Divisão** de **defesa sanitaria animal, Ministério** da **agricultura, Brasil.** Rio de Janeiro. *Bolm Div. Def. sanit. anim., Bras.* [1950–] **L.**V.

7350 **Boletim. Divisão** de **fomento** da **producção mineral, Ministério** da **agricultura, Brasil.** Rio de Janeiro. *Bolm Div. Fom. Prod. min., Bras.* **L.**MI. 34–51 imp.: 52–; **Y.**

7351 **Boletim. Divisão** de **geologia** e **mineralogia, Ministério** da **agricultura, Brasil.** Rio de Janeiro. *Bolm Div. Geol. Miner., Bras.* [1940–] **L.**MI. 40–44 imp.: 46–; **Y.** [*C. of:* 7490]

7352 **Boletim** da **Divisão** de **mecanização agrícola.** Rio de Janeiro. *Bolm Div. Mecaniz. agríc., Rio de J.* [1952–] **Sil.** 53–.

7353 **Boletim** de **divulgação. Instituto** de **cacau.** Bahia. *Bolm Divulg. Inst. Cacau, Bahia* [1945–] **C.**A.

7354 **Boletim** de **endocrinologia** e **clínica.** Lisboa. *Bolm Endocr. Clín.*

7355 **Boletim. Escola agrícola 'Luiz** de **Queiroz.'** Piracicaba. *Bolm Esc. agríc. 'LuisQueiroz.'*

7356 **Boletim. Escola** de **agronomia** e **veterinaria 'Eliseu Maciel'.** Pelotas. *Bolm Esc. Agron. Vet. 'Eliseu Maciel'* [1932–] **L.**BMᴺ. 32: 41– imp.

7357 **Boletim. Escola** de **geologia, Universidade** de **Pôrto Alegre.** *Bolm Esc. Geol. Univ. Pôrto Alegre* [1960–] **Y.**

7358 **Boletim** da **Escola nacional** de **agronomia.** Rio de Janeiro. *Bolm Esc. nac. Agron., Rio de J.* [1938–42] **L.**EB. [*C. as:* 1479]

7359 **Boletim** da **Escola nacional** de **veterinária.** Rio de Janeiro. *Bolm Esc. nac. Vet., Rio de J.* [1945–] **L.**BMᴺ. 46; **Ld.**U. 45.

7360 **Boletim especial** da **Repartição sanitario pan-americana.** Washington. *Bolm espec. Repart. sanit. pan-am.* **L.**TD. 23–26.

7361 **Boletim** da **Estação agrária central.** Lisboa. *Bolm Estaç. agr. cent., Lisb.* **L.**SC. 28–36* imp.; **Rt.** (*a, b, c*) 26–35 imp.

7362 **Boletim** da **Estação climatológica** do **Funchal.** Lisboa. *Bolm Estaç. clim. Funchal* [1936–45] **L.**MO. 40–45. [*C. of:* 18538; *Replaced by:* 7433]

7363 **Boletim** da **Estação climatológica** do **Mont' Estoril.** Lisboa. *Bolm Estaç. clim. Mt Estoril* [1936–37] [*C. of:* 18539; *C. as:* 9810]

7364 **Boletim** da **Estação climatológica** da **Praia** da **Rocha.** Lisboa. *Bolm Estaç. clim. Praia da Rocha* [*C. as:* 7327]

7365 **Boletim** da **Estação experimental** de **agricultura.** Bello Horizonte. *Bolm Estaç. exp. Agric., Bello Horizonte* **L.**BM. 36–.

7366 **Boletim** da **Estação experimental** de **canna** de **assucar.** Escada. *Bolm Estaç. exp. Canna Assuc., Escada* **L.**EB. 13.

7367 **Boletim estatístico agropecuaria.** Buenos Aires. *Bolm estat. agropec., B. Aires* **Abs.**U. 39–42.

7367ᶜ **Boletim estatístico mensal. Instituto Rio Grandense** do **Arroz.** *Bolm estat. mens. Inst. Rio Grand. Arroz* **Y.**

7368 **Boletim** da **Faculdade** de **farmácia** e **odontologia** de **Pelotas.** *Bolm Fac. Farm. Odont. Pelotas* **L.**BMᴺ. 40–.

7369 **Boletim** da **Faculdade** de **filosofia, ciências** e **letras,** Universidade de São Paulo. *Bolm Fac. Filos. Ciênc. Univ. S Paulo* [1937–] **L.**BMᴺ. 37–39; L. (zool.) 40–; Z. (zool.); **C.**B. (zool.); S. (geol.) 45–; **E.**R. (zool.); **Fr.** (bot.) 55–: (zool.) 43–; **Hu.**G. (bot.); **Lv.**U. (zool.); **Pl.**M. (zool.). [*Published in series*]

7370 **Boletim. Federação brasileira** das **sociedades** de **tuberculose.** Rio de Janeiro. *Bolm Fed. bras. Socs Tuberc.* [1953–] **L.**MA.

7371 **Boletim** da **Federação** das **sociedades** de **assistência** aos **lazaros** e **defesa** contra a **lepra.** São Paulo. *Bolm Fed. Socs Assist. Lazaros, S Paulo* **L.**TD. 29–.

7371ᶜ **Boletim. Filmoteca ultramarina portuguesa.** Lisboa. *Bolm Filmoteca ultramar. port.* [1954–] **L.**BM. 55–.

7372 **Boletim fitossanitario.** Divisão de defesa sanitária vegetal. Rio de Janeiro. *Bolm fitossanit.* [1944–] **L.**EB.; MY. 44–55.

7372ᶜ **Boletim fluviométrico.** Rio de Janeiro. *Bolm fluviométr., Rio de J.* **Y.**

7373 **Boletim** de **fomento.** Nova Goa. *Bolm Fom., Nova Goa* **L.**EB. 21. [*C. of:* 7292]

7374 **Boletim forestal.** Rio de Janeiro. *Bolm for., Rio de J.* [1957–] **O.**F.

7375 **Boletim** de **Fundação Gonçalo Moniz.** Bahia. *Bolm Fund. Gonçalo Moniz* [1954–] **L.**BMᴺ. 58–imp.; MA.

7376 **Boletim geográfico.** Rio de Janeiro. *Bolm geogr., Rio de J.* [1943–] **L.**BM.; MO. 56–; QM. 51–; SC. 49–; U. 48–; UC. 51–; **E.**G.; **Wo.** 57–; **Y.** [*C. of:* 7337ᶜ]

7377 **Boletim geomagnético preliminar, Angola.** Luanda. *Bolm geomagn. prelim. Angola* **E.**M. 57– imp.

7378 **Boletim geomagnético preliminar, Lourenço Marques.** *Bolm geomagn. prelim., Lourenço Marq.* **L.**MO. 57–.

7379 **Boletim geral** de **medicina** e **farmácia.** Bastora, Nova Goa. *Bolm ger. Med. Farm., Bastora* [1912–] **L.**TD. imp.

7380 **Boletim geral** de **medicina** e **farmácia.** Rio de Janeiro. *Bolm ger. Med. Farm., Rio de J.*
   Boletim hidrológico. Serviço de aquas, Seccão de pluviometria e inundaçoes. Rio de Janeiro. *See* 51671ᶜ.

7381 **Boletim** de **higiene mental.** São Paulo. *Bolm Hig. ment., S Paulo* [1944–]

7382 **Boletim** de **higiene** e **saúde pública.** Rio de Janeiro. *Bolm Hig. Saúde públ., Rio de J.* [1943–]

7383 **Boletim** do **Horto botânico.** São Paulo. *Bolm Hort. bot., S Paulo* **L.**K.

7384 **Boletim** do **Hospital** das **clínicas** da **Faculdade** de **medicina** da **Universidade** da **Bahia.** Salvador. *Bolm Hosp. Clín. Fac. Med. Univ. Bahia*

7385 **Boletim** do **INT.** Instituto nacional de tecnologia. Rio de Janeiro. *Bolm INT* [1950–] **O.**F. 51– imp.; **Y.**

7386 **Boletim** de **industria animal.** São Paulo. *Bolm Ind. anim.* [1941–] **L.**AM.; BMᴺ.; MA.; V. imp.; **Abd.**R.; **Abs.**A. 54–; **C.**A.; V. 50–56; **E.**AB. 41–54; **Hu.**G.; **R.**D.; **W.** [*C. of:* 46605]

7387 **Boletim** de **informações. Instituto nacional** de **tecnologia.** Rio de Janeiro. *Bolm Inf. Inst. nac. Tecnol., Rio de J.* [1936–]

7388 **Boletim informativo. Instituto geobiológico 'La Salle'.** Canoas, Brazil. *Bolm inf. Inst. geobiol. La Salle* **L.**BMᴺ. 49–.
   Boletim informativo de **sericicultura.** São Paulo. *See* 7389.

7389 **Boletim informativo. Servico** de **sericicultura.** São Paulo. *Bolm inf. Serv. Sericicult., S Paulo* [1952–] **L.**AM.; TP.; **Rt.** 52.

7390 **Boletim** do **inpabo.** Curitiba, Paraná. *Bolm Inpabo* [1954–] **L.**K. 57–.

7391 **Boletim** de **inseminação artificial.** Rio de Janeiro. *Bolm Insem. artif.* [1944–] **L.**V. 44–47: 53; **W.**

7392 **Boletim** da **Inspectoria** de **Serviços públicos.** São Paulo. *Bolm Insp. Servs públ. S Paulo* [1937–]

7393 **Boletim** do **Instituto agronómico** de **Campinas.** *Bolm Inst. agron. Campinas*

7394 **Boletim** do **Instituto agronómico** do **Estado** de **Minas Geraes.** *Bolm Inst. agron. Est. Minas Geraes* [1948–] **C.**A.

7395 **Boletim** do **Instituto** de **Angola.** Luanda. *Bolm Inst. Angola* [1953–] **L.**BMᴺ.; **Y.**

7396 **Boletim** do **Instituto biológico** da **Bahia.** Saõ Salvador. *Bolm Inst. biol. Bahia* [1954–] **L.**BMᴺ.

7397 **Boletim. Instituto biológico** de **defesa agrícola.** Rio de Janeiro. *Bolm Inst. biol. Def. agríc., Rio de J.* [1921–30] **L.**EB.; **Nw.**A. 25–30; **Rt.**

7398 **Boletim** do **Instituto botânico, Universidade** de **Coimbra.** Coimbra. *Bolm Inst. bot. Univ. Coimbra* [1922–] **Db.**

7399 **Boletim** do **Instituto brasileiro** de **sciências.** Rio de Janeiro. *Bolm Inst. bras. Sci.* [1925–27] **L.**BMᴺ. 25–26 imp.; EB.; TD.; **E.**C. 25–26 imp.

7400 **Boletim** do **Instituto** de **café** do **Estado** de **São Paulo.** *Bolm Inst. Café Est. S Paulo*

7401 **Boletim** do **Instituto central** de **fomento económica** da **Bahia.** *Bolm Inst. cent. Fom. econ. Bahia* [1938–48] **L.**BM^N. 38–42 imp.; **C.**A. 38–46; **O.**F. 39–48 imp.

7402 **Boletim** do **Instituto** de **criminologia.** Lisboa. *Bolm Inst. Crim., Lisb.*

7403 **Boletim** do **Instituto** de **ecologia** e **experimentação agrícolos.** Rio de Janeiro. *Bolm Inst. Ecol. Exp. agríc., Rio de J.* [1941–] **Y.** [*C. of:* 7405]

7404 **Boletim. Instituto** de **engenharia.** São Paulo. *Bolm Inst. Engen., S Paulo* **L.**SC. 31–41*. [*C. as:* 18065]

7405 **Boletim** do **Instituto** de **experimentação agrícola.** Rio de Janeiro. *Bolm Inst. Exp. agríc., Rio de J.* [*C. as:* 7403]

7406 **Boletim** do **Instituto geográfico** e **cadastral.** Lisboa. *Bolm Inst. geogr. cadast., Lisb.*

7407 **Boletim** do **Instituto geográfico** e **geológico** do **Estado** de **São Paulo.** *Bolm Inst. geogr. geol. Est. S Paulo* [1941–] **Y.**

7408 **Boletim** do **Instituto** de **história natural.** Curitiba, Paraná. *Bolm Inst. Hist. nat., Curitiba*
　　Ser. Geologia [1958–] **L.**BM^N.
　　Ser. Zoologia [1957–] **L.**BM^N.
　　Ser. Botânica [1959–] **L.**BM^N.; **Y.**

7409 **Boletim** do **Instituto** de **hygiene. Faculdade** de **medicina veterinaria. Universidade** de **São Paulo.** *Bolm Inst. Hyg. Fac. Med. vet. Univ. S Paulo* [1919–] **L.**LI. 19–38 imp.; TD. 27–44 v. imp.
　　Boletim do **Instituto nacional** de **tecnologia.** Rio de Janeiro. *See* 7385.

7410 **Boletim** do **Instituto oceanográfico.** São Paulo. *Bolm Inst. Oceanogr., S Paulo* [1952–] **L.**AM.; BM^N.; L.; Z.; **Abd.**M.; T. 59–; **C.**B.; **Dm.**; **Lo.**; **Lv.**U.; **Pl.**M.; **Wo.** [*C. of:* 7411]

7411 **Boletim** do **Instituto paulista** de **oceanografía.** São Paulo. *Bolm Inst. paul. Oceanogr.* [1950–51] **L.**AM.; BM^N.; L.; Z.; **Abd.**M.; **C.**B.; **Dm.**; **Lo.**; **Lv.**U.; **Pl.**M.; **Wo.** [*C. as:* 7410]

7412 **Boletim** do **Instituto** de **pesquisas technológicas.** São Paulo. *Bolm Inst. Pesq. technol., S Paulo* [1936–] **L.**BM.; **O.**F. imp.; R.

7413 **Boletim** do **Instituto português** de **oncologia.** Lisboa. *Bolm Inst. port. Oncol.* [1934–] **L.**BM. 55–; CB. 46–; H. 34–42: 47–; MD. 39–.

7414 **Boletim** do **Instituo** de **puericultura.** Rio de Janeiro. *Bolm Inst. Pueric., Rio de J.* [1938–] **L.**MA. 38: 46–; MD. 38: 48–; **G.**U. 57–; **O.**R. 55–.

7415 **Boletim** do **Instituto** de **química agrícola.** Rio de Janeiro. *Bolm Inst. Quím. agríc., Rio de J.* [1938–] **L.**BM. 51–; C. 55–; **Br.**A. 54– imp.; **C.**A. 59–; **Rt.**; **Y.**

7416 **Boletim** do **Instituto superior** de **higiene Doctor Ricardo Jorge.** Lisboa. *Bolm Inst. sup. Hig. Dr Ricardo Jorge* [1946–53] **L.**BM. 53; H.; TD. imp. [*C. as:* 7495]

7417 **Boletim** do **Instituto Vital Brazil.** Niteroi. *Bolm Inst. Vital Braz.* [1927–] **L.**BM^N. 27–54; EB.; LI.; v. 35–48 imp.; z. 33–44 imp.; **E.**C. 42–45; **Sal.** 44–; **W.** 44–. [*C. of:* 4584: *Suspended* 1949–1953]

7418 **Boletim** do **Jardim botânico.** Rio de Janeiro. *Bolm Jard. bot., Rio de J.* **O.**F. 42.

7419 **Boletim. Junta nacional** do **azeite.** *Bolm Jta nac. Azeite* [1946–] **Y.**

7420 **Boletim. Junta nacional** da **cortiça.** Lisboa. *Bolm Jta nac. Cortiça* **L.**EB. (ent.) 42–46; **O.**F. 46– imp.; **Y.**

7421 **Boletim. Junta nacional** das **frutas.** Lisboa. *Bolm Jta nac. Frutas* [1941–] **L.**AM. 49– imp.; BM. 55–; **Br.**A. 52–; **Md.**H. 46–; **Y.**

7422 **Boletim** do **Laboratório central** da **producção mineral.** Rio de Janeiro. *Bolm Lab. cent. Prod. min., Rio de J.* [1940–] **L.**MI. 40: 43–.

7423 **Boletim** do **Laboratório** de **pathologia vegetal** do **Estado** da **Bahia.** Bahia. *Bolm Lab. Path. veg. Est. Bahia* [1924–31] **L.**BM^N. 24–29; EB.

7424 **Boletim. Laboratório** da **producção mineral.** Rio de Janeiro. *Bolm Lab. Prod. min., Rio de J.* [1940–] **L.**MI. 40: 43–; **Y.**

7425 **Boletim** do **leite** e **seus derivados.** Rio de Janeiro. *Bolm Leite* [1946–] **L.**AM. 46–48; **R.**D. 47–; **Y.** [*C. of:* 7334]

7426 **Boletim. Liga portuguesa** de **profilaxia** da **cegueira.** Lisboa. *Bolm Liga port. Profilax. Cegueira* [1952–] **L.**MD. 53–.

7427 **Boletim magnético.** Rio de Janeiro. *Bolm magn., Rio de J.* **L.**AS. 26–; MO. 24–28; SC. 29–; UC. 27–28.

7428 **Boletim** de **medicina, hygiene** e **biologia.** São Paulo. *Bolm Med. Hyg. Biol.* **L.**EB. 26.

7428ᵃ **Boletim médico britânico.** London. *Bolm méd. br.* [1943–48] **L.**BM. [*Portuguese edition of:* 8906]

7429 **Boletim mensal. Directoria** de **meteorologia.** Rio de Janeiro *Bolm mens. Dir. Met., Rio de J.* [1924–] **L.**MO. 24–34; **M.**P. 28–33 imp. [*C. of:* 7443]

7430 **Boletim mensal** de **estatística demographo-sanitaria** de **Belem.** Para. *Bolm mens. Estat. demogr.-sanit. Belem* **Lv.**U. 33–.

7431 **Boletim mensal** de **informação. Laboratório** de **engenharia civil.** Lisboa. *Bolm mens. Inf. Lab. Eng. civ., Lisb.* [1949–52] **L.**P. 50–52. [*C. as:* 7432]

7432 **Boletim mensal** de **informação. Laboratório nacional** de **engenharia civil.** Lisboa. *Bolm mens. Inf. Lab. nac. Eng. civ., Lisb.* [1953–] **L.**P. [*C. of:* 7431]

7433 **Boletim mensal** das **observações meteorológicas** no **Arquipélago** da **Madeira.** Funchal, Lisboa. *Bolm mens. Obsçoes met. Arquip. Madeira* [1945–] **L.**BM. 55–; MO.; **Y.** [*C. of:* 7362]

7434 **Boletim mensal** das **observações meteorológicas** feitas nos **postos** da **colónia, Lourenço Marques.** *Bolm mens. Obsções met. Lourenço Marq.* [1934–50] **L.**BM. 50–; MO.; **E.**M.; **O.**G. imp.; **Y.** [*C. as:* 7435]

7435 **Boletim mensal** das **observações meteorológicas** organizad pelo **Serviço meteorológico** de **Moçambique.** Lourenço Marques. *Bolm mens. Obsçoes met. Serv. met. Moçamb.* [1951–] **L.**BM.; MO. 55–; **E.**M.; **Y.** [*C. of:* 7434]

7436 **Boletim mensal** do **Observatório** de **Rio de Janeiro.** Rio de Janeiro. *Bolm mens. Obs. Rio de J.* [1900–08] **L.**MO.; **Abd.**U. 01–08; **C.**O.; UL.; **Db.**; **E.**G.; M. imp.; R.; **O.**G. [*C. as:* 7463]

7436° **Boletim mensal** e **resumo anual. Instituto geofísico, Universidade** do **Porto.** *Bolm mens. Resumo a. Inst. geofís. Porto* **L.**BM. 54–.

7437 **Boletim mensal** e **resumo anual. Observatório** da **Serra do Pilar.** Oporto. *Bolm mens. Resumo a. Obs. Serra Pilar* **L.**MO. 27–; **E.**M. 23–44; **O.**G. 28–.

7438 **Boletim mensal. Secretaria** da **agricultura, commercio** e **obras públicas, São Paulo.** *Bolm mens. Secr. Agric. S Paulo* L.BM^N. 28–30 imp.

7439 **Boletim mensal. Serviço meteorológico, São Tomé** e **Príncipe.** *Bolm mens. Serv. met. S Tomé* L.MO. 57–.

7440 **Boletim meteorológico.** Coimbra. *Bolm met., Coimbra* E.M. 08– imp.

7441 **Boletim meteorológico.** Florianopolis. *Bolm met. Florianopolis*

7442 **Boletim meteorológico.** Macau. *Bolm met., Macau*

7443 **Boletim meteorológico.** Rio de Janeiro. *Bolm met., Rio de J.* [1910–24] L.MO.; SC.; C.O.; UL.; **Db.**; E.G.; M. 10–13: 20–24; O.; R.; **M.P.** 22–24; O.G. 10–24 imp. [*Replaces:* 7463; *C. as:* 7429]

7444 **Boletim meteorológico.** São Paulo. *Bolm met., S Paulo* [1938–42] L.MO. 38–41; SC.

7445 **Boletim meteorológico** para a **agricultura.** Lisboa. *Bolm met. Agric.* L.MO. 51–.

7446 **Boletim meteorológico** do **Observatório** do **Infante D. Luiz.** Lisboa. *Bolm met. Obs. Infante D. Luiz* L.MO. 79–.

7447 **Boletim meteorológico** do **Observatório** da **Serra** do **Pilar.** Gaia. *Bolm met. Obs. Serra Pilar* [1913–] L.MO. 13–35; E.M. 09–19: 28–35; O.G. 35. [*C. of:* 46153]

7448 **Boletim meteorológico, Uruguay.** Montevideo. *Bolm met. Urug.* L.MO. 35–48. [*C. of:* 7941]

7449 **Boletim** de **minas.** Lisboa. *Bolm Minas, Lisb.* L.BM. 15–17.

7450 **Boletim** do **Ministério** da **agricultura.** Lisboa. *Bolm Minist. Agric., Lisb.* **Rt.** 18–23: 30.

7451 **Boletim** do **Ministério** da **agricultura, industria** e **comercio.** Rio de Janeiro. *Bolm Minist. Agric. Ind. Com., Rio de J.* [1912–] L.AM. 15–33 imp.: 47; EB. 12–52 imp.; K. 25–34 imp.; P. 27–40 imp.; TP. 26–47; UC. 26–; **Abs.**A. 34–; **C.**A. 28–47 imp.; **E.**AB. 42–47 imp.; **M.**P. 33–40 imp.; O.G. 30–31; F. 30–46 imp.; **Pl.**M. 33–34; **R.**D. 43–; **Rt.** 12–23: 43–44; **Sil.** 46–47.

7452 **Boletim** do **Ministério** da **viação** e **obras públicas.** Rio de Janeiro. *Bolm Minist. Viaç., Rio de J.* L.G. 09–.

7453 **Boletim** das **missões civilizadores, Sernache** do **Bomjardim.** *Bolm Miss. civiliz. Sernache Bomjardim* L.TD. 20–25 imp.; **Lv.**U. 20–25.

7454 **Boletim** do **Museu** de **biologia Prof. Mello-Leitão.** Santa Teresa. *Bolm Mus. Biol. Prof. Mello-Leitão* [1949–] L.BM^N.; Z.

    Boletim do **Museu Goeldi** de **história natural** e **ethnographia.** *See* 7458.

7455 **Boletim** do **Museu** e **Laboratorio mineralógico** e **geológico** da **Universidade** de **Lisboa.** *Bolm Mus. Lab. miner. geol. Univ. Lisb.* [1931–] L.BM^N.; GL.; GM.; O.R.; **Y.**

7456 **Boletim** do **Museu municipal** do **Funchal.** *Bolm Mus. munic. Funchal* [1945–] L.BM^N. imp.; **C.**B. 46–; **Dm.** 56–; **Lo.** 49–; **Pl.**M.; **Wo.** 45–52 imp.; **Y.**

7457 **Boletim** do **Museu nacional** de **Rio de Janeiro.** *Bolm Mus. nac. Rio de J.* [1923–42: 42– *in series below*] L.AM. 35–41 imp.; AN. 23–35; BM^N.; E. 35–42; EB. (ent.);

GL.; HO. 35–41; L.; Z. 35–42; **Abd.**U. 36–42; **Bl.**U.; **C.**P.; **E.**B.; C. 23–35 imp.; R.; U. 35–41 imp.; W. 35–42; **G.**U. 35–42; **Ld.**U. 36–42; **Lv.**U.; **M.**U.; **Nw.**A. 34–42; **O.**R. 35–42; **Pl.**M. 35–42; **Rt.** 35–42 imp.; **Sa.** 35–42; **Wo.** 32–42 imp.

    Antropologia. L.BM.; BM^N. 44–; **Abd.**U.; **Abs.**U. 43– imp.; **Bl.**U.; **C.**P.; **E.**B.; R.; U. 43– imp.; **G.**U. imp.; **Ld.**U.; **Lv.**U.; **M.**U.; **Nw.**A.; **O.**R.; **Rt.** 44–; **Sa.**; **Y.**

    Botânica. L.BM.; BM^N.; L.; SC.; **Abs.**U.; **Bl.**U.; **C.**B. imp.; P.; **E.**B.; R.; U.; W.; **Fr.** imp.; **G.**U. imp.; **H.**U.; **Ld.**U.; **Lv.**U.; **M.**U.; **Nw.**A.; **O.**R.; **Pl.**M.; **Rt.**; **Sa.**; **Wo.** imp.; **Y.**

    Geologia. L.BM.; BM^N.; GL.; **Abd.**U.; **Abs.**U. 43– imp.; **Bl.**U.; **C.**P.; S.; **E.**B.; R.; U.; W.; **Fr.** 52– imp.; **G.**U. imp.; **Ld.**U.; **Lv.**U.; **M.**U.; **Nw.**A.; **O.**R.; **Rt.**; **Sa.**; **Wo.** imp.; **Y.**

    Zoologia. L.BM.; BM^N.; E.; EB. (ent.); L.; Z.; **Abd.**U.; **Bl.**U.; **C.**B. imp.; P.; **E.**B.; R.; W.; **Fr.** 52– imp.; **G.**U. imp.; **H.**U. imp.; **Ld.**U.; **Lv.**U.; **M.**U.; **Nw.**A.; **O.**R.; Z. 45–47; **Pl.**M.; **Rt.** imp.; **Sa.**; **Wo.** imp.; **Y.**

7458 **Boletim** do **Museu paraense 'Emilio Goeldi.'** Pará. *Bolm Mus. para. 'Emilio Goeldi'* [1957–]
    Ser. Antropologia L.BM^N.; **Cr.**M.; **E.**R.; **G.**U.; **Y.**
    Ser. Botanica L.BM^N.; Z. imp.; **Cr.**M.; **E.**R.; **G.**U.; **Y.**
    Ser. Geologia L.BM^N.; Z. imp.; **Cr.**M.; **E.**R.; **G.**U.; **Y.**
    Ser. Zoologia L.BM^N.; Z.; **Cr.**M.; **E.**R.; **G.**U.; **Y.**
    [*C. of:* 7459]

7459 **Boletim** do **Museu paraense Emilio Goeldi** de **história natural** e **etnografia.** Bélem, Pará. *Bolm Mus. para. Emilio Goeldi Hist. nat. Ethnogr.* [1894–56] L.BM. 94–09; BM^N.; E. 04–12; G. 97–10; K. 10: 33; L. 97–10; SC.; TD. 06–12; UC. 00–12; Z. imp.; **C.**UL. 97–12; **E.**R. imp.; **G.**U. 56; **O.**G. 09; R. 98–12 imp.; **Lv.**U. 08–12; **M.**U. 00–12. [*C. as:* 7458]

7460 **Boletim** do **Museu Rocha.** Cara. *Bolm Mus. Rocha*

7461 **Boletim** das **observações meteorológicas**—e dos **resultados magnéticos.** Rio de Janeiro. *Bolm Obsções met., Rio de J.* [1901–] L.MO. 01–07; U. 03–08; UC. 03–.

7462 **Boletim. Observatório meteorológico** da **Beira.** *Bolm Obs. met Beira* L.MO. 03–15.

7463 **Boletim** do **Observatório nacional.** Rio de Janeiro. *Bolm Obs. nac., Rio de J.* [1909] L.MO.; C.O.; UL.; **Db.**; E.G.; M.; O.; R. [*C. of:* 7436; *Replaced by:* 7443]

7464 **Boletim. Observatório** de **São Paulo.** São Paulo. *Bolm Obs. S Paulo* [1907–] L.BM.; G.; MO. 24–36; SC.; E.G. [*C. of:* 7336]

7465 **Boletim odontológico paulista.** São Paulo. *Bolm odont. paul.*

7465° **Boletim oficial** dos **C.T.T. Administração geral** dos **correios, telégrafos** e **telefones.** Lisboa. *Bolm of. C.T.T.* L.BM. 57–.

7466 **Boletim** da **Ordem** dos **engenheiros.** Lisboa. *Bolm Ord. Engen., Lisb.* [1937–43: 54–] L.MI. 54– imp.; P. 54–56 imp.; **Y.** [*Replaces* 46852; >46325, 1944–51]

7467 **Boletim** da **Ordem** dos **médicos.** Oporto. *Bolm Ord. Méd., Oporto* [1952–] L.MA. 57–.

7468 **Boletim paranaense** de **geografia.** Curitiba. *Bolm parana. Geogr.* [1960–] **Ld.**U.

7469 **Boletim. Parque nacional** do **Itatiáia.** Rio de Janeiro. *Bolm Parq. nac. Itatiáia* [1949–] **L.**BM^N.

7470 **Boletim paulistica** de **geografia.** São Paulo. *Bolm paul. Geogr.* [1949–] **L.**U. imp.; **C.**GG. 50–; **E.**G. (curr.)

7471 **Boletim pecuário.** Lisboa. *Bolm pecuár.* [1933–] **L.**AM. 54–; BM. 57–; MD. 56–; V. 49– imp.; **E.**AB. 56–; **W.** 36–; **Y.**

7472 **Boletim** da **pesca.** Lisboa. *Bolm Pesca* [1944–] **Abd.**M. 52–; **Lo.** 57–; **Y.**

7473 **Boletim** de **pharmacia** do **Porto.** Porto. *Bolm Pharm. Porto*

7474 **Boletim pluviométrico.** São Paulo. *Bolm pluviométr.* [1941–] **L.**MO.; **Rt.** 41–45; **Y.**

7475 **Boletim. R. Associação** dos **architectos** in **Lisboa.** Lisboa. *Bolm R. Ass. Archit. Lisb.*

7476 **Boletim** da **R. Associação central** da **agricultura portugueza.** Lisboa. *Bolm R. Ass. cent. Agric. port.* **Db.** 15–.

7477 **Boletim. Repartição** de **agricultura, Moçambique.** Lourenço Marques. *Bolm Repart. Agric. Moçamb.* **L.**EB. 14–15; K. 10–11.

7478 **Boletim** da **Repartição** de **aguas** e **esgotos Estado** de **São Paulo.** *Bolm Repart. Aguas S Paulo* [1937–]

7479 **Boletim** do **S.E.S.P.** Serviço especiál de saúde pública. Rio de Janeiro. *Bolm S.E.S.P.* **L.**TD. 48–.

7480 **Boletim** do **Sanatorio São Lucas.** São Paulo. *Bolm Sanat S Lucas* [1939–] **L.**MA. 45–; MD.; TD. v. imp.; **Bl.**U. 45–49 imp.; **Lv.**M. 50–; **O.**R. [*Supplement to:* 2270]

7481 **Boletim sanitario.** Rio de Janeiro. *Bolm sanit., Rio de J.* [1922–26] **L.**TD. imp.; **Lv.**U.

7481ᶜ **Boletim sanitario. Direcção** do **serviços** de **saúde** e **higiene, Angola.** Luanda. *Bolm sanit. Angola* **L.**BM. 47–.

7482 **Boletim. Secção** de **fructicultura** do **Estado** de **São Paulo.** *Bolm Secç. Fructic. Est. S Paulo*

7483 **Boletim** da **Secretaria** de **agricultura, industria** e **comercio** do **Estado** de **Pernambuco.** *Bolm Secr. Agric. Ind. Com. Est. Pernambuco* [1936–] **L.**AM. 34–41; MY. 49–; TP. 37–45 imp.; **Br.**A. 46– imp.; **C.**A. 37–; **O.**F. v. imp.; **Rt.** 46–; **Y.**

7484 **Boletim** da **Secretaria geral** de **saúde** e **assistencia.** Rio de Janeiro. *Bolm Secr. ger. Saúde Assist., Rio de J.* [1936–39] **L.**TD.

Boletim. Secretaria da **viaçao** e **obras públicas** do **Estado** de **São Paulo.** *See* 7392.

7485 **Boletim** da **segunda classe. Academia** das **sciências** de **Lisboa.** *Bolm seg. Cl. Acad. Sci. Lisb.* [1910–29] **L.**BM. 10–15; G.; GL. 14–29; UC.; **C.**UL.; **E.**B.; C. 12–29 imp.; R.; U.; **M.**R.; **O.**B. 10–24. [*C. in:* 7284]

7486 **Boletim semestral. Estação central** no **Morro** de **Santo Antonio.** Rio de Janeiro. *Bolm semest. Estaç. cent. Morro S Antonio* **L.**MO. 97–04; UC. 03–06.

7487 **Boletim semestral. Observatório meteorológico 'D. Basco.'** Cuyabá. *Bolm semest. Obs. met. D. Basco* **L.**MO. 03.

Boletim do **Serviço especial** de **saúde pública.** Rio de Janeiro. *See* 7479.

7488 **Boletim. Serviço forestal** do **Brasil.** Rio de Janeiro. *Bolm Serv. for. Bras.* **O.**F. 29–31.

7489 **Boletim. Serviço geológico. Estado** de **Minas Geraes.** Bello Horizonte. *Bolm Serv. geol. Est. Minas Geraes* **L.**BM^N. 33–34.

7490 **Boletim. Serviço geológico** e **mineralógico** do **Brasil.** Rio de Janeiro. *Bolm Serv. geol. miner. Bras.* [1920–39] **L.**BM^N. imp.; GL. 28–39 imp.; GM.; MI. 30–39 imp.; **C.**S. 78–39; **E.**D. 26–39 imp. [*C. as:* 7351]

Boletim. Serviço meteorologico de **São Paulo.** *See* 7336.

7491 **Boletim** do **Serviço nacional** de **lepra.** Rio de Janeiro. *Bolm Serv. nac. Lepra, Rio de J.* [1942–] **L.**TD. 43– imp.

7492 **Boletim** do **Serviço nacional** de **pesquisas agronômicas.** Rio de Janeiro. *Bolm Serv. nac. Pesq. agron., Rio de J.* [1947–] **C.**A.; **Y.**

7493 **Boletim** dos **Serviços** de **agricultura** e **commercio, colonizacão** e **florestas.** Angola. *Bolm Servs Agric. Comm., Angola* **L.**AM. 30–37.

7494 **Boletim. Serviços** de **indústria, minas** e **geologia.** Lourenço Marques. *Bolm Servs Ind. Minas Geol., Lourenço Marq.* Serie de geologia e minas—memorias e comunicações. **L.**BM^N. 37–.

7495 **Boletim** dos **servicos** de **saúde pública.** Lisboa. *Bolm Servs Saúde públ.* [1954–] **L.**BM.; H.; MA.; TD. [*C. of:* 7416]

7496 **Boletim. Setor** de **inventários florestais, Serviço florestal, Brazil.** Rio de Janeiro. *Bolm Setor Invent. flor. Serv. flor. Braz.* [1959–] **O.**F.

7497 **Boletim sismológico.** Rio de Janeiro. *Bolm sism., Rio de J.* **L.**AS. 33–; SC. 26–.

7498 **Boletim** da **Sociedade brasileira** de **agronomía.** Rio de Janeiro. *Bolm Soc. bras. Agron.* [1941–49] **L.**EB.; **Hu.**G. 43–45. [*C. of:* 46973]

7499 **Boletim** da **Sociedade brasileira** de **dermatologia.** Rio de Janeiro. *Bolm Soc. bras. Derm.* [1912–] **L.**TD. 12–19 imp.

7500 **Boletim** da **Sociedade brasileira** de **entomologia.** São Paulo. *Bolm Soc. bras. Ent.* [1948–] **L.**BM^N. 48–50; E. 48 imp.

7501 **Boletim** da **Sociedade brasileira** de **geologia** São Paulo. *Bolm Soc. bras. Geol.* [1952–] **L.**BM^N. 55–; **Y.**

7502 **Boletim** da **Sociedade brasileira** de **medicina veterinaria.** Rio de Janeiro. *Bolm Soc. bras. Med. vet.* [1924–] **L.**TD. 24–29; V. 37–52 imp.; **C.**V. 52–53; **W.** 43–.

7503 **Boletim** da **Sociedade brasileira** de **orquidofilos.** Rio de Janeiro. *Bolm Soc. bras. Orquidof.* **L.**HS. 58–.

7504 **Boletim** da **Sociedade brasileira** de **tuberculose.** Rio de Janeiro. *Bolm Soc. bras. Tuberc.* [1951–] **L.**MA.

7505 **Boletim** da **Sociedade Broteriana.** Coimbra. *Bolm Soc. broteriana* [1880–] **L.**BM. 83–17; BM^N. 83–; HS. 84–; K.; L.; MY. 25–; SC. 22–; UC. 22–31; **Abs.**S. 49–; U. 23–; **Ba.**I. 34–; **Bl.**U. 25– imp.; **Bm.**U. 32–; **Br.**A. 49–; **C.**A. 35–; P. 25–; **Db.** 22–; **E.**B. 80–06; R. 22–; W. 49–; **Hu.**G. 38– imp.; **Lv.**U. 22–; **Nw.**A. 26–; **O.**BO. 51–; F. 22– imp.; **Rt.** 35– imp.; **Y.**

7505ᵃ **Boletim** da **Sociedade cearense** de **agronomia.** Ceará. *Bolm Soc. cearense Agron.* [1960–] **L.**BMᴺ.

7506 **Boletim** da **Sociedade entomologica** do **Brasil.** Rio de Janeiro. *Bolm Soc. ent. Bras.* [1922–23] **L.**E.; EB.

7507 **Boletim** da **Sociedade** de **estudios** (da Colónia) de **Moçambique.** Lourenço Marques. *Bolm Soc. Estud. Moçamb.* [1931–] **L.**BMᴺ. 32– imp.; K. 32–; **Y.**

7508 **Boletim** da **Sociedade** de **geographia** de **Lisboa.** Lisboa. *Bolm Soc. Geogr. Lisb.* [1876–] **L.**AN. 80–96 imp.; BM.; G. 78–; GL. 00–14; SC. 48–; **C.**UL. 83–; **E.**G. 87–; R. 80–92 imp.: 20–; Lv.U. 85–14 imp.; **O.**B. 83–85.

7509 **Boletim** da **Sociedade geológica** de **Portugal.** Porto. *Bolm Soc. geol. Port.* [1941–] **L.**BMᴺ.; GL.; GM.; I. 48–; **Y.**

7510 **Boletim** da **Sociedade** de **matemática** de **São Paulo.** São Paulo. *Bolm Soc. Mat. S Paulo* [1946–] **L.**M.; **C.**P.; **Db.**; **E.**R.; **G.**U.; **Ld.**U. 61–; **Y.**

7511 **Boletim** da **Sociedade** de **medicina** e **cirurgia** de **Rio de Janeiro.** *Bolm Soc. Med. Cirurg. Rio de J.*

7512 **Boletim** da **Sociedade** de **medicina** e **cirurgia** de **São Paulo.** São Paulo. *Bolm Soc. Med. Cirurg. S Paulo* [1895–?] **L.**TD. 19–25 imp.; **Lv.**U. 19–20 imp. [*Replaced by:* 46738]

Boletim da **Sociedade nacional** de **agricultura.** Rio de Janeiro. *See* 28215.

7513 **Boletim** da **Sociedade nacional** de **horticultura** de **Portugal.** Lisboa. *Bolm Soc. nac. Hort. Port.*

7514 **Boletim** da **Sociedade paranaense** de **matemática.** Curitiba. *Bolm Soc. parana. Mat.* [1958–] **Y.**

7515 **Boletim** da **Sociedade paulista** de **medicina veterinaria.** São Paulo. *Bolm Soc. paul. Med. vet.* [1944–] **L.**v.; **W.** [*C. of:* 46979]

7516 **Boletim** da **Sociedade portuguesa** de **ciências naturais.** Lisboa. *Bolm Soc. port. Ciênc. nat.* [1948–] **L.**BMᴺ.; EB.; K.; L.; **Db.**; **Dm.**; **Lv.**U.; **Y.** [*C. of:* 12138]

7517 **Boletim** da **Sociedade portuguesa** de **oftalmologia.** Lisboa. *Bolm Soc. port. Oftal.* **L.**MD. 44–.

7518 **Boletim** da **Superintendencia** dos **serviços** do **café.** São Paulo. *Bolm Suptdcia Serv. Café, S Paulo* **L.**MY. 42–; **Rt.** 42–43 imp.

7519 **Boletim técnico. Instituto agronômico** do **Estado** em **Campinas.** São Paulo. *Bolm téc. Inst. agron. Est. Campinas* [1933–40] **L.**EB. (ent.) 36–40; **C.**A.; **O.**F. 38–40 imp.; **Rt.** 36–40 imp. [*C. as:* 8635]

7520 **Boletim técnico. Instituto agronômico** do **leste.** Cruz das Almas. *Bolm téc. Inst. agron. leste* [1954–] **C.**A. 56–.

7521 **Boletim técnico. Instituto agronômico** do **nordeste.** Recife. *Bolm téc. Inst. agron. NE.* [1954–] **Rt.** 54; **Y.**

7523 **Boletim técnico** do **Instituto agronômico** del **Norte.** Bélem. *Bolm téc. Inst. agron. N.* [1943–] **L.**A. 50– imp.; AM. 46– imp.; BMᴺ. 43–45; K.; MY. 50–; **Br.**A. 50–51: 53–54; **C.**A.; **Hu.**G. 49–; **O.**F.; **Rt.** 48–; **Y.**

7524 **Boletim técnico. Instituto agronômico** do **sul.** Pelotas, Pôrto Alegre. *Bolm téc. Inst. agron. S.* [1947–] **L.**MO. 52– imp.; **C.**A.; **Hu.**G. 53–

7525 **Boletim técnico. Instituto** de **cacau** da **Bahia.** Bahia. Série 'Cultura de cacau'. *Bolm téc. Inst. Cacau Bahia* [1938–] **L.**BMᴺ.; **C.**A.

7526 **Boletim** de **therapeutica.** Rio de Janeiro. *Bolm Ther.*

7527 **Boletim trimestral** da **Clínica** de **doenças tropicais** e da **nutrição** do **Hospital Pedro II.** Recife. *Bolm trimest. Clín. Doenç. trop. Hosp. Pedro II*

7527ᶜ **Boletim** da **Universidade** do **Paraná.** Curitiba. *Bolm Univ. Paraná*
  Botânica [1960–] **L.**BMᴺ.; **Pl.**M.
  Geologia [1959–] **L.**BMᴺ.
  Zoologia [1960–] **L.**BMᴺ.; Z.

7527ᵉ **Boletim veterinario.** Porto Alegre. *Bolm vet., Porto Alegre* **L.**V. 38–39 imp.

7528 **Boletín** de la **Academia** de **ciencias** y **artes** de **Barcelona.** Barcelona. *Boln Acad. Cienc. Artes Barcelona* [1932–33] **L.**BM.; BMᴺ.; **Db.**; Lv.U. 32. [*C. of:* 8034; *C. as:* 12704]

Boletín de la **Academia** de **ciencias, bellas letras** y **nobles artes, Córdoba.** *See* 8034ᵃ.

7529 **Boletín** de la **Academia** de **ciencias exactas, físico-químicas** y **naturales** de **Madrid.** *Boln Acad. Cienc. exact. Madr.* [1935–36] **L.**BMᴺ.; SC.; Z.; **E.**C.

7530 **Boletín** de la **Academia** de **ciencias físicas, matemáticas** y **naturales.** Caracas. *Boln Acad. Cienc. fís., Caracas* [1934–] **L.**BMᴺ. imp.; TP. 41– imp.; **Ld.**U. 61–; **Y.**

7531 **Boletín. Academia colombiana** de **ciencias exactas, físicas** y **naturales.** Bogotá. *Boln Acad. colomb. Cienc.* [1936–]

Boletín de la **Academia** de **Córdoba.** *See* 8034ᵃ.

7532 **Boletín. Academia** de **estomatología** del **Perú.** Lima. *Boln Acad. Estomat. Perú* [1941–] **L.**D.

7533 **Boletín** de la **Academia nacional** de **ciencias** en **Córdoba.** *Boln Acad. nac. Cienc. Córdoba* [1874–] **L.**BMᴺ.; E. 74–23; G. 79–02; GL. 00–; K. 11–46; L. imp.; MO. (meteor.) 83–25 imp.; MY. 21–29 imp.; Z. 74–18 imp.; **Bl.**U. 84–90; **Db.** 84–; **E.**G. 90–; R. 79– imp.; **G.**N. 79–.

7534 **Boletín** de la **Academia nacional** de **medicina** de **Buenos Aires.** *Boln Acad. nac. Med. B. Aires* [1928–] **L.**BM. 45–; MD. 31– imp.; **C.**UL.; **O.**R. 28–29.

7535 **Boletín** de la **Administración nacional** del **agua.** Buenos Aires. *Boln Adm. nac. Agua, B. Aires* [1945] **L.**TD.; **O.**R.; **Wa.**W. [*C. of:* 7984; *C. as:* 46256]

7536 **Boletín administrativo** de la **Secretária (Ministério)** de **salud pública** de la **nación.** Buenos Aires. *Boln adm. Secr. (Minist.) Salud. públ. Nac., B. Aires* [1946–] **L.**H. 46–50; LI. 48–; MA.; TD. imp.

7537 **Boletín** de **aeronáutica.** Buenos Aires. *Boln Aeronaut.*

7539 **Boletín agrícola.** Ciudad Real. *Boln agric., Ciudad Real*

7540 **Boletín agrícola.** Mendoza. *Boln agríc., Mendoza* **L.**AM. 34–44 imp.

7541 **Boletín agrícola.** Palma. *Boln agríc., Palma*

7542 **Boletín agrícola** de **Andalucía oriental.** Granada. *Boln agric. Andalucía orient.*

7543 **Boletín agrícola** para el **campesino cubano.** La Habana. *Boln agríc. Camp. cub.* **L.**AM. (1 yr).

7544 **Boletín agrícola** de la **región agronómica** de **Levante.** Valencia. *Boln agríc. Reg. agron. Levante*

7545 **Boletín agrícola** de la **región** de **Andalucía occidental.** Sevilla. *Boln agríc. Reg. Andalucía occid.*

7546 **Boletín** de **agricultura.** Ambato. *Boln Agric., Ambato* **L.**MO. 20.

7547 **Boletín** de **agricultura.** Bogotá. *Boln Agric.,*
Bogotá [1927–35] **L.**BM. 30–35; **Rt.** 32–33. [*C. as:*
1251]

7548 **Boletín** de **agricultura.** México. *Boln Agric.,*
Méx. **E.**R. 93–01.

7549 **Boletín** de **agricultura.** S. José de Costa Rica.
Boln Agric., S José C. Rica

7550 **Boletín** de **agricultura** y **ganadería.** Buenos
Aires. *Boln Agric. Ganad., B. Aires* [1901–03] [*C. as:*
47034]

7551 **Boletín** de **agricultura** y **ganadería.** Buenos
Aires. *Boln Agric. Ganad., B. Aires* [1958–] **L.**AM.

7552 **Boletín** de **agricultura** y **ganadería.** Corrientes.
Boln Agric. Ganad., Corrientes [1942–]

7553 **Boletín** de **agricultura, industría** y **comercio** de
Guatemala. Guatemala. *Boln. Agric. Ind. Com. Guatem.*
[1921–31] **L.**EB. 21–26; K.; TP. 27–31. [*C. as:* 46260]

7554 **Boletín** de **agricultura técnica** y **económica.**
Madrid. *Boln Agric. téc. econ.* [1909–] **L.**AM. 09–32;
EB. 17–29; MO. 45–48: 51–; **Db.**; **Rt.** 16–32.

7555 **Boletín agro-pecuario.** Barcelona. *Boln agro-*
pec. **Hu.**G. 49–.

7556 **Boletín anatómico.** La Habana. *Boln anat.*

7557 **Boletín anual meteorológico.** La Paz, Bolivia.
Boln a. met., La Paz [1945–] **L.**MO.; **Y.**

7558 **Boletín anual meteorológico.** Lima. *Boln a.*
met., Lima [1939–] **L.**MO. [*C. of:* 46135]

7559 **Boletín anual meteorológico, Uruguay.** Montevideo. *Boln a. met. Urug.* **L.**MO. 39–43.

7560 **Boletín anual** del **Observatorio meteorológico.**
Granada. *Boln a. Obs. met., Granada* **L.**MO. 08–15;
E.M. 08–11: 13–15.

7561 **Boletín anual. Observatorio meteorológico** del
Colegio salesiano. Punta Urenas. *Boln a. Obs.*
met. Col. sales. [1917–] **L.**MO. 17–22. [*C. of:* 7942]

7562 **Boletín anual** del **Servicio meteorológico mexi-**
cano. Tacubaya. *Boln a. Serv. met. mex.* **L.**MO.
19–42 imp.; **Bl.**U. 21: 28–30; **E.**R.; **O.**G. [*C. of:*
7926]

7563 **Boletín anual** del **Servicio** de **obstetricia** en el
Hospital del **Salvador.** Santiago de Chile. *Boln a.*
Serv. Obstet. Hosp. Salvador

7564 **Boletín anual. Sociedad** de **tisiología.** Buenos
Aires. *Boln a. Soc. Tisiol., B. Aires*

7565 **Boletín argentino forestal.** Buenos Aires. *Boln*
argent. for. **O.**R. 57–.

7566 **Boletín** de la **Asociación** de **agricultores** del
Ecuador. Guayaquil. *Boln Asoc. Agric. Ecuador*

7567 **Boletín** de la **Asociación** de **agricultores** de
España. Madrid. *Boln Asoc. Agric. Esp.*

7568 **Boletín** de la **Asociación argentina** de **electro-**
técnicos. Buenos Aires. *Boln Asoc. argent. Electrotéc.*
[1914–27] **L.**EE. imp. [*C. as:* 46480]

7569 **Boletín** de la **Asociación** de **empresas eléctricas**
de **Chile.** Santiago. *Boln Asoc. Empr. eléct. Chile*

7570 **Boletín** de la **Asociación geofísica** de **México.**
Boln Asoc. geofís. Méx.

7571 **Boletín. Asociación** de **ingenieros agronomos.**
Montevideo. *Boln Asoc. Ing. agron* [1929–33] [*C. as:*
46316]

7572 **Boletín** de la **Asociación internacional** de
hidatidologia. Azul. *Boln Asoc. int. Hidatid.*

7573 **Boletín. Asociación international permanente.**
Congreso sudamericano de **ferrocarriles.** *Boln*
Asoc. int. perm. Congr. sudam. Ferroc.

7574 **Boletín** de la **Asociación** de **labradores** de **Zara-**
goza y su **provincia.** Zaragoza. *Boln Asoc. Labrad.*
Zaragoza **L.**AM.; **Db.** 14–.

7575 **Boletín** de la **Asociación médica** de **Bahia**
Blanca. Bahia Blanca. *Boln Asoc. méd. Bahia Blanca*

7576 **Boletín** de la **Asociación médica nacional** de
Panama. *Boln Asoc. méd. nac. Panama* [1938–51]
L.MA. 45–51; TD. 47–51. [*C. as:* 4610]

7577 **Boletín** de la **Asociación médica** de **Puerto Rico.**
San Juan, etc. *Boln Asoc. méd. P. Rico* [1903–] **L.**MA.
30– imp.; TD. 14– imp.; **M.**MS. 41– imp.

7578 **Boletín** de la **Asociación médica** de **Santiago.**
Boln Asoc. méd. Santiago **L.**MA. 46–.

7579 **Boletín** de la **Asociación** de **médicos titulares.**
Madrid. *Boln Asoc. Méd. titul.*

7580 **Boletín** de la **Asociación** de **molineros** de **Chile.**
Santiago. *Boln Asoc. Molin. Chile*

7581 **Boletín** de la **Asociación nacional** de **ingenieros**
agronomos. Madrid. *Boln Asoc. nac. Ing. Agron.*
[1945–] **L.**AM. 49– imp.; **Y.**

7582 **Boletín** de la **Asociación odontológica argentina.**
Buenos Aires. *Boln Asoc. odont. argent.* [1930–] **L.**D.
40–42 imp.: 49–.

7583 **Boletín** de la **Asociación química española** de
la **industría** del **cuero.** Barcelona. *Boln Asoc. quím.*
esp. Ind. Cuero [1950–59] **L.**LE. 54–59; P. 56–59.
[*C. as:* 7788]

7584 **Boletín** de la **Asociación uruguaya** para el **prog-**
reso de la **ciencia.** Montevideo. *Boln Asoc. urug.*
Prog. Cienc. [1952–] **Y.**

7585 **Boletín. Asociación venezolana** de **productores**
de **cacao.** Caracas. *Boln Asoc. venez. Prod. Cacao*
[1936–]

7586 **Boletín astronómico** del **Observatorio astro-**
nómico de **Madrid.** *Boln astr. Obs. astr. Madr.*
[1932–] **L.**AS.; SC. 35–; **E.**O.; **M.**U. imp.; **Y.**

7587 **Boletín azucarero mexicano.** México. *Boln*
azuc. mex. **Y.**

7588 **Boletín** de **bacteriología** e **investigación** (vete-
rinaria). Montevideo. *Boln Bact. Invest.* (vet.) **Lv.**U.;
26–28.

7589 **Boletín bibliográfico agrícola.** Madrid. *Boln*
biblfico agríc. [1948–] **L.**AM. imp.; EB.; **Hu.**G. 48–55; **Sil.**

7590 **Boletín bibliográfico** de **antropología ameri-**
cana. México. *Boln biblfico Antrop. am.* [1937–] **L.**AN.;
BM.; HO.; S. 47–; **Br.**U.; **C.**UL.; **O.**B.; R.

7591 **Boletín bibliográfico artillero.** Madrid. *Boln*
biblfico artill. **L.**P. 32–36.

7592 **Boletín bibliográfico. Facultad** de **agricultura,**
Universidad de **Venezuela.** Maracay. *Boln biblfico*
Fac. Agric. Univ. Venez. **L.**BM^N. 54–.

7593 **Boletín bibliográfico. Facultad** de **medicina.**
Universidad de **Montevideo.** *Boln biblfico Fac. Med.*
Univ. Montev. [1948–]

7593° **Boletín bibliográfico** de **geofísica** y **oceanográfica americanas.** Tacubaya. *Boln biblfico Geofís. Oceanogr. am.* **L.**MO. 58–.

7594 **Boletín bibliográfico. Ministerio** de **agricultura** de la **nación.** Buenos Aires. *Boln biblfico Minist. Agric. Nac., B. Aires* [1934–] **L.**AM. 39–54 imp.; BM.; SC.; **M.**P. 35–41 imp.; **O.**B. 35–; **Sil.** 53–.

7594° **Boletín. Biblioteca nacional** de **aeronáutica.** Buenos Aires. *Boln Bibltca nac. Aeronáut., B. Aires* [1956–] **L.**BM.

Boletín bimensual. Dirección de **algodón.** Buenos Aires. *See* 7896.

Boletín bimensual. Junta de **algodón.** Buenos Aires. *See* 7896.

7595 **Boletín bimestral. Servicio meteorología** y **comunicaciones.** Maracay. *Boln bimest. Serv. Met. Comun., Maracay* **L.**MO. 50–.

7596 **Boletín biológico. Universidad** de **Puebla.** México. *Boln biol. Univ. Puebla* [1942–]

7597 **Boletín** de **bosques, pesca** i **caza** de **Chile.** Santiago. *Boln Bosq. Pesca Caza Chile* **L.**BM^N. 12–14.

7598 **Boletín** del **Centro antirreumático. Facultad** de **ciencias médicas** de **Buenos Aires.** *Boln Cent. antirreum. B. Aires* **L.**MD. 37–39; **Lv.**M. 37–39.

7599 **Boletín. Centro** de **documentación científica** y **técnica** de **México.** México. *Boln Cent. Docum. cient. téc. Méx.* [1952–55: 56– in sections below] **L.**AM.; AV.; C. 55–56; P. 55–; TD.; **Abd.**R. imp.; **Db.**; **Rt.** 54–; **Sy.**R.; **Y.**
 1. Matemáticas, astronomía y astrofísica, física, geología, geofísica, geodesía.
 2. Ingeniera.
 3. Química. ·
 5. Biología, agricultura, zootécnia y industrias de la alimentación.
 L.AM. sect. 5 only; AV. sect. 1, 2, 3 only; **Db.** sect. 1, 3 only.

7600 **Boletín** del **Centro** de **investigaciones especiales** e **Laboratorio** de **estadística.** Madrid. *Boln Cent. Invest. espec. Lab. Estadíst.* **L.**AM. 34–35; BM. 33–; TD. 33–35 imp.

7601 **Boletín** del **Centro nacional** de **agricultura Costa Rica.** San José. *Boln Cent. nac. Agric. C. Rica* **L.**BM. 29–.

7602 **Boletín** del **Centro nacional** de **agricultura.** San Pedro de Montes de Oca. *Boln Cent. nac. Agric., S Pedro*

7603 **Boletín. Centro nacional** de **investigación** y **experimentación agrícola.** Lima. *Boln Cent. nac. Invest. Exp. agric., Lima* [1948–52] **L.**EB.; **C.**A.; **Rt.** [C. of: and *Rec. as:* 7705]

7604 **Boletín** del **Centro naval.** Buenos Aires. *Boln Cent. nav., B. Aires* **Y.**

7605 **Boletín** del **Centro** de **odontología** del **Uruguay.** Montevideo. *Boln Cent. Odont. Urug.* **L.**D. 42–45 imp.

7606 **Boletín** de la **Chacra experimental** de '**La Previsión.**' Tres Arroyos. *Boln Chacra exp. 'La Previsión'* [1933–] **L.**SC. 33–42; **C.**A. 34–42.

7607 **Boletín chileno** de **parasitología.** Santiago de Chile. *Boln chil. Parasit.* [1954–] **L.**L.; MC.; MD.; TD.; Z.; **C.**MO.; **Sal.**; **Y.** [C. of: 7782]

7608 **Boletín** de **ciencia** y **tecnología.** Washington. *Boln Cienc. Tecnol.* [1950–51] **L.**P. imp. [C. as: 14042]

7609 **Boletín** de **ciencia veterinaria.** Madrid. *Boln Cienc. vet.* **W.** 49–.

7610 **Boletín** de **ciencias médicas.** México. *Boln Ciencs méd.*

7611 **Boletín científico.** Lima. *Boln cient., Lima*

7612 **Boletín científico** de la **Sociedad médica** de **Mendoza.** *Boln cient. Soc. méd. Mendoza* [1954–] **L.**MA. imp. [C. of: 8123]

7613 **Boletín científico** y **técnico** del **Museum comercial** de **Venezuela.** Caracas. *Boln cient. téc. Mus. com. Venez.* **L.**K. 27★. [C. as: 53440]

7613° **Boletín** de **circulación limitada. Asociación española** del **hormigon pretensado.** Instituto técnico de la construcción y del cemento. Madrid. *Boln Circul. limit. Asoc. esp. Hormigon pret.* **Y.**

7614 **Boletín** del **Circulo** de **maquinistas** de la **Armada.** Ferrol. *Boln Circ. Maquin. Armada* **L.**MI. 46–.

7615 **Boletín** del **Circulo odontológico** de **Rosario.** *Boln Circ. odont. Rosario* **L.**D. 47–49 imp.

7616 **Boletín** de **cirugía.** Santander. *Boln Cirug., Santander*

7617 **Boletín climatológico.** La Paz. *Boln clim., La Paz* **L.**MO. 58–.

7618 **Boletín** de la **Clínica dental 'Chile'.** Santiago de Chile. *Boln Clín. dent. 'Chile'*

7619 **Boletín** de la **Clínica ginecotocológica.** Montevideo. *Boln Clín. ginecotoc.*

7620 **Boletín** de la **Clínica 'Maternidad Obrera Habana'.** Marianao. *Boln Clín. 'Matern. Obrera Habana'*

7621 **Boletín clínico.** Medellin. *Boln clín., Medellin* [1932–50] **L.**MA. 46–50; TD. 32–34: 41–50 imp. [C. in: 3594]

7623 **Boletín** del **Colegio** de **arquitectos.** Santiago. *Boln Col. Arquit., Santiago* **L.**BA. 46–.

7624 **Boletín** del **Colegio médico** de **Camagüey.** *Boln Col. méd. Camagüey* **L.**MD. 38–42.

7625 **Boletín** del **Colegio médico** de **Holguin.** *Boln Col. méd. Holguin* **L.**MD. 47–.

7626 **Boletín** del **Colegio médico** de **La Habana.** *Boln Col. méd. La Habana*

7627 **Boletín** del **Colegio médico** de **Manzanillo.** Manzanillo. *Boln Col. méd. Manzanillo*

7628 **Boletín** del **Colegio médico-farmacéutico.** Alicante. *Boln Col. méd.-farm., Alicante*

7629 **Boletín** del **Colegio médico-farmacéutico.** Ferrol. *Boln Col. méd.-farm., Ferrol*

7630 **Boletín** del **Colegio** de **médicos.** Castellón de la Plana. *Boln Col. Méd., Castellón*

7631 **Boletín** del **Colegio** de **médicos.** Reus. *Boln Col. Méd., Reus*

7632 **Boletín** del **Colegio oficial** de **farmacéuticos.** Gerona. *Boln Col. of. Farm., Gerona*

7633 **Boletín** del **Colegio oficial** de **médicos.** Cáceres. *Boln Col. of. Méd., Cáceres*

7634 **Boletín** del **Colegio oficial** de **médicos.** Huesca. *Boln Col. of. Méd., Huesca*

7635 **Boletín** del **Colegio oficial** de **médicos.** Palma. *Boln Col. of. Méd., Palma*

7636 **Boletín** del **Colegio oficial** de **médicos.** Tarragona. *Boln Col. of. Méd., Tarragona*

7637 **Boletín. Colegio oficial** de **médicos** de la **provincia** de **Córdoba.** *Boln Col. of. Méd. Prov. Córdoba*

7638 **Boletín** del **Colegio provincial** de **médicos.** Valladolid. *Boln Col. prov. Méd., Valladolid*

7639 **Boletín. Colegio provincial** de **veterinarios** de **Burgos.** Burgos. *Boln Col. prov. Vet. Burgos* **L.**V. 55–57.

7640 **Boletín** de los **Colegios** de **practicantes** de **medicina** y **cirugía.** Madrid. *Boln Cols Pract. Med. Cirug.*

7641 **Boletín** de la **Comisión central** para el **estudio** del **tabardillo.** México. *Boln Comn cent. Estud. Tabard., Méx.*

7642 **Boletín. Comisión honoraria** para la **lucha antituberculosa.** Montevideo. *Boln Comn hon. Lucha antituberc., Montev.*

7643 **Boletín** de la **Comisión** del **mapa geológico** de **España.** Madrid. *Boln Comn Mapa geol. Esp.* [1874–09] **L.**BM.; BM^N.; GL. 00–09; GM.; **Db.**; **E.**R.; **G.**N. 00–09. [*C. as:* 7823]

7644 **Boletín. Comisión nacional** para la **erradicación** del **paludismo.** México. *Boln Comn nac. Errad. Palud., Méx.* [1957–] **L.**BM^N.

7645 **Boletín** de la **Compañia administradora** del **guano.** Lima. *Boln Cia adm. Guano* **L.**AM. 53–; **Lo.** 54–; **Wo.** 53–; **Y.**

7646 **Boletín. Consejo** de **medicamentos, alimentos** y **cosméticos.** La Habana. *Boln Cons. Medic. Alim. Cosmét.* [1956–] **L.**MA. 58–.

7647 **Boletín** del **Consejo nacional** de **higiene.** Montevideo. *Boln Cons. nac. Hig., Montev.*

7648 **Boletín** del **Consejo superior** de **higiene pública.** Santiago de Chile. *Boln Cons. sup. Hig. públ., Santiago*

7649 **Boletín** del **Consejo superior** de **salubridad.** México. *Boln Cons. sup. Salubr., Méx.* **C.**MD. 01–17 imp.

7650 **Boletín** del **Consejo superior** de **salubridad.** San Salvador. *Boln Cons. sup. Salubr., S Salvador*

7651 **Boletín** de **Consultas** sobre **agricultura, ganaderia** e **industrias rurales.** México. *Boln Consult. Agric. Ganad., Méx.* **L.**EB. 11–14*.

7652 **Boletín** del **Cuerpo** de **ingenieros** de **caminos.** Lima. *Boln Cuerpo Ing. Camin., Lima*

7653 **Boletín** del **Cuerpo** de **ingenieros civiles** de **Lima.** Lima. *Boln Cuerpo Ing. civ. Lima*

7654 **Boletín** del **Cuerpo** de **ingenieros** de **minas** del **Perú.** Lima. *Boln Cuerpo Ing. Minas Perú* [1902–] **L.**BM^N. imp.; GL. 04–26: 34–39; GM.; I.; MI. 02–39: 41–48; SC.; UC.; **Bl.**U. imp.; **Bm.**U. 14–38; **C.**P. 34–; **Db.**; **E.**C. 07–38; G. 13–; J. 19–; R. 02–38; U. 34–39; **G.**MG. 15– imp.; **Ld.**U. 03–; **Lv.**U. 04–13 imp.; **M.**U. 19–24 imp.; **Nw.**A. 05–14; **Pl.**M. 02–21 imp.; **Sh.**M. 02–05: 14–38.

7655 **Boletín cultural** e **informativo. Consejo general** de **colegios médicos** de **España.** Madrid. *Boln cult. inf. Cons. gen. Col. méd. Esp.* **L.**MD. 48–.

7656 **Boletín demográfico** de **España.** Madrid. *Boln demogr. Esp.* **L.**TD. 27–33*.

7657 **Boletín demográfico meteorológico.** San Luis Potosi. *Boln demogr. met., S Luis Potosi* **L.**MO. 13.

7658 **Boletín dental argentino.** Buenos Aires. *Boln dent. argent.*

7659 **Boletín dental uruguayo.** Montevideo. *Boln dent. urug.*

7660 **Boletín** del **Departamento** de **agricultura.** Santiago. *Boln Dep. Agric., Santiago* [1929–] **L.**AM. 29–30.

7661 **Boletín** del **Departamento forestal** y de **caza** y **pesca** de **México.** *Boln Dep. for. Caza Pesca Méx.* [1935–39] **L.**BM^N.; MY.; SC.; **O.**F. 36–39. [*C. as:* 7674]

7662 **Boletín** del **Departamento** de **higiene.** Córdoba. *Boln Dep. Hig., Córdoba*

7663 **Boletín** del **Departamento** de **minas** y **petroleo.** Santiago de Chile. *Boln Dep. Minas Petrol., Santiago* **L.**GL. 31–35 imp.

7664 **Boletín** del **Departamento** de **salubridad pública.** México. *Boln Dep. Salubr. públ., Méx.* **L.**EB. 25: 28; MD. 29*; **C.**PA. 17–20. [*C. as:* 48492]

7665 **Boletín** del **Departamento** de **sanidad vegetal.** Santiago de Chile. *Boln Dep. Sanid. veg., Santiago* [1941–43] **L.**EB.; MY.; **C.**A. [*C. as:* 1281]

7666 **Boletín. Departamento técnico, Instituto** de **fomento algodonero.** Bogotá. *Boln Dep. téc. Inst. Fom. algod., Bogotá*

7667 **Boletín diaro. Instituto central meteorológico** Madrid. *Boln diaro Inst. cent. met.* [1893–10] **L.**MO. [*C. as:* 7986]

7668 **Boletín diaro** del **Servicio meteorológico nacional.** Madrid. *Boln diaro Serv. met. nac.* **L.**MO. 52–.

7669 **Boletín** de la **Dirección** de **agricultura, ganadería** y **colonización.** Lima. *Boln Dir. Agric. Ganad., Lima* [1931–] **L.**EB. 42–45; **C.**A.

7670 **Boletín** de la **Dirección** de **estudios biológicos.** México. *Boln Dir. Estud. biol., Méx.* [1915–26] **L.**BM. 15–18; BM^N.; K. 15–18; TD. 15–17; **Bm.**N. 23–26; U.; **Lv.**U. 15–18; **M.**U. 15–16. [*C. of:* 2438]

7671 **Boletín** de la **Dirección general** de **aeronáutica civil.** Lima. *Boln Dir. gen. Aeronáut. civ., Lima* [1936–] **L.**AV. 52–55; BM. 45–.

7672 **Boletín** de la **Dirección general** de **agricultura.** México. *Boln Dir. gen. Agric., Méx.* **L.**EB. 11–16*; **Lv.**U. 11–12 imp. [*C. as:* 46263]

7673 **Boletín. Dirección general** de **estadística** y **estudios geográficos.** La Paz. *Boln Dir. gen. Estadíst. Estud. geogr., La Paz* **L.**MO. 19.

7674 **Boletín** de la **Dirección general forestal** y de **caza.** México. *Boln Dir. gen. for. Caza, Méx.* [1940–44] **O.**F. 42–44. [*C. of:* 7661]

7675 **Boletín** de la **Dirección general** de **ganadería.** Madrid. *Boln Dir. gen. Ganad., Madr.*

7676 **Boletín** de la **Dirección general** de **minas, geología** e **hidrología.** Buenos Aires. *Boln Dir. gen. Minas Geol. Hidrol., B. Aires* **L.**GL. 32–39; MI. (*a*) 14–21 imp.: (*b*) 13–22 imp.: (*c*) 14–21 imp.; UC. 22– imp.

7677 **Boletín. Dirección general** del **Servicio meteorológico nacional.** Montevideo. *Boln Dir. gen. Serv. met. nac., Montev.*

7678 **Boletín. Dirección general** de los **servicios agrícolas.** Santiago de Chile. *Boln Dir. gen. Serv. agríc., Santiago*

7679 **Boletín. Dirección** de **minas** y **geología.** Buenos Aires. *Boln Dir. Minas Geol., B. Aires* **L.**MI. 33–48.

7680 **Boletín. Dirección nacional** de **minería.** Buenos Aires. *Boln Dir. nac. Min., B. Aires* [1914–] **L.**MI. imp.; **Y.**

7681 **Boletín** de la **Dirección** de **tierras** y **colonias, Paraguay.** Asunción. *Boln Dir. Tierr. Colon. Parag.* **L.**BM[N]. 24–26.

7682 **Boletín** de **divulgación. Departamento** de **caza. Dirección general forestal** y de **caza.** México. *Boln Divulg. Dep. Caza, Méx.* [1950–]

Boletín de **divulgación. Departamento** de **investigación agropecuaria, Colombia.** Bogotá. *See* 16254.

7684 **Boletín** de **divulgación ganadería.** Ciudad Real. *Boln Divulg. Ganad.* **L.**V. 49–.

7685 **Boletín** de **divulgación. Instituto** de **fomento algodonero.** Bogotá. *Boln Divulg. Inst. Fom. algod., Bogotá* [1953–] **L.**P. (curr.).

7686 **Boletín** de **divulgación. Oficina** para la **defensa agrícola.** Tacubaya. *Boln Divulg. Of. Def. agríc., Tacubaya* [1927–] **L.**EB. 27–32.

7687 **Boletín** de **divulgación** de la **Sociedad rural argentina.** Buenos Aires. *Boln Divulg. Soc. rur. argent.* **L.**BM. 31–.

7688 **Boletín** de **entomología venezolana.** Caracas. *Boln Ent. venez.* [1941–] **L.**BM[N].; E.; EB. 41–57; TD. 46–49 imp.; **O.**H.; **Rt.** 41–44.

7689 **Boletín epidemiológico.** México. *Boln epidem., Méx.* [1944–] **L.**TD. 48– imp.

7690 **Boletín** de la **Escuela dental.** Santiago. *Boln Esc. dent., Santiago*

7691 **Boletín. Escuela especial** de **ingenieros** de **Lima.** Lima. *Boln Esc. esp. Ing. Lima* [*C. as:* 7694]

7692 **Boletín. Escuela** de **ingenieros** de **Guadalajara.** *Boln Esc. Ing. Guadalajara*

7693 **Boletín. Escuela nacional** de **ciencias biológicas.** México. *Boln Esc. nac. Cienc. biol., Méx.* [1939–] **L.**BM[N]. 40–46; **Db.** 40–.

7694 **Boletín. Escuela nacional** de **ingenieros.** Lima. *Boln Esc. nac. Ing., Lima* [1949–55] **L.**P. [*C. of:* 7691; *C. as:* 8179]

7695 **Boletín** de la **Escuela** de **odontología. Universidad central** de **Ecuador.** Quito. *Boln Esc. Odont. Univ. cent. Ecuad.* **L.**D. 40–44.

7696 **Boletín** de la **Escuela** de **odontología** de la **Universidad nacional.** Bogotá. *Boln Esc. Odont. Univ. nac., Bogotá*

7697 **Boletín** de la **Escuela** de **odontología, Universidad** de **San Marcos.** Lima. *Boln Esc. Odont. Univ. S Marcos* [1937–43] **L.**D. 43. [*C. as:* 7728]

7698 **Boletín** de la **Escuela práctica** de **agricultura.** Santiago de Chile. *Boln Esc. práct. Agric., Santiago*

7699 **Boletín español** de **otorrinolaringología** y **broncoesofagología.** Madrid. *Boln esp. Otorrinolar.* [1948–] **L.**MA. 52–; MD. 52–.

7700 **Boletín. Estación agrícola central.** México. *Boln Estac. agríc. cent., Méx.*

7701 **Boletín. Estación agronómica.** Madrid. *Boln Estac. agron., Madr.* **Rt.** 91–.

7702 **Boletín** de la **Estación agronómica** de **Santiago.** Santiago de Chile. *Boln Estac. agron. Santiago*

7703 **Boletín. Estación central meteorológica, climatológica** y **cosechas.** La Habana. *Boln Estac. cent. met. clim., Habana* [1904–06] **L.**MO. [*C. of:* 46132[a]; *C. as:* 8011]

7704 **Boletín** de la **Estación enológica** de **Chile.** Santiago. *Boln Estac. enol. Chile*

7705 **Boletín. Estación experimental agrícola** de **La Molina.** Lima. *Boln Estac. exp. agríc. La Molina* [1934–47: 53–] **L.**EB.; **C.**A.; **Rt.**; **Y.** [*C. of:* 7706; >7603, 1948–52]

7706 **Boletín. Estación experimental agrícola** de la **Sociedad nacional agraria.** Lima. *Boln Estac. exp. agríc. Soc. nac. agrar., Lima* [1928–29] **L.**EB.; **C.**A.; **Rt.** 29. [*C. as:* 7705]

7706° **Boletín. Estación experimental agrícola** de **Tingo María.** Huanucu. *Boln Estac. exp. agríc. Tingo María* **Y.** 54–.

7707 **Boletín. Estación experimental agrícola** de **Tucumán.** Tucumán. *Boln Estac. exp. agríc. Tucumán* [1924–] **L.**EB. (ent.) 36–49; P. 29–55; **C.**A. imp.; **Rt.** 24: 46–; **Y.**

7708 **Boletín. Estación experimental agronómica** de **Cuba.** Santiago de las Vegas. *Boln Estac. exp. agron. Cuba* [1905–] **L.**EB. 05–52; K. 08–22 imp.; MY. 15–28 imp.; **C.**A. 15–; **O.**F. 46–.

7709 **Boletín** de la **Estación experimental Cinco Saltas,** Rio Negro. Cinco Saltas. *Boln Estac. exp. Cinco Saltas* **Md.**H. 50–. [*C. of:* 51302]

Boletín. Estación experimental insular, Rio Piedras. *See* 11538.

7710 **Boletín** de la **Estación experimental** de **San Pedro** de **Montes** de **Oca.** *Boln Estac. exp. S Pedro* **C.**A. 29–.

Boletín. Estación de **experimentos agriculturales** de **Puerto Rico.** *See* 11537 and 11538.

7711 **Boletín** de la **Estación** de **patología vegetal.** Madrid. *Boln Estac. Patol. veg., Madr.* [1926–27] **L.**AM.; EB.; MY. [*C. as:* 8024]

7712 **Boletín** de la **Estación sismológica** de **Chinchiná.** Bogotá. *Boln Estac. sism. Chinchiná* [1949–]

7713 **Boletín** de la **Estación sismológica. Colegio** de **San Calixte.** La Paz. *Boln Estac. sism. Col. S Calixte*

7714 **Boletín. Estadística agropecuaria. Ministerio** de **agricultura** de la **nación.** Buenos Aires. *Boln Estadíst. agropec., B. Aires* **L.**BM, 34–42*.; BM[N]. 38–42; **E.**W. 39–42; **Rt.** 39–42. [*C. as:* 7901]

7715 **Boletín estadístico. Ministerio** de **agricultura.** Buenos Aires. *Boln estadíst. Minist. Agric., B. Aires* [1945–46] **L.**BM.; BM[N].; **E.**W.; **O.**AEC. [*C. of:* 7901; *C. as:* 49793]

7716 **Boletín** de **estudios geográficos** de la **Universidad nacional** de **Cuyo.** Mendoza. *Boln Estud. geogr. Univ. nac. Cuyo* [1948–] **L.**G.; MO.; **C.**PO. 49–; **Y.**

7716° **Boletín** de **extensión. Facultad** de **agronomía, Universidad** de **Colombia.** Bogotá. *Boln Ext. Fac. Agron. Univ. Colombia* [1948–] **L.**BM[N].

7717 **Boletín** de **extensión. Facultad** de **ciencias agrarias, Universidad nacional** de **Cuyo.** Mendoza. *Boln Ext. Fac. Cienc. agr. Univ. nac. Cuyo* [1952–] **L.**A.; BM[N].; **Bn.**U.; **C.**A.; **G.**U.; **Y.**

7718 **Boletín** de **extensión. Federación nacional** de **cafeteros.** Chinchiná, Colombia. *Boln Ext. Fed. nac. Cafet., Chinchiná* **Md.**H. 50–51 imp.

7719 **Boletín** de **extensión. Instituto** de **fomento algo-donero.** Bogotá. *Boln Ext. Inst. Fom. algod., Bogotá* [1958–] **Y.**

7720 **Boletín** de **extensión. Servicio** de **extensión agrícola.** Mayaguez. *Boln Ext. Serv. Ext. agríc., Mayaguez* [1935–]

7721 **Boletín fabril.** Lima. *Boln fabril*

7722 **Boletín. Facultad** de **agronomía** y **veterinaria** de la **Universidad** de **Buenos Aires.** *Boln Fac. Agron. Vet. Univ. B. Aires* **L.**K. 49–; **C.**A. 57–; **Y.**

7723 **Boletín** de la **Facultad** de **ciencias exactas, físicas** y **naturales, Universidad nacional** de **Córdoba.** *Boln Fac. Cienc. exact. Univ. Córdoba* [1938–] **L.**SC.
Serie ciencias naturales [1954–] **L.**SC.
Serie ingenieria civil [1954–] **L.**SC.

7724 **Boletín** de la **Facultad** de **ciencias físicas** y **matemáticas, Universidad** del **Zulia.** Maracaibo. *Boln Fac. Cienc. fís. mat. Univ. Zulia* [1951–] **O.**R.

7725 **Boletín. Facultad** de **ciencias, Universidad** de **Buenos Aires.** Buenos Aires. *Boln Fac. Cienc. Univ. B. Aires* [1947–] **Db.** 49–.

7725° **Boletín** de la **Facultad** de **ciencias, Universidad nacional** del **Cuzco.** *Boln Fac. Cienc. Univ. nac. Cuzco* [1960–] **L.**BMᴺ.

7726 **Boletín** de la **Facultad** de **ingenieria** y **agrimen-sura** de **Montevideo.** *Boln Fac. Ing. Agrim. Montev.* [1935–] **L.**P. 37– imp.; **Y.**

7727 **Boletín. Facultad** de **ingenieria forestal, Uni-versidad** de los **Andes.** Merida. *Boln Fac. Ing. for. Univ. Andes* [1954–] **O.**F.

7727° **Boletín. Facultad** de **ingenieria, Universidad** de **San Carlos** de **Guatemala.** *Boln Fac. Ing. Univ. S Carlos Guatem.* **Y.**

7728 **Boletín** de la **Facultad** de **odontología, Universi-dad** de **San Marcos.** Lima. *Boln Fac. Odont. Univ. S Marcos* [1943–] **L.**D. 43–45. [*C. of:* 7697]

7729 **Boletín farmacéutico.** Barcelona. *Boln farm.*

7730 **Boletín** de **farmacía militar.** Madrid. *Boln Farm. milit.*

7731 **Boletín** de la **Federación médica** del **Ecuador.** Quito. *Boln Fed. méd. Ecuad.* **L.**MA. 53–.

7732 **Boletín fenológico.** Buenos Aires. *Boln fenol.* [1947–] **L.**MO.; **O.**F.; **Y.**

7733 **Boletín** de **fomento, Costa Rica.** San José. *Boln Fom. C. Rica* [1911–14: 25–] **L.**BMᴺ. 11–14; EB. 13–14: 27; K. 11–14; MO. 12; Z. 11–14; **E.**B. 11–14 imp.; G. 11.

7734 **Boletín fomento ganadero.** Buenos Aires. *Boln Fom. ganad., B. Aires* [1936–] **L.**AM. imp.

7735 **Boletín fomento rural.** Buenos Aires. *Boln Fom. rur., B. Aires* [1936–] **L.**BM.

7736 **Boletín forestal.** Chihuahua. *Boln for., Chihua-hua* [1949–51] **O.**F. imp.

7737 **Boletín forestal. Departamento forestal, Ecuador.** Quito. *Boln for. Ecuad.* [1957–] **O.**F.

7737° **Boletín forestal. F.A.O.** Santiago de Chile. *Boln for. F.A.O.* [1957–] **O.**F. [*C. of:* 20046]

7738 **Boletín forestal. Servicio forestal** y de **caza, Bolivia.** La Paz. *Boln for. Serv. for. Caza Boliv.* [1956–] **L.**BMᴺ.; K.; **O.**F.; T.; **Rt.** 56.

7739 **Boletín forestal. Universidad mayor** de **San Simon.** Cochabamba, Bolivia. *Boln for. Univ. mayor S Simon* [1948–] **O.**F.

7740 **Boletín frutas** y **hortalizas.** Buenos Aires. *Boln Frut. Hort., B. Aires* [1936–] **L.**BM.

7741 **Boletín** de **geología. Dirección** de **geología, Venezuela.** Caracas. *Boln Geol. Dir. Geol. Venez.* [1951–] **L.**MI.; **Y.** [*Also special publications*]

7741° **Boletín** de **geología, Facultad** de **petróleos, Universidad industrial** de **Santander.** Bucura-manga. *Boln Geol. Fac. Petról. Univ. ind. Santander* [1958–] **L.**BMᴺ.

7742 **Boletín** de **geología** y **minería.** Caracas. *Boln Geol. Min., Caracas* [1937–] **L.**BMᴺ. 37–38.

7743 **Boletín** de **geología. Ministerio** de **minas** e **hidrocarburos, Venezuela.** Caracas. *Boln Geol. Min-ist. Minas Venez.* [1951–] **L.**BMᴺ.; GL.; GM.; MI.; **Y.**

7744 **Boletín geológico. Instituto geológico nacional, Colombia.** Bogotá. *Boln geol., Bogotá* [1953–] **L.**BMᴺ. 56–; GL.; MI.

7745 **Boletín geomagnético, Ano geofísico inter-nacional 1957/58.** La Plata. *Boln geomagn. Ano geofís. int.* [1957–] **L.**MO.

7746 **Boletín. Granja experimental algodonera** del **Atlantico.** Barranquilla. *Boln Granja exp. algod. Atlant.* [1938–] **L.**SC.

7747 **Boletín heliofísica** del **Observatorio** del **Ebro.** Tortosa. *Boln heliofís. Obs. Ebro* [1948–] **L.**MO.; **Y.** [*C. from:* 7915]

7748 **Boletín** de **hidroterapía.** Barcelona. *Boln Hid-roter.*

7749 **Boletín** de **higiene.** Jalapa, Veracruz. *Boln Hig., Jalapa* **L.**TD. 43. [*C. as:* 48494ᵃ]

7750 **Boletín** de **higiene** y **demografía.** Santiago de Chile. *Boln Hig. Demogr., Santiago* **O.**R. 02–09.

7751 **Boletín** de **higiene mental.** Lima. *Boln Hig. ment.* [1932–37] [*Replaced by:* 4632]

7752 **Boletín** de **historia natural** de la **Sociedad 'Felipe Poey'.** Habana. *Boln Hist. nat. Soc. Felipe Poey* [1950–] **L.**BMᴺ. 50–51; SC.; Z. 50–51.

7753 **Boletín** del **Hospital Carlos J. Bello.** Caracas. *Boln Hosp. Carlos J. Bello* [1948–] **L.**MA. 54–.

7754 **Boletín** del **Hospital civil** de **San Juan** de **Dios.** Quito. *Boln Hosp. civ. S Juan Dios*

7755 **Boletín. Hospital Melchor Romero.** Buenos Aires. *Boln Hosp. Melchor Romero* [1941–]

7756 **Boletín** del **Hospital militar.** Habana. *Boln Hosp. milit., Habana* [1948–] **L.**MA.

7757 **Boletín** del **Hospital Nuestra Señora** de la **Paz.** Trujillo. *Boln Hosp. Nuestra Señ. Paz*

7758 **Boletín** del **Hospital oftalmológico** de **Nuestra Señora** de la **Luz.** México. *Boln Hosp. oftal. Nuestra Señ. Luz* [1947–] **L.**OP. 51–.

7759 **Boletín** del **Hospital San Juan** de **Dios.** Val-paraíso. *Boln Hosp. S Juan Dios*

7760 **Boletín** del **Hospital sanatorio 'El Peral'.** Santiago. *Boln Hosp. sanat. El Peral* [1941–] **L.**MA. 42– imp.

7761 **Boletín** de los **hospitales.** Caracas. *Boln Hosps, Caracas* [1902–] **L.**H. 41–47; MA. 44–; TD. 06–07: 27: 36– imp.

7762 **Boletín** de los **hospitales municipales** del **distrito federal.** Caracas. *Boln Hosps mun., Caracas*

7763 **Boletín** de la **I.N.E.D.** Institución nacional de la examen y diagnóstico. La Habana. *Boln I.N.E.D.* [1959–] **L.**MD.; **Br.**U.

7764 **Boletín iberoamericano** de **cultura técnica.** *Boln iberoam. Cult. téc.* [1957–] **Y.**

7765 **Boletín indigenista.** México. *Boln indig., Méx.* [1941–] **L.**AN. 45–; **Y.** [*Supplement to:* 1892]

7766 **Boletín** de la **industría** y **comercio** del **papel.** Madrid. *Boln Ind. Com. Papel* [1907–21] **L.**SB. 07–17 imp.

7767 **Boletín** de **información. Colegio nacional** de **veterinarios** de **España.** Madrid. *Boln Inf. Col. nac. Vet. Esp.* **L.**V. 47–48*. [*C. as:* 7768]

7768 **Boletín** de **información. Consejo general** de **colegios veterinarios** de **España.** Madrid. *Boln Inf. Cons. gen. Col. vet. Esp.* [1948–53] **L.**V. [*C. of:* 7767; *C. in:* 7801]

7769 **Boletín** de **información dental.** Madrid. *Boln Inf. dent.* **L.**D.

7770 **Boletín** de **información. Departamento** de **química vegetal, Consejo superior** de **investigaciones científicas, Patronato Juan** de la **Cuerva.** *Boln Inf. Dep. Quím. veg. Patron. Juan Cuerva* **L.**P. (curr.)

7771 **Boletín** de **información** de la **Dirección general** de **arquitectura.** Madrid. *Boln Inf. Dir. gen. Arquit.* [1946–] **L.**BA.

7772 **Boletín** de **información documental** y **bibliográfica. Escuela oficial** de **telecomunicación.** Madrid. *Boln Inf. docum. biblfica Esc. of. Telecomun., Madr.* [1954–] **L.**P. [*Supplement to* and *published in:* 46368]

7773 **Boletín** de **información electronica.** Madrid. *Boln Inf. electron.* [1958] **L.**AV. [*C. as:* 46609]

7774 **Boletín** de **información** de la **Escuela nacional** de **ciencias biológicas.** México. *Boln Inf. Esc. nac. Cienc. biol., Méx.* **L.**BMN. 40–46.

7775 **Boletín** de **información. Laboratorio** del **transporte, Escuela especial** de **ingenieros** de **caminos, canales** y **puertos.** Madrid. *Boln Inf. Lab. Transp. Esc. esp. Ing. Camin., Madr.* [1952–] **L.**P. imp.

7775[a] **Boletín** de **información. Laboratorio** del **transporte** y **mecánica** del **suelo.** Madrid. *Boln Inf. Lab. Transp. Mec. Suelo, Madr.* **Y.**

7776 **Boletín** de **información** del **Ministerio** de **agricultura** (*afterwards* de **industria** y **agricultura**). Madrid. *Boln Inf. Minist. Ind. Agric., Madr.* [1948–] **L.**AM. (4 yr.); **N.**U. 49– imp.; **O.**F. imp.; **Rt.** 49–; **Sil.** imp.

Boletín de **información privada. Laboratorio** del **transporte, Escuela especial** de **ingenieros** de **caminos, canales** y **puertos,** Madrid. *See* 7775.

7777 **Boletín** de **informacion técnica. Departamento** de **parasitología.** Santiago. *Boln Inf. téc. Dep. Parasit., Santiago* [1946–48] **L.**EB.; SC.; TD.; Z.; **C.**MO.; **Sal.** [*C. as:* 7782]

7777[c] **Boletín** de **información técnica** y **estadística. Dirección general** de **minas** y **combustibles.** Madrid. *Boln Inf. téc. estadíst. Dir. gen. Minas Combust., Madr.* **L.**BM. 53–.

7778 **Boletín** de **informaciones** del **agrónomo regional** de la 1ª **zona.** La Serena. *Boln Infs Agrón. reg., La Serena*

7779 **Boletín** de **informaciones** del **agrónomo regional** de la 3ª **zona.** San Fernando. *Boln Infs Agrón. reg., S Fernando*

7780 **Boletín** de **informaciones** del **agrónomo regional** de la 4ª **zona.** Chillan. *Boln Infs Agrón. reg., Chillan*

7781 **Boletín** de **informaciones cientificas nacionales.** Quito. *Boln Infs cient. nac., Quito* [1947–] **L.**BMN.

7782 **Boletín** de **informaciones parasitarias chilenas.** Santiago. *Boln Infs parasit. chil.* [1949–53] **L.**EB.; MA. MD. imp.; SC.; TD.; Z.; **C.**MO.; **Pl.**M. 50–51; **Sal.** [*C. of:* 7777; *C. as:* 7607]

7783 **Boletín** de **informaciones petroleras.** Buenos Aires. *Boln Infs petrol.* [1924–50] **L.**BM. 45–50; SC. 48–50; **O.**B. 34–50. [*C. as:* 47033]

7784 **Boletín** de **informaciones** de los **servicios agrícolas.** Santiago de Chile. *Boln Infs Servs agríc., Santiago*

7785 **Boletín informativo. Actividades europeas** en **paleontología** de **vertebrados.** Museo de Sabadell. *Boln inf. Activid. eur. Paleont. Vertebr.* **L.**BMN. 56–.

7786 **Boletín informativo aerotécnico.** Buenos Aires. *Boln inf. aerotéc.* **L.**AV. 45–46.

7787 **Boletín informativo** de la **Asociación médica peruana 'Daniel A. Carrión'.** Lima. *Boln inf. Asoc. méd. peru.* [1934–] **L.**TD. 35–36 v. imp.

7788 **Boletín informativo. Asociación química española** de la **industria** del **cuero.** Barcelona. *Boln inf. Asoc. quím. esp. Ind. Cuero* [1959] **L.**LE.; P. [*C. of:* 7583; *C. as:* 8148]

7789 **Boletín informativo. Centro nacional** de **investigaciones** de **café, Colombia.** Chinchiná. *Boln inf. Cent. nac. Invest. Café Colombia* [1949–56] **L.**MO. 54–56; **C.**A. 51–56; **Md.**H. [*C. as:* 13525]

7790 **Boletín informativo** de la **Dirección** de **ganadería.** Buenos Aires. *Boln inf. Dir. Ganad., B. Aires* [1943–] **L.**SC.; **O.**R. [*C. of:* 8031]

7791 **Boletín informativo. Dirección nacional** de **minería.** Buenos Aires. *Boln inf. Dir. nac. Min., B. Aires* [1957–] **L.**MI.

7792 **Boletín informativo** de la **Dirección** de **sanidad vegetal.** Buenos Aires. *Boln inf. Dir. Sanid. veg., B. Aires* [1937–43] **L.**EB.

7793 **Boletín informativo. Estación experimental pergamino.** Pergamino. *Boln inf. Estac. exp. Pergamino* **Rt.** 55.

7794 **Boletín informativo** de **estadísticas agropecuarias.** Caracas. *Boln inf. Estadíst. agropec., Caracas* **L.**AM. 48–50.

7795 **Boletín informativo. Instituto cubano** de **investigaciones tecnológicas.** *Boln inf. Inst. cub. Invest. tecnol.*

7796 **Boletín informativo** del **Instituto** de la **fievre aftosa.** Caracas. *Boln inf. Inst. Fievre aftosa, Caracas* [1951–] **L.**AM.

7797 **Boletín informativo. Instituto** de **fitotécnia.** Castelar. *Boln inf. Inst. Fitotéc., Castelar* [1954–] **C.**A.; **Rt.** 54.

7798 **Boletín informativo. Instituto nacional** del **carbón, Oviedo.** Madrid. *Boln inf. Inst. nac. Carb. Oviedo* [1952–] **L.**MIE.; P.; **Sh.**M.; **Y.**

7799 **Boletín informativo. Junta reguladora** de vinos. Buenos Aires. *Boln inf. Jta regul. Vinos, B. Aires* **L.**A. 52–; SC. 36–.

Boletín informativo. Organo de la **biblioteca** del **Centro nacional** de investigaciones de café, **Chinchiná.** *See* 7789.

7799ᶜ **Boletín informativo. Sindicato** de la **construcción vidro** y **cerámica.** Madrid. *Boln inf. Sind. Constr. Vidro Cerám.* **Y.**

7800 **Boletín informativo. Sociedad dasonómica** de la **América tropical.** San José. *Boln inf. Soc. dasonom. Am. trop.* **O.**F. 55–.

7801 **Boletín informativo** del **suplemento científico. Consejo general** de **colegios veterinarios** de España. Madrid. *Boln inf. Supl. cient. Consejo gen. Col. vet. Esp.* [1957–] **L.**V.; **W.** [*C. of:* 7768 and 51455]

7802 **Boletín** de **ingenieros.** México. *Boln Ings*

7803 **Boletín. Inspección** de **geografía** y **minas.** Santiago de Chile. *Boln Insp. Geogr. Minas, Santiago*

7804 **Boletín** de la **Inspección nacional** de **ganadería** y **agricultura** de **Uruguay.** Montevideo. *Boln Insp. nac. Ganad. Agric. Urug.* **L.**AM.; BM. 15–.

7805 **Boletín. Inspección nacional** de **policia sanitaria** de los **animales.** Montevideo. *Boln Insp. nac. Polic. sanit. Anim., Montev.*

Boletín. Institución nacional de la **examen** y **diagnóstico.** La Habana. *See* 7763.

7806 **Boletín** del **Instituto** de **agricultura tropical, Universidad** de **Puerto Rico.** Mayaguez. *Boln Inst. Agric. trop. Univ. P. Rico* [1946–] **C.**A.

7807 **Boletín** del **Instituto antartico argentino.** Buenos Aires. *Boln Inst. antart. argent.* [1957–] **L.**BMᴺ.; **Wo.**

7808 **Boletín** del **Instituto bacteriológico** de **Chile.** Santiago. *Boln Inst. bact. Chile* [1942–] **L.**MD. 43–; TD imp.

7809 **Boletín** del **Instituto botánico** de la **Universidad central** del **Ecuador.** Quito. *Boln Inst. bot. Univ. cent. Equad.* [1942–] **L.**BMᴺ. imp.; **Abs.**A. 42–45.

7809ᶜ **Boletín** del **Instituto caro** y **cuervo.** Bogotá. *Boln Inst. Caro Cuervo, Bogotá* [1945–50] **L.**BM. 49–50. [*C. as:* 53079ᶜ]

7810 **Boletín** del **Instituto** de **ciencias naturales, Universidad central** del **Ecuador.** Quito. *Boln Inst. Cienc. nat. Univ. cent. Ecuad.* [1952–56] **L.**BMᴺ. 52; **Y.** [*C. as:* 14039]

7811 **Boletín** del **Instituto** de **clínica quirúrgica.** Buenos Aires. *Boln Inst. Clín. quir., B. Aires* [1925–] **L.**MA. 43–; MD. 28– imp.; S. 39–50; TD. 25–50; U. 43–50; **Br.**U. 27– imp.; **C.**UL. 28–; **Db.** 28–; **E.**U. 28–; **Lv.**U. 28–; **O.**R. 28–.

7812 **Boletín** del **Instituto español** del **caucho.** Barcelona. *Boln Inst. esp. Caucho* [1955–] **Sy.**R.

7813 **Boletín** del **Instituto español** de **oceanografía.** Madrid. *Boln Inst. esp. Oceanogr.* [1948–] **L.**AM.; BMᴺ.; L. imp.; SC.; UC.; **Abd.**M.; **E.**R.; **Lo.**; **Lv.**U.; **Mi.**; **Pl.**M.; **Wo.**

7814 **Boletín** del **Instituto** de **estudios médicos** y **biológicos, Universidad nacional** de **México.** México. *Boln Inst. Estud. méd. biol. Univ. nac. Méx.* [1945–] **L.**MD.; S.; **Br.**U. 50–; **G.**U. 55– imp.; **O.**R. 50–; **Y.** [*C. of:* 7857]

7815 **Boletín** del **Instituto experimental** de **agricultura. Departamento** de **genética.** El Valle, Venezuela. *Boln Inst. exp. Agric. Dep. Genét., El Valle* [1945–] **C.**A.

7816 **Boletín** del **Instituto experimental** de **agricultura** y **zootecnia.** El Valle, Venezuela. *Boln Inst. exp. Agric. Zootec., El Valle* [1940–]

7817 **Boletín** del **Instituto físico-geográfico** de **Costa Rica.** S José. *Boln Inst. fís.-geogr. C. Rica* [1901–04] **L.**BMᴺ.; G.; K.; MO. 01–03; **E.**G. 03–04; M. 01–03.

7817ᶜ **Boletín. Instituto forestal** de **investigaciones** y **experiencias.** Madrid. *Boln Inst. for. Invest. Exp.* **Y.**

7818 **Boletín. Instituto forestal latino-americano** de **investigación** y **capacitación.** Merida. *Boln Inst. for. lat.-am. Invest. Capacit.* [1957–] **L.**BMᴺ.; **O.**F.

7819 **Boletín. Instituto geofísico** de los **Andes colombianos.** *Boln Inst. geofís. Andes colomb.* [1949–]
Série A. Sismología **Y.**
Série C. Geología **Y.**

7820 **Boletín** del **Instituto geográfico argentino.** Buenos Aires. *Boln Inst. geogr. argent.* [1879–] **L.**G. imp.; **E.**G. 90–.

7821 **Boletín** del **Instituto** de **geología** (*formerly* **geológico**) de **México.** México. *Boln Inst. Geol. Méx.* [1895–] **L.**BM. 95–10; BMᴺ.; GL. 00–27 imp.; GM.; MI. 97–; UC. 99–02; **Bl.**U. 00–31 imp.; **Bm.**N. 99– imp.; **C.**P. 95–; S. 96–; **Cr.**N. 99– imp.; **Db.**; **E.**F. 02–; J. 08–; R. imp.; **G.**MG. 19– imp.; N.; T. 02–; **Ld.**U. 02–19; **Lv.**U. 95–23; **M.**U. 01–55 imp.; **Nw.**A. 12–50 imp.; **O.**R. 98–28; **Y.**

7822 **Boletín** del **Instituto** de **geología** y **perforaciones.** Montevideo. *Boln Inst. Geol. Perfor., Montev.* [1914–37] **L.**BMᴺ. 31–37; GL. 24–31; GM. 31–37; [*C. as:* 7825]

7823 **Boletín** del **Instituto geológico** y **minero** de **España.** Madrid. *Boln Inst. geol. min. Esp.* [1910–] **L.**BM. 11–; BMᴺ.; GL. imp.; GM.; MI. 46–; SC. 20–; **Bl.**U. 20–24; **E.**R. 11–; **Sh.**SC. 60–. [*C. of:* 7643]

7824 **Boletín** del **Instituto geológico** del **Perú.** Lima. *Boln Inst. geol. Perú* [1945–] **L.**BMᴺ.; GL.; SC.

7825 **Boletín** del **Instituto geológico** del **Uruguay.** Montevideo. *Boln Inst. geol. Urug.* [1938–] **L.**BMᴺ.; GL. 38–47; GM.; **Y.** [*C. of:* 7822]

7826 **Boletín** del **Instituto** de **higiene.** México. *Boln Inst. Hig., Méx.* [1923–37] **L.**LI. 32–36; MA. 32–35; TD. 32–36 imp. [*C. in:* 8041]

7827 **Boletín** del **Instituto indigenista nacional, Guatemala.** *Boln Inst. indig. nac. Guatem.* [1945–] **Db.** 47–.

7828 **Boletín** del **Instituto interamericano** del **niño.** Montevideo. *Boln Inst. interam. Niño* [1958–] **L.**U. [*C. of:* 7829]

7829 **Boletín** del **Instituto internacional americano** de **protección** a la **infancia.** Montevideo. *Boln Inst. int. am. Prot. Infanc.* [1927–57] **L.**MA. 47–57; TD. 29–30: 35: 51–53 imp.; U. [*C. as:* 7828]

7830 **Boletín** del **Instituto** de **investigaciones veterinarias.** Caracas. *Boln Inst. Invest. vet., Caracas* [1942–] **L.**V. imp.; **W.**; **Y.**

7830ᶜ **Boletín. Instituto** de **investigaciones veterinarias.** Maracay. *Boln Inst. Invest. vet., Maracay* **Y.**

7831 **Boletín** del **Instituto** de **matemática, astronomía y física, Universidad nacional** de **Córdoba.** Córdoba. *Boln Inst. Mat. Astr. Fís. Univ. nac. Córdoba* [1957-] **Y.**

7832 **Boletín** del **Instituto** de **maternidad.** Buenos Aires. *Boln Inst. Matern., B. Aires*

7833 **Boletín** del **Instituto** de **medicina experimental** para el **estudio** y **tratamiento** del **cáncer.** Buenos Aires. *Boln Inst. Med. exp. Estud. Trat. Cáncer, B. Aires* [1924-48] **L.**LI.; MD. 25-44; S. 24-44; TD. 25-44 imp.; **Bm.**U. 24-30; **Ld.**U. 32-43 imp.; **M.**MS. 43; **O.**P. [*C. as:* 2433]

7834 **Boletín** del **Instituto nacional** de **alimentación.** Montevideo. *Boln Inst. nac. Aliment., Montev.* [1944-] **L.**BM.; MA.; TD. 44-46. [*C. of:* 7905]

7835 **Boletín** del **Instituto nacional** de **colonización** del **Uruguay.** Montevideo. *Boln Inst. nac. Colon. Urug.* [1950-] **L.**AM. imp.; **Hu.**G. 51-52; **Rt.** 52-; **Sil.**

7836 **Boletín** del **Instituto nacional** de **higiene** de **Alfonso XIII.** Madrid. *Boln Inst. nac. Hig. Alfonso XIII* [1908-19] **L.**LI.; MD.; TD. 09-19; **Lv.**U. [*C. of:* 7849; *C. as:* 4579]

7837 **Boletín** del **Instituto nacional** de **higiene Samper Martínez.** Bogotá. *Boln Inst. nac. Hig. Samper Martínez* **L.**TD. 41-42.

7838 **Boletín** del **Instituto nacional** de **investigaciones agronómicas.** Madrid. *Boln Inst. nac. Invest. agron., Madr.* [1935-] **L.**AM. 46- imp.; BM^N.; EB.; K. 54-; TP. 53-; **Abd.**R. (curr.); **Abs.**A. 54-; **Br.**U. 48-; **E.**AB. 45- imp.; AG. 50-; R. 48-; **Hu.**G.; **Md.**H.; **N.**U. 54-; **Rt.** 42-; **Sil.** 48-; **Y.** [*Replaces:* 7839]

7839 **Boletín** del **Instituto nacional** de **investigaciones** y **experiencias agronómicas** y **forestales.** Madrid. *Boln Inst. nac. Invest. Exp. agron. for., Madr.* [1927-29] **L.**P.; **Abs.**A.; **C.**A. 28; **Rt.** [*Replaced by:* 7838]

7839° **Boletín** del **Instituto nacional** de **investigaciones** y **fomento mineros.** Lima. *Boln Inst. nac. Invest. Fom. min., Lima* [1949-] **L.**MI. 52-; **Y.**

7840 **Boletín** del **Instituto nacional** de **radium.** Bogotá. *Boln Inst. nac. Radium, Bogotá*

7841 **Boletín** del **Instituto** de **patología médica.** Madrid. *Boln Inst. Patol. méd., Madr.* [1946-61] **L.**MD. [*C. as:* Boletín de patología médica]

7842 **Boletín** del **Instituto patológico.** México. *Boln Inst. patol., Méx.*

7843 **Boletín. Instituto** de **pesca** del **Pacífico.** Sonora. *Boln Inst. Pesca Pacíf.* [1948-] **Lo.**

7844 **Boletín** del **Instituto psicopedagógico nacional.** Lima. *Boln Inst. psicoped. nac., Lima* **E.**U. 47-.

7845 **Boletín** del **Instituto** de **química** de la **Universidad nacional autónoma** de **México.** México. *Boln Inst. Quím. Univ. nac. Méx.* [1949-] **L.**C. 54-; **C.**CH. 51- imp.; **Y.**

7846 **Boletín** del **Instituto** de **radiología** y **Centro** de **estudio** y **lucha contra** el **cáncer.** Montevideo. *Boln Inst. Radiol., Montev.*

7847 **Boletín** del **Instituto sismológico, Universidad** de **Chile.** Santiago. *Boln Inst. sism. Univ. Chile* **Y.**

7848 **Boletín** del **Instituto sudamericano** del **petroleo.** Montevideo. *Boln Inst. sudam. Petrol.* [1943-] **L.**PT. (curr.); SC.

7849 **Boletín** del **Instituto** de **sueroterapía, vaccinación** y **bacteriología.** Madrid. *Boln Inst. Sueroter., Madr.* [1905-08] **L.**LI. 05-07; MD.; TD.; **Lv.**U. 05-07. [*C. as:* 7836]

7850 **Boletín interna. Instituto nacional** de la **nutrición.** Buenos Aires. *Boln interna Inst. nac. Nutr., B. Aires* [1941-]

7851 **Boletín internacional** de los **servicios** de **sanidad** de los **ejercitos** de **tierra, mar** y **aire.** Lieja. *Boln int. Servs Sanid. Ejerc.* **L.**MA. 48-; MD. 49-55 imp.

7852 **Boletín. Laboratorio** de **bacteriología** de **Tucumán.** *Boln Lab. Bact. Tucumán*

7853 **Boletín** del **Laboratorio** de **biología marina, Universidad católica** de **Santo Tomas** de **Villanueva.** Mariano. *Boln Lab. Biol. mar. Univ. cat. S Tomas, Mariano* [1956-] **L.**BM^N. 57-; **Pl.**M. 57-.

7854 **Boletín** del **Laboratorio** de **botánica.** La Plata. *Boln Lab. Bot., La Plata* [1950-] **Hu.**G. 50-51.

7855 **Boletín** del **Laboratorio** de la **Clínica 'Luis Razetti.'** Caracas. *Boln Lab. Clín. Luis Razetti* [1940-] **L.**BM^N.; MD. 43- imp.; TD.

7856 **Boletín. Laboratorio** de **entomología, Estación nacional agronómica.** Santo Domingo. *Boln Lab. Ent. S Domingo*

7857 **Boletín** del **Laboratorio** de **estudios médicos** y **biológicos.** México, D.F. *Boln Lab. Estud. méd. biol., Méx.* [1942-43] **L.**MD.; S. 42. [*C. as:* 7814]

7858 **Boletín. Laboratorio municipal** de **Guayaquil.** *Boln Lab. mun. Guayaquil* **L.**BM. 20.

7859 **Boletín** del **Laboratorio municipal** de **higiene.** Madrid. *Boln Lab. mun. Hig., Madr.*

7860 **Boletín. Laboratorio químico nacional, Colombia.** Bogotá. *Boln Lab. quím. nac. Colombia* [1954-] **Rt.** imp.; **Y.**

7861 **Boletín** de **laringología, otología** y **rinología.** Madrid. *Boln Lar. Otol. Rinol.*

7862 **Boletín** de la **Liga antileprosa** de **Cuba.** La Habana. *Boln Liga antilepr. Cuba*

7863 **Boletín. Liga argentina** de **profilaxis social.** Buenos Aires. *Boln Liga argent. Profil. soc.*

7864 **Boletín** de la **Liga argentina contra** el **reumatismo.** Buenos Aires. *Boln Liga argent. Reumat.* [1938-] **L.**MA. 44-; MD. 43-.

7865 **Boletín** de la **Liga contra** el **cáncer.** Habana. *Boln Liga Cáncer, Habana* [1926-] **L.**CB. 47-; MA. 46-; MD. 33-36; S. 47-.

7866 **Boletín** de la **Liga español contra** el **cáncer.** Madrid. *Boln Liga esp. Cáncer*

7867 **Boletín** de la **Liga uruguaya contra** el **reumatismo.** Montevideo. *Boln Liga urug. Reumat.* [1944-] **L.**MA.; MD.

7868 **Boletín matemático.** Buenos Aires. *Boln mat.* **L.**BM.

7869 **Boletín** de la **maternidad 'Concepción Palacios'.** Caracas. *Boln Matern. 'Concepción Palacios'* [1950-] **L.**MA.; MD. [*Supplement to:* 46840]

7870 **Boletín** de **medicina.** Santiago de Chile. *Boln Med., Santiago*

7871 **Boletín** de **medicina** y **cirugía.** Guayaquil. *Boln Med. Cirug., Guayaquil* **L.**BM. 12–15.

7872 **Boletín médico.** Caracas. *Boln méd., Caracas* [1948–] **L.**EB. 48–49; TD.

7873 **Boletín médico.** Huesca. *Boln méd., Huesca*

7874 **Boletín médico.** Lérida. *Boln méd., Lérida*

7875 **Boletín médico.** San Sebastian (Guipúzcoa). *Boln méd., Guipúzcoa*

7875ᵃ **Boletín médico británico.** London. *Boln méd. br.* [1943–49] **L.**BM. [*Spanish edition of:* 8906]

7876 **Boletín médico** de **Chile.** Valparaiso. *Boln méd. Chile* **L.**TD. 39–43 imp.

7877 **Boletín médico** del **Hospital infantil.** México. *Boln méd. Hosp. infant., Méx.* **L.**MA. 46–.

7878 **Boletín médico mexicano.** México. *Boln méd. mex.*

7879 **Boletín médico** del **Norte.** Iquique. *Boln méd. N.*

7880 **Boletín médico-farmacéutico extremeño.** Plasencia. *Boln méd.-farm extrem.*

7881 **Boletín médico-quirúrgico.** Santiago. *Boln méd.-quir.*

7882 **Boletín médico-social.** Santiago. *Boln méd.-soc.* **L.**MA. 46–; TD. 41– imp.

7883 **Boletín mensual** de la **Asistencia pública.** Valparaíso. *Boln mens. Asist. públ., Valparaíso*

7884 **Boletín mensual** de la **Asociación nacional** de **medicina veterinaria** de **Cuba.** *Boln mens. Asoc. nac. Med. vet. Cuba* **W.** 33–.

7885 **Boletín mensual. Centro meteorológico Palma** de **Mallorca.** *Boln mens. Cent. met. Palma Mallorca* **L.**MO. 46–.

7886 **Boletín mensual climatológico.** Las Palmas. *Boln mens. clim., Las Palmas* **L.**MO. 47. [*C. as:* 8169]

7887 **Boletín mensual climatológico.** Madrid. *Boln mens. clim., Madr.* **L.**MO. 44–.

7888 **Boletín mensual climatológico.** Santa Cruz de Tenerife. *Boln mens. clim., S Cruz Tenerife* **L.**MO. 45–49*. [*C. as:* 8170]

7889 **Boletín mensual climatológico.** Sidi Ifni. *Boln mens. clim., Sidi Ifni* **L.**MO. 47–51. [*C. as:* 8171]

7890 **Boletín mensual climatológico.** Valencia. *Boln mens. clim., Valencia* **L.**MO. 45–48.

7891 **Boletín mensual climatológico e hidrológico.** Caracas. *Boln mens. clim. hidrol., Caracas* **L.**MO. 58–.

7892 **Boletín mensual** de la **Clínica** de la **Asociación** de **damas** de la **Covadonga.** La Habana. *Boln mens. Clín. Asoc. Damas Covadonga* **L.**MD. 37–41; **E.**R. 37–40.

7893 **Boletín mensual** del **Colegio** de **médicos** de la **provincia** de **Gerona.** Gerona. *Boln mens. Col. Méd. Prov. Gerona*

7894 **Boletín mensual** de la **Comisión nacional agraria.** México. *Boln mens. Comn nac. agr., Méx.*

7895 **Boletín mensual. Defensa agrícola.** México. *Boln mens. Def. agríc., Méx.* **L.**MY. 22–35.

7896 **Boletín mensual. Dirección** de **algodón.** Buenos Aires. *Boln mens. Dir. Algodón, B. Aires* [1944–] **L.**EB. (ent.) 44–45; **M.**C. 44–46 imp.; **Y.** [*C. of:* 7907]

7897 **Boletín mensual. Dirección** de **ganadería.** Montevideo. *Boln mens. Dir. Ganad., Montev.* **E.**AB. 50–52; **W.** 43–.

7898 **Boletín mensual** de la **Direccion general** de **economía (rural) agrícola.** Mexico. *Boln mens. Dir. gen. Econ. (rur.) agríc., Méx.* **L.**AM. 47– imp.

7899 **Boletín mensual. Estación sismológica** de **Cartuja.** *Boln mens. Estac. sism. Cartuja* **L.**AS. 14–35 imp.

7900 **Boletín mensual** de **estadística agrícola.** México. *Boln mens. Estadíst. agríc., Méx.* **L.**AM. 36–38.

7901 **Boletín mensual** de **estadística agropecuaria.** Buenos Aires. *Boln mens. Estadíst. agropec., B. Aires* [1943–44] **L.**BM.; BMᴺ.; **E.**W. [*C. of:* 7714; *C. as:* 7715]

7902 **Boletín mensual dos Estados unidos mexicanos** per la **defensa agrícola.** San Jacinto. *Boln mens. Ests un. mex. Def. agríc.* [1927–]

7903 **Boletín mensual: geoeletricidad** y **meteorología. Observatorio** de **física cósmica.** San Miguel. *Boln mens. Geoelect. Met., S Miguel* [1953–] **L.**MO. [*C. from:* 7917]

7904 **Boletín mensual: heliofísica. Observatorio** de **física cósmica.** San Miguel. *Boln mens. Heliofís. S Miguel* [*C. from:* 7917]

7905 **Boletín mensual. Instituto nacional** de **alimentación.** Montevideo. *Boln mens. Inst. nac. Aliment., Montev.* [1944] **L.**BM.; TD. [*C.as:* 7834]

7906 **Boletín mensual** del **Instituto nacional físico-climatológico** de **Montevideo.** *Boln mens. Inst. nac. fís.-clim. Montev.* **L.**MO. 03–14: 16–20; **Db.** 07–13 imp.

7907 **Boletín mensual. Junta nacional** de **algodón.** Buenos Aires. *Boln mens. Jta nac. Algodón, B. Aires* **L.**EB. 41–43 imp.; **M.**C. 41–43 imp. [*C. as:* 7896]

7908 **Boletín mensual** de la **Liga** contra la **tuberculosis** en **Cuba.** Habana. *Boln mens. Liga Tuberc. Cuba*
 Boletín mensual del **Ministerio** de **agricultura.** Buenos Aires. *See* 7963.

7909 **Boletín mensual** del **Ministerio** de **industrias. Defensa agrícola.** Montevideo. *Boln mens. Minist. Ind. Def. agríc., Montev.* **L.**EB. 20–24.

7909ᵉ **Boletín mensual—observaciones astronómicas** y **microsísmicas. Observatorio** de **Cartuja.** Granada. *Boln mens. Obsnes astr. microsísm. Obs. Cartuja* [1958–] **L.**MO.; **Y.** [*C. from:* 35577]

7909ᶠ **Boletín mensual—observaciones meteorológicas. Observatorio** de **Cartuja.** Granada. *Boln mens. Obsnes mét. Obs. Cartuja* **L.**MO.; **Y.** [*C. from:* 35577]

7910 **Boletín mensual** de las **observaciones sísmicas.** Madrid. *Boln mens. Obsnes sísm., Madr.*

7910ᵉ **Boletín mensual—observaciones sísmicas. Observatorio** de **Cartuja.** Granada. *Boln mens. Obsnes sísm. Obs. Cartuja* [1957–] **L.**MO.; **Y.** [*C. from:* 35577]

7911 **Boletín mensual. Observatorio astronómico** y **meteorológico.** Quito. *Boln mens. Obs. astr. met., Quito* **L.**MO. 14. [*C. of:* 46131]

7912 **Boletín mensual. Observatorio astronómico-meteorológico** del **Colegio** del **Estado** de **Puebla.** *Boln mens. Obs. astr.-met. Col. Est. Puebla* **L.**MO. 03–04: 08–11.

7913 **Boletín [mensual. Observatorio astronómico-meteorológico, Zacatecas.** México. *Boln mens. Obs. astr.-met. Zacatecas* **L.**MO. 06–12.

7914 **Boletín mensual. Observatorio** de **Cartuja.** Granada. *Boln mens. Obs. Cartuja* **L.**AS. 05–30 imp.; MO. 09–11: 23–30: 39–47; **C.**O. 43–; **O.**G. 03–31 imp. [*See also:* 7909°, 7909ᶠ, 7910°, 7950]

7914° **Boletín mensual. Observatorio** del **Colegio San José.** Punta Arenas. *Boln mens. Obs. Col. S José* **L.**MO. 08–12. [*C. as:* 7942]

7915 **Boletín mensual** del **Observatorio** del **Ebro.** Tortosa. *Boln mens. Obs. Ebro* [1910–47] **L.**AS.; MO.; E.O. 10–14; **O.**G. 12–47; O.; **Y.** [*C. as:* 7747; 7949 and 8073]

7916 **Boletín mensual** del **Observatorio** de **El Salto.** Santiago de Chile. *Boln mens. Obs. El Salto* **L.**MO. 25–39 imp.

7917 **Boletín mensual. Observatorio** de **física cósmica.** San Miguel, R. Argentina. *Boln mens. Obs. Fís. cósm., S Miguel* [1946–52] **L.**AS.; MO.; **Db.** 49–52. [*C. as:* 7903 and 7904]

7918 **Boletín mensual. Observatorio meteorológico.** Manila. *Boln mens. Obs. met., Manila* **L.**MO. 95–01; **E.**M. 95–05.

7922 **Boletín mensual. Observatorio meteorológico central** del **Estado** de **Oaxaca.** *Boln mens. Obs. met. cent. Est. Oaxaca* **L.**MO. 97–11.

7923 **Boletín mensual. Observatorio meteorológico** de **Léon.** México. *Boln mens. Obs. met. Léon* **L.**MO. 96–13.

7924 **Boletín mensual. Observatorio meteorológico** dirigido por los **padres** de la **Compañía** de **Jesús.** Sucre. *Boln mens. Obs. met. Padr. Comp. Jesús, Sucre* **L.**MO. 15–23.

7925 **Boletín mensual** del **Observatorio meteorológico** y **sismológico central.** Tacubaya. *Boln mens. Obs. met. sism. cent., Tacubaya* **L.**MO. 17–22 imp.; **E.**M. 17–18. [*C. as:* 8059]

7926 **Boletín mensual** del **Observatorio meteorológico-magnético central** de **México.** *Boln mens. Obs. met.-magn. cent. Méx.* **L.**MO. 88–90: 95–16 imp.; **Bl.**U. 90: 96–14; **E.**C. 11–16; M. 95–18 imp.; R. 88–18; **Ld.**U 90–13; **O.**G. 88–18 imp. [*C. as:* 7562]

7927 **Boletín mensual** del **Observatorio** de **Montevideo.** *Boln mens. Obs. Montev.* **L.**MO. 89–05.

7928 **Boletín mensual** del **Observatorio nacional.** Habana. *Boln mens. Obs. nac., Habana* [1906–28] **L.**MO. 22–28; **E.**M. 25–28; **O.**G. 22–28. [*C. as:* 7991]

7929 **Boletín mensual. Observatorio** del **Seminario conciliar.** Guadalajara. *Boln mens. Obs. Semin. conc., Guadalajara*

7930 **Boletín mensual. Observatorio** del **Seminario conciliar.** Morelia. *Boln mens. Obs. Semin. conc., Morelia* **L.**MO. 09–10: 13 imp.; **E.**C. 09–10.

7931 **Boletín mensual. Oficina meteorológica nacional.** Buenos Aires. *Boln mens. Of. met. nac., B. Aires* **L.**MO. 16–28.

7932 **Boletín mensual** de **olivicultura.** Tortosa. *Boln mens. Olivic.* [1919–]

7933 **Boletín mensual. Organo** de la **Oficina** para la **defensa agrícola.** San Jacinto, D.F. *Boln mens. Org. Of. Def. agríc., S Jacinto* **L.**BMᴺ. 27–29*; EB. 27–29.

7934 **Boletín mensual. Sección meteorológica** del **Estado** de **Michoacan.** Morelia. *Boln mens. Secc. met. Est. Michoacan* **L.**MO. 07–12.

7935 **Boletín mensual** de la **Sección meteorológica** del **estado** de **Yucatán.** Mérida. *Boln mens. Secc. met. Est. Yucatán* **L.**MO. 06–16 imp.

7936 **Boletín mensual. Servicio meteorológico mexicano.** Tacubaya. *Boln mens. Serv. met. mex.*

7937 **Boletín mensual. Servicio meteorológico** del **Uruguay.** *Boln mens. Serv. met. Urug.* **L.**MO. 53–; **Y.**

7938 **Boletín mensual** del **Sindicato** de **médicos** y **professionistas conexos** de **Yucatán.** *Boln mens. Sind. Méd. Profess. conex. Yucatán* **L.**TD. 40–42 imp.

7939 **Boletín mensual** del **tiempo.** La Paz. *Boln mens. Tiempo, La Paz* **L.**MO. 43– imp.; **Y.**

7940 **Boletín** de **meteorología.** Montevideo. *Boln Met., Montev.* [1943–48] **L.**MO.; SC.

7940° **Boletín** de **meteorológia. Observatorio** del **Ebro.** *Boln Met. Obs. Ebro* **Te.**C.; **Y.**

7941 **Boletín meteorológico.** Montevideo. *Boln met., Montev.* **L.**MO. 29–31. [*C. as:* 7448]

7942 **Boletín meteorológico.** Punta Arenas. *Boln met., Punta Arenas* [1913–16] **L.**MO. [*C. of:* 7914°; *C. as:* 7561]

7943 **Boletín meteorológico, Costa Rica.** San José. *Boln met. C. Rica* **L.**MO. 51–55. [*C. as:* 7954]

7944 **Boletín meteorológico diario, Venezuela.** Maracay. *Boln met. diario Venez.* **L.**MO. 51–.

7945 **Boletín meteorológico, Ecuador.** Quito. *Boln met. Ecuad.* **L.**MO. 44–.

7946 **Boletín meteorológico** de **El Salvador.** *Boln met. El Salv.* [1953–] **L.**MO.; **Db.** 54–; **Y.** [*C. of:* 7952]

7947 **Boletín meteorológico. Instituto geofísico, Huancayo.** *Boln met. Inst. geofís. Huancayo* [1955–] **L.**MO. [*C. from:* 8071]

7948 **Boletín meteorológico. Instituto tropical** de **investigaciones científicas.** San Salvador. *Boln met. Inst. trop. Invest. cient., S Salv.* [1953–] **Db.**

7949 **Boletín meteorológico** del **Observatorio** del **Ebro.** Tortosa. *Boln met. Obs. Ebro* [1948–] **L.**MO. [*C. from:* 7747]

7950 **Boletín meteorológico. Observatorio geofísico** de **Cartuja.** Granada. *Boln met. Obs. geofís. Cartuja* [1931–32] **L.**MO.

7951 **Boletín meteorológico. Observatorio nacional, Guatemala.** Guatemala. *Boln met. Obs. nac. Guatom.* **L.**MO. 49–50.

7952 **Boletín meteorológico** de **San Salvador.** *Boln met. S Salvador* **L.**MO. 51–52*. [*C. as:* 7946]

7953 **Boletín meteorológico** y **seismológico.** Quito. *Boln met. seism., Quito* **L.**MO. 30–38. [*C. of:* 46138ᵃ]

7954 **Boletín meteorológico semestral, Costa Rica.** San José. *Boln met. semest. C. Rica* [1956–] **L.**MO. [*C. of:* 7943]
Boletín meteorológico. Servicio meteorológico nacional, San Salvador. *See* 7952.

7955 **Boletín** de **minas.** Habana. *Boln Minas, Habana* **L.**P. 27–29.

7956 **Boletín** de **minas, industrias** y **construcciones.** Lima. *Boln Minas Ind. Constr., Lima* **L.**P. 91–40.

7957 **Boletín** de **minas** y **petroleo.** Bogota. *Boln Minas Petrol., Bogota* [1929-] **L.**BM. 32-; PT. 52-.

7958 **Boletín** de **minas** y **petróleo.** México. *Boln Minas Petrol., Méx.* [1939-] **L.**BM. 46-; **Y.** [*C. of:* 8029]

7959 **Boletín** de **minas** y **petróleo.** Santiago de Chile. *Boln Minas Petrol., Santiago*

7960 **Boletín minero.** Almería. *Boln min., Almería*

7961 **Boletín minero.** México. *Boln min., Méx.* [1916-33] **L.**BM.; **C.**UL.; **E.**J.; **Ld.**U.; **Lv.**U. 16-23 imp.; **O.**R. 18-23.

7962 **Boletín minero** y **comercial.** Madrid. *Boln min. com.* **Nw.**A. 98-05.

7962ᶜ **Boletín minero** y **industrial.** Bilbao. *Boln min. ind., Bilbao* **Y.**

Boletín minero de la **Sociedad nacional** de **minería.** Santiago de Chile. *See* 8128.

7963 **Boletín** del **Ministerio** de **agricultura.** Buenos Aires. *Boln Minist. Agric., B. Aires* [1904-] **L.**AM. 04-21: 50-; BM. 08-imp.; BMᴺ. 13- imp.; E. 29-33; EB. 13-22: 29-35; G. 01-35; GM. 12-35; K. 29-32; MY. 22-35; UC. 22-35 imp.; **Abs.**N. 29-35; **Bm.**U. 29-32; **C.**A. 29-35; **Db.** 11-35; **E.**J. 14-35; U. 29-32; W. 29-34; **Lv.**U. 29-32; **M.**P. 29-35; **O.**R.; **Pl.**M. 29-32; **Sa.** 29-31.

7964 **Boletín** del **Ministerio** de **agricultura.** Guatemala. *Boln Minist. Agric., Guatemala*

7965 **Boletín** del **Ministerio** de **agricultura.** Quito. *Boln Minist. Agric., Quito* **L.**EB. (ent.) 42-43.

7966 **Boletín** del **Ministerio** de **agricultura.** Santiago. *Boln Minist. Agric., Santiago* **L.**AM. 29-30 (imp.).

Boletín. Ministerio de **agricultura** y **cria, Venezuela.** *See* 8025.

7967 **Boletín. Ministerio** de **agricultura** y **ganadería.** Managua. *Boln Minist. Agric. Ganad., Managua* [1954-] **C.**A.

7968 **Boletín** del **Ministerio** de **fomento.** Caracas. *Boln Minist. Fom., Caracas* **L.**BM. 52.

7969 **Boletín** del **Ministerio** de **fomento.** Lima. *Boln Minist. Fom., Lima* **L.**AM. 03-08; **Db.** 01-.

7970 **Boletín** del **Ministerio** de **higiene** y **salubridad.** La Paz. *Boln Minist. Hig. Salubr., La Paz* [1938-] **L.**TD. 39.

7971 **Boletín** del **Ministerio** de **sanidad** y **asistencía social.** Caracas. *Boln Minist. Sanid., Caracas* [1936-39] **L.**MA. 38-39 imp.; TD.; **Br.**U.; **Sal.** imp. [*C. as:* 46913]

7972 **Boletín miscelanea. Departamento** de **investigación agropecuaria.** Bogota. *Boln misc. Dep. Invest. agropec., Bogotá* [1957-] **C.**A.; **Rt.** 58; **Y.**

7973 **Boletín** del **Museo argentino** de **ciencias naturales 'Bernardino Rivadavia'** e **Instituto nacional** de **investigación** de **ciencias naturales.** Buenos Aires. *Boln Mus. argent. Cienc. nat. Bernardino Rivadavía* [1956-] **L.**BMᴺ. 56-58; Z.; **Y.**

7974 **Boletín** del **Museo** de **ciencias naturales.** Caracas. *Boln Mus. Cienc. nat., Caracas* [1955-] **L.**BM.; BMᴺ. 60-; Z.; **G.**U.

7975 **Boletín. Museo** de **ciencias naturales** (de **historia natural**). Tucumán. *Boln Mus. Cienc. nat., Tucumán* **L.**BMᴺ. 24-36* imp.

7976 **Boletín** del **Museo** de **historia natural 'Javier Prado'.** Lima. *Boln Mus. Hist. nat. Javier Prado* [1939-] **L.**BMᴺ. 39-46; E. 39-46 imp.

Boletín. Museo de **historia natural, Tucumán.** *See* 7975.

7977 **Boletín** del **Museo nacional** de **arqueología, historia** y **etnología.** México. *Boln Mus. nac. Arqueol., Méx.* [1911-34] **L.**BM. [*C. of:* 7981]

7978 **Boletín** del **Museo nacional** de **Chile.** Santiago de Chile. *Boln Mus. nac. Chile* [1908-36] **L.**BMᴺ.; Z. imp.; **Db.** 10; **Pl.**M. 08-11; **Y.** [*C. as:* 7980]

7979 **Boletín** del **Museo nacional** de **Costa Rica.** San José. *Boln Mus. nac. C. Rica* [1945-] **L.**BMᴺ.; 45-48 imp.; SC.; **Pl.**M. 43-56 imp.

7980 **Boletín. Museo nacional** de **historia natural, Chile.** Santiago. *Boln Mus. nac. Hist. nat. Chile* [1937-] **L.**BMᴺ.; Z. imp.; **C.**PO. 40-; **Pl.**M. 43-49 imp.; **Y.** [*C. of:* 7978]

7981 **Boletín** del **Museo nacional** de **México.** México. *Boln Mus. nac. Méx.* [1903-04] **L.**BM. 04; BMᴺ. [*C. as:* 7977]

7982 **Boletín** del **Museo** de **Valparaíso.** Valparaíso. *Boln Mus. Valparaíso* **L.**BMᴺ. 99-10 imp.

7983 **Boletín** de los **museos nacionales.** Caracas. *Boln Museos nac., Caracas* **L.**BMᴺ. 21.

7984 **Boletín** de **obras sanitarias** de la **nación.** Buenos Aires. *Boln Obras sanit. Nac., B. Aires* [1937-45] **L.**TD. 39-44; **E.**R. 37-42; **M.**P. 40-41; **O.**R.; **Wa.**W. [*C. as:* 7535]

Boletín. Observatorio astronómico, geodinámico y **meteorológico** de **Cartuja.** *See* 7909ᶜ, 7909ᶠ, 7910ᶜ and 7950.

7985 **Boletín. Observatorio astronómico nacional.** Tacubaya. *Boln Obs. astr. nac., Tacubaya* [1890-42] **L.**AS. 90-01: 12-42; MO. 90-01: 28-31; SC. 12-42; **C.**O. 12-42; **Db.** 12-42; **E.**O.; R. 12-42; **Nw.**A. 12-42 imp. [*C. as:* 7995]

7986 **Boletín** del **Observatorio central meteorológico.** Madrid. *Boln Obs. cent. met., Madr.* [1911-] **L.**MO. 11-36. [*C. of:* 7667]

Boletín del **Observatorio** del **Ebro.** Tortosa. *See* 7915.

Boletín del **Observatorio** de **El Salto.** *See* 7916 and 7940ᶜ.

7987 **Boletín. Observatorio Fabra.** Barcelona. *Boln Obs. Fabra* **L.**AS. (astr.) 19-34; MO 19-; **C.**O. 20-; **E.**O. 19-; R. 23-57; **O.**O. (astr.) 21-; **Y.** (meteor. sism.)

7988 **Boletín** del **Observatorio meteorológico. Colegio** de **Nuestra Señora** del **Recuerdo.** Madrid. *Boln Obs. met. Col. nuest. Señ. Recuerdo* **L.**MO. 03-06.

7989 **Boletín** del **Observatorio meteorológico** de la **Escuela normal** de **varones.** Tegucicalpa. *Boln Obs. met. Esc. norm. Varones, Tegucicalpa* **L.**MO. 20.

7990 **Boletín** del **Observatorio meteorológico. Sociedad geográfica** de **La Paz.** *Boln Obs. met. Soc. geogr. La Paz*

7991 **Boletín. Observatorio meteorológico municipal** de **Montevideo.** *Boln Obs. met. munic. Montev.* [*C. as:* 7993]

7992 **Boletín. Observatorio nacional argentino.** Córdoba. *Boln Obs. nac. argent.* **L.**BM. 11; **C.**O. 11-.

7993 **Boletín. Observatorio nacional físico-climatológico** de **Montevideo.** *Boln Obs. nac. fís.-climat. Montev.* **L.**SC. 10-15 imp. [*C. of:* 7991]

7994 **Boletín** del **Observatorio nacional.** Habana. *Boln Obs. nac., Habana* [1936–] **L.**MO.; **E.**M.; **O.**G. 36–38. [*C. of:* 7928]

7995 **Boletín** de los **observatorios Tonantzintla** y **Tacubaya.** México. *Boln Observs Tonantzintla Tacubaya* [1952–] **L.**AS.; SC.; **C.**O.; **Db.**; **E.**O.; R.; **Ld.**U. 60–; **M.**U. imp.; **Nw.**A.; **Y.** [*C. of:* 7985]

7996 **Boletín** de **oceanografía** y **pescas.** Madrid. *Boln Oceanogr. Pesc.* [1930–32] **L.**AM. 30–31; BM[N]. imp.; MO.; **Abd.**M. imp.; **E.**R. 30; **Lo.** 30–31; **Lv.**U.; **Mi.**; **Pl.**M. imp.; [*C. of:* 8027]

7997 **Boletín** de **odontología.** Bogota. *Boln Odont., Bogota* **L.**D. 40.

7998 **Boletín odontológico mexicano.** México. *Boln odont. mex.* **L.**D. 42– imp.

7999 **Boletín oficial** de la **Asociación** de **técnicos azucareros** de **Cuba.** Habana. *Boln of. Asoc. Téc. azuc. Cuba* [1942–] **L.**P. 55– imp.; **C.**A. (1 yr).

8000 **Boletín oficial** del **C.M.V.N.** Colegio medico veterinario nacional. La Habana. *Boln of. C.M.V.N., Habana* **L.**V. 43–48 imp.

8001 **Boletín oficial** del **Colegio** de **farmacéuticos.** Palencia. *Boln of. Col. Farm., Palencia*

8002 **Boletín oficial** del **Colegio** de **farmacéuticos.** Zaragoza. *Boln of. Col. Farm., Zaragoza*

8003 **Boletín oficial** del **Colegio** de **médicos.** Almería. *Boln of. Col. Méd., Almería*

8004 **Boletín oficial** del **Colegio** de **médicos.** Barcelona. *Boln of. Col. Méd., Barcelona*

8005 **Boletín oficial** des **Consejo general** de **colegios** de **odontologos.** Oviedo. *Boln of. Cons. gen. Col. Odont., Oviedo* **L.**D. 45–.

8006 **Boletín oficial. Facultad** de **ciencias médicas, Universidad** de **Buenos Aires.** *Boln of. Fac. Cienc. méd. Univ. B. Aires* [1944–] **L.**TD. 44.

8007 **Boletín oficial** de **marcas** y **patentes.** Habana. *Boln of. Marc. Pat., Habana* **L.**P. 06–.

8008 **Boletín oficial** de **minas, metalurgia** (y **combustibles).** Madrid. *Boln of. Minas Metal., Madr.* **L.**GL. 27–36; GM. 24–; MI. 27–36 imp.

8009 **Boletín oficial** de **minas** y **petróleo, Peru.** Lima. *Boln of. Minas Petrol. Peru*

8010 **Boletín oficial** del **Ministerio** de **fomento.** Madrid. *Boln of. Minist. Fom., Madr.* **L.**BM. 62–24.

8011 **Boletín oficial** de la **Secretaría** de **agricultura, comercio** y **trabajo.** Habana. *Boln of. Secr. Agric. Com. Trab., Habana* [1906–] **L.**BM.; MO. 06–12; E.M. 23–. [*C. of:* 7703]

8012 **Boletín oficial** de la **Secretaría** de **agricultura** y **fomento.** México. *Boln of. Secr. Agric. Fom., Méx.* [1908–25] **L.**BM[N]. 22–25 imp.; GL. 23–25 imp.; MO. 22–24; E.C. 23–25 imp.; M. 22–25; R. 22–25. [*C. of:* 8051]

8013 **Boletín oficial** de la **Secretaría** de **sanidad** y **beneficiencia.** Habana. *Boln of. Secr. Sanid., Habana* **Lv.**U. 19–.

8014 **Boletín oficial. Servicio meteorológico, climatológico** y de **cosechas** de la **Habana.** Habana. *Boln of. Serv. met. Habana*

8015 **Boletín. Oficina** para la **defensa agrícola.** Tacubaya. *Boln Of. Def. agríc., Tacubaya* **L.**EB. 27–29★.

8016 **Boletín** de la **Oficina meteorológica argentina.** Buenos Aires. *Boln Of. met. argent.* **L.**MO. 11–14; **E.**R. 11–19; **M.**P. 23–; **O.**G. 16–23 imp.

8017 **Boletín. Oficina** de **patología vegetal.** Habana. *Boln Of. Patol. veg., Habana*

8018 **Boletín. Oficina** de **sanidad nacional.** Caracas. *Boln Of. Sanid. nac., Caracas* **L.**BM. 18★; **O.**R. 17–18.

8019 **Boletín. Oficina** de **sanidad vegetal.** Habana. *Boln Of. Sanid. veg., Habana* **L.**EB. 17–23.

8020 **Boletín** de la **Oficina sanitaria pan-americana.** Washington. *Boln Of. sanit. pan-am.* [1923–] **L.**EB. 43–; H. 33–; MA. 31–; MD. 36–; SH. 41–56; TD.; **Y.** [*C. of:* 8023; *also supplements*]

8021 **Boletín** de **oleicultura internacional.** Madrid. *Boln Oleicult. int.* [1951–] **L.**AM. imp.; **Md.**H.

8021ᶜ **Boletín** de **orientación profesional** y **industrial** de la **Revista** de **telecomunicación.** Madrid. *Boln Orient. prof. ind. Revta Telecomun.* **Y.** [*Supplement to:* 46995]

8022 **Boletín paleontológico** de **Buenos Aires.** *Boln paleont. B. Aires* [1934–] **L.**BM[N]. 34–55 imp.; Z. 54–55.

8023 **Boletín pan-americano** de **sanidad** de la **Oficina sanitaria internacional.** Washington. *Boln pan-am. Sanid.* **L.**TD. 22–23★. [*C. as:* 8020]
     Boletín de **patologia medica.** Madrid. *See* 7841.

8024 **Boletín** de **patología vegetal** y **entomología agrícola.** Madrid. *Boln Patol. veg. Ent. agric.* [1927–] **L.**AM. 27–55 imp.; BM[N]. 51–; EB.; MY. 27–41: 44–52; **C.**A. 50–; **Y.** [*C. of:* 7711]

8025 **Boletín** de **pesca. Ministerio** de **agricultura** y **cría.** Caracas. *Boln Pesca Minist. Agric. Cria, Caracas* **L.**BM[N]. 52–.

8026 **Boletín** de **pesca** y **caza.** Madrid. *Boln Pesca Caza* [1916–] **Fr.** 35–36; **Lo.** 16–31.
     Boletín de **pesca** de la **Republica** de **Venezuela.** *See* 8025.

8027 **Boletín** de **pescas. Instituto español** de **oceanografía.** Madrid. *Boln Pescas* [1916–30] **L.**AM.; BM[N].; MO. 21–30; Z. 17–30 imp.; **Abd.**M.; **Lo.**; **Lv.**U.; **Mi.**; **Pl.**M. 21–30; **Wo.** 16–22 imp. [*C. as:* 7996]

8028 **Boletín** del **petróleo.** México. *Boln Petról., Méx.* [1917–33] **L.**BM.; P. 24–33; SC. 26–33; **E.**J.; **Ld.**U.; **Lv.**U. imp.; **O.**B. [*C. as:* 8029]

8029 **Boletín** de **petróleo** y **minas.** México. *Boln Petról. Minas, Méx.* [1933–39] **L.**BM.; GL.; P.; SC.; **E.**J.; **Ld.**U.; **Lv.**U.; **O.**B. [*C. of:* 8028; *C. as:* 7958]

8030 **Boletín platanero** y **agrícola.** México. *Boln platan. agríc.* [1938–39] [*C. as:* 1225ᶜ]

8031 **Boletín** de **policía sanitaria** de los **animales.** Buenos Aires. *Boln Polic. sanit. Anim.* **O.**R. 34–42★. [*C. as:* 7790]

8032 **Boletín** de **Pro-Cultura regional S.C.L. Mazatlan,** Sinaloa. *Boln Pro-cult. reg. S.C.L. Mazatlan* **L.**K. 29–36.

8033 **Boletín** de **producción** y **fomento agrícolo.** Buenos Aires. *Boln Prod. Fom. agríc., B. Aires* [1949–] **L.**AM.; **C.**A.; **Hu.**G.; **Md.**H. 52–; **Rt.**

8034 **Boletín** de la **R. Academia** de **ciencias** y **artes** de **Barcelona.** Barcelona. *Boln R. Acad. Cienc. Artes Barcelona* [1892–31] **L.**BM. 92–94; BM[N].; MO. 16–20 imp.; **Db.** 17–31; **E.**C. 17–19; **Lv.**U. 17–31; **M.**U. 17–28. [*C. as:* 7528]

8034ª **Boletín** de la **R. Academia** de **Córdoba** de **ciencias, bellas letras** y **nobles artes.** Córdoba. *Boln R. Acad. Córdoba* **L.**BM. 52–; **O.**B. 44–.

8035 **Boletín** de la **R. Academia gallega.** Coruña. *Boln R. Acad. gallega* [1906–] **L.**SC. 16–31; **C.**UL.; **Db.** 42–; **O.**B.; 11–35.

8036 **Boletín** de la **R. Academia** de **historia natural.** Madrid. *Boln R. Acad. Hist. nat.* **Abs.**N. 26–.

8037 **Boletín** de la **R. Sociedad española** de **historia natural.** Madrid. *Boln R. Soc. esp. Hist. nat.* [1901–] **L.**BM.; BMᴺ.; E. 20–37; GM. 09–; MY. 22–37; R. 01–19; SC. 26–; Z.; **C.**UL.; **Dm.** 14–33; **E.**C. 01–37; U. 01–04; **G.**N.; **O.**R. 04–. [*From* 1950 *divided into sections*]

8038 **Boletín. R. Sociedad geográfica.** Madrid. *Boln R. Soc. geogr.* [1876–] **L.**BM.; G. imp.; **Db.**; **E.**G. 85–.

8039 **Boletín** de **radiactividad.** Madrid. *Boln Radiactiv.* **Abd.**S. 51–54; **Y.**

8040 **Boletín** de la **Revista** de **medicina** y **cirugía prácticas.** Madrid. *Boln Revta Med. Cirug. práct.*
Boletín de **salubridrad** y **asistencia.** México. *See* 48494ª.

8041 **Boletín** de **salubridad** e **higiene.** México. *Boln Salubr. Hig.* [1937–] **O.**R. 38–. [*C. of:* 7826 *and* 48492]

8042 **Boletín** de **salud pública.** Montevideo. *Boln Salud públ.* [1941–] **L.**TD. 41–45.
Boletín de **sanidad vegetal.** Santiago de Chile. *See* 7665.

8043 **Boletín sanitario.** Buenos Aires. *Boln sanit., B. Aires* [1937–43] **L.**H. 40–43; LI. 37–39; TD.; **Bl.**U.; **Br.**U.; **Dn.**U. 39–40; 42; **M.**MS. imp.; **O.**R.

8044 **Boletín sanitario.** San Salvador. *Boln sanit., S Salv.*

8045 **Boletín sanitario.** Santiago de Chile. *Boln sanit., Santiago* [1927–] **L.**TD.

8046 **Boletín sanitario internacional.** Santiago de Chile. *Boln sanit. int.*

8047 **Boletín sanitorio São Lucas.** São Paulo. *Boln sanit. S Lucas* **Bl.**U. 45–.

8048 **Boletín** de la **Sección** de **geografía** y **minas** de la **Dirección** de **obras públicas.** Santiago de Chile. *Boln Secc. Geogr. Minas, Santiago*

8049 **Boletín** de la **Sección** de **investigaciones geográficas. Instituto** de **estudios superiores** del **Uruguay.** Montevideo. *Boln Secc. Invest. geogr. Inst. Estud. sup. Urug.* **L.**G. 38–.

8050 **Boletín. Secretaría** de **agricultura. Sección** de **publicaciones** y **difusión** de **ensenanza agrícola.** Santo Domingo. *Boln Secr. Agric., S Domingo* [1932–]

8051 **Boletín** de la **Secretaría** de **fomento.** México. *Boln Secr. Fom., Méx.* [1891–08] **L.**BM. 97–03; P. 01–04. [*C. as:* 8012]

8052 **Boletín** de la **Secretaría** de **fomento, obras públicas** y **agricultura.** Tegucicalpa. *Boln Secr. Fom. Obr. públ. Agric., Tegucicalpa* **L.**AM. 13–14.

8053 **Boletín** de **seguridad** e **higiene** del **trabajo.** Madrid. *Boln Segur. Hig. Trab., Madr.* **L.**MA. 45–; TD. 44–46 imp.

8054 **Boletín semanal. Departamento** de **salubridad pública.** México. *Boln sem. Dep. Salubr. públ., Méx.*

8055 **Boletín semestral. Sección fito-meteorológica** de la **Estación experimental** de **Riego.** Montevideo. *Boln semest. Secc. fito-met. Estac. exp. Riego* **L.**MD. 07: 32–37: 40–44.

8056 **Boletín** del **Seminario matemático argentino.** Buenos Aires. *Boln Semin. mat. argent.* [1928–] **L.**M.; UC.; **C.**P. 29–; **E.**C. 28–29; R. 28–38; **Ld.**U. 28–30 imp.

8057 **Boletín. Servicio geológico nacional** de **Nicaragua.** Managua. *Boln Serv. geol. nac. Nicaragua* [1957–] **L.**GM.

8058 **Boletín** del **Servicio meteorológico.** Buenos Aires. *Boln Serv. met., B. Aires*

8059 **Boletín** del **Servicio meteorológico mexicano.** Tacubaya. *Boln. Serv. met. mex.* **L.**MO. 33–39 imp.; **E.**C. 23–30 imp.; **O.**G. 18–38 imp. [*C. of:* 7925]

8060 **Boletín** del **Servicio meteorológico nacional.** Lima. *Boln Serv. met. nac., Lima* [1929–34] **L.**MO. [*C. as:* 46135]

8061 **Boletín** del **Servicio nacional** de **protección materno-infantil.** Lima. *Boln Serv. nac. Prot. materno-infant.* [1941–] **L.**TD. 43–45 imp.

8062 **Boletín** del **Servicio oceanográfico.** Montevideo. *Boln Serv. oceanogr., Montev.* **Dm.** 38; **Pl.**M. 38.

8063 **Boletín** del **Servicio** de **plagas forestales.** Madrid. *Boln Serv. Plagas for.* [1958–] **L.**EB.; **O.**F.; **Y.**

8064 **Boletín. Servicio** de **policía sanitaria vegetal.** Santiago de Chile. *Boln Serv. Polic. sanit. veg., Santiago*

8065 **Boletín. Servicio** de **sanidad pública.** Guayaquil. *Boln Serv. Sanid. públ., Guayaquil*

8066 **Boletín** del **Servicio sismológico** de la **Universidad** de **Chile.** Santiago de Chile. *Boln Serv. sism. Univ. Chile* **L.**BM. 30–36 imp.; SC. 28–38; **O.**O. 06–13.

8067 **Boletín** del **Sindicato** de **médicos** de **Chile.** Valparaiso. *Boln Sind. Méd. Chile*

8068 **Boletín. Sindicato** de **médicos** de la **República Argentina.** Buenos Aires. *Boln Sind. Méd. Repub. Argent.*

8068ᶜ **Boletín. Sindicato nacional** del **metal.** Madrid. *Boln Sind. nac. Metal* **Y.**

8069 **Boletín sísmico. Instituto geofísico** de los **Andes colombianos.** Bogotá. *Boln sísm. Inst. geofís. Andes colomb.* [1949–] **Y.**

8069ᶜ **Boletín sísmico. Instituto geofísico.** Huancayo. *Boln sísm. Inst. geofís., Huancayo* [1955–] **L.**MO. [*C. from:* 8071]

8070 **Boletín sísmico. Instituto** y **Observatorio** de **marina** de **San Fernando.** *Boln sísm. Inst. Obs. Mar. S Fernando*

8071 **Boletín sísmico** y **meteorológico. Instituto geofísico.** Huancayo. *Boln sísm. met. Inst. geofís., Huancayo* **L.**MO. 52–54. [*C. as:* 7947 *and* 8069ᶜ]

8072 **Boletín sísmico. Observatorio geofísico** de **Cartuja.** Granada. *Boln sísm. Obs. geofís. Cartuja*
Boletín sísmico del **Observatorio, La Paz.** *See* 7713.

8073 **Boletín sismológico** del **Observatorio** del **Ebro.** Tortosa. *Boln sism. Obs. Ebro* [1948–] **L.**AS.; MO.; **O.**G.; **Y.** [*C. from:* 7915]

8074 **Boletín sismológico** del **Servicio geológico nacional** de **El Salvador.** Salvador. *Boln sism. Serv. geol. nac. El Salvador* [1954–] **Y.**

8075 **Boletín sismológico. Servicio meteorológico nacional.** San Salvador. *Boln sism. Serv. met. nac., S Salvador* [1954–] **Db.**; **Y.**

8076 **Boletín** de la **Sociedad agrícola** del **Norte.** La Serena. *Boln Soc. agríc. N.*

8077 **Boletín** de la **Sociedad agrícola** del **Sur.** Concepción. *Boln Soc. agríc. S.*

8078 **Boletín** de la **Sociedad Amigos** de las **ciencias naturales 'Kraglievich-Fontana.'** Nueva Palmira. *Boln Soc. Amig. Cienc. nat. Kraglievich-Fontana* [1938-] **L.**BM. 38; BM^N. 38-39.

8079 **Boletín** de la **Sociedad** de **anatomía patológica.** Montevideo. *Boln Soc. Anat. patol., Montev.* **Bm.**U. 30-; **C.**UL. 30-.

8080 **Boletín** de la **Sociedad aragonesa** de **ciencias naturales.** Zaragoza. *Boln Soc. aragon. Cienc. nat.* [1892-18] **L.**BM^N. 02-18. [*C. as:* 8117]

8081 **Boletín** de la **Sociedad argentina** de **angiología.** Buenos Aires. *Boln Soc. argent. Angiol.* [1956-] **L.**MA.; MD.

8082 **Boletín** de la **Sociedad argentina** de **botanica.** La Plata. *Boln Soc. argent. Bot.* [1945-] **L.**BM^N.; K.; **Y.**

8083 **Boletín** de la **Sociedad argentina** de **ciencias naturales.** Buenos Aires. *Boln Soc. argent. Cienc. nat.* **L.**SC. 25-.

8083° **Boletín** de la **Sociedad argentina** de **estudios geográficos.** Buenos Aires. *Boln Soc. argent. Estud. geogr.* **L.**BM. 54-.

8084 **Boletín** de la **Sociedad argentina** de **horticultura.** Buenos Aires. *Boln Soc. argent. Hort.* **L.**HS. 43-; **Y.**

8085 **Boletín** de la **Sociedad astronómica** de **Barcelona.** *Boln Soc. astr. Barcelona* **L.**AS. 10-21; BM. 12.

8086 **Boletín** de la **Sociedad astronómica** de **México.** *Boln Soc. astr. Méx.*

8087 **Boletín** de la **Sociedad** de **biología** de **Concepción** (Chile). *Boln Soc. Biol. Concepción* [1927-] **L.**BM^N.; L.; **C.**P.; UL. 27-28; **Db.**; **E.**R. 27-28; **Y.**

8088 **Boletín** de la **Sociedad** de **biología** de **Santiago** de **Chile.** Santiago de Chile. *Boln Soc. Biol. Santiago Chile* [1942-] **L.**MD. 48-54. [*Supplement to:* 46728]

8089 **Boletín** de la **Sociedad boliviana** de **pediatría.** La Paz. *Boln Soc. boliv. Pediat.* [1947-] **L.**MD. 50-52.

8090 **Boletín** de la **Sociedad chilena** de **obstetricia** y **ginecología.** Santiago. *Boln Soc. chil. Obstet. Ginec.* [1935-] **L.**MA. 46-.

8091 **Boletín** de la **Sociedad chilena** de **química.** Santiago de Chile, Concepción. *Boln Soc. chil. Quím.* [1949-] **L.**C. 50- imp.; P. 58-; **Y.**

8092 **Boletín** de la **Sociedad** de **ciencias naturales** del **Instituto** de **La Salle.** Bogotá. *Boln Soc. Cienc. nat. Inst. La Salle* [1913-18] **L.**BM^N. [*C. as:* 8098]

8093 **Boletín** de la **Sociedad** de **cirugía** de **Barcelona.** *Boln Soc. Cirug. Barcelona*

8094 **Boletín** de la **Sociedad** de **cirugía** de **Chile.** Santiago. *Boln Soc. Cirug. Chile* [1922-]

8095 **Boletín** de la **Sociedad** de **cirugía** del **Montevideo.** *Boln Soc. Cirug. Montev.* **L.**S. 30-34*. [*C. as:* 8097]

8096 **Boletín. Sociedad** de **cirugía** de **Rosario.** Rosario. *Boln Soc. Cirug. Rosario*

8097 **Boletín** de la **Sociedad** de **cirugía** del **Uruguay** Montevideo. *Boln Soc. Cirug. Urug.* [1934-] **L.**MA. 46-; S. 48-; **Nw.**A. 47-. [*C. of:* 8095]

8098 **Boletín. Sociedad colombiana** de **ciencias naturales.** Bogotá. *Boln Soc. colomb. Cienc. nat.* [1918-29] **L.**BM^N.; E. 24-29. [*C. of:* 8092; *C. as:* 46945]

8099 **Boletín** de la **Sociedad cubana** de **dermatología** y **sifilografía.** Habana. *Boln Soc. cub. Derm. Sif.* [1929-] **L.**MA.; MD. 29-30; TD. 51- imp.

8100 **Boletín** de la **Sociedad cubana** de **pediatría.** *Boln Soc. cub. Pediat.* [1929-] **L.**MA. 32-45; MD. [*C. as:* 46458]

8101 **Boletín** de la **Sociedad** de **dermatología** y **sifilografía** de la **Asociación médica argentina.** Buenos Aires. *Boln Soc. Derm. Sif. Asoc. méd. argent.* [1934-] **L.**MD. 34-36; **Bl.**U.

8102 **Boletín** de la **Sociedad entomológica argentina.** Buenos Aires. *Boln Soc. ent. argent.* [1925-31: 38-] **L.**BM^N. 25-31; E. 25-29; EB. 25-31; **O.**H. 25-31.

8103 **Boletín** de la **Sociedad entomológica** de **Chile.** Santiago. *Boln Soc. ent. Chile* [1928] **L.**E.

8104 **Boletín** de la **Sociedad entomológica** de **España.** Zaragoza. *Boln Soc. ent. Esp.* [1918-36] **L.**BM^N. 18-35 imp.; E.; EB.

8105 **Boletín** de la **Sociedad española** de **biología.** Madrid. *Boln Soc. esp. Biol.*

8106 **Boletín** de la **Sociedad española** de **historia** de la **farmacía.** Madrid. *Boln Soc. esp. Hist. Farm.* [1950-] **L.**SC.

8107 **Boletín** de la **Sociedad** de **estudios vascos.** San Sebastian. *Boln Soc. Estud. vascos* **L.**AN. 21-36.

8108 **Boletín** de la **Sociedad** de **fomento fabril.** Santiago de Chile. *Boln Soc. Fom. fabr., Santiago* **L.**P. 10-34*. [*C. as:* 23121]

8109 **Boletín. Sociedad ganadera** del **Paraguay.** Asunción. *Boln Soc. ganad. Parag.*

8110 **Boletín** de la **Sociedad** de **geografía** y **estadística** de la **República mexicana.** México. *Boln Soc. Geogr. Estadíst. Repúb. méx.* [1839-] **L.**BM. 1852-89; G. 63- imp.; **C.**UL. 18-; **E.**G. 13-; L. 79-; R. 73-88 imp.; **Lv.**U. 18-19.

8111 **Boletín** de la **Sociedad geográfica** de **Colombia.** Bogotá. *Boln Soc. geogr. Colombia* [1907: 34-] **Y.**

8112 **Boletín** de la **Sociedad geográfica** de **La Paz.** *Boln Soc. geogr. La Paz* [1898-31: 41-] **L.**BM. 98-11; G. 89-; **E.**G. 02-.

8113 **Boletín** de la **Sociedad geográfica** de **Lima.** Lima. *Boln Soc. geogr. Lima* [1891-] **L.**BM. 91-12; G. 92-[imp.; **C.**UL. 04-; **Cr.**N. 24-; **E.**G. 94-; **Lv.**U. 04; **Y.**

8114 **Boletín. Sociedad geográfica** de **Sucre.** Sucre. *Boln Soc. geogr. Sucre* [1898-] **L.**BM. 04-; G. 04-08 imp.

8115 **Boletín** de la **Sociedad geológica mexicana.** México. *Boln Soc. geol. mex.* [1905-] **L.**BM^N. 05-12; GL. 05-12; GM. 05-12; UC. 05-36 imp.; **Db.** 05-12; **Ld.**U. 05-11; **Lv.**U. 05-48. [*Suspended* 1912-35]

8116 **Boletín** de la **Sociedad geológica** del **Perú.** Lima. *Boln Soc. geol. Perú* [1925-] **L.**BM^N.; GL.; GM.; UC.; **Bl.**U. 26-29; **C.**P. 25-29; S. 50- imp.; **Lv.**U. 25-26; **Y.**

8117 **Boletín. Sociedad ibérica** de **ciencias naturales.** Zaragoza. *Boln Soc. ibér. Cienc. nat.* [1919-] **L.**BM^N. 19-36; **E.**V. 19-20. [*C. of:* 8080]

8118 **Boletín** de la **Sociedad indianista mexicana.** México. *Boln Soc. indian. mex.*

8119 **Boletín** de la **Sociedad** de **ingenieros.** Lima. *Boln Soc. Ing., Lima*

8120 **Boletín** de la **Sociedad malagueña** de **ciencias.** Málaga. *Boln Soc. malag. Cienc.* **L.**MO. 11–12; **E.**V. 19–.

8121 **Boletín** de la **Sociedad matemática mexicana.** México, D.F. *Boln Soc. mat. mex.* **L.**M.; SC. 56–; **E.**R. 43–; **G.**U. 56–; **Y.**

8122 **Boletín** de la **Sociedad médica** del **Centro materno-infantil general Maximino Avila Camacho.** Tacubaya. *Boln Soc. méd. Cent. materno-infant. gen. Maximino Avila Camacho* [1949–] **L.**MA.

8123 **Boletín** de la **Sociedad médica** de **Mendoza.** *Boln Soc. méd. Mendoza* **L.**MA. 47–53. [*C. as:* 7612]

8124 **Boletín** de la **Sociedad mexicana** de **electro-radiología.** México. *Boln Soc. mex. Electro-radiol.*
Boletín de la **Sociedad mexicana** de **geografía** y **estadística.** *See* 8110.

8125 **Boletín** de la **Sociedad michoacana** de **geografía** y **estadística.** Morelia. *Boln Soc. michoac. Geogr. Estadíst.*

8125ᶜ **Boletín** de la **Sociedad nacional agraria.** Lima. *Boln Soc. nac. agr., Lima* **Y.**

8126 **Boletín** de la **Sociedad nacional** de **agricultura.** Santiago de Chile. *Boln Soc. nac. Agric., Santiago* [1869–33] [>1247, 1916–21; *C. as:* 13101]

8127 **Boletín** de la **Sociedad nacional** de **agricultura** de **Costa Rica.** San José. *Boln Soc. nac. Agric. C. Rica* [1906–10] **L.**BMᴺ. 07–10; K.

8128 **Boletín** de la **Sociedad nacional** de **minería.** Santiago de Chile. *Boln Soc. nac. Min., Santiago* [1883–] **L.**GL. 00–; MIE. 08–40; SC. 29–; **Bm.**U. 10–19; **G.**MG. 08– imp.; **M.**U. 06–26; **Sh.**M. 40–41.

8129 **Boletín** de la **Sociedad nacional** de **minería** del **Peru.** Lima. *Boln Soc. nac. Min. Peru* [1898–08: 43–52] **L.**MI. 46–; P. 43–52; PT. (curr.); SC. 43–52. [*C. as:* 8130]

8130 **Boletín.** **Sociedad nacional** de **minería** y **petróleo.** Lima. *Boln Soc. nac. Min. Petrol., Lima* [1952–] **L.**MI.; P.; PT. (curr.); **Y.** [*C. of:* 8129]

8131 **Boletín** de la **Sociedad** de **obstetricia** y **ginecología** de **Buenos Aires.** *Boln Soc. Obstet. Ginec. B. Aires* **L.**MD. 24–40.

8132 **Boletín** de la **Sociedad** de **oceanografía** de **Guipúzcoa.** San Sebastian. *Boln Soc. Oceanogr. Guipúzcoa* **L.**MO. 08.

8133 **Boletín. Sociedad** de **oftalmología.** Buenos Aires. *Boln Soc. Oftal., B. Aires*

8134 **Boletín** de la **Sociedad** de **pediatría** de **Montevideo.** *Boln Soc. Pediat. Montev.* [1927–29] [*Replaced by:* 4631]

8135 **Boletín** de la **Sociedad peruana** de **botanica.** Lima. *Boln Soc. peru. Bot.* [1948–] **L.**K.

8136 **Boletín. Sociedad peruana** de **historia** de la **medicina.** Lima. *Boln Soc. peru. Hist. Med.* [1939–]

8137 **Boletín** de la **Sociedad Physis** para el **cultivo** y **difusión** de las **ciencias naturales** en la **Argentina.** Buenos Aires. *Boln Soc. Physis* [1912–15] **L.**BMᴺ. imp.; EB.; K.; R.; Z.; **E.**R.; **Lv.**U. [*C. as:* 37734]

8138 **Boletín** de la **Sociedad química** del **Perú.** Lima. *Boln Soc. quím. Perú* [1934–] **L.**C.; **Y.**

8139 **Boletín** de la **Sociedad Taguato.** Montevideo. *Boln Soc. Taguato* [1958–] **L.**BMᴺ; Z.

8140 **Boletín** de la **Sociedad tipográfica bonaerense.** Buenos Aires. *Boln Soc. tipogr. bonaer.* **L.**SB. 11–14 imp.

8140ᵒ **Boletín** de la **Sociedad valenciana** de **pediatría.** Valencia. *Boln Soc. valenc. Pediat.* [1959–]

8141 **Boletín** de la **Sociedad venezolana** de **ciencias naturales.** Caracas. *Boln Soc. venez. Cienc. nat.* [1931–] **L.**BM. 48; BMᴺ.; EB.; **Y.**

8142 **Boletín** de la **Sociedad venezolana** de **cirugía.** Caracas. *Boln Soc. venez. Cirug.* **L.**MA. 47–.

8143 **Boletín** de la **Subdirección técnica agropecuaria** del **Litoral.** Guayaquil. *Boln Subdir. téc. agropec. Litoral*

8144 **Boletín tabacalero.** Buenos Aires. *Boln tabac.* [1937–]

8145 **Boletín** de **tabaco.** Buenos Aires. *Boln Tab.* **L.**AM. 44–; TP. 42–48; **Y.**

8146 **Boletín** de **tabaco** y **timbres.** Madrid. *Boln Tab. Timb.*

8147 **Boletín taxonómico** del **Laboratorio** de **pesqueria** de **Caiguire.** Caracas. *Boln taxon. Lab. Pesq. Caiguire* [1948–] **L.**Z. 48.

8148 **Boletín técnico. Asociación química española** de la **industría** del **cuero.** Barcelona. *Boln téc. Asoc. quím. esp. Ind. Cuero* [1960–] **L.**LE.; P. [*C. of:* 7788]

8149 **Boletín técnico. Centro nacional** de **agricultura.** San Pedro de Montes de Oca. *Boln téc. Cent. nac. Agric., S Pedro* **Rt.** 42–45.

8150 **Boletín técnico. Centro nacional** de **investigaciones** de **café, Colombia.** Chinchiná. *Boln téc. Cent. nac. Invest. Café Colombia* [1949–] **C.**A.; **Rt.** 53–.

8151 **Boletín técnico. Departamento** de **genetica fitotécnica.** Santiago de Chile. *Boln téc. Dep. Genet. fitotéc., Santiago* [1941–] **C.**A.; **O.**F. 42–.

Boletín técnico. Departamento de **investigación agropecuaria, Colombia.** *See* 16255.

8152 **Boletín técnico. Departamento** de **investigaciones agrícoles, Chili.** Santiago. *Boln téc. Dep. Invest. agríc. Chili* [1953–] **C.**A.

8153 **Boletín técnico** de la **Dirección general** de **ganadería.** Buenos Aires. *Boln téc. Dir. gen. Ganad., B. Aires* **E.**AB. 44–46.

8154 **Boletín técnico** de la **Dirección general** de **sanidad.** Madrid. *Boln téc. Dir. gen. Sanid., Madr.* [1926–31] **L.**MA. 29–30 imp.; SH. 27–31 imp.; TD. [*C. as:* 46918]

8155 **Boletín técnico. Empresa petrolera fiscal.** Lima. *Boln téc. Empr. petrol. fisc.* [1954–] **L.**GM.

8156 **Boletín técnico. Facultad** de **ciencias agrarias, Universidad nacional** de **Cuyo.** Mendoza. *Boln téc. Fac. Cienc. agrar. Univ. Cuyo* [1952–] **L.**A.; BMᴺ.; **Bn.**U.; **Br.**A. 58– imp.; **C.**A.; **G.**U.; **Md.**H.; **Rt.**; **Y.**

8157 **Boletín técnico. Federación nacional** de **cafeteros** de **Colombia.** Chinchiná. *Boln téc. Fed. nac. Cafet. Colombia* **L.**MO. 56–; **C.**A. 49–58; **Md.**H. 46–; **Rt.** 55.

8158 **Boletín técnico. Instituto científico Paul Hnos. S.A.** *Boln téc. Inst. cient. Paul Hnos* **L.**MY. 57–.

8159 **Boletín técnico. Instituto** de **fomento algodonero.** Bogotá. *Boln téc. Inst. Fom. algod., Bogotá* [1958–] **Y.**

8160 **Boletín técnico. Instituto nacional** de **agri-cultura, Venezuela.** Maracay. *Boln. téc. Inst. nac. Agric. Venez.* [1951–56] **C.**A.; **Y.**

8161 **Boletín técnico. Servicio botanico. Ministe-rio** de **agricultura** y **cría.** Caracas. *Boln téc. Serv. bot., Caracas*

8162 **Boletín tecnológico** de la **Asociación** de **peritos industriales.** Madrid. *Boln tecnol. Asoc. Perit. ind.*

8163 **Boletín** de **terapéutica radiactiva.** Madrid. *Boln Terap. radiact.*

8164 **Boletín tisiológico dispensarial.** Mexico, D.F. *Boln tisiol. dispens.*

8165 **Boletín** y **trabajos. Academia argentina** di **cirugía.** Buenos Aires. *Boln Trab. Acad. argent. Cirug.* [1939–51] **L.**MA. 39–41; S. 45–51; **Br.**U. [*C. of:* 8168; *C. as:* 8166]

8166 **Boletín** y **trabajos. Sociedad argentina** de **cirujanos.** Buenos Aires. *Boln Trab. Soc. argent. Ciruj.* **L.**MA. 56–. [*C. of:* 8165]

8167 **Boletín** y **trabajos** de la **Sociedad argentina** de **ortopedía** y **traumatología.** Buenos Aires. *Boln Trab. Soc. argent. Ortop. Traum.*

8168 **Boletín** y **trabajos** de la **Sociedad** de **cirugía** de **Buenos Aires.** *Boln Trab. Soc. Cirug. B. Aires* [1911–39] **L.**MA. 29–39; **Br.**U. 27–39; **M.**MS. 37–39; **O.**R. 37–39. [*C. as:* 8165]

8169 **Boletín trimestral** del **Centro meteorológico** de **G. Canaria.** Las Palmas. *Boln trim. Cent. met. G. Canaria* [1948–] **L.**MO. 48–52. [*C. of:* 7886]

8170 **Boletín trimestral** del **Centro meteorológico** de **Tenerife.** Santa Cruz de Tenerife. *Boln trim. Cent. met. Tenerife* [1950–] **L.**MO. [*C. of:* 7888]

8171 **Boletín trimestral climatológico, Sidi Ifni.** *Boln trim. clim. Sidi Ifni* [1952–] **L.**MO. [*C. of:* 7889]

8172 **Boletín trimestral. Estación central** de **ensayo** de **semillas.** Madrid. *Boln trim. Estac. cent. Ens. Semillas, Madr.*

8173 **Boletín trimestral** de **experimentación agro-pecuaria.** Lima. *Boln trim. Exp. agropec.* [1952–] **L.**MY. 54–; **C.**A. imp.; **Y.**

8174 **Boletín** de la **Union** de **fabricantes** de **conservas** de **Galicia.** *Boln Un. Fabr. Conserv. Galicia*

8175 **Boletín. Unión sanitaria valenciana.** Valencia. *Boln Un. sanit. valenc.*

8176 **Boletín. Universidad catolica** de **Santo Tomas** de **Villanueva.** Marianao. *Boln Univ. catol. S Tomas de Villanueva* [1958–] **Lo.**

8177 **Boletín** de la **Universidad** de **Granada.** *Boln Univ. Granada* [1928–] **L.**BMN. imp.; **Bl.**U. imp.; **Bm.**U.; **Ld.**U. 28–39: 46–; **O.**B. 31–.

8178 **Boletín** de la **Universidad** de **Madrid.** *Boln Univ. Madr.* [1929–31] **L.**SC.; **Bl.**U. imp.; **C.**UL.; **Ld.**U.; **M.**U.; **O.**B.; **Sa.**

8179 **Boletín. Universidad nacional** de **ingeniera.** Lima. *Boln Univ. nac. Ing., Lima* [1955–] **L.**P. [*C. of:* 7694]

8180 **Boletín** de la **Universidad nacional** de **México.** *Boln Univ. nac. Méx.* [1917–29] **L.**BMN. 20–21 imp.; **Bm.**U. 22–29; **C.**P.; UL. 22–29; **E.**C. 17–18; **Ld.**U. 22–29; **M.**U. 17–22; **O.**B. 17–25 imp.; **Sa.** 22–29. [*C. as:* 46781]

8181 **Boletín** de la **Universidad nacional** de **La Plata.** *Boln Univ. nac. La Plata* [1919–] **Abs.**U. imp.; **Bm.**U. imp.; **Db.** imp.; **Ld.**U.; **M.**U. 19–28 imp.; **O.**B. 19–34 imp.; **Sa.** imp.

8182 **Boletín universitario. Universidad mayor** de **San Marcos.** Lima. *Boln univ. Univ. mayor S Marcos* [1946] [*C. of:* 47020; *C. as:* 2542]

8183 **Boletín** de **veterinaria.** Tarragona. *Boln Vet., Tarragona*

Boletines. *See* **Boletín.**
Boletins. *See* **Boletim.**

8185 **Bolezni rastenii.** S.-Peterburg. Болезни растений. *Bolez. Rast.* [1907–30] **L.**BMN.; EB.; K. 22–30; MY. 14–15: 24–30 imp.; SC. 23–30; **Rt.** 23–30. [*C. of:* 28683]

8186 **Bollettino A.M.D.I.** Organo officiale dell'Asso-ciazione medici dentisti italiani. Roma. *Boll. A.M.D.I.*

8187 **Bollettino A.R.A.** Associazione ricostruzione rinno-vamento agricoltura. Roma. *Boll. A.R.A.* [1946–] **L.**AM. 46–47 imp.

8188 **Bollettino** della **Accademia** di **scienze, lettere** e **belle arti** di **Palermo.** Palermo. *Boll. Accad. Sci. Palermo* **L.**SC. 52–; **Db.** 84–; **E.**R. 91–92.

8189 **Bollettino** dell'**Aero Club** di **Roma.** *Boll. Aero Club Roma* [1914–16] [*C. of:* 47985; *C. as:* 47882]

8190 **Bollettino aerologico giornaliero.** Roma. *Boll. aerol. giorn.* **L.**MO. 14–24 imp.

8191 **Bollettino aeronautico.** Aeroplani Caproni. Milano. *Boll. aeronaut.* **L.**P. 28–33.

8192 **Bollettino agrario** della **Dalmazia.** Zara. *Boll. agr. Dalmazia*

8193 **Bollettino agricolo** e **commerciale** della **Colonia Eritrea.** Asmara. *Boll. agric. comm. Colon. Eritrea* [1903–05] **L.**K.

8194 **Bollettino** dell'**agricoltura.** Milano. *Boll. Agric., Milano*

8195 **Bollettino** di **agricoltura, agronomia** e **chimica agraria.** Firenze. *Boll. Agric. Agron. Chim. agr.*

8195e **Bollettino alliania.** Istituto ed orto botanico dell'Università di Torino. Torino. *Boll. alliania* **G.**N. 54–.

8196 **Bollettino** dell'**alpinista.** Rovereto. *Boll. Alpin.*

8197 **Bollettino annuale. Ufficio idrografico** del **Po.** Parma. *Boll. a. Uff. idrogr. Po* [1923–24] **L.**SC. [*C. of:* 6985; *C. as:* 3039]

8198 **Bollettino annuale. Ufficio idrografico.** Vene-zia. *Boll. a. Uff. idrogr., Venezia* [1923–24] **L.**MO. [*C. as:* 3029]

8199 **Bollettino** dell'**arboricoltura italiana.** Portici, etc. *Boll. Arboric. ital.* **L.**AM. 08–11*; K. 05–11. [*C. as:* 3096]

8200 **Bollettino** dell'**Associazione agraria toscana, sezione provinciale** de **Firenze.** Firenze. *Boll. Ass. agr. tosc. Sez. prov. Firenze*

8201 **Bollettino** dell'**Associazione agraria toscana, sezione provinciale sienese.** Siena. *Boll. Ass. agr. tosc., Sez. prov. sienese*

8202 **Bollettino** dell'**Associazione** degli **agronomi** della **Toscana.** Firenze. *Boll. Ass. Agron. Tosc.*

8203 **Bollettino** dell'**Associazione** dell'**industria laniera italiana.** Biella. *Boll. Ass. Ind. laniera ital.* [1887–25] [*C. as:* 8308]

8204 **Bollettino** dell'**Associazione internazionale** degli **studi mediterranei.** Roma. *Boll. Ass. int. Studi mediterr.* [1930–] **L.**GL. 30–31 imp.; **Db.**; **Ld.**U.; **O.**B.

8205 **Bollettino** dell'**Associazione italiana** dei (di) **chimici tessili** e **coloristi.** Milano. *Boll. Ass. ital. Chim. tess. color.* [1925–] **L.**P. 26–40; **M.**C. 25–40.

8206 **Bollettino** dell'**Associazione italiana gas** e **acqua.** Roma. *Boll. Ass. ital. Gas Acqua* [1912–16] [*C. as:* 23136]

8207 **Bollettino** dell'**Associazione italiana** dell'**industria** di **zucchero** e dell'**alcool.** *Boll. Ass. ital. Ind. Zucch. Alc.*

8208 **Bollettino** dell'**Associazione italiana** pro **piante medicinale, aromatiche** ed **altre utili.** Milano. *Boll. Ass. ital. Piante med.*

8209 **Bollettino** dell'**Associazione italiana** della **stampa tecnica.** Milano. *Boll. Ass. ital. Stampa tec.*

8210 **Bollettino. Associazione italiana tecnici** del **latte.** Modena. *Boll. Ass. ital. tec. Latte* [1954–57] **L.**P. [*C. of:* 49284; *C. as:* 52659]

8211 **Bollettino** dell'**Associazione medica mantovana.** Mantova. *Boll. Ass. med. mantov.*

8212 **Bollettino** dell'**Associazione medica marchigiana.** Loreto. *Boll. Ass. med. marchig.*

8213 **Bollettino** dell'**Associazione medica tridentina.** Trento. *Boll. Ass. med. trident.*

8214 **Bollettino** dell'**Associazione medica triestina.** Trieste. *Boll. Ass. med. triest.*

Bollettino dell'**Associazione medici dentisti italiani.** *See* 8186.

8215 **Bollettino** dell'**Associazione mineraria italiana.** Roma. *Boll. Ass. min. ital.* **L.**GL. 24–25.

8216 **Bollettino** dell'**Associazione mineraria sarda.** Iglesias. *Boll. Ass. min. sarda*

8217 **Bollettino** dell'**Associazione mineraria siciliana** Palermo. *Boll. Ass. min. sicil.*

8218 **Bollettino** dell'**Associazione nazionale** dei **medici condotti.** Milano. *Boll. Ass. naz. Med. cond.*

8219 **Bollettino** dell'**Associazione nazionale** per lo **sviluppo** dell'**illuminazione.** *Boll. Ass. naz. Svil. Illum.* [1926–] **L.**SC. 26–30.

8220 **Bollettino** dell'**Associazione ottica italiana.** Firenze. *Boll. Ass. ottica ital.* [1927–48] **L.**SC. 35–47. [*C. as:* 28838]

Bollettino. Associazione ricostruzione rinnovamento agricoltura, Roma. *See* 8187.

8221 **Bollettino** dell'**Associazione romana** di **entomologia.** Roma. *Boll. Ass. romana Ent.* [1946–] **L.**BM^N.; **E.**; **Y.**

8222 **Bollettino** dell'**Associazione sanitaria milanese.** Milano. *Boll. Ass. sanit. milan.*

8223 **Bollettino astrofilo. Società astronomica udinese.** Udine. *Boll. astrof., Udine*

8224 **Bollettino** e **atti** della **Accademia Lancisiana** di **Roma.** *Boll. Atti Accad. lancis. Roma*

8225 **Bollettino** ed **atti** della **Accademia medica.** Roma. *Boll. Atti Accad. med.* [1923–] **L.**BM. [*C. of:* 8386]

8226 **Bollettino** ed **atti** della **Accademia pugliese** di **scienze.** *Boll. Atti Accad. pugl. Sci.*

Bollettino ed **atti** della **R. Accademia medica.** Roma. *See* 8225.

8227 **Bollettino** di **bibliografia** e **storia** delle **scienze matematiche.** Genova, Torino. *Boll. Biblfia Stor. Sci. mat.* **L.**BM. 98–19*; **C.**UL. 98–19. [*C. in:* 8318]

8228 **Bollettino bibliografico. Association internationale** de la **presse médicale.** Milano. *Boll. biblfico Ass. int. Presse méd.* **L.**MA. 46–.

8229 **Bollettino bibliografico** della **botanica italiana.** Firenze. *Boll. biblfico Bot. ital.* [1904–38] **L.**BM. 04–15; BM^N.; **K.**; **L.**; **Abd.**U. 04–12; **C.**UL.; **E.**B. 04–13.

8230 **Bollettino bibliografico** dell'**Istituto sperimentale** dei **metalli leggeri.** Milano. *Boll. biblfico Ist. sper. Metalli legg.* **L.**P. 54–55.

8231 **Bollettino bibliografico. Stato maggiore aeronautica militare.** *Boll. biblfico Stato maggi. aeronaut. milit.* **L.**AV. 57–.

8232 **Bollettino bimensuale** della **Società meteorologica italiana.** Torino. *Boll. bimens. Soc. met. ital.* [1914–30] **L.**MO.; SC. 25–30; **C.**O.; **E.**M. 14–22 imp. [*C. of:* 8346]

8233 **Bollettino bimestrale. R. Comitato talassografico italiano.** Venezia. *Boll. bimest. R. Com. talassogr. ital.* [1909–24] **L.**AM.; BM^N.; G. 10–24; MO. 09–16; SC.; **Abd.**M. 15–21 imp.; **Dm.** 16–21; **E.**G. 12–24; **Lv.**U. 11–17 imp.; **Pl.**M. imp.

8233^c **Bollettino** dei **brevetti** per **invenzioni, modelli** e **marchi.** Roma. *Boll. Brev. Invenz. Modelli Marchi* **Y.** 60–.

8234 **Bollettino** della **Casa** di **salute Fleurent.** Napoli. *Boll. Casa Salute Fleurent*

8235 **Bollettino** della **Cattedra ambulante** d'**agricoltura** di **Brindisi.** Brindisi. *Boll. Catt. amb. Agric. Brindisi* **L.**EB. 14–15.

8236 **Bollettino** della **Cattedra ambulante** d'**agricoltura** per la **provincia** di **Bergamo.** *Boll. Catt. amb. Agric. Prov. Bergamo*

8237 **Bollettino** della **Cattedra ambulante** d'**agricoltura** per la **provincia** de **Reggio Emilia.** *Boll. Catt. amb. Agric. Prov. Reggio Emilia*

8238 **Bollettino** delle **Cattedre ambulanti** d'**agricoltura** di **Roma.** *Boll. Cattedre amb. Agric. Roma*

8239 **Bollettino. Centro Volpi** di **elettrologia.** Venezia. *Boll. Cent. Volpi Elettrol.* [1938–43] **L.**P.; SC. [*C. as:* 8254]

8240 **Bollettino** di **chimica clinica** e **farmacoterapia.** Napoli. *Boll. Chim. clin. Farmacoter.*

8241 **Bollettino chimico-farmaceutico.** Milano. *Boll. chim.-farm.* [1861–] **L.**C. 07–40 imp.; MA. 46–; P. 60–; PH. 46–; **Y.**

8242 **Bollettino** delle **cliniche.** Napoli. *Boll. Cliniche* [1884–23] **L.**S.

8243 **Bollettino clinico-scientifico** della **Poliambulanza** di **Milano.** Milano. *Boll. clin.-scient. Poliamb. Milano*

8244 **Bollettino** del **Collegio** degl'**ingegneri** ed **architetti, Cagliari.** *Boll. Coll. Ing. Archit. Cagliari*

8245 **Bollettino** del **Collegio** degl'**ingegneri** ed **architetti, Napoli.** *Boll. Coll. Ing. Archit. Napoli*

8246 **Bollettino** del **Collegio** degl'**ingegneri** ed **architetti, Palermo.** *Boll. Coll. Ing. Archit. Palermo*

8247 **Bollettino. Comitato glaciologico italiano** Roma. *Boll. Com. glaciol. ital.* [1914–] **L.**BM^N. 37–38; GL. 14–27 imp.; SC. 14–39: 50–; **C.**P. 47–; PO. 50–; **Y.**

8248 **Bollettino. Comitato nazionale italiano geodetico-geofisico.** Union géodesique et géophysique internationale. Bruxelles. *Boll. Com. naz. ital. geod.-geofis.* L.SC. 27–.

8249 **Bollettino** della **Commissione speciale** d'**igiene** del **Municipio** di **Roma.** *Boll. Comm. spec. Ig. Munic. Roma*

8250 **Bollettino. Corpo forestale** dello **stato.** Roma. *Boll. Corpo for. St.* O.F. 50– imp.

8251 **Bollettino** della **cotoniera.** Milano. *Boll. Coton.* L.P. 13–40 imp.; M.C. 21–40.

8252 **Bollettino** delle **crociere periodiche.** Regio Comitato talassografico italiano. Venezia. *Boll. Croc. period.* [1912–14] L.BM^N.; Pl.M.

8253 **Bollettino demografico-meteorico.** Roma. *Boll. demogr.-met.*

8254 **Bollettino** di **documentazione elettrotecnica.** Padova. *Boll. Docum. elettrotec.* [1947–49] L.P.; SC.; Db. imp.; Nw.A. imp. [*C. of:* 8239; *C. as:* 6557]

8255 **Bollettino** di **documentazione tecnica.** Roma. *Boll. Docum. tec.* Y.

8256 **Bollettino ematologico** e **quaderni** di **dietetica.** Milano. *Boll. emat. Quad. Diet.*

8257 **Bollettino enologico toscano.** Arezzo. *Boll. enol. tosc.*

8258 **Bollettino** di **entomologia agraria** e **patologia vegetale.** Padova. *Boll. Ent. agr. Patol. veg.* [1894–03]
Bollettino della **Facoltà** di **medicina** e **chirurgia Università** di **Padova.** *See* 5259^a.
Bollettino della **Federazione internazionale** delle **associazioni** di **chimica tessile** e **coloristica.** *See* 10235.

8259 **Bollettino** della **Federazione mineraria.** Roma. *Boll. Fed. miner.*

8260 **Bollettino. Federazione nazionale** fra i **brefotrofi.** Roma. *Boll. Fed. naz. Brefotr.*

8261 **Bollettino** della **Federazione nazionale fascista** per la **lotta** contro la **tuberculosi.** Roma. *Boll. Fed. naz. fasc. Lotta Tuberc.*
Bollettino della **Federazione svizzera** allavamento **bovini bruni.** *See* 32726.

8262 **Bollettino Fondazione Sen. Pascale.** Centro per la diagnosi e la cura dei tumori. Napoli. *Boll. Fond. Sen. Pascale* [1954–] L.MA.; MD.

8263 **Bollettino** dei **geodesia** e **scienze affini.** *Boll. Geod.* F.A. 53–; Y.

8264 **Bollettino** di **geofisica teorica** ed **applicata.** Osservatorio geofisico, Trieste. *Boll. Geofis. teor. appl.* [1959–] L.MO.; P.; Y.

8266 **Bollettino geografico.** Governo della Cirenaica. Bengasi. *Boll. geogr. Gov. Cirenaica*

8267 **Bollettino geografico.** Ufficio di studi, Tripolitania. *Boll. geogr. Uff. Studi Tripolit.* [1931–36] L.SC.

8268 **Bollettino giornaliero. R. Istituto geofisico.** Trieste. *Boll. giorn. R. Ist. geofis.* Lv.U. 22–.

8269 **Bollettino giornaliero. Ufficio idrografico** del **Po.** Venezia. *Boll. giorn. Uff. idrogr. Po* L.MO. 49– imp.

8270 **Bollettino** di **idrobiologia, caccia** e **pesca** dell' **Africa orientale italiana.** Addis Abeba. *Boll. Idrobiol. Cacc. Pesca Afr. orient. ital.* [1940] L.BM^N.; Z.; Bl.U.; Fr.

8271 **Bollettino idrografico, Bologna.** *Boll. idrogr. Bologna* L.MO. 22–29. [*C. as:* 3031]

8272 **Bollettino idrografico, Cagliari.** *Boll. idrogr. Cagliari* L.MO. 24–28.

8273 **Bollettino idrografico, Catanzaro.** Monteleone Calabro. *Boll. idrogr. Catanzaro* L.MO. 23–26. [*C. as:* 3033]

8274 **Bolletino idrografico, Chieti.** *Boll. idrogr. Chieti* L.MO. 23–24.

8275 **Bollettino idrografico, Napoli.** *Boll. idrogr. Napoli* L.MO. 23–37. [*C. as:* 3037]

8276 **Bollettino idrografico, Palermo.** *Boll. idrogr. Palermo* L.MO. 24–29. [*C. as:* 3038]

8277 **Bollettino idrografico, Pisa.** *Boll. idrogr. Pisa* L.MO. 22–23.

8278 **Bollettino idrografico, Roma.** *Boll. idrogr. Roma* L.MO. 73–78: 23–33. [*C. as:* 3041^a]

8279 **Bollettino idrologico mensile.** Roma. *Boll. idrol. mens.* L.MO. 39–40: 49–; Y.

8280 **Bollettino idrologico, Supplemento annuale.** Roma. *Boll. idrol. Supp. a.* Y.

8281 **Bollettino** delle **industrie italiane** della **carta,** della **cancelleria,** dell'**arredamento,** dell'**ufficio.** Milano. *Boll. Ind. ital. Carta*

8282 **Bollettino** di **informazione** per l'**industria olearia** e **saponiera.** Catania. *Boll. Inf. Ind. olear. Sapon.* [1955–] L.P. 59–; Y.

8283 **Bollettino** d'**informazioni. Consiglio nazionale** delle **ricerche.** Roma. *Boll. Inf. Cons. naz. Ric.* [1930–] L.SC. 30–60 imp.

8284 **Bollettino** d'**informazioni** agli **iscritti.** Perugia. *Boll. Inf. Iscritti* [1948–] L.MA. 49–.

8285 **Bollettino** di **informazioni** sulla **microriproduzione.** Milano. *Boll. Inf. Microriprod.* [1953–] L.BM.; Sh.U. 58–.

8286 **Bollettino** d'**informazioni. Ordine** degli **ingegneri** della **provincia** di **Torino.** Torino. *Boll. Inf. Ord. Ing. Prov. Torino* L.P. 54–. [*Supplement to:* 5226]

8286° **Bollettino internazionale** delle **opere scientifiche medicina.** Bologna. *Boll. int. Opere scient. med.* L.MA. 58–.

8287 **Bollettino** degli **Istituti** di **zoologia** e **anatomia comparata** della **R. Università** di **Genova.** *Boll. Istituti Zool. Anat. comp. Genova* [1939–40] L.BM^N; SC.; Z.; E.U.; Lv.U. [*C. of:* 8360; *C. as:* 8359]

8288 **Bollettino** dell'**Istituto aero-elettroterapico** di **Torino** per la **cura** delle **malattie** dei **polmoni** e del **cuore.** Torino. *Boll. Ist. aero-elettroter. Torino*

8289 **Bollettino** dell'**Istituto agrario** di **Scandicci.** Firenze. *Boll. Ist. agr. Scandicci* L.SC. 25–; Rt. 96–07.

8289° **Bollettino** dell'**Istituto** di **alimentazione** e **dietologia.** Rome. *Boll. Ist. Aliment. Diet.* Abd.R. 50–51.
Bollettino dell'**Istituto botanico** della **R. Università** di **Modena.** *See* 4385.

8290 **Bollettino** dell'**Istituto botanico.** Palermo. *Boll. Ist. bot., Palermo*

8291 **Bollettino** dell'**Istituto botanico** della **R. Università** di **Sassari.** *Boll. Ist. bot. R. Univ. Sassari*

8292 **Bollettino** dell'**Istituto** di **entomologia agraria** e dell'**Osservatorio** di **fitopathologia** di **Palermo.** Palermo. *Boll. Ist. Ent. agr. Oss. Fitopath. Palermo* [1954–] L.BM^N.

    Bollettino dell'**Istituto** di **entomologia** della **R. Università** degli **studi** di **Bologna.** *See* 8293.

8293 **Bollettino** dell'**Istituto** di **entomologia** della **Università** degli **studi** di **Bologna.** *Boll. Ist. Ent. Univ. Bologna* [1935–] L.AM. 47–; BM^N. imp.; EB.; L.; SC. 35–57; Z. 36–; C.P.; E.R.; Ld.U. 52–57; O.H. [*C. of:* 8303]

8294 **Bollettino** dell'**Istituto** e **Museo** di **zoologia** della **Università** di **Torino.** Torino. *Boll. Ist. Mus. Zool. Univ. Torino* [1943–] L.BM.; BM^N.; SC.; Z.; C.P.; Lv.U.; Y. [*C. of:* 8361]

8295 **Bollettino** dell'**Istituto** di **patologia** del **libro.** Roma. *Boll. Ist. Patol. Libro* [1939–] L.BM. 46–; BM^N. 46–53; EB. 46–; P. 55–; Bm.U. 56–; E.A. 53–; Y.

8296 **Bollettino** dell'**Istituto sieroterapico milanese.** Milano. ¦*Boll. Ist. sieroter. milan.* [1917–] L.LI. 44–; MA. 48–; MD. 39–; S. 17–48; SC. 29–; TD. 17–45 imp.; Y.

8297 **Bollettino** dell'**Istituto storico italiano** dell'**arte sanitaria.** Roma. *Boll. Ist. stor. ital. Arte sanit.* [1921–34] L.MD. [*Supplement to:* 42149; *C. as:* 5211]

    Bollettino dell'**Istituto** di **zoologia** della **R. Università** di **Roma.** *See* 8300.

8298 **Bollettino** dell'**Istituto zoologico.** Messina. *Boll. Ist. zool., Messina* [1925–] Pl.M. 25–28.

8299 **Bollettino** dell'**Istituto zoologico** della **R. Università** di **Palermo.** Palermo. *Boll. Ist. zool. R. Univ. Palermo* [1918–47] L.BM^N.; SC.; Abd.M. 18–36 imp.; Lv.U.; Pl.M. 18–35.

8300 **Bollettino** dell'**Istituto zoologico** della **R. Università** di **Roma.** Roma. *Boll. Ist. Zool. R. Univ. Roma* [1923–30] L.BM^N.; EB.; Z.; Lv.U. [*C. of:* 8479]

8301 **Bollettino** dei **Laboratori chimici provinciali.** Bologna. *Boll. Laboratori chim. prov.* [1950–] L.P. 60–; R.D.; Y.

8302 **Bollettino** del **Laboratorio** di **entomologia agraria 'Filippo Silvestri'.** Portici. *Boll. Lab. Ent. agr. Filippo Silvestri* [1949–] L.BM^N.; E.; L.; SC.; Z.; C.P.; Db.; E.R.; Ld.U. 55–; O.H.; Rt. [*C. of:* 8392]

8303 **Bollettino** del **Laboratorio** di **entomologia** del **R. Istituto superiore agrario** di **Bologna.** *Boll. Lab. Ent. R. Ist. sup. agr. Bologna* [1928–35] L.BM^N.; EB.; L.; SC.; Z. 33–34; C.P.; E.R.; Lv.U.; O.H. [*C. as:* 8293]

8304 **Bollettino** del **Laboratorio sperimentale** e **Osservatorio** di **fitopatologia.** Torino. *Boll. Lab. sper. Oss. Fitopatol.* [1935–42: 56–] L.EB.; MY. 36–39: 56–. [*C. of:* 16971]

    Bollettino del **Laboratorio sperimentale** e **R. Osservatorio** di **fitopatologia.** Torino. *See* 8304.

8305 **Bollettino** del **Laboratorio** di **zoologia agraria** e **bachicoltura** del **R. Istituto superiore agrario** di **Milano.** Parma. *Boll. Lab. Zool. agr. Bachic. R. Ist. sup. agr. Milano* [1928–35] L.BM^N.; E. 28–31; EB.; SC.; E.R. 30–35; Rt. [*C. as:* 8507]

8306 **Bollettino** del **Laboratorio** di **zoologia generale** e **agraria** della **Facoltà agraria** in **Portici.** *Boll. Lab. Zool. gen. agr. Portici* [1939–43: 56–] L.BM^N.; E.; EB.; Z.; Bm.N. 39–43; C.B. 39–43; P. 39–43; Cr.N. 39–43; Db.; E.C. 39–43; R. 39–43; Lv.U.; Rt. [*C. of:* 8307]

8307 **Bollettino** del **Laboratorio** di **zoologia generale** e **agraria** della **R. Scuola superiore** d'**agricoltura.** Portici. *Boll. Lab. Zool. gen. agr. R. Scuola Agric. Portici* [1907–38] L.BM^N.; E.; EB.; L. 07–30; Z.; Bm.N. 08–38; C.B. 08–38; P. 26–38; Cr.N. 15–38 imp.; Db.; Dm. 16–27; E.C. 16–38; R. 13–38; Lv.U.; M.U. 07–15; O.R. 11–19 imp.; Rt. 08–38 imp.; Sal. 32–38. [*C. as:* 8306]

8308 **Bollettino** della **'Laniera'.** Biella. *Boll. 'Laniera'* [1926–37] L.P. 26–35; Ld.W. 32–37 imp.; Y. [*C. of:* 8203; *C. as:* 28127]

8309 **Bollettino** della **Lega italiana** per la **lotta** contro il **cancro.** Roma. *Boll. Lega ital. Lotta Cancro* [1927–34] L.MD. 33–34. [*C. as:* 42163]

    Bollettino della **Lega italiana** per la **lotta** contro i **tumori** e **rassegna** di **oncologia.** *See* 8367 *and* 8433.

8310 **Bollettino magnetico. Osservatorio magnetico** l'**Aquila.** *Boll. magn. Oss. magn. Aquila* E.M. 58–.

8311 **Bollettino malariologico.** Roma. *Boll. malar.* Lv.U. 22–25*. [*C. as:* 47907]

8312 **Bollettino** delle **malattie** dell'**orecchio,** della **gola** e del **naso.** Firenze. *Boll. Mal. Orecch. Gola Naso* [1883–] L.MA. 47–; MD. 00–; G.F. 95: 97–99.

8313 **Bollettino** delle **malattie veneree, sifilitiche** e della **pelle.** Roma. *Boll. Mal. vener.*

8314 **Bollettino** dei **manicomi.** Genova. *Boll. Manicomi, Genova*

8315 **Bollettino** del **Manicomio provinciale** di **Ferrara.** Ferrara. *Boll. Manicomio prov. Ferrara* [1874–02] [*C. as:* 21290]

8316 **Bollettino mareografico mensile.** Istituto idrografico italiano. Genova. *Boll. mareogr. mens.*

8317 **Bollettino marzoli.** Brescia. *Boll. marzoli* [1959–] L.P.

8318 **Bollettino** di **matematica.** Firenze. *Boll. Mat.* [1902–48] L.BM. 23–48; O.R. 22–48. [*Not published* 1944–46]

8319 **Bollettino** di **matematiche** e di **scienze fisiche** e **naturali.** Bologna. *Boll. Mat. Sci. fis. nat.*

    Bollettino dei **medici svizzeri.** *See* 48921.

8320 **Bollettino** di **medicina pratica** e **interessi sindacali.** Cosenza. *Boll. Med. prat.*

8321 **Bollettino medico cremonese.** Cremona. *Boll. med. cremon.*

8322 **Bollettino medico** di **Salsomaggiore.** Parma. *Boll. med. Salsomagg.*

8323 **Bollettino medico** della **Svizzera italiana.** Lugano. *Boll. med. Svizz. ital.*

8324 **Bollettino medico trentino.** Trento. *Boll. med. trent.*

8325 **Bollettino** e **memorie** della **Società piemontese** di **chirurgia.** Biella. *Boll. Memie Soc. piemont. Chir.* [1931–] L.MA. 48–; S. 39; Br.U. 31–41.

8326 **Bollettino** e **memorie** della **Società tosco-umbra** di **chirurgia.** Firenze. *Boll. Memie Soc. tosco-umbra Chir.*

8327 **Bollettino mensile agro-meteorologico** per la **Puglia** e **Lucania.** Bari. *Boll. mens. agro-met. Puglia Lucania* [1953] L.MO. [*C. of:* 8350; *C. as:* 8330]

8328 **Bollettino mensile. Associazione nazionale** degl'**ingegneri** e **architetti italiani.** Sezione di Napoli. *Boll. mens. Ass. naz. Ing. Archit. ital. Sez. Napoli* L.SC. 49–53*. [*C. as:* 42193]

8329 **Bollettino mensile** della **Compagnia generale** di **elettricità.** Milano. *Boll. mens. Comp. gen. Elett.*

8330 **Bollettino mensile ecologico-agrario** per la **Puglia** e **Lucania.** Beri. *Boll. mens. ecol.-agr. Puglia Lucania* [1953–56] L.MO. [*C. of:* 8327; *C. as:* 8354]

8331 **Bollettino mensile** d'**informazione. Istituto geografico polare.** Forli. *Boll. mens. Inf. Ist. geogr. polare* [1945] C.PO. [*C. as:* 38037]

8332 **Bollettino mensile** dei **medici** della **marina mercantile.** Genova. *Boll. mens. Med. Mar. merc.*

8333 **Bollettino mensile. Osservatorio Baldini.** Pisa. *Boll. mens. Oss. Baldini*

8334 **Bollettino mensile. Osservatorio geofisico** del **Seminario patriarcale** di **Venezia.** *Boll. mens. Oss. geofis. Semin. patr. Venezia* [1911–] L.MO. 11–35. [*C. of:* 36480]

8335 **Bollettino mensile** dell'**Osservatorio meteorico geodinamico** in **Mineo.** Caltagirone. *Boll. mens. Oss. meteorico geodin. Mineo*

8336 **Bollettino mensile. Osservatorio meteorico-aerologico-geodinamico** di **Montecassino.** *Boll. mens. Oss. meteorico-aerol.-geodin. Montecassino* L.MO. 38–39. [*C. of:* 31526]

8337 **Bollettino mensile** dell'**Osservatorio meteorologico** del **R. Istituto nautico.** Riposto. *Boll. mens. Oss. met. R. Ist. naut.* L.MO. 76–28.

8338 **Bollettino mensile. Osservatorio meteorologico, Seminario patriarcale** di **Venezia.** *Boll. mens. Oss. met. Venezia* L.MO. 02–04. [*C. as:* 36480]

8339 **Bollettino mensile** delle **osservazioni meteorologiche.** Messina. *Boll. mens. Ossni met., Messina*

8340 **Bollettino mensile** della **R. Stazione** di **patologia vegetale.** Roma. *Boll. mens. R. Staz. Patol. veg.* [1920–25] L.AM.; K.; MY. 20–24; Md.H. [*C. as:* 8483]

8341 **Bollettino mensile** della **Sezione autonoma** del **genio civile** per il **dominio** del **litorale Lazio.** Roma. *Boll. mens. Sez. auton. Gen. civ. Lazio*

8342 **Bollettino mensile. Sezione italiana, Technical Association** of the **Pulp** and **Paper Industry.** *Boll. mens. Sez. ital. tech. Ass. Pulp Pap. Ind.* L.P. [*Supplement to* and *published in:* 23128°]

Bollettino mensile della **Società svizzera** per l'**industria** del **gas** e dell'**acqua potabile.** *See* 33108.

8343 **Bollettino mensile** della **Società zoofila.** Trieste. *Boll. mens. Soc. zoof., Trieste*

8344 **Bollettino mensile. Ufficio idrografico, Parma.** *Boll. mens. Uff. idrogr. Parma* L.G. 13– imp.; MO. 13–25 imp.; Lv.U. 21–.

8345 **Bollettino mensile. Ufficio idrografico.** Venezia. *Boll. mens. Uff. idrogr. Venezia* [1912–] L.G. imp.; MO.; E.G.; Lv.U. 21–. [*C. of:* 8502]

8346 **Bollettino mensuale** pubblicato per cura del **Comitato direttivo, Società meteorologica italiana.** Torino. *Boll. mensu. Com. dir. Soc. met. ital.* L.MO. 81–13* imp.; C.O. 98–13; E.M. 95–13 imp. [*C. as:* 8232]

8347 **Bollettino meteorico giornaliero** dell'**Ufficio centrale** di **meteorologia** e **geodinamica.** Roma. *Boll. meteor. giorn. Uff. cent. met. Geodin.* L.MO. 80–40.

8348 **Bollettino meteorico mensile. Osservatorio meteorologico, Acireale.** *Boll. meteorico mens. Oss. met. Acireale*

8349 **Bollettino meteorico mensile** del **R. Istituto idrografico.** Genova. *Boll. meteorico mens. R. Ist. idrogr.* L.MO. 11–17*. [*C. as:* 19752]

8350 **Bollettino meteorico-agrario** per la **Puglia** e **Lucania.** Bari. *Boll. meteorico-agr. Puglia Lucania* L.MO. 53. [*C. as:* 8327]

8351 **Bollettino meteorico-geodinamico. Osservatorio Pio X.** Valle di Pompei. Napoli. *Boll. meteorico-geodin. Oss. Pio X* L.MO. 11–29.

8352 **Bollettino meteorico-sismico. Osservatorio** di **Chiavari.** *Boll. meteorico-sism. Oss. Chiavari*

8353 **Bollettino meteorologico** dell'**Africa italiana.** Roma. *Boll. met. Afr. ital.* [1935–] L.MO. 35–36. [*C. of:* 8355]

8354 **Bollettino meteorologico agraria. Ufficio centrale meteorologia** e **ecologia.** Roma. *Boll. met. agr.* [1956–] L.MO. [*C. of:* 8330]

8355 **Bollettino meteorologico** delle **colonie italiane.** Roma. *Boll. met. Colon. ital.* [1932–34] L.MO. [*C. as:* 8353]

8356 **Bollettino meteorologico** e **geodinamico. Osservatorio** del **R. Collegio Carlo Alberto** in **Mencaliere.** Torino. *Boll. met. geodin. Oss. R. Coll. Carlo Alberto*
    A. Osservazioni meteorologici. L.MO. 09–17.
    B. Osservazioni sismiche.

8357 **Bollettino meteorologico. Italia, Libia, Egeo, Albania, Ungheria, Romania, Jugoslavia, Bulgaria, Grecia.** Roma. *Boll. met. Ital.* L.MO. 40–41.

8358 **Bollettino meteorologico. Osservatorio Ximeniano** dei **PP.** delle **scuole pie.** Firenze. *Boll. met. Oss. Ximeniano, Firenze* L.MO. 07: 19: 21: 29–39.

Bollettino meteorologico del **R. Osservatorio** di **Palermo.** *See* 21296.

Bollettino del **Ministero** dell' **agricoltura.** *See* 8496.

8359 **Bollettino** dei **musei** e degli **istituti biologici** della **(R.) Università** di **Genova.** *Boll. Musei Ist. biol. Univ. Genova* [1941–] L.BM^N.; SC.; Z.; E.U.; Lv.U. [*C. of:* 8287]

8360 **Bollettino** dei **musei** e **laboratorii** di **zoologia** e di **anatomia comparata** della **R. Università** di **Genova.** *Boll. Musei Lab. Zool. Anat. comp. R. Univ. Genova* [1892–38] L.BM^N.; SC. 26–38; Z. 26–38; Abd.M. 26–28; E.U. 26–38; Lv.U. 26–38 imp.; Y. [*C. as:* 8287]

Bollettino dei **musei** di **zoologia** e di **anatomia comparata** della **R. Università** di **Genova.** *See* 8360

8361 **Bollettino** dei **musei** di **zoologia** e di **anatomia comparata** della **R. Università** di **Torino.** *Boll. Musei Zool. Anat. comp. R. Univ. Torino* [1886–42] L.BM.; BM^N.; EB. 12–32; SC. 24–42; Z.; C.P. 89–42; Db. 86–97; E.R. 86–99; Lv.U. [*C. as:* 8294]

8362 **Bollettino** del **Museo civico** di **storia naturale** di **Venezia.** Venezia. *Boll. Mus. civ. Stor. nat. Venezia* [1954–] L.AM. 55–; BM^N.; Z. 54–imp.; Abd.M. 56–; Bl.U. 57–; Dm. 55–56; Fr. 55–; Ld.U. 56–59; O.H. imp.; Pit.F. 55–; Pl.M. 54–; Y. [*C. of:* 8478]

8363 **Bollettino** del **naturalista.** Siena. *Boll. Nat.* [1890–10] L.BM^N. [*Supplement to:* 47897]

8364 **Bollettino** di **notizie agrarie.** Roma. *Boll. Notiz. agr.* [1879–01] L.A. 89–01; MO. 79–82. [*C. as:* 8496]

8365 **Bollettino** di **oculistica.** Firenze. *Boll. Oculist.* [1922–] L.MA. 47–; MD. 28–; OP. 40–; Y.

8366 **Bollettino** degli **olii** e dei **grassi.** Milano. *Boll. Olii Grassi* [1921–] **L**.P.   [*C. as:* 23154]

8367 **Bollettino** di **oncologia.** Lega italiana per la lotta contro i tumori. Roma. *Boll. Oncol.* [1950–] **L**.CB. imp.; MA. 54–.   [*C. of:* 36182; *see also* 8433]

8368 **Bollettino** dell'**Ordine** dei **medici** della **provincia** di **Firenze.** *Boll. Ord. Med. Prov. Firenze*

8369 **Bollettino** dell'**Ordine** dei **medici** della **provincia** di **Napoli.** *Boll. Ord. Med. Prov. Napoli*

8370 **Bollettino** dell'**Ordine** dei **medici** della **provincia** di **Torino.** *Boll. Ord. Med. Prov. Torino*

8371 **Bollettino** dell'**Ordine** dei **sanitari** di **Catanzaro** e **provincia.** Catanzaro. *Boll. Ord. Sanit. Catanzaro*

8372 **Bollettino** dell'**Ordine** dei **sanitari** della **città** e **provincia** di **Parma.** Parma. *Boll. Ord. Sanit. Città Prov. Parma*

8373 **Bollettino** dell'**Ordine** dei **sanitari** di **Piacenza.** Piacenza. *Boll. Ord. Sanit. Piacenza*

8374 **Bollettino** dell'**Ordine** dei **sanitari** della **provincia** di **Teramo.** *Boll. Ord. Sanit. Prov. Teramo*

8375 **Bollettino** dell'**Ordine** dei **sanitari** della **provincia** di **Trapani.** *Boll. Ord. Sanit. Prov. Trapani*

8376 **Bollettino** dell'**Orto botanico.** Napoli. *Boll. Orto bot., Napoli* [1899–47] **L**.BM^N. 99–36; K.; SC. 31–38. [*C. as:* 16478]

8377 **Bollettino** dell'**Ospedale oftalmico** della **provincia** di **Roma.** Roma. *Boll. Osp. oftal. Prov. Roma* [*C. as:* 38518]

8378 **Bollettino** dell'**Osservatorio. Collegio Pennisi.** Acireale. *Boll. Oss. Coll. Pennisi*

8379 **Bollettino** di **paletnologia italiana.** Parma. *Boll. Paletnol. ital.* [1875–] **L**.AN.; BM. 91–; UC.; **C**.UL. 82–; **E**.R. 75–07 imp.; U. 75–08; V. imp.; **L**v.U. imp.; **O**.B. 84–. [*Suspended* 1918–21]

8380 **Bollettino** di **pesca, piscicoltura** e **idrobiologia.** Roma. *Boll. Pesca Piscic. Idrobiol.* [1925–] **L**.AM. 46– imp.; BM^N. 26– imp.; Z. 46–; **Abd**.M. 26–39: 46–; **Dm.** imp.; **Fr.** 46–; **Lo.**; **L**v.U. imp.; **Mi.** imp.; **Pit**.F. 28–39: 46–; **Pl**.M.; **Y.**

8381 **Bollettino** di **pomologia** e **frutticoltura.** Treviso. *Boll. Pomol. Fruttic.*

8382 **Bollettino quindicinale** del **Comizio agrario.** Mantova. *Boll. quind. Com. agr., Mantova*

8383 **Bollettino quindicinale** della **Società** degli **agricoltori italiani.** Roma. *Boll. quind. Soc. Agric. ital.*

8384 **Bollettino quotidiano tecnico. Servizio meteorologico** dell'**aeronautica.** Roma. *Boll. quotid. tec. Serv. met. Aeronaut.* **L**.MO. 52–.

8385 **Bollettino** della **R. Accademia medica, Genova.** *Boll. R. Accad. med. Genova* [*C. as:* 434]

8386 **Bollettino** della **R. Accademia medica, Roma.** *Boll. R. Accad. med. Roma* [1880–23] **L**.BM. 88–23; **O**.R. 80–01. [*C. as:* 8825]

     Bollettino della **R. Accademia** di **scienze, lettere** e **belle arti** di **Palermo.** *See* 8188.

8387 **Bollettino** del **R. Comitato geologico** d'**Italia.** Roma. *Boll. R. Com. geol. Ital.* [1870–21] **L**.BM. 70–75; BM^N.; GL. 00–21; GM.; R.; **E**.R. 76–21 imp.; **G**.U. 70–83; **M**.U. 73–84; **O**.R. [*C. as:* 8400]

     Bollettino. R. Comitato talassografico italiano Venezia. *See* 8233.

8388 **Bollettino** del **R. Ispettorato agrario provinciale** di **Bergamo.** *Boll. R. Isp. agr. prov. Bergamo*

8389 **Bollettino. R. Istituto superiore agraria, Milano** *Boll. R. Ist. sup. agr. Milano* **E**.R. 30–35.

8390 **Bollettino. R. Istituto superiore agraria, Pisa.** *Boll. R. Ist. sup. agr. Pisa* [1925–37] **L**.SC. imp.; **C**.A.; **Rt.**; **Y.** [*C. as:* 3017]

8391 **Bollettino** del **R. Laboratorio** di **entomologia agraria. R. Scuola superiore** d'**agricoltura** in **Portici.** *Boll. R. Lab. Ent. agr. R. Scuola sup. Agric. Portici* [1917–19] **L**.EB.

8392 **Bollettino** del **R. Laboratorio** di **entomologia agraria** di **Portici.** *Boll. R. Lab. Ent. agr. Portici* [1937–48] **L**.BM^N.; E.; EB.; L.; SC. 38–48; Z.; **C**.P.; **Db.**; **E**.R.; **O**.H.; **Rt.** 39–48; **Sal.** 37–45. [*C. as:* 8302]

8393 **Bollettino** del **R. Orto botanico, Palermo.** *Boll. R. Orto bot. Palermo* [1897–21] **L**.BM^N.; K. imp.

8394 **Bollettino** del **R. Orto botanico, Siena.** *Boll. R. Orto bot. Siena* [1897–06] **L**.K.; L.; **E**.B.

8395 **Bollettino** della **R. Società toscana** d'**orticultura.** Firenze. *Boll. R. Soc. tosc. Ortic.* [1876–38] **L**.HS.; K. 76–31. [*C. as:* 47961]

8396 **Bollettino** della **R. Stazione agraria** di **Modena.** Modena. *Boll. R. Staz. agr. Modena*

     Bollettino della **R. Stazione chimico-agraria sperimentale** di **Roma.** *See* 8481.

     Bollettino della **R. Stazione** di **patologia vegetale.** *See* 8483.

8397 **Bollettino** della **R. Stazione sperimentale** di **agrumicoltura** e **frutticoltura** in **Acireale.** Acireale. *Boll. R. Staz. sper. Agrum. Fruttic. Acireale* [1912–41] **L**.AM. 12–26; EB.; HS. 12–37; K. 12–38 imp.; MY. 19–41 imp.; SC. 14–41; **Rt.** 14–40 imp.

8398 **Bollettino** della **R. Stazione sperimentale** di **gelsicoltura** e **bachicoltura** di **Ascoli Piceno.** *Boll. R. Staz. sper. Gelsic. Bachic. Ascoli Piceno* [1922–42] **L**.EB.; SC. 32–42.

     Bollettino. R. Stazione sperimentale per l'**industria** delle **pelli** e delle **materie concianti.** *See* 8499.

8399 **Bollettino. R. Stazione sperimentale** di **Milano** per l'**industria** della **carta** e lo **studio** delle **fibre tessili vegetali.** Milano. *Boll. R. Staz. sper. Milano Ind. Carta*

     Reparto carta. **L**.P. 28–33*.   [*C. in:* 8251]

     Reparto fibre tessili vegetali. [1929–33] **L**.C. 33; P. 29–33; **M**.C.   [*Supplement to:* 8251; *C. in:* 23128^c]

8400 **Bollettino. R. Ufficio geologico** d'**Italia.** *Boll. R. Uff. geol. Ital.* [1922–44] **L**.BM^N.; GL.; GM.; R. 22–38; SC. 26–44; **E**.R.; **O**.R. 22–33.   [*C. of:* 8387; *C. as:* 8418]

8401 **Bollettino. R. Ufficio meteorologico** della **Tripolitania.** *Boll. R. Uff. met. Tripolit.*

8402 **Bollettino. R. Ufficio** per i **servizi agrari** della **Tripolitania.** Tripoli. *Boll. R. Uff. Serv. agr. Tripolit.* **C**.A. 32–.

     Bollettino della **R. Università italiana** per **stranieri.** *See* 8505.

8403 **Bollettino radiotelegrafico** del **R. Esercito.** Roma. *Boll. radiotelegr. R. Eserc.*

8404 **Bollettino radiotelegrafico** della **R. Marina.** Livorno. *Boll. radiotelegr. R. Mar.* [1918–] **L**.P. 21–31; SC. 23–; UC. 19– imp.

     Bollettino del **Reparto fibre tessili vegetali.** Milano. *See* 8399.

8406 **Bollettino** di **ricerche** e **informazioni** del **Centro regionale sperimentale** per l'**industria enologica 'F. Paulsen'.** Marsala. *Boll. Ric. Inf. Cent. reg. sper. Ind. enol. F. Paulsen* [1955–] **Y.**

8407 **Bollettino** dei **rurali.** Firenze. *Boll. Rurali*

8408 **Bollettino sanitario annuale, Spezia.** *Boll. sanit. a., Spezia*

8409 **Bollettino sanitario. Direzione generale** della **sanità pubblica, Roma.** *Boll. sanit., Roma* **L.**H. 07–13.

8410 **Bollettino sanitario settimanale** del **bestiame.** Roma. *Boll. sanit. settim. Best.*

8411 **Bollettino sanitario trimestrale, Spezia.** *Boll. sanit. trim., Spezia*

8412 **Bollettino sanitario** della **Tripolitania.** Tripoli. *Boll. sanit. Tripolit.* **L.**MA. 44– imp.; TD. 44–53 imp.

8413 **Bollettino schermografico.** Roma. *Boll. scherm.* [1948–] **L.**H. 56–; MA. 49–; MD. 56–; TD. 49– imp.; **Y.**

8414 **Bolletino scientifico** della **Facoltà** di **chimica industriale, Università** di **Bologna.** *Boll. scient. Fac. Chim. ind. Univ. Bologna* [1940–] **L.**C. 50–; P.; **Y.** [*C. of:* 59401]

8415 **Bolletino** delle **scienze mediche.** Bologna. *Boll. Sci. med.* [1829–] **L.**BM.; MA. 29–31; S. 1848–1852: 24–25: 37–39.

8416 **Bollettino** delle **sedute** dell'**Accademia Gioenia** di **scienze naturali** in **Catania.** Catania. *Boll. Sed. Accad. gioenia Sci. nat.* [1888–] **L.**BMN. 88–39; M. 04–; R. 88–52; TD. 11–18; UC. 04–24; **Db.** 89–; **E.**R. imp.

8417 **Bollettino** di **sericoltura.** Roma. *Boll. Seric.*

8418 **Bollettino. Servizio geologico** d'**Italia.** Italia. *Boll. Serv. geol. Ital.* [1945–] **L.**BMN.; GL.; GM.; SC.; [*C. of:* 8400]

8419 **Bollettino** della **Sezione entomologica** del **R. Osservatorio fitopatologico** di **Milano.** *Boll. Sez. ent. R. Oss. fitopatol. Milano* [1935] **L.**BMN.; EB.; SC.; **E.**R.; **Rt.**

8420 **Bollettino** della **Sezione** di **Firenze** dell'**Associazione nazionale** degli **ingegneri italiani.** Collegio toscano degli ingegneri ed architetti. Firenze. *Boll. Sez. Firenze Ass. naz. Ing. ital.*

8421 **Bollettino** della **Sezione italiana. Società internazionale** di **microbiologia.** Milano. *Boll. Sez. ital. Soc. int. Microbiol.* [1929–39] **L.**LI. 29–30; MC. 29–38; MD.; MY. 31–39; TD.; V. 34–39; **Bl.**U.; **E.**U. 31–35; **O.**P.; **R.**D. v. imp.; **Rt.** 30–35 imp.

8422 **Bollettino** della **Sezione meteorologica, Cirenaica.** Tripoli. *Boll. Sez. met. Cirenaica* [1923–31] **L.**MO. [*C. in:* 8355]

8423 **Bollettino** della **Sezione meteorologica, Tripolitania.** Tripoli. *Boll. Sez. met. Tripolit.* [1923–31] **L.**MO. [*C. in:* 8355]

8424 **Bollettino** della **Sezione** di **Trento** del **Consiglio provinciale** d'**agricoltura** pel **Tirolo.** Trento. *Boll. Sez. Trento Cons. prov. Agric. Tirolo*

8425 **Bollettino** delle **sezioni regionali. Società italiana** di **dermatologia** e **sifilografia.** Milano. *Boll. Sezni reg. Soc. ital. Derm. Sif.* [1931–] **L.**MD.; S.

8426 **Bollettino** del **Sindacato** per l'**incremento** dell'**agricoltura** e dell'**industria nazionale.** Rovigo. *Boll. Sind. Increm. Agric. Ind. naz.*

8427 **Bollettino** del **Sindacato provinciale geometri** di **Parma.** *Boll. Sind. prov. geom. Parma*

8428 **Bollettino sismico.** Roma. *Boll. sismico, Roma*

8428° **Bollettino sismico. Osservatorio geofisico.** Trieste. *Boll. sismico Oss. geophys., Trieste* **Y.**

8429 **Bollettino sismografico** dell'**Osservatorio** di **Quarto-Castello.** Firenze. *Boll. sismogr. Oss. Qto-Castello* **O.**O. 98–06.

8430 **Bollettino sismologico** dell'**Osservatorio 'Morabito'** nel **Seminario** di **Mileto.** *Boll. sism. Oss. Morabito*

8431 **Bollettino sismologico** dell'**Osservatorio Ximeniano** dei **PP.** delle **scuole pie** di **Firenze.** Firenze. *Boll. sism. Oss. Ximeniano* [1901–]

8432 **Bollettino sismologico** del **R. Osservatorio geodinamico** di **Catania.** *Boll. sism. R. Oss. geodin. Catania*

8433 **Bollettino** per i **soci** della **Lega italiana** per la **lotta** contro i **tumori.** Roma. *Boll. Soci Lega ital. Lotta Tumori* [1951–] **L.**CB. 55–; MA. 55–.

8434 **Bollettino** della **Società adriatica** di **scienze naturali** in **Trieste.** Trieste. *Boll. Soc. adriat. Sci. nat.* [1874–] **L.**AM. 31–39; BMN. 74–39: 56–; R. 75–; SC. 34–; **E.**C. 78–93; R. 75: 80–86 imp.; **Lo.** 31–39; **Lv.**U. 90–93: 14– imp.; **Pl.**M. imp.; **Y.**

8435 **Bollettino** della **Società aeronautica italiana.** Roma. *Boll. Soc. aeronaut. ital.* [1904–08] **L.**P.; SC. [*C. as:* 47985]

8436 **Bollettino** della **Società africana** d'**Italia. Sezione fiorentina.** Firenze. *Boll. Soc. afr. Ital. Sez. fiorent.*

8437 **Bollettino** della **Società** degli **agricoltori italiani.** Roma. *Boll. Soc. Agric. ital.*

Bollettino della **Società astronomica italiana.** *See* 47828.

8438 **Bollettino** della **Società** di **biologia sperimentale.** Napoli. *Boll. Soc. Biol. sper.* [1925–26] **E.**U. 26. [*C. as:* 8448]

8439 **Bollettino** della **Società botanica italiana.** Firenze. *Boll. Soc. bot. ital.* [1892–26] **L.**BM.; BMN.; K.; L.; R. imp.; **Abd.**U. 92–02: 04–12; **C.**UL.; **E.**B.; **O.**BO. 92–15.

8440 **Bollettino** della **Società** fra i **cultori** di **scienze mediche** e **naturali** in **Cagliari.** *Boll. Soc. Cult. Sci. med. nat. Cagliari* [1896–26] **Lv.**U. 26. [*C. as:* 5237]

8441 **Bollettino** della **Società entomologica italiana.** Firenze, Genova. *Boll. Soc. ent. ital.* [1869–] **L.**BM.; BMN. imp.; E.; EB. 10–; Z.; **Bl.**U. 84–89; **C.**UL. 22–; **G.**N.; **O.**R. 81–; **Y.**

8442 **Bollettino** della **Società Eustachiana.** Camerino. *Boll. Soc. eustach.* **L.**V. 32–40 imp.; **Bn.**U. 38–39.

8443 **Bollettino** della **Società fiorentina** d'**igiene.** Firenze. *Boll. Soc. fiorent. Ig.*

8444 **Bollettino** della **Società generale** dei **viticoltori italiani.** Roma. *Boll. Soc. gen. Vitic. ital.*

8445 **Bollettino** della **Società geografica italiana.** Roma. *Boll. Soc. geogr. ital.* [1868–] **L.**AN. 16–; BM.; G. 86–; QM. 57–; U. 24–41; UC. 05–21; **Db.** 82–; **E.**G.; U. 49–; **G.**U. 50–; **H.**U. 60–; **O.**B.; **Y.**

8446 **Bollettino** della **Società geologica italiana.** Roma. *Boll. Soc. geol. ital.* [1882–] **L.**BM.; BMN.; GL. 00–; GM.; SC. 52–; **Abs.**U. 57–; **C.**S. 83–; **Db.**; **E.**J. 99–; **G.**G. 06–; **Lv.**U. 24–; **Y.**

8447 **Bollettino** della **Società** degli **ingegneri** ed **architetti italiani.** Roma. *Boll. Soc. Ing. Archit. ital.*

8448 **Bollettino** della **Società italiana** di **biologia sperimentale.** Napoli, etc. *Boll. Soc. ital. Biol. sper.* [1927–] **L.**C. 56–; EB. 31–59 imp.; MA. 46–; MC. 35–45: 55–; MD. 46–; OP. 53–; R. 40–; S. 33–40 imp.; SC.; UC. 32–; **Abd.**R. 35–40: 57–; **C.**APH. 49–55: 59–; B. 54–; P. 33–; **E.**U.; **O.**BI.; **Pl.**M. 53–; **R.**D. 51–; **Y.** [*C. of:* 8438]

8449 **Bollettino** della **Società italiana** di **cardiologia.** Roma. *Boll. Soc. ital. Cardiol.* [1956–] **L.**MA.

8450 **Bollettino** della **Società italiana** di **dermatologia** e **sifilografia.** Roma. *Boll. Soc. ital. Derm. Sif.*
Sezioni regionali, Milano. [1931–37] **L.**S.

8451 **Bollettino** della **Società italiana** di **elettricità.** Milano. *Boll. Soc. ital. Elett.*

8452 **Bollettino** della **Società italiana** di **fisica.** Bologna. *Boll. Soc. ital. Fis.* [1951–] **L.**P. (curr.); SC. 60–; **Bn.**U. 56– imp.; **Db.** 56–; **Ld.**U. 57–; **Sh.**U. 59–; **Te.**C. 58–; **Y.**

8453 **Bollettino** della **Società italiana** di **fotogrammetria** e **topografia.** Roma. *Boll. Soc. ital. Fotogramm. Topogr.* **L.**P. 58–.

8454 **Bollettino** della **Società italiana** di **medicina** e **d'igiene coloniale.** Roma. *Boll. Soc. ital. Med. Ig. colon.* [1908–] **L.**TD. 08–11.

8455 **Bollettino** della **Società italiana** di **medicina** e **igiene tropicale. Sezione Eritrea.** Asmara. *Boll. Soc. ital. Med. Ig. trop. Sez. Eritrea* [1942–50] **L.**EB.; MA.; MD. 42–43; TD.; **W.** 47–50.

8456 **Bollettino** della **Società italiana** di **patologia.** Torino. *Boll. Soc. ital. Patol.*

8457 **Bollettino** della **Società italiana** di **pediatria.** Torino. *Boll. Soc. ital. Pediat.* **L.**MD. 33–36.

8458 **Bollettino** della **Società italiana** per lo **studio** dell' **alimentazione.** Firenze. *Boll. Soc. ital. Stud. Aliment.*

8459 **Bollettino** della **Società lancisiana** degli **ospedali.** Roma. *Boll. Soc. lancis. Osp.*

8460 **Bollettino** della **Società lombarda** per la **pesca** e **l'acquicoltura.** Como. *Boll. Soc. lomb. Pesca Acquic.* **Db.** 14. [*C. of:* 47925]

8461 **Bollettino. Società medica 'Lazzaro Spallanzani.'** Reggio Emilia. *Boll. Soc. med. Lazzaro Spallanzani*

8462 **Bollettino** della **Società medica** di **Parma.** Parma. *Boll. Soc. med. Parma* [*C. of:* 42533; *C. as:* 5087]

8463 **Bollettino. Società medica provinciale** di **Bergamo.** *Boll. Soc. med. prov. Bergamo*

8464 **Bollettino** della **Società** di **medicina** e **chirurgia** del **Salento.** Lecce. *Boll. Soc. Med. Chir. Salento*

8465 **Bollettino** della **Società medico-chirurgica.** Cremona. *Boll. Soc. med.-chir., Cremona* [1946–] **L.**D.; MA. 47–; MD.; U.; **Bl.**U. 48– imp.

8466 **Bollettino** della **Società medico-chirurgica bresciana.** Brescia. *Boll. Soc. med.-chir. bresciana*

8467 **Bollettino** della **Società medico-chirurgica** di **Modena.** *Boll. Soc. med.-chir. Modena* [1887–] **L.**MA. 46–; S. 14–20.

8468 **Bollettino** della **Società medico-chirurgica** di **Pavia.** *Boll. Soc. med.-chir. Pavia* [1887–] **L.**MC. 20–39 imp.: 50–; MD. 25–40; S. 20–40.

8469 **Bollettino. Società medico-chirurgica** di **Pisa.** Pisa. *Boll. Soc. med.-chir. Pisa* **L.**MA. 54–; MD. 55–.

8470 **Bollettino** della **Società medico-chirurgica** della **provincia** di **Varese.** Varese. *Boll. Soc. med.-chir. Prov. Varese*

8471 **Bollettino** della **Società medico-chirurgica trevigiana.** Treviso. *Boll. Soc. med.-chir. trevig.* [1934–38] [*C. as:* 21280]

Bollettino della **Società meteorologica italiana.** See 8232 and 8346]

8472 **Bollettino** della **Società** di **naturalisti** i **Napoli.** Napoli. *Boll. Soc. Nat. Napoli* [1887–] **L.**BM.; BM^N.; R. 88–29 imp.; Z.; **C.**P.; **Pl.**M. 89– imp.

8473 **Bollettino** della **Società paleontologica italiana.** Modena. *Boll. Soc. paleont. ital.* [1960–] **L.**BM^N.

8473^c **Bollettino** della **Società piemontese** di **ostetricia** e **ginecologia.** Torino. *Boll. Soc. piemont. Ostet. Ginec.* [1933–34] [*Replaced by:* 21209]

8474 **Bollettino** della **Società** di **scienze naturali** ed **economiche** di **Palermo.** *Boll. Soc. Sci. nat. econ. Palermo* [1877–] **L.**BM^N. 19–42; GM. 19–.

8475 **Bollettino** della **Società sismologica italiana.** Roma. *Boll. Soc. sism. ital.* [1895–] **L.**GL. 00–30; SC. 24–; **C.**P. 07–32 imp.

Bollettino della **Società storico-scientifica maltese.** See 4687.

8476 **Bollettino** della **Società ticinese** di **scienze naturali.** Bellinzona. *Boll. Soc. ticin. Sci. nat.* [1904–] **L.**BM^N. 04–39: 41– imp.; L. 48–; SC. 34–40: 49–.

8477 **Bollettino** della **Società toscana** di **ostetricia** e **ginecologia.** Firenze. *Boll. Soc. tosc. Ostet. Ginec.*

8478 **Bollettino** della **Società veneziana** di **storia naturale** e del **Museo civico** di **storia naturale.** Venezia. *Boll. Soc. veneziana Stor. nat.* [1932–52] **L.**BM^N. imp.; EB. 32–43: 49–52; SC.; **Fr.** 49–52; **O.**H. imp. [*C. as:* 8362]

8479 **Bollettino** della **Società zoologica italiana.** Roma. *Boll. Soc. zool. ital.* [1892–19] **L.**BM.; BM^N.; EB. 13–19; Z.; **Bl.**U.; **C.**P. 01–17; **Dm.**; **G.**N. 92–14; **Lv.**U. 92–14. [*C. as:* 8300]

8480 **Bollettino** delle **specialità medico-chirurgiche.** Milano. *Boll. Spec. med.-chir.*

8481 **Bollettino** della **Stazione chimico-agraria sperimentale** di **Roma.** Roma. *Boll. Staz. chim.-agr. sper. Roma* **C.**A. 32–; **Rt.** 02–.

8482 **Bollettino. Stazione forestale** del **Centro sperimentale agrario** e **forestale.** Trieste. *Boll. Staz. for. Cent. sper. agr. for., Trieste* [1947–]
Ser. 1. Sperimentazioni, studi, richerche. **O.**F.

8483 **Bollettino** della **Stazione** di **patologia vegetale** di **Roma.** Firenze. *Boll. Staz. Patol. veg. Roma* [1926–] **L.**AM.; EB.; MY.; **Abs.**A. 31–40; **C.**A. 31–; **E.**B. 31–39; **Md.**H. 26–29; **Rt.** 26–40 imp.; **Y.** [*C. of:* 8340]

8484 **Bollettino. Stazione sperimentale** di **ortifrutticoltura.** Milano. *Boll. Staz. sper. Ortifruttic., Milano*

8485 **Bollettino** di **studi** e **informazioni. R. Giardino botanico (coloniale).** Palermo. *Boll. Studi Inf. R. Giard. bot., Palermo* **L.**BM^N. 14–20; K. 14–29 imp.

Bollettino tecnico dell'**Amministrazione** dei **telegrafi** e dei **telefoni svizzeri.** Berna. See 52562.

8486 **Bollettino tecnico** della **coltivazione** dei **tabacchi.** R. Istituto sperimentale de Scafati (Salerno)-Portici. *Boll. tec. Colt. Tab.* [1902–] **L.**P. 33–41; **C.**A. 35–41; **Db.** 22–; **Lv.**U. 36–41; **Rt.** 36–40.

8487 **Bollettino tecnico. Direzione sperimentale** dell' **aviazione.** Roma. *Boll. tec. Dir. sper. Aviaz.*

8488 **Bollettino tecnico. Laboratorio elettrotecnico Luigi Magrini.** Bergamo. *Boll. tec. Lab. elettrotec. Luigi Magrini* L.P. 24–32* imp.

8489 **Bollettino tecnico ligure.** Genova. *Boll. tec. ligure*
 Bollettino tecnico PTT. *See* 52557.

8490 **Bollettino tecnico Savigliano.** Torino. *Boll. tec. savigl.* L.P. 28–49. [*Suspended* June 1938–Aug. 1948]

8491 **Bollettino ufficiale** per l'**amministrazione forestale italiana.** Roma. *Boll. uff. Ammin. for. ital.*

8492 **Bollettino ufficiale** dell'**Associazione orticola professionale italiana.** San Remo. *Boll. uff. Ass. ortic. prof. ital.* L.K. 13–15 imp.

8493 **Bollettino ufficiale** del **Comizio agrario biellese.** Biella. *Boll. uff. Com. agr. biell.*

8494 **Bollettino ufficiale** del **controllo chimico permanente italiano.** Genova. *Boll. uff. Controllo chim. perm. ital.*

8494ᶜ **Bollettino ufficiale. Corpo forestale** dello **stato.** Roma. *Boll. uff. Corpo for. St.* [1958–] O.F.

8495 **Bollettino ufficiale** del **Ministero** dell'**agricoltura** e delle **foreste.** Roma. *Boll. uff. Minist. Agric. Foreste* [1929–] L.AM. (4 yr.); BM.; **Abs.**N.; **Y.**

8496 **Bollettino ufficiale** del **Ministero** d'**agricoltura, industria** e **commercio.** Roma. *Boll. uff. Minist. Agric. Ind. Comm.* [1902–21] L.AM.; BM. 09–17; **Abs.**N. imp. [*C. of:* 8364]

8497 **Bollettino ufficiale** del **Ministero** dei **lavori pubblici.** Roma. *Boll. uff. Minist. Lav. pubbl.*

8498 **Bollettino ufficiale** della **R. Stazione sperimentale** per l'**industria** delle **essenze** e dei **derivati** degli **agrumi** in **Reggio Calabria.** *Boll. uff. R. Staz. sper. Ind. Essenze Reggio Calabria* L.C. 33–.

8499 **Bollettino ufficiale R. Stazione sperimentale** per l'**industria** delle **pelli** e delle **materie concianti.** Napoli. *Boll. uff. R. Staz. sper. Ind. Pelli* [1923–43] L.C.; LE. 33–39; P. 26–43; **Y.** [*C. as:* 16150]
 Bollettino ufficiale. R. Stazione sperimentale per la **seta.** Milano. *See* 8500.

8500 **Bollettino ufficiale. Stazione sperimentale** per la **seta.** Milano. *Boll. uff. Staz. sper. Seta, Milano* L.P. 26–39: 51–52; **M.**C. 31–38. [*Suspended* 1940–50; *C. as:* 49585]

8501 **Bollettino. Ufficio centrale** per i **servizi agrari** della **Libia.** Tripoli. *Boll. Uff. cent. Serv. agr. Libia* [1932–36] L.TD. [*C. as:* 1238]

8502 **Bollettino. Ufficio idrografico, Venezia.** *Boll. Uff. idrogr. Venezia* [1908–11] L.G. imp.; MO. [*C. as:* 8345]
 Bollettino dell'**Ufficio veterinario** e della **Divisione** di **agricoltura** [del] **Dipartimento svizzero** dell'**economia pubblica.** *See* 32851.

8503 **Bollettino** dell'**Unione agraria italiana.** Roma. *Boll. Un. agr. ital.*

8504 **Bollettino** dell'**Unione matematica italiana.** Bologna. *Boll. Un. mat. ital.* [1922–] L.SC. 24–39: 52–; U. 57–; UC.; **C.**UL.; E.Q. (curr.); R. 38–52 imp.; O.R. 50–; **Y.**

8505 **Bollettino** dell' **Università italiana** per **stranieri.** Perugia. *Boll. Univ. ital. Stran.* [1929–] L.U. 35–40; **Abs.**U. imp.; **Bm.**U.; **Ld.**U.; **Nw.**A. 29–32.

8506 **Bollettino veterinario italiano.** Torino. *Boll. vet. ital.* [1905–] L.SC. 31–; V. 34–39 imp.

8507 **Bollettino** di **zoologia agraria** e **bachicoltura.** Torino, etc. *Boll. Zool. agr. Bachic.* [1936–] L.BMᴺ.; EB.; SC.; E.R.; **Md.**H. 45– imp.; **Rt.**; **Y.** [*C. of:* 8305]

8508 **Bollettino** di **zoologia,** pubblicato dall' **Unione zoologica italiana.** Napoli, etc. *Boll. Zool.* [1930–] L.BMᴺ.; EB.; SC. 38–; Z. 48–; **Y.**

8509 **Bol'nichnaya gazeta Botkina.** S.-Peterburg Больничная газета Боткина. *Bol'n. Gaz. Botkina* [1890–03]

8510 **Bologna medica.** Bologna. *Bologna med.* [1960–] L.MD. [*C. of:* 47913]

8511 **Bolotovêdênie.** Minsk. Болотовѣдѣніе. *Bolotovêdênie*

8512 **Bombay Cotton Annual.** Bombay. *Bombay Cott. A.* [1919–] **M.**P.; O.I. 45–.

8513 **Bombay Geographical Magazine.** Bombay. *Bombay geogr. Mag.* [1953–] L.G.; C.GG. imp.; E.G. (curr.); **Y.**

8514 **Bombay Medical Journal.** Bombay. *Bombay med. J.* [1932–36] L.TD. 32–35 imp.; Lv.U.
 Bombay Medical and **Physical Society. Reports** of **Meetings.** Bombay. *See* 44485.

8515 **Bombay Technologist.** Bombay. *Bombay Technol.* [1951–] **Y.**

8516 **Bombay Veterinary College Magazine.** Bombay. *Bombay vet. Coll. Mag.* [1949–] L.V. 49.

8517 **Bombus.** Faunistische Mitteilungen aus Nordwestdeutschland und der Nordmark. Hamburg. *Bombus* [1937–] L.BMᴺ. 37–39: 46–; E. 37–39: 46–48; **Y.**

8518 **Bombyx.** Eisenach. *Bombyx* [1925–] L.P.

8519 **Bonderizer.** Brentford. *Bonderizer* [1951–] L.BM. 57–; P.

8520 **Bonds nieuws.** Officieele mededeelingen van den Bond van N. A. F. V. Amsterdam. *Bonds Nieuws N.A.F.V.* L.PG. 27–40 imp.: 47–.

8521 **Bonne terre.** Sainte-Anne de la Pocatière. *Bonne Terre* [1919–43] L.AM. 37–43.

8522 **Bonner geographische Abhandlungen.** Bonn. *Bonn. geogr. Abh.* [1947–] L.G.; UC. imp. [*C. of:* 5979]

8523 **Bonner zoologische Beiträge.** Bonn. *Bonn. zool. Beitr.* [1950–] L.BMᴺ.; SC. 55–; Z.; O.AP.; OR.

8524 **Bonytt.** Oslo. *Bonytt* L.BA. 44–.
 Book of **A.S.T.M. Standards.** *See* 123.
 Book of the **A.S.T.M. Tentative Standards.** *See* 126.

8524ᶜ **Book** of **Normals.** Commonwealth Bureau of Meteorology. Melbourne. *Bk Norm. Commonw. Bur. Met.* [1956–] L.BM.

8525 **Booklet. Forestry Commission.** London. *Bookl. For. Commn* [1947–] L.BMᴺ.; HS. imp.; P.; **Bm.**P.; **Ld.**P.; O.AP.; F.; **Rt.**; **Y.**

8526 **Booklet Series. Agricultural Organisation Society.** London. *Bookl. Ser. agric. Org. Soc.* L.AM. 19–22.

8526ᶜ **Boor** en **spade.** Utrecht. *Boor Spade* [1948–] L.BM.

8527 **Bör** es **cipötechnika.** Budapest. *Bör Cipötech.* **Y.**

8528 **Borászati lapok.** Budapest. *Borász. Lapok*

8529 **Bor'ba** za **khlopok.** Tashkent. Борьба за хлопок. *Bor'ba Khlop.* [1933–37] **L.**BM.; **C.**A.; **Rt.** imp. [*C. as:* 50096]

8530 **Bor'ba** s **silikozom.** Moskva. Борьба с силикозом. *Bor'ba Silik.* [1953–] **L.**BM.; **P.** 59–.

8531 **Bor'ba** s **tuberkulezom.** Moskva. Борьба с туберкулезом. *Bor'ba Tuberk.* [1930–35] **L.**MD. 32–35; TD. 35. [*C. of:* 56942; *C. as:* 38786]

8531° **Borba** protiv **tuberkuloze.** Beograd. *Borba Tuberk.* [1953–] **L.**BM.

8532 **Borbásia,** Dissertationes botanicae. Budapest. *Borbásia* [1938–] **L.**BM^N.; L. 38–39.

8532° **Borbata** sŭs **silikozata** v **Bulgariya.** Sofiya. Борбата със силикозата в България. *Borbata Silik. Bulg.* [1956–] **L.**BM.

8533 **Bordeaux chirurgical.** Bordeaux. *Bordeaux chir.* [1930–] **L.**MA. imp.; MD. 43–; S.; **Br.**U.; **G.**F. 44–.

8534 **Borden's Review** of **Nutrition Research.** New York. *Borden's Rev. Nutr. Res.* [1940–] **L.**AM. 49–; MD. 56–; TP. 46–50; **Abd.**R. 61–; **R.**D. 52–.

8535 **Bórgyógyászati** és **venerologiai szemle.** Budapest. *Bórgyóg. vener. Szle* **Y.**

8536 **Boring Records. Victoria Department** of **Mines.** Melbourne. *Boring Rec. Vict. Dep. Mines* **L.**MI. 49–.

8537 **Böripar.** Budapest. *Böripar*

8538 **Böripari szemle.** Budapest. *Börip. Szle*

8538ᵃ **Bör-** és **bujakortan.** *Bör- és Bujakortan* [*Supplement to:* 29238]

8539 **Bornova Ziraat Mücadele İstasyonu İzmir.** İzmir. *Bornova Zir. Müc. İstas. İzmir* [1940–] **L.**EB. (ent.) 40–41.

8540 **Boron** in **Agriculture.** London. *Boron Agric.* [1957–] **L.**MY.; P. 59–; TP. 59–; **Md.**H.; **Y.** [*C. of:* 1368]

8541 **Boron** in **Glass.** London. *Boron Glass* [1957–] **L.**P.; **Y.**

8542 **Boron** and **Plant Life.** London. *Boron Pl. Life* [1935–] **L.**AM.; **O.**B. 55–.

8543 **Boron** as a **Plant Nutrient.** [Bibliographies.] American Potash Institute. Washington. *Boron Pl. Nutrient* [1936–] **L.**P. 36–53; **O.**BO. 46–; **Y.**

8544 **Borsig Mitteilungen.** Berlin-Tegel. *Borsig Mitt.* **L.**P. 33–35. [*C. of:* 8546; *C. as:* 47686]

8545 **Borsig Technical Review.** Berlin-Tegel. *Borsig tech. Rev.* [1930–34] [*C. as:* 47687]

8546 **Borsig-Zeitung.** Berlin-Tegel. *Borsig-Ztg* [1923–31] **L.**P. [*C. as:* 8544]

8547 **Bortermelők lapja.** Budapest. *Borterm. Lapja*

8548 **Boschbouwkundig tijdschrift.** Semarang. *Boschbouwk. Tijdschr.* [1908–19] [*C. as:* 52670]

8549 **Bosch-Zunder.** Berlin. *Bosch-Zunder* **L.**AV. 37–42 imp.

8550 **Bosco.** Comitato nazionale forestale. Milano. *Bosco* [1925–]

8551 **Bosques** y **maderas** de **Chile.** Santiago de Chile. *Bosq. Maderas Chile* [1957–] **O.**F.

8552 **Boston Medical Quarterly.** Boston. *Boston med. Q.* [1950–] **L.**GH.; MA.; MC.; MD.; S.; TD.

8553 **Boston Medical** and **Surgical Journal.** Boston. *Boston med. surg. J.* [1828–28] **L.**BM.; MA. 93–28; MD. 68–28; S. 1836–28; TD. 15–28; UC. 21–28; **Bm.**U. 84–10: 21–27; **Br.**U. imp.; **C.**PA. 95–09; **Db.** 75–28 imp.; **E.**P.; S. 21–28; U. 88–20; **G.**F. imp.; **Lv.**M. 80–08: 18–27; U. 21–28; **M.**MS. 1829–28 imp.; **O.**R. 70–28. [*C. as:* 34640]

8554 **Boston University Bulletin.** Boston, Mass. *Boston Univ. Bull.* [1918–26] **Abs.**A. 21–26; U. 20–26; **Bm.**U. 24–26; **Db.**; **N.**U. 19–26; **O.**RE. 20–26; **R.**U.

8555 **Botanic Annual.** Bolton. *Botanic A.* [1907–09] **L.**BM.; **O.**R. 07: 09. [*C. of:* 8556]

8556 **Botanic Physician.** Bolton. *Botanic Physn* [1905] **L.**BM.; **O.**R. [*C. as:* 8555]

8557 **Botânica.** Instituto nacional de pesquisas da Amazônia. Rio de Janeiro. *Botânica* [1956–] **L.**BM^N.

8558 **Botanica agraria, tecnologica e merceologica.** Milano. *Botanica agr. tecnol. merceol.* [1934–] **L.**SC. **Botanica experimentalis.** *See* 54489.

8559 **Botanica marina.** International Review for Seaweed Research and Utilization. Internationale Zeitschrift für die Erforschung und Auswertung von Meeresalgen. Hamburg. *Botanica mar.* [1959–] **L.**B.; BM^N.; SC.; **Bl.**U.; **Bn.**U.; **C.**BO.; **G.**U.; **Ld.**U.; **Pl.**M.

8560 **Botanica oeconomica.** Hamburg. *Botanica oecon.* [1948–] **L.**SC.; **Rt.** 48.

8561 **Botanical Abstracts.** Baltimore, Md. *Bot. Abstr.* [1918–26] **L.**AM.; B.; BM^N.; HS. 20–21; K. 18–22; L.; MY. 21–26; P.; SC.; **Abd.**U.; **Abs.**A.; **Bl.**U.; **Bm.**P.; U.; **Bn.**U.; **Br.**A.; U.; **C.**BO.; UL.; **Cr.**U.; **Dn.**U.; **E.**B.; **Fr.**; **G.**M.; U.; **Ld.**U.; **Lv.**U.; **M.**P. 21–26; U.; **Md.**H. 21–26; **N.**U. 19–26; **Nw.**A.; **O.**BO.; F.; RE. 20–26; **Pit.**F. 18–21; **R.**U.; **Rt.**; Sa. 20–26; **Sal.**F. 25–26; **Sw.**U. 21–26. [*C. in:* 7057]

8562 **Botanical Bulletin** of **Academia sinica.** Taipei. *Bot. Bull. Acad. sin., Taipei* [1960–] **L.**BM^N.; **C.**A.

8563 **Botanical Bulletin** of **Academia sinica.** Shanghai. *Bot. Bull. Acad. sin., Shanghai* [1947–49] **L.**BM^N.; K.; MY.; SC.; **Bn.**U.; **C.**A.; P.; BO.; **E.**B.; R. 47; **Fr.**; **O.**BO.; F.; **Pl.**M. 47–48; **Rt.**

8564 **Botanical Bulletin. Board of Commissioners** of **Agriculture** and **Forestry, Hawaii.** Honolulu. *Bot. Bull. Bd Commnrs Agric. For. Hawaii* [1911–17] **L.**BM.; BM^N.; K.; SC. 12–17.

8565 **Botanical Bulletin. Presidency College, Madras.** *Bot. Bull. Pres. Coll. Madras* [1912–21] **L.**BM. imp.; BM^N. 14–21; K.

8566 **Botanical Gazette.** Chicago. *Bot. Gaz.* [1875–] **L.**B. 01– imp.; BM. 11–; BM^N.; IC. 47–; K.; L.; NP. 16–37; PH. 88–; QM. 01– imp.; SC.; UC. 05–; **Abd.**U. 86–; **Abs.**A. 51–; U. 80– imp.; **Ba.**I. 03–; **Bl.**U. 98–; **Bm.**U. 88–89: 96–; **Bn.**U. 98–; **Br.**A. 55–; U.; **C.**BO.; UL. 11–; **Cr.**U. 98–; **Db.** 03–; **Dn.**U. 99–02; **E.**A. 50–57; B. imp.; **Ex.**U. 28–; **G.**U.; **H.**U. 19–; **Hu.**G. 40–; **Je.** 44–; **Ld.**U.; **Lv.**U. imp.; **M.**U. 97–; **Md.**H. 26–; **N.**U. 95–00: 06– imp.; **Nw.**A. 96–; **O.**BO. 86–; **Pl.**M. 10–32 imp.; **R.**U. 08–; **Rt.** 18–; Sa. 75–95; **Sh.**U. 96–; **Sw.**U. 01–03; **Y.**

8567 **Botanical Journal.** London. *Bot. J.* [1910–18] **L.**AM.; BM.; BM^N.; K.; MO.; SC. 12–16; **Abs.**N. 16–18; **O.**BO. imp. [*C. of:* 41593; *C. as:* 41646]

8568 **Botanical Leaflets.** Chicago. *Bot. Leafl.* **L.**BM^N. 50–; **O.**BO. 50–54.
 Botanical Magazine. London. *See* 16210.

8569 **Botanical Magazine.** Tokyo. *Bot. Mag., Tokyo* [1887–] **L.**BM.; BM^N.; K. 89–; L. 90– imp.; MY. 22–; SC. 87–98: 30–; **Abs.**A. 22–32 imp.; **C.**BO. 91–39: 41–; **E.**B. 92–16: 23–; **G.**U. 08–21; **M.**U. 08– imp.; **O.**BO. 28–32 imp.
 Botanical Memoirs. London. *See* 36644.

8570 **Botanical Memoirs. University** of **Bombay.** Bombay. *Bot. Mem. Univ. Bombay* [1951–] **L.**BM^N.

8571 **Botanical Museum Leaflets.** Harvard University. Cambridge, Mass. *Bot. Mus. Leafl. Harv. Univ.* [1932–] **L.**BM^N.; K.; **C.**A.; **E.**B.

8572 **Botanical Notes. Nigerian College** of **Technology,** Ibadan Branch. Ibadan. *Bot. Notes Niger. Coll. Technol. Ibadan* **L.**BM^N. 60–.

8573 **Botanical Review.** Lancaster, Pa. *Bot. Rev.* [1935–] **L.**AM. 37– imp.; B. 46–; BM^N.; HS. 44–; IC. 41–; K.; L.; QM.; SC.; TP. 50–; U. 48–; UC. 39–; VC. 53–; **Abd.**U. 47–; **Abs.**A.; **Ba.**I.; **Bl.**U.; **Bm.**U.; **Bn.**U.; **Br.**A.; U.; **C.**BO.; **Cr.**U.; **Db.** 44–; **E.**AG. 49–; B.; HW. 49–; U. 49–; **Ex.**U. 35–; **Fr.** 46–; **G.**U. imp.; **H.**U.; **Hu.**G. 47–; **Je.**; **Ld.**U.; **Lv.**U. 35– imp.; **M.**U. imp.; **Md.**H.; **N.**T. 49–; U. 37– imp.; **Nw.**A. 37–; **O.**BO.; F.; RE.; **R.**U.; **Rt.** 43–; **Sa.**; **Sh.**U. 46–; **Sw.**U. 37–; **Y.**

8574 **Botanical Series. Mysore Department** of **Agriculture.** Bangalore. *Bot. Ser. Mysore* [1952–] **C.**A.

8575 **Botanical Studies. Butler University.** Indianapolis. *Bot. Stud. Butler Univ.* [1929–] **L.**SC.; **E.**R.

8576 **Botanical Studies** of the **Geological** and **Natural History Society** of **Minnesota.** Minneapolis. *Bot. Stud. geol. nat. Hist. Soc. Minn.* [1892–12] **L.**P.
 Botanical Survey of **Nebraska.** *See* 51161.

8577 **Botanicheskie materialỹ Gerbariya Botanicheskogo instituta V. A. Komarova.** Tashkent. Ботанические материалы Гербария Ботанического института В. А. Комарова. *Bot. Mater. Gerb. bot. Inst. V. A. Komarova* [1940–] **L.**K. 46–54; **C.**P. 57–.

8578 **Botanicheskĭe materialỹ Gerbarĭya Glavnago botanicheskago sada.** Petrograd. Ботаническіе матеріалы Гербарія Главнаго ботаническаго сада. *Bot. Mater. Gerb. glavn. bot. Sada* [1919–26] **L.**BM^N.; K.; **E.**B.; **Rt.** 22–.
 Botanicheskie materialỹ Instituta sporovỹkh rastenii Glavnogo botanicheskogo sada. Petrograd. Ботанические материалы Института споровых растений Главного ботанического сада. *See* 35330.

8580 **Botanicheskii kabinet. Gosudarstvennỹi Nikitskii opỹtnỹi botanicheskii sad.** Yalta. Ботанический кабинет. Государственный Никитский опытный ботанический сад. *Bot. Kab., Yalta* [1916–17]
 Botanicheskii zhurnal. Leningradskoe obshchestvo estestvo-ispỹtatelei. Ботаническій журналъ. Ленинградское общество естество-испытателей. *See* 54588. Sect 3.
 Botanicheskii zhurnal Akademii nauk SSSR. Leningrad. Ботанический журнал Академии наук СССР. *See* 8581.

8581 **Botanicheskii zhurnal SSSR.** Leningrad, Moskva. Ботанический журнал СССР. Ленинград, Москва.

8582 **Botanicheskĭya zapiski, izdanỹya pri Botanicheskom sadê Imperatorskago S.-Peterburgskago universiteta.** Ботаническія записки, изданныя при Ботаническомъ садѣ Императорскаго С.-Петербургскаго университета. *Bot. Zap.* [1886–30] **L.**BM.; BM^N.; K. 86–12; L. 86–09; **C.**UL.; **E.**R. 86–27 imp.

8583 **Botanicheskoe obozrenie. Referiruyushchii organ Glavnogo botanicheskogo sada v Petrograde.** Petrograd. Ботаническое обозрение. Реферирующий орган Главного ботанического сада в Петрограде. *Bot. Oboz.* [1919–23] **L.**BM^N.; K. 22–23.

8584 **Botanichnii zhurnal.** Kỹyiv. Ботанічний журнал. *Bot. Zh., Kỹyiv* [1940–55] **L.**BM.; BM^N. 40: 49–55; SC. 42–45: 51; TP. 44–55 imp.; **C.**A. 40–50; **E.**B.; **Hu.**G. 40–54; **O.**BO. 41–45; **Rt.** [*C. as:* 55484]

8585 **Botanik.** København. *Botanik* **L.**BM^N. 46–.

8586 **Botanika.** Lwów, Warszawa. *Botanika* [1925–] **Abs.**A. 27–38; **C.**BO. 35.

8587 **Botanikai közlemények.** Budapest. *Bot. Közl.* [1909–] **L.**BM^N. 09–39; K. 14–46; L. 24–46; **E.**B. 24–; R. 09–41; **Y.** [*C. of:* 35383]
 Botanikos sodas rastai. Kaunas. *See* 49325.

8588 **Botanisch jaarboek.** Gand. *Bot. Jaarb.* [1889–34] **L.**BM^N.; K. 89–07; L. 89–07; SC. 25–34; **C.**BO. 89–07; **M.**U. 91: 94. [*Replaced by:* 7097]

8589 **Botanische Abhandlungen.** Jena. *Bot. Abh.* [1922–32] **L.**BM^N. 22–28; K.; L.; SC.; **Abd.**U.; **Bl.**U.; **C.**UL.; **G.**U.; **O.**BO.

8590 **Botanische Exkursionen** und **pflanzengeographische Studien** in der **Schweiz.** Zürich. *Bot. Exkurs. pflgeogr. Stud. Schweiz*

8591 **Botanische Garten** und das **Botanische Museum** der **Universität Zürich.** *Bot. Gart. bot. Mus. Univ. Zürich* **L.**BM. 02–; BM^N. 98–07; K. 95–37; SC. 26–; **E.**B. 99– imp.

8592 **Botanische Jahrbücher** für **Systematik, Pflanzengeschichte** und **Pflanzengeographie.** Leipzig, etc. *Bot. Jb.* [1880–] **L.**BM. 86–; BM^N.; HS. 81–39; K.; L. 80–39; SC. 80–40: 45–; **Abd.**U. 94–39; **Bm.**U.; **Br.**U. 90–93: 02–31; **C.**BO.; UL.; **Db.**; **E.**B.; **G.**U. 80–39; **H.**U. 80–19: 29–; **Ld.**U.; **M.**U. 05–; **O.**BO. 80–14: 23–; **Y.**

8593 **Botanische Mitteilungen** aus den **Tropen.** Jena. *Bot. Mitt. Trop.* [1888–01] **L.**BM.; BM^N.; K.; L.; SC.; **Br.**U.; **E.**B.; **O.**BO.

8594 **Botanische Studien.** Jena. *Bot. Stud., Jena* [1952–] **L.**BM. 56–; **Y.**

8595 **Botanische Zeitung.** Berlin & Leipzig. *Bot. Ztg* [1843–10] **L.**BM. 1843–01; BM^N.; K.; L.; SC.; UC. 74–09; **Abd.**U.; **Abs.**U. 72–10; **Bl.**U. 1844–10 imp.; **Bm.**U. imp.; **Bn.**U.; **Br.**U. 75–10; **C.**BO.; UL.; **Db.**; **Dn.**U. 1843–87; **E.**B.; R. imp.; U. 1851–10; **Fr.** 90–04; **G.**U.; **Ld.**U. 76–10; **Lv.**U. 06–10; **M.**U. 71: 77–10; **Nw.**A. 85–10; **O.**BO. 05–10; **Sa.** 00–10; **Sh.**U.
 Botanischer Jahresbericht. *See* 27137.

8596 **Botanisches Archiv.** Berlin, etc. *Bot. Arch.* [1922–44] **L.**BM^N. 22–33: 39–44; K. imp.; L. 22–28; SC. 30–44 imp.; **Abs.**A. 30–31; N.; **C.**UL.; **E.**B.; **Ld.**U.; **M.**U. imp.; **N.**U. 22–37.

8597 **Botanisches Echo.** Königsberg. *Bot. Echo, Königsb.* [1925–27] L.BM^N.; L.; **C.**UL.; **Ld.**U. [*Supplement to* and *C. in:* 8596 *as its* Literaturbesprechungen]

8598 **Botanisches Zentralblatt.** Jena & Dresden. *Bot. Zbl.* [1880–45] **L.**B. 08: 11–16; BM.; BM^N.; C.; L. 80–39; MY. 02–16 imp.; SC.; UC. 99–14; **Abd.**U. 91–43; **Abs.**A. 30–45 imp.; U. 97–45 imp.; **Bl.**U. 92–16; **Bm.**U.; **Bn.**U. 80–18 imp.; **Br.**U.; **C.**BO. 80–17: 22–44; G. 80–16; UL.; **Cr.**U. 92–16; **Db.**; **Dn.**U.; **E.**B.; R. 89–45 imp.; **Fr.** 06–08 imp.; **G.**U. imp. **H.**U. 97–39; **Ld.**U.; **Lv.**U. 06–45; **M.**U. imp.; **N.**U. 80–90: 10–13; **Nw.**A. imp.; **O.**BO.; **R.**U.; **Rt.** 12–27; **Sh.**U. 96–16. [*Supplements at:* 5905]

8599 **Botanisk Tidsskrift.** Kjøbenhavn. *Bot. Tidsskr.* [1866–] **L.**BM.; BM^N.; C.; L.; SC. 37–; **Bm.**U. 39–; **C.**BO. 11–; **E.**B. 67–; **Fr.** 52–; **G.**U. imp.; **M.**U. 77–96 imp.; **O.**BO. 86–99: 46–; **Sa.** 56–; **Y.**

Botaniska darza raksti. *See* 602.

8600 **Botaniska notiser.** Lund. *Bot. Notiser* [1839–] **L.**BM.; BM^N.; K. 1849– imp.; L. imp.; SC. 29–; UC. 48–; **Abs.**A. 35–; U. 47–; **Bl.**U. 30–; **Bn.**U. 50–; **C.**BO. 04–14: 16–; **E.**B. 1839–05 imp.; **H.**U. 60–; **Hu.**G. 30–53; **Lv.**U. 42–; **Nw.**A. 42–; **O.**BO. 21–; **Pit.**F. 57–; **Y.** [*Supplements which are C. as:* 36219]

8601 **Botaniste.** Caen, Poitiers, Paris, etc. *Botaniste* [1888–] **L.**BM.; BM^N.; K.; L.; MY. 88–00: 26; SC. 88–34 imp.; **Abd.**U. 00–10; **Br.**U. 03; **C.**BO. 88–14; UL.; **Db.**; **E.**B.; **G.**U. 10–; **Ld.**U. 49–; **Lv.**U. 26–31; **M.**U.; **Rt.**; **Y.**

8602 **Botany Bulletin.** Department of Agriculture, Queensland. Brisbane. *Botany Bull. Dep. Agric. Qd* [1890–20] **L.**K. imp.; P. 90–03; SC. 93–20; **E.**B.

8603 **Botany. Current Literature.** Bureau of Plant Industry. Washington. *Botany curr. Lit.* **Md.**H. 32–34* imp.; **O.**F. 29–34. [*C. as:* 37870]

8604 **Botany of Iceland.** Copenhagen. *Botany Icel.* [1912–] **O.**BO.

8605 **Botany Pamphlet.** Carnegie Museum. Pittsburgh. *Botany Pamph. Carnegie Mus.* [1935–] **L.**SC.

8606 **Botany** and **Zoology,** theoretical and applied. Tokyo. *Botany Zool., Tokyo* [1933–43] **L.**BM^N. 35–43; **C.**A. 33–41; **E.**AB. 35; **Pl.**M. 35–41.

Botanȳchnii zhurnal. Kȳyiv. Ботанічнїй журнал. *See* 8584.

8608 **Bothalia.** National Herbarium. Pretoria. *Bothalia* [1921–] **L.**AM. 21–50 imp.; BM.; BM^N.; K.; L.; MY.; TP.; **Abs.**A. 21–41; **Br.**A. 60–; **E.**B.; **G.**U.; **Lh.**P. 45–51; **O.**BO.; F.; **Rt.** 50–; **Y.**

8609 **Botteghe oscure.** Roma. *Botteghe osc.* [1948–] **L.**BM.; **E.**U. 49–.

8610 **Bottler** and **Packer.** London. *Bottler Pckr* [1927–57] **L.**AM. 48–57; P. 31–57; TP. 30–57; **Lh.**P. 45–51; **Lv.**P. 52–57; **Sh.**IO. 52–57; **Y.** [*C. as:* 23817]

8611 **Bottlers' Year Book.** Guildford. *Bottlers' Yb.* **L.**BM. 31–; P. (curr.); **G.**M. 52–; **Ld.**P. (curr.); **Lv.**P. 55–; **O.**B. 38–41; **Y.**

8612 **Bottling.** London. *Bottling* [1924–] **L.**AM. 52–; BM. 29–; P.; **Bm.**U. 39–41: 43; **Ld.**P. (5 yr.); **Lh.**P. 49–; **Nu.**B. 51–; **Sh.**IO. (5 yr.); **Y.** [*Supplement to:* 8731]

8613 **Botyu-kagaku.** Scientific Insect Control. Bulletin of the Institute of Insect Control, Kyoto University. Kyoto. *Botyu-Kagaku* [1937–] **L.**C. 51–; EB.; **Je.** 53–; **Md.**H. 55–; **Rt.** 47–; **Wd.** 48–; **Y.**

8614 **Bourges-hygiène.** Bourges. *Bourges-Hyg.*

8615 **Bourgogne médicale.** Dijon. *Bourgogne méd.*

8616 **Bourgogne odontologique.** Dijon. *Bourgogne odont.*

8617 **Bourgogne vinicole.** Beaune. *Bourgogne vinic.*

8618 **Bourgogne viticole, agricole** et **horticole.** Dijon. *Bourgogne vitic. agric. hort.*

8619 **Bouw.** Den Haag. *Bouw* [1946–] **L.**BA.; **Nw.**A. 48–; **Wa.**B.

8620 **Bouwbedrijf.** Antwerpen. *Bouwbedrijf* [1924–] **L.**BA. 36–40; SC. 33–.

8620° **Bouwbedrijvigheid** en **bouwmaterialen.** 's-Gravenhage. *Bouwbedrijv. Bouwmater.* [1947–51] **L.**BM. [*C. as:* 36635°]

8621 **Bouwcentrum.** Den Haag. *Bouwcentrum* [1946–] **L.**BA. 48–.

8621° **Bouwkroniek.** Brussel. *Bouwkroniek* **Y.**

8622 **Bouwkundig weekblad architectura.** 's Gravenhage. *Bouwk. Weekbl. Archit.* [1881–] **L.**BA. 88–01: 24–.

8623 **Bouw-** en **sier-kunst.** Haarlem. *Bouw- en Sier-kunst*

8624 **Bouwwereld.** Amsterdam. *Bouwwereld*

8624° **Bovine Tuberculosis.** Ottawa. *Bovine Tuberc.* [1954–] **L.**BM.

8625 **Bowater Papers.** Birmingham, London. *Bowater Pap.* [1950–] **L.**P.; U.; **Bl.**U. 54–; **Bm.**P.; **Ld.**P.; **M.**P.; **N.**P.; T. 58–; **O.**B.; **Y.**

8626 **Bowdoin College Bulletin.** Brunswick, Me. *Bowdoin Coll. Bull.*

8627 **Bowman Memorial Lectures.** American Geographical Society. New York. *Bowman memor. Lect.* [1951–] **L.**G.; **Bl.**U. 52–53; **Sw.**U. 52–.

8628 **Bowplant.** Willenhall. *Bowplant* **L.**P. (curr.)

8629 **Box Makers' Journal** and **Packaging Review.** London. *Box Mkrs' J.* [1897–44] **L.**P. 10–44; SB. 97–02: 12–13; **O.**B. 98–36. [*C. as:* 36733]

8630 **Boxboard Containers.** Chicago. *Boxbd Cont.* [1950–] **Lh.**P. [*C. of:* 49620]

8631 **Boydell Bulletin.** Manchester. *Boydell Bull.* [1955–] **L.**P.; **Sil.** (1 yr)

8632 **Boyle Lectures.** Oxford. *Boyle Lect.* **O.**B. 92–20; R. 92–38.

8633 **Bradford Scientific Journal.** Bradford. *Bradford scient. J.* [1904–12] **L.**BM.; BM^N.; K. imp.; SC. 05–12; **Bm.**N.; **Bra.**P.; **Ld.**P.; U.; **O.**R. 06–12.

8634 **Bradley's Magazine.** Bradley and Foster, Ltd. Darlaston, Staffs. *Bradley's Mag.* [1930–] **L.**I. (1 yr); P. 31– imp.; **Bm.**C. 30–45; **Y.**

8635 **Bragantia.** Campinas. *Bragantia* [1941–] **L.**AM.; MY. 43–; TP. 41–52; **C.**A.; **Db.** 48–; **E.**D.; **Hu.**G. 47–; **Md.**H.; **O.**BO. 43–; F. imp.; **Rt.**; **Y.** [*C. of:* 7519]

8636 **Brain:** a journal of neurology. London. *Brain* [1878–] **L.**B. 07–; BM.; CB. 50–; GH.; MA.; MC. 22–; MD.; OP. 49–; PS. 14–17: 19: 21; S.; SC.; U. imp.; UC.; UCH. 98–; **Abd.**U.; **Abs.**N. 12–; **Bl.**U. imp.; **Bm.**U. imp.; **Br.**U.; **C.**AN. imp.; PH. 39– imp.; PS.; UL.; **Cr.**MD. 00– imp.; MS. 85–09 imp.; U. 87–10: 52– imp.; **Dn.**U. imp. **E.**A.; P.; S.; U.; **Ex.**U. 56–; **G.**F.; U. imp.; **Ld.**U.; **Lv.**M.; U.; **M.**MS.; **Nw.**A.; **O.**PH.; R.; **Sa.** 78–31; **Sh.**U. 79–; **Y.**

8637 **Brain** and **Nerve.** Tokyo. *Brain Nerve, Tokyo* [1948–]

8637° **Brain Research.** Osaka. *Brain Res., Osaka* [1948–]

8638 **Brake Service.** Akron, Ohio. *Brake Serv.* [1931–]

8639 **Brand Stop.** Stuttgart. *Brand Stop* L.P. (curr.)

8640 **'Brandenburgia.'** Monatsblatt der Gesellschaft für Heimatkunde der Provinz Brandenburg zu Berlin. Berlin. *Brandenburgia*

8641 **Brandenburgische Feuerwehrzeitung.** Berlin. *Brandenb. Feuerwehrztg*

8642 **Brandfare** og **brandværn.** *Brandfare Brandværn* Y.

8643 **Brandwacht.** München. *Brandwacht* [1946–] L.P. 54–; El.FE. 51–.

8644 **Brandweer.** Utrecht. *Brandweer* Y.

8645 **Branntweinwirtschaft.** Berlin. *Branntweinwirtschaft* [1947–] Y.

8646 **Brasil açucareiro.** Rio de Janeiro. *Bras. açuc.* [1938–] L.P. 40–; Y.

8647 **Brasil agricola.** Rio de Janeiro. *Bras. agric.* [1916–] L.EB. (ent.) 20–26.

8648 **Brasil madeireiro.** Rio de Janeiro. *Bras. madeir.* [1945–] O.F. imp.

8649 **Brasil-médico.** Rio de Janeiro. *Bras.-méd.* [1927–] L.MA. 37–; MD. 27–28; TD. imp.; Lv.U. 27–32 imp.; M.MS. [*C. of:* 8692]

8650 **Brasil textil.** São Paulo. *Bras. text.* [1954–] M.C. 55– imp.; Y.

8651 **Brass** and **Bronze Forgings Digest.** New York. *Brass Bronze Forg. Dig.* [1949–] L.NF.; P. 49–60. [*C. of:* 34929]

8652 **Brass Quarterly.** Durham, N.H. *Brass Q.* [1957–] L.BM.

8653 **Brass Tacks.** Bridgeport Brass Company. Bridgeport, Conn. *Brass Tacks* [1927] L.P.

8654 **Brass World.** London. *Brass Wld* [1918–34] L.BM.; Abs.N.; O.B.

8655 **Brass World** and **Plater's Guide.** Bridgeport, Conn. *Brass Wld Plat. Guide* [1905–32] L.MT. 11–32; NF. 23–32; P. 10–32; Bm.P. 07–32; M.U. 10–31 imp. [*C. as:* 37946]

8656 **Brasserie.** Paris. *Brasserie* [1946–] L.SC.; Nu.B. 47–50 imp.: 52–; Y.

8657 **Brasserie française.** Paris. *Brass. fr.* [1937–] L.P.

8658 **Brasserie gauloise.** Paris. *Brass. gaul.*

8659 **Brasserie** et **malterie.** Nancy. *Brass. Malt.* [1910–37] L.P. 24–37; Nu.B. 34–37 imp. [*C. in:* 8665]

8660 **Brasserie** et la **malterie franco-belge.** Paris. *Brass. Malt. fr.-belge*

8661 **Brasserie moderne.** Lille. *Brass. mod.*

8662 **Brasserie** du **Nord.** Lille. *Brass. N.*

8663 **Brasserie pratique.** Lille. *Brass. prat.*

8664 **Brasseur.** Namur. *Brasseur*

8665 **Brasseur français.** Paris. *Brasseur fr.* [1937–] L.P. 37–40.

8666 **Brassey's Annual** and **Armed Forces Yearbook.** London. *Brassey's A.* [1950–] L.BM.; P.; Abs.N.; Bm.P.; Br.P.; Bra.P.; C.UL.; Db.; E.A.; G.E.; M.; U.; Ld.P.; Lv.P.; M.P.; N.P.; Nw.P.; O.B.; Sh.P. [*C. of:* 8667]

8667 **Brassey's Naval Annual.** Portsmouth. *Brassey's nav. A.* [1920–49] L.BM.; P.; Abs.N. imp.; Bm.P.; Br.P.; Bra.P. 40–49; C.UL.; Db.; E.A.; F. 20–39; G.E.; M.; T. 20–24 imp.; U.; Ld.P.; Lv.P. imp.; M.P.; N.P. 42–45: 49; Nw.A. 20–29; P.; O.B.; Sh.P. imp. [*C. of:* 34414; *C. as:* 8666]

Brassey's Naval and **Shipping Annual.** *See* 8667.

8668 **Brastvo.** Knjige Društva Svetog Save. u Beogradu. Брaство. Књиге Друштва Светог Саве. *Brastvo* L.BM. 88–.

Bratislavai (Pozsonyi) orvos- és **természettudomanyi egyesület közlemenyei.** *See* 38280.

8669 **Bratislavské lékařske listy.** Praha. *Bratisl. lék. Listy* [1921–] L.MA. 29–39: 46; MC.; MD.; S. 32–39 imp.; O.R. 35; Y.

8670 **Brauer** und **Mälzer.** München. *Brauer Mälzer* [1948–] Nu.B. 51–.

8671 **Brauerei.** Berlin. *Brauerei* [1947–] L.P. (curr.); Nu.B. 47–50 imp.: 51–.

8672 **Brauerei. Wissenschaftliche Beilage.** Berlin. *Brauerei wiss. Beil.* [1948–59] L.P.; Nu.B. imp. [*Supplement to:* 8671; *C. as:* 33124]

8673 **Brauereibesitzer** und **Braumeister.** Deggendorf. *Brauereibes. Braumeister* Nu.B. 59–.

8674 **Brauereijournale.** Stuttgart. *Brauerei-J.*

8675 **Brauereitechniker.** München. *Brauereitechniker* [1949–] Nu.B. 49 imp.: 51–.

8676 **Brauer-Zeitung.** Cincinnati. *Brauer-Ztg, Cincinnati*

8677 **Brauer-Zeitung.** Hannover. *Brauer-Ztg, Hannover* **Brauer-** und **Hopfenzeitung.** Gambrinus. *See* 20593.

8678 **Brauindustrie.** Hamburg. *Brauindustrie*

8679 **Brau-** und **Malzindustrie.** Wien. *Brau- u. Malzind.* L.P. 38–41.

8680 **Braun** und **Braun Nachrichten.** Wien. *Braun u. Braun Nachr.* L.P. 54–.

8681 **Braunkohle.** Halle a. S. *Braunkohle* [1902–45] L.P. 10–45 imp.; Y. 30–45. [*C. as:* 8682]

8682 **Braunkohle, Wärme** und **Energie.** Düsseldorf. *Braunkohle Wärme Energie* [1949–] L.MIE. 51–; P.; Y. [*C. of:* 8681]

8683 **Braunkohlenarchiv.** Halle a. S. *Braunkohlenarchiv* [1921–] L.P. 21–51; Y. 21–42: 49–.

8684 **Braunkohlen-** und **Brikett-Industrie.** Halle. *Braunkohlen- u. Brikett-Ind.* [*C. as:* 6151]

8685 **Braunschweiger landwirtschaftliche Nachrichten.** Braunschweig. *Braunschw. landw. Nachr.*

8686 **Braunschweigische landwirtschaftliche Zeitung.** Braunschweig. *Braunschw. landw. Ztg*

8687 **Brautechnische Rundschau.** Berlin. *Brautech. Rdsch., Berl.*

8688 **Brautechnische Rundschau.** Mährisch-Ostrau. *Brautech. Rdsch., Mähr.-Ostrau*

8689 **Brauwissenschaft.** Nürnberg. *Brauwissenschaft* [1948–] L.P. 55–; Nu.B. 50–; Y.

8690 **Brazilian Engineering** and **Mining Review.** Rio de Janeiro. *Braz. Engng Min. Rev.* [1905–08] **L.**P. [*C. of:* 8691]

8691 **Brazilian Mining Review.** Rio de Janeiro. *Braz. Min. Rev.* [1902–04] **L.**P. [*C. as:* 8690]

8692 **Brazil-médico.** Rio de Janeiro. *Braz.-méd.* [1887–26] **L.**MD. 12–26 imp.; TD. 09–26 imp.; **Lv.**U. 20–26 imp.; **M.**MS. 26. [*C. as:* 8649]

8693 **Brecon** and **Radnor Agricultural Quarterly Journal.** Brecon. *Brecon Radnor agric. q. J.* [1933–38] **L.**AM.

8694 **Breeder's Gazette.** Chicago. *Breed. Gaz.* [1881–] **L.**SC. 32–42; **Abs.**A. 82–90; **Db.** 05–.

8695 **Breeder's Guide** of **Rare Furbearing.** Bainsville, Ontario. *Breed. Guide rare Furbearing* [1958–] **E.**AB. 58.

8696 **Breeder's Journal.** Cleveland. *Breed. J.*

8697 **Breeders World.** New Albany, Ind. *Breed. Wld* [1925–]

8698 **Breinar.** Societas scientiarum islandica. Reykjavík. *Breinar* [1935–] **Db.**

8699 **Bremer Ärzteblatt.** Bremen. *Bremer Ärztebl.*

8700 **Bremer Baumwoll-Blätter.** Bremen. *Bremer Baumwoll-Bl.*

8701 **Bremer Beiträge** zur **Naturwissenschaft.** Bremen. *Bremer Beitr. Naturw.* [1933–] **L.**BM[N]. (nat. hist.) 33–37.

8702 **Brennereizeitung.** Berlin. *Brennereizeitung*

8703 **Brennstoff-Chemie.** Essen. *Brennst.-Chem.* [1920–] **L.**AV. 20–43 imp.; C. imp.; P. imp.; PT. 32–38: 51–; SC. 20–42: 49–; UC.; **Bm.**T. 37–38: 54–; U.; **Db.** 49–; **Ep.**D. 36–43: 49–; **Ld.**U.; **M.**T. 20– imp.; **Nw.**A. 27–; **Rt.** 20–27; **Sh.**IO. 34–38: 52–; S. 22–39; SC. 49–; **Te.**C. 20–43: 49–; **Y.** [*Contained in:* 35888, Apr. 1943–1948]

8704 **Brennstoff-Untersuchungen.** Thermochemische Prüfungs- und Versuchs-Anstalt Dr. Aufhäuser. Hamburg. *Brennst.-Unters.* **L.**P. 24–30.

8705 **Brennstoff—Wärme—Kraft.** Düsseldorf. *Brennst. —Wärme—Kraft* [1949–] **L.**I. 50–; P.; **G.**ME.; U. 51–; **Rn.**B. 58–; **Y.** [*Incorporates* 4178, 19334 and 57055]

8706 **Brennstoff-** u. **Wärmewirtschaft.** Halle. *Brennst.- u. Wärmew.* [1919–43] **L.**P. 24–43; SC. 28–40. [*C. of:* 32323; *C. in:* 4178]

8707 **Brenthol Pamphlets.** Imperial Chemical Industries. London. *Brenthol Pamph.* **L.**BM. 37–; SC. 36–.

8708 **Brenthurst Papers.** Johannesburg. *Brenthurst Pap.* [1943–44] **L.**MD.; S.; U.; **Bl.**U. 43; **O.**R.

8709 **Bretagne agricole.** Saint-Brieuc. *Bretagne agric.*

8710 **Bretagne agricole** et **industrielle.** Rennes. *Bretagne agric. ind.*

8711 **Bretagne hippique** et **agricole.** Morlaix. *Bretagne hipp. agric.*

8712 **Bretagne médicale.** Rennes. *Bretagne méd.*

8713 **Breveté.** Revue des brevets d'invention et Ingénieur français. Paris. *Breveté*

8714 **Brevets d'invention.** Office national de la propriété industrielle. Paris. *Brev. Invent.* **L.**P. 02–.

8715 **Brevets de sucrerie.** Paris. *Brev. Sucr.* [1898–14] **L.**P.

8716 **Breviora.** Museum of Comparative Zoology. Cambridge, Mass. *Breviora* [1952–] **L.**BM[N].; GL.; L.; Z.; **Bl.**U. imp.; **E.**G. (curr.); R.; **C.**P.; **Cr.**N. 60–; **G.**U.; **Ld.**U. 53–; **Lo.** 52–54 imp.; **Lv.**U.; **M.**U.; **O.**R. imp.; **Pl.**M.

8717 **Breviora geológica astúrica.** Oviedo. *Breviora geol. astúr.* [1957–] **Y.**

8718 **Brewer** and **Maltster.** Chicago & New York. *Brewer Maltst.* [1882–37] [*C. in:* 8723]

8719 **Brewer** and **Wine Merchant** and **Brewers' Guardian.** London. *Brewer Wine Merch.* [1901–47] **L.**BM.; P. 32–47 imp.; **Nu.**B. 38–47 imp. [*C. as:* 8721°]

8720 **Brewer's Art.** St.'Louis. *Brewer's Art* [1923–32] [*C. as:* 32934]

8721 **Brewers' Digest.** Chicago, etc. *Brewers' Dig.* [1937–] **L.**P.; **Nu.**B. 38–50 imp.: 51–; **Y.** [*C. of:* 8727]

8721° **Brewers' Guardian.** London. *Brewers' Guard.* [1948–] **L.**P.; **Lh.**P. 49–; **Nu.**B. imp.; **Sil.** 48–50 imp.; **Y.** [*C. of:* 8719]

8722 **Brewers' Guild Journal.** London. *Brewers' Guild J.* [1950–] **L.**P.; **Bm.**U.; **C.**A. (2 yr.); **E.**A.; **Nu.**B.; **Y.** [*C. of:* 26127]

8723 **Brewers' Journal.** Chicago, etc. *Brewers' J., Chicago* [1934–] **L.**P. 56–; **E.**A.; **Nu.**B. 51. [*C. of:* 57388]

8724 **Brewers' Journal.** New York. *Brewers' J., N.Y.* **L.**P. 92–21; **M.**T. 00–21.

8725 **Brewers' Journal** and **Hop** and **Malt Trades Review.** London. *Brewers' J. Hop Malt Trades Rev.* [1865–] **L.**AM. 43–56 imp.; BM.; C. 28–; P. 53–; **Bm.**U. 98; **Br.**P. (1 yr); **C.**UL. 21–; **M.**T. 97–29; **Nu.**B. 81–14: 51–; **O.**B. 21–.

8726 **Brewers' Technical Journal.** London. *Brewers' tech. J.* **L.**BM. 04–06★; **O.**B. 04.

8727 **Brewers' Technical Review.** Chicago. *Brewers' tech. Rev.* [1934–37] **L.**SC. [*C. of:* 49713; *C. as:* 8721]

8728 **Brewery Age.** Chicago. *Brewery Age*

8729 **Brewing Industry Research Foundation Bulletin.** London. *Brew. Ind. Res. Fdn Bull.* **Sil.** 53–.

8730 **Brewing, Malting** and **Allied Processes.** London. *Brew. Malt. all. Processes* [1955–57] **L.**P.; SC.; **Br.**A. [*C. of:* 42870; *C. as:* 29331]

8731 **Brewing Trade Review.** London. *Brew. Trade Rev.* [1886–] **L.**AM. 98– imp.; BM.; P. (1 yr); **Bm.**U. 87–; **Ld.**P. 87–91: 00–38: 54–; U. 02–19; **Nu.**B. 87–14: 49–; **Sh.**IO. (5 yr.); **Y.**

8732 **Brick Builder.** London. *Brick Bldr* [1925–] **L.**BA.; BM.; P. 25–39: 51–53; SC. 33–.

8733 **Brick Bulletin.** London. *Brick Bull.* [1947–] **L.**BA.; P. 59–; **N.**T. (5 yr.); **Wa.**B.

8734 **Brick** and **Clay Record.** Chicago. *Brick Clay Rec.* [1892–] **L.**P. 15–28: 34–44: 55–; SC. 36–; **Sh.**IO. 45–; **St.**R. 38–; **Wa.**B. 26–40: 46–50.

8735 **Brick** and **Pottery Trades Journal.** London. *Brick Pott. Trades J.* [1896–24] **L.**BM. 00–24; P. 06–24; **O.**B. 22–24. [*C. in:* 29541]

8736 **Brickbuilder.** Boston. *Brickbuilder* [1892–16] **L.**BA. 05–16; P. 11–16. [*C. as:* 3990]

Brief Report. Rubber Research Institute of **Malaya.** *See* 45182.

8737 **Briefe** für den **Lackierernachwuchs** von **W. P.-Hülkenberg.** Hannover. *Briefe LackNachw. W. P.-Hülkenberg* **L.**P. (curr.) [*Supplement to:* 23358]

8738 **Brigham Young University Studies.** *Brigham Young Univ. Stud.* [1925-]

8739 **Brill Magazine.** Philadelphia. *Brill. Mag.*

8740 **Brimstone Brevities.** Freeport Sulphur Company. New York. *Brimst. Brevities* [1935-] L.P.

8741 **Brique.** Organe de l'industrie, etc., briquetière et céramique. Bruxelles. *Brique*

8742 **Bristol Medico-Chirurgical Journal.** Bristol. *Bristol med.-chir. J.* [1883-52] L.BM.; GH. 91-52; MA.; MD.; S. 88-52; TD. 46-52; UCH. 94-01; Abs.N. 12-52; Bl.U. 33-52; Bm.U.; Br.U.; C.UL.; Cr.MS. 83-07; Db.; E.A.; P.; G.F. 83-33; Ld.U. 32-52; Lv.M. imp.; M.MS. 83-21; Nw.A. 25-52; O.B.; R. [*C. in:* 30262]

8743 **Bristol Quarterly.** Bristol Aeroplane Co. Bristol. *Bristol Q.* [1954-59] L.AV.; BM.; P.; QM.; Bl.U. 57-59; Br.U.; E.A.; F.A.; Ld.P.; Nw.A. 57-59; O.B.; Sa. 57-59; Y. [*C. as:* 8745]

8744 **Bristol Review.** Bristol Aeroplane Co. Filton, Bristol. *Bristol Rev.* [1929-59] L.AV. 56-59; BM. 50-59; P. 30-39; SC. (Aircraft issue) 30-37; Br.P. (Engine issue) 32-39; O.R. 32-39.

8745 **Bristol Siddeley Journal.** London. *Bristol Siddeley J.* [1959-] L.AV.; BM.; P.; SC.; Bl.U.; Br.U.; Co.T.; G.ME. (2 yr.); Ld.P. (5 yr.); U.; Y. [*C. of:* 8743]

Bristol and **Somerset Society** of **Architects Journal.** *See* 25692.

8747 **Britain's Forests.** Forestry Commission. London. *Britain's Forests* [1948-] L.BM.; Ld.P.; O.F.

8748 **Britain's Roads.** Bituminous Roads Development Group. London. *Britain's Rds* [1958-] L.P. (curr.); Y.

8749 **British Abstracts.** London. *Br. Abstr.* [1945-53; *C. of:* 8771]
Pure Chemistry
A.1. General, physical and inorganic chemistry. L.AM. 45-49; AV.; B.; BM.; BM^N.; C.; GH.; LE.; LI. 45-48; MC.; P.; PH.; PR.; QM.; R.; SC.; TD.; TP.; UC.; Abd.S.; Abs.N.; Bl.U.; Bm.T.; U.; Bn.U.; Br.A.; P.; U.; C.BI.; CH.; PH.; Cr.P. 45-52; U.; Dn.U.; E.A.; HW.; R. 45-52; T.; U.; W.; Fr. 47-53; G.M.; U.; H.U.; Hu.G. 47-49; Lc.A.; Ld.P.; W.; Lh.P.; Lo.; Lv.U.; M.C.; P.; T.; U.; Md.H.; N.P.; T. 47-53; U.; Nw.A.; O.R.; R.D.; U.; Rt.; Sh.IO.; St.R.; Y. [*Replaced by:* 16167]
A.2. Organic chemistry. L.AV.; B.; BM.; C.; GH.; LE.; LI. 45-48; MC.; P.; PH.; PR.; QM.; R.; SC.; TD.; TP.; UC.; Abd.S.; Abs.N.; Bl.U.; Bm.T.; U.; Bn.U.; Br.A.; P.; U.; C.BI.; CH.; PH.; Cr.P. 45-52; U.; Dn.U.; E.A.; HW.; R. 45-52; T.; U.; W.; Fr. 47-53; G.M.; U.; H.U.; Hu.G. 47-49; Lc.A.; Ld.P.; W.; Lh.P.; Lv.U.; M.C.; P.; T.; U.; Md.H.; N.P.; T. 47-53; U.; Nw.A.; O.R.; R.D.; U.; Rt.; Sh.IO.; St.R.; W.; Y. [*Replaced by:* 16167]
A.3. Physiology and biochemistry. L.AM. 45-47; AV.; BM.; C.; D.; GH.; LE.; LI. 45-48; MA.; MC.; MD.; OP.; P.; PH.; PR.; QM.; R.; S.; SC.; TD.; TP.; UC.; UCH.; Abd.R.; S.; Abs.N.; Bl.U.; Bm.T.; U.; Bn.U.; Br.A.; P.; U.; C.APH.; B.; BI.; CH.; PH.; Cr.P. 45-52; U.; Dn.U.; E.A.; AG. 48-52; HW.; R. 45-52; T.; U.; W.; Fr. 47-53; G.M.; U.; H.U.; Hu.G. 47-49; Lc.A.; Ld.P.; U.; W.; Lh.P.; Lo. 51-52; Lv.U.; M.C.; MS.; P.; T.; U.; Md.H.; N.P.; T.; U.; Nw.A.; O.P.; PH.; R.; Pl.M.; R.D.; U.; Rt.; Sh.IO.; St.R.; W.; Y. [*Replaced by:* 8750]

Applied Chemistry
B.1. Chemical engineering, etc. L.AM. 45-50 imp.; AV.; BM.; C.; GH.; LE.; LI. 45-48; MC.; MD.; NF.; P.; PH.; PR.; QM.; SC.; TD.; UC.; Abd.S.; Abs.N.; Bl.U.; Bm.C.; T.; U.; Bn.U.; Br.A.; P.; U.; C.A. 45-47; CH.; Dn.U.; E.HW.; R. 46-48; U.; W.; Fr. 47-53; G.M.; U.; Hu.G. 47-52; Lc.A.; Ld.P.; W.; Lh.P.; Lv.U.; M.C.; P.; T.; U.; Md.H.; N.P.; T. 47-53; Nw.A.; O.R.; R.D.; U.; Rt.; Sal.F. 45-51; Sh.IO.; Sil. 51-53; St.R.; W.; Y. [*C. in:* 25571]
B.2. Industrial organic chemistry. L.AM. 45-50; AV.; BM.; C.; GH.; LE.; LI. 45-48; MC.; MD.; NF.; P.; PH.; PR.; QM.; SC.; TD.; UC.; Abd.S.; Abs.A. 51-53; N.; Bl.U.; Bm.T.; U.; Bn.U.; Br.A.; P.; U.; C.A. 45-47; CH.; Cr.U.; Dn.U.; E.HW.; R. 46-48; U.; W.; Fr. 47-53; G.M.; U.; Hu.G. 47-52; Lc.A.; Ld.P.; W.; Lh.P.; Lv.U.; M.C.; P.; T.; U.; Md.H.; N.P.; T. 47-53; Nw.A.; O.R.; R.D.; U.; Rt.; Sal.F. 45-51; Sh.IO.; Sil. 51-53; St.R.; Y. [*C. in:* 25571]
B.3. Agriculture, food, sanitation. L.AM. 41-50; AV.; BM.; C.; E. 47-53; EB. 47-53; GH.; LE.; LI. 45-48; MC.; MD.; NF.; P.; PH.; PR.; QM.; SC.; SH.; TD.; UC.; Abd.R.; S.; Abs.A. 51-53; N.; Bl.U.; Bm.T.; U.; Bn.U.; Br.A; P.; U.; C.A. 45-47; CH.; Cr.U.; Dn.U.; E.HW.; R. 46-48; U.; W.; Fr. 47-53; G.M.; U.; Hu.G. 47-52; Lc.A.; Ld.P.; W.; Lh.P.; Lv.U.; M.C.; P.; T.; U.; Md.H.; N.P.; T. 47-53; Nw.A.; O.R.; R.D.; U.; Rt.; Sal.F. 43-51; Sh.IO.; Sil. 51-53; St.R.; W.; Y. [*C. in:* 25571]
C. Analysis and apparatus. L.AM. 45-47: 50 imp.; AV.; BM.; BM^N.; C.; GH.; LE.; LI. 46-48; MA. 50-53; MC. 46-53 imp.; MD.; NF.; P.; PH.; PR.; QM.; R. SC.; TD.; UC.; Abd.R.; S.; Abs.N.; Bl.U.; Bm.C.; T.; U.; Bn.U.; Br.A.; P.; U.; C.A. 45-47; BI.; CH.; Cr.U.; Dn.U. 50-53; E.A.; HW.; R. 46-47; U.; W.; Fr. 47-53; G.M.; U.; H.U.; Hu.G. 47-53; Lc.A.; Ld.P.; W.; Lh.P.; Lv.P.; U.; M.C.; MS.; P.; T.; U.; Md.H.; N.P.; U.; Nw.A.; O.R.; Pl.M. 45-50; R.D.; U.; Rt.; Sal.F. 45-51; Sh.IO.; Sil. 53; St.R.; Y. [*Replaced by:* 2563]

8750 **British Abstracts** of **Medical Sciences.** London. *Br. Abstr. med. Sci.* [1954-56] L.AV.; BM.; CB.; D.; GH.; MA.; MC.; MD.; OP.; P.; PH.; QM.; S.; TD.; U.; UC.; UCH.; Abd.R.; U.; Bl.U.; Bm.P.; T.; U.; Bn.U.; Br.U.; C.APH.; BI.; PH.; UL.; Cr.MD.; U.; Dn.U.; E.A.; T.; U.; Ep.D.; G.F.; M.; U.; Ld.P.; U.; Lv.P.; U.; M.T.; U.; N.U. 56; Nw.A.; O.B.; PH.; R.; Sh.U.; Sw.U.; W. 55-56; Y. [*Replaces* 8749 A.3; *C. as:* 23801]

8751 **British Acetylene** and **Welding Association.** [**Pamphlets.**] London. *Br. Acet. Weld. Ass.* [1923-24] L.BM.; P.; SC. [*C. of:* 23719; *C. as:* 39025]

8752 **British Agricultural Bulletin.** London. *Br. agric. Bull.* [1948-55] L.AM.; BM.; FA.; SC.; TP.; Abd.R.; S. 52-55; U. 48-54; Abs.A.; U. 48-51; Bl.U.; Bn.U.; Br.A.; U.; C.A.; APH.; E.AB.; PO. 50-55 imp.; U.; W.; Hu.G.; Ld.U.; Md.H.; N.U.; Nw.A.; O.AEC.; B.; R.; Rd.; Rt.; Sil. [*C. as:* 1408]

8753 **British Agricultural Chemicals** and **Chemical Weed Control.** London. *Br. agric. Chem.* [1960-] L.AM.; P. [*C. of:* 20452; *Supplement to:* 37385]

8754 **British Aircraft Industry Bulletin.** London. *Br. Aircr. Ind. Bull.* [1928; 47-] L.AV. 50-; P. 58-; SC.; Bm.T. (5 yr.); G.T. (curr. issue); Y.

British Aluminium Company Publications. *See* 40897.

8755 **British Antarctic Terra Nova Expedition, 1910.**
London. *Br. Antarct. Terra Nova Exped. 1910* [1914–]
L.BM.; BM^N.; MO. (meteor. etc.) 19–24; Z. (zool.): (geol.)
imp.; E.R.; Ld.P.; Lv.U. 14–30; O.R.

8756 **British Architect.** London. *Br. Archit.* [1874–
19] L.BM.; P.; **Bm.**P. 86–07; **Db.** 83–19; E.T. 74–15 imp.;
G.M. 77–19; **M.**P.; T. 00–11; **Nw.**P. 94–07; O.B. 17–19.

8757 **British Baker.** London. *Br. Baker* [1887–] L.AM;
39– imp.; BM.; P. (curr.); Ep.D. 43–; G.M.; T. (3 yr.);
Lv.P. 59–; **Y.**
  **British Baking Industries Research Association
  Bulletin.** *See* 9604^a.

8758 **British Bee Journal.** London. *Br. Bee J.* [1873–]
L.AM. imp.; BM. 74–; P. (1 yr); Abs.N. 12–; **Bm.**P. 19–;
Br.P. (1 yr); C.UL.; **Db.**; E.A.; G.M. 09–; Lv.P. 45–;
M.P. 26–; O.B.; R.U. 02–35 v. imp.; **Rt.**; Sa. 86–30 imp.;
Y.
  British Bee Journal and **Beekeepers' Adviser.**
  See 8758.

8759 **British Beet Grower** and **Empire Sugar Producer.** London. *Br. Beet. Grow.* [1927–29] L.BM.;
P.; C.A.; UL.; E.A.; O.R.; Rt. [*C. in:* 51290]

8760 **British Birds.** London. *Br. Birds* [1907–] L.AM.
27–; BM.; BM^N.; HO. 07–13 imp.; NC.; SC. 31–; U. 07–37:
47–; UC. 07–11; Z.; **Abd.**U. 08–28: 47–; Abs.N. 09–;
U. 07–25; **Bm.**N. 17–; P. 26–; U. 48–; **Bn.**U.; **Br.**U.;
Bra.P. 07–22; C.B.; UL.; **Cr.**M.; P. 13–; **Db.**; E.A.; F.;
T.; U. 58–; G.M.; **Ld.**P. 07–28: 36–; U. 46–; Lv.P.; M.P.
17–; U. imp.; **Nw.**A. 38–39: 46–; O.OR.; R.; **Pl.**M. 07–19;
Sa.; T.; **Y.**

8761 **British Builder.** London. *Br. Bldr* [1919–26]
L.BA. 21–26; BM.; GM.; P. 21–26; Abs.N.; C.UL. 24–26;
G.M. 22–26; Lv.P. 23–26; O.R. [*C. in:* 9040]

8762 **British Bulletin** of **Spectroscopy.** London.
Cambridge. *Br. Bull. Spectrosc.* [1951–] L.BM.; C.; G.;
LE. 51–60; MC.; P.; PR.; SC.; SI.; TP. 59–; **Bl.**U.; **C.**CH.
59–; E.A.; F.A. 55–; G.U. 53–; **Ld.**W. 54–; M.C. 54–; D.;
P.; U.; O.B.; R.; Sy.R. 54–; **Y.**

8763 **British Buttons.** London. *Br. Buttons* L.P.
(curr.); **Bm.**P. 48–.

8764 **British Catalogue** of **Plastics.** London. *Br. Cat.
Plast.* [1947–50] L.P.

8765 **British Cattle Breeders Club Digest.** Devizes.
Br. Cattle Breed. Club Dig. [1948–] C.A.; N.U.; R.U. 48–54.

8766 **British Caver.** Mendip Exploration Society. New
Milton, Hants. *Br. Caver* [1940–] L.BM.; NC. 58–;
SC. 43–; **Cr.**M. 41– imp.; P. imp.; G.M. 42; O.B. 46–; **Y.**
[*C. of:* 26451]

8767 **British Ceramic Abstracts.** Stoke-on-Trent. *Br.
Ceram. Abstr.* [1942–] L.AV. 54–; DI. 50– imp.; P.; SC.
54–; SI. 47–; **Bm.**C. 47– imp.; F.A. 43; **Ld.**U. 50–; M.P.
55; **Y.** [*Supplement to* and *issued in:* 53620; *C. of:* 305]

8768 **British Chemical Abstracts.** London. *Br. chem.
Abstr.*
    A. Pure Chemistry [1926–36] L.B.; BM.; BM^N.; C.;
IC.; LE.; LI.; MC.; MD.; MI. 26–30; NF.; P.; PH.; PR.;
QM.; R. 31–37; RI.; S.; SC.; TD.; U.; UC.; **Abd.**R.; S.;
U.; Abs.N.; U.; **Bl.**U.; **Bm.**C.; P.; T.; U.; **Bn.**U.;
Br.P.; U.; C.BI.; CH.; P.; UL.; **Co.**T.; **Cr.**P.; U.;
Db.; **Dn.**U.; E.A.; HW.; T.; U.; W.; Ep.D.; Ex.U.;
G.M.; T.; U.; H.U.; **Ld.**P.; U.; W.; Lv.P.; U.; M.C.;
MS.; P.; T.; U.; **Md.**H.; N.T. 26–30; U.; **Nw.**A.; P.;
O.BS.; R.; **R.**D.; U.; **Rt.**; Sa.; Sal.F.; Sh.P.; S.;
U.; **St.**R.; Sw.U.; Sy.R.; **Y.**

    B. Applied Chemistry [1926–37] L.B.; BM.; BM^N.;
C.; I.; IC.; LE.; LI.; MC.; MD.; MI. 31–37; NF.; P.;
PH.; PR.; QM.; R. 31–37; SC.; U.; UC.; **Abd.**S.;
U.; Abs.N.; U.; **Bl.**U.; **Bm.**C.; P.; T.; U.;
Bn.U.; **Br.**P.; U.; C.BI.; CH.; P.; UL.; **Cr.**P.; U.;
Db.; **Dn.**U.; E.A.; HW.; R.; T.; W.; Ep.D.; Ex.U.;
G.M.; T.; U.; **Ld.**P.; U.; W.; Lv.P.; U.; M.C.; MS.; P.;
T.; U.; **Md.**H.; N.U.; **Nw.**A.; P.; O.BS.; R.; **R.**D.; U.;
Rt.; Sal.F.; Sh.P.; S.; U.; **St.**R.; Sw.U.; Sy.R.;
Y. [*C. of:* 322 and 26920 (*c*); *C. in:* 8771]

8769 **British Chemical Digest.** Beckenham. *Br. chem.
Dig.* [1946–49] L.AV. 47–48; BM.; C.; EE. 47–49; P.; PH.;
Abs.N.; Ep.D. 46–47; M.C. 46–48.

8770 **British Chemical Engineering.** London. *Br.
chem. Engng* [1956–] L.AV.; BM.; C.; LE.; NP.; P.; PH.; PR.;
PT.; RI.; TP.; **Bm.**P.; T. 59–; **C.**CH. 59–; **Db.**; E.A.; CE.
57–; U.; Ep.D.; G.M. 57–; T.; Lc.A.; **Ld.**U. 61–; **Lh.**FO.;
Lv.P.; M.D.; P.; N.U.; O.R.; Rt. 56; Sh.SC. 57–; Ste.
59–; **Wd.**; **Y.**

8771 **British Chemical** and **Physiological Abstracts.**
London. *Br. chem. physiol. Abstr.* [1937–44]
Pure Chemistry and Physiology
    A.1. General, physical and inorganic chemistry
[1937–44] L.AM.; AV.; B.; BM.; BM^N.; C.; GH.; LE.;
LI.; MA.; MC.; MD.; MI.; P.; PH.; QM.; R.; RI.; SC.;
TD.; TP.; U.; **Abd.**R. 40; Abs.N.; **Bl.**U.; **Bm.**T.; U.;
Bn.U.; **Br.**A.; U.; C.BI.; CH.; PH.; **Co.**T.; **Cr.**P.;
U.; **Db.**; **Dn.**U.; E.HW.; R.; T.; U.; W.; Ep.D.; G.M.;
T.; U.; H.U.; Lc.A.; **Ld.**P.; W.; **Lh.**P. 42–44; Lv.P.;
U.; M.C.; P.; T.; U.; **Md.**H.; N.P.; U.; O.BS.; R.; **R.**D.;
U.; **Rt.**; Sal.F.; Sh.P.; Sy.R.; W.; **Y.**
    A.2. Organic chemistry [1937–44] L.AV.; B.; BM.;
C.; GH.; LE.; LI.; MA.; MC.; MD.; MI.; P.; PH.; QM.; R.;
RI.; SC.; TD.; TP.; U.; **Abd.**R. 40; Abs.N.; **Bl.**U.;
Bm.T.; U.; **Bn.**U.; **Br.**A.; P.; U.; C.BI.; CH.; PH.;
Co.T.; **Cr.**P.; U.; **Db.**; **Dn.**U.; E.HW.; R.; T.; U.; W.;
Ep.D.; G.M.; T.; U.; H.U.; Lc.A.; **Ld.**P.; W.; **Lh.**P.
42–44; Lv.P.; U.; M.C.; P.; T.; U.; **Md.**H.; N.P.; U.;
O.BS.; R.; **R.**D.; U.; **Rt.**; Sal.F.; Sh.P.; Sy.R.; W.; **Y.**
    A.3. Biochemistry *later* Physiology and biochemis-
try [1937–44] L.AM.; AV.; B.; BM.; C.; D. 39–44; GH.;
LE.; LI.; MA.; MC.; MD.; MI.; OP.; P.; PH.; QM.; R.;
RI.; S.; SC.; TD.; TP.; U.; UC.; UCH.; **Abd.**R. 40–44;
Abs.N.; **Bl.**U.; **Bm.**T.; U.; **Bn.**U.; **Br.**A.; P.; U.;
C.B.; BI.; CH.; PH.; **Co.**T.; **Cr.**MD.; P.; U.; **Db.**;
Dn.U.; E.AG.; HW.; R.; T.; U.; W.; Ep.D.; G.M.; T.;
U.; H.U.; Lc.A.; **Ld.**P.; U.; W.; **Lh.**P. 42–44; Lv.P.;
U.; M.C.; MS.; P.; T.; U.; **Md.**H.; N.P.; U.; O.BS.;
P.; PH.; R.; **Pl.**M.; **R.**D.; U.; **Rt.**; Sal.F.; Sh.P.;
Sy.R.; W.
Applied Chemistry [1938–40; *then* 41–44 *in sections*]
    B.1. General and industrial inorganic chemistry.
L.AM.; AV.; BM.; C.; GH.; LE.; LI.; MA.; MC.; MD.; MI.;
NF.; P.; PH.; QM.; R.; RI.; SC.; TD.; U.; Abs.N.;
Bl.U.; **Bm.**C.; T.; U.; **Bn.**U.; **Br.**A.; P.; U.; C.CH.;
Cr.P.; U.; **Db.**; **Dn.**U.; E.HW.; R.; T.; U.; W.;
G.M.; T.; U.; H.U.; Lc.A.; **Ld.**P.; W.; **Lh.**P. 42–44;
Lv.P.; U.; M.C.; P.; T.; U.; **Md.**H.; N.P.; U.; O.BS.;
R.; **R.**D.; U.; **Rt.**; Sal.F.; Sh.P.; Sy.R.; **Y.**
    B.2. Industrial organic chemistry. L.AM.; AV.;
BM.; C.; GH.; LE.; LI.; MA.; MD.; MI.; NF.; P.; PH.;
QM.; R.; RI.; SC.; TD.; U.; Abs.N.; **Bl.**U.; **Bm.**T.;
U.; **Bn.**U.; **Br.**A.; P.; U.; C.CH.; **Cr.**P.; U.; **Db.**;
Dn.U.; E.HW.; R.; T.; U.; W.; G.M.; T.; U.; H.U.;
Lc.A.; **Ld.**P.; W.; **Lh.**P. 42–44; Lv.P.; U.; M.C.;
P.; T.; U.; **Md.**H.; N.P.; U.; O.BS.; R.; **R.**D.; U.;
Rt.; Sal.F.; Sh.P.; Sy.R.; **Y.**

B.3. Agriculture, food, sanitation. **L.**AM.; AV.; BM.; C.; GH.; LE.; LI.; MA.; MC.; MD.; MI.; NF.; P.; PH.; QM.; R.; RI.; SC.; SH.; TD.; U.; **Abd.**R.; **Abs.**N.; **Bl.**U.; **Bm.**T.; U.; **Bn.**U.; **Br.**U.; **Bra.**P.; U.; **C.**CH.; **Cr.**P.; U.; **Db.**; **Dn.**U.; **E.**HW.; R.; T.; U.; W.; **G.**M.; T.; U.; **H.**U.; **Lc.**A.; **Ld.**P.; W.; **Lh.**P. 42–44; **Lv.**P.; U.; **M.**C.; P.; T.; U.; **Md.**H.; **N.**P.; U.; **O.**BS.; R.; **R.**D.; U.; **Rt.**; **Sal.**F.; **Sh.**P.; **Sy.**R.; **W.**; **Y.**

C. Analysis and apparatus [1944] **L.**AM.; AV.; BM.; BM^N.; C.; GH.; LE.; MC.; MI.; P.; PH.; QM.; R.; RI.; SC.; U.; **Abs.**N.; **Bl.**U.; **Bm.**T.; U.; **Bn.**U.; **Br.**A.; P.; U.; **C.**CH.; **Db.**; **E.**HW.; R.; T.; W.; **G.**T.; U.; **H.**U.; **Lc.**A.; **Ld.**P.; W.; **Lv.**P.; U.; **M.**C.; P.; T.; U.; **Md.**H.; **N.**P.; U.; **O.**BS.; R.; **Y.** C. of: 8768 and 37114; C. as: 8749]

8771° **British Chemical Plant.** London. Br. chem. Pl. [1947–] **L.**BM.; P.

8772 **British Chemicals,** their manufacturers and users. London. Br. Chemicals [1925–] **L.**P. (curr.); SC. (curr.); U. 46–; **Abs.**N. 25: 27; **Bm.**P. imp.; **G.**M. 25–53 imp.; **Ld.**U. 25; **Lv.**P. imp.; **Y.** (curr.)

8773 **British Chemist.** London. Br. Chemist [1949–] **L.**BM.; C.; UC.; **Abs.**N.; **G.**T. 53–; **Sh.**IO. 53–; **Y.** [C. of: 25693]

8774 **British Chiropody Journal.** London. Br. Chirop. J. [1933–] **L.**BM.; MA.; S.; **Abs.**N. 47–; **C.**UL. 47–; **G.**PH. 51–52; **O.**R. 47–.

8775 **British Clayworker.** London. Br. Claywkr [1892–] **L.**BA. 31–; BM.; GM. 96–; P. IO–; **G.**M. 94– imp.; **Ld.**P. (5 yr.); **Lv.**P. 53–; **M.**P. 35–; **Sh.**IO. (5 yr.); **St.**R.; **Y.**

8776 **British Climatological Branch Memoranda.** London. Br. clim. Brch Memor. **L.**MO. 56–.

8777 **British Clock Manufacturer.** London. Br. Clock Mfr [1933–40] **L.**P.

8778 **British** and **Colonial Druggist.** London. Br. colon. Drugg. [1884–15] **L.**BM. 96–15; P. IO–15; PH. 86–15; **Bm.**U. 12–13 imp.; **N.**U. 05–12. [C. as: 8780]

8779 **British** and **Colonial Mineral Water Trade Journal.** Cardiff. Br. colon. Miner. Wat. Trade J. [1888–46] **L.**BM. 03–46; P. 88–18; **Bm.**P. [C. as: 50006]

8780 **British** and **Colonial Pharmacist.** London. Br. colon. Pharm. [1915–51] **L.**BM.; MA. 29–51; P.; PH.; SC. 33–51; **Abs.**N. 20–51; **Br.**U. 31–51. [C. of: 8778; C. as: 8917]

8781 **British** and **Colonial Pharmacist's Diary.** London. Br. colon. Pharm. Diary [1938–] **L.**P. 39– imp.

British and **Colonial Pharmacist's Yearbook.** See 8781.

8782 **British** and **Colonial Printer** and **Stationer.** London. Br. colon. Print. [1878–53] **L.**BM. 82–53; P. imp.; SB.; **Abs.**N. 12–53 imp.; **G.**M. 84–53; **Ld.**P. 11–53; **Lh.**P. 37–53 mp.; **O.**B. 02–53. [C. as: 38702]

British Columbia Farmer and **Gardener.** See 5637.

British Columbia Forest Service Publications. See 5638.

8783 **British Columbia Fruit Farming Magazine.** Vancouver. Br. Columbia Fruit Fmg Mag.

8783° **British Columbia Government News.** Victoria, B.C. Br. Columbia Gov. News

8784 **British Columbia Lumberman.** Vancouver. Br. Columbia Lumberm. **O.**F. (3 yr.); **Y.** [C. of: 36691]

8785 **British Columbia Medical Journal.** Vancouver. Br. Columbia med. J. [1959–] **L.**MA. [C. of: 12571]

8786 **British Columbia Miner.** Vancouver. Br. Columbia Miner [1928–30] [C. as: 31885]

8787 **British Columbia Mining** and **Engineering Record.** Victoria. Br. Columbia Min. Engng Rec. [1895–12] **L.**BM.; P. 06–12. [C. as: 32010]

8788 **British Columbia Pharmaceutical Record.** Victoria. Br. Columbia pharm. Rec.

British Columbia Professional Engineer. See 5639.

8789 **British Columbia Review** and **North American Mining Journal.** London. Br. Columbia Rev. N. Am. Min. J. [1897–05] **L.**BM.

British Columbia's Health. See 5640.

8790 **British Communications** and **Electronics.** London. Br. Commun. Electron. [1955–] **L.**AV.; BM.; EE.; NP.; SC.; SI. 57–; **Bl.**U.; **Bm.**P.; **Bn.**U.; **Br.**P. (2 yr.); **Bra.**P.; **C.**UL.; **Co.**T.; **Db.**; **Dn.**U. 60–; **E.**A.; O. 60–; HW.; **Ep.**D.; **F.**A.; **G.**M.; T.; U. 56–; **Li.**M.; **Lv.**P. 56–; **M.**C.; P. 56–; T.; **Ma.**T.; **N.**U.; **O.**B.; R.; **Sh.**SC. 60–; **Sil.**; **Y.** [C. of: 15078]

8791 **British Constructional Engineer.** London. Br. constr. Engr [1950–59] **L.**P. 54–59; **C.**UL. 54–59; **E.**A. 54–59; **Lv.**P. 57–59; **O.**B. 54–59; **Wa.**B.

8792 **British Cotton Growing Association.** [Publications.] Manchester. Br. Cott. Grow. Ass. [1903–] **L.**BM.; G. 04–; K.; **M.**C. 06– imp.; P. 13– imp.; U. 13–38 imp.; **Rt.** 06–; **Y.**

8792° **British Delphinium Society's Year Book.** London. Br. Delphinium Soc. Yb. [1930–56] **L.**HS.; SC. 49–56; **R.**U. 42–56. [C. as: 16477]

8793 **British Dental Annual.** London. Br. dent. A. [1952–] **L.**BM.; MD.; **Br.**U.; **Dn.**U.; **E.**A.; U.; **M.**P.

British Dental Assistant. See 8799.

8794 **British Dental Association Newsletter.** Br. dent. Ass. Newsl. **L.**D.

8795 **British Dental Digest.** London. Br. dent. Dig. [1947–49] **L.**BM.; D.; H.; MA.; **Bm.**U.; **C.**UL.; **Dn.**U.; **Ld.**U.; **Nw.**A.

8796 **British Dental Journal.** London. Br. dent. J. [1903–] **L.**BM.; D.; GH. 04–; H. 40– imp.; MA. 09–; MD.; S.; TD. (curr.); U.; UCH. 42–; **Abd.**U.; **Abs.**N. 06– imp.; **Bl.**U. IO– imp.; **Bm.**U.; **Br.**U.; **C.**AN. 50– imp.; UL.; **Cr.**MD. 32–; **Db.**; **Dn.**U.; **E.**A. imp.; S.; T. 34–; U. 47–; **G.**F.; M. 22–; **Ld.**P. (5 yr.); U.; **Lv.**P. 38–; U.; **M.**P. 34–; MS.; **Nw.**A. imp.; U.; **O.**R.; **Sa.**; **Sh.**P. 29–; U. 04–23: 34–; **Y.** [C. of: 25699]

8797 **British Dental Journal** and the **Dentist.** London. Br. dent. J. Dent. [1898–00] **L.**BM.; D.; P.; **Db.**; **O.**B.

8798 **British Dental Review.** London. Br. dent. Rev. [1925–29] **L.**BM.; D. imp.

8799 **British Dental Surgery Assistant.** Leyland. Br. dent. Surg. Asst **L.**D. 46– imp.

British Duck Keepers Association Notes. Crayford, Swanley. See 35198.

8800 **British Electricity.** Journal of the British Electricity Authority. London. Br. Elect. [1948–54] **L.**BM.; EE. 49–54; QM. 53–54 imp.; **Ld.**U. 54; **Sw.**U. 54. [C. of: 5649°; C. as: 17706]

British Electricity Authority. Utilization Research Report. See 55782°.

8801 **British Electricity Laboratories Memoirs.** Leatherhead. *Br. Elect. Lab. Mem.*

8802 **British** and **Empire Confectioner.** London. *Br. Emp. Confect.* [1932–39] L.BM.; P. [*C. of:* 8822; *C. as:* 15384°]

8803 **British Engineer.** London. *Br. Engr* L.P. 55–; SC. 54–; E.U. 29–42 imp.; G.T. 51–; M.P. 39–43; Y.

8804 **British Engineering.** London. *Br. Engng* [1949–54] L.EE. 55–54; P.; RI. (curr.); Abs.N.; E.A. 52–54; G.E. (3 yr.); I.; M.; Lv.P. 52–54; Rn.B. (1 yr); Sh.IO. 51–57; Sil. 54. [*C. of:* 8805; *C. as:* 8807]

8805 **British Engineering Export Journal.** London. *Br. Engng Export J.* [1945–48] L.BM.; P.; G.M.; O.R. [*C. of:* 8814; *C. as:* 8804]

8806 **British Engineering International.** London. *Br. Engng Int.* [1957–59] L.EE.; P.; Abs.N.; G.I.; M.; Lv.P.; Sil. [*C. of:* 8807; *C. as:* 8810]

8807 **British Engineering Overseas.** London. *Br. Engng Overseas* [1955–57] L.EE.; P.; Abs.N.; G.E. (1 yr); I.; M.; Lv.P.; Sil.; Y. [*C. of:* 8804; *C. as:* 8806]

8808 **British Engineering Standards Association.** London. *Br. Engng Stand. Ass.* [1916–31] L.BM.; I.; P. imp.; SC.; UC.; Abs.N.; Bm.P.; T.; Cr.P.; Db.; E.A.; T.; U. 19–31; G.E.; Ld.U.; Lv.P. 16–22; U. 16–22; M.U.; Nw.A.; P.; O.R. 20–31; Sh.P. 20–31. [*C. of:* 18173; *C. as:* 8950]

8809 **British Engineering Standards Coded Lists.** London. *Br. Engng Stand. cod. Lists* [1904–11] L.BM.; Bm.P. 04–05; G.M.; U.; Lv.P.; M.P.; O.R. imp.
British Engineering Standards Committee. *See* 8808.

8810 **British Engineering** and **Transport.** London. *Br. Engng Transp.* [1959–] L.EE.; P.; Abs.N.; G.E. (3 yr.); I.; M.; Lv.P.; Sil.; Y. [*C. of:* 8806]
British Engineers' Export Journal. *See* 8811.

8811 **British Engineers' Home** and **Export Journal.** London. *Br. Engrs' Home Export J.* [1919–31] L.BM.; P. 21–31; Abs.N.; Db. 22–31; G.M. 24–31; O.R. [*C. as:* 8814]

8812 **British Epilepsy Association Journal.** London. *Br. Epilepsy Ass. J.* [1955–] L.H.

8813 **British European Airways Magazine.** London. *Br. Eur. Airw. Mag.* L.AV. 56–.

8814 **British Export Journal.** London. *Br. Export J.* [1931–45] L.BM.; P.; Db.; G.M.; O.R. [*C. of:* 8811; *C. as:* 8805]

8815 **British Farm Mechanisation.** London. *Br. Fm Mechanis.* [1949–50] L.AM.; BM.; P.; Abs.N.; Bn.U. 50; C.UL.; E.A.; N.U.; O.B.; R.; R.U. imp.; Rt.; Sil. [*C. as:* 19071]

8816 **British Farmer.** London. *Br. Fmr* [1948–] L.AM. (curr.); BM.; FA.; HS. 58–; Abs.U. 53–; C.A.; Hu.G. (3 yr.); Ld.U.; Md.H. 48–57; O.AEC.; Rt. (3 yr.); Sil. (1 yr) Y. [*C. of:* 33940]

8817 **British Farmer** and **Journal** of **Agriculture.** London. *Br. Fmr J. Agric.* [1920–23] L.AM.; BM.; Abs.N. 23; Bm.P.; G.U. 21–23 imp.; Ld.U. 21–23; M.U. 21–23 imp.; O.B. 21–23.

8818 **British Fern Gazette.** Kendal, Tunbridge Wells. *Br. Fern Gaz.* [1909–] L.BM.; BM^N.; K. 09–39; L.; Bn.U. 59–; Cr.M. 35–; Db. 12–; G.U. 09–14 imp.; M.P. 09–22; O.BO. 17–36 imp.

8819 **British Film Journal.** London. *Br. Film J.* [1928–29] Bm.U.; O.B.

8820 **British Food Journal** and **Hygienic Review.** London. *Br. Fd J.* [1899–] L.AM. imp.; BM.; H. 20– imp.; P. 10–; MA. 33–; SC. 34–; Abd.U. 06–52 imp.; C.UL.; E.A.; CE. 57–; T. 01–06 imp.; G.PH. 31–; Ld.U. 15–32 imp.; Lh.FO. 32–; M.P. 38–49; O.A. imp.; Y.

8821 **British Food Machinery Export Journal.** London. *Br. Fd Mach. Export J.* [1948–51] L.BM.; P.
British Food Manufacturing Industries Research Association Journal. *See* 25704.

8822 **British** and **Foreign Confectioner.** London. *Br. for. Confect.* [1877–31] L.BM.; P. [*C. as:* 8802]

8823 **British Foundryman.** Manchester. *Br. Foundrym.* [1957–] L.BM.; I.; NF.; P.; SC.; Bm.C.; P.; T.; U.; C.UL.; Co.T. 61–; E.A.; G.T.; Ld.; Lv.P. 59–; M.P.; T.; Nw.A.; O.B.; Sh.IO.; SC.; St.R.; Sw.U.; Y. [*C. of:* 26177 and 39259]

8824 **British Friesian Journal.** Lewes. *Br. Fries. J.* [1919–] L.AM. 49–; BM.; VC. (curr.); Abs.U. 49–; Bn.U. 49–; Br.U. 32– imp.; C.UL. 47–; E.A.; AB. 49–; W. 49–; G.U. 53–; Ld.U.; Nw.A. 23–43 imp.; R.D.; U. 33–41; Y.

8825 **British Fur Farmer.** London. *Br. Fur Fmr* [1923–] L.TD. 30–; Sal. 31–32.

8826 **British Fur Trade.** London. *Br. Fur Trade* [1923–] L.BM.; P. 46– imp.; Y.

8827 **British Fur Trade Year Book.** London. *Br. Fur Trade Yb.* [1933–] L.BM.; P.

8828 **British Furnishing.** London. *Br. Furnish.* [1946–] L.P.; C.UL. 46–50.
British Gelatine and **Glue Research Association Bulletin.** *See* 9613.
British Geon Ltd. Bulletin. *See* 9614.
British Glass Industry Research Association Bulletin. *See* 9615.

8829 **British Glass Packer.** London. *Br. Glass Pckr* [1939–45] L.BM.; P. [*C. as:* 8920]
British Goat Society Monthly Journal. *See* 33531.
British Goat Society Yearbook. *See* 58017.

8830 **British Guiana Medical Annual** and **Hospital Reports.** Demerara. *Br. Guiana med. A.* [1887–] L.BM. 89–02; EB. 13–25; MA. 91–; S. 90–36; TD. 90–47; Bm.U. 15; E.U. 89–08 imp.; G.F. 90; Lv.U. 91–; M.MS. 01– imp.

8831 **British Guiana Timbers.** Georgetown. *Br. Guiana Timb.* [1951–] L.P.; O.F. 51.

8832 **British Gynaecological Journal.** London. *Br. gynaec. J.* [1885–07] L.BM.; MA.; MD.; S.; UCH. 85–06 imp.; Bm.U.; Br.U.; C.UL.; Cr.MS.; Db.; Dn.U.; E.A.; P.; S.; G.F.; Ld.U.; Lv.M.; M.MS.; Nw.A. 91–07; O.R.; Sa. 85–05. [*C. in:* 39643]

8833 **British Health Review.** London. *Br. Hlth Rev.* [1909–10] L.BM.; O.R. imp.

8834 **British Heart Journal.** London. *Br. Heart J.* [1939–] L.BM.; GH.; H. 39–49; MA.; S.; U. 46–48: 50–; UCH.; Abd.U.; Abs.N.; Bl.U. 40– imp.; Bm.U.; Br.U.; C.APH. 56–; UL.; V. 49–; Cr.MD.; MS. 48–; Db.; Dn.U. 46– imp.; E.A.; U.; G.F.; U.; Ld.U.; M.MS.; Nw.A.; O.R.; Sh.U. 44–; Y.

8835 **British Herb Doctor.** Wigan. *Br. Herb Doct.* [1939–] L.BM.

8836 **British Homoeopathic Journal.** London. *Br. homoeop. J.* [1911–] L.BM.; MA. 34–; MD. 34–; S.; U.; C.UL.; Db.; E.A.; M.MS. 54–; O.R. [*Replaces: 25710*]

8837 **British Homoeopathic Review.** London. *Br. homoeop. Rev.* [1907–10] L.BM.; S.; UC.; Abd.U.; C.UL.; Db.; E.A. 07; M.P.; O.R. [*C. of: 33526; C. in: 8836*]

8838 **British Housing** and **Planning Review.** *Br. Hous. Plann. Rev.* [1948–] L.BA.; SH. (1 yr); Wa.B. 53–. [*C. of: 22455*]

British Hydromechanics Research Association Bulletin. *See* 9616.

8839 **British Industrial Equipment.** London. *Br. ind. Equip.* [1948–] L.BM.; E.A.; O.R. [*C. of: 23205*]

British Industrial Finishing. Leighton Buzzard. *See* 23209.

8840 **British Industrial Finishing.** London. *Br. ind. Finish., Lond.* [1930–32] L.BM.; P.; PR. [*C. as: 23210*]

8841 **British Industry** and **Engineering.** London. *Br. Ind. Engng* [1936–] O.B.; Y.

8842 **British Ink Maker.** London. *Br. Ink Maker* [1958–] L.BM.; P.; PR.; Ld.P.; M.D.; P.; Y.

8843 **British Instruments.** Directory and buyers' guide. London. *Br. Instrum.* [1959–] L.P.; SC.; Dn.U. [*Replaces: 8942*]

8845 **British Journal** of **Actino-Therapy** and **Physiotherapy.** London. *Br. J. Actino-Ther. Physiother.* [1926–31] L.BM.; D. 28–31 imp.; MA.; MD.; P.; RA. 29–31; S. 28–30; SC.; Abs.N.; Bn.U. 29–31; Br.U.; C.UL.; E.A.; Nw.A.; P.; O.R. [*C. of: 33011; C. as: 8877*]

8846 **British Journal** of **Addiction** to **Alcohol** and other **Drugs.** London. *Br. J. Addict. Alcohol* [1947–] L.BM.; MA.; MD.; S.; Abs.N.; Br.U.; C.UL.; Db.; E.A.; Ha.RD. 59–; O.B. [*C. of: 8865*]

8847 **British Journal** of **Anaesthesia.** Manchester, etc. *Br. J. Anaesth.* [1923–] L.BM.; CB. 56–; MA.; MD.; S. 50–; UCH. 57–; VC. 58–; Abd.U.; Abs.N.; Bl.U. 40–55 imp.; Bm.U. 23–29; Br.U.; C.APH. 56–; UL.; V. 54–; Cr.MD. 38–; Db.; Dn.U. 23–30: 51–; E.A.; S.; U.; G.F. 48–; U. 63–; Ld.U. imp.; Lv.M.; M.MS.; Nw.A.; O.R.; Sh.U. 46–; Wd. 57–; Y.

8848 **British Journal** of **Animal Behaviour.** London. *Br. J. Anim. Behav.* [1953–57] L.AM.; B.; BM.; BM^N.; KC. 57; L.; MD.; QM.; SC.; U.; UC.; V.; VC.; Z.; Abd.M.; R.; U. 55–; Abs.U.; Bl.U.; Bm.P.; U.; Bn.U.; Br.U.; C.A.; B.; PS.; UL.; V.; Cr.U.; E.A.; AR.; B.; PO.; U.; G.U.; Hu.G.; Ld.U.; Lo.; Lv.U.; M.U.; N.U.; Nw.A.; O.AP.; B.; EP.; F.; OR. imp.; R.; Pl.M.; R.D.; U.; Sw.U. 54–57; W. [*C. of: 9369; C. as: 2610*]

8849 **British Journal** of **Applied Physics.** London. *Br. J. appl. Phys.* [1950–] L.AV.; BM.; C.; DI.; EE.; I.; LE.; NP.; P.; PR.; QM.; RI.; SC.; SI.; TP.; U.; Abd.S. 50–56; U.; Abs.U.; Bl.U. 51– imp.; Bm.C. 56–; T.; Bn.U.; Br.U.; C.ENG.; MS. 58–; R.; UL.; Co.T.; Cr.U.; Db.; E.HW.; U.; Ep.D.; Ex.U.; F.A.; G.M.; T.; U.; H.U.; Hu.G. 54–; Lc.A.; Ld.P.; W.; Lh.P.; Li.M.; Lv.P.; M.C.; D.; P. 55–; T.; U.; Ma.T.; N.T.; U.; Nw.A.; O.B.; R.; R.D.; U.; Rt.; Sa.; Sh.IO.; SC.; U.; Sil.; St.R.; Ste.; Sw.U.; Sy.R.; Wo.; Y. [*Also supplements; C. from: 26865*]

8850 **British Journal** of **Biophysics.** London. *Br. J. Biophys.* [1929–30] L.BM.; S.; Abs.N.; C.UL.; O.R. [*C. of: 851*]

8851 **British Journal** of **Cancer.** London. *Br. J. Cancer* [1947–] L.BM.; CB.; H.; MA.; MC.; MD.; S.; TD. 53–; U.; UCH.; Abd.U.; Abs.N.; Bl.U. imp.; Bm.U.; Br.U.; C.PA. 47–54; R.; UL.; Cr.MD.; Db.; Dn.U.; E.A.; PO.; U.; G.U.; Ld.U.; Lv.M.; M.MS.; P.; Nw.A.; O.P.; R.; Sh.IO.; Y.

8852 **British Journal** of **Children's Diseases.** London. *Br. J. Child. Dis.* [1904–44] L.BM.; GH. 04–19 imp.; MA.; MD.; S.; U. 04: 09–23; Abd.U.; Abs.N. 12–44; Bl.U. 04–14; Bm.U. 04–05; Br.U.; C.PA. 04–09; UL.; Cr.MS.; Db.; Dn.U. 04–31; E.A. 04–15; P.; S. 04–35; G.F. 28–43; Ld.U.; Lv.M.; M.MS.; Nw.A. 17–25; O.R.; Sh.U. 33–44. [*C. in: 4215*]

8853 **British Journal** of **Clinical Practice.** London. *Br. J. clin. Pract.* [1956–] L.BM.; D.; H.; MA.; MD.; P.; S.; TD.; U.; Abs.N.; Bl.U.; C.PA. 57–; UL.; Cr.MD.; Db.; Dn.U.; E.P. 60–; S.; U.; G.F.; Ld.U.; Lv.M.; M.MS.; Nw.A.; O.R.; Sa.; Y. [*C. of: 30479*]

8854 **British Journal** of **Criminology, Delinquency** and **Deviant Social Behaviour.** London. *Br. J. Crim.* [1960–] L.BM.; KC.; MA.; MD.; PS.; U.; Bl.U.; Bm.U.; Br.U.; Cr.U.; Db.; Dn.U.; E.U.; G.U.; H.U.; Ld.U.; Lv.P.; N.U.; Nw.A.; Sh.U. [*C. of: 8855*]

8855 **British Journal** of **Delinquency.** The Official organ of the Institute for the Study and Treatment of Delinquency. *Br. J. Delinq.* [1950–60] L.BM.; KC.; MA.; MD.; PS.; U.; Bl.U. 51–60; Bm.U.; Br.U.; Cr.U.; Db 51–60; Dn.U. 53–60; E.U.; G.U. imp.; H.U.; Ld.U.; Lv.P.; N.U.; Nw.A.; Sh.U. [*C. as: 8854*]

8856 **British Journal** of **Dental Science** and **Prosthetics.** London. *Br. J. dent. Sci. Prosthet.* [1856–35] L.BM.; D.; MD. 01–35; P. 10–35; S.; UCH. 76–95: 04–08; Abs.N. 12–35; Bm.U. 68–35; Br.U.; C.UL.; Db.; Dn.U. 70–83 imp.; E.A. 1856–07; G.F. 79–98; Ld.P. 02–30; U. 64–30 imp.; Nw.A. 67–35; O.R.; Sh.U. 75–83.

8857 **British Journal** of **Dermatology.** London. *Br. J. Derm.* [1888–] L.BM.; CB. 46–; GH. 07–38 imp: 40–; MA.; MD.; S. 88–46; TD. 88–31; U. 52–; UCH.; Abd.U. 96: 46–; Abs.N. 12–; U. 46–; Bl.U. imp.; Bm.U. 94–12: 44–; Br.U.; C.UL.; Cr.MD. 31–; Db.; Dn.U. 17–; E.A.; P.; S. 20–22; U. 96–; G.F.; U. 08– imp.; Ld.U. 92–; Lv.M. 89–; U. 26–; M.D. 57–; MS.; Nw.A. 95–; O.R.; Sh.U. 25–32: 42–; Y.

British Journal of **Dermatology** and **Syphilis.** *See* 8857.

8858 **British Journal** of **Diseases** of the **Chest.** London. *Br. J. Dis. Chest* [1959–] L.BM.; H.; MA.; MD.; S.; SC.; SH. (1 yr); TD.; U. 61–; Abs.N.; Bl.U.; Bm.U.; Br.U.; C.UL.; Db.; Dn.U.; E.A.; P.; G.PH.; U.; Ld.U. 61–; Lv.U.; M.MS.; Nw.A.; O.R.; Sh.U.; Y. [*C. of: 8895*]

8859 **British Journal** of **Educational Psychology.** *Br. J. educ. Psychol.* [1931–] L.B.; BM.; PS.; U.; UC.; Abd.U.; Bl.U. imp.; Bm.P.; T. 46–; U.; Br.U.; Bra.P. 54–; C.PS.; UL.; Cr.P.; U.; Db.; E.T.; U. imp.; Ex.U.; G.M.; U.; H.U.; Ld.P.; U.; Lv.P. 48–; M.P. 46–; N.U.; Nw.A.; O.B.; R.U.; Sa.; Sh.U.; Sw.U.; Y.

8860 **British Journal** of **Experimental Biology.** Edinburgh. *Br. J. exp. Biol.* [1923–29] L.AM.; B.; BM.; BM^N.; L.; LI.; MC.; MD.; P.; QM.; S.; SC.; TD.; U.; UC.; Z.; Abd.U.; Abs.N.; Bl.U. imp.; Bm.U.; Bn.U.; Br.U.; C.A.; AN.; B.; BI.; P. 27–29; PH. 27–29; UL.; Db.; E.AG.; S.; U.; W. 24–26; Ex.U. 25–29; Fr.; G.M.; U.; H.U.; Ld.U.; Lo.; Lv.U.; M.U.; N.U.; Nw.A.; O.R.; Z.; Pl.M.; R.D.; U.; Rt.; Sa.; Sh.U. [*C. as: 25976*]

8861 British Journal of **Experimental Pathology.** London. *Br. J. exp. Path.* [1920–] **L.**BM.; CB.; H.; LI.; MA. 23–; MC.; MD.; OP. 58–; S.; SC. 29–; TD.; U. 48–; UC. 20–29: 42: 48–; UCH.; **Abd.**R. 20–32: 47–; U.; **Abs.**N.; U. 45–; **Bl.**U. 20–30; **Bm.**U.; **Bn.**U. 60–; **Br.**U.; **C.**AN. 23–; APH.; PH. 20–34; R. 47–; UL.; V. 22–; **Cr.**MD.; **Db.**; **Dn.**U.; **E.**A.; AR. 56–; N. 37–; P.; PO. 48–; U.; **Ep.**D. 46–; **G.**T. 53–; U.; **Ld.**U.; **Lv.**M. 28–51; U.; **M.**MS.; **N.**U. 55–; **Nw.**A.; **O.**BI.; P.; PH.; R.; **R.**D.; U. 50–; **Rt.** 38–; **Sh.**U.; **W.** 29–; **Y.**

8862 British Journal of **Haematology.** Oxford. *Br. J. Haemat.* [1955–] **L.**BM.; CB.; GH.; LI.; MA.; MC.; MD.; S. 62–; SC.; TD.; U.; UC.; VC.; **Abs.**N.; **Bl.**U.; **Br.**U.; **C.**APH.; MD.; UL.; V.; **Cr.**MD.; **Db.**; **Dn.**U.; **E.**A.; U.; **G.**F.; U.; **Ld.**U.; **Lv.**M.; **Nw.**A.; **O.**R.; **Sh.**U.; **Y.**

8863 British Journal of **Herpetology.** *Br. J. Herpet.* [1948–] **L.**B. 48–52; BM.; BM^N.; NC.; U. 48–55; UC.; Z.; **C.**UL.; **Cr.**M. 50–; **E.**A.; **O.**R.; **Y.**

8864 British Journal of **Industrial Medicine.** London. *Br. J. ind. Med.* [1944–] **L.**AM.; AV. imp.; BM.; CB. 55–; GH.; H.; IC. 48–; MA.; MC. 44–60 imp.; NF.; P. 57–; SC.; SH. 55–; TD.; U.; UC. 45–; **Abd.**U.; **Abs.**N.; **Bl.**U. 46–; **Bm.**P. 50–; U.; **Br.**U.; **C.**UL.; **Cr.**MD.; MS.; **Db.**; **Dn.**U.; **E.**A.; U.; **Ep.**D. 54–; **F.**A. 53–; **G.**F. 45–; PH. 44–45; U.; **Ld.**U.; W. 45–; **Lv.**M.; **M.**C.; D.; MS.; **Nw.**A.; **O.**R.; **Sh.**IO. 54–; U.; **Wd.**; **Y.**

8864ᶜ British Journal of **Industrial Safety.** London. *Br. J. ind. Saf.* [1946–] **L.**AV. 57–; H. 50–; P. 53–; TD.; **Bm.**P.; T. 56–; **Dn.**U. 59–; **O.**B. 54–; **Sh.**IO. 49–; **Sy.**R.; **Wd.**; **Y.**

8865 British Journal of **Inebriety.** London. *Br. J. Inebr.* [1903–46] **L.**BM.; MA.; MD. 05–46; S.; TD. 26–32; **Abs.**N. 12–46; **Bm.**U. 04–07; **Br.**U. 03–06; **C.**UL.; **Db.**; **Dn.**U. 05–07; **E.**A. 03–15; U. 06–20; **G.**F. 03–33 v. imp.; **M.**MS. 04–18; **O.**R. [*C. of:* 39693; *C. as:* 8846]

8866 British Journal of **Medical Hypnotism.** Hove. *Br. J. med. Hypnot.* [1949–] **L.**D.; MA.; MD.; **Bm.**P. 52–; **C.**UL.; **Db.**; **O.**R.

8867 British Journal of **Medical Psychology.** Cambridge. *Br. J. med. Psychol.* [1923–] **L.**B.; MA.; MD.; PS.; S.; U.; UC.; **Abd.**U. 37–50, **Abs.**N.; U. 37–; **Bl.**U.; **Bm.**P.; U.; **Br.**U.; **C.**MC.; PS.; SJ.; UL.; **Db.**; **Dn.**U. 47–; **E.**A.; U.; **Ex.**U. 23–30; **G.**U.; **H.**U.; **Ld.**U. 23–24; **Lv.**P. 56–; U. 23–31; **M.**MS. 40–; P. 47–; **N.**U. 31–; **Nw.**A. imp.; **O.**EP.; R.; **Sh.**U. 39–. [*C. of:* 8885]

8868 British Journal of **Natural Therapeutics.** Blackpool. *Br. J. nat. Ther.* [1933–] **L.**BM. [*C. of:* 50604]

8868ᶜ British Journal of **Naturopathic Medicine.** London. *Br. J. naturopathic Med.* [1955–] **L.**BM.

8869 British Journal of **Non-Destructive Testing.** Dunmow. *Br. J. non-destr. Test.* [1959–] **L.**AV.; BM.; P.; SC.; **Abs.**N.; **G.**ME.; **Ld.**P.; **Y.**

8870 British Journal of **Nursing.** London. *Br. J. Nurs.* [1902–56] **L.**BM.; H. 45–56; MD. 25–56; **Br.**P. (2 yr.); **G.**M. [*C. of:* 35488]

8871 British Journal of **Nutrition.** Cambridge. *Br. J. Nutr.* [1947–] **L.**AM.; B.; BM.; C.; D.; H.; MA.; MC.; MD.; NP. 52–; P.; SC.; SH.; TD.; U.; UCH.; VC.; **Abd.**R.; U.; S.; **Abs.**A. 52–; U.; **Bl.**U.; **Bm.**U.; **Bn.**U.; **Br.**A.; U.; **C.**A.; APH.; UL.; V. 55–; **Cr.**MD. 58–; **Db.**; **Dn.**U.; **E.**A.; AG. 47–52 imp.; CE. 53–; PO.; U.; W. 53–; **Ep.**D.; **G.**F. 56–; T. 51–; U.; **Hu.**G.; **Ld.**U.; **Lv.**P. 56–; **M.**MS.; **N.**U.; **Nw.**A.; **O.**BI.; RE. 47–59; **Pl.**M. 47–58; **R.**D.; U.; **Rt.**; **Sa.** 53– imp.; **Sal.**F.; **W.**; **Y.** [*From 1948–52 contained* 39552]

8872 British Journal of **Ophthalmology.** London. *Br. J. Ophthal.* [1917–] **L.**BM.; CB. 52–; GH. 54–; H. 39–; LI. 56–; MA.; MD.; OP.; S.; SC. 40–; U. 50–; UCH. 17–23; **Abd.**U. 19– imp.; **Abs.**N.; **Bl.**U.; **Bm.**T. 54–; U. 32–; **Br.**U.; **C.**MS. 59–; UL.; **Cr.**MD. 32–; **Db.**; **Dn.**U.; **E.**A.; S.; U. 40–; **G.**F.; M. 22–36: 53–; **Ld.**U.; **Lv.**M.; **M.**MS.; **Nw.**A.; **O.**R.; **Sa.** 17–46; **Sh.**U.; **Y.** [*C. of:* 36236, 36244 and 48171]

8873 British Journal of **Pharmacology** and **Chemotherapy.** London. *Br. J. Pharmac. Chemother.* [1946–] **L.**C.; CB.; GH.; H.; LI.; MA.; MC.; MD.; PH.; S.; SC.; TD.; TP.; U.; UC.; UCH.; V. 48–; VC.; **Abd.**U.; **Abs.**N.; U.; **Bl.**U.; **Bm.**U.; **Br.**U.; **C.**APH.; CH.; PH.; R.; UL.; **Cr.**MD.; **Db.**; **Dn.**U.; **E.**A.; HW. 50–; N.; U.; **Ep.**D.; **G.**E. 47–; T. 48–52; U.; **Lc.**A. 54–; **Ld.**U.; **Lv.**P. 46–; **M.**MS.; P.; **N.**U.; **Nw.**A.; **O.**P. 48–; R.; **R.**D. 47–; **Sh.**U.; **W.** 47–; **Y.**

8874 British Journal for the **Philosophy** of **Science.** Edinburgh. *Br. J. Phil. Sci.* [1950–] **L.**B.; HQ.; KC. 54–; MO.; P. 55–; QM.; RI.; SC.; U.; VC.; **Abd.**M. 54–; U.; **Abs.**U. 51–; **Bn.**U.; **Br.**U.; **C.**PS. 55–; UL.; **Cr.**U.; **Db.**; **Dn.**U.; **E.**AG.; R.; U.; **Ex.**U.; **G.**T. 57–; U.; **H.**U. 47–; **Ld.**U.; **Lv.**P. 58–; **M.**C. 50–60 imp.; P. 57–; **N.**U.; **Nw.**A.; **O.**R.; **R.**D. 47–52; U.; **Rt.**; **Sa.**; **Sh.**IO. 51–; **Sw.**U. 53–; **Wd.** 51–; **Y.**

8875 British Journal Photographic Almanac. London. *Br. J. photogr. Alm.* [1861–] **L.**BM.; P.; PG.; SC.; 66–26; U. 49–; **Abs.**N. 03– imp.; **Bm.**P. 64– imp.; U. 11–38 imp.; **Br.**P. 05–; **C.**UL. 00–; **Cr.**P. 23– imp.; **E.**F. 83–18 imp.; O. 12– imp.; T. 98–37 imp.: 49–; U. 49–; **G.**M. 79–; **Ld.**P. 82–; **Lh.**P. 41–; **Lv.**P. 29–; **M.**P. 66–; **Nw.**P. 05– imp.; **O.**B. 99–; **Sh.**P. 20–; **We.**K. 64–65: 67–. [–61*]

8876 British Journal of **Photography.** London. *Br. J. Photogr.* [1860–] **L.**AV. 36–55 imp.; BM.; CB. 55–; P. 10–; PG.; RI. 83–52; SC. 07–; U. 44–; **Abs.**N. 12–; **Bm.**P.; **Br.**P. (4 yr.); **C.**APH. 59–; P. 19–21; UL. 62–; V. 55–; **Cr.**MD. 59–; P. 61–00: 45–; **Db.** 67–; **Dn.**U. 48–; **E.**A. 62–; F. 83–14; T. 09– imp.; U. 49–; **Ep.**D. 48–; **F.**A. 46–; **G.**M. 77–; T. (4 yr.) imp.; **H.**U. 60–; **Hu.**G. (4 yr.); **Ld.**P. 65–; U. 82–17 imp.; **Li.**M. (1 yr); **Lv.**P. 40–; **M.**C. (1 yr); P.; T. 02–; **Nw.**A. 49–; P. 95–; **O.**B. 62–; **Rn.**B. (1 yr); **Rt.** (4 yr.); **Sh.**IO. 37–; **Sil.** 50–; **We.**K.; **Y.**

8877 British Journal of **Physical Medicine** and **Industrial Hygiene.** London. *Br. J. phys. Med. ind. Hyg.* [1931–57] **L.**BM.; D.; H. 33–37; IC. 48–57; MA.; MD.; P.; RA. 42–57; S.; SC.; U. 50–57; **Abd.**R. 32–42; **Abs.**N.; **Bl.**U. 51–57; **Bn.**U. 31–34; **Br.**U. 38–57; **C.**A.; UL.; **Cr.**MD. 32–57; **Db.**; **E.**A.; R. 33–42; **F.**A. 53–57; **G.**M. 43–57; PH.; U. 50–57; **Ld.**U. 45–57; **Lv.**M. 35–42: 48–52; **M.**MS. 31–57 imp.; **Nw.**A.; P.; **O.**R.; **Sh.**U. 44–57; **Y.** [*C. of:* 8845]

8878 British Journal of **Physiological Optics.** *Br. J. physiol. Optics* [1925–39: 50–] **L.**BM.; H. 50–; OP.; S. 31–32; SC.; SI. 50–; UC. 31–35 imp.; **Bm.**T. 50–; **C.**UL. 27–39: 50–; **Db.** 27–39: 50–; **E.**A. 25–39; HW. 50–; **H.**U. 25–39; **M.**MS. 25–39; T.; **O.**R.; **Y.** [*From 1940–49 contained in* 17000]

8879 British Journal of **Physiotherapy.** London. *Br. J. Physiother.* [1949–] **L.**BM.; H. 51–; MA.; MD.; **C.**UL. 50–; **O.**B.; R.; **Y.**

8880 British Journal of **Plastic Surgery.** Edinburgh. *Br. J. plast. Surg.* [1948–] **L.**BM.; D.; MA.; MD.; S.; U.; **Abs.**N.; U. 55–; **Bl.**U. imp.; **Bm.**U.; **Br.**U.; **C.**UL.; **Cr.**MD.; **Db.**; **Dn.**U.; **E.**A.; S.; U.; **G.**F.; M.; **Ld.**U.; **Lv.**M.; **M.**MS.; **Nw.**A.; **O.**R.; **Sh.**U.; **Y.**

8881 **British Journal** of **Preventative** and **Social Medicine.** London. *Br. J. prev. soc. Med.* [1953–] **L.**AN.; B. 57–; BM.; CB.; GH.; H.; MA.; MC.; MD.; SC.; SH.; TD.; U.; **Abd.**R. 53–56; U.; **Abs.**N.; **Bl.**U.; **Bm.**U.; **Br.**U.; **C.**UL.; **Cr.**MD.; **Db.**; **Dn.**U.; **E.**A.; U.; **G.**F.; M.; PH.; U.; **Ld.**U.; **M.**MS.; **Nw.**A.; **O.**R.; **Wd.**; **Y.** [*C. of:* 8892]

8882 **British Journal** of **Psychiatric Social Work.** London. *Br. J. psychiat. soc. Wk* [1947–] **L.**B.; BM.; H.; PS.; TD.; U.; **Bm.**U.; **Co.**T. 61–; **Cr.**U.; **Db.**; **E.**U.; **Ex.**U. 54–; **G.**PH. 54–; U. imp.; **H.**U.; **Ld.**U.; **N.**U.; **Nw.**A. 50–.

8883 **British Journal** of **Psychical Research.** London. *Br. J. psych. Res.* [1926–29] **L.**BM.; U.; **Abs.**N.; **C.**PS.; UL.; **Db.**; **E.**A.; **O.**R.

8884 **British Journal** of **Psychology.** Cambridge. *Br. J. Psychol.* [1904–] **L.**AN.; B.; BM.; MA. 21–37 imp.; MC. 19–; MD.; PS.; RI.; S. 04–46; SC. 21–; U.; UC.; **Abd.**U. 05–19: (gen. sect.) 20–; **Abs.**N. 12–; U.; **Bl.**U.; **Bm.**P.; T. 37–39: 45–; U.; **Br.**P. 42–; U.; **C.**P.; PS.; SJ.; UL.; **Cr.**P.; U.; **Db.**; **Dn.**U.; **E.**A.; P.; T.; U.; **Ex.**U.; **G.**M. 09–15: 20–; U.; **H.**U. (suppl.) 11–; **Ld.**U.; **Lh.**P. 53–; **Lv.**M. 04–22; P. 33–; U. 04–31; **M.**MS. 04–33; P.; R.; **N.**U. imp.; **Nw.**A.; P. 04–40; **O.**R.; **R.**U.; **Sa.**; **Sh.**U.; **Sw.**U.; **Y.** [*Also Monograph supplements*]

8885 **British Journal** of **Psychology. Medical Section.** Cambridge. *Br. J. Psychol. med. Sect.* [1920–22] **L.**B.; MA.; MD.; PS.; S. 22; U.; UC.; **Abs.**N.; **Bl.**U.; **Bm.**P.; **Br.**U.; **C.**MC.; SJ.; UL.; **Cr.**P.; **Db.**; **E.**A.; U.; **Ex.**U.; **G.**U.; **H.**U.; **Ld.**U.; **Lv.**U.; **O.**R.; **R.**U. [*C. as:* 8867]

8886 **British Journal** of **Psychology. Statistical Section.** Cambridge. *Br. J. Psychol. statist. Sect.* [1947–52] **L.**MD. 49–52; PS.; TD.; U.; **Abs.**N.; **Br.**U.; **C.**PS.; SL.; **Cr.**U.; **E.**A.; U.; **Ex.**U.; **G.**U.; **Ha.**RD. 49–52; **Ld.**U.; **N.**U.; **Nw.**A.; **O.**EP.; **R.**U.; **Sa.**; **Sh.**U. [*C. as:* 8893]

8887 **British Journal** of **Radiesthesia** (and **Radionics**). *Br. J. Radiesth. Radion.* [1953–] **L.**BM.; **C.**UL.; **E.**A.; **O.**R. [*C. as:* 8934ᵃ]

8888 **British Journal** of **Radiology.** British Association of Radio and Physiotherapy Section. London. *Br. J. Radiol. B.I.R. Sect.* [1924–27] **L.**BM.; CB.; MA.; MC.; MD.; P.; PG.; RA.; S.; SC.; UC.; **Br.**U.; **C.**P.; UL.; **Cr.**MD.; **Db.**; **E.**A.; P.; S.; **G.**U.; **Ld.**U.; **Lv.**M.; **M.**MS.; **Nw.**A.; **O.**R. [*C. of:* 4348; *C. in:* 8889]

8889 **British Journal** of **Radiology. New Series.** London. *Br. J. Radiol.* [1928–] **L.**BM.; C.; CB.; H. 38–48 imp.; IC. 47–; MA.; MC.; MD.; P.; PG.; RI.; RA.; S.; SC.; TD. 56–; U. 33– imp.; UC.; UCH. 33– imp.; **Abd.**U.; **Abs.**N.; **Bl.**U.; **Bm.**P. 40–; U. 32– imp.; **Bn.**U.; **Br.**U.; **C.**APH. 52–54; P.; R. imp.; UL.; V. 54–; **Cr.**MD.; **Db.**; **Dn.**U. imp.; **E.**A.; AG. 50–55; P.; S.; U.; **G.**F. 28–42: 59–; U.; **Ld.**U.; **Lo.** 57–; **Lv.**M.; **M.**MS. imp.; P. 52–; **Ma.**T. 47–; **Nw.**A.; **O.**R.; **Sh.**U.; **We.**K. 30–; **Y.** [*C. of:* 8888 and 8890; *also supplements*]

8890 **British Journal** of **Radiology. Röntgen Society Section.** London. *Br. J. Radiol. Röntg. Soc. Sect.* [1924–27] **L.**BM.; C.; CB.; MA.; MC.; MD.; P.; PG.; RI.; RA.; S.; SC.; UC.; **Abs.**N.; **Bl.**U.; **Bm.**U.; **Bn.**U.; **Br.**U.; **C.**P.; UL.; **Db.**; **Dn.**U.; **E.**A.; **Nw.**A.; **O.**R.; **Sh.**U.; **We.**K. [*C. of:* 26790; *C. in:* 8889]

8891 **British Journal** of **Rheumatism.** London. *Br. J. Rheum.* [1938–40] **L.**BM.; MA.; MD.; **Abs.**N.; **C.**UL.; **Nw.**A.; **O.**R.

8892 **British Journal** of **Social Medicine.** London. *Br. J. soc. Med.* [1947–52] **L.**AN.; CB. 50–52; GH.; H.; MA.; MC.; MD.; SC.; TD.; U.; **Abd.**R. 48–52; U.; **Abs.**N.; **Bl.**U.; **Bm.**U.; **Br.**U.; **C.**UL.; **Cr.**MD.; **Db.**; **Dn.**U.; **E.**A.; U.; **G.**F.; U.; **Ld.**U.; **M.**MS.; **Nw.**A.; **O.**R.; **Wd.** [*C. as:* 8881]

8893 **British Journal** of **Statistical Psychology.** Cambridge, London. *Br. J. statist. Psychol.* [1953–] **L.**B. 56–; MD.; PS.; TD.; U.; **Abd.**U. 57–; **C.**PS.; **Dn.**U.; **E.**A.; U.; **Ex.**U.; **G.**U.; **Ha.**RD.; **Ld.**U.; **M.**P.; **N.**U.; **O.**EP.; **R.**U.; **Y.** [*C. of:* 8886]

8894 **British Journal** of **Surgery.** Bristol. *Br. J. Surg.* [1913–] **L.**BM.; CB. 45–; D. imp.; GH.; KC. 53–; MA.; MD.; RA. 23– imp.; S.; SC. 22–; U. imp.; UCH. imp.; **Abd.**U.; **Abs.**N.; **Bl.**U.; **Bm.**U.; **Br.**U.; **C.**UL.; V. 56–; **Cr.**MD.; **Db.**; **Dn.**U.; **E.**A.; S.; T. 15–17; U.; **G.**F.; M. 31–; U.; **Ld.**U.; **Lv.**M.; U. 15–; **M.**MS.; **Nw.**A.; **O.**R.; **Sh.**U.; **Y.**

8895 **British Journal** of **Tuberculosis** (*afterwards* and **Diseases** of the **Chest**). *Br. J. Tuberc. Dis. Chest* [1907–58] **L.**BM.; H.; MA.; MD.; S.; SC. 35–58; TD. 22–58; U. 52–58; **Abs.**N. 12–58; **Bl.**U. 13–15: 36–58 imp.; **Bm.**U. imp.; **Br.**U.; **C.**UL.; **Db.**; **Dn.**U. imp.; **E.**A.; P.; S. 20–28; **G.**PH. 31–58; U. 13–58 imp.; **Lv.**M. 07–16; U.; **M.**MS. 35–58; P. 12–40 imp.; **Nw.**A. 13–58; **O.**R.; **Sa.** 33–39; **Sh.**U. 44–58; **Y.** [*C. as:* 8858]

8896 **British Journal** of **Urology.** *Br. J. Urol.* [1929–] **L.**BM.; CB.; MA.; MD.; RA. 42–; S.; U. 31– imp.; **Abd.**U.; **Abs.**N. 47–; **Bl.**U.; **Bm.**U.; **Br.**U.; **C.**MS. 58–; UL.; **Cr.**MD.; **Db.**; **Dn.**U.; **E.**A.; S.; U. 35–; **G.**F.; **Ld.**U.; **Lv.**M.; U.; **M.**MS.; **Nw.**A.; **O.**R.; **Sh.**U. imp.; **Y.**

8897 **British Journal** of **Venereal Diseases.** London. *Br. J. vener. Dis.* [1925–] **L.**BM.; GH.; H. 33–; MA.; MD.; TD.; **Abs.**N.; **Bl.**U. imp.; **Bm.**U. 44–; **Br.**U. 28– imp.; **C.**UL.; **Cr.**MD.; **Db.**; **Dn.**U. 25–40; **E.**A.; T. 25–35; U. 43–; **G.**PH.; **Ld.**U.; **Lv.**M. imp.; U.; **M.**MS.; **O.**R.; **Sh.**U. 44–; **Y.**

8898 **British Kinematography.** London. *Br. Kinematogr.* [1947–] **L.**BM.; P.; PG.; RI. (curr.); SC.; **Bm.**P.; **C.**UL.; **E.**A.; **F.**A.; **M.**D. 48–; **Nw.**A.; **O.**B.; **We.**K.; **Y.** [*C. of:* 25715]

British Launderers Research Association Communication. *See* 5673.

8899 **British Launderers Year Book.** London. *Br. Laund. Yb.* **L.**BM. 30–.

8900 **British Limemaster.** Birmingham. *Br. Limemaster* [1926–28] **L.**BM.; **Bm.**P.; **M.**P.; **Sh.**P. [*C. as:* 13511]

8901 **British Machine Tool Engineering.** London. *Br. Mach. Tool Engng* [1920–] **L.**BM.; P.; SC. 31–; U. 41–; **Abs.**N. 47–; **Bm.**U. 59–; **C.**ENG.; **Co.**T. (curr.); **G.**M. 50–; **Ld.**P. (5 yr.); U. 21– imp.; **Lv.**P. 52–; **M.**C. (2 yr.); T. (1 yr); **Nw.**A. 22–; **Sh.**IO. 53–; **Y.**

8902 **British Machinery Gazette.** Leeds. *Br. Mach. Gaz.* [1904–14] **L.**BM.

8903 **British Machinist** and **Patents.** London. *Br. Machst Pat.* [1910–11] **L.**BM.; P. [*C. of:* and *Rec. as:* 37215]

8904 **British Malaya.** London. *Br. Malaya* [1926–] **L.**TP. 32–51; **O.**G. 27–42 imp.; **Sy.**R. 26–41 imp.

8905 **British Medical Booklist.** London. *Br. med. Bklist* [1950–] **L.**BM.; VC. 57–; **Bl.**U.; **Br.**U.; **C.**UL.; **E.**A.; **Ld.**P.; **Sh.**U. 59–.

8906 British Medical Bulletin. London. *Br. med. Bull.* [1943–] L.AM. 47– imp.; BM.; D.; GH.; H.; LI. 44–; MA.; MC.; MD.; PH.; S.; SC.; TD.; U.; UC. 44–; UCH. 44–; VC. 45– imp.; **Abd.**R. 44–; U. 44–; **Abs.**N.; **Bl.**U.; **Bm.**P. 46–; U.; **C.**APH. 45–; MD. 45–; UL.; VC. 45–; **Cr.**MD.; P. 44–50; U. 60–; **Db.**; **Dn.**U. 44–; **E.**A.; AG. 43–51; S. 44–; U. imp.; **Ep.**D. 44–; **G.**F. 44–; M. 53–; T. 44–; U. imp.; **Ld.**U.; **Lv.**M. 44–; P. 56–; U. 44–47 imp.; **M.**MS.; **N.**U. 44–; **Nw.**A. 43–; **O.**BI.; P.; R.; **R.**D. 44–53; U. 44–; **W.** 44–; **Y.** [*Portuguese edition at:* 7428ª; *Spanish edition at:* 7875ª]

8907 British Medical Journal. London. *Br. med. J.* [1857–] L.AM. 25– imp.; B. 19–21: 29–40: 46–; BM.; BMᴺ. 08–; CB. 22–26: 38–; D. 73–; GH.; H.; LI. 91–; MA.; MC. 97–; MD.; P. 75–; PH.; RA. 27–; S.; SH. 33–; SC. 80–; TD. 74–; TP. 50–; U.; UCH. 61–; V.; VC. 37–; Z. 58–; **Abd.**R. 37–; U. 63–; **Abs.**N. 12–; **Bl.**U. 67–; **Bm.**P. 77–; U.; **Br.**P. 80– imp.; U.; **C.**AN. 23–34: 51–; APH. 49–; GE. 43–; MD. 47–; PA. 1860–; R. 44–51; UL.; V. 47–; **Cr.**MD. 14–; MS.; P. 68– imp.; **Db.** 1859–; **Dn.**U.; **E.**A. 81–; I.; N. 12–; P.; S. imp.; T. 68–; U. 1860: 62–; **Ep.**D. 46–; **G.**F.; M. 76–; PH. 16–; T. 51–; U.; **Ld.**P. 83–; U. 68–; **Lv.**M.; P. 76–; U. 84–03: 13–27: 34–; **Nw.**A.; **O.**P. 36–; R. 68–; **R.**D. 13–; U. 44–; **Sa.** 83–; **Sal.**F. 40–; **Sh.**IO. 30–; U.; **W.** 06–; **Wd.** 48–; **Y.** [*Also supplements*]

8908 British Medical Students' Journal. London. *Br. med. Stud. J.* [1946–] L.MA.; MD.; S. 47–; U.; **Bm.**U.; **Br.**U. imp.; **C.**UL.; **Db.**; **Dn.**U.; **E.**A.; I.; **O.**R.

8909 British Metal Finishing Bulletin. London. *Br. Metal Finish. Bull.* [1943–45] L.P. imp. [*C. as:* 28573]

8910 British Meteorologic and Magnetic Year Book. London. *Br. met. magn. Yb.* [1908–21] L.BM. 11–21; G. 11–21; MO.; SC. 11–21; UC. 09–21; **Abs.**N. 11–21; **Bm.**P. 09–21; U. 11–21; **Br.**U. (pt. 5) 10: 14–18; **Cr.**U. 12–21; **E.**F. 11–21 imp.; M. 11–21; O. 10–21; R. 10–21; U. 10–21 imp.; **G.**M. 14–21 imp.; **N.**U. 13–21; **O.**R. 10–21 v. imp. [*C. in:* 22443 *and* 35655]

8911 British New Guinea. Melbourne. *Br. New Guinea* [1886–06] L.AN.; BM.; BMᴺ. 88–06; G.; K. 00–06; MO. 91–06; **O.**RH. [*C. as:* 37139]

8912 British Optical and Photographic Trade Journal. London. *Br. opt. photogr. Trade J.* [1901–07] L.BM.; P.; PG. 05–06; **Db.** 04; **O.**R. 01–05. [*C. in:* 36266]

8913 British Optical Practitioner. London. *Br. opt. Practnr* [1931–33] L.BM. [*C. as:* 36282]

8914 British Orthoptic Journal. Shrewsbury. *Br. orthop. J.* [1939–] L.BM.; MA. 39–45; MD.; OP.; S. 39–60; **Abs.**N.; **C.**UL.; **E.**A.; **Nw.**A. 55–; **O.**R.

8915 British Osteopathic Journal. Sheffield. *Br. osteop. J.* [1934–] L.BM.; **Bm.**P. 34–37.

8916 British Osteopathic Review. London. *Br. Osteop. Rev.* [1934–] L.BM.; **Bm.**U. 34–36; **O.**R.

8917 British and Overseas Pharmacist. London. *Br. Overseas Pharmst* [1952–57] L.BM.; P.; **Y.** [*C of:* 8780; *C. as:* 8918]

8917° British and Overseas Pharmacists Yearbook. London. *Br. Overseas Pharmsts Yb.* **Y.**

8918 British and Overseas Pharmacy and Medicine. London. *Br. Overseas Pharm. Med.* [1958–60] L.BM.; P.; PH.; PT.; SH. (1 yr) **Y.** [*C. of:* 8917; *C. as:* 13856]

8919 British PBMA Testing Method. British Paper and Board Makers Association. Kenley. *Br. PBMA Test. Meth.* [1954–] L.P.; **Y.**

8920 British Packer. London. *Br. Pckr* [1945–] L.AM. 46–; AV. 52–; BM.; P.; **E.**CE. 55–; **F.**A. 48–; **Lh.**P. 46– imp.; **Lv.**P. 48– imp.; **Y.** [*C. of:* 8829]

8921 British Paint and Varnish Production Manager. London. *Br. Paint Varn. Prod. Mgr* [1930–] L.P. [*C. in:* 36760]

8922 British Paper. London. *Br. Pap.* [1933–] L.P. 33–41: 46–50; SB. 47–48. [*Suspended* June 1941–Aug. 42; Sept. 1942–45, *contained in:* 36970]

British Paper Box Industry Yearbook. *See* 58022.

8923 British Patents Abstracts. London. *Br. Pat. Abstr.* [1960–] L.AV.; BM.; C.; P.; PR.; **M.**P.; **Rn.**B.; **Sil.**; **Y.** [*C. of:* 37191°]

8924 British Petroleum Equipment. London. *Br. Petrol. Equip.* [1949–] L.P. imp.; PT.; **G.**M. 51–; **Y.**

8925 British Petroleum Equipment News. London. *Br. Petrol. Equip. News* [1948–] L.AV. 57–; P.; **Bm.**C. (curr.); **G.**E. (3 yr.); **Li.**M. (3 yr.); **Y.**

8926 British Phycological Bulletin. Glasgow. *Br. phycol. Bull.* [1959–] L.BM.; BMᴺ.; QM.; **Abd.**U.; **Abs.**N.; **Bl.**U.; **Bn.**U.; **C.**UL.; **E.**A.; **Fr.**; **Ld.**U.; **Lv.**U.; **Mi.**; **Nw.**A.; **O.**BO.; R.; **Nw.**A.; **Pl.**M.; **Y.** [*C. of:* 37668]

8927 British Plastics. London. *Br. Plast.* [1945–] L.AV.; C. 45–54; DI. 45–51; IC.; NF.; NP. imp.; P.; PL.; PR. 45–59; SC.; SI.; TP.; **Bm.**P.; T.; **Br.**P.; **Bra.**P.; **C.**UL.; **Cr.**M. 61–; **E.**A.; **Ep.**D.; **F.**A.; **G.**M.; T.; **Ld.**P. 48–; U.; W. 45–49; **Lh.**P. 45–56; **Li.**M. (3 yr.); **Lv.**P.; **M.**C.; D.; P.; T.; **Ma.**T.; **N.**P. 46–; T. (10 yr.); **O.**R.; **Sh.**IO.; **Wd.**; **We.**K.; **Y.** [*C. of:* 8928]

8927° British Plastics Federation Abstracts. *Br. Plast. Fed. Abstr.* L.SC.; **Y.**

8928 British Plastics and Moulded Products Trader. London. *Br. Plast. mould. Prod. Trader* [1929–44] L.AV. 39–44; C. 43–44; DI. 44; IC. 32–44; NF. 32–44; NP. 33–44 imp.; P.; PL.; PR. 29–44; SC.; SI.; TP.; **Bm.**P.; T. 43–44; **Br.**P. 40–44; **Bra.**P.; **C.**UL. 37–44; **E.**A.; **Ep.**D. 31–44; **F.**A. 42–44; **G.**M. 30–44; T. 44; **Lv.**U. 43–44; W.; **Lh.**P. 42–44; **M.**C.; D.; P. 31–44; T.; **O.**R. 37–44; **Sh.**IO. 39–44; **Sy.**R. 29–31; **Wd.** 32–44; **We.**K. 40–44. [*C. as:* 8927]

8929 British Plastics Year Book. London. *Br. Plast. Yb.* [1931–] L.BM.; C. 34–; P.; PL.; SC. (curr.); U. 47–; **Abs.**N. 33–; **Bm.**P.; **Br.**P. 37–41; **Bra.**P.; **E.**A.; T. 45–; **G.**M. 33– imp.; **Ld.**P. (curr.); **Lv.**P. 38–; **M.**P.; **Nw.**P. 45–; **O.**B.; **Sh.**P. 35–; **Y.**

8930 British Poultry Science. Edinburgh, London. *Br. Poult. Sci.* [1960–] L.AM.; BM.; VC.; **Abd.**R.; **Bn.**U.; **C.**A.; **Ld.**U.; **Y.**

8931 British Power Engineering. London. *Br. Pwr Engng* [1960–] L.AV.; BM.; P.; SC.; **Bn.**U.; **Br.**U.; **Lv.**P.; **Y.**

8932 British Power Farmer and Agricultural Engineer. Dublin. *Br. Pwr Fmr agric. Engr* [1947–50] L.AM.; SC.; **Nw.**A.; **R.**D.; **Rt.**; **Sil.**; **Sy.**R. [*C. of:* 38238; *C. as:* 38239]

8933 British Printer. Leicester, etc. *Br. Print.* [1888–] L.BM. 92–; P. 00–; PR. 29–; SB.; U. imp.; **Abs.**N. 12–; **Bm.**P. 97– imp.; **Br.**P. 10– imp.; SC. 10–; **Bra.**P.; **E.**A. 91–; HW. 29– imp.; T.; **G.**M.; **Lc.**A. 56–; **Ld.**P. 92–; **Lh.**P. 31–; **Lv.**P. 03–; **M.**P. 09–; imp.; T.; **N.**T. (1 yr.); **O.**B. 91–; **Sh.**IO. (5 yr.); **We.**K. 46–; **Y.**

8934 British Rabbits. Yearbook of the National Rabbit Council. *Br. Rabbits* [1936–] L.AM. 41–51 imp.; BM.; P. 36–40; **Y.** [*C. of:* 41739]

8934ᵃ **British Radiesthesia Journal.** London. *Br. Radiesth. J.* [1953–] **L.**BM.; **C.**UL.; **E.**A.; **O.**R.; **Y.** [*C. of:* 8887]

8934ᵇ **British Radio Maker** and **Exporter.** London. *Br. Radio Maker* [1946–47] **L.**BM. [*C. as:* 8934ᶜ]

8934ᶜ **British Radio** and **Television.** London. *Br. Radio Telev.* [1947–] **L.**BM. [*C. of:* 8934ᵇ]

8934ᵈ **British Railways Magazine.** London. *Br. Rlys Mag.* [1948–] **L.**BM.; **C.**UL.; **E.**A.; **G.**M.

8935 **British Rainfall.** London. *Br. Rainf.* [1860–] **L.**AM. 00–; BM.; G. 65–; GM. 81–; IC. 84–37: 46–; MD. 1860–66; QM. 80–35 imp.; R. 1860–52; UC. 79–35 imp.; **Abd.**M. 02: 10–27: 38–; U. 63–; **Abs.**N.; **Bl.**U. imp.; **Bm.**P. 63–; U. 71– imp.; **Bn.**U. 65–; **Br.**A. 88– imp.; P. 68–; U.; **Bra.**P. 65–; **C.**A.; GG. 66–; UL. 65–; **Cr.**M. 94–03; P. 86– imp.; **Db.**; **E.**A.; F. 19–22; G.; M.; O. 72–; R.; T. 65–38; U. 03–; **Ex.**U. 80–86: 36–; **Fr.** 86–39 imp.; **G.**M. 63: 65–; **Ld.**P. imp.; U. imp.; **Lo.** 02–34: 39–; **Lv.**P. 65– imp.; **M.**P. 65–; U.; **N.**P. 18–; U. 05–25; **Nw.**A. 70–; **O.**G.; R.; RE. 75–27; **R.**U. 63–03 v. imp.: 04–; **Rt.**; **Sa.** 53–; **Sh.**IO. 81– imp.; U. 82–; **Sw.**U. 81–18; **Y.**

8935ᵃ **British Rayon Research Association Publications.** Manchester. *Br. Rayon Res. Ass. Publs* **M.**C. 51–54 imp. [*C. as:* 8935ᵇ]

8935ᵇ **British Rayon Research Association Scientific Reprints.** Manchester. *Br. Rayon Res. Ass. scient. Repr.* [1955–] **M.**C. 55–61. [*C. of:* 8935ᵃ]

8935ᶜ **British Rayon Research Association Technological Reprints.** Manchester. *Br. Rayon Res. Ass. technol. Repr.* **M.**C. 54–61 imp.

8936 **British Rayon** and **Silk Journal.** Manchester. *Br. Rayon Silk J.* [1949–55] **L.**BM.; P.; TP.; **Bra.**P.; **G.**T. 51–55; **Ld.**U.; **M.**C.; D.; P.; T.; **N.**T.; **O.**B. [*C. of:* 49754; *C. in:* 29370]

8936ᶜ **British Refrigeration** and **Air Control Handbook.** London. *Br. Refrig. Air Control Handb.* **Y.**

8937 **British Refrigeration** and **Allied Interests.** London. *Br. Refrig. all. Interests* [1899–04] **L.**BM.; P. 01–04; **E.**A. 02–03; **O.**B. imp.

8938 **British Regional Geology.** London. *Br. reg. Geol.* [1935–] **L.**BM.; BMᴺ.; GM.; **Abd.**U.; **Bra.**P. 48–; **Ld.**P.; **Lv.**U.; **N.**P.; **Nw.**A.; **Rt.**; **Sw.**U.

8939 **British Rheumatic Association Review.** London. *Br. rheum. Ass. Rev.* [1950–] **L.**BM.; H.; MA.; **C.**UL.; **E.**A.; **G.**M. 56–; **Nw.**A.

8940 **British Road Tar Association.** London. *Br. Rd Tar Ass.* [1938–] **L.**P.

8941 **British Science News.** London. *Br. Sci. News* [1947–50] **L.**BM.; BMᴺ.; C.; DI. 47–49 imp.; NF.; P.; PH.; PG. 47–49 imp.; SC.; V.; **Abd.**M.; **Abs.**N.; U.; **Ba.**I.; **Bm.**P.; U.; **Bn.**U.; **C.**A.; GE.; UL.; **Dn.**U.; **E.**A.; R.; W.; **Ep.**D.; **Ex.**U.; **G.**U.; **H.**U.; **Lh.**P. 48–50; **Ld.**W.; **Md.**H.; **N.**U.; **O.**BO.; F.; R.; **Pl.**M.; **R.**D.; U.; **Sil.**; **Sw.**U.; **W.** [*C. of:* 28971]

8942 **British Scientific Instruments.** Scientific Instrument Manufacturers' Association. London. *Br. scient. Instrum.* **G.**U. 56–. [*C. in:* 8843]

8943 **British Sea Anglers' Society's Quarterly.** London. *Br. Sea Angl. Soc. Q.* [1907–] **L.**BM.; P. 07–21; SC. 29–39; **Abs.**N. 07–21 imp.; **C.**UL.; **E.**A. 07–22; **Ld.**U. 20– imp.; **O.**R.; **Pl.**M. 22–39 imp.

8944 **British Soap Manufacturer** and **Soap Trade Review.** London. *Br. Soap Mfr* [1924–31] **L.**BM.; P.

British Society of **Rheology Bulletin.** *See* 9633.

8945 **British Solomon Islands Geological Record.** London. *Br. Solomon Isl. geol. Rec.* [1960–]

British Solomon Islands Protectorate Agricultural Gazette. *See* 1329.

8947 **British Standard Code** of **Practice.** London. *Br. Stand. Code Pract.* [1943–] **L.**BM.; P.; **Ld.**P.; **M.**P.; **O.**R.; **Y.** [*See also* 14457]

8948 **British Standard Specification** for **Aircraft Materials** and **Components.** London. *Br. Stand. Specif. Aircr. Mater. Compon.* [1921–] **L.**I.; P. imp.; **G.**E. imp.; M.; **Ld.**P. 58–.

8949 **British Standard Test Report.** National Institute of Agricultural Engineering. Silsoe. *Br. Stand. Test Rep. natn. Inst. agric. Engng* [1950–] **L.**P. 55–; **O.**R.

British Standards Institution Information Sheet. *See* 5685ᶜ.

British Standards Institution News. *See* 5686.

8950 **British Standards Institution. Reports.** London. *Br. Stand. Instn Rep.* [1931–] **L.**BM.; I.; P. (curr.); SC.; UC.; **Abs.**N.; **Bm.**P.; T.; **Bra.**P. 56–; **Cr.**P.; **Db.**; **E.**A.; T.; **G.**E.; M. 52–; U. 53–; **Ld.**P. 53–; U.; **M.**U.; **Nw.**A.; P.; **O.**B.; R.; **Sh.**P. [*C. of:* 8808]

British Standards Institution. S.T.A. Specification. *See* 48408.

8951 **British Standards Yearbook.** London. *Br. Stand. Yb.* [1932–] **L.**AM. (4 yr.); C. 46–; I.; P.; PG. 46: 49: 51–; SC. (curr.); U. 47–; **Dn.**U. 46– imp.; **E.**T. 33– imp.; U. 58–; **G.**M. 39–43; **Ld.**P. (5 yr.); **Lv.**P. 51–; **M.**U. imp.; **N.**U. 35–; **Nw.**A. 54–; **O.**R. 44–; **R.**U. 51; **Rt.** (curr.)

British Steel Castings Research Association Abstracts. *See* 5684.

8952 **British Steelmaker.** London. *Br. Steelmkr* [1935–] **L.**BM.; I.; P. 37–; SC. 56–; **Bm.**C. 52–; T. 50– imp.; **G.**I. 41– imp.; M. 39–; **Ld.**P. (5 yr.); **Lv.**P. 46–49 imp.: 52–; **Sh.**IO.; **Y.**

8953 **British Sugar Beet Review.** London. *Br. Sug. Beet Rev.* [1930–] **L.**AM. 40– v. imp.; BM.; MY. 50–; P.; **Bn.**U. 46–; **Br.**U. 46–; **E.**A.; W. 38– imp.; **Hu.**G. 46–; **Je.** 47–; **Ld.**U. 39–; **N.**U. 46–; **O.**R.; RE. (1 yr); **Rt.**; **Sil.** 46–; **Y.** [*C. of:* 51290; *Suspended* 1941–45]

8954 **British Surgical Practice (-Surgical Progress).** London. *Br. surg. Pract. (surg. Prog.)* [1947–] **Dn.**U.; **G.**U.; **Nw.**A. 51–; **O.**R. 51–.

British Telecommunications Research Technical Society Papers. *See* 5695.

8955 **British Textiles.** London. *Br. Text.* [1940–] **L.**BM.; **M.**C. 50–52.

British Thomson-Houston Technical Monographs. *See* 5690.

8956 **British Thunderstorms.** Huddersfield. *Br. Thunderstorms* **L.**BM. 46–; MO. 32–.

British Timken Ltd. Bulletin. *See* 9634.

8957 **British Tractors** and **Farm Machinery.** *Br. Tractors Fm Mach.* [1951–] **L.**BM.; AM.

8958 **British Veterinary Association Publications.** London. *Br. vet. Ass. Publs* [1952–] **L.**BM.; V.; **Bn.**U.; **O.**R.; **Y.** [*C. of:* 33961]

8959 **British Veterinary Journal.** London. *Br. vet. J.*
[1949-] L.AM. imp.; BM.; MD.; S. 49–60; SH. (I yr); U.; V.;
VC.; Z. 58–; **Abd.**R.; U.; **Abs.**N.; **Bn.**U. 54–; **Br.**P.; U.;
C.A.; APH. 53–; UL.; **Db.**; **E.**A.; AR. 48–; N.; **Hu.**G. 54–;
Ld.U.; **Lv.**U.; **M.**P.; **O.**B.; **R.**D.; **Sal.** 57–; **W.**; **Y.** [*C.
of:* 56639]

British Waterfowl Association Notes. *See* 35199.

8961 **British Waterworks Year Book.** London. *Br.
WatWks Yb.* [1926-] L.BM.; **O.**R. 26–36; **Y.**

8962 **British Welding Journal.** London. *Br. Weld.
J.* [1954-] L.AV.; BM.; EE.; I.; NF.; P.; **Abs.**N.; **Bl.**U.;
Bm.C.; P.; T. 59–; U.; **Br.**U.; **C.**ENG.; UL.; **Cr.**I.; **E.**A.;
F.A.; **G.**E.; U.; **Ld.**U.; **Li.**M.; **Lv.**P.; **M.**P.; T. (5 yr.);
U.; **N.**U.; **Nw.**A.; **O.**B.; **Rn.**B.; **Sh.**SC.; **Sil.** 59–; **Sw.**U.;
Y. [*C. of:* 53764 and 57312]

8963 **British Westinghouse Gazette.** Manchester. *Br.
Westinghouse Gaz.* [1914–19] L.BM. 19; P. 17–19. [*C. as:*
31701]

8964 **British Year Book** of **Agriculture.** London. *Br.
Yb. Agric.* [1908–14] L.AM.; BM.; P.; **Abd.**U.; **Abs.**N.
09–14; U. 13–14; **Bm.**U. 08–09: 13–14; **Bn.**U.; **C.**UL.;
Db.; **E.**A. imp.; U. 09–10; **M.**P.; **Nw.**P. 08–11; **O.**R.

8965 **Brittonia.** New York. *Brittonia* [1931-] L.BM[N].;
HS.; K.; **E.**B.; **Hu.**G. 31–46; **O.**F.; **R.**U. 57–; **Y.**

8966 **Broad Acres.** Leeds. *Broad Acres* [1935–39]
L.AM.; BM.; P. 35–36; **Abs.**N.; **C.**A.; **Ld.**P.; U.; W.;
Md.H.; **R.**D.; **Rt.**

8967 **Broad Way,** or **Westminster Hospital Gazette.**
London. *Broad Way* [1899–09: 23-] L.BM. 30–; MA.
41–; MD. 23–; S. U. 49–; **Bl.**U. 46– imp.; **Br.**U. 00–05;
C.UL. 99–09; **O.**B. 99–08.

8967° **Broadcast Engineering.** Tokyo. *Broadcast
Engng, Tokyo* **Y.**

8968 **Brochure. Anchor Chemical Co.** Manchester.
Broch. Anchor Chem. Co. [1934–38] L.P.

8969 **Brochure. Applications mécaniques** et **thermiques S.A.** Bruxelles. *Broch. Applic. méc. therm.*

8970 **Brochure. Asphalt Association.** New York.
Broch. Asph. Ass. L.P. 23–25 imp.

8971 **Brochure** du **Groupement professionnel** des
fabricants de **ciment portland artificiel** de **Belgique.**
Broch. Grpmt| prof. Fabr. Cim. portland artif. Belg. L.P.
29–; **C.**UL. 32–.

8972 **Brochure. Société** pour le **perfectionnement** de
l'**éclairage.** Paris. *Broch. Soc. Perf. Éclair.* L.P.
29–37.

8973 **Brochure. Station océanographique** de **Salammb-
bô.** *Broch. Stn océanogr. Salammbô* [1943-] L.BM[N].
43; **Abd.**M. 43–52; **Bn.**U. 43–48; **Dm.** 48–52; **Lv.**U.;
Pl.M. 43–52; **Wo.** 43.

8974 **Brochure technique. Station** de **recherche** et
d'**expérimentation forestières.** Rabat. *Broch. tech.
Stn Rech. Exp. for., Rabat* [1951-] **O.**F.

8975 **Brodogradnja.** Zagreb. *Brodogradnja* [1950-]
L.BM. 51–; **G.**E. (3 yr.); **Y.**

8975° **Broiler Bulletin.** Liverpool. *Broil. Bull.* **C.**A.
59–.

8976 **Broiler Growing.** Mount Morris. *Broil. Grow.*
[1951-] **E.**PO. 57–.

8977 **Broilers.** London. *Broilers* [1957-] L.AM.; BM.;
C.A.; **E.**A.; **W.** (curr.) [–61*: *C. as:* Chicken]

8978 **Brompton Hospital Reports.** London. *Bromp-
ton Hosp. Rep.* [1932-] L.GH.; H.; MA.; MD.; S.; TD. imp.;
UCH.; **Abd.**U.; **Bl.**U.; **Bm.**U.; **Br.**U.; **C.**PA. 32–48; **Dn.**U.;
E.U.; **G.**F. 35– imp.; PH. 32: 44: 46; U. imp.; **Ld.**U.;
Lv.M.; **M.**MS.; **Nw.**A.; **O.**R.; **Sh.**U.; **Y.**

8979 **Bronches.** Paris. *Bronches* [1951-] L.MD.

8980 **Bronchi.** Roma. *Bronchi*

8981 **Bronchoscopie, oesophagoscopie** et **gastroscopie.**
Paris. *Bronchosc. Oesophagosc. Gastrosc.* [1934-] L.MD.
34–40: 47–; **G.**U.

8982 **Bronn's Klassen** und **Ordnungen** des **Tierreichs.**
Leipzig. *Bronn's Kl. Ordn. Tierreichs* [1859-] L.BM.
80–14; BM[N].; L. 1859–33; S. 1859–39; SC.; UC.; Z.;
Abd.U.; **Bm.**U. 80–; **C.**B.; **Cr.**M. 1859–14 imp.; **E.**F.; U.;
G.U.; **Ld.**U.; **Lv.**P. 1859–14; **M.**U. 1859–36 imp.; **Nw.**A.
66–; **O.**R. 80–; **Pl.**M.; **Sa.**; **Sh.**U.; **Wo.** 36–40 imp.

8983 **Bronze.** London. *Bronze* [1954–55] L.BM.; **E.**A.;
O.B.

8984 **Brook.** Brook Motors. Huddersfield. *Brook*
[1937-] L.P. 50–; **F.**A. 53–; **Sil.** (I yr); **Sy.**R. 37–39 imp.
Brookhaven National Laboratory. [**Publications.**]
Upton, N.Y. *See* 5677[a].

8985 **Brookhaven Symposia** in **Biology.** Upton, N.Y.
Brookhaven Symp. Biol. [1948-] L.BM[N]. 52–; **C.**A. imp.;
G.U. 56–; **Y.**

8986 **Brooklyn Botanic Garden Leaflets.** Brooklyn.
Brooklyn bot. Gdn Leafl. [1913-] L.K. 13–34 imp.; SC.;
O.F. 25–.

Brooklyn Botanic Garden Memoirs. *See* 30890.

8987 **Brooklyn Botanic Garden Record.** Brooklyn.
Brooklyn bot. Gdn Rec. [1912–44] L.BM[N]. imp.; K.; L.;
Abs.A. 23–44; **C.**BO. 27–44; **Db.** 14–17; **E.**B.; **Ld.**U. 35–
44 imp.; **Lv.**U. 29–44 imp.; **Md.**H. 31–44; **O.**F. 35–44
imp. [*C. as:* 37896]

8988 **Brooklyn Hospital Journal.** Brooklyn. *Brooklyn
Hosp. J.* [1939-] L.MA. 47–; MD.; S. 39–54.

8989 **Brooklyn Medical Journal.** Brooklyn. *Brooklyn
med. J.* [1888–06] L.MD.; **Br.**U. 97–05 imp.; **G.**F. 98–01
imp.; **Lv.**M. [*C. as:* 28793]

8990 **Brooklyn Museum Bulletin.** Brooklyn. *Brooklyn
Mus. Bull.* [1939-] **Cr.**M. 56–; **E.**A. 56–. [*C. of:* 8992]

8991 **Brooklyn Museum Journal.** Brooklyn. *Brooklyn
Mus. J.* [1942-]

8992 **Brooklyn Museum|Quarterly.** Brooklyn. *Brooklyn
Mus. Q.* [1914–39] L.BM.; BM[N]. 14–36; HO.; SC. 21–39;
Z. 14–32 imp.; **Db.**; **E.**F.; U. imp.; **G.**U.; **M.**U.; **O.**R. 14–
36; **Sa.** [*C. of:* 33858; *C. as:* 8990]

Broomhall's Corn Trade News. *See* 15918.

8993 **Brot** und **Gebäck.** *Brot Gebäck* [1951-] **Sal.**F.
[*C. of:* 21168]

8994 **Broteria.** Lisboa. *Broteria*
Serie botânica [1902–32] L.BM[N].; **E.**B. 02.
Serie zoológica [1902–32] L.BM[N].; E. 07–20; **E.**B.
13–32; Z.; **E.**B.
Serie trimestral: Ciências naturais [1932-] L.BM[N].;
EB.; MY. 43–; SC. 49–; Z.; **Ld.**U. 57–; **M.**U. 52– imp.;
Y.

8995 **Brown Bayley's Journal.** Sheffield. *Brown Bayley's J.* [1924–36] L.P.

8996 **Brown Boveri Mitteilungen.** Baden. *Brown
Boveri Mitt.* [1914-] [*For|the English edition, see* 8997
and 47073]

8997 **Brown Boveri Review.** Baden. *Brown Boveri Rev.* [1922–] **L.**AV. 41–; EE.; I. (4 yr.); NF. 29–; P. imp.; SC. 27–; **Bl.**U. 56–; **Bm.**T. 47–; U. 26– imp.; **Br.**U. 44–; **C.**ENG. 41–46: 51– imp.; **F.**A. 43–; **G.**M. 27–39; **Lc.**A. 51–; **Ld.**P. 49–; U. 46–; **M.**C. (1 yr); P. 40–; T. 27–; U. 54–; **N.**U. 53– imp.; **Rn.**B. (1 yr); **Sw.**U. 27–31; **Y.** [*C. of:* 47073]

8998 **Brown Gazette.** London. *Brown Gaz.* [1931–34] **L.**P. [*C. of:* 8999]

8999 **Brown Marine Gazette.** London. *Brown mar. Gaz.* [1927–30] **L.**P. [*C. as:* 8998]

9000 **Brown University Papers.** Providence, R.I. *Brown Univ. Pap.* [1920–] **E.**U. 26–.

9001 **Brown's Nautical Almanac.** Glasgow. *Brown's naut. Alm.* [1878–] **L.**BM.; **Abs.**N. 09– imp.; **Bm.**P. 32–; **Br.**P. (2 yr.); **Cr.**P. 24– imp.; **E.**A. 94– imp.; **G.**M. 93–; T. 25–; **Lo.** 51–59; **Lv.**P. 36– imp.; **M.**P. 46–; **O.**B.; **Y.**

9002 **Brücke.** Braunschweig. *Brücke, Braunschw.* **L.**P. (curr.)

9003 **Brücke** und **Strasse.** Berlin. *Brücke Str.* **L.**P. 58–; **Ha.**RD. 50–; **Y.**

9004 **Brückenbau.** Zentralorgan für Strassen- u. Eisenbahnbrücken, Fussgänger-, Kanal- u. Gerüstbrücken. Karlsruhe. *Brückenbau* [1912–23] **L.**P. [*C. in:* 50711]

9004° **Brüel** and **Kjaer Technical Review.** Cleveland. *Brüel Kjaer tech. Rev.* [1957–] **L.**AV. imp.; P.; **Bm.**T.; **Co.**T. 58–; **Ld.**P. (5 yr.); **Pl.**M.

9005 **Brünner Monatsschrift** für **Textilindustrie.** Brünn. *Brünn. Mschr. TextInd.*

9006 **Bruinsma Bulletin.** Naaldwijk. *Bruinsma Bull.* [1956–] **C.**A.

Brunnenbau—Tiefbohrtechnik. *See* 7242.

9007 **Brunnenbauer.** Berlin. *Brunnenbauer* [*C. as:* 41376]

Bruns Beiträge. *See* 5975.

9008 **Brush Foundation Publications.** Cleveland. *Brush Fdn Publs* [1929–38] **L.**S.

Brush Group Technical Journal. London. *See* 52107.

9009 **Brush Recorder.** Cleveland. *Brush Rec.* [1957–] **L.**P. [*C. of:* 9010]

9010 **Brush Strokes.** Brush Development Co. Cleveland, Ohio. *Brush Strokes* **L.**P. 35–39: 51–55*. [*C. as:* 9009]

9011 **Bruxelles maritime.** Bruxelles. *Brux. marit.*

9012 **Bruxelles médical.** Bruxelles. *Brux. méd.* [1920–] **L.**MA. 28–40: 45–; MD.; S. 32–36: 47–; TD. (10 yr.); **Lv.**M. 35–40 imp.; **Y.**

9013 **Bryanskiĭ sel'sko-khozyaĭstvennyĭ vêstnik.** Bryansk. Брянскій сельско-хозяйственный вѣстникъ. *Bryansk. sel'.-khoz. Vêst.*

9014 **Brygmesteren.** København. *Brygmesteren* [1944–] **Nu.**B. 48–; **Y.**

9015 **Bryn Mawr College Monographs.** Bryn Mawr, Pa. *Bryn Mawr Coll. Monogr.* [1901–25] **L.**BM.; UC. 05–25 imp.; SC. 02–25; **Abs.**N. 10: 13; **C.**UL.; **E.**U. 04–25; **Lv.**U. 02–23; **M.**U. 02–22; **O.**B.; **Pl.**M. 01–15 imp.

9016 **Bryn Mawr Notes** and **Monographs.** Bryn Mawr, Pa. *Bryn Mawr Notes Monogr.* [1921–40] **C.**UL.; **O.**B. 21–24.

9017 **Bryologische Zeitschrift.** Berlin. *Bryol. Z.* [1916–] **L.**BM^N. 16.

9018 **Bryologist.** Brooklyn, etc. *Bryologist* [1898–] **L.**BM^N. 00–; K. 00–; L. 98–04; **Bl.**U. 12–19; **Bm.**U.; **C.**PO. 44– imp.; **E.**U. 56–; **M.**U. 47–; **O.**BO. 46–; **Y.**

9019 **Buchbinderei** und **Papierverarbeitung.** Berlin. *Buchbind. PapVerarb.* [1952–] **L.**P. 55; **Y.** [*Published in:* 37121]

9019° **Buch-** und **Werbekunst.** Leipzig. *Buch- u. Werbekunst* [1932–37] **L.**SB. [*C. as:* 17231]

9020 **Buckinghamshire Farmer.** Cheltenham. *Bucks. Fmr* [1933–] **L.**AM. 33–40: 46; BM.; **O.**R.; **R.**D.; **Rt.** 45–46 imp.

9021 **Bucureşti medical.** Bucureşti. *Buc. med.* [1929–] **L.**MA. 29–35 imp.

9022 **Budapest székosföváros közkórhazainak évkönyve.** Budapest. *Bpest Szék. Közkór. Évk.*

9023 **Budapesti építészeti szemle.** Budapest. *Bpesti építész. Szle* **E.**R. 61–63.

9024 **Budapesti K. M. T. egyetemi 2. számú sebészeti klinikum betegforgalma.** Budapest. *Bpesti K.M.T. Egy. 2. Sz. sebész. Klin. Betegforg.*

9024° **Budapesti műszaki egyetem Központi könyvtára műszaki tudománytörténeti kiadványok.** Budapest. *Bpesti Műsz. Egy. Közp. Könyv. Műsz. TudomTört. Kiadv.* [1952–] **L.**BM. 53–; **Y.**

9024ᶠ **Budapesti műszaki egyetem Központi könyvtara tudományos műszaki bibliográfiák.** Budapest. *Bpesti Műsz. Egy. Közp. Könyv. Tudom. Műsz. Biblfiák.* [1954–] **L.**BM. 54; **Y.**

9025 **Budapesti orvosegyesület értesítője.** Budapest. *Bpesti Orvosegy. Ért.*

9026 **Budapesti orvosi ujság.** Budapest. *Bpesti orv. Ujs.* [1903–] **L.**MA. 39–41 imp.: 46–; MD. 46–. [*C. of:* 29238]

9027 **Budapesti tejgazdasági lapok.** Budapest. *Bpesti tejgazd. Lapok*

9027ª **Budock's Technical Digest.** Washington. *Budock's tech. Dig.* [1949–] **L.**BM.

9027ᵇ **Budowlani** i **ceramicy.** Warszawa. *Budow. Ceram.* **L.**BM. 52–.

9028 **Bücher** der **Anstrichtechnik.** Berlin. *Büch. Anstrichtech.* [1936–38] **L.**P.; PR.

9029 **Bücher** der **Deutschen keramischen Gesellschaft.** Berlin. *Büch. dt. keram. Ges.* [1921–23] **L.**SC.

9030 **Bücher** von der **Reichsbahn.** Berlin. *Büch. Reichsbahn* [1929–] **L.**SC. 29.

9031 **Bücherei** des **Augenarztes.** Stuttgart. *Bücherei Augenarztes* **L.**MD. 38–39; S. 38–40. [*Supplement to:* 27530]

9032 **Buffalo Medical Journal.** Buffalo. *Buffalo med. J.* [1861–18] **L.**BM. 63–18; **Abs.**N. 97–12 imp.; **Br.**U. 80–06 imp.; **Db.** 84–07; **M.**MS. imp.

9033 **Build.** London. *Build* **L.**P. (curr.)

9034 **Builder.** London. *Builder, Lond.* [1843–] **L.**AV. 50–; BA.; BM. 67–; H. (curr.); IC. 42–; P. 10–; U. 48–; UC. 06–; **Abs.**N. 12–; **Bm.**P.; T. 54–; U. 1848–16; **Br.**P. 1850–; **Bra.**P.; **C.**UL.; **Cr.**P. 1845– imp.; U. 53–; **Db.** 1853–; **E.**A. imp.; CE. 58–; F. 75–21; T.; **Ep.**D. 46–; **F.**A. 53–; **G.**M.; PH. 41–48; **Lc.**A. 56–; **Ld.**P.; U. 28–48 imp.; **Lv.**P. 1848– imp.; U. 04–; **M.**P.; T. 00–; U. 1843–99; **N.**P. 36–; T. (3 yr.); **Nw.**P.; **O.**B.; **Sh.**P.; U. 83–; **Y.**

9035 **Builder.** Pittsburg, Pa. *Builder, Pittsb.*

9036 **Builders' Gazette.** Pittsburg, Pa. *Bldrs' Gaz.*

9037 **Builders' Journal.** London. *Bldrs' J.* [1895–10] **L.**BA.; BM.; P. 06–10; SC. 01–10; **E.**T. 95–00; **G.**M.; **Lv.**P. 97–09; **M.**P. 04–10; **Sh.**U. 08–10. [*C. as:* 3967]

9038 **Builders' Merchants' Journal** and **Builders' Ironmonger.** *Bldrs' Merch.J.* [1920–] **L.**BM.; PR. 30–32; **Y.**

9038ª **Builders' Year Book.** Johannesburg. *Bldrs' Yb.* [1948–] **L.**BM.

9039 **Building.** Johannesburg. *Building, Johannesb.* [1917–23] **L.**BA.; BM. [*C. of:* 25629; *C. as:* 50127]

9040 **Building.** London. *Building, Lond.* [1926–53] **L.**BA.; BM.; NP. 28–53; P. 26–28; SC. 26–53; **Bm.**T. 32–44: 47–52; **C.**UL.; **E.**A.; **G.**M.; **Lc.**A. 39–52; **Lv.**P.; **M.**T.; **Nw.**P. 42–53; **O.**R.; **Sh.**U. 31–53; **Wa.**B. [*C. as:* 4013]

9041 **Building.** Sydney. *Building, Sydney* [1907–42] **L.**BA. 07: 24–42; SC. 37–42. [*C. as:* 9051°]

9042 **Building Age.** New York. *Bldg Age* [1910–21: 29–30] **L.**P. [*C. of:* 13372; > 9043, 1921–24 and > 9044, 1924–29]

9043 **Building Age** and the **Builders' Journal.** New York. *Bldg Age Bldrs' J.* [1921–24] **L.**P. [*C. of:* 9042; *C. as:* 9044]

9044 **Building Age** and **National Builder.** New York. *Bldg Age natn. Bldr* [1924–29] **L.**P. [*C. of:* 9043; *C. as:* 9042]

9045 **Building America.** Philadelphia. *Bldg Am.* **Sy.**R. 35–43 imp.

9046 **Building Bulletin.** London. *Bldg Bull.* [1949–] **L.**BM.; **Db.** 55–; **E.**A.; **Y.**

9047 **Building** in **Canada.** Toronto. *Bldg Can.* [1929–] [*C. of:* 15557]

9047° **Building** and **Construction.** Perth. *Bldg Constr.* **Y.**

9048 **Building Construction** and **Engineering.** Dublin. *Bldg Constr. Engng* [1954–56] **E.**A.; **O.**R. [*C. as:* 9049]

9049 **Building Construction** and **Engineering Survey** and **Directory.** Dublin. *Bldg Constr. Engng Surv. Dir.* [1956–] **E.**A.; **O.**R. [*C. of:* 9048]

9050 **Building Digest.** London. *Bldg Dig.* [1947–53] **L.**BA.; BM.; P.; SC.; **Bm.**T. 51–53; **E.**A. 49–53; HW. 50–53 imp.; T. 48–53; **G.**M.; **Lc.**A. 49–53; **Lv.**P. 49–53 imp.; **M.**P. 49–53; **O.**B.; **Wa.**B. [*C. of:* 34133; *C. as:* 9064]
    Building Digest and the **National House Builder.** London. *See* 9050.
    Building Documentation. *See* 17075.

9051 **Building Economy.** Common Brick Manufacturers' Association of America. Cleveland, Ohio. *Bldg Econ.* **L.**SC. 27–.

9051° **Building** and **Engineering.** Sydney. *Bldg Engng, Sydney* [1942–51] **L.**BA.; SC. [*C. of:* 9041; *C. as:* 9061]

9052 **Building Engineering.** Tokyo. *Bldg Engng, Tokyo* **Y.**

9053 **Building, Engineering** and **Mining Journal.** Melbourne. *Bldg Engng Min. J.*

9054 **Building** and **Engineering News.** San Francisco. *Bldg Engng News*

9055 **Building Equipment News.** London. *Bldg Equip. News* [1955–] **L.**BM.; **C.**UL.; **E.**A.; **O.**B.; R.

9056 **Building Gazette.** Madras. *Bldg Gaz.* [1948–] **L.**BA.

9057 **Building Industries.** Glasgow. *Bldg Inds* [1890–55] **L.**BA. 31–55; BM.; **E.**A. 50–55; **G.**M.; **Y.** [*C. as:* 9058]

9058 **Building Industries** and **Scottish Architect.** Glasgow. *Bldg Inds Scot. Archit.* [1955–] **L.**BA.; BM.; **E.**A.; **G.**M.; **Y.** [*C. of:* 9057]

9059 **Building Industries Survey.** London. *Bldg Inds Surv.* [1936–47] **L.**BM.; **Bm.**P.; **C.**UL.; **E.**A.; **O.**R.

9060 **Building** and **Lighting.** London. *Bldg Ltg* [1930] **L.**P.

9061 **Building, Lighting, Engineering.** Sydney. *Bldg Ltg Engng* [1952–] **L.**BA.; BM.; **Wa.**B. 52–55; **Y.** [*C. of:* 9051°]

9062 **Building Maintenance.** Milwaukee. *Bldg Maint.* [1929–34] **L.**SC.

9063 **Building Materials.** Components and Equipment. London. *Bldg Mater.* [1955–] **L.**AM.; BA.; BM.; P.; **Bm.**T.; **Bra.**P.; **E.**A.; HW.; T.; **F.**A. 57–; **G.**M.; T.; **Lc.**A.; **Lv.**P.; **M.**P.; T. (5 yr.); **N.**T.; **O.**B.; **Sy.**R.; **Y.** [*C. of:* 9064]

9064 **Building Materials Digest.** London. *Bldg Mater. Dig.* [1954–55] **L.**BA.; BM.; H.; P.; **Bm.**T.; **Bra.**P.; **E.**A.; HW.; T.; **G.**M.; T.; **Lc.**A.; **Lv.**P.; **M.**P.; **O.**B.; **Wa.**B. [*C. of:* 9050; *C. as:* 9063]

9065 **Building Materials Export Components** and **Equipment.** London. *Bldg Mater. Export Compon. Equip.* [1958–] **L.**P. 60–; **Y.**

9066 **Building News** and **Engineering Journal.** London. *Bldg News Engng J.* [1854–26] **L.**BM. 1860–26; P. 63–26; SC. 07–09; **Abs.**N. 12–26; **Bm.**P. 1856–26; **Br.**P. 66–92; **Bra.**P. 70–26; **C.**UL. 93–26; **Cr.**P. 66–26 imp.; **Db.** 70–26; **E.**A. 93–26 imp.; T. 1856–26; **G.**M. 71–26; **Ld.**P. 1857–26; **M.**P. 65–26; T. 00–26; **Nw.**A. 66–09; **O.**B. 93–26; **Sh.**P. 1860–26. [*C. in:* 3955]

9067 **Building Notes.** Division of Building Research, National Research Council, Canada. Ottawa. *Bldg Notes* **L.**MO. 54– imp.; P. (curr.).

9068 **Building Plant** and **Materials.** London. *Bldg Pl. Mater.* [1955–] **L.**BM.; P. (curr.); **Y.**

9069 **Building Products.** New York. *Bldg Prod.* [1937–38] [*C. as:* 57489]

9070 **Building Progress.** Dunedin. *Bldg Prog., Dunedin*

9071 **Building Progress.** Pittsburgh. *Bldg Prog., Pittsb.*

9072 **Building References.** Ministry of Works. London. *Bldg Refs* [1944–50] **L.**BA. 45–46; P.; **Y.** [*C. as:* 15500]

9073 **Building Research.** London. *Bldg Res.* [1956–] **L.**BM.; GM.; H.; P.; **Abs.**N.; **Bl.**U.; **Bm.**P.; **Br.**U.; **E.**A.; **Ld.**P.; U.; **Lv.**P.; **M.**P.; U.; **N.**P.; **Nw.**P.; **O.**F.; R.; **Rt.**; **Sh.**P.; **Y.** [*C. of:* 42923]

9074 **Building Research** in **Canada.** Ottawa. *Bldg Res. Can.* [1951–58] **L.**MO. 58; P.; **Wa.**B. [*C. as:* 13126]

9075 **Building Research News.** Division of Building Research, National Research Council, Canada. Ottawa. *Bldg Res. News* **L.**P. (curr.)

9076 **Building Research Station Digest.** Watford. Herts. *Bldg Res. Stn Dig.* [1948–] L.BA.; BM.; H.; P.; PR.; QM. imp.; TD.; Bl.U.; Bm.T.; Br.P.; U.; Bra.P. 50–; Cr.P.; Db.; E.R.; U.; F.A. 56–; G.M. 49–; U.; Lc.A.; Ld.P.; Lv.P.; M.P.; T. 49–; U. 48–57 imp.; N.P.; T.; Nw.P. 57–; Sh.IO (5 yr.); U.; Y.

9077 **Building Review.** New Orleans. *Bldg Rev., New Orl.*

9078 **Building Review.** San Francisco. *Bldg Rev., S Francisco* [1919–23] L.BA 21–23. [*C. of:* 3957; *C. as:* 36687]

9079 **Building Science Abstracts.** London. *Bldg Sci. Abstr.* [1926–] L.BA. 28–; C. 28–; GM.; NF. 40–; P.; PR. 28–; SC.; SH. 32–; TD. 28–; UC. 38–41; Abs.N. 28–; U. 28–39; Bl.U. 28–; Bm.P. 28–; T. 32–; U. 28–; Br.P. 33–; U.; C.ENG. 41–; UL. 28–; Co.T. 61–; Cr.P. 28–; U. 28–; Dn.U. 46–; E.A. 28–; HW.; R. 28–; T. 28–; G.M.; T. 57–; U. 38–; Lc.A. 45– imp.; Ld.P. 28–; U. 28–; W. 28–; Lv.P. 28–; U. 30–; M.C. 28– imp.; P. 28–; T. 40– imp.; U. 51–; N.P. 28–; T. 56–; U. 45– imp.; Nw.A. 28–; P. 28–; Sh.G. 31–; P. 28–; SC. 45–; St.R. 28–; Sy.R. 28–; Y.

9079° **Building Science Questions** and **Answers.** London. *Bldg. Sci. Quest. Answ.* [1933–39] L.P.; Br.U. [*C. of:* 35213]

9080 **Building Standards Monthly.** Los Angeles. *Bldg Stand. Mon.* [1935–] L.BA. 42–; Y. [*C. of:* 15390]

9081 **Building** with **Steel.** London. *Bldg Steel* [1960–] L.P.; Bl.U.; Co.T. (5 yr.); Wa.B.; Y.

9082 **Building Study.** Division of Building Research, C.S.I.R.O., Australia. Melbourne. *Bldg Study* [1960–] L.P.

9083 **Building Times.** London. *Bldg Times* [1933–38] L.BM.; P.; E.A.; M.P.; O.B. [*C. of and Rec. as:* 50961]

9084 **Building Today.** Auckland. *Bldg Today* [1936–?] L.BA. [*C. as:* 22282]

9085 **Building Topics.** London. *Bldg Top.* [1947–] L.BA; P. 54–; M.T. (2 yr.)

9086 **Building Trade.** London. *Bldg Trade* [1906–18] L.BM.; P. 06; G.M. 06–08; Lv.P. 06–08.

9087 **Building Trade News.** London. *Bldg Trade News* [1959–] L.BM.

9088 **Building Witness.** Cincinnati. *Bldg Witn.* [*C. of:* 57383]

9089 **Building World.** London. *Bldg Wld* [1895–20] L.BM.; P.; Abs.N. 12–18; E.A. 95–05; T. 03; Ld.P. 95–09; Lv.P. 05–20; O.B. 95–18.

9090 **Buildings.** Chicago. *Buildings* L.P. 22–26*.

9091 **Bukowinaer landwirtschaftliche Blätter.** Czernowitz. *Bukowin. landw. Bl.*

9092 **Buletin** për **shkencat natyrore.** Tiranë. *Buletin Shkenc. nat.* [1952–57] L.BM. 54–57; BM^N. 56; O.R.; T. [*C. in:* 9094]

9093 **Buletin ştiinţific. Academia republicii populare române (romîne).** Bucureşti. *Buletin şti. Acad. Repub. pop rom.* [*C. of:* 11716]
  Seria: Geologie, geografie, biologie, ştiinţe tehnice şi agricole. Secţiunea de ştiinţe biologice, agronomice, geologice şi geografice [1950–56] L.BM.; BM^N.; MY.; R.; C.A.; E.R.; O.R.; Y.
  Then in sections
  Secţia de biologie şi ştiinţe agricole.

  Seria agronomie [1957–] L.AM.; BM.; BM^N.; MY.; R.; C.A.; E.R.; O.B.; R.; Y.
  Seria botanică [1957] L.AM.; BM.; BM^N.; C.A.; Y. [*C. as:* 51173, Seria vegetală]
  Seria zoologie [1957] L.AM.; BM.; BM^N.; MY.; C.A.; E.R.; O.B.; R.; Y. [*C. as:* 51173, Seria biologie animală]
  Seria: Matematică, fizică, chimie [1950] L.BM.; R.; C.P.; E.R.; O.R.; Y.
  Then in sections
  Secţia de ştiinţe matematice şi fizice [1951–] L.BM. imp.; P. 54–; R.; C.P.; E.R.; O.R.; Y.
  Secţia de ştiinţe tehnice şi chimice [1951–] L.BM.; P. 54–; O.R.; Y.
  Seria: Ştiinţe medicale.
  Secţiunea de ştiinţe medicale [1947–] L.BM.; MA. 53– imp.; R.; C.UL. 48–50; E.R.; O.R.; Y.

9094 **Buletin i Universitetit shtetëror të Tiranës.** Tiranë. *Buletin Univ. shtet. Tiranës* [1957–] L.BM.; BM^N. (Ser. Shkencat natyrore); O.R.; T. [*C. of:* 9092]

9095 **Buletinul Academiei** de **înalte studii agronomice** din **Cluj.** *Bul. Acad. înalte Stud. agron. Cluj* [1930–37] L.AM. 32–34; SC.; Nw.A. [*C. as:* 9111]
  Buletinul agriculturii. Bucureşti. *See* 9128.

9096 **Buletinul apicultorilor.** Iaşi. *Bul. Apic.* [1922–29]

9097 **Buletinul Asociaţiei generăle** a **inginerilor** din **România.** Bucureşti. *Bul. Asoc. gen. Ing. Rom.*

9098 **Buletinul Asociaţiei generăle** a **medicilor veterinari** din **România.** Bucureşti. *Bul. Asoc. gen. Med. vet. Rom.* L.V. 33–39 imp.

9099 **Buletinul Asociaţiunei generăle** a **medicilor** din **România** (*formerly* din **Tara**). Bucureşti. *Bul. Asoc. gen. Med. Rom.* [1897–01] [*C. as:* 46756]
  Buletinul C.E.R. *See* 9103.

9100 **Buletinul căilor ferate.** Bucureşti. *Bul. Căilor fer.*

9101 **Buletinul cărtii. Academia romana.** Bucureşti. *Bul. Cart.* [1923–30] L.SC. 30; E.R.; O.B. 23–24.

9102 **Buletinul** de **chimie pură** şi **aplicată** al **Societăţei Române** de **chimie.** Bucureşti. *Bul. Chim. pură apl.* L.C. 22–36; P. 27–38.

9103 **Buletinul. Comitatul electrotechnic român.** Bucureşti. *Bul. Com. electrotech. rom.* [1933–38]

9104 **Buletinul cultivărei** şi **fermentărei tutunului.** Bucureşti. *Bul. Cult. Ferment. Tutun.* [1906–30] Lv.U. 21. [*Suspended:* 1917–19 and 1922–29; *C. as:* 9105]

9105 **Buletinul culturii tutunului.** Bucureşti. *Bul. Cult. Tutun.* [1930–52] L.C. imp.; SC.; C.A. [*C. of:* 9104; *C. as:* 9152]

9106 **Buletinul demografic** al **României.** Bucureşti. *Bul. demogr. Rom.* L.AM. 38–; H. 38–40 imp.

9107 **Buletinul Direcţiei generăle zootehnice** şi **sanitare veterinare.** Bucureşti. *Bul. Dir. gen. Zooteh. Sanit. vet.* [1924–] L.BM.; V. 24–31 imp.; W.

9108 **Buletinul Direcţiunii generale** a **serviciului sanitar.** Bucureşti. *Bul. Dir. gen. Serv. sanit.*

9109 **Buletinul** de **documentare tehnică.** Bucureşti. *Bul. Docum. teh.* [1949–55] L.AM. 49; BM. 49. [*C. as:* 17072]

9110 **Buletinul Erbarului Institutului botanic** din **Bucureşti.** Bucureşti. *Bul. Erb. Inst. bot. Buc.* [1901–02] L.BM. 01; BM^N. 01; K.

9111 **Buletinul Facultăţii** de **agronomie** din **Cluj.** Cluj. *Bul. Fac. Agron. Cluj* [1938–43] **L.**SC.; **C.**A. 38. [*C. of:* 9095; *C. as:* 2283]

9112 **Buletinul Facultăţii** de **ştiinţe agricole, Chişinău.** Chişinău. *Bul. Fac. Şti. agric. Chişinău* [1936–]

9113 **Buletinul Facultăţii** de **ştiinţe** din **Cernăuţi.** *Bul. Fac. Şti. Cernăuţi* [1927–37] **L.**BM^N^. 27–35; L. 28–37; P.; **Bl.**U. 27–28; **C.**P.

9114 **Buletinul Grădinii botanice** şi al **Muzeului botanic** de la **Universitatea** din **Cluj.** Cluj. *Bul. Grăd. bot. Muz. bot. Univ. Cluj* [1926–] **L.**BM^N^.; K.; MY. 26–47; **E.**B.; **Y.** [*C. of* 9116]

Buletinul I.R.E. *See* 9116.

9115 **Buletinul industriei.** Bucureşti. *Bul. Ind.*

9116 **Buletinul** de **informaţii** al **Grădinii botanice** şi al **Muzeului botanice** de la **Universitatea** din **Cluj.** *Bul. Inf. Grăd. bot. Muz. bot. Univ. Cluj* [1921–25] **L.**BM^N^.; K.; MY.; 23–25; **E.**B. [*C. as:* 9114]

Buletinul de **informaţii Institutului** de **cercetări piscicole.** *See* 9118.

9117 **Buletinul** de **informaţii** al **Ministerului agriculturii** şi **domenilor.** Bucureşti. *Bul. Inf. Minist. Agric. Domen.* [1932–] Rt. 33–40 imp. [*C. of:* 9128]

9118 **Buletinul Institutului** de **cercetări piscicole.** Bucureşti. *Bul. Inst. Cerc. pisc.* [1942–] **L.**BM^N^. 53–; Z. 56–; **Bn.**U. 59–; **Fr.** 50–; **Lo.** 59–; **Pl.**M. 53–; **Wo.** 56–

9119 **Buletinul Institutului** national de **cercetări technologice.** Bucureşti. *Bul. Inst. nat. Cerc. technol.* [1946–] **L.**AM. 48–; C. 46–48; P. 46–48; PT.; SC.

9120 **Buletinul Institutului** de **petrol, gaze** şi **geologie** din **Bucureşti.** Bucureşti. *Bul. Inst. Petrol Gaze Geol. Buc.* [1960–] **L.**P.; **Y.**

9121 **Buletinul Institutului politehnic Bucureşti.** Bucureşti. *Bul. Inst. politeh. Buc.* **L.**C. 56–; **Te.**C.; **Y.**

9122 **Buletinul Institutului politehnic** din **Iaşi.** Iaşi. *Bul. Inst. politeh. Iaşi* [1946–] **L.**AV. 57–; BM. 47–48; C. 55–; **L.**E. 59–; P. 47; R. 46–48; **C.**P.; **E.**R.; **G.**U. 48– imp.; **Md.**H. 48–; **Y.**

9123 **Buletinul Institutului român** de **energie.** Bucureşti. *Bul. Inst. rom. Energ.* [1937–] **L.**P. 37–39.

9124 **Buletinul Institutului romanese** de **organizare ştiinţifică** a **Muncii.** Bucureşti. *Bul. Inst. rom. Org. şti. Muncii*

9125 **Buletinul lunar.** Observatorul astronomic şi meteorologic. Bucureşti. *Bul. lun.* [1892–27] **L.**MO.; **E.**M. 01–09: 14–24; R. 96: 07–09: 21–27; **O.**G. 93–09. [*Suspended:* 1917–20; *C. as:* 9127]

Buletinul medical. Bucureşti. *See* 46756.

9126 **Buletinul** de **mersul epizootilor animalelor domestice.** Bucureşti. *Bul. Mers. Epizoot. Anim. dom.*

9127 **Buletinul meteorologic lunar.** Institutul meteorologic central al României. Bucureşti. *Bul. met. lun.* [1928–] **L.**MO.; **E.**R. 28–38 imp. [*C. of:* 9125]

9128 **Buletinul Ministerului agriculturii, industriei, comerciului** şi **domeniilor.** Bucureşti. *Bul. Minist. Agric. Ind.* [1923–31] **L.**AM.; SC. 28–31; **Abs.**A. 28–31; **C.**A. 28–31; **E.**U. 25–31; **Lv.**U. 28–31 imp.; **M.**U.; **Md.**H. 31; **O.**R.; **R.**D.; Rt. 29–31. [*C. as:* 9117]

9129 **Buletinul Muzeului** national de **istorie naturala** din **Chişinău.** *Bul. Muz. natn. Ist. nat. Chişinău* [1926–] **L.**BM^N^. 26–42; **Rt.** 34–38.

Buletinul Muzeului regional al **Besarabiei** din **Chişinău.** *See* 9129.

9130 **Buletinul** de **normalizare AGIR.** Asociaţie generăla a inginerilor din România. Bucureşti. *Bul. Norm. AGIR* [1948–]

Buletinul oficial al **proprietăţei industriale.** *See* 11409.

Buletinul Politehnica "Gh. Asachi" din **Iaşi.** *Bul. Politeh. 'Gh. Asachi' Iaşi.* *See* 9122.

9131 **Buletinul Şcoaleî centrale** de **agricultură.** Herestrău. *Bul. Şcoal. cent. Agric., Herestrău*

9132 **Buletinul Serviciului antirabic.** Bucureşti. *Bul. Serv. antirab.* [1935–]

9133 **Buletinul Serviciului viticol** din **Basarabia.** Chişinau. *Bul. Serv. vitic. Basarabia*

9134 **Buletinul Societăţii** de **chimie** din **România.** Bucureşti. *Bul. Soc. Chim. Rom.* [1919–] **L.**C. 19–38; P. 28; SC. 34–39.

9135 **Buletinul Societăţii geografice române.** Bucureşti. *Bul. Soc. geogr. rom.* [1876–12] **L.**BM. 76–85; G. imp. [*C. as:* 9141]

9136 **Buletinul Societăţii medicale** din **Chişinău.** Chişinău. *Bul. Soc. med. Chişinău*

9137 **Buletinul Societăţii** de **medici** şi **naturalişti** din **Iaşi.** Iaşi. *Bul. Soc. Med. Nat. Iaşi* [1887–23] **L.**BM^N^.; MD. [*C. as:* 46764]

9138 **Buletinul Societăţii medico-militare.** Sibiiu. *Bul. Soc. med.-milit.*

9139 **Buletinul Societăţii naturalişţor** din **România.** Bucureşti. *Bul. Soc. Nat. Rom.* [1932–] **L.**BM^N^. 32–43; EB. 36–39; Z. 38–39.

9140 **Buletinul Societăţii politechnice.** Bucureşti. *Bul. Soc. politech.*

9141 **Buletinul Societăţii regale române** de **geografie.** Bucureşti. *Bul. Soc. r. rom. Geogr.* [1913–] **L.**G. imp. [*C. of:* 9135]

9142 **Buletinul Societăţii române** de **fizica.** Bucureşti. *Bul. Soc. rom. Fiz.* [1923–] **C.**P. 33–; **E.**R. 33– imp. [*C. of part of:* 9145]

9143 **Buletinul Societăţii române** de **geologie.** Bucureşti. *Bul. Soc. rom. Geol.* [1932–39] **L.**BM.; BM^N^; GM.; SC. 32–37; **Ld.**U. 37–39; **Lv.**U. 32–35.

9144 **Buletinul Societăţii române** de **oftalmologie.** Cluj. *Bul. Soc. rom. Oftal.* [1924] **L.**BM.

9145 **Buletinul Societăţii române** de **ştiinţe.** Bucureşti. *Bul. Soc. rom. Şti.* [1911–15] **L.**BM^N^.; R.; **G.**U.; **Lv.**U. imp. [*C. of:* 9147; *C. as:* 9142, 9146, and 10886]

9146 **Buletinul Societăţii** de **ştiinţe agricole.** Bucureşti. *Bul. Soc. Şti. agric.* [1938–] [*C. of part of:* 9145]

9147 **Buletinul Societăţii** de **ştiinţe** din **Bucureşti.** Bucureşti. *Bul. Soc. Şti. Buc.* [1892–10] **L.**BM. 98–00; BM^N^.; R.; UC. 00–10 imp.; **G.**U. 97–10 imp.; **Lv.**U. 97–10 imp. [*C. as:* 9145]

9148 **Buletinul Societăţii** de **ştiinţe** din **Cluj.** Cluj. *Bul. Soc. Şti. Cluj* [1921–] **L.**BM^N^. 21–48; EB. 21–48; SC. 21–48.

Buletinul Societăţii de **ştiinţe fizice** din **Bucureşti.** *See* 9145.

9149 **Buletinul Societăţii ştiinţelor medicale.** Bucureşti. *Bul. Soc. Şti. med.*

9150 **Buletinul Societății studenților** in **ştiinţe naturale** din **Bucureşti.** Bucureşti. *Bul. Soc. Stud. Şti. nat. Buc.* [1930–36] **L.**z. 34–36.

9151 **Buletinul** de **standardizare.** Bucureşti. *Bul. Stand.* [1949–]

9152 **Buletinul tutunului.** Bucureşti. *Bul. Tutun.* [1953–] **C.**A. [*C. of:* 9105]

9153 **Buletinul Universităților "V. Babeş"** si **"Bolyai".** Cluj. *Bul. Univ. "V. Babes" "Bolyai".* Seria ştiinţele naturii [1956–57] **L.**BM^N. 57; **G.**U. 57. [*C. as:* 51079]

9154 **Bulgarie médicale.** Sofia. *Bulgarie méd.* [1906–]

9155 **Bŭlgarska klinika.** Sofiya. Българска клиника. *Bŭlg. Klin.* [1928–] **L.**MA. 48–; MD. 46–.

9156 **Bŭlgarski farmatsefticheski vestnik.** Druzhestvo 'Galeius'. Sofiya. Български фармацефтически вѣстникъ. Дружество 'Галеиусъ'. *Bulg. farm. Vest.*

9157 **Bŭlgarski lêkar'.** Sofiya. Български лѣкарь. *Bŭlg. Lêk.*

9158 **Bŭlgarski lovets.** Sofiya. Български ловецъ. *Bŭlg. Lovets*

9159 **Bŭlgarsko voenno-sanitarno dêlo.** Vrattsa-Russe, Sofiya, St. Zagora. Българско военно-санитарно дѣло. *Bŭlg. voenno-sanit. Dêlo*

Bulletein. *See* **Bulletijn.**

Bulletijn. Brandstofnavorsingsinstituut van **Suid-Afrika.** *See* 10313.

Bulletijn. Departement van den **Landbouw, Suriname.** *See* 9951.

Bulletijn der **zittingen. Académie royale** des **sciences coloniales.** Bruxelles. *See* 11704.

Bulletijn der **zittingen. K. Belgisch koloniaal instituut.** Brussel. *See* 11705.

9160 **Bulletin. A. T. Still Research Institute.** Cincinnati. *Bull. A. T. Still Res. Inst.* [1911–31] **L.**BM. imp.

Bulletin of the **Abastumani Astrophysical Observatory.** *See* 12737.

9161 **Bulletin** of the **Aberdeen** and **North of Scotland College** of **Agriculture.** Aberdeen. *Bull. Aberd. N. Scotl. Coll. Agric.* [1903–10] **L.**AM.; P.; **Abd.**U.; **Bm.**U.; **C.**A. 04–10; UL.; **Cr.**P. 04–10 imp.; **E.**U.; **M.**U.; **Nw.**A. 03–04; **Rt.**; **Sa.** [*C. as:* 11342]

Bulletin. Abkhasia Agricultural Experimental Station. *See* 24289.

9162 **Bulletin** of **Abstracts. American Gas Association** (*formerly* **Institute**). New York. *Bull. Abstr. Am. Gas Ass.* [1907–30] **L.**P.; SC. [>298, 1911–18]

9164 **Bulletin** of **Abstracts. Bureau** of **Fuel** and **Combustion Records, Ltd.** London. *Bull. Abstr. Bur. Fuel Combust. Rec.* [1911–] **L.**BM.; P.

9165 **Bulletin. Abuyoma Seismological Observatory,** University of Kyoto. Kyoto. *Bull. Abuyoma seism. Obs.* **Db.** 52–.

Bulletin de l'**Académie** de **Belgique.** *See* 9184.

9166 **Bulletin** de l'**Académie delphinale.** Grenoble. *Bull. Acad. delph.* [1846–] **L.**BM. 70–; **C.**UL. 1846–73; **O.**B.

Bulletin de l'**Académie** de **hautes études agronomiques** de **Cluj.** *See* 9095.

9167 **Bulletin** de l'**Académie d'Hippone.** Bône. *Bull. Acad. Hippone* [1865–] **L.**BM. 65–02; BM^N. 65–94; **C.**UL. 65–99.

9168 **Bulletin** de l'**Académie d'hygiène** contre les **maladies** du **premier âge.** Paris. *Bull Acad. Hyg. Mal. prem. Âge* [*C. as:* 25408]

9169 **Bulletin. Académie** de l'**Île de la Réunion.** Saint-Denis. *Bull. Acad. Île Réunion* **L.**BM^N. 22: 38.

Bulletin de l'**Académie impériale** des **sciences** de **St. Petersbourg.** *See* 24372.

9170 **Bulletin** de l'**Académie internationale** de **géographie botanique.** Le Mans. *Bull. Acad. int. Géogr. bot.* [1891–10] **L.**BM.; BM^N.; K.; **E.**B. [*C. as:* 10330]

9171 **Bulletin** de l'**Académie Malgache.** Tananarive. *Bull. Acad. malgache* [1902–] **L.**BM^N. imp.; SC. 41–; TD. 31–; Z. 41–; **O.**B. 02–13; **Y.** [*C. of:* 12432]

9172 **Bulletin** de l'**Académie** de **médecine.** Paris. *Bull. Acad. Méd.* [1836–46] **L.**BM.; H. 01–46; MA. 00–46; MC. 22–46; MD.; S.; TD. 17–46; UC. 34–40; **Bl.**U. 21–24; **Bm.**U. 93–06: 32–40; **Br.**U. 91–46; **C.**UL.; **Db.** 72: 14–18: 36–37: 45–46; **E.**P.; S. 85–46; U.; **G.**F. 77–05 imp.; U.; **Lv.**M. 09–46; **O.**R.; **Y.** [*C. as:* 9174]

Bulletin de l'**Académie** de **médecine** de **Belgique.** *See* 9185.

9173 **Bulletin** de l'**Académie** de **médecine** de **Roumanie.** Paris. *Bull. Acad. Méd. Roum.* [1935–] **L.**D. 36–40: 45–; H. 36–39: 42; MA. 36–45; MD.; S. 35–41 imp.; SC.; TD. 36–39; **Br.**U.; **G.**F. 36–40; **Nw.**A. 36–43: 45–47.

9174 **Bulletin** de l'**Académie nationale** de **médecine.** Paris. *Bull. Acad. natn. Méd.* [1947–] **L.**BM.; H.; MA.; MC.; MD.; PH. 55–; S.; TD.; **Br.**U.; **C.**UL.; **Db.** 47–55 imp.; **E.**P.; S.; U.; **G.**F.; U.; **Lv.**M.; **O.**BI; R.; **R.**D. 47–52. [*C. of:* 9172]

9175 **Bulletin** de l'**Académie navale Nicolas.** St.-Pétersbourg. *Bull. Acad. nav. Nicolas* **L.**MO 11–15.

9176 **Bulletin** de l'**Académie polonaise** des **sciences.** Classe II. Série des sciences biologiques. Varsovie. *Bull. Acad. pol. Sci. Cl. II Sér. Sci. biol.* [1953–] **L.**AM.; AV.; BM^N.; GL.; MA. (med.); MD. (med.); MY. 54; P.; R.; SC.; TD. 57–; U. 59–; UC.; Z.; **Abd.**S.; **Bl.**U.; **Br.**A.; **C.**A.; APH. 60–; BO.; P.; UL.; **Db.**; **Dm.**; **E.**B.; R.; W.; **G.**U.; **Hu.**G.; **Ld.**U.; **Lv.**P.; **Pl.**M.; **R.**D. 56–; **W.**; **Y.** [*C. from:* 10660, Série B]

9177 **Bulletin** de l'**Académie polonaise** des **sciences.** Classe III: Mathématique, astronomie, physique, chimie, géologie et géographie. Varsovie. *Bull. Acad. pol. Sci. Cl. III. Math.* [1953–57] **L.**AV.; BM^N.; C.; GL.; P.; R.; SC.; U.; **Bl.**U.; **C.**B. 56–57; MO.; P.; UL.; **Db.**; **E.**B.; R.; **G.**U. 53; **Ld.**U.; **Lv.**P.; **Nw.**A.; **O.**R.; **Te.**C.; **Y.** [*C. of:* 10660, Série A; *C. as:* 9179, 9180 and 9182]

9178 **Bulletin** de l'**Académie polonaise** des **sciences.** Classe IV: Mécanique appliquée. Varsovie. *Bull. Acad. pol. Sci. Cl. IV. Méc. appl.* [1953–57] **L.**EE. imp.; P. 55–57; R.; SC.; **Lv.**P.; **Y.** [*C. as:* 9183]

9179 **Bulletin** de l'**Académie polonaise** des **sciences.** Série des sciences chimiques. Varsovie. *Bull. Acad. pol. Sci. Sér. Sci. chim.* [1960–] **L.**C.; P.; R.; SC.; U.; **Bl.**U.; **C.**P.; UL.; **Db.**; **E.**B.; R.; **Ld.**U.; **Lv.**P.; **O.**R.; **Y.** [*C. from:* 9177 and 9180]

9180 **Bulletin** de l'**Académie polonaise** des **sciences.** Série des sciences chimiques, géologiques et géographiques. Varsovie. *Bull. Acad. pol. Sci. Sér. Sci. chim. geol. geogr.* [1958–59] **L.**BM^N.; C.; GL.; P.; R.; SC.; U.; **Bl.**U.; **C.**MO.; P.; UL.; **Db.**; **E.**B.; R.; **Ld.**U.; **Lv.**P.; **O.**R.; **Y.** [*C. from:* 9177; *C. as:* 9179 and 9181]

9181 **Bulletin** de l'**Académie polonaise** des **sciences.** Série des sciences géologiques et géographique. Varsovie. *Bull. Acad. pol. Sci. Sér. Sci. géol. géogr.* [1960–] **L.**BM^N.; GL.; P.; SC.; **Ld.**U.; **Lv.**P.; **Y.** [*C. from:* 9180]

9182 **Bulletin** de l'**Académie polonaise** des **sciences.** Série des sciences mathématiques, astronomiques et physiques. Varsovie. *Bull. Acad. pol. Sci. Sér. Sci. math. astr. phys.* [1958–] **L.**AV.; P.; R.; SC.; U.; **Bl.**U.; **C.**P.; UL.; **Db.**; **E.**B.; R.; **Ld.**U. **Lv.**P.; **O.**R.; **Y.** [*C. from:* 9177]

9183 **Bulletin** de l'**Académie polonaise** des **sciences.** Série des sciences techniques. Varsovie. *Bull. Acad. pol. Sci. Sér. Sci. tech.* [1958–] **L.**AV.; EE.; P.; R.; SC.; **E.**R.; **Lv.**P.; **Y.** [*C. of:* 9178]

9184 **Bulletin** de l'**Académie r.** de **Belgique. Classe** des **sciences.** Bruxelles. *Bull. Acad. r. Belg. Cl. Sci.* [1832–] **L.**BM.; BM^N.; C. 1852–; E. 1832–97; G. 63–; GL. 00–; K. (bot.) 76–11; L.; M. 69–; P.; R. 1836–; S.; SC. 1839–; UC. 99–; Z.; **Abd.**U.; **Bm.**N. 85– imp.; **Bn.**U. 96–13 imp.; **C.**P.; UL.; **Db.**; **E.**B. 77–; C. 69–; J. 69–92; P.; R.; **G.**G. 02–; U. 1840– imp.; **Ld.**U. 26–; **Lv.**U. 73–; **M.**U. 36–39; **Nw.**A. 81–14; **O.**R.; **Pl.**M. 54–59; **Sa.** 1832–92; **Y.**

9185 **Bulletin** de l'**Académie r.** de **médecine** de **Belgique.** Bruxelles. *Bull. Acad. r. Méd. Belg.* [1841–] **L.**BM.; CB. 55–; H. 98–40 imp.; MA. 40– imp.; MC. 21–; MD. 08–14: 24–; R. 1841–55; S. 1849–; SC. 23–; UC. 23–39 imp.; **Br.**U. 91–; **C.**UL.; **Db.** 1843–1844: 77–03; **E.**P.; U. 1857–76; **Lv.**M. 30–34 imp.; U. 07– imp.; **M.**MS. 1841–74; **O.**R.; **Y.**

9186 **Bulletin** de l'**Académie** des **sciences, arts** et **belles-lettres** de **Caen.** Caen. *Bull. Acad. Sci. Arts Belles-Lett. Caen*

9187 **Bulletin** de l'**Académie** des **sciences, belles-lettres** et **arts** de **Besançon.** Besançon. *Bull. Acad. Sci. Belles-Lett. Arts Besançon* **L.**BM. 1806–.

9188 **Bulletin** de l'**Académie** des **sciences, inscriptions** et **belles-lettres** de **Toulouse.** Toulouse. *Bull. Acad. Sci. Inscript. Belles-Lett. Toulouse* [1897–00] **L.**BM.; BM^N.; SC.; **C.**UL.; **Db.**; **E.**P.; R.; **O.**B.; **Sa.** [*C. as:* 30699]

Bulletin de l'**Académie** des **sciences** et des **lettres** de **Danemark.** *See* 36629.

Bulletin de l'**Académie** des **sciences** et **lettres** de **Montpellier.** *See* 10961.

9189 **Bulletin** de l'**Académie** des **sciences mathématiques** et **naturelles.** Belgrade. *Bull. Acad. Sci. math. nat., Belgr.* [1933–40]

A. Sciences mathématiques et physiques. **L.**AS.; R.; SC.; **Abs.**U.; **C.**P.; **Db.**; **E.**R.; **G.**U.; **Ld.**U.

B. Sciences naturelles. **L.**BM^N.; GL.; R.; **Abd.**M. 33–37; **C.**S.; **Db.**; **E.**C.; R.; **Fr.**; **G.**U.; **Pl.**M. 33. [*C. as:* 9190]

Bulletin de l'**Académie** des **sciences** de l'**URSS** *See* 24296.

Bulletin de l'**Académie** des **sciences** d'**Ukraine. Classe** des **sciences naturelles** et **techniques.** *See* 58332.

Bulletin de l'**Académie** des **sciences** d'**Ukraine. Classe** des **sciences physiques** et **mathématiques.** *See* 58284^c.

9190 **Bulletin** de l'**Académie serbe** des **sciences. Classe** des **sciences mathématiques** et **naturelles.** Beograd. *Bull. Acad. serbe Sci. Cl. Sci. math. nat.*

Sciences mathématiques [1952–] **L.**AS.; BM.; P.; R.; **C.**P.; **Ld.**U.; **Lv.**U.; **M.**P.; **Y.**

Sciences naturelles [1950–] **L.**BM^N.; GL.; P.; R.; **C.**P.; S.; **Db.**; **E.**C.; **Fr.**; **Lv.**U.; **Y.** [*C. from 9189*]

9191 **Bulletin** de l'**Académie serbe** des **sciences. Classe** des **sciences médicales.** Beograd. *Bull. Acad. serbe Sci. Cl. Sci. méd.* [1951–] **L.**BM.; R.; **C.**P.; **Db.**; **Y.** [*C. from:* 9189]

9192 **Bulletin** de l'**Académie serbe** des **sciences. Classe** des **sciences techniques.** Beograd. *Bull. Acad. serbe Sci. Cl. Sci. tech.* [1951–] **L.**BM.; P.; **C.**P.; **Db.**; **Y.** [*C. from:* 9189]

Bulletin de l'**Académie suisse** des **sciences médicales.** *See* 11663.

9193 **Bulletin** de l'**Académie** du **Var.** Toulon. *Bull. Acad. Var*

9194 **Bulletin** de l'**Académie vétérinaire** de **France.** Paris. *Bull. Acad. vét. Fr.* [1928–] **L.**BM.; LI. 28–32; MC. 28–54 imp.; MD.; V.; **Br.**U.; **C.**V. 33–34: 37– imp.; **Db.** 30–33; **E.**N. 28–45; **Lv.**U.; **W.** imp.; **Y.** [*C. of:* 10935]

9195 **Bulletin** of the **Academy** of **Medicine.** Toronto. *Bull. Acad. Med., Toronto* [1927–] **L.**MA. 32–; MD. 47–.

9196 **Bulletin** of the **Academy** of **Medicine** of **Toledo** and **Lucas County.** Toledo. *Bull. Acad. Med. Toledo Lucas Cty* [1933–] **L.**MA. 47–. [*C. of:* 12415]

9197 **Bulletin. Academy** of **Science** of **St. Louis.** *Bull. Acad. Sci. St Louis* [1935–]

Bulletin. Academy of **Sciences** of **Kazakh SSR.** Alma-Ata. *See* 24293.

Bulletin of the **Academy** of **Sciences, USSR.** *See* 24296.

9198 **Bulletin** of the **Academy** of **Sciences** of the **USSR. Division** of **Chemical Science.** New York. *Bull. Acad. Sci. USSR Div. chem. Sci.* [1952–] **L.**C.; P.; **M.**P. 57–; **Te.**C. 55–; **Y.** [*English translation of:* 24296 Ser. khim.]

9199 **Bulletin** of the **Academy** of **Sciences** of the **USSR. Geophysics Series.** New York, London. *Bull. Acad. Sci. USSR Geophys. Ser.* [1957–] **L.**BM.; MO. 58–; P.; SC. 59–; **E.**A.; **Ld.**U. 59–; **Lv.**U.; **O.**R.; **Wo.**; **Y.** [*English translation of:* 24296 Ser. geofiz.]

9200 **Bulletin** of the **Academy** of **Sciences** of the **USSR. Physical Series.** New York. *Bull. Acad. Sci. USSR phys. Ser.* [1954–] **L.**P.; **M.**U. 59–; **Te.**N.; **Y.** [*English translation of:* 24296 Ser. fiz.]

9201 **Bulletin** of the **Academy** of **Sciences** of the **United Provinces** of **Agra** and **Oudh.** Allahabad. *Bull. Acad. Sci. Un. Prov. Agra Oudh* [1931–34] **L.**BM.; BM^N.; C.; SC.; **Abs.**A.; **C.**A.; P.; **E.**R.; **Md.**H.; **Rt.**; **Sal.** [*C. as:* 38795]

9202 **Bulletin** de l'**acétylène** et de la **soudure autogène.** Paris. *Bull. Acét. Soud. autogène* [1914–18] **L.**P. imp. [*C. as:* 50109]

9203 **Bulletin. Acheson Colloids Ltd.** London. *Bull. Acheson Colloids* **L.**P. 50–.

9204 **Bulletin. Acid Open Hearth Research Association.** Pittsburgh. *Bull. Acid open Hearth Res. Ass.* [1945–] **Y.**

9204^c **Bulletin. Acoustical Materials Association.** New York. *Bull. acoust. Mater. Ass.* **L.**BM. 57–.

9205 **Bulletin actinométrique international.** Observatoire Léon Teisserenc de Bort. Trappes. *Bull. actinom. int.* [1930–37] **L.**MO.; **O.**G.; **Rt.**

9206 Bulletin administratif de l'**Association** des **ingénieurs** de l'**Institut industriel** du **Nord.** Lille. *Bull. adm. Ass. Ingrs Inst. ind. N.*

9207 Bulletin administratif de la **Société** pour le **développement** de l'**enseignement technique.** Grenoble. *Bull. adm. Soc. Dév. Enseign. tech.*

9208 Bulletin administratif du **Syndicat national** de **médecine sociale.** Lille. *Bull. adm. Synd. natn. Méd. soc.*

9209 Bulletin de l'**administration** de l'**agriculture.** Bruxelles. *Bull. Adm. Agric., Brux.* [1908–09] **L.**AM. [*C. of:* 9262; *C. as:* 9263]

9210 Bulletin de l'**Administration** de l'**hygiène.** Liége. *Bull. Adm. Hyg., Liége* [*C. of:* 9212]

9211 Bulletin de l'**Administration sanitaire** des **frontières.** Constantinople. *Bull. Adm. sanit. Front., Constantinople* [1921–22] **L.**MD.; TD.; Lv.U. [*C. as:* 11649]

9212 Bulletin de l'**administration** du **Service** de **santé** et de l'**hygiène.** Bruxelles. *Bull. Adm. Serv. Santé Hyg., Brux.* **L.**H. 08–12; TD. 08. [*C. of:* 11774; *C. as:* 9210]

9213 Bulletin. Admiralty Centre for **Scientific Information** and **Liaison.** London. *Bull. Admty Cent. scient. Inf.* **L.**MO. 50; RI. (curr.); **Sil.** 56–.

9214 Bulletin of the **Advisory Council** of **Science** and **Industry.** Melbourne. *Bull. advis. Coun. Sci. Ind., Melb.* [1917–19] **L.**AM.; BM.; EB. (ent.); K. imp.; P.; SC.; UC.; **Bm.**P.; U.; **C.**A.; **Ld.**U.; **Lv.**U. imp.; **M.**U.; **Nw.**A.; **O.**RH.; **Rt.; Sa.** [*C. as:* 10645]

9215 Bulletin. Advisory Council for **Scientific** and **Industrial Research.** Ottawa. *Bull. advis. Coun. scient. ind. Res., Ottawa* [1918–24] **L.**BM.; EB. (ent.); K.; P.; SC. [*C. as:* 11236]

9216 Bulletin. Advisory and **Research Department, South-Eastern Agricultural College, Wye.** *Bull. advis. Res. Dep. S.-East. agric. Coll., Wye* [1922–28] **L.**AM. imp.; EB.

9217 Bulletin on **Aerial Photogrammetry.** Syracuse University, Syracuse, N.Y. *Bull. aer. Photogram.* **L.**P. 42–49; **O.**F. 38– imp.

9218 Bulletin of the **Aerological Laboratory.** Tateno. *Bull. aerol. Lab., Tateno* [1959–] **Y.**

9218° Bulletin. Aerological Observatory. Tateno. *Bull. aerol. Obs., Tateno* **L.**BM. 50–.

9219 Bulletin aérologique. Observatoire de Zi-ka-Wei. Chang-Hai. *Bull. aérol. Obs. Zi-ka-Wei* [1931] **L.**MO. 31–37; **E.**M. 31–37; **O.**G. 31–37.

Bulletin aérologique de **Hongrie.** *See* 1030.

9220 Bulletin aéronautique. Paris. *Bull. aéronaut.*

9221 Bulletin de l'**aéronautique française.** Paris. *Bull. Aéronaut. fr.*

9222 Bulletin de l'**Afas.** Paris. *Bull. Afas* [1901–03] **L.**GL.; S.; **E.**P. [*C. of:* 23787; *C. as:* 9444]

9223 Bulletin. Affiliated Engineering Societies of **Minnesota.** Minneapolis, Minn. *Bull. affil. Engng Socs Minn.* [*C. of:* 39408]

9224 Bulletin de l'**Afrique** du **nord. Office national météorologique.** Paris. *Bull. Afr. N. Off. natn. mét.* **L.**MO. 29–36. [*C. as:* 35637°]

9225 Bulletin de l'**Agence économique** des **colonies autonomes** et des **territoires africains** sous **mandat.** Paris. *Bull. Ag. écon. Colon. auton. Terr. afr.* [1934–] **L.**BM. [*C. of:* 9227]

9226 Bulletin de l'**Agence économique** de l'**Indochine.** Paris. *Bull. Ag. écon. Indoch.* [1928–] **L.**TP 29–37; **Sy.**R. 30–37 imp.

9227 Bulletin de l'**Agence générale** des **colonies.** Paris. *Bull. Ag. gén. Colon.* [1919–34] **L.**BM.; G.; TP. [*C. of:* 11109; *C. as:* 9225]

9228 Bulletin agricole. Fort-de-France, Martinique. *Bull. agric., Fort-de-Fr.* [1930–] **L.**TP. 30–41; **C.**A. 35–41.

9229 Bulletin agricole. Tananarive. *Bull. agric., Tananarive* [1948–51] **L.**EB.; **C.**A.

9230 Bulletin agricole de l'**Algérie** et de la **Tunisie.** Alger. *Bull. agric. Algér. Tunis.* **L.**EB. 13*. [*C. as:* 9231]

9231 Bulletin agricole de l'**Algérie-Tunisie-Maroc.** Alger. *Bull. agric. Algér.-Tunis.-Maroc* [1914–29] **L.**EB.; MY. 22–29. [*C. of:* 9230]

9232 Bulletin agricole du **Congo belge.** Bruxelles, etc. *Bull. agric. Congo belge* [1910–] **L.**AM.; BM^N. 14–18; EB.; G. 16–55; K.; L. 14–; MO. 48–57; MY. 20–; P. 13–31 imp.; TP.; V. 15–; Z. 15–; **Hu.**G. 40– imp.; **Lv.**U. 14–; **Md.**H. 30–; **N.**U. 38–44 imp.; **O.**F. 30–; RE. 46–; **Rt.; W.; Y.** [*From* 1960 *title is:* Bulletin agricole du Congo]

9234 Bulletin agricole de l'**Institut scientifique** de **Saigon.** Saigon. *Bull. agric. Inst. scient. Saigon* [1919–21] **L.**EB.; K.

9235 Bulletin of the **Agricultural Chemical Society** of **Japan.** Tokyo. *Bull. agric. chem. Soc. Japan* [1926–60] **L.**AM. 59–60; C. 36–39: 56–60; TD. 55–60; **G.**U. 59–60; **Ld.**U. 28–34; **Rt.** 55–60; **Y.** [*C. as:* Agricultural and Biological Chemistry]

Bulletin of the **Agricultural Chemistry Department** of the **University College** of **Wales, Aberystwyth.** *See* 9245.

Bulletin. Agricultural College Experiment Station, Michigan. *See* 11080.

Bulletin. Agricultural College, University of **Tehran.** *See* 12545.

9236 Bulletin of **Agricultural** and **Commercial Statistics.** Rome. *Bull. agric. comm. Statist.* [1910–15] **L.**A. 12–15; AM.; BM.; MO. 11–15; TP.; **Abd.**U. 14–15; **Bn.**U.; **Db.; E.**A. 13–14; B. 13–15; **G.**U. 13–15 imp.; **Ld.**U. 12–15; **M.**P. 13–15; U. 13–15; **O.**B. 13–15; RE. 12–15; **R.**U. 14–15; **Sa.** 14–15 [*C. as:* 23833]

9237 Bulletin of the **Agricultural Department** of the **Armstrong College, Newcastle-on-Tyne.** *Bull. agric. Dep. Armstrong Coll.* [1905 16] **L.**AM.; P.; **Ld.**U. 06–16; **Nw.**A.; **Rt.**

9238 Bulletin of the **Agricultural Department, Assam.** Shillong. *Bull. agric. Dep. Assam* [1894–] **L.**BM. 96–12; P. 94–12: 28–35 imp.; **E.**U. 06–09; **O.**B. 94–12.

9239 Bulletin. Agricultural Department, Bahamas. *Bull. agric. Dep. Bahamas* [1906–11] **L.**AM. 06–10; K. imp.

9240 Bulletin of the **Agricultural Department, British North Borneo.** Jesselton. *Bull. agric. Dep. Br. N. Borneo*

Bulletin of the **Agricultural Department, Eastern Bengal** and **Assam.** *See* 9238.

Bulletin. Agricultural Department, Hyderabad. *See* 10470.

Bulletin. Agricultural Department, Mysore State. *See* 9980.

9242 Bulletin of the **Agricultural Department, Nigeria.** *Bull. agric. Dep. Nigeria* [1921–] L.BM^N. 21–36; Abs.A. 30; **Rt.** 21–36.

9243 Bulletin of the **Agricultural Department, Tasmania.** Hobart. *Bull. agric. Dep. Tasm.* [1904–] L.AM.; EB. (ent.) 05–25: 41; Abs.U. 28–; C.A. 28–; R.D. 12–; **Rt.** 12–; Y.

Bulletin. Agricultural Department, United Provinces of **Agra** and **Oudh.** Allahabad. *See* 10003.

9245 Bulletin of the **Agricultural Department** of the **University College** of **Wales.** Aberystwyth. *Bull. agric. Dep. Univ. Coll. Wales, Aberyst.* [1911–22] L.AM.; P.; Abs.N.; U.; Ld.U.; **Rt.** 11.

9246 Bulletin. Agricultural Development Department, Imperial Chemical Industries. London. *Bull. agric. Dev. Dep. I.C.I.* [1950–55] L.BM.; P. 52–55; Bn.U.; C.UL. 53–55; G.U. [*C. as:* 9720]

9247 Bulletin. Agricultural Directorate, M.E.F. Basrah. *Bull. agric. Dir. M.E.F.* L.EB. 18.

9248 Bulletin. Agricultural Division, Ministry of **Food** and **Agriculture, Ghana.** Accra. *Bull. agric. Div. Ghana* [1959–] L.BM^N.; C.A.

9249 Bulletin. Agricultural Education Advisory Committee for **Banff.** Aberdeen. *Bull. agric. Educ. advis. Comm. Banff* [1932–] C.A.

9250 Bulletin. Agricultural Engineering Division, Department of **Agriculture, British Columbia.** Victoria. *Bull. agric. Engng Div. Br. Columb.* [1954–] L.P. 56–; Y.

Bulletin. Agricultural Experiment Station, Colorado State University. *See* 9845.

Bulletin. Agricultural Experiment Station, Delaware University. *See* 9945.

9251 Bulletin of the **Agricultural Experiment Station, Government General** of **Chosen.** Suigen. *Bull. agric. Exp. Stn Chosen* [1922–] L.BM.; EB. 22–28; Lv.U 28; **Rt.** 22–26.

Bulletin. Agricultural Experiment Station, Illinois University. *See* 10485.

9252 Bulletin. Agricultural Experiment Station, Kyusyu. *Bull. agric. Exp. Stn, Kyusyu* E.R. 53–.

9253 Bulletin. Agricultural Experiment Station, Rehovoth. *Bull. agric. Exp. Stn, Rehovoth* [1934–53] L.BM.; BM^N.; EB (ent.); P.; SC.; Abs.A. 33–53; C.A.; **Rt.** [*C. of:* 9255; *C. in:* 27785]

9254 Bulletin. Agricultural Experimental Station, Tahreer Province, Egypt. *Bull. agric. exp. Stn Tahreer Prov.*

9255 Bulletin. Agricultural Experiment Station, Tel-Aviv. *Bull. agric. Exp. Stn, Tel-Aviv* [1924–30] L.BM.; BM^N.; EB. (ent.); P.; SC.; C.A.; **Rt.** [*C. as:* 9253]

Bulletin. Agricultural Experiment Station, University of **Idaho.** *See* 10483.

Bulletin. Agricultural Experiment Station, University of **Illinois.** *See* 10485.

Bulletin. Agricultural Experiment Station, University of **Maryland.** *See* 10861.

Bulletin. Agricultural Experiment Station, University of **Minnesota.** *See* 11124.

Bulletin. Agricultural Experiment Station, University of **Minnesota School** of **Forestry.** *See* 11655°.

Bulletin. Agricultural Experiment Station, University of **Missouri.** *See* 11139.

Bulletin. Agricultural Experiment Station, University of **Nevada.** *See* 11268.

Bulletin. Agricultural Experiment Station, University of **Puerto Rico. Insular Station Rio Piedras.** *See* 11538.

Bulletin. Agricultural Experiment Station, West Virginia University. *See* 12625.

Bulletin. Agricultural Experiment Station, Wisconsin University. *See* 12631.

Bulletin. Agricultural Experiment Stations, Institute of **Agricultural Sciences, State College** of **Washington.** *See* 12601.

9256 Bulletin. Agricultural and **Forestry College, Suigen, Chosen.** *Bull. agric. For. Coll. Suigen* O.F. 27–31.

Bulletin of **Agricultural Information, Trinidad** and **Tobago.** *See* 10002.

9257 Bulletin. Agricultural Insecticide and **Fungicide Manufacturers Association.** Philadelphia. *Bull. agric. Insect. Fungic. Mfrs Ass.* [1925–]

Bulletin of **Agricultural Intelligence** and **Plant Diseases.** *See* 9647.

9258 Bulletin. Agricultural Research Institute, Pusa. Calcutta. *Bull. agric. Res. Inst. Pusa* [1906–31] L.AM.; BM.; BM^N.; E. (ent.) 11–31; EB. (ent.); HS. 28–31; K. imp.; L.; P. imp.; SC.; TD. 10–31 imp.; UC. 07–24 imp.; Abs.N imp.; U. 06–21 imp.; Bl.U. 07–24 imp.; Bm.U. 07–24 imp.; C.A.;. P. 08–11 imp.; UL.; Cr.P. 08–11 imp.; Dn.U. 06–24 imp.; E.B. 23–31; U. 21–26 imp.; G.U. imp.; Ld.U. 07–25 imp.; Lv.U. 07–25 imp.; M.U. 08–26 imp.; Nw.A. imp.; O.I. 06–25 imp.; RE. 11–29 imp.; **Rt.**; Sa. 06–23 v. imp.

9258° Bulletin. Agricultural Research Service, Department of **Agriculture.** Washington. *Bull. agric. Res. Serv., Wash.* [1960–]

Bulletin. Agricultural Research Station, Jealott's Hill. *See* 10724.

9259 Bulletin of the **Agricultural Section** of the **Department** of **Natural Resources, Newfoundland.** St John's. *Bull. agric. Sect. Dep. nat. Resour. Newfoundl.* [1934–] L.BM.; **Rt.** 34–35.

9260 Bulletin. Agricultural Series. Department of **Land Records** and **Agriculture, Bengal.** Calcutta. *Bull. agric. Ser. Beng.* [1895–05] L.BM.; K. imp.; P.

9261 Bulletin of the **Agricultural Society.** Cairo. *Bull. agric. Soc., Cairo* Technical section [1920–] L.BM^N. 20–38; P. imp.; C.A.; M.C. 36–38; O.RE. 34–38 imp.; **Rt.**; Y.

Bulletin of **Agricultural Statistics.** Rome. *Bull. agric. Statist.* *See* 9236.

Bulletin. Agricultural and **Stock Department, Tasmania.** *See* 9243.

9262 Bulletin de l'**agriculture.** Bruxelles. *Bull. Agric., Brux.* [1885–07] L.AM. [*C. as:* 9209]

Bulletin de l'**agriculture.** Bucarest. *See* 9128.

9263 Bulletin de l'**agriculture** et de **horticulture.** Bruxelles. *Bull. Agric. Hort., Brux.* [1911–33] L.AM. imp.; HS. 30–33; SC. 30–33; **Rt.** 29–33. [*C. of:* 9209]

9263° Bulletin d'**agriculture** du **sud-ouest.** Toulouse. *Bull. Agric. Sud-ouest* Y.

9264 Bulletin of the **Agri-Horticultural Society** of **Western India.** Poona. *Bull. agri-hort. Soc. west. India* [1904–08] L.K.; P.

9265 **Bulletin** of the **Agrogeological Institution** of **Finland.** Helsingfors. *Bull. agrogeol. Instn Finl.* [1924-] **Abs.**N. 24-28.

9266 **Bulletin agronomique. Ministère** de la **France** d'**outre mer.** Nogent-sur-Marne. *Bull. agron. Minist. Fr. d'outre mer* Section technique d'agriculture tropicale [1946-] **L.**EB. 51- imp.; MY 54-; **C.**A.; **Hu.**G.; **Md.**H.; **Rt.**; **Y.**

9267 **Bulletin** of the **Aichi Gakugei University.** Okazaki. *Bull. Aichi Gakugei Univ.*
Natural Science [1952-] **Y.** 56-.

9268 **Bulletin. Air Board, Canada.** Ottawa. *Bull. Air Bd Can.* [1920-21] **L.**P.; SC.; **O.**R. 21.

9268° **Bulletin. Air League** of the **British Empire.** London. *Bull. Air Leag. Br. Emp.* **L.**SC. 26-.

9269 **Bulletin** of the **Airplane Engineering Department, U.S.A.** Dayton, Ohio. *Bull. Airpl. Engng Dep. U.S.A.*
Bulletin. Aktiebolag Atlas Diesel. Stockholm. *See* 9534.

9270 **Bulletin. Alabama Agricultural Experiment Station.** Auburn. *Bull. Ala. agric. Exp. Stn* [1888-] **L.**AM.; BM^N; 98-06; EB. (ent.) 07-; K. 91-08 imp.; P.; **O.**F. 36- imp.; RE. 38- imp.; **Rt.** imp.; **Y.**

9271 **Bulletin** of the **Alabama Dental Association.** Birmingham. *Bull. Ala. dent. Ass.* [1917-] **L.**D. 41-43.

9272 **Bulletin. Alabama Department** of **Agriculture** and **Industries.** Montgomery. *Bull. Ala. Dep. Agric. Ind.* **Abs.**N. 10-11 imp.

9273 **Bulletin. Alabama Engineering Experiment Station.** Auburn. *Bull. Ala. Engng Exp. Stn* [1930-39] **L.**P. [*C. as:* 18085°]
Bulletin. Alabama Geological Survey. *See* 10343.

9274 **Bulletin. Alabama Polytechnic Institute Engineering Experiment Station.** Auburn. *Bull. Ala. polytech. Inst. Engng Exp. Stn* **L.**P. 30-.

9275 **Bulletin** of the **Alabama State Board** of **Health.** Montgomery. *Bull. Ala. St. Bd Hlth*

9276 **Bulletin. Alabama State Commission** of **Forestry.** Montgomery. *Bull. Ala. St. Commn For.* **O.**F. 26-29.

9277 **Bulletin. Alabama State Mine Experiment Station School** of **Mines.** *Bull. Ala. St. Mine Exp. Stn* **L.**P. 25-28★; SC. 25-28.

9278 **Bulletin** of the **Alameda County District Dental Society.** Oakland, Cal. *Bull. Alameda Cty Distr. dent. Soc.*

9279 **Bulletin. Alaska Agricultural Experiment Station.** Washington, etc. *Bull. Alaska agric. Exp. Stn* [1902-] **L.**AM.; BM.; BM^N. 23-26; P.; **Bm.**U.; 02-07; **Cr.**P. 23-26; **G.**M. 23-32; **Lv.**P. 02-26; **M.**P. 05-32; **O.**F. 59- imp.; **Rt.**; **Y.**

9280 **Bulletin. Alexander Blain Hospital.** Detroit. *Bull. Alexander Blain Hosp.* **L.**MA. 45-.

9280° **Bulletin algérien** de **cancérologie.** Alger. *Bull. algér. Cancér.* [1948] [*C. as:* 9281]

9281 **Bulletin algérien** de **carcinologie.** Alger. *Bull. algér. Carcin.* [1948-] **L.**CB. 53-; MA.; MD.; TD. 51-; **G.**F. 51-. [*C. of:* 9280°]

9282 **Bulletin. Allahabad University Mathematical Association.** Allahabad. *Bull. Allahabad Univ. math. Ass.* [1927-] **L.**SC. 28-.
Bulletin of the **All-Union Geological** and **Prospecting Service** of the **U.S.S.R.** *See* 24549.

9283 **Bulletin. Alox Corporation.** Niagara Falls. *Bull. Alox Corp.* **L.**P. 36-41.

9284 **Bulletin** of the **Alpine Garden Society** of **Great Britain.** Wallington. *Bull. alp. Gdn Soc.* [1930-33] **L.**BM.; BM^N.; HS.; K.; **Br.**U.; **E.**B.; **M.**P. 30-31; **R.**U.; **Y.** [*C. as:* 41442]
Bulletin. Aluminium Plant and **Vessel Company.** *See* 98°.

9285 **Bulletin** of the **Amateur Entomologists Society.** London. *Bull. amat. Ent. Soc.* [1939-] **L.**BM.; BM^N.; E. 44-; NC. 51-; **Bn.**U. 46-55 imp.; **C.**UL.; **Ld.**U. 49- imp.; **O.**AP. 52-; H. imp.; R. 35-; **Rt.** imp.; **Y.** [*C. of:* 18266].

9286 **Bulletin** of the **Amateur Orchid Growers' Society.** *Bull. amat. Orchid Grow. Soc.* [1952-57] **L.**HS. [*C. as:* 25489]

9287 **Bulletin** of **Ambulant Proctology.** Youngstown, O. *Bull. ambul. Proct.*

9288 **Bulletin** of the **American Academy** of **Medicine.** Easton, Pa. *Bull. Am. Acad. Med.* [1891-14] [*C. as:* 26956]

9289 **Bulletin. American Academy** of **Ophthalmology** and **Otolaryngology.** St Louis. *Bull. Am. Acad. Ophthal. Otolar.* [1932-40] [*C. in:* 53510]

9290 **Bulletin** of the **American Academy** of **Tuberculosis Physicians.** Denver, Colo. *Bull. Am. Acad. Tuberc. Physns* [1937-42] [*C. as:* 55277]

9291 **Bulletin. American Agricultural Chemical Company.** *Bull. Am. agric. chem. Co.* [1913-23] **L.**P. imp.; **Rt.**

9292 **Bulletin** of the **American Anthropological Association.** Menasha. *Bull. Am. anthrop. Ass.* [1953-59] **L.**BM.; BM^N. 55-59; **Abd.**U. 56-59; **Abs.**N. 54-59; **Br.**U.; **E.**U.; **Ex.**U. 54-59; **H.**U. 56-59; **Ld.**U.; **Nw.**A.; **Sh.**U. 59. [*Supplement to:* 1898; *C. as:* 19277]

9293 **Bulletin. American Arch Co.** New York. *Bull. Am. Arch Co.* [1918-20] **L.**P.
Bulletin. American Association for the **Advancement** of **Science.** *See* 2.

9294 **Bulletin** of the **American Association** for the **Conservation** of **Vision.** New York. *Bull. Am. Ass. Conserv. Vision*
Bulletin. American Association of **Creamery Butter Manufacturers.** *See* 19135.

9295 **Bulletin** of the **American Association** of **Industrial Physicians** and **Surgeons.** Chicago. *Bull. Am. Ass. ind. Physns Surg.* [1926-32] **L.**SC. 29-32. [*C. in:* 23244]

9296 **Bulletin. American Association** of **Medical Record Librarians.** Chicago. *Bull. Am. Ass. med. Rec. Libr.* [1938-] [*C. of:* 9506]

9297 **Bulletin. American Association** of **Nurse Anaesthetists.** *Bull. Am. Ass. Nurse Anaesth.* [1939-] [*C. of:* 11202]

9298 **Bulletin** of the **American Association** of **Petroleum Geologists.** Chicago, etc. *Bull. Am. Ass. Petrol. Geol.* [1918–] **L.**B. 49–; BM^N.; GL. 28–; GM.; KC. 57–; P. 26– imp.; PT.; QM. 56–; SC.; UC. 27–; **Abd.**U. 45–; **Abs.**U. 53–; **Bl.**U. 55–; **Br.**U.; **C.**S. 47–; UL. 40–; **Cr.**U. 50–; **E.**U. 48– imp.; **Ex.**U. 56–; **G.**U. 51–; **H.**U. 48–; **Ld.**U. imp.; **Lv.**P. 59–; U. 49–; **M.**U.; **N.**U. 47–; **Nw.**A. 38–; **O.**R. 25– imp.; **Sh.**SC. 54–; **Sw.**U. 55–; **Y.** [*C. of:* 12272]

9299 **Bulletin** of the **American Association** of **Pharmaceutical Chemists.** New York. *Bull. Am. Ass. pharm. Chem.*

9300 **Bulletin** of the **American Association** of **Public Health Dentists.** Minneapolis. *Bull. Am. Ass. publ. Hlth Dent.*

9301 **Bulletin** of the **American Association** of **School Physicians.** *Bull. Am. Ass. Sch. Physns*

9302 **Bulletin** of the **American Association** of **Soil Survey Workers.** Madison. *Bull. Am. Ass. Soil Surv. Wkrs* [1921–22] [*C. as:* 9357]

9303 **Bulletin. American Association** of **Variable Star Observers.** Cambridge, Mass. *Bull. Am. Ass. var. Star Obsrs* **Y.**

9304 **Bulletin** of the **American Bureau** of **Geography.** Winona, Minn. *Bull. Am. Bur. Geogr.* [*C. in:* 26050]
Bulletin. American Bureau for **Medical Aid** to **China.** *See 6.*

9305 **Bulletin** of the **American Ceramic Society.** Easton, Pa., etc. *Bull. Am. Ceram. Soc.* [1922–] **L.**AV. 57–; C. 57–; DI. 44–; I.; IC.; NF. 44–; P.; SC.; SI. 42–; **Abd.**U. 45–; **Bm.**C. 34–; P.; **Bn.**U. 50– imp.; **Br.**U. 23–27; **C.**P. 48–; **Cr.**U. 59–; **F.**A. 45–; **G.**T. 25–; **Ld.**U.; **Lv.**P. 59–; **M.**D. 46–49; P. 56–; U. 25–48 imp.; **Rn.**B. 56–; **Sh.**IO. 40–; SC. 51–; **St.**R.; **Sw.**U. 34–; **Y.**

9306 **Bulletin. American Chemical Paint Co.** Ambler, Pa. *Bull. Am. chem. Paint. Co.* **L.**P. 29–38.

9307 **Bulletin** of the **American College** of **Physicians.** Lancaster, Pa. *Bull. Am. Coll. Physns* [1960–] **L.**MD. 61–.

9308 **Bulletin** of the **American College** of **Surgeons.** Chicago. *Bull. Am. Coll. Surg.* [1916–] **L.**MA. 38–; MD. 21–; S.; **Bl.**U. 42– imp.; **Br.**U. 28– imp.; **Db.** 33–35: 51–; **G.**F. 51–; **M.**MS. 47–; **Y.**
Bulletin. American Congress on **Surveying** and **Mapping.** *See 51520.*

9309 **Bulletin** of the **American Congress** on **Tuberculosis.** New York. *Bull. Am. Congr. Tuberc.*

9310 **Bulletin. American Dahlia Society.** Newark. *Bull. Am. Dahlia Soc.* [1915–] **L.**HS. 15–34 imp.

9311 **Bulletin. American Dental Association.** Chicago. *Bull. Am. dent. Ass.*

9312 **Bulletin** of the **American Dietetic Association.** Baltimore. *Bull. Am. diet. Ass.* [1924] [*C. of:* 13874; *C. as:* 25507]

9313 **Bulletin. American Electrochemical Society.** Philadelphia. *Bull. Am. electrochem. Soc.* [1904–31] **Ld.**U. 30–31; **Nw.**A. 30–31 [*C. as:* 10154]

9314 **Bulletin** of the **American Electrochemical Society, India Section.** Bangalore. *Bull. Am. electrochem. Soc. India Sect.* [1952–]

9315 **Bulletin. American Engineering Council.** New York. *Bull. Am. Engng Coun.* [*C. of:* 10230]

9316 **Bulletin. American Eugenics Society.** New Haven. *Bull. Am. Eugen. Soc.*

9317 **Bulletin. American Foundrymen's Association.** Chicago. *Bull. Am. Foundrym. Ass.* [1921–38] **Bm.**C. imp. [*Replaced by:* 1963]

9318 **Bulletin** of the **American Game Protective Association.** New York. *Bull. Am. Game prot. Ass.* [1912–25] **L.**SC. 23–25; **O.**AP. 14–25 imp. [*C. as:* 1968]

9319 **Bulletin** of the **American Gastroscopic Club.** Chicago. *Bull. Am. gastrosc. Club* [1942–43] **L.**MD.

9320 **Bulletin** of the **American Geographical Society** of **New York.** New York. *Bull. Am. geogr. Soc. N.Y.* [1901–15] **L.**BM.; BM^N.; G.; UC.; **Abs.**U. imp.; **Bl.**U.; **E.**F.; G.; R.; U. 09–15; **Lv.**U.; **M.**P.; **O.**G. 06–15; **R.**U.; **Sh.**U. 13–15. [*C. of:* 25512; *C. as:* 20969]

9321 **Bulletin** of the **American Heart Association.** New York. *Bull. Am. Heart Ass.* [1925–] **L.**MD. 39–43.

9322 **Bulletin. American Horticultural Society.** Washington. *Bull. Am. hort. Soc.* [1923–26]

9323 **Bulletin** of the **American Hospital Association.** Menasha, Wis. *Bull. Am. Hosp. Ass.* [1927–35] [*C. as:* 22416]

9324 **Bulletin** of the **American Institute** of **Architects.** Washington. *Bull. Am. Inst. Archit.* [1900–57] **L.**BA. 42–57; **Lv.**U. 10–57 imp. [*C. in:* 25515]
Bulletin. American Institute of **Biological Sciences.** *See 59.*

9325 **Bulletin. American Institute** of **Chemical Engineers.** *Bull. Am. Inst. chem. Engrs* [1910–] **Ep.**D. 45–46.

9326 **Bulletin** of the **American Institute** of **Mining** and **Metallurgical Engineers.** New York. *Bull. Am. Inst. Min. metall. Engrs* [1908–19] **L.**MT. 10–16; P. 10–19; **Bm.**T. 18–19; **Db.** 08–10; **G.**M. 14–19; **T.** 08–14 imp.; **M.**U. 09–10; **Nw.**A. imp. [*C. of:* 6994; *C. as:* 32036]

9327 **Bulletin** of the **American Institute** of **Weights** and **Measures.** New York. *Bull. Am. Inst. Wghts Meas.* [1917–] **L.**P. 33–36; SC.

9328 **Bulletin** of the **American Interplanetary Society.** New York. *Bull. Am. interplan. Soc.* [1930–32] **L.**P.; **Bm.**P.; **G.**U. [*C. as:* 5025]

9329 **Bulletin. American Iris Society.** *Bull. Am. Iris Soc.* **L.**HS. 20–.

9330 **Bulletin** of the **American Iron** and **Steel Association.** Philadelphia, Pa. *Bull. Am. Iron Steel Ass.*

9331 **Bulletin** of the **American Mathematical Society.** Lancaster, Pa. & New York, etc. *Bull. Am. math. Soc.* [1891–] **L.**B.; BM.; M.; R. 97–; SC. 27–; U. 50–; UC. 94–; **Abd.**U. 45–; **Abs.**U. 49– imp.; **Bl.**U. 22–; **Br.**U.; **C.**P.; SJ. 98–38; T. 91–; UL. 91–04; **Co.**T. 62–; **Db.**; **Dn.**U. 34–; **E.**Q. imp.; R.; U. 95–04; **Ex.**U. 37–39: 41–; **G.**T. 98–28: 58–; U. 94–; **Ld.**U.; **Lv.**U. 23–27; **M.**P. 33–; U. 23–; **N.**U. 47–; **Nw.**A. 07–; P. 07–36; **O.**R.; **Sa.**; **Sh.**U. 24–31: 47–; **Sw.**U. 18–; **Y.**

9332 **Bulletin. American Meat Institute Foundation.** Chicago. *Bull. Am. Meat Inst. Fdn* **C.**A. 52– imp.

9333 **Bulletin. American Medical Association.** Chicago. *Bull. Am. med. Ass.* [1905–36] [*C. in:* 25520]

9334 **Bulletin** of the **American Medical Temperance Association.** Hartford. *Bull. Am. med. Temp. Ass.*

9335 **Bulletin. American Meteorological Society.** Easton, Pa. *Bull. Am. met. Soc.* [1920–] **L.**MO.; SC.; **Abd.**U. 51–; **Bm.**U. 45–; **C.**PO 33–; **Dn.**U. 55–; **E.**G.; M.; **H.**U. 39–; **Lv.**U. 23–; **O.**R. 47–; **Wo.** 54–; **Y.**

9336 **Bulletin. American Meter Co.** *Bull. Am. Meter Co.* [1929–48] **L.**P. 29–46. [*C. of:* 27920]

9337 **Bulletin** of the **American Mosquito Control Association.** *Bull. Am. Mosq. Control Ass.* [1948–] **Y.**

9338 **Bulletin** of the **American Mosquito Extermination Society.** New York. *Bull. Am. Mosq. Exterm. Soc.*

9339 **Bulletin** of the **American Museum** of **Natural History.** New York. *Bull. Am. Mus. nat. Hist.* [1881–] **L.**AM. 87– imp.; AN. 97–07 imp.; BM. 81–87; BM^N.; GL. 00–; L.; R.; S. 92–96; SC.; UC.; Z.; **Abd.**U. 48– imp.; **Bl.**U.; **Bm.**N. 96–; **C.**P.; **Db.**; **E.**F. 86–22; imp. G. 24–; J.; R.; **G.**M. 97–03; **Lo.** 36–; **Lv.**U.; **M.**U. imp.; **Nw.**A. 52–; **O.**R.; **Pl.**M. 94– imp.; **Sh.**U. 96–07; **Y.**

9340 **Bulletin. American Nature Association.** Washington. *Bull. Am. Nat. Ass.*

9341 **Bulletin. American Orchid Society.** Washington. *Bull. Am. Orchid Soc.* [1932–] **L.**HS. 44–; K.

9342 **Bulletin** of **American Paleontology.** Cornell University, Ithaca. *Bull. Am. Paleont.* [1895–] **L.**BM.; BM^N.; GL. 40–; GM.; SC.; **Abs.**U. 52–; **Bm.**U. 48–; **Br.**U. 95–37; **Ex.**U. 56–.

9343 **Bulletin. American Peony Society.** Clinton, N.Y. *Bull. Am. Peony Soc.* [1925–] **L.**HS. 25–31. [*C. of:* 11493]

9344 **Bulletin** of the **American Petroleum Institute.** New York. *Bull. Am. Petrol. Inst.* [1920–30] **L.**P. [*C. as:* 50806]

9345 **Bulletin. American Pharmaceutical Association.** Baltimore. *Bull. Am. pharm. Ass.* [1906–11] [*C. as:* 25528]

9346 **Bulletin. American Physical Society.** Ithaca, New York, Menasha. *Bull. Am. phys. Soc.* [1899–02: 25–] **L.**BM. 99–02: 49–; B. 56–; P. 56–; QM. 56–; SC. 37–; **Bl.**U. 56–; **Bn.**U. 55–; **C.**UL. 56–; **Db.** (curr.); **Ex.**U. 56–; **F.**A. 56–; **G.**U. 50–; **Lv.**P. 56–; **M.**C. 56–; P. 56–; T. 56–; U. 60–; **Ma.**T. 56–; **N.**U. 56–; **O.**R. 48–; **Rn.**B. 56–57; **We.**K. 25–49; **Y.**

9347 **Bulletin. American Plant Pest Committee.** Boston. *Bull. Am. Pl. Pest Comm.* **L.**EB. 18–20*.

9348 **Bulletin** of the **American Railway Association.** New York. *Bull. Am. Rly Ass.*

9349 **Bulletin** of the **American Railway Engineering Association.** Madison. *Bull. Am. Rly Engng Ass.* **Y.**
    Bulletin of the **American Railway Engineering** and **Maintenance** of **Way Association.** *See* 9349.

9350 **Bulletin** of the **American School** of **Prehistoric Research.** New Haven. *Bull. Am. Sch. prehist. Res.* [1926–] **L.**BM.; BM^N.; S. 27–37; SC.; **Abd.**U. 30–36 imp.; **Cr.**M.

9351 **Bulletin. American Society** of **Clinical Laboratory Technicians.** Detroit. *Bull. Am. Soc. clin. Lab. Techns* [1934–35] [*C. as:* 2024]

9352 **Bulletin. American Society** for the **Control** of **Cancer.** *Bull. Am. Soc. Control Cancer* [1931–] [*C. of:* 13097]

9353 **Bulletin** of the **American Society** for **Hospital Pharmacists.** Washington. *Bull. Am. Soc. Hosp. Pharmsts* [1944–57] **L.**H. 52–57; PH. 46–57 imp. [*C. as:* 2016]

9354 **Bulletin American Society** of **Plant Physiologists.** Chicago. *Bull. Am. Soc. Pl. Physiol.* **Abd.**U. 47–; **Bm.**U. 44–; **Br.**U. 41–; **Rt.** 41–; **Y.** [*Supplement to:* 37861]

9355 **Bulletin** of the **American Society** of **Swedish Engineers.** East Orange, N.J. *Bull. Am. Soc. Swed. Engrs* [*C. as:* 2165]

9356 **Bulletin. American Society** for **Testing Materials.** Philadelphia. *Bull. Am. Soc. Test. Mater.* [1921–60] **L.**AV. 42–60 imp.; DI. 46–60; I. 27–60; IC. 48–60; LE. 46–50; NF. 35–60; P.; PL. 44–60; PR.; PT. 44–60; SC. 28–60; SI. 34–60; **Bm.**C. 34–60 imp.; P. 39–60; T. 59–60; U. 23–60; **Br.**U. 44–60; **C.**ENG. 40–60; **Ep.**D. 45–60; **F.**A. 44–60; **G.**I. 41–60; U.; **Ld.**P. 53–60; U. 27–60; W. 29–60; **Li.**M. 46–60; **Lv.**P. 53–60; **M.**C.; D. 46–60; P. 38–45; T.; U. 28–60; **N.**U. 50–60; **Nw.**A. 55–60; **R.**D. 50–60; **Sh.**IO. 47–60; **Sy.**R. 23–60; **Y.** [*C. as:* Materials, Research and Standards]

9357 **Bulletin** of the **American Soil Survey Association.** Ames, Ia. *Bull. Am. Soil Surv. Ass.* [1923–36] **L.**SC. 24–36; **Abs.**U. 24–36 imp.; **C.**A. 24–35 imp.; **Rt.** 28–36. [*C. of:* 9302; *C. as:* 39698]
    Bulletin. American Standards Association. *See* 102.

9358 **Bulletin. American Statistical Association.** Washington. *Bull. Am. statist. Ass.* [1935–47] **C.**GE. 45–47; P. 37–47; SL. [*C. as:* 2159]

9359 **Bulletin. American Stove Co. Research Department.** *Bull. Am. Stove Co. Res. Dep.*

9360 **Bulletin. American Sugar Cane League** of the **U.S.A.** New Orleans. *Bull. Am. Sug. Cane Leag.* [1922–25] [*C. as:* 51291]

9361 **Bulletin** of the **American Zinc Institute.** New York. *Bull. Am. Zinc Inst.* [1918–28] **L.**MT.; NF. 19–29; P.; PR. 27–28; SC. 21–28. [*C. as:* 25549]

9362 **Bulletin** de l'**Amicale électrique.** Paris. *Bull. Amic. élect.*

9363 **Bulletin** of **Analysis. Wyoming Dairy Food** and **Oil Department.** Helena, Mont. *Bull. Analysis Wyo. Dairy Fd Oil Dep.*

9364 **Bulletin analytique. Centre** de **documentation sidérurgique.** *Bull. analyt. Cent. Docum. sidérurg.* **L.**I. (2 yr.); P. 55–; **Cr.**I. 49–; **G.**I. 48–.

9365 **Bulletin analytique. Centre national** de la **recherche scientifique.** Paris. *Bull. analyt. Cent. natn. Rech. scient.* [1940–55] **L.**AM. 48–55 imp.; AV. 51–55; B. 47–55 imp.; C.; D. 46–55; GM. 47–55; MC. (sect. iv) 51–55; P.; R. 47–55; SC.; SI. 47–55; U. 47–55; Z. imp.; **Abs.**U. 47–55; **Bl.**U. (partie I: sect. 13, 14) 53–55; **Br.**U. 47–55; **C.**P.; **Db.** 47–55; **E.**SW. 48–55; U. (pure and appl. sci.) 47–55; **Ld.**U. 47–55; **Lv.**P. (partie 2) 44–55 imp.; **M.**C. 53–55; **Nw.**A. 54–55; **O.**P. 46–55; R.; **Y.** [*Replaced by:* 11789]
    Bulletin analytique. Coton et **fibres tropicales.** *See* 15981.

9366 **Bulletin** des **anciens élèves** de l'**École française** de **meunerie.** Paris. *Bull. anc. Élev. Éc. fr. Meun.* **Sal.**F. 35–; **Y.**

9367 **Bulletin** des **anciens élèves** de l'**École supérieure** de la **métallurgie** et de l'**industrie** des **mines** de **Nancy.** *Bull anc. Élev. Éc. sup. Métall. Nancy*
    Bulletin für **angewandte Botanik.** St. Petersburg. *See* 54499.

9368 Bulletin of the **Anglo-Egyptian Sudan Geological Survey.** Khartoum. *Bull. Anglo-Egypt. Sudan geol. Surv.* [1911–34] L.BM.; BM^N.; GL.; MI; P. II; SC.

9369 Bulletin of **Animal Behaviour.** London. *Bull. Anim. Behav.* [1938–51] L.AM. 47–48; B.; BM.; BM^N. MC. 47–51; SC.; V. imp; VC.; Z.; **Abd.**R. 48–51; **Bm.**U.; **C.**A. 47–51; B.; UL. imp.; **Cr.**U.; **E.**A.; **Hu.**G. 47–51; **Ld.**U. 47–51; **Lo.**; **Lv.**U. 38–48 imp.; **N.**U.; **O.**AP.; R.; **R.**U.; **W.** 38–41: 47–51. [*C. as:* 8848]

9370 Bulletin. Animal Health Service, Tasmania. Hobart. *Bull. Anim. Hlth Serv. Tasm.* [1938–]

9371 Bulletin of the **Animal Health Station, Yeerongpilly, Queensland.** *Bull. Anim. Hlth Stn Yeerongpilly* L.BM^N. 34.

Bulletin. Animal Husbandry Series, Department of **Veterinary Science** and **Animal Husbandry.** Dar-es-Salaam. *See* 10077.

9372 Bulletin, annales et **comptes rendus** de la **Société belge** des **ingénieurs** et des **industriels.** Bruxelles. *Bull. Annls C.r. Soc. belge Ingrs Ind.* [1920–54] L.AV. 49–53; P. 26–53; SC. 20–40: 48–53. [*C. as:* 47575]

9373 Bulletin et **annales** de la **Société r. entomologique** de **Belgique.** Bruxelles. *Bull. Annls Soc. r. ent. Belg.* [1925–] L.BM^N.; E.; EB.; L.; Z.; **Bn.**U. 50–; **C.**UL.; **Ld.**U. 29–59; **O.**H.; R.; **Y.** [*C. of:* 11908]

Bulletin annexe. Direction de l'**hydraulique agricole.** Paris. *See* 10087.

9374 Bulletin annuaire de la **Station météorologique** du **Gymnase bulgare** de **garçons St. Cyrille** et **Méthode,** Salonique. *Bull. Annu. Stn mét. Salonique* L.MO. 94–11.

9375 Bulletin annuel de l'**Association** des **chimistes** de l'**industrie textile.** Paris. *Bull. a. Ass. Chim. Ind. text.* L.P. 11–30 imp.; SC. 30. [*Incorporated in:* 47238]

9376 Bulletin annuel de l'**Association française** des **ponts** et **charpentes.** Paris. *Bull. a. Ass. fr. Ponts Charp.* L.P. 49–.

Bulletin annuel de l'**Association générale** des **chimistes** de l'**industrie textile.** Paris. *See* 9375.

9377 Bulletin annuel de l'**Association** pour la **lutte anti-tuberculeuse** en **Savoie.** Chambéry. *Bull. a. Ass. Lutte anti-tuberc. Savoie*

9377° Bulletin annuel. Commission départementale de **météorologie** du **Rhône.** Belley. *Bull. a. Commn dép. Mét. Rhône* L.BM. 39–.

9378 Bulletin annuel de la **Commission** de **météorologie** du **Département** des **Bouches-du-Rhône.** Marseille. *Bull. a. Commn Mét. Dép. Bouches-du-Rhône* L.MO. 82–47; E.M. 82–19.

9379 Bulletin annuel de la **Commission** de **météorologie** de l'**Yonne.** Auxerre. *Bull. a. Commn Mét. Yonne*

9380 Bulletin annuel de la **Commission météorologique** des **Côtes-du-Nord.** St. Brieuc. *Bull. a. Commn mét. Côtes-du-N.*

9381 Bulletin annuel de la **Commission météorologique** du **Département** de la **Sarthe.** Le Mans. *Bull. a. Commn mét. Dép. Sarthe*

9382 Bulletin annuel de la **Commission météorologique** de la **Haute-Loire.** Le Puy. *Bull. a. Commn mét. Hte-Loire*

9383 Bulletin annuel des **cotons** et des **graines** de **coton.** Alexandrie. *Bull. a. Cotons*

9384 Bulletin annuel de **liaison** des **organisations météorologiques départementales** et des **correspondants** du **réseau climatologique français.** Paris. *Bull. a. Liaison Orgs mét. dép.* L.MO. 55–.

9385 Bulletin annuel. Météorologie nationale. Tunis. *Bull. a. Mét. natn., Tunis* L.MO. 52.

Bulletin annuel de l'**Observatoire hydro-météorologique Marjan.** Split. *See* 21434^a.

9387 Bulletin annuel. Observatoire météorologique. Séminaire-Collège St. Martial, Port-au-Prince. *Bull. a. Obs. mét. Sémin.-Coll. St Martial* [1917–] L.MO; **Y.** [*C. of:* 11733]

9388 Bulletin annuel. Office nationale météorologique. Paris. *Bull. a. Off. natn. mét.* [1935–?] L.MO. 35–36. [*C. of:* 11009; *C. as:* 9390]

9389 Bulletin annuel. Service météorologique de la **côte française** des **Somalis.** Paris. *Bull. a. Serv. mét. Côte fr. Somalis* L.MO. 46–47.

9390 Bulletin annuel. Service météorologique metropole et de l'**Afrique** du **Nord.** Paris. *Bull. a. Serv. mét. metrop. Afr. N.* [1946–] L.MO. [*C. of:* 9388]

9391 Bulletin annuel. Service météorologique et **Observatoire géophysique, Martinique.** Paris. *Bull. a. Serv. mét. Obs. géophys. Martinique* L.MO. 32–38.

9392 Bulletin annuel. Société astronomique et **météorologique** de **Port-au-Prince.** *Bull. a. Soc. astr. mét. Port-au-Prince* L.MO. 05–10.

9393 Bulletin annuel de la **Société jersiaise.** Jersey. *Bull. a. Soc. jersiaise* [1875–56] L.BM.; BM^N.; SC.; UC. 75–36 imp.; **C.**UL.; **E.**R. 50; **O.**B.; **Pl.**M. 38–56 imp. [*C. as:* 3334]

9394 Bulletin annuel de la **Société pomologique** d'**Ernée.** Argentan. *Bull. a. Soc. pomol. Ernée*

9395 Bulletin annuel de la **Société** des **professeurs spéciaux** d'**agriculture.** Gannat. *Bull. a. Soc. Prof. spéc. Agric., Gannat*

9396 Bulletin annuel de la **Société suisse** de **chronométrie** et du **Laboratoire suisse** de **recherches horlogères.** Lausanne. *Bull. a. Soc. suisse Chronom.* [1943–] L.P. 50–; SC.; **Y.**

Bulletin annuel de **statistique** de l'**énergie éléctrique** pour l'**Europe.** *See* 3332.

9397 Bulletin annuel du **Syndicat** des **pisciculteurs** de **France.** Paris. *Bull. a. Synd. Piscic. Fr.* [*C. as:* 47638]

9398 Bulletin of **Anthropology.** Chicago. *Bull. Anthrop.*

Bulletin. Anti-Locust Research Centre. *See* 3590.

9399 Bulletin of the **Antivenin Institute** of **America.** Philadelphia. *Bull. Antivenin Inst. Am.* [1927–32] L.BM^N.; MD.; SC. 30–31; TD.; Z.; **Lv.**U.

9400 Bulletin of the **Aomori Agricultural Experiment Station.** *Bull. Aomori agric. Exp. Stn* [1954–] C.A.

9401 Bulletin apicole d'**information** et de **documentation scientifique** et **technique.** Nice. *Bull. apic. Inf. Docum. scient. tech.* L.P. 59–.

Bulletin of **Applied Botany.** St. Petersburg. *See* 54499.

Bulletin of **Applied Botany** and **Plant Breeding.** Leningrad. *See* 54987.

9402 **Bulletin** of **Aquatic Biology.** Amsterdam. *Bull. aquat. Biol.* [1957–] **L.**BM^N.; SC.; Z.; **Fr.**; **Pl.**M.

9403 **Bulletin** d'**arboriculture,** de **floriculture** et de **culture potagère.** Gand. *Bull. Arboric., Gand.* **L.**K. 65–05*.

9404 **Bulletin archéologique** et **agricole** de l'**Association bretonne.** Saint-Brieuc. *Bull. archéol. agric. Ass. bret.* **L.**BM. 74–; **Abs.**N. 08; **C.**UL. 1847–.

9405 **Bulletin** of the **Architecture** and **Planning Group** (S.C.R.). London. *Bull. Archit. Plann. Grp* [1948–] **Wa.**B. 49–57. [*C. of:* 50356]

Bulletin of the **Arctic Institute.** Leningrad. *See* 12739.

9406 **Bulletin** of the **Arctic Institute** of **North America.** Montreal. *Bull. arct. Inst. N. Am.* [1946–] **C.**PO.

9407 **Bulletin** of the **Argentine Meteorological Office.** Buenos Aires. *Bull. Argent. met. Off.* **Sh.**U. 12–14.

9408 **Bulletin** of the **Arizona Agricultural Experiment Station.** Tucson. *Bull. Ariz. agric. Exp. Stn* [1889–] **L.**AM.; EB. (ent.) 96–; P. 90–; **Abs.**N. 08; **Bm.**U. 07–42; **Cr.**P. 03–09 imp.; **O.**F. 53– imp.; RE. 43– imp.; **Rt.** imp.; **Y.**

9409 **Bulletin. Arizona Board of Health.** Tucson. *Bull Ariz. Bd Hlth*

Bulletin. Arizona Bureau of **Mines.** *See* 9670.

9410 **Bulletin. Arkansas Agricultural Experiment Station.** Fayetteville. *Bull. Ark. agric. Exp. Stn* [1888–] **L.**AM.; BM^N. 06–16 imp.; EB. (ent.) 96–; K. 02–08 imp.; P.; SC. 21–; **Db.** 02; **Rt.** 93– imp.; **Y.**

9411 **Bulletin. Arkansas Bureau** of **Mines.** *Bull. Ark. Bur. Mines*

Bulletin. Arkansas Geological Survey. *See* 10344.

9412 **Bulletin** of the **Arkansas State Agricultural School.** Jonesboro. *Bull. Ark. St. agric. Sch.*

9413 **Bulletin. Arkansas University Engineering Experiment Station.** *Bull. Ark. Univ. Engng Exp. Stn* **L.**P. 25–; **Y.**

9414 **Bulletin. Arkansas University Medical Department.** Little Rock. *Bull. Ark. Univ. med. Dep.*

9415 **Bulletin** of the **Armour Institute** of **Technology.** Chicago. *Bull. Armour Inst. Technol.*

9416 **Bulletin. Asbestos Mines Ltd.** New York. *Bull. Asbestos Mines Ltd* **L.**P. 24–25.

9417 **Bulletin. Associated Camera Clubs** of **America.** Los Angeles. *Bull. ass. Camera Clubs Am.* **L.**PG. 31–.

9418 **Bulletin** of the **Associated State Engineering Societies.** Madison. *Bull. ass. St. Engng Socs, Madison* [1926–38] **L.**P.; SC. 31–38.

9419 **Bulletin. Associated Technical Societies** of **Detroit.** *Bull. ass. tech. Socs Detroit* [*C. as:* 132]

9420 **Bulletin** de l'**Association** des **actuaires belges.** Bruxelles. *Bull. Ass. Actuair. belg.* **L.**SC. 96–; **E.**E. 96–.

Bulletin de l'**Association** des **actuaires suisses.** *See* 32802.

9421 **Bulletin** de l'**Association agricole** et **viticole** de la **Marne.** Reims. *Bull. Ass. agric. vitic. Marne*

9422 **Bulletin** de l'**Association algérienne** des **adjoints techniques** et **commis** des **ponts** et **chaussées** et des **mines.** Alger. *Bull. Ass. algér. Adj. tech.*

9423 **Bulletin** de l'**Association alsacienne** des **propriétaires** d'**appareils** à **vapeur.** Nancy. *Bull. Ass. alsac. Propr. Appar. Vap.*

9424 **Bulletin** of the **Association** of **American Medical Colleges.** Chicago. *Bull. Ass. Am. med. Coll.* **Nw.**A. 27–28*. [*C. of:* 38965; *C. as:* 25599]

9425 **Bulletin** de l'**Association amicale** des **chimistes, élèves** et **anciens élèves** de l'**Institut polytechnique** de **Bretagne.** Rennes. *Bull. Ass. amic. Chim. Inst. polytech. Bret.*

9426 **Bulletin** de l'**Association amicale** de **médecine** et de **chirurgie.** Paris. *Bull. Ass. amic. Méd. Chir.*

9427 **Bulletin** de l'**Association amicale** des **vétérinaires algériens.** Agha-Alger. *Bull. Ass. amic. Vét. algér.*

9428 **Bulletin** de l'**Association** des **anatomistes.** Paris. *Bull. Ass. Anat., Paris* [1926–] **L.**SC.; **Pl.**M. 32–36 imp.

9429 **Bulletin** de l'**Association astronomique** du **Nord.** Lille. *Bull. Ass. astr. N.*

9430 **Bulletin. Association** of **Auto-Electrical Technicians Ltd.** London. *Bull. Ass. auto-elect. Techns Ltd* **L.**P. 42–49. [*C. as:* 25603]

9431 **Bulletin** de l'**Association belge** des **chimistes.** Gand. *Bull. Ass. belge Chim.* **L.**C. 87–98; P. 90–03; PH. 01–04. [*C. as:* 11885]

9432 **Bulletin** de l'**Association belge** de **photographie.** Bruxelles. *Bull. Ass. belge Photogr.* [1874–14: 20–24] **L.**BM. 75–34; PG. 83–36; SC. 29–36. [*C. as:* 37589]

9433 **Bulletin** de l'**Association belge** de **vinaigriers.** Gand. *Bull. Ass. belge Vinaigr.*

9434 **Bulletin** de l'**Association centrale française** contre la **tuberculose.** Paris. *Bull. Ass. cent. fr. Tuberc.*

Bulletin de l'**Association** des **chimistes** des **industries** du **cuir** et **documents scientifiques** et **techniques** des **industries** du **cuir.** *See* 9446.

9435 **Bulletin** de l'**Association** des **chimistes** de **sucrerie,** de **distillerie** et des **industries agricoles** de **France** et des **colonies.** Paris. *Bull. Ass. Chim. Sucr. Distill. Fr.* [1883–46] **L.**C. 06–46; P. imp.; SC. 22–46; **Rt.** 14–46. [*C. as:* 23365]

9436 **Bulletin. Association cotonnière coloniale.** Paris. *Bull. Ass. cotonn. colon.* **L.**TP. 03–23.

9437 **Bulletin. Association** pour le **développement** des **relations médicales** entre la **France** et les **pays étrangers.** Paris. *Bull. Ass. Dév. Relat. méd. Fr. Pays étrang.* **L.**MA 29–; MD. 29–.

9438 **Bulletin** de l'**Association** des **diplomés** de la **Faculté** de **biologie.** Nancy. *Bull. Ass. Dipl. Fac. Biol., Nancy*

9439 **Bulletin** de l'**Association** des **diplomés** de **microbiologie** de la **Faculté** de **pharmacie** de **Nancy.** Nancy. *Bull. Ass. Dipl. Microbiol., Nancy* **L.**MA. 48–; **Abd.**T. 58–; **R.**D. 32– imp; **Y.**

9440 **Bulletin** de l'**Association** d'**enseignement médical professionnel.** Paris. *Bull. Ass. Enseign. méd. prof.*

9441 **Bulletin** de l'**Association** d'**études physiopathologiques** de **foie** et de la **nutrition.** Paris. *Bull. Ass. Étud. physiopath. Foie Nutr.* [*C. in:* 47333]

9442 **Bulletin** de l'**Association** des **femmes-médecins.** Paris. *Bull. Ass. Femmes-Méd.*

9443 **Bulletin. Association forestière québecoise.** Québec. *Bull. Ass. for. québ.*

9444 **Bulletin de l'Association française** pour l'**avancement** des **sciences.** Paris. *Bull. Ass. fr. Avanc. Sci.* [1904–35] L.BM^N.; GL. 04–12; MO. 20–31; P. 31–35; SC. imp.; **E.P.; Nw.**A. 06–09. [*C. of:* 9222; *C. as:* 49116]

9445 **Bulletin de l'Association française** de **botanique.** Le Mans. *Bull. Ass. fr. Bot.*

9446 **Bulletin de l'Association française** des **chimistes** des **industries** du **cuir** et **documents scientifiques** et **techniques** des **industries** du **cuir.** Paris. *Bull. Ass. fr. Chim. Ind. Cuir* [1939–] L.LE 44–; P. 48–; SC. 49–; **Ld.**U. 49–; **Y.** [*Supplement to:* 16136 and 47604]

9447 **Bulletin de l'Association française** pour le **développement** des **travaux publics.** Paris. *Bull. Ass. fr. Dév. Trav. publ.*

9448 **Bulletin de l'Association française** pour l'**étude** du **cancer.** Paris. *Bull. Ass. fr. Étude Cancer* [1908–] L.CB. imp.; MA. 22–; MD.; S. 08–10; U. 50–; **Abd.**U. 24–32; C.R. 24–; UL. 08–10; **E.**PO. 54–; **G.**F. 51–; **M.**MS. 35–39; **O.**R. 08–14; **Y.**

9449 **Bulletin** de l'**Association française** des **ingénieurs** et **techniciens** du **cinéma.** Paris. *Bull. Ass. fr. Ingrs Techns Cinéma* [1947–] L.P.; **Y.**

9450 **Bulletin de l'Association française** des **ingénieurs-conseils** en matière de **propriété industrielle.** Paris. *Bull. Ass. fr. Ingrs-Cons. Propr. ind.* [1902–11] L.P. [*C. of:* 12329]

9451 **Bulletin de l'Association française** des **observateurs** d'**étoiles variables.** *Bull. Ass. fr. Obsrs Étoiles var.* [1932–] L.AS.; BM.; C.O. [*C. of:* 11362]

9452 **Bulletin de l'Association française pomologique** de l'**Ouest.** Le Mans. *Bull. Ass. fr. pomol. Ouest*

9453 **Bulletin de l'Association française** des **techniciens** du **pétrole.** Paris. *Bull. Ass. fr. Techns Pétrole* L.P. 54–; PT. 36–38: 48–; **Y.**
Bulletin. Association of **Gas Appliance** and **Equipment Manufacturers.** *See* 46.

9454 **Bulletin de l'Association** des **gaziers belges.** Bruxelles. *Bull. Ass. Gaz. belge* L.P. 36–38*. [*C. as:* 47233]

9455 **Bulletin de l'Association générale aéronautique.** Paris. *Bull. Ass. gén. aéronaut.* [*C. as:* 10808]

9456 **Bulletin de l'Association générale automobile.** Paris. *Bull. Ass. gén. auto.*

9457 **Bulletin de l'Association** des **géographes français.** Paris. *Bull. Ass. Géogr. fr.* [1924–] L.AM. 47–53; G.; **C.**PO. 49–; **O.**G. 24–39.

9458 **Bulletin de l'Association** des **gynécologues** et **obstétriciens** de **langue française.** Paris. *Bull. Ass. Gynéc. Obstét. Lang. fr.* [1949–50] L.MA.; MD.; **Dn.**U. [*C. as:* 10239]

9459 **Bulletin. Association** of **Hawaiian Pineapple Canners' Experiment Station.** Honolulu. *Bull. Ass. Hawaiian Pineapple Cann. Exp. Stn* L.EB. (ent.) 26–30*; P. 25–30 imp.; SC. 25–30; C.A. 25–30. [*C. as:* 10197]

9460 **Bulletin of the Association of Indian Geographers.** New Delhi. *Bull. Ass. Indian Geogr.* [1956–] L.G.

9461 **Bulletin de l'Association** des **ingénieurs** de **chauffage** et **ventilation** de **France.** *Bull. Ass. Ingrs Chauff. Vent. Fr.*

9462 **Bulletin** de l'**Association** des **ingénieurs** issus de l'**École** d'**application** de l'**artillerie** et du **génie.** Bruxelles. *Bull. Ass. Ingrs Éc. Applic. Artill., Brux.*

9463 **Bulletin de l'Association** des **ingénieurs** sortis de l'**École** de **Liége.** Liége. *Bull. Ass. Ingrs Éc. Liége* L.I. 78–19 imp.; P. 85–21.

9464 **Bulletin** de l'**Association** des **ingénieurs** de l'**École** des **mines** de **Mons.** Liége. *Bull. Ass. Ingrs Éc. Mines Mons* L.EE. 90– imp.

9465 **Bulletin de l'Association** des **ingénieurs électriciens belges.** Liége. *Bull. Ass. Ingrs Électns belg.* L.P. 10–.

9466 **Bulletin de l'Association** des **ingénieurs électriciens** sortis de l'**Institut électro-technique Montefiore.** Liége. *Bull. Ass. Ingrs Electns Inst. électro-tech. Montefiore* [1886–30] L.EE. 90–30; P. 10–30; SC. 22–30. [*C. as:* 11681]

9467 **Bulletin. Association** des **ingénieurs-chimistes** de l'**Université** de **Caen.** *Bull. Ass. Ingrs-Chim. Univ. Caen*
Bulletin de l'Association des **ingénieurs-conseils** en matière de **propriété industrielle.** *See* 9450.

9468 **Bulletin** de l'**Association internationale** des **chemins de fer.** *Bull. Ass. int. Chem.-de-fer*

9469 **Bulletin** de l'**Association internationale** pour la **destruction rationelle** des **rats.** Copenhague. *Bull. Ass. int. Destr. ration. Rats*

9470 **Bulletin** de l'**Association internationale** du **froid.** Paris. *Bull. Ass. int. Froid* [1910–13] L.AM; P.; TD. imp. [*C. as:* 10965]

9471 **Bulletin. Association internationale** d'**hydrologie scientifique.** Venezia, Louvain, etc. *Bull. Ass. int. Hydrol. scient.* [1931–] L.MO.; U.; **Bl.**U. 31–38 imp.; **C.**GG. 56–; **E.**R. imp.; **G.**T. 56–. [*C. of:* 12492, Section hydrologie. *See also:* 10536 and 10666°]

9472 **Bulletin. Association internationale** de **magnétisme** et **électricité terrestres.** *Bull. Ass. int. Magn. Élect. terr.* L.AS. 56–; BM.; U. [*C. of:* 9481]
Bulletin. Association internationale de **magnétisme terrestre.** *See* 9481.

9473 **Bulletin. Association internationale** des **médecins mécano-thérapeutes.** Bruxelles. *Bull. Ass. int. Méd. méc.-ther.*

9474 **Bulletin. Association internationale** de **pédiatrie préventive.** Genève. *Bull. Ass. int. Pédiat. prév.* L.MA. 33–38.

9475 **Bulletin** de l'**Association internationale permanente** des **congrès** de la **route.** Paris. *Bull. Ass. int. perm. Congr. Route* [1919–] L.P. 25–40; SC. 25–39: 51–; **Ha.**RD. 33–48: 51–; **Lv.**U. 39–; **Y.** [*Not published:* 1941–50]
Bulletin de l'**Association internationale** des **ponts** et **charpentes.** Zürich. *See* 10663.

9477 **Bulletin** de l'**Association internationale** des **sélectionneurs** de **plantes** de **grande culture.** Gembloux. *Bull. Ass. int. Sélect. Pl. gr. Cult.* C.A. 30–32.

9478 **Bulletin. Association internationale** de la **soie.** Lyon. *Bull. Ass. int. Soie* [1949–] L.P. 51–; TP.; **M.**C.

9479 **Bulletin of the Association of Iron and Steel Electrical Engineers.** Pittsburgh. *Bull. Ass. Iron Steel elect. Engrs* [1919–23]

9480 **Bulletin** de l'**Association languedocienne** d'**horticulture pratique.** Montpellier. *Bull. Ass. languedoc. Hort. prat.*

9481 **Bulletin. Association** de **magnétisme terrestre.** Venezia. *Bull. Ass. Magn. terr.* [1931–54] L.AS. 34–54; BM.; MO.; SC.; U. 34–54; E.R. [*C. of:* 12492, Sect. magnét.; *C. as:* 9472]

9482 **Bulletin** de l'**Association maritime.** Paris. *Bull. Ass. marit.*

9483 **Bulletin** de l'**Association** des **médecins** de **langue française.** Paris. *Bull. Ass. Méd. Lang. fr.* [1950–] L.MD. [*Supplement to:* 38635]

9484 **Bulletin** de l'**Association** des **médecins** de **langue française** de l'**Amérique** du **Nord.** Montréal. *Bull. Ass. Méd. Lang. fr. Am. N.* L.MA. 35–37.

9485 **Bulletin** of the **Association** of **Medical Librarians.** Baltimore. *Bull. Ass. med. Libr.* [1902] L.S.; Br.U.; E.P. [*C. of:* 30265; *C. as:* 30266]

9486 **Bulletin** de l'**Association médicale belge** des **accidents** du **travail.** Bruxelles. *Bull. Ass. méd. belge Accid. Trav.*

9487 **Bulletin** de l'**Association médicale corporative.** Paris. *Bull. Ass. méd. corp.*

9488 **Bulletin** de l'**Association médicale haïtienne.** Port-au-Prince. *Bull. Ass. méd. haïti.* [1948–] L.MA.

9489 **Bulletin** de l'**Association médicale internationale** de **Notre-Dame** de **Lourdes.** *Bull. Ass. méd. int. Notre-Dame de Lourdes*

9490 **Bulletin** de l'**Association médico-chirurgicale** des **accidents** du **travail.** Orléans. *Bull. Ass. méd.-chir. Accid. Trav.*

9491 **Bulletin** de l'**Association** des **membres** du **corps enseignant** des **Facultés** de **médecine.** Lyon. *Bull. Ass. Membr. Corps Facs Méd., Lyon*

9492 **Bulletin** de l'**Association** des **naturalistes** de **Levallois-Perret.** Levallois-Perret. *Bull. Ass. Nat. Levall.-Perret* [1906–13] L.BM^N. imp.; E.; Z.

9493 **Bulletin** de l'**Association** des **naturalistes** de la **vallée** du **Loing.** Moret. *Bull. Ass. Nat. Vall. Loing* L.BM^N. 13–39.

9494 **Bulletin** de l'**Association normande** pour **prévenir** les **accidents** du **travail.** Paris. *Bull. Ass. normande Accid. Trav.* [1908–49] [*C. in:* 35010; *Suspended* 1939–47]

9495 **Bulletin** de l'**Association** d'**océanographie physique.** Venezia. *Bull. Ass. Océanogr. phys.* [1930–31] L.BM^N.; SC.; E.R.; Ld.U.; Lo.; Lv.U.; Pl.M. [*C. of:* 12492, Sect. océanographique; *C. as:* 41215]

9496 **Bulletin** de l'**Association** de l'**Ordre national** du **mérite agricole.** Paris. *Bull. Ass. Ordre natn. Mérite agric.* L.AM. 02–07.

9497 **Bulletin** de l'**Association permanente** des **congrès belges** de la **route.** Bruxelles. *Bull. Ass. perm. Congr. belg. Route* [1932–] L.P. 32–36; 49–55; Ha.RD. 33–38:54–58; Y.

9498 **Bulletin** de l'**Association philomathique.** Paris. *Bull. Ass. philomath.*

9499 **Bulletin. Association philomathique** d'**Alsace** et de **Lorraine.** Strasbourg. *Bull. Ass. philomath. Als. Lorr.* Y.

9500 **Bulletin** de l'**Association** des **planteurs** de **caoutchouc** et **autres produits tropicaux** Anvers. *Bull. Ass. Plrs Caoutch.* L.EB. 13–25*; K. 09–25 imp.; Sy.R. 09–25. [*Suspended* 1914–19]

Bulletin of the **Association** of **Polish Technicians** in **Great Britain.** *See* 7201.

9501 **Bulletin** de l'**Association** de la **presse médicale française.** Paris. *Bull. Ass. Presse méd. fr.*

9502 **Bulletin** de l'**Association** des **professeurs** de **mathématiques** de l'**enseignement publics.** Paris. *Bull. Ass. Prof. Math., Paris* Y.

9503 **Bulletin** de l'**Association provinciale** des **architectes français.** *Bull. Ass. prov. Archit. fr.*

9504 **Bulletin** de l'**Association** des **psychiatres roumaines.** Bucarest. *Bull. Ass. Psychiat. roum.* [1922–24] L.SC. [*C. of:* 10954; *C. as:* 12157]

9505 **Bulletin** de l'**Association pyrénéenne** pour l'**échange** des **plantes.** Poitiers. *Bull. Ass. pyrén. Éch. Pl.* L.BM^N. 91–04.

9506 **Bulletin. Association** of **Record Librarians** of **North America.** Chicago. *Bull. Ass. Rec. Libr. N. Am.* [1930–38] [*C. as:* 9296]

9507 **Bulletin** de l'**Association régionale** pour le **développement** des **recherches** de **paléontologie** et **préhistoire.** Lyon. *Bull. Ass. rég. Dév. Rech. Paléont., Lyon* [1927–35]

9508 **Bulletin. Association régionale** pour l'**étude** et la **recherche scientifique.** Reims. *Bull. Ass. rég. Étude Rech. scient., Reims* [1960–] L.P.

9509 **Bulletin** de l'**Association régionale** des **ingénieurs** d'**Alsace** et **Lorraine.** Strasbourg. *Bull. Ass. rég. Ingrs Als. Lorr.*

Bulletin [de l'**Association russe** pour les **recherches scientifiques** à **Prague.** *See* 58321.

9510 **Bulletin** of the **Association** of **Scientific Workers** of **Southern Africa.** Cape Town. *Bull. Ass. scient. Wkrs Sth. Afr.*

9511 **Bulletin** de l'**Association scientifique algérienne.** Alger. *Bull. Ass. scient. algér.*

9512 **Bulletin** de l'**Association séricicole** du **Japon.** Tokyo. *Bull Ass. séricic. Japon*

Bulletin. Association suisse des **électriciens.** *See* 11664.

9513 **Bulletin** de l'**Association technique** de la **fonderie.** Paris. *Bull. Ass. tech. Fond.* [1927–45] L.I.; NF.; P. 27–44; Bm.C. 27–44 imp.; Y. [*C. as:* 19846]

9514 **Bulletin** de l'**Association technique** de **fonderie** de **Liège.** *Bull. Ass. tech. Fond. Liége* Bm.C. 20–22. [*C. as:* 10967]

9515 **Bulletin. Association technique** de l'**industrie papetière.** Paris. [1947–] *Bull. Ass. tech. Ind. pap.* Lh.P. 53–; P. 48–; Y. [*Supplement to:* 37117]

9516 **Bulletin** de l'**Association technique maritime** et **aéronautique.** Paris. *Bull. Ass. tech. marit. aéronaut.* [1890–] L.AV. 48- imp.; P.; SC. imp.; G.E. imp.; Nw.A. 23–39: 45–; Y.

9517 **Bulletin. Association technique** pour la **production** et l'**utilisation** de l'**énergie nucléaire.** Paris. *Bull. Ass. tech. Prod. Util. Énerg. nucl.* [1956–60] L.P.; Y. [*C. as:* 10538]

9518 Bulletin de l'Association vosgienne d'histoire naturelle. Épinal. *Bull. Ass. vosg. Hist. nat.*

Bulletin des associations françaises des propriétaires d'appareils à vapeur. *See* 10416.

9519 Bulletin of the Astronomical Institute. Athens. *Bull. astr. Inst., Athens* L.AS. 50-.

Bulletin. Astronomical Institute of the Kyoto Imperial University. *See* 10764.

9520 Bulletin of the Astronomical Institutes of Czechoslovakia. Prague. *Bull. astr. Insts Csl.* [1947-50: 53-] L.AS.; SC.; **Db.**; **E.R.**; **O.O.**; **Y.** [*International edition of* 13405; >9721, 1951-52]

9521 Bulletin of the Astronomical Institutes of the Netherlands. *Bull. astr. Insts Neth.* [1921-] L.AS.; SC. 43-; **C.O.**; SP.; **E.O.** 22-; **M.U.** imp.; **Nw.A.** 56-; **O.O.**; **Sa.** 39-43; **Y.**

Bulletin of the Astronomical Observatory. Copernicus University. *See* 7187. Sect. I.

9522 Bulletin of the Astronomical Observatory, Erivan. *Bull. astr. Obs. Erivan* L.AS. 41-.

9523 Bulletin. Astronomical Observatory, Harvard University. Cambridge, Mass. *Bull. astr. Obs. Harv. Univ.* [1912-] L.AS. 15- imp.; BM.; SC. 21-52; **C.O.**; UL.; **E.O.** 27-; R.; **M.U.** 12-52; **Nw.A.** 27-; **O.O.**; R.

9524 Bulletin. Astronomical Observatory of Illinois University. Urbana. *Bull. astr. Obs. Ill. Univ.*

Bulletin of the Astronomical Observatory of N. Copernicus University in Torun. *See* 7188.

9525 Bulletin on Astronomical Practice. Washington. *Bull. astr. Pract.*

9526 Bulletin of the Astronomical Society of Tasmania. Hobart. *Bull. astr. Soc. Tasm.* L.AS. 45-.

Bulletin of the Astronomical-Geodetical Society of the U.S.S.R. *See* 12834.

9527 Bulletin d'astronomie. Université de Lausanne. *Bull. Astr. Univ. Lausanne* [1906-18]

9528 Bulletin astronomique. Paris. *Bull. astr., Paris* [1884-] L.AS.; BM.; SC. 84-18; SI. 47-; **C.UL.**; **Db.** 47-; **E.O.**; R.; **O.R.**; **Sw.U.** 18; **Te.N.** 20-31:49-. [*From* 1920 *issued in two parts. For pt.* 2 *see* 47259]

9529 Bulletin astronomique de l'Observatoire de Besançon. Besançon. *Bull. astr. Obs. Besançon* L.AS. 86-96.

9530 Bulletin astronomique. Observatoire r. de Belgique. Gembloux. *Bull. astr. Obs. r. Belg.* [1931-] L.AS.; BM.; SC.; UC.; **C.O.**; **Db.**; **E.O.**; R.; **Ld.U.** 35-39 imp.; **M.U.**; **O.O.**

9531 Bulletin. Atlanta Medical College. Atlanta. *Bull. Atlanta med. Coll.*

9532 Bulletin. Atlanta University. Atlanta. *Bull. Atlanta Univ.* **Lv.P.** 96-07.

9533 Bulletin of the Atlantic Deeper Waterways Association. Philadelphia. *Bull. Atlantic deep. WatWays Ass.* [1908-20] [*C. as:* 5099]

9534 Bulletin of the Atlas Diesel Organisation. Stockholm. *Bull. Atlas Diesel Org.* **L.P.** 30-32*; SC. 28-32. [*C. as:* 5103]

9535 Bulletin of the Atmospheric Radioactivity. Tokyo. *Bull. atmos. Radioact.* **L.MO.** 55-; **Y.**

9536 Bulletin of the Atomic Scientists (of Chicago). *Bull. atom. Scient.* [1946-] L.AV. 47-54; C. 47-; CB. 55-; MC.; P.; RI. 53-; SC.; U. 47-; **Abs.N.**; **Bm.P.** 47-; **Bn.U.**

45- v. imp.; **Br.P.** 48- imp.; U.; **C.C.** 47-; R. 47-; **Cr.U.** imp.; **Db.**; **E.A.** 52-; AG. 58-; T. 48-; **F.A.** 55-; **G.M.** 47-; U. imp.; **Ld.U.** 48-54 imp.; **Lo.** 58-; **Lv.P.** 47-; **O.R.** imp.; **Sa.** 53-; **Y.**

9537 Bulletin. Auckland Institute and Museum. Auckland, N.Z. *Bull. Auckland Inst. Mus.* [1941-] L.BMᴺ.; L.; Z.; **Bl.U.**; **E.F.**; R.; **Pl.M.**; **Y.**

Bulletin. Auckland Lily Society. *See* 5284.

9538 Bulletin of the Auckland Museum Conchology Club. Auckland. *Bull. Auckland Mus. Conch. Club* [1945-52] L.BMᴺ. 51-52. [*C. as:* 9899]

9539 Bulletin of the Auckland University College. Auckland, N.Z. *Bull. Auckland Univ. Coll.* [1927-] L.BMᴺ. 27-36 imp.; SC. (math.) 53-; **Bm.U.** 30-36; **C.A.** 27-49 imp.; **O.B.** (geogr.) 56-.

9540 Bulletin. Australasian Institute of Mining and Metallurgy. Melbourne. *Bull. Australas. Inst. Min. Metall.* L.MI. 48- imp.

9541 Bulletin. Australian Commonwealth Engineering Standards Association. Sydney. *Bull. Aust. Commonw. Engng Stand. Ass.*

9542 Bulletin. Australian Lilum Society. *Bull. Aust. Lilum Soc.* L.HS. 57-.

9543 Bulletin. Australian Tobacco Investigation. Canberra. *Bull. Aust. Tob. Invest.* **C.A.** 32-; **Rt.** 32.

Bulletin of the Austrian National FAO-Committee. *See* 32661.

Bulletin of the Avicultural Society of Australia. Melbourne. *See* 33406ᶜ.

9544 Bulletin of the Ayer Clinical Laboratory of the Pennsylvania Hospital. Philadelphia. *Bull. Ayer clin. Lab.* [1903-] **L.GH.** 03-34; MD.; S.; **Bl.U.** 06-; **Bm.U.** 34-; **Br.U.** 03-24; **Db.** 03-37: 46-; **E.P.**; **Lv.M.** 22-25; U.; **M.MS.** 03-06; **Nw.A.** 41-; **O.R.** 25- imp.

9544ᵃ Bulletin of the Azabu Veterinary College. Kanagawa-Ken. *Bull. Azabu vet. Coll.* [1959-] **W.**

Bulletin of the Azerbaijan Fishery Laboratory. *See* 24312.

9545 Bulletin du B.C.G. Paris. *Bull. B.C.G.* [1949-] **L.MD.** 55-56; TD.

Bulletin. B.G.G.R.A. British Gelatine and Glue Research Association. *See* 9613.

9546 Bulletin. Bacon Development Board. London. *Bull. Bacon Dev. Bd* [1937-38] L.BM.; P.; SC.; **C.A.**; **Rt.**

9547 Bulletin. Baird Associates Inc. Cambridge, Mass. *Bull. Baird Ass.* **L.P.** 51-.

9548 Bulletin. Baldwin-Lima-Hamilton Corporation. Philadelphia. *Bull. Baldwin-Lima-Hamilton Corp.* **L.P.** 51- v. imp.

9549 Bulletin. Barley Improvement (Research) Institute. Winnipeg. *Bull. Barley Improv. Res. Inst.* [1949-55] **L.P.**; **C.A.**; **Rt.** [*C. as:* 9601]

Bulletin. Bartlett Research Laboratories. *See* 9550.

9550 Bulletin. Bartlett Tree Research Laboratories. Stamford, Conn. *Bull. Bartlett Tree Res. Labs* [1928-] **L.K.**; P.; SC.; **C.A.**; **O.F.**; **Rt.** 28.

9551 Bulletin of Basic Science Research. Cincinnati. *Bull. basic Sci. Res.* [1926-33] **L.MC.**; MD. 31-32; P.; SC.; TD. 28-33 imp.; UC.; **Abs.A.**; U. 31-32; **Bl.U.** 31-32; **Bm.U.** 28-30; **Bn.U.** 31-32; **Br.U.** 31-32; **C.A.**; **Cr.MD.** 31-32; **E.U.** 31-32; **G.U.**; **Ld.U.**; **M.U.** 28-32 imp.; **Nw.A.**; **Pl.M.** 31-32; **Sa.**

9552 **Bulletin** of the **Battle Creek Sanitarium.** Battle Creek. *Bull. Battle Creek Sanit.* [1923–31] **L.**MD.; **E.**U. imp. [*Replaces:* 32973]

Bulletin of the **Batum Subtropical Botanical Garden.** Batum. *See* 24510.

9553 **Bulletin. Baylor University College** of Medicine. Dallas, Texas. *Bull. Baylor Univ. Coll. Med.*

9554 **Bulletin** of the **Beach Erosion Board.** Washington. *Bull. Beach Eros. Bd* [1947–] **L.**HQ. 50; **Wl.**H. 50–; **Y.**

9555 **Bulletin. Becco Chemical Division, Food Machinery** and **Chemical Corporation.** Buffalo. *Bull. Becco chem. Div. Fd Mach. Chem. Corp.* [1955–] **L.**P.

Bulletin of the **Belaya-Cerkov Plant-Breeding Station.** *See* 54476.

9556 **Bulletin. Belfast Municipal Art Gallery** and **Museum.** Belfast. *Bull. Belf. munic. Art Gall. Mus.* [1949–] **L.**BM.; SC.; **Db.**; **O.**B. [*C. of:* 41567]

9557 **Bulletin belge** de **métrologie.** Bruxelles. *Bull. belge Métrol.* [1956–] **L.**P.; **Te.**N.; **Y.** [*C. of:* 11079]

9558 **Bulletin belge** des **sciences militaires.** Bruxelles. *Bull. belge Sci. milit.*

9559 **Bulletin** of the **Bernice P. Bishop Museum.** Honolulu. *Bull. Bernice P. Bishop Mus.* [1922–] **L.**AN. (anthrop.); BM. imp.; BMN.; **EB.** (ent.) 23–; HS. 24–33 imp.; K. 23– imp.; I. 24–; R. 22–54; Z. (zool.); **C.**E.; **Db.**; **Dm.** 24– imp.; **E.**R.; **Lv.**U. imp.; **Nw.**A. 24– imp.; **O.**R.; **Pl.**M. imp.

Bulletin of the **Bernice Pauahi Bishop Museum.** *See* 9559.

9560 **Bulletin bibliographique. Association technique** de l'**industrie** de **gaz** en **France.** *Bull. biblphique Ass. tech. Ind. Gaz Fr.* [1950–] **Y.**

9561 **Bulletin bibliographique. Bureau permanent interafricain** de la **tsé-tsé** et de la **trypanosomiase.** Léopoldville. *Bull. biblphique Bur. perm. interafr. Tsé-Tsé* [1949–] **L.**MD.; TD.; V. 50–51 imp.; **C.**GG. 52–57; **W.**

9562 **Bulletin bibliographique** du **C.N.E.E.M.A.** Centre national d'études et d'expérimentation de machinisme agricole. Antony. *Bull. biblphique C.N.E.E.M.A.* [1958–] **L.**P.; **Sil.**; **Y.**

9563 **Bulletin bibliographique. Centre** de documentation, **Institut national** de **bois.** Paris. *Bull. biblphique Cent. Docum. Inst. natn. Bois* **L.**P. 51–52. [*C. as:* 9565]

9564 **Bulletin bibliographique. Centre** d'**études** et de **recherches** des **charbonnages** de **France.** Paris. *Bull. biblphique Cent. Étud. Rech. Charb. Fr.* [1960–] **L.**P.

9565 **Bulletin bibliographique. Centre technique** du **bois.** Paris. *Bull. biblphique Cent. tech. Bois* [1953–] **L.**P.; **Y.** [*C. of:* 9563]

9566 **Bulletin bibliographique hebdomadaire. Institut international** d'**agriculture.** Rome. *Bull. biblphique hebd. Inst. int. Agric.* [1910–15] **L.**AM.; BM.; EB. 12–15; K.; P. 12–15; **Bm.**U. 10–14 imp.; **C.**A.; **M.**U. imp.; **O.**B. 13–15 imp.

9567 **Bulletin bibliographique. Institut provincial** d'**hygiène** et de **bactériologie** du **Hainaut.** Mons. *Bull. biblphique Inst. prov. Hyg. Bact. Hainaut*

9568 **Bulletin bibliographique** des **publications périodiques reçues. Académie** des **sciences** de l'**Institut** de **France.** Paris. *Bull. biblphique Publs périod.*

Acad. Sci. Inst. Fr. **L.**AS. 33– imp.; BM. 37–; MO. 30–40: 48–; **Db.** 28–; **E.**C. 29–39 imp.

9569 **Bulletin bibliographique trimestriel. Union géodésique** et **géophysique internationale. Section** de **séismologie.** Bruxelles. *Bull. biblphique trimest. Un. géod. géophys. int. Sect. Séism.*

9570 **Bulletin bimensuel** de la **Société linnéenne** de **Lyon.** *Bull. bimens. Soc. linn. Lyon* [1922–31] **L.**BMN.; K. 23–31; Z. 30–31 imp. [*C. as:* 11033]

9571 **Bulletin bimensuel. Société** de **médecine militaire française.** Paris. *Bull. bimens. Soc. Méd. milit. fr.*

9572 **Bulletin bimestriel** de l'**Association corporative** des **pharmaciens** de **réserve** et de **territoriale.** Paris. *Bull. bimest. Ass. corp. Pharmns Réserve Territ.* [*C. as:* 11391]

9572a **Bulletin bimestriel** de l'**Association** des **naturalistes** de la **Vallée** du **Loing.** Moret. *Bull. bimest. Ass. Nat. Vall. Loing* [1960–] **L.**BMN. [*C. of:* 10966]

9573 **Bulletin bimestriel. Centre belge** d'**étude** et de **documentation** des **eaux.** Liège. *Bull bimest. Cent. belge Étude Docum. Eaux* [1960–] **L.**P.; **Y.** [*C. of:* 17082]

9574 **Bulletin** of the **Bingham Oceanographic Collection, Yale University.** New Haven. *Bull. Bingham oceanogr. Coll.* [1927–] **L.**AM.; BMN.; L. 27–46; SC. 48–; Z.; **Abd.**M. 30– imp.; **Bm.**N. 28–; **Bn.**U. 36–; **Br.**U. 49–; **C.**B.; P.; **Db.**; **Dm.** 36–; **E.**F. 27–28; R.; **Lo.**; **Lv.**U.; **Mi.**; **Pl.**M.; **Sa.** 48–54 imp.: 56–; **Wo.** 37–56 imp.

9575 **Bulletin** of the **Biogeographical Society** of **Japan.** Tokyo. *Bull. biogeogr. Soc. Japan* [1929–] **L.**BMN. imp.; Z.; **E.**U. 29–35; **O.**AP. 35; R. 36–44; **Y.**

9576 **Bulletin** of the **Biological Board** of **Canada.** Toronto. *Bull. biol. Bd Can.* [1918–38] **L.**AM.; BM.; BMN. 23–38; C.; SC. 23–38; **Abd.**M.; **Br.**U. 23–24: 35–38; **Db.**; **Dm.**; **E.**R. 23–38; **Fr.** 30–38; **Lo.**; **Lv.**U.; **Mi.**; **Nw.**A. 20–38; **Pl.**M.; **Sa.** [*C. as:* 10258]

9577 **Bulletin** of the **Biological Department** of the **College** of **Science, Sun Yat-Sen University.** Canton. *Bull. biol. Dep. Coll. Sci. Sun Yat-Sen Univ.* [1929–] **L.**BMN. 29–31 imp.; K. 30; **Abs.**U.; **E.**U. 29–31 imp.; **Ld.**U. 30–.

9577c **Bulletin** of the **Biological Laboratory.** Milford, Conn. *Bull. biol. Lab., Milford* [1959–] **Pl.**M. [*C. of:* 10253]

Bulletin of the **Biological Research Institute, Molotov.** *See* 24314.

Bulletin of **Biological Research, Nippon Institute** for **Biological Science.** *See* 33942.

9578 **Bulletin. Biological Society** of the **Fukien Christian University.** Foochow. *Bull. biol. Soc. Fukien Christ. Univ.* **L.**BMN. 36–45.

9579 **Bulletin** of the **Biological Society** of **Washington.** Washington, D.C. *Bull. biol. Soc. Wash.* [1918] **L.**BMN.

9580 **Bulletin** of the **Biological Station** of **Asamushi, Tohoku University.** Japan. *Bull. biol. Stn Asamushi* [1949–] **L.**BMN.; **Abd.**M.; **Fr.**; **Lo.** 52–; **Pl.**M.

Bulletin. Biological Survey, Ohio State University. *See* 11420.

9581 **Bulletin. Biological-Dynamic Agricultural Service Scheme, Blairs.** London. *Bull. biol.-dyn. agric. Serv. Scheme* [1943–] **L.**BM.; SC.; **O.**R.

9582 **Bulletin** de **biologie clinique.** Bordeaux. *Bull. Biol. clin.*

9583 **Bulletin** de **biologie** et de **médecine expérimen-tale** de l'**URSS**. Moscou. *Bull. Biol. Méd. exp. URSS* [1936–] L.BM.; BM^N. 36–39; MC. 36–39 imp.; SC. 38; TD. 36–38; **Abd.**R. 36–39; **Bl.**U. 36–38; **E.**AB. 36 imp.; U. 36–38; **Pl.**M. 36. [*French edition of* 12748]

9584 **Bulletin biologique** de la **France** et de la **Belgique**. Paris. *Bull. biol. Fr. Belg.* [1917–] L.BM^N.; E. 54–; L.; SC. 25–; UC.; Z.; **Bn.**U. 35–; **C.**UL.; **E.**R. 19–; **Lv.**U. 17–20; **M.**U.; **O.**R.; **Pl.**M.; **Sh.**U. 33–. [*C. of:* 11691; *also supplements*]

9585 **Bulletin** des **biologistes pharmaciens**. Sens. *Bull. Biol. Pharmns*
    Bulletin of **Biology** of the **U.S.S.R.** *See* 12748.

9586 **Bulletin**. **Bituminous Roads Development Group**. London. *Bull. bitum. Rds Dev. Grp* [1958–] L.BM.; P.; **Lv.**P.

9587 **Bulletin**. **Blue Hill Meteorological Observa-tory**. Milton, Mass. *Bull. Blue Hill met. Obs.* [1898–00] L.BM.; MO. 98–99; **E.**R. imp. [*C. in:* 3150]

9588 **Bulletin**. **Board** of **Agriculture, Isle of Man**. Douglas. *Bull. Bd Agric. Isle Man* [1931–] L.P. 31–32; **C.**A. 31–; **Rt.** 31–32.

9589 **Bulletin**. **Board** of **Commissioners** of **Agri-culture** and **Forestry, Hawaii, Division** of **Entomo-logy**. Honolulu. *Bull. Bd Commnrs Agric. For. Hawaii Div. Ent.* [1903–] L.BM. 03–18; EB. 03–18; K. 11– imp.; P. 03–07; SC.

9590 **Bulletin**. **Board** of **Commissioners** of **Agricul-ture** and **Forestry, Hawaii, Division** of **Forestry**. Honolulu. *Bull. Bd Commnrs Agric. For. Hawaii Div. For.* [1911–] L.BM. 11–17; BM^N. 11; P. 11; SC. 24–.
    Bulletin. **Board** of **Health, British Columbia**. *See* 10046.

9591 **Bulletin**. **Board** of **Science** and **Art, New Zea-land**. Wellington. *Bull. Bd Sci. Art N.Z.* [1918–21] L.BM^N.; P.; SC.; **E.**D.; R.
    Bulletin du **bois** pour l'**Europe**. Geneva. *See* 18920^d.

9592 **Bulletin** of the **Boston Mycological Club**. Cam-bridge, Mass. *Bull. Boston mycol. Club*

9593 **Bulletin** of the **Boston Society** of **Natural His-tory**. Boston. *Bull. Boston Soc. nat. Hist.* [1915–36] L.BM^N.; SC. 26–36; **C.**UL. 26–36; **E.**R.; **O.**R. 26–36. [*C. as:* 11272]

9594 **Bulletin**. **Boston Society** for **Psychic Research**. Boston. *Bull. Boston Soc. psychic Res.* [1925–36] L.U.

9595 **Bulletin** of the **Botanic Gardens, Buitenzorg**. Buitenzorg. *Bull. bot. Gdns Buitenz.* [1941–50] L.BM^N.; K.; L.; SC.; TP.; **Abs.**N.; **C.**BO.; P.; **E.**B.; **Rt.** [*C. of:* 10722; *C. as:* 42481]
    Bulletin of the **Botanic Garden, Erivan**. *See* 12743.

9596 **Bulletin**. **Botanical Department, Jamaica**. Kingston. *Bull. bot. Dep. Jamaica* [1887–02] L.AM. 94–02; BM^N.; K. 94–02; L.; P.; TP. 94–02; **E.**B. imp.; **G.**U.; **O.**BO. 94–02 imp; **Rt.** [*C. as:* 9975]
    Bulletin. **Botanical Department, Trinidad**. *See* 11134.

9597 **Bulletin** of the **Botanical Society** of **Bengal**. Calcutta. *Bull. bot. Soc. Beng.* [1947–] L.BM^N.; K.; L.; SC. 50–; **C.**A.; **O.**BO. 47–53.

9598 **Bulletin** of the **Botanical Society** of the **Univer-sity** of **Sagar**. Sagar. *Bull. bot. Soc. Univ. Sagar* L.BM^N. 48–; **Y**.

9599 **Bulletin** de **botanique liégeois**. Liége. *Bull. Bot. liég.* [1936–] [*Issued with:* 4240]

9600 **Bulletin** of the **Bradford Natural History** and **Microscopical Society**. Bradford. *Bull. Bradford nat. Hist. microsc. Soc.* L.BM^N. 51–.
    Bulletin. **Brewing Industry Research Founda-tion**. *See* 8729.

9601 **Bulletin**. **Brewing** and **Malting Barley Re-search Institute**. Winnipeg. *Bull. Brew. Malt. Barley Res. Inst.* [1957–] L.P.; **C.**A.; **Rt.** [*C. of:* 9549]

9602 **Bulletin** of **Brewing Science**. Tokyo. *Bull. Brew. Sci.* [1955–] L.P. 57–; **C.**A.; **Nu.**B.; **Y**.

9603 **Bulletin**. **British Association** of **Chemists**. London. *Bull. Br. Ass. Chem.* [1922–24] [*C. in:* 49272]

9604 **Bulletin**. **British Astronomical Association, New South Wales Branch**. Sydney. *Bull. Br. astr. Ass. N.S.W. Brch* L.AS. 47–.

9604^a **Bulletin**. **British Baking Industries Research Association**. Chorley Wood. *Bull. Br. Bak. Ind. Res. Ass.* [1948–] L.AM.; H.; **Ep.**D.
    Bulletin. **British Boot, Shoe** and **Allied Trades Research Association**. *See* 48366.

9605 **Bulletin** of the **British Bureau** of **Non-Ferrous Metal Statistics**. Birmingham. *Bull. Br. Bur. non-ferr. Metal Statist.* [1948–54] L.BM.; MI.; NF. [*C. as:* 12651]

9606 **Bulletin**. **British Carnation Society**. London. *Bull. Br. Carnat. Soc.* [1924–] L.HS. 24–36.

9607 **Bulletin** of the **British Cast Iron Research Association**. Birmingham. *Bull. Br. cast Iron Res. Ass.* [1924–59] L.AV. 53–59; BA. 45–59; BM.; I.; MT.; NF. 41–59; P.; SC.; SI. 46–59; **Bm.**C.; P.; T.; U.; **F.**A. 46–59; **G.**I. imp.; M. 55–59; **Li.**M. (1 yr); **Lv.**U. 24–29; **O.**B.; **Rn.**B. 45–59; **Sh.**IO. [*C. of:* 12687; *C. in:* 5643]

9608 **Bulletin**. **British Coke Research Association**. London. *Bull. Br. Coke Res. Ass.* [1945–] **Ld.**P.; U.
    Bulletin. **British Columbia Bureau** of **Mines**. *See* 9666.
    Bulletin of the **British Columbia Department** of **Agriculture**. *See* 9957.

9609 **Bulletin**. **British Columbia Department** of **Health** and **Welfare**. Victoria. *Bull. Br. Columb. Dep. Hlth* L.H. 47– imp.; TD. 36–49.
    Bulletin of the **British Columbia Department** of **Mines**. *See* 10062.

9610 **Bulletin** of the **British Columbia Entomo-logical Society**. Vancouver. *Bull. Br. Columb. ent. Soc.* [1906–08] L.BM^N.; EB.

9611 **Bulletin**. **British Columbia Snow Survey**. Victoria. *Bull. Br. Columb. Snow Surv.* **C.**PO. 50–.

9612 **Bulletin** of the **British Commercial Gas As-sociation**. London. *Bull. Br. comm. Gas Ass.* L.BM. 20–.
    Bulletin. **British Conference** on **Automation** and **Computation**. *See* 5641.

9613 **Bulletin**. **British Gelatine** and **Glue Research Association**. London. *Bull. Br. Gelat. Glue Res. Ass.* [1949–] L.AM.; BM. 52–.

9614 *Bulletin.* **British Geon Ltd.** London. *Bull. Br. Geon.* L.P. ser. G., H., R., S. 47–; **Y.** [*Series start at different dates. Ser. G. ends in 1953 and is C. as:* 23483]

9615 **Bulletin. British Glass Industry Research Association.** Sheffield. *Bull. Br. Glass Ind. Res. Ass.* [1956–] **L.**SI.

Bulletin. British Guiana Geological Survey. *See* 10345.

9616 **Bulletin. British Hydromechanics Research Association.** London, etc. *Bull. Br. Hydromech. Res. Ass.* [1948–] **L.**AV.; BM.; NF.; P. 51–; SC.; SI.; SL.; **Br.**U.; **C.**ENG.; **Co.**T.; **Db.** 61–; **Dn.**U.; F.A.; **Lh.**P.; **Li.**M. (5 yr.); **Ma.**T. 58–; **N.**U.; **Sil.** 53–; **Sy.**R.; **Wo.**; **Y.**

Bulletin. British Insulated Callender's Cables. *See* 5663.

Bulletin. British Internal Combustion Engine Research Association. *See* 5665.

9617 *Bulletin* of the **British Interplanetary Society** Wallasey. *Bull. Br. interplan. Soc.* [1946–47] **L.**BM.; P.; SC.; U. imp.; **Abs.**N.; **Bm.**P.; E.A.; M.P.; U. imp.; **O.**R.

9618 *Bulletin* of the **British Jute Trade Research Association.** Dundee. *Bull. Br. Jute Trade Res. Ass.* **L.**AM. 48–.

Bulletin. British Kinematograph Society. *See* 5670.

Bulletin. British Launderers Research Association. *See* 5672.

9619 *Bulletin* of the **British Museum (Natural History).** London. *Bull. Br. Mus. nat. Hist.*

A. Geology [1949–] **L.**B. imp.; BM.; BM^N.; GL.; L.; R.; RI.; SC.; U.; Z.; **Abd.**M.; U.; **Abs.**U. 56–; **Bl.**U.; **Bn.**U.; **Br.**U.; **C.**P.; S.; UL.; **Cr.**M.; E.R.; **Ex.**U.; **G.**M.; U.;**Ld.**P.; **Lv.** U.; **M.**P.; U.; **N.**U.; **Nw.**A.; **O.**B.; R.; **Sa.**; **Sh.**U.; **Y.**

B. Entomology [1950–] **L.**AM.; BM.; BM^N.; E.; EB.; L.; R.; RI.; SC.; U.; Z.; **Abd.**M.; U.; **Bl.**U.; **Bn.**U.; **C.**B.; P.; UL.; **Cr.**M.; E.R.; **Ex.**U.; **G.**M.; U.; **Ld.**P.; **Lv.**U.; **M.**P.; U.; **Nw.**A.; **O.**B.; H.; R.; **Pl.**M.; **Sa.**; **Sh.**U.; **Sw.**U.; **Y.**

C. Mineralogy [1950–] **L.**BM.; BM^N.; GL.; MI.; R.; RI.; SC.; U.; **Abd.**M.; U.; **Bl.**U.; **Bn.**U.; **Br.**U.; **C.**P.; UL.; **Cr.**M.; E.R.; **Ex.**U.; **G.**M.; U.; **Ld.**P.; **Lv.**U.; **M.**P.; U.; **Nw.**A.; **O.**B.; R.; **Sa.**; **Sh.**U.; **Sw.**U.

D. Zoology [1950–] **L.**AM.; BM.; BM^N.; L.; R.; RI.; SC.; U.; Z.; **Abd.**M.; U.; **Bl.**U.; **Bn.**U.; **C.**B.; P.; UL.; **Cr.**M.; E.R.; **Ex.**U.; **G.**M.; U.; **Ld.**P.; **Lo.**; **Lv.**U.; **M.**P.; U.; **Mi.**; **Nw.**A.; **O.**B.; R.; **Pl.**M.; **Sa.**; **Sh.**U.; **Sw.**U.; **Y.**

E. Botany [1951–] **L.**AM.; BM.; BM^N.; HS.; K.; L.; R.; RI.; SC.; U.; **Abd.**U.; **Bl.**U.; **Bn.**U.; **C.**P.; UL.; **Cr.**M.; E.A.; R.; **G.**M.; U.; **H.**U. 51–52; **Ld.**P ; **Lv.**U.; **M.**P.; U.; **Nw.**A.; **O.**B.; BO.; R.; **Sa.**; **Sh.**U.; **Y.**

F. Historical [1953–] **L.**BM.; BM^N.; L.; R.; RI.; SC.; U.; Z.; **Abd.**U.; **Bl.**U.; **Bn.**U.; **C.**P.; UL.; **Cr.**M.; E.A.; R.; **G.**M.; U.; **Ld.**P.; **Lv.**U.; **M.**U.; **Nw.**A.; **O.**B.; R.; **Sa.**; **Sh.**U.; **Y.**

9620 **Bulletin** of the **British Non-Ferrous Metals Research Association.** Birmingham. *Bull. Br. nonferr. Metals Res. Ass.* [1921–] **L.**AV. 43– imp.; BM.; DI. 44–; I.; MI. 41–; MT.; NF.; P.; PR. 37–; SC.; SI. imp.; U. 46–; UC. 42–46; **Bm.**; P.; T. 45–55; U. 22–; **Br.**U. 37–; **C.**UL.; **Ep.**D. 44– imp.; **F.**A. 43–; **G.**M. 56–; T. 53–; U. 22–57 imp.; **Ld.**P. 38–56; **Lh.**P. 37– imp.; **Li.**M. (1 yr); **Lv.**U.; **M.**C. 32– imp.; P.; T. 30–; U.; **Ma.**T. 53–; **Nw.**A. 22–31 imp.; **Rn.**B. 41–; **Sh.**IO. 32–.

9621 *Bulletin* of the **British Oological Association.** London. *Bull. Br. oolog. Ass.* [1923–46] **L.**BM^N.; **O.**OR. [*C. as:* 10730]

9622 *Bulletin* of the **British Ornithologists' Club.** London. *Bull. Br. Orn. Club* [1892–] **L.**BM. 05–; BM^N.; Z.; **Abs.**N. 11–; **Bm.**P.; **Bn.**U. 07–14 imp.; **Br.**U. 92–18: 42–; **C.**B. 92–14; UL. 06–; **Cr.**P. 10–14 imp.; **Db.** 02–; **E.**A. 06– imp.; F. imp.; **G.**M. imp.; **M.**P. 92–41; U. imp.; **O.**OR.; R.; **Sa.** 54–; **Y.**

9622° *Bulletin.* **British Paper** and **Board Industry Research Association.** Kenley. *Bull. Br. Pap. Bd Ind. Res. Ass.* **Y.**

9623 *Bulletin.* **British Plastics Moulding Trade Association.** London. *Bull. Br. Plast. Mould. Trade Ass.*

9624 *Bulletin* of the **British Psychological Society.** London. *Bull. Br. psychol. Soc.* [1953–] **L.**PS.; U.; **Bl.**U.; **Br.**U.; **Ld.**U. [*C. of* 41447]

9625 *Bulletin.* **British Refractories' Research Association.** Stoke-on-Trent. *Bull. Br. Refract. Res. Ass.* [1923–] **Bm.**C. 23–47 imp. [*C. of:* 41448]

9626 *Bulletin.* **British Research Association** for the **Woollen** and **Worsted Industries.** Leeds. *Bull. Br. Res. Ass. Wooll. Worst. Inds* [1929–30] **Ld.**P.; U. [*C. as:* 12645]

9627 *Bulletin.* **British Rheologists' Club.** London. *Bull. Br. Rheol. Club* [1945–50] **L.**C. 46–50; IC. 47–50; P. 50; PT. 47–50; SC. 47–50; **Ld.**U. 46–50; **Lh.**FO. [*C. as:* 9633]

9628 *Bulletin.* **British Rubber Publicity Association.** London. *Bull Br. Rubb. Publ. Ass.* [1939–40] Rubber and Agricultural Series **L.**BM.; P.; **Bm.**P.; **C.**A.; **G.**U.; **Ld.**P.; **Lv.**P.; **M.**P.; **Md.**H.; **O.**F.; **Rt.** [*C. of:* 11630]

9629 *Bulletin* of the **British Scientific Instrument Research Association.** London, etc. *Bull. Br. scient. Instrum. Res. Ass.* [1946–59] **L.**AM. 50–58; AV. 54–59; DI.; EE.; IC.; NF.; P.; PR.; SC.; U.; **Bm.**C.; P. 47–59; U. 46–52 imp.; **Bn.**U. 46–52; **Br.**U.; **C.**C.; UL.; **E.**A.; **Ep.**D.; F.A.; **G.**M. 56–59; **Lc.**A. 51–59; **Ld.**U.; **Lh.**FO.; P.; **Lv.**P. 54–56 imp.; **M.**C.; **Ma.**T. 49–59; **O.**R.; **Sal.**F.; **Sh.**IO. 49–59; **Sil.** 52–59; **Sy.**R.; **We.**K. [*C. as:* 23722]

Bulletin of the **British Section, World Engineering Conference (Conference technique mondiale).** London. *See* 12647.

9631 *Bulletin* of the **British Society** of **Aviculture.** London. *Bull. Br. Soc. Avicult.* [1924–33] **L.**BM. [*C. of* and *Rec. as:* 25719]

9632 *Bulletin.* **British Society** for the **History** of **Science.** London. *Bull. Br. Soc. Hist. Sci.* [1949–58] **L.**BM.; BM^N.; C.; L.; MD.; P. 55–57; R.; RI.; SC.; U.; **Bm.**U.; **C.**UL.; **Cr.**M.; **Db.**; E.R.; **G.**T. 55–58; **Ld.**U.; **N.**U.; **O.**R.; **Sh.**U. [*From 1955–58 contained in:* 3187]

9633 *Bulletin.* **British Society** of **Rheology.** Farnborough. *Bull. Br. Soc. Rheol.* [1950–57] **L.**C. 50–54; DI.; IC.; P.; PR.; PT. 50–53; SC.; **Ld.**U.; **Lh.**FO.; **M.**D.; **Sil.** 51–53. [*C. of:* 9627; *C. as:* 47691]

Bulletin. British Steel Founders' Association. *See* 5684.

9634 **Bulletin. British Timken Ltd.** Birmingham. *Bull. Br. Timken* [1953–55] **L.**P. [*C. of:* 15421]

9635 **Bulletin. British Trust** for **Ornithology.** Oxford. *Bull. Br. Trust Orn.* [1934–54] **L.**BM. imp.; BM^N.; SC. imp.; U. imp.; Z. imp.; **C.**B. imp.; UL.; **Cr.**M. imp.; **E.**T.; **Ld.**U. imp.; **Lv.**P.; **O.**OR.; **Sa.** [*C. as:* 7139]

9636 **Bulletin. British West Indian Central Sugar Cane Breeding Station.** Barbados. *Bull. Br. W. Indian cent. Sug. Cane Breed. Stn* [1933–] **C.**A.; **O.**RE. 49– imp.; **Rt.**

9637 **Bulletin. British Whiting Research Laboratories.** Bedford. *Bull. Br. Whiting Res. Lab.* [1949–] **L.**BM. 51–; P. 51–56; **Sy.**R. 49–56; **Y.**

9638 **Bulletin. Brooklyn Aquarium Society.** Brooklyn, N.Y. *Bull. Brooklyn Aquar. Soc.* [1914–17] [*C. as:* 3780]

9639 **Bulletin** of the **Brooklyn Entomological Society.** Lancaster, Pa. *Bull. Brooklyn ent. Soc.* [1878–] **L.**BM^N.; E. 81–; EB. 12–; Z. 78–85; **Bn.**U. 53–; **Y.** [*Suspended from 1885 to 1912.*]

9640 **Bulletin** of **Brooklyn Institute** of **Applied Biology.** Brooklyn. *Bull. Brooklyn Inst. appl. Biol.* [1949–] **L.**MD. 49.

Bulletin. Brooklyn Museum. *See* 8990.

9641 **Bulletin** of the **Buffalo General Hospital.** Buffalo. *Bull. Buffalo gen. Hosp.* [1923–29] **L.**MD.; **Bm.**U. imp.; **Br.**U.; **Dn.**U. imp.; **Lv.**U.; **O.**R. 23–25.

9642 **Bulletin** of the **Buffalo Society** of **Natural Sciences.** Buffalo, N.Y. *Bull. Buffalo Soc. nat. Sci.* [1873–] **L.**BM. 73–99; BM^N. 73–53; E. 73–94; GL. 73–06; L. imp.; SC. 28–; Z. 73–01; **Abs.**U. 21–34 imp.; **Bl.**U. 86–; **C.**P. 73–81; UL.; **Cr.**M. 86– imp.; **Db.**; **Dm.** 74–35 imp.; **E.**R. 86– imp.; **G.**N. 73–21; **Ld.**U. 91– v. imp.; **Lv.**U. imp.; **Nw.**A. 36–53 imp.; **Pl.**M. 73–53 imp.; **Y.**

9643 **Bulletin. Building Industries National Council.** London. *Bull. Bldg Inds natn. Coun.* [1946–] **L.**BA.; **C.**UL.

9644 **Bulletin. Building Research. Department** of **Scientific** and **Industrial Research.** London. *Bull. Bldg Res. D.S.I.R.* [1925–38] **L.**BM.; C.; GM.; H. 27–38 imp.; P.; SC.; **Abs.**N.; **Bm.**P. 27–28; **Br.**U. imp.; **E.**A.; R.; **Ld.**P.; U.; **M.**P.; **O.**R.; **Sh.**10 imp. [*Replaced by:* 50538]

Bulletin. Building Research Unit, Roorkee, U.P. *See* 5681.

9645 **Bulletin. Buildings** and **Roads Research Laboratory.** Lahore. *Bull. Bldgs Rds Res. Lab., Lahore* [1952–] **L.**P. 53–; **Ha.**RD. 53–; **Wa.**B. 53–57.

Bulletin. Bulgarian Academy of **Sciences.** *See* 24318.

9646 **Bulletin** of the **Bureau** of **Agricultural Economics, Australia.** Canberra. *Bull. Bur. agric. Econ. Aust.* [1946–] **C.**A.; **O.**RH.

9647 **Bulletin** of the **Bureau** of **Agricultural Intelligence** and **Plant Diseases.** International Institute of Agriculture. Rome. *Bull. Bur. agric. Intell.* [1911–12] **L.**AM.; BM.; C.; EB.; K.; MO.; P.; TD.; U.; UC. 12; V.; **Abs.**U.; **Bm.**U. imp.; **Bn.**U.; **C.**UL. 12; **Cr.**U. 12; **Db.**; **E.**F.; W.; **G.**U. imp.; **Ld.**U. 11–12; **Lv.**U. imp.; **M.**C.; U.; **Nw.**A.; **O.**AEC.; R.; **Rt.**; **Sa.** 12. [*C. of:* and *Rec. as:* 33401]

9648 **Bulletin. Bureau** of **Agriculture, Philippine Islands.** Manila. *Bull. Bur. Agric. Philipp. Isl.* **L.**EB. (ent.); K. 03–24.

9649 **Bulletin** of the **Bureau** of **American Ethnology.** Smithsonian Institution. Washington. *Bull. Bur. Am. Ethnol.* [1887–] **L.**AN.; BM.; BM^N. 94–; G. 03–; HO.; R. 03– imp.; SC.; U.; UC. 88– imp.; **Abd.**U.; **Abs.**N. 01–; **Bl.**U. 88–; **Bm.**P.; U.; **Bn.**U. 03– imp; **Br.**P. 01–39 imp.; **C.**E. 06–; P. 04–; T. 04–; UL. 04–; **E.**A. imp.; F. imp.; G. 89–; R. 88–; U. imp.; **G.**M. 12–27; N. 01–; **Ld.**U. 87–23 imp.; **Lv.**P. 04– imp.; U. 88–23; U.; **Nw.**A. 01– imp.; **O.**R.; RH. 03– imp.; **Sa.** 88–; **Sh.**U. 12–; **Y.**

9650 **Bulletin** of the **Bureau** of **Animal Industry, Philippine Islands.** Manila. *Bull. Bur. Anim. Ind. Philipp. Isl.* [1930–] **L.**BM.

9651 **Bulletin. Bureau** of **Animal Industry. United States Department** of **Agriculture.** Washington. *Bull. Bur. Anim. Ind. U.S. Dep. Agric.* [1893–13] **L.**AM.; BM.; BM^N. 94–13; EB. 98–13 imp.; K. 06–08 imp.; P.; SC.; TD. 98–13 imp.; Z. 94–12 imp.; **Abs.**N. 13; **Bm.**U. 00–13; **Cr.**P. 03–13 imp.; **E.**R. 10; **G.**M. 04–13 imp.; U. 10–13; **Ld.**U. 00–13; **Lv.**P. imp.; U.; **Nw.**A. 02–05 imp.; **Rt.** imp.

Bulletin of the **Bureau** of **Applied Ichthyology.** Leningrad. *See* 24462.

9652 **Bulletin. Bureau** of **Biological Research, Rutgers University.** New Brunswick. *Bull. Bur. biol. Res. Rutgers Univ.* **L.**BM^N. 48–.

9653 **Bulletin. Bureau** of **Biological Survey. United States Department** of **Agriculture.** Washington. *Bull. Bur. biol. Surv. U.S. Dep. Agric.* [1889–13] **L.**AM.; BM.; BM^N.; EB. 98–12 imp.; K. 06–12 imp.; P.; SC. 93–13; UC. 98–11 imp.; Z. 97–09 imp.; **Bl.**U. 89–08; **Bm.**P. imp.; U. 05–12; **C.**A. 97–13 imp.; **Cr.**P. 98–09 imp.; **E.**F. 97–12 imp.; R. imp.; **G.**M. 12–13; N.; **Lv.**P.; U. 89–10; **O.**R.; **Rt.**

9654 **Bulletin** of the **Bureau** of **Biotechnology.** Leeds. *Bull. Bur. Biotechnol.* [1920–29] **L.**AM.; BM.; BM^N.; C.; EB. 20–27; K. 20–27; P.; SC.; **Abs.**N.; **Bm.**U.; **C.**UL.; **G.**U. 20–23; **Ld.**P.; U. 20–23; **M.**C. 20–27; **Nw.**A. 20–27; **Rt.** 20–23.

Bulletin du **Bureau central météorologique suisse.** *See* 57476.

9655 **Bulletin. Bureau** of **Chemistry. United States Department** of **Agriculture.** Washington. *Bull. Bur. Chem. U.S. Dep. Agric.* [1883–13] **L.**AM.; BM.; C. 86–13 imp.; K. 83–12 imp.; P. 84–13 imp.; SC. 87–13; **Bm.**U. 98–13 imp.; **Cr.**P. 98–13 imp.; **E.**R. 98; **G.**M. 87–13 imp.; **Ld.**U. 97–13 imp.; **Lv.**P. 87–12 imp.; **M.**P. 98–12 imp.; **Rt.** imp.

Bulletin. Bureau of **Economic Geology** and **Technology, University** of **Texas.** *See* 12546.

9656 **Bulletin** of the **Bureau** of **Economic** and **Social Intelligence.** International Institute of Agriculture. Rome. *Bull. Bur. econ. soc. Intell.* [1910–12] **L.**AM.; BM.; **Bm.**U. 11–12; **Abd.**U. 11–12; **Bn.**U.; **C.**A.; UL.; **G.**U. 11–12 imp.; **Ld.**U. 11–12; **M.**U.; **O.**AEC.; B.; RE.; **Rt.** [*C. as:* 33427]

9657 **Bulletin. Bureau** of **Entomology. United States Department** of **Agriculture.** Washington. *Bull. Bur. Ent. U.S. Dep. Agric.* [1883–15] **L.**AM.; BM. 83–13; BM^N. 83–13; E. 83–98 imp.; EB.; K. 83–14; P. 84–13 imp.; SC. 03–15; Z. 83–14; **Abs.**N. 10; **Bm.**U. 99–12 imp.; **C.**UL.; **E.**F. 88–93 imp.; **G.**M. 95–14 imp.; **Ld.**U. 00–13 imp.; **Lv.**P. 84–14; **Rt.** 95–15 imp.

Bulletin of the **Bureau** of **Eugenics.** Leningrad. *See* 24323.

Bulletin of the **Bureau** of **Fisheries.** Leningrad. *See* 24463.

9658 **Bulletin** of the **Bureau** of **Fisheries.** Washington. *Bull. Bur. Fish., Wash.* [1904–40] L.AM. 23–40; BM.; BM^N.; P. 10–38; R. 04–28; SC.; U. 29–40; Z.; **Abd.**M.; U. 09–40 imp.; **Bm.**P.; **Bn.**U. v. imp.; **Br.**U. 11–40 imp.; **C.**P.; **Cr.**M.; **Db.**; **Dm.** 08–40; **E.**R.; U. 04–17; **G.**M. 10–40; U. 04–27 imp.; **Lo.**; **Lv.**U.; **Mi.**; **Nw.**A. 22–38; **O.**AP. 12–40; **Pl.**M.; **Sa.** 04–28; **Wo.** 38–40 [*C. of:* 12509; *C. as:* 19549]

9659 **Bulletin** of the **Bureau** of **Forestry, Philippine Islands.** Manila. *Bull. Bur. For. Philipp. Isl.* [1903–] L.BM^N. 03–19 imp.; K. 03–26 imp.; L. 03: 07; **Bn.**U. 10–15; **E.**R. 03: 08; **O.**F. 06–23 imp.

Bulletin of the **Bureau** of **Genetics.** Leningrad. *See* 24323.

9660 **Bulletin** of the **Bureau** of **Government Laboratories, Philippine Islands.** Manila. *Bull. Bur. Gov. Labs Philipp. Isl.* L.P. 04–06*. [*C. in:* 37550]

9661 **Bulletin** of the **Bureau** of **Horticultural Inspection. New York State Department** of **Agriculture.** Albany. *Bull. Bur. hort. Insp. N.Y. St.*

Bulletin. Bureau of **Industrial Research, University** of **Washington.** *See* 12553.

9662 **Bulletin. Bureau international** de **l'édition mécanique.** Paris. *Bull. Bur. int. Édn méc.* [1959–] L.P.

9663 **Bulletin** du **Bureau international** de la **répression** des **fraudes alimentaires** et **pharmaceutiques.** Paris. *Bull. Bur. int. Repress. Fraud. aliment. pharm.*

Bulletin. Bureau of **Labor Statistics, Safety Code Series.** *See* 11636.

9664 **Bulletin. Bureau** de **météorologie.** Québec. *Bull. Bur. Mét., Québ.* L.MO. 47–53; **C.**PO. 49–; **Y.**

9664^c **Bulletin. Bureau** of **Meteorology.** Melbourne. *Bull. Bur. Met., Melb.* **Y.**

9665 **Bulletin. Bureau** of **Mineral Resources, Geology** and **Geophysics, Australia.** Melbourne. *Bull. Bur. Miner. Resour. Geol. Geophys. Aust.* [1932–] L.BM. 60–; BM^N.; GL. 50– imp.; GM.; MI. 45–; **Abs.**U. 55–57 imp.; **C.**S. 32–45 imp.: 52–; **Y.**

9666 **Bulletin** of the **Bureau** of **Mines, British Columbia.** Vancouver. *Bull. Bur. Mines Br. Columb.* [1896–] L.BM. 96; GL. 09–19; SC. 96–02: 17–. [*See also* 10062]

9667 **Bulletin** of the **Bureau** of **Mines** and the **Geological Survey** in **Indonesia.** Bandoeng. *Bull. Bur. Mines geol. Surv. Indones.* [1947–] L.BM^N. 47; SC.

Bulletin. Bureau of **Mines** and **Geology, Idaho.** *See* 10484.

9668 **Bulletin** of the **Bureau** of **Mines, Ontario.** Toronto. *Bull. Bur. Mines Ont.* L.MI. 32– imp.

9669 **Bulletin. Bureau** of **Mines, Philippine Islands.** Manila. *Bull. Bur. Mines Philipp. Isl.* L.P. 02–05.

Bulletin. Bureau of **Mines, United States.** *See* 12505.

9670 **Bulletin. Bureau** of **Mines, University** of **Arizona.** Tucson. *Bull. Bur. Mines Univ. Ariz.* [1915–] L.BM. 59–; BM^N. 27– imp.; GM.; P. 15–; **Y.**

Bulletin du **Bureau permanent** des **Congrès entomophytopathologiques** de **Russie.** *See* 12808.

9671 **Bulletin** du **Bureau permanent interafricain** de la **tsétsé** et de la **trypanosomiase.** Leopoldville. *Bull. Bur. perm. interafr. Tsétsé* L.BM^N. 49–. [*See also* 9561]

9672 **Bulletin. Bureau** of **Plant Industry, Philippine Islands.** Manila. *Bull. Bur. Pl. Ind. Philipp. Isl.*

9673 **Bulletin. Bureau of Plant Industry. United States Department** of **Agriculture.** Washington. *Bull. Bur. Pl. Ind. U.S. Dep. Agric.* [1901–13] L.AM.; BM.; BM^N. imp.; K. 02–13; L. 02–05 imp.; P. imp.; SC.; **Abs.**N. 10; **Bm.**U. imp.; **E.**B. imp.; R. 03; **G.**M. 12–13 imp.; **Lv.**P.; **O.**RE. 05–12 imp.; **Rt.**

Bulletin. Bureau of **Raw Products Research, National Canners' Association.** *See* 11212.

9674 **Bulletin. Bureau** de **recherches minières** de l'**Algérie.** Algér. *Bull. Bur. Rech. min. Algér.* [1955–] **Br.**U.

9675 **Bulletin. Bureau** of **Science, Philippine Islands.** Manila. *Bull. Bur. Sci. Philipp. Isl.* L.BM^N. 02–06; L. 03–06; **E.**G. 12–.

9676 **Bulletin. Bureau** of **Scientific Research. Division** of **Conservation, Department** of **Agriculture, Ohio.** Columbus. *Bull. Bur. scient. Res. Div. Conserv. Ohio* [1927–] **O.**AP. 27–36.

Bulletin of the **Bureau** of **Soils.** Leningrad. *See* 50080.

9677 **Bulletin** of the **Bureau** of **Standards.** Washington. *Bull. Bur. Stand., Wash.* [1904–19] L.BM.; C. 04–18; EE.; I. 04–17 imp.; MO. 07–19 imp.; MT. 09–19; NF. imp.; P.; PR. 04–18; R.; RI.; SC.; UC.; **Abd.**U.; **Abs.**U.; **Bl.**U.; **Bm.**P.; U.; **Bn.**U. 04–18; **Br.**U.; **C.**P.; UL.; **Cr.**U. imp.; **Db.** 06–19; **Dn.**U. imp.; **E.**R.; T. 06–19; **G.**I. 15–18; M. 12–19 imp.; T. imp.; U.; **Ld.**U.; **Lv.**U.; **M.**C.; P. 09–18; T.; U.; **N.**U.; **Nw.**A. imp.; **O.**R.; **Sh.**U.; **Sw.**U.; **Y.** [*C. as:* 49193]

9678 **Bulletin** of the **Bureau** of **Sugar Experiment Stations, Queensland.** Brisbane. *Bull. Bur. Sug. Exp. Stns Qd* [1913–24] L.P. 24; SC.; **C.**A.; **Rt.** 24.

9679 **Bulletin. Bureau** of **Sugar Experiment Stations, Queensland. Division** of **Entomology.** Brisbane. *Bull. Bur. Sug. Exp. Stns Qd Div. Ent.* [1914–] L.EB. 14–35; K. 17–21 imp.; P. 14–35 imp.; **C.**A.

9680 **Bulletin. Bureau** of **Sugar Experiment Stations, Queensland. Division** of **Pathology.** Brisbane. *Bull. Bur. Sug. Exp. Stns Qd Div. Path.* [1923–] L.EB. 23–33; K. 32; P. 23–33; **Rt.** 29–.

Bulletin des **Bureaus** für **angewandte Botanik.** St. Petersburg. *See* 54499.

9681 **Bulletin. Bussey Institution.** Harvard University. Cambridge, Mass. *Bull. Bussey Instn* [1874–06] L.BM. 74–84; BM^N.; **E.**R. 76; **Rt.**

Bulletin du **C.E.R.S.** Centre d'études et de recherches scientifiques, Biarritz. *See* 9741.

Bulletin C.E.T.A. Centres d'études techniques agricole. *See* 9748.

Bulletin du **C.I.B.** Conseil international du bâtiment. *See* 12883.

Bulletin C.S.I.R.O. Melbourne. *See* 9895.

9682 **Bulletin. Calcium Chloride Association.** Detroit. *Bull. Calc. Chlor. Ass.* L.P. 34–.

9683 **Bulletin** of the **Calcutta Mathematical Society.** Calcutta. *Bull. Calcutta math. Soc.* [1909–] L.AV. 50– imp.; BM. imp.; M.; R.; SC.; U. 58–; UC. 14– imp.; **C.**P.; **Db.**; **E.**Q.; R. 09: 17–; **G.**U.; **Y.**

9684 **Bulletin. Calcutta Psychical Society.** Calcutta. *Bull. Calcutta psych. Soc.* [1932–] L.BM.

9685 **Bulletin** of the **Calcutta School** of **Tropical Medicine** (and **Hygiene**). Calcutta. *Bull. Calcutta Sch. trop. Med. Hyg.* [1953–] **L**.C. 56–; EB. 58–; MC. 58–; MD. 57–; TD.; **Br**.U. 58–; **O**.R. 55–.
Bulletin. Calcutta Statistical Association. *See* 13004.

9686 **Bulletin** of the **California Agricultural Experiment Station.** Berkeley. *Bull. Calif. agric. Exp. Stn* [1884–] **L**.AM.; BM. 30–; BM^N. 92– imp.; EB. (ent.) 85–; K. 20– imp.; P. imp.; U. 03– imp.; **Abd**.U. 98–; **Bm**.U. 07–30 imp.; **Br**.A. 17– imp.; **E**.B. 99– imp.; U. 24–34 imp.; **G**.N. 06– imp.; **Ld**.U. 12– imp.; **Lv**.U. 08–; **M**.U. 06– imp.; **Nw**.A. 01– imp.; **O**.F. 15– imp.; R. 94–03; RE. 41– imp.; **Rt**. 88–; **Y**.

9687 **Bulletin** of the **California Board** of **Horticulture.** San Francisco. *Bull. Calif. Bd Hort.*

9688 **Bulletin** of the **California Board** of **Viticulture.** Sacramento. *Bull. Calif. Bd Vitic.*

9689 **Bulletin** of the **California Department** of **Agriculture.** Sacramento. *Bull. Calif. Dep. Agric.* [1936–] **L**.AM.; BM^N.; EB.; K.; P.; **C**.A.; **Hu**.G. 50–; **Je**. 47–; **Md**.H. 50–; **Rt**. 36–44; **Y**. [*C. of:* 33413]
Bulletin. California Department of **Fish** and **Game.** *See* 10032.

9690 **Bulletin. California Department** of **Public Works. Division** of **Engineering** and **Irrigation.** Sacramento. *Bull. Calif. Dep. publ. Wks Div. Engng Irrig.*

9691 **Bulletin** of the **California Insect Survey.** Berkeley, Los Angeles. *Bull. Calif. Insect Surv.* [1950–] **L**.AM.; BM.; BM^N.; E.; TD.; Z.; **C**.P.; **M**.U. 50–57; **Rt**.; **Y**.

9692 **Bulletin. California Institute** of **Technology.** Pasadena. *Bull. Calif. Inst. Technol.* [1921–] **L**.MO. 32–36; **Y**.

9693 **Bulletin** of the **California State Board** of **Forestry.** Sacramento. *Bull. Calif. St. Bd For.*

9694 **Bulletin. California State Board** of **Health.** Sacramento. *Bull. Calif. St. Bd Hlth*

9695 **Bulletin** of the **California State Dental Association.** San Francisco. *Bull. Calif. St. dent. Ass.* [1916–17] [*C. as:* 25732]

9696 **Bulletin. California State Mining Bureau.** San Francisco. *Bull. Calif. Min. Bur.* [1888–26] **L**.BM. 88–00 imp.; GM. 96–26 imp.; MI. 95–26 imp.; P. 10–26 imp.; SC. 94–26; **E**.A. 88: 94: 95 imp. [*C. as:* 10098]

9697 **Bulletin** of the **California State Nurses Association.** San Francisco. *Bull. Calif. St. Nurses Ass.* [1904–] [> 36690, 1912–43]
Bulletin. Calorizing Co., Oil Refining Series. *See* 11426.

9698 **Bulletin** of the **Canadian Army Medical Corps.** London. *Bull. Can. Army med. Cps* [1918–19] **L**.MC.; S. imp.; **Lv**.U.

9699 **Bulletin** of the **Canadian Association** of **Geographers.** Hamilton. *Bull. Can. Ass. Geogr.* [1956–] **L**.G.

9700 **Bulletin. Canadian Dental Research Foundation.** Toronto. *Bull. Can. dent. Res. Fdn* [1921–] **L**.MD.; **Lv**.U. 21–24.
Bulletin. Canadian Engineering Standards Association. *See* 12879.

9701 **Bulletin. Canadian Gladiolus Society.** *Bull. Can. Gladiol. Soc.*

9702 **Bulletin** of the **Canadian Hospital Council.** Toronto. *Bull. Can. Hosp. Coun.* **L**.MD. 37.

9703 **Bulletin. Canadian Institute** of **Mining** and **Metallurgy.** Ottawa. *Bull. Can. Inst. Min. Metall.* **L**.I. (1 yr); PT. (2 yr.)

9704 **Bulletin** of the **Canadian Peat Society.** Ottawa. *Bull. Can. Peat Soc.* [1911] **Br**.U. [*C. as:* 25741]

9705 **Bulletin** of the **Canadian Pulp** and **Paper Association.** Montreal. *Bull. Can. Pulp Pap. Ass.* [1918–]

9706 **Bulletin** of the **Canadian Society** of **Civil Engineers.** Montreal. *Bull. Can. Soc. civ. Engrs* [1907–15] **E**.R. 09–12; **G**.U. 09–12 imp.

9707 **Bulletin. Canadian Society** of **Forest Engineers.** Toronto. *Bull. Can. Soc. Forest Engrs* [1936–]

9708 **Bulletin** of the **Canadian Tuberculosis Association.** Ottawa. *Bull. Can. Tuberc. Ass.* [1922–] **L**.H. 30–53 imp.; MA. 29–; SH. (1 yr.); TD. 40– imp.; **G**.PH. 40–.
Bulletin canadien de **mathématique.** *See* 13194.
Bulletin. Canal de **Suez.** *See* 13266.

9709 **Bulletin** of the **Canebrake Agricultural Experiment Station.** Uniontown, Ala. *Bull. Canebrake agric. Exp. Stn* **L**.P. 88–10*.

9710 **Bulletin. Canterbury Agricultural College.** Lincoln. *Bull. Canterbury agric. Coll.*

9711 **Bulletin** des **caoutchoucs** de l'**Institut colonial** de **Marseille.** *Bull. Caoutch. Inst. colon. Marseille* [1919–21] **L**.P.; **Sy**.R.

9713 **Bulletin** of the **Carmichael Medical College, Belgachia.** Calcutta. *Bull. Carmichael med. Coll.* [1920–] **L**.K. 20–22; **E**.B.

9714 **Bulletin** of the **Carnegie Institute** of **Technology.** Pittsburg, Pa. *Bull. Carnegie Inst. Technol.* **L**.BM. v. imp.; SC. v. imp.; **C**.UL. imp.; **E**.U. 24–37 imp.

9715 **Bulletin. Caroline A. Fox Research** and **Demonstration Forest.** Hillsboro. *Bull. Caroline A. Fox Res. Demonst. Forest* **O**.F. 36–38.

9716 **Bulletin. Carothers Observatory.** Houston, Tex. *Bull. Carothers Obs.*

9717 **Bulletin. Cawthron Institute** of **Scientific Research. Chemistry Department.** Nelson, N.Z. *Bull. Cawthron Inst. scient. Res. Chem. Dep.* [1925–30] **L**.SC. 26–30; **Rt**. 26–27 imp.

9718 **Bulletin** van het **Centraal laboratorium** van de **bloedtransfusiedienst** van het **Nederlandse Rode Kruis.** Amsterdam. *Bull. cent. Lab. BloedtransfDienst ned. Rode Kruis* [1951–52] **L**.MD. imp. [*C. as:* 56974]

9719 **Bulletin** of the **Central Agricultural Committee.** Madras. *Bull. cent. agric. Comm., Madras* **L**.BM. 05–11.

9720 **Bulletin. Central Agricultural Control, Imperial Chemical Industries.** London. *Bull. cent. agric. Control I.C.I.* [1956–] **L**.BM.; P.; **Bn**.U.; **G**.U.; **Ld**.P. [*C. of:* 9246]
Bulletin. Central Asiatic University. *See* 12515.

9721 **Bulletin. Central Astronomical Institute** of **Czechoslovakia.** Prague. *Bull. cent. astr. Inst. Csl.* [1951–52] **L**.AS.; **E**.R.; **O**.O.; **Y**. [*C. of:* and *Rec. as:* 9520]

9722 Bulletin. Central Board of **Irrigation** (and **Power), India.** Simla. *Bull. cent. Bd Irrig. Pwr India* [1942–] **Y.** [*C. of:* 41453]

9723 Bulletin. Central Electrochemical Research Institute. Karaikudi. *Bull. cent. electrochem. Res. Inst., Karaikudi* [1954–] **L.**P. 54–55.

9724 Bulletin. Central Experimental Farm, Ottawa, Canada. Ottawa. *Bull. cent. exp. Fm Ottawa* [1887–13] **L.**AM.; K.; SC.; **Abd.** R.; U.; **Bm.**P.; **Cr.**P. 00–13 imp.; **Db.** 02–13; E.B. imp.; **G.**N. 87–08 imp.; U. 95–13; **Ld.**U. 02–13 imp.; U.; **M.**P. 01–13 imp.; **O.**G. 11–13; R. imp.; **Rt.** [*C. as:* 10201]

9725 Bulletin. Central Food Technological Research Institute, Mysore.' *Bull. cent. Fd technol. Res. Inst., Mysore* [1952–56] **L.**HP. 55–56; P.; TP. 53–56 imp.; **Abd.**R.; T.; **R.**D. 52–54. [*C. of:* 51936; *C. as:* 19899]

9726 Bulletin. Central Glass and **Ceramic Research Institute.** Calcutta. *Bull. cent. Glass Ceram. Res. Inst., Calcutta* [1954–] **L.**P.; **Y.**

9727 Bulletin. Central Leather Research Institute. Madras. *Bull. cent. Leath. Res. Inst., Madras* [1954–] **L.**BM. 57–; LE.; P.; TP.; **Y.**

9728 Bulletin. Central Meteorological Observatory. Tokyo. *Bull. cent. met. Obs., Tokyo* **L.**MO 04–.

9729 Bulletin of the **Central National Museum** of **Manchoukuo.** Hsinking. *Bull. cent. natn. Mus. Manchoukuo* [1939–] **L.**BM^N. 39–44. [*C. of:* 10849]

9731 Bulletin of the **Central Research Institute, University** of **Kerala.** Trivandrum. *Bull. cent. Res. Inst. Univ. Kerala* [1957–]
  A. Physical sciences. **Lv.**U.; **O.**F.; **Rt.** imp.; **Y.**
  B. Statistics. **Y.**
  C. Natural sciences. **L.**BM^N.; Z.; **Bn.**U. imp.; **Lo.**; **Lv.**U.; **Pl.**M.; **Rt.** imp.; **Y.**
  [*C. of:* 9732]

9732 Bulletin of the **Central Research Institute, University** of **Travancore.** Trivandrum. *Bull. cent. Res. Inst. Univ. Travancore* [1950–57]
  A. Physical sciences. **Lv.**U. 51–57; **O.**F. imp.; **Rt.** imp.; **Y.**
  B. Mathematics (*afterwards* Statistics). **Y.**
  C. Natural sciences. **L.**BM^N.; Z.; **Bn.**U. 51–57 imp.; **Lo.** 51–57; **Lv.**U.; **Pl.**M.; **Rt.** imp.; **Y.**
  [*C. as:* 9731]

9733 Bulletin. Central Silk Board, India. *Bull cent. Silk Bd India* **L.**TP. 49–55. [*C. as:* 49755]

9734 Bulletin of the **Central Veterinary Medical Association.** Tokyo. *Bull. cent. vet. med. Ass., Tokyo.*

9735 Bulletin. Centre belge d'**étude** et de **documentation des eaux.** Liège. *Bull. Cent. belge Étud. Docum. Eaux* **L.**P. 54–60*; **Pl.**M. 57–60; **Wa.**W. 48–61; **Y.** [*C. in:* Tribune de CEBEDEAU]

9736 Bulletin. Centre de **documentation aéronautique internationale.** Paris. *Bull. Cent. Docum. aéronaut. int.* [1928–30] **L.**P. [*C. as:* 19376]

9737 Bulletin du **Centre** de **documentation** de **bâtiment.** Bruxelles. *Bull. Cent. Docum. Bâtim.* [1938–] **L.**SC.

9738 Bulletin du **Centre** d'**études économiques** de l'**alimentation.** *Bull. Cent. Étud. écon. Aliment.* **Abd.**R. 34–39.

9739 Bulletin du **Centre** d'**études psychiques** de **Marseille.** Marseille. *Bull. Cent. Étud. psych. Marseille.*

9740 Bulletin du **Centre** d'**études** de **recherches** et d'**essais scientifiques** du **génie civil** et d'**hydrau-**lique fluviale. Liége. *Bull. Cent. Étud. Rech. Essais scient. Génie civ.* [1947–] **L.**P.; **C.**ENG.; **Y.** [*C. of:* 9929]

9741 Bulletin du **Centre** d'**études** et de **recherches scientifiques.** Biarritz. *Bull. Cent. Étud. Rech. scient., Biarritz* [1956–] **L.**AM.; BM^N.; **Db.**; **Dm.**; **Pl.**M.; **Y.**

9742 Bulletin du **Centre** d'**information** de la **couleur.** Paris. *Bull. Cent. Inf. Couleur* [1952–54] **L.**P.; **Y.** [*C. as:* 16010]

9743 Bulletin. Centre international des **engrais chimiques.** Zürich. *Bull. Cent. int. Engrais chim.* [1953–] **L.**P.

9744 Bulletin du **Centre** de **physique nucléaire.** Bruxelles. *Bull. Cent. Phys. nucl., Brux.* [1948–53] **L.**P. imp.; SC.; **Y.**

9745 Bulletin. Centre polonais de **recherches scientifiques** de **Paris.** Académie polonaise des sciences et des lettres. Paris. *Bull. Cent. pol. Rech. scient. Paris* [1948–] **L.**BM. 50–; Z. 48–50.

9746 Bulletin. Centre de **recherches agronomiques** de **Bingerville.** *Bull. Cent. Rech. agron. Bingerville* **L.**MY. 53–.

9747 Bulletin du **Centre technique** du **machinisme agricole.** *Bull. Cent. tech. Mach. agric.* [1947–] **Sil.**

9748 Bulletin des **centres** d'**études techniques agricole.** Paris. *Bull. Cents Étud. tech. agric.* [1954–] **L.**AM. 55–; P. 55–; **Sil.** 54.

Bulletin. Centro Volpi di **elettrologia.** *See* 8239.

Bulletin. Ceramic Experiment Station, New York State College of **Ceramics.** *See* 11299.

Bulletin. Ceramic Society. Easton, Pa. *See* 9305.

9748ᵉ Bulletin. Cercle Benelux d'**histoire** de la **pharmacie.** Amsterdam, Bruges. *Bull. Cercle Benelux Hist. Pharm.* [1951–]

9749 Bulletin du **Cercle botanique congolais.** Bruxelles. *Bull. Cerc. bot. congol.* [1932–] **L.**BM^N. 32–34; **O.**F. [*Supplement to:* 47664]

9750 Bulletin du **Cercle** des **électriciens** de l'**Institut électromécanique** annexé à l'**Université** de **Louvain.** Louvain. *Bull. Cerc. Électns Inst. électroméc. Univ. Louvain*

9751 Bulletin. Cercle d'**études** des **métaux.** Saint-Étienne. *Bull. Cerc. Étud. Métaux, St Étienne* **L.**P. 52–; **Y.**

9752 Bulletin du **Cercle** des **géographes liègeois.** Liège. *Bull. Cerc. Géogr. liège.* **L.**G. 29–32.

9753 Bulletin du **Cercle zoologique congolais.** Gand. *Bull. Cerc. zool. congol.* [1924–] **L.**BM^N.; E. 24–32; EB. 24–28; **Lv.**U.; **O.**F. 28–.

9754 Bulletin des **céréales** ·et des **plantes** à **fécule.** Institut colonial de Marseille. *Bull. Céréal. Pl. Fécule* [1919–22] **L.**P. imp.

9755 Bulletin. Ceylon Coconut Research Scheme. Lunnwila. *Bull. Ceylon Cocon. Res. Scheme* [1934–48] **L.**P. imp.; SC.; **C.**A. [*C. as:* 9823]

9756 Bulletin of the **Ceylon Fisheries.** Ceylon Department of Fisheries. Colombo. *Bull. Ceylon Fish.* [1922–38: 56] **L.**AM.; BM^N.; L. imp.; P. 22–38; SC.; TP. 26–38: 56; UC.; Z.; **Abd.**M.; **Abs.**U. 26–38:56; **Bl.**U.; **Bm.**U.; **Bn.**U.; **Br.**U.; **C.**B.; P.; UL.; **Cr.**U.; **Db.**; **Dm.** 26–38: 56; **E.**R.; U.; **Fr.** 56; **G.**U. 22–38; **Ld.**U. 26–38: 56; **Lo.**; **Lv.**U. 22–38; **M.**U. 24–30; **Mi.** 25–38; **Nw.**A. 26–38: 56; **O.**R. 26–38: 56; **Pit.**F. 56; **Pl.**M.; **R.**U. 26–38: 56; **Sa.** [*Forms Ser.* C. *of:* 13655; *Suspended* 1939–55; *C. in:* 13656]

9757 **Bulletin** of the **Ceylon Geographical Society.** Colombo. *Bull. Ceylon geogr. Soc.* [1945–56] **L.**BM. 46–56; G.; GM. 56; SC. 47–56; **E.**G. [*C. as:* 13652]

9757ᶜ **Bulletin. Ceylon Planters' Society.** Kandy. *Bull. Ceylon Plrs' Soc.* **L.**BM. 55–.

9758 **Bulletin** of the **Ceylon Rubber Research Scheme.** Colombo. *Bull. Ceylon Rubb. Res. Scheme* [1913–20] **L.**MY. 19–20; P. 17–20; SC. 15–20 imp.; **C.**A. [*C. as:* 11633]

9759 **Bulletin** of the **Chamber** of **Horticulture.** London. *Bull. Chamber Hort.* [1922–26] **L.**AM.; EB.; **Abs.**N.; **Md.**H. 22–24 imp.; **Nw.**A. 22–24.

9760 **Bulletin** de la **Chambre française** d'**agriculture** de **Rabat**, du **Rharb** et d'**Ouezzane.** Rabat. *Bull. Chamb. fr. Agric. Rabat* **L.**AM. (curr.)

9761 **Bulletin Chambre syndicale** des **industries aéronautiques.** Paris. *Bull. Chamb. synd. Ind. aéronaut.* **L.**P. 30–31.

9762 **Bulletin** de la **Chambre syndicale** des **mécaniciens, chaudronniers, fondeurs.** Paris. *Bull. Chamb. synd. Mécns*

9763 **Bulletin** de la **Chambre syndicale** des **pharmaciens** du **Forez.** St. Étienne. *Bull. Chamb. synd. Pharmns Forez*

9764 **Bulletin** de la **Chambre syndicale** des **pharmaciens** de la **Gironde.** Bordeaux. *Bull. Chamb. synd. Pharmns Gironde*

9765 **Bulletin** de la **Chambre syndicale** des **produits chimiques** de **Paris.** Paris. *Bull. Chamb. synd. Prod. chim. Paris* [*C. as:* 11046]

9766 **Bulletin** de la **Chambre syndicale** de la **sidérurgie.** Paris. *Bull Chamb. synd. Sidérurg.*
    Série Bleue **L.**I. 46–; **Y.**
    Série Rose **L.**I. 46–; **Y.**
    Série Verte **L.**I. 46–; **Y.**

9767 **Bulletin** de la **Chambre syndicale** et **Société** de **prévoyance** des **pharmaciens** de **Paris.** Paris. *Bull. Chamb. synd. Soc. Prévoy. Pharmns Paris*

9768 **Bulletin** for **Character Figures** of **Solar Phenomena.** I.A.U. Zurich. *Bull. Charact. Fig. sol. Phenom.* [1917–38] **L.**AS.; MO.; SC.; **C.**O.; SP.; **E.**M. 28–38; **O.**O. [*C. as:* 41494]

9769 **Bulletin** of the **Charleston Museum.** Charleston, S.C. *Bull. Charleston Mus.* [1905–22] **L.**BMᴺ. 05–21; SC. [*C. as:* 13684]

9770 **Bulletin. Chekiang Provincial Fisheries Experiment Station.** Tinghai. *Bull. Chekiang prov. Fish. Exp. Stn* **L.**BMᴺ. 35–37; **Abd.**M. 35; **Dm.** 35–37; **Pl.**M. 35–37.

9771 **Bulletin** of the **Chemical Research Institute** of **Non-Aqueous Solutions,** Tohoku University. Sendai. *Bull. chem. Res. Inst. non-aqueous Solut., Tohoku Univ.* [1951–] **L.**P.; **Y.**

9772 **Bulletin** of the **Chemical Society** of **Japan.** Tokyo. *Bull. chem. Soc. Japan* [1926–] **L.**C.; I. 38–41 imp.; IC. 29–38; P.; PT. 50–; R. 26–40; SC. 26–41: 48–; UC.; **Abd.**U. 26–39; **Bm.**U.; **Bn.**U. 26–41 imp.; **Br.**U. imp.; **C.**CH. 52–; P.; UL.; **Cr.**P. 26–28 imp.; U. 26–41 imp.; **Db.**; **Dn.**U.; **E.**U. 26–41; **G.**T. 26–41; U. 26–41 imp.; **Ld.**U. 26–41; W. 56–; **Lv.**P. 60–; U. 26–41; **M.**T. 26–53 imp.; U. 57–; **N.**U. 27–41 imp.; 57–; **Nw.**A. 27–30: 54–; **O.**R.; **Sy.**A. 49–; **Y.** [*Suspended* 1945–46]

9773 **Bulletin** of the **Chemical Society** of the **University** of **Allahabad.** *Bull. chem. Soc. Univ. Allahabad* **L.**BM. 33–.

9774 **Bulletin** of **Chemical Thermodynamics.** Manchester. *Bull. chem. Thermodyn.* [1958–61] **L.**P.; **Y.** [*C. of:* 53077ᵃ and 12556; *C. as:* Bulletin of Thermodynamics and Thermochemistry]

9775 **Bulletin. Chemical Warfare Field Service.** Washington. *Bull. chem. Warf. Fld Serv.* **L.**BM. 31–.
    Bulletin. Chemistry Department, Cawthron Institute for **Scientific Research.** *See* 9717.

9776 **Bulletin. Chemistry Department, University** of **Illinois.** Urbana. *Bull. Chem. Dep. Univ. Ill.* **L.**C 24–.
    Bulletin. Chemistry Division, Department of **Agriculture, New Zealand.** *See* 9984.

9777 **Bulletin** of the **Cheyenne Mountain Museum.** Broadmoor, Colorado. *Bull. Cheyenne Mtn Mus.* **L.**BMᴺ. 38–39.

9778 **Bulletin** of the **Chiba College** of **Agriculture.** Matsudo. *Bull. Chiba Coll. Agric.* **Md.**H. 32–35.

9779 **Bulletin** of the **Chiba College** of **Horticulture.** Matsudo. *Bull. Chiba Coll. Hort.* [1932–] **L.**SC.

9780 **Bulletin** of the **Chicago Academy** of **Sciences.** Chicago. *Bull. Chicago Acad. Sci.* [1883–] **L.**BM. 10–15; BMᴺ.; G. 95– imp.; L. 86– imp.; SC.; Z. 40–; **Bl.**U. 01– imp.; **Bm.**N. 96– imp.; **Db.** 95–; **E.**C. 30–34 imp.; J. 98–10; R.; **G.**N. 83–13; **Ld.**U. 95–13 imp.; **M.**U.; **Y.**

9781 **Bulletin** of the **Chicago Dental Society.** Chicago. *Bull. Chicago dent. Soc.* [1920–40] [*C. as:* 20191]

9782 **Bulletin** of the **Chicago Municipal Tuberculosis Sanatorium.** *Bull. Chicago munic. Tuberc. Sanat.* **L.**MA. 29–34 imp.; **Lv.**U. 22–.

9783 **Bulletin. Chicago School** of **Sanitary Instruction.** Chicago. *Bull. Chicago Sch. sanit. Instruct.* [1906–23] **C.**MD.; **Lv.**U. imp. [*C. as:* 57231]

9784 **Bulletin. Chicago Tuberculosis Institute.** Chicago. *Bull. Chicago Tuberc. Inst.* [*C. as:* 57231]
    Bulletin de **chimie pure** et **appliquée.** Bucarest. *See* 9102.

9785 **Bulletin** de **chimie textile.** St.-Pierre-lès-Elbeuf. *Bull. Chim. text.* [1951–56] **L.**P.

9786 **Bulletin** of the **Chinese Association** for the **Advancement** of **Science.** Taipei. *Bull. Chin. Ass. Advmt Sci.* [1953–] **L.**BM. 57–; BMᴺ.; LI. 57–; P.; **Bl.**U. 55–; **G.**U. 56– imp.; **O.**R. 56–; **Y.**

9787 **Bulletin** of the **Chinese Botanical Society.** Peiping. *Bull. Chin. bot. Soc.* [1935–] **L.**BMᴺ. 35–37 imp.; **Ld.**U.

9788 **Bulletin chirurgical** des **accidents** du **travail.** Paris. *Bull. chir. Accid. Trav.* [*C. of:* 10927]

9789 **Bulletin chirurgical** de **Cannes** et de la **région** du **Sud-Est.** Cannes. *Bull. chir. Cannes*

9790 **Bulletin** des **chirurgiens dentistes indépendants.** Paris. *Bull. Chir. Dent. indép.* **L.**MD. [*C. in:* 47200]

9790ᶜ **Bulletin** of the **Christmas Island Natural History Society.** *Bull. Christmas Isl. nat. Hist. Soc.* [1958–] **L.**BMᴺ.

9791 **Bulletin** et **chronique documentaire** de l'**Association** de **bibliographie** et de **documentation scientifique, industrielle** et **commerciale.** Paris. *Bull. Chron. docum. Ass. Biblphie Docum. scient.* [1911–21] **L.**BM.; P.; SC. [*C. as:* 9792]

9792 **Bulletin** et **chronique documentaire** de l'**Association** de **documentation scientifique, industrielle** et **commerciale.** Paris. *Bull. Chron. docum. Ass. Docum. scient.* [1922–39] **L.**BM.; P.; SC. [*C. of:* 9791]

9793 **Bulletin chronométrique. Université** de **Besançon.** Besançon. *Bull. chronom. Univ. Besançon* [1885–24] **L.**AS. 91–24 imp.; MO. 13; SC. 13–24; **E.**O. 89–10; R. 05–24; **O.**O. 07–24. [*C. as:* 2742]

9794 **Bulletin** of the **Chugoku-Shikoku Agricultural Experimental Station.** Himeji. *Bull. Chugoku-Shikoku agric. exp. Stn* [1952–]
    Ser. A. **L.**AM.; **C.**A.
    Ser. B. **L.**AM.; **C.**A.

9795 **Bulletin** of the **Cicadidae Museum.** Kato Entomological Laboratory. Shakujii, Tokyo. *Bull. Cicadidae Mus.* [1938–40] **L.**BM^N. imp.

9796 **Bulletin** du **ciment.** Wildegg. *Bull. Ciment* [1935–] **L.**P. 52–; **Wa.**B. 37–40.

9797 **Bulletin** of the **Cincinnati Dental Society.** Cincinnati. *Bull. Cincinnati dent. Soc.*

9798 **Bulletin** of the **Citrus Experiment Station, Shizuoka Prefecture.** Shimizu-shi. *Bull. Citrus Exp. Stn Shizuoka* **Md.**H. 56–.
  Bulletin of the **City** of **Chicago Municipal Tuberculosis Sanatorium.** *See* 9782.

9799 **Bulletin** pertaining to **Civil Engineering.** Syracuse University. *Bull. civ. Engng Syracuse Univ.* [1955–] **L.**P.

9800 **Bulletin. Civil Engineering Testing Laboratories, Columbia University.** New York. *Bull. civ. Engng Test. Lab. Columbia Univ.* **L.**P. 29–37.

9801 **Bulletin. Civil Veterinary Department, Burma.** Rangoon. *Bull. civ. vet. Dep. Burma* **L.**P. 29.

9802 **Bulletin** de la **Classe** d'**agriculture** de la **Société** des **arts** de **Genève.** Genève. *Bull. Cl. Agric. Soc. Arts Genève* **L.**AM. 1822–68.
  Bulletin de la **Classe** des **sciences** de l'**Académie r.** de **Belgique.** *See* 9184.

9803 **Bulletin. Clay Products Technical Bureau** of **Great Britain.** London. *Bull. Clay Prod. tech. Bur. Gt Br.* [1937–] **L.**BM.; **O.**B. 39.

9804 **Bulletin. Clemson Agricultural College.** Clemson. *Bull. Clemson agric. Coll.* **O.**F. 26–; **Y.**

9805 **Bulletin. Cleveland Academy** of **Medicine.** Cleveland. *Bull. Cleveland Acad. Med.* **L.**MA. 47–; SC. 28–.

9806 **Bulletin** of the **Cleveland Dental Society.** Cleveland, Ohio. *Bull. Cleveland dent. Soc.*

9807 **Bulletin** of the **Cleveland Medical Library.** Cleveland. *Bull. Cleveland med. Libr.* [1954–] **L.**BM.; MD.; S.; **Bl.**U. 57– imp.; **E.**P.

9808 **Bulletin** of the **Cleveland Museum** of **Natural History.** Cleveland, O. *Bull. Cleveland Mus. nat. Hist.* [1922–31] **L.**BM^N.; SC. [*C. as:* 18779]

9809 **Bulletin. Cleveland Scientific** and **Technical Institute.** Middlesborough. *Bull Cleveland scient. tech.*

Inst. [1921–26] **L.**BM.; C.; NF. 22–26; P.; SC.; UC. 21–23; **Abs.**N.; **Bm.**C. 21–25; **M.**P.; U.; **Nw.**A.; P.; **Sh.**G.
  Bulletin. Cleveland Technical Institute. *See* 9809.

9810 **Bulletin** of the **Climatologic Station** of **Mont Estoril.** Lisbon. *Bull. clim. Stn Mt Estoril* [1938–] **L.**SC. [*C. of:* 7363]

9811 **Bulletin climatologique annuel** du **Congo belge** et du **Ruanda-Urundi.** Bruxelles. *Bull. clim. a. Congo belge Ruanda-Urundi* **L.**MO. 50–; **Ld.**U. 53–; **Md.**H. 50–. [*Forms part of:* 9813]

9812 **Bulletin climatologique mensuel** de l'**Algérie.** Alger. *Bull. clim. mens. Algér.* **L.**MO. 52–.

9813 **Bulletin climatologique mensuel. Institut r. météorologique** de **Belgique.** Bruxelles. *Bull. clim. mens. Inst. r. mét. Belg.* **L.**MO. 28–.

9814 **Bulletin climatologique mensuel. Observatoire** de **Puy-de-Dôme.** Clermont-Ferrand. *Bull. clim. mens. Obs. Puy-de-Dôme* **L.**MO. 20–23.

9815 **Bulletin climatologique mensuel. Service central météorologique.** Koara. *Bull. clim. mens. Serv. cent. mét., Koara* **L.**MO. 28–.

9816 **Bulletin climatologique. Observatoire** de **Puy-de-Dôme.** Clermont-Ferrand. *Bull. clim. Obs. Puy-de-Dôme* [1954–] **L.**MO. 54–55; **Y.** [*C. of* 11364]

9817 **Bulletin** of the **Clinical** and **Scientific Society, Cairo University.** Abbassia. *Bull. clin. scient. Soc. Cairo Univ.*

9818 **Bulletin** de la **Clinique ophthalmologique** d'**Angers.** Angers. *Bull. Clin. ophthal. Angers*

9819 **Bulletin** de la **Clinique** de **physiothérapie** des **docteurs George** et **Hanriot.** Nancy. *Bull. Clin. Physiothér. Drs George et Hanriot*

9820 **Bulletin clinique** du **Poitou.** Niort. *Bull. clin. Poitou*

9821 **Bulletin** de **clinique thérapeutique** à l'**usage** des **médecins praticiens.** Paris. *Bull. Clin. thér.*
  Bulletin du **Club Montanyeux.** Barcelone. *See* 12707.
  Bulletin. Co.S.T.I.C. Comité scientifique et technique de l'industrie du chauffage et de la ventilation. *See* 9862.
  Bulletin. Coal Utilisation Council Technical Department. London. *See* 12342.
  Bulletin. Coal-Mining Investigations. Carnegie Institute of **Technology.** Pittsburgh. *See* 14674.

9822 **Bulletin. Coastguards** and **Fisheries Service, Egypt. Fisheries Research Section.** Cairo. *Bull. Cstgds Fish. Serv. Egypt Fish. Res. Sect.* **L.**BM. 30; BM^N. 30.

9823 **Bulletin. Coconut Research Institute, Ceylon.** Colombo. *Bull. Cocon. Res. Inst. Ceylon* [1947–] **L.**P. 59–; **Br.**A. 57–; **C.**A.; **Y.** [*C. of:* 9755]

9824 **Bulletin. Coleman** and **Appleby.** Birmingham. *Bull. Coleman & Appleby* [1935–36] **L.**P.; **Bm.**P. [*C. as:* 12849]
  Bulletin. College of **Agriculture Agricultural Experiment Station, Wisconsin University.** *See* 12631.

9825 **Bulletin** of the **College** of **Agriculture, Alberta University.** *Bull. Coll. Agric. Alberta Univ.* [1923–44] **L.**P. 28–44 imp.; SC. 26–44; **Abs.**U. 39–44 imp.; **Rt.** [*C. as:* 10206]
    Bulletin. College of **Agriculture** and **Forestry, Mosioka, Japan.** *See* 10501.

9826 **Bulletin, College** of **Agriculture** and **Forestry. University** of **Nanking.** *Bull. Coll. Agric. For. Univ. Nanking* [1924–26: 32–] **L.**BM. 32–; P. 32–; **C.**A. 33–34 imp.; **Rt.** 33–34.

9827 **Bulletin** of the **College** of **Agriculture, Tokyo Imperial University.** Tokyo. *Bull. Coll. Agric. Tokyo imp. Univ.* [1887–09] **L.**AM. 93–08; BM. 93–09; K. 94–08; **Bm.**U. 94–08; **Db.** 09; **Pl.**M. 02; **Rt.** [*C. as:* 25837]

9828 **Bulletin** of the **College** of **Agriculture, Utsonomiya University.** *Bull. Coll. Agric. Utsonomiya Univ.* [1950–] **Lv.**U.; **Y.** [*C. of:* 12570]

9829 **Bulletin** of the **College** of **Arts** and **Sciences, Baghdad.** *Bull. Coll. Arts Sci. Baghdad* [1956–] **O.**B.

9830 **Bulletin** of the **College** of **Engineering, National Taiwan University.** Taipei. *Bull. Coll. Engng natn. Taiwan Univ.* [1956–] **L.**P. 59–; **Y.**

9831 **Bulletin. College** of **Engineering, Ohio State University.** Columbus. *Bull. Coll. Engng Ohio St. Univ.* [1911–20] **L.**P. imp.; SC. [*C. as:* 11421]
    Bulletin. College of **Engineering, Washington State University.** Seattle. *See* 12604.
    Bulletin. College of **Forestry, Belgrade University.** *See* 21357.

9831° **Bulletin. College** of **Forestry, Syracuse.** *Bull. Coll. For. Syracuse* **Y.**

9832 **Bulletin. College** of **Forestry, University** of **Idaho.** Moscow. *Bull. Coll. For. Univ. Idaho* [1955–] **O.**F. [*C. of:* 11659]

9833 **Bulletin. College** of **Forestry, Washington State University.** Seattle. *Bull. Coll. For. Wash. St. Univ.* [1946–] **O.**F. 47– imp.

9834 **Bulletin. College** of **Hawaii.** Honolulu. *Bull. Coll. Hawaii* [1911–16] **L.**BM.; BM^N. imp.; K.; P.; SC. 11–15. [*C. as:* 12520]

9835 **Bulletin. College** of **Industrial Arts.** Denton, Texas. *Bull. Coll. ind. Arts, Denton*
    Bulletin. College of **Medicine, University** of **Nebraska.** *See* 12531.
    Bulletin of the **Colombo Observatory.** *See* 13655 Section E.

9836 **Bulletin. Colonial Forest Air Survey Centre.** Surbiton. *Bull. colon. Forest Air Surv. Cent.* [1955–] **O.**F.

9837 **Bulletin** of the **Colonial Institute** of **Amsterdam.** *Bull. colon. Inst. Amst.* [1937–40] **L.**AN.; BM^N.; EB.; LI.; TD.; **C.**UL.; **Rt.**; **Sy.**R. [*C. as:* 34530]

9838 **Bulletin** of the **Colonial Museum.** Wellington. *Bull. colon. Mus., Wellington* [1905–12] **L.**AN.; BM.; BM^N.; GL.; **E.**R. 11–12; **Pl.**M. [*C. as:* 10129]

9839 **Bulletin. Colorado Bureau** of **Mines.** Denver. *Bull. Colo. Bur. Mines* **L.**SC. 19–.

9840 **Bulletin. Colorado Geological Survey.** Denver. *Bull. Colo. geol. Surv.* [1910–25] **L.**BM^N. 10–24; GM.; SC.; **Ld.**U. 19–25; **Lv.**U. 10.

9841 **Bulletin** of the **Colorado Scientific Society.** Denver. *Bull. Colo. scient. Soc.*

9842 **Bulletin. Colorado State Agricultural College.** Fort Collins. *Bull. Colo. St. agric. Coll.* **L.**BM. 87–95; BM^N. 91–04 imp.

9843 **Bulletin** of the **Colorado State Board** of **Health.** Denver. *Bull. Colo. St. Bd Hlth*

9844 **Bulletin** of the **Colorado State Dental Association.** Denver. *Bull. Colo. St. dent. Ass.* [1915–35] [*C. as:* 25845]

9845 **Bulletin. Colorado State University Agricultural Experiment Station.** Fort Collins. *Bull. Colo. St. Univ. agric. Exp. Stn* [1889–] **L.**AM.; BM^N. 91–04; EB. (ent.) 93–; K. 07–08 imp.; P. 90–46; **Bm.**U. 06; **C.**A.; **O.**F. 26– imp.; **Rt.** imp.

9846 **Bulletin** of the **Colorado Veterinary Medical Association.** Denver. *Bull. Colo. vet. med. Ass.*

9847 **Bulletin. Column Research Council Engineering Foundation.** *Bull. Column Res. Coun. Engng Fdn* [1952–] **Br.**U.
    Bulletin of the **Combined British Astronomical Societies.** *See* 36004.

9848 **Bulletin** des **combustibles.** Paris. *Bull. Combust.*

9850 **Bulletin** du **Comité** de l'**Asie française.** Paris. *Bull. Com. Asie fr.* [1901–10] **L.**BM.; G. 01. [*C. as:* 4985]

9851 **Bulletin** du **Comité** de l'**Association amicale** des **internes** et des **anciens internes** en **médecine** des **hôpitaux** et **hospices civils** de **Paris.** Paris. *Bull. Com. Ass. amic. Internes Hôp. Paris*
    Bulletin du **Comité cotonnier congolais.** *See* 12441.

9852 **Bulletin** du **Comité** d'**études historiques** et **scientifiques** de l'**Afrique occidentale française.** Paris. *Bull. Com. Étud. hist. scient. Afr. occid. fr.* [1918–38] **L.**AN.; BM.; BM^N.; EB.; G.; MO. 21–38 imp.; SC. 29–38; TD. 24–38; TP.; U. 20–38; **Abs.**U. 24–38 imp.; **Bl.**U. 26–38; **Bm.**U. 20–22; **C.**UL. 20–38; **Db.** 24–38; **Ld.**U. 20–22; **O.**RH. 20–38. [*C. of:* 3284; *Replaced by:* 10588]

9853 **Bulletin** du **Comité** des **forêts.** Paris. *Bull. Com. Forêts* [1915–] **O.**F.; **Y.**

9854 **Bulletin** du **Comité** des **forges** de **France.** Paris. *Bull. Com. Forg. Fr.* [1864–] **L.**I. 74–40; P. 85–14.
    Bulletin du **Comité géologique** de **Russie.** *See* 24344.
    Bulletin du **Comité géologique** de **Russie. Section** de l'**Ucraine.** *See* 56756.
    Bulletin du **Comité géologique** de **Russie—Succursale** pour le **Sibérie.** *See* 24563.

9855 **Bulletin** du **Comité** de la **Guyane Française.** *Bull. Com. Guyane fr.*

9856 **Bulletin** du **Comité** de l'**Heure. Observatoire** de **Poulkovo.** Poulkovo. *Bull. Com. Heure Obs. Poulkovo* **L.**AS. 31–41.

9857 **Bulletin** du **Comité international permanent** pour l'**exécution photographique** de la **carte** du **ciel.** Paris. *Bull. Com. int. perm. Exéc. photogr. Carte Ciel* [1888–] **L.**SC. 02–15; **C.**O. 92–; **E.**O. 09–15; R. 09–15 imp.; **O.**R. 92–00.

9858 **Bulletin. Comité maritime international.** Bruxelles. *Bull. Com. marit. int.* [1897–38] **L.**BM.

9859 **Bulletin** du **Comité national** de **défense** contre la **tuberculose.** Paris. *Bull. Com. natn. Déf. Tuberc.* [1920–23] **L.**MD. 21–33. [*C. as:* 47501]
    Bulletin du **Comité pédologique Dokoutchaieff.** *See* 37978.

9860 **Bulletin** du **Comité permanent** du **Congrès international** des **accidents** du **travail.** Paris. *Bull. Com. perm. Congr. int. Accid. Trav.*

9861 **Bulletin. Comité permanent** des **Congrès internationaux** d'**actuaires.** Bruxelles. *Bull. Com. perm. Congr. int. Actu.* **E.**E. 97–.

9862 **Bulletin. Comité scientifique** et **technique** de l'**industrie** du **chauffage** et de la **ventilation.** Paris. *Bull. Com. scient. tech. Ind. Chauff. Vent.* **L.**P. 54*; **Y.** [*C as.* 23378]

9863 **Bulletin** du **Comité technique** contre l'**incendie.** Paris. *Bull. Com. tech. Incend.*

Bulletin du **Comité** des **travaux historiques** et **scientifiques.** Sect. 3. Bulletin de géographie historique et descriptive. Paris. *See* 10331.

9864 **Bulletin** de la **Commission actinométrique permanente.** Léningrad. *Bull. Commn actinom. perm., Léningrad* **L.**MO. 26–33.

Bulletin de la **Commission centrale sismique permanente.** *See* 12810.

9865 **Bulletin** of the **Commission** appointed to **further** the **Study** of **Solar** and **Terrestrial Relationships.** Paris. *Bull. Commn furth. Study sol. terr. Relat.* **Abd.**U. 26–.

9866 **Bulletin** de la **Commission géologique** de la **Finlande.** Helsingfors. *Bull. Commn géol. Finl.* [1895–] **L.**B. 60–; BM.; BM^N.; GL.; GM.; U. 49–imp.; UC. 15–; **Abd.**U. 46–; **Abs.**U. 58–; **Bl.**U. 55–; **Bm.**U. 95–07; **Br.**U. imp.; **C.**P. 99–15; MI.; PO. 33–; S.; SJ.; **Db.**; **Dn.**U. 48–; **E.**C. 41–43; D. imp.; U. 13–; **G.**G. 99–; U. 16–imp.; **Lv.**U. imp.; **M.**U.; **Nw.**A. 98– imp.; **O.**R. 55–; **Sw.**U. 57–; **Y.**

9867 **Bulletin** de la **Commission internationale** du **Congrès** des **chemins de fer.** Bruxelles. *Bull. Commn int. Congr. Chem.-de-fer* [1887–14: 19–] **L.**BM. 87–14; P. 89–93; **M.**U. 94–00. [*For the English edition see* 10689]

9868 **Bulletin** de la **Commission internationale** pour l'**exploration scientifique** de la **mer Méditerranée.** Monaco. *Bull. Commn int. Explor. scient. Mer Méditerr.* [1920–24] **L.**AM. 20–22; BM^N.; MO.; P.; **E.**F.; R.; U. 20–21; **Lo.**; **Lv.**U.; **Pl.**M.; **Wo.** [*C. as:* 42093]

9869 **Bulletin. Commission internationale permanente** pour l'**étude** des **maladies professionelles.** Milan. *Bull. Commn int. perm. Étude Mal. prof.* **L.**S. 08–09.

9870 **Bulletin** de la **Commission internationale** de **télégraphie sans fil.** Bruxelles. *Bull. Commn int. T.S.F.*

Bulletin. Commission internationale du **verre.** *See* 39304.

9871 **Bulletin** de la **Commission météorologique** de **Bar-le-Duc.** Bar-le-Duc. *Bull. Commn mét. Bar-le-Duc*

9872 **Bulletin** de la **Commission météorologique** de **Bordeaux.** Bordeaux. *Bull. Commn mét. Bordeaux* [1907–11] **E.**R. 07–10; **Lv.**U. 07–10. [*C. of:* 35605; *C. as:* 35636]

Bulletin de la **Commission météorologique** des **Côtes** du **Nord.** *See* 9380.

9873 **Bulletin. Commission météorologique** du **département** de l'**Allier.** Moulins. *Bull. Commn mét. Dép. Allier*

9874 **Bulletin** de la **Commission météorologique** du **département** du **Gard** à **Nîmes.** Nîmes. *Bull. Commn mét. Dép. Gard*

Bulletin de la **Commission météorologique** du **département** de la **Gironde.** *See* 9872.

9875 **Bulletin** de la **Commission météorologique** du **département** de la **Haute-Garonne.** Toulouse. *Bull. Commn mét. Dép. Hte-Garonne* **L.**MO. 01–08; SC. 02–11; **Db.**; **E.**R. imp.; **Lv.**U. 03–11 imp.; **O.**G.

9876 **Bulletin** de la **Commission météorologique** du **département** de **Maine-et-Loire.** Angers. *Bull. Commn mét. Dép. Maine-et-Loire*

9877 **Bulletin** de la **Commission météorologique** du **département** de la **Meurthe-et-Moselle.** Nancy. *Bull. Commn mét. Dép. Meurthe-et-Moselle*

9878 **Bulletin** de la **Commission météorologique** du **département** de **Seine-et-Marne.** *Bull. Commn mét. Dép. Seine-et-Marne*

9879 **Bulletin** de la **Commission météorologique** des **Deux-Sèvres.** Niort. *Bull. Commn mét. Deux-Sèvres*

9880 **Bulletin** de la **Commission météorologique** du **Doubs.** Besançon. *Bull. Commn mét. Doubs*

9881 **Bulletin** de la **Commission météorologique** d'**Ille-et-Vilaine.** Rennes. *Bull. Commn mét. Ille-et-Vilaine* **Db.** 93–03.

9882 **Bulletin** de la **Commission météorologique** du **Loiret.** Orléans. *Bull. Commn mét. Loiret*

9883 **Bulletin** de la **Commission météorologique** de la **Lozère.** Mende. *Bull. Commn mét. Lozère*

9884 **Bulletin** de la **Commission météorologique** de la **Marne.** Châlons-sur-Marne. *Bull. Commn mét. Marne*

9885 **Bulletin. Commission météorologique** de la **Nièvre.** Nevers. *Bull. Commn mét. Nièvre*

9886 **Bulletin** de la **Commission météorologique** de la **Somme.** Amiens. *Bull. Commn mét. Somme* **L.**MO. 24–33.

Bulletin de la **Commission** pour les **recherches** du **soleil.** *See* 12777.

9887 **Bulletin. Committee** on **Automatic Train Control.** American Railway Association. Washington. *Bull. Comm. autom. Train Control* [1929–31] **L.**P.

9888 **Bulletin. Committee** for the **Distribution** of **Astronomical Literature.** Harvard College Observatory. Cambridge, Mass. *Bull. Comm. Distrib. astr. Lit. Harv. Coll. Obs.* **L.**AS. 41–45*.

9889 **Bulletin. Committee** against **Malnutrition.** London. *Bull. Comm. Malnutr.* [1934–39] **L.**BM.; MD.; TD.; **Abd.**R.; **Nw.**A.; **O.**AEC. [*C. as:* 57107]

Bulletin. Committee on the **Relationship** of **Electricity** to **Agriculture.** *See* 12900.

9890 **Bulletin** of the **Committee** for the **Study** of **Special Diseases.** Edinburgh and London. *Bull. Comm. Study spec. Dis.* [1904–18] **L.**HO. 05–14; MA.; MD. 05–08; S. 05–14; **Bm.**U. 05–08; **Br.**U. 05–10; **C.**UL.; **E.**P. 05–10; **G.**U. 05–08; **M.**MS. 05–10.

9891 **Bulletin. Commonwealth Bureau** of **Meteorology.** Melbourne. *Bull. Commonw. Bur. Met.* [1908–] **L.**BM. 20; G.; MO. 08–45 imp.; **E.**M. 08–16; **O.**R. 08: 16; **Y.**

9892 **Bulletin. Commonwealth** (*formerly* **Imperial**) **Bureau** of **Pastures** and **Field Crops.** Aberystwyth, Farnham Royal. *Bull. Commonw. Bur. Past. Fld Crops* [1938–] **L**.K. 48–; P.; **Abd**.U. 47–; **Abs**.A.; **Bl**.U. 38–45 imp.; **Bn**.U. 44–; **C**.BO.; **Ld**.U.; **N**.U. 44–; **O**.BO.; RE. imp.; **Rt**.; **Y**. [*C. of:* 10499]
　Bulletin. Commonwealth Bureau of **Pastures** and **Forage Crops.** *See* 9892.

9893 **Bulletin. Commonwealth Experimental Building Station.** Sydney. *Bull. Commonw. exp. Bldg Stn, Sydney* [1946–] **L**.P.; **Y**.

9894 **Bulletin. Commonwealth Forestry** and **Timber Bureau, Australia.** Canberra. *Bull. Commonw. For. Timb. Bur. Aust.* [1931–] **L**.BM. 52–; **O**.BO. 31–38; F.; **Y**.

9894° **Bulletin. Commonwealth Meteorological Bureau, Australia.** *Bull. Commonw. met. Bur. Aust.* **Y**.

9895 **Bulletin. Commonwealth Scientific** and **Industrial Research Organization.** Melbourne. *Bull. Commonw. scient. ind. Res. Org.* [1949–] **L**.AM.; BM.; BM^N.; EB. (ent.); K.; MA.; MD.; P.; R.; SC.; UC.; **Abs**.N.; U.; **Bl**.U.; **Bm**.P.; U.; **Bn**.U.; **Br**.A.; **C**.A.; **Cr**.U. 49–; **E**.U.; **Ld**.U.; **Lv**.U.; **M**.T. imp.; U.; **N**.U.; **Nw**.A.; **O**.BO. (biol.); RH.; **Pl**.M. 49–50; **Rt**.; **Sa**.; **Sw**.U.; **Y**. [*C. of:* 9928]
　Bulletin. Communicable Disease Centre. Atlanta. *See* 12870.

9896 **Bulletin** of **Communicable Diseases** and **Medical Notes.** U.N.O. Health Division. London. *Bull. commun. Dis.* [1944–47] **L**.MA.; SH. 45–47; TD.
　Bulletin. Compagnie internationale d'électricité. *See* 10673.

9897 **Bulletin** of **Comparative Medicine** and **Surgery.** Indianapolis. *Bull. comp. Med. Surg.*

9898 **Bulletin. Compressed Gas Manufacturers Association.** New York. *Bull. compr. Gas Mfrs Ass.* [1921–33] **L**.P. imp.

9899 **Bulletin** of **Conchology Section** of the **Auckland Museum.** Auckland. *Bull. Conch. Sect. Auckland Mus.* [1953–] **L**.BM^N. [*C. of* 9538]

9900 **Bulletin** of the **Conference** of **State** and **Provincial Public Health Laboratory Directors.** *Bull. Conf. St. prov. publ. Hlth Lab. Dir.* **L**.TD.
　Bulletin. Conférence technique mondiale. *See* 12646.
　Bulletin. Conférence technique mondiale. British Section. *See* 12647.

9901 **Bulletin** du **Congrès** des **botanistes tchécoslovaques.** *Bull. Congr. Bot. tchécosl.*
　Bulletin. Congrès international des **chemins** de **fer. Electric Traction** on the **Railways.** *See* 10149.

9902 **Bulletin** du **Congrès permanent** de l'**outillage colonial.** Paris. *Bull. Congr. perm. Outill. colon.* **L**.SC. 23–28.

9903 **Bulletin. Connecticut Agricultural College Extension Service.** Storrs. *Bull. Conn. agric. Coll. Ext. Serv.* **O**.R. 17.

9904 **Bulletin. Connecticut Agricultural Experiment Station.** New Haven. *Bull. Conn. agric. Exp. Stn* **L**.AM.; BM. 05–; BM^N. 91– imp.; EB. (ent.) 95–; K. 98–07 imp.; L. 13–14; MY. 51– imp.; P. 17–; SC. 17– imp.; Z. 18– imp.; **Bn**.U. 45–; **Br**.A. 21– imp.; **C**.A.; **Cr**.P. 17–; **O**.F. 26– imp; RE. 39– imp.; **Rt**. 82–; **Y**.

9905 **Bulletin. Connecticut Arboretum.** New London. *Bull. Conn. Arbor.* [1934–]

9906 **Bulletin. Connecticut Dairy** and **Food Commission.** New Haven. *Bull. Conn. Dairy Fd Commn* **L**.BM. 18–.
　Bulletin. Connecticut Engineering Experiment Station. Storrs. *See* 10161.

9907 **Bulletin. Connecticut Ground Water Survey.** Hartford. *Bull. Conn. Grd Wat. Surv.*

9908 **Bulletin** of the **Connecticut State Dental Association.** Hartford. *Bull. Conn. St. dent. Ass.*

9909 **Bulletin. Connecticut State Geological** and **Natural History Survey.** Hartford. *Bull. Conn. St. geol. nat. Hist. Surv.* [1904–] **L**.BM.; BM^N.; EB. (ent.) 11–; G. 06– imp.; GL. 04–38 imp.; GM.; L. 06–38 imp.; P.; **C**.P. 05– imp.; **G**.N.; U. 04–38 imp.; **O**.R.; **Y**.
　Bulletin. Conseil international du **bâtiment** pour la **recherche**, l'**étude** et la **documentation.** *See* 12883.

9910 **Bulletin** du **Conseil national** de l'**Ordre** des **chirurgien-dentistes,** Paris. *Bull. Cons. natn. Ordre Chir.-Dent.* **L**.D. 46–.

9911 **Bulletin** du **Conseil sanitaire, maritime** et **quarantenaire** d'**Égypte.** *Bull Cons. sanit. marit. quar. Égypte*

9912 **Bulletin** du **Conseil supérieur** de l'**agriculture.** Bruxelles. *Bull. Cons. sup. Agric., Brux.*

9913 **Bulletin** of the **Conservation Department. Nebraska University Conservation** and **Survey Division.** Lincoln. *Bull. Conserv. Dep. Neb. Univ.* [1928–39] **L**.SC.; **C**.A.; **O**.F. 31–39. [*C. of:* 11265; *C. as:* 34441]

9914 **Bulletin** du **Conservatoire national** des **arts** et **métiers.** Paris. *Bull. Conservre natn. Arts Métiers* [1944–] **L**.P.

9914^a **Bulletin** des **constructeurs.** Paris. *Bull. Constr., Paris.* [*Supplement to:* 3966]
　Bulletin de la **construction métallique.** *See* 50720.

9915 **Bulletin. Consultative Committee** for **Development** of **Spectrographic Work.** Aberdeen. *Bull. consult. Comm. Dev. spectogr. Wk* [1957–] **L**.BM.; P.; SC.; **Bn**.U.; **Rt**.; **Y**.

9916 **Bulletin. Co-operative Coal Mining Series. Illinois State Geological Survey.** Urbana. *Bull. co-op. Coal Min. Ser. Ill. St. geol. Surv.* [1916–] **L**.BM.; GM. 16–30 imp.; P. 16–30 imp.; **Bm**.N. imp.; U. 17–29 imp.; **E**.R. 16–30; U. 16–30; **Lv**.U. 16–30 imp.; **M**.U. 16–17; **O**.R. 16–30 imp. [*C. of:* 10486]

9917 **Bulletin. Co-operative Extension Work** in **Agriculture** and **Home Economics, Florida.** *Bull. co-op. Ext. Wk Agric. Fla* **Rt**. 16–38 imp.

9918 **Bulletin** of the **Co-operative Oil-Shale Laboratory.** Boulder, Colorado. *Bull. co-op. Oil-Shale Lab., Boulder*

9919 **Bulletin** of the **Copper** and **Brass Research Association.** New York. *Bull. Copp. Brass Res. Ass.* [1921–46] **L**.NF. imp; P. 24–46; SC. 24–46. [*C. as:* 15903]

9920 **Bulletin. Copper Development Association.** London. *Bull. Copp. Dev. Ass.* [*C. as:* 15899]

9921 **Bulletin. Cornell University Agricultural Experiment Station.** Ithaca, N.Y. *Bull. Cornell Univ. agric. Exp. Stn* [1888–] **L.**AM.; BM. imp.; BMᴺ. 91– imp.; EB. (ent.) 93–; K. 23–; L. 04–11; P. 89–; UC. 14– imp.; **Abs.**N. 16–; **Bm.**U. 98–28 imp.; **Bn.**U. 04– imp.; **Br.**U. 23– imp.; **C.**A.; P. 34–; UL. 27–; **Cr.**P. 97–23; **Db.** 20–; **E.**B. 13–; **G.**N. 17–48; U. 22–; **Ld.**U. 97–; **Lv.**U. 17– imp.; **M.**U. 14–48 imp.; **Nw.**A. 20– imp.; **O.**F. 00– imp.; R. 20–; RE. 11– imp.; **Rt.**; **Y.**

9922 **Bulletin. Cornell University Engineering Experiment Station.** Ithaca. *Bull. Cornell Univ. Engng Exp. Stn* [1923–] **L.**I. 46–; **Y.**

9923 **Bulletin. Corps des Lieutenants honoraires** de **chasse du Congo Belge.** Service des eaux et forêts, chasse et pêche. Léopoldville. *Bull. Cps Lieuts hon. Chasse Congo belge* [1947–] **L.**Z. 47–56.

Bulletin. Council for the **Co-ordination** of **International Congresses** of **Medical Sciences.** *See* 41459.

9924 **Bulletin. Council for International Organizations** of **Medical Sciences.** Paris. *Bull. Coun. int. Orgs med. Sci.* [1952–58] **L.**BM. 54–58; H.; MD.; S. 56–58; TD.; **E.**U. 53–58; **M.**P. 54–58; **O.**R. [*C. of:* 41459; *C. as:* 34827ᶜ]

9925 **Bulletin. Council for the Promotion of Field Studies.** London. *Bull. Coun. Promot. Fld Stud.* **L.**BMᴺ. 44–46; SC. 46–.

9926 **Bulletin. Council for Psychical Investigation, London University.** London. *Bull. Coun. psych. Invest.* [1935–] **L.**BM.; **Br.**U. 35; **O.**B. [*C. of:* 11232]

9927 **Bulletin. Council for Science** of **Indonesia.** Djakarta. *Bull. Coun. Sci. Indonesia* **L.**BMᴺ. 59–.

9928 **Bulletin. Council for Scientific** and **Industrial Research.** Melbourne. *Bull. Coun. scient. ind. Res., Melb.* [1927–48] **L.**AM.; BM.; BMᴺ.; EB. (ent.); K.; MA. 34–48; MD. imp.; MO. (radio) 32–39; P.; R. 34–48; SC.; UC.; **Abs.**N.; U.; **Bl.**U.; **Bm.**P.; U.; **Bn.**U. imp.; **Br.**A. imp.; **C.**A.; **Cr.**U. 20–48; **Dm.** 41–48; **E.**U.; **Ld.**U.; **Lv.**U.; **M.**T. 47–48 imp.; **Nw.**A.; **O.**BO. (biol.); F. (for.); RH.; **Pl.**M. 34–48 imp.; **Rt.**; **Sa.**; **Sw.**U. 31–48; **Wo.** 41–48 imp. [*C. of:* 10645; *C. as:* 9895]

9928ᶜ **Bulletin. Council of Scientific** and **Industrial Research, India.** Delhi. *Bull. Coun. scient. ind. Res. India* [1955–] **O.**F.

Bulletin of the **County Experiment Station, Cockle Park.** *See* 11347.

9929 **Bulletin des cours** et des **laboratoires d'essais** des **constructions** du **génie civil** et **d'hydraulique fluviale.** Liège. *Bull. Cours Labs Essais Constr. Génie civ.* [1940–41] **L.**P. 40. [*C. as:* 9740]

9930 **Bulletin. Cranbrook Institute** of **Science.** Bloomfield Hills, Mich. *Bull. Cranbrook Inst. Sci.* **L.**BMᴺ. 31–; Z. 42–49 imp.; **Y.**

9931 **Bulletin. Creighton University School** of **Medicine.** Omaha, Neb. *Bull. Creighton Univ. Sch. Med.* [1940–]

9931ᶜ **Bulletin** du **cultivateur.** Ottawa. *Bull. Cultivateur* **Y.**

9932 **Bulletin** of **Current Literature. Brewing Industry Research Foundation.** Nutfield. *Bull. curr. Lit. Brew. Ind. Res. Fdn* [1952–] **L.**AM.; P.; **Md.**H.

9933 **Bulletin** on **Current Literature. National Society** for **Crippled Children** and **Adults.** Chicago. *Bull. curr. Lit. natn. Soc. crippl. Child. Adults* [1950–55] **L.**H. [*C. as:* 42468]

9934 **Bulletin. Cyprus Natural History Society.** Nicosia. *Bull. Cyprus nat. Hist. Soc.* [1910] **L.**BM.; BMᴺ.; **Db.**; **O.**R.

Bulletin of the **Czechoslovak Academy** of **Agriculture.** *See* 56422.

9935 **Bulletin** of the **Czechoslovak Medical Association** in **Great Britain.** London. *Bull. Czechosl. med. Ass. Gt Br.* [1941–44] **L.**BM.; D. 42–44; MD. 41–43; S.; **Db.** 41–43; **O.**R. [*C. as:* 35203]

Bulletin des **Dagestaner Laboratoriums** für **Ichtiologie.** *See* 24325.

9936 **Bulletin. Dahlia Society** of **California.** San Francisco. *Bull. Dahlia Soc. Calif.* **L.**HS. 17–24; K. 17–18 imp.

9937 **Bulletin. Dairy** and **Cold Storage Commissioner's Branch** of the **Department of Agriculture.** Ottawa. *Bull. Dairy cold Stor. Commnr's Brch Dep. Agric., Ottawa* [1905–20] **L.**AM. imp.; P.; SC. 06–20 imp.

Bulletin. Dairy Division, Department of **Agriculture, New Zealand.** *See* 9985.

9938 **Bulletin** of the **Dairy Research Bureau, Mathews Company.** Detroit. *Bull. Dairy Res. Bur. Mathews Co.* **R.**D. 35–45.

9939 **Bulletin** of the **Daniel Guggenheim Fund** for the **Promotion** of **Aeronautics.** New York. *Bull. Daniel Guggenheim Fund Promot. Aeronaut.* **L.**P. 27–29.

9940 **Bulletin. Davey Tree Expert Company, Research Department.** Kent, Ohio. *Bull. Davey Tree Expert Co. Res. Dep.* [1920–] **O.**F. 28–39 imp.

9941 **Bulletin** of the **Davis-Fischer Sanatorium,** Atlanta, Georgia. *Bull. Davis-Fischer Sanat.*

9942 **Bulletin décadaire** d'**observations quotidiennes. Météorologie nationale.** Paris. *Bull. décad. Obsns quotid. Mét. natn.* **L.**BM. 58–; MO. 58– [*Supplement to:* 46115]

9943 **Bulletin** of the **Deccan College Research Institute.** Poona. *Bull. Deccan Coll. Res. Inst.* [1939–] **L.**BM.; **E.**U. 48–.

Bulletin dékadaire de l'**Ukrmète.** *See* 16459.

9944 **Bulletin** of the **Delaware State Board** of **Agriculture.** Dover. *Bull. Del. St. Bd Agric.* [1911–] **Y.**

9945 **Bulletin** of the **Delaware University Agricultural Experiment Station.** Newark. *Bull. Del. Univ. agric. Exp. Stn* [1888–] **L.**AM.; BMᴺ. 36– imp.; EB. (ent.) 95–; K. 03–08 imp.; P.; **Bm.**U. 35–; **C.**A.; **Rt.** imp.; **Y.**

9946 **Bulletin** van het **Deli proefstation** te **Medan.** Medan. *Bull. Deli Proefstn Medan* [1914–] **L.**EB. 14–40; P. 14–38 imp.; SC. 25–; **C.**A. 29–: **Rt.** 30–40.

Bulletin démographique et **sanitaire suisse.** *See* 48544.

Bulletin dentaire. Montréal. *See* 16518ᶜ.
Bulletin dentaire. Zurich. *See* 7230.

9947 **Bulletin. Dental Hygienists' Association** of the **City** of **New York.** *Bull. dent. Hyg. Ass. Cy N.Y.* [*C. as:* 25880]

9948 **Bulletin** of the **Dental Society** of the **State** of **New York.** *Bull. dent. Soc. St. N.Y.* [1933–38] [*C. as:* 36006]

9949 **Bulletin** du **Département** de l'**agriculture** aux **Indes néerlandaises.** Buitenzorg. *Bull. Dép. Agric. Indes néerl.* [1906–11] L.BM^N.; K.; L.; MY.; R.; C.P.; E.B.; **Rt.** [*C. of:* 10578; *C. as:* 10722]

9950 **Bulletin** du **Département** de l'**agriculture** et de la **pêche, Seychelles.** Victoria. *Bull. Dép. Agric. Pêche Seychelles* [1923–29] L.BM.; BM^N. 25–29; EB. 26–29; P.; SC. 25–29. [*C. as:* 10082]

9951 **Bulletin. Departement** van den **landbouw, Suriname.** Paramaribo. *Bull. Dep. Landb. Suriname* [1908–25] L.AM.; EB.; K.; P. imp.; SC. 20–25. [*C. of:* 10570; *C. as:* 9952]

9952 **Bulletin. Departement-Landbouwproefstation** in **Suriname.** Paramaribo. *Bull. Dep.-LandbProefstn Suriname* [1932–52] L.AM.; EB.; K.; P. imp.; SC.; **Rt.** 37–52. [*C. of:* 9951; *C. as:* 10796]

9953 **Bulletin. Department** of **Agricultural Research. Campbell Soup Company.** Camden, N.J. *Bull. Dep. agric. Res. Campbell Soup Co.* [1939–42]

9954 **Bulletin. Department** of **Agriculture, Alberta.** Edmonton. *Bull. Dep. Agric. Alberta* **Y.**

    Bulletin. Department of **Agriculture, Assam.** *See* 9238.

    Bulletin. Department of **Agriculture, Bahamas.** *See* 9239.

9955 **Bulletin. Department** of **Agriculture, Bermuda.** Hamilton. *Bull. Dep. Agric. Bermuda* L.EB. (ent.) 28–; **O.F.** 50– imp.; **Y.**

9956 **Bulletin. Department** of **Agriculture, Bihar** and **Orissa.** Patna. *Bull. Dep. Agric. Bihar Orissa* [1932–] C.A. imp.

9957 **Bulletin** of the **Department** of **Agriculture, British Columbia.** Victoria. *Bull. Dep. Agric. Br. Columb.* [1893–] L.AM.; BM^N. 13–20; EB. (ent.) 16–23: 47–; P. 01– imp.; **Abs.**N. 15–24 imp.; **Cr.**P. 01–29 imp.; **Lv.**P. 12–21; **M.**P. 13–38 imp.; **O.F.** 41–; **Rt.** 19–38; **Y.**

9958 **Bulletin. Department** of **Agriculture, British East Africa.** Nairobi. *Bull. Dep. Agric. Br. E. Afr.* [1914–19] L.AM.; BM^N. 19; EB. 17–19; P. 14–17; **Rt.**; **Y.** [*C. as:* 9976]

9959 **Bulletin. Department** of **Agriculture, British East Africa, Division of Entomology.** Nairobi. *Bull. Dep. Agric. Br. E. Afr. Div. Ent.* L.BM^N. 19*; EB. 19; SC. 19. [*C. as:* 9977]

    Bulletin. Department of **Agriculture, British North Borneo.** *See* 9240.

9960 **Bulletin** of the **Department** of **Agriculture, Burma.** Rangoon. *Bull. Dep. Agric. Burma* [1909–] L.BM.; EB. (ent.) 12–; K. 09–37 imp.; P.; **Abs.**N. 13–21; C.A. 10–37 imp.; **E.**A.; **O.**B. 09–26; **Rt.** 10–37.

    Bulletin. Department of **Agriculture, California.** *See* 9689.

9961 **Bulletin** of the **Department** of **Agriculture, Canada, Entomological Branch.** Ottawa. *Bull. Dep. Agric. Can. ent. Brch* [1911–] L.AM.; BM^N. 11–38; EB.; P. 15–20; SC. 12: 24–; C.B. 13–20 imp.; P. 12–20; **O.**R. 11–20 imp.; **Rt.** 15–.

    Bulletin. Department of **Agriculture, Canada. Experimental Farms Branch.** *See* 10201.

9962 **Bulletin. Department** of **Agriculture, Canada. Fruit Branch.** Ottawa. *Bull. Dep. Agric. Can. Fruit Brch* L.SC. 17–.

9963 **Bulletin. Department** of **Agriculture, Canada. Health** of **Animals Branch.** Ottawa. *Bull. Dep. Agric. Can. Hlth Anim. Brch* L.P. 02–20; SC. 11–.

9964 **Bulletin. Department** of **Agriculture, Canada. Live Stock Branch.** Ottawa. *Bull. Dep. Agric. Can. Live Stk Brch* L.AM.; P. 05–16*. [*C. as:* 36875(*a*)]

9965 **Bulletin. Department** of **Agriculture, Canada. Seed Branch.** Ottawa. *Bull. Dep. Agric. Can. Seed Brch* L.AM.; P. 05–15*. [*C. as:* 36875(*b*)]

9966 **Bulletin** of the **Department** of **Agriculture, Cape** of **Good Hope.** Cape Town. *Bull. Dep. Agric. Cape Gd Hope* L.EB. (ent.) 98–10.

9967 **Bulletin** of the **Department** of **Agriculture, Central Provinces.** Nagpur. *Bull. Dep. Agric. cent. Prov.* [1896–] L.BM. 08–16; **O.**B. 97–16; **Rt.** 97–02: 08–10.

9968 **Bulletin** of the **Department** of **Agriculture, Ceylon.** Colombo. *Bull. Dep. Agric. Ceylon* [1912–38] L.BM.; BM^N. 18–27 imp.; EB. (ent.) 13–38; HS. imp.; K.; P.; MY. 14–38; SC. 23–38; C.A.; **Db.**; E.B.; **G.**U. 12–14 imp.; **Lv.**U. 12–14 imp.; **M.**U. 12–14; **Nw.**A. imp.; **O.**F. 13–37 imp.; **Rt.** [*C. of:* 14111; *C. as:* 1309°]

9969 **Bulletin. Department** of **Agriculture, Colony** of the **Gambia.** Bathurst. *Bull. Dep. Agric. Colony Gambia* [1929–] L.BM^N. 29; SC.; C.A.; **Rt.** 29.

9970 **Bulletin. Department** of **Agriculture, Cyprus.** *Bull. Dep. Agric. Cyprus.*

    A. Entomological series [1929–] L.BM^N. 29–39; EB.; SC.; C.A.; **O.**RH. 29–39; **Rt.** 29–37.

    B. Horticultural series [1932–] L.BM^N. 32–33; P. 32–39; C.A.; **O.**RH. 29–39; **Rt.** 32–39.

    C. Mycological series [1933–] L.BM^N. 33; P.; C.A.; **O.**RH. 33; **Rt.** 33.

9971 **Bulletin** of the **Department** of **Agriculture** of the **Dominion** of **Canada.** Ottawa. *Bull. Dep. Agric. Dom. Can.* [1922–] L.AM.; EB. (ent.) 22–33; K.; P. 22–35 imp.; **Abd.**U.; **Bm.**P.; **Br.**A. 22–33 imp.; C.A. 25–; **Db.**; E.B.; **G.**U.; **Ld.**U. 22–34 imp.; U. 30–; **O.**G. 22–23 imp.; R.; **Rt.** 22–25.

9972 **Bulletin** of the **Department** of **Agriculture, Federated Malay States.** Kuala Lumpur. *Bull. Dep. Agric. F.M.S.* [1909–22] L.AM.; BM. 11–12; BM^N. imp.; EB.; K.; MY. imp.; P.; C.A.; P.; **Rt.**; **Y.** [*C. as:* 9999]

9973 **Bulletin** of the **Department** of **Agriculture, Fiji.** *Bull. Dep. Agric. Fiji* [1911–] L.BM^N. 12–; EB. (ent.) 12–; C.A. imp.; **O.**F. 42– imp.; **Rt.** 11–26: 46–; **Y.**

    Bulletin. Department of **Agriculture** and **Fisheries, Travancore.** *See* 10011.

    Bulletin of the **Department** of **Agriculture** and **Forestry, Union** of **South Africa.** *See* 10012.

    Bulletin. Department of **Agriculture** and **Forests, Sudan.** *See* 10014.

    Bulletin. Department of **Agriculture, Gambia.** *See* 9969.

9974 **Bulletin. Department** of **Agriculture, Gold Coast Colony.** Accra. *Bull. Dep. Agric. Gold Cst* [1925–38] L.AM.; BM^N. 26–38 imp.; EB.; K. imp.; MO. 28–38; P. 26–38; SC.; U. 28–38; **Br.**U. 27–38; C.A. 26–38; **E.**U. 27–30 imp.; **G.**U. 27–38 imp.; **O.**R. 27–33; RH. 27–38; **M.**U. 26–38; **Rt.**

    Bulletin. Department of **Agriculture** and **Horticulture, University** of **Bristol.** *See* 10015.

    Bulletin of the **Department** of **Agriculture** for **Ireland.** *See* 10018.

9975 Bulletin of the **Department** of **Agriculture, Jamaica.** *Bull. Dep. Agric. Jamaica* [1903–15: 44–57] **L.**AM. 03–27 imp.; BM. 07–11; BM^N.; EB. 13–15: 44–57; HS. 03–15; K.; MY. 52–57 imp.; P. 03–15: 49–57; **Abd.**S. 49–57; **Br.**A. 49–57 imp.; **E.**B. 03–08 imp.; **G.**U. 07–08; **O.**RE. 44–57; **Rt.**; **Y.** [*C. of:* 9596; *Suspended* 1916–33; > 10074, 1934–43; *C. as:* 11120]

9976 Bulletin. Department of **Agriculture, Kenya Colony.** Nairobi. *Bull. Dep. Agric. Kenya* [1921–] **L.**AM.; BM^N. 21–35; EB. (ent.) 21–34; K. 21–33 imp.; P. 21–35; SC.; **C.**A.; **Lv.**U. 30–35 imp.; **O.**F. 31–35; R. 31; **Rt.** [*C. of:* 9958]

9977 Bulletin. Department of **Agriculture, Kenya. Division** of **Entomology.** Nairobi. *Bull. Dep. Agric. Kenya Div. Ent.* **Rt.** 25–35 imp. [*C. of:* 9959]

Bulletin of the **Department** of **Agriculture** and **Lands, Southern Rhodesia.** *See* 10016.

Bulletin. Department of **Agriculture, Leeds University.** *See* 12522.

9978 Bulletin. Department of **Agriculture, Mauritius.** Reduit. *Bull. Dep. Agric. Maurit.* [1914–] **L.**AM.; BM.; BM^N. 16–49 imp.; EB. (ent.); K.; P. imp.; **Abs.**N.; **Bm.**U. (sci.) 32–34; **Br.**U. 47– imp.; **C.**A.; **O.**RE. 37– imp.; RH.; **Rt.**; **Y.**

9979 Bulletin of the **Department** of **Agriculture, Mozambique.** Lourenço Marques. *Bull. Dep. Agric. Mozamb.* **L.**K. 10–11.

9980 Bulletin. Department of **Agriculture, Mysore State.** Bangalore. *Bull. Dep. Agric. Mysore* [1902–] **L.**BM. 02; **C.**A. 09–.
    Agricultural Series [1952–].
    Botanical Series [1952–] **C.**A.; **Y.**
    Chemistry Series [1955–] **C.**A.; **Y.**
    Entomological Series [1911–] **L.**EB.; P. 18–34; **C.**A.; **Y.**
    Mycological Series [1910–] **L.**K. 10.

9981 Bulletin. Department of **Agriculture, Natal.** Pietermaritzburg. *Bull. Dep. Agric. Natal* [1902–10] **L.**EB. imp.; K. 02–06 imp.

9982 Bulletin. Department of **Agriculture, New Guinea.** Rabaul. *Bull. Dep. Agric. New Guinea* [1931–] **C.**A. 31–34; **Rt.** 34.

9983 Bulletin. Department of **Agriculture, New Zealand.** Wellington. *Bull. Dep. Agric. N.Z.* [1909–] **L.**BM^N.; EB. (ent.) 13–; K. 10–12 imp.; P. 13– imp.; **C.**A. imp.; **O.**G. 46; **Rt.** 09–24: 47– imp.; **Y.**

9984 Bulletin. Department of **Agriculture, New Zealand. Chemistry Division.** Wellington. *Bull. Dep. Agric. N.Z. Chem. Div.* [1906–07] **L.**K. imp.; P. 06. [*C. in:* 9983]

9985 Bulletin. Department of **Agriculture, New Zealand. Dairy Division.** Wellington. *Bull. Dep. Agric. N.Z. Dairy Div.* [1900–09] **L.**AM.; **O.**RH. 08–09. [*C. in:* 9983]

9986 Bulletin. Department of **Agriculture, New Zealand. Division** of **Biology** and **Horticulture.** Wellington. *Bull. Dep. Agric. N.Z. Div. Biol. Hort.* [1904–09] **L.**AM.; BM^N.; K. [*C. in:* 9983]

9987 Bulletin. Department of **Agriculture, New Zealand. Division** of **Veterinary Science.** Wellington. *Bull. Dep. Agric. N.Z. Div. vet. Sci.* [1903–09] **L.**AM. [*C. in:* 9983]

Bulletin. Department of **Agriculture, Nigeria.** *See* 9242.

9988 Bulletin of the **Department** of **Agriculture, Northern Rhodesia.** Lusaka. *Bull. Dep. Agric. Nth. Rhod.* [1950–] **C.**A.

9989 Bulletin of the **Department** of **Agriculture, North-West Territories.** *Bull. Dep. Agric. N.W. Terr.* **L.**BM. 03–05.

9990 Bulletin. Department of **Agriculture, Nova Scotia.** Halifax. *Bull. Dep. Agric. Nova Scotia* [1912–] **L.**BM^N. 17–38: 40–44 imp.; EB. (ent.) 13–33; SC. 13–.

9991 Bulletin. Department of **Agriculture, Nyasaland (Protectorate).** Zomba. *Bull. Dep. Agric. Nyasald (Protect.)* [1918–] **L.**BM.; BM^N. 18–34 imp.; EB. (ent.) 18–32; P. 32–36 imp.; SC. 23–36; **Bm.**U. 30: 32–34; **C.**A. 26–; **O.**RH. 32–; **Rt.** 24–.

9992 Bulletin of the **Department** of **Agriculture, Orange River Colony.** Bloemfontein. *Bull. Dep. Agric. Orange Riv. Colony* **L.**BM. 05–08; EB. (ent.) 10–.

9993 Bulletin of the **Department** of **Agriculture** of the **Province** of **Saskatchewan.** Regina. *Bull. Dep. Agric. Prov. Saskatch.* [1906–] **L.**AM.; P. 09– imp.; SC. 24–; **Rt.** 14–20.

9994 Bulletin of the **Department** of **Agriculture, Punjab.** Lahore. *Bull. Dep. Agric. Punjab* [1896–10] **L.**BM. 07–10; **E.**A. 07: 10 imp.; **O.**B. 07–12; **Rt.**

9995 Bulletin of the **Department** of **Agriculture, Quebec.** *Bull. Dep. Agric. Queb.* [1899–] **L.**EB. (ent.) 16–; SC. 17–.

9996 Bulletin. Department of **Agriculture, Queensland.** Brisbane. *Bull. Dep. Agric. Qd* [1887–] **L.**BM^N. 91–96 imp.; EB. (ent.) 24–; **Rt.** 91–96.

Bulletin. Department of **Agriculture** and **Rural Reconstruction, Newfoundland.** *See* 10017.

Bulletin. Department of **Agriculture, Seychelles.** *See* 9950.

9997 Bulletin of the **Department** of **Agriculture** of **South Australia.** Adelaide. *Bull. Dep. Agric. S. Aust.* [1905–] **L.**AM.; BM^N. 28–40 imp.; EB. (ent.) 07–; SC. 24–; **Abs.**N. 10–19 imp.; **Br.**A. 15–40 imp.; **Cr.**P. 10– imp.; **Ld.**U. 12–40 imp.; **Nw.**A. 12–28 imp.; **Rt.** 24–34 imp.

9998 Bulletin of the **Department** of **Agriculture, Southern Provinces** of **Nigeria.** *Bull. Dep. Agric. Sth. Prov. Nigeria* **L.**K.

Bulletin. Department of **Agriculture, Southern Rhodesia.** *See* 10016.

9999 Bulletin. Department of **Agriculture, Straits Settlements** and **F.M.S.** Kuala Lumpur. *Bull. Dep. Agric. Straits Settl. & F.M.S.* [1923–?] **L.**AM.; BM^N. 23–27; EB. 23–26; K. 23–26; MY. 23–26: (gen.) 30–38; P. (gen.) 30–40: (sci.) 30–39; **C.**A.; P.; **Rt.** 23–27; **Y.** [*C. of:* 9972; *C. as:* 11116^a]

Bulletin. Department of **Agriculture, Tasmania.** *See* 9243.

Bulletin of the **Department** of **Agriculture** and **Technical Instruction** for **Ireland.** *See* 10018.

10000 Bulletin. Department of **Agriculture, Thailand.** Bangkok. *Bull. Dep. Agric. Thailand* [1950–] **Y.**

10001 Bulletin. Department of **Agriculture, Transvaal.** Pretoria. *Bull. Dep. Agric. Transv.*
    A. Horticulture.
    B. Irrigation.
    C. Publications.
    D. Veterinary. **L.**AM.

Bulletin. Department of **Agriculture, Travancore.** *See* 10011.

10002 **Bulletin** of the **Department** of **Agriculture, Trinidad** and **Tobago.** Port-of-Spain. *Bull. Dep. Agric. Trin. Tobago* [1909–] **L.**AM. 12–27; BM. 11–12; BM^N. 11–23: 50–; EB. 09–27: 52–; K.; MY. 11–28: 52– imp.; P. 10–27; TP. 09–10; Z. 13–22 imp.; **Abs.**N. 16–; **Db.** 14–; **Rt.** 09–27: 52–; **Y.**   [*C. of:* 11134]

    Bulletin. Department of **Agriculture, Union** of **S. Africa.**   *See* 10012.

10003 **Bulletin. Department** of **Agriculture, United Provinces** of **Agra** and **Oudh.** Allahabad. *Bull. Dep. Agric. Unit. Prov. Agra Oudh* [1895–16: 21–] **L.**AM.; BM. 95–16; K. 95–16 imp.; P. 95–16; **Abs.**N. 12–16; **C.**A. (genet.) 35–; **E.**A. 11–16 imp.; **O.**B.; **Rt.** 95–16; **Y.**

10004 **Bulletin. Department** of **Agriculture, United Provinces** of **Agra** and **Oudh. Fruit Series.** Allahabad. *Bull. Dep. Agric. Unit. Prov. Agra Oudh Fruit Ser.* [1933–] **L.**BM.; **C.**A. 35–; **O.**B.

    Bulletin. Department of **Agriculture, University** of **Bristol.**   *See* 10015.

    Bulletin. Department of **Agriculture, University** of **Leeds.**   *See* 12522.

10005 **Bulletin** of the **Department** of **Agriculture, University** (College) of **Reading.** *Bull. Dep. Agric. Univ. Reading* [1907–23] **L.**AM.; BM.; P.; SC.; **C.**A.; **Ld.**U.; **Nw.**A. imp.; **R.**D.; **Rt.** imp.   [*C. as:* 10208]

10006 **Bulletin. Department** of **Agriculture, Uttar Pradesh.** Allahabad. *Bull. Dep. Agric. Uttar Pradesh* **Rt.** 53.

10007 **Bulletin** of the **Department** of **Agriculture, Victoria.** Melbourne. *Bull. Dep. Agric. Vict.* [1888–91: 02–] **L.**AM.; BM. 02–10; BM^N. 02–04 imp.; P. 88–91: 02–05; SC. 08–; **Rt.** 88–29 imp.

10008 **Bulletin. Department** of **Agriculture, Western Australia.** Perth. *Bull. Dep. Agric. West. Aust.* [1908–31] **L.**AM.; BM^N. 22–24 imp.; EB. (ent.) 12–26; SC. 24–31; **Rt.** 17–25.

10009 **Bulletin. Department** of **Agriculture, Zanzibar.** *Bull. Dep. Agric. Zanzibar* **L.**TD. 58–; TP.; **O.**RE. 52– imp.

10011 **Bulletin. Department** of **Agriculture** and **Fisheries.** Travancore. *Bull. Dep. Agric. Fish., Travancore.*

10011^a **Bulletin. Department** of **Agriculture, Fisheries** and **Forestry, Hong Kong.** *Bull. Dep. Agric. Fish. For. Hong Kong* **Y.**

10012 **Bulletin** of the **Department** of **Agriculture** and **Forestry, Union** of **South Africa.** Pretoria. *Bull. Dep. Agric. For. Un. S. Afr.* [1911–] **L.**AM.; BM^N. 12– imp.; EB. (ent.) 14–; K. 16– imp.; L. 57–; MY. 21– imp.; P. imp.; U. 17–27; **Br.**A. 22–54 imp.; **C.**A. 25–; **E.**B. 27–; U. 26–27; **Ld.**U. 27– imp.; **Lv.**U. 16– imp.; **Nw.**A. 16– imp.; **O.**RE. 38– imp.; **Rt.** 16–; **Y.**

10013 **Bulletin** of the **Department** of **Agriculture** and **Forests, Palestine.** Jerusalem. *Bull. Dep. Agric. Forests Palest.* **O.**F. 34.

10014 **Bulletin. Department** of **Agriculture** and **Forests, Sudan.** Wad Medani. *Bull. Dep. Agric. Forests Sudan* **O.**F. 41: 49–55*; RE. 51–55.   [*C. as:* 11122]

10015 **Bulletin. Department** of **Agriculture** and **Horticulture, University** of **Bristol.** *Bull. Dep. Agric.*

Hort. Univ. Bristol [1926–] **L.**SC.; **Bm.**U. 28–30 imp.; **Br.**A. 26–38 imp.; U.; **C.**A.; **Rt.** 26–39 imp.

10016 **Bulletin** of the **Department** of **Agriculture** and **Lands, Southern Rhodesia.** Salisbury. *Bull. Dep. Agric. Lds Sth Rhod.* **L.**EB. (ent.) 09–; **O.**F. 29– imp.; **Rt.** 14–25 imp.; **Y.**

    Bulletin. Department of **Agriculture** and **Markets, New York State.**   *See* 11302.

10017 **Bulletin. Department** of **Agriculture** and **Rural Reconstruction, Newfoundland.** St. John's. *Bull. Dep. Agric. rur. Reconstr. Newfoundld* [1934–] **L.**BM.

10018 **Bulletin** of the **Department** of **Agriculture** and **Technical Instruction** for **Ireland.** Dublin. *Bull. Dep. Agric. tech. Instruct. Ire.* [1901–] **L.**AM.; BM. 09; SC.; **Db.**; **Ld.**U.; **Rt.** 01–08 imp.

    Bulletin. Department of **Agriculture, United Provinces** of **Agra** and **Oudh.**   *See* 10003.

10019 **Bulletin. Department** of **Anthropology, India.** Calcutta, Delhi. *Bull. Dep. Anthrop. India* [1952–] **L.**AN.; BM.; **Db.** 53–.

10019° **Bulletin. Department** of **Anthropology, University** of **Bihar.** Ranchi. *Bull. Dep. Anthrop. Univ. Bihar* [1957–] **L.**AN.

10020 **Bulletin. Department** of **Archaeology** and **Anthropology, Taiwan University.** Taipei. *Bull. Dep. Archaeol. Anthrop. Taiwan Univ.* [1953–] **L.**AN.

10020° **Bulletin** of the **Department** of **Biology, Korea University.** Seoul. *Bull. Dep. Biol. Korea Univ.* [1958–] **L.**BM^N. 59–.

10021 **Bulletin. Department** of **Biology, Mineral, Metal** and **By-Product Company.** Denver. *Bull. Dep. Biol. Miner. Metal By-Prod. Co.* **L.**EB. 19–20.

10022 **Bulletin** of the **Department** of **Biology. Yenching University.** Peking. *Bull. Dep. Biol. Yenching Univ.* [1930] **L.**BM^N.; EB.; **Lv.**U.   [*C. in:* 37299]

10023 **Bulletin. Department** of **Ceramic Engineering, University** of **Illinois.** Urbana. *Bull. Dep. Ceram. Engng Univ. Ill.* [1907–14] **L.**BM.; P.; **M.**U. imp.; **O.**B. [*C. of:* 51156]

10024 **Bulletin. Department** of **Chemistry, South Australia.** Adelaide. *Bull. Dep. Chem. S. Aust.* [1916–17] **L.**BM^N. imp.; C.; P.; UC.; **Bm.**U.; **M.**U. imp.

10025 **Bulletin. Department** of **Civil Engineering, King's College Newcastle-upon-Tyne.** Newcastle. *Bull. Dep. civ. Engng King's Coll. Newcastle* [1954–] **L.**P.; **Y.**

10026 **Bulletin. Department** of **Electrical Engineering, North-eastern University.** Boston, Mass. *Bull. Dep. elect. Engng N.East. Univ.* **L.**SC. 40–.

10027 **Bulletin. Department** of **Engineering Research, North Carolina State College** of **Agriculture** and **Engineering.** Raleigh. *Bull. Dep. Engng Res. N. Carol. St. Coll. Agric. Engng* [1946–] **L.**P.; **Y.**   [*C. of:* 11334]

10028 **Bulletin. Department** of **Engineering Research, Pennsylvania State** (College) **University.** State College. *Bull. Dep. Engng Res. Pa St. Univ.* [1949–56] **L.**P. 53–56; **Y.**   [*C. of:* 11491; *C. as:* 18157]

10029 **Bulletin. Department** of **Engineering Research, University** of **Michigan.** Ann Arbor. *Bull. Dep. Engng Res. Univ. Mich.* [1926–42] **L.**BM.; P.; **Abd.**U. 27–42; **Abs.**N.; **Bm.**U.; **C.**UL.; **Dn.**U. imp.; **E.**U.; **G.**U.; **Ld.**U.; **M.**T. 28–42; U.; **O.**R.; **Y.**   [*C. of:* 10176]

10030 **Bulletin.** **Department** of **Entomology, Kansas State University.** Lawrence. *Bull. Dep. Ent. Kans. St. Univ.* **L.**EB. 92–17*.

10031 **Bulletin.** **Department** of **Entomology, Nebraska State University.** Lincoln. *Bull. Dep. Ent. Neb. St. Univ.*

10032 **Bulletin.** **Department** of **Fish** and **Game, State** of **California.** Sacramento. *Bull. Dep. Fish Game St. Calif.* [1913–] **L**o.

10033 **Bulletin.** **Department** of **Fisheries, Baroda State.** *Bull. Dep. Fish. Baroda* **L.**BM^N. 43–49.

10034 **Bulletin** of the **Department** of **Fisheries, Bengal.** Calcutta. *Bull. Dep. Fish Beng.* [1913–24] **L.**BM.; SC.; Z. 14–21 imp.; **Abd.**M. 14–24 imp.; **Abs.**N. 13–15; **E.**A. 13–21 imp.; **Lv.**U. 14–24 imp.; **O.**B. 13–23 imp.; **Pl.**M. 14–24 imp.

10035 **Bulletin.** **Department** of **Fisheries, Israel.** *Bull. Dep. Fish. Israel*

10036 **Bulletin.** **Department** of **Forestry, British North Borneo.** Sandakan. *Bull. Dep. For. Br. N. Borneo* [1916–17] **L.**P.; SC.; **O.**F.

10037 **Bulletin** of the **Department** of **Forestry, Canada.** *Bull. Dep. For. Can.* [1960–] **L.**BM.; P.; **E.**B.; **O.**F.; **Rt.** [*C. of:* 10293]

10038 **Bulletin.** **Department** of **Forestry, Pennsylvania.** Harrisburg. *Bull. Dep. For. Pa* [1902–] **L.**P. 02–17 imp.; **O.**F. 19– imp.

10038^c **Bulletin.** **Department** of **Forestry. Stephen F. Austen State College, Texas.** *Bull. Dep. For. Stephen F. Austen St. Coll. Tex.* [1957–] **O.**F.

10039 **Bulletin.** **Department** of **Forestry, University** of **Adelaide.** *Bull. Dep. For. Univ. Adelaide* [1918–22] **E.**R. [*C. as:* 12643]

10040 **Bulletin.** **Department** of **Forestry** (*formerly* **Forests**), **Union** of **South Africa.** Cape Town. *Bull. Dep. For. Un. S. Afr.* [1920–] **L.**BM. 23–; BM^N. 53–; K.; **O.**F.; **Y.**

10041 **Bulletin.** **Department** of **Geological Surveys, Northern Rhodesia.** Lusaka. *Bull. Dep. geol. Surv. Nth. Rhod.* [1955–] **L.**MI.; **C.**S.

Bulletin. **Department** of **Geology** and **Mineral Industries, Oregon.** *See* 11450.

10042 **Bulletin.** **Department** of **Geology, Santa Barbara Museum** of **Natural History.** Santa Barbara. *Bull. Dep. Geol. S Barbara Mus. nat. Hist.* **L.**BM^N. 57–.

10043 **Bulletin.** **Department** of **Geology, University** of **Alberta.** Edmonton. *Bull. Dep. Geol. Univ. Alberta* [1924] **L.**BM^N.; SC.; **Rt.**

Bulletin of the **Department** of **Geology.** **University** of **California.** *See* 55582.

10044 **Bulletin** of the **Department** of **Health, Australia.** Melbourne. *Bull. Dep. Hlth Aust.* [1923–] **Lv.**U. [*C. of:* 11563]

10045 **Bulletin** of the **Department** of **Health, Kentucky.** Louisville. *Bull. Dep. Hlth Ky* [1934–] **L.**TD. 34–47 imp. [*C. of:* 12283]

10046 **Bulletin.** **Department** of **Health** and **Welfare, British Columbia.** Victoria. *Bull. Dep. Hlth Welf. Br. Columb.* [1936–49] [*C. as:* 21956]

10047 **Bulletin** of the **Department** of **Heating** and **Ventilating Engineering.** **University College, Lon-** **don.** *Bull. Dep. Heat. Vent. Engng Univ. Coll. Lond.* [1918–23] **L.**P.; SC.; U.; UC.; **Br.**U.

10048 **Bulletin** of the **Department** of **Industrial Research, Pittsburgh University.** *Bull. Dep. ind. Res. Pittsburgh Univ.* [1912] **L.**P. [*C. as:* 49969]

10049 **Bulletin.** **Department** of **Industries, Bengal.** Calcutta. *Bull. Dep. Inds Beng.* [1919–] **L.**P. 21–47 imp.

10050 **Bulletin** of the **Department** of **Industries, Bihar** and **Orissa.** Patna. *Bull. Dep. Inds Bihar Orissa* **L.**P. 27–33.

10051 **Bulletin** of the **Department** of **Industries, Bombay.** *Bull. Dep. Inds Bombay* [1920–] **L.**BM.; P. 20–44 imp.; **Rt.** 20–26.

10052 **Bulletin.** **Department** of **Industries** and **Commerce, United Provinces** of **Agra** and **Oudh.** Allahabad. *Bull. Dep. Inds Comm. Unit. Prov. Agra Oudh* **L.**P. 40–48; **Rt.** 27.

10053 **Bulletin** of the **Department** of **Industries, Hyderabad.** *Bull. Dep. Inds Hyderabad* **L.**P. 20–26: 30–32.

10054 **Bulletin** of the **Department** of **Industries, Madras.** *Bull. Dep. Inds Madras* [1918–] **L.**P. 29–33; SC.

10055 **Bulletin** of the **Department** of **Industries, South Australia.** Adelaide. *Bull. Dep. Inds S. Aust.* **Bm.**U. 12–.

10056 **Bulletin** of the **Department** of **Land Records** and **Agriculture, Bengal.** Calcutta. *Bull. Dep. Ld Rec. Agric. Beng.* [1895–] **L.**BM. 12–; BM^N. 01–29 imp.; K. 95–34 imp.; P. 95–05; **O.**B. 95–05: 12–21 imp. [*For Agricultural series See* 9260]

10057 **Bulletin** of the **Department** of **Land Records** and **Agriculture, Bombay.** Bombay. *Bull. Dep. Ld Rec. Agric. Bombay* [1884–] **L.**BM. 09–; P. 85–38 imp.; SC. 08–; **Bm.**U. 10–16; **C.**A. 09–; **E.**U. 25–; **M.**U. 04–18 imp.; **O.**I. 21–39; **Rt.** 00–40.

10058 **Bulletin** of the **Department** of **Land Records** and **Agriculture, Madras.** Madras. *Bull. Dep. Ld Rec. Agric. Madras* [1889–] **L.**BM.; BM^N. 01–29 imp.; EB. (ent.) 13–28; K. 09–29 imp.; P. imp.; SC. 23–; **Abs.**N. 12–21; **C.**A. 17–; **M.**U. 89–18 imp.; **O.**B. 89–23 imp.; **Rt.** 89–29.

10059 **Bulletin.** **Department** of **Lands** and **Forests, Nova Scotia.** Halifax. *Bull. Dep. Lds Forests Nova Scotia* [1951–] **O.**F. imp.

10060 **Bulletin.** **Department** of **Lands** and **Forests.** Ottawa. **Silviculture Series.** *Bull. Dep. Lds Forests, Ottawa Silvic. Ser.* [1960–] **O.**F.

10061 **Bulletin** of the **Department** of **Mathematics** of **Brown University.** Providence. *Bull. Dep. Math. Brown Univ.* **L.**BM. 22.

10062 **Bulletin.** **Department** of **Mines** (*afterwards* and **Petroleum Resources**), **British Columbia.** Victoria. *Bull. Dep. Mines Petrol. Resour. Br. Columb.* [1940–] **L.**BM.; BM^N.; GL.; MI.; **Bm.**P.; **Y.** [*See also:* 9666]

10063 **Bulletin.** **Department** of **Mines, Federation** of **Malaya.** Kuala Lumpur. *Bull. Dep. Mines Fed. Malaya* [1957–] **L.**BM.; **O.**R.

Bulletin. **Department** of **Mines, Geological Survey Division, Union** of **South Africa.** *See* 10353.

10064 **Bulletin** of the **Department** of **Mines** and **Mineral Resources, Western Australia.** Perth. *Bull. Dep. Mines Miner. Resour. West. Aust.* [1945–] **L.**MI.

10065 **Bulletin. Department** of **Mines, Mines Branch, Canada.** Ottawa. *Bull. Dep. Mines, Mines Brch Can.* [1909-] **L.**BM.; GL.; GM.; MT. 19- imp.; P. 09-21; UC. 10- imp.; **Abd.**U. 09-20; **Abs.**N. imp.; **Bl.**U. 09-20 imp.; **Bm.**P. 09-21 imp.; U. 09-21; **Br.**U. 09-18 imp.; **Cr.**U. 18- imp.; **Dn.**U. 10-21 imp.; **E.**C. 15-20 imp.; F. 09-21 imp.; R. 10- imp.; U. 10-21 imp.; **G.**U. 10-; **Lv.**P. 13- imp.; U. 10- imp.; **M.**U. 09-21 imp.; **Nw.**A. 21- imp.; **O.**R. 09-21; **Pl.**M. 22- imp.; **Sa.** 09-21; **Sh.**M. 10-21.

10066 **Bulletin. Department** of **Mines** and **Resources, Newfoundland.** *Bull. Dep. Mines Resour. Newfoundld* [1954-] **L.**BM^N. 54-; MI.

10067 **Bulletin. Department** of **Mines, Southern Rhodesia.** Salisbury. *Bull. Dep. Mines Sth. Rhod.* **L.**MI. 47-.

10068 **Bulletin. Department** of **Mines, Union** of **South Africa. Geological Series.** Pretoria. *Bull. Dep. Mines Un. S. Afr. Geol. Ser.* [1934-] **L.**BM.; GL.; P.; **Bm.**U.; **C.**S.; **E.**D.; R. imp.; **O.**G.; R.

10069 **Bulletin. Department** of **Mining** and **Metallurgy, State College** of **Washington.** Pullman, Wash. *Bull. Dep. Min. Metall. St. Coll. Wash.* [1934-] **L.**P. 34-45; SC. 34-45.

Bulletin. Department of **Neurology, Harvard University Medical School.** *See* 10099.

10070 **Bulletin** of the **Department** of **Psychology, Wyoming University.** Laramie. *Bull. Dep. Psychol. Wyo. Univ.*

Bulletin. Department of **Public Works, California. Division** of **Engineering** and **Irrigation.** *See* 9690.

10071 **Bulletin. Department** of **Public Works. Division** of **Water Rights.** Sacramento. *Bull. Dep. publ. Wks Sacramento Div. Wat. Rights*

10072 **Bulletin. Department** of **Rural Electrification. Foochow Electric Company.** *Bull. Dep. rur. Elect. Foochow elect. Co.* **C.**A. 30-34.

10073 **Bulletin. Department** of **Science** and **Agriculture, Barbados.** *Bull. Dep. Sci. Agric. Barbados* **L.**BM^N. 46- imp.; EB. (ent.) 44-; **O.**G. 47; RH. 44-; **Rt.** 45-; **Y.**

10074 **Bulletin** of the **Department** of **Science** and **Agriculture, Jamaica.** Kingston. *Bull. Dep. Sci. Agric. Jamaica* [1934-43] **L.**AM.; BM^N. imp.; EB.; K.; P. 34-41; SC.; **C.**A.; **O.**F. 38-43; RE.; **Rt.** [*C. of:* and *Rec. as:* 9975]

10075 **Bulletin. Department** of **Scientific** and **Industrial Research.** London. *Bull. Dep. scient. ind. Res.* [1918-22] **L.**BM.; BM^N.; P.; SC.; **Bm.**P.; **C.**UL.; **E.**R.; **Lv.**P.; **O.**R. imp.

Bulletin. Department of **Scientific** and **Industrial Research. Forest Products Research.** *See* 19977.

Bulletin. Department of **Scientific** and **Industrial Research, New Zealand.** *See* 11315.

Bulletin. Department of **Soil** and **Land Use Survey, Gold Coast.** *See* 10404.

10076 **Bulletin** of the **Department** of **State Medicine** and **Public Health, Western Australia.** Perth. *Bull. Dep. St. Med. publ. Hlth West. Aust.* **L.**BM. 08-09.

10077 **Bulletin. Department** of **Veterinary Science** and **Animal Husbandry.** Dar-es-Salaam. *Bull. Dep. vet. Sci. Anim. Husb., Dar-es-Salaam* Animal Husbandry Series [1936-] **C.**A.

10078 **Bulletin** of the **Department** of **Zoology, Panjab University.** Lahore. *Bull. Dep. Zool. Panjab Univ.* [1931-] **L.**BM.; BM^N.; **E.**R. 31-39; **Nw.**A. 31-35; **Pl.**M. 31-39; **Y.**

10079 **Bulletin. Derbyshire Ornithological Society.** *Bull. Derbysh. orn. Soc.* **O.**OR 55 imp.: 58.

10080 **Bulletin. Detroit College** of **Medicine** and **Surgery.** Detroit, Mich. *Bull. Detroit Coll. Med. Surg.*

Bulletin. Development Department, Portland Cement Association. Chicago. *See* 11595.

10081 **Bulletin. Development** and **Welfare** in the **West Indies.** *Bull. Dev. Welf. W. Indies* [1942-] **L.**BM.; BM^N. 45-50 imp.; SC.; **O.**G. 49-; **Pl.**M. (fish.) 42-45 imp.

10082 **Bulletin** du **développement agricole** et **industriel** des **Îles Seychelles.** Victoria. *Bull. Dév. agric. ind. Îles Seychelles* [1931] **L.**BM.; BM^N.; EB.; P.; SC.; **C.**A.; **Rt.** [*C. of:* 9950]

10083 **Bulletin. Dight Institute** of the **University** of **Minnesota.** Minneapolis. *Bull. Dight Inst. Univ. Minn.* [1943-] **L.**BM.; **C.**UL.; **O.**R.; **Y.**

Bulletin. Direction de l'**agriculture,** de l'**élevage** et des **forêts, Section technique** d'**agriculture tropicale. Série technologique.** *See* 11740.

10084 **Bulletin** de la **Direction fédérale** des **mines** et de la **géologie, Afrique occidentale française.** Dakar. *Bull. Dir. féd. Mines Géol. Afr. occid. fr.* [1956-] **L.**BM.; BM^N.; GL.; MI. [*C. of:* 10088]

10085 **Bulletin. Direction générale** de l'**agriculture,** etc. Tunis. *Bull. Dir. gén. Agric. Tunis* **C.**A. 26-35*. [*C. as:* 11748]

10086 **Bulletin. Direction** de l'**hydraulique agricole.** Paris. *Bull. Dir. Hydraul. agric.* **L.**P. 85-02*. [*C. as:* 2714]

10087 **Bulletin** de la **Direction** des **mines** et de la **géologie** de l'**Afrique equatoriale française.** Le Caire. *Bull. Dir. Mines Géol. Afr. equat. fr.* [1952-59] **L.**BM^N.; GL.; MI.; **G.**U.; **Y.** [*C. of:* 11768; *C. as:* 10585]

10088 **Bulletin** de la **Direction** des **mines** et de la **géologie, Afrique occidentale française.** Dakar. *Bull. Dir. Mines Géol. Afr. occid. fr.* **L.**BM. 50-55*; BM^N.; GL.; MI. [*C. of:* 11769; *C. as:* 10084]

10089 **Bulletin. Direction** des **mines** et de la **géologie, Territoire** du **Cameroun.** Paris. *Bull. Dir. Mines Géol. Terr. Cameroun* [1953-] **L.**BM^N.; MI.; **Y.** [*C. of:* 11770]

10090 **Bulletin. Direction** de la **production agricole** de l'**Algérie.** Alger. *Bull. Dir. Prod. agric. Algér.*

10091 **Bulletin. Directorate-General** of **Agriculture, Iraq.** Baghdad. *Bull. Dir.-gen. Agric. Iraq* **L.**BM. 44-; EB. 43-44; **Rt.** 44.

10092 **Bulletin. Disaster Prevention Research Institute, Kyoto University.** *Bull. Disast. Prev. Res. Inst., Kyoto Univ.* [1951-] **E.**R.; **Y.**

Bulletin of the **District Geological Research Administration** in **Ucraina.** *See* 56757.

10093 **Bulletin. Division** of **Agriculture** and **Chemistry, Hawaiian Sugar Planters' Association Experiment Station.** Honolulu. *Bull. Div. Agric. Chem. Hawaiian Sug. Plrs' Ass. Exp. Stn* [1905-45] **L.**K.; P. 14-45; SC. 23-45; **C.**A.; UL.; **M.**P. 20-45; **Rt.**

10094 **Bulletin. Division of Agrostology. United States Department** of **Agriculture.** Washington. *Bull. Div. Agrost. U.S. Dep. Agric.* [1895–01] **L.**BM.; BM^N. 95–00 imp ; K.; P.; SC.; **Bm.**P. 97–00 imp.; U. 00–01 imp.; **Rt.** 97– imp.

    Bulletin. Division of Biology and **Horticulture, Department** of **Agriculture, New Zealand.** *See* 9986.

10095 **Bulletin. Division of Botany. United States Department** of **Agriculture.** Washington. *Bull. Div. Bot. U.S. Dep. Agric.* [1886–01] **L.**AM.; BM.; BM^N. 87–01 imp.; K.; L. 87–01 imp.; P. imp.; SC. 87–01; **Bm.**U. imp.; E.B. imp.; R. 98–01; **G.**M. 88–01 imp.; **Lv.**P. 98: 01; **Rt.** imp.

    Bulletin. Division of Engineering and **Irrigation, California Department** of **Public Works.** *See* 9690.

    Bulletin. Division of Entomology, Board of **Commissioners** of **Agriculture** and **Forestry, Hawaii.** *See* 9589.

    Bulletin. Division of Entomology, Bureau of **Sugar Experiment Stations, Queensland.** *See* 9679.

    Bulletin. Division of Entomology, Department of **Agriculture, British East Africa.** *See* 9959.

    Bulletin. Division of Entomology, Department of **Agriculture, Kenya.** *See* 9977.

10096 **Bulletin. Division of Entomology** and **Plant Pathology, Queensland.** Brisbane. *Bull. Div. Ent. Pl. Path. Qd* [1924–] **L.**EB. (ent.); **C.**A.; **Rt.**

    Bulletin. Division of Forestry, Board of **Commissioners** of **Agriculture** and **Forestry, Hawaii.** *See* 9590.

10097 **Bulletin. Division of Forestry. United States Department** of **Agriculture.** Washington. *Bull. Div. For. U.S. Dep. Agric.* [1887–13] **L.**BM.; BM^N. 98–11 imp.; K. 88–13 imp.; P. imp.; SC. 89–13; **Bm.**U. 92–12 imp.; **C.**A. 89–13 imp.; **G.**M. 12–13 imp.; **Ld.**U. 00–04 imp.; **Lv.**P. 92–13 imp.; **O.**F. imp.

    Bulletin. Division of Geodesy, United States Coast and **Geodetic Survey.** *See* 12506.

    Bulletin. Division of Geology, Tennessee. *See* 12382.

10097° **Bulletin. Division of Hydrography, Hawaii.** Honolulu. *Bull. Div. Hydrogr. Hawaii* [1935–] **L.**GM.; **Abs.**U. imp.; **Bl.**U. 40–47; **Bm.**U.; **O.**R.

    Bulletin. Division of Industrial Research, Washington State Institute of **Technology.** *See* 12609.

10098 **Bulletin. Division of Mines** (and **Mining), Department** of **Natural Resources, State** of **California.** Los Angeles, San Francisco. *Bull. Div. Mines Calif.* [1927–] **L.**BM. 49–; BM^N. 45 ; GM. imp.; MI. imp.; P.; **Y.** [*C. of:* 9696]

10099 **Bulletin. Division of Neurology, Harvard University Medical School.** Boston. *Bull. Div. Neurol. Harv. Univ. med. Sch.* **L.**S. 12–26.

    Bulletin. Division of Pathology, Bureau of **Sugar Experiment Stations, Queensland.** *See* 9680.

10100 **Bulletin. Division of Pathology** and **Physiology, Hawaiian Sugar Planters' Association Experiment Station.** Honolulu. *Bull. Div. Path. Physiol. Hawaiian Sug. Plrs' Ass. Exp. Stn* [1905–12] **L.**BM^N.; EB.; K.; **C.**A.; UL.; **O.**R.; **Rt.** [*C. as:* 10432 Botanical Series]

10101 **Bulletin** of the **Division** of **Plant Breeding** and **Cultivation, Tokai-Kinki National Agricultural Experiment Station.** Tsu-City. *Bull. Div. Pl. Breed. Cult. Tokai-Kinki natn. agric. Exp. Stn* [1954–58] **L.**AM.; MY.; **C.**A.; **Rt.**; **Y.** [*C. as:* 10252]

10102 **Bulletin. Division of Plant Disease Control. Tennessee State Department** of **Agriculture.** Knoxville. *Bull. Div. Pl. Dis. Control Tenn.* [1924–] **L.**EB. 24–31. [*C. of:* 12381]

10102° **Bulletin. Division of Plant Industry, Department** of **Agriculture, Florida.** *Bull. Div. Pl. Ind. Fla* [1961–] **L.**BM^N.; EB.; **C.**A.; **Y.** [*C. of:* 12289]

10103 **Bulletin. Division of Plant Industry, Queensland Department** of **Agriculture** and **Stock.** Brisbane. *Bull. Div. Pl. Ind. Qd* **Y.**

10104 **Bulletin. Division of Pomology. United States Department** of **Agriculture.** Washington. *Bull. Div. Pomol. U.S. Dep. Agric.* [1888–01] **L.**AM.; BM.; K. imp.; P.; SC.; **Bm.**U. 99–01; **Lv.**P.

10105 **Bulletin. Division of Soils. United States Department** of **Agriculture.** Washington. *Bull. Div. Soils U.S. Dep. Agric.* [1895–13] **L.**AM.; BM.; C. 97–13 imp.; K. imp.; P.; SC.; **Abs.**N. 10; **Bm.**U. 98–12 imp.; **G.**M. 12–13 imp.; **Ld.**U. 08–13 imp.; **Lv.**P.; **Nw.**A. 09–13 imp.; **Rt.** imp.

10106 **Bulletin. Division of Statistics. United States Department** of **Agriculture.** Washington. *Bull. Div. Statist. U.S. Dep. Agric.* [1890–13] **L.**AM.; BM.; K. 04–12 imp.; SC. 96–13; **Bm.**U. 01–12 imp.; **G.**M. 12–13 imp.; **Lv.**P. 95–10.

10107 **Bulletin. Division of Surgery, Harvard University Medical School.** Boston. *Bull. Div. Surg. Harv. Univ. med. Sch.* [1905–12] **L.**MD. imp.; S.

10108 **Bulletin. Division of Vegetable Physiology** and **Pathology. United States Department** of **Agriculture.** Washington. *Bull. Div. Veg. Physiol. Path. U.S. Dep. Agric.* [1891–01] **L.**AM.; BM.; BM^N. imp.; K. 91–00; P.; SC.; **Bm.**U. imp.; **E.**B. imp.; **Lv.**P. imp.; **Rt.** imp.

10109 **Bulletin. Division of Veterinary Research, Kenya.** *Bull. Div. vet. Res. Kenya* **Lv.**U. 31– imp.

    Bulletin. Division of Veterinary Science, Department of **Agriculture, New Zealand.** *See* 9987.

    Bulletin. Division of Water Rights, Department of **Public Works, Sacramento.** *See* 10071.

10110 **Bulletin** of the **Division** of **Waters. Illinois Department** of **Public Works.** Chicago. *Bull. Div. Wat. Ill.* **L.**SC. 21–; **Lv.**U. 20–30 imp.

10111 **Bulletin. Division** of **Wood Technology, Forestry Commission, New South Wales.** Sydney. *Bull. Div. Wood Technol. For. Commn N.S.W.* [1942–] **L.**BM.; P. 58–; **Y.**

10112 **Bulletin documentaire. Groupement professionnel** des **fabricants** de **ciment portland artificiel** de **Belgique.** Bruxelles. *Bull. docum. Grpmt prof. Fabr. Cim. Portl. artif. Belg.* **L.**P. 30–.

10113 **Bulletin de documentation. Association internationale** des **fabricants** de **superphosphates.** Paris. *Bull. Docum. Ass. int. Fabr. Superphos.* [1947–] **L.**P.; **Abd.**S. 53–; **Abs.**U. 56–; **Br.**A. 56–; **C.**A. 47– imp.; **Hu.**G. 53–; **Je.**; **O.**RE. (2 yr.); **Y.**

10114 **Bulletin** de **documentation bibliographique. Institut international** de **sécurité** pour la **prévention** des **accidents** du **travail** et des **maladies professionnelles.** Paris. *Bull. Docum. biblphique Inst. int. Sécur. Prév. Accid. Trav.* [1950–] **L.**P. 51–; **Y.**

10115 **Bulletin** de **documentation. Bureau** d'**études industrielles Fernand Courtoy.** Bruxelles. *Bull. Docum. Bur. Étud. ind. Fernand Courtoy* **L.**P.; **Y.**

10116 **Bulletin** de **documentation. Centre** d'**études** et de **recherches** de l'**industrie** des **liants hydrauliques.** Paris. *Bull. Docum. Cent. Étud. Rech. Ind. Liants hydraul.* [1949–] **L.**P. 52–; SC.; **Y.**

10117 **Bulletin** de **documentation. Centre** d'**études** et de **recherches** du **machinisme agricole.** Paris. *Bull. Docum. Cent. Étud. Rech. Mach. agric.* [1950–52] **L.**P. 51–52; SC.; **Sil.** [*C. of:* 10118]

10118 **Bulletin** de **documentation. Centre technique** du **machinisme agricole.** Paris. *Bull. Docum. Cent. tech. Mach. agric.* [1947–49] [*C. as:* 10117]
   Bulletin de **documentation** étrangère technique. Belgrade. *See* 6991ᵃ.

10119 **Bulletin** de **documentation** et d'**information. Syndicat** des **constructeurs français.** Paris. *Bull. Docum. Inf. Synd. Constr. fr.* **Sil.** 46–60*. [*C. as:* Bulletin de documentation technique]

10120 **Bulletin** de **documentation. Institut** d'**hygiène** des **mines, A.S.B.L.** Hasselt. *Bull. Docum. Inst. Hyg. Mines A.S.B.L.* **L.**TD. 52–.
   Bulletin de **documentation. International Superphosphate Manufacturers' Association.** *See* 10113.

10121 **Bulletin** de **documentation médicale. Institut** d'**hygiène** des **mines, A.S.B.L.** Hasselt. *Bull. Docum. méd. Inst. Hyg. Mines A.S.B.L.* [1947–59] **L.**MI.; P. 53–59; **Sh.**S. 55–59. [*C. as:* 47318]
   Bulletin de **documentation** et de **recherches** de l'**industrie** des **liants hydrauliques.** *See* 10116.

10122 **Bulletin** de **documentation** de la **santé publique** et de la **population.** Paris. *Bull. Docum. Santé publ. Pop.* [1935–49] **L.**H. [*C. as:* 42568]
   Bulletin de **documentation scientifique** pour la **médecine,** la **pharmacie** et la **médecine vétérinaire.** Beograd. *See* 6991ʰ.

10123 **Bulletin** de **documentation. Société** de **contrôle** et d'**exploitation** de **transports auxiliaires.** Paris. *Bull. Docum. Soc. Contrôle Exploit. Transp. auxil.* [1949–] **Y.**
   Supplément. **Y.**
   Notice de documentation. **Y.**

10124 **Bulletin** de **documentation** de la **soudure** et des **techniques connexes.** Paris. *Bull. Docum. Soud.* [1943–48] **Y.** [*C. of:* 10980; *C. as:* 6605]
   Bulletin de **documentation technique.** Belgrade. *See* 6991ᵍ.

10125 **Bulletin** de **documentation technique. Centre technique** des **industries** de la **fonderie.** Paris. *Bull. Docum. tech. Cent. tech. Ind. Fond.* **L.**P. 52–.

10126 **Bulletin** de **documentation technique. Institut** d'**hygiène** des **mines, A.S.B.L.** Hasselt. *Bull. Docum. tech. Inst. Hyg. Mines A.S.B.L.* [1947–59] **L.**MI. imp.; P. 53–59. [*C. as:* 47318]

10127 **Bulletin** de **documentation. Union internationale** des **chemins** de **fer.** Paris. *Bull. Docum. Un. int. Chem. de Fer.* [1947–] **L.**P. 56–; SC. 55–; **Y.**
   Bulletin. Dominion Forest Service, Ottawa. *See* 10293.

10128 **Bulletin** of the **Dominion Grain Research Laboratory, Winnipeg.** Ottawa. *Bull. Dom. Grain Res. Lab. Winnipeg* **L.**SC. 18; **Rt.** 43.

10129 **Bulletin** of the **Dominion Museum.** Wellington, N.Z. *Bull. Dom. Mus., Wellington* [1912–29] **L.**AN.; BM.; BMᴺ. 12–25; GL. 12–27; GM. 24–29; SC. 24–29; **C.**UL. 22–29; **E.**R.; **O.**B. 24–29; **Pl.**M. [*C. of:* 9838; *C. as:* 17144ᶜ]

10130 **Bulletin. Dominion Observatory, New Zealand.** *Bull. Dom. Obs. N.Z.* [1925–] **L.**AS. 25–39; BM.; MO. 26–29 imp.; SC. 28–; **C.**O.; **E.**O.; R. 28– imp. [*C. of:* 22025]

10131 **Bulletin** of the **Dominion Water Power** and **Reclamation Service, Irrigation Series.** Ottawa. *Bull. Dom. Wat. Pwr Reclam. Serv. Irrig. Ser.* **L.**SC. 30–; **Rt.** 22–30.

10132 **Bulletin** de la **Droguerie fédérale** de **France.** Paris. *Bull. Drog. féd. Fr.*

10133 **Bulletin. Druggists' Research Bureau.** New York. *Bull. Drugg. Res. Bur.*

10134 **Bulletin. Dry Farming Congress.** Lethbridge, Alberta. *Bull. Dry Fmg Congr.* [1907–15] [*C. as:* 1407]

10135 **Bulletin. Duke University Marine Station.** Durham, N.C. *Bull. Duke Univ. mar. Stn* [1943–] **L.**BMᴺ.; **Abd.**M.; **C.**UL. 45–46; **Dm.** 46–47; **Mi.**; **O.**R. 45–; **Pl.**M. 45–; **Y.**
   Bulletin. Duke University School of **Forestry.** *See* 11657.

10136 **Bulletin. E.I. Du Pont** de **Nemours** and **Company.** Wilmington, Del. *Bull. E.I. Du Pont de Nemours* [1934–] **L.**P. 34–45.

10137 **Bulletin** of the **Earthquake Investigation Committee.** Tokyo. *Bull. Earthq. Invest. Comm., Tokyo* [1907–25] **L.**BM.; G.; GL.; GM.; MO. 11–25; R.; SC. 14–25; **Abs.**N. 14–25; **Bm.**U.; **C.**P.; **Db.**; **E.**O.; R.; U. 11–25; **G.**U. imp.; **Ld.**U. 22–25; **M.**U.; **O.**O.; R. 07–13. [*C. as:* 10138]

10138 **Bulletin** of the **Earthquake Research Institute, Tokyo University.** Tokyo. *Bull. Earthq. Res. Inst. Tokyo Univ.* [1926–] **L.**AS. 39–; BM.; G.; GL.; MO. 26–37; P. 30–; SC.; **Bm.**U. 26–30; **C.**P.; **Db.**; **E.**O.; R.; U. 49–; **G.**U.; **Ld.**U. 31–36; **M.**U.; **O.**O.; **Y.** [*C. of:* 10137]
   Bulletin of the **East Africa Natural History Society.** *See* 34266.

10139 **Bulletin. East Anglian Institute** of **Agriculture.** Chelmsford. *Bull. E. Angl. Inst. Agric.* [1927–28] **L.**AM.; SC.; **Rt.**

10140 **Bulletin** of **Eclectic Medical University.** Kansas City. *Bull. eclect. med. Univ., Kans. Cy*

10141 **Bulletin** de l'**École française** d'**Extrême-Orient.** Hanoï. *Bull. Éc. fr. Extr.-Orient* [1901–] **L.**AN. 01–02: 31–; BM.; G. imp.; **C.**UL.; **Db.** 36–; **O.**B.; I.

10141ᶜ **Bulletin. École** de la **meunerie belge.** Gand. *Bull. Éc. Meun. belge* **Y.** [*C. in:* 19292]

10142 **Bulletin** de l'**École officielle** de la **meunerie belge.** Gand. *Bull. Éc. off. Meun. belg.* **L.**P. 57–58; SC. 39–58; **Sal.**F. 36–58. [*C. in:* 19292]
   Bulletin de l'**École polytechnique** de **Jassy.** *See* 9122.

10143 **Bulletin** de l'**École supérieure** d'**aéronautique** et de **construction mécanique.** Paris. *Bull. Éc. sup. Aéronaut, Paris.*
   Bulletin de l'**École supérieure** d'**agronomie. Faculté** d'**agriculture.** Brunn. *See* 48707 and 48708.
   Bulletin de l'**École supérieure** d'**agronomie. Faculté** de **silviculture.** Brunn. *See* 48707 and 48708.

10144 **Bulletin** of the **Ecological Society** of **America.** Tucson. *Bull. ecol. Soc. Am.* [1917–] **L.**NC. 52–; **Hu.**G. 36–; **O.**AP. 46–48. [*Not published* 1919–22]

10145 **Bulletin** of **Economic Minerals.** Geological Survey of India. Calcutta. *Bull. econ. Miner.* **L.**BMᴺ. 42–.

10146 **Bulletin. Economic Research Institute.** Jewish Agency for Palestine. Jerusalem. *Bull. econ. Res. Inst., Jerusalem* **O.**AEC. 45–.

10147 **Bulletin. Edinburgh** and **East** of **Scotland College** of **Agriculture.** Edinburgh. *Bull. Edinb. E. Scotl. Coll. Agric.* [1902–] **L.**AM. 02–10; **Bn.**U. 52–; **C.**A.; **Dn.**U.; **E.**U. 46–; W.; **Ld.**U. 05–10; **N.**U. 46– imp.; **Nw.**A. 02–06 imp.; **O.**RE. 46–; **Rt.** 46–; **Y.**

10148 **Bulletin. Edison Electric Institute.** New York. *Bull. Edison elect. Inst.* [1934–] **L.**EE.; P. imp.; SC. 37–; **Rn.**B. (1 yr); **Y.** [*Replaces:* 33936]
     Bulletin des **eidgenössischen Gesundheitsamtes.** Bern. *See* 11666.

10149 **Bulletin. Electric Traction** on the **Railways.** International Railway Congress Association. *Bull. elect. Tract. Rlys* [1950–] **L.**EE.; SC. 60–; **E.**A.; **O.**R.
     Bulletin. Electrical Engineering Department Research Division, Massachusetts Institute of **Technology.** *See* 10876.

10150 **Bulletin** of the **Electrical Engineering Department, Tokyo University.** *Bull. elect. Engng Dep. Tokyo Univ.* [1952–60] [*C. as:* 10152]

10151 **Bulletin** of **Electrical Engineering Education.** Manchester. *Bull. elect. Engng Educ.* [1949–] **L.**NP.; P. 53–; **Bm.**T.; **Bn.**U.; **Br.**U.; **C.**ENG.; **Db.** 58–; **Dn.**U.; **F.**A. 53–57; **G.**T.; **Lc.**A.; **M.**P.; T.; U.; **N.**T. 52–; U. 53–; **Sh.**SC.; **Sw.**U.; **Y.** [*C. of:* 10153]

10152 **Bulletin** of the **Electrical Engineering** and **Electronic Engineering Departments, Tokyo University.** Tokyo. *Bull. elect. Engng electronic Engng Dep. Tokyo Univ.* [1960–] **L.**P.; **Y.** [*C. of:* 10150]

10153 **Bulletin** of **Electrical Engineering Laboratory Practice.** Manchester. *Bull. elect. Engng Lab. Pract.* [1948] **L.**SC.; **Br.**U.; **C.**ENG.; **Dn.**U.; **Lc.**A.; **M.**P.; T.; U. [*C. as:* 10151]
     Bulletin of the **Electrochemical Laboratory.** Tokyo. *See* 16498.

10154 **Bulletin** of the **Electrochemical Society.** New York. *Bull. electrochem. Soc.* [1931–47] **L.**P. 35–47; SC.; PR. 35–41; **C.**P. 37–47; **Ld.**U. 31; **M.**U. imp.; **Nw.**A. 31–32: 43–47. [*C. of:* 9313; *Replaced by:* 25936]
     Bulletin of the **Electrochemical Society, India Section.** *See* 10509.
     Bulletin. Electrodepositors' Technical Society. *See* 17325.

10155 **Bulletin. Electron Microscope Society** of **America.** Camden, N.J. *Bull. Electron Microsc. Soc. Am.* [1944–] **L.**P. 44–45.

10156 **Bulletin. Ellen M. Richards Institute. Research Series.** Pennsylvania School of Agriculture. State College. *Bull. Ellen M. Richards Inst. Res. Ser.* [1942–] **C.**A.

10157 **Bulletin. Empire State Forest Products Association.** Albany, N.Y. *Bull. Emp. St. Forest Prod. Ass.*

10158 **Bulletin** of **Endemic Diseases.** Baghdad. *Bull. endem. Dis.* [1954–] **L.**MD.; TD.; **Fr.**; **Rt.** 54; **Y.**
     Bulletin of the **Engelhardt Observatory, Kazan.** *See* 12742.

10159 **Bulletin** of **Engineering** and **Architecture.** Kansas University. Lawrence. *Bull. Engng Archit.* [1952–] **L.**P. [*C. of:* 27242]

10160 **Bulletin. Engineering Department, National Lamp Works.** Cleveland. *Bull. Engng Dep. natn. Lamp Wks* [1907–29] **L.**P. 21–29.

10161 **Bulletin. Engineering Experiment Station, Connecticut.** Storrs. *Bull. Engng Exp. Stn Conn.* [1946–] **L.**P.; **Y.**
     Bulletin. Engineering Experiment Station, Florida. *See* 10167.
     Bulletin. Engineering Experiment Station, Kansas State University of **Agriculture** and **Applied Science.** *See* 10738.

10162 **Bulletin. Engineering Experiment Station, Louisiana State University** and **Agricultural** and **Mechanical College.** Baton Rouge. *Bull. Engng Exp. Stn La St. Univ.* **L.**P. 54–; **Y.**
     Bulletin. Engineering Experiment Station, Minnesota University. *See* 12525.
     Bulletin. Engineering Experiment Station, Montana State College. *See* 11157.

10163 **Bulletin. Engineering Experiment Station, North Carolina State College. Industrial Information Series.** Raleigh. *Bull. Engng Exp. Stn N. Carol. St. Coll. ind. Inf. Ser.* **L.**P. 53–55.

10164 **Bulletin. Engineering Experiment Station, Oregon State College.** Corvallis. *Bull. Engng Exp. Stn Ore. St. Coll.* [1939–] **L.**P.; **M.**T. 49–; **Y.** [*C. of:* 11742]
     Bulletin. Engineering Experiment Station, Pennsylvania. *See* 11491.

10165 **Bulletin. Engineering Experiment Station, Purdue University.** Lafayette. *Bull. Engng Exp. Stn Purdue Univ.* [1918–29] **L.**P.; SC. 18–23; **Bm.**U. 18–28. [*C. in:* 18095]
     Bulletin. Engineering Experiment Station Series, University of **Missouri.** *See* 12527.
     Bulletin. Engineering Experiment Station Series, University of **New Mexico.** *See* 12537.
     Bulletin. Engineering Experiment Station, Tennessee University. *See* 12384.

10166 **Bulletin. Engineering Experiment Station, University** of **Arizona. Mechanical Engineering Series.** Tucson. *Bull. Engng Exp. Stn Univ. Ariz. mech. Engng Ser.* [1954–] **Y.**

10167 **Bulletin. Engineering Experiment Station, University** of **Florida.** Gainesville. *Bull. Engng Exp. Stn Univ. Fla* [1933–49] **L.**P.; SC.; U.; **Abs.**U.; **Br.**U.; **M.**U. imp.; **Nw.**A. 43–49 imp. [*C. in:* 18150]
     Bulletin. Engineering Experiment Station, University of **Illinois.** *See* 10496.

10168 **Bulletin. Engineering Experiment Station, University** of **Kentucky.** Lexington. *Bull. Engng Exp. Stn Univ. Ky* **L.**P. 56–; **Y.**
     Bulletin. Engineering Experiment Station, University of **Minnesota.** *See* 12525.
     Bulletin. Engineering Experiment Station, University of **Missouri.** *See* 12527.

10169 **Bulletin. Engineering Experiment Station, University** of **Nebraska.** Lincoln, Neb. *Bull. Engng Exp. Stn Univ. Neb.* [1952–] **Db.**

   Bulletin. Engineering Experiment Station, University of **Nevada.** *See* 11270.

   Bulletin. Engineering Experiment Station, University of **Utah.** *See* 12565.

   Bulletin. Engineering Experiment Station, University of **Washington.** *See* 12610.

10170 **Bulletin. Engineering Experiment Station, University** of **Wisconsin.** Madison. *Bull Engng Exp. Stn Univ. Wis.* [1927–] **L.**P. 27–39; **C.**UL.; **Db.** [*C. of:* 12554]

   Bulletin. Engineering Experiment Station, Virginia Polytechnic Institute. *See* 12588.

   Bulletin. Engineering Experiment Station, Washington State College. *See* 12604.

   Bulletin. Engineering Experiment Station, Washington University. *See* 12610.

10171 **Bulletin. Engineering Extension Department, Iowa College** of **Agriculture & Mechanic Arts.** Ames. *Bull. Engng Ext. Dep. Iowa Coll. Agric.* **L.**P. 14–.

10172 **Bulletin. Engineering Extension Department, Purdue University.** Lafayette. *Bull. Engng Ext. Dep. Purdue Univ.* [1922–29] **L.**P. [*C. in:* 18095; *Part of:* 40995]

10173 **Bulletin. Engineering Extension Division, Virginia Polytechnic Institute.** Blacksburg, Va. *Bull. Engng Ext. Div. Va polytech. Inst.* [1924–] **L.**P. imp.

   Bulletin. Engineering Extension Service, Iowa College of **Agriculture** and **Mechanic Arts.** *See* 10171.

   Bulletin. Engineering and **Industrial Experiment Station, University** of **Florida.** *See* 10167.

10174 **Bulletin** of **Engineering Information. U.S. Navy Department.** Washington. *Bull. Engng Inf. U.S. Navy Dep.* **L.**BM. 29–.

10175 **Bulletin** of the **Engineering Research Institute, Kyoto University.** Kyoto. *Bull. Engng Res. Inst. Kyoto Univ.* [1952–] **L.**EE. 52–55; **G.**U. 52–55; **Y.**

10176 **Bulletin. Engineering Research Institute, University** of **Michigan.** Ann Arbor. *Bull. Engng Res. Inst. Univ. Mich.* [1948–] **L.**P. 48–55; **Dn.**U.; **M.**T.; U. imp.; **Y.** [*C. of:* 10029]

   Bulletin. Engineering School, North Carolina State College. *See* 18168.

10177 **Bulletin. Engineering Society** of **Buffalo.** Buffalo. *Bull. Engng Soc. Buffalo* **L.**P. 23– imp.

10178 **Bulletin** of the **Engineering Society. University College, London.** *Bull. Engng Soc. Univ. Coll. Lond.* [1923–25] **L.**UC.

10179 **Bulletin. Engineers Club, Baltimore.** *Bull. Engrs Club Baltimore*

10180 **Bulletin. Engineers Club, Cincinnati.** *Bull. Engrs Club Cincinnati* [*C. as:* 14058]

10181 **Bulletin. Engineers Club** of the **Lehigh Valley.** Bethlehem. *Bull. Engrs Club Lehigh Vall.*

10182 **Bulletin** des **engrais.** Paris. *Bull. Engrais* [1928–] **Rt.** 29–38 imp.: 54–; **Y.**

10183 **Bulletin** de l'**enseign ementtechnique.** Paris. *Bull. Enseign. tech.*

   Bulletin. Entomological Branch, Department of **Agriculture, Canada.** *See* 9961.

   Bulletin. Entomological Department, Rhode Island State Board of **Agriculture.** *See* 11614.

10184 **Bulletin** of **Entomological Research.** London. *Bull. ent. Res.* [1910–] **L.**AM.; BM.; BM^N.; E.; EB.; H.; HS. 47–; IC.; K. 10–33: 47–; L.; LE. 33–37; MC. 10–29: 47–; NC. 45–47: 50–; P.; QM. 50–; SC.; SH. 14–19: 21–24 imp.; TD.; TP.; V. 53–; Z.; **Abd.**U.; **Abs.**N. 12–; U. 10–28: 54–; **Bl.**U. 27–44 imp.; **Bm.**P.; U.; **Bn.**U. 21–; **Br.**A.; U. 23–; **C.**B.; MO.; UL.; **Cr.**U.; **Db.**; **E.**A.; F.; P.; T.; U.; **Ex.**U. 28–; **G.**M.; U. 22–; **H.**U. 50–; **Hu.**G. 54–; **Je.**; **Ld.**U.; **Lh.**FO. 49–56; **Lv.**P. 10–32; U.; **M.**P. 10–15; U.; **Md.**H. 23–; **N.**U.; **Nw.**A. 37–; **O.**AP. 47–; F.; H.; R.; **R.**U. 29–; **Rt.**; **Sh.**U. 11–; **Sil.** 47–; **Sw.**U. 60–; **W.** 51–; **Wd.** 48–; **Y.**

   Bulletin. Entomological Service, Ottawa. *See* 11758.

10185 **Bulletin** of the **Entomological Society** of **America.** Washington. *Bull. ent. Soc. Am.* [1955–] **L.**BM^N.; E.; EB. 61–; **Ld.**U.

   Bulletin entomologique de la **Pologne.** *See* 38059.

10186 **Bulletin** of **Entomology. Department** of **Zoology, Loyola College.** Madras. *Bull. Ent. Loyola Coll.* [1960–] **L.**BM^N.; EB.; **Ld.**U.

10187 **Bulletin** of **Epizootic Diseases** of **Africa.** Muguga. *Bull. epizoot. Dis. Afr.* [1953–] **L.**AM.; TD.; VC.; **C.**V.; **O.**RE. (2 yr.); **W.**; **Y.**

10188 **Bulletin** of the **Essex County Ornithological Club.** Salem, Mass. *Bull. Essex Cty orn. Club* [1919–] **L.**BM^N. 19–38; SC. 19–38; **O.**OR. 19–38.

   Bulletin. Estación experimental insular, Puerto Rico. *See* 11538.

10189 **Bulletin** of the **Esterline-Angus Company.** *Bull. Esterline-Angus Co.*

10190 **Bulletin** of the **Ethnological Society.** Addis Ababa. *Bull. ethnol. Soc., Addis Ababa* [1953–] **L.**AN.; BM.

10191 **Bulletin** of the **Ethnological Society** of **China.** Taipei. *Bull. ethnol. Soc. China* [1955–] **L.**AN.

10192 **Bulletin d'études appliquées** de l'**École supérieure** des **sciences** d'**Alger.** Alger. *Bull. Étud. appl. Éc. sup. Sci. Alger*

10193 **Bulletin** des **études** de l'**École** d'**agriculture.** Montpellier. *Bull. Étud. Éc. Agric., Montpellier*

10194 **Bulletin** des **études océaniennes.** Tahiti. *Bull. Étud. océan.*

10195 **Bulletin d'études** et de **recherches techniques.** Bucarest. *Bull. Étud. Rech. tech., Buc.* [1949–] **L.**BM.

10196 **Bulletin. Eugenics Record Office.** Cold Spring Harbor. *Bull. Eugen. Rec. Off.* [1911–33] **L.**BM. 11–22; H. 11–28 imp.; MA. 11–15; SC.; **C.**UL.; **E.**U.; **O.**R. 11–26.

   Bulletin. Experiment Station, Minnesota School of **Mines.** *See* 11131.

10197 **Bulletin** of the **Experiment Station** of the **Pineapple Producers' Cooperative Association, University** of **Hawaii.** Honolulu. *Bull. Exp. Stn Pineapple Prod. coop. Ass. Hawaii* [1931–] **L.**G. 31–39; P. 34; **C.**A. imp. [*C. of:* 9459]

10198 **Bulletin. Experiment Station** of the **South African Sugar Association.** Natal. *Bull. Exp. Stn S. Afr. Sug. Ass.* [1957–] **L.**P.; **C.**A. [*Supplement to* and published in 50185]

10199 **Bulletin** of **Experimental Animals.** Tokyo. *Bull. exp. Anim., Tokyo* [1952–] **Y.**

10200 **Bulletin** of **Experimental Biology** and **Medicine,** **U.S.S.R.** New York. *Bull. exp. Biol. Med. U.S.S.R.* [1956–] L.MC. imp.; MD. imp.; C.APH.; G.T.; U. 59–; Y. [*English translation of:* 12748]

10201 **Bulletin. Experimental Farms Branch. Department** of **Agriculture, Canada.** Ottawa. *Bull. exp. Fms Brch Dep. Agric. Can.* [1913–21] L.AM.; BM^N. 15–21; K.; P.; SC.; Abd.R.; U.; Bm.P.; Cr.P. 13–19; Db.; E.B.; G.U.; Ld.U.; O.G.; R.; Rt. [*C. of:* 9724; *C. in:* 9971]

10202 **Bulletin** of the **Experimental Forests, Tokyo University** of **Agriculture.** Tokyo. *Bull. exp. Forests Tokyo Univ. Agric.* [1958–] O.F.

10203 **Bulletin** of the **Eyesight Conservation Council** of **America.** *Bull. Eyesight Conserv. Coun. Am.*

Bulletin. F.A.O. *See* 18911.

Bulletin de la **Faculté** de **médecine** de l'**Université** d'**Istanbul.** *See* 24249.

Bulletin de la **Faculté** des **sciences agricoles,** **Chişinău.** *See* 9112.

10204 **Bulletin** de la **Faculté** des **sciences, Université franco-chinoise** de **Peiping.** *Bull. Fac. Sci. Univ. fr.-chin. Peiping* [1934–] L.BM^N. 34–35 imp.; P. 34–36; C.UL. 34–44 imp.

10205 **Bulletin. Faculty** of **Agriculture, Ain Shams University.** Cairo. *Bull. Fac. Agric. Ain Shams Univ.* [1950–] C.A. 50–54.

10206 **Bulletin** of the **Faculty** of **Agriculture, Alberta University.** Edmonton. *Bull. Fac. Agric. Alberta Univ.* [1945–] L.P.; Abs.U. imp.; Rt.; Y. [*C. of:* 9825]

10207 **Bulletin** of the **Faculty** of **Agriculture, Hirosaki University.** Hirosaki. *Bull. Fac. Agric. Hirosaki Univ.* [1955–] L.MY.; Ba.I.; Br.A.; C.A.; Md.H.; Rt. 55.

10208 **Bulletin** of the **Faculty** of **Agriculture** and **Horticulture, University** of **Reading.** *Bull. Fac. Agric. Hort. Univ. Reading* [1925–] L.AM.; BM.; P.; SC.; C.A.; Ld.U.; O.R. 31–; R.D.; Rt. imp. [*C. of:* 10005]

10209 **Bulletin** of the **Faculty** of **Agriculture, Kagoshima University.** Kagoshima. *Bull. Fac. Agric. Kagoshima Univ.* [1952–] L.AM.; BM^N. 54–; K.; MY.; Abs.A.; N.; C.A.; Cr.N. imp.; E.R.; Hu.G. 53–; Ld.U.; Md.H.; Rt.; Y. [*C. of:* 10732]

10210 **Bulletin** of the **Faculty** of **Agriculture, Meiji University.** Ikuta. *Bull. Fac. Agric. Meiji Univ.* [1952–]

10211 **Bulletin** of the **Faculty** of **Agriculture, Mie University.** Tsu, Mie. *Bull. Fac. Agric. Mie Univ.* [1947–] C.A. 55–; Rt. 58.

10211° **Bulletin. Faculty** of **Agriculture, Shinshu University.** Ina. *Bull. Fac. Agric. Shinshu Univ.* [1951–]

10212 **Bulletin** of the **Faculty** of **Agriculture, Shizuoka University.** Iwata. *Bull. Fac. Agric. Shizuoka Univ.* [1956–] L.AM.; C.A.; Y. [*C. of:* 43654]

10213 **Bulletin** of the **Faculty** of **Agriculture, Tamagawa University.** Machida City. *Bull. Fac. Agric. Tamagawa Univ.* [1960–] L.AM.; BM^N.; C.A.; Md.H.; Y.

10214 **Bulletin. Faculty** of **Agriculture. Transvaal University College.** Pretoria. *Bull. Fac. Agric. Transv. Univ. Coll.* [1921–31] L.BM^N. 23–31; SC.; C.A.; Nw.A.; Rt. [*C. as:* 10216]

10215 **Bulletin** of the **Faculty** of **Agriculture, University** of **Miyazaki.** Miyazaki. *Bull. Fac. Agri. Univ. Miyazaki* [1955–] L.AM.; Br.A.; C.A.; Hu.G.; Rt.; Y.

10216 **Bulletin. Faculty** of **Agriculture. University** of **Pretoria.** *Bull. Fac. Agric. Univ. Pretoria* [1931–35] L.BM^N.; SC.; C.A.; Nw.A.; Rt.; Sa. 32–35. [*C. of:* 10214; *C. as:* 41281]

10217 **Bulletin** of the **Faculty** of **Agriculture, Yamaguchi University.** Shimonoseki. *Bull. Fac. Agric. Yamaguchi Univ.* [1950–] L.MY.; Hu.G. 57–.

10218 **Bulletin** of the **Faculty** of **Engineering, Cairo University.** Cairo. *Bull. Fac. Engng Cairo Univ.* [1953–] L.P.; Bm.U. 53–55; G.U. 54–; Ld.U. 54.

10218° **Bulletin. Faculty** of **Engineering, Hiroshima University.** Hiroshima. *Bull. Fac. Engng Hiroshima Univ.* Y.

10219 **Bulletin** of the **Faculty** of **Engineering, Ibaraki University.** Taga. *Bull. Fac. Engng Ibaraki Univ.* [1954–] Y.

10220 **Bulletin** of the **Faculty** of **Engineering, Yokohama National University.** Yokohama. *Bull. Fac. Engng Yokohama natn. Univ.* [1951–] L.EE.; P. 55–; QM. 53–; E.R.; G.U.; M.T.; Nw.A.; Te.N. 53–; Y.

10221 **Bulletin** of the **Faculty** of **Fisheries, Hokkaido University.** Hakodate. *Bull. Fac. Fish. Hokkaido Univ.* [1950–] L.AM.; BM^N.; Abd.M.; Bm.N. imp.; Dm. Fr.; Lo.; Lv.U.; Mi.; O.Z. 55–; Pl.M.; Wo. 52–; Y.

10222 **Bulletin** of the **Faculty** of **Fisheries, Nagasaki University.** Sasebo. *Bull. Fac. Fish. Nagasaki Univ.* [1953–] Lo. 55–.

Bulletin of the **Faculty** of **Horticulture** and **Viticulture, University** of **Agricultural Sciences, Budapest.** *See* 1216.

10223 **Bulletin** of the **Faculty** of **Liberal Arts, Ibaraki University.** Ibaraki. *Bull. Fac. lib. Arts Ibaraki Univ.* Natural Science [1951–] L.QM.; Y.

10223ᵃ **Bulletin. Faculty** of **Medicine, Osaka University.** *Bull. Fac. Med. Osaka Univ.* [1954–]

10224 **Bulletin** of the **Faculty** of **Pharmacy, Kinki University.** Fuse. *Bull. Fac. Pharm. Kinki Univ.* [1956–] Y.

10225 **Bulletin** of the **Faculty** of **Science. Egyptian University.** Cairo. *Bull. Fac. Sci. Egypt. Univ.* [1934–] L.BM^N.; MY. 45–47 imp.; C.A. 34–57; B. 39–; P.; Db.; E.C. 34–45 imp.; R. 34–54 imp.; Fr. 34–41; G.U. 34–45 imp.; Pl.M. 34–45 imp.; Rt.; Sa. 51–; Y.

Bulletin of the **Faculty Science. Fouad I University.** *See* 10225.

10226 **Bulletin** of the **Faculty** of **Textile Fibers, Kyoto University** of **Industrial Arts** and **Textile Fibers.** Kyoto. *Bull. Fac. text. Fib. Kyoto Univ. ind. Arts* [1954–] Y.

Bulletin. Fair Isle Bird Observatory. *See* 18991.

10227 **Bulletin** of the **Fan Memorial Institute** of **Biology.** Peking. *Bull. Fan meml Inst. Biol.* [1929–] L.BM^N. 29–48; HO.; K.; L. 29–39; SC. 34–; UC.; Z. 29–40; Abd.M. 29–36; Abs.U.; Bl.U. 29–30; Bm.U. 31–32 imp.; Bn.U. 29–36 imp.; Br.U.; C.UL. 35–; Db.; E.B.; R. 36–39; U. 29–36; G.U. 29–37 imp.; Ld.U.; Lv.U. 29–38; M.U. 29; Mi.; O.F. 29–35; R. 29–36; Pl.M. 29–39 imp.

Bulletin of the **Far Eastern Branch** of the **Academy** of **Sciences** of the **U.S.S.R.** *See* 56432.

Bulletin of the **Farm Implement Bureau** of the **General Direction** of **Agriculture.** Moscow. *See* 24324.

10228 **Bulletin. Farmer Cooperative Service U.S. Department** of **Agriculture.** Washington. *Bull. Fmr co-op. Serv.* [1955–] **C.**A. imp.

10229 **Bulletin fédéral. Fédération européene** des **fabricants** de **carton ondulé.** Paris. *Bull. féd. Féd. eur. Fabr. Carton ond.* **L.**P. 60–.

10230 **Bulletin. Federated American Engineering Societies.** New York. *Bull. fed. Am. Engng Socs* [*C. as:* 9315]

10231 **Bulletin. Fédération aéronautique international.** Paris. *Bull. Féd. aéronaut. int.* **L.**AV. 31–52 imp.; **Y.**

10232 **Bulletin** de la **Fédération dentaire internationale.** Bruxelles, etc. *Bull. Féd. dent. int.* [1925–] **L.**D.; **Ld.**U. 35–36.

10233 **Bulletin** de la **Fédération** des **groupements français** pour la **protection** des **oiseaux.** Paris. *Bull. Féd. Grpmt. fr. Prot. Oiseaux* [*C. of:* 10809]

10234 **Bulletin** de la **Fédération** des **industries chimiques** de **Belgique.** Bruxelles. *Bull. Féd. Inds chim. Belg.* [1921–29] **L.**C.; IC.; P.; SC.; **C.**P.; **Ld.**U. 26–29; **Lv.**U. imp.; **Ste.** [*Issued with* 11885; *C. as:* 23320]

10235 **Bulletin** de la **Fédération internationale** des **associations** des **chimistes** du **textile** et de la **couleur** Bâle. *Bull. Féd. int. Ass. Chim. Text.* [1932–] **L.**P. 32–37; SC.; **M.**C. 32–38.

10236 **Bulletin** de la **Fédération internationale pharmaceutique.** La Haye. *Bull. Féd. int. pharm.* [1912–56] **L.**PH.; **Y.** [*C. as:* 26500]

10237 **Bulletin** de la **Fédération nationale** du **bâtiment** et des **travaux publics.** Paris. *Bull. Féd. natn. Bât. Trav. publ.*

10238 **Bulletin** de la **Fédération normande** des **sociétés** de **pharmacie.** Le Havre. *Bull. Féd. normande Socs Pharm.*

10239 **Bulletin** de la **Fédération** des **sociétés** de **gynécologie** et d'**obstétrique** de **langue française.** Paris. *Bull. Féd. Socs Gynéc. Obstét. Lang. fr.* [1951–] **L.**MA.; MD.; **Dn.**U.; **E.**S. [*C. of:* 9458; *supplement to:* 21683]

10240 **Bulletin** de la **Fédération** des **sociétés savantes** de **Franche-Comté.** Besançon. *Bull. Féd. Socs sav. Franche-Comté* **L.**BM. 51–.

10241 **Bulletin** de la **Fédération** des **sociétiés** et **syndicats vétérinaires** de **France.** Lyon. *Bull. Féd. Socs Synds vét. Fr.*

10242 **Bulletin** de la **Fédération suisse** des **chauffeurs** et **machinistes.** Andelfingen. *Bull. Féd. suisse Chauff. Mach.* [*Supplement to:* 16344]

10243 **Bulletin** de la **Fédération** des **syndicats médicaux** du **Loiret.** Orléans. *Bull. Féd. Synds méd. Loiret*

10244 **Bulletin** de la **Fédération** des **syndicats médicaux** de la **Mayenne.** Mayenne. *Bull. Féd. Synds méd. Mayenne*

10245 **Bulletin** de la **Fédération** des **syndicats pharmaceutiques** de l'**Ouest.** *Bull. Féd. Synds pharm. Ouest*

10246 **Bulletin** of the **Fellowship** for **Freedom** in **Medicine.** London. *Bull. Fellowsh. Freedom Med.* [1948–] **L.**BM.; MA. 54– imp.; MD. 52–; **E.**A. 54–55; **O.**R. 50–.

10247 **Bulletin** of the **Fellowship** of **Medicine.** London. *Bull. Fellowsh. Med.* [1919–25] **L.**BM.; MD.; S. 20–25 imp.; **Lv.**U. 20–24 imp.; **M.**P. 22–25. [*C. as:* 38179]

10248 **Bulletin** de la **ferme.** Québec. *Bull. Ferme*

10249 **Bulletin. Fernando Sanford Terrestrial Electric Observatory.** *Bull. Fernando Sanford terr. elect. Obs.* **L.**BM. 23–.

10250 **Bulletin. Field Seed Institute** of **North America.** Washington. *Bull. Field Seed Inst. N. Am.* [1947–] **C.**A.

10250ª **Bulletin** of **Field Training Programs. Communicable Disease Center.** Atlanta. *Bull. Fld Train. Progms commun. Dis. Cent.* [1951–] **L.**BM. [*See also:* 12870]

Bulletin de **Filiale** de la **Sibérie** d'**Ouest** du **Comité géologique.** *See* 24563.

10251 **Bulletin** des **filiales** de la **Société** de **biologie** de **Paris. Société** de **biologie** d'**Alger.** *Bull. Fil. Soc. Biol. Paris Soc. Biol. Alger* **L.**Z. 42–44.

Bulletin. Fire Research Board. *See* 19488.

10252 **Bulletin** of the **First Agronomy Division, Tokai-Kinki National Agricultural Experiment Station.** Tsu-City. *Bull. first Agron. Div. Tokai-Kinki natn. agric. Exp. Stn* [1959–] **L.**AM.; MY.; **C.**A.; **Rt.**; **Y.** [*C. of:* 10101]

10253 **Bulletin** of the **Fish Biological Laboratory.** Milford, Conn. *Bull. Fish biol. Lab., Milford Conn.* **Pl.**M. 58–59. [*C. as:* 9577ᶜ]

10254 **Bulletin. Fisher Scientific Company.** Pittsburgh. *Bull. Fisher scient. Co.* **L.**P. 53–.

10255 **Bulletin. Fisheries Council** of **Canada.** Ottawa. *Bull. Fish. Coun. Can.* [1959–] **Lo.**

10256 **Bulletin** of the **Fisheries Experiment Station, Canton.** *Bull. Fish. Exp. Stn Canton* **Pl.**M. 29.

10257 **Bulletin** of the **Fisheries** and **Marine Biological Survey, Union** of **South Africa.** *Bull. Fish. mar. biol. Surv. Un. S. Afr.* [1935–] **L.**AM.; **Abd.**M.

10258 **Bulletin. Fisheries Research Board** of **Canada.** Ottawa. *Bull. Fish. Res. Bd Can.* [1939–] **L.**AM.; BMᴺ.; C.; P. 51–; SC.; Z. 50–; **Abd.**M.; **Abs.**U. 51–55 imp.; **Bn.**U. 47– imp.; **C.**B.; P. 51–; PO. 46– imp.; **Db.**; **Dm.**; **E.**R.; **Fr.**; **Lo.**; **Lv.**U.; **Mi.**; **N.**U. 50–; **Pl.**M.; **Sa.** 39–54; **Wo.** 50– imp. [*C. of:* 9576]

Bulletin. Fisheries Research Section, Coastguards and **Fisheries Service, Egypt.** *See* 9822.

10259 **Bulletin** of the **Fisheries Research Station. Department** of **Fisheries, Ceylon.** Colombo. *Bull. Fish. Res. Stn Ceylon* [1952–] **L.**BMᴺ.; Z. 56–; **Abd.**M.; **Dm.**; **Fr.** 55–; **Lo.**; **Pl.**M. 56–; **Y.**

10260 **Bulletin** of the **Fisheries Society** of the **Philippines.** Manila. *Bull. Fish. Soc. Philipp.* [1950–] **Mi. Pl.**M.; **Wo.**

10261 **Bulletin** of the **Fishery Experiment Station, Fusan.** Chosen. *Bull. Fishery Exp. Stn Fusan* [1925–] **L.**AM. 25–33; **Abd.** M. 29–33; **Dm.** 33; **Lo.** 25–33; **Lv.**U. 25– imp.; **Pl.**M. 29–39 imp.

10262 **Bulletin. Fishing Industry Research Institute, Union** of **South Africa.** Cape Town. *Bull. Fishg Ind. Res. Inst. Un. S. Afr.* **Pl.**M. 47.

10263 **Bulletin. Florida Agricultural Experiment Station.** Gainesville. *Bull. Fla agric. Exp. Stn* [1888–] L.AM.; BM^N 06–39 imp.; EB. (ent.) 90–; HS. 26– imp.; K. 44– imp.; P. 13–; SC. 91–; **Br.**A. 11– imp.; **C.**A.; **H.**U. 28–35; **Ld.**U. 12–44 imp.; **O.**RE 37– imp.; **Rt.** 93–; **Y.**

10264 **Bulletin. Florida Agricultural Extension Service.** Gainesville. *Bull. Fla agric. Ext. Serv.*

10264° **Bulletin. Florida Agricultural and Mechanical University.** Tallahassee. *Bull. Fla agric. mech. Univ.* **Y.**

10265 **Bulletin. Florida Department** of **Agriculture.** Tallahassee. *Bull. Fla Dep. Agric.*

    Bulletin. Florida Engineering Experiment Station. *See* 10167.

10266 **Bulletin. Florida Forest** and **Park Service.** Tallahassee. *Bull. Fla Forest Park Serv.* **O.**F. 41–.

10267 **Bulletin. Florida Game** and **Fresh-water Fish Commission.** Gainesville. *Bull. Fla Game Freshwat. Fish Commn*

10268 **Bulletin** of the **Florida State Dental Society.** Clermont. *Bull. Fla St. dent. Soc.* [1922–31] [*C. as:* 19652.

10269 **Bulletin. Florida State Engineering Society.** *Bull. Fla St. Engng Soc.* [1934–]

10270 **Bulletin. Florida State Geological Survey,** Tallahassee. *Bull. Fla St. geol. Surv.* [1908–33] L.BM^N. 08–33; GM.; P.; **C.**S. 30–33; **E.**R. 30; **Y.** [*C. as:* 21006°]

10271 **Bulletin** of the **Florida State Museum: Biological Sciences.** Gainesville. *Bull. Fla St. Mus. biol. Sci.* [1956–] L.BM^N.; L.; Z.; **E.**G. (curr.); R.; **Bl.**U.; **Fr.**; **G.**N. 58–; **M.**U.; **O.**R.; **Pl.**M.

    Bulletin. Florida State Plant Board. *See* 12289.

10272 **Bulletin** of the **Florida State Road Department.** Tallahassee. *Bull. Fla St. Rd Dep.* L.SC. 19–20.

    Bulletin. Flower and **Fifth Avenue Hospitals,** New York Medical College. *See* 11293.

10274 **Bulletin Fokker.** Amsterdam. *Bull. Fokker* [1925–] L.P. 25–36; SC. 28–.

10275 **Bulletin** de la **Fondation** de la **brasserie** et de la **malterie françaises.** Nancy. *Bull. Fondn Brass. Malt. fr.* **Bm.**U. 23–29.

10276 **Bulletin** de la **Fondation documentaire dentaire.** Bruxelles. *Bull. Fondn docum. dent.* [1931–46] L.D. 45–46. [*C. as:* 17080]

10277 **Bulletin. Food** and **Drug Laboratory.** Ottawa. *Bull. Fd Drug Lab., Ottawa*

10277° **Bulletin** of the **Food Manufacturers Federation,** Inc. London. *Bull. Fd Mfrs Fed.* L.AM. 43–58. [*C. as:* 18937]

10278 **Bulletin. Food Production Department. Ministry** of **Agriculture.** London. *Bull. Fd Prod. Dep. Minist. Agric.* L.AM.

10279 **Bulletin** of **Foreign Agricultural Intelligence.** International Institute of Agriculture, Ottawa. *Bull. for. agric. Intell.* L.EB. 11–16; K. 15–16.

10280 **Bulletin** of the **Forest Biological Research Station, Cawthron Institute.** Nelson, N.Z. *Bull. Forest biol. Res. Stn Cawthron Inst.* [1932–] O.F. 32; **Rt.** 32.

10280° **Bulletin. Forest** and **Conservation Experiment Station, University** of **Montana.** *Bull. Forest Conserv. Exp. Stn Univ. Mont.* **Y.**

10281 **Bulletin** of the **Forest Department, British Honduras.** Belize. *Bull. Forest Dep. Br. Honduras* [1946–] O.F.

10281° **Bulletin. Forest Department, Sarawak.** Kuching. *Bull. Forest Dep. Sarawak* [1925–] O.F.

10282 **Bulletin** of the **Forest Department, Uganda.** Entebbe. *Bull. Forest Dep. Uganda* O.F. 34.

10282° **Bulletin. Forest Department, Uttar Pradesh.** Allahabad. *Bull. Forest Dep. Uttar Pradesh* **Y.**

10283 **Bulletin** of the **Forest Department, Western Australia.** Perth. *Bull.'Forest Dep. West. Aust.* O.F. 19– imp.; **Rt.** 24–39; **Y.**

10284 **Bulletin. Forest Experiment Station** of the **Imperial Household.** Tokyo-Fu. *Bull. Forest Exp. Stn imp. Household* O.F. 25–38.

10285 **Bulletin** of the **Forest Experiment Station, Seoul.** *Bull. Forest Exp. Stn Seoul* L.BM^N. 56–.

    Bulletin. Forest Products Laboratory, Oregon State College. *See* 11448.

    Bulletin. Forest Products Research. *See* 19976.

10286 **Bulletin. Forest Products Research Center, Oregon.** Corvallis. *Bull. Forest Prod. Res. Cent. Ore.* [1957–] L.P.; O.F.; **Y.** [*C. of:* 11448]

10287 **Bulletin. Forest Research Institute.** Taipei. *Bull. Forest Res. Inst., Taipei* [1947–] O.F.

10288 **Bulletin, Forest Service, Department** of **Lands** and **Forests, Quebec.** Quebec. *Bull. Forest Serv. Queb.* [1942–] L.P.; O.F.; **Y.**

10289 **Bulletin. Forest Service, Kentucky.** Frankfort, Ky. *Bull. Forest Serv. Ky* [1926–] O.F.

    Bulletin. Forest Service, New Zealand. Wellington. *See* 11316.

10291 **Bulletin forestier** du **Centre.** Le Coteau, Loire. *Bull. for. Cent.*

10292 **Bulletin forestier polonais.** Varsovie. *Bull. for. pol.* [1931–33] L.K.; SC.; O.F.

10293 **Bulletin** of the **Forestry Branch. Department** of **Northern Affairs** and **Natural Resources, Canada.** Ottawa. *Bull. For. Brch Can.* [1904–60] L.BM. 08–60; K. 11–14 imp.; P. 10–60; **E.**B. 23–60; **O.**F. imp.; G. 12–24: 34–38 imp.; **Rt.**; **Y.** [*C. as:* 10037]

10294 **Bulletin** of the **Forestry Commission.** London. *Bull. For. Commn, Lond.* [1919–] L.BM.; BM^N. 20–36 imp.; EB. (ent.); HS. 46–; K. 22–46 imp.; L. 52–; NC. 32–; P. imp.; **Abs.**N.; **Bl.**U. 53–60; **Bm.**P. 36–; **Bn.**U.; **C.**A.; UL.; **Cr.**M. 19–33; P. imp.; **E.**B.; R. 32– imp.; **G.**M.; **Ld.**P.; **Lv.**P. 20–; **M.**P. 22–; **O.**AP. 26–; F.; R.; **Rt.**; **Sw.**U.; **Y.**

10295 **Bulletin** of the **Forestry Commission, New South Wales.** Sydney. *Bull. For. Commn N.S.W.* **Y.**

10296 **Bulletin** of the **Forestry Department, Ghana.** Accra. *Bull. For. Dep. Ghana* L.BM^N.; **Y.** [*C. of:* 10297]

10297 **Bulletin** of the **Forestry Department, Gold Coast.** Accra. *Bull. For. Dep. Gold Cst* L.BM^N. 38: 52–56; O.F. 35–38; **Y.** [*C. as:* 10296]

10298 **Bulletin** of the **Forestry Department, Kenya.** Nairobi. *Bull. For. Dep. Kenya* O.F. 36–.

10299 **Bulletin. Forestry Department, Nigeria.** Lagos. *Bull. For. Dep. Nigeria* [1928–] L.K. 28–36; SC.; O.F.; RH.

10300 **Bulletin. Forestry Department, Tasmania.** Hobart. *Bull. For. Dep. Tasm.* [1955–] O.F.

Bulletin. Forestry Department, United Provinces. Allahabad. *See* 12503.

10301 **Bulletin** of the **Forestry Department, University** of **Edinburgh.** Edinburgh. *Bull. For. Dep. Univ. Edinb.* [1955–] L.BM^N.; Bn.U.; C.UL.; E.A.; O.R.

10302 **Bulletin. Forestry Experiment Station, Chosen.** Keijo. *Bull. For. Exp. Stn Chosen*

Bulletin. Forestry and **Timber Bureau, Australia.** *See* 9894.

10303 **Bulletin. Forests Commission, Victoria.** Melbourne. *Bull. Forests Commn Victoria* [1946–] Y.

10304 **Bulletin** of the **Formosa Agricultural Experiment Station.** Taihoku. *Bull. Formosa agric. Exp. Stn* L.BM^N. 15–20.

10305 **Bulletin. Formosa Bureau** of **Productive Industry.** Taihoku. *Burr. Formosa Bur. prod. Ind.* L.K. 14–15 imp.

Bulletin and **Foundry Abstracts** of the **British Cast Iron Research Association.** Birmingham. *See* 9607.

10306 **Bulletin. Foxboro Company.** Foxboro, Mass. *Bull. Foxboro Co.* L.P. 39– imp.

10307 **Bulletin. Foxboro-Yoxall Ltd.** London. *Bull. Foxboro-Yoxall* L.P. 54– imp.

10308 **Bulletin français** de **pisciculture.** Paris. *Bull. fr. Piscic.* [1928–] L.AM. 30–52 v. imp.; SC. 34–; Abd.M. 50–51; Fr. 32: 49–; Pit.F. 50–. Y.

10309 **Bulletin. Franz Theodore Stone Laboratory,** Ohio University. Columbus. *Bull. Franz Theodore Stone Lab.*

10310 **Bulletin** of the **Free Museum** of **Science** and **Art** of the **University** of **Pennsylvania.** Philadelphia. *Bull. free Mus. Sci. Art Univ. Pa* [1897–02] L.BM.; Br.U. [*Replaced by:* 53720]

10311 **Bulletin** of the **Freshwater Fisheries Research Laboratory.** Tokyo. *Bull. Freshwat. Fish. Res. Lab., Tokyo* [1952–] L.BM^N.; Fr.; Y.

Bulletin. Fruit Branch, Department of **Agriculture, Canada.** *See* 9962.

Bulletin. Fruit Series, Department of **Agriculture, United Provinces** of **Agra** and **Oudh.** *See* 10004.

10312 **Bulletin** of the **Fuel Research Institute, Japan.** Tokyo. *Bull. Fuel Res. Inst. Japan* [1927–] L.P. 27–36.

10313 **Bulletin. Fuel Research Institute** of **South Africa.** Pretoria. *Bull. Fuel Res. Inst. S. Afr.* [1933–] Y.

10314 **Bulletin** of the **Fusion Welding Corporation.** Chicago. *Bull. Fusion Weld. Corp.* L.P. 28.

Bulletin. GPO-Research and **Engineering Council** of the **Graphic Arts Industry** Inc. Washington. *See* 20517.

Bulletin. Game Division, Western Australia. *See* 20596.

Bulletin of the **Game** and **Fish Commission, Wyoming.** Cheyenne. *See* 12653.

10316 **Bulletin. Gas Engine** and **Farm Power Association.** Chicago. *Bull. Gas Eng. Fm Pwr Ass., Chicago*

10317 **Bulletin** für **Gasschutz.** Zürich. *Bull. Gasschutz* L.P. 29–31.

10318 **Bulletin** du **gaz.** Paris. *Bull. Gaz*

10319 **Bulletin général français** du **moulinage** de la **soie.** Paris. *Bull. gén. fr. Moulin. Soie*

Bulletin. General Lighting Information Service. *See* 20510.

10320 **Bulletin** of **General Research** and **Patent Information.** Association of British Insecticide Manufacturers. London. *Bull. gen. Res. Pat. Inf. Ass. Br. Insectic. Mfrs* L.EB. 28–31.

10321 **Bulletin général** de **thérapeutique médicale, chirurgicale, obstétricale** et **pharmaceutique.** Paris. *Bull. gén. Thér. méd. chir.* [1831–39] L.BM.; MA. 75–81; MD. 1855–39; S.; Abd.U. 1838–1843; Dn.U. 03–16; E.P.; G.F. 1852–14; U. 1831–38; Ld.U. 96–16; M.MS. 1833–28; O.R. 83–01 imp.

10322 **Bulletin géodésique.** Section de géodésie, Union géodésique et géophysique internationale. Toulouse, etc. *Bull. géod.* [1922–] L.AS. 28–; BM.; G. 24–; MO. 27–34; P.; R. 23–; SC.; U. 30–; UC. 28–; Abs.N. 28; U. 32– imp.; Bl.U. 28–; Bm.U.; C.GD. 22–47; S.; UL.; Db. 28–; E.A. 27– imp.; O.; R. 24–42; U. 28–; G.U. 28–46; Ld.U. 28–51; M.U. 28– imp; O.R.; R.U. 29–; Sa. 29–; Sh.U. 28–42; Wo. 30–34; Y. [*Suspended:* 1943–45]

10323 **Bulletin** of the **Geographic Society** of **Chicago.** Chicago. *Bull. geogr. Soc. Chicago* L.G. 14–33 imp.; C.UL. 28–.

10324 **Bulletin** of the **Geographical Society** of **America.** Washington. *Bull. geogr. Soc. Am.*

10325 **Bulletin** of the **Geographical Society** of **Ireland.** *Bull. geogr. Soc. Ire.* [1944–46] L.SC.; U.; Abs.N.; Bl.U.; Br.U.; C.GG. 45–46; UL.; E.A.; G.; U.; G.M.; Ld.U. imp.; Nw.A.; Sa. [*C. as:* 24152]

10326 **Bulletin** of the **Geographical Society** of **Philadelphia.** Philadelphia. *Bull. geogr. Soc. Philad.* [1893–38] L.B. 96–38; BM.; BM^N. 94–22; G. 95; SC. 28–38; E.G.; R.; O.G. 04–22 imp.; Sh.U. 10–38.

10327 **Bulletin** of the **Geographical Survey Institute.** Tokyo. *Bull. geogr. Surv. Inst., Tokyo* [1948–] L.BM. 50–; G.; E.M. 49–; Y.

10328 **Bulletin** de **géographie** d'**Aix-Marseille.** *Bull. Géogr. Aix-Marseille* [1955–] L.BM.; G.; E.G. [*C. of:* 11977]

10329 **Bulletin** de **géographie** et d'**archéologie** de la **province** d'**Oran.** Oran. *Bull. Géogr. Archéol. Prov. Oran* L.G. 78– imp.; E.G. 85–.

10330 **Bulletin** de **géographie botanique.** Le Mans. *Bull. Géogr. bot.* [1911–19] L.BM.; BM^N.; K.; E.B. 11–15. [*C. of:* 9170]

10331 **Bulletin** de **géographie historique** et **descriptive.** Paris. *Bull. Géogr. hist. descr.* [1886–12] L.BM.; G.; O.B. [*C. as:* 11715]

Bulletin. Geological and **Biological Survey, South Dakota.** *See* 12262.

10332 **Bulletin** of the **Geological Committee** of **Hokkaido.** Sapporo. *Bull. geol. Comm. Hokkaido* Y.

10333 **Bulletin. Geological Department** of the **Hebrew University.** Jerusalem. *Bull. geol. Dep. Hebrew Univ.* [1936–] L.BM^N.; GL. 36–44; GM.

10334 **Bulletin. Geological Department, Rewa State.**
Calcutta. *Bull. geol. Dep. Rewa St.* [1923–] L.BM.; BM^N.
23.

10335 **Bulletin** of the **Geological Division, Department**
of **Lands** and **Mines. Tanganyika Territory.** Dar es
Salaam. *Bull. geol. Div. Dep. Lds Mines Tanganyika*
[1937–48] L.MI.; Bm.U.; Br.U.; G.U. imp.; Lv.U.; O.R.;
Y. [*C. of:* and *Rec. as:* 10377]
    Bulletin. Geological Division, Moscow Society
of **Naturalists.** *See* 11159^f.

10336 **Bulletin. Geological Division, Research**
Council of **Alberta.** Edmonton. *Bull. geol. Div. Res.*
Coun. Alberta [1958–] L.BM.; BM^N.; E.D.

10337 **Bulletin** of the **Geological Institution** of the
University of **Upsala.** Upsala. *Bull. geol. Instn Univ.*
Upsala [1892–] L.BM.; BM^N.; G.; GL.; GM.; I. 27–; L.;
MI. 93–43: 46; MIE. 92–35 imp.: 53–; P.IO–; R. 92–32;
SC. 92–01: 37–; UC.; Bl.U.; Bm.N. imp.; U.; Br.U.;
C.P.; PO. 16–; S.; UL.; Cr.N.; Db.; Dn.U. 49–; E.D.; J.;
R.; U. 25–; G.N. 92–19; T.; U. 12–; Ld.U. imp.; Lv.U.;
M.U.; Nw.A. 92–35; O.R.; Sh.M. 92–30; SC. 32–; Y.

10338 **Bulletin. Geological, Mining** and **Metallur-**
gical Society of **India.** Calcutta. *Bull. geol. min.*
metall. Soc. India [1937–] L.BM. 57–; BM^N.; GL.; MI. 57–;
P.; UC.; Y.
    Bulletin of the **Geological** and **Prospecting**
Service of **U.S.S.R.** *See* 24350.

10339 **Bulletin** of the **Geological Section** of the **De-**
partment of **Natural Resources, Newfoundland.** St.
John's. *Bull. geol. Sect. Dep. nat. Resour. Newfoundld*
[1934–37] L.BM^N.; GL.; MI.; P.; SC. 37; UC.; Bl.U. imp.;
C.S. imp.; Lv.U. [*C. as:* 11321]
    Bulletin. Geological Series, Auckland Uni-
versity College. *See* 9539.
    Bulletin. Geological Series, Department of
Mines, Union of **South Africa.** *See* 10068.

10341 **Bulletin** of the **Geological Society** of **America.**
Rochester, N.Y., etc. *Bull. geol. Soc. Am.* [1890–]
L.B. 34–; BM.; BM^N.; GL.; GM.; KC. 53–; MI. 47–; SC. 25–;
UC.; Abd.U. 29–; Bm.U. 06–; Br.U. 23–; C.GD. 53–; MI.; S.
25–; Cr.U. 49–; E.D. 38–; R.; U. 10– imp.; Ex.U. 55–; G.U.;
H.U.; Ld.U.; Lv.P. 59–; U. 20–; M.U. 35– imp.; N.U.
47–; Nw.A. 35–; O.R. 90–03: 10–; R.U. 48–; Sa. 47–;
Sh.SC. 32–; U. 32–; Sw.U. 55–; Wo. 54–; Y.

10342 **Bulletin** of the **Geological Society** of **China.**
Peking. *Bull. geol. Soc. China* [1922–] L.BM^N. 22–51;
GL. 22–48; GM.; MI. 38–48 imp.; SC. 22–48; Bm.U. 22–47
imp.; Br.U. 22–48; C.S.; E.R. 40–44 imp.; G.U. 22–48
imp.; Ld.U. 26–; Lv.U. imp.
    Bulletin of the **Geological Society** of **Turkey.**
See 55353.

10343 **Bulletin. Geological Survey** of **Alabama.**
Montgomery. *Bull. geol. Surv. Ala.* [1886–] L.BM^N.; GL.
00–30; GM.; Y.

10344 **Bulletin. Geological Survey** of **Arkansas.**
Little Rock. *Bull. geol. Surv. Ark.* [1929–] L.BM^N.; GM.;
Y.

10345 **Bulletin. Geological Survey** of **British Guiana.**
Georgetown. *Bull. geol. Surv. Br. Guiana* [1933–] L.BM.;
BM^N. 33–49; GL.; MI. 36–; UC.; Bl.U. 57–; Bm.U. 37–; C.S.
imp.; Cr.M. 34–; E.D. 36–; Lv.U. 37–; O.G. 38–; R.;
Sw.U. 56–; Y.

10346 **Bulletin. Geological Survey** of **Canada.**
Ottawa. *Bull. geol. Surv. Can.* [1921–28] L.AN.(anthrop.);
BM.; BM^N.; G.; GL.; GM.; I.; K.; L.; SC.; UC.; Abd.U.; Bl.U.
imp.; Bm.P.; U. 21–26; Bn.U. 21–22; Br.U. 21–22; C.P.;
Db.; Dn.U. 21–25 imp.; E.A.; B.; C. 21–26 imp.; D.; F.;
G.; R.; U.; G.N. imp.; U. 21–26; H.U. (biol.); Ld.U.;
Lv.U.; M.P.; U.; Nw.A. imp.; O.G. 23–25 imp.; R.; Pl.M.
22–28 imp.; Sa. 21–25; Sh.M. 21–25; Sw.U. 21–24: 26;
Y. [*C. of:* 33851; *C. as:* 11233]

10347 **Bulletin. Geological Survey** of **Canada.**
Ottawa. *Bull. geol. Surv. Can.* [1945–] L.BM.; BM^N.; GL.;
MI. imp.; SC.; Bl.U.; Br.U.; C.P.; PO. imp.; UL.; Dn.U.;
E.R.; U. 52–; Lv.U.; O.G.; Sa. 45–53.

10348 **Bulletin** of the **Geological Survey** of **China.**
Peking. *Bull. geol. Surv. China* [1919–] L.BM^N.; GL. 19–
48; GM.; SC.; UC. 20–; Bm.U. 23–32; Br.U.; C.S. 19–25
imp.: 33–; UL.; E.D. 20–40; J. 22–; R. 20–48; G.U.; Lv.U.
[Ser. A. *ended in* 1929; *C. as:* 21009]

10349 **Bulletin** of the **Geological Survey** of **Chosen.**
Keijo. *Bull. geol. Surv. Chosen* [1919–39] L.BM^N. 24–39
imp.; GL. 25–34; GM. 24–39; UC. 31–39; Lv.U. 31–34
imp.
    Bulletin. Geological Survey Department,
British Guiana. *See* 10345.

10350 **Bulletin. Geological Survey Department,**
British Territories in **Borneo.** Kuching. *Bull. geol.*
Surv. Dep. Br. Terr. Borneo [1951–] L.BM.; BM^N.; GL.;
MI.; C.S.; O.R. 55–; Y.

10350° **Bulletin. Geological Survey Department** of
Fiji. Suva. *Bull. geol. Surv. Dep. Fiji* [1958–] L.BM^N.

10351 **Bulletin. Geological Survey Department,**
Jamaica. Kingston. *Bull. geol. Surv. Dep. Jamaica*
[1951–] L.BM^N. 51; GL.; GM.
    Bulletin. Geological Survey Department,
Tanganyika. *See* 10377.

10353 **Bulletin. Geological Survey Division, Depart-**
ment of **Mines. Union** of **South Africa.** *Bull. geol.*
Surv. Div. Un. S. Afr. [1934–] L.BM.; BM^N.; MI.; SC.;
Abd.U. 34–43; Br.U.; Cr.U.; E.D.; R.; Lv.U.; Nw.A.
38– imp.

10354 **Bulletin. Geological Survey** of **Georgia.**
Atlanta. *Bull. geol. Surv. Ga* [1894–] L.BM^N.; GL. 94–11;
GM.; G.U. imp.; Y.

10355 **Bulletin. Geological Survey, Ghana.** Accra.
Bull. geol. Surv. Ghana [1957–] L.BM.; BM^N.; GL.; MI.;
U.; UC.; Bm.U.; C.S.; E.D.; R.; G.U.; O.G.; R.; Y.
[*C. of:* 10356]

10356 **Bulletin. Geological Survey, Gold Coast**
Colony. London. *Bull. geol. Surv. Gold Cst* [1925–56]
L.BM.; BM^N.; GL.; MI. 25–46: 52–56; U.; UC.; Bm.U 25–
30: 37–56; C.S.; E.D. 28–56; R.; G.U. 38–56 imp.;
Lv.U. 25–47; O.G. 27–56 imp.; R.; Rt.; Y. [*C. as:* 10355]

10357 **Bulletin** of the **Geological Survey** of **Great**
Britain. London. *Bull. geol. Surv. Gt Br.* [1939–] L.B.;
BM.; BM^N.; GL.; I.; MI. 54–; P.; QM. 51–; SC.; U.; UC.;
Bm.P.; U.; Bn.U.; Br.U.; C.S.; UL.; Cr.P.; Dn.U. 61–;
E.D.; R.; U.; G.T.; H.U.; Ld.P.; Lv.U.; M.P.; N.P.; U.;
O.R.; R.U.; Rt.; Y.

10358 **Bulletin. Geological Survey** of **Hunan.** Chang-
sha. *Bull. geol. Surv. Hunan* L.BM^N. 29– imp.; Bm.U.
29–34.

10359 **Bulletin** of **the Geological Survey** of **India.** Calcutta. *Bull. geol. Surv. India* [1950–]
    Series A: Economic geology. L.BM^N.; GL.; I. 50–57; SC.; **Bl.**U.; **Br.**U.; **C.**P.; S.; **Db.**; **E.**R.; U. imp.; **Lv.**U.; **M.**U.; **Nw.**A.; **Y.**
    Series B: Engineering geology and ground-water. **L.**I. 50–57; **Bl.**U.; **Br.**U.; **C.**P.; S.; **E.**R.; U. imp.; **Lv.**U.; **Y.**
    Bulletin. Geological Survey of **Iowa.** *See* 10708.

10360 **Bulletin** of **the Geological Survey** of **Israel.** Jerusalem. *Bull. geol. Surv. Israel* [1957–] L.MI.; **C.**S. [*C. of:* 41021ª]

10361 **Bulletin** of **the Geological Survey** of **Japan.** Tokyo, etc. *Bull. geol. Surv. Japan* [1886–37: 50–] L.BM^N.; GL.; GM. 03–37; **Db.** 05–37; **Lv.**U. 22–27; **Y.**

10362 **Bulletin. Geological Survey** of **Kenya.** Nairobi. *Bull. geol. Surv. Kenya* [1954–] L.BM.; GL.; GM.; MI.; **C.**S.; **Lv.**U.; **Y.**

10363 **Bulletin** of **the Geological Survey** of **Kiangsi.** *Bull. geol. Surv. Kiangsi* L.BM^N. 40: 48; GL. 40–.

10364 **Bulletin** of **the Geological Survey** of **Louisiana.** Baton Rouge. *Bull. geol. Surv. La* [1905–08] L.BM^N. imp.; GL. 08; GM.; P.; SC.
    Bulletin. Geological Survey of **Minnesota.** *See* 11129.

10365 **Bulletin** of **the Geological Survey** of **Nebraska.** *Bull. geol. Surv. Neb.* [1927–] L.BM^N.; SC.; **M.**P. 31–; **Bl.**U. 32–47; **Db.** 33–; **Lv.**U. 23–43; **Nw.**A. 27–47; **O.**R. 31–.

10366 **Bulletin** of **the Geological Survey** of **New Jersey.** Trenton. *Bull. geol. Surv. New Jers.* [1911–15] L.BM^N.; GL. 11–13; GM.; P.; SC. 13–15; UC. imp.; **E.**D.; J.; **Lv.**U. 11–13. [*C. as:* 11282]

10367 **Bulletin. Geological Survey** of **New South Wales.** Sydney. *Bull. geol. Surv. N.S.W.* [1922–25] L.BM.; BM^N. 25; GL.; GM.; MI. 23–25; P.; SC.; UC.; **Bm.**U. 23–25 imp.; **C.**S.; **E.**R.; **Lv.**U.; **Sh.**M. 23–24.

10368 **Bulletin. Geological Survey** of **New Zealand.** Wellington, N.Z. *Bull. geol. Surv. N.Z.* [1906–] L.BM.; BM^N.; G.; GL.; GM.; L. 06–08; MI.; R. 06–50; SC.; U.; **Abd.**U. 06–09; **Bl.**U. 06–07; **Bm.**U.; **Br.**U.; **C.**S.; UL.; **Db.**; **E.**D. imp.; R. 06–39; U. 07–39 imp.; **G.**U. 06–21; **Lv.**U. imp.; **M.**U. 08–19 imp.; **O.**R.; **Sa.** 06–09; **Y.**
    Bulletin. Geological Survey of **Newfoundland.** *See* 11321.

10369 **Bulletin. Geological Survey** of **Nigeria.** London. *Bull. geol. Surv. Nigeria* [1921–] L.BM.; BM^N.; G.; GL.; GM.; K. 21–37; MI. imp.; P. 21–37; UC.; **Bl.**U. 48–53; **Br.**U. 22–; **C.**S.; **Db.** 46–; **E.**D. 53–; J.; R. 46– imp.; U.; **G.**U. imp.; **Lv.**U.; **Rt.** 48–; **Sw.**U. 52:55; **Y.**
    Bulletin. Geological Survey, Northern Rhodesia. *See* 10041.

10370 **Bulletin. Geological Survey** of **Nyasaland.** Zomba. *Bull. geol. Surv. Nyasald* [1923–] L.BM^N. 27–37; GL. 27–; MI.; **C.**S. 27– imp.; **E.**D. 27–; **Lv.**U. 27–37 imp.; **Rt.** 47.

10371 **Bulletin** of **the Geological Survey** of **Ohio.** Columbus. *Bull. geol. Surv. Ohio* [1903–] L.BM^N.; GL.; GM. 04–; UC.; **E.**D.; **Lv.**U. 04–; **Nw.**A. 03–28; **Y.**

10372 **Bulletin. Geological Survey** of **Queensland.** Brisbane. *Bull. geol. Surv. Qd* [1895–02] L.BM^N.; GL.; P.; SC.; **E.**D. imp.; **G.**G. [*C. in:* 41023]

10372° **Bulletin. Geological Survey** of **Sierra Leone.** London. *Bull. geol. Surv. Sierra Leone* [1958–] L.BM^N.

10373 **Bulletin. Geological Survey** of **South Australia.** Adelaide. *Bull. geol. Surv. S. Aust.* [1912–] L.BM.; BM^N.; GL.; GM.; MI. 12–54 imp.; P. 12–39; UC.; **Bm.**U.; **C.**S.; **G.**T.; **Lv.**U.; **M.**U. 13–39 imp.; **O.**R. 12–22 imp.: 39–; **Y.**

10374 **Bulletin** of **the Geological Survey** of **Southern Rhodesia.** Salisbury. *Bull. geol. Surv. Sth. Rhod.* [1913–] L.BM^N. 13–16; GL.; GM.; MI.; **Bm.**U imp.; **Br.**U. imp.; **C.**S.; **E.**D. 18– imp.; **G.**U. 14– imp.; **Lv.**U. imp.; **N.**T. 56–; **O.**B. 35–; R. 31–; **Rt.** 19: 31–; **Y.**

10375 **Bulletin. Geological Survey** of **Szechuan.** Chungking. *Bull. geol. Surv. Szechuan*

10376 **Bulletin** of **the Geological Survey** of **Taiwan.** Taipei. *Bull. geol. Surv. Taiwan* [1947–] L.BM^N.; GL. 51–; **C.**S.

10377 **Bulletin. Geological Survey, Tanganyika Territory.** Dar-es-Salaam. *Bull. geol. Surv. Tanganyika* [1927–35: 48–] L.BM. 31–33; BM^N.; GL.; GM.; MI.; P.; UC.; **Abs.**U. 33: 55–57; **Bm.**U.; **Br.**U. 35: 48–; **C.**S.; **Dn.**U. 54–; **G.**U. 31–35: 48–; **Lv.**U. 31–; **O.**G. 31–35; R. 31–35; **Rt.** 48; **Sa.** 54–; **Y.** [> 10335, 1937–48]
    Bulletin. Geological Survey of **Tasmania.** *See* 21025.

10378 **Bulletin. Geological Survey** of **Uganda.** Entebbe. *Bull. geol. Surv. Uganda* [1933–] L.BM.; BM^N.; GL.; MO. 35–39; SC. **Bm.**U. 35–39; **C.**S.; **Lv.**U. 35–39; **O.**R. 35–39. [*Bulletin No.* 1a *published in* 43854]
    Bulletin. Geological Survey, Union of **South Africa.** *See* 10353.
    Bulletin. Geological Survey, United States. *See* 12510.

10379 **Bulletin. Geological Survey** of **Victoria.** Melbourne. *Bull. geol. Surv. Vict.* [1903–] L.BM. 13–; BM^N.; G. 13– imp.; GL. 03–29; GM.; MI. imp.; **Br.**U. 58–; **C.**P. 03–17; S.; **E.**D.; J.; **G.**G.; **Lv.**U. 03–29; **Y.**
    Bulletin. Geological Survey of **West Virginia.** *See* 12621.

10380 **Bulletin, Geological Survey** of **Western Australia.** Perth. *Bull. geol. Surv. West. Aust.* [1898–] L.BM. 99–; BM^N.; G. 08– imp.; GL.; GM.; I. imp.; MI. imp.; P.; R. 98–17 imp.; UC.; **Abs.**U. 12–17; **Bm.**N.; U.; **Br.**U. 10–17; **C.**S. 99–; UL.; **Db.**; **E.**D. imp.; R. imp.; T. 98–17 imp.; U. V. imp.; **G.**G. 06–; T.; **Ld.**U. 04–; **Lv.**U. imp.; **Nw.**A. 03–19 imp.; **Sa.** 99–29 imp.; **Sh.**M. 98–29; **Y.**

10381 **Bulletin. Geological Survey** of **Wyoming.** Laramie. *Bull. geol. Surv. Wyo.* **Y.**

10382 **Bulletin géologique** de **Madagascar.** Tananarive. *Bull. géol. Madagascar* L.BM^N. 49.

10383 **Bulletin géologique** de la **Nouvelle-Calédonie.** Paris. *Bull. géol. Nouv.-Calédonie* [1958–] L.BM^N.; **Y.**
    Bulletin géologique. Zavod za geološka isbrázivanya N. R. Hrvatskoj, Zagreb. *See* 21063.
    Bulletin of the **Geophysical Observatory, Tashkent.** *See* 12826.

10384 **Bulletin** of the **Geophysical Observatory, University College, Addis Ababa.** *Bull. geophys. Obs. Addis Ababa* L.MO 59–.

10385 **Bulletin** de **géophysique. Observatoire** de **géophysique, Collège Jean-de-Brébeuf.** Montréal. *Bull. Géophys. Coll. Jean-de-Brébeuf* L.MO. 57–.

10386 **Bulletin. George Foster Peabody School** of **Forestry.** Athens, Ga. *Bull. George Foster Peabody Sch. For.* [1943–] **O.**F. 43–50.

10387 **Bulletin** of the **George Washington University.** Washington, D.C. *Bull. George Wash. Univ.* **L.**BM^N. 34–48.

10388 **Bulletin** of the **Georgetown University medical Center.** Washington, D.C. *Bull. Georgetown Univ. med. Cent.*

10389 **Bulletin. Georgia Academy** of **Science.** Athens, Ga. *Bull. Ga Acad. Sci.* [1943–] **Db.**

10390 **Bulletin** of the **Georgia Agricultural Experiment Station.** Athens. *Bull. Ga agric. Exp. Stn* [1888–] **L.**AM.; EB. (ent.) 01–47; K. 96–07 imp.; P.; C.A.; **O.**F. 35– imp.; **Rt.** imp.; **Y.**

10390° **Bulletin. Georgia Agricultural Extension Service.** *Bull. Ga agric. Ext. Serv.* **Y.**

10391 **Bulletin. Georgia Board** of **Health.** Augusta. *Bull. Ga Bd Hlth*

10392 **Bulletin. Georgia Coastal Plain Experiment Station.** Tifton. *Bull. Ga cst. Plain Exp. Stn* **L.**EB. (ent.) 47–50; **O.**F. 52–; **Rt.** 34– imp.; **Y.**

10393 **Bulletin. Georgia College** of **Agriculture.** Athens. *Bull. Ga Coll. Agric.* **Rt.** 12– imp.

10394 **Bulletin** of the **Georgia Department** of **Agriculture.** Atlanta. *Bull. Ga Dep. Agric.*

10395 **Bulletin. Georgia Department** of **Entomology.** Atlanta. *Bull. Ga Dep. Ent.* **L.**BM^N. 17– imp.; EB. 99– imp.; **G.**G. 06–; **Y.**

10396 **Bulletin. Georgia Department** of **Game** and **Fish.** Augusta. *Bull. Ga Dep. Game Fish*

10397 **Bulletin** of the **Georgia State Dental Society.** Macon. *Bull. Ga St. dent. Soc.* [1901–32] [*C. as:* 26068]

10398 **Bulletin. Georgia State Engineering Experiment Station.** Atlanta. *Bull. Ga St. Engng Exp. Stn* [1938–] **L.**P.; **Y.**

10399 **Bulletin. Geotechnical Committee. Government Railways** of **Japan.** Tokyo. *Bull. geotech. Comm. Govt Rlys Japan* [1931–] **L.**GM.; P.; SC.

10400 **Bulletin. Geoteknisk institut.** Copenhagen. *Bull. geotek. Inst.* [1956–] **L.**P.; **Y.**

10401 **Bulletin. Geranium Society.** London. *Bull. Geranium Soc.* [1952–] **L.**BM.; HS.; **N.**U. 53–.

10402 **Bulletin** of the **Ghana Geographical Association.** Accra. *Bull. Ghana geogr. Ass.* [1957–] **L.**G.; **E.**U. 57. [*C. of:* 10405]

10403 **Bulletin. Glass Research Association.** London. *Bull. Glass Res. Ass.* [1921–25] **L.**C. 22–25 imp.; P. imp.; SC.; **Bm.**U.; **Nw.**A. 22–25 imp.; **Sh.**G.

10404 **Bulletin. Gold Coast Department** of **Soil** and **Land-Use Survey.** Kumasi. *Bull. Gold Cst Dep. Soil Ld-Use Surv.* [1954–56] **Rt.** 55.

10405 **Bulletin** of the **Gold Coast Geographical Association.** Achimota. *Bull. Gold Cst geogr. Ass.* [1956] **L.**G. [*C. as:* 10402]

10406 **Bulletin. Goldberg's Laboratory** for **Precision Work.** *Bull. Goldberg's Lab. Precis. Wk* [1945–46] **L.**P. [*Supplement to:* 25611]

    Bulletin. Government Botanical Garden, Nikita, Yalta. *See* 12761.

10406° **Bulletin** of the **Government Chemist, Jamaica.** Kingston. *Bull. Govt Chem. Jamaica* [1951–] **L.**BM.

10407 **Bulletin** of the **Government Forest Experiment Station, Meguro.** Tokyo. *Bull. Govt Forest Exp. Stn Meguro* **L.**BM^N. 49–; L. 52–; **Y.**

10408 **Bulletin. Government Hospital** for the **Insane.** Washington. *Bull. Govt Hosp. Insane, Wash.* **L.**BM. 09–; **Lv.**U. 10–12.

    Bulletin. Government Mechanical Laboratory. Tokyo. *See* 21506.

10409 **Bulletin** of the **Government Research Institute.** Taihoku, Formosa. *Bull. Govt Res. Inst., Taihoku* **L.**SC. 24–; **Rt.** 29.

10410 **Bulletin** du **Grand conseil** des **vétérinaires** de **France.** Besançon. *Bull. gr. Cons. Vét. Fr.*

10411 **Bulletin** de la **grand Masse.** Paris. *Bull. gr. Masse* [1949–] **L.**BA.

10412 **Bulletin. Gravure Technical Association.** New York. *Bull. Gravure tech. Ass.* [1950–] **Lh.**P.

10413 **Bulletin** of the **Green Section** of the **United States Golf Association.** Washington. *Bull. Green Sect. U.S. Golf Ass.* **E.**B. 21–; **Ld.**U. 30–.

10414 **Bulletin** du **groupe** d'**études scientifiques.** Paris. *Bull. Grpe Étud. scient.* **L.**BM. 10–13.

10415 **Bulletin** du **groupe français** des **Argiles.** *Bull. Grpe fr. Argiles* [1955–] **L.**P.; **Abd.**S.; **Y.** [*C. of:* 15224]

10416 **Bulletin. Groupement** des **Associations françaises** de **propriétaires** d'**appareils** à **vapeur.** Paris. *Bull. Grpmt Ass. fr. Propr. Appar. Vap.* **L.**P. 54★; **Y.** [*C. of:* 12355]

10417 **Bulletin** du **Groupement international** pour la **recherche scientifique** en **stomatologie.** Paris, etc. *Bull. Grpmt int. Rech. scient. Stomat.* [1958–] **L.**D.; MD. imp.

10418 **Bulletin. Guam Agricultural Experiment Station.** Washington. *Bull. Guam agric. Exp. Stn* [1921–26] **L.**BM^N.; EB. 21–22; SC.; **M.**P.; **Rt.**

10419 **Bulletin** of the **Gulf Biologic Station.** Cameron, La. *Bull. Gulf biol. Stn*

10420 **Bulletin. H. Shaw School** of **Botany.** St. Louis, Mo. *Bull. H. Shaw Sch. Bot.* **C.**UL. 28–.

10421 **Bulletin** of the **Hadley Climatological Laboratory** of the **University** of **New Mexico.** Albuquerque. *Bull. Hadley clin. Lab.* [1899–05] **L.**MO. 00–03; P.; SC. [*C. as:* 12539]

10422 **Bulletin. Halifax River Bird Club.** Daytona. *Bull. Halifax Riv. Bird Club*

10423 **Bulletin. Hannah Dairy Research Institute.** Glasgow, Kirkhill. *Bull. Hannah Dairy Res. Inst.* [1929–] **L.**AM.; C. 32–; P. 29–50; TD.; **Abd.**U. 29–50; **Br.**U. 50–; **C.**A.; **E.**U. 29–33; **G.**PH. 36–; U. 29–42; **Lv.**U. 29–50; **N.**U. imp.; **Nw.**A.; **O.**R.; **R.**D.; **Rt.**; **Y.**

10424 **Bulletin** of the **Hardy Plant Society.** London. *Bull. hardy Pl. Soc.* [1957–] **L.**BM.; BM^N.; HS.; K.; **C.**UL.; **E.**A.; **O.**R.

10425 **Bulletin** of the **Harper-Adams Agricultural College.** Newport, Salop. *Bull. Harper-Adams agric. Coll.* [1903–] **L.**AM.; BM. 18–; P. 07–20; SC. 04–; **Db.** 12–; **Rt.**

10426 **Bulletin. Harpswell Laboratory.** Salisbury Cove, Me. *Bull. Harpswell Lab.* [1950–] **L.**SC.

    Bulletin. Harvard College Observatory. *See* 9523.

10427 **Bulletin. Harvard Forest.** Petersham. Mass. *Bull. Harv. Forest* [1920–] **L.**BM^N. 21–; K. 20–22; P. 22–; **Bn.**U. 47–; **C.**A. 32– imp.; **O.**F.

10428 **Bulletin of the Harvard Medical Alumni Association.** Boston. *Bull. Harv. med. Alumni Ass.* [1891–] **L.**BM. 91–00 imp.; S. 93–00 imp.

Bulletin. Harvard University Medical School. Department of Neurology *See* 10099. **Division of Surgery** *See* 10107.

10429 **Bulletin of the Hatano Tobacco Experiment Station.** Hatano. *Bull. Hatano Tob. Exp. Stn* **C.**A. 52–; **Md.**H. 51–54; **Rt.** 51–.

10430 **Bulletin. Hatch Agricultural Experiment Station.** Hatch, Mass. *Bull. Hatch agric. Exp. Stn* [1888–07] **L.**AM.; BM^N. imp.; EB. (ent.) 01–07; K. 97–07 imp.; P.; **Rt.** imp.; **Y.** [*C. as:* 10866]

10431 **Bulletin. Hawaii Agricultural Experiment Station.** Honolulu. *Bull. Hawaii agric. Exp. Stn* [1901–] **L.**AM.; BM. 04–; BM^N. 14–43 imp.; EB. 04–; K. 03– imp.; P.; UC. 32–; **Bm.**U. 01–08 imp.; **C.**A.; **Cr.**P. 04–24; **G.**M. 12–33 imp.; **Lv.**P. 01–28 imp.; U imp.; **M.**P. 05–; **Nw.**A. 32–44 imp.; **O.**R. 32–; **Rt.**; **Y.**

10432 **Bulletin. Hawaiian Sugar Planters' Association Experiment Station.** Honolulu. *Bull. Hawaiian Sug. Plrs' Ass. Exp. Stn*
    Botanical series [1921–] **L.**BM^N. 21–24; K. 21–24; **C.**A. 21–45; UL.; **O.**R. 21: 24. [*C. of:* 10100]
    Entomological series [1905–36] **L.**BM^N.; EB.; K. 09 imp.; SC. 24–36; **C.**A. 12–36; B. 06–36; UL.; **O.**R.; **Rt.** 05–08.

Bulletin. Hawaiian Sugar Planters' Association Experiment Station. Division of Agriculture and Chemistry *See* 10093. **Division of Pathology and Physiology** *See* 10100.

Bulletin. Hawaiian Volcano Observatory. *See* 21937.

Bulletin. Health of Animals Branch, Department of Agriculture, Canada. *See* 9963.

10433 **Bulletin of the Health Organisation, League of Nations.** Geneva. *Bull. Hlth Org.* [1937–46] **L.**D.; EB.; GH.; LI.; MA.; MC.; PH.; S. 40–46 imp.; SC.; SH.; TD.; **Abd.**R. 37–41; **Bm.**P.; U.; **Dn.**U.; **E.**U.; **G.**PH.; T.; U. 40–44; **Ld.**U.; **M.**P.; **O.**AP.; R.; **R.**D. [*C. of:* 41469; *C. in:* 12649]

10434 **Bulletin of the Heating and Ventilating Research Council.** London. *Bull. Heat. Vent. Res. Coun.* [1956–] **L.**BM.; P. 56–58; **E.**A.; **Lv.**P.; **O.**R.

10435 **Bulletin hebdomadaire. Conseil sanitaire maritime et quarantenaire d'Égypte.** Alexandrie. *Bull. hebd. Cons. sanit. marit. quarant. Égypte* [1900–] **L.**TD. 25–40 imp.

10436 **Bulletin hebdomadaire de documentation. Office central de l'acétylène et de la soudure autogène.** Paris. *Bull. hebd. Docum. Off. cent. Acét. Soud. autog.*

10437 **Bulletin hebdomadaire. Erdbebenwarte der Universität.** Budapest. *Bull. hebd. ErdbWarte Univ. Bpest*

10438 **Bulletin hebdomadaire des observatoires sismiques de la Hongrie et de la Croatie.** *Bull. hebd. Obs. sism. Hong. Croat.*

Bulletin hebdomadaire de la Société des architectes diplômés par le gouvernement. *See* 3966.

Bulletin hebdomadaire. Station sismique d'Irkoutsk. *See* 18905.

Bulletin of the Helicopter Association of Great Britain. *See* 26085.

10439 **Bulletin of the Helwan Observatory.** Cairo. *Bull. Helwan Obs.* [1915–36] **L.**AS.; BM.; SC.; **C.**O.; **E.**O.; R. 33–36; U. 33–36; **O.**R. 20–36. [*C. of:* 10753]

10440 **Bulletin. Hemlock Arboretum.** Germantown, Pa. *Bull. Hemlock Arbor.* **L.**BM^N. 33.

10441 **Bulletin of the Hendry-Connell Research Foundation.** Kingston, Ontario. *Bull. Hendry-Connell Res. Fdn* [1936–] **L.**MA. 36–38; MD. 36–38; **Br.**U.

10442 **Bulletin de l'Herbier Boissier.** Genève & Bâle. *Bull. Herb. Boissier* [1893–08] **L.**BM.; BM^N.; K.; L.; **C.**P.; **E.**B.; **O.**BO. [*C. in:* 11873]

Bulletin de l'Herbier de l'Institut botanique de Bucarest. *See* 9110.

Bulletin de l'Herbier du Jardin botanique de Nikita. *See* 12761.

10443 **Bulletin. Hertfordshire Institute of Agriculture.** St Albans. *Bull. Herts. Inst. Agric.* [1923–] **L.**SC. 24–38; **C.**A. 27–38; **Rt.** 23–29.

Bulletin. High Duty Alloys, Ltd. Slough. *See* 21703.

10444 **Bulletin. Highway Research Board.** Washington. *Bull. Highw. Res. Bd* [1946–] **L.**P.; **Rt.** 55; **Y.**

10445 **Bulletin of the Hill Museum, Witley.** London. *Bull. Hill Mus. Witley* [1921–32] **L.**BM.; BM^N.; E.; Z.; **Abs.**N.; **C.**UL.; **Db.**; **E.**A.; **Lv.**U. 21–22; **O.**H.; R.

10446 **Bulletin. Hill Observatory, Sidmouth.** *Bull. Hill Obs. Sidmouth* [1914–19: 38–] **L.**AS.; BM. 14–19; SC. 14–19; **Db.** 14–19; **E.**O. 14–19; R. 14–19.

10447 **Bulletin of the Hiroshima Agricultural College.** Saijo. *Bull. Hiroshima agric. Coll.* [1958–] **L.**AM.; **C.**A.; **Rt.**

10448 **Bulletin d'histologie appliquée à la physiologie et à la pathologie et de technique microscopique.** Paris. *Bull. Histol. appl. Physiol. Path.* [1924–50] **L.**MD.; U.; UC.; **C.**UL.; **E.**U.; **Ld.**U. 38–50; **M.**MS. 46–50; **O.**R. 26–50; **W.** 47–50. [*C. in:* 11088]

10449 **Bulletin historique et scientifique de l'Auvergne.** Clermont-Ferrand. *Bull. hist. scient. Auvergne* [1881–] **L.**BM.; **G.**T. 24–.

10450 **Bulletin of History of Dentistry.** Chicago. *Bull. Hist. Dent.* [1953–] **L.**D.

10451 **Bulletin of the History of Medicine.** Baltimore. *Bull. Hist. Med.* [1939–] **L.**BM. 52–; MA.; MD.; S.; SC.; TD.; U. 58–; **Abd.**U.; **Bl.**U.; **Bm.**U.; **Cr.**MD.; **Dn.**U. 52–; **E.**S. 45–; U.; **G.**F. 54–; U. imp.; **Ld.**U. 62–; **Lv.**M.; **M.**MS.; **Nw.**A.; **O.**R. 39–44; **Sa.**; **Y.** [*C. of:* 10625]

10452 **Bulletin Hoblitzelle Agricultural Laboratory.** Renner. *Bull. Hoblitzelle agric. Lab.* [1950–] **C.**A.

10453 **Bulletin. Hokkaido Agricultural Experiment Station.** Sapporo. *Bull. Hokkaido agric. Exp. Stn* [1905–] **L.**BM^N. 22–29 imp.; EB. (ent.) 13–37; P.; **Rt.** 06–; **Y.**

10454 **Bulletin of the Hokkaido Forestry Experiment Station.** Napporo. *Bull. Hokkaido For. Exp. Stn* **Rt.** 45. [*C. as:* 11651]

10455 **Bulletin of the Hokkaido Regional Fisheries Research Laboratory.** Yorchi, Hokkaido. *Bull. Hokkaido reg. Fish. Res. Lab.* [1951–] **L.**AM. 52–; **Lo.**; **Pl.**M.

10456 **Bulletin** of the **Hokuriki Agricultural Experiment Station.** Takada. *Bull. Hokuriki agric. Exp. Stn* [1960–] **C.**A.; **Y.**

10456° **Bulletin. Holden Arboretum.** Cleveland. *Bull. Holden Arbor.* [1949–] **O.**F.

10457 **Bulletin. Honan Museum.** Kaifeng. *Bull. Honan Mus.* **L.**BM^N. 33–34.

10458 **Bulletin** of the **Hong Kong Chinese Medical Association.** Hong Kong. *Bull. Hong Kong Chin. med. Ass.*

10459 **Bulletin** de l'**Hôpital civil français de Tunis.** Tunis. *Bull. Hôp. civ. fr. Tunis*

10460 **Bulletin** de l'**Hôpital Saint-Michel.** Paris. *Bull. Hôp. St-Michel* [1929–32] **L.**MA.; **Br.**U. imp.; **Lv.**M. imp. [*C. as:* 4236]

10461 **Bulletin horaire** du **Bureau international** de l'**heure.** Paris. *Bull. horaire* [1921–] **L.**AS. 22–; **SI.** 45–; **C.**O.; **E.**O. 22–; **O.**O.; **Te.**N.; **Y.** [*Divided into series*]

10462 **Bulletin horticole.** Liège. *Bull. hort., Liège* **Md.**H. 52–; **Y.**

10463 **Bulletin. Horticultural Branch (Section), Kanagawa Agricultural Experiment Station,** Minomiya. Kanagawa. *Bull. hort. Brch Kanagawa agric. Exp. Stn* [1953–] **C.**A.; **Md.**H.

10464 **Bulletin. Horticultural Division, Tokai-Kinki Agricultural Experimental Station.** Okitsu. *Bull. hort. Div. Tokai-Kinki agric. exp. Stn* [1952–] **Br.**A.; **C.**A.; **Md.**H.; **Y.**

10465 **Bulletin. Horticultural Society** of **Alexandria.** *Bull. hort. Soc. Alexandria* [1904–10] **L.**K.

10466 **Bulletin** d'**horticulture méditerranéenne.** *Bull. Hort. méditerr.*

10467 **Bulletin** of the **Hospital** for **Joint Diseases.** New York. *Bull. Hosp. Jt Dis., N.Y.* [1940–] **L.**MA. 46–; **MD.** 47–; **S.** 47–; **M.**MS. 57–. [–61*; *C. as:* Journal of the Hospital for Joint Diseases]

10468 **Bulletin** of the **Hospital** for **Sick Children.** Toronto. *Bull. Hosp. sick Child., Toronto* [1952–] **L.**MD.; **Bl.**U.; **G.**U.; **Ld.**U.; **M.**MS. 54–; **Nw.**A. 52–55.

10469 **Bulletin** of the **Hudson County Dental Society.** Woodcliff, N.J. *Bull. Hudson Cty dent. Soc.*

Bulletin of the **Hungarian College of Horticulture.** *See* 29198.

Bulletin of the **Hungarian Geological Society.** *See* 19768.

10470 **Bulletin. Hyderabad Agricultural Department.** Deccan. *Bull. Hyderabad agric. Dep.* [1936–] **C.**A.

10471 **Bulletin. Hyderabad Commerce and Industries Department.** Deccan. *Bull. Hyderabad Comm. Ind. Dep.* **L.**P. 30–32. [*C. of:* 10530]

10472 **Bulletin** of the **Hyderabad Geological Survey.** Deccan. *Bull. Hyderabad geol. Surv.* [1936–] **E.**R. 43–.

Bulletin. Hydraulic Laboratory, National Bureau of **Standards.** Washington. *See* 11210.

10473 **Bulletin** de l'**hydraulique agricole.** Paris. *Bull. Hydraul. agric.*

Bulletin of the **Hydrographic Department** of the **Imperial Japanese Navy.** *See* 10474.

10474 **Bulletin** of the **Hydrographic Department.** Tokyo. *Bull. hydrogr. Dep., Tokyo* [1917–?] **L.**AS. 33; **BM.** 18; **MO.** 26–30; **SC.; O.**B. 33; **Wo.** 33– imp.; **Y.** [*C. as:* 22537]

Bulletin. Hydrographic Office. Tokyo. *See* 10474.

10475 **Bulletin hydrographique. Conseil permanent internationale** pour l'**exploration** de la **mer.** Copenhague. *Bull. hydrogr. Cons. perm. int. Explor. Mer.* [1908–] **L.**AM. 08–47; **BM.; BM**^N.; **G.** 11–; **L.** 27–41 imp.; **MO.** 26–28; **R.** 08–39 imp.; **U.** 08–46; **UC.** 08–11; **Z.** 08–46; **Abd.**M.; **U.; Bm.**U.; **Bn.**U. 08–46 imp.; **C.**B.; **Db.** 10–15; **Dm.** imp.; **E.**M. imp.; **R.; U.** 23–; **G.**U. 08–15: 32–; **Lo.; Lv.**U.; **M.**U. 08–15: 20–46; **Mi.; O.**R.; **Pl.**M.; **Sa.** 08–15: 20–24; **Wo.** imp.; **Y.** [*C. of:* 12456]

10476 **Bulletin hydrographique. République** d'**Haiti.** Port-au-Prince. *Bull. hydrogr. Répub. Haiti* **L.**SC. 24–.

10477 **Bulletin hydrologique mensuel.** Prague. *Bull. hydrol. mens., Prague* **L.**MO. 30–33*. [*C. as:* 38551^a]

10478 **Bulletin** of **Hygiene.** London. *Bull. Hyg., Lond.* [1926–] **L.**AM. 39– imp.; **BM.; D.** (curr.); **EB.; H.; IC.** 37–; **LI.; MA.; MC.; MD.; MY.** 43–; **P.; PH.** 42–; **SC.; SH.; TD.; TP.** 47–; **U.** 45–; **UC.** 26–39; **UCH.; Abd.**R.; **U.; Abs.**N.; **U.** 26–30: 47–; **Bl.**U. imp.; **Bm.**U. 34–; **Br.**U. 31–; **C.**PA.; **UL.; Cr.**MD. 33–; **Db.; Dn.**U. 40–; **E.**A.; **AR.** 56–; **U.; Ep.**D. 46–; **Ex.**U. 48–56; **G.**M.; **PH.** 36–; **T.** 53–; **Ld.**U. 44–; **Lh.**FO. 39–; **Lv.**P. 54–; **U.; M.**C.; **D.** 57–; **MS.; P.** 28–; **Nw.**A. imp.; **O.**B. 35–; **R.; R.**D.; **Sa.; Sh.**IO. 39–; **U.** 42–; **W.** 29–; **Wd.** 45–; **Y.** [*C. of:* 48563]

10479 **Bulletin** d'**hygiène.** Montréal. *Bull. Hyg., Montréal* [1914–] **L.**H. 43–; **SH.** 43–; **TD.; G.**PH. 38–.

10480 **Bulletin** of the **Hygienic Laboratory.** Washington. *Bull. hyg. Lab., Wash.* [1900–30] **L.**BM. 03–30; **BM**^N. 07–30; **EB.** (ent.) 03–30; **H.** 03–30; **LI.** 00–28; **MC.; MD.; P.** 10–28 imp.; **S.** 08–30; **SC.** 11–30; **TD.** 03–30 imp.; **Bm.**U.; **Br.**U. 09–12 imp.; **C.**P. 08–30 imp.; **PA.** 01–30 imp.; **Db.** 08–30; **E.**U. 05–30 imp.; **G.**M. 10–30; **Ld.**U. 19–30 imp.; **Lv.**U. 00–23. [*C. as:* 34135]

10480° **Bulletin. Hyogo Prefectural Medical College.** *Bull. Hyogo pref. med. Coll.* [*C. as:* 10756]

10481 **Bulletin IAI.** Institute for International Collaboration in Agriculture and Forestry. Prague. *Bull. IAI* (1948–) **L.**AM. 48–50; **O.**AEC.; **Rt.** 49–50.

10482 **Bulletin I.O.S.T.A.** Institut pour l'organisation scientifique de travail en agriculture. Paris. *Bull. I.O.S.T.A.* **L.**AM. 51–57; **Sil.** 50–57. [*C. as:* 52884]

Bulletin. Ichthyological Laboratory, Baku. *See* 24312.

10483 **Bulletin. Idaho Agricultural Experiment Station.** Moscow. *Bull. Idaho agric. Exp. Stn* [1892–] **L.**AM.; **EB.** (ent.) 16–; **K.** 98–04 imp.; **P.; C.**A.; **Ld.**U. **Rt.** imp.; **Y.**

10484 **Bulletin** of the **Idaho Bureau** of **Mines** and **Geology.** Moscow. *Bull. Idaho Bur. Mines Geol.* [1920–] **L.**GM.; **MI.** imp.; **P.; Y.**

10485 **Bulletin. Illinois Agricultural Experiment Station.** Urbana. *Bull. Ill. agric. Exp. Stn* [1888–] **L.**AM.; **BM.** 09–; **BM**^N. 91– imp.; **EB.** (ent.) 94–; **K.** 88–09 imp.; **P.; U.** 06– imp.; **UC.** 08– imp.; **Abs.**N. 19– imp.; **Br.**A. 02– imp.; **C.**A.; **UL.** 91–; **Cr.**P. 02– imp.; **Db.** 09– imp.; **E.**B. 10– imp.; **U.** 32–; **G.**U. 08–; **Ld.**U. 95– imp.; **M.**P. 09–; **U.** imp.; **Nw.**A. 10– imp.; **P.** 94– imp.; **O.**F. 51–; **R.** 09–; **RE.** 35–55 imp.; **Rt.** imp.; **Sa.** 09–; **Y.**

10486 **Bulletin. Illinois Coal Mining Investigation.** Urbana. *Bull. Ill. Coal Min. Invest.* [1913–16] **L.**BM.; **GL.** 15–16; **GM.; P.** 15–16; **UC.** 14–16 imp.; **Bm.**N. 14–16; **E.**R. 14–16; **U.** 15–16; **Lv.**U. 14–16 imp.; **M.**U. 14–16; **O.**R. 14–16. [*C. as:* 9916]

10487 **Bulletin** of the **Illinois Department** of **Agriculture.** Springfield. *Bull. Ill. Dep. Agric.*

Bulletin. Illinois Department of **Public Works, Division** of **Waters.** *See* 10110.

10488 **Bulletin. Illinois Food** and **Dairy Commission.** Springfield. *Bull. Ill. Fd Dairy Commn* **G.**U. 14– imp.

10489 **Bulletin. Illinois Highway Commission.** Springfield. *Bull. Ill. Highw. Commn*

10490 **Bulletin. Illinois Miners'** and **Mechanics' Institute.** Urbana. *Bull. Ill. Miners' Mech. Inst.* [1914] **L.**BM.; GL.; **Bm.**N.; **Db.**; E.U. imp.; **Lv.**U.; **M.**U.; O.B.

10491 **Bulletin** of the **Illinois State Dental Society.** Quincy. *Bull. Ill. St. dent. Soc.* [1918–31] [*C. of:* 33441; *Replaced by:* 22757]

10492 **Bulletin. Illinois State Florists' Association.** Urbana. *Bull. Ill. St. Flor. Ass.* **Md.**H. 59–.

10493 **Bulletin. Illinois State Geological Survey.** Urbana. *Bull. Ill. St. geol. Surv.* [1906–] **L.**BM. 08–; BM^N.; G. 07– imp.; GL.; GM.; SC. 07–; U. 07–; UC. 08–25 imp.; **Bm.**N. 08– imp.; **Br.**U. 07– imp.; **C.**S. 56–; UL. 07–; **Db.** 08–; E.J. 10–; R. 08– imp.; U. 08–; **G.**N. 16–38 imp.; U. 08–23; **Lv.**U. 08– imp.; **M.**U. 08– imp.; **O.**R. 08– imp.; **Y.** [*For* Co-operative Coal Mining Series *See* 9916]

10494 **Bulletin** of the **Illinois State Laboratory** of **Natural History.** Urbana. *Bull. Ill. St. Lab. nat. Hist.* [1876–17] **L.**BM^N.; EB.; SC. 84–17; Z.; **Abs.**U. 15–17; **C.**A. 95–17; P.; **Db.** 05–17; E.R. 03–13 imp.; U. 03–10; **G.**N.; U.; **Lv.**U.; O.F. 09–17 imp.; **Pl.**M. [*C. as:* 10495]

10495 **Bulletin** of the **Illinois State Natural History Survey.** Urbana. *Bull. Ill. St. nat. Hist. Surv.* [1918–] **L.**BM^N.; EB.; Z.; **Abs.**U.; **Bm.**N. 22–; **C.**B.; P.; **Db.**; E.R. 21–; **G.**N.; U.; **Ld.**U. 24–; **Lv.**U.; O.F. imp.; **Pl.**M.; **Y.** [*C. of:* 10494]

Bulletin. Illinois State Water Survey. *See* 22773.

10496 **Bulletin. Illinois University Engineering Experiment Station.** Urbana. *Bull. Ill. Univ. Engng Exp. Stn* [1904–39] **L.**AV. 20–39 imp.; BM. 09–39 imp.; I. 07–39 imp.; NF. 07–39 imp.; P.; SC. 08–39; U. imp.; UC. 17–39 imp.; **Bm.**P. 06–39; **Br.**U.; **C.**ENG. 06–39; UL. 06–39; **Db.** 08–39; E.R. 12–39 imp.; U. (pt. 1) 20–39; **G.**E.; **Ld.**P. 08–39; U. 20–39; **Lv.**U. 20–39; **M.**P. 09–39 imp.; T. imp.; U. 06–39 imp.; **N.**U. 08–39 imp.; **Nw.**A. 09–39 imp.; P. 09–39 imp.; **O.**R. 09–39; **Sh.**M. 06–39; IO. 16–39; **Y.** [*C. as:* 11744]

10497 **Bulletin** of **Immediate Information. Connecticut Agricultural Experiment Station.** New Haven. *Bull. immed. Inf. Conn. agric. Exp. Stn* **L.**EB. (ent.) 06–29★; SC. 17–29; **C.**A.; **Rt.** 24–29. [*C. as:* 14168]

10498 **Bulletin** of the **Imperial Agricultural Experiment Station** of **Japan.** Nishigahara, Tokyo. *Bull. imp. agric. Exp. Stn Japan* [1924–32] **L.**AM.; BM^N. imp.; EB.; K.; MY. 24–28; P.; SC.; **Bm.**U.; **C.**A.; **E.**B.; R.; **Lv.**U. 28–32; **M.**U. [*C. of:* 10500; *Replaced by:* 11226]

Bulletin. Imperial Bureau of **Pastures** and **Forage** (*afterwards* and **Field Crops**). *See* 9892.

10499 **Bulletin. Imperial Bureau** of **Plant Genetics. Herbage.** Aberystwyth. *Bull. imp. Bur. Pl. Genet. Herb.* [1930–38] **L.**AM.; K. 30–37 imp.; P.; SC.; **Abs.**A.; N.; U.; **Bl.**U. imp.; **Bn.**U.; **C.**A.; **E.**A.; **Ld.**U. 30–37; O.R.; RE. 31–38 imp.; **R.**U.; **Rt.** 30–37. [*C. as:* 9892]

10500 **Bulletin** of the **Imperial Central Agricultural Experiment Station, Japan.** Nishigahara, Tokyo. *Bull. imp. cent. agric. Exp. Stn Japan* [1905–19] **L.**AM.; BM^N. 19; EB.; MY.; P.; **Bm.**U.; **Db.** 05–14; E.B.; **G.**U. imp.; **Nw.**A. imp.; **Rt.** [*C. as:* 10498]

Bulletin. Imperial Chemical Industries Central Agricultural Control. *See* 9720.

10501 **Bulletin. Imperial College** of **Agriculture** and **Forestry.** Morioka, Japan. *Bull. imp. Coll. Agric. For., Morioka* [1907–53] **L.**AM.; MY. 23–35; **C.**A. imp.; **Db.** 23–53; E.B. 23–13; **Ld.**U. 23–40; **Lv.**U. 07–40; **Nw.**A. 07–24; O.R. 23–30 imp.; **Rt.** 07–40. [*C. as:* 25986]

Bulletin of the **Imperial Earthquake Investigation Committee.** Tokyo. *See* 10137.

10503 **Bulletin** of the **Imperial Forestry Experiment Station, Meguro.** Tokyo. *Bull. imp. For. Exp. Stn Meguro* **O.**F. 31–.

Bulletin of the **Imperial Geological Survey** of **Japan.** *See* 10361.

10504 **Bulletin** of the **Imperial Institute.** London. *Bull. imp. Inst., Lond.* [1903–48] **L.**AM.; B. 20–48; BM.; BM^N.; DI. 43–48; EB. 38–48; FO. 20–48; IC. 27–48; K.; LE. 30–48; MI.; MT. 04–48; MY. 32–48; P.; PH. 23–48; PR. 14–48; PT.; RI.; SC.; SH.; TP.; U.; UC. 03–04; **Abd.**P. 24–48; R. 05–48; U.; **Abs.**A. 28–48; N. 11–48; **Bm.**C. 26–48; P.; U. 03–04: 16–30: 48; **Bn.**U. 26–30; **Br.**P. 19–48; U. 06–48 imp.; **Bra.**P. 12–47; **C.**UL.; **Cr.**M.; P. imp.; **Db.** 04–48; **Dn.**U. 04–48; **E.**A.; B. 22–48; D. 43–46; G.; R. 27–48; T. 03–10 imp.: 36–48; U. 16–48; **G.**M. 05–48; MG. 10–48 imp.; U.; **Hu.**G. 30–48; **Ld.**P. 14–48; U. 05–48 imp.; W. 20–48; **Lv.**P. 05–48; U.; **M.**C. 04–16: 19–48; P.; **Md.**H. 30–48; **N.**P. 46–48; U. 44–48; **Nw.**A. 04–48; P. imp.; **O.**G. 15–48 imp.; R.; **R.**D. 31–48; U. imp.; **Rt.**; **Sa.** 24–48; **Sh.**G. 16–48; M. 26–30; **Sil.** 45–48; **St.**R. 40–48; **Sy.**R. [*C. of:* 22830; *C. as:* 14913 and 14915]

Bulletin of the **Imperial Institute** of **Agricultural Research, Pusa.** *See* 9258.

10505 **Bulletin** of the **Imperial Plant Quarantine Station, Yokohama.** *Bull. imp. Pl. Quarant. Stn Yokohama* **L.**BM^N. 22; EB. 22–24★. [*C. as:* 51980]

10506 **Bulletin** of the **Imperial Sericultural College.** Tokyo. *Bull. imp. seric. Coll., Tokyo* **L.**SC. 16–.

Bulletin of the **Imperial Sericultural Experiment Station, Japan.** *See* 11738.

10507 **Bulletin** of the **Imperial Zootechnical Experiment Station, Chiba-Shi.** *Bull. imp. zootech. Exp. Stn Chiba-Shi*

10508 **Bulletin. Independent Biological Laboratories, Palestine.** Tel-Aviv. *Bull. indep. biol. Labs Palest.* [1932–] **L.**BM^N. imp.; SC.; EB. (ent.); **C.**A.; **Dm.** 34–57; O.F. imp.; **Pl.**M. 32–57 imp.

10509 **Bulletin** of the **India Section** of the **Electrochemical Society.** Bangalore. *Bull. India Sect. electrochem. Soc.* [1952–] **L.**C. 52–55; P. 55–; **Wd.** 56–; **Y.**

10510 **Bulletin. Indian Association** for the **Cultivation** of **Science.** Calcutta. *Bull. Indian Ass. Cult. Sci.* [1909–18] **L.**BM. 14–18; P. 12–18; SC. 12–18; UC. 12–18; **Br.**U. 12–18; **C.**P.; **Db.** 17–18; **E.**R.; **Nw.**A. 12–18.

10511 **Bulletin. Indian Central Coconut Committee.** Ernakulam. *Bull. Indian cent. Cocon. Comm.* [1949–57] **C.**A. 55–57; **Md.**H. [*C. as:* 14695]

10511° **Bulletin. Indian Central Cotton Committee.** Bombay. *Bull. Indian cent. Cott. Comm.* **M.**C. 22–29 imp.

10512 **Bulletin. Indian Central Jute Committee.** Calcutta. *Bull. Indian cent. Jute Comm.* [1938–46] **L.**TP.; **C.**A. 42–46; **Ld.**U. 45–46.   [*C. as*: 27142]

10513 **Bulletin. Indian Coffee Board Research Department.** Balehonnur. *Bull. Indian Coff. Bd Res. Dep.* [1948–] **L.**EB.; **C.**A.; **Rt.**

10514 **Bulletin. Indian Council** of **Agricultural Research.** Delhi. *Bull. Indian Coun. agric. Res.* [1951–] **L.**BM.; EB.; P.; **C.**A.; **Y.**   [*C. of*: 32125]

10515 **Bulletin** of the **Indian Council** of **Ecological Research.** Debra Dun. *Bull. Indian Coun. ecol. Res.* [1955–] **L.**K.; **Rt.** 55.

10516 **Bulletin. Indian Council** for **Scientific Research.** Delhi. *Bull. Indian Coun. scient. Res.* [1955–] **O.**R.

10517 **Bulletin** of **Indian Industrial Research.** Delhi. *Bull. Indian ind. Res.* [1936–41] **L.**P.; SC.

10518 **Bulletin** of **Indian Industries** and **Labour.** Calcutta. *Bull. Indian Inds Labour* **L.**P. 21–22 imp.; **O.**B. 21–23.

10519 **Bulletin** of the **Indian Lac Association** for **Research.** Namkuni. *Bull. Indian Lac Ass. Res.* [1928–31] **L.**BM^N.; C.; EB. (ent.); K. 29–31; U.; **C.**A.; UL.; **E.**U.; **Ld.**U.; **Lv.**U. imp.; **O.**R.; **R.**D.; **Rt.** imp.   [*C. as*: 10520]

10520 **Bulletin** of the **Indian Lac Research Institute.** Namkuni. *Bull. Indian Lac Res. Inst.* [1932–] **L.**BM.; BM^N. 32–48 imp.; C. 32–44; EB. (ent.) imp.; K. 32–43 imp.; P. 32–48; U.; **C.**A. 32–40; UL.; **E.**U. 32–35; **Ld.**U.; **Lv.**U. imp.; **M.**P. 36–42 imp.; **O.**B. 32–40 imp.; R.; **R.**D.; **Rt.** 32–42 imp.; **Y.**   [*C. of*: 10519]

10521 **Bulletin. Indian Rubber Board.** Kottayam. *Bull. Indian Rubb. Bd* [1951–54] **L.**P.   [*C. as*: 11628]

10522 **Bulletin. Indian Society** of **Soil Science.** New Delhi. *Bull. Indian Soc. Soil Sci.* [1938–51] **L.**BM.; **C.**A.; **O.**RE. imp.; **Rt.**; **Y.**

Bulletin. Indian Standards Institution. *See* 22676.

10523 **Bulletin. Indiana Agricultural Experiment Station.** Lafayette. *Bull. Indiana agric. Exp. Stn* [1885–] **L.**AM.; EB. (ent.); K. 89–09 imp.; P. 91–; **Br.**A. 08–44 imp.; **Ld.**U. 12–19: 37–; **O.**RE. 40–; **Rt.** imp.

10524 **Bulletin. Indiana Board** of **Forestry.** Indianapolis. *Bull. Indiana. Bd For.*

10525 **Bulletin. Indiana Department** of **Conservation. Geological Survey.** *Bull. Indiana Dep. Conserv. geol. Surv.* **Y.**

10526 **Bulletin. Indiana Division** of **Geology.** Indianapolis. *Bull. Indiana Div. Geol.* **L.**BM^N. 48–.

Bulletin. Indiana Engineering Experiment Station. *See* 10165.

10527 **Bulletin. Indiana Society** for **Mental Hygiene.** Indianapolis. *Bull. Indiana Soc. ment. Hyg.*

10528 **Bulletin of the Indiana State Dental Association.** Fort Wayne. *Bull. Indiana St. dent. Ass.* [1922–32]   [*C. as*: 26153]

10529 **Bulletin. Indianapolis Dental Society.** Indianapolis. *Bull. Indianapolis dent. Soc.*

10530 **Bulletin. Industrial Laboratory. Hyderabad Department** of **Industries** and **Commerce.** *Bull. ind. Lab. Hyderabad* **L.**P. 20–26*.   [*C. as*: 10471]

10531 **Bulletin** of **Industrial Psychology** and **Personnel Practice.** Melbourne. *Bull. ind. Psychol.* [1945–] **L.**MD.; TD. 46–53 imp.

10531^a **Bulletin. Industrial Recovery Advisory Councils.** Leeds. *Bull. ind. Recov. advis. Coun.* [1951–54] **G.**M.   [*C. as*: 11225]

10532 **Bulletin. Industrial Research Council, Eire.** Dublin. *Bull. ind. Res. Coun. Eire* [1937–] **L.**BM.; P. 37–46 imp.; SC.; **O.**B.

10533 **Bulletin industriel** de **renseignements professionnels** et **techniques** des **pêches maritimes.** Paris. *Bull. ind. Renseign. prof. tech. Pêch. marit.*

10534 **Bulletin d'information. Association française** pour l'**étude** des **eaux.** *Bull. Inf. Ass. fr. Étude Eaux* [1950–] **L.**P. 52–58; **Wa.**W. 52–58.   [*C. as*: 17356]

10535 **Bulletin d'information. Association française** des **ingénieurs** et **techniciens** de l'**aéronautique.** *Bull. Inf. Ass. fr. Ingrs Techns Aéronaut.* **L.**AV. 46.

10535^c **Bulletin d'information. Association internationale** pour le **calcul analogique.** Bruxelles. *Bull. Inf. Ass. int. Calcul analog.* [1956–]

10536 **Bulletin d'information** de l'**Association internationale d'hydrologie scientifique.** London. *Bull. Inf. Ass. int. Hydrol. scient.* [1956–] **L.**NC.; **Rt.** [*English edition at*: 10666^c; *see also* 9471]

10537 **Bulletin d'information** de l'**Association technique** de **fonderie** et du **Centre technique** des **industries** de la **fonderie.** Paris. *Bull. Inf. Ass. tech. Fond.* [1946–48] **L.**SC.   [*C. as*: 10986 and 10987]

10538 **Bulletin d'information. Association technique** pour la **production** et l'**utilisation** de l'**énergie nucléaire.** Paris. *Bull. Inf. Ass. tech. Prod. Util. Énerg. nucl.* [1960–61] **L.**P.; **Y.**   [*C. of*: 9517; *C. as*: Bulletin d'information. Association technique de l'énergie nucléaire]

10539 **Bulletin d'information** du **C.N.E.E.M.A. Centre** national d'études et d'expérimentation de machinisme agricole. Antony. *Bull. Inf. C.N.E.E.M.A.* **Sil.** 58–.

Bulletin d'information. C.O.E.C. Paris. *See* 10542.

10540 **Bulletin d'information CORESTA.** Centre de coopération pour les recherches scientifiques rélatives au tabac. Paris. *Bull. Inf. CORESTA* [1957–] **L.**P.; **C.**A.; **Md.**H.; **Y.**

10541 **Bulletin d'information. Centre** d'information pour le **développement** du **conditionnement** d'**air,** de la **ventilation,** du **filtrage** de l'**air** et du **dépoussiérage.** Paris. *Bull. Inf. Cent. Inf. Dév. Condit. Air* [1957–] **L.**P.

10542 **Bulletin d'information. Comité central** d'**océanographie** et d'**étude** des **côtes.** Paris. *Bull. Inf. Com. cent. Océanogr. Étude Côtes* [1949–57] **C.**PO. 51–57; **Lo.** 52–57; **Lv.**U.; **Wo.** 51–57.   [*C. as*: 12976]

10543 **Bulletin d'information** du **Comité spécial** de l'**Année géophysique internationale, Conseil international** des **unions scientifiques.** *Bull. Inf. Com. spéc. Année geophys. int. Cons. int. Un. scient.* **Wo.** 53–.

10544 **Bulletin d'information** et de **documentation. Association technique** de la **première transformation** de l'**acier** et des **métaux non-ferreux.** Paris. *Bull. Inf. Docum. Ass. tech. prem. Transf. Acier* [1947–] **L.**NF.

10545 **Bulletin** d'**information** et de **documentation**. **Office** des **pêches maritimes**. Paris. *Bull. Inf. Docum. Off. Pêch. mar.* Pl.M. 51–52 imp. [*C. as:* 49058]

10546 **Bulletin** d'**information** de la **Fédération française** des **syndicats patronaux** de l'**imprimerie** et des **industries graphiques**. Paris. *Bull. Inf. Féd. fr. Synds patron. Imprim.* Lh.P. 55–.

10547 **Bulletin** d'**information I.N.E.A.C.** Institut national pour l'étude agronomique du Congo belge. Bruxelles. *Bull. Inf. I.N.E.A.C.* [1952–] L.AM.; K.; MO. 52–57; C.A.; Md.H.; O.F.; **Y.** [*Published in:* 9232]

10548 **Bulletin** d'**information**. Institut de l'**énergie solaire**, Université d'**Alger**. *Bull. Inf. Inst. Énerg. sol. Univ. Alger* **Y.**

Bulletin d'**information** de l'**Institut national** pour l'**étude agronomique** du **Congo belge**. Bruxelles. *See* 10547.

10549 **Bulletin** d'**information**. **Laboratoire central** des **industries électriques**. Paris. *Bull. Inf. Lab. cent. Inds élect.* L.P. 56–. [*Supplement to:* 47230]

10550 **Bulletin** d'**information** sur la **lèpre**. Bruxelles. *Bull. Inf. Lèpre* [1953–] **Y.**

10551 **Bulletin** d'**information** du **Ministère** de la **santé publique** et de la **population**. Paris. *Bull. Inf. Minist. Santé publ.* [1955–] L.MD.; SH. (1 yr); TD.

10552 **Bulletin** of the **Information Service** of the **Association** for the **Study** of the **European Quaternary**. Moscow. *Bull. Inf. Serv. Ass. Study eur. Quatern.* [1931–] L.BM^N. 31–32; UC.; Ld.U. 31–32.

Bulletin. **Information Service**. **Food** and **Agriculture Organisation**. **United Nations**. *See* 18909.

10553 **Bulletin** d'**information** du **Service** de **santé militaire**. Paris. *Bull. Inf. Serv. Santé milit.* [1942–44] L.MD.; SC. 43–44; TD. [*C. of:* 47567; *C. as:* 47130]

10554 **Bulletin** d'**information** de la **Société suisse** des **ingénieurs** et des **architectes**. *Bull. Inf. Soc. suisse Ingrs Archit.*

10555 **Bulletin** d'**information** du **Sous-Secrétariat** de l'**aéronautique**. Paris. *Bull. Inf. Sous-Secr. Aéronaut.*

10556 **Bulletin** d'**information** de l'**U.G.G.I.** Union géodésique et géophysique internationale. Bruxelles, Paris. *Bull. Inf. U.G.G.I.* [1952–] L.MO.; P.; Abd.M.; Bl.U.; C.UL.; E.R.; G.U.; Ld.U. 53–; Lv.U. 53–56; **Wo.** 53– imp.; **Y.**

Bulletin d'**information**. **Union géodésique** et **géophysique internationale**. *See* 10556.

Bulletin d'**information**. **Union internationale** de la **chimie pure** et **appliquée**. *See* 23419.

10557 **Bulletin** d'**informations aéronautiques**. Bruxelles. *Bull. Infs aéronaut.* L.P. (curr.)

10558 **Bulletin** des **informations agricoles**. **Service botanique** de l'**Algérie**. Alger. *Bull. Infs agric. Algér.*

10559 **Bulletin** d'**informations**, de **documentation** et de **statistique**. **Ministère** des **postes**, **télégraphes** et **téléphones**. Paris. *Bull. Infs Docum. Statist. Minist. Postes* [1932–39] L.SC. 36–39. [*C. as:* 47480]

10559° **Bulletin** d'**informations mécanographiques**. *Bull. Infs mécanogr.* [1953–] L.BM.

10560 **Bulletin** d'**informations**. **Météorologie nationale**. Paris. *Bull. Infs Mét. natn.* [1946–] L.MO. 46–48.

10561 **Bulletin** d'**informations pratiques** concernant les **applications** de l'**électricité**. Paris. *Bull. Infs prat. Applic. Élect.*

10562 **Bulletin** d'**informations scientifiques** et **techniques**. **Commissariat** à l'**énergie atomique**. Paris. *Bull. Infs scient. tech. Commt Énerg. atom.* [1957–] L.BM.; P.; SC.; **M.P.**

10563 **Bulletin** d'**informations**. **Soil Zoology Committee**, **International Society** of **Soil Science**. Versailles. *Bull. Infs Soil Zool. Comm. int. Soc. Soil Sci.* [1957–] Rt.

10564 **Bulletin** d'**informations techniques**. **Centre** d'**études** et **recherches** des **charbonnages** de **France**. Paris. *Bull. Infs tech. Cent. Étud. Rech. Charbonn. Fr.* L.MI. 51– imp.

10565 **Bulletin** d'**informations techniques**. **Centre technique** du **bois**. Paris. *Bull. Infs tech. Cent. tech. Bois* [1955–] L.P. 59–; **Y.**

10566 **Bulletin** d'**informations**. **Union internationale** des **architectes**. Paris. *Bull. Infs Un. int. Archit.* L.BA. 48–.

10567 **Bulletin** des **ingénieurs** des **constructions civiles**. Paris. *Bull. Ingrs Constr. civ.*

10568 **Bulletin** des **ingénieurs E.C.A.M.** Bruxelles. *Bull. Ingrs E.C.A.M.*

10569 **Bulletin**. **Inland Waterways Association**. London. *Bull. inld WatWays Ass.* [1946–] Bm.P.

10570 **Bulletin**. **Inspectie** van den **landbouw** in **West-Indie**. Paramaribo. *Bull. Insp. Landb. W.-Indie* L.K. 04–08*; P. 08. [*C. as:* 9951]

10571 **Bulletin**. **Inspection générale** de l'**agriculture**. Alger. *Bull. Insp. gén. Agric., Alger* Br.A. 41–47 imp.

10572 **Bulletin** de l'**Inspection** du **travail** et de l'**hygiène industrielle**. Paris. *Bull. Insp. Trav. Hyg. ind.*

10573 **Bulletin** des **installateurs électriciens** de **Nancy** et de l'**Est** de la **France**. Nancy. *Bull. Install. Élect. Nancy*

10574 **Bulletin** de l'**Institut aérodynamique** de **Koutchino**. St. Pétersbourg & Moscou. *Bull. Inst. aérodyn. Koutchino* [1909–23] L.MO. 09–14; P. 06–12; SC. 09; Ld.U.

10575 **Bulletin** de l'**Institut aérotechnique** de l'**Université** de **Paris**. Paris. *Bull. Inst. aérotech. Univ. Paris* [1911–14] L.P.; SC. 12.

10576 **Bulletin** de l'**Institut agricole** de **Pau**. Pau. *Bull. Inst. agric. Pau*

10577 **Bulletin** de l'**Institut agronomique** et des **stations** de **recherches** de **Gembloux**. Gembloux. *Bull. Inst. agron. Stns Rech. Gembloux* [1932–] L.AM. imp.; BM^N.; EB.; K.; MY.; P. 35–; Abd.R.; Abs.A. 55–; R. imp.; Br.A. 41–; C.A.; E.R. 41–; Hu.G.; Md.H. 38–; R.D. 51–; Rt.; Sil. 34–; **Y.** [*Replaces:* 3311]

Bulletin de l'**Institut astronomique**. Léningrad. *See* 12741.

Bulletin de l'**Institut biologique**. Sofia. *See* 24315.

10578 **Bulletin** de l'**Institut botanique** de **Buitenzorg**. Buitenzorg. *Bull. Inst. bot. Buitenz.* [1898–05] L.BM^N.; K.; L. 04–05; MO. 04; R.; C.P. 98–04; E.B. 04–05; Lv.U. 02–04; Rt. 99–05. [*C. as:* 9949]

10579 **Bulletin** de l'**Institut botanique** de **Caen.** Caen. *Bull. Inst. bot. Caen* L.BM^N. 36–; SC. 48–.

Bulletin de l'**Institut botanique.** Sofia. *See* 24317.

10580 **Bulletin** de l'**Institut botanique** de l'**Université** de **Liége.** *Bull. Inst. bot. Univ. Liége*

10581 **Bulletin** de l'**Institut colonial** et **agricole** de **Nancy.** Nancy. *Bull. Inst. colon. agric. Nancy* [1904–]

10582 **Bulletin** de l'**Institut colonial** de **Marseille. Section** des **matières grasses.** Marseille. *Bull. Inst. colon. Marseille Sect. Matièr. grasses* [1917–46] L.C. 33–40; K. 23–46; P.; SC. 18: TP. 19–46; **Md.**H. 38–46; **Sy.**R. 23–46 imp. [*C. as:* 36169]

10583 **Bulletin** de l'**Institut** du **désert.** Heliopolis. *Bull. Inst. Désert* [1953–] L.BM^N.; SC.; **O.**A.; **Y.** [*C. of:* 10587]

10584 **Bulletin** de l'**Institut** d'**Égypte.** Le Caire. *Bull. Inst. Égypte* [1857–] L.BM. 1859–; BM^N. 80–; G. 72–84 imp.; GL. 37– imp.; SC. 39–49; TP. 06–50 imp.; UC. 86–90 imp.; **C.**P. 02–; UL. 80–; **Db.** 04–.

Bulletin de l'**Institut égyptien.** *See* 10584.

10585 **Bulletin** de l'**Institut équatoriale** de **recherches** des **mines** et de la **géologie.** Le Caire. *Bull. Inst. équat. Rech. Mines Géol.* [1960–] L.BM^N.; GL.; MI.; **G.**U.; **Y.** [*C. of:* 10087]

10586 **Bulletin** de l'**Institut** d'**études centrafricaines.** Brazzaville. *Bull. Inst. Étud. centafr.* [1945–] L.AN.; BM^N. imp.; EB. 50–; K. 50–; TD. 50–; TP. 50–; **C.**A. 50–; **Hu.**G. 51–; **O.**F. 51– imp.; **Y.** [*C. of:* 12154; *not published* 1948–49]

Bulletin de l'**Institut** des **forêts.** Sofia. *See* 24382.

10587 **Bulletin** de l'**Institut Fouad I** du **désert.** Heliopolis. *Bull. Inst. Fouad I Désert* [1951–52] L.BM^N.; **O.**A.; **Y.** [*C. as:* 10583]

10588 **Bulletin** de l'**Institut française** d'**Afrique Noire.** Paris, Dakar. *Bull. Inst. fr. Afr. noire* [1939–53: 54– *in series below*] L.AN. 39–53; BM^N. 54–; EB.; K.; L.; MY. 52–53; SC.; TD.; U.; UC.; Z. 52–53; **E.**G.; **G.**U.; **Nw.**A.; **Pl.**M. 47–53; **Y.**

Série A. Sciences naturelles L.BM^N.; EB.; K.; L.; MY.; SC.; TD.; TP.; U.; UC.; Z.; **E.**G.; **G.**U.; **Nw.**A.; **Pl.**M.; **Y.**

Série B. Sciences humaines L.AM.; TP.; **E.**G.; **G.**U.; **Nw.**A.; **Y.**

[*Replaces:* 9852]

10589 **Bulletin** de l'**Institut général psychologique.** Paris. *Bull. Inst. gén. psychol.* [1903–] L.PS.; U. 05: 27–29; **Abs.**U. 03–08 imp. [*C. of:* 10605]

10590 **Bulletin** de l'**Institut géologique** de **Géorgie.** Tiflis. *Bull. Inst. géol. Géorgie* L.BM^N. 32–38.

Bulletin. Institut géologique de la **République macédonienne.** *See* 54436.

Bulletin de l'**Institut géologique** de **Zagreb.** *See* 56804.

10591 **Bulletin** de l'**Institut** des **hautes études marocaines.** *Bull. Inst. ht. Étud. maroc.* [1920] [*C. in:* 22127]

Bulletin de l'**Institut hydrologique.** Léningrad. *See* 24357.

10592 **Bulletin** de l'**Institut** d'**hygiène** du **Maroc.** Rabat. *Bull. Inst. Hyg. Maroc* [1931–38: 41–] L.EB. 41–; MA. 45–; TD. imp.; **Y.**

Bulletin de l'**Institut international** du **froid.** *See* 10680, 23820 and 33445.

10593 **Bulletin** de l'**Institut international** de **statistique.** Rome. *Bull. Inst. int. Statist.* [1886–] L.AM. 30– imp.; BM.; G. 86–89 imp.; H. 86–38: 54–55 imp.; TD.; U. 86–05; **Abd.**U. 14–; **Br.**U. 89–09; **C.**SL. 32–55; **E.**U. 87– imp.; **Ld.**U. 26–; **M.**R.; **O.**B. 86–15; **Y.**

Bulletin de l'**Institut** et du **Jardin botanique** de l'**Université** de **Belgrade.** *See* 21342.

Bulletin de l'**Institut Leshaft.** *See* 24435.

Bulletin de l'**Institut M. Gorki** pour l'**étude** de la **région** du **Volga-bas.** *See* 24489.

Bulletin de l'**Institut** de **mathématique** et **mécanique** à l'**Université** de **Koubycheff.** *See* 24438.

Bulletin de l'**Institut** de **médecine clinique** et **sociale.** Sofia. *See* 24384.

Bulletin de l'**Institut** de **médecine experimentale.** Sofia. *See* 24378.

10594 **Bulletin** de l'**Institut métapsychique international.** Paris. *Bull. Inst. métapsych. int.* [1920–27] L.U. [*C. as:* 47445]

10595 **Bulletin** de l'**Institut** de **Metchnikoff.** Kharkov. *Bull. Inst. Metchnikoff* **Pl.**M. 36.

Bulletin de l'**Institut météorologique, Université Debreczen.** *See* 29211.

Bulletin de l'**Institut** de **microbiologie** de l'**Académie bulgare** des **sciences.** *See* 24422.

Bulletin de l'**Institut** de **morphologie.** Sofia. *See* 24385.

Bulletin de l'**Institut national agronomique.** Brunn. *See* 48707.

10596 **Bulletin** de l'**Institut national genevois.** Genève. *Bull. Inst. natn. genev.* [1853–] L.BM.; BM^N.; R.; **C.**UL.; **Cr.**M. 14–; **Db.** 77–; **Y.**

10597 **Bulletin** de l'**Institut national** d'**hygiène.** Paris. *Bull. Inst. natn. Hyg.* [1946–] L.H.; MA. 48–; MC. 50–; MD. 51–; SC. 48–; SH. 50–57 imp.; TD.; **Abd.**R.; **R.**D.; **Y.**

Bulletin de l'**Institut national** de **recherches technologiques** de **Roumanie.** *See* 9119.

10598 **Bulletin** de l'**Institut** et **Observatoire** de **physique** du **globe** du **Puy-de-Dôme.** Clermont-Ferrand. *Bull. Inst. Obs. Phys. Globe Puy-de-Dôme* [1929–48] L.MO. 34–48; **E.**U. 31–36; **Y.** [*C. as:* 11364]

10599 **Bulletin** de l'**Institut océanographique** (*formerly* de **Monaco**). *Bull. Inst. océanogr. Monaco* [1906–] L.AM.; BM^N.; G.; L.; MO. 20– imp.; R.; SC.; UC. 06–28; Z.; **Abd.**M.; U.; **Bn.**U. imp.; **C.**B. 21–; P.; **Cr.**M. 11–; **Db.**; **Dm.** 20–; **E.**F.; R.; U. 06–21; **G.**U.; **Lo.**; **Lv.**U.; **M.**U.; **Mi.**; **Pl.**M.; **O.**R. 58–; **Wo.** imp. [*C. of:* 11171]

Bulletin de l'**Institut** d'**organisation scientifique** de **travail** en **agriculture.** *See* 10482.

10600 **Bulletin** de l'**Institut Pasteur.** Paris. *Bull. Inst. Pasteur, Paris* [1903–] L.BM.; BM^N. 03–10; EB. 26–; IC. 03–30; LI.; MA. 09–; MC.; MD.; P.; R. 10–; RI.; S. 03–40: 43–55 imp.; SC.; TD.; UCH.; V. 11–51; VC. 22–47; **Abd.**U. 20–; **Bl.**U. 12–39; **Bm.**U.; **Br.**U. 49–; **C.**PA.; **Cr.**MD. 04–; **Db.** 11–; **Dn.**U. 19–57; **E.**P.; U.; **Ex.**U. 28–33; **G.**M. 27–40; U.; **Ld.**U. 11–; **Lv.**U. 03–11; **M.**U. 10–; **Nw.**A. imp.; **O.**P. 28–; R.; **Pl.**M. 21–46; **R.**D. 06–; **Rt.**; **Sh.**U.; **Ste.** 03–30; **W.**; **Y.**

10601 **Bulletin** de l'**Institut Pasteur palestinien.** Jerusalem. *Bull. Inst. Pasteur palest.* L.LI. 28–29.

Bulletin de l'**Institut** de **pathologie comparée** des **animaux domestiques.** Sofia. *See* 24391.

Bulletin de l'**Institut** des **pêches maritimes** de **Gdynia.** *See* 7186.

10602 **Bulletin de l'Institut des pêches maritimes** du **Maroc.** Rabat, Casablanca. *Bull. Inst. Pêch. marit. Maroc* [1953–] **L.**BM^N.; **Dm.**; **Lo.**; **Lv.**U.; **Pl.**M.; **Y.**

Bulletin de l'Institut pédagogique du **Caucase** du **Nord** (de **Géorgie**). *See* 24355.

Bulletin de l'Institut de pédologie et de **géobotanique** de l'**Université** de l'**Asie Centrale.** *See* 24387.

10603 **Bulletin de l'Institut du pétrole. Université** de **Strasbourg.** *Bull. Inst. Pétrôle Univ. Strasb.* [1923–24] **L.**P.; U.; UC. 23; **Lv.**U. 23 imp. [*C. of:* 10780]

Bulletin de l'Institut physico-mathématique de l'**Académie russe des sciences.** *See* 24340.

10604 **Bulletin de l'Institut du pin.** Bordeaux. *Bull. Inst. Pin* [1924–] **L.**C. 24–38 imp.; P. 34–39 imp.; **Bn.**U. 24–39.

Bulletin de l'Institut polytechnique à Ivanovo-Vosniesensk. *See* 24395.

Bulletin de l'Institut polytechnique Lénine à **Tiflis.** *See* 24360.

10605 **Bulletin de l'Institut psychologique international.** Paris. *Bull. Inst. psychol. int.* [1900–] **L.**PS. [*C. as:* 10589]

10606 **Bulletin de l'Institut r. des sciences naturelles** de **Belgique.** Bruxelles. *Bull. Inst. r. Sci. nat. Belg.* [1949–] **L.**BM^N.; EB. (ent.); GL.; GM.; L.; R.; SC.; UC.; Z.; **Abd.**M.; **Bl.**U. imp.; **Br.**U.; **C.**P.; **Cr.**M. imp.; **Db.**; **Dm.**; E.R.; **G.**U.; H.U.; **Ld.**U.; **Lo.**; M.U.; N.U. **Nw.**A.; **Pl.**M.; **Sh.**U.; **Y.** [*C. of:* 11173]

Bulletin de l'Institut de recherches biologiques et de la **Station biologique** à l'**Université** de **Perm.** *See* 24314.

Bulletin de l'Institut de recherches biologiques de l'**Université** de **Molotov.** *See* 24314.

Bulletin de l'Institut de recherches forestières de la **Suède.** *See* 29864.

Bulletin de l'Institut des sciences et des **arts** de l'**Arménie soviétique.** *See* 34386.

Bulletin de l'Institut scientifique de biologie et de **géographie, Irkoutsk.** *See* 24316.

Bulletin de l'Institut scientifique de Léningrad. *See* 24417.

10607 **Bulletin de l'Institut scientifique de recherches géographiques** et **géochimiques** en **Asie.** Téhéran. *Bull. Inst. scient. Rech. géogr. géochim. Asie* [1930] **L.**BM^N. [*C. as:* 3000]

Bulletin de l'Institut scientifique de Saint Pétersbourg. *See* 24466.

10608 **Bulletin de l'Institut technique roubaisien.** Tourcoing. *Bull. Inst. tech. roubais.*

10609 **Bulletin de l'Institut textile de France.** *Bull. Inst. text. Fr.* [1948–] **L.**P. 49–; **Ld.**W.; **M.**C.; **Y.** [*C. of:* 53001]

10610 **Bulletin de l'Institut du verre.** *Bull. Inst. Verre* [1946] **Sh.**G. [*C. as:* 56271]

Bulletin de l'Institut de zoologie appliquée et de **phytopathologie.** Léningrad. *See* 24416.

Bulletin de l'Institut zoologique de l'**Académie bulgare des sciences.** *See* 24565.

Bulletin de l'Institut de zootechnie. Sofia. *See* 24392.

10610° **Bulletin. Institute of Advanced Architectural Studies.** *Bull. Inst. advd archit. Stud.* **E.**A. 59–.

Bulletin of the Institute of Agricultural Engineering, Oxford University. *See* 10644.

10611 **Bulletin of the Institute of Agricultural Research, Tohoku University.** Sendai. *Bull. Inst. agric. Res. Tohoku Univ.* [1949–] **Abd.**S. 51–; **C.**A.; **Y.**

10612 **Bulletin. Institute of Agriculture, Anand. Botanical Series.** Anand. *Bull. Inst. Agric. Anand bot. Ser.* [1943–] **L.**SC.; **Abs.**A.; **C.**A.

10613 **Bulletin. Institute of Agriculture, Anand. General Series.** Anand. *Bull. Inst. Agric. Anand gen. Ser.* [1942–] **C.**A.

Bulletin of the Institute of Agriculture of East Siberia. *See* 24546.

Bulletin. Institute of Amateur Cinematographers. *See* 22677.

10614 **Bulletin. Institute of Applied Agriculture** on **Long Island.** Farmingdale, N.Y. *Bull. Inst. appl. Agric. Long Isl.* **L.**SC. 20–22.

10615 **Bulletin of the Institute of Applied Biology.** Brooklyn. *Bull. Inst. appl. Biol.* [1949–] **L.**SC.; E.R. 49.

Bulletin of the Institute of Biology. Sofia. *See* 24315.

10616 **Bulletin of the Institute for Chemical Research, Kyoto University.** Kyoto. *Bull. Inst. chem. Res. Kyoto Univ.* [1929–] **L.**C. 50– imp.; P. 53–; RI. 55–; SC. 50–; **Bl.**U. 55–; **Bn.**U. 55–; **Br.**U. 55–; **C.**CH. 55–; P. 55–; **Db.** 55–; E.R. 55–; **G.**U. 50–56; N.U. 55–; **Rt.** 50– imp.; **Y.**

10616° **Bulletin of the Institute of Chemistry, Academia sinica.** Taipei. *Bull. Inst. Chem. Acad. sin.* **L.**C. 61–; **C.**A. 60–.

10617 **Bulletin of the Institute of Commercial Research in the Tropics.** Liverpool. *Bull. Inst. comm. Res. Trop.* [1909] **L.**BM.; BM^N.; K.

Bulletin of the Institute for controlling Pests and **Diseases.** Leningrad. *See* 24376.

10618 **Bulletin. Institute of Cotton Genetics.** Lima. *Bull. Inst. Cott. Genet., Lima* [1944–] **L.**SC.

10619 **Bulletin. Institute of Ethnology.** Taipei. *Bull. Inst. Ethnol., Taipei* [1956–] **L.**AN.

Bulletin of the Institute of Experimental Agriculture of Georgia. *See* 56452.

10620 **Bulletin of the Institute for Fisheries Research, University of Michigan.** Ann Arbor. *Bull. Inst. Fish. Res. Univ. Mich.* [1932–] **L.**BM^N. 32; **Bl.**U. 32; **Bm.**U.; **Dm.** 32: 50; **M.**U. 32.

10621 **Bulletin. Institute of Forest Products, Washington State University.** Seattle. *Bull. Inst. Forest Prod. Wash. St. Univ.* [1950–] **O.**F. imp.

Bulletin of the Institute of Freshwater Fisheries. Leningrad. *See* 24550.

10622 **Bulletin. Institute of Fuel.** London. *Bull. Inst. Fuel* [1946–47] **L.**P.; **Br.**U. [*Supplement to:* 26190; *C. of:* 23692]

10623 **Bulletin. Institute of Gas Technology.** Chicago. *Bull. Inst. Gas Technol.* [1948–] **Y.**

10624 **Bulletin of the Institute of Geology, Academia sinica.** Peking. *Bull. Inst. Geol. Acad. sin.* [1956–] **L.**GM.; **C.**S.; E.R.

Bulletin of the Institute of Geology. Skopje. *See* 54436.

Bulletin of the Institute of Grain Husbandry of the **South-Eastern U.S.S.R.** *See* 12769.

10625 **Bulletin** of the **Institute** of **History** of **Medicine, Johns Hopkins University.** Baltimore. *Bull. Inst. Hist. Med. Johns Hopkins Univ.* [1933–38] L.MD.; S.; SC. 36–38; **Abd.**U.; **Bl.**U. 33–34; **Bm.**U.; **Br.**U.; **Cr.**MD. 34–38; **E.**U.; **G.**F. 33; **Lv.**M.; **M.**MS.; **Nw.**A.; **O.**R.; **Sa.** 34–38; **Sh.**U.   [*C. as:* 10451]

    Bulletin of the **Institute** of **Ichthyology.** Leningrad.   *See* 24418.

10626 **Bulletin** of the **Institute** of **Industrial Research.** Washington. *Bull. Inst. ind. Res., Wash.* [1911–14] L.P.

    Bulletin of the **Institute** of **Insect Control, Kyoto University.**   *See* 8613.

10627 **Bulletin** of the **Institute** of **Jamaica. Science Series.** Kingston. *Bull. Inst. Jamaica Sci. Ser.* [1940–] L.BM^N.; L. 51–; **C.**B. 40–48; UL.; **Db.**; **E.**R.; **O.**R.; **Y.**

10628 **Bulletin** of the **Institute** of **Margarine Manufacturers.** Washington. *Bull. Inst. Marg. Mfrs*

10629 **Bulletin** of the **Institute** of **Marine Biology, Academia sinica.** Peking. *Bull. Inst. mar. Biol. Acad. sin.* [1958–] L.BM^N.

10630 **Bulletin** of the **Institute** of **Marine Medicine** in **Gdansk.** Gdansk. *Bull. Inst. mar. Med. Gdansk* [1957–] L.EB.; LI.; MA.; TD.; **Pl.**M.; **Sh.**U.; **Y.**   [*C. of:* 10631]

10631 **Bulletin** of the **Institute** of **Marine** and **Tropical Medicine, Medical Academy, Gdansk.** *Bull. Inst. mar. trop. Med. Gdansk* [1948–56] L.EB.; LI.; MA.; MD.; TD.; **Pl.**M. 50–56; **Sh.**U.   [*C. as:* 10630]

10632 **Bulletin** of the **Institute** of **Medical** and **Laboratory Technology.** London. *Bull. Inst. med. Lab. Technol.* [1945–50] L.BM.; H. imp.; **Db.** 46–50 imp.; **E.**A.; **R.**D.   [*C. of:* 33446; *C. in:* 26438]

    Bulletin from the **Institute** for **Medical Research, Federated Malay States.**   *See* 10633.

10633 **Bulletin** from the **Institute** for **Medical Research, Federation** of **Malaya.** Kuala Lumpur. *Bull. Inst. med. Res. Fed. Malaya* [1924–] L.BM^N. imp.; EB. (ent.); H. 24–41 imp.; LI. 24–39 imp.; MC.; MD. 24–34 imp.; P. 31–40 v. imp.; TD.; U. 27–; **E.**U. 34–; **Lv.**U.; **Y.**   [*C. of:* 30188]

10634 **Bulletin** of the **Institute** of **Medical Research. University** of **Madrid.** *Bull. Inst. med. Res. Univ. Madr.* [1948–] L.GH.; H.; LI.; MA.; MC.; MD.; S.; TD.; **Abd.**R.; **Bl.**U.; **Bm.**U.; **C.**APH.; UL.; **E.**U.; **G.**U. imp.; **Nw.**A.

10635 **Bulletin** of the **Institute** of **Metal Finishing.** London. *Bull. Inst. Metal Finish.* [1951–58] L.AV.; BM.; C.; **Bm.**P.; T.; **Lh.**P. 54–58; **O.**R. 52–58.   [*C. of:* 17325; *C. in:* 53760]

10636 **Bulletin** of the **Institute** of **Metals.** London. *Bull. Inst. Metals* [1951–] L.EE.; QM. 52–; SC.; **Abd.**U.; **Bm.**T.; **C.**UL.; **Co.**T.; **Cr.**P.; **E.**A.; U.; **G.**U.; **Ld.**P.; **M.**D.; **Nw.**A.; **Sa.**; **Sh.**SC.; **Y.**   [*Issued as part of:* 26197]

10637 **Bulletin. Institute** of **Mining** and **Technology, State Bureau** of **Mines** and **Mineral Resources New Mexico.** Soccoro. *Bull. Inst. Min. Technol. New Mex.* L.BM^N. 61–.

10638 **Bulletin** of the **Institute** of **Nuclear Sciences 'Boris Kidrich'.** Belgrade. *Bull. Inst. nucl. Sci. Boris Kidrich* [1953–] L.C.; P.; **Bl.**U.; **Bn.**U.; **C.**P.; **Db.**; **Ld.**U.; **Te.**N.; **Y.**   [*C. of:* 42376]

10639 **Bulletin** of the **Institute** of **Paper Chemistry.** Appleton, Wis. *Bull. Inst. Pap. Chem.* [1930–58] L.P.; PR. 51–58; **Lh.**P. 35–38 imp.; **M.**C. 51–58; **Y.**   [*C. as:* 316]

10640 **Bulletin** of the **Institute** of **Physical** and **Chemical Research, Japan.** Tokyo. *Bull. Inst. phys. chem. Res. Japan* [1928–48] L.C.; I.; M.; P. 28–41 imp.; SC.; UC.; **Abs.**U.; **Bm.**U.; **Br.**U.; **C.**P.; **E.**R.; U. 28–40; **G.**U. 28–41; **Ld.**U. 28–41; **M.**U. 28–41 imp.; **N.**U. 34–41 imp.; **Nw.**A. 28–37; **O.**R.; **Sa.**; **Sw.**U.   [*C. as:* 45234]

10641 **Bulletin. Institute** of **Physics** (and the Physical Society). London. *Bull. Inst. Phys., Lond.* [1950–] L.AV. 56–; BM.; RI. (curr.); VC. 58–; **Bl.**U. 58–; **Bm.**U. 57–; **Bn.**U. 56–; **Br.**U. 57–; **C.**UL.; **Co.**T. (1 yr); **E.**A.; **Lc.**A. 57–; **M.**T. 58–; U. 58– imp.; **N.**T. (5 yr.); **O.**R.; **Sh.**U.; **Sil.** 61–; **Y.**

10642 **Bulletin Institute** of **Plant Industry, Indore.** *Bull. Inst. Pl. Ind. Indore* [1934–] L.SC. 34–39; **C.**A. 34–55; **Rt.** 34–39.

10643 **Bulletin** of the **Institute** of **Public Health.** Tokyo. *Bull. Inst. publ. Hlth, Tokyo* [1951–] L.H.; LI. 52–; TD.; **Y.**

10644 **Bulletin** of the **Institute** for **Research** in **Agricultural Engineering, Oxford University.** Oxford. *Bull. Inst. Res. agric. Engng Oxf. Univ.* [1926–29] L.AM.; P.; SC.; **Abs.**A.; N.; **Bn.**U.; **C.**A.; UL.; **Db.**; **O.**R.; **Rt.**

10645 **Bulletin** of the **Institute** of **Science** and **Industry.** Melbourne. *Bull. Inst. Sci. Ind., Melb.* [1919–25] L.AM.; BM.; BM^N. 24–25; EB. (ent.); K. 19–22 imp.; P.; SC.; UC.; **Abs.**U. imp.; **Bl.**U. 23–25; **Bm.**P.; U.; **C.**A. imp.; **E.**U.; **Ld.**U. imp.; **Lv.**U.; **M.**U.; **Nw.**A. imp.; **O.**BO. (biol.); F. 21–25 imp.; RH.; **Rt.**; **Sa.**   [*C. of:* 9214; *C. as:* 9928]

10646 **Bulletin. Institute** of **Science Technology.** London. *Bull. Inst. Sci. Technol.* [1955–] L.BM.; CB. 56–; P. (curr.); TD. (2 yr.); **C.**UL. 57–; **E.**A. 57–; **M.**P.; **Y.**   [*C. of:* 48407°]

10646° **Bulletin. Institute** of **Science, University** of **Tehran.** *Bull. Inst. Sci. Univ. Tehran* **Y.**

10647 **Bulletin** of the **Institute** of **Statistics, Oxford University.** Oxford. *Bull. Inst. Statist. Oxf. Univ.* [1940–45] L.B. 41–45 imp.; **Abd.**R.; U.; **Bm.**U.; **C.**UL.; **Cr.**U.; **Db.** 41–45; **Dn.**U.; **E.**A.; U. 43–45; **Ex.**U. imp.; **Ld.**P. 43–45; **M.**P. 41–45; **N.**U. imp.; **O.**AEC.; **R.**U.   [*C. as:* 11467]

10648 **Bulletin** of the **Institute** of **Technicians** in **Venereology.** London. *Bull. Inst. Techns Vener.* [1951–] L.BM.; MA. 53: 58–; SH. (1 yr).

10649 **Bulletin** of the **Institute** of **Vitreous Enamellers.** London. *Bull. Inst. vitr. Enam.* [1948–] L.BM.; P. 51–; **Bm.**C.; **E.**A.; **O.**R. 53–.

    Bulletin of the **Institute** of **Zoology.** Sofia.   *See* 24565.

    Bulletin of the **Institution** of **Civil Engineers** of **Ireland.**   *See* 53767.

10650 **Bulletin** of the **Institution** of **Engineers, India.** Calcutta. *Bull. Instn Engrs India* [1951–] L.EE.; **Br.**U. 55–; **Sil.**

10651 **Bulletin. Institution** of **Highway Engineers.** London. *Bull. Instn Highw. Engrs* [1936–47] L.BM.; P. imp.; SC. 39–46.   [*C. as:* 26226]

10652 **Bulletin** of the **Institution** of **Hydraulics.** Stockholm. *Bull. Instn Hydraul., Stockh.* **Bl.**U. 47–; **Wo.** 48– imp.

10653 **Bulletin** of the **Institution** of **Metallurgists.** London. *Bull. Instn Metall.* [1946–59] L.AV.; BM.; I.; MI. 53–59; NF.; **Bm.**C. 47–59; T. 49–54; **C.**UL.; **O.**B.; **Sh.**IO. 46–59. [*C. as:* 31486]

10654 **Bulletin** of the **Institution** of **Mining** and **Metallurgy.** London. *Bull. Instn Min. Metall.* [1904–] L.AV. 47–53; BM. 18–; BM^N. 47–; EE. 42–; GL.; GM.; I.; MI.; MT. 19–; NF. 40–; P. (curr.); PT.; SC. 17–; U. 49–; **Abs.**N. 15–; **Bm.**C. 23–; U. 14–20: 30–36; **E.**A.; D. 19–; U. 57–; **G.**U. 08–; **Ld.**U. 24–; **Lv.**P. 19–22: 38–42: 47–50 imp.; U. 20–29; **M.**P. 54–; T. 24–; **N.**U. 49– imp.; **Nw.**A.; **O.**R. 36–; **Sh.**M. 24–55; P. 22–; **Y.**

10655 **Bulletin. Institution** of **Production Engineers.** London. *Bull. Instn Prod. Engrs* L.BM. 40–41.

10656 **Bulletin. Institution** of **Radio Engineers, Australia.** Sydney. *Bull. Instn Radio Engrs Aust.*

10657 **Bulletin** of the **Institution** of **Sanitary Engineers.** London. *Bull. Instn sanit. Engrs* [1939–42] L.BM.; P.; SC.; SH.; **Abd.**U.; **G.**U.; **Ld.**U.; **Nw.**A. [*C. of:* and *Rec. as:* 26236]

Bulletin des **institutions r.** d'histoire naturelle. Sofia. *See* 24533.

Bulletin des **instituts** de **médecine.** Sofia. *See* 24421.

Bulletin des **instituts** de **recherches agronomiques** de la République tchécoslovaque. *See* 59344.

10658 **Bulletin. Instituut** voor **plantenziekten, Buitenzorg.** *Bull. Inst. PlZiekt. Buitenz.* L.EB. 21–31*; P. 21–31 imp.; SC. 31; **C.**A. 18–31 imp.; **Rt.** 23–31.

Bulletin des **instruments** de **mésure.** *See* 11763.

10659 **Bulletin. Inter-American Tropical Tuna Commission.** La Jolla. *Bull. inter-Am. trop. Tuna Commn* [1954–] L.BM^N.; **Bn.**U.; **Dm.**; **Fr.** 55–; **Ld.**U. 56– imp.; **Lo.**; **Lv.**U.; **Pl.**M.; **Wo.**

10660 **Bulletin international** de l'**Académie polonaise** des **sciences** et des **lettres.** Cracovie. *Bull. int. Acad. pol. Sci. Lett.*
Classe des sciences mathématiques et naturelles [1919–51]
Série A. Sciences mathématiques. L.BM.; C.; GL.; P. imp.; R.; SC.; **Bl.**U. 21–24: 29–51; **C.**P. 36–51; UL.; **Db.**; **E.**B.; R.; **G.**U.; **Ld.**U. 28–38; **M.**MS. 30–38; **O.**R.
Série B. Sciences naturelles:
   B.I. Botanique. L.AM.; BM.; BM^N.; C.; MY. 19–27 imp.; P. 16–51 imp.; R.; SC. imp.; Z.; **Bl.**U. 21–24: 46–51; **C.**A. 46–51; P. 36–51; UL.; **Db.**; **Dm.** 49–51; **E.**B.; R.; **G.**U.; **Ld.**U. 24–38; **M.**MS. 30–38; **O.**B. 38–31; R.; **Pl.**M. 33–51.
   B.II. Zoologie. L.AM.; BM.; BM^N.; C.; GL.; MY. 19–27 imp.; P. 36–51; R.; SC. imp.; Z.; **Bl.**U. 21–24: 46–51; **C.**A. 46–51; P. 36–51; UL.; **Db.**; **Dm.** 49–51; **E.**B.; R.; **G.**U.; **Ld.**U. 24–38; **M.**MS. 30–38; **O.**B. 38–51; R.; **Pl.**M. 33–51.
Classe de médecine [1930–51] L.BM.; BM^N.; GL.; MA. 30–35; MD.; S.; TD.; UC. 30–36; **Bl.**U.; **C.**UL.; **Db.**; **E.**R.; **G.**U.; **Sal.** [*C. of:* 10660^a]

Bulletin international. Académie des **sciences** de l'**Empereur François Joseph I.** *See* 10661.

10660^a **Bulletin international** de l'**Académie** des **sciences** et des **lettres** de **Cracovie.** Cracovie. *Bull. int. Acad. Sci. Lett. Cracovie* [1889–00: *then in sections*] L.BM.; BM^N.; C.; GL.; MY. imp.; R.; Z.; **Bm.**U. 96–00; **C.**UL.; **Db.**; **E.**B.; R.; **G.**U.; **O.**R.
   Classe des sciences mathématiques et naturelles [1901–18]

Série A. Sciences mathématiques. L.BM.; C.; GL.; P. 16–18; R.; SC. 10–18; **Bm.**U. 07–13; **C.**UL.; **Db.**; **E.**B.; R.; **G.**U.; **O.**R
   Série B. Sciences naturelles: L.BM. 01–13; BM^N.; C.; GL.; MY. P. 16–18; R.; SC. 10–18; Z.; **Bm.**U. 01–13 imp.; **C.**UL.; **Db.**; **E.**B.; R.; **G.**U.; **O.**R [*C. as:* 10660]

10661 **Bulletin international. Académie tchéque** des **sciences.** Prague. *Bull. int. Acad. tchéque Sci.* [1894–] L.BM. imp.; BM^N. (sci. math.) 95–40: 43–53; K. 26–46 imp.; MD. (med.) 30–; R. 95–52; SC. 20–; UC. 06–11 imp.; **C.**P. (med.) 96–04; **E.**R.; **Ld.**U. 28–; **M.**U. 25–52 imp.

10662 **Bulletin international** de l'**Académie yougoslave** des **sciences** et des **beaux-arts.** Zagreb. *Bull. int. Acad. yougosl. Sci.* [1930–]
   Classe des sciences mathématiques et naturelles. L.BM. imp.; BM^N. 30–55; R. 39–45.
   Classe des sciences medicales. L.MD. 51–54. [*C. of:* 24567]

Bulletin. International Air Transport Association. *See* 22594.

10663 **Bulletin** of the **International Association** for **Bridge** and **Structural Engineering.** Zurich. *Bull. int. Ass. Bridge struct. Engng* [1933–] L.P. imp.; SC. 52–; **Br.**U. 33–47; **G.**T. imp.; **Wa.**B. 33–55: 57–.

10664 **Bulletin. International Association** for **Hydraulic Structures Research.** Delft. *Bull. int. Ass. hydraul. Struct. Res.* [1937–38] L.P. 38. [*C. as:* 42270]

10665 **Bulletin** of the **International Association** of **Medical Museums.** Montreal & Washington. *Bull. int. Ass. med. Mus.* [1907–25: 47–] L.BM. 11–18; MD. 13–51 imp.; S.; UC. 11–18 imp.; **Bl.**U. 47–51 imp.; **Bm.**U. 07–22; **Br.**U. 18; **C.**AN. 07–51; UL. 11–25; **Db.** 15–22; **Dn.**U. 09–51 imp.; **G.**U. 09: 13–18; **Ld.**U. 22; **Lv.**U. imp.; **M.**U. 13–18; **O.**R. 13–22; **Sa.** 13–18; **Y.** [>27015, 1926–46]

10666 **Bulletin** of the **International Association** for **Promoting** the **Study** of **Quaternions** and **Allied Systems** of **Mathematics.** Lancaster, Pa. *Bull. int. Ass. Promot. Study Quatern.* [1900–13] L.BM. 13; M. 08: 13; **E.**Q.; **O.**R. imp.

Bulletin of the **International Association** of **Refrigeration.** *See* 10965.

10666° **Bulletin. International Association** of **Scientific Hydrology.** London. *Bull. int. Ass. scient. Hydrol.* **Y.** [*English edition of:* 10536]

10667 **Bulletin. International Association** for **Testing Materials, American Section.** *Bull. int. Ass. Test. Mater. Am. Sect.* L.P. 99–02*; **Bm.**C. 99–02; **G.**M. 02. [*C. as:* 38904]

10668 **Bulletin. International Association** of **Tropical Agriculture.** Paris. *Bull. int. Ass. trop. Agric.*

Bulletin. International Atomic Energy Agency. Vienna. *See* 23811.

10669 **Bulletin international** du **Bureau central météorologique** de **France.** *Bull. int. Bur. cent. mét. Fr.* L.MO. 1857–21*. [*C. as:* 10685]

10669° **Bulletin. International Commission** on **Large Dams.** Paris. *Bull. int. Commn large Dams* L.P. 53– imp.

10670 **Bulletin** of the **International Committee** for **Bird Preservation.** New York, Bruxelles. *Bull. int. Comm. Bird Preserv.* [1928–] L.BM^N.; NC. 39–; SC.; **C.**UL. 52; **E.**A. 52; **O.**R. 52. [*C. of:* 10671]

10671 **Bulletin** of the **International Committee** for **Bird Protection.** New York. *Bull. int. Comm. Bird Prot.* [1927] **L.**BM^N.; SC. [*C. as:* 10670]

Bulletin of the **International Council** for **Bird Preservation.** *See* 10670.

Bulletin. International Council for **Building Research, Studies** and **Documentation.** *See* 12883.

10672 **Bulletin. International Dairy Federation.** La Haye. *Bull. int. Dairy Fed.*

10673 **Bulletin. International Electrical Engineering Company.** London. *Bull. int. elect. Engng Co.* **L.**P. 01–06.

10674 **Bulletin international** de l'**électricité.** Paris. *Bull. int. Élect.* **L.**P. 86–10 imp.

10675 **Bulletin. International Epidemiological Association.** *Bull. int. epidem. Ass.* **Bl.**U. 60–.

10676 **Bulletin** of the **International Federation** for **Housing** and **Town Planning.** London. *Bull. int. Fed. Hous. Town Plann.* [1927–28] **L.**BA. [*C. of:* 10677; *C. as:* 23852]

10677 **Bulletin** of the **International Federation** for **Town** and **Country Planning** and **Garden Cities.** London. *Bull. int. Fed. Town Ctry Plann.* [1924–26] **L.**BA. [*C. of:* 10678; *C. as:* 10676]

10678 **Bulletin** of the **International Garden Cities** and **Town Planning Federation.** London. *Bull. int. Gdn Cit. Town Plann. Fed.* [1923] [*C. as:* 10677]

Bulletin. International Geodetic and **Geophysical Union.** *See* 12492.

Bulletin of the **International Geographical Union.** *See* 22621.

Bulletin international de l'**habitation** et de l'**aménagement** des **villes.** *See* 23852.

10679 **Bulletin. International Institute** for **Land Reclamation** and **Improvement.** Wageningen. *Bull. int. Inst. Ld Reclam.* [1958–] **L.**BM.; P.; Rt.; **Y.**

10680 **Bulletin** of the **International Institute** of **Refrigeration.** Paris. *Bull. int. Inst. Refrig.* [1934–] **L.**AM. IC. 34–40; P.; SC.; SI. 47–; TP. 57–; **Abd.**T.; **Br.**A. 52–; **Ld.**U. 57–; **Lh.**P. 52– imp.; **Lv.**P. 34–40; U.; **Y.** [*C. of:* 23820]

10681 **Bulletin** of the **International Institute** of **Sanitary** and **Municipal Engineering.** London. *Bull. int. Inst. sanit. munic. Engng* **L.**TD. 25–28.

Bulletin of the **International Institute** of **Statistics.** *See* 10593.

Bulletin. International Magazine of **Astronomy** and the related **Sciences** from the **Orient.** Kwasans Observatory, Kyoto Imperial University. *See* 10762.

10682 **Bulletin. International Nickel Company.** New York. *Bull. int. Nickel Co.* **L.**P. 32–. [*Several series issued*]

10683 **Bulletin. International North Pacific Fisheries Commission.** Vancouver. *Bull. int. N. Pacif. Fish. Commn* [1955–] **L.**BM.; BM^N.; Z.; **Bl.**U.; **Bm.**U.; **Bn.**U.; **E.**A.; **Dm.**; **Lo.**; **Lv.**U.; **O.**AP.; **Pl.**M.; **Sa.**; **Wo.**

10684 **Bulletin** of the **International Oceanographic Foundation.** Talahassee. *Bull. int. oceanogr. Fdn* [1954–57] **L.**BM^N. 54–56; **Dm.** 56; **Lv.**U.; **Wo.** 57. [*C. as:* 49335]

10685 **Bulletin international** de l'**Office national météorologique** de France. Paris. *Bull. int. Off. natn. mét. Fr.* [1922–] **L.**MO. 22–26. [*C. of:* 10669]

10686 **Bulletin. International Pacific Salmon Fisheries Commission.** New Westminster, B.C., etc. *Bull. int. Pacif. Salm. Fish. Commn* [1945–] **L.**AM.; BM.; BM^N. 45–51; Z.; **Abd.**M. 45–56 imp.; **Bn.**U. 45–50; **Dm.** 45–48; **Fr.** 54–; **Lo.**; **Lv.**U. imp.; **O.**AP.

Bulletin of the **International Pharmaceutical Federation.** *See* 10236.

10687 **Bulletin. International Photo-Engravers' Union** of **North America.** *Bull. int. Photo-Engrav. Un. N. Am.* [1939–]

10688 **Bulletin international** de la **protection** de l'**enfance.** Bruxelles. *Bull. int. Prot. Enf.* [1925–] **L.**TD. 25–39. [*C. of:* 23924]

Bulletin international de la **protection** de **nature.** *See* 10699.

Bulletin of the **International Railway Association.** Brussels. *See* 10689.

10689 **Bulletin** of the **International Railway Congress Association.** Brussels. *Bull. int. Rly Congr. Ass.* [1896–14: 19–] **L.**BM.; P. 10–; **C.**UL.; **E.**A. 21–; **O.**R.; **Y.** [*For the French edition see* 9867]

Bulletin. International Railway Congress Association. Electric traction on the **railways.** *See* 10149.

10690 **Bulletin international** de la **répression** des **fraudes.** Paris. *Bull. int. Repress. Fraudes* **L.**AM. 10–11; C. 08–16*; P. 08–16.

Bulletin. International Road Federation, Ltd. London. *See* 22672ᵃ.

Bulletin. International Scientific Radio Union. Brussels. *See* 11050.

10692 **Bulletin international** des **services** de **santé** des **armées** de **terre,** de **mer** et de l'**air.** Liège. *Bull. int. Servs Santé Arm.* [1937–57] **L.**H. 53–57; MA.; MD. 37–40; **Br.**U. 37–40. [1928 *to* 1936 *published in* 4290; *C. as:* 47346]

Bulletin of the **International Silk Association.** Lyons. *See* 9478.

Bulletin international de la **Société hongroise** de **géographie.** *See* 19766.

10693 **Bulletin international** des **sociétés** de la **Croix-Rouge.** Genève. *Bull. int. Socs Croix Rouge* **O.**R. 70–18*. [*C. as:* 47327]

10694 **Bulletin** of the **International Society** of **Soil Science.** Amsterdam. *Bull. int. Soc. Soil Sci.* [1952–] **C.**A.; Rt.

10695 **Bulletin. International Society** of **Sugar Cane Technologists.** Sourabaya. *Bull. int. Soc. Sug. Cane Technol.* **L.**EB. (ent.) 29–.

10696 **Bulletin** of the **International Society** for **Tropical Ecology.** Poona. *Bull. int. Soc. trop. Ecol.* [1960] **L.**BM^N.; **Bn.**U.; **Y.** [*C. as:* Tropical Ecology]

10697 **Bulletin** of the **International Tin Research** and **Development Council.** London. *Bull. int. Tin Res. Dev. Coun.* [1935–37] **L.**BM.; C.; P.; SC.; U.; UC.; **Bn.**U.; **E.**R.; **G.**U. imp.; **Ld.**P. imp.; **M.**P.; **Nw.**A.; **O.**R.; **Sw.**U.

10698 **Bulletin** of the **International Union** for **Conservation** of **Nature** and **Natural Resources.** Brussels. *Bull. int. Un. Conserv. Nat.* [1956–] **L.**BM^N.; K. imp.; MY.; NC.; Z. imp.; **C.**UL.; **E.**R.; **Fr.**; **O.**AP.; **Y.** [*C. of:* 10699]

10699 **Bulletin** of the **International Union** for the **Protection** of **Nature.** Brussels. *Bull. int. Un. Prot. Nat.* [1952–56] **L.**BM^N.; MY. 53–56; NC.; Z. imp.; **C.**UL.; E.R.; **Fr.**; **O.**AP.; Pl.M. 55. [*C. as:* 10698]

Bulletin. International Union of **Railways.** *See* 12494.

10700 **Bulletin. International Union** for the **Scientific Investigation** of **Population Problems.** Baltimore. *Bull. int. Un. scient. Invest. Pop. Probl.* [1929–31] **L.**BM.

Bulletin of the **International Union** against **Tuberculosis.** *See* 12497.

Bulletin der **Internationalen Federation** textil-chemischer und kolaristischer **Vereine.** Basel. *See* 10235.

Bulletin. Internationaler Verband für **wasser-bauliches Versuchswesen.** Delft. *See* 10664.

10701 **Bulletin. Inter-Society Color Council.** New York. *Bull. Inter-Soc. Color Coun.* **L.**P. 32*. [*C. as:* 34836]

10702 **Bulletin. Interstate Cotton Seed Crushers' Association.** Atlanta, Ga. *Bull. interst. Cott. Seed Crush. Ass.* **L.**SC. 28–29*. [*C. as:* 11214]

10703 **Bulletin** des **inventeurs.** Bruxelles. *Bull. Inventrs, Brux.*

10703° **Bulletin** on **Inventions.** New York. *Bull. Invent.* **Y.** 57–. [*English abstracts of:* 12770]

10703° **Bulletin** ionosphérique. **Station** de **Lwiro.** *Bull. ionosph. Stn Lwiro* [1953–] **L.**MO.; **Y.**

10704 **Bulletin. Iowa Agricultural Experiment Station.** Ames. *Bull. Ia agric. Exp. Stn* [1888–] **L.**AM.; BM^N. 89–37 imp.; EB. (ent.) 95–39; K. 11–12 imp.; P.; SC. 22–39; UC. 21–39; **Abs.**U. 14–35 imp.; **Br.**A. 40– imp.; **C.**A.; UL. 13–39; Ld.U. 35–39; O.F. 35–39; RE. 43–50 imp.; **Rt.** imp.; **Y.**

10705 **Bulletin. Iowa Dairy** and **Food Department.** Des Moines. *Bull. Ia Dairy Fd Dep.*

10706 **Bulletin** of the **Iowa Department** of **Agriculture.** Des Moines. *Bull. Ia Dep. Agric.* **Y.**

10707 **Bulletin** of the **Iowa Engineering Experiment Station.** Ames. *Bull. Ia Engng Exp. Stn* **L.**P. 05–; **Y.**

10708 **Bulletin** of the **Iowa Geological Survey.** Des Moines. *Bull. Ia geol. Surv.* [1901–] **L.**BM. 13–; BM^N. 05–10; GL. 03–18; GM.; P. 13–18; SC. 13–; UC. 13–; **C.**P. 13–30; UL. 05–; **E.**F. 13 imp.; R. 05–18; U. 13; **G.**U. 09–; Ld.U. 13; Lv.U. 13: 18; M.U. 13–18; **Sa.** 13–18.

Bulletin. Iowa State University. *See* 12290.

10709 **Bulletin** of the **Iris Society.** Tunbridge Wells. *Bull. Iris Soc.* [1924–29] **L.**BM.; HS.; **M.**P. [*C. as:* 24125]

10710 **Bulletin. Iris Society** of **Southern Africa.** *Bull. Iris Soc. sth. Afr.* **L.**HS. 53–.

10711 **Bulletin** of the **Iron** and **Steel Institute.** London. *Bull. Iron Steel Inst.* [1936–46] **L.**P.; SC.; **Bm.**C. 40–46; E.A.; **O.**R. 44–46. [*Also published as section 2 of* 26260]

10712 **Bulletin. Israel Exploration Society.** *Bull. Israel Explor. Soc.* [1951–] **Y.** [*C. of:* 10724°]

10713 **Bulletin** of **J.S.M.E.** Japan Society of Mechanical Engineers. Tokyo. *Bull. J.S.M.E.* [1958–] **L.**BM.; P.; **Br.**U.; **C.**P.; G.ME.; Ld.U.; M.U.; **Sil.**; **Y.**

10714 **Bulletin** of the **Jackson County Medical Society.** Kansas City. *Bull. Jackson Cty med. Soc.*

10715 **Bulletin** of the **Jackson Memorial Hospital** and the **School** of **Medicine** of the **University** of **Florida.** Miami. *Bull. Jackson mem. Hosp.* [1954] **L.**BM.; MD.; **Lv.**M. [*C. of:* 24675; *C. as:* 12523]

10716 **Bulletin** of the **Japan Petroleum Institute.** Tokyo. *Bull. Japan Petrol. Inst.* [1959–] **Ld.**U. 60–; **Y.**

10717 **Bulletin** of the **Japan Sea Regional Fisheries Research Laboratory.** Niigata. *Bull. Japan Sea reg. Fish. Res. Lab.* [1951–] **Bn.**U. 57–; **Dm.** 58–; **Lo.**; **Wo.** 57–; **Y.**

Bulletin. Japan Society of **Mechanical Engineers.** *See* 10713.

10718 **Bulletin** of the **Japan Society** for **Preserving Beautific Sceneries** and **Historical** and **Natural Monuments.** Tokyo. *Bull. Japan Soc. Preserv. beaut. Scen.* [1926–44] **L.**BM^N. 26.

10719 **Bulletin** of the **Japanese Association** of **Leather Technology.** Hiratsuka. *Bull. Jap. Ass. Leath. Technol.* [1955–] **L.**LE.; **Y.**

10720 **Bulletin** of the **Japanese Society** of **Phycology.** Sapporo. *Bull. Jap. Soc. Phycol.* [1953–] **L.**BM^N.; **Y.**

10721 **Bulletin** of the **Japanese Society** of **Scientific Fisheries.** Tokyo. *Bull. Jap. Soc. scient. Fish.* [1932–] **L.**AM. 32–41; BM^N. imp.; **Abd.**M.; T. 32–44: 48–; **Bn.**U. 55–; **Fr.** 32–41; **Lo.**; **Mi.** 43–; Pl.M. imp.; **Y.**

Bulletin du **Jardin botanique** de l'**Académie** des **sciences** de l'**URSS.** *See* 24346.

10722 **Bulletin** du **Jardin botanique** de **Buitenzorg.** Buitenzorg. *Bull. Jard. bot. Buitenz.* [1911–40] **L.**BM^N.; K.; L.; MY. 11–19 imp.; R. 11–27; **Abs.**N. 27–40; **Br.**U. 25–40; **C.**BO. 35–40; P.; **E.**B. imp.; **Rt.** imp. [*C. of:* 9949; *C. as:* 9595]

Bulletin du **Jardin botanique** de **Cluj.** *See* 9114.

10723 **Bulletin** du **Jardin botanique** de l'**État** à **Bruxelles.** Bruxelles. *Bull. Jard. bot. État Brux.* [1902–] **L.**AM. 15–28; BM.; BM^N.; HS.; K.; L. 10– imp.; MY. 20–; SC. 34–; **Abd.**U. 19–20; **Abs.**A. 31–; **Bm.**U. 14: 22–; **Br.**U. 19–20; **C.**BO. 31– imp.; **Db.** 31–; **E.**B.; R. 02–05; **Hu.**G. 51–; **Lv.**U. 03– imp.; **M.**U. 10–30 imp.; **Md.**H. 13– imp.; **N.**U. 22–39 imp.; **O.**BO.; **Rt.** 14–31; **Sw.**U. 32– imp.; **Y.**

Bulletin du **Jardin botanique** de **Kieff.** *See* 56750.

Bulletin du **Jardin botanique** de la **République russe.** *See* 24346.

Bulletin du **Jardin botanique** de **St. Pétersbourg.** *See* 24370.

Bulletin du **Jardin botanique** de l'**URSS.** *See* 24346.

Bulletin du **Jardin colonial.** Paris. *See* 1456.

10724 **Bulletin. Jealott's Hill Research Station.** Bracknell. *Bull. Jealott's Hill Res. Stn* [1940–] **L.**AM.; BM.; K. 47–48; P.; **Abs.**U. 47–48; **Bm.**U. 47–; **Br.**A. 47–; **C.**A.; Ld.U.; **N.**U.; **O.**R. 49–; RE.; **Rt.**; **Y.**

Bulletin. Jerusalem Naturalists' Club. *See* 25329.

Bulletin. Jewish Memorial Hospital. New York. *See* 25339.

10724° **Bulletin. Jewish Palestine Exploration Society.** *Bull. Jew. Palest. Explor. Soc.* [*C. as:* 10712]

10725 **Bulletin** of the **John Sealy Hospital** and the **School** of **Medicine** of the **University** of **Texas.** Galveston. *Bull. John Sealy Hosp. Univ. Tex.* [1939–]

10726 **Bulletin** of the **Johns Hopkins Hospital.** Baltimore. *Bull. Johns Hopkins Hosp.* [1925–] **L.**BM.; GH.; H. 33–; LI.; MA.; MC.; MD.; OP. 51–; S.; TD. 25–28: 48–; U. 47–48: 51–; UC.; UCH.; **Abd.**U.; **Abs.**N. 31–; **Bl.**U.; **Bm.**U. 46–; **Br.**U.; **C.**APH. 49–; MO. 25–37; PA. 27–; UL.; **Cr.**MD. 40–; **Db.** 25–28: 51–; **Dn.**U.; **E.**P.; U.; **G.**F.; U.; **Ld.**U.; **Lv.**M.; U.; **M.**MS.; U. 25–27; **Nw.**A. 28–; **O.**B.; PH. 26–30; R.; **R.**D. 25–28; **Sa.**; **Sh.**U.; **Y.** [*C. of:* 25349]

10727 **Bulletin** of the **Johns Hopkins University.** Baltimore. *Bull. Johns Hopkins Univ.* **E.**G. 86–; I. 43–47; **Lv.**P. 03–.

10728 **Bulletin Joseph Pâquet.** Organe mensuel des cultivateurs de graines. Nice. *Bull. Joseph Pâquet*

10729 **Bulletin** of the **Josselyn Botanical Society** of **Maine.** Portland. *Bull. Josselyn bot. Soc. Me*

10730 **Bulletin** of the **Jourdain Society.** London. *Bull. Jourdain Soc.* [1946–] **L.**BM^N. [*C. of:* 9621]
   Bulletin-journal. *See* 12673, 12674.
   Bulletin. K. Maatschappij voor **dierkunde** van **Antwerpen.** *See* 12152.

10732 **Bulletin. Kagoshima Imperial College** of **Agriculture** and **Forestry.** Kagoshima. *Bull. Kagoshima imp. Coll. Agric. For.* [1914–49] **L.**K. 15–32; **Abs.**N. 26–49 imp.; **Rt.** 15–32. [*C. as:* 10209]

10733 **Bulletin** of the **Kagoshima Tobacco Experiment Station.** Kagoshima. *Bull. Kagoshima Tob. Exp. Stn*

10734 **Bulletin. Kamigano Geophysical Observatory,** University of Kyoto. Kyoto. *Bull. Kamigano geophys. Obs.* [1952–] **Db.**

10735 **Bulletin** of the **Kansas Academy** of **Sciences.** Topeka. *Bull. Kans. Acad. Sci.* [1916–19] [*C. in:* 53798]

10736 **Bulletin** of the **Kansas Agricultural Experiment Station.** Manhattan. *Bull. Kans. agric. Exp. Stn* [1888–] **L.**AM.; BM^N. 90–; EB. (ent.); K. 89–06 imp.; P.; **Bm.**P. 89–; **Br.**A. 24– imp.; **C.**A.; **E.**B. 91– imp.; **O.**F. 39– imp.; **Rt.**; Y.

10737 **Bulletin** of the **Kansas City Testing Laboratory.** Kansas City. *Bull. Kansas Cy Test. Lab.* **L.**P. 18–34 imp.

10738 **Bulletin** of the **Kansas Engineering Experiment Station.** Manhattan. *Bull. Kans. Engng Exp. Stn* **L.**P. 59–; SC. 48–.

10739 **Bulletin. Kansas State Agricultural College.** Manhattan. *Bull. Kans. St. agric. Coll.* **L.**K. 89–06 imp.; **Bm.**P. 06– imp.

10740 **Bulletin** of the **Kansas State Board** of **Health.** Topeka. *Bull. Kans. St. Bd Hlth*

10741 **Bulletin** of the **Kansas State Dental Association.** Kansas City. *Bull. Kans. St. dent. Ass.* [1917–32] [*C. as:* 26312]

10742 **Bulletin** of the **Kansas State Fish** and **Game Warden.** Topeka. *Bull. Kans. St. Fish Game Ward.*

10743 **Bulletin** of the **Kansas University Geological Survey.** Topeka. *Bull. Kans. Univ. geol. Surv.* [1913–] **L.**BM.; BM^N.; GL. 14; GM.; SC. 18–; UC. 18– imp.; **Abs.**U. 45–; **Bm.**U. 20–30 imp.; **E.**R. 13–27; **Lv.**U. imp.

10744 **Bulletin** of the **Karachi Geographical Society.** Karachi. *Bull. Karachi geogr. Soc.* [1949–] **L.**G. 50–52.

10745 **Bulletin. Kent Field Club.** Maidstone. *Bull. Kent Fld Club* **L.**BM^N. 57–; NC. 56–.

10746 **Bulletin** of the **Kentucky Agricultural Experiment Station.** Lexington. *Bull. Ky agric. Exp. Stn* [1888–] **L.**AM.; EB. (ent.) 90–; K. 90–08 imp.; P.; **C.**A.; **Rt.** 94– imp.; **Y.**

10747 **Bulletin** of the **Kentucky Bureau** of **Agriculture.** Frankfort. *Bull. Ky Bur. Agric.*

10748 **Bulletin** of the **Kentucky Department** of **Geology** and **Forestry.** Louisville. *Bull. Ky Dep. Geol. For.* [1919–20] **L.**BM.; BM^N.; GL.; SC.; **G.**U.; **O.**R.; I. [*C. of:* and *Rec. as:* 10749]

10749 **Bulletin** of the **Kentucky Geological Survey.** Lexington. *Bull. Ky geol. Surv.* [1905–] **L.**BM. 20–; BM^N. 05–12 imp.: 20–; GL. 05–13: 20–; SC. 05–13: 20–; **G.**U. 20–; **Lv.**P. 12; U. 05–20 imp.; **Sa.** 51– imp. [> 10748, 1919–20]
   Bulletin of the **Kentucky State Board** of Health. *See* 12283.

10751 **Bulletin** of the **Kentucky State Medical Association.** Louisville. *Bull. Ky St. med. Ass.* [*C. of:* 53803; *C. as:* 27226]

10752 **Bulletin. Keuringsdienst** van **eet-** en **drinkwaren** in **Suriname.** Paramaribo. *Bull. Keuringsdienst Eet- en Drinkwaren Suriname*

10753 **Bulletin. Khedivial Observatory, Helwan.** Helwan. *Bull. khediv. Obs. Helwan* [1911–14] **L.**AS.; BM.; SC.; **C.**O.; **E.**O. [*C. as:* 10439]
   Bulletin. King's College Mining Society, University of **Durham.** *See* 27459.

10754 **Bulletin** of the **King's County Dental Society.** Brooklyn. *Bull. King's Cty dent. Soc.*

10755 **Bulletin** of the **Kobayasi Institute** of **Physical Research.** Tokyo. *Bull. Kobayasi Inst. phys. Res.* [1951–] **L.**C. 54–; P.; **Db.**; **G.**U.; **Ld.**U. 51–52; **Y.**

10755° **Bulletin. Kobe Marine Observatory.** *Bull. Kobe mar. Obs.* **Pl.**M. 60–.

10756 **Bulletin** of the **Kôbe Medical College.** Kusunokicho. *Bull. Kôbe med. Coll.* [1950–] [*C. of:* 10480°]

10757 **Bulletin. Koch Cancer Foundation.** Detroit. *Bull. Koch Cancer Fdn* [*C. as:* 25745]

10758 **Bulletin. Kodaikánal Observatory.** Madras. *Bull. Kodaikánal Obs.* [1905–] **L.**AS.; BM.; MO. 13–; SC.; UC.; **Abd.**U.; **Abs.**N. 11– imp.; **C.**O.; SP.; **Cr.**P. 05–16 imp.; **Db.**; **E.**A. imp.; O.; R.; U. 10– imp.; **M.**U.; **O.**O.; R. 05–06.

10759 **Bulletin** of the **Kolar Gold Field Mining** and **Metallurgical Society.** Ooregum. *Bull. Kolar Gold Fld Min. Metall. Soc.* [1929–39] **L.**MI.; P. imp. [*C. of:* 41476; *C. as:* 53805]

10760 **Bulletin** van het **Koloniaal Museum** te **Haarlem.** Amsterdam. *Bull. kolon. Mus. Haarlem* [1892–13] **L.**BM^N.; K. 93–12; SC. 01–14; **O.**F. 09–11 imp.
   Bulletin van het **Koloniaal-Instituut** te **Amsterdam.** *See* 9837.

10761 **Bulletin. Kwangsi Agricultural Experiment Station.** Shatang. *Bull. Kwangsi agric. Exp. Stn* [1939–] **C.**A. 39; **O.**F. 39.

10762 **Bulletin** published by the **Kwasan Observatory.** Kyoto Imperial University. Kyoto. *Bull. Kwasan Obs.* [1929–36] **L.**AS. [*C. of:* 10764; *C. as:* 36362]

10763 **Bulletin** of the **Kyoto Gakugei University.** Tokyo. *Bull. Kyoto Gakugei Univ.* [1951: *then in series* 1952–] **L.**P.; **Bl.**U.
    Ser. B. Mathematics and Natural Science. **L.**P.; **Br.**U.; **Ld.**U. 61–; **Y.**

10764 **Bulletin** of the **Kyoto University Observatory.** Kyoto. *Bull. Kyoto Univ. Obs.* [1921–29] **L.**AS.; **C.**O. [*C. as:* 10762]

10765 **Bulletin** of the **Kyushu Agricultural Experiment Station.** Hainuzukamachi, Chikugo. *Bull. Kyushu agric. Exp. Stn* [1951–] **L.**P. 53–; **C.**A.; **G.**U. 60–; **Je.** 56–; **Rt.** 53–; **Y.**

10766 **Bulletin** of the **Kyushu Institute** of **Technology.** Fukuoka-ken, Tobata. *Bull. Kyushu Inst. Technol.*
    Science and Technology [1951–] **L.**BM^N.; P.; **C.**UL.; **Ld.**U.; **Y.**
    Mathematics, Natural science [1955–] **L.**BM^N.; P.; SC.; **C.**UL.; **Db.**; **E.**R.; **Ld.**U.; **Y.**

10767 **Bulletin** of the **Kyushu University Forests.** Fukuoka. *Bull. Kyushu Univ. Forests* [1931–] **L.**AM. 51–.

10768 **Bulletin. Laboratoire aérotechnique** de **Belgique.** Bruxelles. *Bull. Lab. aérotech. Belg.* [1922] **L.**P.; SC. [*C. as:* 11777]

10769 **Bulletin** du **Laboratoire d'agronomie coloniale.** Paris. *Bull. Lab. Agron. colon.* **L.**P. 13; K. 21–.
    Bulletin du **Laboratoire d'anthropologie** et **d'ethnologie.** Kieff. *See* 54736, Ser. 2.

10770 **Bulletin** du **Laboratoire Arago.** *Bull. Lab. Arago* [1950–] **L.**SC.

10771 **Bulletin** du **Laboratoire** de **bactériologie** de **l'Institut Pasteur** de la **Loire-inférieure.** Nantes. *Bull. Lab. Bact. Inst. Pasteur Loire-infér.*

10772 **Bulletin** du **Laboratoire** de **biologie appliquée.** Paris. *Bull. Lab. Biol. appl.* [*C. as:* 47509]
    Bulletin du **Laboratoire biologique** de **Saint Pétersbourg.** *See* 24468 and 24484.

10772° **Bulletin. Laboratoire central d'helmintologie, Académie** des **sciences** de **Bulgarie.** Béograd. *Bull. Lab. cent. Helmint., Béogr.* **Y.**

10773 **Bulletin. Laboratoire** d'essais, **Conservatoire national** des **arts** et **métiers.** Paris. *Bull. Lab. Essais Conserv. natn. Arts Métiers* [1944–48] **L.**P.

10774 **Bulletin** du **Laboratoire** d'essais. **École professionelle** des **matières plastiques.** Oyonnax (Ain). *Bull. Lab. Essais Éc. prof. Matièr. plast.* [1933–] **L.**P. 33; SI. 44–.

10775 **Bulletin** du **Laboratoire** d'essais **mécaniques, physiques, chimiques,** et de **machines** du **Conservatoire national** des **arts** et **métiers.** Paris. *Bull. Lab. Essais méc. phys. chim. Conserv. natn. Arts Métiers* **L.**P. 08–24.

10776 **Bulletin** du **Laboratoire expérimental** de **viticulture** et d'**oenologie** de la **Maison Moët** et **Chandon.** Épernay. *Bull. Lab. exp. Vitic. Oenol. Mais. Moët et Chandon*

10777 **Bulletin** du **Laboratoire** de **géologie** de la **Faculté** des **sciences** de **Caen.** Caen. *Bull. Lab. Géol. Fac. Sci. Caen* **L.**BM^N. 90–95.

10778 **Bulletin** du **Laboratoire maritime** de **Dinard.** Rennes. *Bull. Lab. marit. Dinard* [1936–] **L.**BM. 52–;

BM^N.; **Dm.** 56–; **Fr.** 41–42; **Lo.** 55–; **Lv.**U.; **Mi.** 56–; **Pl.**M. [*C. of:* 10779]
    Bulletin du **Laboratoire maritime** de **Gdynia.** *See* 7186.

10779 **Bulletin** du **Laboratoire maritime** du **Muséum d'histoire naturelle** de **Saint-Servan.** *Bull. Lab. marit. Mus. Hist. nat. St-Servan* [1929–35] **L.**BM^N.; **Lv.**U.; **Pl.**M. [*C. of:* 54242; *C. as:* 10778]

10780 **Bulletin** du **Laboratoire** de **pétrole** de l'**Université** de **Strasbourg.** *Bull. Lab. Pétrole Univ. Strasb.* [1922] **L.**U.; UC.; **Bn.**U.; **Lv.**U. [*C. as:* 10603]

10781 **Bulletin** du **Laboratoire** de **plasmogénie.** Mexico. *Bull. Lab. Plasmog., Mex.* [1932–] **L.**C. 32–35; GL. imp.; **C.**UL.; **Lv.**U.; **Pl.**M. 32–42 imp.

10782 **Bulletin** du **Laboratoire provincial** de **chimie agricole** à **Roulers.** *Bull. Lab. prov. Chim. agric. Roulers*

10783 **Bulletin. Laboratoire** de **recherches biologiques. Établissements J. J. Carnaud, Forges** de **Basse-Indre.** Paris. *Bull. Lab. Rech. biol. Établ. J. J. Carnaud Forges Basse-Indre* **L.**P. 31–.

10784 **Bulletin** du **Laboratoire** de **recherches** et du **contrôle** du **caoutchouc.** Paris. *Bull. Lab. Rech. Contrôle Caoutch.* **Sy.**R. 50– imp.

10785 **Bulletin** du **Laboratoire régional** d'**entomologie agricole.** Rouen. *Bull. Lab. rég. Ent. agric., Rouen* **L.**BM^N. 00–11; EB. 06–18* imp.

10786 **Bulletin** des **laboratoires** de **géologie, géographie physique, minéralogie, paléontologie, géophysique** et de la **Musée géologique** de l'**Université** de **Lausanne.** Lausanne. *Bull. Labs Géol. Geogr. phys. Minér. Univ. Lausanne* [1901–] **L.**BM^N.; GL.; SC. 40–46: 50–; **Lv.**U. imp.; **Y.**

10787 **Bulletin** from the **Laboratories** of **Natural History** of the **State University** of **Iowa.** Iowa City. *Bull. Labs nat. Hist. St. Univ. Ia* [1888–18] **L.**BM.; BM^N.; L. 88–04; SC. 15–18; U. 90–18 imp.; **C.**P. 15–18; UL. 13–18; **E.**R. imp.; **G.**U. 96–18; **M.**U. 96–18; **O.**R. 11–18; **Pl.**M. 88–04. [*C. as:* 51138]

10788 **Bulletin. Laboratory** of **Applied Entomology, University** of **Tehran.** *Bull. Lab. appl. Ent. Univ. Tehran* [1950–] **Y.**

10789 **Bulletin** of the **Laboratory** of the **Department** of **Health.** Ottawa. *Bull. Lab. Dep. Hlth, Ottawa* [1919–] **L.**P. [*C. from:* 10790]

10790 **Bulletin** of the **Laboratory** of the **Department** of **Trade** and **Commerce.** Ottawa. *Bull. Lab. Dep. Trade Comm., Ottawa* [1918–19] **L.**P. [*C. of:* 10791; *C. in:* 10789]
    Bulletin of the **Laboratory** of **Genetics.** Leningrad. *See* 54811.

10791 **Bulletin** of the **Laboratory** of the **Inland Revenue Department.** Ottawa. *Bull. Lab. inl. Revenue Dep., Ottawa* **L.**P. 87–18* imp.; SC. 87–18. [*C. as:* 10790]

10792 **Bulletin** and **Laboratory Notes. Baird** and **Tatlock.** London. *Bull. Lab. Notes Baird & Tatlock* **L.**P. 50–56*; **Ld.**P. 55–56; **M.**D. 54–56 imp.; **Sy.**R. 38–46. [*C. as:* 11596]
    Bulletin. Laboratory of **Tree-ring Research. University** of **Arizona.** *See* 12518.

10793 **Bulletin. Lake Survey Office. Corps** of **Engineers, United States Army.** Detroit. *Bull. Lake Surv. Off. Cps Engrs U.S. Army*

10794 **Bulletin. Lancashire** and **Cheshire Coal Research Association.** Manchester. *Bull. Lancs. Chesh. Coal Res. Ass.* [1918–25] L.BM.; C.; GM.; P.; SC.; C.UL.; G.U.; M.P. 22–25; T.; O.B.

10795 **Bulletin** of the **Land Settlement Association.** London. *Bull. Ld Settlem. Ass.* [1935] L.BM. [*C. as:* 27989]

10796 **Bulletin. Landbouwproefstation, Surinam.** Paramaribo. *Bull. LandbProefstn Surinam* [1953–] L.AM.; EB.; P.; R.; Rt.; Y. [*C. of:* 9952]

10797 **Bulletin** de **laryngologie, otologie** et **rhinologie.** Paris. *Bull. Lar. Otol. Rhinol., Paris* L.MD. 07–10. [*C. as:* 11465]

10798 **Bulletin** of the **Laws Observatory.** Columbia, Mo. *Bull. Laws Obs.* [1902–21] L.AS.; BM. 02–08 imp.; TD. 19–21; U. imp.; UC. 19–21; Bm.U.; C.O.; UL.- Db. 03; E.O.; G.U.; Ld.U. imp.; Lv.U. imp.; M.MS. 20; 21; U.; O.O.; R.; Sa. [*C. as:* 41277]

10799 **Bulletin. Lead Industries Development Council.** London. *Bull. Lead Inds Dev. Coun.* L.P. 36–53; M.P. 37– imp.; Y.
Bulletin. Lead Sheet and **Pipe Development Council.** *See* 10799.

10800 **Bulletin. Lederle Laboratories Inc.** New York. *Bull. Lederle Labs* L.P. 39–47*. [*C. as:* 28368]

10801 **Bulletin. Leicester Museum** and **Art Gallery.** Leicester. *Bull. Leics. Mus.* [1924–] L.BM^N.; HO.; imp.; C.FT. 35–44; O.B. 29–.
Bulletin of the **Lenin Academy** of **Agricultural Sciences** of the **U.S.S.R.** *See* 12839.

10802 **Bulletin** of the **Lepidopterological Society** of **Japan.** Kyoto. *Bull. lepidopt. Soc. Japan* L.BM^N. 46.

10803 **Bulletin** of the **Lewis Institute Structural Materials Research Laboratory.** Chicago. *Bull. Lewis Inst. struct. Mater. Res. Lab.* [1919–25] L.P.; SC.; Bm.U. 22–25; Ld.U.; Lv.U. 19–22.

10804 **Bulletin** de **liaison. Comité** du **machinisme agricole** d'**outre-mer.** *Bull. Liais. Com. Mach. agric. Outre-Mer* [1956–] L.EE.; Sil.

10805 **Bulletin** de **liaison** des **laboratoires. Conseil international** pour l'**exploration scientifique** de la **mer mediterrané.** Banyuls-sur-mer. *Bull. Liais Labs Cons. int. Explor. scient. Mer mediterr.* [1952–] L.BM^N. 55–; Br. 56–; Pl.M. 55; Y.

10806 **Bulletin. Liberal Arts College, Wakayama University.** Wakayama. *Bull. lib. Arts Coll. Wakayama Univ.*
Natural Science [1953–] Y. [*C. of:* 20574]

10807 **Bulletin. Library. United States Department** of **Agriculture.** Washington. *Bull. Libr. U.S. Dep. Agric.* [1894–12] L.BM.; EB. (ent.) 06; K. 07 imp.; P.; SC. 96–12; U. 97–12; Bm.U. 01–12 imp.; E.G.

10808 **Bulletin** de la **Ligue aéronautique** de **France.** *Bull. Lig. aéronaut. Fr.* [*C. of:* 9455]

10809 **Bulletin** de la **Ligue française** pour la **protection** des **oiseaux.** Paris. *Bull. Lig. fr. Prot. Oiseaux* [*C. as:* 10233]

10810 **Bulletin. Ligue générale** pour l'**aménagement** et l'**utilisation** des **eaux.** Paris. *Bull. Lig. gén. Amén. Util. Eaux*

10811 **Bulletin** de la **Ligue** d'**hygiène mentale.** Paris. *Bull. Lig. Hyg. ment.* Lv.U. 21.

10812 **Bulletin** de la **Ligue luxembourgeoise** pour la **protection** des **oiseaux utiles.** Esch-sur-Alzette. *Bull. Lig. luxemb. Prot. Oiseaux util.*

10813 **Bulletin. Ligue sanitaire française.** Paris. *Bull. Lig. sanit. fr.* [1914–15] L.EB.; TD.

10814 **Bulletin** de la **Ligue** contre le **trachome.** Paris. *Bull. Lig. Trachome*

10815 **Bulletin** de la **Ligue** contre la **tuberculose** en **Touraine.** Tours. *Bull. Lig. Tuberc. Touraine*

10816 **Bulletin. Lithographic Technical Foundation, Inc. Research Series.** New York. *Bull. lithogr. tech. Fdn Res. Ser.* L.P. 25–.
Bulletin. Live Stock Branch, Department of **Agriculture, Canada.** *See* 9964.

10817 **Bulletin** and **Live Stock Journal. Dutch Belted Cattle Association** of **America.** Covert, Mich. *Bull. live Stk J. Dutch belt. Catt. Ass. Am.*

10818 **Bulletin. Liverpool Botanical Society.** Liverpool. *Bull. Lpool bot. Soc.* L.BM^N. 51–.

10819 **Bulletin** of the **Liverpool Museums.** Liverpool. *Bull. Lpool Mus.* [1897–01] L.BM.; BM^N.; Z.; C.UL.; Db.; E.F. imp.; Ld.P.; Lv.P.; U.; M.P.; U.; O.B.

10820 **Bulletin** of the **Liverpool School** of **Tropical Medicine.** Liverpool, London. *Bull. Lpool Sch. trop. Med.* [1909] L.BM.; EB.; P.; S.; TD.; Lv.U.

10821 **Bulletin** of the **Lloyd Library** of **Botany, Pharmacy** and **Materia Medica.** Cincinnati. *Bull. Lloyd Libr.* [1900–36]
Botany series: L.BM^N.; HS. imp.; K. 11–34; SC. 11–36; UC. imp.; Abs.U. 25; Bm.N. 08–36 imp.; Br.U. 02–12 imp.; E.B. imp.; R. imp.; G.N. 11–36 imp.; Ld.U. 21–36; Lv.U. 11–36 imp.; M.U. 21–36 imp.; Nw.A. 11–34; Pl.M. 00–02 imp.; Rt. 11–34.
Mycological series: L.BM^N.; HS. imp.; K. 02–36; P. 02–33; SC. 02–36; UC. imp.; Abs.U. 27; Bm.N. 08–36 imp.; Br.U. 02–12 imp.; E.B. imp.; R. imp.; G.N. 02–36 imp.; Ld.U. 21–36; Lv.U. 02–36; M.U. 21–36 imp.; Nw.A.; Pl.M. 00–02 imp.; Rt. 02–13: 36.
Pharmacy series: L.BM^N.; K. 02–12; P. 02–12; SC. 02–12; UC. imp.; Bm.N. 08–36 imp.; Br.U. 02–12 imp.; Cr.N. 02–12 imp.; E.B. imp.; R. imp.; G.N. 02–12; Ld.U. 21–36; Lv.U. imp.; M.U. 21–36 imp.
Reproduction series: L.BM^N.; K. 00–31; SC. imp.; UC. imp.; Bm.N. 08–36 imp.; Br.U. 02–12 imp.; Cr.N. 00–09 imp.; E.B. imp.; R. imp.; G.N. 00–17; Ld.U. 21–36; Lv.U. imp.; M.U. 21–36 imp.; Nw.A
Entomological series: L.BM^N.; EB. 21–26; K. 23–26; P. 21–26; SC. 21; UC. imp.; Abs.U. 21–26; Bm.N. imp.; E.B. imp.; R. imp.; G.N. 23–26; Ld.U.; M.U. imp.; Nw.A. 21–26; Rt. 21–26.
[*Replaced by:* 28741]

10822 **Bulletin** of the **Logan Museum.** Beloit, Wis. *Bull. Logan Mus.* [1928–] L.SC.; Bm.N. 30–.
Bulletin. London Computer Group. *See* 15310.

10823 **Bulletin. London Shellac Research Bureau.** London. *Bull. Lond. Shellac Res. Bur.* [1935–45] L.BM. 38–45; BM^N.; P.; PR.; SC.; C.UL.; Lv.P. 38–45; M.P.; O.R. 38–45; Rt.

10824 **Bulletin** of the **Los Angeles Neurological Society.** Los Angeles. *Bull. Los Ang. neurol. Soc.* [1936–] L.MA. 46–; MD.; S.; Bl.U.; Br.U. imp.

10825 **Bulletin** of the **Louisiana Agricultural Experiment Station.** Baton Rouge. *Bull. La agric. Exp. Stn* [1886–] **L.**AM.; EB. (ent.) 89–; K. 86–16 imp.; P. 92–; **C.**A.; **O.**F. 44–51 imp.; R. 44– imp.; **Rt.** imp.; **Y.**

10826 **Bulletin** of the **Louisiana Conservation Department.** Baton Rouge. *Bull. La Conserv. Dep.* **L.**SC. 16–.
Bulletin. Louisiana Engineering Experiment Station. *See* 10162.

10826ᶜ **Bulletin** of the **Louisiana Forestry Commission.** Baton Rouge. *Bull. La For. Commn* [1945–] **O.**F. imp.
Bulletin of the **Louisiana Geological Survey.** *See* 10364.

10827 **Bulletin. Louisiana Society** for **Horticultural Research.** Lafayette. *Bull. La Soc. hort. Res.* [1956–] **L.**BMᴺ.

10828 **Bulletin** of **Lowell Observatory.** Flagstaff, Ariz. *Bull. Lowell Obs.* [1903–] **L.**AS.; BM.; SC. 03–35; **C.**O.; UL.; **Cr.**P. 03–15 imp.; **E.**O. 11–; R. 16–17; **O.**O.; R. 03–27.

10829 **Bulletin** of the **Lowell Technological Institute.** Lowell, Mass. *Bull. Lowell technol. Inst.* [1953–] **Ld.**W.; **M.**C. 54–; **Y.** [*C. of:* 10830]

10830 **Bulletin** of the **Lowell Textile Institute.** Lowell, Mass. *Bull. Lowell Text. Inst.* **Ld.**W. 38–53; **M.**C. 52–53. [*C. as:* 10829]

10831 **Bulletin** of the **Lying-in Hospital** of the **City** of **New York.** New York. *Bull. Lying-in Hosp. Cy N.Y.* [1904–32] **L.**GH. 07–20; MD. 05–32; S. 07–32; UC. 08–32; **Abd.**U. 08–32 imp.; **Br.**U. 08–32; **E.**P.; **Lv.**M. 17–32 imp.; **M.**MS. 08–32.

10832 **Bulletin. Maatschappij** ter **bevordering** van het **natuurkundige onderzoek** der **nederlandse kolonien.** Leiden. *Bull. Maatsch. Bevord. natuurk. Onderz. ned. Kolon.*

10833 **Bulletin** of the **McKillip Veterinary College.** Chicago. *Bull. McKillip vet. Coll.*

10834 **Bulletin. Madjelis Ilmu Pengetahuan Indonesia.** Djakarta. *Bull. Madjelis Ilmu Penget. Indonesia* [1959–] **L.**P.; **Y.**
Bulletin. Madras Fisheries Bureau. *See* 29088.
Bulletin. Madras Fisheries Department. *See* 29088.

10835 **Bulletin** of the **Madras Government Museum.** Madras. *Bull. Madras Govt Mus.* [1894–07] **L.**BM.; BMᴺ.; HO.; L.; P. imp.; SC. 98–07; Z.; **Bl.**U. 97–06; **C.**E.; P. 96–07; UL.; **Db.**; **Dm.** 00; **E.**F. 94–01; R.; **Lv.**U.; **M.**P. 96–06; R.; U. 94–03; **O.**B.; **Pl.**M. 94–00.

10836 **Bulletin** of the **Madras Government Museum. New Series.** Madras. *Bull. Madras Govt Mus. new Ser.* [1927–]
General series: **L.**AN. 29–; SC.; **Abs.**N.; **Bm.**N.; U.; **C.**P.; **Db.**; **E.**F.; R.; U.; **Lv.**U.; **O.**I. 29–.
Natural history series: **L.**BMᴺ.; SC.; Z.; **Abs.**N.; **Bl.**U.; **Bm.**N.; U.; **C.**E.; P.; UL.; **Cr.**M.; **Db.**; **Dm.**; **E.**F.; R.; U.; **Lv.**U.; **M.**P.; R.; **Nw.**A. 31–; **O.**P.; **Pl.**M.

10837 **Bulletin magnétique. Institut géophysique national tchécoslovaque.** Praha. *Bull. magn. Inst. géophys. natn. tchécosl.* **L.**MO. 27–36.

Bulletin de **magnétisme terrestre** et d'**électricité atmosphérique.** Léningrad. *See* 21065.

10838 **Bulletin** of the **Maine Agricultural Experiment Station.** Orono. *Bull. Me agric. Exp. Stn* [1885–] **L.**AM.; BM. 11– imp.; BMᴺ. 02–47 imp.; EB. (ent.) 89–; K. 97–16 imp.; L. 23–; P. 00–32; SC. 06–; **Bm.**U. 08–30; **Br.**A. 20–53; **C.**A.; UL. 11–; **Cr.**P. 07–; **G.**N. 11–; U. 11– imp.; **Ld.**U. 09–41 imp.; **Lv.**U. 11– imp.; **M.**U. 16 imp.; **O.**F. 37–52 imp.; R. 11–30; **Rt.** imp.; **Sa.** 11–30; **Y.**

10839 **Bulletin** of the **Maine Department** of **Agriculture.** Augusta. *Bull. Me Dep. Agric.* **L.**EB. 13–20.

10840 **Bulletin** of the **Maine Department** of **Agriculture, Dairy Division.** Augusta. *Bull. Me Dep. Agric. Dairy Div.*

10841 **Bulletin. Maine Department** of **Health.** Augusta. *Bull. Me Dep. Hlth*

10842 **Bulletin** of the **Maine Department** of **State Lands** and **Forestry.** Augusta. *Bull. Me Dep. St. Lds For.*

10843 **Bulletin** of the **Maine Forest Service.** Augusta. *Bull. Me Forest Serv.* [1923–] **L.**EB. (ent.) imp.; **O.**F. 27– imp.; **Y.**

10844 **Bulletin. Maine University Technology Experiment Station.** *Bull. Me Univ. Technol. Exp. Stn* **L.**P. 16–; **Y.**

10845 **Bulletin** de la **Maison** du **médecin.** Paris. *Bull. Maison Méd.* [*C. as:* 12453]
Bulletin. Malaya Department of **Mines.** Kuala Lumpur. *See* 10063.

10846 **Bulletin. Malayan Dental Association.** Singapore. *Bull. Malay. dent. Ass.* [1947–] **L.**D.

10847 **Bulletin. Mammal Society** of the **British Isles.** Birmingham. *Bull. Mammal Soc. Br. Isl.* [1954–] **L.**BMᴺ.; Z.

10848 **Bulletin. Manchester Interplanetary Society.** Manchester. *Bull. Manchr interplan. Soc.* [1938–] **L.**BM.

10849 **Bulletin. Manchurian Science Museum.** Mukden. *Bull. Manchur. Sci. Mus.* [1937] **L.**BMᴺ.; **Br.**U. [*C. as:* 9729]

10850 **Bulletin. Manila Central Observatory. Weather Bureau.** Manila. *Bull. Manila cent. Obs. Weath. Bur.* **L.**BM. 22–; **O.**G. 03–35 imp.

10851 **Bulletin** of the **Manila Medical Society.** Manila. *Bull. Manila med. Soc.* [1909–13] **L.**MD. 10–12 imp.; TD. 10–13 imp.; **Lv.**U. 10–13.

10852 **Bulletin** of the **Manitoba Agricultural College.** Winnipeg. *Bull. Manitoba agric. Coll.* **L.**SC. 14–15.

10853 **Bulletin. Manufacturers' Association** of **New Jersey.** Trenton. *Bull. Mfrs' Ass. New Jers.*

10854 **Bulletin** of the **Margaret Hague Maternity Hospital.** Jersey City. *Bull. Margaret Hague Matern. Hosp.* [1948–] **L.**MA.; MD. imp.; S. 54–57 imp.; **M.**MS. 54–; **Nw.**A. 53–.
Bulletin. Marine Biological Station of **Asamushi.** *See* 9580.

10855 **Bulletin. Marine Department, New Zealand. Fisheries.** Wellington. *Bull. mar. Dep. N.Z. Fish.* [1927–] **L.**SC.; **Abs.**U.; **Lv.**U.

10856 **Bulletin** of **Marine Ecology.** Edinburgh. *Bull. mar. Ecol.* [1953–] **L.**AM.; BM.; BM^N.; L.; NC.; QM.; U.; UC.; Z.; **Abd.**M.; U.; **Abs.**N.; U.; **Bl.**U.; **Bm.**U.; **Bn.**U.; **Br.**U.; **C.**B.; P.; UL.; **Cr.**U.; Db.; Dm.; E.A.; F.; R.; U.; **Ex.**U.; **Fr.**; G.U.; H.U.; Ld.U.; Lo.; Lv.U.; **M.**U.; **Mi.**; N.U. 54–; **Nw.**A.; O.AP.; R.; Z.; **Pl.**M.; R.U.; Sh.U.; Sw.U.; **Wo.**; Y. [*C. of:* 22473]

10857 **Bulletin** de la **marine marchande.** Paris. *Bull. Mar. march.* [*C. as:* 11258]

10858 **Bulletin. Marine Observatory, Hakodate.** *Bull. mar. Obs. Hakodate* **L.**MO. 56–.

10859 **Bulletin** of **Marine Science** of the **Gulf** and **Caribbean.** Coral Gables. *Bull. mar. Sci. Gulf Caribb.* [1951–] **L.**BM^N.; SC.; Z.; **M.**U. 52–; **Pl.**M.; Y.

10860 **Bulletin** of the **Maryland Academy** of **Sciences.** Baltimore. *Bull. Md Acad. Sci.* [1921–29] **L.**BM^N.; SC.; **Nw.**A. [*C. of:* 53838; *C. as:* 26386]

10861 **Bulletin** of the **Maryland Agricultural Experiment Station.** College Park. *Bull. Md agric. Exp. Stn* [1888–] **L.**AM.; BM^N 95–18; EB. (ent.) 98–; K. 07–09 imp.; P.; **C.**A.; **Ld.**U. 17–25 imp.; **Rt.** imp.; Y.

10862 **Bulletin. Maryland Department** of **Geology, Mines** and **Water Resources.** Baltimore. *Bull. Md Dep. Geol. Mines* **L.**BM^N. 44–; Lv.U.

10863 **Bulletin. Maryland University Extension Service.** College Park. *Bull. Md Univ. Ext. Serv.* **O.**F. 26–43 imp.

10864 **Bulletin. Maryland University School** of **Medicine** and **College** of **Physicians** and **Surgeons.** Baltimore. *Bull. Md Univ. Sch. Med.* [1916–54] **L.**MA. 31–54; MD. imp.; S. 28–54; UCH. 48–54; **Bl.**U. 31–54; **Bm.**U. 38–46; **Bn.**U. 41–54; **Br.**U. 32–50 imp.; **Cr.**MD. 31–33: 42: 45–54; **Dn.**U. 31–54 v. imp.; **Ld.**U. 31–54; **Lv.**M. 38–50 imp.; **Nw.**A. 29–54 imp.; **O.**R. 20–54 imp.; **Sw.**U. 30–50.

10865 **Bulletin** of the **Mason Clinic.** Seattle. *Bull. Mason Clin.* **L.**MA. 48–; S. 52–.

10866 **Bulletin** of the **Massachusetts Agricultural Experiment Station.** Amherst. *Bull. Mass. agric. Exp. Stn* [1907–] **L.**AM.; BM^N. imp.; EB. (ent.); P.; 13–; U. 33–39 imp.; **Br.**A. 16– imp.; **C.**A.; **Ld.**U. 12–17: 33– imp.; **Lv.**U. 33–38; **Nw.**A. 33–39 imp.; **O.**F. 14– imp.; R. 33– imp.; **Rt.**; Y. [*C. of:* 10430]

10867 **Bulletin. Massachusetts Audubon Society.** Boston. *Bull. Mass. Audubon Soc.* **L.**BM^N. 57–.

10868 **Bulletin** of the **Massachusetts College** of **Pharmacy.** Boston. *Bull. Mass. Coll. Pharm.*

10869 **Bulletin** of the **Massachusetts Commission** on **Mental Diseases.** Boston. *Bull. Mass. Commn ment. Dis.* **L.**UC. 20–21; **C.**UL. 18–; **Lv.**U. 18–19 imp.

10870 **Bulletin** of the **Massachusetts Department** of **Agriculture.** Boston. *Bull. Mass. Dep. Agric.* **L.**EB. 11–15; SC. 21–.

10871 **Bulletin** of the **Massachusetts Department** of **Health.** Boston. *Bull. Mass. Dep. Hlth* **Lv.**U. 16–.

10872 **Bulletin** of the **Massachusetts Department** of **Weights** and **Measures.** Boston. *Bull. Mass. Dep. Wghts Meas.*

Bulletin. Massachusetts Forest and **Park Association.** *See* 10873.

10873 **Bulletin** of the **Massachusetts Forestry Association.** Boston. *Bull. Mass. For. Ass.* **O.**F. 29–39.

10874 **Bulletin** of the **Massachusetts Horticultural Society.** Boston. *Bull. Mass. hort. Soc.* [1919–23] **Abd.**U. imp.; **Br.**U. imp. [*C. of part of:* 53839; *C. as:* 58091]

10875 **Bulletin** of the **Massachusetts Institute** of **Technology.** Boston. *Bull. Mass. Inst. Technol.* **L.**SC. 08–10*. [*C. as:* 49015]

10876 **Bulletin. Massachusetts Institute** of **Technology. Electrical Engineering Department Research Division.** Boston. *Bull. Mass. Inst. Technol. elect. Engng Dep. Res. Div.* **L.**SC. 15–19. [*C. as:* 15814]

10877 **Bulletin** of the **Massachusetts Medical Society.** Boston. *Bull. Mass. med. Soc.*

10878 **Bulletin. Massachusetts Meteorological Observatory.** *Bull. Mass. met. Obs.*

10879 **Bulletin** of the **Massachusetts State Dental Society.** Boston. *Bull. Mass. St. dent. Soc.* **L.**D. 27–38 imp.

10880 **Bulletin. Massey Agricultural College.** Palmerston North, N.Z. *Bull. Massey agric. Coll.* [1929–] **C.**A.; **Rt.**; **Sal.** 35–36 imp.

10881 **Bulletin** of **Material** on the **Geography** of the **U.S.S.R.** Nottingham. *Bull. Mater. Geogr. U.S.S.R.* [1958–] **C.**GG.; Y.

10882 **Bulletin** of **Mathematical Biophysics.** Chicago. *Bull. math. Biophys.* [1939–] **L.**BM. 41–; SC.; **Br.**U. 50–; **C.**P. 48–; UL. 41–; E.A.; U.; G.U.; **M.**U. 48–; **Nw.**A. 53–; **O.**R.; Y. [*Supplement to:* 40476]

Bulletin. Mathematical Series, Auckland University College. *See* 9539.

10884 **Bulletin** of **Mathematical Statistics.** Fukuoka. *Bull. math. Statist., Fukuoka* [1947–] **L.**SC. 50–; Y.

10885 **Bulletin mathématique. Faculté** des **sciences** de **Marseille.** *Bull. math. Fac. Sci. Marseille* [1934–]

10886 **Bulletin mathématique** de la **Société roumaine** des **sciences.** Bucarest. *Bull. math. Soc. roum. Sci.* [1923–47] **L.**BM. 28–47 imp.; M. 27–47 imp.; SC. 30; UC.; **C.**P. 26–47 imp.; E.R. 26–47. [*C. of part of:* 9145; *C. as:* 10887]

10887 **Bulletin mathématique** de la **Société** des **sciences mathématiques** et **physiques** de la **République populaire roumaine.** Bucarest. *Bull. math. Soc. Sci. math. phys. Répub. pop. roum.* [1957–] **L.**BM.; M.; SC.; UC.; **C.**P.; Db.; E.R.; G.U.; Y. [*C. of:* 10886]

10888 **Bulletin mathématique** de l'**Université** d'**État** à **Moscou.** Moscou. *Bull. math. Univ. Moscou* Série internationale 1927–; Section A Mathématiques et mécanique 1937–. **L.**SC. (A); **C.**P. (A).

10889 **Bulletin** de **mathématiques élémentaires.** Paris. *Bull. Math. élém.*

10890 **Bulletin** de **mathématiques** et de **physique pures** et **appliquées** de l'**École polytechnique** de **Bucarest.** *Bull. Math. Phys. Éc. polytech. Buc.* [1929–] **L.**SC.; U. 29–39; UC. 36–; **Abs.**U. 33–38; **Br.**U. 29–38; E.R. 33–37; G.U. 29–38; **Ld.**U.; **M.**U. 29–39 imp.; **Nw.**A. 29–38; **O.**R.; **Sa.** 33–38.

10891 **Bulletin** de **mathématiques spéciales.** Paris. *Bull. Math. spéc.* [1894–00] **L.**SC.

Bulletin des **matières grasses** de l'**Institut colonial** de **Marseille.** *See* 10582.

10892 **Bulletin** of the **Mauritius Institute.** Port Lonis. *Bull. Maurit. Inst.* [1937–] L.BM^N.; K.; L.; TP. imp.; Z.; **Abs.**A.; **C.**A.; B.; **Hu.**G.; **M.**U.; **O.**F. 41–; R. 39–; **Pl.**M. 42–; **Y.**

Bulletin. Mauritius Sugar Cane Research Station. *See* 12323.

10893 **Bulletin. Mauritius Sugar Industry Research Institute.** Réduit. *Bull. Maurit. Sug. Ind. Res. Inst.* [1954–] L.P.; **Br.**A. 55– imp.; **C.**A. 55–; **N.**U. 55–; **O.**RE. 55–; **Y.** [*C. of:* 12323]

10894 **Bulletin** de **Mayenne-sciences.** Laval. *Bull. Mayenne-Sci.* L.BM^N. 06–.

10894° **Bulletin. Mechanical and Electrical Engineers Department, British Railways.** *Bull. mech. elect. Engrs Dep. Br. Rlys* [1951–] L.BM.

10895 **Bulletin** of **Mechanical Engineering Education.** Manchester. *Bull. mech. Engng Educ.* [1952–] L.BM.; EE.; KC. 53–; P.; **Bl.**U. 60–; **Bm.**T.; **Bn.**U.; **Br.**U.; **C.**ENG.; **Co.**T.; **Db.**; **G.**E.; T. imp.; U.; **Lc.**A.; **M.**P.; T.; U.; **N.**T. 60–; U. 54–; **Sh.**SC.; **Sw.**U. 53–; **Y.**

10896 **Bulletin** de **médecine** et de **pharmacie dosimétriques burggraeviennes.** Médecine humaine et médecine vétérinaire. Gand, Paris. *Bull. Méd. Pharm-dosimétr. burggraev.*

10897 **Bulletin** de **médecine sanitaire maritime.** Marseille. *Bull. Méd. sanit. marit.*

10898 **Bulletin** de **médecine vétérinaire indo-chinoise.** Hanoï. *Bull. Méd. vét. indo-chin.*

10899 **Bulletin** de **médecine vétérinaire pratique belge.** Anvers. *Bull. Méd. vét. prat. belge*

10900 **Bulletin médical.** Paris. *Bull. méd., Paris* [1887–] L.MA. 26–; MD. 88: 24–.

10901 **Bulletin médical** de l'**A.O.F.** Dakar. *Bull. méd. A.O.F.* [1956–58] L.MC. 57–58; MD.; S; TD. [*C. of:* 10904; *C. as:* 12072]

10902 **Bulletin médical** des **accidents** du **travail** et des **maladies professionnelles.** Bruxelles. *Bull. méd. Accid. Trav. Mal. prof.*

10903 **Bulletin médical** et **administratif** du **Dispensaire général** de **Lyon.** Lyon. *Bull. méd. adm. Dispens. gén. Lyon*

10904 **Bulletin médical** de **Afrique occidentale française.** Dakar. *Bull. méd. Afr. occid. fr.* L.TD. 43–55*. [*C. as:* 10901]

10905 **Bulletin médical** de l'**Aisne.** Saint-Quentin. *Bull. méd. Aisne*

10906 **Bulletin médical** de l'**Algérie.** Alger. *Bull. méd. Algér.* [*C. as:* 26409]

10907 **Bulletin médical annuel. Direction générale** de l'**hygiène** de **Damas.** *Bull. méd. a. Dir. gén. Hyg. Damas*

10908 **Bulletin. Medical Center, Georgetown University.** Washington. *Bull. med. Cent. Georgetown Univ.* [1947–] L.BM. 50–.

Bulletin. Medical Center, Temple University. Philadelphia. *See* 52835.

10909 **Bulletin** of the **Medical** and **Chirurgical Faculty** of **Maryland.** Baltimore. *Bull. med. chir. Fac. Md* [*C. of:* 53845]

10910 **Bulletin médical** de la **Clinique Saint-Vincent-de-Paul** de **Bordeaux.** Bordeaux. *Bull. méd. Clin. St Vincent-de-Paul Bordeaux*

10911 **Bulletin** of the **Medical College** of **Virginia.** Richmond. *Bull. med. Coll. Va*

10912 **Bulletin médical** de **Constantinople.** Constantinople. *Bull. méd. Constantinople*

10913 **Bulletin médical franco-chinois.** Pékin. *Bull. méd. fr.-chin.* L.TD. 21.

10914 **Bulletin médical** de l'**Indochine française.** Hanoï. *Bull. méd. Indochine fr.*

10915 **Bulletin médical** du **Katanga.** Élisabethville. *Bull. méd. Katanga* [1924–38] L.TD. imp.

10916 **Bulletin** of the **Medical Library Association.** Baltimore, etc. *Bull. med. Libr. Ass.* [1911–] L.BM. 38–; CB. 48– imp.; MA. 48–; MC. 45– imp.; PH. 48–; S. 32–; TD. 31–; UC. 38–; **Bl.**U. 38– imp.; **Bm.**U. 44–; **Br.**U. 11–16: 27; **Cr.**MD. 44–; **E.**P. 43: 45: 52–; U. 53–; **G.**F. 48–; **Ld.**U. 53–; **M.**MS. 47–. [*C. of:* 1155]

10917 **Bulletin médical** de **Québec.** Québec. *Bull. méd. Québ.* [1899–31] [*Replaced by:* 28188]

Bulletin. Medical School, Osaka University. *See* 10223^a.

Bulletin. Medical School, Washington University. *See* 11662.

10918 **Bulletin** of the **Medical Section** of the **Library Association.** London. *Bull. med. Sect. Libr. Ass.* [1949–] L.BM.; TD.; **Br.**U. [*C. of:* 10922]

Bulletin. Medical Series, University of Missouri. *See* 12528.

10919 **Bulletin. Medical Society** of the **County** of **King's, Brooklyn.** *Bull. med. Soc. Cty King's* [1924–] L.MA. 48–; **Bl.**U. 58– imp.; **Br.**U. 58–; **Ld.**U. 58–.

10920 **Bulletin** of the **Medical Society** of the **District** of **Columbia.** Washington. *Bull. med. Soc. Distr. Columbia* [1924–31] [*Replaced by:* 30179]

10921 **Bulletin médical** des **stations pyrénéennes.** Toulouse. *Bull. méd. Stns pyrén.*

10922 **Bulletin** of the **Medical Sub-Section, University** and **Research Section** of the **Library Association.** London. *Bull. med. Sub-Sect. Univ. Res. Sect. Libr. Ass.* [1947–48] L.BM.; TD.; **Br.**U. [*C. as:* 10918]

10923 **Bulletin médical** de **Toulouse.** Toulouse. *Bull. méd. Toulouse*

10924 **Bulletin médical** de l'**Université l'Aurore.** Shanghai. *Bull. méd. Univ. Aurore* L.MA. 47–.

10925 **Bulletin médical** des **Vosges.** Épinal. *Bull. méd. Vosges*

10926 **Bulletin. Medical Women's National Association.** Seattle. *Bull. med. Wom. natn. Ass.*

10927 **Bulletin médico-chirurgical** des **accidents** du **travail.** Paris. *Bull. méd.-chir. Accid. Trav.* [*C. as:* 9788]

10928 **Bulletin médico-chirurgical** du **Mans** et de l'**Ouest.** Le Mans. *Bull. méd.-chir. Mans*

10929 **Bulletin. Meehanite Metal Corporation.** New Rochelle. *Bull. Meehanite Metal Corp.* [1951–] L.P. v. imp. [*C. of:* 10930]

10930 **Bulletin. Meehanite Research Institute** of **America.** Pittsburgh. *Bull. Meehanite Res. Inst. Am.* [1934–50] L.P. v. imp. [*C. as:* 10929]

Bulletin of the **Mellon Institute** of **Industrial Research** and **School** of **Specific Industries.** *See* 6601 and 49969.

10931 **Bulletin** et **mémoires** de l'**École préparatoire** de **médecine** et de **pharmacie** de **Dakar**. Dakar. *Bull. Mém. Éc. prép. Méd. Pharm. Dakar* [1952–] **L**.MD.; S. 52–56; TD.; **Cr**.MD.

10932 **Bulletin** et **mémoires** de la **Société anatomique** de **Paris**. *Bull. Mém. Soc. anat. Paris* [1826–25] **L**.BM. 1841–25; MD.; S.; **Br**.U. 20–25; **C**.AN.; UL. 20–25; **Db**. 02–25; **Dn**.U. 66–13; **E**.P.; U. 04–13; **G**.F. 99–12; **O**.R. [*C. in:* 2671]

10933 **Bulletin** et **mémoires** de la **Société** d'**anthropologie** de **Paris**. *Bull. Mém. Soc. Anthrop. Paris* [1860–] **L**.AN.; BM.; BMN. 1860–84; G. 82–93 imp.; MD. 1860–07; R. 1860–09; S. 1860–34; UC. 10– imp.; **Bm**.U. 33–; **Br**.U. 1860–10 imp.; **C**.AN. 02: 09–28; UL. imp.; **Db**. 90–30; **E**.R. 83–; U. 1860–84 imp.; V. 96–28; **Ld**.U. 63–03; **O**.B. 1860–30; R.; **Sa**, 1860–19; **Y**.

10934 **Bulletin** et **mémoires** de la **Société belge** d'**orthopédie** et de **chirurgie** de l'**appareil moteur**. Bruxelles. *Bull. Mém. Soc. belge Orthopéd.* [1929–33] [*C. as:* 11864]

10935 **Bulletin** et **mémoires**. **Société centrale** de **médecine vétérinaire**. Paris. *Bull. Mém. Soc. cent. Méd. vét.* [1844–27] **L**.BM. 83–27; LI. 27; MD. 08–27; SC. 25–27; TD. 09: 13–27: V. imp.; **Lv**.U. 03–27 imp.; **O**.R. 83–01. [*C. as:* 9194]

10936 **Bulletin** et **mémoires** de la **Société** de **chirurgie** de **Bucarest**. *Bull. Mém. Soc. Chir. Buc.* [1898–29] [*C. in:* 46392]

10937 **Bulletin** et **mémoires** de la **Société** de **chirurgie** de **Marseille**. *Bull. Mém. Soc. Chir. Marseille* [1927–47] **L**.SC. 32–47 imp.; U. 32–47. [*C. as:* 29473]

10938 **Bulletin** et **mémoires** de la **Société** de **chirurgie** de **Paris**. *Bull. Mém. Soc. Chir. Paris* [1847–23] **L**.MD. 1848–23; S. 1848–23; **C**.UL. 75–23; **Db**. 1847–1854: 75–18; **E**.S. 98–23; **O**.R. 75–23. [*C. as:* 10953]

10940 **Bulletin** et **mémoires** de la **Société** des **chirurgiens** de **Paris**. *Bull. Mém. Soc. Chirgns Paris* [1924–] **L**.MA. 29–; MD.; S. 25–37: 52–53 imp.; **Bl**.U.; **Bm**.U. 27–37; **Br**.U. 27–37 imp.; **Dn**.U. 29–; **Lv**.M. 30–37 imp.; **M**.MS. 27–37; **O**.R. 28–.

10941 **Bulletin** et **mémoires** de la **Société** d'**électroradiologie médicale** de **France**. Paris. *Bull. Mém. Soc. Électroradiol. méd. Fr.* [1938–39] **L**.MA.; MD.; SC.; **E**.U.; **M**.MS. [*C. of:* 10955]

10942 **Bulletin** et **mémoires** de la **Société** d'**émulation** des **Côtes-du-Nord**. Saint-Brieuc. *Bull. Mém. Soc. Émul. Côtes-du-N.* **L**.BM. 61–; UC. 10–12.

10943 **Bulletin** et **mémoires** de la **Société française** d'**ophtalmologie**. Paris. *Bull. Mém. Soc. fr. Ophtal.* [1883–] **L**.MD. imp.; OP.; **Abd**.U. 29–39; **Dn**.U. 29–; **E**.S. 09–39 imp.; **G**.F. 09–13: 23–39; **Lv**.M. 28–38 imp.

10944 **Bulletin** et **mémoires** de la **Société française** d'**otologie**. Paris. *Bull. Mém. Soc. fr. Otol.* [1883–07] **L**.MD. 93–07; **Bm**.U. 95–07. [*C. as:* 11954]

10945 **Bulletin** et **mémoires** de la **Société** de **laryngologie**, d'**otologie** et de **rhinologie** de **Paris**. *Bull. Mém. Soc. Lar. Otol. Rhinol. Paris*

10946 **Bulletin** et **mémoires** de la **Société** de **médecine** et de **chirurgie** de **Bordeaux**. Paris & Bordeaux. *Bull. Mém. Soc. Méd. Chir. Bordeaux* [1905–] **L**.MD. 14–16: 23–25; R. 05–19; S. 05–37; **Db**. 05–26. [*C. of:* 30708]

10947 **Bulletin** et **mémoires** de la **Société** de **médecine** et de **climatologie** de **Nice**. *Bull. Mém. Soc. Méd. Clim. Nice*

10948 **Bulletin** et **mémoires** de la **Société** de **médecine** de **Paris**. *Bull. Mém. Soc. Méd. Paris* [1865–] **L**.MA. 30– imp.; MD. 37–38; **Br**.U. 30– imp.; **Lv**.M. 30–54 imp.

10949 **Bulletin** et **mémoires** de la **Société** de **médecine** de **Vaucluse**. Avignon. *Bull. Mém. Soc. Méd. Vaucluse*

10950 **Bulletin** et **mémoires** de la **Société médicale** des **hôpitaux** de **Bucarest**. *Bull. Mém. Soc. méd. Hôp. Buc.* [1919–] **L**.MA. 29–40; MC. 47–; MD. 25– imp.; S. 32–40 imp.; **O**.R.

10951 **Bulletin** et **mémoires** de la **Société médicale** des **hôpitaux** de **Paris**. *Bull. Mém. Soc. méd. Hôp. Paris* [1849–] **L**.GH. 84– imp.; MA. 13–; MC. 47–; MD.; S.; TD. (2 yr.); **Cr**.MD. 22–28; **E**.P.; U. 45–; **G**.F. 98–13; **Ld**.U. 84–; **Lv**.M. 06–; **O**.R. 29–; **Sh**.U. 33–39; **Y**.

10952 **Bulletin** et **mémoires** de la **Société médicale** de **Passy**. *Bull. Mém. Soc. méd. Passy* [1932–] **L**.MA. 32–39: 46–.

10953 **Bulletin** et **mémoires** de la **Société nationale** de **chirurgie**. Paris. *Bull. Mém. Soc. natn. Chir.* [1924–35] **L**.MA. 29–35; MD.; S.; U. 31–35; **C**.UL.; **Db**. 28–31 imp.; **Dn**.U. 29–35; **E**.S.; U. 32–35; **Ld**.U. 27–35; **Lv**.U. 28–35; **Nw**.A. 27–35; **O**.R. [*C. of:* 10938; *C. as:* 30672]

10954 **Bulletin** et **mémoires** de la **Société** de **neurologie, psychiatrie** et **psychopathie** de **Jassy**. *Bull. Mém. Soc. Neurol. Psychiat. Psychopath. Jassy* [1919–22] **L**.SC. [*C. as:* 9504]

10955 **Bulletin** et **mémoires** de la **Société** de **radiologie médicale** de **France**. *Bull. Mém. Soc. Radiol. méd. Fr.* [1909–37] **L**.MD. 09–14: 34–37; RA. 22–31; SC. 29–37; **E**.U. 24–37; **M**.MS. 33–37. [*C. as:* 10941]

Bulletin et **mémoires** de la **Société** de **radiologie médicale** de **Paris**. *See* 10955.

10956 **Bulletin** et **mémoires** de la **Société** de **thérapeutique**. Paris. *Bull. Mém. Soc. Thér.* [1867–] **L**.BM. 82–96; MC. 36–; MD. 67–94: 29–40; S. 67–95; **Db**.; **Dn**.U. 03–12; **E**.U. 19–26; **G**.F. 82–89; **O**.R. 83–96.

10957 **Bulletin** of the **Memorial Hospital** for the **Treatment** of **Cancer** and **Allied Diseases**. New York. *Bull. meml Hosp. Treat. Cancer, N.Y.*

10958 **Bulletin** of the **Menninger Clinic**. Topeka, Kans. *Bull. Menninger Clin.* [1936–] **L**.GH.; MA. 46–; MD. 41–; **Abd**.U. 39– imp.; **Bl**.U. 56–; **Bm**.U. 42– imp.; **Cr**.MD. 37–55 imp.; **Db**.; **E**.U.; **Ld**.U. 48–; **M**.MS.; **Nw**.A.; **O**.R.; **Y**.

10959 **Bulletin mensuel** de l'**Académie** de **Clermont**. Clermont. *Bull. mens. Acad. Clermont* **L**.BM. 79–87.

10960 **Bulletin mensuel** de l'**Académie** des **sciences**, **belles-lettres** et **arts** d'**Angers**. *Bull. mens. Acad. Sci. Bell.-Lett. Arts Angers* [1958–] **L**.BM.

10961 **Bulletin mensuel** de l'**Académie** des **sciences** et **lettres** de **Montpellier**. Montpellier. *Bull. mens. Acad. Sci. Lett. Montpellier* [1909–] **L**.L. imp.; R. 09–43: 48–53; **Db**.; **E**.O. 09–15 imp.; R. imp.; U. 09–15 imp.; **Ld**.U. 44–; **Lv**.U.

10962 **Bulletin mensuel** de l'**Académie** de **Vaucluse**. Avignon. *Bull. mens. Acad. Vaucluse*

10963 **Bulletin mensuel** de l'**Agence économique** de l'**Afrique occidentale français**. Paris. *Bull. mens. Ag. écon. Afr. occid. fr.* **L**.TP. 28–39.

10964 **Bulletin mensuel** de l'**Association** des **docteurs** en **pharmacie** des **universités** de **France**. Paris. *Bull. mens. Ass. Doct. Pharm. Univ. Fr.*

Bulletin mensuel de l'**Association française** pour l'**avancement** des **sciences**. *See* 9444.

10965 **Bulletin mensuel** de l'**Association internationale** du **froid**. Paris. *Bull. mens. Ass. int. Froid* [1914–19] **L**.AM.; P.; TD.; **Db**. 17–19. [*C. of:* 9470; *C. as:* 33445]

10966 **Bulletin mensuel** de l'**Association** des **naturalistes** de la **Vallée** du **Loing**. Moret. *Bull. mens. Ass. Nat. Vall. Loing* **L**.BM^N. 26–39: 47–59★. [*C. as:* 9572ª]

10967 **Bulletin mensuel** de l'**Association technique** de **fonderie**. Liège. *Bull. mens. Ass. tech. Fond.* **Bm**.C. 27–. [*C. of:* 9514]

10968 **Bulletin mensuel** des **associations agricoles** de la **région** de **Lannion**. *Bull. mens. Assns agric. Rég. Lannion*

10969 **Bulletin mensuel** de **bibliographie**. **Communauté européenne** du **charbon** et de l'**acier**. Luxembourg. *Bull. mens. Biblphie Commun. eur. Charb. Acier* [1953–55] **Dn**.U. [*C. as:* 6670]

10970 **Bulletin mensuel** de la **Bourgogne apicole**. Dijon. *Bull. mens. Bourgogne apic.*

10971 **Bulletin mensuel** du **Bureau central météorologique** de **France**. Paris. *Bull. mens. Bur. cent. mét. Fr.* **L**.MO. 01–20★; **E**.M. 05–20 imp.; **O**.G. 81–20 imp. [*C. as:* 11009]

10972 **Bulletin mensuel** du **Bureau municipal** d'**hygiène** et de **statistique**. Cité de Montréal. *Bull. mens. Bur. munic. Hyg. Statist. Montréal* [1915–] **L**.TD. 15–16.

Bulletin mensuel du **Cebedeau**. Liège. *See* 10973.

10973 **Bulletin mensuel**. **Centre belge** d'**étude** et de **documentation** des **eaux**. Liège. *Bull. mens. Cent. belge Étude Docum. Eaux* [1950–] **L**.P. 55–; **Wa**.W.; **Y**.

10974 **Bulletin mensuel** du **Cercle horticole** de **Roubaix**. Roubaix. *Bull. mens. Cerc. hort. Roubaix*

10975 **Bulletin mensuel**. **Chambre syndicale** des **constructeurs** de **machines agricoles**. Paris. *Bull. mens. Chamb. synd. Constr. Mach. agric.*

10976 **Bulletin mensuel**. **Chambre syndicale française** de la **photographie** et de ses **applications**. Paris. *Bull. mens. Chamb. synd. fr. Photogr.* **L**.PG. 20–39 imp.

10977 **Bulletin mensuel climatologique**. Athènes. *Bull. mens. clim., Athènes* **L**.MO. 36–40: 50–.

10978 **Bulletin mensuel**. **Commission** de **météorologie** de la **Haute-Savoie**. Annecy. *Bull. mens. Commn Mét. Hte-Savoie*

10979 **Bulletin mensuel** de la **Commission météorologique** du **Calvados**. Caen. *Bull. mens. Commn mét. Calvados*

10980 **Bulletin mensuel** de **documentation**. **Office central** de l'**acétylène** et de la **soudure autogène**. Paris. *Bull. mens. Docum. Off. cent. Acét. Soud. autog.* [1937–40] **L**.SC. [*C. as:* 10124]

10981 **Bulletin mensuel** de **documentation**. **Union technique** de l'**automobile**, du **motocycle** et du **cycle**. Paris. *Bull. mens. Docum. Un. tech. Auto.* **L**.P. 60–; **Li**.M. 52–; **Y**.

10982 **Bulletin mensuel**. **Fédération industrielle** des **matériaux** de **construction**. Paris. *Bull. mens. Féd. ind. Matér. Constr.*

10983 **Bulletin mensuel** de la **Fédération** des **syndicats médicaux** de l'**Aube**. Troyes. *Bull. mens. Féd. Synds méd. Aube*

10984 **Bulletin mensuel** de la **Fédération** des **syndicats pharmaceutiques** de l'**Est**. Dijon. *Bull. mens. Féd. Synds pharm. E.*

10985 **Bulletin mensuel** de la **France hippique**. Paris. *Bull. mens. Fr. hipp.*

10986 **Bulletin mensuel** d'**information**. **Association technique** de **fonderie**. Paris. *Bull. mens. Inf. Ass. tech. Fond.* [1948–] **Y**. [*C. from* 10537]

10987 **Bulletin mensuel** d'**information**. **Centre technique** des **industries** de la **fonderie**. Paris. *Bull. mens. Inf. Cent. tech. Ind. Fond.* [1948–] **L**.SC. [*C. from:* 10537]

10988 **Bulletin mensuel** d'**information**. **Institut technique** d'**études** et de **recherches** des **corps gras**. Paris. *Bull. mens. Inf. Inst. tech. Étud. Rech. Corps gras* [1947–54] **L**.P. 53–54. [*C. as:* 47188]

10989 **Bulletin mensuel** de l'**Institut central bulgare** pour la **météorologie**. Sofia. *Bull. mens. Inst. cent. bulg. Mét.* [1893–] **L**.MO. 15–37; SC. 23–; **E**.M. 07–33; R. imp.

10990 **Bulletin mensuel**. **Institut colonial** de **Bordeaux**. *Bull. mens. Inst. colon. Bordeaux*

10991 **Bulletin mensuel**. **Institut colonial** du **Havre**. *Bull. mens. Inst. colon. Havre*

10992 **Bulletin mensuel** de l'**Institut électro-médical** de la **Tronche**. *Bull. mens. Inst. électro-méd. Tronche*

10993 **Bulletin mensuel**. **Institut français** de la **prévention** du **feu**. Paris. *Bull. mens. Inst. fr. Prévent. Feu*

Bulletin mensuel. **Institut international** de **statistique**. *See* 11010.

10994 **Bulletin mensuel**. **Institut** de **météorologie** et de **physique** du **globe** de l'**Algérie**. *Bull. mens. Inst. Mét. Phys. Globe Algér.* [1932–] **L**.MO. 32–51. [*C. of:* 35646]

Bulletin mensuel de l'**Institut météorologique central** de **Bulgarie**. *See* 10989.

10994° **Bulletin mensuel**. **Institut r. météorologique** de **Belgique**. *Bull. mens. Inst. r. mét. Belg.* **Y**.

10995 **Bulletin mensuel** de la **Ligue agricole** de **France**. Paris. *Bull. mens. Lig. agric. Fr.*

10996 **Bulletin mensuel** du **magnétisme terrestre** de l'**Observatoire r.** de **Belgique**. Bruxelles. *Bull. mens. Magn. terr. Obs. r. Belg.*

10997 **Bulletin mensuel** des **musées** et **collections** de la **ville** de **Genève**. *Bull. mens. Mus. Collect. Ville Genève* **L**.BM^N. 44–58.

Bulletin mensuel. Les **Naturalistes belges**. Bruxelles. *See* 34253.

10998 **Bulletin mensuel** de la **normalisation française**. *Bull. mens. Norm. fr.* **Y**.

10999 **Bulletin mensuel** des **observations**. **Service météorologique** de l'**Indo-Chine**. Phu-Lien. *Bull. mens. Obsns Serv. mét. Indo-Chine* **L**.MO. 30–39; SC. 38–39.

11000 **Bulletin mensuel**. **Observatoire astronomique** et **météorologique** de l'**Université r. Serbe**. Belgrade. *Bull. mens. Obs. astr. mét. Univ. r. Serbe* **E**.M. 69–.

11001 **Bulletin mensuel** de l'**Observatoire central** de **Béograd**. Béograd. *Bull. mens. Obs. cent. Béogr.* [1902–04] **L**.MO. [*C. of:* 11069]

11002 **Bulletin mensuel** de l'**Observatoire Jules Carde.** Tamanrasset. *Bull. mens. Obs. Jules Carde* **L.**MO. 47–51; SC. 47–.

Bulletin mensuel de l'**Observatoire magnétique et météorologique** de **Zi-Ka-Wei.** *See* 11356.

11003 **Bulletin mensuel** de l'**Observatoire météorologique** de l'**Université** d'**Upsal.** Uppsala. *Bull. mens. Obs. mét. Univ. Upsal* [1868–] **L.**AS. 16–17; MO. 69–; R. imp.; **C.**GG. 37–; O. 69–; **Db.**; **E.**C. imp.; M.; R.; **O.**G. 69–; **Y.**

11004 **Bulletin mensuel. Observatoire** de **Montsouris** et de la **Tour St. Jacques.** Paris. *Bull. mens. Obs. Montsouris* **L.**MO. 72–77: 20–39.

11005 **Bulletin mensuel** de l'**œuvre** des **enfants tuberculeux, Hôpital** d'**Ormesson.** Paris. *Bull. mens. Œuvre Enf. tuberc. Hôp. Ormesson*

11006 **Bulletin mensuel** de l'**Office central** de l'**agriculture française.** Paris. *Bull. mens. Off. cent. Agric. fr.*

11007 **Bulletin mensuel. Office international** des **épizooties.** Paris. *Bull. mens. Off. int. Épizoot.* [1927–31] **L.**I.; MC.; SC.; V.; **E.**N. 30–31; **W.** [*C. as:* 11378 and 50854]

11008 **Bulletin mensuel** de l'**Office international** d'**hygiène publique.** Paris. *Bull. mens. Off. int. Hyg. publ.* [1909–46] **L.**EB. 28–46; H.; LI.; MA.; MC.; MD.; S.; SC. 25–46; SH.; TD.; **Bl.**U. 12–40 imp.; **Bm.**U. 27–46; **E.**U.; **G.**F.; PH. 35–40; O.AP. 36–46. [*C. of:* 11379; *C. in:* 12649]

11009 **Bulletin mensuel. Office national météorologique.** Paris. *Bull. mens. Off. natn. mét.* [1921–34] **L.**MO.; **E.**M.; **O.**G. 23–30 imp. [*C. of:* 10971; *C. as:* 9388]

11010 **Bulletin mensuel** de l'**Office permanent. Institut international** de **statistique.** La Haye. *Bull. mens. Off. perm. Inst. int. Statist.* [1920–32] **L.**AM. 28–32. [*C. as:* 47319]

11012 **Bulletin mensuel** de l'**Office** des **renseignements agricoles.** Paris. *Bull. mens. Off. Renseign. agric.* [1902–20] **L.**AM.; BM.; P.; **Bn.**U.; **C.**A. 12–20; UL.; **Db.**; **Ld.**U.; **Nw.**A. 14–20. [*C. as:* 11386]

11013 **Bulletin mensuel** de la **Régalia: Société amicale** des **pharmaciens** du **IX**e et du **XVII**e **arrondissements.** Paris. *Bull. mens. Régalia*

11014 **Bulletin mensuel** de **renseignements agricoles** du **Comptoir français** de l'**azote.** Paris. *Bull. mens. Renseign. agric. Compt. fr. Azote* **Rt.** 32–39.

11015 **Bulletin mensuel** des **renseignements frigorifiques.** Paris. *Bull. mens. Renseign. frigorif.* **L.**AM. 20–.

Bulletin mensuel du **Réseau météorologique, Kasan.** *See* 12783.

11016 **Bulletin mensuel** de la **Réunion médicochirurgicale** de la **VI**e **région.** Châlons-sur-Marne. *Bull. mens. Réun. méd.-chir. VI*e *Rég.*

11017 **Bulletin mensuel** du **Sahara.** Institut de météorologie et de physique du globe de l'Algérie. Alger. *Bull. mens. Sahara Inst. Mét. Phys. Globe Algér.* **L.**MO. 39–51.

Bulletin mensuel. Service central météorologique. Koara. *See* 9815.

11018 **Bulletin mensuel. Service central météorologique** du **Levant.** *Bull. mens. Serv. cent. mét. Levant*

11019 **Bulletin mensuel. Service central météorologique** en **Syrie** et au **Liban.** *Bull. mens. Serv. cent. mét. Syrie Liban* **L.**SC. 32–41.

11020 **Bulletin mensuel. Service météorologique** de **Belgique.** Bruxelles. *Bull. mens. Serv. mét. Belg.* **L.**MO. 50–; **Y.**

11020° **Bulletin mensuel. Service météorologique** du **Congo belge.** *Bull. mens. Serv. mét. Congo belge* [1951–]

11021 **Bulletin mensuel** du **Service national** d'**hygiène** et d'**assistance publique, République** d'**Haiti.** *Bull. mens. Serv. natn. Hyg. Assist. publ. Répub. Haiti* [1931–] **L.**TD. 31–32 imp.

11022 **Bulletin mensuel signalétique.** Service de documentation et d'information technique de l'aéronautique. Paris. *Bull. mens. sign. Serv. Docum. Inf. tech. Aéronaut.* **L.**AV. 51–59. [*C. as:* 11791]

11023 **Bulletin mensuel. Société astronomique** de **Liège.** *Bull. mens. Soc. astr. Liège* **L.**AS. 39–40.

11024 **Bulletin mensuel** de la **Société belge** d'**électriciens.** *Bull. mens. Soc. belge Électns* [1884–59] **L.**EE.; P. 13–59; **E.**F. 95–59; **Y.** [> 47153, 1911–12; *C. as:* 12143ᵃ] [*July* 1928–*Jan.* 1929 *as Bulletin*]

11025 **Bulletin mensuel. Société centrale** d'**agriculture** du **département** de la **Seine-inférieure.** Rouen. *Bull. mens. Soc. cent. Agric. Dép. Seine-inér.* **Md.**H. 39–41* imp. [*C. of:* 18862; *C. as:* 12460]

11026 **Bulletin mensuel. Société centrale** d'**architecture** de **Belgique.** Bruxelles. *Bull. mens. Soc. cent. Archit. Belg.* **L.**BA. 34–40.

11027 **Bulletin mensuel** de la **Société départementale** d'**agriculture** des **Bouches-du-Rhône.** Marseille. *Bull. mens. Soc. dép. Agric. Bouches-du-Rhône*

11028 **Bulletin mensuel** de la **Société** d'**encouragement** à l'**agriculture** de l'**arrondissement** d'**Orléans.** Orléans. *Bull. mens. Soc. Encour. Agric. Arrond. Orléans*

11029 **Bulletin mensuel** de la **Société entomologique** du **nord** de la **France.** Lille. *Bull. mens. Soc. ent. N. Fr.* [1938] **L.**BMᴺ. [*C. as:* 11912]

Bulletin mensuel de la **Société** d'**études scientifiques** sur la **tuberculose.** *See* 11936.

11030 **Bulletin mensuel** de la **Société générale** de **pharmacie** de **France.** Paris. *Bull. mens. Soc. gén. Pharm. Fr.*

11031 **Bulletin mensuel** de la **Société** d'**hygiène** de l'**enfance.** Abbeville. *Bull. mens. Soc. Hyg. Enf., Abbeville*

11032 **Bulletin mensuel** de la **Société industrielle** du **nord** de la **France.** Lille. *Bull. mens. Soc. ind. N. Fr.* [1909–] **L.**P. 09–23; SC. 09–14; **Bm.**U. 09–13. [*C. of:* 12466]

11033 **Bulletin mensuel** de la **Société linnéenne** de **Lyon.** *Bull. mens. Soc. linn. Lyon* [1932–] **L.**AN. 32–47 imp.; BMᴺ.; E. 40–45 imp.; L.; Z.; **Db.**; **E.**B.; R.; **G.**N. 37–38; **Pl.**M.; **Y.** [*C. of:* 9570]

Bulletin mensuel de la **Société linnéenne** du **nord** de la **France.** *See* 12040.

11034 **Bulletin mensuel. Société Lorraine-Dietrich.** Argenteuil. *Bull. mens. Soc. Lorr.-Dietrich* **L.**P. 26–27*. [*C. as:* 12044]

11035 **Bulletin mensuel. Société nantaise** des **amis** de l'**horticulture.** Nantes. *Bull. mens. Soc. nant. Amis Hort.* [1925–] L.HS. 25–39 imp. [*C. of:* 2837]

11036 **Bulletin mensuel** de la **Société nationale** d'**horticulture** de **France.** Paris. *Bull. mens. Soc. natn. Hort. Fr.* [1928–46] L.AM. 28–40; BM.; HS.; K.; SC.; C.UL.; **Md.**H. 30–39. [*C. of:* 26906; *C. as:* 25283]

11037 **Bulletin mensuel** de la **Société** des **naturalistes luxemburgeois.** Luxembourg. *Bull. mens. Soc. Nat. luxemb.* [1907–48] L.BM^N. 07–38; L.; R. 09–48; SC.; Z.; **E.**B.; **G.**N. 14–48 imp. [*C. of:* 15252 and 42364; *C. as:* 12096]

11038 **Bulletin mensuel** de la **Société ornithologique** et **mammalogique** de **France.** Paris. *Bull. mens. Soc. orn. mammal. Fr.* L.BM^N. 30–.

11039 **Bulletin mensuel** de la **Société** des **sciences naturelles** de **Toulon.** Toulon. *Bull. mens. Soc. Sci. nat. Toulon* L.BM^N. 46–51 imp.

11040 **Bulletin mensuel** de la **Société scientifique** des **pharmaciens** de l'**Aveyron** et du **Centre.** Clermont-Ferrand. *Bull. mens. Soc. scient. Pharmns Aveyron*

11041 **Bulletin mensuel** de la **Société** de secours aux **blessés militaires.** Paris. *Bull. mens. Soc. Secours Blessés milit.*

Bulletin mensuel de la **Société suisse** de l'industrie du **gaz** et des **eaux.** *See* 33108.

11042 **Bulletin mensuel** de la **Société vétérinaire pratique** de **France.** Paris. *Bull. mens. Soc. vét. prat. Fr.* L.V. 47–; **W.** 49–.

11043 **Bulletin mensuel. Station météorologique, Port-au-Prince.** *Bull. mens. Stn mét. Port-au-Prince*

11044 **Bulletin mensuel** du **Syndicat général** des **agriculteurs** du **Sud-Ouest.** Toulouse. *Bull. mens. Synd. gén. Agric. Sud-Ouest*

11045 **Bulletin mensuel** du **Syndicat général** des **cuirs** et **peaux** de **France.** Paris. *Bull. mens. Synd. gén. Cuirs Peaux Fr.*

11046 **Bulletin mensuel** du **Syndicat général** des **produits chimiques.** Paris. *Bull. mens. Synd. gén. Prod. chim.* [*C. of:* 9765; *C. as:* 55538]

11047 **Bulletin mensuel** du **Syndicat** des **mécaniciens, chaudronniers** et **fondeurs** de **France.** Paris. *Bull. mens. Synd. Mécns Chaudr. Fond. Fr.*

11048 **Bulletin mensuel. Syndicat professionnel** des **caoutchouc, gutta-percha, tissus, plastiques, toiles cireés, toiles cuir.** Paris. *Bull. mens. Synd. prof. Caoutch.*

11049 **Bulletin mensuel technique** et **documentaire. Chambre syndicale** des **entrepreneurs** de **couverture plomberie.** Paris. *Bull. mens. tech. docum. Chamb. synd. Entrepr. Couvert. Plomb.* L.P. 35–40.

11050 **Bulletin mensuel. Union radio-scientifique internationale.** Bruxelles. *Bull. mens. Un. radioscient. int.* [1938–] L.AS. 38–54 imp.; **E.**R. 47–; **Sw.**U. 59–.

11051 **Bulletin** of **Mental Health, Virgin Islands.** St. Thomas. *Bull. ment. Hlth Virgin Isl.*

11052 **Bulletin** of the **Metallurgical Department** of the **Ontario Research Foundation.** Toronto. *Bull. metall. Dep. Ontario Res. Fdn* **Bm.**C. 30–33.

Bulletin. Metallurgical Research Bureau, State College of **Washington.** *See* 10069.

11053 **Bulletin** of the **Meteorological Bureau.** Quebec. *Bull. met. Bur., Queb.* L.SC. 46–; **O.**F. 46– imp.

Bulletin. Meteorological Institute of the **University, Debrecen.** *See* 31527°.

11054 **Bulletin** of the **Meteorological Society** for **Research** of **Tohoku District.** Sendai. *Bull. met. Soc. Res. Tohoku Distr.* L.MO. 55.

11055 **Bulletin météorologique.** Besançon. *Bull. mét., Besançon* L.MO. 21–53★; **E.**R. 01–32; **O.**G. 03–37: 47; O. 10–26 imp.; **Y.** [*C. as:* 14547]

11056 **Bulletin météorologique** d'**Algérie.** Alger. *Bull. mét. Algér.* L.MO. 77–39. [*C. as:* 11571]

11057 **Bulletin météorologique annuel** des **Pyrénées-orientales.** Perpignan. *Bull. met. a. Pyrén. orient.* L.MO. 72–11.

11058 **Bulletin météorologique** du **département** de l'**Aude.** *Bull. mét. Dép. Aude*

11059 **Bulletin météorologique** du **département** de l'**Hérault.** Montpellier. *Bull. mét. Dép. Hérault* L.MO. 73–74: 19–20: 24–25.

Bulletin météorologique et **hydrographique, Pologne.** *See* 57822.

11060 **Bulletin météorologique** de l'**Indo-Chine.** Saigon. *Bull. mét. Indo-Chine* L.MO. 33–37. [*C. as:* 35623]

11061 **Bulletin météorologique. Institut scientifique chérifien.** Rabat. *Bull. mét. Inst. scient. chérif.* L.MO. 26.

11062 **Bulletin météorologique journalier, Vietnam.** Saigon. *Bull. mét. journ. Vietnam* [1956–] L.MO.

11063 **Bulletin météorologique** du **Maroc.** Casablanca. *Bull. mét. Maroc* L.MO. 22–39.

11064 **Bulletin météorologique** et **médical** de **Leysin.** Leysin. *Bull. mét. méd. Leysin*

Bulletin météorologique mensuel de l'**Observatoire physique** de **Géorgie.** *See* 18901.

11065 **Bulletin météorologique mensuel** de l'**Observatoire** de **Tananarive.** *Bull. mét. mens. Obs. Tananarive* L.MO. 24–; **Y.**

11066 **Bulletin météorologique mensuel, Yougoslavie.** Béograd. *Bull. mét. mens. Yougosl.* L.MO. 51–55.

11067 **Bulletin météorologique, Nijni-Oltchedaef.** Moghilev. *Bull. mét. Nijni-Oltchedaef* L.MO. 06–14.

11068 **Bulletin météorologique** du **Nord.** Copenhague. *Bull. mét. N.* [1874–11] L.MO.; SC. 81–11; **E.**M. 06–11.

11069 **Bulletin météorologique. Observatoire central.** Béograd. *Bull. mét. Obs. cent., Béogr.* [1900] L.MO. [*C. as:* 11001]

11070 **Bulletin météorologique. Observatoire** de **Ksara.** *Bull. mét. Obs. Ksara* L.MO. 10–14.

11071 **Bulletin météorologique. Observatoire météorologique.** Béograd. *Bull. mét. Obs. mét., Béogr.* [1920–47] L.MO.; **E.**M. 20–35. [*C. as:* 35619]

11072 **Bulletin météorologique quotidien** du **Méxique.** Tacubaya. *Bull. mét. quot. Méx.*

11073 **Bulletin météorologique, séismique** et **magnétique.** Istanbul. *Bull. mét. séism. magn. Istanbul* **E.**M. (mét.) 43–45.

11074 **Bulletin météorologique** et **sismologique.** Port-au-Prince. *Bull. mét. sism., Port-au-Prince* L.MO. 07–11.

11075 **Bulletin météorologique. Station agronomique** du **Pas-de-Calais.** Arras. *Bull. mét. Stn agron. Pas-de-Calais*

11076 **Bulletin météorologique. Stations** du **territoire** de l'**Observatoire, Béograd.** *Bull. mét. Stns Terr. Obs. Béogr.* L.MO. 32–33.

11077 **Bulletin météorologique synoptique.** Alger. *Bull. mét. synopt., Alger* [1945–] L.MO. 45–47; SC.
Bulletin météorologique tchécoslovaque. Prague. *See* 31653.

11078 **Bulletin météorologique, Warszawa.** *Bull. mét. Warsz.* L.MO. 23–36.
Bulletin of the **Methodi Popoff Institute** of **Biology.** Sofia. *See* 24375.

11079 **Bulletin** de **métrologie.** Bruxelles. *Bull. Métrol.* L.P. 50–56*; Te.N.; Y. [*C. as:* 9557]
Bulletin of the **Michigan Academy** of **Science.** *See* 28940.

11080 **Bulletin. Michigan Agricultural College Experiment Station.** East Lansing. *Bull. Mich. agric. Coll. Exp. Stn* [1888–] L.AM.; BM[N]. 93–98 imp.; EB. (ent.) 89–21; K. 03–08 imp.; P. 95–22; Cr.U. 14– imp.; Rt. 95–20.

11081 **Bulletin. Michigan Anti-Tuberculosis Association.** Ann Arbor *Bull. Mich. Anti-Tuberc. Ass.* [1915–17] C.UL. imp. [*C. of:* 11082; *C. as:* 31744]

11082 **Bulletin. Michigan Association** for the **Prevention** and **Relief** of **Tuberculosis.** Ann Arbor. *Bull. Mich. Ass. Prev. Relief Tuberc.* [1912–14] C.UL. imp. [*C. as:* 11081]

11083 **Bulletin. Michigan College** of **Mining** and **Technology.** Houghton, Mich. *Bull. Mich. Coll. Min. Technol.* Y.

11084 **Bulletin. Michigan Dairy** and **Food Department.** Lansing. *Bull. Mich. Dairy Fd Dep.*

11085 **Bulletin. Michigan Engineering Experiment Station.** East Lansing. *Bull. Mich. Engng Exp. Stn* [1925–] L.P. 25–53; Bm.P. imp.; Y.

11086 **Bulletin** of the **Michigan Ornithological Club.** Detroit. *Bull. Mich. orn. Club*

11087 **Bulletin** of the **Michigan State Dental Society.** Chicago. *Bull. Mich. St. dent. Soc.* [1919–32] L.D. 19–28 imp. [*C. as:* 26465]
Bulletin of the **Microbiological Institute.** Sofia. *See* 24422.

11088 **Bulletin** de **microscopie appliquée.** Paris. *Bull. Microsc. appl.* [1951–] L.BM[N].; MD.; P.; SC.; SI.; U.; C.P.; UL.; E.U.; G.ME. (5 yr); M.MS.; O.R.; W. 51–54; Y. [*C. of:* 10488 and 31774]

11089 **Bulletin microsismique.** Observatoire sismologique de l'Université de Budapest. *Bull. microsism. Obs. sism. Univ. Bpest*
Bulletin. Middle West Soil Improvement Committee. *See* 11218.

11090 **Bulletin. Midland Agricultural** and **Dairy College,** Sutton Bonington. Loughborough. *Bull. Midl. agric. Dairy Coll.* L.EB. (ent.) 27–34; SC. 28–; C.A. 25–; N.U. 27–40 imp.; R.D. 26–; Rt. 18–28.

11091 **Bulletin** of the **Mie University Forests.** Mie Prefectural University. Tsu. *Bull. Mie Univ. Forests* O.F. 58–.

11092 **Bulletin militaire** du **Corps** de **santé.** Limoges & Paris. *Bull. milit. Cps Santé*
Bulletin. Military Hospitals Commission. Ottawa. *See* 31838.

11093 **Bulletin** of the **Milwaukee County Dental Society.** Milwaukee. *Bull. Milwaukee Cty dent. Soc.*

11094 **Bulletin** of the **Mine Ventilation Society** of **South Africa.** Johannesburg. *Bull. Mine Vent. Soc. S. Afr.* [1948–56] L.MI. 51–56; MIE. 56; Ld.U. 53–56, Sh.SC. 53–56. [*C. as:* 26474]

11095 **Bulletin** of the **Mineral Industries Experiment Station, College of Mineral Industry, Pennsylvania State University.** *Bull. Miner. Inds Exp. Stn Penn. St. Univ.* L.MI. 45– imp.; Y.

11096 **Bulletin. Mineral Research** and **Exploration Institute.** Ankara. *Bull. Miner. Res. Explor. Inst., Ankara* L.BM[N]. 36–; MI. 36– imp.; Y.

11097 **Bulletin. Mineral Resources Survey, Australia.** Canberra. *Bull. Miner. Resour. Surv. Aust.*

11098 **Bulletin. Mineral Resources Survey** of **New Mexico.** School of Mines, Sorocco. *Bull. Miner. Resour. Surv. New Mex.*

11099 **Bulletin** of the **Mineral Survey** of **Chosen.** *Bull. Miner. Surv. Chosen* L.BM[N]. 31– imp.

11100 **Bulletin** of the **Mineralogical Society** of **Southern California.** *Bull. mineral. Soc. sth. Calif.* [1931–34] L.BM[N]. [*C. in:* 31938]

11101 **Bulletin. Minerals Research Laboratory. University** of the **Witwatersrand.** Johannesburg. *Bull. Miner. Res. Lab. Univ. Witwatersrand* [1936–40] L.BM.; SC.
Bulletin. Mines Branch, Department of **Mines, Canada.** *See* 10065.
Bulletin. Mines Experiment Station, Minnesota Institute of **Technology.** *See* 11130.

11102 **Bulletin** des **mines** de **Madagascar.** Tananarive. *Bull. Mines Madagascar* L.MI. 23–25 imp.

11103 **Bulletin** des **mines** d'**or.** Paris. *Bull. Mines Or*

11104 **Bulletin. Mining Bureau, Philippine Islands.** Manila. *Bull. Min. Bur. Philipp. Isl.* L.P. 02–05.
Bulletin. Mining Experiment Station and **State Electrometallurgical Research Laboratories, State College** of **Washington.** *See* 10069.
Bulletin. Mining and **Metallurgical Investigations. Carnegie Institute** of **Technology.** *See* 32033.

11105 **Bulletin** of the **Mining** and **Metallurgical Society** of **America.** New York. *Bull. Min. metall. Soc. Am.* L.MI. 21–31: 32– imp.; Sh.IO. 23–42; Y.

11106 **Bulletin** of the **Mining Society** of **Chosen.** *Bull. Min. Soc. Chosen*
Bulletin du **Ministère** de l'**agriculture.** Bucarest. *See* 9128.

11107 **Bulletin** du **Ministère** de l'**agriculture.** Paris. *Bull. Minist. Agric., Paris* [1882–02] L.AM.; BM.; P.; U. [*C. as:* 2842]

11108 **Bulletin** du **Ministère** de l'**agriculture** de la **République tchécoslovaque.** Prague. *Bull. Minist. Agric. Répub. tchécosl.* [1920–21] L.AM.; BM. [*C. as:* 41144]

11109 **Bulletin** du **Ministère** des **colonies.** Paris. *Bull. Minist. Colon., Paris* [1908–19] L.BM. 17–19; G.; TP. [*C. as:* 9227]

11110 **Bulletin** du **Ministère** de l'**intérieur** et de l'**agriculture.** Bruxelles. *Bull. Minist. Intér. Agric., Brux.* L.AM. 08–10.

Bulletin du **Ministère** de la **santé publique,** Belgrade. *See* 21350.

11111 **Bulletin** du **Ministère** de la **santé publique,** Bruxelles. *Bull. Minist. Santé publ., Brux.* [1936–38] L.H. 37–38; MA.; SC.; TD. 38; Bm.U. 38. [*C. as:* 11650]

11112 **Bulletin** du **Ministère** de la **santé publique,** Paris. *Bull. Minist. Santé publ., Paris* [1936–56] L.H.; SH.; TD. [*C. of:* 42567; *C. as:* 42367]

11113 **Bulletin** du **Ministère** des **sciences** et des **arts,** Bruxelles. *Bull. Minist. Sci. Arts, Brux.*

11114 **Bulletin** du **Ministère** du **travail** et de l'**hygiène,** Paris. *Bull. Minist. Trav. Hyg., Paris* [1894–]

11115 **Bulletin** du **Ministère** des **travaux publics,** Paris. *Bull. Minist. Trav. publ., Paris*

Bulletin van het **Ministerie** van **volksgezondheid.** Brussels. *See* 11111.

Bulletin. Ministry of **Agriculture, Egypt. Petroleum Research.** Cairo. *See* 37428.

11116 **Bulletin. Ministry** of **Agriculture, Egypt. Technical** and **Scientific Service.** Cairo. *Bull. Minist. Agric. Egypt tech. scient. Serv.* [1916–] L.AM.; BM.; EB. (ent.) 16–54 imp.; K. 24–47 imp.; L. 16–40 imp.; MO. 23–24 imp.; MY. 20–48 imp.; P. 25–39 imp.; Abs.N. 17; C.A.; E.R. 16–17; U. 24–40; M.C. imp.; O.R. 23–; Rt.; Y.

11116ᵃ **Bulletin. Ministry of Agriculture, Federation** of **Malaya.** Kuala Lumpur. *Bull. Minist. Agric. Fed. Malaya* [1956–] L.AM.; C.A.; P.; Y. [*C. of:* 9999]

11117 **Bulletin. Ministry of Agriculture, Fisheries** (and **Food**). London. *Bull. Minist. Agric. Fish Fd., Lond.* [1930–] L.AM.; BM.; BMᴺ. imp.; EB. (ent.) 31–; K. imp.; P. imp.; SC.; Abs.N. imp.; Bm.P.; Bn.U. imp.; C.A; E.A.; R.; Ld.P.; U.; Lo. 57–; M.P.; N.P. 39–; R.; O.RE.; R.U.; Rt.; Y.

11118 **Bulletin** of the **Ministry** of **Agriculture** and **Forestry.** Nanking. *Bull. Minist. Agric. For., Nanking* [1941–45] O.F.

11119 **Bulletin. Ministry of Agriculture, Israel.** Tel-Aviv. *Bull. Minist. Agric. Israel* [1949–]

11120 **Bulletin** of the **Ministry** of **Agriculture** and **Lands, Jamaica.** *Bull. Minist. Agric. Lds Jamaica* [1959–] L.EB.; K.; MY.; P.; Abd.S.; Br.A. 47– imp.; O.RE.; Rt.; Y. [*C. of:* 9975]

Bulletin of the **Ministry** of **Agriculture** and **Lands, Southern Rhodesia.** *See* 10016.

11121 **Bulletin** of the **Ministry** of **Agriculture, Quebec.** Quebec. *Bull. Minist. Agric. Queb.* L.EB. (ent.) 16–; SC. 17–; Rt. 30– imp.

11122 **Bulletin. Ministry** of **Agriculture, Sudan.** Khartoum. *Bull. Minist. Agric. Sudan* [1956–] C.A.; O.F. imp.; RE.; Y. [*C. from:* 10014]

Bulletin. Minneapolis Steel Machinery Co. *See* 32065.

11123 **Bulletin** of the **Minnesota Academy** of **Natural Sciences.** Minneapolis. *Bull. Minn. Acad. nat. Sci.* [1873–17] L.BM. 73–89; BMᴺ.; SC. 74–91; Z. 74–91; Bl.U. 91–11; Lv.U. 73–11 imp.; Pl.M. 89–91.

11124 **Bulletin. Minnesota Agricultural Experiment Station.** St. Paul. *Bull. Minn. agric. Exp. Stn* [1888–] L.AM.; BM. 13–; BMᴺ. 08– imp.; EB. (ent.) 92– imp.; GL. 00–19 imp.; K. 96–08 imp.; P. 92–; U. 31– imp.; UC. 14– imp.; Abs.N. 17– imp.; Ba.I. 17–36; Bm.U. 31–33 imp.; Br.A. 11– imp.; U. 47–; C.A.; UL. 13–; E.R. 14– imp.; U. 24– imp.; G.N. 21–49 imp.; U. 14– imp.; Ld.U. 12– imp.; Lv.P. 96– imp.; U. 14– imp.; M.U. 13– imp.; Nw.A. 31– imp.; O.F. 27–39 imp.; R. 13–; Rt. imp.; Sa. 14–22; Sw.U. 31–; Y. [*See also* 11655]

11125 **Bulletin. Minnesota Department** of **Agriculture.** St. Paul. *Bull. Minn. Dep. Agric.* [1919–] L.P. 19–29 imp.; E.A.; G.U.; Y.

11126 **Bulletin** of the **Minnesota Federation** of **Architectural** and **Engineering Societies.** St. Paul, Minn. *Bull. Minn. Fed. archit. Engng Socs* L.P. 27–32.

11127 **Bulletin. Minnesota Forestry Board.** St. Paul. *Bull. Minn. For. Bd*

11128 **Bulletin** of the **Minnesota Geological** and **Natural History Survey. Botanical Series.** Minneapolis. *Bull. Minn. geol. nat. Hist. Surv. bot. Ser.* [1887–] L.GM. 89–94; SC. 15–; UC. 89–94: 14–; Abd.U. 14–; Bl.U. 89–25; C.UL. 17–; E.U. 89–93; Lv.U. 89–23; M.U. 89–23; O.R. 89–; Sa. 89–94.

11129 **Bulletin. Minnesota Geological Survey.** Minneapolis. *Bull. Minn. geol. Surv.* [1887–] L.BM. 14– imp.; BMᴺ.; GL. 89–54; P. 87–04: 15–39; UC. 89–93; Abd.U. 87–94: 14–49 imp.; Abs.U. 24–26 imp.; E.R.; U. 87–32 imp.; Lv.P. 87–39 imp.; U. 14–; M.U. 89–23; O.R. 89–; Sa. 87–89: 15–; Y.

11130 **Bulletin. Minnesota Institute** of **Technology Mines Experiment Station.** Minneapolis. *Bull. Minn. Inst. Technol. Mines Exp. Stn* [1937–]ᵢ L.P. 37. [*C. of:* 11131]

11131 **Bulletin. Minnesota School** of **Mines Experiment Station.** Minneapolis. *Bull. Minn. Sch. Mines Exp. Stn* [1912–27] L.BM. 12–21; GL. imp.; GM. 12–22; P.; SC. 13–27; UC.; Abd.U.; C.UL. 13–21; Ld.U.; Lv.U. 12–21 imp.; M.U. 12–21 imp.; O.R. 12–21. [*C. as:* 11130]

Bulletin. Minnesota University Engineering Experiment Station. Minneapolis. *See* 12525.

11133 **Bulletin** of **Miscellaneous Information. Royal Botanic Gardens, Kew.** London. *Bull. misc. Inf. R. bot. Gdns Kew* [1887–41] L.A. 90–41 imp.; AM.; BM.; BMᴺ.; C.; G.; HS.; K.; L.; MA. 87–16; MY.; P. 10–41; PH.; RI.; SC.; TP.; UC. 15–41 imp.; Z. 87–39; Abd.R. 36–41 imp.; U.; Abs.A. 93–41; N. 01–41; Bm.P.; T. 29–37; Bn.U.; Br.U.; C.A. 36–40; BO.; UL.; Cr.M. 93–41; P. 25–41; Db.; E.A. imp.; B.; R. 87–25; T. 35–39; G.M.; U.; Ld.P. 18: 38–41; U. 87–39; Lv.U. imp.; M.P. imp.; U. imp.; Md.H. 30–41; N.U. 17–18: 29–34; O.BO.; F. 88–41; R.; RE. 00–30; Rt. 93–41; Sa. 93–27 imp. [*C. as:* 27381. *For* Additional series *see* 907]

11134 **Bulletin** of **Miscellaneous Information. Royal Botanic Gardens, Trinidad.** *Bull. misc. Inf. R. bot. Gdns, Trin.* [1888–08] L.AM. 99–08; BM. 93–08; BMᴺ. imp.; EB. 99–08 imp.; HS. 00–08; K.; L.; P. 00–08; SC. 91–08; TP.; E.B. 97–08 imp.; O.BO. imp.; Rt. 91–08. [*C. as:* 10002]

11135 **Bulletin** of the **Mississippi Agricultural Experiment Station.** State College. *Bull. Miss. agric. Exp. Stn* [1888–] L.AM.; BMᴺ. 97–37 imp.; EB. (ent.) 97–; K. 92–08 imp.; P.; Abs.U. 01–11 imp.; C.A.; Rt. 89– imp.; Y.

11136 **Bulletin** of the **Mississippi Agricultural** and **Mechanical College.** *Bull. Miss. agric. mech. Coll.* L.BM^N. 16–20; EB. 15.

11137 **Bulletin. Mississippi Department** of **Agriculture.** Jackson. *Bull. Miss. Dep. Agric.*

11138 **Bulletin** of the **Mississippi State Geological Survey.** Jackson. *Bull. Miss. St. geol. Surv.* [1907–] L.BM^N.; GL. 35–51; GM.; UC. 07–20; E.D. 30– v. imp.; O.R. 20–; **Y.**

11139 **Bulletin. Missouri Agricultural Experiment Station.** Columbia. *Bull. Mo. agric. Exp. Stn* [1888–] L.AM.; BM^N. 36–39 imp.; EB. (ent.) 94–; K. 45–47; P.; U. 20–45 imp.; **Br.**A. 13–45 imp.; U. 94; **C.**A.; **Ld.**U. 29–; O.RE. 47–54 imp.; **Rt.** imp.; **Y.**

11140 **Bulletin. Missouri Botanical Garden.** St. Louis. *Bull. Mo. bot. Gdn* [1913–] L.HS. 28–; K. 29– imp.; SC.; **Bl.**U.; **Bm.**N. 14–.

11141 **Bulletin. Missouri Bureau** of **Geology** and **Mines.** Rolla. *Bull. Mo. Bur. Geol. Mines* **Sh.**M. 03–30.

11142 **Bulletin. Missouri Food Administration.** Columbia. *Bull. Mo. Fd Adm.*

11143 **Bulletin. Missouri Game** and **Fish Department.** Jefferson City. *Bull. Mo. Game Fish Dep.*

11144 **Bulletin. Missouri School** of **Mines.** Rolla. *Bull. Mo. Sch. Mines* [1908–] L.GL. 22; GM. 16–; I.; MI. 09–22: 41– imp.; P. imp.; **Bm.**N. 16– imp.; **Nw.**A. 21– imp.; **Sh.**P. 16– imp.

11145 **Bulletin. Missouri School** of **Mines. Technical Series.** Rolla. *Bull. Mo. Sch. Mines tech. Ser.* [1911–23] L.MI. imp.; P. imp.; UC. imp.; **Abs.**N. 22–23; **Ld.**P.; **Lv.**U. imp.; **Nw.**A. imp. [*C. as:* 52016]

11146 **Bulletin** of the **Missouri State Board** of **Horticulture.** Columbia. *Bull. Mo. St. Bd Hort.* L.EB. 07–13★.

11147 **Bulletin** of the **Missouri State Dental Association.** *Bull. Mo. St. dent. Ass.* [1921–34] [*C. as:* 26495]

11148 **Bulletin** of the **Missouri State Fruit Experiment Station.** Mountain Grove. *Bull. Mo. St. Fruit Exp. Stn* L.EB. 12–14; **Y.**

11149 **Bulletin. Missouri State Poultry Experiment Station.** Mountain Grove. *Bull. Mo. St. Poult. Exp. Stn*

11150 **Bulletin. Missouri State Resources Museum.** Jefferson City. *Bull. Mo. St. Resour. Mus.* [1932–36]

11151 **Bulletin. Miyazaki College** of **Agriculture** and **Forestry.** Miyazaki. *Bull. Miyazaki Coll. Agric. For.* [1929–43] L.AM.; BM^N. 29–38; K. 29–38; SC. 31–43; **C.**A.; **E.**B.; **Hu.**G. 31–38, **Md.**H. 29–38; **Rt.** [*C. as:* 11152]

11152 **Bulletin** of the **Miyazaki University.** Miyazaki. *Bull. Miyazaki Univ.* [1950–]
Natural Science. L.AM. 53–; **C.**A. 50–53.
[*C. of:* 11151]
Bulletin. Miyazaki University, Faculty of **Agriculture.** *See* 10215.

11153 **Bulletin. Miyazaki University Forests.** Miyazaki. *Bull. Miyazaki Univ. Forests* [1954–] O.F.
Bulletin. Mleev Horticultural Experiment Station. *See* 54850.

11154 **Bulletin** of the **Montana Agricultural Experiment Station.** Bozeman. *Bull. Mont. agric. Exp. Stn*

[1894–] L.AM.; BM^N. 07–18 imp.; EB. (ent.); P.; **C.**A. imp.; O.F. 41–; **Rt.**; **Y.**

11155 **Bulletin** of the **Montana Livestock Sanitary Board.** Helena. *Bull. Mont. Livestk sanit. Bd*

11156 **Bulletin. Montana State Board** of **Health.** Helena. *Bull. Mont. St. Bd Hlth*

11157 **Bulletin. Montana State College Engineering Experiment Station.** Bozeman. *Bull. Mont. St. Coll. Engng Exp. Stn* [1936–] L.P.

11158 **Bulletin** of the **Montreal Medico-Chirurgical Society.** Quebec. *Bull. Montreal med.-chir. Soc.*

11159 **Bulletin** of the **Morioka Imperial College** of **Forestry** and **Agriculture.** *Bull. Morioka imp. Coll. For. Agric.* L.AM. 07–30 imp.

11159° **Bulletin. Morkrum-Kleinschmidt Printing Telegraph Systems.** Chicago. *Bull. Morkrum-Kleinschmidt Print. Telegr. Syst.* L.P. 23–25. [*C. as:* 12379]
Bulletin of the **Moscow Naturalists' Society.** *See* 12786.

11159^f **Bulletin** of the **Moscow Society** of **Naturalists, Geological Division.** Washington. *Bull. Mosc. Soc. Nat. geol. Div.* L.SC. 56–; **Y.** 57–. [*English abstracts of:* 12786 Sect. geology]

11160 **Bulletin** of the **Moses Taylor Hospital.** Scranton, Pa. *Bull. Moses Taylor Hosp.* [1923–] L.S. 23–33; **M.**MS. 23–27; **Nw.**A.

11161 **Bulletin. Motor Industry Research Association.** Breantford, etc. *Bull. Mot. Ind. Res. Ass.* [1947–] L.AV. 51–59 imp.; **Bm.**C.; **F.**A. 47–52; **Li.**M.; **Sh.**IO.; **Sil.** 47–55.

11162 **Bulletin. Mount Desert Island Biological Laboratory,** Salisbury Cove, Maine. *Bull. Mt Desert Isl. biol. Lab.* [1933–] L.BM^N. 50–; SC. 50–; **C.**BI. 33–39; **Dm.** 32–41; **Lo.** 31–40; **Lv.**U.; **Pl.**M. 40–41; **Y.** [*C. of:* 44595]

11163 **Bulletin** of the **Mount Weather Observatory.** Washington. *Bull. Mt Weath. Obs.* [1908–14] L.BM.; MO.; R.; **E.**G.; M.; O.; R.; **G.**U.; **N.**U. 09–13; O.R.

11164 **Bulletin. Muirhead** and **Co.** Beckenham. *Bull. Muirhead Co.* L.P. 48–50; **Y.**

11165 **Bulletin** de la **Murithienne.** Société valaisanne des sciences naturelles. Sion. *Bull. Murithienne* L.BM^N. 61–; L. 09–.

11166 **Bulletin** du **Musée** d'**anthropologie préhistorique** de **Monaco.** Fontvieille. *Bull. Mus. Anthrop. préhist. Monaco* [1954–] L.SC.

11167 **Bulletin** du **Musée** de **Beyrouth.** Beirut. *Bull. Mus. Beyrouth* L.BM. 44–.
Bulletin. Musée du **Caucase.** *See* 24399.
Bulletin du **Musée** de **Chersonnèse taurique.** *See* 27388.

11168 **Bulletin** du **Musée** d'**ethnographie** du **Trocadéro.** Paris. *Bull. Mus. Ethnogr. Trocadéro* [1931–35] L.AN.; BM.; HO. [*C. as:* 11169]
Bulletin du **Musée ethnographique** de **Belgrade.** *See* 21345.
Bulletin du **Musée ethnographique national.** Sophia. *See* 24432.
Bulletin du **Musée ethnographique** à **Zagreb.** *See* 56802.
Bulletin du **Musée** de **Georgie.** *See* 11176.
Bulletin. Musée d'**histoire naturelle** du **pays serbe.** *See* 21354.

11169 **Bulletin. Musée** de l'**homme.** Paris. *Bull. Mus. Homme* [1935–] **L.**AN.; BM.; HO. [*C. of:* 11168]

Bulletin du **Musée minéralogique** d'état **Dionýz Štúr, Banska Štiavnica.** *See* 48676.

Bulletin du **Musée national** de **sciences naturelles** de **Kichineff.** *See* 9129.

11171 **Bulletin** du **Musée océanographique** de **Monaco.** Monaco. *Bull. Mus. océanogr. Monaco* [1904–06] **L.**AM.; BM^N.; G.; L.; R.; SC.; UC.; Z.; **Abd.**M.; U.; **Bn.**U. imp.; **C.**P.; **Db.**; **E.**F.; R.; U.; **G.**U. 05–06; **Lv.**U.; **M.**U.; **Mi.**; **Pl.**M.; **Wo.** [*C. as:* 10599]

11173 **Bulletin** du **Musée r.** d'**histoire naturelle** de **Belgique.** Bruxelles. *Bull. Mus. r. Hist. nat. Belg.* [1882–48] **L.**AM.; BM^N.; EB. (ent.) 31–48; GL.; GM.; L. 30–48; R.; SC.; UC. 82–35; Z.; **Abd.**M. 30–48 imp.; **Bl.**U. 30–48; **Bn.**U. 42–48 imp.; **Br.**U.; **C.**P.; **Cr.**M. 30–48; **Db.** 30–48; **Dm.** 30–48; **E.**R.; **Ld.**U. 30–48; **Lo.** 30–48; **M.**U.; **N.**U. 30–48 imp.; **Nw.**A. 30–48; **Pl.**M. 30–48; **Sh.**U. 30–39: 46–48; **Y.** [*Suspended* 1889–29; *C. as:* 10606]

Bulletin du **Musée régional** de **Bessarabie.** *See* 9129.

11173° **Bulletin** des **musées** de **France.** Paris. *Bull. Musées Fr.*

11174 **Bulletin** des **musées royaux** du **cinquantenaire.** Bruxelles. *Bull. Musées r. Cinquant.*

11175 **Bulletin** of the **Museum** of **Comparative Zoology** at **Harvard College.** Cambridge, Mass. *Bull. Mus. comp. Zool. Harv.* [1863–] **L.**BM.; BM^N.; GL.; GM. 67–; L.; R.; SC.; Z.; **Abs.**U. 25–; **Bl.**U. 81– imp.; **Bm.**U. 81–11 imp.; **C.**B. 63–03; P.; **Cr.**U. 56–; **Db.** 76–; **Dn.**U. 63–85; **E.**C. imp.; G. 86–; R.; U.; **G.**N. 97–; U.; **Ld.**U. imp.; **Lo.** 98– imp.; **Lv.**U.; **M.**U. imp.; **O.**R.; **Pl.**M. imp.; **Sa.** 63–76; **Wo.** 14– imp.; **Y.**

11176 **Bulletin** du **Muséum** de **Géorgie.** Tiflis. *Bull. Mus. Géorgie* [1920–52] **L.**BM. 28–52; BM^N.; EB. 20–36; Z. 20–27; **Lv.**U. [*From* 1937 *in series A and B. C. of:* 24399; *C. as:* 56448]

11177 **Bulletin** du **Muséum** d'**histoire naturelle.** Paris. *Bull. Mus. Hist. nat., Paris* [1895–06] **L.**BM.; BM^N.; GL.; HS.; K.; L.; R.; SC.; Z.; **Abd.**M. 00–06; **C.**N.; P.; UL.; **Db.**; **E.**B.; R.; **Ld.**U.; **Lo.**; **Lv.**U.; **O.**R.; **Pl.**M. [*C. as:* 11179]

11178 **Bulletin** du **Muséum** d'**histoire naturelle** de **Marseille.** *Bull. Mus. Hist. nat. Marseille* [1941–] **L.**BM^N.; L.; Z. imp.; **Bm.**U.; **C.**P. 54–; **G.**U.; **Lv.**U.; **M.**U. 41– imp.; **Pl.**M. 46–; **Rt.** 46–; **Y.**

Bulletin du **Muséum** d'**histoire naturelle** du **pays serbe.** *See* 21354.

Bulletin of the **Museum** of the **Manchuria Research Society.** *See* 36581, series E.

11179 **Bulletin** du **Muséum national** d'**histoire naturelle.** Paris. *Bull. Mus. natn. Hist. nat., Paris* [1907–] **L.**BM.; BM^N.; E. 26–; GL.; HS.; K.; L.; MY. 22–37: 48–; R. 07–34; Z.; **Abd.**M.; **Abs.**U. 26– imp.; **Br.**U. 41–; **C.**N.; P.; UL.; **Db.**; **E.**B.; R.; **Ld.**U.; **Lo.**; **Lv.**U.; **O.**R.; **Pl.**M.; **Y.** [*C. of:* 11177]

11180 **Bulletin. Museum** of **Northern Arizona.** Flagstaff. *Bull. Mus. nth. Ariz.* **L.**BM^N. 32–.

11181 **Bulletin. Museum** of **Technology** and **Applied Science.** Sydney. *Bull. Mus. Technol. appl. Sci., Sydney* [1948–] **L.**P. [*C. of:* 12377]

11182 **Bulletin** of the **Museum, Valetta.** *Bull. Mus. Valetta* [1929–35] **L.**BM^N.; SC.; U.; UC.; Z.; **E.**V. 29–34.

11183 **Bulletin** of the **Museums Association** of **China.** Peiping. *Bull. Mus. Ass. China* **L.**BM^N. 35–37.

Bulletin. Mushroom Growers Association. *See* 28960.

11184 **Bulletin** of the **Mysore Coffee Experiment Station.** Department of Agriculture, Bangalore. *Bull. Mysore Coffee Exp. Stn* [1930–] **L.**EB. (ent.) 30–43; P. 33–39; **C.**A. 30–45; **Rt.** 30–39; **Sal.** 31–38.

Bulletin. Mysore Department of **Agriculture.** *See* 9980.

11185 **Bulletin. Mysore Engineers' Association.** Bangalore. *Bull. Mysore Engrs' Ass.* **L.**P. 21–38 imp.

11186 **Bulletin. Mysore Geological Department.** Bangalore. *Bull. Mysore geol. Dep.* [1904–] **L.**BM^N. imp.; GL.; GM.; I. imp.; **G.**U. 40– imp.; **Y.**

11187 **Bulletin. Mysore Geologists' Association.** Bangalore. *Bull. Mysore Geol. Ass.* [1951–] **L.**BM^N. 51–52; GL.; GM.; **Y.**

11188 **Bulletin** of the **Nagano College** of **Agriculture** and **Forestry.** Nagano. *Bull. Nagano Coll. Agric. For.* [1947–] **L.**AM. 50–; **C.**A. 47–50.

11189 **Bulletin** of the **Nagasaki Marine Observatory.** *Bull. Nagasaki mar. Obs.* [1951–] [*C. of:* 44805]

11190 **Bulletin** of the **Nagoya Institute** of **Technology.** Nagoya. *Bull. Nagoya Inst. Technol.* [1949–] **Y.**

11190° **Bulletin** of the **Nagoya University Forests.** Nagoya. *Bull. Nagoya Univ. Forests* [1958–] **O.**F.

11191 **Bulletin** of the **Nagpur Museum.** Allahabad. *Bull. Nagpur Mus.* [1920–] **L.**BM.

11192 **Bulletin** of the **Naikai Regional Fisheries Research Laboratory.** Hiroshima. *Bull. Naikai reg. Fish. Res. Lab.* [1952–] **Lo.**; **Pl.**M.

11193 **Bulletin** of the **Naniwa University.** Sakai. *Bull. Naniwa Univ.*

Ser. A. Engineering and natural sciences [1952–55] **L.**P.; SC.

Ser. B. Agricultural and natural sciences [1952–54] **L.**AM.; BM.; BM^N.; **C.**A. [Ser. B. *C. of:* 49216] [*C. as:* 12542]

11194 **Bulletin** on **Narcotics.** Geneva, New York. *Bull. Narcot.* [1949–] **L.**P. 55–; PH.; S.; TP.; **G.**M.; T.

11195 **Bulletin** of the **Nassau County Dental Society.** Glen Cove, N.Y. *Bull. Nassau Cty dent. Soc.*

11196 **Bulletin. Natal Society** for the **Preservation** of **Wild Life** and **Natural Resources.** Durban. *Bull. Natal Soc. Preserv. wild Life nat. Resour.* **L.**BM. 53–; BM^N. 47–49: 51–52 imp.; **Pl.**M. 48–51 imp.

11197 **Bulletin** of the **National Academy** of **Sciences, Republic** of **Korea.** Seoul. *Bull. natn. Acad. Sci. Repub. Korea* [1958–] **G.**U. 60–.

11198 **Bulletin. National Aniline Division, Allied Chemical** (and **Dye**) **Corporation.** New York. *Bull. natn. Aniline Div. all. Chem. Corp.* **L.**P. 55–.

11199 **Bulletin** of the **National Association** of **Audubon Societies** for the **Protection** of **Wild Birds** and **Animals.** New York. *Bull. natn. Ass. Audubon Socs Prot. wild Birds Anim.*

11200 **Bulletin** of the **National Association** of **Clayworks Managers.** Birmingham. *Bull. natn. Ass. Claywks Mgrs* [1927–28] **L.**BM.; P.; **Bm.**P.; **St.**R. [*C. as:* 14483]

11201 **Bulletin. National Association** of **Cotton Manufacturers.** Boston, Mass. *Bull. natn. Ass. Cott. Mfrs* **M.**C. 20–32.

11202 **Bulletin. National Association** of **Nurse Anaesthetists.** *Bull. natn. Ass. Nurse Anaesth.* [1933–39] [*C. as:* 9297]

    Bulletin. National Association for the **Prevention** of **Tuberculosis.** London. *See* 33918.

11203 **Bulletin. National Association** of **Steel** and **Copper Plate Engravers.** Louisville, Ky. *Bull. natn. Ass. Steel Copp. Plate Engr.* **Ld.**P. 14–.

11204 **Bulletin** of the **National Association** for the **Study** and **Prevention** of **Tuberculosis.** New York. *Bull. natn. Ass. Stud. Prev. Tuberc.* [1914–18] [*C. as:* 11246]

11205 **Bulletin. National Association** of **Tyre Specialists.** London. *Bull. natn. Ass. Tyre Spec.* **Sy.**R. 43–45.

11206 **Bulletin** of the **National Association** of **Wool Manufacturers.** Boston, Mass. *Bull. natn. Ass. Wool Mfrs* [1869–] **L.**BM. 69–90; **Ld.**P. 55–; U. 85–32: 43–; W. 99–; **M.**C. 37–38; **Y.**

11207 **Bulletin. National Botanic Gardens, Lucknow.** *Bull. natn. bot. Gdns Lucknow* [1956–] **L.**BM^N.; K.

11208 **Bulletin. National Building Research Institute, Union** of **South Africa.** Pretoria. *Bull. natn. Bldg Res. Inst. Un. S. Afr.* [1948–] **L.**BM.; P.; **Y.**

11209 **Bulletin. National Building Studies.** Building Research Station, D.S.I.R., Watford. *Bull. natn. Bldg Stud.* [1948–] **L.**AM.; BM.; H.; P. 48–54; **E.**R. 48–51; **Ld.**P.; **Nw.**A.; **Y.**

11210 **Bulletin. National Bureau** of **Standards Hydraulic Laboratory.** Washington. *Bull. natn. Bur. Stand. hydraul. Lab.*

11211 **Bulletin. National Canners' Association.** Washington. *Bull. natn. Cann. Ass.* [1912–] **L.**P. 23–; SC. 27–.

11212 **Bulletin. National Canners' Association Bureau** of **Raw Products Research.** Washington. *Bull. natn. Cann. Ass. Bur. raw Prod. Res.* [1920–]

11213 **Bulletin. National Canners' Association Research Laboratory.** Washington. *Bull. natn. Cann. Ass. Res. Lab. Ass.* [1914–] **L.**H. 17–27 imp.; P. 23–; **Y.**

    Bulletin. National Congress on **Surveying** and **Mapping.** *See* 51520.

11214 **Bulletin. National Cotton Seed Production.** Atlanta, Ga. *Bull. natn. Cott. Seed Prod.* [1929–] [*C. of:* 10702]

11215 **Bulletin** of the **National Crushed Stone Association.** *Bull. natn. crush. Stone Ass.* [1927–] **L.**P.27–42; **Bm.**P.; **Y.**

11216 **Bulletin** of the **National Dental Association.** Manassas, Va. *Bull. natn. dent. Ass.* **L.**D. 46–49 imp.

    Bulletin of the **National Electric Light Association.** New York. *See* 33936.

    Bulletin. National Electrical Lamp Association, Engineering Department. *See* 10160.

11217 **Bulletin. National Farm Chemurgic Council.** Columbus, Ohio. *Bull. natn. Fm chemurg. Coun.* [1940–] **L.**P. 40–42.

11218 **Bulletin** of the **National Fertilizer Association. Middle West Soil Improvement Committee.** *Bull. natn. Fertil. Ass. middle W. Soil Improv. Comm.*

11219 **Bulletin** of the **National Formulary Committee** of the **American Pharmaceutical Association.** Washington. *Bull. natn. Formul. Comm. Am. pharm. Ass.* [1831–51] **L.**PH. 38–51; U. 49–51. [*C. as:* 17243]

11220 **Bulletin** of the **National Froebel Foundation.** London. *Bull. natn. Froebel Fdn* [1940–] **L.**BM.; **Abs.**N.; **C.**UL.; **Lv.**U.; **O.**B. [*C. of:* 13890]

11221 **Bulletin. National Gas Engine Association.** Lakemont, N.Y. *Bull. natn. Gas Eng. Ass.*

11222 **Bulletin** of the **National Geographic Society** of **India.** Benares. *Bull. natn. geogr. Soc. India* [1946–54] **L.**G.; GL.; **E.**G.; **Rt.** [*C. as:* 34123]

11223 **Bulletin** of the **National Home Grown Timber Council.** *Bull. natn. Home grown Timb. Coun.* [1937–] **O.**F. 37.

11224 **Bulletin** of the **National Hygienic Laboratory.** Tokyo. *Bull. natn. hyg. Lab., Tokyo* **L.**MA. 52–59* imp.; MY. 52–53; **G.**U. 52–59 imp.; **O.**R. 52–59; **Y.** [*C. as:* 11229]

11225 **Bulletin. National Industrial Salvage** and **Recovery Council.** Leeds. *Bull. natn. ind. Salv. Recov. Coun.* [1954–55] **L.**BM.; **G.**M. [*C. of:* 10531^a; *C. as:* 23284]

11226 **Bulletin** of the **National Institute** of **Agricultural Sciences.** Tokyo. *Bull. natn. Inst. agric. Sci., Tokyo*

    Ser. A. Physics and Statistics [1951–] **L.**AM.; MY.; P.; **C.**A.; **E.**R.; **R.**D.; **Rt.**; **Y.**

    Ser. B. Soils and Fertilizers [1952–] **L.**AM.; MY.; P.; **C.**A.; **E.**R.; **R.**D.; **Rt.**; **Y.**

    Ser. C. Plant Pathology (*afterwards* Phytopathology) and Entomology [1952–] **L.**AM.; BM^N.; MY.; P.; **Br.**A. 57–; **C.**A.; **E.**R.; **R.**D.; **Rt.**; **Y.**

    Ser. D. Plant Physiology, Genetics and Crops [1951–] **L.**AM.; MY.; P.; **C.**A.; **E.**R.; **R.**D.; **Rt.**; **Y.**

    Ser. E. Horticulture [1952–] **L.**MY. 54–; **Br.**A.; **C.**A.; **Md.**H.; **R.**D.; **Rt.**; **Y.**

    Ser. F. Agricultural Engineering [1951–] **C.**A.; **R.**D.; **Rt.**; **Y.**

    Ser. G. Animal Husbandry [1951–] **L.**AM. 51–53; **Abd.**R.; **C.**A.; **E.**AB. 52–; **R.**D.; **Rt.**; **Y.** [*C. of:* 45788]

    Ser. H. Farm Management and Land Utilization [1951–] **L.**AM.; **C.**A.; **R.**D.; **Rt.**; **Y.** [*C. of:* 10498]

11227 **Bulletin** of the **National Institute** of **Animal Health.** Tokyo. *Bull. natn. Inst. Anim. Hlth, Tokyo* [1956–] **W.** [*C. of:* 18734^a]

11229 **Bulletin** of the **National Institute** of **Hygienic Sciences.** Tokyo. *Bull. natn. Inst. hyg. Sci., Tokyo* [1960–] **L.**MA.; MY.; **G.**U.; **O.**R.; **Y.** [*C. of:* 11224]

    Bulletin. National Institute of **Industrial Psychology.** *See* 33946.

11230 **Bulletin. National Institute** of **Poultry Husbandry.** Newport, Salop. *Bull. natn. Inst. Poult. Husb.* [1928–] **Bm.**P. 29–; **C.**A. 29–.

11230° **Bulletin. National Institute** for **Road Research. C.S.I.R. South Africa.** Pretoria. *Bull. natn. Inst. Rd Res., Pretoria* [1956–] **L.**BM.

11231 **Bulletin** of the **National Institute** of **Sciences** of **India.** New Delhi. *Bull. natn. Inst. Sci. India* [1952–] **L.**BM^N.; K. imp.; P.; SC.; **O.**F.

11232 **Bulletin. National Laboratory** for **Psychical Research.** London. *Bull. natn. Lab. psych. Res.* [1931–33] **L.**BM.; **Nw.**A.; **O.**B. [*Supersedes* 39469; *C. as:* 9926]

11233 **Bulletin. National Museum** of **Canada.** Ottawa. *Bull. natn. Mus. Can.* [1928–] **L.**AN. (anthrop.); BM.; BM^N.; G.; GL. 29–47; I.; K. 28–45 imp.; L.; UC. 38–; Z. (zool.) 32–; **Abd.**U. 45–; **Bl.**U. imp.; **Bm.**P.; U. 45–; **Bn.**U. imp.; **Br.**U.; **C.**P.; PO. imp.; UC.; **Dn.**U. imp.; **E.**A.; B.; C. 32–40 imp.; F.; G.; R.; U. 28–40 imp.; **G.**N. 28–40 imp.; **H.**U. (biol.); **Ld.**U.; **Lv.**P. 28–40; U.; **M.**P.; U. 28–40 imp.; **Nw.**A. imp.; **O.**G. 32– imp.; R.; **Pl.**M. imp.; **Sa.** imp.; **Y.** [*C. of:* 10346]

11233^c **Bulletin** of the **National Museum, State** of **Singapore.** Singapore. *Bull. natn. Mus. St. Singapore* [1961–] **L.**AN.; BM.; BM^N.; EB. (ent.); L.; UC.; Z.; **C.**B.; **Cr.**M.; **O.**H.; R.; **Pl.**M. [*C. of:* 11578]

11234 **Bulletin. National Organization** for **Public Health Nursing.** New York. *Bull. natn. Org. publ. Hlth Nurs.*

Bulletin. National Parks Association. Washington. *See* 34149.

11235 **Bulletin. National Pig Breeders' Association.** London. *Bull. natn. Pig Breed. Ass.* **L.**BM. 24–; **C.**A. 38–41.

11236 **Bulletin** of the **National Research Council, Canada.** Ottawa. *Bull. natn. Res. Coun. Can.* [1926–37] **L.**BM.; BM^N.; K. 29; P.; SC. 26–30; **Ld.**P. 26–30; **M.**C. 26–35 imp.; **Rt.** [*C. of:* 9215]

Bulletin. National Research Council of **Canada.** *For* Bulletins of the various Divisions *See* the **Bulletin** of the **Division.**

11237 **Bulletin. National Research Council** of the **Philippine Islands.** Manila, etc. *Bull. natn. Res. Coun. Philipp. Isl.* [1934–] **L.**BM. 48–; U. 41–; **C.**A. 57–; **E.**AB. 51–; **Ld.**U. 59; **O.**R. 41–; **Y.**

11238 **Bulletin** of the **National Research Council. Washington.** *Bull. natn. Res. Coun., Wash.* [1919–50] **L.**AS. imp.; BM. imp.; BM^N.; M.; MO. 19–46 imp.; NF.; P.; RI. 19–44 imp.; SC.; U.; **Abs.**N.; U. 19–37; **Bl.**U. 19–46 imp.; **Bm.**U. 19–38 imp.; **Bn.**U. 19–46 imp.; **Br.**U. 19–46; **C.**A.; BO.; P.; UL.; **Db.**; **E.**R. imp.; **G.**U.; **Ld.**U.; **Lv.**U. imp.; **M.**C. imp.; U. 19–46 imp.; **N.**U.; **Nw.**A. 20–41 imp.; **O.**R.

Bulletin. National Research Development Corporation. *See* 33955.

11239 **Bulletin** of the **National Research Institute** of **Agriculture.** Tokyo. *Bull. natn. Res. Inst. Agric., Tokyo* [1949–] **L.**AM.; BM.

11240 **Bulletin. National Sand** and **Gravel Association.** Washington. *Bull. natn. Sand Gravel Ass.* **L.**P. 27–30.

11240^c **Bulletin. National Science Board, Philippine Islands.** Manila. *Bull. natn. Sci. Bd Philipp. Isl.* [1957–] **L.**BM.

11241 **Bulletin** of the **National Science Museum.** Tokyo. *Bull. natn. Sci. Mus., Tokyo* [1949–] **L.**BM^N.; SC. imp.; Z. [*C. of:* 12411]

11242 **Bulletin** of the **National Society** of **India** for **Malaria** and other **Mosquito Borne Disease.** Delhi. *Bull. natn. Soc. India Malar.* [1953–] **L.**TD.

11243 **Bulletin** of the **National Society** for **Medical Research.** Chicago. *Bull. natn. Soc. med. Res.* [1946–] **L.**MA. 47–.

11244 **Bulletin. National Speleological Society.** Washington. *Bull. natn. speleol. Soc.* [1940–] **Y.**

11245 **Bulletin. National Sweet Pea Society.** London. *Bull. natn. sweet Pea Soc.* [1952–] **L.**BM.; HS. 55–.

11246 **Bulletin. National Tuberculosis Association.** New York. *Bull. natn. Tuberc. Ass.* [1918–] **L.**MA. 40–; MC. 55–; MD. 52–; TD. 40–; [*C. of:* 11204]

11247 **Bulletin. Natural History Museum, Balboa Park.** San Diego. *Bull. nat. Hist. Mus. Balboa Pk* **L.**BM^N. 22–.

11248 **Bulletin. Natural History Society** of **British Columbia.** Victoria. *Bull. nat. Hist. Soc. Br. Columb.* [1893–10] **L.**BM. 97–10; BM^N. 93–97: 10.

Bulletin. Natural History Society, Christmas Island. *See* 9790^c.

11250 **Bulletin. Natural History Society** of **Maryland.** Baltimore. *Bull. nat. Hist. Soc. Md* [1930–43] **L.**BM^N. [*C. as:* 29480]

11251 **Bulletin** of the **Natural History Society** of **New Brunswick.** St. John's. *Bull. nat. Hist. Soc. New Brunswick* [1882–14] **L.**BM^N.; G. 96–14; GL.; K.; R. 84–13 imp.; **Bl.**U. imp.; **Bm.**U. 85–99; **G.**N. 85–14; **Ld.**U. 97–14; **Lv.**U. 87–14; **Pl.**M. 88–13 imp. [*C. as:* 432]

11252 **Bulletin** of the **Natural History Survey. Chicago Academy** of **Sciences.** Chicago. *Bull. nat. Hist. Surv. Chicago Acad. Sci.* [1896–27] **L.**BM.; BM^N.; GL.; R.; SC.; **Db.**; **E.**C. 96–23; R.; **M.**U. 96–98: 23.

11253 **Bulletin** of the **Natural History Survey, State** of **Louisiana.** New Orleans. *Bull. nat. Hist. Surv. St. La* **L.**BM^N. 10.

11253^c **Bulletin. Natural Resources Research Institute, College** of **Engineering, University** of **Wyoming.** *Bull. nat. Resour. Res. Inst. Univ. Wyo.* **Y.**

11254 **Bulletin** des **naturalistes** de **Mons** et du **Borinage.** Mons. *Bull. Nat. Mons* **L.**BM^N. 18– imp.

11255 **Bulletin** of the **Naturalists' Club** of **Shanghai.** Shanghai. *Bull. Nat. Club Shanghai* **L.**BM^N. 35.

11256 **Bulletin** of the **Naval Medical Association** of **Japan.** Tokyo. *Bull. nav. med. Ass. Japan* [1912–] **L.**MA. 29–41; S. 12–25: 35–39; **G.**U. 13–19 imp.; **Lv.**U. 12–25 imp.

11257 **Bulletin** de la **navigation aérienne.** Paris. *Bull. Navig. aér.* [1920–38] **L.**AV.

11258 **Bulletin** de la **navigation** et des **pêches maritimes.** Paris. *Bull. Navig. Pêch. marit.* [*C. of:* 10857]

11259 **Bulletin** of the **Nawa Entomological Laboratory.** Gifu, Japan. *Bull. Nawa ent. Lab.* [1916–17] **L.**BM^N.

11260 **Bulletin** of the **Nebraska Agricultural Experiment Station.** Lincoln. *Bull. Neb. agric. Exp. Stn* [1887–] **L.**AM.; C. 00–19 imp.; EB. (ent.) 89– imp.; P.; UC. 95–14 imp.; **Abs.**N. 10–20 imp.; **Bm.**U. 91–98; **C.**A.; **E.**R. 90– v. imp.; **G.**U. 91–30 imp.; **Ld.**U. 42–; **O.**RE. 43–53 imp.; **Rt.** 90– imp.; **Sa.** 05– imp.; **Y.**

11261 **Bulletin** of the **Nebraska Board** of **Agriculture.** Lincoln. *Bull. Neb. Bd Agric.* **L.**K. 87– imp.

11262 **Bulletin. Nebraska State Entomologist.** Lincoln. *Bull. Neb. St. Ent.* **L.**EB. 13–20.

11263 **Bulletin. Nebraska State Museum.** Lincoln. *Bull. Neb. St. Mus.* **L.**BM^N. 24–38★. [*C. as:* 12532]

11264 **Bulletin. Nebraska University College** of **Medicine.** Lincoln. *Bull. Neb. Univ. Coll. Med.* [1906–09]

11265 **Bulletin. Nebraska University Conservation** and **Survey Division.** Lincoln. *Bull. Neb. Univ. Conserv. Surv. Div.* [1916–25] L.SC. 18–25. [*C. as:* 9913]

11266 **Bulletin** of the **Netherlands East Indian Volcanological Survey.** Bandoeng. *Bull. Neth. E. Indian volc. Surv.* [1927–] L.B. 27–28; BM^N. 29– imp.; GL. 27–31; GM.; SC. 30–.

11267 **Bulletin** of the **Neurological Institute** of **New York.** *Bull. neurol. Inst. N.Y.* [1931–38] L.GH.; MC.; MD.; S.; U.; UC.; Bl.U.; Bm.U.; Br.U.; Db.; Dn.U. 31–37; E.S. 31–32; U.; G.F.; Ld.U. 31–37; Lv.M.; M.MS.; Sa. 31–37.

11268 **Bulletin** of the **Nevada Agricultural Experiment Station.** Reno. *Bull. Nev. agric. Exp. Stn* [1888–] L.AM.; EB. (ent.) 92–; K. 93–04 imp.; P. imp.; C.A.; Cr.P. 95– imp.; Ld.U. 16– imp.; O.F. 45– imp.; Rt. 92– imp.; Y.

11269 **Bulletin. Nevada Department** of **Agriculture.** Reno. *Bull. Nev. Dep. Agric.* [1936–]

11269° **Bulletin. Nevada State Bureau** of **Mines.** *Bull. Nev. St. Bur. Mines* [1929] [*C. as:* 55651°]

11270 **Bulletin. Nevada University Engineering Experiment Station.** Reno. *Bull. Nev. Univ. Engng Exp. Stn* [1925–38] L.P.; SC.

Bulletin of the **New Bast Fibres Research Institute.** Moscow. *See* 54685.

11271 **Bulletin** of the **New England Medical Centre.** Boston, Mass. *Bull. New Engl. med. Cent.* [1939–54] L.MA. 47–54; MD. 42: 45–54; Bl.U. 49–52. [*C. in:* 12480]

11272 **Bulletin** of the **New England Museum** of **Natural History.** Boston. *Bull. New Engl. Mus. nat. Hist.* [1936–38] L.BM^N.; SC.; Z. 37–38; C.UL.; E.R.; O.R. [*C. of:* 9593; *C. as:* 34643]

11273 **Bulletin** of the **New England Weather Service.** Boston. *Bull. New Engl. Weath. Serv.* L.MO. 92–95 imp.

11274 **Bulletin** of the **New Hampshire Agricultural Experiment Station.** Durham. *Bull. New Hamps. agric. Exp. Stn* [1888–] L.AM.; BM^N. 08–36 imp.; EB. (ent.) 97–; K. 94–08 imp.; P. imp.; C.A.; Cr.P. imp.; Rt. imp.; Y.

11275 **Bulletin. New Hampshire Board** of **Health.** Concord. *Bull. New Hamps, Bd Hlth*

11276 **Bulletin** of the **New Hampshire Dental Society.** Concord. *Bull. New Hamps. dent. Soc.*

11277 **Bulletin** of the **New Hampshire Forestry Commission.** Concord. *Bull. New Hamps. For. Commn*

11278 **Bulletin. New Hampshire Forestry Department.** Concord. *Bull. New Hamps. For. Dep.* [1934–]

11279 **Bulletin** of the **New Jersey Agricultural Experiment Station.** New Brunswick. *Bull. New Jers. agric. Exp. Stn* [1886–] L.AM.; BM^N. 93–31 imp.; EB. (ent.) 99–; K. 90–06 imp.; P. 90–; Br.A. 11– imp.; C.A.; Cr.P. 04–20 imp.; Rt. imp.; Y.

11280 **Bulletin** of the **New Jersey College** of **Agriculture.** New Brunswick. *Bull. New Jers. Coll. Agric.*

11281 **Bulletin** of the **New Jersey Department** of **Agriculture.** Trenton. *Bull. New Jers. Dep. Agric.* L.EB. 17–25; SC. 16–.

11282 **Bulletin** of the **New Jersey Division** of **Geology.** Trenton. *Bull. New Jers. Div. Geol.* [1916–] L.BM^N.; GM.; P.; SC. 23–; E.D. imp.; J. [*C. of:* 10366]

11283 **Bulletin. New Jersey Federation** of **Shade Tree Commissioners.** Kearney. *Bull. New Jers. Fed. Shade Tree Commnrs* [1928] [*C. as:* 49611]

11284 **Bulletin. New Jersey State Soil Conservation Committee.** New Brunswick. *Bull. New Jers. St. Soil Conserv. Comm.* [1938–]

11285 **Bulletin** of the **New Mexico Agricultural Experiment Station.** State College, New Mexico. *Bull. New Mex. agric. Exp. Stn* [1890–] L.AM.; BM. 01–12 imp.; BM^N. 90–12; EB. (ent.) 91–; K. 02–08 imp.; P. imp.; Z. 00–08 imp.; Abs.U. 00–12 imp.; C.A.; Rt. imp.; Y.
Bulletin of the **New Mexico College** of **Agriculture** and **Mechanical Arts.** *See* 11285.

11285° **Bulletin. New Mexico Institute** of **Mining** and **Technology.** *Bull. New Mex. Inst. Min. Technol.* Y.

11286 **Bulletin. New Mexico School** of **Mines.** Socorro. *Bull. New Mex. Sch. Mines*

11287 **Bulletin. New Mexico State Bureau** of **Mines** and **Mineral Resources.** Socorro. *Bull. New Mex. St. Bur. Mines* L.MI. 28– imp.; Y.
Bulletin. New South Wales Branch, British Astronomical Association. *See* 9604.

11288 **Bulletin. New South Wales University** of **Technology.** Kensington, N.S.W. *Bull. N.S.W. Univ. Technol.* [1957–] L.P.

11289 **Bulletin** of the **New York Academy** of **Medicine.** New York. *Bull. N.Y. Acad. Med.* [1860–71: 25–] L.GH. 25–; H. 33–; MA. 28–; MC. 33–; MD. 25–; S. 25–; SC. 25–39 imp.; TD. 25–48 imp.: 57–; Bl.U. 25– imp.; Bm.U. 34–42 imp.: 52–; Br.U.; C.MD. 47–56; Cr.MD. 51–; Db. 25–43; E.U. 46–; G.F. 25–43: 47–; Ld.U. 25– imp.; Lv.M. 25–48: 56–; M.MS. 25–39: 49–; Nw.A. 38–; O.R. 25–35; Y. [> 53899, 1870–01; *Suspended* 1902–24]

11290 **Bulletin** of the **New York Academy** of **Sciences.** New York. *Bull. N.Y. Acad. Sci.* [1906–] [*Replaces:* 11673]

11291 **Bulletin** of the **New York Botanical Garden.** New York. *Bull. N.Y. bot. Gdn* [1896–32] L.BM^N.; K.; L.; C.BO. imp.; Db.; E.B.; Lv.U. 08–32; M.U.; Nw.A.; Pl.M. 21–32.

11292 **Bulletin** of the **New York City Health Department.** New York. *Bull. N.Y. Cy Hlth Dep.* Bm.N. 99–00.

11293 **Bulletin** of the **New York Medical College. Flower** and **Fifth Avenue Hospitals.** New York. *Bull. N.Y. med. Coll.* [1938–56] L.MA. 46–56; MD. 48–56; Bl.U. 44–56. [*C. as:* 26561]

11294 **Bulletin. New York Microscopical Society.** New York. *Bull. N.Y. microsc. Soc.* [1936–] L.BM^N. 36–51; SC.

11295 **Bulletin** of the **New York Mineralogical Club.** New York. *Bull. N.Y. miner. Club* L.BM. 07–14.

11296 **Bulletin** of the **New York Post-Graduate Medical School** and **Hospital.** Cooperstown. *Bull. N.Y. post-grad. med. Sch.* L.S. 15–16.

11297 **Bulletin** of the **New York State Agricultural Experiment Station.** Geneva. *Bull. N.Y. St. agric. Exp. Stn* [1885–] L.AM.; BM[N]. 08– imp.; C. 00– imp.; EB. (ent.) 97–; HS. 49–50; K. 97–21 imp.; L. 33– imp.; P.; UC. 25–; Z. 02– imp.; **Abd.**U. 97–30; **Abs.**U. 00–13 imp.; **Br.**A. 97– imp.; **C.**A.; **Cr.**P. 06– imp.; **Ld.**U.; **Lv.**U. 02–19 imp.; **O.**RE. 48–54 imp.; **Rt.** 88– imp.; **Y.**

11298 **Bulletin. New York State College** of **Agriculture Extension Service.** Ithaca. *Bull. N.Y. St. Coll. Agric. Ext. Serv.* O.F. 37– imp.

11299 **Bulletin. New York State College** of **Ceramics Ceramic Experiment Station.** Alfred, N.Y. *Bull. N.Y. St. Coll. Ceram. ceram. Exp. Stn* [1937–] L.P. imp.; **Y.**

11300 **Bulletin** of the **New York State College** of **Forestry.** Syracuse. *Bull. N.Y. St. Coll. For.* [1913–] L.EB. (ent.) 16: 34–; SC. 15; **C.**A. imp.; **O.**F. imp.

Bulletin of the **New York State Conservation Commission.** *See* 11301.

11301 **Bulletin** of the **New York State Conservation Department.** New York. *Bull. N.Y. St. Conserv. Dep.* O.F. 42– imp.

11302 **Bulletin** of the **New York State Department** of **Agriculture** (and **Markets**). Albany. *Bull. N.Y. St. Dep. Agric.* L.AM. 10–39 imp.; **Y.** [*C. as:* 1298[a]]

11303 **Bulletin. New York State Department** of **Farms** and **Markets.** *Bull. N.Y. St. Dep. Fms Mkts* L.AM. 19–; EB. (ent.) 19–22.

11304 **Bulletin** of the **New York State Department** of **Health.** Albany. *Bull. N.Y. St. Dep. Hlth* [1948–] L.H.

11305 **Bulletin. New York State Food Supply Commission.** Albany. *Bull. N.Y. St. Fd Supply Commn*

11306 **Bulletin** of the **New York State Hospitals.** New York. *Bull. N.Y. St. Hosps*

11307 **Bulletin** of the **New York State Industrial Commission.** Albany. *Bull. N.Y. St. ind. Commn* L.BM. 99–15★ [*C. as:* 50417]

11308 **Bulletin** of the **New York State Museum.** Albany. *Bull. N.Y. St. Mus.* [1887–55] L.BM[N].; EB. (ent.) 88–55; GL. 00–55; GM. 88–03: 19–55; L. 15–55 imp.; P. 87–18; SC.; U. 10–55 imp.; Z. 87–94; **Abs.**N. 96–55 imp.; **Bl.**U. 03–55 imp.; **Bm.**U. 87–25 imp.; **C.**P.; S. (geol.) 88–55 imp.; **Db.**; **E.**C. 87–10 imp.; J. 93–07; R. 87–10 imp.; **G.**N. 23–55 imp.; **Lv.**U. imp.; **M.**P. 18–55; U.; **O.**R. 95–55; **Rt.** 53–55 imp.; **Sw.**U. 92–55; **Y.** [*C. as:* 11309]

Bulletin of the **New York State Museum** of **Natural History.** *See* 11308.

11309 **Bulletin** of the **New York State Museum** and **Science Service.** Albany. *Bull. N.Y. St. Mus. Sci. Serv.* [1956–] L.BM[N].; EB. (ent.); GL.; GM.; L.; SC. imp.; U. imp.; **Abs.**N. imp.; **Bl.**U. imp.; **C.**P.; S. (geol.); **Db.**; **G.**N. imp.; **Lv.**U. imp.; **M.**P.; U.; **O.**R.; **Rt.**; **Sw.**U. [*C. of:* 11308]

11310 **Bulletin** of the **New York State Society** of **Dentistry** for **Children.** *Bull. N.Y. St. Soc. Dent. Child.* L.D.

11311 **Bulletin. New York Tuberculosis** and **Health Association.** New York. *Bull. N.Y. Tuberc. Hlth Ass.* L.TD. 24–26.

11312 **Bulletin** of the **New York Zoological Society.** New York. *Bull. N.Y. zool. Soc.* [1928–41] L.BM[N].; Z.; **O.**AP.; **Pl.**M. 28–35 imp.; **Y.** [*C. of:* 59265; *C. as:* 2620]

11313 **Bulletin** of the **New Zealand Astronomical Society.** Wellington. *Bull. N.Z. astr. Soc.* [1924–37] L.AS. [*C. in:* 50254]

11314 **Bulletin. New Zealand Astronomical Society. Variable Star Section.** Wellington. *Bull. N.Z. astr. Soc. var. Star Sect.* [1927–] L.AS.; SC.

Bulletin of the **New Zealand Board** of **Science** and **Art.** *See* 9591.

Bulletin. New Zealand Department of **Agriculture.** *See* 9983.

11315 **Bulletin** of the **New Zealand Department** of **Scientific** and **Industrial Research.** Wellington. *Bull. N.Z. Dep. scient. ind. Res.* [1927–] L.BM.; EB. (ent.) 30–; MI. 33: 37: 45: 56; P. imp.; SC. 28–; Z. (zool.) 49–; **Br.**A. 28– imp.; **C.**A.; **E.**R. 33– imp.; **O.**RE. 38–55 imp.; **Rt.**

11316 **Bulletin** of **New Zealand Forest Service.** Wellington. *Bull. N.Z. Forest Serv.* [1923–] L.BM. 36–; P.; **O.**F.; **Y.**

Bulletin of the **New Zealand Geological Survey.** *See* 10368.

11317 **Bulletin** of the **New Zealand Institute.** Wellington. *Bull. N.Z. Inst.* [1910–29] L.BM.; BM[N].; K. (bot.) 13–14 imp.; L. 13; SC.; UC.; **C.**P.; **E.**R. [*C. as:* 11626]

11318 **Bulletin. New Zealand Institute** of **Horticulture.** Wellington. *Bull. N.Z. Inst. Hort.* [1925–] [*Suspended* June 1928 *to* May 1939]

11319 **Bulletin. New Zealand Iris Society.** *Bull. N.Z. Iris Soc.* L.HS. 50–.

11320 **Bulletin** of the **New Zealand Society** of **Civil Engineers.** Wellington. *Bull. N.Z. Soc. civ. Engrs* [1914–37] [*C. as:* 11549]

11321 **Bulletin** of the **Newfoundland Geological Survey.** St John's. *Bull. Newfoundld geol. Surv.* [1938–49] L.BM.; BM[N].; MI.; P.; SC.; UC.; **Bl.**U. imp.; **C.**S.; **Lv.**U. [*C. of:* 10339]

11322 **Bulletin. Newfoundland Government Laboratory.** St. Johns. *Bull. Newfoundld Govt Lab.* [1948] L.AM.; BM[N].; **Dm.**; **Lo.**; **Pl.**M.; **Wo.** [*C. of:* 45794]

11323 **Bulletin** of the **Ninth District Dental Society.** White Plains, N.Y. *Bull. ninth Distr. dent. Soc.*

11324 **Bulletin** of the **Nippon Agricultural Research Institute.** Tokyo. *Bull. Nippon agric. Res. Inst.* [1951–] **C.**A.

11325 **Bulletin** of the **Nippon Institute** for the **Scientific Research** of **Pearls.** *Bull. Nippon Inst. scient. Res. Pearls* [1953–] L.AM.; **Pl.**M.

Bulletin. Norman Lockyer Observatory. *See* 10446.

11326 **Bulletin** of the **North American Gladiolus Council.** Havre de Grace. *Bull. N. Am. Gladiolus Coun.* L.HS. 46–.

11327 **Bulletin. North Borneo State Museum.** Sandakan. *Bull. N. Borneo St. Mus.* L.BM. 38–.

11328 **Bulletin** of the **North Carolina Agricultural Experiment Station.** West Raleigh. *Bull. N.Carol. agric. Exp. Stn* [1888–] L.AM.; BM[N]. 07–11 imp.; EB. (ent.) 91–; P.; **C.**A.; **Rt.** imp.; **Y.**

Bulletin. North Carolina Board of **Agriculture.** *See* 11332.

11329 **Bulletin** of the **North Carolina Board** of **Health.** Raleigh. *Bull. N.Carol. Bd Hlth*

11330 **Bulletin. North Carolina College** of **Agriculture** and **Mechanic Arts.** Raleigh. *Bull. N.Carol. Coll. Agric.* L.EB. (ent.) 91–; Rt. 88–.

11331 **Bulletin** of the **North Carolina Dental Society.** Greensboro. *Bull. N.Carol. dent. Soc.*

11332 **Bulletin** of the **North Carolina Department** of **Agriculture.** Raleigh. *Bull. N.Carol. Dep. Agric.* L.EB. (ent.) 08–25; P. 03–27; Rt. 02–15 imp.

11333 **Bulletin. North Carolina Department** of **Conservation** and **Development.** Raleigh. *Bull. N.Carol. Dep. Conserv. Dev.* [1925–] L.BM^N. 25–36; GM.; O.F. 44– imp.; Y. [*C. of:* 11335]

11334 **Bulletin. North Carolina Engineering Experiment Station.** Raleigh. *Bull. N.Carol. Engng Exp. Stn* [1927–45] L.AV. 38–45 imp.; P.; SC. 37–45. [*C. as:* 10027]

11335 **Bulletin** of the **North Carolina Geological** and **Economic Survey.** Chapel Hill. *Bull. N.Carol. geol. econ. Surv.* [1893–23] L.BM^N.; GM.; P. imp.; SC. 06–23; **Bm.**U. 10. [*C. as:* 11333]

Bulletin of the **North Caucasian Plant Protection Station.** Rostov, Don. *See* 24497.

11336 **Bulletin** of the **North Dakota Agricultural Experimental Station.** Fargo. *Bull. N. Dak. agric. Exp. Stn* [1891–] L.AM.; EB. (ent.) 98–; K. 96–08 imp.; P. imp.; Ld.U. 10–35 imp.; Rt. imp.; Y.

11337 **Bulletin** of the **North Dakota Board** of **Health.** Devil's Lake. *Bull. N. Dak. Bd Hlth*

11338 **Bulletin** of the **North Dakota Geological Survey.** Grand Forks. *Bull. N. Dak. geol. Surv.* [1920–] L.BM. 23–; GL. 23; GM.; P. 25–38; Y.

11339 **Bulletin. North Dakota Research Foundation.** Bismarck. *Bull. N. Dak. Res. Fdn* [1946–] Y.

11340 **Bulletin** of the **North Dakota University School** of **Mines.** Grand Forks. *Bull. N. Dak. Univ. Sch. Mines*

11341 **Bulletin. North Negros Sugar Co. Inc.,** Manapla [and] **Victorias Milling Co., Inc.,** Victorias, Philippine Islands. Manila. *Bull. N. Negros Sug. Co.* L.EB. 30–.

11342 **Bulletin. North** of **Scotland College** of **Agriculture.** Aberdeen. *Bull. N. Scotl. Coll. Agric.* [1910–] L.AM.; EB. 27–29 imp.; Abd.U.; Br.U. 10–20; C.UL.; Cr.P. 10–19; U. 13–19; E.U.; Ld.U. 13–20; M.U. 10–20; Rt. 13–35; Sa. [*C. of:* 9161]

11343 **Bulletin. North Staffordshire Mining Students' Association.** Stoke-on-Trent. *Bull. N. Staffs. Min. Stud. Ass.* L.BM. 11–; O.R. 11.

11344 **Bulletin. Northampton County Council Farm Institute.** Moulton. *Bull. Northampt. Cty Coun. Fm Inst.* C.A. 23–.

11345 **Bulletin. Northeastern Wood Utilization Council.** New Haven, Conn. *Bull. N.East. Wood Util. Coun.* L.SC. 45–; O.F. 45; Rt. 45–.

11346 **Bulletin** of the **Northern Territory** of **Australia.** Melbourne. *Bull. Nth. Terr. Aust.* [1912–36] L.AN. 12–13; BM. 12–18; BM^N. imp.; EB. 15–18 imp.; G. 12–18; GL. 12–18; GM. 12–18; TD. 12–15 v. imp.; Lv.U. 12–15 imp.; O.RH. 12–16.

11347 **Bulletin. Northumberland Co. Agricultural Experiment Station, Cockle Park.** *Bull. Northumb. Co. agric. Exp. Stn* [1902–] L.AM.; P.; Br.U. 14–; Ld.U. 05–25 imp.; Nw.A.; P. 05–.

11348 **Bulletin. North-West Line Elevator Association.** Agricultural Department. Winnipeg. *Bull. N.W. Line Elev. Ass.* [1940–] C.A.

11349 **Bulletin** of the **Northwestern University Medical School.** Chicago. *Bull. N.West. Univ. med. Sch.* [*C. as:* 41486]

Bulletin de **nouvelles** de l'**U.G.I.** Union géographique international. *See* 22621.

11350 **Bulletin. Nova Scotia Department** of **Natural Resources.** *Bull. Nova Scotia Dep. nat. Resour.*

11351 **Bulletin** of the **Oberlin College Laboratory.** Oberlin. *Bull. Oberlin Coll. Lab.* [1893–] L.BM. 00– imp.; BM^N. 31; L. 07–08; UC. 22–; E.F. imp.; Lv.U. 01–; M.U. 02–31 imp.; Pl.M. 22–28.

11352 **Bulletin** of the **Observation** of **Upper Air Current.** Osaka. *Bull. Obsn upp. Air Curr.* L.MO. 28–33.

11353 **Bulletin** des **observations magnétiques** et **météorologiques** faites à l'**Observatoire** de **Jersey.** Saint-Hélier. *Bull. Obsns magn. mét. Obs. Jers.* L.MO. 94–13*; SC. 95–13. [*C. as:* 46121^a]

11354 **Bulletin** des **observations météorologiques, Commission météorologique** de la **Haute Loire.** Le Pay-en-Velay. *Bull. Obsns mét. Commn mét. hte Loire* L.MO. 13–28.

11355 **Bulletin** des **observations météorologiques** faites dans le **département** de la **Nièvre.** Nevers. *Bull. Obsns mét. Dép. Nièvre*

11356 **Bulletin** des **observations. Observatoire** de **Zi-Ka-Wei.** Chang-Haï. *Bull. Obsns Obs. Zi-Ka-Wei* L.MO. 74–38; E.M. 86–38 imp.; O.G. 80–35 imp.

Bulletin de l'**Observatoire actinométrique** et **météorologique.** Moscou. *See* 12738.

11357 **Bulletin** de l'**Observatoire astronomique** de **Belgrade.** Belgrade. *Bull. Obs. astr. Belgr.* [1936–] L.AS.; BM. 48–; MO. 55–; C.O.; E.O. 36–39; R. imp.; Y.

11358 **Bulletin** de l'**Observatoire astronomique** de **Libau** (Liépaja). Libau. *Bull. Obs. astr. Libau* L.AS. 31–38.

11359 **Bulletin** de l'**Observatoire astronomique** de **Lisbonne, Tapada.** *Bull. Obs. astr. Lisb. Tapada* M.U. 57.

Bulletin de l'**Observatoire astronomique** de **Tashkent.** *See* 12825.

Bulletin de l'**Observatoire astronomique** de **Vilno.** *See* 7187.

11360 **Bulletin** de l'**Observatoire Carlier** à la **Tour Moncade** d'**Orthez.** Orthez. *Bull. Obs. Carlier* L.MO. 00–02: 03–04 imp.

Bulletin de l'**Observatoire central** de **Russie** à **Poulkovo.** *See* 24352.

Bulletin de l'**Observatoire géophysique.** Odessa. *See* 12746.

Bulletin de l'**Observatoire géophysique centrale.** Leningrad. *See* 24353.

11361 **Bulletin** de l'**Observatoire** de l'**Hôpital** de **Pau.** Pau. *Bull. Obs. Hôp. Pau*

11362 **Bulletin** de l'**Observatoire** de **Lyon.** Lyon. *Bull. Obs. Lyon* [1922–31] L.AS.; SC. 26–31 imp.; C.O.; Pl.M. 22–26 imp. [*C. as:* 9451]

11362e **Bulletin. Observatoire météorologique, Seminaire Collège St Martial.** Port-au-Prince. *Bull. Obs. mét., Port-au-Prince* Y.

Bulletin de l'**Observatoire météorologique** de l'**Université** de **Kasan.** *See* 12783.

11363 **Bulletin** de l'**Observatoire** de **Nice.** *Bull. Obs. Nice*

11364 **Bulletin** de l'**Observatoire** du **Puy** de **Dôme.** *Bull. Obs. Puy de Dôme* [1953] **L.**MO.; **Y.** [*C. of:* 10598; *C. as:* 9816]

Bulletin de l'**Observatoire séismologique** à **Varsovie.** *See* 7189.

11365 **Bulletin** de l'**Observatoire** de **Talence.** Talence. *Bull. Obs. Talence* [1910–12: 28–] **L.**AS. 28–40; MO. 28–40; SC. 38–; **O.**O. 28–.

11366 **Bulletin** de l'**Observatoire** de **Toulouse.** *Bull. Obs. Toulouse* [1922–] **L.**AS. 23–26; **C.**O.; SP.

Bulletin of the **Observers' Corporation** of the **Astronomical-geodetical Society** of the **U.S.S.R.** *See* 12776.

Bulletin of the **Observing Corporation** of the **Society** of **Amateur Astronomers** of **Moscow.** *See* 12775.

11367 **Bulletin** of the **Oceanographical Institute** of **Taiwan.** Taipei. *Bull. oceanogr. Inst. Taiwan* [1946–49] **L.**BM^N.; Z.; **C.**S. 47–49; **Dm.** 46; **Lo.**; **Pl.**M.; **Wo.** 48–49; **Y.**

11368 **Bulletin** on **Oceanography. Tsingtao Observatory.** *Bull. Oceanogr. Tsingtao Obs.* [1930–] **L.**MO. 30–32 imp.; **Pl.**M. 30.

11369 **Bulletin** d'**oculistique.** Toulouse. *Bull. Oculist.* [1888–12]

11370 **Bulletin** of the **Odontological Society** of **Western Pennsylvania.** Pittsburgh. *Bull. odont. Soc. West. Pa*

11371 **Bulletin odontologique** de **Bourgogne** et de **Franche-Comté.** Dijon. *Bull. odont. Bourgogne*

11372 **Bulletin Oerlikon.** Oerlikon. *Bull. Oerlikon* [1921–] **L.**AV. 45–48; EE.; P.; UC. 21–29; **C.**ENG. 40–; **G.**T. (2 yr.); **Ld.**P. 45–; **M.**P. 30–; T. 50–; **Sh.**IO. 49–; **Y.**

11373 **Bulletin** de l'**œuvre** des **sanatoria maritimes** pour **enfants.** Paris. *Bull. Œuvre Sanat. marit. Enf.*

11373° **Bulletin. Office** of **Agricultural Information, Philippine Islands. Extension Series.** Manila. *Bull. Off. agric. Inf. Philipp. Isl. Ext. Ser.* [1955–] **L.**BM.

11374 **Bulletin** de l'**Office centrale** de **bibliographie agricole.** Paris. *Bull. Off. cent. Biblphie agric.* **L.**SC. 31–.

11375 **Bulletin** de l'**Office colonial.** Bruxelles. *Bull. Off. colon., Brux.* [1928–] **L.**TP. 28–40. [*C. of:* 42564]

11376 **Bulletin. Office** of **Experiment Stations, United States Department** of **Agriculture.** Washington. *Bull. Off. Exp. Stns U.S. Dep. Agric.* [1889–13] **L.**AM.; BM.; C. 99–10 imp.; K. 89–11 imp.; P.; SC.; **Bm.**U. 92–13 imp.; **Bn.**U. 89–03 imp.; **Db.** 98–00; **E.**R. 92–10 imp.; **G.**M. imp.; U. 07–13 imp.; **Ld.**U. 91–04; **Lv.**P.; **O.**R. 89–10 imp.; **Rt.**; **Y.**

11377 **Bulletin** de l'**Office** du **gouvernement général** de l'**Algérie.** Paris. *Bull. Off. Gouv. gén. Algér.* **L.**EB. 13–14.

11378 **Bulletin. Office international** des **épizooties.** Paris. *Bull. Off. int. Épizoot.* [1931–] **L.**H. 33– imp.; MC. 31–39: 46–; MD. 49– imp.; TP.; **Br.**U. 59–; **W.** 31–39: 46–; **Y.** [*C. of:* 11007]

11379 **Bulletin** de l'**Office international** d'**hygiène publique.** Paris. *Bull. Off. int. Hyg. publ.* [1909] **L.**H.; LI.; MA.; MD.; S.; SH.; TD. [*C. as:* 11008]

11380 **Bulletin** de l'**Office international** du **vin.** Paris. *Bull. Off. int. Vin* **Md.**H. 48–.

11381 **Bulletin. Office national anti-acridien, Algérie.** Paris. *Bull. Off. natn. anti-acrid. Algér.* [1951–] **L.**EB. 51–56 imp.; Z.; **Rt.**; **Y.** [*C. of:* 11734]

11382 **Bulletin. Office** of **Public Roads. United States Department** of **Agriculture.** Washington. *Bull. Off. publ. Rds U.S. Dep. Agric.* [1894–13] **L.**AM.; BM.; P. imp.; **Bm.**U. imp.

11383 **Bulletin** de l'**Office régional agricole** du **Centre.** Bourges. *Bull. Off. rég. agric. Cent.*

11384 **Bulletin** de l'**Office régional agricole** de l'**Est.** Troyes. *Bull. Off. rég. agric. E.* **C.**A. 29–.

11385 **Bulletin** de l'**Office régional agricole** du **massif central.** Clermont-Ferrand. *Bull. Off. rég. agric. Massif cent.*

11386 **Bulletin** de l'**Office** de **renseignements agricoles.** Paris. *Bull. Off. Renseign. agric.* [1923–] **L.**AM. 23–39 imp. [*C. of:* 11012]

11387 **Bulletin** de l'**Office** des **renseignements cidricoles.** Amiens. *Bull. Off. Renseign. cidric., Amiens*

11388 **Bulletin. Office** of the **Surgeon General, War Department.** Washington. *Bull. Off. Surg. gen. War Dep.* **L.**EB. (ent.) 14; TD. 13–19; **Lv.**U. 13–19.

Bulletin de l'**Office vétérinaire,** etc. Berne. *See* 32851.

11389 **Bulletin officiel** de l'**alimentation.** Paris. *Bull. off. Aliment.*

11390 **Bulletin officiel** de l'**Association belge** des **inventeurs.** Bruxelles. *Bull. off. Ass. belge Invent.*

11391 **Bulletin officiel** de l'**Association corporative** des **pharmaciens** de **réserve** et de **territoriale.** Paris. *Bull. off. Ass. corp. Pharmns Réserve* [*C. of:* 9572]

11392 **Bulletin officiel** de l'**Association française** pour le **département** de l'**outillage national.** Paris. *Bull. off. Ass. fr. Dép. Outill. natn.*

11393 **Bulletin officiel** de l'**Association** des **médecins dentistes** de **France.** Paris. *Bull. off. Ass. Méd. Dent. Fr.*

11394 **Bulletin officiel** de la **Chambre syndicale** des **constructeurs** d'**automobiles.** Paris. *Bull. off. Chamb. synd. Constr. Auto.*

11395 **Bulletin officiel** du **Collège** des **médecins** de l'**agglomération bruxelloise.** Bruxelles. *Bull. off. Coll. Méd. Agglom. brux.*

11396 **Bulletin officiel** du **Comité international permanent** du **carbonne-carburant.** Paris. *Bull. off. Com. int. perm. Carb.-Carbur.*

11397 **Bulletin officiel** du **Comité national français** pour l'**étude** et la **protection** de l'**enfance anormale.** Lyon. *Bull. off. Com. natn. fr. Étude Prot. Enf. anorm.* [*C. as:* 18060]

11398 **Bulletin officiel. Commission internationale** de **navigation aérienne.** Paris. *Bull. off. Commn int. Navig. aér.* [1922–]

11399 **Bulletin officiel** de la **Commission technique** de l'**Automobile-Club** de **France.** Paris. *Bull. off. Commn tech. Auto.-Club Fr.*

11400 **Bulletin officiel** du **Conseil national** de l'**Ordre** des **chirurgiens-dentistes.** Paris. *Bull. off. Cons. natn. Ordre Chir.-Dent.* **L.**D. 46–.

11401 **Bulletin officiel du Département d'agriculture.** Port-au-Prince. *Bull. off. Dép. Agric., Port-au-Prince*

11402 **Bulletin officiel de la Direction des recherches scientifiques et industrielles et des inventions.** Paris. *Bull. off. Dir. Rech. scient. ind.* **L.**NF. 19–22*; SC. 19–22. [*C. as:* 42272]

11403 **Bulletin officiel de la Fédération générale des brasseurs belges.** *Bull. off. Féd. gén. Brass. belg.*

11404 **Bulletin officiel de la Fédération médicale belge.** Bruxelles. *Bull. off. Féd. méd. belge*

11405 **Bulletin officiel du Ministère de l'hygiène.** Paris. *Bull. off. Minist. Hyg.*

11406 **Bulletin officiel. Office international du cacao et du chocolat.** Bruxelles. *Bull. off. Off. int. Cacao Choc.* [1935–39] **L.**MY.; P.; SC.; TP.; Lh.FO. [*C. of:* 11407]

11407 **Bulletin officiel. Office international des fabricants de chocolat et de cacao.** Bruxelles. *Bull. off. Off. int. Fabr. Choc. Cacao* [1931–34] **L.**P. 33–34; SC.; TP.; Lh.FO. [*C. as:* 11406]

11408 **Bulletin officiel de l'Office national d'hygiène sociale.** Paris. *Bull. off. Off. natn. Hyg. soc.* [1928–34] **L.**TD. [*C. in:* 11112]

11409 **Bulletin officiel. Office de la propriété industrielle, Roumanie.** Bucarest. *Bull. off. Off. Propr. ind. Roum.* [1921–] **L.**P.

11410 **Bulletin officiel de l'Office des textiles coloniaux.** Lyon. *Bull. off. Off. Text. colon.*

11411 **Bulletin officiel de la propriété industrielle.** Paris. *Bull. off. Propr. ind.* **L.**P. 08–; **Ld.**P. (part 2) 59–; **M.**P. 56–.

11412 **Bulletin officiel de la Société française d'électrothérapie et de radiologie médicale.** Paris. *Bull. off. Soc. fr. Électrothér.* [1893–] **L.**RA. 23–25: 27–29.

11413 **Bulletin officiel de la Société d'hygiène de France.** Paris. *Bull. off. Soc. Hyg. Fr.*

11414 **Bulletin officiel de la Société médicale des praticiens.** Paris. *Bull. off. Soc. méd. Pratns* **L.**MD. 52–. [*C. as:* 12224; *Supplement to:* 14637]

11415 **Bulletin officiel de la Société de neurologie de Paris.** Paris. *Bull. off. Soc. Neurol. Paris*

11416 **Bulletin officiel de la Société de thérapeutique dosimétrique de Paris.** Paris. *Bull. off. Soc. Thér. dosimétr. Paris*

11417 **Bulletin officiel des sociétés médicales d'arrondissement de Paris.** Paris. *Bull. off. Socs méd. Arrond. Paris*

11418 **Bulletin officiel. Université aérotechnique de France.** Paris. *Bull. off. Univ. aérotech. Fr.*

11419 **Bulletin of the Ohio Agricultural Experiment Station.** Wooster. *Bull. Ohio agric. Exp. Stn* [1888–44] **L.**AM.; BM^N. 90–39 imp.; EB. (ent.) 89–44 imp.; K. 42–44 imp.; P. 10–44; **Abs.**U. 26–30 imp.; **Bm.**U. 06–44; **Br.**A. 09–43 imp.; **Cr.**P. 04–44 imp.; **Ld.**U. 11–44.; **Lv.**P. 89–44 imp.; **M.**U. 12–14 imp.; **O.**F. 10–44 imp.; **Rt.** imp.; **Y.** [*C. as:* 45813]

11420 **Bulletin of the Ohio Biological Survey.** Columbus. *Bull. Ohio biol. Surv.* [1913–54: 59–] **L.**BM^N.; EB. (ent.); L.; U. 34–; UC. 16: 28; Z. (zool.); **Abs.**U. 26–49 imp.; **Bl.**U. 15–54; **Br.**A. 38– imp.; **C.**UL. 21–; **Cr.**M. 13–54 imp.; **E.**C. 16–35 imp.; **Lv.**U.; **O.**R. 35–; **Pl.**M. 16– imp.; **Sa.** 49–; **Y.**

Bulletin. Ohio Division of Geological Survey *See* 10371.

11421 **Bulletin. Ohio Engineering Experiment Station.** *Bull. Ohio Engng Exp. Stn* [1921–] **L.**BM. 32–; P.; **Bm.**U.; **C.**UL. 26–; **G.**U. 26–32 imp.; **Ld.**P. 27–; **Nw.**A. 28– imp.; **O.**R. 26–; **Sa.** 26–28: 33– imp.; **Sh.**M. 28– imp.; **Y.** [*C. of:* 9831]

11422 **Bulletin. Ohio Highway Department.** Springfield. *Bull. Ohio Highw. Dep.*

11423 **Bulletin of the Ohio State Dental Society.** Columbus. *Bull. Ohio St. dent. Soc.* [1927–30] **L.**D. [*C. as:* 26593]

11424 **Bulletin. Ohio State University.** Columbus. *Bull. Ohio St. Univ.* [1913–] **L.**BM^N. 13–34 imp.; EB. (ent.) 13–28; **Db.** 16–17; **Pl.**M. 29–31 imp.

11425 **Bulletin. Ohio State University Agricultural Extension Service.** Columbus. *Bull. Ohio St. Univ. agric. Ext. Serv.* **O.**F. 34– imp.

Bulletin. Ohio State University Engineering Experiment Station. *See* 11421.

11426 **Bulletin. Oil Refining Series. Calorizing Co.** Pittsburgh, Pa. *Bull. Oil Refin. Ser. Calor. Co.* [1926–27] **L.**P.

Bulletin. Oil Shale Research Laboratory, Dorpat University. *See* 11431.

11427 **Bulletin of the Oklahoma Agricultural Experiment Station.** Stillwater. *Bull. Okla. agric. Exp. Stn* [1892–] **L.**AM.; BM^N. 08–39 imp.; EB. (ent.) 08–; K. 99–06 imp.; P.; **O.**R. 33–; RE. 45– imp.; **Rt.**; **Y.**

11428 **Bulletin of the Oklahoma Anthropological Society.** Oklahoma City. *Bull. Okla. anthrop. Soc.* [1953–]

11429 **Bulletin of the Oklahoma Geological Survey.** Norman. *Bull. Okla. geol. Surv.* [1908–] **L.**BM^N.; GL. 08–14; GM.; UC. imp.; **Br.**U. 57– imp.; **Y.**

11430 **Bulletin of the Oklahoma State Dental Society.** Tulsa. *Bull. Okla. St. dent. Soc.*

11431 **Bulletin. Olikividi uurimise laboratoorium. Dorpat University.** Tartu. *Bull. olikividi Uurim. Lab. Dorpat Univ.* **L.**P. 30–32.

11432 **Bulletin. Olympia Agricultural Company Research Department.** Leamington. *Bull. Olympia agric. Co. Res. Dep.* **C.**A. 22*; **Rt.** 22.

11433 **Bulletin of the Ontario Agricultural College.** Toronto. *Bull. Ont. agric. Coll.* [1886–] **L.**AM.; BM^N. 17–23; EB. (ent.) 01–44 imp.; K. 04–31 imp.; P.; **Abs.**N. 22–26; U. 94–20; **C.**UL. 13–; **Cr.**P. 09– imp.; **Ld.**U. 04–31 imp.; **Lv.**U. 02– imp.; **M.**P. 19–32 imp.; **Rt.**; **Y.**

11434 **Bulletin of the Ontario College of Pharmacy.** Toronto. *Bull. Ont. Coll. Pharm.* [1952–] **L.**PH. 54– imp.; **Y.**

11435 **Bulletin. Ontario Department of Lands and Forests.** Toronto. *Bull. Ont. Dep. Lds Forests* [1924–] **O.**F.

11436 **Bulletin of the Ontario Department of Mines.** Toronto. *Bull. Ont. Dep. Mines* [1896–] **L.**MI. 32– imp.; **Lv.**U. 24–30 imp.

11437 **Bulletin of the Ontario Hospitals for the Insane.** Toronto. *Bull. Ont. Hosps Insane*

11438 **Bulletin. Ontario Hydro-Electric Power Commission.** Toronto. *Bull. Ont. hydro-elect. Pwr Commn* [1916–42] **L.**SC. 26–41.

11439 Bulletin. Ontario Medical Association Toronto. *Bull. Ont. med. Ass.* [1923–43] [*C. as:* 36202]

11440 Bulletin. Ontario Province Department of **Game** and **Fisheries.** Toronto. *Bull. Ont. Prov. Dep. Game Fish.* **L.**SC. 28–.

11441 Bulletin. Ontario Research Foundation. Toronto. *Bull. Ont. Res. Fdn* [1936–] **L.**P. 36–41. [*C. of:* 35548]

11442 Bulletin. Operations Research Society of **America.** Baltimore. *Bull. Ops Res. Soc. Am.* **C.**P.; **Sh.**U. 59–; **Te.**N. 59–; **Y.** [*Also supplements*]
Bulletin of the **Ophthalmological Society** of **Egypt.** *See* 12111.

11443 Bulletin opothérapique. Paris. *Bull. opothér.* [*C. as:* 12449]

11444 Bulletin de l'**Ordre** des **médecins.** Paris. *Bull. Ordre Méd.* **L.**H. 46–.

11445 Bulletin de l'**Ordre** des **pharmaciens.** Bruxelles. *Bull. Ordre Pharmns* **L.**PH. 42–44.

11446 Bulletin of the **Oregon Agricultural College.** Corvallis. *Bull. Ore. agric. Coll.* **L.**EB. (ent.) 14.

11447 Bulletin of the **Oregon Agricultural Experiment Station.** Corvallis. *Bull. Ore. agric. Exp. Stn* [1890–13] **L.**AM.; EB. (ent.) 11–13; **K.** 97–06 imp.; **P.** 91–13; **Cr.**P. 08–13 imp.; **Ld.**U.; **Rt.** imp. [*C. as:* 50788]

11448 Bulletin. Oregon Forests Products Laboratory. Corvallis. *Bull. Ore. Forests Prod. Lab.* [1947–57] **L.**P.; **O.**F.; **Y.** [*C. as:* 10286]

11449 Bulletin. Oregon State Board of **Forestry.** Salem. *Bull. Ore. St. Bd For.* **O.**F. 29–; **Y.**

11450 Bulletin. Oregon State Department of **Geology** and **Mineral Industries.** Portland. *Bull. Ore. St. Dep. Geol. miner. Ind.* [1938–] **L.**BM^N.; **Y.**

11451 Bulletin. Oregon State Engineer. Portland. *Bull. Ore. St. Engr*

11452 Bulletin. Oregon State Game Commission. Portland, Ore. *Bull. Ore. St. Game Commn* **L.**BM. 59–; **Pit.**F. 50– imp.

11453 Bulletin. Organisatie voor natuurwetenschappelijk onderzoek. Batavia. *Bull. Org. natuurw. Onderz.* [1948–] **L.**BM^N. 50–55 imp.; **P.** 50–55; SC.

11454 Bulletin. Organisation internationale de **métrologie légale.** Paris. *Bull. Org. int. Métrol. lég.* [1960–] **L.**HQ.; **P.**; **Te.**N.; **Y.**

11455 Bulletin des **organismes officiels** de **petit élevage** du **Hainaut.** Pâturages. *Bull. Organismes off. pet. Élev. Hainaut* [1932–40]
Bulletin. Organization for **Scientific Research** in **Indonesia.** *See* 11453.

11456 Bulletin of the **Ornithological Society** of **Japan.** *Bull. orn. Soc. Japan* **Y.**

11457 Bulletin of the **Ornithological Society** of **New Zealand.** *Bull. orn. Soc. N.Z.* [1941–42] **L.**BM^N. [*C. as:* 34724]

11458 Bulletin ornithologique romand. Genève. *Bull. orn. romand* [1932–35] **L.**BM^N.; Z.; **O.**OR. 32. [*C. of:* 12221]

11459 Bulletin d'**orthopédie.** Bruxelles. *Bull. Orthop., Brux.*

11460 Bulletin of the **Osaka Medical School.** Osaka. *Bull. Osaka med. Sch.* [1954–] **L.**MD. 60–; S.; **Ld.**U.

11461 Bulletin of the **Osaka Municipal Museum** of **Natural History.** Osaka. *Bull. Osaka munic. Mus. nat. Hist.* [1955–56] **L.**BM^N.; **Pl.**M.; **Y.** [*C. as:* 11462^c]

11462 Bulletin of the **Osaka Municipal Technical Research Institute.** Osaka. *Bull. Osaka munic. tech. Res. Inst.* **Y.**

11462^c Bulletin of the **Osaka Museum** of **Natural History.** Osaka. *Bull. Osaka Mus. nat. Hist.* [1959–] **L.**BM^N.; **Pl.**M.; **Y.** [*C. of:* 11461]

11463 Bulletin ostréicole et **maritime** du **quartier** de **Marennes.** *Bull. ostréic. marit. Quart. Marennes*

11464 Bulletin of the **Oto-Laryngological Clinics** of the **Beth-Israel Hospital.** New York. *Bull. oto-lar. Clins Beth-Israel Hosp.*

11465 Bulletin d'**oto-rhino-laryngologie.** Paris. *Bull. Oto-rhino-lar., Paris* **L.**MD. 11–12. [*C. of:* 10797]
Bulletin of **Otorhinolaryngology.** Leningrad. *See* 56492.

11466 Bulletin. Oxford University Exploration Club. Oxford. *Bull. Oxf. Univ. Explor. Club* [1948–] **L.**BM.; BM^N.; G.; K.; Z.; **C.**PO.; **E.**A.; **O.**AP. [*C. of:* 44847]

11467 Bulletin of the **Oxford University Institute** of **Statistics.** Oxford. *Bull. Oxf. Univ. Inst. Statist.* [1945–] **L.**AM. (5 yr.); B. 50–; BM.; U. 46–; UC. 47–; **Abd.**R.; **Bm.**U.; **C.**UL.; **Cr.**U.; **Db.**; **Dn.**U.; **E.**A.; U.; **Ex.**U.; **Ld.**P.; W. 46–49; **M.**C. 53–59; P.; **N.**T. 46–; U.; **O.**AEC.; **R.**U.; **Y.** [*C. of:* 10647]

11468 Bulletin of the **Pacific Coast Society** of **Orthodontists.** Sacramento. *Bull. Pacif. Cst Soc. Orthod.* **L.**D. 23– imp.
Bulletin of the **Pacific Committee** of the **Academy** of **Sciences** of the **U.S.S.R.** *See* 12829.

11469 Bulletin of the **Pacific Marine Fisheries Commission.** Portland, Ore. *Bull. Pacif. mar. Fish. Commn* [1948–] **L.**AM.; BM^N.; **Abd.**M.; **Bl.**U.; **Dm.** 48–54; **H.**U.; **Lo.**; **Lv.**U.; **Pl.**M.; **Sa.**; **Y.**
Bulletin of the **Pacific Ocean Scientific Fishery Research Station.** *See* 24524.

11470 Bulletin of the **Pacific Orchid Society** of **Hawaii.** Honolulu. *Bull. Pacif. Orchid Soc. Hawaii* **L.**K. 41– imp.

11471 Bulletin. Pacific Rocket Society. Glendale. *Bull. Pacif. Rock. Soc.* [1952–] **Y.** [*C. of:* 36718]
Bulletin of the **Pacific Scientific Institute** of **Fisheries** and **Oceanography.** Vladivostock. *See* 24524.

11472 Bulletin. Paint Manufacturers' and **Allied Trades Association.** London. *Bull. Paint Mfrs' all. Trades Ass.* **L.**PR. 45–.

11473 Bulletin. Paint Manufacturers' Association of the **United States. Scientific Section.** Philadelphia. *Bull. Paint Mfrs' Ass. U.S. scient. Sect.* [1908–17] [*C. in:* 14370]

11474 Bulletin des **palplanches.** Paris. *Bull. Palplanches* [1937–] **L.**P. 37–39.

11475 Bulletin. Parasites of **Sheep.** London. *Bull. Parasit. Sheep* **L.**P. 35–38.

11476 Bulletin of the **Parenteral Drug Association.** Philadelphia. *Bull. parent. Drug Ass.* **L.**PH. 60–.

11477 Bulletin of the **Pasteur Institute.** New York. *Bull. Pasteur Inst., N.Y.*

11478 Bulletin of the **Pasteur Institute** of **Southern India.** Madras. *Bull. Pasteur Inst. Sth. India* [1908–10] **L.**BM. 09–10; TD.; **Abs.**N.; **E.**A.; **Lv.**U.; **O.**B.

11479 **Bulletin** of the **Patna Science College Philosophical Society.** Patna. *Bull. Patna Sci. Coll. phil. Soc.* **L.**BM[N]. 31–38.

11480 **Bulletin** of the **Peabody Museum** of **Natural History.** New Haven, Conn. *Bull. Peabody Mus. nat. Hist.* [1926–] **L.**BM. 49–; BM[N].; GL. 26 imp.; Z. 58– imp.; **Dm.** 58; **E.**R. 26–31; **Ld.**U.; **Lv.**U. [*Not published 1936–48*]

11480° **Bulletin** of the **Peak District Mines Historical Society.** Sheffield. *Bull. Peak Distr. Mines hist. Soc.* [1959–] **L.**BM[N].

11481 **Bulletin** des **pêches maritimes.** Paris. *Bull. Pêch. marit.* **Lv.**U. 93–98.

11482 **Bulletin. Peking Society** of **Natural History.** Peking. *Bull. Peking Soc. nat. Hist.* [1926–29] **L.**BM[N].; SC. [*C. in:* 37299]

11483 **Bulletin** of the **Pennsylvania Agricultural Experiment Station.** State College, Pa. *Bull. Pa agric. Exp. Stn* [1887–] **L.**AM.; BM[N]. 37–39; EB. (ent.) 10–; K. 03–07 imp.; P. 87–11: 37–; **Abs.**N. 13–20 imp.; **Br.**A. 14– imp.; **Ld.**U. 94–41 imp.; **O.**F. 29– imp.; **Rt.** imp.; **Y.**

11484 **Bulletin. Pennsylvania Bureau** of **Plant Industry, Technical Series.** Harrisburg. *Bull. Pa Bur. Pl. Ind. tech. Ser.*

11485 **Bulletin** of the **Pennsylvania Department** of **Agriculture.** Harrisburg. *Bull. Pa Dep. Agric.* **L.**AM.; BM[N]. 05–39 imp.; EB. (ent.) 20–37; P. 96–37 imp.; **C.**B. (zool.) 03–08; **Y.**

Bulletin. Pennsylvania Department of **Forestry.** *See* 11486.

11486 **Bulletin. Pennsylvania Department** of **Forests** and **Waters.** Harrisburg. *Bull. Pa Dep. Forests Wat.* [1902–] **O.**F. 19: 22–35 imp.

Bulletin of the **Pennsylvania Engineering Experiment Station.** *See* 11491.

11487 **Bulletin** of the **Pennsylvania Game Commissioners.** Harrisburg. *Bull. Pa Game Commnrs*

11488 **Bulletin** of the **Pennsylvania Geological Survey.** Harrisburg. *Bull. Pa geol. Surv.* [1922–] **L.**BM[N].; GM. 24–; **Lv.**U. 22–39; **C.**UL.; **O.**R.; **Y.** [*Issued in series*]

11489 **Bulletin** of the **Pennsylvania Highway Department.** Harrisburg. *Bull. Pa Highw. Dep.*

11490 **Bulletin** of the **Pennsylvania Museum.** Philadelphia. *Bull. Pa Mus.* [1903–38] **L.**BM. 04–38; **C.**FT. 31–38; **E.**R. 03–34; **O.**A. 10–38. [*C. as:* 37531]

11491 **Bulletin** of the **Pennsylvania State College Engineering Experiment Station.** State College, Pa. *Bull. Pa St. Coll. Engng Exp. Stn* [1910–48] **L.**P. 24–48; SC. 19–48. [*C. as:* 10028]

11492 **Bulletin** of the **Pennsylvania State Dental Society.** Philadelphia. *Bull. Pa St. dent. Soc.* [1930–33] [*Replaced by:* 37327]

Bulletin. Pennsylvania State University Mineral Industries Experiment Station. *See* 11095.

Bulletin of the **Pennsylvania Topographic** and **Geological Survey.** *See* 11488.

Bulletin. Pennsylvania University Agricultural Experiment Station. *See* 11483.

11493 **Bulletin** of **Peony News.** Clinton, N.Y. *Bull. Peony News* [1903–24] **L.**HS.; SC. 14–24. [*C. as:* 9343]

Bulletin périodique de la **Société belge** de **géomètres.** *See* 11861.

11495 **Bulletin périodique** de la **Société** de **géographie** du **Cher.** Bourges. *Bull. périod Soc. Géogr. Cher* **L.**G. 03.

11496 **Bulletin** of the **Permanent International Association** of the **International Navigation Congresses.** *Bull. perm. int. Ass. int. Navig. Congr.* [1926–] **L.**SC.; **Wl.**H. 54–; **Y.**

Bulletin. Permanent International Association of **Road Congresses.** *See* 9475.

11498 **Bulletin** of the **Permanent Wild Life Protective Association.** New York. *Bull. perm. wild Life prot. Ass.* **L.**BM. 15–20.

Bulletin pertaining to ... *See* **Bulletin** ...

11499 **Bulletin** of the **Perth Observatory, Western Australia.** Perth. *Bull. Perth Obs.* [1913] **L.**AS.; BM.; **C.**O.

11500 **Bulletin. Pest Infestation Research Board.** D.S.I.R., London. *Bull. Pest Infest. Res. Bd* [1954–] **L.**BM.; BM[N]. 54; P.; **Ld.**P.; **Y.**

11501 **Bulletin** of the **Petroleum Executive.** London. *Bull. Petrol. Exec.* [1919–21] **L.**BM.; P.; SC.

Bulletin. Petroleum Series, Wyoming University School of **Mines.** *See* 12656.

11502 **Bulletin** of the **Pharmaceutical Research Institute, Takatsuki.** Osaka. *Bull. pharm. Res. Inst., Takatsuki* [1950–] **L.**MC. 50–56; PH.; **Y.**

11503 **Bulletin pharmaceutique** d'**Égypte.** Le Caire. *Bull. pharm. Égypte*

11504 **Bulletin** de **pharmacie** de **Lyon.** Lyon. *Bull. Pharm. Lyon*

11505 **Bulletin** de **pharmacie** du **Sud-Est.** Montpellier. *Bull. Pharm. Sud-Est*

11506 **Bulletin** des **pharmaciens** du **département** du **Nord.** *Bull. Pharmns Dép. N.*

11507 **Bulletin** of **Pharmacy.** Detroit, Mich. *Bull. Pharm., Detroit*

11508 **Bulletin** of the **Philadelphia College** of **Pharmacy** and **Alumni Report.** Philadelphia. *Bull. Philad. Coll. Pharm.*

11509 **Bulletin** of the **Philadelphia County Dental Society.** Philadelphia. *Bull. Philad Cty dent. Soc.*

11510 **Bulletin** of the **Philadelphia Medico-Chirurgical College.** Philadelphia. *Bull. Philad. med.-chir. Coll.*

11511 **Bulletin** of the **Philippine Museum.** Manila. *Bull. Philipp. Mus.* **L.**BM[N]. 03–04.

11512 **Bulletin** of the **Philippine Ophthalmological** and **Otolaryngological Society.** Manila. *Bull. Philipp. ophthal. otolar. Soc.* [1949–54] **L.**MD. imp. [*C. as:* 37548]

11513 **Bulletin** of the **Philippine Public Health Association.** Manila. *Bull. Philipp. publ. Hlth Ass.*

11514 **Bulletin** of the **Philosophical Society** of **Washington.** Washington. *Bull. phil. Soc. Wash.* [1871–10] **L.**AS. 74–10 imp.; BM.; BM[N].; P.; R.; RI. 88–10; SC. 71–88; UC. 71–88; Z. 71–94; **Abd.**U. 92–10; **Bl.**U. 00–10; **Bm.**U. 83–86; **C.**P. 74–13; **Cr.**P. 95–07 imp.; **Db.**; **E.**C. 88–99; Q. 81–07 imp.; R.; **G.**U. imp.; **O.**R.

11515 **Bulletin. Photoelectric Spectrometry Group.** *Bull. photoelect. Spectrom. Grp* [1949–] **L.**P. 52–; **Y.**

11516 **Bulletin** de **photogrammétrie.** Paris. *Bull. Photogramm., Paris* [1931–39] L.C.; P.; PG.; SC.; **Bm.**U. 33–39; **We.**K. [*C. as:* 47204]

11517 **Bulletin** of the **Photographic Society** of **America.** Pittsburgh. *Bull. photogr. Soc. Am.* **L.**PG. 31–34*. [*C. as:* 26678]

11518 **Bulletin** of **Photography.** Philadelphia. *Bull. Photogr.* **L.**PG. 07–19.

11519 **Bulletin** of the **Physiographical Science Research Institute.** Tokyo. *Bull. physiogr. Sci. Res. Inst., Tokyo* **L.**AM. 50–.

11520 **Bulletin. Pictou Academy Scientific Association.** Pictou. *Bull. Pictou Acad. scient. Ass.*

11521 **Bulletin. Pineapple Experiment Station, University** of **Hawaii.** Honolulu. *Bull. Pineapple Exp. Stn Univ. Hawaii* **L.**P. 25–34 imp.

11522 **Bulletin. Pittsburgh Lectrodryer Corporation.** Pittsburgh. *Bull. Pittsb. Lectrodryer Corp.* **L.**P. 50–57. [*C. as:* 11523]

11523 **Bulletin. Pittsburgh Lectrodryer Division, McGraw-Edison Co.** Pittsburgh. *Bull. Pittsb. Lectrodryer Div. McGraw-Edison Co.* [1958–] **L.**P. [*C. of:* 11522]

11524 **Bulletin. Pittsburgh University.** Pittsburgh. *Bull. Pittsb. Univ.*

11525 **Bulletin planktonique.** Conseil permanente internationale pour l'exploration de la mer. Copenhague. *Bull. plankt.* [1908–12] **L.**AM.; BM.; BM^N.; SC.; U.; UC.; Z.; **Abd.**M.; U.; **Bm.**U.; **C.**B.; **Db.**; **E.**M.; R.; U.; **G.**U.; **Lo.**; **Lv.**U.; **M.**U.; **Mi.**; **O.**R.; **Pl.**M.; **Sa.**; **Wo.** [*C. of:* 12456]

Bulletin of the **Plant Physiology Experiment Station** at **Detskoje Selo.** *See* 50082.

Bulletin of **Plant Protection.** Ankara. *See* 7159.

Bulletin of **Plant Protection.** Leningrad. *See* 55238 and 56564.

Bulletin of **Plant Protection** in **Siberia.** *See* 55239.

11526 **Bulletin** of the **Plumbago-Graphite Association.** New York. *Bull. Plumbago-Graph. Ass.*

11527 **Bulletin pluviométrique. Observatoire central** de l'**Indochine.** Phu-Lien. *Bull. pluviom. Obs. cent. Indochine* **L.**MO. 06–30.

11528 **Bulletin pluviométrique. Observatoire météorologique, Séminaire-Collège Saint Martial.** Port au Prince. *Bull. pluviom. Obs. mét. Sémin.-Coll. St Martial* [1948–] **L.**MO.; **Y.**

11529 **Bulletin** des **poids** et **mesures.** Saint-Marcellin. *Bull. Poids Mes.* **L.**P. 07–14 imp.

11530 **Bulletin** of the **Polish Institute** of **Arts** and **Sciences in America.** New York. *Bull. Pol. Inst. Arts Sci. Am.* [1943–] **Db.**

11531 **Bulletin** of **Polish Medical History** and **Science.** Chicago. *Bull. Pol. med. Hist. Sci.* [1956–60] **L.**MA.; MD.; **Dn.**U.; **G.**U.; **Ld.**U.; **Y.** [*C. as:* 11532]

11532 **Bulletin** of **Polish Medical Science** and **History.** Chicago. *Bull. Pol. med. Sci. Hist.* [1960–] **L.**MA.; MD.; **Dn.**U.; **G.**U.; **Ld.**U.; **Y.** [*C. of:* 11531]

Bulletin of the **Polytechnical Institute** of **Tiflis.** *See* 24360.

Bulletin of the **Pomological Experimental Station.** Tiflis. *See* 55241.

Bulletin. Polska akademia nauk. *See* 9176–9183.

11533 **Bulletin populaire** de la **pisciculture.** Toulouse. *Bull. pop. Piscic.* [1907–10] **Pl.**M. [*C. of:* 12305]

11534 **Bulletin** of **Popular Information. Arnold Arboretum.** Cambridge, Mass. *Bull. pop. Inf. Arnold Arbor.* [1911–40] **L.**BM^N. 22–24 imp.; HS. 15–40; K.; SC. 24–40; **E.**B. 24–40. [*C. as:* 4840]

11535 **Bulletin** of **Popular Information. Morton Arboretum.** Lisle, Ill. *Bull. pop. Inf. Morton Arbor.* [1925–] **L.**BM^N. 30 imp.; **Y.**

11536 **Bulletin. Portland Cement Association.** Chicago. *Bull. Portland Cem. Ass.* [1905–11]

11537 **Bulletin Porto Rico Agricultural Experiment Station, Federal Station, Mayaguez.** Washington. *Bull. Porto Rico agric. Exp. Stn fed. Stn Mayaguez* [1902–] **L.**AM.; BM.; BM^N. 02–38 imp.; EB. (ent.); K. 02–41: 47–; P. 03–45: 53–; **Bm.**U. 02–09 imp.; **C.**A.; **Cr.**P. 04–26 imp.; **G.**M. 13–34; **Lv.**P. 02–28; **M.**P. 14–28; **O.**F. 50– imp.; **Rt.**

11538 **Bulletin. Porto Rico Agricultural Experiment Station, Insular Station, Rio Piedras.** *Bull. Porto Rico agric. Exp. Stn insular Stn Rio Piedras* [1911–] **L.**BM^N. 31– imp.; EB. (ent.) 12–; P. 24–; **Br.**A. 32– imp.; **C.**A. 22–; **O.**F. 46– imp.; **Rt.** 19–; **Y.**

11539 **Bulletin. Porto Rico Sugar Producers Association Experiment Station.** *Bull. Porto Rico Sug. Prod. Exp. Stn* **L.**EB. 12–14*. [*C. in:* 11538]

11540 **Bulletin** of the **Post Graduate Committee** in **Medicine, University** of **Sydney.** *Bull. post Grad. Comm. Med. Univ. Sydney* **L.**MA. 46–; MD. 45–; S. 45–.

11541 **Bulletin. Poultry Association** of **British Columbia.** *Bull. Poult. Ass. Br. Columb.*

11542 **Bulletin** of **Practical Ophthalmology.** San Francisco. *Bull. pract. Ophthal.* [1931–] **L.**MA. 41–.

11543 **Bulletin pratique** des **brasseurs.** Bruxelles. *Bull. prat. Brass.*

11544 **Bulletin préliminaire** de l'**Institut séismologique** de l'**Université** de **Béograd.** Béograd. *Bull. prélim. Inst. séism. Univ. Béogr.*

11545 **Bulletin** du **Premier Observatoire astronomique** d'**Odessa.** *Bull. prem. Obs. astr. Odessa* [1938–] **L.**AS. 39.

11546 **Bulletin** of the **Prince** of **Wales Museum** of **Western India.** Bombay. *Bull. Prince Wales Museum west. India* [1950–] **L.**BM.; BM^N. 50–54; **Y.**

Bulletin of the **Principal Botanic Garden, Moscow.** *See* 12754.

11547 **Bulletin. Printing** and **Allied Trades Research Association.** London. *Bull. Print. all. Trades Res. Ass.* [1938–] **L.**BM.; U. 46–; **Lh.**P.

Bulletin. Problems of **Forest Protection.** Leningrad. *See* 48697.

11548 **Bulletin** of **Proceedings** of the **Brooklyn Institute** of **Arts** and **Sciences.** Brooklyn, N.Y. *Bull. Proc. Brooklyn Inst. Arts Sci.* **Db.** 01–; **G.**N. 01–.

11549 **Bulletin** and **Proceedings** of the **New Zealand Institution** of **Engineers.** Wellington. *Bull. Proc. N.Z. Instn Engrs* [1938–46] **L.**SC. 39–46; **Te.**N. 44–46. [*C. of:* 11320]

Bulletin. Production Engineering Research Association. Melton Mowbray. *See* 36669.

11550 **Bulletin** van het **Proefstation** voor **cacao**, **Salatiga.** *Bull. Proefstn Cacao, Salatiga* **L.**EB. 01–04 imp.; K. 01–04 imp.

11551 **Bulletin. Proefstation** voor de **Javasuikerin-dustrie, Technische Afdeeling.** Semarang. *Bull. Proefstn JavasuikInd. tech. Afd.*

11552 **Bulletin. Proefstation** voor **suikerriet** in **West-Java, 'Kagok'.** Tegal. *Bull. Proefstn Suikerriet W.-Java 'Kagok'* **L.**K. 87–06 imp.

11553 **Bulletin** de la **protection** des **végétaux.** Dakar. *Bull. Prot. Vég.* [1954–] **L.**EB. 54–59; MY.

11554 **Bulletin** of the **Provisional International Computation Centre.** Rome. *Bull. provis. int. Comput. Cent.* [1958–] **L.**HQ.; P.; SC.; **Bl.**U.; **Dn.**U.; **G.**U.; **Y.**

11555 **Bulletin** on **Psychiatric Rehabilitation.** New York. *Bull. psychiat. Rehab.* [1944–]

11556 **Bulletin** de **psychologie.** Paris. *Bull. Psychol., Paris* **L.**MD. 55–; PS. 56–; **H.**U. 57–.

11557 **Bulletin psycho-magnétique.** Paris. *Bull.psychomagn.*

11558 **Bulletin** of the **Public Health** and **Marine-Hospital Service.** Washington. *Bull. publ. Hlth Mar.-Hosp. Serv.* **L.**BM. 81–; U. 08–18 imp.; **G.**M. 16– imp.

11559 **Bulletin** of the **Public Museum.** Milwaukee. *Bull. publ. Mus., Milwaukee* [1910–] **L.**BM. 28–; BM^N. 10–52 imp.; HO.; **Bl.**U.; **Db.**; **E.**B.; F.; **Lv.**U. imp.

11560 **Bulletin** of **Publications** dealing with **Power** and **Fuel.** Tokyo. *Bull. Publs Pwr Fuel* [1931] **L.**P. [*C. in:* 38264]

Bulletin. Puerto Rico Agricultural Experiment Station, Federal Station, Mayaguez. *See* 11537.

Bulletin. Puerto Rico University Agricultural Experiment Station, Rio Piedras. *See* 11538.

11561 **Bulletin. Puget Sound Marine Station.** *Bull. Puget Sound mar. Stn* [1912–] **Pl.**M. 12.

11562 **Bulletin** of the **Pusan Fisheries College.** *Bull. Pusan Fish. Coll.* [1956–] **Pl.**M.

11563 **Bulletin** of the **Quarantine Service.** Melbourne. *Bull. Quarant. Serv., Melb.* **Lv.**U. 16–23* imp. [*C. as:* 10044]

Bulletin. Queensland Department of **Agriculture** and **Stock, Division** of **Plant Industry.** *See* 10103.

Bulletin of the **Queensland Forest Service.** Brisbane. *See* 20025.

11564 **Bulletin** of the **Quetta Fruit Experiment Station.** Quetta. *Bull. Quetta Fruit Exp. Stn* **L.**AM.; BM. 13–19; **Rt.** 13–19.

11565 **Bulletin** of the **Quezon Institute.** Manila. *Bull. Quezon Inst.* [1939–] **O.**R. 41–.

11566 **Bulletin quotidien** d'**études. Office national météorologique.** Paris. *Bull. quot. Étud. Off. natn. mét.* [1923–] **L.**MO. 24–.

11567 **Bulletin quotidien** de l'**Institut central météorologique danois.** Copenhague. *Bull. quot. Inst. cent. mét. dan.*

Bulletin quotidien de l'**Institut r. hongrois** de **météorologie.** *See* 29206.

11568 **Bulletin quotidien international. Office national météorologique.** Paris. *Bull. quot. int. Off. natn. mét.*

11569 **Bulletin quotidien** d'**observations. Météorologie national.** Paris. *Bull. quot. Obsns Mét. natn.* **L.**MO. 37–.

11569° **Bulletin quotidien. Observatoire r.** de **Belgique.** Bruxelles. *Bull. quot. Obs. r. Belg.* [1899–08] **L.**MO. [*C. as:* 12379°]

11570 **Bulletin quotidien** de **renseignements** du **Maroc. Service météorologique.** Casablanca. *Bull. quot. Renseign. Maroc Serv. mét.* **L.**MO. 36–39: 48–.

11571 **Bulletin quotidien** de **renseignements météorologiques** de l'**Afrique** du **nord.** Alger. *Bull. quot. Renseign. mét. Afr. N.* [1948–] **L.**MO. [*C. of:* 11056]

11572 **Bulletin quotidien** de **renseignements. Office national météorologique.** Paris. *Bull. quot. Renseign. Off. natn. mét.* **L.**MO. 24–.

11573 **Bulletin quotidien** du **temps.** Athène. *Bull. quot. Temps, Athène* **L.**MO. 32–40: 50–.

11574 **Bulletin R.I.L.E.M.** Réunion internationale des laboratoires d'essais et de recherches sur les matériaux et les constructions. Paris. *Bull. R.I.L.E.M.* [1954–] **L.**P.; **Wa.**B.; **Y.** [*C. of:* 11611]

11575 **Bulletin** of the **Radio** and **Electrical Engineering Division, National Research Council** of **Canada.** Ottawa. *Bull. Radio elect. Engng Div. natn. Res. Coun. Can.* [1955–] **L.**MO. 56–; P.; **Bm.**U.; **Br.**U. 55–; **E.**U.; **Ma.**T.; **Y.** [*C. of:* 40148]

11576 **Bulletin. Radio Inductive Interference.** Radio Branch, Department of Marine (and Fisheries). Ottawa. *Bull. Radio induct. Interfer., Ottawa* **L.**P. 25–34.

Bulletin. Radio Society of **Great Britain.** *See* 41735.

11577 **Bulletin radiographique.** Lausanne. *Bull. radiogr.*

11578 **Bulletin** of the **Raffles Museum.** Singapore. *Bull. Raffles Mus.* [1928–60] **L.**AN. (Ser. B.) 36–49; BM.; BM^N.; E. 28–40; EB. (ent.); L.; UC. 33–60; Z.; **C.**B. 33–60 imp.; UL. (Ser. B.) 36–49; **Cr.**M. 28–60: (Ser. B.) 36–49; **O.**H.; R.; **Pl.**M.; **Y.** [*C. as:* 11233°]

11579 **Bulletin** of the **Railway** and **Locomotive Historical Society.** Taunton, Mass. *Bull. Rly Loco. hist. Soc.* [1921–] **L.**P.; SC. 30–; **Y.**

11580 **Bulletin** of the **Railway Technical Laboratory.** Tokyo. *Bull. Rly tech. Lab., Tokyo*

11581 **Bulletin. Rayon** and **Silk Association.** London. *Bull. Rayon Silk Ass.* **L.**BM. 39–.

11582 **Bulletin. Reading Public Museum** and **Art Gallery.** Reading, Pa. *Bull. Reading publ. Mus.* **L.**BM^N. 24–54 imp.; **Y.**

11583 **Bulletin. Reinforced Concrete Department, Faculty** of **Engineering, Egyptian University.** Cairo. *Bull. reinf. Concr. Dep. Fac. Engng Egypt. Univ.*

11584 **Bulletin** des **relations scientifiques. Institut international** de **cooperation intellectuelle.** Paris. *Bull. Relat. scient. Inst. int. Coop. intell.* [1926–] **L.**P. 27.

11585 **Bulletin** de **renseignements. Chambre syndicale** des **maîtres** de **verrerie** de **France.** Paris. *Bull. Renseign. Chamb. synd. Maîtr. Verr. Fr.*

11586 **Bulletin** de **renseignements** du **Service technique** de l'**aéronautique**. Paris. *Bull. Renseign. Serv. tech. Aéronaut.*

Bulletin. Rensselaer Polytechnic Institute, Engineering and **Science Series.** *See* 18169.

Bulletin. Report of **State Geologist, South Dakota.** *See* 6955.

11587 **Bulletin** of the **Research Association** of **British Flour Millers.** London. *Bull. Res. Ass. Br. Flour Mill.* [1924–27: 50–] L.AM. 50–; C.; **C.**A.; UL.; **Rt.** 24–25.

11588 **Bulletin. Research Association** of **British Paint Colour** and **Varnish Manufacturers.** Teddington. *Bull. Res. Ass. Br. Paint Mfrs* [1936–] L.BM.; P.; **C.**UL. 36–48; **O.**B. 39–.

Bulletin. Research Association of **British Rubber Manufacturers.** *See* 41696.

11589 **Bulletin** of the **Research Association** of **British Rubber** and **Tyre Manufacturers.** London. *Bull. Res. Ass. Br. Rubb. Tyre Mfrs* L.P. 23*; SC. 20–23; **Sy.**R. 20–23.

11589° **Bulletin. Research Branch, Forest Department, United Provinces** of **Agra** and **Oudh.** Allahabad. *Bull. Res. Brch Forest Dep. un. Prov. Agra Oudh* [1928–] L.BM.

11590 **Bulletin. Research Committee, British Bee-Keepers' Association.** Crawborough. *Bull. Res. Comm. Br. Bee-Keep. Ass.* [1951–] L.P.

11591 **Bulletin** of the **Research Council** of **Israel.** Jerusalem. *Bull. Res. Coun. Israel* [1951–] L.AM.; BM^N.; C. 52–; P.; PR. 53–; R.; RI.; TD. imp.; TP.; U.; **C.**P.; UL. 51–52; **Db.**; **E.**R.; **Ld.**U.; **M.**P.; U.; **Md.**H.; **O.**RE.; **Y.**

From 1955 continued in sections:

Sect. A. Mathematics, Physics and Chemistry [1955–] L.C.; M.; P.; R.; RI.; U.; **Abd.**R. 61–; **Ba.**I.; **Bm.**U.; **E.**R.; **Ld.**U. 55–56; **M.**T.; U.; **Md.**H.; **O.**R.; **Y.** [*From 1957 part C. as* Sect. F. *below*]

Sect. B. Biology and Geology [1955–57] L.AM.; B.; BM^N.; C. 55–56; P.; R.; RI.; Z.; **C.**A.; **Bm.**U.; **E.**R.; **Hu.**G.; **Ld.**U. 55–56; **M.**T.; U.; **Md.**H.; **O.**R.; **Y.**

Then C. as: Section B. Zoology *and* Section G. Geosciences.

Sect. B. Zoology [1957–] L.AM.; B.; BM^N.; P.; R.; RI.; Z.; **C.**A.; **Bm.**U.; **E.**R.; **Hu.**G.; **Ld.**U.; **M.**U.; **Md.**H.; **O.**R.; **Y.**

Sect. C. Technology [1955–] L.C. 58–; MC. 55–56; P.; R.; **Bm.**U.; **Hu.**G.; **Ld.**U. 55–56; **M.**T.; U.; **Md.**H.; **O.**R.; **Sil.** 59–; **Y.**

Sect. D. Botany [1955–] L.AM.; BM^N.; HS.; K.; MC. 55–56; MY.; R.; **Bl.**U.; **Bm.**U.; **C.**A.; **E.**R.; **Hu.**G.; **Ld.**U. 55–56; **M.**U.; **Md.**H.; **O.**R.; **Y.** [*Replaces:* 36833 and 33834]

Sect. E. Experimental Medicine [1957–] L.BM^N. 58–; C.; MC.; R.; **Abd.**R. 61–; **Bl.**U.; **E.**R.; **M.**U.; **O.**R.; **Y.**

Sect. F. Mathematics and Physics [1957–] L.C.; M.; P.; U.; **E.**R.; **G.**U. 59–; **Ld.**U.; **M.**U.; **O.**R.; **Y.** *and some other libraries listed under* Sect. A. *above.* [*C. from:* Sect. A *above*]

Sect. G. Geosciences [1957–] L.BM^N. 58–; HQ.; **E.**R.; **M.**U.; **O.**R.; **Y.** *and some other libraries listed under* Sect. B. Biology and Geology [*C. from:* Sect. B. Biology and Geology *above*]

11593 **Bulletin** of the **Research Department, British Coal Utilisation Research Association.** London. *Bull. Res. Dep. Br. Coal Util. Res. Ass.* [1938–] [*C. of:* 342]

Bulletin. Research Department. Davey Tree Expert Company. *See* 9940.

11594 **Bulletin. Research Department, Indian Coffee Board.** Ballehonur. *Bull. Res. Dep. Indian Coff. Bd* [1949–] **Rt.**; **Y.**

Bulletin. Research Department, Olympia Agricultural Company. *See* 11432.

11595 **Bulletin. Research** and **Development Laboratories, Portland Cement Association.** Chicago. *Bull. Res. Dev. Labs Portland Cem. Ass.* L.P. 45–; **Y.**

11596 **Bulletin. Research** and **Development** in the **Laboratory. Baird** and **Tatlock.** London. *Bull. Res. Dev. Lab. Baird & Tatlock* [1956–] L.P.; **Ld.**P.; **M.**D. [*C. of:* 10792]

Bulletin. Research Division, Electrical Engineering Department, Massachusetts Institute of **Technology.** *See* 10876.

11597 **Bulletin. Research** and **Experiments Department, Ministry** of **Home Security.** Princes Risborough. *Bull. Res. Exps Dep. Minist. Home Secur.* L.P. 41–43.

11598 **Bulletin** of the **Research Institute** of **Applied Electricity, Hokkaido University.** Sapporo. *Bull. Res. Inst. appl. Elect. Hokkaido Univ.* [1949–] L.P. 60–; **Y.**

11598° **Bulletin** of **Research Institute** for **Applied Mechanics.** Fukuoka. *Bull. Res. Inst. appl. Mech., Fukuoka* [1952–]

11599 **Bulletin. Research Institute** of **Atmospherics, Nagoya University.** Tokokawa. *Bull. Res. Inst. Atmos. Nagoya Univ.* [1950–] L.MO.

11600 **Bulletin** of the **Research Institute** of **Flax** and **Flax Fibres.** Sapporo. *Bull. Res. Inst. Flax* [1951–]

11601 **Bulletin** of the **Research Institute** for **Food Science, Kyoto University.** Kyoto. *Bull. Res. Inst. Fd Sci. Kyoto Univ.* [1949–] L.P. 52–; SC.; **C.**A.; **Rt.** 55–; **Y.**

11602 **Bulletin** of the **Research Institute** of **Mineral Dressing** and **Metallurgy.** Sendai. *Bull. Res. Inst. Miner. Dress. Metall., Sendai* [1942–] L.MI.; **Y.**

11603 **Bulletin** of the **Research Institute** of the **S.P.A.** Sumatra Planters' Association. Medan. *Bull. Res. Inst. S.P.A.* [1958–] **Md.**H. [*C. of:* 6163]

Bulletin of the **Research Institute** of the **Sumatra Planters' Association.** *See* 11603.

Bulletin of the **Research Institute** of the **Tea Industry** in the **U.S.S.R.** *See* 55184.

11604 **Bulletin** of the **Research Laboratories** of the **National Cash Register Company.** Perivale. *Bull. Res. Labs natn. Cash Register Co.* L.P. 43.

11605 **Bulletin** of the **Research Laboratory. International X-ray Corporation.** New York. *Bull. Res. Lab. int. X-ray Corp.* [1921–24] L.P.

Bulletin. Research Laboratory, National Canners' Association. *See* 11213.

11606 **Bulletin** of the **Research Laboratory** of the **Portland Cement Association.** Chicago. *Bull. Res. Lab. Portland Cem. Ass.* [1939–]

11607 **Bulletin. Research Office, Government Railways, Japan.** Tokyo. *Bull. Res. Off. Govt Rlys Japan* L.P. 37–40.

11608 **Bulletin** of **Research. Underwriter's Laboratories, Inc. Chicago.** *Bull. Res. Underwrit. Labs* [1937–] L.C. 38– imp.; P.; **Y.**

11609 **Bulletin. Resistance Welder Manufacturers' Association.** Philadelphia. *Bull. Resist. Weld. Mfrs' Ass.* **L.**P. 40– imp.

11610 **Bulletin** des **résultats** acquis pendant les **courses périodiques** p.p. le **Bureau** du **conseil. Conseil permanent international** pour l'**exploration** de la **mer.** Copenhague. *Bull. Résult. Cours périod. Bur. Cons. perm. int. Explor. Mer* [1902–05] **L.**AM.; BM.; BM^N.; MO.; R.; SC.; U.; UC.; Z.; **Abd.**M.; U.; **Bm.**U.; **C.**B.; **Dm.**; E.M.; R.; U.; **G.**U.; **Ld.**U.; **Lo.**; **Lv.**U.; **M.**U.; **O.**R.; **Pl.**M.; **Sa.**; **Wo.** [*C. as:* 12456]
   Bulletin. Réunion internationale des **laboratoires** d'**essais** et de **recherches** sur les **matériaux** et les **constructions.** *See* 11574.

11611 **Bulletin. Réunion** des **laboratoires** d'**essais** et de **recherches** sur les **matériaux** et les **constructions.** Paris. *Bull. Réun. Labs Essais Rech. Matér. Constr.* **L.**P. 53–54; **Wa.**B. 53–54. [*C. as:* 11574]
   Bulletin-revue. *See* 12675, 12676.

11612 **Bulletin** on **Rheumatic Diseases.** New York. *Bull. rheum. Dis.* [1950–] **L.**MD.

11613 **Bulletin. Rhode Island Agricultural Experiment Station.** Kingston. *Bull. Rhode Isl. agric. Exp. Stn* [1888–] **L.**AM.; EB. 01–15; K. 93–08 imp.; P. 89–; **Abs.**N. 00–20 imp.; **Br.**A. 21– imp.; **C.**A.; **Cr.**P. 00–14 imp.; **Ld.**U. 12–14; **O.**F. 49– imp.; **Rt.** imp.; **Y.**

11614 **Bulletin. Rhode Island State Board** of **Agriculture, Entomological Department.** Kingston. *Bull. Rhode Isl. St. Bd Agric. ent. Dep.* **L.**EB. 20.

11615 **Bulletin** of the **Rhode Island State Board** of **Health.** Providence. *Bull. Rhode Isl. St. Bd Hlth*
   Bulletin. Richards Institute. Research Series. *See* 10156.

11615° **Bulletin. River** and **Harbour Research Laboratory** of the **Technical University** of **Norway.** *Bull. Riv. Harb. Res. Lab. tech. Univ. Norw.* **Y.**

11616 **Bulletin. Rivers** and **Lakes Commission, State** of **Illinois.** Urbana. *Bull. Riv. Lakes Commn St. Ill.*

11616° **Bulletin. Road Emulsion Association.** *Bull. Rd Emuls. Ass.* [1949–] **L.**BM.; HQ.

11617 **Bulletin. Road Research Board.** London. *Bull. Rd Res. Bd* [1936–46] **L.**BM.; P.; SC.; **Bm.**P.; **Br.**U. 36; **E.**R.; **Ld.**P.; **N.**P.; **O.**R.

11618 **Bulletin. Rochester Medical Association.** Rochester, N.Y. *Bull. Rochester med. Ass.*

11619 **Bulletin. Roger Williams Park Museum.** Providence, R.I. *Bull. Roger Williams Pk Mus.* **M.**U. 09–.

11620 **Bulletin. Ross Institute Information** and **Advisory Service.** London School of Hygiene and Tropical Medicine. London. *Bull. Ross Inst. Inf. advis. Serv.* **L.**MD. 52– imp. [*See also:* 11621]

11621 **Bulletin. Ross Institute Industrial** and **Advisory Committee.** London. *Bull. Ross Inst. ind. advis. Comm.* [1949–] **L.**TD.; **O.**R.; **Y.** [*See also:* 11620]

11622 **Bulletin** of the **Roswell Park Memorial Institute.** Buffalo, N.Y. *Bull. Roswell Pk meml Inst.* [1956–] **Y.**
   Bulletin of the **Royal Agricultural Society** of **Cairo.** *See* 9261.

11623 **Bulletin** of the **Royal Asiatic Society** of **Bengal.** Calcutta. *Bull. R. asiat. Soc. Beng.* **L.**BM^N. 48.

Bulletin of the **Royal Botanic Gardens, Kew.** *See* 11133.
   Bulletin. Royal Botanic Gardens, Trinidad. *See* 11134.
   Bulletin. Royal Greenwich Observatory. *See* 48168.

11624 **Bulletin. Royal Naval Birdwatching Society.** *Bull. R. nav. Birdwatch. Soc.* **O.**OR. 55–.

11625 **Bulletin** of the **Royal Ontario Museum** of **Zoology.** Toronto. *Bull. R. Ont. Mus. Zool.* **L.**BM^N. 28–; **O.**AP. 28–40 imp.; OR. 28–38.
   Bulletin of the **Royal School** of **Forestry.** Stockholm. *See* 27811.

11626 **Bulletin** of the **Royal Society** of **New Zealand.** Wellington. *Bull. R. Soc. N.Z.* [1934–] **L.**BM.; BM^N. 54–; P. 56–; Z. 54–; **Bl.**U. 55–56; **C.**P.; **Pl.**M. 54–; **Rt.** imp.; **Y.** [*C. of:* 11317]

11627 **Bulletin** of the **Royal Victoria Hospital, Montreal.** *Bull. R. Vict. Hosp. Montreal* **L.**MD. 12.

11628 **Bulletin. Rubber Board, India.** Kottayam. *Bull. Rubb. Bd India* [1956–] **L.**P. [*C. of:* 10521]

11629 **Bulletin** of the **Rubber Growers' Association.** London. *Bull. Rubb. Grow. Ass.* [1919–49] **L.**BM. 20–49; K.; MY. 22–41; P. 23–49; SC.; TP. 19–41; **C.**A. 31–39; **E.**A. 23–49; **Ld.**U. 36–49 imp.; W. 35–49; **M.**P. 38–49; **O.**B. 38; **Sy.**R.

11630 **Bulletin. Rubber Growers' Association. Rubber** and **Agriculture Series.** London. *Bull. Rubb. Grow. Ass. Rubb. Agric. Ser.* [1936–38] **L.**BM.; P.; SC.; **Bm.**P.; **C.**A.; **G.**U.; **Ld.**P.; **Lv.**P.; **M.**P.; **Md.**H.; **O.**F.; **Rt.** [*C. as:* 9628]

11631 **Bulletin** of the **Rubber Research Institute** of **Ceylon.** Dartonfield, Agalawatta. *Bull. Rubb. Res. Inst. Ceylon* [1955–] **L.**BM.; MY.; P.; **C.**A.; **Y.** [*Replaces:* 11633]

11632 **Bulletin. Rubber Research Institute** of **Malaya.** Kuala Lumpur. *Bull. Rubb. Res. Inst. Malaya* [1929–] **L.**K. 39–41 imp.; P. 29–34; SC. 29–34; **C.**A.; **O.**F. 29–34; **Rt.** 29–34.

11633 **Bulletin** of the **Rubber Research Scheme, Ceylon.** Dartonfield, Agalawatta. *Bull. Rubb. Res. Scheme Ceylon* [1921–37] **L.**MY.; P.; SC.; **C.**A. [*C. of:* 9758; *Replaced by:* 11631]

11634 **Bulletin** of the **Russian Translation Service, University** of **Delhi.** Delhi. *Bull. Russ. Transl. Serv. Univ. Delhi* [1950–] **L.**BM. 51–; **G.**U. 51–; **M.**U. 51; **Y.**
   Bulletin SCAR. Special Committee on Antarctic Research. *See* 48721.

11635 **Bulletin S.I.A.** Société suisse des ingénieurs et architectes. Genève. *Bull. S.I.A.* [1952–] **L.**P.; **Y.** [*Published in:* 12371]

11636 **Bulletin. Safety Code Series. Bureau** of **Labor Statistics, United States.** Washington. *Bull. Saf. Code Ser. Bur. Lab. Statist. U.S.* **L.**P. 23–36.

11637 **Bulletin** of the **St. Francis Hospital** and **Sanatorium.** Roslyn, N.Y. *Bull. St Francis Hosp. Sanat., Roslyn* **L.**LI. 55–.

11638 **Bulletin** of **St. Louis College** of **Pharmacy.** St. Louis, Mo. *Bull. St Louis Coll. Pharm.*

11639 **Bulletin** of the **St. Louis Dental Society.** St. Louis, Mo. *Bull. St Louis dent. Soc.*

11640 **Bulletin. St. Louis Health Department.** St. Louis, Mo. *Bull. St Louis Hlth Dep.* [1912–] **L**.TD. 12–15 imp.

11641 **Bulletin** of the **St. Louis Medical Society.** St. Louis, Mo. *Bull. St Louis med. Soc.*

11642 **Bulletin** of the **San Diego County Dental Society.** San Diego. *Bull. S Diego Cty dent. Soc.*

11643 **Bulletin** of the **San Juan** de **Dios Hospital** of **Manila.** *Bull. S Juan de Dios Hosp. Manila* [1927–] **L**.MD. 30–31; TD. 30–37 imp.; **Lv**.U. 30–.

11644 **Bulletin. Sandal Spike Investigation Committee.** Mysore. *Bull. Sandal Spike Invest. Comm.* **L**.P. 33–34; **C**.A. 30–34.

11645 **Bulletin sanitaire.** Bruxelles. *Bull. sanit., Brux.* **W**. 30–.

11646 **Bulletin sanitaire.** Montréal. *Bull. sanit., Montréal*

11647 **Bulletin sanitaire.** Paris. *Bull. sanit., Paris*

11648 **Bulletin sanitaire** de l'**Algérie.** Alger. *Bull. sanit. Algér.* [1906–]

11649 **Bulletin sanitaire** de **Constantinople.** *Bull. sanit. Constantinople* [1922–23] **L**.MD.; TD.; **Lv**.U. [*C. of:* 9211]

11650 **Bulletin** de la **santé publique.** Bruxelles. *Bull. Santé publ., Brux.* [1939–] **L**.BM. 51–; H.; MA.; TD.; **Bm**.U.; **Y**. [*C. of:* 11111]

11651 **Bulletin** of the **Sapporo Branch** of the **Government Forest Experiment Station.** Sapporo. *Bull. Sapporo Brch Govt Forest Exp. Stn* [1953–] **O**.F. imp.; **Rt**. [*C. of:* 10454]

11652 **Bulletin. Saskatchewan University College** of **Agriculture, Extension Department.** *Bull. Sask. Univ. Coll. Agric. Ext. Dep.*

11653 **Bulletin** of the **School** of **Agriculture** and **Forestry, Taihoku Imp. University.** *Bull. Sch. Agric. For. Taihoku imp. Univ.* [1940–] **L**.BM^N. 40; SC.; **C**.A.; **G**.U. 40–41; **Md**.H. 40–41; **O**.F. 40–41; **Rt**. 40–41.

Bulletin. School of **Engineering Research, University** of **Toronto.** *See* 12550.

11654 **Bulletin** of the **School** of **Fishery, Hokkaido Imperial University.** Sapporo. *Bull. Sch. Fish. Hokkaido imp. Univ.* [1927–] **L**.AM. 32–34; **Abd**.M. 27–34 imp.; **Dm**. 27; **Lo**. 32–34; **Lv**.U. 27; **Pl**.M. 32–34.

11655 **Bulletin. School** of **Forestry Agricultural Experiment Station, University** of **Minnesota.** *Bull. Sch. For. agric. Exp. Stn Univ. Minn.* **O**.F. 49–. [*See also:* 11124]

11656 **Bulletin** of the **School** of **Forestry** and **Conservation, University** of **Michigan.** Ann Arbor. *Bull. Sch. For. Conserv. Univ. Mich.* [1932–49] **L**.BM^N.; EB. 33–49; P.; **Bl**.U.; **Bm**.U. imp.; **C**.P. 32–44; **Db**.; **E**.U. 33–39; **Lv**.U. 32–44; **M**.U. 32–44 imp.; **O**.F. 33–49; R.

11657 **Bulletin. School** of **Forestry, Duke University.** Durham, N.C. *Bull. Sch. For. Duke Univ.* [1935–] **O**.F.; **Y**. [*C. of:* 20026]

11658 **Bulletin. School** of **Forestry, Montana State University.** Missoula. *Bull. Sch. For. Montana St. Univ.* [1948–] **O**.F. 49–.

Bulletin. School of **Forestry, University** of **Cambridge.** *See* 55601.

11659 **Bulletin. School** of **Forestry, University** of **Idaho.** Moscow. *Bull. Sch. For. Univ. Idaho* **O**.F. 21–54*. [*C. as:* 9832]

11660 **Bulletin. School** of **Forestry. University** of **Melbourne.** Melbourne. *Bull. Sch. For. Univ. Melb.* [1960–] **O**.F.

11661 **Bulletin. School** of **Forestry. Yale University.** New Haven. *Bull. Sch. For. Yale Univ.* [1912–] **L**.K. 13–.

Bulletin. School of **Medicine** and **Jackson Memorial Hospital, University** of **Miami.** *See* 12523.

Bulletin of the **School** of **Medicine, Maryland University.** *See* 10864.

11662 **Bulletin** of the **School** of **Medicine, Washington University.** Saint-Louis. *Bull. Sch. Med. Wash. Univ.* [1912–27] **L**.MA. 16–18; S. 16–27; UC. 16–17; **Abd**.U. 12–16; **Bm**.U. 16–27; **Br**.U. 23–27; **C**.UL.; **E**.P.; U. 14–16: 22–27; **G**.U. 14–21 imp.; **Ld**.U. 20–27; **Lv**.U. imp.; **O**.R. 15–27; **Sa**. 12–21.

Bulletin. School of **Mines, Alabama State Mine Experiment Station.** *See* 9277.

Bulletin. School of **Mines** and **Geology** and **State Metallurgical Research Laboratory, State College** of **Washington.** *See* 10069.

Bulletin. School of **Mines, Wyoming University.** *See* 12656.

Bulletin. School of **Mining** and **Metallurgy, University** of **Otago.** *See* 12543.

11663 **Bulletin** der **Schweizerischen Akademie** der **medizinischen Wissenschaften.** Basel. *Bull. schweiz. Akad. med. Wiss.* [1944–] **L**.D. 45–; H.; LI.; MA.; MC. imp.; MD.; S.; SH. (1 yr); TD. 44: 54–; UC. 44–52; **Bm**.U.; **E**.U.; **G**.U. imp.; **Ld**.U. 48–61; **O**.R.; **Y**.

Bulletin der **Schweizerischen astronautischen Arbeitsgemeinschaft.** *See* 48354.

11664 **Bulletin** des **Schweizerischen elektrotechnischen Vereins.** Zürich. *Bull. schweiz. elektrotech. Ver.* [1910–] **L**.EE. imp.; P. 23– imp.; SC. 28–; **F**.A. 47–; **G**.T. 25–; **Sh**.SC. 46–; **Te**.N. 50–; **Y**.

11665 **Bulletin** der **Schweizerischen Gesellschaft** für **Anthropologie** und **Ethnologie.** Bern. *Bull. schweiz. Ges. Anthrop. Ethnol.* [1924–] **L**.AN. 31–.

11666 **Bulletin** des **Schweizerischen Gesundheitsamtes.** Bern. *Bull. schweiz. GesundhAmt.* **L**.H. 33–55 imp.; MA. 46–; SC. 24–; SH. 32– imp. [*C. of:* 48544]

11667 **Bulletin** der **Schweizerischen Vereinigung** für **Krebsbekämpfung.** Bern. *Bull. schweiz. Verein. Krebsbekämpf.* **L**.MD. 33–35; SC. 36–.

11667ᶜ **Bulletin. Science Clubs** of **India.** Baroda. *Bull. Sci. Clubs India* **L**.BM. 55–.

11668 **Bulletin** of **Science** and **Engineering Research Laboratory, Waseda University.** Waseda, Tokyo. *Bull. Sci. Engng Res. Lab. Waseda Univ.* [1955–] **L**.P.; **G**.U.; **Ld**.U. 58–; **M**.P.; T.; **O**.R.; **Y**.

Bulletin. Science Technologists Association. *See* 49104ᵃ.

11669 **Bulletin** des **sciences mathématiques.** Paris. *Bull. Sci. math.* [1870–] **L**.BM.; M.; QM. 12–24; R. 70–32; SC.; U. 21–35: 57–; UC.; **Abd**.U. 97–35; **Abs**.N.; U. 95–96: 40–50 imp.; **C**.UL.; **Db**.; **Dn**.U. 29–37 imp.; **E**.R.; **Ex**.U. 48–; **G**.U.; **Lv**.U. 08–31 imp.; **O**.R.; **Sa**. 21–; **Sh**.U. 49–; **Y**.

Bulletin des **sciences mathématiques pures** et **appliquées** de la **Société roumaine** des **sciences.** *See* 10886.

11670 **Bulletin** des **sciences médicales.** Paris. *Bull. Sci. méd.* **E.**R. 24–31.

11671 **Bulletin** des **sciences pharmacologiques.** Paris. *Bull. Sci. pharmac.* [1899–42] **L.**PH.; SC. 32–42; **E.**R.; U.; **Lv.**U. 08–14 imp. [*C. in:* 2886]

11672 **Bulletin** des **sciences physiques** et **naturelles.** Budapest. *Bull. Sci. phys. nat.*

Bulletin. Sciences Series, University of Missouri. *See* 12529.

11673 **Bulletin** of the **Scientific Alliance** of **New York.** New York. *Bull. scient. Alliance N.Y.* [1891–06] [*Replaced by:* 11290]

11674 **Bulletin. Scientific Film Association.** London. *Bull. scient. Film Ass.* [1949–] **E.**A. 49–50.

Bulletin. Scientific and **Industrial Research Department, London.** *See* 10075.

11675 **Bulletin** of the **Scientific Laboratories** of **Denison University.** Granville, Ohio. *Bull. scient. Labs Denison Univ.* [1885–19] **L.**BM.; BM^N.; P.; R. 05–19 imp.; SC. 88–19; Z. 85–05; **C.**P.; **Db.**; **E.**R. imp.; **G.**N. 05–19. [*C. as:* 26866]

11676 **Bulletin** of the **Scientific Research Committee, Jamaica.** Kingston. *Bull. scient. Res. Comm. Jamaica* [1960–] **Ld.**U.

Bulletin of the **Scientific Research Cotton Institution.** Tashkent. *See* 12790.

11677 **Bulletin** of the **Scientific Researches** of the **Alumni Association** of the **Morioka College** of **Agriculture** and **Forestry.** *Bull. scient. Res. Alumni Ass. Morioka Coll. Agric. For.* **C.**A. 37–39.

11678 **Bulletin** of the **Scientific Section** of the **Paint Manufacturers' Association** of the **U.S.** Philadelphia. *Bull. scient. Sect. Paint Mfrs' Ass. U.S.* **L.**P. 08–17* imp.

11679 **Bulletin. Scientific Society** of **San Antonio.** San Antonio, Tex. *Bull. scient. Soc. S Antonio* **L.**BM^N. 22.

11680 **Bulletin. Scientific** and **Technical Documentation Centre, National Research Council** of **Egypt.** Cairo. *Bull. scient. tech. Docum. Cent. Egypt* [1955–57] **L.**BM.; BM^N.; P.; SC.; TD.; **C.**A.; **Rt.** [*C. of:* 28673; *C. as:* 17079: *For Part 2 see:* 404, 405]

11681 **Bulletin scientifique A.I.M.** Liège. *Bull. scient. A.I.M., Liège* [1930–] **L.**EE.; P.; **Y.** [*C. of:* 9466; *Suspended* Mar. 1940–Dec. 1945]

11682 **Bulletin scientifique. Association** des **élèves** et **anciens élèves** de l'**Université** de **Paris.** *Bull. scient. Ass. Élèv. anc. Élèv. Univ. Paris*

11683 **Bulletin scientifique** de l'**Association** des **élèves** des **écoles spéciales** de l'**Université** de **Liège.** *Bull. scient. Ass. Élèv. Éc. spéc. Univ. Liège* **L.**P. 30–40*; SC. 26–40.

11683^c **Bulletin scientifique. Association** des **ingénieurs électriciens** sortis de l'**Institut électrotechnique.** Montefiore. *Bull. scient. Ass. Ingrs Électns Inst. électrotech., Montefiore* **Y.**

11684 **Bulletin scientifique** de **Bourgogne.** Dijon. *Bull. scient. Bourgogne* [1931–] **L.**BM^N.; L.; **E.**R. [*C. of:* 11878]

11685 **Bulletin scientifique** du **Comité** d'**océanographie** et d'**études** des **côtes** du **Maroc.** Casablanca. *Bull. scient. Com. Océanogr. Étud. Côt. Maroc* **Wo.** 54– imp.

11686 **Bulletin scientifique** du **Comité** des **travaux historiques** et **scientifiques.** Paris. *Bull. scient. Com. Trav. hist. scient.* [1956–] **L.**BM.; SC.; **O.**R.

11687 **Bulletin scientifique. Conseil** des **académies** de la **RPF Yougoslavie.** Béograd, etc. *Bull. scient. Cons. Acads RPF Yougosl.* [1953–] **L.**C.; MA.; P.; R.; RI.; TD.; U.; **Bl.**U.; **C.**A.; P.; UL.; **Db.**; **E.**AB.; R.; **G.**U.; **Ld.**U. 56–; **Md.**H.; **Nw.**A.; **R.**D.; **Rt.** 53; **Y.**

11688 **Bulletin scientifique** du **Dioradin** pour le **traitement** de la **tuberculose.** Paris. *Bull. scient. Dioradin Trait. Tuberc.*

11689 **Bulletin scientifique** de l'**École polytechnique.** Timişoara. *Bull. scient. Éc. polytech., Timişoara* [1925–] **L.**UC.; **C.**P.; **Ld.**U.; **Nw.**A. 25–29.

11690 **Bulletin scientifique** et **économique** du **B.M.R.A. Bureau** des **recherches minières** de l'Algérie. Alger. *Bull. scient. écon. B.M.R.A.* [1955–] **L.**MI.; **Y.**

11691 **Bulletin scientifique** de la **France** et de la **Belgique.** Londres, Paris, Berlin. *Bull. scient. Fr. Belg.* [1887–17] **L.**BM^N.; L.; UC.; Z.; **C.**B. 87–04; UL.; **Dn.**U. 88–90; **E.**B. 99–06; C. 88–91 imp.; **Lv.**U.; **M.**U. 91–93: 11–16; **O.**R. 90–16; **Pl.**M. imp. [*C. as:* 9584]

11692 **Bulletin scientifique** des **ingénieurs** sortis de l'**Institut polytechnique** de **Liège.** Liège. *Bull. scient. Ingrs Inst. polytech. Liège*

Bulletin scientifique. Institut d'amélioration des **plantes** à **Salonique.** *See* 18310.

Bulletin scientifique de l'**Institut** de l'**exploration régional** du **Caucase** du **Nord.** *See* 55434.

Bulletin scientifique de l'**Institut polytechnique** d'**Azerbaidjane** d'**Azisbékoff.** *See* 24310.

11693 **Bulletin scientifique** du **Laboratoire microbiologique** de **Vitré.** *Bull. scient. Lab. microbiol. Vitré*

11694 **Bulletin scientifique** de la **Maison Roure-Bertrand fils** de **Grasse.** Evreux. *Bull. scient. Maison Roure-Bertrand*

11695 **Bulletin scientifique. Ministère** des **colonies** de la **France** d'**outre mer. Section technique** d'**agriculture tropicale.** Nogent-sur-Marne. *Bull. scient. Minist. Colon. Fr. outre Mer Sect. tech. Agric. trop.* [1947–] **C.**A.; **Y.**

11696 **Bulletin scientifique roumain.** Paris. *Bull. scient. roum.* [1952–] **L.**MA.; MD. 52–57; P.; **Y.**

Bulletin scientifique. Station d'**amélioration** des **plantes** à **Salonique.** *See* 18310.

Bulletin scientifique de l'**Université** d'**État** de **Kieff.** *See* 34393.

Bulletin scientifique. Beograd. *See* 11687.

11698 **Bulletin. Scripps Institution** for **Biological Research.** University of California. Berkeley, Cal. *Bull. Scripps Instn biol. Res.* [1916–23] **L.**BM^N.; SC.; **Abs.**U.; **Dm.** 18–23; **E.**R. 17–23; **Lv.**U. imp.; **Mi.**; **Pl.**M. [*C. as:* 11699 and 11700]

11699 **Bulletin** of the **Scripps Institution** of **Oceanography. Non-technical series.** La Jolla, Cal. *Bull. Scripps Instn Oceanogr. non-tech. Ser.* [1925–] **L.**BM^N. 25–30; MO. 57–; SC.; **Abs.**U.; **Dm.**; **E.**R.; **Mi.**; **Pl.**M.; **Wo.** 57–; **Y.** [*C. from:* 11698]

11700 **Bulletin. Scripps Institution** of **Oceanography. Technical Series.** La Jolla, Cal. *Bull. Scripps Instn Oceanogr. tech. Ser.* [1927–] **L.**AM.; BM 31–; BM^N. imp.; L. 27–36 imp.; MO. 57–; P. 27–28; SC.; **Abd.**M.; **Abs.**U.; **Bl.**U. imp.; **Bn.**U. 51–; **C.**B.; P.; **Dm.** 27–45; **E.**R.; V. 41– imp.; **Lo.**; **Lv.**U.; **Mi.**; **Pl.**M.; **Sa.** 51–; **Wo.** imp.; **Y.** [*C. from:* 11698]

11701 **Bulletin. Sea Fisheries Research Station, Israel.** Caesarea, Haifa. *Bull. Sea Fish. Res. Stn Israel* [1951–] **L.**BM^N.; **Bn.**U.; **C.**B. 58–; **Dm.**; **Lo.**; **Pl.**M.; **Wo.** 53–.

11702 **Bulletin** of **Sea View Hospital.** Staten Island. New York. *Bull. Sea View Hosp.* [1954–60] **L.**H.; MA.; MD.; **Br.**U. [*C. of:* 41493]

11703 **Bulletin. Seafood Processing Laboratory, University** of Maryland. Crisfield. *Bull. Seafd Process. Lab. Univ. Maryland* [1957–] **L.**P.

11704 **Bulletin des séances. Académie r.** des **sciences coloniales** (d'outre mer). Bruxelles. *Bull. Séanc. Acad. r. Sci. colon. (outre Mer)* [1954–] **L.**AN.; BM^N.; GM.; K.; TD.; TP.; **Bl.**U.; **Db.**; **Y.** [*C. of:* 11705]

11705 **Bulletin** des **séances. Institut r. colonial belge.** Bruxelles. *Bull. Séanc. Inst. r. colon. belge* [1930–54] **L.**AN. 47–54; BM.; BM^N. 37–54; GM.; K. 45–54; SC.; TD. 45–54; TP. 44–54; **Bl.**U. imp.; **Db.** 49–54. [*C. as:* 11704]

11706 **Bulletin** des **séances** de la **Société française** de **physique.** Paris. *Bull. Séanc. Soc. fr. Phys.* [1902–10] **L.**EE.; P.; R.; SC.; **Bn.**U. 02–06 imp.; **C.**P. 05–10; **E.**R.; **G.**U. 08–10; **M.**U. 05–10. [*C. of:* 49341; *Replaced by:* 39871]

11707 **Bulletin** des **séances** de la **Société nationale d'agriculture** de **France.** Paris. *Bull. Séanc. Soc. natn. Agric. Fr.* [1877–15] **L.**AM.; BM. 06–15; P. 81–15; **C.**A. 06–15; **Db.** 07–15; **E.**R. 80–15 imp.; **Rt.** 79–15. [*C. as:* 15206]

11708 **Bulletin** des **séances** de la **Société r. malacologique** de **Belgique.** *Bull. Séanc. Soc. r. malac. Belg.* [1863–03] **L.**BM. 65–02; BM^N.; L.; R.; Z.; **Bl.**U. 78–02 imp.; **Db.** 00–03; **E.**C.; **G.**N. 75–02; **Lv.**U. 80–02; **M.**U. imp. [*Contained in:* 2962]

11709 **Bulletin** des **séances** de la **Société r.** des **sciences médicales** et **naturelles** de **Bruxelles.** *Bull. Séanc. Soc. r. Sci. méd. nat. Brux.* [1840–10] **L.**MC. 00–10; S. 96–10; **C.**P. 00–10; **Lv.**U. 97–10. [*C. in:* 2963]

11710 **Bulletin** des **séances** de la **Société** des **sciences** de **Nancy** et de la **Réunion biologique** de **Nancy.** Paris. *Bull. Séanc. Soc. Sci. Nancy* [1868–29: 36–60] **L.**BM. 74–29; BM^N.; MY. 83–14 imp.; R. 73–10; Z. 47–60; **Lv.**U. 89–29 imp. [*Replaced by:* 30852, 1930–35; *C. as:* 12043^c]

11711 **Bulletin Sécheron.** Genève. *Bull. Sécheron* **L.**P. 44–; **Bm.**U. 44–; **Y.**

11712 **Bulletin** of the **Second Agronomy Division, Tokai-Kinki National Agricultural Experiment Station.** Tsu-City. *Bull. second Agron. Div. Tokai-Kinki natn. agric. Exp. Stn* [1959–] **L.**AM.; MY.; **C.**A.; **Rt.**; **Y.**

11713 **Bulletin** of the **Second District Dental Society** of the **State** of **New York.** Brooklyn. *Bull. second Dist. dent. Soc. St. N.Y.* [1915–37] [*C. as:* 26881]

11714 **Bulletin** de la **Section** d'**agriculture coloniale. Société française** de **colonisation** et d'**agriculture coloniale.** Paris. *Bull. Sect. Agric. colon. Soc. fr. Colon.*

Bulletin de la **Section entomologique** du **Musée national** de **Prague.** *See* 48611.

Bulletin. Section de **géodésie, Union géodesique** et **géophysique internationale.** *See* 10322.

11715 **Bulletin** de la **Section** de **géographie** du **Comité** des **travaux historiques** et **scientifiques.** Paris. *Bull. Sect. Géogr. Com. Trav. hist. scient.* [1913–] **L.**BM. 13–21; G.; **O.**B.; G. 32–43; **Y.** [*C. of:* 10331]

Bulletin. Section d'**hydrologie scientifique, Union géodesique** et **géophysique internationale.** *See* 12492.

Bulletin. Section de **magnétisme terrestre, Union géodesique** et **géophysique internationale.** *See* 12492.

Bulletin. Section d'**océanographie, Union géodesique** et **géophysique internationale.** *See* 12492.

11716 **Bulletin** de la **Section scientifique** de l'**Académie roumaine.** Bucarest. *Bull. Sect. scient. Acad. roum.* [1912–46] **L.**BM.; BM^N.; C.; GL. 12–31; GM.; MO. 12–39 imp.; P. 12–31; R. 12–31: 40–45; SC. 24–46; U.; UC. 12–33 imp.; **Bm.**U. 12–16 imp.; **Br.**U. imp.; **C.**P.; UL.; **Db.**; **E.**C. 16–39 imp.; D. 12–32: 40–45; R.; **G.**U. 12–30: 40–46; **M.**U. 12–32: 39–40; **O.**R. 12–45. [*Replaced by:* 9093]

Bulletin. Section technique d'**agriculture tropicale, Direction** de l'**agriculture,** de l'**élevage** et des **forêts.** Série technologique. *See* 11740.

Bulletin. Section technique d'**agriculture tropicale, Ministère** des **colonies** de la **France** d'**outre mer.** *See* 11695.

11717 **Bulletin** de la **Section vosgienne. Club alpin français.** Nancy. *Bull. Sect. vosg. Club alp. fr.*

Bulletin. Seed Branch, Department of **Agriculture, Canada.** *See* 9965.

11718 **Bulletin** of the **Seikai Region Fisheries Research Laboratory.** Nagasaki. *Bull. Seikai Reg. Fish. Res. Lab.* [1954–] **Lo.**; **Pl.**M. 57–.

Bulletin séismique. *See* **Bulletin sismique.**

11719 **Bulletin. Seismographic Station, Florissant.** *Bull. seismogr. Stn Florissant* **L.**SC. 35–.

11720 **Bulletin. Seismographic Station, St. Louis University.** St. Louis, Mo. *Bull. seismogr. Stn St Louis Univ.* **L.**SC. 35–.

Bulletin of the **Seismographic Stations, University** of **California.** *See* 55583.

11721 **Bulletin** of the **Seismological Committee** of the **British Association.** London. *Bull. seism. Comm. Br. Ass.* [1918–20] **L.**AS.; BM.; MO.; **Abs.**N.; **C.**UL.; **E.**O.; **Ld.**U.; **O.**O.; R. [*C. of:* 33488; *C. as:* 23943]

11722 **Bulletin** of the **Seismological Observations. Central Meteorological Observatory.** Tokyo. *Bull. seism. Obsns cent. met. Obs., Tokyo* [*C. of:* 49386]

11723 **Bulletin. Seismological Observatory, John Carroll University.** Cleveland, Ohio. *Bull. seism. Obs. John Carroll Univ.* **Y.**

11724 **Bulletin. Seismological Observatory.** Little Rock, Arkansas. *Bull. seism. Obs., Little Rock*

11725 **Bulletin. Seismological Observatory, Rathfarnham Castle.** Rathfarnham. *Bull. seism. Obs. Rathfarnham* [1950–] **Db.**; **Y.**

Bulletin of the **Seismological Observatory, St. Ignatius College.** Cleveland, Ohio. *See* 11723.

11725^c **Bulletin. Seismological Observatory, Wellington.** *Bull. seism. Obs., Wellington* **Y.** [*Several series*]

11726 **Bulletin. Seismological Observatory. Weston College.** Weston, Mass. *Bull. seism. Obs. Weston Coll.* [1937–] **L.**MO. 38–39; SC.

11727 **Bulletin** of the **Seismological Society** of **America.** Stanford, Cal. *Bull. seism. Soc. Am.* [1911–] **L.**AS. 37–; BM.; G.; P. 59–; SC.; **Abd.**U. 14–26 imp: 49–; **C.**GD. 56–; P. 26–; UL. 27–; **Ld.**U.; **Lv.**U. 53–; **O.**O.; **Wo.** 55–; **Y.**

11728 **Bulletin** of the **Seismological Station, Harvard.** Cambridge, Mass. *Bull. seism. Stn Harvard* **E.**R. 47–50.

11729 **Bulletin** of the **Seismological Station, Ivigtut.** Copenhagen. *Bull. seism. Stn Ivigtut* **C.**PO. 29–30; **Y.**

11730 **Bulletin** of the **Seismological Station Nord.** Copenhagen. *Bull. seism. Stn Nord* [1957–] **L.**BM.; **Y.**

11731 **Bulletin** of the **Seismological Station, Scoresby-Sund.** *Bull. seism. Stn Scoresby-Sund* [1928–] **C.**PO. 28; **Y.**

11732 **Bulletin semestriel** des **huiles essentielles, parfums synthétiques,** etc. Schimmel et Cie. Leipzig. *Bull. semest. Huil. essent.* [*For English edition see* 49503]

11733 **Bulletin semestriel** de l'**Observatoire météorologique** du **Séminaire Collège Saint-Martial.** Port-au-Prince. Haïti. *Bull. semest. Obs. mét. Coll. St-Martial* [1905–16] **L.**MO. 10–16. [*C. as:* 9387]

11734 **Bulletin semestriel** de l'**Office national anti-acridien.** Alger. *Bull. semest. Off. natn. anti-acrid.* [1945–46] **L.**EB.; SC.; Z.; **Rt.** [*C. as:* 11381]

11735 **Bulletin** of the **Semet-Solvay** and **Piette Coke Oven Co., Ltd.** Sheffield. *Bull. Semet-Solvay* **L.**P. 24–28; **B.**MC. 22–28.

11736 **Bulletin séricicole français.** Paris. *Bull. séric. fr.*

11737 **Bulletin** of the **Sericultural Experiment Station, Government General** of **Chosen.** Suigen. *Bull. seric. Exp. Stn Chosen* **L.**EB. 26; LI. 26; **Rt.** 26.

11738 **Bulletin** of the **Sericultural Experiment Station, Japan.** Tokyo. *Bull. seric. Exp. Stn Japan* **L.**EB. 16–27; **Rt.** 16– imp.; **Y.**

11739 **Bulletin** of **Sericulture** and **Silk Industry.** Uyeda. *Bull. Seric. Silk Ind.* **L.**BM^N. 37–41; C. 30–41; LI. 20–37.

11740 **Bulletin. Série technologique. Direction** de l'**agriculture,** de l'**élevage** et des **forêts. Section technique** d'**agriculture tropicale.** Nogent-sur-Marne. *Bull. Sér. technol. Dir. Agric. Élev. Forêts Sect. tech. Agric. trop.*

11741 **Bulletin Series. British Railways. Performance** and **Efficiency Tests.** London. *Bull. Ser. Br. Rlys Perform. Effic. Tests* **Ld.**P. 51– imp.

11741° **Bulletin Series. Florida Engineering** and **Industrial Experiment Station.** *Bull. Ser. Fla Engng ind. Exp. Stn* **Y.**

Bulletin Series. Oregon State Agricultural College Engineering Experiment Station. *See* 11742.

11742 **Bulletin Series. Oregon State College Engineering Experiment Station.** Corvallis. *Bull. Ser. Ore. St. Coll. Engng Exp. Stn* [1929–39] **L.**P.; **O.**F. imp.; **Y.** [*C. as:* 10164]

11743 **Bulletin Series. South African Ornithologists' Union.** Pretoria. *Bull. Ser. S. Afr. Orn. Un.* [1908–14] **L.**BM. 14; BM^N.; Z.; **Abs.**N. 14.

11744 **Bulletin Series. University** of **Illinois Engineering Experiment Station.** Urbana. *Bull. Ser. Univ. Ill. Engng Exp. Stn* [1939–] **L.**BM. imp.; I. imp.; NF. imp.; P.; U. imp.; UC.; **Bm.**P.; **Br.**U.; **C.**ENG.; UL. 39–52; **Db.**; **E.**R. imp.; U.; **G.**E.; **Ld.**P.; U.; **Lv.**U.; **M.**P. imp.; T.; U. imp.; **Nw.**A. 39–43; P.; **O.**R.; **Sh.**IO.; M. 39–51; **Y.** [*C. of:* 10496]

11745 **Bulletin Series. Welding Research Council.** New York. *Bull. Ser. Weld. Res. Coun.* [1949–53] **L.**AV. imp.; P.; SC.; **Br.**U.

11746 **Bulletin. Serological Museum.** New Brunswick. *Bull. serol. Mus., New Brunsw.* [1948–] **L.**BM^N.; **Y.**

11747 **Bulletin** du **sérum antituberculeux** du **Dr. Aiguillère.** Willemur. *Bull. Sérum antituberc. Dr Aiguillère*

11748 **Bulletin. Service** de l'**agriculture** de **Tunisie.** Tunis. *Bull. Serv. Agric. Tunis* [1935–] **C.**A. 35–39. [*C. of:* 10085]

11749 **Bulletin** du **Service** de l'**arboriculture** de la **province** de **Québec.** Québec. *Bull. Serv. Arboric. Prov. Québ.* **L.**BM. 16–.

11750 **Bulletin** du **Service** de **biogéographie, Université** de **Montréal.** *Bull. Serv. Biogéogr. Univ. Montréal* [1945–] **L.**BM^N.; NC. 48–; **O.**F. imp.

11751 **Bulletin** du **Service botanique** et **agronomique** de **Tunisie.** Tunis. *Bull. Serv. bot. agron. Tunis* [1945–51] **L.**AM. 47–51; BM^N. 46–51 imp.; **C.**A. 47–51; **Ld.**U. 46–51; **Rt.** [*C. as:* 42125]

11752 **Bulletin** du **Service** de la **carte géologique** de l'**Algérie.** Alger. *Bull. Serv. Carte géol. Algér.* [1902–51] **L.**BM^N.; GL.; GM. 02–33 imp.; MI. 32: 37: 38; **Br.**U. 50–51; **Y.** [*C. of:* Ser. 2 of 29642]

11753 **Bulletin** du **Service** de la **carte géologique** de l'**Algérie. Travaux récents** des **collaborateurs.** *Bull. Serv. Carte géol. Algér. Trav. réc.* [1924–52] **L.**BM^N. 24; SC. [*C. as:* 12424]

11754 **Bulletin** du **Service** de la **carte géologique** d'**Alsace** et de **Lorraine.** Strasbourg. *Bull. Serv. Carte géol. Als. Lorr.* [1920–] **L.**BM.; BM^N.; GL.; GM.; **C.**UL.; **E.**D. 28–; **Y.** [*C. of:* 32453]

Bulletin. Service de la **carte géologique** de la **France.** See 11778.

11755 **Bulletin** du **Service** de la **carte phytogéographique.** Paris. *Bull. Serv. Carte phytogéogr.* [1956–] Sér. A. Carte de la végétation. **L.**BM^N.; **Y.** Sér. B. Carte des groupements végétaux. **L.**K.; NC.; **C.**BO.; **Hu.**G.; **Y.**

11756 **Bulletin. Service** des **eaux** et **forêts** en **Algérie.** Alger. *Bull. Serv. Eaux Forêts Algér.* **O.**F. 12–38.

Bulletin. Service des **eaux** et **forêts, chasse** et **pêche, Congo belge.** See 9923.

11757 **Bulletin. Service** d'**électricité, Institut** de **physique, Université libre** de **Bruxelles.** Bruxelles. *Bull. Serv. Élect. Inst. phys. Univ. Brux.* [1958–] **L.**P.; **Y.**

11758 **Bulletin** du **Service** d'**entomologie.** Québec. *Bull. Serv. Ent., Québ.* [1937–40] **L.**EB.; **O.**F.

Bulletin du **Service fédéral** de l'**hygiène publique.** Berne. See 11666.

11759 **Bulletin. Service forestier, Québec.** Québec. *Bull. Serv. for. Québ.* **Bn.**U. 48–; **Y.**

11760 **Bulletin** du **Service géologique** du **Congo belge**
et du **Ruanda-Urundi.** Léopoldville. *Bull. Serv. géol.*
Congo belge [1945–] **L.**BM.; BM^N.; GL.; MI. 46–; **C.**S.; **E.**D.
imp.; **Lv.**U.

11761 **Bulletin** du **Service géologique** de l'**Indo-Chine.**
Hanoï-Haïphong. *Bull. Serv. géol. Indochine* [1913–]
L.BM^N. 13–50; G.; GL. 13–52; GM.; **C.**S. 13–38 imp.
Bulletin du **Service géologique** de la **Pologne.**
See 7190.
Bulletin du **Service géologique** du **Royaume** de
Yougoslavie. *See* 56410.

11762 **Bulletin** du **Service hydrologique** et **météoro-**
logique de **Pologne.** Varsovie. *Bull. Serv. hydrol.*
mét. Pol. **L.**MO. 47–; **Fr.** 51; **Lv.**U.   [*C. of:* 57522]

11763 **Bulletin. Service** des **instruments** de **mesure.**
Bull. Serv. Instrum. Mesure [1958–] **L.**P.   [*Supplement*
to: 47447]

11764 **Bulletin** du **Service médical** du **travail.** Gand.
Bull. Serv. méd. Trav. **L.**TD. 26–30*.

11765 **Bulletin** du **Service météorologique** de l'**A.O.F.**
Dakar. *Bull. Serv. mét. A.O.F.* [1931–] **L.**MO. 31–36;
SC. 36–.   [*C. of:* 46124]

11766 **Bulletin** du **Service météorologique algérien.**
Alger. *Bull. Serv. mét. algér.*

11767 **Bulletin** du **Service météorologique** en **Syrie**
et au **Liban.** Beyrouth. *Bull. Serv. mét. Syrie Liban*
Bulletin. Service des **mines** du **Cameroun.** *See*
11770.

11768 **Bulletin** du **Service** des **mines. Gouvernement**
général de l'**A.E.F.** Le Caire. *Bull. Serv. Mines*
A.E.F. [1943–48] **L.**BM^N. 47–48; GL.; MI.; SC.; **G.**U. 48.
[*C. as:* 10087]

11769 **Bulletin** du **Service** des **mines. Gouvernement**
général de l'**A.O.F.** Dakar. *Bull. Serv. Mines A.O.F.*
[1938–42] **L.**BM^N.; GL.; MI.; SC.   [*C. as:* 10088]

11770 **Bulletin** du **Service** des **mines, Territoire** du
Cameroun. Paris. *Bull. Serv. Mines Terr. Cameroun*
[1953–] **L.**BM^N.; MI.; **Y.**   [*C. of:* 10089]

11771 **Bulletin Service. National Association** of
Dyers and **Cleaners.** Silver Spring. *Bull. Serv.*
natn. Ass. Dyers Clean. [1933–45] **L.**P. 35–45 imp.   [*C.*
as: 11771^c]

11771^c **Bulletin Service. National Institute** of **Dry-**
cleaning. Silver Spring. *Bull. Serv. natn. Inst. Dry-*
clean. **Y.**   [*Issued in several series; C. of:* 11771]

11772 **Bulletin. Service national** de la **production**
agricole, Haïti. Port-au-Prince. *Bull. Serv. natn.*
Prod. agric. Haïti **C.**A. 34– imp.

11773 **Bulletin** du **Service** de la **police sanitaire** des
animaux domestiques. Bruxelles. *Bull. Serv. Police*
sanit. Anim. dom.

11774 **Bulletin** du **Service** de **santé** et de l'**hygiène.**
Bruxelles. *Bull. Serv. Santé Hyg., Brux.* [1893–07]
L.H.; **Lv.**U. 04–06.   [*C. as:* 9212]

11775 **Bulletin** du **Service** de **santé militaire.** Paris.
Bull. Serv. Santé milit.
Bulletin du **Service suisse** de l'**hygiène publique.**
See 11666.

11776 **Bulletin** du **Service** de **surveillance** de la **fabri-**
cation et du **commerce** de **denrées alimentaires.**
Bruxelles. *Bull. Serv. Surveill. Fabr. Commerce Denr.*
aliment., Brux.

11777 **Bulletin** du **Service technique** de l'**aéronauti-**
que. Bruxelles. *Bull. Serv. tech. Aéronaut., Brux.*
[1924–] **L.**AV. 27–53 imp.; P. 24–53; SC. 26–53.   [*C. of:*
10768]

11778 **Bulletin** des **Services** de la **carte géologique** de
la **France** et des **topographies souterraines.** Paris.
Bull. Servs Carte géol. Fr. [1889–] **L.**BM.; BM^N.; GL. 33–;
GM.; SC. 21–; **Abd.**U. 45–; **E.**D.; **G.**U. 19–; **Y.**

11779 **Bulletin** des **Services** de l'**élevage** et des **indus-**
tries animales de l'**A.O.F.** Dakar. *Bull. Servs Élev.*
Ind. anim. A.O.F. [1948–52] **L.**SC.; V.; **C.**V.; **E.**AB.; **W.**
[*C. of:* 11781]

11780 **Bulletin** des **Services techniques. Service** des
recherches de l'**aéronautique, Ministère** de l'**air.**
Paris. *Bull. Servs tech. Serv. Rech. aéronaut.* [1937–]
L.AV. imp.; P.; SC.; **Y.**   [*C. of:* 12364]

11781 **Bulletin** des **Services zootechniques** et des **épi-**
zooties de l'**Afrique occidental française.** Dakar.
Bull. Servs zootech. Épizoot. Afr. occid. fr. [1938–43]
L.V.; **E.**AB.; **W.**   [*C. as:* 11779]

11782 **Bulletin** of the **Seto Marine Biological Labora-**
tory. Sirohama. *Bull. Seto mar. biol. Lab.*

11783 **Bulletin. Severn Wildfowl Trust.** Slimbridge,
Gloucester. *Bull. Severn Wildfowl Trust* [1950–54]
L.BM^N.; Z.; **O.**OR.   [*C. as:* 12630]

11784 **Bulletin** of the **Shanghai Science Institute.**
Shanghai. *Bull. Shanghai Sci. Inst.* [1929–] **L.**BM^N.
29–37; **Pl.**M. 29–31 imp.; **Sh.**M. 29–35.

11785 **Bulletin** of the **Shikoku Agricultural Experi-**
ment Station. Zentsuji. *Bull. Shikoku agric. Exp.*
Stn [1954–] **C.**A. imp.

11786 **Bulletin** of the **Shimane University.** Matsue.
Bull. Shimane Univ.
Natural science [1951–] **Y.**

11787 **Bulletin** of the **Shizuoka Agricultural College.**
Iwata. *Bull. Shizuoka agric. Coll.* [1949–50] **C.**A.   [*C.*
as: 43654]

11788 **Bulletin. Sierra Leone Lands** and **Forests De-**
partment. Freetown. *Bull. Sierra Leone Lds Forests*
Dep.

11789 **Bulletin signalétique. Centre national** de la
recherche scientifique. Paris. *Bull. signal. Cent. natn.*
Rech. scient. [1956–]
Issued as: Partie I, Sections: Astronomie, chimie,
mathématiques, physique, etc.; Partie II, Sections:
Agriculture, sciences biologiques, etc. Partie III,
Sections: Philosophie, sciences humaines, etc. *The*
holdings by libraries of particular sections is not
specified; some libraries hold only one or two sections of a
Partie **L.**AV. (Pt. I): (Pt. 4) 61–; B.; BM.; BM^N.; MY.
(Pt. II); P. (Pt. I, II); R. (Pt. II); SC.; U.; Z.; **Bl.**U.
(Pt. I) 59–; **C.**MI. (Pt.I); P.; **Ld.**U.; **Lv.**P.; **M.**C.
(Pt. IV); **N.**U.; **Nw.**A.; **Sh.**U. (Pt. III); **Wo.**; **Y.**
[*C. of:* 9365; *from* 1961 *sections subdivided*]

11790 **Bulletin signalétique** d'**entomologie médicale**
et **vétérinaire.** Paris. *Bull. signal. Ent. méd. vét.*
[1954–] **L.**BM^N.; TD.; **Db.** 61–; **Rt.**; **Y.**

11791 **Bulletin signalétique. Service** de **documen-**
tation et d'**information technique** de l'**aéronautique.**
Bull. signal. Serv. Docum. Inf. tech. Aéronaut. [1960–]
L.AV.   [*C. of:* 11002]

11792 **Bulletin signalétique** des **télécommunications.** Paris. *Bull. signal. Télécommun.* [1958-] **L.**AV. 59-; P.; SC. 61-; **Y.** [*Supplement to* and *before 1958 published in* 2982]

11793 **Bulletin. Silk Association.** London. *Bull. Silk Ass.* **L.**BM. 20-.

11794 **Bulletin. Silk** and **Rayon Users' Association.** London. *Bull. Silk Rayon Us. Ass.* **M.**C. (2 yr.).

11795 **Bulletin** of **Silk Technical College.** Uyeda. *Bull. Silk tech. Coll., Uyeda*

11796 **Bulletin** de la **Silva mediterranea.** Firenze. *Bull. Silva mediterr.* **O.**F. 25-35.

Bulletin sismique. Irkoutsk. *See* 18905.

11797 **Bulletin sismique.** Parc Saint-Maur. *Bull. sism., Parc St-Maur* [1921-] [*C. of:* 35647]

11798 **Bulletin sismique.** Prague. *Bull. sism., Prague*
Bulletin sismique. Zagreb. *See* 24568.

11799 **Bulletin sismique mensuel. Institut séismologique** de **Béograd.** Béograd. *Bull. sism. mens. Inst. séism. Béogr.* **L.**BM. 54-; **Y.**

11800 **Bulletin sismique** de l'**Observatoire national.** Athènes. *Bull. sism. Obs. natn., Athènes*

11801 **Bulletin sismique** de l'**Observatoire r.** de **Belgique.** Bruxelles. *Bull. sism. Obs. r. Belg.* **L.**UC. 15- imp.; **E.**R. 14-41.

11802 **Bulletin sismique** de l'**Observatoire** de l'**Université** d'**Aix-Marseille.** *Bull. sism. Obs. Univ. Aix-Marseille*

11803 **Bulletin sismique** de l'**Observatoire** de **Zi-Ka-Wei.** Chang-Haï. *Bull. sism. Obs. Zi-Ka-Wei*

11804 **Bulletin sismique** du **Service sismologique** de la **Serbie.** Belgrade. *Bull. sism. Serv. sismol. Serb.* [*C. of:* 35632]

11805 **Bulletin sismique** de la **Station internationale** de **Reykjavik.** *Bull. sism. Stn int. Reykjavik*

11806 **Bulletin sismique** de la **Station sismologique** de **Stará Dala.** Stará Dala. *Bull. sism. Stn sismol. Stará Dala* [1937-]

11807 **Bulletin sismique** des **Stations sismologiques** de **Praha** et de **Cheb.** Praha. *Bull. sism. Stns sismol. Praha Cheb*

11808 **Bulletin sismographique** de l'**Institut météorologique centrale** de **Bulgarie.** Sofia. *Bull. sismogr. Inst. mét. cent. Bulg.* [1905-11] **L.**SC.; **E.**E. 10-11.

11809 **Bulletin sismologique.** Bucarest. *Bull. sismol., Buc.*

Bulletin sismologique de l'**Observatoire** de **Zi-Ka-Wei.** *See* 11803.

11810 **Bulletin. Sleeping Sickness Bureau.** London. *Bull. Sleep. Sickn. Bur.* [1908-12] **I.**.BM.; BM^N.; EB.; H.; L.; MA.; MD.; R.; S.; TD.; Z.; **Br.**U.; **C.**B.; PA.; **C.**P.; **Db.**, E.A.; P.; U.; **G.**M.; U.; **Lv.**P.; U.; **M.**MS.; **O.**R.; **W.** 09-12. [*C. in:* 54400]

11811 **Bulletin** of the **Sloane Hospital** for **Women** in the **Columbia-Presbyterian Medical Center.** New York. *Bull. Sloane Hosp. Women* [1955-] **L.**MA.; MD.; S.; **Bl.**U. imp.

Bulletin. Smithsonian Institution, United States National Museum. *See* 12512.

11812 **Bulletin** de la **Société académique** d'**agriculture belles-lettres, sciences** et **arts** de **Poitiers.** *Bull. Soc. acad. Agric. Belles-Lett. Sci. Poitiers*

11813 **Bulletin** de la **Société académique** d'**archéologie, sciences** et **arts** du **département** de l'**Oise.** Beauvais. *Bull. Soc. acad. Archéol. Sci. Arts Dép. Oise*

11814 **Bulletin** de la **Société académique** de l'**arrondissement** de **Boulogne-sur-Mer.** *Bull. Soc. acad. Arrond. Boulogne* **L.**BM. 73-12.

11815 **Bulletin** de la **Société académique** de **Brest.** *Bull. Soc. acad. Brest* [1861-] **L.**BM. 61-12.

11816 **Bulletin** de la **Société académique** du **Centre.** Châteauroux. *Bull. Soc. acad. Cent.*

11817 **Bulletin** de la **Société académique** de **Laon.** Laon. *Bull. Soc. acad. Laon* [1852-13] **L.**BM. 65-13; **C.**UL. 1852-72; **O.**B.

11818 **Bulletin** de la **Société** d'**acclimatation** du **golfe** de **Gascogne.** Biarritz. *Bull. Soc. Acclim. Golfe Gascogne*

11819 **Bulletin** de la **Société agricole, scientifique** et **littéraire** des **Pyrénées-orientales.** Perpignan. *Bull. Soc. agric. scient. litt. Pyrén.-orient.* **L.**BM^N. 1835-12.

11820 **Bulletin** de la **Société** des **agriculteurs** d'**Algérie.** Alger. *Bull. Soc. Agricrs Algér.* **Y.** [*C. of:* 11822]

11821 **Bulletin** de la **Société** des **agriculteurs** de **France.** Paris. *Bull. Soc. Agricrs Fr.* [1869-27] **L.**A. 85-27 imp.; AM. 85-27; EB. 13-27; **Db.** 07-27; **Rt.** 77-01. [*C. as:* 12487 and 47057]

11822 **Bulletin** de la **Société** d'**agriculture** d'**Alger.** *Bull. Soc. Agric. Alger* **Y.** [*C. as:* 11820]

11823 **Bulletin** de la **Société** d'**agriculture** de **Brignoles.** Carcès. *Bull. Soc. Agric. Brignoles* **Rt.** 21-33 imp.

11823^c **Bulletin** de la **Société** d'**agriculture, sciences** et **arts** de la **Sarthe.** Le Mans. *Bull. Soc. Agric. Sci. Arts Sarthe* **L.**BM. 1850- imp.

11824 **Bulletin** de la **Société alsacienne** de **constructions mécaniques.** Mulhouse. *Bull. Soc. als. Constr. méc.* **L.**P. 23-; **Y.** [*Suspended* May 1939-June 1951]

11825 **Bulletin** de la **Société amicale** des **pharmaciens** de l'**Étoile.** Paris. *Bull. Soc. amic. Pharmns Étoile*

11826 **Bulletin** de la **Société** des **amis** et **anciens élèves** de l'**École nationale** des **eaux** et **forêts.** Nancy. *Bull. Soc. Amis anc. Élèv. Éc. natn. Eaux Forêts* [1927-34] **O.**F. [*C. in:* 47147]

11827 **Bulletin** de la **Société** des **amis** de l'**Institut océanographique** du **Havre.** *Bull. Soc. Amis Inst. océanogr. Havre* [1934-37] **Abd.**M. imp.; **Lo.**; **Lv.**U.

11828 **Bulletin** de la **Société** des **amis** du **Musée** d'**ethnographie.** Paris. *Bull. Soc. Amis Mus. Ethnogr.*

11829 **Bulletin** de la **Société** des **amis** des **sciences** et **arts** de **Rochechouart.** *Bull. Soc. Amis Sci. Arts Rochechouart* **Db.** 93-.

11830 **Bulletin. Société** des **amis** des **sciences** et des **lettres** de **Poznań.** *Bull. Soc. Amis Sci. Lett. Poznań*
Sér. B. Sciences mathématiques et naturelles [1925-] **L.**BM.; BM^N. 25-60; MD.; **Db.**; **E.**R. 25-32; **Lv.**U.; **Y.**
Sér. C. Médecine [1949-] **L.**MD.; **Db.**; **Y.**
Sér. D. Sciences biologiques [1960-] **L.**BM^N.; **Db.**; **Y.**

11831 **Bulletin** de la **Société** des **amis** des **sciences naturelles** et du **Muséum** de **Rouen.** *Bull. Soc. Amis Sci. nat. Mus. Rouen* [1936-] **L.**BM^N. 36-49; Z. 41-52 imp. [*C. of:* 11832]

11832 **Bulletin** de la **Société** des **amis** des **sciences naturelles** de **Rouen**. *Bull. Soc. Amis Sci. nat. Rouen* [1865–35] **L.**BM. 68–15; BM^N.; SC. 30–35.   [*C. as:* 11831]

11833 **Bulletin** de la **Société** des **amis** des **sciences naturelles** de **Vienne**. Miribel-les-Échelles. *Bull. Soc. Amis Sci. nat. Vienne*

11834 **Bulletin** de la **Société** des **amis** de l'**Université** de **Lyon**. *Bull. Soc. Amis Univ. Lyon* [1887–14] **Abd.**U.; 93–03; **C.**UL.; **Db**. 88–06; **E.**U. 88–93; **G.**U. 95–06; **O.**B. 89–06.

11835 **Bulletin** de la **Société** d'**anatomie** et de **physiologie normales** et **pathologiques** de **Bordeaux**. *Bull. Soc. Anat. Physiol. norm. path. Bordeaux* [1880–10] **L.**S. 90–98; GH. 90–10.   [*C. as:* 11837]

11836 **Bulletin** de la **Société anatomique** de **Nantes**. *Bull. Soc. anat. Nantes*

11837 **Bulletin** de la **Société anatomo-clinique** de **Bordeaux**. *Bull. Soc. anat.-clin. Bordeaux* [1911–13] **L.**GH.   [*C. of:* 11835]

11838 **Bulletin** de la **Société anatomo-clinique** de **Lille**. *Bull. Soc. anat.-clin. Lille*

11839 **Bulletin** de la **Société** d'**anthropologie** et de **biologie** de **Lyon**. *Bull. Soc. Anthrop. Biol. Lyon* [1881–22] **L.**AN.; BM.; BM^N. 81–87; G. 81–91; R. 81–95; **Db**. 96–12 imp.; **E.**V. 81–11 imp.   [*C. in:* 2950]

11840 **Bulletin** de la **Société** d'**anthropologie** de **Bruxelles**. *Bull. Soc. Anthrop. Brux.* [1882–] **L.**AN.; BM. 82–14; BM^N. 82–87; **Br.**U. 83–85; **O.**R. 82–83.
   Bulletin de la **Société** d'**anthropologie** de **Lyon**. *See* 11839.

11841 **Bulletin** de la **Société** d'**archéologie, sciences, lettres** et **arts** du **département** de **Seine-et-Marne**. Melun. *Bull. Soc. Archéol. Sci. Dép. Seine-et-Marne* **L.**BM. 65–.

11842 **Bulletin** de la **Société archéologique, historique** et **scientifique** de la **région** de **Bonnières**. *Bull. Soc. archéol. hist. scient. Rég. Bonnières*

11843 **Bulletin** de la **Société archéologique, historique** et **scientifique** de **Soissons**. *Bull. Soc. archéol. hist. scient. Soissons* [1847–] **L.**BM.; **O.**B. 1847–35.

11844 **Bulletin** de la **Société archéologique, scientifique** et **littéraire** de **Béziers**. *Bull. Soc. archéol. scient. litt. Béziers*

11845 **Bulletin** de la **Société archéologique, scientifique** et **littéraire** de **Sens**. *Bull. Soc. archéol. scient. litt. Sens*

11846 **Bulletin** de la **Société archéologique, scientifique** et **littéraire** de **Sousse**. *Bull. Soc. archéol. scient. litt. Sousse* **L.**SC. 26–.

11847 **Bulletin** de la **Société archéologique, scientifique,** et **littéraire** du **Vendômois**. Vendôme. *Bull. Soc. archéol. scient. litt. Vendômois* [1862–] **L.**BM. 30–.

11848 **Bulletin** de la **Société ariégoise** des **sciences, lettres** et **arts**. Foix. *Bull. Soc. ariég. Sci. Lett. Arts*

11849 **Bulletin** de la **Société** d'**astronomie populaire** de **Toulouse**. *Bull. Soc. Astr. pop. Toulouse*

11850 **Bulletin** de la **Société astronomique amiénoise**. Amiens. *Bull. Soc. astr. amién.*

11851 **Bulletin** de la **Société astronomique** de **Bordeaux**. *Bull. Soc. astr. Bordeaux* [1913–] **L.**AS. 21–32; MO. 21–24.

11852 **Bulletin** de la **Société astronomique Flammarion** de **Genève**. *Bull. Soc. astr. Flammarion Genève* **L.**AS. 28–37.

11853 **Bulletin** de la **Société astronomique** de **France**. Paris. *Bull. Soc. astr. Fr.* [1887–10] **L.**AS.; BM. 95–10; SC. 02–10; **Cr.**P. 95–10 imp.; **Db**. 95–08; **E.**R. 95–10; **G.**M. 96–03 imp.; **Ld.**U. 98–06; **Sh.**P. 10.   [*C. as:* 5057]

11854 **Bulletin** de la **Société astronomique** du **Rhône**. Lyon. *Bull. Soc. astr. Rhône*
   Bulletin de la **Société astronomique russe**. *See* 24480.

11855 **Bulletin** de la **Société** des **aviculteurs français**. Paris. *Bull. Soc. Avic. fr.*

11855° **Bulletin** de la **Société belfortaine** d'**émulation**. Belfort. *Bull. Soc. belfort. Émul.* **L.**BM. 56–.

11856 **Bulletin** de la **Société belge** d'**astronomie**. Bruxelles. *Bull. Soc. belge Astr.* [1895–09] **L.**AS.; BM.; SC.; **Cr.**P.; **E.**G. 96–09; R.   [*C. in:* 14029]

11857 **Bulletin. Société belge** de **dermatologie** et de **syphiligraphie**. Bruxelles. *Bull. Soc. belge Derm. Syph.*
   Bulletin de la **Société belge** d'**électriciens**. Bruxelles. *See* 11024 and 12143^a.

11858 **Bulletin** de la **Société belge** d'**études coloniales**. Bruxelles. *Bull. Soc. belge Étud. colon.* [1894–25] **L.**AN. 02–19; BM.; BM^N. 04–19; G. 94; K. 00–19 imp.; **E.**G. 01.   [*C. in:* 15427]

11859 **Bulletin** de la **Société belge** des **études géographiques**. Bruxelles, Louvain. *Bull. Soc. belge Étud. géogr.* [1931–] **L.**BM.; G. 31; QM. 56–; **Abs.**U. 58–; **C.**UL. 37–; **E.**U. 50–; **O.**G.; **R.**U.

11860 **Bulletin** de la **Société belge** de **géologie**, de **paléontologie** et d'**hydrologie**. Bruxelles. *Bull. Soc. belge Géol. Paléont. Hydrol.* [1887–] **L.**BM.; BM^N.; G. 89– imp.; GL.; GM.; R. 87–14; SC.; UC.; Z. 02–; **Abs.**U. 94– imp.; **Br.**U.; **C.**S.; UL. 26–; **Db**. 19–; **E.**D. 93–v. imp.; F. 95–12; J. 88–; U.; **G.**U.; **Ld.**U.; **Lv.**U.; **Pl.**M.; **R.**U. 20–; **Y**.

11861 **Bulletin** de la **Société belge** des **géomètres** à **Anvers**. *Bull. Soc. belge Géom. Anvers*

11862 **Bulletin** de la **Société belge** de **gynécologie** et d'**obstétrique**. Bruxelles. *Bull. Soc. belge Gynéc. Obstét.* [1889–] **L.**MD. imp.; **Lv.**M. 25–33 imp.

11863 **Bulletin** de la **Société belge** d'**ophtalmologie**. Bruxelles. *Bull. Soc. belge Ophtal.* [1896–] **L.**MA. 46– imp.; MD. 05–; OP. 11; S. 49–.

11864 **Bulletin** de la **Société belge** d'**orthopédie** et de **chirurgie** de l'**appareil moteur**. Bruxelles. *Bull. Soc. belge Orthop.* [1934–39]   [*C. of:* 10934; *C. as:* 686]

11865 **Bulletin** de la **Société belge** d'**otologie**, de **laryngologie** et de **rhinologie**. Bruxelles. *Bull. Soc. belge Otol. Lar. Rhinol.* [1896–46] **L.**MD. 33–46.   [*C. as:* 692]

11866 **Bulletin** de la **Société belge** de **photogrammetrie**. Bruxelles. *Bull. Soc. belge Photogramm.* **L.**P. 57–; SC. 56–.

11867 **Bulletin. Société belge** de **physique**. Loverval. *Bull. Soc. belge Phys.* **L.**P. 56–.

11868 **Bulletin** de la **Société belge** de **stomatologie.**
Anvers. *Bull. Soc. belge Stomat.* [1903–07] [*C. as:*
47633]

Bulletin. Société de **biologie** d'**Alger.** Alger.
See 10251.

Bulletin de la **Société** de **biologie** de **Lettonie.**
See 28164.

11869 **Bulletin** de la **Société biologique** d'**Arcachon.**
Arcachon. *Bull. Sci. biol. Arcachon* [1956] **L.**BM.; BM^N.;
SC.; Z.; **C.**P.; UL.; **E.**U.; **Lo.**; **Lv.**U.; **O.**R.; **Pl.**M. [*C. of:*
and *Rec. as:* 12301]

11870 **Bulletin** de la **Société** de **Borda.** Dax. *Bull.
Soc. Borda* [1876–] **L.**BM^N. 76–07; UC. 85–07.

Bulletin de la **Société** de **botanique** d'**Auch.**
See 12595.

Bulletin de la **Société botanique** de **Belgique.**
See 12145.

Bulletin de la **Société botanique** de **Bulgarie.**
See 24319.

11871 **Bulletin** de la **Société botanique** des **Deux-
Sèvres, Vienne** et **Vendée.** Niort. *Bull. Soc. bot.
Deux-Sèvres*

11872 **Bulletin. Société botanique** de **France.** Paris.
Bull. Soc. bot. Fr. [1854–] **L.**BM.; BM^N.; K.; L.; PH.
1854–90; SC.; **Bl.**U. 1857–15; **Bm.**U. 1854–33 imp.;
C.BO.; UL.; **Cr.**M.; **Db.**; **E.**B.; **Ex.**U. 54–; **G.**U.; **H.**U.;
Ld.U.; **M.**U.; **O.**BO.; **Rt.** 1854–11; **Y.**

11873 **Bulletin** de la **Société botanique** de **Genève.**
Bull. Soc. bot. Genève [1879–51] **L.**BM. 79–21; BM^N.;
HS. 25–33; K. 09–41; SC. 27–51; **C.**A. 29–41; P. 09–51;
UL. 09–51; **E.**B. 09–51; **M.**U. 25–42; **Rt.** 91–05: 09–51.
[*C. as:* 54296]

11874 **Bulletin** de la **Société botanique** du **Limousin.**
Limoges. *Bull. Soc. bot. Limousin*

11875 **Bulletin** de la **Société** de **botanique** du **nord**
de la **France.** Lille. *Bull. Soc. Bot. N. Fr.* **L.**BM^N. 51–.

Bulletin de la **Société botanique suisse.** *See*
6341.

Bulletin de la **Société botanique tchécoslovaque**
à **Prague.** *See* 38612.

11876 **Bulletin** de la **Société** de **botanique** et de **zoologie congolaises.** Léopoldville. *Bull. Soc. Bot. Zool.
congol.* [1940–42] **L.**BM^N. [*C. of:* and *Rec. as:* 59253]

11877 **Bulletin** de la **Société bourguignonne** d'**histoire**
et de **géographie.** Dijon. *Bull. Soc. bourguign. Hist.
Géogr.*

11878 **Bulletin** de la **Société bourguignonne** d'**histoire
naturelle** et de **préhistoire.** Dijon. *Bull. Soc.
bourguign. Hist. nat.* [*C. as:* 11684]

11879 **Bulletin. Société bretonne** de **géographie.**
Lorient. *Bull. Soc. bretonne Géogr.* **L.**G. 89–02 imp.

11880 **Bulletin** de la **Société centrale** d'**aquiculture** et
de **pêche.** Paris. *Bull. Soc. cent. Aquic. Pêche* [1889–
39] **L.**AM. 26–39; P. 01–14; SC. 25–39; **Db.** 05–39; **Pl.**M.
94–39 imp.; **Sa.** 89–28.

11881 **Bulletin** de la **Société centrale forestière** de
Belgique. Bruxelles. *Bull. Soc. cent. for. Belg.*
[1893–50] **L.**MY. 28–50; **C.**FO. 11–13; **O.**F. [*Suspended*
1941–44; *C. as:* 12146]

11882 **Bulletin** de la **Société centrale** d'**horticulture** du
département de la **Seine-inférieure.** Rouen. *Bull.
Soc. cent. Hort. Dép. Seine-infér.* [1950–] **Md.**H. 50–53.
[*C. of:* 12460]

11883 **Bulletin** de la **Société** de **chimie biologique.**
Paris. *Bull. Soc. Chim. biol.* [1914–] **L.**C. imp.; CB. 48–;
IC. 14–30; LE. 46–; LI. 20–; MA. 36–; MC. 45–; MD. 36–;
P. 28–41: 46–; PH. 54– imp.; SC.; TD.; U. 50–; UC.;
Abd.U. 47–; **Bl.**U. 20: 53–; **Bm.**U.; **Br.**U.; **C.**APH.; BI.;
MO. 36–; PH. 23–37; **Cr.**U. 56–; **Db.** 20–25: 53–; **E.**U.
20–; **Ep.**D. 37–; **G.**U. 20–; **Ld.**U. 49–; **Lv.**U.; **M.**MS.
20–; **O.**BI.; R.; **R.**D. 38–; **Sal.**F. 47–49: 51–; **Sh.**U. 39–47;
Ste. 14–30; **Y.**

11884 **Bulletin** de la **Société** de **chimie industrielle.**
Paris. *Bull. Soc. Chim. ind.* **L.**P. (curr.)

11885 **Bulletin. Société chimique** de **Belgique.** Gand.
Bull. Soc. chim. Belg. [1904–44] **L.**C. 06–44; IC. 11–44;
P. 10–44; SC. 23–44; **Bra.**D. 41–44 imp.; **C.**P. 13–44;
Ld.U. 26–44; **Lv.**U. 09–29 imp.; **O.**R. 40–44; **Ste.** 11–44.
[*C. of:* 9431; *C. as:* 12222]

Bulletin de la **Société chimique** de **Belgrade.**
See 21346.

11886 **Bulletin. Société chimique** de **France.** Paris.
Bull. Soc. chim. Fr. [1907–] **L.**B. 47–; BM.; C.; CB. 53–;
FO. 36–39; IC. 11–; KC. 53–; MA. 47–; MC. 61–; QM. 51–;
P. imp.; PH. 07–20; RI.; SC. 07–46; TP. 47–; U. 46–;
UC. 10–; **Abd.**U.; **Abs.**U. 07–29; **Bl.**U. 36– imp.; **Bm.**U.;
Bn.U. 49–; **Br.**U.; **C.**CH. 57–; P. 23–; UL.; **Cr.**U. 25: 30–
39; **Db.**; **Dn.**U. 22–; **E.**U.; **Ep.**D. 47–; **Ex.**U. 48–; **F.**A.
46–; **G.**T.; U.; **Ld.**U. 26–; **Lv.**P. 51–; **M.**C. 34–38: 50–;
T. 28–41 v. imp.: 47–; U.; **N.**U. 97–13: 47–; **Nw.**A.; **O.**R.;
R.D. 55–; **Sa.**; **Ste.** 11–; **Sy.**R. 46–52; **Te.**C.; **Wd.** 51–; **Y.**
[*C. of:* 11889: Sect. 2 > 11887, 1933–45]

11887 **Bulletin** de la **Société chimique** de **France.
Documentation.** Paris. *Bull. Soc. chim. Fr. Docum.*
[1933–45] **L.**C. 33–40 imp.; P.; **Abd.**U.; **M.**C. 33–38.

11888 **Bulletin** de la **Société chimique** du **Nord** de la
France. Lille. *Bull. Soc. chim. N. Fr.*

11889 **Bulletin** de la **Société chimique** de **Paris.** *Bull.
Soc. chim. Paris* [1863–06] **L.**BM.; BM^N. 63–02; C.; P.;
PH. imp.; RI.; SC.; **Abd.**U. 95–06; **Abs.**U.; **Bm.**U. 95–06;
Br.U. 73–06; **C.**UL.; **Db.**; **E.**U.; **G.**U.; **Ld.**U. 96–06;
M.U.; **N.**U. 97–06; **Nw.**A. 06; **O.**R.; **Sa.** [*C. as:* 11886]

Bulletin de la **Société chimique** du **Royaume** de
Yougoslavie. *See* 21347.

11890 **Bulletin** de la **Société** des **chimistes** de **Maurice.**
Bull. Soc. Chimts Maurice

11891 **Bulletin** de la **Société** de **chirurgie** de **Bordeaux.**
Bull. Soc. Chir. Bordeaux **L.**S. 32–34.

11892 **Bulletin** de la **Société** de **chirurgie** de **Lyon.**
Bull. Soc. Chir. Lyon

11893 **Bulletin** de la **Société clinique** de l'**Hôpital civil**
de **Charleroi.** Charleroi. *Bull. Soc. clin. Hôp. civ.
Charleroi* [1950–] **L.**MA. 51–.

11894 **Bulletin** de la **Société clinique** des **hôpitaux** de
Bruxelles. *Bull. Soc. clin. Hôp. Brux.*

11895 **Bulletin** de la **Société clinique** de **médecine mentale.** Paris. *Bull. Soc. clin. Méd. ment.*

11896 **Bulletin** de la **Société dauphinoise** d'**ethnologie**
et d'**anthropologie.** Grenoble. *Bull. Soc. dauphin.
Ethnol. Anthrop.*

11897 **Bulletin. Société dauphinoise** d'**études biologiques.** Grenoble. *Bull. Soc. dauphin. Étud. biol.*

11898 **Bulletin. Société dendrologique** de **France.**
Paris. *Bull. Soc. dendrol. Fr.* [1906–] **L.**K.; L. 06–37;
SC. 34–; **C.**UL.; **E.**B. 08–; **O.**F. 06–12.

11899 **Bulletin** de la **Société départementale** d'**agriculture** de l'**Orne**. Alençon. *Bull. Soc. dép. Agric. Orne*

11900 **Bulletin** de la **Société départementale démocratique** d'**encouragement** à l'**agriculture** de l'**Aude**. Carcassonne. *Bull. Soc. dép. démocr. Encour. Agric. Aude*

11901 **Bulletin** de la **Société départementale** d'**horticulture** de la **Dordogne**. Périgueux. *Bull. Soc. dép. Hort. Dordogne*

11902 **Bulletin** de la **Société départementale** d'**horticulture** de la **Seine**. Saint-Maur. *Bull. Soc. dép. Hort. Seine*

11903 **Bulletin** de la **Société dunkerquoise** pour l'**encouragement** des **sciences** des **lettres** et des **arts**. Dunkerque. *Bull. Soc. dunkerq. Encour. Sci.*

11904 **Bulletin** de la **Société** d'**élevage** d'**Anjou**. Angers. *Bull. Soc. Élev. Anjou*

11905 **Bulletin**. **Société** d'**émulation** d'**Abbeville**. *Bull. Soc. Émul. Abbeville* L.BM. 88–; C.UL. 77–.

11906 **Bulletin** de la **Société** d'**émulation** du **Bourbonnais**. Moulins. *Bull. Soc. Émul. Bourbonn.* [1903–] L.BM.; O.B. [*C. of:* 12675]

11907 **Bulletin** de la **Société** d'**encouragement** pour l'**industrie nationale**. Paris. *Bull. Soc. Encour. Ind. natn., Paris* [1802–40] L.BM.; I. 92–40; P.; SC. 96–40; TP. 95–38 imp.; **Bm**.U. 72–20 imp.; C.UL.; **Db**.; E.F. 75–05; R. 1824–1840: 07–40; G.U. 1802–1857; **Ld**.U. 14–27: 37; O.B. 1802–19; **Rt**. 90–27; **Ste**. 13–30. [*Suspended* 1941–48; *Replaced by:* 23338]

11908 **Bulletin** de la **Société entomologique** de **Belgique**. Bruxelles. *Bull. Soc. ent. Belg.* [1919–24] L.BM^N.; EB.; L.; C.UL.; O.H. [*C. as:* 9373]

Bulletin de la **Société entomologique** de **Bulgarie**. *See* 24320.

11909 **Bulletin**. **Société entomologique** d'**Égypte**. Le Caire. *Bull. Soc. ent. Égypte* [1908–] L.BM^N.; E.; EB.; SC. 24–; Z.; C.B.; P.; O.H. [>11940, 1938–54]

11910 **Bulletin** de la **Société entomologique** de **France**. *Bull. Soc. ent. Fr.* [1896–] L.BM^N.; E.; EB. 13–; L.; NC. 54–; SC.; Z.; **Bn**.U. 50–; C.P. 19–; UL.; **Db**.; **Fr**. 28–55; **G**.N. 96–40; U. 50–; **N**.U. 51–; O.H.; R. 20–21; **Rt**. 18–31; **Y**. [1832–95 *forms part of* 2943]

Bulletin de la **Société entomologique** de **Moscou**. *See* 24425.

11911 **Bulletin** de la **Société entomologique** de **Mulhouse**. *Bull. Soc. ent. Mulhouse* [1945–] L.BM^N.; E. 48–; **Y**.

11912 **Bulletin** de la **Société entomologique** du **Nord** de la **France**. Lille. *Bull. Soc. ent. N. Fr.* [1939–] L.BM^N.; **Y**. [*C. of:* 11029]

Bulletin de la **Société entomologique suisse**. *See* 32727.

11913 **Bulletin** de la **Société** d'**ethnographie**. Paris. *Bull. Soc. Ethnogr., Paris* [1887–03] L.BM. [*C. as:* 18585]

11914 **Bulletin** de la **Société** pour l'**étude** de la **flore franco-helvétique**. Pamiers. *Bull. Soc. Étude Flore fr.-helv.*

11915 **Bulletin** de la **Société** d'**étude** des **formes humaines**. Paris. *Bull. Soc. Étude Formes hum.* L.AN. 27–32.

11916 **Bulletin** de la **Société** d'**étude** des **sciences naturelles** de **Béziers**. *Bull. Soc. Étude Sci. nat. Béziers* L.BM^N. 76–37; R. 77– imp.

11917 **Bulletin** de la **Société** d'**étude** des **sciences naturelles** d'**Elbeuf**. *Bull. Soc. Étude Sci. nat. Elbeuf* L.BM. 82–91; BM^N. 81–47.

11918 **Bulletin** de la **Société** d'**étude** des **sciences naturelles** de la **Haute-Saône**. Vesoul. *Bull. Soc. Étude Sci. nat. Hte-Saône*

11919 **Bulletin** de la **Société** d'**étude** des **sciences naturelles** de **Nîmes**. *Bull. Soc. Étude Sci. nat. Nîmes* L.BM^N. 74–.

11920 **Bulletin** de la **Société** d'**étude** des **sciences naturelles** de **Reims**. *Bull. Soc. Étude Sci. nat. Reims* L.BM^N. 92–14: 23–37: 46–47: 56–.

11921 **Bulletin** de la **Société** d'**études camerounaises**. Doula. *Bull. Soc. Étud. cameroun.* [1935–47] L.AN.; BM^N.; Z.; E.G.; O.RH. [*C. as:* 18625]

Bulletin de la **Société** d'**études coloniales**. Bruxelles. *See* 11858.

11922 **Bulletin**. **Société** des **études coloniales** et **maritimes**. Paris. *Bull. Soc. Étud. colon. marit.* [*C. as:* 47535]

11923 **Bulletin** de la **Société** d'**études** des **Haute-Alpes**. Gap. *Bull. Soc. Étud. Ht.-Alpes*

11924 **Bulletin** de la **Société** d'**études historiques** et **géographiques** de **Bretagne**. Rennes. *Bull. Soc. Étud. hist. géogr. Bretagne*

11925 **Bulletin** de la **Société** d'**études historiques** et **géographiques** de l'**Isthme** de **Suez**. Le Caire. *Bull. Soc. Étud. hist. géogr. Isthme Suez* [1947–] L.BM.; U. 47–54; C.UL. 47–54; E.A.

11925° **Bulletin** de la **Société** d'**études historiques**, **géographiques** et **scientifiques** de la **région parisienne**. Paris. *Bull. Soc. Étud. hist. géogr. scient. Rég. paris.* [1927–] L.BM. 56–.

11926 **Bulletin** de la **Société** des **études historiques** et **scientifiques** de l'**Oise**. Beauvais, Paris. *Bull. Soc. Étud. hist. scient. Oise*

11927 **Bulletin** de la **Société** des **études indo-chinoises** de **Saïgon**. Paris. *Bull. Soc. Étud. indo-chin. Saïgon* L.AN. 50–; BM. 89–15.

11928 **Bulletin** de la **Société** d'**études** de l'**industrie** de l'**engrenage**. Paris. *Bull. Soc. Étud. Ind. Engren.* Li.M. 46–.

11929 **Bulletin** de la **Société** d'**études océaniennes** (**Polynésie orientale**). Papeete, Tahiti. *Bull. Soc. Étud. océanien.* [1917–] L.AN.; BM.; BM^N.; G.; SC. 28–.

11930 **Bulletin** de la **Société** d'**études psychiques** de **Marseille**. *Bull. Soc. Étud. psych. Marseille*

11931 **Bulletin** de la **Société** d'**études psychiques** de **Nancy**. *Bull. Soc. Étud. psych. Nancy*

11932 **Bulletin** de la **Société** d'**études scientifiques** d'**Angers**. *Bull. Soc. Étud. scient. Angers* [1871–] L.BM^N. 71–46: 58–; EB. 12–28; P. 72–09.

11933 **Bulletin** de la **Société** des **études scientifiques** et **archéologiques** de **Draguignan** du **Var**. *Bull. Soc. Étud. scient. archéol. Draguignan* L.BM. 56–.

11934 **Bulletin** de la **Société** d'**études scientifiques** de l'**Aude**. Carcassonne. *Bull. Soc. Étud. scient. Aude* L.BM^N. 90–49.

11935 **Bulletin** de la **Société** d'**études scientifiques** de **Lyon**. *Bull. Soc. Étud. scient. Lyon* L.BM^N. 74–79.

11936 **Bulletin** de la **Société** d'**études scientifiques** sur la **tuberculose.** Paris. *Bull. Soc. Étud. scient. Tuberc.* **C.**MD. 07–.

11937 **Bulletin** de la **Société** d'**études** et de **vulgari-sation** de la **zoologie agricole.** Bordeaux. *Bull. Soc. Étud. Vulg. Zool. agric., Bordeaux* **L.**EB. 03–20*. [*C. as:* 49663]

11938 **Bulletin** de la **Société fédérale** des **pharmaciens** de **France.** Paris. *Bull. Soc. féd. Pharmns Fr.*

11939 **Bulletin** de la **Société forestière** de **Franche-Comté** et **Belfort** (et des **provinces** de l'est). Besançon. *Bull. Soc. for. Franche-Comté* [1891–] **O.**F.; **Y.**

11940 **Bulletin** de la **Société Fouad** Ier d'**entomologie.** Le Caire. *Bull. Soc. Fouad I. Ent.* [1938–54] **L.**BM^N.; E.; EB.; Z.; **C.**B.; P.; **O.**H. [*C. of:* and *Rec. as:* 11909]

11941 **Bulletin** de la **Société française** des **amis** des **arbres.** Nice. *Bull. Soc. fr. Amis Arbres*

11942 **Bulletin** de la **Société française** de **botanique** de **Courrensan.** Condom. *Bull. Soc. fr. Bot. Courrensan*

11943 **Bulletin** de la **Société française** de **céramique.** Paris. *Bull. Soc. fr. Céram.* [1948–] **L.**P.; SC. 52–; **Ld.**U. 62–; **St.**R.; **Y.**

11944 **Bulletin** de la **Société française** du **dahlia.** *Bull. Soc. fr. Dahlia* [1954–] **L.**HS. [*C. of:* 26903]

11945 **Bulletin** de la **Société française** de **dermatolo-gie** et de **syphiligraphie.** Paris. *Bull. Soc. fr. Derm. Syph.* [1890–] **L.**MA. 24– imp.; MD. 07–41; S. 07–41: 48– imp.; U. 07–11: 57–; UCH. 20–41; **Bl.**U. 29–41 imp.; **Br.**U. 07–15 imp.; **Db.** 48–49; **Dn.**U. 21–31 imp.; **E.**P. 07–41; S. 08–22; **G.**U. 52–; **Ld.**U. 12–41; **Lv.**M. 07–20 imp.: 53–56; **Nw.**A. 28–36 imp.; **M.**MS. 19–33; **Y.**

11946 **Bulletin. Société française** pour l'**échange** des **plantes vasculaires.** Versailles. *Bull. Soc. fr. Éch. Pl. vasc.* **L.**BM^N. 47–.

11947 **Bulletin** de la **Société française** d'**économie rurale.** Paris. *Bull. Soc. fr. Écon. rur.* [1949–52] **L.**AM.; **O.**AEC. [*C. as:* 17442]

11948 **Bulletin** de la **Société française** des **électriciens.** Paris. *Bull. Soc. fr. Électns* [1918–] **L.**BM.; EE.; P.; SC.; SI. 46–; **C.**P. 35–38; **E.**HW. 48–; **G.**U. 19–; **Lv.**U. 21–; **N.**U. 51– imp.; **Y.** [*C. of:* 12025]

11949 **Bulletin** de la **Société française** d'**histoire** de la **médecine.** Paris. *Bull. Soc. fr. Hist. Méd.* [1902–40] **L.**BM. 02–22; D. 31–29 imp.; MD. 13–40; S. 13–39; V. 22–40; **G.**U. 20–40; **O.**R. [*C. as:* 30810]

11950 **Bulletin** de la **Société française** d'**horticulture.** Tours. *Bull. Soc. fr. Hort.*

11951 **Bulletin** de la **Société française** des **ingénieurs coloniaux.** Paris, etc. *Bull Soc. fr. Ingrs colon.* **L.**P. 12 18 imp.

11952 **Bulletin** de la **Société française** de **microscopie.** Paris. *Bull. Soc. fr. Microsc.* [1932–] **L.**BM^N. 32–39; **Dm.** 32–34; **Lv.**U. 32–38.

11953 **Bulletin** de la **Société française** de **minéralogie** (et de **cristallographie**). Paris. *Bull. Soc. fr. Minér. Cristallogr.* [1878–] **L.**BM.; BM^N.; GL.; GM.; R. 86–32; SC.; **Abd.**U.; **C.**MI.; UL. 20–; **Db.**; **E.**U. 07–; **G.**U.; **Ld.**U. 48–; **Lv.**U. 20–23; **M.**U. 79–; **O.**R.; **Sa.** 20–22; **Y.**

11954 **Bulletin. Société française** d'**oto-rhino-laryn-gologie.** Paris. *Bull. Soc. fr. Oto-rhino-lar.* [1907–22] **L.**MD.; S. 07–21; **Bm.**U. imp.; **Br.**U. 21–22 imp. [*C. of:* 10944; *C. as:* 15445]

11955 **Bulletin** de la **Société française** de **phlébologie.** Paris. *Bull. Soc. fr. Phlébol.* [1948–] **L.**MA. 50–; MD. 50–.

11956 **Bulletin** de la **Société française** de **photographie** et de **cinématographie.** Paris. *Bull. Soc. fr. Photogr.* [1855–53] **L.**BM.; C. 27–39; P. imp.; PG.; SC. 25–38; **We.**K. [*Suspended* Aug. 1939–Dec. 1946: Oct. 1947–Apr. 1951]

11957 **Bulletin** de la **Société française** de **physiologie végétale.** Paris. *Bull. Soc. fr. Physiol. vég.* [1955–] **L.**SC.; **Br.**A. 57–.

11958 **Bulletin** de la **Société française** de **physiothé-rapie.** Paris. *Bull. Soc. fr. Physiothér.*

    Bulletin de la **Société française** de **physique.** See 11706.

11959 **Bulletin** de la **Société française** de **prophylaxie sanitaire** et **morale.** Paris. *Bull. Soc. fr. Prophyl. sanit. mor.* [1901–28] **L.**UC. 05. [*C. as:* 40234]

11960 **Bulletin** de la **Société française** d'**urologie.** Paris. *Bull. Soc. fr. Urol.* [1919–] **L.**MD. 35–.

11961 **Bulletin** de la **Société fribourgeoise** d'**horti-culture.** Fribourg. *Bull. Soc. fribourg. Hort.*

11962 **Bulletin** de la **Société fribourgeoise** des **sciences naturelles.** Fribourg. *Bull. Soc. fribourg. Sci. nat.* [1879–] **L.**BM^N.; GL. 00–; **E.**J. 03–; **Y.**

11963 **Bulletin** de la **Société** des **gens** de **science.** Paris. *Bull. Soc. Gens Sci.*

11964 **Bulletin** de la **Société** de **géographie** de l'**Afrique occidentale française.** Dakar. *Bull. Soc. Géogr. Afr. occid. fr.*

11965 **Bulletin** de la **Société** de **géographie** de l'**Ain.** Bourg. *Bull. Soc. Géogr. Ain*

11966 **Bulletin** de la **Société** de **géographie** de l'**Aisne.** Laon. *Bull. Soc. Géogr. Aisne*

11967 **Bulletin** de la **Société** de **géographie** d'**Alger** et de l'**Afrique** du **Nord.** Alger. *Bull. Soc. Géogr. Alger Afr. N.* [1896–45] **L.**BM. 80; G. 96–39 imp.; **E.**G. 22–45; **O.**G. 22–33 imp.

11968 **Bulletin** de la **Société** de **géographie** d'**Anvers.** *Bull. Soc. Géogr. Anvers* [1876–40: 46–] **L.**BM. 78; G. 87–; **E.**G. 78–50.

    Bulletin de la **Société** de **géographie** et d'**archéo-logie** de la **province** d'**Oran.** See 12463.

    Bulletin de la **Société** de **géographie** de **Béograd.** See 21355.

11969 **Bulletin** de la **Société** de **géographie commer-ciale** de **Bordeaux.** *Bull Soc. Géogr. comm. Bordeaux* [1874–11] **L.**BM.; G. 75–11; **E.**R. 78–11 imp. [*C. as:* 47263]

11970 **Bulletin** de la **Société** de **géographie commer-ciale** du **Havre.** Le Havre. *Bull. Soc. Géogr. comm. Havre* [1882–40] **L.**B. 84–03; G. imp.; SC. 24–40.

11971 **Bulletin** de la **Société** de **géographie commer-ciale** de **Nantes.** *Bull. Soc. Géogr. comm. Nantes* [1893–14] **L.**G. 85–86 imp.; **E.**G.

11972 **Bulletin** de la **Société** de **géographie commer-ciale** de **Paris.** *Bull. Soc. Géogr. comm. Paris* [1878–18] **L.**BM. 98–18; G. 83–18 imp.; **E.**G. 84. [*C. as:* 47150]

11973 **Bulletin** de la **Société** de **géographie commer-ciale** de **Paris. Section tunisienne.** *Bull. Soc. Géogr. comm. Paris Sect. tunis.* [1908–14]

11974 **Bulletin** de la **Société** de **géographie** de **Dijon.**
Bull. Soc. Géogr. Dijon

11975 **Bulletin** de la **Société** de **géographie** de **Dunkerque.** *Bull. Soc. Géogr. Dunkerque*

11976 **Bulletin** de la **Société** de **géographie** d'**Égypte.**
Le Caire. *Bull. Soc. Géogr. Égypte* [1922–] **L.**AN.; B.
56–; G.; **Abs.**N. 39–; **C.**UL.; **E.**G.; **Y.** [*C. of:* 12029]

11977 **Bulletin** de la **Société** de **géographie** et d'**études coloniales** de **Marseille.** *Bull. Soc. Géogr. Étud. colon.*
Marseille [1903–54] **L.**BM.; G.; TP. 03–37 imp.; **E.**G.;
O.G. 05–10 imp. [*C. of:* 11982; *C. as:* 10328]
      Bulletin de la **Société** de **géographie** de **Finlande.**
See 19282.

11978 **Bulletin** de la **Société** de **géographie** de **Hanoï.**
Bull. Soc. Géogr. Hanoï

11979 **Bulletin** de la **Société** de **géographie** de **Lille.**
Bull. Soc. Géogr. Lille [1882–14] **L.**BM.; **E.**G. 87–14.

11980 **Bulletin** de la **Société** de **géographie** de **Lyon.**
Bull. Soc. Géogr. Lyon [1875–41] **L.**BM.

11981 **Bulletin** de la **Société** de **géographie** du **Maroc.**
Casablanca. *Bull. Soc. Géogr. Maroc* **E.**G. 16. [*C. as:*
47266]

11982 **Bulletin** de la **Société** de **géographie** de
Marseille. *Bull. Soc. Géogr. Marseille* [1877–02] **L.**BM.;
G. 87–02; TP. 97–02; **E.**G. 85–02. [*C. as:* 11977]

11983 **Bulletin** de la **Société** de **géographie** et du
Musée commercial de **St-Nazaire.** *Bull. Soc. Géogr.*
Mus. comm. St-Nazaire
      Bulletin de la **Société** de **géographie** de **Paris.**
See 20974.

11984 **Bulletin** de la **Société** de **géographie** de **Poitiers.**
Bull. Soc. Géogr. Poitiers
      Bulletin de la **Société** de **géographie** de **Québec.**
See 53722.

11985 **Bulletin** de la **Société** de **géographie** de **Rochefort.** *Bull. Soc. Géogr. Rochefort* [1879–30] **L.**G. imp.

11986 **Bulletin** de la **Société** de **géographie** de **Toulouse**
Bull. Soc. Géogr. Toulouse [1882–] **E.**G. 94–.

11987 **Bulletin** de la **Société** de **géographie** de **Tours.**
Bull. Soc. Géogr. Tours

11988 **Bulletin** de la **Société** **géologique** de **France.**
Paris. *Bull. Soc. géol. Fr.* [1830–] **L.**BM.; BM^N.; GL.;
GM.; R. 1830–28; SC. 66–; UC. imp.; **Abd.**U. 46–; **Abs.**U.
17: 20: 30–; **Bl.**U. imp.; **Bm.**P.; U. 00–; **Br.**U.; **C.**S.;
UL.; **Cr.**M. 1830–20; **Db.**; **E.**C. 80–; D. 1830–25: 46–;
G. 88–; J. 23–; R. imp.; U. 81–; **G.**G. 1860– imp.; U.;
Lv.U. 03–; **M.**P. 1843–13 imp.; U. 97–30 imp.; **N.**U. 01–
imp.; **Nw.**A. imp.; **O.**R.; R.U. 1844–72: 27–; **Y.**

11989 **Bulletin** de la **Société** **géologique** et **minéralogique** de **Bretagne.** Rennes. *Bull. Soc. géol. minér.*
Bretagne [1920–] **L.**BM^N. 20–36; GL. imp.; GM.; UC.;
Bl.U.; **C.**P.; **Db.** 23–; **E.**D.; R. 20: 23: 30–; **Pl.**M. 21–22;
Y.

11990 **Bulletin** de la **Société** **géologique** de **Normandie.**
Le Havre. *Bull. Soc. géol. Normandie* [1873–] **L.**BM.
06–12 imp.; BM^N. 73–36; GL. 73–11; GM.; **E.**R. 31–; **Y.**
      Bulletin de la **Société** **géophysique** de **Varsovie.**
See 7202.

11991 **Bulletin** de la **Société** **grayloise** d'**émulation.**
Gray. *Bull. Soc. grayl. Émul.* **L.**BM^N. 98–36.

11992 **Bulletin** de la **Société** de **gynécologie** et d'**obstetrique** de **Paris.** Paris. *Bull. Soc. Gynéc. Obstet.*

Paris [1938–41] **L.**MA.; MD. 38–40; S. 38–40; **Bm.**U.;
Dn.U.; **E.**P.; S.; **G.**F.; **Lv.**M.; **M.**MS. [*C. of:* and *Rec. as:*
12106; *Contained in* 21683 *for* 1940–48 *and in* 9458 *for*
1949–50]

11993 **Bulletin** de la **Société hellénique** d'**ophtalmologie.** Athène. *Bull. Soc. hell. Ophtal.* [1932–] **L.**MD.
51–54 imp.; OP. 49–.

11994 **Bulletin** de la **Société** d'**histoire naturelle** de
l'**Afrique** du **Nord.** Alger. *Bull. Soc. Hist. nat. Afr.*
N. [1909–] **L.**BM^N.; EB.; K.; L.; MY. 22–; Z.; **Lv.**U.; **Pl.**M.
20–.

11995 **Bulletin** de la **Société** d'**histoire naturelle** des
Ardennes. Charleville. *Bull. Soc. Hist. nat. Ardennes*
L.BM^N. 94–53.

11996 **Bulletin** de la **Société** d'**histoire naturelle**
d'**Autun.** *Bull. Soc. Hist. nat. Autun* [1888–] **L.**BM^N.
88–30; SC. imp.

11997 **Bulletin** de la **Société** d'**histoire naturelle**
d'**Auvergne.** Clermont-Ferrand. *Bull. Soc. Hist. nat.*
Auvergne **L.**BM^N. 21–34*. [*C. as:* 47555]

11998 **Bulletin** de la **Société** d'**histoire naturelle** de
Colmar. Colmar. *Bull. Soc. Hist. nat. Colmar* [1860–]
L.BM^N.; **Y.**
      Bulletin. **Société** d'**histoire naturelle** du **Creusot.** *See* 49996.

11999 **Bulletin** de la **Société** d'**histoire naturelle** du
Doubs. Besançon. *Bull. Soc. Hist. nat. Doubs* **L.**BM^N.
14–. [*C. of:* 30819]

12000 **Bulletin** de la **Société** d'**histoire naturelle** du
Jura. Lons-le-Saunier. *Bull. Soc. Hist. nat. Jura*
L.BM^N. 19–36.

12001 **Bulletin** de la **Société** d'**histoire naturelle** de
Loir-et Cher. Blois. *Bull. Soc. Hist. nat. Loir-et-Cher*

12002 **Bulletin** de la **Société** d'**histoire naturelle** de
Metz. *Bull. Soc. Hist. nat. Metz* **L.**BM. 1844–; BM^N.
1844–38; **G.**N. 76–21.

12003 **Bulletin** de la **Société** d'**histoire naturelle** de
l'**Ouest.** *Bull. Soc. Hist. nat. Ouest*

12004 **Bulletin** de la **Société** d'**histoire naturelle** et de
palethnographie de la **Haute-Marne.** Chaumont.
Bull. Soc. Hist. nat. Palethnogr. Hte-Marne

12005 **Bulletin** de la **Société** d'**histoire naturelle** de
Reims. *Bull. Soc. Hist. nat. Reims* **L.**BM^N. 77–82.

12006 **Bulletin** de la **Société** d'**histoire naturelle** de
Savoie. Chambery. *Bull. Soc. Hist. nat. Savoie* **L.**BM^N.
1850–34; GL. 87–50.

12007 **Bulletin** de la **Société** d'**histoire naturelle** de
Toulouse. *Bull. Soc. Hist. nat. Toulouse* [1867–] **L.**BM^N.;
E. 67–38: 54–; GL. 79–; L. 26–; SC. 38–; Z. 74–; **E.**B. 01–;
G.N. 23–37; **Lv.**U. 00–.

12008 **Bulletin** de la **Société** d'**histoire** de la **pharmacie.**
Paris. *Bull. Soc. Hist. Pharm.* [1913–27] **L.**PH. [*C. as:*
47279]

12009 **Bulletin** de la **Société historique, littéraire,**
artistique et **scientifique** du **département** du **Cher.**
Bourges. *Bull. Soc. hist. litt. artist. scient. Dép. Cher*

12010 **Bulletin.** **Société historique** et **scientifique** des
Deux-Sèvres. Niort. *Bull. Soc. hist. scient. Deux-*
Sèvres [1905–] **L.**BM. 55–.
      Bulletin de la **Société hongroise** de **géographie.**
See 19766.

12011 **Bulletin. Société** de l'**horticulture** de **Genève.** Genève. *Bull. Soc. Hort. Génève* [1879–] **L.**HS. 79–46 imp.

12012 **Bulletin** de la **Société** de l'**Industrie minérale** de **St-Étienne.** *Bull. Soc. Ind. minér.* St-Étienne [1855–20] **L.**I.; MIE. 00–20; P.; SC. imp.; **Cr.**U. 78–14 imp.; **Ld.**U. 98–15; **Nw.**A. 89–91: 14–20. [*C. in:* 47307]

12013 **Bulletin** de la **Société industrielle** d'**Angers** et du **département** de **Maine-et-Loire.** Angers. *Bull. Soc. ind. Angers*

12014 **Bulletin** de la **Société industrielle** de l'**Est.** Nancy. *Bull. Soc. ind. E.* [1883–] **L.**P. 03–11 imp.; SC. 25–.

12015 **Bulletin** de la **Société industrielle** de **Mulhouse.** *Bull. Soc. ind. Mulhouse* [1826–] **L.**BM. 1836–87; C. 1845–1853: 67–89 imp.; P. 10–; **Db.** 1853–; **G.**E. 10–; U. 95–33; **Ld.**U. 63–; **M.**C. 1826–39; D. 28–39: 46– imp.; P. 35–; **O.**B. 1836–05; **Y.**

Bulletin. Société industrielle du **Nord** de la **France.** *See* 11032 and 12466.

12016 **Bulletin** de la **Société industrielle** de **Rouen.** *Bull. Soc. ind. Rouen* [1873–39] **L.**BM. 73–91; P.; SC. 73–02: 30–39; **Ld.**U. 73–10; **M.**C. 73–03: 22–39; P. 73–23. [*C. in:* 35010]

12017 **Bulletin** de la **Société industrielle** de **St-Quentin** et de l'**Aisne.** St-Quentin. *Bull. Soc. ind. St-Quentin* **L.**P. 69–11 imp.

12018 **Bulletin** de la **Société** des **ingénieurs** et **architectes sanitaires** de **France.** Paris. *Bull. Soc. Ingrs Archit. sanit. Fr.*

12019 **Bulletin** de la **Société** des **ingénieurs civils** de **France.** Paris. *Bull. Soc. Ingrs civ. Fr.* [1909–59] **L.**AV. 57–59; EE. 36–39 imp.; I. 09–59 imp.; MI. 50–59 imp.; P. 41–59; SC. 39–59; **C.**UL. 49–59; **G.**U. 41–59 imp.; **M.**U. 36–50 imp. [*C. in:* 30718]

12020 **Bulletin** de la **Société** des **ingénieurs** sortis de l'**École** d'**industrie** et des **mines** du **Hainaut.** Liège. *Bull. Soc. Ingrs Éc. Ind. Mines Hainaut*

12021 **Bulletin** de la **Société** des **ingénieurs soudeurs.** Paris. *Bull. Soc. Ingrs Soud.* [1930–39] **L.**P. imp.; SC. 38–39. [*C. in:* 50112]

12022 **Bulletin** de la **Société** de l'**internat** des **hôpitaux** de **Paris.** *Bull. Soc. Internat Hôp. Paris*

12023 **Bulletin** de la **Société internationale** des **amis** des **arbres** de **Tunisie.** Paris. *Bull. Soc. int. Amis Arbres Tunis.*

12024 **Bulletin** de la **Société internationale** de **chirurgie.** Bruxelles. *Bull. Soc. int. Chir.* [1955–] **L.**MA.; MD.; S.; **Bl.**U.; **E.**S.; **Lv.**M.; **M.**MS. [*C. of:* 26244]

12025 **Bulletin** de la **Société internationale** des **électriciens.** Paris. *Bull. Soc. int. Électns* [1884–18] **L.**BM.; O. 88–89; EE.; P.; SC. imp.; **G.**U.; **Te.**N. 06–18. [*C. as:* 11948]

12025ᶜ **Bulletin. Société internationale** d'**histoire** de la **médecine.** Bruxelles. *Bull. Soc. int. Hist. Méd.* [1954–]

12026 **Bulletin** de la **Société internationale** de **prophylaxie sanitaire** et **morale.** Bruxelles. *Bull. Soc. int. Prophyl. sanit. mor.* [1901–02] **L.**MD.; TD.; **Bm.**U. 01.

12027 **Bulletin** de la **Société** des **inventeurs français.** Paris. *Bull. Soc. Invent. fr.*

12028 **Bulletin** de la **Société** des **inventeurs réunis** de **Lyon.** *Bull. Soc. Invent. réun. Lyon*

Bulletin de la **Société japonaise** de **syphiligraphie.** *See* 28861.

Bulletin de la **Société jersiaise.** *See* 9393.

12029 **Bulletin** de la **Société khédiviale** de **géographie** du **Caire.** Le Caire. *Bull. Soc. khéd. Géogr. Caire* [1876–22] **L.**AN. 98–22; BM. 94–11; G.; SC. 17–22; **C.**UL. 82–22; **E.**G. 05–22. [*C. as:* 11976]

12030 **Bulletin** de la **Société languedocienne** de **géographie.** Montpellier. *Bull. Soc. languedoc. Géogr.* [1878–] **L.**BM.; G.; **E.**G. 92–; **Nw.**A. 54–.

12031 **Bulletin** de la **Société lépidoptérologique** de **Genève.** *Bull. Soc. lépidopt. Genève* [1905–45] **L.**BMᴺ.; E. 05–24; EB. 27–30; **Bn.**U. 14–21; **O.**H.

12032 **Bulletin** de la **Société** des **lettres, sciences** et **arts** de **Bar-le-Duc.** *Bull. Soc. Lett. Sci. Arts Bar-le-Duc*

12033 **Bulletin** de la **Société** des **lettres, sciences** et **arts** de la **Corrèze.** Tulle. *Bull. Soc. Lett. Sci. Arts Corrèze* [1879–]

12034 **Bulletin** de la **Société** des **lettres, sciences** et **arts** du **département** de l'**Aveyron.** Villefranche. *Bull. Soc. Lett. Sci. Arts Dép. Aveyron*

12035 **Bulletin** de la **Société** des **lettres, sciences** et **arts** de la **Flèche.** *Bull. Soc. Lett. Sci. Arts Flèche*

12036 **Bulletin** de la **Société** des **lettres, sciences** et **arts** de la **Haute-Auvergne.** Aurillac. *Bull. Soc. Lett. Sci. Arts Hte-Auvergne*

12037 **Bulletin. Société** des **lettres, sciences** et **arts** du **Saumurois.** Saumur. *Bull. Soc. Lett. Sci. Arts Saumur.*

12038 **Bulletin** de la **Société libre** pour l'**étude psychologique** de l'**enfant.** Paris. *Bull. Soc. libre Étude psychol. Enf.*

12039 **Bulletin** de la **Société libre** des **pharmaciens** de **Rouen.** *Bull. Soc. libre Pharmns Rouen*

12040 **Bulletin** de la **Société linnéenne** du **nord** de la **France.** Amiens. *Bull. Soc. linn. N. Fr.* [1872–18: 27–36] **L.**BM.; BMᴺ.; SC. 72–81; **Bl.**U. 89–09 imp.; **E.**B. 82–36; J. 74–36.

12041 **Bulletin** de la **Société linnéenne** de **Normandie.** Caen. *Bull. Soc. linn. Normandie* [1855–] **L.**BM. 90–; BMᴺ.; E. 1855–13; GL. 00– imp.; L.; R. 94–50; UC. 96–; Z.; **C.**P. 28–; S. 81–; UL.; **Cr.**N. 14–58 imp.; **Db.** 1855–24; **E.**C. 86–37 imp.; **Lv.**U. 98–; **M.**U. 93–04: 12–24: 37; **Pl.**M. 21–38.

12042 **Bulletin Société linnéenne** de **Provence.** Marseille. *Bull. Soc. linn. Provence* [1909–] **L.**BM. 13–; BMᴺ. 13–; EB. 09–31: 38.

12043 **Bulletin** de la **Société linnéenne** de la **Seine-maritime.** Le Havre. *Bull. Soc. linn. Seine-marit.* [1913–] **L.**BMᴺ. 13–39.

12043ᶜ **Bulletin. Société lorraine** des **sciences.** Paris. *Bull. Soc. lorr. Sci.* **L.**BMᴺ.; Z.; **Y.** [*C. of:* 11710]

12044 **Bulletin. Société Lorraine-Dietrich.** Argenteuil. *Bull. Soc. Lorr.-Dietrich* **L.**P. 26–29. [*C. of:* 11034]

Bulletin de la **Société lunaire internationale.** *See* 46956.

Bulletin de la **Société** des **mathématiciens** et **physiciens** de la **R.P.** de **Serbie.** *See* 5641.

Bulletin de la **Société** des **mathématiciens** et **physiciens** de la **R. P.** de **Macédoine.** *See* 6991ʰ.

12045 **Bulletin** de la **Société mathématique** de **Belgique.** Brussels. *Bull. Soc. math. Belg.* [1947–] **L.**M.; SC. 58–; **C.**P.; **G.**U.

12046 **Bulletin** de la **Société mathématique** de **France.** Paris. *Bull. Soc. math. Fr.* [1872–] **L.**BM. 75–; M.; R.; SC. 72–05: 15–19: 25– imp.; U. 50–; UC. 73–; **Abd.**U. 50–; **Abs.**U.; **C.**P.; UL.; **Db.** 36–; **Dn.**U. 30–; **E.**Q.; R.; **F.**A. 53–54; **G.**U. 53–; **Ld.**U. 26–; **Lv.**U. imp.; **Nw.**A. 09– imp. P. 09–36 imp.; **O.**R.; **Sa.** 21–22; **Y.**

12047 **Bulletin** de la **Société mathématique** de **Grèce.** Athènes. *Bull. Soc. math. Grèce* [1919–] **L.**M.; SC.; UC. 19–38; **Y.**

12048 **Bulletin** de la **Société** de **médecine** d'**Alger.** *Bull. Soc. Méd. Alger*

12049 **Bulletin** de la **Société** de **médecine** d'**Angers.** *Bull. Soc. Méd. Angers*

12050 **Bulletin** de la **Société** de **médecine** du **Bas-Rhin.** Strasbourg. *Bull. Soc. Méd. Bas-Rhin*

12051 **Bulletin** de la **Société** de **médecine** et de **chirurgie** de **La Rochelle.** *Bull. Soc. Méd. Chir. La Rochelle*

12052 **Bulletin** de la **Société** de **médecine** du **département** de la **Sarthe.** Le Mans. *Bull. Soc. Méd. Dép. Sarthe*

12053 **Bulletin** de la **Société** de **médecine** d'**Haïti.** Port-au-Prince. *Bull. Soc. Méd. Haïti* **L.**TD. 26–27.

12054 **Bulletin** de la **Société** de **médecine légale** de **France.** Paris. *Bull. Soc. Méd. lég. Fr.* [1869–22] **L.**MD. 04–22.

12055 **Bulletin. Société** de **médecine** de **Loiret.** Orléans. *Bull. Soc. Méd. Loiret*

12056 **Bulletin** de la **Société** de **médecine mentale** de **Belgique.** Bruxelles. *Bull. Soc. Méd. ment. Belg.*

12057 **Bulletin. Société** de **médecine** de **Nancy.** *Bull. Soc. Méd. Nancy* [*C. of:* 15155]
    Bulletin de la **Société** de **médecine** de **Paris.** *See* 10948.

12058 **Bulletin** de la **Société** de **médecine** des **praticiens** de **Lille.** *Bull. Soc. Méd. Pratns Lille*

12059 **Bulletin** de la **Société** de **médecine** de **Rouen.** *Bull. Soc. Méd. Rouen* **L.**MD. 08–11.

12060 **Bulletin** de la **Société** de **médecine sanitaire maritime.** Marseille. *Bull. Soc. Méd. sanit. marit.*

12061 **Bulletin** de la **Société** de **médecine** de **Toulouse.** *Bull. Soc. Méd. Toulouse*

12062 **Bulletin** de la **Société** de **médecine vétérinaire** des **Basses-Pyrénées.** Orthez. *Bull. Soc. Méd. vét. Basses-Pyrén.*

12063 **Bulletin** de la **Société** de **médecine vétérinaire** du **département** de l'**Oise.** Clermont. *Bull. Soc. Méd. vét. Dép. Oise*

12064 **Bulletin** de la **Société** de **médecine vétérinaire** des **départements** du **Centre.** Nevers. *Bull. Soc. Méd. vét. Déps Cent.*

12065 **Bulletin** de la **Société** de **médecine vétérinaire** d'**Eure-et-Loir.** Chartres. *Bull. Soc. Méd. vét. Eure-et-Loir*

12066 **Bulletin** de la **Société** de **médecine vétérinaire** de **Lot-et-Garonne.** Agen. *Bull. Soc. Méd. vét. Lot-et-Gar.*

12067 **Bulletin** de la **Société** de **médecine vétérinaire** de **Lyon** et du **Sud-Est.** Lyon. *Bull. Soc. Méd. vét. Lyon*

12068 **Bulletin** de la **Société** de **médecine vétérinaire pratique.** Paris. *Bull. Soc. Méd. vét. prat.*

12069 **Bulletin** de la **Société** de **médecine vétérinaire** de la **Somme.** Abbeville. *Bull. Soc. Méd. vét. Somme*

12070 **Bulletin** de la **Société** de **médecine** de la **Vienne.** Poitiers. *Bull. Soc. Méd. Vienne*

12071 **Bulletin** de la **Société** des **médecins** des **dispensaires antituberculeux** de l'**Office public** d'**hygiène sociale** du **département** de la **Seine.** Paris. *Bull. Soc. Médns Dispens. antituberc. Dép. Seine*
    Bulletin de la **Société** des **médecins** et **naturalistes** de **Jassy.** *See* 9137.

12072 **Bulletin** de la **Société médicale** d'**Afrique noire** de **langue française.** Dakar. *Bull. Soc. méd. Afr. noire Lang. fr.* [1959–] **L.**MA.; MC.; S.; TD. [*C. of:* 10901]

12073 **Bulletin** de la **Société médicale** d'**Amiens.** *Bull. Soc. méd. Amiens*

12074 **Bulletin** de la **Société médicale** de **Bayonne-Biarritz** et de la **côte basque.** Bayonne. *Bull. Soc. méd. Bayonne*

12075 **Bulletin** de la **Société médicale belge** de **tempérance.** Liège. *Bull. Soc. méd. belge Tempér.*

12076 **Bulletin** de la **Société médicale** de **Charleroi.** *Bull. Soc. méd. Charleroi*

12077 **Bulletin** de la **Société médicale** d'**éducation physique** et de **sport.** Paris. *Bull. Soc. méd. Éduc. phys.*

12078 **Bulletin** de la **Société médicale** des **hôpitaux** de **Lyon.** *Bull. Soc. méd. Hôp. Lyon*

12079 **Bulletin** de la **Société médicale** de l'**Île Maurice.** Port Louis. *Bull. Soc. méd. Île Maurice* **L.**MD. 09–13; TD. 08–30 v. imp.; **Lv.**U. 06–30 imp.

12080 **Bulletin** de la **Société médicale** de **Pau.** *Bull. Soc. méd. Pau*

12081 **Bulletin** de la **Société médicale** de l'**Yonne.** Auxerre. *Bull. Soc. méd. Yonne*

12082 **Bulletin** de la **Société médico-chirurgicale** d'**Athènes.** Athènes. *Bull. Soc. méd.-chir. Athènes* **L.**TD. 32–33.

12083 **Bulletin** de la **Société médico-chirurgicale** de la **Drôme** et de l'**Ardèche.** Valence. *Bull. Soc. mèd.-chir. Drôme*

12084 **Bulletin. Société médico-chirurgicale française** de l'**Ouest africain.** *Bull. Soc. méd.-chir. fr. Ouest afr.* **L.**TD. 19–21. [*C. in* :12116]

12085 **Bulletin** de la **Société médico-chirurgicale** de l'**Indochine.** Hanoï. *Bull. Soc. méd.-chir. Indochine* [1910–37] **L.**EB. 34–37; MD. 10–13; TD. 10–22: 29–37; **Lv.**U. [*C. as:* 47405]

12086 **Bulletin** de la **Société médico-chirurgicale** de **Paris.** *Bull. Soc. méd.-chir. Paris*

12087 **Bulletin** de la **Société médico-historique.** Paris. *Bull. Soc. méd.-hist.* **L.**BM. 09–10*.
    Bulletin de la **Société minéralogique** de **France.** *See* 11953.

12088 **Bulletin** de la **Société minière** de **Colombie britannique.** Paris. *Bull. Soc. min. Colomb. br.*

12089 **Bulletin** de la **Société** du **Musée** d'**ethnographie** du **Bas-Limousin.** Tulle. *Bull. Soc. Mus. Ethnogr. Bas-Limousin*

12090 **Bulletin** de la **Société mutuelle médico-pharmaceutique liégeoise.** Liége. *Bull. Soc. mut. méd.-pharm. liége.*

12091 **Bulletin** de la **Société mycologique** de la **Côte-d'Or.** Dijon. *Bull. Soc. mycol. Côte-d'Or* **L.**BM. 03.

12092 **Bulletin** de la **Société mycologique** de **France.** Paris. *Bull. Soc. mycol. Fr.* [1885–03] **L.**AM.; BM.; BM^N.; K.; L.; MY. 91–03; **C.**BO.; UL.; **Db.** 99–03; **Ld.**U.; **Y.** [*C. as:* 12468]

12093 **Bulletin** de la **Société mycologique** de **Genève.** *Bull. Soc. mycol. Genève* [1914–]
    Bulletin. Société mycologique de l'**ouest.** Le Mans. *See* 49998.

12094 **Bulletin** de la **Société nationale** d'**acclimatation** de **France.** Paris. *Bull. Soc. natn. Acclim. Fr.* [1854–46] **L.**BM. 96–46; BM^N. 1854–90; EB. 13–28; K. 61–42 imp.; SC. 30–34; Z.; **E.**B. 20–46; **M.**P. 88–36 imp.; **O.**OR. 28–46. [*C. in:* 52886]
    Bulletin de la **Société nationale** d'**agriculture** de **France.** *See* 11707.
    Bulletin de la **Société** des **naturalistes** et des **amis** de la **nature** en **Crimée.** *See* 58311.

12095 **Bulletin** de la **Société** des **naturalistes** et des **archéologues** de l'**Ain.** Bourg. *Bull. Soc. Nat. Archéol. Ain* [1886–] **L.**BM. 56–.

12096 **Bulletin** de la **Société** des **naturalistes luxembourgeois.** Luxemburg. *Bull. Soc. Nat. luxemb.* [1949–] **L.**BM^N. imp.; L.; R.; Z.; **Db.**; **E.**B.; **G.**N. 49–55; **Y.** [*C. of:* 11037]
    Bulletin de la **Société** des **naturalistes** de **Moscou.** *See* 12786.

12097 **Bulletin** de la **Société** des **naturalistes** d'**Oyonnax** pour l'**étude** et la **diffusion** des **sciences naturelles** dans la **région.** Bourg. *Bull. Soc. Nat. Oyonnax* **L.**BM^N. 47–.

12098 **Bulletin** de la **Société** des **naturalistes parisiens.** Paris. *Bull. Soc. Nat. paris.* [1904–] **L.**BM^N. 04–35.
    Bulletin de la **Société** des **naturalistes** de **Voronèje.** *See* 12803.

12099 **Bulletin** de la **Société neuchâteloise** de **géographie.** Neuchâtel. *Bull. Soc. neuchâtel. Géogr.* [1885–] **L.**AN. 91–; G.; **Abs.**N. 97–19 imp.; **E.**C. 89–19 imp.; R. 94– imp.; U. 91–01; **O.**B. 02–04.

12100 **Bulletin** de la **Société neuchâteloise** des **sciences naturelles.** Neuchâtel. *Bull. Soc. neuchâtel. Sci. nat.* [1844–] **L.**BM^N.; MO.; R.; Z. 1844–70: 76–; **C.**UL.; **Db.**; **E.**C. 04– imp.; R. 1856–; **G.**N. 95–; **M.**U. 89–; **O.**R. 1844–84 imp.; **Y.**

12101 **Bulletin** de la **Société nivernaise** des **lettres, sciences** et **arts.** Nevers. *Bull. Soc. nivern. Lett. Sci.* [1854–] **L.**BM.

12102 **Bulletin** de la **Société normande** d'**entomologie.** Caen. *Bull. Soc. normande Ent.* [1925–] **L.**BM^N. 26–27; E. 25.

12103 **Bulletin** de la **Société normande** d'**études préhistoriques.** Louviers. *Bull. Soc. normande Étud. préhist.*

12104 **Bulletin** de la **Société normande** de **géographie.** Rouen. *Bull. Soc. normande Géogr.* **L.**BM. 79–12; G. 79–95.

12105 **Bulletin** de la **Société normande** d'**hygiène pratique.** Rouen. *Bull. Soc. normande Hyg. prat.*

12106 **Bulletin** de la **Société** d'**obstétrique** et de **gynécologie** de **Paris.** *Bull. Soc. Obstét. Gynéc. Paris* [1912–37: 51–] **L.**MA. 29–37; MD.; S. 23–37; **Bm.**U. 27–37; **Db.** 24–37; **Dn.**U. 23–37; **E.**P.; S.; **G.**F. 12–14: 23–37; **Lv.**M. 28–38 imp.; **M.**MS. 23–37. [> 11992, 1938–41]

12107 **Bulletin** de la **Société** d'**obstétrique** et de **gynécologie** de la **Suisse romande.** Genève. *Bull. Soc. Obstét. Gynéc. Suisse romande* **L.**MD. 06–11.

12108 **Bulletin** de la **Société** des **océanistes.** Paris. *Bull. Soc. Océanistes* [1937] **L.**AN.; BM^N. [*C. as:* 26907]

12109 **Bulletin** de la **Société** d'**océanographie** de **France.** Paris. *Bull. Soc. Océanogr. Fr.* [1921–38] **L.**BM^N. 26–28; MO. 26–38; SC. 29–38; **Abd.**M. imp.; **C.**B.; GG. 31–37; **Lo.**; **Lv.**U. imp.; **Pl.**M.

12110 **Bulletin. Société océanophile** de **France.** *Bull. Soc. océanoph. Fr.*

12111 **Bulletin. Société** d'**ophtalmologie** d'**Égypte.** Alexandrie & Le Caire. *Bull. Soc. Ophtal. Égypte* [1902–] **L.**BM. 14– imp.; H. 36–; MA. 26: 28–41; MD. 06–; OP. 21–; S. 04– imp.; TD. 04–05: 12–; U. 37–; **C.**UL. 14–; **Db.** 30–38; **Lv.**U. 30–; **O.**R. 14– imp.

12112 **Bulletin** de la **Société** d'**ophtalmologie** de **France.** Paris. *Bull. Soc. Ophtal. Fr.* [1949–56] **L.**MD.; OP. [*C. of:* 12114; *C. as:* 12225]

12113 **Bulletin** de la **Société** d'**ophtalmologie** de **Lyon.** *Bull. Soc. Ophtal. Lyon*

12114 **Bulletin** de la **Société** d'**ophtalmologie** de **Paris.** *Bull. Soc. Ophtal. Paris* **L.**MD. 12–48* imp.; OP. 13–48. [*C. as:* 12112]
    Bulletin de la **Société ouralienne** d'**amateurs** des **sciences naturelles.** *See* 58350.

12115 **Bulletin** de la **Société** de **pathologie comparée.** Paris. *Bull. Soc. Path. comp.*

12116 **Bulletin** de la **Société** de **pathologie exotique.** Paris. *Bull. Soc. Path. exot.* [1908–] **L.**BM.; EB.; MA. 47–; MC.; MD.; S. 08–60 imp.; TD.; UCH. 12–18; **Bm.**U.; **C.**MO.; **E.**P.; U. 39–; **G.**U.; **Lv.**U.; **Nw.**A. 05–15 imp.; **O.**R. 19–36; **Sal.** imp.; **W.** 23–; **Y.**

12117 **Bulletin** de la **Société** de **pathologie végétale** de **France.** Paris. *Bull. Soc. Path. vég. Fr.* [1914–22] **L.**BM^N.; EB.; MY.; **C.**UL.; **Db.**; **Rt.** 22. [*C. as:* 47490]

12118 **Bulletin** de la **Société** de **pêche** et de **pisciculture,** les **Pêcheurs chambériens.** Chambéry. *Bull. Soc. Pêche Piscic., Chambéry*

12119 **Bulletin** de la **Société** de **pédiatrie** de **Jassy.** Jassy. *Bull. Soc. Pédiat. Jassy* [1930–] **L.**MA. 32–39; MD. 33–39.

12120 **Bulletin** de la **Société** de **pédiatrie** de **Paris.** *Bull. Soc. Pédiat. Paris* [1899–] **L.**MD.

12121 **Bulletin** de la **Société pharmaceutique** d'**Indre-et-Loire.** Tours. *Bull. Soc. pharm. Indre-et-Loire*
    Bulletin de la **Société** de **pharmacie** de **Bruxelles.** *See* 12150.

12122 **Bulletin** de la **Société** de **pharmacie** du **Loiret.** Orléans. *Bull. Soc. Pharm. Loiret* [1890–]

12123 **Bulletin** de la **Société** de **pharmacie** du **Lot.** Cahors. *Bull. Soc. Pharm. Lot*

12123^c **Bulletin** de la **Société** de **pharmacie** de **Marseille.** Marseille. *Bull. Soc. Pharm. Marseille* **Y.**

12124 **Bulletin** de la **Société** de **pharmacie** de **Strasbourg.** Strasbourg. *Bull. Soc. Pharm. Strasb.* [1955–] **L**.P.; **Y.**

12125 **Bulletin** de la **Société** de **pharmacie** du **Sud-Ouest.** Toulouse. *Bull. Soc. Pharm. Sud-Ouest*

12126 **Bulletin** de la **Société** de **pharmacie** de **Tours.** *Bull. Soc. Pharm. Tours*

12127 **Bulletin** de la **Société** de **pharmacie** des **Vosges.** Épinal. *Bull. Soc. Pharm. Vosges*

12128 **Bulletin** de la **Société** des **pharmaciens** du **Calvados.** Caen. *Bull. Soc. Pharmns Calvados*

12129 **Bulletin** de la **Société** des **pharmaciens** de l'**Eure.** Evreux. *Bull. Soc. Pharmns Eure*

12130 **Bulletin** de la **Société philomathique** de **Bordeaux.** *Bull. Soc. philomath. Bordeaux*

12131 **Bulletin** de la **Société philomathique** de **Paris.** *Bull. Soc. philomath. Paris* [1791–] **L**.BM. 80–; BM^N. 1791–37; P. 1791–13 imp.; R. 1791–18; S. 1791–1833; Z. 1791–43 imp.; **C**.UL. 88–16; **E**.R. 1797–1826: 79–39; **O**.R. 1791–1825.

12132 **Bulletin** de la **Société philomathique vosgienne.** St-Dié. *Bull. Soc. philomath. vosg.* **L**.BM 39–.

12133 **Bulletin. Société phycologique** de **France.** Paris. *Bull. Soc. phycol. Fr.* [1955–] **L**.BM^N.

Bulletin de la **Société physico-mathématique** de **Kasan.** *See* 24341.

Bulletin de la **Société polonaise** d'**anatomie** et de **zoologie.** *See* 19807.

12134 **Bulletin** de la **Société polonaise** pour l'**avancement** des **sciences.** Léopol. *Bull. Soc. pol. Avanc. Sci.* [1901–13] **L**.BM. 01–11; **C**.UL.; **Db.**; **G**.U. imp.; **O**.B.

12135 **Bulletin. Société polonaise** d'**ethnographie.** Léopol. *Bull Soc. pol. Ethnogr.*

12136 **Bulletin** de la **Société polymathique** du **Morbihan.** Vannes. *Bull. Soc. polymath. Morbihan* [1857–] **L**.AN. 66–21; BM. 68–; BM^N. 1857–93; **C**.E. 95–; UL. 1857–93; **E**.R. 86; U. 12–13; **M**.U. 1860–79 imp.

12137 **Bulletin** de la **Société pomologique** de **France.** Lons-le-Saunier. *Bull. Soc. pomol. Fr.*

12138 **Bulletin** de la **Société portugaise** des **sciences naturelles.** Lisbonne. *Bull. Soc. port. Sci. nat.* [1907–43] **L**.AM. 07–31 imp.; BM^N.; EB.; GL. 07–15; K.; L.; UC. 07–16; Z. 07–08; **Abd**.M. 07–21 imp.; **Bm**.U. 07; **Db.**; **Dm.**; **Lo.** 07–31; **Lv**.U.; **Pl**.M. 11–31; **Y.** [*C. as:* 7516]

12139 **Bulletin** de la **Société pratique** d'**horticulture** d'**Yvetot.** *Bull. Soc. prat. Hort. Yvetot*

12140 **Bulletin** de la **Société** de **préhistoire** du **Maroc.** Casablanca. *Bull. Soc. Préhist. Maroc* [1927–]

12141 **Bulletin** de la **Société préhistorique** de l'**Ariège.** *Bull. Soc. préhist. Ariège* **L**.BM^N. 61–; **Bm**.U. 46–.

12142 **Bulletin** de la **Société préhistorique française.** Paris. *Bull. Soc. préhist. fr.* [1904–] **L**.AN. 09–; BM^N. 48– imp.; GL. 49–; SC. 36–; **Db.**; **E**.V. 10–; **G**.M. 08–15; U. 57–; **Y.**

12143 **Bulletin** de la **Société** de **psychiatrie** de **Bucarest.** Bucarest. *Bull. Soc. Psychiat. Buc.* [1936–] **L**.MA. 36–37; MD. 36–38. [*C. of part of:* 12157]

Bulletin. Société r. d'**agriculture** du **Caire. Technical Section.** *See* 9261.

12143^a **Bulletin. Société r. belge** des **électriciens.** Bruxelles. *Bull. Soc. r. belge Électns* **L**.EE.; P.; **Y.** [*C. of:* 11024]

12144 **Bulletin** de la **Société r. belge** de **géographie.** Bruxelles. *Bull. Soc. r. belge Géogr.* [1877–] **L**.AN. 04–36; B. 77–26; BM.; G.; MO. 00; SC. 33–; **Abs**.U. 02–04: 07–11; **C**.S. 87–; **E**.G. 85–; **G**.U. 55–; **N**.U. 39–; **Y.**

12145 **Bulletin. Société r.** de **botanique** de **Belgique.** Bruxelles. *Bull. Soc. r. Bot. Belg.* [1862–] **L**.BM.; BM^N.; HS. 1862–39; K.; L.; MY. 27–; SC. 33–; **Bl**.U. 80– imp.; **Bm**.N. 01– imp.; **Br**.U. 21–31 imp.; **C**.BO. 62–35 imp.; P. 01–; **Db.**; **E**.B.; C. 11–; **G**.U. 69–86: 96–00 imp.; **Ld**.U.; **Lv**.U. 03– imp.; **M**.U. 62–89; **Nw**.A. 10–; **O**.BO. 85–08: 11– imp.; **Y.**

Bulletin. Société r. entomologique d'**Égypte.** *See* 11909.

12146 **Bulletin. Société r. forestière** de **Belgique.** Bruxelles. *Bull. Soc. r. for. Belg.* [1950–] **L**.MY.; **O**.F.; **Y.** [*C. of:* 11881]

Bulletin de la **Société r.** de **géographie** d'**Égypt.** *See* 11976.

12147 **Bulletin** de la **Société r. linnéenne** de **Bruxelles.** *Bull. Soc. r. linn. Brux.* [1872–34] **L**.BM^N. 72–06; Z. 72–04. [*C. as:* 12148]

12148 **Bulletin** de la **Société r. linnéenne** et de **flore.** Bruxelles. *Bull. Soc. r. linn. Flore, Brux.* [1935–] [*C. of:* 12147]

Bulletin de la **Société r. malacologique** de **Belgique.** *See* 11708.

12149 **Bulletin** de la **Société r.** de **médecine publique** du **royaume** de **Belgique.** Bruxelles. *Bull. Soc. r. Méd. publ. Belg.* **L**.TD. 83–12.

12150 **Bulletin** de la **Société r.** de **pharmacie** de **Bruxelles.** *Bull. Soc. r. Pharm. Brux.* [1857–12] **L**.PH. 1859–78.

12151 **Bulletin** de la **Société r.** des **sciences** de **Liége.** *Bull. Soc. r. Sci. Liége* [1932–] **L**.C. 55–; E. 32–40: 47–48; GL. imp.; L.; P. imp.; R. 32–54; **C**.P.; **Db.** 47–; **E**.Q. (curr.); **Ld**.U.; **Y.**

Bulletin de la **Société r.** des **sciences médicales** et **naturelles** de **Bruxelles.** *See* 11709.

12152 **Bulletin** de la **Société r.** de **zoologie** d'**Anvers.** Anvers. *Bull. Soc. r. Zool. Anvers* [1953–] **L**.BM^N.; Z.; **Bl**.U. 58–; **Db.**; **E**.R.; U.; **G**.U.; **Lv**.U.

Bulletin de la **Société Ramond.** Explorations pyrénéennes. Toulouse. *See* 18778.

12153 **Bulletin** de la **Société Rateau.** Paris. *Bull. Soc. Rateau* [1924–29] **L**.EE. 28–29; P.; **G**.M. 27–28. [*C. as:* 12368]

12154 **Bulletin** de la **Société** des **recherches congolaises.** Brazzaville. *Bull. Soc. Rech. congol.* **L**.BM^N. 22–36. [*C. as:* 10586]

12155 **Bulletin** de la **Société romande** d'**apiculture.** Daillens, Vaud. *Bull. Soc. romande Apic.* [1904–] **L**.AM. 18–23.

12156 **Bulletin** de la **Société roumaine** d'**endocrinologie.** Bucarest. *Bull. Soc. roum. Endocr.* [1935–?] **L**.MD. [*C. of part of:* 12157; *C. as:* 557]

Bulletin de la **Société roumaine** de **géologie.** *See* 9143.

12157 **Bulletin** de la **Société roumaine** de **neurologie, psychiatrie, psychologie** et **endocrinologie.** Bucarest. *Bull. Soc. roum. Neurol.* [1924–35] **L**.MD. 26–28: 30–35; S. 34–35; SC. [*C. of:* 9504; *C. as:* 12143 and 12156]

Bulletin de la **Société roumaine** de **physique.** *See* 9141.

Bulletin de la **Société roumaine** des **sciences.** *See* 9145.

Bulletin de la **Société russe** de **géographie.** *See* 24364.

12158 **Bulletin. Société** des **sciences anciennes.** Paris. *Bull. Soc. Sci. ancienn.*

12159 **Bulletin** de la **Société** des **sciences** et **arts** de **Bayonne.** *Bull. Soc. Sci. Arts Bayonne*

12160 **Bulletin de la Société** des **sciences, arts** et **belles-lettres** du **département** du **Tarn.** Albi. *Bull. Soc. Sci. Arts Belles-Lett. Dép. Tarn* [1921–34]

12161 **Bulletin** de la **Société** des **sciences** et **arts** de l'**Île de la Réunion.** Saint-Denis. *Bull. Soc. Sci. Arts Île Réunion* L.BM^N. 70–23 imp.

12162 **Bulletin** de la **Société** des **sciences** et **arts** de **Rochechouart.** *Bull. Soc. Sci. Arts Rochechouart*

12163 **Bulletin** de la **Société** de **sciences** et **arts** de **Vitry-le-François.** *Bull. Soc. Sci. Arts Vitry-le-Franç.*

12164 **Bulletin** de la **Société** des **sciences historiques** et **naturelles** de la **Corse.** Bastia. *Bull. Soc. Sci. hist. nat. Corse* L.BM. 81–; BM^N. 81–26 imp.

12165 **Bulletin** de la **Société** des **sciences historiques** et **naturelles** de **Sémur-en-Auxois.** *Bull. Soc. Sci. hist. nat. Sémur* L.BM^N. 65–23.

12166 **Bulletin** de la **Société** des **sciences historiques** et **naturelles** de l'**Yonne.** Auxerre. *Bull. Soc. Sci. hist. nat. Yonne* [1847–] L.BM^N.; C.UL. imp.; O.B.

12167 **Bulletin** de la **Société** des **sciences, lettres** et **beaux-arts** de **Cholet.** *Bull. Soc. Sci. Lett. Beaux-Arts Cholet*

12168 **Bulletin** de la **Société** des **sciences** et des **lettres** de **Łódź.** Łódź. *Bull. Soc. Sci. Lett. Łódź*
Classe III: Sciences mathématiques et naturelles [1946–] L.BM^N. 50–; P. 50–; **Db.** 55–; **G.**U. 50– imp.; **Ld.**U. 50–; **O.**R. 50–; **Y.**
Classe IV: Sciences médicales [1950–] **Db.** 55–; **G.**U. 52–; **Ld.**U. 52–; **Y.**

12169 **Bulletin** de la **Société** des **sciences médicales** et **biologiques** de **Montpellier** et du **Languedoc méditerranéen.** *Bull. Soc. Sci. méd. biol. Montpellier* [1919–27] L.LI. 26–27; MD.; U.; UC.; **Bl.**U. 22–27; **Bm.**U. imp.; **Br.**U. 22–27; **Db.** 24–27; **E.**U. 22–27; **G.**U. 22–27; **Ld.**U. imp.; **M.**MS.; **Nw.**A. 23–27. [*C. as:* 4367]

12170 **Bulletin** de la **Société** des **sciences médicales** de **Constantine.** *Bull. Soc. Sci. méd. Constantine*

12171 **Bulletin** de la **Société** des **sciences médicales** du **Grand-duché** de **Luxembourg.** *Bull. Soc. Sci. méd. Gr.-Duché Luxemb.* L.MD. 59–.

12172 **Bulletin** de la **Société** des **sciences médicales** de **Lille.** *Bull. Soc. Sci. méd. Lille*

12173 **Bulletin. Société** des **sciences médicales** de **Madagascar.** Tananarive. *Bull. Soc. Sci. méd. Madagascar*

Bulletin de la **Société** des **sciences médicales** de **Tunis.** *See* 12430.

Bulletin de la **Société** des **sciences** de **Nancy.** *See* 11710.

12174 **Bulletin** de la **Société** des **sciences naturelles** et d'**archéologie** de l'**Ain.** Bourg. *Bull. Soc. Sci. nat. Archéol. Ain* [1894–14]

12175 **Bulletin** de la **Société** des **sciences naturelles** et **arts** de **St-Étienne.** *Bull. Soc. Sci. nat. Arts St-Étienne*

12176 **Bulletin** de la **Société** des **sciences naturelles** d'**Autun.** *Bull. Soc. Sci. nat. Autun*

12177 **Bulletin** de la **Société** des **sciences naturelles** de la **Charente-inférieure.** La Rochelle. *Bull. Soc. Sci. nat. Charente-infér.*

12178 **Bulletin** de la **Société** des **sciences naturelles** de la **Haute-Marne.** Langres. *Bull. Soc. Sci. nat. Hte-Marne*

12179 **Bulletin** de la **Société** des **sciences naturelles** de **Mâcon.** *Bull. Soc. Sci. nat. Mâcon*

12180 **Bulletin** de la **Société** des **sciences naturelles** du **Maroc.** Rabat. *Bull. Soc. Sci. nat. Maroc* [1921–52] L.BM^N; E. 25–31 imp.; EB.; GL.; GM. imp.; L.; TP. 48–52; Z.; **C.**P. 43–52; **Dm.** 48–52; **E.**R. 43–52; **Lo.**; **Mi.** 48–52; **Pl.**M. 29–52; **Y.** [*C. as:* 12183]

12181 **Bulletin** de la **Société** des **sciences naturelles** et **médicales** de **Seine-et-Oise.** Versailles. *Bull. Soc. Sci. nat. méd. Seine-et-Oise* [1919–48] L.BM^N.; SC. [*C. of:* 30855; *C. in:* 12476]

Bulletin de la **Société** des **sciences naturelles** de **Neuchâtel.** *See* 12100.

12182 **Bulletin** de la **Société** des **sciences naturelles** de l'**ouest** de la **France.** Nantes. *Bull. Soc. Sci. nat. Ouest Fr.* [1891–] L.BM^N.; L.; R. 91–52; Z. 93–; **Abs.**U. 25–35 imp.; **Bl.**U. 93–05; **C.**P.; **Dm.** 11–; **E.**R.

12183 **Bulletin** de la **Société** des **sciences naturelles** et **physiques** du **Maroc.** Rabat. *Bull. Soc. Sci. nat. phys. Maroc* [1953–] L.BM^N.; EB.; GL.; GM.; L.; TP.; Z.; **C.**P.; **Dm.**; **E.**R.; **Lo.**; **Mi.**; **Pl.**M.; **Y.** [*C. of:* 12180]

12184 **Bulletin** de la **Société** des **sciences naturelles** et **physiques** de **Montpellier.** *Bull. Soc. Sci. nat. phys. Montpellier* **Lv.**U. 22– imp.

12185 **Bulletin** de la **Société** des **sciences naturelles** de **Rouen.** *Bull. Soc. Sci. nat. Rouen*

12186 **Bulletin** de la **Société** des **sciences naturelles** de **Saône-et-Loire.** Châlon-sur-Saone. *Bull. Soc. Sci. nat. Saône-et-Loire* [1875–] L.BM.; BM^N. 82–29; L. 82– imp.; Z. 75–04.

12187 **Bulletin** de la **Société** des **sciences naturelles** du **Sud-Est.** Grenoble. *Bull. Soc. Sci. nat. Sud-E.*

12188 **Bulletin** de la **Société** des **sciences naturelles** de **Tarare.** *Bull. Soc. Sci. nat. Tarare*

12189 **Bulletin** de la **Société** des **sciences naturelles** de **Tunisie.** Tunis. *Bull. Soc. Sci. nat. Tunis.* [1948–55] L.BM^N.; EB.; GL.; K.; L.; SC.; Z.; **Abd.**M.; **C.**UL.; **Db.**; **Dm.**; **Lo.**; **Mi.**; **O.**OR.; **Pl.**M.

12190 **Bulletin** de la **Société** des **sciences vétérinaires** et de **médecine comparée** de **Lyon.** *Bull. Soc. Sci. vét. Méd. comp. Lyon* [1898–] L.V. 28–38: 47–; **E.**AB. 47–; **W.** 33– imp.; **Y.**

Bulletin de la **Société scientifique** d'**Abkhazie.** *See* 24288.

Bulletin de la **Société scientifique** d'**Arcachon.** *See* 12301.

12191 **Bulletin** de la **Société scientifique, artistique** et **littéraire** de **Châlon-sur-Saône.** *Bull. Soc. scient. artist. litt. Châlon-s.-Saône*

Bulletin de la **Société scientifique** d'**Azerbaidjan.** *See* 24453.

12192 **Bulletin** de la **Société scientifique** de **Bretagne.**
Rennes. *Bull. Soc. scient. Bretagne* [1924–] L.BM^N.;
L. 36–; R. 24–53; RI.; SC.; Bl.U. 40–; C.P.; Db.; E.R.;
Ld.U. 36–; Lv.U.; Y. [*C. of:* 12201]

12193 **Bulletin** de la **Société scientifique** de **Dauphiné.**
Grenoble. *Bull. Soc. scient. Dauphiné* [1925–] L.BM^N.
25–49; SC. 33–; O.B. [*C. of:* 12199]

12194 **Bulletin** de la **Société scientifique Flammarion.**
Argentan. *Bull. Soc. scient. Flammarion, Argentan*

12195 **Bulletin** de la **Société scientifique Flammarion.**
Marseille. *Bull. Soc. scient. Flammarion, Marseille*

12196 **Bulletin** de la **Société scientifique, historique** et
archéologique de la **Corrèze.** Brive. *Bull. Soc. scient.
hist. archéol. Corrèze* [1878–15] L.BM.; M.R.

12197 **Bulletin** de la **Société scientifique** d'**hygiène
alimentaire** et d'**alimentation rationelle** de l'**homme.**
Paris. *Bull. Soc. scient. Hyg. aliment.* [1911–] L.MA.
47–; P. imp.; TD. 27–48 imp.; U. 11–23; Abd.R. 30–;
C.A. 29–48; R.D. 47–; Y. [*C. of:* 47576]

12198 **Bulletin** de la **Société scientifique industrielle.**
Marseille. *Bull. Soc. scient. ind.* [1872–30] L.P. 10–30;
Db. 79–30; E.R. imp.; Sh.M. 72–82. [*C. as:* 12200]

12199 **Bulletin** de la **Société scientifique** de l'**Isère.**
Grenoble. *Bull. Soc. scient. Isère* [1921–24] L.BM^N.;
O.B. [*C. of* 12205; *C. as:* 12193]

12200 **Bulletin. Société scientifique** de **Marseille**
pour la **vulgarisation industrielle.** Marseille. *Bull.
Soc. scient. Marseille Vulg. ind.* [1931–] L.P. 31–38; Db.;
E.R. 31–38. [*C. of:* 12198]

12201 **Bulletin** de la **Société scientifique** et **médicale**
de l'**Ouest.** Rennes. *Bull. Soc. scient. méd. Ouest* [1892–
23] L.BM^N.; EB.; GL.; R.; C.P.; Db.; E.R.; Lv.U.; O.R.
[*C. as:* 12192]

12202 **Bulletin** de la **Société scientifique** des **pharmaciens** de l'**Auvergne** et du **Centre.** Clermont-Ferrand.
Bull. Soc. scient. Pharms Auvergne

Bulletin de la **Société scientifique** de **Skopje.**
See 21355.

12203 **Bulletin. Société sélestadienne** des **lettres,
sciences** et **arts.** Sélestat. *Bull. Soc. sélestad.*

Bulletin de la **Société serbe** de **géographie.** *See*
21356.

12204 **Bulletin** de la **Société séricole.** Alais. *Bull. Soc.
séric., Alais*

Bulletin de la **Société** de **spéléologie.** *See* 50591.

12205 **Bulletin** de la **Société** de **statistique,** des **sciences
naturelles** et des **arts industriels** du **département** de
l'**Isère.** Grenoble. *Bull. Soc. Statist. Sci. nat. Arts ind.
Dép. Isère* [1838–20] L.BM. 1840–86; BM^N.; O.B. [*C. as:*
12199]

Bulletin de la **Société suisse** de l'**acétylène.** *See*
32725.

Bulletin de la **Société suisse** d'**anthropologie** et
d'**ethnologie.** *See* 11665.

Bulletin. Société suisse des **ingénieurs** et
des **architectes.** *See* 11635.

Bulletin de la **Société sultanieh** de **géographie.**
Le Caire. *See* 12029.

12206 **Bulletin** de la **Société** de **topographie** de **France.**
Paris. *Bull. Soc. Topogr. Fr.* [1876–] L.G. 83–93 imp.;
SC. 22–.

12207 **Bulletin** de la **Société tourangelle** d'**horticulture.** Tours. *Bull. Soc. tourang. Hort.*

Bulletin de la **Société turque** de **médecine.** *See*
55340.

12208 **Bulletin** de la **Société vaudoise** d'**agriculture** et
de **viticulture.** Lausanne. *Bull. Soc. vaud. Agric.
Vitic.*

12209 **Bulletin** de la **Société vaudoise** des **ingénieurs**
et des **architectes.** Lausanne. *Bull. Soc. vaud. Ingrs
Archit.* [1875–00] L.SC. 84–96 imp. [*C. as:* 12371]

12210 **Bulletin** de la **Société vaudoise** des **sciences
naturelles.** Lausanne. *Bull. Soc. vaud. Sci. nat.*
[1842–] L.BM^N.; GL. 00–; K. 79–13; L. 1846–; MO. 22–;
R. 64–; SC. 1842–68: 35–; Z. 1856–; Bl.U. 80–; Bm.N.
89– imp.; C.S. 66–81; Db.; E.J. 71–; P.; R. imp.; Ld.U.
27–; M.U. 74–25 imp.; O.R. 1846–21; Y.

12211 **Bulletin** de la **Société vaudoise** des **vétérinaires.**
Lausanne. *Bull. Soc. vaud. Vét.* W. 33–.

12212 **Bulletin** de la **Société vétérinaire hellénique.**
Athène. *Bull. Soc. vét. hell.* [1950–] L.V. 51–.

12213 **Bulletin** de la **Société vétérinaire** du **Loiret.**
Orléans. *Bull. Soc. vét. Loiret*

12214 **Bulletin** de la **Société vétérinaire** de la **Seine-
inférieure** et de l'**Eure.** Rouen. *Bull. Soc. vét. Seine-
infér.* W. 32–.

12215 **Bulletin** de la **Société vétérinaire** de **zootechnie**
d'**Algérie.** Alger. *Bull. Soc. vét. Zootech. Algér.*

12216 **Bulletin** de la **Société** des **vétérinaires** de **Seine-
et-Oise.** Neauphle-le-Château. *Bull. Soc. Véts Seine-
et-Oise*

12217 **Bulletin** de la **Société** de **viticulteurs** de **France.**
Paris. *Bull. Soc. Vitics Fr.* [1899–27] [*C. as:* 56791]

12218 **Bulletin** de la **Société** de **viticulture** et d'**horticulture** d'**Arbois.** *Bull. Soc. Vitic. Hort. Arbois*

12219 **Bulletin** de la **Société** de **viticulture, horticulture** et **sylviculture** de l'**arrondissement** de **Reims.**
Bull. Soc. Vitic. Hort. Sylvic. Arrond. Reims

Bulletin de la **Société** de la **zoologie agricole.**
Bordeaux. *See* 11937.

12220 **Bulletin** de la **Société zoologique** de **France.**
Paris. *Bull. Soc. zool. Fr.* [1876–] L.BM.; BM^N.; L.; SC.
97–; Z.; Bn.U. 55–; C.B. 76–88; UL.; Db.; Dm. 30–41:
46–; Dn.U. 96–04 imp.; E.C.; P.; R.; G.N. 76–21 imp.;
U. 56–; Lv.U. 88–; M.U. imp.; Mi. 76–96; O.R.; Pl.M.;
Sa. 96–04; Y.

12221 **Bulletin** de la **Société zoologique** de **Genève.**
Bull. Soc. zool. Genève [1907–32] L.BM^N.; Z.; O.OR.
[*C. as:* 11458]

12222 **Bulletin** des **sociétés chimiques belges.** Bruxelles. *Bull. Socs chim. belg.* [1945–] L.C.; IC.; I. 49–; P.;
PH.; QM. 50–; SC.; Bra.D.; C.P.; G.U. 48–; Ld.U.;
Lv.P. 48– imp.; M.D. 48–; U. 58–59; N.T. 45–51; Nw.A.
52–; O.R.; Ste.; Wd. 51–; Y. [*C. of:* 11885]

12223 **Bulletin** des **sociétés** de **géographie** de **Québec** et
de **Montréal.** Québec. *Bull. Socs Géogr. Québ. Montréal* [1942–] L.BM.; E.G.

12224 **Bulletin** des **sociétés médicales** d'**arrondissement** etc., du **département** de la **Seine.** Paris. *Bull.
Socs méd. Arrond. Dép. Seine* [*C. as:* 11414]

12225 **Bulletin** des **sociétés** d'**ophtalmologie** de **France.**
Paris. *Bull. Socs Ophtal. Fr.* [1957–] L.MA.; Y. [*C. of:*
12112]

12226 **Bulletin** des **sociétés** de **pharmacie** du **Sud-Ouest** et du **Centre.** Toulouse. *Bull. Socs Pharm. Sud-Ouest Cent.*

12227 **Bulletin** of the **Society** of **Alaskan Natural History** and **Ethnology.** Sitka. *Bull. Soc. Alask. nat. Hist. Ethnol.*

12228 **Bulletin. Society** of **American Military Engineers.** Washington. *Bull. Soc. Am. milit. Engrs* **L.**SC. 40–41.

12229 **Bulletin** of the **Society** for **Analytical Chemistry.** Cambridge, London. *Bull. Soc. analyt. Chem.* [1951–] **L.**BM.; P. (curr.); **Abs.**U. 54–; **Y.** [*Supplement to:* 2560]

12230 **Bulletin** of the **Society** for **Applied Spectroscopy.** Plainfield. *Bull. Soc. appl. Spectrosc.* [1947–51] **L.**AV. 51; SI. 51. [*C. as:* 3759]

12231 **Bulletin** of the **Society** of **Astronomical Friends.** Kyoto. *Bull. Soc. astr. Friends, Kyoto* **E.**R. 21–.

Bulletin. Society of **Automotive Engineers.** *See* 48360.

12231° **Bulletin. Society** for **Cultural Relations** with the **U.S.S.R. Science** and **Engineering Section.** *Bull. Soc. cult. Relat. U.S.S.R. Sci. Engng Sect.* [1952–54] **L.**BM. [*C. as:* 50359]

12232 **Bulletin. Society** of **Industrial Artists.** *Bull. Soc. ind. Art.* [1945–48] **L.**BA. [*C. as:* 26932]

12233 **Bulletin** of the **Society** of **Industrial Engineers.** Chicago. *Bull. Soc. ind. Engrs* [1918–32] **L.**P. 23–32.

12234 **Bulletin** of the **Society** of **Medical History.** Chicago. *Bull. Soc. med. Hist.* [1911–] **L.**MD.; **O.**R. 11–17.

12235 **Bulletin. Society** of **Naval Architects** and **Marine Engineers.** New York. *Bull. Soc. nav. Archit. mar. Engrs* [1947–48] **L.**P.; **Te.**N. [*C. as:* 52393]

12236 **Bulletin** of the **Society** for **Plant Ecology.** Tokyo. *Bull. Soc. Pl. Ecol., Tokyo* [*C. as:* 25227]

12237 **Bulletin. Society** for the **Promotion** of **Engineering Education.** Lancaster, Pa. *Bull. Soc. Promot. Engng Educ.*

12238 **Bulletin. Society** for **Research** in **Chinese Architecture.** Peiping. *Bull. Soc. Res. Chin. Archit.* **L.**BA. 33–37.

12239 **Bulletin** of the **Society** of **Salt Science.** Tokyo. *Bull. Soc. Salt Sci., Tokyo* **Y.**

12240 **Bulletin** of the **Society** of **Scientific Photography** of **Japan.** Tokyo. *Bull. Soc. scient. Photogr. Japan* [1951–] **L.**PG.; **We.**K.

12241 **Bulletin** of the **Society** of **Weight Engineers.** London. *Bull. Soc. Wght Engrs* **L.**P. 53–59. [*C. as:* 20445]

12242 **Bulletin** des **soies** et des **soieries.** Lyon. *Bull. Soies*

12243 **Bulletin. Soil Bureau, D.S.I.R., New Zealand.** *Bull. Soil Bur. N.Z.* **Y.**

12244 **Bulletin** of the **Soil Conservation Board, Palestine.** Jerusalem. *Bull. Soil Conserv. Bd Palest.* [1942–] **O.**F.; **Rt.** 42.

12245 **Bulletin. Soil Conservation** and **Rivers Control Council, New Zealand.** Wellington. *Bull. Soil Conserv. Rivers Control Coun. N.Z.* [1944–] **C.**A.; **O.**RE. 44–45; **Rt.**

Bulletin. Soil and **Land-use Survey, Gold Coast.** *See* 10404.

12246 **Bulletin. Soil Mechanics** and **Foundation Research Laboratory, Egyptian University.** Cairo. *Bull. Soil Mech. Fdn Res. Lab. Egypt. Univ.* **L.**SC. 37.

12247 **Bulletin** of the **Soil Science Society** of **China.** *Bull. Soil Sci. Soc. China* [*C. as:* 709]

12248 **Bulletin** of **Solar Phenomena. Tokyo Astronomical Observatory.** Tokyo. *Bull. sol. Phenom., Tokyo* [1949–] **L.**AS. imp.; SC.; **M.**U. 51–; **Y.**

12249 **Bulletin. Solvay Technical** and **Engineering Service.** New York. *Bull. Solvay tech. Engng Serv.* [1936–] **L.**P. imp.

Bulletin de la **Sous-Section** pour **combattre** les **ennemis** des **plantes** du **Comité** d'**agriculture** à **Pétrograd.** *See* 24472.

12250 **Bulletin. South African Association** for the **Advancement** of **Science.** Johannesburg. *Bull. S. Afr. Ass. Advmt Sci.* [1936–] **L.**BM.; SC. 38–; **C.**P.

12250° **Bulletin. South African Association** of **Marine Biological Research.** *Bull. S. Afr. Ass. mar. biol. Res.* [1960–] **Pl.**M.

12251 **Bulletin. South African Biological Society.** Pretoria. *Bull. S. Afr. biol. Soc.* **L.**BMᴺ. 18*; K. 18. [*C. as:* 50162]

12252 **Bulletin. South African Museums Association.** Durban. *Bull. S. Afr. Mus. Ass.* [1936–] **L.**BMᴺ.; SC. 48–; **Y.**

12252° **Bulletin. South African Sugar Association Experiment Station.** Durban. *Bull. S. Afr. Sug. Ass. Exp. Stn* [1956–] **L.**BM.

12253 **Bulletin. South African Wool Textile Research Institute.** Grahamstown. *Bull. S. Afr. Wool Text. Res. Inst.* [1952–] **L.**P. 52–54; **Y.**

12254 **Bulletin. South Carolina Agricultural Experiment Station.** Clemson College. *Bull. S. Carol. agric. Exp. Stn* [1888–] **L.**AM.; BMᴺ. 36–38; EB. (ent.) 04–; K. 93–06 imp.; P. imp.; **O.**F. 26–; **Rt.** 94: 02– imp.; **Y.**

12255 **Bulletin. South Carolina Department** of **Agriculture.** Columbia. *Bull. S. Carol. Dep. Agric.*

12256 **Bulletin. South Carolina Engineering Experiment Station.** Clemson College. *Bull. S. Carol. Engng Exp. Stn* [1931–] **L.**P.

12257 **Bulletin** of the **South Carolina Geological Survey.** Columbia. *Bull. S. Carol. geol. Surv.*

12258 **Bulletin** of the **South Carolina State Board** of **Health.** Columbia. *Bull. S. Carol. St. Bd Hlth*

12259 **Bulletin. South Carolina State Commission** of **Forestry.** Columbia. *Bull. S. Carol. St. Commn For.* **O.**r. 44.

Bulletin. South Carolina State Planning Board. *See* 12288.

12260 **Bulletin. South Dakota Agricultural Experiment Station.** Brookings. *Bull. S. Dak. agric. Exp. Stn* [1887–] **L.**AM.; EB. (ent.) 90–; K. 97–16 imp.; P.; **C.**A.; **Cr.**P. 09–25 imp.; **O.**RE. 34– imp.; **Rt.** imp.; **Y.**

12261 **Bulletin. South Dakota Food** and **Drug Department.** *Bull. S. Dak. Fd Drug Dep.* **L.**SC. 13–23.

12262 **Bulletin. South Dakota Geological Survey.** Vermilion. *Bull. S. Dak. geol. Surv.* [1894–] **L.**BM. 08–; BMᴺ. 94–23 imp.; GM.; SC. 98–.

12263 **Bulletin** of the **South Dakota Live Stock Sanitary Board.** Pierre. *Bull. S. Dak. live Stk sanit. Bd* **L.**SC. 24–.

12264 **Bulletin** of the **South Dakota School** of **Mines.** Rapid City. *Bull. S. Dak. Sch. Mines* [1888–29] **L.**BM^N. 99–29 imp.; GL. 20–29; P. 99–29; SC. 18–29; **Abs.**N. 20–29; U. 27–29; **Bl.**U. 20–29; **Bm.**U. 20–29; **E.**U. 20–29; **Ld.**U. 20–29; **O.**R. 29–29.

12265 **Bulletin** of the **South Eastern Union** of **Scientific Societies.** London. *Bull. S.-East. Un. scient. Socs* [1912–] **L.**BM.; BM^N. 12–46 imp; SC.; **C.**UL. 36–; **Ld.**U. 33–47 imp. [*C. of:* 15452]

12266 **Bulletin.** **South Essex Natural History Society.** Southend-on-Sea. *Bull. S. Essex nat. Hist. Soc.* **L.**BM^N. 38–39. [*C. of:* 34814]

12267 **Bulletin** of the **South Indian Medical Union.** Madras. *Bull. S. Indian med. Un.* [1929–34] [*Replaced by:* 26979]

12268 **Bulletin** of the **Southern California Academy** of **Sciences.** Los Angeles. *Bull. Sth. Calif. Acad. Sci.* [1902–] **L.**BM^N.; E. 04–; Z. 33–; **Y.**

12269 **Bulletin.** **Southern California Camellia Society.** Pasadena. *Bull. Sth. Calif. Camellia Soc.* **L.**K. [*C. as:* 13076]

12270 **Bulletin** of **Southern California University.** Los Angeles. *Bull. Sth.Calif. Univ.*

12271 **Bulletin** of the **Southern Dental Society** of **New Jersey.** Camden. *Bull. Sth. dent. Soc. N.Jers.*

12272 **Bulletin** of the **Southwestern Association** of **Petroleum Geologists.** *Bull. S.-west. Ass. Petrol. Geol.* [1917] **L.**BM^N.; GM.; PT.; SC.; **M.**U. [*C. as:* 9298]

12273 **Bulletin** of the **Southwestern University Medical College.** Dallas, Tex. *Bull. S.-west. Univ. med. Coll.*

12274 **Bulletin spécial.** **Comité technique, Société hydrotechnique** de **France.** Lyon. *Bull. spéc. Com. tech. Soc. hydrotech. Fr.* **L.**P. 15–19.

12275 **Bulletin spécial** du **Service** de **santé** et de **l'hygiène publique.** Bruxelles. *Bull. spéc. Serv. Santé Hyg. publ., Brux.* **L.**H. 93–12.

Bulletin spécial. **Société hydrotechnique** de **France.** **Comité technique.** Lyon. *See* 12274.

12276 **Bulletin** of **Spectrum Analysis.** London. *Bull. Spectrum Analysis* [1929–] **L.**BM.; NF.; **Abs.**N.; **E.**R.; **Nw.**A.

12277 **Bulletin.** **Sport Fishing Institute.** Washington. *Bull. Sport Fish. Inst.* **L.**Z. 57–60. [*C. as:* 48381]

12278 **Bulletin.** **Spring Washer Industry.** Chicago. *Bull. Spring Washer Ind.* [1939–] **L.**P. 39–40.

12279 **Bulletin** of the **Springfield Museum** of **Natural History.** Springfield, Mass. *Bull. Springfield Mus. nat. Hist.* [1904–] **L.**BM.; **G.**N. 04: 10.

12280 **Bulletin** of **Staff Meetings.** **Hospitals** of the **University** of **Minnesota.** Minneapolis. *Bull. Staff Meet. Hosps Univ. Minn.* [1929–36] [*C. as:* 50714]

Bulletin. **Standards Association** of **Australia.** *See* 48355.

12281 **Bulletin.** **Standards Institution** of **Israel.** Tel-Aviv. *Bull. Stand. Instn Israel* [1950–] **L.**P.; **Y.** [*C. of:* 12282; *From* 1950–57 *published in* 25611 *and from* 1958 *in* 21777]

12282 **Bulletin.** **Standards Institution** of **Palestine.** Tel-Aviv. *Bull. Stand. Instn Palest.* [1943–48] **L.**P.; **Y.** [*Published in:* 25611; *C. as:* 12281]

Bulletin. **State Board** of **Forestry, Oregon.** *See* 11449.

12283 **Bulletin** of the **State Board** of **Health** of **Kentucky.** Louisville. *Bull. St. Bd Hlth Ky* **L.**TD. 31–33. [*C. as:* 10045]

Bulletin. **State Bureau** of **Mines** and **Mineral Resources, New Mexico Institute** of **Mining** and **Technology.** *See* 10637.

Bulletin. **State** of **Connecticut.** **State Geological** and **Natural History Survey.** *See* 9909.

12284 **Bulletin.** **State Division** of **Conservation.** **Department** of **Mines, Mining** and **Geology, Georgia.** Atlanta, Ga. *Bull. St. Div. Conserv. Dep. Mines Ga*

12285 **Bulletin.** **State Electricity Commission, Victoria.** Melbourne. *Bull. St. Elect. Commn Vict.* [1926–27] **L.**P.; SC.

Bulletin. **State Electrometallurgical Research Laboratories.** **State College** of **Washington.** *See* 10069.

12286 **Bulletin** of the **State Geological Survey, Tennessee.** Nashville. *Bull. St. geol. Surv. Tenn.* [1910–21] **L.**BM^N.; SC.; **G.**U. 10–12 imp.; **Lv.**U. 10–11; **O.**R. 10–12. [*C. as:* 12382]

Bulletin of the **State Institute** of **Marine** and **Tropical Medicine** in **Gdansk.** *See* 10631.

Bulletin. **State Institute** for **Tobacco Investigations.** Krasnodar. *See* 54687.

12287 **Bulletin** of the **State** of **Israel Sea Fishing Research Station.** *Bull. St. Israel Sea Fish. Res. Stn* **Dm.** 52–.

Bulletin of the **State Oceanographical Institute.** Moscow. *See* 12762.

12288 **Bulletin.** **State Planning Board, South Carolina.** Columbia. *Bull. St. Plann. Bd S. Carol.* **O.**F. 41– imp.

12289 **Bulletin.** **State Plant Board** of **Florida.** Gainesville. *Bull. St. Pl. Bd Fla* [1953–60] **L.**BM^N.; EB. (ent.); **C.**A. [*C. as:* 10102^c]

12290 **Bulletin** of the **State University** of **Iowa.** Iowa City. *Bull. St. Univ. Iowa* **Db.** 16–; **O.**B.

12291 **Bulletin** de la **Station agricole** du **Pas de Calais.** Arras. *Bull. Stn agric. Pas de Calais*

12292 **Bulletin.** **Station d'agriculture** et de **pêche** de **Castiglione.** Alger. *Bull. Stn Agric. Pêche Castiglione* [1926–] **L.**AM. 33–40 imp.; BM^N. 27–36; **Abd.**M. 50–; **Lo.** 33–36 imp: 40–; **Pl.**M. 40–; **Y.**

12293 **Bulletin** de la **Station agronomique** du **département** de **l'Aisne.** Laon. *Bull. Stn agron. Dép. Aisne* **Rt.** 12–13.

12294 **Bulletin** de la **Station agronomique** de l'**état** à **Gembloux.** Bruxelles. *Bull. Stn agron. État Gembloux* **Rt.** 75–08.

12295 **Bulletin.** **Station agronomique** de **Guadeloupe.** Pointe-à-Pitre. *Bull. Stn agron. Guadeloupe* **L.**EB. 19–27; K. 19–27 imp.

12296 **Bulletin.** **Station agronomique** et **Laboratoire départemental** de **Finistère.** Quimper. *Bull. Stn agron. Lab. dép. Finistère*

12297 **Bulletin** de la **Station agronomique** de la **Loire-inférieure.** Nantes. *Bull. Stn agron. Loire-infér.*

12298 **Bulletin** de la **Station agronomique** de **Maurice.** *Bull. Stn agron. Maurice* [1900–] **L.**K. 01–imp.; **Lv.**U. 03–05; **Rt.** 00–13.

12299 **Bulletin** de la **Station agronomique** de la **Somme.** *Bull. Stn agron. Somme* **Rt.** 21 imp.

12301 **Bulletin** de la **Station biologique** d'**Arcachon**. Bordeaux. *Bull. Stn biol. Arcachon* [1909-38: 49-] L.AM. 09-12; BM.; BMᴺ.; R. 25-37; SC. 31-; UC. 09-38 imp.; Z.; Bn.U. 58-; **C.P.** 15-; UL. 14-; **Db.** 25-34; **Dm.** 14-37; **E.**C. 21-37 imp.; U.; **G.**U. 25-37; Lo.; Lv.U.; M.U. 14-37; O.R. 14-; Pl.M. [*C. of:* 54254: >11869 *for* 1956]

    Bulletin de la **Station biologique** de la **Société** des **amis** des **sciences naturelles**, d'**anthropologie** et d'**ethnographie**. Moscou. *See* 58278.

    Bulletin de la **Station** pour la **défense** des **plantes**. Stavropol. *See* 24508.

12302 **Bulletin** de la **Station ionosphérique** de **Lwiro, Congo belge**. Bruxelles. *Bull. Stn ionosph. Lwiro* L.MO. 52-53; **Y.**

    Bulletin. **Station marine** d'**Endoume**. *See* 42384.

    Bulletin de la **Station maritime** de **Hel**. *See* 7199.

12304 **Bulletin**. **Station océanographique** de **Salammbô**. Tunis. *Bull. Stn océanogr. Salammbô* [1924-] L.AM.; BMᴺ.; Z. 24-29; **Abd.**M.; Bn.U. 25-49; **Dm.** 25-56; **E.**U. 25; Lv.U.; **Mi.**; Pl.M.; **Wo.** 37-56 imp.; **Y.**

12305 **Bulletin** de la **Station** de **pisciculture** et d'**hydrobiologie** de l'**Université** de **Toulouse**. Paris. *Bull. Stn Piscic. Hydrobiol. Univ. Toulouse* [1903-06] Pl.M. 04-05. [*C. as:* 11533]

    Bulletin of the **Station** for **Plant Acclimatisation**. Leningrad. *See* 54512.

12306 **Bulletin** de la **Station** des **recherches forestières** du **Nord** de l'**Afrique**. Alger. *Bull. Stn Rech. for. N. Afr.* O.F. 12-38*; R. 12-32 imp.

    Bulletin de la **Station régionale protectrice** des **plantes** à **Léningrad**. *See* 24494.

    Bulletin de la **Station séismique** de **Tiflis**. *See* 12827.

12307 **Bulletin** de la **Station séricole** du **Caucase**. Tiflis. *Bull. Stn séric. Caucase* L.EB. 12-14 imp.

12308 **Bulletin** de la **Station séricole** de **Montpellier**. *Bull. Stn séric. Montpellier*

    Bulletin des **stations agronomiques hongroises**. *See* 27475.

12309 **Bulletin** des **stations** de la **classe** du **réseau séismique** de l'**U.R.S.S.** *Bull. Stns Cl. Réseau séism. U.R.S.S.*

    Bulletin des **stations séismiques régionales** du **Caucase**. *See* 12812.

12310 **Bulletin** des **stations séismographiques**. **Institut** pour la **recherche scientifique** en **Afrique centrale**. Bruxelles. *Bull. Stns séismogr. Inst. Rech. scient. Afr. cent.* [1955-] Lv.U.; **Y.**

12311 **Bulletin** de **statistique agricole**. **Institut internationale** d'**agriculture**. Rome. *Bull. Statist. agric. Inst. int. Agric.* L.BM. 10-.

12312 **Bulletin** de **statistique agricole** à l'**usage** des **services** de l'**agriculture**. Paris. *Bull. Statist. agric. Us. Serv. Agric.* O.AEC. 42-44.

12314 **Bulletin statistique**. **Communauté européene** du **charbon** et de l'**acier, Haute autorité**. Luxembourg. *Bull. statist. Commun. eur. Charb. Acier* [1953-] Dn.U. 57-; **G.**U. 57- imp.; Ld.P. 57-; **M.**P.; **Sa.** 57-.

    Bulletin statistique. **European Coal** and **Steel Community**. *See* 12314.

12315 **Bulletin statistique mensuel**. **Comité** des **forges** de **France**. Paris. *Bull. statist. mens. Com. Forges Fr.* L.I. 30-39.

    Bulletin statistique des **pêches maritimes** de **Lettonie**. *See* 28167.

12316 **Bulletin statistique** des **pêches maritimes** des **pays** du **nord** de l'**Europe**. Copenhagen. *Bull. statist. Pêch. marit. Pays N. Eur.* [1903-22] L.AM.; BM.; BMᴺ.; MO.; Z.; **Abd.**M.; U.; **Bm.**U.; Bn.U. 07-22; **C.**B.; UL. 08-22; **Db.**; **E.**M.; R.; U.; **G.**U.; Ld.U.; Lo.; Lv.U.; M.U.; **Mi.** 05-22; **Nw.**A.; **O.**G. 03-09; R.; Pl.M.; **Sa.** 11-22; **Wo.** 06-22 imp.; **Y.** [*C. as:* 12317]

12317 **Bulletin statistique** des **pêches maritime** des **pays** du **nord** et de l'**ouest** l'**Europe**. Copenhagen. *Bull. statist. Pêch. marit. Pays N. Ouest Eur.* [1923-] L.AM.; BM.; BMᴺ.; L. 26-; MO.; R. 28-; U.; Z.; **Abd.**M.; U.; **Bm.**U.; Bn.U. 07-47 imp.; **C.**B.; U.; **Db.**; **E.**M.; R.; U.; Ld.U. Lo.; Lv.U.; M.U.; **Mi.**; **Nw.**A. 22-37 imp.; O.R.; Pl.M.; **Sa.** 22-39; **Wo.**; **Y.** [*C. of:* 12316]

12318 **Bulletin** du **Stéréo-Club français**. Paris. *Bull. Stéréo-Club fr.*

    Bulletin. **Sternberg State Astronomical Institute**, Moscow University. *See* 12760.

12319 **Bulletin** of the **Stoneham Museum, Kitale, Kenya Colony**. Nairobi. *Bull. Stoneham Mus.* [1931-] L.BMᴺ.; E. 31-35; EB.

12320 **Bulletin** of the **Storrs Agricultural Experiment Station**. Storrs, Conn. *Bull. Storrs agric. Exp. Stn* [1888-] L.AM.; BM. 13-17; BMᴺ. 08-12 imp.; EB. (ent.) 95-22 imp.; K. 89-06 imp.; P. 88-23; SC. 14-; Br.A. 22- imp.; **C.**A.; **Cr.**P. 95-11 imp.; **G.**U. 11-19 imp.; **Rt.** 07-.

12321 **Bulletin**. **Structural Materials Research Laboratory, Portland Cement Association**. Chicago. *Bull. struct. Mater. Res. Lab. Portland Cem. Ass.* [1919-25]

12322 **Bulletin** of the **Sugar Cane Expert**. Istanbul. *Bull. Sug. Cane Expert, Istanbul* [1947-] L.SC.; **C.**A.

12323 **Bulletin**. **Sugar Cane Research Station, Mauritius**. Port Louis. *Bull. Sug. Cane Res. Stn Mauritius* [1933-47] L.P.; **C.**A.; **Rt.**; **Y.** [*C. as:* 10893]

    Bulletin. **Sugar Industry Research Association, Mauritius**. *See* 10893.

12324 **Bulletin**. **Suid-Afrikaanse Woltekstiel Navorsingsinstituut**. *Bull. Sd-Afr. Woltekst. NavorsInst.* [1952-] **Y.**

    Bulletin suisse de **minéralogie** et de **pétrographie**. *See* 48950.

    Bulletin suisse de **mycologie**. *See* 48977.

12325 **Bulletin suisse** de **pêche** et de **pisciculture**. Neuchâtel. *Bull. suisse Pêche Piscic.* [1901-36] Db. 03-10; Pl.M. 03-19 imp. [*C. as:* 37265]

12325° **Bulletin** of **Sunspot Observations**. **Geofizički institut**. Zagreb. *Bull. Sunspot Obsns, Zagreb* L.MO. 49-50.

12326 **Bulletin** of the **Swedish Engineers Society** of **Chicago**. *Bull. Swed. Engrs Soc. Chicago* [1933-] L.P. 33-45. [*C. of:* 33491; *Suspended:* 1939-42]

12327 **Bulletin** du **Syndicat** des **chirurgiens dentistes** de **France**. Paris. *Bull. Synd. Chir. Dent. Fr.* L.MD. 07-13*. [*C. as:* 38634]

12328 **Bulletin** du **Syndicat** des **chirurgiens français**. Paris. *Bull. Synd. Chir. fr.*

12329 **Bulletin** du **Syndicat** des **ingénieurs-conseils** en matière de **propriété industrielle.** Paris. *Bull. Synd. Ingrs-Cons. Propr. ind.* **L.**P. 85–02*. [*C. as:* 9450]

12330 **Bulletin** du **Syndicat national** des **vétérinaires.** Paris. *Bull. Synd. natn. Vét.* [1949–] **L.**V.

12331 **Bulletin** du **Syndicat national** des **vétérinaires** de **France** et des **colonies.** Paris. *Bull. Synd. natn. Vét. Fr. Colon.* **W.** 32–.

12332 **Bulletin. Syndicat** des **planteurs** de **caoutchouc** de l'**Indo-Chine.** Saigon. *Bull. Synd. Plrs Caoutch. Indochine* **L.**SC. 35–; **Sy.**R. 18–39 imp. [*C. of:* 2894]

12333 **Bulletin. Taichung Sugarcane Improvement Station.** Taichung. *Bull. Taichung SugCane Improv. Stn* [1952–] **Y.**

12334 **Bulletin. Taihoku Agricultural Experiment Station.** Taihoku. *Bull. Taihoku agric. Exp. Stn*

12335 **Bulletin. Taiwan Agricultural Research Institute.** Taipeh. *Bull. Taiwan agric. Res. Inst.* [1946–] **L.**BM^N. 46–47; EB. 46–47; **C.**A.; **Rt.** 50; **Y.** [*C. of:* 43946]
 Bulletin. Tashkent Astronomical Observatory. *See* 12825.

12336 **Bulletin. Taylor Forge** and **Pipe Works.** Chicago. *Bull. Taylor Forge Pipe Wks* **L.**P. 49– imp.

12337 **Bulletin. Taylor Society.** New York. *Bull. Taylor Soc.* **L.**P. 22–34*. [*C. as:* 12338]

12338 **Bulletin** of the **Taylor Society** and the **Society** of **Industrial Engineers.** New York. *Bull. Taylor Soc.* [1934–35] **L.**P. [*C. of:* 12339; *C. as:* 26912]

12339 **Bulletin** of the **Tea Division, Tôkai-Kinki Agricultural Experiment Station.** Kanaya. *Bull. Tea Div. Tôkai-Kinki agric. Exp. Stn* [1953–61] **C.**A. 58–61; **Md.**H.; **Y.** [*C. in:* Bulletin of the Tea Research Station, Ministry of Agriculture and Forestry, Japan. Kanaya]

12340 **Bulletin. Tea Research Institute** of **Ceylon.** Talawakella. *Bull. Tea Res. Inst. Ceylon* [1926–] **L.**EB. 27–; K. 27–47; P. 33–; **Br.**A. 59–; U. 30–; **C.**A.; **Rt.**; **Y.**
 Bulletin of the **Tea Research Station. Ministry** of **Agriculture** and **Forestry, Japan.** *See* 12339.

12341 **Bulletin** of **Technical Data** for the **Plywood Industry.** Philadelphia. *Bull. tech. Data Plywood Ind.* [1942–] **L.**P. 42–45 imp.

12342 **Bulletin. Technical Department. Coal Utilisation Council.** London. *Bull. tech. Dep. Coal Util. Coun.* [1933–36] **L.**P.; **Bm.**P.; **M.**P. 35–36. [*C. as:* 51937]

12343 **Bulletin** of the **Technical** and **Engineering Society** of the **Colorado School** of **Mines.** Denver. *Bull. tech. Engng Soc. Colo. Sch. Mines* [1900–10] **L.**P.

12344 **Bulletin. Technical Information Service, London Master Builders' Association.** London. *Bull. tech. Inf. Serv. Lond. Master Bldrs' Ass.* [1951–] **L.**P. imp.
 Bulletin of **Technical** and **Medicinal Plants.** Saratov. *See* 54822.
 Bulletin. Technical Publications Committee, Association of **Teachers** of **Printing** and **Allied Subjects.** *See* 131°.

 Bulletin. Technical and **Scientific Service, Ministry** of **Agriculture, Egypt.** *See* 11116.

12344° **Bulletin. Technical Service** of the **Department** of **Agriculture** and **Professional Education. Republic** of **Haïti.** Port-au-Prince. *Bull. tech. Serv. Dep. Agric. Haïti*
 Bulletin of the **Technical University** of Istanbul. *See* 24242.
 Bulletin technique de l'**administration** des **postes, télégraphes** et **téléphones suisses.** *See* 52562.

12345 **Bulletin technique** des **aéroplanes Henry Potez.** Paris. *Bull. tech. Aéropl. Henry Potez* [1929–36] **L.**P. 30–36; SC.

12346 **Bulletin technique** de l'**Association** des **ingénieurs** et **conducteurs** sortis de l'**Institut électrotechnique** de **Grenoble 'La Nouvelle Blanche'.** Lyon. *Bull. tech. Ass. Ingrs Conduct. Inst. électrotech. Grenoble*

12347 **Bulletin technique** de l'**Association** des **ingénieurs** sortis de l'**École polytechnique** de l'**Université libre** de **Bruxelles.** *Bull. tech. Ass. Ingrs Éc. polytech. Brux.* [1902–52] **L.**P. 33. [*C. as:* 47252]

12348 **Bulletin technique** de l'**Association** des **ingénieurs** de l'**Institut industriel** du **nord** de la **France.** Lille. *Bull. tech. Ass. Ingrs Inst. ind. N. Fr.*
 Bulletin technique des **avions Henry Potez.** *See* 12345.

12349 **Bulletin technique** du **Bureau Veritas.** Paris. *Bull. tech. Bur. Veritas* [1919–] **L.**P. imp.; **Nw.**A. 33–; **Y.**

12350 **Bulletin technique** de la **Chambre syndicale** des **fabricants** d'**appareils électriques** à **bas voltage.** Paris. *Bull. tech. Chamb. synd. Fabr. Appar. élect. bas Volt.*

12351 **Bulletin technique** de la **Chambre syndicale** des **fabricants** et **négociants** de la **photographie.** Paris. *Bull. tech. Chamb. synd. Fabr. Négoc. Photogr.*

12351° **Bulletin technique. Chambre syndicale** des **mines** de **fer** de **France.** *Bull. tech. Chamb. synd. Mines Fer Fr.* **Y.**

12352 **Bulletin technique châtaignier.** Nancy. *Bull. tech. châtaign.* [1949–] **L.**P.; **O.**F.; **Y.**

12353 **Bulletin technique** et **chimique. Comité central** des **fabricants** de **sucre** de **France.** Paris. *Bull. tech. chim. Com. cent. Fabr. Sucre Fr.* **L.**P. 34–38.

12354 **Bulletin technique** et **commercial** de l'**industrie** des **pâtes alimentaires.** Marseille. *Bull. tech. comm. Ind. Pâtes aliment.*

12355 **Bulletin technique. Groupement** des **associations** de **propriétaires** d'**appareils** à **vapeur** et **électriques.** Paris. *Bull. tech. Grpmt Ass. Propr. Appar. Vap. élect.* [1955–] **L.**P.; **Y.** [*C. of:* 10416]

12356 **Bulletin technique. Groupement professionnel** des **fabricants** de **ciment portland artificiel** de **Belgique.** Bruxelles. *Bull. tech. Grpmt prof. Fabr. Cim. Portland artif. Belg.* **L.**P.; **Y.**

12357 **Bulletin technique—houille** et **dérivés. Institut national** de l'**industrie charbonnière.** Liége. *Bull. tech. Houille Dériv. Inst. natn. Ind. charb.* **L.**P. 50–; **Y.**

12358 **Bulletin technique** de l'**industrie papetière.** Paris. *Bull. tech. Ind. pap.* [1947–] **Lh.**P.

12359 **Bulletin technique** d'information des **ingénieurs** des **services agricoles.** Paris. *Bull. tech. Inf. Ingrs Servs agric.* **L.**AM. 49–; P. 57–; **C.**A. 49–; **Hu.**G. 47– imp.
    Bulletin technique. Institut national de l'**Industrie charbonnière.** Liège.
      Houille et derivés. *See* 12357.
      Mines. *See* 12360.
      Préparation des minerais. *See* 12361.

12360 **Bulletin technique—mines. Institut national** de l'**industrie charbonnière.** Liège. *Bull. tech. Mines Inst. natn. Ind. charb.* **L.**MI. 56–; P. 50–; **Y.**
    Bulletin technique PTT. *See* 52557.

12361 **Bulletin technique—Préparation** des **minerais. Institut national** de l'**industrie charbonnière.** Liège. *Bull. tech. Prép. Miner. Inst. natn. Ind. charb.* [1951–] **L.**P.; **Y.**

12362 **Bulletin technique** de la **route silicatée.** Paris. *Bull. tech. Route silic.* **L.**P. 27–32 imp.

12363 **Bulletin technique séricicole. Station** de re**cherches séricicoles.** Alès. *Bull. tech. séric. Stn Rech. séric. Alès*

12364 **Bulletin technique** du **Service technique** de l'**aérotechnique.** Paris. *Bull. tech. Serv. tech. Aérotech.* **L.**AV. 28–29 imp.; P. 27–31* imp.; SC. 22–31. [*C. as:* 11780]

12365 **Bulletin technique** de la **Société belge radioéléctrique.** Bruxelles. *Bull. tech. Soc. belge radio-élect.*

12366 **Bulletin technique. Société française** des **constructions Babcock** et **Wilcox.** Paris. *Bull. tech. Soc. fr. Constr. Babcock et Wilcox* **L.**P. 27–; **Y.**

12367 **Bulletin technique** de la **Société r. belge** des **ingénieurs** et des **industriels.** Bruxelles. *Bull. tech. Soc. r. belge Ingrs Inds* **L.**MI. 45–.

12368 **Bulletin technique. Société Rateau.** Paris. *Bull. tech. Soc. Rateau* [1929–] **L.**AV. 43–48; EE. 29–30 imp.; P.; **G.**M. 29–30. [*C. of:* 12153]

12369 **Bulletin technique. Société Standard française** des **pétroles.** *Bull. tech. Soc. Standard fr. Pétrol.* [1936–39] **L.**C.; P.; SC. [*C. of:* 29272]

12370 **Bulletin technique. Station agronomique** de la **Guadeloupe.** Pointe-à-Pitre. *Bull. tech. Stn agron. Guadeloupe* **L.**EB. 25–26; **Rt.** 25–26.

12371 **Bulletin technique** de la **Suisse romande.** Lausanne. *Bull. tech. Suisse romande* [1900–] **L.**AV. 45– imp.; BA. 32–; P. 10–; **Te.**N. 47–59; **Wa.**B. 47–56; **Y.** [*C. of:* 12209]

12372 **Bulletin technique trimestriel. Union professionnelle** des **inspecteurs techniques** et des **chefs** de **section** des **chemins** de **fer belges.** Schaerbeck. *Bull. tech. trimest. Un. prof. Insp. tech. Chem.-de-Fer belg.* **L.**P. 32–39.

12373 **Bulletin technique** de l'**Union** des **ingénieurs** sortis des **écoles spéciales** de **Louvain.** *Bull. tech. Un. Ingrs Éc. spéc. Louvain* **L.**P. 34–39; SC. 30; **Nw.**A. 47.

12374 **Bulletin technique. Union** des **ingénieurs techniques** sortis de l'**Institut Gramme** de **Liége.** *Bull. tech. Un. Ingrs tech. Inst. Gramme Liége*

12375 **Bulletin technique Vevey.** Vevey. *Bull. tech. Vevey* **L.**P. 55–.

12376 **Bulletin. Technological Laboratory, Indian Central Cotton Committee.** Bombay. *Bull. technol. Lab. Indian cent. Cott. Comm.* [1927–29] **L.**P.; SC.; **Abs.**N.; **O.**B. 28–29; **Rt.** (tech. ser.). [*C. as:* 52616]

12377 **Bulletin** of the **Technological Museum.** Sydney. *Bull. technol. Mus., Sydney* [1923–46] **L.**BM.; BM^N imp.; EB. 23: 29; P.; SC. 31–42. [*C. as:* 11181]
    Bulletin. Technology Experiment Station, Maine University. *See* 10844.

12378 **Bulletin** of the **Telecommunication Engineering Bureau** of **Japan.** Tokyo. *Bull. Telecommun. Engng Bur. Japan*

12379 **Bulletin. Teletype Printing Telegraph Systems.** Chicago. *Bull. Teletype Print. Telegr. Syst.* [1929–] **L.**P. [*C. of:* 11159°]

12379° **Bulletin** du **temps. Observatoire r.** de **Belgique.** Bruxelles. *Bull. Temps Obs. r. Belg.* [1909–] **L.**MO. [*C. of:* 11569°]

12380 **Bulletin** of the **Tennessee Agricultural Experiment Station.** Knoxville. *Bull. Tenn. agric. Exp. Stn* [1888–] **L.**AM.; BM^N. 06–38 imp.; EB. (ent.) 91–; K. 91–06 imp.; P.; **C.**A.; **Cr.**P. 06–13 imp.; **Rt.** imp.; **Y.**

12381 **Bulletin. Tennessee Board** of **Entomology.** Knoxville. *Bull. Tenn. Bd Ent.* [1905–22] **L.**BM^N. 06–17; EB.; SC. 16–22. [*C. as:* 10102]

12382 **Bulletin. Tennessee Division** of **Geology.** Nashville. *Bull. Tenn. Div. Geol.* [1923–] **L.**BM^N.; GM.; P.; **E.**D.; **G.**U. 31–32 imp.; **Y.** [*C. of:* 12286]
    Bulletin. Tennessee State Geological Survey. *See* 12286.

12383 **Bulletin** of the **Tennessee State Horticultural Society.** Knoxville. *Bull. Tenn. St. hort. Soc.*

12384 **Bulletin. Tennessee University Engineering Experiment Station.** Knoxville. *Bull. Tenn. Univ. Engng Exp. Stn* [1922–] **L.**P. imp.

12385 **Bulletin** de **terminologie.** Bureau des traductions, Canada. Ottawa. *Bull. Terminol.* [1954–] **L.**SC.

12386 **Bulletin** of the **Terrestrial Electric Observatory** of **Fernando Sanford.** Palo Alto. *Bull. terr. elect. Obs. Fernando Sanford* [1920–30] **L.**BM.; MO.; SC.; **E.**R. 23–30; U. 23–30; **O.**R. 23–30; **Pl.**M. 23.

12387 **Bulletin** of the **Territory** of **Papua.** Melbourne. *Bull. Terr. Papua* [1913–21] **L.**BM^N.; G.; GL. 15–21; GM.; SC.; UC. 13–18; **Lv.**U. 15–20.

12388 **Bulletin. Texas Agricultural Experiment Station.** College Station. *Bull. Tex. agric. Exp. Stn* [1888–] **L.**AM.; EB. (ent.) 91–; K. 96–21 imp.; P.; **Br.**A. 10– imp.; **C.**A.; **M.**U. 36–47 imp.; **O.**F. 32– imp.; RE. 33–53 imp.; **Rt.** imp.; **Y.**

12389 **Bulletin** of the **Texas Agricultural** and **Mechanical College.** College Station. *Bull. Tex. agric. mech. Coll.* **Ld.**U. 36–.

12390 **Bulletin. Texas Agricultural** and **Mechanical College Extension Service.** College Station. *Bull. Tex. agric. mech. Coll. Ext. Serv.* **O.**F. 44– imp.

12391 **Bulletin** of the **Texas Archaeological** and **Palaeontological Society.** Abilene. *Bull. Tex. archaeol. palaeont. Soc.* [1929–] **L.**BM^N. 38.

12392 **Bulletin. Texas Department** of **Agriculture.** Austin. *Bull. Tex. Dep. Agric.* **L.**EB. (ent.) 08–25; **Cr.**P. 10–13 imp.

12393 **Bulletin. Texas Engineering Experiment Station.** College Station. *Bull. Tex. Engng Exp. Stn* [1915–] **L.**P. imp.; **Y.**

12394 **Bulletin. Texas Forest Service.** *Bull. Texas Forest Serv.* **O.**F. 56–; **Y.**

12395 **Bulletin. Texas Game** and **Fish Commission.** Austin. *Bull. Texas Game Fish Commn* **Lo.** 58–.

12396 **Bulletin** of the **Texas Health Department.** Austin. *Bull. Tex. Hlth Dep.*

12397 **Bulletin. Texas Reclamation Department.** Austin. *Bull. Tex. Reclam. Dep.* [1913–] **L.**P. 13–31.

12398 **Bulletin** of the **Texas State Forester.** College Station. *Bull. Tex. St. Forester* **L.**SC. 17–.

12399 **Bulletin** of the **Textile Research Institute.** Yokohama. *Bull. Text. Res. Inst., Yokohama* **L.**P. 60–; **Ld.**W. 54–; **M.**C. 54–; **Y.**

12400 **Bulletin** of the **Theory** of **Differential Periodicity.** Avoca. *Bull. Theory diff. Period.* [1951–] **L.**BM^N. 53– imp.

12401 **Bulletin thérapeutique** de la **tuberculose.** Paris. *Bull. thér. Tuberc.*
    Bulletin of **Thermodynamics** and **Thermochemistry.** *See* 9774.

12402 **Bulletin. Thorne Ecological Research Station.** Boulder. *Bull. Thorne ecol. Res. Stn* [1956–] **L.**BM^N.

12403 **Bulletin. Tobacco Experiment Station. Connecticut Agricultural Experiment Station.** New Haven. *Bull. Tob. Exp. Stn Conn.* [1922–27] **L.**BM.; P.; **Rt.** [*C. in:* 9904]

12404 **Bulletin. Tobacco Research Board** of **Rhodesia** (and **Nyasaland**). Salisbury, Kutsaga. *Bull. Tob. Res. Bd Rhod. Nyasald* [1952–] **L.**BM. 53–; MY.; P. 55– imp.; **Br.**A. 55– imp.; **O.**RE.; **Rt.**; **Y.**

12405 **Bulletin** of the **Tohoku National Agricultural Experimental Station.** Morioka. *Bull. Tohoku natn. agric. exp. Stn* [1946 ?–] **Md.**H. 58–; **Rt.** 58; **Y.**

12406 **Bulletin** of the **Tokai Regional Fisheries Research Laboratory.** Tokyo, etc. *Bull. Tokai reg. Fish. Res. Lab.* [1950–] **L.**AM.; BM^N.; **Abd.**M.; T. 53–; **Lo.**; **Pl.**M. imp.; **Y.**
    Bulletin of the **Tokai-Kinki National Agricultural Experiment Station.** Tsu, Kanaya.
        Horticultural Division. *See* 10464.
        Division of Plant Breeding and Cultivation. *See* 10101.
        First Agronomy Division. *See* 10252.
        Second Agronomy Division. *See* 11712.
        Tea Division. *See* 12339.
    Bulletin of the **Tokyo Anthropological Society.** Tokyo. *See* 25566.

12408 **Bulletin. Tokyo Dental College.** *Bull. Tokyo dent. Coll.* [1960–] **Bl.**U.
    Bulletin of the **Tokyo Imperial University Forests.** *See* 12414.

12409 **Bulletin** of the **Tokyo Institute** of **Technology.** Tokyo. *Bull. Tokyo Inst. Technol.*
        Series A: [1949–] **L.**AV.; BM.; **C.**UL. 49; **G.**ME. 60–; U. 49; **M.**U. 49; **Sa.** 49; **Y.**
        Series B: [1950–] **L.**BM.; MI. 50–51 imp.; **C.**UL. 50–51; **G.**ME. 60–; U. 50–51; **M.**U. 50–51; **Sa.** 50–51 imp.; **Y.**
        Series C. *See* 27562.

12410 **Bulletin** of **Tokyo Medical** and **Dental University.** Tokyo. *Bull. Tokyo med. dent. Univ.* [1954–] **L.**D.; LI.; MA.; MD. 55– imp.; S.; TD.; **Ld.**U. 58–; **Nw.**A.; **Y.**

12411 **Bulletin** of the **Tokyo Science Museum.** Tokyo. *Bull. Tokyo Sci. Mus.* [1939–49] **L.**BM^N.; SC. imp.; Z. imp.; **Pl.**M. 39. [*C. as:* 11241]

12412 **Bulletin** of the **Tokyo University** of **Agricultural** and **Textile Industry.** Tokyo. *Bull. Tokyo Univ. agric. Text. Ind.* [1950–] **L.**AM.

12413 **Bulletin** of the **Tokyo University** of **Engineering.** Tokyo. *Bull. Tokyo Univ. Engng* [1932–]

12414 **Bulletin** of the **Tokyo University Forests.** Tokyo. *Bull. Tokyo Univ. Forests* **O.**F. 28–37 imp.; **Y.**

12415 **Bulletin** of the **Toledo Academy** of **Medicine.** Toledo, Ohio. *Bull. Toledo Acad. Med.* [*C. as:* 9196]
    Bulletin of the **Tomsk State University.** *See* 55084.

12416 **Bulletin** of the **Topographical Survey** of **Canada.** Ottawa. *Bull. topogr. Surv. Can.* **L.**SC. 05–; **O.**G. 29.

12417 **Bulletin** of the **Torrey Botanical Club** (and **Torreya**). New York. *Bull. Torrey bot. Club* [1870–] **L.**BM^N.; HS. 28–55; K.; L.; SC. 38–; **Bl.**U. 61–; **Bm.**U. 46–; **Bn.**U. 59–; **C.**BO. 94–; **Cr.**U. 37–; **Db.** 94–; **E.**B.; **G.**U.; **Ld.**U. 70–83: 86–87: 99–21: 29–39: 45–; **Lv.**U. 38–; **M.**U.; **Md.**H. 51–; **O.**BO. 86–; **Sh.**U. 37–43 imp.; **Y.**

12418 **Bulletin** of the **Tottori University Forests.** Tottori. *Bull. Tottori Univ. Forests* [1958–] **C.**A.; **O.**F.

12419 **Bulletin** des **transports.** Paris. *Bull. Transp., Paris*

12420 **Bulletin** des **transports** en **commun** à **traction mécanique** et **électrique.** Paris. *Bull. Transp. Commun Tract. méc. élect.*

12421 **Bulletin** des **transports internationaux** par **chemins** de **fer.** Berne. *Bull. Transp. int. Chem.-de-Fer* **Y.**

12422 **Bulletin** of the **Transvaal Museum.** Pretoria. *Bull. Transv. Mus.* [1955–] **L.**BM.; BM^N.; TP. 59–; **Dm.**; **E.**R.; **Ld.**U. 60–; **O.**R.; **Pl.**M.
    Bulletin. Transvaal University College. Pretoria. *See* 10214.

12423 **Bulletin** des **travaux** de **chimie** executés par les **ingénieurs** des **mines.** Paris. *Bull. Trav. Chim. Ingrs Mines*

12424 **Bulletin. Travaux** des **collaborateurs, Service** de la **carte géologique** de l'**Algérie.** Alger. *Bull. Trav. Collab. Serv. Carte géol. Algér.* [1953–] **L.**BM^N. [*C. of:* 11753]

12425 **Bulletin** des **travaux** du **Conseil** d'**hygiène** et de **salubrité** de l'**arrondissement** de **Saint-Nazaire.** *Bull. Trav. Cons. Hyg. Salubr. Arrond. St-Nazaire*

12426 **Bulletin** et **travaux. Fondation ophtalmologique Adolphe de Rothschild.** Paris. *Bull. Trav. Fondn ophtal. Adolphe de Rothschild* **L.**MD. 11.

12427 **Bulletin** et **travaux. Institut indochinois** pour l'**étude** de l'**homme.** Hanoi. *Bull. Trav. Inst. indochin. Étude Homme* [1938–44] **L.**AN.

12428 **Bulletin** des **travaux** de la **Société** de **pharmacie** de **Bordeaux.** *Bull. Trav. Soc. Pharm. Bordeaux* [1860–] **L.**PH. 73–90: 34–40: 45–; **Y.**

12429 **Bulletin** des **travaux. Société** de **pharmacie** de **Lyon.** Lyon. *Bull. Trav. Soc. Pharm. Lyon* [1957–] **L.**P.; **Y.**

12430 **Bulletin** et **travaux** de la **Société** des **sciences médicales** de **Tunis.** *Bull. Trav. Soc. Sci. méd. Tunis* [1903–13] [*C. as:* 47641]
    Bulletin des **travaux** publiés par la **Station** d'**aquiculture** et de **pêche** de **Castiglione.** *See* 12292.

12431 **Bulletin. Trelawny Tobacco Research Station.** Salisbury, S. Rhodesia. *Bull. Trelawny Tob. Res. Stn* **C.**A. 41–.

12432 **Bulletin trimestriel de l'Académie Malgache.** Tananarive. *Bull. trimest. Acad. Malgache* [1902–04] **L.**BM.; BM^N. [*C. as:* 9171]

12433 **Bulletin trimestriel. Alliance d'hygiène sociale.** Bordeaux. *Bull. trimest. Alliance Hyg. soc.*

12434 **Bulletin trimestriel. Amis du Musée océanographique** de **Monaco.** *Bull. trimest. Amis Mus. océanogr. Monaco* [1947–] **L.**BM^N. 47; Z. 47–54; **G.**U.

12435 **Bulletin trimestriel. Association** des **amis** du **Musée** de la **Marine.** Paris. *Bull. trimest. Ass. Amis Mus. Mar.* [1931–] **L.**P.

12436 **Bulletin trimestriel de l'Association des anciens élèves** de l'**École supérieure** de **brasserie de l'Université** de **Louvain.** *Bull. trimest. Ass. anc. Élèv. Éc. sup. Brass. Univ. Louvain*

12437 **Bulletin trimestriel Association centrale** des **vétérinaires.** Paris. *Bull. trimest. Ass. cent. Vét.*

12438 **Bulletin trimestriel. Association internationale** des **congrès** de la **route.** Paris. *Bull. trimest. Ass. int. Congr. Route*

Bulletin trimestriel du Centre belge d'**étude** et de **documentation** des **eaux.** *See* 9735.

12439 **Bulletin trimestriel. Centre** d'études et de **documentation paléontologiques.** Paris. *Bull. trimest. Cent. Étud. Docum. paléont.* [1948–57] **L.**BM^N.; SC. [*C. as:* 12457°; *See also* 12446]

12440 **Bulletin trimestriel. Centre textile** de con**trôle** et de **recherche scientifique.** Roubaix. *Bull. trimest. Cent. text. Contrôle Rech. scient.* **L.**P. 54–.

12441 **Bulletin trimestriel du Comité cotonnier congolais.** Bruxelles. *Bull. trimest. Com. cotonn. congol.* [1936–] **L.**SC.; TP. 36–49; **M.**C. 36–49.

Bulletin trimestriel de la **Commission** du **Pacifique** du **sud.** *See* 41496.

12442 **Bulletin trimestriel** de documentation signalé**tique** de **chronométrie générale.** Besançon. *Bull. trimest. Docum. signal. Chronom. gén.* [1952–53] **L.**P. [*C. from:* 2742; *C. as:* 12458]

12443 **Bulletin trimestriel** de la **Droguerie vétérinaire Renault** aîné. Paris. *Bull. trimest. Drog. vét. Renault*

12444 **Bulletin trimestriel** de l'**enseignement professionel** et **technique** des **pêches maritimes.** Orléans. *Bull. trimest. Enseign. prof. tech. Pêch. marit.* **Abd.**M. 11:17–19; **Pl.**M. 98–19 imp.

12445 **Bulletin trimestriel, Fédération française** des **sociétés** de **sciences naturelles.** Versailles. *Bull. trimest. Féd. fr. Socs Sci. nat.* [1956–] **L.**BM^N.; **Y.** [*C. of:* 12476]

12446 **Bulletin trimestriel** d'**information** du **C.E.D.P.** Centre d'études et de documentation paléontologiques. Paris. *Bull. trimest. Inf. C.E.D.P.* **L.**BM^N. 48–; GL. 50–. [*See also* 12439]

12447 **Bulletin trimestriel** d'**information** du **carbure** de **calcium** et de l'**acétylène.** Paris. *Bull. trimest. Inf. Carbure Calc. Acét.* [1939] **L.**P.; SC. [*C. of:* 25411]

12448 **Bulletin trimestriel. Laboratoire** d'**analyses** et de **recherches industrielles.** Roubaix. *Bull. trimest. Lab. Analyses Rech. ind., Roubaix* [1929–] **Ld.**W. 29–39; 49–; **M.**C. 29–39; **Y.**

12449 **Bulletin trimestriel** du **Laboratoire Chaix.** Paris. *Bull. trimest. Lab. Chaix* [*C. of:* 11443]

12450 **Bulletin trimestriel. Ligue algérienne** de **lutte** contre le **cancer.** Alger. *Bull. trimest. Lig. algér. Lutte Cancer* [1951–] **L.**MA. 55–; TD. 52– imp.

12451 **Bulletin trimestriel. Ligue** des **amis** de la **forêt** de **Soignes.** Linkebeek. *Bull. trimest. Lig. Amis Forêt Soignes* **O.**F. 52–.

12452 **Bulletin trimestriel** de la **Ligue** du **Nord** contre la **tuberculose.** Lille. *Bull. trimest. Lig. N. Tuberc.*

12453 **Bulletin trimestriel** de la **Maison** du **médecin.** Paris. *Bull trimest. Maison Méd.* [*C. of:* 10845]

12454 **Bulletin trimestriel** de l'**Office forestier** du **Centre** et de l'**Ouest.** Le Mans. *Bull. trimest. Off. for. Cent. Ouest*

12455 **Bulletin trimestriel. Office régional agricole** du **Midi.** Marseille. *Bull. trimest. Off. rég. agric. Midi* **C.**A. 32–36*.

Bulletin trimestriel du rayonnement, Organisation météorologique mondiale. *See* 41591^a.

12456 **Bulletin trimestriel** des **résultats** acquis pendant les **croisières périodiques,** etc. **Conseil permanent international** pour l'**exploration** de la **mer.** Copenhague. *Bull. trimest. Résult. Crois. périod. Cons. perm. int. Explor. Mer* [1905–08] **L.**AM.; BM.; BM^N.; MO.; R.; SC.; U.; UC.; Z.; **Abd.**M.; U.; **Bm.**U.; **Db.**; **Dm.**; **E.**M.; R.; U.; **G.**U.; **Ld.**U.; **Lo.**; **Lv.**U.; **M.**U.; **Mi.**; **O.**R.; **Pl.**M.; **Sa.**; **Wo.** [*C. of:* 11610; *C. as:* 10475 and 11525]

12457 **Bulletin trimestriel** de la **Section A. M. A.** de la **Société forestière française** des **amis** des **arbres.** Reims. *Bull. trimest. Sect. A. M. A. Soc. for. fr.*

12457° **Bulletin trimestriel** du **Service** d'**information géologique** du **Bureau** de **recherches géologiques, géophysiques** (et **minières**). Paris. *Bull. trimest. Serv. Inf. géol. Bur. Rech. géol. géophys.* [1958–] **L.**BM^N.; SC. [*C. of:* 12439]

12457° **Bulletin trimestriel. Service météorologique, Belgique.** *Bull. trimest. Serv. mét. Belg.* **Y.**

12458 **Bulletin trimestriel signalétique** de **documentation** de **chronométrie générale.** Besançon. *Bull. trimest. signal. Docum. Chronom. gén.* [1954–] **L.**P. 54–58. [*C. of:* 12442]

12459 **Bulletin trimestriel** de la **Société antituberculeuse** de l'**enseignement primaire** du **département** de la **Seine.** Paris. *Bull. trimest. Soc. antituberc. Dép. Seine*

Bulletin trimestriel de la **Société de Borda.** *See* 11870.

12460 **Bulletin trimestriel** de la **Société centrale** d'**agriculture** du **département** de la **Seine-inférieure.** Rouen. *Bull. trimest. Soc. cent. Agric. Dép. Seine-infér.* [1942–50] **Md.**H. [*C. of:* 11025; *C. as:* 11882]

Bulletin trimestriel de la **Société** d'**émulation** d'**Abbeville.** *See* 11905.

12461 **Bulletin trimestriel. Société** d'**émulation** du **département** des **Vosges.** Épinal. *Bull. trimest. Soc. Émul. Dép. Vosges* **L.**BM. 20–.

12462 **Bulletin trimestriel. Société forestière française.** Paris. *Bull. trimest. Soc. for. fr.* [1893–14] [*C. as:* 3933]

12462° **Bulletin trimestriel. Société forestière** de **Franche Comté** et des **provinces** de l'**est.** *Bull. trimest. Soc. for. Franche Comté* **Y.**

12463 **Bulletin trimestriel** de la **Société** de **géographie** et d'**archéologie** d'**Oran.** *Bull. trimest. Soc. Géogr. Archéol. Oran* [1878–] **L.**G. imp.; **E.**G. 85–.

Bulletin trimestriel. Société de **géographie** d'**Égypte.** *See* 11976.

12464 **Bulletin trimestriel** de la **Société** de **géographie** de l'**Est.** Paris & Nancy. *Bull. trimest. Soc. Géogr. E.* [1879–14] **L.**BM. 79–13; G. 95; **E.**G. 93–14.

12465 **Bulletin trimestriel** de la **Société** d'**hygiène** de **Vichy.** *Bull. trimest. Soc. Hyg. Vichy*

12466 **Bulletin trimestriel** de la **Société industrielle** du **Nord** de la **France.** Lille. *Bull. trimest. Soc. ind. N. Fr.* [1873–09] **L.**P. 94–09; **Bm.**U. 92–09. [*C. as:* 11032]

12467 **Bulletin trimestriel** de la **Société** de **médecine vétérinaire** de la **Gironde.** Bordeaux. *Bull. trimest. Soc. Méd. vét. Gironde*

12468 **Bulletin trimestriel** de la **Société mycologique** de **France.** Paris. *Bull. trimest. Soc. mycol. Fr.* [1903–] **L.**AM. 13–39; BM.; BMᴺ.; K. 04–; L.; MY.; SC. 20–; U. 20–; UC. 20–23; **Abs.**N. 24–; **Br.**U. 52–; **C.**BO. 03–10; UL.; **Cr.**U. 27–; **E.**B. 08–; U. 20–23; **G.**U. 20–21 imp.; **Ld.**U.; **M.**U. 20– imp.; **O.**BO. 28–; R. 20–23; **Rt.** 24–39; **Y.** [*C. of:* 12092]

12469 **Bulletin trimestriel** de la **Société** des **sciences, lettres** et **arts** de **Pau.** Pau. *Bull. trimest. Soc. Sci. Lett. Arts Pau*

Bulletin trimestriel de la **Société scientifique** de **Borda.** *See* 11870.

12470 **Bulletin trimestriel** de la **Société** des **vétérinaires lorrains.** Lunéville. *Bull. trimest. Soc. Vét. lorr.*

12471 **Bulletin trimestriel** de la **Société** des **vétérinaires** du **Nord.** Lille. *Bull. trimest. Soc. Vét. N.*

Bulletin trimestriel de la **Station séismique** de **Tiflis.** *See* 27863.

12472 **Bulletin trimestriel** du **Syndicat** des **fabricants** de **sucre.** Paris. *Bull. trimest. Synd. Fabr. Sucre*

12473 **Bulletin trimestriel** du **Syndicat médical** d'**Angers.** *Bull. trimest. Synd. méd. Angers*

12474 **Bulletin trimestriel** des **syndicats médicaux** du **département** du **Maine-et-Loire.** Angers. *Bull. trimest. Synds méd. Dép. Maine-et-Loire*

12475 **Bulletin trimestriel** de l'**Union** pour la **coordination** de la **production** et du **transport** de l'**électricité.** Laufenburg. *Bull. trimest. Un. Coord. Prod. Transp. Élect.* **L.**P. 60–.

12476 **Bulletin trimestriel. Union** des **sociétés françaises** d'**histoire naturelle.** Versailles. *Bull. trimest. Un. Socs fr. Hist. nat.* [1950–55] **L.**BMᴺ.; K.; SC. [*C. as:* 12445]

12477 **Bulletin. Tropical Plant Research Foundation.** Washington. *Bull. trop. Pl. Res. Fdn* [1925–29] **L.**EB. (ent.) 26–29; P.; SC.; **C.**A.; **Rt.**

12478 **Bulletin. Tufts College.** Boston. *Bull. Tufts Coll.* **L.**G. 98– imp.

12479 **Bulletin** of the **Tufts Dental Club** of **New York.** *Bull. Tufts dent. Club N.Y.*

12480 **Bulletin** of **Tufts—New England Medical Center.** Boston. *Bull. Tufts New Engl. med. Cent.* [1955–] **L.**MA. [*C. of:* 11271 and 55308]

12481 **Bulletin** of the **Tulane Medical Faculty.** New Orleans. *Bull. Tulane med. Fac.* [1941–] **L.**MA.; **M.**MS. 51–.

Bulletin. Turkestan Section, Imperial Russian Geographical Society. *See* 24536.

Bulletin of the **Turkish Physical Society.** *See* 55333.

Bulletin. Tuskegee Agricultural Experiment Station. *See* 55360.

Bulletin. USSR Central Forestry Research Institute. Leningrad. *See* 48697.

12482 **Bulletin** of the **Uganda Society.** Kampala. *Bull. Uganda Soc.* [1943–45] **L.**BMᴺ.; SC. 44–45. [*Temporarily replaced:* 55450]

Bulletin of the **Ukrainian Scientific Institute** of **Grain Culture.** *See* 55116.

12483 **Bulletin** of the **Umeno Entomological Laboratory.** Kurume. *Bull. Umeno ent. Lab.* [1935–] **L.**BMᴺ. 35–38.

12484 **Bulletin** de l'**Union agricole calédonienne.** Nouméa. *Bull. Un. agric. calédon.*

12485 **Bulletin** de l'**Union agricole** de **Jodoigne.** *Bull. Un. agric. Jodoigne*

12486 **Bulletin** de l'**Union** des **agriculteurs** d'**Égypte.** Le Caire. *Bull. Un. Agricrs Égypte* [1901–] **L.**EB. 13–28; SC. 29–; **C.**A. 48–; **Db.** 19–; **Rt.** 22–.

12487 **Bulletin** de l'**Union centrale** des **syndicats** de la **Société** des **agriculteurs** de **France.** Paris. *Bull. Un. cent. Synds Soc. Agricrs Fr.* [1928–] [*C. from:* 11821]

12488 **Bulletin** de l'**Union** de **charbonnages, mines** et **usines métallurgiques** de la **province** de **Liège.** Liège. *Bull. Un. Charb. Mines Us. métall. Prov. Liège* **Sh.**M. 69–24.

12489 **Bulletin** de l'**Union** des **chimistes** et **naturalistes** d'**Haiti.** Port-au-Prince. *Bull. Un. Chim. Nat. Haiti* [1955–] **L.**BMᴺ.

12490 **Bulletin. Union coloniale française.** Paris. *Bull. Un. colon. fr.* **L.**SC. 23–27*.

12491 **Bulletin** de l'**Union** des **exploitations électriques** en **Belgique.** Bruxelles. *Bull. Un. Exploit. élect. Belg.* [1931–54] **Y.** [*Not published* 1939–46; *C. as:* 56971]

12492 **Bulletin. Union géodesique** et **géophysique internationale.** Venezia. *Bull. Un. géod. géophys. int.*
Section de magnétisme terrestre [1919–30] **L.**AS. 27–30; BM.; MO.; SC. 23–30; **E.**R. imp. [*C. as:* 9481]
Section d'océanographie [1921–31] **L.**BMᴺ.; MO. 28–29; SC.; **Abd.**M.; **E.**R. imp.; **Ld.**U. 28–30; **Lo.**; **Lv.**U.; **Pl.**M. [*C. as:* 9495]
Section d'hydrologie scientifique [1924–30] **L.**MO. imp.; SC.; **E.**R. 27–30 imp.; **Ld.**U. 27–30; **Lv.**U. 27–30. [*C. as:* 9471]
Section de géodesie [1922–] *See* 10322.
[*For Bulletin d'information See* 10556]

12493 **Bulletin** de l'**Union géographique** du **nord** de la **France.** Douai. *Bull. Un. géogr. N. Fr.* **L.**G. 80–.

12494 **Bulletin** de l'**Union internationale** des **chemins** de **fer.** Paris. *Bull. Un. int. Chem.-de-fer* **L.**P. 24–39: 52–.

Bulletin de l'**Union internationale** pour l'**étude** des **insectes sociaux.** *See* 23666.

Bulletin. Union internationale pour la **protection** de la **nature.** *See* 10699.

12495 **Bulletin** de l'**Union internationale** de **secours** aux **enfants.** Genève. *Bull. Un. int. Secours Enf.* **L.**BM. 20–21.

12496 **Bulletin.** Union internationale de **tramways,** de **chemins** de **fer** d'intérêt **local,** et de **transports** publics automobiles. Bruxelles. *Bull. Un.int. Tramways* [1933–34] **L.**P.

12497 **Bulletin** de l'**Union internationale** contre la **tuberculose.** Paris. *Bull. Un. int. Tuberc.* [1924–] **L.**MA. 24–40; MD.; S. 24–40; **G.**PH. 32–48.

12498 **Bulletin** de l'**Union pharmaceutique** de l'**arrondissement judiciaire** de **Charleroi.** *Bull. Un. pharm. Arrond. Charleroi*

12499 **Bulletin** de l'**Union** des **physiciens.** Paris. *Bull. Un. Physns* **L.**P. 08– imp.; **Y.**
　　Bulletin of the **Union** of **Socialist Soviet Republics Tobacco Investigations.** Krasnodar. *See* 54687.
　　Bulletin de l'**Union** des **sociétés savantes** polonaises de **Léopol.** *See* 50679.
　　Bulletin de l'**Union suisse** des **papeteries.** *See* 27677.

12500 **Bulletin** de l'**Union thermale.** Paris. *Bull. Un. therm.*

12501 **Bulletin.** **United Gas** and **Electrical Engineering Corporation.** New York. *Bull. un. Gas. elect. Engng Corp.*

12502 **Bulletin.** **United Planters' Association** of **Southern India.** Coimbatore. *Bull. un. Plrs Ass. Sth. India* **L.**C. 34–36; EB. 53–; SC. 34–; **O.**RE. 36– imp.

12503 **Bulletin.** **United Provinces Forestry Department.** Allahabad. *Bull. un. Prov. For. Dep.* **L.**SC. 39–; **O.**F. 28–.

12504 **Bulletin** of the **United States Army Medical Department.** Carlisle Barracks, Pa. *Bull. U.S. Army med. Dep.* [1943–49] **L.**EE. 44–49; H. 45–49; MA. 44–49; MC.; MD.; TD.; V. 43–47; **Br.**U.; **Db.** 47–49; **Ld.**U. 43–44; **O.**R.; **W.** 44–49. [*C. of:* 4832; *C. in:* 55551]
　　Bulletin of the **United States Bureau** of **Fisheries.** *See* 9658.

12505 **Bulletin** of the **United States Bureau** of **Mines.** Washington. *Bull. U.S. Bur. Mines* [1910–] **L.**BM.; BM^N. 11– imp.; C. 17–; GM. imp.; I. 12– imp.; MI. 12–56 imp.: 57–; NF. 11– imp.; P. imp.; **Abs.**N. imp.; **Bm.**U. imp.; **Db.** 11–; **G.**M. 12–35 imp.; MC. 21– imp.; U. 16–; **Ld.**P. 27– imp.; **M.**U. 13–50 imp.; **Nw.**A. 20– imp.; **Sh.**10. 24–; M. imp.; **Y.**
　　Bulletin. **United States Bureau** of **Standards.** *See* 9677.

12506 **Bulletin** of the **United States Coast** and **Geodetic Survey.** Washington. *Bull. U.S. Cst geod. Surv.* [1888–02] **L.**AS. 88–01; BM. 88–01; G. 94–00; SC. 88–01; UC. 93–00; **Db.** 88–00; **E.**G. 02; R. 88–99; **G.**M. 88–00 imp.

12507 **Bulletin.** **United States Coast Guard.** Washington. *Bull. U.S. Cst Guard* **L.**AM. 29–39; BM. 13–; MO. 13– imp.; **Abd.**M. 20– imp.; **Abs.**N. 22–; **C.**PO. 14– imp.; **Dm.** 15–39 imp.; **G.**M. 15–35; **Lo.** 14– imp.; **O.**AP. 14–39 imp.: 41–; **Pl.**M. 26–40 imp.; **Wo.** 13– imp. [*Not issued* 1917, 1918, 1942–45]

12508 **Bulletin.** **United States Department** of **Agriculture.** Washington. *Bull. U.S. Dep. Agric.* [1913–

23] **L.**AM.; BM.; BM^N.; C. imp.; EB. (ent.); K. imp.; MD. imp.; P.; SC.; Z.; **Abs.**N. 13: 15: 22–23 imp.; **Br.**A. imp.; **C.**UL.; **Cr.**P. 13–22 imp.; **E.**B. imp.; F. v. imp.; R.; **G.**M. imp.; **Ld.**U.; **Lv.**P.; U. imp.; **M.**P. imp.; **O.**R. 15–23 imp.; RE. 15–23 imp.; **Rt.** imp. [*C. as:* 16587]
　　Bureau of **Animal Industry.** *See* 9651.
　　Bureau of **Biological Survey.** *See* 9653.
　　Bureau of **Chemistry.** *See* 9655.
　　Bureau of **Entomology.** *See* 9657.
　　Bureau of **Plant Industry.** *See* 9673.
　　Division of **Agrostology.** *See* 10094.
　　Division of **Biological Survey.** *See* 9653.
　　Division of **Botany.** *See* 10095.
　　Division of **Chemistry.** *See* 9655.
　　Division of **Entomology.** *See* 9657.
　　Division of **Forestry.** *See* 10097.
　　Division of **Pomology.** *See* 10104.
　　Division of **Soils.** *See* 10105.
　　Division of **Statistics.** *See* 10106.
　　Division of **Vegetable Physiology** and **Pathology.** *See* 10108.
　　　Library. *See* 10807.
　　　Office of **Experiment Stations.** *See* 11376.
　　　Office of **Public Roads.** *See* 11382.
　　　Office of **Road Enquiry.** *See* 11382.
　　　Weather Bureau. *See* 12612.

12509 **Bulletin** of the **United States Fish Commission.** Washington. *Bull. U.S. Fish Commn* [1881–03] **L.**AM.; BM.; BM^N.; P. imp.; R.; SC.; Z.; **Abd.**M.; **Bm.**P.; **Bn.**U. 87–03 imp.; **C.**B. 81–01; P. 02–04; **Cr.**M. 89–03; **Db.**; **E.**F. 87–03; R.; U. imp.; **G.**M. 81–86; U. 83–03 imp.; **Lo.**; **Lv.**U.; **M.**U. 89–02 imp.; **Pl.**M. imp.; **Sa.**; **Wo.** 84–97 imp. [*C. as:* 9658]

12510 **Bulletin** of the **United States Geological Survey.** Washington. *Bull. U.S. geol. Surv.* [1883–] **L.**BM.; BM^N.; C.; G.; GL.; GM.; I. imp.; MI. 84–43 imp.: 44–; SC.; UC.; Z. 83–15 imp.; **Abd.**U. 03–; **Abs.**N. imp.; U. imp.; **Bl.**U. 91– imp.; **Bm.**N. 06–; U. 85–; **Br.**U.; **C.**P. imp.; S. 85–; UL. 03–; **Cr.**N. 91– imp.; **Db.**; **Dn.**U. 03– imp.; **E.**A. 83–03; B. 83–03 imp.; C. 10– imp.; D. imp.; G.; J.; R.; U. 02– imp.; **G.**M. 11–37; MG. 87– imp.; N.; T.; U. imp.; **Ld.**U. imp.; **Lv.**U. imp.; **M.**U. 83–25 imp.; **Nw.**A. imp.; **O.**G. 98–36 imp.; R.; **Sh.**M. 91–; U. 03–23 imp.; **Sw.**I. 90–02; U. 94–37 imp.; **Y.**

12511 **Bulletin** of the **United States Institute** for **Textile Research.** Lancaster, Pa. *Bull. U.S. Inst. Text. Res.* [1931–32] **Ld.**W.; **M.**C. [*C. as:* 52988]

12512 **Bulletin.** **United States National Museum.** Smithsonian Institution. Washington. *Bull. U.S. natn. Mus.* [1875–] **L.**BM.; BM^N.; EB. (ent.) 82–; G. imp.; GL. 00–; GM. (geol.); L.; R.; SC. 78–; U. 76–46 imp.; UC.; Z.; **Abd.**U.; **Abs.**N. imp.; **Bl.**U. 87–; **Bm.**N. 01–; P.; U. 83–33 imp.; **Bn.**U. 96–; **Br.**P. 89–04 imp.; U. 05–41 imp.; **C.**B.; P.; UL. 87–; **Cr.**N. 92– imp.; P. imp.; **Db.**; **Dm.** 05– imp.; **Dn.**U. imp.; **E.**C. 93– imp.; F.; R.; U. imp.; **G.**M. 12– imp.; N. 93–; U.; **Ld.**P. 79– imp.; U. 08–; **Lv.**U. 89– imp.; **M.**U. 91–; **N.**P. 91–; U.; **Nw.**A. 02: 11–32 imp.; **O.**R.; **Pl.**M. 89– imp.; **Rt.** 42–; **Sh.**M. 91–; U. imp.; **Sw.**U. 07–23 imp.; **Y.**

12513 **Bulletin.** **United States War Department Engineer School.** Washington. *Bull. U.S. War Dep. Engr Sch.*

12514 **Bulletin.** **United Typothetae** of **America.** Chicago. *Bull. un. Typoth. Am.* [1907–16] **L.**SB. 09–16. [*C. as:* 55391]

12515 **Bulletin** de l'**Université** de l'**Asie centrale.** Tachkent. *Bull. Univ. Asie cent.* [1923–] L.AS. 25–27; BM.; BM^N. 23–45; C. 29–38; GL. 23–38; L. 25–; SC.; TD. 25–; UC.; **Bl.**U. 24–26; **Bm.**N. 24–; **C.**P. 23–35; **E.**B. 24–; R. 23–45; U. 24–; **G.**U. 25–38: 45; **Lv.**U.; **O.**B. 23–29.

12516 **Bulletin** de l'**Université** l'**Aurore.** Shanghai. *Bull. Univ. Aurore* L.BM^N. 20–38 imp.

Bulletin de l'**Université** de **Bakou.** *See* 24311.

Bulletin de l'**Université** d'état de la **R.S.S.** d'**Arménie.** *See* 24361.

Bulletin de l'**Université** de **Nijni-Novgorod.** *See* 24441.

12517 **Bulletin** de l'**Université** de **Toulouse.** Toulouse. *Bull. Univ. Toulouse* **Abd.**U. 12–; **O.**B. 97–08.

12517° **Bulletin.** **University** of **Alaska Extension Service.** College. *Bull. Univ. Alaska Ext. Serv.* **Y.**

Bulletin of the **University** of **Arizona.** **Bureau** of **Mines.** *See* 9670.

12518 **Bulletin.** **University** of **Arizona Laboratory** of **Tree-ring Research.** Tucson. *Bull. Univ. Ariz. Lab. Tree-ring Res.* [1941–] L.SC.; U. 41–53.

Bulletin. **University** of **Cambridge School** of **Forestry.** *See* 55601.

Bulletin. **University** of **Connecticut Engineering Experiment Station.** *See* 10161.

Bulletin. **University** of **Florida Engineering Experiment Station.** *See* 10167.

Bulletin. **University Geological Survey** of **Kansas.** *See* 10743.

12519 **Bulletin** of the **University Geological Survey** of **Wyoming.** Laramie. *Bull. Univ. geol. Surv. Wyo.* L.BM^N. 34–39; SC. 29–.

12520 **Bulletin.** **University** of **Hawaii.** Honolulu. *Bull. Univ. Hawaii* [1917–19] L.BM.; P. [*C. of:* 9834; *C. as:* 41499]

Bulletin of the **University** of **Illinois.**
　Agricultural Experiment Station. *See* 10485.
　Chemistry Department. *See* 9776.
　Department of Ceramic Engineering. *See* 10023.
　Engineering Experiment Station. *See* 10496.
　Water Survey Series. *See* 57184.

12521 **Bulletin** of the **University** of **Kansas.** Lawrence. *Bull. Univ. Kans.* [1900–02] L.BM^N.; M. imp.; **Lv.**U. imp. [*C. in:* 27244]

12521° **Bulletin.** **University** of **Kentucky Research Club.** *Bull. Univ. Ky Res. Club* **Y.**

12522 **Bulletin.** **University** of **Leeds Department** of **Agriculture.** Leeds. *Bull. Univ. Leeds Dep. Agric.* [1898–] **Ld.**U.; **Rt.** 99–.

Bulletin. **University** of **London Council** for **Psychical Investigation.** *See* 9926.

12523 **Bulletin.** **University** of **Miami School** of **Medicine** and **Jackson Memorial Hospital.** Miami. *Bull. Univ. Miami Sch. Med.* [1955–] L.BM.; MD. [*C. of:* 10715]

12524 **Bulletin.** **University** of **Minnesota.** Minneapolis. *Bull. Univ. Minn.* L.BM. 13; GM. 13–; SC. 13–; **E.**R. 12–21; **G.**U. 14–15; **O.**B.

Bulletin of the **University** of **Minnesota Agricultural Experiment Station.** *See* 11124.

12525 **Bulletin** of the **University** of **Minnesota Engineering Experiment Station.** Minneapolis. *Bull. Univ. Minn. Engng Exp. Stn* [1923–52] L.P.; SC.; **Bm.**U. 15–28 imp.; **Ld.**P. imp.; **M.**T. 30: 39–52 imp.

12526 **Bulletin** of the **University** of **Minnesota Hospitals** and **Minnesota Medical Foundation.** Minneapolis. *Bull. Univ. Minn. Hosps* **Bm.**U. 48–.

Bulletin. **University** of **Minnesota School** of **Forestry Agricultural Experiment Station.** *See* 11655.

12527 **Bulletin.** **University** of **Missouri.** **Engineering Experiment Station Series.** *Bull. Univ. Mo. Engng Exp. Stn Ser.* [1910–] L.PH. 28; U. 10–15 imp.; **Bm.**U. 10–13; **C.**UL.; **G.**MG. imp.; U. 11–; **M.**U. 10–13 imp.; **O.**B. 11–13; **Sh.**M. 35–; **Y.**

12528 **Bulletin.** **University** of **Missouri.** **Medical Series.** Columbia. *Bull. Univ. Mo. med. Ser.* [1913–16] L.U.; **Abd.**U.; **Bm.**U.; **G.**U.; **Lv.**U. imp.; **M.**U.; **O.**R.

12529 **Bulletin.** **University** of **Missouri.** **Science Series.** Columbia. *Bull. Univ. Mo. Sci. Ser.* [1911–14] L.BM.; P.; **C.**UL.; **E.**B.; **G.**U. imp.; **Lv.**U.; **M.**U.; **O.**R.

12530 **Bulletin** of the **University** of **Montana.** Missoula. *Bull. Univ. Mont.* L.BM^N. 99–23 imp.; **Bl.**U. 01–10 imp.; **Db.** (biol.) 02–11 imp.

12531 **Bulletin** of the **University** of **Nebraska College** of **Medicine.** Lincoln. *Bull. Univ. Neb. Coll. Med.* [1906–09] **Lv.**U. 06–07; **M.**MS. 07–09.

12532 **Bulletin** of the **University** of **Nebraska State Museum.** Lincoln. *Bull. Univ. Neb. St. Mus.* [1939–] L.BM^N.; **C.**P. 55–; **Y.** [*C. of:* 11263]

Bulletin. **University** of **Nevada.** *See* 55651°.

Bulletin. **University** of **Nevada Agricultural Experiment Station.** *See* 11268.

Bulletin. **University** of **Nevada Engineering Experiment Station.** *See* 11270.

12533 **Bulletin** of the **University** of **New Mexico.** **Anthropological Series.** Albuquerque. *Bull. Univ. New Mex. anthrop. Ser.* [1936–43] L.AN. imp.; SC.; U.; **O.**B. [*C. as:* 55652]

12534 **Bulletin** of the **University** of **New Mexico.** **Biological Series.** Albuquerque. *Bull. Univ. New Mex. biol. Ser.* [1899–41] L.BM^N. imp.; P. imp.; SC.; **Db.** 07–19; **Lv.**U. 08–41 imp. [*C. as:* 55653]

12535 **Bulletin** of the **University** of **New Mexico.** **Chemistry Series.** Albuquerque. *Bull. Univ. New Mex. Chem. Ser.* [1913–38] L.GL. 14; P. 14–38; SC.; **Db.**

12536 **Bulletin** of the **University** of **New Mexico.** **Conservation Series.** Albuquerque. *Bull. Univ. New Mex. Conserv. Ser.* [1933–] L.SC.; U.

12537 **Bulletin** of the **University** of **New Mexico.** **Engineering Experiment Station Series.** Albuquerque. *Bull. Univ. New Mex. Engng Exp. Stn Ser.* [1937–] L.U. 37–40.

12538 **Bulletin** of the **University** of **New Mexico.** **Engineering Series.** Albuquerque. *Bull. Univ. New Mex. Engng Ser.* [1931–] L.SC.; U. 34–35.

12539 **Bulletin** of the **University** of **New Mexico.** **Geological Series.** Albuquerque. *Bull. Univ. New Mex. geol. Ser.* [1906–] L.BM^N. 22–37 imp.; GL. 14; P. 06–23 imp.; SC. 06–39; **Db.** 09–. [*C. of:* 10421]

12540 **Bulletin** of the **University** of **New Mexico.** **Monograph Series.** Albuquerque. *Bull. Univ. New Mex. Monogr. Ser.* [1934–] L.SC.

12541 **Bulletin** of the **University** of **New Mexico.** **Physics Series.** Albuquerque. *Bull. Univ. New Mex. Phys. Ser.* [1912–] L.P. 12; SC. 12; U. 12: 34–; **Db.** 12. [*Suspended* 1913–33]

12542 **Bulletin** of **University** of **Osaka Prefecture.**
Sakai, Osaka. *Bull. Univ. Osaka Prefect.*
　　　Ser. A.　Engineering and natural sciences [1956–]
L.P.; SC.; **C.**CH.; **Y.**
　　　Ser. B.　Agriculture and biology [1955–] **L.**AM.;
BM.; BM^N.; TP. 57–; **C.**A.; **Hu.**G.; **Md.**H. 56–; **Y.**
[*C. of:* 11193]

12543 **Bulletin** of the **University** of **Otago School** of
Mining and **Metallurgy.** Otago. *Bull. Univ. Otago
Sch. Min. Metall.* **L.**MI. 46– imp.
　　　Bulletin. **University** of **Pennsylvania Museum**
See 55650.

12544 **Bulletin.** **University** of **South Carolina.**
Columbia. *Bull. Univ. S. Carol.* **L.**SC. (phys. sci.) 50–.

12545 **Bulletin.** **University** of **Tehran Agricultural
College.** Karaj. *Bull. Univ. Tehran agric. Coll.* **O.**F.
56–.

12546 **Bulletin.** **University** of **Texas.** **Bureau** of
Economic Geology and **Technology.** *Bull. Univ. Tex.
Bur. econ. Geol. Technol.* **L.**BM^N. 17– imp.; SC. 15– imp.
　　　Bulletin of the **University** of **Texas.** **Engineer-
ing Research Series.** *See* 18159.

12547 **Bulletin.** **University** of **Texas.** **Medical Series.**
Austin. *Bull. Univ. Tex. med. Ser.* [1905–11] **O.**R.

12548 **Bulletin.** **University** of **Texas.** **Mineral Survey Series.** Austin. *Bull. Univ. Tex. Miner. Surv.
Ser.* [1900–04] **L.**BM^N.; GM.; P.

12549 **Bulletin.** **University** of **Texas.** **Scientific
Series.** Austin. *Bull. Univ. Tex. scient. Ser.* [1905–14]
L.BM. imp.; GL. 12–14; GM. 07–14 imp.; P.; **Bm.**U. 12–14;
G.U. 09–14 imp.; **Lv.**P. 12–14; **M.**U. imp.; **O.**R. imp.

12550 **Bulletin.** **University** of **Toronto.** **School** of
Engineering Research. Toronto. *Bull. Univ.
Toronto Sch. Engng Res.* [1919–] **L.**BM.; NF.; P. 21–57;
Br.U. 19–32; **C.**UL.; **M.**U. 19–32; **Nw.**A. 19–32; **O.**R.
19–28; **Y.**

12551 **Bulletin** of the **University** of **Utah.** **Biological
Series.** Salt Lake City. *Bull. Univ. Utah biol. Ser.*
[1929–49] **L.**BM^N.; **Db.** [*C. as:* 55693]

12552 **Bulletin** of the **University** of **Utah.** **Geological
Series.** Salt Lake City. *Bull. Univ. Utah geol. Ser.*
L.BM^N. 44.
　　　Bulletin. **University** of **Vermont Agricultural
Experiment Station.** *See* 12575.

12553 **Bulletin.** **University** of **Washington.** **Bureau**
of **Industrial Research.** Seattle. *Bull. Univ. Wash.
Bur. ind. Res.* [1917–18] **L.**BM.; U.; **C.**UL.; **E.**U.; **G.**U.
imp.; **M.**U.; **O.**B. [*C. as:* 12610]
　　　Bulletin. **University** of **Washington College** of
Engineering. *See* 12604.

12554 **Bulletin** of the **University** of **Wisconsin.
Engineering Series.** Madison. *Bull. Univ. Wis.
Engng Ser.* [1894–26] **L.**BM. 94–05 imp.; P. 09–26; **C.**UL.;
Db.; **G.**U.; **Ld.**P.; **M.**U. 94–04. [*C. as:* 10170]

12555 **Bulletin** of the **University** of **Wisconsin.** **Science
Series.** Madison. *Bull. Univ. Wis. Sci. Ser.* [1894–17]
L.BM. 94–07; GL. 07; P.; **C.**UL. 96–17; **Db.**; **E.**R. 95; **M.**U.
94–01. [*C. as:* 55702]

12556 **Bulletin** of **Unpublished Thermal Data.** Ann
Arbor. *Bull. unpubld therm. Data* [1955] **L.**P. [*C. as:*
9774]

12557 **Bulletin** of the **Upper Air Current Observations.** Academia sinica. Shanghai. *Bull. upp. Air
Curr. Obsns, Shanghai* [1930–] **L.**MO. 30–34; **E.**R. 30–32.

12558 **Bulletin.** **Urban Land Institute.** Chicago.
Bull. urb. Ld Inst. [1942–43] [*C. as:* 55739]

12559 **Bulletin** des **usines électriques.** Paris. *Bull.
Usin. élect.* [1896–07] **L.**P.

12560 **Bulletin** des **usines** de **guerre.** Paris. *Bull.
Usin. Guerre*

12561 **Bulletin** des **usines Renault.** *Bull. Usin. Renault*

12562 **Bulletin** of **Utah Agricultural College.** Logan.
Bull. Utah agric. Coll.

12563 **Bulletin** of the **Utah Agricultural Experiment
Station.** Logan. *Bull. Utah agric. Exp. Stn* [1891–]
L.AM.; BM^N. 18–34; EB. (ent.) 99– imp.; K. 98–08 imp.; P.
(2 yr.); **C.**A.; **Ld.**U. 10–22 imp.; **O.**RE. 48– imp.; **Rt.**
imp.; **Y.**

12564 **Bulletin.** **Utah Crop Pest Commission.** Salt
Lake City. *Bull. Utah Crop Pest Commn*

12565 **Bulletin** of the **Utah Engineering Experiment
Station.** Salt Lake City. *Bull. Utah Engng Exp. Stn*
L.P. 16–27: 57–; **Y.** [*C. in:* 32034]

12566 **Bulletin.** **Utah Geological** and **Mineralogical
Survey.** Salt Lake City. *Bull. Utah geol. miner. Surv.*

12567 **Bulletin** of **Utah Health Board.** Salt Lake City.
Bull. Utah Hlth Bd
　　　Bulletin. **Utah State Agricultural Experiment
Station.** *See* 12563.

12568 **Bulletin.** **Utah State Live Stock Board.** Salt
Lake City. *Bull. Utah St. live Stk Bd*

12569 **Bulletin.** **Utah-Idaho Sugar Co.** Salt Lake
City. *Bull. Utah-Idaho Sug. Co.* [1940–] **C.**A.

12570 **Bulletin** of the **Utsonomiya Agricultural
College.** *Bull. Utsonomiya agric. Coll.* [1931–34: *then
in sections below*] **L.**AM.; BM.; BM^N.; SC.; **Bm.**U.; **Db.**;
E.U.; **G.**U.; **Lv.**P.; **M.**U.; **Sa.**
　　　Section A.　Agricultural sciences, forestry and
veterinary science [1934–48] **L.**AM. 34–39; BM.;
BM^N.; SC.; **Bm.**U. 34–39; **Db.**; **E.**U. 34–37; **G.**U.
34–39; **Lv.**U.; **M.**U. 34–39; **Sa.** 34–39.
　　　Section B.　Agricultural and forestry economics
[1937–48] **L.**AM. 37–39; BM.; SC.; **Bm.**U. 37–39;
C.A.; **Db.**; **E.**U. 37–39 imp.; **G.**U. 37–39; **Lv.**U.;
M.U. 37–39; **Sa.** 37–39.
　　　[*C. as:* 9828]
　　　Bulletin of the **Valetta Museum.** *See* 11182.
　　　Bulletin. **Van der Grinten N.V.** Venlo. *See*
55862.

12571 **Bulletin** of the **Vancouver Medical Association.**
Bull. Vancouver med. Ass. [1924–58] **L.**MA. 46–58. [*C.
as:* 8785]

12572 **Bulletin** of the **Vanderbilt Marine Museum.**
Huntington, L.I. *Bull. Vanderbilt mar. Mus.* [1930–38]
L.BM^N.; L.; UC. 34–38; Z.; **C.**B. 30–35; P.; **Dm.**; **E.**R.;
Lv.U. imp.; **O.**R.; **Pl.**M. [*C. of:* 12573]

12573 **Bulletin** of the **Vanderbilt Oceanographic
Museum.** Huntington, L.I. *Bull. Vanderbilt oceano-
gr. Mus.* [1928] **L.**BM^N.; L.; Z.; **C.**P.; **Dm.**; **E.**R.; **Lv.**U.;
O.R.; **Pl.**M. [*C. as:* 12572]

　　　Bulletin. **Variable Star Section, New Zealand
Astronomical Society.** *See* 11314.
　　　Bulletin. '**The Variable Stars.**' Moscow. *See*
37341.

12574 **Bulletin** des **variations** des **éléments** du **magnétisme terrestre.** Tsingtao. *Bull. Var. Élém. Magn. terr.* **L.**MO. 30–33.

Bulletin of **Venerology** and **Dermatology.** Moscow. *See* 56549.

12574° **Bulletin. Vereinigung schweizer Petroleum-Geologen** und **-Ingenieure.** *Bull. Verein. schweiz. Petrol.-Geol. u. -Ing.*

12575 **Bulletin** of the **Vermont Agricultural Experiment Station.** Burlington. *Bull. Vt agric. Exp. Stn* [1887–] **L.**AM.; BM[N]. 94–37 imp.; EB. 88–17 imp.; K. 91–07 imp.; P.; **C.**A.; **Ld.**U. 30–41; **O.**F. 14– imp.; **Rt.** 88– imp.; **Y.**

12576 **Bulletin. Vermont Bird Club.** Rutland. *Bull. Vt Bird Club*

12577 **Bulletin** of the **Vermont Board** of **Health. Montpelier.** *Bull. Vt Bd Hlth*

12578 **Bulletin** of the **Vermont Botanical Club.** Burlington. *Bull. Vt bot. Club*

12579 **Bulletin. Vermont Department** of **Agriculture.** *Bull. Vt Dep. Agric.* **Y.**

12580 **Bulletin. Vermont Development Commission.** Montpelier. *Bull. Vt Dev. Commn* [1950–] **Y.**

12581 **Bulletin. Vermont Geological Survey.** Montpelier. *Bull. Vt geol. Surv.* [1950–] **L.**BM[N].; GL.; **E.**R.; **Y.**

Bulletin vétérinaire. Lisbonne. *See* 7471.

12582 **Bulletin vétérinaire.** Orléans. *Bull. vét., Orléans* **L.**MD. 00–04.

Bulletin of **Veterinary Research, Nippon Institute** for **Biological Science.** *See* 33943.

12583 **Bulletin. Victoria Memorial Museum** of the **Geological Survey** of **Canada.** Ottawa. *Bull. Victoria meml Mus.* [1913] **L.**BM.; BM[N].; GL.; GM.; K.; P.; SC.; UC.; **Abd.**U.; **Bm.**P.; U.; **Bn.**U.; **Br.**U.; **C.**P.; **Dm.**U.; **E.**A.; D.; G.; U.; **G.**U.; **Ld.**U.; **Lv.**U.; **M.**U.; **Nw.**A.; **O.**G.; R.; **Sa.**; **Sh.**M. [*C. as:* 33851]

12584 **Bulletin. Virgin Islands Agricultural Experiment Station.** St. Croix. Washington. *Bull. Virgin Isl. agric. Exp. Stn* [1921–26] **L.**AM.; BM.; BM[N].; EB.; P. 26; SC.; **C.**A.; **G.**M.; **M.**P.; **Rt.**; **Y.**

12585 **Bulletin** of the **Virginia Agricultural Experiment Station.** Blacksburg. *Bull. Va agric. Exp. Stn* [1889–] **L.**AM.; BM. 33–34; BM[N]. 08–34 imp.; EB. (ent.) 96–; K. 02–08 imp.; P.; UC. 33–34; **Abs.**U. 99–11 imp.; **C.**A.; **Db.** 99–; **O.**R. 22–; **Rt.**; **Y.**

12585° **Bulletin. Virginia Department** of **Agriculture** and **Immigration.** Richmond. *Bull. Va Dep. Agric.*

12586 **Bulletin** of the **Virginia Geological Survey, University** of **Virginia.** Charlottesville. *Bull. Va geol. Surv.* [1905–] **L.**BM[N]. 12– imp.; GM.; **Y.**

12587 **Bulletin** of **Virginia Medical College.** Richmond. *Bull. Va med. Coll.*

12588 **Bulletin. Virginia Polytechnic Institute Engineering Experiment Station.** Blacksburg. *Bull. Va polytech. Inst. Engng Exp. Stn* **L.**P. 24–54; **Y.**

12589 **Bulletin** of the **Virginia State Dental Association.** Richmond. *Bull. Va St. dent. Ass.* **L.**D. 31–43 imp.

12590 **Bulletin** of the **Virginia State Forester.** Charlottesville. *Bull. Va St. Forester* **L.**SC. 17–.

12591 **Bulletin. Virginia Truck Experiment Station.** Norfolk. *Bull. Va Truck Exp. Stn* [1909–] **L.**AM.; EB. (ent.); P. imp.; **Br.**A. 12–42 imp.; **C.**A.; **Cr.**P. imp.; **Ld.**U. 09–12; **Rt.**; **Y.**

12592 **Bulletin** of **Visual Education.** Exeter. *Bull. vis. Educ.* [1944–] **L.**PG. 44–46 imp. [*C. of:* 56771]

12593 **Bulletin** of the **Volcanological Society** of **Japan.** *Bull. volcan. Soc. Japan* **C.**UL. 37–; **Y.**

12594 **Bulletin volcanologique.** Union géodésique et géophysique internationale. Bruxelles. *Bull. volcan.* [1924–] **L.**BM. 37–; BM[N]. 37–; GL.; I. (1 yr); MO. 30–; SC. 24–40: 49–; U. 49–; **Bl.**U. 37–58 imp.; **Bm.**U. 37–; **C.**GD.; **Db.** 37–60; **E.**D.; R. 37–; U. imp.; **G.**U. 24–31: 37–; **Ld.**U. 37–; **Lv.**U.; **M.**U. 37–; **Nw.**A.; **O.**R.; **R.**U. 37–; **Sa.** 37–39: 50–; **Sh.**SC. 37–; **Y.**

12595 **Bulletin** de **vulgarisation** des **sciences naturelles.** Auch. *Bull. Vulg. Sci. nat.* **L.**BM[N]. 01–23.

12596 **Bulletin** of the **Wagner Institute** of **Science** of **Philadelphia.** Philadelphia. *Bull. Wagner Inst. Sci. Philad.* [1926–58] **L.**BM[N].; SC. 31–58; **C.**P.; **E.**C. imp.; D. 32–58 imp.; R.; **Ld.**U. imp.

12597 **Bulletin. Wahl-Henius Institute** of **Fermentology.** Chicago. *Bull. Wahl-Henius Inst. Ferment.* [1937–] **L.**P. 37–41; SC.

12598 **Bulletin** of **War Medicine.** Medical Research Committee. London. *Bull. War Med.* [1940–46] **L.**AV. 40–45; D.; GH.; H.; LI.; MC.; MD.; P.; PH.; RA.; S.; SC.; TD.; U.; UCH.; **Abd.**R.; U.; **Abs.**N.; **Bl.**U.; **Bm.**P.; U.; **Bn.**U.; **Br.**U.; **C.**BI.; PS. 41–46; UL.; V.; **Cr.**MD.; P.; **Db.**; **Dn.**U. imp.; **E.**A.; I.; S.; U.; **G.**F.; M.; PH.; U.; **Ld.**P.; U.; **Lv.**M.; **M.**MS.; P.; **Nw.**A.; **O.**R.; **Sh.**U.; **W.** 40–44.

12599 **Bulletin** of the **Warren Anatomical Museum, Harvard Medical School.** Boston. *Bull. Warren anat. Mus. Harv.* **L.**MD. 10.

12600 **Bulletin. Waseda Applied Chemical Society.** Tokyo. *Bull. Waseda appl. chem. Soc.* [1924–] **L.**SC. 39–.

12601 **Bulletin** of the **Washington Agricultural Experiment Station.** Pullman. *Bull. Wash. agric. Exp. Stn* [1891–] **L.**AM.; BM. 06– imp.; BM[N]. 06– imp.; EB. (ent.) 98–; HS. 34–; P. imp.; **Br.**A. 16– imp.; **C.**A.; **Db.** 31–; **Ld.**U. 06– imp.; **Nw.**A. 01–16: 34– imp.; **O.**F. 25–47 imp.; RE. 41–52 imp.; **Rt.** imp.; **Y.**

12602 **Bulletin** of the **Washington Geological Survey.** Seattle. *Bull. Wash. geol. Surv.* [1910–] **L.**BM[N].; GL. 10–14; GM.; P. 10–24 imp.; SC.

Bulletin of the **Washington State Agricultural Experiment Station.** *See* 12601.

12603 **Bulletin** of **Washington State Board** of **Health.** Seattle. *Bull. Wash. St. Bd Hlth*

Bulletin. Washington State College Electrometallurgical Research Laboratories. *See* 10069.

12604 **Bulletin. Washington State College Engineering Experiment Station.** Pullman. *Bull. Wash. St. Coll. Engng Exp. Stn* [1943–] **L.**P.; SC. [*C. of:* 18098]

12605 **Bulletin. Washington State College Extension Service.** Pullman. *Bull. Wash. St. Coll. Ext. Serv.* [1914–] **L.**BM[N].; **Rt.** 15–20.

12606 **Bulletin. Washington State Dental Association.** Seattle. *Bull. Wash. St. dent. Ass.* [1934] [*C. as:* 57119]

12607 **Bulletin. Washington State Department** of **Agriculture.** Olympia. *Bull. Wash. St. Dep. Agric.* [1943–]

12608 **Bulletin** of the **Washington State Department** of **Conservation** and **Development.** Olympia. *Bull. Wash. St. Dep. Conserv. Dev.*

12609 **Bulletin** of the **Washington State Institute** of **Technology, Division** of **Industrial Research.** Pullman. *Bull. Wash. St. Inst. Technol. Div. ind. Res.* **L.**P. 48–; **Y.**

12610 **Bulletin** of the **Washington University Engineering Experiment Station.** Seattle. *Bull. Wash. Univ. Engng Exp. Stn* [1918–] **L.**AV. 35–51 imp.; BM.; P. 19–; U.; **C.**UL.; **E.**U.; **G.**U.; **M.**U. 18–51 imp.; **O.**R.; **Y.** [*C. of:* 12553]

Bulletin of the **Washington University Medical School.** Saint-Louis. *See* 11662.

12611 **Bulletin. Water Resources Branch, Department** of **Northern Affairs** and **National Resources** (*formerly* Department of Resources and Development), **Canada.** *Bull. Wat. Resour. Brch Can.* **Y.**

12611ᶜ **Bulletin. Waterways Experiment Station, Vicksburg.** Vicksburg. *Bull. WatWays Exp. Stn Vicksb.* **L.**P. 51–55 imp.

Bulletin. Weather Bureau, Manila Central Observatory. *See* 10850.

12612 **Bulletin. Weather Bureau, United States Department** of **Agriculture.** Washington. *Bull. Weath. Bur. U.S. Dep. Agric.* [1892–13] **L.**BM.; G. imp.; MO. imp.; P. 94–13 imp.; SC. 94–13; **E.**G. 07–13; R. 92–04 imp.; **O.**G. 92–96 imp.; R. imp.; **Rt.** imp.

12613 **Bulletin** of **Weekly Rainfall** in **Kenya.** Nairobi. *Bull. wkly Rainf. Kenya* **L.**MO. 51–55.

12614 **Bulletin. Welding Research Council.** New York. *Bull. Weld. Res. Coun.* [1949–]

12615 **Bulletin. Wellcome Tropical Research Laboratories.** Khartoum. *Bull. Wellcome trop. Res. Labs* [1914–33]
Chemical section. **L.**SC. 24–33; **Rt.** 14–15.
Entomological section. **L.**BMᴺ. 18–30; EB.; SC. 17–33; **C.**A. 18–33; **M.**C. 17–33 imp.

12616 **Bulletin** of the **Wellington Botanical Society.** Wellington, N.Z. *Bull. Wellington bot. Soc.* **L.**BMᴺ. 50–; K. 49–.

12617 **Bulletin. Welsh Plant Breeding Station. University College** of **Wales.** Aberystwyth. *Bull. Welsh Pl. Breed. Stn*
Series C. [1920–23] **L.**AM.; BM.; P.; **Abs.**A.; N.; **C.**A.; **Ld.**U.; **N.**U. 21–23; **O.**R.; RE. 22–23; **Rt.** 20–22; **Sw.**U.
Series H. [1919–] **L.**AM.; BM.; K. 22–45; P.; **Abs.**A.; N.; **Bl.**U. 23–45 imp.; **C.**A.; **Ld.**U.; **N.**U. 22–; **O.**R.; RE. 22–; **Rt.** 26–; **Sw.**U.; **Y.**
Series S. [1928–] **L.**BM.
[*See also:* 28327]

12618 **Bulletin** of the **West** of **Scotland Agricultural College.** Glasgow. *Bull. W. Scotl. agric. Coll.* [1899–] **L.**AM.; P. 00–; **Abs.**A. 11–; N. 17; **Br.**A. 40– imp.; **Cr.**P. 00–12 imp.; **G.**U. 00– imp.; **N.**U. 40– imp.; **O.**RE. 52– imp.; **Rt.**; **Y.**

Bulletin. West Virginia Agricultural Experiment Station. *See* 12625.

12619 **Bulletin. West Virginia Crop Pest Commission.** Morgantown. *Bull. W. Va Crop Pest Commn* **L.**EB. 13–14*; P. 13–14; SC. 13–14.

12620 **Bulletin. West Virginia Department** of **Agriculture.** Charleston. *Bull. W. Va Dep. Agric.* **L.**EB. (ent.) 16–48; SC. 24–.

12621 **Bulletin** of the **West Virginia Geological Survey.** Morgantown. *Bull. W. Va geol. Surv.* [1901–] **L.**BMᴺ.; GL. 12; GM. 03–28; P. 11–37; SC.; **Bm.**U. 17–23 imp.

12622 **Bulletin. West Virginia Public Health Council.** Morgantown. *Bull. W. Va publ. Hlth Coun.*

12623 **Bulletin. West Virginia State Dental Society.** Charleston. *Bull. W. Va St. dent. Soc.* [1926–35] [*C. as:* 57371]

12624 **Bulletin. West Virginia University.** Morgantown. *Bull. W. Va Univ.* **Sh.**S. 47–.

12625 **Bulletin** of the **West Virginia University Agricultural Experiment Station.** Morgantown. *Bull. W. Va Univ. agric. Exp. Stn* [1888–] **L.**AM.; BM. 22–34; BMᴺ. 09–11; EB. (ent.) 91–; P. (selected issues) 20– imp.; UC. 99–28 imp.; **Bm.**U. 22–43 imp.; **Br.**A. 04–34; **Lv.**U. 22–44 imp.; **O.**F. 91– imp.; **Rt.** imp.; **Sw.**U. 31; **Y.**

12626 **Bulletin. West Virginia University Resources Committee.** Morgantown. *Bull. W. Va Univ. Resour. Comm.* [1940–]

12627 **Bulletin** of the **West Virginia University Scientific Association.** Morgantown. *Bull. W. Va Univ. scient. Ass.* [1922–30] **L.**SC. 23–30; **Abs.**N. [*C. of:* 57375]

12628 **Bulletin. Western Society** of **Engineers.** Chicago. *Bull. West. Soc. Engrs* [1929–]

12629 **Bulletin. Western Washington Experiment Station, Puyallup.** Pullman. *Bull. West. Wash. Exp. Stn Puyallup* **L.**SC. 27–28.

Bulletin. Weston College Seismological Observatory. *See* 11726.

12630 **Bulletin. Wildfowl Trust.** *Bull. Wildfowl Trust* [1954–] **L.**BMᴺ.; Z.; **O.**OR. [*C. of:* 11783]

12631 **Bulletin. Wisconsin Agricultural Experiment Station.** Madison. *Bull. Wis. agric. Exp. Stn* [1883–] **L.**AM.; EB. (ent.) 93–; HS. 53–; K. 05–06 imp.; P.; **Abs.**N. 16– imp.; **Br.**A. 11–53 imp.; **C.**A.; **Cr.**P. 02–15 imp.; **Ld.**U. 90–41 imp.; **Lv.**U. 09–14 imp.; **O.**F. 29– imp.; **Rt.** 85–; **Y.**

12632 **Bulletin. Wisconsin Board** of **Health.** Madison. *Bull. Wis. Bd Hlth*

12633 **Bulletin. Wisconsin Department** of **Agriculture.** Madison. *Bull. Wis. Dep. Agric.* **L.**BMᴺ. 16–20; EB. (ent.) 16–42; SC. 16 ; **O.**F. 31– imp.

12634 **Bulletin. Wisconsin Farmers' Institutes.** Madison. *Bull. Wis. Fmrs' Inst.* [1887–24] **L.**P. 92–24; **Rt.** 87.

12635 **Bulletin** of the **Wisconsin Geological** and **Natural History Survey.** Madison. *Bull. Wis. geol. nat. Hist. Surv.* [1898–] **L.**BM.; BMᴺ. imp. GL. 98–04; GM.; P.; UC. 98–04 imp.; **Bl.**U. 98–29 imp.; **Bm.**N. imp.; U. 98–01; **C.**P. 98–05; UL.; **Db.**; **E.**R. 92–29 imp.; **G.**N. 98–15; **Lv.**P. 98–12; U. 98–29 imp.; **M.**U. 98–28 imp.; **O.**R. 06– imp.; **Rt.** 11–27; **Y.**

12636 **Bulletin** of the **Wisconsin Mining School.** Platteville. *Bull. Wis. Min. Sch.*

12637 **Bulletin** of the **Wisconsin Natural History Society.** Milwaukee. *Bull. Wis. nat. Hist. Soc.* [1900–15] **L.**BMᴺ.; HO. 00–09; K. 00; SC. 05–15; **Bl.**U.; **Bm.**N. 13–15; U. 09; **Cr.**N.; **Db.**; **E.**B.; **G.**N.; **Lv.**P. 00–09; U.

12638 **Bulletin. Wisconsin State Conservation Commission.** Madison. *Bull. Wis. St. Conserv. Commn*

12639 **Bulletin** of the **Wistar Institute** of **Anatomy.** Philadelphia. *Bull. Wistar Inst. Anat.* **M.**U. 05–16.

12640 **Bulletin** of the **Woman's Hospital, Cathedral Parkway.** New York. *Bull. Woman's Hosp. N.Y.* **L.**MA. 12–15; S. 12–15; **M.**MS. 12–15; **Pl.**M. 16–25.

12641 **Bulletin** of the **Woman's Medical College.** Philadelphia. *Bull. Woman's med. Coll., Philad.*

12642 **Bulletin 'Wood Research' Institute, Kyoto University.** Kyoto. *Bull. Wood Res. Inst. Kyoto* [1949–] **O.**F.

12643 **Bulletin. Woods** and **Forests Department, South Australia.** Adelaide. *Bull. Woods Forests Dep. S. Aust.* **L.**SC. 28–; **O.**F. 28–. [*C. of:* 10039]

12644 **Bulletin** of the **Woods** and **Forests Department, Western Australia.** Perth. *Bull. Woods Forests Dep. West. Aust.*

12645 **Bulletin. Woollen Industries Research Association.** Leeds. *Bull. Wool. Inds Res. Ass.* [1930–] **Ld.**U. 30–40. [*C. of:* 9626]

12646 **Bulletin** of the **World Engineering Conference.** Paris. *Bull. Wld Engng Conf.* [1948–] **L.**P.; SC.

12647 **Bulletin** of the **World Engineering Conference. British Section.** London. *Bull. Wld Engng Conf. Br. Sect.* [1947–48] **L.**P.; SC.; **G.**E.; I.

12648 **Bulletin** of the **World Federation** for **Mental Health.** London. *Bull. Wld Fed. ment. Hlth* [1949–52] **L.**BM.; H.; MD.; TD.; **E.**A.; **O.**B.; R. [*C. as:* 57881]

12649 **Bulletin** of the **World Health Organization.** Geneva. *Bull. Wld Hlth Org.* [1947–] **L.**AM. 50–; BM^N. 60–; D.; EB.; LI.; MA.; MC.; MD.; PH.; SH.; TD.; TP. 49– imp.; U.; **Abd.**R.; **Bl.**U. 49–; **Bm.**P.; U.; **Br.**U.; **C.**UL.; V. 53–56 imp; **Cr.**MD.; **Db.**; **Dn.**U.; **E.**A.; U.; **G.**F. 56–; PH.; T. 50–; **Ld.**P.; U.; **Lv.**P.; **M.**P.; **Nw.**A.; **O.**AP.; **R.**D.; **Sh.**U.; **W.** 52–; **Y.** [*C. of:* 10433 and 11008; *also supplements*]

12650 **Bulletin. World Medical Association.** Mount Morris, Ill. *Bull. Wld med. Ass.* [1949–53] **L.**MA. [*C. as:* 57879]
Bulletin. World Meteorological Organization. *See* 57045.

12651 **Bulletin. World Non-Ferrous Metal Statistics.** Birmingham. *Bull. Wld non-ferr. Metal Statist.* [1955–] **L.**BM.; MI.; NF.; **Bm.**C.; P.; **C.**UL.; **E.**A.; **Lv.**P.; **M.**P.; **O.**R. [*C. of:* 9605]

12652 **Bulletin. Wyoming Agricultural Experiment Station.** Laramie. *Bull. Wyo. agric. Exp. Stn* [1891–] **L.**AM.; BM^N. 94–19 imp.; EB. (ent.) 92–; K. 93–08 imp.; **C.**A.; **E.**B. 96– imp.; **Ld.**U. 02–19 imp.; **M.**U. 08–19 imp.; **Rt.** imp.; **Y.**

12653 **Bulletin. Wyoming Game** and **Fish Commission.** Laramie. *Bull. Wyo. Game Fish Commn* [1955–] **L.**BM^N.; **Bm.**U. 55–56; **Y.** [*C. of:* 12654]

12654 **Bulletin. Wyoming Game** and **Fish Department.** Laramie. *Bull. Wyo. Game Fish Dep.* [1942–54] **L.**BM^N.; **Bm.**U. imp.; **Y.** [*C. as:* 12653]

12655 **Bulletin** of the **Wyoming State Geologist.** Cheyenne. *Bull. Wyo. St. Geol.* [1908–] **L.**BM^N. 17–32 imp.; GM. 11–; P. 08–16; SC. 17–.
Bulletin. Wyoming University Geological Survey. *See* 12519.

12656 **Bulletin. Wyoming University School** of **Mines. Petroleum Series.** Laramie. *Bull. Wyo. Univ. Sch. Mines Petrol. Ser.* **L.**P. 96–03*.

12657 **Bulletin. Yale College Observatory.** New Haven. *Bull. Yale Coll. Obs.* **C.**O. 96–.

12658 **Bulletin** of **Yale University.** New Haven. *Bull. Yale Univ.* **Ld.**P. 01–23; U. 05–.

12659 **Bulletin** of the **Yama Farms Mycological Club.** Napanoch, N.Y. *Bull. Yama Fms mycol. Club*

12660 **Bulletin** of the **Yamagata Agricultural College.** Tsuruoka. *Bull. Yamagata agric. Coll.* [1949–51] **L.**AM.; **C.**A. [*C. as:* 12661, Agric. Sciences]

12661 **Bulletin** of the **Yamagata University.** Yamagata. *Bull. Yamagata Univ.* [1952–]
Agricultural Sciences. **L.**AM.; **C.**A. [*C. of:* 12660]
Engineering. **L.**P. 58–; **Y.**
Natural Science. **L.**P. 57–; **Y.**

12662 **Bulletin** of the **Yamaguchi Medical School.** Ube. *Bull. Yamaguchi med. Sch.* [1953–] **L.**LI.; MA.; MD. imp.; TD.; **G.**U. imp.; **Lv.**M. imp.; **Y.**
Bulletin. Yellow Fever Bureau. Liverpool. *See* 58184.

12663 **Bulletin. Yellow Fever Institute.** Washington. *Bull. yell. Fev. Inst., Wash.* [1902–09] **L.**BM. 02–07; MD. 02–07; **Lv.**U.

12664 **Bulletin. Yerkes Observatory, University** of **Chicago.** *Bull. Yerkes Obs.* [1896–03] **L.**AS.; BM.; SC.; **Bl.**U. 96–01; **C.**O.; **Cr.**P. 97–03 imp.; **E.**O.; R.; **O.**O.; R. 99–03.

12665 **Bulletin. York Institute** of **Architectural Study.** York. *Bull. York Inst. archit. Study* [1954–56] **L.**BM.; **Ld.**P.; **O.**B.
Bulletin. Zinc Development Association. Oxford. *See* 59220.

12666 **Bulletin** of **Zoological Nomenclature.** London. *Bull. zool. Nom.* [1943–] **L.**AM.; BM^N.; E. 43–55; EB.; GL.; L.; SC.; TD.; Z.; **Abs.**N.; **Bl.**U. 43–54; **Bm.**U. 56–; **Br.**U.; **C.**B. 43–58; UL.; **E.**A.; U.; **G.**U.; **H.**U.; **Lv.**U.; **M.**U. 43–; N.U. 55–; **Nw.**A.; **O.**R.; **Sal.** 43–54; **Sh.**U.; **Y.**

12667 **Bulletin. Zoological Society** of **Egypt.** *Bull. zool. Soc. Egypt* [1927–] **L.**BM^N.; Z.; **O.**OR. 39–.

12668 **Bulletin** of the **Zoological Society** of **India.** Nagpur. *Bull. zool. Soc. India* [1947–] **L.**Z.; **Ld.**U.

12669 **Bulletin. Zoological Society** of **Philadelphia.** *Bull. zool. Soc. Philad.* [1926–37] [*Replaced by:* 37532]

12670 **Bulletin** of the **Zoological Society** of **San Diego.** *Bull. zool. Soc. S Diego* [1924–] **L.**BM^N.; Z.; **Y.**

12671 **Bulletin** der **zootechnischen** und **experimentellen Züchtungsstation** im **staatlichen Naturschüzpark Tschapli (Askania Nova).** Moskau. *Bull. zootech. exp. ZüchtStn Tschapli* [1926–]

12672 **Bulletin-annexe** des **Annales** du **Ministère** de l'**agriculture.** Paris. *Bull.-annexe Annls Minist. Agric.*

12673 **Bulletin-journal** de l'**Association générale** des **dentistes** du **sud-est** de la **France.** Nice. *Bull.-J. Ass. gén. Dent. S.-E. Fr.*

12674 **Bulletin-journal** des **fabricants** de **papier.** Paris. *Bull.-J. Fabr. Pap.* [1854–14] **L.**P. 93–14; SB. 02–11.

12675 **Bulletin-revue. Société d'émulation** et des **beaux-arts** du **Bourbonnais.** Moulins. *Bull.-Rev. Soc. Émul. Beaux-Arts Bourbonn.* [1892–02] **L.**BM.; **O.**B. [*C. as:* 11906]

12676 **Bulletin-revue** du **Syndicat** des **pharmaciens** de la **Drôme.** Valence. *Bull.-Rev. Synd. Pharmns Drôme*
Bulletins. *See* **Bulletin.**
Bullettino. *See* **Bollettino.**
Bülteni. Türkiye jeoloji kurumu. *See* 55353.

12678 **Bulteno** de la **Aerologia observatorio** de **Tateno.** *Bult. aerol. Obs. Tateno* **L.**MO. 27–36: 48–.

12679 **Bulteno** de la **Internacia scienca asocio esperantista.** Paris. *Bult. int. sci. Asoc. esperant.* [*There is a copy* (1926–) *in the library of the British Esperanto Association.*]

12680 **Bulteno scienca** de la **Fakultato terkultura, Kjuŝu imperia universitato.** *Bult. sci. Fak. terk. Kjuŝu Univ.* [1924–44] **L.**BM^N. 24–41; **Abs.**A. 44; **C.**A. 34–44. [*Suspended* 1945–49; *C. as:* 49006]

12681 **Bumazhnaya promȳshlennost'.** Moskva. Бумажная промышленность. *Bumazh. Prom.* [1922–] **L.**BM. 51–; P. 48– imp.; **Y.** [*Not published* 1942–44]

12682 **Bumed Gazette.** Bureau of Medicine and Surgery. Navy Department. Washington. *Bumed Gaz.* [1943–] [*C. of:* 57255]

12683 **Bumed News Letter.** Bureau of Medicine and Surgery. Navy Department. Washington. *Bumed News Lett.* **L.**MD. 43–46.

12684 **Búnaðarrit.** Reykjavík. *Búnaðarrit* [1887–] **L.**BM. **Ld.**U.; **Y.**

12685 **Bundesmitteilungen deutscher Photo-** und **Kinohändler-Bunde** von **Berlin.** *Bundesmitt. dt. Photo- u. KinohändlBunde* **L.**PG. 32–33. [*Supplement to:* 37666]

12686 **Bur.** Chicago. *Bur* **L.**D. 36–39 imp.

12687 **Bureau Bulletin** of the **British Cast Iron Research Association.** Birmingham. *Bur. Bull. Br. cast Iron Res. Ass.* [1923–24] **L.**BM.; MT.; P.; SC.; **Bm.**C.; P.; U.; **G.**I.; **Lv.**U. [*C. as:* 9607]

12688 **Bureau Bulletin. Steel Castings Development Bureau.** Philadelphia. *Bur. Bull. Steel Cast. Dev. Bur.* [1930–31] **L.**P. imp.
Bureau permanent interafricain de la **tsé-tsé** et de la **trypanosomiase,** Leopoldville. *See* 40910.

12689 **Bureau** of **Ships Journal.** Washington. *Bur. Ships J.* [1952–] **L.**P. imp.; **Y.**

12690 **Bureau** of **Standards Journal** of **Research.** Washington. *Bur Stand. J. Res.* [1928–34] **L.**AV.; C.; EE. imp.; I.; IC.; NF.; P.; PR.; QM. imp.; R.; RA.; RI.; SC.; SI. 29–34; U.; UC.; **Abd.**U.; **Abs.**U.; **Bl.**U.; **Bm.**C.; P.; U.; **Bn.**U. 29–34 imp.; **Br.**U.; C.; P.; UL.; **Db.**E.; **E.**R.; U.; **Ex.**U.; **F.**A.; **G.**E.; I.; M.; T.; U.; **H.**U.; **Ld.**P. imp.; U.; W.; **Lv.**P.; U.; **M.**C.; D. imp.; P. 32–34; T.; U.; **N.**U.; **Nw.**A; **O.**R.; **R.**U. 29–34; **Sa.**; **Sh.**IO.; SC.; **Sw.**U. 32–34; **Sy.**R.; **Te.**N.; **We.**K. [*C. of:* 49193; *C. as:* 26785]

12691 **Burma Forest Bulletin.** Rangoon. *Burma Forest Bull.* [1921–40] **L.**EB. (ent.) 23–36; K. 21–32 imp.; P. 26–36 imp.; SC.; **C.**A.; P.; **O.**B. 25–26 imp.; F.

12692 **Burma Medical Journal.** Rangoon. *Burma med. J.* [1953–] **L.**MA.; TD.

12693 **Burma Monthly Weather Review.** Rangoon. *Burma mon. Weath. Rev.* [1938–40] **L.**MO.; **O.**B.; G.

12694 **Burma Weather Review. Annual Summary.** Rangoon. *Burma Weath. Rev. a. Summ.* **L.**MO. 48–49.

12695 **Burmese Forester.** Rangoon. *Burm. Forester* [1951–] **L.**BM^N.; TP.; **Bn.**U.; **E.**U.; **O.**F.

12695^a **Burning Glass Miscellany.** Shorne. *Burning Glass Misc.* [1947–] **L.**BM.

12695^b **Burning Glass Papers.** Shorne. *Burning Glass Pap.* [1946–] **L.**BM. imp.

12696 **Burns Engineering Magazine.** Howrah. *Burns Engng Mag.* **L.**P. 12–32*. [*C. as:* 18076]
Burntisland Group Journal. *See* 12697.

12697 **Burntisland Shipbuilding Group Journal.** Burntisland. *Burntisland Shipbldg Grp J.* **L.**P. (curr.); **E.**A. 21– imp.; **G.**E. (1 yr); **Y.**

12698 **Buryatovedcheskiĭ sbornik.** Irkutsk. Бурятоведческий сборник. *Buryat. Sb.* [1926–30]

12699 **Bus** and **Coach.** London. *Bus Coach* [1929–] **L.**P. 30–; **Bm.**P. 48–; **Br.**P. (2 yr.); **Bra.**P. 55–; **C.**UL.; **E.**A. 30–; **G.**M. 49–; **Ld.**P. (5 yr.); **Li.**M. 46–; **M.**P. 31–; **O.**B.; **Sh.**IO. (5 yr.); **Y.**

12700 **Bus Transportation.** Electric Railway Journal. Sect. 2. New York. *Bus Transpn* [1921–] **L.**BM. 35–; P. 21–56.

12701 **Business Screen Magazine.** Chicago. *Busin. Screen Mag.* **L.**PG. 46– imp.

12702 **Buskap** og **avdrått.** Tidsskrift for svin- og storfehold. Gjøvik. *Buskap Avdrått* [1949–] **L.**A. 52–; **Hu.**G. 56–; **Y.**

12702^c **Busseiron kenk-yū.** Osaka. *Busseiron kenk-yu* **M.**C. 54–61 imp.; **Y.**

12702^d **Butane, propane.** Paris. *Butane, Propane* **Y.**

12703 **Butler University Botanical Studies.** Indianapolis. *Butler Univ. bot. Stud.* [1929–] **L.**BM^N.; **Abs.**A. 41–45: 54–; **E.**R.; **Hu.**G.; **O.**BO.; **Y.**

12704 **Butlletí** de l'**Acadèmia** de **ciències i arts** de **Barcelona.** Barcelona. *Butll. Acad. Ciènc. Arts Barcelona* [1934–] **L.**BM^N. 34–36. [*C. of:* 7528]

12705 **Butlletí** de l'**Associació catalana d'antropología, etnología i prehistória.** Barcelona. *Butll. Ass. catal. Antrop. Etnol.* **E.**V. 23–25.

12706 **Butlletí** del **Centro excursionista** de **Catalunya.** Barcelona. *Butll. Cent. excurs. Catal.* **L.**BM^N. 23–31.

12707 **Butlletí** del **Club montanyenc.** Associació de ciencias naturals, excursions. Barcelona. *Butll. Club montanyenc* **L.**BM^N. 12–36; GM. 12–25; **Bl.**U. 22–25; **Pl.**M. 12.

12708 **Butlletí** del **Departament d'agricultura, Barcelona.** *Butll. Dep. Agric.* **L.**AM. 36–37.

12709 **Butlletí d'informació. Institut botánic.** Barcelona. *Butll. Inf. Inst. bot.* [1937–]

12710 **Butlletí** de la **Institució catalana d'historia natural.** Barcelona. *Butll. Inst. catal. Hist. nat.* [1901–35] **L.**BM^N. 01–34; EB.; Z. 04–29 imp.

12711 **Butlletí** del **Sindicat** de **metges** de **Catalunya.** Barcelona. *Butll. Sind. Metges Catal.* **L.**MA. 31–36 imp.

12712 **Butlletí** de la **Societat catalana** de **pediatria.** *Butll. Soc. catal. Pediat.* [1928–36] **L.**MA. 31–36 imp.; MD.
Butlletí de la **Societat** de **ciencias naturals** de **Barcelona.** 'Club Montanyenc.' *See* 12707.

12713 **Butlletí** de la **Societat protectora** dels **animals** i de les **plantes** de **Cataluña.** Barcelona. *Butll. Soc. prot. Anim. Pl. Catal.*

12714 **Butonia.** Zentralorgan für die gesamte Knopf-industrie. Naunhof. *Butonia*

12715 **Butter, Cheese** and **Egg Journal.** Milwaukee. *Butt. Cheese Egg J.* [1910–28] [*C. as:* 12716]

12716 **Butter, Cheese Journal.** Milwaukee. *Butt. Cheese J.* [1928–30] **R.**D. 29–30. [*C. of:* 12715; *C. as:* 34102]

12717 **Butter, Cheese** and **Milk Products Journal.** Milwaukee. *Butt. Cheese Milk Prod. J.* [1950–53] **L.**P.; **R.**D.; **Y.** [*C. of:* 34102; *C. as:* 31849]

12718 **Butter Fat** and **Solids.** Sydney. *Butter Fat Solids* **R.**D. 46–; **Y.**
      Butter-Fat. Vancouver. *Butter-Fat* **R.**D. 52–.

12719 **Butterfield News.** W. P. Butterfield Ltd. Shipley. *Butterfield News* **L.**P. (curr.)

12720 **Butterflies** and **Moths.** Kyoto. *Butterfl. Moths* **L.**BM^N. 49–.

12721 **Butterley Foundry News.** *Butterley Fdry News* [1958–] **L.**P. (curr.)

12722 **Buxbaumia.** Mededelingen van de Nederland-sche natuurhistorische vereeniging, Bryologische werk-groep. Zaandam. *Buxbaumia* [1947–] **L.**BM^N.; K.; **Y.**

12722ᵉ **By Gum!** Reichhold Chemicals Inc. Detroit, Mich. *By Gum* **L.**P. 38–; PR. 47–; **Y.**

12723 **Bygg.** Oslo. *Bygg* [1953–] **L.**P. 57–.

12724 **Byggaren.** Helsingfors. *Byggaren* **Y.**

12725 **Bygge** og **Bo.** København. *Bygge Bo* **L.**BA. 45–.

12725ᶜ **Bygge industrien.** *Bygge Ind.* **Wa.**B. 54–; **Y.**

12726 **Byggekunst.** Kristiania (Oslo). *Byggekunst* **L.**BA. 26–; SC. 31–.

12726ᶜ **Bygget.** *Bygget* **Y.**

12727 **Bygglitteratur.** Stockholm. *Bygglitteratur* [1948–] **L.**BA.; SC. 48–51; **Nw.**A.; **Wa.**B. [*C. of:* 48579]

12728 **Byggmästaren.** Stockholm. *Byggmästaren* [1922–57]
      Upplaga A. Arkitektur. **L.**BA. 37–57; **Nw.**A. 44–57 imp.; **Wa.**B. 43–51; **Y.** [*C. as:* 4801ᶜ]
      Upplaga B. Byggnadstenik. **L.**BA. 37–57; **Nw.**A. 44–57 imp.; **Wa.**B. 43–51; **Y.** [*C. as:* 12729]

12729 **Byggmästaren.** Stockholm. *Byggmästaren* [1958–] **L.**BA.; BM.; P. 59–; **Wa.**B.; **Y.** [*C. of:* 12728, Upplaga B]

12730 **Byggnadsindustrin.** Stockholm. *Byggnadsindus-trin* **L.**BA. 48–; **Y.**
      Byggnadsteknik. *See* 12728.

12731 **Byggnadsvärlden.** Stockholm. *Byggnadsvärlden* **L.**SC. 31–.

12733 **Bygmesteren.** København. *Bygmesteren* **L.**BA. 37–; **Y.**
      Byuleten' Kabinetu antropolohiyi ta **etnolo-hiyi.** Kiyiv. Бюлетень Кабінету антропології та етнології. *See* 54736.

12735 **Byuletin'** za **industrialna sobstvennost'.** Sofiya. Бюлетинъ за индустриална собственность. *Byul. ind. Sobst.* **L.**P. 18–.

12736 **Byuletin'** po **rastitelna zashchita.** Sofiya. Бюлетин по растителна защита. *Byul. Rast. Zashch.* [1952–58] **L.**EB. [*C. as:* 42198]

12737 **Byulleten'. Abastumanskaya astrofizicheskaya observatoriya.** Tbilissi. Бюллетень. Абастуманская астрофизическая обсерватория. *Byull. abastuman. astrofiz. Obs.* [1937–] **L.**AS.; SC. 42–; **E.**R. imp.; **M.**U. 52–59.

12738 **Byulleten' Aktinometricheskoĭ** i **meteorologi-cheskoĭ observatorii** im. **Mikhel'sona.** Moskva. Бюллетень Актинометрической и метеорологической обсерватории им. Михельсона. *Byull. aktinom. met. Obs. Mikhel'sona* **L.**MO. 35–37.

12739 **Byulleten' Arkticheskogo instituta SSSR.** Leningrad. Бюллетень Арктического института СССР. *Byull. arktich. Inst. SSSR* [1931–36] **L.**AM. imp.; BM^N.; GL.; L. imp.; MO. 33–36; SC.; **Abd.**M.; **C.**PO.; **Dm.** 31–35; **Lo.** imp.; **Lv.**U.; **O.**AP.; **Pl.**M. [*C. in:* 38764]

12740 **Byulleten'. Assotsiatsiya** po **izucheniyu proiz-voditel'nykh sil severa** pri **Arkhangel'skom gub-plane.** Arkhangel. Бюллетень. Ассоциация по изучению производительных сил севера при Архан-гельском губплане. *Byull. Ass. Izuch. proizvod. Sil Severa Arkhang. Gubpl.* **L.**SC. 27–.

12741 **Byulleten' Astronomicheskogo teoreticheskogo instituta.** Leningrad. Бюллетень Астрономического теоретического института. *Byull. astr. teor. Inst., Leningr.* [1924–] **L.**AS.; SC.; **M.**U. 52– imp.; **O.**O.

12742 **Byulleten' Astronomicheskoĭ observatorii** im. **V. P. Éngel'gardta.** Imperatorskiĭ Kazanskiĭ universitet. Kazan'. Бюллетень Астрономической обсерватории им. В. П. Энгельгардта. Императорский Казанский университет. *Byull. astr. Obs. V. P. Éngel'gardta* [1934–] **L.**AS.

12743 **Byulleten' Botanicheskogo sada.** Erevan. Бюл-летень Ботанического сада. *Byull. bot. Sada, Erevan* **L.**BM^N. 41; **C.**BO. 54–57.

12744 **Byulleten' Dagestanskogo muzeya.** Makhach-Kala. Бюллетень Дагестанского музея. *Byull. dagest. Muz.* [1924–26] **L.**BM.; BM^N.

12745 **Byulleten' Dal'nevostochnogo promyshlen-nogo byuro V.S.N.Kh.** Chita. Бюллетень Дальне-восточного промышленного бюро В.С.Н.Х. *Byull. dal'nevost. prom. Byuro V.S.N.Kh.* **L.**BM. 23–.

12746 **Byulleten'. Derzhavna geofizichna observa-voriya.** Odessa. Бюллетень. Державна геофі-зична обсерваторія. *Byull. derzh. geofiz. Obs., Odessa* **L.**MO. 24–29.

12747 **Byulleten' Éksperimental'nago instituta puteĭ soobshenĭya.** Moskva. Бюллетень Эксперименталь-наго института путей сообщенія. *Byull. eksp. Inst. Put. Soobshch.* **L.**BM. 18.

12748 **Byulleten' éksperimental'noĭ biologii** i **medi-tsinȳ.** Moskva. Бюллетень экспериментальной био-логии и медицины. *Byull. eksp. Biol. Med.* [1936–] **L.**BM^N. 46–47; MA. 43–44; MC. 43–45: 57–; MD. 36; UC. 36–37; TD. 43–45 imp.; **Abd.**R. 36–38; **C.**BI. 36–39; **Y.** [*For French edition see* 9583; *English translation at:* 10200]
      Byulleten'. Éngel'gardtovskaya astronomiche-skaya observatoriya. Kazan'. Бюллетень. Энгель-гардтовская астрономическая обсерватория. *See* 12742.

12750 **Byulleten'. Éntomologicheskiĭ otdel, Poltav-skaya s.-kh. opȳtnaya stantsiya.** Poltava. Бюлле-тень. Энтомологический отдел. Полтавская с.-х. опытная станция. *Byull. ent. Otd. poltav. s.-kh. opȳt. Sta.* **L.**EB. 23–25.

12751 **Byulleten' po fiziologii rastenii.** Kiev. Бюллетень по физиологии растений. *Byull. Fiziol. Rast* [1957–] **Y.**

12753 **Byulleten' Geograficheskogo instituta.** Leningrad. Бюллетень Географического института. *Byull. geogr. Inst.* [1921] [*C. as*: 20940]

12753ª **Byulleten' Glavnogo botanicheskogo sada.** Leningrad. Бюллетень Главного ботанического сада. *Byull. glavn. bot. Sada, Leningr.* [1948–] **L.**к. 52: 55–; **C.**A. 52–59 imp.; P. 56–.

12754 **Byulleten' Glavnogo komiteta po dělam bumazhnoi promyshlennosti i torgovli pri Vysshom sovete narodnago khozyaistva.** Moskva. Бюллетень Главного комитета по дѣламъ бумажной промышленности и торговли при Высшемъ совете народнаго хозяйства. *Byull. glavn. Kom. Dělam bumazh. Prom.*

12755 **Byulleten' Glavnogo komiteta Vsesoyuznoi sel'skokhozyaistvennoi vystavki.** Moskva. Бюллетень Главного комитета Всесоюзной сельскохозяйственной выставки. *Byull. glavn. Kom. vses. sel'.khoz. Vyst.* **L.**вм.; **Abs.**A. 39– imp.

12756 **Byulleten' Glavnogo torfyanogo komiteta Otděla topliva vysshago sověta narodnago khozyaistva.** Moskva. Бюллетень Главного торфяного комитета Отдѣла топлива высшаго совѣта народнаго хозяйства. *Byull. glavn. torf. Kom.*

12757 **Byulleten' Glavnogo upravleniya nauchnykh, khudozhestvennykh i muzeinykh uchrezhdenii Akademichskogo tsentra Narkomprosa** (Glavnauka). Moskva. Бюллетень Главного управленія научныхъ, художественныхъ и музейныхъ учрежденій Академического центра Наркомпроса (Главнаука). *Byull. glavn. Uprav. nauch. khudozh. muz. Uchrezh.*

12758 **Byulleten' Glavnogo voenno-veterinarnago komiteta.** Petrograd. Бюллетень Главного военно-ветеринарнаго комитета. *Byull. glavn. voenno-vet. Kom.* **L.**вм. 17–18.

12760 **Byulleten' Gosudarstvennogo astronomicheskogo instituta** imeni **Shternberga.** Moskva. Бюллетень Государственного астрономического института имени Штернберга. *Byull. gosud. astr. Inst. Shternberga* [1940–] **L.**AS. 40–41.

12761 **Byulleten' Gosudarstvennogo nikitskogo opytnogo botanicheskogo sada.** Бюллетень Государственного никитского опытного ботанического сада. *Byull. gosud. nikitsk. opyt. bot. Sad* [1929–] **L.**к. 29–35 imp.; MO. 34; **E.**в.

12762 **Byulleten' Gosudarstvennogo okeanograficheskogo instituta.** Moskva. Бюллетень Государственного океанографического института. *Byull. gosud. okeanogr. Inst.* [1931–34] **L.**AM. 31–32 imp.; вм.; вмᴺ.; **Abd.**M. 31–32; **E.**R. 31–32; **Lo.** 31–32; **Lv.**U.; **Pl.**M. 31–32.

12762ᶜ **Byulleten' Gosudarstvennoi komissii po élektrifikatsii Rossii.** Moskva. Бюллетень Государственной комиссии по электрификации России. *Byull. gosud. Kom. Elektrif. Ross.* **L.**вм. 20–.

Byulleten' Imperatorskago Moskovskago obshchestva ispytatelei prirody. Moskva. Бюллетень Императорскаго Московскаго общества испытателей природы. *See* 12786.

12763 **Byulleten' Instituta astrofiziki.** Stalinabad. Бюллетень Института астрофизики. *Byull. Inst. Astrofiz., Stalinabad* [1952–] **L.**SC.

12764 **Byulleten' Instituta biologii. Belaruskaya akademiya navuk.** Minsk. Бюллетень Института биологии. Беларуская академія навук. *Byull. Inst. Biol., Minsk* [1955–] **L.**вмᴺ. 56–; **O.**R. 56–; **Y.**

12765 **Byulleten' Instituta biologii vodokhranilishch.** Moskva. Бюллетень Института биологии водохранилищ. *Byull. Inst. Biol. Vodokhran.* [1958–] **L.**вмᴺ.; **Y.**

12766 **Byulleten' Instituta épidemiologii i mikrobiologii i nauchnogo obshchestva épidemiologov, mikrobiologov, parazitologov i sanitarnykh vrachei.** Tashkent. Бюллетень Института эпидемиологии и микробиологии и научного общества эпидемиологов, микробиологов, паразитологов и санитарных врачей. *Byull. Inst. Épidem. Mikrobiol., Tashkent* [1935–38] **L.**TD. 35–37. [*C. of*: 54611]

12767 **Byulleten' Instituta mekhanizatsii sel'skogo khozyaistva.** Leningrad. Бюллетень Института механизации сельского хозяйства. *Byull. Inst. Mekhaniz. sel'. Khoz.* [1930–31]

Byulleten' Instituta teoreticheskoi astronomii. Leningrad. Бюллетень Института теоретической астрономии. *See* 12741.

12769 **Byulleten' Instituta zernovogo khozyaistva Yugo-vostoka SSSR.** Saratov. Бюллетень Института зернового хозяйства Юго-востока СССР. *Byull. Inst. zern. Khoz. Yugo.-Vost. SSSR* [1942–] **L.**AM. 42–46 imp.; **Abs.**A. 43–; **Rt.** 43–45. [*C. of*: 50099]

12770 **Byulleten' izobretenii.** Moskva. Бюллетень изобретений. *Byull. Izobr.* [1950–] **L.**вм. 58–; **Y.** [*C. of*: 18895; *English translation at*: 55414; *English abstracts at*: 10703ᶜ]

12771 **Byulleten' Kazanskago okruga putei soobshcheniya.** Kazan'. Бюллетень Казанскаго округа путей сообщенія. *Byull. kazan. Okruga Put. Soobshch.*

12772 **Byulleten' Khar'kovskago obshchestva lyubitelei prirody.** Khar'kov. Бюллетень Харьковскаго общества любителей природы. *Byull. khar'kov. Obshch. Lyub. Prir.* **L.**EB. 12–18*.

12773 **Byulleten' khlopkovodcheskoi kooperatsii.** Tashkent. Бюллетень хлопководческой кооперации. *Byull. khlopkovod. Koop.* [1928–30]

12774 **Byulleten' Kievskago politekhnicheskago obshchestva inzhenerov i agronomov.** Kiev. Бюллетень Кіевскаго политехническаго общества инженеровъ и агрономовъ. *Byull. kiev. politekh. Obshch. Inzh. Agron.*

12775 **Byulleten' Kollektiva nablyudatelei Moskovskogo obshchestva lyubitelei astronomii.** Moskva. Бюллетень Коллектива наблюдателей Московского общества любителей астрономии. *Byull. Koll. Nablyud. mosk. Obshch. Lyub. Astr.* [1925–32] **L.**AS. 27–32; **O.**O. imp. [*Supplement to*: 32106; *suspended* 1929–31; *C. as*: 12776]

12776 **Byulleten' Kollektiva nablyudatelei Vsesoyuznogo astronomo-geodezicheskogo obshchestva Akademii nauk SSSR.** Moskva. Бюллетень Коллектива наблюдателей всесоюзного астрономо-геодезического общества Академии наук СССР. *Byull. Koll. Nablyud. vses. astr.-geod. Obshch.* [1932–37] **L.**AS.; **O.**O. imp. [*Supplement to*: 32106; *C. of*: 12775; *C. as*: 12834]

12777 **Byulleten' Komissii po issledovaniyu solntsa.** Leningrad. Бюллетень Комиссии по исследованию солнца. *Byull. Kom. Issled. Sol.* [1932–35] **L.**AS.

12778 **Byulleten' Komissii po izucheniyu chetver-tichnogo perioda.** Leningrad. Бюллетень Комиссии по изучению четвертичного периода. *Byull. Kom. Izuch. chetvert. Perioda* [1929–] **L.**ʙᴍ.; ʙᴍᴺ. 51–; **Lv.**ᴜ. 53–.

12779 **Byulleten' Komissii po kometam i meteoram.** Stalinabad. Бюллетень Комиссии по кометам и метеорам. *Byull. Kom. Komet. Meteor.* [1952–] **L.**ᴀꜱ.

12780 **Byulleten' Komissii po okhrane prirody.** Moskva. Бюллетень Комиссии по охране природы. *Byull. Kom. Okhr. Prir.* **L.**ʙᴍᴺ. 56–.

12781 **Byulleten' Kruzhka tekhnologov Moskovskago raĭona.** Moskva. Бюллетень Кружка технологовъ Московскаго района. *Byull. Kruzhka Tekhnol. mosk. Raiona*

12782 **Byulleten' Kubanskoĭ sel'sko-khozyaĭstven-noĭ opỹtnoĭ stantsii.** Rostov na Donu. Бюллетень Кубанской сельско-хозяйственной опытной станции. *Byull. kuban. sel'.-khoz. opỹt. Sta.* **Rt.** 25–26.

12783 **Byulleten' Meteorologicheskoĭ observatorii Kazanskago universiteta.** Kazan'. Бюллетень Метеорологической обсерватории Казанскаго университета. *Byull. met. Obs. Kazan. Univ.* **L.**ᴍᴏ. 99–15.

12784 **Byulleten' Mezhdunarodnoĭ sektsii Vỹsshago tekhnicheskago sovêta Narodnago komissarĭata puteĭ soobshcheniya.** Moskva. Бюллетень Международной секции Высшаго техническаго совѣта народнаго комиссаріата путей сообщенія. *Byull. mezhdunar. Sek. vỹssh. tekh. Sov. nar. Kom. Put. Soobshch.*

12784ᶜ **Byulleten' Mezhduvedomstvennoĭ okeanogra-ficheskoĭ Kommissii.** Moskva. Бюллетень Междуведомственной океанографической коммиссии. *Byull. mezhduved. okeanogr. Komm.* [1958–] **L.**ʙᴍᴺ.

12785 **Byulleten' Moskovskago gorodskogo prodo-vol'stvennago komiteta.** Moskva. Бюллетень Московскаго городского продовольственнаго комитета. *Byull. mosk. gorod. prodovol'. Kom.* **L.**ʙᴍ. 18* imp. [*C. as:* 12811]

12786 **Byulleten' Moskovskogo obshchestva ispỹtate-leĭ prirody.** Moskva. Бюллетень Московского общества испытателей природы. *Byull. mosk. Obshch. Ispỹt. Prir.* [1829–] **L.**ʙᴍ. 1829–95; ʙᴍᴺ.; ᴇ. imp.; ᴇʙ. 40–; ɢʟ. imp.; ɢᴍ. (geol.) 17–; ᴋ. 1829–15: (biol.) 17–imp.; ʟ. (biol.) 17–; (geol.) 22–46 imp.; ᴩ. 1829–26; ꜱ. 1829–79 imp.; ꜱᴄ. imp.; ᴢ.; **Bl.**ᴜ. 54– imp.; **Bm.**ɴ. 85–15; **C.**ᴀ. (biol.) 40–46; ᴩ.; ᴜʟ. 1829–95: 27–; **Db.** 1829–81: (biol.) 17–46; **E.**ʙ. 85–16; ᴄ. 84–; ᴅ. (geol.) 22–34 imp.; ᴊ. 85–16; ʀ. imp.; **G.**ɴ. 67–46 imp.; ᴜ. 89– imp.; **Ld.**ᴜ. 85– imp.; **Lv.**ᴜ. imp.; **M.**ᴜ. 1853–61: 84–86: 91–16 imp. (biol.) 17–40: 45–58 imp. (geol.) 22–40: 45–46; **O.**ᴀᴩ. (biol.) 45–46; ʜ. 1829–81 imp.; ʀ.; **Rt.** (biol.) 37–40; **Y.** [*Published in Biology and Geology sections; English abstracts at:* 11159ᵇ]

Byulleten' Moskovskogo obshchestva lyubite-leĭ astronomii. Бюллетень. Московского общества любителей астрономии. *See* 12834.

12787 **Byulleten' Moskovskogo obshchestva vozdu-khoplavaniya.** Moskva. Бюллетень Московского общества воздухоплавания. *Byull. mosk. Obshch. Vozdukhopl.*

Byulleten' Muzeya obshchestva izucheniya Man'chzhurskago kraya. Бюллетень Музея общества изученія Маньчжурскаго края. *See* 36581.

12788 **Byulleten' Narodnago komissarĭata truda.** Moskva. Бюллетень Народнаго комиссаріата труда. *Byull. nar. Kom. Truda* [1918–] **L.**ʙᴍ.

12789 **Byulleten' Narodnogo komissariata zdravo-okhraneniya.** Moskva. Бюллетень Народного комиссариата здравоохранения. *Byull. nar. Kom. Zdravookh.* [1922–27] **L.**ʙᴍ. 22. [*C. as:* 56945]

12790 **Byulleten' Nauchno-issledovatel'skogo insti-tuta po khlopkovodstvu.** Tashkent. Бюллетень Научно-исследовательского института по хлопководству. *Byull. nauchno-issled. Inst. Khlopkov., Tashkent* [1930–36] **L.**ʙᴍ.; ᴋ.; **C.**ᴀ.; **Rt.** 32–36 imp.

Byulleten' Nauchno-issledovatel'skogo insti-tuta sel'skogo khozyaĭstva Yugo-vostoka. Saratov. Бюллетень Научно-исследовательского института сельского хозяйства Юго-востока. *See* 12805.

12791 **Byulleten' Nauchno-issledovatel'skogo insti-tuta tekstil'noĭ promỹshlennosti.** Moskva. Бюллетень Научно-исследовательского института текстильной промышленности. *Byull. nauchno-issled. Inst. tekst. Prom.* **L.**ᴩ. 34.

12792 **Byulleten' Nauchno-issledovatel'skogo insti-tuta zoologii Moskovskogo gosudarstvennogo universiteta.** Moskva. Бюллетень Научно-исследовательского института зоологии Московского государственного университета. *Byull. nauchno-issled. Inst. Zool. mosk. gosud. Univ.* [1931–32] **L.**ꜱᴄ. [*C. as:* 48637]

12793 **Byulleten' nauchno-tekhnicheskoĭ informatsii po agronomicheskoĭ fizike.** Leningrad. Бюллетень научно-технической информации по агрономической физике. *Byull. nauchno-tekh. Inf. agron. Fiz.* [1956–] **Rt.**

12794 **Byulleten' nauchno-tekhnicheskoĭ informatsii Milyutinskoĭ gosudarstvennoĭ selektsionnoĭ stantsii.** Samarkand. Бюллетень научно-технической информации Милютинской государственной селекционной станции. *Byull. nauchno-tekh. Inf. Milyutin. gosud. selekt. Sta.* [1956–] **Rt.**

12795 **Byulleten' nauchno-tekhnicheskoĭ informatsii po sel'skokhozyaĭstvennoĭ mikrobiologii.** Leningrad. Бюллетень научно-технической информации по сельскохозяйственной микробиологии. *Byull. nauchno-tekh. Inf. sel'.khoz. Mikrobiol.* [1956–] **Rt.**

12796 **Byulleten' nauchno-tekhnicheskoĭ informatsii soyuznikov.** Tashkent. Бюллетень научно-технической информации союзников. *Byull. naucho-tekh. Inf. Soyuz.* [1957–] **Rt.** 57.

Byulleten' nauchno-tekhnicheskoĭ informatsii. Tsentral'naya geneticheskaya laboratoriya imeni I. V. Michurina. Бюллетень научно-технической информации. Центральная генетическая лаборатория имени И. В. Мичурина. *See* 12830.

12798 **Byulleten' nauchno-tekhnicheskoĭ informatsii Vsesoyuznogo nauchno-issledovatel'skogo instituta agrolesomelioratsii.** Moskva. Бюллетень научно-технической информации Всесоюзного научно-исследовательского института агролесомелиорации. *Byull. nauchno-tekh. Inf. vses. nauchno-issled. Inst. Agrolesomel.* [1956–] **O.**ꜰ.; **Y.**

12799 **Byulleten' nauchno-tekhnicheskoĭ informatsii Vsesoyuznogo nauchno-issledovatel'skogo instituta sakharnoĭ sveklỹ.** Kiev. Бюллетень науно-технической информации Всесоюзного научно-исследовательского института сахарной свеклы. *Byull. nauchno-tekh. Inf. vses. nauchno-issled. Inst. sakh. Sveklỹ* [1956–] **Rt.**

Byulleten' nauchno-tekhnicheskoĭ informatsii Vsesoyuznogo nauchno-issledovatel'skogo instituta udobreniĭ agrotekhniki i agropochvovedeniya. *See* 12836.

12801 **Byulleten' nauchno-tekhnicheskoĭ informatsii po zashchite rasteniĭ.** Leningrad. Бюллетень научно-технической информации по защите растений. *Byull. nauchno-tekh. Inf. Zashch. Rast.* [1956-] **Rt.**

12802 **Byulleten' Obshchestva élektrotekhnikov.** Moskva. Бюллетень Общества электротехников. *Byull. Obshch. Elektrotekh.*

12803 **Byulleten' Obshchestva estestvoispȳtateleĭ pri Voronezhskom gosudarstvennom universitetê.** Бюллетень Общества естествоиспытателей при Воронежскомъ государственномъ университетѣ. *Byull. Obshch. Estest. voronezh. gosud. Univ.* [1925-29] **L.**BM^N. 25-29; EB.; GL.; **E.**R.

12804 **Byulleten' Okeanograficheskoĭ komisii.** Moskva. Бюллетень Океанографической комиссии. *Byull. okeanogr. Kom.* [1958-] **L.**BM^N. imp.

12805 **Byulleten' Ordena trudovogo krasnogo znameni nauchno-issledovatel'skogo instituta sel'skogo khozyaĭstva Yugo-vostoka.** Saratov. Бюллетень Ордена трудового красного знамени научно-исследовательского института сельского хозяйства Юго-востока. *Byull. Ord. trudov. krasn. Znam. nauchno-issled. Inst. sel'. Khoz. Yugo-Vost.* [1956-] **Rt.**

12806 **Byulleten' Politekhnicheskago obshchestva, sostoyashchago pri Imperatorskom tekhnicheskom uchilishchê.** Moskva. Бюллетень Политехническаго общества, состоящаго при Императорскомъ техническомъ училищѣ. *Byull. politekh. Obshch. imp. tekh. Uchil.*

12807 **Byulleten' Poltavskoĭ sel'sko-khozyaĭstvennoĭ stantsii.** Poltava. Бюллетень Полтавской сельскохозяйственной станции. *Byull. poltav. sel'.-khoz. Sta.* **L.**BM^N. 23-25 (ent.)

12808 **Byulleten' Postoyannago byuro Vserossiĭskikh éntomo-fitopatologicheskikh s"ēzdov.** Leningrad. Бюллетень Постояннаго бюро Всероссійскихъ энтомо-фитопатологическихъ съѣздовъ. *Byull. post. Byuro vseross. ént.-fitopatol. S"ēzd.* [1921-24] **L.**EB.; **Rt.** 21. [*C. as:* 58367]

12809 **Byulleten' Postoyannoĭ aktinometricheskoĭ komissii pri Glavnoĭ geograficheskoĭ observatorii.** Leningrad. Бюллетень Постоянной актинометрической комиссии при Главной геофизической обсерватории. *Byull. post. aktinom. Kom.* **L.**SC. 25-.

12810 **Byulleten' Postoyannoĭ tsentral'noĭ seĭsmicheskoĭ komissii.** S.-Peterburg. Бюллетень Постоянной центральной сейсмической комиссии. *Byull. post. tsent. seism. Kom.* [1902-] **L.**MO. 07-12 imp.; **C.**UL. 14-; **E.**R. 08: 11; **O.**O. 02-07.

12811 **Byulleten' Prodovol'stvennago otdêla Moskovskago sovêta rabochikh i krasnoarmeĭskikh deputatov.** Moskva. Бюллетень Продовольственнаго отдѣла Московскаго совѣта рабочихъ и красноармейскихъ депутатовъ. *Byull. prodov. Otd. mosk. Sov. rab. krasnoarm. Deput.* [1918-] **L.**BM. 18. [*C. of:* 12785]

12812 **Byulleten' regional'nȳkh seĭsmicheskikh stantsiĭ Kavkaza.** Moskva. Бюллетень региональных сейсмических станций Кавказа. *Byull. reg. seism. Sta. Kavk.* [1933-] **L.**SC.

12813 **Byulleten' Rossïĭskago gidrologicheskago Instituta.** Petrograd. Бюллетень Россійскаго гидрологическаго института. *Byull. ross. gidrol. Inst.* [1922]

12814 **Byulleten'. Rostov-nakhichevanskaya na Donu raĭonnaya (oblastnaya) sel'sko-khozyaĭstvennaya opȳtnaya stantsiya.** Rostov na Donu. Бюллетень. Ростовъ-нахичеванская на Дону районная (областная) сельско-хозяйственная опытная станція. *Byull. rost.-nakhich. Donu raĭonn. sel'.-khoz. opȳt. Sta.* **L.**EB. (ent.) 18-30; **Rt.** 19-26 imp.

12815 **Byulleten' rȳbnogo khozyaĭstva.** Moskva. Бюллетень рыбного хозяйства. *Byull. rȳbn. Khoz.* [1921-30] [*C. as:* 58232]

12816 **Byulleten' sakharotresta.** Moskva. Бюллетень сахаротреста. *Byull. Sakharotr.* [1923-29] [*C. as:* 50317]

12817 **Byulleten'. Severno-vostochnoe byuro kraevedeniya.** Arkhangel'. Бюллетень. Северно-восточное бюро краеведения. *Byull. sev.-vost. Byuro Kraeved.* **L.**SC. 26-.

12818 **Byulleten'. Solnechnȳie dannȳie.** Бюллетень. Солнечные данные. *Byull. soln. Dann.* [1956-] **L.**AS.

12819 **Byulleten' Soveta po seĭsmologii.** Moskva. Бюллетень совета по сейсмологии. *Byull. Sov. Seĭsm.* **L.**P. 57-.

12820 **Byulleten' spravochnoĭ chasti po vnêshneĭ torgovli.** S.-Peterburg. Бюллетень справочной части по внѣшней торговли. *Byull. sprav. Chasti vnêsh. Torg.*

Byulleten' Sredne-aziatskago gosudarstvennago universiteta. Бюллетень Средне-азіатскаго государственнаго университета. *See* 12515.

12821 **Byulleten' Sredne-aziatskogo raĭonnogo upravleniya, Glavnoe geologo-razvedochnoe upravlenie.** Moskva. Бюллетень. Средне-азиатского районного управления, Главное геолого-разведочное управление. *Byull. sredne-aziat. raĭonn. Upr. glav. geol.-razved. Upr.* [1930-]

12822 **Byulleten' Stalinabadskoĭ astronomicheskoĭ observatorii.** Stalinabad. Бюллетень сталинабадской астрономической обсерватории. *Byull. stalinabad. astr. Obs.* [1952-] **L.**AS.; **M.**U. 52-57.

12823 **Byulleten'. Stantsiya zashchitȳ rastenii yuzhnogo berega Krȳma.** Yalta. Бюллетень. Станция защиты растений южного берега Крыма. *Byull. Sta. Zashch. Rast. yuzh. Berega Krȳma* [1927-] **L.**EB. 27-28.

12824 **Byulleten' stroitel'noĭ tekhniki.** Moskva. Бюллетень строительной техники. *Byull. stroit. Tekh.* [1944-] **L.**BM. 53-; P. 57-; **Wa.**B. 46-; **Y.**

12825 **Byulleten' Tashkentskoĭ astronomicheskoĭ observatorii.** Tashkent. Бюллетень Ташкентской астрономической обсерватории. *Byull. tashkent. astr. Obs.* [1933-] **E.**R.

12826 **Byulleten' Tashkentskoĭ geofizicheskoĭ observatorii.** Tashkent. Бюллетень Ташкентской геофизической обсерватории. *Byull. tashkent. geofiz. Obs.* [1928-] **L.**G. 28-30; MO. 28: 30.

12827 **Byulleten' Tbilisskoĭ seĭsmicheskoĭ stantsii.** Tbilissi. Бюллетень Тбилисской сейсмической станции. *Byull. tbiliss. seĭsm. Sta.* **L.**SC. 28-33*. [*C. as:* 27863]

12828 **Byulleten' tekhnicheskoĭ informatsii** (po **stroi-tel'stvu**). Leningrad. Бюллетень технической информации по строительству. *Byull. tekh. Inf. Stroit.* [1955–59] **L.**вм. 58–59; P. 58–59. [*C. in:* 4777]

12828° **Byulleten' tekhniko-ékonomicheskoĭ informa-tsii.** Moskva. Бюллетень технико-экономической информации. *Byull. tekh.-ékon. Inf.*

12829 **Byulleten' Tikhookeanskogo komiteta Akade-mii nauk SSSR.** Leningrad. Бюллетень Тихоокеанского комитета Академии наук СССР. *Byull. tikhookean. Kom.* [1929–34] **L.**вм.; GM.; MO.; SC.; **Pl.**м. 29.

12829° **Byulleten' tovarnȳkh znakov.** Komitet po delam izobreteniĭ i otkrytiĭ pri Sovete ministrov SSSR. Moskva. Бюллетень товарных знаков. Комитет по делам изобретений и открытий при Совете министров СССР. *Byull. tovarn. Znak. Kom. Delam Izobr. Otkrȳt.* [1959–] **L.**P.

12830 **Byulleten' Tsentral'noĭ geneticheskoĭ labora-torii** imeni **I. V. Michurina.** Michurinsk. Бюллетень Центральной генетической лаборатории имени И. В. Мичурина. *Byull. tsent. genet. Lab. I. V. Michurina* [1956–] **C.**A.

12830° **Byulleten' Uchenogo meditsinskogo soveta Ministerstva zdravookhraneniya RSFSR.** Бюллетень Ученого медицинского совета Министерства здравоохранения РСФСР. *Byull. uchen. med. Sov.*

12831 **Byulleten' Uzbekistanskogo instituta éksperi-mental'noĭ meditsinȳ.** Tashkent. Бюллетень Узбекистанского института экспериментальной медицины. *Byull. uzbek. Inst. éksp. Med.* [1934–] **L.**TD. 34–37 imp.

12832 **Byulleten' o vreditelyakh sel'skago khozyaĭstva** i **mêrakh bor'bȳ** c **nimi.** Khar'kov. Бюллетень о вредителяхъ сельскаго хозяйства и мѣрахъ борьбы съ ними. *Byull. Vred. sel'. Khoz.* **L.**EB. 13–16.

12833 **Byulleten' Vserossiĭskago éntomo-fitopato-logicheskago sovêshchanīya (s"êzda)** v **Petrogradê.** Бюллетень Всероссійскаго энтомо-фитопатологическаго совѣщанія (съѣзда) въ Петроградѣ. *Byull. vseross. ént.-fitopatol. Sovêshch.* **L.**EB. 20–22.

Byulleten' Vserossiĭskogo tekstil'nogo sindikata. Бюллетень Всероссийского текстильного синдиката. *See* 24521.

12834 **Byulleten' Vsesoyuznogo astronomo-geode-zicheskogo obshchestva,** Akademiya Nauk SSSR. Leningrad. Бюллетень Всесоюзного астрономо-геодезического общества, Академия наук СССР. *Byull. vses. astr.-geod. Obshch.* [1938–] **L.**AS. imp.; **M.**U. 47–58 imp.; **O.**O. imp.; **Y.** [*Supplement to:* 32106; *C. of:* 12776]

12835 **Byulleten' Vsesoyuznogo instituta (morskogo) rȳbnogo khozyaĭstva** i **okeanografii.** Moskva. Бюллетень Всесоюзного института (морского) рыбного хозяйства и океанографии. *Byull. vses. Inst. rȳb. Khoz. Okeanogr.* [1934–] **L.**вм.; вм^N. 34; **Abd.**м. 34; **E.**R.

12836 **Byulleten' Vsesoyuznogo instituta rastenievod-stva.** Leningrad. Бюллетень Всесоюзного института растениеводства. *Byull. vses. Inst. Rasteniev.* **L.**AM.; **C.**A. 56–.

12837 **Byulleten' Vsesoyuznogo nauchno-issledova-tel'skogo geologicheskogo instituta 'Vsegei'.** Mosk-va. Бюллетень Всесоюзного научно-исследовательского геологического института 'Всегеи'. *Byull. vses. nauchno-issled. geol. Inst. 'Vsegei'* [1958–] **L.**вм^N.

12838 **Byulleten' Vsesoyuznogo nauchno-issledova-tel'skogo instituta svinovodstva.** Poltava. Бюллетень Всесоюзного научно-исследовательского института свиноводства. *Byull. vses. nauchno-issled. Inst. Svinov.* [1930–]

12839 **Byulleten' Vsesoyuznogo nauchno-issledova-tel'skogo instituta tsementov.** Leningrad. Бюллетень Всесоюзого научно-исследовательского института цементов. *Byull. vses. nauchno-issled. Inst. Tsem.* [1937–]

12840 **Byulleten' Vsesoyuznogo nauchno-issledova-tel'skogo instituta udobreniĭ agrotekhniki** i **agro-pochvovedeniya.** Moskva. Бюллетень Всесоюзного научно-исследовательского института удобрений агротехники и агропочвоведениия *Byull. vses. nauchno-issled. Inst. Udobr. Agrotekh. Agropochvov.* [1956–] **E.**AB. 57–; **Rt.**

12841 **Byulleten' Vsesoyuznogo s"ezda** po **kurortnomu delu.** Moskva. Бюллетень Всесоюзного съезда по курортному делу. *Byull. vses. S"ezda kurort. Delu* **L.**вм. 24–.

12842 **Byulleten' Vsesoyuznoĭ akademii sel'skokho-zyaĭstvennȳkh nauk** im. **V. I. Lenina.** Moskva. Бюллетень Всесоюзной академии сельскохозяйственных наук имени В. И. Ленина. *Byull. vses. Akad. sel'.-khoz. Nauk V. I. Lenina* [1935–37] **L.**AM.; **C.**A.; **E.**AB. 35; **Hu.**G.; **R.**D. [*C. as:* 17121]

12843 **Byulleten' Vseukrainskogo obshchestva seme-novodstva.** Kharkov. Бюллетень Всеукраинского общества семеноводства. *Byull. vseukr. Obshch. Seme-nov.* [1927 ?–]

12844 **Byulleten' Vseukrainskoĭ gosudarstvennoĭ chernomorsko-azovskoĭ nauchno-promȳslovoĭ opȳt-noĭ stantsii 'Bugchanpos.'** Ochakov. Бюллетень Все-украинской государственной черноморско-азовской научно-промысловой опытной станции 'Бугчаннос'. *Byull. vseukr. gosud. chernomorsko-azov. nauchno-promȳsl. opȳt. Sta. Bugchanpos*

12845 **Byulleten' Vul'kanologicheskoĭ stantsii** na **Kam-chatke.** Moskva. Бюллетень Вулканологической станции на Камчатке. *Byull. vul'kan. Sta. Kamchatke* **L.**вм. 46–; GM. 46–; P. 57–; **C.**PO. 46.

12846 **Byulleten' yarovizatsii.** Odessa. Бюллетень яровизации. *Byull. Yaroviz.* [1932] [*C. as:* 57976]

12847 **Byulleten' Zootekhnicheskoĭ opȳtnoĭ** i **plemen-noĭ stantsii Gosudarstvennogo nauchno-issledo-vatel'skogo stepnogo instituta goszapovednika 'Chapli'.** Moskva. Бюллетень Зоотехнической опытной и племенной станции Государственного научно-исследовательского степного института госзаповедника 'Чапли'. *Byull. zootekh. opȳt. plem. Sta. gosud. nauchno-issled. stepn. Inst. Goszap. 'Chapli'* [1926–] **E.**AB. 26–32.

C

12848 **C.A.** Bulletin of Cancer Progress. New York. *C.A.* [1950–] **L.**H. 56–; MA. 55–; MD.; **Dn.**U. 58–; **G.**U. 58–; **Ld.**U. 59–.

12849 **C. and A. Bulletin.** Coleman and Appleby, Ltd. Birmingham. *C. & A. Bull.* [1936–] **L.**P.; **Bm.**P. [*C. of:* 9824]

12850 **C.A.A. Journal.** Civil Aeronautics Authority. *C.A.A. Jl* [1945–] **L.**AV.; P. 45–52. [*C. of:* 14445]

12851 **C.A.A. Publications.** Civil Aeronautics Authority. *C.A.A. Publs* **L.**AV.

C.A.A. Report. Civil Aeronautics Authority. Washington. *See* 43051.

12852 **CAC Magazine.** Cape Asbestos Co. London. *CAC Mag.* [1952–] **L.**BM. 57–; **G.**E. (1 yr)

12853 **C.A.C.A. Library Abstract.** Cement and Concrete Association. London. *C.A.C.A. Libr. Abstr.* [1951–] **L.**BM.; P.; **Bl.**U.; **Br.**U.; **Dn.**U.; **Ld.**P. 53–; **M.**T.; U.; **Y.**

12854 **C.A.C.A. Library Bibliography.** Cement and Concrete Association. London. *C.A.C.A. Libr. Biblphy* [1960–] **L.**BA.; P.; **Bl.**U.; **Br.**U.; **Dn.**U.; **Ld.**P.; **M.**U.; **Nw.**A.; **Y.** [*C. of:* 12855]

12855 **C.A.C.A. Library Record.** Cement and Concrete Association. London. *C.A.C.A. Libr. Rec.* [1948–59] **L.**BA. 49–59; P.; **Bl.**U.; **Br.**U.; **Dn.**U.; **Ld.**P. 51–59 imp.; **M.**U. 49–59; **Nw.**A. 49–59; **Y.** [*C. as:* 12854]

12856 **C. A. C. A. Library Translation.** Cement and Concrete Association. London. *C. A. C. A. Libr. Transl.* [1948–] **L.**BM.; P.; **Bl.**U.; **Br.**U. imp.; **M.**P. 57–; T. 51–; U. 50–; **N.**T.; **Y.**

12857 **C. A. C. A. Library Translation Loan Series.** Cement and Concrete Association. London. *C. A. C. A. Libr. Transl. Loan Ser.* [1952–] **L.**BM.; **Br.**U.; **Ld.**P. imp.

C.A.C.A. Research Notes. Cement and Concrete Association. *See* 45883.

12857ᵃ **C.A.E. News.** Canadian Aviation Electronics. St. Laurent. *C.A.E. News* **Y.**

12858 **C.A.L.** Certified Akers Laboratory. Chicago. *C.A.L.* [1938–]

12859 **C.A.M.** Orgão do Centro academico de medicina. Pôrto Alegre. *C.A.M.* [1938–]

12860 **CAMEP.** Centro de asistencia médica para enfermos pobres. México. *CAMEP* [1936–43] [*C. as:* 38594]

12861 **CAMSI.** Canadian Association of Medical Students and Internees. Montreal. *CAMSI* [1942–]

12862 **CARDE Technical Memorandum.** Canadian Armament Research and Development Establishment. Valcartier. *CARDE tech. Memor.* **L.**P. (Public issues) 60–.

CATC Electronics News. London. *See* 14449.

12863 **C. A. V.-Bosch Bulletin.** London. *C.A. V.-Bosch Bull.* [1934–38] **L.**P.

12864 **C. A. V. Engineering Review.** C. A. V. Ltd. London. *C. A. V. Engng Rev.* [1954–] **L.**AV. 58–; BM.; P.; **Y.**

12865 **CBCC Positive Data Series.** Chemical-Biological Coordination Center. Washington. *CBCC posit. Data Ser.* [1955–] **L.**P.

12866 **C. C. Schmidts Jahrbücher** der in- und ausländischen gesamten Medizin. Bonn. *C. C. Schmidts Jb. in- u. ausl. ges. Med.* [1834–22] **L.**BM. 1834–14; GH.; MD.; S.; U. 93–06 imp.; UCH. 66–14 imp.; **Abd.**U.; **Bl.**U. 81–15; **Bm.**U.; **Br.**U. 1858–22 imp.; **C.**MD. 92–22; PH. 02–14; UL. 1848–22; **Cr.**MS. 62–87 imp.; **Db.** 1856–93; **E.**P.; **G.**F. 1834–14; **Lv.**U. 94–13 imp.; **M.**MS.; **Sa.** 1834–64.

12867 **C. C. H.** Mykologický sborník. v Praze. *C. C. H.* [1935–] [*C. of:* 13403]

12868 **CCHE Information Digest.** Central Council for Health Education. London. *CCHE Inf. Dig.* [1952–53] **L.**BM. 52; H.; MD.; TD. [*C. as:* 21970]

12868ᵉ **C.C.T.A. Report.** Commission for Technical Cooperation in Africa South of the Sahara. London. *C.C.T.A. Rep.* [1950–] **L.**BM.; **O.**RE. 52– imp.; **Rt.** 54– imp.

C.D.A. Bulletin. Copper Development Association. *See* 9920.

12869 **C. D. A. Publications.** Copper Development Association. London. *C. D. A. Publs* [1934–] **L.**BM.; P. 56–; **Bm.**U.; **Bn.**U. imp.; **Dn.**U. imp.; **E.**U. imp.; **Ld.**P. imp.; **Lv.**P.; **N.**P.; **O.**B.; **Sw.**U.; **Y.**

12870 **C.D.C. Bulletin.** Communicable Disease Centre. Atlanta. *C. D. C. Bull.* [1948–51] **L.**H.; MA.; TD. [*See also:* 10250ᵃ]

12871 **C.E. Bib.** Central Electricity Authority, Central Electricity Generating Board. London. *C.E. Bib.* [1955–] **L.**BM.; P.; SC. [*Replaces:* 5650]

C.E.C. Napoli. *See* 13314.

12871ᵃ **C.E. Trans.** Central Electricity Generating Board (*formerly* Central Electricity Authority). London. *C.E. Trans* [1955–] **L.**BM.; P. [*C. of:* 5651]

12872 **CEA.** Cambridge Electron Accelerator. Cambridge, Mass. *CEA* [1956–] **L.**SC.

12873 **CEC Recordings.** Consolidated Engineering Corp. Pasadena. *CEC Record.* **L.**AV. 50–56 imp.; P. 50–.

12874 **CEG-Berichte.** Continental-Elektroindustrie-Gesellschaft. Düsseldorf. *CEG-Ber.* [1955–56] **L.**P. [*C. as:* 12875]

369

12875 **CEIG-Berichte.** Continental-Elektroindustrie-Gesellschaft. Düsseldorf. *CEIG-Ber.* [1957–58] **L**.P. [*C. of:* 12874; *C. as:* 15549]

12876 **CENCO News Chats.** Central Scientific Company. Chicago. *CENCO News Chats* **L**.P. 32– imp.

12876° **C.E.R.A.M.I.C.A.** Barcelona. *C.E.R.A.M.I.C.A.* [1952–] **L**.BM.

12876° **CERCHAR Publications.** Centre d'études et recherches des charbonnages de France. Paris. *CERCHAR Publs* **L**.MI. 53– imp.; **Sh**.S. 53–.

12877 **CERN Bibl.** Conseil européen de recherche nucléaire. Genève. *CERN Bibl.* [1958–] **L**.BM.; P.; SC.; **Y**.

12878 **CERN Courier.** Conseil européen de recherche nucléaire. *CERN Cour.* **L**.P. 59–; SC. 55–; **Y**.

12879 **C. E. S. A. Bulletin.** Canadian Engineering Standard Association. Ottawa. *C. E. S. A. Bull.* **L**.SC. 27–38; **Br**.P. (1 yr). [*C. as:* 41451]

12879° **C.F.F.** Chemins de fer fédéraux. Berne. *C.F.F.* **Y**.

12880 **CFT informations.** Compagnie française de télévision. Paris. *CFT Infs* [1959–] **L**.P.

12881 **C. G. A.** Organe de la Confédération générale des agriculteurs de France. Paris. *C. G. A.*

12882 **CGR.** Compagnie générale de radiologie. Paris. *CGR* [1959–]

12883 **C. I. B. Bulletin.** Conseil international du bâtiment pour la recherche, l'étude et la documentation. Rotterdam. *C. I. B. Bull.* [1954–] **L**.P. 54; **O**.B.; **Wa**.B.; **Y**.

CIBA. *See* **Ciba.**

12884 **C. I. E. Journal.** Chinese Institute of Engineers. Shanghai. *C. I. E. Jl* [1943–] **L**.P. 43–49; SC. 46–. [*C. of:* 25800]

12885 **C. I. E. Journal. American Section.** Chinese Institute of Engineers. New York. *C. I. E. Jl Am. Sect.* [1943–] **L**.P. 43–49.

12886 **C. I. L. Explosives Bulletin.** Canadian Industries, Ltd. Montreal. *C. I. L. Explos. Bull.* [1950–] **L**.P. [*C. of:* 18782]

12887 **C-I-L Oval.** Canadian Industries, Ltd. Montreal. *C-I-L Oval* [1932–] **L**.P. (1 yr).

12888 **C. I. T. Technical Journal.** Carnegie Institute of Technology. Pittsburg. *C. I. T. tech. J.* [*C. as:* 13364]

12889 **C. L. A. Journal.** Central Landowners Association. London. *C. L. A. J.* [1930–46] **L**.AM. 40–46; BM.; **E**.A.; **O**.R.; **R**.D.; **Rt**. 43–45. [*C. of:* 25758; *C. as:* 25757]

12889° **C.L.A.I.R.A. News.** Chalk Lime and Allied Industries Research Association. Welwyn. *C.L.A.I.R.A. News* **Y**.

12890 **C. M. B. Newsletter.** Ghana Cocoa Marketing Board. Accra. *C. M. B. Newsl.* [1955–] **L**.TP. 57–.

12891 **C. M. P. A. Bulletin.** Hartford, Conn. *C. M. P. A. Bull.*

12892 **C. M. U. A. Journal.** Commercial Motor Users' Association. London. *C. M. U. A. Jl* [1927–40] **L**.P.; **C**.UL. 28–40; **E**.U. 30–40 imp.; **Sy**.R. [*C. as:* 15031]

12893 **C. N. A.** Revista del Centro nacional de agricultura. San Pedro de Montes de Oca. *C. N. A.* [1936–40] **L**.SC.; **Md**.H. 39–40 imp. [*C. as:* 16262]

12894 **CNEP boletín.** Comisión nacional para la erradicación del paludismo. Piso. *CNEP Boln* [1957–] **L**.BM^N.; **Y**.

12895 **CNRN notiziario.** Comitato nazionale per le ricerche nucleari. Roma. *CNRN Notiz.* [1955–] **L**.BM.; P.; **Ld**.P. 60–; **Y**. (*From* 1955 *to* 1957 *issued in:* 47739)

12896 **CO₂ the Dry Ice Journal.** Horb. *CO₂* [1951–] **L**.P. [*C. of:* 17249]

CoA Note. College of Aeronautics, Cranfield. *See* 35201.

CORESTA Bulletin d'information. *See* 10540

12897 **C.P. Forest Bulletin.** Nagpur. *C.P. Forest Bull.* [1938–] **O**.F.

C.P.F.S. Report. Council for the Promotion of Field Studies. *See* 43204.

12898 **CQ.** The radio amateurs' journal. New York. *CQ* [1945–] **L**.AV. 58–; P. 59–; SC. 49–; **Y**.

12899 **C. and R. Bulletin.** Bureau of Construction and Repair. Navy Department. Washington. *C. & R. Bull.* [1931–] **L**.BM.; U.

12900 **C. R. E. A. Bulletin.** Committee on the Relationship of Electricity to Agriculture. Chicago. *C. R. E. A. Bull.* [1924–37] **L**.P. 25–37 imp.

12901 **C. R. E. A. News Letter.** Committee on the Relationship of Electricity to Agriculture. Chicago. *C. R. E. A. News Lett.* [1928–38] **L**.P.

12902 **CSA Bulletin.** Canadian Standards Association. Ottawa. *CSA Bull.* [1955–] **L**.BM.; **Y**. [*C. of:* 41451]

12903 **C. S. I. R. Information.** South African Council of Scientific and Industrial Research. Pretoria. *C. S. I. R. Inf.* [1946–] **L**.SC.

12903° **C.S.I.R. Research Report.** South African Council of Scientific and Industrial Research. Pretoria. *C.S.I.R. Res. Rep.* [1960–] **L**.BM.

12904 **C. S. I. R. Research Review.** South African Council of Scientific and Industrial Research. Pretoria. *C. S. I. R. Res. Rev.* [1952–] **L**.AV. imp.; BM.; HQ.; TP.; **Hu**.G.; **Sil**. 55–; **Y**. [*C. of:* 46006]

12904° **C.S.I.R. Technical Note.** South African Council of Scientific and Industrial Research. Durban. *C.S.I.R. tech. Note* **Y**.

12905 **C.S. & I.R. Ore Dressing Investigations Information sheet.** Council for Scientific and Industrial Research. Melbourne. *C.S. & I.R. Ore Dress. Invest. Inf. Sh., Melb.* [1945] **L**.P. [*C. as:* 12909]

12906 **C.S.I.R.O. Abstracts.** Commonwealth Scientific and Industrial Research Organization. Melbourne. *C.S.I.R.O. Abstr.* [1958–] **L**.BM. 60–; P.; **Abd**.R.; **C**.A.; **Hu**.G.; **Ld**.W.; **Md**.H. 59–; **R**.D.; **Rt**.; **Y**. [*C. of:* 12910]

C.S.I.R.O. Abstracts of Published Papers and List of Translations. *See* 393.

C.S.I.R.O. Coal Research. Melbourne. *See* 14678.

C.S.I.R.O. Land Research Series. Melbourne. *See* 27987.

12907 **C.S.I.R.O. Leaflet Series.** Melbourne. *C.S.I.R.O. Leafl. Ser.* [1951–] **C**.A. imp.; **Rt**. (curr.); **Y**.

12908 **C.S.I.R.O. Ore Dressing Investigations Information Circular.** Commonwealth Scientific and Industrial Research Organization. Melbourne. *C.S.I.R.O. Ore Dress. Invest. Inf. Circ.* [1956–] **L**.P. [*C. of:* 12909]

12909 **C.S.I.R.O. Ore Dressing Investigations Information Sheet.** Commonwealth Scientific and Industrial Research Organization. Melbourne. *C.S.I.R.O. Ore Dress. Invest. Inf. Sh.* [1949] **L**.P. [*C. of:* 12905; *C. as:* 12908]

C.S.I.R.O. Rural Research. Melbourne. *See* 48282.

12910 **C.S.I.R.O. Science Index.** Melbourne. *C.S.I.R.O. Sci. Index* [1957] **L.**P.; **Abd.**R.; **C.**A.; **Hu.**G.; **R.**D.; **Rt.**; **Y.** [*Contains* vol. 1 *of:* 5419; *C. of:* 393; *C. as:* 12906]
   C.S.I.R.O. Soil Publication. *See* 50023.
   C.S.I.R.O. Technical Paper. *See* **Technical Paper** of the **Divisions.**

12911 **C.S.I.R.O. Wildlife Research.** Melbourne. *C.S.I.R.O. Wildl. Res.* [1956–] **L.**AM.; BM^N.; NC.; Z.; **Abd.**R.; **Bm.**U.; **C.**A.; B.; **E.**A.; AB.; **Hu.**G.; **Ld.**U.; **M.**U.; **O.**AP.; OR.; R.; **Sal.**; **Y.**

12912 **C. S. T. A. Review.** Canadian Society of Technical Agriculturists. Ottawa. *C. S. T. A. Rev.* [1934–45] **L.**P.; SC. 39–45; **Hu.**G. 39–45. [*C. as:* 1344]

12913 **C. T. and F. C. D. Circular.** Office of Cotton, Truck and Forest Crop Disease. Washington. *C. T. & F. C. D. Circ.* **L.**SC. 18–.

12914 **C. U. C. News.** Coal Utilisation Council. London. *C. U. C. News* [1956–] **L.**BM.; P. (curr.)
   C.U.R.-rapport. Commissie voor uitvoering van research, Betonvereniging. *See* 42008.

12915 **C. V. Magazine.** Clyde Valley Electrical Power Co. *C. V. Mag.* **O.**R. 26–32.

12916 **C Y M.** Revista de ciencia y medicina. Medellín. *C Y M* [1941–]

12916° **Cable.** General Cable Works. Southampton. *Cable* [1956–] **Sy.**R. 58–.

12917 **Câbles** et **transmission.** Revue trimestrielle publié par Sotelec. Paris. *Câbles Transm.* [1947–] **L.**EE.; P.; SC.; **Bm.**P.; **Br.**U.; **C.**ENG. (3 yr.); **G.**U.; **Y.**

12918 **Cacao.** Inter-American Cacao Center. Turrialba. *Cacao, Turrialba* [1950–] **L.**H.; TP. 53– imp.; **Lh.**FO.; **Md.**H. [*C. of:* 12920]

12919 **Cacao** en **Colombia.** Palmira. *Cacao Colomb.* [1952–] **L.**AM.; **Md.**H. 52–56.

12920 **Cacao Information Bulletin.** Turrialba, Costa Rica. *Cacao Inf. Bull.* [1947–50] **C.**A.; **Lh.**FO.; **Md.**H. 48–50. [*C. as:* 12918]

12920° **Cacao-chocolade-suikerwerken.** Bussum. *Cacao-Choc.-SuikWkn* **Y.**

12921 **Caccia** e la **pesca.** Torino. *Caccia Pesca*

12922 **Cacciatore italiano.** Milano. *Cacciatore ital.*

12923 **Cacciatore trentino.** Trento. *Cacciatore trent.*

12924 **Cactaceae.** Jahrbücher der Deutschen Kakteen-gesellschaft. Berlin. *Cactaceae* [1937–] **L.**BM^N. 37–44 imp.; K. 37–39. [*C. of:* 24710]

12925 **Cactaceas** y **suculentas mexicanas.** México City. *Cactaceas Sucul. mex.* [1955–] **L.**K.

12926 **Cactus.** Mont St-Amand. *Cactus* [1931–] **L.**SC. 34–.

12927 **Cactus Journal.** London. *Cactus J.* [1898–00] **L.**BM.; BM^N.; K.; **Bm.**U.; **Cr.**P.; **E.**A.; B.; **G.**M.; **O.**R.

12928 **Cactus Journal.** Cactus and Succulent Society of Great Britain. London. *Cactus J.* [1932–39] **L.**BM.; BM^N. imp.; HS.; K.; L.; SC. 34–39; **E.**B.; **Y.** [*C. as:* 12930]

12929 **Cactus** and **Succulent Journal.** Los Angeles. *Cactus Succ. J., Los Ang.* [1931–] **L.**K.; SC. 36–. [*C. of:* 25728]

12930 **Cactus** and **Succulent Journal** of **Great Britain.** Elstree. *Cactus Succ. J. Gt Br.* [1946–] **L.**BM.; BM^N.; HS.; K.; L.; **E.**B.; **Y.** [*C. of:* 12928]

12931 **Cactussen** en **vetplanten.** Amsterdam. *Cactussen Vetpl.* **L.**K. 35–43.

12932 **Cadalyte Service Bulletin.** Grasselli Chemical Company. Cleveland, Ohio. *Cadalyte Serv. Bull.* [1933–35] **L.**SC. 35. [*C. as:* 49558]

12933 **Cadernos científicos.** Instituto Pasteur de Lisboa. *Cadern. cient. Inst. Pasteur Lisb.* [1946–] **L.**H.; MA. 46–55; MD.; TD.; **Y.**

12934 **Cádiz médico.** Cádiz. *Cádiz méd.*

12935 **Caducée.** Journal de chirurgie et de médecine d'armée. Paris. *Caducée* [1901–20] **L.**MA. 13–19; MD. 01–09; **Lv.**U. 11–20.

12936 **Caduceus.** Hongkong University Medical Society. Hongkong. *Caduceus* [1922–] **L.**MA. 30–41; MD. 32–; S. 22–26 imp.: 27–41; TD. 22–41 imp.; **Bl.**U. 31–41; **Bm.**U. 26– imp.; **Br.**U. 26–; **Db.** 28–; **Nw.**A. 27–; **O.**R. 26–.

12937 **Café.** Turrialba. *Café, Turrialba* [1959–] **C.**A.; **Md.**H. [*English edition at:* 14700]

12938 **Café-cacao-thé.** Nogent-sur-Marne. *Café-Cacao-Thé* [1957–] **L.**K.; P.; TP.; **C.**A.; **Md.**H.; **R.**U.; **Rt.** 57; **Sil.**; **Y.** [*Supplement to:* 1491]

12939 **Cage Birds Annual.** London. *Cage Birds A.* [1903–] **L.**BM.; **O.**B. 11– imp.

12940 **Cage-Birds** and **Bird World** (**Fancy**). London. *Cage-Birds* [1902–] **L.**BM.; **Abs.**N. 15– imp.; **E.**A. 02–06 imp.; **G.**M. 07–; **O.**B. 02–36.

12941 **Cahiers** d'**acoustique.** Centre national d'étude des télecommunications. Paris. *Cah. Acoust.* [1949–] **L.**SC. 51–.

12942 **Cahiers** d'**aérodynamique.** Paris. *Cah. Aérodyn.* **L.**AV. 46–47.

12943 **Cahiers agricoles** et **économiques** de l'**École nationale** d'**agriculture** de **Grignon.** Grignon. *Cah. agric. écon. Éc. natn. Agric. Grignon* [1954–] **C.**A.

12944 **Cahiers algériens** de la **santé.** Alger. *Cah. algér. Santé* [1946–] **L.**TD. 46–47.

12945 **Cahiers** d'**anesthésiologie.** Paris. *Cah. Anesth.* [1953–] **L.**MD.; S.

12946 **Cahiers apicoles.** Lyon. *Cah. apic.* [1950–] **Rt.**

12947 **Cahiers** de **biologie marine.** Roscoff. *Cah. Biol. mar.* [1960–] **L.**AM.; BM^N.; Z.; **Bn.**U.; **Y.**

12948 **Cahiers.** Bureau universitaire de **recherche opérationnelle,** Université de **Paris.** Paris. *Cah. Bur. univ. Rech. opér. Univ. Paris* [1957–] **L.**P.; **Y.**

12949 **Cahiers** de la **C.F.A.** Compagnie française d'audiologie. Paris. *Cah. C.F.A.* **L.**P. 56–.

12949° **Cahiers CIBA.** Basle. *Cah. CIBA* [1946–] **L.**BM. 52–.

12950 **Cahiers** du **Centre** de **recherches** et **études océanographiques.** Paris. *Cah. Cent. Rech. Étud. océanogr.* [1950–] **L.**MO. 50; **Lv.**U. 50.

12951 **Cahiers** du **Centre scientifique** et **technique** du **bâtiment.** Paris. *Cah. Cent. scient. tech. Bâtim.* [1948–] **L.**BA.; P.; **R.**U. 55; **Wa.**B. 60–; **Y.**

12952 **Cahiers.** Centre technique du **bois.** Paris. *Cah. Cent. tech. Bois* [1954–] **L.**P.; **Y.**

12952° **Cahiers** de la **céramique,** du **verre** et des **arts** du **feu.** Sèvres. *Cah. Céram.* [1955–] **Y.**

12953 **Cahiers** du **cessid.** Metz. *Cah. Cessid* [1952–] **L.**P.

12954 **Cahiers** de **climatologie.** Paris. *Cah. Clim.* [1933–] [*Supplement to:* 20755]

12955 **Cahiers coloniaux. Supplément technique.** Institut colonial de Marseille. Marseille. *Cah. colon. Supp. tech., Marseille* **L.**P. 18–20: 27–51*; TP. 38–51.

12956 **Cahiers. Comité français** de l'**éclairage** et du **chauffage.** Paris. *Cah. Com. fr. Éclair. Chauff.* **Y.**

12956[b] **Cahiers. Comités** de **prévention,** du **bâtiment** et des **travaux publics.** Paris. *Cah. Coms Prév. Bâtim.* **Y.**

12956[c] **Cahiers. Commission** du **bassin** de la **Seine.** Paris. *Cahiers Commn Bass. Seine* [1941–]

12957 **Cahiers** de **gastro-entérologie.** Paris. *Cah. Gastro-ent.* [1931–] [*Supplement to:* 20755]

12958 **Cahiers** de **géographie.** Université Laval, Québec. *Cah. Géogr. Univ. Laval* [1952–56] **L.**G. [*C. as:* 12959]

12959 **Cahiers** de **géographie** de **Québec.** Québec. *Cah. Géogr. Québ.* [1956–] **L.**G.; **E.**G. (curr.); **Ld.**U. 61–; **O.**B. [*C. of:* 12958]

12960 **Cahiers géologiques** de **Thoiry.** *Cah. géol. Thoiry* **L.**BM[N]. 50–.

12961 **Cahiers** du **Groupe français** d'**études** de **rhéologie.** Paris. *Cah. Grpe fr. Étud. Rhéol.* [1955–] **L.**BM.; **P.**; **SC.**

12962 **Cahiers. Hôtel-Dieu** de **Québec.** Québec. *Cah. Hôt.-Dieu Québ.* [1946–] **L.**S. imp.

12963 **Cahiers I. R. C. I.** Institut de recherches sur le caoutchouc en Indochine. Paris. *Cah. I. R. C. I.* [1944–] **Md.**H. 44–49; **Rt.**; **Sy.**R. 46–48.

12964 **Cahiers** de l'**information géographique.** Paris. *Cah. Inf. géogr.* [1952–54] **L.**G.; **O.**B. [*Supplement to:* 23463]

12964[c] **Cahiers** de l'**information. Station biologique marine Grande-Rivière.** *Cah. Inf. Stn biol. mar. Grande-Rivière* **Pl.**M. 61– imp.

12965 **Cahiers** des **ingénieurs agronomes.** Paris. *Cah. Ingrs agron.* [1945–] **L.**AM. 59–; **R.**U. 56–; **Y.**

12966 **Cahiers** de l'**Institut technique** de la **betterave.** Paris. *Cah. Inst. tech. Betterave* [1946–] **C.**A. 46–51.

12967 **Cahiers. Laboratoire** du **froid** et de la **conserve.** Casablanca. *Cah. Lab. Froid Conserve, Casablanca* [1951–] **L.**P. 51–57.

12968 **Cahiers Laënnec.** Paris. *Cah. Laënnec* [1934–] **L.**BM. 54–; **MA.** 53–. [*Not published* 1940–45]

12969 **Cahiers ligures** de **préhistoire** et d'**archéologie.** Montpellier. *Cah. ligur. Préhist. Archéol.* [1953–] **L.**BM[N]. [*C. of:* 12983]

12970 **Cahiers lyonnais** d'**histoire** de la **médecine.** Lyon. *Cah. lyonn. Hist. Méd.* [1956–] **L.**MD. imp.

12971 **Cahiers** de **médecine vétérinaire.** Paris. *Cah. Méd. vét.* **W.** 36–; **Y.**

12972 **Cahiers médicaux** d'**Auvergne.** Paris. *Cah. méd. Auvergne* [1950–] **L.**MA. [*C. of:* 5526]

12973 **Cahiers médicaux** de l'**Union française.** Alger. *Cah. méd. Un. fr.* [1946–] **L.**MA.; **MD.**

12974 **Cahiers** des **naturalistes.** Paris. *Cah. Nat.* [1953–] **L.**BM.; BM[N].; Z.; **O.**H. 53–54; **Y.** [*C. of:* 19347]

12975 **Cahiers** de **notes documentaires. Institut national** de **sécurité** pour la **prévention** des **accidents** du **travail** et des **maladies professionnelles.** Paris. *Cah. Notes docum. Inst. natn. Sécur. Prév. Accid. Travail* [1955–] **L.**P.; **Y.**

12976 **Cahiers océanographiques.** Paris. *Cah. océanogr.* **Lo.**; **Pl.**M. 59–; **Wl.**H. 58– **Wo.** [*C. of:* 10542]

12977 **Cahiers odonto-stomatologiques.** Marseille. *Cah. odonto-stomat.* [1951–] **L.**D.; **MD.**; **Bl.**U. imp.; **C.**AN.

12978 **Cahiers** d'**outre-mer.** Revue de géographie de Bordeaux et de l'Atlantique. Bordeaux. *Cah. d'outre-mer* [1948–] **L.**G.; SC. 49–; **Bl.**U. 58–; **Br.**U.; **E.**U. 50–; **G.**U.; **Ld.**U. 55–; **N.**U.; **O.**G. 48–52; **Y.**

12979 **Cahiers** du **Pacifique.** Paris. *Cah. Pacif.* [1958–] **L.**BM[N].; SC.; Z.; **Bn.**U.; **Dm.**; **Lo.**; **Pl.**M.; **Wo.**

12980 **Cahiers** de **pathologie végétale** et **entomologie agricole.** Paris. *Cah. Path. vég. Ent. agric.* [1942–43] **L.**SC. 42. [*Issued during suspension of* 47490]

12981 **Cahiers** du **pharmacien** de **France.** Paris. *Cah. Pharmn Fr.* **L.**PH. 47–.

12982 **Cahiers** de **physique.** Paris. *Cah. Phys.* [1941–] **L.**P.; R. 45–; SC. 44–; **N.**U. 51–; **Nw.**A.; **Te.**N. 52–; **Y.**

12983 **Cahiers** de **préhistoire** et d'**archéologie.** Montpellier. *Cah. Préhist. Archéol.* [1952] **L.**BM[N]. [*C. as:* 12969]

12984 **Cahiers Pyrénéistes.** Société Ramond. Bagnères-de-Bigorre. *Cah. pyrén.* **L.**BM[N]. 22–24.

12985 **Cahiers** de **radiologie.** Paris. *Cah. Radiol.* [1930–] [*Supplement to:* 20755]

12986 **Cahiers** de la **recherche agronomique.** Rabat. *Cah. Rech. agron.* [1948–] **Hu.**G. 49–; **Md.**H. 60–; **O.**F.; **Rt.**

12987 **Cahiers** de la **recherche théorique** et **expérimentale** sur les **matériaux** et les **structures.** Paris. *Cah. Rech. théor. exp. Matér. Struct.* [1957–] **L.**P.

12988 **Cahiers** du **Service géographique** de l'**armée.** Paris. *Cah. Serv. géogr. Armée*

12989 **Cahiers** du **Service météorologique.** Alger. *Cah. Serv. mét., Alger* **L.**MO. 23.

12989[c] **Cahiers. Société** d'**études historiques** et **géographiques** de l'**Isthme** de **Suez.** *Cah. Soc. Étud. hist. géogr. Isthme Suez* [1955–] **L.**BM.

12990 **Cahiers** de la **Société** de **géographie** de **Hanoï.** *Cah. Soc. Géogr. Hanoï*

12991 **Cahiers techniques** du **Centre national** de **coordination** des **études** et **recherches** sur la **nutrition** et l'**alimentation.** Paris. *Cah. tech. Cent. natn. Coord. Étud. Rech. Nutr. Aliment.* [1958–] **L.**BM.; **P.**; **Y.**

12992 **Cairngorm Club Journal.** Aberdeen. *Cairngorm Club J.* [1893–] **L.**BM. 94– imp.; **Abd.**R.; U.; **Abs.**N. 16– imp; **C.**UL.; **E.**A. imp.; G. 94–; T. 93–11: 36–; U. 93–37; **G.**M. 94–; **O.**B. 38–.

12993 **Cairo Scientific Journal.** Cairo. *Cairo scient. J.* [1908–26] **L.**BM.; G.; MO. 08–25; R. 08–25; SC.; **Abs.**N. 18; **Br.**U. 09; **C.**P. 08–21; UL. 08–25; **Rt.** 08–17 imp. [*C. of:* 51504]

12993[c] **Cal.** *Cal* **L.**D.

12994 **Călăuza sanitară** şi **igienică.** Bucureşti. *Călăuza sanit. ig.*

12995 **Calavo News.** Los Angeles. *Calavo News* **Md.**H. 31–41 imp.

12996 **Calcium Chloride Association News.** Detroit. *Calc. Chlor. Ass. News* [1935–50] **L.**P.; SC. 42–50; **Wa.**B. 50. [*C. as:* 12997]

Calcium Chloride Bulletin. *See* 9682.

12997 **Calcium Chloride Institute News.** Detroit. *Calc. Chlor. Inst. News* [1951–] **L.**P.; **Y.** [*C. of:* 12996]

12998 **Calco Technical Bulletin.** American Cyanamid Co. Bound Brook, N.J. *Calco tech. Bull.* **M.**C. 42–53 imp.; **Y.**

Calculo automático y **cibernética.** *See* 46368.

12999 **Calculo previsométrico universal, meteorológico, sísmico** et **patológico.** Faro. *Calculo previsom. univ. met. sísm. patol.* **L.**MO. 58–.

13000 **Calcutta Geographical Review.** Calcutta. *Calcutta geogr. Rev.* [1936–50] **L.**BM.; G. imp.; **Bm.**U. 36–45 imp.; **E.**U. [*C. as:* 20970]

13001 **Calcutta Journal** of **Medicine.** Calcutta. *Calcutta J. Med.* [1868–19] **L.**BM. 87–19; MD. 68–82 imp.

13002 **Calcutta Medical Journal.** Calcutta. *Calcutta med. J.* [1904–] **L.**MA. 28– imp.; MD. 22–; S. 34–55 imp.; TD. 22– imp.; UC. 34–; **Abd.**R. 35– imp.; **Br.**U. 33– imp.; **Ld.**U. 33–46 imp.; **Lv.**M. 36–40: 47–49 imp.; **M.**MS. 36–40: 49–; **O.**R. 32–.

13003 **Calcutta Medical Review.** Calcutta. *Calcutta med. Rev.* [1938–] **L.**MA.

13004 **Calcutta Statistical Association Bulletin.** Calcutta. *Calcutta statist. Ass. Bull.* [1947–] **C.**SL.; **E.**R.

13005 **Caldasia.** Boletín del Instituto de ciencias naturales. Universidad nacional de Colombia. Bogota. *Caldasia* [1940–] **L.**BM^N. 43–; K.; Z. 43–; **Rt.** 41–44; **Y.**

13006 **Caledonian Medical Journal.** Glasgow. *Caledon. med. J.* [1893–] **L.**BM. 94–; MA.; MD. 02–; **Abd.**U. 91–39; **Abs.**N. 02–; **Bm.**U. 18–; **Br.**U. 99– imp.; **C.**UL.; **Dn.**U. 99–40 imp.; **E.**A.; P. 01–40; U.; **G.**F. 01–40; M. 04–40; U. 93–40; **Lv.**M. 94–37 imp.; **M.**MS. 13–39; **Nw.**A. 14–36; **O.**R. 99–; **Sa.** 99–36.

13007 **Calendar. Meteorological Office. London.** *Calendar met. Off.* [1913–] **L.**BM. 16–; MO.; SC. 16–; **Abs.**N. 13–21; **E.**M. 13–21; **G.**M. 13–21; **Rt.** 17–21 imp.

13008 **Calendario astronomico** delle **colonie italiane** d'**Africa.** Firenze. *Cal. astr. Colon. ital. Afr.*

13009 **Calendario astronómico** del **Observatorio astronómico** de la **Plata.** Buenos Aires. *Cal. astr. Obs. astr. La Plata* **L.**BM. 08–12; **C.**O. 11–.

13010 **Calendario astronómico** para le **parte austral** de la **América** del **Sur.** Buenos Aires. *Cal. astr. Parte austral Am. S.*

13011 **Calendario atlante** de **Agostini.** Novara. *Cal. atlante Agostini* **L.**G. 15–; **O.**G. 17– imp.

13012 **Calendario forestale italiano.** Roma. *Cal. for. ital.*

13013 **Calendario meteoro-fenológico. Servicio meteorológico nacional.** Madrid. *Cal. meteoro-fenol., Madr.* **L.**MO. 45–.

13014 **Calendario** del **R. Osservatorio astronomico** al **Collegio romano** in **Roma.** *Cal. R. Oss. astr. Coll. romano Roma*

13015 **Calendrier annuaire. Observatoire** de **Zi-Ka-Wei.** Chang-Haï. *Calendrier a. Obs. Zi-Ka-Wei* **L.**MO. 04; **C.**UL. 08–.

13015° **Calendrier astronomique** et **climatologique. Institut météorologique central** de **Bulgarie.** Sofia. *Cal. astr. clim., Sofia* **L.**MO. 30–31.

13016 **Caliche.** Instituto científico e industrial del salitre. Santiago de Chile. *Caliche* [1919–30] **L.**C. imp.; UC.; **Lv.**U. 28–30.

13017 **California Agricultural Journal.** Fresno. *Calif. agric. J.*

13018 **California Agriculture.** Berkeley. *Calif. Agric.* [1946–] **L.**AM. 48– imp.; EB. 49– imp.; MY. 49–; P. 49–; TP. 50–; V. 51; **Abs.**U. 49–; **Ba.**I. 49–; **C.**A.; **E.**AB. 53–; **Hu.**G. 51–; **Md.**H. 48– imp.; **O.**RE. 52–; **R.**D. 53–; **Rt.** 48–; **Sal.** 50–; **Sil.** 50– imp.; **Y.**

13019 **California Arts** and **Architecture.** San Francisco. *Calif. Arts Archit.* [1929–] **L.**BA. [*C. of:* 36687]

13020 **California Bean Growers' Journal.** San Francisco. *Calif. Bean Grow. J.*

13021 **California Citrograph.** Los Angeles. *Calif. Citogr.* [1915–] **L.**AM. 54–; EB. 41–48; IC. 48–; MY. 22–; SC. 29–; TP. 51–; **Je.** 48–; **Md.**H. 29–.

13022 **California Conservationist.** *Calif. Conserv.* **L.**SC. 37–.

13023 **California Cultivator.** Los Angeles. *Calif. Cultiv.* **L.**SC. 29–42.

13024 **California Dairyman.** Los Angeles. *Calif. Dairym.*

13025 **California Eclectic Medical Journal.** Los Angeles. *Calif. ecl. med. J.*

13026 **California Farm Reporter.** Santa Clara. *Calif. Fm Reptr* [1941–]

13027 **California Farmer.** Los Angeles. *Calif. Fmr*

13028 **California Fish** and **Game.** Sacramento. *Calif. Fish Game* [1914–] **L.**AM. 49–; BM. imp.; BM^N. 18– imp.; NC.; TP. 50– imp.; Z. 14–32: 41–; **Abd.**M. 48–; **Bn.**U. 48–; **C.**B. 48–; **Db.** 21–; **Dm.** 23–26: 33–38: 42–; **E.**U. 48–; **Fr.** 49–; **Ld.**U. 27–32 imp.; **Lv.**U. 17– imp.; **Mi.** 43–; **O.**AP. 15–; **Pl.**M. 23– imp.; **Sa.** 19–54; **Sal.** 45– imp.; **Wo.** 53–; **Y.**

13029 **California Forestry.** Berkeley. *Calif. For.*

13030 **California Forestry** and **Forest Products.** Berkeley. *Calif. For. Forest Prod.* [1957–] **O.**F.

13031 **California Fruit** and **Grape Grower.** San Francisco. *Calif. Fruit Grape Grow.* [1947–50] **L.**SC. 48–50. [*C. as:* 57412]

13032 **California Fruit Grower.** San Francisco. *Calif. Fruit Grow.*

13033 **California Fruit News.** San Francisco. *Calif. Fruit News* **L.**TP. 52–61.

13034 **California Grape Grower.** San Francisco. *Calif Grape Grow.* [1919–34] [> 13035, 1929–33; *C. as:* 57624]

13035 **California Grower.** San Francisco. *Calif. Grow.* [1929–33] [*C. of:* and *Rec. as:* 13034]

13036 **California Highways** and **Public Works.** Sacramento. *Calif. Highw. publ. Wks* **Ha.**RD. 42–; **Y.**

13037 **California Journal** of **Development.** San Francisco. *Calif. J. Dev.*

13038 **California Journal** of **Mines** and **Geology.** Sacramento. *Calif. J. Mines Geol.* [1923–] **L.**BM^N. 41– imp.; GL. 31–; MI. 33–; P. 33–58. [*C. of:* 42949]

13039 **California Journal** of **Technology.** Berkeley. *Calif. J. Technol.*

13040 **California Livestock News.** San Francisco. *Calif. Livestk News* [1951–] **Ld.**W. [*C. of:* 13054]

13041 **California Medical Bulletin.** San Francisco. *Calif. med. Bull.*

13042 **California Medical Journal.** San Francisco. *Calif. med. J.* [*C. of:* 53851]

13043 **California Medical** and **Surgical Reporter.** Los Angeles. *Calif. med. surg. Reptr*

13044 **California Medicine.** San Francisco. *Calif. Med.* [1946–] **L.**MA. 47–; MD.; **Br.**U. imp.; **Y.** [*C. of:* 13053]

13044° **California Mental Health News.** Sacramento. *Calif. ment. Hlth News* [1956–] **L.**BM.

13045 **California Natural History Guides.** Berkeley. *Calif. nat. Hist. Guides* [1959–] **Y.**

13046 **California Oil World.** Bakersfield. *Calif. Oil Wld*

13047 **California Pear Grower.** San Francisco. *Calif. Pear Grow.*

13048 **California Polytechnic Journal.** San Luis Obispo. *Calif. polytech. J.*

13049 **California Poultry Journal.** Hamilton. *Calif. Poult. J.*

13050 **California Poultry Tribune.** Los Angeles. *Calif. Poult. Trib.*

13050° **California Safety News.** Sacramento. *Calif. Saf. News* [1917–] L.BM. 45–.

13051 **California State Journal** of **Medicine.** San Francisco. *Calif. St. J. Med.* [1902–24] **Br.**U. 05–24 v. imp. [*C. as:* 13053]

13052 **California Veterinarian.** San Francisco. *Calif. Vet.* [1947–] **L.**V. 48–; **W.** 49–.

13053 **California** and **Western Medicine.** San Francisco. *Calif. west. Med.* [1924–46] **L.**MD. 28–46; TD. 26–34; **Br.**U. imp.; **Nw.**A. 24: 27–28: 32–38. [*C. of:* 13051; *C. as:* 13044]

13054 **California Wool Grower.** San Francisco. *Calif. Wool Grow.* [1925–51] **Ld.**W. 40–51 imp.; **E.**AB. 43–45. [*C. as:* 13040]

13055 **California's Health.** San Francisco. Berkeley. *Calif.'s Hlth* **L.**TD. 53–.

13056 **Calore.** Roma. *Calore* [1928–] **L.**I. (2 yr.); **P.** 28–40: 55–; **Y.** [*C. of:* 55872]

13057 **Caltex Lubrication.** New York. *Caltex Lubric.* **Li.**M. 46–.

13058 **Calzatura.** Napoli. *Calzatura*

13059 **Calzatura vigevanese.** Vigevano. *Calzatura vigevanese*

13060 **Camara textil** de **México.** México. *Camara text. Méx.* [1953–] **Y.**

13061 **Camborne School** of **Mines Magazine.** Camborne. *Camborne Sch. Mines Mag.* [1900–] **L.**BM. 05–; MI. 49–.

13062 **Cambrian Natural Observer.** Cardiff. *Cambrian nat. Obsr* [1898–10] **L.**AS.; BM.; **Abs.**N.; **Cr.**M. imp.; P.; **Lv.**P.; **M.**P. 98–06; **O.**R. 00–10; **Sw.**U. 98–02. [*C. of:* and *Rec. as:* 25635]

13063 **Cambridge Biological Studies.** London. *Camb. biol. Stud.* [1938–] **L.**BM.; **C.**UL.

Cambridge Electron Accelerator. See 12872.

13064 **Cambridge Engineering Tracts.** Cambridge. *Camb. Engng Tracts* [1910–13] **L.**BM.; **Abs.**N. 13; **Bm.**P.; T.; **C.**UL.; **Db.**; **Nw.**A.; **O.**R. 10.

13065 **Cambridge Mountaineering.** *Camb. Mountg* [1925–26: 32–] **C.**PO. 32–. [>36645, 1928–29]

13066 **Cambridge Papers** in **Social Anthropology.** Cambridge. *Camb. Pap. soc. Anthrop.* [1958–] **L.**AN.; **C.**UL.

13067 **Cambridge Physical Tracts.** Cambridge. *Camb. phys. Tracts* **C.**UL. 38–; **E.**U. 38–41.

13068 **Cambridge Tracts** in **Mathematics** and **Mathematical Physics.** Cambridge. *Camb. Tracts Math.* [1905–] **L.**BM. 07–; M.; SC.; U.; UC. 13–; **Abd.**U. 13–; U.; **Bl.**U.; **Bm.**P.; T.; U.; **Br.**U.; **C.**UL.; **Cr.**U.; **Db.**; **E.**U.; **G.**T. 05–20; U.; **Ld.**P.; U.; **Lv.**P.; U.; **N.**U.; **Nw.**A.; **O.**N.; R.; **Sa.**; **Sh.**U. 06–16; **Sw.**U. imp.; **Y.**

13069 **Cambridge University Agricultural Society Magazine.** Cambridge. *Camb. Univ. agric. Soc. Mag.* [1924–] **L.**AM. 24–39; P. 24–39; **Abs.**N.; **C.**A.; UL.; **Db.**; **O.**R.; **Rt.** 24–38.

13070 **Cambridge University Engineering** and **Aeronautical Societies Journal.** Cambridge. *Camb. Univ. Engng aeronaut. Socs J.* [1926–46] **L.**P.; QM.; SC. 27–46; **Bm.**U.; **C.**UL. [*C. as:* 13071]

13071 **Cambridge University Engineering Society Journal.** Cambridge. *Camb. Univ. Engng Soc. J.* [1921: 47–] **L.**P. 47–; QM. 47–; SC. 47–; **Bm.**U. 47–; **C.**ENG. 47–; UL. 47–; **Y.** 47–. [*C. as:* and *Rec. of:* 13070]

Cambridge University Engineers' Association Yearbook. See 58028.

13073 **Cambridge University Medical Society Magazine.** Cambridge. *Camb. Univ. med. Soc. Mag.* [1922–] **L.**BM.; MA. 40–; MD. 29–; S. imp.; **Abs.**N.; **Br.**U. 23–26: 48–; **C.**PA.; UL.; **M.**MS. 39– imp.; **O.**B. imp.

13074 **Cambridge Wire.** Cambridge Md. *Camb. Wire* [1956–] **L.**P.

13075 **Camellia.** Australian and New Zealand Camellia Research Society. Gordon, N.S.W. *Camellia* [1954–] **L.**HS.; K.

13076 **Camellia Review.** Pasadena. *Camellia Rev.* [1950–] **L.**HS.; K. [*C. of:* 12269]

13077 **Camellian.** Columbia, S. Carolina. *Camellian* [1950–] **L.**HS.; K.

13078 **Camera.** Dublin. *Camera, Dublin* [1921–] **L.**BM. 25–; PG. 21–40 imp.

13079 **Camera.** Dundee. *Camera, Dundee* [1911–16] **L.**PG. 14–16.

13080 **Camera.** 's Gravenhage. *Camera, 's Grav.* **L.**PG. 12–14. [*C. in:* 28914]

13081 **Camera.** London. *Camera, Lond.* **L.**BM. 19–; TP. 60–; **Db.** 23–; **M.**P. 36–40; **O.**B. 28–.

13082 **Camera.** Luzern, Zürich. *Camera, Luzern* [1922–] **L.**PG. imp.

13083 **Camera Club Journal.** London. *Camera Club J.* **L.**PG. 45– imp.

13084 **Camera Craft.** San Francisco. *Camera Craft* [1900–42] **L.**PG. 10–42 imp.; SC. 32–42. [*C. in:* 2118]

13085 **Camera** and **Dark Room.** New York. *Camera dark Rm* [1899–06] **L.**PG. 01–06. [*C. in:* 1895]

13086 **Camera Magazine.** Philadelphia, etc. *Camera Mag.* [1897–53] **L.**P. 23–26 imp.; PG. 99–53; **We.**K. 36–53. [*C. in:* 37646°]

13087 **Camera News** and **Technique.** London. *Camera News Tech.* [1946–48] **L.**BM.; PG. imp.

13088 **Camera Notes.** Official organ of the Camera Club of New York. New York. *Camera Notes* [1897–09] **L.**PG. 97–02. [*C. in:* 2118]

13089 **Camera obscura.** Haarlem, etc. *Camera obsc.* **We.**K. 50–.

13090 **Camera World.** London. *Camera Wld* [1955–58] **L.**BM.; PG.; **We.**K. [*C. of:* 31995; *C. as:* 53088]

13091 **Cameras** and **Equipment.** London. *Cameras Equip.* [1960–] **L.**BM.

13092 **Caminos.** Revista técnica. Buenos Aires. *Caminos*

13093 **Caminos** de **México.** México. *Caminos Méx.* **Sy.**R. 53–.

13094 **Campagna.** Como. *Campagna* **L.**EB. 14–15.

13095 **Campagne antipaludique.** Alger. *Campagne antipalud.* [1908–14] **L.**BM^N. 10–14; EB.; TD. 08–10.

13096 **Campagne harenguière.** Ostende. *Campagne hareng.* [1954–] **Lo.** [*C. of:* 35607]

13097 **Campaign Notes. American Society** for the **Control** of **Cancer.** New York. *Campgn Notes Am. Soc. Control Cancer* [1918–30] [*C. as:* 9352]

13098 **Campaign** against **Tuberculosis** in **Iowa.** Anamosa. *Campgn Tuberc. Iowa*

13099 **Campbell's Scientific Farmer.** Millings, Mont. *Campbell's scient. Fmr*

13100 **Campesino.** Guatemala. *Campesino, Guatemala* **L.**AM. 45– imp.

13101 **Campesino.** Sociedad nacional de agriculture. Santiago de Chile. *Campesino, Santiago* [1933–] **L.**AM. [1 yr); **Abs.**A. 43–; **Rt.** 36: 41–43; **Y.** [*C. of:* 8126]

13102 **Campo.** Agricultura, industria, commercio. Rio de Janeiro. *Campo, Rio de J.* **L.**BM^N. 30–; EB. (ent.) 30–37.

13103 **Campo.** Liga nacional de agricultores catoncos. Quito. *Campo, Quito*

Canada Lancet and **National Hygiene.** *See* 13104.

13104 **Canada Lancet** and **Practitioner.** Toronto. *Canada Lancet Practnr* [1868–34] **L.**S. 73–34; **Br.**U. 04–21. [*C. in:* 13178]

13105 **Canada Medical Record.** Montreal. *Canada med. Rec.* [1872–04] **O.**R. 72–01.

13106 **Canada Poultryman.** Victoria, B.C. *Canada Poultrym.* [1928–] [*C. of:* 13236]

13107 **Canada's Health** and **Welfare.** Ottawa. *Canada's Hlth Welf.* [1945–] **L.**H. imp.; TD. 45–49; TP. 58–.

13108 **Canada's Mental Health.** Ottawa. *Canada's ment. Hlth*

13109 **Canadian Aeronautical Journal.** Ottawa. *Can. aeronaut. J.* [1955–] **L.**AV. 56–; P. 57–; **Bl.**U. 60–; **Br.**U. 60–; **F.**A.; **Y.** [–61★; *C. as:* Canadian Aeronautics and Space Journal]

13110 **Canadian Agriculture.** Ottawa. *Can. Agric.* **O.**AEC. 56–; F. 56–.

13111 **Canadian Air Review.** Whitby. *Can. Air Rev.*

13112 **Canadian Aircraft Industries.** Ottawa. *Can. Aircr. Ind.* [1958–59] **L.**AV. imp.

13113 **Canadian Alpine Journal.** Winnipeg, etc. *Can. alp. J.* [1907–] **L.**BM.; G. 07; **Bm.**P.; **C.**PO. 50–; **Nw.**A. 09; **Y.**

13114 **Canadian Anaesthetists' Society Journal.** Toronto. *Can. Anaesth. Soc. J.* [1954–] **L.**MA.; MD.; S.; **Abd.**U.; **Cr.**MD.; **Ld.**U.; **Lv.**M. 59–; **M.**MS.

13115 **Canadian Architect.** Toronto. *Can. Archit.* [1955–] **L.**BA.; BM.

13116 **Canadian Architect** and **Builder.** Toronto. *Can. Archit. Bldr* [1888–08] [*C. as:* 15554]

Canadian Association of **Medical Students** and **Internees.** *See* 12861.

13117 **Canadian Astronomical Handbook.** Toronto. *Can. astr. Handb.* **E.**R. 07–08★; **O.**O. 07–08. [*C. as:* 35663]

13118 **Canadian Atlantic Fauna.** Fisheries Research Board. Ottawa. *Can. Atlant. Fauna* [1921–] **L.**SC. 29–; **Abd.**M. 21–48 v. imp.; **Db.** 29–; **Dm.**; **E.**R. 29–48; **Pl.**M. imp.

13119 **Canadian Audubon.** Toronto. *Can. Audubon* [1958–] **L.**BM^N.; SC.; **Y.** [*C. of:* 13218]

13120 **Canadian Automotive Trade.** Toronto. *Can. automot. Trade*

13121 **Canadian Aviation.** Toronto. *Can. Aviat.* [1928–] **L.**AV. 32– imp.; **F.**A. 45–56; **Y.**

13122 **Canadian Ayrshire Review.** Huntingdon. *Can. Ayrsh. Rev.* **L.**BM. 23–.

13123 **Canadian Bee Journal.** Brantford, Ont. *Can. Bee J.* [1885–] **L.**AM. 85–92; **Rt.** 47– imp.; **Sa.** 34–36. [> 13161, 1913–21 and 5882, 1921–33]

13124 **Canadian Building Abstracts.** Ottawa. *Can. Bldg Abstr.* [1960–] **L.**P.; **Ha.**RD. (2 yr.); **Wa.**B.; **Y.**

13125 **Canadian Building Digest.** Ottawa. *Can. Bldg Dig.* [1960–] **L.**P.; **Y.**

13126 **Canadian Building Research.** Ottawa. *Can. Bldg Res.* [1958–] **L.**MO.; P.; [*C. of:* 9074]

13127 **Canadian Bulletin** on **Nutrition.** Ottawa, Halifax. *Can. Bull. Nutr.* [1948–] **L.**AM. 53–56 imp.; BM. 56–; **Y.** [*C. of:* 35493]

13128 **Canadian Chemical Journal.** Toronto. *Can. chem. J.* [1917–20] **L.**C.; I. 18–20; P. 19–20; **Ste.** [*C. as:* 13130]

13129 **Canadian Chemical Processing.** Toronto. *Can. chem. Process.* [1951–] **L.**C.; IC.; P.; **Br.**U.; **C.**CH.; **Ep.**D.; **Ld.**U.; **Lv.**P. 59–; **M.**D.; **Ste.**; **Sy.**R.; **Wd.**; **Y.** [*C. of:* 13131]

13130 **Canadian Chemistry** and **Metallurgy.** Toronto. *Can. Chem. Metall.* [1921–45] **L.**C.; I. 21–37; IC. 31–45; NF. 25–44; P.; PR. 29–43; SC. 25–45; **Br.**U. 23–45; **C.**CH. 22–45; **Ep.**D. 40–45; **Ld.**U. 42–45; **Nw.**A. 37–39; **Ste.**; **Sy.**R. 44–45; **Wd.** 31–45; **Y.** [*C. of:* 13128; *C. as:* 13131]

13131 **Canadian Chemistry** and **Process Industries.** Toronto. *Can. Chem. Process Ind.* [1946–50] **L.**C.; IC.; P.; SC.; **Br.**U.; **C.**CH.; **Ep.**D.; **Ld.**U.; **M.**D.; **Ste.**; **Sy.**R.; **Wd.**; **Te.**C.; **Y.** [*C. of:* 13130; *C. as:* 13129]

13132 **Canadian Coarse Grains Quarterly Review.** Ottawa. *Can. coarse Grains q. Rev.* **O.**AEC. 41–.

13133 **Canadian Colorist** and **Textile Processor.** Toronto. *Can. Color. Text. Processor*

13134 **Canadian Dairy** and **Ice Cream Journal.** Toronto. *Can. Dairy Ice Cream J.* [1923–] **Abs.**U. 59–; **R.**D. 36–; **Y.**

13135 **Canadian Diesel Power.** Toronto. *Can. Diesel Pwr* **L.**P. (curr.); **Y.**

Canadian Diesel Power and **Traction.** *See* 13135.

13136 **Canadian Druggist.** Toronto. *Can. Drugg.*

13137 **Canadian Electrical News** and **Steam Engineering Journal.** Toronto & Montreal. *Can. elect. News* [1891–09] **L.**BM. 08–09. [*C. as:* 17667]

13138 **Canadian Electronics.** Toronto. *Can. Electron.* **Y.**

13139 **Canadian Electronics Engineering.** Toronto. *Can. Electron. Engng* [1957–] **L.**P. 59–; **Y.**

13140 **Canadian Engineer.** Toronto. *Can. Engr* [1893–39] **L.**P. 10–31; SC. 25–39; **Lv.**U. 10–39 imp. [*C. as:* 48028 and 57180]

13141 **Canadian Entomologist.** Guelp., Ont., etc. *Can. Ent.* [1869–] **L.**AM. 30–; BM.; BM^N.; E.; EB. 70–72: 08–; L.; SC. 25–; TP. 54–; Z.; **Bn.**U. 13–; **C.**A. (1 yr); B. 20–35; **Db.** 19–; **E.**U. 56–; **G.**H. 69–51 imp.; U. 52–; **Je.** 49–; **Lv.**U. 06–; **Md.**H. 51–; **N.**U. 39–; **O.**H. 12– imp.; R. 83–; **Rt.** 20–31: 51–; **Y.** [*Also supplements*]

13142 **Canadian Farm Implements.** Winnipeg. *Can. Fm Impl.* **Rt.** 47–; **Sil.** 39–47: 50–.

13143 **Canadian Farmer.** Ottawa. *Can. Fmr*

13144 **Canadian Field Naturalist.** Ottawa. *Can. Fld Nat.* [1919–] **L.**BM^N.; z.; **C.**PO. 42–; **O.**AP. 20–; z. 20–; **Y.** [*C. of:* 36503]

13145 **Canadian Fish Culturist.** Ottawa. *Can. Fish Cult.* [1946–] **L.**AM. 52–; BM. 54–; **Fr.** 49–; **Mi.** 51–; **Pit.**F. 50– imp.; **Pl.**M. 52–.

13146 **Canadian Fish** and **Game.** Toronto. *Can. Fish Game*

13147 **Canadian Fisherman.** Montreal. *Can. Fisherm.* [1914–] **L.**BM. 19–; P. 14–23; **Abd.**T. 54; **Abs.**N. 15– imp.

13148 **Canadian Food Bulletin.** Ottawa. *Can. Fd Bull.*

13149 **Canadian Food Industries.** Gardenvale, Quebec. *Can. Fd Ind.* [1947–] **L.**AM. 51–; **Ld.**U. 62–; **Lh.**FO. 56–; **Md.**H. 47–50 imp.; **Y.** [*C. of:* 13150]

13150 **Canadian Food Packer.** Gardenvale, Quebec. *Can. Fd Pack.* [1937–47] **Md.**H. 41–47. [*C. as:* 13149]

13151 **Canadian Forester.** Guelph. *Can. Forester*

13152 **Canadian Forestry Journal.** Ottawa. *Can. For. J.* [1905–20] **L.**P.; **O.**F. 10–20 imp.; RE. 09–15. [*C. as:* 22784]
     Canadian Foundryman and **Electroplater.** See 13153.

13153 **Canadian Foundryman** and **Metal Industry.** Toronto. *Can. Foundrym. Metal Ind.* [1909–32] **L.**MT. 24–32; P. 22–28; **Bm.**C. 21–26. [*C. in:* 13192]

13154 **Canadian Gas Journal.** Hamilton. *Can. Gas J.* [1939–] **Y.** [*C. of:* 23766]

13155 **Canadian Geographer.** Manotick. *Can. Geogr.* [1951–] **L.**G.; **Bl.**U. 59–; **C.**PO.; **Ld.**U. 61–; **O.**B.; G.; **Sw.**U. 59–.

13156 **Canadian Geographical Journal.** Montreal. *Can. geogr. J.* [1930–] **L.**B.; BM. 37–; G.; SC. 38–; U. 50–; **Abd.**U. 48–; **Abs.**N. 37–; U. 49–; **Bm.**U. 46–; **Br.**P. 32–; **C.**GG. 49–50; PO.; **Dn.**U.; **E.**G.; T. 30–40; **Ex.**U. 47–; **G.**M.; U. 37–; **H.**U. 48–; **Lv.**P.; **M.**P. 36–; **N.**U. 47–; **Nw.**A. 30–39 imp.; **O.**G.; RH.; **Sa.** 39–; **Y.**

13157 **Canadian Geophysical Bulletin.** Ottawa. *Can. geophys. Bull.* [1947–] **L.**AS. 49–; MI.; MO.; P. 52–; SC. 50–; **Abd.**U. 53–; **Bn.**U. 53–; **Br.**U. 53–; **C.**PO.; **E.**U. 52–; **Ex.**U. 53–; **G.**U. 53–; **Ld.**U. 52–; **Lo.** 52–; **Lv.**U. 52–; **M.**U. 53: 58; **N.**U. 53–; **O.**R. 53–; **Pl.**M. 48–; **Sa.** 53–; **Y.**

13158 **Canadian Grain Journal.** Winnipeg. *Can. Grain J.* [1945–] **C.**A. (1 yr).

13159 **Canadian Grower.** Toronto. *Can. Grow.* [1947–] **Md.**H. 47–51. [*C. of* 13160 (*Fruit ed.*)]

13160 **Canadian Horticulture** and **Home Magazine.** *Can. Hort. Home Mag.* [1877–47]
     Floral edition. **Md.**H. 43–47.
     Fruit *afterwards* Growers' edition.
     [Floral ed. *C. as:* 58197^b; Fruit ed. *C. as:* 13159]

13161 **Canadian Horticulturist** and **Beekeeper.** Peterboro, Ont. *Can. Hortst Beekeep.* [1913–21] **L.**AM.; EB. (ent.) 16–21. [*C. of:* 13123; *C. as:* 5882]

13162 **Canadian Hospital.** Toronto. *Can. Hosp.* [1924–] **L.**H. 54–.

13163 **Canadian Implement Trade** and **Power Farming Equipment Journal.** Toronto. *Can. Impl. Trade Pwr Fmg Equip. J.* [1900–35] **L.**SC. 29–35.

13164 **Canadian Insect Pest Review.** Ottawa. *Can. Insect Pest Rev.* **L.**AM. 48– imp.; BM. 54–; EB. 47– imp.; TP. 53–; **Bl.**U. 43–; **Bn.**U. 52–; **N.**U. 54–; **O.**H. 48–53 imp.; **Rt.** 37–.

13165 **Canadian Journal** of **Agricultural Economics.** Toronto. *Can. J. agric. Econ.* [1952–] **Br.**U.; **C.**A.; **O.**AEC. 53–; **R.**U.

13166 **Canadian Journal** of **Agricultural Science.** Ottawa. *Can. J. agric. Sci.* [1953–56] **L.**AM.; IC.; MY.; P.; V.; VC. 54–56; **Abd.**R.; **Abs.**A.; U. 56; **Bl.**U.; **Bm.**U.; **Br.**A.; **C.**A.; **Db.**; **E.**AB.; W.; **G.**U.; **Hu.**G.; **Je.**; **Ld.**U.; **Md.**H.; **N.**U.; **Nw.**A.; **O.**RE.; **R.**D.; U.; **Rt.**; **Sal.**; **Sil.**; **W.**; **Y.** [*C. of:* 49139; *C. in:* 13167, 13184 and 13188]

13167 **Canadian Journal** of **Animal Science.** Ottawa. *Can. J. Anim. Sci.* [1957–] **L.**AM.; P.; V.; VC.; **Abd.**R.; S.; **Abs.**A.; U.; **Bl.**U.; **Bm.**U.; **C.**A.; **Db.**; **E.**AB.; AR. 58–; **G.**U.; **Hu.**G.; **Je.**; **Ld.**U.; **N.**U.; **Nw.**A.; **O.**RE.; **R.**D.; U.; **W.**; **Y.** [*C. from:* 13166]

13168 **Canadian Journal** of **Biochemistry** and **Physiology.** Ottawa. *Can. J. Biochem. Physiol.* [1954–] **L.**AM.; AV. imp.; BM^N.; C.; CB.; LI.; MA.; MC.; MD.; MY.; P.; R.; RI.; SC.; TD.; TP.; U.; UC.; **Abd.**R.; S.; U.; **Bl.**U. 56–; **Bm.**U.; **Bn.**U.; **Br.**U. 60–; **C.**A.; APH.; BI. 57–; P.; **Cr.**U. 58–; **Db.**; **E.**AB.; U.; W.; **Ep.**D.; **G.**T.; U.; **Je.** 56–; **Ld.**U.; **Lv.**U.; **M.**C.; U.; **Md.**H. 55–; **N.**U.; **Nw.**A.; **Pl.**M.; **R.**D.; U.; **Rt.**; **Sa.** 56–; **Sal.**; **Sh.**U.; **W.**; **Y.** [*C. of:* 13176]

13169 **Canadian Journal** of **Botany.** Ottawa. *Can. J. Bot.* [1951–] **L.**AM.; AV. 51–55 imp.; BM.; BM^N.; C. 51–56; IC.; KC. 53–; L.; LI.; MA.; MY.; QM. 53–; P.; PR.; R.; RI.; SC.; TP.; UC.; **Abd.**R.; S.; U.; **Abs.**A.; N.; U. 56–; **Bl.**U. imp.; **Bn.**U.; **Br.**A.; **Bra.**D.; **C.**A.; P.; PO.; **Db.**; **E.**R.; W.; **Ep.**D.; **Fr.** 51–52; **G.**T. 51–52 imp.; U.; **Hu.**G.; **Je.**; **Ld.**U.; W. 51–52; **Lv.**P.; U.; **M.**C.; D.; U.; **Md.**H.; **Mi.** 57–; **N.**T. 51–53; U.; **Nw.**A.; **O.**BO.; R.; **Pl.**M.; **Pr.**FT.; **R.**D.; U.; **Rt.**; **Sa.**; **Sal.**; **Sh.**U. 59–; **Sw.**U. 58–; **Y.** [*C. of:* 13187, Sect C]

13170 **Canadian Journal** of **Chemical Engineering.** Ottawa. *Can. J. chem. Engng* [1957–] **L.**AM.; AV.; BM.; C.; IC.; LI.; P.; PR.; SC.; TP.; **Abd.**S.; U.; **Abs.**N.; **Bm.**U.; **Bn.**U.; **Db.**; **E.**R.; U.; W.; **Ep.**D.; **F.**A.; **G.**T.; U.; **Ld.**U.; W.; **Lh.**FO.; P.; **Li.**M.; **Lv.**P.; U.; **M.**C.; D.; P.; U.; **N.**T.; U.; **Nw.**A. 57; **O.**R.; **Pl.**M. 57; **R.**D.; U.; **Rt.**; **Sal.**; **Sy.**R.; **Y.** [*C. of:* 13190]

13171 **Canadian Journal** of **Chemistry.** Ottawa. *Can. J. Chem.* [1951–] **L.**AM.; AV.; BM.; C.; HQ.; IC.; LE.; LI.; MA.; MC.; NF.; P.; PR.; R.; RI.; SC.; TP.; UC.; **Abd.**R.; S.; U.; **Abs.**N.; **Bl.**U.; **Bm.**C. 51–55; **Bn.**U.; **Br.**A.; U.; **Bra.**D.; **C.**APH. 51–59; CH.; **Cr.**U. 55–; **Db.**; **Dn.**U.; **E.**U. 59–; W.; **Ep.**D.; **Ex.**U.; **F.**A.; **G.**T. 53–; U.; **H.**U. 59–; **Hu.**G. 51–54; **Je.** 56–; **Ld.**U.; W.; **Lv.**P.; U.; **Lh.**P.; **M.**C.; D.; P. 54–; U.; **Md.**H.; **N.**T. 51–59; U.; **O.**R.; **Pl.**M.; **Pr.**FT.; **R.**D.; U.; **Rt.**; **Sa.**; **Sal.**; **Sh.**U.; **Ste.** 52–; **Sw.**U.; **Sy.**R.; **Y.** [*C. of:* 13187, Sect. B]

13172 **Canadian Journal** of **Comparative Medicine** (and **Veterinary Science**). Quebec. *Can. J. comp. Med.* [1937–] **L.**LI. 37–46; MA. 38–41; SC. 46–; TD. (10 yr.); V.; **Abd.**R. imp.; **Abs.**U. 45–; **Br.**U. 57–; **C.**V. 46–; **Db.**; **E.**AB. 37–42 imp.: 43–; **R.**D.; **Sal.**; **W.**; **Y.**

13173 **Canadian Journal** of **Fabrics.** Montreal. *Can. J. Fabr.* [1883–06] **L.**P. 90–06. [*C. as:* 13254]

13174 **Canadian Journal** of **Genetics** and **Cytology.** Ottawa. *Can. J. Genet. Cytol.* [1959–] **L.**SC.; **C.**A.; **Dn.**U. 62–; **E.**AB.; **G.**U. 61–; **O.**BO.; **Y.** [*C. of:* 39215]

13175 **Canadian Journal** of **Mathematics.** Toronto. *Can. J. Math.* [1949–] **L.**B. 59–; BM.; M.; QM.; R.; SC.; U.; **Abd.**U.; **Abs.**U.; **Bl.**U. 49–52; **Bm.**U.; **Bn.**U.; **C.**P.; **Db.**; **E.**R.; U.; **G.**U.; **H.**U. 60–; **Ld.**U.; **M.**U.; **N.**U.; **O.**R.; **Sw.**U. 57–; **Y.**

13176 **Canadian Journal** of **Medical Sciences.** Ottawa. *Can. J. med. Sci.* [1951–53] **L.**AM.; AV.; BM.; BM^N.; C.; CB.; LI.; MA.; MC.; MD.; P.; R.; RI.; SC.; TD.; U.; **Abd.**R.; S.; U.; **Bm.**U.; **Bn.**U.; **C.**A.; P.; **Db.**; **E.**AB.; R.; W.; **Ep.**D.; **G.**T.; U.; **Ld.**U.; W. 51–52; **Lv.**U.; **M.**C.; U.; **N.**U.; **O.**R.; **Pl.**M.; **R.**D.; U. 52–53; **Sal.**; **W.**; **Y.** [*C. of:* 13187, Sect. E; *C. as:* 13168]

13177 **Canadian Journal** of **Medical Technology.** Hamilton. *Can. J. med. Technol.* **Y.**

13178 **Canadian Journal** of **Medicine** and **Surgery.** Toronto. *Can. J. Med. Surg.* [1897–36] **L.**MA. 30–36; **Lv.**M. 35–36; **M.**MS. 06–09.

13179 **Canadian Journal** of **Mental Hygiene.** Toronto. *Can. J. ment. Hyg.* [1919–22] **L.**PS.

13180 **Canadian Journal** of **Microbiology.** Ottawa. *Can. J. Microbiol.* [1954–] **L.**AM.; LI.; MA. 57–; MC.; MD.; MY.; NC.; P.; SC.; TD.; TP.; U.; **Abd.**R.; S.; **Bm.**P.; **Bn.**U.; **Br.**A.; **C.**A.; APH.; **Db.**; **E.**HW.; W.; **G.**T.; U.; **H.**U. 60–; **Hu.**G.; **Je.**; **Ld.**U.; **Lv.**U.; **M.**C.; **Md.**H.; **N.**U.; **Pl.**M.; **Rt.**; **R.**D.; U.; **Sa.**; **Sh.**U.; **W.**; **Y.**

13181 **Canadian Journal** of **Occupational Therapy.** Toronto. *Can. J. occup. Ther.* **L.**MA. 33–34.

13182 **Canadian Journal** of **Optometry.** Toronto. *Can. J. Optom.*

13183 **Canadian Journal** of **Physics.** Ottawa. *Can. J. Phys.* [1951–] **L.**AM.; AV. imp.; BM.; BM^N.; C. 51– imp.; HQ.; IC.; LI.; MA.; MC.; P.; PR.; QM. 56–; R.; RI.; SC.; SI.; TP.; U.; UC.; **Abd.**R.; S. 51–56; U.; **Abs.**N.; **Bl.**U.; **Bm.**C. 51–55; U.; **Bn.**U.; **Br.**U.; **Bra.**D.; **C.**P.; PO.; **Db.**; **E.**R.; W.; **Ep.**D.; **Ex.**U.; **F.**A.; **G.**T.; U.; **Hu.**G. 51–54; **Ld.**U.; W.; **Lv.**P.; U.; **M.**C.; D.; P.; U.; **Ma.**T. 59–; **N.**T.; U.; **Nw.**A.; **O.**R.; **Pl.**M.; **Pr.**FT.; **R.**D.; U.; **Sa.**; **Sal.**; **Sh.**U.; **Sy.**R.; **Y.** [*C. of:* 13187, Sect. A]

13184 **Canadian Journal** of **Plant Science.** Ottawa. *Can. J. Pl. Sci.* [1957–] **L.**AM.; BM^N.; K.; MY.; P.; **Abd.**R.; S.; **Abs.**A.; U.; **Bl.**U.; **Bm.**U.; **Bn.**U. 59–; **C.**A.; **Dn.**U. 63–; **G.**U.; **Hu.**G.; **Je.**; **Ld.**U.; **Md.**H.; **N.**U.; **O.**RE.; **R.**U.; **Rt.**; **Y.** [*C. from:* 13166]

13185 **Canadian Journal** of **Psychology.** Toronto. *Can. J. Psychol.* [1947–] **L.**BM.; **Bl.**U. 61–; **C.**PS. 55–; **O.**EP. 48–; **Sh.**U. 53–; **Y.**

13186 **Canadian Journal** of **Public Health.** Toronto. *Can. J. publ. Hlth* [1943–] **L.**H.; MA.; MD.; SH.; TD.; **Abd.**R. 43–50; U.; **Bl.**U. 48–; **Br.**U. 44– imp.; **Cr.**MD. 43–53; **Dn.**U.; **E.**U.; **M.**MS.; **R.**D.; **Sw.**U. 55– imp.; **Y.** [*C. of:* 13242]

13187 **Canadian Journal** of **Research.** Ottawa. *Can. J. Res.* [1929–35: *from 1935–50 in series below*] **L.**AM. 29–32; BM. imp.; BM^N.; C.; EB. 34–35; L.; LI.; P.; PR. 34–35; R.; SC.; **Abs.**A.; N.; R.; **Bm.**U.; **C.**A.; P.; **Db.**; **E.**AB.; AG.; R.; U. 29–30 imp.; W.; **Ep.**D. 31–35 imp.; **Fr.** imp.; **G.**T.; U.; **Hu.**G.; **Ld.**U. imp.; **Lv.**P.; U.; **M.**C.; U.; **N.**U.; **Nw.**A.; **O.**R.; **Pl.**M.; **R.**D.; **Rt.**; **Sa.**; **Sal.**; **Y.**

A. Physical sciences [1935–50] **L.**AM. imp.; AV. 47–50; BM. imp.; BM^N.; C.; HQ.; IC. 47–50; L.; LE.; MC. 47–50; MY.; NF.; P.; PR.; R.; RI.; SC.; SI. 46–50; UC. 49–50; **Abs.**N.; **Bl.**U. 40–43; **Bm.**C. 39–50; U.; **Bn.**U. 44–50; **Br.**A. 40–43; U.; **Bra.**D. 48–50; **C.**A.; P.; **Db.**; **E.**AB. 35–44; R.; W.; **Ep.**D.; **F.**A. 44–50;

G.T.; U.; **Hu.**G.; **Ld.**U. imp.; W.; **Lv.**P.; U.; **M.**C.; D. 45–50; U.; **Md.**H. imp.; **N.**T.; U.; **Nw.**A.; **O.**R.; **Pl.**M.; **Pr.**FT.; **Sa.**; **Sal.**F.; **Y.** [*C. as:* 13183]

B. Chemical sciences [1935–50] **L.**AM.; AV.; BM. imp.; BM^N.; C.; HQ.; IC. 47–50; LE.; MC. 47–50; MY. 44–50; NF.; P.; PR.; R.; RI.; SC.; TP.; UC. 49–50; **Abs.**N.; **Bl.**U.; **Bm.**C. 39–50; U.; **Bn.**U. 44–50; **Br.**A.; U.; **Bra.**D. 48–50; **Db.**; **E.**AB. 35–43; R.; W.; **Ep.**D.; **F.**A. 44–50; **G.**T.; U.; **Hu.**G.; **Ld.**U.; W.; **Lv.**P.; U.; **M.**C.; D. 45–50; U.; **Md.**H.; **N.**U.; **Nw.**A.; **O.**R.; **Pr.**FT.; **Rt.**; **Sa.**; **Sal.**F.; **Y.** [*C. as:* 13171]

C. Botanical sciences [1935–50] **L.**AM.; AV. 48–50; BM. imp.; BM^N.; HQ.; IC. 36–50; L.; MC. 47–50; MY. 47–50; P.; PR.; R.; RI.; SC.; TP.; UC. 49–50; **Abs.**N.; **Bm.**U.; **Bn.**U. 44–50; **Bra.**D. 48–50; **C.**A.; P.; **Db.**; **E.**AB. 35–43; R.; W.; **Ep.**D.; **F.**A. 46–47; **Fr.**; **G.**T.; U.; **Hu.**G.; **Je.** 36–50; **Ld.**U.; W.; **Lv.**P.; U.; **M.**C.; D. 45–50; **Md.**H.; **N.**T. 48–50; U.; **Nw.**A.; **O.**R.; **Pl.**M.; **Pr.**FT.; **Rt.**; **Sa.**; **Sal.**F.; **Y.** [*C. as:* 13169]

D. Zoological sciences [1935–50] **L.**BM. imp.; BM^N.; EB.; HQ.; L.; MC. 47–50; MY. 47–50; P.; PR.; R.; RI.; SC.; TD. 48–50; TP.; Z.; **Abs.**N.; **Bm.**U.; **Bn.**U. 44–50; **Bra.**D. 48–50; **E.**AB.; R.; W.; **Ep.**D.; **F.**A. 46–47; **Fr.**; **G.**T.; U.; **Hu.**G.; **Je.** 36–50; **Ld.**W.; **Lv.**P.; U.; **M.**C.; U.; **Md.**H. imp.; **N.**U.; **Nw.**A.; **O.**R.; **Pl.**M.; **Pr.**FT.; **Rt.**; **Sa.**; **W.** 41–50; **Y.** [*C. as:* 13191]

E. Medical sciences [1944–50] **L.**AM.; BM. imp.; BM^N.; C.; HQ.; IC. 47–50; MA.; MC. 47–50; MD. 48–50; MY. 47–50; R.; RI.; SC.; TD. 48–50; U. 50; **Bm.**U.; **Bn.**U.; **Db.**; **E.**R.; **G.**T.; U.; **Ld.**U.; W.; **Lv.**P.; **M.**C.; D.; U.; **N.**U.; **O.**R.; **Rt.**; **Y.** [*C. as:* 13176]

F. Technology [1944–50] **L.**AM.; AV. 46–50; BM.; BM^N.; IC. 45–50; MC. 47–50; MY. 47–50; NF.; P.; PR.; RI.; SC.; **Abs.**N.; **Bm.**C.; U.; **Bn.**U.; **Br.**A. 44–45; **Db.**; **E.**AB. 44–48; R.; W.; **F.**A. 46–50; **G.**T.; U.; **Hu.**G.; **Ld.**U.; W.; **Lh.**FO. 46–50; P. 46–50; **Lv.**P.; U.; **M.**C.; D.; U.; **N.**T.; U.; **O.**R.; **Rt.**; **Sal.**F.; **Y.** [*C. as:* 13190]

13188 **Canadian Journal** of **Soil Science.** Ottawa. *Can. J. Soil Sci.* [1957–] **L.**AM.; P.; SC. 63–; **Abd.**S.; **Abs.**U.; **Bm.**U.; **Bn.**U. 59–; **C.**A.; **Db.**; **G.**U.; **Hu.**G.; **Je.**; **Ld.**U.; **Md.**H.; **N.**U.; **O.**RE.; **Rt.**; **Y.** [*C. from:* 13166]

13189 **Canadian Journal** of **Surgery.** Toronto. *Can. J. Surg.* [1957–] **L.**MD.; S.; **Bl.**U. 59–; **E.**S.; **G.**F.; **M.**MS.; **Y.**

13190 **Canadian Journal** of **Technology.** Ottawa. *Can. J. Technol.* [1951–57] **L.**AM.; AV. imp.; BM.; C. 52–56; IC.; LI.; MA.; P.; PR.; RI.; SC.; **Abd.**R.; S.; U.; **Abs.**N.; **Bm.**C. 51–55; **Bn.**U.; **Db.**; **E.**R.; W.; **Ep.**D.; **F.**A.; **G.**T., U.; **Hu.**G. 51–54; **Ld.**U.; W.; **Lh.**FO.; P.; **Li.**M. 52–57; **Lv.**P.; U.; **M.**C.; D.; U.; **Md.**H.; **N.**T.; U.; **O.**R.; **Pl.**M.; **R.**D.; T.; U. 52–57; **Sal.**; **Sy.**R.; **Y.** [*C. of:* 13187, Sect. F.; *C. as:* 13170]

13191 **Canadian Journal** of **Zoology.** Ottawa. *Can. J. Zool.* [1951–] **L.**AV. 51–55 imp.; BM.; BM^N.; C.; EB.; HQ.; L.; LI.; MA.; P.; R.; RI.; SC.; TD.; TP.; Z.; **Abd.**R.; S.; U.; **Abs.**N.; U. 58–; **Bm.**U.; **Bn.**U.; **Br.**A.; **Bra.**D.; **C.**APH.; PO.; **Db.**; **E.**AB.; R.; W.; **Ep.**D. 51–54; **Fr.**; **G.**T.; U.; **Je.**; **Ld.**W. 51–52; **Lv.**P.; U.; **M.**C.; P. 54–; U.; **Md.**H.; **Mi.** 57–; **N.**U.; **O.**R.; **Pl.**M.; **Pr.**FT.; **R.**D.; U. 52–; **Rt.**; **Sa.**; **Sal.**; **Sw.**U. 60–; **W.**; **Y.** [*C. of:* 13187 Sect. D.]

13192 **Canadian Machinery** and **Manufacturing News.** Montreal. *Can. Mach. Mfg News* [1905–] **L.**BM. 09– imp.; DI. 44– imp.; NF. 25–28 imp.; P. 15–28; **Y.**

13194 **Canadian Mathematical Bulletin.** Montreal, Toronto. *Can. math. Bull.* [1958–] L.SC.; **C.**P.; **G.**U.; **Nw.**A.; **Sa.**; **Y.**

13195 **Canadian Meat** and **Produce Journal.** Toronto. *Can. Meat Prod. J.* [1907–] L.BM.

13196 **Canadian Medical Association Journal.** Toronto. *Can. med. Ass. J.* [1911–] L.AM. 52–; BM. 23–; D. 39–; GH. 25–; H. 33–; MA.; MC. 40–; MD.; S.; U. 52–; UC. 28–55 imp.; **Abd.**U. 48–; **Abs.**N. 23–; R. 35–; **Bl.**U. 28–; **Bm.**U. 39–43: 46–; **Br.**U. 11–33; **C.**UL. 23–; **Db.** 11–19; **Dn.**U. 47–; **E.**I. 43–50; P.; S. 58–; U. 32–; **G.**F. 33–; U. 39– imp.; **Lv.**M. 31–; U. 19–26 imp.; **M.**MS. imp.; **Nw.**A. 31–34: 40: 47–; **O.**R.; **Sa.** 38–46; **Sh.**U. 44–; **Y.** [*C. of:* 29460 and 33669]

13197 **Canadian Medical Bulletin.** Toronto. *Can. med. Bull.*

Canadian Medical Monthly. *See* 13198.

13198 **Canadian Medical Quarterly.** Toronto. *Can. med. Q.* [1918–20]

13199 **Canadian Medical Record.** Montreal. *Can. med. Rec.*

13200 **Canadian Medical Services Journal.** Hamilton. *Can. med. Servs J.* [1943–57] L.MA. 46–57; MD. 54–57; S. 43–47; TD. [*C. as:* 30351]

13201 **Canadian Metals** and **Metallurgical Industries.** Toronto. *Can. Metals metall. Ind.* [1938–57] L.I.; NF.; P.; **Bm.**C. 39–57; **Sh.**IO. 53–57; **Y.** [*C. as:* 13202]

13202 **Canadian Metalworking.** Toronto. *Can. Metalwkg* [1957–] L.I.; MI. (curr.); NF.; P. 59–; **Bm.**C.; **Sh.**IO.; **Y.** [*C. of:* 13201]

13203 **Canadian Meteorological Memoirs.** Ottawa. *Can. met. Mem.* [1935–38] L.MO.; **Y.**

Canadian Miller and **Cerealist.** *See* 13204.

13204 **Canadian Miller** and **Grain Elevator.** Montreal. *Can. Miller* L.P. 11–16⋆.

13205 **Canadian Milling** and **Grain Journal.** Montreal. *Can. Mill. Grain J.* [1920–] L.BM. 21–.

13206 **Canadian Mineral Industry.** Ottawa. *Can. Miner. Ind.* [1934–] L.BM.; P. 34–39: 45–; **Bm.**P.; **Ld.**P. imp.; **M.**P.; **Y.**

13207 **Canadian Mineralogist.** Ottawa, Toronto. *Can. Mineralogist* [1957–] L.BM^N.; GM.; **Br.**U.; **C.**MI.; **E.**R.; **Ld.**U.; **M.**U.; **Y.** [*C. of:* 15636]

13208 **Canadian Mining Journal.** Toronto, etc. *Can. Min. J.* [1907–] L.BM 12–; GM.; I.; MI.; MIE. 49– imp.; P. 10–; **C.**PO. 52–; **G.**MG. 21–; T. 56–; **Nw.**A. 17: 26–36; **Sh.**M. 13–20; **Y.** [*C. of:* 13214]

13209 **Canadian Mining Manual** (and Mining Companies Year Book). Toronto. *Can. Min. Man.* L.MI. 46–49: 51–; P. 97–03; **Bm.**P. 27–; **G.**M. 52–.

13210 **Canadian Mining** and **Metallurgical Bulletin.** Ottawa. *Can. Min. metall. Bull.* [1927–] L.MI.; NF.; P.; PT.; SC.; **Bm.**T. 38–39 imp.: 49–; **Ld.**U. 47–; **O.**R. 38–; **Sh.**S.; **Y.** [*C. of:* 33414]

13211 **Canadian Mining** and **Metallurgical Notes.** London. *Can. Min. metall. Notes* L.MIE. 50– imp.; **O.**G. 30–40 imp.

13212 **Canadian Mining Monthly Review.** London. *Can. Min. mon. Rev.* **O.**R. 24–27.

13213 **Canadian Mining Record.** Toronto. *Can. Min. Rec.*

13214 **Canadian Mining Review.** Ottawa. *Can. Min. Rev.* [1882–07] L.MI. 06–07; P. 95–07; **G.**M. 89–05 imp. [*C. as:* 13208]

13214° **Canadian Missiles** and **Rockets.** Toronto. *Can. Missiles Rock.* [1958–]

13215 **Canadian Motor Tractor** and **Implement Trade Journal.** *Can. Mot. Tract. Impl. Trade J.*

13216 **Canadian Municipal Utilities.** Toronto. *Can. munic. Util.* [1959–] L.P.; **Wa.**W. 60–; **Y.** [*C. of:* 33835]

13217 **Canadian Natural Resources** and **Industrial Notes.** London. *Can. nat. Resour. ind. Notes* **O.**G. 29–39 imp.

13218 **Canadian Nature.** Toronto. *Can. Nat.* [1939–57] L.SC. 40–57. [*C. as:* 13119]

13219 **Canadian Nurse** and **Hospital Review.** Vancouver. *Can. Nurse Hosp. Rev.*

13220 **Canadian Nutrition Notes.** Ottawa. *Can. Nutr. Notes* [1945–] L.AM.; BM. 57–.

13221 **Canadian Official Mining News Letter.** London. *Can. off. Min. News Lett.* **O.**G. 30–39 imp.

13222 **Canadian Oil** and **Gas Industries.** Quebec. *Can. Oil. Gas Inds*

13223 **Canadian Optometrist** and **Optician.** Toronto. *Can. Optom. Optn* [1919–]

13224 **Canadian Pacific Fauna.** Fisheries Research Board. Ottawa. *Can. Pacif. Fauna* [1937–] L.BM^N.; **Abd.**M. 37–52; **Db.**; **Dm.**; **E.**R.; **Pl.**M. imp.; **Sa.** 37–43: 48 imp.

13225 **Canadian Packaging.** Toronto. *Can. Pckgng* **Lh.**P. 53–.

13226 **Canadian Paint** and **Varnish Magazine.** Toronto. *Can. Paint Varn. Mag.* [1927–] L.PR. 47–.

13227 **Canadian Patent Office Record.** Ottawa. *Can. Pat. Off. Rec.* [1873–] L.BM.; P.; SC. 25–; **Br.**P. 38–58; **Ld.**P. 28–; **Lv.**P. 40–; **M.**P.; **Sh.**P. 19–; **Sy.**R. (10 yr.)

13228 **Canadian Patent Reporter.** Toronto. *Can. Pat. Reptr* [1941–] L.P. 52–.

13229 **Canadian Pharmaceutical Journal.** Toronto. *Can. pharm. J.* [1868–] L.PH. 71–83: 35–; **Y.**

13230 **Canadian Photography.** Toronto. *Can. Photogr.* [1950–] L.PG. imp.

13231 **Canadian Phytopathological Society News.** Ottawa. *Can. phytopath. Soc. News* L.MY. 50–.

13232 **Canadian Plant Disease Survey.** Ottawa. *Can. Pl. Dis. Surv.* [1960–] **Br.**A.; **Ld.**U.; **Md.**H.; **Y.** [*C. of:* 42959]

13233 **Canadian Plastics.** Toronto. *Can. Plast.* [1943–] L.IC. 46–; NP. 57–; P. 59–; PL. 46–; **Lh.**P. 49–; **Sy.**R. 46–; **Y.**

13234 **Canadian Poultry Journal.** Toronto. *Can. Poult. J.* [1915–34]

13235 **Canadian Poultry Review.** Toronto. *Can. Poult. Rev.* [1877–]

13236 **Canadian Poultry World.** Victoria, B.C. *Can. Poult. Wld* [1912–28] [*C. as:* 13106]

13237 **Canadian Power Farmer.** Winnipeg. *Can. Pwr Fmr* [*C. as:* 13256]

13238 **Canadian Practitioner** and **Review.** Toronto. *Can. Practnr Rev.* [1883–24] L.MD. 98–24; S. 84–24; **Br.**U. 94–06; **E.**P. 94–12; **M.**MS. 06–21. [*C. in:* 13104]

13239 **Canadian Progress.** Montreal. *Can. Prog.* [1924–] **Abs.**U.; **Br.**U.; **E.**R. 24–31; U. 24–31 imp.; **G.**M. 25–31; U.; **Ld.**U.; **Nw.**A. 25–27; **O.**RH. 24–31.

13240 **Canadian Psychiatric Association Journal.** Ottawa. *Can. psychiat. Ass. J.* [1956–] **L.**MD.

13241 **Canadian Psychological Journal.** Toronto. *Can. psychol. J.* [1947–] **C.**PS.

13242 **Canadian Public Health Journal.** Toronto. *Can. publ. Hlth J.* [1929–42] **L.**H. 33–42; MA. 33–42; MD.; SC. 30–42; SH. 31–42; TD.; **Abd.**R. 36–42; **Bm.**U. 36–42; **Br.**U. 35–42 imp.; **Cr.**MD. 36–42; **Dn.**U. 36–42; **E.**U. 39–42; **Ld.**U. 36–42; **M.**MS.; **O.**R. 41–42; **R.**D. 42. [*C. of:* 40609; *C. as:* 13186]

13243 **Canadian Railway** and **Marine World.** Toronto. *Can. Rly mar. Wld* [1912–36] **L.**BM.; **Lv.**U. 13–20. [*C. of:* 41926°; *C. as:* 13257]

13244 **Canadian Record** of **Science.** Montreal. *Can. Rec. Sci.* [1884–16] **L.**BM.; BM^N. 84–05; GL. 00–16; GM.; K.; Z. 84–05; **C.**UL.; **Db.**; **E.**B.; C.; D.; R. 85–16 imp.; **M.**U.; **O.**R.

13245 **Canadian Refrigeration** and **Air Conditioning.** Quebec. *Can. Refrig. Air Condit.* [1956–] **L.**P. [*C. of:* 13246]

13246 **Canadian Refrigeration** and **Air Conditioning Journal.** Quebec. *Can. Refrig. Air Condit. J.* [1955] **L.**P. [*C. of:* 13247; *C. as:* 13245]

13247 **Canadian Refrigeration Journal.** Gardenvale, Que. *Can. Refrig. J.* [1943–55] **L.**P. 52–55. [*C. of:* 42433; *C. as:* 13246]

13248 **Canadian Resources Bulletin.** Ottawa. *Can. Resour. Bull.* [1937–42]

13249 **Canadian Services Medical Journal.** Ottawa. *Can. Servs med. J.* [1954–57] **L.**BM.; H.; MD. [*C. of:* 54320; *C. as:* 30351]

13250 **Canadian Shipping** and **Marine Engineering News.** Toronto. *Can. Shipp. mar. Engng News* [1920–] **G.**E. (3 yr.) [*C. of:* 29430; *Suspended* 1922–41]

13251 **Canadian Short Horn Journal.** Ottawa. *Can. Short Horn J.*

13252 **Canadian Statistical Review.** Dominion Bureau of Statistics. Ottawa. *Can. statist. Rev.* [1948–] **Bm.**U.; **C.**UL.; **Cr.**U. 54–; **Lv.**P. 60–.

13253 **Canadian Surveyor.** Ottawa. *Can. Surveyor* [1936–] **C.**PO. 48–. [*C. of:* 25608]

13254 **Canadian Textile Journal.** Montreal. *Can. Text. J.* [1907–] **L.**P. (1 yr); **Ld.**W. 21–24: 31– imp.; **M.**C. 50–; D. 49–; P. 53–; **Y.** [*C. of:* 13173]

13255 **Canadian Textile Seminar.** Montreal. *Can. Text. Semin.* [1949–] **L.**P. 50–.

13256 **Canadian Thresherman** and **Power Farmer.** Winnipeg. *Can. Thresherm. Pwr Fmr* [*C. of:* 13237]

13257 **Canadian Transportation.** Toronto. *Can. Transpn* [1936–] **L.**BM. [*C. of:* 13243]

13258 **Canadian Veterinary Journal.** Ottawa. *Can. vet. J.* [1960–] **L.**VC.; **Abd.**R.

13259 **Canadian Veterinary Record.** Toronto. *Can. vet. Rec.* [1920–25]

13260 **Canadian Weed Survey Report.** Ottawa. *Can. Weed Surv. Rep.* **C.**A. 48–.

13261 **Canadian Welding Journal.** Toronto. *Can. Weld. J.*

13262 **Canadian Woodlands Review.** Gardenvale, Que. *Can. Woodlds Rev.* [1929–31] [*Supplement to* 41370; *Replaces:* 57807; *C. as:* 57809]

13263 **Canadian Woodman.** London, Ontario. *Can. Woodm.* [1895–]

13264 **Canadian Woodworker.** Toronto. *Can. Woodwkr* [1901–] **L.**P. 56–.

13265 **Canal Record.** Balboa Heights. *Canal Rec.* [1907–16] **L.**SC. 15; **Bm.**U. 09–16; **G.**M. 07–11; **Lv.**U. 10–16. [*C. as:* 36937]

13266 **Canal** de **Suez.** Bulletin. Paris. *Canal Suez* [1870–] **L.**G. 85–93 imp.; **Bm.**U. 47–; **Cr.**P. 11–14.

13267 **Canals** and **Waterways Journal.** Birmingham. *Canals WatWays J.* [1919–24] **L.**BM.; **Bm.**P.; U. 19.

13268 **Canapa.** Roma. *Canapa* [1933–] **L.**TP. 33–40.

13269 **Cancer.** Berlin. *Cancer, Berl.* [1908–14] **L.**S. 09.

13270 **Cancer.** Bruxelles. *Cancer, Brux.* [1923–37] **L.**MA. 31–35; MD. 27–37.

13271 **Cancer.** Edinburgh. *Cancer, Edinb.* [1934–37] **L.**BM.; MD.; S.; **C.**UL.; **E.**U.; **O.**R.

13272 **Cancer.** London. *Cancer, Lond.* [1901–02] **L.**BM.; **O.**R.

13273 **Cancer.** New York, Philadelphia, etc. *Cancer, N.Y.* [1948–] **L.**CB.; MA.; MC. 52–55: 58–; MD.; S.; U. 52–; UC. 52–; **Abd.**U.; **Bm.**U.; **C.**PA. 48–54; R.; UL.; **Cr.**MS.; **Db.** 51–; **Dn.**U.; **E.**P. imp.; PO.; U.; **G.**F.; U.; **Ld.**U.; **Lv.**M.; **M.**MS.; **Nw.**A. 56–; **Sh.**IO.; U. 55–; **Y.**

13274 **Cancer.** Philadelphia. *Cancer, Philad.* [1923–28] **L.**MD. 23–25.

13275 **Cancer.** Santiago de Chile. *Cancer, Santiago* [1930–]

13276 **Cancer.** Toronto. *Cancer, Toronto* [1939–]

13277 **Cancer Bulletin.** Houston. *Cancer Bull., Houston* [1949–] **L.**CB. (curr.); MD.; **Br.**U. [*C. of:* 52917]

13278 **Cancer Bulletin.** Washington. *Cancer Bull., Wash.* [*Supplement to:* 30179]

13279 **Cancer Chemotherapy Abstracts.** Bethesda. *Cancer Chemother. Abstr.* [1959–] **L.**CB.; MD.; **Bl.**U. imp. [*C. of:* 16198]

13279° **Cancer Chemotherapy Reports.** *Cancer Chemother. Rep.* **Bl.**U. 60–.

13280 **Cancer Crusade Leaflet.** London. *Cancer Crus. Leafl.* [1919] **L.**BM.; **Abs.**N.

13281 **Cancer Crusade Series.** London. *Cancer Crus. Ser.* [1912–19] **L.**BM.; **Abs.**N.

13282 **Cancer Current Literature.** Amsterdam, New York. *Cancer curr. Lit.* [1947–55] **L.**CB.; MC. 50–52; MD.; S.; **Bl.**U. 51; **C.**PA. 50–51; R. 50–55; **Dn.**U. imp.; **G.**F. 50–55; U. 50–55; **Lv.**M. 50–55.

13283 **Cancer Current Literature Index.** Amsterdam. *Cancer curr. Lit. Index* [1959–60] **L.**MD.; **G.**U.; **Ld.**U.

13284 **Cancer Cytology.** New York. *Cancer Cytol.* [1958–] **L.**MD.

13285 **Cancer Digest** of **America.** Indianapolis. *Cancer Dig. Am.* [1898–34]

13285° **Cancer Morbidity Series.** National Cancer Institute. Washington. *Cancer Morb. Ser.* [1950–] **L.**BM.

13286 **Cancer News.** New York. *Cancer News* [1947–] **L**.CB. (curr.); MA.

Cancer Report. United Birmingham Hospitals. *See* 3335.

13287 **Cancer Research.** Baltimore, etc. *Cancer Res.* [1941–] **L**.CB.; MA.; MC. 50–55: 59–; MD.; S.; U. 49–; UCH.; **Abd.**R. 48–; U. 53–; **Bm.**U.; **Br.**U.; **C.**PA. 41–54; R. 42–; UL. 49–; **Db.** 49–; **E.**A. 49–; P. imp.; PO.; S.; U.; **G.**F. 54–; U.; **Ld.**U. 50–; **M.**MS. 41–51; **Nw.**A. 56–; **O.**P.; R.; **W.** 45–57; **Y.** [*C. of:* 1998]

13288 **Cancer Research Memoirs.** Edinburgh. *Cancer Res. Mem.* [1940–] **L**.BM.

13289 **Cancer Review.** Bristol. *Cancer Rev.* [1926–32] **L**.CB.; H.; MA.; MC.; MD.; RA. 28–31; S.; SC.; TD.; UCH.; V. 27–32; **Abd.**U.; **Abs.**N.; **Bm.**U.; **Br.**U.; **C.**PA.; **Cr.**MD.; **Db.**; **E.**A.; S.; **Lv.**M.; **M.**MS.; O.R.

13290 **Cancer Series.** U.S. Public Health Service. Washington. *Cancer Ser.* [1949–] **L**.BM.

13291 **Cancérologie.** Lille. *Cancérologie* [1953–57] **L**.CB.; H.

13292 **Cancro.** Torino. *Cancro*

13293 **Candollea.** Organe du Conservatoire et du Jardin botaniques de la ville de Genève. *Candollea* [1922–] **L**.BM^N.; HS. 22–52; K. 22; L.; **Bl.**U. 43–; **C.**BO. 22–29; P.; **E.**B. [*C. of:* 3259]

13294 **Cane Growers' Quarterly Bulletin.** Brisbane. *Cane Grow. q. Bull.* [1933–] **L**.P. 57–; **C.**A.; **Md.**H. 48–; **Rt.**; **Sil.** 59– imp.; **Y.**

13295 **Canned** and **Dried Fruit Notes.** London. *Canned dried Fruit Notes* [1931–39] **L**.AM.; BM.; **O.**AEC.; B. [*C. of:* 57236]

13296 **Canner.** Chicago. *Canner* [1895–55] **L**.AM. 47–55; **Br.**U. 26–31; **Lh.**FO. 48–52 imp.: 53–55. [*C. as:* 13297]

13297 **Canner** and **Freezer.** Chicago. *Canner Freez.* [1955–57] **L**.AM.; **Lh.**FO. [*C. of:* 13296; *C. in:* 13298]

13298 **Canner/Packer.** Chicago. *Canner/Pckr* [1958–] **L**.AM.; P.; TP.; **G.**U. 62–; **Lh.**FO.; **Y.** [*C. of:* 13297, 19888 and 57395]

13299 **Canners' Bulletin.** Fruit and Vegetable Preservation Research Station. Campden. *Canners' Bull.* [1930–] **L**.BM.; P. 30–31; **Br.**U.; **C.**A.

13300 **Canners' Information Letter. British Food Manufacturing Industries Research Association.** Leatherhead. *Canners' Inf. Lett. Br. Fd Mfg Ind. Res. Ass.* [1957–] **L**.AM.; BM.; P.

13301 **Canners' Information Letter. Fruit** and **Vegetable Canning** and **Quick Freezing Research Association.** Chipping Campden. *Canners' Inf. Lett. Fruit Veg. Cann. quick Freez. Res. Ass.* [1957–] **L**.AM.; BM.; P.

13302 **Cannery Notes.** Buffalo. *Cannery Notes*

13303 **Cannes médical.** Cannes. *Cannes méd.*

13304 **Canning Age.** New York. *Cann. Age* [1920–43] **L**.P. 25–43; **Br.**U. 21–43; **Lh.**FO. 27–43. [*C. as:* 19888]

13305 **Canning** and **Food Trade Journal.** London. *Cann. Fd Trade J.* [1934–35] **L**.BM.; P.; **C.**UL.; **O.**B. [*C. of:* 13310]

13306 **Canning Industry** and **Food Packing Trades Gazette.** London. *Cann. Ind.* **L**.P. 33–39; **Br.**U. 32–39. [*Incorporated* Oct. 1939–Sept. 1952 *in:* 53283; *C. as:* 13308]

13307 **Canning Journal.** Birmingham. *Cann. J.* [1960–] **L**.P.

13308 **Canning** and **Packing.** London. *Cann. Pckg* [1953–] **L**.AM. imp.; P.; SH. (1 yr); TP. 54–; **Lh.**FO.; **Lv.**P. 54–; **Y.** [*C. of:* 13306]

13309 **Canning Trade.** Baltimore. *Cann. Trade* [1878–] **L**.I. (curr.); P. 15–21; TP. 54–; **Y.**

13310 **Canning Trade Journal.** London. *Cann. Trade J.* [1931–33] **L**.BM.; P.; **C.**UL.; **O.**B.; **Sh.**P. [*C. as:* 13305]

13311 **Cantal agricole.** Aurillac. *Cantal agric.* **Y.**

Canterbury Agricultural College Annual Review. *See* 3434.

13312 **Canterbury Agricultural College Magazine.** Christchurch, N.Z. *Canterbury agric. Coll. Mag.*

13313 **Canterbury Museum Bulletin.** Wellington. *Canterbury Mus. Bull.* [1950–] **L**.BM^N.; Z.; **Pl.**M. 54–; **Y.**

13314 **Cantieri** e **costruzioni.** Napoli. *Cantieri Costr.* **L**.P. 55–57.

13315 **Cantor Lectures.** Royal Society of Arts. London. *Cantor Lect.* **L**.BM. 69–; C. 1853–; P. 72–; **Br.**P. 77–17; **Cr.**P. 69–92 imp.; U. 84–12; **E.**F. 63–; **G.**T. 81–93; **Ld.**P.; **Lv.**P. 11–22: 36.

13316 **Canvas.** London. *Canvas* [1936–39] **L**.P.; SC. [*Supplement to* and *C. in:* 27143]

13317 **Caoutchouc cellulaire étanche 'Mousse' informations.** Paris. *Caoutch. cell. étanche 'Mousse' Infs* [1954–] **L**.P.

13318 **Caoutchouc** et la **gutta-percha.** Paris. *Caoutch. Gutta-percha* [1904–39] **L**.P. 10–39; TP.; **M.**D. 29–39; **Sy.**R.

13319 **Caoutchouc moderne.** Paris. *Caoutch. mod.* **L**.P. 26–30*. [*Supplement to:* 47238]

13320 **Caoutchouc: Série Indochine.** Saigon. *Caoutch. Sér. Indochine* [1948–] **Md.**H. 49–; **C.**A. 55–.

13321 **Caoutchoucs** et **latex artificiels.** Paris. *Caoutchs Latex artif.* [1947–] **L**.P. 47–51. [*Supplement to:* 47238]

13322 **Caoutchoucs** et **plastiques.** Bruxelles. *Caoutchs Plast.* **Sy.**R. 38–41.

13323 **Cape Astrographic Zones.** Royal Observatory, Cape Town. *Cape astrogr. Zones* [1913–] **L**.AS.; BM.; SC. 13–26; **Abd.**U.; **Abs.**N.; **Bm.**P.; **C.**O.; **Db.**; **E.**O.; R. 13–26; U. 13–26; **G.**M. 13–26; **Lv.**U.; **M.**P.; **O.**R. 13–26; **Sa.** 13–26.

13324 **Cape Expedition Series Bulletin.** Department of Scientific and Industrial Research. Wellington N.Z. *Cape Exped. Ser. Bull.* **L**.BM^N. 47–; EB. (ent.) 49–.

Cape Meridian Observations. *See* 46091.

13325 **Cape Mimeograms.** Cape of Good Hope. *Cape Mimeogr.* [1953–] **L**.AS.

13326 **Cape Naturalist.** Cape Town. *Cape Nat.* [1934–39] **L**.BM.; BM^N.

13326° **Cape Wild Life.** Cape Town. *Cape wild Life* [1951–] **L**.BM.

13327 **Capita zoologica.** 's Gravenhage. *Capita zool.* [1921–39] **L**.BM^N.; SC.; Z.; **C.**UL.; **M.**U.; **O.**R.; **Pl.**M. 21–34 imp.

13328 **Capper's Farmer.** Topeka, Kans. *Capper's Fmr* **R.**U. 44–57 v. imp.

13329 **Car Mechanics.** London. *Car Mech.* [1958–] **L**.BM.; P. 59–; **O.**R.

13330 **Caractère.** Industries et technique papetières et graphiques. Paris. *Caractère* [1949–] **L.**HP. 50–; P. 50–; SB. 51–; **Y.**

13331 **Caractère magnétique** pour **chaque jour** du **mois.** Commission internationale de magnétisme terrestiale. *Caract. magn. chaque Jour Mois* **L.**MO. 06–39; **C.**SP. 06–.

13332 **Caractère magnétique numérique** des **jours.** U.G.G.I. Bruxelles. *Caract. magn. num. Jours* **L.**MO. 30–39.

13333 **Caractères climatologiques** en **Nouvelle Calédonie** et **Dépendances.** Nouméa. *Caracts clim. Nouv. Caléd.* **L.**MO. 57–.
   Caractéristique géophysique de l'**Ukraine.** See 22082.

13334 **Caratteristiche** del **tempo** nell'**Africa orientale italiana.** Roma. *Caratt. Tempo Afr. orient. ital.* **L.**MO. 37.

   Carbid und **Acetylen.** Berlin. *See* 27249.

13335 **Carbide Engineering.** Wheaton, Ill. *Carbide Engng* [1949–] **L.**DI. 54–.

13336 **Carbón.** Oviedo. *Carbón, Oviedo* **O.**R. 42–.

13337 **Carbon.** The Magazine of Manchester Collieries, Ltd. Manchester. *Carbon, Manchr* **M.**U. 32– imp.

13338 **Carbon Black Abstracts.** Boston, Mass. *Carb. Black Abstr.* [1952–] **L.**P. 53–; PR. 54–; Lv.P. 56–; Sy.R.

13339 **Carbon News.** Cleveland. *Carb. News*

13340 **Carbon** and its **Uses.** London. *Carb. Uses* [1960–] **L.**P.

13341 **Carbonic Acid.** New York. *Carbonic Acid*

13342 **Carbonic Acid** and **Carbonated Beverages.** Chicago. *Carbonic Acid carbd Bev.*

13343 **Carbons.** Society of Carbon Research. Tokyo. *Carbons, Tokyo* [1950–] **Y.**
   Carborundum's Refractories. Carborundum Co. *See* 42425°.

13344 **Carderelli.** Napoli. *Carderelli* [1959–] **L.**MD.

13345 **Cardiac.** Toronto. *Cardiac*

13346 **Cardiac News Letter.** Chest and Heart Association. London. *Cardiac News Lett.* [1960–] **L.**BM.

13347 **Cardiganshire Natural History Bulletin.** *Cardigansh. nat. Hist. Bull.* [1951–] **O.**OR. 51.

13348 **Cardinal.** Audubon Society of the Sewickley Valley. Sewickley, Pa. *Cardinal*

13349 **Cardiologia.** Basel. *Cardiologia* [1937–] **L.**MA. 46–; MD.; E.U. 57–; **M.**MS. 53–; **Y.**

13350 **Cardiologica pratica.** Milano. *Cardiol. prat.* [1949–] **L.**MA. 52–.

13351 **Care, Maintenance** and **Instruction Leaflet. National Institute** of **Agricultural Engineering.** Askham Bryan. *Care Maint. Instruct. Leafl. natn. Inst. agric. Engng* [1948–] **Rt.** [*C. as:* 19055]

13352 **Cargill Crop Bulletin.** *Cargill Crop Bull.* **R.**U. 51–.

13353 **Cargo Handling.** London. *Cargo Handl.* [1953–] **L.**BM.; P.; **C.**UL.; E.A.; Lv.P. 54–; O.B.; **Y.**

13354 **Caribbean Forester.** Rio Piedras, Puerto Rico. *Caribb. Forester* [1939–] **L.**BM^N.; EB.; K.; TP.; **C.**A.; **O.**F.

13354° **Caribbean Journal** of **Science.** *Carrib. J. Sci.* **Y.**

13355 **Caribbean Medical Journal.** Port-of-Spain. *Caribb. med. J.* [1938–] **L.**MA.; MD. imp.; TD. imp.; **Br.**U. imp.; E.P. imp.; **G.**F. 41– imp.

13356 **Caribbean Quarterly.** Trinidad, B.W.I. *Caribb. Q.* [1949–] **L.**BM^N.; E.U. 55–.

13357 **Caribbean Technological Abstracts.** *Caribb. technol. Abstr.* [1954–] **L.**TP. 54–60; E.A. 57–.

13358 **Carinthia II.** Mitteilungen des Naturhistorischen Landesmuseums für Kärnten. Klagenfurt. *Carinthia II* **L.**BM^N. 91–; **Rt.** 01; **Y.**

13359 **Carle** and **Montanari News.** Milano. *Carle Montanari News* [1960–] **L.**P.
   Carlsberg Foundation's Oceanographical Expedition round the **World.** *See* 16348.

13359ª **Carlswerk-Rundschau.** Köln-Mülheim. *Carlswerk-Rdsch* **L.**P. 27*. [*C. as:* 19279]

13360 **Carmarthen Antiquary.** Transactions of the Carmarthenshire Antiquarian Society and Field Club. Carmarthen. *Carmarthen Antiq.* [1941–] **L.**BM.; **Abs.**N.; **C.**UL.; E.V.; Lv.U.; **M.**P.; O.B.; Sw.U.

13361 **Carnation Year Book.** Burnley, etc. *Carnation Yb.* [1910–] **L.**BM.; HS.; **Abs.**N. 18–; **Br.**U. 50–57; **M.**P. 35–; O.R. 10–12; R.D. 38– imp.; U. 38–39: 41: 43–.

13362 **Carnegie Graduate Study** in **Engineering** and **Science.** Washington. *Carnegie Grad. Study Engng Sci.* **Y.**

13363 **Carnegie Scholarship Memoirs.** Iron and Steel Institute. London. *Carnegie Schol. Mem. Iron Steel Inst.* [1909–38] **L.**BM.; C.; GM.; IC.; NF.; P.; SC.; UC.; **Abs.**N.; **Bm.**C.; P.; T.; U.; **Bn.**U. 20–38; **Br.**U.; **C.**UL.; **Cr.**U.; **Db.**; E.A.; U.; **G.**E.; I.; M. imp.; T.; **Ld.**P.; U. imp.; Lv.P.; U. 09–17; **M.**P. imp.; U. imp.; **N.**U. 09–25 imp.; **Nw.**A.; P.; O.R.; **Sh.**P.; SC.; **St.**R. 09–34; Sw.U.; **Wd.** [*C. in:* 26260]

13364 **Carnegie Technical Journal.** Pittsburgh. *Carnegie tech. J.* [*C. of:* 12888]

13365 **Carnet** de l'**architecture,** de l'entrepreneur et du conducteur de travaux. Paris. *Carnet Archit.*

13366 **Carnets.** Publiés par la Société zoologique de Québec. *Carnets Soc. zool. Québ.* [1940–] **L.**Z. imp.

13367 **Carniola.** Izvestja Muzejskego društva za Kranjsko. v Ljubljani. *Carniola* [1908–19] **L.**BM.; BM^N. [*C. of:* 32624; *C. as:* 21354°]

13368 **Carobronze Mitteilungen.** Berlin. *Carobronze Mitt.* **L.**P. 32–33.

13369 **Carolina Chemist.** Chapel Hill, N.C. *Carol. Chem.*

13370 **Carolina Journal** of **Pharmacy.** Chapel Hill. *Carol. J. Pharm.* [1915–17: 22–]

13371 **Carolina Medical Journal.** Charlotte, S.C. *Carol. med. J.*

13372 **Carpentry** and **Building.** New York. *Carp. Bldg* [1879–09] **L.**BM.; P. 91–09. [*C. as:* 9042]

13373 **Carriage Builders' Journal, Wheelwright** and **Saddlery & Harness Record.** London. *Carr. Bldrs' J.* [1898–02] **L.**P. 00–02. [*C. as:* 5485]

13373° **Carrier Cable Communication.** *Carrier Cable Commun.* **M.**T. 36–40.

13374 **Carron Cupola.** Falkirk. *Carron Cupola* [1950–] **L.**BM.; **Bm.**C.; E.A. 52–.

13375 **Carrosserie automobile.** Paris. *Carross. auto.* [1911–21] [*C. as:* 18319]

13375° **Carta, stampa** e **cartotecnica.** Milano. *Carta Stampa Cartotec.* **Y.**

13376 **Carta** del **tiempo, Argentina.** Buenos Aires. *Carta Tiempo Argent.* [1902–] **L.**BM. 59–; MO. 02–47.

13377 **Carta** del **tiempo, Chile.** Santiago. *Carta Tiempo Chile* **L.**MO. 30– imp.

13378 **Cartas geológicas** y **mineras** de la **República mexicana.** México. *Cartas geol. min. Repúb. mex.* [1931–] **L.**BM[N].; **C.**S.; **E.**R. imp.; **Y.**

13379 **Carte annuali** delle **piogge.** Venezia. *Carte a. Piogge* [1909–21] **L.**MO.

13380 **Carte** des **sols** et de la **végétation** du **Congo belge** et du **Ruanda-Urundi.** Bruxelles. *Carte Sols Vég. Congo belge* [1953–] **L.**BM.; **K.**; **O.**F. 54–.
Carte du **temps** à **Davos.** *See* 16428.

13381 **Cartes synoptiques** de la **chromosphère solaire** et **catalogue** des **filaments** de la **couche supérieure.** Paris. *Cart. synopt. Chromosph. sol.* **L.**AS. 31–.

13382 **Cartes synoptiques journalières** du **temps.** Copenhague. *Cart. synopt. journ. Temps* **L.**MO. 73–76.

13383 **Cartillas rurales.** Madrid. *Cartillas rur.* **L.**AM. 49–.

13383° **Cartografía** de **ultramar.** Madrid. *Cartogr. Ultramar* [1949–55] **L.**BM.

13384 **Cartographical Progress.** London. *Cartogr. Prog.* [1960–] **L.**BM.

13385 **Cartography.** Journal of the Australian Institute of Cartographers. Melbourne. *Cartography* [1954–] **L.**BM.; **G.**; **N.**C.; **U.**; **Bm.**U.; **G.**U.; **Sw.**U.

13386 **Carus Mathematical Monographs.** Chicago. *Carus math. Monogr.* [1925–] **L.**BM.; **Bl.**U. 51–56; **C.**UL.; **Sw.**U.

13387 **Carworth Farms Quarterly Letter.** *Carworth Fms q. Lett.* [1946–] **E.**U.

13388 **Caryologia.** Giornale de citologia, citosistematica e citogenetica. Torino, etc. *Caryologia* [1948–] **L.**BM[N].; **C.**B.; **S.**C.; **U.**; **Ba.**I.; **C.**A.; **G.**E. 55–; **M.**U.; **O.**R.; **Y.**

13389 **Čas.** Znanstvena revija 'Leonove Družbe'. v Ljubljani. *Čas*

13390 **Casa** del **médico.** Madrid. *Casa Méd.* **L.**MA. 44–48*; MD. 44–48; **E.**P. 44–45 imp. [*C. as:* 17152]

13391 **Casabella.** Roma. *Casabella* [1928–40] **L.**BA. 30–40. [*C. as:* 17151]

13392 **Case.** Reed Corrugated Cases Ltd. London. *Case* [1958–] **L.**AV.; BM.; **P.** 59–; **Ld.**P. (5 yr.); **Lv.**P. 59–.

13393 **Case** d'**oggi.** Milano. *Case Oggi* **L.**BA. 34–37.

13394 **Case Reports** of the **Children's Memorial Hospital, Chicago.** *Case Rep. Child. meml Hosp. Chicago* **L.**MA. 48–.

13395 **Case Studies. National Institute** of **Agricultural Engineering.** Silsoe. *Case Stud. natn. Inst. agric. Engng* [1949–52] **L.**P. 50–52 imp.; **N.**U.; **O.**R. 50–52; **O.**RE.

13396 **Case Technologist.** Cleveland. *Case Technol.*

13397 **Caslon Circular** and **Type-founder.** London. *Caslon Circ.* [1875–] **L.**BM.; **P.** 04–34; SB. 75–33; **Abs.**N. 09–; **Bm.**U. 21–; **O.**B. 75–95 imp. [*Suspended* 1915–20]

13398 **Časopis České společnosti entomologické.** Praha. *Čas. české Spol. ent.* [1904–18] **L.**BM[N].; **E.**; EB.; **Z.**; **O.**H. [*C. as:* 13401]

13399 **Časopis českého lékárnictva.** v Praze. *Čas. česk. Lék.* [1880–15] [*C. as:* 13402]

13400 **Časopis českého ovocnictva.** Troja. *Čas. česk. Ovocn.*

13401 **Časopis. Československé společnosti entomologické.** Praha. *Čas. čsl. Spol. ent.* [1919–52: 57–] **L.**BM[N].; **E.**; EB.; **S.**C. 34–; **Z.**; **Br.**A. 45–; **C.**B. 49–; **Db.** 41–; **Ld.**U. 39–; **Lv.**U. 20–21; **O.**H.; **Y.** [*C. of:* 13398; >48038, 1953–56]

13402 **Časopis československého lékárnictva.** Praha. *Čas. čsl. Lék.* [1921–] **L.**PH. 46–. [*C. of:* 13399]
Časopis Československého žímného sdružení. *See* 25626.

13403 **Časopis československých houbařů.** Praha. *Čas. čsl. Houb.* [1919–34] [*C. as:* 12867]

13404 **Časopis československých inženýrův a architektův.** Praha. *Čas. čsl. Inž. Archit.* **L.**BA. 07–12.

13405 **Časopis československých ústavů astronomických.** Praha. *Čas. čsl. Úst. astr.* [1951–57] **L.**BM. 55–57. [*International edition at:* 9520]

13406 **Časopis československých veterinařů.** v Brne. *Čas. čsl. Vet.* [1946–] **L.**V.; **W.**

13407 **Časopis českých lékařův.** Praha. *Čas. českých Lék.*

13408 **Časopis českých zvěrolékářů.** v Třebící, Val. Meziříčí. *Čas. českých Zvěrolék.* [1902]

13409 **Časopis** pro **dějiny venkova.** Praha. *Čas. Děj. Venk.* [*C. of:* 1208]
Časopis Kvas. *See* 37821.

13411 **Časopis lékařů českých.** v Praze. *Čas. Lék. česk.* [1862–] **L.**MA. 47–; MC. 53– imp.; MD. 30–; TD. (10 yr.) V. 55–; **Y.**

13412 **Časopis lesného hospodárstva a drevárskeho priemyslu.** Bratislava. *Čas. lesn. Hospod. drev. Priem.*

13413 **Časopis maćicy serbskeje.** Budyšin. *Čas. Mać serb.* [1848–] **L.**BM. 1848–18; **O.**B. 1848–36.

13413° **Časopis** pro **mineralogii** a **geologii.** Praha. *Čas. Miner. Geol.* [1956–] **L.**BM. 60–; **Y.**

13414 **Časopis Moravského musea** v **Brne.** Brno. *Čas. morav. Mus. Brne* [1946–51: 52– in series] **L.**BM. 53–; BM[N].; **E.** 54–; **Db.**; **Lv.**U. 47–; **O.**H. imp.; **Y.** [*C. of:* 13415]

13415 **Časopis Moravského zemského musea.** v Brné. *Čas. morav. zemsk. Mus.* [1901–43] **L.**BM. 01–19; BM[N].; **O.**H. 04–43 imp. [*C. as:* 13414]

13416 **Časopis Musea království českého.** v Praze. *Čas. Mus. Král. česk.* [1827–22] **L.**BM. [*C. as:* 13418]

13417 **Časopis Museálnej slovenskej společnosti.** Turčiansky Sv. Martin. [1898–01] *Čas. mus. slov. Spol.*

13418 **Časopis Národního musea.** Praha. *Čas. národ. Mus.* [1923–] **L.**BM.; BM[N]. 54–; GL. 49–; GM.; SL. 23: 26–; **E.**R. 53–; **V.**; **Y.** (přírod.) [*C. of:* 13416]

13419 **Časopis** pro **pěstování fysiky.** Praha. *Čas. Pěst. Fys.* [1951–] **L.**BM.; **P.** imp.; **U.**; UC.; **Bm.**U. 55–; **C.**P.; **E.**R.; **G.**U. 56–; **Ld.**U.; **Y.** [*C. from:* 13421; *International edition at:* 16241]

13420 **Časopis** pro **pěstování matematiky.** Praha. *Čas. Pěst. Mat.* [1951–] **L.**BM.; **M.**; **U.**; UC.; **Bm.**U. 55–; **C.**P.; **E.**R.; **G.**U. 56–; **Ld.**U.; **O.**R. 51–52; **Y.** [*C. from:* 13421; *International edition at:* 16242]

13421 **Časopis** pro **pěstování matematiky** a **fysiky.** Praha. *Čas. Pěst. Mat. Fys.* [1872–50] **L.**BM.; M. 10–50 imp.; UC. 10–50 imp.; **C.**P. 21–50; **E.**R. 35–50; **Ld.**U. 46–50; **Y.** [*C. as:* 13419 and 13420]

13422 **Časopis Slezského musea** v **Opavě.** *Čas. slezsk. Mus. Opavě*
Ser. A. Hist. nat. [1951–] **L.**BM^N.; **Ld.**U. 51–59; **Y.**
Časopis Spolku muzejního v **Olomouci.** *See* 13425.

13423 **Časopis** pro **tělesnou výchovu.** Praha. *Čas. těl. Vých.*

13424 **Časopis** pro **veřejné zdravotnictví.** v Praze. *Čas. veř. Zdrav.* [1899–08]

13425 **Časopis Vlasteneckého muzejního spolku Olomuckého.** Olomouc. *Čas. vlast. muz. Spolku olomuck.* [1884–]

13426 **Časopis** pro **Vlastivědu** a **nauku občanskou.** Velké Meziříčí. *Čas. Vlast. Nauku občansk.* **Bm.**P. 00–.

13427 **Časopis** pro **zdravotnictvo.** Bratislava. *Čas. Zdrav.* [1899–33] **L.**LI. 21–23; SC. 26–33; TD. 26: 28–33; **M.**MS. 21–23.
Časopis Zemského musea v **Brně.** *See* 13415.

13428 **Časopis** za **zgodovino** in **narodopisjo.** Maribor. *Čas. Zgod. Narod.* [1906–32]

13429 **Časové otázky zemědělské.** Praha. *Časové Otáz. zeměd.* [1926–] **C.**A. imp.; **Hu.**G. 27–38 imp.; **Rt.** 32.

13430 **Časové spisky.** Ministerstvo zemědělství. Praha. *Časové spisky Minist. Zeměd.* **L.**SC. 24–.

13431 **Cassel Salt Bath Furnaces Data Sheet.** London. *Cassel salt Bath Furnaces Data Sh.* [1953–] **L.**P.

13432 **Cassier's Engineering Monthly.** New York. *Cassier's Engng Mon.* [1913–18] **L.**BM.; EE.; I.; P.; **Bm.**P.; T.; **C.**UL.; **Db.**; **E.**A. 13–15; L.; T. imp.; **G.**M.; U.; **Lv.**P.; U. 13–16; **M.**P.; T.; U.; **N.**P.; **Nw.**P.; **O.**R.; **Sh.**P. [*C. of:* 13434; *C. as:* 18125]

13433 **Cassier's Industrial Management.** London. *Cassier's ind. Mgmt* [1924–29] **L.**BM.; EE.; MT.; NF.; P.; SC.; **Abs.**N.; **Bm.**P.; T.; U.; **Br.**U. 28–29; **C.**UL.; **Db.**; **E.**L.; **G.**M.; U.; **Lv.**P.; **M.**P.; T.; U.; **Nw.**P.; **O.**R. [*C. of:* 23242; *C. as:* 13435]

13434 **Cassier's Magazine.** New York. *Cassier's Mag.* [1891–13] **L.**BM.; EE. 95–13; I. 93–13; P. 09–13; SC.; **Bm.**P. 00–13; T.; U. 95–13; **Br.**U. 97–09; **C.**UL.; **Db.**; **E.**A. imp.; F. 95–06; L. 95–13; T. 94–13 imp.; **G.**M.; U. 96–13; **Lv.**P. 94–13; U. 09–13; **M.**P. 97–13; T. 94–13; U. 02–13; **N.**P. 98–13; **Nw.**A. 95–11; P. 01–13; **O.**R.; **Sh.**P. 05–13. [*C. as:* 13432]

13435 **Cassier's Mechanical Handling, Works Management** and **Equipment.** London. *Cassier's mech. Handl.* [1930] **L.**BM.; EE.; MT.; NF.; P.; SC.; **Abs.**N.; **Bm.**P.; T.; U.; **Br.**U.; **C.**UL.; **Db.**; **E.**L.; T.; **G.**M.; U.; **Lv.**P.; **M.**P.; T.; U.; **Nw.**P.; **O.**R. [*C. of:* 13433; *C. as:* 29762]

13436 **Cassinia.** Proceedings of the Delaware Valley Ornithological Club. Philadelphia. *Cassinia* [1901–] **L.**BM^N. 11–; Z.; **Y.**

13437 **Cast Iron Pipe News.** Chicago. *Cast Iron Pipe News* [1935–] **L.**P. (curr.)

13438 **Cast Stone Architecture** and **Concrete Design.** London. *Cast Stone Archit.* **L.**BM. 31–.

13439 **Castanea.** The Journal of the Southern Appalachian Botanical Club. Morgantown, W. Va. *Castanea* [1937–] **L.**BM^N.; K.; **E.**B.; **O.**F. 42–; **Y.** [*C. of:* 26984]

13440 **Castella médica.** Valladolid. *Castella méd.*

13441 **Castings.** London. *Castings, Lond.* [1910–12] **L.**BM.; P. 10–11; **O.**B.

13442 **Castings.** Cleveland. *Castings, Cleveland* [1907–15] **L.**P. 11–12.

13443 **Castings.** Sydney. *Castings, Sydney* [1955–] **L.**P; **Bm.**C.; **Y.** [*C. of:* 20288]

13444 **Casualties Union Journal.** Whyteleafe, Surrey. *Casualt. Un. J.* **L.**MA. 46–58*. [*C. as:* 13445]

13445 **Casualty Simulation.** London. *Casualty Simul.* [1958–] **L.**BM.; MA. 58–; **Do.**F. [*C. of:* 13444]

13446 **Casuistica medico-chirurgica.** Milano. *Casuist. med.-chir.*

13447 **Catalógo** e **estatística** dos **gêneros botânicos fanerogâmicos.** Curitiba. *Catalógo Estatíst. Gên. bot. fanerog.* [1956–] **L.**K.

13448 **Catalogue** of the **Active Volcanoes** of the **World** including **Solftara Fields.** International Volcanological Association. Napoli. *Cat. act. Volc. Wld* **E.**D. 51–.

13449 **Catalogue** of the **Annual Exhibition** of **Scientific Instruments.** Physical Society. London. *Cat. a. Exhib. scient. Instrum., Lond.* **L.**P. 32–48; **Bn.**U. 27–48; **Ld.**P. 33–37: 46: 48; **O.**R. 36–48. [*C. as:* 21796]

13450 **Catalogue** of **Charts, Coast Pilots** and **Tide Tables.** Washington. *Cat. Charts Cst Pilots Tide Tables, Wash.* **L.**BM. 67–; **G.**M. 92– imp.

13451 **Catalogue** of **Disturbances** in **Ionosphere, Geomagnetic Field, Field Intensity** of **Radio Wave, Cosmic Ray, Solar Phenomena** and **other** related **phenomena.** Tokyo. *Cat. Disturb. Ionosph.* [1950–54] **L.**MO. [*C. in:* 44227]

13452 **Catalogue** d'**essais** d'**hélices.** Grande soufflerie de Paris. Paris. *Cat. Ess. Hélices* [1933–] **L.**P. 33–34.

13453 **Catalogue** de l'**Exposition** d'**instruments** et **matériel scientifiques.** Société française de physique. Paris. *Cat. Expos. Instrum. Matér. scient.* **L.**P. 49–; SC. 49–; **E.**R. 50–.

13454 **Catalogue. Institut français** d'**Afrique noire.** Dakar. *Cat. Inst. fr. Afr. noire* [1947–] **L.**BM^N. 48– imp.; **Dm.** imp.; **Y.**

13454^a **Catalogue mensuel** des **traductions** du **C.N.R.S.** Centre national de la recherche scientifique. Paris. *Cat. mens. Traduct. C.N.R.S.* **L.**HQ. (1 yr); **Y.**

13454^b **Catalogue** des **normes françaises.** Paris. *Cat. Norm. fr.* **L.**P. (curr.); **Y.**

13455 **Catalogue officiel. Salon international** des **inventeurs.** Paris. *Cat. off. Salon int. Invent.* [1952–] **L.**P. imp.

13456 **Catalogue** of the **Parasites** and **Predators** of **Insect Pests.** Institute of Entomology, Parasite Service. Ottawa. *Cat. Parasites Predat. Insect Pests* [1943–] **L.**BM^N.; EB.; Z.; **O.**AP.

13457 **Catalogue photographique** du **ciel.** Observatoire astronomique d'Alger. *Cat. photogr. Ciel* [1886–13] **L.**SC. 05–13. [*C. as:* 41166]

13458 **Catalogue** de **profils** d'**ailes.** Service des recherches de l'aéronautique. Paris. *Cat. Profils Ailes* [1930–] **L.**P. 30–31.

13459 **Catalogue** des **publications. Office national d'études** et de **recherches aéronautiques.** Chatillon-sous-Bagneux. *Cat. Publs Off. natn. Étud. Rech. aéronaut.* [1951–] **L.**P.

13460 **Catalogue** of **Scientific Papers.** London. *Cat. scient. Pap.* [1867–25] **L.**AS.; BM.; BM^N. imp.; C.; E.; G.; GL.; K.; L.; MO.; P.; R.; S.; SC.; TD.; UC.; Z.; **Abd.**U.; **Abs.**N. 09–16; **Bm.**U. 02–20; T. 02–11; U.; **Bn.**U.; **Br.**U.; **C.**PH. 67–02; **Cr.**P. 67–02; U.; **Dn.**U.; **E.**A. 02–20; B.; F.; R.; U. 03–25; **G.**M.; U.; **Ld.**P.; U.; **Lv.**P. 67–00; U.; **M.**P.; U.; **Nw.**A.; P.; **O.**R.; **Sa.**; **Sh.**U.   [*C. as:* 23825]

13461 **Catalogue** des **thèses** et **écrits académiques.** Ministère de l'instruction publique. Paris. *Cat. Thèses Écrits acad., Paris*

13461^c **Catalogus** van **normen.** Nederlands normalisatie-instituut. 's-Gravenhage. *Cat. Norm. Ned.* **L.**P. (curr.) [*Supplement to:* 35006]

13462 **Cataluña textil.** Badalona. *Cataluña text.* **L.**SC. 25–; **M.**C. 23–27.

13463 **Catalyst.** American Chemical Society. Easton, Pa. *Catalyst, Easton* [1916–] **L.**P. 26–28; **Y.**

13464 **Catalyst.** Research Institute for Catalysts, Hokkaido Imperial University. Tokyo. *Catalyst, Hokkaido* [1946–] **Y.**

13465 **Catalyst.** Shell Chemical Company. London. *Catalyst, Lond.* [1959–] **L.**AV.; BM.; P. (curr.); **Co.**T. (curr.); **E.**R. 59–; **H.**U.; **Ld.**P. (5 yr.); **Y.**

13466 **Cathode Press.** Machlett Laboratories. Springdale, Conn. *Cathode Press* **L.**P. 60–; **Y.**

13467 **Catholic Medical Guardian.** London. *Cath. med. Guard.* [1923–41] **L.**BM.; MA. 29–41; MD. 38–40; **Abs.**N. 24–41; **C.**UL.; **Db.** 32–36: 40; **O.**R.   [*C. in:* 13468]

13468 **Catholic Medical Quarterly.** Cambridge. *Cath. med. Q.* [1947–] **L.**MA. 51–; **C.**UL.; **Db.**; **M.**MS.

13469 **Catholic Nurse.** Journal of the Catholic Nurses Guild. London. *Cath. Nurse* [1933–] **L.**BM.

13470 **Catholic Pharmacist.** Croydon. *Cath. Pharmst* **L.**BM. 37–.

Catholic University of **America Biological Series.** *See* 7079.

13471 **Cattle Breeder.** Cambridge. *Cattle Breed.* [1952–] **C.**A.; **E.**AB.; **N.**U. 54– imp.

13472 **Cattleman.** Fort Worth, Tex. *Cattleman* **E.**AB. 26: 39: 51 imp.

13473 **Caucho.** Boletín de información del consorcio de fabricantes de artículos de caucho. Madrid. *Caucho* [1958–] **Sy.**R.

13474 **Cavanillesia.** Barcinone. *Cavanillesia* [1928–38] **L.**BM^N.; K.; L.; **E.**B.

13475 **Cave Notes.** Cave Research Associates. San Franciso. *Cave Notes* [1959–] **L.**BM^N.

13476 **Cave Science.** Settle, Yorks. *Cave Sci.* [1947–] **L.**BM.; BM^N.; GM.; U.; **Bm.**P.; **Br.**P.; U.; **C.**UL.; **Cr.**M. 47–51; U.; **E.**A.; **Ex.**U.; **G.**M. 47–51; **Ld.**P.; **M.**P.; **N.**T. (5 yr.); **O.**R.; **Sh.**P.; **Y.**

13477 **Cave Studies.** Cave Research Associates. San Francisco. *Cave Stud.* [1953–] **L.**BM^N.; **Y.**

13478 **Caves** and **Caving.** Settle, Yorks. *Caves Caving* [1937–38] **L.**BM.; GM.; SC.; **C.**UL.; **Ld.**P.; **M.**P.; **O.**R

13479 **Caving.** Westminster Speleological Group. London. *Caving* [1951–] **L.**BM.; BM^N. 51.

13480 **Cawthron Institute Monographs.** Nelson, N.Z. *Cawthron Inst. Monogr.* [1939–] **L.**BM.; SC.; **Br.**A. imp.; **C.**A.

13481 **Cawthron Institute Pasture** and **Soils Research Publications.** Nelson, N.Z. *Cawthron Inst. Past. Soils Res. Publs* [1929–44] **L.**BM. 36–44; SC. 32–44 imp.; **Br.**A. 34–43 imp.

13482 **Cawthron Institute Publications.** Nelson, N.Z. *Cawthron Inst. Publs* [1935–] **L.**BM. 36–; SC.; **Br.**A. 36– imp.; **O.**RE. 47–51 imp.

13483 **Cawthron Institute** of **Scientific Research.** Nelson, N.Z. *Cawthron Inst. scient. Res.* **L.**EB. (ent.) 21–; P. 21–33.

Cawthron Institute Soil and **Pasture Research Publications.** *See* 13481.

13484 **Cawthron Lectures Series.** Cawthron Institute of Scientific Research. Nelson, N.Z. *Cawthron Lect. Ser.* [1916–] **L.**BM. 20–; BM^N. 27– imp.; **Abs.**A. 25–; **C.**A.; **E.**R. 28–; **Rt.**; **Y.**

13485 **Caxton Magazine** (and British Stationer). London. *Caxton Mag.* [1901–58] **L.**BM.; P.; SB.; **Abs.**N. 12–58; **E.**A.; HW. 29–58; T. 01–37; **G.**M.; **Lh.**P. 29–58 imp.; **M.**T. (1 yr); **N.**P. 01–15; **Nw.**A. 01–36 imp.; **O.**B. 01–36; **Y.**   [*C. in:* 28713]

13486 **Ceará agrícola.** Ceará. *Ceará agric.* [1937–]

13487 **Cedara Memoirs.** Cedara School of Agriculture. *Cedara Mem.* **Rt.** 09–12.

13488 **Cedro.** Revista del Instituto de estudios de jardinería y arte paisajista. Madrid. *Cedro* [1956–] **L.**HS.; K. imp.

13489 **Ceiba.** A scientific journal issued by the Escuela agrícola panamerica. Tegucigalpa. *Ceiba* [1950–] **L.**BM^N.; HS.; K.; TP. 62– (English ed.); **Y.**

13490 **Celanese Plastics.** New York. *Celan. Plast.* **L.**P. (curr.); **Lh.**P. 46–.

13491 **Cellon Bulletin.** Kingston-on-Thames. *Cellon Bull.* [1956–] **L.**P. (curr.); **Lv.**P.

13492 **Cellotex-meddelelser.** Oslo. *Cellotex-Meddr* **L.**P. 28–.

13493 **Cellule.** Lierre, etc. *Cellule* [1884–] **L.**BM.; BM^N.; L.; S. 84–38; SC.; UC. 00–13: 30; **Ba.**I. 24–37; **Bl.**U. 52–; **Bm.**U. 39–; **Bn.**U. 49–; **C.**B. 84–04; P. 25–; UL.; **Db.**; **Dn.**U. 85–11; **E.**AG. 48–50; P. 87–13; U.; **G.**U.; **Ld.**U. 85–98: 48–; **Lv.**U. 00–; **M.**U. 23–; **N.**U. 47–; **Nw.**A. 28–; **O.**R.; **Pl.**M. 95–; **Sa.** 84–13; **Y.**

13493^a **Celluloid** und **plastische Massen.** *Celluloid plast. Mass.* [*Supplement to:* 21663]

13493^b **Celluloid-Industrie.** *Celluloid-Ind.* [*Supplement to:* 21663]

13494 **Cellulosa.** Roma. *Cellulosa* **L.**P. 38–40.

13495 **Cellulosa** e **carta.** *Cellulosa Carta* [1950–] **L.**TP. 53–; **O.**F. 53– imp.; **Y.**

13496 **Cellulose.** Grenoble. *Cellulose, Grenoble*

13497 **Cellulose.** New York. *Cellulose, N.Y.* **L.**P. 30.

13498 **Cellulose Industry.** Tokyo. *Cellulose Ind., Tokyo* [1925–] **L.**C. 29–41; P. 25–41 imp.; SC. 35–; **M.**C. 25–41.

13499 **Cellulose Plastics.** Wilmington, Del. *Cellulose Plast.* [1946–]

13500 **Cellulose-Chemie.** Berlin. *Cellulose-Chem.* [1920–36: 40–44] **L.**C. 25–36; IC.; P.; SC. 31–36; **Bm.**U. 31–36 imp.; **M.**C.; T.; **Pr.**FT. 29–36: 40–43; **Ste.** [*From 1920–36 as supplement to:* 37123; *from 1937–39 combined with:* 37123]

13501 **Celuloză şi hîrtie.** Bucureşti. *Celuloză Hîrt.* [1952–] **L.**BM. 56–; **O.**F.; **Y.** [*Until 1956 issued in:* 23147]

13502 **Cement.** Amsterdam. *Cement, Amst.* [1949–] **L.**P. 55–; **Wa.**B.; **Y.**
Cement. Moscow. *See* 55254.

13503 **Cement.** New York. *Cement, N.Y* [1900–13]

13504 **Cement.** New York. *Cement, N.Y.* [1956–] **L.**P. 58–; **Wa.**B. 56–57; **Y.** [*English translation of:* 55254]

13504° **Cement.** Washington. *Cement, Wash.* **Y.** 57–. [*English abstracts of:* 55254]

13505 **Cement Age.** New York. *Cem. Age* [1904–12] **L.**P. 10–12. [*C. in:* 15379°]

13506 **Cement och betong.** Stockholm, Malmo. *Cem. Betong* [1926–] **L.**P. 51–; **Wa.**B. 54–; **Y.**

13507 **Cement and Cement Manufacture.** London. *Cem. & Cem. Mf.* [1929–37] **L.**BM.; C. 30–37 imp.; P.; SC. 32–37; UC.; **Bm.**P.; **E.**A.; **G.**M. 36–37; **M.**P. 32–37; **O.**B.; **Sh.**P. 30–34; **Wa.**B. [*C. as:* 13512]

13507° **Cement and Concrete.** Tokyo. *Cem. Concr., Tokyo* **Y.**
Cement and Concrete Association. For titles beginning with the name of the Association: *See also* C.A.C.A.

13508 **Cement and Concrete Association Specifications.** London. *Cem. Concr. Ass. Specif.* **L.**P. 35–44: 54–.

13509 **Cement and Engineering News.** Chicago. *Cem. Engng News* [1896–24] **L.**P. 10–24. [*Merged in:* 48045]

13510 **Cement Era.** Chicago. *Cem. Era* [1903–17]

13511 **Cement, Lime and Gravel.** Birmingham. *Cem. Lime Gravel* [1928–] **L.**BM.; GL. 44–; GM.; IC. 29–; MI. 55–; P. 29–; **Bm.**P. imp.; U.; **E.**A. 57–; D. 45–; **G.**M. 37–; **Ld.**P. (5 yr.); **Lv.**P. 60– imp.; U. 29– imp.; **M.**P.; **Sh.**IO. 55–; **Wa.**B.; **Y.** [*C. of:* 8900]

13512 **Cement and Lime Manufacture.** London. *Cem. Lime Mf.* [1937–] **L.**BM.; IC. 37–39; P.; **Bm.**P.; **E.**A.; **G.**M.; **Lv.**P. 53–; **M.**P.; U. 56–; **O.**B.; **Sh.**IO. (5 yr.); **Y.** [*C. of:* 13507]

13513 **Cement Products.** Chicago. *Cem. Prod.* **L.**P. 24–43. [*Supplement to:* 48045]

13514 **Cement, wapno, gips.** Kraków, Warszawa. *Cem. Wapno Gips* [1930–] **Y.**

13515 **Cement World.** Chicago. *Cem. Wld* [1907–17] [*C. as:* 18099]

13516 **Cementer.** Duncan, Okla. *Cementer* **L.**P. 31.

13517 **Cement-, Ziegel-** u. **Künststeinindustrie.** Nürnberg. *Cem.-, Zieg. u. KünststInd.*

13518 **Cementindustrien.** Vejle. *Cementindustrien*

13519 **Cemento.** Milano. *Cemento, Milano* **L.**P.; **Wa.**B. 48–; [*C. of:* 13522]

13520 **Cemento.** Torino. *Cemento, Torino* [1904–23] **L.**P. 12–23. [*C. as:* 13521]

13521 **Cemento armato.** Torino, etc. *Cemento arm.* [1924–35] **L.**P.; **Wa.**B. 29–35. [*C. of:* 13520; *C. as:* 13522]

13522 **Cemento armato**—le **industrie** del **cemento.** Milano. *Cemento arm.—Ind. Cemento* [1936–40] **L.**P.; **Wa.**B. [*C. of:* 13521 and 23315; *C. as:* 13519]

13523 **Cemento fuso.** Trieste. *Cemento fuso*

13524 **Cemento-hormigon.** Barcelona. *Cemento-Horm.* **L.**P. 55–; **Y.**
Cenco News Chats. *See* 12876.

13525 **Cenicafé.** Chinchiná. *Cenicafé* [1957–] **L.**MO.; P.; **C.**A.; **Md.**H.; **Rt.** [*C. of:* 7789]

13526 **Census Report. Forestry Commission.** London. *Cens. Rep. For. Commn* [1952–53] **L.**BM.; **Ld.**P.; **O.**AP.; F.; R.; **Y.**

13527 **Census** of **Thunderstorms** in the **British Islands.** Huddersfield. *Cens. Thunderst. Br. Isl.* [1925–36] **L.**SC.; **Ld.**P.; **Rt.** 31–34. [*C. as:* 51516]

13528 **Centaur.** Sydney University Veterinary Society. Sydney. *Centaur* [1937–]

13529 **Centaurus.** Copenhagen. *Centaurus* [1950–] **L.**BM.; BM^N.; MA.; MD.; MO.; R.; SC.; U.; UC.; **Abd.**U.; **E.**P. 51–; U.; **G.**F. 50–53; **Ld.**U. 56–; **Nw.**A.; **O.**R.; **Sh.**U.; **Y.**

13530 **Centennial Review** of Arts and **Science.** College of Science and Arts, Michigan State University. East Lansing. *Centenn. Rev. Arts Sci. Mich. St. Univ.* [1957–] **L.**SC.

13531 **Centraalblad** der **bouwbedrijven** voor **Nederland** en **koloniën.** *Centraalbl. Bouwbedr. Ned. Kolon.*

13532 **Central.** Organ of the Central Technical College Old Students' Association. London. *Central* [1903–] **L.**BM.; **Abs.**N. 16–; **O.**B. 03–08; **Y.**

13533 **Central African Journal** of **Medicine.** Salisbury. *Cent. Afr. J. Med.* [1955–] **L.**MA.; MD.; S.; SH. (1 yr); TD.; **Br.**U.; **E.**P. 55–; S; **O.**R.; **Y.**

13534 **Central African Pharmaceutical Journal.** Bulawayo. *Cent. Afr. pharm. J.* [1956–] **L.**PH. [*C. of:* 47708]

13535 **Central African Planter.** Songani, Zomba. *Cent. Afr. Plr* **L.**K.

13536 **Central Asian Review.** London. *Cent. Asian Rev.* [1953–] **L.**BM.; G.; **Abs.**U. 57–; **C.**UL.; **E.**A.; G. 54–59; **H.**U.; **Lv.**P.; **O.**B.
Central Asiatic Medical Journal. *See* 50698.

13537 **Central Association Bulletin.** Central Association of Photographic Societies. London. *Cent. Ass. Bull.* [1932–] **L.**PG. imp.

13537° **Central Nervous System** and **Behaviour.** Transactions of the Conferences. Josiah Macy Jr. Foundation. New York. *Central nerv. Syst. Behav. Trans. Confs Josiah Macy Jr Fdn* [1958–] **L.**MD. 58–60.

13538 **Central Provinces Veterinary Journal.** Nagpur. *Cent. Prov. vet. J.* **L.**V. 32–36 imp.

13539 **Central Review** of **Sericulture** and **Raw Silk Industry.** Tokyo. *Cent. Rev. Seric. raw Silk Ind.*

13540 **Central States Medical Magazine (Monitor).** Indianapolis. *Cent. St. med. Mag. (Monit.)* [*C. as:* 23096]
Centralblatt. *See* **Zentralblatt.**
Centralorgan. *See* **Zentralorgan.**

13541 **Centralstyrelsens** för **hästavelsförbunden** i **Finland publikationer.** Lahtis. *CentStyr. Hästavelsförb. Finl. Publr*

Centralzeitung. *See* **Zentralzeitung.**

Centre de **chimie théorique** de **France.** Publications. *See* 40928.

13542 **Centre** de **documentation sidérurgique.** Paris. *Centre Docum. sidérurg.* [1953–] **Cr.**I.

Centro academico de **medicina.** Pôrto Alegre. *See* 12859.

Centro de **asistencia médica para enfermos pobres.** México. *See* 12860.

13543 **Centro-América intelectual.** Revista científico-literaria. San Salvador. *Centro-Am. intelect.*

Centuria. Brno. *See* 48727.

13544 **Centurion.** Engineering Supplement. London. *Centurion* [1938–40] **L.**P.; **Sy.**R. [*C. of:* 13545]

13545 **Century Works Quarterly Review.** Engineering Supplement. London. *Century Wks q. Rev.* [1936–38] **L.**P.; **Sy.**R. [*C. as:* 13544]

13546 **Ceramic Abstracts.** Easton, Pa. *Ceramic Abstr.* [1922–] **L.**AV. 61–; DI. 44–; I.; P.; SC.; SI. 42–; **Abd.**U. 45–; **Br.**U. 22–27 imp.; **Ld.**U.; **M.**U. 25–40 imp.; **N.**U. 58–; **Sh.**IO. 48–; **Y.**

13547 **Ceramic Age.** Trenton, N.J. *Ceramic Age* [1927–] **L.**P.; **Bm.**P. 41–; **St.**R. 46–; **Y.** [*C. of:* 13564]

13548 **Ceramic Digest.** St. Albans. *Ceramic Dig.* **Bm.**C. (curr.).

13549 **Ceramic Forum.** Pittsburgh. *Ceramic Forum* [1934–]

13550 **Ceramic Industry.** Chicago. *Ceramic Ind.* [1923–] **L.**P. 54–; **Lv.**P. 59–; **Sh.**G.; **St.**R. 44–; **Y.**

13551 **Ceramic News.** Beverley Hills. *Ceramic News* [1952–] **St.**R. 55–; **Y.**

13552 **Ceramica.** Barcelona. *Ceramica, Barcelona* [1931–]

13553 **Ceramica.** Milano. *Ceramica, Milano* [1952–] **L.**DI. 58–; **St.**R. [*C. of:* 23129]

13554 **Ceramica.** Roma. *Ceramica, Roma* [1939–] **L.**P. 55–; **St.**R. 51–; **Y.**

13555 **Ceramiche e laterizi.** Milano. [1938–] *Ceramiche Laterizi* [*Replaces:* 23169]

13557 **Ceramics.** Leighton Buzzard, etc. *Ceramics* [1947–] **L.**C. 50–; I. (1 yr); P. 56–; **Lv.**P. 53– imp.; **M.**P. 56–; **Sh.**IO.; **St.**R.; **Y.**

13558 **Ceramics** in **Art** and **Industry.** Doulton & Co. London. *Ceramics Art Ind.* [1938–] **L.**BM.; P. 38–53; **Ld.**U. 45–; **M.**P.; **Y.** [*Suspended:* 1941–44]

Ceramics and **Glass.** Moscow. *See* 27339.

13559 **Céramique.** Paris. *Céramique* [1908–10] **L.**P. [*C. as:* 13560]

Céramique (*afterwards* et les matériaux de construction). Paris. *See* 13561.

13560 **Céramique** et **architecture.** Paris. *Céramique Archit.* [1912] **L.**P. [*C. of:* 13559]

13561 **Céramique** et les **matériaux** de **construction.** Paris. *Céramique Matér. Constr.* [1898–] **L.**P. 10–39.

13561° **Céramique moderne.** Paris. *Céramique mod.* **Y.**

13562 **Céramique** et **verrerie.** Paris. *Céramique Verr.* [1925–32] **Sh.**G. [*C. as:* 13563]

13563 **Céramique, verrerie, émaillerie.** Stockholm. *Céramique Verr. Émaill.* [1933–] **L.**SC. 34–39; **Sh.**G. 33–39. [*C. of:* 13562]

13564 **Ceramist.** Trenton, N.J. *Ceramist* [1921–26] **L.**P. 25–26; [*C. as:* 13547]

13565 **Céramiste limousin.** Limoges. *Céramiste limousin*

13566 **Cerberus Elektronik.** Bad Ragaz. *Cerberus Elektron.* [1951–] **L.**P. 58–.

13567 **Cereal Chemistry.** St. Paul, Minn., etc. *Cereal Chem.* [1924–] **L.**AM. 46– imp.; C.; P.; SC. 32–; TP. 46–; **Abd.**R. 35–; **Abs.**A. 52–; **Bm.**U.; **Bn.**U. 48–; **E.**CE. 42–; HW. 48–; **Ep.**D. 24–37 imp.; 46–; **G.**T.; **Hu.**G. 48–; **Lh.**FO. 44–; **Lv.**P. 38– imp.; **M.**C.; P. 56–; T. 47–; **R.**D. 47–; **Sal.**F.; **Sil.**; **Y.** [*Supersedes:* 25491]

13568 **Cereal News.** Ottawa. *Cereal News* [1952–] **C.**A. imp.

13569 **Cereal Science Today.** Minneapolis. *Cereal Sci. Today* [1956–] **L.**C.; P.; SC.; TP.; **C.**A.; **E.**CE.; **G.**T.; **Hu.**G.; **Lh.**FO.; **Lv.**P.; **R.**D. 56–59; **Sal.**F.; **Y.** [*C. of:* 53513]

13570 **Cerealia.** Rotterdam. *Cerealia*

13571 **Cerebral Palsy Bulletin.** London. *Cerebr. Palsy Bull.* [1958–61] **L.**BM.; H.; MA.; **Br.**U.; **Cr.**MD. [*C. as:* Developmental Medicine and Child Neurology]

13572 **Ceres.** Blätter für fortschrittlichen Gemüse- und Obstbau. Hamburg. *Ceres, Hamburg* **Md.**H. 48–49.

13573 **Ceres.** Revista bi-mensal de divulgação de ensinamentos teóricos e prácticos sobre agricultura, veterinária, indústrias rurais. Minas Gerais. *Ceres, Minas Gerais* [1939–43] **L.**TP. imp.; **C.**A.; **Md.**H. imp.; **Y.** [*C. as:* 46382]

Cern. Conseil européen de recherche nucléaire. *See* **CERN.**

13574 **Certainty.** Hubbard Association of Scientologists. London. *Certainty* [1954–] **L.**BM.; **C.**UL.; **E.**A. 54–55; **O.**R.

13575 **Certificated Engineer.** Johannesburg. *Certifd Engr* [1959–] **L.**BM.; EE.; **Y.** [*C. of:* 26217]

13576 **Certificates** and **Reports. Agricultural Machinery Testing Committee.** London. *Certifs Rep. agric. Mach. Test. Comm.* [1926–] **L.**P. 26–42; **C.**A. 31–; **O.**R. 31–. [1926–30 *issued with* 42673]

Certified Akers Laboratory. Chicago. *See* 12858.

13577 **Certified Milk.** Scranton, Pa., etc. *Certified Milk* **R.**D. 28– imp.

13578 **Certified Milk Conferences.** American Association of Medical Milk Commissioners. *Certified Milk Confs* [1907–35] **L.**MD. 27–31; S. 25–35; SC. 26–35; TD. 26–35; **G.**F. 25–35; **M.**MS. 25–35; **R.**D. 11: 27–35.

13579 **Cervello.** Giornale di neurologia. Napoli. *Cervello* [1922–] **L.**MA. 43–; MD. 58–.

13580 **Cesalpino.** Giornale medico della Provincia di Arezzo. Arezzo. *Cesalpino*

13581 **Česká dermatologie.** Praha. *Česká Derm.* **L.**MD. imp. [*C. as:* 13590]

13582 **Česká flora.** Praha-Vršovice. *Česká Flora*

13582° **Česká hospodyně.** *Česká Hospod.* [*Supplement to:* 22431]

13583 **Česká mykologie.** Praha. *Česká Mykol.* [1947–] **L.**BM. 53– imp.; BM[N].; K.; MY.; **Y.**

13584 **Česká neurologie a psychiatrie.** Praha. *Česká Neurol. Psychiat.*

13584° **Česká stomatologie.** *Česká Stomat.* [*Supplement to:* 13411]

13585 **Česká zemědělská bibliografie.** Praha. *Česká zeměd. Biblfie* [1941–] **L.**AM. 43–; SC.; **C.**A. 41–49; RT. 42–49 imp.

13585° **České listy hospodářské.** Věstník ustřední společnosti hospodářské pro království české. Praha. *České Listy hospod.* [1893–13]

13586 **České zahradnické listy.** Praha. *České zahr. Listy*

13587 **Českobrodsko a černokostelecko.** *Českobrod. Černokost.*

13588 **Českomoravský rybář.** Velké Mezeříčí. *Českomorav. Rybář*

13589 **Československá biologie.** Praha. *Čslká Biol.* [1952–58] **L.**BM. 53–58; C. 54–58; MA.; UC.; **Br.**A. 54; **C.**A. 53–58; **Pl.**M.; **Sal.** 54. [*International edition at:* 13704; *C. in:* 7049, 19779 and 19806]

13590 **Československá dermatologie.** Praha. *Čslká Derm.* **L.**MA. 46–; MD. [*C. of:* 13581]

13591 **Československá epidemiologie, mikrobiologie, imunologie.** Praha. *Čslká Epidem. Mikrobiol. Imunol.* [1956–] **L.**MC. 57; TD.; **Y.** [*C. of:* 13599]

13592 **Československá ethnografie.** Praha. *Čslká Ethnogr.* [1953–] **L.**AM.; BM. 55–; **O.**B.

13593 **Československá farmacie.** Praha. *Čslká Farm.* [1952–] **L.**C. 55–; MA.; PH. imp.; **Y.**

13594 **Československá fotografie.** Praha. *Cslká Fotogr.* [1931–50: 53–] **L.**PG. imp. [> 35361, 1950–52]

13595 **Československá fysiologie.** Praha. *Čslká Fysiol.* [1952–55] **L.**BM. 55; MA.; R. 53–55; UC. imp.; **Y.** [*International edition at:* 13705; *C. in:* 37711]

13596 **Československá gastroenterologie a výživa.** Praha. *Čslká Gastroent. Výž.* [1947–] **L.**MD. 60–; **Y.** [*C. of:* 20685]

13597 **Československá gynekologie** (*formerly* **gynaekologie**). *Čslká Gynek.* [1936–] **L.**MA. 47–; U. 48–; **M.**MS. 47–.

13598 **Československá hygiena.** Praha. *Čslká Hyg.* [1956–] **L.**TD.; **Y.**

13599 **Československá hygiena, epidemiologie, mikrobiologie.** Praha. *Čslká Hyg. Epidem. Mikrobiol.* [1952–55] **L.**TD. [*C. as:* 13591]

13600 **Československá matice rolnická.** Chrudim. *Čslká Matice roln.*

13601 **Československá mikrobiologie.** Praha. *Čslká Mikrobiol.* [1956–58] **Ld.**U. [*C. as:* 19806]

13602 **Československá morfologie.** Praha. *Čslká Morf.* [1953–] **L.**BM. 55–; **Y.**

13603 **Československá nemocnice.** Praha. *Čslká Nemocn.* [1929–]

13604 **Československá neurologie.** Praha. *Čslká Neurol.* [1956–] **L.**MA. [*C. from:* 34606]

13605 **Československá oftalmologie.** v Praze. *Čslká Oftal.* [1935–] **L.**OP. 51–.

13606 **Československá onkológia.** Bratislava. *Čslká Onkol.* [1954–56] **L.**CB.; MA. [*C. as:* 34511]

13607 **Československá otolaryngologie.** Praha. *Čslká Otolar.* [1952–] **L.**MA.

13608 **Československá parasitologie.** Praha. *Čslká Parasit.* [1954–] **L.**BM[N].; EB. 55–; TD. 55–; **Sal.** 55–.

13609 **Československá pediatrie.** Praha. *Čslká Pediat.* [1955–] **L.**MA. [*C. of:* 37286]

13610 **Československá psychiatrie.** Praha. *Čslká Psychiat.* [1956–] **L.**MA. [*C. from:* 34606]

13610° **Československá psychologie.** Praha. *Čslká Psychol.* **L.**BM. 60–.

13611 **Československá rentgenologie.** Praha. *Čslká Rentg.* [1955–] **L.**CB.; MD. 58–; **C.**R.; **E.**P. 56–. [*C. of:* 749]

13612 **Československá sbirka mikrobiologická.** Holesov. *Čslká Sbirka mikrobiol.* [1921–24]

13613 **Československá stomatologie.** Praha. *Čslká Stomat.* [1901–] **L.**D.; MA. 47–. [*Supplement to:* 13411]

13615 **Československé botanické listy.** Praha. *Čslké bot. Listy* [1948–] **L.**K. 48–52; **Bl.**U. 48–53; **Md.**H. 48–53.

13616 **Československé lesnicko-lovecké listy.** Brno. *Čslké lesn.-lov. Listy*

13617 **Československé letopisy musejní.** Čáslav. *Čslké Let. Mus.* **L.**BM. 02–.

13617° **Československé rybarstvi.** *Čslké Ryb.* **L.**AM. (1 yr) [*C. of:* 13631]

13618 **Československé spoje.** Praha. *Čslké Spoje* [1956–] **L.**BM. 57–; **Y.**

13618° **Československé státni lázne a zřidla.** Praha. *Čslké St. Lázne Zřidla* [1949–]

13619 **Československé zahradnické listy.** Praha. *Čslké zahr. Listy*

13620 **Československé zdravotnictví.** Praha. *Čslké Zdrav.* [1953–] **L.**BM. 57–.

13620° **Československý architekt.** Praha. *Čslký Archit.* **Y.**

Československý časopis pro **fysiku.** *See* 13421.

13621 **Československý Červený Kříž.** Praha. *Čslký červ. Kříž* [1953–]

13622 **Československý dřevařský věstník.** Česká Trebová. *Čslký dřev. Věst.*

13623 **Československý dřevoprůmysl.** Praha-Vršovice. *Čslký Dřevoprům.* [*C. of:* 17205]

13624 **Československý fotograf.** Praha. *Čslký Fotogr.*

13625 **Československý hornik.** Praha. *Čslký Hornik* **Y.**

13626 **Československý les.** Praha. *Čslký Les* **O.**F. 51. [*C. in:* 28449]

13627 **Československý lesnik.** Praha. *Čslký Lesn.*

13628 **Československý lnář.** Jindř. Hradec. *Čslký Lnář*

13629 **Československý odborný časopis opráv.** Chrudim. *Čslký odb. Čas. Opr.*

13630 **Ceskoslovenský ornitholog.** Přerov. *Čslký Orn.* [1934–] **O.**OR. 35: 45–49.

13631 **Československý rybář.** Vodnany, etc. *Čslký Rybář* [*C. as:* 13617°]

13631ª **Československý sborník lesnický.** *Čslký Sb. lesn.* [*Supplement to:* 21737]

13632 **Československý strojník a elektrotechnik.** Praha. *Čslký Strojník Elektrotech.*

13633 **Československý trh strojů a technických potřeb.** Frenštát p. R. *Čslký Trh Strojů tech. Potřeb*

13634 **Československý zemědělec.** Praha. *Čslký Zeměd.* [1920–39] [*C. as:* 13639]

13635 **Český drogista.** Praha. *Český Drog.*

13636 **Český obuvník.** Praha. *Český Obuv.*

13637 **Český včelař.** Praha. *Český Včel.* [1867–]

13638 **Český zahradník.** Písek. *Český Zahr.*

13639 **Český zemědělec.** Praha. *Český Zeměd.* [1940–] [*C. of:* 13634]

13640 **Český zvěrolékař.** v Hořici. *Český Zvěrolék.* [1891–]

13641 **Ceste i mostovi.** Zagreb. *Ceste Mostovi* **Ha.**RD.; **Y.**

13642 **Ceylon Administration Reports. Agriculture.** Colombo. *Ceylon Adm. Rep. Agric.* **L.**AM. 11–; BM.; BM^N. 24– imp.; EB. 11–; SC. 23–.

13643 **Ceylon Administration Reports** of the **Director of Fisheries.** Colombo. *Ceylon Adm. Rep. Dir. Fish.* [1940–] **L.**AM.; BM.; BM^N.; **Abd.**M.; **Dm.**; **Fr.** 40–54; **Pl.**M. 40–52. [*C. of:* 13646]

13644 **Ceylon Administration Reports. Mineralogical Survey.** Colombo. *Ceylon Adm. Rep. miner. Surv.* [1903–08] **L.**BM.; BM^N. 03–06; **Br.**U.; **Lv.**U.

13645 **Ceylon Administration Reports. Miscellaneous.** Colombo. *Ceylon Adm. Rep. misc.* **L.**BM^N. 83–15.

13646 **Ceylon Administration Reports. Report** of the **Marine Biologist.** Colombo. *Ceylon Adm. Rep. mar. Biol.* [1908–39] **L.**AM. 22–39; BM.; BM^N. 08–39 imp.; G. 27–31; SC. 28–39; Z. 10–38 imp.; **Abd.**M. 10–39 imp.; **Bn.**U. 29–39 imp.; **Dm.** 11–39; **Lo.** 22–39 imp.; **Lv.**U. 09–39 imp.; **M.**U. 10–38; **Mi.** 11–29; **Pl.**M. 09–39 imp. [*C. as:* 13643]

13647 **Ceylon Administration Reports. Veterinary.** Colombo. *Ceylon Adm. Rep. vet.* **L.**BM. 01–; EB. 11–; SC. 29–; **Lv.**U. 21–. [*From* 1930 *included in* 13642]

13648 **Ceylon Coconut Planters' Review.** Lunuwila. *Ceylon Cocon. Plrs Rev.* [1960–] **L.**P.; TP.; **Br.**A.; **C.**A.; **Md.**H.; **Y.**

13649 **Ceylon Coconut Quarterly.** Lunnwila. *Ceylon Cocon. Q.* [1950–] **L.**P.; TP.; **Br.**A. 51–; **C.**A.; **Md.**H.; **Rt.**; **Y.**

13651 **Ceylon Forester.** Colombo. *Ceylon Forester* [1895–98: 1953–] **L.**BM. 95–98; BM^N.; K.; TP.; **Bn.**U.; **E.**U.; **O.**F.; **Y.**

13652 **Ceylon Geographer.** Colombo. *Ceylon Geographer* [1957–] **L.**BM.; **E.**G.; **G.**M.; **Y.** [*C. of:* 9757]

13653 **Ceylon Health News.** Colombo. *Ceylon Hlth News* **L.**MA. 44–52★; TD. 40–47 imp. [*C. as:* 21974]

13654 **Ceylon Journal** of **Medical Science.** Colombo. *Ceylon J. med. Sci.* [1949–] **L.**BM. 54–; EB.; MC.; MD.; P.; S. 49–56; TD.; TP.; U.; UC.; **Abd.**U. 49–51; **Abs.**N.; **Bl.**U.; **Bm.**U.; **Br.**U.; **C.**P.; UL.; **Db.**; **E.**R.; U.; **G.**U.; **Ld.**U.; **Lv.**U.; **M.**U. 50–53 imp.; **Nw.**A.; **O.**R.; **R.**U.; **Sa.**; **Y.** [*C. of:* 13655 Sect. D.]

13655 **Ceylon Journal** of **Science.** Colombo. *Ceylon J. Sci.*

Section A. Botany. *See* 3183.

Section B. Zoology and geology. [*For* 1924–40 *see* 50633: 1944–57] **L.**AM.; BM.; BM^N.; EB.; G.; L.; P.; SC.; UC.; Z.; **Abd.**M.; **Abs.**N.; U. 44–53 imp.; **Bl.**U.; **Bm.**N.; U.; **Bn.**U. 44–47; **Br.**U.; **C.**B.; P.; UL.; **Cr.**M.; U.; **E.**C.; R.; U.; **G.**U.; **Ld.**U.; **Lo.** 44–46; **Lv.**U.; **M.**U.; **Nw.**A.; **O.**B.; H.; Z. 57; **Pl.**M.; **Sa.**; **Sh.**U.; **Sy.**R.; **Y.** [*C. in:* 13656]

Section C. Fisheries. *See* 9756.

Section D. Medical science [1924–41] **L.**BM^N.; EB.; LI. 24–39; MD.; P.; S.; TD.; TP.; UC.; **Abd.**U. 24–38; **Abs.**N.; **Bl.**U.; **Bm.**U.; **Bn.**U. 25–41 imp.; **Br.**U.; **C.**P.; UL.; **Db.**; **E.**R.; U. imp.; **G.**U.; **Ld.**U.; **Lv.**U.; **M.**U.; **Nw.**A.; **O.**R.; **R.**U. 27–41; **Sa.**; **Y.** [*C. as:* 13654]

Section E. Mathematics, physics and meteorology. [1926–57] **L.**MO. 26–29; P.; SC.; **Abs.**N.; **Bl.**U.; **Bm.**U.; **Bn.**U. 26–36; **Br.**U.; **C.**P.; UL.; **Cr.**U.; **Db.**; **E.**R.; U.; **G.**U.; **Ld.**U.; **M.**U.; **Nw.**A. 26–29; **O.**R.; **R.**U.; **Sa.**; **Sh.**U.; **Y.** [*C. in:* 13657]

Section F. [*Not published*]

Section G. Archaeology, ethnology (anthropology). [1924–33: 40–57] **L.**AN.; BM.; MO.; UC.; **Abs.**N.; **Bm.**U.; **Bn.**U. imp.; **Br.**U.; **C.**P. imp.; UL.; **Cr.**U.; **Db.**; **E.**R.; U.; **G.**U.; **Ld.**U.; **Lv.**U.; **Nw.**A. 26–29; **O.**R.; **R.**U.; **Sa.**; **Sh.**U.; **Y.** [*C. in:* 13657]

13656 **Ceylon Journal** of **Science. Biological Sciences.** Colombo. *Ceylon J. Sci. biol. Sci.* [1957–] **L.**AM.; BM.; BM^N.; EB.; G.; L.; P.; SC.; TP.; UC.; Z.; **Abd.**M.; **Abs.**N.; U.; **Bl.**U.; **Bm.**N.; U.; **Br.**U.; **C.**A.; B.; P.; UL.; **Cr.**M.; U.; **Dm.** 57; **E.**R.; U.; **G.**U.; **Ld.**U.; **Lo.**; **Lv.**U.; **M.**U.; **Md.**H.; **Nw.**A.; **O.**B.; H.; R.; **Pit.**F.; **Pl.**M.; **R.**U.; **Rt.**; **Sa.**; **Sh.**U.; **Y.** [*C. of:* 13655, Sections A, B, and C.]

13657 **Ceylon Journal** of **Science. Physical Sciences.** Colombo. *Ceylon J. Sci. phys. Sci.* [1958–] **L.**AM.; BM.; MO.; SC.; UC.; **Abs.**N.; **Bl.**U.; **Bm.**U.; **Bn.**U.; **Br.**U.; **C.**P.; UL.; **Cr.**U.; **Db.**; **E.**R.; U.; **G.**U.; **Ld.**U.; **Lv.**U.; **O.**R.; **R.**U.; **Sa.**; **Y.** [*C. of:* 13655 Sections E and G.]

13658 **Ceylon Journal** of **Veterinary Science.** Colombo. *Ceylon J. vet. Sci.* [1941–] **L.**BM. 45– imp.; V. 46–52.

Ceylon Marine Biological Reports. *See* 42995.

13659 **Ceylon Medical Journal.** Colombo. *Ceylon med. J.* [1952–] **L.**BM. 56–; MA.; MD.; TD.; **G.**U.; **Ld.**U.; **Lv.**M.; **Sal.** 57–; **Y.** [*C. of:* 25763]

13660 **Ceylon Tea Quarterly.** *Ceylon Tea Q.* **L.**MY. 28–.

13661 **Ceylon Veterinary Journal.** Colombo, Peradeniya. *Ceylon vet. J.* [1953–] **L.**BM. 55–; V.; VC.; **Sal.**; **W.**

13662 **Chacaras e quintaes.** São Paulo. *Chacaras Quint.* **L.**EB. 14–32.

13663 **Chacra.** Revista mensual de agricultura, ganadería e industria. Buenos Aires. *Chacra*

13664 **Chaldean.** Chaldean Society. *Chaldean* [1917–27] **L.**AS.; BM. 18–27; **O.**B. 18–27.

13665 **Chaleur** et **climats.** Bruxelles. *Chal. Clim.* **L.**P. 58–.; **Y.**

13666 **Chaleur** et **industrie.** Lyon. *Chal. Ind.* [1920–] **L.**NF. 23–26; I. (2 yr.); P.; SC. 23–; **G.**U. 58–; **Ld.**U. 20–31; **Nw.**A. 23–32 imp.; **Sh.**G. 23–40; **Y.** [*Suspended:* May 1940–Dec. 1944]

13667 **Chalmers tekniska högskolas handlingar.** Göteborg. *Chalmers tek. Högsk. Handl.* [1941–] **L.**AV. 41–46: 56– imp.; C. 42–; EE. 47– imp.; P. 50–; SC.; **Db.**; **G.**E. 56–; U. 52–; **Wo.** 48–; **Y.**

13667° **Changes** in **Farm Production** and **Efficiency.** Agricultural Research Administration. Washington. *Changes Fm Prod. Effic.* [1956–] **L.**BM.

13668 **Changing Scene.** Eden Field Club, Penrith & District Natural History Society, Kendal Natural History Society. *Changing Scene* **L.**BM^N. 57–.

13668° **Chanic revue.** Bruxelles. *Chanic Revue* [1959–] **L**.P.

13669 **Channel.** Official Journal of the Scientific Society of the R. Technical College. Glasgow. *Channel* [1917–23] **L**.P. imp.

13670 **Chanousia.** Torino. *Chanousia* **L**.BM^N. 28–37.

13671 **Chanteclair.** Romainville. *Chanteclair* **L**.MD. 08–09.

13672 **Chantiers.** Alger. *Chantiers, Alger* **L**.BA. 36–38.

13673 **Chantiers.** Boulogne-sur-Seine. *Chantiers, Boulogne* **L**.BA. 33–35.

13674 **Chantiers** dans le **monde.** Bruxelles. *Chantiers Monde* **L**.BA. 48–.

13675 **Chapingo.** Sociedad de alumnos de la Escuela nacional de agricultura. Chapingo. *Chapingo* [1947–] **Hu**.G. 49–51; **Rt**. 55.

    Character Figures of **Solar Phenomena.** *See* 9768.

13676 **Character** and **Personality.** London. *Character Person.* [1932–45] **L**.BM.; MA. 32–39; MD.; PS.; U.; **Abd**.U. 40–45; **Bl**.U. 32–42 imp.; **Bm**.U.; **Br**.U.; **C**.PS.; **E**.U. imp.; **Ld**.U. 34–42; **Lv**.M.; **O**.B.; **R**.U. [*C. as:* 26652]

13677 **Charbon.** Paris. *Charbon*

13678 **Charbon** et **chauffage.** Neuilly-sur-Seine. *Charb. Chauff.* [1954–] **L**.P. 57–; **Y**.

13679 **Charing Cross Hospital Gazette.** London. *Charing Cross Hosp. Gaz.* [1899–] **L**.BM.; MA.; MD. 29–; S. 99–28 imp.: 34–; U. 46–; **Br**.U. imp; **M**.MS. 30–42 imp.; **Nw**.A. 30–.

13680 **Charité-annalen.** Berlin. *Charité-Annln* [1874–13] **L**.MD. 01–13; S.; **Bm**.U. 75–85; **Dn**.U.; **E**.P.; **G**.U. 75–13; **M**.MS.; **O**.R.

13681 **Charleroi-Jeumont.** Jeumont, Charleroi. *Charleroi-Jeumont* [1939–47] **L**.EE. 46–47; P.; SC.; **Br**.U. 46–47; **M**.P.; **Nw**.A. 39: 46–47. [*C. of:* 12 and 25332; *C. as:* 9 and 47355]

13682 **Charles Innes's Diary.** Animal Health Trust. London. *Charles Innes's Diary* [1952–] **E**.A. 52–57.

13683 **Charleston Museum Leaflet.** Charleston, S.C. *Charleston Mus. Leafl.* **L**.BM^N. 30–; z. (zool.) 33–45; **Db**. 33–; **Y**.

13684 **Charleston Museum Quarterly.** Charleston, S.C. *Charleston Mus. Q.* [1923–32] **L**.BM^N.; SC. [*C. of:* 9769]

13685 **Charlotte Medical Journal.** Charlotte, N.C. *Charlotte med. J.*

13686 **Chartered Civil Engineer.** London. *Chart. civ. Engr* [1949–57] **L**.AV. 56–57, BM.; P.; QM. 50–57; RI.; SC.; U.; **Abd**.U.; **Bl**.U.; **Bm**.T. 56–57; **Bn**.U.; **Br**.U.; **C**.ENG. (3 yr.); UL.; **Cr**.U.; **Db**.; **E**.A.; U.; **G**.U.; **Ld**.U.; **M**.P.; T.; U. imp.; **Nw**.A.; **O**.R.; **Sh**.IO.; **Y**.

13687 **Chartered Marine Engineer.** London. *Chart. mar. Engr* [1950–51] **L**.EE.; P.; QM.; SC.; U.; **Bm**.C.; **Br**.U.; **E**.U. imp.; **G**.U.; **Ld**.U.; **Nw**.A. [*C. in:* 53759]

13688 **Chartered Mechanical Engineer.** London. *Chart. mech. Engr* [1954–] **L**.AV.; BA.; BM.; DI. 54–57; EE.; IC.; MT.; NF.; P.; QM.; RI.; SC.; U.; **Abd**.U.; **Abs**.N.; **Bl**.U.; **Bm**.C.; P.; T. 56–; U.; **Bn**.U.; **Br**.P.; U.; **Bra**.P.; **C**.ENG.; UL.; **Co**.T.; **Cr**.P.; **Db**.; **Dn**.U.; **E**.A.; HW.; R.; T. imp.; U.; **F**.A.; **G**.E.; I.; M.; T.; U.; **Lc**.A.; **Ld**.P. U.; **Li**.M (1 yr); **Lv**.P.; **M**.C.; D. 54–57; P.; T.; U.; **N**.T.;

Nw.A.; P.; **O**.R.; **Rn**.B.; **Sh**.M.; **Sil**.; **St**.R.; **Ste**.; **Sw**.U.; **Wd**.; **Y**. [*C. of:* 26228°]

13689 **Chartered Surveyor.** London. *Chart. Surv.* [1955–] **L**.AM.; BA.; BM.; EE.; MIE.; NC. 61–; P.; SC.; SH. (1 yr); **Abs**.N.; U.; **Bm**.P.; **Br**.U.; **C**.UL.; **Cr**.P.; **Db**.; **E**.A.; U.; **G**.U. 57–; **Ld**.U.; **M**.P.; **N**.T. 56–; **Nw**.A.; **O**.AEC.; B.; R.; **Rt**.; **Sh**.M.; **Sil**.; **Y**. [*C. of:* 26817 and 53984]

13690 **Chase Diamond.** Waterbury, Conn. *Chase Diam.* **L**.NF. 23–; P. 23–27.

13691 **Chat.** Bulletin of the Carolina Bird Club Inc. Columbia. *Chat* **L**.BM^N. 56– imp.

13692 **Châtel-Guyon journal.** Clermont-Ferrand. *Châtel-Guyon J.*

13692° **Chaud—froid—plomberie.** Paris. *Chaud—Froid—Plomb.* **Y**.

13693 **Chaudesaigues thermal.** Saint-Flour. *Chaudesaigues therm.*

13693° **Chaudronnerie-tolerie.** Paris. *Chaudronn.-Tolerie* **Y**.

13694 **Chauffage industriel moderne.** Paris. *Chauff. ind. mod.*

13695 **Chauffage** et **industries sanitaires.** Paris. *Chauff. Ind. sanit.*

13696 **Chauffage** au **mazout.** Paris. *Chauff. Mazout* [1956–60] **L**.P. 57–60. [*C. as:* 20698]

13697 **Chauffage moderne pratique.** Paris. *Chauff. mod. prat.*

13698 **Chauffage** et **ventilation.** Paris. *Chauff. Vent.* **L**.P. 28–36* [*C. as:* 13699]

13699 **Chauffage-ventilation-conditionnement.** Paris. *Chauff.-Vent.-Condit.* [1937–] **L**.P. imp.; **Y**. [*C. of:* 13698]

13700 **Chaufferie.** Paris. *Chaufferie*

13701 **Cheap Steam.** London, etc. *Cheap Steam* [1916–56] **L**.BM.; EE. 16–42 imp.; P.; SC. 30–56; **Bm**.P.; **Br**.P. (2 yr.); **Cr**.P. 16–30; **G**.PH. 42–56; **M**.P. imp.; **N**.U. 54–56; **Nw**.A. 25–26; **Sw**.U. 20–56 imp.

13702 **Cheese Abstracts.** Milwaukee. *Cheese Abstr.* [1955–] **L**.P.

13703 **Cheiron.** Veterinär-historisches Jahrbuch. Leipzig. *Cheiron* [1936–38] [*C. of:* 56583; *Replaced by:* 5959]

13704 **Chekhoslovatskaya biologiya.** Praha. Чехословацкая биология. *Chekh. Biol.* [1952–54] **L**.BM^N.; Z.; **C**.A. 53–54 imp.; **Rt**. 53–54 [*International edition of* 13589. *C. as:* 19779]

13705 **Chekhoslovatskaya fiziologiya.** Praga. Чехословацкая физиология. *Chekh. Fiziol.* [1952–?] **L**.BM. 55– imp. [*International edition of:* 13595; *C. in:* 37711]

    Chekhoslovatskiĭ fizicheskiĭ zhurnal. Чехословацкий физический журнал. *See* 16241.

    Chekhoslovatskiĭ matematicheskiĭ zhurnal. Чехословацкий математический журнал. *See* 16242.

13705° **Chekhoslovatskoe meditsinskoe obozrenie.** Praha. Чехословацкое медицинское обозрение. *Chekh. med. Obozr.* [1955–]

13706 **Chelověk.** Leningrad. Человѣкъ. *Chelověk* [1928] **L**.AN.; BM.

13707 **Chelověk i priroda.** Petrograd. Человѣкъ и природа. *Chelověk Prir.* [1920–26]

13708 **Cheltenham College Natural History Magazine.** Cheltenham. *Cheltenham Coll. nat. Hist. Mag.*

13709 **Cheltenham** and **District Naturalists' Society Journal.** Cheltenham. *Cheltenham Distr. Nat. Soc. J.* O.OR. [*C. as:* 35085]

13709ᶜ **Chemia.** Buenos Aires. *Chemia, B. Aires* **Y.**

13710 **Chemia analityczna.** Warszawa. *Chemia analit.* [1956–] **L.**C.; **Y.**

13711 **Chemia stosowana.** Warszawa. *Chemia stosow.* [1957–] **L.**BM.; C.; **Y.**

13712 **Chemical Abstracts.** Easton, Pa., etc. *Chem. Abstr.* [1907–] **L.**AM. 40–; AV. 38– imp.; B. 24–; C.; CB. imp.; H. 39–55; I. 12–; IC.; LE. 46–; LI. 07–15: 37–; MC. 15–; MD. 26– imp.; MY. 49–55; NF. 23–; NP. 25–; P.; PH. 17–; PL. 45–; PR. 26–; PT. 45–54; QM. 26–; RI.; SC.; SH. 46–; SI. 33–; TD.; TP. 20–; U. 33–; UC. 09–; UCH.; **Abd.**M. 47–; R. 25–; U. 20–; **Abs.**U. 09–; **Ba.**I. 28–; **Bl.**U. 18–; **Bm.**C.; P.; T. 12– imp.; U. 17–; **Bn.**U. 09–; **Br.**A. 46–; P. 20–50; U.; **C.**A. 21–; APH. 20–; BI. 20–; CH. 19–; HO. 19–; P.; R. 44–; **Co.**T. 47–; **Cr.**MD. 53–; U. 20–; **Db.** 09–; **Dn.**U. 35–; E.CE. 17–; HW. 12–; SW. 16–; U.; W. 22–; **Ep.**D. 07–09: 17–; **Ex.**U.; **F.**A.; FR. 46–55; **G.**M. 13–; T. 10–; U.; **H.**U.; **Je.** 28–; **Lc.**A. 46–; **Ld.**P. 36–; U. 20–; W. 11–; **Lo.** 51–; **Lv.**P. 11– imp.; U.; **M.**C.; P. 16–; T. 20–; U. 18–; **Md.**H. 28–31; **Mi.** 46–; **N.**T.; U. 20–; **Nw.**A. 26–; **O.**BI.; P. 41–; PC. 28–; PH. 48–; R.; **Pl.**M. 15–60; **R.**D. 20–; **Rt.** 20–; **Sa.** 30–; **Sal.**F. 10–; **Sh.**IO. 20–; SC. 39–; U. 21–; **Sw.**U. 21–; **Sy.**R.; **W.**; **We.**K. 18–; **Y.** [*C. of:* 46183]

13713 **Chemical Abstracts. Thornton Research Centre.** Chester, Ellesmere Port. *Chem. Abstr. Thornton Res. Cent.* **L.**P. (curr.); **Y.**

13714 **Chemical Age.** London. *Chem. Age, Lond.* [1919–] **L.**AV. 38–39: 52–; BM.; C.; DI. 51–52; H. (curr.); I. (1 yr); MA. 50–; MC. 55–; P.; PR. 56–; TP. 26–; UC. 39–; **Abs.**N.; **Bm.**C. (1 yr); P. 20–; U.; **C.**UL.; **Db.**; **E.**A.; U. 23– imp.; **Ep.**D. 37–; **G.**M.; T. 19–54; U.; **Ld.**P. 52–; U. 19–40; **Lv.**U. 24–; **M.**C. (2 yr.); D. 25– imp.; P.; T. 20–51: (5 yr.); **N.**U. 36–39; **Nw.**A. 39–52 imp.; P. 52–; **O.**R.; **R.**D. 19–41 v. imp.: 47–; **Sh.**IO. 45–; **Sw.**U. 19–32 imp.; **Sy.**R. 23–; **Wd.**; **Y.**

13715 **Chemical Age.** New York, etc. *Chem. Age, N.Y.* [1920–25] **L.**C.; P. [*C. of:* 13726; *C. in:* 13764]

13716 **Chemical Age** of **India.** Bombay. *Chem. Age India* **L.**P. 60–; **Y.**

13717 **Chemical Age Year Book.** London. *Chem. Age Yb.* [1922–] **L.**BM. 24–; P. 29–; SC. (1 yr); UC. 31–; **Abs.**N. 23– imp.; **Abs.**U. 23–; **Bm.**P. 25–; **E.**A. 32–; **G.**M. 35–; **Ld.**P. (curr.); U. 23–; **Lv.**P. 24–; **O.**B. 24–43.
Chemical Annual. See 55762.
Chemical and **Biological Survey** of the **Waters** of **Illinois.** See 22773 and 57184.

13718 **Chemical Bulletin.** Chicago. *Chem. Bull., Chicago* [1919–] **L.**MT. [*C. of:* 13871]

13719 **Chemical Bulletin. Department** of **Agriculture, British Guiana.** Georgetown. *Chem. Bull. Dep. Agric. Br. Guiana* [1930–] **Rt.**

13719ᶜ **Chemical Buyers Guide.** Toronto. *Chem. Buy. Guide* **L.**P. (curr.)

13720 **Chemical, Color** and **Oil Record.** New York. *Chem. Color Oil Rec.* [*C. in:* 13764]

13721 **Chemical Corps Journal.** Washington. *Chem. Cps J.* [1946–]

13722 **Chemical Data Bulletin Series.** Climax Molybdenum Company. New York. *Chem. Data Bull. Ser. Climax Molybdenum Co.* [1954–] **L.**P.

13723 **Chemical Developments Abroad.** Washington. *Chem. Dev. abroad* **M.**P. 36–.

13724 **Chemical Digest.** New York. *Chem. Dig.* **L.**P. (curr.)

13725 **Chemical Engineer.** London. *Chem. Engr, Lond.* [1956–] **L.**BM.; PR.; SC.; **Ld.**P.; **Y.** [*C. of:* 41473]

13726 **Chemical Engineer.** New York, etc. *Chem. Engr, N.Y.* [1904–20] **L.**C. 19–20; P. 10–20. [*C. as:* 13715]

13727 **Chemical Engineering.** Albany, N.Y. *Chem. Engng, Albany* [1946–] **L.**AM.; AV. imp.; BM.; C.; I.; IC.; MI. 48–50; NF.; P.; PR.; PT.; SC.; SI.; U. 48–; **Bm.**C. 59–; T. 46–57 imp.; C.ENG.; **Db.** 57–; E.CE. 55–; SW.; U.; **G.**T.; U. 47– imp.; **Ld.**U.; **Lh.**FO. 46–49; **Lv.**P. imp.; **M.**D. 47–; P.; T.; U.; **Nw.**A. 30–32: 46–; **Sh.**P.; **Ste.**; **Wd.**; **We.**K. 47–; **Y.** [*C. of:* 13752]

13728 **Chemical Engineering.** Dover. *Chem. Engng, Dover* [1911–35] **L.**BM.; C. 11–23 imp.; P. 11–25; SC. 14–29; **G.**M. 11–16; **Ld.**U. 11–25; **M.**D. 17–21; U. 11–25 imp.; **O.**R. 11–24. [*Suspended* 1925–29]
Chemical Engineering. Kharkov, Moscow. See 27394ª.

13729 **Chemical Engineering.** Society of Chemical Engineers, Japan. Tokyo. *Chem. Engng, Tokyo* **L.**C. 53–; P. 60–; **Y.**

13729ᶜ **Chemical Engineering Bulletin. Tennessee Valley Authority.** *Chem. Engng Bull. T.V.A.* **Y.**

13730 **Chemical Engineering Catalog.** New York. *Chem. Engng Cat.* [1916–] **L.**C. 18–19; P. 16–40; **G.**M. 19: 23–32: 36– imp.; **Y.**

13731 **Chemical Engineering** and **Chemical Catalogue.** London. *Chem. Engng chem. Cat.* [1925–34] **L.**P.; **Bm.**P. 29–33; **Ld.**U.; **O.**B. [*C. as:* 13745]

13732 **Chemical Engineering Costs Quarterly.** Dover, U.S.A. *Chem. Engng Costs Q.* [1951–] **Ep.**D. 55–.

13733 **Chemical Engineering Data Book.** London. *Chem. Engng Data Bk* **L.**P. 58–; SC. 49–; **Ld.**P.

13734 **Chemical** and **Engineering Data Series.** Washington. *Chem. Engng Data Ser.* [1956–58] **L.**C. 56–57; P.; **Ld.**P.; **M.**T.; U.; **Sh.**IO.; **Ste.**; **Wd.** [*Contained in:* 23197; *C. as:* 25773]

13735 **Chemical Engineering** and **Mining Review.** Melbourne. *Chem. Engng Min. Rev.* [1917–60] **L.**BM.; C. 28–53 imp.; I (2 yr.); MI.; P.; **Y.** [*C. of:* 32011; *C. as:* 32001]

13736 **Chemical** and **Engineering News.** Easton, Pa., etc. *Chem. Engng News* [1942–] **L.**AV.; BM. 49–; C.; H. (curr.); LE. 56–; P.; PH. 48–; PL. 46–; PR.; SC.; TP.; UC.; **Bm.**U.; **Br.**P.; **C.**CH. 57–; P.; UL.; **Cr.**U. 42–55; **Db.**; **E.**SW. 48–; U. 47–; **Ep.**D.; **F.**A.; **G.**M.; T (1 yr); **H.**U. 53–; **Ld.**P. 51–; U.; W.; **Lh.**FO.; P. 45–49; **Lv.**P. 41–; U.; **M.**C. (curr.); D.; P.; T (5 yr.); U.; **N.**U.; **Nw.**A.; **R.**D.; **Rt.**; **Sa.**; **Sal.**F. 49–; **Sh.**G.; P.; **Sy.**R.; **Wd.**; **We.**K.; **Y.** [*C. of:* 1926]

13737 **Chemical Engineering Progress.** New York. *Chem. Engng Prog.* [1947–] **L.**AV. 61–; C.; I.; IC.; KC. 52–; P.; QM. 50–; SC.; UC.; **Bm.**P.; T. 58–; U.; **Db.** 49–; E.U. 47–58; **Ep.**D.; **F.**A. 52–; **G.**M.; T.; **Lc.**A. 54–; **Ld.**U.; **Lv.**P. 47– imp.; **M.**C. 47–61 imp.; D.; P. imp.; T.; **N.**T. 55–; U.; **Nw.**A. 48–; **Sh.**SC. 51–; **St.**R.; **Ste.** 51–; **Wd.**; **Y.** [*C. of:* 53543]

13738 **Chemical Engineering Progress Monograph Series.** New York. *Chem. Engng Prog. Monogr. Ser.* [1951–] **L.**C.; P.; **Sw.**U.; **Wd.**; **Y.**

13739 **Chemical Engineering Progress Symposium Series.** New York. *Chem. Engng Prog. Symp. Ser.* [1951–] **L.**C.; P.; SC.; **Bm.**U.; **M.**D.; **Sw.**U.; **Wd.**; **Y.**

13740 **Chemical Engineering Report. Tennessee Valley Authority.** *Chem. Engng Rep. T. V. A.* **L.**BM. 42–; **Y.**

13741 **Chemical Engineering Science:** Génie chimique. London. *Chem. Engng Sci.* [1951–] **L.**BM.; C.; P.; SC.; **Abs.**N.; **Bm.**P.; T. 55–; **C.**UL.; **Db.**; **E.**A.; U.; **G.**T.; **Ld.**P.; U.; **Lv.**P. 53–; **M.**C. 51–57; D.; T.; P. 55–; U.; **N.**T. 54–57; **Nw.**A.; **O.**R.; **Sh.**SC.; **Ste.**; **Sw.**U.; **Wd.**; **Y.** **Chemical Engineering** and the **Works Chemist.** *See* 13728.

13742 **Chemical Engineers Digest.** *Chem. Engrs Dig.* **Y.**

13743 **Chemical Equipment Preview.** Chicago. *Chem. Equip. Preview* [1941–] **L.**SC. [*C. of:* 18323]

13744 **Chemical Facts** and **Fancies.** Philadelphia. *Chem. Facts Fancies* **Chemical Fibres U.S.S.R.** *See* 27393.

13744° **Chemical Industrial Economy.** Tokyo. *Chem. ind. Econ., Tokyo* **Y.**

13745 **Chemical Industries.** London. *Chem. Inds, Lond.* [1935–] **L.**BM.; IC.; P.; **Abs.**N. 38–; **Bm.**P. imp.; **G.**M.; **Ld.**P. 52; **M.**P.; imp.; **O.**B.; **Y.** [*C. of:* 13731]

13746 **Chemical Industries.** Philadelphia. *Chem. Inds, Philad.* [1933–50] **L.**C. 38–50; **Ep.**D. 47–50; **M.**D. 37–50; **Wd.**; **Y.** [*C. of:* 13751; *C. as:* 13747]

13747 **Chemical Industries Week.** Philadelphia. *Chem. Inds Week* [1951] **L.**C.; **Ep.**D.; **M.**D.; **Wd.**; **Y.** [*C. of:* 13746; *C. as:* 13774]

13747° **Chemical Industry.** New York. *Chem. Ind.* **Y.** 57–. [*English abstracts of:* 27392]

13748 **Chemical Industry** and **Engineering.** Sydney. *Chem. Ind. Engng* [1951–59] **L.**P. 55–59; **Y.** [*C. as:* 13762]

13749 **Chemical Industry** in **Europe.** O.E.E.C. Paris. *Chem. Ind. Eur.* [1954–] **L.**BM.; SC.; **Bm.**P.; **Y.**

13750 **Chemical Literature.** Detroit. *Chem. Lit.* [1949–] **L.**P. 51–.

13751 **Chemical Markets.** New York. *Chem. Mkts* [1926–33] **L.**IC. 32–33; SC. 33; **Wd.** 32. [*C. from:* 17239; *C. as:* 13746] **Chemical Messenger.** Zagreb. *See* 27307.

13752 **Chemical** and **Metallurgical Engineering.** New York. *Chem. metall. Engng* [1918–46] **L.**BM. 35–46; C.; EE.; I.; IC.; MI.; NF.; P.; PR. 26–46; PT. 30–46; QM. 19–22 imp.; SC.; UC. 24–37; **Bm.**C. 21–32; T.; U.; **Br.**U.; **C.**ENG.; **Cr.**U. 19–35; **E.**HW. 21–27; **Ep.**D. 37–46; **G.**T. 30–46 imp.; **Ld.**U. 18–46; **Lv.**U.; **M.**D.; P. 23–46; R.; U.; **Sal.**F. 24–44; **Sh.**P. 22–46; **Ste.**; **Sw.**U. 18–41; **Sy.**R. 19–36 imp.; **Wd.**; **Y.** [*C. of:* 31474; *C. as:* 13727]

13753 **Chemical News** and **Journal of Physical (Industrial) Science.** London. *Chem. News, Lond.* [1860–32] **L.**BM.; BM^N.; C.; GL. 00–32; GM.; I. 95–23; IC.; MI. 21–28; P. 10–32; PH. 1860–20; RI.; S.; SC.; 1860–28; U.; TP. imp.; UC. 93–23; **Abd.**P. 75–32; U. 1860–28; **Abs.**N. 12–32; U. 1860–19; **Bl.**U. 67–32; **Bm.**P.; T. 61–31; U. 1860–28; **Bn.**U. 70–23; **Br.**P. 76–32; U. 61–15;

Bra.P. 72–32; **C.**P. 1860–21; UL. 63–21; **Cr.**P. 62–32 imp.; U. 69–21; **Db.** 68–32; **Dn.**U. 1860–22; **E.**A. imp.; F.; T. 02–32 imp.; U. 1860–26; **Ex.**U. 22–29; **G.**M.; T. 1860–20 imp.; U. 1860–23 imp.; **Ld.**U. 1860–03; **Lv.**M. 71–84; P.; U.; **M.**D. 70–31; P.; T. 92–32; U. imp.; **N.**P. 83–27; **Nw.**A. 1860–22; P.; **O.**BS. 79–20; R.; **Rt.** 1860–25; **Sa.**; **Sh.**IO. 63–32; **Ste.**; 73–82 imp.: 96–31; **Sw.**U. 1860–28; **Sy.**R. 00–29 imp.; **Wd.** 1860–31; **Y.** [*Replaced by:* 13763]

13754 **Chemical News. Manufacturing Chemists Association.** Washington. *Chem. News, Wash.* **L.**P. (curr.)

13755 **Chemical Papers** from the **Research Laboratory** of the **Pharmaceutical Society.** London. *Chem. Pap. Res. Lab. pharm. Soc.* **L.**BM. 92; PH. 04–14; **O.**R. 92; **Rt.** 92–95.

13756 **Chemical Patents.** Washington. *Chem. Pat.*

13757 **Chemical Pathways** of **Metabolism.** *Chem. Pathw. Metab.* [1954–] **L.**VC.

13758 **Chemical** and **Pharmaceutical Bulletin.** Tokyo. *Chem. pharm. Bull., Tokyo* [1958–] **L.**C.; PH.; SC.; **C.**CH. 60–; **G.**U.; **Ld.**U. 61–; **M.**U.; **O.**R.; **Y.** [*C. of:* 37473]

13759 **Chemical Practitioner.** London. *Chem. Practnr* [1927–42] **L.**BM.; C.; SC.; **O.**R.; **Sa.** 37–41; **Sh.**IO. 30–42 [*C. as:* 25693]

13760 **Chemical** and **Process Engineering.** London. *Chem. Process Engng* [1951–] **L.**AV. 53– imp.; BM.; C.; LE. 53–; P.; PR.; SC.; **Bn.**U. 59–; **C.**UL.; **E.**A. 54–; CE. 57–; U. 56–; **Ep.**D. 53–; **Ld.**P. 57–; **Lo.** 59–; **M.**C. 53–55; D. 53–; P. 55–; U. 55–; **N.**T.; U. 53–; **Nw.**A.; **O.**R.; **Sh.**IO.; **Sil.**; **Sw.**U. 57–; **Sy.**R. 52–58 imp.; **Y.** [*C. of:* 23826]. **Chemical** and **Process Engineering Abstracts.** *See* 55965.

13761 **Chemical Processing.** London. *Chem. Process., Lond.* [1954–] **L.**BM.; C. 62–; P. 55–; PR. 55–; **C.**UL. imp.; **E.**A. 56–; **Lv.**P. 59–; **O.**R.; **Sy.**R.; **Y.**

13762 **Chemical Processing.** Sydney. *Chem. Process., Sydney* [1959–61] **L.**P.; TP.; **Y.** [*C. of:* 13748; *C. as:* Australian Chemical Processing]

13763 **Chemical Products** and the **Chemical News.** London. *Chem. Prod.* [1938–] **L.**BM.; C.; LE. 55–62; MA.; MD.; P.; PH. 39–; TP. 58– imp.; U. 39– imp.; **Abs.**N. 48–; **Bm.**P.; **C.**CH.; PH.; UL.; **E.**A.; R.; **Ep.**D. 41–; **G.**M. 54–; **Ld.**P. (5 yr.); **M.**C. (2 yr.); P. imp.; **O.**R.; **R.**D. 41–48; **Wd.** 48–; **Y.** [*Replaces:* 13753]

13764 **Chemical Record-Age.** New York. *Chem. Rec.-Age* **L.**P. 25 [*C. of:* 13715 and 13720; *C. in:* 13777] **Chemical Research.** Athens. *See* 22070°.

13765 **Chemical Researches.** Tokyo. *Chem. Res., Tokyo* [1948–] **L.**C. 48–51.

13765° **Chemical Residues.** New York. *Chem. Resid.* [1958–]

13766 **Chemical Reviews.** Baltimore, etc. *Chem. Rev.* [1924–] **L.**B.; C.; CB. 46–; IC.; LI.; MC. 44–; NP. 53–; P.; PH. 39–; PR. 28–; QM. 27–; RI.; SC.; TD. imp.; TP. 44–; U.; UC. **Abd.**U. 26– imp.; **Abs.**U. 24–42: 45–; **Bl.**U.; **Bm.**P. 42–; T. 52– imp.; U.; **Bn.**U.; **Br.**U.; **C.**BI.; CH.; P. 26– imp.; R. 47–; **Co.**T. 61–; **Cr.**U.; **Db.**; **Dn.**U.; **E.**HW.; U.; W.; **Ep.**D.; **Ex.**U.; **F.**A. 46–; **G.**M.; T.; U.; **H.**U. 25–; **Lc.**A. 48–; **Ld.**P. 60–; U.; W. 29–; **Lh.**P. 44–54; **Lv.**P. 53–; U.; **M.**C.; D.; P. 47–; T.; U.; **Md.**H. 28–31; **Mi.** 44–; **N.**T. 48–; U.; **Nw.**A.; **O.**BS. 32–; N. 40–; R.; **Pl.**M. 50–; **R.**D. 45–; U.; **Rt.**; **Sa.**; **Sal.**F. 32–; **Sh.**SC. 46–; **Ste.**; **Sw.**U.; **Sy.**R.; W. 61–; **Wd.**; **We.**K. 29–; **Y.**

13767 **Chemical** and **Rubber Industry Report.** Washington. *Chem. Rubb. Ind. Rep.* [1954–] **Ep.**D. 55–; **Sy.**R.

13767° **Chemical Science** and **Industry.** *Chem. Sci. Ind.* **Y.** [*English abstracts of:* 27390]

13768 **Chemical Technology.** Kiriu, Japan. *Chem. Technol.* [1928–41] **L.**MT.; P. 28–40; SC.

13769 **Chemical Titles.** Washington. *Chem. Titles* [1960–] **Abd.**R.; **Bn.**U.; **Y.**

13770 **Chemical Topics.** Spirax Manufacturers Company. Cheltenham. *Chem. Top.* [1946–] **Sy.**R. [*C. of:* 53372]

13771 **Chemical Trade Journal** and **Chemical Engineer.** Manchester, etc. *Chem. Trade J.* [1887–] **L.**AV. 37– imp.; BM.; C.; H. 44–; I. 03–25; IC.; LE. 45–; MI. 22–; NF. 22–25; P. 10–; PL. 45–; PR. 27–; TP. 09–; **Abd.**U. 01–31; **Abs.**N. 12–; U. 21–; P. 18–; U. 88–26; **Bm.**U. 88–27: 48–; **Br.**P. (2 yr.); **C.**UL.; **Db.** 19–; **E.**A. 87–05; **Ep.**D. 37–; **G.**M. 88–; T.; **Ld.**P. (5 yr.); U. 46–; W. 40–; **Lv.**P. 00–; **M.**D. 16–21: 30–; P. 94–; T (1 yr) **Nw.**A. 88–25: 41–51; **O.**B.; **Sh.**10. 47–; **Ste.** 04–; **Sy.**R. 14–44 imp.; **Wd.**; **Y.**

13772 **Chemical Trade Review** and **Dyer's Journal.** Philadelphia. *Chem. Trade. Rev.*

13773 **Chemical Warfare.** Edgewood, Md. *Chem. Warfare*

Chemical Week. Philadelphia. *See* 13774.

13774 **Chemical Weekly.** Philadelphia, New York. *Chem. Wkly* [1951–] **L.**C.; **Ep.**D.; **M.**P. 53–; T. 54–57; **Wd.**; **Y.** [*C. of:* 13747]

13775 **Chemical World.** London. *Chem. Wld* [1912–14] **L.**BM.; C.; P.; SC.; **Db.**; **Ld.**U.; **Lv.**U.; **M.**P. imp.; **Nw.**A.; **O.**B.; **Rt.**; **Sw.**U.

13776 **Chemicalia.** Berlin. *Chemicalia*

13777 **Chemicals.** New York. *Chemicals* [1925–34] **L.**C. 26–31; P. 25–29; PR. 30; SC.; **M.**P. 26–31. [*C. of:* 13764 and 14928]

13778 **Chemické Listy.** Praha. *Chemické Listy* [1906–] **L.**BM. 55–; C. 21– imp.; I. 48–; P. 60–; **C.**P. 21–59; **E.**U. 54–; **G.**N. 53–; **Te.**C. 49–; **Y.**

13779 **Chemické zvesti.** Bratislava. *Chemické Zvesti* [1947–] **L.**BM. 53–; C. 55–; P. 54–; PL. 55–; PR. 56–; **Bm.**U. 55–; **Db.** 57–; **Te.**C. 49–61; **Y.**

13780 **Chemický obzor.** Praha. *Chemický Obz.* [1926–51] **L.**P. 26–39: 46–50; SC. [*C. as:* 13781]

13781 **Chemický průmysl.** Praha. *Chemický Prům.* [1951–] **L.**BM. 53–; C. 54–; P. 56–; PR. 55–; **Sy.**R. 54–; **Y.** [*C. of:* 13780]

13782 **Chemico Bulletin.** London. *Chemico Bull.* **L.**P. 59–.

13783 **Chemie.** Berlin. *Chemie* [1942–45] **L.**AV.; C. imp.; IC. 42–44; P.; **Bm.**U.; **C.**CH.; **Ep.**D. 42–44; **Ld.**U. 42–43; **M.**D.; T.; **Ste.** 42; **Te.**C. [*C. of:* and *Rec. as:* 2594]

13784 **Chemie** in **Einzeldarstellungen.** Stuttgart. *Chemie Einzeldarst.* [1912–34] **L.**C.; P. imp.; SC.; **Ld.**U.; **M.**U.; **O.**B.

13785 **Chemie** der **Erde.** Beiträge zur chemischen Mineralogie, Petrographie u. Geologie. Jena. *Chemie Erde* [1914–] **L.**BM^N.; C.; GM.; P. 27–; SC. 31–43: 52–; **Abd.**S. 30–31: 34–; **C.**MI. 19–38; **Rt.**; **Y.** [*Suspended* 1946–51]

13786 **Chemie** en **industrie.** Amsterdam. *Chemie Ind.* [1923–30] **L.**C.; P.; SC. 24–30. [*Supplement to:* 13803; *C. as:* 48251]

13787 **Chemie** für **Labor** und **Betrieb.** Frankfurt am Main. *Chemie Labor Betrieb* [1950–] **L.**P. 55–; **Y.**

13788 **Chemie** und **Medizin.** Berlin. *Chemie Med.* [1957–] **L.**P.

13789 **Chemie** en **Techniek.** Leiden. *Chemie Tech.* [1959–] **Y.** [*C. of:* 2561]

13790 **Chemie** en **Technik** der **Gegenwart.** Leipzig. *Chemie Tech. Gegenw.* [1923–] **L.**P.; SC.

13791 **Chemie** der **Zelle** und **Gewebe.** Leipzig. *Chemie Zelle Gewebe* [1925–26] **L.**IC.; P.; SC.; TD.; UC.; **Br.**U.; **C.**BI.; **Ste.** [*C. of:* 58833]

13791ᵃ **Chemiearbeit—Schützen** und **Helfen.** Düsseldorf. *Chemiearbeit* **L.**P. 60–. [*Supplement to:* 13808]

13792 **Chemiefasern.** Berlin, Frankfurt/Main. *Chemiefasern* [1960–] **L.**P.; SC.; **M.**C.; T.; **Y.** [*C. of:* 47672]

13793 **Chemie-Ingenieur-Technik.** Berlin. *Chemie-Ingr-Tech.* [1949–] **L.**BM.; C.; IC.; P.; SC.; **Bm.**U.; **Ep.**D. 50–; **F.**A.; **G.**T. 57–; U.; **Ld.**U.; **Lv.**P.; **M.**D.; P. 54–; T.; U.; **Ste.**; **Sw.**U. 57–; **Wd.**; **Y.** [*C. of:* 2595]

13794 **Chemie-Rundschau.** Berlin. *Chemie-Rdsch.* [1960–] **Y.**

13795 **Chemik.** Gliwice, Warszawa. *Chemik* [1948–] **L.**BM. 53–.

Chemik polski. *See* 48060.

Chēmika chronika. Athenai. *See* 22070ᵃ.

13796 **Chemikalien-** und **Drogenmarkt.** B. Leipa. *Chemikal.- u. Drogenmarkt*

Chēmike. Athenais. *See* 22070°.

13798 **Chemikerkalender.** Berlin. *Chemikerkalender* [1880–] **L.**SC. 26–; **E.**U. 02–12; **Ld.**U. 13–27 imp.; **Lv.**U. 81–90 imp.

13799 **Chemikerzeitung.** Cöthen, etc. *Chemikerzeitung* [1877–58] **L.**AV. 92–45 imp.; C. imp.; I. 88–32; IC. 82–40: 43–58; P. 80–58; PR. 27–39; SC. 81–44: 50–58; **C.**CH. 80–35; **Ld.**U. 93–58 imp.; **Lv.**U. 84–13; **M.**D. 94–45: 50–58; P. 24–39; T. 90–58 imp.; U. 81–58 imp.; **Sh.**S. 23–29; **Ste.** 50–58; **Sy.**R. 27–34 imp.; **Te.**C. 26–58; **Wd.** 82–58 imp.; **Y.** [*C. as:* 13800]

13800 **Chemikerzeitung — Chemische Apparatur.** *Chemikerzeitung—chem. Appar.* [1959–] **L.**C.; IC.; P.; SC.; **Ld.**U.; **M.**D.; T.; U.; **Ste.**; **Te.**C.; **Wd.**; **Y.** [*C. of:* 13799]

13800° **Chemins** de **fer.** Paris. *Chem. de Fer* **Y.**

13801 **Chemins** de **fer** et les **tramways.** Paris. *Chemins de Fer Tramw.* **L.**SC. 34–38*.

13802 **Chemisch jaarboekje** voor **Nederland, België** en **Nederlandsch Indië.** Amsterdam. *Chem. Jaarb. Ned.* **Y.**

13803 **Chemisch weekblad.** Amsterdam, Hilversum. *Chem. Weekbl.* [1903–] **L.**C. 07–40: 46– imp.; I. 20–31: 48–; MT. 20–; P.; PT. (1 yr); SC. 24–; UC. 28–38; **C.**CH. 28–; **M.**D. 32– imp.; T. 37–; **R.**D. 51–52; **Y.** [*Suspended between:* May 1943–August 1945]

13804 **Chemische Analyse.** Sammlung von Einzeldarstellungen aus dem Gebiet der chemischen, technischen-chemischen u. physikal-chemischen Analyse. Stuttgart. *Chem. Analyse* **L.**C. 07–.

13805 Chemische Apparatur. Leipzig. *Chem. Appar., Lpz.* [1914–42] **L.**C. 39–42; P.; SC. 31–42; UC. 32–41 imp.; **M.**T. 33–42. [*C. in:* 13816]

13806 Chemische Berichte. Heidelberg und Berlin, etc. *Chem. Ber.* [1947–] **L.**AV. 47–56 imp.; BM.; C.; CB.; IC.; LE.; LI.; MC.; MD.; NP.; P.; PH.; R.; RI.; SC.; SI.; TD.; TP.; U.; UC.; **Abd.**U.; **Abs.**N.; **Bl.**U.; **Bm.**P.; T. 58–; U.; **Bn.**U.; **Br.**U.; **C.**BI.; CH.; P.; UL.; **Cr.**U. 49–; **Db.**; **Dn.**U.; E.HW.; U.; **Ep.**D. 49–; **Ex.**U.; **F.**A. 47–50; **G.**T.; U.; **H.**U. 48–; **Je.**; **Ld.**U.; **Lv.**P. 52–; U.; **M.**C.; P. 55–; T.; U.; **Md.**H. 50–; **N.**U.; **Nw.**A.; **O.**R.; **R.**U.; **Rt.**; **Sa.**; **Sh.**W.; **Ste.**; **Sw.**U.; **Wd.**; **We.**K. 56–; **Y.** [*C. of:* 6192]

13807 Chemische Fabrik. Berlin. *Chem. Fabr., Berl.* [1928–41] **L.**AV. 28–38; C.; U.; UC. 28–37; **Bm.**U.; **C.**CH. 31–38; **G.**U.; **Ld.**U. 28–32; W.; **Lv.**U.; **M.**D. 32–38; T.; U. imp.; **O.**R. 28–33; **Ste.** 28–40; **Wd.** imp. [*See also* 5917; >16439, 1939–41 and *C. as:* 13816]

13808 Chemische Industrie. Berlin, Düsseldorf. *Chem. Ind., Düsseld.* [1874–44: 49–] **L.**A. 26–44; C. imp.; IC. 78–40; P. 95–33: 60–; PR. 35–39; SC. 21–44: 49–; TP. 32– imp.; UC. 21–40 imp.; **Bm.**U. 22–; **C.**C. 49–; CH. 78–24: 31–44; **Ep.**D. 49–; **G.**U. 23–33; **Ld.**U. 31–32; W. 26–29; **Lv.**U. 23–; **M.**D. 78–19: 37–; T. 21–38: 50–; U. 21– imp.; **O.**R. 21–33; **Ste.** 01– imp.; **Wd.**; **Y.**
    English edition **L.**C.; P.; **Ep.**D.; **M.**D. 54–55*; **Ste.** 54–55; **Y.** [*C. as:* 13809]
    Chemische Industrie. Budapest. *See* 55933.

13809 Chemische Industrie International. Düsseldorf. *Chem. Ind. int., Düsseld.* [1956–] **L.**C.; P.; **Ep.**D.; **M.**D.; **Ste.**; **Y.** [*C. of:* 13808 English edition]

13810 Chemische Mitteilungen. Augsburg. *Chem. Mitt.*

13812 Chemische Novitäten. Leipzig. *Chem. Novit., Lpz.* [1904–] **L.**C. 04–13; P. 11–32; SC. 34–; **O.**R. 04–25.

13813 Chemische en pharmaceutische techniek. Dordrecht. *Chem. pharm. Techn., Dordrecht* [1945–58] **L.**P. 57–58; SC. 48–58. [*Replaced by:* 34479]

13814 Chemische Revue über die **Fett-** u. **Harzindustrie.** Hamburg. *Chem. Revue Fett- u. Harzind.* [1894–15] **L.**C. 01–11 imp.; P.; TP. 12–15. [*C. as:* 13819]

13815 Chemische Rundschau für **Mitteleuropa** und den **Balkan.** Budapest. *Chem. Rdsch. Mitteleur.* [1924–32] **L.**P. 28–32 imp.; SC. 30–32; **C.**UL. 28–32.
    Chemische techniek. *See* 13813.

13816 Chemische Technik. Berlin. *Chem. Tech., Berl.* [1942–45] **L.**AV.; C.; IC.; P. imp.; SC. 42–43; U.; **G.**U.; **Ld.**W. 42–44; **Lv.**P.; **M.**D. 42 imp.; U. imp.; **Y.** [*C. of* 13805 and 13807; *C. as:* 2595]

13817 Chemische Technik. Kammer der Technik. Berlin. *Chem. Tech., Berl.* [1949–] **L.**C.; P.; **M.**D.; **Wd.**; **Y.**

13818 Chemische und **technische Untersuchungen** der **Landwirtschaftlichen Versuchsstation in Münster.** Münster. *Chem. tech. Unters. landw. VersStn Münster*

13819 Chemische Umschau auf dem **Gebiete** der **Fette, Oele, Wachse** u. **Harze.** Stuttgart. *Chem. Umsch. Geb. Fette* [1919–32] **L.**C.; P.; PR. 27–32; TP.; **M.**D. 28–32. [*C. of:* 13814; *C. as:* 19326]

13820 Chemische Zeitschrift. Berlin. *Chem. Z.* [1901–20] **L.**C. 13–20; IC. 01–12; P. 10–20; **M.**T. 02–09; U. 01–18; **Ste.** 01–12.

13821 Chemischen neuesten Nachrichten. Berlin. *Chemn neu. Nachr.* [1908–10] **L.**P.

13822 Chemisches Repertorium. Cöthen. *Chem. Repert.* [1885–07] **L.**C. 87–02; IC. 96–07; P. 86–07; **C.**UL.; **Ld.**U. 93–07; **M.**T. 03–07; U. 86–07; **Ste.** [*C. as:* 13832]

13823 Chemisches Zentralblatt. Berlin. *Chem. ZentBl.* [1856–] **L.**AV. 10–53 imp.; B. 13–23; BM^N. 1856–31; C.; I. 23–42; IC. 97–; LI. 89–; MC. 97–54 imp.; P. imp.; PH. 90–14; PR. 34–39; RI. 87–; SC. 97–44: 49–; TP. 97– imp.; UC. 97– imp.; **Abd.**U. 00–32: 40–43: 45–; **Bl.**U. 97–40; **Bm.**P. 01–12: 25–; U. 79–81: 97–; **Bn.**U. 97–48; **Br.**U. 97–; **C.**CH. 97–; P. 28–; **Cr.**U. imp.; **Db.** 15–; **Dn.**U. 97–; E.U. 70–; **Ep.**D. 97– imp.; **G.**T. 00– imp.; U. 70– imp.; **Ld.**U. 97–; **Lv.**P. 53–; U. 97–; **M.**C. 97–39: 42–44 imp.; P. 97–22; T. 85–; U.; **N.**U. 97–50 imp.; **Nw.**A. 97–; **O.**R.; **Rt.** 97–39: 42–44 imp.; **Sh.**U. 97–10; **Y.**
    Chemisch-metallurgische Zeitschrift. *See* 31450.

13824 Chemischreiniger und **Färber.** München. *Chemischrein. Färb.* [1957–] **L.**P. [*C. of:* 18980]

13825 Chemisch-technische Industrie. Berlin. *Chem.-tech. Ind.* **L.**SC. 27–44: 47–.

13826 Chemisch-technische Mitteilungen der **Versuchsanstalten** an der **K.K. Staatsgewerbeschule Wien.** Wien & Leipzig. *Chem.-tech. Mitt. VersAnst. K.K. StaatsgewSch.* [1911–12] **L.**P. [*C. as:* 32553]

13827 Chemisch-technische Rundschau. Ludwigshafen a. Rh. *Chem.-tech. Rdsch., Ludwigshafen* [1885–32] **L.**P. 25–27.

13828 Chemisch-technische Rundschau. Wien. *Chem.-tech. Rdsch., Wien* [1932–39] **L.**SC. [*C. in:* 19328]

13829 Chemisch-technische Übersicht. Cöthen. *Chem.-tech. Übers.* [1917–45] **L.**C.; IC. 17–38; P.; SC.; **C.**UL.; **Ld.**U. 17–38; **M.**T.; U. 17–43 imp.; **Ste.** 17–39. [*C. of:* 13832]

13830 Chemisch-technische Wochenschrift. Berlin. *Chem.-tech. Wschr.*

13831 Chemisch-technische Zeitschrift. Erfurt. *Chem.-tech. Z.*

13832 Chemisch-technisches Repertorium. Berlin. *Chem.-tech. Repert.* [1908–16] **L.**C.; IC.; P.; **C.**UL.; **Ld.**U.; **M.**T.; U.; **Ste.** [*C. of:* 13822; *C. as:* 13829]

13833 Chemisch-technisches Repertorium (Jacobsen). Berlin. *Chem.-tech. Repert. (Jacobsen)* [1862–01] **L.**BM.; C. 76–01; P.; SC.

13834 Chemist. Cornell University, Ithaca, N.Y. *Chemist, Cornell Univ.*

13835 Chemist. Bulletin of the American Institute of Chemists. Easton, Pa. New York. *Chemist, Am. Inst. Chem.* **Y.**

13836 Chemist Analyst. J. T. Barker Chemical Co. Philipsburg, N.J. *Chemist Analyst* [1911–] **L.**C. 43–; I. 23–; MT. 24–; NP. 58–; P. 14– imp.; PH. 48–; PR. 56–; SC. 35–; TP. 56–; **Ld.**P. (5 yr.); U. 52–; **Lv.**P. 55–; **Sh.**IO. 55–; **Y.**

13837 Chemist and **Druggist.** London. *Chemist Drugg.* [1859–] **L.**BM.; H. 46–; MA. 48–; MD. 27–; P. 10–; PH.; TP. 27–; UC. 29–; **Bm.**T (curr.); **Br.**P. (1 yr); U. 31–; **Db.** 76–82; **G.**M. 79–05: 08–32: 51–; PH. 48–; T. 52–; **Lc.**A. 89– imp.; **Ld.**P. (5 yr.); U. 38–47 imp.; **M.**MS. 78–; **N.**U. V. imp.; **O.**B. 82–; **Sh.**IO. 49–; **Y.**

13838 **Chemist** and **Druggist** of **Australasia.** Melbourne. *Chemist Drugg. Austral.* [1886–] **L.**BM.; C. 27–; PH. 86–15 imp.
    Chemist and **Druggist Diary.** *See* 13840.

13839 **Chemist** and **Druggist Export Review.** London. *Chemist Drugg. Export Rev.* [1948–51] **L.**BM. 49–51; MA. 47–51 [*C. as:* 18788]

13840 **Chemist** and **Druggist Yearbook.** London. *Chemist Drugg. Yb.* **L.**BM. 74–; P. (curr.); PH. 00–; **Abs.**N. 20; **Bra.**D. 40– imp.; **E.**A. 57–; **G.**M. 81–96: 29–32: 51–; **Ld.**P. (curr.); **O.**B. 96–26 imp.; **Y.**

13841 **Chemist-Optician.** London. *Chemist-Optn* [1926–39] **L.**BM. [*C. as:* 22608]
    Chemistry. Kyoto. *See* 27165.

13842 **Chemistry.** Chinese Chemical Society. Taipei. *Chemistry, Taipei* [1954–] **L.**C. 55–; **Y.**

13843 **Chemistry Bulletin. Special Libraries Association.** New York. *Chemy Bull. spec. Libr. Ass.*

13844 **Chemistry** in **Canada.** Ottawa. *Chemy Can.* [1949–] **L.**C.; P. 53–; **Lv.**P. 51–58 v. imp.; **Y.**

13844° **Chemistry** and **Chemical Industry.** Tokyo. *Chemy chem. Ind., Tokyo* **Y.**

13845 **Chemistry Collection.** New York. *Chemy Collect.* [1957–] **L.**P.

13846 **Chemistry** in **Commerce.** London. *Chemy Comm.* [1934–35] **L.**C.

13847 **Chemistry** of **High Polymers.** Tokyo. *Chemy high Polym.* [1944–] **L.**C. 52–53: 57– imp.; P. 55–; **M.**C. 53–; **Y.**

13848 **Chemistry** and **Industry.** London. *Chemy Ind.* [1932–] **L.**AM.; AV. 37– imp.; B. 37– imp.; BM.; C.; CB.; EE.; GM.; H. 43–; I.; IC.; LE.; LI.; MA. 44–; MC.; MD. 58–; NF.; NP.; P.; PH.; PL. 44–; PR.; PT.; QM.; RI.; SC.; SI. 37–; TP. 39–; UC.; **Abd.**R. 41–; **Abs.**N. 36–; R. 41–; **Bm.**C. 59–; T.; **Bn.**U. 43–; **Br.**A. 49–; P.; **Bra.**D. 48–; P. 47–; **C.**CH. (curr.); UL.; **Cr.**U.; **Db.**; **Dn.**U.; **E.**A.; CE. 43–; HW. 38–; SW. 48; U. 41; **Ep.**D.; **Ex.**U.; **F.**A.; **G.**T.; U. 37–; **Je.**; **Lc.**A.; **Ld.**P.; W. 44–; **Lh.**P. 41– imp.; **Lv.**P.; **M.**C. 48–; D.; P.; T.; U.; **Md.**H.; **N.**P.; T.; U.; **Nw.**P.; **O.**R.; **R.**D.; **Sal.**F. 35–; **Sh.**G. 44– IO.; SC.; U.; **Sil.** 32–58; **Sw.**U.; **Sy.**R.; **Wd.**; **We.**K. 46–; **Y.** [*C. of:* 13849]

13849 **Chemistry** and **Industry Review.** London. *Chemy Ind. Rev.* [1923–31] **L.**AM.; C.; CB. 29–31; EE.; GM.; I.; IC.; LE.; LI. 27–31; MC.; NF. 24–31; NP.; P.; PH.; PR.; PT.; QM.; RI.; SC.; UC.; **Abs.**U.; **Bm.**T.; U.; **Br.**P.; **C.**CH.; UL.; **Cr.**P.; U.; **Db.**; **Dn.**U.; **E.**A.; R. 23–25; **Ep.**D.; **Ex.**U.; **G.**M.; **Je.** 25–31; **Lc.**A. imp.; **Ld.**P.; **Lv.**P.; U.; **M.**P.; T.; U.; **Md.**H.; **N.**P.; U.; **Nw.**A.; P.; **O.**R.; **R.**D.; **Sal.**F. 25–31; **Sh.**IO.; SC. 26–31; U.; **Sw.**U.; **Sy.**R.; **Wd.**; **Y.** [*C. of:* 26920 (a); *C. as:* 13848]

13850 **Chemistry** and **Pharmacy.** University of Colorado. Boulder. *Chemy Pharm.* [1952–] **Db.**

13851 **Chemistry Research.** Report of the Chemistry Research Board. London. *Chemy Res.* [1957–58] **L.**C.; P.; **Bm.**P.; U.; **E.**R.; **G.**U.; **O.**R. [*C. of:* 43017; *C. as:* 44629]
    Chemistry Research, Special Report. *See* 50511.

13852 **Chemistry** and **Technology** of **Fuels** and **Oils.** *Chemy Technol. Fuels Oils* **L.**P.; **Y.** 57–. [*English abstracts of:* 27407]

13853 **Chemists' Annual.** London. *Chemists' A.* **L.**P. 06–15; PH. 06–17; **G.**M. 15–16.

13854 **Chemists' Year Book.** London. *Chemists' Yb.* [1915–] **L.**BM.; C. 16– imp.; P.; SC. 16: 18–; U. 47–; **Abs.**N. imp.; **Bm.**P. 19–; **Br.**P. (3 yr.); **C.**UL.; **E.**A. imp.; **G.**M.; **Ld.**P. 27– imp.; **Lv.**P. 18– imp.; **M.**P.; **O.**R.; **Sh.**P. 26–.

13854° **Chemmunique.** Atlas Powder Company. Wilmington. *Chemmunique* **L.**P. (curr.)

13855 **Chemotherapia.** Basel, New York. *Chemotherapia* [1960–] **L.**MD.; **Y.**

13856 **Chemotherapy Review.** London. *Chemother. Rev.* [1960–] **L.**BM.; MD.; P.; PH.; PT.; SH. (1 yr); TP.; **Y.** [*C. of:* 8918]

13857 **Chemurgic Digest.** Columbus, Ohio. *Chemurg. Dig.* [1942–] **L.**AM. 50–; P. 42–49 imp.; SC. 46–; TP. 52–; **Rt.** 46–. [*Replaces:* 34785]

13858 **Chemurgic Papers.** National Farm Chemurgic Council. Columbus, O. *Chemurg. Pap.* **L.**P. 41–; SC. 46–.

13859 **Chêne.** Société forestière provençale. Marseille. *Chêne*

13860 **Chêne-liége.** Bône. *Chêne-liége*

13861 **Chercheur.** Journal illustré des inventions nouvelles. Paris. *Chercheur*

13862 **Chernigovskiĭ selyanin.** Chernigov. Черниговский селянин. *Chernig. Selyanin* [1919]

13862° **Chernomorskiĭ selyanin.** Черноморскій селянинъ. *Chernomorsk. Selyanin* [*Supplement to:* 13863]

13863 **Chernomorskoe sel'skoe khozyaĭstvo.** Novorossiĭsk, Sukhum. Черноморское сельское хозяйство. *Chernomorsk. sel'. Khoz.* **L.**EB. 15 imp.

13864 **Chesapeake Science.** Solomons. *Chesapeake Sci.* [1960–] **L.**AM.; BM^N.; Z.; **Bn.**U.; **Y.** [*C. of:* 29493]

13865 **Cheshire** and **North** (and **Mid-**) **Wales Natural History.** Chester. *Cheshire N. Wales nat. Hist.* [1947–] [*Contained in:* 39082]

13866 **Chest Disease Index** and **Abstracts** including **Tubercolosis.** London. *Chest. Dis. Index Abstr.* [1959–] **L.**BM.; H.; MA.; MC.; MD.; S.; TD.; U.; UCH.; V.; **Bl.**U.; **C.**PA.; UL.; **Cr.**MD.; **Db.**; **Dn.**U.; **E.**A.; P.; U.; **G.**PH.; U.; **Nw.**A.; **O.**R.; W.; **Y.** [*C. of:* 55288]

13867 **Chest** and **Heart Bulletin.** London. *Chest Heart Bull.* [1959–] **L.**BM.; H.; LI.; MA.; MD.; S.; TD.; **Bm.**U.; **Br.**U.; **C.**UL.; **Db.**; **E.**A.; U.; **G.**PH.; **Lv.**M.; **M.**MS.; **O.**R.; **Y.** [*C. of:* 33918]

13868 **Chetvertichnyĭ period.** Kiyiv. Четвертичный період. *Chetv. Period* [1930–] **L.**BM.; BM^N. 30–35.

13869 **Chiasma.** Saint Andrews University Medical Society. Saint Andrews. *Chiasma* [1949–] **L.**BM.; **Sa.**
    Chiba igakkai zasshi. *See* 32611.

13870 **Chicago Academy** of **Sciences Natural History Miscellanea.** Chicago. *Chicago Acad. Sci. nat. Hist. Misc.* [1946–] **L.**BM^N.; SC.; Z.; **Bl.**U.; **Db.** imp.; **E.**R.; **G.**N. 49–59; **Y.**

13871 **Chicago Chemical Bulletin.** Chicago. *Chicago chem. Bull.* [1914–19] **L.**MT. [*C. as:* 13718]

13872 **Chicago Clinic.** Chicago. *Chicago Clin.* **Db.** 17–20.

13873 **Chicago Dairy Produce.** Chicago. *Chicago Dairy Prod.* [1894–27] [*C. as:* 16316]

13874 **Chicago Dietician.** Baltimore. *Chicago Dietn* [1924] [*C. as:* 9312]

13875 **Chicago Medical Recorder.** Chicago. *Chicago med. Rec.* **L.**s. 91–27 imp. [*C. in:* 41853]

13876 **Chicago Medical School Quarterly.** *Chicago med. Sch. Q.* [1941–] **L.**H. 50–; MD. 48–; S. 48–; TD. 49–; **G.**F. 49–.

13877 **Chicago Medical Times.** Chicago. *Chicago med. Times* [1869–10] **L.**MD. 08–10.

13878 **Chicago Natural History Museum Bulletin.** Chicago. *Chicago nat. Hist. Mus. Bull.* [1944–] **L.**BMᴺ. [*C. of:* 19398]

13879 **Chicago Naturalist.** Chicago. *Chicago Nat.* [1938–48] **L.**BMᴺ.; NC.; Z. 40–48; **Bl.**U.; **E.**R.; **M.**U. imp.

13880 **Chicago's Health.** Chicago. *Chicago's Hlth* [1924–] **L.**MA. 29–31 imp.; **Lv.**U. [*C. of:* 57231]

13881 **Chief Engineer's Reports** of the **British Engine Boiler** and **Electrical Insurance Co.** *Chf Engrs Rep. Br. Eng. Boil. elect. Insur. Co.* **L.**P. 79–10*; **Cr.**P. 79–09 [*C. as:* 52329]

13882 **Chiesa** e **quartiere.** Bologna. *Chiesa Quart.* [1957–] **L.**BA.

13883 **Child.** London. *Child, Lond.* [1910–28] **L.**BM.; S. 21–28; **Abs.**N. 12; U. 10–27; **C.**UL.; **Db.**; **E.**A.; P. 17–20; **G.**F. 17–20 imp.; **Ld.**P. 10–26; **Lv.**U.; **O.**B.

13884 **Child.** Washington. *Child, Wash.* [1936–53] **L.**BM. [*C. as:* 13893]

13885 **Child Development.** Baltimore, etc. *Child Dev.* [1930–] **L.**MD.; **Abd.**R. 30–51: 53–; **Bm.**U. 47–; **Br.**U.; **C.**UL.; **E.**U. 47–; **G.**U. 62–.

13886 **Child Development Abstracts** and **Bibliography.** Washington, etc. *Child Dev. Abstr. Biblphy* [1930–] **L.**MA. 33–; MD. 33–; UC. 30–; 35 imp.; **Abd.**R. 32–; **Br.**U. 48–; **R.**U. 40– imp.; **O.**Z. 43– imp.; **Sh.**U. 53–. [*C. of:* 49427]
   Child Development Series. University of **Toronto.** *See* 55681.

13887 **Child Guidance Inter-Clinic Conferences.** National Association for Mental Health. London. *Child Guid. inter-Clin. Confs* **L.**MD. 51–.

13888 **Child Health Bulletin.** New York. *Child Hlth Bull.* [1925–35] **Br.**U. 30–35. [*C. of:* 13889]

13889 **Child Health Magazine.** Washington. *Child Hlth Mag.* [1924–25] **G.**PH. [*C. of:* 33698; *C. as:* 13888]

13890 **Child Life.** London. *Child Life* [1899–39] **L.**BM.; **Abs.**N. 13–39 imp.; **Br.**P. (1 yr) **C.**UL.; **E.**A. 99–05; **Lv.**U.; **Nw.**A. 18–31; P. 07–19 imp.; **O.**B. [*C. as:* 11220]

13891 **Child Psychology.** Bulletin of the Institute of Child Psychology. London. [1937–] *Child Psychol.* **L.**BM.

13892 **Child Study.** London. *Child Study* [1908–20] **L.**B. 11–17 imp.; BM.; MA. 08–16; **Abs.**N. 14–20; U. 12–20; **Bm.**P. 08–18; **C.**UL.; **Db.**; **E.**A.; **G.**U. 08–17 imp.; **N.**U. 08–13 imp.; **O.**B. 08–19; **Sw.**U. 08–17. [*C. of:* 36754]

13893 **Children.** Washington. *Children* [1954–] **L.**BM.; MA. imp. [*C. of:* 13884]

13894 **Children's Museum Bulletin.** Brooklyn, N.Y. *Childn's Mus. Bull., Brooklyn* [1902–04] **L.**BMᴺ.; **Cr.**M. [*C. as:* 13895]

13895 **Children's Museum News.** Brooklyn, N.Y. *Childn's Mus. News, Brooklyn* [1904–] **L.**BMᴺ. 04–46; **Cr.**M. 04–05. [*C. of:* 13894: Apr. 1905–May 1913; *Contained in:* 33857]

13896 **Chile maderero.** Santiago. *Chile mader.* [1951–] **O.**F. 53–.

13897 **Chilton Tractor Journal.** Philadelphia. *Chilton Tract. J.*

13898 **Chimia.** Zürich. *Chimia* [1947–] **L.**C.; P.; SC.; **C.**CH.; **M.**D.; **Y.** [*C. of:* 48911]

13899 **Chimica.** Milano. *Chimica, Milano* [1946–] **L.**P.; **Y.**

13900 **Chimica.** São Paulo. *Chimica, S Paulo* [1933] **L.**C.; P.; **Sh.**G.; **Sy.**R. [*C. as:* 13901]

13901 **Chimica e industria.** São Paulo. *Chimica Ind., S Paulo* [1934–38] **L.**C.; P.; **Sh.**G.; **Sy.**R. [*C. of:* 13900; *C. as:* 41685]

13902 **Chimica e l'industria.** Milano. *Chimica Ind., Milano* [1935–] **L.**C.; I.; IC.; P.; PT. (5 yr.); TP. 35–55 imp.; **Ep.**D. 35–40; **M.**C. 35–40; U. 60–; **Sh.**G. 46–; **Ste.** imp.; **Sy.**R. 35–40 imp.: 46–; **Y.** [*C. of:* 21233 and 23131]

13903 **Chimica nell'industria nell'agricoltura, nella biologia** e altre sue **applicazioni.** *Chimica Ind. Agric. Biol.* [1925–] **L.**P. 25–40. [*C. of:* 13905]

13904 **Chimica industriale.** Torino. *Chimica ind.* [1899–03] **L.**P. [*C. as:* 23132]

13905 **Chimica industriale e applicata.** Milano. *Chimica ind. appl.* [1924] **L.**P. [*C. as:* 13903]

13906 **Chimica e la medicina moderna.** Milano. *Chimica Med. mod.*

13907 **Chimico italiano.** Roma. *Chimico ital.* [1928–] **L.**C. 28–29; **C.**P.

13908 **Chimie et agriculture.** Bruxelles. *Chim. Agric.* [1954–] **L.**P.; **Y.**

13909 **Chimie analytique.** Paris. *Chim. analyt.* [1947–] **L.**C.; I.; P.; PT. (5 yr.); SC.; **Bm.**C. 49–52; **Db.**; **Nw.**A.; **Y.** [*C. of:* 2697]

13910 **Chimie et bâtiment.** Bruxelles, Ruisbroek. *Chim. Bâtim.* **L.**P. 56–; **Y.**

13910° **Chimie des hautes températures.** Compte rendu du colloque national, Centre national de la recherche scientifique. Paris. *Chim. htes Temp.* [1954–] **L.**P.

13911 **Chimie et industrie.** Paris. *Chim. Ind.* [1918–] **L.**C.; HQ. 25–; I.; IC.; NF. 26–29; P. imp.; PH. 26–; PR. (5 yr.); SC.; TD. 36–; TP.; **Bm.**U. 18–20 imp.; **Br.**U. 24–; **Db.**; **E.**HW. 49–; R. 18–60; **Ep.**D. 20–40: 45–; **G.**I. 40–51 imp.; **Ld.**U. 26–59; **Lv.**P. 18–35: 40: 42: 52–; **M.**C. 18–43: 45– imp.; D. 19: 23– imp.; P. 56–; **N.**T. 40–; **Nw.**A. 20–21: 53–; **Sh.**G. 24–; **Ste.** imp.; **Sy.**R. 27–; **Te.**C. 18–35; **Wd.** 22–; **Y.** [*For supplement see* 20896]

13912 **Chimie industrielle** et **financière.** Shanghaï. *Chim. ind. financ.*

13913 **Chimie mathématique.** Paris. *Chim. math.* [1938–] **L.**SC. 38–42.

13914 **Chimie médicale.** Paris. *Chim. méd.*

13915 **Chimie des peintures.** Bruxelles. *Chim. Peint.* [1938–] **L.**P. 51–; PR.; **Sl.**I. 48–; **Sy.**R. 38–40; **Y.**

13916 **Chimie des peintures** et **vernis.** Aarau. *Chim. Peint. Vernis* [1947–] **L.**SC.

Chimika chronika. Athens. *See* 22070ᵃ.

13918 **Chimiste.** Journal des distillateurs. Paris. *Chimiste*

13919 **Chimiste** au **laboratoire** et à l'**usine.** Bruxelles. *Chimiste Lab. Usine* [1910–14] **L.**P.

13920 **Chimiste** de la **ville** et des **champs.** Paris. *Chimiste Ville Champs*

13921 **China Clay Trade Review.** London. *China Clay Trade Rev.* [1919–29] **L.**BM. 19–22; C. 23–29; P.; SC. 24–29; **O.**B. 19–22.

13922 **China Coast Meteorological Register.** Hongkong Observatory. Hongkong. *China Cst met. Reg.* **L.**BM. 94–12⋆; MO. 73–12; **E.**M. 96–12.

13923 **China Dental Journal.** Shanghai. *China dent. J.* [1935–36] **L.**D.

13924 **China, Glass** and **Lamps.** Pittsburg. *China Glass Lamps*

China Imperial Maritime Customs. Medical Reports. Shanghai. *See* 30304.

13925 **China Journal.** Shanghai. *China J.* [1927–41] **L.**BM.; BMᴺ.; G.; MT.; P. 27–28; SC.; Z.; **Abs.**N.; **C.**UL.; **Cr.**P.; **G.**U.; **M.**U. [*C. of:* 13926]

13926 **China Journal** of **Science** and **Arts.** Shanghai. *China J. Sci. Arts* [1923–26] **L.**BM.; BMᴺ.; E.; G.; MT.; P. 24–26; Z. imp.; **Abs.**N.; **C.**UL.; **Cr.**P. 26; **G.**U. 24–26; **M.**U. [*C. as:* 13925]

13927 **China Medical Journal.** Shanghai. *China med. J.* [1887–31] **L.**BM.; EB. 19–26; MA. 30–31; MD. 14–31; TD. 06–31; **Bm.**U. 30–31; **Br.**U. 88–05 imp.; **E.**S. 28–31; U. 24–31; **Lv.**U. 07–31. [*C. in:* 13937]

China Medical Missionary Journal. Shanghai. *See* 13927.

Chinese Institute of **Engineers Journal.** *See* 12884 and 12885.

13928 **Chinese Journal** of **Agricultural Research.** Peking. *Chin. J. agric. Res.* **L.**P. 52. [*C. as:* 478]

13929 **Chinese Journal** of **Civil Engineering.** Peking. *Chin. J. civ. Engng* **L.**P. 59–; **Sil.** 59–.

13930 **Chinese Journal** of **Experimental Biology.** Shanghai. *Chin. J. exp. Biol.* [1950–51] **L.**SC.; **E.**R. 50–51; **Fr.** 50–51; **Pl.**M. 50–51; **Rt.** 50–51. [*C. as:* 506]

13931 **Chinese Journal** of **Nutrition.** Anshun, etc. *Chin. J. Nutr.* [1946–] **L.**MD.; TD. 46–48 imp.; **Abd.**R. 46–48.

13932 **Chinese Journal** of **Physics.** Shanghai. *Chin. J. Phys.* [1933–50] **L.**BM.; P.; RI.; **Bm.**U. imp.; **C.**P. 35–50; **E.**R. 33–36: 44–49; U. imp.; **G.**U. 33–36: 44–50; **Ld.**U.; **O.**R. [*C. as:* 723]

13933 **Chinese Journal** of **Physiology.** Peking. *Chin. J. Physiol.* [1927–54] **L.**MC. 27–41; MD. 27; S. 27–28; **Abs.**N; R. 35–41; **Bl.**U. 28; **Bm.**U. 27–28; **Br.**U. 27–41 imp.; **C.**PH.; **E.**R. 27–40; U. 27–34; **M.**MS. 27–37; **Nw.**A. 27–38; **O.**PH.27–38; R.; **Pl.**M. 31. [*C. as:* 730]

13934 **Chinese Journal** of **Physiology. Report Series.** Peking. *Chin. J. Physiol. Rep. Ser.* [1928–31] **L.**MD. 28; **Abs.**N.; **Bl.**U.; **Bm.**U.; **C.**PH.; **E.**R. 28.

13935 **Chinese Journal** of **Scientific Agriculture.** Chungking. *Chin. J. scient. Agric.* [1943–] **C.**A. 43–44; **Rt.** 43–44.

13936 **Chinese Journal** of **Zoology.** Nanking. *Chin. J. Zool.* [1935] **L.**BMᴺ.

13937 **Chinese Medical Journal.** Shanghai, etc. *Chin. med. J.* [1932–] **L.**BM.; CB. 57–; LI. 57– imp.; MA.; MC. 52–; MD.; S. 32–; SH. 34–41 imp.: 50–; TD.; **Abd.**R. 50–53; **Bl.**U. 58–; **Bm.**U. 32–38; **E.**A. 55–; P. 57–; U. imp.; **Lv.**M. 34–39 imp.; U.; **M.**MS. 32–39; **Nw.**A. 33– imp.; **O.**R.; **Y.** [*C. of:* 13927 and 34141]

13938 **Chinese Medical Journal. Chengtu edition.** Chengtu. *Chin. med. J. Chengtu Edn* [1942–] **L.**S. 42–45 imp.

13939 **Chinese Medical Journal. Free China Edition.** Taiwan. *Chin. med. J. free China Edn* [1954–] **L.**TD.; **Y.**

13940 **Chinese Review** of **Tropical medicine.** Taipeh, Taiwan. *Chin. Rev. trop. Med.* [1948] **L.**BMᴺ.; EB.; TD.; **E.**R.; **Ld.**U.

Chinese-American Joint Committee on **Rural Reconstruction.** Taipei.
Animal industry series. *See* 2619.
Economic digest series. *See* 17416.
Fishery series. *See* 19556ᶜ.
Forestry series. *See* 20060.
General report. *See* 20860.
Plant industry series. *See* 37854.

13941 **Chiropodist.** London. *Chiropodist* [1914–] **L.**BM.; H. 50–; MA. 38–; MD. 35–; S. 38–; SH. (1 yr); **Bm.**P. 36–; **G.**M. 47–; PH. 43–48; **M.**MS. 48–.

13942 **Chiropody Practitioner.** London. *Chirop. Practnr* [1934–] **L.**BM.; **Abs.**N. 35–; **E.**A.; **O.**R. 35–37.

13943 **Chiropody Review.** London. *Chirop. Rev.* [1930–] **L.**H. 50–; MA. 46–.

13944 **Chirurg.** Zeitschrift für alle Gebiete der operativen Medizin. Berlin. *Chirurg* [1928–] **L.**MA. 34–35: 46–; MD.; S. imp.; **E.**S.; **Y.**

13945 **Chirurg polski.** Warszawa. *Chirurg pol.*

13946 **Chirurgia.** Bucureşti. *Chirurgia, Buc.* [1952–] **L.**BM. 55–; MA. 54–; MD. 54– v. imp.; S. 56–; **E.**S. 58–.

13947 **Chirurgia.** Milano. *Chirurgia, Milano* [1946–] **L.**MA. 47–; MD. 47–; S. imp.

Chirurgia. Sofia. *See* 27416.

13948 **Chirurgia clinica polonica.** Krakow. *Chir. clin. pol.* [1929–31] **L.**S.

13949 **Chirurgia** dell' **ernia.** Napoli. *Chir. Ernia*

13950 **Chirurgia generale.** Perugia. *Chir. gen., Perugia* [1951–] **L.**S. 57–.

13951 **Chirurgia italiana.** Belluno, etc. *Chir. ital.* [1948–] **L.**MA.; MD. 57–; **M.**MS. 55–.

13952 **Chirurgia maxillofacialis & plastica.** Zagreb. *Chir. maxillofac. plast.* [1956–] **L.**BM.; MA.; MD.

Chirurgia narządów ruchu i ortopedia polska. *See* 13963.

13953 **Chirurgia** degli **organi** di **movimento.** Bologna. *Chir. Org. Mov.* [1917–] **L.**BM.; MA. 28–; MD.; S. 17–40: 46–; **Br.**U. 24–39 imp.

Chirurgia et **orthopedia.** Sofia. *See* 27417.

13954 **Chirurgia** e **patologia sperimentale.** Milano *Chir. Patol. sper.* [1953–] **L.**MA.; MD. [*C. of:* 37234]

13955 **Chirurgia speciale.** Rivista di oculistica, ostetricia, ginecologia e malattie urinarie. Napoli. *Chir. spec.*

13956 **Chirurgia toracica.** Roma. *Chir. torac.* [1948–] **L.**MA.; MD.; S.

13957 **Chirurgie** des **aliénés.** Paris. *Chirurgie Aliénés* **E.**P. 01–.

13958 **Chirurgie contemporaine** des **organes génito-urinaires.** Paris. *Chirurgie contemp. Org. génito-urin.* [1891–]

Chirurgie réparatrice et **traumatologie.** *See* 57537.

13959 **Chirurgie-Mechanik.** Berlin. *Chirurgie-Mech.*

13960 **Chirurgien-dentiste français.** Paris. *Chirurgien-Dent. fr.* **L.**D. 47–.

13961 **Chirurgisch-technisches Korrespondenzblatt** für **Chirurgie-Mechanik.** Berlin. *Chir.-tech. KorrBl.* [1879–35] **L.**P. 23–35 [*C. as:* 30587]

13962 **Chirurgja kliniczna.** Kraków. *Chirurgja klin.* **L.**S. 27–34.

13963 **Chirurgja narządów ruchu** i **ortopedja polska.** Warszawa. *Chirurgja narz. Ruchu Ortop. pol.* [1928–] **L.**MA. 29–38: 52–; **Y.**

Chiryô. Tokyo. *See* 53052ᵃ.

13964 **Chloride Chronicle** (and **Exide News**). Manchester. *Chlor. Chron.* [1917–] **L.**EE. 17–21; **Ld.**U. 38–40.

13965 **Chlorination Topics.** Newark, N.J. *Chlorin. Top.* [1938–39] **L.**SC.

13966 **Chmelařské listy.** Rakonice. *Chmel. Listy*

13966ᶜ **Chmelarstvi.** Praha. *Chmelarstvi* **Y.**

13967 **Choroby roślin.** Warszawa. *Chor. Rośl.* [1931] **L.**EB. [*C. of:* 13968]

13968 **Choroby i szkodniki roślin.** Warszawa. *Chor. Szkodn. Rośl.* [1925–27] **L.**BMᴺ. 25–26; EB.; MY.; **E.**U. [*C. as:* 13967]

Chosen igakkai zasshi. *See* 25809.

13969 **Chosen Sotoku-Fu igakkai.** Keijo. *Chosen Sotoku-Fu Igak.* **L.**TD. 19.

13970 **Chov hospodářských zvířat.** Brno. *Chov hospod. Zvíř.*

13971 **Chovatelsky pokrok.** Praha. *Chovat. Pokrok* [1950–] **R.**D.

13972 **Christ Hospital Medical Bulletin.** Cincinnati. *Christ Hosp. med. Bull.*

13973 **Christ's Hospital Science Journal** and **Natural History Society Report.** Horsham. *Christ's Hosp. Sci. J. nat. Hist. Soc. Rep.* [1950–] **L.**BMᴺ. 50–51: 54; **Y.**

13974 **Christiaan Huygens.** Internationaal mathematisch tijdschrift. Groningen. *Christiaan Huygens* [*C. in:* 49779]

13975 **Christianstads läns hushållnings-sällskaps tidskrift.** Christianstad. *Christianstads Läns Hushålln-Sällsk. Tidskr.*

13976 **Chromatographic Data.** Amsterdam. *Chromat. Data* [1958–] **L.**P.; **Bn.**U.; **G.**U.; **Y.** [*Supplement and published with* 25812]

13977 **Chromatographic Methods.** New York. *Chromat. Meth.* [1956–] **L.**P. 56–57.

13978 **Chromatographic Reviews.** Amsterdam, London. *Chromat. Rev.* [1959–] **L.**BMᴺ.; SC.; UC.; **Bn.**U.; **Br.**A.; **Dn.**U. 60–; **G.**U.; **Ld.**U.; **M.**U.; **Y.**

13979 **Chromatography.** *Chromatography* [1958–] **L.**VC.

13980 **Chrome dur.** Paris. *Chrome dur* [1948–] **L.**I.; NF.; P.; **Y.**

13981 **Chromosoma.** Zeitschrift für Zellkern- und Chromosomenforschung. Berlin, Wien. *Chromosoma* [1939–] **L.**BMᴺ.; CB. 47–; MC. 39–54; MD.; QM. 52–; SC.; U.; UC. 47–; Z.; **Abs.**A. 55–; **Ba.**I.; **Bm.**U. 41–; **C.**A. 41–; B.; BO. 49–; GE.; **Cr.**M. 45–54; **E.**AG.; U.; **G.**U. imp.; **Ld.**U.; **M.**U. imp.; **Nw.**A. 48–; **Sa.**; **Y.** [*C. from:* 58906]

13982 **Chronic Rheumatic Diseases.** London. *Chronic rheum. Dis.* [1937–38] **L.**S.; **Ld.**U. [*C. of:* 43048; *C. as:* 47695]

13983 **Chronica botanica.** Leiden, Waltham, Mass. *Chronica bot.* [1935–] **L.**AM. 38–41 imp.; B. 35–57; BM. 38–; BMᴺ.; HS.; K.; L.; NP. 35–47; SC.; **Abs.**A.; U.; **Ba.**I. 42–54; **Bm.**P.; U.; **Bn.**U.; **C.**A. 38–47; BO.; **Cr.**U. 35–37: 49–50; **E.**A.; **Ex.**U. 37–; **Fr.** 38–39; **G.**U.; **H.**U.; **Ld.**U. 41–; **M.**U.; **Md.**H. 35–59; **N.**U. 46–51: 57–; **Nw.**A.; **O.**BO. 35–54; R. 44–; **R.**U.; **Rt.**; **Sa.** 35–39.

13984 **Chronica botanica Reprints.** Waltham, Mass. *Chronica bot. Repr.* [1943–]

13985 **Chronica naturae.** Kolff, Batavia. *Chronica Nat.* [1947–50] **L.**BMᴺ.; K.; L.; MO.; **Abd.**R.; **C.**P.; **E.**R.; **Md.**H. 48–50. [*C. of:* 34329; *C. as:* 23118]

13986 **Chronica nicotiana.** Bremen. *Chronica nicot.* [1940–] **L.**P. 42–43; **C.**A. [*C. of:* 51753]

13987 **Chronicle** of the **Health Organisation, League** of **Nations.** Geneva. *Chronicle Hlth Org.* [1939–45] **L.**BM.; H.; MC.; MD.; S.; SC.; SH.; TD.; **Bl.**U.; **G.**PH. 39–40; U.; **O.**R. [*C. as:* 13989]

Chronicle. **International Union** of **Geodesy** and **Geophysics.** *See* 14003.

13988 **Chronicle** of the **Omaha District Dental Society.** *Chronicle Omaha Distr. dent. Soc.* **L.**D.

13989 **Chronicle** of the **World Health Organisation.** Geneva. *Chronicle Wld Hlth Org.* [1947–58] **L.**AM.; BM.; H.; LI.; MA.; MC.; MD.; PH.; S.; SC.; SH.; TD.; TP.; U.; UC.; UCH.; V.; **Abd.**R.; **Bl.**U. imp.; **Bm.**P.; U.; **Br.**U.; **C.**V. 57–58; **Cr.**MD. 47–53; **Db.**; **Dn.**U.; **E.**A.; **E.**P. 47–56 v. imp.; U.; **G.**F. 48–58 imp.; PH.; **Ld.**U.; **Lh.**FO. 50–58; **M.**P.; **Nw.**A. imp.; U.; **O.**R.; **R.**D. 50–58; **Sa.** 51–53 imp.; **W.** 51–58. [*C. of:* 13987; *C. as:* 57041]

Chronik der **Ruthenischen Ševčenko-Gesellschaft** der **Wissenschaften in Lemberg.** *See* 13990.

13990 **Chronik** der **Ukrainischen Ševčenko-Gesellschaft** der **Wissenschaften in Lemberg.** Lemberg. *Chronik ukr. Ševčenko-Ges. Wiss. Lemberg* [1900– **E.**R. 00–11 imp. [*For Ukrainian edition see* 27775]

Chronika. **Mpenakeion phutopathologikon institouton.** Χρονικα. Μπενακειον φυτοπαθολογικον ινστιτουτον. *See* 2791.

13991 **Chronique** de l'**A.I.Lg.** Association des ingénieurs sortis de l'École de Liège. *Chron. A.I.Lg.* **L.**SC. 37–40.

13992 **Chronique agricole** de l'**Ain.** Bourg. *Chron. agric. Ain*

13993 **Chronique agricole** du **canton** de **Vaud.** Lausanne. *Chron. agric. Canton Vaud* **Rt.** 88–08*. [*C. as:* 52885]

Chronique de la **Association** des **ingénieurs** sortis de l'**Ecole** de **Liège.** *See* 13991.

13994 **Chronique** des **avions Louis Breguet.** Paris. *Chron. Avions Louis Breguet* [1925–36] **L.**AV. 27–32; P. 27–36.

13995 **Chronique géographique** des **pays celtes.** Poitiers. *Chron. géogr. Pays celt.* [1947–53] **L.**G. [*C. as:* 35015]

13996 **Chronique industrielle.** Métallurgie, mécanique, machines outils, manutention. Bruxelles. *Chron. ind.* **L.**P. 57–.

13997 **Chronique médicale.** Paris. *Chron. méd.* [1894–40] **L.**MA. 96–28; MD.; **O.**R. 95–22.

13998 **Chronique mensuelle** de la **Société française** de **photographie** et de **cinématographie.** Paris. *Chron. mens. Soc. fr. Photogr. Cinématogr.* [1948–] **L.**PG. 49–51; SC. 49–51. [*C. of:* 37394]

13999 **Chronique mensuelle technique** de l'**Association générale** des **chimistes** de l'**industrie textile.** Paris. *Chron. mens. tech. Ass. gén. Chim. Ind. text.*

14000 **Chronique** des **mines coloniales.** Paris. *Chron. Mines colon.* [1932–55] **L.**BM^N.; GL. 48–55; GM. 41–55; MI.; SC.; **O.**R. [*C. of:* 14002; *C. as:* 14001]

14001 **Chronique** des **mines** d'**outre mer.** Paris. *Chron. Mines d'outre Mer* [1956–] **L.**BM^N.; GM.; MI.; **O.**R. [*C. of:* 14000]

14001° **Chronique** des **mines** et de la **recherche minière.** Paris. *Chron. Mines Rech. min.* **Y.**

14002 **Chronique minière coloniale.** Paris. *Chron. min. colon.* [1932] **L.**BM^N.; **O.**R. [*C. as:* 14000]
Chronique de l'**Organisation** d'**hygiène.** Genève. *See* 13987.
Chronique de l'**Organisation mondiale** de la **santé.** Genève. *See* 13989.

14003 **Chronique** de l'**U.G.G.I.** Union géodésique et géophysique internationale. Paris. *Chron. U.G.G.I.* [1957–] **L.**BM. 60–; GM.; MO.; P.; SC.; U.; **Abd.**M.; **Bl.**U.; **Br.**U.; **E.**R.; **Lo.**; **Y.** [*Also supplements*]
Chronique de l'**Union géodesique** et **géophysique internationale.** *See* 14003.

14004 **Chrońmy przyrodę ojczystą.** Kraków. *Chrońmy Przyr. ojcz.* [1945–] **L.**BM^N. imp.; E. 47–48 imp.; NC. 48–; **O.**AP.; **Y.**

14004° **Chronos.** De Bilt. *Chronos* **Y.**

14005 **Chrysanthème.** Lyon. *Chrysanthème* **L.**HS. 19–.

14006 **Chrysanthemum.** London. *Chrysanthemum, Lond.* [1950–55] **L.**AM.; BM.; HS.; **C.**UL.; **E.**A.; **O.**R. [*C. as:* 14008]

4007 **Chrysanthemum.** Lucknow. *Chrysanthemum, Lucknow* **L.**BM^N. 56–.

14008 **Chrysanthemum** and **Dahlia.** London. *Chrysanth. Dahlia* [1955–] **L.**AM.; BM.; HS.; **C.**UL.; **E.**A.; **O.**R. [*C. of:* 14006]

14009 **Chrysanthemum Year Book.** London. *Chrysanth. Yb.* [1895–07] **L.**BM. 95–96: 07; K. 95: 07; **E.**A. imp.

14010 **Chūhō.** Japanese Society for the Study of Insects. Tokyo. *Chūhō* [1949–] **L.**BM^N.; Z.

14011 **Church Builder.** London. *Church Bldr* [1862–16] **L.**BM.; **Abs.**N.; **E.**A. 62–02 imp.; **Ld.**P.; **N.**P. 63–88; **O.**B.

14012 **Churchill's Journal** of **Modern Production Practice.** London. *Churchill's J. mod. Prod. Pract.* [1935–40] **L.**P.

14013 **Churn Bulletin.** London. *Churn Bull.* **L.**AM. (curr.); **Abs.**U. 54–57 imp.

14014 **Chymia.** Annual Studies in the History of Chemistry. Philadelphia. *Chymia* [1948–] **L.**BM.; C.; P.; PH.; R.; RI.; SC.; UC.; **Abd.**U.; **Bm.**P.; U.; **Bra.**P.; **C.**UL.; **G.**U.; **Ld.**P.; U.; **M.**D.; P.; **O.**R.; **Sa.**; **Y.**

14015 **Ciba-A.R.L.-Ltd Technical Notes.** Duxford. *Ciba-A.R.L.-Ltd tech. Notes* [1958–] **L.**AV.; BM.; LE.; P.; SC.; **Bm.**P.; **Fr.**; **Lc.**A.; **Ld.**P.; **Lv.**P.; **M.**C.; P. (5 yr.); **N.**T. (5 yr.); U.; **Sy.**R. [*C. of:* 1024]

14015° **Ciba-Blätter.** Basel. *Ciba-Bl.* **L.**P. 60–.

14016 **Ciba Clinical Symposia.** Ciba Pharmaceutical Products Inc. Summit. *Ciba clin. Symp.* [1948–] **L.**UC.; **Br.**U. 50–55; **M.**MS.; **Nw.**A.; **Y.**

14017 **Ciba Foundation Colloquia** on **Ageing.** London. *Ciba Fdn Colloq. Ageing* [1955–] **L.**CB.; MD.; **Abd.**U.

14018 **Ciba Foundation Colloquia** on **Endocrinology.** London. *Ciba Fdn Colloq. Endocr.* [1952–] **L.**CB.; MD.; VC.; **Abd.**U.; **C.**APH.; **Dn.**U.; **N.**U.

14019 **Ciba Foundation Study Groups.** London. *Ciba Fdn Study Grps* [1959–] **L.**MD.; **Dn.**U. 60–.

14019° **Ciba Foundation Symposia.** Ciba Foundation for the Promotion of International Cooperation in Medical and Chemical Research. *Ciba Fdn Symp.* [1950–] **L.**BM.; **Y.**

14020 **Ciba Journal.** Basel. *Ciba J.* [1957–] **L.**P. 59–; **M.**P.; **Y.**

14020° **Ciba Lectures** in **Microbial Biochemistry.** Institute of Microbiology. New York. *Ciba Lect. microb. Biochem.* [1956–] **L.**BM.

14021 **Ciba Review.** Society of Chemical Industry in Basle. *Ciba Rev.* [1937–] **L.**AN.; BM.; C.; I. (curr.); LE.; P. 52–; PL. 52–; PR. 40–; SC.; U.; **Bm.**U.; **Br.**U.; **Bra.**D.; P.; **C.**GG.; P. 50–; UL.; **Db.**; **Lc.**A.; **Ld.**U.; W.; **Lv.**P. 56–; **M.**C.; P. 39–; T. 53–; U.; **N.**T.; U.; **Y.** [*For the German edition, see* 14022]

14022 **Ciba-Rundschau.** Basel. *Ciba-Rdsch.* [1936–52] **L.**BM. 51–52; P.; U. 50–52; **M.**C.; P. 39–52; T. 36–40. [*For the English edition, see* 14021]

14023 **Ciba Symposia.** Ciba Pharmaceutical Products, Inc. Summit, N.J. *Ciba Symp., Summit, N.J.* [1939–51] **L.**BM.; C. 47–51; MD. imp.; SC.; U. imp.; **Bm.**U.; **C.**UL. 49–51; **E.**P imp.; **M.**MS. 47–49; **Nw.**A. 48–51.

14024 **Ciba-Symposium.** Basel. *Ciba-Symposium* [1953–] **L.**BM.; MA.; SC.; U.; **C.**UL.; **Dn.**U.; **E.**P.; **G.**F. imp.; **M.**MS.; **Nw.**A. [*There is a German edition and an English edition*]

14025 **Ciba-Zeitschrift.** Basel. *Ciba-Z.* [1933–52] **L.**HO.; MA. 48–52; MD.; PH. 50–52. [*Superseded by:* 14024]

14026 **Cidre** et le **poiré.** Paris. *Cidre Poiré* [1889–19] **Br.**U. 00–19. [*C. as:* 14027]

14027 **Cidrerie française.** *Cidrerie fr.* [1920–] **Br.**A. 30–40; U. 20–41. [*C. of:* 14026]

14028 **Ciel étoilé.** Rossenges, Vaud. *Ciel étoilé*

14029 **Ciel** et **terre.** Bruxelles. *Ciel Terre* [1880–] **L.**AS. 83–; BM. 81–; G. 01–06 imp.; MO.; SC. 10–; **E.**G. 96–10; M. 80–13 imp.; R. 85–; **Y.**

14030 **Ciencia.** Revista catalana de ciencia i tecnología. Barcelona. *Ciencia, Barcelona* **Sy.**R. 26–33.

14031 **Ciencia.** Revista hispano-americana de ciencias puras y aplicados. México. *Ciencia, Méx.* [1940–] **L.**BM^N.; C. 41– imp.; CB. 54–; EB.; MA. 43–; MD. 43–; TD. 40–45 imp.; Z. 44– imp.; **C.**A.; **O.**R. 53–; **Pl.**M. 59– imp.; **Sal.** 54–; **W.**; **Y.**

14032 **Ciencia aeronáutica.** Caracas. *Cienc. aeronáut.* [1954–] **L.**AV. 58– imp.; **Br.**U. 59–.

14033 **Ciencia** y **cultura.** Maracaibo. *Cienc. Cult.,* *Maracaibo* [1956–] **L.**BM.; MD. 57; **Y.**

14034 **Ciência** e **cultura.** São Paulo. *Ciênc. Cult.,* *S Paulo* [1949–]

14035 **Ciencia interamericana.** Washington. *Cienc. interam.* [1960–] **Y.**

14036 **Ciencia** e **investigación.** Buenos Aires. *Cienc. Invest.* [1945–] **L.**MA. 48–; **Ba.**I. 45–54; **Hu.**G. 45–54; **Y.**

14037 **Ciencia médica.** Rio de Janeiro. *Cienc. méd., Rio de J.* **L.**TD. 44–48 imp.

14038 **Ciencia médica alemana.** Berlin. *Cienc. méd. alemana*

14039 **Ciencia** y **naturaleza.** Quito. *Cienc. Nat.* [1957–] **L.**BM^N.; **Md.**H. [*C. of:* 7810]

14040 **Ciencia** y **técnica.** Buenos Aires. *Cienc. Téc.* **Y.**

14041 **Ciencia** y **técnica** de la **soldadura.** Madrid. *Cienc. Téc. Soldad.* [1951–] **Y.**

14042 **Ciencia** y **tecnologia.** Washington. *Cienc. Tecnol.* [1950–] **L.**BM. 56–; P. 52–57. [*C. of:* 7608]

14043 **Ciencia veterinaria.** Madrid. *Cienc. vet.* **L.**V. 47–48 imp.

14044 **Ciencia** y **vida.** Habana. *Cienc. Vida* [1943–]

14045 **Ciencias.** Anales de la Asociación española para el progreso de las ciencias. Madrid. *Ciencias* [1934–] **L.**BM^N. 34–; P. 56–; **O.**B. 53–; **Y.**

14046 **Ciencias** y **letras.** Guayaquil. *Ciencs Letr., Guayaquil*

14047 **Ciencias** e **letras.** Rio de Janeiro. *Ciencs Letr., Rio de J.* [1937–]

14048 **Ciencias** y **letras.** Santiago de Chile. *Ciencs Letr., Santiago*

14049 **Ciencias médicas hispano-americanas.** Madrid. *Ciencs méd. hisp.-am.* [1948–] **L.**MA.

14050 **Ciencias veterinarias.** México. *Ciencs vet.* [1956–] **W.**

14051 **Çiftçiye öğütler.** Yüksek ziraat enstitüsü. Ankara. *Çiftç. Ogütl.* [1934–]

14052 **Cigar** and **Tobacco World.** London. *Cigar Tob. Wld* [1889–] **L.**BM. 99–; P. (1 yr); **Abs.**N. 25–; **Br.**P. (1 yr); **O.**B. 91–36.

14053 **Ciment.** Paris. *Ciment* **L.**P. 10–36; **Wa.**B. 26–36.

14054 **Ciment armé.** Paris. *Cim. armé* [1932–39?]

14055 **Cimentier français.** Bordeaux. *Cimentier fr.*

14056 **Cimentier moderne.** La Roche-sur-Yon. *Cimentier mod.*

14057 **Cimes.** Círculo médico del sud. Buenos Aires. *Cimes* [1934–] **L.**MD. 38.

14058 **Cincinnati Engineer.** Cincinnati. *Cincinn. Engr* [*C. of:* 10180]

14059 **Cincinnati Journal** of **Medicine.** Cincinnati. *Cincinn. J. Med.* [1921–] **L.**MA. 42–; **G.**F. 47–50 imp. [> 26443, 1926–42]

14060 **Cincinnati Lancet-Clinic.** Cincinnati. *Cincinn. Lancet-Clin.* [1842–04] **Br.**U. 1859–04. [*C. as:* 27977]

14061 **Cincinnati Medical News.** Cincinnati. *Cincinn. med. News* [*C. of:* 30276]

14062 **Cincinnati Sanitary Bulletin.** Cincinnati. *Cincinn. sanit. Bull.*

14063 **Cincinnati Telephone Bulletin.** Cincinnati. *Cincinn. Teleph. Bull.*

14064 **Cine Camera.** London. *Cine Camera* [1960–] **L.**P.

14065 **Cinema Construction.** London. *Cinema Constr.* [1929–30] **L.**BA.; BM. [*C. as:* 14067]
Cinema Theatre and **allied Construction.** *See* 14067.

14066 **Cinema** and **Theatre Construction.** London. *Cinema Theatre Constr.* [1935–48] **L.**BM. [*C. of:* 14067]

14067 **Cinema Theatre** and **general Construction.** London. *Cinema Theatre gen. Constr.* [1930–34] **L.**BA. 30–31; BM. [*C. of:* 14065; *C. as:* 14066]

14068 **Cinematograph Times.** London. *Cinemat. Times* [1928–] **L.**BM.; **Abs.**N.; **O.**B. 28–30.

14069 **Cinématographie française.** Paris. *Cinémat. fr.* [1919–] **L.**PG. 45–47.

14070 **Cinéopse.** Revue technique. Paris. *Cinéopse* **L.**PG. 31–51 imp.

14071 **Cine-Technician.** London. *Cine-Techn* [1937–56] **L.**BM.; P.; PG.; **Abs.**N.; **C.**UL.; **E.**A.; **O.**R.; **We.**K. [*C. of:* 25606; *C. as:* 19425]

14072 **Circle News. Goodrich Co.** Akron, Ohio. *Circle News Goodrich Co.* [1944–] **Sy.**R. [*C. of:* 21466]

14073 **Circolare. Fenomeni solari.** Roma. *Circol. Fenom. sol.* [1958–] **L.**AS.

14074 **Circolare** del **Laboratorio** di **entomologia generale** e **agraria** della **R. Scuola sup.** di **agricoltura** in **Portici.** *Circol. Lab. Ent. gen. agr. R. Scu. Agric. Portici* **L.**EB. 21–41*.

14075 **Circolare. Osservatorio astronomica** di **Roma.** Roma. *Circol. Oss. astr. Roma* **M.**U. 58– imp.

14076 **Circolare. Osservatorio** per le **malattie** delle **piante** delle **provincie** di **Genova** e **La Spezia.** Genova. *Circol. Oss. Mal. Piante Prov. Genova* [1948–] **L.**EB. 48–53

14077 **Circolare. Osservatorio regionale** di **fitopatologia** per la **Calabria.** Catanzaro. *Circol. Oss. reg. Fitopatol. Calabria* [1947–] **L.**EB. (ent.)

14078 **Circolare. R. Istituto** di **entomologia** della **R. Università** di **Bologna.** *Circol. R. Ist. Ent. R. Univ. Bologna* [1935–42] **L.**EB.

14079 **Circolare. R. Osservatorio** di **fitopatologia** per le **Puglie.** Taranto. *Circol. R. Oss. Fitopatol. Puglie* **L.**EB. 24–31.

14080 **Circolo matematico.** Palermo. *Circolo mat.* **L.**QM. 11–25.
Circulaire. Afdeling corrosie, **Centraal instituut** voor **material-onderzoek.** *See* 14084.
Circulaire. Afdeling hout, Centraal instituut voor **material-onderzoek.** *See* 14085.
Circulaire. Afdeling metalen, Centraal instituut voor **material-onderzoek.** *See* 14086.
Circulaire. Afdeling verf en **corrosie, Centraal instituut** voor **material-onderzoek.** *See* 14087.

14081 **Circulaire bibliographique. Association technique** de l'**industrie** du **gaz** en **France.** Paris. *Circul. biblphique Ass. tech. Ind. Gaz Fr.* [1950–]

14082 **Circulaire. Bureau central international** des **télégrammes astronomiques.** Uccle, etc. *Circul. Bur. cent. int. Télégr. astr.* **L.**AS. 20–; **O.**O. 20–.

14083 **Circulaire. Bureau international** de l'**heure.** Paris. *Circul. Bur. int. Heure* [1921–] **L.**AS. 21–25.

14084 **Circulaire. Centraal instituut** voor **material-onderzoek. Afdeling corrosie.** 's-Gravenhage. *Circul. cent. Inst. MaterOnderz. Afd. Corros.* [1950] **L.**P.; **Y.** [*C. as:* 14092]

14085 **Circulaire. Centraal instituut** voor **material-onderzoek. Afdeling hout.** Delft. *Circul. cent. Inst. MaterOnderz. Afd. Hout* [1947–] **Y.**

14086 **Circulaire. Centraal instituut** voor **material-onderzoek. Afdeling metalen.** Delft. *Circul. cent. Inst. MaterOnderz. Afd. Metal.* [1949] **L.**C. [*C. as:* 14095ᶜ]

14087 **Circulaire. Centraal instituut** voor **material-onderzoek. Afdeling verf** en **corrosie.** 's-Gravenhage. *Circ. cent. Inst. MaterOnderz. Afd. Verf Corros.* [1947–] **L.**C. 49; **PR.**; **Y.** [*Partly C. as:* 14084]

14088 **Circulaire** du **Centre** des **recherches** et **études océanographiques.** Paris. *Circul. Cent. Rech. Étud. océanogr.* [1949–] **Lo.**; **Lv.**U. 49–53; **Pl.**M. [*Published in two sections:* Sect. I. *Renseignements techniques et bibliographiques;* Sect. II. *Instructions techniques.*]

14089 **Circulaire. Chambre syndicale** des **fabricants** et **constructeurs** de **matériel** pour **chemins** de **fer** et **tramways.** Paris. *Circul. Chamb. synd. Fabr. Constr. Matér. Chem.-de-fer*

14090 **Circulaire** du **Comité central** des **houillères** de **France.** Paris. *Circul. Com. cent. Houill. Fr.*

14091 **Circulaire** du **Comité** des **forges** de **France.** Paris. *Circul. Com. Forg. Fr.* **L.**I. 05–19★. [*C. as:* 17104]

14092 **Circulaire. Corrosie-institut T.N.O.** Delft. *Circul. Corros.-Inst. T.N.O.* [1951–] **L.**P. 51–54; **Y.** [*C. of:* 14084]

14092ᶜ **Circulaire** d'**information. Fédération aéronautique internationale.** Paris. *Circ. Inf. Féd. aéronaut. int.* **Y.**

14093 **Circulaire** d'**informations techniques. Centre** de **documentation sidérurgique.** Paris. *Circul. Infs tech. Cent. Docum. sidérurg.* **L.**I. 47–; **G.**I. 49–.

14094 **Circulaire. Institut technique** du **bâtiment** et des **travaux publics.** Paris. *Circul. Inst. tech. Bâtim.*

14095 **Circulaire. Ligue sanitaire française.** Paris. *Circul. Lig. sanit. fr.* **L.**EB. 15–16★.

14095ᶜ **Circulaire. Metaalinstituut T.N.O.** Delft. *Circ. Metaalinst. T.N.O.* **L.**P. 51–53★. [*C. of:* 14086; *C. as:* 40829ᵃ]

14096 **Circulaire** de l'**Observatoire** de **Cracovie.** *Circul. Obs. Cracovie* **L.**AS. 21–30; **E.**O. 21–.

14097 **Circulaire** de l'**Observatoire** de **Marseille.** Marseille. *Circul. Obs. Marseille* [1918–26] **L.**AS.; **O.**O. 18–21.

14098 **Circulaire périodique.** Paris. *Circul. périod.* **L.**EE. 50–54. [*C. as:* 17440]

14099 **Circulaire. Société helvétique** des **sciences naturelles.** Fribourg. *Circul. Soc. helvét. Sci. nat.*

14100 **Circulaire** du **Syndicat** des **fabricants** de **sucre.** Paris. *Circul. Synd. Fabr. Sucre*

14101 **Circulaire-annuaire. Chambre syndicale française** des **mines métalliques.** Paris. *Circul.-Annu. Chamb. synd. fr. Mines métall.*

14101ᵃ **Circular AGC.** Alaska Game Commission. *Circ. AGC* [1940–43] **L.**BM. [*C. of:* 14116]

Circular. Advisory Committee on **Atmospheric Pollution.** *See* 31613.

14102 **Circular. Advisory Council** of **Science** and **Industry, Australia.** Melbourne. *Circ. advis. Coun. Sci. Ind. Aust.* [1919–20] **L.**BM. 19; **P.** imp. [*C. as:* 14269]

14103 **Circular. Aerological Division, U.S. Weather Bureau.** Washington. *Circ. aerol. Div. U.S. Weath. Bur.* **L.**MO. 28– imp.

14104 **Circular** on **Agricultural Economic Entomology, Indian Museum.** Calcutta. *Circ. agric. econ. Ent. Indian Mus.* **L.**EB. 03.

Circular. Agricultural Experiment Station, Cornell University. *See* 14174.

Circular. Agricultural Experiment Station, Nevada State University. *See* 14322.

Circular. Agricultural Experiment Station, University of **California.** *See* 14153.

Circular. Agricultural Experiment Station, University of **Florida.** *See* 14242.

14105 **Circular. Agricultural Experiment Station, University** of **Georgia.** Athens, Ga. *Circ. agric. Exp. Stn Univ. Ga* **O.**F. 51–.

Circular. Agricultural Experiment Station, University of **Nebraska.** *See* 14320.

14107 **Circular. Agricultural Experiment Station, Washington State Institute** of **Agricultural Sciences.** *Circ. agric. Exp. Stn Wash. St. Inst. agric. Sci.* **C.**A. 57–.

14108 **Circular. Agricultural Experiment Station. Zionist Organisation Institute** of **Agriculture** and **Natural History.** Tel-Aviv. *Circ. agric. Exp. Stn Zion. Org. Inst. Agric.* [1925–] **L.**EB. (ent.) 26–27; **P.** 25–28; **SC.** 25; **C.**A. imp.; **Rt.** 25–29.

Circular. Agricultural Experiment Stations, University of **Florida.** Gainesville. *See* 14242.

Circular. Agricultural Extension Division, University of **Minnesota.** *See* 14233.

Circular. Agricultural Extension Service, University of **Wisconsin.** *See* 14416.

14109 **Circular. Agricultural Extension Service, Virginia Polytechnic** and **U.S. Department** of **Agriculture.** *Circ. agric. Ext. Serv. Va Polytech. U.S. Dep. Agric.* **Y.**

14110 **Circular. Agricultural Extension Service, Wyoming University.** Laramie. *Circ. agric. Ext. Serv. Wyo. Univ.* **O.**F. 41– imp.

14111 **Circular** and **Agricultural Journal** of the **Royal Botanic Gardens, Peradeniya, Ceylon.** Colombo. *Circ. agric. J. R. bot. Gdns Peradeniya* [1897–12] **L.**BM.; BMᴺ. imp.; **K.**; **P.**; 03–12; **C.**A.; **E.**B. 00–12; **M.**U. 05–11; **Nw.**A.; **Rt.** [*C. as:* 9968]

14112 **Circular** of the **Agricultural Settlement Service, British Columbia.** Vancouver. *Circ. agric. Settlem. Serv. Br. Columb.* **L.**SC. 46–; **O.**RH. 48–.

14113 **Circular. Alabama Agricultural Experiment Station.** Auburn. *Circ. Ala. agric. Exp. Stn* [1906–] **L.**AM.; EB. (ent.); **P.** 31–; **O.**F. 42– imp.; **Rt.** imp.; **Y.**

14114 **Circular. Alabama Geological Survey.** Montgomery. *Circ. Ala. geol. Surv.* **L.**BMᴺ. 28– imp.; GL. 27–29; GM. 28–; **Y.**

14115 **Circular. Alaska Agricultural Experiment Stations.** Washington. *Circ. Alaska agric. Exp. Stns* [1916–] **L.**AM. 23–32; BM.; BM^N. 16–49 imp.; P.; SC.; **G.**M.; **Lv.**P. 23; **Rt.** 23– imp.; **Y.**

14116 **Circular. Alaska Game Commission.** Washington. *Circ. Alaska Game Commn* [1925–39] **L.**BM.; **M.**P. 28–29. [*C. as:* 14101^a]

14117 **Circular. American Agricultural Chemical Company.** Boston. *Circ. Am. agric. chem. Co.* [1913–19] **L.**P. 13; **Rt.** 15–19.

14118 **Circular. American Meat Institute Foundation.** Chicago. *Circ. Am. Meat Inst. Fdn* [1949–] **C.**A. 52– imp.

14119 **Circular. American Paint and Varnish Manufacturers' Association.** Washington. *Circ. Am. Paint Varn. Mfrs' Ass.* [1926–33] **L.**P.; PR.; SC. 28–33. [*C. of:* 14370; *C. as:* 14316]

Circular. American Railroad Association, Engineering Section. *See* 14222.

14120 **Circular. American Refractories Institute.** Pittsburgh. *Circ. Am. Refract. Inst.* **L.**P. 28.

Circular. American Society of Refrigerating Engineers. *See* 117.

14121 **Circular of the American Society for Testing Materials.** Philadelphia. *Circ. Am. Soc. Test. Mater.* **Bm.**U. 23–; **Ld.**U. 44–; **M.**P. 25– imp.

14121^c **Circular. Arctic Unit, Fisheries Research Board of Canada.** Nanaimo. *Circ. Arct. Unit Fish. Res. Bd Can.* **Dm.** 58–.

14122 **Circular. Arizona College of Agriculture and Agricultural Experiment Station.** Tucson. *Circ. Ariz. Coll. Agric. agric. Exp. Stn*

14123 **Circular. Arizona Commission of Agriculture and Horticulture.** Tucson. *Circ. Ariz. Commn Agric. Hort.*

14124 **Circular. Arkansas Agricultural Experiment Station.** Fayetteville. *Circ. Ark. agric. Exp. Stn* [1909–] **L.**AM. 09–18; EB. (ent.) 09–24; P. 09–24 imp.; **Rt.** 09–18 imp.

14125 **Circular. Arkansas Engineering Experiment Station, Arkansas University.** Fayetteville. *Circ. Ark. Engng Exp. Stn* **L.**P. 24–.

14126 **Circular. Arkansas State Plant Board.** Little Rock. *Circ. Ark. St. Pl. Bd* **L.**EB. (ent.) 17–25.

14127 **Circular. Asphalt Association.** New York. *Circ. Asph. Ass.* [1922–29] **L.**P. [*C. as:* 14128]

14128 **Circular. Asphalt Institute.** New York. *Circ. Asph. Inst.* [1930–] [*C. of:* 14127]

14129 **Circular. Association of Hawaiian Pineapple Canners Experiment Station.** Honolulu. *Circ. Ass. Hawaii. Pineapple Cann. Exp. Stn* [1925–26] **L.**SC.

14130 **Circular of the Astronomical Institute of the University of Amsterdam.** *Circ. astr. Inst. Univ. Amst.* [1950–] **L.**SC.; **M.**U. 50–57 imp.

14131 **Circular. Astronomical Observatory of Harvard College.** Cambridge, Mass. *Circ. astr. Obs. Harv.* [1895–] **L.**AS. 00–; BM.; SC. 17–; **C.**O. 00–; UL. 96–; **E.**R. 05–; **M.**U. 05–52; **Nw.**A. 27–; **O.**R.; O.

Circular of the Astronomical Observatory of the Jozef Pilsudski University. Warsaw. *See* 36162.

Circular of the Astronomical Observatory of the University of Warsaw. *See* 36162.

14132 **Circular. Atlantic Biological Station. General Series.** Saint Andrews, New Brunswick. *Circ. Atlant. biol. Stn* [1942–] **L.**SC. 47–; **Abd.**M. 45–; **Dm.** 45– imp.; **E.**U. 49–; **Lo.** 52–; **Lv.**U. 50–.

14133 **Circular. Australian Museum.** Sydney. *Circ. Aust. Mus.*

14134 **Circular. Board of Agriculture and Forestry, Territory of Hawaii.** Honolulu. *Circ. Bd Agric. For. Hawaii*

14135 **Circular. Board of Agriculture, Trinidad and Tobago.** *Circ. Bd Agric. Trin.* [1911–15] **L.**Z.

14136 **Circular of the British Astronomical Association.** London. *Circ. Br. astr. Ass.* [1923–] **L.**AS.; **C.**UL. 50–; **E.**A. 50– imp.; **O.**R. 50–.

14137 **Circular. British Lichen Society.** Cardiff. *Circ. Br. Lichen Soc.* [1958–] **L.**K.

14138 **Circular. British Mosquito Control Institute.** Hayling Island. *Circ. Br. Mosq. Control Inst.* [1927–] **L.**EB. 27–33; SC. [*C. of:* 14253]

14139 **Circular. British Rheologists' Club.** Reading. *Circ. Br. Rheol. Club* **Sy.**R. 43–44.

14140 **Circular of the British Westinghouse Electric Company.** London. *Circ. Br. Westinghouse elect. Co.* **L.**P. 99–07.

14141 **Circular. British Wood Preserving Association.** London. *Circ. Br. Wood Preserv. Ass.* [1933–] **L.**BM.; P. 33–37; **O.**F. 33–37.

14142 **Circular Bulletin. Department of Agriculture, British Columbia.** Victoria. *Circ. Bull. Dep. Agric. Br. Columb.* [1913–] **L.**AM.; SC. 24–; **Abs.**N. 15–19 imp.; **Rt.** 13–21 imp.

14143 **Circular Bulletin. Live Stock Branch. Department of Agriculture, British Columbia.** Victoria. *Circ. Bull. Live Stk Brch Dep. agric. Br. Columb.*

14144 **Circular Bulletin. Michigan State University Agricultural Experiment Station.** East Lansing. *Circ. Bull. Mich. St. Univ. agric. Exp. Stn* [1921–] **L.**AM. 22– imp.; EB. (ent.); P. 33– imp.; SC. 22–; **C.**A.; **O.**F. 31– imp.; **Rt.** 22– imp.; **Y.** [*C. of:* 14294]

14145 **Circular Bulletin. Oregon Agricultural College and Experiment Station.** Corvallis. *Circ. Bull. Ore. agric. Coll. Exp. Stn* **L.**EB. (ent.) 13; P. 08–19* imp. [*C. as:* 50790]

14146 **Circular of the Bureau of Agriculture, Philippine Islands.** Manila. *Circ. Bur. Agric. Philipp. Isl.*

14147 **Circular. Bureau of Animal Industry. United States Department of Agriculture.** *Circ. Bur. Anim. Ind. U.S. Dep. Agric.* [1895–13] **L.**AM.; BM.; BM^N.; EB. imp.; MD. 07–13 imp.; P. imp.; SC. 08–13; Z. 96–13; **Bm.**U. 00–13; **G.**M. 12–13; U. 10–13 imp.; **Lv.**P. imp.; U. imp.; **M.**P. 99–11; **Rt.**

14148 **Circular. Bureau of Engineering Research, University of Texas.** Austin. *Circ. Bur. Engng Res. Univ. Tex.* **L.**P. 54–.

14149 **Circular. Bureau of Entomology. United States Department of Agriculture.** *Circ. Bur. Ent. U.S. Dep. Agric.* [1891–13] **L.**AM.; BM.; BM^N.; EB.; K. imp.; P.; Z. 06–13; **Bm.**U. 94–12 imp.; **G.**M. 12–13; **Ld.**U. 08–13; **Lv.**P.; **Rt.** 93–13 imp.

14150 **Circular of the Bureau of Forestry, Philippine Islands.** Manila. *Circ. Bur. For. Philipp. Isl.* **L.**BM^N. 08.

14151 **Circular. Bureau** of **Plant Industry. United States Department** of **Agriculture.** *Circ. Bur. Pl. Ind. U.S. Dep. Agric.* [1908–13] L.AM.; BM.; BM^N. imp.; K. 08–12; P. imp.; **Bm.**U. imp.; **E.**B. imp.; **G.**M. 12–13; **Lv.**P.; **M.**P. imp.; **Rt.** imp. [*C. of:* 14204 and 14207]

14152 **Circular. Bureau** of **Sport, Fisheries** and **Wildlife.** Washington. *Circ. Bur. Sport Fish. Wildl.* [1956–] O.AP.

14153 **Circular. California Agricultural Experiment Station.** Berkeley. *Circ. Calif. agric. Exp. Stn* [1903–] L.AM.; BM^N. 28–; EB. (ent.); HS. imp.; K. 10–21 imp.; P.; U. 34– imp.; **C.**A.; **E.**B. imp.; U. 28–34 imp.; **G.**U. 03–05: 08; **Ld.**U. 26– imp.; **Lv.**U. 13– imp.; **M.**U. 15– imp.; **Nw.**A. imp.; **O.**RE. 39– imp.; **Rt.** 14– imp.; **Y.**

14154 **Circular. California Agricultural Experiment Station Extension Service.** Berkeley. *Circ. Calif. agric. Exp. Stn Ext. Serv.* [1952–] L.AM.; BM.; BM^N. imp.; EB. (ent.); P.; U.; **Br.**A. imp.; **C.**A.; **Lv.**U.; **Nw.**A.; **Rt.** [*C. of:* 14155]

14155 **Circular. California Agricultural Extension Service,** California University. Berkeley. *Circ. Calif. agric. Ext. Serv.* [1926–52] L.AM.; BM. 34–52; BM^N. 34–52 imp.; EB. (ent.) 27–52; P.; U. 34–52; **Br.**A. imp.; **E.**U. 29–34 imp.; **Lv.**U.; **Nw.**A.; **O.**RE. 39–51 imp.; **Rt.** [*C. as* 14154]

Circular. California Department of **Fish** and **Game.** *See* 14196^c.

14156 **Circular** of the **California State Board** of **Forestry.** Sacramento. *Circ. Calif. St. Bd For.*

14157 **Circular. Canadian Seed Growers' Association.** Ottawa. *Circ. Can. Seed Grow. Ass.* **C.**A. 35–; **Y.**

14158 **Circular. Central Agricultural Board, Trinidad** and **Tobago.** *Circ. cent. agric. Bd Trin.* [1911–15] L.BM^N.; EB.; P.; **Rt.**

14159 **Circular. Centro nacional** de **investigación** y **experimentación agrícola.** Lima. *Circ. Cent. nac. Invest. Exp. agríc., Lima* [1948–52] L.EB.; **C.**A. [*C. of:* and *Rec. as:* 14226]

14160 **Circular. Clemson Agricultural College Extension Service.** Clemson, S.C. *Circ. Clemson agric. Coll. Ext. Serv.* **O.**F. 30– imp.; **Y.**

14161 **Circular. Colegio provincial** de **veterinarios** de **Burgos.** *Circ. Col. prov. Vet. Burgos* L.V. 48–50.

14162 **Circular** of the **College** of **Agriculture, Alberta University.** *Circ. Coll. Agric. Alberta* [1923–44] L.AM.; P. 30–44; SC. 29–44; **C.**A. 24–44; **Rt.** 23–39. [*C. as:* 14237]

14163 **Circular** of the **College** of **Agriculture, Nova Scotia.** Halifax. *Circ. Coll. Agric. Nova Scotia* L.EB. (ent.) 17.

14164 **Circular. College** of **Agriculture, University** of **Illinois.** Urbana. *Circ. Coll. Agric. Univ. Ill.* **O.**F. 32–.

14165 **Circular. Colorado College** of **Agriculture Extension Service.** Fort Collins. *Circ. Colo. Coll. Agric. Ext. Serv.*

14166 **Circular** of the **Colorado State Entomologist.** Fort Collins. *Circ. Colo. St. Ent.* [1910–] L.BM^N. 10–23 imp.; EB. 10–35; SC.

14167 **Circular. Comisión** de **parasitología agrícola.** México. *Circ. Comn Parasit. agríc., Méx.* [1903–08] L.EB. imp.

14168 **Circular. Connecticut Agricultural Experiment Station.** New Haven. *Circ. Conn. agric. Exp. Stn* [1930–] L.EB. (ent.); BM^N. 43– imp.; P.; Z. (zool.) 43–; **Bn.**U. 46–; **Br.**A. 38– imp.; **O.**F. 31–39 imp.; RE. 49– imp.; **Rt.**; **Y.** [*C. of:* 10497]

14169 **Circular. Cooperative Extension Service, New Mexico State University.** *Circ. coop. Ext. Serv. New Mex. St. Univ.* **Y.**

14169^c **Circular. Cooperative Extension Service, University** of **Georgia.** *Circ. coop. Ext. Serv. Univ. Ga* **Y.**

14170 **Circular. Cooperative Extension Service, University** of **Hawaii.** *Circ. coop. Ext. Serv. Univ. Hawaii* **Y.**

14171 **Circular. Cooperative Extension Service, University** of **Kentucky.** *Circ. coop. Ext. Serv. Univ. Ky* **Y.**

14172 **Circular. Co-operative Extension Work** in **Agriculture** and **Home Economics,** Florida. *Circ. co-op. Ext. Wk Agric. Fla* **Rt.** 17–19.

14173 **Circular. Co-operative Extension Work** in **Agriculture** and **Home Economics. Missouri College** of **Agriculture.** *Circ. co-op. Ext. Wk Agric. Mo. Coll. Agric.*

14174 **Circular. Cornell University Agricultural Experiment Station.** Ithaca, N.Y. *Circ. Cornell Univ. agric. Exp. Stn* [1908–] L.AM.; EB. (ent.) 10–15; P. 08–16 imp.; **M.**U. 14–16; **Rt.** 08–15.

14175 **Circular. Cornell University College** of **Agriculture.** Ithaca, N.Y. *Circ. Cornell Univ. Coll. Agric.* L.BM. 13–16.

14176 **Circular. Cotton Worm** and **Boll Worm Commission.** Cairo. *Circ. Cott. Worm Boll Worm Commn* L.BM^N. 12*; EB. 12.

14177 **Circular. Council** for **Scientific** and **Industrial Research, Australia.** Melbourne. *Circ. Coun. scient. ind. Res. Aust.* [1927–] L.P. 27; UC.; **Abs.**U. 27; **Bm.**U. 27–29; **C.**A. 34–. [*C. of:* 14269]

Circular. Crop Protection Institute. Purdue University. *See* 16097.

14178 **Circular** of the **Dairy** and **Cold Storage Commissioner.** Ottawa. *Circ. Dairy cold Stor. Commnr, Ottawa* L.P. 12–21 imp.

14179 **Circular. Defence Standards Laboratories, Maribyrnong.** *Circ. Def. Stand. Labs Maribyrnong* **Y.**

Circular. Department of **Agriculture, Alberta.** *See* 9954.

14181 **Circular** of the **Department** of **Agriculture, British Columbia.** Victoria. *Circ. Dep. Agric. Br. Columb.* L.P. 27–; SC. 23–; **Abs.**N. 19–24 imp.; **O.**RH. 45–; **Rt.** 18–27. imp.

Circular of the **Department** of **Agriculture, British Columbia. Horticultural Branch.** *See* 14254.

14182 **Circular** of the **Department** of **Agriculture, Canada.** Ottawa. *Circ. Dep. Agric. Can.* [1922–] L.AM. 35–; EB. (ent.) 22–33; P. 23–33 imp.; SC. 36–; **C.**A. 32–; **Lv.**P. 36–; **O.**R. 35–.

Circular. Department of **Agriculture** and **Commerce. Porto Rico.** *See* 14185.

Circular. Department of **Agriculture, Federated Malay States.** *See* 20878 and 49263.

Circular. Department of **Agriculture, Fiji.** *See* 1305.

Circular. Department of **Agriculture** and **Immigration, Manitoba.** *See* 14291.

14183 **Circular** of the **Department** of **Agriculture, Jamaica.** Kingston. *Circ. Dep. Agric. Jamaica* [1921–22] **L.**BM^N.; **Y.**

14184 **Circular** of the **Department** of **Agriculture, Kenya.** Nairobi. *Circ. Dep. Agric. Kenya*

14185 **Circular. Department** of **Agriculture** and **Labor, Porto Rico.** *Circ. Dep. Agric. Labor P. Rico*

14186 **Circular. Department** of **Agriculture** and **Markets, New York State.** Albany. *Circ. Dep. Agric. Mkts N.Y. St.* **Y.**

14187 **Circular** of the **Department** of **Agriculture, Mysore.** Bangalore. *Circ. Dep. Agric. Mysore* **C.**A. 34–; **Rt.** 17–39 imp.

14188 **Circular. Department** of **Agriculture, Nyasaland.** Zomba. *Circ. Dep. Agric. Nyasald* [1926–] **L.**BM^N. 26; EB. (agron.) 26; P. 26–30; **C.**A. (agron.); **Rt.** (agron.).

14189 **Circular** of the **Department** of **Agriculture, Ontario.** Toronto. *Circ. Dep. Agric. Ont.* [1916–28] **L.**AM.; EB. (ent.) 20–27; P. 17–18.

14190 **Circular. Department** of **Agriculture, Quebec.** *Circ. Dep. Agric. Queb.*

14191 **Circular. Department** of **Agriculture, Saskatchewan.** Regina. *Circ. Dep. Agric. Sask.*

14192 **Circular. Department** of **Agriculture, Tasmania.** Hobart. *Circ. Dep. Agric. Tasm.* **Rt.** 29–.

14193 **Circular** of the **Department** of **Agriculture, Trinidad** and **Tobago.** Trinidad. *Circ. Dep. Agric. Trin.* [1909–14] **L.**BM. 12; BM^N. 11–14; EB. 11–14; P.; Z. 09–13; **Rt.** 11–14.

14194 **Circular** of the **Department** of **Agriculture, Uganda Protectorate.** Entebbe. *Circ. Dep. Agric. Uganda* [1914–] **L.**BM^N. 14–26; EB. (ent.) 22–24; P. 14–36 imp.; **C.**A.; **O.**G. 21–23 imp.; **Rt.** 14–30.

14194ᶜ **Circular. Department** of **Conservation** and **Development, North Carolina.** Raleigh. *Circ. Dep. Conserv. Dev. N. Carol.* **O.**F. 39– imp.

14195 **Circular. Department** of **Economic Zoology, University** of **Birmingham.** Birmingham. *Circ. Dep. econ. Zool. Univ. Bgham* [1904–06] **L.**BM. 06; **Bm.**U.

Circular. Department of **Engineering Research, University** of **Michigan.** *See* 14403.

14196 **Circular. Department** of **Entomology, Nebraska State University.** Lincoln. *Circ. Dep. Ent. Neb. St. Univ.*

14196ᶜ **Circular. Department** of **Fish** and **Game, State** of **California.** Sacramento. *Circ. Dep. Fish Game Calif.* **Lo.** 51–.

14197 **Circular. Department** of **Forestry, New Zealand.** *Circ. Dep. For. N. Z.*

14198 **Circular. Department** of **Mines. Board** of **Trade.** London. *Circ. Dep. Mines Bd Trade* **O.**B. 34–.

14199 **Circular. Department** of **Sugar Technology, Imperial College** of **Tropical Agriculture.** Saint Augustine, Trinidad. *Circ. Dep. Sug. Technol. imp. Coll. trop. Agric.* [1938–] **Y.**

14200 **Circular. Departamento forestal.** Quito. *Circ. Depto for., Quito* **O.**F. 49– imp.

14201 **Circular. Departamento** de **genética. Instituto experimental** de **agricultura** y **zootecnia.** El Valle, Venezuela. *Circ. Depto Genét. Inst. exp. Agric. Zootec. Venez.* [1940–] **L.**SC. 42–; **C.**A. 42–.

14202 **Circular. Dirección** de **agricultura, ganaderia** y **colonización, Peru.** Lima. *Circ. Dir. Agric. Ganad. Colon. Peru*

14203 **Circular. Division** of **Agriculture, New York Department** of **Farms** and **Markets.** Albany. *Circ. Div. Agric. N.Y. Dep. Fms Mkts* **L.**EB. 20–27.

14204 **Circular. Division** of **Agrostology. United States Department** of **Agriculture.** *Circ. Div. Agrost. U.S. Dep. Agric.* [1895–01] **L.**AM.; BM. 97–01; BM^N. imp.; K. imp.; P.; **Bm.**U. 01; E.B. 99–01 imp.; **Lv.**P. imp. [*C. in:* 14151]

14205 **Circular. Division** of **Animal Industry. California Department** of **Agriculture.** Sacramento. *Circ. Div. Anim. Ind. Calif. Dep. Agric.*

14206 **Circular. Division** of **Biological Survey. United States Department** of **Agriculture.** *Circ. Div. biol. Surv. U.S. Dep. Agric.* [1886–13] **L.**AM.; BM. 89–13; EB. 01–11 imp.; P.; SC. 08–13; **G.**M. 12–13; **Lv.**P. imp.

14207 **Circular. Division** of **Botany. United States Department** of **Agriculture.** *Circ. Div. Bot. U.S. Dep. Agric.* [1886–00] **L.**AM.; BM. 94–00; BM^N. 94–00; K. 95–00 imp.; L. 96–98; P. 89–00; **E.**B. imp.; **G.**M. 96–00 imp.; **Lv.**P. 98–00. [*C. in:* 14151]

14208 **Circular. Division** of **Chemistry, Department** of **Agriculture, Canada.** *Circ. Div. Chem. Dep. Agric. Can.* **Rt.** 14–15.

14209 **Circular. Division** of **Chemistry. United States Department** of **Agriculture.** *Circ. Div. Chem. U.S. Dep. Agric.* [1894–13] **L.**AM.; BM. imp.; C. 08–13 imp.; K. 05–13 imp.; P. imp.; **G.**M. 12–13; **Lv.**P. 94–12; **Rt.** 03–13 imp.

14210 **Circular. Division** of **Communicable Diseases, Department** of **Public Health, Philadelphia.** *Circ. Div. commun. Dis. Philad.* **L.**H. 47.

14211 **Circular. Division** of **Entomology, Board** of **Agriculture** and **Forestry, Territory** of **Hawaii.** Honolulu. *Circ. Div. Ent. Bd Agric. For. Hawaii*

14212 **Circular. Division** of **Entomology. Department** of **Agriculture, Canada.** Ottawa. *Circ. Div. Ent. Dep. Agric. Can.* [1913–21] **L.**AM.; BM^N.; EB.; P. 14–21 imp.; SC. 18–21; Z. imp.; **O.**R.; **Rt.** [*C. in:* 14182]

14212ᶜ **Circular. Division** of **Fisheries** and **Oceanography, C.S.I.R.O.** Australia. *Circ. Div. Fish. Oceanogr. C.S.I.R.O.* [1940–] **Y.**

14213 **Circular. Division** of **Forestry. United States Department** of **Agriculture.** *Circ. Div. For. U.S. Dep. Agric.* [1886–13] **L.**BM. 92–13; BM^N. 97–13 imp.; K. 95–13 imp.; P. 96–13 imp.; SC. 05–13; **Bm.**U. 96–12 imp.; **C.**A. 04–12 imp.; **G.**M. 12–13; **Lv.**P. 98–13 imp.; **O.**F. 96–13 imp.

14214 **Circular. Division** of **Pomology. United States Department** of **Agriculture.** *Circ. Div. Pomol. U.S. Dep. Agric.* **L.**P. 97.

14215 **Circular. Division** of **Soils. United States Department** of **Agriculture.** *Circ. Div. Soils U.S. Dep. Agric.* [1894–13] **L.**AM.; BM.; P.; **Bm.**U. 02–13; **G.**M. 12–13 imp.; **Lv.**P. 00–13 imp.; **Nw.**A. 11–13; **Rt.** 00–13 imp.

14215ᶜ **Circular. Division** of **Systematic Biology, Stanford University.** *Circ. Div. syst. Biol. Stanford Univ.* [1962–] **L.**BM^N.; Z. [*C. of:* 14318]

14216 **Circular** de **divulgación. Estación experimental, Pergamino.** *Circ. Divulg. Estac. exp. Pergamino* [1954–] **C.**A.

14217 **Circular** of the **Electrotechnical Laboratory, Ministry** of **Communications, Japan.** Tokyo. *Circ. electrotech. Lab. Japan* **L.**P. 25–40 imp.; **Y.**

14218 **Circular. Engineering Experiment Station, Kansas State College** of **Agriculture** and **Applied Science.** Manhattan. *Circ. Engng Exp. Stn Kans. St. Coll. Agric. appl. Sci.* [1950–] **L.**P. 56–; **Y.**
    Circular. Engineering Experiment Station, Ohio State University. *See* 14350.

14219 **Circular. Engineering Experiment Station, Oregon State College.** *Circ. Engng Exp. Stn Ore St. Coll.* **M.**T. 50–; **Y.** [*See also:* 14376]

14220 **Circular. Engineering Experiment Station, Purdue University.** Lafayette. *Circ. Engng Exp. Stn Purdue* [1918–20] **L.**P.; **Bm.**U. [*Forms part of:* 40995]
    Circular. Engineering Experiment Station, University of **Arkansas.** *See* 14125.
    Circular. Engineering Experiment Station, University of **Illinois.** *See* 14263.

14221 **Circular. Engineering Extension Department, Purdue University.** Lafayette. *Circ. Engng Ext. Dep. Purdue* [1923–] **L.**P. 23–29; **Bm.**U. 23–29. [*Part of:* 40995]

14222 **Circular** of the **Engineering Section, American Railroad Association.** New York, Chicago. *Circ. Engng Sect. Am. Railr. Ass.*

14223 **Circular. Engineering Section, Commonwealth Scientific** and **Industrial Research Organization, Australia.** Melbourne. *Circ. Engng Sect. C.S.I.R.O. Aust.* [1959–] **L.**P.

14224 **Circular. Entomological Department, Rhode Island Board** of **Agriculture.** Providence. *Circ. ent. Dep. Rhode Isl. Bd Agric.*
    Circular. Estación central agronómica de **Cuba.** *See* 14230.

14225 **Circular. Estación experimental agrícola, Cañete.** *Circ. Estac. exp. agríc. Cañete* **C.**A. 49– imp.

14226 **Circular. Estación experimental agrícola** de **La Molina.** Lima. *Circ. Estac. exp. agríc. La Molina* [1931–47: 53–] **L.**EB.; **C.**A.; **Rt.** 31–41 imp. [*C. of:* 14227; >14159, 1948–52]

14227 **Circular. Estación experimental agrícola** de la **Sociedad nacional agraria.** Lima. *Circ. Estac. exp. agríc. Soc. nac. agr., Lima* [1927–30] **L.**EB.; **C.**A. 28–30 imp.; **Rt.** 29. [*C. as:* 14226]

14228 **Circular. Estación experimental agrícola, Tucumán.** Buenos Aires. *Circ. Estac. exp. agríc. Tucumán* [1915–] **L.**EB. (ent.) 33–58; P. imp.; **C.**A. imp.; **Rt.** 46–; **Y.**

14229 **Circular. Estación experimental agroforestal** de **San Lorenzo.** *Circ. Estac. exp. agrofor. S Lorenzo* [1959–] **O.**F.

14230 **Circular. Estación experimental agronómica** de **Cuba.** Santiago de las Vegas. *Circ. Estac. exp. agron. Cuba* [1904–] **L.**EB. 07–46; **K.** 08–11 imp.; **MY.** 15–29 imp.; **C.**A. 15–.
    Circular. Estación experimental insular, Rio Piedras. *See* 14361.

14231 **Circular. Estación experimental, Quinta normal.** Ambato. *Circ. Estac. exp. Quinta normal, Ambato*

14232 **Circular. Experimental Farms** of **Canada.** Ottawa. *Circ. exp. Fms Can.* **M.**P. 15– imp.

14233 **Circular. Extension Division. Minnesota University College** of **Agriculture.** *Circ. Ext. Div. Minn. Univ. Coll. Agric.* **L.**BM. 35–; BM^N. 35–36; EB. (ent.) 28–36; **Abs.**A. 23.

14234 **Circular** de **extensión. Instituto** de **producción animal, Universidad central** de **Venezuela.** Maracay *Circ. Ext. Inst. Prod. anim. Univ. cent. Venez.* [1957–]

14235 **Circular. Extension Service. Ministry** of **National Economy, Syria.** Damascus. *Circ. Ext. Serv. Minist. natn. Econ. Syria* [1947–] **L.**EB. (ent.)
    Circular. Extension Service, Missouri College of **Agriculture.** *See* 14307.
    Circular. Extension Service, University of **Arizona College** of **Agriculture.** *See* 14401.
    Circular. Extension Service, Wisconsin University of **Agriculture.** *See* 14416.

14236 **Circular** de **extensión. Servicio** de **extensión agrícola.** Mayaguez. *Circ. Ext. Serv. Ext. agríc., Mayaguez* [1935–]

14237 **Circular** of the **Faculty** of **Agriculture, Alberta University.** Edmonton. *Circ. Fac. Agric. Alberta Univ.* [1945–] **L.**P.; **Y.** [*C. of:* 14162]

14238 **Circular farmacéutica.** Barcelona. *Circ. farm.* **L.**PH. 52–58 imp.
    Circular. Federal Experiment Station in **Puerto Rico.** *See* 14360.
    Circular. Federal Station, Porto Rico Experiment Station. *See* 14360.

14238° **Circular. Field Crops Branch, Department** of **Agriculture, British Columbia.** Victoria. *Circ. Fld Crops Brch Br. Columb.* **Y.**

14239 **Circular. Fish** and **Wildlife Service.** United States Department of Agriculture. Washington. *Circ. Fish Wildl. Serv., Wash.* [1941–] **L.**BM.; L. 53– imp.; NC. 45–; SC.; Z. (zool.) imp.; **Abd.**M. imp.; **C.**A.; **E.**R.; **G.**N. 54–56 imp.; **Lo.** 53–; **Lv.**U. imp.; **Pl.**M.; **Sa.** 53– imp.; **Wo.** 53– imp.; **Y.** [*C. of:* 57603]

14239° **Circular. Florida Agricultural Extension Service.** Gainesville. *Circ. Fla agric. Ext. Serv.*

14240 **Circular. Florida Forest** and **Park Service.** Gainesville. *Circ. Fla Forest Pk Serv.*

14241 **Circular. Florida State Plant Board.** Gainesville. *Circ. Fla St. Pl. Bd*

14242 **Circular. Florida University Agricultural Experiment Station.** Gainesville. *Circ. Fla Univ. agric. Exp. Stn* [1949–] **L.**EB. (ent.); HS.; **Br.**A. imp.; **O.**RE. 50–54 imp.; **Rt.**; **Y.** [*Replaces:* 38618]

14243 **Circular. Forest Products Laboratories, Canada.** Ottawa. *Circ. Forest Prod. Labs Can.* **Y.**

14244 **Circular** of the **Forest Service. Department** of the **Interior, Canada.** Ottawa. *Circ. Forest Serv. Can.* [1901–] **L.**BM. 13–15; P. 09–48 imp.; UC. 33–; **O.**F. 04–; G. 14–35 imp.; **Rt.** 15–48 imp.
    Circular. Forestry Branch, Department of the **Interior, Canada.** *See* 14244.

14244ª **Circular. Geological Society** of **London.** London. *Circ. geol. Soc. Lond.* [1952–] **L.**BM^N.; G.; GL.

14244^b **Circular. Geological Survey** of **Alabama.** *Circ. geol. Surv. Ala* **L.**BM^N. 27–49.

Circular. Geological Survey, United States. *See* 14396.

14245 **Circular** of the **Geologists' Association.** London. *Circ. Geol. Ass.* **L.**BM^N. 75–; GL. 71–.

Circular. Georgia Agricultural Experiment Station. *See* 14105.

14246 **Circular. Georgia Coastal Plain Experiment Station.** Tifton. *Circ. Ga cstl Plain Exp. Stn* [1922–] **C.**A.; **O.**F. 42–; **Rt.** 40–.

14247 **Circular. Georgia Geological Survey.** Atlanta. *Circ. Ga geol. Surv.* [1953–] **L.**BM^N.

Circular. Georgia State Board of **Entomology.** *See* 14248.

14248 **Circular. Georgia State Department** of **Entomology.** Atlanta. *Circ. Ga St. Dep. Ent.* **L.**EB. 99–32 imp.

14249 **Circular. Georgia State Engineering Experiment Station.** Atlanta. *Circ. Ga St. Engng Exp. Stn* **Y.**

14250 **Circular. Guam Agricultural Experiment Station.** Washington. *Circ. Guam agric. Exp. Stn* [1921–] **L.**BM.; SC. 21; **C.**A.; **G.**M.; **M.**P.; **Rt.** 21–23.

Circular. Harvard College Astronomical Observatory. *See* 14131.

Circular. Harvard Observatory. *See* 14131.

14251 **Circular. Hawaii Agricultural Experiment Station.** Honolulu. *Circ. Hawaii agric. Exp. Stn* [1931–] **L.**BM.; BM^N. 53–; EB. (ent.) 37–; **Br.**A. 48– imp.; **C.**A.; **M.**P. 37–45 imp.; **Rt.** 42–; **Y.**

14252 **Circular. Hawaiian Sugar Planters' Association Experiment Station.** Honolulu. *Circ. Hawaii. Sug. Plrs Ass. Exp. Stn* **L.**BM^N. 15–46 imp.; **C.**A. 36–39; **Rt.** 25–41.

14253 **Circular. Hayling Mosquito Control.** Hayling Island. *Circ. Hayling Mosq. Control* [1922–27] **L.**EB.; SC. [*C. as:* 14138]

14254 **Circular. Horticultural Branch. Department** of **Agriculture, British Columbia.** Victoria. *Circ. hort. Brch Dep. Agric. Br. Columb.* [1910–] **L.**AM. 44–; EB. (ent.) 18–36; P. 21–; SC. 12–; **Abs.**N. 21–23 imp.; **Lv.**P. 21–26 imp.; **Rt.** 12: 18–27 imp.

14255 **Circular. Idaho Agricultural Experiment Station.** Moscow. *Circ. Idaho agric. Exp. Stn* **L.**AM. 44–; EB. (ent.) 18–45; **C.**A.; **Rt.** 44; **Y.**

14256 **Circular. Illinois Agricultural Experiment Station.** Urbana. *Circ. Ill. agric. Exp. Stn* **L.**AM.; BM. 10– imp.; BM^N. 15– imp.; EB. (ent.) 98–; P. 04–45; U. 06–21; **Abs.**N. 07– imp.; **Bm.**U. 20–; **C.**UL. 09–; **E.**B. 10– imp.; **G.**U. 06–22 imp.; **Ld.**U. 20–; **M.**P. 09– imp.; **Nw.**A. 10–17 imp.; **O.**R. 10– imp.; **Rt.** 03– imp.; **Y.**

14257 **Circular. Illinois Department** of **Agriculture.** Urbana. *Circ. Ill. Dep. Agric.*

14258 **Circular. Illinois Division** of **Natural History Survey. Botanical Series.** Urbana. *Circ. Ill. Div. nat. Hist. Surv. bot. Ser.* **L.**BM^N. 29.

14259 **Circular. Illinois Division** of **Natural History Survey. Entomological Series.** Urbana. *Circ. Ill. Div. nat. Hist. Surv. ent. Ser.* **L.**BM^N. 18– imp.; EB. 18– imp.

Circular. Illinois Engineering Experiment Station. *See* 14263.

14260 **Circular. Illinois Miners'** and **Mechanics' Institute.** Urbana. *Circ. Ill. Miners' Mech. Inst.*

14261 **Circular. Illinois Natural History Survey.** Urbana. *Circ. Ill. nat. Hist. Surv.* **L.**BM^N. 39– imp.; **Db.** 37–; **E.**R. 34–; **Pl.**M. 38–49 imp.

14262 **Circular. Illinois State Geological Survey.** Urbana. *Circ. Ill. St. geol. Surv.* [1906–] **L.**BM^N.; GM. 06–09; SC. 38–; U. 55–; **Br.**U. 38–; **Lv.**U. 48– imp.; **M.**U. 55–; **O.**R. 55–; **Y.**

14262^a **Circular. Illinois State Water Survey.** Urbana. *Circ. Ill. St. Wat. Surv.* **Y.**

14263 **Circular. Illinois University Engineering Experiment Station.** Urbana. *Circ. Ill. Univ. Engng Exp. Stn* [1905–] **L.**AV. 44– imp.; BM.; I.; P.; U. 34–; **Bm.**P. 08–; U. 24– imp.; **Br.**U. imp.; **E.**R. 35–; U. 24– imp.; **Ld.**P. imp.; U. 21–; **M.**P. 09–; T. 17–; U. 39– imp.; **Nw.**A. 21–30 imp.; **O.**R.; **Sh.**10. 23–29 imp.; M. 21–38; **Y.**

14264 **Circular. Indiana Agricultural Experiment Station.** Lafayette. *Circ. Indiana agric. Exp. Stn* [1906–] **L.**AM.; EB. (ent.); P. 08– imp.; **Br.**A. 12–43 imp.; **Ld.**U. 13–18; **O.**RE. 43–52 imp.; **Rt.** 06–18 imp.; **Y.**

14265 **Circular** de **informação técnica. Laboratório** de **engenharia civil.** Lisboa. *Circ. Inf. téc. Lab. Engenh. civ., Lisb.* [1951–52] **L.**P. [*C. as:* 14266]

14266 **Circular** de **informação técnica. Laboratório nacional** de **engenharia civil.** Lisboa. *Circ. Inf. téc. Lab. nac. Engenh. civ., Lisb.* [1952–] **L.**BM. 54–; P. [*C. of:* 14265]

14267 **Circular** de **información. Servicio** de **extensión agrícola.** Mayaguez. *Circ. Inf. Serv. Ext. agríc., Mayaguez* **O.**F. 45– imp.

Circular. Institute of **Forest Products, Washington State University.** New Wood-Use Series. *See* 14332.

14268 **Circular. Institute** of **Research. Lehigh University.** Bethlehem. *Circ. Inst. Res. Lehigh Univ.* [1924–] **L.**SC.; U. 24–42 imp.; UC. imp.; **G.**U. 24–42 imp.; **O.**R.

14269 **Circular** of the **Institute** of **Science** and **Industry.** Melbourne. *Circ. Inst. Sci. Ind., Melbourne* [1922–27] **L.**P.; **Bm.**U. 22. [*C. of:* 14102; *C. as:* 14177]

14270 **Circular. Institution** of **Mechanical Engineers** London. *Circ. Instn mech. Engrs* **L.**BM. 37–.

14271 **Circular. Institution** of **Mining** and **Metallurgy.** London. *Circ. Instn Min. Metall.* [1955–] **L.**BM.

14272 **Circular. Instituto agronômico, Bello Horizonte.** Bello Horizonte. *Circ. Inst. agron. Bello Horizonte* **Rt.** 53.

14272^c **Circular. Instituto agronómico** do **nordeste.** Recife, Pernambuco. *Circ. Inst. agron. NE.* [1954–]

14273 **Circular. Instituto agronómico** do **Norte.** Belem. *Circ. Inst. agron. N., Belem* [1943–] **L.**K.

Circular. Instituto experimental de **agricultura** y **zootecnia, Departamento** de **genetica.** El Valle. *See* 14201.

Circular. Instrument Room, Weather Bureau. United States Department of **Agriculture.** *See* 14409.

Circular. Insular Station, Porto Rico Experiment Station. *See* 14361.

14274 **Circular. Iowa Agricultural Experiment Station.** Ames. *Circ. Ia agric. Exp. Stn* [1913–] **L.**AM.; EB. (ent.) 14–32; P. 13–33 imp.; SC.

Circular. Johns Hopkins University. *See* 25351.

14275 **Circular. Kansas Agricultural Experiment Station.** Manhattan. *Circ. Kans. agric. Exp. Stn* [1909-] L.AM. 25-; BM^N. imp.; EB. (ent.); P. imp.; Br.A. 20- imp.; E.B. imp.; O.F. 40- imp.; Rt. imp.; Y.

14276 **Circular. Kansas State Entomological Commission.** Topeka. *Circ. Kans. St. ent. Commn* L.EB. 08-47.

14277 **Circular. Kansas State Geological Survey.** Topeka. *Circ. Kans. St. geol. Surv.* L.BM. 22-.

14278 **Circular. Kentucky Agricultural Experiment Station.** Lexington. *Circ. Ky agric. Exp. Stn* [1915-] L.AM. 16-; EB. (ent.); P. 15-17; C.A.; O.F. 45- imp.; Rt. imp.; Y.

14279 **Circular. Kentucky Agricultural Extension Division.** Lexington. *Circ. Ky agric. Ext. Div.* Y.

14280 **Circular** of the **Kwasan Observatory.** Kyoto. *Circ. Kwasan Obs.* [1940-] L.AS. 40.

14281 **Circular. Laboratório** de **entomología. Estación nacional agronómica.** Santo Domingo. *Circ. Lab. Ent. Est. nac. agron., S Domingo* L.EB. 27-28.

14282 **Circular Letter. U.S. Weather Bureau.** Washington. *Circ. Lett. U.S. Weath. Bur.* L.MO. 41-49 (imp.)

14283 **Circular. London Master Builders Association Information Service.** London. *Circ. Lond. Master Bldrs Ass. Inf. Serv.* L.BA. 48-.

14284 **Circular. Louisiana Agricultural Experiment Station.** Baton Rouge. *Circ. La agric. Exp. Stn* L.EB. (ent.) 03.

14285 **Circular. Louisiana State Crop Pest Commission.** Baton Rouge. *Circ. La St. Crop Pest Commn* L.EB. 04-09.

14286 **Circular. Maine Agricultural Experiment Station.** Orono. *Circ. Me agric. Exp. Stn*

14287 **Circular** of the **Maine Department** of **Health.** Augusta. *Circ. Me Dep. Hlth*

14288 **Circular. Maine State Forest Service.** Augusta. *Circ. Me St. Forest Serv.* [1930-] O.F. imp.; Y.

14289 **Circular. Malaria Advisory Board, Federation** of **Malaya.** Kuala Lumpur. *Circ. Malar. advis. Bd Fedn Malaya* L.BM^N. 54-; Y.

14290 **Circular** of the **Manitoba Agricultural College.** Winnipeg. *Circ. Manitoba agric. Coll.* L.EB. (ent.) 14-21.

14291 **Circular. Manitoba Department** of **Agriculture.** Winnipeg. *Circ. Manitoba Dep. Agric.*

14292 **Circular** of the **Massachusetts State Board** of **Agriculture.** Boston. *Circ. Mass. St. Bd Agric.* L.EB. (ent.) 13-18; P. 13-17 imp.

14293 **Circular** of the **Meteorological Division, Department** of **Transport.** Toronto. *Circ. met. Div. Dep. Transp., Toronto* L.MO. 46- imp.

14294 **Circular. Michigan Agricultural Experiment Station.** East Lansing. *Circ. Mich. agric. Exp. Stn* [1908-20] L.AM.; EB. (ent.) 11-20; P. imp.; Cr.U. 16-20 imp.; Rt. [*C. as*: 14144]

14294° **Circular. Mineral Industries Experiment Station, Pennsylvania State University.** University Park. *Circ. Miner. Inds Exp. Stn Pa* Y.

14295 **Circular. Ministerio** de **agricultura** de la **nación.** Buenos Aires. *Circ. Minist. Agric. Nac., B. Aires* L.EB. (ent.) 24-30.

14296 **Circular** of the **Ministry** of **Agriculture, Egypt.** Cairo. *Circ. Minist. Agric. Egypt* L.SE. 11-14; E.R. 12-17.

14297 **Circular. Ministry** of **Agriculture, Northern Ireland.** Belfast. *Circ. Minist. Agric. Nth. Ire.*

14298 **Circular. Ministry** of **Health.** London. *Circ. Minist. Hlth* [1919-] L.H. 20-; M.P. 46-; O.B.

14299 **Circular. Ministry** of **Town** and **Country Planning.** London. *Circ. Minist. Town Country Plann.* [1943-] L.BM.; Br.U.; O.B.

14300 **Circular. Minnesota Agricultural Experiment Station.** St. Paul. *Circ. Minn. agric. Exp. Stn* C.A.; Nw.A. 35-36.

14301 **Circular** of the **Minnesota State Entomologist.** St. Paul. *Circ. Minn. St. Ent.* L.BM^N. 09-20*; EB. 14-20 imp.

Circular. Minnesota University College of **Agriculture, Extension Division.** *See* 14233.

14302 **Circular. Mississippi Agricultural Experiment Station.** State College. *Circ. Miss. agric. Exp. Stn* [1904-] L.EB. (ent.); C.A.; Rt. 04-12: 44-; Y.

14303 **Circular. Mississippi Agricultural** and **Mechanical College Extension Division.** *Circ. Miss. agric. mech. Coll. Ext. Div.* L.BM^N. 16-19.

14304 **Circular. Mississippi State Plant Board.** Agricultural College. *Circ. Miss. St. Pl. Bd* L.EB. 18-20.

14305 **Circular. Missouri Agricultural Experiment Station.** Columbia. *Circ. Mo. agric. Exp. Stn* L.BM^N. 16-19 imp.; EB. (ent.) 06-; P. 11-; U. 35-46 imp.; Abs.U. 08-11 imp.; C.A. 38-; Ld.U. 33-; O.F. 36-40 imp.; Rt. 22- imp.; Y.

14306 **Circular. Missouri College** of **Agriculture.** Columbia. *Circ. Mo. Coll. Agric.*

14307 **Circular. Missouri College** of **Agriculture Extension Service.** Columbia. *Circ. Mo. Coll. Agric. Ext. Serv.* O.F. 36- imp.; Y.

14308 **Circular** of the **Missouri State Fruit Experiment Station.** Mountain Grove. *Circ. Mo. St. Fruit Exp. Stn* Y.

14309 **Circular. Missouri State Poultry Experiment Station.** *Circ. Mo. St. Poult. Exp. Stn*

14310 **Circular. Montana Agricultural Experiment Station.** Bozeman. *Circ. Mont. Agric. Exp. Stn* [1908-] L.AM.; BM^N. 10-18 imp.; E.B. (ent.) 08-41; Rt. 39-; Y.

14311 **Circular. Montana State Board** of **Entomology.** Helea. *Circ. Mont. St. Bd Ent.* L.EB. 19-21.

14312 **Circular. Museo** y **biblioteca** de **malacologia** de la **Habana.** Habana. *Circ. Mus. Bibltca Malac. Habana* [1950-54] L.BM^N.; Z.; Pl.M. 50-54 imp. [*C. of*: 14377; *C. as*: 14313]

14313 **Circular. Museo** y **biblioteca** de **zoologia** de la **Habana.** *Circ. Mus. Bibltca Zool. Habana* [1954-] L.BM^N.; Z.; Db. [*C. of*: 14312]

Circular. Museo de **malacologia, Habana.** *See* 14312.

14314 **Circular** of the **Museum** of **Zoology, University** of **Michigan.** *Circ. Mus. Zool. Univ. Mich.* L.BM^N. 32-35.

14315 **Circular. Mysore Coffee Experiment Station.** Bangalore. *Circ. Mysore Coffee Exp. Stn* [1934-] L.BM.; P. 34-36; C.A. 34-39; Rt. 34-36.

Circular. National Bureau of **Standards, United States.** *See* 14398.

14316 **Circular** of the **National Paint Varnish** and **Lacquer Association.** Washington. *Circ. natn. Paint Varn. Lacq. Ass.* [1933–] **L.**IC. 46– imp.; P.; PR.; **Y.** [*C. of:* 14119]

14317 **Circular. National Sand** and **Gravel Association.** Washington. *Circ. natn. Sand Gravel Ass.* **L.**P. 29–44: 49– imp.; **Y.**

14318 **Circular. Natural History Museum, Stanford University.** *Circ. nat. Hist. Mus. Stanford Univ.* [1956–61] **L.**BMᴺ.; Z.; **Cr.**M. [*C. as:* 14215°]

14319 **Circular. Naval Meteorological Branch.** London. *Circ. nav. met. Brch* **L.**MO. 44–48* imp. [*C. as:* 14319°]

14319° **Circular. Naval Weather Service.** London. *Circ. Nav. Weath. Serv.* [1949–52] **L.**MO. [*C. of:* 14319]

14320 **Circular. Nebraska Agricultural Experiment Station.** Lincoln. *Circ. Neb. agric. Exp. Stn* [1917–] **L.**EB. (ent.) 22–; SC. imp.; **C.**A. imp.; **E.**R. 19–22 imp.; **Rt.** 39–; **Y.**

14321 **Circular. Nebraska Insect Pest** and **Plant Disease Bureau.** Lincoln. *Circ. Neb. Insect Pest Pl. Dis. Bur.* **L.**EB. 08–09; SC. 08–09.

14322 **Circular** of the **Nevada Agricultural Experiment Station.** Reno. *Circ. Nev. agric. Exp. Stn*

14324 **Circular. New Hampshire Agricultural Experiment Station.** Durham. *Circ. New Hamps. agric. Exp. Stn* **L.**P. 19–42 imp.

14325 **Circular. New Hampshire Department** of **Agriculture. State Moth Work.** Concord. *Circ. New Hamps. Dep. Agric. St. Moth Wk* **L.**EB. 13–15.

14326 **Circular. New Jersey Agricultural Experiment Station.** New Brunswick. *Circ. New Jers. agric. Exp. Stn* [1912–] **L.**AM.; BMᴺ. 18–31 imp.; EB. (ent.); P.; **Br.**A. 14–43 imp.; **C.**A.; **O.**F. 39– imp.; **Rt.**; **Y.**

14327 **Circular. New Jersey Board** of **Health.** Trenton. *Circ. New Jers. Bd Hlth*

14328 **Circular. New Jersey Bureau** of **Plant Industry.** Trenton. *Circ. New Jers. Bur. Pl. Ind.* **O.**F. 41– imp.

14329 **Circular. New Jersey Department** of **Agriculture.** Trenton. *Circ. New Jers. Dep. Agric.* **L.**EB. (ent.) 17–45; **Y.**

14330 **Circular. New Mexico Oil Conservation Commission.** Socorro. *Circ. New Mex. Oil Conserv. Commn* [1935–] **L.**SC.

14331 **Circular. New Mexico State Bureau** of **Mines** and **Mineral Resources.** Socorro. *Circ. New Mex. St. Bur. Mines Miner. Resour.* **L.**MI. 30–53 imp.: 54–; **Y.**
Circular. New Mexico State University Cooperative Extension Service. *See* 14169.

14332 **Circular. New Wood-Use Series. Institute** of **Forest Products, Washington State University.** Seattle. *Circ. new Wood-Use Ser. Inst. Forest Prod. Wash. St. Univ.* **O.**F. 49– imp.

14333 **Circular. New York State Agricultural Experiment Station.** Geneva. *Circ. N.Y. St. agric. Exp. Stn* **L.**EB. (ent.) 13–44; **C.**A. 34–; **O.**F. 13– imp.

14334 **Circular. New York State College** of **Forestry.** Syracuse. *Circ. N.Y. St. Coll. For.* [1913–] **O.**F. imp.

14335 **Circular. New York State Department** of **Health.** Albany. *Circ. N.Y. St. Dep. Hlth*

14336 **Circular. New York State Museum.** Albany. *Circ. N.Y. St. Mus.* [1928–] **L.**BMᴺ. 30–56; GL. 51– imp.; L. 51–56 imp.; **Bl.**U. 51–; **Lv.**U. 53–; **M.**U. 51–56; **Rt.** 53– imp.; **Sw.**U. imp.
Circular. New York State Museum of **Natural History.** *See* 14336.

14337 **Circular. New Zealand Dairy Board.** Wellington. *Circ. N.Z. Dairy Bd.* [1934–]
Circular. New Zealand Department of **Forestry.** *See* 14197.

14338 **Circular** of the **New Zealand State Forest Service.** Wellington. *Circ. N.Z. St. Forest Serv.* **L.**P. 26–; SC. 22–; **O.**F. 22–38.

14339 **Circular. North Carolina Agricultural Experiment Station.** West Raleigh. *Circ. N. Carol. agric. Exp. Stn*

14340 **Circular. North Carolina Division** of **Forestry** and **Parks.** Raleigh. *Circ. N. Carol. Div. For. Pks*

14341 **Circular. North Carolina Geological** and **Economic Survey.** Chapel Hill. *Circ. N. Carol. geol. econ. Surv.* **L.**BMᴺ. 21–31 imp.

14342 **Circular. North Dakota Agricultural Experiment Station.** Fargo. *Circ. N. Dak. agric. Exp. Stn* [1914–46] **L.**EB. (ent.) 25–36; P.; SC. 17–46; **Ld.**U. 17–35; **Rt.** 22–34.

14343 **Circular Notes, New Zealand Meteorological Service.** Wellington. *Circ. Notes N.Z. met. Serv.* **L.**MO. 44–51 imp. [*C. as:* 52184]
Circular. Office of **Cotton, Truck** and **Forest Crop Disease.** Washington. *See* 12913.

14344 **Circular. Office** of **Experiment Stations. United States Department** of **Agriculture.** *Circ. Off. Exp. Stns U.S. Dep. Agric.* [1889–13] **L.**AM.; BM.; P. imp.; **Bm.**U. 02–12; **Lv.**P. 91–13 imp.; **M.**P. 06–13 imp.; **Rt.** 06–13 imp.

14345 **Circular. Office** of **Public Roads. United States Department** of **Agriculture.** Washington. *Circ. Off. publ. Rds U.S. Dep. Agric.* **L.**BM. 96–13*; P. 94–13 imp.; **Bm.**U. 96–13 imp.

14346 **Circular. Office** of the **Secretary. United States Department** of **Agriculture.** *Circ. Off. Secr. U.S. Dep. Agric.* [1896–19] **L.**AM.; BM. 04–19; BMᴺ. 11–19; EB. 11–19 imp.; K. 96–16 imp.; **Bm.**U. 03–10; **E.**F. 15–16 imp.; **G.**M. 12–19 imp.; **Lv.**P. 98–19 imp.; **M.**P. 06–19 imp.; **Rt.** 06–19 imp.

14347 **Circular. Oficina** de **sanidad vegetal** de **Cuba.** Habana. *Circ. Ofic. Sanid. veg. Cuba* **L.**EB. 17–19.

14348 **Circular. Ohio Agricultural Experiment Station.** Wooster. *Circ. Ohio agric. Exp. Stn* [1888–15] **L.**AM.; EB. (ent.) 05–15; L. 13–14; P.; **Bm.**U. 07–15 imp.; **Ld.**U. 10–15; **Lv.**P. imp.; **Rt.** 06–15.

14349 **Circular. Ohio Department** of **Agriculture.** Wooster. *Circ. Ohio Dep. Agric.*

14350 **Circular. Ohio State University Engineering Experiment Station.** Columbus. *Circ. Ohio St. Univ. Engng Exp. Stn* [1921–] **L.**P. 21–57; **Ld.**P.; **M.**U. 36–55 imp.; **Nw.**A. imp.; **O.**R. 32–; **Sa.** 34–55 imp.; **Sh.**M.

14351 **Circular. Oklahoma Agricultural Experiment Station.** Stillwater. *Circ. Okla. agric. Exp. Stn* **L.**EB. (ent.) 16–; P. 26–; SC. 15– imp.; **O.**R. 39–; **Rt.** 16–.

14352 **Circular. Oklahoma Geological Survey.** Norman. *Circ. Okla. geol. Surv.* [1908–] **L.**BM[N]. 11–30; **GM.**; **P.** 08–30; **UC.** 11– imp.; **Br.**U. 59–; **Y.**

    Circular. Oregon Agricultural Experiment Station. *See* 50790.

14353 **Circular. Oregon State Board** of **Forestry.** Salem. *Circ. Ore. St. Bd For.* [1940–] **O.**F.

    Circular. Oregon State College Engineering Experiment Station. *See* 14219 and 14376.

    Circular. Oregon State College School of **Forestry.** *See* 14369.

14354 **Circular. Pennsylvania Agricultural Experiment Station.** State College, Pa. *Circ. Pa agric. Exp. Stn* **Br.**A. 48– imp.; **Rt.** 28– imp.

14355 **Circular. Pennsylvania Bureau of Economic Zoology.** Harrisburg. *Circ. Pa Bur. econ. Zool.* **L.**EB. 17–19*.

14356 **Circular. Pennsylvania Bureau** of **Plant Industry.** Harrisburg. *Circ. Pa Bur. Pl. Ind.* **L.**EB. (ent.) 20–; **SC.** 27– imp.

14357 **Circular. Pennsylvania Department of Agriculture.** Harrisburg. *Circ. Pa Dep. Agric.* **L.**EB. (ent.) 25; **SC.** 25–.

14358 **Circular. Pennsylvania Department** of **Forests** and **Waters.** Harrisburg. *Circ. Pa Dep. Forests Wat.*

14359 **Circular. Pennsylvania State College Mineral Industries Experiment Station.** *Circ. Pa St. Coll. Miner. Ind. Exp. Stn* **L.**MI. 53–56 imp.: 57–; **Y.**

14360 **Circular. Porto Rico Agricultural Experiment Station, Federal Station, Mayaguez.** Washington. *Circ. P. Rico agric. Exp. Stn fed. Stn Mayaguez* [1903–] **L.**BM. 06–; BM[N]. 18–21: 31–38; EB. (ent.) 04–; **K.** 03–47 imp.; **P.** 04–47 imp.; **C.**A.; **G.**M. 15–30; **M.**P. 20–21; **O.**F. 48–; **Rt.** 04– imp.

14361 **Circular. Porto Rico Agricultural Experiment Station, Insular Station, Rio Piedras.** *Circ. P. Rico agric. Exp. Stn insular Stn Rio Piedras* [1912–] **L.**EB. 12–34; **P.** 25–43; **C.**A. 31–; **Rt.** 16– imp.

    Circular. Porto Rico Insular Experiment Station. *See* 14361.

14362 **Circular. Porto Rico Sugar Producers' Association Experiment Station.** *Circ. P. Rico Sug. Prod. Ass. Exp. Stn*

    Circular. Poulkovo Observatory. *See* 38200.

    Circular. Puerto Rico Agricultural Experiment Station, Mayaguez. *See* 14360.

    Circular. Puerto Rico University Agricultural Experiment Station, Rio Piedras. *See* 14361.

14363 **Circular. Radio. United States Weather Bureau.** Washington. *Circ. Radio U.S. Weath. Bur.* [1933–35] **L.**BM.; MO. imp. [*C. as:* 41783]

14364 **Circular. Research Association** of **British Rubber** and **Tyre Manufacturers' Information Bureau.** London. *Circ. Res. Ass. Br. Rubb. Tyre Mfrs' Inf. Bur.* **L.**P. 26– imp.; **Y.**

14365 **Circular. Research Branch Library, Post Office Engineering Department.** London. *Circ. Res. Brch Libr. P.O. Engng Dep.*

    Circular. Royal New Zealand Astronomical Society. Solar Section. *See* 14380. **Variable Star Section.** *See* 14406.

14366 **Circular. Royal Observatory.** Edinburgh. *Circ. R. Obs., Edinb.* [1889–] **L.**AS. 89–01.

14367 **Circular. Rubber Growers' Association.** London. *Circ. Rubb. Grow. Ass.* **Sy.**R. 31–39.

14368 **Circular. Rubber Research Institute** of **Malaya.** Kuala Lumpur. *Circ. Rubb. Res. Inst. Malaya* [1939–] **L.**K. 39–52 imp.; **P.**; **SC.**; **O.**F. imp.; **Rt.** 41–.

    Circular. School of **Forestry** and **Conservation, University** of **Michigan.** *See* 14404.

14369 **Circular. School** of **Forestry, Oregon State College.** Corvallis. *Circ. Sch. For. Ore. St. Coll.* [1949–] **O.**F.

14370 **Circular. Scientific Section, Paint Manufacturers' Association** of the **United States.** Philadelphia. *Circ. scient. Sect. Paint Mfrs' Ass. U.S.* **L.**P. 22–26*; **PR.** 13–26. [*C. as:* 14119]

14371 **Circular. Secção** de **fructicultura. Departamento** de **fomento** da **producção vegetal.** São Paulo. *Circ. Secc. Fructic. Dep. Fom. Prod. veg., S Paulo* [1936–]

14372 **Circular. Secretaria** de **agricultura** y **fomento.** México. *Circ. Secr. Agric. Fom., Méx.* **L.**EB. (ent.) 21.

14373 **Circular. Section** of **Food Preservation** and **Transport, Council** for **Scientific** and **Industrial Research, Australia.** *Circ. Sect. Fd Preserv. Transp. C.S.I.R. Aust.* [1938–] **L.**P. 38–42.

14374 **Circular. Seismological Committee** of the **British Association.** Newport, I.W. *Circ. seism. Comm. Br. Ass.* [1899–12] **L.**BM.; MO. imp.; **E.**D. 01; **Ld.**U.; **O.**O. [*C. as:* 33488]

14375 **Circular Series. Department** of **Engineering Research, University** of **Michigan.** Ann Arbor. *Circ. Ser. Dep. Engng Res. Univ. Mich.* [1927–31] **L.**BM.; **P.**; **Abs.**N.; **Bm.**U.; **E.**U.; **G.**U. 28–31; **Ld.**U.

    Circular Series. Engineering Experiment Station. University of **Illinois.** *See* 14263.

    Circular Series. Oregon Agricultural College Engineering Experiment Station. *See* 14219 and 14376.

14376 **Circular Series. Oregon State College Engineering Experiment Station.** Corvallis. *Circ. Ser. Ore. St. Coll. Engng Exp. Stn* [1929–] **L.**P.; **O.**F. imp.; **Y.** [*See also:* 14219]

14377 **Circular. Sociedad malacologica 'Carlos de la Torre'.** La Habana. *Circ. Soc. malac. Carlos de la Torre* **L.**BM[N]. 49–50*; **Pl.**M. 49–50. [*C. as:* 14312]

14378 **Circular** of the **Society** of **Entomologists.** Sydney. *Circ. Soc. Ent., Sydney* **L.**BM[N]. 54–.

14379 **Circular. Society** for the **Prevention** and **Relief** of **Cancer.** London. *Circ. Soc. Prev. Relief Cancer* **L.**BM. 12*.

14380 **Circular** of the **Solar Section** of the **Royal New Zealand Astronomical Society.** Wellington. *Circ. sol. Sect. R.N.Z. astr. Soc.* **L.**AS. 29.

14381 **Circular. South Carolina Agricultural Experiment Station.** Clemson College. *Circ. S. Carol. agric. Exp. Stn* **L.**EB. (ent.) 13–; **Rt.** 33–; **Y.**

14382 **Circular. South Dakota Agricultural Experiment Station.** Brookings. *Circ. S. Dak. agric. Exp. Stn* [1931–] **L.**EB. (ent.) 42–; **P.** 40–; **C.**A.; **O.**RE. 47– imp.; **Rt.** 51–; **Y.**

14383 **Circular. South Dakota Department** of **Agriculture.** Pierre. *Circ. S. Dak. Dep. Agric.*

14384 **Circular** of the **South Dakota Geological** and **Natural History Survey.** Vermillion. *Circ. S. Dak. geol. nat. Hist. Surv.* **L.**BM^N. 19–27 imp.; GM. 18–; **C.**A.

14385 **Circular** of the **South Dakota State Entomologist.** Brookings. *Circ. S. Dak. St. Ent.* **L.**EB. 18–22.

Circular. Stanford University Natural History Museum. *See* 14318.

Circular. State Moth Work, New Hampshire Department of Agriculture. *See* 14325.

Circular. Tadjik Astronomical Observatory. *See* 55261.

14386 **Circular. Tennessee Agricultural Experiment Station.** Knoxville. *Circ. Tenn. agric. Exp. Stn* **L.**EB. (ent.) 26–; **Y.**

14387 **Circular** of the **Tennessee State Dairy Commissioner.** Nashville. *Circ. Tenn. St. Dairy Commnr*

14388 **Circular. Tennessee State Division** of **Forestry.** Nashville. *Circ. Tenn. St. Div. For.* **O.**F. 26–27.

14389 **Circular. Texas Agricultural Experiment Stations.** College Station. *Circ. Tex. agric. Exp. Stns* [1913–] **L.**EB. (ent.) 15–; P.; **C.**A.; **Ld.**U. 36–; **M.**U. 38–47 imp.; **Rt.** 23–; **Y.**

14390 **Circular trimestral.** Asociación de **productores** de **salitre** de **Chile.** Valparaíso. *Circ. trimest. Asoc. Prod. Salitre Chile*

14391 **Circular** on **Tropical Diseases.** Manila. *Circ. trop. Dis.* **E.**R. 09–19.

14391° **Circular. Union géographique international.** Washington. *Circ. Un. géogr. int.* [1952–] **L.**BM.

14392 **Circular** of the **Union Observatory.** Republic of South Africa. Johannesburg. *Circ. Un. Obs.* [1912–] **L.**AS.; SC.; **C.**O.; **E.**O.; R.; **M.**U. imp.; **Nw.**A.; **O.**O.; **Y.** [*C. of:* 54151]

Circular. United States Bureau of **Standards.** *See* 14397.

14393 **Circular. United States Coast** and **Geodetic Survey.** Washington. *Circ. U.S. Cst geod. Surv.*

14394 **Circular. United States Department** of **Agriculture.** Washington. *Circ. U.S. Dep. Agric.* [1927–] **L.**BM^N.; EB. (ent.); HS. 27–51 imp.; SC.; U.; UC. 34– imp.; Z. (zool.); **Abs.**N. imp.; **Bm.**U. 30– imp.; **Br.**A. 27–55 imp.; **E.**F. 27–39 imp.; **Lv.**P. imp.; **Nw.**A. imp.; **O.**F.; RE. 29–55 imp.; **Rt.** [*C. of:* 16590]

Circular. United States Department of **Agriculture, Bureau** of **Animal Industry.** *See* 14147.

Circular. United States Department of **Agriculture, Bureau** of **Entomology.** *See* 14149.

Circular. United States Department of **Agriculture, Bureau** of **Plant Industry.** *See* 14151.

Circular. United States Department of **Agriculture, Division** of **Agrostology.** *See* 14204.

Circular. United States Department of **Agriculture, Division** of **Biological Survey.** *See* 14206.

Circular. United States Department of **Agriculture, Division** of **Botany.** *See* 14207.

Circular. United States Department of **Agriculture, Division** of **Chemistry.** *See* 14209.

Circular. United States Department of **Agriculture, Division** of **Forestry.** *See* 14213.

Circular. United States Department of **Agriculture, Division** of **Pomology.** *See* 14214.

Circular. United States Department of **Agriculture, Division** of **Soils.** *See* 14215.

Circular. United States Department of **Agriculture, Office** of **Experiment Stations.** *See* 14344.

Circular. United States Department of **Agriculture, Office** of **Public Roads.** *See* 14345.

Circular. United States Department of **Agriculture, Office** of **Road Inquiry.** *See* 14345.

Circular. nited UStates Department of **Agriculture, Office** of the **Secretary.** *See* 14346.

Circular. United States Department of **Agriculture, Weather Bureau, Instrument Room.** *See* 14409.

Circular of the **United States Fish** and **Wildlife Service.** Washington. *See* 14239.

14396 **Circular. United States Geological Survey.** Washington. *Circ. U.S. geol. Surv.* [1933–] **L.**BM^N. imp.; C.; GL. 33–54 imp.; GM.; P.; SC. 33–34: 51–; **Bl.**U. 33–34; **Bm.**U. 33–34; **C.**P.; **Db.**; **E.**C. 33–34; R.; U. 33–34; **Lv.**U.; 33–34: 53– imp.; **M.**U. 33–34: 52–54; **Nw.**A. 33–34; **O.**R.; **Y.**

14397 **Circular. United States National Bureau** of **Standards.** Washington. *Circ. U.S. natn. Bur. Stand.* **L.**BM. 08–; C. 16– imp.; I. 17– imp.; MI. 24– imp.; MO. 12– imp.; NF. 11– imp.; P. 03–59; RI. 11–; SC. 17–; UC. 10– imp.; **Abs.**U. 13– imp.; **Bm.**P. 11– imp.; U. 16–; **Bn.**U. 11 imp.; **C.**P. 18–; UL. 20–; **Dn.**U. 14–22 imp.; **E.**R. 14– imp.; **G.**I. 16– imp.; M. 12–36; U. 13–16 imp.; **Ld.**U. 16–; **Lv.**U. 11– imp.; **M.**C. 18– imp.; P. 11–33 imp.; U. 12– imp.; **Y.**

14398 **Circular. United States National Museum.** Smithsonian Institution. Washington. *Circ. U.S. natn. Mus.*

14399 **Circular. United States Naval Observatory.** Washington. *Circ. U.S. nav. Obs.* [1949–] **L.**AS.; SC.; **C.**P.; **Db.**; **E.**R.; **M.**U. imp.

14400 **Circular** of the **United States Signal Service.** Washington. *Circ. U.S. Sign. Serv.*

14401 **Circular** of the **University** of **Arizona College** of **Agriculture Extension Service.** Tucson. *Circ. Univ. Ariz. Coll. Agric. Ext. Serv.* [*C. as:* 18835]

Circular. University of **Arkansas Engineering Experiment Station.** *See* 14125.

Circular. University Astronomical Observatory. Leningrad. *See* 55263.

Circular. University of **Birmingham Department** of **Economic Zoology.** Birmingham. *See* 14195.

Circular. University of **Florida Agricultural Experiment Stations.** *See* 14242.

Circular. University of **Georgia Agricultural Experiment Station.** *See* 14105.

Circular. University of **Georgia Cooperative Extension Service.** *See* 14169°.

Circular. University of **Hawaii Agricultural Experiment Station.** *See* 14251.

Circular. University of **Hawaii Cooperative Extension Service.** *See* 14170.

Circular. University of **Kentucky Cooperative Extension Service.** *See* 14171.

14402 **Circular** of the **University** of **London Observatory.** London. *Circ. Univ. Lond. Obs.* **L.**AS. 47–.

14403 **Circular. University** of **Michigan Department** of **Engineering Research.** Ann Arbor. *Circ. Univ. Mich. Dep. Engng Res.* **Bm.**U. 27–31.

Circular. University of **Michigan Museum** of **Zoology.** *See* 14314.

14404 **Circular. University** of **Michigan School** of **Forestry** and **Conservation.** Ann Arbor. *Circ. Univ. Mich. Sch. For. Conserv.* [1937–] **L.**BM^N. 37–42; EB. (ent.); SC.; **Bl.**U.; **Bm.**U. 37–42 imp.; **C.**P.; **E.**U. 37–39 imp.; **M.**U. 37–42 imp.

    Circular. University of **Minnesota Agricultural Extension Division.** *See* 14233.

    Circular. University of **Wyoming Agricultural Extension Service.** *See* 14110.

14405 **Circular** of the **Utah Agricultural Experiment Station.** Logan. *Circ. Utah. agric. Exp. Stn* [1904–] **L.**AM. 12–; BM^N. 16–37; EB. (ent.) 13–; P.; **C.**A.; **Ld.**U. 12–21 imp.; **O.**RE. 49– imp.; **Rt.** 12–24: 41–; **Y.**

14406 **Circular** of the **Variable Star Section** of the **Royal New Zealand Astronomical Society.** Wellington. *Circ. var. Star Sect. R.N.Z. astr. Soc.* **L.**AS. 33–; SC. 45–; **Y.**

14407 **Circular. Vermont Agricultural Experiment Station.** Burlington. *Circ. Vt agric. Exp. Stn* **L.**AM. 42– imp.; EB. 10–15.

14408 **Circular. Virginia State Crop Pest Commission.** Blacksburg. *Circ. Va St. Crop Pest Commn* **L.**EB. 06–14.

14409 **Circular. Weather Bureau, Instrument Room. United States Department** of **Agriculture.** *Circ. Weather Bur. Instrum. Rm U.S. Dep. Agric.* **L.**BM. 94–; P. 92–11; SC. 14–; **G.**M. 14– imp.

14410 **Circular. Wellcome Tropical Research Laboratories.** Khartoum. *Circ. Wellcome trop. Res. Labs*

14411 **Circular. West India Committee.** London. *Circ. W. India Comm.* **L.**BM. 03–; K. 41–; SC. 24–; **Md.**H. 39–43; **O.**RH. 03– imp.; **Rt.** 23–.

14412 **Circular. West Norfolk Farmers' Manure** and **Chemical Co.** *Circ. W. Norf. Fmrs' Manure Chem. Co.* **Rt.** 05–15: 33–.

14413 **Circular. West Virginia Agricultural Experiment Station.** Morgantown. *Circ. W. Va agric. Exp. Stn* [1903–] **L.**AM.; EB. (ent.) 13–; **O.**F. 30– imp.; **Rt.** 51–; **Y.**

14414 **Circular. Wild Flower Preservation Society, Inc.** Washington. *Circ. wild Flower Preserv. Soc.* **L.**BM^N. 34 imp.

14415 **Circular. Wisconsin Agricultural Experiment Station.** Madison. *Circ. Wis. agric. Exp. Stn* [1909–14] **L.**AM.; P.; **C.**A. [*C. as:* 14416]

    Circular of the **Wisconsin College** of **Agriculture Extension Service.** *See* 14416.

14415^c **Circular. Wisconsin Department** of **Agriculture.** Madison. *Circ. Wis. Dep. Agric.* **L.**BM^N. 16–18 imp.; EB. (ent.) 15–26; SC. 16–.

14416 **Circular** of the **Wisconsin University** of **Agriculture Extension Service.** Madison. *Circ. Wis. Univ. Agric. Ext. Serv.* [1915–] **L.**EB. (ent.) 16–; P.; **Abs.**N. 21– imp.; **Ld.**U. 30–40 imp.; **Rt.** 20–; **Y.** [*C. of:* 14415]

14417 **Circular. Wolsingham Observatory.** Darlington. *Circ. Wolsingham Obs.* **L.**AS. 87–02 imp.

14418 **Circular. Wyoming Agricultural Experiment Station.** Laramie. *Circ. Wyo. agric. Exp. Stn* **Rt.** 51–.

    Circulares. *See* **Circular.**
    Circulars. *See* **Circular.**

14419 **Circulation.** Journal of the American Heart Association. New York. *Circulation* [1950–] **L.**GH.; MA.; MD.; S.; U. 51–; UC.; UCH. 53–; **Abd.**U.; **Bl.**U.; **Br.**U.; **C.**APH.; MS.; **G.**U.; V. 56–; **Cr.**MD.; **Db.**; **Dn.**U.; **E.**P.; U.; **G.**F.; U.; **Lv.**M.; **M.**MS.; **Nw.**A.; **O.**R.; **Sh.**U.; **Y.**

14420 **Circulation Research.** New York. *Circulation Res.* [1953–] **L.**GH.; MA.; MC.; MD.; S.; U.; UC.; UCH.; **Abd.**U.; **Bl.**U.; **Br.**U.; **C.**APH.; MS. 59–; PH. 63–; UL. 55–; **Cr.**MD. 58–; **Dn.**U.; **E.**A. 55–; P.; U.; **Ld.**U.; **M.**MS.; **Sh.**U.; **Y.**

14421 **Cirenaica.** Rapporti e monografie coloniale. Roma. *Cirenaica* **C.**A. imp.

14422 **Cirillo.** Rivista mensile di medicina e scienze affini. Aversa. *Cirillo*

14423 **Cirkulär. Jordbrukstekniska institutet.** Uppsala. *Cirk. jordbrtek. Inst.* [1947–] **L.**P.; **C.**A. 50–; **Rt.** 48–.

14424 **Cirkulär. Statens provningsanstalt.** Stockholm. *Cirk. St. ProvnAnst.* [1922–] **L.**I.; P.; **Y.**

14425 **Cirkulär** från **Telegrafstyrelsens tekniska byrå.** Stockholm. *Cirk. TelegrStyr. tek. Byrå*

14426 **Cirkulär. Trätekniska avdelningen, Svenska träforskningsinstitutet.** Stockholm. *Cirk. trätek. Avd. svenska TräforskInst.* **L.**SC. 46–47.

14427 **Cirugía.** Guadalajara. *Cirugía, Guadalajara* [1935–]

14428 **Cirugía.** Madrid. *Cirugía, Madr.* [1954–] **L.**MA.; TD.

14429 **Cirugía** del **aparato locomotor.** Madrid. *Cirug. Apar. locom.* [1944–52] **L.**MA.; MD. 48–52; S. 44–46; TD.; **E.**P. 48–50 imp. [*C. as:* 689]

14430 **Cirugía** y **cirujanos.** México. *Cirug. Ciruj.* [1933–] **L.**MA.; MD. 33–44 imp.: 60–; S. imp.; TD. 41–42 imp.

14431 **Cirugía contemporánea.** México. *Cirug. contemp.*

14432 **Cirugía, ginecologia** y **urologia.** Madrid. *Cirug. Ginec. Urol.*

14433 **Cirugía menor.** Madrid. *Cirug. menor*

14434 **Cirugía ortopédica** y **traumatologia.** Habana. *Cirug. ortop. Traum.* **L.**MD. 34: 40–41; S. 48–49 imp.: 55–56.

14435 **Cirurgia** no **sanatoria.** São Lucas. *Cirurg. Sanat.* [1939–] **L.**MD.; **Br.**U.

14436 **Cita-Post.** Internationale Zeitschrift für den Fortschritt in der Landwirtschaft. München. *Cita-Post* [1953–]

14437 **Cité.** Bruxelles. *Cité* [1919–35] **L.**P. 19–24.

14438 **Citrus Grower.** Port Elizabeth, etc. *Citrus Grow.* [1925–] **L.**AM. 50– imp.; BM. 59–; TP. 55–; **Md.**H.

14439 **Citrus Industry.** Tampa, etc. *Citrus Ind.* [1920–] **L.**TP. 56–; **Md.**H. 30–39: 54–.

14440 **Citrus Leaves.** Los Angeles. *Citrus Leaves* **Md.**H. 53–37.

14441 **Citrus Magazine.** Tampa, Fla. *Citrus Mag.* **L.**TP. 50–; **Md.**H. 52–.

14442 **Citrus News.** Melbourne. *Citrus News* **L.**TP. 55–; **Md.**H. 45–.

    Civil Aeronautics Authority Reports. Washington. *See* 43051.

14444 **Civil Aeronautics Bulletin.** Washington. *Civ. Aeronaut. Bull.*

14445 **Civil Aeronautics Journal.** Washington. *Civ. Aeronaut. J.* [1940–45] L.BM.; P.; F.A. 40–45. [*C. of:* 1526; *C. as:* 12850]

14446 **Civil Aircraft Accident Reports.** London. *Civ. Aircr. Accid. Rep.* Y.

14447 **Civil Aviation.** *Civ. Aviat.* Y. 57–. [*English abstracts of:* 21549]

14448 **Civil Aviation Journal.** Wellington. *Civ. Aviat. J.* [1949–] L.AV. 51–57 imp.; BM.

14449 **Civil Aviation Radio News.** London. *Civ. Aviat. Radio News* [1954–] L.AV.; BM.; P.; F.A.; Ma.T. [*C. of:* 14450; –61*; *C. as:* CATC Electronics News]

14450 **Civil Aviation Radio News Letter.** London. *Civ. Aviat. Radio News Lett.* [1950–54] L.AV.; BM.; P.; F.A. 52–54. [*C. of:* 28947; *C as:* 14449]

14451 **Civil Aviation Statistical** and **Technical Review.** London. *Civ. Aviat. statist. tech. Rev.* [1937–] L.AV. 40–52 imp.; P.; Bm.P.; G.M. 37–38; M.P.; O.R. 38.

14452 **Civil Engineer.** London. *Civ. Engr* [1958–] L.BA.; BM.; P.; SC.; U.; Bl.U. 60–; C.UL.; Cr.I.; E.A.; Lv.P.; M.P.; O.R.; Y. [*C. of:* 14463]

14453 **Civil Engineer Corps Bulletin. U.S. Navy Department.** Washington. *Civ. Engr Cps Bull. U.S. Navy Dep.* L.P. (curr.)

14454 **Civil Engineer** in **South Africa.** South African Institution of Civil Engineers. Johannesburg. *Civ. Engr S. Afr.* [1959–] L.BM.; P.; Ha.RD.; Y. [*C. of:* 14455]

14455 **Civil Engineer** in **Southern Africa.** South African Institution of Civil Engineers. Johannesburg. *Civ. Engr sth. Afr.* [1959] L.P.; Y. [*Replaces* 54051; *C. as:* 14454]

14456 **Civil Engineering.** Easton, Pa., etc. *Civ. Engng, Easton, Pa* [1930–] L.EE. 50–; KC. 57–; P.; SC.; Bm.U.; Br.U.; C.ENG. 45–; Co.T. 54–; Db. 56–; G.M. 49–53 imp.; PH. 56–; T. (4 yr.); U. imp.; Ld.U. 46–; N.U. 56–; Nw.A.; Wa.B.; Y.

Civil Engineering. London. *See* 14458.
Civil Engineering Abstracts. *See* 20247.

14457 **Civil Engineering Code** of **Practice.** London. *Civ. Engng Code Pract.* [1950] L.P.; Ld.P.; Y. [*See also* 8947]

14458 **Civil Engineering** and **Public Works Review.** London. *Civ. Engng publ. Wks Rev.* [1905–] L.AM. 42–; BA. 46–; BM.; P. 34–; QM. 35– imp.; SC. 25–; SH. (1 yr); UC. 29–; Abs.N. 12–; Bl.U. 31–imp.; Bm.T. 48–; Br.P. (1 yr); U. 32–; Bra.P. 50–; C.ENG. 46–; UL. 38–; Db. 33–; Dn.U. 31– imp.; E.A. 06–; HW. 49–; R. 31–51; U. 54–; F.A. 54–; G.E. (3 yr.); M. 22–25: 28–; T. 34–; U. 46–; Ha.RD. 38–; Ld.U. 48–; Lv.P. 47–; U. 31–; M.P. 21–; T. 50–; U. 58–; N.T. 56–; U. 52–; Nw.A. 42–; P. 52–; O.R. 38–; Sh.SC. 42–; Sw.U. 35–; Wl.H. 53–; Y.

14459 **Civil Engineering Series. Engineering Experiment Station, Arizona.** *Civ. Engng Ser. Engng Exp. Stn Ariz.* L.P. 58–.

14459° **Civil Engineering Studies. University** of **Illinois. Soil Mechanics Series.** *Civ. Engng Stud. Univ. Ill. Soil Mech. Ser.* Y.

14459ᶠ **Civil Engineering Studies. University** of **Illinois. Structural Research Series.** *Civ. Engng Stud. Univ. Ill. struct. Res. Ser.* Y.

14460 **Civil Engineering Transactions. Institution** of **Engineers, Australia.** Sydney. *Civ. Engng Trans. Instn Engrs Aust.* [1959–] L.AV.; BM.; HG.; I.; NF.; P.; UC.; Bm.C.; Br.U.; Cr.I.; G.E.; Lv.P.; Nw.A.; Sh.M.; Wl.H.; Y. [*C. from:* 26222]

14461 **Civil Engineers' Review.** London. *Civ. Engrs' Rev.* [1947–53] L.BA.; BM.; SC.; U. 48–53; C.UL.; Cr.I. 50–53; E.A.; Lv.P. 53; M.P.; O.R.; Y. [*C. as:* 14463]

14462 **Civil Specifications** of the **Air Ministry.** London. *Civ. Specif. Air Minist.* [1936–] L.P.

14463 **Civil** and **Structural Engineers' Review.** London. *Civ. struct. Engrs' Rev.* [1953–58] L.BA.; BM.; P.; SC.; U.; C.UL.; Cr.I.; E.A.; Lv.P.; M.P.; O.R.; Y. [*C. of:* 14461; *C. as:* 14452]

14464 **Civila veterinärväsendet.** Stockholm. *Civila VetVäs.* L.AM. 25–37; W. 17–27.

14465 **Civile veterinaervesen.** Oslo. *Civile VetVes.* [1923–] L.AM.; W. 24–. [*C. of:* 56584]

14466 **Civiltà** delle **macchine.** Roma. *Civiltà Macch.* [1953–] L.BM.; P.; SC.; Lv.P. 56–; Y.

14467 **Clad News.** Lukens Steel Company. Coatesville, Pa. *Clad News* L.P. 38–49 imp.

14468 **Clairon médical.** Neuilly-sur-Seine. *Clairon méd.*

14469 **Clarke-Built Messenger.** *Clarke-Built Messgr* [1957–] L.P. (curr.); Br.U.; Ld.U. 57–58; R.D.; Y. [*C. of:* 31845]

14470 **Classeur médical** des **spécialités pharmaceutiques.** Paris. *Classeur méd. Spéc. pharm.*

14471 **Classeur périodique médical** pour **faciliter** les **recherches** du **docteur.** Paris. *Classeur périod. méd.*

14472 **Classification Bulletin** of the **United States Patent Office.** Washington. *Classifn Bull. U.S. Pat. Off.* L.BM. 06–; P. 00–; U. 25–; G.M. 12– imp.

14473 **Classified Accessions List. Ministry** of **Town** and **Country Planning.** London. *Classifd Access. List Minist. Town Country Plann.* L.BA.

14474 **Classified List of Egyptian Scientific Papers.** Cairo. *Classifd List. Egypt. scient. Pap.* [1952–54] L.BM.; P.; U.; Db.; O.B.; Y. [*C. in:* 404]

14475 **Classified Subject-Matter Index** to **Specifications** of **Inventions.** Patent Office, Australia. *Classifd Subj.-Matter Index Specif. Invent. Pat. Off. Aust.*

14476 **Clay.** Columbus, Ohio. *Clay, Columbus.*

14477 **Clay Minerals Bulletin.** Galashiels, London. *Clay Miner. Bull.* [1947–] L.BM.; P.; QM. 53–; SC. 53–; Abd.S.; Br.U.; C.MI.; E.A. 47–55; Ld.U. 56 ; N.U.; O.RE.; R.U.; Rt.; Sh.SC.; St.R.; Y.

14478 **Clay Products Bulletin.** Lower Hutt, N.Z. *Clay Prod. Bull.* [1954–] L.P.; Y.

14479 **Clay Products Journal** of **Australia.** Sydney. *Clay Prod. J. Aust.* [1933–] St.R.

14480 **Clay Products News** and **Ceramic Record.** Toronto. *Clay Prod. News Ceram. Rec.* [1928–] St.R. 45–.

14481 **Clay Record.** Chicago. *Clay Rec.*

14482 **Clay Tile Bulletin.** National Federation of Clay Industries. London. *Clay Tile Bull.* [1955–] L.P. imp.

14483 **Claycraft.** Birmingham, etc. *Claycraft* [1928–] L.BM.; I. (2 yr.); P.; Bm.P.; C.UL. 48–; Cr.I. 52–; M.P. 32–; T. (1 yr); Sh.G. 42–; P. 30–; St.R.; Wa.B. 42–; Y. [*C. of:* 11200]

14484 **Claycrafter.** Dayton. *Claycrafter* **L.**P. 10–11.

14485 **Clays** and **Clay Minerals.** Proceedings of the National Conference on Clays and Clay Minerals. Washington, London. *Clays Clay Miner.* [1953–] **L.**SC.; **Bn.**U. 59–; **N.**U. 54–.

14486 **Clayworker.** Indianapolis. *Clayworker* [1884–33] **L.**P. 10–33; **Sh.**G. 17–.

14487 **Clean Air.** Manchester. *Clean Air* [1929–30] **L.**BM.; EE.; MA.; P.; **Abs.**N.; **Bm.**P.; **C.**UL.; **G.**M.; **O.**R. [*C. as:* 26530]

14488 **Clean Air Quarterly.** Los Angeles. *Clean Air Q.* [1957–] **L.**TD.

14489 **Clean Air Yearbook.** National Society for Clean Air. London. *Clean Air Yb.* [1957–] **L.**BM.; H.; MD. 58; P.; SC.; **Bm.**P.; **E.**T.; **G.**M.; PH.; **Ld.**P.; **M.**MS.; **O.**R.; **Sh.**P.; **Y.** [*C. of:* 58112]

14490 **Cleaning** and **Maintenance.** London. *Clean. Maint.* [1953–] **L.**BM.; H.; P.; TD.; **C.**UL. 54–; **Co.**T. (curr.); **E.**A. 54–; **Lv.**P.; **M.**P. 54–; **O.**B. 54–; **Y.**

14491 **Cleaning** and **Maintenance Yearbook.** London. *Clean. Maint. Yb.* [1956–] **L.**BM.; P.; **E.**A.; **Lv.**P. 57–; **Y.**

14492 **Cleansing Superintendent.** Glasgow. *Cleans. Supdt* **L.**P. 24–28*. [*C. as:* 40597]

14493 **Clearing-House Bulletin** of **Research** in **Human Organization.** Chicago. *Clearing-Ho. Bull. Res. hum. Org.* [1951–54] **L.**AN.; U.; **Bm.**U.; **G.**U.; **O.**R. [*C. as:* 22485]

14494 **Cleaver-Hume Technical Article Index.** London. *Cleaver-Hume tech. Art. Index* [1952] **L.**P.; **E.**A. [*Issued in sections*]

Clebsch's Annalen. *See* 29696.

14494ᶜ **Cleft Palate Bulletin.** *Cleft Palate Bull.* **L.**D.

14495 **Clemson Agricultural College Extension Work.** Clemson College, S.C. *Clemson agric. Coll. Ext. Wk*

14496 **Clemson Agricultural Journal.** Clemson College, S.C. *Clemson agric. J.*

14497 **Clermont médical.** Clermont-Ferrand. *Clermont méd.* **L.**MD. 56–.

14498 **Cleveland Bird-Life.** Cleveland. *Cleveland Bird-Life* [1944–] [*C. of:* 7142]

14499 **Cleveland Clinic Quarterly.** Cleveland. *Cleveland Clin. Q.* [1931–] **L.**MA. 35–; MD. 35–; S.; **Abd.**U. 55–; **Cr.**MD. 58–; **Nw.**A. 38–.

14500 **Cleveland Engineering.** Cleveland. *Cleveland Engng* [1917–]

14501 **Cleveland Medical Gazette.** Cleveland. *Cleveland med. Gaz.*

14502 **Cleveland Medical Journal.** Cleveland. *Cleveland med. J.* [1902–18] **L.**MD. 09–18; S. 03–18; **Db.** 12–18 imp.; **E.**P. 09–12; **M.**MS. 09–18.

14503 **Cleveland Medical** and **Surgical Reporter.** Cleveland. *Cleveland med. surg. Reptr*

14504 **Clifton Medical Bulletin.** Clifton Springs, N.Y. *Clifton med. Bull.* [1913–36] **L.**MA. 22–35; MD. 22–36; **Lv.**U. 23–36 imp.; **O.**R. 25–36 imp.

14505 **Clima** de **Portugal.** Observatório central meteorológico Infante D. Luiz. Lisboa. *Clima Port.* **L.**MO. 42–.

Climat. St. Pétersbourg. *See* 27508.

14506 **Climat** de la **Belgique.** Bruxelles. *Climat Belg.* **L.**MO. 86: 92: 97–01; **E.**M. 86–99; SC. 98.

14507 **Climate.** London. *Climate, Lond.* [1899–05] **L.**BM. 99–03; BMᴺ.; G.; MD.; S.; TD.; **C.**UL.; **E.**A. 00–05 imp.; **O.**R.

14508 **Climate.** St. Louis. *Climate, St Louis*

14509 **Climate** of **British Columbia.** Victoria. *Climate Br. Columb.* **L.**BM. 44–46*; MO. 16–46; **Md.**H. 24–46 imp.; **Rt.** 27–45; **Y.**

14510 **Climate** and **Crop Bulletin.** Washington. *Climate Crop Bull., Wash.*

14511 **Climate Information Sheets, Rhodesia** and **Nyasaland.** Salisbury. *Climate Inf. Sh. Rhod. Nyasald* **L.**MO. 57–.

14512 **Climate. Meteorological Bureau.** Fukiei. *Climate met. Bur., Fukiei* **L.**MO. 41–42.

14513 **Climate** in **Palestine** and the **Neighbouring Countries.** Tel-Aviv. *Climate Palest.* **L.**MO. 32–36. [*C. as:* 43066ᵃ]

14514 **Climatic Observations** at **University College Ibadan.** Ibadan. *Climatic Obsns Univ. Coll. Ibadan* [1952–] **L.**BM. 54–; MO. 53–; U.; **C.**GG.; **E.**U.; **G.**U.; **O.**R.; **Rt.**

14515 **Climatología aeronáutica.** Oficina central meteorologica. Madrid. *Climatología aeronáut., Madr.* **L.**MO. 47–49 imp.

14516 **Climatological Bulletin** of **Monte Estoril.** Lisbon. *Clim. Bull. Mt. Estoril* **L.**BM. 55–; MO. 40–; **Y.**

14517 **Climatological Charts** of the **North Atlantic.** London. *Clim. Charts N. Atlant.* **L.**BM.; MO.

14518 **Climatological Data. Alaska Section.** Washington. *Clim. Data Alaska Sect.* **L.**MO. 15–; **E.**M. 41–48.

14519 **Climatological Data** for **Djakarta.** *Clim. Data Djakarta* **L.**MO. 56–.

14520 **Climatological Data. Hawaiian Section.** Washington. *Clim. Data Hawaii. Sect.* **L.**MO. 10–; **E.**M. 34–45.

14521 **Climatological Data** for **Manila.** Manila. *Clim. Data Manila*

14522 **Climatological Data. National Summary.** Washington. *Clim. Data natn. Summ., Wash.* [1950–] **L.**MO.; **Db.**; **E.**R.; **H.**U.; **R.**U.; **Y.**

14523 **Climatological Data, Pacific.** U.S. Weather Bureau. Asheville. *Clim. Data Pacif.* **L.**MO. 56–.

14524 **Climatological Data. Puerto Rico** and **Virgin Islands.** Asheville, Washington. *Clim. Data P. Rico Virgin Isl.* [1955–] **L.**MO.; **Y.** [*C. from:* 14526]

14525 **Climatological Data** for **U.S.** Washington. *Clim. Data U.S.* [1914–] **L.**BM.; G.; MO.; **C.**PO. 49–; **E.**M.; R.; **G.**M. 14–36 imp.; **Rt.** 28–; **Y.**

14526 **Climatological Data. West Indies** and **Caribbean Service.** San Juan. *Clim. Data W. Indies Caribb. Serv.* [1921–] **L.**MO.; **E.**M. 21–47 imp.; **H.**U. 21–47 imp.; **O.**G.; **Rt.**; **Y.**

14527 **Climatological Note. Oregon Forest Lands Research Center.** *Clim. Note Ore. Forest Lds Res. Cent.* [1959–] **O.**F.

14527ᶜ **Climatological Notes. Meteorological Department, Ghana.** *Clim. Notes met. Dep. Ghana* [1959–]

14528 **Climatological Notes, South Pacific Region.** Wellington. *Clim. Notes S. Pacif. Reg.* **L.**MO. 43–44.

14529 **Climatological Observations** at **Colonial** and **Foreign Stations.** London. *Clim. Obsns colon. foreign Stns* [1904] **L.**BM.; MO.; SC.; **O.**G.

14530 **Climatological Report. Dugway Proving Ground,** Utah. Dugway. *Clim. Rep. Dugway Proving Grd* **L.**MO. 55–.

14531 **Climatological Report. States** of **Jersey.** *Clim. Rep. Sts Jersey* **L.**MO. 56–.

14532 **Climatological** and **Sea Surface Current Charts** of the **North Atlantic.** London. *Clim. Sea Surf. Curr. Charts N. Atlant.* **L.**MO. 57–.

14533 **Climatological Summaries. British Caribbean Meteorological Service.** Port of Spain. *Clim. Summs Br. Caribb. met. Serv.* [1955–] **L.**BM.

14534 **Climatological Summaries. West Indies Meteorological Service.** Trinidad. *Clim. Summs W. Indies met. Serv.* [1954–] **L.**MO.; **Y.** [*C. of:* 51351]

14535 **Climatological Summary. Alert, North West Territories, Canada.** Toronto. *Clim. Summ. Alert N.W. Terr. Can.* **L.**MO. 50–.

14536 **Climatological Summary. Federated Malay States.** *Clim. Summ. F.M.S.*

14537 **Climatological Summary, Isachsen, North West Territories, Canada.** Toronto. *Clim. Summ. Isachsen N.W. Terr. Can.* **L.**MO. 48–.

14538 **Climatological Summary, Mould Bay, North West Territories, Canada.** Toronto. *Clim. Summ. Mould Bay N.W. Terr. Can.* **L.**MO. 48–.

14539 **Climatological Summary, Northern Rhodesia** and **Nyasaland.** Salisbury. *Clim. Summ. Nth. Rhod. Nyasald* [1948–] **L.**MO.; SC.

14540 **Climatological Summary, Singapore.** *Clim. Summ. Singapore* **Y.** 46–.

14541 **Climatological Summary, Southern Rhodesia,** Salisbury. *Clim. Summ. Sth. Rhod.* [1948–]

14542 **Climatological Tables.** Wellington, N.Z. *Clim. Tabl. N.Z. Bn.*U. 46–.

14543 **Climatologie aéronautique.** Bruxelles. *Climatologie aéronaut., Brux.* **L.**MO. 46–49*. [*C. in:* 11020]

14544 **Climatologie aéronautique.** Ksara. *Climatologie aéronaut., Ksara* [1937–] **L.**MO.

14545 **Climatologie aéronautique.** Paris. *Climatologie aéronaut., Paris* **L.**MO. 25–36.

14546 **Climatologie** de l'**Afrique occidentale française.** Dakar. *Climatologie Afr. occid. fr.* [1949–52] **L.**MO. [*C. as:* 46113ª]

14547 **Climatologie comtoise** et **jurassienne.** Besançon. *Climatologie comt. jurass.* [1954–] **L.**BM.; MO.; **E.**R.; **Y.** [*C. of:* 11055]

14548 **Clincher Magazine.** Edinburgh. *Clincher Mag.* [1918–30] **Sy.**R. [*C. as:* 35075]

14549 **Clinic.** Adelaide. *Clinic* **L.**MA. 41–.

14550 **Clinic Bulletin** of the **University College** of **Medicine.** Richmond, Va. *Clinic Bull. Univ. Coll. Med., Richmond, Va* [*C. of:* 6998]

14551 **Clínica.** Barcelona. *Clínica, Barcelona* **L.**MA. 29–.

14552 **Clinica.** Bologna. *Clinica, Bologna* [1935–] **L.**MA. 45–.

14553 **Clínica.** Madrid. *Clínica, Madr.*

14554 **Clínica.** Montevideo. *Clínica, Montev.*
Clinica bulgara. *See* 9155.

14555 **Clínica castellana.** Valladolid. *Clínica castell.*

14556 **Clinica chimica acta.** Amsterdam, London. *Clinica chim. Acta* [1956–] **L.**C.; CB.; MC.; MD.; UC.; **Abd.**R.; U.; **Bl.**U.; **Br.**U.; **C.**APH.; V. 57–; **Cr.**MD.; **Dn.**U.; **E.**U.; **Ld.**U.; **M.**MS.; **O.**R.; **R.**D.; **Sh.**U.; **Y.**

14557 **Clinica chirurgica.** Milano. *Clinica chir.* [1893–] **L.**MD. 48–; **Br.**U. 27–40.

14558 **Clinica contemporanea.** Lisboa. *Clinica contemp.* [1947–] **L.**MA. 49–; MD. 49–56.

14559 **Clinica dermosifilopatica** della **R. Università** di **Roma.** Roma. *Clinica dermosif. R. Univ. Roma* **L.**S. 96–98.

14560 **Clinica, higiene** e **hidrologia.** Lisboa. *Clinica Hig. Hidrol.*

14561 **Clínica hispánica.** Madrid. *Clínica hisp.* **L.**MA. 46–.

14562 **Clinica** e **igiene infantile.** Torino. *Clinica Ig. infant.*

14563 **Clínica** y **laboratorio.** Zaragoza. *Clínica Lab.* [1905–] **L.**MA. 46–; MD. 45–; **E.**P. 48; **Y.**

14564 **Clinica latina.** Torino. *Clinica lat.* [1951–] **L.**MA. 53–.

14565 **Clinica medica italiana.** Milano. *Clinica med. ital.* [1898–15: 24–] **L.**MD. 98–14: 36–; S. 24–25; **G.**F. 98–07.

14566 **Clinica medica specializzata.** Milano. *Clinica med. spec.*

14567 **Clínica médico-quirúrgica.** Merida. *Clínica méd.-quir.* [1944]

14568 **Clinica moderna.** Firenze. *Clinica mod., Firenze* [1895–07] **L.**MD. 04–05: 07; **E.**U. 02–07.

14569 **Clínica moderna.** Zaragoza. *Clínica mod., Zaragoza*

14570 **Clinica nuova.** Roma. *Clinica nuova* [1945–?] **L.**BM. 48– imp.; MA.; MD. 48–. [*C. as:* 42261]

14571 **Clinica oculistica.** Palermo. *Clinica oculist.* [1900–15] **L.**MD. 06–15; OP. 01–15. [*C. in:* 3088]

14572 **Clinica odontoiatrica** e **ginecologia.** Roma. *Clinica odontoiat. ginec.* [1946–] **L.**D.; MA.; MD. 47–.

14573 **Clinica odonto-protesia.** Pisa. *Clinica odontoprotes.* **L.**D.

14574 **Clinica ortopedica.** Parma, Padova. *Clinica ortop.* **L.**MD. 60– imp.

14575 **Clinica ostetrica.** Roma. *Clinica ostet.* [1899–] **L.**MA. 46–; MD. 37–.

14576 **Clinica otorino-laringo-iatrica.** Roma. *Clinica otorino-lar.-iatr.* [1949–] **Br.**U.

14577 **Clinica pediatrica.** Modena, Bologna. *Clinica pediat.* [1919–] **L.**MA. 28–40: 46–; MD. 22–34; **Y.**

14578 **Clinica** e **pratica.** Treviglio. *Clinica Prat.*

14579 **Clínica psicopedagógica;** organo del Instituto psicopedagógico para niños nerviosos. Buenos Aires. *Clínica psicopedag.*

14580 **Clinica terapeutica.** Roma. *Clinica terap.* [1951–] **L.**MA. 53–.

14581 **Clinica** e **terapia fisica** delle **malattie** dei **polmoni** e del **cuore.** Torino. *Clinica Terap. fis. Mal. Polm. Cuore*

14582 **Clinica** e **terapia** dei **tumori.** Napoli. *Clinica Terap. Tumori*

14583 **Clinica termale.** Roma. *Clinica term.*

14584 **Clínica tisiológica.** Rio de Janeiro. *Clínica tisiol.* [1946–] **L.**MA.; MD.

14585 **Clinica** del **torax.** Buenos Aires. *Clinica Torax* [1949–] **L.**MA. 52–; S. 49–57.

14586 **Clínica** del **trabajo.** Buenos Aires. *Clínica Trab.*

14587 **Clinica** per **tutti.** Roma. *Clinica tutti*

14588 **Clínica urológica.** Barcelona. *Clínica urol.*

14589 **Clínica veterinaria.** Madrid. *Clínica vet., Madr.*

14590 **Clinica veterinaria** e **rassegna** di **polizia sanitaria** e di **igiena.** Milano. *Clinica vet., Milano* [1878–] **L.**AM. 48– imp.; EB. 22–40; V. 80– imp.; **Br.**U. 20–35; **C.**V. 24–35; **E.**N. 16–23 imp.; U. 13–20; **W.** 15–; **Y.**

14591 **Clinical Archives** of the **Gulf Hospital, Maracaibo.** Maracaibo. *Clin. Archs Gulf Hosp. Maracaibo* [1936–38] **L.**TD. imp.

14592 **Clinical Calorimetry.** Russell Sage Institute of Pathology. New York. *Clin. Calorim.* **L.**MD. 15–; **E.**U. 15–20.

14593 **Clinical Chemistry.** Baltimore, New York. *Clin. Chem.* [1955–] **L.**C.; MA.; MD.; P.; UC. 55: 57–; **Abd.**U.; **Bn.**U. 62–; **C.**UL.; **Dn.**U. 60–; **E.**U. imp.; **Ld.**U.; **Sh.**U. 58–; **Y.**

14594 **Clinical Endocrinology.** New York, London. *Clin. Endocr.* [1960–] **L.**MD.; **G.**U.; **Y.** [*C. of:* 39993]

14595 **Clinical Excerpts.** London. *Clin. Excerpts, Lond.* [1897–] **L.**BM. 09–; MA. 30– imp.; MC. 36–40; MD. 34–; S. 97–55 imp.; TD. 31–; **Br.**U. 30–; **Db.** 45: 53–; **Dn.**U. 97–14 imp.; **M.**MS. 11–13: 27–; **Nw.**A. 30–53 imp.; **O.**R. 09–14 imp.

14596 **Clinical Excerpts.** Winthrop Chemical Co. New York. *Clin. Excerpts, N.Y.* [1927–]

14596° **Clinical Gynecology** and **Obstetrics.** Tokyo. *Clin. Gynec. Obstet., Tokyo* [1946–]

14597 **Clinical Journal.** London. *Clin. J.* [1892–51] **L.**BM.; GH.; MA.; MD.; S.; U. 93–20: 35–51; UCH. 92–06; **Abd.**U. 30–32; **Abs.**N. 12–51 imp.; **Bl.**U. 92–51 imp.; **Bm.**U. 92–34 imp.; **Br.**U.; **C.**UL.; **Cr.**MD. 00–46 imp.; MS. imp.; **Db.**; **Dn.**U. 92–13; **E.**A.; I.; P.; T. 40–51; U. 48–51; **G.**F.; M. 92–19; **Ld.**U. 21–51 imp.; **Lv.**M. 92–17: 19–51 imp.; U. 92–01; **M.**MS.; **Nw.**A. 07–13: 31–51; **O.**R.; **Sh.**U. 93–97.

14598 **Clinical Journal** of **Chiropody, Podiatry** and **Pedic Surgery.** Chicago. *Clin. J. Chirop. Podiat. Pedic Surg.*

Clinical Medicine. Moscow. *See* 27516.

14599 **Clinical Medicine** and **Surgery.** Chicago. *Clin. Med. Surg.* [1924–] **L.**MA. 47–; MD. 34: 37–; **M.**MS. 26–51 imp. [*C. of:* 2002]

14600 **Clinical Neurosurgery.** Proceedings of the Congress of Neurological Surgeons. New Orleans. *Clin. Neurosurg.* [1955–] **L.**MD.; S.

14601 **Clinical Obstetrics** and **Gynecology.** New York. *Clin. Obstet. Gynec.* [1958–] **L.**MD.; **Bl.**U. 60–.

14602 **Clinical Orthopaedics.** Philadelphia, London, etc. *Clin. Orthop.* [1953–] **L.**MD.; S.; **C.**UL.; **Dn.**U. 55– imp.; **E.**A.; U.; **Ld.**U. 57–; **O.**R.

14603 **Clinical Pathologic Conferences** of **Cook County Hospital.** *Clin. path. Confs Cook Cty Hosp.* [1955–] **Dn.**U.

14604 **Clinical** and **Pathological Papers** from the **Lakeside Hospital.** Cleveland. *Clin. path. Pap. Lakeside Hosp.* [1901–14] **L.**S. 01–12; **Lv.**U.

14605 **Clinical** and **Pathological Reports** of the **Liverpool Royal Infirmary.** Liverpool. *Clin. path. Rep. Lpool R. Infirm.* **Lv.**U. 96–.

14606 **Clinical** and **Pathological Reports. Montreal General Hospital.** Montreal. *Clin. path. Rep. Montreal gen. Hosp.* **L.**S. 76–02; **E.**U. 80.

14607 **Clinical Pediatrics.** New York. *Clin. Pediat.*

14608 **Clinical Pharmacology** and **Therapeutics.** St. Louis. *Clin. Pharmac. Ther.* [1960–] **L.**MC. 61–; MD.; PH.; S. 62–; TD.; UC.; **Bl.**U.; **Ld.**U.; **Y.**

14609 **Clinical Proceedings.** Journal of the Cape Town Post-Graduate Medical Association. Cape Town. *Clin. Proc., Cape Town* [1942–49] **L.**C. 42–43; GH.; MA.; MD.; S.; TD. imp.; **Abd.**R.; **Bl.**U.; **Bm.**U.; **Br.**U.; **E.**U. 45–49; **G.**F. imp.; **Ld.**U. 48–49; **Lv.**M.; **Nw.**A. [*C. in:* 50156]

14610 **Clinical Proceedings** of the **Children's Hospital, Washington.** *Clin. Proc. Child. Hosp. Wash.* **L.**MA. 55–; MD. 45–.

14611 **Clinical Radiology.** Edinburgh, London. *Clin. Radiol.* [1960–] **L.**BM.; MA.; S.; **Br.**U.; **Dn.**U.; **E.**A.; **G.**U. 63–; **Ld.**U.; **Y.** [*C. of:* 25998]

14612 **Clinical Report** of the **Adelaide Children's Hospital.** Adelaide. *Clin. Rep. Adelaide Child. Hosp.* [1947–] **L.**MA.; MD.; S.; **E.**P.; **M.**MS.

14613 **Clinical Report** of the **Alfred Hospital, Melbourne.** Melbourne. *Clin. Rep. Alfred Hosp. Melb.* [1949–] **L.**MA.; MD. 49: 51–; S.; **Ld.**U. 53–.

14614 **Clinical Report** of the **Council's Obstetric Service. Croydon Public Health Department.** Croydon. *Clin. Rep. Coun. obstet. Serv. Croydon* **L.**MD. 33–.

14615 **Clinical Report. East End Maternity Hospital.** London. *Clin. Rep. E. End Matern. Hosp.* **L.**MD. 29–.

14616 **Clinical Report. Farnborough Hospital.** Farnborough. *Clin. Rep. Farnborough Hosp.* [1958–] **L.**MD.

14617 **Clinical Report. Guy's Hospital Maternity Department.** London. *Clin. Rep. Guy's Hosp. Matern. Dep.* **L.**MD. 28–31.

14618 **Clinical Report. Government Maternity Hospital, Madras.** Madras. *Clin. Rep. Govt Matern. Hosp. Madras* **Br.**U. 98–07: 12–19.

14619 **Clinical Report. Maternity Department, Our Lady** of **Lourdes Hospital.** Drogheda. *Clin. Rep. Matern. Dep. Our Lady Lourdes Hosp.* **L.**MD. 50–.

14620 **Clinical Report. Maternity Department, Paddington General Hospital.** Shrewsbury. *Clin. Rep. Matern. Dep. Paddington gen. Hosp.* [1950–] **L.**MD. 52–.

14621 **Clinical Report** of the **Queen Charlotte Lying-in** (*later* maternity) **Hospital.** London. *Clin. Rep. Queen Charl. lying-in Hosp.* [1905–] **L.**GH. imp.; MD. 05–21; S. 05–12: 48–58; **Abs.**N. 06–16 imp.; **Bm.**U. 25–30; **Lv.**U. 07–12; **M.**MS. 25–39.

14622 **Clinical Report** of the **Rotunda Hospital.** Dublin. *Clin. Rep. Rotunda Hosp.* **Bl.**U. 21–; **Br.**U. 96–97: 22–30; **Db.** 69–; **Dn.**U. 08: 12: 27–29: 34; **M.**MS. 17–.

Clinical Report. Royal Melbourne Hospital. See 48172.

14623 **Clinical Reporter.** St. Louis, Mo. *Clin. Reptr*
Clinical Reports. See **Clinical Report.**

14624 **Clinical Research.** American Federation for Clinical Research. New York. *Clin. Res.* [1958–] **L.**MA.; MD.; **Bl.**U. 61–; **Dn.**U. 60–; **E.**O.; **Y.** [C. of: 14625]

14625 **Clinical Research Proceedings.** New York. *Clin. Res. Proc.* [1953–57] **L.**MA.; MD.; **E.**U. 57; **Y.** [C. as: 14624]

14626 **Clinical Review.** Chicago. *Clin. Rev.*

14627 **Clinical Science,** incorporating Heart. London. *Clin. Sci.* [1933–] **L.**B.; BM.; CB. 58–; GH.; MA.; MC.; MD.; S.; TD. 59–; U.; UC.; UCH.; **Abd.**U.; **Abs.**N.; **Bl.**U.; **Bm.**U.; **Bn.**U. 61–; **Br.**U.; **C.**APH. 51–; MD. 49–; PA.; PH.; UL.; **Cr.**MD.; **Db.**; **Dn.**U.; **E.**A.; P.; U.; **G.**F.; U.; **Ld.**U.; **Lv.**M.; **M.**MS.; **Nw.**A.; **O.**PH.; R.; **Sh.**U.; **Y.** [C. of: 21992]

14628 **Clinical Statistical Report. Royal Cancer Hospital.** London. *Clin. statist. Rep. R. Cancer Hosp.* [1945–] **L.**MD.; UCH. 52–; **Bl.**U. 45–49; **O.**R.

14629 **Clinical Studies.** Edinburgh. *Clin. Stud.* [1902–10] **L.**BM.; MA. 03–10; MD.; S.; **Bm.**U. 03; **Br.**U. 02–08; **C.**UL.; **Db.**; **Dn.**U. 02–09; **E.**A.; P.; T.; U. 05–10; **G.**F.; **Lv.**U. 02–08; **M.**MS.; **Nw.**A.; **O.**R.

Clinical Symposia. Ciba Pharmaceutical Products Inc. See 14016.

14630 **Clinics.** Philadelphia. *Clinics* [1942–46] **L.**MA.; MD.; S.; **Abd.**U.; **C.**UL.; **Db.**; **E.**P.; U.; **G.**U.; **O.**R. [C. of: 34661]

14631 **Clinics** and **Collected Papers. St. Elizabeth's Hospital,** Richmond, Va. *Clinics Coll. Pap. St Eliz. Hosp.* [1922] **L.**BM.; MD.; **E.**S.; **O.**R.

14632 **Clinics** of **John B. Murphy, M.D.,** at **Mercy Hospital.** Chicago. *Clinics John B. Murphy Mercy Hosp.* [1914–16] **L.**MD.; S.; UCH.; **Bl.**U.; **Bm.**U.; **Br.**U.; **E.**U.; **G.**F.; U.; **Lv.**M.; U.; **Nw.**A. [C. of: 51482; C. as: 51481]

14633 **Clinics** of **Tuberculosis.** Tokyo. *Clinics Tuberc., Tokyo* [1953–]

14634 **Clinique.** Bruxelles. *Clinique, Brux.*

14635 **Clinique.** Chicago. *Clinique, Chicago* [1880–26]

14636 **Clinique.** Montréal. *Clinique, Montréal* [1894–23]

14637 **Clinique.** Paris. *Clinique, Paris* [1906–] **L.**MD. 48–.

14638 **Clinique européenne.** Paris. *Cliniq. eur.*

14639 **Clinique française.** Paris. *Cliniq. fr.*

14640 **Clinique générale** de **chirurgie.** Paris. *Cliniq. gén. Chir.*

14641 **Clinique infantile.** Paris. *Cliniq. infant.* [1903–] **E.**P. 03–14.

14642 **Clinique internationale.** Paris. *Cliniq. int.*

14643 **Clinique** et **laboratoire.** Paris. *Cliniq. Lab.* [1922–]

14644 **Clinique médicale** de l'**Hôtel-Dieu** de **Paris.** *Cliniq. méd. Hôtel-Dieu Paris* [1896–09] **L.**MD.; S.; **O.**R. 98–09.

14645 **Clinique ophtalmologique.** Paris. *Cliniq. ophtal.* [1895–28] **L.**MD. 95–15: 22; OP. 97–28; **O.**R. 97.

14646 **Clinique ophtalmologique** de la **Faculté** de **médecine** de **Bordeaux.** Bulletin. Paris. *Cliniq. ophtal. Fac. Méd. Bordeaux*

14647 **Clinique pratique** des **maladies** des **yeux,** du **larynx,** du **nez** et des **oreilles.** Paris. *Cliniq. prat. Mal. Yeux* [1905–]

14648 **Clinique pratique médico-chirurgicale.** Paris. *Cliniq. prat. méd.-chir.* [1905–14]

14649 **Clothing Institute Journal.** London. *Cloth. Inst. J.* [1951–] **L.**HQ. 59–; **Lc.**A. 53–; **Ld.**W. 54–; **Y.**

14650 **Clothing Machine Engineer.** London. *Cloth. Mach. Engr* [1953–] **L.**P. 54–.

14651 **Clujul medical.** Bucureşti. *Clujul med.* [1920–]

14652 **Clyde.** Harland and Wolff, Ltd., Magazine. *Clyde* **O.**R. 46–.

14652ª **Coach Builders'** and **Wheelwrights'** and **Motor Car Manufacturers' Art Journal.** London. *Coach Bldrs' J.* [1880–09] **L.**P. 98–09; **C.**UL.; **G.**M. 98–07; **O.**R. [C. as: 15886]

14653 **Coal.** London. *Coal* [1947–] **L.**AM. (curr.); BM.; FA.; U.; **Bra.**P. 51–; **C.**UL.; **E.**A.; U. 49–; **G.**M.; **H.**U.; **Ld.**U. 49–; **N.**T. (1 yr); **O.**B.; **Y.**

14654 **Coal Age.** New York. *Coal Age* [1911–15] **L.**BM. imp.; P. [C. as: 14655]

14655 **Coal Age** and **Colliery Engineer.** New York. *Coal Age Colliery Engr* [1915–] **L.**BM. 35–; I. 20–; MIE. 34–39 imp.: 45–; P. imp.; **Bm.**U. 16–; **Cr.**U. 37–; **G.**U. 23–; **Ld.**U. 16–52 imp.; **M.**P. 32–40; **N.**U. 47–; **Nw.**A. 31– imp.; **Sh.**M. 18–36; P. 30–; S. 48–; SC. 45–; **Y.** [C. of: 14654]

14656 **Coal Analysis Reports.** Chicago. *Coal Analysis Rep.*

14657 **Coal** and **Appliances Trade Digest.** London. *Coal Appl. Trade Dig.* [1953–] **L.**BM.; **Abs.**N.; **Y.** [C. of: 14662]

14658 **Coal** and **Base Minerals** of **Southern Africa.** Johannesburg. *Coal base Miner. sth. Afr.* [1953–] **Y.**

14659 **Coal Carbonisation.** London. *Coal Carbonis.* [1935–39] **L.**MIE. imp.; P.; SC.; **Bm.**P.; U.; **Sh.**IO. 36–39; SC. [Supplement to: 14890; C. in: 14710]

14660 **Coal** and **Coke.** Baltimore. *Coal Coke* [1894–11] **Cr.**P. 07–11.

14661 **Coal** and **Coke Operator.** Pittsburg. *Coal Coke Oper.* [1905–17] [C. as: 14667]

14662 **Coal** and **Colliery News (-Digest).** London. *Coal Coll. News (-Dig.)* [1937–52] **L.**BM.; **Abs.**N.; **Y.** [C. of: 35839; C. as: 14657]

14663 **Coal Dust Research Reports.** Midland Counties Colliery Owners' Association. Derby. *Coal Dust Res. Rep.* [1941–] **L.**P.

14664 **Coal Exploration Record** of **Boreholes. Bechuanaland Protectorate Geological Survey Department.** Lobatsi. *Coal Explor. Rec. Boreholes Bechuanald* [1957–] **C.**S.

14665 **Coal Figures.** National Coal Board. London. *Coal Fig.* [1949–53] **L.**BM.; **G.**U.; **H.**U.; **Ld.**U.; **N.**U.; **O.**B.

14665ᶜ **Coal Heat** and **Building Materials.** Chicago. *Coal Heat Bldg Mater.* **Y.**

14666 **Coal Herald-Stoker** and **Airconditioner Journal.** New York. *Coal Her.-Stok. Aircondit. J.* [1927–]

14667 **Coal Industry.** Pittsburg. *Coal Ind.* [1918–24] **L.**P. 19–24. [*C. of:* 14661]

14668 **Coal** and **Iron** and **By-Products Journal.** London. *Coal Iron By-Prod. J.* [1891–24] **L.**BM.; **Abs.**N. 12–24; **Cr.**P. 97–03 imp. [*C. as:* 35839]

14669 **Coal** and **Iron Diary.** London. *Coal Iron Diary* **L.**BM. 97–; **Abs.**N. 18–21.

14670 **Coal Mine Management.** Chicago. *Coal Mine Mgmt* [1922–29] **L.**P. 26–28.

14671 **Coal Mine Modernization Year Book.** Washington, D.C. *Coal Mine Modern. Yb.* [1940–55] **L.**MIE. 42: 48–55; P.; **Ld.**P. 48–55; U. 49–52; **Sh.**U. 40–42. [*C. of:* 58037]

14671ᶜ **Coal Mines** in **Canada.** Department of Mines and Technical Surveys. Ottawa. *Coal Mines Can.* **Y.**

14672 **Coal Mines Monthly Bulletin.** Cleveland. *Coal Mines mon. Bull.*

14673 **Coal Mining.** Pittsburg. *Coal Min.* [1928–] **L.**P. [*C. of:* 32984]

14674 **Coal Mining Investigations.** Carnegie Institute of Technology. Pittsburg. *Coal Min. Invest.* [1922–25] **L.**P.; **Abs.**N. 22–24; **Bm.**P. 24–25; **M.**P. 23–25. [*C. as:* 32019]

14675 **Coal Mining Review.** Columbus, O. *Coal Min. Rev.* [1913–]

14676 **Coal Preparation Review.** Fuel Research Institute. Kawaguchi, Japan. *Coal Prep. Rev., Kawaguchi* [1951–] **Y.**

14677 **Coal Research.** British Coal Utilisation Research Association. London. *Coal Res.* [1944–48] **Bm.**C.; **Sy.**R.

14678 **Coal Research** in **C.S.I.R.O.** Melbourne. *Coal Res. C.S.I.R.O.* [1957–] **L.**P.; **Ld.**U. 61–; **Y.**

14679 **Coal Survey Memoirs.** Department of Mines, Union of South Africa. Pretoria. *Coal Surv. Mem. S. Afr.* [1940–] **L.**GL.; **Br.**U. 40–52; **C.**S.; **Lv.**U.; **O.**G. 40.

14680 **Coal Tar.** Osaka. *Coal Tar* **Y.**

14680ᶜ **Coal Tar Data Book.** Gomershall. *Coal Tar Data Bk* [1953–] **L.**BM.

14681 **Coal Technology.** New York. *Coal Technol.* [1946–48] **L.**C.; I.; P.; **Bm.**U. imp. ⋆[*Replaced by:* 32007]

14682 **Coal Utilization.** Washington, D.C. *Coal Util.* **Y.**

14683 **Coalfield Papers** of the **Geological Survey** of **Great Britain.** Edinburgh, London. *Coalfld Pap. geol. Surv.* [1956–] **L.**BM.; BMᴺ.; SC.; **Bm.**U.; **E.**R.; **O.**R.; **Y.**

14684 **Coarse Grain Situation.** Canberra. *Coarse Grain Situ.* [1954–] **L.**AM.; BM.; **Abs.**U.; **E.**U.

14685 **Coarse Grains Quarterly.** Ottawa. *Coarse Grains Q.* **L.**AM. 44–54.

14686 **Coated Paper Bulletin.** Toronto. *Coated Pap. Bull.* [1953–] **L.**P.

14687 **Coates Inklings.** Coates Brothers & Co. London. *Coates Inklings* [1948–] **L.**BM. imp.; HP.; P. 53–.

14688 **Cobalt.** Brussels. *Cobalt* [1958–] **L.**AV. 59–; P.; **Bl.**U.; **Bm.**T.; **Bn.**U. 59–; **Dn.**U. 59–; **Li.**M.; **Te.**C; **Y.**

14689 **Cobbler.** Huddersfield Local Centre of the Guild of Technical Dyers. Huddersfield. *Cobbler* [1948–] **L.**P. 51–; **Ld.**W.

14690 **Cochrane Bulletin.** Cochrane Corporation. Philadelphia. *Cochrane Bull.* **L.**P. 25–31.

14691 **Cochrane Reprints.** Cochrane Corporation. Philadelphia. *Cochrane Repr.* [1936–]

14692 **Cocoa** and **Chocolate.** New York. *Cocoa Choc.* [1934–]

14693 **Cocoa Statistics.** F.A.O. Rome. *Cocoa Statist.* [1958–] **L.**TP.; **Abd.**R.; **C.**A.; **E.**A.; **G.**M.; **O.**B.

14694 **Cocobro jaarboek.** Wageningen. *Cocobro Jaarb.* [1951–55] **L.**AM.; **C.**A. [*C. as:* 24604]

14695 **Coconut Bulletin** issued by the **Indian Central Coconut Committee.** Ernakulam. *Cocon. Bull.* [1957–] **L.**TP. 60–; **C.**A.; **Md.**H. [*C. of:* 10511]

14696 **Coconut Journal.** Manila. *Cocon. J.* [1941–]

14697 **Coconut Situation.** F.A.O. Rome. *Cocon. Situ.* [1959–] **Abd.**R.; **C.**A.

14698 **Coedwigwr.** Magazine of the Forestry Society of North Wales. *Coedwigwr* [1949–] **Bn.**U.; **O.**F. 49–.

14699 **Coelum.** Bologna. *Coelum* [1931–] **L.**SC. 57–; **Y.**

14700 **Coffee.** Turrialba. *Coffee* **L.**P. 60–. [*Spanish edition at:* 12937]

14701 **Coffee** and **Tea Industries** and the **Flavour Field.** New York. *Coff. Tea Ind.* [1949–] **L.**TP.; **Y.** [*C. of:* 50601]

14701ᶜ **Coil Spring Journal.** *Coil Spring J.* **L.**AV. 47–61⋆ imp.; **F.**A. 47–61. [*C. as:* Spring Journal]

14702 **Coimbra médica.** Coimbra. *Coimbra méd.* [1881–01] **L.**MA. 86–87.

14703 **Coimbra médica.** Coimbra. *Coimbra méd.* [1934–]

14704 **Coir.** Ernakulam. *Coir* [1956–] **L.**P. 58–.

14704ᵃ **Coke** and **Chemistry.** Washington. *Coke Chem., Wash.* **L.**HQ. 59–; **Y.** 57–. [*English abstracts of:* 27589]

14705 **Coke** and **Chemistry U.S.S.R.** Leeds. *Coke Chem. U.S.S.R.* [1959–] **L.**BM.; C.; SC.; **E.**A.; **H.**U.; **Ld.**P.; **Y.** [*English translation of:* 27589]

14706 **Coke** and **Gas.** London. *Coke Gas* [1947–] **L.**BM.; C.; P.; **Abs.**N.; **Bm.**C.; P.; T. 51–52: 56–; U.; **C.**UL.; **E.**A.; **Ld.**U.; **N.**U.; **Sh.**P.; SC.; **Y.** [*C. of:* 14710]

14707 **Coke News.** British Coke Research Association. Chesterfield. *Coke News* [1960–] **L.**BM.; P.; **Ld.**P.; U.; **Y.**

14708 **Coke Research Report.** British Coke Research Association. Chesterfield. *Coke Res. Rep.* [1959–] **L.**P.; **Co.**T.; **Y.**

14709 **Coke Review.** British Coke Research Association London, Chesterfield. *Coke Rev.* [1952–] **L.**C.; P.; **Co.**T. 57–; **Ld.**P.; U. 57–; **M.**C. 52–57; **Sy.**R.; **Y.**

14710 **Coke** and **Smokeless Fuel Age.** London. *Coke Smokel. Fuel Age* [1939–46] **L.**BM.; C. 46; P.; **Bm.**C. (curr.); P.; U.; **C.**UL.; **Ld.**U. 46; **Sh.**P.; SC.; **Y.** [*C. as:* 14706]

14711 **Col. William B. Greeley Lectures** in **Industrial Forestry.** Washington University. Seattle. *Col. William B. Greeley Lect. ind. For.* [1957–] **O.**F.

14712 **Cold.** Madison Cooper Co., Calcium, N.Y. *Cold*

14713 **Cold Injury. Transactions** of **Conferences.** Josiah Macy Jr. Foundation. New York. *Cold Injury Trans. Confs Josiah Macy jr Fdn* [1951–] **L.**MD.; **Dn.**U.; **E.**U. 52–; **O.**R.

14714 **Cold Spring Harbor Monographs.** Brooklyn, N.Y. *Cold Spring Harb. Monogr.* [1903–26] **L.**BM. 03–09; BM^N. 03–09; L. 03–09; Z. 03–21; **Bl.**U. 03–09; **Bm.**U. 03–09; **Bn.**U. 03–09; **C.**P. 03–09; **Db.**; **E.**F. 03–09; R. 03–09; U. 05–09; **Lv.**U. 03–21; **O.**R. 03–09; **Pl.**M.; **Sa.**

14715 **Cold Spring Harbor Symposia** on **Quantitative Biology.** Cold Spring Harbor. *Cold Spring Harb. Symp. quant. Biol.* [1933–] **L.**B. 34–36: 38; C. 46–; CB. 41– imp.; LI. 46: 53; MA. 46– imp.; MC.; MD.; RI. 42–; SC.; U. 48– imp.; UC.; Z. 54–; **Abd.**U. imp.; **Bl.**U. imp.; **Bm.**P. 42–; U.; **Bn.**U. 35– imp.; **Br.**U. 35–47 imp.; **C.**APH. 44– imp.; B.; BI.; BO. 40– imp.; **Cr.**MD. 51–; U. 41: 46–; **Dn.**U. 35– imp.; **E.**U.; **G.**U. imp.; **H.**U. 46– imp.; **Ld.**U.; **M.**C. 33–42; U.; **N.**U. 34– imp.; **Nw.**A. 35–37: 40–; **O.**BO. 34–53 imp.: 57–; R. 35–; **Pl.**M.; **R.**U. 41– imp.; **Rt.**; **Sa.** imp.; **Sw.**U. 50: 56–; **Y.**

14716 **Cold Storage** and **Distribution.** Kansas City. *Cold Stor. Distrib.*

Cold Storage and **Ice Association Proceedings.** London. *See* 39092.

14717 **Cold Storage Publications.** Cawthron Institute of Scientific Research. Nelson, N.Z. *Cold Stor. Publs Cawthron Inst.* [1925–33] **L.**P. 30–33.

14718 **Cold Storage Report.** Washington. *Cold Stor. Rep.* **L.**AM. 45–.

14719 **Colecção natura.** Societas scientiarum naturalium portucalensis. Lisboa. *Colecç. nat.* **L.**BM^N. 22–28.

14719^c **Colectanea. Missão** de **biologia maritima.** Lisboa. *Colnea Miss. Biol. marit.* [1956–] **L.**AM.; **Pl.**M.

14720 **Colegio farmacéutico.** Santiago. *Col. farm.*

14721 **Colegio médico.** Santiago de Chile. *Col. méd.* **L.**MA. 54– imp.

14722 **Coleopterists' Bulletin.** Dryden, N.Y. *Coleopts Bull.* [1947–] **L.**BM^N.; E.; **Y.**

14723 **Coleopterological Contributions.** Chicago. *Coleopt. Contr.* [1927–30] **L.**BM^N.; E.; EB.; Z.; **Bm.**U.; **Bn.**U.; **C.**UL.; **E.**R. 27; **Ld.**U.; **M.**U.

Coleopterologische Rundschau. *See* 27593.

14724 **Coleopterologisches Zentralblatt.** Berlin. *Coleopt. Zbl.* [1926–32] **L.**BM^N. 26–31.

14725 **Coleopterorum catalogus.** Berlin. *Coleoptm Cat.* [1910–] **L.**BM^N.; E.; EB. 10–22 imp.; Z.; **E.**F.; **G.**U.; **O.**R.

14725^c **Collagen Currents.** Somerville, N.J. *Collagen Curr.* [1960–] **L.**LE. 61–; MD.; S.; **C.**APH.

14726 **Collectanea botanica** a **Barcinonensi Botanico Instituto edita.** Barcinone. *Collnea bot., Barcinone* [1946–] **L.**BM^N.; K.; L.; **Bl.**U.; **C.**BO.; **O.**BO.; **Y.**

14727 **Collectanea friburgensia.** Fribourg. *Collnea friburg.* [1893–] **L.**BM.; **O.**B. 95–07 imp.

14728 **Collectanea mathematica.** Barcelona. *Collnea math.* [1948–] **L.**M.; SC. 59–; **C.**P.; **E.**R.; **G.**U.; **Y.**

14729 **Collectanea pharmaceutica suecica.** Stockholm. *Collnea pharm. suec.* [1947–] **L.**MA.; P. 49–; **Y.**

14730 **Collectanea** dos **trabalhos** do **Instituto** de **Butantan.** *Collnea Trab. Inst. Butantan* [1917–24: 51–] **L.**MC. 18–24; **C.**V. 51–52; **E.**R. 27–.

14730^c **Collected Abstracts** on **Trends** in **Diesel Engine Technology.** Motor Industry Research Association. Lindley. *Coll. Abstr. Trends Diesel Eng. Technol.* **Y.**

14731 **Collected Addresses** and **Laboratory Studies. London School** of **Hygiene** and **Tropical Medicine.** London. *Coll. Addr. Lab. Stud. Lond. Sch. Hyg.* [1924–31] **L.**BM.; BM^N. 24–29; EB. 25–31; L.; MA.; MC.; MD.; 24–29; S.; SC.; SH.; TD.; UC.; Z.; **Abd.**U.; **Bm.**U.; **Br.**U.; **Db.**; **E.**U.; **Lv.**U.; **M.**U.; **O.**R.; **Rt.** [C. of and *Rec. as:* 14785]

14732 **Collected Clinical** and **Radiological Papers.** Middlesex Hospital Medical School. London. *Coll. clin. radiol. Pap. Middx Hosp.* [1930–] **L.**MD.; **Bn.**U. 30–39 imp.; **Br.**U.; **Cr.**MD.; **E.**U.; **Ld.**U. 49–50; **M.**MS. [C. of: 41358]

14733 **Collected Contributions** from the **Massachusetts State Board** of **Insanity.** *Coll. Contr. Mass. St. Bd Insan.* **C.**UL. 15–16.

14734 **Collected Leaflets. Ministry** of **Agriculture** and **Fisheries.** London. *Coll. Leafl. Minist. Agric. Fish.* **L.**EB. (ent.) 21–; P. 28–30; SC. 34–; **Abs.**U. 21–; **Bm.**P. 21–; **Br.**U. 21; **O.**R. 33–36; **Rt.** 36–39.

14735 **Collected Meteorological Papers. Geophysical Institute, University** of **Tokyo.** Tokyo. *Coll. met. Pap. geophys. Inst., Tokyo* [1949–] **L.**MO.

14736 **Collected Oceanographical Papers. Geophysical Institute, University** of **Tokyo.** Tokyo. *Coll. oceanogr. Pap. geophys. Inst., Tokyo* [1949–] **Lv.**U.; **Pl.**M. 51–; **Wo.**

14737 **Collected Papers. Associate Committee** on **Grain Research.** National Research Council, Canada. Ottawa. *Coll. Pap. ass. Comm. Grain Res. Can.* [1929–] **C.**A.; **Rt.**

14738 **Collected Papers. Associate Committee** on **Weed Control.** National Research Council, Canada. Ottawa. *Coll. Pap. ass. Comm. Weed Control Can.* [1932–37] **C.**A.

14739 **Collected Papers** on **Atmospheric Turbulence** Tokyo. *Coll. Pap. atmosph. Turbul.* **L.**MO. 56–.

14740 **Collected Papers. Australian Institute** of **Tropical Medicine.** Townsville, Queensland. *Coll. Pap. Aust. Inst. trop. Med.* [1914–30] **L.**BM.; EB. 14; MD. 14: 30; TD. 14–17; **E.**R. 22–30. [*Replaced by:* 14748]

14741 **Collected Papers. Bacteriological Laboratory. Guy's Hospital Medical School.** London. *Coll. Pap. bact. Lab. Guy's Hosp.* **Lv.**U. 02–07.

14742 **Collected Papers. Baker Medical Research Institute** and the **Clinical Research Unit.** Melbourne. *Coll. Pap. Baker med. Res. Inst.* **L.**MC. 30–; MD. 30–34 imp.; S. 31–; **Nw.**A. 30–; **Y.**

14743 **Collected Papers** on **Bibliography** and **History** of **Medicine.** Laboratory of Physiology. Yale University. *Coll. Pap. Biblphy Hist. Med.* [1930–] **L.**S. 30–34.

14744 **Collected Papers. Biological Laboratory** of the **University** of **Western Australia.** *Coll. Pap. biol. Lab. Univ. West. Aust.* [1923–] **Pl.**M. 23–26.

14745 **Collected Papers. British Post-graduate Medical School.** London. *Coll. Pap. Br. post-grad. med. Sch.* **L.**TD. 36–42; U. 38–43; **Abd.**U. 35–42; **Bm.**U. 36–38; **Br.**U. 36–37; **E.**S. 36–39.

14746 **Collected Papers** of the **Canadian Committee** on **Food Preservation.** Ottawa. *Coll. Pap. Can. Comm. Fd Preserv.* **Md.**H. 38–.

14747 **Collected Papers. Chemical Defence Experimental Establishment.** Porton. *Coll. Pap. chem. Def. exp. Establ.* [1959–] **L.**P.; **Y.**

14748 **Collected Papers. Commonwealth School** of **Public Health** and **Tropical Medicine** of **Sydney University.** Sydney. *Coll. Pap. Commonw. Sch. publ. Hlth trop. Med. Sydney Univ.* [1937] **L.**BM^N.; MD.; SH.; **Abd.**R.; **E.**R. [*Replaces:* 14740]

14749 **Collected Papers** of the **County Pottery Laboratory.** Stoke-on-Trent. *Coll. Pap. Cty Pott. Lab., Stoke* **L.**BM. 14–; P. 14.

    Collected Papers from the **Danish State Vitamin Laboratory.** *See* 29952.

    Collected Papers. Department of **Animal Nutrition, Pennsylvania State University.** *See* 14800.

14750 **Collected Papers** from the **Department** of **Coal, Gas** and **Fuel Industries** with **Metallurgy, University** of **Leeds.** *Coll. Pap. Dep. Coal Gas Fuel Ind. Univ. Leeds* [1908–] **Ld.**U.

14751 **Collected Papers. Department** of **Diseases** of the **Nervous System, Harvard Medical School.** Boston. *Coll. Pap. Dep. Dis. nerv. Syst. Harvard* [1931–] **L.**MD.; S. 31–39: 41; **Db.** 31–41 imp. [*C. of:* 15680]

14752 **Collected Papers. Department** of **Neurology, Harvard Medical School.** Boston. *Coll. Pap. Dep. Neurol. Harvard* **L.**MD. 06–12. [*C. as:* 15680]

14753 **Collected Papers. Department** of **Neuropathology, Harvard Medical School.** Boston. *Coll. Pap. Dep. Neuropath. Harvard* [1904–09] **L.**MD. 09.

14754 **Collected Papers** from the **Department** of **Pathology** in the **University** of **Oxford.** *Coll. Pap. Dep. Path. Univ. Oxf.* [1909–] **L.**MC. 11–; MD. 09–11; S. 09–13: 35–38; TD. 14–34; UCH. 14–38; **Bm.**U. 09–34; **Br.**U. 09–13; **C.**PA. 09–38; **E.**S. 11–13; **Ld.**U. 14–34; **Lv.**U.; **O.**R. 09–35.

14755 **Collected Papers** from the **Department** of **Pharmacology. Peiping Union Medical College.** Peiping. *Coll. Pap. Dep. Pharmac. Peiping Un. med. Coll.* **L.**K. 27; **E.**U. 25–.

14755° **Collected Papers. Department** of **Physiology, Edinburgh University.** *Coll. Pap. Dep. Physiol. Edinb. Univ.* **Abd.**R. 32–33: 57–60.

14756 **Collected Papers** from the **Department** of **Physiology, Peking Union Medical College.** Peking. *Coll. Pap. Dep. Physiol. Peking Un. med. Coll.* **E.**U. 27–39 imp.

14757 **Collected Papers. Department** of **Physiology, Pharmacology** and **Biochemistry, University College, London.** London. *Coll. Pap. Dep. Physiol. Pharmac. Biochem. Univ. Coll. Lond.* **L.**UC.; **E.**U.; **Y.**

14758 **Collected Papers** from the **Department** of **Physiology** of the **University** of **Pennsylvania.** *Coll. Pap. Dep. Physiol. Univ. Pa* [1922–] **L.**MC.; S. 22–37; UC. 34–; **Br.**U. imp.; **E.**U. 22–30; **G.**U. 22–30; **O.**R. 22–37.

14759 **Collected Papers** of the **Department** of **Physiology, University** of **Western Ontario.** London, Canada. *Coll. Pap. Dep. Physiol. Univ. west. Ont.* [1931–] **L.**S. 31.

14760 **Collected Papers** from the **Department** of **Physiology, Western Reserve University School** of **Medicine.** Cleveland, O. *Coll. Pap. Dep. Physiol. west. Res. Univ.* **L.**MC. 19–; S. 23–27: 39–41; **E.**U. 19– imp.

14761 **Collected Papers** from the **Department** of **Surgical Research, University** of **Edinburgh.** *Coll. Pap. Dep. surg. Res. Univ. Edinb.* [1909–] **L.**S.; **E.**S.

14762 **Collected Papers** of the **Division** of **Animal Health** and **Production, C.S.I.R.O., Australia.** Melbourne. *Coll. Pap. Div. Anim. Hlth Prod. C.S.I.R.O., Aust.* **Abd.**R. 46–.

14762° **Collected Papers. Division** of **Medicine** and **Public Health** of the **Rockefeller Foundation.** New York. *Coll. Pap. Div. Med. publ. Hlth Rockefeller Fdn* [1951–] **L.**TD. [*C. of:* 14775]

    Collected Papers. Division of **Pathological Science, Henry Lester Institute** of **Medical Research.** Shanghai. *See* 14769.

14763 **Collected Papers** from the **Faculty** of **Medicine, Osaka Imperial University.** Osaka. *Coll. Pap. Fac. Med. Osaka imp. Univ.* [1936–42] **L.**C. 37–42; LI. 36–37; S. imp.; Z. 38; **Bl.**U. 36–38; **Bm.**U. 36–38; **Br.**U. 36–38; **Cr.**MD. 37–38; **E.**R. 36–38; **G.**U. 36–38; **Lv.**M. 36–39; **Nw.**A. 36–38; **O.**R. 36–38; **Sa.** 36–38.

14764 **Collected Papers** from the **Faculty** of **Science, Osaka Imperial University.** Osaka. *Coll. Pap. Fac. Sci. Osaka imp. Univ.*

    Mathematics [1933–48] **L.**BM.; LI.; TD. 36: 39; UC.; **Bl.**U. 33–38; **Cr.**U. 33–39 imp.; **E.**R.; U. 33–37; **G.**U. 33–39; **N.**U. 33–39; **Nw.**A. 33–38: 40–47. [*C. as:* 36446]

    Physics [1933–52] **L.**BM.; LI. 36–37; QM. 38–40 imp.; RI. 43–51; SC.; TD. 36–39; **Bl.**U. 33–37: 40–42; **Br.**U.; **E.**R.; **G.**U. imp.; **M.**T.; **Nw.**A. 33–37: 40–51. [*C. in:* 45239]

    Chemistry [1933–52] **L.**BM.; C. 33–42; LI. 36–37; QM. 37–51 imp.; RI. 43–51; SC.; TD. 36–39; UC.; **E.**R.; **G.**U. 33–39 imp. [*C. in:* 45239]

14765 **Collected Papers. Field Service School** for **Medical Officers.** Fort Leavenworth. *Coll. Pap. Fld Serv. Sch. med. Offrs*

14766 **Collected Papers. Freshwater Biological Association.** Ambleside, Windermere. *Coll. Pap. Freshwat. biol. Ass.* **L.**NC. 50–; U. 50–; **Fr.** 49–; **Lo.** 49–; **Pl.**M. 49–. [*See also:* 14843°]

    Collected Papers on **Grain Research.** National Research Council. Ottawa. *See* 14737.

14767 **Collected Papers. Gynæcological Department** of the **Johns Hopkins Hospital** and **University.** Baltimore. *Coll. Pap. gynæc. Dep. Johns Hopkins Hosp.* [1916–] **L.**S. 16–38; **Bm.**U. 16–22; **E.**S. 16–22: 29–38; **O.**R.

14768 **Collected Papers** from the **H. K. Cushing Laboratory** of **Experimental Medicine.** Western Reserve University. Cleveland. *Coll. Pap. H. K. Cushing Lab. exp. Med.* [1901–] **L.**MC. 16–; MD. 12–28; S. 01–31; U. 01–20; **Abd.**U. 11–13; **Br.**U. 11–31; **C.**P. 11–31; **E.**U.; **Lv.**U.; **M.**MS. 18–20; **O.**R. 13–17.

    Collected Papers. Henry Ford Hospital. New York. *See* 14820.

14769 **Collected Papers. Henry Lester Institute** of **Medical Research.** Shanghai. *Coll. Pap. Henry Lester Inst. med. Res.* [1932–] L.MD. 35–; PH. 32–40; TD. 32–39; **Abd.**R. 32–40.

Collected Papers from the **Hygienic Institute** of the **Jagellonian University** in **Cracow.** *See* 58381.

14770 **Collected Papers. Institute** of **Animal Physiology.** Babraham. *Coll. Pap. Inst. Anim. Physiol., Babraham* [1948–] **Abd.**R. 57–; **C.**APH.; **Pl.**M. 50–.

14771 **Collected Papers. Institute** for **Biological Research, Johns Hopkins University.** Baltimore. *Coll. Pap. Inst. biol. Res. Johns Hopkins Univ.* [1928–41] **L.**BM.; LI.; MC.; Z.; **Ba.**I.; **C.**UL.; **O.**R.; **Rt.**

14772 **Collected Papers. Institute** of **Medical** and **Veterinary Science.** Adelaide. *Coll. Pap. Inst. med. vet. Sci., Adelaide* [1938–] **L.**TD.; **Abd.**R. 38–47; **Bm.**U.; **E.**R.; U.; **G.**U. 38–47; **Ld.**U. 38–47; **M.**MS.; **O.**R.; **Sa.**

14773 **Collected Papers** from the **Institute** of **Pharmacology, Tokyo University.** Tokyo. *Coll. Pap. Inst. Pharmac. Tokyo Univ.* **E.**U. 27–37 imp.

14773° **Collected Papers** of the **Institute** of **Physiology, University College, London.** *Coll. Pap. Inst. Physiol. Univ. Coll. Lond.* [1874–] **L.**BM. 12–24; S.; U. 95–19; UC.; UCH. 79–24 imp.; **Bm.**U. 92–37; **Br.**U. 09–39; **E.**U.; **Lv.**U. 91–13; **Pl.**M. 27–34; **Y.**

14774 **Collected Papers** from the **Institute** of **Physiology** of the **University** of **Glasgow.** *Coll. Pap. Inst. Physiol. Univ. Glasg.* [1910–] **L.**BM. 34–; MC.; S. 12–28; **Abd.**R. 10–24: 34: 56; **Bl.**U. 34–; **Bm.**U. 34; **Bn.**U. 34–; **E.**U. 10–13; **Br.**U. 34–; **Dn.**U. 34–; **E.**A.; R.; S. 10–28; U. 18–; **G.**U.; **Lv.**U. 10–13; **M.**MS. 18–24; **N.**U. 34–; **O.**R. 34–; **R.**D. 48–; **Sa.** 10–28: 34–; **Y.**

Collected Papers. International Health Board of the **Rockefeller Foundation.** *See* 14775.

14775 **Collected Papers. International Health Division** of the **Rockefeller Foundation.** New York. *Coll. Pap. int. Hlth Div. Rockefeller Fdn* [1925–50] **L.**TD.; **Bm.**U. 25–26. [*C. as:* 14762°]

14776 **Collected Papers. Jane Coffin Childs Memorial Fund** for **Medical Research.** *Coll. Pap. Jane Coffin Childs meml Fund med. Res.* [1938–]

14777 **Collected Papers. Laboratory Animals Bureau.** London. *Coll. Pap. Lab. Anim. Bur.* [1953–] **L.**BM.; LI.; MD.; TD.; UC.; **Abs.**U.; **Bm.**U.; **C.**UL.; **Cr.**U. 53–59; **G.**U.; **N.**U.; **O.**AP.; R.; **Y.**

14778 **Collected Papers** of the **Laboratory** of **Comparative Physiology** of the **Timiriasev Biological Institute.** Moscow. *Coll. Pap. Lab. comp. Physiol. Timiriasev biol. Inst.* **E.**R. 34.

14779 **Collected Papers. Laboratory** of **Comparative Physiology, Utrecht.** *Coll. Pap. Lab. comp. Physiol. Utrecht* **L.**S. 32–34; UC. 28; **Pl.**M. 30– imp.

14780 **Collected Papers** from the **Laboratory** of **Physiological Chemistry** of **Yale University.** *Coll. Pap. Lab. physiol. Chem. Yale* [1919–] **Abd.**R. 33–35. [*C. of:* 14818]

14781 **Collected Papers** from the **Laboratory** of **Physiology** and **Biochemistry, Middlesex Hospital Medical School.** London. *Coll. Pap. Lab. Physiol. Biochem. Middx Hosp.* **E.**U. 29–.

14782 **Collected Papers. Lister Institute** of **Preventive Medicine.** London. *Coll. Pap. Lister Inst.*

[1904–47] **L.**K. 04; LI.; MA.; MC.; MD. 04: 11–13; P.; S.; SH.; TD.; U. 04–12: 18–38 imp.; UC. 07–26 imp.; UCH.; **Bm.**U. 04–34 imp.; **C.**MO.; PA. 04–20; **Cr.**MD. 09–21; **Db.**; **E.**U. 04–25; **Lv.**U.; **M.**MS. 31–47 imp.; **Nw.**A. 07–26; **O.**R. 04–17.

14783 **Collected Papers. Liverpool School** of **Tropical Medicine.** Liverpool. *Coll. Pap. Lpool Sch. trop. Med.* [1945–] **L.**TD.

14784 **Collected Papers** of the **Lockwood Clinic.** Toronto. *Coll. Pap. Lockwood Clin.* **L.**S. 29.

14785 **Collected Papers** from the **London School** of **Hygiene** and **Tropical Medicine.** London. *Coll. Pap. Lond. Sch. Hyg. trop. Med.* [1922–24: 31–]
    Clinical and Pathological. **L.**BM^N.; MC.; MD.; S.; SH. imp.; TD.; **Abd.**U.; **Bm.**U.; **Br.**U.; **C.**UL.; **Dn.**U.; **E.**U.; **Lv.**U.; **Sa.**
    Department of Helminthology. **L.**BM^N.; MC.; MD.; S.; SH. imp.; TD.; Z.; **Abd.**U.; **Abs.**U.; **Bm.**U.; **Br.**U.; **C.**UL.; **Dn.**U.; **E.**U.; **Lv.**U.; **M.**U.; **Rt.**; **Sa.** [> 14731, 1924–31]

14786 **Collected Papers. Macaulay Institute** for **Soil Research.** Craigiebuckler. *Coll. Pap. Macaulay Inst. Soil Res.* [1930–] **L.**SC.; **Abd.**R.; S.; U.; **Bm.**U. 32–48; **Br.**U. 30–38; **C.**A.; **E.**D.; R.; W. 38–; **G.**U.; **Md.**H.; **O.**F. 30–54; RE. 48–; **Rt.**; **Y.** [*Also supplements*]

14787 **Collected Papers** of the **Mathematical Institute, Nagoya University.** *Coll. Pap. math. Inst. Nagoya Univ.* [1942–] **L.**R.

14788 **Collected Papers** of the **Mayo Clinic.** Rochester, Minn. *Coll. Pap. Mayo Clin.* [1905–] **L.**GH. 05–42; MA. 05–16: 18–21: 23–; MD.; S. 14–; U. 49–; UCH. 05–13: 18; **Abd.**U. 06–46 imp.; **Bl.**U. imp.; **Bm.**U.; **Br.**U.; **Cr.**MD.; **Db.**; **Dn.**U. 05–30: 56; **E.**I. 05–10: 14–48; P.; S. imp.; U. 05–21: 31–; **G.**F.; **Lv.**M. 05–51: 54–; U.; **M.**MS.; **Nw.**A.; **O.**R. 42–.

Collected Papers from the **Medical Department B, Rigshospitalet.** Copenhagen. *See* 3794.

Collected Papers from the **Medical Research Laboratories, Parke Davis & Co.** Detroit. *See* 14810.

Collected Papers by **Members** of the **Staff** of the **Division** of **Medicine** and **Public Health** of the **Rockefeller Foundation.** New York. *See* 14762°.

Collected Papers by **Members** of the **Staff** of the **International Health Division** (**Board**) of the **Rockefeller Foundation.** New York. *See* 14775.

14793 **Collected Papers. Microbiological Research Establishment.** Porton. *Coll. Pap. microbiol. Res. Establ.* [1956–] **L.**P.; UCH.; **Abd.**R.; **Br.**U.; **Rt.**; **Y.**

14794 **Collected Papers** of the **Middlesex Hospital Medical School.** London. *Coll. Pap. Middx Hosp. med. Sch.* **L.**LI. 46–; MD. 29–; S. 23–; U. 50–.

14795 **Collected Papers** from the **Museum** of **Natural History.** Aarhus. *Coll. Pap. Mus. nat. Hist., Aarhus* [1948–] **L.**BM^N.; **O.**AP.; **Y.**

14796 **Collected Papers. National Foundation** for **Infantile Paralysis.** New York. *Coll. Pap. natn. Fdn infant. Paralysis* **L.**MD. 50–.

14797 **Collected Papers. Osborn Zoological Laboratory, Yale University.** New Haven. *Coll. Pap. Osborn zool. Lab.* [1914–] **L.**UC. 14–43; **E.**U.; **O.**Z.; **Pl.**M. 14–55.

14798 **Collected Papers** from the **Pathological Department** of the **University** of **Manchester.** *Coll. Pap. path. Dep. Univ. Manchr* **L.**LI. 16–21; **M.**MS. 21–.

14799 **Collected Papers. Pathological Institute Glasgow Royal Infirmary.** Glasgow. *Coll. Pap. path. Inst. Glasg. R. Infirm.* **G.**U. 09–11.

14800 **Collected Papers. Pennsylvania State University Institute** of **Animal Nutrition.** State College, Pa. *Coll. Pap. Pa St. Univ. Inst. Anim. Nutr.* **Abd.**R. 36–46.

14801 **Collected Papers** from the **Pharmacological Laboratory, Cambridge.** *Coll. Pap. pharmac. Lab. Camb.* **L.**LI. 06–09; MD. 06; UC. 08–09; **Abd.**U. 08–09.

14802 **Collected Papers** from the **Pharmacology Department** of **Edinburgh University.** Edinburgh. *Coll. Pap. Pharmac. Dep. Edinb. Univ.* [1919–] **E.**U.

14803 **Collected Papers** in **Physiological** and **Biological Physico-Chemistry.** Kyoto. *Coll. Pap. physiol. biol. Physico-Chem.* [1925–] **L.**C. 27; LI.; MC.; MD.; **Br.**U. 25–28; **E.**U.

Collected Papers from the **Physiological Department** of the **University** of **Glasgow.** *See* 14774.

14804 **Collected Papers** of the **Physiological Laboratory** of **King's College, London.** *Coll. Pap. physiol. Lab. King's Coll. Lond.* [1893–27] **L.**BM.; MD. 93–24 imp.; R.; S. 93–24; U. 93–24; UC.; **Br.**U. 10–22; **C.**PA. 93–05; **E.**U. 93–25; **Lv.**U. 08–27; **M.**MS. 05–24.

14806 **Collected Papers** from the **Physiological Laboratory. London Hospital Medical College.** London. *Coll. Pap. physiol. Lab. Lond. Hosp.* **L.**MD. 97–00; **Br.**U. 97–04; **Lv.**U. 97–04.

Collected Papers of the **Physiological Laboratory, University College, London.** *See* 14773ᶜ.

14807 **Collected Papers. Physiology Laboratory, Guy's Hospital Medical School.** London. *Coll. Pap. Physiol. Lab. Guy's Hosp.* **E.**U. 94–29; **Lv.**U. 05–10.

14808 **Collected Papers. Quick Laboratory, University** of **Cambridge.** *Coll. Pap. Quick Lab.* [1913–18] **L.**LI.; MD. 13–14; TD.; **C.**UL.

Collected Papers. Research Department, University College Hospital Medical School. *See* 14824.

Collected Papers from the **Research Laboratory** of the **Department** of **Health, New York City.** *See* 14866.

14810 **Collected Papers** from the **Research Laboratory, Parke, Davis** & **Co.** Detroit. *Coll. Pap. Res. Lab. Parke Davis Co.* [1913–20] **L.**MC.; MD.; P.; SC. 14–20; TD.; U.; **Abd.**R. 14–20; **Br.**U. 13–14; **C.**PA.; **E.**U.; **G.**U.; **Lv.**U.; **O.**R.

14811 **Collected Papers** on **Research** of the **Millbank Memorial Fund.** New York. *Coll. Pap. Res. Millbank meml Fund* **Abd.**R. 42–.

14812 **Collected Papers. Rowett Research Institute.** Aberdeen. *Coll. Pap. Rowett Res. Inst.* [1925–] **L.**AM.; BM.; P. 25–33: 54–; **Abd.**S. 33– imp.; U.; **Abs.**A.; N. 30–; **Br.**U. 56–; **C.**A.; APH. 51–; UL.; **Db.**; **E.**A.; R. 25–30; T.; U.; **O.**R.; RE. 55–; **R.**D. 25–33: 49–; **Rt.** imp.; **Y.**

14813 **Collected Papers. School** of **Hygiene** and **Public Health. Johns Hopkins University.** Baltimore. *Coll. Pap. Sch. Hyg. publ. Hlth Johns Hopkins Univ.* [1919–34] **L.**BM.; EB.; MC.; MD.; S. 20–34; SH. 20–34; TD.; UC.; **Abd.**U.; **Bl.**U.; **Bm.**U. 19–33; **C.**UL.; **Db** 19–33; **E.**P.; U.; **G.**U.; **Lv.**U.; **O.**R.; **Sa.**

14814 **Collected Papers. School** of **Physiology, Trinity College, Dublin.** *Coll. Pap. Sch. Physiol. Trin. Coll. Dubl.* **O.**R. 18.

14815 **Collected Papers. School** of **Tropical Medicine, Porto Rico.** *Coll. Pap. Sch. trop. Med. P. Rico* [1926–] **L.**TD. 32–37; **C.**PA. 32–38.

14816 **Collected Papers. School** of **Veterinary Medicine, University** of **Cambridge.** Cambridge. *Coll. Pap. Sch. vet. Med. Univ. Camb.* **Abd.**R. 57–; **C.**A. 57–.

14817 **Collected Papers** from the **Science Laboratories** of the **University** of **Melbourne.** *Coll. Pap. Sci. Labs Univ. Melb.* [1906–] **L.**S. 10–28; UC. 06–09; **Abd.**U.; **Bm.**U. 06–09; **C.**UL. 06–09; **Cr.**U. 06–09; **Db.**; **E.**R. 10–; U. 06–09; **G.**U. 06–28; **Ld.**U. 06–28; **Lv.**U. 06–09; **M.**U. 06–09; **Rt.** 10–28.

14818 **Collected Papers. Sheffield Laboratory** of **Physiological Chemistry, Yale University.** *Coll. Pap. Sheff. Lab. physiol. Chem. Yale* [1901–18] **L.**S. 13–14; **E.**U. 04–18; **O.**R. 04–16. [*C. as:* 14780]

14819 **Collected Papers. Squibb Institute** for **Medical Research.** New Brunswick, N.J. *Coll. Pap. Squibb Inst. med. Res.* [1938–]

14820 **Collected Papers** by the **Staff** of the **Henry Ford Hospital.** New York. *Coll. Pap. Staff Henry Ford Hosp.* **L.**S. 15–25; TD. 15–25.

Collected Papers by the **Staff** of **St. Mary's Hospital, Mayo Clinic.** *See* 14788.

Collected Papers by the **Staff** of the **State Institute** of **Public Health** in **Prague.** *See* 50103.

Collected Papers. State Veterinary Medical Institute. Stockholm. *See* 29870.

14821 **Collected Papers** of **Thyroid Gland.** University of Kyoto. *Coll. Pap. Thyroid Gland* [1925] **C.**BI.; **E.**U. [*C. as:* 19790]

14822 **Collected Papers. Universitets dyrefysiologiske Laboratorium.** Copenhagen. *Coll. Pap. Univ. dyrefysiol. Lab., Copenh.* [1911–] **L.**MC.; S. 19–33 imp.; UC. 17–22; **E.**U. 12–; **Pl.**M. imp.

Collected Papers. Universitets zoofysiologiske Laboratorium. Copenhagen. *See* 14822.

14823 **Collected Papers** from the **University** of **Adelaide.** *Coll. Pap. Univ. Adelaide* [1919–] **E.**R. 36–46 imp.; **M.**U. 32–38.

14824 **Collected Papers. University College Hospital Medical School Research Department.** London. *Coll. Pap. Univ. Coll. Hosp. med. Sch. Res. Dep.* [1910–] **L.**MD. 12– imp.; S.; TD.; U. imp.; UC. 10–23; UCH.; **Bm.**U. 10–20; **Br.**U. 10–31; **C.**PA. 10–33; **Cr.**MD. 12–20; **Dn.**U. 10–14; **E.**U. 10–31; **Lv.**U.; **O.**P. 10–22.

14825 **Collected Papers. University College Psychological Laboratory.** London. *Coll. Pap. Univ. Coll. psychol. Lab., Lond.* **L.**BM. 12–; UC. 12–.

Collected Papers from the **University Institute** of **Hygiene, Copenhagen.** *See* 29956.

14826 **Collected Papers** from the **University** of **Queensland.** Brisbane. *Coll. Pap. Univ. Qd* [1916–18] **L.**BM.; GM.; P.; **Abs.**N.; **C.**UL.; **Db.**; **E.**U.; **G.**U.; **Lv.**U.; **M.**U.; **O.**R.

Collected Papers from the **Veterinary Institute, Stockholm.** *See* 29894.

14827 **Collected Papers. Veterinary School, Glasgow University.** Glasgow. *Coll. Pap. vet. Sch. Glasg. Univ.* [1951–] **Abd.**R.; **Br.**U. 51–55; **R.**D.

14828 **Collected Papers. Walter** and **Eliza Hall Institute** of **Research** in **Pathology** and **Medicine.** Melbourne. *Coll. Pap. Walter Eliza Hall Inst. Res. Path. Med.* [1920–] **L.**LI.; MC.; MD. 20–29; S. 20–45; TD.; **Bl.**U. 23–44; **C.**PA. 23–29 imp.; **G.**U. 23–44; **O.**R. 26–27.

14829 **Collected Papers. Washington University School** of **Medicine.** St. Louis. *Coll. Pap. Wash. Univ. Sch. Med.* **L.**BM. 23–; **C.**UL. 21; **O.**R. 21–22.

14830 **Collected Papers. Wellcome Chemical Research Laboratories.** London. *Coll. Pap. Wellcome chem. Res. Labs* **L.**S. 13–38.

14831 **Collected Papers. Wellcome Physiological Research Laboratories.** London. *Coll. Pap. Wellcome physiol. Res. Labs* **L.**S. 13–38.

14832 **Collected Papers** on **Yellow Fever** by members of the staff of the **International Health Division** of the **Rockefeller Foundation.** New York. *Coll. Pap. yell. Fev.* **L.**TD. 27–.

14833 **Collected Papers. Zoological Laboratory** and **State University** of **Iowa.** *Coll. Pap. zool. Lab. St. Univ. Ia* **Nw.**A. 27–28; **Pl.**M. 27–28.

14833ᶜ **Collected Reprints. Agricultural** and **Mechanical College** of **Texas.** *Coll. Repr. agric. mech. Coll. Tex.* **Wo.** 50–.

14834 **Collected Reprints** and **Annual Reports. Marine Biological Station, University College** of **North Wales.** Bangor. *Coll. Repr. a. Rep. mar. biol. Stn Univ. Coll. N. Wales* **Bn.**U. 50–57. [*C. as:* 15771]

14835 **Collected Reprints** from **Brady Urological Institute.** Baltimore. *Coll. Repr. Brady urol. Inst.* [1911–] **L.**MD.

14836 **Collected Reprints. Chesapeake Bay Institute.** Baltimore. *Coll. Repr. Chesapeake Bay Inst.* [1951–] **Bn.**U.; **Dm.** 53–; **Lv.**U. 53–; **Pl.**M.; **Wo.**; **Y.**

14837 **Collected Reprints** from the **Department** of **Experimental Surgery** of **New York University.** New York. *Coll. Repr. Dep. exp. Surg. N.Y. Univ.* [1915–] **L.**MD. 15–27; S. 15–27; **Br.**U. 15–27; **E.**S. 15–27; **M.**MS. 15–25. [*C. of:* 51158]

14838 **Collected Reprints** of the **Department** of **Ophthalmology, West China Union University College** of **Medicine** and **Dentistry.** Chengtu. *Coll. Repr. Dep. Ophthal. W. China Un. Univ.* **Br.**U. 38–45.

14839 **Collected Reprints** of the **Department** of **Pathology** and **Bacteriology** of the **University** of **Illinois College** of **Medicine.** Chicago. *Coll. Repr. Dep. Path. Bact. Univ. Ill.* [1926–] [*C. of:* 14863]

14840 **Collected Reprints. Department** of **Pathology, Columbia University.** New York. *Coll. Repr. Dep Path. Columbia Univ.* [1928–] **L.**LI.; UC.; **Br.**U.; **C.**UL.; **E.**U.; **Lv.**U. [*C. of:* 51112]

14841 **Collected Reprints. Department** of **Pharmacology** and **Therapeutics, University** of **Illinois.** Urbana. *Coll. Repr. Dep. Pharmac. Ther. Univ. Ill.* **Lv.**U. 17–26 imp.

14842 **Collected Reprints. Department** of **Physiology** and **Biochemistry, Cornell University Medical College.** Ithaca, N.Y. *Coll. Repr. Dep. Physiol. Biochem. Cornell Univ.* **Br.**U. 17–23.

14843 **Collected Reprints** from the **Department** of **Physiology, University** of **Edinburgh.** *Coll. Repr. Dep. Physiol. Univ. Edinb.* [1899–] **Abd.**R. 23–33; **Br.**U. 28–; **E.**U.; **Pl.**M. 24–33 imp.

14843ᶜ **Collected Reprints. Freshwater Biological Association.** Ambleside. *Coll. Repr. Freshwat. biol. Ass.* **Wo.** 52–. [*See also:* 14766]

14844 **Collected Reprints** from the **George Williams Hooper Foundation** for **Medical Research, University** of **California.** Berkeley. *Coll. Repr. George Williams Hooper Fdn med. Res.* [1915–] **L.**MD. 15–21; S. 15–31; TD. 15–46; UC. 15–22; **Bm.**U. 15–31; **C.**PA. 16–23; **E.**P.; U.; **G.**PH. 16–23; **Lv.**U. 15–29 imp.; **M.**MS. 20–23; U. 15–31; **O.**R.

14844ᶜ **Collected Reprints. German Hydrographic Institute.** Hamburg. *Coll. Repr. Germ. hydrogr. Inst.* **Wo.** 50–.

14845 **Collected Reprints** from the **Laboratories. Philadelphia General Hospital.** Philadelphia. *Coll. Repr. Labs Philad. gen. Hosp.* [1920–28] **L.**BM.; MC. 25–28; MD.; S.; UCH.; **Abd.**U.; **Bm.**U.; **Br.**U.; **C.**UL.; **Db.**; **E.**U. 24–28; **Lv.**U. imp.; **M.**MS. 24–26; **O.**P. [*C. of:* and *Rec. as:* 37527]

14846 **Collected Reprints. Lerner Marine Laboratory.** Miami. *Coll. Repr. Lerner mar. Lab.* [1948–] **Dm.**; **E.**U.; **Pl.**M.

14846ᶜ **Collected Reprints. Marine Laboratory, Florida State Board** of **Conservation.** *Coll. Repr. mar. Lab. Fla* [1955–] **Pl.**M.

14847 **Collected Reprints. Montefiore Hospital, New York.** *Coll. Repr. Montefiore Hosp.* [1917–] **L.**GH. 17–39; MD.; S. 17–39; U.; **C.**PA. 22–24; UL.; **Dn.**U. 23–42; **E.**U.; **O.**R.

14848 **Collected Reprints. Narragansett Marine Laboratory** of the **University** of **Rhode Island.** Kingston. *Coll. Repr. Narragansett mar. Lab.* [1952–] **Bn.**U.; **Dm.**; **Pl.**M.; **Wo.**

14849 **Collected Reprints. National Foundation** for **Infantile Paralysis.** New York. *Coll. Repr. natn. Fdn infant. Paralysis* [1939–61] **L.**S. 46–61; UCH. 51–61.

14850 **Collected Reprints. National Institute** of **Oceanography.** Wormley, Surrey. *Coll. Repr. natn. Inst. Oceanogr.* [1953–] **L.**BM.; BMᴺ.; MO.; SC.; U.; Z.; **Bl.**U.; **Bn.**U.; **Br.**U.; **C.**GG.; PO.; **Dm.** 54–; **Dn.**U.; **E.**R.; U.; **Fr.**; **G.**U.; **Lo.**; **Lv.**U.; **Mi.**; **Nw.**A.; **O.**R.; **Pl.**M.; **Sa.**; **Wo.**

14851 **Collected Reprints. New York State Department** of **Health.** Albany. *Coll. Repr. N.Y. St. Dep. Hlth* **L.**SC. 27–.

14851ᵃ **Collected Reprints. New Zealand Oceanographic Commission.** Wellington. *Coll. Repr. N.Z. oceanogr. Commn* **Dm.** 57–.

14851ᵇ **Collected Reprints. New Zealand Oceanographic Institute.** Wellington. *Coll. Repr. N.Z. oceanogr. Inst.* **L.**Z. 58–; **Wo.** 52–.

14852 **Collected Reprints. Oceanographical Laboratory, Meteorological Research Institute, Mabashi.** Tokyo. *Coll. Repr. oceanogr. Lab. met. Res. Inst. Mabashi* [1954–] **L.**MO. 54; **Lv.**U.; **Wo.**

Collected Reprints. Plant Protection Service of the **Netherlands.** *See* 56406ᵃ.

14852ᶜ **Collected Reprints. Port Erin Biological Station.** *Coll. Repr. Port. Erin biol. Stn* **Pl.**M. 52–.

14853 **Collected Reprints. Portobello Marine Biological Station.** *Coll. Repr. Portobello mar. biol. Stn* [1957–] **Pl.**M.

14854 **Collected Reprints. Scottish Marine Biological Association.** Millport. *Coll. Repr. Scott. mar. biol. Ass.* [1948–] **L.**L. 51–; Z.; **Abd.**M.; U.; **Bn.**U.; **Dm.**; **E.**R.; U.; **Fr.**; **H.**U.; **Lo.**; **Lv.**U.; **Pl.**M.; **Wo.** 53–.

14854° **Collected Reprints. Scripps Institution of Oceanography.** La Jolla. *Coll. Repr. Scripps Instn Oceanogr.* **Wo.** 49–.

14855 **Collected Reprints. Tokai Regional Fisheries Research Laboratory.** Tokyo. *Coll. Repr. Tokai reg. Fish. Res. Lab.* **Pl.**M. 58–; **Y.**
    Collected Reprints. Tokyo Meteorological Research Institute. *See* 14852.

14856 **Collected Reprints** from the **University** of **Oregon Medical School.** Eugene. *Coll. Repr. Univ. Ore. med. Sch.* **L.**U. 23–24.

14857 **Collected Reprints. University** of **Sheffield School** of **Medicine.** Sheffield. *Coll. Repr. Univ. Sheffield Sch. Med.* [1934–] **Abd.**U. 34–36; **Br.**U. 34–36; **Cr.**MD. 34–36.

14858 **Collected Reprints** from the **Wilmer Ophthalmological Institute** of the **Johns Hopkins University.** Baltimore. *Coll. Repr. Wilmer ophthalm. Inst. Johns Hopkins Univ.* [1925–] **L.**BM.; GH.; MD.; OP. 25–45; S.; **Bl.**U.; **Bm.**U.; **Br.**U.; **Db.**; **E.**P. 25–49; S. imp.; U. 33–; **G.**F.; **M.**MS. imp.; **O.**R.; **Y.**

14859 **Collected Reprints** from the **Woods Hole Oceanographic Institution.** Woods Hole, Mass. *Coll. Repr. Woods Hole oceanogr. Instn* [1933–] **L.**AM.; BM^N.; L.; MO. 44–; UC.; **Bn.**U.; **Br.**U. 33–43; **Dm.**; **E.**R. 44–; **Fr.** 39–; **Lv.**U.; **Pl.**M.; **Sh.**SC. 58–; **Wo.** 44–46: 49–.

14860 **Collected Research Papers** from the **Division** of **Agricultural Biochemistry, University** of **Minnesota.** St. Paul. *Coll. Res. Pap. Div. agric. Biochem. Univ. Minn.* [1923–] **L.**C. 23–49.

14861 **Collected Researches. National Physical Laboratory.** London. *Coll. Res. natn. phys. Lab.* [1905–35] **L.**AV. 05–30; BM. 06–35; C.; EE.; GM. 06–35; I.; M.; MO. 15: 27; NF. 20–35; P.; R.; SC. 08–35; U. 06–35; UC.; **Abs.**N. 07–35; **Bm.**P. 07–35; U.; **Br.**U. 05–21; **C.**P.; UL.; **Cr.**P. 07–35; **Db.**; **Dn.**U. 05–30; **E.**A.; R.; T. 08–35; U. 06–15: 27; **Ex.**U. 05–20; **G.**E.; I. 15–35; M. 07–35; T. 12–35; U. 30–35; **H.**U. 15–29; **Ld.**P. 08–35; U.; **Lv.**U. 05–21; **M.**C. 05–32: 35; P. 13–35; T. 07–35; U.; **N.**U. 22–29 imp.; **Nw.**A. 07–35; P. 19–35; **O.**R.; **Sh.**IO. 08–35; U. 05–21. [*Replaced by:* 372]
    Collected Studies from the **Bureau** of the **Laboratory** of the **Department** of **Health, New York City.** *See* 14866.
    Collected Studies from **Chicago Tuberculosis Sanatorium Research Laboratory.** *See* 14867.
    Collected Studies. Department of **Health, New York City. Bureau** of **Laboratories.** *See* 14866.

14863 **Collected Studies** from the **Department** of **Pathology** and **Bacteriology, Illinois University College** of **Medicine.** Chicago. *Coll. Stud. Dep. Path. Bact. Ill. Univ.* [1914–25] **C.**PA. 17–25. [*C. as:* 14839]

14864 **Collected Studies. Laboratory** of **Physiological Chemistry, Illinois University.** *Coll. Stud. Lab. physiol. Chem. Ill. Univ.*

14865 **Collected Studies. Long Island College** of **Medicine.** Brooklyn. *Coll. Stud. Long Isl. Coll. Med.* **L.**UCH. 37–47.

14866 **Collected Studies** from the **Research Laboratory, Department** of **Health, New York City.** *Coll. Stud. Res. Lab. Dep. Hlth N.Y. Cy* [1905–] **L.**BM. 05–15; H. 07–; MC.; MD. 05–26; S. 05–26; SC. 16–; SH. 07: 12–15; TD. 05–26; U.; UC. 08–; **Abd.**U. 06–26; **Bm.**U. 05–20; **Br.**U. 07–15; **C.**PA. 06–11; **Dn.**U. 20–26; **E.**P.; U. 07–26; **G.**PH. 12–15; U. 05–10; **Lv.**U. imp.; **M.**MS. 11–19; P. 08–13; **O.**R. 12–15.

14867 **Collected Studies** from the **Research Laboratory** of the **Municipal Tuberculosis Sanatorium.** Chicago. *Coll. Stud. Res. Lab. munic. Tuberc. Sanat., Chicago* [1923–] **L.**BM. 43–; GH. 23–24; S. 23–25: 41–; **C.**PA. 26–33; **M.**MS. 23–25; **O.**R.

14868 **Collecting** and **Breeding.** Tokyo. *Collecting Breed., Tokyo* **L.**BM^N. 55–; **Y.**

14869 **Collecting Leaflet. San Diego Society** of **Natural History.** San Diego. *Collecting Leafl. S Diego Soc. nat. Hist.* **L.**BM^N. 35.

14870 **Collecting Net.** Woods Hole, Mass. *Collecting Net* [1926–] **Bm.**U. 30–43; **Pl.**M. 31–37 imp.

14871 **Collectio Theron.** University of Seoul. Seoul. *Collectio Theron*
    Scientia naturalis [1954–] **O.**F.

14872 **Collection** of **Czechoslovak Chemical Communications. English Edition.** Praha. *Colln Czech. chem. Commun. Engl. Edn* [*Some libraries listed under* 14877 *will hold this edition*]

14873 **Collection** in 4° de **spectroscopie** et **astrophysique. Institut** d'astrophysique. Liège. *Colln 4° Spectrosc. Astrophys. Inst. Astrophys., Liège* [1936–] **L.**AS.; **M.**U.

14873° **Collection** de **logique mathématique.** *Colln Log. math.* [1952–] **L.**BM. [*Issued in series*]

14874 **Collection** de **mémoires** in 8°. **Institut** d'**astrophysique** de l'**Université** de **Liège.** *Colln Mém. 8° Inst. Astrophys. Univ. Liège* [1924–] **M.**U. imp.

14875 **Collection** de **mémoires** relatifs à la **physique.** Société française de physique. Paris. *Colln Mém. Phys.* [1884–91: 05–14] **L.**BM.; **C.**UL.; **Db.**; **E.**R. 84–91: 05; U. 84–91: 05.

14876 **Collection** de **monographies ethnographiques.** Bruxelles. *Colln Monogr. ethnogr.* [1907–13] **L.**AN.
    Collection of **Scientific Papers. Agricultural College** in **Prague.** *See* 48709.

14877 **Collection** de **travaux chimiques** de **Tchécoslovaquie (tchèques).** Prague. *Colln Trav. chim. Tchécosl.* [1929–39: 47–] **L.**BM.; C.; I. (2 yr.); IC. 29–38: 47–; MC.; P.; PH. 53–; PR. 54–; R. 53–; SC.; UC.; **Abd.**U.; **Bm.**U.; **Br.**A. 56–; **C.**P.; UL. 29–36; **Cr.**U.; **E.**R.; U. 54–; **Ep.**D. 47–; **G.**U.; **Ld.**U.; **Lv.**U. 37–; **M.**C. 50–52: 54–; D. 47–; P. 56–; U.; **Nw.**A. 51–; **O.**R.; **Wd.** 47–; **Y.** [*See also:* 14872]

14878 **Collections** du **Musée** de **zoologie.** Nancy. *Collns Mus. Zool., Nancy* **L.**BM^N. 46–47; Z. 46–.
    Collective Farm Production. Moscow. *See* 27597.

14879 **Collectivité médicale.** Paris. *Collectivité méd.*

14880 **College** of **Aeronautics Gazette.** Cranfield. *College Aeronaut. Gaz.* [1958–] **L.**AV.; P. (curr.); QM.; **E.**A.; **Ld.**U.; **O.**B.; **Y.**

College of **Aeronautics Note.** Cranfield. *See* 35201.

College Bulletin. Agricultural Department, Armstrong College. *See* 9237.

College Bulletin. College of **Industrial Arts, Denton, Tex.** *See* 9835.

College of **General Practitioners Newsletter.** London. *See* 25841.

College of **General Practitioners Research Newsletter.** London. *See* 45880.

College Note. College of **Aeronautics, Cranfield.** *See* 35201.

College of **Nursing Bulletin.** *See* 14882.

14882 **College** of **Nursing Quarterly Bulletin.** London. *College Nurs. q. Bull.* [1920–26] **L.**BM.; **O.**B. [*C. in:* 35490]

14883 **Collégien figeacois.** Revue mensuelle, littéraire et scientifique du Collège Champollion. Cahors. *Collégien figeac.*

14884 **Collegium. International Association** of **Leather Trades Chemists, British Section.** London. *Collegium, Lond.* [1915–17] **L.**BM.; P.; SC.; **Abs.**N. 16–17; **Ld.**U. [*C. as:* 26934]

14885 **Collegium. Zentralorgan des Internationalen Vereins der Lederindustrie-Chemiker.** Haltingen, etc. *Collegium, Haltingen* [1902–43] **L.**C. 05–13: 23–40; LE. 03–43; P.; SC. 05–43 v. imp.; TP. 09–41; **Ld.**U. 02–42. [*Replaced by:* 28364]

14886 **Collezione miscellanea. Osservatorio astronomico** di **Capodimonte.** Napoli. *Collezione misc. Oss. astr. Capodimonte* [1951–] **L.**AS.; **M.**U. 51–56.

14887 **Collezione** di **pubblicazioni scientifiche** sull' **Eritrea.** Asmara. *Collezione Pubbl. scient. Eritrea* **L.**TD. 14.

14888 **Colliery Engineer.** London. *Colliery Engr, Lond.* [1924] **L.**BM.; P.; **Abs.**N.; **Bm.**U.; **C.**UL.; **Cr.**P.; **E.**A.; D.; **G.**M.; **Nw.**A.; **O.**R. [*C. as:* 14890]

14889 **Colliery Engineer.** Scranton. *Colliery Engr, Scranton* [1912–15] **L.**I.; MIE. 13–14; **Bm.**U.; **G.**E.; M. imp.; **Ld.**U. 14–15. [*C. of:* 31988; *C. in:* 14665]

14890 **Colliery Engineering.** London. *Colliery Engng* [1924–] **L.**BM.; GM.; MI.; MIE.; P.; SC.; **Abs.**N.; **Bm.**P.; T.; U.; **C.**UL.; **Cr.**P.; U. 43: 45: 51–; **E.**D. 24–27; **G.**M.; T.; **Ld.**U.; **M.**P. 38–; **N.**T. (5 yr.); U.; **Nw.**A.; P. 52–; **O.**R.; **Sh.**M. 24–36; P.; S. (3 yr.); SC.; **Y.** [*C. of:* 14888]

14891 **Colliery Guardian.** London. *Colliery Guard.* [1858–] **L.**BM.; GM. 74–; I. 80–; MIE.; P. 10–; SC.; UC. 05–; **Abs.**N. 12–; **Bm.**P. 61– imp.; U. 84–40: 48–; **Br.**P. (1 yr); **C.**UL. 21–; **Cr.**M. 22–; P. 61– imp.; U. 88– imp.; **E.**A. 07–; **G.**M. 67–68: 80–; MG. 12–; T. 39–; U. 05–40; **Ld.**P. 51–; U. 09–; **Lv.**P. 40–51 imp.: 52–; **M.**P. 73–; T. 00–50 (5 yr.); U. 96–49; **N.**T. (5 yr.); U. 40– imp.; **Nw.**A. 09–; P. 50–; **O.**B. 90–; **Sh.**M. 1858–64: 10–16; P. 28–; S. (1 yr); SC. 92–42; **Ste.** 13–; **Sw.**I.; **Y.**

14892 **Colliery Guardian Overseas.** London. *Colliery Guard. overseas* **L.**P. 59–. [*Supplement to:* 14891]

14893 **Colliery Manager.** London. *Colliery Mgr* [1884–04] **L.**BM. 87–04; MIE. 96–99; P. 85–04; **Cr.**P. 91–93; **G.**M.

14894 **Colliery Year Book,** etc. London. *Colliery Yb.* [1922–] **L.**BM.; MIE. 38–; P. (curr.); **Ex.**U. 43–53; **G.**M. 23–; **H.**U. 46– imp.; **Ld.**P. (curr.); U. 26–; **M.**P. 23–; **O.**B. 22–24; **Sh.**P. 24–; SC. 27– imp.; **Sw.**U. 24–38 imp.

14895 **Colloid Journal.** New York. *Colloid J., N. Y.* **L.**C. 52–; P. 57–; **G.**T. 57–; **M.**C. 57–60; **N.**U. 58–. [*English translation of:* 27606]

14896 **Colloid Journal.** Washington. *Colloid J., Wash.* **Te.**C. 55–; **Y.** 57–. [*English abstracts of:* 27606]

14897 **Colloid Symposium Annual.** New York. *Colloid Symp. A.* [1929–36] **L.**C. 29; P. 29–31; SC.; UC.; **C.**BI. 29–35; UL.; **E.**U. 29–31; **H.**U. 29–30; **Ld.**U.; **O.**R.; **Pl.**M. 29. [*C. of:* 14898; *C. in:* 26682]

14898 **Colloid Symposium Monograph.** New York. *Colloid Symp. Monogr.* [1923–28] **L.**C.; P.; SC.; UC.; **Bl.**U. imp.; **C.**BI.; UL.; **E.**U.; **H.**U.; **Ld.**U.; **O.**R.; **Pl.**M.; **Rt.** [*C. as:* 14897]

14899 **Colloques internationaux** du **Centre national** de la **recherche scientifique.** Paris. *Colloques int. Cent. natn. Rech. scient.* [1946–] **L.**BM. 54– imp.; MO. 49–53 imp.; P. imp.; RI.; SC.; **G.**U. 49–; **O.**BO. 49– imp.; **R.**

14900 **Colloques** du **Laboratoire** de l'**Hôpital Saint-Jean** à **Bruges.** Bruges. *Colloques Lab. Hôp. St Jean Bruges* [1953–56] **L.**MD. [*C. as:* 40259]

14901 **Colloques nationaux** du **Centre national** de la **recherche scientifique.** Paris. *Colloques natn. Cent. natn. Rech. scient.* [1952–] **L.**BM. 54–; RI.

14901° **Colloques. Union internationale** des **sciences biologiques.** Paris. *Colloques Un. int. Sci. biol.* [1948–] **C.**A. 49–; **O.**F. 49–.

14902 **Colloqui** del **Centro** di **astrofisica** del **Consiglio nazionale** delle **richerche.** Paria. *Colloqui Cent. Cons. naz. Rich.* [1956–] **L.**SC. [*Supplement to:* 31310]

Colloquia on **Ageing.** Ciba Foundation. *See* 14017.

Colloquia on **Endocrinology.** Ciba Foundation. *See* 14018.

14903 **Colloquia. Papers** published by the **American Mathematical Society.** New York. *Colloquia* **L.**BM. 93–13.

14904 **Colloquium geographicum.** Bonn. *Colloquium geogr.* [1951–] **L.**G.; **O.**B.

14905 **Colloquium. Gesellschaft** für **physiologische Chemie.** Berlin. *Colloquium Ges. physiol. Chem.* **L.**P. 53–.

14906 **Colloquium Lectures. American Mathematical Society.** New York. *Colloquium Lect. Am. math. Soc.* [1903–] **L.**M. 27–; SC.; UC. 05– imp.; **Abs.**U. 10–; **C.**UL.; **Sw.**U.; **Y.**

14907 **Colloquium mathematicum.** Wrocław. *Colloquium math.* [1947–] **L.**BM.; M.; R.; SC.; U.; **C.**P.; **Db.**; **E.**G.; R.; **G.**U. 56–; **Sh.**U.; **Y.**

Colloquium Publications. American Mathematical Society. *See* 14903 and 14906.

14908 **Colombia ganadera.** Bogotá. *Colombia ganad.*

14909 **Colombia médica.** Bogotá. *Colombia méd.* [1939–] **L.**TD. 43–46 imp. [*Suspended* 1940–43]

14910 **Colombo Museum Natural History Series.** Colombo. *Colombo Mus. nat. Hist. Ser.* **L.**BM. 39–.

14911 **Colonial Building Notes.** Watford. *Colon. Bldg Notes* [1950–58] **L.**TD.; **Wa.**B. [*C. as:* 36617]

14912 **Colonial Development.** London. *Colon. Dev.* [1950–56] L.AM.; C.; TP.; **Abs.**U.; **Br.**A.; U.; **C.**A.; **E.**AB.; **G.**M.; U.; **Hu.**G.; **Nw.**A. 53–56; **O.**B.; **Pl.**M. 50–53 imp.; **R.**D.; **Rt.**; **Sa.**; **Sil.** 50–51; **Y.** [*C. as:* 15044]

14913 **Colonial Geology** and **Mineral Resources.** London. *Colon. Geol. Miner. Resour.* [1950–56] L.BM^N.; GL.; KC.; MI.; MIE. 55–56; P.; PR. 55–56; QM.; SC.; **Abs.**U.; **Bm.**P.; **Br.**P.; U.; **C.**GG.; MI.; UL.; **Cr.**M.; P.; U.; **Dn.**U.; **E.**D.; U.; **Ex.**U.; **G.**M.; U.; **H.**U.; **Ld.**P.; U.; **Lv.**P.; U.; **M.**P.; **N.**P.; U.; **Nw.**A.; **O.**B.; R.; G.; **R.**U.; **Rt.**; **Sa.**; **Sh.**SC.; **St.**R.; **Y.** [*C. from:* 10504; *C. as:* 36620]

14914 **Colonial Meteorological Observations. British Colonies.** London. *Colon. met. Obsns Br. Colon.* L.MO. 09–38.

14915 **Colonial Plant** and **Animal Products.** London. *Colon. Pl. Anim. Prod.* [1950–56] L.AM.; BM.; BM^N.; C.; EB.; HS.; K.; LE.; MY.; PH.; PR. 51–56; P.; TP.; **Abd.**R.; **Abs.**A.; **Bl.**U.; **Bm.**P.; **Br.**P.; U. 50–54; **Bra.**P.; **C.**A.; GG.; **Cr.**M.; P.; **Dn.**U.; **E.**R.; U.; **G.**M.; T. 54–56; U.; **Hu.**G.; **Ld.**P.; U.; W.; **Lh.**FO.; **Lv.**P.; **M.**C.; P.; **Md.**H.; **Mi.**; **N.**U.; **Nw.**A. 51–56; P.; **O.**B.; F.; G. 50–56; R.; RE.; **Pl.**M. 51; **R.**D.; U.; **Rt.**; **Sa.**; **Sil.**; **Sy.**R.; **W.**; **Y.** [*C. from:* 10504; *C. as:* 54409]

14916 **Colonial Reports. Miscellaneous Series.** Colonial Office. London. *Colon. Rep. misc. Ser.* [1891–21] L.BM.; BM^N. imp.; G. imp.; GL.; P.; SC.; **Bm.**P.; **Db.**; **E.**A.; F.; V. imp.; G. 11–21; **G.**M.; **Ld.**U. 11; **Lv.**P. 91–16 imp.; **M.**P. 02–21; **Nw.**P.; **O.**RH.; **Rt.** 05–14 imp.

14917 **Colonial Research.** London. *Colon. Res.* [1944–56] L.BM.; BM^N. 48–56; C. 44–46; EB.; K. 47–56; P.; **Bl.**U.; **Bm.**P.; **G.**M. 45–46; **Ld.**P.; U.; **Lo.** 46–56; **M.**P.; **Md.**H. 48–50: 53–56; **O.**G.; RE. 46–56; **Pl.**M. 50–56; **Rt.** 45–56; **Y.** [*C. of:* 43108]

14918 **Colonial Research Publications.** London. *Colon. Res. Publs* [1948–] L.BM.; EB. (ent.) 50–; **Ld.**P.; **O.**G. 48; RE. 48–52 imp.; RH.; **Y.**

14920 **Colonial Research Studies.** London. *Colon. Res. Stud.* [1950–] L.BM.; **Ld.**P.; **O.**RE. 51– imp.; **Rt.** imp.; **Y.**

14921 **Colonial Road Note.** Road Research Board. London. *Colon. Rd Note* **Ld.**P. 55–.

14922 **Colonial Shipbuilding, Ship Repairing** and **Engineering.** Liverpool. *Colon. Shipbldg* L.I. (curr.); **G.**E. [*Supplement to:* 57355]

14923 **Colonies** et **marine.** Paris. *Colonies Mar.* E.G. 17–.

14924 **Colonización** y **agricultura.** La Paz. *Coloniz. Agric., La Paz* L.BM^N. 36–37. [*C. as:* 46440]

14925 **Colonizer.** London. *Colonizer* [1903–37] L.BM.; **Lv.**U. 06–17; **O.**B. 06–32; RH. 16–32.

14926 **Coloquio** realizado na **Junta** de **investigações coloniais.** Lisboa. *Coloquio Jta Invest. colon.*

14927 **Color Photographic Journal.** New Westminster B.C. *Color photogr. J.* L.PG. 53–.

14928 **Color Trade Journal** and **Textile Chemist.** New York. *Color Trade J.* [1917–25] L.P. 20–25; SC. 25; **M.**C. 23–25 imp.; D. 18–25; P. 23–25. [*C. in:* 13777]

14929 **Colorado Agricultural Bulletin.** Fort Collins. *Colo. agric. Bull.*

14930 **Colorado College Bulletin.** Colorado Springs. *Colo. Coll. Bull.* **Bm.**U. 11– imp.

14931 **Colorado College Publications. Education** and **Psychology Series.** Colorado Springs. *Colo. Coll. Publs Educ. Psychol. Ser.* L.BM. 19*; **E.**R. 19 imp.

14932 **Colorado College Publications. Engineering Series.** Colorado Springs. *Colo. Coll. Publs Engng Ser.* [1906–17] L.BM.; P.; **Bl.**U.; **Bm.**U. 06–08; **Db.**; **E.**R. 06–08 imp.

14933 **Colorado College Publications. Science Series.** Colorado Springs. *Colo. Coll. Publs Sci. Ser.* [1904–26] L.BM.; G. 04–10 imp.; **Bl.**U.; **Bm.**U. 04–08; **C.**P.; UL. 05–26; **Db.** 07–26; **E.**R.; **Nw.**A.

14934 **Colorado College Publications. Semi-annual Bulletin** of the **Colorado College Observatory.** Colorado Springs. *Colo. Coll. Publs semi-a. Bull. Colo. Coll. Obs.* L.MO. 04–07; **Bm.**U. 07– imp.; **E.**M. 04–07; R. 04–08 imp.

14935 **Colorado College Publications. Studies Series.** Colorado Springs. *Colo. Coll. Publs Stud. Ser.* **Bl.**U. 29–.

14936 **Colorado College Studies.** Colorado Springs. *Colo. Coll. Stud.* [1890–03] L.UC. 94–03 imp.; **Bl.**U. 96–03; **Bm.**U. 96–03; **C.**P. 99–03; **Db.** 00–03; **E.**B. 94–03; R. 99–03; **Nw.**A. 02–03.

14937 **Colorado College Studies.** Colorado Springs. *Colo. Coll. Stud.* [1958–] **Bl.**U.; **Db.**; **Ld.**U.

14938 **Colorado Conservation.** Denver. *Colo. Conserv.*

14939 **Colorado Engineer.** Boulder. *Colo. Engr* **Y.**

14940 **Colorado Engineers' Magazine.** Boulder. *Colo. Engrs' Mag.*

14941 **Colorado Farm Bulletin.** Fort Collins. *Colo. Fm Bull.* [1939–46] **C.**A.; **O.**F. 41–46; **Rt.** imp.

14942 **Colorado Farm** and **Home Research.** Fort Collins. *Colo. Fm Home Res.* [1951–] L.P. (curr.); **C.**A. 55–; **Y.**

14943 **Colorado Forester.** Fort Collins. *Colo. Forester*

14944 **Colorado Highways.** Denver. *Colo. Highw.*

14945 **Colorado Medical Journal.** Denver. *Colo. med. J.*

14946 **Colorado Medicine.** Denver. *Colo. Med.* L.MD. 30–37*; **Lv.**M. 35–37. [*C. as:* 48052]

14947 **Colorado School** of **Mines Alumni Magazine.** Golden. *Colo. Sch. Mines Alumni Mag.* [1921–31] L.P [*C. of:* and *Rec. as:* 31984]

14948 **Colorado School** of **Mines Mineral Industries Bulletin.** Golden. *Colo. Sch. Mines Miner. Ind. Bull.* [1958–] L.MI.; P.

14949 **Colorado School** of **Mines Quarterly.** Golden. *Colo. Sch. Mines Q.* [1906–] L.BM^N. 22– imp.; GL. 41– imp.; GM. 21–; MI. 42–56 imp.: 57–; MT.; P. imp.; PT. 46–; UC. 24–; **Bm.**C. (curr.); P. 44–; **Ld.**U. 26–; **Lv.**U. 50–; **Nw.**A. 14– imp.; **Sa.** 27–; **Y.**

14950 **Colorado Seed Laboratory Bulletin.** Fort Collins. *Colo. Seed Lab. Bull.*

Colorado University Studies. [1890–03] *See* 14936.

Colorado University Studies. Series in Anthropology. Colorado Springs. *See* 55614.

Colorado University Studies. Series in Biology. Colorado Springs. *See* 55615.

Colorado University Studies. Series in Chemistry and **Pharmacy.** Colorado Springs. *See* 55616.

14951 **Colorado Wheat Grower.** Denver. *Colo. Wheat Grow.*

14952 **Colorado Wool Grower** and **Marketer.** Denver. *Colo. Wool Grow.* [1929–]

14953 **Colores** y **pinturas.** Madrid. *Colores Pint.* [1952–] **L.**P.; PR.

14954 **Colour Index Report. Star Colour Section** of the **New Zealand Astronomical Society.** Wellington. *Colour Index Rep. N.Z. astr. Soc.* **L.**AS. 30–.

14955 **Colour Photography.** London. *Colour Photogr.* [1907–35] **L.**P. 07–34; PG. [*Supplement to:* 8876]

14956 **Colour Photography.** London. *Colour Photogr.* [1959–] **L.**BM.; P.; **E.**A.; **O.**B.

14957 **Colour Photography Annual.** New York. *Colour Photogr. A.* [1956–] **L.**BM.

14960 **Colourage.** Bombay. *Colourage* **L.**P. 58–.

14961 **Colston Papers.** Colston Research Society. Bristol. *Colston Pap.* [1949–] **Br.**U.

14962 **Coltivatore.** Milano. *Coltivatore* **L.**MY. 23–29; **Y.**

14963 **Coltivatore siciliano.** *Coltiv. sicil.*

14964 **Coltura avicola.** Genova. *Coltura avic.* [1936–] [*C. of:* 5780]

14965 **Coltura geografica.** Trieste. *Coltura geogr.*

14966 **Coltura medica moderna.** Palermo. *Coltura med. mod.* [1922] [*C. as:* 16143]
Columbia Biological Series. *See* 14976.

14968 **Columbia College Natural Science Series.** New York. *Columbia Coll. nat. Sci. Ser.* [1941–]

14969 **Columbia Dental Review.** New York. *Columbia dent. Rev.* [1932–] **L.**D. 38–. [*C. of:* 16563]

14970 **Columbia Engineer.** New York. *Columbia Engr*

14971 **Columbia Engineering Quarterly.** New York. *Columbia Engng Q.* [1948–] **Y.**

14972 **Columbia Geomorphic Studies.** New York. *Columbia geomorph. Stud.* [1931–] **L.**BM.

14973 **Columbia Optometrist.** New York. *Columbia Optom.*

14974 **Columbia River** and **Oregon Timberman.** Portland. *Columbia Riv. Ore. Timberm.* [1899–04] [*C. as:* 53268]

14975 **Columbia Studies** in **Archaeology** and **Ethnology.** New York. *Columbia Stud. Archaeol. Ethnol.* [1943–] **L.**AN. 44–.

14976 **Columbia University Biological Series.** New York. *Columbia Univ. biol. Ser.* [1894–] **L.**BM. 94–10, BM^N. 94–19; **Abd.**U.; **Bl.**U. 95–08 imp.; **Bm.**U. imp.; **Db.**; **Lv.**U.; **M.**U. 94–59; **O.**R.

14977 **Columbia University Contributions** to **Anthropology.** New York. *Columbia Univ. Contr. Anthrop.* [1910–] **L.**AN.; HO. 10–37 imp.; **Bm.**P.; **C.**UL. 28–; **O.**B. 13–39.
Columbia University Contributions to **Philosophy, Psychology** and **Education.** *See* 4346.

14978 **Columbia University Quarterly.** New York. *Columbia Univ. Q.* [1898–41] **L.**BM.; U.; **C.**UL.; **G.**U. 98–19: 30–32 imp. [*Suspended* 1920–29]

14979 **Columbia University School** of **Mines Quarterly.** New York. *Columbia Univ. Sch. Mines Q.* [1879–15] **L.**BM. 84–15; BM^N.; P.; U. 94–15 imp.; **Cr.**P. 89–03 imp.; **Db.** 80–15; **G.**MG. 81–15; **Nw.**A. 10–15.

14980 **Columbia University Studies** in the **History** of **American Agriculture.** New York. *Columbia Univ. Stud. Hist. Am. Agric.* [1934–] **L.**BM.

14981 **Columbian Colloidal Carbons.** Columbian Carbon Co. New York. *Columbian colloid. Carb.* [1938–] **L.**C.; P. imp.; **Y.**

14982 **Columbia-Southern Chemicals.** Pittsburgh. *Columbia-Sth. Chem.* [1958–] **L.**P. (curr.); **Sy.**R.

14983 **Combined Annual Reports. Potlatch Timber Protective Association.** Potlatch, Idaho. *Comb. a. Rep. Potlatch Timb. prot. Ass.* [1925–40] **L.**SC. [*C. as:* 6945]
Combined Conference Proceedings. National Shade Tree Conference. *See* 14984.

14984 **Combined Proceedings. National Shade Tree Conference.** Wooster, Ohio. *Comb. Proc. natn. Shade Tree Conf.* [1942–] **L.**EB.; SC.; **Md.**H.; **O.**F. [*C. of:* 39482]

14984° **Combined Quarterly Circulars. Rubber Research Board, Ceylon.** *Comb. q. Circ. Rubb. Res. Bd Ceylon* [1944–] **L.**BM.

14985 **Combined Report. Akyab Agricultural Station** and **Kyaukpyu Coconut Farm.** Rangoon. *Comb. Rep. Akyab agric. Stn Kyaukpyu Cocon. Fm* **L.**SC. 28–; **Abs.**N. 26–; **Md.**H. 29–33.

14986 **Combustibili** e **combustione.** Bibliografia italiana e straniera. Milano. *Combustibili Combustione* **L.**P. 54–; SC. 49–.

14987 **Combustibles.** Madrid. *Combustibles* [1941–] **L.**P. 54–; PT. 49–; **Y.**

14988 **Combustion.** New York. *Combustion, N.Y.* [1919–29] **L.**BM. 24–29; NF. 25–29; P. 21–29; **Bm.**U. 23–29; **Br.**U. 24–29; **G.**M. 24–29; **M.**P. 24–29; **O.**B.; **Sh.**SC. 26–29; **Y.** [*C. as:* 18119]

14989 **Combustion.** International Combustion Engineering Corporation. New York. *Combustion int. Combust. Engng Corp.* [1929–] **L.**P.; **G.**U. 48–; U. 48–; **Lv.**P. 46– imp.; **M.**D. 53–; **Rn.**B. 38–; **Sh.**SC.; **Y.**

14990 **Combustion.** Paris. *Combustion, Paris* **L.**P. 31–32*.

14991 **Combustion, Boiler House** and **Nuclear Review.** London. *Combust. Boiler Ho. nucl. Rev.* [1957–58] **L.**BA.; BM.; P.; U.; **C.**UL.; **Cr.**I.; **E.**A.; **Lv.**P.; **O.**B.; Sil.; **Y.** [*C. of:* 14992; *C. as:* 35424]

14992 **Combustion** and **Boilerhouse Engineering.** London. *Combust. Boilerh. Engng* [1953–56] **L.**BA.; BM.; P.; U.; **C.**UL.; **Cr.**I.; **E.**A.; **Lv.**P.; **O.**B.; Sil.; **Y.** [*C. of:* 14995; *C. as:* 14991]

14993 **Combustion économique.** Bruxelles. *Combust. écon.*

14994 **Combustion Engine Progress.** London. *Combust. Engine Prog.* [1957–] **L.**BM.; P.; **O.**R.; **Y.** [*C. of:* 16958]

14995 **Combustion Engineering.** London. *Combust. Engng* [1950–53] **L.**BA.; BM.; U.; **C.**UL.; **Cr.**I. 51–53; **E.**A.; **Lv.**P. 52–53; **O.**B.; Sil. [*C. of:* 14997; *C. as:* 14992]

14996 **Combustion Engineering Association Journal.** London. *Combust. Engng Ass. J.* **L.**P. 51–52; **Y.**

14997 **Combustion Engineering** and **Power Review.** London. *Combust. Engng Pwr Rev.* [1947–50] L.BA.; BM.; SC.; U. 49–53; C.UL.; E.A.; O.B.; Sil. 49–50. [*C. as:* 14995]

14998 **Combustion** and **Flame.** London. *Combust. Flame* [1957–] L.AV.; BM.; C.; P.; SC.; Bm.P.; T. 59–; U.; C.CH.; ENG.; Dn.U.; E.A.; F.A.; G.M.; T.; U.; Ld.P.; U.; M.C.; P.; T.; O.R.; Rn.B.; Sh.S.; SC.; Ste.; Y.

14999 **Combustion Researches** and **Reviews.** London. *Combust. Res. Rev.* Bl.U. 55–57; Bm.P. 55–.

15000 **Comet Journal.** Mastabar Mining Equipment Company (Belt Fastener Co.). Accrington, Hull. *Comet J.* [1955–] L.BM. 57–; P. (curr.); Y.

Comisión nacional para la **erradicación** del **paludismo.** Boletín. *See* 12894.

15001 **Comité électro-technique français.** Commission électrotechnique internationale. Paris. *Com. électro-tech. fr.*

15002 **Commentari** dell'**Ateneo** di **Brescia.** *Comment. Aten. Brescia* L.BM. 1812–; BM^N. 1812–86.

Commentarii Instituti Astrachensis ad **defensionem plantarum.** *See* 58275.

15003 **Commentarii mathematici helvetici.** Zürich. *Comment. math. helvet.* [1928–] L.M.; R. 50–; SC.; U. 50–; UC. 29–; Abd.U. 41–; Bl.U.; Br.U.; C.P.; Dn.U. 61–; E.R.; Ex.U. 59–; G.U. 55–; Ld.U.; M.U.; N.U. 53–; O.R.; R.U.; Sh.U. 49–; Sw.U. 60–; Y.

15004 **Commentarii mathematici Universitatis Sancti Pauli.** Tokyo. *Comment. math. Univ. S Pauli, Tokyo* [1952–] L.M.; SC.; E.A.; O.R.; Y.

15005 **Commentationes balticae.** Bonn. *Commentat. balt.* [1954–] L.BM.; O.B.; Y.

15006 **Commentationes biologicae.** Societas scientiarum fennica. Helsingfors. *Commentat. biol.* [1922–] L.BM.; BM^N.; R.; SC.; Z.; Abd.M. imp.; U.; Abs.U.; Bm.U. 27–; C.A. 22–51; P.; Db.; Dm. 54–; E.R.; G.U. imp.; Ld.U.; Lv.U.; Mi. 40–; O.R.; Sh.U.; Y. [*C. of part of:* 36052]

15007 **Commentationes forestales.** Societas scientiarum fennica. Helsingfors. *Commentat. for.* [1928–33] L.BM^N.; K.; SC.; Bn.U. 31–33; C.P.; E.B.; O.F.

15007° **Commentationes mathematicae Universitatis Carolinae.** Prague. *Commentat. math. Univ. Carol.* [1960–] C.P.

15008 **Commentationes physico-mathematicae.** Societas scientiarum fennica. Helsingfors. *Commentat. physico-math.* [1922–] L.BM.; BM^N.; C. 48–; K. 28–38; M.; MO. 22–37 imp.: 52–; P. 57–; R.; SC.; U. 50– imp.; UC.; Abd.U.; Abs.U.; Bm.U.; C.P.; Db.; Dm. 28–33 imp.; E.R.; G.U.; Ld.U.; Lv.U.; O.R.; Sh.U. 22–38 imp.; Wo. 30– imp.; Y. [*C. of part of:* 36052]

15009 **Commentationes Pontificiae academiae scientiarum.** Roma. *Commentat. pontif. Acad. Scient.* [1937–] L.BM.; BM^N. 37–56; R. 39: 44–; Br.U. 44–; Db.; E.C. 39–40 imp.; R. [*C. of:* 31271]

15010 **Commercial Art** and **Industry.** London. *Comml Art Ind.* [1922–36] L.BM.; Cr.P. 26–36; G.M.; M.P. 26–36; Sh.IO. 23–36 imp. [*C. as:* 4925]

15011 **Commercial Auto Engineer.** New York. *Comml Auto Engr*

15012 **Commercial Camera Magazine.** Rochester. *Comml Camera Mag.*

15013 **Commercial Engineering News.** Westinghouse Lamp Co. Bloomfield, N.J. *Comml Engng News*

15014 **Commercial Fertilizer.** Atlanta. *Comml Fertil., Atlanta* Rt. 47–48.

15015 **Commercial Fertilizer.** Charleston. W. Va. *Comml Fertil., Charleston*

15016 **Commercial Fisheries Abstracts.** Fish and Wildlife Service. Washington. *Comml Fish. Abstr.* [1948–] L.AM. imp.; P. 54–; TP.; Abd.M.; Bn.U. 51–; E.SW.; Fr. 55–; Lo.; Pl.M. 61–; Y.

15017 **Commercial Fisheries Review.** Fish and Wildlife Service. Washington. *Comml Fish. Rev.* [1946–] L.AM.; BM^N. 50–; P. 55–; TP. 56–; Abd.M. 50–; T.; Bn.U. 51–; Dm. 58–; E.SW.; Lo. 52–; Pl.M.; Y.

15018 **Commercial Fisherman.** Vancouver, B.C. *Comml Fisherm.*

15019 **Commercial Grower.** London. *Comml Grow.* [1952–] L.AM.; BM.; P.; TP. 58–; Abs.U.; Bl.U.; Br.A. (5 yr.); C.A. (6 mo.); E.A.; Md.H.; N.U.; O.AEC.; Sil. [*C. of:* 20382]

15020 **Commercial Grower Handbook** and **Diary.** London. *Comml Grow. Handb. Diary* [1957–] Bl.U.; Bm.P.; Br.A.; E.A.; Md.H. 57–61; N.U. 58–; O.R. [*C. of:* 15021]

15021 **Commercial Grower Year Book.** London. *Comml Grow. Yb.* [1954–56] L.AM. (curr.); Bl.U.; Bm.P.; Br.A.; E.A.; Md.H.; N.U. 54; O.R. [*C. of:* 20383; *C. as:* 15020]

15022 **Commercial Horticultural Review.** Worcester. *Comml hort. Rev.* L.BM. 34–.

15023 **Commercial Horticulture** and **Garden Craftsman.** London. *Comml Hort. Gdn Craftsm.* [1953] L.BM.; Sil. [*C. of:* 20611]

15024 **Commercial Motor.** London. *Comml Mot.* [1905–] L.AV. 50– imp.; BM.; P. 05–13: 17–; Abs.N. 13–; Bm.U. 20–; Br.P. (1 yr) C.UL.; E.A.; CE. 57–; F.A. 51–; G.M. 29–; Ld.P. (5 yr.); Li.M. 46–; Lv.P. 40–; N.T. (5 yr.); O.B.; Y.

15025 **Commercial Outboarder.** Nassau. *Comml Outboarder* [1960–] L.BM.; P. (curr.)

15026 **Commercial Photographer.** Cleveland. *Comml Photogr.* [1925–50] L.PG. 27–50. [*C. in:* 39951]

15027 **Commercial Refrigeration** and **Air Conditioning.** Cleveland. *Comml Refrig. Air Condit.* L.P. 57–58. [*C. as:* 42434]

15028 **Commercial Standard. Standards Association** of **Australia.** Sydney. *Comml Stand.* [1932–] L.P. [*C. of:* 49780]

15029 **Commercial Standards Monthly. U.S. Bureau** of **Standards.** *Comml Stand. Mon.* L.BM. 29–33*; SC. 28–33; Bm.P. 29–33; G.M. 29–33. [*C. in:* 23288]

15031 **Commercial Vehicles.** Manchester. *Comml Vehs* [1941–] L.AV. 49–53; P.; Lv.P. 60–; M.P.; Sy.R.; Y. [*C. of:* 12892]

Commercial Vehicles Users Journal. *See* 15031.

15032 **Commercio metallurgico.** Roma. *Commercio metall.* L.BM. 34–.

15033 **Commission Leaflets. American Telephone** and **Telegraph Company.** New York. *Commn Leafl. Am. Teleph. Telegr. Co.*

15034 **Commission météorologique** du **département des Vosges.** Épinal. *Commn mét. Dép. Vosges*

15035 **Commission permanente** de **standardisation.** Paris. *Commn perm. Standard.*

Commission for the **Scientific Survey** of the **Mongolian** and the **Tannu-Tuvin Republics.** *See* 27616.

15036 **Commodity Bulletin. Department** of **Agriculture, Jamaica.** Kingston. *Commod. Bull. Dep. Agric. Jamaica* [1955–] **C.**A.; **Y.**

15037 **Commodity Policy Studies. F.A.O.** Rome. *Commod. Policy Stud.* [1952–] **L.**BM.; **C.**A.; **Ld.**P.; **O.**B.

15038 **Commodity Reports. F.A.O.** Washington. *Commod. Rep. F.A.O.* [1950–] **L.**BM.; **Ld.**P.

15039 **Commodity Series. Commonwealth Economic Committee.** (Empire Marketing Board, *later* Imperial Economic Committee.) London. *Commod. Ser. commonw. econ. Comm.* **Cr.**U. 35–; **O.**AEC. 32–; **G.** 36–37: 47–; **Ld.**P. 32–.

Commodity Series. F.A.O. *See* 18912.

15040 **Commonhealth.** Massachusetts Department of Health. Boston. *Commonhealth* **L.**TD. 18–42 imp.; **G.**PH. 35–41. [*C. of:* 40603]

15041 **Commonwealth Agriculturist.** Melbourne. *Commonw. Agricst* [1931–] **C.**A. 36–; **Hu.**G. 42–.

Commonwealth Air Transport Council Newsletter. London. *See* 34827.

15043 **Commonwealth Dental Review.** Sydney. *Commonw. dent. Rev.* [1903–20] **L.**D. 12–13. [*Replaced by:* 16564]

15044 **Commonwealth Development.** London. *Commonw. Dev.* [1957–] **L.**AM.; **C.**; **TP.**; **Abs.**U.; **Br.**A.; **P.** (1 yr); **U.**; **C.**A. (3 yr.); **E.**AB.; **G.**M.; **U.**; **Hu.**G.; **Nw.**A.; **O.**B.; **R.**D.; **Rt.**; **Sa.**; **Y.** [*C. of:* 14912]

15045 **Commonwealth Engineer.** Melbourne. *Commonw. Engr* [1913–60] **L.**BM. 20–60; **I.** (2 yr.); **NF.** 48–60; **P.** 14–60 imp.; **Bm.**C. (curr.); **Ha.**RD. 53–60. [*C. as:* 5396]

Commonwealth Forestry Review. London. *See* 17983.

Commonwealth Health Messenger, National Association for the Prevention of Tuberculosis. *See* 33919.

15046 **Commonwealth Journal** of the **Society** for **growing Australian Plants.** Padslois. *Commonw. J. Soc. grow. Aust. Pl.* [1959–] **L.**BM^N.; **Y.**

Commonwealth Messenger, National Association for the Prevention of Tuberculosis. *See* 33920.

15047 **Commonwealth Phytopathological News.** London. *Commonw. phytopath. News* [1955–] **L.**AM.; BM.; BM^N.; K.; MY.; TP.; **Bn.**U.; **Br.**A.; **C.**A.; UL.; **Db.**; **Dn.**U. 61–; **E.**A.; **Ep.**D. 56–; **Ex.**U.; **Hu.**G.; **Md.**H.; **N.**U.; **O.**BO.; F.; R.; RE.; **Y.**

15048 **Commonwealth Weather Chart.** Adelaide. *Commonw. Weath. Chart*

Communicações da **Commissão** dos **trabalhos geológicos** de **Portugal.** *See* 15335.

15050 **Communicações** da **Secção** de **estudos zootécnicos. Estação agraria nacional.** Lisboa. *Communçoes Secç. Estud. zootéc. Estaç. agr. nac.* **Rt.** (Ser. A.) 28–.

Communication. For Communications issued by institutions etc. *See* **Communications.**

15052 **Communication** and **Broadcast Engineering.** New York. *Commun. Broadc. Engng* [1934–37] **L.**P.; SC. 37; **Bm.**U. [*C. in:* 15057]

15053 **Communication Engineering.** Great Barrington, Mass. *Commun. Engng, Gt Barrington* [1953–54] **L.**P. [*C. from:* 18938; *C. in:* 41790]

Communication Engineering. London. *See* 26219, pt. 3.

15054 **Communication News.** N.V. Philips Radio. Eindhoven. *Commun. News* [1947–56] **L.**P.; **Bm.**P.; **Db.** 50–56. [*C. of:* 37574; *C. as:* 37573]

15055 **Communication Review.** Communication Engineering Pty., Ltd. Sydney. *Commun. Rev.* [1945–] **L.**P. 45–59; **F.**A. 48–51; **O.**F. 46–; **Y.**

Communicationes ex **Bibliotheca historiae medicae hungarica.** *See* 36419.

Communicationes ex **Instituto quaestionum forestalium Finlandiae.** *See* 31711.

15056 **Communicationes veterinariae.** Bogor. *Communicationes vet.* [1957–] **L.**V.; **C.**A.; **E.**AB. 57–58; **W.**

15057 **Communications.** New York. *Communications* [1937–49] **L.**AV. 44–49; P.; **Bm.**U.; **F.**A.; **Ma.**T. 40–49 imp. [*C. of:* 15052 and 41793; *C. as:* 52819]

Communications. Académie de **marine** de **Belgique.** *See* 30024.

15058 **Communications. Académie** des **sciences coloniales.** Paris. *Communs Acad. Sci. colon.* **L.**Z. 31–40.

15059 **Communications** on **Applied Mathematics.** New York University. New York. *Communs appl. Math.* [1948] **L.**AV.; IC.; SC.; **Abs.**U.; **Bl.**U.; **Bm.**U.; **C.**P.; **Db.**; **E.**R.; **Ex.**U.; **F.**A.; **G.**T.; U.; **M.**T.; U.; **N.**U.; **Nw.**A.; **Sw.**U.; **Wo.**; **Y.** [*C. as:* 15109]

15060 **Communications. Association** for **Computing Machinery.** New York, Philadelphia. *Communs Ass. comput. Mach.* [1958–] **L.**AV.; P.; SC.; **Co.**T. 61–; **E.**U.; **Ha.**RD. 62–; **Ld.**U.; **Ma.**T.; **Sh.**U.; **Y.**

15061 **Communications. Association internationale** pour l'**essai** des **matériaux.** Paris. *Communs Ass. int. Essai Matér.* **L.**P. 10–13.

15062 **Communications. Balai penjelidikan** dan **pemakaian karet.** Bogor. *Communs Balai Penjel. Pemak. Karet* [1954–] **Y.**

Communications of the **Botanical Institute** of the **Hungarian University,** Sopron. *See* 41050.

15063 **Communications. Building Research Station.** Watford. *Communs Bldg Res. Stn*

Communications Bulletin. Moscow. *See* 56533.

15064 **Communications** du **Bureau climatologique. Institut national** pour l'**étude agronomique** du **Congo belge.** Bruxelles. *Communs Bur. clim. Inst. natn. Étude agron. Congo belge* [1950–] **L.**BM.; BM^N.; MO.; **Md.**H., **Rt.** 51–; **Y.**

15065 **Communications. Centre** de **cartographie phytosociologique** et **Centre** de **recherches écologiques.** Gembloux. *Communs Cent. Cartogr. phytosoc., Gembloux* **O.**F. 46–47. [*C. as:* 15066]

15066 **Communications. Centre** de **recherches écologiques** et **phytosociologiques** de **Gembloux.** Bruxelles. *Communs Cent. Rech. écol. phytosoc. Gembloux* [1948–] **O.**BO. imp. [*C. of:* 15065]

15067 **Communications. Cercle hydrobiologique** de **Bruxelles.** Bruxelles. *Communs Cercle hydrobiol. Brux.* Pl.M. 50–53 imp.

15068 **Communications** du **Clinic neurologique** de l'**Université** de **Copenhague.** *Communs Clin. neurol. Univ. Copenh.* L.MD. 33; S. 33.

15069 **Communications** du **Comité** d'**études** de la **Société belge** des **ingénieurs** et des **industriels.** Bruxelles. *Communs Com. Étud. Soc. belge Ingrs Ind.* L.P. 10–11.

15070 **Communications** of the **Committee** for **Plastic Water Pipes.** Don Haag. *Communs Comm. plast. Wat. Pipes* [1956–] L.P.

15071 **Communications. Congrès belge** de l'**emballage.** Bruxelles. *Communs Congr. belge Emball.* [1956–] L.P.

15072 **Communications** from the **County Pottery Laboratory, Staffordshire.** London. *Communs Cty Pott. Lab. Staffs.* L.P. 07–19*.

15073 **Communications. David Dunlap Observatory.** University of Toronto. *Communs David Dunlap Obs.* [1938–] L.AS.; UC.; E.O.; M.U.; Y.

15074 **Communications** of the **Department** of **Astronomy** of **Ankara University.** *Communs Dep. Astr. Ankara Univ.* [1954–] L.AS.; SC.

15074ᶜ **Communications. Department** of **Mathematical** and **Natural Sciences.** Poznań. *Communs Dep. math. nat. Sci., Poznań* L.BM^N. 59–.

15075 **Communications. Division** of **Geology** and **Geography, National Research Council.** Washington, D.C. *Communs Div. Geol. Geogr. natn. Res. Coun.*

15076 **Communications. Division** of **Silviculture, Institute** of **Forestry Research.** Wageningen. *Communs Div. Silvic. Inst. For. Res., Wageningen* [1960–] O.F.

15077 **Communications** of the **Dublin Institute** of **Advanced Studies.** Dublin. *Communs Dubl. Inst. advd Stud.* [1943–]
Series A. L.SC.; U. 46–; Bl.U.; Br.U.; C.P.; UL.; Db.; E.R. 43; O.R.; Y.

15078 **Communications** and **Electronics.** London. *Communs Electron., Lond.* [1954–55] L.AV.; BM. 55; EE.; NP.; P.; Bl.U.; Bm.P.; Bn.U.; Br.P. (2 yr.); Bra.P.; C.UL.; Co.T.; E.A.; HW.; Ep.D.; F.A.; G.M.; T.; Li.M. imp.; M.C.; T.; Ma.T. imp.; N.U.; O.B.; R.; Sil.; Y. [*C. as:* 8790]
Communications and **Electronics, American Institute** of **Electrical Engineers.** *Communs Electron. Am. Inst. elect. Engrs See* 53544. Part 1.

15079 **Communications** de la **Faculté** des **sciences** de l'**Université** d'**Ankara.** *Communs Fac. Sci. Univ. Ankara* [1948–]
Série A. Mathématiques-physique L.BM^N.; P.; U. 52–56; C.P.; Db.; E.Q.; R.; G.U. 52–; O.R. 52–; Y.
Série B. Chimie L.C. 52–; P.; C.P.; Db.; E.R.; Y.
Série C. Sciences naturelles L.BM^N.; P.; C.P.; Db.; E.R.; G.U. 54–; Rt. 54–; Y.
[*Foreign language edition of:* 2633]
Communications. Fédération internationale de **documentation.** *See* 18931.

15080 **Communications** of the **Forest Research Institute.** Bogor. *Communs Forest Res. Inst., Bogor* [1951–] L.BM^N.; Y.

15081 **Communications. Gas Research Board.** London. *Communs Gas Res. Bd* [1940–]
Communications from the **General Experiment Station** of the **A. V. R. O. S.** *See* 30025.
Communications. General Experiment Station for **Agriculture.** Buitenzorg. *See* 30027.

15082 **Communications géologiques. Muséum** de **minéralogie** et de **géologie** de l'**Université** de **Copenhague.** *Communs géol., Mus. Minér. Géol. Univ. Copenh.* [1907–] L.BM^N. imp.; SC.
Communications. Groenendael Station des **recherches.** *See* 15118.

15084 **Communications** from the **Hill Observatory.** Salcome Regis. *Communs Hill. Obs.* [1920–] [*Nos.* 1–41 *were issued without the title*]

15085 **Communications hors-série. Institut** d'**hygiéne** des **mines ASBL.** Hasselt. *Communs hors-Sér. Inst. Hyg. Mines ASBL* L.MI. 54–.

15086 **Communications** from the **Horticultural Institute, Taihoku Imperial University.** Taiwan. *Communs hort. Inst. Taihoku imp. Univ.* L.BM^N. 32–34 imp.; K. 29–; C.A. 32–40 imp.
Communications de l'**Institut** de **géophysique** et de **météorologie** de l'**Université** de **Lemberg.** *See* 27618.

15087 **Communications** de l'**Institut** d'**hygiène** des **mines ASBL.** Hasselt. *Communs Inst. Hyg. Mines ASBL* L.MI. 46–59*; P. 53–59; TD. 50–59 imp.; Sh.S. 52–59. [*C. in:* 47318; *For* Communications hors-série *see* 15085]

15088 **Communications** de l'**Institut médical** de l'**état.** Stockholm. *Communs Inst. méd. État, Stockh.* [1910–] L.LI. 10–17; TD. 10–13.

15089 **Communications** de l'**Institut national** pour l'**étude agronomique** du **Congo belge.** Yangambi. *Communs Inst. natn. Étude agron. Congo belge* [1943–] C.A.

15090 **Communications** de l'**Institut sérothérapique** de l'**État danois.** Extraits. Copenhague. *Communs Inst. sérothér. État. dan.* [1907–48] L.TD.; C.V.; Dn.U. 45–48. [*Extracts in French translation from:* 29950; *C. as:* 15116]

15091 **Communications. Institute** for the **Study** of **Mental Images.** Church Crookham. *Communs Inst. Study ment. Imag.* [1957–] L.BM.; O.R.

15092 **Communications. Institution** of **Gas Engineers.** London. *Communs Instn Gas Engrs* Y. [*Discarded by libraries as numbers are reprinted in:* 53771]

15093 **Communications. International Association** of **Theoretical** and **Applied Limnology.** Stuttgart. *Communs int. Ass. theor. appl. Limnol.* [1953–] L.P.; SC.

15094 **Communications** from the **Kamerlingh Onnes Laboratory** of the **University** of **Leiden.** Leiden. *Communs Kamerlingh Onnes Lab.* [1931–] L.P.; R.; RI.; SC.; Abd.U.; Bl.U. 52–; Bn.U.; Br.U.; C.P.; SJ.; Db.; E.R.; U. 39–; G.U.; Ld.U.; M.U.; N.U. 31–34; O.R.; Rt.; Y. [*C. of:* 15108; *also supplements*]

15095 **Communications. Kodak Research Laboratories.** Hayes. *Communs Kodak Res. Labs* L.P. 44–51.
Communications du **Laboratoire bactériologique** de l'**état suédois.** *See* 29849.

15096 **Communications du Laboratoire des produits végétaux** et de l'**Herbier** du **Service forestier** du **Kivu.** Bruxelles. *Communs Lab. Prod. vég. Herb. Serv. for. Kivu* **O.**F. 30–32*. [*Replaced by:* 47059]

15097 **Communications des laboratoires** de l'**Institut** d'**optique.** Paris. *Communs Labs Inst. Opt., Paris* [1944–] **L.**AS. 44–46; PG. 44–46.

15098 **Communications** from the **Low Temperature Division** of the **McLennan Laboratory.** Toronto. *Communs low Temp. Div. McLennan Lab.* [1935–] **L.**P. 35–39; **Bn.**U. 35–39; **O.**R. [*Part of:* 55690]
 Communications magnétiques. Copenhague. *See* 41347.

15099 **Communications. Marine Biological Station.** Millport. *Communs mar. biol. Stn, Millport* [1900] **L.**BM.; BM^N.; **Abd.**U.; **E.**R.; **Lv.**U.

15100 **Communications** of the **Master Brewers' Association** of **America.** Chicago. *Communs Master Brew. Ass. Am.* **Nu.**B. 51–.

15101 **Communications** et **mémoires. Académie** de **marine.** Paris. *Communs Mém. Acad. Mar.* **L.**BM. 23–.
 Communications. Mount Wilson Solar Observatory. *See* 15102.

15102 **Communications** to the **National Academy** of **Sciences. Mount Wilson Solar Observatory.** Washington. *Communs natn. Acad. Sci. Mt Wilson sol. Obs.* [1915–] **L.**AS. 15–38; BM.; SC.; **C.**O.; **E.**O.; R. 15–38; **Ld.**U. 27–; **M.**U. 26–28 imp.; **Nw.**A.; **O.**O.
 Communications from the **National Museum** of the **History** of **Science** at **Leiden.** *See* 30137.

15103 **Communications** of the **New International Association** for the **Testing** of **Materials.** Zurich. *Communs new int. Ass. Test. Mater.* [1930] **L.**C.; NF.; P.; **Br.**U.; **Lv.**U.

15104 **Communications. Norman Lockyer Observatory.** Salcombe Regis. *Communs Norman Lockyer Obs.* [1937–] **L.**AS.; BM. 38–; SC.

15105 **Communications** de l'**Observatoire r.** de **Belgique.** Bruxelles. *Communs Obs. r. Belg.* [1948–] **L.**AS.; BM.; SC.; **Db.**; **E.**R.; **M.**U.

15106 **Communications paléontologiques. Muséum** de **minéralogie** et de **géologie** de l'**Université** de **Copenhague.** *Communs paléont. Mus. Minér. Géol. Univ. Copenh.* [1902–] **L.**BM^N.; SC.

15107 **Communications périodiques. Ateliers** de **construction Oerlikon.** Oerlikon. *Communs périod. Atel. Constr. Oerlikon*

15108 **Communications** from the **Physical Laboratory** at the **University** of **Leiden.** *Communs phys. Lab. Univ. Leiden* [1885–31] **L.**IC.; P. 10–31; QM. 00–18; R. 13–31 imp.; RI.; SC.; UC.; **Abd.**U. 28–31; **Bn.**U.; **Br.**U.; **C.**P. 11–31; SJ. imp.; **Db.** 99–31; **E.**R. 13–31; U. 85–01; **Ex.**U.; **G.**U. imp.; **Ld.**U. 14–31; **M.**U.; **N.**U. 94–31; **O.**R. 89–31 imp.; **Rt.** [*C. as:* 15094]
 Communications of the **Poznań Society** of **Friends** of **Science.** *See* 38388ᵃ.

15109 **Communications** on **Pure** and **Applied Mathematics.** New York University. New York. *Communs pure appl. Math.* [1949–] **L.**AV.; IC. 54–; SC.; U.; **Abs.**U.; **Bl.**U. 49–51; **Bm.**U.; **Cr.**U. 60–; **Db.**; **E.**R.; **Ex.**U.; **F.**A.; **G.**T.; U.; **M.**T.; U.; **Ma.**T. 53–57; **N.**U.; **Sa.** imp.; **Sh.**U.; **Sw.**U.; **Wo.**; **Y.** [*C. of:* 15059]

15110 **Communications** from the **Radcliffe Observatory.** Pretoria. *Communs Radcliffe Obs.* [1939–] **L.**AS.; SC.; **C.**P., UL.; **Db.** 50–; **E.**R.; **M.**U. 50– imp.

15110° **Communications. Rekenafdeling, Mathematisch centrum.** Amsterdam. *Communs Rekenafd. math. Cent.*

15111 **Communications. Rhodes-Livingstone Institute.** Livingstone. *Communs Rhodes-Livingstone Inst.* **L.**U. 50–; **O.**RH. 43–.

15112 **Communications** from the **Royal Observatory, Edinburgh.** *Communs R. Obs. Edinb.* [1949–] **L.**AS.; **Db.**; **E.**R. 51–; **M.**U. 51–58.
 Communications from the **Rubber Foundation.** Amsterdam. *See* 30145.

15113 **Communications. Rubber Research Institute** of **Malaya.** Kuala Lumpur. *Communs Rubb. Res. Inst. Malaya* **L.**P. 31–. [*Supplement to:* 26835]

15114 **Communications** from the **School** of **African Studies** in the **University** of **Cape Town.** *Communs Sch. Afr. Stud. Univ. Cape Town* **L.**AN. 42–; **Db.** 43–.

15115 **Communications** on the **Science** and **Practice** of **Brewing.** New York. *Communs Sci. Pract. Brew.* [1937–38] **L.**C.; P.; SC.; **Bm.**P.; **Br.**U. [*C. as:* 57079]
 Communications du **Service** des **eaux.** Berne. *See* 32254.
 Communications de la **Société mathématique** de **Kharkoff.** *See* 50081.

15116 **Communications** de **Statens seruminstitut.** Extraits. København. *Communs St. Seruminst.* [1949–] **L.**TD.; **C.**V.; **Dn.**U. [*Extracts in French translation from:* 29950; *C. of:* 15090]

15117 **Communications** de la **Station internationale** de **géobotanique méditerranéenne** et **alpine.** Montpellier. *Communs Stn int. Géobot. médit. alp.* [1931–] **C.**BO.

15118 **Communications** de la **Station** de **recherches** de **Groenendael.** Bruxelles. *Communs Stn Rech. Groenendael* [1947–] **O.**F. (Sér. B, C imp.)

15119 **Communications** from the **Testing** and **Observation Institute** of the **Danish National Association** for **Infantile Paralysis.** Hellerup. *Communs Test. Obsn Inst. Dan. natn. Ass. infant. Paralysis* [1958–] **Y.**

15120 **Communications** from the **University** of **London Observatory.** London. *Communs Univ. Lond. Obs.* **L.**AS. 49–; **M.**U. 38–.

15121 **Communications** from the **University Observatory.** Oxford. *Communs Univ. Obs., Oxf.* [1933–] **L.**AS.; BM.; **Bm.**U.; **E.**A.; R. 33–39 imp.; U. 33–39; **G.**U. 33–39; **M.**U., **Nw.**A. 33–39; **O.**R. [*C. of:* 32145]

15122 **Communications. Wallerstein Laboratories.** New York. *Communs Wallerstein Labs* **Y.**

15123 **Communications** from the **Wrocław Astronomical Observatory.** Wrocław. *Communs Wrocl. astr. Obs.* [1953–] **M.**U. 53–54.

15125 **Communiqués** de la **Société** des **architectes diplomés** par le **gouvernement.** Paris. *Communiqués Soc. Archit. dipl.* **L.**BA. 48–.

15126 **Community Planning Review.** Ottawa. *Community Plann. Rev.* **L.**BA. 51–; **Bl.**U. 62–.

15127 **Comparative Biochemistry** and **Physiology.** London. *Comp. Biochem. Physiol.* [1960–] **L.**BM.; MD.; NC.; UC.; SC.; Z.; **Bl.**U. 61–; **Bn.**U.; **E.**A.; **Ld.**U.; **Lo.**; **M.**U.; **Y.**

15128 **Comparative Oologist.** Santa Barbara, Cal. *Comp. Oolog.* [1924–] O.OR. 24. [*C. of:* 26508]

15129 **Comparative Psychology Monographs.** Cambridge, Mass. *Comp. Psychol. Monogr.* [1922–51] L.AM. 46–51; B. imp.; PS.; S. 28–35 imp.; SC. imp.; Z. 42–51; **Bm.**U.; **C.**PS.; **G.**U.; **O.**EP. 22–42 imp. [*C. of:* 5897]

15130 **Compas.** Journal à l'usage des géomètres, des architectes, etc. Tirlemont. *Compas*

15131 **Compass.** Magazine of the Cambridge University Geographical Society. Cambridge. *Compass, Cambr.* [1948–] L.BM.; E.U.; N.U.; O.G.

15132 **Compass.** Socony-Vacuum Oil Company. New York. *Compass Socony-Vacuum Oil Co.* L.P. 53–.

15133 **Compendium médical.** Revue bi-mensuelle. Paris. *Compend. méd.*

15134 **Compensation Medicine.** New York. *Compens. Med.* L.MA. 55–.

15135 **Compilación de los estudios geológicos oficiales en Colombia.** Bogota. *Compilac. Estud. geol. of. Colomb.* [1933–] L.BM.; BM^N.; Y.

15135° **Compilacion de trabajos del Departamento de zoologia vertebrados.** Universidad de la Republica. Montevideo. *Compilac. Trab. Dep. Zool. vert.* [1960–]

15136 **Compilation of Committee Reports for the Annual Convention. Philippine Sugar Association.** Manila. *Compil. Comm. Rep. a. Conv. Philipp. Sug. Ass.* L.P. 23–26; SC. 26–.

15137 **Complete Abstracts of Japanese Chemical Literature.** Tokio. *Complete Abstr. Jap. chem. Lit.*

15138 **Complete Chemical Abstracts of Japan.** Sendai. *Complete chem. Abstr. Japan* Y.

15139 **Complete Papers and Talks. National Telemetering Conference.** Chicago. *Complete Pap. Talks natn. Telemeter. Conf.* [1953–] L.P.

Components News. Standard Telephone and Cables Ltd. *See* 48409.

15140 **Composite Catalog of Oil-field and Pipe-line Equipment.** Houston, Tex. *Compos. Cat. Oil-Fld Pipe-line Equip.* L.P. 36: 40.

15141 **Composite Catalog of Oil-refinery and Natural Gasoline Plant Equipment including the Process Handbook.** Houston, Tex. *Compos. Cat. Oil-Refin. nat. Gasol. Pl. Equip.* L.P. 34–36.

15142 **Composite Wood.** Dehra Dun. *Compos. Wood* [1953–] L.P.; F.A.; Pr.FT.; Y.

15143 **Compositio mathematica.** Groningen. *Compositio math.* [1934–] L.BM.; M.; R. 50–; SC.; U. 56–; Bl.U.; **Br.**U.; **C.**P.; UL.; **Cr.**U.; Db.; E.R.; U.; G.U. 34–40; Ld.U. imp.; M.U.; N.U. 52–; Nw.A. 38–; O.R.; Sa.; Sh.U.; Y. [*Suspended* 1941–49]

15144 **Comprehensive Psychiatry.** New York. *Compreh. Psychiat.* [1960–] L.MD.; Dn.U. 61–; Ld.U.

Compressed Air. *See* 15146.

15145 **Compressed Air Comments.** Milano. *Compress. Air Comments* [1958–] Y. [*Replaces:* 5102]

Compressed Air Engineering. *See* 15147.

15146 **Compressed Air and Hydraulic Engineering.** London. *Compress. Air hydraul. Engng* [1935–56] L.AV. 48–56; EE. 45–56; P.; **Bm.**U. 45–56; **G.**M. 54–56; **Lv.**P. 52–56; **M.**P. 39–56; **Sh.**IO. 53–56; Y. [*C. as:* 15147]

15147 **Compressed Air and Hydraulics.** London. *Compress. Air Hydraul.* [1956–] L.AV. imp.; EE.; MI. (curr.); P.; **Bm.**U.; **Br.**P. (2 yr.); **G.**M.; ME. 57–62; **Lv.**P.; **M.**P.; **Sh.**IO.; **Sil.** 59–; Y. [*C. of:* 15146]

15148 **Compressed Air Magazine.** New York. *Compress. Air Mag.* [1896–] L.AV. 52–54; P. 96–08; **Bm.**P. 45–; U. 14–19 imp.; **Cr.**U. 37–; **G.**E. (1 yr); M. 29–53; **Lv.**P. 53–; **Nw.**A. 98– imp.; Y.

15149 **Compressed Air Mining.** London. *Compress. Air Min.* [1938–41] L.P.; SC. [*Supplement to:* 15147]

Compte rendu de l'Académie d'agriculture de France. *See* 15206.

15150 **Compte rendu de l'Académie bulgare des sciences.** Sofia. *C. r. Acad. bulg. Sci.* [1948–]
Sciences mathématiques et naturelles L.AM.; BM^N. 48–51; C. 48–50: 58–; MA.; MD. imp.; P. 59–; R.; SC.; U.; UC. 58–; Bl.U. imp.; **Br.**A. 48–50; **C.**P.; UL.; Db.; G.U.; Md.H.; Y.

Compte-rendu de l'Académie de la république populaire roumaine. *See* 15339.

15151 **Compte rendu de l'Académie des sciences, belles-lettres et arts de Clermont-Ferrand.** *C. r. Acad. Sci. Belles-lett. Arts Clermont-Ferrand* G.M. 1837–1841: 78; Sw.U. 21–.

Compte rendu de l'Académie des sciences. Paris. *See* 15207.

Compte rendu de l'Académie des sciences de l'U.R.S.S. *See* 17112.

15152 **Compte-rendu de l'activité. Institut textile de France.** Paris. *C. r. Activ. Inst. text. Fr.* [1952–] L.P.; Y. [*From* 1954 *forms supplement to:* 10609]

15152° **Compte rendu d'activité et recueil des travaux. Station biologique de la Tour du Valat.** *C. r. Activ. Rec. Trav. Stn biol. Tour Valat* [1950–] L.BM^N.; Z. 56–57; **C.**B.; Fr. 55–.

Compte rendu annuel et Archives de la Société turque des sciences physiques et naturelles. *See* 55334.

15153 **Compte rendu annuel des observations météorologiques.** Alençon *C. r. a. Obsns mét., Alençon*

15154 **Compte rendu annuel des opérations pratiquées à la Clinique chirurgicale de Clermont-Ferrand.** Montluçon. *C. r. a. Opér. prat. Clin. chir. Clermont-Ferrand*

15155 **Compte rendu annuel et procès-verbaux des séances de la Société de médecine de Nancy.** *C. r. a. P.-v. Séanc. Soc. Méd. Nancy* [*C. as:* 12057]

15156 **Compte rendu annuel du Service de chirurgie du Dr. A. Depage à l'Hôpital Saint-Jean de Bruxelles.** *C. r. a. Serv. Chir. Dr A. Depage, Brux.*

15157 **Compte rendu de l'assemblée annuelle. Association des ingénieurs forestiers de la province de Québec.** Québec. *C. r. Assemb. a. Ass. Ingrs for. Prov. Québ.* O.F. 40– imp.

15158 **Compte rendu. Assemblée générale du Comité national français. Union géodésique et géophysique internationale.** Paris. *C. r. Assembl. gén. Com. natn. fr. U.G.G.I.* L.MO. 50–; SC. 26– imp.

15159 **Compte rendu des assemblées générales et des séances de discussions techniques. Société technique de l'industrie du gaz en France.** Paris. *C. r. Assembls gén. Séanc. Discuss. tech. Soc. tech. Ind. Gaz Fr.* [*See also:* 15180]

15160 **Compte rendu** de l'**Association** des **anatomistes.** Paris & Nancy. *C. r. Ass. Anat.* [1899–] **L.**SC. 25–; UC.; **Bl.**U. 30–37; **Bm.**U. 29–; **Br.**U. 47; **C.**AN. imp.; UL.; **Cr.**U. 24–; **E.**U. 31–39; **M.**MS. 26–39: 47–; **O.**R.; **Pl.**M. 24–36 imp.; **Sa.** 33–; **Y.**

15161 **Compte rendu** de l'**Association française** pour l'**avancement** des **sciences.** Paris. *C. r. Ass. fr. Avanc. Sci.* [1872–] **L.**BM.; imp.; BM^N. 72–36: 38– imp.; GL. 72–14; GM.; MO. 72–22; P. 72–36; R. 72–23; S. 75–24; SC.; UC. 80– imp.; **Abd.**U. 72–14; **C.**UL.; **E.**R. 72–25; U. 72–14; **G.**U. 72–36; **M.**U. 72–80 imp.: 99–04; **Nw.**A. 72–15.

15162 **Compte rendu** de l'**Association française** de **pédiatrie.** Paris. *C. r. Ass. fr. Pédiat.* **Lv.**M. 10–12. [*C. as*: 15442]

Compte rendu de l'**Association internationale** d'**essais** de **semences.** *See* 39307.

Compte rendu de l'**Association libre** des **physiologistes suisses.** *See* 56020.

15163 **Compte rendu** de l'**Association lyonnaise** des **amis** des **sciences naturelles.** Lyon. *C. r. Ass. lyonn. Amis Sci. nat.* **L.**BM. 74–86 imp.

15164 **Compte rendu. Association** pour **prévenir** les **accidents** de **machines.** Mulhouse. *C. r. Ass. prév. Accid. Mach.*

15165 **Compte rendu** de l'**Aunis. Commission** de **météorologie** de la **Charente.** Angoulême. *C. r. Aunis Commn Mét. Charente*

15166 **Compte rendu bimensuel. Société** d'**encouragement** pour l'**industrie nationale.** Paris. *C. r. bimens. Soc. Encour. Ind. natn.*

15167 **Compte rendu** de la **Clinique obstétricale** et **gynécologique** de l'**Université** de **Turin.** *C. r. Clin. obstét. gynéc. Univ. Turin* [1903–]

15168 **Compte rendu** du **Club médical** de **Constantinople.** Constantinople. *C. r. Club méd. Constantinople*

Compte rendu. Comité international de **thermodynamique** et **cinétique électrochimiques.** *See* 15223.

15169 **Compte rendu. Comité national français** et **Comité national marocain** de **géodésie** et **géophysique.** Bruxelles. *C. r. Com. natn. fr. Com. natn. maroc. Géod. Géophys.* **L.**MO. 37–38; P. 33–46* imp.; SC. 26–46; U. 39–46; **Bl.**U. 33–36; **C.**UL. 33–46; **Db.** 33–46; **E.**R. 33–46; **Ld.**U. 33–46; **Lv.**U. 39–45. [*C. as*: 15170]

15170 **Compte rendu** du **Comité national français** de **géodésie** et **géophysique.** Paris. *C. r. Com. natn. fr. Géod. Géophys.* [1947–] **L.**MO. 51–; P.; SC.; U.; **C.**UL.; **Db.**; **E.**R.; **Ld.**U.; **Lv.**U.; **Y.** [*C. of*: 15169]

15171 **Compte rendu** de la **Commission géodésique baltique.** Stockholm, Riga. *C. r. Commn géod. balt.* [1926–38] **L.**AS.; BM. 28–38; P.; SC.; **C.**GD.; **E.**R.; **O.**R. [*C. of*: 15174; *C. as*: 865]

15172 **Compte rendu. Commission météorologique** du **département** des **Ardennes.** Mézières. *C. r. Commn mét. Dép. Ardennes*

15173 **Compte rendu. Commission météorologique** du **département** de **Vaucluse.** Avignon. *C. r. Commn mét. Dép. Vaucluse* **L.**MO. 78–03.

15174 **Compte rendu. Conférence géodésique.** Helsingfors. *C. r. Conf. géod., Helsingf.* [1924] **L.**AS.; P.; **C.**GD. [*C. as*: 15171]

15175 **Compte rendu** des **conférences. Association internationale** de **pédiatrie préventive.** Genève. *C. r. Confs Ass. int. Pédiat. prév.* [1931–] **L.**SH. 32–33.

15176 **Compte rendu** du **Congrès annuel** des **sociétés** de **pharmacie** de **France.** *C. r. Congr. a. Socs Pharm. Fr.*

15177 **Compte rendu** du **Congrès antipesteux** organisé à **Saratov** par l'**Institut** de **microbiologie** et d'**épidémiologie** d'état du **Sud-Est** de la **Russie.** Saratov. *C. r. Congr. antipest. Saratov* [1924–25] **L.**EB.; SC. 25; TD. 25; **C.**UL. 24; **E.**U.; **Lv.**U.; **O.**R. [*C. as*: 15178]

15178 **Compte rendu** du **Congrès antipesteux** de l'**U.R.S.S.** *C. r. Congr. antipest. U.R.S.S.* [1927] **L.**EB.; TD.; **E.**U.; **Lv.**U.; **O.**R. [*C. of*: 15177]

15179 **Compte rendu. Congrès** d'**assainissement** et de **salubrité** de l'**habitation.** *C. r. Congr. Assain. Salub. Habit.* **L.**P. 97–10 imp.

15180 **Compte rendu** du **Congrès** de l'**Association technique** de l'**industrie** du **gaz.** Paris. *C. r. Congr. Ass. tech. Ind. Gaz* [1927–] **L.**P.; **Y.** [*C. of*: 15272; *see also*: 15159]

15181 **Compte rendu. Congrès dentaire national.** Paris. *C. r. Congr. dent. natn., Paris*

15182 **Compte rendu. Congrès dentaire national belge.** Bruxelles. *C. r. Congr. dent. natn. belge*

15183 **Compte rendu. Congrès** des **dermatologistes** et **syphiligraphes** de **langue française.** Paris. *C. r. Congr. Derm. Syph. Lang. fr.*

15184 **Compte rendu. Congrès égyptien** de **médecine.** Le Caire. *C. r. Congr. égypt. Méd.* **L.**S. 02; TD. 04.

15185 **Compte rendu. Congrès** de la **Faculté catholique** et **française** de **médecine** de **Beyrouth.** Beyrouth. *C. r. Congr. Fac. cath. fr. Méd. Beyrouth*

15186 **Compte rendu. Congrès français** de **climatothérapie** et d'**hygiène urbaine.** *C. r. Congr. fr. Climatothér. Hyg. urb.* **L.**BM. 04–08.

15187 **Compte rendu** du **Congrès français** du **froid.** Paris. *C. r. Congr. fr. Froid* [1909–12] **L.**P. [*C. as*: 15196]

15188 **Compte-rendu. Congrès** du **froid tropicale.** Marseille. *C. r. Congr. Froid trop.* [1951–] **L.**P.

15189 **Compte-rendu. Congrès** des **grands barrages.** *C. r. Congr. gr. Barrages* [1934–] **L.**P.

15191 **Compte rendu. Congrès** de la **houille blanche.** Grenoble, etc. *C. r. Congr. Houille blanche* **L.**P. 02: 25.

Compte rendu du **Congrès** de l'**industrie** du **gaz** en **France.** Paris. *See* 15272.

15192 **Compte rendu. Congrès** de la **machine agricole.** Paris. *C. r. Congr. Mach. agric.* **C.**A. 33.

15193 **Compte rendu. Congrès** des **mathématiciens scandinaves.** Stockholm. *C. r. Congr. Math. scand.* **L.**BM. 09: 11; **Abd.**U. 09–29 v. imp.; **Bl.**U. 29: 46: 57; **Sw.**U. 16.

15194 **Compte rendu. Congrès** de **médecine légale** de **langue française.** Paris. *C. r. Congr. Méd. lég. Lang. fr.*

15195 **Compte rendu** du **Congrès national** de la **culture** des **plantes médicinales.** Paris. *C. r. Congr. natn. Cult. Pl. méd.* **L.**PH. 24–25.

15196 **Compte rendu. Congrès national** du **froid.** Paris. *C. r. Congr. natn. Froid* [1920–] **L.**P. 20–23. [*C. of:* 15187]

15197 **Compte rendu. Congrès national** de **laiterie.** Brecht. *C. r. Congr. natn. Lait.*

15198 **Compte rendu** du **Congrès national** de **navigation intérieure.** Paris. *C. r. Congr. natn. Navig. intér.* **L.**P. II.

15199 **Compte rendu. Congrès national** des **sciences.** Bruxelles. *C. r. Congr. natn. Sci., Brux.* **L.**BM^N. 30–; P. 30: 35.

15200 **Compte rendu. Congrès national** des **sociétés françaises** de **géographie.** Lyon. *C. r. Congr. natn. Socs fr. Géogr.* **L.**BM. 94.

15201 **Compte rendu. Congrès** des **naturalistes** et **médecins** du **Nord** tenu à **Helsingfors.** *C. r. Congr. Nat. Méd. N. Helsingf.*

15202 **Compte rendu. Congrès préhistorique** de **France.** Paris. *C. r. Congr. préhist. Fr.* **L.**BM. 05–08; SC. 10–26; UC. 06–13; **Db.** 12–13; **E.**U. 06–12; V. 31: 36.

15203 **Compte rendu. Congrès provincial. Association forestière québecoise.** Québec. *C. r. Congr. prov. Ass. for. québ.* [1944–] **Y.**

15203^c **Compte rendu** du **Congrès quinquennial. Association forestière québecoise.** Québec. *C. r. Congr. quinq. Ass. for. québ.* **Y.**

15204 **Compte rendu** du **Congrès** des **sociétés savantes** de **Paris** et des **départements. Section** des **sciences.** Paris. *C. r. Congr. Socs sav. Paris Sect. Sci.* **L.**BM. 96; BM^N. 96–39: 56–; GL. 50–; **C.**UL. 30: 33–; **E.**R. 20–38; **Y.**
Compte rendu, discussions et **communications diverses. Congrès français** de **médecine.** *See* 39869.

15205 **Compte-rendu** de l'**expérimentation fruitière** et de l'**activité** du **Service** de l'**arboriculture** en **Algérie.** Alger. *C. r. Expn fruit. Activ. Serv. Arboric. Algér.* **Md.**H. 41–46 imp.

15206 **Compte rendu hebdomadaire** des **séances** de l'**Académie** d'**agriculture** de **France.** Paris. *C. r. hebd. Séanc. Acad. Agric. Fr.* [1915–] **L.**A. v. imp.; AM.; BM.; EB.; IC. 28–40: 47–; MY. 48–; P.; **Abs.**A. 52–54; **C.**A. 32–; P. 30–; **Db.**; **E.**R.; **Hu.**G. 48–; **Je.** 28–; **Md.**H. 35–; **O.**R. 54–; **R.**D. 57–; **Rt.**; **Sal.**F. 50–; **Y.** [*C. of:* 11707]

15207 **Compte rendu hebdomadaire** des **séances** de l'**Académie** des **sciences.** Paris. *C. r. hebd. Séanc. Acad. Sci., Paris* [1835–] **L.**AS. imp.; B. 13–; BM.; BM^N.; C.; CB. 50–; EE. 88–; G. 1837–; GL.; GM. 97–; H. 93–39 imp.; HQ. 25–; I. 47–; IC. 79–; K. 88–31; L.; LI. 98–40; MC. 93– imp.; MD.; MO. 70–; P.; PH. 1843–; QM. 50–; R.; RI.; S.; SC.; TD. 10–; U. imp.; UC.; Z. imp.; **Abd.**U.; **Abs.**N. 1858–12 imp.: 25–; U. 69– imp.; **Bl.**U.; **Bm.**P.; T. 59–; U.; **Bn.**U. 23–; **Br.**U.; **C.**APH. 57–61; C. 15–; P.; UL.; **Cr.**U. 84–; **Db.**; **Dn.**U.; **E.**B. 92–05; C. 85–91 imp.; O. imp.; P. 1835–56; R.; U.; **Ep.**D. 48–; **Ex.**U. 38–; **F.**A. 19–39: 43–; **G.**F. 1854–02; M. 1831–1841: 70–40: 49–; T. 93–; U.; **H.**U. 48–; **Ld.**U. imp.; **Lv.**P. 1835–19 imp.: 47–; U.; **M.**C. 20–40: 51–; D. 09– imp.; P. 24–; U. 1840–; **N.**P. 04–09; U. 18–; **Nw.**A.; **O.**R.; **Pl.**M. 81– imp.; **R.**D. 47–; U. 05–; **Rt.** 67–; **Sa.**; **Sh.**S. 50–; U. 73–; **Ste.** 93–; **Sw.**U. 31–34; **Wd.** 45–; **Wo.** 1835–19; **Y.**

15208 **Compte rendu hebdomadaire** des **séances** de l'**Académie** des **sciences** de **Jekaterinoslaw.** *C. r. hebd. Séanc. Acad. Sci. Jekaterinoslaw*

Compte rendu hebdomadaire des **séances** et **mémoires** de la **Société** de **biologie.** Paris. *See* 15247.

15209 **Compte rendu** de l'**Hôpital général** d'**Uleåborg.** Helsingfors. *C. r. Hôp. gén. Uleåborg*

15210 **Compte rendu. Inspection générale** des **services agricoles.** Alaotra. *C. r. Insp. gén. Servs agric., Alaotra* **C.**A. 52–.
Compte rendu de l'**Institut** de **géographie** de l'**Université** de **Varsovie.** *See* 50676.

15210^c **Compte rendu** des **journées internationales** de **sciences aéronautiques.** Office nationale d'études et de recherches aéronautiques. Paris. *C. r. Journées int. Sci. aéronaut.* [1957–]

15211 **Compte rendu mensuel. Centre technique** des **industries** de la **fonderie.** Paris. *C. r. mens. Cent. tech. Ind. Fond.* **Bm.**C. 46–49★. [*C. as:* 15307]

15212 **Compte rendu mensuel** des **réunions** de la **Société** de l'**industrie minérale.** St-Étienne. *C. r. mens. Réun. Soc. Ind. minér.* [1874–20] **L.**I. 93–20; P. 87–20; SC. 77–20; **Cr.**U. 94–13 imp. [*C. in:* 47307]

15212^c **Compte rendu mensuel** des **séances** de l'**Académie** des **sciences coloniales.** Paris. *C. r. mens. Séanc. Acad. Sci. colon.* [1948–] **L.**SC.; Z. 48–49 imp. [*C. of:* 15225^c]

15213 **Compte rendu mensuel** des **séances** de la **Classe** de **médecine. Académie polonaise** des **sciences** et des **lettres.** Cracovie. *C. r. mens. Séanc. Cl. Méd. Acad. pol. Sci. Lett.* [1930–] **L.**S. 30–48 imp.; **Bl.**U. 45–52; **Sal.** 32–38 imp.

15214 **Compte rendu mensuel** des **séances** de la **Classe** des **sciences mathématiques** et **naturelles. Académie polonaise** des **sciences** et des **lettres.** Cracovie. *C. r. mens. Séanc. Cl. Sci. math. nat. Acad. pol. Sci. Lett.* [1929–51] **L.**BM.; BM^N. imp.; C.; GL.; P.; R. 45–51; S. 30–31: 47–48; SC.; Z. 31–51; **Bl.**U. 46–51; **C.**B. 45–51; UL.; **Db.** (biol.); **Dm.**; **E.**R. imp.; **G.**U. imp.; **Ld.**U.; **O.**R.; **Pl.**M. 33–51 imp.; **Sal.** 45–51. [*Suspended* July 1939–Jan. 1945]

15215 **Compte rendu mensuel** des **séances. Institut technique** du **bâtiment** et des **travaux publics.** Paris. *C. r. mens. Séanc. Inst. tech. Bâtim. Trav. publ.*
Compte rendu du **Musée** de **Carniola.** *See* 13367.

15216 **Compte rendu officiel** des **congrès. Fédération** des **sociétés** de **pêche** et de **pisciculture** du **Sud-Ouest.** *C. r. off. Congr. Féd. Socs Pêche Piscic. Sud-Ouest*

15217 **Compte rendu, procès-verbaux,** etc. **Congrès** des **médecins aliénistes** de **France** et des **pays** de **langue française.** *C. r. P.-v. Congr. Méd. Alién. Fr.* **L.**BM. 23–.

15218 **Compte rendu, procès-verbaux, mémoires. Association bretonne.** St-Brieuc. *C. r. P.-v. Mém. Ass. breton.* **L.**BM. 73–08★; **C.**UL. 73–08.

15219 **Compte rendu provisoire. Société** d'**encouragement** pour l'**industrie nationale.** Paris. *C. r. provis. Soc. Encour. Ind. natn.* **Db.** 99–.

15220 **Compte rendu** des **recherches effectuées. Laboratoires** du **bâtiment** et des **travaux publics.** Paris. *C. r. Rech. Labs Bâtim. Trav. publ.* **Y.**

15221 **Compte rendu** de **recherches. Institut** pour l'**encouragement** de la **recherche scientifique** dans l'**industrie** et l'**agriculture**. Bruxelles. *C. r. Rech. Inst. Encour. Rech. scient. Ind. Agric.* [1950–] **L.**AM.; HQ.; P.; SC.; **Rt.** imp.; **Y.**

15222 **Compte rendu** des **réunions** de l'**Académie** d'**Hippone**. Bône. *C. r. Réun. Acad. Hippone* **C.**UL. 88–98.

15223 **Compte-rendu** des **réunions. Comité international** de **thermodynamique** et de **cinétique électrochimiques**. *C. r. Réun. Com. int. Thermodyn. Cinét. électrochim.* [1949–] **L.**BM. 54–; C. 50–; P. 50–; **C.**UL. 54–; **E.**A. 54–.

15224 **Compte-rendu** des **réunions** d'**études. Groupe français** des **argiles**. Paris. *C. r. Réun. Étud. Grpe fr. Argiles* [1949–53] **L.**P. 51–53; **Abd.**S. [*C. as:* 10415]

Compte rendu des séances de l'Académie d'agriculture de France. *See* 15206.

15225 **Compte rendu** des **séances** de l'**Académie nationale** des **sciences** de **Bordeaux**. *C. r. Séanc. Acad. natn. Sci. Bordeaux*

15225° **Compte rendu** des **séances. Académie** des **sciences coloniales**. Paris. *C. r. Séanc. Acad. Sci. colon.* **L.**LI. 22–27; SC. 41–46; UC. 22–24; **C.**UL. 22–24; **O.**B. 22–; **Sy.**R. 23–24. [*C. as:* 15212°]

15226 **Compte rendu** des **séances** de l'**Académie** des **sciences** de **Roumanie**. Bucarest. *C. r. Séanc. Acad. Sci. Roum.* [1936–38] **L.**BM^N.; R.; **C.**P.; **E.**R. [*C. as:* 15242]

15227 **Compte rendu** des **séances annuelles** de la **Société** des **pharmaciens** de l'**Aisne**. Laon. *C. r. Séanc. a. Soc. Pharmns Aisne*

15228 **Compte rendu** des **séances. Association française** pour le **développement** des **travaux publics**. Paris. *C. r. Séanc. Ass. fr. Dév. Trav. publ.*

15229 **Compte rendu** des **séances. Association** des **propriétaires** d'**appareils** à **vapeur**. Paris. *C. r. Séanc. Ass. Propr. Appar. Vap.*

15230 **Compte rendu** des **séances. Association** de **séismologie, U.G.G.I.** *C. r. Séanc. Ass. Séism. U.G.G.I.* **Lv.**U. 47–54. [*C. of:* 15245]

15231 **Compte rendu** des **séances** du **Cercle pharmaceutique** de la **Marne**. Reims. *C. r. Séanc. Cercle pharm. Marne*

15232 **Compte rendu** des **séances** du **Cercle zoologique** de **Cluj**. Cluj. *C. r. Séanc. Cercle zool. Cluj* **L.**BM^N. 45–.

15233 **Compte rendu** des **séances. Comité** d'**études** sur l'**éclairage** pour la **navigation aérienne**. Commission internationale de l'éclairage. *C. r. Séanc. Com. Étud. Éclair. Navig. aér.* **L.**P. 30–32.

15234 **Compte rendu** des **séances** de la **Commission centrale sismique permanente**. St. Pétersbourg. *C. r. Séanc. Commn cent. sism. perm., St-Pétersb.* [1902–24] **L.**MO. 10–19 imp.; R. 02–19; **C.**UL. 13–24; **E.**O. 04–13; R. 02–13; **O.**O. 06–09.

15236 **Compte rendu** des **séances. Conférence général** des **poids** et **mésures**. Paris. *C. r. Séanc. Conf. gén. Poids Més.* **L.**P. 89–; **Y.**

15237 **Compte rendu** des **séances. Congrès national** des **naturalistes** de **Roumanie**. Cluj. *C. r. Séanc. Congr. natn. Nat. Roum.* **L.**BM^N. 28; EB. 28.

15238 **Compte rendu** des **séances** du **Conseil** d'**hygiène publique** et de **salubrité** du **département** de la **Seine**. Paris. *C. r. Séanc. Cons. Hyg. publ. Salub. Dép. Seine* **L.**H. 95–38 imp.; P. 11–31.

15239 **Compte rendu** des **séances générales** de la **Société professionelle** des **pharmaciens** du **nord** de la **France**. Lille. *C. r. Séanc. gén. Soc. prof. Pharmns N. Fr.*

15240 **Compte rendu** des **séances. Institut français** d'**anthropologie**. Paris. *C. r. Séanc. Inst. fr. Anthrop.* [1911–14] **L.**S. 11–13; **C.**UL. 11–12; **E.**R.; **G.**U.; **O.**R. 11–12.

15241 **Compte rendu** des **séances** de l'**Institut géologique** de **Roumanie**. Bucarest. *C. r. Séanc. Inst. géol. Roum.* [1910–] **L.**BM^N. 10–40; GL.; GM.; UC. imp.; E.D. 11–51 imp.; J. 15–16; **Lv.**U. 10–44 imp.; **Y.**

15242 **Compte rendu** des **séances** de l'**Institut** des **sciences** de **Roumanie**. Bucarest. *C. r. Séanc. Inst. Sci. Roum.* [1939–] **L.**BM^N. 39; **C.**P.; **E.**R. 39. [*C. of:* 15226]

Compte rendu des séances et mémoires de la Société de biologie. Paris. *See* 15247.

15243 **Compte rendu** des **séances mensuelles. Société** des **sciences naturelles** (*afterwards* et **physiques**) du **Maroc**. Rabat. *C. r. Séanc. mens. Soc. Sci. nat. phys. Maroc* [1935–] **L.**BM^N. 53–; EB. 50–; GL. 50–; K. 50–; L. 50–; TP. 51–; Z. 50–; **C.**P. 50–; **Dm.** 50–; **Pl.**M. 57–; **Y.**

15244 **Compte rendu** des **séances scientifiques** de la **Société internationale** de **médecine** du **Caire**. *C. r. Séanc. scient. Soc. int. Méd. Caire* **L.**MD. 08–13.

15245 **Compte rendu** des **séances. Section** de **séismologie, U.G.G.I.** Toulouse. *C. r. Séanc. Sect. Séism. U.G.G.I.* **L.**MO. 22–31. [*C. as:* 15230]

Compte rendu des séances du Service géologique de la Pologne. *See* 38150.

15246 **Compte rendu** des **séances** de la **Société académique** d'**archéologie, sciences** et **arts** du **département** de l'**Oise**. Beauvais. *C. r. Séanc. Soc. acad. Archéol. Sci. Arts Dép. Oise* **L.**BM. 93–.

15247 **Compte rendu** des **séances** de la **Société** de **biologie**. Paris. *C. r. Séanc. Soc. Biol.* [1849–] **L.**BM.; BM^N.; C. 65–04 imp.: 30–; CB. 22–; EB. 14–; H. 35–40; LI. 01–; MA. 23– imp.; MC. 02– imp.; MD.; NC. 59–; R. 1849–39; S.; SC. 1849–78: 17–; SI. 37–40; TD. 03–; U. 49–; UC. 02–; UCH. 31–; Z. 84–; **Abd.**U. 02–11: 27–; **Abs.**U. 55–; **Bl.**U. 14– imp.; **Bm.**U. 12– imp.; **Bn.**U. 49–; **Br.**U. 32– imp.; **C.**APH. 48–; MO. 24–; P. 07–; PH. 67–; R. 54–; UL.; V. 24–; **Cr.**MD. 25–; **Db.** 02–; **Dn.**U. 21– imp.; **E.**P.; PO. 55–; R. 92–; U. 95–; **Ex.**U. 41–; **G.**T. 53–; U. 03–; **Ld.**U. 05–; **Lv.**M. 84–; U. 00– imp.; **M.**MS. 1855–; **Nw.**A. 14– imp.; **O.**R.; **Pl.**M. 94– imp.; **R.**D. 14–; **Sa.** 1849–78; **Sal.** 32–; **Sh.**U. 10–; **W.** 23–40: 46–; **Y.**

Compte rendu des séances de la Société botanique de Genève. *See* 11873.

15248 **Compte rendu** des **séances** de la **Société** d'**ethnographie américaine** et **orientale**. Paris. *C. r. Séanc. Soc. Ethnogr. am. orient.*

15249 **Compte rendu** des **séances. Société géologique** de **France**. Paris. *C. r. Séanc. Soc. géol. Fr.* **L.**BM. [*Previously contained in:* 11988]

15250 **Compte rendu** des **séances. Société géologique** et **minéralogique** de **Bretagne**. Rennes. *C. r. Séanc. Soc. géol. minér. Bretagne* [1935–] **L.**BM^N. 35–37; UC.; **Bl.**U. 37.

Compte rendu des séances de la Société géologique de Serbie. *See* 58361.

Compte rendu des séances. Société imperiale des naturalistes de St. Pétersbourg. *See* 54588.

Compte rendu des séances de la Société lépidoptérologique de Genève. *See* 12031.

15251 **Compte rendu** des **séances** de la **Société mathématique** de **France.** Paris. *C. r. Séanc. Soc. math. Fr.* [1912–38] **L.**M. imp.; SC. 15–38 imp.; **Abs.**U. imp.; **E.**R.; **Ld.**U. 26–38; **O.**R. [*C. in:* 12046]

15252 **Compte rendu** des **séances** de la **Société** des **naturalistes luxembourgeois.** Luxembourg. *C. r. Séanc. Soc. Nat. luxemb.* [1891–06] **L.**BM.ᴺ.; L. 98–06; Z. [*C. as:* 11037]

15253 **Compte rendu** des **séances** de la **Société d'odontologie** de **Paris.** *C. r. Séanc. Soc. Odont. Paris* **L.**MD. 40–41.

15254 **Compte rendu** des **séances** de la **Société paléontologique** et **palethnographique** de **Provence.** Marseille. *C. r. Séanc. Soc. paléont. palethnogr. Provence* **L.**BMᴺ. 48–.

15255 **Compte rendu** des **séances** de la **Société** de **physique** et d'**histoire naturelle** de **Genève.** *C. r. Séanc. Soc. Phys. Hist. nat. Genève* [1884–47] **L.**AS. 10–47 imp.; BMᴺ.; C. 01–47; E. 17–47; GL. 00–47; L. 13–47; MO. 96–47; RI.; UC. 10–47; Z. 10–47; **Abs.**U. 26–47; **Bm.**N. 02–47 imp.; **C.**P. 13–47; **Db.**; **Dm.** 26–43 imp.; **E.**C. 85–47; J. 86–47; R. 10–47; **Ld.**U. 26–47; **Lv.**U. 10–45; **Nw.**A. 22–47; **Pl.**M. 29–47 imp. [*From* 1948 *contained in:* 4356]

15256 **Compte rendu** des **séances** de la **Société polonaise** de **physique.** Varsovie. *C. r. Séanc. Soc. pol. Phys.* [1920–31] **L.**P.; R. 23–31; UC.; **C.**P. 22–31; UL.; **E.**R. 27–31. [*C. as:* 722]
   Compte rendu des **séances** de la **Société r.** de **botanique** de **Belgique.** *See* 12145, pt. 2.
   Compte rendu des **séances** de la **Société scientifique** de **Varsovie.** *See* 50669.
   Compte rendu des **séances** de la **Société serbe** de **géologie.** Beograd. *See* 58361.

15257 **Compte-rendu** des **séances** et des **travaux** de la **Société** de **médecine** et d'**hygiène tropicales** d'**Égypte.** Alexandrie. *C. r. Séanc. Trav. Soc. Méd. Hyg. trop. Égypte* [1929–] **L.**TD. 33–37 v. imp.

15258 **Compte rendu** des **séances** de l'**Union coloniale.** Paris. *C. r. Séanc. Un. colon.* (*a*) Section de l'A. E. F. (*b*) Section de l'A. O. F.

15259 **Compte rendu** des **séances** de l'**Union française** des **acétylénistes.** Paris. *C. r. Séanc. Un. fr. Acét.*

15260 **Compte rendu** du **Secrétariat** de l'**Organisation météorologique internationale.** Lausanne. *C. r. Secr. Org. mét. int.* **L.**MO. 39–48.

15261 **Compte rendu** des **sessions. Institut colonial international.** Bruxelles. *C. r. Sess. Inst. colon. int.* **L.**BM. 94–09.
   Compte rendu de la **Société** de **biogéographie.** *See* 15273.
   Compte rendu de la **Société** de **biologie.** Paris. *See* 15247.

15262 **Compte rendu** de la **Société** de **chirurgie** de **Marseille.** *C. r. Soc. Chir. Marseille*

15263 **Compte rendu** de la **Société française** de **gynécologie.** Paris. *C. r. Soc. fr. Gynéc.* [1931–] **L.**MA. 48–; MD.

15264 **Compte rendu** de la **Société française** d'**orthopédie dento-faciale.** Lyon. *C. r. Soc. fr. Orthop. dento-fac.* [1921–] **L.**D. 21–37.

15265 **Compte rendu** de la **Société fribourgeoise** des **sciences naturelles.** Fribourg. *C. r. Soc. fribourg. Sci. nat.*
   Compte rendu de la **Société** de **génétique** du **Canada.** *See* 39215.
   Compte rendu de la **Société géologique** de **France.** *See* 15274.

15266 **Compte rendu** de la **Société** d'**histoire naturelle** de **Saône-et-Loire** à **Autun.** *C. r. Soc. Hist. nat. Saône-et-Loire*

15267 **Compte-rendu. Société** de l'**industrie minérale.** St. Etienne. *C. r. Soc. Ind. minér.* [1887–14] **L.**P.

15268 **Compte rendu** de la **Société médicale** d'**émulation** de **Montpellier.** *C. r. Soc. méd. Émul. Montpellier*
   Compte rendu de la **Société** des **naturalistes** de **Varsovie.** *See* 55125.

15269 **Compte rendu** de la **Société** d'**obstétrique,** de **gynécologie** et de **pédiatrie** de **Paris.** *C. r. Soc. Obstét. Gynéc. Pédiat. Paris* [1898–11] **L.**MD.; **Bm.**U. 99–06; **E.**P. 98–05. [*C. in:* 12106]
   Compte rendu des **physiologistes suisses.** *See* 56082.
   Compte rendu. Société r. des **lettres** et des **sciences** de **Bohème.** *See* 57031.
   Compte rendu de la **Société** des **sciences** de **Bohème.** *See* 57031.

15270 **Compte rendu** de la **Société** des **sciences** et des **lettres** de **Wrocław.** Wrocław. *C. r. Soc. Sci. Lett. Wrocł.* [1946–] **L.**BM.; BMᴺ.; **G.**U. 52–56; **Y.**

15271 **Compte rendu** de la **Société** de **stomatologie** de **Paris.** Paris. *C. r. Soc. Stomat. Paris*
   Compte rendu de la **Société suisse** de **biologie médicale.** *See* 56066°.

15271° **Compte rendu** de la **Société suisse** de **physiologie** et **pharmacologie.** *C. r. Soc. suisse Physiol. Pharmac.* [*Contained in:* 22066]
   Compte rendu de la **Société tchécoslovaque** de **cardiologie.** *See* 48037.

15272 **Compte rendu** de la **Société technique** de l'**industrie** du **gaz** en **France.** Paris. *C. r. Soc. tech. Ind. Gaz Fr.* **L.**P. 10–27*. [*C. as:* 15180]
   Compte rendu sommaire et **bulletin** de la **Société géologique** de **France.** *See* 11988 and 15274.

15273 **Compte rendu sommaire** des **séances. Société** de **biogéographie.** Paris. *C. r. somm. Séanc. Soc. Biogéogr.* [1923–] **L.**BMᴺ.; SC. 39–; Z. 57–; **C.**UL.; **Y.**

15274 **Compte rendu sommaire** des **séances** de la **Société géologique** de **France.** Paris. *C. r. somm. Séanc. Soc. géol. Fr.* **L.**BMᴺ. 90–; SC. 24–; **Abd.**U. 46–; **Abs.**U. 30–; **Br.**U. 11–; **C.**S. 15; UL. 24–; **Db.** 15–; **E.**C. 15–39 imp.; R. 93–97: 15–; **G.**U. 12–; **Ld.**U. 59–; **Lv.**U. 03–; **N.**U. 11– imp.; **Nw.**A. 27–; **O.**R. 23–; **R.**U. 27–38; **Sh.**SC. 11–; **Y.**
   Compte-rendu de la **Station biologique** de la **Tour** du **Valat.** *See* 15152°.

15276 **Compte-rendu. Station hydrobiologique Lac** de **Wigry.** *C. r. Stn hydrobiol. Lac de Wigry* [1925–] **Pl.**M. 25.

15277 **Compte rendu** des **travaux** de l'**Association générale** des **médecins** de **France.** Toulouse. *C. r. Trav. Ass. gén. Méd. Fr.*

15278 **Compte rendu** des **travaux** du **Comité central** de **culture mécanique.** Paris. *C. r. Trav. Com. cent. Cult. méc.* **L.**SC. 24–.

15279 **Compte rendu** des **travaux. Commission météorologique** de la **Haute-Vienne.** Limoges. *C. r. Trav. Commn mét. Hte-Vienne*

15280 **Compte-rendu** des **travaux** effectués par les **Congrès** de l'**agriculture française.** Paris. *C. r. Trav. Congr. Agric. fr.* **L.**AM. 30–36.

15280° **Compte rendu** des **travaux. Congrès** de l'**habitation.** Lyon. *C. r. Trav. Congr. Habit.*

15281 **Compte rendu** des **travaux. Congrès national** des **travaux publics français.** Paris. *C. r. Trav. Congr. natn. Trav. publ. fr.*

15282 **Compte rendu** des **travaux. Congrès** de **physiothérapie.** Paris. *C. r. Trav. Congr. Physiothér.*

15283 **Compte rendu** des **travaux. Congrès** de la **technique** du **bureau.** Paris. *C. r. Trav. Congr. Tech. Bur.* **L.**P. 35–36.

15284 **Compte rendu** des **travaux. Conseil central** d'**hygiène publique** et de **salubrité** du **département** d'**Eure-et-Loir.** Chartres. *C. r. Trav. Cons. cent. Hyg. publ. Salub. Dép. Eure-et-Loir*

15285 **Compte rendu** des **travaux** du **Conseil central** d'**hygiène publique** et de **salubrité** du **département** de la **Loire.** *C. r. Trav. Cons. cent. Hyg. publ. Salub. Dép. Loire*

15286 **Compte rendu** des **travaux** du **Conseil départemental** d'**hygiène** et des **commissions sanitaires** du **département** des **Basses-Alpes.** Digne. *C. r. Trav. Cons. dép. Hyg. Commns sanit. Dép. Basses-Alpes*

15287 **Compte rendu** des **travaux. Conseil d'hygiène** du **département** de l'**Ardèche.** Aubenas. *C. r. Trav. Cons. Hyg. Dép. Ardèche*

15288 **Compte rendu** des **travaux** du **Conseil d'hygiène publique** et de **salubrité** du **département** d'**Alger.** Alger. *C. r. Trav. Cons. Hyg. publ. Salub. Dép. Alger.*

15289 **Compte rendu** des **travaux** du **Conseil d'hygiène publique** et de **salubrité** de **Vaucluse.** Avignon. *C. r. Trav. Cons. Hyg. publ. Salub. Vaucluse*

15290 **Compte rendu** des **travaux** des **conseils** d'**hygiène** et de **salubrité** des **Bouches-du-Rhône.** Marseille. *C. r. Trav. Conseils Hyg. Salub. Bouches-du-Rhône*

15291 **Compte rendu** des **travaux** des **conseils** d'**hygiène** et de **salubrité** de la **Côte d'Or.** Dijon. *C. r. Trav. Conseils Hyg. Salub. Côte d'Or*

15292 **Compte rendu** des **travaux** des **conseils** d'**hygiène** et de **salubrité** de l'**Hérault.** Montpellier. *C. r. Trav. Conseils Hyg. Salub. Hérault*

15293 **Compte rendu** des **travaux** de la **Faculté** des **sciences** de **Marseille.** *C. r. Trav. Fac. Sci. Marseille* [1941–] **L.**BM^N. 41–43; **L.** 47–; SC.; **E.**R. 41.

15294 **Compte rendu** des **travaux** des **facultés** et de l'**École** de **médecine** et de **pharmacie** de l'**Université** de **Grenoble.** Grenoble. *C. r. Trav. Facs Éc. Méd. Pharm. Univ. Grenoble* [1949–] **L.**BM. 51–.

15295 **Compte rendu** des **travaux** des **facultés** de **Toulouse.** *C. r. Trav. Facs Toulouse*

15296 **Compte rendu** des **travaux** des **facultés** de l'**Université** de **Bordeaux.** *C. r. Trav. Facs Univ. Bordeaux*

15297 **Compte rendu** des **travaux. Institut** de **recherches agronomiques** de l'**Indochine.** Hanoï. *C. r. Trav. Inst. Rech. agron. Indochine* **L.**SC. 32–; **C.**A. 32–; **Rt.** 34: 37.

15298 **Compte rendu** des **travaux** du **Laboratoire** de **Carlsberg.** Copenhague. *C. r. Trav. Lab. Carlsberg* [1878–] **L.**BM^N.; C.; K. 52–; LI.; MA. (chim.) 41–: (phys.) 40–; MC.; MD. 47–; P. 09–; R. (chim.) 37–39: (phys.) 36–40; RI. (chim.) 51–: (phys.) 50–; SC.; UC. 00–03; **Abd.**R. 35–; **Abs.**U. 17– imp.; **Ba.**I. 27–; **Bm.**U.; **Bn.**U. (phys.) 50–57; **Br.**U. (chim.) 38–; **C.**A. (phys.) 35–58: 58–; B. 07–; BI. 35–; P. 17–; PH. 09–25: 30 imp.; **Dm.** 09–30 imp.; **E.**R. 17–; U. 14–; **Ep.**D. 47–; **G.**U. 07– imp.; **H.**U. (phys.) 40–51; **Ld.**U. 10–; **Lv.**U.; **M.**T. 03–15: 40–; **N.**U. 12–35 imp.; **Nu.**B. (chim.) 51–: (phys.) 50–; **Nw.**A. 49–; **O.**R.; **Pl.**M.; **R.**D. 49–; **Rt.** 07–; **Sh.**U. (chim.) 38–: (phys.) 40–; **Y.** [From 1935–58 *divided into Série chimique* and *Série physiologique; French edition of:* 29898]

15299 **Compte rendu** des **travaux** effectués par les **offices agricoles régionaux** et **départementaux.** Paris. *C. r. Trav. Offs agric. rég. dép.* **L.**AM. 30–33.

15300 **Compte rendu** des **travaux** de la **Société** des **agriculteurs** de **France.** Paris. *C. r. Trav. Soc. Agric. Fr.* [1869–] **L.**AM. 69–05 imp.; EB. 13–27; **Rt.** 90–99.

     Compte rendu des **travaux** de la **Société helvétique** des **sciences naturelles.** *See* 56067.

15301 **Compte rendu** des **travaux** de la **Société** de **médecine** d'**Angers.** *C. r. Trav. Soc. Méd. Angers*

15302 **Compte rendu** des **travaux** de la **Société** de **médecine** de **Toulouse.** *C. r. Trav. Soc. Méd. Toulouse*

15303 **Compte rendu** des **travaux** de la **Société médicale** des **Alpes-maritimes.** Nice. *C. r. Trav. Soc. méd. Alpes-marit.*

15304 **Compte rendu** des **travaux** de la **Société médicale** de **Chambéry.** *C. r. Trav. Soc. méd. Chambéry*

15305 **Compte rendu** des **travaux** de la **Société médicale** de l'**Yonne.** Auxerre. *C. r. Trav. Soc. méd. Yonne*

15306 **Compte rendu** des **travaux** de la **Société** des **sciences médicales** de **Gannat.** *C. r. Trav. Soc. Sci. méd. Gannat*

     Compte rendu des **travaux spéciaux** de l'**Institut vétérinaire** à **Kharkoff.** *See* 48690.

15307 **Compte rendu trimestriel. Centre technique** des **industries** de la **fonderie.** Paris. *C. r. trimest. Cent. tech. Ind. Fond.* [1950–] **Bm.**C. 50–52. [*C. of:* 15211]

     Compte rendu. Wrocławskie towarzystwo naukowe. *See* 15270.

     Comptes rendus. *See* **Compte rendu.**

15308 **Computer Abstracts.** London. *Comput. Abstr.* [1960–] **L.**AV.; P.; SC.; **E.**A.; **Ha.**RD.; **Ld.**U.; **Ma.**T.; **Y.** [*C. from:* 15309]

15309 **Computer Bibliography.** London. *Comput. Biblphy* [1959] **L.**AV.; P.; SC.; **Ld.**U.; **Ma.**T.; **Y.** [*C. of:* 15313; *C. as:* 15308 and 15312]

15310 **Computer Bulletin.** London. *Comput. Bull.* [1957–] **L.**AV.; BM.; C. 58–; MO. 58–; P.; SC.; **Bm.**P.; **Bn.**U. 58–; **Co.**T. 61–; **Cr.**U.; **E.**A.; **G.**T.; **H.**U.; **Ld.**U.; **Te.**N.; **W.** 58–; **Wl.**H. 62–; **Y.**

15311 **Computer Journal.** London. *Comput. J.* [1958–] L.AV.; BM.; C.; EE.; MO. 58–; P.; SC.; **Bm.**P.; **Bn.**U.; **Co.**T.; **Cr.**U.; **Dn.**U.; E.A.; O. 60–; **Ex.**U.; **G.**T. H.U.; **Ld.**P.; U.; W.; **M.**P.; **Ma.**T.; O.R.; Rt.; **Sw.**U.; **Y.**

15312 **Computer News.** London. *Comput. News* [1960–] L.AV.; P.; SC.; **Ld.**U. 61–; **Y.** [*C. from:* 15309]

15313 **Computers.** Iota Services Ltd. Monthly Bibliographical Series. *Computers* [1957–58] L.AV.; P.; **Ld.**U.; **Y.** [*C. as:* 15309]

15314 **Computers** and **Automation.** New York. *Computers Automn* [1953–] L.AV. imp.; P.; SC. 54–; F.A. 54–; **Ld.**U. 53–60 imp.; **M.**T. 54–; Rt.; **Sh.**U. 59–; **Y.** [*C. of:* 15315]

15315 **Computing Machinery Field.** New York. *Computg Mach. Fld* [1952–53] L.AV.; P. imp.; **Ld.**U. imp. [*C. as:* 15314]

15316 **Computing Reviews.** New York. *Computg Rev.* [1960–] L.P.; **Ld.**U.; **Y.**

15317 **Computor News.** Short Brothers and Harland Ltd. London. *Computor News* [1957–] L.P.

15318 **Comtat agricole.** Carpentras. *Comtat agric.*

15319 **Comunicaciones antropologias** del **Museo** de **historia natural** de **Montevideo.** Montevideo. *Comun. antrop. Mus. Hist. nat. Montev.* [1956–] L.BMᴺ.; C.P.

15320 **Comunicaciones botanicas** del **Museo** de **historia natural** de **Montevideo.** *Comun. bot. Mus. Hist. nat. Montev.* [1942–] L.BMᴺ. 42–45; K.; L. 46–; C.P. **Pl.**M. 58–.

15321 **Comunicaciones científicas agrícolas.** Turrialba. *Comun. cient. agríc.* [1955–] C.A. 56–; O.F. 57–.

15322 **Comunicaciones científicas** del **Museo** de la **Plata.** *Comun. cient. Mus. La Plata* [1951–] L.BMᴺ. 51; Z. 51–52; E.R.

15323 **Comunicaciones. Herbarium Cornelius Osten.** Montevideo. *Comun. Herb. Cornelius Osten* L.BMᴺ. 25: 32; **Lv.**U. 25–.

15324 **Comunicaciones. Instituto forestal** de **investigaciones y experiencias.** Madrid. *Comun. Inst. for. Invest. Exp.* [1955–] O.F.; **Y.**

15325 **Comunicaciones** del **Instituto nacional** de **investigación** de las **ciencias naturales** y **museo argentino** de **ciencias naturales 'Bernardino Rivadavia'.** Buenos Aires. *Comun. Inst. nac. Invest. Cienc. nat., B. Aires* [1948–56]
   Ciencias botánicas: L.BMᴺ.; R.; **Bl.**U.; **Wo.** 48–54; **Y.**
   Ciencias geológicas: L.BMᴺ.; R.; **Bl.**U.; **C.**PO.; **Wo.** 48–54; **Y.**
   Ciencias zoológicas: L.BMᴺ.; EB. (ent.); R.; Z.; **Bl.**U.; **C.**PO. 51–56; **Wo.** 49–54; **Y.** [*C. as:* 15327]

15325° **Comunicaciones. Instituto nacional** de **investigaciones agronómicas.** Madrid. *Comun. Inst. nac. Invest. agron.* [1955–]

15326 **Comunicaciones** del **Instituto tropical** de **investigaciones científicas.** San Salvador. *Comun. Inst. trop. Invest. cient. S Salv.* [1952–] L.BMᴺ. 52– imp.; SC.; **Db.**

15327 **Comunicaciones** del **Museo argentino** de **ciencias naturales Bernardino Rivadavia** e **Instituto nacional** de **investigación** de las **ciencias naturales.** Buenos Aires. *Comun. Mus. argent. Cienc. nat. Bernardino Rivadavia*

Ciencias botánicas [1957–] L.BMᴺ.; R.; **Bl.**U.; **Y.**
Ciencias zoológicas [1957–] L.BMᴺ.; EB. (ent.); R.; Z.; **Bl.**U.; **Pl.**M.; **Wo.**; **Y.**
Ciencias geológicas [1957–] L.BMᴺ.; R.; **Bl.**U.; **Y.** [*C. of:* 15325]

15328 **Comunicaciones** del **Museo** de **Concepción.** *Comun. Mus. Concepción* L.BMᴺ. 36.

15329 **Comunicaciones** del **Museo nacional** de **Buenos Aires.** *Comun. Mus. nac. B. Aires* [1898–01] L.BMᴺ.; E.; GL.; R.; SC.; Z.; **Bl.**U.; **Bm.**N.; **Db.**; E.R.; G.N.; **Lv.**U.; **Pl.**M. [*C. as:* 15330]

15330 **Comunicaciones** del **Museo nacional** de **historia natural Bernardino Rivadavia.** Buenos Aires. *Comun. Mus. nac. Hist. nat. Bernardino Rivadavia* [1923–25] L.BMᴺ.; L.; Z.; E.R. [*C. of:* 15329]

15331 **Comunicaciones** del **Observatorio** de **Santiago.** *Comun. Obs. Santiago* L.AS. 47–.

15332 **Comunicaciones técnicas. Dirección general** de **fomento agrícola.** Buenos Aires. *Comun. téc. Dir. gen. Fom. agríc.* [1946–] **Y.**

15332° **Comunicaciones técnicas. División hortalizas, Dirección general** de **fomento agrícola.** Buenos Aires. *Comun. téc. Div. hort., B. Aires* **Y.**

15333 **Comunicaciones** de **Turrialba.** Turrialba. *Comun. Turrialba* [1952–] C.A. imp.

15334 **Comunicaciones zoológicas** del **Museo** de **historia natural** de **Montevideo.** *Comun. zool. Mus. Hist. nat. Montev.* [1943–] L.BMᴺ.; L. 49–; Z. 39–; C.P. 43–; **Pl.**M. 56–.

15335 **Comunicações** da **Commissão** dos **trabalhos** do **Serviço geológico** de **Portugal.** Lisboa. *Comunçoes Comm. Trab. Serv. geol. Port.* [1883–17] L.BM.; BMᴺ.; GL.; GM. 85–17; UC. 83–07; **Br.**U.; C.P.; S.; E.D.; G.G.; O.R. [*C. as:* 15336]

15336 **Comunicações** dos **serviços geológicos** de **Portugal.** Lisboa. *Comunções Servs geol. Port.* [1919–] L.BM.; BMᴺ.; GL.; GM.; MI.; C.P.; S.; **Db.** 43–; E.D.; G.G.; **Lv.**U. 46; O.R. [*C. of:* 15335]

15336ᵃ **Comunicado científico. Instituto** de **micologia, Universidade** do **Recife.** Recife. *Comunicado cient. Inst. Micol. Univ. Recife* [1957–] Rt. 57.

15337 **Comunicado técnico. Instituto** de **ecologia** e **experimentação agrícolas.** Rio de Janeiro. *Comunicado téc. Inst. Ecol. Exp. agríc., Rio de J.* [1957–] **Y.**

15338 **Comunicado técnico. Universidade rural** de **Pernambuco.** *Comunicado téc. Univ. rur. Pernamb.* [1956–]

15339 **Comunicările Academiei republicii populare române.** București. *Comunle Acad. Rep. pop. rom.* [1951–] L.BMᴺ.; P. 55–; SC. 55–; Fr.; **Y.**

15340 **Comunicările** de **botanică.** București. *Comunle Bot.* L.BMᴺ. 60–.

15341 **Comunicările Laboratorului** de **chimie agricola.** Iași. *Comunle Lab. Chim. agric.* L.SC. 36–; Rt. 37.

15342 **Comunicările** de **zoologie.** București. *Comunle Zool.* L.BMᴺ. 57–.

15343 **Comunicazioni aeree.** Roma. *Comunicaz. aeree*

15343° **Comunicazioni e rassegne. Osservatorio astronomico** di **Padova.** Padova. *Comunicaz. Rass. Oss. astr. Padova* M.U. 56–58.

15344 **Comunicazioni** della **Specola (astronomica) vaticana.** Roma. *Comunicaz. Spec. astr. vatic.* L.AS. 37–; SC. 54–; E.R. 56–; M.U. 54–59.
Série 1. **Y.**

15345 **Concentrated Milk Industries.** Milwaukee. *Concent. Milk Ind.*

15346 **Conchological Magazine.** Kyoto. *Conch. Mag.* L.BM^N. 07–09; SC. 08–09.

15347 **Conciatore.** Torino. *Conciatore*

15348 **Concord.** Liverpool. *Concord* L.P. 28–39.

15349 **Concours médical.** Paris. *Concours méd.* [1879–] L.MA. 49–; MD. 79–07: 59– imp.

15350 **Concours pharmaceutique.** Paris. *Concours pharm.*

15351 **Concrete.** Detroit. *Concrete, Detroit.* [*C. as:* 15379^c]

15352 **Concrete.** New York. *Concrete, N.Y.* [1916–] L.P. 18–57 imp.; SC. (Cement Mill edition) 34–; Bm.U. 22–36; Wa.B. 26–61. [*C. of:* 15379^c]

15353 **Concrete Age.** Atlanta, Ga. *Concr. Age, Atlanta* [1905–23] L.BM. 23.

15354 **Concrete Age.** London. *Concr. Age, Lond.* L.P. 29–31.

15355 **Concrete** in **Architecture.** London. *Concr. Archit.* [1936] L.P.

15356 **Concrete Builder.** Chicago. *Concr. Bldr, Chicago* [1918–] [*Suspended* 1923–31]

15357 **Concrete** for the **Builder.** London. *Concr. Bldr, Lond.* [1926–28] L.BM.; SC. imp.; Abs.N.; O.B. [*C. as:* 15358]

15358 **Concrete Building** and **Concrete Products.** London. *Concr. Bldg Concr. Prod.* [1929–] L.BM.; P. 40–; Abs.N.; O.B.; Wa.B. (1 yr); Y. [*C. of:* 15357]

15360 **Concrete** in **Collieries.** London. *Concr. Collier.* [1947–] L.SC.
Concrete Construction. *See* 33963.

15361 **Concrete** and **Constructional Engineering.** London. *Concr. constr. Engng* [1906–] L.AV. 46–; BA.; BM.; IC. 29–; P.; QM. 48–; SC. 21–; UC. 39–; Abd.U. 27– imp.; Bl.U. 18– imp.; Br.P. 17–; T. 07–; U. 45–; Br.P. (1 yr); U.; C.ENG. 41–; UL.; Cr.U. 29–; Db. 26–; Dn.U. 52–; F.A. 53–; G.M. 07–; T. 33–; U. 31–; Ld.P. 52–; U. 34–; Lv.P. 09–; U. 10– imp.; M.P. 24–; T. 07; U. 58–; N.T. 18–; U. 34–; Nw.A. 37–; O.R.; Sh.SC.; U. 06–29 imp.: 38–; Sw.U. 48–; Y.

15362 **Concrete Craft.** New York. *Concr. Craft* [1919]

15363 **Concrete Engineering.** Cleveland, O. *Concr. Engng* [1907–10] [*C. in:* 13505]

15364 **Concrete Era.** Los Angeles. *Concr. Era*

15365 **Concrete Highway Magazine.** Chicago. *Concr. Highw. Mag.*

15366 **Concrete Highways.** Philadelphia. *Concr. Highws* Ha.RD. (2 yr.) [*C. of:* 15375]

15367 **Concrete Information.** Portland Cement Association. Chicago. *Concr. Inf.* [1934–] **Y.**

15368 **Concrete Manufacturer.** Chicago. *Concr. Mfr* L.P. 54–. [*Supplement to:* 37808]

15369 **Concrete Masonry Review.** Beverley Hills. *Concr. Mason. Rev.* [1953–] L.P. imp.

15370 **Concrete Memoranda.** Cement and Concrete Association. London. *Concr. Memor.* [1937–] L.BM.; P. 37–40 imp.; SC.; Ld.P. imp.

15371 **Concrete Products.** Chicago. *Concr. Prod.* [1918–36] L.SC. 27–28.

15372 **Concrete Quarterly.** London. *Concr. Q.* [1947–] L.AM. 50–; BA.; BM.; LE. 62–; NP. (2 yr.); P.; QM. 50–; Bl.U. 50–; Bm.T. 48–; U.; Br.U.; Cr.M. 59– imp.; Dn.U.; E.HW. 49–; U. 49–; Lc.A.; Ld.P. (5 yr.); Lv.P. 52–; M.U. 49–; N.T. (5 yr.); Nw.A. 49–; Sh.IO. 51–; Sil. (1 yr); Sw.U. 52–; Y.

15373 **Concrete** for **Railways.** Chicago. *Concr. Rlys* **Y.**

15373^a **Concrete** and **Reinforced Concrete.** *Concr. reinf. Concr.* **Y.** 57–. [*English abstracts of:* 6503]

15374 **Concrete Research.** London. *Concr. Res.* [1949–] L.BA.

15375 **Concrete Review.** Philadelphia. *Concr. Rev.* [*C. as:* 15366]

15376 **Concrete Road Surfacing. Leaflets.** Cement and Concrete Association. London. *Concr. Rd Surf. Leafl.* [1938–] L.BM.; P.; SC.
Concrete and **Steel.** Berlin. *See* 6499.

15377 **Concrete Structure** and **Technology Reports.** Imperial College of Science and Technology. London. *Concr. Struct. Technol. Rep.* L.P. 60– imp.

15378 **Concrete Way.** London. *Concr. Way* [1928–37] L.P.; Cr.P.; M.U. [*C. of:* 48026]

15379 **Concrete Year Book.** London. *Concr. Yb.* [1924–] L.BM. 25–; KC. 53–; P. (curr.); Abs.N.; Bm.P.; Br.U. 29–; E.A.; T. 32– imp.; G.M. 29– imp.; Ld.P. 35– imp.; U. 34– imp.; Lv.P. 31– imp.; M.P. imp.; O.B.; Sh.P.; Sw.U. 48–; Y.

15379^c **Concrete-Cement Age.** Detroit. *Concr.-Cem. Age* [1912–15] L.P. [*C. of:* 15351; *C. as:* 15352]

15380 **Concreto.** Valparaíso. *Concreto*

15381 **Condensed Catalogue** of **Mechanical Equipment.** New York. *Cond. Cat. mech. Equip.* L.P. 12–29*. [*C. as:* 29750]

15382 **Conditions** for **Industrial Health** and **Efficiency.** Industrial Health Research Board. London. *Condit. ind. Hlth Effic.* [1943–45] L.P.; SC.; Bm.U.

15383 **Condon Lectures.** Eugene. *Condon Lect.*

15384 **Condor.** Santa Clara, Cal. *Condor* [1900–] L.BM^N.; NC. 38–50 imp.: 59–; SC. 03–; Z.; Abd.U. 26–; Br.U. 03–; C.B. 28–40 imp.: 44–; E.PO. 55–; O.AP. 42–50 imp.: 57–58; OR. 15–; Y.

15384^c **Confectioner, Baker** and **Restaurateur.** London. *Confectr Bak. Restaur.* [1939–] L.BM.; P. [*C. of:* 8802]

15385 **Confectionery Manufacture.** London. *Confect. Mf.* [1955–] L.AM.; BM.; Ld.U. 61–; Lh.FO.; Y.

15386 **Confectionery Production.** London. *Confect. Prod.* [1935–] L.BM.; P.; TP. 57–; Lh.FO. 38–; P. 46–; Lv.P. 50– imp.; M.P. 54–; Sh.IO. 42–; Y.

15387 **Confectionery Studies.** National Confectioners' Association. Chicago. *Confect. Stud.* [1930–]
Confédération générale des **agriculteurs** de **France.** *See* 12881.
Conference on **Administrative Medicine.** *See* 53672.
Conference on the **Adrenal Cortex.** *See* 925.
Conference. All-India Conference of **Medical Research Workers.** *See* 38814.

15388 **Conférence. Association française** des **chimistes** des **industries** du **cuir.** Paris. *Conf. Ass. fr. Chim. Ind. Cuir* [1948–] **L.**P.; **Y.**

15389 **Conference** of the **British Coke Research Association.** London. *Conf. Br. Coke Res. Ass.* [1944–] **L.**P. 44–53; **Y.**

15390 **Conference Bulletin. Pacific Coast Building Officials Conference.** Los Angeles. *Conf. Bull. Pacif. Cst Bldg Off. Conf.* [1933–35] [*C. as:* 9080]
Conference on **Central Nervous System** and **Behaviour.** *See* 13537ᶜ.
Conference on **Cold Injury.** *See* 14713.

15391 **Conference** on **Cotton-Growing Problems.** Empire Cotton Growing Corporation. London. *Conf. Cott.-Grow. Probl.* [1930–38] **L.**BM.; P.; **M.**C.; **Rt.**; **Y.**

15392 **Conference** on **Extremely High Temperatures.** Air Force Cambridge Research Center. New York, London. *Conf. extrem. high Temp.* [1958–] **L.**P.; SC.

15393 **Conférence forestier interafricaine. C.C.T.A.** Nogent-sur-Marne. *Conf. for. interafr.* [1951–] **O.**F.
Conference on **Glaucoma.** *See* 21382.
Conference of **Group Processes.** *See* 21585.
Conference on **Magnetism** and **Magnetic Materials.** *See* 39741.

15394 **Conference** on **Mechanical Wood Technology.** F.A.O., Rome. *Conf. mech. Wood Technol.* [1949–] **O.**F.

15395 **Conference** on **Mechanized Farming.** Oxford. *Conf. mechd Fmg* [1936–37] **L.**BM. 37; P.; **C.**A.; **Rt.** [*C. as:* 36646]
Conference on **Neuropharmacology.** *See* 34612.

15396 **Conference. Oil** and **Colour Chemists Association.** London. *Conf. Oil Colour Chem. Ass.* [1937–] **L.**P.

15397 **Conference Papers. Chicago Medical Society.** Chicago. *Conf. Pap. Chicago Med. Soc.* **L.**MD. 46–.

15397ᶜ **Conference Papers. Conference** on **Electronic Computation,** American Society of Civil Engineers. New York. *Conf. Pap. Conf. electron. Comput.* [1959–] **L.**P.
Conference on **Polysaccharides** in **Biology.** *See* 38069.
Conference on **Problems** of **Aging.** *See* 53678.
Conference on **Problems** of **Consciousness.** *See* 38753.
Conference on **Problems** of **Infancy** and **Childhood.** *See* 38757.
Conference Proceedings. British Coke Research Association. *See* 15389.

15398 **Conference** on **Pulverised Fuel.** London. *Conf. pulv. Fuel* [1947–] **L.**SC.

15398ᵃ **Conference Report. Air Pollution Research Seminar.** Washington. *Conf. Rep. Air. Pollut. Res. Semin.* **L.**P. 60–.
Conference Reports. Botanical Society of the **British Isles.** *See* 5683ᵃ.

15399 **Conference Reports. South-Eastern Agricultural College.** Wye, Kent. *Conf. Rep. S.-East. agric. Coll.* [1946–] **C.**A.

15400 **Conference** of **Scientific Research Workers** on **Cotton** in **India.** Bombay. *Conf. scient. Res. Wkrs Cott. India* [1937–] **L.**P. 37.
Conference on **Shock** and **Circulatory Homeostasis.** *See* 49668.

15400ᵃ **Conference** on **Silicosis** and **Aluminium Therapy.** McIntyre Research Foundation. Toronto. *Conf. Silicosis Alumin. Ther.* **Y.**

15401 **Conférence. Société** de **technique pharmaceutique.** Paris. *Conf. Soc. Tech. pharm.* **L.**P. 53–. [*Issued as section of:* 52497]

15402 **Conference** on **Weights** and **Measures** of the **U.S. Bureau** of **Standards.** Washington. *Conf. Wghts Meas. U.S. Bur. Stand.* [1905–07] **L.**BM.; P.; SC.; **Bm.**P.; **M.**U. [*C. as:* 57274]

15403 **Conférences d'actualités scientifiques** et **industrielles.** Paris. *Confs Actual. scient. ind.* [1929–31] **L.**SC. 30–31; **C.**UL.; **E.**C. 30–31; **O.**R. imp. [*C. as:* 901]
Conférences. Association française des **chimistes** des **industries** du **cuir.** *See* 15388.

15405 **Conférences. Centre** de **recherches** et d'**études océanographiques.** Paris. *Confs Cent. Rech. Étud. oceanogr.* [1950–] **L.**MO. 50–53 imp.; **Lv.**U.
Conferences. Empire Cotton Growing Corporation. London. *See* 15391.

15406 **Conférences I.F.A.C.** Institut des fruits et agrumes coloniaux. Paris. *Confs I.F.A.C.* [1944–] **L.**SC.

15407 **Conférences internationales** de **sciences mathématiques** organisées à l'**Université** de **Genève.** *Confs int. Sci. math. Univ. Genève* **L.**BM. 38–.

15408 **Conférences** du **Palais** de la **découverte.** Paris. *Confs Palais Découv.*
Ser. D. Histoire des sciences **L.**BM. 52–.

15409 **Conférences** faites à la **Société chimique** de **Paris.** *Confs Soc. chim. Paris* [1883–] **L.**BM. 87–00; C. 04–; P. 83–00; SC.

15410 **Conférences. Société** d'**encouragement** pour l'**industrie nationale.** Paris. *Confs Soc. Encour. Ind. natn.* [1946–] **L.**P. 46–48. [*Replaced by:* 23338]

15410ᶜ **Conférences. Société** de **technique pharmaceutique.** Paris. *Confs Soc. Tech. pharm.* **L.**P. 53–.

15411 **Conferencia sanitaria nacional** de **Venezuela.** Caracas. *Confcia sanit. nac. Venez.* **L.**EB. 31; TD. 30–31.

15412 **Conferencia** de la **Sección** de **ciencias naturales. Sociedad científica argentina.** Buenos Aires. *Confcia Secc. Cienc. nat. Soc. cient. argent.* **L.**BM. 16–.

15413 **Conferencia sul-americana** de **hygiene, microbiologia** e **pathologia.** *Confcia sul-am. Hyg. Microbiol. Path.* **L.**TD. 31.

15414 **Conferencias clínicas** de **urología.** Madrid. *Confcias clín. Urol.*

15415 **Conferencias** de **divulgación científica. Universidad** de **Chile.** Santiago. *Confcias Divulg. cient. Univ. Chile* **Sa.** 30–.

15416 **Conferencias. Escuela especial** de **ingenieros** de **caminos canales** y **puertos.** Madrid. *Confcias Esc. esp. Ing. Camin. Canal. Puertos* **L.**P. 26–34⋆.

15416ᶜ **Conferencias. Instituto nacional** de **investigaciones agronómicas.** Madrid. *Confcias Inst. nac. Invest. agron.* [1958–] **L.**BMᴺ. 59–; **Y.**

15417 **Conferencias** y **reseñas científicas** de la **R. Sociedad española** de **historia natural.** Madrid. *Confcias Reseñ. cient. R. Soc. esp. Hist. nat.* [1926–30] **L.**BMᴺ.; SC.; Z.; **C.**UL.; **O.**R. [*C. as:* 46037]

15418 **Conferencias** de la **Sociedad meteorológica** de **Bolivia.** La Paz. *Confcias Soc. met. Boliv.* [1944–] **L.**sc.

15419 **Conferenze tecniche. Scuola** di **applicazione** per gli **ingegneri, Università** di **Padova.** *Confze tec. Scu. Applic. Ing. Univ. Padova* **C.**UL. 09–13*.

15420 **Confiance.** Bulletin de l'oeuvre nationale belge de lutte contre le cancer. Bruxelles. *Confiance* [1947–] **L.**H. 55–.

15421 **Confidential Bulletin. British Timken Ltd.** Birmingham. *Confid. Bull. Br. Timken* [1949–52] **L.**BM.; P. [*C. as:* 9634]

15422 **Confidential Summaries** of **Road Research.** Road Research Board. D.S.I.R. London. *Confid. Summ. Rd Res.* [1946–] **Bl.**U.

15423 **Confinia neurologica.** Basel. etc. *Confinia neurol.* [1938–] **L.**MA. 46–; MD.; S. 38–50; UC. 39–45; **C.**AN. 39; **E.**P.; **O.**R.

15424 **Confinia psychiatrica.** Basel, N.Y. *Confinia psychiat.* [1958–] **L.**MD.

15425 **Confluence.** Cambridge, Mass. *Confluence* [1952–] **L.**BM.; U. 52–58; **Bl.**U.; **Bm.**U.; **C.**UL.; **Ld.**U. 52–57; **M.**P.; **N.**U.; **O.**B.

15426 **Confrontations radio-anatomo-cliniques.** Paris. *Confront. radio-anat.-clin.* [1946–54] **L.**S.

15427 **Congo.** Revue générale de la colonie belge. Bruxelles. *Congo* [1920–39] **L.**AN.; BM. 23–39; G. [*C. as:* 58263]

15427° **Congo-Tervuren.** Amis du Musée r. du Congo belge. Tervuren. *Congo-Tervuren* [1955–60] **L.**BM^N.; Z. [*C. as:* Africa-Tervuren]

15428 **Congrès agricole. Association bretonne.** Paris. *Congrès agric. Ass. breton.*

15429 **Congrès** de l'**alimentation.** Liège. *Congrès Aliment.*

15430 **Congrès annuel** de l'**Association parisienne** des **propriétaires** d'**appareils à vapeur.** Paris. *Congrès a. Ass. paris. Propr. Appar. Vap.*

15431 **Congrès** de l'**Association** des **gynécologues** et d'**obstétriciens** de **langue française.** Paris. *Congrès Ass. Gynéc. Obstét. Lang. fr.* [1920–50] **Dn.**U. [*Issue for* 1950 *contained in* 21683; *C. as:* 15435]

15432 **Congrès** pour l'**avancement** des **études** de **stratigraphie carbonifère.** Heerlen. *Congrès Avanc. Étud. Stratigr. carb.* [1927–] **Br.**U. 35; **G.**U. 27–35; **O.**R.

15433 **Congrès belge** de **chirurgie.** Bruxelles. *Congrès belge Chir.*

Congrès belge de **neurologie** et de **psychiatrie.** *See* 42030.

15434 **Congrès** de **chimie industrielle.** Paris, etc. *Congrès Chim. ind.* [1921–] **L.**C. 23–; P. 23–; SC. 24–41; **Rt.** 23. [1921–22 *published in* 13911]

Congrès dentaire national. Paris. *See* 15181.
Congrès dentaire national belge. *See* 15182.
Congrès égyptien de **médecine.** *See* 15184.
Congrès de la **Faculté catholique** et **française** de **médecine** de **Beyrouth.** *See* 15185.

15435 **Congrès** de la **Fédération** des **sociétés** de **gynécologie** et d'**obstétrique.** Paris. *Congrès Féd. Socs Gynéc. Obstét.* [1952–] **Dn.**U. [*C. of:* 15431]

Congrès du **froid tropicale.** Marseille. *See* 15187.

15436 **Congrès** du **G. A. M. S.** Groupement pour l'avancement des méthodes d'analyse spectrographique des produits métallurgiques. Paris. *Congrès G. A. M. S., Paris* [1946–] **L.**I.; NF.; P. 46: 49–; SC.; **Bm.**C. 46–48; **G.**U.

Congrès des **grands barrages.** *See* 15189.

15437 **Congrès** de l'**hygiène** et de la **securité** des **travailleurs** et des **ateliers.** Paris. *Congrès Hyg. Secur. Travaill. Atel.*

15438 **Congrès inter-départemental algérien, commercial, agricole** et **industriel.** Alger. *Congrès inter.-dép. algér. comml agric. ind.*

Congrès de **médecins aliénistes** de **France** et des **pays** de **langue française.** *See* 15218.

Congrès de **médecine légale** de **langue française.** *See* 15194.

15439 **Congrès** de **médecine** des **pays** du **Nord.** *Congrès Méd. Pays N.* **L.**TD. 21–27. [*Supplement to:* 648]

15440 **Congrès national** de l'**aviation française.** Paris. *Congrès natn. Aviat. fr.* **O.**R. (sect. 3) 45–.

15441 **Congrès national** des **syndicats agricoles.** *Congrès natn. Synds agric.* **C.**UL. 04–07.

Congrès national des **travaux publics français.** *See* 15281.

15442 **Congrès** des **pédiatres** de **langue française.** Paris. *Congrès Pédiat. Lang. fr.* [*C. of:* 15162]

15443 **Congrès pomologique. Société pomologique** de **France.** Villefranche-sur-Saône. *Congrès pomol.* **Md.**H. 50: 52–.

15444 **Congrès** des **practiciens. Assemblée nationale** des **médecins** de **France.** Paris. *Congrès Practns Assembl. natn. Méd. Fr.*

15445 **Congrès** de la **Société française** d'**oto-rhino-laryngologie.** Paris. *Congrès Soc. fr. Oto-rhino-lar.* [1923–] **L.**MD. 23–36 imp.; **Bm.**U. 23–25; **E.**S. 37–48 imp. [*C. of:* 11954]

Congrès de la **Société internationale** de **chirurgie.** *See* International Congress Section.

15446 **Congrès** des **sociétés normandes scientifiques, artistiques** et **littéraires.** Le Havre. *Congrès Socs normandes scient.*

15447 **Congreso argentino** de **cirugia.** Buenos Aires, etc. *Congreso argent. Cirug.* [1928–] **L.**S. 30–49: 52: 57; **Bm.**U. 30–33: **Br.**U. 30–31; **E.**U. 28–37; **O.**R.

15448 **Congreso español** de **geografía colonial** y **mercantil.** Madrid. *Congreso esp. Geogr. colon. merc.*

15449 **Congreso médico pan-americano. Sesiones generales.** Habana. *Congreso méd. pan-am.*

15450 **Congreso nacional** de **pesquerias maritímas** e **industrias derivadas.** Buenos Aires. *Congreso nac. Pesq. marit., B. Aires* [1949–] **L.**BM.; BM^N.

15451 **Congreso sudamericano** de **dermatología** y **sifilografía.** *Congreso sudam. Derm. Sif.* **L.**TD. 21.

15452 **Congress Bulletin. South Eastern Union** of **Scientific Societies.** London. *Congress Bull. S.-East. Un. scient. Socs* **L.**BM. 12*. [*C. as:* 12265]

Congress of the **World Meteorological Organisation.** *See* 19437.

15453 **Congresso brasileiro** e **americano** de **cirurgia.** Rio de Janeiro. *Congresso bras. am. Cirurg.* [1938–] **L.**S. 38–42.

15454 **Congresso brasileiro** de **hygiene.** Rio de Janeiro. *Congresso bras. Hyg.* **L.**TD. 23–29 imp.

15455 **Congresso nazionale** della **Federazione 'Arti tessili'.** Milano. *Congresso naz. Fed. 'Arti tess.'*

15456 **Congresso** della **Società freniatrica italiana.** Reggio nell'Emilia. *Congresso Soc. freniat. ital.*

15457 **Congresul. Asociaţiunea română** pentru înaintarea şi respândirea ştiinţelor. Bucureşti. *Congresul Asoc. rom. Înaint. Respând. ştiinţ.*

Conjoint Board of **Scientific Societies. Proceedings.** *See* 39126.

15458 **Connaissance** de l'**homme.** Paris. *Connaiss. Homme* [1953–] **L.**MD. 54–. [*C. of:* 47458]

15459 **Connaissance** du **monde.** Paris. *Connaiss. Monde* [1956–] **L.**G.; **Ld.**U. 59–.

15460 **Connaissance** des **temps** ou des **mouvements célestes.** Paris. *Connais. Temps* [1679–] **L.**AS.; BM. 79–; MO. 27–; SC. 1835–48; **Abd.**U. 1849–22; **C.**O. 1760–; UL. 1750–; **Db.** 1790–; **E.**O. 1681– imp.; R. 23–; U. 1779–70; **G.**U. 1839–; **O.**B. 1831–; O. 76–.

15461 **Connaître.** Cahiers de l'humanisme medical. Paris. *Connaître*

15462 **Connecticut Health Bulletin.** Hartford. *Conn. Hlth Bull.* [1887–] **L.**H. 36–; TD. 26– imp.

15463 **Connecticut Medicine.** New Haven. *Conn. Med.* [1958–] **L.**MA.; MD. [*C. of:* 15466]

15464 **Connecticut Occupational Therapy Bulletin.** Stamford. *Conn. occup. Ther. Bull.*

15465 **Connecticut Pharmacist.** New Haven. *Conn. Pharmst* [1944–]

15466 **Connecticut State Medical Journal.** New Haven. *Conn. St. med. J.* [1940–58] **L.**MA. 46–58; MD. [*C. of:* 25860; *C. as:* 15463]

15467 **Connective Tissues.** Transactions of Conferences, Josiah Macy Jr. Foundation. New York. *Connect. Tissues, Trans. Confs Josiah Macy Jr Fdn* [1950–] **L.**MD.; SC.

15468 **Connollian Quarterly Magazine.** Connollys (Blackley) Ltd. Manchester. *Connollian q. Mag.* [1945–] **Sy.**R.

15469 **Conquest.** Johannesburg. *Conquest, Johannesb.* [1957–]

15470 **Conquest.** London. *Conquest, Lond.* [1919–26] **L.**BM.; P.; SC. 26; **Abs.**N.; **Db.**; **E.**A.; **G.**M.; **O.**R. [*C. as:* 33007]

15471 **Conquest.** Research Defence Society. London. *Conquest, Res. Def. Soc.* [1950–] **L.**AM.; BM.; H.; LI.; MA.; MD.; S. 50–56; TD. imp.; U.; UC.; VC. 52–; **C.**APH. 51–; UL.; **Cr.**P. 53–; **E.**U.; **G.**M.; PH.; **Ld.**U.; **M.**P.; U.; **O.**R.; W. [*C. of:* 19415]

15472 **Conquest** by **Healing.** London. *Conquest Healing* [1924–] **L.**BM.; **Abs.**N.; **C.**AN. 37–; **E.**A. 35–; **O.**B. [*C. of:* 30273]

15473 **Conquest Pamphlet.** Research Defence Society. London. *Conquest Pamph.* [1956–] **L.**U.; **O.**R.

15474 **Conquête** de l'**air** et de l'**espace.** Bruxelles. *Conquête Air Espace* **Y.**

Conseil européen de **recherche nucléaire CERN Bibliographie.** *See* 12877.

Conseil national polonais pour la **protection** de la **nature.** *See* 36949.

15475 **Conseils pratiques.** Inventions nouvelles, sciences pratiques. Paris. *Conseils prat.*

15476 **Consejo general** de **colegios médicos** de **España.** Madrid. *Consejo gen. Cols méd. Esp.* [1946–] **L.**MA. imp.; S. 50–51: 56–59 imp.; **E.**P. 46–50 imp.

15477 **Consejos agrícolas.** San Rafael, R.A. *Consejos agríc., S Rafael* [1941–]

15478 **Conserva.** Den Haag. *Conserva* **L.**P. 57–; **Y.**

15478° **Conservación** en las **Americas.** Washington. *Conservac. Am.* [1946–47] **L.**NC. [*C. as:* 15484]

15479 **Conservas** de **peixe.** Lisboã. *Conservas Peixe*

15480 **Conservation.** Monthly bulletin published by the Commission of Conservation. Ottawa. *Conservation, Ottawa* **Abs.**N. 19–21 imp.

15481 **Conservation.** St. Louis, Mo. *Conservation, St Louis* [1912]

15482 **Conservation.** American Forestry Association. Washington. *Conservation, Am. For. Ass.* [1935–42]

15483 **Conservation** in **Action.** Fish and Wildlife Service. Washington. *Conserv. Action* **L.**BM.; Z. 53–54.

15484 **Conservation** in the **Americas.** Washington. *Conserv. Am.* [1947–] **L.**BM^N. 47–52 imp.; NC. 47–53; **O.**AP. imp.; F. 48–55. [*C. of:* 15478°]

15485 **Conservation Bulletin.** Minnesota. St. Paul. *Conserv. Bull., Minn.*

15486 **Conservation Bulletin** of the **Fish** and **Wildlife Service.** Washington. *Conserv. Bull. Fish Wildl. Serv., Wash.* [1940–] **L.**BM.; BM^N.; Z. 40–45 imp.; **Abd.**M. 41–50 imp.; **E.**R. 43–; **Pl.**M. 42–44 imp.; **Y.**

15487 **Conservation Bulletin. Missouri Conservation Commission.** Jefferson City. *Conserv. Bull., Jefferson Cy* **O.**F. 40.

15488 **Conservation** and **Industry.** Raleigh, N.C. *Conserv. Ind.* [1928–] **L.**BM^N. 28–31; GM. [*C. of:* 34227]

15489 **Conservation** of **Life.** Commission of Conservation, Ottawa. *Conserv. Life* [1914–19] **L.**BM. 14–15. [*C. as:* 53402]

15490 **Conservation News.** National Wildlife Federation. Washington. *Conserv. News*

15491 **Conservation Volunteer.** St. Paul, Minn. *Conserv. Volunt.* **L.**NC. 46–49 imp.

15492 **Conservationist.** New York State Conservation Commission. Albany. *Conservationist* **Y.**

15493 **Conservatory.** New York. *Conservatory*

15494 **Conserve alimentaire.** Meulan. *Conserve aliment.* **L.**P. 03–14*.

15495 **Conserve** e **derivati agrumari.** Palermo. *Conserve Deriv. agrum.* [1952–] **L.**P. 54–; TP. 59–; **Br.**A. 53– imp.; **Lh.**FO. imp.; **Y.**

15496 **Conserverie belge.** Anvers. *Conserverie belge* [1934–35] **L.**P. [*C. as:* 15497]

15497 **Conserverie** et l'**industrie alimentaire belges.** Anvers. *Conserverie Ind. aliment. belg.* [1935–] **L.**P. 35–40. [*C. of:* 15496]

15498 **Consigliere** dell'**agricoltore.** Torino. *Consigl. Agric.* **L.**EB. 14–21.

15499 **Consolidated Accession Lists. Ministry of Works Library.** London. *Consol. Access. Lists Minist. Wks Libr.* [1944–] **L.**BA.; P.; **Cr.**P. 45–; **Lc.**A. 49–; **Ld.**P. 49–; **Y.**

15500 **Consolidated Building References** to **Articles** in **Periodicals.** Ministry of Works Library. London. *Consol. Bldg Refs Art. Period.* [1951–] **L.**AV.; P.; **Ld.**P.; **Y.** [*C. of:* 9072]

15501 **Conspectus florae angolensis.** Coimbra. *Conspectus Flor. angol.* [1937–] **Db.**; **E.**R.; **Y.**
  Conspectus literaturae botanicae. *See* 3584.

15502 **Constantine médical.** Constantine, Algérie. *Constantine méd.*

15503 **Constants** for the **Observing Stations. Seismology Committee, British Association** for the **Advancement** of **Science.** London. *Constants obsg Stns Seism. Comm. Br. Ass. Advmt Sci.* **L.**AS. 29–.

15504 **Constitutional Medicine, Endocrinology** and **Allergy.** *Constit. Med. Endocr. Allergy* **C.**UL. 44–.

15505 **Construcción.** México. *Construcción, Méx.* [1941–]

15505° **Construcción.** New York. *Construcción, N.Y.* [1942–] **L.**BM. 55–. [*C. from:* 23590]

15506 **Construcción moderna.** Madrid. *Construcc. mod.* **Wa.**B. 55–57; **Y.**

15506° **Construcciones.** Buenos Aires. *Construcciones, B. Aires* **Y.**

15507 **Constructeur.** Paris. *Constructeur, Paris.*

15508 **Constructeur.** St-Quentin. *Constructeur, St-Quentin*

15509 **Constructeur** de **ciment armé.** Paris. *Constructeur Cim. armé* **L.**P. 21–39; **Wa.**B. 36–39.

15510 **Constructeur. Moniteur spécial** des **industries** du **fer.** Paris. *Constructeur Monit. spéc. Ind. Fer*

15511 **Constructeur** des **usines** à **gaz.** Paris. *Constructeur Us. Gaz* **L.**P. 94–06★.

15512 **Construction.** Dijon. *Construction, Dijon*

15513 **Construction.** New York. *Construction, N.Y.*

15514 **Construction.** Paris. *Construction, Paris* [1946–] **L.**P. 57–; **Y.**

15515 **Construction.** Pittsburg. *Construction, Pittsb.*

15516 **Construction.** Toronto. *Construction, Toronto* **L.**BA. 10–34.

15517 **Construction Bulletin. British Insulated Callenders Construction Company.** London. *Constr. Bull. Br. insul. Callenders* [1950–] **L.**P. imp.; **Y.**

15518 **Construction Glues.** Seattle. *Constr. Glues*

15519 **Construction** and **Industry.** Tel-Aviv. *Constr. Ind.*

15520 **Construction lyonnaise.** Lyon. *Constr. lyonn.*

15521 **Construction mécanique internationale.** Paris. *Constr. méc. int.* [*C. as:* 23789]

15522 **Construction moderne.** Paris. *Constr. mod.* [1885–] **L.**BA.; BM. 95–28; P. 95–28 imp.; **C.**UL. 26–; **Nw.**A. 39–; **Y.**

15523 **Construction News.** Chicago. *Constr. News*

15524 **Construction Series. Asphalt Institute.** New York. *Constr. Ser. Asph. Inst.* [1930–] **L.**P. 30–54 imp.

15525 **Construction Specifications. Asphalt Association.** New York. *Constr. Specifs Asph. Ass.*

15526 **Construction Specifier.** Washington. *Constr. Specifier* **L.**P. 56–.

15527 **Construction** et **travaux publics.** Paris. *Constr. Trav. publ.* [1933–34] **L.**SC. [*C. from:* 49032; *C. as:* 54162]

15528 **Constructional Research Bulletin.** Timber Research Association. London. *Constrl Res. Bull.* [1948–] **L.**P. 48–50; **Bn.**U.; **Ld.**P.; **O.**B.; **Y.**

15528° **Constructional Review.** Sydney. *Constrl Rev.* **Y.**
  Constructions en **fer.** Leipzig. *See* 17562.

15529 **Constructive Medicine.** North Carolina State Board of Health. Raleigh, N.C. *Constructive Med.*

15530 **Constructor.** Associated General Contractors of America. Washington. *Constructor* **Y.**

15531 **Constructores civis.** Lisboa. *Constructores Civis* **L.**BA. 47–.

15531° **Constructorul.** Bucureşti. *Constructorul* **Y.**

15532 **Construmag.** London. *Construmag* [1933–34] **L.**P.

15533 **Consultation médicale.** Paris. *Consultn méd.*

15534 **Consulting Engineer.** London. *Consult. Engr, Lond.* [1946–] **L.**AV. 49–60; BA. 47–; BM.; P. 56–; U. 48–; **Bl.**U. 60–; **C.**UL.; **Cr.**I. 49–; **E.**A.; **G.**M. 54–; **Lv.**P. 51–; **M.**P. 47–; **O.**R.; **Y.**

15535 **Consulting Engineer.** St. Joseph, Mich. *Consult. Engr, St Joseph* **L.**P. 55–.

15536 **Consulting Engineer Who's Who** and **Yearbook** London. *Consult. Engrs Who's Who Yb.* [1951–] **L.**BM.; **Bm.**P.; **Dn.**U. 60–; **E.**T.; **G.**M.; **Ld.**P. 55–; **M.**P. 53–; **O.**R. [*C. of:* 15537]

15537 **Consulting Engineer Yearbook.** London. *Consult. Engr Yb.* [1947–50] **L.**U. 48; **Bm.**P. 48–50; **E.**T. 48; **G.**M. 48–50; **O.**R. [*C. as:* 15536]

15538 **Consultor** de los **agricultores.** Ciudad Real. *Consultor Agric.*

15539 **Consultor terapéutico.** Paris. *Consultor terap.*

15540 **Contact.** London. *Contact, Lond.* [1922–31] **L.**BM.; EE. 24–31 imp.; P.; SC. 30–31; **M.**P. 27–31. [*C. as:* 17680]

15541 **Contact.** School of Aviation medicine. Pensacola. *Contact, Pensacola*

15542 **Contact Point.** School of Dentistry. College of Physicians and Surgeons. San Francisco. *Contact Pt* [1924–] **L.**D. 46–; **M.**MS. 32– imp.; **Y.**

15543 **Contactblad.** Zeebrugge. *Contactblad* **Abd.**T. 54–56.

15544 **Contacto.** The contact lens journal. Chicago. *Contacto* [1957–] **L.**P. 59–.

15544° **Containers.** International Container Bureau. Paris. *Containers* **Y.**

15545 **Contemporary Physics.** London. *Contemp. Phys.* [1959–] **L.**AV.; BM., P.; SC.; U.; **Abs.**N.; **Bl.**U.; **Dn.**U. 60–; **Co.**T.; **Dn.**U.; **H.**U.; **Ld.**P.; **Lv.**P.; **M.**U.; **N.**T. 60–; **Sw.**U. **Y.**

15546 **Contemporary Psychology.** Washington, Baltimore. *Contemp. Psychol.* [1956–] **L.**B.; MD.; PS.; **Bl.**U.; **Bm.**U.; **Dn.**U.; **E.**U.; **O.**B.

15547 **Contents Lists** of **Biological Journals.** London. *Contents Lists biol. J.* **G.**T. 51–53; U. 48–53.

15548 **Contents** of the **Publications** of the **Earthquake Research Institute.** University of Japan. Tokyo. *Contents Publs Earthq. Res. Inst., Tokyo* **L.**SC. 52–.

15549 **Conti Elektro Berichte.** Continental-Elektroindustrie. Düsseldorf. *Conti Elektro Ber.* [1959–] **L.**AV. 61–; P.; **Y.** [*C. of:* 12875]
  Foreign edition. **L.**P. 60–; **Y.**

15550 **Contigeactualités.** Bruxelles. *Contigeactualités* [1959–] **L.**P. [*C. of:* 17309]

15551 **Continental Metallurgical** and **Chemical Engineering.** Berlin. *Contin. metall. chem. Engng* [1926–27] **L.**P.; **Bm.**C.

15552 **Continental Paints** and **Resins.** London. *Contin. Paints Resins* [1957–] **L.**BM.

15553 **Contract Journal** and **Specification Record.** London. *Contract J. Specif. Rec.* [1879–] **L.**BM.; **P.** (1 yr); **SH.** (1 yr); **Br.**P. (1 yr); **G.**M. 84–; **Ha.**RD. 59–; **Lc.**A. 57–; **Ld.**P. (5 yr.); **Lv.**P. 46–56.

15554 **Contract Record** and **Engineering Review.** Toronto. *Contract Rec. Engng Rev.* [1908–36] [*C. of:* 13116; *C. as:* 18103]

15555 **Contracting.** New York. *Contracting*

15556 **Contracting Builders' Magazine.** Freeport, Ill. *Contract. Bldrs' Mag.*

15557 **Contractor;** the Canadian Building Construction Magazine. Toronto. *Contractor* [1920–29] [*C. as:* 9047]

15558 **Contractors'** and **Engineers' Monthly.** New York. *Contractors' Engrs' Mon.* [1920–] **G.**M. 23–; **Y.**

15559 **Contractors' Record** and **Municipal Engineering.** London. *Contractors' Rec. munic. Engng* [1908–] **L.**BM.; **P.** (1 yr); **SC.** 46–; **SH.** (1 yr); **Br.**P. (1 yr); **Co.**T. 62–; **Ld.**P. (5 yr.); **Lv.**P. 48–; **M.**P. 32–; **Sw.**U. 44–; **Y.**

15560 **Contractors' Record** and **Public Works Engineer. Overseas Edition.** London. *Contractors' Rec. publ. Wks Engr Overseas Edn* [1949–57] **L.**P.; **Ha.**RD. 53–57. [*C. as:* 23829]

Contribución. *See* **Contribuciones.**

15561 **Contribuciones. Centro** de **investigaciones pesqueras, Habano.** Mayo. *Contrnes Cent. Invest. pesq. Habano* [1952–] **L.**BM^N. 54– imp.; **Dm.** 53–54; **Lo.** 53–; **Pl.**M. 53–.

15562 **Contribuciones científicas. Facultad** de **ciencias exactas, físicas** y **naturales, Universidad** de **Buenos Aires.** Buenos Aires. *Contrnes cient. Fac. Cienc. exact. fís. nat. Univ. B. Aires* [1950–]
    Ser. A. Matematica [1950–] **L.**P.; **Bl.**U.; **C.**P.; **UL.** 50–56; **Db.**; **E.**R.; **M.**U. 56–; **Y.**
    Ser. B. Física [1950–] **L.**P.; **Bl.**U.; **C.**UL. 50–56; **Db.**; **E.**R.; **M.**U.; **Y.**
    Ser. C. Química [1956–] **L.**C.; **P.**; **C.**P.; **UL.** 50–56; **Db.**; **E.**R.; **M.**U. 56; **Y.**
    Ser. E. Geología [1950–] **L.**BM^N.; **GM.**; **P.**; **Bl.**U.; **C.**P.; **UL.** 50–56; **E.**R.; **M.**U.; **Y.**
    Ser. Botánica [1956–] **L.**BM^N.; **P.**; **Ld.**U.; **M.**U.; **Y.**
    Ser. Zoología [1957–] **L.**BM^N.; **Z.**; **Bl.**U.; **C.**P.; **Y.**

15563 **Contribuciones. Estación experimental agronómica.** Santiago de las Vegas. *Contrnes Estac. exp. agron, Santiago de las Vegas* [1947–] **L.**SC.

15564 **Contribuciones** al **estudio** de la **antropología chilena.** Santiago. *Contrnes Estud. Antrop. chil.* [1932–] **L.**AN. 33–41.

15565 **Contribuciones** al **estudio** de la **ciencias físicas** y **matemáticas.** La Plata. *Contrnes Estud. Cienc. fís. mat.* [1914–38] **L.**M.; **C.**P.; **UL.**; **Cr.**U. 14–19; **E.**C. imp.; **Q.**; **R.** 14–38; **U.** 15–16 imp.; **G.**U. 14–19 imp.; **Ld.**U.; **M.**U. 14–19 imp.; **O.**R. 14–25; **Sa.** 14–19. [*C. in:* 40677]

15566 **Contribuciones geofísicas. Observatorio astronómico** de la **Universidad** de **La Plata.** *Contrnes geofís. Obs. astr. Univ. La Plata* [1926–36] **L.**AS.; **C.**O. [*C. as:* 49543]

15566° **Contribuciones** a la **historia natural colombiana.** Barranquila. *Contrnes Hist. nat. colomb.* [1938–] **L.**BM^N. 38 imp.

15567 **Contribuciones** del **Instituto antarctico argentino.** Buenos Aires. *Contrnes Inst. antarct. argent.* **L.**BM^N. 59–; **Wo.** 59.

15568 **Contribuciones. Instituto ecuatoriano** de **ciencias naturales.** Quito. *Contrnes Inst. ecuat. Cienc. nat.*

15569 **Contribuciones ocasionales** de la **colección ictiológica** del **Laboratorio** de **pesqueria.** Caiguire. *Contrnes ocas. Col. ictiol. Lab. Pesq., Caiguire* [1949–] **L.**BM^N. 49.

15570 **Contribuciones ocasionales** del **Museo** de **historia natural** del **Colegio 'de la Salle.'** Vedado, Habana. *Contrnes ocas. Mus. Hist. nat. Col. 'de la Salle'* **L.**BM^N. 44– imp.

15571 **Contribuciones técnicas. Instituto** de **pesca** del **Pacifico.** Sonora. *Contrnes téc. Inst. Pesca Pacif.*

15572 **Contribuïções** para o **estudo** da **antropologia portuguesa.** Coimbra. *Contrçoes Estudo Antrop. port.* [1936–] **L.**AN.

15573 **Contribuições** do **Instituto geobiológico La Salle** de **Canõas.** *Contrções Inst. geobiol. La Salle Canõas* **L.**BM^N. 51–.

15574 **Contribuições** avulsas do **Instituto oceanográfico, Universidade** de **São Paulo.** São Paulo. *Contrções Inst. oceanogr. Univ. S Paulo*
    Ser. Oceanográfia biológica [1955–] **L.**BM^N. imp.; **Z.**; **Dm.**; **Lo.**; **Lv.**U.; **Pl.**M.; **Wo.** imp.
    Ser. Oceanográfia física [1956–] **L.**BM^N. imp.; **Dm.**; **Lo.**; **Lv.**U.; **Pl.**M.; **Wo.**
    Ser. Tecnologia [1960–] **L.**BM^N.; **Z.**; **Dm.**; **Lo.**; **Lv.**U.; **Pl.**M.; **Wo.**

15575 **Contributed Technical Papers. Katmai Series.** National Geographical Society. Washington. *Contrd tech. Pap. Katmai Ser.* [1923–24] **L.**GL.

15576 **Contributed Technical Papers. Mexican Archeology Series.** National Geographic Society. Washington. *Contrd tech. Pap. Mex. Archeol. Ser.* [1940–]

15577 **Contributed Technical Papers. Pueblo Bonito Series.** National Geographic Society. Washington. *Contrd tech. Pap. Pueblo Bonito Ser.* [1935–] **L.**BM.

15578 **Contributed Technical Papers. Solar Eclipse Series.** National Geographic Society. Washington. *Contrd tech. Pap. sol. Eclipse Ser.* [1939–] **L.**BM.; **SC.** 39–42.

15579 **Contributed Technical Papers. Stratosphere Series.** National Geographic Society. Washington. *Contrd tech. Pap. Stratosph. Ser.* [1935–36] **L.**BM.

15580 **Contributi astronomici. Osservatorio astronomico** di **Capodimonte.** Napoli. *Contrti astr. Oss. astr. Capodimonte* [1913–] **L.**AS. 14– imp.; **SC.** 27–34; **C.**O.; **E.**O.; **M.**U. 47–58 imp.; **O.**O.
    Contributi astronomici. R. Osservatorio astronomico di **Capodimonte.** *See* 15580.

15581 **Contributi astronomici. R. Osservatorio astronomico** al **Collegio Romano.** Roma. *Contrti astr R. Oss. astr. Coll. romano* [1920–21] **L.**AS.; **C.**O.; **E.**O.; **O.**O.

15582 **Contributi astronomici** della **R. Specola** di **Brera** in **Milano.** *Contrti astr. R. Specola Brera* [1923–37] **L.**AS.; **C.**O.; **E.**O.; R. 24–37; **M.**U. 34–36 imp.; **O.**O.

15583 **Contributi astronomici** della **R. Specola** di **Merate.** Milano. *Contrti astr. R. Specola Merate* [1924–37] **L.**AS.; **E.**R.; **M.**U. 36; **O.**O. [*C. as:* 15589]

15584 **Contributi astrofisici. Osservatorio astrofisico, Catania.** *Contrti astrofis. Oss. astrofis. Catania* **L.**AS. 33–; **M.**U. 55– imp.

15584° **Contributi fuori serie. Osservatorio astronomico** di **Capodimonte.** Napoli. *Contrti fuori Ser. Oss. astr. Capodimonte* **L.**SC. 54–55.

15585 **Contributi geofisici. Osservatorio astronomico** di **Capodimonte.** Napoli. *Contrti geofis. Oss. astr. Capodimonte* [1914–] **L.**AS. imp.; MO. 30–; SC. 28–; **M.**U. 50–54; **O.**G. 14–32 imp.; O. imp.

15585° **Contributi. Istituto** di **ricerche agrarie.** Milano. *Contrti Ist. Ric. agr., Milano* [1956–]

15586 **Contributi meteorologici. Osservatorio astronomico** di **Capodimonte.** Napoli. *Contrti met. Oss. astr. Capodimonte* **L.**MO. 14–29; SC. 29–; **O.**G. 29.

15587 **Contributi. Osservatorio astrofisico** di **Arcetri.** Firenze. *Contrti Oss. astrofis. Arcetri* **M.**U. 56–; **Y.**

15588 **Contributi** dell'**Osservatorio astrofisico** dell' **Università** di **Padova** in **Asiago.** Pavia. *Contrti Oss. astrofis. Univ. Padova* [1944–] **L.**AS.; **M.**U. imp.

15589 **Contributi** del **Osservatorio astronomico** di **Milano-Merate.** *Contrti Oss. astr. Milano-Merate* [1938–] **L.**AS.; SC. 55–; **E.**R.; **M.**U. 38–58 imp.; **Y.** [*C. of:* 15583]

15590 **Contributi psicologici. Laboratorio** di **psicologia sperimentale, Università** di **Roma.** *Contrti psicol. Lab. Psicol. sper. Univ. Roma* **L.**BM. 10–17.

Contributi. R. Osservatorio astronomico di **Milano-Merate.** *See* 15589.

15591 **Contributi scientifici. Osservatorio astronomico** di **Capodimonte.** Napoli. *Contrti scient. Oss. astr. Capodimonte* **M.**U. 56–59; **Y.**

15592 **Contributi scientifici. Osservatorio astronomico** di **Roma** su **succursal** sul **Gran Sasso.** Roma. *Contrti scient. Oss. astr. Roma Gran Sasso* [1951–] **L.**AS.; **M.**U. 51–58 imp.; **O.**O. [*C. of:* 15594]

15593 **Contributi scientifici. R. Osservatorio astronomico** di **Roma** sul **Campidoglio.** Roma. *Contrti scient. R. Oss. astr. Roma Campidoglio* [1929–37] **L.**AS. 36–37; **O.**O. [*C. as:* 15594]

15594 **Contributi scientifici** del **R. Osservatorio** e **Museo astronomico** di **Roma** su **Monte Mario.** Roma. *Contrti scient. R. Oss. Mus. astr. Roma Mte Mario* [1937–51] **L.**AS.; **M.**U. 49–51; **O.**O. [*C. of:* 15593; *C. as:* 15592]

15595 **Contributi scientifico-pratici** per una **miglione conoscenza** ed **utilizzazione** del **legno.** Roma. *Contrti scient.-prat. migl. Conosc. Util. Legno* [1957–] **O.**F.

15596 **Contributi** di **scienze geologiche.** Roma. *Contrti Sci. geol.* [1950–] **Y.** [*Supplement to:* 8284]

15597 **Contributi teorici** e **sperimentali** di **polarografia.** Roma. *Contrti teor. sper. Polarogr.* [1951–] **L.**P.; **Y.** [*Supplement to:* 47739]

Contribution. *See* **Contributions**

15598 **Contributions. Agricultural Experiment Station, Massachusetts State College.** Amsherst. *Contr. agric. Exp. Stn Mass. St. Coll.* **O.**F. 41– imp.

15599 **Contributions. Agricultural Experiment Station, Rhode Island State College.** Kingston. *Contr. agric. Exp. Stn Rhode Isl. St. Coll.* **O.**F. 49– imp.

15600 **Contributions** from the **Akkeshi Marine Biological Station.** Sapporo. *Contr. Akkeshi mar. biol. Stn* **Dm.** 40; **Lo.** 51–; **Pl.**M. 54– imp.

15601 **Contributions. Allan Hancock Foundation.** Los Angeles. *Contr. Allan Hancock Fdn* **Dm.** 53– imp.; **Lv.**U. 49; **Pl.**M. 46– imp.

15602 **Contributions** to **American Anthropology** and **History.** Washington. *Contr. Am. Anthrop. Hist.* [1939–] **L.**AN.; BM.N. 52–; **Bn.**U.; **Br.**U.; **C.**UL.; **M.**P.; **N.**U.

15603 **Contributions. American Institute** of **Mining** and **Metallurgical Engineers.** New York. *Contr. Am. Inst. Min. metall. Engrs* [1932–] **L.**I. 32–45 imp.; **P.** 33–.

15604 **Contributions** of the **Ames Botanical Laboratory.** North Easton, Mass. *Contr. Ames bot. Lab.* [1904–] **L.**BM. 04; BM.N. 04–09 imp.; K. 04–09 imp.

15605 **Contributions** from the **Anatomical Laboratory** of **Brown University.** Providence, R.I. *Contr. anat. Lab. Brown Univ.* [1898–08] **L.**UC. 98–03; **Lv.**U.; **Pl.**M. [*C. as:* 15616]

15606 **Contributions** from the **Anna M. R. Lauder Department** of **Public Health, Yale University School** of **Medicine.** *Contr. Anna M. R. Lauder Dep. publ. Hlth Yale* [1917–] **L.**H. 20–48; TD. 24– imp.; **Bm.**U. 17–39; **Cr.**MD. 23–39.

15607 **Contributions** of the **Annual Mineral Industries Conference, Illinois Geological Survey.** *Contr. a. Miner. Ind. Conf. Ill.* **L.**P. 37.

15608 **Contributions** of the **Arctic Institute, Catholic University** of **America.** Washington. *Contr. Arct. Inst. cath. Univ. Am.* [1948–] **L.**K. 53–.

Contributions. Armagh Observatory. *See* 4815.

15609 **Contributions** from the **Arnold Arboretum** of **Harvard University.** Cambridge, Mass. *Contr. Arnold Arbor.* [1932–38] **L.**BM.N.; K. [*C. as:* 48585]

15610 **Contributions** from the **Astronomical Institute** of the **Charles University, Prague.** Prague. *Contr. astr. Inst. Charles Univ.* [1949–] **L.**AS.

Contributions from the **Astronomical Institute** of **Lwów University.** *See* 38307.

15611 **Contributions** from the **Astronomical Institute, Masaryk University.** Brno. *Contr. astr. Inst Masaryk Univ.* [1947–56] **L.**AS.; SC.; **E.**O.; **M.**U. imp.

Contributions. Astronomical Observatory, Skalnote Pleso. *See* 38283.

Contributions to **Astrophysics.** Smithsonian Institute. *See* 49961.

15612 **Contributions** of the **Baltic University.** Hamburg, Pinneberg. *Contr. Baltic Univ.* [1946–49] **L.**AS. imp.; MO.; SC. imp.; **Bl.**U. imp.; **M.**U. 47–48 imp.; **Rt.** imp.; **Sw.**U. imp.

15613 **Contributions** from the **Baylor University Museum.** Waco, Texas. *Contr. Baylor Univ. Mus.* [1925–] **L.**BM.N. 25–39.

15613° **Contributions** from **Bears Bluff Laboratories.** Wadmalew Island. *Contr. Bears Bluff Labs* [1947]– **L.**AM.

15614 **Contributions** from the **Bermuda Biological Station.** St. George's West. *Contr. Bermuda biol. Stn* [1904–] L.AM. imp.; BM^N. 32– imp.; L. imp.; S. 04–22; SC.; UC. 32– imp.; Z. 31–; **Abd.**M. 46– imp.; **Abs.**U. 37; **Bm.**U. 04–19 imp.; **Dm.** imp.; **E.**R. 32– imp.; U. 32– imp.; **H.**U. 31–; **Lo.** imp.; **Lv.**U. imp.; **M.**I.; **Pl.**M. imp.; **Wo.** 32–.

15615 **Contributions** from the **Biological Laboratories** in **Princeton University, N.J.** *Contr. biol. Labs Princeton Univ.* [1912–49] L.BM^N.; HS. 25–49 imp.; U. 25–49; UC.; Z.; **Abd.**U.; **Bm.**U.; **C.**UL.; **Db.**; **Dm.** 12–38; **Dn.**U.; **E.**U.; **G.**U.; **Lv.**U.; **M.**U.; **O.**R.; **Pl.**M.; **Sa.** 25–49.

15616 **Contributions** from the **Biological Laboratory** of **Brown University.** Providence, R.I. *Contr. biol. Lab. Brown Univ.* [1909–] **Lv.**U. 09–33; **Pl.**M. 09–40. [C. of: 15605]

15617 **Contributions** from the **Biological Laboratory. Catholic University** of **America.** Washington. *Contr. biol. Lab. Cath. Univ. Am.* [1915–43] L.BM.; SC. 21–36. [C. as: 7079]

15617° **Contributions** from the **Biological Laboratory, Kyoto University.** Kyoto. *Contr. biol. Lab. Kyoto Univ.* [1955–] L.BM^N.

15618 **Contributions** from the **Biological Laboratory** of the **Science Society** of **China.** Shanghai, etc. *Contr. biol. Lab. Sci. Soc. China* [1925–29: *then in series below*] L.BM.; BM^N.; K.; L. 27–29; SC.; Z.; **Br.**U.; **C.**P.; **Db.** 27–29; **E.**R. 27–29; U. **Ld.**U. 27–29; **M.**U.
　　Botanical series [1930–39] L.BM.; BM^N.; K.; L. 30–35; LI. 30–35; MY. 32–38; QM. 32–35 imp.; SC.; **Bl.**U.; **Bm.**U. imp.; **Bn.**U. imp.; **C.**A.; UL. imp.; **E.**B.; R.; **G.**U. 30–35; **Ld.**U. 30–35; **Lv.**U. 30–35; **N.**U. imp.; **Pl.**M. 31–38; **Rt.** imp.
　　Zoological series [1930–47] L.BM.; BM^N.; L. 30–35; LI. 30–35; QM. 32–35 imp.; SC.; TD. imp.; UC.; Z.; **Abd.**M. imp.; **Bl.**U.; **Bm.**U. imp.; **Bn.**U. imp.; **Br.**U.; **C.**UL.; **E.**B.; R.; U.; **G.**U.; **Ld.**U.; **Lv.**U.; **M.**U.; **Mi.** imp.; **N.**U.; **O.**R. 33–35; **Pl.**M.; **Rt.** imp. [*Many libraries may not have received volume 16 dated* 1947]

15619 **Contributions. Biological Laboratory, Weir Mitchell Station, Mount Desert Island.** Bar Harbor. *Contr. biol. Lab. Weir Mitchell Stn* **Lv.**U. 26–.

15620 **Contributions** from the **Biological** and **Microscopical Section** of the **Academy** of **Natural Sciences** of **Philadelphia.** *Contr. biol. microsc. Sect. Acad. nat. Sci. Philad.* L.BM^N. 22.

15621 **Contributions** to **Biology** from the **Hopkins Seaside Laboratory** of the **Leland Stanford Jr University.** Palo Alto. *Contr. Biol. Hopkins Seaside Lab.* [1895–04] L.BM. 95–03; BM^N.; SC. 95–01; Z.; **Br.**U. 03; **Db.** 95–99; **E.**U.; **M.**U. imp.; **O.**R. 95–98.

15622 **Contributions** from the **Bosscha Observatory.** Lembany. *Contr. Bosscha Obs.* **M.**U. 52–58; **Y.**

15623 **Contributions. Botanical Department, Iowa State College** of **Agriculture.** Ames. *Contr. bot. Dep. Ia St. Coll. Agric.* L.BM^N. 01–07 imp.; K. 96–25.

15624 **Contributions** from the **Botanical Laboratory, Johns Hopkins University.** Baltimore. *Contr. bot. Lab. Johns Hopkins Univ.* L.BM. 01.

15625 **Contributions** from the **Botanical Laboratory** and the **Morris Laboratory University** of **Pennsylvania.** Philadelphia. *Contr. bot. Lab. Morris Lab. Univ. Pa* [1892–38] L.BM. imp.; BM^N.; K.; L.; **C.**P. 04–38;

UL.; **Db.** 01–38; **E.**B.; F. 92–08 v. imp.; R.; **G.**U. 11–20 imp.; **M.**U. 92–07; **O.**BO. 92–20 imp.; R. 92–20 imp.; **Pl.**M. 98–30 imp.; **Rt.** 92–97: 29–38.

15626 **Contributions** from the **Botanical Laboratory** of **Ohio State University.** Columbus. *Contr. bot. Lab. Ohio St. Univ.* L.BM^N. 21: 26.

15627 **Contributions** from the **Botanical Laboratory, University** of **Michigan.** Ann Arbor. *Contr. bot. Lab. Univ. Mich.*
　　Contributions. Botanical Laboratory, University of **Montreal.** *See* 15759.
　　Contributions from the **Botanical Laboratory, University** of **Pennsylvania.** *See* 15625.

15628 **Contributions** from the **Botanical Laboratory, University** of **Tennessee.** Knoxville. *Contr. bot. Lab. Univ. Tenn.* [1935–] **Y.**
　　Contributions botaniques de **Cluj.** *See* 15867.

15629 **Contributions. Boyce Thompson Institute** for **Plant Research.** Menasha, Wis., etc. *Contr. Boyce Thomson Inst. Pl. Res.* [1925–] L.AM.; C. 40–; EB. 31–; IC. 32–; K.; MY.; P. 25–37; SC.; TP.; UC. 25–30; **Abs.**A.; U. 29– imp.; **Ba.**I. 25–30; **Bl.**U.; **Bm.**U. 47–; **Bn.**U.; **Br.**A.; U.; **C.**A.; AB. 30–; BO.; **Db.**; **E.**B.; **Ex.**U.; **G.**U.; **Hu.**G.; **Je.** 36–; **Ld.**U.; **Lv.**U.; **M.**U.; **Md.**H.; **N.**U. imp.; **O.**F.; **Pl.**M.; **R.**U.; **Rt.**; **Wd.** 32–; **Y.**

15630 **Contributions** from the **Brooklyn Botanic Garden.** Brooklyn. *Contr. Brooklyn bot. Gdn* [1911–] L.BM^N.; L.; **Abs.**A.; **C.**A. 32–; P. 49–; **Lv.**U. 27– imp.; **Md.**H.; **O.**F. 45– imp.

15631 **Contributions** from the **Burakan Observatory.** Erivan. *Contr. Burakan Obs.* L.AS. 46–.

15632 **Contributions** from the **Bureau** of **British Marine Biology.** London. *Contr. Bur. Br. mar. Biol.* [1910] L.BM.; BM^N.; **E.**R.

15633 **Contributions** to the **Calculus** of **Variations.** University of Chicago. *Contr. Calculus Var.* [1930–] **O.**R.

15634 **Contributions** from the **Cambridge Observatories.** Cambridge. *Contr. Camb. Obs.* [1948–] L.SC.; **Db.**; **E.**Q.; **M.**U.

15635 **Contributions** to **Canadian Biology** and **Fisheries.** Ottawa. *Contr. Can. Biol. Fish.* [1901–34] L.AM.; BM.; BM^N.; SC. 25–34; Z. 01–15; **Abd.**M.; **Br.**U. imp.; **Cr.**M. 01–18; U. 22–34; **Dm.**; **E.**F. 01–16; R. 06–34; **Fr.** 06–17: 22–34; **Ld.**U. 01–17; **Lo.**; **Lv.**U.; **Mi.**; **Nw.**A. 01–16: 21–27; **O.**Z. 06–10; **Pl.**M.; **Sa.** 23–34; **Wo.** 06–34. [C. as: 25665]

15636 **Contributions** to **Canadian Mineralogy.** Lancaster, Pa. *Contr. Can. Miner.* [1949–55] L.BM^N.; SC.; **M.**U. [C. of: 55682; C. in: 13207]

15637 **Contributions** to **Canadian Palaeontology.** Ottawa. *Contr. Can. Palaeont.* [1885–10] L.BM.; BM^N.; GL. 85–01; L. 89–10; SC.; UC.; **Abd.**U. 85–98; **Br.**U.; **C.**P. 85–01; **Db.**; **E.**F. 85–01 imp.; R. imp.; U. 85–08; **G.**U. 85–08; **Lv.**U.; **M.**U. imp.; **O.**R.; **Sa.** 85–01.

15638 **Contributions** from the **Cancer Research Laboratories. Washington University School** of **Medicine.** St. Louis. *Contr. Cancer Res. Labs Wash. Univ.* L.MD. 26–27.
　　Contributions. Carnegie Institute of **Technology, Coal Research Laboratory.** *See* 15651.

15639 **Contributions** à la **carte géologique** de l'**Indo-Chine.** Hanoï-Haïphong. *Contr. Carte géol. Indo-chine*

15640 **Contributions. Central Fisheries Station** of **Japan.** Tokyo. *Contr. cent. Fish. Stn Japan* [1946–] **L.**SC.; **Abd.**R.; T.; **Pl.**M. 48–51.

15641 **Contributions. Centre** des **recherches** et **études océanographiques.** *Contr. Cent. Rech. Étud. océanogr.* **Pl.**M. 48–54.

15642 **Contributions** from the **Charleston Museum.** Charleston, S.C. *Contr. Charleston Mus.* [1910–] **L.**BM^N.; Z. (zool.) 13–49; **Db.**; **Y.**

15643 **Contributions** to **Chemical Education.** Easton, Pa. *Contr. chem. Educ.* [1941–] **L.**SC. 41–44; 51.

15644 **Contributions** from the **Chemical Laboratory** of the **Case School** of **Applied Science.** Cleveland, O. *Contr. chem. Lab. Case Sch. appl. Sci.*

15645 **Contributions** from the **Chemical Laboratory** of **Harvard University.** Cambridge. *Contr. chem. Lab. Harv.*

15646 **Contributions** from the **Chemical Laboratory** of the **Massachusetts Institute** of **Technology.** Boston. *Contr. chem. Lab. M. I. T.*

15647 **Contributions** from the **Chemical Laboratory** of the **Rose Polytechnic Institute.** Terre Haute, Ind. *Contr. chem. Lab. Rose polytech. Inst.*

15648 **Contributions** from the **Chemical Laboratory, University** of **Nebraska.** Lincoln. *Contr. chem. Lab. Univ. Neb.*

Contributions of the **Chemist** to **Insulation Research.** See 16980.

15649 **Contributions. Chesapeake Biological Laboratory, Solomon's Island, Maryland.** *Contr. Chesapeake biol. Lab.* **L.**AM. 32– imp.; **Bn.**U. 37–; **Lo.**; **Pl.**M. 36– imp.; **Y.**

15650 **Contributions** to **Clinical Practice** in **Medicine** and **Surgery.** Southend General Hospital. Southend. *Contr. clin. Pract. Med. Surg.* **L.**MD. 36; **C.**UL. 36; **O.**R. 36.

15651 **Contributions. Coal Research Laboratory. Carnegie Institute** of **Technology.** Pittsburgh. *Contr. Coal Res. Lab. Carnegie Inst. Technol.* **Y.**

15652 **Contributions. College** of **Engineering, New York University.** New York. *Contr. Coll. Engng N.Y. Univ.* [*C. of:* 40941]

Contributions. College of **Fisheries. University** of **Washington.** Seattle. *See* 15849.

15653 **Contributions** from the **Colombo Fisheries Research Station.** Colombo. *Contr. Colombo Fish. Res. Stn* **Dm.** 59–.

15654 **Contributions** from the **Columbia University Observatory.** New York. *Contr. Columbia Univ. Obs.* [1892–15] **L.**AS. 95–06; **Bl.**U. 92–10 imp.; **C.**O.; **E.**O. imp.; **O.**O. 06–15. [*C. as:* 15820]

15655 **Contributions. Committee** on **Abstracts** and **Bibliography. Technical Association** of the **Pulp** and **Paper Industry.** New York. *Contr. Comm. Abstr. Biblphy tech. Ass. Pulp Pap. Ind.* [1916–24]

Contributions à la **connaissance** de la **faune** et de la **flore** de l'**URSS.** *See* 29626.

15656 **Contributions** from the **Cryptogamic Laboratory** of **Harvard University.** Cambridge, Mass. *Contr. cryptog. Lab. Harv.* [1883–] **L.**UC. 83–29 imp.

15657 **Contributions** from the **Cushman Foundation** for **Foraminiferal Research.** Sharon, Mass, etc. *Contr. Cushman Fdn foramin. Res.* [1950–] **L.**BM^N.; GL.; GM.; SC.; UC.; **Abs.**U. 52–; **C.**S.; **Db.**; **Ex.**U.; **H.**U.; **Sw.**U. 58–; **Y.** [*C. of:* 15658]

15658 **Contributions** from the **Cushman Laboratory** for **Foraminiferal Research.** Sharon, Mass. *Contr. Cushman Lab. foramin. Res.* [1925–49] **L.**BM^N.; GL.; GM.; **Abs.**U. imp.; **C.**S.; **G.**N. 25–38. [*C. as:* 15657]

15659 **Contributions** from the **Dearbon Observatory.** Evanston. *Contr. Dearbon Obs.* [1951–] **L.**AS.; **M.**U. 51–55; **Y.**

15660 **Contributions** du **Département** de **biologie, Université Laval.** Québec. *Contr. Dép. Biol. Univ. Laval* [1952–] **L.**BM^N.; Z. imp.; **Db.**; **Dm.**; **Lo.**; **Y.** [*C. of:* 15836]

15661 **Contributions** du **Département** des **pêcheries.** Québec. *Contr. Dép. Pêch., Québ.* **L.**BM^N. 54– imp.; Z. 60– imp.; **Bn.**U. 38– imp.; **Dm.** 44– imp.; **E.**R. 38–; **Lo.** 38–; **Pl.**M. 56–; **Y.**

15662 **Contributions** from the **Department** of **Anatomy, Minnesota University.** Minneapolis. *Contr. Dep. Anat. Minn. Univ.* [1909–] **L.**BM. 09–20; S. 24–56; UC.; **C.**UL.; **Db.** imp.; **E.**R.; U. 26– imp.; **M.**U. 09–20; **O.**R.

15663 **Contributions. Department** of **Anatomy, Peking Union Medical College.** Peking. *Contr. Dep. Anat. Peking Un. med. Coll.* [1918–] **L.**S. 18–30; UC. 18–22; **Br.**U. 23–27.

15664 **Contributions** of the **Department** of **Biological Sciences, Loyola University.** Chicago. *Contr. Dep. biol. Sci. Loyola Univ.* **L.**BM^N. 49–52.

15665 **Contributions. Department** of **Biology, Hamilton College,** McMaster University. *Contr. Dep. Biol. Hamilton Coll.* **Bl.**U. 54–.

Contributions. Department of **Biology, Laval University.** Quebec. *See* 15660.

15666 **Contributions** from the **Department** of **Botany, Columbia University.** New York. *Contr. Dep. Bot. Columbia Univ.* [1886–] **L.**K. 86–14; **E.**B. 86–02 imp.

15667 **Contributions** from the **Department** of **Botany, Pennsylvania State College.** *Contr. Dep. Bot. Pa St. Coll.*

15668 **Contributions** from the **Department** of **Botany, University** of **Nebraska.** Lincoln. *Contr. Dep. Bot. Univ. Neb.* **L.**K. 92–01; **Rt.** 34–36.

15669 **Contributions** from the **Department** of **Chemical Engineering, Massachusetts Institute** of **Technology.** Boston. *Contr. Dep. chem. Engng M.I.T.* **L.**P. 21– imp.

15670 **Contributions** from the **Department** of **Electrical Engineering, Columbia University.** New York. *Contr. Dep. elect. Engng Columbia Univ.*

15671 **Contributions** from the **Department** of **Entomology, University** of **Nebraska.** Lincoln. *Contr. Dep. Ent. Univ. Neb.* **L.**EB. 08–22.

15672 **Contributions** from the **Department** of **Fisheries** and the **Fishery Research Laboratory, Kyushu University.** *Contr. Dep. Fish. Fishery Res. Lab. Kyushu Univ.* [1942–] **L.**BM^N.

Contributions from the **Department** of **Fisheries, Quebec.** *See* 15661.

15673 **Contributions** from the **Department** of **Geology** of **Columbia University.** New York. *Contr. Dep. Geol. Columbia Univ.*

15674 **Contributions** from the **Department** of **Geology** of **Stanford University.** Palo Alto. *Contr. Dep. Geol. Stanford Univ.* [1930–36] **L.**BM.; BM^N.; SC.; **E.**R.; U.; **M.**U.; **Nw.**A.; **O.**R.; **Pl.**M. 30–31.

15675 **Contributions** from the **Department** of **Hygiene** and **Bacteriology** and the **Department** of **Clinical Bacteriology** and **Serology, Hebrew University** (Hadassah Medical School). *Contr. Dep. Hyg. Bact. Dep. clin. Bact. Serol. Hebrew Univ.* [1926–] **L.**MC.; TD. imp.

15676 **Contributions** from the **Department** of **Mathematics, Massachusetts Institute** of **Technology.** Boston. *Contr. Dep. Math. M.I.T.* [1920–32] **L.**U.; UC. 20–23 imp.; **Bn.**U. imp.; **C.**P.; UL.; **M.**U. imp.; **O.**R

15677 **Contributions. Department** of **Meteorology** and **Climatology, University** of **Washington.** Seattle. *Contr. Dep. Met. Clim. Univ. Wash.* **L.**MO. 49–.

15678 **Contributions** from the **Department** of **Mineralogy** of **Columbia University.** New York. *Contr. Dep. Miner. Columbia Univ.*

15679 **Contributions** from the **Department** of **Mineralogy** and **Petrography, Harvard University.** Cambridge, Mass. *Contr. Dep. Miner. Petrogr. Harv.* **L.**GM. 25–.

15680 **Contributions** from the **Department** of **Neurology, Harvard University Medical School.** Boston. *Contr. Dep. Neurol. Harv.* **L.**S. 12–26. [*C. of:* 14752; *C. as:* 14751]

15681 **Contributions** from the **Department** of **Neurology** and **Laboratory** of **Neuropathology, Medicochirurgical College** of **Pennsylvania.** University of Pennsylvania. Philadelphia. *Contr. Dep. Neurol. Lab. Neuropath. med.-chir. Coll. Pa* [1905–14] **L.**MD. 06–12; S. 06–12; **Bm.**U. 06–12; **E.**P. 05–12; **Lv.**U. 06–12.

15682 **Contributions** from the **Department** of **Obstetrics** and **Gynecology** of **Michigan University.** Ann Arbor. *Contr. Dep. Obstet. Gynec. Mich. Univ.* [1923–28] **L.**S.; **Bm.**U.; **C.**UL.; **G.**U.; **O.**R. [*C. of:* 15796]

15683 **Contributions** from the **Department** of **Pathology** and **Bacteriology, Iowa University.** Iowa. *Contr. Dep. Path. Bact. Ia Univ.* [1908] **L.**BM.; **M.**U.

15684 **Contributions** from the **Department** of **Pathology, Bacteriology** and **Public Health, Minnesota University.** Minneapolis. *Contr. Dep. Path. Bact. publ. Hlth Minn. Univ.* [1913–] **L.**BM. 13–19; UC.; **C.**UL.; **Db.** imp.; **M.**U. 13–19; **O.**R.

15685 **Contributions** from the **Department** of **Pharmacology, Peking Union Medical College.** Peking. *Contr. Dep. Pharmac. Peking Un. med. Coll.* **L.**PH. 20–25.

15686 **Contributions** from the **Department** of **Physiology, Minnesota University.** Minneapolis. *Contr. Dep. Physiol. Minn. Univ.* **L.**S. 30–39.

15687 **Contributions. Department** of **Research, Fisheries Commission, Oregon.** Salem. *Contr. Dep. Res. Fish. Commn Ore.* **Dm.** 39– imp.

15688 **Contributions** from the **Department** of **Zoology** and **Entomology, Ohio State University.** Columbus. *Contr. Dep. Zool. Ent. Ohio St. Univ.* **L.**BM^N. 19–46; EB. 00–36 imp.; SC. 99–.

15689 **Contributions** from the **Department** of **Zoology, Smith College.** Northampton, Mass. *Contr. Dep. Zool. Smith Coll.* **L.**BM^N. 19– imp.

15689° **Contributions. Department** of **Zoology, University** of **Illinois.** Urbana. *Contr. Dep. Zool. Univ. Ill.* [1950–]

Contributions from the **District Research Administration** in the **Ukraine.** Kiev. *See* 29655.

15690 **Contributions** from the **Division** of **Entomology, Department** of **Agriculture, Canada.** Ottawa. *Contr. Div. Ent. Can.* **L.**BM^N 1911–15*. [*C. as:* 15702]

15691 **Contributions. Division** of **Forest Biology Department** of **Agriculture, Canada.** Ottawa. *Contr. Div. Forest Biol. Can.* **L.**MO. 51–52 imp.

15692 **Contributions. Division** of **Zoology** and **Palaeontology, Royal Ontario Museum.** Toronto. *Contr. Div. Zool. Palaeont. R. Ont. Mus.* [1955–59] **L.**BM^N.; SC.; **C.**PO.; **Cr.**M.; **E.**F. [*C. of:* 15819; *C. as:* 15768]

15693 **Contributions** from the **Dominion Astrophysical Observatory.** Victoria, B.C. *Contr. Dom. astrophys. Obs., Victoria B.C.* [1946–] **L.**AS.; BM.; RI. (curr.); SC.; **E.**R.; U. imp.; **M.**U.

15694 **Contributions** from the **Dominion Observatory.** Ottawa. *Contr. Dom. Obs., Ottawa* [1947–] **L.**AS.; MO. (meteor.); **Bl.**U.; **M.**U. 48– imp.; **Y.**

15695 **Contributions** from the **Dove Marine Laboratory.** Cullercoats. *Contr. Dove mar. Lab.* [1955–] **L.**AM.; BM.; BM^N.; L.; P.; UC.; Z.; **Abs.**N.; U.; **Bl.**U.; **Bn.**U.; **Br.**U.; **C.**B.; **Cr.**M.; **Db.**; **Dm.**; **E.**R.; U.; **G.**T.; **Lo.**; **Lv.**U.; **Mi.**; **Nw.**A.; P.; **O.**R.; **Pl.**M.; **Wo.**; **Y.** [*C. of:* 43539]

15696 **Contributions** from the **Dudley Herbarium.** Stanford University. Palo Alto. *Contr. Dudley Herb.* [1927–] **L.**BM^N.; K.; L. 27–37; **Abd.**U.; **Bl.**U. 50–; **Bm.**U.; **E.**R. 28–; U. 27–41; **G.**U.; **Lv.**U. 27–43; **M.**U.; **Nw.**A. 40–; **O.**R.; **Pl.**M. 27–57 imp.; **Y.**

15697 **Contributions** from the **Duke University Marine Laboratory.** Beaufort. *Contr. Duke Univ. mar. Lab.* Ser. A. **Bn.**U. 55–.

15698 **Contributions** from the **Dunsink Observatory.** Dublin. *Contr. Dunsink Obs.* [1951–] **L.**AS.; SC.; **C.**UL.; **E.**R.; **M.**U. 51–55.

15699 **Contributions** de l'**École supérieure** de **chimie** de l'**Université Laval.** Québec. *Contr. Éc. sup. Chim. Univ. Laval* **Dm.** 33–34; **Pl.**M. 33–34.

15700 **Contributions** to **Economic Geology.** Kueiyang, China. *Contr. econ. Geol.* [1944–] **Rt.** 44.

15701 **Contributions** to **Embryology.** Washington. *Contr. Embryol.* [1915–] **L.**B. 26–; BM.; BM^N. imp.; MD.; S.; SC.; U.; UC.; VC. 45–; Z. 32– imp.; **Abd.**U.; **Abs.**N. 25–; **Bl.**U.; **Bm.**P.; U.; **Bn.**U.; **Br.**U.; **C.**AN.; P.; UL.; **Db.**; **Dn.**U. 21– imp.; **E.**R.; U.; **G.**U.; **Ld.**U. imp.; **Lv.**U.; **M.**P.; U.; **N.**U. 35– imp.; **Nw.**A.; **O.**R.; Z. 15–20; **Sa.**; **Sh.**U.; **Y.**

Contributions to **Engineering Chemistry** by **members** of the **Staff** of **A. D. Little, Inc.** *See* 39939.

15702 **Contributions** from the **Entomological Branch. Department** of **Agriculture, Canada.** Ottawa. *Contr. Ent. Brch Can.* [1915–] **O.**R. 15–21. [*C. of:* 15690: *see also* 15825]

15703 **Contributions** from the **Entomological Laboratory, Taihoku University.** *Contr. ent. Lab. Taihoku Univ.* **L.**BM^N. 36–38.

Contributions to **Ethnology.** Leningrad. *See* 29592.

15704 **Contributions. Faculté** des **sciences, Université Laval.** Québec. *Contr. Fac. Sci. Univ. Laval* Géologie et minéralogie. **L.**BM^N. 48– imp.; **Y.**

15705 **Contributions** à la **faune** des **Indes néerlandaises.** Buitenzorg. *Contr. Faune Indes néerl.* [1915–18] **L.**EB.; **L.**; **Z.**; **E.**F.   [*C. as:* 54350]

15705° **Contributions. Fish Commission of Oregon.** *Contr. Fish Commn Ore.* **Y.**

15706 **Contributions. Fisheries Experimental Station.** Canton. *Contr. Fish. exp. Stn, Canton* **Pl.**M. 32–34 imp.

15707 **Contributions. Fisheries Research Station, Ceylon.** Colombo. *Contr. Fish. Res. Stn Ceylon*

15708 **Contributions** to the **Flora** of **Australia.** Melbourne. *Contr. Flora Aust.* **L.**K. 06–.

15709 **Contributions** towards a **Flora** of **Nevada.** Washington. *Contr. Flora Nev.* **L.**BM^N. 40–41 imp.; **O.**BO. 40– imp.

15710 **Contributions. Fonds** de **recherches forestières** de l'**Université Laval.** Québec. *Contr. Fonds Rech. for. Univ. Laval* [1958–] **L.**BM^N.

Contributions. Forest Research Foundation, Laval University. Québec. *See* 15710.

15711 **Contributions. Franz Theodore Stone Institute** of **Hydrobiology.** Columbus. *Contr. Franz Theodore Stone Inst. Hydrobiol.* [1950–] **L.**BM^N. 50. [*C. of:* 15712]

15712 **Contributions. Franz Theodore Stone Laboratory.** Ohio State University. Columbus. *Contr. Franz Theodore Stone Lab.* [1928–49] **L.**BM^N. [*C. as:* 15711]

15713 **Contributions** from the **General Agricultural Research Station, Bogor.** *Contr. gen. agric. Res. Stn Bogor* [1950–51] **L.**AM. imp.; EB. (ent.); K.; **C.**A.; **Md.**H.; **Rt.**   [*C. of:* 30027; *C. as:* 37305]

15714 **Contributions** to **Geochemistry.** U.S. Geological Survey. Washington. *Contr. Geochem.* [1942–] **L.**P. SC.; **E.**R. [*Contained in:* 12510]

15715 **Contributions** in **Geographical Exploration.** Ohio State University. Columbus. *Contr. geogr. Explor.* **L.**BM^N. 20.

15716 **Contributions** from the **Geological Department, Yale University.** New Haven. *Contr. geol. Dep. Yale* **Sa.** 23–.

15717 **Contributions** from the **Geological Institute** of the **National University, Peking.** *Contr. geol. Inst. natn. Univ. Peking* **L.**BM^N. 24–48 imp.; GL. 24–48 imp.; **Bm.**U. 23–24.

15718 **Contributions** from the **Geological Laboratory, Indiana University.** Bloomington. *Contr. geol. Lab. Indiana Univ.*

15719 **Contributions. Geophysical Institute, University** of **Alaska.** College. *Contr. geophys. Inst. Univ. Alaska* [1950–]
Series A. **L.**MO.; **C.**PO.; **M.**U. 55–58 imp.
Series B. **L.**MO. 52–; **C.**PO.; **M.**U. 54– imp.

15720 **Contributions** from the **Giannini Foundation** of **Agricultural Economics.** Berkeley. *Contr. Giannini Fdn agric. Econ.* **O.**AEC. 30–; **R.**U. 30–.

15721 **Contributions** from the **Gray Herbarium** of **Harvard University.** Cambridge, Mass. *Contr. Gray Herb. Harv.* [1891–] **L.**BM^N.; K.; L. 17–; **Bl.**U. 77–49; **E.**B.; **Lv.**U. 24–49; **M.**U. 94–36 imp.; **O.**B. 99– imp.; BO. 99– imp.

15721° **Contributions. Great Lakes Research Division.** *Contr. Gt Lakes Res. Div.* **Pl.**M. 56–.

15722 **Contributions** of the **Harvard Institute** for **Tropical Biology** and **Medicine.** Cambridge, Mass. *Contr. Harv. Inst. trop. Biol. Med.* [1925–34] **L.**BM^N.; EB. (ent.); SC.; TD.; **Abs.**N. 26; **O.**R. 25–30 imp.

15723 **Contributions** from the **Harvard Mineralogical Museum.** Cambridge, Mass. *Contr. Harv. miner. Mus.*

15724 **Contributions** from the **Havemeyer Laboratories, Columbia University.** New York. *Contr. Havemeyer Labs Columbia Univ.*

15725 **Contributions. Hawaii Institute** of **Geophysics,** University of Hawaii. Honolulu. *Contr. Hawaii Inst. Geophys.* [1957–] **L.**MO.; **Wo.**

15726 **Contributions. Hawaii Marine Laboratory,** University of Hawaii. Honolulu. *Contr. Hawaii mar. Lab.* [1950–] **Bn.**U. 54–; **Dm.** 54–; **Lo.**; **Pl.**M. 54–.

15727 **Contributions** from the **Herbarium** of **Taihoku Imperial University.** Taihoku. *Contr. Herb. Taihoku imp. Univ.* [1930–] **L.**BM^N. 30–36; K. 30–38 imp.; L.; **Br.**U.; **Lv.**U. 30–37; **O.**F. 30–36.

Contributions from the **Herbarium, University** of **Michigan.** *See* 15846.

15728 **Contributions** from the **Horticultural Institute, Taihoku Imperial University.** Taiwan, Japan. *Contr. hort. Inst. Taihoku imp. Univ.* [1929–] **L.**BM^N. 29–32 imp.; K. 29–36 imp.; **C.**A. 33–41 imp.

15729 **Contributions** from the **Hull Botanical Laboratory.** University of Chicago. *Contr. Hull bot. Lab. Univ. Chicago*

15730 **Contributions** to **Indiana Palæontology.** New Albany. *Contr. Indiana Palæont.* **L.**GL. 00–05 imp.; **E.**R. 98–06; **Lv.**U. 99–06.

Contributions of the **Inland Fisheries Research Stations.** Djakarta-Bogor. *See* 37305.

15731 **Contributions** de l'**Institut agricole** d'**Oka.** Montréal. *Contr. Inst. agric. Oka* [1911–47] **Rt.** 15–37 imp. [*C. as:* 15736]

15732 **Contributions** de l'**Institut** d'**astrophysique.** Paris. *Contr. Inst. astrophys., Paris* [1946–] **L.**AS.; SI.; **C.**O. (Sér. B.); UL.; **M.**U. (Sér. A.) 47–56 imp.; (Sér. B.) imp.

15733 **Contributions** de l'**Institut** de **biologie** de l'**Université** de **Montréal.** *Contr. Inst. Biol. Univ. Montréal* [1941–45: 48–] **L.**BM^N.; **Lo.**; **Rt.** [>15738, 1946–47]

15734 **Contributions** de l'**Institut botanique** de l'**Université** de **Montréal.** *Contr. Inst. bot. Univ. Montréal* [1938–] **L.**BM^N.; HS.; K.; L.; SC.; UC.; **Abs.**A.; **Bl.**U.; **Bm.**U.; **Bn.**U.; **E.**B.; **Hu.**G.; **Lv.**U.; **O.**BO.; F.; **Rt.** [*C. of:* 15759]

15735 **Contributions. Institut océanographique** de l'**Indochine.** Saigon. *Contr. Inst. océanogr. Indochine* [1949–] **L.**BM^N.; **Lo.** 53–; **Pl.**M.

15736 **Contributions** de l'**Institut** d'**Oka.** Université de Montréal. La Trappe. *Contr. Inst. Oka* [1948–] **L.**K.; **Rt.** [*C. of:* 15731]

15737 **Contributions. Institut r. météorologique** de **Belgique.** Bruxelles. *Contr. Inst. r. mét. Belg.* [1951–] **L.**BM. 58–; MO.; SC.

15738 **Contributions** de l'**Institut** de **zoologie** de l'**Université** de **Montréal.** *Contr. Inst. Zool. Univ. Montréal* [1937–40: 46–47] **L.**BM^N.; **Dm.** 39; **Lo.** 38–47; **Rt.** [>15733, 1941–45; *C. as:* 15733]

15738° **Contributions** of the **Institute** of **Acarology. Department** of **Zoology, University** of **Maryland.** *Contr. Inst. Acarol. Univ. Md* [1957–]

15739 **Contributions** from the **Institute** of **Astrophysics, Kyoto University.** Kyoto. *Contr. Inst. Astrophys. Kyoto Univ.* **L.**AS. 38–39; SC. 49–; **M.**U. 48– imp.

15740 **Contributions** from the **Institute** of **Botany, National Academy** of **Peiping.** *Contr. Inst. Bot. natn. Acad. Peiping* [1933–34] **L.**BM^N.; MY. [*C. of:* 15760]

15741 **Contributions** from the **Institute** of **Chemistry, National Academy** of **Peiping.** *Contr. Inst. Chem. natn. Acad. Peiping* [1934–36] **L.**P.; SC.

Contributions. Institute of **Fisheries Research, University** of **North Carolina.** *See* 15848.

15742 **Contributions** from the **Institute** for **General Pathology, Copenhagen University.** Copenhagen. *Contr. Inst. gen. Path. Copenh. Univ.* [1923–] **L.**LI. 44–; UCH. 44–; MD. 31; **C.**APH. 35–36: 48–; **Cr.**MD. 44–47.

15743 **Contributions** from the **Institute** of **Geology** and **Paleontology, Tohoku University.** Sendai. *Contr. Inst. Geol. Paleont. Tohoku Univ.* [1921–] **L.**BM^N. imp.; GL. 51–; Z. 51–; **Br.**U. 51–; **C.**P. 51–; S. 52–; **G.**U. 51–; **Lv.**U. 51–; **Y.**

15744 **Contributions** from the **Institute** of **Low Temperature Science, Hokkaido University.** Sapporo. *Contr. Inst. low Temp. Sci. Hokkaido Univ.* [1952–] **L.**MO.; P.; SC.; **C.**PO.; **Y.**

15745 **Contributions. Institute** of **Marine Biology, Puerto Rico.** *Contr. Inst. mar. Biol. P. Rico* [1958–] **Pl.**M.

Contributions. Institute of **Oceanography, Florida State University.** *See* 15796°.

15746 **Contributions** from the **Institute** of **Physiology, National Academy** of **Peiping.** *Contr. Inst. Physiol. natn. Acad. Peiping* [1934–37] **L.**BM^N. 34; **C.**UL.; **O.**R.

15747 **Contributions** from the **Institute** for **Regional Exploration.** Ann Arbor. *Contr. Inst. reg. Explor.* **L.**BM^N. 54.

15748 **Contributions** from the **Institute** of **Zoology, National Academy** of **Peiping.** *Contr. Inst. Zool. natn. Acad. Peiping* [1932–49] **L.**BM^N.; Z. (zool.); **C.**UL.; **E.**U.; **O.**R. 34–36; **Pl.**M. 34–49.

15749 **Contributions** to **Invertebrate Palaeontology.** *Contr. invertebr. Palaeont.* **E.**R. 55–.

15750 **Contributions** from the **Iowa Corn Research Institute.** Ames. *Contr. Ia Corn Res. Inst.* [1935–51] **L.**P.; SC.; **C.**A.; **Rt.** 39–51.

15751 **Contributions** from the **Iowa Engineering Experiment Station.** Ames. *Contr. Ia Engng Exp. Stn* **L.**P. 16–21; SC. 16–20.

15752 **Contributions** du **Jardin botanique** de **Rio** de **Janeiro.** *Contr. Jard. bot. Rio de J.* [1901–07] **L.**BM. 01–02; BM^N. 01–02; K.; **E.**B.

15753 **Contributions** from the **Jefferson Physical Laboratory** of **Harvard University.** Cambridge, Mass. *Contr. Jefferson phys. Lab. Harv.* [1903–29] **L.**BM.; EE.; R.; RI.; SC. 11–29; U.; **Abd.**U. 04–25; **Bl.**U. 28–31; **Bm.**U.; **Br.**U.; **C.**P.; UL.; **G.**U. 03–10; **Ld.**U.; **M.**T. 03–15; U.; **O.**R. 03–15. [*C. as:* 15804]

15754 **Contributions** from the **John Harrison Laboratory** of **Chemistry, University** of **Pennsylvania.** Philadelphia. *Contr. John Harrison Lab. Chem. Univ. Pa*

15755 **Contributions** from the **Kansu Science Education Institute.** Lanchow. *Contr. Kansu Sci. Educ. Inst.* **L.**BM^N. 43–45.

15756 **Contributions** from the **Kent Chemical Laboratory** of **Yale University.** New Haven. *Contr. Kent chem. Lab. Yale* **O.**R. 09–17 imp.

15757 **Contributions. Kiruna Geophysical Laboratory.** *Contr. Kiruna geophys. Lab.* **Bl.**U. 60–.

Contributions from the **Konkoly Observatory.** *See* 32562.

15758 **Contributions** du **Laboratoire** d'**astronomie** de **Lille.** Lille. *Contr. Lab. Astr. Lille* [1951–] **L.**AS.; **M.**U. 51–58.

15759 **Contributions** du **Laboratoire** de **botanique** de l'**Université** de **Montréal.** *Contr. Lab. Bot. Univ. Montréal* [1922–38] **L.**BM^N.; HS.; K.; L.; SC. 23–38; UC.; **Abs.**A.; **Bl.**U.; **Bm.**U.; **Bn.**U. 27–38; **E.**B.; **Hu.**G.; **Ld.**U.; **Lv.**U.; **O.**BO.; **Rt.** [*C. as:* 15734]

15760 **Contributions** from the **Laboratory** of **Botany, National Academy** of **Peiping.** *Contr. Lab. Bot. natn. Acad. Peiping* **L.**BM^N. 31–32*; MY. 31–32. [*C. as:* 15740]

15761 **Contributions** from the **Laboratory** of **Entomology, Bussey Institution** of **Applied Biology, Harvard University.** *Contr. Lab. Ent. Bussey Instn appl. Biol. Harv.* **O.**H. 09–26.

15762 **Contributions** from the **Laboratory** and **Museum** of **Comparative Pathology, Zoological Society** of **Philadelphia.** *Contr. Lab. Mus. comp. Path. zool. Soc. Philad.* **L.**MD. 21–36; Z. 22–29.

15763 **Contributions** from the **Laboratory** of **Neuropathology, University** of **Pennsylvania.** Philadelphia. *Contr. Lab. Neuropath. Univ. Pa* [1905] **L.**MD.; **Bm.**U.; **Lv.**U. [*C. in:* 15681]

15764 **Contributions** from the **Laboratory** of **Systematic Botany** and **Plant Oecology, Taihoku Imperial University.** Taihoku. *Contr. Lab. syst. Bot. Pl. Oecol. Taihoku imp. Univ.* **L.**BM^N. 37.

15765 **Contributions** from the **Laboratory** of **Vertebrate Biology** of the **University** of **Michigan.** Ann Arbor. *Contr. Lab. vertebr. Biol. Univ. Mich.* [1943–] **L.**BM^N.; UC.; Z.; **Abd.**U.; **Bl.**U.; **Bm.**U.; **C.**A.; P.; UL.; **Db.**; **Dm.**; **E.**R.; U.; **G.**N. 43–46; U.; **Lv.**U.; **M.**U.; **Nw.**A.; **O.**R.; **Y.** [*C. of:* 15766]

15766 **Contributions** from the **Laboratory** of **Vertebrate Genetics** of the **University** of **Michigan.** Ann Arbor. *Contr. Lab. vertebr. Genet. Univ. Mich.* [1936–42] **L.**BM^N.; UC.; Z.; **Abd.**U.; **Bl.**U.; **Bm.**U.; **C.**A.; P.; UL.; **Db.**; **E.**R.; U.; **G.**U.; **Lv.**U.; **M.**U.; **Nw.**A.; **O.**R.; **Y.** [*C. as:* 15765]

15766° **Contributions. Lamont Geological Observatory.** *Contr. Lamont geol. Obs.* **Pl.**M. 50– imp.

15767 **Contributions** from the **Lick Observatory.** Mount Hamilton, Cal. *Contr. Lick Obs.* [1889–95: 42–] **L.**AS.; **Cr.**P. 92–95; **E.**R. 89–95: 56–; **M.**U.; **Y.**

15768 **Contributions. Life Sciences Division, Royal Ontario Museum.** Toronto. *Contr. Life Sci. Div. R. Ont. Mus.* [1960–] L.BM^N.; SC.; C.PO.; Cr.M.; E.F. [*C. of:* 15692]
Contributions of the **Los Angeles Astronomical Department.** *See* 55586.

15768° **Contributions. Marine Biological Laboratory.** Helsingfors. *Contr. mar. biol. Lab., Helsingf.* [1960–] Pl.M.

15769 **Contributions** of the **Marine Biological Station.** Asamushi. *Contr. mar. biol. Stn, Asamushi* Pl.M. 52–54.

15770 **Contributions** on **Marine Biology. Stanford University.** Palo Alto. *Contr. mar. Biol. Stanford Univ.* Pl.M. 30.

15771 **Contributions** to **Marine Biology** from the **University** of **Wales.** Bangor. *Contr. mar. Biol. Univ. Wales* [1957–] Bn.U.; Dm. [*C. of:* 14834]

15772 **Contributions** of the **Marine Botanical Institute.** Göteborg. *Contr. mar. bot. Inst., Göteborg* [1950–] Pl.M.

15772° **Contributions. Marine Laboratories, University** of **Delaware.** *Contr. mar. Labs Univ. Delaware* [1954–] Pl.M. imp.
Contributions from the **Marine Laboratory, Duke University.** *See* 15697.

15773 **Contributions. Marine Laboratory, Florida State Board** of **Conservation.** *Contr. mar. Lab. Fla St. Bd Conserv.* Pl.M. 58–.

15774 **Contributions** from the **Marine Laboratory, University** of **Miami.** Coral Gables. *Contr. mar. Lab. Univ. Miami* L.AM. 54–; Bn.U. 51–; Pl.M. 45–.

15775 **Contributions** from the **Massachusetts General Hospital.** Cambridge, Mass. *Contr. Mass. gen. Hosp.* Br.U. 06–12; Lv.U. 06–08.

15775° **Contributions. Metals Research Laboratory, Carnegie Institute.** Pittsburgh. *Contr. Metals Res. Lab. Carnegie Inst.* [1924–]

15776 **Contributions** of the **Meteoritical Society.** Northfield, Minn. *Contr. meteorit. Soc.* [1947–] L.AS.; BM^N.; U. 47–51; Bm.U.; E.U.; O.R. [*C. of:* 15835]

15777 **Contributions** from the **Mineralogical Laboratory** of the **Sheffield Scientific School, Yale University.** New Haven. *Contr. miner. Lab. Sheffield scient. Sch. Yale* O.R. 09–15 imp.

15778 **Contributions** to **Mineralogy. Mineralogisk** og **geologisk Museum, Kjøbenhavns Universitet.** *Contr. Miner. miner. geol. Mus, Kbh.* [1902–] L.sC.

15779 **Contributions** to the **Mineralogy** of **Western Australia.** Perth. *Contr. Miner. West. Aust.*

15780 **Contributions** of the **Misaki Marine Biological Station.** *Contr. Misaki mar. biol. Stn* [1940–] Bn.U. 59–; Pl.M.

15781 **Contributions** from the **Mitsui Institute** of **Marine Biology.** Susaki, Japan. *Contr. Mitsui Inst. mar. Biol.* [1933–] Dm. 33–38; Lv.M. 33–38; Pl.M. 33–38.

15782 **Contributions** from the **Mount Hakkoda Botanical Laboratory.** Sendai. *Contr. Mt Hakkoda bot. Lab.* L.K. 30– imp.

15783 **Contributions** from the **Mount Wilson Solar Observatory.** Washington. *Contr. Mt Wilson sol. Obs.* [1905–] L.AS. 05–49; BM.; MO. 05; SC.; Abs.N. 07–16 imp.; Bl.U. 05–07; C.O.; P.; UL.; Cr.P 05–07; Db.; E.O.; R. 05–49; Ld.U. 25–; M.U. 21–49 imp.; Nw.A. 08–49; O.O.; R. 05–07.

15783° **Contributions. Mukaishima Marine Biological Station.** *Contr. Mukaishima mar. biol. Stn* Pl.M. 54–.

15784 **Contributions** from the **Museum** of the **American Indian, Heye Foundation.** New York. *Contr. Mus. Am. Indian* [1913–] L.AN.; BM. 18–; SC. 19–; C.UL.; E.U. 16–; O.RH.

15785 **Contributions** from the **Museum** of **Geology, University** of **Michigan.** Ann Arbor. *Contr. Mus. Geol. Univ. Mich.* [1924–27] L.BM^N.; GM.; SC.; Z.; Abd.U.; Bl.U.; Br.U.; C.P.; UL.; E.R.; U.; G.N. 25–27; U.; Ld.U.; Lv.U.; M.U.; O.R. [*C. as:* 15787]

15786 **Contributions. Museum** of **History** and **Technology, United States National Museum.** Washington. *Contr. Mus. Hist. Technol., Wash.* [1959–] Bl.U.; Bn.U. [*Issued in:* 12512]

15787 **Contributions** from the **Museum** of **Paleontology, University** of **Michigan.** Ann Arbor. *Contr. Mus. Paleont. Univ. Mich.* [1928–] L.BM^N.; GM.; UC. 32–37; Z.; Abd.U.; Bl.U.; Bm.U.; Br.U.; C.P.; UL.; Db.; E.R.; U.; G.N. 28–49; U.; Ld.U.; Lv.U.; M.U.; O.R.; Y. [*C. of:* 15785]

15788 **Contributions. National Research Institute** of **Chemistry.** Shanghai. *Contr. natn. Res. Inst. Chem., Shanghai* [1934–]

15789 **Contributions** from the **National Research Institute** of **Geology.** Shanghai. *Contr. natn. Res. Inst. Geol., Shanghai* [1931–] L.BM^N. 31–36: 48; GL. 31–48 imp.; SC.; UC.; Bm.U. 31–33; E.R. 38; Lv.U. imp.

15790 **Contributions. National Research Institute** of **Psychology.** Peiping. *Contr. natn. Res. Inst. Psychol., Peiping* [1932–]

15791 **Contributions** from the **New South Wales National Herbarium.** Sydney. *Contr. N.S.W. natn. Herb.* [1939–] L.BM^N.; HS.; K. imp.; L.; Abs.U. 40; Hu.G. 39–51; O.BO. 55–57; Y.

15792 **Contributions** from the **New York Botanical Garden.** New York. *Contr. N.Y. bot. Gdn* [1899–33] L.BM^N. 03–26 imp.; K.

15793 **Contributions. New Zealand Oceanographic Institute.** Wellington. *Contr. N.Z. oceanogr. Inst.* [1954–] L.MO. 55–; Dm. 57–; Pl.M. [*C. of:* 41160]

15794 **Contributions** from the **Nyström Institute** for **Scientific Research** in **Taiyuanhu.** Shansi. *Contr. Nyström Inst. scient. Res. Taiyuanhu* L.BM. 25–27*; BM^N. 21–27. [*C. as:* 15833]
Contributions. Observatoire géophysique, Kiruna. *See* 15757.

15795 **Contributions** from the **Observatory, University** of **Saint Andrews.** Saint Andrews. *Contr. Obs. Univ. St Andrews* [1953–] L.AS.; BM. imp.; E.R.; M.U. 53–56; Y.

15796 **Contributions. Obstetrics** and **Gynaecology. University** of **Michigan.** Ann Arbor. *Contr. Obstet. Gynaec. Univ. Mich.* [1893–22] L.BM.; Bm.U. 19–22; C.UL. 19–22; O.R. 19–22. [*C. as:* 15682]

15796° **Contributions. Oceanographic Institute, Florida State University.** Talahassee. *Contr. oceanogr. Inst. Fla St. Univ.* L.AM. 52–; Dm. 52– imp.; Lo. 56– imp.; Pl.M. 54–.
Contributions. Oceanographic Institute of **New Zealand.** *See* 15793.

15796⁰ **Contributions** in **Oceanography** and **Meteorology.** Agricultural and Mechanical College, Texas. *Contr. Oceanogr. Met. agric. mech. Coll. Tex.* [1950–] **Lo.**; **Pl.**M.

15797 **Contributions** from the **Osborn Botanical Laboratory, Yale University.** New Haven. *Contr. Osborn bot. Lab. Yale* [1916–] **L.**BMᴺ. 16–32 imp.; K.

15798 **Contributions** from the **Palaeontological Laboratory, Peabody Museum, Yale University.** New Haven. *Contr. palaeont. Lab. Peabody Mus.* **O.**R. 09–21 imp.; **Sa.** 18–.

15799 **Contributions** to **Palaeontology.** Washington. *Contr. Palaeont.* [1925–] **L.**U.; **Bn.**U.; **Br.**U.; **C.**P. imp.; **E.**R.; **N.**U. imp.; **Nw.**A. 25–49.

15800 **Contributions** to the **Palaeontology** of **Kansas.** State Geological Survey. Lawrence. *Contr. Palaeont. Kans.* [1932–33] **L.**BM.; BMᴺ.; GM.; SC.; UC.

15801 **Contributions** from the **Pathological Laboratory, University** of **Michigan.** Ann Arbor. *Contr. path. Lab. Univ. Mich.* [1896–] **L.**BM. imp.; **Bm.**U. 13–29; **C.**PA. 96–12: 15–; **E.**U. 15–; **G.**U. 22–46 imp.; **Lv.**U. 22–; **O.**R. 20–.

15802 **Contributions** from the **Peking Union Medical College.** Peking. *Contr. Peking Un. med. Coll.* [1921–24] **L.**LI.; MA.; MC.; TD.; **Abd.**U.; **Bm.**U.; **Br.**U. imp.; **C.**UL.; **E.**U.; **Lv.**U.; **M.**MS. 24; U. 21–22; **O.**R. [*C. as:* 49429]

15803 **Contributions** from the **Perkins Observatory.** Ohio Wesleyan University. Delaware. *Contr. Perkins Obs.* [1935–] **L.**AS.; SC.; **C.**O.; **M.**U. (Ser.I) imp.: (Ser. II) 53–; **Y.** (Ser. I & II)

15804 **Contributions** from the **Physical Laboratories** of **Harvard University.** Cambridge, Mass. *Contr. phys. Labs Harv.* [1930–] **L.**EE. 33–37; R. 30–45; SC. imp.; **Br.**U.; **M.**U. 30–45. [*C. of:* 15753]

15805 **Contributions** from the **Physical Laboratory** of **Iowa University.** Iowa City. *Contr. phys. Lab. Ia Univ.* [1907–17] **L.**BM. 15; **C.**P. 13–17; UL. 11–17; **E.**R.; **G.**U. imp.; **M.**U. 07–15; **O.**R. [*C. as:* 55632]

15806 **Contributions** from the **Physical Laboratory, University** of **Michigan.** Ann Arbor. *Contr. phys. Lab. Univ. Mich.* [1913–] **L.**BM.; P. 13–27; **Bm.**U. 13–27; **C.**UL.; **E.**U. 13–27 imp.; **Ld.**U. 25–; **Lv.**U. 25–; **M.**U. 13–26 imp.; **O.**R. 13–27 imp.; **Sa.** 27.

15807 **Contributions** from the **Physiological Laboratory, Medico-Chirurgical College** of **Philadelphia.** *Contr. physiol. Lab. med.-chir. Coll. Philad.* **E.**U. 97–12.

15808 **Contributions.** **Phytopathological Laboratory, Taihoku Imperial University.** Taihoku. *Contr. phytopath. Lab. Taihoku imp. Univ.* [1929–] **L.**AM. 32–41; BMᴺ. 41–; LI. 29–39; **Abs.**U. 29–; **Br.**A. 30–38 imp.; **Lv.**U. 29–41; **Nw.**A. 29–37.

15809 **Contributions.** **Plant Research Institute, Department** of **Agriculture, Canada.** Ottawa. *Contr. Pl. Res. Inst. Can.* **O.**F. 60– imp.

15810 **Contributions** from the **Princeton University Observatory.** Princeton. *Contr. Princeton Univ. Obs.* [1911–] **L.**AS.; M. 11–15; SC.; UC.; **C.**O.; P.; **Db.**; **E.**O. imp.; R. 11–24; **M.**U. 11–53; **O.**O.

15811 **Contributions** to **Psychological Theory.** Duke University. Durham, N.C. *Contr. psychol. Theory* [1934–] **L.**SC.; **C.**UL.; **E.**A.; **O.**B. [*Replaces:* 17258]

15812 **Contributions** in **Psychology.** Ohio State University. Columbus. *Contr. Psychol.* [1922–34] **L.**BM.; UC. [*C. of:* 36085]

15813 **Contributions** from the **Psychopathic Hospital.** Boston. *Contr. psychopath. Hosp., Boston* **C.**UL. 13–19*. [*C. in:* 14733]

15813⁰ **Contributions** of the **Research Council** of **Alberta.** Edmonton. *Contr. Res. Coun. Alberta* **L.**BM. 45– imp.

15814 **Contributions** from the **Research Division, Electrical Engineering Department, Massachusetts Institute** of **Technology.** Boston. *Contr. Res. Div. elect. Engn Dep. M.I.T.* [*C. of:* 10876]

15815 **Contributions** from the **Research Laboratory** of **Physical Chemistry, Massachusetts Institute** of **Technology.** Boston. *Contr. Res. Lab. phys. Chem. M.I.T.*

15816 **Contributions** of the **Royal Ontario Museum** of **Geology.** Toronto. *Contr. R. Ont. Mus. Geol.* [1939–] **L.**BMᴺ. 39; **C.**S. 39–46.

15817 **Contributions** of the **Royal Ontario Museum** of **Palaeontology.** Toronto. *Contr. R. Ont. Mus. Palaeont.* [1939–47] **L.**BMᴺ.; **G.**U. 39–46 imp. [*C. in:* 15818]

15818 **Contributions** of the **Royal Ontario Museum** of **Zoology.** Toronto. *Contr. R. Ont. Mus. Zool.* [1928–51] **L.**BMᴺ.; **C.**PO. 39–51 imp.; **Cr.**M.; **E.**F. 43–51; **Y.** [*C. as:* 15819]

15819 **Contributions** of the **Royal Ontario Museum** of **Zoology** and **Palaeontology.** Toronto. *Contr. R. Ont. Mus. Zool. Palaeont.* [1952–55] **L.**BMᴺ.; **C.**PO.; **Cr.**M.; **E.**F.; **Y.** [*C. of:* 15818; *C. as:* 15692]

15820 **Contributions** from the **Rutherfurd Observatory** of **Columbia University.** New York. *Contr. Rutherfurd Obs. Columbia Univ.* [1937–] **L.**AS.; SC. 38–; **C.**O.; **E.**O.; **M.**U. 37 imp.; **O.**O. [*C. of:* 15654]

15821 **Contributions** from the **Sanitary Research Laboratory** and **Sewage Experiment Station, Massachusetts Institute** of **Technology.** Boston. *Contr. sanit. Res. Lab. Sewage Exp. Stn M.I.T.* **L.**TD. 05–10 imp.; **Lv.**U. 05–14.

Contributions. **School** of **Fisheries, University** of **Washington.** *See* 15849.

Contributions. **School** of **Forestry** and **Conservation, University** of **Michigan.** *See* 15846.

15823 **Contributions** in **Science.** Los Angeles County Museum. Los Angeles. *Contr. Sci.* [1957–] **L.**BMᴺ.; K. (bot.); Z.; **O.**BO. imp.; **Y.**

15824 **Contributions.** **Scripps Institution** of **Oceanography.** La Jolla, Cal. *Contr. Scripps Instn Oceanogr.* [1937–] **L.**AM. 38–; BMᴺ. 39–; MO.; SC. 40–; **Bn.**U. 51–; **C.**P. 39–; **Cr.**M. 53–; **Dm.** 39–; **E.**R.; **Fr.** 46–; **Lo.** 38–; **Lv.**U. 39–; **Mi.**; **Pl.**M. imp.; **Sa.** 54–; **Sh.**SC. 54–; **Y.**

15825 **Contributions** du **Service** d'**entomologie.** Québec. *Contr. Serv. Ent., Québ.* **O.**F. 41–. [*See also* 15702]

15826 **Contributions.** **Service océanographique** des **pêches** de l'**Indochine.** Nhatrang. *Contr. Serv. océanogr. Pêch. Indochine*

15827 **Contributions.** **Seto Marine Biological Laboratory.** Kyoto. *Contr. Seto mar. biol. Lab.* **L.**SC. 52–; **Bn.**U. 31–36; **Dm.** 31–; **Lo.** 30– imp.; **Lv.**U. 30– imp.; **Pl.**M. 31– imp.

15828 **Contributions** from the **Shaw School** of **Botany.** Urbana, Illinois. *Contr. Shaw Sch. Bot., Urbana* **L.**K. 88–06*.

15829 **Contributions** from the **Sheffield Chemical Laboratory** of **Yale University.** New Haven. *Contr. Sheffield chem. Lab. Yale*

15830 **Contributions** from the **Shellac Research Bureau** of the **Polytechnic Institute** of **Brooklyn.** *Contr. Shellac Res. Bur. polytech. Inst. Brooklyn* [1929–]

15831 **Contributions. Shimonoseki College** of **Fisheries.** Yoshima, Shimonoseki City. *Contr. Shimonoseki Coll. Fish.* [1951–] **L.**BM^N.; **E.**R.; **Pl.**M. 51.

15832 **Contributions** from the **Sin Yuan Fuel Laboratory, Geological Survey** of **China.** Peking. *Contr. Sin Yuan Fuel Lab.* [1930–] **L.**GM.; **P.** 30–37 imp.

15833 **Contributions** from the **Sino-Swedish Scientific Research Association.** Taiyüanfu. *Contr. Sino-Swed. scient. Res. Ass.* [1928–] **L.**BM.; BM^N. 28–30 [*C. of:* 15794]

15834 **Contributions** from the **Sloane Physical Laboratory, Yale University.** New Haven. *Contr. Sloane phys. Lab. Yale* **O.**R. 12–20 imp.; **Sa.** 20–.

15835 **Contributions** of the **Society** for **Research** on **Meteorites.** Northfield, Minn. *Contr. Soc. Res. Meteorites* [1935–46] **L.**AS.; BM^N.; U.; **Bm.**U.; **E.**U. 38–46; **O.**R. 37–46. [*C. as:* 15776]

15836 **Contributions** de la **Station biologique** du **St Laurent** à **Trois Pistoles.** Québec. *Contr. Stn biol. St Laurent* [1932–52] **L.**BM^N.; SC.; Z. imp.; **Db.**; **Dm.**; **E.**R.; **Lo.** 35–52; **Lv.**U.; **Pl.**M. [*C. as:* 15660]

15837 **Contributions** to **Stellar Statistics.** Washington. *Contr. stell. Statist.* [1904–] **L.**SC.; **Bm.**P. 10–; **G.**U. 04; **Ld.**U.; **Sa.**

15838 **Contributions** from the **Sterling Chemical Laboratory** of **Yale University.** New Haven. *Contr. Sterling chem. Lab. Yale* **Sa.** 23–.

15839 **Contributions** to the **Study** of **Tuberculosis** by the **Research Department, National Jewish Hospital, Denver.** *Contr. Study Tuberc. Res. Dep. natn. Jewish Hosp. Denver* [1920–32] **L.**MD. 25–29; **Bm.**U. 27–29; **E.**U. 26–29.

Contributions suisses à la **dendrologie.** *See* 48926.

15840 **Contributions** from the **Tamano Marine Laboratory.** Okayama University. Okayama. *Contr. Tamano mar. Lab.* **L.**BM^N. 60–; **Bn.**U. 56– imp.

15841 **Contributions. Texas Game** and **Fish Commission.** Austin. *Contr. Tex. Game Fish Commn* **Lo.** 58–.

15842 **Contributions** from the **Texas Research Foundation.** Renner. *Contr. Tex. Res. Fdn* **L.**BM^N. 50–.

15843 **Contributions** from the **Third Division Neurological Institute** of **New York.** *Contr. third Div. neurol. Inst. N.Y.* **L.**MD. 19; S. 19; **M.**MS. 19.

15844 **Contributions** from the **United States National Herbarium.** Washington. *Contr. U.S. natn. Herb.* [1890–] **L.**AM.; BM.; BM^N.; GL. 90–24; HS. 03–; K.; L.; P.; R. 05–22; UC. 05–32 imp.; **Abd.**U. 02–; **Abs.**N. 09–; **Bl.**U. 92–; **Bm.**U. 05–; P.; U.; **Bn.**U. 05–24; **Br.**U. 06: 19–28; **C.**BO. imp.; P.; UL. 92–; **Cr.**N. 09–; P. 05–24; **Db.**; **E.**B.; C. 95–23 imp.; F. imp.; R. 96– imp.; U. 93–24 imp.; **G.**M. 12–33; N. 05–24; U. 89–24 imp.; **Ld.**U. 05–40 imp.; **Lv.**P. imp.; U. 05–; **M.**P.; U. 05– imp.; **N.**P. 05–; U. 05–25; **Nw.**A. 99–; **O.**BO.; R. 05–; **Pl.**M. 05–24 imp.; **Sh.**U. 92– imp.; **Y.**

Contributions. University of **Illinois Department** of **Zoology.** *See* 15689^c.

Contributions from the **University Institute** for **Human Genetics** in **Copenhagen.** *See* 36221.

15845 **Contributions** from the **University** of **Iowa Observatory.** Iowa City. *Contr. Univ. Ia Obs.* [1931–] **L.**AS. 31–38; **C.**O.

15846 **Contributions** from the **University** of **Michigan Herbarium.** Ann Arbor. *Contr. Univ. Mich. Herb.* [1939–42] **L.**BM^N.; K.; SC.; **Bl.**U.; **Bm.**U.; **G.**U.; **Lv.**U.; **M.**U.; **Nw.**A.; **O.**F.; R.

15847 **Contributions** from the **University** of **Michigan School** of **Forestry** and **Conservation.** Ann Arbor. *Contr. Univ. Mich. Sch. For. Conserv.* **O.**F. 29–33 imp.

15848 **Contributions. University** of **North Carolina Institute** of **Fisheries Research.** Chapel Hill. *Contr. Univ. N. Carol. Inst. Fish. Res.* **Pl.**M. 53–.

Contributions. University Observatory, Saint Andrews. *See* 15795.

15849 **Contributions. University** of **Washington College** (*formerly* **School**) of **Fisheries.** Seattle. *Contr. Univ. Wash. College* (*Sch.*) *Fish.* [1952–] **L.**Z. 60– imp.; **Dm.** imp.; **Lo.** 53–; **Lv.**U.; **Pl.**M.; **Y.**

15850 **Contributions** in **Veterinary Medicine. Ohio State University.** Columbus. *Contr. vet. Med. Ohio St. Univ.* **L.**BM^N. 26.

15851 **Contributions. Virginia Fisheries Laboratory.** Gloucester Point. *Contr. Va Fish. Lab.* **Dm.** 57–; **Lo.** 51–; **Y.**

15852 **Contributions** from the **W. J. Macdonald Observatory, Texas University.** Fort Davis. *Contr. W. J. Macdonald Obs.* [1936–] **L.**AS.; **E.**O.; R. 36–47.

15853 **Contributions** from the **Walker Museum.** Chicago. *Contr. Walker Mus.* [1901–30] **L.**BM.; BM^N.; GM.; SC. 30; **C.**UL. 17–30.

15854 **Contributions** from the **William Pepper Laboratory** of **Clinical Medicine, University** of **Pennsylvania.** Philadelphia. *Contr. Wm Pepper Lab. clin. Med.* [1900–] **L.**BM. 23–; MA. 00–28; MD. 00–03: 25–37; S. 02–40; TD. 37–40; U. 00–03; **Abd.**U. 00–03 imp.; **Bm.**U. 00–03; **Br.**U. 09–14; **C.**PA. 00: 02–25; UL.; **E.**U. 00–03; **G.**U. 00–37; **O.**R. 00–37 imp.

15855 **Contributions** from the **Woods Hole Oceanographic Institution.** Woods Hole. *Contr. Woods Hole oceanogr. Instn* [1933–56] **Wo.**

15856 **Contributions** from the **Wrocław Astronomical Observatory.** *Contr. Wrocław astr. Obs.* [1948–] **L.**AS.; SC. [*Part C. of:* 27494]

15857 **Contributions. Yorkton Natural History Society.** Yorkton. *Contr. Yorkton nat. Hist. Soc.* **L.**BM^N. 43.

15858 **Contributions** from the **Zoological Laboratory** of the **Indiana University.** Bloomington. *Contr. zool. Lab. Indiana Univ.* **L.**SC. 22.

15859 **Contributions** from the **Zoological Laboratory** of the **Museum** of **Comparative Zoology** at **Harvard College.** Cambridge, Mass. *Contr. zool. Lab. Mus. comp. Zool. Harv.* **L.**SC. 96–; **Bm.**U. 94–18 imp.; **M.**U. 01–14 imp.

15860 **Contributions. Zoological Laboratory, Syracuse University.** *Contr. zool. Lab. Syracuse Univ.* [1906–] **Pl.**M. 08–37.

15861 **Contributions** from the **Zoological Laboratory** of the **University** of **Illinois.** Urbana. *Contr. zool. Lab. Univ. Ill.* **L.**BM^N. 33–35.

15862 **Contributions** from the **Zoological Laboratory, University** of **Michigan.** Ann Arbor. *Contr. zool. Lab. Univ. Mich.*

15863 **Contributions** from the **Zoological Laboratory** of the **University** of **Missouri.** Columbia. *Contr. zool. Lab. Univ. Mo.*

15864 **Contributions** from the **Zoological Laboratory, University** of **Pennsylvania.** Philadelphia. *Contr. zool. Lab. Univ. Pa* [1893–] **L.**BM.; L. 24–; UC. 20–24; Z. 95–36 imp.; **Br.**U. 33–; **C.**P.; UL.; **Db.** 01–; **Dm.** 10–60; **E.**R. 00–; U. 04–; **Ld.**U. 49–58; **Lv.**U. 04– imp.; **M.**U. 93–58 imp.; **O.**R. 95–; Z. 95–54 imp.; **Pl.**M. 04–59; **Rt.** 27–32 imp.: 39–; **Sa.** 02– imp.

15865 **Contributions** from the **Zoological Laboratory** of the **University** of **Texas.** Austin. *Contr. zool. Lab. Univ. Tex.* [1900–] **C.**P.; UL.

Contributions in **Zoology** and **Entomology. Ohio State University.** *See* 15688.

15866 **Contributions** on **Zoology. University College** of **Swansea.** *Contr. Zool. Univ. Coll. Swansea* [1957–] **L.**AM.; **Pl.**M.

15867 **Contributiuni botanice** din **Cluj.** *Contrtiuni bot. Cluj* [1921–37] **L.**BM^N.; K.; **E.**B.

15868 **Contributiuni** la **studiul chimioterapia tuberculosei.** Bucureşti. *Contrtiuni Stud. Chimioter. Tuberc.*

15869 **Contribuzioni** alla **biologia vegetale.** R. Istituto botanico de Palermo. *Contrzioni Biol. veg.* **L.**BM^N. 94–09*; K. 94–09.

15870 **Contro** la **tuberculosi** e le altre **malattie sociali.** Lentini. *Contro Tuberc.*

15871 **Control.** London. *Control* [1958–] **L.**AV.; BM.; DI.; EE.; P.; QM. 59–; SI.; **Bl.**U. 60–; **Bn.**U.; **Co.**T.; **Cr.**U. 61–; **Db.**; **Dn.**U.; **Ep.**D.; **G.**M.; U.; **H.**U.; **Ld.**U.; **Ld.**W.; **Lv.**P.; **M.**C. 59–; P.; U.; **Ma.**T.; **N.**T. 60–; U.; **O.**R.; **Sh.**SC.; **Sil.** 58–59; **Ste.**; **Sw.**U.; **Wd.**; **Y.**

15872 **Control Engineering.** New York. *Control Engng* [1954–] **L.**AV. 55– imp.; EE.; NP. 56–; P.; QM.; SI.; **Bl.**U. 59–; **Bm.**P. 55–; T. 55–; **Bn.**U.; **Br.**U. 56–; **C.**ENG. (5 yr.); **Co.**T. 60–; **Ep.**D.; **F.**A. 55–; **G.**T.; U. imp.; **Ld.**U. 59–; **Lv.**P.; **M.**P. 56–; T.; U.; **N.**T. 60–; U. 58–; **Sh.**SC. 60–; **Sw.**U. 57–; **Y.**

15873 **Control Series Bulletin. Massachusetts Agricultural Experiment Station.** Amherst. *Control Ser. Bull. Mass. agric. Exp. Stn* [1914–] **L.**P. 14; **Rt.**; **Y.**

15873° **Controlling Chemical Hazards.** Washington. *Controlling Chem. Haz.* **L.**BM. 54–.

15874 **Convegni biologici.** Consiglio nazionale delle ricerche. Comitato nazionale per la biologia e Comitato talassografico. Roma. *Convegni biol.* **L.**BM^N. 31: 33.

15875 **Convegno** di **genetica.** Roma. *Convegno Genet.* **L.**BM^N. 52–56; SC. 53–.

15876 **Convegno nazionale ortofrutticolo.** Roma. *Convegno naz. ortofrutt.* **L.**BM. 34–.

15877 **Convention Record** of the **Institute** of **Radio Engineers.** New York. *Conv. Rec. Inst. Radio Engrs N.Y.* [1953–55] **L.**AV.; P. imp.; SC.; **Bm.**T. 54–55; **F.**A.; **G.**U. imp.; **M.**U.; **Te.**N. [*C. as:* 22638]

15878 **Converter Notes.** London. *Converter Notes* [1949–]

15879 **Conveying.** London. *Conveying* [1918–25] **L.**P. [*Supplement to:* 13433]

15880 **Conveyor.** Journal of the Burnley and District Mining Society. Burnley. *Conveyor* **L.**P. 52–.

15881 **Convorbiri ştiinţifice.** Orăştie. *Convorb. ştiinţ.*

15882 **Cook Technical Review.** Cook Research Laboratories. Chicago. *Cook tech. Rev.* [1954–] **L.**EE.; P.

15883 **Coolia.** Contactblad van de Nederlandse mycologische vereniging. Leiden. *Coolia* [1954–] **L.**BM^N.; K.; MY.; **Y.**

Cooper Research Laboratory Journal. *See* 25864.

15885 **Cooper Union Bulletin. Engineering** and **Science Series.** New York. *Cooper Un. Bull. Engng Sci. Ser.* [1930–] **L.**P. 46–; **Y.**

15886 **Cooper's Vehicle Journal.** London. *Cooper's Veh. J.* [1909–22] **L.**BM.; P. 10–13; **Abs.**N. 12–22; **Bm.**P. 21–22; **C.**UL.; **G.**M. 09–13; **O.**R. [*C. of:* 14652^a; *C. as:* 33720]

15887 **Coopération.** Périodique dentaire. Bruxelles. *Coopération, Brux.* [1936]

15888 **Co-operation** in **Agriculture.** London. *Co-opn Agric., Lond.* [1910–15] **L.**AM.; BM.; SC. 12–15; **Abs.**N. 12–14; **Ld.**U.; **O.**R. 15. [*C. of:* 92]

15889 **Cooperativa** dos **armadores** da **pesca** da **Baleiro.** Lisboa. *Cooperativa Armad. Pesca Baleiro* **Wo.** 57–58.

Co-operative Bulletin. Mining and **Metallurgical Investigations. Carnegie Institute** of **Technology.** *See* 32033.

Co-operative Coal Mining Series. Bulletin. Illinois State Geological Survey. *See* 9916.

15890 **Co-operative Economic Insect Report. Bureau** of **Entomology** and **Plant Quarantine, U.S. Department** of **Agriculture.** Washington. *Co-op. econ. Insect Rep.* [1951–] **L.**AM.; **E.**B.; **O.**H.; **Rt.** [*C. of:* 23661, 33678 and 51349]

15891 **Co-operative Electrical Research.** Leatherhead. *Co-op. elect. Res.* [1956–] **L.**AV. 57–; BM.; EE.; P.; SI.; **Abs.**N.; **Bl.**U.; **Bm.**T.; **Br.**U.; **C.**UL.; **Co.**T.; **E.**A.; HW. 57–; **Ld.**U.; **M.**C.; P.; T.; U. 56–58; **Ma.**T.; **O.**R.; **Rt.** 56; **Sh.**S.; **Sil.**; **Y.**

Co-operative Extension Work in **Agriculture** and **Home Economics,** Florida. *See* 14172.

Co-operative Extension Work in **Agriculture** and **Home Economics, Missouri College** of **Agriculture.** *See* 14173.

15892 **Co-operative Ground Water Report. Illinois State Water Survey.** Urbana. *Co-op. Grnd Wat. Rep. Ill.* [1959–] **E.**R.; **Y.**

15893 **Co-operative Ore-Dressing Investigations. South Australia School** of **Mines** and **Industries.** *Co-op. Ore-Dress. Invest. S. Aust. Sch. Mines* [1935–]

15894 **Co-operative Ore-Dressing Investigations. University** of **Melbourne.** *Co-op. Ore-Dress. Invest. Univ. Melbourne* [1935–]

15895 **Co-operative Russian Translations. D.S.I.R.** London. *Co-op. Russ. Transl.* **Ld.**P. 56–59 imp. [*Supplement to:* 54105; *C. in:* 27891]

15896 **Cooper-Bessemer Monthly.** Grove City, Pa. *Cooper-Bessemer Mon.* [1930–31] [*C. of:* 6490]

15897 **Coordination Report. Department** of **Tsetse Research, Tanganyika Territory.** Dar-es-Salaam. *Co-ord. Rep. Dep. Tsetse Res. Tanganyika* **L.**EB. 28–30*; Z. 28–30.

15898 **Copeia.** New York, etc. *Copeia* [1913–] L.BM^N.; L. 24–32; SC. 39–; UC.; Z. imp.; Bn.U. 55–; C.B.; **Dm.** 30–37; E.U.; **Fr.** 52–; **Lo.** 39–; **Mi.** 52–; **Pl.**M. 37–; **Y.**

15899 **Copper.** Copper Development Association. London. *Copper, Lond.* [1957–] L.AV. 59–; BM.; MI.; P.; **Bm.**T.; **Bn.**U.; **Br.**U.; **Bra.**P. 58–; **Co.**T. 59–; **Cr.**U.; E.A.; **Ld.**P.; U. 58–; **M.**P.; U.; **Ma.**T.; **N.**T. (I yr); O.R.; **Sil.** (I yr); **Y.** [*C. of:* 9920]

15900 **Copper.** New York. *Copper, N.Y.*

15901 **Copper Abstracts.** London. *Copper Abstr.* [1959–] L.AV.; P.; SC.; **Abs.**U.; **Bm.**P.; T.; **Bn.**U.; **Br.**U.; **Co.**T.; **Cr.**U.; **Dn.**U.; G.U.; **Ld.**P.; U.; **Li.**M.; **M.**P.; **Ma.**T. N.T.; O.R.; **Sil.**; **Y.**

15902 **Copper** and **Brass.** Detroit. *Copper Brass*

15903 **Copper** and **Brass Bulletin.** New York. *Copper Brass Bull.* [1946–] L.NF.; P. (curr.); **Y.** [*C. of:* 9919]

15904 **Copper** and **Copper Alloys:** a survey of technical progress. Radlett. *Copper & Copper Alloys* [1946–51: 59–]L.BM. 59–; MI.; P. 49–51: 59–; **Bm.**T.; E.U. 59–; G.U.; **Ld.**P.; U. 59–; **M.**P. 59–; O.R.; **Y.** [>52418, 1953–59]
Copper Development Association Publications. *See* 12869.

15905 **Copper Handbook.** Houghton, Mich. *Copper Handb.* [1900–13] L.BM. 00–11 imp.; P. 00–08 imp.; SC. 11–13; G.M. 10–13. [*C. as:* 31983]

15906 **Copper Industry Report.** *Copper Ind. Rep.* [1955–] E.A.

15907 **Copyright Communications.** Incorporated Institution of Gas Engineers. London. *Copyr. Commun. inc. Instn Gas Engrs* G.U. 51– imp.; **Y.**

15907° **Copyright Publication. Gas Research Board.** *Copyr. Publ. Gas Res. Bd* L.P. 49–52*; G.U. 40–52 imp. [*Replaced by:* 45837]

15908 **Cor** et **vasa.** Praha. *Cor Vasa* [1959–] L.MD.; **Y.**

15909 **Cord.** Journal of the Paraplegic Branch of the British Legion. London, etc. *Cord* [1947–] L.MA.; H. 47–48.

15910 **Cord Age.** New York. *Cord Age*

15911 **Cordage, Canvas** and **Jute World.** London. *Cordage Canv. Jute Wld* [1939–48: 58–] L.BM.; P.; TP.; **Y.** [*C. of:* 15913; > 15914, 1949–52; > 19361, 1953–57]

15912 **Cordage Trade Journal.** New York. *Cordage Trade J.*

15913 **Cordage World.** London. *Cordage Wld* [1919–39] L.P. 35–39; TP. 27–39. [*C. as:* 15911]

15914 **Cordage World** and **Industrial Textiles.** London. *Cordage Wld ind. Text.* [1949–52] L.BM.; P.; TP. [*C. of:* 15911; *C. as:* 19361]
Cordage World and **Wire Rope Maker.** *See* 15913.

15915 **Cordoba médica.** Cordoba. *Cordoba méd.* [1927–29] L.C. 27–28 imp.
Coresta Information Bulletin. Cooperation Centre for Scientific Research relative to Tobacco. Paris. *See* 10540.

15916 **Coridon.** Bourne End. *Coridon* [1960–] L.BM^N.

15917 **Corn.** Corn Industries Research Foundation. New York. *Corn* [1945–] **Y.**

15918 **Corn Trade News.** Liverpool. *Corn Trade News* [1890–] L.AM.; C.UL. 22–; E.CE. (I yr); Lv.P. 36– imp.; O.AEC. 33–; B.

15919 **Cornbelt Farmer.** Waterloo, Ia. *Cornbelt Fmr*

15920 **Cornell Architect.** Ithaca. *Cornell Archit.*

15921 **Cornell Chemist.** Ithaca. *Cornell Chemist*

15922 **Cornell Civil Engineer.** Ithaca. *Cornell civ. Engr* [1907–35] L.P. 10–31; SC. 25–35. [*C. of:* 53599; *C. in:* 15924]

15923 **Cornell Conferences** on **Therapy.** New York. *Cornell Confs Ther.* [1946–] L.MD.; Dn.U. 47–55; E.U. 49–51.

15924 **Cornell Engineer.** Ithaca. *Cornell Engr* [1935–] L.P. imp.; SC. 37–39. [*C. of:* 15922 and 49702]

15925 **Cornell Extension Bulletin.** Ithaca. *Cornell Ext. Bull.* [1916–] L.BM. 26–; Nw.A. 43– imp.; Rt. 55.

15925° **Cornell Nutrition Conference.** *Cornell Nutr. Conf.* Bl.U. 59–.

15926 **Cornell Plantations.** Ithaca. *Cornell Plantns* [1944–] L.K. 50–; O.F.

15927 **Cornell Rural School Leaflet.** Ithaca. *Cornell rur. Sch. Leafl.* L.BM^N. 53– imp.; Rt. 07–16: 25–33.

15928 **Cornell University Medical Bulletin.** New York. *Cornell Univ. med. Bull.* [1911–32] L.MA. 11–22; MC. 12–32 imp.; MD. 12–32; SC. 14–17; U. 11–19; **Db.** imp.; E.U. 15–24; Lv.U. 12–32.

15929 **Cornell Veterinarian.** Ithaca. *Cornell Vet.* [1911–] L.MD. 43–; TD. 17–30; V.; VC. 45– imp.; Z. 58–; **Abd.**R. 38–; **Br.**U. 46–; C.APH. 35–; V. 38–; **Db.** 52–; E.N. 16– imp.; PO. 49–; Lv.U. 22–; R.D. 44–; W. 29–; **Y.**

15930 **Cornerstone.** Dunstable. *Cornerstone* [1953–] L.BM.; P.; **Lh.**P. imp.; **Y.**

15931 **Cornue.** Bulletin de l'Association des élèves et anciens élèves de l'Institut de chimie de l'Université de Rennes. Rennes. *Cornue* [1949–] **Y.**

15932 **Corona.** London. *Corona* [1949–] L.TD.; **Ha.**RD.; N.U.

15933 **Corps gras industriels.** Paris. *Corps gras ind.* L.P. 27–28*.

15934 **Corpuscle.** Chicago. *Corpuscle*

15935 **Correio agrícola.** Organo da Sociedade bahiana de agricultura. Bahia. *Correio agríc.* [1923–32] L.EB. imp.; SC. 29–32.

15936 **Correio médico.** Lisboa. *Correio méd.*

15937 **Correo médico** de **Paris.** Paris. *Correo méd. Paris*

15938 **Correo odontológico internacional.** Madrid. *Correo odont. int.*

15939 **Correo terapéutico.** Caracas. *Correo terap.*

15940 **Correspondance** de **médecine** et d'**hygiène.** Oran. *Corresp. Méd. Hyg.*

15941 **Correspondance médicale.** Paris. *Corresp. méd.* [1902–]

15942 **Correspondance minière** et **métallurgique.** Paris. *Corresp. min. métall.*

15943 **Correspondance** d'**Orient.** Paris. *Corresp. Orient* E.G. 11–.

15944 **Correspondant médical.** Paris. *Correspt méd.* [1893–]

15945 **Correspondence. Agricultural Association** of **China.** *Corresp. agric. Ass. China* **Abs.**A. 46–; O.F. 45–.

15946 **Correspondencia médica.** Madrid. *Correspcia méd.*
Correspondenzblatt. *See* **Korrespondenzblatt.**

15947 **Corriere agricola.** Lugano. *Corr. agric.*

15948 **Corriere** dei **ceramisti.** Rivista tecnica. Perugia. *Corr. Ceram.* **L.**P. 27–40; **Wa.**B. 27–38.

15949 **Corriere** delle **macchine.** Milano. *Corr. Macch.* **L.**P. 59–.

15950 **Corriere nucleare.** Milano. *Corr. nucl.* **L.**P. (curr.)

15951 **Corriere** della **pesca.** Roma. *Corr. Pesca*

15952 **Corriere** dei **sanitari.** Faenza. *Corr. Sanit.*

15953 **Corriere sanitario.** Milano. *Corr. sanit.*

15954 **Corriere silvano.** Roma. *Corr. silv.*

15955 **Corrosion.** National Association of Corrosion Engineers. Houston, Tex. *Corrosion* [1945–] **L.**AV. 50–; C. 58–; I.; IC.; NF.; P. 52–; PR. 47–; SC.; **Bm.**C. 46–; P. 53–; T. 59–; **C.**UL.; **F.**A. 46–; **G.**U.; **Li.**M. 50–; **M.**D. 56–; T. 56–; **Ma.**T. 56–; **Nw.**A. 54–; **Rn.**B. 54–; **Sh.**IO. SC. 60–; **Sl.**I. 53–; **Te.**C.; **Wd.**; **Y.**

15956 **Corrosion Abstracts.** National Association of Corrosion Engineers. Houston, Tex. *Corros. Abstr.* [*Issued with:* 15955]

15957 **Corrosion** et **anti-corrosion.** Paris. *Corros. Anti-Corros.* [1953–] **L.**AV. 56– imp.; P.; **Y.**

15958 **Corrosion Commentary.** London. *Corros. Comment.* **L.**P. 57–.

15959 **Corrosion Engineer.** London. *Corros. Engr* [1959–] **L.**AV.; BM.; EE.; P.; PT.; **Br.**U.; **Db.**; **E.**A.; **G.**M.; **Lh.**FO.; **Lv.**P.; **Rn.**B.; **Sil.**; **Sl.**I.; **Sy.**R.; **Y.** [*Supplement to* and *published in:* 15961]

15960 **Corrosion** and **Material Protection.** Pittsburgh. *Corros. Mater. Prot.* [1945–48] **L.**I. 46–48; NF.; SC. 47–48; **Bm.**C. 46; **Te.**C.

15961 **Corrosion Prevention** and **Control.** London. *Corros. Prev. Control* [1954–] **L.**AV.; BM.; EE.; P.; PR. 54–59; PT. 57–; SC.; SI. 54–58; **Bm.**C. 54–58; **Br.**U.; **Db.** 55–; **E.**A.; **G.**M.; **Lh.**FO. 55–; **Lv.**P.; **Rn.**B.; **Sil.**; **Sl.**I.; **Sy.**R. 54–56; **Y.**

15962 **Corrosion Reporter.** Toronto. *Corros. Reptr* [1946–] **Y.**

15963 **Corrosion Science.** *Corros. Sci.* [1961–] **L.**SC.; **Y.**

15964 **Corrosion Technology.** London. *Corros. Technol.* [1954–] **L.**AV. imp.; BM.; SC.; LE.; P.; PR.; PT. 55–; **Bm.**C. 57–; P.; T.; U. 55– imp.; **C.**UL.; **E.**A.; **Ep.**D.; **F.**A. 55–; **G.**T.; U. 55–; **Lh.**P.; **Lv.**P. (imp.); **M.**D. 57–; P. 56–; **Ma.**T. 55–; **O.**R.; **Rn.**B.; **Sl.**I.; **Sy.**R.; **Y.** [Nos. 1–3 of 1954 issued as supplement to: 13760]

15965 **Corrosioneering News.** Rochester. *Corrosg News* [1954–] **L.**P. [*C. of:* 21367]

15966 **Corse agricole.** Ajaccio. *Corse agric.*

15967 **Cortijos** y **rascacielos.** Madrid. *Cortijos Rascac.* [1945–] **L.**BA.

15968 **Cortisone Investigator.** Rahway. *Cortis. Invest.* [1950–54] **L.**MA.; MC. 52–54; **Lv.**P. 54.

15969 **Cosmétologie.** Paris. *Cosmétologie* [1957–] **L.**P. **Cosmétologie, Körperpflege, Wissenschaft.** *See* 37161.

Cosmic Data. Moscow. *See* 27708.

15970 **Cosmopolitan Osteopath.** Des Moines. *Cosmop. Osteop.*

15971 **Cosmopolitan Sanatorium Journal.** Cleveland. *Cosmop. Sanat. J.*

15972 **Cosmos.** Geographical and Geological Societies, Queen Mary College. London. *Cosmos, Lond.* [1949–] **L.**QM.; U.; **C.**GG. 51–55; **O.**G. 52–.

15973 **Cosmos.** Revue des sciences et de leurs applications. Paris. *Cosmos, Paris* [1863–14] **L.**BM.; P.; RI.; SC. 63–95; **Db.**; **E.**R. 63–66: 81–82; **O.**R. 85–10.

15974 **Cosmos.** Comunicazioni sui progressi più recenti e notevoli della geografia e delle scienze affini. Torino. *Cosmos, Torino* [1873–13] **L.**BM. 73–02; G.; **MO.** 73–77; Z. 73–79.

15975 **Cospar Information Bulletin.** Committee on Space Research. The Hague. *Cospar Inf. Bull.* [1960–] **L.**AV.; BM.; P.

15976 **Costa azzurra agricola-floreale.** San Remo. *Costa azzurra agric.-flor.* **L.**K. 26; MY. 26–42.

15977 **Costruttore edile.** Torino. *Costrutt. edile* **L.**P. 24–28.

15978 **Costruzioni metalliche.** Milano. *Costruz. metall.* [1949–54: 59–] **L.**I. 59–; P.; **Y.** [>438, 1955–59]

15978ᶜ **Côte d'azur agricole** et **horticole.** Nice. *Côte d'azur agric. hort.* **Y.**

15979 **Coton** et **culture cotonnière.** Paris. *Coton Cult. cotonn.* [1926–] **L.**BMᴺ. 26–29; TP. 26–39; **C.**A. 26–28; **M.**C. 26–39; **Y.**

15980 **Coton** et **fibres tropicales.** Paris. *Coton Fibr. trop.* [1946–] **L.**AM.; EB. 46–47; P.; TP.; **Hu.**G.; **M.**C.; **Y.**

15981 **Coton** et **fibres tropicales. Bulletin analytique.** Paris. *Coton Fibr. trop. Bull. analyt.* [1952–] **L.**P.; MC.; TP.; **Y.** [*Previously issued as part of:* 15980]

15982 **Cotton.** Atlanta, Ga. *Cotton, Atlanta* [1899–46] **L.**P. 11–46; SC. 24–26; **M.**C. 20–46; T. 32–46. [*C. as:* 52966]

15983 **Cotton.** Manchester. *Cotton, Manchr* [1895–] **L.**BM.; **E.**A.; **Lv.**P. 17–; **M.**C. 38– imp.; P.; **O.**B. **Cotton.** Monthly review of the world situation. *See* 15994. World statistics. *See* 16006.

15984 **Cotton Board Trade Letter.** Manchester. *Cott. Bd Trade Lett.* **M.**C. 48–52. **Cotton Campaign.** Tashkent. *See* 8529.

15985 **Cotton** and **Cotton Oil News.** Dallas, Tex. *Cott. & Cott. Oil News* [1904–35] **L.**SC. 25–35. [*C. in:* 15986]

15986 **Cotton** and **Cotton Oil Press.** Dallas, Tex. *Cott. & Cott. Oil Press* [1936–49] **L.**SC.; TP. 43–45. [*C. of:* 15985 and 15997; *C. as:* 15990]

15987 **Cotton Digest.** *Cott. Dig.* **Y.**

15988 **Cotton Farmer** and **Dairyman.** Rockhampton, Qd. *Cott. Fmr Dairym.* [1923–24]

15989 **Cotton Gazette.** Liverpool. *Cott. Gaz.* [1894–] **L.**BM.

15990 **Cotton Gin** and **Oil Mill Press.** Dallas, Tex. *Cott. Gin Oil Mill Press* [1950–] **L.**TP.; **Y.** [*C. of:* 15986]

15991 **Cotton Ginner.** Dallas, Tex. *Cott. Ginner*

15992 **Cotton Literature.** Washington. *Cott. Lit.* [1931–42] **L.**P.; **M.**C.

15993 **Cotton Mill Year Book.** Boston, Mass. *Cott. Mill Yb.* **L.**P. 18–21.

15994 **Cotton. Monthly Review** of the **World Situation.** Washington. *Cott. mon. Rev. Wld Situ.* **M.**C. 51–58; **Y.** [*C. in:* 16006]

15995 **Cotton News.** Columbia, S.C. *Cott. News*

15996 **Cotton News Weekly.** Durban. *Cott. News Wkly* [1924–] **L.**BM.

15997 **Cotton Oil Press.** Washington. *Cott. Oil Press* [1917–35] **L.**PR. 27–30; TP. [*C. in:* 15986]

15998 **Cotton Plant.** Greenville, S.C. *Cott. Pl.* [1882–04]

15999 **Cotton. Quarterly Statistical Bulletin.** Washington. *Cotton q. statist. Bull.* [1949–57] **M.**C. 50–57; **Y.** [*C. as:* 16006]

16000 **Cotton Record.** Savannah, Ga. *Cott. Rec.* [1907–]

16001 **Cotton Region Climate** and **Crop Bulletin.** Washington. *Cott. Reg. Clim. Crop Bull.*

16002 **Cotton Report. Department** of **Agriculture, Uganda.** *Cott. Rep. Dep. Agric. Uganda* **Rt.** 49–.

16003 **Cotton Review.** Liverpool. *Cott. Rev.* **L.**BM. 15–18*.

16004 **Cotton Seed Oil Magazine.** Atlanta. *Cott. Seed Oil Mag.* [1900–]

16005 **Cotton Situation.** Washington. *Cott. Situ.* [1931–] **L.**BM. 52–; **M.**C. 53–.

16005° **Cotton Trade Journal.** Savannah, Ga. *Cott. Trade J.* **M.**C. (2 yr.)

16005ᶠ **Cotton Trade Journal. International Edition.** Memphis. *Cott. Trade J. int. Edn* **M.**C. 33–.

16006 **Cotton: World Statistics.** Washington. *Cotton Wld Statist.* [1957–] **M.**C.; **Y.** [*C. of:* 15999]

16007 **Cotton Year Book.** New York. *Cott. Yb., N.Y.* **M.**P. 31– imp.; **Y.**

16008 **Cotton Yearbook** and **Diary.** Manchester. *Cott. Yb. Diary, Manchr* [1909–] **L.**BM.; P.; **Abs.**N. 14– imp.; **Bm.**P. 18–; **Br.**P. (5 yr.); **Br.**A. 09–; **C.**UL. 11–; **E.**A. 11–; **G.**M. 13–25: 37– imp.; **Ld.**P. 28–; **Lv.**P. 17–; **M.**P. 10–; **O.**B. 11–; **Y.** [*C. of:* 52998]

16009 **Coturnix.** Report of Bishop's Stortford college Natural History Society. Bishop's Stortford. *Coturnix* **L.**BMᴺ. 54–.

16010 **Couleurs.** Centre d'information de la couleur. Paris. *Couleurs* [1954–] **L.**P.; **Y.** [*C. of:* 9742]

16011 **Council** for the **Coordination** of **International Congresses** of **Medical Sciences.** Paris. *Coun. Coord. int. Congr. med. Sci.* [1950–51] **L.**TD.

16012 **Council Paper. Legislative Council, Fiji.** Suva. *Coun. Pap. Fiji* **L.**EB. (ent.) 14–; **C.**A. (agr.) 31–.

16013 **Council Paper. Legislative Council, Trinidad** and **Tobago.** *Coun. Pap. Trin.* **L.**EB. (agr. & med.) 15–33; SC. 05– imp.

16014 **Council's Report. British Boot Shoe** and **Allied Trades Research Association.** Kettering. *Coun.'s Rep. Br. Boot Shoe all. Trades Res. Ass.* **L.**P. 47–.

16015 **Country Landowner.** London. *Ctry Ldowner* [1950–] **L.**AM.; BM.; NC. 53–; **C.**A. 57– imp.; **E.**A.; **O.**R.; **R.**D. [*C. of:* 25757]

16016 **Countryman.** Idbury. *Countryman, Idbury* [1927–] **L.**AM.; BM.; MY. 49–; NC. 33–44; Z. 46–; **Abs.**A. 50–; N.; P. 36–; U. 52–; **Ba.**I. (curr.); **Bra.** 44–; P. 50–; U. 44–; **C.**UL.; **Cr.**P.; **E.**A.; AR. (curr.); **G.**M. 44–; U. 44–54 imp.; **Hu.**G. 52–; **Ld.**U. 33–53 imp.; **Lv.**P. 37–; **M.**P.; **N.**U. imp.; **Nw.**A. 27–48; **O.**AEC.; BO. 61–; R.; **Rt.** 29–39 imp.

16016° **Countryman.** Nicosia. *Countryman, Nicosia* **L.**AM. 49–; TP. 47–; **Abs.**A. 55–; **C.**A. (3 yr.); **E.**A. 49–; W. 57–; **Hu.**G. 49–; **Md.**H. 49–; **O.**F. 56–; RE. 49–55 imp.; **R.**D. 49–; **Rt.** 50– imp.; **Sil.** 50–.

16017 **Country-side.** London. *Country-side* [1905–] **L.**BMᴺ.; HO. 05–14; L. 49–; NC. 55–; U.; Z. 05–24; **Bn.**U. 31–49 imp.; **C.**UL.; **M.**P. 05–06: 51–; **O.**OR. 10–; R.; **Rt.** 34–45 imp.; **Y.**
 Country-side Leaflet. *See* 16017.
 Country-side Monthly. *See* 16017.

16018 **County Agricultural Surveys. Royal Agricultural Society** of **England.** London. *Cty agric. Survs* [1954–] **L.**BM.; **Rt.**

16019 **County Council** and **Agricultural Record.** London. *Cty Coun. agric. Rec.* [1906–07] **L.**AM. 07; BM.; P.; **Bm.**P.; **C.**UL. [*C. as:* 1385]

16019° **County Gentleman** and **Land** and **Water Illustrated.** London. *Cty Gent. Ld Wat. illustr.* [1880–15] **L.**BM.; UC. 14–15; Z. 80–05; **Db.** 97–02; **E.**A. 93–15 imp.; **G.**M. 80–14; **O.**B. 93–05. [*C. as:* 27993]

16020 **County Reports. Geological Survey** of **Alabama.** University of Alabama. Alabama. *Cty Rep. geol. Surv. Ala.* [1923–] **L.**BMᴺ.

16021 **County Reports. Idaho Bureau** of **Mines** and **Geology.** Moscow, Ida. *Cty Rep. Idaho Bur. Mines Geol.* [1956–] **L.**MI.

16022 **County Reports. Ornithological Section, Leicester Literary** and **Philosophical Society.** Leicester. *Cty Rep. orn. Sect. Leicester lit. phil. Soc.* **O.**OR. 41–.

16023 **Courrier apicole.** Limoges. *Courr. apic.*
 Courrier CERN. *See* 12878.

16023° **Courrier** du **Centre internationale** de l'**enfance.** Paris. *Courr. Cent. int. Enf.* [1950–] **L.**H.; MA.; MC.; MD.; TD. imp.; **Abd.**R. 55–; **C.**UL. 50–53; **E.**P. 51–54; U.; **O.**R. 56–.

16024 **Courrier** des **chercheurs. Office** de la **recherche scientifique** (et **technique**) d'**outre-mer.** Paris. *Courr. Cherch.* [1949–] **L.**BM. 50–; BMᴺ. 53–56; TD. 52–; **Pl.**M. 49–56 imp.; **Rt.** 54.

16025 **Courrier chirurgical.** Alger. *Courr. chir.*

16026 **Courrier** de l'**eau,** du **gaz** et de l'**électricité.** Paris. *Courr. Eau Gaz Élect.*

16027 **Courrier—H.E.C.** H. Ernst & Cie. Berne. *Courr.—H.E.C.* **L.**P. (curr.)

16028 **Courrier horticole.** Bruxelles, Belsele. *Courr. hort.* **Md.**H. 45–60.

16029 **Courrier** de l'**hygiène.** Paris. *Courr. Hyg.*

16030 **Courrier** de l'**I.M.C. Institut international** de mécano-culture. Lausanne. *Courr. I.M.C.* **L.**AM. 31–37; SC. 35–36; **C.**A. 34–.
 Courrier. International Children's Centre. Paris. *See* 16023°.

16031 **Courrier médical.** Paris. *Courr. méd.* [1850–]

16032 **Courrier médical** et **pharmaceutique.** Bruxelles. *Courr. méd. pharm.* **L.**MA. 36–39. [*C. of:* 16033]

16033 **Courrier médico-pharmaceutique.** Bruxelles. *Courr. méd.-pharm.* **L.**MA. 29–35*. [*C. as:* 16032]

16034 **Courrier métallurgique.** Bruxelles. *Courr. métall.* **L.**P. (curr.); **Y.**

16035 **Courrier** de la **normalisation.** Paris. *Courr. Norm.* [1934–] **L.**P. 50–; **Y.**

16036 **Courrier** des **pétroles** et des **combustibles liquides.** Paris. *Courr. Pétrol.* [1920–] **L.**PT. 50–.

16037 **Courrier pharmaceutique belge.** Bruxelles. *Courr. pharm. belge*
　　Cours d'**eau** et **énergie.** *See* 57145.

16038 **Couverture, plomberie.** *Couv. Plomb.*

16039 **Coventry Engineering Society Journal.** Coventry. *Coventry Engng Soc. J.* [1919–] **L.**BM.; P. 26–60; **Bm.**P.; U. 20–; **M.**P. 23–; **Sh.**IO. (5 yr.); **Y.**

16040 **Cow Testing Circular.** Department of Agriculture, Saskatchewan. Regina. *Cow Test. Circ. Sask.*

16041 **Cowkeeper** and **Dairyman's Journal.** London. *Cowkeep. Dairym. J.* [1879–04] **L.**BM. [*C. as:* 16336]

16042 **Cowry.** St. Austell. *Cowry* [1960–] **L.**BM^N.

16043 **Crabtree.** J. A. Crabtree and Co. Walsall. *Crabtree* **L.**P. (curr.); **E.**A. 57–; **Sil.** (1 yr.).

16044 **Cracow Reprints.** Observatoryum, Uniwersytet Jagielloński. Kraków. *Cracow Repr.* [1927–] **L.**AS.; **E.**O.

16045 **Craigleith Hospital Chronicle.** Edinburgh. *Craigleith Hosp. Chron.* [1914–19] **L.**BM.; MA. imp.; MD.; **E.**A. 14–15; **O.**B. 15–19.

16046 **Crane Valve World.** Crane Co. Chicago. *Crane Valve Wld* **L.**NF. 45–; **F.**A.; **Y.**
　　Cranfield College of **Aeronautics Reports.** *See* 43088.

16048 **Cravache.** Journal hippique de Marseille. Marseille. *Cravache*

16049 **Craven Machine Tool Gazette.** Reddish. *Craven Mach. Tool Gaz.* **L.**I. (curr.); P. 33–59; **Bm.**C. (curr.); **Sh.**IO. 47–; **Y.**

16050 **Creamery Gazette.** Des Moines, Ia. *Cream. Gaz.*

16051 **Creamery Manager.** Dublin. *Cream. Mgr* [1903–32] **L.**BM. 04–32; **Abs.**N. 28–32; **Db.**; **O.**B. 27–32. [*C. as:* 24126]

16052 **Creamery** and **Milk Plant Monthly.** Chicago. *Cream. Milk Pl. Mon.* [1912–30] **L.**SC. 29–30; **R.**D. 26–30. [*C. as:* 31847]

16053 **Creighton Medical Bulletin.** Omaha. *Creighton med. Bull.* [1898–]
　　Crelles Journal. *See* 26767.

16054 **Crerar Metals Abstracts.** Chicago. *Crerar Metals Abstr.* [1952–] **L.**P.; RI. 54–; **Y.**

16055 **Criação** e **veterinária.** Porto Alegre. *Criação Vet.* **L.**V. 47–48; **E.**AB. 48: 56–.

16056 **Criança portuguesa.** Lisboa. *Criança port.* [1942–] **L.**MA.; MD. 46–.

16057 **Cripple.** Oswestry. *Cripple* [1928–30] **L.**MD.; **Abs.**N.; **Br.**U.; **C.**UL.; **Db.**; **O.**R. 28–29. [*C. of:* 16060]

16058 **Crippled Child.** Battle Creek, Mich., etc. *Crippl. Child* [1923–] **L.**H. 50–; MD. 30–; **G.**PH. 24–.

16059 **Crippled Child Bulletin.** Elyria. *Crippl. Child Bull.* **L.**MD. 42–.

16060 **Cripples Journal.** Oswestry. *Cripples J.* [1924–28] **L.**MD.; **Abs.**N.; **Br.**U.; **C.**UL.; **Db.**; **Nw.**A. 24–27; **O.**R. [*C. as:* 16057]

16061 **Criterio católico** en las **ciencias médicas.** Barcelona. *Criter. catól. Cienc. méd.*

16062 **Criterio médico-quirúrgico.** Pamplona. *Criter. méd.-quir.*

16063 **Critica.** Giornale di medicina omiopatica scientifica e chirurgia. Firenze. *Critica*

16064 **Critica medica.** Milano. *Critica med.*

16065 **Critica sanitaria.** Napoli. *Critica sanit.* [1910–13: 24–36] **C.**UL. 24–36; **O.**R. 24–36.

16066 **Critica zootecnica.** Roma. *Critica zootec.*

16067 **Croatica chemica acta.** Zagreb. *Croat. chem. Acta* [1956–] **L.**BM.; C.; P.; RI.; **C.**CH.; P.; **Db.**; **Ld.**U.; **Lv.**P.; **O.**R.; **Y.** [*C. of:* 4750]

16067° **Croce azzurra.** Teramo. *Croce azzurra* [1950–53] [*C. as:* 56594]

16068 **Crockery** and **Glass Journal.** New York. *Crock. Glass J.*

16069 **Croda Product Users Digest.** Goole. *Croda Prod. Us. Dig.* [1957] **L.**P. imp. [*C. as:* 16070]

16070 **Croda User's Digest.** Goole. *Croda Us. Dig.* [1958–] **L.**P. [*C. of:* 16069]

16071 **Croisade moderne.** Journal de médecine. Paris *Croisade mod.*

16072 **Cronaca** della **clinica medica.** Genova. *Cronaca Clin. med.*

16073 **Cronaca** della **Congregazione** di **carità** e del **Manicomio** di **Teramo.** *Cronaca Congreg. Carità Manicom. Teramo*

16074 **Cronaca** del **Manicomio** di **Siena.** Siena. *Cronaca Manicom. Siena*

16075 **Cronaca** del **R. Manicomio** di **Alessandria.** Alessandria. *Cronaca R. Manicom. Alessandria*

16076 **Cronache agrarie.** Firenze. *Cronache agr.*

16077 **Cronache** di **chirurgia.** Napoli. *Cronache Chir., Napoli*

16078 **Cronache** di **chirurgia** dell'**Ospedale civile** di **Chieti.** *Cronache Chir. Osp. civ. Chieti*

16079 **Cronache** dell'**I.D.I.** Istituto dermopatico dell' immacolata. Roma. *Cronache I.D.I.* **L.**MD. 59–.

16080 **Cronache mediche.** Roma. *Cronache med.*

16081 **Crónica agrícola.** Buenos Aires. *Crón. agríc.*

16082 **Crónica dental.** Lima. *Crón. dent.*

16083 **Crónica médica.** Lima. *Crón. méd., Lima* [1884–] **L.**MA. 41–; MD. 41–; TD. 04: 13– imp.; **Abd.**R. 40– imp.; **Br.**U. 23– imp.

16084 **Crónica médica.** Valencia. *Crón. méd., Valencia* [1878–] **L.**MA. 32–; MD. 28–37; **Lv.**M. 35–39 imp.

16085 **Crónica médica.** Valparaiso, *Crón. méd., Valparaiso*

16086 **Crónica médica mexicana.** México. *Crón. méd. mex.* [1897–36] **L.**TD. 14; **Lv.**U. 10–14.

16087 **Crónica médico-quirúrgica.** Habana. *Crón. méd.-quir.* [1875–35] **L.**LI. 22–35 imp.; TD. 22–35 v. imp.; **Lv.**U. 22–35 imp.

16088 **Crónica** de **vinos** y **cereales.** Madrid. *Crón. Vinos Cer.*

16089 **Crookes' Digest.** London. *Crookes' Dig.* [1939–] **L.**AM. 40– imp.; C.; MD.; **Abs.**N. 46–; **Bm.**P.; **M.**P.

16090 **Crop Bulletin. Department** of **Agriculture, Manitoba.** Winnipeg. *Crop Bull. Dep. Agric. Manitoba.* **Rt.** 15–; **Y.**

16091 **Crop Bulletin. Grain Research Laboratory.** Ottawa. *Crop Bull. Grain Res. Lab.* [1943–] **Rt.**

16092 **Crop Bulletin. Ontario Department** of **Agriculture.** Ottawa. *Crop Bull.* **L.**AM.; **Br.**U. 25–; **Ld.**U. 04– imp.; **Lv.**U. 05– imp.; **M.**P. 19–43; **Rt.** 09–30.

16093 **Crop Experiments. Department** of **Agriculture, Bombay.** Bombay. *Crop Exp. Dep. Agric. Bombay* **L.**BM. 79–98; **E.**A. 79–98; **Rt.** 84–08.

16094 **Crop Inquiry Series. Caribbean Research Council.** Washington. *Crop. Inq. Ser. Caribb. Res. Coun.* [1946–] **L.**SC.; **C.**A.; **O.**G. imp.; **Rt.** 46–47.

16095 **Crop Pest** and **Horticultural Reports. Oregon Agricultural Experiment Station.** Corvallis. *Crop Pest hort. Rep. Ore. agric. Exp. Stn* [1915–20] **L.**AM.; EB.; P.; **Br.**U.; **Md.**H.; **Rt.** [*C. of:* 6858]
Crop Production. Budapest. *See* 35384.

16096 **Crop Protection Digest.** Washington. *Crop Prot. Dig.*

16097 **Crop Protection Institute Circular. Purdue University.** Lafayette. *Crop. Prot. Inst. Circ. Purdue Univ.* **Md.**H. 37–48 imp.

16098 **Crop Protection Leaflets. Department** of **Agriculture, Canada.** Ottawa. *Crop Prot. Leafl. Can.* [1917–21] **L.**AM.; BM^N.; EB.; **O.**R. [*C. in:* 14182]

16099 **Crop Report.** Dublin. *Crop Rep., Dubl.* **Db.** 1860–.

16100 **Crop Report.** Enkhuizen, Holland. *Crop Rep., Enkhuizen*

16101 **Crop Report. Grain Research Laboratory.** Ottawa. *Crop Rep. Grain Res. Lab., Ottawa* [1941–] **L.**AM. (curr.); **C.**A.

16102 **Crop Reporter.** Washington. *Crop Reptr, Wash.* [1899–13] **L.**AM. 00–13 imp.; BM. 01–13 imp.; **Bm.**U. imp.

16103 **Crop Talk.** Ohio Department of Agriculture. Columbus. *Crop Talk*

16104 **Crops** and **Markets. Department** of **Agriculture, Union** of **South Africa.** Pretoria. *Crops Mkts, Pretoria* [1922–41] **L.**AM.; BM. 32–41; **R.**D. 27–41. [*C. in:* 19177]

16105 **Crops** and **Markets. U.S. Department** of **Agriculture.** Washington. *Crops Mkts, Wash.* [1924–57] **L.**BM^N. 31–57 imp.; MO. 24–54 imp.; **Abs.**N. 26–57 imp.; U. 49–57 imp.; **Lv.**P. 41–57; **O.**AEC. 47–57; **R.**D. 43–57. [*C. of:* 57207^g]

16106 **Crops** and **Soils.** Madison. *Crops Soils* [1958–] **L.**AM.; C.A.; **Rt.**; **Y.** [*C. of:* 57490]

16107 **Cross-Hatch.** Micromatic Hone Corporation. Detroit. *Cross-Hatch* [1949–] **L.**P.; **Lv.**P.

16108 **Crossley Chronicles.** Crossley Brothers Ltd. Manchester. *Crossley Chron.* **L.**P. 33–; **G.**E. (1 yr); **Lv.**P. 54–; **Y.**

16109 **Crown Colonist.** London. *Crown Colon.* [1931–50] **L.**AM. 48–50; TD. 31–41; TP.; **Abs.**A. 42–50; **C.**A. 36–50; GG. 47–56; **E.**AB. 48–50; **Ex.**U. 48–50; **Md.**H. 40–50; **O.**B.; G. 42–50.

16110 **Crucible Titanium Review.** *Crucible Titan. Rev.* [1958–] **L.**AV. [*C. of:* 42528]

16111 **Crushed Stone Journal.** Washington. *Crushed Stone J.* [1925–] **L.**P. 31– imp.; **Y.**

16112 **Crushing, Grinding, Mining** and **Quarrying Journal.** London. *Crush. Grind. Min. Quarr. J.* [1931–36] **L.**P.; **Abs.**N.; **Bm.**P. 32–36; U.; **C.**UL.; **Nw.**A. 31–35; **O.**R. [*Superseded by:* 31885]
Crushing and **Grinding Trades Journal.** *See* 16112.

16113 **Crustaceana.** Leiden. *Crustaceana* [1960–] **L.**AM.; BM^N.; SC.; Z.; **Bl.**U.; **Bn.**U.; **M.**U.; **Pl.**M.

16114 **Cryogenics.** London, New York. *Cryogenics* [1960–] **L.**AV.; BM.; P.; SC.; **Bn.**U.; **Ld.**U.; **Y.**

16115 **Crystal-ized Facts** about **Sugar Beets.** *Crystal. Facts Sug. Beets Sil.* 53–.

16115^a **Crystallography.** Washington. *Crystallography, Wash.* **Te.**C. 59–; N. 59–; **Y.** 57–. [*English abstracts of:* 27764]
Crystallography U.S.S.R. *See* 50348.

16116 **Csillagászati lapok.** Budapest. *Csillag. Lap.* [1938–] **L.**AS.

16117 **Csillagok világa.** Budapest. *Csillag. Vil.*

16117^c **Csomagolastechnika.** Budapest. *Csomagolastechnika* **Y.**

16118 **Cuadernos** de **arquitectura.** Barcelona. *Cuad. Arquit.* [1944–] **L.**BA.

16119 **Cuadernos. Centro** de **estudios** del **tabaco.** Santiponce. *Cuad. Cent. Estud. Tab., Santiponce* **C.**A. 44–imp.; **Rt.** 43.

16120 **Cuadernos** de **geografía** de **Colombia.** Bogotá. *Cuad. Geogr. Colombia* **Y.** [*Supplement to:* 8111]

16121 **Cuadernos** de **historia primitiva.** Madrid. *Cuad. Hist. primit.* [1946–] **L.**AN.

16122 **Cuadernos** de **historia sanitaria.** La Habana. *Cuad. Hist. sanit.* [1949–] **L.**MD. 54– imp.; **O.**R. 52–.
Monograph Series [1952–]

16122^a **Cuadernos** del **Instituto** de **historia.** México. *Cuad. Inst. Hist., Méx.*
Seria antropológica [1957–]

16123 **Cuadernos. Laboratorio** de **física cósmica, Universidad mayor** de **San Andres.** La Paz. *Cuad. Lab. Fís. cósm. Univ. may. S Andres* **L.**MO. 52–.

16124 **Cuadernos médicos.** Mexico, D.F. *Cuad. méd., Méx.*

16125 **Cuadernos médicos** y de **divulgación científica.** Valencia. *Cuad. méd. Divulg. cient.* [1944–]

16126 **Cuadernos de mineralogía** y **geología. Universidad** de **Tucuman.** *Cuad. Miner. Geol. Univ. Tucuman* [1938–] **L.**BM.; GL. 38–46 imp.; GM.; U. 38–46 UC.; **Bm.**U.; **Br.**U.; **C.**S. 38–39.

16127 **Cuadernos** de **seminaria. Universidad nacional** de **Córdoba.** Córdoba. *Cuad. Semin. Univ. nac. Córdoba*
Serie ciencias físico-naturales [1931–] **L.**U. 31–36.

16128 **Cuadernos. Seminario** de **problemas científicos** y **filosoficas. Universidad nacional** de **México.** *Cuad. Semin. Probl. cient. filos. Univ. nac. Méx.* **L.**BM. 57–; U. 57–.

16129 **Cuadernos** del **Servicio** de **hematología** del **Hospital general** de **Miraflores.** La Paz. *Cuad. Serv. Hemat. Hosp. gen. Miraflores* [1955–] **L.**MA.

16130 **Cuadros** de **frequencía** de los **differentes elementos meteorológicos** en **'El Bosque'.** Santiago. *Cuadr. Freq. differ. Elem. met. El Bosque* [1930–32] **L.**MO. [*C. of:* 35580; *C. as:* 46134]

16131 **Cuba agrícola.** Habana. *Cuba agríc.*

16132 **Cuenca minera.** Córdoba. *Cuenca min.*

16133 **Cuenta** del **Ministerio** de **salubridad** y de **agricultura** y **cria.** Caracas. *Cuenta Minist. Salubr. Agric., Caracas* **L.**BM. 32–.

16134 **Cuenta** del **Ministerio** de **trabajo** y de **comunicaciones.** Caracas. *Cuenta Minist. Trab. Comun., Caracas* **L.**BM. 38–.

16135 **Cuir.** Paris. *Cuir* [1906–23] **Ld.**U. 08–23. [*C. as:* 16136]

16136 **Cuir technique.** Paris. *Cuir tech.* [1923–47] **L.**BM.; LE. 46–47; P. 25–40; **Ld.**U. [*C. of:* 16135; *C. as:* 47604]

16137 **Cuivre** et **laiton.** Paris. *Cuivre Laiton* **L.**NF. 28–39.

16138 **Cuivre, laitons, alliages.** Paris. *Cuivre Laitons Alliages* [1951–] **L.**P. 53– imp.; **Y.**

16139 **Cukoripar.** Budapest. *Cukoripar* **L.**P. 55–; **Y.**
Cultivators' Leaflet. Agricultural Department, Burma. *See* 28257.

16140 **Cultura.** 's Gravenhage. *Cultura, 's Grav.* [1902–23] **Db.** 03–21. [*C. as:* 28015]

16141 **Cultura médica.** Rio de Janeiro. *Cultura méd., Rio de J.* [1939–] **L.**MA. 46–.

16142 **Cultura medica.** Roma. *Cultura med., Roma* **L.**MA. 58– imp.

16143 **Cultura medica moderna.** Palermo. *Cultura med. mod.* [1923–] **L.**MD. 29–40. [*C. of:* 14966]

16144 **Cultura stomatologica.** Roma. *Cultura stomat.* [1914–30] [*C. as:* 3011]

16145 **Culture.** Paris. *Culture, Paris* [1948–53] **L.**AM.; **Sil.**

16146 **Cultureel Indië.** Leiden. *Cult. Indië* [1939–] **L.**AN. 39–46; **C.**UL.

16146a **Cultures marines.** Rivages de France. Paris. *Cultures mar.* **L.**AM. 59–.

16147 **Cultus.** Colégio Anglo Latino. São Paulo. *Cultus*

16148 **Cultuur** en **handel.** Kortenberg. *Cultuur Handel* **Md.**H. 39–.

16149 **Cumulated index medicus.** Chicago. *Cumul. Index med.* [1960–] **L.**BM.; MC.; MD.; S.; SC.; **Y.** [*Annual cumulation of:* 22895]

16150 **Cuoio, pelli, materie concianti.** Napoli. *Cuoio Pelli* [1947–] **L.**LE. 48–; P. 51–; TP.; **Y.** [*C. of:* 8499]

16151 **Cuore** e **circulazione.** Roma. *Cuore Circul.* [1924–] **L.**MA. 46–; MD.; S. 35–40. [*C. of:* 29303]

16152 **Cura Kneipp.** Torino. *Cura Kneipp*

16153 **Curator.** American Museum of Natural History. New York. *Curator* [1958–] **L.**BM^N.; K.; **E.**R. 38–59.

16154 **Cure marine.** Ostende. *Cure mar.* [1931–] **L.**MA.; MD.

16155 **Curette.** Journal médical. Bruxelles. *Curette*

16156 **Curity Research Notes.** Chicago. *Curity Res. Notes* [1942–]

16157 **Current Abstracts. Research** and **Development Department. General Foods Corporation.** Hoboken. *Curr. Abstr. Res. Dev. Dep. gen. Fds Corp.* [1954–] **L.**P. [*C. of:* 16158]

16158 **Current Abstracts** of **Scientific** and **Technical Literature.** Hoboken. *Curr. Abstr. scient. tech. Lit.* **L.**P. 52–54. [*C. as:* 16157]

16159 **Current Affairs Bulletin. Indo-Pacific Fisheries Council, F.A.O.** Bangkok. *Curr. Aff. Bull. Indo-Pacif. Fish. Coun.* **L.**TP. 58–; **Wo.** 52–.

16160 **Current Agricultural Literature.** London. *Curr. agric. Lit.* [1953–] **L.**AM.; P.; TP. 54–; V. 54–; **N.**U. (curr.); **Sil.**

16161 **Current Anthropological Literature.** Lancaster, Pa. *Curr. anthrop. Lit.* [1912–13] **L.**AN.; **Abs.**N.

16162 **Current Anthropology.** Chicago. *Curr. Anthrop.* [1960–] **L.**BM.; BM^N.; **Abs.**N.; **Bl.**U.; **H.**U.

16163 **Current Bibliography. Administration** and **Organisation** of **Scientific Research** and **Technical Development.** D.S.I.R. London. *Curr. Biblphy Adm. Org. scient. Res. tech. Dev.* **L.**MO. 53–57.
Current Bibliography of **Applied Geophysics.** *See* 49050.

16164 **Current Bibliography** for **Aquatic Sciences** and **Fisheries.** F.A.O. Rome. *Curr. Biblphy aquat. Sci. Fish.* [1959–] **L.**AM.; BM^N.; NC.; SC.; Z.; **Bn.**U.; **Dm.**; **Fr.**; **G.**U.; **Ld.**U.; **Lo.**; **Mi.**; **Pl.**M.; **Y.** [*Also supplements; C. of:* 16165]

16165 **Current Bibliography** for **Fisheries Science.** F.A.O. Rome. *Curr. Biblphy Fish. Sci.* [1958–59] **L.**BM^N.; NC.; SC.; Z.; **Bn.**U.; **Dm.**; **Fr.**; **G.**U.; **Lo.**; **Pl.**M.; **Y.** [*C. as:* 16164]

16166 **Current Bibliography** on **Science** and **Technology, Japan.** *Curr. Biblphy Sci. Technol. Japan*
Chemistry and Chemical Industry. **Y.**
Civil Engineering and Architecture. **Y.**
Electrical Engineering. **Y.**
Geology, Mining and Metallurgy. **Y.**
Physics and Applied Physics. **Y.**

16166c **Current Caribbean Bibliography.** Port-of-Spain. *Curr. Caribb. Biblphy* **Y.**

16167 **Current Chemical Papers.** Chemical Society. London. *Curr. chem. Pap.* [1954–] **L.**AM.; AV.; BM.; C.; CB. (2 yr.); LI.; MC. 54–55; NP.; P.; PH.; PR.; QM.; RI. 57–; SC.; TD.; TP.; U.; UC.; **Abd.**U.; **Bl.**U.; **Bm.**P.; T. (1 yr); **Bn.**U.; **Br.**A.; P.; **C.**CH.; UL.; **Co.**T. (curr.); **Dn.**U.; **E.**A.; U.; **Ep.**D.; **F.**A.; **G.**T. 54–56; U. (curr.); **H.**U.; **Lc.**A.; **Ld.**P.; U.; **Lo.**; **Lv.**P. 59–; U.; **M.**C. (2 yr.); P.; T.; U.; **Md.**H. 54–55; **N.**T.; **O.**R.; **Pit.**F.; **R.**D.; U.; **Sh.**S. 55–; **Sw.**U.; **Y.** [*Replaces:* 8749, A.I & II]

16168 **Current Contents.** Philadephia. *Curr. Cont.* [1959–] **L.**BM.; MD.; **G.**U. 60–; **Y.** [*C. of:* 16169]

16169 **Current Contents** of **Pharmaco-Medical Publications.** Philadelphia. *Curr. Cont. pharm.-med. Publs* [1958–59] **L.**BM. 59; MD.; **Bn.**U.; **Y.** [*C. as:* 16168]

16170 **Current Engineering Practice.** *Curr. Engng Pract.* **Y.**

16171 **Current Farm Economics.** Stillwater, Okla. *Curr. Fm Econ.* [1928–] **L.**AM. 33–; BM^N. 36–39; **N.**U. 52–; **O.**AEC. 30–; **R.**D. 39–.

16172 **Current Food Additives Legislation.** F.A.O. Rome. *Curr. Fd Addit. Legisl.* [1956–] **L.**AM.; BM.; H.; TP.; **E.**CE.; **Lh.**FO.

16173 **Current Forestry Literature.** Ottawa. *Curr. For. Lit.* O.F. 26–.

16174 **Current Geographical Publications.** New York. *Curr. geogr. Publs* [1938–] L.B. 39–51 imp.; SC. 48–; U. 48–; **Abs.**U. 42–43: 55– imp.; **Bm.**U. 46–; **Br.**U. 47–; **C.**GG. 50–; PO. 46–; UL. 43–; **E.**G. 40–; U. 48–; **G.**U. 45–; **H.**U. 46–; **Ld.**U. 55–; **N.**U. 51–; **Nw.**A. 48–; **O.**B.; G. imp.; **R.**U. 54–; **Sw.**U. 49–; **Y.**

16175 **Current Index** of Anesthesia and **Analgesia.** *Curr. Index Anesth. Analg.* **Y.**

16176 **Current Iodine Literature.** London. *Curr. Iodine Lit.* [1954–60] **L.**A.; AM.; BM.; K.; MY.; P.; PH.; TP.; UC.; UCH. imp.; V.; **Abd.**U.; **Abs.**U.; **Bn.**U.; **Br.**U.; **C.**APH.; V.; **Cr.**U.; **Db.**; **Dn.**U.; **E.**U.; **G.**U. 54–60; **Ld.**P. (5 yr.); W.; **Lh.**FO.; **M.**C.; **O.**B.; **R.**U.; **Rt.**; **Sw.**U.; **Y.**

16177 **Current List** of Medical Literature. Washington. *Curr. List med. Lit.* [1941–59] **L.**CB. 50–59; D. 47–59; H. 47–59; GH. 47–59; H. 47–59; LI. 53–59; MA.; MC. 43–59; MD.; MY. 52–59; OP. 50–59; P. 47–59; PH. 47–59; S.; SC. 45–59; SH. 47–59; TD.; UCH. 50–59; VC. 58–59; **Bl.**U. 47–59; **Bm.**U. 46–59; **Br.**U. 47–59; **C.**APH. 53–59; PA. 49–59; UL. 47–59; V. 54–59; **Cr.**MD. 47–59; U. 54–59; **Db.** 47–59; **Dn.**U. 47–59; **E.**P. 50–59; R. 47–59; U. 47–59; **G.**F. 50–59; U. 46–59; **Ld.**U. 47–59; **Lv.**M. 47–59; **M.**MS. 46–59; **Nw.**A. 47–59; **O.**AP. 42–53; R.; **R.**U. 49–51; **Sa.** 47–59; **Sh.**U. 55–59; **W.** 55–59. [*C. in:* 22895]

16178 **Current Literature** on Coal Mining. London. *Curr. Lit. Coal Min.* [1952–] **L.**MIE.; P. [*C. of:* 22911]

16179 **Current Literature: Congenital Anomalies.** *Curr. Lit. congen. Anom.* [1960–] **Br.**U.; **G.**U.

Current Literature List. Documentation of **Molecular Spectroscopy.** *See* 16261.

16180 **Current Literature: Poliomyelitis** and **Related Diseases.** *Curr. Lit. Poliomyelitis* **L.**BM.; H.; TD. [*C. of:* 38015]

16181 **Current Literature Review. Battelle Memorial Library.** Columbus, O. *Curr. Lit. Rev. Battelle meml Libr.* **L.**SC. 38–51* imp. [*C. as:* 5792]

16182 **Current Literature** on **Venereal Disease.** Washington. *Curr. Lit. ven. Dis.* [1952–] **L.**TD.; **Db.**; **E.**P. 52–53; **G.**F.; **Ld.**O.

16183 **Current Medical Abstracts** for **Practitioners.** Wilmslow. *Curr. med. Abstr. Practnrs* [1960–] **L.**BM.; **E.**P. [*C. of:* 350]

16184 **Current Medical Digest.** Washington. *Curr. med. Dig.*

16185 **Current Medical Practice.** Bombay. *Curr. med. Pract.* [1957–] **L.**MA.; MD. imp.

16186 **Current Medical Research.** London. *Curr. med. Res.* [1957–] **L.**BM. 58–; P. 58–; **Bl.**U.; **M.**P.; **Y.**

16187 **Current Medicine.** Johannesburg. *Curr. Med.* **L.**MD. 47–.

16188 **Current Medicine** and **Drugs.** London. *Curr. Med. Drugs* [1960–] **L.**BM.; MD.; **Bl.**U.; **Dn.**U.; **Ld.**P.

16189 **Current Metallurgical Abstracts.** Pittsburg. *Curr. metall. Abstr.* [1930–39] **L.**C. 33–39. [*C. as:* 31476]
Current Metallurgical Literature. *See* 16189.

16190 **Current Metallurgy.** Maribyrnong. *Curr. Metall.*

16191 **Current Monthly Record** of Forestry Literature. Oxford. *Curr. mon. Rec. For. Lit.* [1936–39] **L.**BM.; **C.**A.; **Md.**H. 38–39; **O.**F.; R.

16192 **Current Nitrofuran Publications.** Norwich, N.Y. *Curr. Nitrofuran Publs* [1958–] **L.**MD.

16193 **Current Notes** of the **Manchester Astronomical Society.** Manchester. *Curr. Notes Manchr astr. Soc.* **L.**AS. 51–; **M.**T. 51–.

16194 **Current Papers. Aeronautical Research Council.** London. *Curr. Pap. aeronaut. Res. Coun.* [1950–] **L.**P.; QM. imp.; SC.; 52–; **Bl.**U. imp.; **Br.**U.; **Ld.**U. 60–; **M.**U. 51–; **Y.**

16195 **Current Problems** in **Dermatology.** Basel, New York. *Curr. Probl. Derm.* [1959–] **L.**MD.
Current Quarterly Bibliography of **Applied Physics.** *See* 49050.

16196 **Current Radiological Literature.** London. *Curr. radiol. Lit.* **L.**CB. 55–; P. 59–; **Dn.**U. 56–.

16197 **Current Report. Garside Cotton Service.** Boston. *Curr. Rep. Garside Cott. Serv.* **C.**UL. 27–; **O.**B. 27–30.

16198 **Current Research** in **Cancer Chemotherapy.** Bethesda. *Curr. Res. Cancer Chemother.* [1954–59] **L.**CB. 55–59. [*C. as:* 13279]

16199 **Current Research** and **Development** in **Scientific Documentation.** Washington. *Curr. Res. Dev. scient. Docum.* [1957–] **L.**BM. 58–; P.; TP. 58–.

16200 **Current Researches** in **Anesthesia** and **Analgesia.** Rocky River, Ohio. *Curr. Res. Anesth. Analg.* [1922–56] **L.**D. 25–56 imp.; GH. 30–56; MA. 29–56; MC. 24–49; MD.; S. imp.; SC. 26–56; UC. 25–56 imp.; UCH. 24–56; **Abd.**U. 37–56; **Bl.**U. 24–56 imp.; **Bm.**U. 27–; **Br.**U. 25–56; **Cr.**MD. 29–56; **Db.** 32–56 imp.; **Dn.**U. 27–56 imp.; **E.**P. 40–55 imp.; U. 26–56; **G.**U. 27–56 imp.; **Ld.**U. 28–56 imp.; **Lv.**M.; **M.**MS. 24–56; **Nw.**A. 27–56; **O.**R. 27–56; **Sh.**U. 28–56. [*C. as:* 2585]

16201 **Current Review** of **Agricultural Conditions** in **Canada.** Ottawa. *Curr. Rev. agric. Condit. Can.* **L.**AM. 44– imp.; BM. 56–; MO. 49–54; **O.**AEC. 58–.

16202 **Current Review** of the **Soviet Technical Press.** Washington. *Curr. Rev. Sov. tech. Press* [1960–] **L.**P.; **Y.**

16203 **Current Road Problems.** Highway Research Board, National Research Council. Washington. *Curr. Rd Probl.* [1946–] **L.**P.; **Y.** [*C. of:* 57111]

16203° **Current Rubber Information.** London. *Curr. Rubb. Inf.* [1953–] **Sy.**R.
Current Safety Topics. *See* 53884.

16204 **Current Science.** Bangalore. *Curr. Sci.* [1932–] **L.**BM^N.; C. imp.; IC. 48–; KC. 56–; LI.; MA. 47–; MY. imp.; P.; RI.; SC.; TP. 45–; **Abs.**A. 52–; **Bm.**U. 32–41; **C.**A.; P. 35–; **Db.** 37–; **E.**R. 38– imp.; **Ex.**U. 47–; **G.**U. 45–; **Je.** 48–; **Lo.** 53–; **M.**U. 55–; **Md.**H. 41–; **Pl.**M. 32–33; **R.**D. 47–; U. 46– imp.; **Rt.** 32–38: 46–; **Y.**

16205 **Current Technical Papers. Bell Telephone Laboratories, Inc.** New York. *Curr. tech. Pap. Bell Teleph. Labs* **L.**P. (2 yr.)

16206 **Current Therapeutic Research, Clinical** and **Experimental.** New York. *Curr. ther. Res.* [1959–] **L.**MD.; S. 60– imp.; **Bl.**U. 60–; **Ld.**U. 60–.

16207 **Current Therapy.** Philadelphia. *Curr. Ther.* [1949–] **L.**BM.; MD. 56; **C.**UL.; **E.**A.; P. 51–52: 55–56; **G.**M. 56–; **Lv.**P. 55–; **M.**P. 55–; **O.**B.

16208 **Current Work** in the **History** of **Medicine.**
London. *Curr. Wk Hist. Med.* [1954–] **L.**BM.; CB.; GH.;
H.; MA.; MC. imp.; MD.; PH.; RI.; SC.; TD.; UC. 56–; V.;
Bl.U.; **Bn.**U.; **Br.**U.; **C.**PA.; UL.; **Db.**; **Dn.**U.; **G.**F.; U.;
H.U.; **Ld.**P.; U.; **M.**MS.; **N.**U.; **Sh.**U.; **W.** 55–; **Y.**

16209 **Currents** in **Biochemical Research.** New York,
London. *Currents biochem. Res.* **L.**P. 56–.

16209ᶜ **Cursillos** y **conferencias. Instituto 'Lucas
Mallada'** de **investigaciones geológicas.** *Curs.
Confs Inst. Lucas Mallada Invest. geol.* **Sh.**SC. 60–.

16210 **Curtis's Botanical Magazine.** London. *Curtis's
bot. Mag.* [1787–] **L.**BM. 1801–; BMᴺ.; HS.; K.; L.; P.
1801–13; SC. 25–; U.; UC. 1787–02; **Abd.**U. 1787–81;
Abs.N.; **Ba.**I.; **Bm.**P. 1793–; U. 1787–94: 48–; **Bn.**U. 31–
49 imp.; **Br.**P. 1827–1832; U. 1787–1826: 1845–; **C.**BO.;
UL.; **Cr.**M. 1793– imp.; **Db.**; **E.**A. 1793– imp.; B. 1793–;
P. 1787–97; R. 1787–1848: 90–92: 10–16; T. 91–20: 48–;
U.; **G.**M. 1787–1826: 77–; U. 1787–23: 49–; **Ld.**P.
1787–21: 37–; U.; **Lv.**P.; U. imp.; **M.**P. 1787–24 imp.;
N.U. 48–; **Nw.**A. 1787–1826; P. 1787–42; **O.**BO.; R.; **R.**U.
1787–1816: 48–; **Sa.** imp.; **Sil.** 53–; **Y.**

16211 **Curtis-Wright Review.** New York. *Curtis-
Wright Rev.* [1930–32] **L.**P.; SC.

16212 **Cutlery Journal.** New York. *Cutlery J.* **Sh.**P.
22–.

16213 **Cutlery Journal.** New York. *Cutlery J.* [1931–
34] **Sh.**IO. [*C. of:* 36756]

16213ᶜ **Cutting Tool Engineering.** Wheaton, Ill.
Cutting Tool Engng **Y.**

16214 **Cyanamid International Newsletter.** London.
Cyanamid int. Newsl. **L.**P. (curr.)

16215 **Cyanamid New Product Bulletin.** New York.
Cyanamid new Prod. Bull. [1949–] **L.**P.

16216 **Cyanamid Rubber Chem Lines.** Bound Brook.
Cyanamid Rubb. Chem Lines [1952–] **Sy.**R.

16217 **Cyanamid's Nitrogen Chemicals Digest.** New
York. *Cyanamid's Nitrog. Chem. Dig.* [1947–] **L.**P. 48–
53.

16218 **Cybele columbiana.** Providence, etc. *Cybele
columb.* [1914] **L.**BMᴺ.

16219 **Cybernetica.** Namur. *Cybernetica* [1958–] **L.**BM.;
P.; SC.; **Te.**N.; **Y.**

16220 **Cybernetics.** Transactions of the Conferences,
Josiah Macy Jr. Foundation. New York. *Cybernetics
Trans. Confs Josiah Macy Jr Fdn* [1949–53] **L.**MD.; SC.
[*Transactions of Conferences 1–5 were not published*]

16221 **Cybium.** Bulletin de l'Association des amis du
Laboratoire des pêches coloniales. Paris. *Cybium*
L.BMᴺ. 47–.

16222 **Cyprus Agricultural Journal.** Nicosia. *Cyprus
agric. J.* [1904–40] **L.**AM. imp.; BMᴺ. 30–40; EB. 14–40;
K.; MY. 32–40; P. 29–40; SC. 23–40; TP. 04–39; **Abd.**R.
31–40; **Br.**U. 34–40; **C.**A. 30–40; **Db.** 21–40; **E.**AB.
33–40; **Hu.**G. 34–39; **Md.**H. 30–40; **O.**RE. 29–40 imp.;
R.D. 33–40; **Rt.** 06–40; **Sal.** 37–40 imp.
Cyprus Journal. See 16222.

16223 **Cyprus Medical Journal.** Nicosia. *Cyprus med.
J.* [1947–] **L.**MA. 48–; TD. 48–49.

16224 **Cyprus Ornithological Society Bulletin.** Nicosia. *Cyprus orn. Soc. Bull.* [1957–] **O.**OR.

16225 **Cyprus Public Health.** Nicosia. *Cyprus publ.
Hlth* [1936–] **L.**TD. 36–39 imp.

16226 **Cytologia.** Tokyo. *Cytologia* [1929–] **L.**CB. 52–;
L. 32–36; MC. 55–58; QM. 50–; SC. 38–; UC. 30–41;
Abs.A. imp.; U. 56–; **Ba.**I.; **Bl.**U. 56–; **C.**A.; BO. 29–33;
GE. 53–; UL.; **Cr.**U. 60–; **E.**AG. 34–; U. 34–; **Lv.**U.; **M.**U.
imp.; **N.**U. 56–; **O.**BO.; **R.**U.; **Y.**

16227 **Cytological** and **Neurological Studies.** Faculty
of Medicine, University of Kanazawa. Kanazawa. *Cytol.
neurol. Stud., Kanazawa* [1951–54] **L.**S.; **Bn.**U.; **Ld.**U.
51–52; **Pl.**M. [*C. of:* 16228]

16228 **Cytological Studies.** Faculty of Medicine, University of Kanazawa. Kanazawa. *Cytol. Stud., Kanazawa*
Bn.U. 49*. [*C. as:* 16227]

16229 **Czasopismo Galicyjskiego towarzystwa aptekarskiego.** we Lwowie. *Czas. galic. Tow. aptek.*
[1903–07] [*C. of:* 16236]

16230 **Czasopismo geograficzne.** Łódź, etc. *Czas.
geogr.* [1923–] **L.**BM. 52–; G. 39–; **E.**G.; **Y.**

16231 **Czasopismo lekarskie.** Łódź. *Czas. lek.* [1899–
08] [*C. in:* 40358]
Czasopismo lotnicze. *See* 28918.

16232 **Czasopismo rolnicze.** Kutno. *Czas. roln.*
[1922–]

16233 **Czasopismo sadowo-lekarskie.** Warszawa. *Czas.
sadowo-lek.* [1928–]

16234 **Czasopismo stomatologiczne.** Miesięcznik.
Warszawa. *Czas. stomat.* **L.**D. 48–; **Y.**
Czasopismo techniczne. Kraków. *See* 16237.

16235 **Czasopismo techniczne.** Organ Towarzystwa
politechnicznego. Lwów. *Czas. tech., Lwów* [1883–]

16236 **Czasopismo Towarzystwa aptekarskiego.**
Lwów. *Czas. Tow. aptek., Lwów* [1872–02] [*C. as:*
16229]

16237 **Czasopismo Towarzystwa technicznego kra-
kowskiego.** Kraków. *Czas. Tow. tech. krakow.* [1880–]
Czech Agricultural Bibliography. *See* 13585.

16238 **Czechoslovak Glass** and **Pottery Journal.**
Prague. *Czech. Glass Pott. J.* [1927] **L.**SE. [*C. of:*
16244]

16239 **Czechoslovak Glass Review.** Prague. *Czech.
Glass Rev.* [1946–] **L.**BM. 54–; P. 55–; SC. 48–; SI. 50–; **Y.**

16240 **Czechoslovak Heavy Industry.** Praha. *Czech.
heavy Ind.* **G.**ME. 55–; **Y.**

16241 **Czechoslovak Journal** of **Physics.** Praha. *Czech.
J. Phys.* [1952–] **L.**BM.; P.; R. 53–; SC.; SI. 53–; **Bm.**U.
55–; **Bn.**U. (Sect. B) 62–; **C.**P.; **Db.**; **E.**R.; **G.**T. 57–;
U. 54–; **N.**U. 57–; **O.**R. 56–; **Sa.**; **Y.** [*International edition
of:* 13419]

16242 **Czechoslovak Mathematical Journal.** Praha.
Czech. math. J. [1951–] **L.**BM.; M.; R. 53–; SC.; U.; **Bm.**U.
55–; **C.**P.; **Db.**; **E.**Q. 58–; R.; **G.**U. 55– imp.; **Y.** [*International edition of:* 13420]

16243 **Czechoslovak Research Work.** Prague. *Czech.
Res. Wk* [1919–31] **L.**BM.; MD. (sect. 2) 22–24; SC.
(sect. 2); SL.; **E.**U. 21–24.

16244 **Czechoslovak Trade Journal.** Prague. *Czech.
Trade J.* [1920–27] [*C. as:* 16238]

16245 **Czipész.** Budapest. *Czipész*

16246 **Czipész szaklap.** Budapest. *Czipész Szak.*

16247 **Czukorrépa.** Budapest. *Czukorrépa*
Czukorrépa-termelő. *Supplement to:* 29162.

D

16248 **D.A.T.A.'S Microwave Tube Characteristics Tabulation.** West Orange, N.J. *D.A.T.A.'S microwave Tube Charact. Tabul.* **L.**P. 60–.

DATZ. *See* 16659.

16249 **D.D.S.** Digest of Dental Science. New York. *D.D.S.* [1952–53] **L.**MA.; MD.

16250 **DDT News.** Manchester. *DDT News* [1946–]

16251 **DEG Information Series.** Development and Engineering Group, United Kingdom Atomic Energy Authority. Risley. *DEG Inf. Ser.* [1959–] **L.**P. 59–60; SC. 60–.

16252 **DEG Report.** Development and Engineering Group, United Kingdom Atomic Energy Authority. Risley. *DEG Rep.* [1959–] **L.**SC. 60–.

DEMAG News. *See* 16486.

16253 **DFL-Bericht.** Deutsche Forchungsanstalt für Luftfahrt. Braunschweig. *DFL-Ber.* **L.**SC. 57–.

16254 **D.I.A. boletín** de **divulgación.** Departamento de investigación agropecuaria, Colombia. Bogotá. *D.I.A. Boln Divulg.* [1957–] **L.**AM. 58–; HS.; P. 58–; **C.**A.; **Rt.** 57; **Y.**

D.I.A. boletín miscelanea. *See* 7972.

16255 **D.I.A. boletín técnico.** Departamento de investigación agropecuaria, Colombia. Bogotá. *D.I.A. Boln téc.* [1957–] **L.**P.; **Rt.**

16255° **D.I.A. Quarterly Journal.** Design and Industries Association. London. *D.I.A. q.J.* [1927–32] **L.**P.; **C.**UL.; **O.**B. [*C. of:* 25898; *C. as:* 16633]

16256 **DIN Normenhefte.** Deutscher Normenausschuss. Berlin. *DIN NormHft.* [1947–55] **L.**P.

16257 **DIPAN.** Diretoria da producão animal. Rio de Janeiro. *DIPAN* [1949–] **L.**TP. 57– imp.; **Y.**

16258 **DK-Mitteilungen.** Ausschuss für Klassifikation im Deutschen Normenausschuss. Berlin. *DK-Mitt.* [1956–] **L.**SC.

16259 **D.L. Report.** Dominion Laboratory, New Zealand. Lower Hutt. *D.L. Rep.* **L.**P. 59–.

16260 **DM:** Disease a month. Chicago. *DM* [1954–] **Dn.**U.; **Ld.**U.

16261 **D.M.S. Current Literature List.** Documentation of Molecular Spectroscopy. London. *D.M.S. curr. Lit. List* [1958–] **L.**QM.; **H.**U. 59–.

16262 **D.N.A.** Revista del Departamento nacional de agricultura. San Pedro de Montes de Oca. *D.N.A.* [1940–] **Md.**H. 40–41. [*C. of:* 12893]

16263 **DNZ.** Deutsche Nähmaschinen-Zeitung. Dresden. *DNZ* [1939–] **L.**P.; **Y.** [*C. of:* 16782]

16264 **D.P.G. Research Report.** Dugway Proving Ground, Utah. Dugway. *D.P.G. Res. Rep.* [1956–] **L.**MO. imp.

16265 **DRTE Report.** Defence Research Telecommunications Establishment, Canada. Ottawa. *DRTE Rep.* **L.**P. 59– imp.

16266 **D. & S. Sawmill Magazine.** Sheffield. *D. & S. Sawmill Mag.* [1925–] **L.**BM.; P. 25–31; **Sh.**IO. 25–36.

16267 **DSH Abstracts.** Washington. *DSH Abstr.* [1960–] **L.**MD.

16268 **D.S.I. Bulletin.** Dairy Society International. Washington. *D.S.I. Bull.* **L.**AM. 57–.

16268° **D.S.I.R. Booklets.** Wallington. *D.S.I.R. Bklets* [1948–] **L.**SC.

D.S.I.R. Colonial Building Notes, Watford. *See* 14911.

D.S.I.R. L.L.U. Translations Bulletin. *See* 27891.

D.S.I.R. Monthly Summary. *See* 33644.

D.S.I.R. Overseas Technical Reports. London. *See* 36626.

D.S.I.R. Report. *See* 43445.

16268ᶠ **D.S.I.R. Technical Digest.** Department of Scientific and Industrial Research. London. *D.S.I.R. tech. Dig.* **L.**P. 59–; **Y.**

D.S.I.R. Translated Contents Lists of **Russian Periodicals.** *See* 54105.

16269 **D.T.D. Specifications.** Ministry of Supply. London. *D.T.D. Specif.* **Ld.**P. 58–; **Y.**

16269° **D.U.S.A.** Durham University School of Architecture. Durham. *D.U.S.A.* **L.**BM. 35–.

16270 **DVL-Nachrichten.** *DVL-Nachr.* [1956–] **L.**AV.

16271 **DVL-Warte.** *DVL-Warte* [1940–] **L.**AV. 40–44 imp. [*C. of:* 16272]

16272 **DVL Werk-Zeitschrift.** *DVL Werk-Z.* [1939] **L.**AV. [*C. as:* 16271]

16273 **Daaglikse weerbulletin.** Pretoria. *Daagl. Weerbull.* [1950–] **L.**MO.; **Y.** [*C. of:* 57207ᵈ]

16274 **Dacca University Bulletin.** Lahore. *Dacca Univ. Bull.* [1925–38] **L.**U. 25–27; **Br.**U. 25–31; **Db.**; **Ld.**U.; **Lv.**U. 25–27; **Nw.**A. 25–27; **O.**B. 25–31; **Sa.**

16275 **Dachdeckerzeitung.** Frankfurt a. M. *Dachdeckerzeitung*

16276 **Dactylography.** Hanley. *Dactylography* [1921–22] **L.**BM.; **Abs.**N.; **O.**B.

16277 **Dados astrónomicos. R. Observatorio astrónómico** de **Lisboa.** *Dados astr. R. Obs. astr. Lisb.* **L.**BM. 16–17.

16278 **Dados climatológicos. Serviço meteorológico.** São Paulo. *Dados clim. Serv. met., S Paulo* **L.**BM. 93–03; MO. 87–12.

16279 **Dados meteorológicos. Instituto astronómico** e **meteorológico** da **Escola** de **engenharia** de **Porto-Alegre.** *Dados met. Inst. astr. met. Esc. Eng. Porto-Alegre* **L.**MO. 12–17. [*C. as:* 7298]

16280 **Dados meteorológicos. Serviço** de **meteorologia.** Bello Horizonte. *Dados met. Serv. Met., Bello Horizonte* **L.**MO. 10–18*. [*C. as:* 7299]

16281 **Daedalus.** Ingeniörs-vetenskaps-akademi. Stockholm. *Daedalus, Stockh.* [1931–] **L.**P. 32–; SC.

16282 **Daedalus.** Proceedings of the American Academy of Arts and Sciences. Boston, Mass. *Daedalus, Boston, Mass.* [1955–] **L.**AV.; BM.; BM^N.; GL.; K.; M.; P.; R.; RI.; SC.; UC.; Z.; **Bl.**U.; **Bm.**U.; **C.**P.; UL.; **Db.**; **E.**C.; G.; L.; O.; R.; **Ex.**U.; **F.**A.; **G.**U.; **Lv.**U.; **M.**U.; **O.**R.; **Y.** [*C. of:* 38819]

16283 **Daffodil Bulletin.** American Daffodil Society. *Daffodil Bull.* **L.**HS. 57–.

16284 **Daffodil** and **Tulip Year Book.** London. *Daffodil Tulip Yb.* [1946–] **L.**AM.; BM.; HS.; K.; **Abs.**N.; **Ba.**I. 46–56; **Bl.**U. 47; **Bm.**U. 47–; **C.**UL.; **Cr.**P.; **E.**A.; **Ex.**U. 39–; **Ld.**P.; **M.**P. 46–49; **Md.**H. 53–; **N.**U.; **O.**R.; **R.**U.; **Y.** [*C. of:* 16285]

16285 **Daffodil Yearbook.** London. *Daffodil Yb.* [1913–15: 33–40] **L.**AM. 39–40; BM.; HS.; K. 14: 33; S.; **Abs.**N. 13–15: 39–40; **Ba.**I. 34–40; **C.**UL.; **Cr.**P. 14–15: 33–40; **E.**A.; **M.**P. 33–40; **N.**U. 14–15: 33–40; **O.**R.; **R.**U. 33–40. [*C. as:* 16284]

16286 **Daglig vejr-budstikke.** Norsk meteorologisk institut. Kristiania. *Dagl. Vejr-Budst. norsk met. Inst.* **L.**MO. 12–31.

16287 **Dahlia Year Book.** London. *Dahlia Yb.* **L.**BM. 31–; **Cr.**P. 25–35; **R.**U. 40–.

16287° **Daildarznieciba.** *Daildarznieciba* **Y.**

16288 **Daily Aerological Record. Meteorological Office.** London. *Dly aerol. Rec.* [1950–] **L.**BM.; MO.; **M.**P.; **O.**R. 56–. [*C. from* 16301]

16289 **Daily Maps** of the **Sun.** Fraunhofer-Institut. Freiburg. *Dly Maps Sun* [1956–] **L.**AS. [*C. of:* 56143]

16290 **Daily Meteorological Record. Freeman Meteorological Observatory.** Canton. *Dly met. Rec. Freeman met. Obs.* [1919–] **L.**BM.; MO. 19–37; SC.; **E.**M.

    Daily Observations in **Wrocław.** Meteorological and Climatological Institute of the University, Wrocław. *See* 38408°.

16290° **Daily Rainfall** recorded in **Burma.** *Dly Rainf. Burma* **Y.**

16291 **Daily Readings** at **Stations** of the **First** and **Second Orders. Meteorological Office.** London. *Dly Readings, Lond.* [1911–21] **L.**BM.; G.; MO.; SC.; UC.; **Abs.**N.; **Bm.**P.; U.; **C.**UL.; **Db.**; **E.**F.; M.; O.; R.; U.; **G.**M. 14–21; **O.**G.; **Rt.** [*C. of:* 31599; *C. in:* 35655]

    Daily Review of the **Foreign Press. Medical Supplement.** *See* 30357.

    Daily Review of the **Foreign Press. Technical Supplement.** *See* 18858.

16291° **Daily Series. Synoptic Weather Maps, Northern Hemisphere.** Washington. *Dly Ser. synopt. Weath. Maps nth. Hemisph.* [1949–]
    A. Sea Level. **L.**MO.
    B. Upper Air. **L.**MO.
    [*C. of:* 22213]

16292 **Daily Synoptic Charts.** Meteorological Office. Pretoria. *Dly synopt. Charts, Pretoria* **L.**MO. 37–41.

    Daily Synoptic Map of the **Royal Hungarian Meteorological Institute.** *See* 29209.

16292° **Daily Upper Air Bulletin.** Washington. *Dly upper Air Bull., Wash.* **L.**MO. 48–54. [*C. in:* 16291°]

16293 **Daily Weather Bulletin. Antarctic Section, New Zealand Meteorological Service.** Wellington, N.Z. *Dly Weath. Bull. Antarct. Sect. N.Z. met. Serv.* **L.**MO. 56–.

16294 **Daily Weather Bulletin. New Zealand Meteorological Service.** Wellington, N.Z. *Dly Weath. Bull. N.Z. met. Serv.* **L.**MO. 44–.

16295 **Daily Weather Bulletin. Pacific Islands Section, New Zealand Meteorological Service.** Wellington, N.Z. *Dly Weath. Bull. Pacif. Isl. Sect. N.Z. met. Serv.* **L.**MO. 49–58. [*C. in:* 16294]

    Daily Weather Bulletin, Pretoria. *See* 16273.

16296 **Daily Weather Chart** of the **North Pacific Ocean.** Imperial Marine Observatory. Kobe. *Dly Weath. Chart N. Pacif. Ocean* **L.**MO. 23–37; **C.**SP. 25–; **Lv.**U. 23–.

16297 **Daily Weather Map.** Peking. *Dly Weath. Map, Peking* **L.**MO. 57–.

16298 **Daily Weather Map, Japan.** Tokyo. *Dly Weath. Map Japan* [1958–] **L.**MO. [*C. of:* 57210^d]

16299 **Daily Weather Maps.** Weather Bureau. Washington. *Dly Weath. Maps, Wash.* **L.**MO. 71–41: 48–.

16300 **Daily Weather Reports.** Meteorological Office. Cairo. *Dly Weath. Rep., Cairo* **L.**MO. 02–58*. [*C. in:* 16301°]

16301 **Daily Weather Reports.** Meteorological Office. London. *Dly Weath. Rep., Lond.* [1868–] **L.**AM. 21– imp.; BM. 77–; MO.; **Abd.**M. 07–39 imp.: 49–; **Abs.**N. 11–; **Bm.**U. 01–; **Br.**U. 06–10: 23–; **C.**UL. 25–36: 56–; **Db.** 98–; **E.**A.; G. 24–; M. 05–; R. 73–39 imp.; **H.**U. 29–; **Lv.**U. 47–49: 52–; **M.**P. 75– imp.; **N.**U. 81–26; **O.**G.; R. 73–27; **Pl.**M. 97– imp.; **Rt.** (5 yr.); **Sa.** 24–; **Sh.**P. 85– imp.

16301° **Daily Weather Reports United Arab Republic.** Cairo. *Dly Weath. Rep. Un. Arab Repub.* [1959–] **L.**MO. [*C. of:* 16300]

16302 **Daimler-Werkzeitung.** Stuttgart-Untertürkheim. *Daimler-Werkztg*

    Dainihon jibiinkôkakai kaihô. *See* 58756.

    Dainippon yogyo kyokwai zasshi. *See* 26290.

16303 **Dairy.** London. *Dairy* [1889–38] **L.**AM. 95–22 imp.; BM.; SC. 34–38.

16304 **Dairy Bulletin.** Sydney. *Dairy Bull.*

16305 **Dairy Circular.** British Columbia Department of Agriculture. Victoria, B.C. *Dairy Circ.* [1921–] **L.**P. 21–33; **Rt.** 21–26.

16306 **Dairy Engineering.** London. *Dairy Engng* [1955–] **L.**AM.; BM.; H.; P.; **Abd.**U.; **Abs.**U.; **E.**A.; **G.**PH.; **N.**U.; **O.**R.; **R.**D.; **Y.** [*C. of:* 16337]

16307 **Dairy Exporter** and **Farm** and **Home Journal.** Wellington, N.Z. *Dairy Exporter* [1932–39] **R.**D. [*C. of:* 16332 and 34730; *C. as:* 34729]

16308 **Dairy Farmer.** Ipswich. *Dairy Fmr, Ipswich* [1929–] **L.**AM. 39– imp.; P. 34–; VC. (1 yr); **Abd.**R.; **Bl.**U. 53–; **Bn.**U. 59–; **Br.**P. (1 yr); **E.**A. 57–; AR. (curr.); **Hu.**G. 41–; **Ld.**U. 48–; **Nw.**A. 47–; **O.**RE. (2 yr.); **R.**D.; **Sil.** (1 yr); **W.** (6 mo.); **Y.**

16310 **Dairy Farmer.** Waterloo, Ia. *Dairy Fmr, Waterloo, Ia* [1919–29] [*C. of:* 27444; *C. in:* 51225°]

16311 **Dairy Goat Journal.** Columbia, Mo. *Dairy Goat J.* **R.**D. 41–59.

16312 **Dairy Industries.** London. *Dairy Inds* [1936–] **L.**AM. 40–; BM.; P.; SH. (1 yr); **Abs.**U.; **Br.**U.; **C.**UL.; **E.**A.; W. 51–; **Ld.**U. 45–; **Lh.**FO. 38–; **Lv.**P. 42– imp.; **N.**U. 39– imp.; **Nw.**A. 47–; **O.**B.; **R.**D.; **Y.**

16313 **Dairy Industries Catalog.** Milwaukee. *Dairy Inds Cat.* **L.**P. (curr.)

16314 **Dairy Information Bulletin.** Sacramento. *Dairy Inf. Bull.* [1945–] **R.**D.

16315 **Dairy News Letter.** Ottawa. *Dairy News Lett.* **R.**D. 41–50*. [*C. as:* 16320]

16316 **Dairy Produce.** Chicago. *Dairy Prod.* [1927–] [*C. of:* 13873]

16317 **Dairy Produce Notes.** Empire Marketing Board. London. *Dairy Prod. Notes* **L.**AM. 29–39.

16318 **Dairy Produce Supplies.** London. *Dairy Prod. Suppl.* **G.**M. 33–38; **R.**D. 33–38. [*Supplement to:* 57238]

16319 **Dairy Production Abstracts.** Melbourne. *Dairy Prodn Abstr.* [1947–] **R.**D.

16320 **Dairy Products Review.** Ottawa. *Dairy Prods Rev.* [1951–] **R.**D. [*C. of:* 16315]

16321 **Dairy Record.** St. Paul, Minn. *Dairy Rec.* [1900–]

16322 **Dairy Report.** Elgin, Ill. *Dairy Rep.*

16323 **Dairy Research Digest.** Baton Rouge. *Dairy Res. Dig.* [1943–] **R.**D.

16324 **Dairy Science Abstracts.** Shinfield, Farnham Royal. *Dairy Sci. Abstr.* [1939–] **L.**AM.; BM.; H. imp.; MC. 46–; MD. 55–; P.; SC.; TD.; TP.; V. 46–; VC. 53–; **Abd.**R.; U. 46–; **Abs.**N.; U. 46–47; **Bl.**U. imp.; **Bm.**P.; U.; **Bn.**U.; **C.**A.; **Db.**; **E.**A.; AB.; AR. 48–; N.; W.; **Hu.**G.; **Je.**; **Ld.**U.; **Lh.**FO. 53–; **M.**P.; U. 51–56 imp.; **N.**U.; **Nw.**A. 46–; **O.**R.; RE.; **R.**D.; U.; **Rt.**; **Sil.** 39–49; **W.**; **Y.**

16325 **Dairy Shorthorn Journal.** London. *Dairy Shorth. J.* [1932–] **L.**AM. 49–; BM.; **Abs.**U. 53–; **Bn.**U. 49–; **Br.**U. 50–; **C.**A. (3 yr.); **E.**AB. 50–; AR. (curr.); W. 50–; **G.**U. 53– imp.; **Ld.**U. 49–; **O.**RE. 32–36; **R.**D. [>49688, 1937–48]

16326 **Dairy Situation.** Canberra. *Dairy Situ., Canberra* [1953–] **Abs.**U.; **Bn.**U.; **E.**U. imp.; **R.**D.

16327 **Dairy Situation.** Washington. *Dairy Situ., Wash.* **O.**AEC. 46–.

16328 **Dairy Technology.** *Dairy Technol.* [1947–] **G.**PH.

16328ᶜ **Dairy Technology Bulletin.** Melbourne. *Dairy Technol. Bull.* [*C. as:* 51923ᶜ]

16329 **Dairy World.** Chicago. *Dairy Wld, Chicago* [1884–05] [*C. in:* 25325]

16330 **Dairy World.** Chicago. *Dairy Wld, Chicago* [1922–]

16331 **Dairy World.** London. *Dairy Wld, Lond.* [1892–39] **L.**AM.; BM. 98–39; **R.**D. 12–32 v. imp.

16332 **Dairyfarmer.** Official Organ of the N.Z. Co-operative Dairy Co., Ltd. Hamilton, N.Z. *Dairyfarmer* [1920–32] **R.**D. [*C. in:* 16307]

16333 **Dairyfarmer's Digest.** Melbourne. *Dairyfmr's Dig.* [1954–55] **E.**AB.; **R.**D. [*C. as:* 16335]

16334 **Dairyfarming Annual.** Massey Agricultural College. Palmerston North, N.Z. *Dairyfmg A.* [1948–] **L.**AM.; **Abs.**U. 50–57 imp.; **Bl.**U. 49–; **Bn.**U. 50–; **C.**A.; **E.**AB.; **Ld.**U.; **N.**U. 54– imp.; **O.**RE.; **R.**D.; U.

16335 **Dairyfarming Digest.** Melbourne. *Dairyfmg Dig.* [1956–] **E.**AB.; **R.**D. [*C. of:* 16333]

16336 **Dairyman.** London. *Dairyman* [1904–40: 44–53] **L.**AM. 47–53 imp.; BM.; P. 45–53; **Abd.**U. 44–53; **E.**A. 45–53; **G.**M. 20–40; **O.**R. 45–53; **R.**D. 19–53. [*C. of:* 16041; *C. as:* 16337]

16337 **Dairyman** and **Dairy Engineering.** London. *Dairym. Dairy Engng* [1953–54] **L.**AM.; BM.; P.; **Abd.**U.; **E.**A.; **O.**R.; **R.**D. [*C. of:* 16336; *C. as:* 16306]

16338 **Dalgety's Annual Wool Digest.** Sydney. *Dalgety's a. Wool Dig.* [1957–] **Bra.**P.; **C.**A. (5 yr.); **E.**AB.; **Ld.**P.; **O.**AEC. [*C. of:* 16339]

16339 **Dalgety's Annual Wool Review** for **Australia** and **New Zealand.** Sydney. *Dalgety's a. Wool Rev.* [1897–56] **Bra.**P. 16–56; **E.**AB. 45–56; **Ld.**P. 26–56; **O.**AEC. 30–56. [*C. as:* 16338]

16340 **Dallas Medical Journal.** Dallas. *Dallas med. J.* [1901–] **L.**MA. 48–; MD. 31–35: 46– imp.

16341 **Dal'nevostochnȳǐ vrachebnȳǐ vestnik.** Shanghai. Дальневосточный врачебный вестник. *Dal'nevost. vrach. Vest.* [1932–34]

16342 **Dalton Memorial Lecture.** London. *Dalton meml Lect.* [1945–48] **L.**BM. [*C. in:* 28356]

16343 **Damião.** Rio de Janeiro. *Damião* **L.**TD. 54–55.

16344 **Dampf.** Andelfingen. *Dampf, Andelfingen*

16345 **Dampf.** Berlin. *Dampf, Berl.* [*C. as:* 27733]

16346 **Dampfmühle.** Neusalz. *Dampfmühle*

16347 **Dân Việt Nam.** Hanoi. *Dân Việt Nam* [1948–]

16348 **Dana Reports.** Carlsburg Foundation. Copenhagen. *Dana Rep.* [1932–] **L.**BM.; BMᴺ.; L.; SC.; Z.; **Abd.**M.; **C.**B.; **E.**U.; **Lo.**; **Lv.**U.; **O.**R.; **Pl.**M.; **Wo.**; **Y.** [*See also* 35823]

16349 **Danfoss Journal.** Danfoss Manufacturing Co. *Danfoss J.* [1953–] **Bm.**T. 56–; **Sil.** (1 yr); **Y.**

16350 **Dania polyglotta.** Copenhagen. *Dania polygl.* [1945–] **L.**AM.; LI.; MO.; P.; SC.; **Br.**U.; **C.**A.; PA. 46–; **Cr.**U.; **Db.**; **Dm.**; **Dn.**U.; **E.**C.; G.; M. 45–55 imp.; R.; **Fr.** 51– imp.; **G.**M.; **Pl.**M.; **R.**U. 47–48; **Sa.**; **Sh.**U.

16351 **Danish Arctic Research.** Charlottenlund. *Dan. Arct. Res.* [1955–] **L.**BM.

   Danish 'Dana' Expeditions 1920–22. *See* 16348 and 35823.

16352 **Danish Ingolf-Expedition.** Copenhagen. *Dan. Ingolf-Exped.* [1898–] **L.**AM. imp.; BM.; BMᴺ.; L. imp.; MO. 99–00; Z.; **Abd.**M.; **C.**B.; **Dm.** 13– imp.; **Lo.** imp.; **Lv.**U. 98–35; **O.**R.; **Pl.**M.; **Wo.**

16353 **Danish Medical Bulletin.** Copenhagen. *Dan. med. Bull.* [1954–] **L.**BM.; CB.; H.; LI.; MA.; MC.; MD.; S.; TD.; UCH.; **Abd.**R. 57–; **Bl.**U. imp.; **Br.**U.; **C.**PA.; **Cr.**MD.; **Db.**; **Dn.**U. 57–; **E.**P.; S. 56–; U.; **G.**U. imp.; **Ld.**U.; **M.**MS.; **Nw.**A.; **O.**R.; **Y.** [*Also bibliographical supplement*]

16354 **Danish Review** of **Game Biology.** Copenhagen. *Dan. Rev. Game Biol.* [1945–] **L.**AM.; BMᴺ.; **O.**AP.; OR.

16355 **Danish Scientific Investigations** in **Iran.** Copenhagen. *Dan. scient. Invest. Iran* [1939–50] **L.**BMᴺ. 39–49; Z.; **Pl.**M. 39–44.

16356 **Danish Seed Culture** and **Seed Trade.** Copenhagen. *Dan. Seed Cult.*

16357 **Danmarks Fauna.** Kjøbenhavn. *Danm. Fauna* [1907–] **L.**BMᴺ.; E. (ent.); Z.; **Pl.**M. 10–48 imp.

16358 **Danmarks geologiske undersøgelse.** Kjøbenhavn. *Danm. geol. Unders.*

    Raekke 1. [1893–] **L.**BMᴺ.; GL.; GM.; UC. imp.; **Abs.**U. 40–45 imp.; **Bm.**U.; **Br.**U.; **C.**S.; **Db.** 99–; **E.**D. 99–; v. imp.; J. 21–; **Y.**

    Raekke 2. [1890–] **L.**BMᴺ.; GL.; GM.; UC. imp.; **Abs.**U. 40–45 imp.; **Bm.**U.; **Br.**U.; **C.**S.; **Db.** 99–; **E.**D. 99– v. imp.; J. 21–; **Y.**

    Raekke 3. [1896–] **L.**BMᴺ.; GL.; GM.; UC. imp.; **Bm.**U.; **Br.**U. imp.; **C.**S.; **Db.** 99–; **E.**D. 99– v. imp.; J. 21–; **Y.**

    Raekke 4. [1915–] **L.**BMᴺ.; GL.; GM.; UC. imp.; **Bm.**U.; **Br.**U. imp.; **C.**S.; **Db.**; **E.**J.; **Y.**

    Raekke 5. [1916–] **L.**BMᴺ.; GL.; GM.; UC. imp.; **Bm.**U.; **Br.**U.; **C.**S.; **Db.**; **E.**J.; **Y.**

16359 **Dansk Arkitektforenings Tidsskrift.** Kjøbenhavn. *Dansk ArkitForen. Tidsskr.*

16360 **Dansk botanisk Arkiv.** Kjøbenhavn. *Dansk bot. Ark.* [1913–] **L.**BM.; BMᴺ.; K.; L.; SC. 36–; **Bn.**U. 40– imp.; **C.**BO.; **E.**B.; **G.**U. 57–; **Ld.**U. 48–; **Lv.**U. 52–; **O.**BO.; **Sa.** 56–; **Y.**

16361 **Dansk Bryggeritidende.** Kjøbenhavn. *Dansk BryggTid.*

16362 **Dansk dendrologisk Årsskrift.** Kjøbenhavn. *Dansk dendrol. Årsskr.* [1950–] **O.**F.
   Dansk dermatologisk Selskabs Forhandlinger. København. *Supplement to:* 22418.

16363 **Dansk Emballage Tidende.** Lynby. *Dansk Emball. Tid.* **Lh.**P. 53– imp.

16364 **Dansk farmaceutisk Aarbog.** København. *Dansk farm. Aarb.* [1930–]

16365 **Dansk Fiskeriforenings Medlemsblad.** Kjøbenhavn. *Dansk FiskForen. MedlBl.* [1892–02] **L.**AM. 99– 01 imp.; **Abd.**M. 95–02 imp. [*C. as:* 16366]

16366 **Dansk Fiskeritidende.** Kjøbenhavn. *Dansk FiskTid.* [1903–] **L.**AM. 12– imp.; **Abd.**M. 47–; **Db.** 06–; **Y.** [*C. of:* 16365]

16367 **Dansk fotografisk Tidsskrift.** Kjøbenhavn. *Dansk fotogr. Tidsskr.* [1903–] **L.**PG. 03–48 imp. [*C. of:* 6085]

16368 **Dansk Frøavl.** Kjøbenhavn. *Dansk Frøavl* [1918–] **Abs.**A. 52–; **Hu.**G. 29–; **Y.**
   Dansk Frøkontrol. *See* 6086.

16369 **Dansk Frugtavl.** København. *Dansk Frugtavl* **L.**HS. 35–40; **Md.**H. 35–39; **Y.**

16370 **Dansk Havebrug.** København. *Dansk Havebr.* **Md.**H. 47–50.

16371 **Dansk Havetidende.** København. *Dansk Havetid.* [1918–39] **L.**SC. 37–39.

16372 **Dansk Husdyravl.** København. *Dansk Husdyravl* **L.**AM. 46–58* imp. [*C. in:* 16379]

16373 **Dansk Ingeniørforeningens Aarbog.** Kjøbenhavn. *Dansk IngForen. Aarb.* [1924–]

16374 **Dansk Ingeniørforenings teknisk Vejkomités Publikationer.** Kjøbenhavn. *Dansk IngForen. tek. Vejkom. Publr*

16375 **Dansk Jærnbaneblad.** Kjøbenhavn. *Dansk JærnbBl.*

16375° **Dansk kemi.** København. *Dansk Kemi* **Y.**
   Dansk kirurgisk Selskabs Forhandlinger. København. *Supplement to:* 22418.

16376 **Dansk Klinik.** Kjøbenhavn. *Dansk Klin.*

16377 **Dansk Kunsthaandvaerk.** Kjøbenhavn. *Dansk Kunsthaandv.* [1948–] **L.**BA. [*C. of:* 35530]

16378 **Dansk Landbrug.** Aarhus. *Dansk Landbr., Aarhus* [1937–] [*C. of:* 56952°]

16379 **Dansk Landbrug.** København. *Dansk Landbr, Kbh.* [1958–] **L.**AM.; **Y.**

16380 **Dansk Maanedskrift for Dyrlaeger.** København. *Dansk Maanedskr. Dyrlaeg.* [1949–55] **L.**V.; **Abs.**U.; **W.** [*C. of:* 29001]
   Dansk medicinsk Selskabs Forhandlinger. København. *Supplement to:* 22418.

16381 **Dansk Mejeritidende.** København. *Dansk Mejeritid.* **R.**D. 46–49: 53–55 imp.; **Y.**
   Dansk meteorologisk Årbog. *See* 31675.

16381° **Dansk Naturfredning.** København. *Dansk Naturfredn.* **Y.**

16382 **Dansk ornithologisk Forenings Tidsskrift.** Kjøbenhavn. *Dansk orn. Foren. Tidsskr.* [1906–] **L.**BMᴺ.; NC. 38–; Z.; **Br.**U. 11–; **C.**B. 48–; **O.**OR.; **Y.**
   Dansk otolaryngologisk Selskabs Forhandlinger. København. *Supplement to:* 22418.

16383 **Dansk Patenttidende.** Kjøbenhavn. *Dansk PatTid.* **L.**P. 94–; **Y.**

16383° **Dansk pelsdyravl.** København. *Dansk Pelsdyravl* **Abd.**R. 56–; **Y.**

16384 **Dansk Radio Industri.** København. *Dansk Radio Ind.* [1950–] **Y.**
   Dansk radiologisk Selskabs Forhandlinger. København. *Supplement to:* 22418.
   Dansk røntgenologisk Forening. København. *Supplement to:* 22418.

16385 **Dansk Skovforeningens Tidsskrift.** Kjøbenhavn. *Dansk Skovforen. Tidsskr.* [1916–] **O.**F. 16: 21; **Y.**

16386 **Dansk Søfartstidende.** København. *Dansk Søfartstid.* [1894–]

16387 **Dansk Standards.** København. *Dansk Stand.*

16388 **Dansk Sundhedstidende.** Kjøbenhavn. *Dansk SundhTid.*

16388° **Dansk Svejsetidende.** *Dansk Svejsetid.* **Y.**

16389 **Dansk Tandlægeblad.** Kjøbenhavn. *Dansk TandlBl.*

16390 **Dansk teknisk Tidsskrift.** Kjøbenhavn. *Dansk tek. Tidsskr.* **L.**P. 48–; **Y.** [*C. of:* 52753]

16391 **Dansk Telegraftidende.** Kjøbenhavn. *Dansk TelegrTid.*

16392 **Dansk Textilindustri-Tidende.** Fredericia. *Dansk TextIndTid.*

16393 **Dansk Tidsskrift for Farmaci.** Kjøbenhavn. *Dansk Tidsskr. Farm.* [1926–] **L.**MA. 46–; PH.; **Y.**

16394 **Dansk Vejtidsskrift.** København. *Dansk Vejtidsskr.* [1924–] **Ha.**RD. 34–; **Y.**

16395 **Dansk veterinærhistorisk Aarbog.** Skive. *Dansk vet.-hist. Aarb.* [1934–] **W.** 39–.

16396 **Dansk Vildtundersøgelser.** Rønde, København. *Dansk Vildtunders.* [1953–] **O.**AP.; OR.

16397 **Danske Biavls-Tidende.** Roskilde. *Danske Biavls-Tid.*

16398 **Danske Fugle.** Viborg. *Danske Fugle* [1920–]

16399 **Danske Gradmaaling.** Kjøbenhavn. *Danske Gradm.* [1867–84: 08–23] **L.**BM.; SC. imp.; **Bl.**U. 67–84: 08–16; **C.**O. 08–23; UL. 08–23; **E.**O. imp. [*C. as:* 20911]
   Danske Ingolf-Expedition. *See* 16352.
   Danske Landhusholdningsselskab. Aarsberetning. *See* 4876.

16400 **Danube international.** Journal officiel de la Commission internationale du Danube. *Danube int.* [1920–22] **Ld.**U.

16401 **Danziger meteorologische Forschungsarbeiten.** Danzig. *Danzig. met. ForschArb.* [1937–42] **L.**MO. [*C. of:* 20137]

16401° **Dapim laboker.** Tel Aviv. *Dapim Labok.* **Y.**

16402 **Dapim reffuim.** Tel Aviv. *Dapim Reffuim* [1935–] **L.**MD. 54–; TD. 36–38, 50–.
   Darbai Eksperimentinės medicinos ir onkologijos instituto, Vilnius. *See* 17588.
   Darbai Lietuvos TSR mokslų akademijos. *See* 28558°.

Darbai Lietuvos TSR mokslų akademijos biologijos instituto. *See* 28558.

16403 **Dare** de **seamă** despre **mișcarea bolnavilor.** București. *Dare Seamă Mișc. Bolnav.*

Dare de **seamă** a **lucrărilor.** Congresul national al naturaliștilor din România. *See* 15237.

Dări de **seamă** ale **sedinţelor.** Institutul geologic al României. *See* 15241.

Darülfünüm coğrafya enstitüsü neşriyate. *See* 24245.

Darülfünüm geologi enstitüsü neşriyate. *See* 24247.

16404 **Darwiniana.** Revista del Instituto de botánica Darwinion. Buenos Aires, etc. *Darwiniana* [1922–] **L.**BM.; BM^N.; L. 40–; SC. 22–30: 37–; **Bl.**U. 37– imp.; **C.**P.; R. 28–; **Hu.**G. 45–; **Md.**H. 41–; **O.**BO.; **Y.**

16405 **Dasika hronika.** Athēnai. Δασικα χρονικα. *Dasika Hron.* [1958–] **O.**F.; **Y.**

16406 **Dasiki zōē.** en Athēnais. Δασικὶ Ζωή. *Dasiki Zōē* [1933–]

16407 **Dasos.** Athenai. Δασος. *Dasos* [1947–54] **O.**F.

16408 **Data Processing.** Detroit. *Data Process., Detroit* [1959–] **G.**ME.; **Te.**N.; **Y.** [*C. of:* 41378]

16409 **Data Processing** in **Business** and **Industry.** London. *Data Process. Business Ind.* [1959–] **L.**AM.; AV.; BM.; **Bn.**U.; **E.**A.; **M.**P.; **O.**B.; **Y.**

16410 **Data Processing Digest.** *Data Process. Dig.* **L.**AV. 60–; **Y.**

16411 **Data Record** of **Oceanographic Observations** and **Exploratory Fishing.** Hokkaido. *Data Rec. oceanogr. Obsns explor. Fishg* [1957–] **Abd.**M.; **Dm.**; **Lo.**; **Lv.**U.; **Pl.**M.

16412 **Data** and **Records** of **Researches. Laboratory** of **Land Reclamation, University** of **Tokyo.** Tokyo. *Data Rec. Res. Lab. Ld Reclam. Univ. Tokyo* **Y.**

16413 **Data Report. Chesapeake Bay Institute.** Baltimore. *Data Rep. Chesapeake Bay Inst.* **Pl.**M. 53–.

16414 **Data Report. Scripps Institution** of **Oceanography.** La Jolla. *Data Rep. Scripps Instn Oceanogr.* **Lo.** 56–.

Data Sheet. Cassel Salt Bath Furnaces. *See* 13431.

Data Sheets. Association of **Engineering** and **Shipbuilding Draughtsmen.** *See* 43°.

16415 **Data Sheets. Bureau** of **Information** on **Nickel, Ltd.** London. *Data Sh. Bur. Inf. Nickel* **L.**L. 40–; P. 29; **C.**P. 37–; **O.**BO. 40–.

16416 **Data Sheets. National Sand** and **Gravel Association.** Washington. *Data Sh. natn. Sand Grav. Ass.* **L.**MO. 31–; SC. 29–.

16417 **Data Sheets. Provisional Standards. Institution** of **Automobile Engineers.** London. *Data Sh. provis. Stand. Instn Auto. Engrs* [1931–38] **L.**P. [*C. of:* 16418]

16418 **Data Sheets. Provisional Standards. Society** of **Motor Manufacturers** and **Traders.** London. *Data Sh. provis. Stand. Soc. Mot. Mfrs* [1923–31] **L.**P. [*C. as:* 16417]

16419 **Data** från **Stockholms högskolas Geokronologiske institut.** Stockholm. *Data Stockh. Högsk. geokron. Inst.* **L.**BM^N. 25–43.

16420 **Datamation.** Chicago, New York. *Datamation* [1959–] **L.**AV.; P.; **Y.** [*C. of:* 45845]

16421 **Date climatologici.** București. *Date clim.* **L.**MO. 31; **E.**R. 31.

16421° **Daten Review.** Division of Atomic Energy, Ministry of Supply. Risley. *Daten Rev.* [1949–] **L.**BM.

16422 **Dati** e **memorie** sulle **radio communicazioni.** Roma. *Dati Memie Radio Commun.* **L.**SC. 30–31.

16423 **Dati meteorologici. Osservatorio principale** de **Mogadiscio.** *Dati met. Oss. princ. Mogadiscio* **L.**MO. 46.

16424 **David Brown Tractor News.** Huddersfield. *David Brown Tract. News* **L.**P. (curr.)

16425 **Datos** para la **materia médica mexicana.** México. *Datos Mater. méd. mex.* **L.**BM. 94; K. 94–08*.

16426 **Datos** del **Observatorio central** de **Montevideo.** *Datos Obs. cent. Montev.* **L.**MO. 06–15: 18–28; SC. 28–.

16427 **Dauphiné médical.** Grenoble. *Dauphiné méd.*

16428 **Davoser Wetterkarte.** Davos. *Davoser WettKarte* **L.**MO. 92–20.

16429 **Davy-United Engineering.** Sheffield. *Davy-United Engng* [1954–] **L.**BM.; P.; **Bm.**T. 57–; **Y.**

16430 **Dawe Digest.** London. *Dawe Dig.* [1958–] **L.**AV. 61–; P.; **Y.**

16431 **Dax médical** et **thermal.** Dax. *Dax méd. therm.*

16432 **Debreceni mezögazdsági akadémia tudományos évkönyve.** Budapest. *Debreceni mezög. Akad. Tudom. Évk.* [1955–] **C.**A.; **Rt.** 56–. [*C. of:* 16433]

16433 **Debreceni mezögazdsági kisérléti intezet évkönyve.** Budapest. *Debreceni mezög. Kisérl. Intez. Évk.* [1950] **C.**A. [*C. as:* 16432]

Debreceni tudományegyetem biológiai intézeteinek évkönyve. *See* 2681.

Decadal Bulletin of **Cosmic Data.** Moscow. *See* 16459.

16434 **Décades botaniques** de la **Mission scientifique permanente** d'**exploration** en **Indo-Chine.** Hanoï. *Décad. bot. Miss. scient. perm. Explor. Indochine*

16435 **Décades zoologiques.** Hanoï. *Décad. zool., Hanoï*

16436 **Decca Navigator News.** London. *Decca Navig. News* [1951–] **L.**AV. 57–; P. (curr.); **Abd.**M.; **Lv.**P. 55–.

16437 **Dechema Mitteilungen.** Frankfurt am. M. *Dechema Mitt.* [1953–]

16438 **Dechema-Monographien.** Berlin. *Dechema-Monogr.* [1930–] **L.**C. 37–; P. 50–; **Y.**

16439 **Dechema-Werkstoffberichte.** Berlin *Dechema-Werkstoffber.* [1939–44] **L.**AV; P.; **G.**U.; **Lv.**P. 40–41; **M.**T. [*C. of:* 16440]

16440 **Dechema-Werkstoffblätter.** Berlin. *Dechema-Werkstoffbl.* [1935–38] **L.**P.; SC. [*Supplement to:* 13807; *C. as:* 16439]

16441 **Dechema-Werkstoff-Tabelle.** Deutsche Gesellschaft für chemisches Apparatewesen. Frankfurt a. M. *Dechema-Werkstoff-Tab.* **L.**P. 53–.

16442 **Decheniana.** Verhandlungen des Naturhistorischen Vereins der Rheinlande und Westfalens. Bonn. *Decheniana* [1935–] **L.**BM.; BM^N.; EB. 35–37; GL.; L.; SC.; Z.; **C.**UL.; **Db.**; **E.**B.; C.; R.; **G.**N.; **Lv.**U.; **Y.** [*C. of:* 56055; *also supplements*]

16443 **Dechets** et **regénérés.** Paris. *Dechets Regén.* **Sy.**R. 29–30.

16444 **Deciduous Fruit Grower.** Cape Town. *Decid. Fruit Grow.* [1951–] **L**.BM.; TP.; **Md**.H. 52–. [*Afrikaans edition at:* 48463]

Decision List. United States Board on **Geographic Names.** *See* 16446.

16445 **Decisions. Geographic Board** of **Canada.** Ottawa. *Decis. geogr. Bd Can.* **C**.PO. 44–; **O**.B. 19–22.

16446 **Decisions** of the **United States Geographic Board.** Washington. *Decis. U.S. geogr. Bd* **L**.BM. 06–; **G**. 22–23; SC. 20–; **C**.PO. 32–44; **G**.M. 90–36; **Y**.

16447 **Declassified documents** from **Manhattan Project, U.S. Atomic Energy Commission.** Washington. *Declass. Docum. Manhattan Proj.* **L**.P. 46–; SC. 46–.

16448 **Declassified Reports. United States Atomic Energy Commission.** Oak Ridge. *Declass. Rep. U.S. atom. Energy Commn* [1946–] **L**.P.; **Y**. [*Issued in various series.*]

16449 **Deco Trefoil.** Denver Equipment Co. Denver, Colo. *Deco Trefoil* **L**.MI. 45–; P. (curr.); **Y**.

16450 **Decoration** and **Glass.** Sydney. *Decor. Glass* [1935–] **Sh**.G. 39–.

16451 **Decorator.** London. *Decorator* [1902–] **L**.BM.; P. 10–; PR. 28–; **Abs**.N. 12– imp.; **Br**.P. 29–; **C**.UL.; **E**.A.; **G**.M. 06–; **Lv**.P. 02–12; **O**.B.; **Sh**.P. 29–; **Sl**.I. 43–; **Y**.

16452 **Deep Sea Research.** London. *Deep Sea Res.* [1953–] **L**.BM.; BM^{N}.; GL.; P.; SC.; **Abd**.M.; U.; **Abs**.N.; **Bn**.U.; **Br**.U.; **C**.GG.; **E**.A.; R.; U.; **Lo**.; **Lv**.U.; **Mi**.; **N**.U.; **Nw**.A.; **O**.R.; **Pl**.M.; **R**.D.; **Sh**.SC.; **Wo**.; **Y**.

16452° **Defence** against **Hail** in **Italy.** Verona. *Def. Hail Italy* **L**.MO. 55–.

16453 **Defensa odontológica.** Montevideo. *Defensa odont.* [1937–]
Défense des **plantes.** Leningrad. *See* 58367.

16454 **Defesa** contro la **tisica.** São Paulo. *Defesa Tisica*

16454° **Degussa Newsletter.** Frankfurt. *Degussa Newsl.* **M**.C. 59– imp.

16455 **Degussa-Brief.** Frankfurt. *Degussa-Brief* **L**.P. 31–39.

16456 **De Havilland Gazette.** Hatfield. *De Havilland Gaz.* [1937–] **L**.AV. 48–; P. 37–39: 57–; **F**.A. 46–; **Sa**. 56–; **Sh**.IO. 38–.

16456° **Dehydration.** United Kingdom Progress Reports. D.S.I.R. London. *Dehydration* **L**.SC. 43.

16457 **Dekadenmonatsberichte** der **K. Sächsischen Landeswetterwarte.** Dresden. *DekadMber. K. sächs. Landeswetterw.* [1905–17] **L**.MO.; **O**.G. [*C. of:* 16458]

16458 **Dekadenmonatsberichte. Vorläufige Mitteilungen** des **K. Sächsischen meteorologischen Instituts** zu **Chemnitz.** *DekadMber. K. sächs. met. Inst.* [1898–04] **L**.MO.; **Db**.; **O**.G. [*C. as:* 16457]

16459 **Dekadniyi byuleten' ukrmetu.** Ukrayins'ka meteorolohýchna sluzhba. Декаднії бюлетень Укрмету. Українська метеорологична служба. *Dekad. Byul. Ukrmetu* [1925–30] **L**.MO.

16460 **Dekadnýĭ obzor. Kosmicheskie dannýe.** Moskva. Декадный обзор. Космические данные. *Dekad. Obz. kosm. Dann.* **L**.MO. 44–47.

16461 **Deklinationskurven. Magnetische Warte** der **Westfälischen Berggewerkschaftskassen** zu **Bochum.** Bochum. *DeklinKurven magn. Warte Bochum*

16462 **Deklinationskurven. Magnetisches Observatorium** d. **Oberschlesischen Steinkohlen-Bergbau-Hilfskasse** in **Beuthen.** *DeklinKurven magn. Obs. Beuthen*

16462° **Dekra.** Zeitschrift des Verbandes der deutschen Kraftfahrzeugüberwachungs-Vereine e. V. Berlin. *Dekra*

16463 **De Laval Centrifugal Review.** New York. *De Laval centrif. Rev.* **L**.P. 27–32.

16464 **De Laval Monthly.** New York. *De Laval Mon.*

16464^{a} **Dela. Institut** za **biologijo.** Slovenska akademija znanosti in umetnosti. Beograd. *Dela Inst. Biol., Beogr.* **C**.P. 51–.

16464^{b} **Dela. Institut** za **elektrisko gospodarstvo.** Slovenska akademija znanosti in umetnosti. Beograd. *Dela Inst. elekt. Gospod., Beogr.* **C**.P. 53–.

16465 **Dela. Institut** za **geografijo.** Slovenska akademija znanosti in umetnosti. Ljubljana. *Dela Inst. Geogr., Ljubl.* [1950–] **L**.G. 50–55; **C**.P. 59–.

16465° **Dela. Institut** za **geologijo.** Slovenska akademija znanosti in umetnosti. Beograd. *Dela Inst. Geol., Beogr.* **C**.P. 59–.

16466 **Dela. Matematično-prirodoslovni razred. Slovenska akademija znanosti** in **umetnosti** v **Ljubljani.** *Dela mat.-prirod. Razr. Ljubl.* **L**.BM^{N}. 44. [*C. as:* 16467]

16467 **Dela. Razred** za **prirodoslovne** in **medicinske vede. Slovenska akademija znanosti** in **umetnosti.** Ljubljana. *Dela Razr. prirod. med. Vede, Ljubl.* [1950–] **L**.BM^{N}.; **Y**. [*C. of:* 16466]

16468 **Delaware County Dairying.** Franklin, N.Y. *Delaware Cty Dairy.*

16469 **Delaware Health News.** Denver. *Delaware Hlth News*

16470 **Delaware State Medical Journal.** Wilmington. *Delaware St. med. J.* [1909–] **L**.MA. 47–; MD. 36–. [*C. of:* 25876; > 5096, 1923–28]

16471 **Delectus seminum** quae **Hortus botanicus sarajevoensis Instituti biologici** pro **mutua commutatione offert.** Sarajevo. *Delectus Semin. Hort. bot. sarajev.* **L**.BM. 50–.

16472 **Déli kárpátók.** Temesvár. *Déli Kárp.*

16473 **Délkeleti fürdölapok.** Oravicza. *Délkel. Fürdöl.*

16474 **Delle.** Ateliers de constructions électriques de Delle. Villeurbanne. *Delle* [1935–39] **L**.P. imp. [*C. of* 5084; *C. as:* 21923]

16475 **Délmagyaroszági természettudományi füzetek.** Temesvár. *Délmag. természettud. Füz.*

16476 **Delphinium.** Chicago. *Delphinium* **L**.HS. 36–49 imp.; SC. 42–46 imp.

16477 **Delphinium Society's Year Book.** London. *Delphinium Soc. Yb.* [1957–] **L**.HS.; SC.; **R**.U. [*C. of:* 8792°]

16478 **Delpinoa.** Bollettino dell'Orto botanico di Napoli. *Delpinoa* [1948–] **L**.K.; SC. [*C. of:* 8376]

16479 **Delta Power Tool Instructor.** Pittsburgh. *Delta Pwr Tool Instruct.* **L**.P. (curr.)

16480 **Deltion** tēs en **Athēnais biomēhanikēs** kai **emporikēs akadēmias.** en Athēnais Δελτίον τῆς ἐν Ἀθήναις βιομηχανικῆς καὶ ἐμπορικῆς ἀκαδημίας. *Delt. Athen. biomeh. empor. Akad.*

16481 **Deltion** tēs **'Ellēnikēs geōgrafikēs 'etaireias.** en Athēnais. Δελτίον τῆς Ἑλληνικῆς γεωγραφικῆς ἑταιρείας. *Delt. 'ell. geogr. 'Etair.* [1922–]
Deltion tēs **'Ellēnikēs mathematikēs 'etaireias.** Δελτίον τῆς Ἑλληνικῆς μαθηματικῆς ἑταιρείας. *See* 12047.

16482 **Deltion. 'Ellenikes mikrobiologikes** kai **'ugieinologikes 'etaireias.** Athenai. Δελτίον ἑλληνικῆς μικροβιολογικῆς καὶ ὑγιεινολογικῆς ἑταιρείας. *Delt. 'ell. mikrobiol. 'ug. 'Etair.* [1956–] **L.**MA.

16483 **Deltion geōrgikon. 'Ellēnikē geōrgikē 'etairia.** en Athēnais. Δελτίον γεωργικόν. Ἑλληικὴ γεωργικὴ ἑταιρία. *Delt. geōrg. 'ell. geōrg. 'Etair.* [1909–] **L.**AM. 38– imp.; BM. 22–; EB. 12–15 imp.; SC. 28–; **Rt.** 19– imp.

16484 **Deltion geōrgikon** tou **geōrgikou tmēmatos** tou **'upourgeiou** tōn **esōterikōn.** en Athēnais. Δελτίον γεωργικὸν τοῦ γεωργικοῦ τμήματος τοῦ ὑπουργείου τῶν ἐσωτερικῶν. *Delt. georg. Georg. Tmēmat. 'Upourg. Esōter.*

16485 **Deltion** tēs **'istorikēs** kai **ethnologikēs 'etairias** tēs **'Ellados.** en Athēnais. Δελτίον τῆς Ἱστορικῆς καὶ ἐθνολογικῆς ἑταιρίας τῆς Ἑλλάδος. *Delt. 'ist. ethnol. 'Etair. 'Ell.* [1883–29] **L.**BM. 83–10. [*Suspended* 1904–09]
Demag Nachrichten. *See* 16486.

16486 **Demag News.** Demag Aktiengesellschaft. Duisburg. *Demag News* **L.**BM. 61–; P. 28–39: 49– imp.; **Bm.**U. 27–39 imp.; **Ld.**U. 61–; **Sh.**IO. 51–; **Y.**

16487 **Demag-Courrier.** Duisberg. *Demag-Courr.* **L.**P. (curr.)

16488 **Dementia Praecox Studies.** Chicago. *Dementia Praecox Stud.* [1918–22] **L.**MD.; **Bl.**U. 18; **O.**R.

16488° **Demir** ve **celik.** Ankara. *Demir Celik* **Y.**

16489 **Demiryollar dergisi.** Ankara. *Demiry. Derg.*

16490 **Demiryollar mecmuasi.** Haidarpaşa. *Demiry. Mecm.* [1925–]

16491 **Demographe.** Paris. *Demographe* [1955–] **E.**AG.

16491° **Demographic Yearbook.** U.N. New York. *Demogr. Yb.* [1949–] **L.**CB. 50–; MD. 50–; QM. 52–; TD.; **Br.**U. 51–; **G.**M.

16492 **Demonstrační pokusy** s **hubením ohnice dusikatým vápnem.** Praha. *Demonst. Pokusy* [*C. as:* 59325]

16493 **Denaturized Alcohol Journal Magazine.** Minneapolis. *Denat. Alcoh. J. Mag.*

16494 **Dendrokomikē ereuna.** en Athēnais. Δενδροκομικὴ ἔρευνα. *Dendrok. Ereuna* [1936–] **L.**MY. 36–39; **Md.**H. 36–40.

16495 **Dendrological Notes. Imperial Forestry Institute.** Oxford. *Dendrol. Notes* [1936–39] **Bn.**U. 38–39; **O.**F.
Dendrologiya i **dekorativnoe sadovodstvo.** Leningrad. Дендрология и декоративное садоводство. *See* 54987, ser. 10.

16496 **Dendron.** International Dendrology Union. Oisterwijk. *Dendron* [1954–] **L.**BM^{N}.; K.
Denison University Bulletin. *See* 26866.

16497 **Deniz tip bülteni.** Ankara. *Deniz Tip Bült* [1955–] **L.**MA.; MD.
Denki-gakkwai zasshi. *See* 26193.

16498 **Denkisikenjo iho.** Tokyo. *Denkisikenjo iho* **L.**EE. 52– imp.; **Y.**
Denkschrift. *See* Denkschriften

16499 **Denkschriften** der **Akademie** der **Wissenschaften.** Wien. *Denkschr. Akad. Wiss., Wien* [1850–46] Math.-nat. Kl. **L.**AS. 1850–18; BM.; BM^{N}.; GL.; GM.; L.; P. 1856–09 imp.; R.; S. 1850–14 imp.; SC.; UC. imp.; Z.; **Abs.**N. 33–46; **C.**P. 1854–46; UL.; **Db.**; **E.**R. imp.; U. 1852–24 imp.; **G.**U. 83–07 imp.; **Lv.**U. imp.; R.; **Sa.**; **Y.** [*C. as:* 16504]

16500 **Denkschriften** betr. die **Bekämpfung** der **Reblauskrankheit.** Berlin. *Denkschr. Bekämpf. Reblauskrankh.* **L.**EB. 75–92.
Denkschriften der **K. Akademie** der **Wissenschaften.** Wien. *See* 16499.

16501 **Denkschriften** der **K. Bayerischen botanischen Gesellschaft** zu **Regensburg.** *Denkschr. K. bayer. bot. Ges. Regensb.* [1815–36] **L.**BM. 1815–65; BM^{N}. imp.; **C.**A. 22–36; **E.**B. 98–05. [*C. as:* 16505]

16502 **Denkschriften** der **Medizinisch-naturwissenschaftlichen Gesellschaft** zu **Jena.** *Denkschr. med.-naturw. Ges. Jena* [1879–32] **L.**BM. 79–28; BM^{N}.; L.; R. 79–13; S. 80–13; SC. 89–32; UC. 79–13 imp.; Z.; **C.**UL.; **E.**R.; **O.**R. 79–29.
Denkschriften des **Naturhistorischen Hofmuseums.** Wien. *See* 16503.

16503 **Denkschriften** des **Naturhistorischen Staatsmuseums.** Wien. *Denkschr. naturh. Staatsmus., Wien* [1917–] **L.**BM^{N}. 17–34; UC. (geol.-paleont.) 17–23; **E.**R.

16504 **Denkschriften** der **Österreichischen Akademie** der **Wissenschaften.** Wien. *Denkschr. öst. Akad. Wiss.* [1948–] Math.-nat. Kl. **L.**BM.; BM^{N}.; GL.; GM.; L.; P.; R.; SC.; UC.; Z.; **Abs.**N.; **C.**P.; UL.; **Db.**; **E.**R.; U.; **Lv.**U.; **O.**R.; **Sa.** 48–51; **Y.** [*C. of:* 16499]

16505 **Denkschriften** der **Regensburgischen botanischen Gesellschaft.** Regensburg. *Denkschr. regensb. bot. Ges.* [1940–] **L.**BM^{N}. 40. [*C. of:* 16501]

16506 **Denkschriften. Reichsarbeitsgemeinschaft 'Windkraft'.** Berlin. *Denkschr. ReichsarbGemeinsch. 'Windkraft'* **L.**MO. 40–43.

16507 **Denkschriften** der **Schweizerischen naturforschenden Gesellschaft.** Zürich. *Denkschr. schweiz. naturf. Ges.* [1920–] **L.**BM.; BM^{N}.; GL.; GM. (geol.); L.; R.; SC.; **C.**P.; **Db.**; **E.**R.; **Y.** [*C. of:* 34544]

16508 **Denkschriften** des **Verbandes deutscher Architekten- u. Ingenieurvereine.** Berlin. *Denkschr. Verb. dt. Archit.- u. IngVer.*

16509 **Denkschriften** über die **Versuchsstrasse.** Deutscher Strassenbauverband. Braunschweig. *Denkschr. Versuchsstr.* **L.**P. 36–.

16509° **Denni přehled pocasi.** Praha. *Denni Prěhl. Pocasi* **L.**MO. 50–.

16510 **Dens.** Osaka. *Dens* **L.**D. 48–.

16511 **Denshi-kembikyo.** *Denshi-kembikyo* [1950–] **Y.** [*English edition at:* 25940]

16512 **Dental Abstracts.** Chicago. *Dent. Abstr., Chicago* [1956–] **L.**GH.; MA.; MD.; S.; **Br.**U.; **Dn.**U.; **E.**U.; **Ld.**U.; **M.**MS.

16513 **Dental Abstracts.** Los Angeles. *Dent. Abstr., Los Angeles* [1939]

16514 **Dental Abstracts.** New York. *Dent. Abstr., N.Y.* [1945–] **L**.D.; S. 45–50; **Br**.U. 47–50; **Ld**.U.

16515 **Dental Annual.** London. *Dent. A.* **O**.R. 03–06.

16516 **Dental Assistant.** New York. *Dent. Assist.* [1931–]

16517 **Dental Brief.** Philadelphia. *Dent. Brief* [1896–13] **L**.D.

16518 **Dental Bulletin.** Houston, Tex. *Dent. Bull., Houston* [1929–34]   [*C. as:* 26109]

16518ᵈ **Dental Bulletin.** Montreal. *Dent. Bull., Montreal*

16519 **Dental Bulletin.** Washington. *Dent. Bull., Wash.* [1929–41] **L**.D. 39–41. [*Supplement to:* 4832; *C. as:* 4831]

16520 **Dental Century.** Madison, Wis. *Dent. Century*

16521 **Dental Clinics** of **North America.** Philadelphia. *Dent. Clin. N. Am.* [1957–] **L**.D.; S. 57–60; **Dn**.U.; **M**.MS. 57–.

16522 **Dental Cosmos.** Philadelphia. *Dent. Cosmos* [1859–36] **L**.BM.; D.; GH. 98–36; MA. 30–36; MD.; MT. 24–36; P. 10–31; S. 1860–36 imp.; **Bl**.U. imp.; **Bm**.U.; **Br**.U. 69–36 imp.; **C**.UL. 21–36; **Db**. 81–94 imp.; **Dn**.U. 1860–36 imp.; **E**.S.; **G**.F. 23–35 imp.; **Ld**.U. 67–36 imp.; **Lv**.U. 22–36; **M**.MS.; **Nw**.A. 28–36. [*C. in:* 25503]

16522ᶜ **Dental Courier.** London. *Dent. Cour.* [1951–] **L**.D.

16523 **Dental Craftsman.** Chicago. *Dent. Craftsm.*

16524 **Dental Delineator.** London. *Dent. Delin.* [1934–] **L**.BM.; D. 35–39 imp.: 50–; S. 50– imp.; **Abs**.N.; **O**.R. 34–38.

16525 **Dental Digest.** Chicago, etc. *Dent. Dig.* [1895–] **L**.D. imp.; GH. 16–31 imp.; MA. 48–; MD. 01–17: 27–; **Dh**.U. 43–46; **Bm**.U. 46–; **Dn**.U. 51–; **Ld**.U. 33– imp.; **M**.MS. 41–; **Nw**.A. 46–54.

16526 **Dental Echo.** Berlin. *Dent. Echo* [1926–41] **L**.D. 40–41 imp.

16527 **Dental Era.** St. Louis, Mo. *Dent. Era* **L**.D. 08–10.

16528 **Dental Examiner.** Athens, Ga. *Dent. Examr, Athens* [1924–30]   [*C. as:* 21556]

16529 **Dental Forum.** Pittsburgh. *Dent. Forum* [1924] **L**.MD.   [*C. of:* 25505]

16530 **Dental Gazette.** London. *Dent. Gaz.* [1934–49] **L**.BM.; D.; GH. 35–49 imp.; H. 39–49; MA. 35–49; S. 46–49; **Bm**.U. 37–49; **C**.UL.; **Db**.; **E**.A.; **Ld**.U. 46–49; **M**.MS. 43–49 imp.; **Nw**.A. 42–49; **O**.R.   [*C. of:* 40598]

16531 **Dental Headlight.** Nashville, Tenn. *Dent. Headlight*

16532 **Dental Hygiene Quarterly.** Philadelphia. *Dent. Hyg. Q.* [1925–]

16533 **Dental Hygienist.** San Francisco. *Dent. Hygst* [1943–]

16534 **Dental Items** of **Interest.** New York. *Dent. Items* [1916–53] **L**.D.; MA. 48–53; MD. 18: 21–53; S.; **Bm**.U. 46–53; **Br**.U. imp.; **G**.F. 49–53; **Ld**.U. imp.; **Nw**.A.   [*C. of:* 24269]

16535 **Dental Journal.** Ann Arbor, Mich. *Dent. J., Ann Arbor*

16536 **Dental Journal** of **Australia.** Sydney. *Dent. J. Aust.* [1929–55] **L**.D. 29–55; S. 34–55; **Abd**.R. 50–55; **Ld**.U. 49–55 imp.; **Nw**.A. 46–55.   [*C. of:* 5365 and 16564; *C. in:* 5363]

Dental Journal of **Japan.** *See* 34912.

Dental Laboratory. Köln. *See* 16576.

16537 **Dental Laboratory Review.** Minneapolis. *Dent. Lab. Rev.* **L**.D. 46– imp.

16538 **Dental Magazine.** London. *Dent. Mag.* [1919–28] **L**.BM. 21–28; D.; MD. imp.; **Abs**.N.; **Bm**.U. 21–28. [*C. of:* 4976; *C. as:* 16539]

16539 **Dental Magazine** and **Oral Topics.** London. *Dent. Mag. oral Top.* [1929–] **L**.BM.; D.; GH. 31–; H. 38–; MA. 46–; MD. imp.; S. 46– imp.; **UCH**. 51–; **Abs**.N.; **Bl**.U. 36– imp.; **Bm**.U. 29–38; **Br**.U. 29–40 imp.; **E**.S. 52–; **G**.F. 50–; PH. 44–; U. imp.; **Ld**.U. 32– imp.; **M**.MS. 40–. [*C. of:* 16538]

16540 **Dental Mail.** London. *Dent. Mail* [1921–22] **L**.BM.

16541 **Dental Monthly** of **Japan.** *Dent. Mon. Japan*

16542 **Dental News.** Huntington. *Dent. News, Huntington* [1927]

16543 **Dental News.** London. *Dent. News, Lond.* [1909] **L**.BM.; D.

16544 **Dental News.** Minneapolis. *Dent. News, Minneap.* [1918–] **L**.D. 29: 33.

16545 **Dental News.** New York University. New York. *Dent. News, N.Y.*

16546 **Dental Observer.** New York. *Dent. Obsr* [1937–40]   [*C. as:* 16558]

16547 **Dental Office** and **Laboratory.** Philadelphia. *Dent. Off. Lab.* [1868–08]

16548 **Dental Outlook.** New York. *Dent. Outl.* [1914–] **L**.D. 28–43 imp.

16549 **Dental Practice.** Toronto. *Dent. Pract.* [1906–12] **Bm**.U. 06.   [*C. as:* 26717]

16550 **Dental Practitioner.** Bristol. *Dent. Practnr, Bristol* [1950–55] **L**.BM.; D.; H.; MD.; P. 54–55; S.; **UCH**.; **Bl**.U. imp.; **Br**.U. 53–55; **Db**.; **Dn**.U.; **E**.A.; U. 53–55; **M**.MS.; **Nw**.A. 53–55; **O**.B.; R.   [*C. as:* 16552]

16551 **Dental Practitioner.** London. *Dent. Practnr, Lond.* [1918–26] **L**.BM. imp.; **O**.R. 19–26.

16552 **Dental Practitioner** and **Dental Record.** Bristol. *Dent. Practnr dent. Rec.* [1955–] **L**.BM.; D.; H.; MD.; P.; S.; **UCH**.; **Bl**.U. imp.; **Br**.U.; **Db**.; **Dn**.U.; **E**.A.; U.; **Ld**.U.; **M**.MS.; **Nw**.A.; **O**.B.; R.; **Sh**.U. 59–.   [*C. of:* 16550]

16553 **Dental Progress.** Chicago. *Dent. Prog.* [1960–] **L**.MD.; S.; **Bl**.U.; **Dn**.U.; Y.

16554 **Dental Quarterly.** Milford, Del. *Dent. Q.* [1913–20]

16555 **Dental Radiography** and **Photography.** Rochester. *Dent. Radiogr. Photogr.* [1927–] **L**.D. 28–; MD. 48–; P. 27–39; PG.; S.; **UCH**. 49–; **Ld**.U. 49: 52–; **We**.K.; Y.

16556 **Dental Rays.** Pittsburgh. *Dent. Rays* [1926–]

16557 **Dental Record.** London. *Dent. Rec.* [1881–55] **L**.BM.; D.; GH. 99–54 imp.; H. 46–55; MA. 46–55; MD.; P. 14–55; S.; **UCH**. 81–91 imp.: 50–55; **Abs**.N. 12–55; **Bl**.U. 23–55 imp.; **Bm**.U. imp.; U. 22–55; **Br**.U. 85–55; **C**.UL.; **Db**.; **Dn**.U. 81: 00–34: 45–55; **E**.A. 86–55; **G**.F. 04–36; **Ld**.U. 24–55; **Lv**.U. 22–55; **M**.MS. 91–55; **Nw**.A. 14–55; **O**.R.   [*Incorporated with:* 16550]

16558 **Dental Reflector.** New York. *Dent. Refl.* [1940–] **L.**D. 46–47 imp. [*C. of:* 16546]

16559 **Dental Register.** Cincinnati. *Dent. Register* [1847–23] **L.**D. 81–22 imp.

16560 **Dental Research** and **Graduate Study Quarterly.** Northwestern University. Chicago. *Dent. Res. Grad. Study Q.* **L.**D. 35–; MD. 35–; S. 46–54 imp.; **M.**MS. 37–48. [*Part of:* 11349]

16561 **Dental Review.** Chicago. *Dent. Rev., Chicago* [1886–18] **L.**D. 87–18 imp.; MD. 88–18; MT.; P. 10–18; S. 07–18.

16562 **Dental Review.** Chicago. *Dent. Rev., Chicago* [*C. of:* 23836]

16563 **Dental Review.** Columbia University. New York. *Dent. Rev., N.Y.* [1930–31] [*C. as:* 14969]

16564 **Dental Science Journal** of **Australia.** Sydney. *Dent. Sci. J. Aust.* [1921–29] **L.**D.; GH. 21. [*Replaces:* 15043; *C. in:* 16536]

16565 **Dental Student.** Chicago. *Dent. Stud.* [1923–25] [*C. as:* 16566]

16566 **Dental Student Magazine.** Chicago. *Dent. Stud. Mag.* [1925–26] [*C. of:* 16565; *C. as:* 16567]

16567 **Dental Students' Magazine.** Chicago. *Dent. Stud's Mag.* [1926–] **Dn.**U. 51–. [*C. of:* 16566]

16568 **Dental Summary.** Toledo, O. *Dent. Summ.* [1902–25] **L.**D. imp.; GH. 20–23; MD. [*C. of:* 36065; *C. in:* 1938]

16569 **Dental Surgeon.** London. *Dent. Surg.* [1904–32] **L.**BM.; D. 21–32 imp.; MD. 04–07: 26–32; S. 04–05; **Abs.**N. 12–32; **Bm.**U. 04–18; **Lv.**U. 04–21; **O.**B.

16570 **Dental Survey.** Minneapolis. *Dent. Surv.* [1929–] **L.**D. imp.; MD. 46–. [*C. of:* 38097]

16571 **Dental Technician.** London. *Dent. Techn* [1947–] **L.**BM.; D.; P. 50–; **C.**UL.; **Dn.**U. 49–; **Ld.**U. 49–; **M.**MS. 54–; **O.**B.; R.

16572 **Dental World.** La Grange, Ga. *Dent. Wld, La Grange*

16573 **Dental World.** Minneapolis. *Dent. Wld, Minneap.* **L.**D. 47–.

16574 **Dentalfabrikant.** Berlin. *Dentalfabrikant*

16575 **Dental-journal.** Weingelden. *Dental-J.* [1912–] **L.**D. 38–40 imp.

16576 **Dental-Labor.** Köln. *Dental-Labor* [1953–] **L.**P. 59–.

16576ᶜ **Dental-Revue.** Wien. *Dental-Revue* [1951–] **L.**D. [*C. of:* 35911]

16577 **Dental-Revy** for **Skandinavien.** Kjøbenhavn. *Dental-Revy Skand.*

16578 **Dental-Universum.** Reichenberg. *Dental-Univ.*

16579 **Dentista.** Torino. *Dentista*

16580 **Dentiste belge.** Bruxelles. *Dent. belge*

16581 **Dentiste** de **France.** Paris. *Dent. Fr.* **L.**D.; MA. 48–.

16582 **Dentisten.** Kjøbenhavn. *Dentisten* **Dentisten-Blatt.** Budapest. *See* 19754.

16583 **Dentistry:** a digest of practice. Philadelphia. *Dentistry* [1940–] **L.**D. 40–48.

16584 **Dentists' Magazine.** Cleveland, O. *Dentists' Mag.*

16585 **Denver Medical Times.** Denver. *Denver med. Times* [1883–15] **L.**MD. 93–06 imp. [*C. as:* 57425]

16586 **Department Bulletin. Massachusetts Department** of **Agriculture.** Boston. *Dep. Bull. Mass. Dep. Agric.* **L.**SC. 21–.

16587 **Department Bulletin. United States Department** of **Agriculture.** Washington. *Dep. Bull. U.S. Dep. Agric.* [1923–27] **L.**AM.; BM.; BMᴺ.; C. imp.; EB. (ent.); K. imp.; MD. imp.; P.; SC.; Z.; **Abs.**N. imp.; **Br.**A.; **C.**UL.; **E.**B. imp.; R.; **G.**M. imp.; **Ld.**U.; **Lv.**P.; U. imp.; **M.**P. imp.; **O.**F.; RE. imp.; **Rt.** imp.; **Sa.** imp.; **Sh.**U. [*C. of:* 12508; *Replaced by:* 52029]

16588 **Department Circular. Forestry Department, Gold Coast.** Accra. *Dep. Circ. For. Dep. Gold Cst* **O.**F. 36–37.

16589 **Department Circular. Massachusetts Department** of **Agriculture.** Boston. *Dep. Circ. Mass. Dep. Agric.*

16590 **Department Circular. United States Department** of **Agriculture.** Washington. *Dep. Circ. U.S. Dep. Agric.* [1919–27] **L.**AM.; BM.; BMᴺ.; EB. (ent.); K.; P.; Z. 20–27; **Abs.**N. 23–27 imp.; **Ba.**I.; **E.**R. 20–21; **G.**M. imp.; **Lv.**P. imp.; **M.**P. imp.; **O.**F.; RE. imp.; **Rt.** imp.; **O.**F. [*C. as:* 14394]

Department of **Mines, Canada.**
Explosives Branch Publications. *See* 41004.
Geological Survey Branch Reports. *See* 43861.
Mines Branch Reports. *See* 44543.

16591 **Department Publications. Indiana Department** of **Conservation.** Indianapolis. *Dep. Publs Indiana Dep. Conserv.* **O.**F. 21–30 imp.

16592 **Departmental Annual Report. East African Medical Survey.** Mwanza, Tanganyika, etc. *Depl a. Rep. E. Afr. med. Surv.* [1949] **L.**Z. [*C. as:* 43551ᵃ]

16593 **Departmental Annual Report. Filariasis Research.** East Africa High Commission. Mwanza, Tanganyika, etc. *Depl a. Rep. Filar. Res. E. Afr.* [1949–50] **L.**EB.; MD. [*C. as:* 43692]

16593ᶜ **Departmental Note. Ghana Meteorological Department.** Accra. *Depl Note Ghana met. Dep.* [1958–] **L.**MO.

16593ᵈ **Departmental Notes. Department** of **Agriculture, Trinidad** and **Tobago.** Port of Spain. *Depl Notes Dep. Agric. Trin.* [1947–] **L.**BM.

16594 **Departmental Papers. Survey** of **India. Geodetic Branch.** Dehra Dun. *Depl Pap. Surv. India geod. Brch* **L.**BM. 31–.

16595 **Departmental Records. Department** of **Agriculture, Bengal.** Calcutta. *Depl Rec. Dep. Agric. Beng.* [1907–12] **L.**BM.; E.A. imp.; **O.**B. imp.

16596 **Departmental Records. Department** of **Agriculture, Bihar** and **Orissa.** Paris. *Depl Rec. Dep. Agric. Bihar Orissa* **L.**BM. 12–13; **O.**B. 12–13.

Departmental Report. Acting Director of **Agriculture, Fisheries** and **Forestry, Hong Kong.** *See* 16596ᶜ.

16596ᶜ **Departmental Report. Director** of **Agriculture, Fisheries** and **Forestry, Hong Kong.** *Depl Rep. Dir. Agr. Fish. For. Hong Kong* **L.**Z. 55–59.

16597 **Departmental Research Bulletin. Department** of **Civil** and **Municipal Engineering, University College, London.** *Depl Res. Bull. Dep. civ. munic. Engng Univ. Coll. Lond.* [1950–] **L.**P.

16598 **Dependable Highways.** Cleveland. *Depend. Highw.* **L.**P. 28–41.

16599 **Derbyshire Farmer.** Derby. *Derbysh. Fmr* [1928–39] **L.**AM. 30–39; **Abs.**A. 38–39; **Bn.**U. 30–39; **Ld.**U.; **N.**U.; **Nw.**A. 28–36; **R.**D.; **Rt.** [*C. of:* 16600]

16600 **Derbyshire Young Farmer.** Monthly Bulletin of the County Agricultural Education Department. Derby. *Derbysh. young Fmr* [1925–28] **Ld.**U. 26–28; **N.**U.; **R.**D. 26–28; **Rt.** [*C. as:* 16599]

16601 **Derevenskaya gazeta.** Moskva. Деревенская газета. *Derev. Gaz.*
Derevenskoe khozyaĭstvo. Деревенское хозяйство. *Supplement to:* 49461.

16602 **Derevnya.** S.-Peterburg. Деревня. *Derevnya*

16603 **Derevoobrabatÿvayushchaya promÿshlennost'.** Moskva. Деревообрабатывающая промышленность. *Derevoob. Prom.* [1955–] **L.**BM.; P.; **Y.** imp. [*English translation at:* 23302; *C. from:* 16604]

16604 **Derevopererabatÿvayushchaya i lesokhimiche-skaya promÿshlennost'.** Moskva. Деревоперерабатывающая и лесохимическая промышленность. *Derevop. lesokhim. Prom.* [1952–54] **L.**BM. 53–54; P. 54; **Y.** 53–54. [*C. as:* 16603]
Dergisi. Ormancılık araştirma enstitüsü. Ankara. *See* 36385.

16607 **Deri hastılıkları ve frengi klinigi arşivi.** Istanbul. *Deri hastılik. frengi Klin. Arşivi* [1934–]

16608 **Dermatologia.** Budapest. *Dermatologia, Bpest* [1928–]

16609 **Dermatología.** México. *Dermatología, Méx.* [1956–] **L.**MA.; MD.

16610 **Dermatologia.** Napoli. *Dermatologia, Napoli* **L.**MA. 55 imp., 58–.

16611 **Dermatologica.** Basel, etc. *Dermatologica* [1939–] **L.**MA. 46–; MD.; S. 39–50 imp.; U. 50–; UCH. 56–; **Bl.**U. 59–; **Dn.**U. 62–; **E.**P.; **G.**U. imp.; **Ld.**U. 54–; **O.**R.; **Y.** [*C. of:* 16615]
Dermatologie und **Urologie.** Fukuoka. *See* 22181.

16612 **Dermatologische Gutachten.** Aulendorf. *Derm. Gutachten* [1952] **L.**TD. imp. [*C. as:* 6479]

16613 **Dermatologische Studien.** Hamburg. *Derm. Studien* [1886–] **L.**BM.; S. 86–03; **Br.**U. 86–94; **E.**P. 86–89; **O.**R. 86–94. [*Supplement to:* 16614 and 33115]

16614 **Dermatologische Wochenschrift.** Leipzig. *Derm. Wschr.* [1912–] **L.**BM.; MA. 12–14; 24–42; MD.; S. 12–40: 43–44: 47–51; UCH. 12–33; **Db.** 12–28; **Dn.**U. 12–27; **E.**P. 12–39: 43– imp.; U. 12–33; **Lv.**U. 24–29; **Y.** [*C. of:* 33115]

16615 **Dermatologische Zeitschrift.** Berlin. *Derm. Z.* [1893–38] **L.**BM. 94–38; MA. 10–14; MD. 08–38; S. 94–38; **E.**P.; **G.**F. 98–99; U. 23–38 imp.; **O.**R. 37–38. [*C. as:* 16611]

16616 **Dermatologischer Jahresbericht.** Wiesbaden. *Derm. Jber.* [1905–08] **L.**MA. 05–07; MD.; **E.**P.

16617 **Dermatologisches Zentralblatt.** Leipzig. *Derm. Zbl.* [1897–20] **L.**MD. 06–20; UCH. 09–14.

16618 **Dermatologĭya.** S.-Peterburg. Дерматологія. *Dermatologĭya* [1913–14]

16619 **Dermato-venerologia.** Bucureşti. *Dermato-Vener.* [1959–] **L.**MA.; MD. [*C. of:* 16620]

16620 **Dermato-venerologie.** Bucureşti. *Dermato-Vener.* [1956–59] **L.**MA.; MD. [*C. as:* 16619]

16621 **Dermosifilografo.** Torino. *Dermosifilografo* [1926–50] **L.**MA. 46–50. [*C. as:* 31958]

16621° **Derwent Russian Patents Report.** *Derwent Russ. Pat. Rep.* **Y.**

16622 **Descrierca invenţiei.** Bucureşti. *Descrierca Invent.* **L.**P. 56–.

16623 **Descripciones** de **arboles forestales.** Instituto forestal latino-americano. Merida. *Descrnes Arboles for.* [1957–] **O.**F.

16624 **Description** des **machines** et **procédés** pour lesquels des **brevets** d'**inventions** ont été pris. Paris. *Descrn Mach. Proc. Brev. Invent.* **L.**BM. 1850–05; P. 1844–; SC. 1811–1833.

16625 **Descriptive Leaflet. Airmec Laboratories Ltd.** High Wycombe. *Descrve Leafl. Airmec Labs* **L.**P. imp. [*C. of:* 51919; *C. as:* 16626]

16626 **Descriptive Leaflet. Airmec Ltd.** High Wycombe. *Descrve Leafl. Airmec* [1954–] **L.**P. [*C. of:* 16625]

16627 **Descriptive List** of **Varieties** of **Field Crops.** Wageningen. *Descrve List Var. Fld Crops*
Cereals. **Y.**
Flax Varieties. **Y.**
Potato Varieties. **Y.**
Pulses Varieties. **Y.**

16628 **Desert.** Pasadena, Cal. *Desert* [1929–32] **L.**K.; [*C. as:* 16629]

16629 **Desert Plant Life.** Pasadena, Cal. *Desert Pl. Life* [1932–] **L.**K.; SC. 33–. [*C. of:* 16628]

16630 **Design.** Council of Industrial Design. London. *Design, Lond.* [1949–] **L.**AV.; BA.; BM.; NP. (2 yr.); P.; SI.; U.; **Bm.**P.; T. imp.; U.; **Br.**P. (2 yr.); U.; **Cr.**P.; **E.**A.; HW.; U. 56–; **F.**A. 53–; **G.**M.; U. 58– imp.; **Ld.**P.; **Li.**M. (1 yr); **M.**P.; T. (5 yr.); **Nw.**P. 58–; **Sh.**IO.; U. 58–; **Y.**

16631 **Design.** Syracuse, N.Y. *Design, Syracuse* **L.**P. 24–28. [*C. of:* 27338]

16632 **Design Engineering.** Toronto. *Design Engng* [1955–] **L.**P. 59–.

16633 **Design** in **Industry.** London. *Design in Ind., Lond.* [1932–33] **L.**BM.; P.; **Bm.**P.; **C.**UL.; **O.**B. [*C. of:* 16255°; *C. in:* 16638]

16634 **Design** for **Industry.** London. *Design for Ind.* [1959–] **L.**BA.; BM.; P.; U.; **Bm.**C.; **Bra.**P.; **Cr.**P.; **E.**A.; **G.**M.; **Ld.**P. imp.; **Lv.**P.; **M.**P.; **N.**P.; **Sh.**IO.; **Sil.**; **Y.** [*C. of:* 4925]

16635 **Design** in **Industry.** Newark, N.J. *Design in Ind., Newark* [1930–32] **L.**P.

16636 **Design** for **Living.** London. *Design Liv.* [1937–38] **L.**BM.; P.; **Bm.**P.; **C.**UL.; **Ld.**P. [*C. of:* 53400ᵃ]

16636° **Design News.** Englewood. *Design News, Englewood* **Lv.**P. 56; **Sil.** 54–56.

16637 **Design News.** Detroit. *Design News, Detroit* [1946–] **L.**AV. 54–; P. 52–; **Y.**
Design Sheet. Timber Development Association. *See* 51722.

16638 **Design** for **To-day.** London. *Design to-day* [1933–36] **L.**BM.; C.; P.; **Abs.**N. 34–36; **Bm.**P.; **C.**UL.; **Cr.**P.; **Ld.**P.; **O.**B. [*C. as:* 53400ᵃ]

16638° **Design Work Sheets.** New York. *Design Wk Sh.* **L.**P. 56–.

16639 **Designers** in **Britain.** London. *Designers Br.* [1947–] **L.**P. 49–; **Bra.**P.; **Ld.**P.; **Lv.**P.

16640 **Désinfection.** Paris. *Désinfection*

16641 **Desinfektion.** Berlin. *Desinfektion* [1908–27] **L.**P. 08–12. [*Suspended* 1912–21]

16642 **Desinfektion** und **Gesundheitswesen.** Staufen. *Desinfekt. GesundhWes.* [1953–60] **L.**AM. 57–60; P. 55–60; TD. [*Supplement to:* 58658 *and* 58487; *C. of:* 38493; *C. as:* 21167°]

16642° **Desinfektion** und **Schädlingsbekämpfung.** Staufen. *Desinfekt. SchädlBekämpf.* [1943–44: 49–50] **L.**TD. [*Supplement to:* 58658 *and* 58647; *C. of: and Rec. as:* 38493]

16643 **Dessins** et **modèles internationaux.** Berne. *Dessins Modèl. int.* [1928–] **L.**P.

16644 **Destillateur** u. **Liqueur-Fabrikant.** *Destill. Liqu.-Fabr.* [*C. as:* 1717]

Deterioration of **Structures** of **Timber, Metal** and **Concrete** exposed to the **Action** of **Sea Water.** See 43140.

16645 **Detroit Chemist.** Detroit. *Detroit Chem.* **Y.**

16645° **Detroit Dental Bulletin.** Detroit. *Detroit dent. Bull.* [1933–]

16646 **Detroit Edison Synchroscope.** Detroit. *Detroit Edison Synchrosc.* **L.**UC. 24–30.

16647 **Detroit Medical Journal.** Detroit. *Detroit med. J.* **Br.**U. 05. [*C. in:* 30267]

16648 **Dêtskaya meditsina.** Moskva. Дѣтская медицина. *Dêtsk. Med.* [1896–1903]

16649 **Deutsch-amerikanische Apothekerzeitung.** New York. *Dt.-am. ApothZtg* [1880–18] [*C. as:* 3727]

16650 **Deutsch-amerikanische Naturarzt.** Chicago. *Dt.-am. Naturarzt*

16651 **Deutsche Aero-Revue.** Frankfurt/Main. *Dt. Aero-Revue* **L.**P. 57–; **Y.**

16653 **Deutsche Ärztezeitung.** Berlin. *Dt. Ärzteztg* [1925–37] [*C. as:* 1141]

16654 **Deutsche Agrarpolitik.** Berlin. *Dt. Agrarpol.* [1942–]

16655 **Deutsche Agrartechnik.** Berlin. *Dt. Agrartech.* [1951–] **L.**P. 52–; **Sil.** 56–; **Y.**

16656 **Deutsche Agrarzeitung.** Berlin. *Dt. Agrarztg* **Y.**

16658 **Deutsche Apothekerzeitung.** Berlin, Stuttgart. *Dt. ApothZtg* [1934–48: 50–] **L.**P. 58–; PH. 35–48: 51– imp.; **Y.**

16659 **Deutsche Aquarien-** und **Terrarien-Zeitschrift.** Stuttgart. *Dt. Aquar.-Terrar.-Z.* [1948–50] **L.**BM[N].; Z. [*C. as:* 3772]

16660 **Deutsche Architektur.** Berlin. *Dte Archit.* [1952–] **L.**BA. 58–; BM. 56–.

16660° **Deutsche Arzt.** Mainz. *Dte Arzt* [1951–] **L.**MA. 53– imp.

16661 **Deutsche Badewesen.** Osterwieck. *Dte Badewes.* [*C. of:* 58798]

16662 **Deutsche Bauerntechnik.** Berlin. *Dt. Bauerntech.* [1946–50] **L.**AM.; P. 50. [*C. in:* 16748]

16662° **Deutsche Bauernzeitung.** Köln. *Dt. Bauernztg* **L.**AM. (curr.)

16663 **Deutsche Bauhütte.** Hannover. *Dt. Bauhütte*

16664 **Deutsche Baukunst.** Lübeck. *Dt. Baukunst*

16665 **Deutsche Baumeister.** München. *Dte Baumeist.* **L.**BA. 39.

16666 **Deutsche Baumschule.** Aachen. *Dt. Baumsch.* **L.**HS. 49–57; **Md.**H. 50–; **Y.**

16667 **Deutsche Baumwollindustrie.** Berlin. *Dt. Baumwollind.*

16668 **Deutsche Bauten.** Stuttgart. *Dt. Bauten*

16669 **Deutsche Bauzeitschrift.** Gütersloh. *Dt. Bauz.* [1953–] **L.**BA.; **Sh.**U. 57–; **Wa.**B. 53–.

16670 **Deutsche Bauzeitung.** Berlin. *Dt. Bauztg* [1867–] **L.**BM. 67–19; P. 67–28; SC. 74–42 v. imp.; **Bm.**U. 73–04; **Wa.**B. 60–.

16671 **Deutsche Bergwerkszeitung.** Essen. *Dt. Bergwksztg*

16672 **Deutsche Bienenwirtschaft.** Nürnberg. *Dt. Bienenwirt.* [1950–] **L.**AM.; P. 55–; **Rt.** 51; **Y.** [*Forms* Teil 2 *of:* 58516]

16673 **Deutsche Bierbrauer.** Stuttgart. *Dte Bierbrauer* [*C. as:* 1751]

16674 **Deutsche Blechindustriezeitung.** Hamburg. *Dt. BlechindZtg*

16675 **Deutsche botanische Monatsschrift.** Arnstadt. *Dt. bot. Mschr.* [1883–12] **L.**BM[N].; K.; **E.**B. 83–03; **G.**U. 91–03; **M.**U. 83–02 imp.

16676 **Deutsche Brauindustrie.** Berlin. *Dt. Brauind.* [1888–10]

16677 **Deutsche Brauwirtschaft.** München. *Dt. Brauwirt.* [1891–] **Nu.**B. 51–.

16678 **Deutsche Chemikerzeitschrift.** Berlin. *Dt. ChemZ.* [1949–50] [*C. in:* 13799]

16679 **Deutsche Chemikerzeitung.** Berlin. *Dt. ChemZtg* [1886–00] **L.**BM. 87–00.

16680 **Deutsche Chirurgie.** Stuttgart. *Dt. Chir.* [1879–29] **L.**BM.; MA. 79–98; MD. 01–13; S.; U. 79–07; **C.**UL.; **E.**U.; **G.**F.

16681 **Deutsche Dentist.** Berlin. *Dte Dent.*

16682 **Deutsche dentistische Wochenschrift.** München. *Dt. dent. Wschr.* [*C. of:* 58260]

16683 **Deutsche dentistische Zeitschrift.** München. *Dt. dent. Z.* **L.**D. 48–.

16684 **Deutsche Destillateurzeitung.** Berlin. *Dt. DestillZtg*

16685 **Deutsche Draht-Zeitung.** Halle a. S. *Dt. Drahtztg* [1944] **L.**P. [*C. of: and Rec. as:* 17192]

16686 **Deutsche Drogist.** Berlin. *Dte Drog.*

16687 **Deutsche Drogistenzeitung.** Leipa. *Dt. DrogZtg*

16688 **Deutsche Edelmetallkunst.** Stuttgart. *Dt. Edelmetallkunst*

16689 **Deutsche Eisenbahntechnik.** Berlin. *Dt. Eisenb-Tech.* [1954–] **L.**P.; **Y.** [*C. of:* 17551]

16690 **Deutsche Eisenbahnwoche.** Berlin. *Dt. Eisenb-Woche*

16691 **Deutsche Elektrotechnik.** Berlin. *Dt. Elektrotech.* [1952–59] **L.**EE.; P.; SI.; **Y.** [*C. of:* 17872; *C. as:* 17808]

16692 **Deutsche entomologische National-Bibliothek.** Berlin. *Dt. ent. Natn-Biblthk* [1910–11] **L.**BM[N].; E.; **Lv.**U.; **O.**H. [*C. as:* 18245]

16693 **Deutsche entomologische Zeitschrift.** Berlin. *Dt. ent. Z.* [1875–] **L.**BM. 75–15; BM^N.; E.; SC. 35–; L. 75–38; Z.; **C.**UL.; **E.**F. 75–37; **Ld.**U. 34–57; **M.**U. 99–43; **O.**H. 75–14 imp.; R.; **Y.**

16694 **Deutsche entomologische Zeitschrift, Iris.** Dresden. *Dt. ent. Z. Iris* [1884–43] **L.**BM^N.; E. 84–39; EB. 28–43 imp.; SC. 35–43; Z. 84–39; **C.**UL.; **N.**P. 89–00; **O.**H. 84–25.

16695 **Deutsche Erde.** Gotha. *Dt. Erde* [1902–14] **L.**G.

16696 **Deutsche Erfinder Post.** Berlin. *Dt. Erfinder Post* [1950–] **L.**P.; **Y.**

16697 **Deutsche Erfinderfreund.** Bremen. *Dte Erfinderfreund*

16698 **Deutsche Essigindustrie.** Berlin. *Dt. Essigind.* [1897–] **L.**P. 10–39.

16699 **Deutsche Färberzeitung.** Wittenberg. *Dt. Färberztg* [1869–43] **L.**P. 14–40; SC. 39–40; **Ld.**U. 35–40; W. 39–40; **M.**C. 73–14: 21–40 imp.; D. 25–40.

16700 **Deutsche Fahrzeugtechnik.** Gera-Reuss. *Dt. FahrzTech.* [1904–] **L.**P. 11–40.

16701 **Deutsche Farben-Zeitschrift.** Stuttgart. *Dt. Farben-Z.* [1951–] **L.**C. 47–48; IC. 49–50; P.; PR.; SC.; **Bm.**T. 56–; **M.**D.; **Sl.**I.; **Y.** [*Also supplements; C. of:* 19008]

16702 **Deutsche Farmer.** St. Paul. *Dte Fmr*

16703 **Deutsche Faserstoffe** und **Spinnpflanzen.** München. *Dt. Faserstoffe Spinnpfl.* [1919–22] **L.**P.; **M.**C. [*C. of:* 34548; *C. as:* 19188]

16704 **Deutsche Feuerwehrzeitung.** Stuttgart. *Dt. Feuerwehrztg*

16705 **Deutsche Fischereirundschau.** Bremerhaven. *Dt. FischRdsch.* [1931–] [*Replaces:* 16707]

16706 **Deutsche Fischereizeitung.** Radebeul, Berlin. *Dt. FischZtg, Radebeul* [1954–] **Lo.**; **Y.**

16707 **Deutsche Fischereizeitung.** Stettin. *Dt. FischZtg, Stettin* [1878–31] [*Replaced by:* 16705]

16708 **Deutsche Fischwirtschaft.** Berlin. *Dt. Fischwirt.* [1934–43] **L.**AM. 34–37 imp.; SC. 34–37; **Abs.**U. 34–38 imp.; **Lv.**U. imp.; **Pl.**M. 34–38. [*Replaces:* 32373]
Deutsche Fisch- u. **Konservenzeitung.** *Supplement to:* 16785.

16709 **Deutsche Flughafen.** *Dte Flughafen* **L.**AV. 38. [*C. of:* 16757; *C. as:* 19693]

16710 **Deutsche Flugtechnik.** Berlin. *Dt. Flugtech.* [1957–] **L.**AV. 60–; P. 59–; **Y.**

16710° **Deutsche Forscherarbeit** in **Kolonie** und **Ausland.** *Dte ForschArb. Kolon. Ausld* [1940–43] **Hu.**G.

16711 **Deutsche Forst-** u. **Jagdblätter.** Berlin. *Dte Forst- u. Jagdbl.*

16712 **Deutsche Forstmann.** Hannover. *Dte Forstm.* [1950–] **L.**P. 50–53.

16713 **Deutsche Forstwirt.** Neudamm. *Dte Forstwirte* [1918–] **O.**F. 28–38.

16714 **Deutsche Forstzeitung.** Brüx. *Dt. Forstztg, Brüx*

16715 **Deutsche Forstzeitung.** Neudamm. *Dt. Forstztg, Neudamm* [1886–33] **O.**F. 21–33. [*C. in:* 16713]

16716 **Deutsche Fussbodenzeitung.** Ichenhausen. *Dt. Fussbodenztg* [1953–] **L.**P. 58–.

16717 **Deutsche Gartenbau.** Berlin. *Dte Gartenb.* [1954–] **C.**A. 55–; **Md.**H. imp.; **Y.**

16717° **Deutsche Gartenbauwirtschaft.** *Dt. GartenbWirt.* **Y.**

16718 **Deutsche Geflügelzeitung.** *Dt. GeflZtg* **Y.**

16718° **Deutsche geodätische Kommission.** *Dt. geod. Kommn*
  Reihe A. Höhere Geodäsie. München. **L.**SC. 53–.
  Reihe B. Angewandte Geodäsie. **L.**SC. 53–; **Y.**
  Reihe C. Dissertationen. Frankfurt a. M. **L.**SC. 54–.
  Reihe D. Tafelwerke. München. [1956–] **L.**SC.
  Reihe E. Geschichte und Entwicklung der Geodäsie. **L.**SC. 61–.

16719 **Deutsche geographische Blätter.** Bremen. *Dte geogr. Bl.* [1877–41: 49–] **L.**BM.; G. 87–; **E.**G. 85–14; **Y.**

16719° **Deutsche Gesundheitswesen.** Berlin. *Dte GesundhWes.* [1946–] **L.**MA.; MD.; TD. 46–52; **Abd.**R. 48–; **Y.**

16720 **Deutsche gewässerkundliche Mitteilungen.** Koblenz. *Dt. gewässerk. Mitt.* [1957–] **L.**MO.; **Wa.**W.; **Y.**

16721 **Deutsche Glasermeister.** Pössneck. *Dte Glaserm.*

16722 **Deutsche Glaserzeitung.** Berlin. *Dt. Glaserztg* [1890–]

16723 **Deutsche Goldschmiedezeitung.** Stuttgart. *Dt. Goldschmiedeztg* **L.**DI. 50–.

16724 **Deutsche Graveur, Ziseleur** und **Emailleur.** Berlin. *Dte Graveur Zisel. Emaill.* [1926–]

16725 **Deutsche Graveur-** u. **Stempelzeitung.** Leipzig. *Dt. Graveur- u. StempZtg* [1875–]

16726 **Deutsche Gummi-Industrie.** Dresden. *Dt. Gummi-Ind.* **Sy.**R. 99–02.

16727 **Deutsche Hebe-** und **Fördertechnik.** Ludwigsburg. *Dt. Hebe- u. Fördertech.* [1957–] **L.**P.; **Y.**

16728 **Deutsche Heilpflanze.** Stollberg i. E. *Dt. Heilpfl.* [1934–] **L.**SC. 34–35; **Md.**H. 42–44. [*Supplement to:* 16658]

16729 **Deutsche Holzbau.** Berlin. *Dte Holzb.* **O.**F. 43–44.

16730 **Deutsche Holzwarenzeitung.** Nürnberg. *Dt. HolzwarZtg*

16731 **Deutsche Holzzeitung.** Königsberg i. Pr. *Dt. Holzztg*

16732 **Deutsche Hopfenbauer.** Spalt. *Dte Hopfenb.*

16733 **Deutsche hydrographische Zeitschrift.** Hamburg. *Dt. hydrogr. Z.* [1948–] **L.**AM.; AS.; BM.; BM^N.; MO.; P. 50–; SC.; **C.**PO.; **Db.**; **Dm.**; **E.**G.; R.; **Fr.**; **Lo.**; **Lv.**U.; **Pl.**M.; **Wo.**; **Y.** [*C. of:* 2646; *also Supplements*]
Deutsche Industrie. Düsseldorf. *See* 40203.

16733° **Deutsche** u. **internationale Patentkalender.** München. *Dte int. PatKal.*

16734 **Deutsche Kieferchirurgie.** Leipzig. *Dt. Kieferchir.* [1934] [*C. of:* 20253; *C. in:* 16852]

16735 **Deutsche Klinik am Eingange des zwanzigsten Jahrhunderts.** Berlin & Wien. *Dt. Klin.* [1901–13] **L.**BM.; MD. 06–13; **E.**P.

16736 **Deutsche klinisch-therapeutische Wochenschrift.** Berlin-Wilmersdorf. *Dt. klin.-ther. Wschr.* [*C. of:* 6469]

16737 **Deutsche Kohlenzeitung.** Berlin. *Dt. Kohlenztg* [1883–] **Nw.**A. 30–31.

16738 **Deutsche Kolonialzeitung.** Berlin. *Dt. Kolon-Ztg* [1884–22] **L.**BM. 88–22; G. 84–13; **C.**UL. 88–22; **E.**G. 88–12; **G.**U. 12–22 imp.

16739 **Deutsche Korbweidenzüchter.** Berlin. *Dte Korbweidenzüchter* **L.**P. 26–31.

16740 **Deutsche Kraftfahrtforschung.** Berlin, etc. *Dt. KraftfForsch.* [1938–56] **L.**P.; SC. 38–44 imp.; **Li.**M. 54–56. [*C. of:* 27734; *C. as:* 16741]

16741 **Deutsche Kraftfahrtforschung** und **Strassenverkehrstechnik.** Düsseldorf. *Dt. KraftfForsch. Strass-VerkTech.* [1956–] **L.**P.; SC.; **Li.**M.; **Y.** [*C. of:* 16740]

16742 **Deutsche Krankenpflegezeitung.** Berlin. *Dt. Krankenpflegeztg*

16743 **Deutsche Kunststoffe.** Wiesbaden. *Dt. Kunststoffe* **L.**PL. 52–.

16744 **Deutsche Lackiererzeitung.** München. *Dt. Lack-Ztg*

16745 **Deutsche Landeskulturzeitung.** Berlin. *Dt. LandeskultZtg* [1932–] **Abs.**A. 35–.

16746 **Deutsche landtechnische Zeitschriftenschau.** Frankfurt/Main. *Dt. landtech. Znschau* [1956] [*C. as:* 28053]

16747 **Deutsche Landwirtschaft.** Berlin. *Dt. Landwirt.* [1947–] **L.**AM.; BM.; P. 50–; **C.**A. 53–; **O.**F. 51–; **Sil.** 56–; **Y.**

16748 **Deutsche Landwirtschaft.** Berlin. *Dt. Landwirt.* [1950–] **L.**AM.; BM.; **O.**F. 51–; **Y.** [*C. of:* 16662]

16749 **Deutsche landwirtschaftliche Geflügelzeitung.** Berlin. *Dt. landwirt. GeflZtg*

16750 **Deutsche landwirtschaftliche Presse.** Berlin. *Dt. landwirt. Presse* [1874–] **L.**AM. 91–43 imp.: 53–; MY. 27–39; P. 91–05; **Db.** 10–; **O.**AG. 29–; **Rt.** 25–39 imp.; **Sil.** 29–30.

16751 **Deutsche landwirtschaftliche Rundschau.** Neudamm. *Dt. landwirt. Rdsch.* [1927–35] **C.**A.; **Md.**H. 30–35. [*C. as:* 20146]

16752 **Deutsche landwirtschaftliche Tierzucht.** Hannover. *Dt. landwirt. Tierzucht* [1897–] **E.**AB. 32–44 v. imp.; **Ld.**W. 28–31.

16753 **Deutsche Lebensmittel-Rundschau.** Nürnberg, etc. *Dt. LebensmittRdsch.* **L.**AM. 53–; C. 50–; P. 47–48; TP. 58–; **R.**D. 50–; **Y.** [*C. of:* 16783]

16754 **Deutsche Leinenindustrielle.** Bielefeld. *Dte Leinenindlle*

16755 **Deutsche Lichtbild.** Berlin. *Dte Lichtbild* [1927–] **L.**PG. 27–38; **Bm.**P. 35–; **Lv.**P. 30– imp.

16756 **Deutsche Luftfahrerzeitschrift.** Berlin. *Dt. LuftfahrZ.* [1912–18] **L.**AV.; P.; SC. 12–13. [*C. of:* 16858; *C. as:* 28865]

16757 **Deutsche Luftfahrt.** Berlin. *Dt. Luftfahrt* [1930–31] **L.**AV. 30; P. 30; **C.**UL. 30 [*C. of:* 19679, 22797 and 28865; *C. as:* 16709]

16758 **Deutsche Luftwacht.** Berlin. *Dt. Luftwacht* (*a*) Ausgabe Luftwehr [1934–39]; (*b*) Ausgabe Luftwelt [1934–42]; (*c*) Ausgabe Luftwissen [1934–42]; (*d*) Ausgabe Modellflug [1936–44] **L.**AV.; SC. (*c*); **F.**A. (*c*). [*Replaces:* 28881]

16759 **Deutsche Marinezeitung.** Bremen. *Dt .MarZtg*

16760 **Deutsche Maschinisten-** u. **Heizerzeitschrift.** Chemnitz. *Dt. Masch.- u. HeizZ.*

16761 **Deutsche Mathematik.** Berlin. *Dt. Math.* [1936–43] **L.**AV.; BM.; SC. 36–40; **C.**UL.

16762 **Deutsche Mechanikerzeitung.** Berlin. *Dt. Mech-Ztg* [1898–16] **L.**BM.; C.; P. 10–16; SC.; UC. 08–16; **Bn.**U. 10–16; **Dn.**U. 00–13; **E.**U.; **Lv.**P. imp.; **O.**R. [*Supplement to:* 58667; *C. as:* 58540]

16763 **Deutsche Medizinalzeitung.** Berlin. *Dt. Med-Ztg* [1880–13] **L.**MD. 90: 92: 05; **G.**F. 92–03; **Lv.**M. 05–11; **M.**MS. 86–10.

16764 **Deutsche medizinische Rundschau.** Baden. *Dt. med. Rdsch.* **L.**MA. 47–.

16765 **Deutsche medizinische Wochenschrift.** Leipzig, etc. *Dt. med. Wschr.* [1875–] **L.**BM.; H. 47–; MA. 93–13: 29–; MC. 15–55; MD. 77–; PH. 51–; S.; TD. (10 yr.); U. 50–; UCH. 50–; **Abd.**R. 48–; U. 10–39; **Bl.**U. 94– imp.; **Bm.**U. 94–13; **Br.**U. 85–56 imp.; **C.**MD. 91–; **Cr.**MD. 00– imp.; MS. 00–09; **Db.** 98–12 imp.; **Dn.**U. 86–; **E.**P.; S. 02–53 imp.; U. 37–; **G.**F. 79: 88–25: 32–39: 49–; **Ld.**U. 05– imp.; **Lv.**U. 77–; **M.**MS.; **Nw.**A. 28–; **O.**P. 28–; R. 91–; **R.**D. 14–23; **Sh.**U. 95–39; **Y.** [*Suspended* Oct. 1944–May 1946; *For English edition see* 21135]

16766 **Deutsche Meiereizeitung.** Königsberg i. Pr. *Dt. Meiereiztg*

16767 **Deutsche Metallindustriezeitung.** Remscheid. *Dt. MetallindZtg*

16768 **Deutsche Metallwarenindustrie.** Leipzig. *Dt. MetallwarInd.*

16769 **Deutsche Milchwirtschaft.** Berlin. *Dt. Milchwirt.* [1954–] **L.**P. 55–; **Y.**

16770 **Deutsche milchwirtschaftliche Zeitung.** Bunzlau. *Dt. milchwirt. Ztg*

16771 **Deutsche Militärarzt.** Berlin. *Dte Militärarzt* [1936–44] **L.**MC. 42–44 imp.

16772 **Deutsche militärärztliche Zeitschrift.** Berlin. *Dt. militärärztl. Z.* [1872–20] **L.**MA. 03–13.

16773 **Deutsche Mineralwasserzeitung.** Lübeck. *Dt. MinerWassZtg* [1935–] [*C. of:* 31942]

16774 **Deutsche Molkerei-** und **Fettwirtschaft.** Hildesheim. *Dt. Molk.- u. Fettwirt.* [1943–]

16775 **Deutsche Molkerei-Zeitung.** Kempten. *Dt. Molk.-Ztg* **L.**AM. 53– imp.; **R.**D. 51–; **Y.**

16776 **Deutsche Monatsschrift** für **Zahnheilkunde.** Berlin. *Dt. Mschr. Zahnheilk.* [1883–33] **L.**D. 86–33; GH. 20–33; MD. 95–33; **Bm.**U. 01–05 imp.

16777 **Deutsche Montanlndustrie.** Berlin. *Dt. Montanind.*

16778 **Deutsche Motor-Zeitschrift.** Dresden. *Dt. Mot.-Z.* [1924–40] **L.**AV. 25–40 imp.; SC. 34–40; **Li.**M. 30–39.

16779 **Deutsche Mühlenindustrie** u. **Deutsche Müller-** u. **Mühlenbauerzeitung, 'Glück zu'.** Berlin. *Dt. Mühlenind.*

16780 **Deutsche Müllerei.** Leipzig. *Dte Müll.* [1943–]

16781 **Deutsche Müller-Zeitung.** München. *Dt. Müller-Ztg* **L.**P. 55–.

16782 **Deutsche Nähmaschinenzeitung.** Bielefeld. *Dt. NähmaschZtg* [1875–39] **L.**P. 08–39. [*C. as:* 16263]

16783 **Deutsche Nahrungsmittelrundschau.** Mainz. *Dt. NahrMittRdsch.* **L.**P. 08–14; **Abd.**U. [*C. as:* 16753]

16784 **Deutsche Nahrungsmittelzeitung.** Leipzig. *Dt. NahrMittZtg*

16785 **Deutsche Nahrungs- u. Genussmittelzeitung.** Hamburg. *Dt. Nahr.- u. GenussmittZtg*

16786 **Deutsche Naturwissenschaftliche Gesellschaft.** Leipzig. *Dt. naturw. Ges.*

16787 **Deutsche Normen.** Berlin. *Dte Norm.* **L.**P. 24– imp.

16788 **Deutsche Obst- u. Gemüsebauzeitung.** Stuttgart. *Dt. Obst- GemüsebZtg* [1906–25] **L.**BM.; SC. 24–25. [*C. as:* 35670]

16789 **Deutsche Optiker-Zeitung.** Berlin. *Dt. OptZtg* [1925–42] **L.**P.; PG. 31–39; SC. 36–40. [*C. in:* 36274]

16790 **Deutsche optische Wochenschrift.** Berlin. *Dt. opt. Wschr.* [1914–52] **L.**P. imp.; PG. 31–39. [*1943–44 contained in:* 36274; *Suspended* 1945–47; *C. as:* 33128]

16791 **Deutsche Papierzeitung.** Baden. *Dt. PapZtg* [1947–48] **Lh.**P. [*C. as:* 34547]

16792 **Deutsche Parfümeriezeitung.** Berlin, etc. *Dt. ParfümZtg* [1925–43] **L.**P. 25–40 imp. [*Suspended* 1943–49; *C. as:* 37159]

16793 **Deutsche Patentanmeldungen.** Berlin. *Dt. PatAnmeld.* **L.**C. 31–46.

16794 **Deutsche Pelztierzüchter.** München. *Dte Pelztierzüchter* [1926–] **E.**AB. 37–40: 48–; **Sal.** 34–35; **Y.**

16795 **Deutsche Photographenzeitung.** Weimar. *Dt. PhotogrZtg* [1876–25] **L.**P. 06–23 imp.; PG. 87–14; SB. 04.

16796 **Deutsche Praxis.** München. *Dt. Praxis* [1898–06] **L.**BM. 98–01. [*C. as:* 28394]

16797 **Deutsche Psychologie.** Langensalza. *Dt. Psychol.*

16798 **Deutsche Rundschau** für **Geographie.** Wien & Leipzig. *Dt. Rdsch. Geogr.* [1878–15] **L.**BM. 80–15; G. 79–14; **E.**G. 88–14; **M.**P. 08–15; **O.**G. 11–15.

16799 **Deutsche Sattlerzeitung. Wagenbaukunst.** Berlin. *Dt. Sattlerztg* **L.**P. 07–28.

16800 **Deutsche Schiffahrt.** Berlin. *Dt. Schiffahrt*

16801 **Deutsche Schlachthofzeitung.** München. *Dt. SchlachthZtg* **W.** 31–32 imp.

16802 **Deutsche Schlosser- u. Schmiedezeitung. Bayerische Schmiedezeitung.** Nürnberg. *Dt. Schlosser- u. Schmiedeztg*

16803 **Deutsche Schmiedemeister.** Leipzig. *Dte Schmiedem.*

16804 **Deutsche Schmiedezeitung.** Berlin. *Dt. Schmiedeztg*

16805 **Deutsche Seilerzeitung.** Berlin. *Dt. Seilerztg* **L.**P. 94–33*.

16806 **Deutsche Spirituosenzeitung.** Neustadt, Haardt. *Dt. SpiritZtg*

16807 **Deutsche Steinbildhauer, Steinmetz u. Steinbruchbesitzer.** München. *Dte Steinbildhauer*

16808 **Deutsche Steinsetzer- und Strassenbauerzeitung.** Oranienburg. *Dt. Steinsetz.- u. StrassenbZtg*

16809 **Deutsche Strassen- u. Kleinbahnzeitung.** Berlin. *Dt. Strass.- u. KleinbZtg*

16810 **Deutsche Strassenbauer-Zeitschrift.** Hannover, Leipzig. *Dt. Strassenb.-Z.*

16811 **Deutsche Südpolar-Expedition,** 1901–03. Berlin. *Dt. Südpol.-Exped.* [1905–31] **L.**BM.; BM^N.; MO. 11–25 imp.; z. (zool.); **G.**U.; **Lv.**U.; **Pl.**M.; **Wo.**

16812 **Deutsche Tabakgewerbe.** Frankfurt a. M. *Dt. Tabakgew.*

16813 **Deutsche Tabakzeitung.** Berlin. *Dt. Tabakztg*

16814 **Deutsche Technik.** Berlin. *Dt. Tech., Berl.* **L.**P. 13–22*.

16815 **Deutsche Technik.** München. *Dt. Tech., München*

16816 **Deutsche Techniker.** Giessen. *Dte Techniker* [1933–] [*C. of:* 16817]

16817 **Deutsche Technikerzeitung.** Giessen. *Dt. TechZtg* [1884–33] **L.**BM. 16–18 imp. [*C. as:* 16816]

16818 **Deutsche technische Rundschau.** Berlin. *Dt. tech. Rdsch.*

16819 **Deutsche Textilindustrie** im **Besitze von Aktiengesellschaften.** Berlin & Leipzig. *Dt. TextInd.*

16820 **Deutsche Textiltechnik.** Berlin. *Dt. TextTech.* [1957–] **L.**P.; **Ld.**W. 58–; **M.**C.; **Y.** [*C. of:* 53018]

16821 **Deutsche Textilwirtschaft.** Berlin. *Dt. TextWirt.* [1934–] **Ld.**W. 38–39.

16822 **Deutsche Tiefbauzeitung.** Berlin. *Dt. TiefbZtg*

16823 **Deutsche tierärztliche Wochenschrift.** Hannover. *Dt. tierärztl. Wschr.* [1893–] **L.**AM. 47–50; EB. 13: 21–26 imp.; MC. 24–38; MD. 37–40: 47–; P. 05–31; v. 99– imp.; **Abs.**U. 46–47; **Br.**U. 24–35; **C.**V. 27–40: 46– imp.; **Db.** 06–43; **E.**N.; **Lv.**U. 05–09: 20–; **Sal.** 24– imp.; **W.**; **Y.** [*1943–44 contained in* 16824]

16824 **Deutsche tierärztliche Wochenschrift: Tierärztliche Rundschau.** Hannover. *Dt. tierärztl. Wschr. tierärztl. Rdsch.* [1943–44] **L.**MC.; SC.; TD.; V.; **Db.**; **E.**N.; **Lv.**U.; **Sal.** imp.; **W.** [*C. of:* 16823 and 53179]

16825 **Deutsche Tierzeitung.** Düsseldorf. *Dt. Tierztg*

16826 **Deutsche Töpfer-Zeitung.** Leipzig, etc. *Dt. Töpferztg* [1877–] **L.**P. 55–.

16827 **Deutsche Töpfer- und Zieglerzeitung.** Halle. *Dt. Töpfer- u. Zieglerztg* [1870–25] **L.**P. 01–25. [*C. as:* 59213]

16828 **Deutsche Tonindustrie.** Berlin-Neukölln. *Dt. Tonind.*

16829 **Deutsche Torfindustriezeitung.** Königsberg. *Dt. TorfindZtg*

16830 **Deutsche tropenmedizinische Zeitschrift.** Leipzig. *Dt. tropenmed. Z.* [1941–44] **L.**EB. imp.; LI. 43–44; MC. imp.; MD. 43–44; TD.; **E.**U. imp. [*C. of:* 4159; *C. as:* 58847]

16831 **Deutsche überseeische meteorologische Beobachtungen.** Hamburg. *Dt. übersee. met. Beob.* [1887–] **L.**BM.; MO. 87–22.

16832 **Deutsche Uhrmacherzeitung.** Berlin. *Dt. UhrmZtg* [1877–] **L.**DI. 57–; P. 05–39.

16834 **Deutsche Verbands-Feuerwehrzeitung.** Brünn. *Dt. Verb.-FeuerwZtg*

16835 **Deutsche Vermessungstechnikerzeitschrift.** Berlin. *Dt. VermessTechZ.* [*C. as:* 58861]

16836 **Deutsche Vierteljahrsschrift** für **öffentliche Gesundheitspflege.** Braunschweig. *Dt. Vjschr. öff. GesundhPflege* [1869–15] **L.**BM.; H. 69–94 imp.; MD. 79–99; TD. 92–04 v. imp.; UCH. 69–75; **C.**UL.; **E.**P.; **Lv.**U. 69–07; **O.**R. [*C. as:* 35884]

16837 **Deutsche Vierteljahrsschrift** f. **Zahnchirurgie.** München. *Dt. Vjschr. Zahnchir.*

16838 **Deutsche Vogelwelt.** Berlin. *Dt. Vogelwelt* [1938–44] **L.**Z. [*C. of:* 36399; *C. as:* 56846]

16839 **Deutsche Wasserwirtschaft.** Charlottenburg. *Dt. WassWirt.* [1923–43] **L.**P. 32–39; SC. 33–39. [*C. of:* 59075; *C. as:* 57143]

16840 **Deutsche Weinbau.** Berlin. *Dte Weinb.* [1921–] **Y.**

16841 **Deutsche Weinrundschau.** Trier. *Dt. Weinrdsch.*

16842 **Deutsche Weinzeitung.** Mainz am Rhein. *Dt. Weinztg* **L.**P. 55–; **Y.**

16843 **Deutsche Werkzeugmaschinenbau.** Leipzig. *Dte WerkzMaschb.* [1911–21] **L.**P.

16844 **Deutsche Wirker-Zeitschrift.** *Dt. Wirker-Z.* [1952–53] **L.**P. [*C. of:* 16845]

16845 **Deutsche Wirkerzeitung.** Apolda. *Dt. Wirkerztg* [1880–51] **L.**P. 07–51 imp. [1943–44 *contained in:* 53016; *C. as:* 16844]

16846 **Deutsche wissenschaftliche Zeitschrift** für **Polen.** Posen. *Dt. wiss. Z. Pol.* [1923–39] **L.**BM. [*C. as:* 16847]

16847 **Deutsche wissenschaftliche Zeitschrift** im **Wartheland.** Posen. *Dt. wiss. Z. Wartheland* [1940–43] [*C. of:* 16846]

16848 **Deutsche Wollengewerbe.** Grünberg i. Schl. *Dt. Wollengew.* [1869–] **L.**P. 91–39; **Ld.**W. 37–39. [*C. in:* 53016]

16849 **Deutsche zahnärztliche Wochenschrift.** Berlin. *Dt. zahnärztl. Wschr.* [1898–43] **L.**D. 30–40. [*C. in:* 58253]

16850 **Deutsche zahnärztliche Zeitschrift.** München. *Dt. zahnärztl. Z.* [1946–] **L.**D.; **Nw.**A. 50: 56–.

16851 **Deutsche zahnärztliche Zeitung.** Berlin. *Dt. zahnärztl. Ztg* [1902–]

16852 **Deutsche Zahn-, Mund- und Kieferheilkunde.** Leipzig. *Dt. Zahn- Mund- u. Kieferheilk.* [1934–] **L.**D. 34–40: 43: 48–; MA. 48–; MD. 38–40; **Y.** [*C. of:* 16734, 20237 and 56706]

16853 **Deutsche Zahnheilkunde** in **Vorträgen.** Leipzig. *Dt. Zahnheilk. Vortr.* **L.**D. 16: 25–34 imp.

16854 **Deutsche Zeitschrift** für **Akupunktur.** Ulm. *Dt. Z. Akupunktur* [1952–]

16855 **Deutsche Zeitschrift** für **Chirurgie.** Leipzig, etc. *Dt. Z. Chir.* [1872–44] **L.**BM.; MA. 20–30; MD.; S.; UCH. 20–36; **Bm.**U. 94–14; **Br.**U. 09–18 imp.; **C.**PA. 98–00; UL.; **Dn.**U. 03–20; **E.**S. imp.; U. 08–13 imp.; **G.**F. 09–13; U. 15–44; **Ld.**U. 99–44; **M.**MS. 72–24 imp.; **O.**R. 72–33. [*C. in:* 4104]

16856 **Deutsche Zeitschrift** für die **gesamte gerichtliche Medizin.** Berlin. *Dt. Z. ges. gericht. Med.* [1922–] **L.**MA. 50–; MD.; P. 22–28; S. 22–40; **Abd.**U.; **C.**UL.; **Dn.**U.; **E.**P. imp.; U. [*C. of:* 56702]

16857 **Deutsche Zeitschrift** für **Homöopathie.** Berlin. *Dt. Z. Homöop.* [*C. of:* 6466]

16858 **Deutsche Zeitschrift** für **Luftschiffahrt.** Berlin. *Dt. Z. Luftschiff.* [1910–11] **L.**AV.; P.; SC. [*C. of:* 22794; *C. as:* 16756]

16859 **Deutsche Zeitschrift** für **Nervenheilkunde.** Leipzig. *Dt. Z. NervHeilk.* [1891–] **L.**MA. 47–; MD.; S.; **Bm.**U. 07–25; **C.**PH. 21–24; **Dn.**U. 91–98; **E.**P.; **Lv.**U. 91–31; **M.**MS. 92–22; **O.**R. 91–01.

16860 **Deutsche Zeitschrift** für **öffentliche Gesundheitspflege.** Berlin. *Dt. Z. öff. GesundhPflege*

16861 **Deutsche Zeitschrift** für **Verdauungs-** und **Stoffwechselkrankheiten.** Leipzig. *Dt. Z. Verdau.-u. StoffwechsKrankh.* [1938–] **L.**MA. 50–; MD. 38–39; **Abd.**R. 38–57; **Y.**

16862 **Deutsche Ziegelmeisterzeitung.** Detmold. *Dt. ZiegelmZtg.*

16863 **Deutsche Ziegel-** u. **Zementzeitung.** Berlin. *Dt. Ziegel- u. ZemZtg*

16864 **Deutsche Zinngiesser.** München. *Dte Zinngiess.*

16865 **Deutsche zoologische Zeitschrift.** Hannover. *Dt. zool. Z.* [1950–51] **L.**BM^N.; Z.; **Pl.**M.

16866 **Deutsche Zuckerindustrie.** Berlin. *Dt. Zuck-Ind.* [1876–43] **L.**AM. 38–40; P. 18–43 imp. [*From* 1943–45 *contained in:* 59363; *Replaced by:* 58909]

16867 **Deutsche Zündwarenzeitung.** Kassel. *Dt. ZündwarZtg*

16868 **Deutschen elektrischen Strassenbahnen.** Berlin, Leipzig, Hamburg. *Dtn elekt. Strassenb.*

16869 **Deutschen Schutzgebiete** in **Afrika** und der **Südsee.** Berlin. *Dtn Schutzgeb. Afr. Südsee* **L.**BM. 10–13. [*C. of:* 24921; *Supplement to:* 16900]

16871 **Deutscher Amerikanischer Farmer.** Lincoln, Neb. *Dt. am. Fmr*

16872 **Deutscher Baukalender.** *Dt. Baukal.* **L.**P. (pt. 2) 27–29.

16873 **Deutscher Bau-Markt.** Düsseldorf. *Dt. Bau-Markt* **L.**P. [*C. as:* 5821]

16874 **Deutscher Brauereianzeiger.** München. *Dt. BrauAnz.*

16875 **Deutscher Buch-** und **Steindrucker.** Berlin. *Dt. Buch- u. Steindrucker* [1894–26] **L.**P. 10–26; SB. 99–24; SC. 09–13. [*C. as:* 16876]

16876 **Deutscher Drucker.** Berlin. *Dt. Drucker* [1926–] **L.**P. 26–31; SB. 30–39; SC. 36–; **Lh.**P. 37–39: 52–54. [*C. of:* 16875]

16877 **Deutscher Eisenhandel.** Mainz. *Dt. Eisenhand.*

16878 **Deutscher Färberkalender.** München. *Dt. Färberkal.* **L.**P. 51–; **Ld.**P. 57–; W. 30–35; **M.**C. 22–41 imp.: 51–.

16879 **Deutscher Faserstoffkalender.** Berlin. *Dt. Faserstoffkal.*

16880 **Deutscher Kalender** für **Elektrotechniker.** München. *Dt. Kal. Elektrotech.* [1904–27] **L.**P. imp.; **Bm.**U. 07. [*C. of:* 27187]

16881 **Deutscher Maschinenbau.** Würzburg. *Dt. MaschBau*

16882 **Deutscher Maschinist** u. **Heizer.** Berlin. *Dtr Masch. Heiz.*

16883 **Deutscher Metallarbeiter.** Berlin. *Dtr Metallarb.*

16884 **Deutscher militärärztlicher Kalender.** Hamburg. *Dt. militärärztl. Kal.*

16885 **Deutscher Naturschutztag.** Berlin. *Dt. Naturschutztag* **L.**BM^N. 25–31.

16886 **Deutscher Verband** für die **Materialprüfungen** der **Technik.** Berlin. *Dt. Verb. MaterPrüf. Tech.* **L.**P. 25–30; SC. 25–.

16887 **Deutscher Witterungsbericht.** Reichsamt für Wetterdienst. Berlin. *Dtr WittBer.* **L.**MO. 21–39. [*C. of:* 34943]

16888 **Deutscher Zieglerkalender.** Halle a. S. *Dt. Zieglerkal.* **L.**P. 10–14.

16889 **Deutsches Ärzteblatt.** Potsdam. *Dts Ärztebl.* **L.**MA. 37–39.

16890 **Deutsches Agrarblatt.** Kgl. Weinberge. *Dts Agrarbl.*

16891 **Deutsches Archiv** für **klinische Medizin.** Leipzig. *Dt. Arch. klin. Med.* [1866–] **L.**MA. 47–; MD.; S. 66–45 imp.; UC. 05–16 imp.; **Abd.**U. 86–52; **Bl.**U. 81–03; **Bm.**U. 66–30 imp.; **Br.**U. 18; **C.**PA. 88–94: 97–00; UL.; **Dn.**U. 99–20 imp.; **E.**P. 66–42: 47–; **G.**F. 66–15: 35–39; **Ld.**U.; **M.**MS.; **O.**R.; **Sh.**U. 95–39; **Y.**

16892 **Deutsches Baujahrbuch.** Berlin. *Dt. Baujb.*

16893 **Deutsches Bergbaujahrbuch.** Halle. *Dt. Bergb-Jb.* [1930–] [*C. of:* 24705]

16894 **Deutsches Dachdecker-Handwerk.** Berlin. *Dt. DachdeckHandwk* **L.**P. 26–29.

16895 **Deutsches Eisenbahnwesen.** Berlin. *Dt. Eisenb-Wes.*

16896 **Deutsches gewässerkundliches Jahrbuch.** Berlin, etc. *Dt. gewässerk. Jb.* [1941–]
Allgemeiner Teil. *See* 16897.
Donaugebiet [1941–] **L.**MO. [*C. from:* 16898]
Elbegebiet [1956–] **L.**MO. [*C. from:* 16898]
Emsgebiet [1941–56] **L.**MO. [*C. below in:* Weser- und Emsgebiet]
Ergänzungsband. Odergebiet und Wesergebiet [1957–] **L.**MO. [*C. from:* 16898]
Gebiet der Deutschen Demokratischen Republik. *See* 16898.
Hoch- und Oberrheingebiet. [1941–55] **L.**MO. [*C. below in:* Rheingebiet]
Küstengebiet der Nord- und Ostsee westlich Travemünde [1941–] **L.**MO.; **Abd.**M. 48–55 imp.
Maingebiet [1941–]
Mittelrheingebiet [1941–55] **L.**MO. [*C. below in:* Rheingebiet]
Neckargebiet und württemburgisches Donau- und Oberrheingebiet [1941–55] **L.**MO. [*C. below in:* Rheingebiet]
Niederrheingebiet unterhalb der Ahr [1941–55] **L.**MO. [*C. below in:* Rheingebiet]
Rheingebiet [1956–] **L.**MO.
Unteres Elbegebiet unterhalb der Sude [1941–] **L.**MO. [*C. from:* 21176]
Wesergebiet [1941–56] **L.**MO. [*C. below in:* Weser- und Emsgebiet]
Weser- und Emsgebiet [1957–] **L.**MO. [*C. of:* 24750]

16897 **Deutsches gewässerkundliches Jahrbuch. Allgemeiner Teil.** Koblenz. *Dt. gewässerk. Jb. allg. Tl* [1948–] **L.**MO. [*C. of:* 24750]

16898 **Deutsches gewässerkundliches Jahrbuch** für das **Gebiet** der **Deutschen demokratischen Republik.** Berlin. *Dt. gewässerk. Jb. Geb. dt. demokr. Repub.* [1941–55] **L.**MO.; **Y.** [*C. of:* 21176; *C. as:* 16896 Elbegeb. and Ergänzungsband Odergeb. u. Wesergeb.]

16899 **Deutsches Jahrbuch** für die **Industrie** der **plastischen Massen.** Berlin. *Dt. Jb. Ind. plast. Mass.* [1935–] **L.**P. 35–42: 45–; **Y.**

16900 **Deutsches Kolonialblatt.** Berlin. *Dts KolonBl.* [1890–21] **L.**BM.; G. 90–20; TD. 08–13 imp.

16901 **Deutsches medizinisches Journal.** Berlin. *Dt. med. J.* [1951–] **L.**MA.; MD. [*C. of:* 6472]

16902 **Deutsches meteorologisches Jahrbuch.** Reichsamt für Wetterdienst. Berlin. *Dt. met. Jb., Berl.* [1934–] **L.**MO.; SC.; **Db.** 46–; **E.**M. 34–40; R. 34–40: 53–; **O.**G. [*C. of:* 16905–16907, 16910, 16912, 16913, 16916; *C. as:* 16908, and 16915]

16903 **Deutsches meteorologisches Jahrbuch.** Bundesrepublik. Bad Kissingen, Offenbach a. M. *Dt. met. Jb., Bad. Kissingen* [1953–] **L.**MO.; **Y.** [*C. of:* 16908 and 16915]

16904 **Deutsches meteorologisches Jahrbuch.** Deutscher meteorologischer Dienst in der Sowjetisch besetzten Zone. Potsdam. *Dt. met. Jb., Potsdam* [1946–] **L.**MO.

16905 **Deutsches meteorologisches Jahrbuch, Baden.** *Dt. met. Jb. Baden* **L.**MO. 86–33*; **E.**M. 85–13: 29–33. [*C. in:* 16902]

16906 **Deutsches meteorologisches Jahrbuch, Bayern.** München. *Dt. met. Jb. Bayern* **L.**MO. 79–34*; SC. 25–34; U. 34; **E.**M. 01–34; R. 80–05. [*C. in:* 16902]

16907 **Deutsches meteorologisches Jahrbuch. Beobachtungssystem** der **Deutschen Seewarte.** Hamburg. *Dt. met. Jb. BeobSyst. dt. Seew.* **L.**MO. 76–33*; SC. 24–33; **E.**M. 78–33. [*C. in:* 16902]

16908 **Deutsches meteorologisches Jahrbuch, Britische Zone.** Hamburg. *Dt. met. Jb. Br. Zone* [1945–52] **L.**MO.; SC. [*C. from:* 16902; *C. in:* 16903]

16909 **Deutsches meteorologisches Jahrbuch, Elsass-Lothringen.** Strassburg i. E. *Dt. met. Jb. Els.-Loth.* [1890–15] **L.**MO.; **Db.** 90–96; **E.**M.; **O.**G. 05–14. [*C. in:* 3270]

16910 **Deutsches meteorologisches Jahrbuch, Freie Hansestadt Bremen.** Bremen. *Dt. met. Jb. Bremen* **L.**MO. 91–33*; SC. 28–33; UC. 19–33 imp.; **E.**M. 93–33 imp. [*C. in:* 16902]

16911 **Deutsches meteorologisches Jahrbuch** für das **Grossherzogtum Hessen.** Darmstadt. *Dt. met. Jb. Hessen* **L.**MO. 01–33*; SC. 01–33. [*C. in:* 16902]

16912 **Deutsches meteorologisches Jahrbuch, Preussen** u. d. **übrigen norddeutschen Staaten.** Berlin. *Dt. met. Jb. Preuss.* **L.**BM. 93–33*; MO. 79–33; **Db.** 86–06; **E.**M. 87–06 imp.; R. 85–94 imp. [*C. in:* 16902]

16913 **Deutsches meteorologisches Jahrbuch, Sachsen, Chemnitz** und **Dresden.** *Dt. met. Jb. Sachs.* **L.**MO. 83–33*. [*C. in:* 16902]

16914 **Deutsches meteorologisches Jahrbuch, Station Aachen.** Karlsruhe. *Dt. met. Jb. Stn Aachen* **L.**MO. 95–29*; SC. 15–18; **E.**M. 95–11: 16–29. [*C. in:* 16913]

16915 **Deutsches meteorologisches Jahrbuch, U.S.-Zone.** Bad Kissingen. *Dt. met. Jb. U.S.-Zone* [1945–52] **L.**SC.; **E.**R. [*C. from* 16902; *C. in:* 16903]

16916 **Deutsches meteorologisches Jahrbuch, Württemberg.** Stuttgart. *Dt. met. Jb. Württ.* **L.**MO. 87–33*; **E.**M. 87–12. [*C. in:* 16902]

16917 **Deutsches Seiler-Gewerbe.** Berlin. *Dt. Seiler-Gew.* [1933–] **L.**P. 33–44 v. imp.

16918 **Deutsches Steinbildhauerjournal.** Liegnitz. *Dt. Steinbildhj.*

16918° **Deutsches Textilgewerbe.** Düsseldorf. *Dt. Text-Gew.* [1951] **L.**P.; **M.**C. [*C. of:* 27504; *C. as:* 58629]

16919 **Deutsches Tierärzteblatt.** Berlin. *Dts Tierärztebl.* [1934–45] **L.**V. 35–44 imp.

16920 **Deutsches Tuberkulose-Blatt.** Leipzig. *Dts TuberkBl.* [1934–45] **L.**H. 34–40; MD.; S. 34–44 imp.; SC. 40–44; TD. 34–44 imp.; **Br.**U.; **Cr.**MD. 34–39; **E.**P. 34–38; U. 37–45 imp.; **Ld.**U. 34–44 imp.; **M.**MS. 34–39; **Hw.**A.; **O.**R. 37–45. [*Supplement to:* 16765; *C. of:* 38508]

16921 **Deutsches Warmblut.** Hannover. *Dt. Warmblut* [1939–] **E.**AB. 39–40. [*C. of:* 58637]

16922 **Deutschmährisches Ärzteblatt.** Brünn. *Dt.-mähr. Ärztebl.*

16923 **Deutschösterreichische Monatsschrift** für **naturwissenschaftliche Fortbildung.** Wien. *Dt.-öst. Mschr. naturw. Fortbild.*

16923° **Deutsch-österreichische tierärztliche Wochenschrift.** Wien. *Dt.-öst. tierärztl. Wschr.* [1919–27] [*C. of:* 35949; *C. as:* 35944]

16924 **Deutschösterreichische Wochenschrift** für **Tierheilkunde.** Graz. *Dt.-öst. Wschr. Tierheilk.*

16925 **Development Bulletin. Aluminium Laboratories Ltd.** Banbury. *Dev. Bull. Alumin. Labs* [1958–] **L.**BM.

16925ᵃ **Development Leaflets. Timber Development Association.** London. *Dev. Leafl. Timb. Dev. Ass.* [1952–] **L.**BM.

16925ᵇ **Development Notes. Plant Protection Ltd.** *Dev. Notes Pl. Prot.* [1952–] **L.**BM.

16926 **Developmental Biology.** New York, London. *Devl Biol.* [1959–] **L.**BMᴺ.; MC.; MD.; NC.; UC.; Z.; **Bl.**U.; **Bn.**U.; **C.**AN.; APH. 61–; **Cr.**U.; **H.**U.; **Ld.**U.; **M.**U.; **O.**BI.; **Y.**

Developmental Medicine and **Child Neurology.** See 13571.

16927 **Developments** in **Industrial Microbiology.** New York. *Devs ind. Microbiol.* [1960–] **L.**P.; SC.; **Y.**

16928 **Devise médicale.** Paris. *Devise méd.*

16929 **Dexion Angle.** London. *Dexion Angle* [1955–] **L.**BM.; P. (curr.); **Br.**P. (1 yr); **Lv.**P.; **Sil.** (1 yr)

16930 **Dexion News.** London. *Dexion News* **L.**BM. 49; P. (curr.)

16931 **Día médico.** Buenos Aires. *Día méd.* [1928–] **L.**MA. 44– imp.; MD. 39–51 imp.; S. 31–34 imp.; TD. 43– imp.; **E.**U. 30– imp.; **M.**MS. 30– imp.; **Y.**

16932 **Diabète.** Le Rainey, Paris. *Diabète* [1953–] **L.**MA.; MD.

16933 **Diabetes.** American Diabetes Association. New York. *Diabetes* [1952–] **L.**GH. 57–; MA. imp.; MD.; SC.; **Bl.**U. 58–; **Br.**U. 56–; **C.**BI. 54–; **Dn.**U. 59–; **E.**U.; **G.**U.; **Ld.**U.; **Wd.** 54–; **Y.** [*C. of:* 16934 and 38846]

16934 **Diabetes Abstracts.** Cincinnati. *Diabetes Abstr.* [1942–51] **G.**U. [*C. in:* 16933]

16935 **Diabetic Digest.** Philadelphia. *Diabet. Dig.* [1941–]

16936 **Diabetic Journal.** London. *Diabet. J., Lond.* [1935–] **L.**BM.; MA. 46–; SH. (1 yr); **G.**M.

16937 **Diabetic Journal.** St. Louis, Mo. *Diabet. J., St Louis* [1941–]

Diaetás és **physikai gyógyítómódok.** *Supplement to:* 9026.

16938 **Diagnosi.** Pisa. *Diagnosi, Pisa* [1921–37]

16939 **Diagnosi:** rivista di medicina pratica. Napoli. *Diagnosi, Napoli* [1945–] **L.**MA. 46–; MD. 47–; SH. (1 yr)

16940 **Diagnostica** e **tecnica** di **laboratorio.** Napoli. *Diagnostica Tec. Lab.* [1930–] **L.**MD. 30–39. [*C. of:* 19783]

16941 **Diagnostics** et **traitements.** Lyon. *Diagnostics Trait.* [1942–] **L.**MA. 46–; MD. 45–47.

16942 **Diamant.** Antwerp. *Diamant, Antwerp* [1958–] **L.**DI.

16943 **Diamant.** Glasindustrie-Zeitung. Leipzig. *Diamant, Lpz.* [1879–] **L.**P. 07–42 imp.; SC. 33–; **Sh.**G. 18–.

16944 **Diamond** in **Industry.** New York. *Diam. Ind.* **L.**DI. 44–58 imp.

16945 **Diamond News** and **South African Watchmaker** and **Jeweller.** Kimberley. *Diam. News* [1937–] **L.**DI. 42–44: 48–.

16946 **Diamond Tool Industry.** London. *Diam. Tool Ind.* [1951–56] **L.**P.; **E.**A.; **Y.** [*C. of:* 23188]

16947 **Diario radiologico.** Torino. *Diario radiol.*

16948 **Diary** for the **Brewing** and **Syrup Rooms.** A. Boake Roberts & Co. London. *Diary Brew. Syrup Rms* [1884–53]

Dichdjilik alémi. Constantinople. *See* 17010.

16949 **Dickcissel.** Sioux City Bird Club. Sioux City. *Dickcissel* [1934–]

16950 **Didier-Feuerfest-Technik.** Wiesbaden. *Didier-Feuerfest-Tech.* [1955–] **L.**P.

16951 **Die Casting News.** London. *Die Cast. News* [1958–] **L.**BM.; P.; **Y.**

16952 **Die Castings.** Cleveland, Ohio. *Die Cast.* [1943–51] **L.**NF. 44–51; SC. 47–51. [*C. as:* 38556]

16953 **Diebeners Goldschmiede-Jahrbuch.** Stuttgart. *Diebeners Goldschm.-Jb.* [1954–] **L.**P.

16954 **Diebeners Uhrmacher-Jahrbuch.** Stuttgart. *Diebeners Uhrm.-Jb.* **L.**P. 54–.

16955 **Diergeneeskundig jaarboekje.** Utrecht. *Diergeneesk. Jaarb.* **W.** 30–.

16956 **Dicsel.** Jersey City. *Diesel* [1938–] **Y.**

16957 **Diesel Digest.** Los Angeles. *Diesel Dig.* [1934–39]

16958 **Diesel Engine Progress.** London. *Diesel Eng. Prog.* [1955–56] **L.**BM.; P.; **O.**R.; **Y.** [*C. as:* 14994]

16959 **Diesel Engine Specification.** New York. *Diesel Eng. Specif.* **L.**P. [*Supplement to:* 16963]

Diesel Engineers and **Users' Association. Proceedings.** *See* 39151.

16960 **Diesel** and **Gas Engine Progress.** New York. *Diesel Gas Eng. Prog.* **Y.** [*C. of:* 16965; *C. as:* 16961]

16961 **Diesel** and **Gas Turbine Progress.** New York. *Diesel Gas Turb. Prog.* **Y.** [*C. of:* 16960]

16962 **Diesel** and **Oil Engine Journal.** Los Angeles. *Diesel Oil Eng. J.* [1925–27]

16963 **Diesel Power.** New York. *Diesel Pwr* [1930–35: 54–] **L.**P.; **Li.**M.; **Sil.** [*C. of:* 36104; > 16964, 1935–53]

16964 **Diesel Power** and **Diesel Transportation.** New York. *Diesel Pwr Diesel Transpn* [1935–53] **L.**P.; **Li.**M. 51–53; **Sil.** 45–53. [*C. of:* and *Rec. as:* 16963]

16965 **Diesel Progress.** New York. *Diesel Prog.* **Y.** [*C. as:* 16960]

16966 **Diesel Railway Traction.** London. *Diesel Rly Tract.* [1939–] **L.**BM.; EE. 46–; P.; SC.; **Abs.**N. 47–; **C.**UL. 49–; **Db.** 55–; **E.**A.; **G.**M. 57–; **Ld.**P. 58–; **Lv.**P. 47–48 imp.: 54–; **M.**P.; T.; **Sh.**IO. 45–; **Y.** [1935–38 *issued as supplement to* 41912]

16967 **Diesel Times.** Cleveland, Ohio. *Diesel Times* [1944–] **Y.**

16968 **Diesel Transportation.** New York. *Diesel Transpn* [1934–35] **L.**P. [*Supplement to:* 16963]

16968° **Diesel-lehti.** *Diesel-lehti* **Y.**

16969 **Dieselmaschinen.** Berlin. *Dieselmaschinen* [1924–] [*Supplement to:* 58863]

16970 **Dietary Administration** and **Therapy.** Cleveland. *Diet. Adm. Ther.*

16971 **Difesa** delle **piante** contra le **malattie** ed i **parassiti.** Torino. *Dif. Piante Mal. Parass.* [1924–35] **L.**MY. 29–35. [*C. of:* 40560; *C. as:* 8304]

16972 **Digest** of **Agricultural Economics.** Oxford. *Dig. agric. Econ.* [1957–] **L.**AM.; **Abs.**N.; U.; **Bn.**U.; **C.**A.; **E.**A.; **Ld.**U.; **O.**B.; **Rt.**

16973 **Digest** of the **Annual Report. Southwestern Forest** and **Range Experiment Station.** Flagstaff. *Dig. a. Rep. SWest. Forest Range Exp. Stn*

   Digest. Building Research Station, D.S.I.R. *See* 9076.

16974 **Digest. Central Electricity Authority.** London. *Dig. cent. Elect. Auth.* [1955–57] **L.**P.; **Bm.**T.; **O.**R.; **Y.** [*C. as:* 16975]

16975 **Digest. Central Electricity Generating Board.** London. *Dig. cent. Elect. gener. Bd* [1958–] **L.**AV. imp.; P.; **Bm.**T.; **Y.** [*C. of:* 16974]

16976 **Digest. Commonwealth Bureau** of **Horticulture** and **Plantation Crops.** East Malling, Farnham Royal. *Dig. Commonw. Bur. Hort. Plantn Crops* [1958–] **L.**BM.; P.; **C.**A.; **R.**T.; **Y.**

   Digest of **Current Russian Literature, International Physical Index.** *See* 17768.

16977 **Digest** of **Current Scientific Literature** on **Lubrication.** Ragosine and Co. London. *Dig. curr. scient. Lit. Lubric.* [1921–26] **L.**P.; **C.**UL.; **O.**R. 22–25.

16978 **Digest** of **Electric Melting News** Detroit, Mich. *Dig. elect. Melt. News* **L.**P. 34★.

16979 **Digest** of **Information. British Glass Industry Research Association.** Sheffield. *Dig. Inf. Br. Glass Ind. Res. Ass.* [1955–] **L.**SI.

16980 **Digest** of **Literature** on **Dielectrics.** Washington. *Dig. Lit. Dielect.* [1948–] **L.**B. 49–; P.; SC.; **Br.**U. 51–55; **M.**C. 50–60; **Y.**

16981 **Digest** des **matières plastiques.** Bruxelles. *Dig. Matièr. plast.* [1954–] **L.**PL. [*C. of:* 29714]

16982 **Digest** of **Neurology** and **Psychiatry.** Hartford. *Dig. Neurol. Psychiat.* [1932–] **L.**MA. 44–; MD. 49; **Bl.**U. 57–; **Nw.**A. 51–.

16983 **Digest** of **Ophthalmology** and **Otolaryngology.** Omaha, Neb., etc. *Dig. Ophth. Otolar.* [1938–] **L.**MA. 49– imp.; **M.**MS. 49–.

16984 **Digest Reports. Society** for the **Advancement** of **Anaesthesia** in **Dentistry.** *Dig. Rep. Soc. Advmt Anaesth. Dent.* **L.**D.

16985 **Digest** of **Soviet Technology.** Kirkham, Preston. *Dig. Sov. Technol.* [1959–60] **Bl.**U.; **Ld.**P.; **M.**P.; **O.**R.; **Wd.**; **Y.** [*C. as:* 50362]

16986 **Digest** of **Statistics. Pneumoconiosis** in the **Mining** and **Quarrying Industries.** London. *Dig. Statist. Pneumoconiosis Min. Quarr. Inds* [1953–] **L.**MD.; **Bm.**U.

16987 **Digest** of **Treatment.** Denton, Md., etc. *Dig. Treat.* [1937–49] **L.**BM.; D. 45–49; MA. imp.; MD. 37–38; **E.**U. 37–45 [*C. in:* 2131]

16988 **Digest** of **War Medicine.** Johannesburg. *Dig. War Med.* [1941–] **L.**TD. [*C. as:* 50137]

16989 **Digeste** de la **presse brassicole mondiale.** Bruxelles. *Digeste Presse brassic. mond.* [1952–] **L.**P. 54–.

16990 **Digital Computer Newsletter.** Washington. *Digit. Comput. Newsl.* [1950–53] **L.**P. imp. [*From* 1954 *forms supplement published in:* 25607 *and from* 1958 *in:* 15060]

16991 **Dignell-Johnson Quarterly.** Fish and Wildlife Service. Washington. *Dignell-Johnson Q.* [1953–] **Fr.**

16992 **Dillinger-Technik.** Dillingen-Saar. *Dillinger-Tech.* **L.**P. 28.

16993 **Dimafon-Blätter.** Bad Homburg. *Dimafon-Bl.* **L.**P. (curr.)

16994 **Dinglers polytechnisches Journal.** Berlin, etc. *Dinglers polytech. J.* [1820–31] **L.**BM.; C. imp.; IC. 70–99: 03–24; P.; SC.; **Bm.**U. 81–85; **Db.** 1845–31; **E.**F. 1841–06 imp.; R.; **G.**U. 1825–31; **Ld.**U. 77–27; **M.**C. 85–13; P. 1859–14; T. 73–89; U. 84–09; **Sw.**U. 1820–97; **Wd.** 76–99.

16995 **Dioptric Bulletin.** London. *Diopt. Bull.* [1910–30] **L.**BM. imp.; S. 26–30; SC.; **G.**T. 21–30; **M.**T. 21–26; **O.**R. 27–30; **Te.**N. 21–23. [*C. of:* 16998; *C. as:* 16999]

16996 **Dioptric News.** London. *Diopt. News* [1930–] **L.**BM.; H. 47–; P. (curr.); SH. (1 yr); **C.**UL. 40–; **Db.** 55–; **M.**MS. 43–; T. 46–; **Y.**

16997 **Dioptric** and **Ophthalometric Review.** Rochdale. *Diopt. ophthalom. Rev.* [1896–03] **L.**BM. 00–03; P. 01–03; PG. 02–03; SC. [*C. as:* 16998]

16998 **Dioptric** and **Optological Review.** Rochdale. *Diopt. optol. Rev.* [1903–09] **L.**BM.; P.; PG. 03–08; SC.; **C.**UL. 06–09; **O.**R. [*C. of:* 16997; *C. as:* 16995]

16999 **Dioptric Review.** London. *Diopt. Rev.* [1930–39] **L.**BM.; SC.; **Bm.**T. 37–39; **E.**A.; **M.**T. 32–39; **O.**R. [*C. of:* 16995; *C. in:* 17000]

17000 **Dioptric Review** and **British Journal** of **Physiological Optics.** London. *Diopt. Rev. Br. J. physiol. Opt.* [1940–49] **L.**BM.; MD. 42–49; S. 41–47 imp.; SC.; SI. 45–49; **Bm.**T.; **E.**A.; HW. 47–49; **H.**U.; **M.**MS.; T.; **O.**R. [*C. of:* 16999 and 8878 and *Rec. as:* 8878]

   Dipan. Diretoria da produção animal. Rio de Janeiro. *See* 16257.

17001 **Dir hilft** die **Landmaschine.** Wolfratshausen, München. *Dir hilft Landmasch.* [1950–] **Sil.**

17002 **Dirección general** de **enseñanza** e **investigaciones agrícolas.** Buenos Aires. *Direcc. gen. Enseñ. Invest. agríc., B. Aires*

17003 **Dirección** de **investigaciones. Instituto** de **sanidad vegetal.** Buenos Aires. *Direcc. Invest. Inst. Sanid. veg., B. Aires* L.BM^N. 45-.

17004 **Direct Current.** London. *Direct Curr.* [1952-] L.BM.; EE.; P.; Bl.U. 61-; Bn.U. 61-; Br.U.; C.UL.; Co.T. 61-; Dn.U. 58-; E.A.; HW.; Ld.U. 63-; M.T.; N.U.; O.R.; Y.

17005 **Director's Quarterly Report. High Altitude Observatory, Boulder** and **Climax.** *Dirtr's q. Rep. high Altit. Obs. Boulder Climax* L.MO. 56-.
Directory of **Graduate Research, American Chemical Society.** *See* 1925.

17005^c **Directory. Indiana Geological Survey.** Bloomington. *Dir. Indiana geol. Surv.* [1951-] L.BM^N. [*C. of:* 17006]

17005^d **Directory** of **Nuclear Reactors.** International Atomic Energy Agency. Vienna. *Dir. nucl. React.* [1959-] L.P.

17006 **Directory Series. Indiana Division** of **Geology.** Bloomington. *Dir. Ser. Indiana Div. Geol.* L.BM^N. 48. [*C. as:* 17005^c]

17007 **Diritto veterinario.** Torino. *Diritto vet.*

17008 **Disaster Studies.** Committee on Disaster Studies, National Research Council. Washington. *Disaster Stud.* [1956-] L.MD.; Y.

17009 **Discharges** of the **Nile.** Cairo. *Discharges Nile* [1956-] L.MO. [*C. from:* 45614^a]

17010 **Dişçilik âlemi.** Le monde dentaire. Istanbul. *Dişç. Âlemi* [1925-29] Abs.N. 26-29.

17011 **Discovery.** London, etc. *Discovery, Lond.* [1920-] L.AM. 43- imp.; AV. 43-; B. 38- imp.; BM.; BM^N. 20-28: 43- imp.; CB. (2 yr.); G.; H. 45-; IC. 43-; MA. 54- imp.; MC. 47- imp.; NP. 50-; P.; PL. 45-; PR. 44-; QM. 43-; R. 56-; RI. 47-; SC.; TP. 38-; U.; UC. 20-36 imp.; VC. 51- imp.; Abd.M. 50-; U. 20-21: 39-45; Abs.N.; U. 20-21; Ba.I. 43-; Bm.P.; T. 26-28: 49-; U.; Bn.U.; Br.P. 20-; U. 32-; Bra.P. 57-; C.A. (3 yr.); UL.; Co.T. 58-; Cr.M.; P. 25-; U. 46-; Db. 35-; Dn.U. 20-27: 56-; E.B. 22-; D. 45-; N. 43-; R. 35-; U. 55-; Ex.U. 21-33: 47-; F.A. 38-; G.M.; U.; H.U. 21-24: 38- imp.; Hu.G. 52-; Je. 44-; Lc.A. 52-; Ld.P.; U. 20-28: 47-; Lh.P. 44-; Lv.P. 20-38: 43-; M.C. (1 yr); MS. 20-39 imp.; P. 20-40; R.; U. 20-39; N.P. 20-37; U. 28-40; Nw.A. imp.; P. 20-35: 53-; O.R.; R.U. 27-31; Rt. 20-43; Sh.IO.; S. 48-; Sy.R. 43-; Wd. 45-; We.K. 46-; Wo. 53-; Y. [*Suspended between* March, 1940 *and* January, 1943]

17012 **Discovery.** University of Melbourne. Melbourne. *Discovery, Melb.* [1955-] L.BM.; BM^N.; P.; G.U.; Ld.U. 55; Y.

17013 **'Discovery' Reports.** Cambridge. *'Discovery' Rep.* [1929-] L.AM.; BM^N.; L.; MO. (met.); R.; SC.; Z.; Abd.M.; U.; Bm.P.; Bn.U.; Br.U.; C.B.; PO.; Cr.M.; U.; Db.; Dm.; Dn.U.; E.A.; F.; U.; Ex.U.; Fr. 25-55 imp.; G.M.; U. 29-; Ld.P.; Lo.; Lv.P.; U.; M.P.; U.; Mi.; N.P.; U.; Nw.A.; O.AP. imp.; R.; Z.; Pl.M.; Sa.; Sw.U. 55-; Y.

17014 **Discussions** of the **Faraday Society.** London. *Discuss. Faraday Soc.* [1947-] L.AV.; B.; BM.; C.; IC.; LE.; LI.; MC.; NF.; P.; PR.; QM.; R.; RI.; SC.; U.; Abd.U.; Abs.U.; Bl.U.; Bm.P.; T.; U.; Bn.U.; Br.U.; C.APH.;

CH.; P.; Co.T.; Cr.U.; Dn.U.; E.A.; HW.; R.; Ex.U.; F.A. 47-53; G.T.; U.; H.U.; Ld.P.; U.; W.; Lh.FO.; P.; Lv.P. 47-48: 51-; U.; M.C.; D.; T.; U.; N.T.; U.; Nw.A.; O.BS.; PC.; R.; Pl.M.; R.D. imp.; U.; Rt.; Sh.IO.; S. 51-; SC.; U.; St.R.; Sw.U.; Sy.R.; Wd.; We.K.; Y.
Disease a Month. Chicago. *See* 16260.

17015 **Diseases** of the **Chest.** El Paso, Texas, etc. *Dis. Chest* [1935-] L.MA. 45-; MD.; RA. 45-; U. 52-; Abd.U. 53-; Bl.U. 45- imp.; Bm.U. 44-; Cr.MD. 51-; E.U. 49-; M.MS. 47-; Nw.A. 48-56; Y.

17016 **Diseases** of the **Colon** and **Rectum.** Philadelphia. *Dis. Colon Rectum* [1958-] L.BM.; MA.; MD.; E.S.; Ld.U.

17017 **Diseases** of the **Eye.** London. *Dis. Eye* [1955-] L.TD.

17018 **Diseases** of the **Eye, Ear, Nose** and **Throat.** Chicago. *Dis. Eye Ear Nose Throat* [1941-42] L.MD. [*C. in:* 18871]

17019 **Diseases** of the **Nervous System.** Chicago. *Dis. nerv. Syst.* [1940-] L.MA. 45-; MD.; S. 41- imp.; Y.

17020 **Diskussionsbericht. Eidgenossische Materialprüfungsanstalt.** Zürich. *DiskussBer. eidg. MaterPrüfAnst.* L.SC. 25-.

17021 **Dispensary** and **Society.** Survey Report. Tuberculosis League. Pittsburgh. *Dispensary Soc.*

17022 **Dispensing Optician.** London. *Dispens. Optn* [1934-] L.BM.; G.F. 54-.

17023 **Disposiciones oficiales sanitarias.** Madrid. *Dispos. of. sanit., Madr.* L.TD. 26- imp.

17024 **Dissertation Abstracts.** Ann Arbor. *Diss. Abstr.* [1952-] L.BM.; C.; CB.; P.; SC.; U.; Abd.R.; Bl.U. 53- imp.; Bm.P.; T. 58-; Bn.U. 55-; C.UL.; Cr.U. 59-; Db.; E.U.; Ex.U. 59-; G.T. (5 yr.); H.U. 60-; Ld.U.; M.C. 52-; P.; T. 54-; Md.H. 58-; N.U. 59-; O.B.; R.; R.D. 56-; Sy.R. 54-; Y.

17025 **Dissertationen. Badische technische Hochschule Fridericiana.** Carlsruhe. *Dissn bad. tech. Hochsch. fridericiana* L.P. 56-.

17026 **Dissertationen** zur **Erlangung** des **Doktorgrades** bei der **Naturwissenschaftlichen Fakultät, Justus Liebig Hochschule.** Giessen. *Dissn Erlang. Doktorgr. naturw. Fak. Justus Liebig Hochsch.* Y.

17027 **Dissertationen. Technische Hochschule, Hannover.** *Dissn tech. Hochsch. Hannover* [1956-] L.P.; Y.
Dissertationes. Academiae scientiarum et artium slovenica: Classis IV: Historia naturalis. *See* 42238.

17028 **Dissertationes Instituti botanici systematici Universitatis Budapestiensis.** Budapestini. *Dissnes Inst. bot. syst. Univ. Bpest* L.BM^N. 48-.

17029 **Dissertationes pharmaceuticae.** Warszawa. *Dissnes pharm., Warsz.* [1949-] L.BM. 42-52; PH. 57-; Y.

17029^c **Dissertatsii. Akademiya meditsinskikh nauk SSSR.** Moskva. Диссертации. Академия медицинских наук СССР. *Disstsii Akad. med. Nauk SSSR* [1951-] L.BM.

17030 **Distillateur.** Paris. *Distillateur*

17031 **Distillation Literature Index** and **Abstracts.** Philadelphia. *Distill. Lit. Index Abstr.* [1953-] L.P.

17032 **Distillatore.** Treviso. *Distillatore*

17033 **Distribution** of **Electricity.** Leeds, etc. *Distrib. Elect.* [1928–60] **L.**AV. 59–60; BM. 38–60; EE. imp.; P. imp.; **Br.**U. 32–60; **C.**ENG. 45–60; **F.**A. 46–57; **Lv.**P. 42–60; **N.**U. 54–60; **Nw.**A. 31–60 imp.; **Sy.**R. 29–60; **Y.** [*C. as:* 17647]

17034 **Distribution Maps** of **Insect Pests.** London. *Distrib. Maps Insect Pests* [1951–] **L.**BMᴺ.; EB.; **Je.**; **Md.**H.; **Nw.**A.; **O.**AP.; F.; RE.; **Rt.**

17035 **Distribution Maps** of **Plant Diseases.** London. *Distrib. Maps Pl. Dis.* [1942–] **L.**SC.; **Je.** 53–; **Md.**H.; **Nw.**A.; **O.**AP.; BO.; F.; RE.; **Rt.**; **Y.**

17036 **Distribuzione** ed **utilizzazione** dei **gas naturali.** Bibliografia internazionale. Roma. *Distribuz. Util. Gas nat.* **L.**P. 57–. [*Supplement to:* 8255]

17036ᶜ **District Heating.** *Distr. Heat.* **Y.**

17037 **Disturbances** in **Aeronautical Phenomena** during the **International Geophysical Year.** Tokyo. *Disturb. aeronaut. Phenom. int. geophys. Year* [1957–] **L.**MO.

    Division Technical Papers. C.S.I.R.O., Australia. *See* **Technical Papers** of the **Divisions.**

17039 **Divisional Reports** of the **Department** of **Agriculture, British Guiana.** Georgetown. *Divl Rep. Dep. Agric. Br. Guiana* [1931–38] **L.**EB. imp.; **Md.**H.; **Rt.**; **Sal.** [*C. as:* 43533]

17040 **Divisional Reports. Division** of **Soils, Commonwealth Scientific** and **Industrial Research Organization.** Adelaide. *Divl Rep. Div. Soils CSIRO* **Rt.** 55– imp.

17041 **Divisional Reports. Faculty** of **Agriculture, Ibadan University College.** *Divl Rep. Fac. Agric. Ibadan Univ. Coll.* [1954–] **L.**BM.; **C.**A.

    Divulgación. *See also* **Divulgaciónes**

17042 **Divulgación agrícola. Estación experimental agrícola** de la **Molina.** Lima. *Divulg. agríc. Estac. exp. agríc. La Molina* [1946–] **L.**EB.

    Divulgaciónes Estación de **fitopatología agrícola** de **La Coruña.** *See* 40671.

17044 **Divulgaciónes Estación** de **patología vegetal** de **Barcelona.** Barcelona. *Divulgs Estac. Patol. veg. Barcelona* **L.**EB. 25–28.

17045 **Divulgaciónes etnológicas. Universidad** del **Atlantico.** Barranquilla. *Divulgs etnol. Univ. Atlant.* [1953–] **L.**AN. [*C. of:* 17046]

17046 **Divulgaciónes. Instituto** de **investigación etnológica, Universidad** del **Atlantico.** Barranquilla. *Divulgs Inst. Invest. etnol. Univ. Atlant.* [1950–51] **L.**AN. imp. [*C. as:* 17045]

17047 **Divulgaciónes. Laboratório** de **biología marina, Universidad católica** de **Santo Tomas** de **Villanueva, Habana.** *Divulgs Lab. Biol. mar. Univ. catól., Habana* [1958–] **Pl.**M. 58.

17048 **Djahané-pézéchki.** Téhéran. *Djahané-pézéchki* **L.**TD. 52–; **Bl.**U. 48– imp.; **Y.**

17049 **Djåwå.** Weltevreden. *Djåwå* **L.**AN. 21–41.

17050 **Djela Jugoslavenske akademije znanosti** i **umjetnosti.** Zagreb. *Djela jugosl. Akad. Znan. Umjetn.* [1882–] **L.**BM.; BMᴺ. (nat. hist.) 82–13.

17050ᶜ **Dnepropetrovskiĭ meditsinskiĭ zhurnal.** Dnepropetrovsk. Днепропетровский медицинский журнал. *Dnepropetrov. med. Zh.* [1927–] **L.**TD. 27–30; **E.**U. [*C. of:* 17577]

17051 **Dnevnik Obshchestva vracheĭ** pri **Imperatorskom Kazanskom universitetê.** Kazan'. Дневникъ Общества врачей при Императорскомъ Казанскомъ университетѣ. *Dnev. Obshch. Vrach. imp. kazan. Univ.* [1868–04]

17052 **Dnevnik XI S''êzda russkikh estestvoispȳtateleĭ** i **vracheĭ.** S.-Peterburg. Дневникъ XI Съѣздъ русскихъ естествоиспытателей и врачей. *Dnev. S''êzda russk. Estestvoisp. Vrach.*

17053 **Dnevnik Otdêla ikhtĭologĭi Imperatorskago Russkago obshchestva akklimatizatsĭi zhivotnȳkh** i **rastenĭi.** Moskva. Дневникъ Отдѣла ихтіологіи Императорскаго Русскаго общества акклиматизаціи животныхъ и растеній. *Dnev. Otd. Ikhtiol. imp. russk. Obshch. Akklim. Zhivot. Rast.* [1907–08]

17054 **Dnevnik S''êzda russkikh zodchikh.** S.-Peterburg. Дневникъ Съѣзда русскихъ зодчихъ. *Dnev. S''êzda russk. Zodch.*

    Dnevnik tkacha, pryadil'nika i **inzhenera.** Дневникъ ткача, прядильника и инженера. *See* 48297.

17055 **Dnevnik Vozdukhoplavatel'nago s''êzda.** S.-Peterburg. Дневникъ Воздухоплавательнаго съѣзда. *Dnev. vozdukh. S''êzda*

17056 **Dnevnik Vserossĭiskago élektricheskago s''êzda.** S.-Peterburg. Дневникъ Всероссійскаго электрическаго съѣзда. *Dnev. vseross. elekt. S''êzda*

17057 **Dnevnik Zoologicheskago otdêlenĭya Imperatorskago Obshchestva lyubiteleĭ estestvoznanĭya, antropologĭi** i **étnografĭi.** Moskva. Дневникъ Зоологическаго отдѣленія Императорскаго Общества любителей естествознанія, антропологіи и этнографіи. *Dnev. zool. Otd. imp. Obshch. Lyub. Estestvozn. Antrop. Étnogr.*

17058 **Doble cruz.** Revista de la Liga argentina contra la tuberculosis. Buenos Aires. *Doble Cruz* [1936–] **L.**BM. 38; MA. 52– imp.

    Doboku-gakkai-shi. *See* 26275.

    Dobutsugaku zasshi. *See* 59259.

17059 **Docaéro.** Paris. *Docaéro* [1950–] **L.**AV. imp.; **F.**A. 56–.

17060 **Dock** and **Harbour Authority.** London. *Dock Harb. Auth.* [1920–] **L.**BM.; P. 21– imp.; **C.**UL.; **E.**A. 50–; **G.**M.; T. 50–; **Lv.**P.; **M.**P. 50–; U. 20–26 imp.; **Nw.**A. 51–; **O.**R.; **Pl.**M. 30; **Sh.**SC. 20–55; **Wo.** 53–; **Y.**

17061 **Doctor.** London. *Doctor* [1938–47] **L.**BM.; **O.**R. 38–39. [*C. as:* 21969]

17062 **Doctoral Dissertations** accepted by **American Universities.** New York, etc. *Doct. Diss. Am. Univs* [1933–55] **L.**BMᴺ.; CB. 49–55; SC. 52–55; **E.**U. 39–55; **Ld.**U. [*C. as:* 22877ᶜ]

17063 **Doctoral Dissertations** and **Master's Theses, Washington University.** St. Louis. *Doct. Diss. Mast. Theses Wash. Univ.* **O.**B. 56–.

17064 **Doctors** of **Philosophy** and **Doctors** of **Science, Harvard University** and **Radcliffe College,** with titles of their theses. Cambridge, Mass. *Doct. Phil. Doct. Sci. Harv. Univ. Radcliffe Coll.* [1945–] **Y.** [*C. of:* 51331]

17065 **Document scientifique** et **médical.** Paris. *Document scient. méd.*

    Documenta cerealia. *See* 5658.

17066 **Documenta Geigy.** Series chirurgica. Basle. *Documenta Geigy Ser. chir.* [1956–] **L.**MD.; S. 56–59.

17067 **Documenta** de **medicina geographica** et **tropica.** Amsterdam. *Documenta Med. geogr. trop.* [1952–57] **L.**EB.; MA.; MD.; SC.; TD.; TP.; **E.**U.; **G.**U. imp. [*C. of:* 17068; *C. as:* 54404]

17068 **Documenta neerlandica** et **indonesica** de **morbis tropicis.** Amsterdam. *Documenta neerl. indones. Morb. trop.* [1949–51] **L.**EB.; MA.; MD.; SC.; TD.; TP. 51; **E.**U.; **G.**U. imp. [*C. as:* 17067]

17069 **Documenta ophthalmologica.** Zurich, Paris, 's Gravenhage. *Documenta ophth.* [1938–] **L.**MD.; OP.; S.; **M.**MS. 51–.
Documenta physiographica Poloniae. *See* 29593.

17070 **Documentación psicopedagógica.** *Documción psicoped.* **L.**PS. 55 imp.

17071 **Documentaire médical.** Paris. *Documentaire méd.* [1935–]

17072 **Documentare tehnică.** Bucureşti. *Documentare teh.* [1956–] **L.**AM.; P.; PR.; **Abd.**S.; **Sil.**; **Y.** [*C. of:* 9109]

17073 **Documentary Leaflets. Institut internationale d'agriculture.** Rome. *Documentary Leafl. Inst. int. Agric.* [1917–22] **L.**AM.; BM.; **Abs.**N.; U. imp.; **E.**B. imp.; **G.**U. imp.; **M.**P.; U. imp.; **O.**AEC. imp.; **Sa.**

17074 **Documentatie** van de **Afdeling tropische producten, Indisch instituut.** Amsterdam. *Documtie Afd. trop. Prod. indisch Inst.* [1949–52] **Md.**H. 50–52; **Rt.** 52. [*C. as:* 17076]

17075 **Documentatië bouwwezen.** Rotterdam. *Documtië Bouww.* **L.**P. 54–.

17075° **Documentatië oosteuropese landbouwkundige literatur.** Wageningen. *Documtië oosteur. landbouwk. Lit.* [1960–] **L.**P.

17076 **Documentatieblad** van de **Afdeling tropische production, K. Instituut** voor de **tropen.** Amsterdam. *Documtiebl. Afd. trop. Prod. K. Inst. Trop.* [1952] **Rt.** [*C. of:* 17074; *C. as:* 54394]

17077 **Documentation agricole BP.** Paris. *Documn agric. BP* [1957–] **L.**P. imp.

17078 **Documentation** du **bâtiment.** Genève. *Documn Bâtim.* **L.**P. 52–. [*Supplement to:* and *issued with:* 12371]
Documentation bibliographique. Centre d'**études** et de **recherches** de l'**industrie** des **liants hydrauliques.** Paris. *See* 10116.
Documentation for the **Building Industry.** Rotterdam. *See* 17075.

17079 **Documentation Bulletin. National Research Centre.** Cairo. *Documn Bull. natn. Res. Cent., Cairo* [1957–] **L.**BM.; BM^N.; P.; SC.; TD.; **C.**A.; **Rt.**; **Y.** [*C. of:* 11680; *For Part 2, see* 404 *and* 405]

17080 **Documentation. Bulletin périodique** de la **Fondation documentaire dentaire.** Bruxelles. *Documn Bull. périod. Fondn docum. dent.* [1948–] **L.**D. [*C. of:* 10276]

17081 **Documentation céramique.** Paris. *Documn céram.* [1957–] **L.**P. [*Supplement to:* 22944]

17082 **Documentation** sur l'**eau** et sur la **corrosion.** Liège. *Documn Eau Corros.* [1957–60] **L.**P. [*C. as:* 9573; *Issues for* 1957 *form supplement to:* 10973]

17083 **Documentation** in **Food** and **Agriculture.** Paris. *Documn Fd Agric.* [1959–] **Bl.**U. 59; **C.**A.; **Y.**

17083° **Documentation mécanique.** Paris. *Documn méc.* **Bm.**C. 49–56.
Documentation médicale. Bruxelles. *See* 6031.

17084 **Documentation médicale.** Comité international de la Croix Rouge. Genève. *Documn méd., Genève* [1946–] **L.**MA. 47–; MD. 48–; S. 46–48.

17085 **Documentation médicale.** Paris. *Documn méd., Paris*

17086 **Documentation médicale française.** Paris. *Documn méd. fr.* [1956–] **L.**MD.

17087 **Documentation métallurgique.** Saint-Étienne. *Documn métall.* [1949–] **L.**MI. 49–50 imp.: 52–; P.; **Y.** [*C. of:* 47307]
Documentation of **Molecular Spectroscopy Current Literature List.** London. *See* 16261.

17088 **Documentation technique. Centre** de **documentation.** Paris. *Documn tech. Cent. Documn* Sér. A. Documentation analytique [1947–] **L.**BM. 51–; **Y.**

17089 **Documentation technique. Centre** d'**information** du **nickel.** *Documn tech. Cent. Inf. Nickel* **L.**P. 28–.

17090 **Documentation technique. Institut technique** du **bâtiment.** Paris. *Documn tech. Inst. tech. Bâtim.* **L.**BA. 46–.

17090° **Documentation** and **Terminology** of **Science.** UNESCO. Paris. *Documn Termin. Sci.* [1951–] **L.**BM.

17091 **Documentazione tessile.** Milano. *Documzne tess.* [1956–] **L.**P.; **M.**C. 56–57; P. [*C. of:* 6571]

17092 **Documentez vous** l'**électricité moderne.** *Documentez vous Élect. mod.* **Y.**

17093 **Documenti** di **architettura** e **industria edilizia.** *Documenti Archit. Ind. edil.* [1950–] **Wa.**B. 50–53; **Y.**

17094 **Documentreproductie.** Oegstgeest. *Documentreproductie* [1947–] **L.**P.; PG. 48–; SC. 49–; **We.**K. 50–.

17095 **Documents** of the **Bureau** of **Fisheries.** Washington. *Docums Bur. Fish., Wash.* **L.**BM. 06–; SC. 24–; **Dm.** 13–30 imp.; **G.**M. 12–30 imp.; U. 10– imp.; **O.**AP. 20–30 imp.; **Wo.** 12–27 imp. [> *Appendix to:* 45515]

17096 **Documents cartographiques** de **géographie économique.** Berne. *Docums cartogr. Géogr. écon.*
Documents ethnographiques congolais. *See* 2849. Ethnographie. Sér. 3.

17097 **Documents** et **informations. Centre technique** du **cuir brut.** Paris. *Docums Inf. Cent. tech. Cuir brut* [1958–] **L.**P.

17098 **Documents pédotechniques.** Société belge de pédotechnie. Bruxelles. *Docums pédotech.*

17099 **Documents** et **rapports** de la **Société paléontologique** et **archéologique** de **Charleroi.** *Docums Rapp. Soc. paléont. archéol. Charleroi* **L.**BM^N. 64–95.

17100 **Documents** et **renseignements agricoles. Algérie bulletin.** *Docums Renseign. agric. Algér.* **Y.**

17101 **Documents** de la **réunion. Comité consultatif international** des **radiocommunications.** *Docums Réun. Com. consult. int. Radiocommun.* **L.**P. 34–.

17102 **Documents** de la **réunion. Comité consultatif international télégraphique.** *Docums Réun. Com. consult. int. télégr.* **L.**P. 34–.

17103 **Documents scientifiques** du **XVe siècle.** Paris. *Docums scient. XVe Siècle* [1925–28] **O.**B.

17104 **Documents** de l'**Union** des **industries métallurgiques.** Paris. *Docums Un. Inds métall.* **L.**I. 20–26. [*C. of:* 14091]

17105 **Documents. Union radio-scientifique internationale.** Bruxelles. *Docums Un. radio-scient. int.*

17106 **Doerfleria.** Wien. *Doerfleria* [1909] **L.**BM[N].; K.

17107 **Dohanyipar.** Budapest. *Dohanyipar* **Y.**

17108 **Dohrniana.** Stettin. *Dohrniana* [1930–42] **L.**BM[N]. 31–37. [*C. of:* 172]

    Dokladhoi. Akademiyai fanhoi RSS Tocikiston. *See* 17113.

    Doklady of the **Academy** of **Sciences** of the **U.S.S.R.** New York, Washington. *See* 17112.

17109 **Dokladȳ Akademii nauk Armyanskoĭ SSR.** Erevan. Доклады Академии наук Армянской ССР. *Dokl. Akad. Nauk armyan. SSR* [1944–] **L.**BM[N]. 58–; C. 56–; **E.**R. 44–47; U. 44–47 imp.; **O.**R.; **Y.** imp.

17110 **Dokladȳ Akademii nauk Azerbaĭdzhanskoĭ SSR.** Baku. Доклады Академии наук Азербайджанской ССР. *Dokl. Akad. Nauk azerb. SSR* [1945–] **L.**BM. 54–; BM[N]. 47: 52–; C. 61–; P. 57–; **Db.** 47: 52–; **O.**R. 54–; **Y.** 55– imp.

17111 **Dokladȳ Akademii nauk Belorusskoĭ SSR.** Minsk. Доклады Академии наук Белорусской ССР. *Dokl. Akad. Nauk belorussk. SSR* [1957–] **L.**BM. 59–; BM[N].; P.; SC.; **O.**B.; **Y.**

17112 **Dokladȳ Akademii nauk SSSR.** Moskva, Leningrad. Доклады Академии наук СССР. *Dokl. Akad. Nauk SSSR* [1922–] **L.**AM. 43–61 imp.; AV. 43–54; BM.; BM[N]. imp.; C. 33–; EB. (ser. A.) 22–; GL. 33–; I. 33–46 imp.: 48–49: 54–; IC. 48–; L. 33–46 imp.; LI. 34–37; MA. 41– imp.; MD. 41– imp.; MO. 49–; MY. 33– imp.; NF. 44–; P. 32–; PG. 54–; R. 23–47 imp.; RI. 27–; S. 34–46 imp.; SC. 33–46; TP. 33–48 imp.; U. 42– imp.; UC. 41– imp.; Z. 33– imp.; **Abd.**M. 58–; U.; **Abs.**U. 41–47 imp.; **Bl.**U. 57–; **Bn.**U. 58–; **Br.**U. 37–47 imp.; **C.**A. 35–48 imp.; APH. (biol.) 59–; P.; U.; **Cr.**U. 43–46 v. imp.: 58–; **Db.** 46–47; **E.**AB. 44–; C. 42; D. 46; R. 24–46 imp.; U. 54– imp.; **Ex.**U. 46: 49; **Fa.** 46–; **G.**T. 58–; U.; **Hu.**G. 38–; **Ld.**U. 42–; **Lv.**P. 56– imp.; **M.**C. 50–; U. 24– imp.; **Md.**H. 41–47; N.U. 42–; **Nw.**A. 35– imp.; **O.**R.; Z. 39–45; **Pl.**M. 33–46 imp.; **R.**U. 46–; **Rt.** 38– imp.; **Sa.** 43–46 imp.: 53–; **Sal.** 45–54 imp.; **Sy.**R. 59–; **Wo.** 57–; **Y.** 43– imp.

Some holdings are possibly of the Foreign language edition or of the English translations shown below:

    (**Foreign language edition.**) Moscow. *Dokl. Akad. Nauk SSSR for. Lang. Edn* [1935–47] **L.**BM.; **Y.**

    Doklady (**Proceedings**) of the **Academy** of **Sciences** of the **U.S.S.R.** New York, Washington. *Dokl. (Proc.) Acad. Sci. U.S.S.R.*

    Agrochemistry section [1956–] **L.**C.; **Te.**N. 57–; **Y.**

    Applied Physics section [1957–] **L.**P.; **Te.**N.; **Y.**

    Biochemistry section [1957–] **L.**C.; P.; TP.; **Abd.**T. 59–; **C.**UL. 58–; **Y.**

    Biological Sciences sections [1957–] **L.**BM[N].; MC. 60–; **Abd.**T.; **Bl.**U.; **C.**U.; **Lo.**; **Y.**

    Botanical Sciences sections [1957–] **L.**BM[N].; **Bl.**U.; **Sw.**U. 58–; **Y.**

    Chemical Technology section [1956–] **L.**C.; P.; **Lv.**P.; **M.**U.; **Te.**C. 57–; **Y.**

    Chemistry section [1956–] **L.**C.; P. 57–; **M.**U.; **Y.**

    Earth Sciences sections **L.**BM[N]. 59–; P. 60–; **Ld.**U. 60–; **Y.**

    Geochemistry section [1956–] **L.**C.; P. 57–; **M.**U.; **Te.**C. 57–; **Y.**

    Geological Sciences section [1957–] **L.**BM[N].; **Y.**

    Mathematics section. *See* 50343.

    Physical Chemistry section. [1957–] **L.**C.; P.; **C.**CH.; **Lv.**P.; **M.**U.; **Te.**C.; **Y.**

    Physics section. *See* 50349.

    [*English abstracts at:* 42598[a]]

17113 **Dokladȳ Akademii nauk Tadzhikskoĭ SSR.** Stalinabad. Доклады Академии наук Таджикской ССР. *Dokl. Akad. Nauk tadzhik. SSR* [1951–] **L.**BM. imp.; BM[N]. 59–; P. 54–; **O.**B. 57–; R. 57–; **Y.** 52–58 imp.

    Dokladȳ Akademii nauk Ukrainskoĭ RSR. Доклады Академии наук Украинской РСР. *See* 17156.

17114 **Dokladȳ Akademii nauk Uzbekskoĭ SSR.** Tashkent. Доклады Академии наук Узбекской ССР. *Dokl. Akad. Nauk uzbek. SSR* [1948–] **L.**BM. 57–; **Y.** 55: 58–.

    Dokladȳ. Bŭlgarska akademiya na naukite. Доклады Българска академия на науките. *Dokl. bulg. Akad. Nauk. See* 15150.

17115 **Dokladȳ Gosudarstvennogo okeanograficheskogo instituta.** Moskva. Доклады Государственного океанографического института. *Dokl. gosud. okeanogr. Inst.* [1931–33] **L.**BM[N].; **E.**R.; **Lv.**U.

17116 **Dokladȳ Moskovskoĭ gubernskoĭ zemskoĭ upravȳ po vrachebno-sanitarnoĭ organizatsii.** Moskva. Доклады Московской губернской земской управы по врачебно-санитарной организации. *Dokl. mosk. gub. zemsk. Upr. vrach.-sanit. Org.*

17117 **Dokladȳ Moskovskoĭ sel'sko-khozyaĭstvennoĭ akademii im. K. A. Timiryazeva.** Moskva. Доклады Московской сельско-хозяйственной академии им. К. А. Тимирязева. *Dokl. mosk. sel'.-khoz. Akad. K. A. Timiryazeva* [1943–] **L.**EB. 46; **C.**A. 44–46; **E.**AB. 45–46 imp.; **Rt.** 55–; **Y.** 45–57 imp.

17118 **Dokladȳ na obshchem sobranii.** Leningrad. Доклады на общем собрании. *Dokl. obshchem Sobran.* **L.**P. 44.

17119 **Dokladȳ Pereyaslavl'-zalêsskago nauchno-prosvêtitel'nago obshchestva.** Pereyaslavl'-Zalêsskiĭ. Доклады Переяславль-залѣсскаго научно-просвѣтительнаго общества. *Dokl. pereyasl.-zalêssk. nauchno-prosvêt. Obshch.*

17119° **Dokladȳ na pervom ezhegodnom chtenii pamyati N. A. Kholodkovskogo.** Moskva. Доклады на первом ежегодном чтении памяти Н. А. Холодковского. *Dokl. perv. ezheg. Chten. N.A. Kholodkovskogo* [1949–] **L.**BM. 51–.

17120 **Dokladȳ pravleniya Obshchestva russkikh vracheĭ v pamyat' N. I. Pirogova.** Moskva. Доклады правленія Общества русскихъ врачей въ память Н. И. Пирогова. *Dokl. Pravl. Obshch. russk. Vrach. Pamyat' N. I. Pirogova* **G.**U. 22–46 imp.

    Dokladȳ i soobshcheniya. Lvov'skiĭ derzhavnȳĭ universitet. Доклады и сообщения. Львовский державный университет. *See* 17157.

17121 **Dokladȳ Vsesoyuznoĭ akademii sel'sko-khozyaĭstvennȳkh nauk im. V. I. Lenina.** Доклады Всесоюзной академии сельско-хозяйственных наук им. В. I. Ленина. *Dokl. vses. Akad. sel'.-khoz. Nauk* [1938–59] **L.**AM. 41–59 imp.; BM. 45–59; EB. 44–59; P. 58–59; **Abd.**S. 39–47 imp.; U. 41; **Ba.**I. 44–47; **C.**A. 39–47; **E.**AB. 39–46 imp.; R. 41; **Hu.**G.; **Md.**H. imp.; **N.**U. 41: 57–59; **R.**D. imp.; **Rt.** imp.; **Sal.** 41 imp.; **Sil.** 57–59 imp.; **Y.** 41–59 imp. [*C. of:* 12842; *C. in:* 56518]

17122 **Dokladȳ Vsesoyuznoĭ konferentsii po molochnomu delu.** Moskva. Доклады Всесоюзной конференции по молочному делу. *Dokl. vses. Konf. moloch. Delu* **E.**AB. 58.

Dokladỹ Vsesoyuznoĭ ordena Lenina akademii sel'sko-khozyaĭstvennỹkh nauk im. **V. I. Lenina.** Доклады Всесоюзной ордена Ленина академии сельскохозяйственных наук им. В. И. Ленина. *See* 17121.

17122° **Doktoravhandlinger. Norges tekniske høgskole.** Oslo. *Doktoravh. Norg. tek. Høgsk.* **Y.**

17123 **Doktordisputatser.** Kjøbenhavn. *Doktordisputatser, Kbh.*

17124 **Doktorsavhandlingar** vid **Chalmers tekniska högskola.** Göteborg. *Doktorsavh. Chalmers tekn. Högsk.* [1942–] **L.**P. 57–; **Y.**

17124° **Doktorske disertacije. Sveučilište u Zagrebu.** Zagreb. *Dokt. Disert. Sveuč. Zagr.* [1950–52] **L.**BM.; **G.**U.

17125 **Dokumentace zemedelská** a **lesnická zahraniční literatura.** Praha. *Dokumce zemed. lesn. zahran. Lit.* **L.**AM. 55. [*C. as:* 38573]

17126 **Dokumentation.** Leipzig. *Dokumentation* [1953–] **L.**BM.; **Y.**

17127 **Dokumentation** und **Arbeitstechnik.** Berlin. *Dokum. ArbTech.*

17128 **Dokumentation. Prüfdienststelle** für **Klimaschutz. Deutsches Amt** für **Material-** und **Warenprüfung.** Berlin. *Dokum. Prüfdienststelle Klimaschutz* **L.**P. 59–.

17129 **Dokumentationsdienst Giessereitechnik.** Zentralinstitut für Giessereitechnik, Leipzig. *DokumDienst GiessTech.*

     Grundausgabe. **Y.**
     Ergänzungsausgabe. **Y.**

17130 **Dokumentationsdienst. Gruppe Faserstoffe.** Zentralstelle für wissenschaftliche Literatur. Berlin. *DokumDienst Gruppe Faserstoffe* [1954–] **L.**P. [*Replaces:* 19189]

     Dolgozatok az **egyetemi borkórtani intézetből.** *Supplement to:* 36433.

17131 **Dolgozatok** az **Erdélyi nemzeti muzeum éremés régiségtárából.** Kolozsvár. *Dolg. erd. nemz. Muz. éremés Régiségt.* [1910–19] **L.**AN.; **E.**V. 11–16. [*C. as:* 17132]

17132 **Dolgozatok** am **Kir. Ferencz József tudományegyetem archæologiai intézetéből.** Szeged. *Dolg. Kir. Ferencz József Tudomány. archæol. Intéz.* [1925–] **L.**AN. [*C. of:* 17131]

17133 **Dolgozatok** a **szegedi** m. **kir. Ferencz József tudományegyetem anatomiai** és **szövettani intézetéből.** Szeged. *Dolg. Szegedi Kir. Ferencz József-Tudomány. anat. szöv. Intéz.* **L.**UC. 33.

17134 **Dom—osiedle—mieszkanie.** Warszawa. *Dom Osiedle Miexzh.* [1928–] **L.**BA. 31–.

17135 **Domar.** Ottawa. *Domar* [1948–] **C.**PO.

17136 **Domashno zdrave.** Plovdiv. Домашно здраве. *Domashno Zdr.*

     Domestic and **Commercial Refrigerator Guide.** *See* 17139ᵃ.

17137 **Domestic Electrical Appliances.** London. *Domest. elect. Appliances* [1960–] **L.**BM.

17138 **Domestic Engineering.** Chicago. *Domest. Engng, Chicago* **Lv.**P. 56–.

     Domestic Engineering and **Estate Engineer.** *See* 17139.

17139 **Domestic Engineering, Heat** and **Ventilation.** London. *Domest. Engng, Lond.* [1895–32] **L.**BM. 11–32; P. 24–32; SC. 26–32; TD. 26–32; **Abs.**N. 16–32; **Bm.**U. 29–32; **O.**R. 16–32.

17139ᵃ **Domestic Refrigerator Guide.** London. *Domest. Refrig. Guide* [1955–58] **L.**BM.; P. [*C. as:* 42439]

17140 **Domez.** Kharkov. Домез. *Domez* [1929–35] [*C. as:* 52847]

17141 **Dominion Dental Journal.** Toronto. *Dom. dent. J.* [1889–34] **L.**D. 02–34; MD. 97–14. [*C. as:* 25737]

17142 **Dominion Engineer.** Montreal. *Dom. Engr* [1934–] **L.**P. imp.; **Y.**

17143 **Dominion Foundryman.** Toronto. *Dom. Foundrym.*

17144 **Dominion Medical Journal.** Toronto. *Dom. med. J.* [1895–21] **Bm.**U. 98–02; **M.**MS. 06–21. [*C. in:* 13104]

17144° **Dominion Museum Bulletin.** Wellington. N.Z. *Dom. Mus. Bull.* [1929–] **L.**AN.; BM.; BMᴺ.; GM.; SC.; **C.**UL.; **E.**R.; **O.**R. 29; Pl.M. [*C. of:* 10129]

17145 **Dominion Museum Monographs.** Wellington, N.Z. *Dom. Mus. Monogr.* [1922–24] **L.**AN.; BMᴺ.; **C.**UL.; **E.**R.

17146 **Dominion Museum Records** in **Entomology.** Wellington. *Dom. Mus. Rec. Ent.* [1946–53] **L.**BM.; BMᴺ.; EB.; K.; SC.; **C.**UL.; **Db.**; **E.**R.; **M.**U.; Pl.M. [*C. from:* and *Rec. in:* 42301]

17147 **Dominion Museum Records** in **Ethnology.** Wellington. *Dom. Mus. Rec. Ethnol.* **Y.**

17148 **Dominion Museum Records** in **Zoology.** Wellington, N.Z. *Dom. Mus. Rec. Zool.* [1946–52] **L.**BM.; BMᴺ.; K.; SC.; Z.; **C.**UL.; **Db.**; **E.**R.; **M.**U.; Pl.M. [*C. from:* and *Rec. in:* 42301]

17149 **Dominion Observatory Pamphlet.** Ottawa. *Dom. Obs. Pamph.* [1929–] **L.**SC. 29–35.

17150 **Dominion Observatory Reprints.** Ottawa. *Dom. Obs. Repr.* **L.**AS. 32–.

17151 **Domus.** Architettura e arredamento dell'abitazione moderna. Milano. *Domus* [1940–] **L.**BA. 46–; BM. 55–; NP. (3 уг.); **G.**T. 57–; **Lv.**P. 57–; **N.**U. 58–; **Nw.**A. 55–. [*C. of:* 13391]

17152 **Domus medici.** Madrid. *Domus Med.* [1949–] **L.**MA. [*C. of:* 13390]

17153 **Don.** Journal of Sheffield University geographical Society. Sheffield. *Don* [1957–] **L.**BM.; **C.**GG.; **Sh.**U.

17154 **Donauländisches Textil-Journal.** Wien. *Donauländ. Text.-J.*

17154° **Données climatologiques** de **Lithuanie.** Kaunas. *Données clim. Lith.* **L.**MO. 26–37.

17155 **Dopovidi Akademiyi nauk Ukrayins'koyi RSR.** Kiev. Доповіді Академії наук Української РСР. *Dopov. Akad. Nauk ukr. RSR* [1957–] **L.**BM.; BMᴺ.; **G.**M.; I. 59–; P.; **C.**A.; **O.**R.; **Y.** [*C. of:* 17156; *English abstracts at:* 42598ᵇ]

17156 **Dopovidi Akademiyi nauk URSR.** Kiev. Доповіді Академії наук УРСР. *Dopov. Akad. Nauk URSR* [1939–56] **L.**BM. 39–40; BMᴺ. 39–40: 50–56 imp.; GM. 56; **C.**A. 56; **Db.** (biol.) 42–56; **Y.** [*C. as:* 17155]

17157 **Dopovidi** ta **povidomlennya. L'vivskўї der-zhavnўї universўtet** im. **I. Franka.** Kharkov. Доповіді та повідомлення. Львівский державний университет ім. I. Франка. *Dopov. Povidom. l'viv. derzh. Univ.* [1949–] **L.**BM.; **Y.** 53–55: 57–.

Dopovidi Vseukrayins'koyi akademiyi nauk. Доповіді Всеукраїнської академії наук. *See* 17156.

17158 **Doriana.** Genova. *Doriana* [1949–] **L.**BM^N.; **E.**; EB.; L. 55–; Z.; **Cr.**N. 49–58; **Ld.**U. 49–58 imp.; **O.**H.; **Pl.**M. 51–; **Y.** [*Supplement to:* 3074]

17159 **Dornier Post.** *Dornier Post* [1935–] **L.**AV. 35–42 imp.

17160 **Dorost knihtiskařský.** Praha. *Dorost kniht.* **L.**SC. 29–38.

17161 **Doshisha Engineering Review.** Kyoto. *Doshisha Engng Rev.* [1950–59] **L.**EE. (imp.); P. [*C. as:* 17163]

17162 **Doshisha Engineering Review Special Papers.** Kyoto. *Doshisha Engng Rev. spec. Pap.* [1952–] **L.**EE. imp.

Doshisha kogakkai shi. *See* 17161.

17163 **Doshisha University Science** and **Engineering Review.** Kyoto. *Doshisha Univ. Sci. Engng Rev.* [1959–] **L.**EE.; P. [*C. of:* 17161]

17164 **Dosimetría.** Barcelona. *Dosimetría, Barcelona*

17165 **Dosimetria.** Porto. *Dosimetria, Porto*

17166 **Dosimetric Medical Review.** New York. *Dosimetric med. Rev.* [1887–01]

17167 **Dosimétrie.** Paris. *Dosimétrie*

17168 **Dosimétrie** au **Canada.** Montréal. *Dosimétrie Can.*

17169 **Doslidi** nad **volohўstyu soyuznoyi varovni.** Kўyiv. Досліді над вологистю союзної варовні. *Dosl. Volog. soyuz. Varov.* [1932]

17170 **Dostizheniya nauki** i **peredovogo opўta** v **sel'skom khozyaĭstve.** Moskva. Достижения науки и передового опыта в сельском хозяйстве. *Dostizh. Nauki pered. Opўta sel'. Khoz.* [1951–55] **L.**BM. 53–55; **E.**AB.; **Rt.** 54–55. [*C. as:* 34374]

17171 **Dosug tekhnika.** S.-Peterburg. Досугъ техника. *Dosug Tekh.*

17172 **Doświadczalnictwo leśne.** Warszawa. *Doświad. leś.* [1932–] **O.**F. 33.

17173 **Doświadczalnictwo rolnicze.** Warszawa. *Doświad. roln.* [1925–33] **L.**AM. 28–33 imp.; **Rt.**

17173^a **Douglas Service.** *Douglas Serv.* **L.**AV. 55– imp.

17173^b **Douglas Service News.** *Douglas Serv. News* [1958–] **L.**AV.

Dove Marine Laboratory Contributions. *See* 15695.

17174 **Dover Museum Bulletin.** Dover. *Dover Mus. Bull.* [1932–] **L.**BM.; BM^N. 32–35.

17175 **Dovidkovo-tekhnyichna literatura.** Kўyiv. Довідково-технічна література *Dovidk.-tekh. Lit.*

17176 **Dow Corning Silastic Facts.** Midland, Mich. *Dow Corning silast. Facts* **L.**P. 50– imp.

17177 **Dow Corning Silastic Notes.** Midland, Mich. *Dow Corning silast. Notes* **L.**P. 54–.

17178 **Dow Corning Silicone News.** Midland, Mich. *Dow Corning Silic. News* **L.**P. (curr.)

17179 **Dow Corning Silicone Notes.** Midland, Mich. *Dow Corning Silic. Notes* **L.**P. 52–.

17180 **Dow Diamond.** Dow Chemical Company. *Dow Diam.* **L.**P. (curr.); **Sy.**R. 49–.

17181 **Down to Earth.** Dow Chemical Co. Midland, Michigan. *Down to Earth* [1945–] **L.**AM. 55–; MY. 46–; P. 55–; **C.**A.; **Hu.**G. 48–; **Lv.**P. 60–; **Md.**H. 46–; **Rt.**; **Sil.** 54–; **Y.**

17182 **Draeger Atemschutz.** Lübeck. *Draeger Atemschutz* [1951–] **L.**P. 51–58; **Y.**

17183 **Draeger Bulletin.** Lübeck. *Draeger Bull.* [1912–43] **L.**BM. 34–38 imp.; P. imp.; **Ld.**U. 21–26.

17183^a **Draeger Hefte.** Lübeck. *Draeger Hft.* **Y.**

17183^b **Draeger Review.** Lübeck. *Draeger Rev.* **Y.**

17184 **Draeger-Gasschutz-Mitteilungen.** Lübeck. *Draeger-Gasschutz-Mitt.* [1928–] **L.**P. 28–33. [*C. of:* 20680]

17185 **Draeger-Mitteilungen.** Lübeck. *Draeger-Mitt.* [*Supplement to:* 17183]

17186 **Draftsman.** New York. *Draftsman* [1942–]

17187 **Dragoco Berichte.** English edition. Holzminden. *Dragoco Ber. Engl. Edn* [1954–] **L.**P.; PH. 55–.

Dragoco Report. *See* 17187.

17188 **Draht.** Coburg. *Draht* [1950–] **L.**DI. 51–; P.; **Y.** [*English edition at:* 57630]

17189 **Draht** und **Aether.** Illustrierte Monatsschrift für angewandte Fernmeldtechnik. Berlin. *Draht Aether*

17190 **Drahtgewerbe.** Heidenheim a. Br. *Drahtgewerbe*

17191 **Drahtindustrie.** Halle a. S. *Drahtindustrie*

17192 **Drahtwelt.** Halle, etc. *Drahtwelt* [1908–] **L.**MT. 33–42; P. 34– imp.; **Bm.**P. 34–42. [>16685, 1944; *not published* Nov. 1944–March 1951; *English edition at:* 57640]

17193 **Drahtwelt. Export-Ausgabe.** Halle. *Drahtwelt Export-Ausg.* **L.**MT. 33–42.

17194 **Dralowid-Nachrichten.** Berlin. *Dralowid-Nachr.* **L.**P. 31–39.

17195 **Drapers' Company Research Memoirs. Biometric Series.** London. *Drap. Co. Res. Mem. biom. Ser.* [1904–22] **L.**AN. 04–13; BM.; MD. 11–19; SC.; U. 04–13; UC. 04–19; **Abd.**U.; **Abs.**N. 13–22 imp.; **Bm.**P.; U.; **C.**UL.; **Db.**; **E.**A. 06–11; P.; U. imp.; **G.**PH. 06–11; U. 11–13 imp.; **M.**P.; **Nw.**A. 04–13; **O.**R.

17196 **Drapers' Company Research Memoirs. Studies** in **National Deterioration.** London. *Drap. Co. Res. Mem. Stud. natn. Deterior.* [1906–24] **L.**MD. 07–24; SC. 08–24; U. 06–14; UC.; **Abd.**U. 07–24; **Abs.**N. 13–24 imp.; **Bm.**U. 08–24; **C.**UL.; **Db.**; **E.**U.; **O.**R.

17197 **Drapers' Company Research Memoirs. Technical Series.** London. *Drap. Co. Res. Mem. tech. Ser.* [1904–18] **L.**BM.; U. 04–09; UC.; **Abs.**N.; **Bm.**P.; **C.**UL. 04–09; **Db.**; **E.**A. 06–11; P.; **G.**T. 04–09; U.; **M.**P.; U. 04–09; **Nw.**A.; **O.**R.

17198 **Draughtsman.** London. *Draughtsman* [1918–] **L.**BM. imp.; P. (3 yr.); **Abs.**N. 24–; **Bm.**U. 55–; **E.**A. 24–; **G.**M. 27–; **O.**R. 38–.

17199 **Drawing Board.** London. *Draw. Bd* [1957] **L.**BM.; P. [*C. as:* 17200]

17200 **Drawing Board** and **Technical Design.** London. *Draw. Bd tech. Des.* [1957–58] **L.**BM.; P. [*C. of:* 17199; *C. as:* 52074]

17201 **Dredging** and **Dock Engineering.** New York. *Dredg. Dock Engng*
Dredging Engineer. *See* 17201.

17202 **Dresdener geographische Studien.** Dresden. *Dresdener geogr. Stud.* **L.**G. 31.

17203 **Dresdner Blätter** für **Geflügelzucht.** Dresden. *Dresdner Bl. GeflZucht*

17204 **Dřevařské listy.** Brno. *Dřev. Listy*

17205 **Dřevařský věstník.** Kr. Vinohrady. *Dřev. Věst.* [*C. as:* 13623]

17206 **Dřevársky výskum.** Bratislava. *Dřev. Výsk.* [1956–] **L.**P.; **Pr.**FT

17207 **Dřevo.** Praha. *Dřevo* **L.**P. 57–; **Pr.**FT. 56–; **Y.**

17208 **Dřevoprůmysl.** Praha. *Dřevoprůmysl*

17209 **Dried Yeasts** and their **Derivatives.** St. Louis, Mo. *Dried Yeasts Deriv.* [1948–]

17209ª **Driemaandelijks bericht Deltawerken.** Den Haag. *Driemaand. Ber. Deltawerken* [1957–] **L.**BM.

17209ᵇ **Driemaandelijks bericht** betreffende de **Zuiderzeewerken.** *Driemaand. Ber. Zuiderzeewerken* **Y.**

17210 **Driftsgranskinger** i **jordbruket.** Norges landbruksøkonomiske institutt. Oslo. *Driftsgransk. Jordbr.* **Y.**

17211 **Drilling.** Dallas, Tex. *Drilling* [1939–] **L.**PT. 55–.

17212 **Drilling Mud.** National Lead Company. Los Angeles. *Drill. Mud* [1931–] **L.**P.

17213 **Drilling** and **Production Practice.** American Petroleum Institute. New York. *Drill. Prod. Pract.* **L.**P. 34; PT. 34– imp.; **Y.**

17214 **Drobny przemysł** i **chałupnictwo.** Instytut gospodarstwa społecznego. Warszawa. *Drobny Przem. Chałup.* [1931–34] **L.**BM.

17215 **Droga** do **zdrowia.** Kraków. *Droga Zdrowia* **L.**TD. 32.

17216 **Drogenrundschau.** Hamburg. *Drogenrundschau*

17217 **Drogerzysta.** Poznań. *Drogerzysta*

17218 **Drogheria.** Torino. *Drogheria*

17219 **Drogista.** Warszawa. *Drogista*

17220 **Drogistenwoche.** Berlin. *Drogistenwoche*

17221 **Drogistenzeitung.** Wien. *Drogistenzeitung*

17222 **Drogownictwo.** Warszawa. *Drogownictwo* [1946–] **L.**BM. 51–; **Y.**

17223 **Droguerie moderne.** Paris. *Drog. mod.*

17224 **Drop Forger.** Birmingham. *Drop Forger* [1921–48] **L.**P.; SC.; **Bm.**C. 24–28; P.; U.; **G.**I. 40–48; M. 28–47 imp.; **Sh.**IO. [*C. in:* 31435]

17225 **Drop Forging Topics.** Cleveland, Ohio. *Drop Forg. Top.* [1936–] **L.**P. 40–55; **Bm.**C. (curr.); **Sh.**IO. 48–53.

17226 **Drosophila Information Service.** Cold Spring Harbour. *Drosoph. Inf. Serv.* [1934–] **L.**CB. 35–52; **Ba.**I.; **C.**GE. 34–39; **E.**AG.; U.; **O.**BO. 52; Z. 41–55 imp.

17227 **Druck** und **Reproduktion.** Berlin. *Druck Reprod.* [1952–] **L.**P. 55–; **Y.** [*Published in:* 37121]

17228 **Druckblatt. Informationsdienst, Aluminium-Zentrale G.m.b.H.** Berlin. *Druckbl. InfDienst AluminZent.* **L.**NF.

17229 **Druckfarbe.** *Druckfarbe* [1959–] **L.**P. [*Supplement to:* 809]

17230 **Druckgewerbe.** Berlin. *Druckgewerbe* **Lh.**P. 49–.

17231 **Druck-** und **Werbekunst.** Leipzig. *Druck- u. Werbekunst* [1937–42] **L.**SB. 37–39. [*C. of:* 9019ᶜ]

17232 **Druckluft.** Berlin-Charlottenburg. *Druckluft* [1934–] **L.**P. 34–35.
Drucksachen. Deutscher Verband für die **Materialprüfungen** der **Technik.** *See* 16886.

17233 **Drucksachen** des **Gesamt-Wasserstrassenbeirats.** K. Preussisches Wasserbauverwaltung, Berlin. *Drucks. Gesamt-WasserstrBeir.*

17234 **Drucksachen. Preussischer Feuerwehrbeirat.** München. *Drucks. preuss. FeuerwBeir.*

17235 **Druckschriften. Siemens** und **Halske Aktien-Gesellschaft.** Berlin. *Druckschr. Siemens Halske* **L.**P. 96–12 imp.

17236 **Druckspiegel.** Stuttgart. *Druckspiegel* **L.**P. 55–; **Lh.**P. 48–.

17237 **Drug** and **Allied Industries.** Atlanta, Ga. *Drug all. Inds* **Lh.**P. 40–.

17238 **Drug** and **Chemical Exports.** London. *Drug Chem. Exports* [1957–59] **L.**BM.; MA.; P.; PH. [*C. of:* 18788]

17239 **Drug** and **Chemical Markets.** New York. *Drug Chem. Mkts* [1914–26] [*C. as:* 13751 and 17242]

17240 **Drug** and **Cosmetic Industry.** New York. *Drug Cosmet. Ind.* [1932–] **L.**P. 36–; PH. 36–; TP. 36–49; **G.**T. 53–56; **Lv.**P. 59–; **Y.** [*C. of:* 17242]

17241 **Drug** and **Cosmetic Review.** New York. *Drug Cosmet. Rev.* **Y.**

17242 **Drug Markets.** New York. *Drug Mkts* [1926–32] [*C. from:* 17238; *C. as:* 17240]

17243 **Drug Standards.** Washington. *Drug Stand.* [1951–60] **L.**P. 59–60; PH.; U.; **G.**T. 54–60; **Lc.**A. 54–60; **Y.** [*C. of:* 11219; *C. in:* Journal of Pharmaceutical Sciences]

17244 **Drug Trade Weekly.** New York. *Drug Trade Wkly* [1918–22] [*C. in:* 37474]

17245 **Drugs** made in **Germany.** Aulendorf. *Drugs Germ.* [1958–] **L.**MD. 61–; P.; PH.; **Y.**

17246 **Drugs, Oils** and **Paints.** Philadelphia. *Drugs Oils Paints* [1885–39] **L.**P. 10–39; PR. 25–39; SC. 33–39. [*C. as:* 36762]

17246ᶜ **Drvarski glasnik.** *Drvarski Glasn.* **Y.**

17247 **Drvna industrija.** Zagreb. *Drvna Ind.* [1950–] **L.**BM. 51–; **Y.**

17248 **Dryad Quarterly.** Leicester. *Dryad Q.* [1931–39] **L.**P. imp.

17249 **Dry-Ice Journal.** Sigmaringen. *Dry-Ice J.* [1935–37: 50] **L.**P. imp. [> 43539ᵇ, 1938: *Suspended* Mar. 1938–Dec. 1949; *C. as:* 12896]

17250 **Drzewo polskie.** Warszawa. *Drzewo pol.*
Du Mont. *See as* DuMont.
Du Pont. *See as* DuPont.

17251 **Dublin Journal** of **Medical Science.** Dublin. *Dubl. J. med. Sci.* [1832–21] **L.**BM.; GH. 1842–21; MA. imp.; MD.; S.; U. 1847–07: 20–21 imp.; UC. 71–19; **Abs.**N. 12–21; **Bl.**U.; **Bm.**U. 1849–07; **Br.**U.; **C.**PA. 1846–72; UL. 1846–21; **Db.**; **Dn.**U. 1832–71 imp.; **E.**A. 1842–21; P. 1842–21; S. 72–21; U.; **G.**F. 1855–20; U.; **Ld.**U. 68–21; **Lv.**M.; **M.**MS.; **Nw.**A. imp.; **O.**R. 72–21. [*C. as:* 24155]

17252 **Dünger-** u. **Leimzeitung.** Berlin. *Dünger- u. Leimztg*

17253 **Düngungsversuche** in den **Deutschen Kolonien.** Berlin. *Düngungsvers. dt. Kolon.* **L.**K. 13–14.

17254 **Düsseldorfer Bauzeitung.** Düsseldorf. *Düsseldorfer Bauztg*

17255 **Düsseldorfer geographische Vorträge.** Düsseldorf. *Düsseldorfer geogr. Vortr.*

17256 **Dugonics társaság évkönyv.** Szeged. *Dugonics Társ. Évk.* **L.**BM. 98–99; SC. 94–96.

17257 **Duke Mathematical Journal.** Durham, N.C. *Duke math. J.* [1935–] **L.**M.; QM. 50–; R.; SC. 39–; U. 41–50: 52–; **Abd.**U. 49–; **Bl.**U.; **Br.**U.; **C.**P.; **Cr.**U. 51–; **Db.**; **E.**Q.; R.; **Ex.**U. 48–; **G.**U. 53–; **H.**U.; **Ld.**U.; **M.**U.; **N.**U.; **Nw.**A.; **O.**R.; **Sh.**U.; **Sw.**U. 46–; **Y.**

17258 **Duke University Psychological Monographs.** Durham, N.C. *Duke Univ. psychol. Monogr.* [1931–34] **Bl.**U. 31–32; **C.**UL.; **E.**U. 31–32; **O.**R. [*Replaced by:* 15811]

17259 **Du Mont Instrument Journal.** Clifton, N.J. *Du Mont Instrum. J.* [1957–60] **L.**P.; **Y.** [*C. of:* 36448; *C. as:* 17260]

17260 **Du Mont Journal** of **Instruments** and **Tubes.** Clifton, N.J. *Du Mont J. Instrum. Tubes* [1960–] **L.**P.; **Y.** [*C. of:* 17259]

17261 **Du Mont Oscillographer.** Upper Montclair, N.J., etc. *Du Mont Oscillogr.* [1937–45] **L.**P.; SC. 45. [*C. as:* 36448]

17262 **Dunantuli szemle.** Szombothely. *Dunant. Szle* [1939–] [*C. of:* 55890]

17262ᶜ **Dunglison's College** and **Clinical Record.** Philadelphia. *Dunglison's Coll. clin. Rec.*

17263 **Dunlop Bulletin.** Wellington. *Dunlop Bull., Wellington* **Sy.**R. 53–.

17264 **Dunlop Gazette.** Birmingham. *Dunlop Gaz., Bgham* **Sy.**R. 22–. [>21553, 1930–33]

17265 **Dunlop Gazette.** Calcutta. *Dunlop Gaz., Calcutta* **Sy.**R. 52–.

17266 **Dunlop Gazette.** Durban. *Dunlop Gaz., Durban* [1942–] **Sy.**R.

17267 **Dunlop Gazette.** Melbourne. *Dunlop Gaz., Melb.* **Sy.**R. 39– imp.

17268 **Dunlop News.** Toronto. *Dunlop News* [1943–] **Sy.**R.

17269 **Dunlop News Sheet.** Sahaganj. *Dunlop News Sh.* **Sy.**R. 41–.

17270 **Dunlop Spur.** Hanau. *Dunlop Spur* **Sy.**R. 51–.

17270ᶜ **Dunsink Observatory Publications.** Dublin. *Dunsink Obs. Publs* [1960–] **L.**BM.; **C.**P.

17271 **Dunsink Observatory Reprints.** Dublin. *Dunsink Obs. Repr.* [1950–] **L.**BM.; **M.**U. 51–56.
  Dünya tip dersleri. *See* 40205.

17272 **Dünyada tip.** İstanbul. *Dünyada Tip* [1952–] **L.**MA. 53– imp.

17273 **Duodecim.** Kirjoituksia lääketieteen ja lääkärintoiminnan aloilta. Helsinki. *Duodecim* [1885–]

17274 **Duodecimal Bulletin.** Staten Island. *Duodec. Bull.* [1945–] **L.**BM. 50–; **Y.**

17275 **Duplicated Document. Commonwealth Experimental Building Station.** Sydney. *Dupl. Docum. Commonw. exp. Bldg Stn* [1947–50] **L.**MO. 50; P.; SC. [*C. as:* 52412]

17276 **Du Pont Dyes** and **Chemicals Technical Bulletin.** Wilmington. *Du Pont Dyes Chem. tech. Bull.* [1957–] **Ld.**P.; W.; **M.**C.; **Y.** [*C. of:* 17283]

17277 **Du Pont Elastomers Notebook.** Wilmington. *Du Pont Elast. Notebk* **L.**P.; **Li.**M. (1 yr); **Sy.**R.; **Y.** [*C. of:* 34514]

17277ᶜ **Du Pont Elastomers Review.** Wilmington. *Du Pont Elast. Rev.* [1958–] **L.**P.; **Sy.**R.; **Y.**

17278 **Du Pont Explosives Service Bulletin.** Wilmington, Del. *Du Pont Explos. Serv. Bull.*

17279 **Du Pont Fumigation Pointers** for **Pest Control.** Wilmington, Del. *Du Pont Fum. Pointers Pest Control* **L.**P. 39–40.

17280 **Du Pont Magazine.** Wilmington, Del. *Du Pont Mag.* [1913–] **L.**AV. 58–; C. 44–; I. (curr.); P. 27–; **Lh.**P. 46–; **M.**C. (selected copies); **Sy.**R. 52–.

17281 **Du Pont Plastics Bulletin.** Arlington, N.J. *Du Pont Plast. Bull.* [1939–51] **L.**P. 42–51; **Sy.**R.; **Y.** [*C. as:* 17282]

17282 **Du Pont Product Engineering Bulletin.** Wilmington. *Du Pont Prod. Engng Bull.* [1954–] **L.**P. 54–57; **Sy.**R.; **Y.** [*C. of:* 17281]

17283 **Du Pont Technical Bulletin.** Wilmington. *Du Pont tech. Bull.* [1945–56] **Ld.**W. 51–56; **M.**C. [*C. as:* 17276]

17284 **Durban Museum novitates.** Durban. *Durban Mus. Novit.* [1952–] **L.**BMᴺ.; E.; EB.; L.; R.; Z.; **Abs.**N.; **C.**UL.; **Cr.**M.; **Dm.**; **E.**F.; **M.**U.; **Pl.**M.; **Y.** [*C. of:* 3144]

17285 **Durez Molder.** North Tonawanda. *Durez Mold.* **L.**P. (curr.)

17286 **Durez Plastic News.** North Tonawanda, N.Y. *Durez Plast. News* [1936–] **L.**P. 47–.

17287 **Durferrit-Hausmitteilungen.** Frankfurt a. M. *Durferrit-Hausmitt.* **L.**P. 31–39.

17288 **Durham Colleges Natural History Society Journal.** Durham. *Durham Colleges nat. Hist. Soc. J.* [1953–] **L.**BMᴺ.

17289 **Duroc Bulletin.** Des Moines, Ia. *Duroc Bull.*

17290 **Duroc Digest.** Minneapolis. *Duroc Dig.*

17291 **Duroc Swine Breeders' Journal.** Indianapolis. *Duroc Swine Breed. J.* [1922–]

17292 **Dusenia.** Curitibá. *Dusenia* [1950–] **L.**BMᴺ.; SC.

17293 **Dust Engineering.** Louisville. *Dust Engng* **L.**P. 44–53 imp.

17294 **Dust Prevention** and **Suppression.** Instructional Pamphlet. London. *Dust Prev. Suppress.* [1955–] **L.**P.

17295 **Dutch Belted Cattle Bulletin** and **Livestock Journal.** Rockville, Conn. *Dutch belted Catt. Bull.*

17296 **Duvan.** Prilepu. Дуван. *Duvan* [1951–] **L.**BM. 58–; **Y.**

17297 **Dvigatel'.** S.-Peterburg. Двигатель. *Dvigatel'* [1907–14]

17297° **Dvigateli boevӯkh mashin.** Moskva. Двигатели боевых машин. *Dvig. boev. Mash.* [1946–] **L.**BM.

     Dyer, Calico Printer, Bleacher, Finisher and **Textile Review.** *See* 17298.

17298 **Dyer, Textile Printer, Bleacher** and **Finisher.** London. *Dyer, Lond.* [1879–] **L.**BM.; C. 27–29; LE. 48–; P. 10–; TP. 43–46; **Abs.**N. 25–; **Bm.**P. 26–30; **Br.**P. (1 yr); **Bra.**P. 10–; **C.**UL. 91–; **E.**A. 92–; **G.**M. 94–; T.; **Ld.**P. 43: 47–; U. 83–; W. 00–; **Lv.**P. 52–; **M.**C. 20– imp.; D. 05: 14–; P. 81– imp.; T. 98–; **N.**T. 33–; **O.**B. 91–; **Y.**

17299 **Dyers' Bulletin.** Philadelphia, Pa. *Dyers' Bull.*

     Dyes and **Chemicals Technical Bulletin,** Du Pont. *See* 17276.

17300 **Dyestuffs.** New York. *Dyestuffs* [1898–] **L.**C. 45–; P. 30–; PR. 33–; **Bra.**P. 21– imp.; **Ld.**P. 56–; W. 37–; **M.**D. 20: 41–51 imp.; **Y.**

17301 **Dyestuffs Division Chemicals Pamphlet.** Imperial Chemical Industries. Manchester. *Dyestuffs Div. Chems Pamph.* **L.**BM. 52–; P. 55–; **Y.**

17302 **Dyna.** Bilbao. *Dyna* [1926–] **L.**EE. 47–; **Y.**

17303 **Dynamo.** Budapest. *Dynamo*

17304 **Dyr** i **Natur** og **Museum.** København. *Dyr Nat. Mus.* [1941–] **L.**BM^N.; Z. [*Suspended* 1946]

17304ᵃ **Dziennik.** Główny urząd geodezji i kartografii. Warszawa. *Dzienn. głów. Urząd Geod. Kartogr.* **L.**BM. 58–.

17304ᵇ **Dziennik urzędowy.** Ministerstwo zdrowia. Warszawa. *Dzienn. urzęd. Minist. Zdrow.* **L.**BM. 58–.

17304ᶜ **Dziennik urzędowy.** Ministerstwo budownictwa. Warszawa. *Dzienn. urzęd. Minist. Budow.* [1957–] **L.**BM.

17305 **Dziennik zdrowia.** Warszawa. *Dzienn. Zdrow.* [1945–] **L.**MD. 45–46.

E

17306 **E.B.U. Review.** European Broadcasting Union. Brussels. *E.B.U. Rev.*
>Part A. Technical **L.**AV. 58–; EE. 58–; P. 58–; **N.**U. 58–59; **Y.**
>Part B. **L.**AV. 58–; **Y.**

17307 **E.D.**—Equipment Development—**Report.** Forest Service. Washington. *E.D. Rep . Forest Serv., Wash.* [1944–] **O.**F.

17307ª **E.D.A. Bulletin.** British Electrical Development Association. London. *E.D.A. Bull.* **L.**BM. 40–.
>**E.E.G. Journal.** *See* 17728.

17308 **E.F.F.I. Bulletin.** Electronic Forum for Industry. London. *E.F.F.I. Bull.* [1959–] **L.**P.; **G.**ME. (1 yr)

17309 **E.G.E. actualités.** Eau-gaz-électricité et applications. Bruxelles. *E.G.E. Actual.* **L.**P. 56–59. [*C. as:* 15550]

17310 **E.I.C. News.** Engineering Institute of Canada. Montreal. *E. I. C. News*
>**E. I. C. Transactions.** Engineering Institute of Canada. *See* 53703.

17311 **E. K. E.** Erdélyi karpát egyesület székesfővárosi osztályának hivatalos lapja. Budapest. *E. K. E.*
>**E. und M.** Wien. *See* 17877.
>**E.M.B.** Empire Marketing Board. *See* 40994.

17312 **E. M. F. Electrical Year Book.** New York. *E. M. F. elect. Yb.*

17312ᶜ **EMI Electronics Post.** *EMI Electron. Post* [1960–] **L.**AV.
>**EMI Electronics Technical Report.** *See* 52345.

17313 **E. and M.J. Metal and Mineral Markets.** Engineering and Mining Journal. New York. *E. & M.J. Metal Miner. Mkts* [1937–] **L.**BM. 40–. [*C. of:* 31419]

17314 **E.N.S.A.** Revue technique de l'aéronautique. Paris. *E.N.S.A.* [1937–] **L.**P. 37–38; SC. 37–38. [*C. of:* 47214]

17315 **E.P.A. Activities.** European Productivity Agency Paris. *E.P.A. Activ.* **L.**HQ. 61–; **Y.**
>**E.P.A. Russian Technical Literature.** European Productivity Agency. *See* 48296.

17316 **E.P.A. Technical Digests.** European Productivity Agency. Paris. *E.P.A. tech. Dig.* [1955–56] **L.**P. **E.**A. 56–; **Y.** [*American edition at:* 17317; *C. as:* 18681]

17317 **E.P.A. Technical Digests:** United States Edition. European Productivity Agency. Paris. *E.P.A. tech. Dig. U.S. Edn* [1956] **L.**P.; **O.**R. [*English edition at:* 17316; *C. as:* 18682]

17318 **E.P.E.A. Technical Series.** Electrical Power Engineers' Association. London. *E.P.E.A. tech. Ser.* **L.**SC. 27–; **Ld.**P. 36.
>**ERA.** Förening för elektricitetens rationella användning. Stockholm. *See* 18325.

17319 **E.R.A. Abstracts.** British Electrical and Allied Industries Research Association. London. *E.R.A. Abstr.* **L.**BM. 57–; SI. 46–; **Bm.**C. 46–; **E.**A. 57–; **N.**U. 57–; **O.**B. 57–; **Sy.**R. 49–.
>**E.R.A. Weekly Abstracts.** British Electrical and Allied Industries Research Association. *See* 17319.

17320 **ERBA Nachrichten.** Baumwollindustrie Erlangen-Bamberg. *ERBA Nachr.* **L.**P. (curr.)
>**E.R.D.E. Translations. Explosives Research and Development Establishment, Waltham Abbey.** *See* 54112.

17321 **ESAB revue.** Elektriska svetningsaktiebolaget. Göteborg. *ESAB Revue* [1948–]
>Deutsche Ausgabe **L.**P. 55–.

17322 **E.S.C. News.** English Steel Corporation, Limited. Sheffield. *E. S. C. News* [1947–] **L.**I. (4 yr.); **G.**E. (1 yr)

17323 **ESL Bibliography.** Engineering Societies Library. New York. *ESL Biblphy* [1948–] **L.**SC.

17323ᶜ **E. T. Browne Monograph.** Marine Biological Association of the United Kingdom. Cambridge. *E. T. Browne Monogr.* [1953–] **L.**BM.

17324 **E.T.J.** Electrotechnical Journal. Institute of Electrical Engineers of Japan. Tokyo. *E.T.J.* [1937–39] **L.**P. imp.; SC.; U.; **Bm.**U. imp.; **Br.**U.; **C.**UL. imp.; **M.**T.; **Ma.**T. imp. [*C. as:* 17785]

17325 **E. T. S. Bulletin.** Electrodepositors' Technical Society. London. *E. T. S. Bull.* [1941–50] **L.**BM. 42–50; SI. [*C. as:* 10635]
>**ETZ.** *See* 17890.

17326 **Earl Grey Memorial Lecture.** Armstrong College. Newcastle-upon-Tyne. *Earl Grey meml Lect.* **L.**BM. 22–; **Abs.**N. 23–; **Nw.**A. 20–; P. 21– imp.

17327 **Early Geophysical Papers** of the **Society** of **Exploration Geophysicists.** Houston, Texas. *Early geophys. Pap. Soc. Explor. Geophys.* **Bm.**U. 47–.

17328 **Earth Mover** and **Road Builder.** Aurora, Ill. *Earth Mover Rd Bldr* [1916–41]

17328ᶜ **Earth Science.** Tokyo. *Earth Sci., Tokyo* **Y.**

17329 **Earth Science Digest.** Omaha. *Earth Sci. Dig.* **L.**BMᴺ. 46– imp.

17330 **Earthquake Register. Seismological Station, Valletta, Malta.** *Earthq. Register Valletta*

17331 **East Africa Agricultural** and **Horticultural Society Quarterly.** Nairobi. *E. Africa agric. hort. Soc. Q.* [1905–07] L.AM.; BM^N.; K. [*C. of:* 17332]
  East Africa Medical Survey Annual Report. *See* 43551^a.

17332 **East Africa Quarterly.** Nairobi. *E. Africa Q.* [1904] L.AM.; BM^N.; K. [*C. as:* 17331]

17333 **East African Agricultural** and **Forestry Journal.** Nairobi. *E. Afr. agric. For. J.* [1960–] L.AM.; BM^N.; EB.; IC.; K.; MY.; TP.; **Abd.**R.; S.; **Br.**A.; U.; **C.**A. **E.**AB.; **Hu.**G.; **Je.**; **Md.**H.; **O.**F.; RE.; **R.**D.; Rt.; Sal.; Sil.; W.; Y. [*C. of:* 17334]

17334 **East African Agricultural Journal.** Nairobi. *E. Afr. agric. J.* [1935–60] L.AM.; BM^N.; EB.; IC. 47–60; K.; MY.; TP.; **Abd.**R.; S. 47–60; **Br.**A.; U.; **C.**A.; **E.**AB.; **Hu.**G.; **Je.**; **Md.**H.; **O.**F.; RE.; **R.**D. 40–60; U. 54–57 imp.; Rt. Sal.; Sil. 47–60; W. 47–60; Y. [*C. as:* 17333]

17335 **East African Engineer.** Nairobi. *E. Afr. Engr*

17336 **East African Farmer** and **Planter.** Nairobi. *E. Afr. Fmr Plr* [1956–] **Hu.**G.; Sil.
  East African Institute for **Medical Research Report.** *See* 43549^c.

17337 **East African Medical Journal.** Nairobi. *E. Afr. med. J.* [1932–] L.BM. 52–; EB.; MD.; TD.; **Bm.**U.; **Br.**U.; **Dn.**U. imp.; **Lv.**M. 35–; U.; **O.**R. 42; Y. [*C. of:* 27330]
  East African Medical Survey and **Research Institute Annual Report.** *See* 43551^a.

17338 **East Anglian Farming World.** Norwich. *E. Anglian Fmg Wld* **C.**A. (6 mon.); Sil. 59–.

17338° **East China Journal** of **Agricultural Science.** Shanghai. *E. China J. agric. Sci.* **C.**A. 58–59.

17339 **East Midland Geographer.** Nottingham. *E. Midld Geogr.* [1954–] L.AM.; B. 57–; BM.; G.; KC.; NC.; QM.; SC.; U.; **Abs.**N.; U.; **Bl.**U.; **Br.**U.; **C.**GG.; **E.**A.; U.; **G.**U.; **H.**U.; **N.**U.; **O.**B.; G.; Y.

17340 **East Riding Medical Journal.** Hull. *E. Riding med. J.* [1933–] L.BM.; **Abs.**N.

17341 **East Sussex Farmer.** Lewes. *E. Suss. Fmr* [1933–] L.AM. 33–40 imp.; BM.; **C.**A. 33–40; **Md.**H. 33–44; **O.**R.

17342 **Eastern Anthropologist.** Lucknow. *East. Anthrop.* [1947–] L.AN.; BM.

17343 **Eastern Area Leprosy News.** New York. *East. Area Lepr. News* [1948–] L.TD. 48–52.

17344 **Eastern Breeder.** Warrenton, Va. *East. Breed.* [1941–] [*C. of:* 56731]

17345 **Eastern Canadian Anthropological Series.** McGill University. Montreal. *East. Can. anthrop. Ser.* [1955–] L.AN.; BM^N. 55.

17346 **Eastern Engineering.** London. *East. Engng* [1910–37] L.BM. 10–21: 30–37; **O.**B.

17347 **Eastern Fruit Grower.** Charles Town, W. Va. *East. Fruit Grow.* [1938–]

17348 **Eastern Geologist.** New York. *East. Geol.* [1936–] L.BM^N. 36.

17349 **Eastern Medical Journal.** Madras. *East. med. J.* [1936–] L.BM.

17350 **Eastern Metals Review.** Calcutta. *East. Metals Rev.* L.MI. 50– imp.; Y.

17351 **Eastern Pharmacist.** New Delhi. *East. Pharmst* [1958–] L.PH.; Y.

17352 **Eaton Engineering Forum.** Cleveland. *Eaton Engng Forum* Li.M. 48–.

17353 **Eau.** Asnières. *Eau* L.P. 13– imp.; **Wa.**W. 30–; Y.

17354 **Eau** et **hygiène.** Paris. *Eau Hyg.*

17355 **Eau pure.** Paris. *Eau pure* [1911–12] L.P. imp.

17356 **Eaux** et **industrie.** Paris. *Eaux Ind.* [1959–] L.P.; **Wa.**W.; Y. [*C. of:* 10534]

17357 **Eaux minérales.** Issoire. *Eaux minér.*

17358 **Ebtenyésztési ertesítö.** Budapest. *Ebten. Ert.*

17359 **Echa leśne.** Warszawa. *Echa leśne* [1924–]

17360 **Échange.** Revue linnéenne. Lyon. *Échange* [1885–] L.BM^N. 85–50; E. 85–04 imp.; Z. 85–50.

17361 **Écho** des **Alpes.** Genève. *Écho Alpes* [1865–24] L.G. 21–24; **Cr.**P. 10–24; **Lv.**U. 19–24.

17362 **Écho** de la **brasserie.** Louvain. *Écho Brass.* **Nu.**B. 47– imp.

17363 **Echo continental.** Hausmitteilungen der Continental Caoutchouc-Cie, G.m.b.h., Hannover. *Echo contin.* Sy.R. 37–39.

17364 **Écho** de la **cordonnerie moderne.** Paris. *Écho Cord. mod.*
  Echo of the **Forest.** Chicago. *See* 21307.

17365 **Écho forestier.** Paris. *Écho for.*

17366 **Écho** für **Kleintierzüchter.** Blankenburg. *Echo Kleintierzüchter*

17367 **Écho** du **laboratoire** de la **fabrique** de **produits pharmaceutiques** de **Courville.** Chartres. *Écho Lab. Fabr. Prod. pharm. Courville*

17368 **Écho** des **laboratoires.** Paris. *Écho Labs*

17369 **Écho** du **magnétisme.** Nice. *Écho Magn.*

17370 **Écho** de la **médecine** et de la **chirurgie.** Lyon. Paris. *Écho Méd. Chir.*

17371 **Écho médical** des **Cévennes.** Nîmes. *Écho méd. Cévennes* [1900–14]

17372 **Écho médical** de **Lyon.** Lyon. *Écho méd. Lyon*

17373 **Écho médical** du **Nord.** Lille. *Écho méd. N.* [1897–] L.MA. 29– imp.; MD. 97–01; S. 34–37 imp.: 44; **Br.**U. 97–39 imp.; **Lv.**M. 35–40 imp.

17374 **Écho médical** de **Paris.** Paris. *Écho méd. Paris*

17375 **Écho médical** et **pharmaceutique.** Paris. *Écho méd. pharm.*

17376 **Écho** du **mentalisme.** Paris. *Écho Ment.*

17377 **Écho** des **mines** et de la **métallurgie.** Paris. *Écho Mines Métall.* [1874–59] L.MI. 50–59; P. 57–59; SC. 35–59; Y. [*C. as:* 31985]

17378 **Écho minier** et **industriel.** Bruxelles. *Écho min. ind.*

17379 **Écho** de la **parfumerie.** Bordeaux. *Écho Parfum.*

17380 **Écho pharmaceutique** du **Midi.** Nîmes. *Écho pharm. Midi*

17381 **Écho pharmaceutique vendéen.** La Roche-sur-Yon. *Écho pharm. vendéen*

17382 **Écho** des **recherches. Centre national** d'**études** des **télécommunications.** Issy-les-Moulineaux. *Écho Rech. Cent. natn. Étud. Télécommun.* **L.**SC. 56–.

17383 **Écho** de la **santé.** Paris. *Écho Santé*

17384 **Écho** des **sociétés** et **associations vétérinaires** de **France.** Lyon. *Écho Socs Ass. vét. Fr.*

17385 **Écho thérapeutique.** Paris. *Écho thér.*

17386 **Écho vétérinaire.** Gembloux. *Écho vét., Gembloux* **W.** 32–.

17387 **Écho vétérinaire.** Liége. *Écho vét., Liége* [1871–08] **L.**V. 76–08.

17388 **Echo** vom **Walde.** Blätter für Forstwarte. Stuttgart. *Echo Walde*

17389 **Echos Solvic.** Brussels. *Echos Solvic* [1953–] **Sy.**R.

17390 **Éclairage.** Paris. *Éclairage*

17391 **Éclairage** et **chauffage.** Marseille. *Éclair. Chauff.*

17392 **Éclairage électrique.** Paris. *Éclair. élect.* [1894–07] **L.**BM.; EE.; P. 97–07; SC.; **Abd.**U.; **G.**U. imp.; **Lv.**U.; **M.**T. 06–07; **Te.**N. 00–07. [*C. as:* 28894]

17393 **Éclairage** et **force motrice.** Bruxelles. *Éclair. Force mot.* [1913–] **L.**EE. 36–40 imp.

17394 **Eclectic Medical Gleaner.** Cincinnati. *Eclect. med. Glean.*

17395 **Eclectic Medical Journal.** Cincinnati. *Eclect. med. J.*

17396 **Eclectic Review.** New York. *Eclect. Rev.*

17396ᶜ **Eclipsing Binaries Circulars.** *Eclips. Binar. Circ.* **Y.**

17397 **Eclogae geologicae Helvetiae.** Lausanne. *Eclog. geol. Helv.* [1888–] **L.**BMᴺ.; GL. 00–; GM.; UC. 88–98; **Abd.**U. 46–; **Bm.**U. 37–; **Br.**U. 24–; **C.**S. 50–; **Cr.**M. 88–36 imp.; **G.**U. 23–; **Lv.**U. 13–15: 52–; **M.**U. 88–08 imp.; **R.**U. 56–; **Y.**

17398 **Eco científico.** Ciego de Avila. *Eco cient.*

17399 **Eco** del **consultorio.** Revista quincenal de medicina y cirugía. Madrid. *Eco Consult.*

17400 **Eco** de la **industria manufacturera textil.** Barcelona. *Eco Ind. mfr. text.*

17401 **Eco** delle **industrie** del **cuoio.** Milano. *Eco Ind. Cuoio*

17402 **Eco** degli **ingegneri** e **periti agrimensori.** Pescia. *Eco Ing. Periti agrim.*

17403 **Eco médico-quirúrgico.** Valladolid. *Eco méd.-quir.*

17403ᶜ **Eco speleologica.** Firenze. *Eco speleol.* [1955–]

17404 **Ecological Monographs.** Durham, N.C. *Ecol. Monogr.* [1931–] **L.**AM. 48–; BM.; BMᴺ.; L. 52–; NC. 31–32: 48–; SC.; Z. 49–; **Abd.**N.; U. 49–; **Abs.**U. 59–; **Bl.**U. 51– imp.; **Bn.**U. 49–; **Br.**U.; **C.**B. 55–; BO.; UL.; **Cr.**M.; **Db.**; **E.**A.; R.; U. 56–; **Ex.**U.; **Fr.** 49–; **G.**U. 31– imp.;

H.U. 45–; **Hu.**G.; **Ld.**U. 57–; **Lo.** 51–; **Mi.**; **O.**AP.; F.; R.; Z.; **Pit.**F. 31–48 imp.: 49–; **Pl.**M.; **R.**U. 55–; **Sw.**U. 56–; **Y.**

17405 **Ecological Review.** Mount Hokkada Botanical Laboratory. Sendai, etc. *Ecol. Rev., Sendai* [1935–] **L.**BMᴺ. 51–; K. 54–; L.; SC. 55–; **C.**A.; P. 52–; **E.**AG. 52– imp.; R. 52–; **O.**B. 52–; BO. 52–; **Pl.**M. 52–; **Rt.**; **Y.**

17406 **Ecology.** Brooklyn, etc. *Ecology* [1920–] **L.**AM. 49–; BMᴺ.; K.; L. 37–; MY. 22–30; NC. 26– imp.; QM. imp.; SC.; U. 47–; **Abd.**M. 52–; S. 54–; U. 20–32: 36–; **Abs.**A. 52–; N. 31–; **Bl.**U. 28–; **Bm.**U. 25–; **Bn.**U. imp.; **Br.**U. 26–29: 38–; **C.**B. 37–; BO.; P. 37–; **Cr.**M.; U. 57–; **Db.**; **E.**B.; SW. 47–56; U. 54–; **Ex.**U. 28–; **Fr.** 39–; **G.**U.; **H.**U. 47–; **Hu.**G. 30–; **Ld.**U.; W. 31–35; **Lo.**; **Lv.**U. imp.; **M.**U.; **Md.**H. 54–; **Mi.**; **Nw.**A.; **O.**AP. imp.; BO. 30–; F.; R.; **Pl.**M.; **Rt.** 29–; **Sa.** 48–; **Sh.**U. 36–; **Sw.**U. 57–; **Wo.** 54–; **Y.** [*C. of:* 37872]

17407 **Econometrica.** Menasha, Wis. *Econometrica* [1933–] **L.**AM. 49–; UC.; **Abd.**U.; **Br.**U.; **C.**SL. 50–; UL.; **Cr.**U.; **Db.** 48–; **Dn.**U.; **E.**R.; U. 48–50: 56–; **Ep.**D. 55–; **Ex.**U. 33–36: 39–; **G.**U. 37–; **Lc.**A. 57–; **M.**C. 49–57; **N.**T. 49–; U.; **Nw.**A.; **R.**U. 48–50; **Rt.** 50–; **Sw.**U.; **Y.**

17408 **Economic Annalist.** Department of Agriculture, Canada. Ottawa. *Econ. Annalist* [1931–] **L.**AM.; TP.; U. 48–; **Abd.**R.; **Abs.**U.; **Bn.**U. imp.; **Ld.**U. 37– imp.; **N.**U. imp.; **O.**AEC.; **R.**D. 31–39; U.

17409 **Economic Biology Bulletin.** Massachusetts Board of Agriculture. Boston. *Econ. Biol. Bull. Mass. Bd Agric.*

17410 **Economic Botany.** Lancaster, Pa., etc. *Econ. Bot.* [1947–] **L.**BMᴺ.; HS.; IC.; L.; SC.; TP.; U.; **Abd.**U.; **Abs.**A. 52–54; U.; **Bl.**U.; **Br.**U. 47–57; **C.**A.; AB.; **Cr.**U.; **Db.**; **E.**B.; SW.; **Ex.**U.; **Hu.**G.; **Je.**; **Lv.**U.; **M.**U.; **Md.**H.; **N.**U.; **Nw.**A.; **O.**F.; RE.; **R.**U.; **Rt.**; **Sw.**U.; **Y.**

17411 **Economic Branch Projects. Forest Research Institute.** Dehra Dun. *Econ. Brch Proj. Forest Res. Inst., Dehra Dun* **O.**F. 22–.

17412 **Economic Bulletin. Department** of **Agriculture, British Guiana.** Georgetown. *Econ. Bull. Dep. Agric. Br. Guiana* [1947–] **C.**A.; **O.**AEC.; RT.

17413 **Economic Bulletin** of the **Department** of **Natural Resources, Newfoundland.** St. Johns. *Econ. Bull. Dep. nat. Resour. Newfoundl.* [1931–] **L.**BMᴺ. 31–42 v. imp.

17414 **Economic Bulletin. Geological Survey Department, Federation** of **Malaya.** Ipoh. *Econ. Bull. geol. Surv. Dep. Fed. Malaya* [1958–] **L.**BM.; BMᴺ.; **Y.**

17415 **Economic Circular. Bureau** of **Fisheries.** Washington. *Econ. Circ. Bur. Fish., Wash.* [1912–31] **L.**BM.; P.; **Abd.**M. 17–31 imp.; **Dm.** 15–28 imp.; **G.**M.; **Lv.**U. 13–18 imp.; **Pl.**M. 13–28 imp. [*Replaced by:* 19551]

17416 **Economic Digest Series. Chinese-American Joint Committee** on **Rural Reconstruction.** Taipei. *Econ. Dig. Ser. Chin.-Am. jt Comm. rur. Reconstr.* [1952–] **C.**A.

17417 **Economic Geography.** Worcester, Mass., etc. *Econ. Geogr.* [1925–] **L.**B.; BM. 51–; G.; QM.; U.; UC.; **Abd.**S. 36–50; U.; **Abs.**A. 52–57; N.; U.; **Bl.**U.; **Bm.**P. 32–; U.; **Br.**U.; **C.**GG.; UL. 46–; **Db.** 51–; **Dn.**U.; **E.**G.; U.; **Ex.**U.; **G.**U. 31–; **H.**U.; **Hu.**G. 42–; **Ld.**U.; W. 26–34; **Lv.**U.; **N.**U. 26–; **Nw.**A. **O.**G.; **R.**U.; **Rt.**; **Sa.** 38–; **Sh.**IO. 51–; U.; **Sil.**; **Sw.**U.; **Y.**

17418 **Economic Geology** and **Bulletin** of the **Society** of **Economic Geologists.** Lancaster, Pa., etc. *Econ. Geol.* [1905–] **L.**B. 48–; BM.; BM^N.; DI. 44–53 imp.; GL.; KC. 57–; MI.; MIE. 58–; P. 10–; PT. 27–; QM. 20–; SC.; U.; **Abd.**U. 42–; **Abs.**U. 55–; **Bl.**U. 55–; **Bm.**U. 09–09: 16–; **Br.**U.; **C.**MI. 21–; S.; **Cr.**U. 49–; **Db.** 20–; **Dn.**U. 49–; **E.**D.; U. 35–; **Ex.**U. 05–13: 37–; **G.**M.; T. 26– imp.; U. 07–; **H.**U. 48–; **Ld.**U.; **Lv.**P. 59–; U. 19–; **M.**U.; **N.**U.; **Nw.**A.; **O.**R.; **Sa.** 19–; **Sh.**10. 53–; SC.; **Sw.**U.; **Y.** [*C. of:* 1973]

17419 **Economic Geology Series. Geological Survey, Canada.** Ottawa. *Econ. Geol. Ser. Can.* [1926–] **L.**BM.; BM^N.; GL.; GM.; I. 26–52 imp.; MI.; **Abd.**U. 26–47; **Abs.**U. 47–52 imp.; **Bl.**U. 26–34; **Bm.**P.; U.; **Br.**U.; **C.**P.; S.; **Db.**; **Dn.**U.; **E.**C. 26–34 imp.; U. 26–34 imp.; **G.**N.; U.; **Ld.**U.; **Lv.**U. imp.; **M.**P.; U. 26–34; **O.**G. 26–34 imp.; R.; **Sa.**; **Sh.**M. 26–30; **Y.**

17420 **Economic Leaflets. British Museum, Natural History.** London. *Econ. Leafl. Br. Mus. nat. Hist.* [1925–] **L.**BM^N.; E.; EB. (ent.); **Bn.**U.; **Ld.**P. (curr. ed.); **Lv.**P. (zool.) 40–48; **O.**AP. 25–40: 51; R.; **Pl.**M. 30–57; **Sw.**U.; **Y.** [*Several editions*]

17421 **Economic Memorandum. Ministry** of **Works.** London. *Econ. Memor. Minist. Wks* [1942–] **L.**P.

17422 **Economic Notes. Lake States Forest Experiment Station.** St. Paul, Minn. *Econ. Notes Lake Sts Forest Exp. Stn* [1935–] **O.**F. imp.

17423 **Economic Papers. Kentucky Geological Survey.** *Econ. Pap. Ky geol. Surv.*

17424 **Economic Papers. North Carolina Department** of **Conservation** and **Development.** Raleigh. *Econ. Pap. N. Carol. Dep. Conserv. Dev.* [1926–] **L.**BM^N. 26–30; P. 26–37; **Y.** [*C. of:* 17425]

17425 **Economic Papers** of the **North Carolina Geological** and **Economic Survey.** Chapel Hill. *Econ. Pap. N. Carol. geol. econ. Surv.* [1897–25] **L.**BM^N.; P.; SC.; **Bm.**U. 08–11; **Y.** [*C. as:* 17424]

17426 **Economic Papers. United States Bureau** of **Mines.** Washington. *Econ. Pap. U.S. Bur. Mines* [1928–40] **L.**BM.; MI.; P.; SC.; **Abs.**N.; **Bm.**U. 29–40 imp.; **G.**M.; U.; **Ld.**P.; **Sh.**M.

17427 **Economic Proceedings** of the **Royal Dublin Society.** Dublin. *Econ. Proc. R. Dubl. Soc.* [1899–59] **L.**AM.; BM.; BM^N.; C.; E. 02–59; EB.; GL.; GM.; L.; LI. 46–59; MD.; MY. 51–59; P.; PH. 99–09; SC.; U.; UC.; Z.; **Abd.**R. 26–50; U.; **Abs.**A. 10–59; N. 10–59; U. imp.; **Bl.**U.; **Bm.**P.; U.; **Bn.**U.; **Br.**A. imp.; U.; **C.**A.; P.; UL.; **Cr.**N.; U.; **Db.**; **Dn.**U.; **E.**A.; B.; C.; F.; O. imp.; P. imp.; R.; U.; **G.**E. 10–59; M.; U.; **Hu.**G. 50–59 imp.; **Ld.**U.; **Lv.**P.; U.; **M.**P.; **N.**P.; **Nw.**A.; **O.**R.; **Pl.**M.; **R.**U. 10–59; **Rt.**; **Sa.** 99–14; **Sh.**U.; **Y.** [*C. in:* 49196, Ser. B]

17428 **Economic Report. Commonwealth Fisheries Office, Department** of **Commerce** and **Agriculture.** Sydney. *Econ. Rep. Commonw. Fish. Off.* [1946–] **L.**Z. 46; **Bn.**U.; **Pl.**M. 46.

17429 **Economic Report. North** of **Scotland College** of **Agriculture.** Aberdeen. *Econ. Rep. N. Scotl. Coll. Agric.* [1946–] **Abs.**U. v. imp.; **C.**A.; **Dn.**U. 56–; **Rt.** imp.

17430 **Economic Review** of **Food** and **Agriculture. F.A.O.** Washington. *Econ. Rev. Fd Agric.* [1947–48] **L.**AM.; BM.; U.; **Bm.**P.; **Br.**U.; **C.**A.; **O.**AEC.; G.; **R.**U. 48; **Rt.**

17431 **Economic Series. British Museum Natural History.** London. *Econ. Ser. Br. Mus. nat. Hist.* [1913–] **L.**AM.; BM.; BM^N.; E.; EB.; K. 16– imp.; Z.; **Abd.**U. 15–; **Bm.**P.; U. 14–; **Bn.**U.; **Br.**P.; **Cr.**U.; **Db.**; **Dn.**U.; **E.**F.; R. 13–32; U.; **G.**M. imp.; U.; **Ld.**P.; **Lv.**P.; U. 13–18; **M.**P. imp.; **N.**P. 16–; **Nw.**A.; P. imp.; **O.**AP. imp.; R.; **Pl.**M. 19–; **Sa.**; **Sh.**U. 13–25; **Sw.**U.; **Y.**

17432 **Economic Series. Department** of **Agriculture, Federation** of **Malaya.** *Econ. Ser. Dep. Agric. Fed. Malaya* [1932–] **L.**BM^N. imp.; **Rt.** 32–41; **Sal.** 38–40; **Y.**

Economic Series. Department of **Agriculture, Straits Settlements** and **Federated Malay States.** *See* 17432

17433 **Economic Series. Ministry** of **Agriculture** and **Fisheries.** London. *Econ. Ser. Minist. Agric. Fish.* [1925–] **L.**FA.; SC.; **Bl.**U. 25–34 imp.; **Bn.**U.; **C.**A.; **G.**U. 27–35 imp.; **Ld.**P.; U.; **N.**P. 25–38 imp.; **Nw.**A. 25–36 imp.; **O.**AEC.; B.; G. 47–; RE.; **Rt.**; **Sw.**U. 34–39: 44–46.

17434 **Economic Series Pamphlet. Utilization Circle, Forest Department, Burma.** Rangoon. *Econ. Ser. Pamph. Util. Circle Forest Dep. Burma* [1929–37] **O.**F.

17435 **Economic Series. Scottish National Development Council.** Glasgow. *Econ. Ser. Scot. natn. Dev. Coun.* [1933–] **L.**BM.; **Bn.**U. 33–34; **C.**A.; **O.**RE. 33–37.

17436 **Economic Studies** in **Sheep Farming** in **Wales.** Aberystwyth. *Econ. Stud. Sheep Fmg Wales* [1957–] **Bn.**U.

17437 **Economics** of **Dried Fruit Production** in the **Sunraysia District.** Canberra. *Economics dried Fruit Prod. Sunraysia Distr.* [1960–] **Ld.**U.

17438 **Economics** of **Fruit Farming.** South-Eastern Agricultural College. Wye. *Economics Fruit Fmg* [1949–] **L.**U.; **Bn.**U.; **E.**A. 50–55; **Rt.**; **Y.**

Economics of **Nuclear Power.** *See* 40019.

17439 **Économie alpestre.** Paris. *Écon. alp.* [1928–39] **O.**F. [*C. of:* 3303]

17440 **Économie électrique.** Paris. *Écon. élect.* [1955–] **L.**EE.; **Y.** [*C. of:* 14098]

17441 **Économie** et **médecine animales.** Paris. *Écon. Méd. anim.* [1960–] **W.**; **Y.**

17442 **Économie rurale.** Paris. *Écon. rurale* **Y.** [*C. of:* 11947]

17443 **Ecos españoles** de **dermatología y sifilología.** Madrid. *Ecos esp. Derm. Sif.* **L.**MD. 31– imp.

17444 **Ecos veterinarios.** Lisboa. *Ecos vet.*

17445 **Ectoparasites.** London & Aylesbury. *Ectoparasites* [1915–24] **L.**BM.; BM^N.; E.; EB.; TD.; **C.**UL.; **O.**R. imp.

17446 **Edel-Erden** und **-Erze.** München. *Edel-Erden u. -Erze* [1919–23] **L.**C.; P. 21–23.

17447 **Edelmetallindustrie.** Wien. *Edelmetallindustrie* [1890–]

17447° **Edesipar.** Budapest. *Edesipar* **Y.**

17448 **Edgar Allen News.** Sheffield. *Edgar Allen News* [1919–] **L.**AV. 51– imp.; BM.; I. 47–; MT.; P. (curr.); **Bm.**C. 45–; T. 56–; **Br.**P. (1 yr); **Cr.**U. 36– imp.; **G.**E. (3 yr.); **Ld.**U. 24– imp.; W. (curr.); **M.**C. (curr.); P. 47–; **Rn.**B. (1 yr); **Sh.**P. 21–; **Sil.** 55–; **Y.** Special Machinery Edition [1940–]

17449 **Edgar Allen-Buell Gazette.** London. *Edgar Allen-Buell Gaz.* **L.**BM. 34–; P. 34–36.

17450 **Edilité technique.** Paris. *Edilité tech.* **L.**P. 08–14.

17451 **Edilizia moderna.** Milano. *Ediliz. mod.* **Wa.**B. 48–; **Y.**

17452 **Edinburgh Bird Bulletin.** Edinburgh. *Edinb. Bird Bull.* [1950–] **L.**BM. 52–; BMN. 51–; NC. 51–59; **E.**A. 50–55; T. 53–.

17453 **Edinburgh Dental Student.** Edinburgh. *Edinb. dent. Stud.* [1910–23] **L.**BM.; D. 21–25 imp.; **E.**A. 00–14 imp.

17454 **Edinburgh Hospital Reports.** Edinburgh. *Edinb. Hosp. Rep.* [1893–00] **L.**BM.; MA.; MD.; S.; **Bl.**U.; **Bm.**U.; **Br.**U.; **C.**PA.; UL.; **Db.**; **Dn.**U.; **E.**A.; P.; S.; U.; **G.**F.; U.; **Ld.**U.; **Lv.**M.; U. 93–96; **M.**MS.; **Nw.**A.; **O.**R.

17455 **Edinburgh Journal** of **Science, Technology** and **Photographic Art.** Edinburgh. *Edinb. J. Sci. Technol. photogr. Art* [1926–] **L.**BM.; P. 26–52; PG. 26–44; R. 26–52; **Abd.**U.; **C.**UL.; **Db.**; **E.**A.; B.; D. 26–44; F.; G.; L.; R. 26–53; U.; **G.**E. 37–52; M. 26–52 imp.; T. 26–52; **Ld.**U.; **Lv.**U.; **M.**U. 26–52 imp.; **Nw.**A. 26–32; **Sa.** [*C. of:* 53991]

17456 **Edinburgh Mathematical Notes.** Edinburgh. *Edinb. math. Notes* [1939–57] **L.**BM.; R.; SC.; U. 43–57; UC.; **Abd.**U.; **Abs.**N.; **Bl.**U.; **Br.**U.; **C.**P.; **Dn.**U.; **E.**A.; Q.; R.; **Ex.**U. 41–49; **G.**T.; U.; **Ld.**U.; **M.**U.; **O.**R.; **Sa.** [*C. of:* 29676; *C. in:* 39162]

17457 **Edinburgh Mathematical Tracts.** London. *Edinb. math. Tracts* [1915] **L.**SC.; **Abs.**N.; **Bl.**U.; **Db.**; **Ld.**U.; **O.**R.; **Sa.**

17458 **Edinburgh Medical Journal.** Edinburgh. *Edinb. med. J.* [1855–54] **L.**BM.; GH. 1855–96; H. 33–39; MA.; MD.; S.; SC. 35–54; TD. 08–54; U. 08–54; VC. 1855–79; **Abd.**U.; **Abs.**N. 12–54; **Bl.**U. 1855–22: 36–54; **Bm.**U.; **Br.**U.; **C.**P. 97–18; PA. 1855–89; UL.; **Cr.**MS. 81–53 imp.; **Db.**; **Dn.**U.; **E.**A.; I.; P.; S.; T. imp.; U.; **G.**F.; U.; **Ld.**U.; **Lv.**M.; U. 97–00: 29–54; **M.**MS.; **Nw.**A. imp.; **O.**R.; **Sa.**; **Sh.**U. 69–39: 44–54. [*Incorporated in:* 49311]

17459 **Edinburgh Medical Monographs.** Edinburgh. *Edinb. med. Monogr.* **L.**BM. 38–.

17460 **Edinburgh Post-Graduate Lectures** in **Medicine.** Edinburgh. *Edinb. Post-Grad. Lect. Med.* [1937–] **L.**S.; **Br.**U. 52–; **E.**S.; U.; **G.**F. 44–; **O.**R.

17461 **Edinburgh University Publications.** Edinburgh. *Edinb. Univ. Publs*

    Geography and Sociology [1952–] **L.**BM.; U.; **Bl.**U. 52–55; **E.**U.

    Science and Mathematics [1948–] **L.**BM.; U.; **C.**UL.; **E.**U.

17462 **Edison Monthly.** New York. *Edison Mon.* [1908–] **L.**P. 08–28.

17463 **Edison Service News.** Boston. *Edison Serv. News* [*C. of:* 17607]

    Éditions séparates du **Musée ethnographique** á **Zagreb.** *See* 38139.

    Éditions spéciales de la **Société serbe** de **géographie.** *See* 38140.

17464 **Éducation mathématique.** Paris. *Éduc. math.* [1898–] **Y.**

17465 **Educational Bulletin. Bartlett Tree Research Laboratories.** Stamford, Conn. *Educ. Bull. Bartlett Tree Res. Labs* [1928–33] **C.**A. 30–33; **O.**F. 30: 33.

17466 **Educational Focus.** Bausch and Lomb Optical Co. Rochester. *Educ. Focus* **L.**P. 59–.

17467 **Educational Leaflet Series. New York State Museum.** Albany. *Educ. Leafl. Ser. N.Y. St. Mus.* [1947–49] **L.**BMN.; **Y.**

17468 **Educational Leaflets. National Association of Audubon Societies.** Harrisburg. Pa. *Educ. Leafl. natn. Ass. Audub. Socs* **E.**F. 03– imp.

    Educational Pamphlets. Division of Forestry, Louisiana Department of **Conservation.** *See* 17469.

17469 **Educational Pamphlets** of the **Louisiana Department** of **Conservation, Division** of **Forestry.** *Educ. Pamph. La Dep. Conserv. Div. For.*

17470 **Educational Pamphlets. Post Office Research Station.** London. *Educ. Pamph. P.O. Res. Stn* [1938–] **L.**SC.; **Ld.**P. 38– imp.; **O.**R.

17471 **Educational** and **Psychological Measurement.** Lancaster, Pa., Baltimore. *Educ. psychol. Measur.* [1941–] **L.**PS.; U. 45–; **Br.**U. 47–; **E.**U. 50–; **Sh.**U. 52–; **Sw.**U. 59–.

17471° **Educational Series. Commonwealth of Pennsylvania Topographic** and **Geologic Survey.** *Educ. Ser. Commonw. Pa topogr. geol. Surv.* **Y.**

17472 **Educational Series. Florida State Board** of **Conservation.** Jacksonville. *Educ. Ser. Fla St. Bd Conserv.* [1948–] **L.**AM.; **Abd.**M.; **Bn.**U.; **Pl.**M. 55–; **Wo.** 55– imp.; **Y.**

    Educational Series. Illinois State Geological Survey. *See* 17475.

17473 **Educational Series. Maryland Board** of **Natural Resources.** Solomons. *Educ. Ser. Md Bd nat. Resour.* [1944–] **L.**AM.; **Bn.**U.; **Lo.**; **Lv.**U.

17474 **Educational Series. Peking Society** of **Natural History.** Peking. *Educ. Ser. Peking Soc. nat. Hist.*

17475 **Educational Series. State** of **Illinois Geological Survey.** Urbana. *Educ. Ser. St. Ill. geol. Surv.* [1927–] **E.**R. 29–31; **Y.**

17476 **Educazione sanitaria.** Perugia. *Educaz. sanit.* [1956–] **L.**TD.

17477 **Edwards' Dental Quarterly.** London. *Edwards' dent. Q.* [1912–15] **L.**BM.

17478 **Eesti arst.** Tartu. *Eesti Arst* [1922–] **L.**BM. 23–; H.

17478ᵃ **Eesti geograafia seltsi aastaraamat.** Tallinn. *Eesti geogr. Seltsi Aastar.* [1957–] **L.**BM.

17478ᵃᵃ **Eesti geograafia seltsi publikatsioonid.** Tallinn. *Eesti geogr. Seltsi Publ.* **Y.**

17478ᵇ **Eesti geoloogia: bibliograafia.** Tallinn. *Eesti Geol. Biblfia* [1960–] **L.**P.

17478ᶜ **Eesti loodusteaduse arhiiv.** Tartu. *Eesti Loodustead. Arh.* [1924:28–] **L.**BMN.; GL.; **E.**R. [*C. of* 4133; *not published* 1938–59]

17480 **Eesti loodus.** Tallinn. *Eesti Loodus* [1958–] **L.**BMN. 59–; **Y.**

17481 **Eesti loomaarstlik ringvaade:** revue vétérinaire estonienne. Tartu. *Eesti loomaarst. Ringv.* [1925–] **W.** 31–.

17482 **Eesti meteoroloogia aastaraamat.** *Eesti met. Aastar.* **E.**M. 77– imp.

17483 **Eesti metsanduse aastaraamat.** Tartu. *Eesti metsand. Aastar.* [1926–] **O.**F. 26–37.

17483ª **Eesti NSV floora.** Tallinn. *Eesti NSV Floora* [1953–] **L.**BM.

17484 **Eesti NSV teaduste akadeemia Füüsika** ja **astronoomia instituudi uurimused.** Tartu. *Eesti NSV Tead. Akad. Füüs. Astr. Inst. Uurim.* [1955–] **L.**BM.; P.; **Bm.**U. 55; **G.**U.; **Y.**

17485 **Eesti NSV teaduste akadeemia toimetised.** Tallinn. *Eesti NSV Tead. Akad. Toim.* [1952–55: 56– in series below] **L.**BM.; BM^N.; P.; **Y.**
　　Bioloogiline seer. [1956–] **L.**BM.; BM^N.; P.; **Y.**
　　Tehniliste ja füüsikalis-matemaatiliste teaduste seer. [1956–] **L.**BM. 57–; P.; **Y.**
　　[*English abstracts at:* 34775ª]

17486 **Eesti põllumajandus.** Tallin. *Eesti Põllum.* **L.**AM. 24–38.

17487 **Eesti põllumajanduse akadeemia teaduslike tööde koguteos.** Tallin. *Eesti põllum. Akad. tead. Tööde Kogut.* [1955–] **L.**AM.

17488 **Eesti rahva muuseumi aastaraamat.** Tartu. *Eesti Rahva Muus. Aastar.* [1925–] **L.**AN. 25–34; UC. 29–.

17489 **Eesti tehnika.** Tallin. *Eesti Tehn.* [1919–] **Eesti vabariigi tartu ulikooli toimetused.** *See* 549.

17490 **Efemeride astronomice** pentru **Bucureşti.** Bucureşti. *Efem. astr. Buc.*

17491 **Efemérides astronómicas.** Observatorio astronómico da Universidade de Coimbra. *Efems astr., Coimbra* [1850–] **M.**U. 52–; **Y.**

17492 **Éfemeridȳ malȳkh planet.** Leningrad, Moskva. Эфемериды малых планет. *Éfem. malȳkh Planet* **L.**AS. 47–; SC. 47; **M.**U. 50: 52–.

17493 **Effemeridi astronomiche** ad **uso** dei **naviganti.** Genova. *Effem. astr. Uso Navig.* [1916–] **C.**O. 18; **E.**O. 18–.

17494 **Effemeridi astronomico-nautiche.** Trieste. *Effem. astr.-naut.*

17495 **Effemeridi** del **sole** e della **lune.** Venezia. *Effem. Sole Lune*

17496 **Efficience textile.** Tournai. *Effic. text.* [1946–] **M.**C. 53– imp.

17497 **Efficiency.** Industrial Mineral Wool Institute. New York. *Efficiency* [1942–]

17498 **Efterretninger** for **sjöfarende.** Kristiania. *Efterretn. Sjöfar.*

17499 **Egatea.** Revista da Escola de engenharia de Porto-Alegre da Universidade technica do Rio Grande do Sul. Porto-Alegre. *Egatea* **L.**EB. 25–34★.

17500 **Egészség.** Budapest. *Egészség, Bpest.* [1887–] **L.**MA. 54–; **Y.**

17502 **Egészséges élet.** Budapest. *Egészséges Élet* [1942–]

17503 **Egészségőr.** Budapest. *Egészségőr*

17504 **Egészségtudomány.** Budapest. *Egészégtudomány* [1957–] **L.**MA.; TD.; **Y.**

17505 **Egészségtudományi közlemények.** Budapest. *Egészségtud. Közl.* [1942–]

17506 **Egészségügyi értesitö.** Budapest. *Egészség. Ért.* [1931–]

17507 **Egészségügyi közlöny.** Budapest. *Egészség. Közl.* [1951–]

17508 **Egészségügyi lapok.** Budapest. *Egészség. Lap.* [1901–]

17509 **Egészségügyi munka.** Középfokú egészsegügyi dolgozók lapja. Budapest. *Egészség. Munka* **Y.**

17510 **Egészségügyőr.** Budapest. *Egészségügyőr*

17511 **Egészségvedelem.** Budapest. *Egészségvedelem* [1947–]

17512 **Eggs.** Rudgwick. *Eggs* [1919–41] **L.**AM.; SC. 33–41; **Abd.**R. 34–38. [*C. as:* 32994]

17513 **Egretta.** *Egretta* [1958–] **O.**OR.

17514 **Egyesitett gyogyszerészi lapok.** Budapest. *Egyesit. gyogysz. Lap.* [1944–]

17515 **Egyetemes bőrujság.** Budapest. *Egyet. Bőrujság*

17516 **Egyházi műipar.** Budapest. *Egyh. Műip.*

17517 **Égypte médicale.** Alexandrie. *Égypte méd.*

17518 **Égypte scientifique.** Marseille. *Égypte scient.*

17519 **Egyptian Agricultural Products.** Cairo. *Egypt. agric. Prod.* [1915–17] **L.**K.; **E.**R. imp.

17520 **Egyptian Agricultural Review.** Cairo. *Egypt. agric. Rev.* [1923–] **C.**A. 41–.

17521 **Egyptian Cotton Gazette.** Alexandria. *Egypt. Cott. Gaz.* **M.**C. 47–.

17522 **Egyptian Cotton Year Book.** Alexandria. *Egypt. Cott. Yb.* [1931–] **M.**P. 31–39 imp.

17523 **Egyptian Insect Pests.** Cairo. *Egypt. Insect Pests* **L.**EB. 20–21.

17524 **Egyptian Journal** of **Botany.** Cairo. *Egypt. J. Bot.* [1958–59] **L.**BM^N.; K.; **Bl.**U.; **Bn.**U.; **Ld.**U.; **Rt.**; **Y.** [*C. as:* 25685]

17525 **Egyptian Journal** of **Chemistry.** Cairo. *Egypt. J. Chem.* [1958–59] **L.**C.; P.; **Bl.**U.; **Bn.**U.; **Ld.**U.; **Rt.**; **Y.** [*C. as:* 25787]

17526 **Egyptian Journal** of **Geology.** Cairo. *Egypt. J. Geol.* [1957–59] **L.**BM^N.; GM.; UC.; **Bl.**U.; **Bn.**U.; **Br.**U.; **C.**S.; **E.**G. (curr.); **G.**U.; **Ld.**U.; **Rt.** 57; **Y.** [*C. as:* 26058ª]

17526ª **Egyptian Journal** of **Neurology, Psychiatry** and **Neurosurgery.** Cairo. *Egypt. J. Neurol. Psychiat. Neurosurg.* [1960–] **L.**MD.

17527 **Egyptian Journal** of **Psychology.** Cairo. *Egypt. J. Psychol.* [1945–55] **L.**PS.
　　Egyptian Medical Review. *See* 29100.

17528 **Egyptian Pharmaceutical Reports.** Cairo. *Egypt. pharm. Rep.* **L.**PH. 50–. [*C. of:* 39590]

17529 **Egyptian Reviews** of **Science.** Cairo. *Egypt. Revs Sci.* [1957–] **L.**BM^N.; GM.; UC.; **Bl.**U.; **Ld.**U.; **Y.**

17530 **Eickhoff Bulletin.** Gebr. Eickhoff Maschinenfabrik. Bochum. *Eickhoff Bull.* **L.**P. 38–.

17531 **Eickhoff-Mitteilungen.** Bochum. *Eickhoff-Mitt.* **L.**P. 30–39.

17532 **Eimreiðin.** Kaupmannahöfn. *Eimreiðin* [1895–] **L.**BM.; **C.**UL.

17533 **Einheimische Tiere.** Bern. *Einheim. Tiere* **L.**BM^N. 55.

17534 **Einzeldarstellungen** auf dem **Gebiet** der **angewandten Naturwissenschaften.** München. *Einzeldarst. Geb. angew. Naturw.*

17535 **Einzeldarstellungen. Kaiser-Wilhelm Institut für Faserstoffchemie.** Berlin. *Einzeldarst. Kais.-Wilhelm Inst. Faserstoffchem.* [1925–] **L.**P. 25– imp.; SC. 25.

17536 **Einzelschriften** zur **chemischen Technologie.** Leipzig. *Einzelschr. chem. Technol.* **L.**P. 11–21.

17537 **Einzelveröffentlichungen. Seewetteramt, Deutscher Wetterdienst.** Hamburg. *Einzelveröff. Seewett-Amt* [1953–] **L.**MO.; **E.**R.; **Lo.** imp.; **Wo.** 56–; **Y.**

17538 **Eir.** Reykjavík. *Eir*

17539 **Eira.** Stockholm. *Eira* [1877–03] [*C. as:* 1802]

17540 **Eisbericht** der **Deutschen Seewarte.** Hamburg. *Eisber. dt. Seew.* **L.**MO. 28–39*. [*C. as:* 17541]

17541 **Eisbericht. Deutsches Hydrographisches Institut.** Hamburg. *Eisber. dt. hydrogr. Inst.* **L.**MO. 48–. [*C. of:* 17540]

Eisei shikenjo hokoku. *See* 11224.

17542 **Eisenbahn.** Leipzig. *Eisenbahn, Lpz.* **Lv.**U. 10–15.

17543 **Eisenbahn.** Wien. *Eisenbahn, Wien* [1948–]

17544 **Eisenbahn** u. **Industrie.** Wien. *Eisenb. Ind.*

17545 **Eisenbahnbau.** Berlin. *Eisenbahnbau*

17546 **Eisenbahnfachschule.** Berlin. *Eisenbahnfachschule*

17547 **Eisenbahnindustrie.** Berlin. *Eisenbahnindustrie*

17548 **Eisenbahningenieur.** Frankfurt am Main. *Eisenbahningenieur* [1950–] **L.**P.; **Y.**

17549 **Eisenbahnkunde.** München. *Eisenbahnkunde*

17550 **Eisenbahnnachrichtenblatt.** Berlin. *Eisenbahnnachrichtenblatt*

17551 **Eisenbahntechnik.** Berlin. *Eisenbahntechnik, Berl.* [1953] **L.**P. [*C. as:* 16689]

17552 **Eisenbahntechnik.** Karlsruhe. *Eisenbahntechnik, Karlsruhe* [1947–51] **L.**P. 48–51; **Y.** [*C. in:* 17548]

17553 **Eisenbahntechnik** der **Gegenwart.** Berlin. *Eisenb-Tech. Gegenw.* [1921–] **L.**BM.

17554 **Eisenbahn-, Maschinen-** u. **Electrotechnik.** Berlin. *Eisenb.-, Masch.- u. Electrotech.*

17555 **Eisenbahntechnische Rundschau.** Köln. *Eisenbtech. Rdsch.* [1952–] **L.**P. 54–; SC.; **Y.**

17556 **Eisenbahntechnische Zeitschrift** für das **Gesamtgebiete** der **Voll-, Klein-** u. **Strassenbahn.** Berlin. *Eisenbtech. Z.* [1905–07] **L.**P. [*C. of:* 22801]

17557 **Eisenbahntierseuchenanzeiger.** Berlin. *Eisenbahntierseuchenanzeiger*

17558 **Eisenbahnwärter.** Berlin. *Eisenbahnwärter*

17559 **Eisenbahnwerkmeister.** Berlin. *Eisenbahnwerkmeister*

17560 **Eisenbahnzahnrad.** Berlin. *Eisenbahnzahnrad*

17561 **Eisenbau.** Berlin. *Eisenbau, Berl.* [1925–29] **L.**P. [*Supplement to:* 48740]

17562 **Eisenbau.** Leipzig. *Eisenbau, Lpz.* [1910–22] **L.**P.; **Bm.**U. 21–22; **Lv.**U. 10–15.

17563 **Eisenbetonliteratur.** Berlin. *Eisenbetonliteratur* [1911] **L.**P. [*C. as:* 58914]

17564 **Eisengewerbe.** Heidenheim a. Br. *Eisengewerbe*

17565 **Eisengiesser.** Gröbzig. *Eisengiesser*

17566 **Eisen-** u. **Metallgiesser.** Wolfenbüttel & Braunschweig. *Eisen- u. Metallgiesser*

17567 **Eisenindustrie-** und **Geschäftszeitung.** Budapest. *Eisenind.- u. Geschäftsztg*

17568 **Eisenkonstrukteur.** Kattowitz. *Eisenkonstrukteur*

17569 **Eisenzeitung.** Berlin. *Eisenzeitung* [1879–15] [*C. as:* 58613]

17570 **Eis-** u. **Kälteindustrie.** Wittenberg. *Eis- u. Kälteind.* **L.**P. 13–19*. [*C. as:* 57059]

17571 **Eisübersichtskarte** der **Deutscher Seewarte.** Hamburg. *EisübersKarte dt. Seew.* **L.**MO. 28–39.

17572 **Eiszeit.** Organ des Instituts für Eiszeitforschung in Wien. Leipzig. *Eiszeit* [1924–27] **L.**GM.; **Ld.**U. [*C. as:* 17573]

17573 **Eiszeit** und **Urgeschichte.** Organ des Instituts für Eiszeitforschung in Wien. *Eiszeit Urgesch.* [1928–30] **L.**BM^N.; GM.; **Ld.**U. [*C. of:* 17572]

17574 **Eiszeitalter** und **Gegenwart.** Hannover, Öhringen. *Eiszeitalter Gegenw.* [1951–] **L.**BM.; BM^N.; GM. 54–; MO. 51; SC. 55–; **C.**BO.; PO.; **Db.**; **Y.**

17575 **Eitanim.** Tel Aviv. *Eitanim* [1952–] **L.**TD.

17576 **Eiweiss-Forschung.** Hamburg. *Eiweiss-Forsch.* [1948–]

Eiyô to **shokuryô.** *See* 26296.
Eiyôgaku zasshi. *See* 25247.

17577 **Ekaterinoslavskiĭ meditsinskiĭ zhurnal.** Ekaterinoslav. Екатеринославский медицинский журнал. *Ekaterinosl. med. Zh.* [1922–26] **L.**TD. 26. [*C. as:* 17050^c]

17578 **Ékho pivovarenīya** i **pivotorgovli.** S.-Peterburg. Эхо пивоваренія и пивоторговли. *Ékho Pivov. Pivotorg.*

17579 **Ekologia polska.** Warszawa. *Ekol. pol.*
Ser. A. [1953–] **L.**BM^N.; NC. 60–; **Bl.**U.; **C.**A.; **Fr.**; **Ld.**U.; **O.**AP.; H.; **Pl.**M.; **Y.**
Ser. B. [1955–] **L.**NC. 60–; **Y.**

17580 **Ékonomicheskiĭ vêstnik Man'chzhurīi.** Kharbin. Экономическій вѣстникъ Маньчжуріи. *Ekon. Vêst. Man'chzhurīi* [1923–24] [*C. of:* and *Rec. as:* 56465]

17581 **Ekonomika** i **organizacja rolnictwa.** Warszawa. *Ekon. Org. Roln.* [1957–] **L.**AM.; **Y.**

17582 **Ékonomika sel'skogo khozyaistva.** Moskva. Экономика сельского хозяйства. *Ékon. sel'. Khoz.* [1957–] **L.**BM.; **Hu.**G.; **Y.** [*C. of:* 50095]

17583 **Ékonomika stroitel'stva.** Экономика строительства. *Ékon. Stroit.* [1959–] **Wa.**B. 59–61; **Y.**

17584 **Ékskursīonnoe dêlo.** Nauchno-pedagocheskiĭ zhurnal. Petrograd. Экскурсіонное дѣло. Научно-педагогическій журналъ *Ékskurs. Dêlo*

17585 **Eksperimentaalbioloogia instituudi uurimused.** Tallinn. *Eksp. Inst. Uurim.* **L.**BM^N. 60–.

Éksperimental'naya botanika. Экспериментальная ботаника. *See* 54489, ser. 4.

17586 **Éksperimental'naya khirurgiya.** Moskva. Экспериментальная хирургия. *Éksp. Khir.* [1956–] **L.**BM.; **Ld.**U. 57–; **Y.** imp.

17587 **Eksperimentinés medicinos instituto darbai.** Vilnius. *Eksp. Med. Inst. Darb.* [1955–] **L.**BM. **Y.** [*C. of:* 17588]

17588 **Eksperimentines medicinos ir onkologijos instituto darbai.** Lietuvos TSR mokslų akademija. Vilnius. *Eksp. Med. Onkol. Inst. Darb.* [1948–55] **L.**BM. 53–55; **Y.** 48–53. [*C. as:* 17587]

17589 **Éksperȳmental'na** ta **klȳnȳchna renthenolo-hiya.** Kharkyiv. Экспериментальна та клінична рентгенологія. *Éksp. klȳn. Renthen.* [1931–]

17590 **Éksperȳmental'na medȳtsȳna.** Kharkiv. Экспериментальна медицина. *Éksp. Med., Kharkiv* [1935–] **L.**мa. 37–41 imp.; тd. 35 imp.

17591 **Éksperȳmental'na medȳtsȳna.** Kȳyiv. Экспериментальна медицина. *Éksp. Med., Kȳyiv.*

17591° **Ekspres informacja.** Poznań. *Ekspres Inf.* **G.**мe. (1 уг); **Sil.** 60–.

17592 **Ékspress-informatsiya.** Moskva. Экспресс-информация.

Issued in separate subject groups:

Astronavtika i raketodinamika. Астронавтика и ракетодинамика. *Ékspress-Inf. Astronav. Raketodinam.*

Atomnaya énergiya. Атомная энергия. *Ékspress-Inf. atom. Énerg.*

Avtomaticheskie linii i metallorezhushchie stanki. Автоматические линии и металлорежущие станки. *Ékspress-Inf. avtom. Linii metallorezh. Stanki*

Avtomobil'nȳĭ transport. Автомобильный транспорт. *Ékspress-Inf. avto. Transp.*

Chernaya metallurgiya. Черная металлургия. *Ékspress-Inf. chern. Metall.* [1958–] **L.**i.

Detali mashin. Детали машин. *Ékspress-Inf. Detali Mash.*

Élektricheskie mashinȳ i apparatȳ. Электрические машины и аппараты. *Ékspress-Inf. élekt. Mash. Appar.*

Élektricheskie stantsii, seti i sistemȳ. Электрические станции, сети и системы. *Ékspress-Inf. élekt. Sta. Seti Sist.*

Élektronika. Электроника. *Ékspress-Inf. Élektron.*

Fizika i tekhnika plazmȳ. Физика и техника плазмы. *Ékspress-Inf. Fiz. Tekh. Plazmȳ*

Foto-kinoapparatura. Nauchnaya i prikladnaya fotografiya. Фото-киноаппаратура. Научная и прикладная фотография. *Ékspress-Inf. Foto-kino-appar.*

Garazhi i garazhnoe oborudovanie. Гаражи и гаражное оборудование. *Ékspress-Inf. Garazhi garazh. Oborud.*

Gidroénergetika. Гидроэнергетика. *Ékspress-Inf. Gidroénerg.*

Gornorudnaya promȳshlennost'. Горнорудная промышленность. *Ékspress-Inf. gornorud. Prom.*

Gorodskoĭ transport. Городской транспорт. *Ékspress-Inf. gorod. Transp.*

Ispȳtatel'nȳe priborȳ i stendȳ. Испытательные приборы и стенды. *Ékspress-Inf. ispȳt. Priborȳ Stendȳ*

Khimiya i pererabotka nefti i gaza. Химия и переработка нефти и газа. *Ékspress-Inf. Khim. Pererab. Nefti Gaza*

Khimiya i tekhnologiya neorganicheskikh veshchestv. Химия и технология неорганических веществ. *Ékspress-Inf. Khim. Tekhnol. neorg. Veshch.*

Kontrol'no-izmeritel'naya tekhnika. Контрольно-измерительная техника. *Ékspress-Inf. kontrol'.-izmer. Tekh.*

Korroziya i zashchita metallov. Коррозия и защита металлов. *Ékspress-Inf. Korroz. Zashch. Metall.*

Metallovedenie i termoobrabotka. Металлове-дение и термообработка. *Ékspress-Inf. Metallov. Termoobrab.* [1958–] **L.**i.

Myasnaya i molochnaya promȳshlennost'. Мясная и молочная промышленность. *Ékspress-Inf. myas. moloch. Prom.*

Neftepromȳslovoe delo. Нефтепромысловое дело. *Ékspress-Inf. nefteprom. Delo*

Organizatsiya perevozok, avtomatika, telemekhanika i svyaz' na zheleznȳkh dorogakh. Организация перевозок, автоматика, телемеханика и связь на железных дорогах. *Ékspress-Inf. Org. Perevoz. Avtom. Telemekh.*

Organizatsiya vozdushnȳkh perevozok i oborudo-vanie aéroportov. Организация воздушных перевозок и оборудование аэропортов. *Ékspress-Inf. Org. vozdush. Perevoz.*

Pishchevaya promȳshlennost'. Пищевая промышленность. *Ékspress-Inf. pishch. Prom.*

Pod"emno-transportnȳe sooruzheniya. Подъёмно-транспортные сооружения. *Ékspress-Inf. pod".-transp. Sooruzh.*

Podvizhnoĭ sostav zheleznȳkh dorog i tyaga poez-dov. Подвижной состав железных дорог и тяга поездов. *Ékspress-Inf. podvizh. Sostav zhelez. Dorog*

Porshnevȳe i gazoturbinnȳe dvigateli. Поршневые и газотурбинные двигатели. *Ékspress-Inf. porsh. gazoturb. Dvigat.*

Pribori i élementȳ avtomatiki. Прибори и элементы автоматики. *Ékspress-Inf. Pribori Élem. Avtom.*

Prokatka i prokatnoe oborudovanie. Прокатка и прокатное оборудование. *Ékspress-Inf. Prokatka prokat. Oborud.*

Promȳshlennȳĭ organicheskiĭ sintez. Промышленный органический синтез. *Ékspress-Inf. prom. org. Sint.* [1960–] **L.**c.

Promȳshlennȳĭ transport. Промышленный транспорт. *Ékspress-Inf. prom. Transp.*

Protsessȳ i apparatȳ khimicheskikh proizvodstv. Процессы и аппараты химических производств. *Ékspress-Inf. Prots. Appar. khim. Proizv.*

Put' i stroitel'stvo zheleznȳkh dorog. Путь и строительство железных дорог. *Ékspress-Inf. Put' Stroit. zhelez. Dorog*

Radiolokatsiya, televidenie, radiosvyaz'. Радиолокация, телевидение, радиосвязь. *Ékspress-Inf. Radiolok. Telev. Radiosv.*

Rezhushchie instrumentȳ. Режущие инструменты. *Ékspress-Inf. rezh. Instrum.*

Rȳbnaya promȳshlennost'. Рыбная промышленность. *Ékspress.-Inf. rȳb. Prom.*

Sel'skokhozyaĭstvennȳe mashinȳ i orudiya. Механизатsiya sel'skokhozyaĭstvennȳkh rabot. Сельскохозяйственные машины и орудия. Механизация сельскохозяйственных работ. *Ékspress-Inf. sel'.-khoz. Mash. Orud.*

Silikatnȳe materialȳ. Силикатные материалы. *Ékspress-Inf. silik. Mater.*

Sinteticheskie vȳsokopolimernȳe materialȳ. Синтетические высокополимерные материалы. *Ékspress-Inf. sint. vȳsokopolim. Mater.*

Sistemȳ avtomaticheskogo upravleniya. Системы автоматического управления. *Ékspress-Inf. Sist. avtom. Uprav.*

Stroitel'stvo i ékspluatatsiya avtomobil'nȳkh dorog. Строительство и эксплуатация автомобильных дорог. *Ékspress-Inf. Stroit. Ékspluat. avto. Dorog* **Ha.**rd. 62–.

Sudostroenie i vodnȳĭ transport. Судостроение и водный транспорт. *Ékspress-Inf. Sudostr. vod. Transp.*

Tara i upakovka. Тара и упаковка. *Ékspress-Inf. Tara Upakovka*

Tekhnologiya i oborudovanie kuznechno-shtampovochnogo proizvodstva. Технология и оборудование кузнечно-штамповочного производства. *Ékpress-Inf. Tekhnol. Oborud. kuzn.-shtampov. Proiz.*

Tekhnologiya i oborudovanie liteĭnogo proizvodstva. Технология и оборудование литейного производства. *Ékspress-Inf. Tekhnol. Oborud. liteĭn. Proiz.* [1958–] **L.**I.

Tekhnologiya i oborudovanie mekhano-sborochnogo proizvodstva. Технология и оборудование механо-сборочного производства. *Ékspress-Inf. Tekhnol. Oborud. mekh.-sboroch. Proiz.*

Tekstil'naya i trikotazhnaya promȳshlennost'. Текстильная и трикотажная промышленность. *Ékspress-Inf. tekst. trikot. Prom.*

Teploénergetika. Теплоэнергетика. *Ékspress-Inf. Teploénerg.*

Traktorostroenie. Тракторостроение. *Ékspress-Inf. Traktorostr.*

Transport i khranenie nefti i gaza. Транспорт и хранение нефти и газа. *Ékspress-Inf. Transp. Khran. Nefti Gaza*

Transportnȳe samoletȳ, vertoletȳ i ikh obsluzhivanie. Транспортные самолеты, вертолеты и их обслуживание. *Ékspress-Inf. transp. Samol. Vertol. Obsluzh.*

Tsellyulozno-bumazhnaya promȳshlennost'. Целлюлозно-бумажная промышленность. *Ékspress-Inf. tsell.-bumazh. Prom.*

Tsvetnaya metallurgiya. Цветная металлургия. *Ékspress-Inf. tsvet. Metall.*

Ugol'naya promȳshlennost'. Угольная промышленность. *Ékspress-Inf. ugol'. Prom.*

Vȳchislitel'naya tekhnika. Вычислительная техника. *Ékspress-Inf. vȳchisl. Tekh.*

17593 **Elarc Jahrbuch.** Hannover. *Elarc Jb.* **L.**P. 32.

Elastomer Notebook. E.I. Du Pont de Nemours. Wilmington. *See* 17277.

Elastomers Review. E.I. Du Pont de Nemours. Wilmington. *See* 17277°.

17596 **Elder Dempster Magazine.** London. *Elder Dempster Mag.* [1922–29] **L.**BM.; **O.**B. [*C. as:* 17597]

17597 **Elders Review** of **West African Affairs.** Liverpool. *Elders Rev. W. Afr. Aff.* [1929–31] **L.**BM.; **O.**B. [*C. of:* 17596; *C. as:* 17598]

17598 **Elders West African Review.** Liverpool. *Elders W. Afr. Rev.* [1931–] **L.**BM.; **O.**B. [*C. of:* 17597; *C. as:* 57355]

17598° **Electra.** Conférence internationale des grands réseaux électriques. Paris. *Electra* [1931–] **Y.**

17599 **Electragist.** Utica, N.Y. *Electragist* [1923–28] [*C. of:* 34109; *C. as:* 17641]

17600 **Électric.** Paris. *Électric*

17601 **Electric Accumulator.** London. *Elect. Accum.* [1906–08] **L.**BM.; C.; P.; SC. 06; **O.**R.

17602 **Electric Club Journal.** Pittsburg. *Elect. Club J.* [1904–05] **L.**EE.; **Br.**U.; **G.**M.; **M.**P.; U.; **Sw.**U. [*C. as:* 17608]

17603 **Electric Dehydrator.** Los Angeles. *Elect. Dehydr.* [1931–39] **L.**P. 38–39.

17604 **Electric Field.** London. *Elect. Fld* **L.**BM. 23–.

17605 **Electric Heat.** London. *Elect. Heat* [1934–38] **L.**P.

17606 **Electric Heat** and **Air conditioning.** Baltimore. *Elect. Heat Air Condit.* [1955–] **Y.**

17607 **Electric Heat** in **Industry.** Boston. *Elect. Heat Ind.* [*C. as:* 17463]

17608 **Electric Journal.** Pittsburg, London. *Elect. J.* [1905–39] **L.**BM. 09–39; EE.; P. 10–39; **Bm.**T. 08–18; **Br.**U.; **Db.** 13–39; **G.**M. 05–19; **Ld.**U. 30–39; **Lv.**U. 13–39 imp.; **M.**P. 05–20; T. 06–39; U.; **Nw.**A. 09–39 imp.; **Sw.**U. 05–13. [*C. of:* 17602; *C. as:* 57448]

17609 **Electric Light** and **Power.** Chicago. *Elect. Lt Pwr, Chicago* [1923–] **L.**P. 54–; **Y.**

17610 **Electric Light** and **Power.** London. *Elect. Lt Pwr, Lond.* [1904–07] **L.**BM.; **O.**R.

17611 **Electric Lighting.** London. *Elect. Ltg* [1958–] **L.**BM.; P. (curr.); **Y.**

17612 **Electric Medical College Bulletin.** Cincinnati. *Elect. med. Coll. Bull.*

17612ᵃ **Electric Power.** Tokyo. *Elect. Pwr, Tokyo* **Y.**

17612ᵇ **Electric Power Bulletin.** Economic Commission for Asia and the Far East. New York. *Elect. Pwr Bull.* **L.**BM. 53–.

17612ᶜ **Electric Railway.** London. *Elect. Rly* [1946–55] **L.**BM. [*C. as:* 17616ᶜ]

17613 **Electric Railway Bus** and **Tramway Journal.** London. *Elect. Rly Bus Tramw. J.* [1928–36] **L.**BM.; EE.; P.; **Abs.**N.; **E.**A.; **G.**E.; M.; **O.**R.; **Sh.**P. [*C. of:* 17618; *C. as:* 37186]

17614 **Electric Railway Journal.** New York. *Elect. Rly J.* [1908–31] **L.**EE.; P. 10–31; SC.; **Bm.**P.; **G.**T.; **Ld.**U. 20–21; **Lv.**U. imp.; **M.**T. [*C. of:* 17616 and 51007, *C. as:* 54103]

17615 **Electric Railway Journal News.** New York. *Elect. Rly J. News* **Bm.**P. 29–31*. [*C. as:* 54104]

17616 **Electric Railway Review.** Chicago. *Elect. Rly Rev.* [1906–08] **L.**P. [*C. of:* 51008; *C. in:* 17614]

17616ᶜ **Electric Railway Society Journal.** Sidcup. *Elect. Rly Soc. J.* [1956–] **L.**BM.; P. (curr.); SC.; **Y.** [*C. of:* 17612ᶜ]

17617 **Electric Railway Traction.** London. *Elect. Rly Tractn* [1939–] **L.**SC. 39–40; **M.**T. 39–40. [1935–38 issued as supplement to 41912]

17618 **Electric Railway** and **Tramway Journal.** London. *Elect. Rly Tramw. J.* [1914–28] **L.**BM.; EE.; P.; **Abs.**N.; **E.**A.; **G.**E.; M.; **O.**B.; **Sh.**P. [*C. of:* 28579; *C. as:* 17613]

17619 **Electric Refrigeration News.** Detroit. *Elect. Refrig. News* [1926–36] [*C. as:* 1532]

17620 **Electric Technology USSR.** New York, London. *Elect. Technol. USSR* [1958–] **L.**BM.; P.; QM.; UC.; **G.**T.; U. 58–; **Lv.**P. 60–; **M.**U.; **O.**R. 59–; **Sw.**U.; **Y.** [*English translation of selections from:* 17805]

17621 **Electric Tool User.** London. *Elect. Tool User* [1936–] **L.**BM. 51–; P. imp. [*Suspended* 1942–48]

17622 **Electric Traction.** Chicago. *Elect. Tractn* [1912–32] **L.**P. 24–31. [*C. of:* 17624; *C. as:* 17623]

17623 **Electric Traction** and **Bus Journal.** Chicago. *Elect. Tractn Bus J.* [1932–35] [*C. of:* 17622; *C. as:* 29531]

    Electric Traction on the **Railways.** *See* 10149.

17624 **Electric Traction Weekly.** Cleveland. *Elect. Tractn Wkly* [1906–12] [*C. as:* 17622]

17625 **Electric Vehicle.** London. *Elect. Veh.* [1914–30] **L.**BM.; EE. 22–24 imp.; P.; **Abs.**N. 17–30; **C.**UL. 14–29; **M.**P. 19–30; **O.**R. [*C. as:* 17628]

17626 **Electric Vehicles.** Chicago. *Elect. Vehs, Chicago* [1913–18] **L.**P. [*C. of:* 22747]

17627 **Electric Vehicles.** London. *Elect. Vehs, Lond.* [1936–] **L.**BM.; EE.; P.; **Abs.**N.; **C.**UL.; **Li.**M. 46–49; **M.**P. 36–52; **O.**R.; **Y.** [*C. of:* 17628; *not published in* 1953]

17628 **Electric Vehicles** and **Batteries.** London. *Elect. Vehs Batt.* [1930–36] **L.**BM.; EE. 32–36; P.; **Abs.**N.; **C.**UL.; **M.**P.; **O.**R. [*C. of:* 17625; *C. as:* 17627]

17629 **Electric Welding.** Cleveland. *Elect. Weld., Cleveland* [1930–33] [*C. as:* 23385]

17630 **Electric Welding.** London. *Elect. Weld., Lond.* [1931–40] **L.**BM.; EE.; NF.; P.; SC.; **Bm.**P.; U.; **G.**M.

17631 **Electrica.** Stockholm. *Electrica* [1927–32] **L.**EE. 27–31 imp.; P.

    Electrical Accidents and their **Causes.** London. *See* 43577.

17632 **Electrical Age.** London. *Electl Age, Lond.* [1932–] **L.**EE.; H. 49–; P.; RI. (curr.); **Bm.**P.; **Br.**P. (1 yr); **E.**T. 54–; **G.**M. 36–40: 49–; **M.**P.; **O.**R.; **Y.** [*C. of:* 17634]

17633 **Electrical Age.** New York. *Electl Age, N.Y.*

17634 **Electrical Age** for **Women.** London. *Electl Age Wom.* [1926–31] **L.**BM.; EE. 30–31 imp.; P.; **M.**P.; **O.**R. [*C. as:* 17632]

17635 **Electrical Bulletin.** London. *Electl Bull.* [1906–09] **L.**BM.; EE. 06–08; **O.**R.

17636 **Electrical Canada.** Toronto. *Electl Can.*

17637 **Electrical Communication.** International Telephone and Telegraph Company. New York. *Electl Commun.* [1922–] **L.**AV. 36–; BM. 27–; EE.; NF. 40–; P.; QM. 48–; RI. (curr.); SC. 62–; SI. 44–; **Bm.**T. 56–; **Bn.**U. 24– imp.; **Br.**U.; **C.**ENG. 40–; **Co.**T. 37–; **Dn.**U. 52–; **E.**U.; **Ex.**U. 40–; **F.**A. 31–50; **G.**N. 26–40 imp.; U. 23– imp.; **Ld.**U. 24–; **Lv.**P. 54– imp.; **Ma.**T. 33– imp.; **N.**U. 57–; **Nw.**A. 27–39: 48–; **R.**U. 48–; **Sa.**; **Sh.**SC. 49–; **Sw.**U. 25–26; **Y.**

17638 **Electrical Communication Laboratory Reports.** Nippon Telegraph and Telephone Public Corporation. Tokyo. *Electl Commun. Lab. Rep., Tokyo* [1953–59] **L.**DI.; EE. imp.; P.; PL. 56–59; **Lv.**P. 56–59; **Y.** [*Replaces:* 17369; *C. as:* 46201]

17639 **Electrical Communication Laboratory Technical Journal.** Nippon Telegraph and Telephone Public Corporation. Tokyo. *Electl Commun. Lab. tech. J., Tokyo* [1952–53] **L.**QM.; **Y.** [*Replaced by:* 17638]

17639° **Electrical Communications.** Washington. *Electl Communs* **Y.** 57–. [*English abstracts of:* 17869]

17640 **Electrical Construction** and **Maintenance.** New York, etc. *Electl Constr. Maint.* [1947–] **L.**BM.; P. 58–; **Lv.**P. 59–; **M.**P. 56–; **Y.** [*C. of:* 17641]

17641 **Electrical Contracting.** Utica, N.Y. *Electl Contracting* [1928–47] **L.**BM. 35–47; SC. 37–47; **Y.** [*C. of:* 17599; *C. as:* 17640]

17642 **Electrical Contractor.** London. *Electl Contractor* [1903–] **L.**BM.; EE. 22– imp.; **O.**R.; **Y.**

17643 **Electrical Contractor-Dealer.** Utica, N.Y. *Electl Contractor-Dlr* [1918–21] [*C. of:* 34111; *C. as:* 34109]

17644 **Electrical Contractors Year Book.** London. *Electl Contractors Yb.* **M.**P. 25– imp.; **Y.**

17645 **Electrical Design News.** Chicago. *Electl Des. News* [1956–] **L.**P. 57–.

17646 **Electrical Digest.** Toronto. *Electl Dig.* [1932–]

17647 **Electrical Distribution.** London. *Electl Distrib.* [1960–] **L.**AV.; BM.; EE.; P.; **Br.**U.; **C.**ENG.; **Co.**T.; **Ld.**P. (5 yr.); **Lv.**P.; **N.**U.; **Nw.**A.; **Sy.**R.; **Y.** [*C. of:* 17033]

    Electrical and **Electronic Insulation.** Lake Forest, Ill. *See* 23749.

17648 **Electrical Energy.** London. *Electl Energy* [1956–59] **L.**AV.; EE.; KC.; P.; QM.; SI.; **Br.**U.; **C.**UL.; **Co.**T.; **Dn.**U.; **E.**HW.; T. 58–59; **F.**A.; **G.**T.; U.; **Ld.**U.; **Lv.**P.; **M.**P.; T.; **N.**T. 56–58; U.; **O.**R.; **Sil.**; **Y.**

17649 **Electrical Engineer.** London. *Electl Engr, Lond.* [1883–12] **L.**BM.; C. 88–12 imp.; EE. 88–12; P. 10–12; SC. 88–11; UC. 88–12; **Bm.**P. 98–08; T. 98–09; U. 88–12; **Cr.**U. 88–12; **Db.**; **E.**A. 88–12; R. 88–12 imp.; T. 98–12 imp.; **G.**M. 92–12; U. 88–09; **Lv.**U. 88–12; **M.**P. 93–09; T. 00–11; U. 90–08; **Nw.**A. 88–11 imp.; **O.**B.; **Y.**

17650 **Electrical Engineer.** Manchester, etc. *Electl Engr, Manchr* [1935–] **L.**P. 36–41; SC.; **Abs.**N.; **Bn.**U. 35–39 imp.; **M.**P. 35–41: 57–; **O.**R. 35–37; **Y.**

17651 **Electrical Engineer** of **Australia** and **New Zealand.** Melbourne. *Electl Engr Aust. N. Z.* [1924–31] **L.**P. 27–31; SC. 25–31. [*C. as:* 17652]

17652 **Electrical Engineer** (and **Merchandiser**). Melbourne. *Electl Engr Merch.* [1931–] **L.**I. (curr.); P.; **Y.** [*C. of:* 17651]

17653 **Electrical Engineering.** Chicago. *Electl Engng, Chicago*

17654 **Electrical Engineering.** London. *Electl Engng, Lond.* [1907–16] **L.**BM.; EE.; P.; SC. imp.; UC. 12–16; **Abs.**N. 12–16; **Bm.**U. 07–14; **Cr.**P. 07–08; **Db.** 07–12 imp.; **E.**T. 12–16; **G.**M.; **Lv.**U. 07–15; **M.**T.; **O.**B.

17655 **Electrical Engineering.** American Institute of Electrical Engineers. New York, etc. *Electl Engng, N.Y.* [1931–] **L.**AV. 43–; P.; QM. imp.; SC.; SI. 47–; **Bl.**U. 47–59; **Bm.**P. 36–; T.; U.; **Bn.**U. 34– imp.; **Br.**U.; **C.**ENG. 39–; P. 34–; UL.; **Co.**T. 60–; **Db.**; **Dn.**U. 34–; **F.**HW. 36–; R.; **F.**A.; **G.**T.; U.; **Lc.**A. 55–; **Ld.**U. 38–; W. 49–; **M.**P.; T.; U. 31–52; **Ma.**T. 34–41: 43–; **N.**U. 35–; **Nw.**A.; P. 53–; **O.**R. 48–; **Sh.**SC.; **Y.** [*C. of:* 25516]

    Electrical Engineering Abstracts. *See* 48992.

17656 **Electrical Engineers' Club Journal.** King's College, Newcastle-upon-Tyne. *Electl Engrs' Club J. King's Coll. Newcastle* [1938–] **Ld.**U.

17657 **Electrical Equipment.** New York. *Electl Equip.* **L.**HQ. 61–; **G.**ME. (1 yr); **Y.**

17658 **Electrical Experimenter.** New York. *Electl Expr* [1913–20] **L.**BM. 19–20. [*C. as:* 49041]

17659 **Electrical Field.** London. *Electl Fld* [1908–11] **L.**BM.; P.; **G.**M. 09–11; **O.**R.

17660 **Electrical Industries.** London. *Electl Inds* [1901–53] **L.**BM. 05–53; EE. 34–53 imp.; NF. 25–53; P. 27–53; **Abs.**N. 17–53; **Br.**P. (1 yr); **E.**A. 12–53; **Ld.**U. 27–53; **Nw.**A. 03–34 imp.; **O.**B. 01–06: 12–53; **Y.** [*C. as:* 17661]

17661 **Electrical Industries Export.** London. *Electl Inds Export* [1954–] **L.**AV.; BM.; EE.; NF.; P.; **Abs.**N.; **Br.**P. (1 yr); **E.**A.; **Ld.**U.; **O.**B.; **Y.** [*C. of:* 17660]

Electrical Industries and **Investments.** *See* 17660.

Electrical Industry Bulletin. Moscow. *See* 56438.

17662 **Electrical Journal.** London. *Electl J.* [1952–] **L.**AV.; BM.; EE.; NF.; QM. 52–56; P.; RI.; SC.; UC.; **Abs.**N.; P.; **Bm.**P.; T.; **Bn.**U.; **Br.**U.; **Bra.**P.; **C.**P.; UL.; **Db.**; **Dn.**U.; **E.**A.; F.; U.; **F.**A.; **G.**M.; T.; U.; **Ld.**P.; U. 52–54; **Lv.**P.; U.; **M.**P.; T. (5 yr.); U.; **Ma.**T.; **Nw.**A.; P.; **O.**B.; **Sh.**IO.; SC.; **Sy.**R. (1 yr); **Y.** [*C. of:* 17688; –61* incorporated in:* 17676]

17662° **Electrical Machinery** and **Apparatus.** British Thomson-Houston Co. Rugby. *Electl Mach. Appar.* [1950–] **L.**BM.

17663 **Electrical Magazine** and **Engineering Monthly.** London. *Electl Mag. Engng Mon.* [1904–10] **L.**BM.; EE.; P.; **Bm.**U. 04; **C.**UL.; **Db.**; **Dn.**U. 04–08; **E.**A.; **O.**R.

17663° **Electrical Manufacturer.** London. *Electl Mfr* [1945–] **L.**EE. 56–; P. 46–; SI. 55–; **E.**A. 56–; **F.**A. 51–57; **O.**R.; **Y.**

17664 **Electrical Manufacturing.** New York. *Electl Mfg* [1928–60] **L.**EE. 56–60; P. 51–60; SC. 39–41: 45–60; **Te.**N. 57–60; **Y.** [*C. as:* 17792]

17665 **Electrical and Mechanical Engineering Transactions. Institution** of **Engineers, Australia.** Sydney. *Electl mech. Engng Trans. Instn Engrs Aust.* [1959–] **L.**AV.; BM.; I.; NF.; P.; UC.; **Bm.**C.; **Br.**U.; **C.**RI.; **G.**E.; **Lv.**P.; **Nw.**A.; **Sh.**M.; **Y.** [*C. from:* 26222]

17666 **Electrical Mining.** Chicago. *Electl Min.* [1904–28] **L.**P. imp.

17667 **Electrical News.** Toronto. *Electl News* [1910–28] [*C. of:* 13137; *C. as:* 17668]

17668 **Electrical News** and **Engineering.** Toronto. *Electl News Engng* [1929–] **L.**EE. 35– imp.; **Y.** [*C. of:* 17667]

17669 **Electrical Patents, Reissues, Trade-marks,** and **Designs.** Washington. *Electl Pat., Wash.* **L.**P. 99–00.

17670 **Electrical Power.** London. *Electl Pwr* [1902–05] **L.**BM.; **O.**R. 03–05.

17671 **Electrical Power Engineer.** Manchester, London. *Electl Pwr Engr* [1919–] **L.**BM.; P. 25–; **Bm.**U. 26–; **Ld.**P. (5 yr.); **M.**P. 22–; **Sh.**P. (5 yr.); **Y.**

17672 **Electrical and Power Plant Register.** London. *Electl Pwr Pl. Regist.* **Abd.**T. 48–53; **Sy.**R. 43–.

17673 **Electrical Progress** and **Monthly Register.** London. *Electl Prog.* **L.**BM. 06–15; P. 99–12; **Abs.**N. 12–16 imp.; **O.**R. 97–15.

17674 **Electrical Record.** Johannesburg. *Electl Rec., Johannesb.* [1946–] **L.**BM. [*Supplement to:* 18075]

17675 **Electrical Record.** New York. *Electl Rec., N.Y.* [1907–32]

Electrical Review. Belgrade. *See* 17865.
Electrical Review. Chicago. *See* 17677.

17676 **Electrical Review.** London. *Electl Rev., Lond.* [1872–] **L.**AV. 42–; BM.; EE.; I. (6 mo.); IC. 39–; NF.; P. 10–; QM. 48–; RA. 22–32; RI. 72–31; SC.; U. 92–03; UC. 38–; **Abs.**N. 12–; U. 86–88; **Bl.**U. 72–92: 59–; **Bm.**C. 15–; P.; T. 97–46: 52–56 imp.; U. 78–81: 19–; **C.**UL. 82–; **Cr.**P. 15–18; U. 91–18; **Db.**; **Dn.**U. 60–; **E.**A.; CE. 57–; P. 88–08; T. 02–04 imp.; U. 76–20; **F.**A. 48–; **G.**M. 78–; T. (2 yr.); U. 84–; **Ld.**P. (5 yr.); U. 72–51 v. imp.; **Li.**M. (1 yr); **Lv.**P. 83–95: 04–; U. 72–13 imp.; **M.**C. (1 yr); P. 94–; U. 92–28 imp.; **Ma.**T. 59–; **O.**B. 92–; **Rn.**B. (1 yr); **Sh.**IO. 51–; SC. 21–; **Ste.** 96–; **Sw.**U. 10–37; **Sy.**R. 82–; **Wd.** 42–; **Y.**

17677 **Electrical Review** and **Industrial Engineer.** Chicago. *Electl Rev. ind. Engr* [1883–22] **L.**EE.; P. 10–22; **Bm.**U. 03–06; **M.**T. 06–13. [*C. as:* 23192]

Electrical Review and **Western Electrician.** *See* 17677.

Electrical Service. Zürich. *See* 17827.

17678 **Electrical Specifications.** New York. *Electl Specif.*

17679 **Electrical Storage.** London. *Electl Stor.* [1932–36] **L.**EE.; P.; **Bm.**U.; **C.**UL.; **Ld.**U.; **Nw.**A. 32–34; **O.**R.; **Sh.**U.

17680 **Electrical Supervisor.** London. *Electl Superv.* [1932–] **L.**BA.; BM.; EE.; P.; **Br.**P. (1 yr); **C.**UL. 35–; **E.**A. 57–; **Ld.**P. (5 yr.); **Lv.**P. 47–; **M.**P.; **O.**R. 57–; **Sh.**P. (5 yr.); **Y.** [*C. of:* 15540]

17681 **Electrical Times.** London. *Electl Times* [1902–] **L.**AV. 42–; BM.; EE.; H. 49–; I. (6 mo.); P. 10–; SC. 26–; U. 50–; UC. 04–31; **Abs.**N. 12–; **Bm.**P.; T. 51– imp.; U. 30–; **Br.**P. (1 yr); **C.**UL. 48–; **Cr.**I. 51–; **E.**A.; **G.**M.; T. (1 yr); **Ld.**P. (5 yr.); **Lv.**P. 13– imp.; **M.**P. 02–06: 32–; **N.**T. (5 yr.); **Nw.**A. 02–39; **Sh.**IO. 06: 09: 12: 20–; **Sil.** 45–; **Y.** [*C. of:* 28593]

17682 **Electrical Trades.** London. *Electl Trades* **L.**MT. 24–.

17683 **Electrical Translators' Bulletin.** *Electl Transl. Bull.* [1955–] **Br.**U.

17684 **Electrical Weekly.** Sydney. *Electl Wkly* [1953–] **L.**EE. 53–56 imp. [*C. of:* 41788]

17685 **Electrical World.** New York. *Electl Wld* [1887–] **L.**EE.; P. 10–; QM. 07–38 imp.; SC. 99–; U. 89–01; **Bm.**T. 91–; T. 91–31; U. 05–; **C.**ENG. 99–; **Db.** 01–22; **G.**U. 02–13; **Ld.**U. 28–54; **Lv.**P. 25–29 imp.: 46–47: 56–; U. 97–; **M.**P. 96–41; T. 06–; U. 21–25; **Nw.**A. 96–34 imp.; **Sh.**SC. 21–35; **Y.**

Electrical World and **Electrical Engineer.** *See* 17685.

Electrical World and **Engineer.** *See* 17685.

17686 **Electrical World** and **Record.** London. *Electl Wld Rec.* [1908–09] **L.**P.; **O.**B.

17687 **Electrical Year Book.** London. *Electl Yb.* [1908–] **L.**P. 52: 56–; **E.**T. 48; **G.**M. 16– imp.; **M.**P. 32–; **O.**B. 38–46; **Y.**

17688 **Electrician.** London. *Electrician* [1878–52] **L.**AV. 99–52 imp.; BM.; EE.; NF. 28–52; P.; RI.; SC.; UC. 42–52; **Abs.**N. 20–52; P. 94–52; U. 90–94; **Bm.**P.; T. 81–52; **Bn.**U. 89–52 imp.; **Br.**U. 90–52; **Bra.**P. 09–52; **C.**P. 94–52; UL. 86–52; **Cr.**U. 81–49; **Db.** 80–52; **Dn.**U. 83–52; **E.**A.; F. 81–52; R. 87–17; T. 78–08 imp.; U. 01–52; **F.**A. 46–52; **G.**M. 81–52; T. 81–52; U. 87–52; **Ld.**P. 82–52; U. 85–52; **Lv.**P. 81–52 imp.; U. 81–52; **M.**P. 82–52; T. 95–50; U. imp.; **Ma.**T. 37–52; **N.**U. 16–19; **Nw.**A.; P.; **O.**B. 91–52; ED. 88–07; R. 78–01; **Sh.**IO. 91–52; SC. 95–52; **Ste.** 14–31; **Sw.**U. 26–44; **Sy.**R. 29–52; **Y.** [*C. as:* 17662]

17689 **'Electrician' Annual Tables** of **Electricity Undertakings.** London. *'Electrician' a. Tabl.* **L.**BM. 18–50*; EE. 98–50; P. (curr.); **Abs.**N. 21–50; **Bm.**P. 34–50: **Lv.**P. 36–50; **M.**P. 31–50; **O.**B. 21–25; **Sh.**P. 25–50. [*C. as:* 17690]

17690 **'Electrician' Red Book.** Electricity Undertakings of the World. *'Electrician' red Bk* [1951–] **L.**BM.; EE.; P. (curr.); **Abs.**N.; **Bm.**P.; **Lv.**P.; **M.**P.; **Sh.**P. [*C. of:* 17689]

17691 **Electricidad** y **mecánica.** Valencia. *Electd Mec.*

17692 **Electricidade** e **mecánica.** Lisboa. *Electde Mec.*

17693 **Électricien.** Paris. *Électricien* [1881–] **L.**BM.; EE. 91–42; P. 10–42: 47–; **Db.** 09–; **Y.**

17694 **Electricista.** Madrid. *Electricista*

17695 **Électricité.** Paris. *Électricité* [1934–58] **L.**EE. 34–36: 46–58; P.; **Ld.**U. 46–47; **Lv.**P. 53–58; **N.**U. 53–58; **Sh.**SC.; **Y.** [*C. from:* 49032; *C. in:* 47242]

17695ᵃ **Électricité.** Revue mensuelle des inventions électriques. Paris. *Électricité, Revue mens. Invent. élect.*

17695ᶜ **Électricité.** **Société hydro-électrique** des **Basses-Pyrénées.** Paris. *Électricité, Soc. hydro-élect. Basses-Pyrén.*

17996 **Électricité automobile.** Paris. *Élect. auto.* [1947–] **L.**P. 57–.

17696ᶜ **Électricité belge.** Anvers. *Élect. belge*

17697 **Électricité industrielle** et **commerciale.** Paris. *Élect. ind. comm.*

17698 **Électricité** et **mécanique.** Revue périodique publiée par la compagnie française Thomson-Houston. Paris. *Élect. Méc.* [1924–28] **L.**P. [*C. as:* 47155]

17699 **Électricité médicale.** Tours, Paris. *Élect. méd.*

17700 **Électricité médicale lyonnaise.** Lyon. *Élect. méd. lyonn.*

17701 **Électricité médicale** du **Sud-Est.** Grenoble. *Élect. méd. S.-E.*

17702 **Electricity.** Washington. *Electricity, Wash.* **Y.** 57–. [*English abstracts of:* 17805]

17703 **Electricity.** London. *Electricity, Lond.* [1890–07] **L.**BM.; EE.; **Db.** 90–96; **G.**M. 01–07; **O.**B. 90–96. [*C. as:* 17707]

17704 **Electricity.** New York. *Electricity, N.Y.* [1891–06] **L.**BM. 97–06; EE.; P.; **Bm.**U. 00–06.

17705 **Electricity.** Electricity Council. London. *Electricity, Electy Coun.* [1947–] **L.**EE.; P.; SC.; **Bl.**U. 62–; **Co.**T. (curr.); **Cr.**I. 54–; **Lv.**P. 54–; **N.**T. (5 yr.); **Nw.**A. 54–; **Sy.**R.

17706 **Electricity.** British Electricity Authority. London. *Electricity, Br. Electy Auth.* [1955–] **L.**BM.; EE.; QM.; **Ld.**U. 54–55; **N.**T. (5 yr.); **Sw.**U. 54–55; **Y.** [*C. of:* 8800]

17707 **Electricity** and **Electrical Engineering.** London. *Electy electl Engng* [1908–29] **L.**BM.; EE.; P. 10–29. [*C. of:* 17703]

17708 **Electricity** and **Engineering.** Chicago. *Electy Engng*

17709 **Electricity** on the **Farm.** New York. *Electy Fm* [1927–] **L.**P. 27–48; **Y.**

17710 **Electricity** in **Industry.** Lancashire Dynamo Group. London. *Electy Ind.* [1953–] **L.**BM.; EE.; P.; QM.

17710ᶜ **Electricity** and **Productivity Series.** British Electrical Development Association. London. *Electy Prod. Ser.* [1953–] **L.**BM.; **Ld.**P.; **Y.**

17711 **Electrics.** London. *Electrics* [1905–] **L.**BM.; **Abs.**N. 16–; **Bm.**U. 05–06 imp.; **Nw.**A. 22–31 imp.; **O.**R. 05–34.

       Electrification of **Agriculture.** Moscow. *See* 17810.

17712 **Electrified Production.** London. *Electd Prod.* **L.**P. (curr.)

17713 **Électrique.** Paris. *Électrique*
       Électrique. Zürich. *See* 17827.

17714 **Électro.** Bruxelles. *Électro*

17715 **Électro Magazine.** Paris. *Électro Mag.* **L.**EE. 53–55.

17715ᶜ **Electro Technology.** Bangalore. *Electro Technol.* **Y.**

17715ᵉ **Électroacoustique.** Liège. *Électroacoustique* [1959–] **Y.**
       Electrochemical Industry. *See* 17716.

17716 **Electrochemical** and **Metallurgical Industry.** New York. *Electrochem. metall. Ind.* [1902–09] **L.**C. 06–08 imp.; EE. 06–09; I.; IC.; NF.; P.; SC.; **Bm.**T.; U. 06–09; **Cr.**U. 06–09 imp.; **E.**U. 06–09; **Ex.**U. 02–08; **Lv.**U.; **M.**T.; U.; **Ste.**; **Wd.** [*C. as:* 31474]

17717 **Electrochemical Review.** Manchester. *Electrochem. Rev.* [1900] **L.**BM.; P.; **O.**B.

17718 **Electro-Chemist** and **Metallurgist.** London. *Electro-Chem. Metall.* [1901–04] **L.**BM.; C. imp.; EE.; I.; P.; **Bm.**U.; **C.**UL. 03–04; **Db.** 04; **E.**A. imp.; **G.**U. 03–04; **M.**U. 03–04; **O.**B.

17719 **Electrochimica acta.** Oxford. *Electrochim. Acta* [1959–] **L.**BM.; C.; P.; SC.; **G.**U.; **O.**R.; **Sh.**SC.; **Wd.**; **Y.**

17720 **Électrochimie.** Paris. *Électrochimie* **L.**P. 95–06.

17721 **Électrocorrespondance.** Zurich. *Électrocorrespondance* [*For the German edition, see* 17844]

17722 **Electrocraft.** Detroit. *Electrocraft*

17723 **Électroculture.** Abbeville. *Électroculture, Abbeville*

17724 **Électroculture.** Paris. *Électroculture, Paris* **L.**P. 13–14. [*Supplement to:* 20898]

17725 **Électrode.** Sécheron. *Électrode* **L.**P. (curr.); **Y.**

17726 **Electrodepositors Technical Bulletin.** *Electrodep. tech. Bull.* **O.**R. 40–.

17727 **Électro-documentation.** Bruxelles. *Électro-Docum.* [1935–]

17728 **Electroencephalography** and **Clinical Neurophysiology.** Montreal. *Electroenceph. clin. Neurophysiol.* [1949–] **L.**MA.; MC. 58–; MD.; S.; U.; UC.; **Abd.**U.; **Bl.**U. imp.; **Bm.**U.; **Br.**U.; **C.**APH. 60–; PH.; **Dn.**U. 54–; **E.**U.; **G.**U.; **H.**U. 59–; **Ld.**U.; **M.**MS.; **Nw.**A.; **O.**R.; **Y.** [*Also supplements*]

17729 **Electro-Farming.** London. *Electro-Fmg* [1925–28] **L.**AM.; BM.; EE. 25–27; P.; **Abs.**N.; **E.**A.; **Ld.**U.; **O.**R.; **Sil.** [*C. as:* 48278]

17730 **Electro-homeopathia.** Lisboa. *Electro-Homeop., Lisb.*

17731 **Electro-Industry.** London. *Electro-Ind.* **L.**P. 49.

17732 **Électro-journal** et **mécanic-revue.** Paris. *Électro-J. Méc.-Revue*

17733 **Électrologie médicale.** Paris. *Électrol. méd.*

17734 **Electromechanical Design.** Components and Systems. West Newton. *Electromech. Des.* [1957–] **Y.**

17735 **Electro-Medical Review.** Holliston, Mass. *Electro-med. Rev.* [1937] **L.**P.

17736 **Electromet Review.** Electro Metallurgical Company. New York. *Electromet Rev.* [1935–] **L.**P. 35–58.

17737 **Electrometallurgy.** London. *Electrometallurgy* [1930] **L.**BM.; **Abs.**N.; **Sh.**IO.

17738 **Electron.** Madrid. *Electron, Madrid*

17739 **Electron.** Rotterdam. *Electron, Rotterdam* [1946–50] [*C. as:* 17852]

17740 **Electron.** Stafford. *Electron, Stafford* [1908–09] **Bm.**U.; **Ld.**U.; **O.**R.

17741 **Electron Microscopy Abstracts.** London. *Electron Microsc. Abstr.* [1949–60] **L.**AV. 56–60; **Ld.**U.; **M.**C. 49–58; D. [*Reprinted from:* 26821]

17742 **Electronews.** Karachi. *Electronews* [1947–]

17743 **Electronic Age.** *Electron. Age* **L.**AV. 57– imp.

17744 **Electronic Applications.** Eindhoven. *Electron. Applic.* [1955–] **L.**AV.; EE.; P.; **Co.**T. 61–; **Li.**M. 57–; **Y.** [*C. of:* 17745]

17745 **Electronic Applications Bulletin.** Eindhoven. *Electron. Applic. Bull.* [1948–55] **L.**AV.; EE. 51–55; P.; **Y.** [*C. of:* 32062; *C. as:* 17744]
　　Electronic Data Processing. Braunschweig. *See* 17860.

17746 **Electronic Design.** New York. *Electron. Des.* [1953–] **L.**AV. 58– imp.; P. 59–; **Te.**N. 59–; **Y.**

17747 **Electronic Engineering.** London. *Electron. Engng* [1941–] **L.**AV. imp.; BM.; EE.; IC. 45–; MA. 47–; MC. 45–; NF. 45–; NP. 49–; P.; PR. 55–58; QM. 43–; RI. 41–; SC.; SI. 46–; U. 50–; UC. 47–; **Abd.**M. 51–; U. 46–; **Abs.**U. 42– imp.; **Bl.**U. 40– imp.; **Bm.**C. (curr.); P.; T.; U.; **Bn.**U. imp.; **Br.**P. 53–; U. 44–; **Bra.**P. 40–; **C.**APH. 43–; C. 42–; CH. 56–; ENG. 46–; PH. 62–; UL.; **Co.**T. 43–; **Cr.**I. 55–; P. 44–; U. 50–; **Db.** 52–; **Dn.**U. 48–; **E.**A.; HW. 42–; O. 60–; T. 42–; U. 49–; **Ex.**U. 44–; **F.**A. 43–; **Fr.** 47–; **G.**M.; T. 42–; **Hu.**G. 59–; **Lc.**A. 53– imp.; **Ld.**P. 44–; U.; W. 46–; **Lh.**P. 49–; **Li.**M. 47–; **Lo.** 58–; **Lv.**P.; **M.**C. 44–; D.; P.; T. 41–; U. 47–; **Ma.**T.; **Mi.** 59–; **N.**P. 54–; T. 49–; U. 47–; **Nw.**A. imp.; P. 46–; **O.**EP. 47–; **Pl.**M. 48–59; **R.**U. 47–; **Rn.**B. 42–; **Rt.** 56–; **Sa.** 42–; **Sh.**IO. 41–; SC. 46–; **Sil.** 48–; **Ste.** 45–; **Sw.**U. 46–; **Sy.**R. 43–50 imp.: 58–; **Wd.** 42– imp.; **We.**K. 44–; **Wo.** 53–; **Y.** [*C. of:* 17772]

17748 **Electronic Engineering Master Index.** New York. *Electron. Engng Master Index* **L.**P. 45–; SC. 45–47; **Br.**U. 49; **F.**A.; **G.**ME. 45–49.

17749 **Electronic Engineering Monographs.** London *Electron. Engng Monogr.* **L.**BM. 42–.

17750 **Electronic Equipment.** White Plains. *Electron. Equip.* [1953–58] **L.**AV. 57; **Y.** [*C. as:* 17751]

17751 **Electronic Equipment Engineering.** White Plains. *Electron. Equip. Engng* [1959–] **L.**AV. 59– imp.; **Y.** [*C. of:* 17750]

17752 **Electronic Equipment News.** London. *Electron. Equip. News* [1959–] **L.**AV.; BM.; P.; **E.**A.; **O.**R.; **Y.**

17753 **Electronic Guide.** Burbank, Calif. *Electron. Guide* [1959–] **L.**P.

17754 **Electronic Industries.** Philadelphia. *Electron. Inds, Philad.* [1958–] **L.**AV.; EE.; NP. (3 yr.); P.; SI.; **M.**T.; **Ma.**T.; **Y.** [*C. of:* 17757]

17755 **Electronic Industries,** including Industrial Electronics. New York. *Electron. Inds, N.Y.* [1942–46] **L.**AV. 46; EE. 44–46 imp.; P. 46; SC. 46. [*C. as:* 17756 and 52811]

17756 **Electronic Industries** and **Electronic Instrumentation.** New York. *Electron. Inds electron. In-strum.* [1947–48] **L.**AV.; EE. imp.; P.; SI. [*C. from:* 52811 and 17755]

17757 **Electronic Industries** and **Tele-Tech.** New York. *Electron. Inds Tele-Tech* [1956–57] **L.**AV.; EE.; P.; SI. 57; **M.**T.; **Ma.**T.; **Y.** [*C. of:* 52811; *C. as:* 17754]

17758 **Electronic News.** New York. *Electron. News* [1956–] **L.**AV. 58–.

17758ᶜ **Electronic Progress.** *Electron. Prog.* **Y.**

17759 **Electronic** and **Radio Engineer.** London. *Electron. Radio Engr* [1957–59] **L.**AV.; BM.; EE.; IC.; MC.; NP.; P.; QM.; RI.; SC.; SI.; U.; **Abs.**U.; **Bl.**U.; **Bm.**C.; P.; T.; U.; **Bn.**U.; **Br.**P.; U.; **Bra.**P.; **C.**ENG.; P.; UL.; **Co.**T.; **Cr.**U.; **Db.**; **Dn.**U.; **E.**A.; HW; U.; **Ep.**D.; **Ex.**U.; **F.**A.; **G.**M.; T.; **H.**U.; **Lc.**A. 58–59; **Ld.**P.; U.; W. 58–59; **Li.**M.; **Lv.**P.; **M.**C.; P.; T.; U. 58–59; **Ma.**T.; **N.**P.; T.; U.; **Nw.**A.; P.; **O.**R.; **Rt.** 59; **Sh.**IO.; SC.; **Sw.**U.; **Wd.**; **Y.** [*C. of:* 57645; *C. as:* 17761]

17760 **Electronic** and **Radio Engineer: Abstracts** and **References.** London. *Electron. Radio Engr Abstr. Ref.* [1957–59] **L.**AV.; **F.**A. [*C. of:* 57645; *C. as:* 17762]

17761 **Electronic Technology.** London. *Electron. Technol.* [1960–] **L.**AV.; BM.; EE.; IC.; MC.; NP.; P.; QM.; RI.; SC.; SI.; U.; **Abs.**U.; **Bl.**U.; **Bm.**C.; P.; T.; U.; **Bn.**U.; **Br.**P.; U.; **Bra.**P.; **C.**ENG.; P.; UL.; **Co.**T.; **Cr.**U.; **Db.**; **Dn.**U.; **E.**A.; HW; O.; U.; **Ep.**D.; **Ex.**U.; **F.**A.; **G.**M.; T.; **H.**U.; **Lc.**A.; **Ld.**P.; U.; W.; **Li.**M.; **Lv.**P.; **M.**C.; P.; T.; U.; **Ma.**T.; **N.**P.; T.; U.; **Nw.**A.; P.; **O.**R.; **Rt.**; **Sh.**IO.; SC.; **Sw.**U.; **Wd.**; **Y.** [*C. of:* 17759; *after 1962 merged in* Industrial Electronics]

17762 **Electronic Technology: Abstracts** and **References.** London. *Electron. Technol. Abstr. Ref.* [1960–] **L.**AV.; BM.; EE.; P.; QM.; RI.; SC.; SI.; U.; **Abs.**U.; **Bl.**U.; **Bm.**C.; P.; T.; U.; **Bn.**U.; **Br.**P.; U.; **Bra.**P.; **C.**ENG.; P.; UL.; **Co.**T.; **Cr.**U.; **Db.**; **Dn.**U.; **E.**A.; HW; U.; **Ep.**D.; **Ex.**U.; **F.**A.; **G.**M.; T.; **H.**U.; **Lc.**A.; **Ld.**P.; U.; W.; **Li.**M.; **Lv.**P.; **M.**C.; P.; T.; U.; **Ma.**T.; **N.**P.; T.; U.; **Nw.**A.; P.; **O.**R.; **Rt.**; **Sh.**IO.; SC.; **Sw.**U.; **Wd.**; **Y.** [*C. of:* 17760]

17763 **Electronica.** Amsterdam. *Electronica, Amst.* [1948–] **L.**P. 55–; SC. 50–; **Sl.**RI. 54–61; **Y.** [*Part of:* 5873]
　　Electrónica. Barcelona. *See* 46493.

17764 **Electrónica internacional.** New York. *Electrón. int.* [1960–] [*Spanish edition of:* 23841]

17765 **Electronics.** New York. *Electronics* [1930–] **L.**AV. 40–; BM. 35–; EE.; IC.; MC. 47–50: 59–; NF. 45–; NP. (3 yr.); P. imp.; QM. 51–; SC.; SI. 34–; U. 58–; UC. 48–; **Abd.**U. 48–; **Abs.**U. 47– imp.; **Bl.**U. 46–; **Bm.**C. (curr.); P. 44–; T. 36– imp.; U. 38–; **Bn.**U. 41– imp.; **Br.**U. 47–; **C.**APH. 52–; P. 35–; **Co.**T. 48–; **Cr.**U. 43–; **Db.** 37– imp.; **Dn.**U. 54–; **E.**HW. 46–57; O. 60–; U. 55–; **Ep.**D. 48– imp.; **F.**A. 33–; **Fr.** 56–; **G.**M. 47–; T. 47–; U.; **H.**U. 47–; **Lc.**A. 53– imp.; **Ld.**P. 54–; U.; W. 49– imp.; **Lh.**P. 49–; **Li.**M. 46–; **Lv.**P. 37– imp.; **M.**C. 34–; D. 46– imp.; T. 47–; U. 52– imp.; **Ma.**T. 37–; **N.**T. 60–; U. 56–; **Nw.**A. 39–; P. 53–; **O.**R. 37–; **Sh.**P. 45–; SC. 47–; **Ste.** 46–; **We.**K. 46–; **Y.** [*In 1957 alternating 'engineering' and 'business' editions were issued*]

17766 **Electronics Buyers' Guide.** New York. *Electronics Buy. Guide* **L**.P. (curr.)
Reference Sheet Section [1950–57] **L**.P. [*C. as:* 17770]

17766° **Electronics** and **Communications, Canada.** *Electronics Communs Can.* **L**.AV. 60–.

17767 **Electronics Digest.** Pittsburgh. *Electronics Dig.* [1945–47]

17768 **Electronics Express.** New York. *Electronics Express* [1958–] **L**.P.; **Sh**.SC. 59–; **Y.** [*Abstracts from various Soviet journals*]

17769 **Electronics Forum.** London. *Electronics Forum* [1946–52] **L**.EE.; P.; SC.; SI.; **Bm**.P.; **E**.A.; **F**.A. 48–53; **O**.B.; R.; **Wa**.B. 49–52. [*C. of:* 49026; *C. as:* 39285]

17770 **Electronics Handbook** for **Design Engineers.** New York. *Electronics Handb. Des. Engrs* [1958–] **L**.P. [*C. of:* 17766]

17771 **Electronics Illustrated.** Greenwich, Conn. *Electronics Illust.* **L**.P. 59–.

17772 **Electronics** and **Television** and **Short-Wave World.** London. *Electronics Telev. short-wave Wld* [1939–41] **L**.EE.; P.; SC.; **Bm**.P.; T. 40–41; U.; **Bn**.U. imp.; **C**.UL.; **E**.T.; **G**.M.; **Ld**.U. 40–41; **M**.D. 40–41; P.; **Ma**.T.; **Sh**.P. [*C. of:* 52824; *C. as:* 17747]

17773 **Electronics Weekly.** London. *Electronics Wkly* [1960–] **L**.AV.; BM.; P. (curr.); **C**.CH. (2 yr.); **Y.**

17774 **Electronics World.** New York. *Electronics Wld* [1959–] **L**.AV.; BM.; P.; SC.; **Br**.A.; **Lv**.P.; **M**.P.; **Y.** [*C. of:* 41811]

17775 **Électronique.** Paris. *Électronique* [1950–] **L**.EE.; **Y.** [*C. from:* 52820]

17776 **Électronique appliquée.** Paris. *Électronique appl.* [1955–57] **L**.P. 57. [*C. as:* 17780]

17777 **Électronique** et **automatisme.** Paris. *Électronique Autom.* [1960–] **L**.AV.; **Y.**

17778 **Électronique** et **industrie.** Paris. *Électronique Ind.* **L**.P. 56–.

17779 **Électronique industrielle.** Paris. *Électronique ind.* [1955–] **L**.P.; **Te**.N.; **Y.**

17780 **Électronique professionelle appliquée.** Paris. *Électronique prof. appl.* [1957–] **L**.P. [*C. of:* 17776]

17781 **Electroplater** and **Electroplating.** London. *Electroplr, Electroplg* [1930] **L**.BM.; **Abs**.N.
Electroplating. Teddington. *See* 17783.

17782 **Electroplating.** Bombay. *Electroplating, Bombay* [1959–] **L**.P.; **Y.**

17783 **Electroplating** and **Metal Finishing.** Teddington. *Electroplg Metal Finish.* [1947–] **L**.AV.; BM.; DI, 49–58; I.; NF.; P.; PR.; SI.; U.; **Bm**.P.; T.; **C**.UL.; **E**.A.; **F**.A. 49–; **G**.M. imp.; **Lh**.P.; **Lv**.P. 49– imp.; **M**.P.; T. (5 yr.); **Sh**.IO.; **Y.**

17784 **Electrosoudure.** Bruxelles. *Electrosoudure* [1937–38] **L**.P. [*C. of:* 53077]

17785 **Electrotechnical Journal.** Tokyo. *Electrotech. J., Tokyo* [1941–42] **L**.P. 41; SC. 41; U. 41; **Bm**.U.; **C**.UL. imp.; **M**.T. 41; **Ma**.T. 41. [*C. of:* 17324; *Suspended 1943–54; Replaced by:* 17786]

17786 **Electrotechnical Journal** of **Japan.** Tokyo. *Electrotech. J. Japan* [1955–] **L**.BM. 57–; EE.; P.; QM. 57–; SC.; U.; **Bm**.U.; **Br**.U.; **C**.UL.; **G**.U. imp.; **M**.T.; **Ma**.T.; **Y.** [*Replaces:* 17785; *Overseas edition of:* 26187]

17787 **Electrotechnical Papers. Institute** of **Electrical Engineers** of **Japan.** Tokyo. *Electrotech. Pap., Tokyo* [1949–] **L**.EE. 54; SC.

17788 **Electrotechnics.** Bangalore. *Electrotechnics* [1926–] **L**.EE. 26–41; P. 26–55; SC. 39: 50; **Bm**.U. 36–38.

17789 **Electrotechnik.** Den Haag. *Electrotechnik* [1927–] **L**.EE. 46–; P. imp.; **Y.** [*C. of:* 50926]

17790 **Electrotechnisch** en **werktuigkundig weekblad.** Amsterdam. *Electrotech. werktuigk. Weekbl.*

17791 **Electrotechnology.** Bangalore. *Electrotechnology, Bangalore* [1957–] **L**.P.; **Te**.N.; **Y.**

17792 **Electro-Technology.** New York. *Electro-Technology, N.Y.* [1960–] **L**.AV. 62–; EE.; P.; SC.; **Y.** [*C. of:* 17664]

17793 **Electrotehnica.** Bucureşti. *Electrotehnica* [1953–] **L**.BM. 55–; EE. 55–; **Y.**

17794 **Electro-Therapeutist.** Lima, O. *Electro-Therapeutist*

17795 **Électrothérapie.** Paris. *Électrothérapie*

17796 **Electrotypers'** and **Stereotypers' Bulletin.** Cleveland, Ohio. *Electrotyp. Stereotyp. Bull.* [1915–51] **Lh**.P. 36–51 imp. [*C. as:* 17798]

17797 **Electrotypers'** and **Stereotypers' Journal.** London. *Electrotyp. Stereotyp. J.* [1938–56] **L**.BM.; SB. 42–56; **Abs**.N.; **E**.A.; **Lh**.P. imp.; **O**.B.; **Y.** [*C. in:* 38701]

17798 **Electrotypers'** and **Stereotypers' Magazine.** Cleveland. *Electrotyp. Stereotyp. Mag.* [1952–] **Lh**.P. [*C. of:* 17796]

17799 **Elefant.** Metzeler Gummiwerke. München. *Elefant* **Sy**.R. 52–56.

17800 **Élektricheskaya énergíya.** Moskva. Электрическая энергія. *Élekt. Énerg., Mosk.*

17801 **Élektricheskaya i teplovoznaya tyaga.** Moskva. Электрическая и тепловозная тяга. *Élekt. teplov. Tyaga* [1957–] **L**.BM. 58–; P. 58–; **Y.** 58–.

17802 **Élektricheskie stantsii.** Moskva. Электрические станции. *Élekt. Sta., Mosk.* [1930–] **L**.AV. 43–49 imp.; BM. 50–; P. 54–; **G**.ME. 62–; **Y.** imp.

17803 **Élektricheskoe dêlo.** Moskva. Электрическое дѣло. *Élekt. Dêlo*

17804 **Élektricheskoe obozrênie.** Moskva. Электрическое обозрѣніе. *Élekt. Obozr.*

17805 **Élektrichestvo.** S.-Peterburg. Электричество. *Élektrichestvo, S-Peterb.* [1880–] **L**.AV. 40: 59–; BM. 50–; P. 10–16: 22–; SC. 24–39: 49–; **Y.** 46– imp. [*Suspended: 1918–21; English abstracts at:* 17702; *English translations of selected articles at:* 17620]

17806 **Élektrichestvo.** Sofiya. Электричество. *Élektrichestvo, Sof.*

17807 **Élektrichestvo i zhizn'.** Nikolaev. Электричество и жизнь. *Élektvo Zhizn'*

17808 **Elektrie.** Berlin. *Elektrie* [1959–] **L**.EE.; P.; **Y.** [*C. of:* 16691]

17809 **Élektrifikatsīya i élektromonter.** Moskva. Электрификація и электромонтер. *Élektrif. Élektromonter* [1923–33] [*C. as:* 17848]

17810 **Élektrifikatsiya sel'skogo khozyaĭstva.** Moskva. Электрификация сельского хозяйства. *Élektrif. sel'. Khoz.* [1931–37] **L**.AM. 34–37 imp.; SC. 36–37. [*C. as:* 30630]

17810° **Elektrik muhendisligi mecmuasi.** *Elektrik Muhend. Mecm.* **Y.**

17811 **Elektrikkeren.** Kristiania. *Elektrikkeren*

17812 **Elektris.** Praha. *Elektris* [1928–39] **L.**P. 32–39. [*Supplement to* and *issued with:* 17871]

17812° **Elektrische Anzeiger.** *Elekt. Anz.* **Y.**

17813 **Elektrische Arbeit.** Bodenbach. *Elekt. Arb.* [1929–] [*C. of:* 54417]

17813° **Elektrische Ausrüstung.** *Elekt. Ausrüst.* **Y.**

17814 **Elektrische Bahnen.** Charlottenburg, etc. *Elekt. Bahn.* [1925–] **L.**EE. 31–44 imp.; P. imp.; **Bm.**T. 56–58 imp.; **M.**P. 29–36; **Y.** [*Suspended* 1945–49]

17815 **Elektrische Bahnen** und **Betriebe.** München. *Elekt. Bahn. Betr.* [1903–06] **L.**EE. 06; P. [*C. as:* 17817]

17816 **Elektrische Betrieb.** München & Berlin. *Elekt. Betr.* [1923–] **L.**EE.; P. 23–39; **Ld.**U. [*C. of:* 17817; >42242, 1926–37]

17817 **Elektrische Kraftbetriebe** u. **Bahnen.** München & Berlin. *Elekt. Kraftbetr. Bahn.* [1907–22] **L.**BM. 18–19 imp.; EE.; P.; **Ld.**U. 22. [*C. of:* 17815; *C. as:* 17816]

17818 **Elektrische** u. **maschinelle Betriebe.** Leipzig. *Elekt. masch. Betr.* **L.**P. 10–13. [*C. of:* 48265]

17819 **Elektrische Nachrichten-Technik.** Berlin. *Elekt. NachrTech.* [1924–44] **L.**EE. 24–43 imp.; P.; SC. 30–44 imp.; **Br.**U. 24–30; **C.**P. 31–44 imp.; **G.**U. imp.; **Ma.**T. 26–43; **Te.**N.

17820 **Elektriska installatörtidningen.** Stockholm. *Elekt. InstallTidn.* [1929–]

17821 **Elektrizität.** Berlin. *Elektrizität, Berl.* [1892–23]

17822 **Elektrizität.** Zeitschrift für Abnehmerberatung. Frankfurt a. M. *Elektrizität, Frankf. a. M.* [1951–] **Y.**

17823 **Elektrizität.** Zürich. *Elektrizität, Zürich*

17824 **Elektrizität** im **Bergbau.** München. *Elektriz. Bergb.* [1926–43] **L.**EE. 26–39; P.; SC.; **Sh.**S. 31–32. [*C. in:* 21407]

17825 **Elektrizität** im **Förderwesen.** Wittenberg. *Elektriz. Förderw.* [1939–44] **L.**P. [*Supplement to:* 19747]

17826 **Elektrizität** in **industriellen Betrieben.** Leipzig. *Elektriz. ind. Betr.* [1924–] **L.**SC. 25.

17827 **Elektrizitätsverwertung.** Zürich. *Elektrizitätsverwertung* **L.**EE. 50–; **Y.**

17828 **Elektrizitätswerk.** Wien. *Elektrizitätswerk* **L.**SC. 25–27. [*Supplement to:* 17877]

17829 **Elektrizitätswirtschaft.** Berlin. *Elektrizitätswirtschaft* [1926–] **L.**EE. 39–44 imp.; P. 26–44: 49–; **Y.** [*C. of:* 32799; *also supplement at:* 5113]

17829ᵃ **Elektro Nachrichten.** *Elektro Nachr.* **Y.**

17830 **Elektrobote.** Graz. *Elektrobote* **L.**P. 59–.

17831 **Elektrochemie.** Berlin. *Elektrochemie* [1893–11] **L.**P. [*Reprinted from:* 13808]

17832 **Elektrochemische Zeitschrift.** Berlin. *Elektrochem. Z.* [1894–22] **L.**C. 19–22; IC. 94–14; MT.; P. 10–22; **Abd.**U. 04–06; **E.**U. 02–20 imp.

17833 **Élektroénergetika.** Электроэнергетика. *Élektroénergetika* [1959–] **L.**SC.; **Y.**

17834 **Élektroénergiya.** Sofiya. Электроэнергия. *Élektroénergiya* [1952–] **L.**BM. [*C. of:* 18055]

17835 **Elektrofahrzeug.** Berlin. *Elektrofahrzeug* **L.**P. 36–39.

17836 **Elektrofertigung.** Berlin. *Elektrofertigung* [1947–] **L.**P. [*Supplement to:* 16691]

17837 **Elektro-Handel.** Heidelberg. *Elektro-Handel* **L.**P. 58*; **Y.** [*C. in:* 17908]

17838 **Elektro-industri.** Kristiania. *Elektro-Industri*

17839 **Elektroindustrie.** Zürich. *Elektroindustrie* **Y.**

17840 **Elektroingeniøren.** København. *Elektroingeniøren*

17841 **Elektro-Installateur.** Berlin. *Elektro-Install.* **L.**P. 26–27.

17842 **Elektroiskrovaya obrabotka metallov.** Moskva. Электроискровая обработка металлов. *Elektroisk. Obrab. Metall.* [1957–] **L.**P.; **Y.**

17843 **Elektro-Journal.** Charlottenburg. *Elektro-J.* [1921–30] **L.**P. 26–30.

17844 **Elektrokorrespondenz.** Zürich. *Elektrokorrespondenz* [*French edition at:* 17721]

17845 **Elektro-Medizin.** Berlin. *Elektro-Med.* [1955–] **L.**MA.; MD.

17846 **Elektromeister.** München. *Elektromeister* [1948–] **L.**P. 58–; **Y.**

17847 **Elektromobil.** Zürich. *Elektromobil*

17848 **Élektromonter.** Moskva. Электромонтер. *Élektromonter* [1934–] **L.**SC. 40–; **Y.** [*C. of:* 17809]

17849 **Elektromonteur.** Aaran. *Elektromonteur, Aaran* [1949–] **L.**P. 55–.

17850 **Elektromonteur.** Berlin. *Elektromonteur, Berl.*

17851 **Elektromotor.** Stuttgart. *Elektromotor*

17852 **Elektron.** Amsterdam. *Elektron, Amst.* [1950–] **Y.** [*C. of:* 17739]

17853 **Elektron.** Berlin. *Elektron, Berl.* [1907–08] **L.**P.

17854 **Elektron.** Linz. *Elektron, Linz* **L.**AV. 47– imp.; P. 55–; **Y.**

17855 **Elektron.** Reykjavík. *Elektron, Reyk.* [1915–21] [*C. as:* 49776°]

17856 **Elektron Review** and **Abstracts.** *Elektron Rev. Abstr.* [1940–41] **L.**NF.; **Bm.**P.; **C.**UL. [*C. as:* 29119]

17857 **Elektron** in **Wissenschaft** und **Technik.** München. *Elektron Wiss. Tech.* [1947–] **L.**AV. 47–51 imp.; P. 48–51.

17858 **Elektronentechnische Berichte.** Wien. *Elektronentech. Ber.*

17859 **Elektronik.** München. *Elektronik* [1952–] **L.**AV. 57–; EE. 54–; **Te.**N. 57–; **Y.**

17859° **Elektroniker.** Aarau. *Elektroniker* **Y.**

17860 **Elektronische Datenverarbeitung.** Braunschweig. *Elektron. Datenverarb.* [1959–] **L.**P.; **Te.**N.; **Y.**

17861 **Elektronische Rechenanlagen.** München. *Elektron. Rechenanl.* [1959–] **L.**P.

17862 **Elektronische Rundschau.** Berlin. *Elektron. Rdsch.* [1955–] **L.**AV. 58– imp.; EE.; P.; SC.; **Y.** [*C. of:* 20455]

17862° **Elektronorm.** *Elektronorm* **Y.**

17863 **Elektrophysikalische Rundschau.** Berlin. *Elektrophys. Rdsch.*

17864 **Elektro-Post.** Mindelheim. *Elektro-Post* [1948–] **L.**P. 55.

17864ᵃ **Elektro-Praktiker.** *Elektro-Prakt.* **Y.**

17865 **Elektroprivreda.** Beograd. *Elektroprivreda* [1948–] **L.**BM. 56–; EE. 57– imp.; **Y.**

17866 **Elektro-Radio Lloyd.** Budapest. *Elektro-Radio Lloyd* [1931–38] [*C. in:* 29060]

17867 **Elektroschweisser.** Berlin. *Elektroschweisser* [1936–42] **L.**P. 36–39 imp.

17868 **Elektroschweissung.** Braunschweig. *Elektroschweissung* [1930–44] **L.**AV. 34–44 imp.; P. imp.; SC. 32–44.

17869 **Élektrosvyaz'.** Leningrad, Moskva. Электросвязь. *Élektrosvyaz'* [1934–] **L.**AV. 59–; P. 57–; **Sw.**U. 58–; **Y.** 56–. [*English abstracts at:* 17639°; *English translation at:* 52768]

17870 **Elektrotechnický časopis.** Bratislava. *Elektrotech. Čas.* [1959–] **L.**P.; **Y.** [*C. from:* 51026]

17871 **Elektrotechnický obzor.** Praha. *Elektrotech. Obz.* [1912–] **L.**AV. 58–; EE. 36– imp.; P. 31–40: 55–; SC. 28–; **M.**T. 54–; **Y.**

17872 **Elektrotechnik.** Berlin. *Elektrotechnik, Berl.* [1947–52] **L.**EE.; P.; SC.; SI. [*C. as:* 16691]

17873 **Elektrotechnik.** Praha. *Elektrotechnik, Praha* **L.**EE. 48–; I. 55–; P. 57–; **Y.**

17874 **Elektrotechnik in Einzeldarstellungen.** Braunschweig. *Elektrotechnik Einzeldarst.* [1902–12] **L.**P.; SC.; **M.**U. imp.

17875 **Elektrotechnik** und **Elektrotechnischer Anzeiger.** Pössneck. *Elektrotechnik elektrotech. Anz.* **L.**P. 44–. [*C. of:* 17895]

17876 **Elektrotechnik in der Industrie** und im **Maschinenbau.** Goldach. *Elektrotechnik Ind. MaschBau* **L.**P. [*Supplement to* and *issued with:* 48917]

17877 **Elektrotechnik** und **Maschinenbau.** Wien. *Elektrotechnik MaschBau* [1906–] **L.**AV. 46– imp.; EE. imp.; I. 56–; P. 10–; SC. 25–44: 47–; **Bm.**U. 11–14; **E.**HW. 49–; **G.**T.; U. 22–; **Lv.**P. imp.; U. 21–28; **M.**P. 29–39; T. 06–14: 50–; **N.**U. 55–; **Y.** [*C. of:* 58564; *From* 1944–46 *contained in* 17890]

17878 **Elektrotechnika.** Budapest. *Elektrotechnika* [1908–] **L.**AV. 58–; BM. 50–; EE. 31–36: 47–; P. 46–; **Y.** [*Also supplements*]

17879 **Elektrotechniker.** Wien. *Elektrotechniker, Wien* [1882–19] **L.**P. 82–14.

17880 **Elektrotechniker.** Wuppertal-Elberfeld. *Elektrotechniker, Wuppertal* [1949–52] **L.**P.; SC. 50–52; **Br.**U.; **N.**U. 52; **Y.** [*C. as:* 17892]

17881 **Elektrotechnische Berichte.** Berlin. *Elektrotech. Ber.* [1937–44] **L.**AV. 39–42; P.; SC.

17882 **Elektro-technische Bibliothek.** Wien. *Elektrotech. Biblthk* [1883–11] **L.**BM.

17883 **Elektrotechnische Mitteilungen.** Halle. *Elektrotech. Mitt.* [1901–02] **L.**P.

17884 **Elektrotechnische Nachrichten.** Berlin. *Elektrotech. Nachr.*

17885 **Elektrotechnische Patentblätter.** Berlin. *Elektrotech. PatBl.* [1906] **L.**P.

17886 **Elektrotechnische Ratgeber.** Berlin. *Elektrotech. Ratg.*

17888 **Elektrotechnische Umschau.** Halle. *Elektrotech. Umsch.*

17889 **Elektrotechnische Vorträge.** *Elektrotech. Vortr.* [1899–07] **M.**T.

17890 **Elektrotechnische Zeitschrift.** Berlin. *Elektrotech. Z.* [1880–52] **L.**AV. 80–45; BM.; C. 28–37; EE. imp.; P. imp.; QM. 09–45 imp.; SC. 02–45: 48–52; **Bm.**P. 99–39; T. 22–38; U.; **Bn.**U. 99–52 imp.; **Db.** 10–52; **G.**T. 21–45 imp.; U.; **Ld.**U. 28–52; **Lv.**P. 30–39; U. 80–14; **M.**P. 27–52; T. 85–48 imp.; U. imp.; **Ma.**T. 40–44; **N.**U. 01–14: 29–52; **Nw.**A. imp.; P.; **Sh.**S. 50–52; SC. 21–52 imp.; **Sw.**U. 23–25; **Y.** [*C. as:* 17891]

17891 **Elektrotechnische Zeitschrift. Ausgabe A.** Berlin. *Elektrotech. Z. Ausg. A.* [1952–] **L.**AV. 57–; BM.; EE.; P.; SC.; U.; **Bn.**U.; **Db.**; **G.**U.; **Ld.**U.; **Lv.**P.; **M.**P.; U.; **N.**U.; **Nw.**A.; P.; **Sh.**S.; SC.; **Sw.**U.; **Y.** [*C. of:* 17890]

17892 **Elektrotechnische Zeitschrift. Ausgabe B.** Berlin. *Elektrotech. Z. Ausg. B* [1952–] **L.**AV. 57–; EE.; P.; SC.; **Br.**U.; **N.**U.; **Y.** [*C. of:* 17880]

17893 **Elektrotechnische Zeitschriftenschau.** Mannheim. *Elektrotech. Znschau*

17894 **Elektrotechnische Zeitung.** Frankenthal. *Elektrotech. Ztg*

17895 **Elektrotechnischer Anzeiger.** Berlin. *Elektrotech. Anz.* [1884–39] **L.**EE. 84–13; P. 10–39; SC. 37–39. [*C. as:* 17875]

17896 **Elektrotechnischer Neuigkeits-Anzeiger** u. **maschinentechnische Rundschau.** Wien. *Elektrotech. NeuigkAnz.*

17897 **Elektrotechnisches Echo.** Magdeburg. *Elektrotech. Echo* [1888–04] **L.**P. 90–04 imp.

17898 **Elektrotechnisches Journal.** Berlin. *Elektrotech. J.*

17898ª **Elektrotehnika.** Beograd. *Elektrotehnika, Beograd* [1952–] **L.**P. 60–. [*Issued as section of:* 52678]

17898ᵇ **Elektrotehnika.** Zagreb. *Elektrotehnika, Zagreb* **Y.**

17899 **Elektrotehniški vestnik.** Ljubljana. *Elektroteh. Vest.* [1933–] **L.**P. 56–; **Y.**

17900 **Élektrotekhnicheskiǐ vêstnik.** Sankt-Peterburg. Электротехническій вѣстникъ. *Élektrotekh. Vêst.*

17901 **Élektrotekhnicheskoe dêlo.** Moskva. Электротехническое дѣло. *Élektrotekh. Dêlo*

17902 **Élektrotekhnik.** S.-Peterburg. Электротехникъ. *Élektrotekhnik*

17903 **Elektroteknikeren.** Kjøbenhavn. *Elektroteknikeren* [1904–] **L.**EE. 52–; P.; **Y.**

17904 **Elektroteknisk Tidsskrift.** Kjøbenhavn. Kristiania. *Elektrotek. Tidsskr.* [1896–] **L.**EE. 33– imp.; P. 26–; **Y.**

17905 **Elektrowärme.** Düsseldorf, Essen. *Elektrowärme, Düsseldorf* [1931–] **L.**EE. 31–40; P. 33–43: 57–; SC. 34–40; **M.**U. 36–43 imp.; **Y.** [1943–44 *contained in:* 20690; –61* *C. as:* Internationale Zeitschrift für Elektrowärme]

17905° **Elektrowärme.** Wien. *Elektrowärme, Wien* [1953–] **Y.** [*Supplement to:* 35553]

17906 **Elektrowärme-Technik.** Mindelheim. *Elektrowärme-Tech.* [1950–] **L.**P. 51–55.

17907 **Elektrowelt.** Brandenburg. *Elektrowelt, Brandenburg*

17908 **Elektro-Welt.** Heidelberg. *Elektro-Welt, Heidelb.* [1956–58: *then in editions below*] **L.**P. 58.
    A. Elektro-Handel. [1959–60] **L.**P.; **Y.** [*C. as:* 17909]
    B. Industrielle Elektrotechnik. [1959–60] **L.**AV. 60; P. [*C. as:* 17910]
    C. Fachausgabe. **L.**AV. 60–; P.; **Y.**

17909 **Elektro-Welt, Elektro-Handel.** Heidelberg. *Elektro-Welt, Elektro-Handel* [1960–] **L.**P.; **Y.** [*C. of:* 17908, A]

17910 **Elektro-Welt, Industrie-Elektrik.** Heidelberg. *Elektro-Welt Ind.-Elekt.* [1960–] **L.**AV.; P.; **Y.** [*C. of:* 17908, B]

17911 **Élelmezési ipar.** Budapest. *Élelm. Ipar* [1950–] **L.**BM.; P. 55–; **Y.** [*C. of:* 31726]

17912 **Élelmiszervizsgalati közlemenyek.** Budapest. *Élelmiszerv. Közl.* [1955–] **L.**TP. 56–.

17912° **Elementa.** Stockholm. *Elementa* **Y.** [*C. of:* 53120]

17913 **Elemente** der **Mathematik.** Basel, Zürich. *Elem. Math., Basel* [1946–] **L.**M.; **C.**P. 55–; SC.; **G.**U. 56–; **Sh.**U. 59–; **Y.**

17914 **Elementos climatológicos.** Serviço meteorológico de Guiné. Bissan. *Elem. clim. Serv. met. Guiné* **L.**MO. 57–58*. [*C. as:* 46057ª]

17915 **Elementos meteorológicos** e **climatológicos.** Loanda. *Elem. met. clim., Loanda* [1937–52] **L.**BM.; MO. 37–52. [*C. of:* 46150; *C. as:* 3657]

17916 **Elements.** Philippine Weather Bureau. Manila. *Elements* **L.**MO. 50–54.

17917 **Elenco** delle **pubblicazioni UNI.** Ente nazionale per l'unificazione nell'industria. Milano. *Elenco Pubbl. UNI* **L.**SC. 36–.

17918 **Élet** és **egészség.** Budapest. *Élet Egészség* [1922–31 ?]

17919 **Eletronica popular.** Buenos Aires. *Eletronica pop.* [1955–] **L.**AV. 58–.

17920 **Elettricista.** Roma. *Elettricista* [1892–32] **L.**P. 10–32; UC. 30–32 imp.

17921 **Elettricità.** Milano. *Elettricità* [1886–08] **L.**EE. 98–08; P.; SC. 87–08. [*C. as:* 47990]

17922 **Elettricità** nel **campo medico.** Novara. *Elett. Campo med.*

17922° **Elettricità** e **vita moderna.** Torino. *Elett. Vita mod.* [1954–] **L.**BM.

17923 **Elettrificazione.** Milano. *Elettrificazione* **L.**P. 55–.

17924 **Elettrochimica.** Milano. *Elettrochimica* **L.**P. 55–. [*Supplement to* and *issued with:* 17923]

17925 **Elettronica.** Torino. *Elettronica* [1946–50] **L.**P.; **Y.**

    Elettronica e **televisione.** *See* 17925.

17926 **Elettrotecnica.** Milano. *Elettrotecnica* [1914–] **L.**AV. 49–; EE. 14–43; P. 21– imp.; SC. 14–18: 25–; **Ld.**U. 28–38; **Y.** [*C. of:* 5168]

    Elettrotecnica. Bibliografia italiana. *See* 6557.

17927 **Elettrotecnica bibliografia straniera.** Milano. *Elettrotec. Biblfia stran.* [1947–48] [*C. as:* 6546]

17928 **Elettrotecnica pratica.** Roma. *Elettrotec. prat.*

17929 **Elettrotrazione.** Roma. *Elettrotrazione* [1922–23] **L.**P. 23.

17930 **Élevage.** Dieghem. *Élevage*

17931 **Élevage français.** Paris. *Élevage fr.* [1904–06] **L.**AM.

17932 **Élevage** et **insemination.** Paris. *Élevage Insem.* **E.**AB. 52–; **Y.**

17933 **Élevage** et la **laiterie pratiques.** Bruxelles. *Élevage Lait. prat.*

17934 **Élevage moderne.** Paris. *Élevage mod.*

17935 **Élevage scientifique.** Paris. *Élevage scient.*

17936 **Elevator.** Manchester. *Elevator*

17937 **Elevator Constructor.** Philadelphia. *Elevator Constr.*

17938 **Éleveur belge.** Zootechnie, etc. Bruxelles. *Éleveur belge*

17939 **Éleveur français.** Fontenay-aux-Roses. *Éleveur fr.*

17940 **Éleveur limousin.** Saint-Priest-Taurion. *Éleveur limousin*

17941 **Éleveur moderne** de **Beaulieu** en **Bignan.** Vannes. *Éleveur mod. Beaulieu* [1951–] **L.**V. 55–.

17942 **Éleveur** et la **revue cynégétique réunis.** Paris. *Éleveur Revue cynég.*

17943 **Éleveur suisse.** Saignelégier. *Éleveur suisse*

17944 **Elfsborgs läns Norra hushållningssällskaps tidskrift.** Venersborg. *Elfsborgs Läns N. Hushålln-Sällsk. Tidskr.*

17945 **Elfsborgs läns Södra hushållningssällskaps qvartallsskrift.** Borås. *Elfsborgs Läns S. Hushålln-Sällsk. QSkr.* [1920–]

17946 **Elimination** of **Waste Series. Commercial Standards.** Department of Commerce, United States. Washington. *Elim. Waste Ser. comm. Stand.* **L.**P. 28–; SC. 28–.

17947 **Elimination** of **Waste Series. Limitation** of **Variety Recommendation.** Department of Commerce, United States. Washington. *Elim. Waste Ser. Limit. Var. Recomm.* **L.**P. 24–; SC. 24–.

17948 **Elimination** of **Waste Series. Report** of **Building Code Committee.** Department of Commerce, United States. Washington. *Elim. Waste Ser. Rep. Bldg Code Comm.* **L.**P. 24–; SC. 24–.

17949 **Elimination** of **Waste Series. Simplified Practice Recommendation.** Department of Commerce, United States. Washington. *Elim. Waste Ser. simpl. Pract. Recomm.* [1923–] **L.**BM.; P.; SC.; UC. 36–; **Bm.**U.; **Lv.**U.

17950 **Elin-Zeitschrift.** Wien. *Elin.-Z.* [1949–] **L.**P. imp.; **Y.**

17951 **Elixir.** Journal of the Hong-Kong University Medical Society. Hong Kong. *Elixir* [1950–] **L.**BM.; **G.**U. 55–.

    Ellenberger-Schütz Jahresbericht. *See* 25031.

17952 **'Ellēnikē heirourgike.** Athenai. Ἑλληνικὴ Χειρουργική. *'Ell. Heirourg.* [1954–] **L.**MD.

17953 **'Ellēnikē iatrikē.** Thessalonikē. Ἑλληνική Ἰατρική. *'Ell. Iatr.* [1927–]

17954 **Ellingwood's Therapeutist.** Chicago. *Ellingwood's Ther.*

17955 **Elliott Journal.** Elliott Brothers. London. *Elliott J.* [1951–] **L.**BM.; EE. 51–53; MO. 51–54; P. 51–54; QM. 52–; **M.**P.; T. (10 yr.); **R.**U.; **Sil.** imp.; **Y.**

17956 **Elliott MEI Bulletin.** Microwave and Electronic Instruments Division, Elliott Brothers. Borehamwood. *Elliott MEI Bull.* [1958–] **L.**P. **Y.**

17957 **Elsässisches Textilblatt.** Gebweiler. *Elsäss. TextBl.*

17958 **Elsners Maschinen-Revue.** Darmstadt. *Elsners Masch.-Revue* **L.**P. 57–.

17959 **Elteknik.** Stockholm. *Elteknik* [1958–] **L.**EE.; P.; SC.; **Y.**

17959° **Elytron.** Washington. *Elytron* [1953–] **L.**E. [*Supplement to:* 14722]

17960 **Émail.** Valenciennes. *Émail* [1929–32] [*Replaced by:* 17961]

17961 **Émaillerie.** Paris. *Émaillerie* [1933–] **Bm.**C. 38–39. [*Replaces:* 17960]

17962 **Emailletechnische Monats-Blätter.** Halberstadt. *Emailletech. Mbl.* **L.**P. 26–39.
Emaillewaren-Industrie. *See* 17964.

17963 **Email-Reporter.** Leverkusen. *Email-Reptr* [1957–] **L.**P.

17964 **Emailwaren-Industrie.** Meissen, Duisberg. *Emailwaren-Ind.* [1924–] **L.**P. 29–40 imp.

17965 **Emasculator.** Quezon City. *Emasculator* [*C. as:* 55400]

17966 **Embalajes.** Madrid. *Embalajes* **Lh.**P. 55– imp.

17967 **Emballage moderne.** Paris. *Emballage mod.* [1955–] **Lh.**P. imp.

17968 **Emballages.** Paris. *Emballages* **L.**P. 53–; imp.; **Y.**

17969 **Emballages** et leur **transport.** Paris. *Emball. Transp.* [1932–] **Lh.**P. 48–.

17970 **Embouteillage informations.** Revue de l'embouteillage et des industries connexes. Paris. *Embouteill. Infs* [1960–] **L.**P.

17971 **Embryologia.** Nagoya. *Embryologia* [1950–] **L.**SC. 58–; UC.; **C.**B.; **E.**AG.; U. 51–.

17972 **Emergency Bulletin. Department** of **Entomology. Nebraska State University.** Lincoln. *Emerg. Bull. Dep. Ent. Neb. St. Univ.* **L.**EB. 17 imp.

17973 **Emergency Period Pamphlets. Geological Survey** of **Ireland.** Dublin. *Emerg. Period Pamph. geol. Surv. Ire.* **E.**R. 43–48; **O.**G. 47–.

17974 **Emergency Reports. Industrial Health Research Board.** London. *Emerg. Rep. ind. Hlth Res. Bd* [1940–44] **L.**BM.; MD.; SC.; **Bl.**U.; 41–44; **Bm.**U. **E.**U.; **M.**P.; **N.**P.41–44; **O.**R.

17976 **Emory Medical Review.** Atlanta. *Emory med. Rev.*

17977 **Emory University Museum Bulletin.** Emory University, Georgia. *Emory Univ. Mus. Bull.* [1943–] **L.**EB. 43–55.

17978 **Empire Cotton Growing Review.** London. *Emp. Cott. Grow. Rev.* [1924–] **L.**AM. 35– imp.; EB.; K.; L. 32–53 imp.; MY.; P.; TP.; UC.; **Abs.**A. 53–; N.; U. imp.; **Bm.**U.; **Bn.**U.; **Br.**U.; **C.**A.; BO. 24–35; UL.; **Cr.**U. 25–; **E.**A.; **Ex.**U. 47–; **G.**U.; **Hu.**G. 52–; **Je.** 27–36: 49–; **Ld.**P. (3 yr.); U.; **Lv.**U.; **M.**C.; P.; T.; U.; **Md.**H. 39–; **N.**U. 40–; **Nw.**A. 25–; **O.**B.; RE. 51–; **R.**U.; **Rt.; Sa.; Sh.**U. 45–; **Sil.** 56–; **Y.**

17979 **Empire Forester.** Syracuse, N.Y. *Emp. Forester*

17980 **Empire Forestry.** London. *Emp. For.* [1922–23] **L.**A.; BM.; BM[N].; EB.; K.; P.; SC.; **Abs.**N.; **Bn.**U.; **C.**A.; UL.; **Db.; E.**A.; B.; **O.**F.; R. [*C. as:* 17982]

17981 **Empire Forestry Handbook.** London. *Emp. For. Handb.* [1930–] **L.**BM.; K. 30–46; **Abs.**N.; **C.**UL.; **Cr.**M. 53– imp.; **Lv.**P. 33– imp.; **M.**P.; **O.**F.; RH.

17982 **Empire Forestry Journal.** London. *Emp. For. J.* [1923–45] **L.**A. 23–36; AM. 23–27; BM.; BM[N].; EB. 23–30; HS. 32–41; K.; L. 28–37; P.; SC.; TP.; **Abd.**U.; **Abs.**N.; P. 29–45; **Bm.**U.; **Bn.**U.; **C.**UL.; **Cr.**M.; **Db.; E.**A.; B.; **O.**F.; R.; **Rt.** imp. [*C. of:* 17980; *C. as:* 17983]

17983 **Empire Forestry Review.** London. *Emp. For. Rev.* [1946–] **L.**BM.; BM[N].; K.; P.; TP.; **Abd.**U.; **Abs.**N.; **Bm.**U.; **Bn.**U.; **C.**A. (3 yr.); UL.; **Cr.**M. 46–52; **Db.; E.**A.; **M.**P.; **O.**B.; F.; **Rt.; Y.** [*C. of:* 17982]

17984 **Empire Journal** of **Experimental Agriculture.** Oxford. *Emp. J. exp. Agric.* [1933–] **L.**A.; AM.; BM.; IC.; K.; P.; TP.; U. 52–; VC. 44–; **Abd.**R.; S.; U. 47–; V. 47–54; **Abs.**A.; **Bl.**U. 52–; **Bm.**U.; **Bn.**U.; **Br.**A.; U.; **C.**A.; AB.; UL.; V.; **Db.; E.**A.; AB. 37–; AR.; B.; PO. 48–; U.; W.; **G.**U. 48– imp.; **Hu.**G.; **Je.; Ld.**U.; W. 36–50; **Md.**H.; **N.**U.; **Nw.**A.; **O.**AEC.; R.; RE.; **R.**D.; U.; **Rt.; Sal.; Sil.** W. 38–; **Y.**
Empire Marketing Board. [Publications.] London. *See* 40994.

17985 **Empire Mining Review.** Johannesburg. *Emp. Min. Rev.* [1930] **L.**P.

17986 **Empire Pork Review.** London. *Emp. Pork Rev.* **C.**A. 31–.

17987 **Empire Social Hygiene Year-Book.** London. *Emp. soc. Hyg. Yb.* [1934–40] **L.**BM.; MD. 34–35: 37; **Bm.**P.; **M.**P.; **O.**B.

17988 **Empire Survey Review.** London. *Emp. Surv. Rev.* [1931–] **L.**AS.; AV. 50–; G.; NC. 57–61; P.; QM. 59–; SC.; U. 49–; **Abs.**N.; U. 57–; **Bl.**U. 46–; **Bm.**U. 32– imp.; **Br.**U. 31–58; **C.**ENG. 46–; GD.; **Cr.**U. 45–; **Db.; Dn.**U. 47–; **E.**A.; U.; **G.**U. 46–; **H.**U. 53–; **Ld.**U. 46–53; **M.**T. 55–; **N.**U. 46–; **Nw.**A. 47–; **O.**R.; **Sa.** 46–; **Sw.**U. imp.; **Y.**

17989 **Emplois industriels** du **gaz.** Paris. *Empl. ind. Gaz* **L.**P. 29–37*.

17990 **Emu.** Melbourne. *Emu* [1901–] **L.**BM[N].; Z.; **Br.**U.; **C.**N.; **O.**OR.; **Y.**

17991 **Émulation.** Société centrale d'architecture de Belgique. Louvain. *Émulation* [1874–?] **L.**BA. 86–13: 22–*. [*Suspended* 1914–18] [*C. as:* 4023]

17992 **Enamel Bibliography** and **Abstracts.** Columbus. *Enam. Biblphy Abstr.* **L.**P. 44–.

17993 **Enamelers' Reference.** Porcelain Enamel and Manufacturing Co. Baltimore. *Enamrs' Ref.* [1938–]

17994 **Enamelist.** Cleveland, Ohio. *Enamelist* [1926–50] **L.**P.; **Bm.**C. 38–50; P. 45–50. [*C. as:* 23842]

17995 **Enamelist Bulletin.** Cleveland. *Enamelist Bull.* [1951–55] **L.**P.

17996 **Enamelling Abstracts.** Birmingham. *Enamg Abstr.* [1939–43] **L.**P.; **Bm.**P.; **O.**R. [*C. in:* 9607]

17997 **Encéphale.** Journal de psychiatrie. Paris. *Encéphale* [1906–] **L.**MA. 37–42; MD. 07–; PS. 27–; S. 06–50; **Dn.**U. 61–; **E.**P.; U. 42–; **Lv.**M. 28–31; **M.**MS. 22–24; **O.**R. 58–.
Encéphale et **hygiène mentale.** *See* 17997.

17998 **Enchiridion.** Sheffield. *Enchiridion* **L.**P. (curr.)

17999 **Enciclopedia annuario** delle **materie plastiche.** Milano. *Encicl. a. Mater. plast.* [1957–] **L.**P. 58–; PL.

18000 **Enciclopedia** di **chimica scientifica** e **industriale.** Torino. *Encicl. Chim. scient. ind.* [1867–18] **L.**C.; P. [*Also supplements*]

18001 **Enciclopedia zoológica** y **agrícola.** Vitoria. *Encicl. zool. agríc.*

18002 **Encilion.** Journal of the Carmarthenshire Antiquarian Society and Field Club. Carmarthen. *Encilion* [1912–13] **Abs.**N.; **Lv.**U.; **Sw.**U.

Encyclopedia of **Plant Physiology.** Berlin. *See* 21829.

18003 **Encyclopédie** de l'**aviation.** Revue mensuelle des publications aéronautiques. Paris. *Encycl. Aviat.* [1904–13] **L.**P.

18004 **Encyclopédie biologique.** Paris. *Encycl. biol.* [1927–] **L.**BM[N].

18005 **Encyclopédie entomologique.** Paris. *Encycl. ent.* [1924–] **L.**BM[N]; E.; EB.; Z. imp.; **C.**B.

18006 **Encyclopédie mycologique.** Paris. *Encycl. mycol.* [1931–] **L.**BM[N].

18007 **Encyclopédie ornithologique.** Paris. *Encycl. orn.* [1924–] **L.**BM[N]. 24–49.

18008 **Encyclopédie pratique** du **naturaliste.** Paris. *Encycl. prat. Nat.* [1913–] **L.**BM[N].; EB. (ent.) 21–24.

18009 **Encyclopédie** des **sciences mathématiques pures** et **appliquées.** Paris. *Encycl. Sci. math. pures appl.* [1904–] **Abs.**N. imp.; **E.**U. 04–14 imp.; **Lv.**U. 04–23 imp.; **Sa.** [*French edition of:* 18280]

18010 **Encyclopédie scientifique.** Paris. *Encycl. scient.* [1908–] **L.**BM[N].; EB. (ent.) 09–31.

18011 **Encyclopédie vétérinaire périodique.** Lyon. *Encycl. vét. périod.* [1944–] **L.**V.; **W.**; **Y.**

18012 **Endeavour.** London. *Endeavour* [1942–] **L.**AM.; AS.; AV.; B.; BM[N].; C.; CB.; E.; FO.; GL.; HS.; IC.; K.; LE. 43–; LI.; MA.; MC.; MD.; MI. 54–; MO. 56–; MY. 44– imp.; NF.; NP.; P.; PC. 49– imp.; PH.; PL.; QM. imp.; R.; RI.; SC.; SH. (1 yr); SI.; TD.; TP.; U.; UC.; UCH. imp.; V. (2 yr.); VC.; **Abd.**A.; R.; S.; U.; **Abs.**A. 50–; U. imp.; **Ba.**I.; **Bl.**U.; **Bm.**C.; P.; U.; **Bn.**U.; **Bra.**P. 46–; U.; **C.**AN. 49–; APH. 50–; B.; BI. 56–; BO. 53–; CH.; GE. 50–; P.; PO. 53–; R. 49–; UL.; V. 53–; **Co.**T.; **Cr.**M.; P.; U.; **Db.**; **Dm.**; **Dn.**U.; **E.**AB.; AG.; AR. 56–; HW. 43– imp.; O.; P.; PO. 52–; R.; S.; TD.; U.; W. imp.; **Ep.**D.; **Ex.**U.; **F.**A.; **Fr.**; **G.**F.; T. 53–; U.; **H.**U.; **Hu.**G.; **Je.**; **Lc.**A.; **Ld.**P.; U.; W.; **Lh.**P.; **Li.**M. (5 yr.); **Lo.** 55–; **Lv.**P.; **M.**C.; D.; MS.; P.; T.; U. imp.; **Ma.**T. imp.; **Md.**H.; **Mi.**; **N.**T. 52–; U.; **Nw.**A.; **O.**AP.; BI. (curr.); BO.; CH. 56–; F. 51– imp.; G. 53– imp.; P.; R.; RE. (2 yr.); Z. 49–; **Pl.**M.; **R.**D.; U. imp.; **Rt.**; **Sa.**; **Sal.**; **Sh.**IO.; U.; **Sil.** 57–; **St.**R.; **Ste.**; **Sy.**R.; **W.**; **Wd.**; **We.**K.; **Wo.** 47–; **Y.**

18013 **Endemic Diseases Bulletin. Nagasaki University.** Nagasaki. *Endem. Dis. Bull. Nagasaki Univ.* [1959–] **L.**EB.; MA.; TP.

18015 **Endocrine Survey.** Glendale, Cal. *Endocrine Surv.* [1923–39] **L.**MA. 29; S. [*C. of:* 23840; *C. in:* 30243]

18016 **Endocrinologia.** Bucureşti. *Endocrinologia, Buc.* [*C. of:* 557]

18017 **Endocrinología.** Buenos Aires. *Endocrinología, B. Aires*

18017° **Endocrinologia japonica.** Tokyo. *Endocr. jap.* [1954–] **L.**MA.; MC.; MD.; SC.; TD.; **Ld.**U. 61–; **R.**D.

18018 **Endocrinologia** e **patologia costituzionale.** Bologna. *Endocr. Patol. costit.* [1922–40] **L.**MD. 33–40. [*C. as:* 18019]

18019 **Endocrinologia** e **scienza** delle **costituzione.** Bologna. *Endocr. Sci. Costit.* [1941–] **L.**MA. 46–; MD. [*C. of:* 18018]

18020 **Endocrinology.** Glendale, Cal., etc. *Endocrinology* [1917–] **L.**B. 51–; C. 45–; CB. 43–; LI.; MA. 34–; MC.; MD.; PH. 35–; S.; U. imp.; UC. 20–; UCH. 47–; VC. 33–; Z. 39–42; **Abd.**R. 47–; U. 38–; **Abs.**N. 49–; U. 59–; **Bl.**U. 38–; **Bm.**U. 34–; **C.**APH. 37–; BI. 39–42: 50–; MD.; PH. 17–31: 50–; UL.; V. 53–; **Cr.**U. 50–; **Db.**; **Dn.**U. 52–; **E.**A.; AG. 38–; P.; PO. 38–; U.; **G.**F. 38: 44–; U.; **Ld.**U. 21–; **Lv.**M.; **M.**MS.; **N.**U. 49–; **Nw.**A. 36–; **O.**R. 18–; **Pl.**M. 51–; **R.**D. 40–; U. 51–; **Sa.**; **Sh.**U. 27–; **W.** 43–; **Y.**

18021 **Endokrinologia polska.** Warszawa. *Endokr. pol.* [1950–] **L.**MA. 59–; MC. 58–; **Y.**

18022 **Endokrinologie.** Leipzig. *Endokrinologie* [1928–] **L.**LI. 28–39; MA. 49–; MC. 36–46: 50–55; MD.; S. 33–50; SC. 30–40: 60–; **C.**UL.; **Y.**

18023 **Endüstri, fen, sanat** ve **teknik.** Istanbul. *Endüstri Fen Sanat Tek.* **Y.**

18024 **Energetica.** Bucureşti. *Energetica* [1953–] **L.**BM. 56–; EE. 55–; **Y.**

18025 **Énergeticheskiĭ byulleten' Ministerstva neftyanoĭ promȳshlennosti.** Moskva. Энергетический бюллетень Министерства нефтяной промышленности. *Énerg. Byull. Minist. neft. Prom.* **L.**BM. 47–58*; P. 54–58 imp.; **Y.** 47–58.

18026 **Énergeticheskiĭ byulleten' narkomnefti.** Moskva. Энергетический бюллетень наркомнефти. *Énerg. Byull. Narkomnefti* [1947–] **L.**BM.

18027 **Énergeticheskiĭ vestnik.** Kharkov. Энергетический вестник. *Énerg. Vest.* [1926–]

18028 **Énergeticheskoe obozrenie.** Vȳpusk teplotekhnicheskiĭ. Moskva. Энергетическое обозрение. Выпуск теплотехнический. *Énerg. Obozr.* [1930–38] [*C. as:* 52852]

18029 **Énergeticheskoe stroitel'stvo.** Энергетическое строительство. *Énerg. Stroit.* [1958–] **Y.** imp.

18030 **Énergetik.** Moskva. Энергетик. *Énergetik* [1953–] **L.**BM. 54–; EE.; P. 54–; SC. 54–; **Y.** 54– imp. [*C. of:* 40217; *English abstracts at:* 28235ª]

18031 **Énergetika.** Kharkov. Энергетика. *Énergetika, Kharkov* [1930–]

18032 **Energetika.** Praha. *Energetika, Praha* [1951–] **L.**BM. 57–59; EE. 54– imp.; P. 58–; **Y.**

18032° **Énergetika** i **avtomatika.** Moskva. Энергетика и автоматика. *Énerg. Avtom.* [1959–] **L.**AV.; I.; SC.; **F.**A.; **M.**P.; **Sh.**S.; **Sw.**U.; **Y.** [*C. from:* 24296]

18033 **Energetyka.** Warszawa. *Energetyka* **L.**EE. 52–.

18034 **Energia.** Bucureşti. *Energia, Buc.* [1921–]

18035 **Energia.** Napoli. *Energia, Napoli* [1946]

18036 **Energia** és **atomtechnika.** Budapest. *Energia Atomtech.* [1957–] **L.**BM.; **Y.** [*C. of:* 29166]

18037 **Energía eléctrica.** Madrid. *Energía eléct.* [1899–] **L.**P. 04–32.

18038 **Energia elettrica.** Milano. *Energia elett.* [1924–] **L.**EE. 26–47 imp.; P. 27–; **Y.**

18039 **Energía nuclear.** Madrid. *Energía nucl., Madrid* [1957–] **L.**P.; **Y.**

18040 **Energia nucleare.** Milano. *Energia nucl., Milano* [1951–] **L.**AV. 58–; EE. 55–; P.; **Y.**

18041 **Energia termica.** Milano. *Energia term.* [1933–] **L.**P. 33–42 imp.; SC. 34–.

18042 **Energie.** Berlin. *Energie, Berl.* [1900–04] **L.**P. [*C. of:* 53249]

18043 **Énergie.** Bruxelles. *Énergie, Brux.* **L.**P. 57–; **Y.**

18044 **Energie.** München. *Energie, Münch.* [1949–] **L.**P. 50–.

18045 **Énergie.** Paris. *Énergie, Paris* [1947–48] **L.**P. 48; SC.; **Ld.**U.; **Li.**M. [*C. in:* 47241]

18046 **Energie** aus dem **Atom.** Zürich. *Energie Atom* [1958–] **L.**P. [*Supplement to* and *issued with:* 17829]

18047 **Énergie électrique.** Paris. *Énergie élect.*

18048 **Énergie nucléaire.** Paris. *Énergie nucl.* [1956–] **L.**P.; SC. 59–; **M.**P. 57–; **N.**U. 58–; **Nw.**A. 57–; **Wd.**; **Y.**

18049 **Energie** und **Technik.** Hamburg. *Energie Tech.* [1949–] **L.**P. 55–; **Y.**

18050 **Énergie végétale** et ses **applications.** Paris. *Énergie vég.*

18051 **Energiebibliographie.** Berlin. *Energiebibliographie* [1931–34] **L.**NF.; P.; **Bm.**P. 34.

18052 **Energietechnik.** Berlin. *Energietechnik* [1951–] **L.**P.; **G.**U. 58–; **Y.** [*C. from:* 6129]

18053 **Energieverwendung.** Berlin. *Energieverwendung* [1943–44] [*C. of:* 57326]

18053° **Energija.** Zagreb. *Energija* **Y.**

18054 **Énergiya.** S.-Peterburg. Энергия. *Énergiya* [1913–14]

18055 **Énergiya** i **voda.** Sofiya. Энергия и вода. *Energiya Voda* [1950–51] **L.**BM. 51. [*C. as:* 17834]

18056 **Énergomashinostroenie.** Leningrad, Moskva. Энергомашиностроение. *Énergomashinostroenie* [1955–] **L.**BM.; P. 57–; **G.**ME. (2 yr); **Y.** imp.

18057 **Énergotekhnologicheskoe ispol'zovanie topliva.** Энерготехнологическое использование топлива. *Énergotekhnol. Ispol'. Topl.* **Y.**

18058 **Enfance.** Paris. *Enfance* [1960–] **Lv.**P.

18059 **Enfance.** Pédiatrie, puériculture. Paris. *Enfance, Pédiat. Puéric.*

18059° **Enfance.** Psychologie, pédagogie, neuro-psychiatrie, sociologie. Paris. *Enfance, Psychol. Pédag.* [1948–] **L.**UC.

18060 **Enfance anormale.** Lyon. *Enf. anorm., Lyon* [*C. of:* 11397]

18061 **Enfance anormale.** Paris. *Enf. anorm., Paris*

18062 **Enfances.** Alger. *Enfances* [1956–] **L.**MA.

18063 **Enfant.** Athènes. *Enfant, Athènes* **L.**TD. 31–34.

18064 **Enfant.** Paris. *Enfant, Paris*

Engelmann's Archiv für **Anatomie** und **Physiologie.** *See* 4044.

18065 **Engenharia.** São Paulo. *Engenharia* [1942–] **Y.** [*C. of:* 7404]

18066 **Engenharia, mineração** e **metalurgia.** Rio de Janeiro. *Engenh. Miner. Metal.* [1951–] **L.**GL.; MI. [*C. of:* 31887]

18067 **Engenharia** e **química.** Rio de Janeiro. *Engenh. Quím.* [1949–] **O.**R. 56–; **Y.**

Engineer. Chicago. *See* 18077.

18068 **Engineer.** Cleveland. *Engineer, Cleveland*

18069 **Engineer.** London. *Engineer, Lond.* [1856–] **L.**AV. 00–; BA. 49–; BM.; EE.; I.; IC. 17–; MT. 22–; NF. 42–; P.; PL. 46–; QM. 48–; SC.; SI. 47–; U. imp.; UC. 36–; **Abd.**U. 48– imp.; **Abs.**N. 12–; P.; U. 48–; **Bl.**U. 63– imp.; **Bm.**C. 24–; P.; T. 1860–69: 80– imp.; **Bn.**U. 1856–68 imp.; **Br.**P.; U. imp.; **Bra.**P. 10–; **C.**ENG. 73–; UL. 94–; **Cr.**P. 69–; U. 91– imp.; **Db.** 72–; **Dn.**U. 84–; **E.**A. 94–; F.; L. 95–23; SW. 47–; T. 1857–50; U. 57–; **F.**A. 39–; **G.**E. 1857– imp.; M.; T. 1856–08: 25–; U. 14–40: 61–; **Lc.**A. 55–; **Ld.**P.; U.; W. 54–; **Li.**M. 22–; **Lv.**P. imp.; U.; **M.**C. 23–; P.; T.; U. 67–; **Ma.**T. 39–; **N.**P.; T. 54–; U. 68– v. imp; **Nw.**A. imp.; P. imp.; **O.**R. 94–; **Sh.**IO.; M. 1857–64: 09–13; SC.; **Sil.** 43–; **Sw.**U. 66– imp.; **Wd.** 30–; **Y.**

18070 **Engineer.** State College, Pa. *Engineer, St. Coll. Pa*

18071 **Engineer Apprentice.** London. *Engr Apprent.* [1947–] **L.**P. 47–59; **F.**A. 53; **Te.**N. (1 yr). [*Suspended* 1951–52]

18072 **Engineer** and **Builder.** Washington. *Engr Bldr*

18073 **Engineer Buyers Guide.** London. *Engr Buy. Guide* **L.**P. (curr.); **Y.**

18074 **Engineer** in **Charge** and **Works Manager.** London. *Engr in Charge* [1906–12] **L.**BM.; P.; SC.; **M.**P. 06–08. [*C. as:* 38262]

18075 **Engineer** and **Foundryman.** Johannesburg. *Engr Foundrym.* [1936–] **L.**BM. 46–; I. 53–; P. 58–; **Bm.**C. 36– imp.; **Sh.**IO. 53–; **Y.**

18076 **Engineer** in **India.** Howrah. *Engr India* [1933–39] **L.**BM.; P. [*C. of:* 12696]

18077 **Engineer** and **Steam Engineering.** Chicago. *Engr Steam Engng* [1888–08] **L.**P.; **Bm.**U. 03–06. [*C. in:* 38230]

18078 **Engineer's Year Book** of Formulae, rules, tables, etc. London. *Engr's Yb.* [1894–] **L.**BM.; **Bm.**P. 18– imp.; U. 08: 13–; **Br.**P. 09–; **Cr.**P. 16– imp.; **E.**A.; R. 23–29; **G.**T. 12–; **Ld.**P. 30–; U. 14– imp.

18079 **Engineering.** The journal of the Chinese Institute of Engineers, Wu-Han Branch. Hankow. *Engineering, Hankow* [1946–]

18080 **Engineering.** London. *Engineering, Lond.* [1866–] **L.**AV. 01–; BA. 49–; BM.; EE. 80– imp.; I.; IC. 10–; MI. 42–48 imp.; NF. 23–; P.; PL. 46–; PT.; QM. 48–; RI. 88–94: 97–; SC.; SI. 46–; U.; UC. imp.; **Abd.**P. 88–; U.; **Abs.**N. 52–; **Bl.**U. 86– imp.; **Bm.**C. 24–; P.; T. imp.; U. 86–; **Bn.**U. imp.; **Br.**P.; U.; **Bra.**P. 72–; **C.**APH. 50–52; ENG. 77–; P. 13–; UL.; **Cr.**P. 67– imp.; U. imp.; **Db.**; **Dn.**U. 84–; **E.**A.; F. 72– imp.; HW. imp.; L. 99–23; SW. 47–; T.; U. 76–; **F.**A. 26–; **G.**E.; M.; T.; U.; **Lc.**A. 53–; **Ld.**P.; U.; W. 42–55; **Li.**M. 21–; **Lv.**P. imp.; U.; **M.**C. 23–; P.; T.; U.; **N.**P. 66–27; T. 47–; U. 76–; **Nw.**A. imp.; P. imp.; **O.**R.; **Rn.**B. 39–; **Sh.**G. 18–; P.; SC.; **Sil.** 43–; **St.**R. 47–; **Ste.** 40–; **Wd.** 16–; **Y.**

18081 **Engineering Abstracts.** London. *Engng Abstr.* [1910–13] **L.**BM. 12; P. 11–13; SC. 11; **M.**P. 10. [*C. of:* 20247]

18081° **Engineering Abstracts.** London. *Engng Abstr.* [1938–40] **L.**P.; **E.**R.; **M.**U. 38–39. [*C. in:* 53759 and 26218]

18082 **Engineering Abstracts. Institution of Civil Engineers.** London. *Engng Abstr. Instn civ. Engrs* [1921–37: *then in section below*] L.AV. 21–24 imp.; MT.; P.; U. 23–37; UC.; **Bm.**C. 22–37; P. 24–37; T. 25–37; U. 25–37; **Br.**U.; **C.**UL.; **E.**R. 28–37; **G.**E.; T. 26–37; U. 23–37; **Ld.**U.; **Lv.**P. 21–35; U.; **M.**U.; **Nw.**A.; **O.**R.; **Sh.**IO. 36–37; **Sw.**U. [*C. of:* 375]

    Section 1. Engineering construction [1938–39] L.BM.; P.; U.; **Bm.**P.; U.; **C.**UL.; **E.**R.; **G.**T.; U.; **Ld.**U.; **M.**U.; **N.**U.; **O.**R.; **Sh.**IO.; **Sw.**U. [*C. in:* 26218]

    Section 2. Mechanical engineering [1939] L.BM.; P.; U.; **Bm.**P.; U.; **C.**UL.; **E.**R.; **G.**T.; U.; **Ld.**U.; **M.**U.; **N.**U.; **O.**R.; **Sh.**IO.; **Sw.**U. [*C. in:* 26218]

    Section 3. Shipbuilding and marine engineering [1938–53] L.BM. imp.; P.; U.; **Bm.**P.; U. imp.; **C.**UL.; **E.**A.; R.; **G.**T.; U. imp.; **Ld.**U.; **M.**U.; **N.**U.; **O.**R.; **Sh.**IO.; **Sw.**U. [*C. as:* 29430ᵃ]

    Section 4. Mining engineering [1938–39] L.BM.; P.; U.; **Bm.**P.; **C.**UL.; **E.**R.; **Ld.**U.; **N.**U.; **O.**R.; **Sw.**U.; **Y.** [*C. in:* 26218]

18083 **Engineering Abstracts. Thornton Research Centre.** Chester. *Engng Abstr. Thornton Res. Cent.* L.P. (2 yr.); **Y.**

18084 **Engineering and Allied Trades Review.** London. *Engng all. Trades Rev.* L.P. 45–58; **F.**A. 48–.

18085 **Engineering and Boiler House Review.** London. *Engng Boil. House Rev.* [1923–] L.BM.; I. (6 mo.); P.; **Abs.**N.; **Bm.**U. 35–41 imp.; **Bra.**P. 23–39; 44–; **E.**A.; **G.**M.; P. 39–; PH. 39–; **Ld.**P. 50–; U. 35–; **Lv.**P. 38– imp.; **M.**P.; T.; **O.**R.; **Sh.**IO. 43–; **St.**R. 47–; **Y.** [*C. of:* 18165]

18085° **Engineering Bulletin. Alabama Engineering Experiment Station.** Auburn. *Engng Bull. Ala. Engng Exp. Stn* [1939–] L.P.; **Y.** [*C. of:* 9273]

18086 **Engineering Bulletin. American Oil Burner Association,** Inc. New York. *Engng Bull. Am. Oil Burner Ass.* L.P. 31–33.

18087 **Engineering Bulletin. Automatic Telephone Manufacturing Electric Company.** Liverpool. *Engng Bull. autom. Teleph. Mfg elect. Co.* L.P. (curr.)

18088 **Engineering Bulletin. Carnegie Institute** of **Technology.** Pittsburg. *Engng Bull. Carnegie Inst. Technol.* [1937–] L.P.; **Abs.**N.; **Bm.**P. [*C. of:* 32033]

18089 **Engineering Bulletin. Department** of **Health, Michigan.** Lansing. *Engng Bull. Dep. Hlth Mich.* L.P. 13–37.

18090 **Engineering Bulletin, Extension Series. Purdue University.** Lafayette. *Engng Bull. Ext. Ser. Purdue Univ.* [1931–] L.AV. 56–; P.; **Bm.**U.; **M.**U. [*C. of:* 10172; *Part of:* 18094]

18091 **Engineering Bulletin. Georgia State Board** of **Health.** Atlanta. *Engng Bull. Ga St. Bd Hlth*

    Engineering Bulletin. Michigan State Board of **Health.** *See* 18089.

18092 **Engineering Bulletin. Ministry** of **Labour.** London. *Engng Bull. Minist. Lab.* [1941–42] L.BM.; P.; SC.; U.; **Bm.**P.; **C.**UL.; **Cr.**P.; **G.**M.; **Ld.**U. 42; **O.**R. [*C. as:* 39904]

18093 **Engineering Bulletin. National Lumber Manufacturers' Association.** Chicago. *Engng Bull. natn. Lumber Mfr's Ass.* L.P. 16.

18094 **Engineering Bulletin. Purdue University.** Lafayette. *Engng Bull. Purdue Univ.* [1930–55] L.P.; **Bm.**U.; **M.**U.; **Y.** [*C. of:* 40995; *C. in:* 45819 and 18847; *Extension series at:* 18090; *Research bulletin at:* 18095]

18095 **Engineering Bulletin, Research Bulletin. Purdue University.** Lafayette. *Engng Bull. Res. Bull. Purdue Univ.* [1931–] L.AV. 49–; P.; **Bm.**U.; **Y.** [*C. of:* 10165 and 10172; *Part of:* 18094]

    Engineering Bulletin. Research Series, Purdue University. *See* 18095.

18096 **Engineering Bulletin. Siemens Brothers** and **Company.** London. *Engng Bull. Siemens* [1945–] L.AV. 49–56; P. 45–57; **G.**E. (3 yr.); **Lv.**P. imp.; **Wd.** 57–58; **Y.** [*C. of:* 18174]

18097 **Engineering Bulletin** of the **Speed Scientific School, Louisville University.** Louisville, Ky. *Engng Bull. Speed scient. Sch. Louisville* L.P. 30–.

18098 **Engineering Bulletin. Washington State College Engineering Experiment Station.** Pullman, Wash. *Engng Bull. Wash. St. Coll. Engng Exp. Stn* [1914–43] L.P. 22–43; SC. 21–43. [*C. as:* 12604]

18098° **Engineering Capacity Register.** Birmingham. *Engng Capac. Register* [1959–] L.BM.

18099 **Engineering** and **Cement World.** Chicago. *Engng Cem. Wld* [1918] [*C. of:* 13515; *C. as:* 18177]

18100 **Engineering** and **Chemical Digest.** Johannesburg. *Engng Chem. Dig.* [1949–52] L.BM.; EE.; **Db.**

18101 **Engineering College Research Review.** Urbana. *Engng Coll. Res. Rev.* L.P. (curr.)

18102 **Engineering Construction** in the **Far West.** San Francisco. *Engng Constr. far W.*

18103 **Engineering** and **Contract Record.** Toronto. *Engng Contract Rec.* [1937–] **Ha.**RD. 55–. [*C. of:* 15554]

18104 **Engineering** and **Contracting.** Chicago. *Engng Contrg* [1911–32] L.P.; **Lv.**U. 21–32. [*C. of:* 18105]

18105 **Engineering Contracting.** Chicago. *Engng Contrg* L.P. 11*. [*C. as:* 18104]

18106 **Engineering Contractor.** New York. *Engng Contractor* [*C. of:* 25535]

18107 **Engineering Departmental Reports** and **Theses. Engineering Experiment Station, University** of **Illinois.** Urbana. *Engng depl Rep. Theses Univ. Ill.* L.P. 59–; **Y.**

18108 **Engineering Designer.** London. *Engng Desr* [1955–] L.BM.; P.; **Y.**

18109 **Engineering Digest.** Los Angeles. *Engng Dig., Los Angeles* [1928–]

18110 **Engineering Digest.** New York. *Engng Dig., N.Y.* [1908–09] L.BM.; P.; SC.; **Br.**P.; **C.**UL.; **E.**T.; **Ld.**P.; **O.**R. [*C. of:* 52112; *C. as:* 23199]

18111 **Engineering Digest.** Toronto. *Engng Dig., Toronto* [1954–] L.EE. 55–.

    Engineering Division, British Broadcasting Corporation Monographs. *See* 5634.

18112 **Engineering Drawing** and **Design.** London. *Engng Draw. Des.* [1947–] L.NF. 49–; P. 47–51; SC. 48–51 imp.; **Bm.**P.; **G.**M. 47–51; **St.**R.

18113 **Engineering Education.** Lancaster, Pa. *Engng Educ.* [*C. as:* 25953]

18114 **Engineering Equipment.** Birmingham. *Engng Equip.* [1957–58] **L.**BM. [*C. in:* 39898]

Engineering Experiment Station Bulletin, Connecticut. *See* 10161.

18115 **Engineering Experiment Station News. Louisiana State University.** Baton Rouge. *Engng Exp. Stn News La St. Univ.* [1945–] **Wa.**W. 46–.

18116 **Engineering Experiment Station News. Ohio State University.** Columbus, O. *Engng Exp. Stn News Ohio St. Univ.* [1929–54] **L.**EE. 34–54; NF. 45–54; P.; **G.**U.; **M.**U. 32–52 imp.; **Nw.**A. 32–54 imp.; **O.**R. 32–54; **Wa.**B. 34–54. [*C. as:* 34799]

18117 **Engineering Experiment Station Series. Virginia Polytechnic Institute.** *Engng Exp. Stn Ser. Va polytech. Inst.* [1923–] **Y.**

Engineering Extension Division Series. Virginia Polytechnic Institute. *See* 18118.

18118 **Engineering Extension Series Bulletin. Virginia Polytechnic Institute.** Blacksburg. *Engng Ext. Ser. Bull. Va polytech. Inst.* **Y.**

18119 **Engineering** and **Finance.** New York. *Engng Finance* [1929–32] **L.**P.; **Bm.**U. 29–31; **Br.**U. 29–31; **M.**P. 29–31; **O.**R. 29–31. [*C. of:* 14988]

18120 **Engineering Gazette.** London. *Engng Gaz.* [1912–] **L.**BM.; P. 25–.

18121 **Engineering Geology Case Histories.** *Engng Geol. Case Hist.* [1957–] **Br.**U.; **E.**R. 58–.

18122 **Engineering Graphic.** Chicago. *Engng Graphic* [1929–30] **L.**P. [*Replaces:* 31882]

18123 **Engineering Index.** London, New York. *Engng Index* [1884–] **L.**BM. 99–19; EE. 96–; KC. 31–; MT. 22–; P.; QM. 46–; SC.; **Bl.**U. 45–50: 58–; **Bm.**C. 19–; P. 92– imp.; T. 43–; U. 92–11 imp.; 44–; **Br.**P. 01–05; U. 54–; **Bra.**P. 19–27; **C.**ENG. 96–; **Co.**T. 46–49: 54–; **Cr.**P. 02–05; U. 59–; **Db.** 50–; **G.**M. 92–27: 44–; T. 20–; U. 46–; **Ld.**P. 52–; U. 20–; **Lv.**P. 36–47; **M.**D. 44–48: 56–; P. 92–; T. imp.; U. 96–00; **N.**T. 56–; U. 55–; **Nw.**A. 96–06: 19–; P. 92–05: 50–; **O.**R. 99–19: 49–; **Rn.**B. 39–; **Sh.**IO. 20–27: 48–; SC. 96–26: 41–; **Y.** [>18124, 1906–18]

18124 **Engineering Index Annual.** New York & London. *Engng Index A.* [1906–18] **L.**BM.; P.; SC. 06–16; **Bm.**P.; U. 06–11; **Cr.**P. 06–11; **G.**M.; **Lv.**P.; **M.**P.; T.; **Nw.**P. 06–13; **O.**R. 11–12. [*C. of:* and *Rec. as:* 18123]

18125 **Engineering** and **Industrial Management.** London. *Engng ind. Mgmt* [1919–22] **L.**BM.; EE.; P.; SC.; **Abs.**N.; **Bm.**P.; T.; U.; **C.**UL.; **Db.**; **E.**L.; T.; **G.**M.; U.; **Lv.**P.; **M.**P.; T.; U.; **Nw.**P.; **O.**R. [*C. of:* 13432; *C. as:* 23242]

18126 **Engineering Industries Bulletin.** Engineering Industries Association. *Engng Inds Bull.* **L.**BM. 46–56★ imp.; **Sil.** 56. [*Also* Export supplement; *C. as:* 18127]

18127 **Engineering Industries Journal.** Engineering Industries Association. *Engng Inds J.* [1957–] **L.**BM.; **Sil.** [*C. of:* 18126]

18128 **Engineering, Industry** and **Commerce.** London. *Engng Ind. Comm.* **L.**BM. 29–.

18129 **Engineering Inspection.** London. *Engng Inspn* [1935–55] **L.**AV. 44–55 imp.; BM.; EE. 52–55; P.; SC.; **Bm.**P. 41–55; U. 35–39 imp.; **G.**E. 48–55; **Lv.**P. 53–55; **M.**T. 52–55; **Nw.**A. 35–40 imp.; **O.**R.; **Sh.**IO.; **Y.** [*Replaces:* 23672; *C. as:* 23676]

18130 **Engineering Journal. Aeronautical Section Reprint.** Montreal. *Engng J. aeronaut. Sect. Repr.* [1931–] **L.**BM.; **Ld.**U. 35–; **O.**R. 35–.

18131 **Engineering Journal** of **Canada.** Toronto. *Engng J. Can.* [1905–10] **L.**BM.

18132 **Engineering Journal. Canadian Society** of **Civil Engineers.** Montreal. *Engng J. Can. Soc. civ. Engrs* [1922–] **L.**AV. 45–; BM.; EE. 39– imp. I. (yr); P.; TD. (1 yr); **Bm.**U. 31: 35–; **Br.**U. 50–; **Db.**; **Dn.**U. 52–; **E.**R.; T. 22–25; **G.**E.; T. 47–; U. 55–; **Ld.**U. 37–; **Lv.**P. 59–; **Sil.** 47–; **Y.** [*C. of:* 25955]

18133 **Engineering Magazine.** New York and London. *Engng Mag.* [1891–16] **L.**BM. 94–16; EE. 01–16 imp.; I. 93–16; P. 10–16; SC. 97–16; **Abs.**N. 12–16; **Bm.**P. 00–16; **Br.**P. 13–15; **Bra.**P. 04–16; **C.**UL. 97–16; **Cr.**P. 04–15 imp.; **Db.**; **E.**A. 97–16; T. imp.; **G.**M. 97–16; **Ld.**P. 04–16; **Lv.**P. 98–16; U. 97–16; **M.**P. 94–15; T. 01–16; **O.**R. 97–16; **Sh.**IO. 98–15. [*C. as:* 23241]

18134 **Engineering Materials Annual.** London. *Engng Mater. A.* [1944–] **L.**SC.; **Abs.**N.; **M.**P.; **O.**R.

18135 **Engineering Materials** and **Design.** London. *Engng Mater. Des.* [1958–] **L.**AV.; BM.; LE.; P.; TP.; **Bn.**U.; **Br.**U. 60–; **Dn.**U.; **G.**M.; T.; **Ld.**P.; U.; W. 59–; **Li.**M.; **Lo.** 59–; **Lv.**P.; **M.**C. 62–; P.; U. imp.; **Ma.**T.; **N.**U.; **Sh.**SC.; **Sil.**; **Sy.**R.; **Wd.**; **Y.**

Engineering Materials and **International Power Review.** *See* 18136.

18136 **Engineering Materials** and **Processes.** London *Engng Mater. Process.* [1944–47] **L.**DI. imp.; P. imp.; **O.**R. [*C. of:* 23919; *C. in:* 49650]

18137 **Engineering** and **Mining Journal.** New York. *Engng Min. J.* [1869–22] **L.**GM. 04–22; I. 75–22 imp.; MI. 79–22 imp.; MIE. 06–14: 19–22 imp.; P. 10–22; **Bm.**T. 20–22; U. 03–22 imp.; **G.**M. 80–22; U. 77–80; **Lv.**U. 21–22; **M.**U. 09–22 imp.; **Nw.**A. 11–22; **Sw.**U. 19–20. [*C. as:* 18138]

18138 **Engineering** and **Mining Journal-Press.** New York. *Engng Min. J.-Press* [1922–] **L.**BM. 35–; DI. 47–; GM. 22–29; I. 22–29 imp.: 48–; IC. 38–; MI. 22–29 imp.: 32–; MIE. imp.; P. 22–29: 32–; **Bm.**T.; U. imp.; **G.**M.; T. 34– imp.; U. 23–29: 32–53; **Ld.**U. 32–; **Lv.**U. 22–29; **M.**U. imp.; **N.**U. 49–; **Nw.**A.; **Sh.**IO. 47–; SC. 61–; **Wd.** 32– imp.; **Y.** [*C. of:* 18137]

18139 **Engineering** and **Mining World.** New York. *Engng Min. Wld* [1930–31] **L.**GM.; P.; MI.; MIE.; SC.; **Bm.**U.; **G.**M.; U.; **Ld.**U.; **Lv.**U.; **M.**U. [*C. in:* 18137]

Engineering Monographs. British Broadcasting Corporation. *See* 5634.

18140 **Engineering Monographs. U.S. Reclamation Service (Bureau).** Denver. *Engng Monogr. U.S. Reclam. Serv. (Bur.)* [1948–] **Y.**

18141 **Engineering News.** New York. *Engng News, N.Y.* [1875–17] **L.**EE. 05–17; I. 92–09; P. 10–17; QM. 09–15; **Dl.**U. 07–17; **Bm.**U. 06–17; **Db.** 08–17; **Dn.**U. 13–17; **G.**U. 95–17; **Ld.**U. 77–17; **Lv.**U. 10–17; **M.**T. 08–17; U. 09–17. [*C. in:* 18143]

18142 **Engineering News.** West Pakistan Engineering Congress. Lahore. *Engng News, Lahore* [1956–] **Rt.** 56; **Y.**

18142c **Engineering News** of **India.** *Engng News India* **Y.**

18143 **Engineering News Record.** New York, etc. *Engng News Rec.* [1917–] **L.**AV. 50– imp.; BA. 41–; EE.; I. 50–58; P. imp.; TD. 25–31; UC. 38–; **Abd.**U. 27–; **Bl.**U. 07–29: 32–36 imp.; **Bm.**P. 27–; U.; **Br.**U. 30–51 imp.; **C.**ENG. (3 yr.); **Db.**; **Dn.**U. 17–40: 47–; **E.**U. 44–46; **G.**M.; T. (5 yr.); U.; **Ld.**U.; **Lv.**P. 29–38: 55– imp.; U.; **M.**P.; T. 17–48 (1 yr); U.; **Nw.**A. 46–; **Sh.**SC. 34–; **Y.** [*C. of:* 18141 and 18152]

18144 **Engineering Notes.** London. *Engng Notes* [1911–14] **O.**R.

18145 **Engineering Outlook** at the **University** of **Illinois.** Urbana. *Engng Outl. Univ. Ill.* [1960–] **L.**BM.; P.; **Ld.**U.; **Y.** [*Forms part of:* 55626]

Engineering Press Monthly Index Review. *See* 22907.

18145° **Engineering Proceedings. College** of **Engineering** and **Architecture, Pennsylvania State College.** University Park. *Engng Proc. Coll. Engng Archit. Pa* [1960–] **L.**P. [*C. of:* 51940]

18146 **Engineering Production.** London. *Engng Prod.* [1920–25] **L.**BM.; NF. 22–23; P.; **Abs.**N. 21–25; **G.**M.; **Lv.**P.; **M.**P. 23–25; **O.**B. [*C. in:* 5490]

18147 **Engineering Production Annual.** London. *Engng Prod. A.* [1944–] **L.**BM.; SC.; **Abs.**N.; **M.**P. 44; **O.**R.

18148 **Engineering Progress.** Berlin. *Engng Prog.* [1920–41] **L.**P. 20–39; SC. 25–41; **Bm.**C. 29–39 imp.; P.; **Br.**U. 29–39; **C.**ENG. 31–41; **E.**U. 27–28; **Ld.**U.; **Lv.**U. 24–41; **M.**P. 31–39; U. 26–27; **Sw.**U. 31–41.

Engineering Progress. Düsseldorf. *See* 40203.

18149 **Engineering Progress** at the **University** of **Florida.** Gainesville. *Engng Prog. Univ. Fla* [1949–] **L.**U.; **G.**U. 53– imp.; **M.**U. imp.; **N.**U.; **Y.** [*C. of:* 18150]

18150 **Engineering Publications. Florida Engineering Experiment Station.** Gainesville. *Engng Publs Fla Engng Exp. Stn* [1949] **L.**SC.; **M.**U. imp. [*C. of:* 10167, 28278 *and* 52244; *C. as:* 18149]

18151 **Engineering Quarterly** of the **University** of **Missouri.** Columbia. *Engng Q. Univ. Mo.*

18152 **Engineering Record.** New York. *Engng Rec.* [1877–17] **L.**BM. 05–10; P. 10–17; **Db.** 02–17; **G.**M. 83–17; **M.**P. 92–17; U. 11–17; **O.**R. 92–00. [*C. in:* 18143]

18153 **Engineering Reports. Central Standing Committee** for **Coordination** of **Power** and **Telecommunication Systems.** Delhi. *Engng Rep. cent. standing Comm. Coord. Pwr Telecommun. Syst.* [1951–] **L.**P.

18154 **Engineering Reports. Iowa Engineering Experiment Station.** Ames. *Engng Rep. Ia Engng Exp. Stn* [1949–] **L.**P.; **Y.**

18155 **Engineering Reports. Joint Subcommittee** on **Development** and **Research. National Electric Light Association** and **American Telephone** and **Telegraph Company.** New York. *Engng Rep. jt Subcomm. Dev. Res. natn. elect. Lt Ass. Am. Teleph. Telegr. Co.* **L.**P. 30–.

18156 **Engineering Reports** of the **National Tsing Hua University.** Peiping. *Engng Rep. natn. Tsing Hua Univ.* [1944–] **L.**HQ. 47–50; P. 47–50; **G.**U. 47–; **Ld.**U. 47–.

18157 **Engineering Research Bulletin. College** of **Engineering** and **Architecture, Pennsylvania State University.** State College. *Engng Res. Bull. Coll. Engng Archit. Pa* [1957–] **L.**P.; **Y.** [*C. of:* 10028]

Engineering Research Bulletin. University of **Michigan.** *See* 10029.

Engineering Research Circular. University of **Michigan.** *See* 14375.

18158 **Engineering Research News. North Carolina State College.** Raleigh, N.C. *Engng Res. News N. Carol. St. Coll.* [1948–] **L.**AV. 61–; HQ. (1 yr); P.

Engineering Research Review. College of **Engineering, New York University.** *See* 33962.

18159 **Engineering Research Series. University** of **Texas.** Austin. *Engng Res. Ser. Univ. Tex.* [1902–] **L.**BM. 38–; P. 15– imp.; **Y.**

18160 **Engineering Research. Special Report.** Engineering Research Board. London. *Engng Res.* [1927–] **L.**BM.; SC.; **Abd.**U.; **Ld.**P.; **Nw.**A.

18161 **Engineering Review.** London. *Engng Rev., Lond.* [1904–19] **L.**BM.; EE.; I. 04–18; P. 10–19; SC. 04–17; **Abs.**N. 12–19; **Bm.**P. 17–19; **Bra.**P. 06–19; **C.**UL.; **Cr.**P. 04–17; **Db.**; **E.**A. 04–07; **G.**M.; T.; **Ld.**P. 04; **M.**P.; U. 04–05 imp.; **Nw.**P. 04–10; **O.**R. [*C. of:* 19266; *C. as:* 18165]

Engineering Review. Moscow. *See* 24080.

18162 **Engineering Review.** New York. *Engng Rev., N.Y.* [1900–12] **L.**P. 10–12. [*C. of:* 22021]

18163 **Engineering Review.** Purdue University. Lafayette, Ind. *Engng Rev., Purdue Univ.*

Engineering Review. C.A.V. *See* 12864.

18164 **Engineering Review** of the **Czechoslovak Metal** and **Engineering Industries.** Prague. *Engng Rev. Czech. Metal Engng Inds* [1950–51]

18165 **Engineering Review** and **Trader.** London. *Engng Rev. Trader* [1919–23] **L.**BM.; EE. 19–21; P. 19–22; **Abs.**N.; **Bm.**P.; **Bra.**P.; **C.**UL.; **Db.**; **G.**M.; T.; **M.**P.; **O.**R. [*C. of:* 18161; *C. as:* 18085]

18166 **Engineering** for **Safety.** American Society of Safety Engineers. Chicago. *Engng Saf.* **L.**P. (curr.)

18167 **Engineering School Bulletin. North Carolina State College.** Raleigh. *Engng Sch. Bull. N. Carol. St. Coll.* [1948–] **L.**AV.

18168 **Engineering School Bulletin. North Carolina State College. Facts** for **Industries Series.** Raleigh. *Engng Sch. Bull. N. Carol. St. Coll. Facts Ind. Ser.* [1955–] **L.**AV. 55–56.

18169 **Engineering** and **Science Series. Rensselaer Polytechnic Institute.** Troy, N.Y. *Engng Sci. Ser. Rensselaer polytech. Inst.* [1911–] **L.**P. 11–35; imp.; UC. 28–; **Bm.**U. 28–33 imp.; **C.**UL.; **Ld.**P. 27– imp.; **Nw.**A. 27–38 imp.; **Sh.**M. 28–40; **Y.**

18170 **Engineering** and **Scientific Papers** of the **Schools** of **Mines, Engineering** and **Chemistry, Columbia University.** New York. *Engng scient. Pap. Schs Mines Engng Chem. Columbia Univ.* **L.**P. 19–24* imp.

18170° **Engineering Series Bulletin. Engineering Experiment Station, University** of **Missouri.** *Engng Ser. Bull. Engng Exp. Stn Univ. Mo.* **Y.**

18171 **Engineering Societies Yearbook.** Engineers' Joint Council. New York. *Engng Socs Yb.* [1948–] **L.**SC.; **Bm.**P.; **M.**P.

18171° **Engineering Society Journal** of **Leeds University.** Leeds. *Engng Soc. J. Leeds Univ.* [1951–] **L.**BM.; **C.**UL.; **Ld.**P. 58–; U.; **O.**R. [*C. of:* 26337]

18172 **Engineering Society Journal. University College London.** *Engng Soc. J. Univ. Coll. Lond.* [1951–58] **L.**BM.; U.; UC.; **Bm.**U.; **Bn.**U.; **C.**UL.; **Dn.**U.; **G.**U.; **Ld.**U.; **Nw.**A. 55–58; **O.**R. [*C. of:* 25961; *C. as:* 55608]

18173 **Engineering Standards Committee.** [Reports.] London. *Engng Stand. Comm.* [1903–16] **L.**BM.; I. 05–16; P.; UC. 04–16; **Abs.**N. 09–16; **Bm.**P.; T.; U. 03–11; **Cr.**P. 04–16; **Db.** 04–16; **E.**A.; T.; U. 10–16; **G.**E. 05–16; M. 04–08; T.; **Ld.**U.; **Lv.**P. 04–16 imp.; U.; **M.**P.; U.; **Nw.**A.; P. [*C. as:* 8808]

18174 **Engineering Supplement** to the **Siemens Magazine.** London. *Engng Suppl. Siemens Mag.* **L.**P. 31–45*; SC. 31–45 imp.; **Lv.**P. 34–45 imp. [*C. as:* 18096; *Supplement to:* 49720]

18175 **Engineering Times.** London. *Engng Times* [1898–10] **L.**BM.; P.; **G.**M.; **Nw.**P. 98–05; **O.**B. 01: 04–08.

18176 **Engineering Trader.** London. *Engng Trader* [1925–] **L.**BM.; **Br.**P. (1 yr); **Sh.**IO. 54–56.

18177 **Engineering World.** Chicago. *Engng Wld, Chicago* [1918–29] [*C. of:* 18099; *C. in:* 22158]

18178 **Engineering World.** London. *Engng Wld, Lond.* [1902–07] **L.**BM.; **O.**R. 03–07.

18179 **Engineering World.** Manchester. *Engng Wld, Manchr* [1921–22] **L.**BM.; P.; **M.**P.; **O.**B.

18179° **Engineering** for **Youth.** Washington. *Engng Youth* **Y.** 57–. [*English abstracts of:* 52711]

18180 **Engineering-Science News.** College of Engineering and Balcones Research Center, University of Texas. Austin. *Engng-Sci. News* **L.**P. 59–.

18181 **Engineers' Bulletin.** Tucson, Ariz. *Engrs' Bull., Tucson* [1922–]

18182 **Engineers' Bulletin. Colorado Society** of **Engineers.** Denver. *Engrs' Bull. Colo. Soc. Engrs* [1918–]

18183 **Engineers' Digest.** New York. *Engrs' Dig., N.Y.* [1943–48] [*American edition of:* and *C. in:* 18184]

18184 **Engineers' Digest.** London. *Engrs' Dig., Lond.* [1940–] **L.**AV. 43–; BM.; DI. 44–; I.; IC. 45–; NF. 42–; P.; QM. 47–; SC. 41–; SI. 46–; U. 40–56; **Abd.**U. 46–; **Bm.**C. 43–; P.; T. 49–; U. imp.; **Br.**P.; **C.**ENG. 44–; UL.; **Cr.**I. 53–; P. 40–50; U. 61–; **E.**A.; SW. 47–; T.; U.; **F.**A.; **G.**E. 41–; M.; T.; U. 50– imp.; **Lc.**A. 43–; **Li.**M. 46–; **Lv.**P. 43–; **M.**C. 45– imp.; P.; T. 43–; **Ma.**T. 55– imp.; **N.**P. 46–; T. (5 yr.); U. 41– imp.; **Nw.**A.; **O.**R.; **Rn.**B. imp.; **Sh.**P.; **Sil.** 43–; **St.**R. 47–; **Sw.**U. 48–55; **Wd.** 47–; **Y.**

18185 **Engineers** and **Engineering.** Engineers' Club of Philadelphia. Chicago, etc. *Engrs Engng* [1922–32] **L.**P. 22–31; SC. 24–32; **Nw.**A. 22–31. [*C. of:* 25966]

18186 **Engineers' Gazette.** London. *Engrs' Gaz.* [1888–03] **L.**BM.; P. imp.; **Nw.**A. 95–03; **O.**B.

18187 **Engineers' Gazette Annual.** London. *Engrs' Gaz. A.* [1889–06] **L.**BM. imp.; **O.**R.

18188 **Engineers' Journal.** Dublin. *Engrs' J.* [1940–] **Bl.**U. 59–; **Db.**

18189 **Engineers' Monthly.** New York. *Engrs' Mon.*
Engineers' and Technicians' Bulletin. Moscow.
See 56453.

18190 **Engineers' Yearbook.** London. *Engrs' Yb.* [1894–] **L.**BM.; EE. 06– imp.; SC. 09–; **Abs.**N. 13–; **Bm.**P. 18– imp.; U. 13–27: 29: 47–; **C.**UL.; **Db.** 12: 17: 19–; **E.**R. 23–29; U. 17–18; **Ld.**P. 30– imp.; U. 13– imp.; **Lv.**P. 05– imp.; **M.**P. 05– imp.; U. 22– imp.; **Nw.**A. 14–19; P. (5 yr.); **O.**R.; **Sw.**U. 21: 35: 52.

18191 **Engines Note.** Melbourne. *Engs Note* **L.**P. 43–52*. [*C. as:* 29756]

18192 **Engelhard Industries Technical Bulletin.** Newark, N.J. *Engelhard Inds tech. Bull.* [1960–] **L.**P. (Overseas edn); **G.**ME. (1 yr.)

18193 **Englebert Magazine.** Liège. *Englebert Mag.* **L.**P. 52–; **Sy.**R. 50–.

18194 **English Abstracts** of **Selected Articles** from **Soviet Bloc** and **Mainland China Technical Journals.** *Engl. Abstr. select. Art. Sov. Bloc Mainld China tech. Js*
Ser. 1. Physics, Geophysics, Astrophysics, Astronomy, Astronautics and Applied Mathematics. **Ld.**U. 61–; **Y.**
Ser. 2. Chemistry, Chemicals and Chemical Products. **Ld.**U. 61–; **Y.**
Ser. 3. Metallurgy, Metals, Metal Products and Non-metallic Minerals. **Ld.**U. 61–; **Y.**
Ser. 4. Mechanical, Electrical, Aeronautical, Nuclear, Petroleum, Structural and Civil Machinery and Equipment—General and Special Purpose. **Ld.**U. 61–; **Y.**
Ser. 5. Communications, Transportation, Navigation, Electrical and Electronic Equipment Systems and Devices. **Ld.**U. 61–; **Y.**
Ser. 6. General Science and Miscellaneous. **Ld.**U. 61–; **Y.**

18195 **English** and **Amateur Mechanics.** London. *Engl. Amat. Mech.* [1926–29] **L.**AS.; BM.; P.; SC.; **Abs.**N.; **Bm.**U. 27–28; **Br.**P.; **Bra.**P.; **C.**UL.; **E.**T.; **G.**M.; **M.**P.; **N.**U.; **Nw.**P.; **O.**B.; **Sh.**P. [*C. of:* 1877 and 18197; *C. as:* 18198]

English Dairy Farmer. *See* 16309.

18196 **English Electric Journal.** Stafford. *Engl. elect. J.* [1920–] **L.**AV. 53–; BM.; EE. imp.; I. (4 yr.); NF. 44–; P.; SC. 30–; UC.; **Bl.**U. 55–; **Bm.**T. 53–; U.; **Bn.**U. imp.; **Br.**U.; **Bra.**P. 55–; **C.**ENG. (3 yr.); **G.**E. (1 yr); I. 42–; M. 25–52; T. (1 yr); U. 29– imp.; **Lc.**A. 51–; **Ld.**P. 55–; U. 33–; **Lv.**P. 48– imp.; **M.**P. 27–41; T. 29– imp.; **Nw.**A. 22– imp.; **Sh.**IO. 52–; **Y.**

18197 **English Mechanic** and **World** of **Science.** London. *Engl. Mech. Wld Sci.* [1865–26] **L.**AS. 70–26; BM.; EE. 81–26; P. 10–26; RI. 81–26; SC.; U. 98–03; **Abd.**U. 83–01 imp.; **Abs.**N. 85–26; **Bm.**P.; U.; **Br.**P. 72–26; U. 65–70: 73–07; **Bra.**P.; **C.**UL.; **Cr.**P. 65–20; **Db.** 70–26; **E.**A.; L. 71–26; O. 13–26; R. 95–26; T. imp.; **G.**M.; **Ld.**U. 81–19 imp.; **Lv.**P. 65–13; U. 02–07; **M.**P.; T. 02–22 imp.; **N.**P. 65–21; U. 00–16: 25–26; **Nw.**P. imp.; **O.**B. [*C. in:* 18195]

18198 **English Mechanics.** London. *Engl. Mechs* [1929–42] **L.**AS. 29–34; BM.; P.; SC.; **Abs.**N.; **Bm.**U. 32–42; **Br.**P.; **Bra.**P.; **C.**UL.; **E.**T. 29–40; **G.**M.; **Lv.**P. 39–42; **M.**P.; **Ma.**T. 37–42; **Nw.**P. 29–34; **O.**B.; **Sh.**P. [*C. of:* 18195; *C. as:* 29770]

18198° **Engrais.** Lille. *Engrais* **L.**P. 01–28; **Db.** 09–.

18199 **Engraver** and **Die Stamper.** London. *Engraver Die Stamper* **L.**BM. 53–.

18200 **Engraver** and **Electrotyper.** Chicago. *Engraver Electrotyper* [1897–16] **L.**SB. 97–14 imp.

18201 **Engravers Bulletin.** New York. *Engravers Bull.* [1939–43]

18202 **Enka** and **Breda Rayon Review.** Arnhem. *Enka Breda Rayon Rev.* [1947–] **Ld.**P. 57–; **M.**C. 47–59; T. 56–; **Y.**

English edition. **M.**C. 47–51: 53–54; **Y.**

18203 **Enlarged Abstracts** of **Papers** presented by the **Electronics Division, Electrochemical Society, Spring Meeting.** New York. *Enlarg. Abstr. Pap. Electron. Div. electrochem. Soc. Spring Meet.* **L.**P. 56–.

18204 **Enología argentina.** Mendoza. *Enol. argent.*

18205 **Enquiry.** London. *Enquiry* [1948–] **L.**U.; **Bm.**U.; **C.**UL.; **G.**M. 48–50 imp.; U.

18206 **Enregistrements** des **instruments enregistreurs** de l'**Observatoire** à **Prague, Karlov.** Praha. *Enregmts Instrum. enreg. Obs. Prag.* L.MO. 21–49. [*C. as:* 58247]
Ensatsu zasshi. *See* 33580.

18207 **Ensayos. Estación experimental** de **Aula Dei.** Departamento de Mejora. Zaragoza. *Ensayos Estac. exp. Aula Dei* Abs.A. 55–; **Br.**A. 56–; **C.**A. 54–; **Md.**H. 55–.

18208 **Enseignement mathématique.** Paris & Genève. *Enseign. math.* [1899–] L.M.; SC. 99–50; UC.; **C.**P. 37–; **G.**T. 99–28; U. 55–; **N.**U. 57–; **Y.**

18209 **Enseignement médical** à **Paris.** Paris. *Enseign. méd. Paris*

18210 **Enseignement médico-mutuel international.** Paris. *Enseign. méd.-mut. int.* L.TD. 09–12. [*C. as:* 49275]

18211 **Enseignement scientifique.** Paris. *Enseign. scient.* **Br.**U. 29–.

18212 **Enseignement technique.** Morlanwecz. *Enseign. tech.*

18213 **Entente médicale.** Paris. *Entente méd.* [*C. of:* 23405]

18214 **Entomologbladet.** Populär bilaga till Entomologisk tidskrift. Stockholm. *Entomologbl.* [1937–38] L.BM.; E.; EB. 37.

18215 **Entomologia** et **ars.** Institutum entomologicum Choui. Wukung, Shensi. *Entomologia Ars* [1946] L.BM.; E.; Ld.U.; O.H. [*C. as:* 18216].

18216 **Entomologia sinica.** Wukung, Shensi. *Entomologia sin.* [1947–51] L.BM.; E.; O.H. 47–51. [*C. of:* 18215]

18217 **Entomologia experimentalis** et **applicata.** Amsterdam. *Entomologia exp. appl.* [1958–] L.AM.; BM.; E.; NC.; TD.; TP. 59–; Z.; **Bl.**U. 62–; **Bn.**U.; **C.**B.; **E.**W.; **G.**U.; **Hu.**G.; **Md.**H.; **N.**U.; **O.**R.; **Rt.**; W. 62–; **Y.**

18218 **Entomologica americana.** Lancaster, Pa. *Entomologica am.* [1885–] L.BM.; E.; EB.; SC.; Z. 85–90; **C.**UL. 26–; **Y.** [*Suspended from* 1890 *to* 1926]

18219 **Entomological Bulletin. Department** of **Agriculture, British Guiana.** Georgetown. *Ent. Bull. Dep. Agric. Br. Guiana* [1930–] L.P. 30–33; **C.**A. 30–; **Rt.** 30.

  Entomological Bulletin. Department of **Agriculture, Cyprus.** *See* 9970 (*a*).

18220 **Entomological Bulletin. Department** of **Agriculture, Jamaica.** Kingston. *Ent. Bull. Dep. Agric. Jamaica* [1921–32] L.BM.; EB.; K. 23–26; P. 26–32; **C.**A.; **Rt.**

18221 **Entomological Bulletin. Wellcome Tropical Research Laboratories, Sudan.** Khartoum. *Ent. Bull. Wellcome trop. Res. Labs Sudan* [1914–36] L.EB.

18222 **Entomological Circular. Department** of **Agriculture, British Columbia.** Victoria, B.C. *Ent. Circ. Dep. Agric. Br. Columb.* [1953–] L.BM.; **Y.**

  Entomological Circular. Department of **Agriculture, Canada.** *See* 14212.

18223 **Entomological Circular. Department** of **Agriculture, Jamaica.** Kingston. *Ent. Circ. Dep. Agric. Jamaica* [1921–34] L.BM.; EB.; P. 24–34; SC.; **C.**A.; **Rt.**

18224 **Entomological Leaflet. Department** of **Agriculture, Queensland.** Brisbane. *Ent. Leafl. Dep. Agric. Qd* [1926–35] L.EB. [*C. as:* 18225ᶜ]

18225 **Entomological Leaflet. Department** of **Agriculture, Tanganyika.** Dar-es-Salaam. *Ent. Leafl. Dep. Agric. Tanganyika* [1930–] L.BM. imp.; BM. 37–38; EB. 36–; **C.**A.

18225ᶜ **Entomological Leaflet. Division** of **Plants, Department** of **Agriculture, Queensland.** Brisbane. *Ent. Leafl. Div. Pl. Qd* [1935–] L.EB. [*C. of:* 18224]

18226 **Entomological Magazine.** Kyoto. *Ent. Mag., Kyoto* [1915–19] L.BM. 15–16; E. 16–17; EB. 16–17; **C.**UL.

18227 **Entomological News.** Academy of Natural Sciences, Philadelphia. *Ent. News* [1890–] L.BM.; BM.; E.; EB. 14–; Z.; **C.**UL. 15–; **M.**U. 97–22; **O.**H.; **Rt.** 18–33.

18228 **Entomological Notes. Department** of **Agriculture. Territory** of **Papua.** Port Moresby. *Ent. Notes Dep. Agric. Papua* L.EB. (Ser. A) 11–13.

18229 **Entomological Papers. Maine Agricultural Experiment Station.** Orono. *Ent. Pap. Me agric. Exp. Stn* L.EB. 88–.

18230 **Entomological Review.** Washington. *Ent. Rev., Wash.* L.NC. 59–; **Y.** [*English translation of:* 18235]

18231 **Entomological Review** of **Japan.** Osaka. *Ent. Rev. Japan* [1946–] L.BM. 49–; **Y.**

18232 **Entomological Student.** Entomological Students' Association, Philadelphia, Pa. *Ent. Student* L.BM. 00–01.

18233 **Entomological World.** Tokyo. *Ent. Wld, Tokyo* [1933–43] L.BM. 33–40; E. 36–38.

18234 **Éntomologicheskïi vêstnik.** Kiev. Энтомологическій вѣстникъ. *Ént. Vest.* [1912–14] L.BM. 12. EB.

18235 **Éntomologicheskoe obozrenie.** Moskva. Энтомологическое обозрение. *Ént. Obozr.* [1933–] L.BM.; E.; EB.; SC. 56–; Z.; **C.**B. 49–; UL.; **G.**N.; U. 58–; **O.**H.; **Rt.** 56–; **Y.** 50– imp. [*C. of:* 48335ᵃ; *English translation at:* 18230]

18236 **Entomologické listy.** v Brné. *Ent. Listy* [1937–51] L.BM.; E. 37: 43–51; EB. 38–51; Z. 48–51; Ld.U. 46–51. [*C. as:* 59271]

18237 **Entomologické přiručky.** Praha. *Ent. Přiručky* [1905–33] L.E. 26: 30. [*Supplement to:* 13398]

18238 **Entomologie** et **phytopathologie appliquées.** Téhran. *Entomologie phytopath. appl.* [1946–] L.BM.; EB.; MY.; **C.**B.; **Md.**H.; **Rt.** 47–48.

18239 **Entomologische Arbeiten** aus dem **Museum Georg Frey.** München. *Ent. Arb. Mus. Georg Frey* [1950–] L.BM.; E.; Z.; Ld.U. 50–52; **O.**H.; **Y.**

18240 **Entomologische Beihefte** aus **Berlin-Dahlem.** Berlin. *Ent. Beih. Berl.-Dahlem* [1934–43] L.BM.; E.; EB.; Z.; **Bl.**U. 34–38; **E.**R.; **O.**H. 34–39.

18241 **Entomologische berichten.** Nederlandsche entomologische vereeniging. Amsterdam. *Ent. Ber., Amst.* [1901–] L.BM.; E.; EB.; L. 05–; Z.; **C.**B. 38–; **Nw.**A. 40– imp.; **O.**H.; **Y.**

18242 **Entomologische Blätter** für **Biologie** und **Systematik** der **Käfer.** Berlin. *Ent. Bl. Biol. Syst. Käfer* [1908–] L.BM.; E.; EB. 09–; Z. 34– imp.; **C.**UL.; **Y.**

18243 **Entomologische Literaturblätter.** Berlin. *Ent. LitBl.* [1901–14] L.BM.; BM.; E.; EB.; **C.**UL. 02–03. [*C. of:* 18247; *C. as:* 42590]

18244 **Entomologische mededeelingen** van **Nederlandsch-Indië.** Buitenzorg. *Ent. Meded. Ned.-Indië* [1935–41] **L.**BM^N.; E.; EB.; SC. [*C. of:* 56383; *C. as:* 22725]

18245 **Entomologische Mitteilungen.** Berlin-Dahlem. *Ent. Mitt.* [1912–28] **L.**BM^N.; E.; EB.; **C.**B. 15–28; **Db.**; **Lv.**U.; **M.**U. 13–28 imp.; **O.**H. [*C. of:* 16692]

18246 **Entomologische Mitteilungen** aus dem **Zoologischen Staatsinstitut** und **Zoologischen Museum Hamburg.** Hamburg. *Ent. Mitt. zool. StInst. zool. Mus. Hamb.* [1952–] **L.**BM^N. 53–; E.; Z.; **Y.**

18247 **Entomologische Nachrichten.** Berlin. *Ent. Nachr.* [1875–00] **L.**AM. 88–94; BM.; BM^N.; E.; Z.; **C.**UL. 81–00; **O.**H. imp. [*C. as:* 18243]

18248 **Entomologische Rundschau.** Stuttgart. *Ent. Rdsch.* [1909–39] **L.**BM^N.; E. 21–39; Z. 27–39. [*C. of:* 18256; *C. in:* 18249]
    Entomologische Zeitschrift. Berlin. *See* 18251.

18249 **Entomologische Zeitschrift.** Frankfurt a. M. *Ent. Z. Frankf. a. M.* [1887–] **L.**BM^N.; EE.; Z. 10– imp.; **Bm.**U. 07; **Bn.**U. 49–57; **O.**H. 11– imp.; **Y.**
    Entomologische Zeitung. Stettin. *See* 50932.

18250 **Entomologischer Anzeiger.** Wien. *Ent. Anz.* [1921–36] **L.**BM^N.; E.

18251 **Entomologischer Jahresbericht.** Berlin. *Ent. Jber.* **L.**Z. 14 imp.

18252 **Entomologisches Jahrbuch.** Frankfurt-am-M. *Ent. Jb.* [1892–37] **L.**BM^N.; E. 94: 12–17: 19–26: 32–40; EB. 12–37; Z. 92–26 imp.

18253 **Entomologisches Nachrichtenblatt.** Burgdorf. *Ent. NachrBl., Burgdorf* [1947–50] **L.**AM.; BM^N.; E. 48–50; **Y.** [*C. in:* 18255]

18254 **Entomologisches Nachrichtenblatt.** Troppau. *Ent. NachrBl., Troppau* [1927–30] **L.**BM^N. 27–38; E.; EB.; **O.**H. 27–39; **Rt.** 28. [*C. in:* 32623]

18255 **Entomologisches Nachrichtenblatt.** Arbeitsgemeinschaft österreichischer und schweizer Entomologen. Wien. *Ent. NachrBl., Wien* [1950–59] **L.**BM^N.; E. 54–57; **Rt.** 56; **Y.** [*C. of:* 18253 and 57555; *C. as:* 58492]

18256 **Entomologisches Wochenblatt.** Stuttgart. *Ent. Wbl.* [1907–08] **L.**BM^N.; E. [*C. as:* 18248]

18257 **Entomologisk tidskrift.** Stockholm. *Ent. Tidskr.* [1880–] **L.**BM.; BM^N.; E.; EB.; L.; Z.; **Bn.**U. 96– imp.; **C.**UL.; **Db.** 47–; **E.**R. 46–; **Ld.**U. 39–58; **N.**U. 16–28: 29: 48; **O.**H.; R.; **Y.**

18258 **Entomologiske Meddelelser.** Kjøbenhavn. *Ent. Meddr* [1887–] **L.**BM.; BM^N.; E.; EB.; SC.; Z.; **N.**U. 21–25; **O.**AP. 50–; H. imp.; **Y.**

18259 **Entomologist.** London. *Entomologist* [1840–] **L.**AM. imp.; BM.; BM^N.; E.; L. 1840–24; NC. 03–13: 27–; SC. 64–; UC. 77–42 imp.; Z.; **Abd.**U.; **Abs.**N. 12–; **Bm.**N. 74–; P.; **Bn.**U. 78–19; **Br.**U. 60–; **C.**B.; UL.; **Cr.**M.; P. 72–50; U. 60–; **Db.**; **Dn.**U. 70–; **E.**A.; F. 64–; U. 47–; **Fr.** 85– imp.; **G.**M. 64–73: 77–; U. 32– imp.; **H.**U. 60–; **Ld.**P. 72–; U. 75–48; **Lv.**U. 05–; **M.**P. 64–; U. 1840–37 imp.; **Md.**H. 64– imp.; **N.**P. 74–; **Nw.**A. 85–90: 93–; **O.**AP. 48–; H.; R.; **Pit.**F. 55–; **Rt.** 72–; **Y.**

18260 **Entomologist's Gazette.** London. *Entomologist's Gaz.* [1950–] **L.**AM. 62–; BM.; BM^N.; E.; EB. 55–; NC.; SC.; Z.; **Abs.**U. 58–; **Bl.**U. 51– imp.; **C.**UL.; **E.**A.; U. 55–; **Fr.**; **M.**P. 53–; **O.**B.; H.; R.; **Pit.**F.; **Y.**

18261 **Entomologist's Monthly Magazine.** London. *Entomologist's mon. Mag.* [1864–] **L.**AM. imp.; BM.; BM^N.; E.; I.; IC. 46–; KC. 53–; L. 64–38; NC. 68–91: 14–; QM. 50–; U. 64–00: 18–31; Z.; **Abd.**U. 67–; **Abs.**N. 12–; U. 67–28: 58–; **Bm.**N. 64–18; U. 74–99 imp.: 48–; **Bn.**U. imp.; **Br.**A. 28–47; U. 28–47; **C.**B.; UL.; **Cr.**M.; P. 69–51; U. 54–; **Db.**; **Dn.**U.; **E.**A. imp.; F.; U.; **Ex.**U. 47–; **Fr.** 79–81: 15– imp.; **G.**M. imp.; U. 72– imp.; **H.**U. 51–; **Ld.**P. 71–; U. 64–48 imp.; **Lv.**U. 05–; **M.**P.; U. 64–20: 44–55 imp.; **Md.**H. 73–; **N.**P. 38–; U. 77–14: 21–; **Nw.**A. 67– imp.; **O.**AP. 68–78: 26– imp.; B.; F. 24–; H.; R.; Z. 02–12; **Pit.**F. 50–; **R.**U.; **Rt.**; **Sh.**P. 82–13; **Y.**

18262 **Entomologist's Record** and **Journal** of **Variation.** London. *Entomologist's Rec. J. Var.* [1890–] **L.**BM.; BM^N.; E.; L.; NC. 90–20: 48–; SC. 34–; TD. 92–02; Z.; **Abs.**N. 57–; **Bl.**U. 05–19 imp.; **Bm.**N.; **Bn.**U. 90–49 imp.; **C.**B.; UL.; **Cr.**M.; P. 90–51 imp.; **Db.**; **Dn.**U. 98–; **E.**A.; **Fr.** 90–41 imp.; **G.**M. 90–11: 14–; U. 44–50; **Ld.**U. 90–51; **Lv.**U. 08–18; **M.**U. 90–47 imp.; **Nw.**A.; **O.**AP. 48–; H.; R.; **R.**U. 90–95 imp.; **Rt.**; **Sh.**P. 90–13; **Y.**

18263 **Entomologist's Report. Department** of **Agriculture, Tanganyika.** *Entomologist's Rep. Dep. Agric. Tanganyika* **Md.**H. 37–38; **Sal.** 34: 37–38.

18264 **Entomologiste.** Paris. *Entomologiste* [1944–] **L.**BM^N.; E. 45–; Z. 46– imp.; **Ld.**U. 46– imp.; **Y.**

18265 **Entomologisto brasileiro.** São Paulo. *Entomologisto bras.* **L.**BM^N. 08–09; E. 23–; EB. 08–09.

18266 **Entomologists' Bulletin.** London. *Entomologists' Bull.* [1937–38] **L.**BM.; BM^N.; E.; **C.**UL.; **O.**H.; R.; **Rt.** [*C. of:* 25970; *C. as:* 1876 and 9285]

18267 **Entomology Memoirs. Department** of **Agriculture, Union** of **South Africa.** Pretoria. *Entomology Mem. Dep. Agric. Un. S. Afr.* [1923–] **L.**AM.; BM^N.; EB.; K. 47–; **Br.**A. 40– imp.; **C.**A. 24–; **Rt.** 24–; **Y.**

18268 **Entomology Memoirs. Department** of **Agricultural Technical Services. Republic** of **South Africa.** *Entomology Mem. Dep. agric. tech. Serv. Repub. S. Afr.* **L.**BM^N.

18269 **Entomology** and **Phytopathology.** Hangchow. *Entomology Phytopath.* [1933–37] **L.**BM^N.; EB.; **Ld.**U. 34–37.

18270 **Entomon.** Internationale Zeitschrift für die gesamte Insektenkunde. München. *Entomon* [1949] **L.**BM^N.; E.; EB.

18271 **Entomophaga.** Paris. *Entomophaga* [1956–] **L.**BM^N.; E.; **Cr.**U.; **O.**H.; **Rt.**; **Y.**
    Mémoires hors série. [1960–]

18272 **Entopath News.** Wrecclesham, Farnham. *Entopath News* **L.**AM. 53–; K. 56–.

18273 **Entopath Newsletter.** Alice Holt, Farnham. *Entopath Newsl.* [1954–] **O.**F.

18274 **Entwicklung** der **Landwirtschaft** der **Provinz Posen.** Posen. *Entw. Landwirt. Prov. Posen*

18275 **Entwicklungs-Berichte. Siemens** und **Halske** A. G. *Entw.-Ber. Siemens u. Halske* **Y.** 55–.

18276 **Enumeratio insectorum Fenniae** et **Sueciae.** Helsinki. *Enum. Insect. Fenn. Suec.* [1944–] **L.**BM.

18277 **Envelope Industry.** Flushing, N.Y. *Envel. Ind.* [1927–31] [*C. as:* 18277^b]

18277^a **Envelope** and **Paper Converting Industry.** Flushing. *Envel. Pap. Convert. Ind.* [1933] [*C. of:* 18277^b; *C. as:* 26640^a]

18277[b] **Envelope** and **Specialty Paper Industry.** Flushing. *Envel. Spec. Pap. Ind.* [1931–33] [*C. of:* 18277; *C. as:* 18277[a]]

18278 **Environment,** a magazine of science. Sydney. *Environment* [1934–37]

18278[c] **Environmental Quarterly.** *Envir. Q.* **L.**AV. 58: 60–; **Y.**

18279 **Environmental Radioactivity at Risö.** Danish Atomic Energy Commission. Copenhagen. *Envir. Radioact. Risö* **L.**MO. 57–.

18280 **Enzyklopädie** der **mathematischen Wissenschaften.** Leipzig. *Enzykl. math. Wiss.* [1898–] **L.**BM.; SC.; UC.; **Abd.**U.; **Cr.**U.; **Db.**; **Dn.**U. 98–35; **E.**R.; **Lv.**U.; **O.**R. 98–34; **Sa.**; **Sh.**U.; **Sw.**U.

18281 **Enzyklopädische Jahrbücher** der **gesamten Heilkunde.** Berlin & Wien. *Enzykl. Jb. ges. Heilk.* [1891–11] **L.**MD. 03–11; S. 91–00; **C.**UL. 91–00; **E.**S. 91–05.

18282 **Enzymologia:** Acta biocatalytica. Den Haag. *Enzymologia* [1936–] **L.**B. 36–37 imp.; C.; CB. 48–; IC. 46–; LI.; MA. 36–40 imp.; MD. 48–; P.; SC.; TD.; U. 50–; UC.; **Abd.**U.; **Bl.**U.; **Bm.**U.; **Bn.**U. 40– imp.; **Br.**U. 56–; **C.**APH. 52–; BI.; MO.; **Cr.**U. 57–; **E.**U. 48–; **Ep.**D. 48–; **G.**U.; **Ld.**U. 43–; **M.**T. imp.; U. 58–; **N.**U.; **Nw.**A.; **O.**R.; **R.**D.; U.; **W.** 49–; **Y.**

18283 **Eos.** Revista española de entomología. Madrid. *Eos, Madr.* [1925–] **L.**BM[N].; E.; EB.; **Db.** 47–; **E.**U. 50–; **Ld.**U. 30–36; **N.**U. 50–; **O.**H.; **Y.**

18284 **Eos.** Vierteljahrschrift für die Erkenntnis und Behandlung jugendlicher Abnormer. Wien. *Eos, Wien*

18284[a] **Eőtvős Loránd tudományegyetem értesitője.** Budapest. *Eőtvős Loránd TudomEgy Ért.* **L.**BM. 56–.

18284[b] **Eőtvős Loránd tudományegyetem évkőnyve.** Budapest. *Eőtvős Loránd TudomEgy. Évk.* [1956–] **L.**BM.

18285 **Epetēris** tou **sullogou Parnassou.** en Athēnais. Ἐπετηρὶς τοῦ συλλόγου Παρνάσσου. *Epet. Sullog. Parnassou* [1896–18] **L.**BM. 96–06.

18286 **Ephemeriden-Zirkular** der **astronomischen Nachrichten.** Kiel. *Ephem.-Zirk. astr. Nachr.*

18287 **Éphémérides aéronautiques.** Bureau des longitudes. Paris. *Éphém. aéronaut.* [1936–] **L.**BM. 51–; MO. 39–43 (3 yr.)

18288 **Ephemerides astronomicas.** Coimbra. *Ephem. astr., Coimbra* **L.**AS. 1804– imp.; **E.**O. 1854– imp.; **G.**U. 16–17.

18289 **Éphémérides astronomiques** et **annuaire** des **marées.** Paris. *Éphém. astr. Annu. Marées*

18290 **Éphémérides** des **étoiles** de **culmination lunaire** et de **longitude.** Paris. *Éphém. Étoil. Culmin. lun. Longit.* **L.**AS. 1888–02.

18291 **Éphémérides** des **étoiles** pour la **détermination** de l'**heure** et de l'**azimut.** St. Pétersbourg. *Éphém. Étoil. Déterm. Heure Azimut, S Pétersb.* **L.**BM. 96–98; **E.**R. 95–99.

18292 **Éphémérides maritimes.** Saint-Brieuc. *Éphém. marit.*

18293 **Éphémérides nautiques.** Bureau des longitudes. Paris. *Éphém. naut.* [1920–] **L.**MO. 38– imp.

18294 **Éphémérides** de l'**Observatoire** de **Marseille.** *Éphém. Obs. Marseille* [1918–] **L.**AS. 18–26.

18294[c] **Éphémérides** de l'**Office** de **biologie.** Ministère de la chasse et des pêcheries, Province de Québec. *Éphém. Off. Biol. Québ.* [1953–]

Éphémérides des **petites planètes.** Moscou. *See* 17492.

18295 **Éphémérides. Petites planètes. Observatoire** de l'**Université** de **Belgrade.** *Éphém. petites Planètes Obs. Univ. Belgr.* **L.**AS. 47–.

18296 **Éphémérides sismiques** et **volcaniques.** Bruxelles. *Éphém. sism. volc.*

18297 **Ephemeris** of **Materia Medica, Pharmacy,** etc. Brooklyn. *Ephem. Mater. med.* [1882–04] **L.**MD. 82–00 imp.; **M.**MS. 83–04.

18298 **Epidemiological Information Bulletin.** U.N.O. Health Division. Washington. *Epidem. Inf. Bull.* [1945–46] **L.**H.; MA.; MD.; SC.; SH.; TD.; U.; **Abd.**U.; **Bl.**U.; **Bm.**U.; **Br.**U.; **Db.**; **Ld.**U.; **Sa.** [*C. in:* 57241]

18299 **Epidemiological Intelligence.** League of Nations. Geneva. *Epidem. Intell.* [1922–25] **L.**H. 23–25; MC.; MD.; SH.; **Bl.**U.; **Dn.**U. 23–25; **G.**PH. 24–25; **O.**R.; **Sh.**U. 24–25. [*C. as:* 18300]

18300 **Epidemiological Report.** League of Nations. Geneva. *Epidem. Rep.* [1926] **L.**H.; MC.; MD.; SH.; **Bl.**U.; **O.**AP.; **Sh.**U. [*C. of:* 18299; *C. as:* 50848]

18301 **Epidemiological Report.** League of Nations Health Section. Geneva. *Epidem. Rep.* [1937–40] **L.**H.; SH.; **Bl.**U.; **Db.** imp.; **E.**U.; **G.**U. imp.; **M.**MS.; **O.**AP.; R. 37–38. [*C. of:* 33522; *C. as:* 18302]

18302 **Epidemiological and Vital Statistics Report.** World Health Organization. Geneva. *Epidem. vit. Statist. Rep.* [1947–] **L.**CB. 52–; H.; MA.; MC.; MD.; SH.; TD.; **Bl.**U.; **Bm.**P.; **Br.**U.; **Cr.**MD.; **Db.**; **Dn.**U.; **E.**U.; **G.**PH.; **Ld.**U.; **M.**MS.; **Nw.**A.; **O.**AP.; R.; **Sa.** imp. [*C. of:* 18301; *Supplement to:* 57241]

18303 **Epigeica.** Milano. *Epigeica* [1955–] **Rt.** 56.

18304 **Epikote Age.** Shell International Chemical Co. London. *Epikote Age* **L.**P. (curr.)

18305 **Epikote Today.** Shell International Chemical Co. London. *Epikote today* **L.**P. (curr.)

18306 **Epilepsia.** Amsterdam, Boston, Copenhagen, Leipzig. *Epilepsia* [1905–15: 37–] **L.**MA. 37–; MD. 09–15: 37–; S. 37–; **Ld.**U. 59–; **O.**R. 09–15; **Y.**

18307 **Epione.** Helsinki. *Epione*

18308 **Epistēmonikē epetēris.** en Athēnais. Ἐπιστημονική ἐπετηρίς. *Epistēm. Epet.* [1902–22] **L.**BM. 12–22 imp.; **Abd.**U. 02–11; **Br.**U. 07–22; **Db.**; **E.**R. 13–17; **Lv.**U.; **Sa.** 02–12.

18309 **Epistēmonikon deltion.** Sindos. Ἐπιστημονικὸν δελτίον. *Epistēm. Delt.* [1947–] **C.**A.; **Y.**

18310 **Epistēmonikon deltion** tou **Institoutou Kallitereuseōs Futōn.** en Thessaloniki. Ἐπιστημονικὸν Δελτίον τοῦ Ἰνστιτούτου Καλλιτερευσέως Φυτῶν. *Epistēm. Delt. Inst. Kallit. Fut.* [1929–] **L.**AM. 33–38; P.; **C.**A. 31; **Rt.** imp.

18310[c] **Építés-építészet.** Budapest. *Építés-Épít.* [1949–] **L.**BM. 50–. [*Also supplements*]

18311 **Építési** és **műszaki közlöny.** Budapest. *Épít. Műsz. Közl.*

18311[c] **Építésügyi szemle.** Budapest. *Épit. Szle* **Y.**

18312 **Építő ipar.** Budapest. *Építő Ipar*

18313 **Épitőanyag.** Budapest. *Épitőanyag* **L.**BM. 51–; **Y.**

18314 **Építőipari lapok.** Budapest. *Építőip. Lap.*

18315 **Épizooticheskiĭ listok Saratovskago gubern-skago zemstva.** Saratov. Эпизоотическiй листокъ Саратовскаго губернскаго земства. *Épizoot. List. saratov. gub. Zemst.*

18316 **Epocha.** Rozhledy a uvahy časové z oboru techniky a vynálezů. Praha. *Epocha*

18317 **Épreuve photographique.** Paris. *Épreuve photogr.*

18317ᵃ **Epuletgepeszet.** Budapest. *Epuletgepeszet* **Y.**

18318 **Équerre.** Bulletin mensuel à l'usage des géomètres, architectes, etc. Anvers. *Équerre*

18319 **Équipement automobile.** Paris. *Équip. auto.* [1921–] **Bm.**U. 36–39. [*C. of:* 13375]

18319ᶜ **Équipement mécanique.** *Équip. méc.* **Y.**

18320 **Équipement rural.** Bruxelles. *Équip. rur.* [1948–49] **L.**AM.; **Sil.**

18321 **Équipements.** Ateliers de constructions électriques de Delle. Villeurbanne. *Équipements* [1948–51] **L.**P. [*Replaced by:* 3730]

18322 **Equipment Notes. F.A.O.** Rome. *Equip. Notes F.A.O.* [1953–54] **L.**P.; **Bn.**U. 54. [*C. as:* 20037]

18323 **Equipment Preview** of **Chemical Process Industries.** Chicago. *Equip. Preview chem. Process Ind.* [1938–40] [*C. as:* 13743]

18324 **Equipment Review.** Chicago. *Equip. Rev.* **L.**P. 23–25*. [*Part of:* 18105]

18325 **Era.** Förening för elektricitetens rationella anvädning. Stockholm. *Era, Stockh.* [1928–] **L.**P. 29–; **R.**U. 47– imp.; **Y.**

18326 **Erasmus:** speculum scientiarum. Amsterdam, Basle. *Erasmus* [1947–] **L.**B.; BM.; U.; **Bm.**P.; **Br.**P.; **E.**A. 53–; U.; **Ex.**U.; **Ld.**U.; **N.**U.; **O.**B.; **R.**U.

Erba Nachrichten. Baumwoll-industrie Erlangen-Bamberg. *See* 17320.

18327 **Erda.** Electrical and Radio Development Association of New South Wales. Sydney. *Erda*

18328 **Erdball.** Berlin. *Erdball*

Erdbeben in **Ungarn.** *See* 29269.

Erdbebenbericht. Zagreb. *See* 24568.

18329 **Erdbebenbericht. Badische Landes-Sternwarte.** Heidelberg. *ErdbBer. bad. Landes-Sternw.*

18330 **Erdbebenbericht** des **Geophysikalischen Observatoriums.** Appia. *ErdbBer. geophys. Obs., Appia*

18331 **Erdbebenbericht. Observatorium, Batavia.** *ErdbBer. Obs. Batavia* **L.**BM. 09*; **G.**U. 09. [*C. as:* 49393]

18332 **Erdbebenstation.** Agram. *Erdbebenstation, Agram*

18333 **Erdbebenwarte.** Laibach. *Erdbebenwarte, Laibach* [1901–10] **L.**BM.; **O.**O.

18334 **Erde.** Berlin. *Erde, Berl.* [1949–] **L.**BM.; MO.; SC.; U.; **C.**GG.; PO.; **Db.**; **E.**G.; U.; **G.**U.; **H.**U. 60–; **Ld.**U.; **N.**U.; **O.**G.; **Sh.**U.; **Y.** [*C. of:* 58636]

18335 **Erde.** Weimar. *Erde, Weimar*

18336 **Erdélyi múzeum.** Kolozsvár. *Erdélyi Múz.* [1874–] **L.**BMᴺ. 74–82; GL. 30–.

18337 **Erdészeti kisérletek.** Sopron. *Erdész. Kisérl.* [1899–49] **L.**EB. 99–18 imp.; K. 26–40 imp.; **O.**F. 26–49; **Rt.** 25–40. [*C. as:* 1214]

18338 **Erdészeti kutatások.** Budapest. *Erdész. Kutat.* [1954–] **C.**A.; **O.**F.; **Y.** [*Foreign edition of summaries from* 1955 *at:* 19992]

18339 **Erdészeti lapok.** Budapest. *Erdész. Lap.* [1862–50] **L.**SC. 28–50; **O.**F. 36–50 imp. [*C. as:* 18351]

18340 **Erdészeti tudományos intezet évkönyve** Budapest. *Erdész. Tudom. Intez. Évk.* [1951–] **O.**F.; **Y.**

18341 **Erdészeti ujság.** Szászsebes. *Erdész. Ujs.*

18342 **Erdészettudományi közlemények.** Sopron. *Erdészettud. Közl.* [1958–] **Bn.**U.; **Rt.** [*C. of:* 18361]

18343 **Erdgeschichtliche** und **landeskundliche Abhandlungen** aus **Schwaben** und **Franken.** Öhringen. *Erdgesch. landesk. Abh. Schwab. Frank.*

18344 **Erdkunde.** Bonn. *Erdkunde* [1947–] **L.**BM.; G.; MO. 51–; NC. 56–; **Bl.**U.; **C.**PO.; **E.**G.; **Ex.**U.; **G.**U.; **H.**U. 60–; **Ld.**U. 50–; **Nw.**A.; **Sh.**U.; **Y.**

18345 **Erdkundliches Wissen.** Remagen. *Erdk. Wissen* [1952–] **L.**G.

18346 **Erdmagnetische Berichte.** Wien. *Erdmagn. Ber.* **L.**MO. 57–.

18347 **Erdmagnetische Kennziffern Ki, Wingst.** Hamburg. *Erdmagn. Kennziff. Ki Wingst* **L.**MO. 48–.

18348 **Erdmagnetische Kennziffern Kp, Wingst.** Hamburg. *Erdmagn. Kennziff. Kp Wingst* **L.**MO. 50–.

18349 **Erdmagnetische Messungen** in den **Ländern** der **ungarischen Krone.** *Erdmagn. Mess. Länd. ung. Kr.* **L.**MO. 92–94.

18350 **Erdmagnetische Untersuchungen** in **Finnland.** Helsingfors. *Erdmagn. Unters. Finnl.* [1910–] **L.**MO. 10–13; P.; SC.; **E.**R. 10; **O.**R. 10.

18351 **Erdő.** Budapest. *Erdő* [1952–] **O.**F.; **Y.** [*C. of:* 18339]

18352 **Erdöl.** Wien. *Erdöl* [1950] **L.**P.; SC. [*C. from:* 7273; *C. as:* 18359]

18353 **Erdöl** und **Kohle.** Berlin, Hamburg. *Erdöl Kohle* [1948–60] **L.**AV. 57–60; BM.; C.; P.; PT.; SC. 49–60; **Bm.**U.; **Ep.**D. 55–60; **Ld.**U.; **Li.**M. 49–60; **Y.** [*C. of:* 35888; *C. as:* 18354]

18354 **Erdöl** und **Kohle, Erdgas, Petrochemie.** Berlin. *Erdöl Kohle Erdgas Petrochem.* [1960–] **L.**AV.; BM.; C.; P.; PT.; SC.; **Bm.**U.; **Ep.**D.; **Ld.**U.; **Li.**M.; **Y.** [*C. of:* 18353]

18355 **Erdöl** und **Teer.** Berlin. *Erdöl Teer* [1925–34] **L.**PT. 32–34; SC. 33–34; **Bm.**U. 27–34. [*C. in:* 35887]

18356 **Erdölchronik** und **-statistik.** Berlin. *Erdölchronik u. -Statist.* **L.**C. 30–33.

18357 **Erdölinformationsdienst.** *Erdölinformationsdienst* **L.**PT. (curr.)

18358 **Erdöl-Zeitschrift** für **Bohr-** und **Fördertechnik.** Wien. *Erdöl-Z. Bohr- u. Fördertech.* [1955–] **L.**DI. 56–57; P.; SC.; **Y.** [*C. of:* 18359]

18359 **Erdöl-Zeitung.** Wien. *Erdöl-Ztg* [1951–55] **L.**P.; SC.; **Y.** [*C. of:* 18352; *C. as:* 18358]

18359ᵃ **Erdögazdaság.** Budapest. *Erdögazdaság* **L.**BM. 50–.

18359ᵇ **Erdögazdaság** és **faipar.** *Erdögazd. Faipar* **Y.**

18360 **Erdömérnöki föiskola évkönyve.** Sopron. *Er-Erdömérn. Föisk. Évk., Sopron* [1950–53] **Db.**; **O.**F.; **Rt.** [*C. of:* 1214; *C. as:* 18361]

18361 **Erdömérnöki föiskola közleményei.** Sopron. *Erdömérn. Föisk. Közl., Sopron* [1954–57] **Bn.**U. 57; **O.**F.; **Rt.** [*C. of:* 18360; *C. as:* 18342]

18362 **Ereunai** epi tou **oruktou** tēs **'Ellados.** Athēnai. Ερευναι επι του 'ορυκτου της 'Ελλαδος. *Ereun. Orukt. 'Ell.* [1951–] **L.**MI.; **E.**R. 51; **Y.**

18363 **Erfahrung** und **Forschung** und **Jahresberichte. Textilingenieurschule, Aachen.** *Erfahr. Forsch. Jber. TextIngrsch. Aachen* **L.**P. 44–50; **M.**C. 51–60.

18364 **Erfahrungen** im **naturwissenschaftlichen Unterricht.** Bern. *Erfahr. naturw. Unterr.*

18365 **Erfahrungsberichte** des **Deutschen Flugwetterdienstes.** Berlin. *ErfahrBer. dt. FlugwettDienst.* **L.**MO. 28–36.

18366 **Erfahrungs-Heilkunde.** Ulm. *Erfahr.-Heilk.* [1952–]

18367 **Erfelijkheid** in **praktijk.** Soesterberg. *Erfelijkh. Prakt.* [1936–55] **C.**A. [*C. as:* 20834]

18368 **Erfinderrundschau.** München. *Erfinderrundschau*

18369 **Erfindung.** Internationale Zeitschrift für Patentwesen. Berlin. *Erfindung* **L.**P. 26*.

18370 **Erfindungen** und **Erfahrungen.** Brünn. *Erfind. Erfahr.* [1938] **L.**P. [*C. as:* 57343]

18371 **Erfindungswesen** in der **U.d.S.S.R.** Moskau. *ErfindWes. U.S.S.R.* **L.**P. 31*.

18372 **Erfindungs-** und **Vorschlagswesen.** Berlin. *Erfind.- u. VorschlWes.* [1952–] **L.**P.; **Ld.**P. 59–; **M.**P. 55–; **Y.**

18373 **Ergänzungshefte** für **angewandte Geophysik.** Leipzig. *ErgänzHft. angew. Geophys.* [1930–33] **L.**AM.; MO.; SC. 31–32; **Abd.**U.; **Ld.**U.; **Lo.**; **M.**U. [*C. as:* 5926; *Supplement to:* 5949]

18374 **Ergänzungshefte. Zeitschrift** für **Spiritusindustrie.** Berlin. *ErgänzHft. Z. SpiritInd.* **L.**P. 87–19.

18375 **Ergänzungsmessungen** zum **bayerischen Präzisionsnivellement.** München. *ErgänzMess. bayer. PräzisNivell.*

18376 **Ergebnisse** der **Aerodynamischen Versuchsanstalt** zu **Göttingen.** *Ergebn. aerodyn. VersAnst. Göttingen* [1921–32] **L.**MO. 23–27; P.; SC. 23–32; **Bl.**U.

18377 **Ergebnisse** aerologischer beobachtungen. K. Nederlandsch meteorologisch instituut. Utrecht. *Ergebn. aerolog. Beob., Utrecht* [1909–40] **L.**BM. 13–40; MO.; SC. 21–40; UC.; **E.**M.; R. [*C. as:* 55719°]

18378 **Ergebnisse** der **Agrikulturchemie.** Berlin. *Ergebn. AgrikChem.* [1929–35] **L.**P. [*Replaced by:* 20147]

18379 **Ergebnisse** der **allgemeinen Pathologie** und **pathologischen Anatomie** des **Menschen** und der **Tiere.** Wiesbaden, etc. *Ergeben. allg. Path. path. Anat.* [1894–] **L.**BM.; MD. 96–; S. 94–58; UCH. 95–15; **Abd.**U. 09–17 imp.; **Bl.**U.; **Bm.**U.; **Br.**U. 94–43; **C.**PA. 97–98: 04–39: 54; UL.; **Db.** 94–39; **Dn.**U. imp.; **E.**P.; S. 94–39; U.; **G.**U. 25– imp.; **M.**MS. 94–12; **O.**R.

18380 **Ergebnisse** der **Anatomie** und **Entwicklungsgeschichte.** Wiesbaden. *Ergebn. Anat. EntwGesch.* [1891–] **L.**BM.; MD.; R.; S. 21–44; SC.; UC. 92–38; Z.; **Abd.**U.; **Bl.**U.; **Bm.**U.; **Br.**U. 94–14; **C.**AN.; B.; MD. 91–14; UL.; **Dn.**U. 91–13; **E.**P. 91–05; S. 00–14; U. 91–38; **G.**F.; U.; **Ld.**U.; **M.**MS. 56–; **O.**R.; **Pl.**M. 91–97; **Sa.** 24–; **Y.**

18381 **Ergebnisse** der **angewandten Mathematik.** Berlin. *Ergebn. angew. Math.* [1952–] **L.**P.; **Sw.**U.

18382 **Ergebnisse** der **angewandten physikalischen Chemie.** Leipzig. *Ergebn. angew. phys. Chem.* [1931–40] **L.**SC. 31–38; **Abd.**U. 31–38.

18383 **Ergebnisse** der **Arbeiten** am **Aeronautischen Observatorium, Berlin.** Berlin. *Ergebn. Arb. aeronaut. Obs. Berl.* **L.**MO. 00–04*; SC. 02; **E.**M. 00–04. [*C. as:* 18385]

18384 **Ergebnisse** der **Arbeiten** der **Drachenstation** am **Bodensee.** Stuttgart. *Ergebn. Arb. Drachenstn Bodensee* **L.**BM. 12; MO. 08–15; **E.**M. 10–13. [*C. of:* 33986]

18385 **Ergebnisse** der **Arbeiten** des **K. Preussischen aeronautischen Observatoriums, Lindenberg.** *Ergebn. Arb. K. preuss. aeronaut. Obs.* [1905–16] **L.**BM. 05–10; MO.; **E.**M. 05–13. [*C. of:* 18383; *C. as:* 3854]

Ergebnisse der **Arbeiten** des **Samoa-Observatoriums** der **K. Gesellschaft** der **Wissenschaften** zu **Göttingen.** *See* 232.

18386 **Ergebnisse** der im **Atlantischen Ozean Planktonexpedition** der **Humboldt-Stiftung, 1889.** Kiel. *Ergebn. Atlant. Ozean Planktonexped. Humboldt-Stift.* [1892–26] **L.**AM. imp.; BM^N.; Z.; **Abd.**M. 95–11 imp.; **C.**B.; **Lo.** 92–11; **Lv.**U.; **Pl.**M.

18387 **Ergebnisse** der **Beobachtungen** am **Adolf Schmidt-Observatorium** für **Erdmagnetismus** in **Niemegk.** Potsdam. *Ergebn. Beob. Adolf Schmidt-Obs. Erdmagn.* [1932–] **L.**MO. [*See also* 18415]

18388 **Ergebnisse** der **Beobachtungen** der **amtlichen meteorologischen Station.** Davos. *Ergebn. Beob. amtl. met. Stn, Davos* [1945–] **L.**MO.; **Y.** [*C. of:* 25177 and 55441]

18389 **Ergebnisse** der **Beobachtungen** des **Magnetischen Observatoriums** zu **Lovö.** Stockholm. *Ergebn. Beob. magn. Obs. Lovö* [1928–] **L.**MO.; **E.**M.; R. 28–32; **Y.**

18390 **Ergebnisse** der **Beobachtungen** des **Magnetischen Observatoriums** zu **Sodankylä.** Helsingfors. *Ergebn. Beob. magn. Obs. Sodankylä* **L.**MO. 14–; **E.**M. 14–35.

Ergebnisse der **Beobachtungen** am **Observatorium Aachen** und dessen **Nebenstationen.** *See* 16914.

Ergebnisse der **Beobachtungen** an den **Stationen 2. u. 3. Ordnung.** *See* 16911.

18391 **Ergebnisse** der **Beobachtungsstationen** an den **deutschen Küsten.** Berlin. *Ergebn. BeobStnen dt. Küst.* **L.**MO. 73–93; **C.**UL. 77–; **E.**M. 87–93 imp.; R. 73–95; **Lv.**U. 74–95; **Pl.**M. 73–93.

18392 **Ergebnisse** der **Biologie.** Berlin. *Ergebn. Biol.* [1926–] **L.**BM^N.; QM. 58–; SC. 30–; UC. 26–43 imp.; Z.; **Bl.**U. 60–; **C.**B.; P.; **E.**U. 26–39: 42; Z.; **Nw.**A.; **O.**R.; **Pl.**M. imp.; **Rt.** 26–28; **Y.**

18393 **Ergebnisse** von **Bohrungen. Preussische geologische Landesanstalt.** Berlin. *Ergebn. Bohr. preuss. geol. Landesanst.*

18394 **Ergebnisse** der **Chirurgie** und **Orthopädie.** Berlin. *Ergebn. Chir. Orthop.* [1910–43: 49–] **L.**MD. 29–; S. 10–31: 43: 49–59; **E.**S. 22–; U. 10–33; **G.**U.

18395 **Ergebnisse** der **Deklinationsbeobachtungen** des **Erdmagnetischen Observatoriums** der **Westf. Berggewerkschaftkasse** zu **Bochum.** Bochum. *Ergebn. DeklinBeob. erdmagn. Obs. Bochum*

18396 **Ergebnisse** der **Enzymforschung.** Leipzig. *Ergebn. Enzymforsch.* [1932–43: 49–54] L.C.; LI. imp.; MC. 32–39; P. 35–54; SC.; U. 50–54; UC. 33–54; **Abd.**U.; **Bl.**U. 32–39; **Bm.**U.; **Bn.**U. 49–54 imp.; **C.**BI. 32–49; BO. 32–39; UL.; **E.**U. 32–39; **G.**U. 32–39: 49–54; **Ld.**U. 32–34; **M.**MS. 32–39; T.; **Nw.**A.; **O.**BO. 35–36; PH.; R.; **Pl.**M. 32–54 imp.; **R.**D. 32–39–; **Sa.**

18397 **Ergebnisse** der **Erdbodentemperaturmessungen** im **Garten** der **Landeswetterwarte** zu **Dresden.** Dresden. *Ergebn. ErdbodentempMess. Landeswetterw. Dresden*

18398 **Ergebnisse** der **erdmagnetischen Beobachtungen** im **Observatorium Wingst.** Hamburg. *Ergebn. erdmagn. Beob. Obs. Wingst* L.MO. 43–; E.M. 49–.

18399 **Ergebnisse** der **exakten Naturwissenschaften.** Berlin. *Ergebn. exakt. Naturw.* [1922–] L.C. 53–; P.; QM. 33– imp.; SC. 31–39: 45–; UC.; **Bl.**U. 22–45 imp.; **Br.**U.; **C.**UL.; **E.**O.; U. 28–; **G.**U. 53–; **H.**U. 22–29: 49–; **M.**U.; **N.**U. imp.; **Nw.**A. imp.; **O.**R.; **R.**U.; **Sa.** 23– imp.; **Y.** [*Not published* 1943–44]

18400 **Ergebnisse** der **Forstverwaltung** im **Reg.-Bez. Bromberg.** *Ergebn. Forstverwalt. Bromberg*

18401 **Ergebnisse** der **Forstverwaltung** d. **Reg.-Bez. Düsseldorf.** *Ergebn. Forstverwalt. Düsseldorf* [*C. of:* 46060]

18402 **Ergebnisse** der **Forstverwaltung** im **Reg.-Bez. Köln.** *Ergebn. Forstverwalt. Köln*

18403 **Ergebnisse** und **Fortschritte** des **Krankenhauswesens.** Jena. *Ergebn. Fortschr. Krankenhausw.* [1912–20]

18404 **Ergebnisse** und **Fortschritte** der **Zoologie.** Jena. *Ergebn. Fortschr. Zool.* [1907–35] L.BM[N].; LI. 07–31; SC.; UC.; Z.; **Abd.**U. 07–32; **Abs.**U. 13–35; **Br.**U. 07–31; **C.**B.; **Db.**; **G.**U.; **Ld.**U.; **M.**U.; **Nw.**A. 07–23; **O.**R.; Z. 07–26; **Pl.**M. 07–14; **Sh.**U. 07–25. [*C. as:* 20254]

18405 **Ergebnisse** der **gesamten Medizin.** Berlin. *Ergebn. ges. Med.* [1920–38] L.MD.

18406 **Ergebnisse** der **gesamten Tuberkulose-Forschung.** Leipzig. *Ergebn. ges. TuberkForsch.* [1930–41] L.MA. 30–34; MD.; **Db.**

18407 **Ergebnisse** der **gesamten Zahnheilkunde.** Wiesbaden. *Ergebn. ges. Zahnheilk.* [1910–24] L.D. 18–22.

18408 **Ergebnisse** der **Gewitterbeobachtungen.** Berlin. *Ergebn. Gewitterbeob.* [1891–] L.BM.; MO. 91–25; E.M. 91–10.

18409 **Ergebnisse** der **Hygiene, Bakteriologie, Immunitätsforschung** u. **experimentellen Therapie.** Berlin. *Ergebn. Hyg. Bakt.* [1917–55] L.LI. 17–43; MC. 17–30; MD.; TD.; **C.**PA. 17–49; **Lv.**U. 22–24; **O.**P. 28–35; **Y.** [*C. of:* 18410; *C. as:* 18428]

18410 **Ergebnisse** der **Immunitätsforschung, experimentellen Therapie, Bakteriologie** und **Hygiene.** Berlin. *Ergebn. ImmunForsch. exp. Ther.* [1914] L.LI.; MC.; MD.; TD. [*C. of:* 24924; *C. as:* 18409]

18411 **Ergebnisse** der **inneren Medizin** und **Kinderheilkunde.** Berlin. *Ergebn. inn. Med. Kinderheilk.* [1908–45: 49–] L.GH. 08–36; MD.; **Abd.**U. 08–52 imp.; **Bm.**U. 08–13; **Db.** 24–32; **Dn.**U. 08–14; **E.**P.; U. 08–33; **Lv.**M. 08–14: 29–33; **Nw.**A. 27–; **O.**R. 08–29; **Y.**

18412 **Ergebnisse** des **Internationalen Breitendienstes.** Preussisches geodätisches Institut. Potsdam. *Ergebn. int. Breitendienst.* [1912–22] L.AS.; SC.; **C.**O. [*C. of:* 56257; *C. as:* 46085]

18413 **Ergebnisse** der **Ionosphäresbeobachtungen.** Köln. *Ergebn. IonosphBeob.* L.MO. 57–.

18414 **Ergebnisse** der **kosmischen Physik.** Leipzig. *Ergebn. kosm. Phys.* [1931–39] L.MO.; **Abd.**U.; **E.**U.; **Ld.**U.; **M.**U. 31–35. [*Supplement to:* 5949]

18414° **Ergebnisse** der **landwirtschaftlichen Forschung** an der **Justus Liebig-Universität.** Giessen. *Ergebn. landwirt. Forsch. Justus Liebig-Univ.* **C.**A. 60–.

18415 **Ergebnisse** der **magnetischen Beobachtungen** im **Adolf Schmidt Observatorium.** Niemegk. *Ergebn. magn. Beob. Adolf Schmidt Obs.* [1932–] L.MO.; E.M. imp. [*C. of:* 18417; *See also* 18387]

Ergebnisse der **magnetischen Beobachtungen** a. d. **K. Observatorium** in **Wilhelmshaven.** *See* 56188.

18416 **Ergebnisse** der **magnetischen Beobachtungen** in **Potsdam.** Berlin. *Ergebn. magn. Beob. Potsdam* [1890–30] L.BM.; MO.; E.M. [*C. as:* 18417]

18417 **Ergebnisse** der **magnetischen Beobachtungen** in **Seddin.** *Ergebn. magn. Beob. Seddin* [1931] L.MO.; E.M. [*C. of:* 18416; *C. as:* 18415]

18418 **Ergebnisse** der **Mathematik** und ihrer **Grenzgebiete.** Berlin. *Ergebn. Math.* [1932–] L.SC. 32–42: 55–; UC. 32–38; **Bl.**U. 32–38: 55–58 imp.; **C.**P.; UL.; **Cr.**U. 32–37; **Dn.**U.; **H.**U. 55–; **M.**U. 32–42: 55–; **Sw.**U.; **Y.**

18419 **Ergebnisse** eines **mathematischen Kolloquiums.** Leipzig. *Ergebn. math. Kolloq.* [1928–36] L.SC.; **C.**P. [*For a second series, see* 44424]

18420 **Ergebnisse** der **medizinischen Strahlenforschung.** Leipzig. *Ergeb. med. StrahlForsch.* [1925–36] L.MD. imp.; RA. 25–31.

Ergebnisse der **meteorologischen Beobachtungen.** Bremen. *See* 16909.

Ergebnisse der **meteorologischen Beobachtungen.** Brünn. *See* 6286.

Ergebnisse der **meteorologischen Beobachtungen** in **Elsass-Lothringen.** *See* 16909.

Ergebnisse der **meteorologischen Beobachtungen.** **K. meteorologisches Institut.** Berlin. *See* 16904.

18421 **Ergebnisse** der **meteorologischen Beobachtungen** an den **Landesstationen** in **Bosnien-Hercegovina.** Wien. *Ergebn. met. Beob. Landesstnen Bosn.-Herc.* [1894–12] L.MO.; E.M.; R.

18422 **Ergebnisse** der **meteorologischen Beobachtungen** in **Litauen.** Kaunas. *Ergebn. met. Beob. Litauen* [1924–] L.MO. 24–30. [*C. of:* 31560[a]]

18423 **Ergebnisse** der **meteorologischen Beobachtungen** in **Pola.** *Ergebn. met. Beob. Pola* L.MO. 64–10; E.M. 1847–10 imp. [*From* 1895 *contained in* 56162]

18424 **Ergebnisse** der **meteorologischen Beobachtungen** in **Potsdam.** Berlin. *Ergebn. met. Beob. Potsdam* L.BM. 93–; MO. 93–33; SC. 02; E.M. 93–12; R. 85–02; **O.**G. 79–34 imp.

18425 **Ergebnisse** der **meteorologischen Beobachtungen.** **Staatliches Observatorium, Danzig.** *Ergebn. met. Beob. st. Obs. Danzig* L.MO. 30–38.

18426 **Ergebnisse** der **meteorologischen Beobachtungen** auf dem **Tzukubazan.** Tokyo. *Ergebn. met. Beob. Tzukubazan* L.MO. 02–12.

Ergebnisse der **meteorologischen Beobachtungen** in **Württemberg.** *See* 16916.

Ergebnisse der **meteorologischen Beobachtungen** an **10 Stationen 2. Ordnung,** etc. *See* 16904.

18427 **Ergebnisse** der **meteorologischen** u. **magnetischen Beobachtungen** zu **Clausthal.** Saarbrücken. *Ergebn. met. magn. Beob. Clausthal*

18428 **Ergebnisse** der **Mikrobiologie, Immunitätsforschung** und **experimentellen Therapie.** Berlin. *Ergebn. Mikrobiol. ImmunForsch. exp. Ther.* [1956–] **L.**LI.; MD.; TD.; **Ld.**U.; **O.**P.; **Y.** [*C. of:* 18409]

18429 **Ergebnisse** der **Neurologie** und **Psychiatrie.** Jena. *Ergebn. Neurol. Psychiat.* [1912–17] **L.**MD.; UC.; **E.**P.

18430 **Ergebnisse** der **Niederschlagsbeobachtungen. Preussisches meteorologisches Institut.** Berlin. *Ergebn. Niederschlagsbeob. preuss. met. Inst.* [1891–] **L.**MO. 91–33.

18431 **Ergebnisse** der **österreichischen Waldbestandsaufnahme.** Mariabrunn-Schönbrunn. *Ergebn. öst. WaldbestAufn.* [1956–] **O.**F. 57–.

Ergebnisse der **pflanzengeographischen Durchforschung** von **Württemberg, Baden** u. **Hohenzollern.** *Supplement to* 25172.

18432 **Ergebnisse** der **phänologischen Beobachtungen** aus **Mähren** u. **Schlesien.** Brünn. *Ergebn. phänol. Beob. Mähren Schles.* **G.**U. 02–06*.

18433 **Ergebnisse** phänologischer **Beobachtungen** im **Deutschen Reich.** Berlin. *Ergebn. phänol. Beob. dt. Reich* **L.**BM. 38–.

18434 **Ergebnisse** der **Physiologie (biologischen Chemie** und **experimentellen Pharmakologie).** Wiesbaden. *Ergebn. Physiol.* [1902–44: 50–] **L.**LI. 02–40; MC.; MD.; SA. 02–44; SC. 26–; U. 02–21; UC.; **Abd.**U. 02–39 imp.; **Br.**U.; **C.**APH. 02–19: 50–; PH. 02–39; 50–; UL.; **Cr.**P. 29–; **Db.** 02–39 imp.: 43–; **Dn.**U.; **E.**P. 02–39: 50–; U. 02–44; **G.**U. 02–39; **Lv.**U.; **M.**MS. 02–40: 50–; **O.**R.; **Pl.**M. 10– imp.; **Sa.**; **Sh.**U.; **Y.**

18435 **Ergebnisse** der **Registrierballonfahrten** ausgeführt vom **Geophysikalischen Institut.** Leipzig. *Ergebn. RegistBallonf. geophys. Inst.* **L.**MO. 26–29; SC. 28–.

18436 **Ergebnisse** der **Säuglingsfürsorge.** Leipzig. *Ergebn. SäuglFürs.* [1908–11] **L.**MD.

18437 **Ergebnisse** der **Schlachtvieh-** u. **Fleischbeschau** im **Deutschen Reiche.** Berlin. *Ergebn. Schlachtvieh- u. FleischBeschau* **W.** 33–.

18438 **Ergebnisse** der **sozialen Hygiene** und **Gesundheitsfürsorge.** Leipzig. *Ergebn. soz. Hyg. GesundhFürs.* [1929–30]

18439 **Ergebnisse** der **Strahlungsregistrierungen** am **Staatlichen Observatorium, Danzig.** *Ergebn. StrahlRegist. st. Obs. Danzig* **L.**MO. 31–38.

18440 **Ergebnisse** der **täglichen Niederschlagsmessungen** auf den **meteorologischen** und **Regenmess-Stationen** in der **Schweiz.** Zürich. *Ergebn. tägl. NiederschlMess. met. Regenmess-Stnen Schweiz* **L.**MO. 36–; **Y.**

18441 **Ergebnisse** der **technischen Röntgenkunde.** Leipzig. *Ergebn. tech. Röntgenk.* [1930–]

18442 **Ergebnisse** für **Terminbeobachtungen. Institut** für **kosmische Physik der Deutschen Universität, Prag.** *Ergebn. Terminbeob. Inst. kosm. Phys. dt. Univ. Prag* **L.**MO. 14–25.

18443 **Ergebnisse** der **theoretischen** und **angewandten Mikrobiologie.** Neudamm. *Ergebn. theor. angew. Mikrobiol.* [1943–] **O.**R.; **Rt.**

18444 **Ergebnisse** der **Triangulierungen** d. **K. K. Militärgeographischen Instituts.** Wien. *Ergebn. Triangul. K. K. militärgeogr. Inst.* [1901–06] **L.**AS.; BM.; **E.**R.

18445 **Ergebnisse** der **Tuberkuloseforschung.** Leipzig. *Ergebn. TuberkForsch.* [1916–20] **L.**BM.

Ergebnisse der **Vegetationsversuche.** Moskau. *See* 47677.

18446 **Ergebnisse** der **Vitamin-** und **Hormonforschung.** Leipzig. *Ergebn. Vitam.- u. Hormonforsch.* [1938–39] **L.**B.; C.; LI.; MD.; P.; SC.; **Abd.**R.; **Bl.**U.; **Bm.**U.; **C.**BI.; **E.**P.; U.; **M.**MS.; **O.**PH.; R.; **R.**D.

18447 **Ergebnisse** der **wissenschaftlichen Medizin.** Leipzig. *Ergebn. wiss. Med.* [1909–11]

18448 **Ergebnisse** der **wissenschaftlichen Untersuchung** des **Schweizerischen Nationalparks.** *Ergebn. wiss. Unters. schweiz. NatnParks* **L.**BM^N. 20–; SC. 29–51; **O.**AP. 20–.

18449 **Ergonomics.** London. *Ergonomics* [1957–] **L.**AV.; BM.; MC.; MD.; TD.; UC.; **Bl.**U. 61–; **Bm.**P.; **E.**A.; U.; **G.**T.; **H.**U.; **Lc.**A.; **Ld.**P.; U.; **Li.**M.; **M.**C.; **O.**B.; **R.**U.; **Sil.**; **Y.**

18450 **Erhvervsfrugtavleren.** Odense. *Erhvervsfrugtavleren* [1934–] **L.**HS. 34–40; **Md.**H. 34–39: 46– imp.

18451 **Erhvervsliv.** København. *Erhvervsliv* **L.**PL. 48–.

18452 **Ericsson Bulletin.** Ericsson Telephones, Ltd. Beeston, Notts. *Ericsson Bull.* [1932–] **L.**AV. 48–56: 59–; P.; **Lv.**P. 53–; **Ma.**T. 59–; **Sh.**IO. 48–54.

18453 **Ericsson Engineering Bulletin.** Stockholm. *Ericsson Engng Bull.* **Ma.**T.

18454 **Ericsson News.** Stockholm. *Ericsson News* [1927–31] **L.**P.

18455 **Ericsson Review.** Stockholm. *Ericsson Rev.* [1935–] **L.**AV. 35–51 imp.; EE.; P.; QM. 49–; **Abs.**U. 45– imp.; **Bl.**U. 50– imp.; **Bm.**C. (curr.); P.; T. 48–; **Bn.**U.; **C.**ENG. 47–; **Co.**T. 45–; **Cr.**U. imp.; **Dn.**U. 46–; **G.**T. (1 yr); U.; **Lc.**A. 50–; **Ld.**U.; **Lv.**P. 45–50 imp.: 53–; **M.**P.; T. (5 yr.); **Ma.**T. 35–37: 47–50: 59–; **N.**U. (curr.); **Nw.**A. imp.; **Sa.** 47–; **Y.** [*C. of:* 27894]

18456 **Ericsson Technics.** Stockholm. *Ericsson Tech.* [1933–] **L.**AV. imp.; P. imp.; SC.; **Bm.**P.; T. 48–; **Bn.**U. imp.; **Co.**T. 53–; **Cr.**U. imp.; **G.**U. 33–44 imp.; **Lc.**A. 53– imp.; **M.**T. 48–; **Ma.**T. 35–37: 48–50: 59–; **N.**U. (curr.); Nw.A. 33–37; **Sa.** 48–50: 58–; **Y.** [*Suspended:* 1939–43]

18457 **Erkens-Rundschau.** Düren. *Erkens-Rdsch.* **L.**P. 30.

18458 **Erkrankungen** des **Bewegungsapparates.** Wien. *Erkrank. BewegAppar.*

18459 **Erläuterungen** zur **geognostischen Karte** des **Königreichs Bayern.** München. *Erläut. geogn. Karte Bayern* [1887–] **L.**GM.; SC. 38–; **E.**D. 87–16 v. imp.

Erläuterungen zu den **geologischen** und **bodenkundlichen Karten Ungarns.** *See* 29266.

18460 **Erläuterungen** zur **geologischen Karte** von **Bayern.** München. *Erläut. geol. Karte Bayern* [1938–] **L.**BM^N. 27–38; SC.

18460° **Erläuterungen** zur **geologischen Karte** von **Preussen** und **benachbarten (Bundesstaaten) deutschen Ländern.** Berlin. *Erläut. geol. Karte Preuss.* [1901–] **L.**BM^N. 01–39; GL.; GM. [*C. of:* 18465]

18461 **Erläuterungen** zur **geologischen Karte** der **Schweiz.** Bern. *Erläut. geol. Karte Schweiz* [1899–] **L.**BM^N. 99–12; GL.; GM.; **E.**R.

18462 **Erläuterungen** zur **geologischen Spezialkarte** von **Elsass-Lothringen.** Strassburg. *Erläut. geol. SpezKarte Els.-Loth.* [1887–] **L.**BM^N. 87–04; GL. OO–19; GM.; **E.**D.

18463 **Erläuterungen** zur **geologischen Spezialkarte** des **Grossherzogthums Baden.** Heidelberg. *Erläut. geol. SpezKarte Baden* [1894–] **L.**BM^N. 94–37; GL. OO–31 imp.; GM.

18464 **Erläuterungen** zur **geologischen Spezialkarte** des **Grossherzogthums Hessen.** Darmstadt. *Erläut. geol. SpezKarte Hessen* [1886–] **L.**BM^N. 86–13; GL. OO–36; GM.

Erläuterungen zur **geologischen Spezialkarte** des **Königreichs Sachsen.** See 18466.

18465 **Erläuterungen** zur **geologischen Spezialkarte** von **Preussen** und den **thüringischen Staaten.** Berlin. *Erläut. geol. SpezKarte Preuss. thüring. St.* **L.**BM^N. 70–00*; GM. 70–00. [*C. as:* 18460°]

18466 **Erläuterungen** zur **geologischen Spezialkarte** des **Sachsen.** Leipzig. *Erläut. geol. SpezKarte Sachs.* [1877–] **L.**BM^N. 77–29; GL. OO–; GM. 79–; MO. 49–.

18467 **Erläuterungen** zur **geologischen Spezialkarte** der **Ungarischen Krone.** Budapest. *Erläut. geol. SpezKarte ung. Kr.* [1885–] **L.**GL. OO–37 imp.; GM.; SC. 85–16.

18468 **Erläuterungen** zur **geologischen Spezialkarte** von **Württemberg.** Stuttgart. *Erläut. geol. SpezKarte Württ.* [1906–] **L.**BM^N. 06–34; GM.

18469 **Erlafthal-Bote.** Wochenschrift für Gewerbe, Industrie u. Landwirtschaft. Scheibbs. *Erlafthal-Bote*

18470 **Erlanger Forschungen.** Erlangen. *Erlanger Forsch.* Reihe B. Naturwissenschaften [1955–] **O.**R.; **Y.**

18471 **Erlanger geologische Abhandlungen.** Erlangen. *Erlanger geol. Abh.* [1952–] **L.**BM^N.; GM.; **Br.**U.

18472 **Erlanger Jahrbuch** für **Bienenkunde.** Freiburg i. B. *Erlanger Jb. Bienenk.* [1923–30] **Rt.**

18473 **Ermak.** Omsk. Ермакъ. *Ermak*

18474 **Ernährung.** Berlin. *Ernährung* [1936–44] **L.**MD.; **Abd.**R. 36–39; **R.**D. 36–43 imp.; **Sal.**F. 36–39; **Y.** [*Replaces:* 58574; *For supplement see* 5913]

18475 **Ernährung** und **Gesundheit.** Leipzig. *Ernähr. Gesundh.*

18476 **Ernährung** der **Pflanze.** Mitteilungen des Kali Syndikats. Berlin. *Ernähr. Pfl.* [1905–43: 52–53] **L.**AM. 52–53; P. 10–40; SC. 32–53; TP. 30–40; **Abd.**U. 29–38; **Abs.**A. 27–43 imp.; S. 27–38; **Br.**P. 32–37; U. 30–53; **C.**A. 28–39: 52–53; **Ld.**U. 27–53; **Md.**N. 31–43: 52–53; **O.**RE. 27–39 imp.; **R.**U. 52–53; **Rt.** 24–53; **Y.**

18477 **Ernährung** und **Verpflegung.** *Ernähr. Verpfleg.* [1949–50] **Abd.**R.; **R.**D.

18478 **Ernährungsforschung.** Berlin. *Ernährungsforschung* [1956–] **L.**C. 59–; SC.; **Abd.**R.; **N.**U. 57–; **Rt.**; **Y.**

Ernährungsindustrie. Hamburg. See 19329

18479 **Ernährungs-Umschau.** Frankfurt am Main. *Ernähr.-Umsch.* **L.**AM. 57–.

18480 **Ernährungswirtschaft.** Berlin. *Ernährungswirtschaft*

18481 **Ernteergebnisse** auf den **Versuchsfeldern** der **Landwirtschaftskammer** f. d. **Prov. Pommern.** Stettin. *Ernteergebn. VersFeld. LandwirtKamm. Prov. Pommern*

18482 **Erő** és **egészség.** Budapest. *Erő Egészség* [1911–]

18483 **Erosion Survey.** Washington. *Eros. Surv.* [1938–41] **Rt.**

18484 **Ertesítő** az **Erdélyi múzeum-egyesület** orvos-természet-tudományi szakosztályából. Kolozsvár. *Ért. erdél. Múz.-Egyes. Orvos.-Term.-Tudom. Szakoszt.* [1875–05] **L.**BM^N. 79–05. [*C. as:* 33888]

18485 **Értesítő** az **Erdélyi múzeum-egyesület** orvos-tudományi szakosztályából. Kolozsvár. *Ért. erdél. Múz.-Egyes. Orvos.-Tudom. Szakoszt.* [1879–12] **Db.** 89–10.

Értesítő. Trencsénvármegyei muzeum-egyesület. Trencsén. See 25169.

18486 **Eruption** of **Hekla.** *Erupt. Hekla* **L.**BM^N. 50–57; **E.**R. 49–.

18487 **Erwerbobstbau.** Berlin. *Erwerbobstbau* [1959–] **Md.**H.; **Sil.**

18488 **Erythea.** A journal of botany. Berkeley, Cal. *Erythea* [1893–22: 38–] **L.**BM^N. 93–22; K. 93–22; L. 93–00.

Erzmetall. See 58577.

18489 **Esakia.** Hikosan biological Laboratory in Entomology. Hikosan. *Esakia* [1960–] **L.**BM^N.; **O.**H.; **Y.**

18490 **Escalpello.** Chaves. *Escalpello*

18491 **Escher Wyss News.** Zurich. *Escher Wyss News* [1928–] **L.**AV. 40–; EE. 29–43 imp.; I. 44–; P.; SC.; **Bm.**P. 50–; **Ld.**P. 44–; **Sh.**IO. (5 yr.); **Y.**

18492 **Escuela** de **ingenieros.** Lima. *Esc. Ing., Lima* **L.**P. 10–40.

18493 **Escuela** de **medicina.** Guatemala. *Esc. Med., Guatem.* **L.**MA. 49–.

18494 **Escuela** de **medicina.** México. *Esc. Med., Méx.*

18495 **Escuela médico-militar.** México. *Esc. méd.-milit., Méx.* [*C. as:* 46402]

18496 **Esculapio.** Madrid. *Esculapio*

18497 **Esercitazioni matematiche.** Circolo matematico di Catania. Catania. *Esercit. mat., Catania* [1921–] **L.**M.; SC. [>35177, 1927–31]

18498 **Esercizio** dell'**Associazione** fra gli **utenti** di **caldaie** a **vapore.** Milano. *Eserc. Ass. Ut. Cald. Vap.*

18499 **Eskimo.** Churchill, Manitoba. *Eskimo, Churchill* [1946–] **C.**PO. [*C. of:* 28623]

18500 **Eskimo.** Eugene, Oregon. *Eskimo, Eugene* [1916–18: 36–47] **C.**PO. 36–47.

18501 **Éskulap.** S.-Peterburg. Эскулапъ. *Éskulap*

18502 **Éspaces.** Paris. *Éspaces* [1946–] **L.**AV. 46–47 imp.

18503 **España agrícola.** Madrid. *Esp. agríc.*

18504 **España automóvil** y **aeronáutica.** Madrid. *Esp. auto. aeronáut.*

18505 **España cartófila.** Barcelona. *Esp. cartóf.*

18506 **España farmacéutica.** Oviedo. *Esp. farm.*

18507 **España forestal.** Madrid. *Esp. for.* [1915–30] **L.**SC. 29–30.

18508 **España futura.** Ciencia, etc. Madrid. *Esp. futura*

18509 **España médica.** Madrid. *Esp. méd.*

18510 **España oftalmológica.** Malaga. *Esp. oftal.*

18510ᵉ **Especificações. Laboratório nacional** de **engenharia civil.** Lisboa. *Especif. Lab. nac. Engenh. civ.* **L.**BM. 54–.

18511 **Esperienze** e **ricerche** dell'**Istituto agrario** della **R. Università, Pisa.** *Esper. Ric. Ist. agr. R. Univ. Pisa* [1888–22] **L.**BM. 96–00.

18512 **Esperienze** e **ricerche** dell'**Istituto** di **agronomia generale** e **coltivazionzi erbacee** della **R. Università, Pisa.** *Esper. Ric. Ist. Agron. gen. Colt. erb. R. Univ. Pisa* [1942–] **C.**A.; **Rt.**

18513 **Esplorazione commerciale.** Milano. *Esplor. comm.* [1886–28] **L.**BM. 86–13; **G.** imp.; **TP.** 16–28; **E.**G. 98–28.

18514 **Esprit médical.** Paris. *Esprit méd.* [1928–] **Essai** d'une **bibliographie générale** des **sciences** de la **mer.** Venezia. *See* 6587.

18515 **Essais pratiquées. Station provinciale** des **recherches scientifiques** de **viticulture.** La Hulpe. *Essais prat. Stn prov. Rech. scient. Vitic.* **Md.**H. 47–.

18516 **Essencias florestais** da **Guiné portuguesa.** Lisboa. *Essenc. flor. Guiné port.* [1953–] **O.**F.

18517 **Essenoil News.** Shanghai Essential Oils Corporation. Shanghai. *Essenoil News* [1958–] **L.**PT.; TP. **Essential Oils** and **Aromatics.** *See* 23912.

18518 **Essenze,** derivati agrumari. Reggio Calabria. *Essenze* **L.**P. 54–; TP. 59–.

18519 **Essex.** Essex Rubber Co. Trenton, N.J. *Essex* [1942–] **Sy.**R. imp.

18520 **Essex Bird Report.** Chelmsford. *Essex Bird Rep.* [1953–] **L.**AM. 56; BMᴺ.; Z. [*C. of:* 18521]

18521 **Essex Bird Watching** and **Preservation Society,** Chelmsford. *Essex Bird Watch. Pres. Soc.* **L.**BMᴺ. 51–52*; Z. 50–52. [*C. as:* 18520]

18522 **Essex Farmers' Journal.** Chelmsford. *Essex Fmrs' J.* [1922–] **L.**AM. imp.; BM.; **Abs.**N.; **C.**A. (1 yr); **Hu.**G. 52–; **Md.**H. 45–; **O.**R.; **Rt.** 23–39: 45– imp.; **Sil.** 54–.

18523 **Essex Field Club Special Memoirs.** London. *Essex Fld Club spec. Mem.* [1885–30] **L.**BM.; BMᴺ.; **Abs.**N.; **C.**UL.; **O.**B.

18524 **Essex Field Experiments.** Education Committee, Chelmsford. *Essex Fld Exp.* [1896–] **L.**AM.; P.; **Rt.** 96–03.

18525 **Essex Naturalist.** Buckhurst Hill. *Essex Nat.* [1887–] **L.**BM.; BMᴺ.; E. 87–34 imp.; GL.; GM. 87–13; K.; L.; NC.; QM. imp.; R.; SC.; UC.; Z.; **Abd.**M. 87–40 imp.; U. 87–93 imp.; **Abs.**N.; U. 87–18; **Bl.**U.; **Bm.**N.; **C.**P.; UL. 87–92; **Cr.**N.; **Db.**; **Dm.** 92: 97: 15–; **E.**A.; B. imp.; J.; R.; **Ld.**U.; **Lv.**U.; **M.**U.; **O.**AP. 56–; H. 87–42 imp.; OR.; R.; **Y.**

18526 **Esso.** Anglo-American Oil Co. London. *Esso* [1938–39] **L.**BM. [*C. as:* 18529]

18527 **Esso Air World.** New York. *Esso Air Wld* [1947–] **L.**BM.; P. (curr.); **Bm.**P.

18528 **Esso Farmer.** London. *Esso Fmr* [1949–] **L.**AM. 58; BM.; P.; **Abs.**U. imp.; **C.**A. 53–; **Db.** 50–; **O.**RE. (3 yr.); **Sil.** (1 yr)

18529 **Esso Magazine.** London. *Esso Mag.* [1949–] **L.**AM. 55–; AV. 56–; BM.; LE. 51–; P. (curr.); **Bm.**C. (curr.); **Br.**P. (2 yr.); **Dn.**U. 54– imp.; **F.**A. 53–; **G.**M. 56–; **Ld.**P. (5 yr.); **Lv.**P. 53–; **M.**C. (curr.); **Nw.**A. 53–; **Sa.** 51– imp; **Sh.**IO. 55–; **Y.** [*C. of:* 18526]

18530 **Esso Oilways.** London. *Esso Oilways* [1948–] **L.**AV. 54– imp.; P. (curr.); **Abs.**U. 50– imp.; **Co.**T. (curr.); **Ld.**P. (curr.); **Y.**

18531 **Essor agricole.** Belfort. *Essor agric.*

18532 **Essor frigorifique français.** Paris. *Essor frig. fr.* [1933–] **L.**SC. 37–.

18533 **Essor médical.** Paris. *Essor méd.*

18534 **Est européen agricole.** Varsovie. *Est eur. agric.* [1932–39] **L.**AM.; **C.**A.; **Rt.** imp. [*C. of:* 1454]

18535 **Est forestier.** Nancy. *Est for.*

18536 **Est métallurgique.** Besançon. *Est métall.*

18537 **Esta.** Revista mensual. Colonización y agricultura. Ministerio del ramo en Bolivia. La Paz. *Esta* **L.**BMᴺ. 36–37 imp.

18538 **Estação climatologica** do **Funchal.** Lisboa. *Estaç. clim. Funchal* **L.**SC. 34–36*. [*C. as:* 7362]

18539 **Estação climatologico** do **Mont' Estoril.** Lisboa. *Estaç. clim. Mt' Estoril* [*C. as:* 7363]

18540 **Estadística forestal** de **España.** Madrid. *Estadíst. for. Esp.* **O.**F. 46–.

18541 **Estadística foto-heliográfica. Observatorio astronómico** de **Cartuja.** *Estadíst. foto-heliogr. Obs. astr. Cartuja* **C.**SP. 05–.

18542 **Estadística** de **pesca.** Madrid. *Estadíst. Pesca, Madr.* **Abd.**M. 52–; **Lo.** 45– imp.

18544 **Estadística sanitaria.** Washington. *Estadíst. sanit.* [1952–] **L.**TD.

18545 **Estancia.** Porto Alegre. *Estancia*

18546 **Estate Clerk** of **Works** and **Country Builder.** London. *Estate Clk Wks Ctry Bldr* [1923–41] **L.**BM.; P. 23–41; SC. 34–; **O.**R. 23–41. [*C. of:* and *Rec. as:* 26928]

18547 **Estate Pamphlet. Prang Besar Rubber Estate, Ltd.** Selangor. *Estate Pamph. Prang Besar Rubb. Est.* **C.**A. 29–.

18548 **Estates Gazette.** London. *Estates Gaz.* [1858–] **L.**AM. 48–; BM.; **Abs.**N. 12–; **Br.**P. (1 yr); **C.**UL. 49–; **E.**A. 12–; CE. 58–; **Lv.**P. 00–; **Nw.**A. 57–; **O.**AEC. 49–.

18549 **Estatística** das **pescas maritimas, Portugal.** Lisboa. *Estatíst. Pesc. mar. Port.* **Wo.** 38–.

18550 **Estestvennoe dvizhenie naseleniya Soyuza SSR.** Moskva. Естественное движение населения Союза ССР. *Estestvennoe Dvizh. Nasel. SSSR* **L.**BM. 29–.

18551 **Estestvenno-istoricheskïe ékskursïi** po **Petrogradu.** Moskva. Естественно-историческіе экскурсіи по Петрограду. *Estestvenno-ist. Ékskurs. Petrogr.* **L.**BM. 23–.

18552 **Estestvennȳya proizvoditel'nȳya silȳ Rossïi.** Petrograd. Естественныя производительныя силы Россіи. *Estestvenn. proizvod. Silȳ Ross.* [1917–24] **L.**BM. 19–24; **Rt.** 22–24.

18553 **Estestvovêdênïe** i **naglyadnoe obuchenïe.** Moskva. Естествовѣдѣніе и наглядное обученіе. *Estestvov. nagl. Obuch.*

18554 **Estestvoznanïe** i **geografīya.** Moskva. Естествознаніе и географія. *Estestvoz. Geogr.*

18555 **Estestvoznanïe** v **shkolê.** Petrograd. Естествознаніе въ школѣ. *Estestvoz. Shk., Petrogr.* [1918–29]

18555° **Estestvoznanie** v **shkole.** Leningrad, Moskva. Естествознание в школе. *Estestvoz. Shk. Leningr.* [1946–56] **L.**BM. 52–56.

18556 **Estestvoznanie** v **sovetskoĭ shkole.** Moskva. Естествознание в советской школе. *Estestvoz. sov. Shk.* [1927–32]

Estländisches forstwirtschaftliches Jahrbuch. See 17483.

18557 **Estomatología.** Bilbao. *Estomatología*

18558 **Estratti. Accademia italiana** di **scienze forestali.** Firenze. *Estr. Accad. ital. Sci. for.* **O.**F. 55–.

18559 **Estratto** dai **rendiconti. R. Istituto lombardo** di **scienze** e **lettre.** Milano. *Estr. Rc. R. Ist. lomb. Sci. Lett.*

18560 **Estratto semestrale** dell' **indice bibliografico.** Milano. *Estr. semest. Indice biblfico* **L.**P. 15–20* imp. [*C. as:* 23102; *Supplement to:* 17926]

18561 **Estrischen Terminfahrten.** Tartu ulikooli ilmade observatorium. Dorpat. *Estrischen Terminfahrten* **L.**MO. 23–28.

18562 **Estuarine Bulletin.** University of Delaware Marine Laboratory. Newark. *Estuar. Bull.* [1955–] **L.**BM^N.; **Bn.**U.; **Pl.**M.; **Y.**

18563 **Estuario.** Revista de geografia e historia. Montevideo. *Estuario* [1958–] **L.**G. 58.

18564 **Estudios geográficos.** Madrid. *Estudios geogr.* [1940–] **L.**BM.; G.; **Bm.**U. 56–; **C.**GG. 55–; **Db.** 48–; **E.**G. 50–; **Rt.**

18565 **Estudios geológicos. Instituto** de **investigaciones geológicas 'Lucas Mallada'.** Madrid. *Estudios geol. Inst. Invest. geol. Lucas Mallada* [1945–] **L.**BM^N.; **Sh.**SC.; **Y.**

18566 **Estudios geológicos** y **paleontológicos** sobre la **Cordillera oriental** de **Colombia.** Bogota. *Estudios geol. paleont. Cordill. orient. Colombia* **L.**BM^N. 38–.

18567 **Estudios** e **informaciones oftalmológicas.** Barcelona. *Estudios Infs oftal.* [1949–] **L.**MD. 54.

18568 **Estudios** de la **Oficina federal** para la **defensa agrícola.** San Jacinto, México. *Estudios Of. fed. Def. agríc. Méx.* **L.**BM^N. 27–29*; EB. 27–29.

18569 **Estudios. Seminario** de **historia** de la **medicina.** Salamanca. *Estudios Semin. Hist. Med.* [1956–] **Db.**

18569° **Estudios** sobre **trabajos** de **investigación. Instituto cubano** de **investigaciones tecnológicas.** Habana. *Estudios Trab. Invest. Inst. cub. Invest. tecnol.* **L.**BM^N. 58– imp.

18570 **Estudos actinométricos.** Coimbra. *Estudos actinom.* **L.**MO. 38–40; SC. 38–.

18571 **Estudos agronómicos.** Lisboa. *Estudos agron.* [1960–] **L.**BM^N.; **Br.**A.; **C.**A.; **Ld.**U.; **Md.**H.; **O.**F. imp.

18572 **Estudos brasileiros** de **geologia.** Fundacão Getûlio Vargas. Rio de Janeiro. *Estudos bras. Geol.* **L.**BM^N. 46.

18573 **Estudos** sobre as **doenças** e **parasitas** do **cacaueiro** e de outras plantas cultivadas em **S. Tomé.** Lisboa. *Estudos Doenç. Parasit. Cacaueiro S Tomé* **L.**EB. 16–21.

18574 **Estudos, ensaios** e **documentos. Junta** de **investigacões** do **ultramar.** Lisboa. *Estudos Ensaios Docum. Jta Invest. Ultramar* [1950–] **L.**BM^N.; **O.**F. imp.; **Y.**

18574° **Estudos etnográficos.** Lisboa. *Estudos etnogr.* [1943–45] **L.**BM.

18575 **Estudos** e **informação. Direcção geral** dos **serviços florestais** e **aquícolos.** Lisboa. *Estudos Inf. Dir. ger. Servs flor. aquíc.* [1953–] **O.**F.

18576 **Estudos, notas** e **trabalhos** do **Serviço** de **fomento mineiro.** Lisboa. *Estudos Notas Trab. Serv. Fom. min.* [1945–] **L.**BM^N.; GL.; GM.; MI.; **Abd.**S.; **Bm.**U.; **E.**D.; U.; **G.**U. 49–; **Lv.**U.; **Nw.**A.; **Y.**

18577 **Estudos psiquicos.** Lisboa. *Estudos psiq.* [1940–]

18578 **Észák magyarországi Kárpat-egylet évkönyvei.** Budapest. *Észák Magyarorsz. Kárp.-Egyl. Évk.*

18579 **Eteenpäin.** Ylioppilaiden raittiusyhdistyksen vuosikirja. Helsinki. *Eteenpäin*

18580 **Ethnographia.** Budapest. *Ethnographia* [1890–22] **L.**BM. [*C. as:* 34518]

18581 **Ethnographia-népélet.** Budapest. *Ethnographia-Népél.* [1927–] **L.**AN.; U. 28–35. [*C. of:* 34518]

18582 **Ethnographic Survey** of **Africa.** London. *Ethnogr. Surv. Afr.* [1950–] **L.**AN.; BM.; BM^N.; **G.**U.

18583 **Ethnographical Survey** of **India.** Burma. [Memoirs.] Rangoon. *Ethnogr. Surv. India* [1906–10] **L.**AN.; BM.; **E.**R.; **G.**U.; **M.**R. 09–10; **O.**I.

18584 **Ethnographical Survey** of **Mysore.** Bangalore *Ethnogr. Surv. Mysore* **L.**AN. 06–14 imp.

Ethnographical Transactions. Committee of **Silesian Publications.** See 38294.

18585 **Ethnographie.** Paris. *Ethnographie* [1913–] **L.**AN.; BM.; **Bm.**U. 46–; **E.**G. (curr.); U. 30–; **Lv.**U. 30–; **O.**B. 31–; **Y.** [*C. of:* 11913]

18586 **Ethnographisch-archäologische Forschungen.** Berlin. *Ethnogr.-archäol. Forsch.* [1953–55] **L.**AN.; **Db.**

18587 **Ethnographisch-archäologische Zeitschrift.** Berlin. *Ethnogr.-archäol. Z.* [1960–] **L.**BM.

Ethnographische Sammlung. Ševčenko-Gesellschaft der **Wissenschaften** in **Lemberg.** See 18611.

Ethnographische Sammlungen des **Ungarischen Nationalmuseums.** See 59229.

18588 **Ethnologia cranmorensis.** Chislehurst. *Ethnologia cranmor.* [1937–39] **L.**AN.; HO.

18589 **Ethnologica.** Leipzig. *Ethnologica* [1909–30] **L.**AN.; BM. 09–16; **Abs.**N.; **C.**UL.; **O.**B.

18590 **Ethnological Publications. Native Affairs Department. Union** of **South Africa.** Pretoria. *Ethnol. Publs Un. S. Afr.* **L.**AN.; **O.**RH. 30–.

18591 **Ethnological Survey Publications, Philippine Islands.** Manila. *Ethnol. Surv. Publs Philipp. Isl.* [1904–17] **L.**AN.; BM.; SC.; **C.**E. 04–08; **E.**R. 04–08; **M.**P. 04–05; **O.**RH. 04–09.

18592 **Ethnologische Mitteilungen** aus **Ungarn.** Budapest. *Ethnol. Mitt. Ung.* [1887–11] **L.**AN. 97–95 imp.; BM. 87–00; **E.**R. 87–89; **O.**B. 87–95.

18593 **Ethnologische Studien.** Leipzig. *Ethnol. Stud., Lpz.* [1929–31] **L.**AN.

18594 **Ethnologischer Anzeiger.** Stuttgart. *Ethnol. Anz.* [1926–44] **L.**AN.; **O.**B.

18595 **Ethnologisches Notizblatt.** Berlin. *Ethnol. Notizbl.* [1894–04] **L.**AN.; BM.; HO. 94–03; UC.; **C.**E.; **E.**F. 99; **O.**R.

18596 **Ethnos.** Lisboa. *Ethnos, Lisb.* [1935–] **C.**UL.; **O.**B.

18597 **Ethnos.** Estudios antropológicos sobre México y Centro-América. México. *Ethnos, Méx.* [1920–25] **L.**AN.; BM.; **Bm.**U. 20; **E.**F. 22–23.

18598 **Ethnos.** Statens etnografiska museum. Stockholm. *Ethnos, Stockh.* [1936–] **L.**AN.; BM.; HO. 50–; **C.**E.
Ethyl Corporation Technical Papers. *See* 52239.

18599 **Ethyl News.** New York. *Ethyl News* **L.**C. 46–; **Y.**

18600 **Étincelle électrique.** Paris. *Étinc. élect.*

18601 **Etlik veteriner bakterioyoloji enstitüsü dergisi.** Ankara. *Etlik vet. Bakt. Enstit. Derg.* [1960–] **W.**

18602 **Etna agricolo.** Acireale. *Etna agric.*

18603 **Etnografia brasileira** e **lingua tupí-guaraní.** *Etnogr. bras.* [1939–] **L.**AN.

18604 **Étnograficheskiĭ byulleten'.** Irkutsk. Этно-графическій бюллетень. *Étnogr. Byull.*

18605 **Étnograficheskoe obozrênie.** Izdaniе étnografi-cheskago otdêla Imperatorskago obshchestva lyubiteleĭ estestvoznanīya. Moskva. Этнографическое обо-зрѣніе. Изданіе Этнографическаго отдѣла Импера-торскаго общества любителей естествознанія. *Étnogr. Obozr.* [1889–16] **L.**BM. 94–95.
Etnografichnyĭ visnyk. Kyyiv. *See* 18610.
Etnografichnyĭ zbirnyk. L'vov. *See* 18611.

18606 **Etnografische Anketes.** Yiddish Scientific Insti-tute. Wilno. *Etnogr. Anketes* **L.**BM. 28–.

18607 **Étnograf-issledovatel'.** Leningrad. Этнограф-исследователь. *Étnograf-Issled.* [1927–28]

18608 **Étnografiya.** Moskva. Leningrad. Этнография. *Étnografiya* [1926–30] **L.**AN. [*C. as:* 50289]

18609 **Etnografska istraživanja** i **građa.** Zagreb. *Etnogr. Istraž. Građa* [1934–] **L.**AN. 34–42.

18610 **Etnohrafichnyĭ visnyk.** u Kyyivi. Етногра-фічний вісник. *Etnohr. Visn.* [1921–30] **L.**BM. 26–30; **C.**UL. 27–30; **L.**AN. 28.

18611 **Etnohrafichnyĭ zbirnyk.** u L'vovi. Етногра-фічний збірник. *Etnohr. Zbirn.* [1895–] **L.**AN. 98.

18612 **Etnolog.** Glasnik Kr. Etnografskega muzeja v Ljubljani. Ljubljana. *Etnolog* [1926–45] **L.**AN.; BM. [*C. as:* 49947]

18613 **Etnología valenciana.** Valencia. *Etnol. valenc.* [1955–] **O.**B.

18614 **Etnologiska studier.** Göteborg. *Etnol. Studier* [1935–] **L.**AN.; BM.

18614° **Etnol'ohichni materyyaly.** u L'vovi. Етно-льогічні матеріяли. *Etnol'. Mater.*

18615 **Etnološka biblioteka.** Zagreb. *Etnol. Bibltka* [1925–34] **L.**AN. 28–34.

18616 **Etnološka** i **etnografska građa.** Beograd. Етно-лошка и етнографска грађа *Etnol. etnogr. Građa*

18617 **Étoile médicale.** Paris. *Étoile méd.*

18618 **Etruria agricola.** Cortona. *Etruria agric.*

18619 **Études agronomiques.** Paris. *Étud. agron., Paris*

18620 **Études agronomiques.** Ministère de l'agriculture, République Libanaise. Rayak. *Étud. agron., Rayak* [1954–] **C.**A.

18621 **Études** publiées par les **Annales** de **médecine sociale.** Lyon. *Étud. Annls Méd. soc.* [1944–] **L.**MD.

18622 **Études anti-alcooliques.** Nantes. *Étud. anti-alcool.* [1947–52] **L.**MA. 51–52; TD. [*C. as:* 47062]

18623 **Études bibliographiques. Union technique** de l'**automobile,** du **motocycle** et du **cycle.** Paris. *Étud. biblphiq. Un. tech. Auto.* [1950–] **L.**P. 50–55.

18624 **Études** de **biologie agricole.** Bruxelles. *Étud. Biol. agric.* [1915–18] **L.**BMN.; EB.; L.; Z.

18625 **Études camerounaises.** Douala. *Étud. cameroun.* [1948–] **L.**AN.; BMN.; Z.; **E.**G.; **O.**RH.; **Y.** [*C. of:* 11921]

18626 **Études climatologiques.** Varsovie. *Étud. clim., Vars.* **L.**MO. 23–38.

18627 **Études** sur les **coléoptères lucanidés** du **globe.** Paris. *Étud. Coléopt. lucan. Globe* [1928–] **L.**BMN. 28–31; E.
Études de **conservation.** *See* 51109.
Études de **conservation: Abstracts.** London. *See* 22629.

18628 **Études dahoméennes.** Porto Novo. *Étud. dahom.* [1948–] **L.**AN.; BM.; BMN.; G. 57; **Y.**

18629 **Études éburnéennes.** Abidjan. *Étud. éburn.* [1950–] **L.**AN. 51–; BM. 51–; BMN. 51– imp.; G. 54–; **Y.**

18630 **Études géographiques.** Fribourg. *Étud. géogr., Fribourg*
Études géographiques de la **Pologne** du **Nord-Ouest.** *See* 5705.
Études géophysiques. Varsovie. *See* 38297.

18631 **Études** des **gîtes minéraux** de la **France.** Paris. *Étud. Gîtes minér. Fr.* [1881–] **L.**BM. 86–; BMN. 86–; GL. 00–; GM. 86–; SC. 91–; UC. 90–03 imp.; **C.**S.; **E.**D. 06–51 imp.; R. 06; 30–; **G.**U. 81–10; **O.**R. 89–.

18632 **Études glaciologiques.** Paris. *Étud. glaciol.* [1909–] **L.**GM. 09–33; MO. 22–47; SC. 25–.

18633 **Études guinéennes.** Conakry. *Étud. guiné.* [1947–] **L.**AN.; BM. 48–; BMN.

18634 **Études** du **Laboratoire** de **recherches** du **Service vétérinaire** de **Tananarive.** *Étud. Lab. Rech. Serv. vét. Tananarive*

18635 **Études** sur le **magnétisme terrestre. Obser-vatoire** de **Zi-Ka-Wei.** *Étud. Magn. terr. Obs. Zi-Ka-Wei* [1918–] **L.**AS. 47–; MO. 18–37.
Études sur les **maladies** et les **parasites** du **cacaoyer** et d'**autres plantes cultivées** à **S. Thomé.** *See* 18575.

18636 **Études mauritaniennes.** Saint-Louis du Sénégal. *Étud. maurit.* [1948–] **L.**AN.; BM.; G. 48–55; **Y.**

18637 **Études mélanésiennes.** Nouméa. *Étud. mélanés.* [1938–] **L.**AN.
Études météorologiques et **hydrographiques.** Varsovie. *See* 38363.

18638 **Études monographiques** sur la **coopération agricole** dans **quelques pays.** Institut international d'agriculture. Rome. *Étud. monogr. Coop. agric.*

18639 **Études néo-natales.** Paris. *Étud. néo-natal.* [1952–58] **L.**H.; MC. 55–58; MD.; **Br.**U.; **C.**AN.; **Cr.**MD. 56–58; **E.**U. 54–58; **Y.** [*C. as:* 7048]

18640 **Études** de **neuro-psycho-pathologie infantile.** Marseille. *Étud. Neuro-psycho-Path. infant.* [1946–] **O.**R. 50–.

18641 **Études** de la **Néva.** *Étud. Néva* [1926–] **Pl.**M. 27–30 imp.

18642 **Études** des **orages** et des **tirs** contre la **grêle** en **Saint-Étienne.** *Étud. Orages Tirs Grêle St-Étienne*

18643 **Études professionnelles. Bâtiments** et **travaux publics.** Paris. *Étud. prof. Bâtim. Trav. publ.*

18644 **Études** de **psychologie.** Louvain, Paris. *Étud. Psychol.*

Études sur les **questions forestières** de la **Lettonie.** *See* 28174.

18646 **Études rhodaniennes.** Revue de géographie régionale. Lyon. *Étud. rhodan.* [1925–?] **L.**G. 25–42; **Y.** [*C. as:* 47265]

18647 **Études sénégalaises.** Dakar. *Étud. sénégal.* [1949–] **L.**AV. 51–; BM.; **E.**G.; **Y.**

18648 **Études soudaniennes.** Koulouba. *Étud. soudan.* [1953–] **Y.**

18649 **Études techniques. Centre national** du **bois** (*formerly* Institut national du bois). Paris. *Étud. tech. Cent. natn. Bois* [1949–] **L.**P.

18650 **Études voltaïques.** Ouagadougou. *Étud. voltaïq.* [1950–]
Mémoire [1960–] **Y.**

18651 **Étyudy̆** po **mikropaleontologii.** Moskva. Этюды по микропалеонтологии. *Étyudy̆ Mikropaleont.* [1937–] **L.**BM^N. 37.

18652 **Euclides.** Revista mensual de ciencias exactas, físicas, etc. Madrid. *Euclides, Madr.* [1941–] **Bl.**U. 49–; **Y.**

18653 **Euclides.** Tijdschrift voor de didactiek der exacte vakken. Groningen. *Euclides, Groningen*

18654 **Eudemus.** An international journal devoted to the History of Mathematics and Astronomy. Copenhagen. *Eudemus* [1941] **L.**U.

18655 **Eugenesia.** Sociedad mexicana de eugenesia. Acapulco. *Eugenesia* [1939–]

18656 **Eugenical News.** Cold Spring Harbor. *Eugenl News* [1916–38?] **C.**UL.; **E.**U. 28–38. [*C. as:* 18659]

18657 **Eugenics Laboratory Lecture Series.** Francis Galton Laboratory. London. *Eugen. Lab. Lect. Ser.* [1909–] **L.**BM.; SC. 09–12; U.; UC. 09–27; **Abs.**N. 15–imp.; **Bm.**U. 11–27; **C.**UL. 09–15; **Db.**; **E.**P.; U. 09–27; **M.**P. 09–21; **O.**R.; **Y.**

18658 **Eugenics Laboratory Memoirs.** Francis Galton Laboratory. London. *Eugen. Lab. Mem.* [1907–35] **L.**BM.; MD.; U.; UC. 07–25; **Abd.**U. 07–14; **Abs.**N. 12–35; **Bm.**P.; **C.**UL.; **Db.**; **E.**A. 07–14; P.; U. 07–33; **M.**P. 07–28; **O.**R.; **Y.**

Eugenics Lecture Series. *See* 18657.

18659 **Eugenics Quarterly.** Baltimore. *Eugen. Q.* [1954–] **L.**BM.; MA.; MD.; TD.; **C.**GE.; **E.**AG.; U.; **Ld.**U.; **Lv.**M. 58–; **Y.** [*C. of:* 18656]

18660 **Eugenics Review.** London. *Eugen. Rev.* [1909–] **L.**AN.; B. 12– imp.; BM.; D. 28–39 imp.; GH. 30–; MA. 10–21: 37; MD.; PS. 22–; RI. 19–; SH. 33–56; TD. 15– imp.; U.; UC. imp.; **Abs.**N. 12–; U. 10– imp.; **Ba.**I. 50–; **Bm.**P. 10–; U. 09–33: 42–; **Br.**U. 17–22: 43–; **C.**A. (5 yr.); AN. 32–52 imp.; E.; UL.; **Cr.**P. 12–; U. 51–; **Db.**; **E.**A.; AG. 19–44: 48–; P. 09–24; R. 30–33; T. 09–13; U. 31–; **Ex.**U. 57–; **G.**M. 09–21 imp.; U. 41–; **H.**U. 30–; **Ld.**P. 32–; U. 50–; **Lv.**M. 52– imp.; P.; U.; **M.**P.; U. 19–; **N.**U. 09–22: 26–; **O.**R.; **Sh.**IO. 22–; **Y.**

18661 **Eugenics Society Broadsheet.** London. *Eugen. Soc. Broadsh.* [1958–] **L.**BM.; U.; **G.**U.; **O.**R.; **Y.**

18662 **Eugénique.** Paris. *Eugénique*

18663 **Euphytica.** Wageningen. *Euphytica* [1952–] **L.**AM.; BM^N.; HS.; **Abs.**A.; U.; **Ba.**I.; **Br.**A. 62–; **C.**A.; **Dn.**U. 62–; **G.**U.; **Hu.**G.; **Ld.**U.; **Md.**H.; **N.**U.; **Nw.**A.; **O.**RE.; **R.**U.; **Y.**

18664 **Eure agricole.** Pacy-sur-Eure. *Eure agric.*

18665 **Eureka.** The Archimedeans' Journal. Cambridge. *Eureka* [1939–] **L.**B. 48–; SC.; U. 44–; **C.**SJ.; UL.; **E.**A.; H.U. 48–; **O.**R. 44–; **Y.**

18666 **Euréka.** Revue de l'invention. Paris. *Euréka*

18667 **Euro-Ceramik.** Düsseldorf. *Euro-Ceram.* [1954–] **L.**P. 57–; **St.**R.; **Y.** [*C. of:* 18670]

18668 **Europa nucleare.** Commissione per l'Euratom della Confederazione internazionale dei dirigenti d'azienda. Roma. *Europa nucl.* [1958–] **L.**P. 59; **Y.**

18669 **Europa orientale.** Roma. *Europa orient.* [1921–]

18670 **Europäische Tonindustrie.** Düsseldorf. *Eur. Tonind.* [1951–53] **St.**R. 53; **Y.** [*C. as:* 18667]

18671 **Europäischer Fernsprechdienst.** Berlin. *Eur. Fernsprechdienst* [1926–44] **L.**EE.; SC.; **Bm.**U. 28–31; **Ld.**U. 28–31; **M.**U. 26–31; **O.**R. 28–31. [*C. of:* 19297]

18671° **Europair.** *Europair* **L.**AV. 62–.

18672 **Europe médicale.** Paris. *Europe méd.* [1936–39] **L.**MA.; MD.; **Br.**U. 37–39 imp.

Europe nucléaire. *See* 18668.

18673 **European Bulletin—Zinc Alloy Die Casting.** Oxford. *Eur. Bull.—Zinc Alloy Die Cast.* [1954–] **L.**P.; **G.**U.; **O.**R.; **Y.**

18674 **European Chiropractic Bulletin.** Belfast. *Eur. chiropr. Bull.* [1932–] **L.**BM.

18675 **European Cotton Industry Statistics.** Manchester. *Eur. Cott. Ind. Statist.* [1958–] **L.**TP.; **Abs.**N.; **M.**C.

18676 **European Engineering.** London. *Eur. Engng* [1960–] **L.**BM.; **Bl.**U.; **Y.**

18677 **European Handling Congress.** *Eur. Handl. Congr.* [1953–]
1. Paris 1953.
2. London 1954. **L.**P.

European Organization for **Nuclear Research.** CERN Bibl. *See* 12877.

18678 **European Potato Journal.** Wageningen. *Eur. Potato J.* [1958–] **L.**AM.; P.; **C.**A.; **Dn.**U. 61–; **Hu.**G.; **Je.**; **Rt.**; **Sil.**; **Y.**

18679 **European Railways.** Sutton. *Eur. Rlys* [1950–] **L.**BM. imp.

18680 **European Shipbuilding.** Oslo. *Eur. Shipbldg* [1952–] **L.**P. 57–; **G.**E. 54–; U. 58–; **Lv.**P. 59–; **Y.**

18681 **European Technical Digests.** Paris. *Eur. tech. Dig.* [1958–61] **L.**P.; **E.**A.; **Y.** [*United States edition at:* 18682; *C. of:* 17316; *C. as:* Technological Digests]

18682 **European Technical Digests. United States Edition.** *Europ. tech. Dig. U.S. Edn* [1957–61] **L.**P. 57; **O.**R. [*English edition at:* 18681; *C. of:* 17317; *C. as:* Technological Digests, U.S. Edn]

18683 **European Trader. Textiles** from **Britain.** London. *Eur. Trader Text. Br.* [1957–] **L.**BM.; P. (curr.)

18684 **Eutectic Welder.** New York. *Eutectic Weld.* [1943–]

18685 **Evans' Analytical Notes.** Liverpool. *Evans' analyt. Notes* [1907–13] **L.**C. 08–12; P.

18686 **Evans' Journal.** Medicine, Pharmacy, Therapy, Bacteriology. Liverpool & London. *Evans' J.* [1912–21: 28–] **L.**BM.; **Lv.**M. 12–15; U. 12–21 imp.; **O.**R. 12–18.

18686° **Evans Medical Gazette.** Liverpool. *Evans med. Gaz.* [1957–] **L.**BM.

18687 **Evaporator.** Webster, N.Y. *Evaporator*

18688 **Éveil médical.** Nanterre. *Éveil méd.*

18689 **Evencias.** Contribuciones ocasionales de la colección ictiológica de Agustin Fernandez-Yepez. Cumaná, Venezuela. *Evencias* **L.**BM^N. 48–49; Z. 48–49.

18690 **Evening Sky Map.** New York. *Even. Sky Map*

18691 **Evershed News.** London. *Evershed News* [1953–] **L.**AV. 58–; BM.; P. 54–; **Ma.**T. 58–; **Sil.** (1 yr)

18692 **Évi jelentés a Magyar Kir földtani intézet.** Budapest. *Évi Jelent. magy. K. földt. Intéz.* [1882–] **L.**BM^N. 82–16; GL.; GM. 91–; **C.**UL.

18693 **Évi jelentés a Magyar szent korona orszagainak földrengesi.** Budapest. *Évi Jelent. magy. Szent Korona Orszag. földr.*
   Évkönyve. Agrártudományi egyetem erdömérnöki kar. *See* 1214.

18694 **Évkönyve. Csillagok világa.** Budapest. *Évk. Csill. Világa* [*C. as:* 29160]
   Évkönyve. Erdészeti tudományos intezet. *See* 18340.
   Évkönyve. Erdömérnöki föiskola, Sopron. *See* 18360.
   Évkönyve. Magyar állami földtani intezet. *See* 29150.
   Évkönyve. Trencsén vármegyei természettudományi egylet. *See* 25168.

18695 **Évkönyve vasvármegye és szombathely Város kulturegyesülete és a Vasvármegyei muzeum.** Szombathely. *Évk. Vasv. Szombath.* **L.**BM^N. 25–29. [*C. as:* 19822]

18696 **Evolução agrícola.** São Paulo. *Evoluç. agríc.*

18697 **Evolución,** revista mensual de ciencias y letras. Montevideo. *Evolución*

18698 **Evolution.** International Journal of Organic Evolution. Lancaster, Pa. *Evolution, Lancaster, Pa.* [1947–] **L.**BM^N.; CB.; L.; NC. imp.; QM.; SC.; U.; Z.; **Abd.**U. 58–; **Abs.**A.; U. 56–; **Ba.**I.; **Bl.**U.; **Bm.**U.; **Bn.**U.; **Br.**U.; **C.**B.; GE.; P.; **Cr.**U.; **E.**AG.; AR.; U.; **Ex.**U.; **G.**U.; **H.**U.; **Ld.**U.; **M.**U.; **N.**U.; **Nw.**A. 49–; **O.**AP.; BO.; Z. 51–; **Pl.**M.; **R.**U. 50–; **Y.**

18699 **Evolution;** a journal of nature. New York. *Evolution, N.Y.* [1927–38]

18700 **Évolution électronique.** Bruxelles. *Évolut. électron.* **L.**AV. 59– imp.

18701 **Évolution médicale.** Paris. *Évolut. méd.*

18702 **Évolution médico-chirurgicale.** Paris. *Évolut. méd.-chir.* [1920–25] [*C. as:* 18705]

18703 **Évolution pharmaceutique.** Poitiers. *Évolut. pharm.*

18704 **Évolution psychiatrique.** Paris. *Évolut. psychiat.* [1948–] **L.**MD.; U.

18705 **Évolution thérapeutique.** Paris. *Évolut. thér.* [1926–] [*C. of:* 18702]

18706 **Evreĭskyiĭ medytsynskyiĭ holos.** Odessa. Еврейскій медицинскій голосъ. *Evreĭsk. med. Holos* [1908–11]

18707 **Excavating Engineer.** Milwaukee. *Excav. Engr* [1912–] **L.**MI. 35–52 imp.: 53–; P. 42–; **Br.**U. 47–; **Nw.**A. 25–; **Y.**

18708 **Excerpta botanica.** Stuttgart. *Excerpta bot.* [1959–]
   Sectio A. Taxonomica et chorologica. **L.**BM^N.; L.; NC. 61–; SC.; **Bn.**U.; **G.**U. 59; **Ld.**U.; **O.**BO.; **Y.**
   Sectio B. Sociologica. **L.**BM^N.; L.; NC. 61–; SC.; **Bn.**U.; **Ld.**U.; **Y.**

18709 **Excerpta medica.** Amsterdam. *Excerpta med.*
   Section 1. Anatomy, anthropology, embryology and histology [1947–] **L.**AN.; CB.; MA.; MD.; UC.; VC.; **Abd.**U.; **Bl.**U.; **Bm.**U.; **Br.**U. 47–51; **C.**APH. 55–; MD.; **Cr.**U.; **Db.**; **Dn.**U. 53–; **E.**U.; **G.**U.; **Ld.**U.; **M.**MS.; **O.**R.; **Sa.**; **Y.**
   Section 2. Physiology, biochemistry and pharmacology [1948–] **L.**CB.; MD.; UC.; VC.; **Abd.**U.; **Bl.**U.; **Bm.**U.; **Br.**U. 48–57; **C.**APH. 55–56; BI. 49–; **Cr.**U.; **Db.**; **Dn.**U. imp.; **E.**U.; **G.**U.; **Ld.**U.; **M.**MS.; **Sa.** 54–; **Y.**
   Section 3. Endocrinology (experimental and clinical) [1947–] **L.**CB.; MA.; MD.; UC.; VC.; **Abd.**U.; **Bl.**U. imp.; **Bm.**U.; **Br.**U. 47–57; **C.**APH. (curr.); BI. 49–; MD.; **Db.**; **E.**U.; **G.**U.; **Ld.**U.; **M.**MS.; **O.**R.; **Pl.**M. 53–; **Y.**
   Section 4. Medical microbiology, immunology and serology (*formerly* Medical microbiology and hygiene) [1948–] **L.**AM. 51–; CB.; MD.; TD.; **Abd.**U.; **Bl.**U.; **Bm.**U.; **Br.**U.; **C.**APH. 55–57: BI. 49–; MD.; **Db.**; **Dn.**U.; **E.**U. 49–; **G.**U.; **Ld.**U.; **M.**MS.; **Nw.**A. 54–; **O.**R.; **Sa.** 52–; **Y.**
   Section 5. General pathology and pathological anatomy [1948–] **L.**CB.; MD.; TD.; **Abd.**U.; **Bl.**U.; **Bm.**U.; **C.**APH. 55–56; MD.; PA.; **Cr.**MD. 60–; **Db.**; **Dn.**U.; **E.**U.; **G.**U.; **Ld.**U.; **M.**MS.; **Nw.**A. 51–; **O.**R.; **Y.**
   Section 6. Internal medicine [1947–] **L.**CB.; MA.; MD.; TD.; UCH. 50–; **Abd.**U.; **Bl.**U. imp.; **Bm.**U.; **Cr.**MS. 57–; **Db.**; **Dn.**U. 48–; **E.**U.; **G.**U.; **Ld.**U.; **M.**MS.; **O.**R.; **Y.**
   Section 7. Pediatrics [1947–] **L.**CB.; MA.; MD.; **Abd.**U.; **Bl.**U.; **Bm.**U.; **Br.**U. 47–57; **C.**MD.; **Cr.**MS. 60–; **Db.**; **Dn.**U.; **E.**U.; **G.**U.; **Ld.**U.; **M.**MS.; **O.**R.; **Y.**
   Section 8. Neurology and psychiatry [1948–] **L.**MD.; UC.; **Abd.**U.; **Bl.**U.; **Bm.**U.; **Br.**U. 48–57; **C.**MC. 58–; MD.; **Db.**; **E.**U.; **G.**U.; **Ld.**U.; **M.**MS.; **Nw.**A.; **O.**R.; **Y.**
   Section 9. Surgery [1947–] **L.**MA.; MD.; S.; **Abd.**U.; **Bl.**U.; **Bm.**U.; **Db.**; **Dn.**U.; **E.**S. 53–; **G.**F. 49–; U.; **Ld.**U.; **Lv.**M. 57–; **M.**MS.; **O.**R.; **Y.**
   Section 9B. Orthopaedics and traumatology [1956–] **L.**MD.; VC.; **Abd.**U.; **Bl.**U. 56–57; **C.**MD.; **Db.**; **E.**S.; **G.**U.; **Ld.**U.; **M.**MS.; **O.**R.; **Y.**
   Section 10. Obstetrics and gynaecology [1948–] **L.**MA.; MD.; **Abd.**U.; **Bl.**U.; **Bm.**U.; **C.**MD.; **Db.**; **Dn.**U. 57–; **E.**S. 55–; U.; **G.**U.; **Ld.**U.; **M.**MS.; **O.**R.; **Y.**
   Section 11. Oto-, rhino-, laryngology [1948–] **L.**MD.; **Abd.**U.; **Bl.**U.; **Bm.**U.; **Br.**U. 49–56; **C.**MD.; **Db.**; **Dn.**U.; **E.**S. 53–; U.; **G.**U.; **Ld.**U.; **M.**MS.; **O.**R.; **Y.**

Section 12. Ophthalmology [1947–] **L.**MA.; MD.; OP.; **Abd.**U.; **Bl.**U.; **Bm.**U.; **Br.**U. 47–56; **C.**MD.; **Db.**; **E.**U.; **G.**U.; **Ld.**U.; **M.**MS.; **O.**R.; **Y.**

Section 13. Dermatology and venereology [1947–] **L.**MA.; MD.; **Abd.**U.; **Bl.**U.; **Bm.**U.; **Br.**U. 47–57; **C.**MD.; **Db.**; **Dn.**U.; **E.**U.; **G.**F. 59–; U.; **Ld.**U.; **M.**MS.; **O.**R.; **Y.**

Section 14. Radiology [1947–] **L.**CB.; MA.; MD.; UC. 51– imp.; **Abd.**U.; **Bl.**U.; **Bm.**U.; **Br.**U. 47–57; **C.**MD.; R.; **Db.**; **E.**S.; U.; **G.**U.; **Ld.**U.; **M.**MS.; **O.**R.; **Y.**

Section 15. Tuberculosis (*formerly* Chest diseases) [1948–] **L.**MD.; MD.; **Abd.**U.; **Bl.**U.; **Bm.**U.; **Br.**U. 48–57; **C.**MD.; **Db.**; **G.**U.; **Ld.**U.; **M.**MS.; **O.**R.; **Y.**

Section 16. Cancer (experimental and clinical) [1953–] **L.**CB.; MD.; S.; TD.; **Abd.**U.; **Bl.**U.; **Bm.**U.; **Br.**U.; **C.**MD.; R.; **Db.**; **Dn.**U.; **E.**P.; S.; U.; **G.**U.; **Ld.**U.; **Lv.**M. 53–56; **M.**MS.; **O.**R.; **Y.**

Section 17. Public health, social medicine and hygiene [1955–] **L.**AM.; CB.; MD.; TD.; **Bl.**U.; **Bm.**U.; **Br.**U.; **C.**MD.; **Db.**; **Dn.**U.; **G.**U.; **Ld.**U.; **M.**MS.; **Nw.**A.; **O.**R.; **Y.**

Section 18. Cardiovascular diseases [1957–] **L.**MD.; S.; **Abd.**U.; **Bl.**U.; **Bm.**U.; **C.**MD.; **Cr.**MD. 60–; **Dn.**U.; **E.**U.; **G.**U.; **Ld.**U.; **M.**MS.; **O.**R.; **Y.**

Section 19. Rehabilitation [1958–] **L.**MD.; **Abd.**U.; **Bl.**U.; **Bm.**U.; **C.**MD.; **Db.**; **Dn.**U.; **E.**U.; **G.**U.; **Ld.**U.; **M.**MS.; **O.**R.; **Y.**

Section 20. Gerontology and geriatrics [1958–] **L.**MA.; MD.; **Abd.**U.; **Bl.**U.; **Bm.**U.; **C.**APH. 60–; MD.; **Db.**; **G.**U.; **Ld.**U.; **M.**MS.; **O.**R.; **Y.**

Abstracts of **Soviet medicine.** *See* 412.

18711 **Excerta médica.** México. *Excerta méd.* [1942–]

18712 **Exhaust Steam.** London. *Exhaust Steam* [1928–29] **L.**BM.

18713 **Exide Ironclad Topics.** Philadelphia. *Exide Ironclad Top.* [1927–53] **L.**P. [*C. as:* 18714]

18714 **Exide Topics.** Philadelphia. *Exide Top.* [1954–] **L.**P. (curr.) [*C. of:* 18713]

18715 **Exide Topics** and **Storage Battery Power.** Philadelphia. *Exide Top. Stor. Batt. Pwr* [1960–] **L.**P. (curr.)

18716 **Exotic Microlepidoptera.** London. *Exot. Microlepidopt.* [1912–37] **L.**BMN.; E.; EB.; **Abd.**N.

18717 **Expanded Shale Concrete Facts.** Washington. *Expanded Shale Concr. Facts* **L.**P. (curr.)

18718 **Expansion** de la **recherche scientifique.** Paris. *Expans. Rech. scient.* **L.**P. 60–.

18719 **Expedition.** University of Pennsylvania Museum. Philadelphia. *Expedition* [1958–] **L.**BM, 59–; **O.**B.

Expériences acquises dans l'**enseignement** des **sciences naturelles.** *See* 18364.

18720 **Experiențe** cu **varietați** de **plante** și cu **ingrășeminte chimice.** Stațiune agronomică. București. *Expțe Var. Pl. Ingrăș. chim.*

18721 **Experientia.** Basel. *Experientia* [1945–] **L.**B.; BM.; BMN.; C.; CB.; IC.; LI.; MA.; MC.; MD.; P.; QM. 55–; RI. 49–; S. 62–; SC.; TD. 48–; TP.; U. 50–; UC.; VC. 53–; **Abd.**U.; **Abs.**U. 48–; **Ba.**I. 48–; **Bl.**U.; **Bm.**P.; U.; **Bn.**U. imp.; **Br.**U. 48–; **C.**A.; APH. 58–; B. 49–; BI. 55–; CH.; P.; R.; **Cr.**MD.; U. 51–; **Db.** 49–; **E.**AG. 47–; U.; **Ep.**D. 48–; **Ex.**U. 49–; **G.**T. 46–; U.; **Ld.**U.; W. 45–49; **M.**C.; D.; T.; U.; **N.**U.; **Nw.**A.; **O.**P.; R.; **R.**D. 53–; **Sa.**; **Sw.**U. 57–; **Wd.**; **Y.** [*Also supplements*]

18722 **Experiment Station Bulletin, Hydraulics.** U.S. Waterways Experiment Station. Vicksburg. *Exp. Stn Bull. Hydraul., Vicksburg* [1939–] [*See also* 12611c]

Experiment Station Bulletin. Office of **Experiment Stations.** Washington. *See* 11376.

Experiment Station Bulletin, Oklahoma. *See* 11427.

18723 **Experiment Station Bulletin, Soil Mechanics.** U.S. Waterways Experiment Station. Vicksburg. *Exp. Stn Bull. Soil Mech. Vicksburg* [1939–] [*See also* 12611c]

18724 **Experiment Station Record.** Office of Experiment Stations, Washington. *Exp. Stn Rec.* [1889–46] **L.**A. 42–46; AM.; BM.; BMN. 02–46; EB. 93–46; K.; LI. 26–46; MC. 20–46; MY.; P. 10–46; SC. 02–46; TD. 08–46; U.; V. 34–46; **Abd.**R. 93–46; S. 39–46; TP.; U. 97–46; **Abs.**A.; N. 09–46 imp.; **Ba.**I. 42–46; **Bl.**U. 01–96 imp.; **Bm.**P. 39–46; U. 00–21 imp.; **Bn.**U.; **Br.**A. 93–46; U. 93–46; **C.**A.; P. 04–46; **Cr.**P. 08–46; U. 08–46 imp.; **Db.**; **Dn.**U. 23–32 imp.: 46; **E.**AB. 21–46; B. imp.; F. 22–39 imp.; N. 17–23 imp.; U.; W. 90–46; SC. 89–36 imp.; **Je.**; **Ld.**U.; W. 28–46; **Lv.**P. imp.; U. 06–11 imp.; **M.**C. 91–46; P. 05–46 imp.; U. 13–46 imp.; **Md.**H. 93–46; **N.**U. 08–46; **Nw.**A. 97–46; **O.**F. 37–46; R. 02–46; RE.; **R.**D. 04–46; U.; **Rt.**; **Sal.** 25–46; F. 25–46; **Sil.** 24–46; **W.** 25–46.

18725 **Experiment Station Work.** Office of Experiment Stations, Washington. *Exp. Stn Wk* [1900–13] **L.**BM. 02–13; P. 04–13 imp.; SC. 12–13; **Db.** 01–13 imp.; **Rt.**

18726 **Experimenta.** Mendoza. *Experimenta* [1948–] **L.**AM. 49–54; **C.**A. 49–.

18727 **Experimental Cell Research.** New York. *Expl Cell Res.* [1950–] **L.**B. 60–; CB.; LI.; MA.; MC.; MD.; QM.; S.; SC.; UC.; UCH.; VC. 57–; **Abd.**U. 58–; **Abs.**U. 56–; **Ba.**I.; **Bl.**U.; **Bn.**U.; **Br.**U.; **C.**APH.; B.; BI.; R.; **Cr.**U.; **Db.**; **Dn.**U. 56–; **E.**AG. 52–; AR. 56–; SW. 50–54; U.; **Ep.**D.; **G.**U.; **Ld.**U.; **M.**MS.; **N.**U.; **Nw.**A. 55–; **O.**BI.; BO.; **Pl.**M.; **R.**D. 59–; U.; **Sa.**; **Sh.**U.; **W.** 59–; **Y.** [*Also supplements*]

18727c **Experimental Eye Research.** *Expl Eye Res.* **Ha.**RD.; **Y.**

18728 **Experimental Farm Highlights** in the **Atlantic Provinces.** Ottawa. *Expl Fm Highlts Atlant. Prov.* **L.**BM. 54–58*; **Br.**A. 57–58; **C.**A. 55–58; **Y.**

18729 **Experimental Horticulture.** London. *Expl Hort.* [1957–] **L.**AM.; BM.; K.; P.; TP.; **Ba.**I.; **Bm.**P.; **Bn.**U.; **Br.**A.; **C.**A.; **Cr.**P.; **Db.**; **G.**M.; **Je.**; **Ld.**P.; U.; **M.**P.; **N.**U.; **O.**R.; **Re.**; **Sil.**; **Y.**

18730 **Experimental Husbandry.** London. *Expl Husb.* [1956–] **L.**AM.; BM.; **Abd.**R.; S.; **Bl.**U.; **Bm.**P.; **Bn.**U.; **C.**A.; **Cr.**P.; **Db.**; **E.**AB.; **G.**U.; **Hu.**G.; **Je.**; **Ld.**P.; **M.**P.; **N.**U.; **O.**R.; **Re.**; **R.**D.; **Rt.**; **Sil.**; **Y.**

18731 **Experimental Medicine** and **Surgery.** New York, etc. *Expl Med. Surg.* [1943–] **L.**MA. 46–; MD.; S.; **Bm.**U.; **Br.**U. 43–44; **E.**U.; **Nw.**A.; **Sh.**U. 59–; **Y.**

18732 **Experimental Neurology.** New York, London. *Expl Neurol.* [1959–] **L.**MC.; MD.; UC.; **Bl.**U.; **Br.**U.; **C.**AN.; APH.; **G.**U.; **Ld.**U.; **Y.**

18733 **Experimental Parasitology.** New York. *Expl Parasit.* [1951–] **L.**BMN.; EB. 51–58 imp.; KC. 53–; MA.; MC.; MD.; SC.; TD.; Z.; **Abd.**R.; U. 58–; **Abs.**U.; **Bl.**U.; **Bn.**U.; **Br.**U.; **C.**MO.; V.; **Cr.**U. 60–; **E.**U.; **G.**T. 54–; U.; **H.**U.; **Hu.**G.; **Ld.**U.; **M.**MS. 58–; **N.**U.; **Nw.**A.; **Sal.**; **Sh.**U.; **W.**; **Y.**

18734 **Experimental Report. Fuel Research Institute.** Department of Commerce and Industry, Japan. *Expl Rep. Fuel Res. Inst. Japan* [1927–33] [*C. as:* 43819]

18734ᵃ **Experimental Report** of the **National Institute** of **Animal Health.** Tokyo. *Expl Rep. natn. Inst. Anim. Hlth, Tokyo* **W.** 49–55*. [*C. as:* 11227]

18735 **Experimental Researches** and **Reports. Department** of **Glass Technology, University of Sheffield** *Expl Res. Rep. Dep. Glass Technol. Univ. Sheff.* [1917–] **L.**P. 22–42; **Abs.**N. 22; **Bm.**T. 17–38 imp.; U. 18–37; **Sh.**G.; U. 18–.

18736 **Experimental Stress Analysis.** Cambridge, Mass. *Expl Stress Analysis* [1943–45] **L.**AV.; I.; NF.; P.; SC.; UC.; **Bm.**C.; P. 44–45; U.; **Bn.**U.; **Cr.**U.; **G.**T.; U.; **Ld.**U.; **Li.**M.; **M.**D.; T.; U. 43; **Nw.**A.; **Sh.**IO.; SC.; **Wd.**; **Y.** [*C. as:* 39684]

18737 **Experimental Studies** in **Psychology** and **Pedagogy.** Philadelphia. *Expl Stud. Psychol. Pedag.*

18738 **Experimental Wireless** and the **Wireless Engineer.** London. *Expl Wireless* [1923–31] **L.**BM.; EE.; NP. imp.; P.; QM.; SC.; UC.; **Bl.**U. 28–31; **Bm.**P.; U.; **Bn.**U.; **Br.**U.; **C.**ENG.; P.; UL.; **Co.**T. 24–31; **Db.**; **E.**A.; **F.**A.; **G.**M. imp.; U. 26–31; **H.**U.; **Ld.**U.; **Lv.**U.; **M.**P. 23–31; T. 24–31; **Ma.**T.; **Nw.**A.; **O.**R. [*C. as:* 57646]
    Experimental Work on **Roads.** London. *See* 45422.
    Experimental Works of the **Institute** of **Pomology.** Skierniewice. *See* 38327.
    Expérimentation agricole. Varsovie. *See* 17172.

18739 **Expérimentation agricole. Service botanique** de **Tunisie.** *Expn agric. Serv. bot. Tunis.*

18740 **Experimentelle Beiträge** zur **Morphologie.** Leipzig. *Explle Beitr. Morph.* [1906–14]
    Experimentelle und **klinische Roentgenologie.** Charkow. *See* 17590.

18741 **Experimentelle Technik** der **Physik.** Berlin. *Explle Tech. Phys.* [1953–] **L.**P.; **Y.**

18742 **Experimentelle Veterinärmedizin.** Leipzig. *Explle VetMed.* [1950–51] **L.**V. [*C. as:* 4072]

18742° **Experimenter.** Hales Corner, Wis. *Experimenter, Hales Corner* [*C. as:* 18744]

18743 **Experimenter.** New York. *Experimenter, N.Y.* [1924–26] **L.**BM. [*C. in:* 49041]

18744 **Experimenter** and **Sports Aviation.** Hales Corner, Wis. *Experimenter Sports Aviat.* [1957] [*C. of:* 18742°; *C. as:* 50641]

18745 **Experiments** at the **College Farm, Bangor.** *Exps Coll. Fm, Bangor* **L.**AM.; **Abs.**N. 10–.

18746 **Experiments** in **Crops** and **Livestock** in **Progress** at the **Experimental Husbandry Farms. N.A.A.S.** London. *Exps Crops Livest. Prog. exp. Husb. Fms* [1954–] **Bn.**U.; **Br.**A.

18746° **Experiments** in **Fish Culture.** Game Tsetse Control Department, Northern Rhodesia. Lusaka. *Exps Fish Cult.*

18747 **Experiments** in **Horticulture** in **Progress** at the **Experimental Horticulture** and **Demonstration Stations. N.A.A.S.** London. *Exps Hort. Prog. exp. Hort. Demonstr. Stns* [1954–] **Bn.**U.; **Br.**A.

18748 **Experiments Leaflet** of the **Aberdeen** and **North** of **Scotland College** of **Agriculture.** Aberdeen. *Exps Leafl. Aberd. N. Scotl. Coll. Agric.* [1905–10] **L.**AM.; P.; **Rt.** 05–10. [*C. as:* 18749]

18749 **Experiments Leaflet** of the **North** of **Scotland College** of **Agriculture.** Aberdeen. *Exps Leafl. N. Scotl. Coll. Agric.* [1910–] **L.**AM.; P.; **Abs.**N. 20–; **Rt.** [*C. of:* 18748]

18750 **Experiments. National Agricultural Advisory Service, Wales.** Trawscoed. *Exps N.A.A.S. Wales* **Bn.**U. 51–; **Br.**A. 58–.

18750° **Experiments. National Agricultural Advisory Service, Yorkshire** and **Lancashire Region.** Leeds. *Exps N.A.A.S. Yorks. Lancs.* **Br.**A. 58–.

18751 **Experiments** in **Progress. Grassland Improvement** (*afterwards* **Research**) **Station.** Stratford-on-Avon. *Exps Prog. Grassld Improv. Stn* [1948–55] **L.**BM.; K.; NC. 54–; P.; **Abd.**S. 50–55; **Abs.**A.; **Br.**A.; **C.**A.; **Db.** 50–; **Md.**H. 50–; **N.**U.; **O.**R. imp.; **R.**U. 50–; **Rt.**; **Y.** [*C. as:* 18752]

18752 **Experiments** in **Progress. Grassland Research Institute, Hurley.** *Exps Prog. Grassld Res. Inst.* [1955–] **L.**BM.; K.; P.; **Abd.**S.; **Abs.**A.; **Br.**A.; **C.**A.; **Db.**; **Md.**H.; **N.**U.; **O.**BO. 54–; R. imp.; **R.**U.; **Rt.**; **Y.** [*C. of:* 18751]

18753 **Experiments Summary. Pea Growing Research Organisation Ltd.** Yaxley. *Exps Summ. Pea Grow. Res. Org.* **Rt.** 57–.

18754 **Explanatory Notes. Bureau of Mineral Resources, Geology** and **Geophysics, Australia.** *Explan. Notes Bur. Miner. Resour. Geol. Geophys. Aust.* **L.**BMᴺ. 55–; **Abs.**U. 57–.

18755 **Exploração do Rio.** Commissão geographica e geologica de São Paulo. *Exploração Rio* **L.**GM. 89–13.
    Exploratie van het **Nationaal Albert Park.** *See* 18756–18766.
    Exploratie van het **Nationaal Garamba Park.** *See* 18766.
    Exploratie van het **Nationaal Kagera Park.** *See* 18768–18769.
    Exploratie van het **Nationaal Upemba Park.** *See* 18770.
    Exploratie der **nationale parken** van **Belgisch Congo.** *See* 18771–18773.

18755° **Exploration** and **Conservation** of **National Resources.** Washington. *Explor. Conserv. natn. Resour.* **Y.** 57–. [*English abstracts of:* 42240]

18756 **Exploration** du **Parc National Albert. Deuxième Série.** Bruxelles. *Explor. Parc natn. Albert deux. Sér.* [1953–] **L.**BM.; BMᴺ.; z.

18757 **Exploration** du **Parc National Albert. Mission F. Bourlière** et **J. Verschuren.** Bruxelles. *Explor. Parc natn. Albert Miss. F. Bourlière J. Verschuren* [1960–] **L.**BM.; BMᴺ.; z.

18758 **Exploration** du **Parc National Albert. Mission G. F. de Witte** (1933–35). Bruxelles. *Explor. Parc natn. Albert Miss. G. F. de Witte* [1937–] **L.**BM.; BMᴺ.; E. (ent.) 37–50; z.

18759 **Exploration** du **Parc National Albert. Mission H. Damas** (1935–36). Bruxelles. *Explor. Parc natn. Albert Miss. H. Damas* [1937–] **L.**BM.; BMᴺ.; z.

18760 **Exploration** du **Parc National Albert. Mission J. de Heinzelin** de **Braucourt** (1950). Bruxelles. *Explor. Parc natn. Albert Miss. J de Heinzelin de Braucourt* [1955–] **L.**BM.; BMᴺ.; z.

18761 **Exploration** du **Parc National Albert. Mission J. Lebrun** (1937–38). Bruxelles. *Explor. Parc natn. Albert Miss. J. Lebrun* [1947–] **L.**BM.; BMᴺ.; z.

18762 **Exploration** du **Parc National Albert. Mission J. Verhoogen** (1938 et 1940). Bruxelles. *Explor. Parc natn. Albert Miss J. Verhoogen* [1948–] L.BM.; BM[N].; Z.

18764 **Exploration** du **Parc National Albert. Mission P. Schumacher** (1933–36). Bruxelles. *Explor. Parc natn. Albert Miss. P. Schumacher* [1939–] L.BM.; BM[N].; Z.

18765 **Exploration** du **Parc National Albert. Mission S. Frechkop** (1937–38). Bruxelles. *Explor. Parc natn. Albert Miss. S. Frechkop* [1943–] L.BM.; BM[N].; Z.

18766 **Exploration** du **Parc National Albert** et du **Parc National** de la **Kagera. Mission L. van den Berghe** (1936). Bruxelles. *Explor. Parc natn. Albert Parc natn. Kagera Miss. L. v. d. Berghe* [1942–] L.BM.; BM[N].; Z.

18767 **Exploration** du **Parc National** de la **Garamba. Mission H. de Saeger.** Bruxelles. *Explor. Parc natn. Garamba Miss. H. de Saeger* [1954–] L.BM.; BM[N].; Z.

18768 **Exploration** du **Parc National** de la **Kagera. Mission J. Lebrun** (1937–38). Bruxelles. *Explor. Parc natn. Kagera Miss. J. Lebrun* [1948–] L.BM.; BM[N].; Z.

18769 **Exploration** du **Parc National** de la **Kagera. Mission S. Frechkop** (1938). Bruxelles. *Explor. Parc natn. Kagera Miss. S. Frechkop* [1944–] L.BM.; BM[N].; Z.

18770 **Exploration** du **Parc National** de l'**Upemba. Mission G. F. de Witte.** Bruxelles. *Explor. Parc natn. Upemba Miss. G. F. de Witte* [1951–] L.BM. 54–; BM[N].; Z.

18771 **Exploration** des **parcs nationaux** du **Congo belge. Mission d'études vulcanologiques.** Bruxelles. *Explor. Parcs natn. Congo belge Miss. Étud. vulc.* [1955–] L.BM[N].; Z.

18772 **Exploration** des **parcs nationaux** du **Congo belge. Mission H. Hediger, J. Verschuren.** Bruxelles. *Explor. Parcs natn. Congo belge Miss. H. Hediger J. Verschuren* [1951–] L.BM.; BM[N].; Z.

18773 **Exploration** des **parcs nationaux** du **Congo belge. Mission J. G. Baer, W. Gerber.** Bruxelles. *Explor. Parcs natn. Congo belge Miss. J. G. Baer W. Gerber* [1959–] L.BM.; BM[N].; Z.

18774 **Exploration** and **Scientific Research.** Pan American Society for Tropical Research. Quito. *Explor. scient. Res.*

18775 **Exploration scientifique** du **Maroc.** Paris. *Explor. scient. Maroc* L.BM. 13–; Z. 20.

18776 **Exploration scientifique** de la **Tunisie.** Paris. *Explor. scient. Tunis.* [1884–] L.GL. 07: 09 imp.; K. (bot.) 96–97 imp.

18777 **Explorations** and **Field Work** of the **Smithsonian Institution.** Washington. *Explors Fld Wk Smithsonian Instn* [1927–40] L.AN.; BM.; BM[N].; GL. 33–40; MO.; SC.; U.; Z.; Abs.N.; Bl.U.; Bm.U.; Bn.U.; C.P. 29–40; E.F.; Ld.U. 27–36; M.P.; O.B.; R.U.; Sa. 27–39. [1910–26 *published in:* 49964]

Explorations géologiques et **minières** sur la **ligne** du **chemin** de **fer** de **Sibérie.** *See* 21031.

Explorations géologiques dans les **régions aurifères** de la **Sibérie.** *See* 21032.

Explorations des **mers russes.** *See* 24282.

18778 **Explorations pyréneennes.** Bulletin de la Société Ramond. Toulouse. *Explors pyrén.* [1866–] L.BM[N]. 66–38; Bl.U. 94: 07–08.

18779 **Explorer.** Bulletin of the Cleveland Museum of Natural History. Cleveland, O. *Explorer* [1938–] L.BM[N].; Z. 61–; O.F. 49– imp. [*C. of:* 9808]

18780 **Explorers' Journal.** New York. *Explorers' J.* [1921–] L.BM.; C.PO. 46–; E.G.

18781 **Explosifs.** Bruxelles, Liège. *Explosifs* L.P. 52; Sh.S. 54–; Ste. 50–; Y.

18782 **Explosive Bulletin.** Explosions Division, Canadian Industries, Ltd. Montreal. *Explosive Bull.* [1927–49] L.P. [*C. as:* 12886]

18782[c] **Explosives Accident Reports.** Home Office. London. *Explos. Accid. Rep.* Y.

18783 **Explosives Engineer.** Wilmington, Del. *Explos. Engr* [1923–] L.BM. 59–; P.; SC.; Ha.RD. (2 yr.); Ld.U. 49–61; Sh.S. 40–; Ste.; Y.

18784 **Explosives Progress.** New York. *Explos. Prog.* [1930–31] L.P.

Explosives Service Bulletin. Wilmington, Del. *See* 17278.

18786 **Explosivstoffe.** Mannheim. *Explosivstoffe* [1953–] L.P.; Y. [*C. of:* 50690]

18787 **Export News** about **Neoprene** and **Rubber Chemicals** and **Colors.** Wilmington. *Export News Neoprene Rubb. Chem.* [1951–53] Sy.R.

18788 **Export Review** of the **British Drug** and **Chemical Industries.** London. *Export Rev. Br. Drug Chem. Ind.* [1951–57] L.BM.; MA.; P. [*C. of:* 13839; *C. as:* 17238]

18789 **Export-Polygraph.** Frankfurt am Main. *Export-Polygr.* [1953–57] L.P.; M.T. 56–57. [*C. as:* 18790]

18790 **Export-Polygraph International.** Frankfurt am Main. *Export-Polygr. int.* [1958–] L.P.; M.T. [*C. of:* 18789]

18792 **Exposé** des **travaux** de l'**Institut géographique national.** Paris. *Exposé Trav. Inst. géogr. natn., Paris* [*C. of:* 41964]

18793 **Exposés actuels** de **biologie cellulaire.** Paris. *Exposés act. Biol. cell.* [1955–] L.S.

18794 **Exposés annuels** de **biochimie médicale.** Paris. *Exposés a. Biochim. méd.* [1939–] L.CB. 45–; S. 39–50; Y.

18795 **Extension Bulletin. Clemson Agricultural College.** Clemson College, S.C. *Ext. Bull. Clemson agric. Coll.*

18796 **Extension Bulletin. College** of **Engineering, University** of **West Virginia.** Morgantown. *Ext. Bull. Coll. Engng Univ. W. Va* L.P. 33–; Y. [*See also:* 18818]

18797 **Extension Bulletin. Colorado Agricultural College.** Fort Collins. *Ext. Bull. Colo. agric. Coll.*

18798 **Extension Bulletin. Cornell Agricultural Experiment Station.** Ithaca, N.Y. *Ext. Bull. Cornell agric. Exp. Stn* L.BM[N]. 53–; Br.A. 49–; C.A.; O.RE. 50–55 imp.

18799 **Extension Bulletin. Florida Agricultural Experiment Station.** Gainesville. *Ext. Bull. Fla agric. Exp. Stn* C.A.

18800 **Extension Bulletin. Hawaii Agricultural Experiment Station.** Honolulu. *Ext. Bull. Hawaii agric. Exp. Stn* L.BM. 26–; EB. (ent.) 17–27; Lv.P. 17–26; U. 17–26 imp.

18801 **Extension Bulletin. Idaho Agricultural Experiment Station.** Moscow. *Ext. Bull. Idaho agric. Exp. Stn* L.EB. (ent.) 13–36.

18802 **Extension Bulletin. Maine College** of **Agriculture.** Orono. *Ext. Bull. Me Coll. Agric.* O.F. 42– imp.

18803 **Extension Bulletin. Manitoba Department** of **Agriculture.** Winnipeg. *Ext. Bull. Manitoba Dep. Agric.* **C.**A. 17–.

18804 **Extension Bulletin. Michigan Agricultural College.** Lansing. *Ext. Bull. Mich. agric. Coll.* **L.**AM. 37–; **C.**A.; **O.**F. 35–45 imp.

18804[c] **Extension Bulletin. Michigan State University Cooperative Extension Service.** *Ext. Bull. Mich. St. Univ. coop. Ext. Serv.* **Y.**

18805 **Extension Bulletin. Mississippi Agricultural Experiment Station.** Jackson. *Ext. Bull. Miss. agric. Exp. Stn* **Rt.** 17–19.

18806 **Extension Bulletin. Nebraska Agricultural Experiment Station.** Lincoln, Neb. *Ext. Bull. Neb. agric. Exp. Stn* [1911–] **L.**P.; **Abs.**N. 11–20 imp.; **E.**R. 12–21 imp.

18807 **Extension Bulletin. New Hampshire College** and **Experiment Station.** Durham, N.H. *Ext. Bull. New Hamps. Coll. Exp. Stn* [1914–] **L.**P.; **O.**F. 14–30 imp.; **Rt.** 14–26. [*See also* 18815[b]]

18808 **Extension Bulletin. New Jersey College** of **Agriculture.** New Brunswick. *Ext. Bull. New Jers. Coll. Agric.* [1915–] **L.**P. 25–; **Br.**A. 26– imp.; U. 34–; **Rt.** 15: 25– imp.; **Y.**

18809 **Extension Bulletin. New Jersey State Agricultural Experiment Station.** New Brunswick. *Ext. Bull. New Jers. St. agric. Exp. Stn*

18810 **Extension Bulletin. New Jersey State University College** of **Agriculture.** Newark. *Ext. Bull. New Jers. St. Univ. Coll. Agric.* **O.**F. 59–.

18811 **Extension Bulletin. Ohio Agricultural College.** Columbus. *Ext. Bull. Ohio agric. Coll.*

18812 **Extension Bulletin. Oregon Agricultural College Extension Service.** Corvallis. *Ext. Bull. Ore. agric. Coll. Ext. Serv.* **L.**EB. (ent.) 17–23.

18813 **Extension Bulletin. Purdue University Department** of **Agricultural Extension.** Lafayette. *Ext. Bull. Purdue Univ. Dep. agric. Ext.* **L.**EB. (ent.) 19–; **O.**F. 37–42 imp.

18814 **Extension Bulletin. Rhode Island State College.** Kingston. *Ext. Bull. Rhode Isl. St. Coll.* **C.**A. imp.

18815 **Extension Bulletin. University** of **Delaware Extension Service** in **Agriculture.** *Ext. Bull. Univ. Del. Ext. Serv. Agric.*

18815[a] **Extension Bulletin. University** of **Idaho College** of **Agriculture.** Moscow. *Ext. Bull. Univ. Idaho Coll. Agric.* **Y.**

18815[b] **Extension Bulletin. University** of **New Hampshire.** Durham. *Ext. Bull. Univ. New Hamps.* **Y.** [*See also* 18807]

18816 **Extension Bulletin. University** of **North Carolina.** Chapel Hill. *Ext. Bull. Univ. N. Carol.*

18817 **Extension Bulletin. Washington State College Extension Service.** Pullman. *Ext. Bull. Wash. St. Coll. Ext. Serv.* **L.**BM[N]. 55– imp.; **Rt.** 57.

18818 **Extension Bulletin. West Virginia University.** Morgantown. *Ext. Bull. W. Va Univ.* **L.**P. 33–; **Y.** [*See also:* 18796]

18819 **Extension Circular. Alberta University College** of **Agriculture.** Edmonton. *Ext. Circ. Alberta Univ. Coll. Agric.*

18820 **Extension Circular. Clemson Agricultural College.** Clemson College, S.C. *Ext. Circ. Clemson agric. Coll.*

18821 **Extension Circular. Department** of **Agriculture, Jamaica.** Kingston. *Ext. Circ. Dep. Agric. Jamaica* [1946–] **L.**BM[N]. 47–; K. 53–.

18822 **Extension Circular. Division** of **Agricultural Research, Louisiana State University** and **Agricultural** and **Mechanical College.** Baton Rouge. *Ext. Circ. Div. agric. Res. La St. Univ.* **O.**F. 39– imp.

18823 **Extension Circular. Federal Cooperativ Extension Service, Oregon State College.** Corvallis. *Ext. Circ. fed. coop. Ext. Serv. Ore. St. Coll.* **O.**F. 41– imp.

18824 **Extension Circular. Guam Agricultural Experiment Station.** Washington. *Ext. Circ. Guam agric. Exp. Stn* **M.**P. 21–23.

18825 **Extension Circular. Idaho Agricultural Experiment Station.** Moscow. *Ext. Circ. Idaho agric. Exp. Stn* **L.**EB. (ent.) 20–21.

18826 **Extension Circular. Kentucky Agricultural Experiment Station.** Lexington. *Ext. Circ. Ky agric. Exp. Stn*

18827 **Extension Circular. Louisiana Agricultural Experiment Station.** Baton Rouge. *Ext. Circ. La agric. Exp. Stn*

18828 **Extension Circular. Mississippi Agricultural Experiment Station.** Jackson. *Ext. Circ. Miss. agric. Exp. Stn* **C.**A.; **Rt.** 16–18.

18829 **Extension Circular. Nebraska Agricultural College.** *Ext. Circ. Neb. agric. Coll.*

18830 **Extension Circular. Nebraska Agricultural Experiment Station.** Lincoln, Neb. *Ext. Circ. Neb. agric. Exp. Stn*

18831 **Extension Circular. New Jersey College** of **Agriculture.** New Brunswick. *Ext. Circ. New Jers. Coll. Agric.* **Br.**U. 33– imp.; **C.**A.

18832 **Extension Circular. New Mexico Agricultural Experiment Station.** *Ext. Circ. New Mex. agric. Exp. Stn* **Rt.** 26–36 imp.

18832[c] **Extension Circular. New Mexico College** of **Agriculture** and **Mechanic Arts.** *Ext. Circ. New Mex. Coll. Agric. mech. Arts* **Y.**

18833 **Extension Circular. North Carolina Agricultural Experiment Station.** West Raleigh. *Ext. Circ. N. Carol. agric. Exp. Stn* **L.**AM. 25–; EB. (ent.) 16–; **O.**F. 42– imp.; **Rt.** 42– imp.

18833[c] **Extension Circular. North Carolina State College** of **Agriculture** and **Engineering.** *Ext. Circ. N. Carol. St. Coll. Agric. Engng* **Y.**

18834 **Extension Circular. Pennsylvania State College School** of **Agriculture.** Centre County. *Ext. Circ. Pa St. Coll. Agric.* **Abs.**N. 15–20 imp.

18835 **Extension Circular. University** of **Arizona College** of **Agriculture.** Tucson. *Ext. Circ. Univ. Ariz. Coll. Agric.* [1922–] [*C. of:* 14401]

18836 **Extension Circular. University** of **Arkansas College** of **Agriculture Extension Service.** Little Rock. *Ext. Circ. Univ. Ark. Coll. Agric. Ext. Serv.* **L.**EB. (ent.) 24–27.

18837 **Extension Circular. University** of **Delaware Service** in **Agriculture.** *Ext. Circ. Univ. Del. Serv. Agric.*

18838 **Extension Circular. University** of **Illinois College** of **Agriculture.** Urbana. *Ext. Circ. Univ. Ill. Coll. Agric.* [1916–21] **L.**BM. 21; EB. (ent.) 19–21; **Abs.**N. 17–21 imp.

18838° **Extension Circular. Washington State University Institute** of **Agricultural Sciences.** Pullman. *Ext. Circ. Wash. St. Univ. Inst. agric. Sci.* **Y.**

18839 **Extension Farm News. North Carolina State College** of **Agriculture.** Raleigh. *Ext. Fm News N. Carol. St. Coll. Agric.* **L.**AM. (curr.)

18840 **Extension Folder. Agricultural Extension Service, North Carolina State College** of **Agriculture** and **Engineering.** Raleigh. *Ext. Folder agric. Ext. Serv. N. Carol. St. Coll. Agric. Engng* **O.**F. 52– imp. **Y.**

18841 **Extension Leaflet. Kirton Agricultural Institute.** Kirton. *Ext. Leafl. Kirton agric. Inst.* [1923–] **C.**A. imp.; **Rt.** 23–28.

18842 **Extension Leaflet. Massachusetts Agricultural College.** Amherst. *Ext. Leafl. Mass. agric. Coll.*

18843 **Extension Leaflet. University** of **Alberta.** Edmonton. *Ext. Leafl. Univ. Alberta* **Rt.** 39–.

18844 **Extension Leaflet. University** of **North Carolina.** Chapel Hill. *Ext. Leafl. Univ. N. Carol.*

18845 **Extension Miscellaneous Pamphlet. North Carolina State College** of **Agriculture.** Raleigh. *Ext. misc. Pamph. N. Carol. St. Coll. Agric.*

18846 **Extension Miscellaneous Publication. Institute** of **Agricultural Sciences, Washington State College.** Pullman. *Ext. misc. Publ. Inst. agric. Sci. Wash. St. Coll.* **Rt.** 56.

18847 **Extension Series. Engineering Extension Department, Purdue University.** Lafayette. *Ext. Ser. Engng Ext. Dep. Purdue Univ.* [1956–] **L.**P.; **Bm.**U.; **M.**U. [*C. from:* 18094]

18848 **Extension Service Bulletin. Washington State College** of **Agriculture.** Pullman. *Ext. Serv. Bull. Wash. St. Coll. Agric.* **L.**BM. 16– imp.; **Bm.**P. 13–; **Nw.**A. 54– imp.; **R.**D. 43–.

18849 **Extension Service Circular. Missouri Agricultural Experiment Station.** Columbia. *Ext. Serv. Circ. Mo. agric. Exp. Stn* **L.**EB. (ent.) 15–26.

18850 **Extension Service Leaflet. College** of **Agriculture, Rutgers University.** New Brunswick. *Ext. Serv. Leafl. Coll. Agric. Rutgers Univ.* **O.**F. 52– imp.

18851 **Extension Service Review. U.S. Department** of **Agriculture.** Washington. *Ext. Serv. Rev. U.S. Dep. Agric.* [1930–] **L.**AM.; BM^N. 32– imp.; TP.; U.; **Abs.**N.; **C.**A. (3 yr.); **G.**M.; **Lv.**P. 41–; **O.**AEC. 49–; **R.**D. 43–; **Y.**

18852 **Exterminators Log.** Kansas City, Mo. *Exterm. Log* [1933–38] **O.**AP. [*C. as:* 37389]

18853 **Extra Publication. Natural Science** and **Archaeological Society.** Littlehampton. *Extra Publ. nat. Sci. archaeol. Soc., Littlehampton* [1929–] **L.**BM.

18854 **Extra Publication. Newcomen Society** for the **Study** of the **History** of **Engineering** and **Technology.** London. *Extra Publ. Newcomen Soc.* [1928–] **L.**P.; SC.; U.; **Abs.**N.; **Br.**P. 28–38; U.; **C.**UL.; **E.**A.; **G.**M. 28–54; **Ld.**P.; **O.**R.

18855 **Extract** of **Meteorological Observations. Royal Observatory, Hongkong.** *Extract met. Obsns R. Obs. Hongkong* **L.**MO. 95–12: 33–; **E.**B. 95–96; R. 95–96: 33–41; **Y.** [>33550, 1913–32]

18856 **Extract-Notulen** van de **algemeene vergadering** van **directeuren. Maatschappij** ter **bevordering** van het **natuurkundig onderzoek** der **nederlandsche koloniën.** Leiden. *Extract-Not. alg. Vergad. Dir. Maatsch. Bevord. natuurk. Onderz. ned. Kolon.*

18857 **Extract-Notulen** der **bestuursvergadering. Maatschappij** ter **bevordering** van het **natuurkundig onderzoek** der **nederlandsche koloniën.** Leiden. *Extract-Not. BestVerg. Maatsch. Bevord. natuurk. Onderz. ned. Kolon.*

18858 **Extracts** from the **Foreign Technical Press. War Office.** London. *Extr. for. tech. Press War Off.* [1918] **L.**BM.; P.; SC.; **Abs.**N. [*C. as:* 52417]

18859 **Extracts** from the **Narrative Reports** of **Officers** of the **Survey** of **India.** Calcutta. *Extr. narr. Rep. Offrs Surv. India* [1900–09] **L.**AS.; BM.; G. 03–09; U.; **C.**GD.; **E.**A.; R.; **O.**B. [*C. as:* 42349]

18859° **Extracts** from the **Proceedings** of the **Royal Horticultural Society.** London. *Extr. Proc. R. hort. Soc.* [1953–] **L.**BM. [*Previously issued in:* 26811]

18860 **Extracts** from the **Scientific** and **Technical Press. Air Ministry.** London. *Extr. scient. tech. Press Air Minist.* [1926–39] **L.**MO. [*C. as:* 407]

18861 **Extracts** from **Statistics** of **New Zealand: Meteorology.** Wellington. *Extr. Statist. N.Z. Met.* **L.**MO. 21–27. [*C. of:* 31582ª; *C. as:* 31607]
    Extrait des **comptes rendus** des **séances** de la **Société linnéenne** de **Bordeaux.** *See* 39885.
    Extrait des **mémoires** du **Musée d'histoire naturelle** de **Belgique.** *See* 30754.

18862 **Extrait** des **travaux** de la **Société centrale** d'**agriculture** du **département** de la **Seine-Inférieure.** Rouen. *Extrait Trav. Soc. cent. Agric. Dép. Seine-inf.* [*C. as:* 11025]

18863 **Extraits** d'**astronomie** et de **géophysique** du **Bulletin analytique** du **Centre national** de la **recherche scientifique.** Paris. *Extraits Astr. Géophys. Bull. analyt. Cent. natn. Rech. scient.* [1948–] **L.**AS. 53–; MO. 53–; **Bl.**U.; **Bm.**P.; **E.**R. [*C. of:* 6665]

18864 **Extraits** du **Bulletin analytique** du **Centre national** de la **recherche scientifique.** Paris. *Extraits Bull. analyt. Cent. natn. Rech. scient.* **C.**MI. 48–; **Ep.**D. 42–.

18865 **Extraits** des **comptes rendus** et des **mémoires** du **Comité** d'**investigation sismique** du **Japon.** Tokyo. *Extraits C. r. Mém. Com. Invest. sism. Japon*

18866 **Extrapulmonale Tuberkulose.** Berlin. *Extrapulm. Tuberk.* [1925–]

18867 **Extrême-Orient médicale.** Hanoi. *Extrême-Orient méd.* [1949–53] **L.**TD. [*C. of:* 54191]

18868 **Extruderitems.** Plastics Department, Union Carbide Plastics Co. New York. *Extruderitems* **L.**P. 60–.

18869 **Eye.** St. Joseph, Missouri. *Eye*

18870 **Eye Comfort.** Chicago. *Eye Comfort*

18871 **Eye, Ear, Nose** and **Throat Monthly.** Chicago. *Eye Ear Nose Throat Mon.* [1922–] **L.**MA. 35–36: 46–; MD. 22–23: 29– imp.; OP. 49–; **Lv.**M. 34–; **Y.**

18872 **Eye Health** and **Safety News.** New York. *Eye Hlth Saf. News* [1943–]

18873 **Ezhednevnȳĭ meteorologicheskĭ byulleten'
Nikolaevskoĭ glavnoĭ fizicheskoĭ observatorĭ.** S.-
Peterburg.　Ежедневный метеорологическій бюллетень Николаевской главной физической обсерваторіи.　*Ezhedn. met. Byull. nikolaev. glav. fiz. Obs.*

18874 **Ezhegodnik agrarnoĭ literaturȳ.**　Moskva.
Ежегодник аграрной литературы.　*Ezheg. agr. Lit.*
[1926–28] **E.**AB. 28 imp.　[*C. in:* 1207]

18875 **Ezhegodnik Byuro** po **mikologĭ i fitopatologĭ
uchenago komiteta.**　Petrograd.　Ежегодникъ бюро
по микологіи и фитопатологіи ученаго комитета.
Ezheg. Byuro Mikol. Fitopatol. uchen. Kom.

18876 **Ezhegodnik fiziko-terapevticheskago obshchestva.**　Moskva.　Ежегодникъ физико-терапевтиче-
скаго общества.　*Ezheg. fiz.-terap. Obshch.*

18877 **Ezhegodnik** po **geologĭ i mineralogĭ Rossĭ.**
Varshava, Novaya Aleksandrĭya.　Ежегодникъ по гео-
логіи и минералогіи Россіи.　*Ezheg. Geol. Miner.
Ross.* [1896–17] **L.**BM^N.; G.; GM.; **C.**S.; UL. 96–12.

18878 **Ezhegodnik Glavnago upravlenĭya zemleu-
stroĭstva (i zemledêlĭya po departamentu zeml-
dêlĭya i lêsnomu departamentu).**　Sankt-Peterburg.
Ежегодникъ Главнаго управленія землеустройства
(и земледѣлія по департаменту земледѣлія и лѣсному
департаменту).　*Ezheg. glav. Uprav. Zemleustr.* [1907–
12] **L.**BM.; EB. 08–12; SC.　[*C. of:* and *Rec. as:* 49463]

18879 **Ezhegodnik Gosudarstvennogo muzeya** imeni
N. M. Mart'yanova.　Minusinsk.　Ежегодникъ
государственного музея имени Н. М. Мартьянова.
Ezheg. gosud. Muz. N.M. Mart'yanova [1923–29] **L.**BM.
27–29; BM^N.　[*C. as:* 24429]

18880 **Ezhegodnik Kavkazskago gornago obshchestva.**
Pyatigorsk.　Ежегодникъ Кавказскаго горнаго общества.　*Ezheg. kavkaz. gorn. Obshch.*

18880° **Ezhegodnik. Leningradskoe otdelenie Obshchestva arkhitektov i khudozhnikov.**　Leningrad,
Moskva.　Ежегодник.　Ленинградское отделение
Общества архитектовъ и художниковъ.　*Ezheg.
leningr. Otd. Obshch. Arkhit. Khudozh.* **L.**BM. 53–.

18881 **Ezhegodnik Magnito-meteorologischeskoĭ observatorĭ Imperatorskago Novorossĭskago universiteta.**　Odessa.　Ежегодникъ Магнито-метеоро-
логической обсерваторіи Императорскаго Новорос-
сійскаго университета.　*Ezheg. magn.-met. Obs. imp.
novoross. Univ.* [1894–12] **L.**MO.; **E.**M.

18882 **Ezhegodnik Meteorologicheskago byuro Amur-
skago raĭona.**　Blagovêshchensk.　Ежегодникъ Мете-
орологическаго бюро Амурскаго района.　*Ezheg. met.
Byuro amursk. Raĭona*

18883 **Ezhegodnik. Muzeĭ** imeni **Akademika F. N.
Chernȳsheva.**　Leningrad.　Ежегодник.　Музей имени
Академика Ф. Н. Чернышева.　*Ezheg. Muz. Akad.
F. N. Chernȳsheva* [1938–] **L.**BM^N. 38.

　　　Ezhegodnik Obshchestva estestvoispȳtateleĭ.
Tallinn.　Ежегодник Общества естествоиспытателей.
See 28797.

18884 **Ezhegodnik Russkago antropologicheskago obshchestva** pri **Imperatorskom S.-Peterburgskom
universitetê.**　Ежегодникъ Русскаго антропологиче-
скаго общества при Императорском С.-Петербург-
скомъ университетѣ.　*Ezheg. russk. antrop. Obshch.
imp. S-Peterb. Univ.* **L.**BM. 05–15 imp.; GL. 17–.

18885 **Ezhegodnik Russkago astronomicheskago obshchestva.**　S.-Peterburg.　Ежегодникъ Русскаго
астрономическаго общества.　*Ezheg. russk. astr. Obshch.*

18886 **Ezhegodnik Russkago gornago obshchestva.**
Moskva.　Ежегодникъ Русскаго горнаго общества.
Ezheg. russk. gorn. Obshch. **E.**R. 11 : 14 : 16 : 17.

18887 **Ezhegodnik Russkago paleontologicheskago
obshchestva.**　Petrograd.　Ежегодник Русскаго пале-
онтологическаго общества.　*Ezheg. russk. paleont.
Obshch.* [1917–30] **L.**BM^N.　[*C. as:* 18891]

18888 **Ezhegodnik Russkikh sel'sko-khozyaĭstvennȳkh
opȳtnȳkh uchrezhdenĭ.**　S.-Peterburg.　Ежегодникъ
Русскихъ сельско-хозяйственныхъ опытныхъ учрежденій.　*Ezheg. russk. sel'.-khoz. opȳt. Uchrezh.*

18889 **Ezhegodnik** po **sakharnoĭ promȳshlennosti
Rossĭskoĭ imperĭ.**　Kiev.　Ежегодникъ по сахарной
промышленности Россійской имперіи.　*Ezheg. sakh.
Prom. ross. Imp.*

　　　**Ezhegodnik Sel'skokhozyaĭstvenno-lesnogo fa-
kulteta, Belgradskĭ universitet.**　Ежегодник Сель-
скохозяйственно - лесного факултета, Белградский
университет.　*See* 21430.

　　　**Ezhegondik Vengerskogo geologicheskogo insti-
tuta.**　Budapest.　Ежегодник Венгерского геологического института.　*See* 29150.

18890 **Ezhegodnik Volzhskoĭ biologicheskoĭ stantsĭ**
v **Saratovê.**　Saratov.　Ежегодникъ Волжской біоло-
гической станціи въ Саратовѣ.　*Ezheg. volzh. biol.
Sta. Saratovê*

18891 **Ezhegodnik Vsesoyuznogo paleontologiche-
skogo obshchestva.**　Leningrad, Moskva.　Ежегодник
Всесоюзного палеонтологического общества.　*Ezheg.
vses. paleont. Obshch.* [1931–] **L.**BM^N.　[*C. of:* 18887]

18892 **Ezhegodnik zemel'nȳkh uluchshenĭ Ministerstva zemledêlĭya.**　Sankt-Peterburg.　Ежегодникъ
земельныхъ улучшеній Министерства земледѣлія.
Ezheg. zemel'. Uluchsh. Minist. Zemled.

18893 **Ezhegodnik Zoologicheskago muzeya** (*formerly*
Imperatorskoĭ Akademĭ Nauk).　S.-Peterburg,
Leningrad.　Ежегодникъ зоологическаго музея Импе-
раторской Академіи наукъ.　*Ezheg. zool. Muz.* [1896–
32] **L.**BM.; BM^N.; E.; EB. 10–32; R.; SC. 14–32; Z. imp.;
C.UL.; **Lv.**U.; **O.**R.　[*C. as:* 55243]

18894 **Ezhemêsyachnik gorlovȳkh, nosovȳkh i ushnȳkh bolêzneĭ.**　S.-Peterburg.　Ежемѣсячникъ горловыхъ, носовыхъ и ушныхъ болѣзней.　*Ezhemk
gorl. nosov. ushn. Bolêz.* [1913–16]　[*C. of:* 18895]

18895 **Ezhemêsyachnik ushnȳkh gorlovȳkh i nosovȳkh
bolêzneĭ.**　S.-Peterburg.　Ежемѣсячникъ ушныхъ,
горловыхъ и носовыхъ болѣзней.　*Ezhemk ushn. gorl.
nosov. Bolêz.* [1906–12]　[*C. as:* 18894]

18896 **Ezhemesyachnȳĭ byulleten'.**　Komitet po delam
izobretenĭ i otkrȳtĭ.　Moskva.　Ежемесячный бюллетень.　Комитет по делам изобретений и открытий.
Ezhem. Byull. Kom. Del. Izobr. [1937–46] [*C. as:* 18897]

18897 **Ezhemesyachnȳĭ byulleten' izobretenĭ.**　Moskva.　Ежемесячный бюллетень изобретений.　*Ezhem.
Byull. Izobr.* [1946–49] **L.**AV. 47–49 imp.; Y.　[*C. of:*
18896; *C. as:* 12770]

18898 **Ezhemêsyachnȳĭ byulleten' Meteorologicheskoĭ observatorĭ MGU.**　Moskva.　Ежемесячный
бюллетень Метеорологической обсерватории МГУ.
Ezhem. Byull. met. Obs. MGU **L.**MO. 56–.

18899 **Ezhemêsyachnȳĭ byulleten' Glavnoĭ fizicheskoĭ
observatorĭ.**　Petrograd.　Ежемѣсячный бюллетень
Главной физической обсерваторіи.　*Ezhem. Byull.
glav. fiz. Obs.*

18900 **Ezhemêsyachnŷĭ meteorologicheskiĭ byulleten'** dlya **Evropeĭskoĭ Rossii.** S.-Peterburg. Ежемѣсячный метеорологическій бюллетень для Европейской Россіи. *Ezhem. met. Byull. evrop. Ross.*

18901 **Ezhemêsyachnŷĭ meteorologicheskiĭ byulleten' Tiflisskoĭ fizicheskoĭ observatorii.** Tiflis. Ежемѣсячный метеорологическій бюллетень Тифлисской физической обсерваторіи. *Ezhem. met. Byull. tifliss. fiz. Obs.* [1898–] **L.**мо. 98–16: 23–38.

18902 **Ezhemêsyachnŷĭ seĭsmicheskiĭ byulleten' Tiflisskoĭ fizicheskoĭ observatorii.** Tiflis. Ежемѣсячный сейсмическій бюллетень Тифлисской физической обсерваторіи. *Ezhem. seism. Byull. tifliss. fiz. Obs.* [1903–09] [*C. of:* 18903]

18903 **Ezhemêsyachnŷya svêdênĭya.** Tiflis. Ежемѣсячныя свѣдѣнія. *Ezhem. Svêdênĭya* [1901–02] [*C. as:* 18902]

18904 **Ezhenedêl'nik zhurnala Prakticheskaya meditsina.** Sankt-Peterburg. Еженедѣльникъ журнала Практическая медицина. *Ezhenk Zh. prakt. Med.* [1894–01] [*C. as:* 56980; *Supplement to:* 38477]

18905 **Ezhenedêl'nŷĭ byulleten' Seĭsmicheskoĭ stantsĭi.** Irkutsk. Еженедѣльный бюллетень Сейсмической станціи. *Ezhen. Byull. seism. Sta., Irkutsk*

18906 **Ezhenedêl'nŷĭ byulleten' Tiflisskoĭ seĭsmicheskoĭ stantsĭi.** Tiflis. Еженедѣльный бюллетень Тифлисской сейсмической станціи. *Ezhen. Byull. tifliss. seism. Sta.* [1912–15]

18907 **Ezhenedêlnŷĭ meteorologicheskiĭ byulleten' Nikolaevskoĭ glavnoĭ fizicheskoĭ observatorii.** Sankt-Peterburg. Еженедѣльный метеорологическій бюллетень Николаевской главной физической обсерваторіи. *Ezhen. met. Byull. nikolaev. glav. fiz. Obs.*